CHAMBERS

OFFICIAL

SCRABBLE®

L I S T S

CHAMBERS

OFFICIAL

L I S T S

3rd EDITION

Compiled by
Allan Simmons
Darryl Francis

CHAMBERS

SCRABBLE® is a registered trademark of J W Spear & Sons PLC, Leicester, England, a Mattel Company, and is used under licence from Mattel Europa B.V.

CHAMBERS
An imprint of Chambers Harrap Publishers Ltd
7 Hopetoun Crescent
Edinburgh EH7 4AY

www.chambersharrap.com

This edition first published by Chambers 2000
First edition published by Chambers 199; second edition published 1995

Copyright © Chambers Harrap Publishers Ltd 2000

Reprinted 2001, 2003

A CIP catalogue record for this book is available from the British Library.

ISBN 0-550-12001 7

Designed and typeset by Chambers Harrap Publishers Ltd
Printed and bound in Great Britain by Cox & Wyman Ltd, Reading, Berkshire

Preface to the third edition

This new edition of *Official Scrabble® Lists* (OSL) brings these essential word lists in line with the 1998 edition of *The Chambers Dictionary* and the 4th edition of *Official Scrabble® Words*. By studying OSL, all Scrabble players will improve their game by adding to their word knowledge and honing their skills and strategies.

The lists included in OSL are based on years of Scrabble-playing experience and contain words that are useful in a variety of situations. These lists have been carefully arranged to make learning words as easy as possible. Many of the lists are new to this edition, and new players will find the Beginners' Starter Set of 1,400 essential Scrabble words particularly valuable.

OSL also includes informative introductions to each section as well as guidance on how to make best use of the wealth of words found in *The Chambers Dictionary*, plus hints on tactics and strategy.

I am sure that OSL, along with its companion OSW, will increase your enjoyment of Scrabble and enhance your play.

Philip Nelkon
Manager Scrabble Clubs
Spear's Games

Contents

Hints

Introduction

Official Scrabble® Lists (OSL) is the ideal companion to *Official Scrabble® Words* (OSW), which is the definitive authority for all Scrabble players. OSL is a unique and thorough collection derived from the wealth of words within OSW, and is organized into useful sections by Allan Simmons and Darryl Francis, two of the UK's top Scrabble players. The lists are an invaluable aid, acting as a convenient vocabulary-building guide for newcomers to the game and a specialist reference for the more experienced players.

The third edition of OSL reflects the changes in OSW (4th edition) resulting from the publication of the latest edition of *The Chambers Dictionary* in 1998. In OSL3 there are also new and improved lists, making the book even more valuable than before. The 'Starter Lists' section serves as a quick introduction to an army of essential vocabulary, giving all the valid 2-, 3- and 4-letter words, plus lists of words containing the high-scoring letters. It also now contains a handy package of over 1,400 particularly useful words to help new players on their way.

There are lists to help players get out of tricky situations: words with many vowels; words with many consonants; words containing V, K etc. There is also a section concentrating on word-endings, including useful suffixes, unusual vowel endings and alternative spellings, as well as one on beginnings including useful prefixes and even '5 to 8's' which are 3-letter extensions of 5-letter words.

The next section concentrates on the 7- and 8-letter 'bonus words'. This includes the 250 most fruitful 6- and 7-letter combinations which yield thousands of likely 'bonuses'. In addition to these, there are suggested mnemonic phrases to help memorize the letters which go with each combination and a list of 6-letter sets which combine with all the vowels, as well as worthwhile high-probability 'bonus word' lists.

Then comes the 'hooks and blockers' section, which now details every hook letter that can be added to the front or back of words from two to eight letters to form valid longer words. As well as normal examples like VOID to AVOID and MORAL to AMORAL, there are some fascinating novelties to unearth, such as ZYGOSES to AZYGOSES, AQUATINT to AQUATINTA and even MELINITE to GMELINITE, as well as common but unthought-of extensions such as VINY to VINYL and UNFAIR to FUNFAIR. If you're feeling mean, the blockers list will make life difficult for your opponent.

OSL also of course contains anagrams, as every Scrabble book should. It lists every valid 7- and 8-letter word according to its

constituent letters in alphabetical order. Thousands of anagrams are there at your fingertips, from the exotic AMRITAS/TAMARIS to the more down to earth OUTSIDE/TEDIOUS and it gives immediate solutions to jumbles of letters such as AAAGMNR – it has to be ANAGRAM!

With lots of tips and hints on strategic secrets of success and learning words to help improve your vocabulary, what more could the Scrabble player want?

Official Scrabble® Lists certainly helped me on my way to winning the World Championship in 1993 and coming runner-up in 1999 and I definitely recommend this new updated edition as the ultimate single-volume Scrabble players' ready-reckoner.

Mark Nyman

Contributors

Compilers
Allan Simmons
Darryl Francis

Computer compilation and project consultancy
Peter Schwarz

Managing Editor
Catherine Schwarz

Publishing Manager
Elaine Higgleton

Acknowledgements

The Compilers and Publishers would like to thank the following for their contribution to this edition of *Official Scrabble® Lists*:

Mike Baron, for developing the algorithm upon which the top bonus stems are based and *The Wordbook* (1988), which played a part in the OSL project; Mark Watkins, for the top 7- and 8-letter empirical bonus lists (used in part for the Beginners' Starter Set); Phil Appleby, Danny McMullan, Elie Dangoor and David Webb for help with the mnemonics; Rich Baker; Kenneth Lawley.

Section One

Starter Lists

Introduction

This section contains a variety of 'starter' lists, a knowledge of which will give every player a firm foundation of useful Scrabble words. There are:

☆ the basic words – a complete listing of all the valid 2-, 3- and 4-letter words

☆ words with many vowels ('light' words) and words with many consonants ('heavy' words) – ammunition for helping you to use up vowels or consonants when you have too many of them

☆ words containing more than one of the same vowel or consonant – awkward vowel dumps and awkward consonant dumps

☆ all the words up to five letters long containing a K or a V

☆ all the words up to eight letters long containing a J, Q, X or Z

☆ a handy package of 1,400 or so particularly useful words to help newer players get started

Each of these lists has an introduction that describes it in more detail.

Basic Words

The following lists contain all the valid 2-, 3- and 4-letter words. There are just over 6,000 words in these three lists, and while it is not essential to know all of them, it will certainly help your game to know as many as possible.

2-letter words

2-letter words, all 110 of which are listed here, can be considered as the backbone words of any Scrabble game. They are very important, not necessarily for the scores which they themselves achieve, but also for the scores of other words they enable to be played.

The 2-letter words:

☆ provide a means of playing words parallel to other words already on the board

☆ can resolve surplus vowel problems (they include AA, EE and OO)

☆ can squeeze scores out of tight board situations

☆ can open the board for future scoring opportunities

Also, many of the 2-letter words can have letters added before or after them, making valid 3-letter words. See Section Six (Hooks) for these.

Make a list of the 2-letter words that you are not familiar with and try to introduce them into your games. Knowing what your words mean can really cement them into your mind, and it is a good idea to check *The Chambers Dictionary* or the Appendix of *Official Scrabble®️ Words* (4th edition) for meanings. Top-flight Scrabble players will know all of these words and will also know most of their meanings!

3-letter words

3-letter words (there are over 1,100 of these here) are also important, as they:

☆ provide a means of discarding unwanted letters

☆ can squeeze scores out of difficult board situations

☆ provide a means of playing higher-scoring words (perhaps bonuses) by turning 2-letter words into 3-letter words

Try to familiarize yourself with some of the 3-letter words that you don't know, and see if you can play them in your games. Leading Scrabble players will be aware of most of the 3-letter words and will be able to call on them when they are needed. But many of the top players will occasionally be uncertain about some of them, possibly recalling FAY and FEY, but being unsure of FOY; they may know HAH and HOH, but could wonder about HEH and HUH. As with the 2-letter words, meanings can be helpful, and are easily found in *The Chambers Dictionary* or *Official Scrabble®️ Words* (4th edition).

4-letter words

There are almost 4,800 of these here. 4-letter words are less important than the 2- and 3-letter words, but they do still provide a useful pool of words to dip into for scoring or rack-balancing purposes.

2-LETTER WORDS

AA	AY	EF	GU	KA	NA	ON	PO	UM	YU
AD	BA	EH	HA	KO	NE	OO	QI	UN	ZO
AE	BE	EL	HE	KY	NO	OP	RE	UP	
AH	BI	EM	HI	LA	NU	OR	SH	UR	
AI	BO	EN	HO	LI	NY	OS	SI	US	
AM	BY	ER	ID	LO	OB	OU	SO	UT	
AN	CH	ES	IF	MA	OD	OW	ST	WE	
AR	DA	EX	IN	ME	OE	OX	TA	WO	
AS	DI	FA	IO	MI	OF	OY	TE	XI	
AT	DO	FY	IS	MO	OH	PA	TI	XU	
AW	EA	GI	IT	MU	OI	PH	TO	YE	
AX	EE	GO	JO	MY	OM	PI	UG	YO	

Two's Company

There are 110 2-letter words and they are all fundamental to the game. The importance of knowing all the 2-letter words can't be emphasized enough; they are vital for parallel word play and maximizing scoring on tight boards and should be learnt off by heart. Write out the complete list over and over again. Play a few solo games allowing yourself to 'cheat' by referring to the list, but don't rely on the lists for too long. If you don't exercise your memory you won't recall them during actual play.

Score or Strategy?

The highest-scoring move is not always the best play. Always consider lower-scoring alternatives that might be better for your strategy. A lower-scoring move might not give so many points away to your opponent, or might leave you with a better balance of letters on your rack, or might enable you to set yourself up for a good score the next turn. Losing 10 points one turn may provide an extra 20 points the following turn or, if your emphasis had been on rack balance rather than score, it may even yield a 50-point bonus play.

3-LETTER WORDS

AAS	BAM	COO		FID	GUE	ILL	LAB	MEN	NUB	
ABA	BAN	COP	EAN	FIE	GUM	IMP	LAC	MES	NUN	
ABB	BAP	COR	EAR	FIG	GUN	INK	LAD	MET	NUR	
ABY	BAR	COS	EAS	FIL	GUP	INN	LAG	MEU	NUS	
ACE	BAS	COT	EAT	FIN	GUR	INS	LAH	MEW	NUT	
ACH	BAT	COW	EAU	FIR	GUS	ION	LAM	MHO	NYE	
ACT	BAY	COX	EBB	FIT	GUT	IOS	LAP	MID	NYS	
ADD	BED	COY	ECH	FIX	GUV	IRE	LAR	MIL		
ADO	BEE	COZ	ECU	FIZ	GUY	IRK	LAS	MIM		
ADS	BEG	CRU	EDH	FLU	GYM	ISH	LAT	MIR	OAF	
ADZ	BEL	CRY	EEK	FLY	GYP	ISM	LAV	MIS	OAK	
AFT	BEN	CUB	EEL	FOB		ISO	LAW	MIX	OAR	
AGA	BET	CUD	EEN	FOE	HAD	ITA	LAX	MIZ	OAT	
AGE	BEY	CUE	EFF	FOG	HAE	ITS	LAY	MNA	OBA	
AGO	BEZ	CUM	EFS	FOH	HAG	IVY	LEA	MOA	OBI	
AHA	BIB	CUP	EFT	FON	HAH		LED	MOB	OBO	
AHS	BID	CUR	EGG	FOP	HAJ	JAB	LEE	MOD	OBS	
AIA	BIG	CUT	EGO	FOR	HAM	JAG	LEG	MOE	OCA	
AID	BIN	CUZ	EHS	FOU	HAN	JAK	LEI	MOG	OCH	
AIL	BIO	CWM	EIK	FOX	HAP	JAM	LEK	MOI	ODA	
AIM	BIS		EKE	FOY	HAS	JAP	LEP	MOM	ODD	
AIN	BIT	DAB	ELD	FRA	HAT	JAR	LES	MON	ODE	
AIR	BIZ	DAD	ELF	FRO	HAW	JAW	LET	MOO	ODS	
AIS	BOA	DAE	ELK	FRY	HAY	JAY	LEU	MOP	OES	
AIT	BOB	DAG	ELL	FUB	HEM	JEE	LEV	MOR	OFF	
AKE	BOD	DAH	ELM	FUD	HEN	JET	LEW	MOT	OFT	
ALA	BOG	DAK	ELS	FUG	HEP	JEU	LEX	MOU	OHM	
ALB	BOH	DAL	ELT	FUM	HER	JEW	LEY	MOW	OHO	
ALE	BOK	DAM	EME	FUN	HES	JIB	LEZ	MOY	OIK	
ALL	BON	DAN	EMS	FUR	HET	JIG	LIB	MOZ	OIL	
ALP	BOO	DAP	EMU		HEW	JIZ	LID	MUD	OKE	
ALS	BOP	DAS	END	GAB	HEX	JOB	LIE	MUG	OLD	
ALT	BOR	DAW	ENE	GAD	HEY	JOE	LIG	MUM	OLE	
AMI	BOS	DAY	ENG	GAE	HIC	JOG	LIN	MUN	OLM	
AMP	BOT	DEB	ENS	GAG	HID	JOR	LIP	MUS	OMS	
ANA	BOW	DEE	EON	GAL	HIE	JOT	LIS	MUX	ONE	
AND	BOX	DEF	ERA	GAM	HIM	JOW	LIT		ONS	
ANE	BOY	DEI	ERE	GAN	HIN	JOY	LOB	NAB	OOF	
ANI	BRA	DEL	ERF	GAP	HIP	JUD	LOD	NAE	OOH	
ANN	BRO	DEN	ERG	GAR	HIS	JUG	LOG	NAG	OOM	
ANT	BUB	DEW	ERK	GAS	HIT	JUS	LOO	NAM	OON	
ANY	BUD	DEY	ERN	GAT	HOA	JUT	LOP	NAN	OOP	
APE	BUG	DIB	ERR	GAU	HOB		LOR	NAP	OOR	
APT	BUM	DID	ERS	GAY	HOC	KAE	LOS	NAS	OOS	
ARB	BUN	DIE	ESS	GED	HOD	KAI	LOT	NAT	OPE	
ARC	BUR	DIG	EST	GEE	HOE	KAM	LOW	NAY	OPS	
ARD	BUS	DIM	ETA	GEL	HOG	KAS	LOX	NEB	OPT	
ARE	BUT	DIN	ETH	GEM	HOH	KAT	LOY	NED	ORB	
ARK	BUY	DIP	EUK	GEN	HOI	KAW	LUD	NEE	ORC	
ARM	BYE	DIT	EVE	GEO	HON	KAY	LUG	NEF	ORD	
ARS	BYS	DIV	EWE	GET	HOO	KEA	LUM	NEK	ORE	
ART		DOB	EWK	GEY	HOP	KEB	LUR	NEP	ORF	
ARY	CAB	DOC	EWT	GHI	HOS	KED	LUV	NET	ORS	
ASH	CAD	DOD	EYE	GIB	HOT	KEF	LUX	NEW	ORT	
ASK	CAM	DOE		GID	HOW	KEG	LUZ	NIB	OUD	
ASP	CAN	DOG	FAB	GIE	HOX	KEN	LYE	NID	OUK	
ASS	CAP	DOH	FAD	GIF	HOY	KEP	LYM	NIE	OUP	
ATE	CAR	DON	FAG	GIG	HUB	KET		NIL	OUR	
AUF	CAT	DOO	FAH	GIN	HUE	KEX	MAA	NIM	OUT	
AUK	CAW	DOP	FAN	GIO	HUG	KEY	MAC	NIP	OVA	
AVA	CAY	DOR	FAP	GIP	HUH	KID	MAD	NIS	OWE	
AVE	CEE	DOS	FAR	GIS	HUI	KIF	MAE	NIT	OWL	
AWA	CEL	DOT	FAS	GIT	HUM	KIN	MAG	NIX	OWN	
AWE	CEP	DOW	FAT	GJU	HUP	KIP	MAK	NOB	OWT	
AWL	CHA	DRY	FAW	GNU	HUT	KIR	MAL	NOD	OYE	
AWN	CHE	DSO	FAX	GOA	HYE	KIT	MAM	NOG	OYS	
AXE	CHI	DUB	FAY	GOB	HYP	KOA	MAN	NOH		
AYE	CID	DUD	FED	GOD		KOB	MAP	NOM	PAD	
AYS	CIG	DUE	FEE	GOE	ICE	KOI	MAR	NON	PAH	
AYU	CIT	DUG	FEN	GON	ICH	KON	MAS	NOR	PAL	
	CLY	DUN	FET	GOO	ICY	KOP	MAT	NOS	PAM	
	COB	DUO	FEU	GOS	IDE	KOS	MAW	NOT	PAN	
BAA	COD	DUP	FEW	GOT	IDS	KOW	MAX	NOW	PAP	
BAC	COG	DUX	FEY	GOV	IFF	KYE	MAY	NOX	PAR	
BAD	COL	DYE	FEZ	GOY	IFS	KYU	MEG	NOY	PAS	
BAG	CON	DZO	FIB	GUB	ILK		MEL	NTH	PAT	
BAH								MEN		PAW

PAX	PRO	REN	SAC	SKI	TAG	TOO		WEM	YEW
PAY	PRY	REP	SAD	SKY	TAI	TOP	VAC	WEN	YEX
PEA	PSI	RES	SAE	SLY	TAJ	TOR	VAE	WET	YGO
PEC	PST	RET	SAG	SMA	TAK	TOT	VAN	WEX	YIN
PED	PUB	REV	SAI	SNY	TAM	TOW	VAS	WEY	YIP
PEE	PUD	REW	SAL	SOB	TAN	TOY	VAT	WHA	YOB
PEG	PUG	REX	SAM	SOC	TAP	TRY	VAU	WHO	YOD
PEN	PUH	REZ	SAN	SOD	TAR	TUB	VEE	WHY	YOK
PEP	PUN	RHO	SAP	SOG	TAT	TUG	VEG	WIG	YON
PER	PUP	RHY	SAR	SOH	TAU	TUI	VET	WIN	YOS
PET	PUR	RIA	SAT	SOL	TAW	TUM	VEX	WIS	YOU
PEW	PUS	RIB	SAW	SON	TAX	TUN	VIA	WIT	YOW
PHI	PUT	RID	SAX	SOP	TAY	TUP	VID	WOE	YUG
PHO	PUY	RIG	SAY	SOS	TEA	TUT	VIE	WOG	YUK
PHS	PYE	RIM	SAZ	SOT	TED	TUX	VIM	WOK	YUP
PIA	PYX	RIN	SEA	SOU	TEE	TWA	VIN	WON	YUS
PIC		RIP	SEC	SOV	TEF	TWO	VIS	WOO	
PIE	QAT	RIT	SED	SOW	TEG	TWP	VLY	WOP	ZAG
PIG	QIS	RIZ	SEE	SOX	TEL	TYE	VOE	WOS	ZAP
PIN	QUA	ROB	SEG	SOY	TEN	TYG	VOL	WOT	ZAX
PIP		ROC	SEI	SPA	TES		VOR	WOW	ZEA
PIR	RAD	ROD	SEL	SPY	TEW	UDO	VOW	WOX	ZED
PIS	RAG	ROE	SEN	STY	THE	UDS	VOX	WRY	ZEE
PIT	RAH	ROK	SET	SUB	THO	UEY	VUG	WUD	ZEK
PIU	RAI	ROM	SEW	SUD	THY	UFO	VUM	WUS	ZEL
PIX	RAJ	ROO	SEX	SUE	TIC	UGH		WYE	ZEX
PLY	RAM	ROT	SEY	SUI	TID	UGS		WYN	ZHO
POA	RAN	ROW	SEZ	SUK	TIE	UKE	WAD		ZIG
POD	RAP	RUB	SHE	SUM	TIG	ULE	WAE		ZIP
POH	RAS	RUC	SHY	SUN	TIL	UNI	WAG	XIS	ZIT
POI	RAT	RUD	SIB	SUP	TIN	UNS	WAN		ZIZ
POM	RAW	RUE	SIC	SUQ	TIP	UPS	WAP	YAH	ZOA
POO	RAX	RUG	SIM	SUR	TIS	URD	WAR	YAK	ZOO
POP	RAY	RUM	SIN	SUS	TIT	URE	WAS	YAM	ZOS
POS	REC	RUN	SIP	SWY	TOC	URN	WAT	YAP	ZUZ
POT	RED	RUT	SIR	SYE	TOD	USE	WAW	YAW	
POW	REE	RYA	SIS		TOE	UTE	WAX	YEA	
POX	REF	RYE	SIT	TAB	TOG	UTS	WAY	YEN	
POZ	REH		SIX	TAD	TOM	UTU	WEB	YEP	
PRE	REM	SAB	SKA	TAE	TON	UVA	WED	YES	
							WEE	YET	

Tackling the Threes

To the uninitiated the number of allowable 3-letter words is quite daunting. However, if you ignore the everyday words the lists begin to become a little more manageable. Pay particular attention to those that can be made by extending 2-letter words (see the Hooks section) and those containing tiles worth three points or more. Write out those you don't know. Many players also find it helpful to know the definitions. These you will find in *The Chambers Dictionary* or in the Appendix of *Official Scrabble® Words* (4th edition).

Open Play

Most people play Scrabble to win, which is natural and should not be discouraged. However, if you are keen to improve your scoring power and vocabulary, try playing the occasional more open game. This will enable you to concentrate on strengthening your rack-balancing, bonus-spotting and hook-word skills. Here are a few tips on open play:

☆ Try to ensure vowels are next to premium squares to provide scoring opportunities for high-scoring consonants.

☆ Experiment with playing the first word to the left of the board to enable easier access to the otherwise awkward top left.

☆ Play conservatively and consider points per tile gained each move rather than points per move.

☆ Don't be afraid to open up the triple-word squares and equally don't think you have to take a triple-word square as soon as it is available.

☆ Change tiles if your rack gets imbalanced and the only moves available block the openings on the board.

☆ Whenever you get the opportunity start a game with a 3-letter word consisting of vowel-consonant-vowel played centrally to open up all four areas of the board, eg ADO, EGO, IRE, OCA, UDO etc.

Fours Feeding

Very few top players are actually familiar with all the 4-letter words. The ones they tend to concentrate on are those that are formed from 3-letter words (see the Hooks section), those that contain the higher-scoring consonants, and those that are useful for sorting out those vowel problems. Work through the 4-letter list and highlight those you don't know, then play a solo game restricting yourself to just 4-letter words as far as you are able. Initially consult the list whilst playing but also try to play from memory. After a while oddities such as BAPU, COFT, DHAL and EUOI become second nature to your game, and impress your opponents!

4-LETTER WORDS

ABAC	ALBE	AREW	BAGS	BENI	BOBA	BRIT	CAME	CHIT	COLL
ABAS	ALBS	ARIA	BAHT	BENJ	BOBS	BROD	CAMP	CHIV	COLS
ABBA	ALEE	ARID	BAIL	BENS	BOCK	BROG	CAMS	CHIZ	COLT
ABBE	ALES	ARIL	BAIT	BENT	BODE	BROO	CANE	CHOC	COMA
ABBS	ALEW	ARIS	BAJU	BERE	BODS	BROS	CANG	CHON	COMB
ABED	ALFA	ARKS	BAKE	BERG	BODY	BROW	CANN	CHOP	COME
ABET	ALGA	ARLE	BALD	BERK	BOFF	BRRR	CANS	CHOU	COMP
ABID	ALIT	ARMS	BALE	BERM	BOGS	BRUT	CANT	CHOW	COMS
ABLE	ALKY	ARMY	BALK	BEST	BOGY	BUAT	CANY	CHUB	COND
ABLY	ALLS	ARNA	BALL	BETA	BOHS	BUBA	CAPA	CHUG	CONE
ABUT	ALLY	AROW	BALM	BETE	BOIL	BUBO	CAPE	CHUM	CONF
ABYE	ALMA	ARSE	BALU	BETH	BOKE	BUBS	CAPI	CHUT	CONK
ACED	ALME	ARTS	BAMS	BETS	BOKO	BUCK	CAPO	CIAO	CONN
ACER	ALMS	ARTY	BANC	BEVY	BOKS	BUDO	CAPS	CIDE	CONS
ACES	ALOD	ARUM	BAND	BEYS	BOLD	BUDS	CARB	CIDS	CONY
ACHE	ALOE	ARVO	BANE	BHEL	BOLE	BUFF	CARD	CIGS	COOF
ACHY	ALOW	ARYL	BANG	BIAS	BOLL	BUFO	CARE	CILL	COOK
ACID	ALPS	ASAR	BANI	BIBS	BOLO	BUGS	CARK	CION	COOL
ACME	ALSO	ASCI	BANK	BICE	BOLT	BUHL	CARL	CIRE	COOM
ACNE	ALTO	ASHY	BANS	BIDE	BOMA	BUIK	CARP	CIRL	COON
ACRE	ALTS	ASKS	BANT	BIDS	BOMB	BUKE	CARR	CIST	COOP
ACTA	ALUM	ASPS	BAPS	BIEN	BONA	BULB	CARS	CITE	COOS
ACTS	AMAH	ATAP	BAPU	BIER	BOND	BULK	CART	CITO	COOT
ACYL	AMBO	ATOC	BARB	BIFF	BONE	BULL	CASA	CITS	COPE
ADAW	AMEN	ATOK	BARD	BIGA	BONG	BUMF	CASE	CITY	COPS
ADDS	AMID	ATOM	BARE	BIGG	BONK	BUMP	CASH	CIVE	COPY
ADIT	AMIE	ATOP	BARF	BIGS	BONY	BUMS	CASK	CLAD	CORD
ADOS	AMIR	AUFS	BARK	BIKE	BOOB	BUNA	CAST	CLAG	CORE
ADRY	AMIS	AUKS	BARM	BILE	BOOH	BUND	CATE	CLAM	CORF
ADZE	AMLA	AULA	BARN	BILK	BOOK	BUNG	CATS	CLAN	CORK
AEON	AMMO	AULD	BARP	BILL	BOOL	BUNK	CAUF	CLAP	CORM
AERO	AMOK	AUNE	BARS	BIND	BOOM	BUNS	CAUK	CLAT	CORN
AERY	AMPS	AUNT	BASE	BINE	BOON	BUNT	CAUL	CLAW	CORS
AESC	AMYL	AURA	BASH	BING	BOOR	BUOY	CAUM	CLAY	CORY
AFAR	ANAL	AUTO	BASK	BINK	BOOS	BURD	CAUP	CLEF	COSE
AFFY	ANAN	AVAL	BASS	BINS	BOOT	BURG	CAVE	CLEG	COSH
AFRO	ANAS	AVAS	BAST	BINT	BOPS	BURK	CAVY	CLEM	COSS
AGAR	ANCE	AVER	BATE	BIOG	BORA	BURL	CAWK	CLEW	COST
AGAS	ANDS	AVES	BATH	BIOS	BORD	BURN	CAWS	CLIP	COSY
AGED	ANES	AVID	BATS	BIRD	BORE	BURP	CAYS	CLOD	COTE
AGEE	ANEW	AVOW	BATT	BIRK	BORN	BURR	CEAS	CLOG	COTH
AGEN	ANIL	AWAY	BAUD	BIRL	BORS	BURS	CECA	CLOP	COTS
AGES	ANIS	AWDL	BAUK	BIRR	BORT	BURY	CEDE	CLOT	COTT
AGHA	ANKH	AWED	BAUR	BISE	BOSH	BUSH	CEDI	CLOU	COUP
AGIN	ANNA	AWES	BAWD	BISH	BOSK	BUSK	CEES	CLOW	COUR
AGIO	ANNO	AWLS	BAWL	BISK	BOSS	BUSS	CEIL	CLOY	COVE
AGMA	ANNS	AWNS	BAWN	BITE	BOTH	BUST	CELL	CLUB	COWL
AGOG	ANOA	AWNY	BAWR	BITO	BOTS	BUSY	CELS	CLUE	COWP
AGON	ANON	AWRY	BAYE	BITS	BOTT	BUTE	CELT	COAL	COWS
AGUE	ANOW	AXED	BAYS	BITT	BOUK	BUTS	CENS	COAT	COXA
AHED	ANTA	AXEL	BAYT	BLAB	BOUN	BUTT	CENT	COAX	COXY
AHEM	ANTE	AXES	BEAD	BLAD	BOUT	BUYS	CEPS	COBB	COZE
AHOY	ANTI	AXIL	BEAK	BLAE	BOWL	BUZZ	CERE	COBS	COZY
AIAS	ANTS	AXIS	BEAM	BLAG	BOWR	BYES	CERT	COCA	CRAB
AIDE	ANUS	AXLE	BEAN	BLAH	BOWS	BYKE	CESS	COCH	CRAG
AIDS	APAY	AXON	BEAR	BLAT	BOXY	BYRE	CETE	COCK	CRAM
AILS	APED	AYAH	BEAT	BLAY	BOYG	BYTE	CHAD	COCO	CRAN
AIMS	APES	AYES	BEAU	BLEB	BOYO		CHAI	CODA	CRAP
AINE	APEX	AYRE	BECK	BLED	BOYS	CABA	CHAL	CODE	CRAW
AIRN	APOD	AYUS	BEDE	BLEE	BOZO	CABS	CHAM	CODS	CRED
AIRS	APSE	AZAN	BEDS	BLET	BRAD	CADE	CHAP	COED	CREE
AIRT	APTS	AZYM	BEEF	BLEW	BRAE	CADI	CHAR	COFF	CREW
AIRY	AQUA		BEEN	BLEY	BRAG	CADS	CHAS	COFT	CRIB
AITS		BAAS	BEEP	BLIN	BRAN	CAFE	CHAT	COGS	CRIM
AITU	ARAK	BABA	BEER	BLIP	BRAS	CAFF	CHAW	COHO	CRIT
AJAR	ARAR	BABE	BEES	BLOB	BRAT	CAGE	CHAY	COIF	CROC
AJEE	ARBA	BABU	BEET	BLOC	BRAW	CAGY	CHEF	COIL	CROP
AKED	ARBS	BACH	BEGO	BLOT	BRAY	CAIN	CHER	COIN	CROW
AKEE	ARCH	BACK	BEGS	BLOW	BRED	CAKE	CHEW	COIR	CRUD
AKES	ARCO	BACS	BEIN	BLUB	BREE	CAKY	CHEZ	COIT	CRUE
AKIN	ARCS	BACK	BELL	BLUE	BREN	CALF	CHIC	COKE	CRUS
ALAE	ARDS	BADE	BELS	BLUR	BRER	CALK	CHID	COKY	CRUX
ALAP	AREA	BADS	BELT	BOAK	BREW	CALL	CHIK	COLA	CUBE
ALAR	ARED	BAEL	BEMA	BOAR	BRIG	CALM	CHIN	COLD	CUBS
ALAS	ARES	BAFF	BEND	BOAS	BRIM	CALP	CHIP	COLE	CUDS
ALAY	ARET	BAFT	BENE	BOAT	BRIO	CALX	CHIS	COLL	CUED

CUES	DEAL	DISS	DRAD	EATH	ERNE	FATE	FLAG	FRIT	GAUP
CUFF	DEAN	DITA	DRAG	EATS	ERNS	FATS	FLAK	FRIZ	GAUR
CUIF	DEAR	DITE	DRAM	EAUS	ERRS	FAUN	FLAM	FROG	GAUS
CUIT	DEAW	DITS	DRAP	EAUX	ERST	FAUX	FLAN	FROM	GAVE
CULL	DEBS	DITT	DRAT	EBBS	ESKY	FAVE	FLAP	FROW	GAWD
CULM	DEBT	DIVA	DRAW	EBON	ESNE	FAWN	FLAT	FUBS	GAWK
CULT	DECK	DIVE	DRAY	ECAD	ESPY	FAWS	FLAW	FUCI	GAWP
CUNT	DECO	DIVI	DREE	ECCE	ESSE	FAYS	FLAX	FUCK	GAYS
CUPS	DEED	DIVS	DREG	ECCO	ESTS	FAZE	FLAY	FUDS	GAZE
CURB	DEEK	DIXI	DREK	ECHE	ETAS	FEAL	FLEA	FUEL	GAZY
CURD	DEEM	DIXY	DREW	ECHO	ETAT	FEAR	FLED	FUFF	GEAL
CURE	DEEN	DOAB	DREY	ECHT	ETCH	FEAT	FLEE	FUGS	GEAN
CURL	DEEP	DOAT	DRIB	ECOD	ETEN	FECK	FLEG	FULL	GEAR
CURN	DEER	DOBS	DRIP	ECRU	ETHE	FEDS	FLEW	FUME	GEAT
CURR	DEES	DOCK	DROP	ECUS	ETHS	FEED	FLEX	FUMS	GECK
CURS	DEEV	DOCS	DROW	EDDO	ETNA	FEEL	FLEY	FUMY	GEDS
CURT	DEFT	DODO	DRUB	EDDY	ETUI	FEER	FLIC	FUND	GEED
CUSH	DEFY	DODS	DRUG	EDGE	EUGE	FEES	FLIP	FUNG	GEEK
CUSK	DEID	DOEK	DRUM	EDGY	EUGH	FEET	FLIT	FUNK	GEEP
CUSP	DEIL	DOEN	DSOS	EDHS	EUKS	FEGS	FLIX	FUNS	GEES
CUSS	DELE	DOER	DUAD	EDIT	EUOI	FEHM	FLOE	FURL	GEIT
CUTE	DELF	DOES	DUAL	EECH	EURO	FEIS	FLOG	FURR	GELD
CUTS	DELI	DOFF	DUAN	EELS	EVEN	FELL	FLOP	FURS	GELS
CWMS	DELL	DOGE	DUAR	EELY	EVER	FELT	FLOR	FURY	GELT
CYAN	DELS	DOGS	DUBS	EERY	EVES	FEME	FLOW	FUSC	GEMS
CYMA	DELT	DOGY	DUCE	EEVN	EVET	FEND	FLUB	FUSE	GENA
CYME	DEME	DOHS	DUCK	EFFS	EVIL	FENI	FLUE	FUSS	GENE
CYST	DEMO	DOIT	DUCT	EFTS	EVOE	FENS	FLUS	FUST	GENS
CYTE	DEMY	DOJO	DUDE	EGAD	EWER	FENT	FLUX	FUZE	GENT
CZAR	DENE	DOLE	DUDS	EGAL	EWES	FEOD	FOAL	FUZZ	GENU
	DENS	DOLL	DUED	EGER	EWKS	FERE	FOAM	FYKE	GEOS
DABS	DENT	DOLT	DUEL	EGGS	EWTS	FERM	FOBS	FYLE	GERE
DACE	DENY	DOME	DUES	EGGY	EXAM	FERN	FOCI	FYRD	GERM
DADO	DERE	DOMY	DUET	EGIS	EXES	FESS	FOEN		GEST
DADS	DERM	DONA	DUFF	EGMA	EXIT	FEST	FOES	GABS	GETA
DAES	DERN	DONE	DUGS	EGOS	EXON	FETA	FOGS	GABY	GETS
DAFF	DERV	DONG	DUKE	EHED	EXPO	FETE	FOGY	GADE	GEUM
DAFT	DESK	DONS	DULE	EIKS	EXUL	FETS	FOHN	GADI	GHAT
DAGO	DEUS	DOOB	DULL	EILD	EYAS	FETT	FOHS	GADS	GHEE
DAGS	DEVA	DOOK	DULY	EINE	EYED	FEUD	FOID	GAED	GHIS
DAHL	DEWS	DOOL	DUMA	EKED	EYES	FEUS	FOIL	GAES	GIBE
DAHS	DEWY	DOOM	DUMB	EKES	EYNE	FEYS	FOIN	GAFF	GIBS
DAIS	DEYS	DOOR	DUMP	EKKA	EYOT	FIAR	FOLD	GAGA	GIDS
DAKS	DHAK	DOOS	DUNE	ELAN	EYRA	FIAT	FOLK	GAGE	GIED
DALE	DHAL	DOPA	DUNG	ELDS	EYRE	FIBS	FOND	GAGS	GIEN
DALI	DHOL	DOPE	DUNK	ELFS	EYRY	FICO	FONE	GAID	GIES
DALS	DHOW	DOPS	DUNS	ELKS		FIDS	FONS	GAIN	GIFT
DALT	DIAL	DOPY	DUNT	ELLS	FACE	FIEF	FONT	GAIR	GIGA
DAME	DIBS	DORK	DUOS	ELMS	FACT	FIER	FOOD	GAIT	GIGS
DAMN	DICE	DORM	DUPE	ELMY	FADE	FIFE	FOOL	GAJO	GILA
DAMP	DICH	DORP	DUPS	ELSE	FADO	FIGO	FOOT	GALA	GILD
DAMS	DICK	DORR	DURA	ELTS	FADS	FIGS	FOPS	GALE	GILL
DANG	DICT	DORS	DURE	EMES	FADY	FIKE	FORA	GALL	GILT
DANK	DIDO	DORT	DURN	EMEU	FAFF	FIKY	FORB	GALS	GIMP
DANS	DIEB	DORY	DURO	EMIR	FAGS	FILE	FORD	GAMB	GING
DANT	DIED	DOSE	DUSH	EMIT	FAHS	FILL	FORE	GAME	GINK
DAPS	DIES	DOSH	DUSK	EMMA	FAIK	FILM	FORK	GAMP	GINN
DARE	DIET	DOSS	DUST	EMUS	FAIL	FILO	FORM	GAMS	GINS
DARG	DIGS	DOST	DUTY	EMYS	FAIN	FILS	FORT	GAMY	GIOS
DARI	DIKA	DOTE	DWAM	ENDS	FAIR	FIND	FOSS	GANE	GIPS
DARK	DIKE	DOTH	DYAD	ENES	FAIX	FINE	FOUD	GANG	GIRD
DARN	DILL	DOTS	DYED	ENEW	FAKE	FINI	FOUL	GANT	GIRL
DART	DIME	DOTY	DYER	ENGS	FALL	FINK	FOUR	GAOL	GIRN
DASH	DIMS	DOUC	DYES	ENOW	FALX	FINO	FOUS	GAPE	GIRO
DATA	DINE	DOUP	DYKE	ENVY	FAME	FINS	FOWL	GAPO	GIRR
DATE	DING	DOUR	DYNE	EOAN	FAND	FIRE	FOXY	GAPS	GIRT
DAUB	DINK	DOUT	DZHO	EONS	FANE	FIRK	FOYS	GARB	GISM
DAUD	DINO	DOVE	DZOS	EORL	FANG	FIRM	FOZY	GARE	GIST
DAUR	DINS	DOWD		EPEE	FANK	FIRN	FRAB	GARS	GITE
DAUT	DINT	DOWF	EACH	EPHA	FANS	FIRS	FRAE	GART	GITS
DAWD	DIPS	DOWL	EALE	EPIC	FARD	FISC	FRAG	GASH	GIVE
DAWK	DIRE	DOWN	EANS	EPOS	FARE	FISH	FRAP	GASP	GIZZ
DAWN	DIRK	DOWP	EARD	ERAS	FARL	FISK	FRAS	GAST	GJUS
DAWS	DIRL	DOWS	EARL	ERED	FARM	FIST	FRAU	GATE	GLAD
DAWT	DIRT	DOWT	EARN	ERES	FARO	FITS	FRAY	GATH	GLAM
DAYS	DISA	DOXY	EARS	ERGO	FARS	FITT	FREE	GATS	GLED
DAZE	DISC	DOZE	EASE	ERGS	FART	FIVE	FRET	GAUD	GLEE
DEAD	DISH	DOZY	EAST	ERIC	FASH	FIZZ	FRIG	GAUM	GLEG
DEAF	DISK	DRAB	EASY	ERKS	FAST	FLAB	FRIS	GAUN	GLEI

GLEN	GRIS	HANK	HILI	HUED	INTI	JOEY	KEDS	KOAS	LAVS
GLEY	GRIT	HAPS	HILL	HUER	INTO	JOGS	KEEK	KOBS	LAWK
GLIA	GROG	HARD	HILT	HUES	IONS	JOHN	KEEL	KOFF	LAWN
GLIB	GROT	HARE	HIND	HUFF	IOTA	JOIN	KEEN	KOHL	LAWS
GLID	GROW	HARK	HING	HUGE	IRES	JOKE	KEEP	KOLA	LAYS
GLIM	GRUB	HARL	HINS	HUGS	IRID	JOKY	KEFS	KOLO	LAZE
GLIT	GRUE	HARM	HINT	HUGY	IRIS	JOLE	KEGS	KOND	LAZO
GLOB	GRUM	HARN	HIPS	HUIA	IRKS	JOLL	KEIR	KONK	LAZY
GLOM	GUAN	HARO	HIPT	HUIS	IRON	JOLT	KEKS	KONS	LEAD
GLOP	GUAR	HARP	HIRE	HULA	ISLE	JOMO	KELL	KOOK	LEAF
GLOW	GUBS	HART	HISH	HULE	ISMS	JOOK	KELP	KOPH	LEAK
GLUE	GUCK	HASH	HISN	HULK	ISOS	JORS	KELT	KORA	LEAL
GLUG	GUDE	HASK	HISS	HULL	ITAS	JOSH	KEMB	KORE	LEAM
GLUM	GUES	HASP	HIST	HUMA	ITCH	JOSS	KEMP	KOSS	LEAN
GLUT	GUFF	HAST	HITS	HUMF	ITEM	JOTA	KENO	KOTO	LEAP
GNAR	GUGA	HATE	HIVE	HUMP	IURE	JOTS	KENS	KOWS	LEAR
GNAT	GUID	HATH	HIYA	HUMS	IWIS	JOUK	KENT	KRAB	LEAS
GNAW	GULA	HATS	HIZZ	HUNG	IXIA	JOUR	KEPI	KRIS	LEAT
GNUS	GULE	HAUD	HOAR	HUNK		JOWL	KEPS	KSAR	LECH
GOAD	GULF	HAUL	HOAS	HUNT		JOWS	KEPT	KUDU	LEED
GOAF	GULL	HAUT	HOAX	HUPS	JABS	JOYS	KERB	KUKU	LEEK
GOAL	GULP	HAVE	HOBO	HURL	JACK	JUBA	KERF	KURI	LEEP
GOAS	GULY	HAWK	HOBS	HURT	JADE	JUBE	KERN	KURU	LEER
GOAT	GUMP	HAWM	HOCK	HUSH	JAGS	JUDO	KESH	KUZU	LEES
GOBO	GUMS	HAWS	HODS	HUSK	JAIL	JUDS	KEST	KYAT	LEET
GOBS	GUNK	HAYS	HOED	HUSO	JAKE	JUDY	KETA	KYLE	LEFT
GOBY	GUNS	HAZE	HOER	HUSS	JAKS	JUGA	KETS	KYND	LEGS
GODS	GUPS	HAZY	HOES	HUTS	JAMB	JUGS	KEYS	KYNE	LEHR
GOEL	GURL	HEAD	HOGG	HWYL	JAMS	JUJU	KHAN	KYTE	LEIR
GOER	GURN	HEAL	HOGH	HYED	JANE	JUKE	KHAT	KYUS	LEIS
GOES	GURS	HEAP	HOGS	HYEN	JANN	JUMP	KHOR		LEKE
GOEY	GURU	HEAR	HOHS	HYES	JAPE	JUNK	KHUD		LEKS
GOFF	GUSH	HEAT	HOIK	HYKE	JAPS	JURA	KIBE	LABS	LEME
GOGO	GUST	HEBE	HOKE	HYLE	JARK	JURE	KICK	LACE	LEND
GOLD	GUTS	HECH	HOKI	HYMN	JARL	JURY	KIDS	LACK	LENG
GOLE	GUVS	HECK	HOLD	HYPE	JARS	JUST	KIER	LACS	LENO
GOLF	GUYS	HEED	HOLE	HYPO	JASP	JUTE	KIFS	LACY	LENS
GOLP	GYAL	HEEL	HOLM	HYPS	JASS	JUTS	KIKE	LADE	LENT
GONE	GYBE	HEFT	HOLP		JASY	JUVE	KILD	LADS	LEPS
GONG	GYMP	HEID	HOLS	IAMB	JATO	JYNX	KILL	LADY	LERE
GONK	GYMS	HEIL	HOLT	IBEX	JAUP		KILN	LAER	LERP
GONS	GYNY	HEIR	HOLY	IBIS	JAWS	KADE	KILO	LAGS	LESS
GOOD	GYPS	HELD	HOME	ICED	JAYS	KADI	KILP	LAHS	LEST
GOOF	GYRE	HELE	HOMO	ICER	JAZY	KAED	KILT	LAIC	LETS
GOOK	GYRI	HELL	HOMY	ICES	JAZZ	KAES	KINA	LAID	LEVA
GOOL	GYRO	HELM	HOND	ICKY	JEAN	KAGO	KIND	LAIK	LEVE
GOON	GYTE	HELP	HONE	ICON	JEAT	KAID	KINE	LAIN	LEVY
GOOP	GYVE	HEME	HONG	IDEA	JEED	KAIE	KING	LAIR	LEWD
GOOR		HEMP	HONK	IDEE	JEEL	KAIF	KINK	LAKE	LEYS
GOOS	HAAF	HEMS	HONS	IDEM	JEER	KAIL	KINO	LAKH	LEZZ
GORE	HAAR	HEND	HOOF	IDES	JEES	KAIM	KINS	LAKY	LIAR
GORM	HACK	HENS	HOOD	IDLE	JEFF	KAIN	KIPE	LAMA	LIBS
GORP	HADE	HENT	HOOK	IDLY	JELL	KAIS	KIPP	LAMB	LICE
GORY	HADJ	HEPS	HOON	IDOL	JERK	KAKA	KIPS	LAME	LICH
GOSH	HADS	HEPT	HOOP	IDYL	JESS	KAKI	KIRK	LAMP	LICK
GOUK	HAEM	HERB	HOOT	IFFY	JEST	KALE	KIRN	LAMS	LIDO
GOUT	HAET	HERD	HOPE	IGAD	JETE	KALI	KIRS	LANA	LIDS
GOVS	HAFF	HERE	HOPS	IKAT	JETS	KAMA	KISH	LAND	LIED
GOWD	HAFT	HERL	HORE	IKON	JEUX	KAME	KIST	LANE	LIEF
GOWF	HAGG	HERM	HORN	ILEA	JEWS	KAMI	KITE	LANG	LIEN
GOWK	HAGS	HERN	HORS	ILEX	JIAO	KANA	KITH	LANK	LIER
GOWL	HAIK	HERO	HOSE	ILIA	JIBE	KANG	KITS	LANT	LIES
GOWN	HAIL	HERS	HOSS	ILKA	JIBS	KANS	KIVA	LANX	LIEU
GOYS	HAIN	HERY	HOST	ILKS	JIFF	KANT	KIWI	LAPS	LIFE
GRAB	HAIR	HESP	HOTE	ILLS	JIGS	KAON	KNAG	LARD	LIFT
GRAD	HAJI	HEST	HOTS	ILLY	JILL	KARA	KNAP	LARE	LIGS
GRAM	HAJJ	HETE	HOUF	IMAM	JILT	KARK	KNAR	LARK	LIKE
GRAN	HAKA	HETS	HOUR	IMPI	JIMP	KART	KNAR	LARN	LILL
GRAT	HAKE	HEWN	HOUT	IMPS	JINK	KATA	KNEE	LASE	LILO
GRAY	HALE	HEWS	HOVE	INBY	JINN	KATI	KNEW	LASH	LILT
GREE	HALF	HEYS	HOWE	INCH	JINX	KATS	KNIT	LASS	LILY
GREN	HALL	HICK	HOWF	INFO	JIRD	KAVA	KNOB	LAST	LIMA
GREW	HALM	HIDE	HOWK	INGO	JISM	KAWS	KNOP	LATE	LIMB
GREY	HALO	HIED	HOWL	INIA	JIVE	KAYO	KNOT	LATH	LIME
GRID	HALT	HIES	HOWS	INKS	JIZZ	KAYS	KNOW	LATS	LIMN
GRIG	HAME	HIGH	HOYA	INKY	JOBE	KAZI	KNUB	LAUD	LIMO
GRIM	HAMS	HIKE	HOYS	INLY	JOCK	KEAS	KNUR	LAUF	LIMP
GRIN	HAND	HILA	HUBS	INNS	JOCO	KEBS	KNUT	LAVA	LIMY
GRIP	HANG	HILD	HUCK	INRO	JOES	KECK	KOAN	LAVE	LIND

LINE	LOWT	MARC	MIDS	MOPE	NAOI	NOGS	OFFS	OURN	PEAN
LING	LOYS	MARD	MIEN	MOPS	NAOS	NOIL	OGAM	OURS	PEAR
LINK	LUAU	MARE	MIFF	MOPY	NAPA	NOLE	OGEE	OUST	PEAS
LINN	LUCE	MARG	MIKE	MORA	NAPE	NOLL	OGLE	OUTS	PEAT
LINO	LUCK	MARK	MILD	MORE	NAPS	NOMA	OGRE	OUZO	PEBA
LINS	LUDO	MARL	MILE	MORN	NARC	NOME	OHMS	OVAL	PECH
LINT	LUDS	MARM	MILK	MORS	NARD	NOMS	OHOS	OVEN	PECK
LINY	LUES	MARS	MILL	MORT	NARE	NONE	OIKS	OVER	PECS
LION	LUFF	MART	MILO	MOSE	NARK	NONG	OILS	OVUM	PEDS
LIPS	LUGE	MARY	MILS	MOSS	NARY	NOOK	OILY	OWED	PEED
LIRA	LUGS	MASA	MILT	MOST	NATS	NOON	OINK	OWER	PEEK
LIRE	LUIT	MASE	MIME	MOTE	NAVE	NOOP	OINT	OWES	PEEL
LIRK	LUKE	MASH	MINA	MOTH	NAVY	NOPE	OKAY	OWLS	PEEN
LISK	LULL	MASK	MIND	MOTS	NAYS	NORI	OKES	OWLY	PEEP
LISP	LULU	MASS	MINE	MOTT	NAZE	NORM	OKRA	OWNS	PEER
LIST	LUMP	MAST	MING	MOTU	NEAL	NORK	OKTA	OWRE	PEES
LITE	LUMS	MASU	MINI	MOUE	NEAP	NOSE	OLDS	OWTS	PEGH
LITH	LUNA	MATE	MINK	MOUP	NEAR	NOSH	OLDY	OXEN	PEGS
LIVE	LUNE	MATH	MINO	MOUS	NEAT	NOSY	OLEO	OXER	PEIN
LOAD	LUNG	MATS	MINT	MOVE	NEBS	NOTA	OLID	OYER	PEKE
LOAF	LUNT	MATT	MINX	MOWA	NECK	NOTE	OLIO	OYES	PELA
LOAM	LURE	MATY	MINY	MOWN	NEDS	NOTT	OLLA	OYEZ	PELE
LOAN	LURK	MAUD	MIRE	MOWS	NEED	NOUL	OLMS		PELF
LOBE	LURS	MAUL	MIRI	MOXA	NEEM	NOUN	OLPE	PACA	PELL
LOBI	LUSH	MAUN	MIRK	MOYA	NEEP	NOUP	OMBU	PACE	PELT
LOBO	LUSK	MAWK	MIRS	MOYL	NEFS	NOUS	OMEN	PACK	PEND
LOBS	LUST	MAWR	MIRV	MOYS	NEIF	NOUT	OMER	PACO	PENE
LOCH	LUTE	MAWS	MIRY	MOZE	NEKS	NOVA	OMIT	PACT	PENI
LOCI	LUTZ	MAXI	MISE	MOZZ	NEMN	NOWL	ONCE	PACY	PENK
LOCK	LUVS	MAYA	MISO	MUCH	NENE	NOWN	ONER	PADS	PENS
LOCO	LUXE	MAYS	MISS	MUCK	NEON	NOWS	ONES	PAGE	PENT
LODE	LYAM	MAZE	MIST	MUDS	NEPS	NOWT	ONLY	PAHS	PEON
LODS	LYES	MAZY	MITE	MUFF	NERD	NOWY	ONST	PAID	PEPO
LOFT	LYME	MEAD	MITT	MUGS	NERK	NOYS	ONTO	PAIK	PEPS
LOGE	LYMS	MEAL	MITY	MUID	NESH	NUBS	ONUS	PAIL	PERE
LOGO	LYNE	MEAN	MIXT	MUIL	NESS	NUDE	ONYX	PAIN	PERI
LOGS	LYNX	MEAT	MIXY	MUIR	NEST	NUFF	OOFS	PAIR	PERK
LOGY	LYRE	MEED	MIZZ	MULE	NETE	NUKE	OOHS	PAIS	PERM
LOID	LYSE	MEEK	MNAS	MULL	NETS	NULL	OOMS	PALE	PERN
LOIN	LYTE	MEER	MOAN	MUMM	NETT	NUMB	OONS	PALL	PERT
LOIR		MEET	MOAS	MUMP	NEUK	NUNS	OONT	PALM	PERV
LOKE	MAAR	MEGA	MOAT	MUMS	NEUM	NURD	OOPS	PALP	PESO
LOLL	MAAS	MEGS	MOBS	MUNT	NEVE	NURL	OOSE	PALS	PEST
LOMA	MACE	MEIN	MOCH	MUON	NEVI	NURR	OOSY	PALY	PETS
LOME	MACK	MELA	MOCK	MURE	NEWS	NURS	OOZE	PAMS	PEWS
LONE	MACS	MELD	MODE	MURK	NEWT	NUTS	OOZY	PAND	PHAT
LONG	MADE	MELL	MODI	MURL	NEXT	NYAS	OPAH	PANE	PHEW
LOOF	MADS	MELS	MODS	MUSE	NIBS	NYED	OPAL	PANG	PHIS
LOOK	MAGE	MELT	MOES	MUSH	NICE	NYES	OPED	PANS	PHIZ
LOOM	MAGG	MEME	MOGS	MUSK	NICK		OPEN	PANT	PHOH
LOON	MAGI	MEMO	MOHR	MUSO	NIDE		OPES	PAPA	PHON
LOOP	MAGS	MEND	MOIL	MUSS	NIDI	OAFS	OPPO	PAPE	PHOS
LOOR	MAID	MENE	MOIT	MUST	NIDS	OAKS	OPTS	PAPS	PHOT
LOOS	MAIK	MENG	MOJO	MUTE	NIED	OAKY	OPUS	PARA	PHUT
LOOT	MAIL	MENT	MOKE	MUTI	NIEF	OARS	ORAL	PARD	PIAS
LOPE	MAIM	MENU	MOKI	MUTT	NIES	OARY	ORBS	PARE	PICA
LOPS	MAIN	MEOW	MOKO	MYAL	NIFE	OAST	ORBY	PARK	PICE
LORD	MAIR	MERC	MOLA	MYNA	NIFF	OATH	ORCA	PARP	PICK
LORE	MAKE	MERE	MOLD	MYTH	NIGH	OATS	ORCS	PARR	PICS
LORN	MAKO	MERI	MOLE	MZEE	NILL	OBAS	ORDS	PARS	PIED
LORY	MAKS	MERK	MOLL		NILS	OBEY	ORES	PART	PIER
LOSE	MALE	MERL	MOLT		NIMB	OBIA	ORFE	PASH	PIES
LOSH	MALI	MESA	MOLY		NIMS	OBIS	ORFS	PASS	PIET
LOSS	MALL	MESE	MOME		NINE	OBIT	ORGY	PAST	PIGS
LOST	MALM	MESH	MOMS		NIPA	OBOE	ORLE	PATE	PIKA
LOTA	MALS	MESS	MONA		NIPS	OBOL	ORRA	PATH	PIKE
LOTE	MALT	METE	MONG		NIRL	OBOS	ORTS	PATS	PILA
LOTH	MAMA	METS	MONK		NISI	OCAS	ORYX	PAUA	PILE
LOTO	MAMS	MEUS	MONO		NITE	OCHE	ORZO	PAUL	PILI
LOTS	MANA	MEVE	MONY		NITS	OCTA	OSSA	PAVE	PILL
LOUD	MAND	MEWL	MOOD		NIXY	ODAL	OTIC	PAWA	PIMP
LOUN	MANE	MEWS	MOOI		NOBS	ODAS	OTTO	PAWK	PINA
LOUP	MANG	MEZE	MOOK		NOCK	ODEA	OUCH	PAWL	PINE
LOUR	MANI	MHOS	MOOL		NODE	ODES	OUDS	PAWN	PING
LOUT	MANO	MICA	MOON		NODI	ODIC	OUKS	PAWS	PINK
LOVE	MANS	MICE	MOOP		NODS	ODOR	OULD	PAYS	PINS
LOWE	MANY	MICK	MOOR		NOEL	ODSO	OULK	PEAG	PINT
LOWN	MAPS	MICO	MOOS		NOES	ODYL	OUPH	PEAK	PINY
LOWS	MARA	MIDI	MOOT		NOGG	OFAY	OUPS	PEAL	PION

PIOY	POSE	PUTT	RAVE	RIOT	RUED	SAWS	SHAM	SKEW	SOHO
PIPA	POSH	PUTZ	RAWN	RIPE	RUES	SAYS	SHAN	SKID	SOHS
PIPE	POSS	PUYS	RAWS	RIPP	RUFF	SCAB	SHAT	SKIM	SOIL
PIPI	POST	PYAT	RAYS	RIPS	RUGS	SCAD	SHAW	SKIN	SOJA
PIPS	POSY	PYES	RAZE	RIPT	RUIN	SCAG	SHAY	SKIO	SOKE
PIPY	POTE	PYET	RAZZ	RISE	RUKH	SCAM	SHEA	SKIP	SOLA
PIRL	POTS	PYNE	READ	RISK	RULE	SCAN	SHED	SKIS	SOLD
PIRN	POTT	PYOT	REAK	RISP	RULY	SCAR	SHES	SKIT	SOLE
PIRS	POUF	PYRE	REAM	RITE	RUME	SCAT	SHET	SKOL	SOLI
PISE	POUK	PYRO	REAN	RITS	RUMP	SCAW	SHEW	SKRY	SOLO
PISH	POUR		REAP	RITT	RUMS	SCOG	SHIM	SKUA	SOLS
PISS	POUT		REAR	RIVA	RUND	SCOP	SHIN	SKUG	SOMA
PITA	POWN	QADI	RECK	RIVE	RUNE	SCOT	SHIP	SKYR	SOME
PITH	POWS	QATS	RECS	RIVO	RUNG	SCOW	SHIR	SLAB	SONE
PITS	POXY	QOPH	REDD	ROAD	RUNS	SCRY	SHIT	SLAE	SONG
PITY	POZZ	QUAD	REDE	ROAM	RUNT	SCUD	SHIV	SLAG	SONS
PIUM	PRAD	QUAG	REDO	ROAN	RURP	SCUG	SHMO	SLAM	SOOK
PIXY	PRAM	QUAT	REDS	ROAR	RURU	SCUL	SHOD	SLAP	SOOM
PIZE	PRAT	QUAY	REED	ROBE	RUSA	SCUM	SHOE	SLAT	SOON
PLAN	PRAU	QUEP	REEF	ROBS	RUSE	SCUP	SHOG	SLAW	SOOP
PLAP	PRAY	QUEY	REEK	ROCH	RUSH	SCUR	SHOO	SLAY	SOOT
PLAT	PREE	QUID	REEL	ROCK	RUSK	SCUT	SHOP	SLED	SOPH
PLAY	PREP	QUIM	REEN	ROCS	RUST	SCYE	SHOT	SLEE	SOPS
PLEA	PREX	QUIN	REES	RODE	RUTH	SEAL	SHOW	SLEW	SORA
PLEB	PREY	QUIP	REFS	RODS	RUTS	SEAM	SHUL	SLEY	SORB
PLED	PRIG	QUIT	REFT	ROED	RYAL	SEAN	SHUN	SLID	SORD
PLIE	PRIM	QUIZ	REGO	ROES	RYAS	SEAR	SHUT	SLIM	SORE
PLIM	PROA	QUOD	REHS	ROIL	RYES	SEAS	SHWA	SLIP	SORI
PLOD	PROB	QUOP	REIF	ROIN	RYFE	SEAT	SIAL	SLIT	SORN
PLOP	PROD		REIK	ROJI	RYKE	SECO	SIBB	SLOB	SORT
PLOT	PROF	RABI	REIN	ROKE	RYND	SECS	SIBS	SLOE	SOSS
PLOW	PROG	RACA	REIS	ROKS	RYOT	SECT	SICE	SLOG	SOTS
PLOY	PROM	RACE	REKE	ROKY	RYPE	SEED	SICH	SLOP	SOUK
PLUG	PROO	RACH	RELY	ROLE		SEEK	SICK	SLOT	SOUL
PLUM	PROP	RACK	REMS	ROLL	SABS	SEEL	SICS	SLOW	SOUM
PLUS	PROS	RACY	REND	ROMA	SACK	SEEM	SIDA	SLUB	SOUP
POAS	PROW	RADE	RENS	ROMP	SACS	SEEN	SIDE	SLUE	SOUR
POCK	PRUH	RADS	RENT	RONE	SADE	SEEP	SIEN	SLUG	SOUS
POCO	PRYS	RAFF	RENY	RONG	SAFE	SEER	SIFT	SLUM	SOUT
PODS	PSIS	RAFT	REPO	RONT	SAGA	SEGO	SIGH	SLUR	SOVS
POEM	PSST	RAGA	REPP	ROOD	SAGE	SEGS	SIGN	SLUT	SOWF
POET	PUBS	RAGE	REPS	ROOF	SAGO	SEIF	SIJO	SMEE	SOWL
POGO	PUCE	RAGG	REST	ROOK	SAGS	SEIK	SIKA	SMEW	SOWM
POIS	PUCK	RAGI	RETE	ROOM	SAGY	SEIL	SIKE	SMIR	SOWN
POKE	PUDS	RAGS	RETS	ROON	SAIC	SEIR	SILD	SMIT	SOWP
POKY	PUDU	RAHS	REVS	ROOP	SAID	SEIS	SILE	SMOG	SOWS
POLE	PUER	RAID	REWS	ROOS	SAIL	SEKT	SILK	SMUG	SOYA
POLK	PUFF	RAIK	RHEA	ROOT	SAIM	SELD	SILL	SMUR	SOYS
POLL	PUGH	RAIL	RHOS	ROPE	SAIN	SELE	SILO	SMUT	SPAE
POLO	PUGS	RAIN	RHUS	ROPY	SAIR	SELF	SILT	SNAB	SPAG
POLT	PUIR	RAIS	RIAL	RORE	SAIS	SELL	SIMA	SNAG	SPAM
POLY	PUJA	RAIT	RIAS	RORT	SAKE	SELS	SIMI	SNAP	SPAN
POME	PUKE	RAJA	RIBS	RORY	SAKI	SEME	SIMP	SNAR	SPAR
POMP	PUKU	RAKE	RICE	ROSE	SALE	SEMI	SIMS	SNEB	SPAS
POMS	PULA	RAKI	RICH	ROST	SALP	SENA	SIND	SNED	SPAT
POND	PULE	RAKU	RICK	ROSY	SALS	SEND	SINE	SNEE	SPAW
PONE	PULK	RALE	RICY	ROTA	SALT	SENS	SING	SNIB	SPAY
PONG	PULP	RAMI	RIDE	ROTE	SAMA	SENT	SINK	SNIG	SPEC
PONK	PULU	RAMP	RIDS	ROTI	SAME	SEPS	SINS	SNIP	SPED
PONS	PULY	RAMS	RIEL	ROTL	SAMP	SEPT	SIPE	SNOB	SPEK
PONT	PUMA	RANA	RIEM	ROTS	SAND	SERA	SIPS	SNOD	SPET
PONY	PUMP	RAND	RIFE	ROUE	SANE	SERE	SIRE	SNOG	SPEW
POOD	PUMY	RANG	RIFF	ROUL	SANG	SERF	SIRI	SNOT	SPIC
POOF	PUNA	RANI	RIFT	ROUM	SANK	SERK	SIRS	SNOW	SPIE
POOH	PUNK	RANK	RIGG	ROUP	SANS	SERR	SISS	SNUB	SPIK
POOK	PUNS	RANT	RIGS	ROUT	SANT	SESE	SIST	SNUG	SPIN
POOL	PUNT	RAPE	RILE	ROUX	SAPS	SESS	SITE	SNYE	SPIT
POON	PUNY	RAPS	RILL	ROVE	SARD	SETA	SITH	SOAK	SPIV
POOP	PUPA	RAPT	RIMA	ROWS	SARI	SETS	SITS	SOAP	SPOT
POOR	PUPS	RARE	RIME	ROWT	SARK	SETT	SIZE	SOAR	SPRY
POOS	PURE	RASE	RIMS	RUBE	SARS	SEWN	SIZY	SOBS	SPUD
POOT	PURI	RASH	RIMU	RUBS	SASH	SEWS	SKAG	SOCA	SPUE
POPE	PURL	RASP	RIMY	RUBY	SASS	SEXT	SKAS	SOCK	SPUN
POPS	PURR	RAST	RIND	RUCK	SATE	SEXY	SKAT	SOCS	SPUR
PORE	PURS	RATA	RINE	RUCS	SATI	SEYS	SKAW	SODA	STAB
PORK	PUSH	RATE	RING	RUDD	SAUL	SHAD	SKEG	SODS	STAG
PORN	PUSS	RATH	RINK	RUDE	SAUT	SHAG	SKEO	SOFA	STAP
PORT	PUTS	RATS	RINS	RUDS	SAVE	SHAH	SKEP	SOFT	STAR
PORY		RATU			SAWN		SKER	SOGS	STAW
		RAUN							

STAY	TABS	TEER	TIPI	TRAM	TYTE	VEER	WAES	WELT	WONT
STED	TABU	TEES	TIPS	TRAP	TZAR	VEES	WAFF	WEMB	WOOD
STEM	TACE	TEFF	TIPT	TRAT		VEGA	WAFT	WEMS	WOOF
STEN	TACH	TEFS	TIRE	TRAY	UDAL	VEHM	WAGE	WEND	WOOL
STEP	TACK	TEGG	TIRL	TREE	UDOS	VEIL	WAGS	WENS	WOON
STET	TACO	TEGS	TIRO	TREF	UEYS	VEIN	WAID	WENT	WOOS
STEW	TACT	TEGU	TIRR	TREK	UFOS	VELA	WAIF	WERE	WOOT
STEY	TADS	TEHR	TITE	TRES	UGHS	VELD	WAIL	WERT	WOPS
STIE	TAED	TEIL	TITI	TRET	UGLY	VELE	WAIN	WEST	WORD
STIR	TAEL	TELA	TITS	TREW	UKES	VELL	WAIT	WETA	WORE
STOA	TAES	TELD	TIZZ	TREY	ULES	VENA	WAKA	WETS	WORK
STOB	TAGS	TELL	TOAD	TREZ	ULEX	VEND	WAKE	WEXE	WORM
STOP	TAHA	TELS	TOBY	TRIE	ULNA	VENT	WAKF	WEYS	WORN
STOT	TAHR	TELT	TOCK	TRIG	UMBO	VERB	WALD	WHAM	WORT
STOW	TAIL	TEME	TOCO	TRIM	UMPH	VERS	WALE	WHAP	WOST
STUB	TAIS	TEMP	TOCS	TRIN	UNAU	VERT	WALI	WHAT	WOTS
STUD	TAIT	TEMS	TODS	TRIO	UNBE	VERY	WALK	WHEE	WOVE
STUM	TAKA	TEND	TODY	TRIP	UNCE	VEST	WALL	WHEN	WOWF
STUN	TAKE	TENE	TOEA	TROD	UNCI	VETO	WALY	WHET	WOWS
STYE	TAKI	TENS	TOED	TROG	UNCO	VETS	WAME	WHEW	WRAP
SUBS	TAKS	TENT	TOES	TRON	UNDE	VEXT	WAND	WHEY	WREN
SUCH	TAKY	TERF	TOEY	TROT	UNDO	VIAE	WANE	WHID	WRIT
SUCK	TALA	TERM	TOFF	TROW	UNIS	VIAL	WANG	WHIG	WUDS
SUDD	TALC	TERN	TOFT	TROY	UNIT	VIAS	WANK	WHIM	WULL
SUDS	TALE	TEST	TOFU	TRUE	UNTO	VIBE	WANS	WHIN	WUSS
SUED	TALI	TETE	TOGA	TRUG	UPAS	VIBS	WANT	WHIP	WYCH
SUER	TALK	TEWS	TOGE	TRYE	UPBY	VICE	WANY	WHIR	WYES
SUES	TALL	TEXT	TOGS	TRYP	UPGO	VIDE	WAPS	WHIT	WYND
SUET	TAME	THAE	TOHO	TSAR	UPON	VIDS	WAQF	WHIZ	WYNN
SUID	TAMP	THAN	TOIL	TUAN	UPSY	VIED	WARD	WHOA	WYNS
SUIT	TAMS	THAR	TOKE	TUBA	URAO	VIER	WARE	WHOM	WYTE
SUKH	TANA	THAT	TOKO	TUBE	URDE	VIES	WARK	WHOP	
SUKS	TANE	THAW	TOLA	TUBS	URDS	VIEW	WARM	WHOW	XYST
SULK	TANG	THEE	TOLD	TUCK	URDY	VILD	WARN	WHOT	
SULU	TANH	THEM	TOLE	TUFA	UREA	VILE	WARP		YACK
SUMO	TANK	THEN	TOLL	TUFF	URES	VILL	WARS	WICE	YAFF
SUMP	TANS	THEW	TOLT	TUFT	URGE	VIMS	WART	WICH	YAHS
SUMS	TAPA	THEY	TOLU	TUGS	URIC	VINA	WARY	WICK	YAKS
SUNG	TAPE	THIG	TOMB	TUIS	URNS	VINE	WASE	WIDE	YALD
SUNK	TAPS	THIN	TOME	TULE	URUS	VINO	WASH	WIEL	YALE
SUNN	TAPU	THIR	TOMS	TUMP	URVA	VINS	WASM	WIFE	YAMS
SUNS	TARA	THIS	TONE	TUMS	USED	VINT	WASP	WIGS	YANG
SUPE	TARE	THON	TONG	TUNA	USER	VINY	WAST	WILD	YANK
SUPS	TARN	THOU	TONK	TUND	USES	VIOL	WATE	WILE	YAPP
SUQS	TARO	THRO	TONS	TUNE	UTAS	VIRE	WATS	WILI	YAPS
SURA	TARP	THRU	TONY	TUNS	UTES	VIRL	WATT	WILL	YARD
SURD	TARS	THUD	TOOK	TUNY	UTIS	VISA	WAUK	WILT	YARE
SURE	TART	THUG	TOOL	TUPS	UTUS	VISE	WAUL	WILY	YARN
SURF	TASH	THUS	TOOM	TURD	UVAE	VITA	WAUR	WIMP	YARR
SUSS	TASK	TIAR	TOON	TURF	UVAS	VITE	WAVE	WIND	YATE
SWAB	TASS	TICE	TOOT	TURM	UVEA	VIVA	WAVY	WINE	YAUD
SWAD	TATE	TICH	TOPE	TURN		VIVE	WAWE	WING	YAUP
SWAG	TATH	TICK	TOPI	TUSH		VIVO	WAWL	WINK	YAWL
SWAM	TATS	TICS	TOPS	TUSK	VACS	VIZY	WAWS	WINN	YAWN
SWAN	TATT	TIDE	TORC	TUTS	VADE	VLEI	WAYS	WINO	YAWP
SWAP	TATU	TIDS	TORE	TUTU	VAES	VOAR	WEAK	WINS	YAWS
SWAT	TAUS	TIDY	TORI	TUZZ	VAGI	VOES	WEAL	WINY	YAWY
SWAY	TAUT	TIED	TORN	TWAE	VAIL	VOID	WEAN	WIPE	YBET
SWEE	TAVA	TIER	TORR	TWAL	VAIN	VOLA	WEAR	WIRE	YEAD
SWEY	TAWA	TIES	TORS	TWAS	VAIR	VOLE	WEBS	WIRY	YEAH
SWIG	TAWS	TIFF	TORT	TWAT	VALE	VOLK	WEDS	WISE	YEAN
SWIM	TAWT	TIFT	TOSA	TWAY	VALI	VOLS	WEED	WISH	YEAR
SWIZ	TAXA	TIGE	TOSE	TWEE	VAMP	VOLT	WEEK	WISP	YEAS
SWOB	TAXI	TIGS	TOSH	TWIG	VANE	VORS	WEEL	WIST	YECH
SWOP	TAYS	TIKA	TOSS	TWIN	VANG	VOTE	WEEM	WITE	YEDE
SWOT	TEAD	TIKE	TOST	TWIT	VANS	VOWS	WEEN	WITH	YEED
SWUM	TEAK	TIKI	TOTE	TWOS	VANT	VRIL	WEEP	WITS	YEGG
SYBO	TEAL	TILE	TOTS	TYDE	VARA	VROW	WEER	WIVE	YELD
SYCE	TEAM	TILL	TOUK	TYED	VARE	VUGS	WEES	WOAD	YELK
SYED	TEAR	TILS	TOUN	TYES	VARY	VULN	WEET	WOCK	YELL
SYEN	TEAS	TILT	TOUR	TYGS	VASA	VUMS	WEFT	WOES	YELM
SYES	TEAT	TIME	TOUT	TYKE	VASE		WEID	WOGS	YELP
SYKE	TECH	TIND	TOWN	TYMP	VAST	WACK	WEIL	WOKE	YELT
SYNC	TEDS	TINE	TOWS	TYND	VATS	WADD	WEIR	WOKS	YENS
SYND	TEDY	TING	TOWT	TYNE	VATU	WADE	WEKA	WOLD	YEPS
SYNE	TEED	TINK	TOWY	TYPE	VAUS	WADI	WELD	WOLF	YERD
SYPE	TEEL	TINS	TOYS	TYPO	VAUT	WADS	WELK	WOMB	YERK
	TEEM	TINT	TOZE	TYRE	VEAL	WADT	WELL	WONK	YESK
TABI	TEEN	TINY	TRAD	TYRO	VEEP	WADY		WONS	YEST

YETI	YIRK	YOGI	YORE	YUGA	YWIS	ZEDS	ZIGS	ZOBO	ZOUK
YETT	YITE	YOKE	YORK	YUGS		ZEES	ZILA	ZOBU	ZULU
YEUK	YLEM	YOKS	YOUK	YUKE	ZACK	ZEIN	ZIMB	ZOEA	ZUPA
YEVE	YLKE	YOLD	YOUR	YUKO	ZAGS	ZEKS	ZINC	ZOIC	ZURF
YEWS	YMPE	YOLK	YOWE	YUKS	ZANY	ZELS	ZINE	ZONA	ZYGA
YGOE	YMPT	YOMP	YOWL	YUKY	ZAPS	ZERO	ZING	ZONE	ZYME
YIKE	YOBS	YOND	YOWS	YULE	ZARF	ZEST	ZIPS	ZONK	
YILL	YOCK	YONI	YUAN	YUMP	ZATI	ZETA	ZITE	ZOOM	
YINS	YODE	YONT	YUCA	YUNX	ZEAL	ZEZE	ZITI	ZOON	
YIPS	YOGA	YOOF	YUCK	YUPS	ZEAS	ZHOS	ZITS	ZOOS	
YIRD	YOGH	YOOP	YUFT	YURT	ZEBU	ZIFF	ZIZZ	ZORI	

Think Big – Think Bonus

One of the reasons that some players struggle to play all seven letters for a 50-point bonus is that they don't believe they can achieve such plays and are reluctant to look very hard. The letter distribution of the Scrabble set is such that, if you concentrate on using the higher-scoring consonants and keep the flexible letters (such as those in RETAINS), you are likely to have a bonus word sooner or later. But you must train yourself to believe there could always be a bonus word to find and constantly ask yourself with each fresh rack 'Is there a bonus word here?' before looking for alternative plays.

Your expectation should be particularly high if you have, say, seven different letters including an E and two other vowels. For example, would you bother to look for a bonus with AEFILNT or DEGILUV? The words are the common words INFLATE and DIVULGE of course!

Sometimes even the most unlikely of racks can yield a surprise bonus word. Would you be inspired to look for a bonus with the racks GHORTUW or AACCNVY for example? Check the Anagram Section for the answers to these!

So, get into the habit of *thinking big* every turn. If nothing leaps out at you then move the tiles around on your rack, or try making common endings and beginnings. You never know when a FOGHORN or a VIADUCT is going to turn up on your rack. Also, don't forget that knowledge of the 2-letter words can be vital for finding somewhere to slot in your bonus. There's nothing more disappointing than finding a brilliant MUGWUMP and not knowing the word MI, say, to slot it in.

Practising with Plates

A convenient way to practise Scrabble vocabulary whilst travelling by car is to find words from car number plates. There are a number of Scrabble games playable (if you're not the driver!):

☆ Find the shortest word containing the three letters of the number plate (ignoring the letter denoting the year).

☆ Look for 7-letter words by converting the numerals to letters thus (1=I, 2=Z, 3=E, 4=A, 5=S, 6=G, 7=T, 8=B, 9=G, 0=O) eg DGF 105H makes DOGFISH!

☆ Look for 7-letter words by taking the four letters and adding the letters A E I, or I E S, or similar, to give a good 'rack'.

Suspicious Minds

Don't be suspicious of all your opponent's moves. It is often better to play to the strength of your own rack and think about your scoring potential than to worry too much about whether your opponent's play is a set-up for a good score next turn. Even amongst top players there are few occasions when there is a deliberate set-up play.

Tile Turnover

An additional consideration when deciding upon the best move is the number of tiles you use. Although other factors such as the score, the balance of the letters left on your rack and the openness of the move, are just as important, the basic philosophy that using more tiles than your opponent increases your chances of getting any of the good tiles remaining in the bag cannot be completely ignored.

When faced with a choice of moves with a poor rack, more often than not the play using most tiles is the one to favour. The exception is when the only tiles remaining are the awkward tiles that you would rather avoid (eg the Q and the V's). Keeping track of the tiles played is advantageous in judging the value of a high turnover play but ultimately you are at the mercy of your own discretion.

Light and Heavy Words

Light words

Light words are those with many vowels, excluding Y. These words are useful for using up excessive vowels on your rack, in an attempt to return to a more balanced rack. The numbers of vowels for words of various lengths in these lists are given here:

2-letter words, 2 vowels (eg AE, OI)

3-letter words, 3 vowels (AIA, EAU)

4-letter words, 3 vowels or more (eg EUOI, IOTA)

5-letter words, 4 vowels (eg AUDIO, QUEUE)

6-letter words, 4 vowels or more (eg COOKIE, LEAGUE)

7-letter words, 5 vowels or more (eg ANAEMIA, EVACUEE)

8-letter words, 5 vowels or more (eg ALIENATE, ORATORIO)

To help you learn and recall words with many vowels, words of four or more letters are listed according to the vowel groups they contain. For example, ANEMIA and AVIATE are both listed in the group of 6-letter words having the vowels AAEI.

Heavy words

Heavy words are those with many consonants. These are useful for discarding excessive consonants from your rack, again in an attempt to return to a more balanced rack. The numbers of vowels for words of various lengths in these lists are given here:

2-letter words, no vowels except Y (eg MY, SH)

3-letter words, no vowels except Y (eg FRY, NTH)

4-letter words, no vowels except Y (eg HYMN, YMPT)

5-letter words, no vowels except Y (eg CRWTH, NYMPH)

6-letter words, 1 vowel (eg CHINTZ, RHYTHM)

To avoid the heavy word lists ballooning in size, inflections ending in -S have been omitted.

When you want to recall words with many consonants, try to home in on words with frequently-occurring clumps of letters – for example, CH, GHT, NCH, PH, SCH, SCR, TCH and TH. Of course, there are many others.

Light Words (Many Vowels)

2-letter words – 2 vowels

AA	AE	AI	EA	EE	IO	OE	OI	OO	OU

3-letter words – 3 vowels

AIA   EAU

4-letter words – 3 vowels or more (by vowel content)

AAE: ALAE, AREA
AAI: AIAS, ARIA
AAO: ANOA
AAU: AQUA, AULA, AURA, PAUA
AEE: AGEE, AJEE, AKEE, ALEE, EALE, EASE
AEI: AIDE, AINE, AMIE, IDEA, ILEA, KAIE, VIAE
AEO: AEON, AERO, ALOE, EOAN, ODEA, TOEA, ZOEA
AEU: AGUE, AUNE, BEAU, EAUS, EAUX, UREA, UVAE, UVEA
AII: ILIA, INIA, IXIA
AIO: AGIO, CIAO, IOTA, JIAO, NAOI, OBIA
AIU: AITU, HUIA
AOU: AUTO, URAO
AUU: LUAU, UNAU
EEE: EPEE
EEI: EINE, IDEE
EEO: EVOE, OGEE
EEU: EMEU, EUGE
EIOU: EUOI
EIU: ETUI, IURE, LIEU
EOO: OBOE, OLEO, OOSE, OOZE
EOU: EURO, MOUE, ROUE
IOO: MOOI, OLIO
OOU: OUZO

5-letter words – 4 vowels or more (by vowel content)

AAEI: AECIA
AAEU: AQUAE, AURAE
AEEI: AERIE, AINEE
AEEO: ZOEAE
AEIU: ADIEU, AUREI, URAEI
AEOO: ZOOEA
AIIO: AIDOI, AIOLI, OIDIA
AIOU: AUDIO, AULOI, OUIJA
EEEI: EERIE
EEOO: COOEE
EEUU: QUEUE
EIOO: OORIE
EIOU: OURIE

6-letter words – 4 vowels or more (by vowel content)

AAAE: AGAPAE, AZALEA
AAAI: ACACIA, ALALIA, ARALIA, ATAXIA, TAIAHA
AAAU: UJAMAA
AAEE: AERATE, AMEBAE, EATAGE, GALEAE, PALEAE, PERAEA, TALEAE
AAEI: ABELIA, ACEDIA, AERIAL, ALEXIA, AMELIA, ANEMIA, ARAISE, AVAILE, AVIATE, LAMIAE, REALIA, TAENIA
AAEO: AMOEBA, AORTAE, APNOEA, AREOLA, OARAGE, OZAENA
AAEU: ALULAE, AUBADE, AURATE, BATEAU, BAUERA, CADEAU, CAUSAE, FAUNAE, GATEAU, NAUSEA
AAII: HAIKAI, KAIKAI
AAIO: ADAGIO, AIKONA, ALOGIA, ANOXIA, APORIA, ATOCIA, COAITA, ORARIA, ZOARIA
AAIU: ABULIA, ANURIA, AUMAIL, IGUANA, QUALIA, UAKARI
AAOO: MANOAO
AAOU: ACAJOU, AGOUTA, AMADOU, AOUDAD, AURORA
AAUU: AUCUBA
AEEI: AEDILE, AERIER, AERIES, APIECE, BAILEE, BEANIE, DEARIE, DEAWIE, EASIER, EPEIRA, FAERIE, HEARIE, IDEAED, IDEATE, KEAVIE, LAESIE, MEALIE, MEANIE, MEDIAE, PEREIA, REDIAE, SEMEIA, TENIAE
AEEO: AEROBE, APOGEE, AREOLE, COATEE, EVOVAE, FOVEAE, GOATEE, OCREAE, OEDEMA, OLEATE
AEEOO: ZOOEAE
AEEOUU: EUOUAE
AEEU: AEMULE, AVENUE, ELUATE, EPAULE, EQUATE, EUREKA, FEAGUE, HEAUME, LEAGUE, QUAERE, QUELEA, RESEAU, UNEASE
AEII: AIRIER, BAILIE, LIAISE, SAIKEI, TIBIAE
AEIO: ANOMIE, AZIONE, BOATIE, EIDOLA, EPIZOA, FEIJOA, GOALIE, IODATE, LEIPOA, OAKIER, OARIER, OBELIA, OPIATE, ROADIE, ROARIE, SOAPIE
AEIU: ACULEI, ADIEUS, ADIEUX, AECIUM, AGUISE, AGUIZE, AUDILE, AUGITE, AUNTIE, CAIQUE, CURIAE, DAUTIE, ELUVIA, EUCAIN, GAUCIE, GUINEA, HAIQUE, SAIQUE, SAULIE, TAUPIE, UREDIA, UREMIA
AEOO: AMOOVE, ZOOEAL, ZOOEAS
AEOU: AROUSE, AVOURE, COTEAU, DOUANE, OPAQUE, OUTAGE, OUTATE, OUTEAT
AEUU: AUREUS, AUTEUR, BUREAU, URAEUS, UVULAE
AIIO: AIKIDO, AIOLIS, ARIOSI, DAIMIO
AIOO: ARIOSO, OOIDAL, OOMIAC, OOMIAK, OORIAL
AIOU: AGOUTI, AUDIOS, BAGUIO, GIAOUR, OUIJAS, OURALI, OURARI, QUINOA, SOUARI, UTOPIA
AOOU: VAUDOO
AOUU: AUROUS
EEEE: PEEWEE, TEEPEE
EEEI: DEEPIE, EELIER, EERIER, FEERIE, HEEZIE, JEELIE, KEELIE, MEEMIE, PEERIE, REEKIE, WEEPIE
EEEO: EPOPEE
EEEU: EKUELE, EMEUTE
EEII: KIERIE, MEINIE, WIENIE
EEIO: ETOILE, OREIDE, SOIREE, TOEIER, VOIDEE
EEIU: ECURIE, EPUISE, EQUINE, EQUIPE, UREIDE
EEOO: BOOTEE, COOEED, COOEES, SOOGEE, TOETOE
EEOU: COULEE, COUPEE, EVOLUE, OEUVRE, TOUPEE
EEUU: QUEUED, QUEUES
EIIO: IODIDE, IODINE, IODISE, IODIZE, IOLITE, IONISE, IONIZE, OILIER
EIIU: EURIPI

MILIEU	HOODIE	ROOMIE	TOURIE	KOUROI
QUINIE	IONONE	SOOGIE	TOUTIE	ODIOUS
EIOO BOODIE	KOOKIE	TOORIE	EIUU UBIQUE	OOOO BOOBOO
BOOGIE	LOONIE	WOODIE	UNIQUE	GOOROO
BOOKIE	NOOKIE	WOOPIE	EOOO HOOPOE	HOODOO
COOKIE	OOLITE	EIOU BOUGIE	EOOU QUOOKE	HOOROO
COOLIE	OORIER	MOUSIE	EOOU UVEOUS	KOODOO
COOTIE	OOSIER	OUGLIE	IIOO OPIOID	VOODOO
DOOLIE	OOZIER	OUREBI	TOITOI	ZOOZOO
FOODIE	ORIOLE	OURIER	IIOU IONIUM	OOUU ROUCOU
FOOTIE	OROIDE	OUTLIE	OIDIUM	VOUDOU
GOOIER	OTIOSE	OUTVIE	IIUU PIUPIU	
GOOLIE	ROOKIE	POURIE	IOOU IODOUS	

7-letter words – 5 vowels or more (by vowel content)

AAAEI ANAEMIA	OLEARIA	RAOULIA	EXUVIAE	MOINEAU
AAAIU AQUARIA	AAEIU AURELIA	SAOUARI	AEEOU AENEOUS	SEQUOIA
AAEEI TAENIAE	CAMAIEU	AEEEI ALIENEE	AUREOLE	AEOUU AQUEOUS
AAEEO AMOEBAE	URAEMIA	AEEEU EVACUEE	AEEOUU EUOUAES	AUTOCUE
AREOLAE	AAEOU AUREOLA	AEEII AIERIES	AEIIU EQUINIA	NOUVEAU
AAEEU AUREATE	AURORAE	AEEIO ETAERIO	AEIOO IPOMOEA	ROULEAU
AAEII AECIDIA	AAIOU ABOULIA	AEEIU EUCAINE	ZOOECIA	AIOOO OOGONIA
AAEIO AEOLIAN	OUABAIN	EUGENIA	AEIOU DOULEIA	EEEIU EPUISEE
AEONIAN	OUAKARI	EUTEXIA	EULOGIA	QUEENIE

8-letter words – 5 vowels or more (by vowel content)

AAAAI ARAPAIMA	SEAQUAKE	AUTOCADE	AMEIOSES	HEMIOLIA
ATARAXIA	AAEII ACTINIAE	AUTOMATE	ETAERIOS	HEMIOPIA
AAAEI ACADEMIA	AKINESIA	OCEANAUT	ETIOLATE	IDEATION
ACHAENIA	APIARIES	AAIII MILIARIA	FOEDARIE	NOTITIAE
ANAEMIAS	AVIARIES	NIRAMIAI	OEILLADE	TAENIOID
ASSEGAAI	CAVIARIE	AAIIO APOSITIA	PAEONIES	AEIIU ACUITIES
AAAEO PARANOEA	HETAIRAI	AVIATION	AEEIOO EPOPOEIA	AECIDIUM
AAAEU ACAUDATE	HETAIRIA	MAIOLICA	AEEIU AUDIENCE	AIGUILLE
AGUACATE	LACINIAE	AAIIU AUXILIAR	BANLIEUE	AQUILINE
AQUACADE	VIRAEMIA	BAUHINIA	BEAUTIED	AUDITIVE
AAAII APIARIAN	AAEIO AERATION	UNIAXIAL	BEAUTIES	AURIFIED
RADIALIA	AGIOTAGE	AAIOO APOLOGIA	BEAUXITE	AURIFIES
AAAIO PARANOIA	ALOPECIA	AAIOU ABOULIAS	CAUSERIE	AURITIES
AAAIU ADULARIA	ANOREXIA	AUTACOID	DECIDUAE	EQUINIAS
AQUARIAN	APOGAEIC	AUTOPSIA	EQUALISE	INDUCIAE
AULARIAN	CAPOEIRA	AZOTURIA	EQUALIZE	INDUVIAE
AVIFAUNA	EGOMANIA	CARIACOU	EQUIPAGE	MAIEUTIC
SAPUCAIA	METANOIA	OUABAINS	EQUISETA	MINUTIAE
AAAOU AUTOMATA	OLEARIAS	OUAKARIS	EUCAINES	UINTAITE
AAAUU AQUANAUT	PAROEMIA	PAROUSIA	EUGENIAS	UREDINIA
AAEEE HETAERAE	TOXAEMIA	RAOULIAS	EUPEPSIA	AEIOO AEROFOIL
AAEEI ACIERAGE	ZABAIONE	SAOUARIS	EUTAXIES	AMOEBOID
ACIERATE	AAEIOU ABOIDEAU	AQUARIUM	EUTAXITE	COENOBIA
AGACERIE	ABOITEAU	AURICULA	EUTEXIAS	IPOMOEAS
ALIENAGE	AAEIU ACAULINE	GUAIACUM	EXEQUIAL	OOGAMIES
ALIENATE	ALLELUIA	AEEEE RELEASEE	EXUVIATE	OVARIOLE
AWEARIED	AUBRETIA	AEEEI ALIENEES	LEUKEMIA	AEIOU AGOUTIES
EMACIATE	AUBRIETA	DETAINEE	MAUVEINE	CAESIOUS
ENCAENIA	AUMAILED	EARPIECE	QUEASIER	DIALOGUE
EPIGAEAL	AURELIAN	EATERIES	QUEAZIER	DOUANIER
EPIGAEAN	AURELIAS	EXAMINEE	UNEASIER	DOULEIAS
ERADIATE	CAMAIEUX	AEEEU EMERAUDE	AEEOO AEROTONE	EDACIOUS
FACETIAE	DIAPAUSE	EVACUEES	FOVEOLAE	EQUATION
HAEREMAI	EPIFAUNA	SEQUELAE	PAHOEHOE	EUPHOBIA
TAENIATE	INAURATE	AEEII AEGIRINE	PEEKABOO	EUPHONIA
AAEEO ANAEROBE	INFAUNAE	AEGIRITE	AEEOU AEGLOGUE	EUPHORIA
AREOLATE	MAUVAISE	ASEITIES	ALEURONE	JALOUSIE
OEDEMATA	PERIAGUA	EPICEDIA	AUREOLED	MOINEAUS
AAEEU ACULEATE	TAQUERIA	GAIETIES	AUREOLES	ODALIQUE
ADEQUATE	URAEMIAS	IDEALISE	FEATEOUS	POULAINE
CAESURAE	AAEOU ACAULOSE	IDEALIZE	JEALOUSE	SEQUOIAS
ECAUDATE	AERONAUT	IDEATIVE	OUTEATEN	THIOUREA
EVACUATE	ANALOGUE	INFERIAE	REAROUSE	AEIUU AUGURIES
EVALUATE	ARACEOUS	METAIRIE	URAEUSES	AUTUNITE
LAUREATE	ARANEOUS	AEEIO ACOEMETI	AEIII INITIATE	FAUTEUIL
NAUSEATE	AUREOLAS	AEROLITE	RETIARII	AEOOO ZOOGLOEA
PAENULAE	AUROREAN		AEIIO AMEIOSIS	AEOOU APOLOGUE
				AUTOSOME

	POACEOUS		ORAGIOUS		EOLIPILE		EULOGISE		OUTVOICE
AEOUU	AUTOCUES		OVARIOUS		ERIONITE		EULOGIZE		ZOOECIUM
	FEATUOUS	AIOUU	CAUTIOUS		MEIONITE		OBSEQUIE	EIOUU	BOUTIQUE
	HUAQUERO		SUBAUDIO		MOIETIES		OUVRIERE		EULOGIUM
	NAUSEOUS	AOOOU	OOGAMOUS		OILERIES	EEIUU	EUPHUISE		EUROPIUM
	OUTVALUE	AOOUU	ANOUROUS		OSIERIES		EUPHUIZE		EXIGUOUS
	ROULEAUS	EEEEU	SQUEEGEE	EEIIU	EQUITIES		QUEUEING		TENUIOUS
	ROULEAUX	EEEIO	EOLIENNE		QUIETIVE		QUIETUDE	EOOOO	HOODOOED
AIIIO	OITICICA	EEEIU	EUXENITE		UBIETIES	EIIIO	IDIOCIES		VOODOOED
AIIIU	DAIQUIRI		EXEQUIES	EEIOO	COOEEING	EIIOO	ONIONIER	EOOUU	DUOLOGUE
AIIOO	AVOISION		MEUNIERE		OOGENIES	EIIOU	EXIMIOUS		OUTHOUSE
AIIOU	AUDITION		QUEENIER	EEIOU	BOUDERIE		FILIOQUE		VOUDOUED
	OLIGURIA		QUEENIES		EPIGEOUS		UNIONISE	IIIOU	OUISTITI
AIOOO	OOGONIAL		QUEENITE		EPILOGUE		UNIONIZE	IOOOU	OOGONIUM
	ORATORIO	EEIIO	EBIONISE		EQUIVOKE	EIOOO	FORHOOIE	IOOUU	BOUZOUKI
	ZOONOMIA		EBIONIZE		ETOURDIE		OOLOGIES		UXORIOUS
AIOOU	AUTOGIRO		EGOITIES		EULOGIES	EIOOU	ISOLOGUE	IOUUU	USURIOUS

Vowel Advice

Once you have more than two of any vowel on your rack (except perhaps E's) it is all too easy to accumulate more because of the difficulty in sorting out the initial problem. Try the following exercise to become more familiar with those words that solve your multiple vowel imbalance.

Select three A's and then repeatedly pick up any four consonants and see how many A-words you can think of for the first move. Try to find the highest-scoring first move and then consult the Awkward Vowel lists for added inspiration. Do not actually play words on the board but treat each fresh rack as if it were the first move. Repeat the exercise with the O's, I's and U's.

Triple Tactics

Every player recognizes the need to avoid giving the opponent easy access to the triple-word squares. However it is important not to be obsessive about giving away triple-word scores. Playing a word out to the edge of the board such that the word covers the double-letter square between two triple-word squares with a low-scoring tile, does not make it that easy for the opponent to score highly from the triple-word square. In fact, it may force the opponent to use his or her best tiles to block your use of the triple-word square next turn.

Valuing the S and Blank

The blank and the S are the most valuable tiles in the Scrabble set. Treat them as if they are worth a potential 50 points each. They are the ingredients of most 7- and 8-letter bonus plays and as such should be used wisely. It is rarely worth playing an S for just a few extra points unless the move is essential for blocking the opponent in a game where winning is all important. A blank retained on the rack, even if not utilized in a bonus play, will provide that extra degree of flexibility of choice for endgame strategy.

ING Addiction

Every Scrabble player has retained ING on their rack at some time or another in the hope of getting an -ING bonus word. The usefulness of this strategy is frequently overrated amongst less experienced players. Although it is a common ending, unless you have the fortune to pick up the right letter for an -ING 7-letter word you will find the G more of a hindrance. Furthermore, if you religiously cling on to the ING you are severely limiting your choice of play for each move and are effectively playing with only four tiles. The advice is to avoid any ING addiction and concentrate on just keeping any subset of the letters RETAIN that you may have. This will be more fruitful.

Looking at Hooks

The 2-, 3- and 4-letter hook words are probably the most important of the hook words. Try to learn a few useful ones at a time and attempt to introduce them into your game. An interesting exercise to assist is as follows:
Take each letter of the alphabet and find a 2-, 3- and 4-letter word that takes that letter before or after as a hook to make a longer word. There may be none for some of the more awkward letters. This will give you a balanced variety of some 100 hook words to study. Note that, for ruthless blocking strategies, the 3- and 4-letter words that do not take hook letters before or after as just as important.

HEAVY WORDS (Many Consonants) except -S inflections

2-letter words – no vowels except Y

BY	CH	FY	KY	MY	NY	PH	SH	ST

3-letter words – no vowels except Y

CLY	FLY	HYP	PLY	RHY	SNY	THY	VLY
CRY	FRY	LYM	PRY	SHY	SPY	TRY	WHY
CWM	GYM	NTH	PST	SKY	STY	TWP	WRY
DRY	GYP	NYS	PYX	SLY	SWY	TYG	WYN

4-letter words – no vowels except Y

BRRR	GYMP	HYMN	LYNX	PSST	SKRY	SYNC	TYMP	WYND	YMPT
CYST	GYNY	JYNX	MYTH	RYND	SKYR	SYND	TYND	WYNN	
FYRD	HWYL	KYND	PRYS	SCRY	SPRY	TRYP	WYCH	XYST	

5-letter words – no vowels except Y

CHYND	DRYLY	GRYPT	GYPSY	LYNCH	PSYCH	SLYLY	SYNTH	WRYLY
CRWTH	GHYLL	GYNNY	KYDST	MYRRH	PYGMY	SYLPH	THYMY	XYLYL
CRYPT	GLYPH	GYPPY	LYMPH	NYMPH	SHYLY	SYNCH	TRYST	

6-letter words – one vowel

BLANCH	CRANCH	FROWST	PLINTH	SCRAMB	SHROFF	SNITCH	SPRUNG	STROMB	THRILL
BLENCH	CRANTS	GLITCH	PLONGD	SCRAWL	SHROWD	SPARTH	SPRUSH	STROND	THRIPS
BLIGHT	CRATCH	GLUMPS	PRANCK	SCRAWM	SHRUNK	SPERST	STANCH	STRONG	THRIST
BLINTZ	CROTCH	GROWTH	PROMPT	SCRIMP	SHTCHI	SPETCH	STANCK	STROWN	THRONG
BLOTCH	CRUNCH	GRUMPH	PUTSCH	SCRIPT	SHTETL	SPHINX	STARCH	STRUCK	THROWN
BORSCH	CRUTCH	GRUTCH	RHYTHM	SCROLL	SHTICK	SPIGHT	STENCH	STRUNG	THRUSH
BRANCH	CULTCH	HIGHTH	SCARPH	SCROWL	SHTUCK	SPILTH	STITCH	STRUNT	THRUST
BRIGHT	DIRNDL	KIRSCH	SCARTH	SCRUFF	SHTUMM	SPLASH	STOWND	SWARTH	THWACK
BROWST	DRACHM	KITSCH	SCATCH	SCRUMP	SKARTH	SPLENT	SWATCH	SWATCH	THWART
BRUNCH	DRENCH	KLATCH	SCHELM	SCRUNT	SKETCH	SPLIFF	STRAFF	SWOWND	TRENCH
CATCHT	FLANCH	KLEPHT	SCHISM	SCULPT	SKLENT	SPLINT	STRAMP	SWITCH	TROGGS
CHINCH	FLENCH	KNICKS	SCHIST	SCUTCH	SKLIFF	SPLOSH	STRAND	TCHICK	TWIGHT
CHINTZ	FLETCH	KNIGHT	SCHLEP	SHLOCK	SKRIMP	SPRACK	STRATH	THATCH	TWITCH
CHRISM	FLIGHT	KNITCH	SCHORL	SHMOCK	SKRUMP	SPRANG	STRAWN	THETCH	WARMTH
CHURCH	FLINCH	KRANTZ	SCHUSS	SHMUCK	SLATCH	SPRAWL	STRESS	THIRST	WHILST
CLASTS	FLYSCH	KVETCH	SCLAFF	SHRANK	SLIGHT	SPREDD	STREWN	THRALL	WHISHT
CLATCH	FRATCH	LENGTH	SCLIFF	SHREWD	SMATCH	SPRENT	STRICH	THRANG	WRENCH
CLENCH	FRENCH	MENSCH	SCORCH	SHRIFT	SMIGHT	SPRING	STRICT	THRASH	WRETCH
CLINCH	FRICHT	PHLEGM	SCOTCH	SHRILL	SMIRCH	SPRINT	STRIFT	THRAWN	WRIGHT
CLUNCH	FRIGHT	PLANCH	SCOWTH	SHRIMP	SMUTCH	SPRITZ	STRING	THRESH	
CLUTCH	FRIGHT	PLIGHT	SCOWTH	SHRINK	SNATCH	SPRONG	STROLL	THRIFT	

Fishing

It is rarely worth holding on to a set of letters hoping to pick up that one tile that will transform your rack into a wonderful high-scoring bonus word. However, if the six letters you are holding on to are likely to yield a bonus play with *many* of the tiles that you are likely to pick up (see Bonus Word Sets section) then 'fishing' could be strategically beneficial. Always consider the chances of actually getting the tile or tiles you hope for and balance this against any alternative scoring plays. Knowledge of the letter distribution and the most fruitful 6-letter combinations is mandatory for timely 'fishing'.

Mind Your Changing

Since it is permissible to change any number of your letters instead of a turn during a game (unless there are fewer than seven tiles in the bag), it can be a wise decision to change some or all of your letters even if you can find a word to play on the board. You should consider changing when:

☆ You have an imbalance of vowels and consonants and the available dump words do not solve your rack problems, score very little, or provide too many scoring opportunities for your opponent.

☆ There are no scoring opportunities on the board and you don't wish to block your opponent with a low-scoring play.

☆ You have a Q with no U and none of the U-less Q words is playable. Note that the existence of QI makes the Q less of a problem, and it may be worth forgoing changing if you can score well with your other letters and there are still I's left.

☆ You have a promising 6-letter combination that combines well with many other letters to make a 7-letter word – but not with the seventh letter on your rack. Changing the odd letter in this situation is often not the best strategic move but the time for such a change may be ripe if you desperately need the bonus to catch up or there are no other worthwhile alternatives.

Bonus Hunting

Faced with a rack of seven letters in any order it is not always easy to spot even common 7-letter words. Moving the tiles around will often enable an otherwise hidden 7-letter word to come to light. But rather than frantic shuffling and reshuffling in the hope of inspiration a more organized approach is recommended. Form beginnings and endings with the letters on your rack and check the remaining tiles to see if they form a word with that beginning or ending. For example, with the rack EEFGLOR making the prefix FORE will lead you to FORELEG. With ACEORTV, the prefix OVER will inspire OVERACT. Similarly with the racks AINOORT, AGEINOS and AEFHLTU it may only be by forming the endings -TION, -ISE and -FUL that you will stumble across ORATION, AGONISE and HATEFUL respectively. Also, splitting your rack into two shorter words may enable you to spot an allowable compound word. For example, the unlikely ADEEESW yields SEA and WEED (SEAWEED) and AADORWY makes ROAD and WAY (ROADWAY).

Awkward Vowel Dumps

Having two of the same vowel on your rack, except perhaps when they are two E's, is often a problem; it can be a nightmare when you are confronted with more than two, especially if they are I's or U's.

Playing just one of the multiple vowels does not always solve the problem, and you can go on being faced with the same problem on subsequent turns. This of course does not help your game. Ideally the solution needs to be found in one turn.

The following lists of words containing multiple A's, E's, I's, O's or U's will be very helpful in such situations.

The lists are summarized below:

A words:	3-letter words, 2 A's (eg ABA, BAA)
	4-letter words, 2 A's (eg AWAY, LAVA)
	5- letter words, 3 A's (eg ABACA, KAAMA)
	6-letter words, 3 A's (eg BANANA, BAZAAR)
E words:	4-letter words, 3 E's (EPEE)
	5-letter words, 3 E's (eg GEESE, MELEE)
	6-letter words, 4 E's (eg PEEWEE, TEEPEE)
I words:	4-letter words, 2 I's (eg IRIS, KIWI)
	5-letter words, 2 I's (eg ICING, RIGID)
	6-letter words, 3 I's (eg BIKINI, IRITIC)
O words:	5-letter words, 3 O's (OVOLO)
	6-letter words, 3 O's or more (eg COCOON, VOODOO)
U words:	3-letter words, 2 U's (UTU)
	4-letter words, 2 U's (eg GURU, LUAU)
	5-letter words, 2 U's or more (eg AUGUR, QUEUE)
	6-letter words, 3 U's (eg MUTUUM, UHURUS)

Note that there is no list of 4-letter words with two O's – it is not too difficult to play a couple of O's in a 4-letter word. As a start, think of all the words (such as FOOD) with a double O in them.

3-letter words with two E's or two O's are also not difficult, and there are no 3-letter words with two I's.

AWKWARD VOWEL DUMPS – A's

3-letter words – 2 A's

AAS	AGA	AIA	ANA	AWA	MAA
ABA	AHA	ALA	AVA	BAA	

4-letter words – 2 A's

ABAC	AGHA	ALAY	ANAS	ARBA	AVAL	CAPA	KAKA	LAVA	NAAM
ABAS	AGMA	ALFA	ANNA	AREA	AVAS	CASA	KAMA	MAAR	NAAN
ABBA	AIAS	ALGA	ANOA	ARIA	AWAY	DATA	KANA	MAAS	NADA
ACTA	AJAR	ALMA	ANTA	ARNA	AYAH	GAGA	KARA	MAMA	NAGA
ADAW	ALAE	AMAH	APAY	ASAR	AZAN	GALA	KATA	MANA	NALA
AFAR	ALAP	AMLA	AQUA	ATAP	BAAS	HAAF	KAVA	MARA	NANA
AGAR	ALAR	ANAL	ARAK	AULA	BABA	HAAR	LAMA	MASA	NAPA
AGAS	ALAS	ANAN	ARAR	AURA	CABA	HAKA	LANA	MAYA	PACA

PAPA	PAWA	RAJA	SAGA	TAKA	TAPA	TAWA	VASA
PARA	RACA	RANA	SAMA	TALA	TARA	TAXA	WAKA
PAUA	RAGA	RATA	TAHA	TANA	TAVA	VARA	

5-letter words – 3 A's

ABACA	ABAYA	AFARA	ALAAP	ALAPA	ANANA	ARABA	ASANA	KAAMA

6-letter words – 3 A's

ABACAS	ALAPAS	ARABAS	ATAMAN	BANANA	DAGABA	KANAKA	NAGANA	SAMAAN
ABAYAS	ALBATA	ARALIA	ATAXIA	BARAZA	JACANA	KARAKA	PALAMA	SAMARA
ACACIA	ALPACA	ARCANA	AVATAR	BATATA	JATAKA	KATANA	PANADA	SATARA
AFARAS	ANABAS	ARGALA	AZALEA	BAZAAR	KAAMAS	LABARA	PANAMA	TAIAHA
AGAPAE	ANANAS	ARMADA	BAHADA	CABALA	KABALA	MANANA	PAPAYA	TAMARA
ALAAPS	ANATTA	ASANAS	BAJADA	CABANA	KABAYA	MARACA	PATACA	UJAMAA
ALALIA	ANTARA	ATABAL	BALATA	CANADA	KAMALA	MASALA	SALAAM	ZAPATA

AWKWARD VOWEL DUMPS – E's

4-letter words – 3 E's

EPEE

5-letter words – 3 E's

BELEE	EERIE	EMEER	EXEME	HEEZE	MELEE	PEECE	REEVE	WEEKE
BESEE	EEVEN	EPEES	FEESE	KEEVE	NEELE	PEEPE	SEMEE	WEETE
DEERE	ELPEE	ETWEE	FEEZE	LEESE	NEESE	PEEVE	TEENE	
DEEVE	EMCEE	EXEEM	GEESE	LEVEE	NEEZE	REEDE	TEPEE	

6-letter words – 4 E's

PEEWEE   TEEPEE

AWKWARD VOWEL DUMPS – I's

4-letter words – 2 I's

DIVI	HILI	IMPI	IRID	IXIA	MINI	NISI	SIMI	TIPI	ZITI
DIXI	IBIS	INIA	IRIS	KIWI	MIRI	PILI	SIRI	TITI	
FINI	ILIA	INTI	IWIS	MIDI	NIDI	PIPI	TIKI	WILI	

5-letter words – 2 I's

ACINI	CIRRI	ICILY	IMPIS	ISSEI	LIKIN	NIHIL	PIRAI	TIKIS	VIZIR
AIDOI	CIVIC	ICING	IMSHI	IVIED	LIMIT	NIMBI	PIXIE	TIMID	WIFIE
AIOLI	CIVIL	ICTIC	INDIE	IVIES	LININ	NISEI	RADII	TIPIS	WILIS
ALIBI	DIGIT	IDIOM	INDRI	IXIAS	LIPID	NITID	REIKI	TITIS	ZIMBI
BIFID	DILLI	IDIOT	INFIX	JINNI	LIVID	NIXIE	RICIN	TORII	
BIKIE	DINIC	ILIAC	INION	KIKOI	MEDII	OBIIT	RIGID	VIGIA	
BIVIA	DIVIS	ILIUM	INTIL	KILIM	MIDIS	OIDIA	RISHI	VIGIL	
BLINI	DIXIE	IMARI	INTIS	KININ	MIMIC	ORIBI	SIGIL	VILLI	
CEILI	FINIS	IMIDE	INWIT	KIRRI	MINIM	ORIBI	SIMIS	VIRID	
CHILI	GENII	IMINE	IODIC	KIWIS	MINIS	PILEI	SIRIH	VISIE	
CILIA	IAMBI	IMMIT	IONIC	LICHI	MIRIN	PILIS	SIRIS	VISIT	
CIPPI	ICIER	IMMIX	IRIDS	LICIT	MODII	PIPIT	TIBIA	VIVID	

6-letter words – 3 I's

BIKINI IMIDIC IRIDIC IRITIC IRITIS MIRITI

AWKWARD VOWEL DUMPS – O's

5-letter words – 3 O's

OVOLO   POTOO

6-letter words – 3 O's or more

BOOBOO	COMODO	DOOCOT	GOOGOL	HOODOO	HOOROO	OOLOGY	POTOOS	ROTOLO	ZOOZOO
COCOON	COROZO	FORHOO	GOOROO	HOOPOE	KOODOO	OOLONG	ROCOCO	VOODOO	

AWKWARD VOWEL DUMPS – U's

3-letter words – 2 U's

UTU

4-letter words – 2 U's

GURU	KUDU	KURU	LUAU	PUDU	PULU	SULU	UNAU	UTUS
JUJU	KUKU	KUZU	LULU	PUKU	RURU	TUTU	URUS	ZULU

5-letter words – 2 U's or more

AUGUR	DURUM	JUGUM	KURUS	MUCUS	QUEUE	TUQUE	UNCUT	URUBU	UVULA
BUCHU	FUCUS	JUJUS	KUZUS	MUNTU	QUIPU	TUTUS	UNDUE	USUAL	VOULU
BUCKU	FUGUE	KUDUS	LUAUS	PUDUS	RURUS	UHURU	UNDUG	USURE	WUSHU
BUNDU	GURUS	KUDZU	LULUS	PUKUS	SULUS	UNAUS	UNGUM	USURP	ZULUS
BUSSU	HUMUS	KUKUS	LUPUS	PULUS	SUNUP	UNCUS	UPRUN	USURY	

6-letter words – 3 U's

MUTUUM   UHURUS   URUBUS

Flashcards

A popular way of testing Scrabble vocabulary is a system called flashcards. Small index cards are used which have 'questions' on one side and the 'answer words' on the reverse. For example if you were using flashcards to learn 2-letter words you may have on one card A=13, with the 13 2-letter words beginning with A on the reverse. On another card B=5, and another C=1, would reveal BA, BE, BI, BO, BY and CH on the reverse respectively. Whenever you get a moment you can quickly flick through the cards and test yourself. The system can be used for many categories such as five-vowelled 7-letter words, words containing J Q X Z, and so on. A good use of flashcards is to log every 7-letter word played against you that you didn't know, thus naturally building up your personal testing library.

Fighting Back

Don't trade off catching up with poor rack retention. A more balanced rack will enable a greater choice of strategic plays in subsequent turns. Initially concentrate on not slipping any further behind and be wary of scoring opportunities open only to yourself. Perhaps you have the last S or the last A for an (A)JAR hook, and so on. Try to keep the board open unless you can block and catch up in a single play. If your opponent is in front it is likely their rack is worsening whilst they are blocking. Keeping the board open and maintaining your rack balance will keep your hopes alive whereas playing too defensively will only assist your opponent to keep their lead.

 Passing Thoughts

It is allowable to pass in Scrabble, that is, to not play a word or change any tiles. This is in effect what a player does at the end of the game if stuck with any unplayable tiles. However, it is rarely worth passing during the game in the hope that the opponent will give you that vital opening or letter you need.

An example of an occasion where passing may be of advantage is if you have a good rack such as TAILEND and it is your play first, or your opponent has just changed letters instead of playing first. Since TAILEND combines with each of the four vowels (A E O U) to make an 8-letter word (DENTALIA, ENTAILED or LINEATED, DELATION, UNTAILED), it is likely your opponent may give you a bonus play next turn.

 Learn As You Play

Always have a scrap of paper with you other than the scoresheet. Jot down any promising racks you find yourself with, 7-letter words you played that might have anagrams, and any words you think of playing but are unsure of. After the game spend a few minutes with *Official Scrabble® Lists* and check out your words and racks, noting any new discoveries. Going through this exercise after every game will gradually strengthen your vocabulary without too much effort.

Awkward Consonant Dumps

The following lists are of words of three to five letters containing one of the following consonants at least twice – B, C, F, H, V, W and Y. (Note that Y is considered here as a consonant, regardless of whether it is acting as a vowel or a consonant in any individual word.) It is usually not too difficult to dump one of these awkward consonants in an attempt to achieve a reasonable score and balance your rack. Dumping two F's, H's, and so on is more of a problem. These lists should help with your awkward consonant racks.

The lists are arranged so that all the B words come together, then the C words, and so on. The 3-letter B words come before the 4-letter B words, which come before the 5-letter B words. Similarly for the other awkward consonants.

There are no 3-letter words having two C's, two V's or two Y's.

AWKWARD CONSONANT DUMPS – B's

3-letter words – 2 B's

ABB	BIB	BOB	BUB	EBB

4-letter words – 2 B's

ABBA	BABA	BABY	BLAB	BLUB	BOMB	BUBO	COBB
ABBE	BABE	BARB	BLEB	BOBA	BOOB	BUBS	EBBS
ABBS	BABU	BIBS	BLOB	BOBS	BUBA	BULB	SIBB

5-letter words – 2 B's or more

ABBAS	BABUL	BIMBO	BOBAS	BUBAL	COBBS	FUBBY	KEBAB	REBBE	WEBBY
ABBES	BABUS	BLABS	BOBBY	BUBAS	COBBY	GABBY	KEBOB	RIBBY	YABBY
ABBEY	BARBE	BLEBS	BOMBE	BUBBY	CUBBY	GOBBI	LOBBY	SIBBS	YOBBO
ABBOT	BARBS	BLOBS	BOMBO	BULBS	CUBEB	GOBBO	MOBBY	SLUBB	ZEBUB
BABAS	BEBOP	BLUBS	BOMBS	BUMBO	DEBBY	HOBBY	NABOB	SUBBY	
BABEL	BEROB	BLURB	BOOBS	BUSBY	DIBBS	HUBBY	NOBBY	SYBBE	
BABES	BIBLE	BOBAC	BOOBY	CABBY	DOBBY	KABAB	NUBBY	TABBY	
BABOO	BILBO	BOBAK	BRIBE	CABOB	EBBED	KABOB	RABBI	TUBBY	

AWKWARD CONSONANT DUMPS – C's

4-letter words – 2 C's

CECA	CHIC	CHOC	COCA	COCH	COCK	COCO	CROC	ECCE	ECCO

5-letter words – 2 C's or more

ACCOY	CACHE	CHACE	CHOCK	CIVIC	COCCI	CONIC	CULCH	ICTIC	TICCA
ACOCK	CACTI	CHACK	CHOCO	CLACK	COCCO	COSEC	CUMEC	OCCAM	WICCA
BACCA	CAECA	CHACO	CHOCS	CLECK	COCKS	COUCH	CURCH	OCCUR	YACCA
BACCO	CASCO	CHECK	CHUCK	CLICK	COCKY	CRACK	CUSEC	PICCY	YUCCA
BACCY	CATCH	CHICA	CINCH	CLOCK	COCOA	CRICK	CUTCH	RECCE	ZOCCO
BICCY	CECAL	CHICH	CINCT	CLUCK	COCOS	CROCK	CYCAD	RECCO	
BOCCA	CECUM	CHICK	CIRCA	COACH	COLIC	CROCS	CYCLE	RECCY	
CABOC	CERCI	CHICO	CIRCS	COACT	COMIC	CRUCK	CYCLO	SECCO	
CACAO	CERIC	CHICS	CISCO	COCAS	CONCH	CUBIC	CYNIC	SUCCI	

AWKWARD CONSONANT DUMPS – F's

3-letter words – 2 F's

EFF   IFF   OFF

4-letter words – 2 F's or more

AFFY	CAFF	DUFF	FUFF	HUFF	LUFF	NUFF	RUFF	WAFF
BAFF	COFF	EFFS	GAFF	IFFY	MIFF	OFFS	TEFF	YAFF
BIFF	CUFF	FAFF	GOFF	JEFF	MUFF	PUFF	TIFF	ZIFF
BOFF	DAFF	FIEF	GUFF	JIFF	NAFF	RAFF	TOFF	
BUFF	DOFF	FIFE	HAFF	KOFF	NIFF	RIFF	TUFF	

5-letter words – 2 F's or more

AFFIX	CAFFS	DRAFF	FLAFF	GUFFS	LUFFS	OFFER	SCAFF	STUFF	WHIFF
BAFFS	CHAFF	DUFFS	FLUFF	HAFFS	MIFFS	PLUFF	SCOFF	TAFFY	YAFFS
BAFFY	CHUFF	EFFED	FUFFS	HOUFF	MIFFY	PUFFS	SCUFF	TEFFS	ZIFFS
BIFFS	CLIFF	FAFFS	FUFFY	HOWFF	MUFFS	PUFFY	SKIFF	TIFFS	
BLUFF	CLOFF	FEOFF	GAFFE	HUFFS	NAFFS	QUAFF	SKOFF	TOFFS	
BOFFS	COFFS	FIEFS	GAFFS	HUFFY	NIFFS	QUIFF	SNIFF	TOFFY	
BUFFA	CUFFO	FIFED	GLIFF	JEFFS	NIFFY	RAFFS	SNUFF	TRIFF	
BUFFE	CUFFS	FIFER	GOFFS	JIFFS	NUFFS	REFFO	SOWFF	TUFFE	
BUFFI	DAFFS	FIFES	GRAFF	JIFFY	NYAFF	RIFFS	SPIFF	TUFFS	
BUFFO	DAFFY	FIFTH	GRIFF	KOFFS	OFFAL	RUFFE	STAFF	WAFFS	
BUFFS	DOFFS	FIFTY	GRUFF	LUFFA	OFFED	RUFFS	STIFF	WAUFF	

AWKWARD CONSONANT DUMPS – H's

3-letter words – 2 H's

HAH   HOH   HUH

4-letter words – 2 H's

HASH	HATH	HECH	HIGH	HISH	HOGH	HOHS	HUSH	PHOH	SHAH

5-letter words – 2 H's

AHIGH	HANCH	HAUGH	HEUCH	HIGHT	HOGHS	HOTCH	HUSHY	PHOHS	SHUSH
CHICH	HARSH	HEATH	HEUGH	HILCH	HOHED	HOUGH	HUTCH	SHAHS	THIGH
EPHAH	HASHY	HECHT	HEWGH	HITCH	HOOCH	HUMPH	HYPHA	SHASH	WHICH
HAITH	HATCH	HEIGH	HIGHS	HITHE	HOOSH	HUNCH	HYTHE	SHCHI	WHISH

AWKWARD CONSONANT DUMPS – V's

4-letter words – 2 V's

VIVA   VIVE   VIVO

5-letter words – 2 V's

BEVVY	CIVVY	LUVVY	SAVVY	VARVE	VIVAS	VIVDA	VIVES	VOLVA	VULVA
BIVVY	DIVVY	NAVVY	VALVE	VERVE	VIVAT	VIVER	VIVID	VOLVE	

AWKWARD CONSONANT DUMPS – W's

3-letter words – 2 W's

WAW   WOW

4-letter words – 2 W's

WAWE	WAWL	WAWS	WHEW	WHOW	WOWF	WOWS

5-letter words – 2 W's

EWHOW	PAWAW	WAWES	WAWLS	WHEWS	WIDOW	WOWED	WOWEE	WRAWL

AWKWARD CONSONANT DUMPS – Y's

4-letter words – 2 Y's

EYRY	GYNY	YAWY	YUKY

5-letter words – 2 Y's

AZYGY	DOYLY	GYNNY	PYGMY	SLYLY	XYLYL	YAWEY	YIPPY	YUKKY
BYWAY	DRYLY	GYPPY	SHYLY	THYMY	YABBY	YAWNY	YOLKY	YUMMY
COYLY	DYKEY	GYPSY	SKYEY	WRYLY	YAPPY	YESTY	YUCKY	YUPPY

Rack Balancing

Always try to keep a balanced rack of vowels and consonants. The more balanced your rack the more choice of words you will have each turn and the more chance you will have of being able to play a bonus-scoring 7-letter word. It helps to be aware that there are 42 vowels to 56 consonants (and 2 blanks) in the Scrabble set. That's three vowels for every four consonants. Counting how many vowels and consonants already played at any stage of a game will serve as a useful guide as to the vowel/consonant distribution remaining in the bag. If there is a surplus of consonants left you might wish to counteract your likely consonant pickup by retaining vowels on your rack when you play, or vice versa.

See the Awkward Vowel Dumps list and the Light and Heavy Words list for some words that will help you keep a balanced rack.

Edging the Endgame

In a tight game where the scores are close there is an advantage in being the player to be the first to play out and finish the game, thus gaining any points remaining on your opponent's rack and depriving him or her of another scoring opportunity. Playing out first is often the difference between winning and losing. A handy tip, whenever you have the opportunity or choice near the end of a game, is to ensure there is a single tile in the bag after your turn. This means that, next turn, you have the first opportunity to play with no tiles remaining in the bag, thus giving you an advantage in planning a 2-move finish. There is further advantage if you have been keeping track of the tiles since you can then have the benefit of the endgame initiative knowing your opponent's exact tiles.

Combination Management

If you have one of the promising 6-letter combinations given under the Bonus Sets section but unfortunately do not have an appropriate seventh letter to make a bonus word, or the bonus word you have does not fit on the board, then it is wiser not to be overly concerned about holding on to your useful 6-letter combination. Rather than just playing the one letter and hoping for a playable bonus word next turn, play two or three tiles. This will probably enable you to score more whilst still retaining the makings of a bonus word. The skill is in making sure you play off the right letters.

For example, with OILERS and an F on your rack there is no bonus word. Rather than just play the F, in the hope of picking a B for BOILERS or a U for LOUSIER perhaps, it is better to play IF or OF. The retention of OLERS and ILERS with a vowel pickup next turn is likely to produce another good 6-letter combination such as AILERS, OILERS or RELIES, and hopefully an obliging seventh letter to make a bonus play. If it doesn't, well at least you've scored some points meanwhile.

Unusual Clues

In browsing through the Anagram section you will find an abundance of unusual 7- and 8-letter words. Some of these are more useful than others, depending on their constituent letters. Those consisting of just the 1- and 2-point Scrabble tiles (ie A D E G I L N O R S T U) are more likely to appear on your rack and are the ones to concentrate on. A good way to remember these words is by making up a non-existent anagram that you are more likely to form on your rack and that will act as an aide-mémoire. For example, the likely rack ELNOSTU yields the bonus word LENTOUS which may best be recalled as the anagram of the non-existent OUTLENS. Similarly, SEERING makes GREISEN and LOOTIER makes TROOLIE. Both SEERING and LOOTIER are not actual words but merely the clues to GREISEN and TROOLIE. Where there is a more common anagram of an unusual word then this naturally serves as a clue, eg OUTLINE gives ELUTION and AGAINST gives GITANAS.

K and V Words

The following lists contain all the words of length two to five letters which have one or more of either a K or a V in them. Words with K or V can be particularly useful for scoring perhaps 40 or so points, helping you at the same time to offload otherwise awkward letters.

If a word contains both K and V, it will appear in both the K and V lists.

K-WORDS

K – 2-letter words

KA   KO   KY

K – 3-letter words

AKE	EIK	INK	KAT	KEG	KIF	KOI	LEK	ROK	WOK
ARK	EKE	IRK	KAW	KEN	KIN	KON	MAK	SKA	YAK
ASK	ELK	JAK	KAY	KEP	KIP	KOP	NEK	SKI	YOK
AUK	ERK	KAE	KEA	KET	KIR	KOS	OAK	SKY	YUK
BOK	EUK	KAI	KEB	KEX	KIT	KOW	OIK	SUK	ZEK
DAK	EWK	KAM	KED	KEY	KOA	KYE	OKE	TAK	
EEK	ILK	KAS	KEF	KID	KOB	KYU	OUK	UKE	

K – 4-letter words

AKED	BUKE	DORK	GOWK	JERK	KATS	KHAT	KNAR	KYLE	MERK
AKEE	BULK	DREK	GUCK	JINK	KAVA	KHOR	KNEE	KYND	MICK
AKES	BUNK	DUCK	GUNK	JOCK	KAWS	KHUD	KNEW	KYNE	MIKE
AKIN	BURK	DUKE	HACK	JOKE	KAYO	KIBE	KNIT	KYTE	MILK
ALKY	BUSK	DUNK	HAIK	JOKY	KAYS	KICK	KNOB	KYUS	MINK
AMOK	BYKE	DUSK	HAKA	JOOK	KAZI	KIDS	KNOP	LACK	MIRK
ANKH	CAKE	DYKE	HAKE	JOUK	KEAS	KIER	KNOT	LAIK	MOCK
ARAK	CAKY	EIKS	HANK	JUKE	KEBS	KIFS	KNOW	LAKE	MOKE
ARKS	CALK	EKED	HARK	JUNK	KECK	KIKE	KNUB	LAKH	MOKI
ASKS	CARK	EKES	HASK	KADE	KEDS	KILD	KNUR	LAKY	MOKO
ATOK	CASK	EKKA	HAWK	KADI	KEEK	KILL	KNUT	LANK	MONK
AUKS	CAUK	ELKS	HECK	KAED	KEEL	KILN	KOAN	LARK	MOOK
BACK	CAWK	ERKS	HICK	KAES	KEEN	KILO	KOAS	LAWK	MUCK
BAKE	CHIK	ERKS	HIKE	KAGO	KEEP	KILP	KOBS	LEAK	MURK
BALK	COCK	ESKY	HOCK	KAID	KEFS	KILT	KOFF	LEEK	MUSK
BANK	COKE	EUKS	HOIK	KAIE	KEGS	KINA /	KOHL	LEKE	NABK
BARK	COKY	EWKS	HOKE	KAIF	KEIR	KIND	KOLA	LEKS	NAIK
BASK	CONK	FAIK	HOKI	KAIL	KEKS	KINE	KOLO	LICK	NARK
BAUK	COOK	FAKE	HONK	KAIM	KELL	KING	KOND	LIKE	NECK
BEAK	CORK	FANK	HOOK	KAIN	KELP	KINK	KONK	LINK	NEKS
BECK	CUSK	FECK	HOWK	KAIS	KELT	KINO	KONS	LIRK	NERK
BERK	DAKS	FIKE	HUCK	KAKA	KEMB	KINS	KOOK	LISK	NEUK
BIKE	DANK	FIKY	HULK	KAKI	KEMP	KIPE	KOPH	LOCK	NICK
BILK	DARK	FINK	HUNK	KALE	KENO	KIPP	KOPS	LOKE	NOCK
BINK	DAWK	FIRK	HUSK	KALI	KENS	KIPS	KORA	LOOK	NOOK
BIRK	DECK	FISK	HYKE	KAMA	KENT	KIRK	KORE	LUCK	NORK
BISK	DEEK	FLAK	ICKY	KAME	KEPI	KIRN	KOSS	LURK	NUKE
BOAK	DESK	FOLK	IKAT	KAMI	KEPS	KIRS	KOTO	LUSK	OAKS
BOCK	DHAK	FORK	IKON	KANA	KEPT	KISH	KOWS	MACK	OAKY
BOKE	DICK	FUCK	ILKA	KANG	KERB	KISS	KRAB	MAIK	OIKS
BOKO	DIKA	FUNK	ILKS	KANS	KERF	KIST	KRIS	MAKE	OINK
BOKS	DIKE	FYKE	INKS	KANT	KERN	KITE	KSAR	MAKO	OKAY
BONK	DINK	GAWK	INKY	KAON	KESH	KITH	KUDU	MAKS	OKES
BOOK	DIRK	GECK	IRKS	KARA	KEST	KITS	KUKU	MARK	OKRA
BOSK	DISK	GEEK	JACK	KARK	KETA	KIVA	KURI	MASK	OKTA
BOUK	DOCK	GINK	JAKE	KART	KETS	KIWI	KURU	MAWK	OUKS
BUCK	DOEK	GONK	JAKS	KATA	KEYS	KNAG	KUZU	MEEK	OULK
BUIK	DOOK	GOUK	JARK	KATI	KHAN	KNAP	KYAT	MEEK	PACK

PAIK	PONK	REEK	SAKI	SKEO	SOCK	TAKY	TUCK	WICK	YOCK
PARK	POOK	REIK	SANK	SKEP	SOKE	TALK	TUSK	WINK	YOKE
PAWK	PORK	REKE	SARK	SKER	SOOK	TANK	TYKE	WOCK	YOKS
PEAK	POUK	RICK	SEEK	SKEW	SOUK	TASK	UKES	WOKE	YOLK
PECK	PUCK	RINK	SEIK	SKID	SPEK	TEAK	VOLK	WOKS	YORK
PEEK	PUKE	RISK	SEKT	SKIM	SPIK	TICK	WACK	WONK	YOUK
PEKE	PUKU	ROCK	SERK	SKIN	SUCK	TIKA	WAKA	WORK	YUCK
PENK	PULK	ROKE	SICK	SKIO	SUKH	TIKE	WAKE	YACK	YUKE
PERK	PUNK	ROKS	SIKA	SKIP	SUKS	TIKI	WAKF	YAKS	YUKO
PICK	RACK	ROKY	SIKE	SKIS	SULK	TINK	WALK	YANK	YUKS
PIKA	RAIK	ROOK	SILK	SKIT	SUNK	TOCK	WANK	YELK	YUKY
PIKE	RAKE	RUCK	SINK	SKOL	SYKE	TOKE	WARK	YERK	ZACK
PINK	RAKI	RUKH	SKAG	SKRY	TACK	TOKO	WAUK	YESK	ZEKS
POCK	RAKU	RUSK	SKAS	SKUA	TAKA	TONK	WEAK	YEUK	ZONK
POKE	RANK	RYKE	SKAT	SKUG	TAKE	TOOK	WEEK	YIKE	ZOUK
POKY	REAK	SACK	SKAW	SKYR	TAKI	TOUK	WEKA	YIRK	
POLK	RECK	SAKE	SKEG	SOAK	TAKS	TREK	WELK	YLKE	

K – 5-letter words

ABACK	BISKS	CAWKS	DARKY	FAKED	GUCKY	JINKS	KARRI	KEXES	KLANG
ABASK	BLACK	CHACK	DAWKS	FAKER	GUNKS	JOCKO	KARST	KEYED	KLOOF
ACKEE	BLANK	CHALK	DECKO	FAKES	HACEK	JOCKS	KARSY	KHADI	KLUTZ
ACOCK	BLEAK	CHANK	DECKS	FAKIR	HACKS	JOKED	KARTS	KHAKI	KNACK
AKEES	BLINK	CHARK	DEKKO	FANKS	HAICK	JOKER	KARZY	KHANS	KNAGS
AKENE	BLOCK	CHECK	DESKS	FECKS	HAIKS	JOKES	KASHA	KHATS	KNAPS
AKING	BLOKE	CHEEK	DHAKS	FENKS	HAIKU	JOKEY	KATAS	KHAYA	KNARL
AKKAS	BLUNK	CHEKA	DICKS	FIKED	HAKAM	JOKOL	KATIS	KHEDA	KNARS
ALACK	BOAKS	CHICK	DICKY	FIKES	HAKAS	JOOKS	KATTI	KHOJA	KNAVE
ALIKE	BOBAK	CHIKS	DIKAS	FINKS	HAKES	JOUKS	KAUGH	KHORS	KNEAD
ALKIE	BOCKS	CHINK	DIKED	FIRKS	HAKIM	JUKED	KAURI	KHUDS	KNEEL
ALKYD	BOINK	CHIRK	DIKER	FISKS	HANKS	JUKES	KAVAS	KIANG	KNEES
ALKYL	BOKED	CHOCK	DIKES	FLACK	HANKY	JUNKS	KAWED	KIBES	KNELL
AMUCK	BOKES	CHOKE	DIKEY	FLAKE	HARKS	JUNKY	KAYAK	KICKS	KNELT
ANKER	BOKOS	CHOKO	DINKS	FLAKS	HASKS	KAAMA	KAYLE	KIDDO	KNIFE
ANKHS	BONKS	CHOKY	DINKY	FLAKY	HAWKS	KABAB	KAYOS	KIDDY	KNISH
ANKLE	BOOKS	CHOOK	DIRKE	FLANK	HECKS	KABOB	KAZIS	KIDEL	KNITS
ANKUS	BOOKY	CHUCK	DIRKS	FLASK	HICKS	KACHA	KAZOO	KIDGE	KNOBS
APEAK	BORAK	CHUNK	DISKS	FLECK	HOCKS	KADES	KEBAB	KIERS	KNOCK
APEEK	BOSKS	CLACK	DOCKS	FLICK	HOICK	KADIS	KEBOB	KIEVE	KNOLL
ARAKS	BOSKY	CLECK	DOEKS	FLISK	HOIKS	KAGOS	KECKS	KIGHT	KNOPS
ARKED	BOUKS	CLEEK	DOOKS	FLOCK	HOKED	KAHAL	KEDGE	KIKES	KNOTS
ASKED	BRACK	CLERK	DORKS	FLUKE	HOKES	KAIAK	KEDGY	KIKOI	KNOUT
ASKER	BRAKE	CLICK	DORKY	FLUNK	HOKEY	KAIDS	KEECH	KILEY	KNOWE
ASKEW	BRAKY	CLINK	DRAKE	FOLKS	HOKIS	KAIES	KEEKS	KILIM	KNOWN
ATOKE	BRANK	CLOAK	DRANK	FORKS	HOKKU	KAIFS	KEELS	KILLS	KNOWS
ATOKS	BREAK	CLOCK	DRECK	FORKY	HOKUM	KAIMS	KEENS	KILNS	KNUBS
AWAKE	BRICK	CLOKE	DREKS	FRACK	HONKS	KAING	KEEPS	KILOS	KNURL
AWOKE	BRINK	CLONK	DRINK	FRANK	HONKY	KAINS	KEEVE	KILPS	KNURR
AWORK	BRISK	CLUCK	DROOK	FREAK	HOOKA	KAKAS	KEFIR	KILTS	KNURS
BACKS	BROCK	CLUNK	DROUK	FRISK	HOOKS	KAKIS	KELIM	KILTY	KNUTS
BAKED	BROKE	COCKS	DRUNK	FROCK	HOOKY	KALES	KELLS	KIMBO	KOALA
BAKEN	BROOK	COCKY	DUCKS	FUCKS	HOWKS	KALIF	KELLY	KINAS	KOANS
BAKER	BUCKO	COKED	DUCKY	FUNKS	HUCKS	KALIS	KELPS	KINDA	KOBAN
BAKES	BUCKS	COKES	DUKED	FUNKY	HULKS	KALPA	KELPY	KINDS	KOFTA
BALKS	BUCKU	CONKS	DUKES	FYKED	HULKY	KAMAS	KELTS	KINDY	KOHLS
BALKY	BUIKS	CONKY	DUMKA	FYKES	HUNKS	KAMES	KELTY	KINGS	KOINE
BANKS	BUKES	COOKS	DUMKY	GAWKS	HUNKY	KAMIK	KEMBO	KININ	KOKER
BARKS	BULKS	COOKY	DUNKS	GAWKY	HUSKS	KAMIS	KEMBS	KINKS	KOKRA
BARKY	BULKY	CORKS	DUSKS	GECKO	HUSKY	KAMME	KEMPS	KINKY	KOKUM
BASKS	BUNKO	CORKY	DUSKY	GECKS	HYKES	KANAE	KEMPT	KINOS	KOLAS
BATIK	BUNKS	CRACK	DYKED	GEEKS	ICKER	KANAH	KENAF	KIOSK	KOLOS
BAUKS	BURKA	CRAKE	DYKES	GEEKY	IKATS	KANAS	KENDO	KIPES	KOMBU
BAULK	BURKE	CRANK	DYKEY	GINKS	IKONS	KANDY	KENOS	KIPPA	KONKS
BEAKS	BURKS	CREAK	EIKED	GLAIK	INKED	KANEH	KENTS	KIPPS	KOOKS
BEAKY	BUSKS	CREEK	EIKON	GLEEK	INKER	KANGA	KEPIS	KIRKS	KOOKY
BECKE	BUSKY	CRICK	EKING	GLIKE	INKLE	KANGS	KERBS	KIRNS	KOORI
BECKS	BYKED	CROAK	EKKAS	GLISK	IRKED	KANJI	KERFS	KIRRI	KOPHS
BEKAH	BYKES	CROCK	ENOKI	GONKS	IROKO	KANTS	KERNE	KISAN	KOPJE
BERKS	CAKED	CRONK	ENSKY	GOOKS	JACKS	KANZU	KERNS	KISTS	KOPPA
BIKED	CAKES	CROOK	ERICK	GOPAK	JAKES	KAONS	KETAS	KITED	KORAS
BIKER	CAKEY	CRUCK	ESKAR	GOUKS	JARKS	KAPOK	KETCH	KITES	KORES
BIKES	CALKS	CUSKS	ESKER	GOWKS	JERKS	KAPPA	KEVEL	KITHE	KORMA
BIKIE	CARKS	DAKER	EUKED	GRIKE	JERKY	KAPUT		KITHS	
BILKS	CASKS	DANKS	EVOKE	GRYKE		KARAS		KITTY	
BINKS	CAUKS	DARKS	EWKED	GUCKS		KARAT		KIVAS	
BIRKS	CAULK		FAIKS			KARKS		KIWIS	

KOSES	LEEKS	NARKS	PINKY	RANKE	SINKS	SKYEY	STEEK	TOKOS	WICKS
KOTOS	LICKS	NARKY	PISKY	RANKS	SINKY	SKYRE	STICK	TONKS	WICKY
KOTOW	LIKED	NEBEK	PLACK	REAKS	SKAGS	SKYRS	STINK	TOPEK	WINKS
KRAAL	LIKEN	NECKS	PLANK	RECKS	SKAIL	SKYTE	STIRK	TORSK	WOKEN
KRABS	LIKER	NERKA	PLINK	REEKS	SKALD	SLACK	STOCK	TOUKS	WOCKS
KRAFT	LIKES	NERKS	PLONK	REEKY	SKANK	SLAKE	STOKE	TRACK	WONKS
KRAIT	LIKIN	NEUKS	PLOOK	REIKI	SKART	SLEEK	STONK	TRAIK	WONKY
KRANG	LINKS	NICKS	PLOUK	REIKS	SKATE	SLICK	STOOK	TRECK	WORKS
KRANS	LIRKS	NIKAU	PLUCK	REKED	SKATS	SLINK	STORK	TREKS	WRACK
KRANZ	LISKS	NOCKS	PLUNK	REKES	SKATT	SLUNK	STUCK	TRICK	WREAK
KRAUT	LOCKS	NOOKS	POAKA	RICKS	SKAWS	SMACK	STUNK	TRIKE	WRECK
KRENG	LOKES	NOOKY	POAKE	RINKS	SKEAN	SMAIK	SUCKS	TROCK	WRICK
KRILL	LOOKS	NORKS	POCKS	RISKS	SKEAR	SMEEK	SUKHS	TROKE	WROKE
KRONA	LUCKS	NUKED	POCKY	RISKY	SKEER	SMIRK	SULKS	TRUCK	YACKS
KRONE	LUCKY	NUKES	POKAL	ROCKS	SKEET	SMOCK	SULKY	TRUNK	YAKKA
KSARS	LURKS	OAKEN	POKED	ROCKY	SKEGG	SMOKE	SUNKS	TUCKS	YAKOW
KUDOS	LUSKS	OAKER	POKER	ROKED	SKEGS	SMOKO	SUKHS	TUPEK	YANKS
KUDUS	MACKS	OAKUM	POKES	ROKER	SKEIN	SMOKY	SWACK	TUPIK	YAPOK
KUDZU	MAIKO	OCKER	POKEY	ROKES	SKELF	SNACK	SWANK	TUSKS	YELKS
KUKRI	MAIKS	OINKS	POLKA	ROOKS	SKELL	SNAKE	SWINK	TUSKY	YERKS
KUKUS	MAKAR	OKAPI	POLKS	ROOKY	SKELM	SNAKY	SYKER	TWANK	YESKS
KULAK	MAKER	OKAYS	PONKS	RUCKS	SKELP	SNARK	SYKES	TWEAK	YEUKS
KULAN	MAKES	OKRAS	POOKA	RUKHS	SKENE	SNEAK	TACKS	TWINK	YIKES
KURIS	MAKOS	OKTAS	POOKS	RUSKS	SKEOS	SNECK	TACKY	TYKES	YIRKS
KURRE	MALIK	ONKUS	POOKS	RYKED	SKEPS	SNICK	TAKAS	UKASE	YLIKE
KURTA	MANKY	OTAKU	PORKS	RYKES	SKERS	SNOEK	TAKEN	UMIAK	YLKES
KURUS	MARKS	OULKS	PORKY	SACKS	SKEWS	SNOKE	TAKER	UNKED	YOCKS
KUTCH	MASKS	OZEKI	POUKE	SAICK	SKIDS	SNOOK	TAKES	UNKET	YOICK
KUZUS	MAWKS	PACKS	POUKS	SAKER	SKIED	SNOWK	TAKHI	UNKID	YOKED
KVASS	MAWKY	PAIKS	PRANK	SAKES	SKIER	SNUCK	TAKIN	UPTAK	YOKEL
KWELA	MELIK	PAKKA	PRICK	SAKIA	SKIES	SOAKS	TAKIS	VAKIL	YOKES
KYANG	MERKS	PALKI	PRINK	SAKIS	SKIEY	SOCKO	TALAK	VODKA	YOKUL
KYATS	MICKS	PARKA	PROKE	SANKO	SKIFF	SOCKS	TALKS	VOLKS	YOLKS
KYDST	MICKY	PARKI	PRONK	SARKS	SKILL	SOKAH	TALKY	VOLKS	YOLKY
KYLES	MIKRA	PARKS	PUCKA	SARKY	SKIMP	SOKEN	TALUK	WACKE	YONKS
KYLIE	MIKVA	PARKY	PUCKS	SCULK	SKIMS	SOKES	TANKA	WACKO	YORKS
KYLIN	MILKO	PAWKS	PUKED	SEEKS	SKINK	SOOKS	TANKS	WACKY	YOUKS
KYLIX	MILKS	PAWKY	PUKER	SEKOS	SKINS	SOUKS	TANKY	WAKAS	YUCKS
KYLOE	MILKY	PEAKS	PUKES	SEKTS	SKINT	SPAKE	TAROK	WAKED	YUCKY
KYNDE	MINKE	PEAKY	PUKKA	SKIOS	SKIPS	SPANK	TASKS	WAKEN	YUKED
KYNDS	MINKS	PECKE	PULKA	SERKS	SKIRL	SPARK	TEAKS	WAKER	YUKES
KYTES	MIRKS	PECKS	PULKS	SHACK	SKIRR	SPEAK	TEREK	WAKES	YUKKY
KYTHE	MOCKS	PEEKS	PUNKA	SHAKE	SKIRT	SPECK	THACK	WAKFS	YUKOS
LACKS	MOKES	PEKAN	PUNKS	SHAKO	SKITE	SPEKS	THANK	WALKS	ZACKS
LAIKA	MOKIS	PEKES	QUACK	SHAKT	SKITS	SPELK	THEEK	WANKS	ZAKAT
LAIKS	MOKOS	PEKOE	QUAKE	SHANK	SKIVE	SPELL	THICK	WANKY	ZINKE
LAKED	MONKS	PENKS	QUAKY	SHARK	SKIVY	SPICK	THILK	WARKS	ZINKY
LAKER	MOOKS	PERKS	QUARK	SHEIK	SKLIM	SPIKE	THINK	WAUKS	ZONKS
LAKES	MUCKS	PERKY	QUICK	SHIRK	SKOAL	SPIKS	TICKS	WAUKT	ZOOKS
LAKHS	MUCKY	PESKY	QUIRK	SHMEK	SKOFF	SPIKY	TICKY	WAULK	ZOUKS
LAKIN	MUJIK	PICKS	QUONK	SHOCK	SKRAN	SPINK	TIKAS	WEEKE	
LANKS	MURKS	PICKY	RACKS	SHOOK	SKRIK	SPOKE	TIKES	WEEKS	
LANKY	MURKY	PIKAS	RAIKS	SHUCK	SKUAS	SPOOK	TIKIS	WEKAS	
LARKS	MUSKS	PIKED	RAKED	SICKO	SKUGS	SPUNK	TIKKA	WELKE	
LARKY	MUSKY	PIKER	RAKEE	SICKS	SKULK	STACK	TINKS	WELKS	
LATKE	NABKS	PIKES	RAKER	SIKAS	SKULL	STAKE	TOCKS	WELKT	
LAWKS	NAIKS	PIKUL	RAKES	SIKES	SKUNK	STALK	TOKAY	WHACK	
LEAKS	NAKED	PINKO	RAKIS	SILKS	SKYER	STANK	TOKED	WHELK	
LEAKY	NAKER	PINKS	RAKUS	SILKY	STEAK	STARK	TOKEN	WHELM	
								WHILK	
								WHISK	

V-WORDS

V – 3-letter words

AVA	GOV	LEV	SOV	VAN	VEE	VIA	VIN	VOL	VUG
AVE	GUV	LUV	UVA	VAS	VEG	VID	VIS	VOR	VUM
DIV	IVY	OVA	VAC	VAT	VET	VIE	VLY	VOW	
EVE	LAV	REV	VAE	VAU	VEX	VIM	VOE	VOX	

V – 4-letter words

ARVO	AVID	CHIV	DEVA	DOVE	EVES	FIVE	GYVE	JUVE	LAVS
AVAL	AVOW	CIVE	DIVA	EEVN	EVET	GAVE	HAVE	KAVA	LEVA
AVAS	BEVY	COVE	DIVE	ENVY	EVIL	GIVE	HIVE	KIVA	LEVE
AVER	CAVE	DEEV	DIVI	EVEN	EVOE	GOVS	HOVE	LAVA	LEVY
AVES	CAVY	DERV	DIVS	EVER	FAVE	GUVS	JIVE	LAVE	LIVE

LOVE	PAVE	URVA	VANE	VEAL	VENT	VICE	VINS	VLEI	VUGS
LUVS	PERV	UVAE	VANG	VEEP	VERB	VIDE	VINT	VOAR	VULN
MEVE	RAVE	UVAS	VANS	VEER	VERS	VIDS	VINY	VOES	VUMS
MIRV	REVS	UVEA	VANT	VEES	VERT	VIED	VIOL	VOID	WAVE
MOVE	RIVA	VACS	VARA	VEGA	VERY	VIER	VIRE	VOLA	WAVY
NAVE	RIVE	VADE	VARE	VEHM	VEST	VIES	VIRL	VOLE	WIVE
NAVY	RIVO	VAES	VARY	VEIL	VETO	VIEW	VISA	VOLK	WOVE
NEVE	ROVE	VAGI	VASA	VEIN	VETS	VILD	VISE	VOLS	YEVE
NEVI	SAVE	VAIL	VASE	VELA	VEXT	VILE	VITA	VOLT	
NOVA	SHIV	VAIN	VAST	VELD	VIAE	VILL	VITE	VORS	
OVAL	SOVS	VAIR	VATS	VELE	VIAL	VIMS	VIVA	VOTE	
OVEN	SPIV	VALE	VATU	VELL	VIAS	VINA	VIVE	VOWS	
OVER	TAVA	VALI	VAUS	VENA	VIBE	VINE	VIVO	VRIL	
OVUM	ULVA	VAMP	VAUT	VEND	VIBS	VINO	VIZY	VROW	

V – 5-letter words

ABOVE	CIVVY	EVERY	KERVE	NAVEW	REIVE	TAVAS	VEEPS	VIGIA	VOARS
ADVEW	CLAVE	EVETS	KEVEL	NAVVY	REVEL	TAVER	VEERS	VIGIL	VOCAB
AGAVE	CLEVE	EVHOE	KIEVE	NEIVE	REVET	TRAVE	VEERY	VIGOR	VOCAL
ALIVE	CLOVE	EVICT	KIVAS	NERVE	REVIE	ULVAS	VEGAN	VILDE	VOCES
AMOVE	CONVO	EVILS	KNAVE	NERVY	REVUE	URVAS	VEGAS	VILER	VODKA
ANVIL	COVED	EVITE	KNIVE	NEVEL	RIEVE	UVEAL	VEGES	VILLA	VOGIE
ARVAL	COVEN	EVOHE	KVASS	NEVER	RIVAL	UVEAS	VEGIE	VILLI	VOGUE
ARVOS	COVER	EVOKE	LARVA	NEVES	RIVAS	UVULA	VEHME	VILLS	VOICE
AVAIL	COVES	FAVEL	LAVAS	NEVUS	RIVED	VACUA	VEILS	VINAL	VOIDS
AVALE	COVET	FAVER	LAVED	NIEVE	RIVEL	VADED	VEILY	VINAS	VOILA
AVANT	COVEY	FAVOR	LAVER	NIVAL	RIVEN	VADES	VEINS	VINCA	VOILE
AVAST	COVIN	FAVUS	LAVES	NOVAE	RIVER	VAGAL	VEINY	VINED	VOLAE
AVENS	CRAVE	FEVER	LAVRA	NOVAS	RIVES	VAGUE	VELAR	VINER	VOLAR
AVERS	CRUVE	FIVER	LEAVE	NOVEL	RIVET	VAGUS	VELDS	VINES	VOLED
AVERT	CURVE	FIVES	LEAVY	NOVUM	RIVOS	VAILS	VELDT	VINEW	VOLES
AVGAS	CURVY	FOVEA	LEVEE	OAVES	ROVED	VAIRE	VELES	VINOS	VOLET
AVIAN	CUVEE	GAVEL	LEVEL	OGIVE	ROVER	VAIRS	VELLS	VINTS	VOLKS
AVINE	DAVEN	GIVED	LEVER	OLIVE	ROVES	VAIRY	VELUM	VINYL	VOLTA
AVION	DAVIT	GIVEN	LEVIN	OLLAV	SALVE	VAKIL	VENAE	VIOLA	VOLTE
AVISE	DEAVE	GIVER	LEVIS	ORVAL	SALVO	VALES	VENAL	VIOLD	VOLTS
AVISO	DEEVE	GIVES	LIEVE	OVALS	SAVED	VALET	VENDS	VIOLS	VOLVA
AVIZE	DEEVS	GLOVE	LIVED	OVARY	SAVER	VALID	VENEY	VIPER	VOLVE
AVOID	DELVE	GRAVE	LIVEN	OVATE	SAVES	VALIS	VENGE	VIRAL	VOMER
AVOWS	DERVS	GRAVY	LIVER	OVENS	SAVEY	VALOR	VENIN	VIRED	VOMIT
AVYZE	DEVAS	GREVE	LIVES	OVERS	SAVIN	VALSE	VENOM	VIREO	VOTED
AWAVE	DEVEL	GROVE	LIVID	OVERT	SAVOR	VALUE	VENTS	VIRES	VOTER
BAVIN	DEVIL	GUAVA	LIVOR	OVINE	SAVOY	VALVE	VENUE	VIRGA	VOTES
BEVEL	DEVOT	GYVED	LIVRE	OVIST	SAVVY	VAMPS	VENUS	VIRGE	VOUCH
BEVER	DIVAN	GYVES	LOAVE	OVOID	SELVA	VANED	VERBS	VIRID	VOUGE
BEVUE	DIVAS	HALVA	LOVAT	OVOLI	SENVY	VANES	VERGE	VIRLS	VOULU
BEVVY	DIVED	HALVE	LOVED	OVOLO	SERVE	VANGS	VERRY	VIRTU	VOWED
BIVIA	DIVER	HAVEN	LOVER	OVULE	SERVO	VANTS	VERSE	VIRUS	VOWEL
BIVVY	DIVES	HAVER	LOVES	PAVAN	SEVEN	VAPID	VERSO	VISAS	VOWER
BLIVE	DIVIS	HAVES	LOVEY	PAVED	SEVER	VAPOR	VERST	VISED	VOXEL
BOVID	DIVOT	HAVOC	LURVE	PAVEN	SHAVE	VARAN	VERTS	VISES	VOZHD
BRAVA	DIVVY	HEAVE	LUVVY	PAVER	SHEVA	VARAS	VERTU	VISIE	VRAIC
BRAVE	DOVED	HEAVY	MALVA	PAVES	SHIVE	VARDY	VERVE	VISIT	VRILS
BRAVI	DOVER	HELVE	MAUVE	PAVID	SHIVS	VAREC	VESPA	VISNE	VROOM
BRAVO	DOVES	HEVEA	MAVEN	PAVIN	SHOVE	VARES	VESTA	VISON	VROUW
BREVE	DOVIE	HIVED	MAVIN	PAVIS	SIEVE	VARIX	VESTS	VISOR	VROWS
CALVE	DRAVE	HIVER	MAVIS	PEAVY	SILVA	VARNA	VETCH	VISTA	VUGGY
CARVE	DRIVE	HIVES	MEVED	PEEVE	SIVER	VARUS	VEXED	VISTO	VULGO
CARVY	DROVE	HOOVE	MEVES	PERVE	SKIVE	VARVE	VEXER	VITAE	VULNS
CAVED	DUVET	HOVED	MIEVE	PERVS	SKIVY	VASAL	VEXES	VITAL	VULVA
CAVEL	EAVES	HOVEL	MIRVS	PIVOT	SLAVE	VASES	VEZIR	VITAS	VYING
CAVER	EEVEN	HOVEN	MOOVE	POOVE	SLIVE	VASTS	VIALS	VITEX	WAIVE
CAVES	EEVNS	HOVER	MOVED	POOVY	SLOVE	VASTY	VIAND	VITTA	WAVED
CAVIE	ELVAN	HOVES	MOVER	PREVE	SOLVE	VATIC	VIBES	VIVAS	WAVER
CAVIL	ELVER	IVIED	MOVES	PRIVY	SPIVS	VATUS	VIBEX	VIVAT	WAVES
CHAVE	ELVES	IVIES	MOVIE	PROVE	STAVE	VAULT	VICAR	VIVDA	WAVEY
CHEVY	EMOVE	IVORY	MURVA	RAVED	STIVE	VAUNT	VICED	VIVER	WEAVE
CHIVE	ENVOI	JAVEL	MVULE	RAVEL	STIVY	VAUTE	VICES	VIVES	WIVED
CHIVS	ENVOY	JIVED	NAEVE	RAVEN	STOVE	VAUTS	VICHY	VIVID	WIVES
CHIVY	ERVEN	JIVER	NAEVI	RAVER	SUAVE	VAWTE	VIDEO	VIXEN	WOLVE
CIVES	EVADE	JIVES	NAIVE	RAVES	SWIVE	VEALE	VIERS	VIZIR	WOVEN
CIVET	EVENS	JUVES	NAVAL	RAVIN	SYLVA	VEALS	VIEWS	VIZOR	YEVEN
CIVIC	EVENT	KAVAS	NAVEL	REAVE	SYVER	VEALY	VIEWY	VLEIS	YEVES
CIVIL	EVERT	KEEVE	NAVES	REEVE	TAVAH	VEENA	VIFDA	VLIES	YRIVD

Q But No U

If you are not familiar with *Official Scrabble*® *Words* you may be unaware that there are quite a few words that contain Q with no U. These are all to be found in the Q lists but it is worth highlighting them separately. You should certainly write down and learn the shorter ones as they are so vital in situations that would otherwise necessitate a change.

QI, QAT, QADI, QOPH, WAQF, QANAT, QIBLA, TALAQ,
QASIDA, QAWWAL, QIGONG, QINDAR, QINTAR, QWERTY, YAQONA,
INQILAB, QABALAH, QAWWALI, QAWWALS, QINDARS, TSADDIQ, TZADDIQ,
MBAQANGA, QAIMAQAM, QALAMDAN, QAWWALIS,
TSADDIQIM, TZADDIQIM.

Note that -S plural forms are all allowed except for TSADDIQIM and TZADDIQIM, which are already plural. QWERTY has the plural QWERTIES as well as QWERTYS. Also note that the following Q words and their corresponding -S plural forms have a U, but not after the Q.

BURQA, MUQADDAM, QIVIUT, QINGHAOSU, SUQ.

Knowing Non-Words

Much time can be wasted in a game when you have a promising-looking set of seven letters on your rack but can't remember whether they make a 7-letter word or not. Therefore it is also beneficial to be familiar with those common sets of seven letters that *don't* make a 7-letter word. Some examples are: ENRAISE, ROGATED, and TAILEND. Note that by forming 'non-words' with these racks they can be more easily recognized during play. Having armed yourself with a selection of non-words the next task is to learn the possible 8-letter plays so that you can be aware of possible bonus plays using available letters on the board. For example, the TAILEND set makes 8-letter words with the letters A B D E F G O P U V. These words and those of other non-words mentioned above can be readily unearthed from the 8-Letter Bonus Sets. For other non-words you might create, such as IRELAND, that don't appear in the top 8-Letter Bonus Sets, you will be able to use the 8-Letter Anagram lists to discover the relevant 8-letter words.

High Scorers

All the words of length two to eight letters which contain any of the four high-scoring letters J, Q, X and Z are listed below. While most Scrabble players know the obvious words, such as JUDGE, QUEEN, EXALT and ZEROS, how many know the more obscure POOJA, SQUEG, SIXTE and NIZAM?

Knowing these words will enable you to be more adventurous when it comes to grabbing the odd triple-word-score square for 50 or so points. It could also help you to play a bonus word with six single-point letters and a high-scoring letter, such as NAARTJE, LASQUES, ANOXIAS and LAIRIZE. You might even be able to play a bonus word using a letter on the board, with words such as REJONEOS, EQUITANT, XENURINE and LAZURITE.

If a word contains two of these four high-scoring letters (as do, for example, JYNX, QUIZ, BANJAX and ZOOTAXY), then it will appear in two lists.

J-WORDS

J – 2-letter words

JO

J – 3-letter words

GJU	JAG	JAP	JAY	JEU	JIG	JOE	JOT	JUD	JUT
HAJ	JAK	JAR	JEE	JEW	JIZ	JOG	JOW	JUG	RAJ
JAB	JAM	JAW	JET	JIB	JOB	JOR	JOY	JUS	TAJ

J – 4-letter words

AJAR	JADE	JARL	JEAT	JEUX	JINX	JOHN	JOTA	JUGA	JUVE
AJEE	JAGS	JARS	JEED	JEWS	JIRD	JOIN	JOTS	JUGS	JYNX
BAJU	JAIL	JASP	JEEL	JIAO	JISM	JOKE	JOUK	JUJU	MOJO
BENJ	JAKE	JASS	JEER	JIBE	JIVE	JOKY	JOUR	JUKE	PUJA
DOJO	JAKS	JASY	JEES	JIBS	JIZZ	JOLE	JOWL	JUMP	RAJA
GAJO	JAMB	JATO	JEFF	JIFF	JOBE	JOLL	JOWS	JUNK	ROJI
GJUS	JAMS	JAUP	JELL	JIGS	JOBS	JOLT	JOYS	JURA	SIJO
HADJ	JANE	JAWS	JERK	JILL	JOCK	JOMO	JOSH	JURE	SOJA
HAJI	JANN	JAYS	JESS	JILT	JOCO	JOOK	JUBA	JURY	
HAJJ	JAPE	JAZY	JEST	JIMP	JOES	JORS	JUBE	JUST	
JABS	JAPS	JAZZ	JETE	JINK	JOEY	JOSH	JUDO	JUTE	
JACK	JARK	JEAN	JETS	JINN	JOGS	JOSS	JUDS	JUTS	
								JUDY	

J – 5-letter words

AFLAJ	FALAJ	JABOT	JAMMY	JATOS	JELAB	JEUNE	JIMPY	JOCKS	JOLLY
AJWAN	FJORD	JACKS	JANES	JAUNT	JELLO	JEWED	JINGO	JODEL	JOLTS
BAJAN	GADJE	JADED	JANNS	JAUPS	JELLS	JEWEL	JINKS	JOEYS	JOLTY
BAJRA	GAJOS	JADES	JANTY	JAVEL	JELLY	JHALA	JINNI	JOHNS	JOMOS
BAJRI	GANJA	JAGER	JAPAN	JAWAN	JEMMY	JIAOS	JINNS	JOINS	JONTY
BAJUS	GAUJE	JAGGY	JAPED	JAWED	JENNY	JIBED	JIRDS	JOINT	JOOKS
BANJO	HADJI	JAGIR	JAPER	JAZZY	JERID	JIBER	JIRGA	JOIST	JORAM
BIJOU	HAJES	JAILS	JAPES	JEANS	JERKS	JIBES	JISMS	JOKED	JORUM
BUNJE	HAJIS	JAKES	JARKS	JEATS	JERKY	JIFFS	JIVED	JOKER	JOTAS
BUNJY	HAJJI	JALAP	JARLS	JEBEL	JERRY	JIFFY	JIVER	JOKES	JOTUN
CAJUN	HEJAB	JAMBE	JARTA	JEELS	JESTS	JIGOT	JIVES	JOKEY	JOUAL
DJINN	HEJRA	JAMBO	JARUL	JEELY	JESUS	JIHAD	JNANA	JOKOL	JOUGS
DOJOS	HIJAB	JAMBS	JASEY	JEERS	JETES	JILLS	JOBED	JOLED	JOUKS
EJECT	HIJRA	JAMBU	JASPE	JEFFS	JETON	JILTS	JOBES	JOLES	JOULE
ENJOY	HODJA	JAMES	JASPS	JEHAD	JETTY	JIMMY	JOCKO	JOLLS	JOURS

JOUST	JUBES	JUICY	JUMBY	JUNTO	JUTTY	MOJOS	PUJAS	SAJOU	UPJET
JOWAR	JUDAS	JUJUS	JUMPS	JUPON	JUVES	MUJIK	RAJAH	SHOJI	WILJA
JOWED	JUDGE	JUKED	JUMPY	JURAL	KANJI	NINJA	RAJAS	SIJOS	YOJAN
JOWLS	JUDOS	JUKES	JUNCO	JURAT	KHOJA	OBJET	RAJES	SOJAS	ZANJA
JOWLY	JUGAL	JULEP	JUNKS	JUROR	KOPJE	OJIME	REJIG	SUJEE	
JOYED	JUGUM	JUMAR	JUNKY	JUSTS	LAPJE	OUIJA	REJON	TAJES	
JUBAS	JUICE	JUMBO	JUNTA	JUTES	MAJOR	POOJA	ROJIS	THUJA	

J – 6-letter words

ABJECT	FINJAN	JACKSY	JARGON	JELABS	JIGJIG	JOGGER	JOVIAL	JUNCUS	OBJECT
ABJURE	FJORDS	JADERY	JAROOL	JELLED	JIGOTS	JOGGLE	JOWARI	JUNGLE	OBJETS
ACAJOU	FRIJOL	JADING	JARRAH	JELLOS	JIGSAW	JOHNNY	JOWARS	JUNGLI	OBJURE
ADJOIN	GADJES	JADISH	JARRED	JEMIMA	JIHADS	JOINED	JOWING	JUNGLY	OJIMES
ADJURE	GAIJIN	JAEGER	JARTAS	JENNET	JILGIE	JOINER	JOWLED	JUNIOR	OUIJAS
ADJUST	GANJAS	JAGERS	JARULS	JERBOA	JILLET	JOINTS	JOWLER	JUNKED	OUTJET
AJOWAN	GARJAN	JAGGED	JARVEY	JERBIL	JIMINY	JOISTS	JOYFUL	JUNKER	OUTJUT
AJWANS	GAUJES	JAGGER	JARVIE	JEREED	JIMJAM	JOJOBA	JOYING	JUNKET	PAJOCK
BAJADA	GIDJEE	JAGHIR	JASEYS	JERIDS	JIMPER	JOKERS	JOYOUS	JUNKIE	POOJAH
BAJANS	GURJUN	JAGIRS	JASIES	JERKED	JIMPLY	JOKIER	JUBATE	JUNTAS	POOJAS
BAJRAS	HADJES	JAGUAR	JASPER	JERKER	JINGAL	JOKING	JUBBAH	JUNTOS	POPJOY
BAJREE	HADJIS	JAILED	JASPES	JERKIN	JINGLE	JOLING	JUDDER	JUPATI	RAJAHS
BAJRIS	HAJJES	JAILER	JASPIS	JERQUE	JINGLY	JOLLED	JUDGED	JUPONS	RAMJET
BANJAX	HAJJIS	JAILOR	JASSES	JERSEY	JINKED	JOLLEY	JUDGES	JURANT	REJECT
BANJOS	HANJAR	JALAPS	JATAKA	JESSED	JINKER	JOLTED	JUDIES	JURATS	REJIGS
BEJADE	HEJABS	JALOPY	JAUNCE	JESSES	JINNEE	JOLTER	JUDOGI	JURIES	REJOIN
BEJANT	HEJRAS	JAMBEE	JAUNSE	JESSIE	JINXED	JOOKED	JUDOKA	JURIST	SAJOUS
BENJES	HIJABS	JAMBER	JAUNTS	JESTED	JINXES	JORAMS	JUGALS	JURORS	SANJAK
BHAJAN	HIJACK	JAMBES	JAUNTY	JESTEE	JIRBLE	JORDAN	JUGATE	JUSTED	SEJANT
BHAJEE	HIJRAH	JAMBOK	JAUPED	JESTER	JIRGAS	JORUMS	JUGFUL	JUSTER	SHOJIS
BIJOUX	HIJRAS	JAMBOS	JAVELS	JETONS	JISSOM	JOSEPH	JUGGED	JUSTLE	SOOJEY
BUNJEE	HOBJOB	JAMBUL	JAWANS	JETSAM	JITNEY	JOSHED	JUGGLE	JUSTLY	SUJEES
BUNJES	HODJAS	JAMBUS	JAWARI	JETSOM	JITTER	JOSHER	JUGLET	JUTTED	SWARAJ
BUNJIE	INJECT	JAMJAR	JAWBOX	JETSON	JIVERS	JOSHES	JUICED	JYMOLD	TAJINE
CAJOLE	INJERA	JAMMED	JAWING	JETTED	JIVING	JOSKIN	JUICER	JYNXES	TINAJA
COJOIN	INJURE	JAMMER	JAZIES	JETTON	JIZZES	JOSSER	JUICES	KANJIS	UJAMAA
CONJEE	INJURY	JAMPAN	JAZZED	JEWELS	JNANAS	JOSSES	JUJUBE	KHODJA	UNJUST
DEEJAY	JABBED	JAMPOT	JAZZER	JEWING	JOANNA	JOSTLE	JUKING	KHOJAS	UPJETS
DEJECT	JABBER	JANDAL	JAZZES	JEZAIL	JOBBED	JOTTED	JULEPS	KOPJES	WILJAS
DJEBEL	JABBLE	JANGLE	JEBELS	JHALAS	JOBBER	JOTTER	JUMARS	LAPJES	WILTJA
DJINNI	JABERS	JANGLY	JEEING	JIBBAH	JOBBIE	JOTUNN	JUMART	MAJLIS	YOJANA
DONJON	JABIRU	JANKER	JEELED	JIBBED	JOBING	JOTUNS	JUMBAL	MAJORS	YOJANS
EJECTA	JABOTS	JANSKY	JEELIE	JIBBER	JOCKEY	JOUALS	JUMBIE	MASJID	ZANJAS
EJECTS	JACANA	JANTEE	JEERED	JIBERS	JOCKOS	JOUKED	JUMBLE	MATJES	
ENJAMB	JACENT	JAPANS	JEERER	JIBING	JOCOSE	JOULED	JUMBLY	MEJLIS	
ENJOIN	JACKAL	JAPERS	JEFFED	JIGGED	JOCUND	JOULES	JUMBOS	MOJOES	
ENJOYS	JACKED	JAPING	JEHADS	JIGGER	JODELS	JOUNCE	JUMPED	MOUJIK	
EVEJAR	JACKET	JAPPED	JEJUNA	JIGGLE	JOGGED	JOURNO	JUMPER	MUJIKS	
FEIJOA		JARFUL	JEJUNE	JIGGLY		JOUSTS	JUNCOS	NINJAS	

J – 7-letter words

ABJECTS	BEJADES	CONJURY	GIDJEES	JABIRUS	JAGGERY	JAMBOOL	JAPPING	JAVELIN
ABJOINT	BEJANTS	DEEJAYS	GOUJONS	JACAMAR	JAGGIER	JAMBULS	JARFULS	JAWARIS
ABJURED	BEJEWEL	DEJECTA	GURJUNS	JACANAS	JAGGING	JAMDANI	JARGONS	JAWBONE
ABJURER	BHAJANS	DEJECTS	HANDJAR	JACCHUS	JAGHIRE	JAMESES	JARGOON	JAWFALL
ABJURES	BHAJEES	DISJECT	HANJARS	JACINTH	JAGHIRS	JAMJARS	JARKMAN	JAWHOLE
ACAJOUS	BLOWJOB	DISJOIN	HEJIRAS	JACKALS	JAILERS	JAMMERS	JARKMEN	JAWINGS
ADJOINS	BONJOUR	DJEBELS	HIJACKS	JACKDAW	JAILING	JAMMIER	JAROOLS	JAZZERS
ADJOINT	BRINJAL	DJIBBAH	HIJINKS	JACKEEN	JAILORS	JAMMING	JARRAHS	JAZZIER
ADJOURN	BUNJEES	DONJONS	HIJRAHS	JACKETS	JAKESES	JAMPANI	JARRING	JAZZILY
ADJUDGE	BUNJIES	EJECTED	HOBJOBS	JACKING	JALAPIC	JAMPANS	JARVEYS	JAZZING
ADJUNCT	CAJEPUT	EJECTOR	IJTIHAD	JACKMAN	JALAPIN	JAMPOTS	JARVIES	JAZZMAN
ADJURED	CAJOLED	ENJAMBS	INJECTS	JACKMEN	JALOPPY	JANDALS	JASMINE	JAZZMEN
ADJURES	CAJOLER	ENJOINS	INJELLY	JACKPOT	JALOUSE	JANGLED	JASPERS	JEALOUS
ADJUSTS	CAJOLES	ENJOYED	INJERAS	JACKSIE	JAMADAR	JANGLER	JASPERY	JEELIED
AJOWANS	CAJUPUT	ENJOYER	INJOINT	JACOBIN	JAMBEAU	JANGLES	JATAKAS	JEELIES
AJUTAGE	CARJACK	EVEJARS	INJUNCT	JACOBUS	JAMBEES	JANITOR	JAUNCED	JEELING
ALFORJA	COJOINS	FAJITAS	INJURED	JACONET	JAMBERS	JANIZAR	JAUNCES	JEEPERS
AZULEJO	COJONES	FEIJOAS	INJURER	JACUZZI	JAMBEUX	JANNOCK	JAUNSED	JEEPNEY
BAJADAS	CONJEED	FINJANS	INJURES	JADEDLY	JAMBIER	JANSKYS	JAUNSES	JEERERS
BAJREES	CONJEES	FRIJOLE	JABBERS	JADEITE	JAMBIYA	JANTIER	JAUNTED	JEERING
BANJOES	CONJOIN	GARJANS	JABBING	JAEGERS	JAMBOKS	JANTIES	JAUNTEE	JEFFING
BASENJI	CONJURE		JABBLED	JAGGERS	JAMBONE	JAPINGS	JAUPING	JEJUNUM
BEJADED			JABBLES					

JELLABA	JESTERS	JIMJAMS	JOGGERS	JORDANS	JUDOGIS	JUNGLIS	LOCKJAW	PYJAMAS
JELLIED	JESTFUL	JIMMIED	JOGGING	JOSEPHS	JUDOIST	JUNIORS	MAATJES	RAMJETS
JELLIES	JESTING	JIMMIES	JOGGLED	JOSHERS	JUDOKAS	JUNIPER	MAJESTY	REJECTS
JELLIFY	JETFOIL	JIMPEST	JOGGLES	JOSHING	JUGFULS	JUNKERS	MAJORAT	REJOICE
JELLING	JETSAMS	JIMPIER	JOGTROT	JOSKINS	JUGGING	JUNKETS	MAJORED	REJOINS
JEMADAR	JETSOMS	JINGALS	JOHNNIE	JOSSERS	JUGGINS	JUNKIER	MANJACK	REJONEO
JEMIDAR	JETSONS	JINGLED	JOINDER	JOSTLED	JUGGLED	JUNKIES	MASJIDS	REJONES
JEMIMAS	JETTIED	JINGLER	JOINERS	JOSTLES	JUGGLER	JUNKING	MISJOIN	REJOURN
JEMMIED	JETTIER	JINGLES	JOINERY	JOTTERS	JUGGLES	JUNKMAN	MOUJIKS	REJUDGE
JEMMIER	JETTIES	JINGLET	JOINING	JOTTING	JUGHEAD	JUNKMEN	MUDEJAR	SANJAKS
JEMMIES	JETTING	JINGOES	JOINTED	JOTUNNS	JUGLETS	JUPATIS	MUNTJAC	SAPAJOU
JENNETS	JETTONS	JINJILI	JOINTER	JOUKERY	JUGULAR	JURALLY	MUNTJAK	SEJEANT
JENNIES	JEWELRY	JINKERS	JOINTLY	JOUKING	JUICERS	JURANTS	NAARTJE	SJAMBOK
JEOFAIL	JEWFISH	JINKING	JOISTED	JOULING	JUICIER	JURIDIC	NARTJIE	SKYJACK
JEOPARD	JEZAILS	JINXING	JOJOBAS	JOUNCED	JUICING	JURISTS	OBJECTS	SOJOURN
JERBILS	JIBBAHS	JIPYAPA	JOKIEST	JOUNCES	JUJUBES	JURYMAN	OBJURED	SOOJEYS
JERBOAS	JIBBERS	JIRBLED	JOLLEYS	JOURNAL	JUKSKEI	JURYMEN	OBJURES	SUBJECT
JEREEDS	JIBBING	JIRBLES	JOLLIED	JOURNEY	JUMARTS	JUSSIVE	OUTJEST	SUBJOIN
JERKERS	JIFFIES	JISSOMS	JOLLIER	JOURNOS	JUMBALS	JUSTEST	OUTJETS	TAJINES
JERKIER	JIGAJIG	JITNEYS	JOLLIES	JOUSTED	JUMBIES	JUSTICE	OUTJUMP	TINAJAS
JERKIES	JIGAJOG	JITTERS	JOLLIFY	JOUSTER	JUMBLED	JUSTIFY	OUTJUTS	TRAJECT
JERKING	JIGGERS	JITTERY	JOLLILY	JOWARIS	JUMBLER	JUSTING	OVERJOY	UJAMAAS
JERKINS	JIGGING	JOANNAS	JOLLING	JOWLERS	JUMBLES	JUSTLED	PAJAMAS	UNJADED
JERQUED	JIGGISH	JOANNES	JOLLITY	JOWLIER	JUMBUCK	JUSTLES	PAJOCKE	UNJOINT
JERQUER	JIGGLED	JOBBERS	JOLLYER	JOWLING	JUMELLE	JUTTIED	PAJOCKS	WILTJAS
JERQUES	JIGGLES	JOBBERY	JOLTERS	JOYANCE	JUMPERS	JUTTIES	PERJINK	YOJANAS
JERRIES	JIGJIGS	JOBBIES	JOLTIER	JOYLESS	JUMPIER	JUTTING	PERJURE	ZANJERO
JERSEYS	JIGSAWS	JOBBING	JOLTING	JUBBAHS	JUMPILY	JUVENAL	PERJURY	
JESSAMY	JILGIES	JOBLESS	JONQUIL	JUBILEE	JUMPING	KAJAWAH	POOJAHS	
JESSANT	JILLETS	JOCKEYS	JONTIES	JUDASES	JUNCATE	KHANJAR	POPJOYS	
JESSIES	JILLION	JOCKNEY	JOOKERY	JUDDERS	JUNCOES	KHODJAS	PREJINK	
JESTEES	JILTING	JOCULAR	JOOKING	JUDGING	JUNGLES	KILLJOY	PROJECT	

J – 8-letter words

ABJECTED	COJOINED	IJTIHADS	JAMBIYAS	JAYWALKS	JIGAJIGS	JOHNNIES	JUGHEADS
ABJECTLY	CONJECTS	INJECTED	JAMBOLAN	JAZERANT	JIGAJOGS	JOINDERS	JUGULARS
ABJOINTS	CONJOINS	INJECTOR	JAMBONES	JAZZIEST	JIGGERED	JOININGS	JUGULATE
ABJURERS	CONJOINT	INJOINTS	JAMBOOLS	JEALOUSE	JIGGINGS	JOINTERS	JUICIEST
ABJURING	CONJUGAL	INJUNCTS	JAMBOREE	JEALOUSY	JIGGLIER	JOINTING	JUKSKEIS
ADJACENT	CONJUNCT	INJURERS	JAMDANIS	JEANETTE	JIGGLING	JOINTURE	JULIENNE
ADJOINED	CONJURED	INJURIES	JAMMIEST	JEELYING	JIGSAWED	JOISTING	JUMARRED
ADJOINTS	CONJURER	INJURING	JAMPANEE	JEEPNEYS	JILLAROO	JOKESOME	JUMBLERS
ADJOURNS	CONJURES	JABBERED	JAMPANIS	JEERINGS	JILLIONS	JOKINGLY	JUMBLIER
ADJUDGED	CONJUROR	JABBERER	JANGLERS	JEJUNELY	JIMCRACK	JOLLEYER	JUMBLING
ADJUDGES	CRACKJAW	JABBLING	JANGLIER	JEJUNITY	JIMMYING	JOLLIEST	JUMBOISE
ADJUNCTS	CUNJEVOI	JACAMARS	JANGLING	JELLABAS	JIMPIEST	JOLLIERS	JUMBOIZE
ADJURING	DEEJAYED	JACINTHS	JANITORS	JELLYING	JIMPNESS	JOLLYING	JUMBUCKS
ADJUSTED	DEJECTED	JACKAROO	JANITRIX	JELUTONG	JINGBANG	JOLTHEAD	JUMELLES
ADJUSTER	DEJEUNER	JACKBOOT	JANIZARS	JEMADARS	JINGLERS	JOLTIEST	JUMPABLE
ADJUSTOR	DEJEUNES	JACKDAWS	JANIZARY	JEMIDARS	JINGLETS	JONCANOE	JUMPIEST
ADJUTAGE	DEMIJOHN	JACKEENS	JANNOCKS	JEMMIEST	JINGLIER	JONGLEUR	JUNCATES
ADJUTANT	DISJECTS	JACKEROO	JANTIEST	JEMMYING	JINGLING	JONQUILS	JUNCTION
ADJUVANT	DISJOINS	JACKETED	JAPANNED	JEOFAILS	JINGOISH	JORDELOO	JUNCTURE
AJUTAGES	DISJOINT	JACKPOTS	JAPANNER	JEOPARDS	JINGOISM	JOSTLING	JUNCUSES
ALFORJAS	DISJUNCT	JACKSIES	JAPONICA	JEOPARDY	JINGOIST	JOTTINGS	JUNGLIER
AZULEJOS	DISJUNES	JACOBINS	JARARACA	JEREMIAD	JINJILIS	JOUNCING	JUNGLIST
BANJAXED	DJELLABA	JACONETS	JARARAKA	JERKIEST	JIPYAPAS	JOURNALS	JUNIPERS
BANJAXES	DJIBBAHS	JACQUARD	JARGONED	JERKINGS	JIRBLING	JOURNEYS	JUNKANOO
BANJOIST	EJECTING	JACULATE	JARGOONS	JEROBOAM	JIRKINET	JOUSTERS	JUNKETED
BASENJIS	EJECTION	JACUZZIS	JAROSITE	JERQUERS	JITTERED	JOUSTING	JUNKIEST
BEJABERS	EJECTIVE	JADEITES	JARRINGS	JERQUING	JOBATION	JOVIALLY	JURATORY
BEJADING	EJECTORS	JADERIES	JASMINES	JERRICAN	JOBBINGS	JOWLIEST	JURISTIC
BEJESUIT	ENJAMBED	JAGGEDER	JASPISES	JERRYCAN	JOBSHARE	JOYANCES	JURYMAST
BEJEWELS	ENJOINED	JAGGEDLY	JAUNCING	JESTBOOK	JOCKETTE	JOYFULLY	JUSSIVES
BENJAMIN	ENJOINER	JAGGIEST	JAUNDICE	JESTINGS	JOCKEYED	JOYOUSLY	JUSTICER
BIJWONER	ENJOYERS	JAGHIRES	JAUNSING	JETFOILS	JOCKNEYS	JUBILANT	JUSTICES
BLOWJOBS	ENJOYING	JALAPENO	JAUNTIER	JETLINER	JOCOSELY	JUBILATE	JUSTLING
BRINJALS	FLAPJACK	JALAPINS	JAUNTIES	JETPLANE	JOCOSITY	JUBILEES	JUSTNESS
CAJEPUTS	FORJUDGE	JALOPIES	JAUNTILY	JETTIEST	JOCUNDLY	JUDDERED	JUTTYING
CAJOLERS	FRABJOUS	JALOUSED	JAUNTING	JETTISON	JODELLED	JUDGMENT	JUVENALS
CAJOLERY	FRIJOLES	JALOUSES	JAVELINS	JETTYING	JODHPURS	JUDICIAL	JUVENILE
CAJOLING	GOUJEERS	JALOUSIE	JAWBONED	JEWELLED	JOGGINGS	JUDOISTS	KABELJOU
CAJUPUTS	HANDJARS	JAMADARS	JAWBONES	JEWELLER	JOGGLING	JUGGINGS	KAJAWAHS
CARCAJOU	HIGHJACK	JAMBEAUX	JAWBOXES	JIBBERED	JOGPANTS	JUGGLERS	KHANJARS
CARJACKS	HIJACKED	JAMBIERS	JAWFALLS	JIBBINGS	JOGTROTS	JUGGLERY	KILLJOYS
CARJACOU	HIJACKER	JAMBIYAH	JAWHOLES	JICKAJOG	JOHANNES	JUGGLING	KINKAJOU

KOMITAJI	MARJORAM	NONJUROR	PERJURER	REJECTED	REJUDGED	SUBJECTS	UNJUSTER
LOCKJAWS	MEJLISES	OBJECTED	PERJURES	REJECTER	REJUDGES	SUBJOINS	UNJUSTLY
LOGJUICE	MISJOINS	OBJECTOR	POPINJAY	REJECTOR	SAPAJOUS	SUCURUJU	UPJETTED
MAHARAJA	MISJUDGE	OBJURING	POPJOYED	REJIGGED	SCRAMJET	SUPERJET	VERJUICE
MAJESTIC	MUNTJACS	OUTJESTS	PREJUDGE	REJIGGER	SERJEANT	SWARAJES	WHIPJACK
MAJLISES	MUNTJAKS	OUTJUMPS	PROJECTS	REJOICED	SJAMBOKS	TJANTING	ZANJEROS
MAJOLICA	NAARTJES	OVERJOYS	PULSEJET	REJOICER	SKIPJACK	TRAJECTS	
MAJORATS	NARTJIES	OVERJUMP	PULSOJET	REJOICES	SKYJACKS	TURBOJET	
MAJORING	NIGHTJAR	PAJOCKES	PYJAMAED	REJOINED	SLAPJACK	UNJOINTS	
MAJORITY	NINJITSU	PEJORATE	RAJASHIP	REJONEOS	SOJOURNS	UNJOYFUL	
MANJACKS	NINJUTSU	PERJURED	READJUST	REJOURNS	STICKJAW	UNJOYOUS	

Q-WORDS

Q – 2-letter words

QI

Q – 3-letter words

QAT	QIS	QUA	SUQ

Q – 4-letter words

AQUA	QATS	QUAD	QUAT	QUEP	QUID	QUIN	QUIT	QUOD	SUQS
QADI	QOPH	QUAG	QUAY	QUEY	QUIM	QUIP	QUIZ	QUOP	WAQF

Q – 5-letter words

AQUAE	QANAT	QUAKE	QUASI	QUENA	QUIDS	QUINT	QUITS	QUOTA	SQUEG
AQUAS	QIBLA	QUAKY	QUATS	QUERN	QUIET	QUIPO	QUOAD	QUOTE	SQUIB
BURQA	QOPHS	QUALE	QUAYD	QUERY	QUIFF	QUIPS	QUODS	QUOTH	SQUID
EQUAL	QUACK	QUALM	QUAYS	QUEST	QUILL	QUIPU	QUOIF	QUYTE	SQUIT
EQUID	QUADS	QUANT	QUEAN	QUEUE	QUILT	QUIRE	QUOIN	ROQUE	SQUIZ
EQUIP	QUAFF	QUARE	QUEEN	QUEYN	QUIMS	QUIRK	QUOIT	SQUAB	TALAQ
MAQUI	QUAGS	QUARK	QUEER	QUEYS	QUINA	QUIRT	QUOLL	SQUAD	TOQUE
PIQUE	QUAIL	QUART	QUELL	QUICH	QUINE	QUIST	QUONK	SQUAT	TUQUE
QADIS	QUAIR	QUASH	QUEME	QUICK	QUINS	QUITE	QUOPS	SQUAW	WAQFS

Q – 6-letter words

ACQUIT	EQUATE	PIQUED	QUAIGH	QUASAR	QUESTS	QUINOL	QUOIST	SACQUE	SQUIER
ASQUAT	EQUIDS	PIQUES	QUAILS	QUATCH	QUETCH	QUINSY	QUOITS	SAIQUE	SQUIFF
BARQUE	EQUINE	PIQUET	QUAINT	QUAVER	QUETHE	QUINTA	QUOKKA	SEQUEL	SQUILL
BASQUE	EQUIPE	PLAQUE	QUAIRS	QUEACH	QUEUED	QUINTE	QUOLLS	SEQUIN	SQUINT
BISQUE	EQUIPS	PULQUE	QUAKED	QUEANS	QUEUES	QUINTS	QUONKS	SQUABS	SQUINY
BURQAS	EQUITY	QANATS	QUAKER	QUEASY	QUEYNS	QUINZE	QUOOKE	SQUADS	SQUIRE
CAIQUE	EXEQUY	QASIDA	QUAKES	QUEAZY	QUICHE	QUIPOS	QUORUM	SQUAIL	SQUIRM
CALQUE	FAQUIR	QAWWAL	QUALIA	QUEENS	QUICKS	QUIPUS	QUOTAS	SQUALL	SQUIRR
CASQUE	HAIQUE	QIBLAS	QUALMS	QUEENY	QUIDAM	QUIRED	QUOTED	SQUAMA	SQUIRT
CHEQUE	JERQUE	QIGONG	QUALMY	QUEERS	QUIETS	QUIRES	QUOTER	SQUAME	SQUISH
CHEQUY	LASQUE	QINDAR	QUANGO	QUEEST	QUIFFS	QUIRKS	QUOTES	SQUARE	SQUITS
CINQUE	LIQUID	QINTAR	QUANTA	QUEINT	QUIGHT	QUIRKY	QUOTHA	SQUARK	TALAQS
CIRQUE	LIQUOR	QIVIUT	QUANTS	QUELCH	QUILLS	QUIRTS	QUOTUM	SQUATS	TOQUES
CLAQUE	LOQUAT	QUACKS	QUARER	QUELEA	QUILTS	QUISTS	QUYTED	SQUAWK	TORQUE
CLIQUE	MANQUE	QUAERE	QUARKS	QUELLS	QUINAS	QUITCH	QUYTES	SQUAWS	TUQUES
CLIQUY	MAQUIS	QUAFFS	QUARRY	QUEMED	QUINCE	QUITED	QWERTY	SQUEAK	UBIQUE
CLOQUE	MARQUE	QUAGGA	QUARTE	QUEMES	QUINES	QUITES	REQUIT	SQUEAL	UNIQUE
COQUET	MASQUE	QUAGGY	QUARTO	QUENAS	QUINIC	QUIVER	RISQUE	SQUEGS	YANQUI
EQUALS	MOSQUE	QUAHOG	QUARTS	QUENCH	QUINIE	QUOIFS	ROQUES	SQUIBS	YAQONA
EQUANT	OPAQUE	QUAICH	QUARTZ	QUERNS	QUINOA	QUOINS	ROQUET	SQUIDS	

Q – 7-letter words

ACQUEST	CIRQUES	INQUIRY	PULQUES	QUARTAN	QUEYNIE	QUINTES	REQUERE	SQUEALS
ACQUIRE	CLAQUES	JERQUED	QABALAH	QUARTER	QUIBBLE	QUINTET	REQUEST	SQUEEZE
ACQUIST	CLIQUES	JERQUER	QASIDAS	QUARTES	QUIBLIN	QUINTIC	REQUIEM	SQUEEZY
ACQUITE	CLIQUEY	JERQUES	QAWWALI	QUARTET	QUICHED	QUINZES	REQUIRE	SQUELCH
ACQUITS	CLOQUES	JONQUIL	QAWWALS	QUARTIC	QUICHES	QUIPPED	REQUITE	SQUIDGE
ALFAQUI	COEQUAL	KUMQUAT	QIGONGS	QUARTOS	QUICKEN	QUIRING	REQUOTE	SQUIDGY
ALIQUOT	COMIQUE	LACQUER	QINDARS	QUARTZY	QUICKER	QUIRKED	RISQUES	SQUIERS
ANTIQUE	CONQUER	LACQUEY	QINTARS	QUASARS	QUICKIE	QUIRTED	ROCQUET	SQUIFFY
AQUAFER	COQUETS	LASQUES	QIVIUTS	QUASHED	QUICKLY	QUITING	ROQUETS	SQUILLA
AQUARIA	COQUINA	LIQUATE	QUACKED	QUASHEE	QUIDAMS	QUITTAL	RORQUAL	SQUILLS
AQUATIC	COQUITO	LIQUEFY	QUACKER	QUASHES	QUIDDIT	QUITTED	SACQUES	SQUINCH
AQUAVIT	CROQUET	LIQUEUR	QUACKLE	QUASHIE	QUIDDLE	QUITTER	SAIQUES	SQUINNY
AQUEOUS	CROQUIS	LIQUIDS	QUADDED	QUASSIA	QUIESCE	QUITTOR	SEQUELA	SQUINTS
AQUIFER	CUMQUAT	LIQUORS	QUADRAT	QUAVERS	QUIETED	QUIVERS	SEQUELS	SQUIRED
AQUILON	DAQUIRI	LOQUATS	QUADRIC	QUAVERY	QUIETEN	QUIVERY	SEQUENT	SQUIRES
AQUIVER	DOCQUET	MACAQUE	QUAERED	QUAYAGE	QUIETER	QUIZZED	SEQUINS	SQUIRMS
ASQUINT	ENQUIRE	MADOQUA	QUAERES	QUEACHY	QUIETLY	QUIZZER	SEQUOIA	SQUIRMY
BANQUET	ENQUIRY	MARQUEE	QUAFFED	QUEECHY	QUIETUS	QUIZZES	SILIQUA	SQUIRRS
BAROQUE	EQUABLE	MARQUES	QUAFFER	QUEENED	QUIGHTS	QUODDED	SILIQUE	SQUIRTS
BARQUES	EQUABLY	MARQUIS	QUAGGAS	QUEENIE	QUILLAI	QUODLIN	SQUABBY	SQUISHY
BASQUED	EQUALLY	MASQUER	QUAHAUG	QUEENLY	QUILLED	QUOIFED	SQUACCO	SQUITCH
BASQUES	EQUANTS	MASQUES	QUAHOGS	QUEERED	QUILLET	QUOINED	SQUADDY	SUBAQUA
BEQUEST	EQUATED	MESQUIN	QUAICHS	QUEERER	QUILLON	QUOISTS	SQUAILS	TEQUILA
BEZIQUE	EQUATES	MESQUIT	QUAIGHS	QUEERLY	QUILTED	QUOITED	SQUALID	TORQUED
BISQUES	EQUATOR	MOSQUES	QUAILED	QUEESTS	QUILTER	QUOITER	SQUALLS	TORQUES
BOSQUET	EQUERRY	OBLIQUE	QUAKERS	QUELEAS	QUINARY	QUOKKAS	SQUALLY	TSADDIQ
BOUQUET	EQUINAL	OBLOQUY	QUAKIER	QUELLED	QUINATE	QUONDAM	SQUALOR	TZADDIQ
BRIQUET	EQUINIA	OBSEQUY	QUAKING	QUELLER	QUINCES	QUONKED	SQUAMAE	UNEQUAL
BRUSQUE	EQUINOX	OPAQUED	QUALIFY	QUEMING	QUINCHE	QUOPPED	SQUAMES	UNIQUER
CACIQUE	EQUIPES	OPAQUER	QUALITY	QUERIED	QUINIES	QUORATE	SQUARED	UNIQUES
CAIQUES	ESQUIRE	OPAQUES	QUAMASH	QUERIES	QUININE	QUORUMS	SQUARER	UNQUEEN
CALQUED	FAQUIRS	PARQUET	QUANGOS	QUERIST	QUINNAT	QUOTERS	SQUARES	UNQUIET
CALQUES	GRECQUE	PERIQUE	QUANNET	QUESTED	QUINOAS	QUOTING	SQUASHY	UNQUOTE
CASQUES	HAIQUES	PICQUET	QUANTAL	QUESTER	QUINOID	QUOTUMS	SQUATTY	VAQUERO
CAZIQUE	INQILAB	PIQUANT	QUANTED	QUESTOR	QUINOLS	QUYTING	SQUAWKS	YANQUIS
CHARQUI	INQUERE	PIQUETS	QUANTIC	QUETHES	QUINONE	QWERTYS	SQUAWKY	YAQONAS
CHEQUER	INQUEST	PIQUING	QUANTUM	QUETSCH	QUINTAL	RACQUET	SQUEAKS	
CHEQUES	INQUIET	PLAQUES	QUAREST	QUETZAL	QUINTAN	RELIQUE	SQUEAKY	
CINQUES	INQUIRE	PREQUEL	QUARREL	QUEUING	QUINTAS	REPIQUE		

Q – 8-letter words

ACQUAINT	BASQUINE	COQUITOS	EXEQUIES	LIQUIDUS	PAROQUET	QUAGMIRY	QUARTZES
ACQUESTS	BEQUEATH	COTQUEAN	FILIOQUE	LIQUORED	PARQUETS	QUAHAUGS	QUASHEES
ACQUIGHT	BEQUESTS	CRITIQUE	FREQUENT	LOQUITUR	PERIQUES	QUAILING	QUASHIES
ACQUIRAL	BEZIQUES	CROQUETS	GRECQUES	LUSTIQUE	PERRUQUE	QUAINTER	QUASHING
ACQUIRED	BLANQUET	CUMQUATS	HAQUETON	MACAQUES	PETANQUE	QUAINTLY	QUASSIAS
ACQUIRES	BOSQUETS	DAIQUIRI	HENEQUEN	MADOQUAS	PHYSIQUE	QUAKIEST	QUATCHED
ACQUISTS	BOUQUETS	DAQUIRIS	HENEQUIN	MAQUETTE	PICQUETS	QUAKINGS	QUATCHES
ACQUITES	BOUTIQUE	DETRAQUE	HENIQUIN	MAROQUIN	PIQUANCY	QUALMIER	QUATORZE
ADEQUACY	BRELOQUE	DISQUIET	HUAQUERO	MARQUEES	PIQUETED	QUALMING	QUATRAIN
ADEQUATE	BRIQUETS	DOCQUETS	ILLIQUID	MARQUESS	PRATIQUE	QUALMISH	QUAVERED
ALFAQUIS	BRUSQUER	ELOQUENT	INEQUITY	MARQUISE	PREQUELS	QUANDARY	QUAVERER
ALIQUANT	CACIQUES	EMBUSQUE	INIQUITY	MASQUERS	QABALAHS	QUANDONG	QUAYAGES
ANTIQUED	CALQUING	ENQUIRED	INQILABS	MBAQANGA	QAIMAQAM	QUANNETS	QUAYSIDE
ANTIQUES	CAZIQUES	ENQUIRER	INQUERED	MESQUINE	QALAMDAN	QUANTICS	QUEACHES
APPLIQUE	CHARQUIS	ENQUIRES	INQUERES	MESQUITE	QAWWALIS	QUANTIFY	QUEASIER
AQUACADE	CHEQUERS	EQUALISE	INQUESTS	MESQUITS	QUACKERS	QUANTING	QUEASILY
AQUAFERS	CINQUAIN	EQUALITY	INQUIETS	MISQUOTE	QUACKERY	QUANTISE	QUEAZIER
AQUALUNG	CLAQUEUR	EQUALIZE	INQUIRED	MOQUETTE	QUACKING	QUANTITY	QUEENDOM
AQUANAUT	CLINIQUE	EQUALLED	INQUIRER	MOSQUITO	QUACKLED	QUANTIZE	QUEENIER
AQUARIAN	CLIQUIER	EQUATING	INQUIRES	MUQADDAM	QUACKLES	QUANTONG	QUEENIES
AQUARIST	CLIQUISH	EQUATION	JACQUARD	MUSQUASH	QUADDING	QUARRELS	QUEENING
AQUARIUM	CLIQUISM	EQUATORS	JERQUERS	MYSTIQUE	QUADRANS	QUARRIED	QUEENITE
AQUATICS	COEQUALS	EQUINIAS	JERQUING	NARQUOIS	QUADRANT	QUARRIER	QUEENLET
AQUATINT	COLLOQUE	EQUINITY	JONQUILS	OBLIQUED	QUADRATE	QUARRIES	QUEERDOM
AQUEDUCT	COLLOQUY	EQUIPAGE	KUMQUATS	OBLIQUER	QUADRATS	QUARTANS	QUEEREST
AQUIFERS	COMIQUES	EQUIPPED	LACQUERS	OBLIQUES	QUADRICS	QUARTERN	QUEERING
AQUILINE	CONQUERS	EQUISETA	LACQUEYS	OBLIQUID	QUADRIGA	QUARTERS	QUEERISH
AQUILONS	CONQUEST	EQUITANT	LIQUABLE	OBSEQUIE	QUADROON	QUARTETS	QUEERITY
ARQUEBUS	COQUETRY	EQUITIES	LIQUATED	ODALIQUE	QUAESTOR	QUARTETT	QUELCHED
BANQUETS	COQUETTE	EQUIVOKE	LIQUATES	OLDSQUAW	QUAFFERS	QUARTICS	QUELCHES
BARBEQUE	COQUILLA	ESQUIRES	LIQUESCE	OPAQUELY	QUAFFING	QUARTIER	QUELLERS
BAROQUES	COQUILLE	ESQUISSE	LIQUEURS	OPAQUEST	QUAGGIER	QUARTILE	QUELLING
	COQUINAS	EXEQUIAL	LIQUIDLY	OPAQUING	QUAGMIRE		QUENCHED

QUENCHER	QUIDDLER	QUINSIED	QUODLINS	REQUOTES	SQUAMOUS	SQUEGGER	TAQUERIA
QUENCHES	QUIDDLES	QUINSIES	QUOIFING	REQUOYLE	SQUAMULA	SQUELCHY	TEQUILAS
QUENELLE	QUIDNUNC	QUINTAIN	QUOINING	ROCQUETS	SQUAMULE	SQUIBBED	TEQUILLA
QUERISTS	QUIESCED	QUINTALS	QUOITERS	ROQUETED	SQUANDER	SQUIDDED	TOQUILLA
QUERYING	QUIESCES	QUINTETS	QUOITING	ROQUETTE	SQUARELY	SQUIDGED	TORQUATE
QUESTANT	QUIETENS	QUINTETT	QUONKING	RORQUALS	SQUARERS	SQUIDGES	TRANQUIL
QUESTERS	QUIETERS	QUINTILE	QUOPPING	SEAQUAKE	SQUAREST	SQUIFFER	TRUQUAGE
QUESTING	QUIETEST	QUIPPING	QUOTABLE	SEQUELAE	SQUARIAL	SQUIGGLE	TRUQUEUR
QUESTION	QUIETING	QUIPPISH	QUOTABLY	SEQUENCE	SQUARING	SQUIGGLY	TSADDIQS
QUESTORS	QUIETISM	QUIPSTER	QUOTIENT	SEQUENTS	SQUARISH	SQUILGEE	TZADDIQS
QUETCHED	QUIETIST	QUIRKIER	QWERTIES	SEQUINED	SQUARSON	SQUILLAS	UBIQUITY
QUETCHES	QUIETIVE	QUIRKILY	RACQUETS	SEQUOIAS	SQUASHED	SQUINIED	UMQUHILE
QUETHING	QUIETUDE	QUIRKING	RAMEQUIN	SILIQUAS	SQUASHER	SQUINIES	UNEQUALS
QUETZALS	QUIGHTED	QUIRKISH	RELIQUES	SILIQUES	SQUASHES	SQUINTED	UNIQUELY
QUEUEING	QUILLAIS	QUIRTING	REMARQUE	SQUABASH	SQUATTED	SQUINTER	UNIQUEST
QUEUINGS	QUILLETS	QUISLING	REPIQUED	SQUABBED	SQUATTER	SQUIRAGE	UNQUEENS
QUEYNIES	QUILLING	QUITCHED	REPIQUES	SQUABBER	SQUATTLE	SQUIREEN	UNQUIETS
QUIBBLED	QUILLMAN	QUITCHES	REQUERED	SQUABBLE	SQUAWKED	SQUIRELY	UNQUOTED
QUIBBLER	QUILLMEN	QUITTALS	REQUERES	SQUACCOS	SQUAWKER	SQUIRESS	UNQUOTES
QUIBBLES	QUILLONS	QUITTERS	REQUESTS	SQUADDIE	SQUAWMAN	SQUIRING	VANQUISH
QUIBLINS	QUILTERS	QUITTING	REQUIEMS	SQUADRON	SQUAWMEN	SQUIRMED	VAQUEROS
QUICHING	QUILTING	QUITTORS	REQUIGHT	SQUAILED	SQUEAKED	SQUIRRED	VEHMIQUE
QUICKENS	QUINCHED	QUIVERED	REQUIRED	SQUAILER	SQUEAKER	SQUIRREL	VERQUERE
QUICKEST	QUINCHES	QUIXOTIC	REQUIRER	SQUALENE	SQUEALED	SQUIRTED	VERQUIRE
QUICKIES	QUINCUNX	QUIXOTRY	REQUIRES	SQUALLED	SQUEALER	SQUIRTER	
QUICKSET	QUINELLA	QUIZZERS	REQUITAL	SQUALLER	SQUEEGEE	SQUISHED	
QUIDDANY	QUININES	QUIZZERY	REQUITED	SQUALOID	SQUEEZED	SQUISHES	
QUIDDITS	QUINNATS	QUIZZIFY	REQUITER	SQUALORS	SQUEEZER	SQUIZZES	
QUIDDITY	QUINOIDS	QUIZZING	REQUITES	SQUAMATE	SQUEEZES	SUBEQUAL	
QUIDDLED	QUINONES	QUODDING	REQUOTED	SQUAMOSE	SQUEGGED	SURQUEDY	

X-WORDS

X – 2-letter words

AX	EX	OX	XI	XU

X – 3-letter words

AXE	FAX	HOX	LOX	MUX	PIX	REX	SOX	VOX	XIS
BOX	FIX	KEX	LUX	NIX	POX	SAX	TAX	WAX	YEX
COX	FOX	LAX	MAX	NOX	PYX	SEX	TUX	WEX	ZAX
DUX	HEX	LEX	MIX	PAX	RAX	SIX	VEX	WOX	ZEX

X – 4-letter words

APEX	AXON	DIXI	EXON	FLEX	IXIA	MAXI	ONYX	ROUX	VEXT
AXED	BOXY	DIXY	EXPO	FLIX	JEUX	MINX	ORYX	SEXT	WAXY
AXEL	CALX	DOXY	EXUL	FLUX	JINX	MIXT	OXEN	SEXY	WEXE
AXES	COAX	EAUX	FAIX	FOXY	JYNX	MIXY	OXER	TAXA	XYST
AXIL	COXA	EXAM	FALX	HOAX	LANX	MOXA	PIXY	TAXI	YUNX
AXIS	COXY	EXES	FAUX	IBEX	LUXE	NEXT	POXY	TEXT	
AXLE	CRUX	EXIT	FLAX	ILEX	LYNX	NIXY	PREX	ULEX	

X – 5-letter words

ADDAX	AXONS	CODEX	EXALT	EXPOS	HEXAD	LAXLY	MUREX	PAXES	REDOX
ADMIX	BEAUX	COXAE	EXAMS	EXTOL	HEXED	LEXES	MUXED	PHLOX	RELAX
AFFIX	BOLIX	COXAL	EXCEL	EXTRA	HEXES	LEXIS	MUXES	PIXEL	REMEX
ANNEX	BORAX	COXED	EXEAT	EXUDE	HOXED	LIMAX	NEXTS	PIXES	REMIX
ATAXY	BOXED	COXES	EXEEM	EXULS	HOXES	LOXES	NEXUS	PIXIE	SALIX
AUXIN	BOXEN	CULEX	EXEME	EXULT	HYRAX	LUXES	NIXED	PODEX	SAXES
AXELS	BOXER	CYLIX	EXERT	EXURB	IMMIX	MALAX	NIXES	POXED	SEXED
AXIAL	BOXES	DESEX	EXIES	FAXED	INDEX	MAXES	NIXIE	POXES	SEXER
AXILE	BRAXY	DETOX	EXILE	FAXES	INFIX	MAXIM	NOXAL	PREXY	SEXES
AXILS	BUXOM	DIXIE	EXINE	FIXED	IXIAS	MAXIS	NOXES	PROXY	SEXTS
AXING	CALIX	DRUXY	EXIST	FIXER	IXTLE	MIXED	OXERS	PYXED	SILEX
AXIOM	CALYX	DUXES	EXITS	FIXES	KEXES	MIXEN	OXIDE	PYXES	SIXER
AXLES	CAREX	EMBOX	EXODE	FLAXY	KYLIX	MIXER	OXIME	PYXIS	SIXES
AXMAN	CAXON	ENFIX	EXONS	FOXED	LATEX	MIXES	OXLIP	RADIX	SIXTE
AXMEN	CHOUX	EPOXY	EXPAT	FOXES	LAXER	MOXAS	OXTER	RAXED	SIXTH
AXOID	CIMEX	EXACT	EXPEL	HELIX	LAXES	MOXIE	PANAX	RAXES	SIXTY

SOREX	TAXOL	TEXTS	UNFIX	VEXER	VOXEL	WEXED	XENON	XYLOL	YEXES
TAXED	TAXON	TOXIC	UNSEX	VEXES	WAXED	WEXES	XERIC	XYLYL	ZAXES
TAXER	TAXOR	TOXIN	UNTAX	VIBEX	WAXEN	WOXEN	XOANA	XYSTI	ZEXES
TAXES	TELEX	TUXES	VARIX	VITEX	WAXER	XEBEC	XYLEM	XYSTS	
TAXIS	TEXAS	UNBOX	VEXED	VIXEN	WAXES	XENIA	XYLIC	YEXED	

X – 6-letter words

ADIEUX	CALXES	EFFLUX	EXODES	EXUDES	HOAXED	MIXENS	PIXIES	SIXAIN	VOLVOX
AFFLUX	CARFAX	ELIXIR	EXODIC	EXULTS	HOAXER	MIXERS	PLEXOR	SIXERS	VORTEX
ALEXIA	CARFOX	EUTAXY	EXODUS	EXURBS	HOAXES	MIXIER	PLEXUS	SIXTES	VOXELS
ALEXIC	CAUDEX	EXACTS	EXOGEN	FAXING	HOXING	MIXING	POLLEX	SIXTHS	WAXERS
ALEXIN	CAXONS	EXALTS	EXOMIS	FIXATE	IBEXES	MOXIES	POXIER	SMILAX	WAXIER
ANNEXE	CERVIX	EXAMEN	EXONIC	FIXERS	ICEBOX	MUXING	POXING	SPADIX	WAXILY
ANOXIA	CHENIX	EXARCH	EXONYM	FIXING	ILEXES	MYXOMA	PRAXES	SPHINX	WAXING
ANOXIC	CLIMAX	EXCAMB	EXOPOD	FIXITY	IMBREX	NEXTLY	PRAXIS	STORAX	WEXING
APEXES	COAXED	EXCEED	EXOTIC	FIXIVE	IMPLEX	NIXIES	PREFIX	STYRAX	WRAXLE
ATAXIA	COAXER	EXCELS	EXPAND	FIXURE	INFLUX	NIXING	PREMIX	SURTAX	XEBECS
ATAXIC	COAXES	EXCEPT	EXPATS	FLAXEN	IXTLES	ONYXES	PREXES	SUFFIX	XENIAL
ATWIXT	COCCYX	EXCESS	EXPECT	FLAXES	JAWBOX	OREXIS	PROLIX	SYNTAX	XENIAS
AUXINS	CONFIX	EXCIDE	EXPELS	FLEXED	JINXED	ORIFEX	PTYXES	SYRINX	XENIUM
AXEMAN	CONVEX	EXCISE	EXPEND	FLEXES	JINXES	ORYXES	PTYXIS	TAXERS	XENONS
AXEMEN	CORTEX	EXCITE	EXPERT	FLEXOR	JYNXES	OUTBOX	PYXING	TAXIED	XEROMA
AXILLA	COWPOX	EXCUSE	EXPIRE	FLIXED	KLAXON	OUTFOX	RAXING	TAXIES	XOANON
AXIOMS	COXIER	EXEATS	EXPIRY	FLIXES	LARNAX	OXALIC	REFLEX	TAXING	XYLEMS
AXISES	COXING	EXEDRA	EXPORT	FLUXED	LARYNX	OXALIS	REFLUX	TAXMAN	XYLENE
AXOIDS	CRUXES	EXEEMS	EXPOSE	FLUXES	LAXEST	OXFORD	RHEXES	TAXMEN	XYLOID
BANJAX	DEFLEX	EXEMED	EXPUGN	FORFEX	LAXISM	OXGANG	RHEXIS	TAXOLS	XYLOLS
BAXTER	DEIXES	EXEMES	EXSECT	FORNIX	LAXIST	OXGATE	SAXAUL	TAXORS	XYLOMA
BEMBEX	DEIXIS	EXEMPT	EXSERT	FOXIER	LAXITY	OXHEAD	SAXONY	TETTIX	XYLOSE
BEMBIX	DENTEX	EXEQUY	EXTANT	FOXING	LEXEME	OXIDES	SCOLEX	THORAX	XYLYLS
BIAXAL	DEXTER	EXERTS	EXTEND	FRUTEX	LUMMOX	OXIMES	SEXERS	TOXINS	XYSTER
BIJOUX	DIAXON	EXEUNT	EXTENT	GALAXY	LUXATE	OXLAND	SEXFID	TOXOID	XYSTOI
BOLLIX	DIOXAN	EXHALE	EXTERN	HALLUX	LUXURY	OXLIPS	SEXIER	TUTRIX	XYSTOS
BOMBAX	DIOXIN	EXHORT	EXTINE	HATBOX	LYNXES	OXSLIP	SEXING	TUXEDO	XYSTUS
BONXIE	DIPLEX	EXHUME	EXTIRP	HAYBOX	MAGNOX	OXTAIL	SEXISM	ULEXES	YEXING
BOXCAR	DIXIES	EXILED	EXTOLD	HEXACT	MATRIX	OXTERS	SEXIST	UNISEX	YUNXES
BOXERS	DOGFOX	EXILES	EXTOLS	HEXADS	MAXIMA	OXYGEN	SEXPOT	VERTEX	
BOXFUL	DUPLEX	EXILIC	EXTORT	HEXANE	MAXIMS	OXYMEL	SEXTAN	VEXERS	
BOXIER	EARWAX	EXINES	EXTRAS	HEXENE	MAXIXE	PAXWAX	SEXTET	VEXING	
BOXING		EXISTS	EXUDED	HEXING	MENINX	PINXIT	SEXTON	VIXENS	
BOYAUX		EXITED		HEXOSE	MINXES	PIXELS	SEXUAL		

X – 7-letter words

ABAXIAL	AXIALLY	COAXERS	EPAXIAL	EXCITOR	EXHUMES	EXPLOIT	EXTREME	FOXINGS
ABRAXAS	AXILLAE	COAXIAL	EPITAXY	EXCLAIM	EXIGENT	EXPLORE	EXTRUDE	FOXSHIP
ADAXIAL	AXILLAR	COAXING	EPOXIDE	EXCLAVE	EXILIAN	EXPORTS	EXUDATE	FOXTROT
ADDAXES	AXINITE	COEXIST	EPOXIES	EXCLUDE	EXILING	EXPOSAL	EXUDING	GATEAUX
ADMIXED	AXOLOTL	COMPLEX	EQUINOX	EXCRETA	EXILITY	EXPOSED	EXULTED	GEARBOX
ADMIXES	BATEAUX	CONFLUX	EUTEXIA	EXCRETE	EXISTED	EXPOSER	EXURBAN	GRAVLAX
AFFIXED	BAUXITE	CONTEXT	EXACTED	EXCUDIT	EXITING	EXPOSES	EXURBIA	HELIXES
AFFIXES	BAXTERS	COTEAUX	EXACTER	EXCURSE	EXOCARP	EXPOUND	EXUVIAE	HEXACTS
ALEXIAS	BEESWAX	COXCOMB	EXACTLY	EXCUSAL	EXODERM	EXPRESS	EXUVIAL	HEXADIC
ALEXINS	BETWIXT	COXIEST	EXACTOR	EXCUSED	EXODIST	EXPUGNS	FIREBOX	HEXAGON
ANAXIAL	BIAXIAL	CURTAXE	EXALTED	EXCUSER	EXOGAMY	EXPUNCT	FIXABLE	HEXANES
ANNEXED	BOLIXED	DESEXED	EXAMENS	EXCUSES	EXOGENS	EXPUNGE	FIXATED	HEXAPLA
ANNEXES	BOLIXES	DESEXES	EXAMINE	EXECUTE	EXOMION	EXPURGE	FIXATES	HEXAPOD
ANOREXY	BONXIES	DETOXED	EXAMPLE	EXEDRAE	EXONYMS	EXSCIND	FIXEDLY	HEXARCH
ANOXIAS	BORAXES	DETOXES	EXARATE	EXEEMED	EXOPODS	EXSECTS	FIXINGS	HEXENES
ANTEFIX	BOSTRYX	DEXTERS	EXARCHS	EXEGETE	EXORDIA	EXSERTS	FIXTURE	HEXINGS
ANTHRAX	BOXCARS	DEXTRAL	EXARCHY	EXEMING	EXOTICA	EXTATIC	FIXURES	HEXOSES
ANXIETY	BOXFULS	DEXTRAN	EXCAMBS	EXEMPLA	EXOTICS	EXTENDS	FLAXIER	HOAXERS
ANXIOUS	BOXIEST	DEXTRIN	EXCEEDS	EXEMPLE	EXPANDS	EXTENSE	FLEXILE	HOAXING
APOPLEX	BOXINGS	DIAXONS	EXCEPTS	EXEMPTS	EXPANSE	EXTENTS	FLEXING	HYDROXY
APRAXIA	BOXROOM	DIOXANE	EXCERPT	EXERGUE	EXPECTS	EXTERNE	FLEXION	HYPOXIA
APTERYX	BOXWOOD	DIOXANS	EXCHEAT	EXERTED	EXPENDS	EXTERNS	FLEXORS	HYPOXIC
ASEXUAL	BRAXIES	DIOXIDE	EXCIDED	EXHALED	EXPENSE	EXTINCT	FLEXURE	HYRAXES
ASPHYXY	BRUXISM	DIOXINS	EXCIDES	EXHALES	EXPERTS	EXTINES	FLIXING	IMMIXED
ATARAXY	BUREAUX	DRUXIER	EXCISED	EXHAUST	EXPIATE	EXTIRPS	FLUMMOX	IMMIXES
ATAXIAS	BUXOMER	ELIXIRS	EXCISES	EXHEDRA	EXPIRED	EXTORTS	FLUXING	INDEXAL
ATAXIES	CACHEXY	EMBOXED	EXCITED	EXHIBIT	EXPIRES	EXTRACT	FLUXION	INDEXED
AUXESES	CADEAUX	EMBOXES	EXCITER	EXHORTS	EXPLAIN	EXTRAIT	FLUXIVE	INDEXER
AUXESIS	CALYXES	ENFIXED	EXCITES	EXHUMED	EXPLANT	EXTREAT	FOXHOLE	INDEXES
AUXETIC	CHOENIX	ENFIXES	EXCITON	EXHUMER	EXPLODE		FOXIEST	INDOXYL

INEXACT	MAXILLA	OXGATES	PICKAXE	RESEAUX	SIMPLEX	TELEFAX	UNSEXES	XANTHAN
INFIXED	MAXIMAL	OXHEADS	PLANXTY	SALPINX	SIXAINE	TELETEX	UNTAXED	XANTHIC
INFIXES	MAXIMIN	OXIDANT	PLEXORS	SALTBOX	SIXAINS	TELEXED	UNTAXES	XANTHIN
INVEXED	MAXIMUM	OXIDASE	PLEXURE	SANDBOX	SIXFOLD	TELEXES	UNVEXED	XERAFIN
JAMBEUX	MAXIXES	OXIDATE	PODEXES	SAXAULS	SIXTEEN	TEXASES	URTEXTS	XERARCH
JINXING	MAXWELL	OXIDISE	POSTBOX	SAXHORN	SIXTIES	TEXTILE	UXORIAL	XERASIA
KLAXONS	MILIEUX	OXIDIZE	POSTFIX	SEALWAX	SIXTHLY	TEXTUAL	VAUDOUX	XEROMAS
LATEXES	MINIMAX	OXLANDS	POXIEST	SEEDBOX	SOAPBOX	TEXTURE	VEXEDLY	XEROSES
LAXATOR	MIXABLE	OXONIUM	PRETEXT	SEXFOIL	SOREXES	TOOLBOX	VEXILLA	XEROSIS
LAXISMS	MIXEDLY	OXSLIPS	PREXIES	SEXIEST	SPANDEX	TORTRIX	VEXINGS	XEROTES
LAXISTS	MIXIEST	OXTAILS	PRINCOX	SEXISMS	SUBTEXT	TOXEMIA	VICTRIX	XEROTIC
LAXNESS	MIXTION	OXTERED	PROXIES	SEXISTS	SYNAXES	TOXEMIC	VITEXES	XIPHOID
LEXEMES	MIXTURE	OXYGENS	PROXIMO	SEXLESS	SYNAXIS	TOXICAL	VITRAUX	XYLENES
LEXICAL	MONAXON	OXYMELS	PYREXIA	SEXPERT	TAXABLE	TOXOIDS	VIXENLY	XYLENOL
LEXICON	MUREXES	OXYTONE	PYREXIC	SEXPOTS	TAXABLY	TRIAXON	WAXBILL	XYLITOL
LEXISES	NARTHEX	PANAXES	PYXIDES	SEXTANS	TAXICAB	TRIPLEX	WAXIEST	XYLOGEN
LIXIVIA	NOXIOUS	PANCHAX	PYXIDIA	SEXTANT	TAXIING	TUBIFEX	WAXINGS	XYLOMAS
LOXYGEN	ORATRIX	PARADOX	REANNEX	SEXTETS	TAXIMAN	TUXEDOS	WAXWING	XYLONIC
LUXATED	OVERTAX	PAXIUBA	RECTRIX	SEXTETT	TAXIMEN	UNBOXED	WAXWORK	XYLOSES
LUXATES	OXALATE	PERPLEX	RELAXED	SEXTILE	TAXINGS	UNBOXES	WOODWAX	XYSTERS
MAILBOX	OXAZINE	PHALANX	RELAXES	SEXTONS	TAXIWAY	UNFIXED	WORKBOX	ZEUXITE
MALAXED	OXBLOOD	PHARYNX	RELAXIN	SEXTUOR	TAXLESS	UNFIXES	WRAXLED	ZOOTAXY
MALAXES	OXFORDS	PHLOXES	REMIXED	SHOWBOX	TAXYING	UNMIXED	WRAXLES	
MARTEXT	OXGANGS	PHOENIX	REMIXES	SILEXES	TECTRIX	UNSEXED	XANTHAM	

X – 8-letter words

ADMIXING	BUXOMEST	DEXTRANS	EXCEPTOR	EXERGUAL	EXPANDER	EXSERTED	FOXINESS
AFFIXING	CACHEXIA	DEXTRINE	EXCERPTA	EXERGUES	EXPANDOR	EXTASIES	FOXSHARK
AFFLUXES	CACODOXY	DEXTRINS	EXCERPTS	EXERTING	EXPANSES	EXTENDED	FOXSHIPS
AMPLEXUS	CACOMIXL	DEXTROSE	EXCESSES	EXERTION	EXPECTED	EXTENDER	FOXTROTS
ANNEXING	CAMAIEUX	DEXTROUS	EXCHANGE	EXERTIVE	EXPECTER	EXTENSOR	GALAXIES
ANNEXION	CARBOXYL	DIOXANES	EXCHEATS	EXHALANT	EXPEDITE	EXTERIOR	GENETRIX
ANNEXURE	CARFAXES	DIOXIDES	EXCIDING	EXHALING	EXPELLED	EXTERNAL	GENITRIX
ANOREXIA	CARFOXES	DISANNEX	EXCISING	EXHAUSTS	EXPELLEE	EXTERNAT	GEOTAXES
ANOREXIC	CARNIFEX	DOGFOXES	EXCISION	EXHEDRAE	EXPENDED	EXTERNES	GEOTAXIS
ANTEFIXA	CATHEXES	DOXOLOGY	EXCITANT	EXHIBITS	EXPENDER	EXTIRPED	GIAMBEUX
ANTHELIX	CATHEXIS	DRUXIEST	EXCITERS	EXHORTED	EXPENSES	EXTOLLED	GLOXINIA
APOMIXES	CAUDEXES	DUPLEXER	EXCITING	EXHORTER	EXPERTED	EXTOLLER	HARUSPEX
APOMIXIS	CERVIXES	DUPLEXES	EXCITONS	EXHUMATE	EXPERTLY	EXTORTED	HATBOXES
APOPLEXY	CHAPEAUX	DUXELLES	EXCITORS	EXHUMERS	EXPIABLE	EXTRACTS	HAYBOXES
APPENDIX	CHATEAUX	DYSLEXIA	EXCLAIMS	EXHUMING	EXPIATED	EXTRADOS	HERITRIX
APRAXIAS	CHENIXES	DYSLEXIC	EXCLAVES	EXIGEANT	EXPIATES	EXTRAITS	HEXAFOIL
APYREXIA	CICATRIX	EARTHWAX	EXCLUDED	EXIGENCE	EXPIATOR	EXTRANET	HEXAGLOT
ASPHYXIA	CINEPLEX	EARWAXES	EXCLUDEE	EXIGENCY	EXPIRANT	EXTREATS	HEXAGONS
ATARAXIA	CLACKBOX	ECOTOXIC	EXCLUDER	EXIGENTS	EXPIRIES	EXTREMER	HEXAGRAM
ATARAXIC	CLANGBOX	EFFLUXES	EXCLUDES	EXIGIBLE	EXPIRING	EXTREMES	HEXAPLAR
AUXETICS	CLIMAXED	EMBOXING	EXCRETAL	EXIGUITY	EXPLAINS	EXTRORSE	HEXAPLAS
AUXILIAR	CLIMAXES	ENDEIXES	EXCRETED	EXIGUOUS	EXPLANTS	EXTRUDED	HEXAPODS
AVIATRIX	COEXISTS	ENDEIXIS	EXCRETER	EXIMIOUS	EXPLICIT	EXTRUDER	HEXAPODY
AXIALITY	COEXTEND	ENFIXING	EXCRETES	EXISTENT	EXPLODED	EXTRUDES	HEXYLENE
AXILLARY	COMMIXED	EPICALYX	EXCUBANT	EXISTING	EXPLODER	EXUDATES	HOMEOBOX
AXINITES	COMMIXES	EPOXIDES	EXCURSED	EXITANCE	EXPLODES	EXULTANT	HYDROXYL
AXIOLOGY	CONFIXED	EUTAXIES	EXCURSES	EXOCARPS	EXPLOITS	EXULTING	HYPOXIAS
AXOLOTLS	CONFIXES	EUTAXITE	EXCURSUS	EXOCRINE	EXPLORED	EXURBIAS	ICEBOXES
AXOPLASM	CONTEXTS	EUTEXIAS	EXCUSALS	EXODERMS	EXPLORER	EXUVIATE	IMMIXING
BANDEAUX	CONVEXED	EUXENITE	EXCUSERS	EXODISTS	EXPLORES	FABLIAUX	IMPLEXES
BANJAXED	CONVEXES	EXACTERS	EXCUSING	EXODUSES	EXPONENT	FIXATING	INDEXERS
BANJAXES	CONVEXLY	EXACTEST	EXCUSIVE	EXOERGIC	EXPORTED	FIXATION	INDEXING
BANXRING	CORTEXES	EXACTING	EXECRATE	EXOGAMIC	EXPORTER	FIXATIVE	INDOXYLS
BAUXITES	COWPOXES	EXACTION	EXECUTED	EXOMIONS	EXPOSALS	FIXATURE	INEXPERT
BAUXITIC	COXALGIA	EXACTORS	EXECUTER	EXOMISES	EXPOSERS	FIXITIES	INFIXING
BEAUXITE	COXCOMBS	EXALTING	EXECUTES	EXOPHAGY	EXPOSING	FIXTURES	INFLEXED
BEMBEXES	COXINESS	EXAMINED	EXECUTOR	EXOPLASM	EXPOSURE	FLAXIEST	INFLUXES
BEMBIXES	COXSWAIN	EXAMINEE	EXECUTRY	EXOSMOSE	EXPOUNDS	FLEXIBLE	INTERMIX
BERCEAUX	CREATRIX	EXAMINER	EXEEMING	EXOSPORE	EXPRESSO	FLEXIBLY	INTERREX
BICONVEX	CRUCIFIX	EXAMINES	EXEGESES	EXOTERIC	EXPUGNED	FLEXIONS	INTERSEX
BISEXUAL	CURATRIX	EXAMPLAR	EXEGESIS	EXOTOXIC	EXPULSED	FLEXUOSE	JAMBEAUX
BOLIXING	CURTALAX	EXAMPLED	EXEGETES	EXOTOXIN	EXPULSES	FLEXUOUS	JANITRIX
BOLLIXED	CURTAXES	EXAMPLES	EXEGETIC	EXPANDED	EXPUNCTS	FLEXURAL	JAWBOXES
BOLLIXES	CYBERSEX	EXANTHEM	EXEMPLAR		EXPUNGED	FLEXURES	KLAXONED
BOMBAXES	DEFLEXED	EXARCHAL	EXEMPLES		EXPUNGER	FORFEXES	LARYNXES
BOXINESS	DEFLEXES	EXCAMBED	EXEMPLUM		EXPUNGES	FOXBERRY	LAXATIVE
BOXROOMS	DENTEXES	EXCAVATE	EXEMPTED		EXPURGED	FOXGLOVE	LAXATORS
BOXWOODS	DESEXING	EXCEEDED	EXEQUIAL		EXPURGES	FOXHOLES	LAXITIES
BRAINBOX	DETOXIFY	EXCELLED	EXEQUIES		EXSCINDS	FOXHOUND	LEXICONS
BRUXISMS	DETOXING	EXCEPTED	EXERCISE		EXSECTED		LEXIGRAM

LIXIVIAL	NALOXONE	OXYTONES	QUIXOTIC	SEXUALLY	TAXIWAYS	UNBOXING	XANTHINE
LIXIVIUM	NEOTOXIN	PANMIXIA	QUIXOTRY	SIXAINES	TAXONOMY	UNFIXING	XANTHINS
LOXYGENS	NEXTNESS	PANMIXIS	REFLEXED	SIXPENCE	TEGUEXIN	UNFIXITY	XANTHOMA
LUMMOXES	NITROXYL	PARADOXY	REFLEXES	SIXPENNY	TELETEXT	UNIAXIAL	XANTHOUS
LUXATING	OPOPANAX	PARALLAX	REFLEXLY	SIXSCORE	TELEXING	UNSEXING	XENOGAMY
LUXATION	OREXISES	PAROXYSM	REFLUXED	SIXTEENS	TETRAXON	UNSEXIST	XENOLITH
LUXMETER	ORIFEXES	PAXIUBAS	REFLUXES	SIXTIETH	TETTIXES	UNSEXUAL	XENOPHYA
LUXURIES	ORTHODOX	PAXWAXES	RELAXANT	SMALLPOX	TEXTBOOK	UNTAXING	XENOTIME
LUXURIST	OUTBOXED	PEROXIDE	RELAXING	SMILAXES	TEXTILES	UXORIOUS	XENURINE
MAGNOXES	OUTBOXES	PHORMINX	RELAXINS	SNUFFBOX	TEXTLESS	VERTEXES	XERAFINS
MALAXAGE	OUTFOXED	PICKAXES	REMIXING	SPARAXIS	TEXTUARY	VEXATION	XERANSES
MALAXATE	OUTFOXES	PLATEAUX	RHEXISES	SPHINXES	TEXTURAL	VEXATORY	XERANSIS
MALAXING	OXALATES	PLEXURES	RONDEAUX	SPINIFEX	TEXTURED	VEXILLUM	XERANTIC
MANTEAUX	OXALISES	PLEXUSES	ROULEAUX	SPINTEXT	TEXTURES	VEXINGLY	XERAPHIM
MARTEXTS	OXAZINES	POLYAXON	SARDONYX	STORAXES	THORAXES	VIDEOTEX	XERASIAS
MATCHBOX	OXBLOODS	PONCEAUX	SAUCEBOX	STYRAXES	THYROXIN	VIXENISH	XEROMATA
MATRIXES	OXIDANTS	PONTIFEX	SAXATILE	SUBOXIDE	TOADFLAX	VOLVOXES	XYLENOLS
MAXILLAE	OXIDASES	POXVIRUS	SAXHORNS	SUBTEXTS	TONNEAUX	VORTEXES	XYLITOLS
MAXIMINS	OXIDATED	PREFIXED	SAXONIES	SUFFIXAL	TOXAEMIA	WATCHBOX	XYLOCARP
MAXIMISE	OXIDATES	PREFIXES	SAXONITE	SUFFIXED	TOXAEMIC	WATERPOX	XYLOGENS
MAXIMIST	OXIDISED	PREMIXED	SCRUMPOX	SUFFIXES	TOXEMIAS	WAXBERRY	XYLOIDIN
MAXIMIZE	OXIDISER	PREMIXES	SEXFOILS	SUPERTAX	TOXICANT	WAXBILLS	XYLOLOGY
MAXWELLS	OXIDISES	PRETEXTS	SEXINESS	SURTAXED	TOXICITY	WAXCLOTH	XYLOMATA
MIREPOIX	OXIDIZED	PROLIXLY	SEXOLOGY	SURTAXES	TOXOCARA	WAXINESS	XYLONITE
MIXTIONS	OXIDIZER	PROXIMAL	SEXPERTS	SYNTAXES	TRACTRIX	WAXWINGS	ZELATRIX
MIXTURES	OXIDIZES	PTYXISES	SEXTANTS	SYNTEXIS	TRANSFIX	WAXWORKS	ZEUXITES
MONAXIAL	OXIMETER	PYREXIAL	SEXTETTE	SYRINXES	TRIAXIAL	WRAXLING	ZOOTOXIN
MONAXONS	OXONIUMS	PYREXIAS	SEXTETTS	TABLEAUX	TRIAXONS	XANTHAMS	
MONOXIDE	OXTERING	PYROXENE	SEXTILES	TAXATION	TRIOXIDE	XANTHANS	
MORCEAUX	OXYMORON	PYROXYLE	SEXTOLET	TAXATIVE	TRUMEAUX	XANTHATE	
MYXEDEMA	OXYTOCIC	PYXIDIUM	SEXTUORS	TAXIARCH	TUTRIXES	XANTHEIN	
MYXOMATA	OXYTOCIN	QUINCUNX	SEXTUPLE	TAXICABS	TUXEDOES	XANTHENE	

Z-WORDS

Z – 2-letter words

ZO

Z – 3-letter words

ADZ	CUZ	JIZ	MOZ	SAZ	ZAX	ZEK	ZIG	ZOA
BEZ	DZO	LEZ	POZ	SEZ	ZEA	ZEL	ZIP	ZOO
BIZ	FEZ	LUZ	REZ	ZAG	ZED	ZEX	ZIT	ZOS
COZ	FIZ	MIZ	RIZ	ZAP	ZEE	ZHO	ZIZ	ZUZ

Z – 4-letter words

ADZE	DOZY	HAZE	LUTZ	OUZO	SWIZ	ZARF	ZETA	ZITI	ZOOS
AZAN	DZHO	HAZY	MAZE	OYEZ	TIZZ	ZATI	ZEZE	ZITS	ZORI
AZYM	DZOS	HIZZ	MAZY	PHIZ	TOZE	ZEAL	ZHOS	ZIZZ	ZOUK
BOZO	FAZE	JAZY	MEZE	PIZE	TREZ	ZEAS	ZIFF	ZOBO	ZULU
BUZZ	FIZZ	JAZZ	MIZZ	POZZ	TUZZ	ZEBU	ZIGS	ZOBU	ZUPA
CHEZ	FOZY	JIZZ	MOZE	PUTZ	TZAR	ZEDS	ZILA	ZOEA	ZURF
CHIZ	FRIZ	KAZI	MOZZ	QUIZ	VIZY	ZEES	ZIMB	ZOIC	ZYGA
COZE	FUZE	KUZU	MZEE	RAZE	WHIZ	ZEIN	ZINC	ZONA	ZYME
COZY	FUZZ	LAZE	NAZE	RAZZ	ZACK	ZEKS	ZINE	ZONE	
CZAR	GAZE	LAZO	OOZE	RIZA	ZAGS	ZELS	ZING	ZONK	
DAZE	GAZY	LAZY	OOZY	SIZE	ZANY	ZERO	ZIPS	ZOOM	
DOZE	GIZZ	LEZZ	ORZO	SIZY	ZAPS	ZEST	ZITE	ZOON	

Z – 5-letter words

ABUZZ	AZOIC	BAZAR	BRAZE	COLZA	DAZER	DZHOS	FURZY	GAZES	GRAZE
ADZES	AZOTE	BEZEL	BRIZE	COZED	DAZES	FADED	FUZEE	GAZON	GRIZE
AGAZE	AZOTH	BEZES	BUAZE	COZEN	DIAZO	FAZES	FUZES	GAZOO	HAMZA
AIZLE	AZURE	BLAZE	BUZZY	COZES	DITZY	FEEZE	FUZZY	GHAZI	HAZAN
AMAZE	AZURN	BLITZ	BWAZI	CRAZE	DIZEN	FEZES	GAUZE	GIZMO	HAZED
AVIZE	AZURY	BONZA	CAPIZ	CRAZY	DIZZY	FIZZY	GAUZY	GLAZE	HAZEL
AVYZE	AZYGY	BONZE	CEAZE	CROZE	DOZED	FRIZE	GAZAL	GLAZY	HAZER
AZANS	AZYME	BOOZE	CHIZZ	CZARS	DOZEN	FRIZZ	GAZAR	GLITZ	HAZES
AZIDE	AZYMS	BOOZY	CLOZE	DARZI	DOZER	FROZE	GAZED	GLOZE	HEEZE
AZINE	BAIZE	BOZOS	COBZA	DAZED	DOZES	FURZE	GAZER	GONZO	HERTZ

HIZEN	LEAZE	MZEES	PUZEL	SIZER	UNZIP	ZAMIA	ZEZES	ZIZEL	ZOOMS
HUZZA	LEZES	NAZES	PZAZZ	SIZES	VEZIR	ZANJA	ZHOMO	ZLOTY	ZOONS
HUZZY	LEZZY	NAZIR	RAZED	SPAZZ	VIZIR	ZANTE	ZIBET	ZOBOS	ZOPPA
IZARD	LOZEN	NEEZE	RAZEE	SPITZ	VIZOR	ZANZE	ZIFFS	ZOBUS	ZOPPO
IZZAT	MAIZE	NIZAM	RAZES	SQUIZ	VOZHD	ZAPPY	ZILAS	ZOEAE	ZORIL
JAZZY	MATZA	OOZED	RAZOO	TAZZA	WALTZ	ZARFS	ZILCH	ZOEAL	ZORIS
KANZU	MATZO	OOZES	RAZOR	TAZZE	WANZE	ZATIS	ZIMBI	ZOEAS	ZORRO
KARZY	MAZED	ORZOS	RITZY	TEAZE	WAZIR	ZAXES	ZIMBS	ZOISM	ZOUKS
KAZIS	MAZER	OUZEL	RIZAS	TIZZY	WEIZE	ZEALS	ZINCO	ZOIST	ZULUS
KAZOO	MAZES	OUZOS	ROZET	TOAZE	WHIZZ	ZEBEC	ZINCS	ZOMBI	ZUPAN
KLUTZ	MAZUT	OZEKI	ROZIT	TOPAZ	WINZE	ZEBRA	ZINEB	ZONAE	ZUPAS
KRANZ	MEZES	OZONE	SADZA	TOUZE	WIZEN	ZEBUB	ZINES	ZONAL	ZURFS
KUDZU	MEZZE	PEAZE	SAZES	TOUZY	WOOTZ	ZEBUS	ZINGS	ZONDA	ZUZIM
KUZUS	MEZZO	PEIZE	SCUZZ	'TOWZE	WOOZY	ZEINS	ZINGY	ZONED	ZYGAL
LAZAR	MILTZ	PIEZO	SEAZE	TOWZY	ZABRA	ZERDA	ZINKE	ZONES	ZYGON
LAZED	MIZEN	PIZES	SEIZE	TOZED	ZACKS	ZEROS	ZINKY	ZONKS	ZYMES
LAZES	MOTZA	PIZZA	SENZA	TOZES	ZAIRE	ZESTS	ZIPPO	ZOOEA	ZYMIC
LAZOS	MOZED	PLAZA	SIZAR	TOZIE	ZAKAT	ZESTY	ZIPPY	ZOOID	
LAZZI	MOZES	POZZY	SIZED	TZARS	ZAMAN	ZETAS			
LAZZO	MUZZY	PRIZE	SIZEL	ULZIE	ZAMBO	ZEXES			

Z – 6-letter words

ABLAZE	BLAZES	DIZAIN	GAZOON	JIZZES	MOZZIE	RAZORS	TEAZED	ZAGGED
ABRAZO	BLAZON	DIZENS	GAZOOS	KAIZEN	MOZZLE	RAZURE	TEAZEL	ZAKATS
AGAZED	BLINTZ	DONZEL	GAZUMP	KAMEEZ	MUZAKY	RAZZED	TEAZES	ZAMANG
AGNIZE	BLOWZE	DORIZE	GEEZER	KANZUS	MUZHIK	RAZZES	TEAZLE	ZAMANS
AGRIZE	BLOWZY	DOZENS	GHAZAL	KAZOOS	MUZZLE	RAZZIA	TENZON	ZAMBOS
AGRYZE	BONZER	DOZERS	GHAZEL	KIBITZ	MZUNGU	RAZZLE	TIZWAS	ZAMBUK
AGUIZE	BONZES	DOZIER	GHAZIS	KRANTZ	NAZIRS	REZONE	TIZZES	ZAMIAS
AIZLES	BOOZED	DOZING	GIZMOS	KUDZUS	NEEZED	REZZES	TOAZED	ZANDER
ALTEZA	BOOZER	DRAZEL	GIZZEN	KWANZA	NEEZES	RHIZIC	TOAZES	ZANIED
AMAZED	BOOZES	DZEREN	GLAZED	LAZARS	NIZAMS	RIZARD	TOLZEY	ZANIER
AMAZES	BOOZEY	ECZEMA	GLAZEN	LAZIER	NOZZER	RIZZAR	TOUZED	ZANIES
AMAZON	BORZOI	ENTREZ	GLAZER	LAZILY	NOZZLE	RIZZER	TOUZES	ZANJAS
APOZEM	BRAIZE	ENZIAN	GLAZES	LAZING	NUZZER	RIZZOR	TOUZLE	ZANTES
ASSIZE	BRAZED	ENZONE	GLITZY	LAZOED	NUZZLE	ROZETS	TOWZED	ZAPATA
AVIZED	BRAZEN	ENZYME	GLOZED	LAZOES	NYANZA	ROZITS	TOWZES	ZAPPED
AVIZES	BRAZES	EPIZOA	GLOZES	LEAZES	OOZIER	ROZZER	TOZIES	ZAPPER
AVYZED	BRAZIL	ERSATZ	GOZZAN	LEZZES	OOZILY	SADZAS	TOZING	ZARAPE
AVYZES	BREEZE	EVZONE	GRAZED	LIZARD	OOZING	SAZHEN	TREZES	ZAREBA
AZALEA	BREEZY	FAZING	GRAZER	LOZELL	OUZELS	SAZZES	TUZZES	ZARIBA
AZIDES	BRIZES	FEEZED	GRAZES	LOZENS	OYEZES	SCAZON	TWEEZE	ZARNEC
AZINES	BRONZE	FEEZES	GRIZES	LUTZES	OZAENA	SCHIZO	TZETSE	ZEALOT
AZIONE	BRONZY	FEZZED	GUIZER	LUZERN	OZEKIS	SCRUZE	ULZIES	ZEBECK
AZOLLA	BROUZE	FEZZES	GUTZER	LUZZES	OZONES	SCUZZY	UNZIPS	ZEBECS
AZONAL	BUAZES	FIZGIG	GUZZLE	MAHZOR	PANZER	SEAZED	UPGAZE	ZEBRAS
AZONIC	BUZZED	FIZZED	HAMZAH	MAIZES	PATZER	SEAZES	VEZIRS	ZEBUBS
AZOTES	BUZZER	FIZZEN	HAMZAS	MAMZER	PAZAZZ	SEIZED	VIZARD	ZELANT
AZOTHS	BUZZES	FIZZER	HAZANS	MATZAH	PEAZED	SEIZER	VIZIED	ZELOSO
AZOTIC	BWAZIS	FIZZES	HAZARD	MATZAS	PEAZES	SEIZES	VIZIER	ZENANA
AZURES	BYZANT	FIZZLE	HAZELS	MATZOH	PEIZED	SEIZIN	VIZIES	ZENDIK
AZYGOS	CEAZED	FLOOZY	HAZERS	MATZOS	PEIZES	SIZARS	VIZIRS	ZENITH
AZYMES	CEAZES	FOOZLE	HAZIER	MATZOT	PEZANT	SIZELS	VIZORS	ZEPHYR
BAIZED	CHAZAN	FOZIER	HAZILY	MAZARD	PHEEZE	SIZERS	VIZSLA	ZERDAS
BAIZES	CHINTZ	FRANZY	HAZING	MAZERS	PHIZOG	SIZIER	VIZZIE	ZEREBA
BANZAI	CIZERS	FRAZIL	HAZZAN	MAZHBI	PIAZZA	SIZING	VOZHDS	ZERIBA
BARAZA	COBZAS	FREEZE	HEEZED	MAZIER	PIZAZZ	SIZISM	WANZED	ZEROED
BAZAAR	COLZAS	FRENZY	HEEZES	MAZILY	PIZZAS	SIZIST	WANZES	ZEROTH
BAZARS	COROZO	FRIEZE	HEEZIE	MAZOUT	PIZZLE	SIZZLE	WAZIRS	ZESTED
BAZAZZ	CORYZA	FRIZES	HIZENS	MAZUMA	PLAZAS	SLEAZE	WEAZEN	ZESTER
BEDAZE	COZENS	FRIZZY	HIZZED	MAZUTS	PODZOL	SLEAZY	WEIZED	ZEUGMA
BENZAL	COZIER	FROWZY	HIZZES	MEAZEL	PRIZED	SLEEZY	WEIZES	ZHOMOS
BENZIL	COZIES	FROZEN	HOWZAT	MEZAIL	PRIZER	SNAZZY	WEZAND	ZIBETS
BENZOL	COZING	FURZES	HUZOOR	MEZUZA	PRIZES	SNEEZE	WHEEZE	ZIGANS
BENZYL	COZZES	FUZEES	HUZZAS	MEZZES	PUTZES	SNEEZY	WHEEZY	ZIGGED
BEZANT	CRAZED	FUZZED	IODIZE	MEZZOS	PUZELS	SNOOZE	WINZES	ZIGZAG
BEZAZZ	CRAZES	FUZZES	IONIZE	MIZENS	PUZZEL	SNOOZY	WIZARD	ZILLAH
BEZELS	CROZES	FUZZLE	IZARDS	MIZZEN	PUZZLE	SOZZLE	WIZENS	ZIMBIS
BEZOAR	CUZZES	GAUZES	IZZARD	MIZZES	QUARTZ	SOZZLY	WIZIER	ZIMMER
BEZZLE	CZAPKA	GAZALS	IZZATS	MIZZLE	QUEAZY	SPRITZ	WUZZLE	ZINCED
BIZAZZ	DARZIS	GAZARS	JAZIES	MIZZLY	QUINZE	STANZA	YAKUZA	ZINCKY
BIZONE	DAZERS	GAZEBO	JAZZED	MOMZER	RANZEL	STANZE	ZABETA	ZINCOS
BIZZES	DAZING	GAZERS	JAZZER	MOZING	RAZEED	STANZO	ZABRAS	ZINEBS
BLAIZE	DAZZLE	GAZIER	JAZZES	MOZZES	RAZEES	SUIVEZ	ZADDIK	ZINGED
BLAZED	DEFUZE	GAZING	JEZAIL		RAZING	SYZYGY	ZAFFER	ZINGEL
BLAZER	DIAZOS	GAZONS			RAZOOS	TAZZAS	ZAFFRE	

ZINGER	ZIPTOP	ZOARIA	ZOMBIS	ZONULA	ZOOMED	ZOSTER	ZYGOSE
ZINKED	ZIRCON	ZOCCOS	ZONARY	ZONULE	ZOONAL	ZOUNDS	ZYGOTE
ZINKES	ZITHER	ZODIAC	ZONATE	ZONURE	ZOONIC	ZUFOLI	ZYMASE
ZINNIA	ZIZELS	ZOETIC	ZONDAS	ZOOEAE	ZOOZOO	ZUFOLO	ZYMITE
ZIPPED	ZIZZED	ZOISMS	ZONING	ZOOEAL	ZORILS	ZUPANS	ZYMOID
ZIPPER	ZIZZES	ZOISTS	ZONKED	ZOOEAS	ZORINO	ZYDECO	ZYMOME
ZIPPOS	ZLOTYS	ZOMBIE	ZONOID	ZOOIDS	ZORROS	ZYGOMA	ZYTHUM

Z – 7-letter words

ABRAZOS	BENZYLS	COZENER	FAHLERZ	GUTZERS	MAMZERS	PHEEZED	SEIZINS	TRIZONE
ADONIZE	BEZANTS	COZIERS	FANZINE	GUZZLED	MATZAHS	PHEEZES	SEIZURE	TUILZIE
AGNIZED	BEZIQUE	COZIEST	FAZENDA	GUZZLER	MATZOON	PHIZOGS	SELTZER	TWEEZED
AGNIZES	BEZOARS	CRAZIER	FEEZING	GUZZLES	MATZOTH	PHIZZES	SHIATZU	TWEEZER
AGONIZE	BEZZLED	CRAZIES	FILAZER	HAMZAHS	MAZARDS	PIAZZAS	SHMALTZ	TWEEZES
AGRIZED	BEZZLES	CRAZILY	FIZGIGS	HAZANIM	MAZEFUL	PIZZLES	SHMOOZE	TWIZZLE
AGRIZES	BIZARRE	CRAZING	FIZZENS	HAZARDS	MAZHBIS	PODZOLS	SHOWBIZ	TZADDIK
AGRYZED	BIZONAL	CROZIER	FIZZERS	HAZELLY	MAZIEST	POETIZE	SIAMEZE	TZADDIQ
AGRYZES	BIZONES	CRUZADO	FIZZGIG	HAZIEST	MAZOUTS	POLYZOA	SIZABLE	TZETSES
AGUIZED	BLAZERS	CYANIZE	FIZZIER	HAZINGS	MAZUMAS	POZZIES	SIZEISM	TZIGANY
AGUIZES	BLAZING	CZAPKAS	FIZZING	HAZZANS	MAZURKA	PRENZIE	SIZEIST	TZIMMES
ALCAZAR	BLAZONS	CZARDAS	FIZZLED	HEEZIES	MAZZARD	PRETZEL	SIZIEST	UNFAZED
ALCORZA	BLINTZE	CZARDOM	FIZZLES	HEEZING	MEAZELS	PREZZIE	SIZINGS	UNFROZE
ALFEREZ	BLITZED	CZARINA	FLOOZIE	HEROIZE	MESTIZA	PRIZERS	SIZISMS	UNITIZE
ALIZARI	BLITZES	CZARISM	FOOZLED	HERTZES	MESTIZO	PRIZING	SIZISTS	UNSIZED
ALTEZAS	BLOWZED	CZARIST	FOOZLER	HIZZING	METAZOA	PUZZELS	SIZZLED	UNZONED
ALTEZZA	BLOWZES	DAMOZEL	FOOZLES	HOATZIN	MEZAILS	PUZZLED	SIZZLER	UPGAZED
AMAZING	BONANZA	DAZEDLY	FORZATI	HORIZON	MEZUZAH	PUZZLER	SIZZLES	UPGAZES
AMAZONS	BOOZERS	DAZZLED	FORZATO	HUMBUZZ	MIDSIZE	PUZZLES	SLEAZES	UTILIZE
ANALYZE	BOOZIER	DAZZLER	FOZIEST	HUTZPAH	MILTZES	PZAZZES	SNEEZED	VIZARDS
ANODIZE	BOOZILY	DAZZLES	FRAZILS	HUZOORS	MITZVAH	QUINZES	SNEEZER	VIZIERS
ANZIANI	BOOZING	DEFROZE	FRAZZLE	HUZZAED	MIZMAZE	QUIZZED	SNEEZES	VIZORED
APOZEMS	BORAZON	DEFUZED	FREEZER	HUZZIES	MIZZENS	QUIZZER	SNOOZED	VIZSLAS
APPRIZE	BORZOIS	DEFUZES	FREEZES	ICONIZE	MIZZLED	QUIZZES	SNOOZER	VIZYING
ARABIZE	BRAIZES	DENIZEN	FRIEZED	IDOLIZE	MIZZLES	RANZELS	SNOOZES	VIZZIED
ASSIZED	BRAZENS	DIALYZE	FRIEZES	IODIZED	MOMZERS	RAZURES	SNOOZLE	VIZZIES
ASSIZER	BRAZIER	DIARIZE	FRIZING	IODIZES	MOZETTA	RAZZIAS	SNUZZLE	WALTZED
ASSIZES	BRAZILS	DIAZOES	FRIZZED	IONIZED	MOZZIES	RAZZING	SOZZLED	WALTZER
ATHEIZE	BRAZING	DITZIER	FRIZZES	IONIZER	MOZZLES	RAZZLES	SOZZLES	WALTZES
ATOMIZE	BREEZED	DIZAINS	FRIZZLY	IONIZES	MUEZZIN	REALIZE	SPAZZED	WANZING
AVIZING	BREEZES	DIZENED	FURZIER	IRIDIZE	MUZHIKS	REFROZE	SPAZZES	WEAZAND
AVYZING	BRITZKA	DIZZARD	FUZZIER	IRONIZE	MUZZIER	REPRIZE	SPITZES	WEAZENS
AZALEAS	BRONZED	DIZZIED	FUZZILY	ITEMIZE	MUZZILY	RESEIZE	SPREAZE	WEIZING
AZIMUTH	BRONZEN	DIZZIER	FUZZING	IZZARDS	MUZZLED	REZONED	SPREEZE	WEZANDS
AZIONES	BRONZER	DIZZIES	FUZZLED	JACUZZI	MUZZLER	REZONES	SPULZIE	WHAIZLE
AZOLLAS	BRONZES	DIZZILY	FUZZLES	JANIZAR	MUZZLES	RHIZINE	SQUEEZE	WHEEZED
AZOTISE	BROUZES	DOCKIZE	GALLIZE	JAZZERS	MYTHIZE	RHIZOID	SQUEEZY	WHEEZER
AZOTIZE	BRULZIE	DONZELS	GAUZIER	JAZZIER	MZUNGUS	RHIZOME	STANZAS	WHEEZES
AZOTOUS	BUMBAZE	DORIZED	GAZANIA	JAZZILY	NEEZING	RHIZOPI	STANZES	WHEEZLE
AZULEJO	BUZZARD	DORIZES	GAZEBOS	JAZZING	NETIZEN	RIOTIZE	STANZOS	WHIZZED
AZUREAN	BUZZERS	DOZENED	GAZEFUL	JAZZMAN	NOZZERS	RITZIER	STARETZ	WHIZZER
AZURINE	BUZZIER	DOZENTH	GAZELLE	JAZZMEN	NOZZLES	RIZARDS	STYLIZE	WIZARDS
AZURITE	BUZZING	DOZIEST	GAZETTE	JEZAILS	NUZZERS	RIZZARS	SUBZERO	WIZENED
AZYGIES	BYZANTS	DOZINGS	GAZIEST	KAIZENS	NUZZLED	RIZZART	SUBZONE	WIZIERS
AZYGOUS	CADENZA	DRAZELS	GAZOOKA	KARZIES	NUZZLES	RIZZERS	SWAZZLE	WOOTZES
AZYMITE	CALZONE	DRIZZLE	GAZOONS	KIBBUTZ	NYANZAS	RIZZORS	SWIZZED	WOOZIER
AZYMOUS	CALZONI	DRIZZLY	GAZUMPS	KLEZMER	OBELIZE	ROZELLE	SWIZZES	WOOZILY
BAIZING	CANZONA	DZERENS	GEEZERS	KLUTZES	ODZOOKS	ROZETED	SWIZZLE	WRIZLED
BANZAIS	CANZONE	EBONIZE	GENIZAH	KOLKHOZ	OOZIEST	ROZITED	SWOZZLE	WUZZLED
BAPTIZE	CANZONI	ECHOIZE	GHAZALS	KRANZES	ORGANZA	ROZZERS	TAILZIE	WUZZLES
BARAZAS	CAPIZES	ECTOZOA	GHAZELS	KUNZITE	OUTSIZE	SAZERAC	TEAZELS	ZABETAS
BAZAARS	CAPSIZE	ECZEMAS	GIZZARD	KWANZAS	OXAZINE	SAZHENS	TEAZING	ZABTIEH
BAZOOKA	CAZIQUE	EGOTIZE	GIZZENS	KYANIZE	OXIDIZE	SCAZONS	TEAZLED	ZADDIKS
BAZOUKI	CEAZING	ELEGIZE	GLAZERS	LAICIZE	OZAENAS	SCHANZE	TEAZLES	ZAFFERS
BEDAZED	CHALAZA	EMBLAZE	GLAZIER	LAIRIZE	OZONISE	SCHERZI	TENDENZ	ZAFFRES
BEDAZES	CHALUTZ	ENDOZOA	GLAZING	LAZARET	OZONIZE	SCHERZO	TENZONS	ZAGGING
BEDIZEN	CHAZANS	ENFROZE	GLITZES	LAZIEST	PALAZZI	SCHIZOS	TIZZIES	ZAITECH
BEMAZED	CHINTZY	ENTOZOA	GLOZING	LAZOING	PALAZZO	SCHMELZ	TOAZING	ZAKUSKA
BENZALS	CHIZZED	ENZIANS	GOZZANS	LEZZIES	PANZERS	SCHMOOZ	TOLZEYS	ZAKUSKI
BENZENE	CHIZZES	ENZONED	GRAZERS	LIONIZE	PARAZOA	SCHERZO	TOPAZES	ZAMANGS
BENZILS	CHORIZO	ENZONES	GRAZIER	LIZARDS	PATZERS	SCHMOOZ	TOUZIER	ZAMARRA
BENZINE	CITIZEN	ENZYMES	GRAZING	LOZELLS	PEAZING	SCRUZED	TOUZING	ZAMARRO
BENZOIC	COALIZE	ENZYMIC	GRIZZLE	LOZENGE	PECTIZE	SCRUZES	TOUZLED	ZAMBUCK
BENZOIN	COGNIZE	EPIZOAN	GRIZZLY	LOZENGY	PEIZING	SCUZZES	TOUZLES	ZAMBUKS
BENZOLE	COROZOS	EPIZOIC	GUEREZA	LUZERNS	PEPTIZE	SEAZING	TOWZIER	ZAMOUSE
BENZOLS	CORYZAS	EPIZOON	GUIZERS	MACHZOR	PEZANTS	SEIZERS	TOWZING	ZAMPONE
BENZOYL	COZENED	EVZONES	GUIZERS	MADZOON	PHEAZAR	SEIZING	TRAPEZE	ZAMPONI
								ZANDERS

ZANELLA	ZEALANT	ZENANAS	ZIGANKA	ZINGELS	ZIZZING	ZONURES	ZOOZOOS	ZYMOGEN
ZANIEST	ZEALFUL	ZENDIKS	ZIGGING	ZINGERS	ZOARIUM	ZOOECIA	ZORGITE	ZYMOMES
ZANJERO	ZEALOTS	ZENITHS	ZIGZAGS	ZINGIER	ZOCCOLO	ZOOGAMY	ZORILLE	ZYMOSES
ZANYING	ZEALOUS	ZEOLITE	ZILCHES	ZINGING	ZODIACS	ZOOGENY	ZORILLO	ZYMOSIS
ZANYISM	ZEBECKS	ZEPHYRS	ZILLAHS	ZINKIER	ZOEFORM	ZOOGONY	ZORINOS	ZYMOTIC
ZAPPERS	ZEBRASS	ZEREBAS	ZILLION	ZINKIFY	ZOISITE	ZOOIDAL	ZOSTERS	ZYMURGY
ZAPPIER	ZEBRINA	ZERIBAS	ZIMMERS	ZINKING	ZOMBIES	ZOOLITE	ZUFFOLI	ZYTHUMS
ZAPPING	ZEBRINE	ZEROING	ZIMOCCA	ZINNIAS	ZOMBIFY	ZOOLITH	ZUFFOLO	
ZAPTIAH	ZEBROID	ZESTERS	ZINCIER	ZIPLOCK	ZONATED	ZOOLOGY	ZYDECOS	
ZAPTIEH	ZEBRULA	ZESTFUL	ZINCIFY	ZIPPERS	ZONINGS	ZOOMING	ZYGOMAS	
ZARAPES	ZEBRULE	ZESTIER	ZINCING	ZIPPIER	ZONKING	ZOONITE	ZYGOSES	
ZAREBAS	ZEDOARY	ZESTING	ZINCITE	ZIPPING	ZONULAE	ZOONOMY	ZYGOSIS	
ZAREEBA	ZELANTS	ZETETIC	ZINCKED	ZIRCONS	ZONULAR	ZOOPERY	ZYGOTES	
ZARIBAS	ZELATOR	ZEUGMAS	ZINCODE	ZITHERN	ZONULAS	ZOOTAXY	ZYGOTIC	
ZARNECS	ZEMSTVA	ZEUXITE	ZINCOID	ZITHERS	ZONULES	ZOOTOMY	ZYMASES	
ZARNICH	ZEMSTVO	ZIFFIUS	ZINCOUS	ZIZANIA	ZONULET	ZOOTYPE	ZYMITES	

Z – 8-letter words

ADONIZED	BANALIZE	BUMBAZES	DEMONIZE	ENZONING	GAZETTES	ITEMIZES	METAZOIC
ADONIZES	BAPTIZED	BUZZARDS	DENAZIFY	ENZOOTIC	GAZOGENE	IZVESTIA	METAZOON
AGNIZING	BAPTIZES	BUZZIEST	DENIZENS	EPIZOANS	GAZOOKAS	JACUZZIS	MEZEREON
AGONIZED	BAROMETZ	BUZZINGS	DEPUTIZE	EQUALIZE	GAZPACHO	JANIZARS	MEZEREUM
AGONIZES	BARTIZAN	BUZZWORD	DIALYZED	ERGOTIZE	GAZUMPED	JANIZARY	MEZUZAHS
AGRIZING	BAZAZZES	CADENZAS	DIALYZER	ERSATZES	GAZUNDER	JAZERANT	MEZUZOTH
AGRYZING	BAZOOKAS	CALZONES	DIALYZES	ETERNIZE	GENIZAHS	JAZZIEST	MINIMIZE
AGUIZING	BAZOUKIS	CANALIZE	DIARIZED	ETHERIZE	GIZZARDS	JUMBOIZE	MISPRIZE
ALBITIZE	BEDAZING	CANONIZE	DIARIZES	ETHICIZE	GIZZENED	KAMEEZES	MITZVAHS
ALCAZARS	BEDAZZLE	CANZONAS	DIAZEPAM	EULOGIZE	GLAZIERS	KAMIKAZE	MITZVOTH
ALCORZAS	BEDIZENS	CANZONET	DIGITIZE	EUPHUIZE	GLAZIEST	KAZATZKA	MIZMAZES
ALGUAZIL	BENZENES	CAPONIZE	DIMERIZE	EXORCIZE	GLAZINGS	KIBITZED	MIZZLIER
ALIZARIN	BENZOATE	CAPSIZAL	DIPLOZOA	FABULIZE	GLITZIER	KIBITZER	MIZZLING
ALIZARIS	BENZOINS	CAPSIZED	DISPRIZE	FANZINES	GLITZILY	KIBITZES	MOBILIZE
ALKALIZE	BENZOLES	CAPSIZES	DISSEIZE	FARADIZE	GLOZINGS	KRANTZES	MOMZERIM
ALTEZZAS	BENZOYLS	CATALYZE	DITZIEST	FAZENDAS	GOLDSIZE	KREUTZER	MONAZITE
AMAZEDLY	BEZAZZES	CAZIQUES	DIVINIZE	FEMINIZE	GRAZIERS	KUNZITES	MONETIZE
AMORTIZE	BEZIQUES	CHALAZAE	DIZENING	FILAZERS	GRAZINGS	KYANIZED	MORALIZE
ANALYZED	BEZONIAN	CHALAZAS	DIZZARDS	FINALIZE	GRAZIOSO	KYANIZES	MOTORIZE
ANALYZER	BEZZLING	CHALAZIA	DIZZIEST	FIZZGIGS	GRIZZLED	LAICIZED	MOZETTAS
ANALYZES	BITESIZE	CHAZANIM	DIZZYING	FIZZIEST	GRIZZLER	LAICIZES	MOZZETTA
ANNALIZE	BIZAZZES	CHINTZES	DOCKIZED	FIZZINGS	GRIZZLES	LAIRIZED	MUEZZINS
ANODIZED	BIZCACHA	CHIZZING	DOCKIZES	FIZZLING	GUEREZAS	LAIRIZES	MUZZIEST
ANODIZES	BLAZERED	CHORIZOS	DORIZING	FLOOZIES	GUZZLERS	LAZARETS	MUZZLERS
ANTICIZE	BLAZONED	CHUTZPAH	DOUZEPER	FLUIDIZE	GUZZLING	LAZINESS	MUZZLING
APHETIZE	BLAZONER	CIVILIZE	DOWNSIZE	FOCALIZE	HAZARDED	LAZULITE	MYTHIZED
APHORIZE	BLAZONRY	COALIZED	DOZENING	FOOZLERS	HAZARDRY	LAZURITE	MYTHIZES
APPETIZE	BLINTZES	COALIZES	DOZENTHS	FOOZLING	HAZELNUT	LEGALIZE	NASALIZE
APPRIZED	BLITZING	COENZYME	DOZINESS	FORZANDI	HAZINESS	LIONIZED	NEBULIZE
APPRIZER	BLIZZARD	COGNIZED	DRIZZLED	FORZANDO	HAZZANIM	LIONIZES	NETIZENS
APPRIZES	BLOWZIER	COGNIZES	DRIZZLES	FORZATOS	HEPATIZE	LOCALIZE	NODALIZE
ARABIZED	BONANZAS	COLONIZE	DYNAMIZE	FOZINESS	HEROIZED	LOGICIZE	NOMADIZE
ARABIZES	BORAZONS	COZENAGE	EBENEZER	FRANZIER	HEROIZES	LOZENGED	NOTARIZE
ARCHAIZE	BOTANIZE	COZENERS	EBIONIZE	FRAZZLED	HOACTZIN	LOZENGES	NOVELIZE
ARMOZEEN	BOUZOUKI	COZENING	EBONIZED	FRAZZLES	HOATZINS	LYSOZYME	NUZZLING
ARMOZINE	BOZZETTI	CRAZIEST	EBONIZES	FREEZERS	HOLOZOIC	MACARIZE	OBELIZED
ASSIZERS	BOZZETTO	CREDENZA	ECHOIZED	FREEZING	HORIZONS	MADERIZE	OBELIZES
ASSIZING	BRAZENED	CREUTZER	ECHOIZES	FRENZIED	HOWITZER	MADZOONS	OOZINESS
ATHEIZED	BRAZENLY	CROZIERS	ECTOZOAN	FRENZIES	HUMANIZE	MAGAZINE	OPALIZED
ATHEIZES	BRAZENRY	CRUZADOS	ECTOZOIC	FRIEZING	HUTZPAHS	MAHZORIM	OPTIMIZE
ATHETIZE	BRAZIERS	CRUZEIRO	ECTOZOON	FRIZZIER	HUZZAING	MAMZERIM	ORGANIZE
ATMOLYZE	BRAZILIN	CURARIZE	EGOTIZED	FRIZZING	HYDROZOA	MANZELLO	ORGANZAS
ATOMIZED	BREEZIER	CUTINIZE	EGOTIZES	FRIZZLED	ICONIZED	MARZIPAN	OUTPRIZE
ATOMIZER	BREEZILY	CYANIZED	ELEGIZED	FRIZZLES	ICONIZES	MATZOONS	OUTSIZED
ATOMIZES	BREEZING	CYANIZES	ELEGIZES	FROWZIER	IDEALIZE	MAXIMIZE	OUTSIZES
ATRAZINE	BRITZKAS	CZARDOMS	EMBEZZLE	FURZIEST	IDOLIZED	MAZARINE	OVERSIZE
AUTOLYZE	BRITZSKA	CZAREVNA	EMBLAZED	FUZZIEST	IDOLIZER	MAZELTOV	OXAZINES
AZIMUTHS	BRONZERS	CZARINAS	EMBLAZES	FUZZLING	IDOLIZES	MAZEMENT	OXIDIZED
AZOTISED	BRONZIER	CZARISMS	EMBLAZON	GADZOOKS	IMMUNIZE	MAZINESS	OXIDIZER
AZOTISES	BRONZIFY	CZARISTS	ENDOZOIC	GALLIZED	INFAMIZE	MAZURKAS	OXIDIZES
AZOTIZED	BRONZING	CZARITSA	ENDOZOON	GALLIZES	IODIZING	MAZZARDS	OZONISED
AZOTIZES	BRONZITE	DAMOZELS	ENERGIZE	GARBANZO	IONIZERS	MELODIZE	OZONISER
AZOTURIA	BRUILZIE	DAZZLERS	ENFREEZE	GAUZIEST	IONIZING	MEMORIZE	OZONISES
AZULEJOS	BRULZIES	DAZZLING	ENFROZEN	GAZANIAS	IRIDIZED	MESPRIZE	OZONIZED
AZURINES	BULLDOZE	DEFREEZE	ENTOZOAL	GAZEBOES	IRIDIZES	MESTIZAS	OZONIZER
AZURITES	BUMBAZED	DEFROZEN	ENTOZOIC	GAZELLES	IRONIZED	MESTIZOS	OZONIZES
AZYGOSES		DEFUZING	ENTOZOON	GAZEMENT	IRONIZES	METALIZE	PAGANIZE
AZYMITES				GAZETTED	ITEMIZED	METAZOAN	PAPALIZE

PARALYZE	REALIZER	SELTZERS	SPRITZER	TRIZONES	WHEEZILY	ZELATRIX	ZOOGENIC
PARAZOAN	REALIZES	SFORZATI	SPRITZES	TUILZIED	WHEEZING	ZEMINDAR	ZOOGLOEA
PARAZOON	REFREEZE	SFORZATO	SPRITZIG	TUILZIES	WHEEZLED	ZEMSTVOS	ZOOGRAFT
PARTIZAN	REFROZEN	SHIATZUS	SPUILZIE	TUTORIZE	WHEEZLES	ZENITHAL	ZOOLATER
PAZAZZES	REGULIZE	SHMALTZY	SPULZIED	TWEEZERS	WHIZBANG	ZEOLITES	ZOOLATRY
PECTIZED	RENDZINA	SHMOOZED	SPULZIES	TWEEZING	WHIZZERS	ZEOLITIC	ZOOLITES
PECTIZES	REPRIZED	SHMOOZES	SQUEEZED	TWIZZLED	WHIZZING	ZEPPELIN	ZOOLITHS
PENALIZE	REPRIZES	SIAMEZED	SQUEEZER	TWIZZLES	WIZARDLY	ZERUMBET	ZOOLITIC
PEPTIZED	RESEIZED	SIAMEZES	SQUEEZES	TZADDIKS	WIZARDRY	ZESTIEST	ZOOMANCY
PEPTIZES	RESEIZES	SIMAZINE	SQUIZZES	TZADDIQS	WIZENING	ZETETICS	ZOOMETRY
PETUNTZE	RESINIZE	SIMILIZE	STANZAIC	TZATZIKI	WOMANIZE	ZEUXITES	ZOOMORPH
PEZIZOID	REZONING	SINICIZE	STANZOES	UNAMAZED	WOOZIEST	ZIBELINE	ZOONITES
PHEAZARS	RHIZINES	SIRENIZE	STRELITZ	UNDAZZLE	WURTZITE	ZIGANKAS	ZOONITIC
PHEEZING	RHIZOBIA	SIZEABLE	STYLIZED	UNFREEZE	WUZZLING	ZIGGURAT	ZOONOMIA
PIAZZIAN	RHIZOIDS	SIZEISMS	STYLIZES	UNFROZEN	YOKOZUNA	ZIGZAGGY	ZOONOMIC
PIROZHKI	RHIZOMES	SIZEISTS	SUBERIZE	UNGLAZED	ZABAIONE	ZIKKURAT	ZOONOSES
PIZAZZES	RHIZOPOD	SIZINESS	SUBITIZE	UNGRAZED	ZABTIEHS	ZILLIONS	ZOONOSIS
PIZZERIA	RHIZOPUS	SIZZLERS	SUBSIZAR	UNIONIZE	ZADDIKIM	ZIMOCCAS	ZOONOTIC
POETIZED	RIBOZYME	SIZZLING	SUBZONAL	UNITIZED	ZAITECHS	ZINCIEST	ZOOPATHY
POETIZES	RIGIDIZE	SLEAZIER	SUBZONES	UNITIZES	ZAMARRAS	ZINCITES	ZOOPERAL
POLARIZE	RIOTIZES	SLEAZILY	SUZERAIN	UNMUZZLE	ZAMARROS	ZINCKIER	ZOOPHAGY
POLEMIZE	RITZIEST	SLEEZIER	SWAZZLES	UNPRIZED	ZAMBOMBA	ZINCKIFY	ZOOPHILE
POLONIZE	RIVALIZE	SMORZATO	SWIZZING	UNSEIZED	ZAMBUCKS	ZINCKING	ZOOPHILY
POLYZOAN	RIZZARED	SNAZZIER	SWIZZLED	UNVIZARD	ZAMINDAR	ZINCODES	ZOOPHORI
POLYZOIC	RIZZARTS	SNEEZERS	SWIZZLES	UNZIPPED	ZAMOUSES	ZINGIBER	ZOOPHYTE
POLYZOON	RIZZERED	SNEEZIER	SWOZZLES	UPGAZING	ZAMPOGNA	ZINGIEST	ZOOSCOPY
PRETZELS	RIZZORED	SNEEZING	SYZYGIAL	URBANIZE	ZANELLAS	ZINKIEST	ZOOSPERM
PREZZIES	ROBOTIZE	SNOOZERS	SYZYGIES	UTILIZED	ZANINESS	ZIPPERED	ZOOSPORE
PRIZABLE	ROYALIZE	SNOOZIER	TAILZIES	UTILIZER	ZANJEROS	ZIPPIEST	ZOOTHOME
PRIZEMAN	ROZELLES	SNOOZING	TEAZELED	UTILIZES	ZANYISMS	ZIRCALOY	ZOOTOMIC
PRIZEMEN	ROZETING	SNOOZLES	TEAZLING	VALORIZE	ZAPPIEST	ZIRCONIA	ZOOTOXIN
PROTOZOA	ROZITING	SNUZZLED	TERRAZZO	VAPORIZE	ZAPTIAHS	ZIRCONIC	ZOOTROPE
PTYALIZE	RURALIZE	SNUZZLES	TERZETTA	VELARIZE	ZAPTIEHS	ZITHERNS	ZOOTYPES
PUZZLERS	SAMIZDAT	SOBERIZE	TERZETTI	VITALIZE	ZARATITE	ZIZANIAS	ZOOTYPIC
PUZZLING	SANITIZE	SODOMIZE	TERZETTO	VIZAMENT	ZAREEBAS	ZIZYPHUS	ZOPILOTE
PYRITIZE	SARRAZIN	SOLARIZE	TETANIZE	VIZARDED	ZARNICHS	ZOCCOLOS	ZORGITES
PYROLYZE	SATIRIZE	SOLECIZE	THEORIZE	VIZCACHA	ZARZUELA	ZODIACAL	ZORILLES
QUANTIZE	SAZERACS	SOLONETZ	THIAZIDE	VIZIRATE	ZASTRUGA	ZOETROPE	ZORILLOS
QUARTZES	SCHANTZE	SORORIZE	THIAZINE	VIZIRIAL	ZASTRUGI	ZOIATRIA	ZUCCHINI
QUATORZE	SCHANZES	SOZZLIER	TIZWASES	VIZORING	ZEALANTS	ZOISITES	ZUCHETTA
QUEAZIER	SCHERZOS	SOZZLING	TOPAZINE	VOCALIZE	ZEALLESS	ZOMBIISM	ZUCHETTO
QUETZALS	SCHIZOID	SPAZZING	TOTALIZE	VOLUMIZE	ZEALOTRY	ZOMBORUK	ZUGZWANG
QUIZZERS	SCHIZONT	SPETSNAZ	TOUZIEST	VOWELIZE	ZEBRINAS	ZONATION	ZYGAENID
QUIZZERY	SCHMALTZ	SPETZNAZ	TOUZLING	WALTZERS	ZEBRINNY	ZONELESS	ZYGANTRA
QUIZZIFY	SCHMOOZE	SPREAZED	TOWZIEST	WALTZING	ZEBRULAS	ZONULETS	ZYGODONT
QUIZZING	SCRUZING	SPREAZES	TRAPEZED	WEAZANDS	ZEBRULES	ZOOBLAST	ZYGOMATA
RACEMIZE	SCUZZIER	SPREEZED	TRAPEZES	WEAZENED	ZECCHINE	ZOOCHORE	ZYLONITE
RAZEEING	SEIZABLE	SPREEZES	TRAPEZIA	WHAIZLED	ZECCHINI	ZOOCHORY	ZYMOGENS
RAZMATAZ	SEIZINGS	SPREEZES	TRAPEZII	WHAIZLES	ZECCHINO	ZOOCYTIA	ZYMOLOGY
REALIZED	SEIZURES	SPRITZED	TRIZONAL	WHEEZIER	ZELATORS	ZOOECIUM	ZYMOTICS

Hint   **Managing the Big Four**

It is rarely worth holding on to the J, Q, X or Z in the hope of a very high score later in the game unless you are aware of the letters you are likely to pick up and you are not sacrificing scores in the process. Generally, keeping the high-score letters back will hinder future opportunities and rack balance. It is often wiser to score what you can rather than wait for something better. But if you are to hold on to any of the big four the X is probably the safest and most flexible simply because of the 2-letter words playable. It is also the one your opponent is most likely unwittingly to provide a scoring opportunity for.

Learning the J Q X Z Words

If you have trouble remembering those useful words containing the J, Q, X or Z then try the following solo game as a learning exercise. Take the J, X, Z, Q and one U out of the letter bag and put to one side. Take six letters at random from the letter bag and place on your rack. Then give yourself a couple of minutes with each of J, Q, X and Z to see how many different words you can make by combining them with the six letters on your rack. When playing with the Q, if you haven't also picked a U, utilize the U you've put to one side. Make a note of the highest-scoring play you found with each of J, Q, X and Z and then check with the lists in this book to see if there was anything you missed. Having completed the exercise with the first rack, play any word from your six letters on the board, keeping the J, Q, X, Z and U to one side, and return any remaining letters to the bag. Select another six letters at random for the second turn. Repeat the exercise with the fresh rack and so on.

Do-It-Yourself 6-Letter Sets

The 250 6-letter combinations (stems) in this book represent those most useful to the Scrabble player. There are many more stems that are useful to study and, as is nearly always the case, compiling lists yourself not only helps you memorize the words but is also more interesting than simply learning from those readily provided. Try deriving your own six-letter stem lists based on names (SHEILA, DANIEL, etc) or fictitious words (INCORE, POSIER, etc) as mnemonics. The Anagram section will be your ideal hunting-ground for this exercise.

Tile-Tracking

It is acceptable in tournament Scrabble to have a note of the letter distribution and to use it during play as a checklist of what letters are still to come. Most top players use this method to enable them to work out what tiles their opponents have at the end of the game. Such a checklist, when used skilfully, can also provide mid-game information about likely pickups and enable the right combination of tiles to be kept on the rack to give the greatest possibility of playing a bonus word. If you practise tile-tracking whilst playing you will soon find you are more aware of the letter distribution which in turn will assist you to maintain a balanced rack. Even if you don't track all the tiles, keeping a note of the vowels, the S's and blanks, the J, Q, X, Z and the awkward consonants C, V and K will help improve your rack management.

Beginners' Starter Sets

To help newer players to improve their game rapidly, the following two pages contain a selection of around 1,400 words specifically chosen for their usefulness and likelihood of occurring. The lists include:

List 1: 2-letter words

This list includes *all* the 2-letter words, which underlines how useful they are, especially for parallel plays.

List 2: 3-letter words

An extensive list of 3-letter words, excluding the very common words that will be in most people's everyday vocabulary. Familiarity with some of the more unusual 3-letter words will improve your ability to score with fewer letters and give you a greater chance of extending 2-letter words on the board.

List 3: Vowel-heavy words

All the 4- and 5-letter words that contain no more than one consonant. These are essential for rapid resolution of racks abounding in vowels – one of the most common rack difficulties.

List 4: JQXZ words

A selection of words containing one of the power tiles, J, Q, X or Z, combined only with tiles having a value of less than 3. The more common everyday words have been excluded so that you can focus more easily on the words to learn. We have also excluded words that are -S, -ES, -D or -ED extensions of shorter words.

List 5: 7-letter words

Over two hundred 7-letter words that are most likely to crop up in the game. Some of these are common words, others more unusual, but all are worth being familiar with. They will help you achieve those 50-point bonus scores for playing all your tiles.

List 6: 8-letter words

It may seem strange to include 8-letter plays in a list for beginners, but a knowledge of just a few likely 8-letter words can be extremely useful for playing bonus words when there is no scope for 7's. It's important for newer players to 'think big' and explore the full spectrum of possibilities to improve scoring. For this reason, a hundred of the most likely 8-letter words have been selected. Some are common words, some more unusual, but all are likely to crop up more often than you might think.

List 1: 2-letter words

AA	AW	DI	ES	HO	KY	NA	OI	OY	ST	US
AD	AX	DO	EX	ID	LA	NE	OM	PA	TA	UT
AE	AY	EA	FA	IF	LI	NO	ON	PH	TE	WE
AH	BA	EE	FY	IN	LO	NU	OO	PI	TI	WO
AI	BE	EF	GI	IO	MA	NY	OP	PO	TO	XI
AM	BI	EH	GO	IS	ME	OB	OR	QI	UG	XU
AN	BO	EL	GU	IT	MI	OD	OS	RE	UM	YE
AR	BY	EM	HA	JO	MO	OE	OU	SH	UN	YO
AS	CH	EN	HE	KA	MU	OF	OW	SI	UP	YU
AT	DA	ER	HI	KO	MY	OH	OX	SO	UR	ZO

List 2: 3-letter words

AAS	BRO	DUO	FOY	HOC	KOA	MEU	OCA	POO	SEC	TOD	WIS
ABA	BUB	DUP	FRA	HOH	KOB	MHO	OCH	POS	SED	TOG	WOK
ABB	BUR	DUX	FRO	HOI	KOI	MIL	ODA	POW	SEG	TOR	WOS
ABY	BYS	DZO	FUB	HON	KON	MIM	ODS	POX	SEI	TUI	WOT
ACH	CAM	EAN	FUD	HOO	KOP	MIR	OES	POZ	SEL	TUM	WOW
ADO	CAW	EAS	FUG	HOS	KOS	MIS	OFT	PRE	SEN	TUN	WOX
ADS	CAY	EAU	FUM	HOX	KOW	MIZ	OHM	PSI	SEY	TUP	WUD
ADZ	CEE	ECH	GAB	HOY	KYE	MNA	OHO	PST	SEZ	TUT	WUS
AGA	CEL	ECU	GAD	HUE	KYU	MOA	OIK	PUD	SIB	TUX	WYE
AHA	CEP	EDH	GAE	HUH	LAC	MOD	OKE	PUH	SIC	TWA	WYN
AHS	CHA	EEK	GAL	HUI	LAH	MOE	OLE	PUR	SIM	TWP	XIS
AIA	CHE	EEN	GAM	HUP	LAM	MOG	OLM	PUY	SIS	TYE	YAH
AIN	CHI	EFF	GAN	HYE	LAR	MOI	OMS	PYE	SKA	TYG	YAM
AIS	CID	EFS	GAR	HYP	LAS	MOM	ONS	PYX	SMA	UDO	YAW
AIT	CIG	EFT	GAT	ICH	LAT	MON	OOF	QAT	SNY	UDS	YEA
AKE	CIT	EHS	GAU	IDE	LAV	MOR	OOH	QIS	SOC	UEY	YEN
ALA	CLY	EIK	GED	IDS	LEA	MOT	OOM	QUA	SOG	UFO	YEP
ALB	COL	EKE	GEE	IFF	LEE	MOU	OON	RAD	SOH	UGH	YEX
ALP	COR	ELD	GEO	IFS	LEI	MOY	OOP	RAH	SOL	UGS	YGO
ALS	COS	ELL	GEY	ILK	LEK	MOZ	OOR	RAI	SOS	UKE	YIN
ALT	COZ	ELS	GHI	INS	LEP	MUN	OOS	RAJ	SOT	ULE	YIP
AMI	CRU	ELT	GIB	ION	LES	MUS	OPE	RAS	SOU	UNI	YOD
ANA	CUD	EME	GID	IOS	LEU	MUX	OPS	RAX	SOV	UNS	YOK
ANE	CUM	EMS	GIE	IRK	LEV	NAE	ORC	REC	SOX	UPS	YON
ANI	CUR	ENE	GIF	ISH	LEW	NAM	ORD	REE	SOY	URD	YOS
ANN	CUZ	ENG	GIO	ISM	LEX	NAN	ORF	REH	SUD	URE	YOW
ARB	CWM	ENS	GIP	ISO	LEY	NAS	ORS	REM	SUI	UTE	YUG
ARD	DAE	EON	GIS	ITA	LEZ	NAT	ORT	REN	SUK	UTS	YUK
ARS	DAG	ERE	GJU	JAG	LIG	NAY	OUD	RES	SUP	UVA	YUP
ARY	DAH	ERF	GOA	JAK	LIN	NEB	OUK	RET	SUQ	VAC	YUS
ASP	DAK	ERG	GON	JAP	LIS	NED	OUP	REW	SUR	VAE	ZAG
AUF	DAL	ERK	GOS	JEE	LOD	NEE	OVA	REX	SUS	VAS	ZAP
AUK	DAN	ERN	GOV	JEU	LOR	NEF	OWT	REZ	SWY	VAU	ZAX
AVA	DAP	ERS	GOY	JIB	LOS	NEK	OYE	RHO	SYE	VEE	ZEA
AVE	DAS	ESS	GUB	JIZ	LOX	NEP	OYS	RHY	TAD	VEG	ZED
AWA	DAW	EST	GUE	JOE	LOY	NID	PAH	RIA	TAE	VIA	ZEE
AWN	DEB	ETA	GUP	JOR	LUD	NIE	PAM	RIN	TAI	VID	ZEK
AYE	DEE	ETH	GUR	JOW	LUM	NIM	PAP	RIT	TAJ	VIM	ZEL
AYS	DEF	EUK	GUS	JUD	LUR	NIS	PAS	RIZ	TAK	VIN	ZEX
AYU	DEI	EWK	GUV	JUS	LUV	NIX	PAX	ROC	TAM	VIS	ZHO
BAC	DEL	EWT	GYP	KAE	LUX	NOB	PEC	ROK	TAT	VLY	ZIG
BAH	DEY	FAH	HAE	KAI	LUZ	NOH	PED	ROM	TAU	VOE	ZIT
BAM	DIB	FAP	HAH	KAM	LYE	NOM	PEP	ROO	TAW	VOL	ZIZ
BAS	DIT	FAS	HAJ	KAS	LYM	NON	PER	RUC	TAY	VOR	ZOA
BEL	DIV	FAW	HAN	KAT	MAA	NOS	PHI	RUD	TED	VOX	ZOS
BEN	DOB	FAY	HAP	KAW	MAC	NOX	PHO	RUE	TEF	VUG	ZUZ
BEY	DOC	FET	HAW	KAY	MAG	NOY	PHS	RYA	TEG	VUM	
BEZ	DOD	FEU	HEP	KEA	MAK	NTH	PIA	SAB	TEL	WAE	
BIO	DOH	FEY	HES	KEB	MAL	NUB	PIC	SAC	TES	WAP	
BIS	DOO	FID	HET	KED	MAM	NUR	PIR	SAE	TEW	WAT	
BIZ	DOP	FIE	HEW	KEF	MAS	NUS	PIS	SAI	THO	WAW	
BOH	DOR	FIL	HEX	KEN	MAW	NYE	PIU	SAL	TIC	WEM	
BOK	DOS	FIZ	HIC	KEP	MAX	NYS	PIX	SAM	TID	WEN	
BON	DOW	FOH	HIE	KET	MEG	OBA	POA	SAN	TIG	WEX	
BOR	DSO	FON	HIN	KEX	MEL	OBI	POH	SAR	TIL	WEY	
BOS	DUB	FOP	HOA	KIF	MES	OBO	POI	SAX	TIS	WHA	
BOT	DUN	FOU		KIR		OBS	POM	SAZ	TOC		

List 3: Vowel-heavy words

AEON	AGIO	AIDE	AJEE	ALEE	ANOA	ARIA	AURA	CIAO	EAUS
AERO	AGUE	AINE	AKEE	ALOE	AQUA	AULA	AUTO	EALE	EAUX
AGEE	AIAS	AITU	ALAE	AMIE	AREA	AUNE	BEAU	EASE	EINE

EMEU	HUIA	IXIA	OBIA	OUZO	UVEA	AINEE	EERIE	ZOOEA
EOAN	IDEA	JIAO	OBOE	PAUA	VIAE	AIOLI	OIDIA	
EPEE	IDEE	KAIE	ODEA	ROUE	ZOEA	AQUAE	OORIE	
ETUI	ILEA	LIEU	OGEE	TOEA		AUDIO	OUIJA	
EUGE	ILIA	LUAU	OLEO	UNAU	ADIEU	AULOI	OURIE	
EUOI	INIA	MOOI	OLIO	URAO	AECIA	AURAE	QUEUE	
EURO	IOTA	MOUE	OOSE	UREA	AERIE	AUREI	URAEI	
EVOE	IURE	NAOI	OOZE	UVAE	AIDOI	COOEE	ZOEAE	

List 4: JQXZ words

AJEE	JOUR	JINGO	AQUA	QUIST	LANX	LAXER	UNTAX	ZING	GAZER	SIZEL
DOJO	JUGA	JINNI	QADI	QUOAD	LUXE	LEXIS	XENIA	ZITE	GAZON	SIZER
GAJO	JURA	JIRGA	QUAD	QUOIN	OXER	NEXUS	XENON	ZITI	GAZOO	TEAZE
JANE	JURE	JNANA	QUAG	QUOIT	ROUX	NIXIE	XOANA	ZOEA	GLITZ	TOAZE
JANN	RAJA	JODEL	QUAT	QUOLL	SEXT	NOXAL		ZONA	GLOZE	TOUZE
JARL	ROJI	JOTUN	QUIN	ROQUE	TAXA	OXIDE	ADZE	ZOON	GONZO	TOZIE
JASS	SIJO	JOUAL	QUOD	SQUEG	ULEX	OXTER	AZAN	ZORI	GRIZE	ULZIE
JATO	SOJA	JOUGS	QUAE	SQUIT	ADDAX	RADIX	LAZO	ZULU	IZARD	ZAIRE
JEAN	DJINN	JOULE	EQUID	TALAQ	ANNEX	REDOX	LUTZ	AGAZE	LAZAR	ZANTE
JEAT	GADJE	JUDAS	QANAT	TOQUE	AUXIN	SALIX	NAZE	AIZLE	LEAZE	ZERDA
JEEL	GANJA	JUGAL	QUAIR	TUQUE	AXIAL	SEXER	ORZO	AZIDE	LOZEN	ZIGAN
JELL	GAUJE	JUNTA	QUALE		AXILE	SILEX	OUZO	AZINE	NAZIR	ZOEAE
JESS	JAGER	JUNTO	QUANT	AXED	AXOID	SIXER	RAZE	AZOTE	NEEZE	ZOEAL
JETE	JAGIR	JURAL	QUARE	AXEL	DESEX	SIXTE	RIZA	AZURE	OUZEL	ZOIST
JIAO	JARTA	JURAT	QUASI	AXIL	DETOX	SOREX	TOZE	AZURN	RAZEE	ZONAE
JILL	JARUL	NINJA	QUEAN	AXON	DIXIE	TAXER	TREZ	DARZI	RAZOO	ZONAL
JINN	JELLO	OUIJA	QUENA	DIXI	EXEAT	TAXOL	TZAR	DAZER	ROZET	ZONDA
JIRD	JERID	REJIG	QUERN	EAUX	EXIES	TAXON	ZATI	DIAZO	ROZIT	ZOOEA
JOLE	JESUS	REJON	QUINA	EXON	EXINE	TAXOR	ZEIN	DIZEN	SADZA	ZOOID
JOLL	JETON	SAJOU	QUINE	EXUL	EXODE	TELEX	ZETA	DOZER	SEAZE	ZORIL
JOSS	JEUNE	SUJEE	QUINT	ILEX	IXTLE	TEXAS	ZILA	GAZAL	SENZA	ZORRO
JOTA	JIGOT		QUIRT	IXIA	LATEX	UNSEX	ZINE	GAZAR	SIZAR	

List 5: 7-letter words

AENEOUS	AUREOLE	ELATION	HAIRNET	LATRINE	ORIGANE	ROUTINE	SPINATE	TINDERS
AEOLIAN	AUSTERE	ELOINED	IDEATES	LENTORS	OSTIATE	RUINATE	STAINED	TINWARE
AEONIAN	AWNIEST	ELOINER	INANEST	LIERNES	OTARIES	SAINTED	STAINER	TISANES
AERATES	BASINET	ENATION	INEARTH	LINEATE	OTARINE	SALIENT	STANIEL	TOENAIL
AERIALS	BESAINT	ENTAILS	INERTIA	MAINEST	PAINTER	SAPIENT	STARNIE	TORNADE
AERIEST	BESTAIN	ENTASIS	INGATES	MANTIES	PANTIES	SARDINE	STEARIN	TRAINED
AGONISE	CANIEST	ENTRAIL	INGESTA	MINARET	PATINES	SATINED	STONIED	TRAINEE
AIERIES	CANTIER	ERASION	INGRATE	NACRITE	PERTAIN	SATINET	SUETIER	TRAINER
AILERON	CERTAIN	EROSION	INMATES	NAIADES	RAIMENT	SAUTOIR	TAENIAE	TRANNIE
AIRIEST	CINEAST	EROTICA	INSTATE	NAIFEST	RATINES	SEALINE	TAENIAS	TRENAIL
AIRLINE	CREATIN	ETAERIO	INSTEAD	NAIVEST	RATLINE	SEATING	TAJINES	TROELIE
ALIENEE	CRINATE	ETALONS	INTAKES	NARTJIE	REGINAE	SENARII	TAMINES	TSIGANE
ALIENOR	DARIOLE	ETESIAN	INTREAT	NASTIER	RELIANT	SENATOR	TANGIER	URALITE
ALSOONE	DAUTIES	EUGENIA	IODATES	NASTIES	REPAINT	SEQUOIA	TANGIES	URANITE
ANEROID	DEARIES	EVASION	IRISATE	NATIVES	RESIANT	SERIATE	TANKIES	URINATE
ANESTRA	DENARII	FAINEST	ISATINE	NATTIER	RESIDUA	SESTINA	TANSIES	URINOSE
ANESTRI	DETAINS	FAINTER	ISOLATE	NEAREST	RETAINS	SINUATE	TARTINE	VAINEST
ANISEED	DIORITE	FENITAR	ISOTONE	NEONATE	RETINAE	SITULAE	TAURINE	WANIEST
ANTSIER	DOUANES	GAINEST	ITERANT	NEROLIS	RETINAL	SLAINTE	TAWNIER	WANTIES
AREOLAE	DOULEIA	GENISTA	JANTIER	NITRATE	RETINAS	SNARIER	TAWNIES	ZANIEST
AREOLES	DAUTIES*	GOATEES	JANTIES	OARIEST	RETINOL	SOCIATE	TEARING	
ARISTAE	EASTING	GOATIER	KENTIAS	OESTRAL	RETRAIN	SODAINE	TEASING	
AROINTS	EASTLIN	GODETIA	KERATIN	OLEARIA	RETSINA	SOILIER	TENAILS	
ATEBRIN	EATINGS	GRANITE	LAIRISE	OLEATES	RIOTISE	SOLIER	TERRAIN	
ATONIES	EERIEST	GRATINE	LAITIES	ORDINEE	ROADIES	SOREDIA	TERTIAN	
AUNTIES	ELASTIN			OREADES	ROSEATE	SOUTANE	THERIAN	

List 6: 8-letter words

ABOITEAU	ARANEOUS	DEVIATOR	ERADIATE	INTERIOR	ORIENTED	RITORNEL	TOLERATE
ACIERATE	AREOLATE	DONATIVE	ERGATOID	INTERNAL	OUTEATEN	SEROTINE	TONALITE
ADROITER	ARTERIAL	DOUANIER	ERIONITE	JAROSITE	OUTLEARN	SIDENOTE	TREENAIL
AEGIRINE	ATROPINE	EATERIES	ETAERIOS	LITERATI	PAEONIES	TAENIATE	TROTLINE
AEGIRITE	AURELIAN	EGESTION	ETIOLATE	LITERATO	RAINDATE	TAENIOID	UINTAITE
AERATION	AUROREAN	EGOITIES	ETOURDIE	METANOIA	RAISONNE	TAILERON	UNEASIER
AEROLITE	DAINTIER	ELOIGNER	FOEDARIE	NAUSEATE	RATOONER	TAILORED	UREDINIA
AERONAUT	DELATION	ELOINERS	GAIETIES	NEGATION	REORDAIN	TAINTURE	URINATOR
ALEURONE	DENTALIA	ELONGATE	IDEATION	NEONATES	REORIENT	TENEBRIO	YEASTIER
ALIENATE	DENTARIA	ENDOSTEA	IDOLATER	OILERIES	RETAINED	TENORITE	
ALIENEES	DERATION	ENTAILER	INAURATE	OLEARIAS	RETAINER	TENTORIA	
ANOESTRA	DEROGATE	ENTOILED	INERTIAL	ORANGIER	RETIARII	TERATOID	
ANTERIOR	DETAINEE	EQUATION	INFERIAE	ORIENTAL	RETINOID	THIOUREA	

Section Two

Beginnings

Introduction

Beginnings of words are what you naturally think about when you are looking for a play. Is there a word playable beginning with BE-, DIS-, OUT-, RE- or UN- ? Sometimes you may be hoping to prefix a word already on the board with letters from your rack. Is there a good score available through adding some letters to the front of an existing word?

In this section there are two categories of lists, each focusing on beginnings of words. The first is a set of lists arranged according to a variety of common prefix letters. These are the Prefix lists.

The second set, the 5 to 8's, is a little more specialist and contains useful 3-letter extensions of 5-letter words. More about this set later on.

Useful Prefixes

The following lists are of 7- and 8-letter words starting with these prefixes:

AB-	EM-	MIS-	SUB-
AD-	EN-	OUT-	SUN-
AIR-	EX-	OVER-	TRI-
BE-	FOOT-	PER-	UN-
BI-	FOR-	PRE-	UP-
COM-	IM-	PRO-	WAR-
CON-	IN-	RE-	
DE-	ISO-	RED-	
DIS-	MAN-	SEA-	

These prefixes have been chosen because each provides a reasonable selection of words. Some of the prefixes, eg MAN- and SEA-, are used for forming compound words, and others are more common prefixes such as RE- and UN-. All are likely to turn up on your rack on a regular basis and if your remaining tiles form a valid word to go with the prefix then, board permitting, you'll be able to play a bonus word.

All the lists contain only those words where, if the prefix is removed, a valid word remains. This eliminates the many words that happen to begin with the prefix but which are not of interest; for example, TRICKING and TRIBUNE are not on the TRI- list because 'CKING' and 'BUNE' are not valid words. However, in the lists there will be some words that coincidentally qualify for inclusion, even though the prefix in question is not strictly used as such. For example, REACHED appears on the RE- list because RE- can be added to the front of ACHED. Similarly, as WAR- can be added at the beginning of BLED, WARBLED appears on the WAR- list. All the words, though, are of genuine interest.

WORDS PREFIXED WITH AB-

7-letter words

ABACTOR	ABDUCES	ABOLLAS	ABRAYED	ABROACH	ABSOLVE	ABUSAGE	ABVOLTS
ABALONE	ABDUCTS	ABOMASA	ABREACT	ABROADS	ABSORBS	ABUSERS	
ABASHES	ABJOINT	ABOUGHT	ABREAST	ABSEILS	ABSTAIN	ABUSING	
ABAXIAL	ABLATED	ABRAIDS	ABRIDGE	ABSENTS	ABTHANE	ABUTTER	

8-letter words

ABACTORS	ABERRANT	ABNORMAL	ABRAIDED	ABRIDGER	ABSENTED	ABSOLVES	ABSTRICT
ABAMPERE	ABESSIVE	ABOMASAL	ABRAYING	ABRIDGES	ABSOLUTE	ABSONANT	ABTHANES
ABDUCTED	ABJOINTS	ABOMASUM	ABREACTS	ABROOKED	ABSOLVED	ABSORBED	ABUSAGES
ABEARING	ABNEGATE	ABORIGIN	ABRIDGED	ABSEILED	ABSOLVER	ABSTAINS	ABUTTERS

WORDS PREFIXED WITH AD-

7-letter words

ADAGIOS	ADDEEMS	ADDUCES	ADJUSTS	ADMIXES	ADREADS	ADVERSE	ADVISOR
ADAPTED	ADDICTS	ADDUCTS	ADNOUNS	ADRENAL	ADVERTS	ADWARDS	
ADAPTER	ADDOOMS	ADJOINS	ADMIRED	ADOPTED	ADSORBS	ADVICES	
ADAWING	ADDRESS	ADJOINT	ADMIRES	ADOPTER	ADVENTS	ADVISED	
ADAXIAL	ADDREST	ADJUDGE	ADMIXED	ADPRESS	ADVERBS	ADVISES	

8-letter words

ADAPTING	ADDOOMED	ADJACENT	ADJUDGES	ADMIRING	ADOPTING	ADUNCATE	ADVISORS
ADDEBTED	ADDUCTED	ADJOINED	ADJUSTED	ADMIXING	ADOPTION	ADVERSER	ADWARDED
ADDEEMED	ADEQUATE	ADJOINTS	ADJUSTER	ADNATION	ADSCRIPT	ADVERTED	
ADDICTED	ADESSIVE	ADJUDGED	ADMASSES	ADOPTERS	ADSORBED	ADVISING	

WORDS PREFIXED WITH AIR-

7-letter words

AIRBASE	AIRGAPS	AIRHOLE	AIRLINE	AIRPORT	AIRSIDE	AIRTING	AIRWAYS
AIRFLOW	AIRGLOW	AIRLESS	AIRLOCK	AIRSHIP	AIRSTOP	AIRWARD	
AIRFOIL	AIRHEAD	AIRLIFT	AIRMAIL	AIRSICK	AIRTIME	AIRWAVE	

8-letter words

AIRBASES	AIRDROME	AIRGLOWS	AIRLINER	AIRPORTS	AIRSPACE	AIRTIMES
AIRBORNE	AIRFIELD	AIRGRAPH	AIRLINES	AIRSCREW	AIRSPEED	AIRWARDS
AIRBURST	AIRFLOWS	AIRHEADS	AIRLOCKS	AIRSHAFT	AIRSTOPS	AIRWAVES
AIRCRAFT	AIRFOILS	AIRHOLES	AIRMAILS	AIRSHIPS	AIRSTRIP	AIRWOMAN
AIRDRAWN	AIRFRAME	AIRLIFTS	AIRPLANE	AIRSIDES	AIRTIGHT	AIRWOMEN

WORDS PREFIXED WITH BE-

7-letter words

BEACHED	BEDEMAN	BEGNAWS	BEJADED	BEMEANS	BEPAINT	BESINGS	BESTILL	BETITLE
BEACHES	BEDEVIL	BEGOING	BEJADES	BEMEANT	BEPEARL	BESLAVE	BESTING	BETOILS
BEADMAN	BEDEWED	BEGONIA	BEJEWEL	BEMEDAL	BEPELTS	BESMEAR	BESTIRS	BETOKEN
BEADMEN	BEDIGHT	BEGORED	BEKNAVE	BEMETED	BEPROSE	BESMUTS	BESTORM	BETRAYS
BEARISH	BEDIZEN	BEGRIME	BEKNOWN	BEMETES	BEPUFFS	BESORTS	BESTOWS	BETREAD
BEAVERS	BEDROPS	BEGUILE	BELABOR	BEMIRED	BEQUEST	BESPAKE	BESTREW	BETRIMS
BEBUNGS	BEDUCKS	BEGUNKS	BELACED	BEMIRES	BERATED	BESPATE	BESTUCK	BETROTH
BECALLS	BEDUNGS	BEHAVES	BELACES	BEMOANS	BERATES	BESPEAK	BESTUDS	BEWAILS
BECALMS	BEDUSTS	BEHEADS	BELATED	BEMOCKS	BERAYED	BESPEED	BETAKEN	BEWARED
BECAUSE	BEDWARF	BEHESTS	BELAUDS	BEMOILS	BEREAVE	BESPICE	BETAKES	BEWARES
BECHARM	BEECHES	BEHIGHT	BELIEFS	BEMOUTH	BESAINT	BESPITS	BETEEMS	BEWEEPS
BECLOUD	BEFALLS	BEHINDS	BELIERS	BEMUSED	BESEEMS	BESPOKE	BETHINK	BEWHORE
BECOMES	BEFOAMS	BEHOLDS	BELIEVE	BEMUSES	BESHAME	BESPORT	BETHUMB	BEWITCH
BECURLS	BEFOOLS	BEHOOFS	BELONGS	BENAMED	BESHINE	BESPOTS	BETHUMP	
BEDAUBS	BEFOULS	BEHOOVE	BELOVED	BENAMES	BESHONE	BESPOUT	BETIDED	
BEDAZED	BEGIFTS	BEHOVED	BELOVES	BENEATH	BESHREW	BESTAIN	BETIDES	
BEDAZES	BEGILDS	BEHOVES	BELYING	BENEMPT	BESIDES	BESTARS	BETIGHT	
BEDECKS	BEGIRDS	BEHOWLS	BEMAULS	BENIGHT	BESIEGE	BESTEAD	BETIMED	
BEDELLS	BEGLOOM	BEINKED	BEMAZED	BENUMBS	BESIGHS	BESTICK	BETIMES	

8-letter words

BEACHIER	BEDIZENS	BEGOTTEN	BELABOUR	BENETTED	BESEEING	BESPICES	BETHWACK
BEACHING	BEDRENCH	BEGRIMED	BELACING	BENIGHTS	BESEEMED	BESPOKEN	BETIDING
BEARABLE	BEDUCKED	BEGRIMES	BELAUDED	BENUMBED	BESEEMLY	BESPORTS	BETIMING
BEBOPPED	BEDUNGED	BEGRUDGE	BELAYING	BEPAINTS	BESETTER	BESPOUTS	BETITLED
BECALLED	BEDUSTED	BEGUILED	BELEEING	BEPATTED	BESHADOW	BESPREAD	BETITLES
BECALMED	BEDWARFS	BEGUILER	BELIEVER	BEPEARLS	BESHAMED	BESPRENT	BETOILED
BECHANCE	BEDYEING	BEGUILES	BELITTLE	BEPELTED	BESHAMES	BESTAINS	BETOKENS
BECHARMS	BEFALLEN	BEHALVES	BELONGED	BEPEPPER	BESHINES	BESTEADS	BETONIES
BECLOUDS	BEFINNED	BEHAPPEN	BELONGER	BEPESTER	BESHREWS	BESTICKS	BETOSSED
BECOMING	BEFITTED	BEHATTED	BELOVING	BEPITIED	BESIEGED	BESTILLS	BETOSSES
BECURLED	BEFLOWER	BEHAVING	BEMADDED	BEPITIES	BESIEGER	BESTORMS	BETREADS
BEDABBLE	BEFOAMED	BEHEADED	BEMAULED	BEPLUMED	BESIEGES	BESTOWED	BETROTHS
BEDAGGLE	BEFOGGED	BEHIGHTS	BEMEANED	BEPOMMEL	BESIGHED	BESTOWER	BEWAILED
BEDARKEN	BEFOOLED	BEHOLDEN	BEMEDALS	BEPOWDER	BESLAVED	BESTREAK	BEWARING
BEDASHED	BEFOULED	BEHOLDER	BEMETING	BEPRAISE	BESLAVER	BESTREWN	BEWETTED
BEDASHES	BEFRIEND	BEHOOVED	BEMIRING	BEPROSED	BESLAVES	BESTREWS	BEWHORED
BEDAUBED	BEFRINGE	BEHOOVES	BEMOANED	BEPROSES	BESMEARS	BESTRIDE	BEWHORES
BEDAZING	BEFUDDLE	BEHOVING	BEMOANER	BEPUFFED	BESMIRCH	BESTRODE	BEWIGGED
BEDAZZLE	BEGEMMED	BEHOWLED	BEMOCKED	BEQUESTS	BESMUTCH	BESTROWN	BEWILDER
BEDEAFEN	BEGETTER	BEJABERS	BEMOILED	BERATING	BESORTED	BESUITED	
BEDECKED	BEGIFTED	BEJADING	BEMOUTHS	BERAYING	BESOTTED	BETAKING	
BEDESMAN	BEGILDED	BEJEWELS	BEMUDDED	BEREAVES	BESOUGHT	BETEEMED	
BEDEVILS	BEGINNER	BEKISSED	BEMUDDLE	BEROBBED	BESOULED	BETHINKS	
BEDEWING	BEGIRDED	BEKISSES	BEMUFFLE	BESAINTS	BESPEAKS	BETHRALL	
BEDIGHTS	BEGLOOMS	BEKNAVES	BEMUSING	BESCRAWL	BESPEEDS	BETHUMBS	
BEDIMMED	BEGNAWED	BELABORS	BENAMING	BESCREEN	BESPICED	BETHUMPS	

WORDS PREFIXED WITH BI-

7-letter words

BIASSES	BICARBS	BICYCLE	BIFILAR	BILOBAR	BIOLOGY	BIPOLAR	BITINGS	BIZONAL
BIAXIAL	BICHORD	BIDENTS	BIFOCAL	BILOBED	BIPEDAL	BISECTS	BITONAL	BIZONES
BIBLIST	BICORNS	BIDINGS	BIKINGS	BIMODAL	BIPLANE	BISHOPS	BIVALVE	

8-letter words

BIANNUAL	BICYCLED	BIELDING	BILANDER	BIOBLAST	BIPLANES	BISERIAL	BISTOURY
BICONVEX	BICYCLES	BIFACIAL	BILOBATE	BIPHASIC	BIRAMOUS	BISEXUAL	BIVALVES
BICUSPID	BIDENTAL	BILABIAL	BIMANUAL	BIPHENYL	BISECTOR	BISTABLE	

WORDS PREFIXED WITH COM-

7-letter words

COMARBS	COMBING	COMICES	COMMODE	COMPACT	COMPASS	COMPERE	COMPONY	COMPOTS
COMARTS	COMBUST	COMMAND	COMMOTE	COMPAGE	COMPAST	COMPILE	COMPORT	COMRADE
COMBATS	COMFIER	COMMEND	COMMOTS	COMPAND	COMPEAR	COMPING	COMPLOT	COMUSES
COMBIER	COMFITS	COMMENT	COMMOVE	COMPARE	COMPEER	COMPLOT	COMPOST	
COMBINE	COMFORT	COMMERE	COMMUTE	COMPART	COMPEND	COMPONE	COMPOTE	

8-letter words

COMBATED	COMFORTS	COMMONER	COMMUTES	COMPARTS	COMPILES	COMPLOTS	COMPOUND
COMBINES	COMMENDS	COMMONEY	COMPACTS	COMPEARS	COMPINGS	COMPORTS	COMPRESS
COMBINGS	COMMERES	COMMOTES	COMPADRE	COMPEERS	COMPLAIN	COMPOSED	COMPRINT
COMBLESS	COMMERGE	COMMOVED	COMPAGES	COMPENDS	COMPLEAT	COMPOSER	COMPRISE
COMBUSTS	COMMIXED	COMMOVES	COMPANDS	COMPERES	COMPLIED	COMPOSES	COMPULSE
COMETHER	COMMIXES	COMMUTED	COMPARED	COMPILED	COMPLIER	COMPOSTS	
COMFIEST	COMMODES	COMMUTER	COMPARES	COMPILER	COMPLIES	COMPOTES	

WORDS PREFIXED WITH CON-

7-letter words

CONACRE	CONCORD	CONDORS	CONFITS	CONGEES	CONJURE	CONSIGN	CONTENT	CONURES
CONARIA	CONCREW	CONDUCE	CONFLUX	CONGEST	CONJURY	CONSIST	CONTEST	CONVENT
CONCAVE	CONCURS	CONDUCT	CONFORM	CONGREE	CONKIER	CONSOLE	CONTEXT	CONVERT
CONCEDE	CONCUSS	CONFESS	CONFUSE	CONGRUE	CONKING	CONSOLS	CONTORT	CONVIVE
CONCENT	CONDIES	CONFEST	CONGAED	CONJEED	CONNOTE	CONSORT	CONTOUR	
CONCERT	CONDOLE	CONFINE	CONGEAL	CONJEES	CONSEIL	CONTACT	CONTRAT	
CONCHAL	CONDONE	CONFIRM	CONGEED	CONJOIN	CONSENT	CONTEND	CONTUND	

8-letter words

CONACRED	CONCORDS	CONFIRMS	CONGENIC	CONJUROR	CONSOLER	CONTEXTS	CONVERGE
CONACRES	CONCOURS	CONFIXED	CONGESTS	CONNOTED	CONSOLES	CONTORTS	CONVERSE
CONCAUSE	CONCREWS	CONFIXES	CONGLOBE	CONNOTES	CONSORTS	CONTOURS	CONVERTS
CONCAVED	CONDENSE	CONFOCAL	CONGREED	CONQUEST	CONSPIRE	CONTRACT	CONVEXED
CONCAVES	CONDOLED	CONFORMS	CONGREES	CONSEILS	CONSTATE	CONTRAIL	CONVEXES
CONCEDED	CONDOLES	CONFOUND	CONGREET	CONSENTS	CONTACTS	CONTRATS	CONVIVES
CONCEDES	CONDUCES	CONFRERE	CONGRUED	CONSERVE	CONTANGO	CONTRIST	CONVOLVE
CONCENTS	CONDUCTS	CONFRONT	CONGRUES	CONSIDER	CONTEMPT	CONTRITE	
CONCERTS	CONFINED	CONFUSED	CONJOINS	CONSIGNS	CONTENDS	CONTUNDS	
CONCLAVE	CONFINER	CONFUSES	CONJOINT	CONSISTS	CONTENTS	CONURBAN	
CONCOLOR	CONFINES	CONGEALS	CONJUGAL	CONSOLED	CONTESTS	CONVENTS	

WORDS PREFIXED WITH DE-

7-letter words

DEBARKS	DECIDES	DECURVE	DEFOULS	DELAYER	DEMOTED	DEPOSIT	DESINED	DETRAIN
DEBASED	DECLAIM	DEDUCES	DEFRAGS	DELIGHT	DEMOTES	DEPRESS	DESINES	DETUNED
DEBASER	DECLASS	DEDUCTS	DEFRAUD	DELIMIT	DEMOUNT	DERAILS	DESIRED	DETUNES
DEBASES	DECLINE	DEFACED	DEFRAYS	DELIVER	DEMURED	DERANGE	DESIRES	DEVALUE
DEBATED	DECODED	DEFACER	DEFROCK	DELOPED	DEMURES	DERATED	DESISTS	DEVESTS
DEBATES	DECODER	DEFACES	DEFROST	DELOPES	DENOTED	DERATES	DESKILL	DEVICES
DEBRIDE	DECODES	DEFAMED	DEFROZE	DELOUSE	DENUDES	DERAYED	DESORBS	DEVISED
DEBRIEF	DECOKED	DEFAMES	DEFUSED	DELUGED	DENYING	DERIDER	DESPITE	DEVISES
DEBUNKS	DECOKES	DEFAULT	DEFUSES	DELUGES	DEPAINT	DERIDES	DESPOIL	DEVISOR
DECADES	DECOLOR	DEFEATS	DEFUZES	DEMAINS	DEPARTS	DERIVED	DESPOTS	DEVOICE
DECAFFS	DECOYED	DEFENCE	DEGAUSS	DEMARKS	DEPENDS	DERIVES	DESTROY	DEVOLVE
DECAMPS	DECREED	DEFENDS	DEGOUTS	DEMEANE	DEPLANE	DESALTS	DESYNED	DEVOTED
DECANAL	DECREES	DEFILED	DEGRADE	DEMEANS	DEPLOYS	DESCALE	DESYNES	DEVOTES
DECANES	DECREWS	DEFILER	DEGREES	DEMERGE	DEPLUME	DESCANT	DETAILS	DEWATER
DECANTS	DECRIED	DEFILES	DEGUSTS	DEMERIT	DEPONES	DESCEND	DETENTS	
DECARBS	DECRIER	DEFINED	DEHORNS	DEMERSE	DEPORTS	DESCENT	DETENUE	
DECARES	DECRIES	DEFINER	DEICTIC	DEMESNE	DEPOSED	DESERVE	DETESTS	
DECEASE	DECROWN	DEFINES	DEJEUNE	DEMISES	DEPOSER	DESEXED	DETORTS	
DECIDED	DECRYPT	DEFORCE	DELAPSE	DEMISTS	DEPOSES	DESIGNS	DETOURS	
DECIDER	DECURIA	DEFORMS	DELATED	DEMOSES	DEPOSES	DESIGNS	DETRACT	

8-letter words

DEARLING	DECERNED	DEFACING	DEFRAYED	DELIVERY	DEPAINTS	DESALTED	DESPOILS
DEBAGGED	DECIDERS	DEFAMING	DEFREEZE	DELOPING	DEPARTED	DESCALED	DESTROYS
DEBARKED	DECIDING	DEFATTED	DEFROCKS	DELOUSED	DEPARTER	DESCALES	DESYNING
DEBARRED	DECIPHER	DEFAULTS	DEFROSTS	DELOUSES	DEPEINCT	DESCANTS	DETACHES
DEBASING	DECLAIMS	DEFEATED	DEFROZEN	DELUGING	DEPENDED	DESCENDS	DETAILED
DEBATING	DECLINES	DEFENCED	DEFUSING	DEMANDED	DEPLANED	DESCENTS	DETENUES
DEBELLED	DECLUTCH	DEFENCES	DEGASSED	DEMARKED	DEPLANES	DESCHOOL	DETESTED
DEBITING	DECODERS	DEFENDED	DEGASSES	DEMEANED	DEPLUMED	DESCRIBE	DETHRONE
DEBOSHES	DECODING	DEFENDER	DEGENDER	DEMEANES	DEPLUMES	DESCRIED	DETOURED
DEBOSSED	DECOKING	DEFIANCE	DEGRADED	DEMERGED	DEPONENT	DESCRIES	DETRACTS
DEBOSSES	DECOLORS	DEFILERS	DEGRADES	DEMERGER	DEPORTED	DESCRIVE	DETRAINS
DEBOUCHE	DECOLOUR	DEFILING	DEGREASE	DEMERGES	DEPOSERS	DESELECT	DETUNING
DEBRIDED	DECOUPLE	DEFINERS	DEGUMMED	DEMERITS	DEPOSING	DESERVED	DEVALUED
DEBRIDES	DECOYING	DEFINING	DEGUSTED	DEMERSES	DEPOSITS	DESERVER	DEVALUES
DEBRIEFS	DECREASE	DEFINITE	DEHORNED	DEMISTED	DERAILED	DESERVES	DEVESTED
DEBUGGED	DECREWED	DEFLEXED	DEHORNER	DEMISTER	DERAILER	DESEXING	DEVIATOR
DEBUNKED	DECRIERS	DEFLEXES	DELAPSED	DEMOBBED	DERANGED	DESIGNED	DEVISING
DEBUSSED	DECROWNS	DEFLOWER	DELAPSES	DEMONISM	DERANGER	DESIGNER	DEVISORS
DEBUSSES	DECRYING	DEFLUENT	DELAYERS	DEMONIST	DERANGES	DESILVER	DEVOICED
DECADENT	DECRYPTS	DEFORCED	DELAYING	DEMOTION	DERATING	DESINING	DEVOICES
DECAMPED	DECURIAS	DEFORCES	DELEGACY	DEMOUNTS	DERAYING	DESIRING	DEVOLVED
DECANTED	DECURIES	DEFOREST	DELEGATE	DEMURING	DERELICT	DESISTED	DEVOLVES
DECANTER	DECURVED	DEFORMED	DELIBATE	DENATURE	DERIDERS	DESKILLS	DEVOTING
DECEASED	DECURVES	DEFORMER	DELIGHTS	DENETTED	DERIDING	DESORBED	DEWATERS
DECEASES	DEDUCTED	DEFOULED	DELIMITS	DENOTATE	DERIGGED	DESPIGHT	DEWITTED
DECENTER	DEFACERS	DEFRAUDS	DELIVERS	DENOTING	DERIVING	DESPITES	

WORDS PREFIXED WITH DIS-

7-letter words

DISABLE	DISBARK	DISCARD	DISCURE	DISFORM	DISHING	DISLEAF	DISLINK	DISMAST
DISALLY	DISBARS	DISCASE	DISCUSS	DISGEST	DISHOME	DISLEAL	DISLOAD	DISMAYS
DISARMS	DISBUDS	DISCIDE	DISEASE	DISGOWN	DISHORN	DISLIKE	DISMALS	DISMISS
DISAVOW	DISCAGE	DISCOED	DISEDGE	DISGUST	DISJOIN	DISLIMB	DISMANS	DISNEST
DISBAND	DISCANT	DISCORD	DISFAME	DISHELM	DISKING	DISLIMN	DISMASK	DISOBEY

DISOWNS	DISPEND	DISPORT	DISRANK	DISSEAT	DISTEND	DISTILS	DISUSES
DISPACE	DISPLAY	DISPOSE	DISRATE	DISSECT	DISTENT	DISTORT	DISYOKE
DISPARK	DISPLED	DISPOST	DISROBE	DISSENT	DISTICH	DISTUNE	
DISPART	DISPONE	DISPRAD	DISROOT	DISSING	DISTILL	DISUSED	

8-letter words

DISABLED	DISCAGES	DISEASES	DISHELMS	DISLOADS	DISPENDS	DISRATES	DISTRAIL
DISABLES	DISCANDY	DISEDGED	DISHINGS	DISLODGE	DISPERSE	DISROBED	DISTRAIN
DISABUSE	DISCANTS	DISEDGES	DISHOMED	DISLOYAL	DISPLACE	DISROBES	DISTRAIT
DISADORN	DISCARDS	DISENDOW	DISHOMES	DISMASKS	DISPLANT	DISROOTS	DISTRESS
DISAGREE	DISCASED	DISENROL	DISHONOR	DISMASTS	DISPLAYS	DISSEATS	DISTRUST
DISALLOW	DISCASES	DISFAMES	DISHORNS	DISMAYED	DISPLING	DISSECTS	DISTUNED
DISANNEX	DISCIDED	DISFAVOR	DISHORSE	DISMOUNT	DISPLUME	DISSEISE	DISTUNES
DISANNUL	DISCIDES	DISFLESH	DISHOUSE	DISNESTS	DISPONES	DISSEIZE	DISUNION
DISAPPLY	DISCINCT	DISFORMS	DISINTER	DISOBEYS	DISPORTS	DISSENTS	DISUNITE
DISARMED	DISCLAIM	DISFROCK	DISINURE	DISORBED	DISPOSED	DISSERVE	DISUNITY
DISARRAY	DISCLOSE	DISGAVEL	DISJOINS	DISORDER	DISPOSER	DISSEVER	DISUSAGE
DISASTER	DISCOLOR	DISGESTS	DISJOINT	DISOWNED	DISPOSES	DISSIGHT	DISUSING
DISAVOWS	DISCORDS	DISGORGE	DISLEAFS	DISOWNER	DISPOSTS	DISSOLVE	DISVALUE
DISBANDS	DISCOUNT	DISGOWNS	DISLEAVE	DISPACED	DISPRIZE	DISTALLY	DISVOUCH
DISBARKS	DISCOURE	DISGRACE	DISLIKED	DISPACES	DISPROOF	DISTASTE	DISYOKED
DISBENCH	DISCOVER	DISGRADE	DISLIKEN	DISPARKS	DISPROVE	DISTENDS	DISYOKES
DISBOSOM	DISCROWN	DISGUISE	DISLIKES	DISPARTS	DISPURSE	DISTILLS	
DISBOWEL	DISCURED	DISGUSTS	DISLIMBS	DISPATCH	DISQUIET	DISTINCT	
DISBURSE	DISCURES	DISHABIT	DISLIMNS	DISPEACE	DISRANKS	DISTORTS	
DISCAGED	DISEASED	DISHABLE	DISLINKS	DISPENCE	DISRATED	DISTRACT	

WORDS PREFIXED WITH EM-

7-letter words

EMAILED	EMBARKS	EMBLAZE	EMBOWEL	EMBREAD	EMMOVED	EMPARES	EMPLOYS
EMBAILS	EMBASED	EMBLOOM	EMBOWER	EMBROIL	EMMOVES	EMPARTS	EMPLUME
EMBALED	EMBASES	EMBOILS	EMBOXED	EMBROWN	EMPAIRE	EMPEACH	EMPOWER
EMBALES	EMBASSY	EMBOLUS	EMBOXES	EMBRUTE	EMPALED	EMPERCE	EMPRESS
EMBALLS	EMBASTE	EMBOSOM	EMBRACE	EMENDED	EMPALES	EMPIGHT	EMPRISE
EMBALMS	EMBATHE	EMBOUND	EMBRAID	EMIRATE	EMPANEL	EMPLACE	EMPUSES
EMBANKS	EMBAYED	EMBOWED	EMBRAVE	EMMEWED	EMPARED	EMPLANE	

8-letter words

EMAILING	EMBATTLE	EMBOILED	EMBRACED	EMBUSIED	EMPAIRES	EMPHASES	EMPOISON
EMBAILED	EMBAYING	EMBOLDEN	EMBRACER	EMBUSIES	EMPALING	EMPHASIS	EMPOLDER
EMBALING	EMBEDDED	EMBORDER	EMBRACES	EMBUSSED	EMPANELS	EMPHATIC	EMPOWERS
EMBALLED	EMBEZZLE	EMBOSOMS	EMBRAIDS	EMBUSSES	EMPARING	EMPIERCE	EMPRISES
EMBALMED	EMBITTER	EMBOSSED	EMBRAVED	EMENDING	EMPARLED	EMPLACED	EMPURPLE
EMBANKED	EMBLAZED	EMBOSSER	EMBRAVES	EMMARBLE	EMPARTED	EMPLACES	
EMBANKER	EMBLAZES	EMBOSSES	EMBREADS	EMMESHED	EMPATHIC	EMPLANED	
EMBARKED	EMBLAZON	EMBOUNDS	EMBREWED	EMMESHES	EMPATRON	EMPLANES	
EMBARRED	EMBLOOMS	EMBOWELS	EMBROILS	EMMEWING	EMPEOPLE	EMPLEACH	
EMBASING	EMBODIED	EMBOWERS	EMBROWNS	EMMOVING	EMPERCED	EMPLONGE	
EMBATHED	EMBODIES	EMBOWING	EMBRUTED	EMPACKET	EMPERCES	EMPLUMED	
EMBATHES	EMBOGGED	EMBOXING	EMBRUTES	EMPAIRED	EMPERISH	EMPLUMES	

WORDS PREFIXED WITH EN-

7-letter words

ENABLED	ENCHANT	ENDEMIC	ENFILED	ENGILDS	ENGUARD	ENLIVEN	ENRINGS	ENSKIES
ENABLER	ENCHARM	ENDEWED	ENFIRED	ENGIRDS	ENGULFS	ENLOCKS	ENRIVEN	ENSLAVE
ENABLES	ENCHASE	ENDINGS	ENFIRES	ENGLOBE	ENGULPH	ENMEWED	ENROBED	ENSNARE
ENACTED	ENCHEER	ENDITED	ENFIXED	ENGLOOM	ENHALOS	ENMOVED	ENROBES	ENSNARL
ENACTOR	ENCLASP	ENDITES	ENFIXES	ENGLUTS	ENHANCE	ENMOVES	ENROLLS	ENSOULS
ENAMOUR	ENCLAVE	ENDIVES	ENFLAME	ENGORED	ENISLED	ENNOBLE	ENROOTS	ENSTAMP
ENARMED	ENCLOSE	ENDORSE	ENFLESH	ENGORES	ENISLES	ENOUNCE	ENROUGH	ENSTEEP
ENCAGED	ENCLOUD	ENDOWED	ENFOLDS	ENGORGE	ENJAMBS	ENPLANE	ENROUND	ENSTYLE
ENCAGES	ENCODED	ENDOWER	ENFORCE	ENGRACE	ENJOINS	ENPRINT	ENSEALS	ENSUING
ENCALMS	ENCODES	ENDUING	ENFORMS	ENGRAFF	ENJOYED	ENQUIRE	ENSEAMS	ENSURED
ENCAMPS	ENCORED	ENDURED	ENFRAME	ENGRAFT	ENLACED	ENRACED	ENSEARS	ENSURER
ENCASED	ENCORES	ENDURES	ENFREED	ENGRAIL	ENLACES	ENRACES	ENSEWED	ENSURES
ENCASES	ENCRUST	ENDUROS	ENFREES	ENGRAIN	ENLARDS	ENRAGED	ENSHELL	ENSWEEP
ENCAVED	ENCRYPT	ENFACED	ENFROZE	ENGRAMS	ENLARGE	ENRAGES	ENSIGNS	ENSWEPT
ENCAVES	ENCYSTS	ENFACES	ENGAGED	ENGRASP	ENLIGHT	ENRANGE	ENSILED	ENTAILS
ENCHAFE	ENDARTS	ENFELON	ENGAGES	ENGRAVE	ENLINKS	ENRANKS	ENSILES	ENTAMED
ENCHAIN	ENDEARS	ENFEOFF	ENGAOLS	ENGROSS	ENLISTS	ENRHEUM	ENSKIED	ENTAMES

ENTICED	ENTOILS	ENTRAIN	ENTREES	ENTWINE	ENVIERS	ENWINDS	ENZONED
ENTICES	ENTOMBS	ENTRANT	ENTRIES	ENTWIST	ENVYING	ENWOMBS	ENZONES
ENTIRES	ENTOPIC	ENTRAPS	ENTRIST	ENVAULT	ENWALLS	ENWOUND	ENZYMES
ENTITLE	ENTRAIL	ENTREAT	ENTRUST	ENVENOM	ENWHEEL	ENWRAPS	ENZYMIC

8-letter words

ENABLING	ENCIRCLE	ENDORSES	ENGILDED	ENHYDROS	ENRACING	ENSIGNED	ENTITLES
ENACTING	ENCLASPS	ENDOSSED	ENGIRDLE	ENISLING	ENRAGING	ENSILAGE	ENTOILED
ENACTION	ENCLAVES	ENDOSSES	ENGLOBED	ENJOINED	ENRANGED	ENSILING	ENTOMBED
ENACTIVE	ENCLITIC	ENDOWERS	ENGLOBES	ENJOINER	ENRANGES	ENSKYING	ENTRAILS
ENACTORS	ENCLOSED	ENDOWING	ENGLOOMS	ENJOYING	ENRANKED	ENSLAVED	ENTRAINS
ENACTURE	ENCLOSER	ENDURING	ENGORGED	ENKERNEL	ENRAUNGE	ENSLAVER	ENTRANCE
ENAMOURS	ENCLOSES	ENFACING	ENGORGES	ENKINDLE	ENRAVISH	ENSLAVES	ENTRANTS
ENARCHED	ENCLOTHE	ENFEEBLE	ENGORING	ENLACING	ENRHEUMS	ENSNARED	ENTREATS
ENARCHES	ENCLOUDS	ENFELONS	ENGRACED	ENLARDED	ENRICHED	ENSNARES	ENTREATY
ENARMING	ENCODING	ENFEOFFS	ENGRACES	ENLARGED	ENRICHES	ENSNARLS	ENTRENCH
ENAUNTER	ENCOLOUR	ENFETTER	ENGRAFFS	ENLARGEN	ENRIDGED	ENSOULED	ENTROPIC
ENCAGING	ENCOLURE	ENFIERCE	ENGRAFTS	ENLARGER	ENRINGED	ENSPHERE	ENTRUSTS
ENCALMED	ENCORING	ENFIRING	ENGRAILS	ENLARGES	ENROBING	ENSTAMPS	ENTWINED
ENCAMPED	ENCRADLE	ENFIXING	ENGRAINS	ENLIGHTS	ENROLLED	ENSTEEPS	ENTWINES
ENCARPUS	ENCREASE	ENFLAMED	ENGRAMMA	ENLINKED	ENROLLER	ENSTYLED	ENTWISTS
ENCASHED	ENCRINAL	ENFLAMES	ENGRASPS	ENLISTED	ENROOTED	ENSTYLES	ENURESES
ENCASHES	ENCRUSTS	ENFLOWER	ENGRAVED	ENLIVENS	ENROUGHS	ENSURING	ENURESIS
ENCASING	ENCRYPTS	ENFOLDED	ENGRAVEN	ENLOCKED	ENROUNDS	ENSWATHE	ENURETIC
ENCAVING	ENCUMBER	ENFORCED	ENGRAVER	ENLUMINE	ENSAMPLE	ENSWEEPS	ENVASSAL
ENCHAFED	ENCYCLIC	ENFORCER	ENGRAVES	ENMESHED	ENSCONCE	ENTAILED	ENVAULTS
ENCHAFES	ENDAMAGE	ENFORCES	ENGRIEVE	ENMESHES	ENSEALED	ENTAMING	ENVENOMS
ENCHAINS	ENDANGER	ENFOREST	ENGROOVE	ENMEWING	ENSEAMED	ENTANGLE	ENVIABLE
ENCHANTS	ENDARTED	ENFORMED	ENGUARDS	ENMOSSED	ENSEARED	ENTELLUS	ENVISAGE
ENCHARGE	ENDEARED	ENFRAMED	ENGULFED	ENMOVING	ENSEMBLE	ENTENDER	ENVISION
ENCHARMS	ENDEIXES	ENFRAMES	ENGULPHS	ENNOBLES	ENSEWING	ENTHETIC	ENWALLED
ENCHASED	ENDEIXIS	ENFREEZE	ENHALOED	ENOUNCES	ENSHEATH	ENTHRALL	ENWALLOW
ENCHASES	ENDERMIC	ENFROZEN	ENHALOES	ENPLANED	ENSHELLS	ENTHRONE	ENWHEELS
ENCHEERS	ENDEWING	ENGAGING	ENHANCES	ENPLANES	ENSHIELD	ENTHUSES	ENWOMBED
ENCHORIC	ENDITING	ENGAOLED	ENHEARSE	ENPRINTS	ENSHRINE	ENTICING	ENZONING
ENCIPHER	ENDORSER	ENGENDER	ENHUNGER	ENQUIRED	ENSHROUD	ENTITLED	

WORDS PREFIXED WITH EX-

7-letter words

EXACTED	EXCHEAT	EXCITES	EXHALES	EXPLAIN	EXPOSES	EXSECTS	EXTERNS	EXTRAIT
EXACTOR	EXCIDED	EXCLAIM	EXODIST	EXPLANT	EXPOUND	EXTENDS	EXTINCT	EXTREAT
EXAMENS	EXCIDES	EXCLAVE	EXPANDS	EXPORTS	EXPRESS	EXTENSE	EXTINES	EXURBAN
EXAMINE	EXCITED	EXCURSE	EXPENDS	EXPOSED	EXPULSE	EXTENTS	EXTORTS	
EXAMPLE	EXCITER	EXHALED	EXPERTS	EXPOSER	EXPURGE	EXTERNE	EXTRACT	

8-letter words

EXACTING	EXCESSES	EXCLAIMS	EXODISTS	EXPLAINS	EXPOSING	EXTENDED	EXTOLLER
EXACTION	EXCHANGE	EXCLAVES	EXOGAMIC	EXPLANTS	EXPOUNDS	EXTENDER	EXTRACTS
EXACTORS	EXCHEATS	EXCURSED	EXOSMOSE	EXPONENT	EXPULSED	EXTENSOR	EXTRAITS
EXAMINES	EXCIDING	EXCURSES	EXPANDER	EXPORTED	EXPULSES	EXTERNAL	EXTREATS
EXANTHEM	EXCITERS	EXCURSUS	EXPENDED	EXPORTER	EXPURGED	EXTERNES	
EXCELLED	EXCITING	EXHALING	EXPERTLY	EXPOSERS	EXPURGES	EXTOLLED	

WORDS PREFIXED WITH FOOT-

7-letter words

| FOOTAGE | FOOTBOY | FOOTLED | FOOTMAN | FOOTPAD | FOOTROT |
| FOOTBAR | FOOTERS | FOOTLES | FOOTMEN | FOOTRAS | FOOTWAY |

8-letter words

FOOTAGES	FOOTFALL	FOOTLESS	FOOTNOTE	FOOTPATH	FOOTRULE	FOOTWAYS	FOOTWORN
FOOTBALL	FOOTGEAR	FOOTLING	FOOTPACE	FOOTPOST	FOOTSLOG	FOOTWEAR	
FOOTBARS	FOOTHILL	FOOTMARK	FOOTPADS	FOOTREST	FOOTSORE	FOOTWELL	
FOOTBOYS	FOOTHOLD	FOOTMUFF	FOOTPAGE	FOOTROTS	FOOTSTEP	FOOTWORK	

WORDS PREFIXED WITH FOR-

7-letter words

FORAGED	FORBODE	FORDONE	FORGETS	FORHOWS	FORLORE	FORPINE	FORSLOE	FORWARD
FORAGES	FORBORE	FORESTS	FORGING	FORKIER	FORLORN	FORPITS	FORSLOW	FORWARN
FORAMEN	FORCATS	FOREVER	FORGIVE	FORKING	FORMATE	FORRAYS	FORSOOK	FORWENT
FORBADE	FORCEPS	FORFAIR	FORGOES	FORLANA	FORMATS	FORSAID	FORTIES	FORWORN
FORBEAR	FORDING	FORFEND	FORGONE	FORLEND	FORMING	FORSAKE	FORTING	FORZATI
FORBIDS	FORDOES	FORGAVE	FORHENT	FORLENT	FORPETS	FORSAYS	FORTUNE	

8-letter words

FORAGING	FORELAND	FORGIVEN	FORLENDS	FORPINES	FORSOOTH	FORSWINK	FORTUNES
FORBEARS	FORESTER	FORGIVES	FORLESES	FORRAYED	FORSPEAK	FORSWORE	FORWARDS
FORBODES	FORFAIRS	FORGOING	FORMATED	FORSAKES	FORSPEND	FORSWORN	FORWARNS
FORBORNE	FORFAULT	FORHENTS	FORMATES	FORSLACK	FORSPENT	FORTHINK	FORWASTE
FORDOING	FORFENDS	FORJUDGE	FORMINGS	FORSLOES	FORSPOKE	FORTRESS	FORWEARY
FOREKING	FORGINGS	FORLANAS	FORPINED	FORSLOWS	FORSWEAR	FORTUNED	

WORDS PREFIXED WITH IM-

7-letter words

IMAGING	IMBOSKS	IMMENSE	IMMURES	IMPARKS	IMPEACH	IMPLEAD	IMPOSTS	IMPULSE
IMAGIST	IMBOSOM	IMMERGE	IMPACTS	IMPARTS	IMPEARL	IMPLIED	IMPOUND	IMPURER
IMAMATE	IMBOWER	IMMERSE	IMPAINT	IMPASSE	IMPENDS	IMPLIES	IMPRESA	
IMARETS	IMBRAST	IMMEWED	IMPAIRS	IMPASTE	IMPERIL	IMPONES	IMPRESE	
IMBARKS	IMBROWN	IMMIXED	IMPALAS	IMPAVED	IMPIETY	IMPORTS	IMPRESS	
IMBASED	IMBRUTE	IMMIXES	IMPALED	IMPAVES	IMPIOUS	IMPOSED	IMPREST	
IMBASES	IMBURSE	IMMORAL	IMPALES	IMPAVID	IMPLANT	IMPOSER	IMPRINT	
IMBATHE	IMMASKS	IMMURED	IMPANEL	IMPAWNS	IMPLATE	IMPOSES	IMPROVE	

8-letter words

IMAGINGS	IMBORDER	IMMATURE	IMMOMENT	IMPASSES	IMPLEACH	IMPOSERS	IMPROVES
IMAGISTS	IMBOSOMS	IMMERGED	IMMORTAL	IMPASTED	IMPLEADS	IMPOSING	IMPUDENT
IMBARKED	IMBOSSED	IMMERGES	IMMURING	IMPASTES	IMPLEDGE	IMPOSTER	IMPULSED
IMBARRED	IMBOSSES	IMMERSES	IMPAINTS	IMPAVING	IMPLUNGE	IMPOTENT	IMPULSES
IMBASING	IMBOWERS	IMMESHED	IMPAIRED	IMPAWNED	IMPLYING	IMPOUNDS	IMPURELY
IMBATHED	IMBROWNS	IMMESHES	IMPALING	IMPEARLS	IMPOCKET	IMPRESES	IMPUREST
IMBATHES	IMBRUTED	IMMEWING	IMPANELS	IMPENDED	IMPOLDER	IMPRESTS	IMPURITY
IMBEDDED	IMBRUTES	IMMINGLE	IMPARITY	IMPERILS	IMPOLICY	IMPRINTS	IMPURPLE
IMBITTER	IMBURSES	IMMINUTE	IMPARKED	IMPINGED	IMPOLITE	IMPRISON	
IMBODIED	IMMANENT	IMMIXING	IMPARLED	IMPLANTS	IMPONENT	IMPROPER	
IMBODIES	IMMANTLE	IMMOBILE	IMPARTED	IMPLATED	IMPORTED	IMPROVED	
	IMMASKED	IMMODEST	IMPARTER	IMPLATES	IMPORTER	IMPROVER	

WORDS PREFIXED WITH IN-

7-letter words

INAPTLY	INCITER	INDOLES	INFILLS	INGROUP	INLOCKS	INSIDER	INSWING	INVADES
INARMED	INCITES	INDOORS	INFIXED	INGROWN	INLYING	INSIDES	INTAKES	INVALID
INBEING	INCIVIL	INDORSE	INFIXES	INGULFS	INMATES	INSIGHT	INTENDS	INVENTS
INBOARD	INCLASP	INDRAFT	INFLAME	INGULPH	INNARDS	INSINEW	INTENSE	INVERSE
INBOUND	INCLINE	INDRAWN	INFLOWS	INHABIT	INNERVE	INSISTS	INTENTS	INVERTS
INBREAK	INCLIPS	INDUCES	INFOLDS	INHALED	INORBED	INSNARE	INTERNE	INVESTS
INBREED	INCLOSE	INDUCTS	INFORCE	INHALER	INPHASE	INSOLES	INTERNS	INVEXED
INBRING	INCOMER	INDUING	INFORMS	INHALES	INQUEST	INSOOTH	INTINES	INVOICE
INBURST	INCOMES	INDWELL	INFRACT	INHAULS	INQUIET	INSOULS	INTOMBS	INVOLVE
INCAGED	INCROSS	INDWELT	INFUSED	INHOOPS	INQUIRE	INSPANS	INTONED	INWALLS
INCAGES	INCRUST	INEARTH	INFUSES	INHUMAN	INROADS	INSPIRE	INTONER	INWARDS
INCASED	INCURVE	INEXACT	INGATES	INISLED	INSANER	INSTALL	INTONES	INWEAVE
INCASES	INDARTS	INFALLS	INGENUS	INISLES	INSCAPE	INSTARS	INTRANT	INWICKS
INCAVED	INDENES	INFAMED	INGESTS	INJELLY	INSCULP	INSTATE	INTREAT	INWINDS
INCAVES	INDENTS	INFAMES	INGLOBE	INJOINT	INSEAMS	INSTEAD	INTRONS	INWORKS
INCEDED	INDEWED	INFANCY	INGOING	INLACED	INSECTS	INSTEPS	INTRUST	INWOUND
INCEDES	INDICES	INFARES	INGRAFT	INLACES	INSEEMS	INSTILL	INTWINE	INWOVEN
INCENSE	INDICTS	INFAUNA	INGRAIN	INLANDS	INSHELL	INSURED	INTWIST	INWRAPS
INCHASE	INDITED	INFESTS	INGRATE	INLAYER	INSHIPS	INSURER	INURNED	
INCITED	INDITES	INFIELD	INGROSS	INLIERS	INSHORE	INSURES	INVADED	

8-letter words

INACTION	INACTIVE	INARABLE	INARCHED	INARCHES	INARMING	INAURATE	INBEINGS

INBREAKS	INCREASE	INERRANT	INFORMER	INJOINTS	INSCIENT	INSTATES	INTWINED
INBREEDS	INCREATE	INESSIVE	INFRACTS	INJURIES	INSCONCE	INSTILLS	INTWINES
INBRINGS	INCRUSTS	INEXPERT	INFRINGE	INLACING	INSCRIBE	INSTRESS	INTWISTS
INBURSTS	INCURRED	INFAMING	INFUSING	INLANDER	INSCROLL	INSUCKEN	INUNDATE
INCAGING	INCURVED	INFAMOUS	INFUSION	INLAYERS	INSCULPS	INSURING	INURBANE
INCASING	INCURVES	INFAUNAE	INGATHER	INLAYING	INSCULPT	INSWATHE	INURNING
INCAVING	INDARTED	INFAUNAL	INGLOBED	INLOCKED	INSEAMED	INSWINGS	INUSTION
INCEDING	INDEBTED	INFAUNAS	INGLOBES	INMESHED	INSECURE	INTARSIA	INVADING
INCENSED	INDECENT	INFECUND	INGOINGS	INMESHES	INSEEMED	INTENDED	INVENTED
INCENSER	INDENTED	INFIELDS	INGRAFTS	INNATIVE	INSHELLS	INTENDER	INVERSES
INCENSES	INDEWING	INFILLED	INGRAINS	INNERVED	INSHRINE	INTENSER	INVERTED
INCENSOR	INDICTED	INFINITE	INGRATES	INNERVES	INSIDERS	INTERNAL	INVESTED
INCENTRE	INDIGEST	INFIRMER	INGROOVE	INNOCENT	INSIGHTS	INTERNED	INVIABLE
INCHASED	INDIRECT	INFIRMLY	INGROUPS	INORBING	INSINEWS	INTERNES	INVOICED
INCHASES	INDITING	INFIXING	INGROWTH	INORNATE	INSISTED	INTHRALL	INVOICES
INCITERS	INDOCILE	INFLAMED	INGULFED	INPUTTER	INSNARED	INTIMIST	INVOLUTE
INCITING	INDOLENT	INFLAMES	INGULPHS	INQUESTS	INSNARES	INTITULE	INVOLVED
INCIVISM	INDORSES	INFLATUS	INHABITS	INQUIETS	INSOULED	INTOMBED	INVOLVES
INCLASPS	INDRAFTS	INFLEXED	INHALERS	INQUIRED	INSPHERE	INTONERS	INWALLED
INCLINES	INDRENCH	INFLUENT	INHALING	INQUIRES	INSPIRED	INTONING	INWEAVES
INCLOSED	INDUCTED	INFLUXES	INHAULER	INRUSHES	INSPIRES	INTRANTS	INWICKED
INCLOSER	INDWELLS	INFOLDED	INHEARSE	INSANELY	INSPIRIT	INTREATS	INWORKED
INCLOSES	INEARTHS	INFORCED	INHOLDER	INSANEST	INSTABLE	INTRENCH	
INCOMERS	INEDIBLE	INFORCES	INHOOPED	INSANIES	INSTALLS	INTREPID	
INCOMING	INEDITED	INFORMAL	INHUMANE	INSANITY	INSTANCE	INTRUSTS	
INCORPSE	INEQUITY	INFORMED	INISLING	INSCAPES	INSTATED	INTUBATE	

WORDS PREFIXED WITH ISO-

7-letter words

ISOBARE	ISOBATH	ISOGRAM	ISOMERE	ISOTONE	ISOTYPE
ISOBARS	ISOGAMY	ISOLATE	ISOPODS	ISOTOPE	
ISOBASE	ISOGONS	ISOLINE	ISOSPIN	ISOTRON	

8-letter words

ISOBARES	ISOCHASM	ISOGAMIC	ISOLINES	ISOSPINS	ISOTONIC	ISOTYPES
ISOBARIC	ISOCHIME	ISOGLOSS	ISOMERES	ISOTHERE	ISOTOPES	
ISOBASES	ISOCHORE	ISOGRAMS	ISOMORPH	ISOTHERM	ISOTOPIC	
ISOBATHS	ISOCLINE	ISOLATED	ISONOMIC	ISOTONES	ISOTRONS	

WORDS PREFIXED WITH MAN-

7-letter words

MANAGED	MANDATE	MANGLED	MANHOOD	MANKIND	MANPACK	MANTEEL	MANTOES
MANAGES	MANGALS	MANGOES	MANHUNT	MANLIER	MANREDS	MANTELS	MANTRAM
MANAKIN	MANGELS	MANGOLD	MANJACK	MANNITE	MANRENT	MANTIDS	MANTRAP
MANANAS	MANGING	MANHOLE	MANKIER	MANNOSE	MANSARD	MANTIES	MANURES

8-letter words

MANAGING	MANDRILL	MANHOLES	MANKINDS	MANPOWER	MANSHIFT	MANTRAPS
MANDATED	MANFULLY	MANHOODS	MANNITES	MANRENTS	MANSWORN	MANURIAL
MANDATES	MANGOLDS	MANHUNTS	MANNOSES	MANRIDER	MANTEELS	
MANDRAKE	MANGROVE	MANJACKS	MANPACKS	MANSARDS	MANTRAMS	

WORDS PREFIXED WITH MIS-

7-letter words

MISAIMS	MISDEED	MISERES	MISGIVE	MISKNEW	MISMATE	MISSEEM	MISSUIT	MISUSED
MISALLY	MISDEEM	MISFALL	MISGOES	MISKNOW	MISNAME	MISSEEN	MISTAKE	MISUSER
MISBORN	MISDIAL	MISFARE	MISGONE	MISLAID	MISPLAY	MISSEES	MISTELL	MISUSES
MISCALL	MISDIET	MISFEED	MISHAPS	MISLAYS	MISPLED	MISSELS	MISTERM	MISWEEN
MISCAST	MISDOER	MISFELL	MISHEAR	MISLEAD	MISRATE	MISSEND	MISTIER	MISWEND
MISCOPY	MISDOES	MISFILE	MISHITS	MISLIKE	MISREAD	MISSENT	MISTIME	MISWENT
MISCUED	MISDONE	MISFIRE	MISJOIN	MISLIVE	MISRULE	MISSETS	MISTING	MISWORD
MISCUES	MISDRAW	MISFITS	MISKENS	MISLUCK	MISSAID	MISSILE	MISTOLD	MISYOKE
MISDATE	MISDREW	MISFORM	MISKENT	MISMADE	MISSALS	MISSING	MISTOOK	
MISDEAL	MISEASE	MISGAVE	MISKEYS	MISMAKE	MISSAYS	MISSTEP	MISTUNE	

8-letter words

MISAIMED	MISDEALS	MISFAITH	MISGUIDE	MISMARRY	MISQUOTE	MISSPENT	MISTRESS
MISALIGN	MISDEALT	MISFALLS	MISHEARD	MISMATCH	MISRATED	MISSPOKE	MISTRIAL
MISALLOT	MISDEEDS	MISFARED	MISHEARS	MISMATED	MISRATES	MISSTATE	MISTRUST
MISAPPLY	MISDEEMS	MISFARES	MISJOINS	MISMATES	MISREADS	MISSTEPS	MISTRYST
MISARRAY	MISDEMPT	MISFEEDS	MISJUDGE	MISMETRE	MISROUTE	MISSUITS	MISTUNED
MISBEGOT	MISDIALS	MISFEIGN	MISKEYED	MISNAMED	MISRULED	MISSUSES	MISTUNES
MISBIRTH	MISDIETS	MISFIELD	MISKNOWN	MISNAMES	MISRULES	MISTAKEN	MISUSAGE
MISCALLS	MISDIGHT	MISFILED	MISKNOWS	MISOLOGY	MISSABLE	MISTAKES	MISUSERS
MISCARRY	MISDOERS	MISFILES	MISLEADS	MISORDER	MISSEEMS	MISTEACH	MISUSING
MISCASTS	MISDOING	MISFIRED	MISLIGHT	MISPLACE	MISSENDS	MISTELLS	MISWEENS
MISCHIEF	MISDONNE	MISFIRES	MISLIKED	MISPLAYS	MISSHAPE	MISTERMS	MISWENDS
MISCOLOR	MISDOUBT	MISFORMS	MISLIKER	MISPLEAD	MISSILES	MISTHINK	MISWORDS
MISCOUNT	MISDRAWN	MISGIVEN	MISLIKES	MISPOINT	MISSISES	MISTIMED	MISWRITE
MISCREED	MISDRAWS	MISGIVES	MISLIVED	MISPRINT	MISSPEAK	MISTIMES	MISWROTE
MISCUING	MISDREAD	MISGOING	MISLIVES	MISPRISE	MISSPELL	MISTINGS	MISYOKED
MISDATED	MISEASES	MISGRAFF	MISLUCKS	MISPRIZE	MISSPELT	MISTITLE	MISYOKES
MISDATES	MISENTRY	MISGRAFT	MISMAKES	MISPROUD	MISSPEND	MISTREAT	

WORDS PREFIXED WITH OUT-

7-letter words

OUTAGES	OUTDURE	OUTGREW	OUTLAST	OUTNAME	OUTRATE	OUTSITS	OUTTOLD	OUTWEPT
OUTBACK	OUTEATS	OUTGROW	OUTLAWS	OUTNESS	OUTREDS	OUTSIZE	OUTTOOK	OUTWICK
OUTBARS	OUTEDGE	OUTGUNS	OUTLAYS	OUTPACE	OUTRIDE	OUTSOAR	OUTTOPS	OUTWIND
OUTBIDS	OUTFACE	OUTGUSH	OUTLEAP	OUTPART	OUTROAR	OUTSOLD	OUTTURN	OUTWING
OUTBRAG	OUTFALL	OUTHAUL	OUTLETS	OUTPEEP	OUTRODE	OUTSOLE	OUTVIED	OUTWINS
OUTBRED	OUTFITS	OUTHIRE	OUTLIED	OUTPEER	OUTROOP	OUTSPAN	OUTVIES	OUTWITH
OUTBURN	OUTFLEW	OUTHITS	OUTLIER	OUTPLAY	OUTROOT	OUTSTAY	OUTVOTE	OUTWITS
OUTCAST	OUTFLOW	OUTJEST	OUTLIES	OUTPORT	OUTROPE	OUTSTEP	OUTWALK	OUTWORE
OUTCOME	OUTFOOT	OUTJETS	OUTLINE	OUTPOST	OUTRUNS	OUTSUMS	OUTWARD	OUTWORK
OUTCROP	OUTGATE	OUTJUMP	OUTLIVE	OUTPOUR	OUTRUSH	OUTSWAM	OUTWASH	OUTWORN
OUTDARE	OUTGAVE	OUTJUTS	OUTLOOK	OUTPRAY	OUTSAIL	OUTSWIM	OUTWEAR	
OUTDATE	OUTGIVE	OUTLAID	OUTMANS	OUTPUTS	OUTSELL	OUTSWUM	OUTWEED	
OUTDOES	OUTGOER	OUTLAIN	OUTMODE	OUTRACE	OUTSETS	OUTTAKE	OUTWEEP	
OUTDONE	OUTGOES	OUTLAND	OUTMOST	OUTRAGE	OUTSHOT	OUTTALK	OUTWELL	
OUTDOOR	OUTGONE	OUTLASH	OUTMOVE	OUTRANK	OUTSIDE	OUTTELL	OUTWENT	

8-letter words

OUTBACKS	OUTDATED	OUTFLOWN	OUTLAWED	OUTPLACE	OUTROARS	OUTSPEAK	OUTVENOM
OUTBOARD	OUTDATES	OUTFLOWS	OUTLEAPS	OUTPLAYS	OUTROOPS	OUTSPEND	OUTVOICE
OUTBOUND	OUTDOING	OUTFLUSH	OUTLEAPT	OUTPOINT	OUTROOTS	OUTSPENT	OUTVOTED
OUTBOXED	OUTDOORS	OUTFOOTS	OUTLEARN	OUTPORTS	OUTROPER	OUTSPOKE	OUTVOTER
OUTBOXES	OUTDRANK	OUTFOXED	OUTLIERS	OUTPOSTS	OUTROPES	OUTSPORT	OUTVOTES
OUTBRAGS	OUTDRINK	OUTFOXES	OUTLINED	OUTPOURS	OUTSAILS	OUTSTAND	OUTVYING
OUTBRAVE	OUTDRIVE	OUTFROWN	OUTLINES	OUTPOWER	OUTSCOLD	OUTSTARE	OUTWALKS
OUTBREAK	OUTDROVE	OUTGATES	OUTLIVED	OUTPRAYS	OUTSCORN	OUTSTAYS	OUTWARDS
OUTBREED	OUTDRUNK	OUTGIVEN	OUTLIVES	OUTPRICE	OUTSELLS	OUTSTEPS	OUTWATCH
OUTBROKE	OUTDURED	OUTGIVES	OUTLOOKS	OUTPRIZE	OUTSHINE	OUTSTOOD	OUTWEARS
OUTBURNS	OUTDURES	OUTGLARE	OUTLYING	OUTRACED	OUTSHONE	OUTSTRIP	OUTWEARY
OUTBURNT	OUTDWELL	OUTGOERS	OUTMARCH	OUTRACES	OUTSHOOT	OUTSWEAR	OUTWEEDS
OUTBURST	OUTDWELT	OUTGOING	OUTMATCH	OUTRAGED	OUTSHOTS	OUTSWELL	OUTWEEPS
OUTCASTE	OUTEATEN	OUTGROWN	OUTMODES	OUTRAGES	OUTSIDER	OUTSWIMS	OUTWEIGH
OUTCASTS	OUTEDGES	OUTGROWS	OUTMOVED	OUTRANCE	OUTSIDES	OUTSWING	OUTWELLS
OUTCLASS	OUTFACED	OUTGUARD	OUTMOVES	OUTRANKS	OUTSIGHT	OUTSWORE	OUTWICKS
OUTCOMES	OUTFACES	OUTHAULS	OUTNAMED	OUTRATED	OUTSIZED	OUTSWORN	OUTWINDS
OUTCRIED	OUTFALLS	OUTHIRED	OUTNAMES	OUTRATES	OUTSIZES	OUTTAKEN	OUTWINGS
OUTCRIES	OUTFIELD	OUTHIRES	OUTNIGHT	OUTREACH	OUTSLEEP	OUTTAKES	OUTWORKS
OUTCROPS	OUTFIGHT	OUTHOUSE	OUTPACED	OUTREIGN	OUTSLEPT	OUTTALKS	OUTWORTH
OUTCROSS	OUTFLANK	OUTJESTS	OUTPACES	OUTRIDER	OUTSMART	OUTTELLS	OUTWOUND
OUTDANCE	OUTFLASH	OUTJUMPS	OUTPARTS	OUTRIDES	OUTSOARS	OUTTHINK	OUTWREST
OUTDARED	OUTFLIES	OUTLANDS	OUTPEEPS	OUTRIGHT	OUTSOLES	OUTTURNS	
OUTDARES	OUTFLING	OUTLASTS	OUTPEERS	OUTRIVAL	OUTSPANS	OUTVALUE	

WORDS PREFIXED WITH OVER-

7-letter words

OVERACT	OVERAWE	OVERDYE	OVERFLY	OVERLAP	OVERNET	OVERREN	OVERSET	OVERUSE
OVERAGE	OVERBID	OVEREAT	OVERGET	OVERLAY	OVERPAY	OVERRUN	OVERSEW	
OVERALL	OVERBUY	OVEREYE	OVERGOT	OVERLIE	OVERPLY	OVERSAW	OVERSOW	
OVERARM	OVERDID	OVERFAR	OVERHIT	OVERMAN	OVERRAN	OVERSEA	OVERTAX	
OVERATE	OVERDUE	OVERFED	OVERJOY	OVERMEN	OVERRED	OVERSEE	OVERTOP	

8-letter words

OVERACTS	OVERCLAD	OVERFISH	OVERHELD	OVERLENT	OVERPLUS	OVERSHOE	OVERTOOK
OVERAGES	OVERCLOY	OVERFLEW	OVERHENT	OVERLIER	OVERPOST	OVERSHOT	OVERTOPS
OVERALLS	OVERCOAT	OVERFLOW	OVERHITS	OVERLIES	OVERRACK	OVERSIDE	OVERTRIP
OVERARCH	OVERCOME	OVERFOLD	OVERHOLD	OVERLIVE	OVERRAKE	OVERSIZE	OVERTURN
OVERAWED	OVERCOOK	OVERFOND	OVERHUNG	OVERLOAD	OVERRANK	OVERSKIP	OVERTYPE
OVERAWES	OVERCRAW	OVERFREE	OVERHYPE	OVERLOCK	OVERRASH	OVERSLIP	OVERUSED
OVERBEAR	OVERCROP	OVERFULL	OVERJOYS	OVERLONG	OVERRATE	OVERSOLD	OVERUSES
OVERBEAT	OVERCROW	OVERFUND	OVERJUMP	OVERLOOK	OVERREAD	OVERSOUL	OVERVEIL
OVERBIDS	OVERDOER	OVERGALL	OVERKEEP	OVERLORD	OVERREDS	OVERSOWN	OVERVIEW
OVERBITE	OVERDOES	OVERGANG	OVERKEPT	OVERLOUD	OVERRENS	OVERSOWS	OVERWASH
OVERBLEW	OVERDONE	OVERGAVE	OVERKEST	OVERMANS	OVERRIDE	OVERSPIN	OVERWEAR
OVERBLOW	OVERDOSE	OVERGETS	OVERKILL	OVERMAST	OVERRIPE	OVERSTAY	OVERWEEN
OVERBOIL	OVERDRAW	OVERGIVE	OVERKIND	OVERMUCH	OVERRODE	OVERSTEP	OVERWENT
OVERBOLD	OVERDREW	OVERGOES	OVERKING	OVERNAME	OVERRUFF	OVERSWAM	OVERWIND
OVERBOOK	OVERDUST	OVERGONE	OVERKNEE	OVERNEAT	OVERRULE	OVERSWAY	OVERWING
OVERBORE	OVERDYED	OVERGREW	OVERLADE	OVERNETS	OVERRUNS	OVERSWIM	OVERWISE
OVERBRIM	OVERDYES	OVERGROW	OVERLAID	OVERNICE	OVERSAIL	OVERSWUM	OVERWORD
OVERBROW	OVEREATS	OVERHAIR	OVERLAIN	OVERPAGE	OVERSEAS	OVERTAKE	OVERWORE
OVERBULK	OVEREYED	OVERHALE	OVERLAND	OVERPAID	OVERSEEN	OVERTALK	OVERWORK
OVERBURN	OVEREYES	OVERHAND	OVERLAPS	OVERPART	OVERSEER	OVERTASK	OVERWORN
OVERBUSY	OVERFALL	OVERHANG	OVERLARD	OVERPASS	OVERSEES	OVERTEEM	OVERYEAR
OVERBUYS	OVERFEED	OVERHAUL	OVERLAYS	OVERPAST	OVERSELL	OVERTIME	
OVERCALL	OVERFELL	OVERHEAD	OVERLEAF	OVERPAYS	OVERSETS	OVERTIRE	
OVERCAME	OVERFILL	OVERHEAR	OVERLEAP	OVERPEER	OVERSEWN	OVERTOIL	
OVERCAST	OVERFINE	OVERHEAT	OVERLEND	OVERPLAY	OVERSEWS	OVERTONE	

WORDS PREFIXED WITH PER-

7-letter words

PERAEON	PERDURE	PERFUSE	PERJURY	PERMING	PERSANT	PERSUES	PERUSED
PERCASE	PEREGAL	PERHAPS	PERKIER	PERMUTE	PERSING	PERTAKE	PERUSER
PERCHER	PERFORM	PERICON	PERKING	PERONES	PERSIST	PERTEST	PERUSES
PERCUSS	PERFUME	PERJINK	PERKINS	PERPEND	PERSONS	PERTOOK	PERVADE
PERDUES	PERFUMY	PERJURE	PERLITE	PERPENT	PERSUED	PERUKES	PERVERT

8-letter words

PERACUTE	PERFORCE	PERFUSES	PERMUTED	PERPENDS	PERSISTS	PERUSERS	PERVERTS
PERAEONS	PERFORMS	PERIODIC	PERMUTES	PERPENTS	PERSPIRE	PERUSING	
PERCOLIN	PERFUMED	PERISHES	PERNANCY	PERRADII	PERSUING	PERVADED	
PERDURED	PERFUMES	PERLITES	PERORATE	PERSAUNT	PERTAKEN	PERVADES	
PERDURES	PERFUSED	PERMEASE	PEROXIDE	PERSEITY	PERTAKES	PERVERSE	

WORDS PREFIXED WITH PRE-

7-letter words

PREACED	PRECEDE	PREDIAL	PREFADE	PRELATE	PREPARE	PRESETS	PRETORS	PREWARN
PREACES	PRECESS	PREDICT	PREFARD	PREMISE	PREPAYS	PRESIDE	PREVAIL	PREWYNS
PREACHY	PRECOOK	PREDIED	PREFORM	PREMISS	PREPONE	PRESTED	PREVENT	
PREAMPS	PRECOOL	PREDIES	PREHEAT	PREMOVE	PREPOSE	PRETEND	PREVERB	
PREBEND	PRECUTS	PREDOOM	PREHEND	PREORAL	PREPUCE	PRETERM	PREVIEW	
PREBORN	PREDATE	PREEVES	PREJINK	PREPACK	PRESAGE	PRETEST	PREVISE	
PRECAST	PREDAWN	PREFACE	PRELACY	PREPAID	PRESENT	PRETEXT	PREWARM	

8-letter words

PREACHED	PRECOOKS	PREDYING	PREHENDS	PREMOVED	PREPONES	PRESIDED	PREVERBS
PREACHES	PRECOOLS	PREFACED	PREHUMAN	PREMOVES	PREPOSED	PRESIDES	PREVIEWS
PREACING	PRECURSE	PREFACES	PREJUDGE	PRENASAL	PREPOSES	PRESTING	PREVISED
PREAMBLE	PREDATED	PREFADED	PREMEDIC	PRENATAL	PREPUCES	PRETENDS	PREVISES
PREASSES	PREDATES	PREFADES	PREMISES	PREORDER	PRESAGER	PRETENSE	PREWARMS
PREBENDS	PREDAWNS	PREFIXED	PREMIXED	PREPACKS	PRESAGES	PRETESTS	PREWARNS
PRECEDED	PREDIALS	PREFIXES	PREMIXES	PREPARED	PRESCUTA	PRETEXTS	
PRECEDES	PREDICTS	PREFORMS	PREMOLAR	PREPARER	PRESENTS	PREVAILS	
PRECINCT	PREDOOMS	PREHEATS	PREMORSE	PREPARES	PRESERVE	PREVENTS	

WORDS PREFIXED WITH PRO-

7-letter words

PROBALL	PROBANG	PROBING	PROCESS	PRODUCE	PROFACE	PROFESS	PROFITS	PROGRAM
PROBAND	PROBATE	PROBITS	PROCURE	PRODUCT	PROFANE	PROFILE	PROFUSE	PROKING

PROLATE	PROLONG	PRONAOS	PROOTIC	PROPEND	PROPOSE	PROTEAS	PROTORE	PROVERS
PROLEGS	PROMISE	PRONEST	PROPAGE	PROPENE	PRORATE	PROTEND	PROVANT	PROVIDE
PROLINE	PROMOTE	PRONOTA	PROPALE	PROPINE	PROSAIC	PROTEST	PROVEND	PROVINE
PROLING	PRONAOI	PRONOUN	PROPANE	PROPONE	PROSING	PROTONS	PROVERB	

8-letter words

PROBANDS	PRODUCES	PROLATED	PRONATES	PROPENES	PROPYLON	PROTEASE	PROVINES
PROBANGS	PRODUCTS	PROLINES	PRONOTAL	PROPHAGE	PRORATED	PROTENDS	PROVIRAL
PROBATED	PROFANES	PROLONGE	PRONOTUM	PROPHASE	PRORATES	PROTENSE	PROVIRUS
PROBATES	PROFILED	PROLONGS	PRONOUNS	PROPINED	PROROGUE	PROTESTS	PROVISOR
PROCINCT	PROFILER	PROMETAL	PROPAGED	PROPINES	PROSAIST	PROTONIC	
PROCLAIM	PROFILES	PROMISER	PROPAGES	PROPONES	PROSEMEN	PROTORES	
PROCURED	PROFOUND	PROMISES	PROPALED	PROPOSED	PROSINGS	PROTRACT	
PROCURER	PROGRADE	PROMOTED	PROPALES	PROPOSER	PROSODIC	PROVENDS	
PROCURES	PROGRAMS	PROMOTES	PROPANES	PROPOSES	PROSTATE	PROVERBS	
PRODROME	PROLAPSE	PROMOTOR	PROPENDS	PROPOUND	PROSTYLE	PROVINED	

WORDS PREFIXED WITH RE-

7-letter words

REACHED	REBUSES	REDIALS	REGIVEN	REMARRY	REPLAYS	RESENTS	RETAILS	REUSING
REACHES	RECALLS	REDOING	REGIVES	REMATCH	REPLICA	RESERVE	RETAKEN	REUTTER
REACTED	RECANTS	REDOUBT	REGORGE	REMEADS	REPLIED	RESHAPE	RETAKER	REVALUE
REACTOR	RECASTS	REDRAFT	REGRADE	REMERCY	REPLIER	RESHIPS	RETAKES	REVAMPS
READAPT	RECATCH	REDRAWN	REGRANT	REMERGE	REPLIES	RESIDED	RETELLS	REVEALS
READMIT	RECEDED	REDRAWS	REGRATE	REMINDS	REPOINT	RESIDER	RETENES	REVENGE
READOPT	RECEDES	REDRESS	REGREET	REMINTS	REPONES	RESIDES	RETHINK	REVENUE
REAGENT	RECENSE	REDRIVE	REGRIND	REMISES	REPORTS	RESIGNS	RETILED	REVERBS
REAKING	RECHART	REDROVE	REGROUP	REMIXED	REPOSED	RESILED	RETILES	REVERSE
REALIGN	RECHEAT	REDUCES	REGULAR	REMIXES	REPOSES	RESILES	RETIMED	REVERSO
REALLOT	RECHECK	REECHED	REHANGS	REMODEL	REPOSIT	RESINED	RETIMES	REVERTS
REAMEND	RECITAL	REECHES	REHEARD	REMORAS	REPOSTS	RESISTS	RETIRED	REVESTS
REANNEX	RECITED	REEKING	REHEARS	REMORSE	REPRESS	RESKEWS	RETIRES	REVIEWS
REAPING	RECITER	REELMEN	REHEATS	REMOTES	REPRIME	RESKILL	RETITLE	REVILER
REAPPLY	RECITES	REFACED	REHEELS	REMOULD	REPRINT	RESOLED	RETOOLS	REVISED
REARISE	RECLAIM	REFACES	REHOUSE	REMOUNT	REPRISE	RESOLES	RETORTS	REVISES
REARMED	RECLAME	REFILLS	REINTER	REMOVED	REPRIZE	RESOLVE	RETOUCH	REVISIT
REAROSE	RECLIMB	REFINED	REISSUE	REMOVER	REPROOF	RESORBS	RETOURS	REVISOR
REAVERS	RECLINE	REFINER	REJOINS	REMOVES	REPROVE	RESORTS	RETRACE	REVIVER
REAWAKE	RECLOSE	REFINES	REJUDGE	RENAMED	REPULPS	RESOUND	RETRACT	REVIVES
REAWOKE	RECODED	REFLAGS	RELAPSE	RENAMES	REPULSE	RESPEAK	RETRAIN	REVOLTS
REBACKS	RECODES	REFLOAT	RELATED	RENEWED	REPURED	RESPELL	RETRAIT	REVOLVE
REBADGE	RECOILS	REFLOWS	RELATER	RENEWER	REPURES	RESPELT	RETREAD	REVYING
REBATED	RECOINS	REFOCUS	RELAXES	RENYING	REQUEST	RESPIRE	RETREAT	REWARDS
REBATES	RECORDS	REFOOTS	RELEASE	REOPENS	REQUIRE	RESPITE	RETREES	REWEIGH
REBECKS	RECOUNT	REFORMS	RELIEFS	REORDER	REQUITE	RESPOKE	RETRIAL	REWINDS
REBINDS	RECOUPS	REFOUND	RELIERS	REPACKS	REQUITS	RESPRAY	RETRIED	REWIRED
REBIRTH	RECOURE	REFRACT	RELIEVE	REPAINT	REQUOTE	RESTAFF	RETRIES	REWIRES
REBITES	RECOVER	REFRAME	RELIGHT	REPAIRS	RERAILS	RESTAGE	RETRIMS	REWORDS
REBLOOM	RECOWER	REFRESH	RELINED	REPAPER	REREADS	RESTART	RETUNDS	REWORKS
REBOILS	RECROSS	REFROZE	RELINES	REPASTS	REREDOS	RESTATE	RETUNED	REWOUND
REBOOTS	RECURED	REFUELS	RELIVED	REPEALS	REROUTE	RESTEMS	RETUNES	REWRAPS
REBORED	RECURES	REFUNDS	RELIVER	REPEATS	RESALES	RESTIFF	RETURFS	REWRITE
REBORES	RECURVE	REFUSED	RELIVES	REPENTS	RESCALE	RESTING	RETURNS	REWROTE
REBOUND	RECYCLE	REFUSES	RELOADS	REPINED	RESCORE	RESTIVE	RETYING	REZONED
REBRACE	REDATED	REGAINS	RELYING	REPINES	RESEALS	RESTOCK	REUNIFY	REZONES
REBUFFS	REDATES	REGALES	REMAINS	REPIQUE	RESEATS	RESTORE	REUNION	
REBUILD	REDEALS	REGALLY	REMAKES	REPLACE	RESECTS	RESTYLE	REUNITE	
REBUILT	REDEALT	REGENTS	REMANET	REPLANS	RESEIZE	RESURGE	REURGED	
REBUKES	REDEEMS	REGESTS	REMARKS	REPLANT	RESELLS	RETABLE	REURGES	

8-letter words

REABSORB	REAGENCY	REAROUSE	REAWAKEN	REBITTEN	REBURIED	RECENSED	RECITING
REACHING	REAGENTS	REARREST	REAWAKES	REBLOOMS	REBURIES	RECENSES	RECLAIMS
REACTING	REALIGNS	REASCEND	REAWOKEN	REBOILED	REBUTTED	RECENTER	RECLAMES
REACTION	REALLIED	REASCENT	REBACKED	REBOOTED	REBUTTER	RECENTRE	RECLIMBS
REACTIVE	REALLIES	REASSERT	REBADGED	REBORING	REBUTTON	RECESSED	RECLINES
REACTORS	REALLOTS	REASSESS	REBADGES	REBORROW	RECALLED	RECESSES	RECLOSED
READAPTS	REAMENDS	REASSIGN	REBATING	REBOUNDS	RECANTED	RECHARGE	RECLOSES
READJUST	REANSWER	REASSUME	REBELLED	REBRACED	RECANTER	RECHARTS	RECLOTHE
READMITS	REAPPEAR	REASSURE	REBELLOW	REBRACES	RECAPPED	RECHEATS	RECODING
READOPTS	REARISEN	REATTACH	REBIDDEN	REBUFFED	RECAPTOR	RECHECKS	RECOILED
READVISE	REARISES	REATTAIN	REBIRTHS	REBUILDS	RECAUGHT	RECITALS	RECOINED
REAFFIRM	REARMING	REAWAKED	REBITING	REBURIAL	RECEDING	RECITERS	RECOLLET

RECOMMIT	REFLOWER	REIMPORT	REMERGED	REPLYING	RESCORES	RESTARTS	REUNIONS
RECONVEY	REFLUENT	REIMPOSE	REMERGES	REPOINTS	RESCRIPT	RESTATED	REUNITED
RECORDED	REFLUXED	REINFORM	REMINDED	REPORTED	RESEALED	RESTATES	REUNITES
RECOUNTS	REFLUXES	REINFUSE	REMINDER	REPORTER	RESEARCH	RESTINGS	REURGING
RECOUPED	REFOOTED	REINSERT	REMINTED	REPOSING	RESEATED	RESTOCKS	REUSABLE
RECOURED	REFOREST	REINSURE	REMIXING	REPOSITS	RESEIZED	RESTORED	REUTTERS
RECOURES	REFORMAT	REINTERS	REMODELS	REPOSTED	RESEIZES	RESTORER	REVALUED
RECOURSE	REFORMED	REINVEST	REMODIFY	REPOTTED	RESELECT	RESTORES	REVALUES
RECOVERS	REFORMER	REISSUED	REMORSES	REPOUSSE	RESEMBLE	RESTRAIN	REVAMPED
RECOWERS	REFOUNDS	REISSUES	REMOTION	REPREEVE	RESENTED	RESTRICT	REVEALER
RECREANT	REFRACTS	REJIGGED	REMOULDS	REPRIEFE	RESERVED	RESTRING	REVENGED
RECREATE	REFRAMED	REJIGGER	REMOUNTS	REPRIEVE	RESERVES	RESTRUNG	REVENGER
RECURING	REFRAMES	REJOINED	REMOVERS	REPRIMED	RESETTER	RESTYLED	REVENGES
RECURRED	REFREEZE	REJUDGED	REMOVING	REPRIMES	RESETTLE	RESTYLES	REVENUES
RECURVED	REFRINGE	REJUDGES	REMURMUR	REPRINTS	RESHAPED	RESUBMIT	REVERIST
RECURVES	REFROZEN	REKINDLE	RENAMING	REPRISED	RESHAPES	RESUPINE	REVERSAL
RECYCLED	REFUNDED	RELACHES	RENEGATE	REPRISES	RESIDERS	RESURGED	REVERSED
RECYCLES	REFUNDER	RELAPSED	RENEWING	REPRIZED	RESIDING	RESURGES	REVERSER
REDATING	REFUSING	RELAUNCH	RENUMBER	REPRIZES	RESIGNED	RESURVEY	REVERSES
REDEEMED	REFUSION	RELAYING	REOCCUPY	REPROOFS	RESIGNER	RETABLES	REVERSOS
REDEFINE	REGAINED	RELEASED	REOFFEND	REPROVED	RESILING	RETAILED	REVERTED
REDEPLOY	REGAINER	RELEASER	REOPENED	REPROVER	RESINING	RETAKERS	REVESTED
REDESIGN	REGATHER	RELEASES	REOPENER	REPROVES	RESISTED	RETAKING	REVESTRY
REDIALED	REGIVING	RELEGATE	REORDAIN	REPUBLIC	RESKEWED	RETELLER	REVETTED
REDIPPED	REGORGED	RELEVANT	REORDERS	REPULPED	RESKILLS	RETHINKS	REVIEWED
REDIRECT	REGORGES	RELIABLE	REORIENT	REPULSED	RESOLING	RETILING	REVIEWER
REDISTIL	REGRADED	RELIEVER	REPACKED	REPULSES	RESOLUTE	RETIMING	REVISING
REDIVIDE	REGRADES	RELIGHTS	REPAINTS	REPURIFY	RESOLVED	RETIRING	REVISION
REDOLENT	REGRANTS	RELINING	REPAIRED	REPURING	RESOLVER	RETITLED	REVISITS
REDOUBLE	REGRATED	RELIVERS	REPAPERS	REQUESTS	RESOLVES	RETITLES	REVISORS
REDOUBTS	REGRATER	RELIVING	REPASSED	REQUIGHT	RESONANT	RETOOLED	REVIVERS
REDRAFTS	REGRATES	RELOADED	REPASSES	REQUIRED	RESORBED	RETOURED	REVIVIFY
REDRIVEN	REGREETS	RELOCATE	REPASTED	REQUIRES	RESORTED	RETRACED	REVOLUTE
REDRIVES	REGRINDS	RELUCENT	REPAYING	REQUITED	RESORTER	RETRACES	REVOLVED
REECHING	REGROUND	RELUMINE	REPEALED	REQUITES	RESOUNDS	RETRACTS	REVOLVES
REFACING	REGROUPS	REMAINED	REPEOPLE	REQUOTED	RESOURCE	RETRAINS	REWARDED
REFELLED	REGROWTH	REMAKING	REPERUSE	REQUOTES	RESPEAKS	RETRAITS	REWARDER
REFIGURE	REHANDLE	REMANENT	REPHRASE	RERAILED	RESPELLS	RETREADS	REWEIGHS
REFILLED	REHASHED	REMANIES	REPINING	REREVISE	RESPIRED	RETREATS	REWIRING
REFINERS	REHASHES	REMANNED	REPIQUED	REREWARD	RESPIRES	RETRENCH	REWORDED
REFINERY	REHEARSE	REMARKED	REPIQUES	REROUTED	RESPITED	RETRIALS	REWORKED
REFINING	REHEATED	REMARKER	REPLACED	REROUTES	RESPITES	RETRYING	REWRITES
REFITTED	REHEATER	REMARQUE	REPLACER	RESALUTE	RESPOKEN	RETUNDED	REZONING
REFLEXED	REHEELED	REMASTER	REPLACES	RESAYING	RESPRAYS	RETUNING	
REFLEXES	REHOUSED	REMEDIAL	REPLANTS	RESCALED	RESTAFFS	RETURFED	
REFLOATS	REHOUSES	REMEMBER	REPLAYED	RESCALES	RESTAGED	RETURNED	
REFLOWED	REILLUME		REPLIERS	RESCORED	RESTAGES	RETURNER	

WORDS PREFIXED WITH RED-

7-letter words

REDACTS	REDBUDS	REDDENS	REDFISH	REDNECK	REDRAFT	REDRIVE	REDSEAR	REDWING
REDBACK	REDCAPS	REDDING	REDHEAD	REDNESS	REDRAWN	REDROOT	REDSKIN	REDWOOD
REDBIRD	REDCOAT	REDDISH	REDLEGS	REDPOLL	REDRAWS	REDROVE	REDTOPS	

8-letter words

REDACTED	REDBELLY	REDDINGS	REDPOLLS	REDROOTS	REDSHORT	REDWINGS
REDACTOR	REDBIRDS	REDHEADS	REDRAFTS	REDSHANK	REDSKINS	REDWOODS
REDARGUE	REDBRICK	REDNECKS	REDRIVEN	REDSHARE	REDSTART	
REDBACKS	REDCOATS	REDOLENT	REDRIVES	REDSHIRE	REDWATER	

WORDS PREFIXED WITH SEA-

7-letter words

SEABANK	SEAFOLK	SEAHAWK	SEALINE	SEAMING	SEARING	SEASONS	SEAWARE	SEAWORM
SEABEDS	SEAFOOD	SEAHOGS	SEALING	SEAPORT	SEASICK	SEASURE	SEAWAYS	SEAZING
SEABIRD	SEAFOWL	SEAKALE	SEAMAID	SEARATS	SEASIDE	SEATING	SEAWEED	
SEACOCK	SEAGULL	SEALANT	SEAMARK	SEAREST	SEASING	SEAWARD	SEAWIFE	

8-letter words

SEABANKS	SEABLITE	SEABORNE	SEACOCKS	SEADROME	SEAFOODS	SEAFRONT	SEAHAWKS
SEABIRDS	SEABOARD	SEACOAST	SEACRAFT	SEAFOLKS	SEAFOWLS	SEAGULLS	SEAHORSE

SEAHOUND	SEALINGS	SEAMOUNT	SEARINGS	SEASIDES	SEAWARDS	SEAWIVES
SEAKALES	SEAMAIDS	SEAPLANE	SEASCAPE	SEASPEAK	SEAWARES	SEAWOMAN
SEALANTS	SEAMANLY	SEAPORTS	SEASHELL	SEASURES	SEAWATER	SEAWOMEN
SEALINES	SEAMARKS	SEAQUAKE	SEASHORE	SEATINGS	SEAWEEDS	SEAWORMS

WORDS PREFIXED WITH SUB-

7-letter words

SUBACID	SUBBASE	SUBDUCE	SUBFEUS	SUBLATE	SUBSERE	SUBTACK	SUBUNIT
SUBACTS	SUBBING	SUBDUCT	SUBFUSC	SUBLETS	SUBSETS	SUBTEEN	SUBVERT
SUBAQUA	SUBCOOL	SUBDUED	SUBGOAL	SUBLIME	SUBSIDE	SUBTEND	SUBWAYS
SUBAREA	SUBDEAN	SUBDUES	SUBGUMS	SUBMISS	SUBSIST	SUBTEXT	SUBZERO
SUBARID	SUBDEWS	SUBEDIT	SUBHEAD	SUBPLOT	SUBSOIL	SUBTILE	SUBZONE
SUBATOM	SUBDUAL	SUBERIC	SUBJOIN	SUBRING	SUBSONG	SUBTYPE	

8-letter words

SUBABBOT	SUBBREED	SUBDUING	SUBGOALS	SUBMENTA	SUBSHRUB	SUBTEENS	SUBUNITS
SUBACRID	SUBCASTE	SUBDUPLE	SUBGRADE	SUBMERGE	SUBSIDED	SUBTENDS	SUBURBAN
SUBACTED	SUBCHIEF	SUBDURAL	SUBGROUP	SUBMERSE	SUBSIDES	SUBTENSE	SUBVERSE
SUBACUTE	SUBCHORD	SUBEDITS	SUBHEADS	SUBORDER	SUBSISTS	SUBTEXTS	SUBVERST
SUBADULT	SUBCLAIM	SUBEQUAL	SUBHUMAN	SUBOVATE	SUBSIZAR	SUBTIDAL	SUBVERTS
SUBAGENT	SUBCLASS	SUBERECT	SUBHUMID	SUBOXIDE	SUBSOILS	SUBTILER	SUBVIRAL
SUBAREAS	SUBCOSTA	SUBEROSE	SUBIMAGO	SUBPHYLA	SUBSOLAR	SUBTITLE	SUBVOCAL
SUBATOMS	SUBCRUST	SUBFEUED	SUBJOINS	SUBPLOTS	SUBSONGS	SUBTONIC	SUBZONAL
SUBAUDIO	SUBDEANS	SUBFIELD	SUBLATED	SUBPOLAR	SUBSONIC	SUBTOTAL	SUBZONES
SUBAURAL	SUBDEWED	SUBFLOOR	SUBLEASE	SUBPRIOR	SUBSTAGE	SUBTRACT	
SUBBASAL	SUBDUALS	SUBFRAME	SUBLIMED	SUBRINGS	SUBSTATE	SUBTRIBE	
SUBBASES	SUBDUCES	SUBGENRE	SUBLIMES	SUBSERES	SUBSTYLE	SUBTRIST	
SUBBINGS	SUBDUCTS	SUBGENUS	SUBLUNAR	SUBSERVE	SUBTACKS	SUBTYPES	

WORDS PREFIXED WITH SUN-

7-letter words

SUNBAKE	SUNBEDS	SUNBURN	SUNDEWS	SUNFAST	SUNHATS	SUNLIKE	SUNSETS	SUNTRAP
SUNBATH	SUNBELT	SUNDAES	SUNDIAL	SUNFISH	SUNKETS	SUNRAYS	SUNSPOT	SUNWARD
SUNBEAM	SUNBIRD	SUNDARI	SUNDOGS	SUNGARS	SUNLAMP	SUNRISE	SUNSUIT	SUNWISE
SUNBEAT	SUNBOWS	SUNDECK	SUNDOWN	SUNGLOW	SUNLESS	SUNROOF	SUNTANS	

8-letter words

SUNBAKED	SUNBEAMY	SUNBLOCK	SUNDECKS	SUNDRIES	SUNLIGHT	SUNSHINE	SUNTRAPS
SUNBAKES	SUNBELTS	SUNBURNS	SUNDERED	SUNDROPS	SUNPROOF	SUNSHINY	SUNWARDS
SUNBATHE	SUNBERRY	SUNBURNT	SUNDIALS	SUNGLASS	SUNRISES	SUNSPOTS	
SUNBATHS	SUNBIRDS	SUNBURST	SUNDOWNS	SUNGLOWS	SUNROOFS	SUNSTONE	
SUNBEAMS	SUNBLIND	SUNDARIS	SUNDRESS	SUNLAMPS	SUNSHADE	SUNSUITS	

WORDS PREFIXED WITH TRI-

7-letter words

TRIABLE	TRIBADE	TRICORN	TRIFLED	TRILITH	TRIONES	TRISECT	TRITIDE	TRIVIAL
TRIACID	TRIBLET	TRICOTS	TRIFORM	TRILOBE	TRIPIER	TRISEME	TRITONE	TRIZONE
TRIAGES	TRIBUTE	TRIDARN	TRIGAMY	TRILOGY	TRIPLED	TRISHAW	TRITONS	
TRIARCH	TRICARS	TRIDENT	TRIGONS	TRINARY	TRIPODS	TRISOME	TRIUMPH	
TRIAXON	TRICEPS	TRIDUAN	TRIGRAM	TRIODES	TRIPSIS	TRITEST	TRIVETS	

8-letter words

TRIANGLE	TRIBRACH	TRICYCLE	TRIGLYPH	TRILOBES	TRIPLIED	TRISHAWS	TRIVALVE
TRIAXIAL	TRIBUTES	TRIDARNS	TRIGRAMS	TRIMETER	TRIPLIES	TRISTICH	TRIZONAL
TRIAXONS	TRICHINA	TRIDENTS	TRIGRAPH	TRIOXIDE	TRIPLING	TRITICAL	TRIZONES
TRIBALLY	TRICHORD	TRIETHYL	TRILEMMA	TRIPEDAL	TRIPODAL	TRITIDES	
TRIBASIC	TRICOLOR	TRIFLING	TRILITHS	TRIPHONE	TRIPOSES	TRITONES	
TRIBLETS	TRICORNS	TRIFOCAL	TRILOBED	TRIPLANE	TRISECTS	TRIUNITY	

WORDS PREFIXED WITH UN-

7-letter words

UNACTED	UNAIRED	UNALIVE	UNASKED	UNBARED	UNBATED	UNBEGOT	UNBELTS	UNBITTS
UNAIDED	UNAKING	UNAPTLY	UNAWARE	UNBARES	UNBEARS	UNBEGUN	UNBENDS	UNBLENT
UNAIMED	UNALIKE	UNARMED	UNBAKED	UNBARKS	UNBEGET	UNBEING	UNBINDS	UNBLESS

UNBLEST	UNCOLTS	UNFITLY	UNHINGE	UNLUCKY	UNQUEEN	UNSENSE	UNSTICK	UNTURFS
UNBLIND	UNCOPED	UNFIXED	UNHIRED	UNMAKES	UNQUIET	UNSEWED	UNSTOCK	UNTURNS
UNBLOCK	UNCOPES	UNFIXES	UNHITCH	UNMANLY	UNQUOTE	UNSEXED	UNSTOPS	UNTWINE
UNBLOWN	UNCORDS	UNFLESH	UNHIVED	UNMARRY	UNRACED	UNSEXES	UNSTOWS	UNTWIST
UNBOLTS	UNCORKS	UNFLUSH	UNHIVES	UNMASKS	UNRAKED	UNSHALE	UNSTRAP	UNTYING
UNBONED	UNCOUTH	UNFOLDS	UNHOARD	UNMATED	UNRAKES	UNSHAPE	UNSTRIP	UNURGED
UNBONES	UNCOVER	UNFOOLS	UNHOODS	UNMEANT	UNRATED	UNSHELL	UNSTUCK	UNUSUAL
UNBOOTS	UNCOWLS	UNFORMS	UNHOOKS	UNMETED	UNRAVEL	UNSHENT	UNSUITS	UNVAILS
UNBORNE	UNCRATE	UNFOUND	UNHOOPS	UNMEWED	UNREADY	UNSHEWN	UNSUNNY	UNVEILS
UNBOSOM	UNCROSS	UNFREED	UNHOPED	UNMIXED	UNREAVE	UNSHIPS	UNSURED	UNVEXED
UNBOUND	UNCROWN	UNFROCK	UNHORSE	UNMOORS	UNREELS	UNSHOED	UNSURER	UNVISOR
UNBOWED	UNCURED	UNFROZE	UNHOUSE	UNMORAL	UNREEVE	UNSHOES	UNSWEAR	UNVITAL
UNBOXED	UNCURLS	UNFUMED	UNHUMAN	UNMOULD	UNREINS	UNSHOOT	UNSWEET	UNVOCAL
UNBOXES	UNCURSE	UNFUNNY	UNHUSKS	UNMOUNT	UNRESTS	UNSHORN	UNSWEPT	UNVOICE
UNBRACE	UNDATED	UNFURLS	UNIDEAL	UNMOVED	UNRIGHT	UNSHOUT	UNSWORE	UNWAGED
UNBROKE	UNDEALT	UNGEARS	UNJADED	UNNAILS	UNRIMED	UNSHOWN	UNSWORN	UNWAKED
UNBUILD	UNDECKS	UNGILDS	UNJOINT	UNNAMED	UNRIPER	UNSHUTS	UNTACKS	UNWARES
UNBUILT	UNDEIFY	UNGIRDS	UNKEMPT	UNNEATH	UNRISEN	UNSIGHT	UNTAKEN	UNWATER
UNBURNT	UNDERNS	UNGIRTH	UNKINGS	UNNERVE	UNRIVEN	UNSINEW	UNTAMED	UNWAYED
UNCAGED	UNDIGHT	UNGLOVE	UNKNITS	UNNESTS	UNRIVET	UNSIZED	UNTAMES	UNWEALS
UNCAGES	UNDINES	UNGLUED	UNKNOTS	UNNOBLE	UNROBED	UNSLAIN	UNTAXED	UNWEARY
UNCANNY	UNDOCKS	UNGLUES	UNKNOWN	UNNOTED	UNROBES	UNSLING	UNTAXES	UNWEAVE
UNCAPED	UNDOERS	UNGODLY	UNLACED	UNOFTEN	UNROLLS	UNSLUNG	UNTEACH	UNWHIPT
UNCAPES	UNDOING	UNGORED	UNLACES	UNOILED	UNROOFS	UNSMART	UNTEAMS	UNWILLS
UNCARTS	UNDRAWN	UNGOWNS	UNLADED	UNORDER	UNROOST	UNSMOTE	UNTENTS	UNWINDS
UNCASED	UNDRAWS	UNGROWN	UNLADEN	UNOWNED	UNROOTS	UNSNAPS	UNTENTY	UNWIPED
UNCASES	UNDRESS	UNGUARD	UNLADES	UNPACED	UNROPED	UNSNARL	UNTHAWS	UNWIRED
UNCHAIN	UNDRIED	UNGYVED	UNLATCH	UNPACKS	UNROPES	UNSNECK	UNTHINK	UNWIRES
UNCHARM	UNDRUNK	UNGYVES	UNLAWED	UNPAGED	UNROUGH	UNSOLID	UNTILED	UNWISER
UNCHARY	UNDYING	UNHABLE	UNLEADS	UNPAINT	UNROUND	UNSONSY	UNTILES	UNWITCH
UNCHECK	UNEARED	UNHAIRS	UNLEARN	UNPANEL	UNROYAL	UNSOOTE	UNTIRED	UNWIVED
UNCHILD	UNEARTH	UNHANDS	UNLEASH	UNPAPER	UNRUFFE	UNSOULS	UNTOMBS	UNWIVES
UNCITED	UNEASES	UNHANDY	UNLIKES	UNPARED	UNRULED	UNSOUND	UNTONED	UNWOMAN
UNCIVIL	UNEATEN	UNHANGS	UNLIMED	UNPAVED	UNRULES	UNSPARS	UNTRACE	UNWOOED
UNCLASP	UNEDGED	UNHAPPY	UNLINED	UNPERCH	UNSAFER	UNSPEAK	UNTREAD	UNWORKS
UNCLEAN	UNEDGES	UNHARDY	UNLINES	UNPICKS	UNSAINT	UNSPELL	UNTRIDE	UNWORTH
UNCLEAR	UNEQUAL	UNHASPS	UNLINKS	UNPLACE	UNSATED	UNSPENT	UNTRIED	UNWOUND
UNCLEWS	UNFACTS	UNHASTY	UNLIVED	UNPLAIT	UNSAVED	UNSPIDE	UNTRIMS	UNWOVEN
UNCLING	UNFADED	UNHEADS	UNLIVES	UNPLUGS	UNSCALE	UNSPIED	UNTRUER	UNWRAPS
UNCLIPT	UNFAIRS	UNHEALS	UNLOADS	UNPLUMB	UNSCARY	UNSPILT	UNTRULY	UNWRITE
UNCLOAK	UNFAITH	UNHEARD	UNLOCKS	UNPLUME	UNSCREW	UNSPOKE	UNTRUSS	UNWROTE
UNCLOGS	UNFAMED	UNHEART	UNLOOSE	UNPOPES	UNSEALS	UNSTACK	UNTRUST	UNWRUNG
UNCLOSE	UNFAZED	UNHEEDY	UNLORDS	UNPOSED	UNSEAMS	UNSTAID	UNTRUTH	UNYOKED
UNCLOUD	UNFEUED	UNHELED	UNLOVED	UNPRAYS	UNSEATS	UNSTATE	UNTUCKS	UNYOKES
UNCOCKS	UNFILED	UNHELES	UNLOVES	UNPROPS	UNSEELS	UNSTEEL	UNTUNED	UNZONED
UNCOILS	UNFIRED	UNHELMS		UNPURSE	UNSELFS	UNSTEPS	UNTUNES	

8-letter words

UNABATED	UNBEGGED	UNBRACES	UNCHASTE	UNCORDED	UNDINTED	UNFAIRED	UNFORGOT
UNACHING	UNBEINGS	UNBREECH	UNCHECKS	UNCORKED	UNDIPPED	UNFAIRER	UNFORMAL
UNACTIVE	UNBELIEF	UNBRIDLE	UNCHEWED	UNCOSTLY	UNDIVINE	UNFAIRLY	UNFORMED
UNADORED	UNBELTED	UNBROKEN	UNCHILDS	UNCOUPLE	UNDOCKED	UNFAITHS	UNFOUGHT
UNAFRAID	UNBENDED	UNBUCKLE	UNCHOSEN	UNCOVERS	UNDOINGS	UNFALLEN	UNFRAMED
UNALLIED	UNBENIGN	UNBUDDED	UNCHURCH	UNCOWLED	UNDOOMED	UNFANNED	UNFREEZE
UNAMAZED	UNBEREFT	UNBUILDS	UNCIPHER	UNCRATED	UNDOUBLE	UNFASTEN	UNFRIEND
UNAMUSED	UNBESEEM	UNBUNDLE	UNCLASPS	UNCRATES	UNDRAPED	UNFAULTY	UNFROCKS
UNANCHOR	UNBIASED	UNBURDEN	UNCLASSY	UNCREATE	UNDREAMT	UNFEARED	UNFROZEN
UNANELED	UNBIASES	UNBURIED	UNCLENCH	UNCROWNS	UNDRIVEN	UNFELLED	UNFUNDED
UNARGUED	UNBIDDEN	UNBURIES	UNCLEWED	UNCULLED	UNDROSSY	UNFENCED	UNFURLED
UNARISEN	UNBISHOP	UNBURNED	UNCLOAKS	UNCURBED	UNDUBBED	UNFETTER	UNFURRED
UNARMING	UNBITTED	UNBURROW	UNCLOSED	UNCURLED	UNDULLED	UNFEUDAL	UNGAGGED
UNARTFUL	UNBLAMED	UNBUTTON	UNCLOSES	UNCURSED	UNEARNED	UNFILIAL	UNGAINLY
UNATONED	UNBLINDS	UNCAGING	UNCLOTHE	UNCURVED	UNEARTHS	UNFILLED	UNGALLED
UNAVOWED	UNBLOCKS	UNCALLED	UNCLOUDS	UNDAMMED	UNEASIER	UNFILMED	UNGAUGED
UNBACKED	UNBLOODY	UNCANDID	UNCLOUDY	UNDAMNED	UNEASILY	UNFISHED	UNGEARED
UNBAGGED	UNBLOWED	UNCAPING	UNCLOVEN	UNDAMPED	UNEDGING	UNFITTED	UNGENIAL
UNBAITED	UNBODIED	UNCAPPED	UNCLUTCH	UNDASHED	UNEDITED	UNFITTER	UNGENTLE
UNBANDED	UNBODING	UNCARING	UNCOATED	UNDAZZLE	UNELATED	UNFIXING	UNGENTLY
UNBANKED	UNBOLTED	UNCARTED	UNCOCKED	UNDECENT	UNENVIED	UNFIXITY	UNGIFTED
UNBARBED	UNBONING	UNCASHED	UNCOILED	UNDECKED	UNEQUALS	UNFLAWED	UNGILDED
UNBARKED	UNBONNET	UNCASING	UNCOINED	UNDEEDED	UNERRING	UNFOLDED	UNGIRDED
UNBARRED	UNBOOKED	UNCAUGHT	UNCOLTED	UNDEFIED	UNESPIED	UNFOLDER	UNGIRTHS
UNBATHED	UNBOOTED	UNCAUSED	UNCOMBED	UNDESERT	UNEVENER	UNFOOLED	UNGIVING
UNBEATEN	UNBOSOMS	UNCHAINS	UNCOMELY	UNDEVOUT	UNEVENLY	UNFOOTED	UNGLAZED
UNBEDDED	UNBOUGHT	UNCHANCY	UNCOMMON	UNDIGHTS	UNFABLED	UNFORBID	UNGLOVED
UNBEGETS	UNBRACED	UNCHARGE	UNCOOKED	UNDIMMED	UNFADING	UNFORCED	UNGLOVES
		UNCHARMS	UNCOPING			UNFORGED	UNGLUING

UNGODDED	UNJOINTS	UNMELTED	UNPOLLED	UNROUSED	UNSINEWS	UNTANGLE	UNVERSED
UNGORGED	UNJOYFUL	UNMEWING	UNPOSTED	UNRUBBED	UNSLAKED	UNTANNED	UNVETTED
UNGOTTEN	UNJOYOUS	UNMILKED	UNPRAISE	UNRUFFLE	UNSLICED	UNTAPPED	UNVIABLE
UNGOWNED	UNJUSTER	UNMILLED	UNPRAYED	UNRULIER	UNSLINGS	UNTARRED	UNVIEWED
UNGRACED	UNJUSTLY	UNMINDED	UNPREACH	UNSADDLE	UNSLUICE	UNTASTED	UNVIRTUE
UNGRADED	UNKENNED	UNMISSED	UNPRETTY	UNSAFELY	UNSMOOTH	UNTAUGHT	UNVISORS
UNGRAZED	UNKENNEL	UNMOANED	UNPRICED	UNSAFEST	UNSNARLS	UNTAXING	UNVIZARD
UNGROUND	UNKINDER	UNMODISH	UNPRIEST	UNSAFETY	UNSNECKS	UNTEAMED	UNVOICED
UNGUARDS	UNKINDLY	UNMONIED	UNPRIMED	UNSAILED	UNSOAPED	UNTEMPER	UNVOICES
UNGUIDED	UNKINGED	UNMOORED	UNPRISON	UNSAINED	UNSOCIAL	UNTENANT	UNVULGAR
UNGUILTY	UNKINGLY	UNMOULDS	UNPRIZED	UNSAINTS	UNSOCKET	UNTENDED	UNWALLED
UNGUMMED	UNKISSED	UNMOUNTS	UNPROPER	UNSALTED	UNSODDEN	UNTENDER	UNWANTED
UNGYVING	UNKISSES	UNMOVING	UNPROVED	UNSAPPED	UNSOILED	UNTENTED	UNWARDED
UNHACKED	UNKNIGHT	UNMUFFLE	UNPROVEN	UNSASHED	UNSOLDER	UNTESTED	UNWARIER
UNHAILED	UNKNOWNS	UNMUZZLE	UNPRUNED	UNSATING	UNSOLEMN	UNTETHER	UNWARILY
UNHAIRED	UNLACING	UNNAILED	UNPULLED	UNSAYING	UNSOLVED	UNTHATCH	UNWARMED
UNHALLOW	UNLADING	UNNATIVE	UNPURGED	UNSCALED	UNSORTED	UNTHAWED	UNWARNED
UNHALSED	UNLASHED	UNNEEDED	UNPURSED	UNSCALES	UNSOUGHT	UNTHINKS	UNWARPED
UNHANDED	UNLASHES	UNNERVED	UNPURSES	UNSCREWS	UNSOULED	UNTHREAD	UNWASHED
UNHANGED	UNLAWFUL	UNNERVES	UNQUEENS	UNSEALED	UNSOURED	UNTHRIFT	UNWASHEN
UNHARMED	UNLAWING	UNNESTED	UNQUIETS	UNSEAMED	UNSPARED	UNTHRONE	UNWASTED
UNHASPED	UNLAYING	UNNETTED	UNQUOTED	UNSEASON	UNSPEAKS	UNTIDIED	UNWATERS
UNHATTED	UNLEADED	UNNOBLES	UNQUOTES	UNSEATED	UNSPELLS	UNTIDIER	UNWATERY
UNHEADED	UNLEARNS	UNOBEYED	UNRACKED	UNSECRET	UNSPHERE	UNTIDIES	UNWEANED
UNHEALED	UNLEARNT	UNOPENED	UNRAISED	UNSEEDED	UNSPOILT	UNTIDILY	UNWEAPON
UNHEALTH	UNLEASED	UNORDERS	UNRAKING	UNSEEING	UNSPOKEN	UNTILING	UNWEAVES
UNHEARSE	UNLICKED	UNPACKED	UNRAVELS	UNSEELED	UNSPRUNG	UNTILLED	UNWEBBED
UNHEARTS	UNLIDDED	UNPACKER	UNREALLY	UNSEEMLY	UNSTABLE	UNTIMELY	UNWEDDED
UNHEATED	UNLIKELY	UNPAINED	UNREAPED	UNSEIZED	UNSTACKS	UNTINGED	UNWEEDED
UNHEDGED	UNLIMBER	UNPAINTS	UNREASON	UNSELDOM	UNSTARCH	UNTINNED	UNWEENED
UNHEEDED	UNLIMING	UNPAIRED	UNREAVES	UNSELFED	UNSTATED	UNTIRING	UNWETTED
UNHELING	UNLINEAL	UNPANELS	UNRECKED	UNSELVES	UNSTATES	UNTITLED	UNWIELDY
UNHELMED	UNLINING	UNPANGED	UNREELED	UNSENSED	UNSTAYED	UNTOMBED	UNWIFELY
UNHELPED	UNLINKED	UNPAPERS	UNREEVED	UNSENSES	UNSTEADY	UNTOWARD	UNWIGGED
UNHEROIC	UNLISTED	UNPATHED	UNREEVES	UNSETTLE	UNSTEELS	UNTRACED	UNWILFUL
UNHIDDEN	UNLIVELY	UNPAYING	UNREINED	UNSEWING	UNSTICKS	UNTRACES	UNWILLED
UNHINGED	UNLIVING	UNPEELED	UNREPAID	UNSEXING	UNSTITCH	UNTRADED	UNWINGED
UNHINGES	UNLOADED	UNPEERED	UNREPAIR	UNSEXIST	UNSTOCKS	UNTREADS	UNWIRING
UNHIVING	UNLOADER	UNPEGGED	UNRHYMED	UNSEXUAL	UNSTOWED	UNTRUEST	UNWISDOM
UNHOARDS	UNLOCKED	UNPENNED	UNRIBBED	UNSHADED	UNSTRAPS	UNTRUISM	UNWISELY
UNHOLIER	UNLOOKED	UNPEOPLE	UNRIDDEN	UNSHADOW	UNSTRING	UNTRUSTS	UNWISEST
UNHOLILY	UNLOOSED	UNPERSON	UNRIDDLE	UNSHAKED	UNSTRIPS	UNTRUSTY	UNWISHED
UNHOLPEN	UNLOOSEN	UNPICKED	UNRIFLED	UNSHAKEN	UNSTRUCK	UNTRUTHS	UNWISHES
UNHOMELY	UNLOOSES	UNPINKED	UNRIGGED	UNSHALED	UNSTRUNG	UNTUCKED	UNWITTED
UNHONEST	UNLOPPED	UNPINNED	UNRIGHTS	UNSHALES	UNSTUFFY	UNTUNING	UNWIVING
UNHOODED	UNLORDED	UNPITIED	UNRINGED	UNSHAMED	UNSUBTLE	UNTURBID	UNWOMANS
UNHOOKED	UNLORDLY	UNPLACED	UNRIPEST	UNSHAPED	UNSUCKED	UNTURFED	UNWONTED
UNHOOPED	UNLOVELY	UNPLACES	UNRIPPED	UNSHAPEN	UNSUITED	UNTURNED	UNWOODED
UNHORSED	UNLOVING	UNPLAITS	UNRIVETS	UNSHAPES	UNSUMMED	UNTWINED	UNWORDED
UNHORSES	UNMAILED	UNPLAYED	UNROBING	UNSHARED	UNSUNNED	UNTWINES	UNWORKED
UNHOUSED	UNMAIMED	UNPLIANT	UNROLLED	UNSHAVED	UNSUPPLE	UNTWISTS	UNWORMED
UNHOUSES	UNMAKING	UNPLUMBS	UNROOFED	UNSHAVEN	UNSUREST	UNUSABLE	UNWORTHS
UNHUNTED	UNMANNED	UNPLUMED	UNROOSTS	UNSHELLS	UNSWATHE	UNUSABLY	UNWORTHY
UNHUSKED	UNMANTLE	UNPLUMES	UNROOTED	UNSHOOTS	UNSWAYED	UNUSEFUL	UNWRITES
UNIMBUED	UNMARKED	UNPOETIC	UNROPING	UNSHOUTS	UNSWEARS	UNVAILED	UNYEANED
UNINURED	UNMARRED	UNPOISED	UNROTTED	UNSHROUD	UNTACKED	UNVALUED	UNYOKING
UNIONISE	UNMASKED	UNPOISON	UNROTTEN	UNSICKER	UNTACKLE	UNVARIED	UNZIPPED
UNIONIZE	UNMASKER	UNPOLISH	UNROUGED	UNSIFTED	UNTAILED	UNVEILED	
UNIRONED	UNMEETLY	UNPOLITE	UNROUNDS	UNSIGNED	UNTAMING	UNVENTED	

WORDS PREFIXED WITH UP-

7-letter words

UPBEARS	UPBURST	UPDRAWS	UPHAUDS	UPLEAPS	UPREARS	UPSPAKE	UPSWEEP	UPTYING
UPBINDS	UPCASTS	UPENDED	UPHEAPS	UPLEAPT	UPRESTS	UPSPEAK	UPSWELL	UPVALUE
UPBLOWN	UPCATCH	UPFILLS	UPHEAVE	UPLIFTS	UPRIGHT	UPSPEAR	UPSWEPT	UPWAFTS
UPBLOWS	UPCHEER	UPFLOWS	UPHILLS	UPLINKS	UPRISEN	UPSPOKE	UPSWING	UPWARDS
UPBOILS	UPCHUCK	UPFLUNG	UPHOARD	UPLOADS	UPRISES	UPSTAGE	UPTAKEN	UPWELLS
UPBORNE	UPCLIMB	UPFRONT	UPHOIST	UPLOCKS	UPRIVER	UPSTAIR	UPTAKES	UPWHIRL
UPBOUND	UPCLOSE	UPFURLS	UPHOLDS	UPLOOKS	UPROARS	UPSTAND	UPTEARS	UPWINDS
UPBRAID	UPCOAST	UPGANGS	UPHOORD	UPLYING	UPROLLS	UPSTARE	UPTHREW	UPWOUND
UPBRAST	UPCOILS	UPGAZED	UPHURLS	UPMAKER	UPROOTS	UPSTART	UPTHROW	UPWRAPS
UPBRAYS	UPCOMES	UPGAZES	UPKEEPS	UPMAKES	UPROUSE	UPSTATE	UPTIGHT	
UPBREAK	UPCURLS	UPGOING	UPKNITS	UPPILED	UPSCALE	UPSTAYS	UPTILTS	
UPBRING	UPDATED	UPGRADE	UPLANDS	UPPINGS	UPSENDS	UPSTOOD	UPTOWNS	
UPBROKE	UPDATES	UPGROWN	UPLEADS	UPRAISE	UPSHOOT	UPSURGE	UPTRAIN	
UPBUILD	UPDRAGS	UPGROWS	UPLEANS	UPRATED	UPSHOTS	UPSWARM	UPTREND	
UPBUILT	UPDRAWN	UPHANGS	UPLEANT	UPRATES	UPSIDES	UPSWAYS	UPTURNS	

8-letter words

UPBOILED	UPCOILED	UPGRADER	UPJETTED	UPRATING	UPSPEAKS	UPSTREAM	UPTRAINS
UPBRAIDS	UPCOMING	UPGRADES	UPLANDER	UPREARED	UPSPEARS	UPSTROKE	UPTRENDS
UPBRAYED	UPCURLED	UPGROWTH	UPLAYING	UPRIGHTS	UPSPOKEN	UPSURGED	UPTURNED
UPBREAKS	UPCURVED	UPGUSHED	UPLEANED	UPRISING	UPSPRANG	UPSURGES	UPVALUED
UPBRINGS	UPDATING	UPGUSHES	UPLEAPED	UPROARED	UPSPRING	UPSWARMS	UPVALUES
UPBROKEN	UPENDING	UPHEAPED	UPLIFTED	UPROLLED	UPSPRUNG	UPSWAYED	UPWAFTED
UPBUILDS	UPFILLED	UPHEAVED	UPLIFTER	UPROOTED	UPSTAGED	UPSWEEPS	UPWELLED
UPBURSTS	UPFLOWED	UPHEAVES	UPLOADED	UPROOTER	UPSTAGES	UPSWELLS	UPWHIRLS
UPCAUGHT	UPFOLLOW	UPHOARDS	UPLOCKED	UPROUSED	UPSTAIRS	UPSWINGS	
UPCHEERS	UPFURLED	UPHOISTS	UPLOOKED	UPROUSES	UPSTANDS	UPTAKING	
UPCHUCKS	UPGATHER	UPHOLDER	UPMAKERS	UPRUSHED	UPSTARED	UPTHROWN	
UPCLIMBS	UPGAZING	UPHOORDS	UPMAKING	UPRUSHES	UPSTARES	UPTHROWS	
UPCLOSED	UPGOINGS	UPHUDDEN	UPRAISED	UPSETTER	UPSTARTS	UPTHRUST	
UPCLOSES	UPGRADED	UPHURLED	UPRAISES	UPSHOOTS	UPSTAYED	UPTILTED	

WORDS PREFIXED WITH WAR-

7-letter words

WARBIER	WARDING	WARFARE	WARLING	WARMING	WARRAND	WARRENS	WARSLED	WARWOLF
WARBLED	WARDOGS	WARHEAD	WARLOCK	WARPATH	WARRANT	WARRING	WARTIER	
WARDENS	WARDROP	WARLIKE	WARLORD	WARPING	WARRAYS	WARSHIP	WARTIME	

8-letter words

WARDERED	WARDROPS	WARHABLE	WARLINGS	WARMINGS	WARPLANE	WARRAYED	WARTIMES
WARDINGS	WARFARED	WARHEADS	WARLOCKS	WARPATHS	WARRANDS	WARSHIPS	WARTWEED
WARDRESS	WARFARES	WARHORSE	WARLORDS	WARPINGS	WARRANTS	WARSLING	

-------------------------------- **5 to 8's** --------------------------------

5 to 8's describes the addition of any three letters at the front or end of a 5-letter word to form a valid 8-letter word. Why are such additions of special interest to the Scrabble player?

Many games will start with a 5-letter play in order to cover one of the double-letter squares. Such plays will either start or end on the centre square. If such a play starts on the centre square it could have the potential to be extended by three letters to reach the triple word square to the right. Note that, as it is easier to spot extensions to the right (we read from left to right, so it is more natural to look at extending a word in this direction) we have not listed here any words formed by adding a suffix such as -ING, -FUL or -EST, though 8-letter words ending in the last two can be found in Section Three in the 'Useful Suffixes' list.

If a 5-letter play ends on the centre square then it is possible that it could be extended by three letters at the front to reach the triple word square to the left. These formations are of particular interest because they are not so easy to spot. As we have noted, it is more natural to see extensions to the right, and it takes extra effort to think about how a word might be extended to the left. Such plays can therefore surprise your opponent and rope in some great triple word scores through clever use of just three letters.

The following is a list of all the possible 8-letter words that can be formed by adding three letters to the front of an existing 5-letter word. Although quite a few of the words will be formed with recognizable prefixes (eg SUB-SOILS, OUT-RAGED) there is also an abundance of more surprising extensions to introduce into your game (eg CLU-BLAND, PEN-CHANT).

You may be amazed at how many possibilities there sometimes are. If a game starts with CABLE with the E on the centre square then there are no less than five possible front extensions (AMI-CABLE, EDU-CABLE, EVO-CABLE, PEC-CABLE, PLA-CABLE). That's between 39 and 48 points for just three letters.

SAR-ABAND	BEM-ADDED	CLO-AKING	TRI-ANGLE	VAG-ARISH	POS-AUNES
DAT-ABASE	SEP-ADDED	CRE-AKING	UNT-ANGLE	DEB-ARKED	PES-AUNTS
CAL-ABASH	STR-ADDLE	CRO-AKING	BOT-ANISE	DEM-ARKED	ROM-AUNTS
SQU-ABASH	UNS-ADDLE	FRE-AKING	HUM-ANISE	EMB-ARKED	TAL-AUNTS
SUB-ABBOT	MAT-ADORE	KAI-AKING	ORG-ANISE	IMB-ARKED	BIN-AURAL
DIS-ABLED	DIS-ADORN	KAY-AKING	PAG-ANISE	IMP-ARKED	MON-AURAL
PAR-ABLED	SUB-ADULT	REM-AKING	TET-ANISE	REM-ARKED	SUB-AURAL
UNF-ABLED	GYN-AECIA	RET-AKING	URB-ANISE	UNB-ARKED	PAR-AVAIL
CAP-ABLER	PER-AEONS	SNE-AKING	WOM-ANISE	UNM-ARKED	PAR-AVANT
BUY-ABLES	PIN-AFORE	SPE-AKING	CAR-ANNAS	EMP-ARLED	CAD-AVERS
DIS-ABLES	DIV-AGATE	TWE-AKING	HOS-ANNAS	IMP-ARLED	CLE-AVERS
DUR-ABLES	IND-AGATE	UNM-AKING	RAB-ANNAS	DIS-ARMED	PAL-AVERS
EAT-ABLES	RUN-AGATE	UNR-AKING	SAV-ANNAS	UNH-ARMED	DIS-AVOWS
MOV-ABLES	SUB-AGENT	UPM-AKING	DIS-ANNEX	UNW-ARMED	THR-AWARD
NOT-ABLES	DAM-AGING	UPT-AKING	DIS-ANNUL	ALG-AROBA	ARE-AWAYS
PAR-ABLES	ENC-AGING	WRE-AKING	INF-ANTAS	ZAM-ARRAS	CAR-AWAYS
POT-ABLES	ENG-AGING	ESC-ALATE	TAR-ANTAS	DIS-ARRAY	CUT-AWAYS
RET-ABLES	ENR-AGING	ALF-ALFAS	ASK-ANTED	MIS-ARRAY	FAR-AWAYS
VOC-ABLES	FOR-AGING	REG-ALIAS	DEC-ANTED	SQU-ARSON	GET-AWAYS
GAD-ABOUT	GAR-AGING	ROS-ALIAS	LEV-ANTED	LAB-ARUMS	LAY-AWAYS
LAY-ABOUT	HOM-AGING	VED-ALIAS	REC-ANTED	UNW-ASHEN	RUN-AWAYS
MAR-ABOUT	INC-AGING	MIS-ALIGN	TEN-ANTED	BED-ASHES	UNL-AWFUL
RUN-ABOUT	MAN-AGING	ALK-ALINE	TRU-ANTED	CAL-ASHES	PAW-AWING
DIS-ABUSE	MAR-AGING	BUB-ALINE	TYR-ANTED	CAM-ASHES	PSH-AWING
DEF-ACERS	MEN-AGING	PET-ALINE	UNW-ANTED	ENC-ASHES	STR-AWING
FIL-ACERS	RAV-AGING	SEP-ALINE	AND-ANTES	FOG-ASHES	THR-AWING
MEN-ACERS	SAV-AGING	PAR-ALLEL	INF-ANTES	GAM-ASHES	UNL-AWING
ARE-ACHED	SIL-AGING	TOM-ALLEY	VOL-ANTES	POT-ASHES	IMP-AWNED
ATT-ACHED	ULL-AGING	MIS-ALLOT	GIG-ANTIC	REH-ASHES	MON-AXIAL
BLE-ACHED	UNC-AGING	DIS-ALLOW	PED-ANTIC	SIW-ASHES	TRI-AXIAL
BRE-ACHED	VOY-AGING	ENW-ALLOW	ROM-ANTIC	SPL-ASHES	UNI-AXIAL
BRO-ACHED	GAR-AGIST	UNH-ALLOW	SEM-ANTIC	SQU-ASHES	MAL-AXING
DET-ACHED	VIS-AGIST	ENH-ALOED	XER-ANTIC	THR-ASHES	REL-AXING
PLE-ACHED	PAR-AGOGE	CAT-ALOES	SEM-ANTRA	UNL-ASHES	UNT-AXING
PRE-ACHED	DEC-AGONS	ENH-ALOES	ZYG-ANTRA	ATT-ASKED	MON-AXONS
ARE-ACHES	HEX-AGONS	PED-ALOES	CAR-APACE	DAM-ASKED	TRI-AXONS
ATT-ACHES	NON-AGONS	PAL-AMATE	MAL-APERT	IMM-ASKED	EMP-AYRES
BLE-ACHES	OCT-AGONS	SQU-AMATE	AWH-APING	UNM-ASKED	THI-AZIDE
BRE-ACHES	PAR-AGONS	PRE-AMBLE	ESC-APING	UNM-ASKER	ATR-AZINE
BRO-ACHES	DIS-AGREE	SCR-AMBLE	SCR-APING	BIO-ASSAY	MAG-AZINE
DET-ACHES	FIL-AGREE	DUR-AMENS	SNE-APING	ADM-ASSES	SIM-AZINE
EAR-ACHES	REN-AGUED	ARM-AMENT	UNC-APING	BAD-ASSES	THI-AZINE
GOU-ACHES	REN-AGUES	ATR-AMENT	ESC-APISM	BAG-ASSES	TOP-AZINE
PAN-ACHES	TRE-AGUES	FIL-AMENT	PRI-APISM	BEC-ASSES	MET-AZOIC
PLE-ACHES	OBE-AHING	LIG-AMENT	SIN-APISM	BYP-ASSES	CUT-BACKS
PRE-ACHES	ABR-AIDED	ORN-AMENT	MEG-APODE	CAM-ASSES	DIE-BACKS
QUE-ACHES	ALC-AIDES	PAR-AMENT	DEC-APODS	CAV-ASSES	FIN-BACKS
REL-ACHES	ASS-AILED	VIZ-AMENT	HEX-APODS	DEG-ASSES	HOG-BACKS
ANT-ACIDS	AUM-AILED	SOD-AMIDE	SCR-APPLE	FIL-ASSES	LAY-BACKS
BEL-ACING	BEW-AILED	BEL-AMIES	THR-APPLE	HAR-ASSES	OUT-BACKS
DEF-ACING	DER-AILED	BIG-AMIES	DIS-APPLY	IMP-ASSES	PAY-BACKS
EFF-ACING	DET-AILED	DIG-AMIES	MIS-APPLY	KAV-ASSES	RED-BACKS
EMB-ACING	EMB-AILED	GOR-AMIES	DEL-APSES	MEG-ASSES	RUN-BACKS
ENF-ACING	ENT-AILED	INF-AMIES	ILL-APSES	MOL-ASSES	SET-BACKS
ENL-ACING	RER-AILED	OCC-AMIES	REL-APSES	MOR-ASSES	SOW-BACKS
ENR-ACING	RET-AILED	OOG-AMIES	SYN-APSES	POT-ASSES	TIE-BACKS
INL-ACING	SQU-AILED	STE-AMIES	SYN-APSIS	PRE-ASSES	WET-BACKS
MEN-ACING	UNH-AILED	CAL-AMINE	SUB-AREAS	REP-ASSES	SUN-BAKED
PRE-ACING	UNM-AILED	COR-AMINE	CAB-ARETS	STR-ASSES	SUN-BAKES
REF-ACING	UNN-AILED	DOP-AMINE	LAZ-ARETS	TIR-ASSES	CAB-BALAS
SOL-ACING	UNS-AILED	IND-AMINE	MIN-ARETS	VAK-ASSES	FAL-BALAS
UNL-ACING	UNT-AILED	KET-AMINE	TAB-ARETS	VIN-ASSES	KAB-BALAS
PAR-ACMES	UNV-AILED	MEL-AMINE	ESC-ARGOT	CAN-ASTER	TIM-BALES
CON-ACRED	MIS-AIMED	SYC-AMINE	RED-ARGUE	DIS-ASTER	EYE-BALLS
CON-ACRES	UNM-AIMED	THI-AMINE	POD-ARGUS	OLE-ASTER	ICE-BALLS
POL-ACRES	DET-AINEE	VIT-AMINE	DAT-ARIAS	PIL-ASTER	NET-BALLS
SUB-ACRID	APP-AIRED	CAL-AMITY	FIL-ARIAS	PIN-ASTER	ODD-BALLS
IMP-ACTED	EMP-AIRED	PAR-AMOUR	MAL-ARIAS	REM-ASTER	PAT-BALLS
OLF-ACTED	IMP-AIRED	ENS-AMPLE	OLE-ARIAS	SUB-ATOMS	PIN-BALLS
RED-ACTED	REP-AIRED	IMM-ANENT	TIM-ARIOT	CAT-ATONY	GLO-BALLY
SUB-ACTED	UNF-AIRED	REM-ANENT	CUR-ARISE	GEM-ATRIA	TRI-BALLY
COF-ACTOR	UNH-AIRED	ARR-ANGER	MAC-ARISE	ZOI-ATRIA	VER-BALLY
RED-ACTOR	UNP-AIRED	END-ANGER	NOT-ARISE	SUB-AUDIO	ARM-BANDS
VAR-ACTOR	IMP-AIRER	ETR-ANGER	POL-ARISE	ARR-AUGHT	DIS-BANDS
PER-ACUTE	REP-AIRER	STR-ANGER	SOL-ARISE	REC-AUGHT	HAT-BANDS
SUB-ACUTE	UNF-AIRER	ENT-ANGLE	VEL-ARISE	STR-AUGHT	HAY-BANDS
FAR-ADAYS	ASL-AKING	SPR-ANGLE	SQU-ARISH	UNC-AUGHT	HUS-BANDS
ILK-ADAYS	BET-AKING	STR-ANGLE	TOV-ARISH	UNT-AUGHT	PRO-BANDS
NOW-ADAYS	BRE-AKING			UPC-AUGHT	RIB-BANDS

SAL-BANDS	HAU-BERKS	HUM-BLEST	ICE-BOUND	TRU-CAGES	TEU-CHEST
TUR-BANDS	BAR-BERRY	NIM-BLEST	MAW-BOUND	PAN-CAKED	FIT-CHEWS
TUR-BANED	BAY-BERRY	STA-BLEST	OUT-BOUND	CAR-CAKES	COL-CHICA
BUG-BANES	BIL-BERRY	BOM-BLETS	FAU-BOURG	CUP-CAKES	DAB-CHICK
COW-BANES	COW-BERRY	DOU-BLETS	DIS-BOWEL	OAT-CAKES	DIP-CHICK
DOG-BANES	DOG-BERRY	DRI-BLETS	OUT-BOXED	PAN-CAKES	DOB-CHICK
FLY-BANES	FOX-BERRY	HER-BLETS	HAT-BOXES	CAT-CALLS	PSY-CHICS
HEN-BANES	HAG-BERRY	TRI-BLETS	HAY-BOXES	MIS-CALLS	KER-CHIEF
MIR-BANES	INK-BERRY	GOR-BLIMY	ICE-BOXES	EPI-CALYX	MIS-CHIEF
MYR-BANES	MUL-BERRY	PUR-BLIND	JAW-BOXES	DIS-CANDY	SUB-CHIEF
LUM-BANGS	NIS-BERRY	SUN-BLIND	OUT-BOXES	CHI-CANED	GOD-CHILD
PRO-BANGS	PEA-BERRY	ICE-BLINK	VAM-BRACE	CHI-CANES	MER-CHILD
SHE-BANGS	SUN-BERRY	QUI-BLINS	TRI-BRACH	JON-CANOE	TWI-CHILD
CAN-BANKS	TAY-BERRY	SEA-BLITE	SHA-BRACK	ALI-CANTS	ISO-CHIME
SEA-BANKS	TEA-BERRY	SUN-BLOCK	OUT-BRAGS	DES-CANTS	TRI-CHINA
TUR-BANTS	WAX-BERRY	FLY-BLOWS	MAD-BRAIN	DIS-CANTS	ZEC-CHINE
RHU-BARBS	GIB-BETED	CUP-BOARD	MID-BRAIN	INS-CAPES	ZEC-CHINO
BOM-BARDS	RAB-BETED	DAM-BOARD	OUT-BRAVE	BAC-CARAT	KIN-CHINS
GAB-BARDS	DIA-BETES	FUN-BOARD	RYE-BREAD	BRO-CARDS	SCU-CHINS
LIB-BARDS	CAR-BIDES	GAR-BOARD	SOW-BREAD	DIS-CARDS	PUT-CHOCK
LUB-BARDS	GAM-BIERS	KEY-BOARD	WAY-BREAD	PLA-CARDS	MOU-CHOIR
ISO-BARES	JAM-BIERS	LAR-BOARD	DAY-BREAK	EPI-CARPS	FAU-CHONS
BAR-BARIC	STA-BILES	LOG-BOARD	OUT-BREAK	EXO-CARPS	TOR-CHONS
ISO-BARIC	SAW-BILLS	MOP-BOARD	PAR-BREAK	SYN-CARPS	ULI-CHONS
DIS-BARKS	TWI-BILLS	OUT-BOARD	OUT-BREED	MIS-CARRY	SUB-CHORD
TAN-BARKS	WAX-BILLS	PEG-BOARD	SUB-BREED	DOG-CARTS	TRI-CHORD
SUB-BASAL	WAY-BILLS	SEA-BOARD	RED-BRICK	CAR-CASED	URO-CHORD
SUR-BASED	WRY-BILLS	TEA-BOARD	SOM-BRING	DIS-CASED	ISO-CHORE
AIR-BASES	HOP-BINDS	WAY-BOARD	DAM-BRODS	CAR-CASES	ZOO-CHORE
ANA-BASES	CAR-BINES	CAT-BOATS	OUT-BROKE	DIS-CASES	SAL-CHOWS
DIA-BASES	COM-BINES	FLY-BOATS	PEM-BROKE	NUT-CASES	DIS-CIDED
ISO-BASES	HOP-BINES	GUN-BOATS	CLU-BROOM	PIN-CASES	PLA-CIDER
SUB-BASES	STI-BINES	ICE-BOATS	CRI-BROSE	URI-CASES	RAN-CIDER
SUR-BASES	TUR-BINES	PIG-BOATS	EYE-BROWS	OUT-CASTE	BIO-CIDES
DIA-BASIC	COM-BINGS	ROW-BOATS	CLU-BRUSH	SUB-CASTE	DEI-CIDES
TRI-BASIC	CUB-BINGS	TOW-BOATS	HAT-BRUSH	MET-CASTS	DIS-CIDES
ANA-BASIS	DAU-BINGS	TUG-BOATS	HAW-BUCKS	MIS-CASTS	ECO-CIDES
LAM-BASTE	DUB-BINGS	KEB-BOCKS	JUM-BUCKS	OUT-CASTS	OVI-CIDES
BOM-BASTS	JIB-BINGS	FOR-BODES	KEB-BUCKS	SEE-CATCH	SUI-CIDES
LAM-BASTS	JOB-BINGS	GAR-BOILS	ROE-BUCKS	EDU-CATES	DIS-CINCT
BAR-BATED	MOB-BINGS	ROE-BOILS	SAW-BUCKS	EMI-CATES	PRE-CINCT
COM-BATED	RIB-BINGS	GUM-BOILS	ZAM-BUCKS	EVO-CATES	PRO-CINCT
GLO-BATED	RUB-BINGS	PAR-BOILS	KEY-BUGLE	JUN-CATES	SUC-CINCT
PRO-BATED	SOB-BINGS	KEM-BOING	GEE-BUNGS	PLA-CATES	EPI-CISTS
SUR-BATED	SUB-BINGS	KIM-BOING	CAR-BURET	PLI-CATES	FAS-CISTS
UNA-BATED	TUB-BINGS	MAM-BOING	TAM-BURIN	CON-CAUSE	ELI-CITED
NIO-BATES	WEB-BINGS	BAR-BOLAS	MOW-BURNS	CON-CAVED	CIR-CITER
PRO-BATES	SYM-BIONT	TOM-BOLAS	OUT-BURNS	CON-CAVES	BRU-CITES
SOR-BATES	ANT-BIRDS	SYM-BOLES	SUN-BURNS	SUR-CEASE	CAL-CITES
SUR-BATES	AWL-BIRDS	DIA-BOLOS	MOW-BURNT	CON-CEDED	DUL-CITES
SUN-BATHE	CAT-BIRDS	TOM-BOLOS	OUT-BURNT	PRE-CEDED	LEU-CITES
ISO-BATHS	COW-BIRDS	DOG-BOLTS	SUN-BURNT	CON-CEDES	ZIN-CITES
MUD-BATHS	RED-BIRDS	EYE-BOLTS	DIS-BURSE	EPI-CEDES	DIS-CLAIM
SUN-BATHS	SEA-BIRDS	HAG-BOLTS	AIR-BURST	PRE-CEDES	PRO-CLAIM
CIA-BATTA	SUN-BIRDS	RAG-BOLTS	OUT-BURST	MAR-CELLA	SUB-CLAIM
SUN-BEAMS	WOS-BIRDS	TUR-BONDS	SUN-BURST	SEI-CENTO	OUT-CLASS
SUN-BEAMY	MIS-BIRTH	JAW-BONED	NIM-BUSED	TRE-CENTO	SUB-CLASS
BOG-BEANS	ARA-BISES	RAW-BONED	IAM-BUSES	CON-CENTS	CON-CLAVE
ANT-BEARS	SOU-BISES	RIB-BONED	MOR-BUSES	DES-CENTS	ISO-CLINE
BUG-BEARS	RAB-BITER	JAM-BONES	NIM-BUSES	PIN-CERED	SYN-CLINE
CUD-BEARS	NIO-BITES	JAW-BONES	SOR-BUSES	GLY-CERIA	CIR-CLING
FOR-BEARS	SOR-BITES	SAW-BONES	COM-BUSTS	GLY-CERIC	MUS-CLING
DRY-BEATS	BAB-BITTS	BOO-BOOKS	TRI-BUTES	CON-CERTS	ORA-CLING
OFF-BEATS	BOB-BITTS	FLY-BOOKS	AMI-CABLE	ARM-CHAIR	CIR-CLIPS
JAM-BEAUX	SAW-BLADE	LOG-BOOKS	EDU-CABLE	BRE-CHAMS	TOE-CLIPS
LIM-BECKS	CLU-BLAND	JAM-BOOLS	EVO-CABLE	BAC-CHANT	DIS-CLOSE
MIS-BEGOT	SLO-BLAND	TOL-BOOTH	PEC-CABLE	COU-CHANT	PAR-CLOSE
COW-BELLS	BIO-BLAST	GUM-BOOTS	PLA-CABLE	MER-CHANT	OIL-CLOTH
RED-BELLY	EPI-BLAST	SLY-BOOTS	BRO-CADES	PEN-CHANT	WAX-CLOTH
TUN-BELLY	MYO-BLAST	BOM-BORAS	CAS-CADES	CLO-CHARD	SEA-COAST
FUR-BELOW	NEO-BLAST	HAR-BORED	FAL-CADES	MOU-CHARD	RED-COATS
RUM-BELOW	ZOO-BLAST	JAM-BOREE	SAC-CADES	PIL-CHARD	SUR-COATS
FLY-BELTS	COM-BLESS	HAR-BORER	SUC-CADES	PET-CHARY	TOP-COATS
SUN-BELTS	CUR-BLESS	AIR-BORNE	DIS-CAGED	PUR-CHASE	BAW-COCKS
ALE-BENCH	HER-BLESS	FOR-BORNE	BOS-CAGES	ISO-CHASM	BIB-COCKS
DIS-BENCH	LIM-BLESS	SEA-BORNE	BRO-CAGES	TEU-CHATS	DAW-COCKS
PRE-BENDS	TOM-BLESS	DIS-BOSOM	DIS-CAGES	TOR-CHERE	GOR-COCKS
SOR-BENTS	VER-BLESS	CHA-BOUKS	RIB-CAGES	BUT-CHEST	HAY-COCKS
ICE-BERGS	FEE-BLEST	CHI-BOUKS	SOC-CAGES	GAU-CHEST	MEA-COCKS
		FOG-BOUND			

PEA-COCKS	UNS-CREWS	MIS-DATES	ABI-DINGS	HOR-DOCKS	SUB-DUALS
PET-COCKS	DES-CRIED	OUT-DATES	BAN-DINGS	MAD-DOCKS	OVI-DUCAL
SEA-COCKS	OUT-CRIED	OXI-DATES	BEA-DINGS	PAD-DOCKS	CON-DUCES
PEA-COCKY	DES-CRIES	PRE-DATES	BED-DINGS	PID-DOCKS	PRO-DUCES
SAR-CODES	OUT-CRIES	PRE-DAWNS	BEN-DINGS	PUD-DOCKS	SUB-DUCES
ZIN-CODES	APO-CRINE	MIS-DEALS	BID-DINGS	RUD-DOCKS	TRA-DUCES
BRI-COLES	CAN-CRINE	MIS-DEALT	BIN-DINGS	WIN-DOCKS	HEY-DUCKS
GLY-COLIC	EXO-CRINE	SUB-DEANS	BIR-DINGS	MIS-DOERS	CON-DUCTS
PER-COLIN	OUT-CROPS	SUN-DECKS	BON-DINGS	FOR-DOING	OVI-DUCTS
CON-COLOR	OUT-CROSS	MIS-DEEDS	BUD-DINGS	MIS-DOING	PRO-DUCTS
DIS-COLOR	DIS-CROWN	MIS-DEEMS	CHI-DINGS	OUT-DOING	SUB-DUCTS
MIS-COLOR	GOR-CROWS	GON-DELAY	COR-DINGS	CON-DOLED	VIA-DUCTS
TRI-COLOR	PIL-CROWS	URO-DELES	EIL-DINGS	CON-DOLES	SUB-DUING
UNI-COLOR	PIE-CRUST	SON-DELIS	FAR-DINGS	MIS-DONNE	SCE-DULES
LEU-COMAS	SUB-CRUST	BRI-DEMAN	FEE-DINGS	PUN-DONOR	SUB-DUPLE
SAR-COMAS	MIS-CUING	SPA-DEMAN	FEU-DINGS	BAN-DOOKS	EPI-DURAL
BUN-COMBE	RES-CUING	ACA-DEMES	FIN-DINGS	BUN-DOOKS	SUB-DURAL
COX-COMBS	BIS-CUITS	ACA-DEMIC	FOL-DINGS	PRE-DOOMS	BAN-DURAS
NEW-COMER	CIR-CUITS	EPI-DEMIC	FUN-DINGS	OUT-DOORS	PAN-DURAS
WEL-COMER	CUR-CUMIN	PAN-DEMIC	GEL-DINGS	PAN-DOORS	OUT-DURED
OUT-COMER	DIS-CURED	MIS-DEMPT	GIL-DINGS	TAN-DOORS	PER-DURED
WEL-COMES	OBS-CURED	CON-DENSE	GIR-DINGS	ACI-DOSES	VER-DURED
BEA-CONED	PRO-CURED	ERO-DENTS	GLI-DINGS	APO-DOSES	BOR-DURED
DRA-CONES	OBS-CURER	EVI-DENTS	GUI-DINGS	LOR-DOSES	OUT-DURES
MUS-CONES	PRO-CURER	MOR-DENTS	HEA-DINGS	EPI-DOTES	PER-DURES
ZIR-CONIA	DIS-CURES	PEN-DENTS	HIL-DINGS	MIS-DOUBT	RON-DURES
ANI-CONIC	EPI-CURES	STU-DENTS	HOL-DINGS	HAN-DOUTS	VER-DURES
DRA-CONIC	OBS-CURES	TRI-DENTS	HYL-DINGS	HOL-DOUTS	COR-DUROY
GLY-CONIC	PRO-CURES	BOR-DERED	LAN-DINGS	HAN-DOVER	SAW-DUSTS
ZIR-CONIC	PRE-CURSE	CIN-DERED	LEA-DINGS	HOL-DOVER	SAW-DUSTY
CHA-CONNE	EXE-CUTER	DAN-DERED	LEN-DINGS	PAN-DOWDY	WOO-DWALE
OLY-COOKS	ELO-CUTES	DID-DERED	LOA-DINGS	SHA-DOWED	OUT-DWELL
PRE-COOKS	EXE-CUTES	DOD-DERED	LOR-DINGS	WIN-DOWED	OUT-DWELT
PRE-COOLS	EPI-CYCLE	DON-DERED	MEN-DINGS	SHA-DOWER	BAN-DYING
PUC-COONS	TRI-CYCLE	FOD-DERED	MIN-DINGS	HAG-DOWNS	BOO-DYING
RAC-COONS	UNI-CYCLE	GEN-DERED	NOD-DINGS	HOE-DOWNS	CAD-DYING
SYN-COPAL	OTO-CYSTS	HIN-DERED	PAD-DINGS	PIN-DOWNS	CAN-DYING
APO-COPES	VEN-DACES	JUD-DERED	PUD-DINGS	RUB-DOWNS	GID-DYING
SYN-COPES	SOL-DADOS	LAD-DERED	REA-DINGS	RUN-DOWNS	KID-DYING
CON-CORDS	FRE-DAINE	MOI-DERED	RED-DINGS	SUN-DOWNS	MAR-DYING
DIS-CORDS	MON-DAINE	MUR-DERED	REE-DINGS	HAN-DRAIL	MOO-DYING
RES-CORED	UPA-DAISY	PAN-DERED	ROA-DINGS	HEA-DRAIL	MUD-DYING
SUC-CORED	PAR-DALES	POL-DERED	ROD-DINGS	LAN-DRAIL	PAN-DYING
RES-CORES	RUN-DALES	PON-DERED	SAN-DINGS	MAN-DRAKE	PRE-DYING
PIL-CORNS	PAR-DALIS	POW-DERED	SEE-DINGS	FIN-DRAMS	REA-DYING
POP-CORNS	FEU-DALLY	PUD-DERED	SEN-DINGS	OUT-DRANK	RUD-DYING
TRI-CORNS	BEL-DAMES	REN-DERED	SHA-DINGS	QUA-DRANT	STU-DYING
UNI-CORNS	MES-DAMES	SAW-DERED	SIN-DINGS	AIR-DRAWN	TAR-DYING
ARC-COSES	ABI-DANCE	SOL-DERED	SLI-DINGS	MIS-DRAWN	TOA-DYING
DUL-COSES	GUI-DANCE	SUN-DERED	SYN-DINGS	MIS-DRAWS	WAD-DYING
GLU-COSES	OUT-DANCE	TEN-DERED	TRA-DINGS	MIS-DREAD	VAN-DYKED
GLY-COSES	RID-DANCE	WAN-DERED	VOI-DINGS	DAY-DREAM	VAN-DYKES
NAR-COSES	TEN-DANCE	WAR-DERED	WAD-DINGS	SUN-DRESS	ANO-DYNES
SAC-COSES	VOI-DANCE	WED-DERED	WAR-DINGS	WAR-DRESS	INV-EAGLE
VIS-COSES	MRI-DANGS	WIL-DERED	WED-DINGS	HEA-DREST	BEM-EANED
SUB-COSTA	SLA-DANGS	WON-DERED	WEE-DINGS	TAW-DRIER	DEM-EANED
ALE-COSTS	YAR-DANGS	EXO-DERMS	WEL-DINGS	BAW-DRIES	UNW-EANED
BOY-COTTS	FON-DANTS	MIL-DEWED	WIL-DINGS	FOU-DRIES	UNY-EANED
HIC-COUGH	GAR-DANTS	SUB-DEWED	WIN-DINGS	SUN-DRIES	UPL-EANED
DIS-COUNT	MOR-DANTS	WOO-DHOLE	WOR-DINGS	TAW-DRIES	AFF-EARED
MIS-COUNT	OXI-DANTS	COR-DIALS	PUD-DINGY	MAN-DRILL	APP-EARED
VIS-COUNT	PEN-DANTS	MIS-DIALS	RON-DINOS	TAW-DRILY	END-EARED
DIS-COURE	OUT-DARED	PRE-DIALS	TON-DINOS	OUT-DRINK	ENS-EARED
CON-COURS	PAN-DARED	STA-DIALS	CRE-DITED	OUT-DRIVE	PAS-EARED
RAN-COURS	OUT-DARES	SUN-DIALS	INE-DITED	AIR-DROME	UNF-EARED
SUC-COURS	PIN-DARIS	CAD-DICES	UNE-DITED	PRO-DROME	UNG-EARED
SEL-COUTH	SUN-DARIS	CAU-DICES	COR-DITES	SEA-DROME	UPR-EARED
BED-COVER	TRI-DARNS	SPA-DICES	CRU-DITES	SYN-DROME	BEP-EARLS
DIS-COVER	CAU-DATED	PRE-DICTS	ERU-DITES	EAR-DROPS	IMP-EARLS
GIM-CRACK	GRA-DATED	VER-DICTS	LYD-DITES	GUM-DROPS	LIN-EARLY
JIM-CRACK	MAN-DATED	MIS-DIETS	VER-DITES	SUN-DROPS	UNL-EARNS
AIR-CRAFT	MIS-DATED	MIS-DIGHT	KHE-DIVAS	WAR-DROPS	APP-EASED
PEN-CRAFT	OUT-DATED	COR-DINER	SAN-DIVER	OUT-DROVE	DEC-EASED
SEA-CRAFT	OXI-DATED	GRA-DINES	SKY-DIVER	WIN-DROWS	DIS-EASED
EXE-CRATE	PRE-DATED	NAN-DINES	KHE-DIVES	DOL-DRUMS	REL-EASED
FUL-CRATE	DEO-DATES	NUN-DINES	BUR-DOCKS	EAR-DRUMS	UNL-EASED
BES-CRAWL	EXU-DATES	SAR-DINES	CAN-DOCKS	HUM-DRUMS	APP-EASES
MIS-CREED	GRA-DATES	URE-DINES	DAD-DOCKS	OUT-DRUNK	DEC-EASES
CON-CREWS	MAN-DATES	URI-DINES	HAD-DOCKS	GRA-DUALS	DIS-EASES

MIS-EASES	DEV-ELOPS	NID-ERING	STR-ESSES	CAR-FAXES	BAR-FLIES
REL-EASES	ENV-ELOPS	OCH-ERING	VOW-ESSES	MIS-FEEDS	BOT-FLIES
CIN-EASTS	UNS-ELVES	OFF-ERING	ARR-ESTER	PIG-FEEDS	GAD-FLIES
OUT-EATEN	REM-EMBER	ORD-ERING	ATT-ESTER	MIS-FEIGN	MAY-FLIES
THR-EATEN	DIL-EMMAS	OTT-ERING	BEP-ESTER	MAT-FELON	MED-FLIES
UNB-EATEN	MAR-EMMAS	OXT-ERING	DIG-ESTER	FOR-FENDS	OUT-FLIES
ANT-EATER	ALI-ENATE	PAP-ERING	FOR-ESTER	PIL-FERER	BAF-FLING
REH-EATER	ARS-ENATE	PET-ERING	GAM-ESTER	SUF-FERER	CUF-FLING
REP-EATER	CAT-ENATE	POW-ERING	HON-ESTER	SAL-FERNS	HAL-FLING
SPR-EATHE	SEL-ENATE	QUE-ERING	MIM-ESTER	GAB-FESTS	MAF-FLING
BER-EATHE	SER-ENATE	REV-ERING	MOD-ESTER	TAF-FETAS	MUF-FLING
INW-EAVES	ACC-ENDED	ROG-ERING	MOL-ESTER	BUF-FETED	OUT-FLING
THR-EAVES	APP-ENDED	RUL-ERING	SEM-ESTER	SUF-FETES	PIF-FLING
UNR-EAVES	ASC-ENDED	SAB-ERING	NAM-ETAPE	SUB-FEUED	PUR-FLING
UNW-EAVES	ATT-ENDED	SAL-ERING	QUI-ETENS	AIR-FIELD	RAF-FLING
UPH-EAVES	DEF-ENDED	SEV-ERING	SWE-ETENS	CAN-FIELD	RIF-FLING
UNW-EBBED	DEP-ENDED	SEW-ERING	COM-ETHER	GAS-FIELD	RUF-FLING
BRE-ECHED	EXP-ENDED	SHE-ERING	TOG-ETHER	HAY-FIELD	SIF-FLING
FLE-ECHED	EXT-ENDED	SKE-ERING	UNT-ETHER	ICE-FIELD	STI-FLING
SME-ECHED	FRI-ENDED	SNE-ERING	DIM-ETHYL	MID-FIELD	TRI-FLING
SPE-ECHED	IMP-ENDED	SOB-ERING	TRI-ETHYL	MIS-FIELD	WAF-FLING
WHE-ECHED	INT-ENDED	SPE-ERING	RES-ETTLE	OIL-FIELD	WOL-FLING
BRE-ECHES	OBT-ENDED	SPH-ERING	UNS-ETTLE	OUT-FIELD	GUN-FLINT
DEP-ECHES	OFF-ENDED	STE-ERING	HEB-ETUDE	SUB-FIELD	SUB-FLOOR
FLE-ECHES	UNB-ENDED	TAP-ERING	QUI-ETUDE	URN-FIELD	RYE-FLOUR
SLE-ECHES	UNT-ENDED	TAS-ERING	ANT-EVERT	BEE-FIEST	OUT-FLOWN
SME-ECHES	DIS-ENDOW	TAV-ERING	THI-EVERY	COM-FIEST	AIR-FLOWS
SPE-ECHES	DIS-ENROL	TOW-ERING	BED-EVILS	DAF-FIEST	OUT-FLOWS
MYX-EDEMA	ASS-ENTER	TWE-ERING	REN-EWERS	FUF-FIEST	OUT-FLUSH
ALL-EDGED	CEM-ENTER	ULC-ERING	SCR-EWERS	GOO-FIEST	CON-FOCAL
DIS-EDGED	DEC-ENTER	UMB-ERING	STR-EWERS	GUL-FIEST	EPI-FOCAL
UNH-EDGED	FOM-ENTER	USH-ERING	UNS-EXIST	HUF-FIEST	TRI-FOCAL
ALL-EDGES	IND-ENTER	UTT-ERING	BOG-EYING	LEA-FIEST	AIR-FOILS
DIS-EDGES	REC-ENTER	WAF-ERING	COO-EYING	MIF-FIEST	JET-FOILS
OUT-EDGES	REP-ENTER	WAG-ERING	HON-EYING	NIF-FIEST	MIL-FOILS
BEN-EDICT	RES-ENTER	WAT-ERING	MOS-EYING	POO-FIEST	SEX-FOILS
MAL-EDICT	SCI-ENTER	WAV-ERING	REN-EYING	PUF-FIEST	TIN-FOILS
REA-EDIFY	SIL-ENTER	CAV-ERNED	SAV-EYING	ROO-FIEST	TRE-FOILS
SUB-EDITS	DEM-ENTIA	DEC-ERNED	OUT-FACED	SUR-FIEST	PEN-FOLDS
AQU-EDUCT	MIS-ENTRY	INT-ERNED	PRE-FACED	TOF-FIEST	PIN-FOLDS
ALL-EGERS	CAN-EPHOR	SEC-ERNED	SUR-FACED	TUR-FIEST	KIN-FOLKS
INT-EGERS	SUB-EQUAL	ALT-ERNES	SUR-FACER	WOO-FIEST	MEN-FOLKS
REN-EGERS	YTT-ERBIA	CAS-ERNES	OUT-FACES	DOG-FIGHT	MER-FOLKS
ALL-EGGED	SUB-ERECT	EXT-ERNES	PRE-FACES	GUN-FIGHT	SEA-FOLKS
SQU-EGGED	PAR-ERGON	INT-ERNES	SUR-FACES	OUT-FIGHT	PLA-FONDS
UNB-EGGED	LIM-ERICK	LUC-ERNES	GEO-FACTS	UNI-FILAR	SEA-FOODS
UNP-EGGED	MAV-ERICK	LIT-EROSE	PRE-FADED	MIS-FILED	TOM-FOOLS
SQU-EGGER	ENT-ERICS	SCL-EROSE	PRE-FADES	PRO-FILED	OUT-FOOTS
STR-EIGHT	GEN-ERICS	SUB-EROSE	JEO-FAILS	PRO-FILER	PER-FORCE
STR-EIGNE	ICT-ERICS	TUB-EROSE	FOR-FAIRS	MIS-FILES	REN-FORCE
SHR-EIKED	SPH-ERICS	DEF-ERRED	FUN-FAIRS	PRO-FILES	HAY-FORKS
CHE-EKING	ADH-ERING	DET-ERRED	FUR-FAIRS	FUL-FILLS	CON-FORMS
CLE-EKING	ALT-ERING	INF-ERRED	MIS-FAITH	HAW-FINCH	DIS-FORMS
FOR-EKING	ANG-ERING	INT-ERRED	JAW-FALLS	COF-FINED	MIS-FORMS
GLE-EKING	BOW-ERING	REF-ERRED	MIS-FALLS	CON-FINED	PER-FORMS
GRE-EKING	BRE-ERING	ASP-ERSES	OUT-FALLS	CON-FINER	PRE-FORMS
SLE-EKING	CAP-ERING	DEM-ERSES	PIT-FALLS	CON-FINES	UNI-FORMS
SME-EKING	CAT-ERING	DIV-ERSES	DIS-FAMES	OLE-FINES	COM-FORTS
STE-EKING	CHE-ERING	IMM-ERSES	PRO-FANES	RAT-FINKS	CON-FOUND
THE-EKING	COH-ERING	INV-ERSES	GON-FANON	MIS-FIRED	DUM-FOUND
FOR-ELAND	COP-ERING	OBV-ERSES	FAN-FARED	BON-FIRES	PRO-FOUND
HOM-ELAND	COV-ERING	REV-ERSES	MIS-FARED	GUN-FIRES	PEA-FOWLS
LAK-ELAND	COW-ERING	DEM-ESNES	WAR-FARED	MIS-FIRES	SEA-FOWLS
TID-ELAND	DAK-ERING	ABB-ESSES	WAY-FARED	CON-FIRMS	OUT-FOXED
GAM-ELANS	DOV-ERING	ACC-ESSES	CAR-FARES	SEL-FISTS	CAR-FOXES
REG-ELATE	DOW-ERING	ALT-ESSES	EEL-FARES	CON-FIXED	DOG-FOXES
VEG-ELATE	EFF-ERING	ASS-ESSES	FAN-FARES	PRE-FIXED	OUT-FOXES
STE-ELBOW	ENT-ERING	CAR-ESSES	MIS-FARES	SUF-FIXED	DIF-FRACT
SHI-ELDER	FEV-ERING	CIT-ESSES	WAR-FARES	CON-FIXES	TAF-FRAIL
DES-ELECT	FLE-ERING	DUR-ESSES	WAY-FARES	PRE-FIXES	AIR-FRAME
RES-ELECT	HAV-ERING	EGR-ESSES	WEL-FARES	SUF-FIXES	SUB-FRAME
UNS-ELFED	HOV-ERING	EXC-ESSES	SIT-FASTS	OUT-FLANK	ECO-FREAK
NOS-ELITE	INH-ERING	FIN-ESSES	TUB-FASTS	EAR-FLAPS	CON-FRERE
GAV-ELMEN	LAY-ERING	IDL-ESSES	SUL-FATED	MUD-FLAPS	COF-FRETS
STE-ELMEN	LEG-ERING	IVR-ESSES	SUL-FATES	OUT-FLASH	POM-FRETS
WHE-ELMEN	LEV-ERING	OBS-ESSES	FOR-FAULT	MUD-FLATS	BEL-FRIED
ANT-ELOPE	LOW-ERING	OGR-ESSES	AVI-FAUNA	DIS-FLESH	BEL-FRIES
DEV-ELOPE	MET-ERING	REC-ESSES	EPI-FAUNA	CAL-FLICK	DIS-FROCK
ENV-ELOPE	MIT-ERING		DIS-FAVOR	WAF-FLIER	CON-FRONT

SEA-FRONT	TAN-GENTS	MIS-GIVES	SHA-GREEN	PIN-HEADS	POT-HOLED
SHO-FROTH	SUB-GENUS	OUT-GIVES	CON-GREES	PIT-HEADS	AIR-HOLES
OUT-FROWN	BER-GERES	GAN-GLAND	PUG-GREES	RAG-HEADS	ARM-HOLES
SYN-FUELS	ETA-GERES	OUT-GLARE	CON-GREET	RAW-HEADS	ASS-HOLES
ART-FULLY	GOU-GERES	BUR-GLARY	DIA-GRIDS	RED-HEADS	BOT-HOLES
FIT-FULLY	LAR-GESSE	CUT-GLASS	CHA-GRINS	SAP-HEADS	CAT-HOLES
IRE-FULLY	BAR-GESTS	EYE-GLASS	SUB-GROUP	SUB-HEADS	DOG-HOLES
JOY-FULLY	CON-GESTS	SPY-GLASS	MAN-GROVE	WAR-HEADS	FOX-HOLES
LAW-FULLY	DIS-GESTS	SCA-GLIAS	OUT-GROWN	ALL-HEALS	JAW-HOLES
MAN-FULLY	SUG-GESTS	SUN-GLASS	OUT-GROWS	COW-HEARD	KEY-HOLES
RUE-FULLY	BAR-GHEST	SON-GLIKE	CON-GRUED	MIS-HEARD	LUG-HOLES
SIN-FULLY	LAI-GHEST	CON-GLOBE	CON-GRUES	UPC-HEARD	MAN-HOLES
USE-FULLY	ROU-GHEST	ISO-GLOSS	HAT-GUARD	MIS-HEARS	MUD-HOLES
WIL-FULLY	TEU-GHEST	FOX-GLOVE	MUD-GUARD	ENS-HEATH	PIN-HOLES
WOE-FULLY	TOU-GHEST	AIR-GLOWS	OUT-GUARD	ESC-HEATS	POT-HOLES
PER-FUMED	ZIN-GIBER	SUN-GLOWS	VAN-GUARD	EXC-HEATS	SPY-HOLES
PER-FUMES	WER-GILDS	ANA-GLYPH	COU-GUARS	PRE-HEATS	DIS-HOMED
FUR-FURAL	NAR-GILLY	DIA-GLYPH	MIS-GUIDE	REC-HEATS	FAT-HOMED
FUR-FURAN	BAG-GINGS	TRI-GLYPH	DIS-GUISE	REC-HECKS	DIS-HOMES
FUR-FUROL	BAN-GINGS	SUB-GOALS	LIN-GULAR	UNC-HECKS	SIP-HONED
CON-FUSED	BEG-GINGS	OUT-GOERS	SIN-GULAR	COW-HEELS	SYP-HONED
DIF-FUSED	BUG-GINGS	CAR-GOING	ARU-GULAS	ENW-HEELS	DIP-HONES
PER-FUSED	COG-GINGS	FOR-GOING	LIN-GULAS	DIT-HEIST	DIS-HONOR
SUF-FUSED	DAG-GINGS	MIS-GOING	TRA-GULES	ANT-HELIX	APE-HOODS
CON-FUSES	DIG-GINGS	OUT-GOING	VIR-GULES	ENS-HELLS	BOY-HOODS
DIF-FUSES	DOD-GINGS	TAN-GOING	SEA-GULLS	INS-HELLS	CAT-HOODS
PER-FUSES	DOG-GINGS	MAN-GOLDS	BUR-GUNDY	MOC-HELLS	CUB-HOODS
SUF-FUSES	FAG-GINGS	DOG-GONER	DIS-GUSTS	MUC-HELLS	ELF-HOODS
DIG-GABLE	FOR-GINGS	WAG-GONER	DIS-HABIT	UNS-HELLS	GOD-HOODS
HAN-GABLE	GAN-GINGS	DRA-GOONS	DIS-HABLE	DIS-HELMS	HOG-HOODS
HUG-GABLE	GAU-GINGS	JAR-GOONS	FIS-HABLE	NOW-HENCE	MAN-HOODS
LUG-GABLE	HAN-GINGS	BAR-GOOSE	OAT-HABLE	SIT-HENCE	NUN-HOODS
SIN-GABLE	HED-GINGS	CAR-GOOSE	TIT-HABLE	PRE-HENDS	EYE-HOOKS
BRI-GADES	HOG-GINGS	MON-GOOSE	WAR-HABLE	FOR-HENTS	MUD-HOOKS
FOU-GADES	IMA-GINGS	MUN-GOOSE	WAS-HABLE	PSC-HENTS	POT-HOOKS
RHA-GADES	JIG-GINGS	WAY-GOOSE	UNS-HADED	COW-HERBS	SKY-HOOKS
BAG-GAGES	JOG-GINGS	DIS-GORGE	ENC-HAINS	COW-HERDS	TYP-HOONS
BUR-GAGES	JUG-GINGS	HAN-GOUTS	UNC-HAINS	CIT-HERNS	UNS-HOOTS
FOG-GAGES	LAG-GINGS	DIS-GOWNS	MAC-HAIRS	LUT-HERNS	UPS-HOOTS
LUG-GAGES	LEG-GINGS	BON-GRACE	UNS-HALED	ZIT-HERNS	BIS-HOPED
BAR-GAINS	LIG-GINGS	DIS-GRACE	UNS-HALES	EST-HETES	WAN-HOPES
GRE-GALES	LOD-GINGS	DIS-GRADE	OMP-HALOS	MAC-HETES	ALP-HORNS
CUP-GALLS	LOG-GINGS	PRO-GRADE	ASP-HALTS	ESC-HEWED	ALT-HORNS
GIN-GALLS	LON-GINGS	SUB-GRADE	BES-HAMED	UNC-HEWED	BIG-HORNS
NUT-GALLS	MUG-GINGS	MIS-GRAFF	UNS-HAMED	ESC-HEWER	COE-HORNS
FRU-GALLY	NOG-GINGS	MIS-GRAFT	BES-HAMES	CAT-HEXES	DIS-HORNS
END-GAMES	PEG-GINGS	ZOO-GRAMS	BEC-HANCE	COW-HIDED	FOG-HORNS
APO-GAMIC	PIG-GINGS	ANA-GRAMS	COW-HANDS	COW-HIDES	INK-HORNS
EPI-GAMIC	PUG-GINGS	DIA-GRAMS	BEG-HARDS	RAC-HIDES	LEG-HORNS
EXO-GAMIC	PUR-GINGS	EPI-GRAMS	ORC-HARDS	RAP-HIDES	SAX-HORNS
ISO-GAMIC	RAG-GINGS	GRO-GRAMS	POC-HARDS	RAW-HIDES	TIN-HORNS
PAN-GAMIC	RID-GINGS	ISO-GRAMS	UNS-HARED	BAS-HINGS	BAT-HORSE
SYN-GAMIC	RIG-GINGS	MYO-GRAMS	FUT-HARKS	BUS-HINGS	DIS-HORSE
SIR-GANGS	RIN-GINGS	PAN-GRAMS	BEC-HARMS	DIS-HINGS	PIL-HORSE
BIO-GASES	RUG-GINGS	PRO-GRAMS	ENC-HARMS	ETC-HINGS	SAW-HORSE
SYN-GASES	SAG-GINGS	TAN-GRAMS	UNC-HARMS	FIS-HINGS	SEA-HORSE
FRI-GATES	SIN-GINGS	TRI-GRAMS	REC-HARTS	LAS-HINGS	WAR-HORSE
OUT-GATES	SOG-GINGS	EMI-GRANT	UNC-HASTE	LAT-HINGS	UNC-HOSEN
VIR-GATES	STA-GINGS	FLA-GRANT	NUT-HATCH	MAS-HINGS	BAT-HOSES
VUL-GATES	SUG-GINGS	FRA-GRANT	UNT-HATCH	MES-HINGS	KYP-HOSES
ARM-GAUNT	SUR-GINGS	AIR-GRAPH	LIT-HATES	MIC-HINGS	ORT-HOSES
DIS-GAVEL	TAG-GINGS	APO-GRAPH	REC-HATES	MOS-HINGS	PAT-HOSES
CON-GEALS	TUG-GINGS	BIO-GRAPH	OUT-HAULS	NIT-HINGS	ALT-HOUGH
BAR-GEESE	WED-GINGS	DIA-GRAPH	UNS-HAVEN	NOT-HINGS	ELK-HOUND
CAR-GEESE	WIG-GINGS	EPI-GRAPH	HEE-HAWED	RUC-HINGS	FOX-HOUND
GIN-GELLY	BUS-GIRLS	MYO-GRAPH	UNT-HAWED	TIT-HINGS	SEA-HOUND
PAN-GENES	COW-GIRLS	ODO-GRAPH	DOR-HAWKS	WAS-HINGS	BUG-HOUSE
BIO-GENIC	IMA-GISMS	SYN-GRAPH	GOS-HAWKS	WIS-HINGS	CAT-HOUSE
CON-GENIC	LEG-GISMS	TRI-GRAPH	SEA-HAWKS	OUT-HIRED	COW-HOUSE
DYS-GENIC	ELE-GISTS	COW-GRASS	SAS-HAYED	JAG-HIRES	DIS-HOUSE
ERO-GENIC	ELO-GISTS	EEL-GRASS	AIR-HEADS	OUT-HIRES	GIN-HOUSE
MYO-GENIC	IMA-GISTS	LOP-GRASS	BOW-HEADS	MYT-HISTS	GUN-HOUSE
ORO-GENIC	OLI-GISTS	MAT-GRASS	CAT-HEADS	SOP-HISTS	HOT-HOUSE
PYO-GENIC	TER-GITES	ROT-GRASS	CUP-HEADS	TAC-HISTS	MAD-HOUSE
ZOO-GENIC	ZOR-GITES	EMI-GRATE	EGG-HEADS	ARC-HIVED	NUT-HOUSE
SUB-GENRE	FOR-GIVEN	BUR-GRAVE	GOD-HEADS	ARC-HIVES	OUT-HOUSE
EXI-GENTS	MIS-GIVEN	MAR-GRAVE	HOT-HEADS	BEE-HIVES	POT-HOUSE
MAR-GENTS	OUT-GIVEN	CON-GREED	JUG-HEADS	PAT-HOGEN	UNS-HOUTS
REA-GENTS	FOR-GIVES	SEN-GREEN	MOP-HEADS	TOE-HOLDS	WAS-HOUTS

UPC-HUCKS	END-IRONS	ARC-KINGS	BYR-LAKIN	OVU-LATED	KIL-LICKS
PRE-HUMAN	ENV-IRONS	AWA-KINGS	ENF-LAMED	PRO-LATED	NIB-LICKS
SUB-HUMAN	MID-IRONS	BAC-KINGS	INF-LAMED	REF-LATED	ROL-LICKS
SUB-HUMID	SAD-IRONS	BAL-KINGS	UNB-LAMED	SUB-LATED	APP-LIERS
BET-HUMPS	ARR-ISHES	BAN-KINGS	INF-LAMER	ULU-LATED	ATE-LIERS
MAN-HUNTS	BAN-ISHES	BOO-KINGS	ENF-LAMES	UNE-LATED	COL-LIERS
YOG-HURTS	EAD-ISHES	BRO-KINGS	INF-LAMES	VIO-LATED	DAL-LIERS
MET-HYLIC	EDD-ISHES	BUC-KINGS	REC-LAMES	DEF-LATER	DOL-LIERS
BOT-HYMEN	FAM-ISHES	BUS-KINGS	SUN-LAMPS	IDO-LATER	HAU-LIERS
OMO-HYOID	FET-ISHES	DEC-KINGS	FOR-LANAS	VIO-LATER	HEL-LIERS
ENT-ICERS	FIN-ISHES	DOC-KINGS	FUR-LANAS	ZOO-LATER	OUT-LIERS
OFF-ICERS	GAR-ISHES	DUC-KINGS	PAR-LANCE	APP-LAUDS	RAL-LIERS
SPL-ICERS	LAV-ISHES	FUC-KINGS	BAD-LANDS	BAC-LAVAS	REP-LIERS
ENR-ICHED	LIN-ISHES	HAC-KINGS	BOG-LANDS	BAK-LAVAS	TAB-LIERS
AFF-ICHES	MAR-ISHES	HAW-KINGS	COT-LANDS	BES-LAVED	TAL-LIERS
BAB-ICHES	MIN-ISHES	HUS-KINGS	ELF-LANDS	ENC-LAVED	PUR-LIEUS
CAL-ICHES	NEB-ISHES	JER-KINGS	FEN-LANDS	ENS-LAVED	AIR-LIFTS
CEV-ICHES	PAP-ISHES	KIR-KINGS	GAR-LANDS	BES-LAVER	HOO-LIGAN
ENR-ICHES	PAR-ISHES	LEK-KINGS	GOL-LANDS	ENS-LAVER	MUL-LIGAN
FET-ICHES	PER-ISHES	LIC-KINGS	GOW-LANDS	BES-LAVES	DAY-LIGHT
MOR-ICHES	POL-ISHES	LUR-KINGS	HOL-LANDS	ENC-LAVES	FAN-LIGHT
POT-ICHES	PUN-ISHES	MAR-KINGS	LAW-LANDS	ENS-LAVES	GAS-LIGHT
STR-ICHES	RAD-ISHES	MIL-KINGS	LOW-LANDS	EXC-LAVES	LOW-LIGHT
SLU-ICIER	RAV-ISHES	MOC-KINGS	MID-LANDS	OUT-LAWED	MIS-LIGHT
ENT-ICING	REL-ISHES	NEC-KINGS	NOR-LANDS	UNF-LAWED	PEN-LIGHT
MAL-ICING	SQU-ISHES	PAC-KINGS	OUT-LANDS	SMI-LAXES	SKY-LIGHT
NOT-ICING	UNW-ISHES	PAR-KINGS	WET-LANDS	GUN-LAYER	SUN-LIGHT
POL-ICING	VAN-ISHES	PEC-KINGS	BIP-LANES	WAY-LAYER	TWI-LIGHT
PUM-ICING	WHA-ISLED	PIC-KINGS	DEP-LANES	EMB-LAZED	DIS-LIKED
SLU-ICING	WHA-ISLES	PIN-KINGS	EMP-LANES	UNG-LAZED	MIS-LIKED
SPL-ICING	THR-ISTLE	QUA-KINGS	ENP-LANES	EMB-LAZES	DIS-LIKEN
MIM-ICKER	OMN-IVORY	RAC-KINGS	BAL-LANTS	EMP-LEACH	MIS-LIKER
MON-ICKER	UNV-IZARD	RAN-KINGS	CAL-LANTS	IMP-LEACH	DIS-LIKES
MUS-ICKER	CAR-JACKS	ROC-KINGS	COO-LANTS	IMP-LEADS	MIS-LIKES
UNS-ICKER	MAN-JACKS	SAC-KINGS	EXP-LANTS	MIS-LEADS	SPI-LIKIN
VRA-ICKER	SKY-JACKS	SAR-KINGS	GAL-LANTS	DIS-LEAFS	DIS-LIMBS
HEL-ICONS	GOU-JEERS	SHA-KINGS	IMP-LANTS	OUT-LEAPS	REC-LIMBS
LEX-ICONS	OUT-JESTS	SIN-KINGS	REP-LANTS	OUT-LEAPT	UPC-LIMBS
LYR-ICONS	CON-JOINS	SMO-KINGS	SEA-LANTS	OUT-LEARN	SUB-LIMED
RUB-ICONS	DIS-JOINS	SOA-KINGS	ZEA-LANTS	NUC-LEASE	MIL-LIMES
SER-ICONS	MIS-JOINS	SUC-KINGS	COL-LAPSE	SUB-LEASE	SUB-LIMES
SIL-ICONS	SUB-JOINS	TAC-KINGS	PRO-LAPSE	DIS-LEAVE	DIS-LIMNS
DIV-IDANT	CON-JOINT	TAL-KINGS	PHY-LARCH	WAY-LEAVE	UNB-LINDS
SUB-IMAGO	DIS-JOINT	TAN-KINGS	BOL-LARDS	IMP-LEDGE	DEC-LINED
SCR-IMPED	BAN-JOIST	TAS-KINGS	COL-LARDS	COL-LEGER	INC-LINED
SHR-IMPED	FRI-JOLES	TIC-KINGS	DUL-LARDS	COL-LEGES	MUS-LINED
SKR-IMPED	MAR-JORAM	TUS-KINGS	FOU-LARDS	FUG-LEMAN	OUT-LINED
SCR-IMPLY	POP-JOYED	WAL-KINGS	MAL-LARDS	NOB-LEMAN	REC-LINED
IMM-INGLE	FOR-JUDGE	WIN-KINGS	POL-LARDS	RIF-LEMAN	TOP-LINED
SPR-INGLE	MIS-JUDGE	WOR-KINGS	POU-LARDS	WHA-LEMAN	AIR-LINER
DOM-INION	PRE-JUDGE	CHE-KISTS	TAI-LARDS	EMB-LEMED	EYE-LINER
ENL-INKED	CON-JUGAL	PEN-KNIFE	DEC-LARES	ANA-LEMMA	JET-LINER
UNL-INKED	LOG-JUICE	BOW-KNOTS	MUD-LARKS	TRI-LEMMA	MIL-LINER
UNP-INKED	VER-JUICE	TOP-KNOTS	SKY-LARKS	FOR-LENDS	REC-LINER
SHR-INKER	OUT-JUMPS	MIS-KNOWN	TIT-LARKS	AMY-LENES	TOP-LINER
SPR-INKLE	CON-JUROR	MIS-KNOWS	MUL-LARKY	ANT-LERED	AIR-LINES
STR-INKLE	NON-JUROR	SAK-KOSES	AMY-LASES	ASH-LERED	ANI-LINES
CHA-INLET	COC-KADES	SHA-KUDOS	DOW-LASES	BUL-LERED	BEE-LINES
BEF-INNED	SEA-KALES	GAL-LABIA	EUC-LASES	BUT-LERED	BER-LINES
UNP-INNED	SER-KALIS	EMP-LACED	INU-LASES	GOL-LERED	BOW-LINES
UNT-INNED	CHI-KARAS	REP-LACED	KIL-LASES	HOL-LERED	CAR-LINES
BEG-INNER	FLO-KATIS	UNP-LACED	ARB-LASTS	TEL-LERED	CHO-LINES
ANO-INTER	BUC-KEENS	ANE-LACES	BAL-LASTS	TIL-LERED	CUT-LINES
DIS-INTER	JAC-KEENS	BUL-LACES	OUT-LASTS	FOR-LESES	DEC-LINES
QUA-INTER	NAN-KEENS	BYP-LACES	POT-LATCH	BUP-LEVER	DYE-LINES
SPL-INTER	COC-KEYED	EMP-LACES	ADU-LATED	REP-LEVIN	HOT-LINES
SPR-INTER	JOC-KEYED	REP-LACES	AFF-LATED	DEF-LEXES	HYA-LINES
SQU-INTER	LAC-KEYED	UNP-LACES	BAL-LATED	DUP-LEXES	INC-LINES
RET-INULA	MIC-KEYED	PEL-LACKS	CHE-LATED	IMP-LEXES	ISO-LINES
VAG-INULA	MIS-KEYED	POL-LACKS	COL-LATED	REF-LEXES	KAO-LINES
DIS-INURE	MON-KEYED	BAL-LADED	DEF-LATED	KAO-LIANG	KEY-LINES
PER-IODIC	BAR-KHANS	BAL-LADES	EMU-LATED	BIL-LIARD	LOG-LINES
NEP-IONIC	SAB-KHATS	PHO-LADES	EPI-LATED	GAL-LIARD	MAR-LINES
TAL-IONIC	CHI-KHORS	ROU-LADES	FEL-LATED	HAL-LIARD	OPA-LINES
ASP-IRATE	MAR-KHORS	SCA-LADES	IMP-LATED	MIL-LIARD	OUT-LINES
LEV-IRATE	ROC-KIERS	PIL-LAGER	INF-LATED	PAL-LIARD	PRA-LINES
VIZ-IRATE	DES-KILLS	SCH-LAGER	ISO-LATED	EXP-LICIT	PRO-LINES
EPE-IRIDS	RES-KILLS	VIL-LAGER	IMP-LICIT	IMP-LICIT	PUR-LINES
AND-IRONS	MAN-KINDS	UNS-LAKED	OCU-LATED	COW-LICKS	RAT-LINES

REC-LINES	RIF-LINGS	URO-LITHS	MYE-LOMAS	BEF-LOWER	SEA-MAIDS
SEA-LINES	RIG-LINGS	ZOO-LITHS	SLA-LOMED	BEL-LOWER	AIR-MAILS
SET-LINES	ROL-LINGS	MIS-LIVED	CAU-LOMES	CAL-LOWER	GER-MAINS
SKY-LINES	SAI-LINGS	OUT-LIVED	COE-LOMES	DEF-LOWER	BED-MAKER
TOP-LINES	SAP-LINGS	MIS-LIVES	EMP-LONGE	ENF-LOWER	FLY-MAKER
TOW-LINES	SCA-LINGS	OUT-LIVES	PRO-LONGE	FAL-LOWER	GUN-MAKER
AIS-LINGS	SEA-LINGS	CAR-LOADS	ANK-LONGS	FOL-LOWER	HAY-MAKER
AMB-LINGS	SEE-LINGS	DIS-LOADS	FUR-LONGS	HOL-LOWER	TOP-MAKER
ANG-LINGS	SIB-LINGS	OFF-LOADS	PRO-LONGS	MEL-LOWER	MIS-MAKES
BAL-LINGS	SMI-LINGS	UNI-LOBAR	HAL-LOOED	REF-LOWER	ANI-MALIC
BAW-LINGS	SOI-LINGS	ENG-LOBED	WIT-LOOFS	SAL-LOWER	SIA-MANGS
BIL-LINGS	SPI-LINGS	ING-LOBED	OUT-LOOKS	WAL-LOWER	EGO-MANIA
BIR-LINGS	SWA-LINGS	TRI-LOBED	BEG-LOOMS	YEL-LOWER	SHA-MANIC
BOI-LINGS	TAB-LINGS	UNI-LOBED	EMB-LOOMS	FEL-LOWLY	SEA-MANLY
BOW-LINGS	TAI-LINGS	EAR-LOBES	ENG-LOOMS	HOL-LOWLY	YEO-MANLY
BUL-LINGS	TAN-LINGS	ENG-LOBES	REB-LOOMS	MEL-LOWLY	OUT-MARCH
CAB-LINGS	TEL-LINGS	ING-LOBES	BAL-LOONS	DIS-LOYAL	DAY-MARKS
CAL-LINGS	TIL-LINGS	TRI-LOBES	GAL-LOONS	HAL-LUCES	EAR-MARKS
CAR-LINGS	TIT-LINGS	RAP-LOCHS	GAL-LOPED	PEL-LUCID	SEA-MARKS
CAT-LINGS	TOI-LINGS	YEL-LOCHS	GOL-LOPED	MIS-LUCKS	WAY-MARKS
CEI-LINGS	TOL-LINGS	AIR-LOCKS	LOL-LOPED	CIS-LUNAR	MIS-MARRY
CIE-LINGS	TOO-LINGS	ARM-LOCKS	WAL-LOPED	SUB-LUNAR	FOU-MARTS
COD-LINGS	UNS-LINGS	BAL-LOCKS	GAL-LOPER	CAL-LUNAS	DIS-MASKS
COL-LINGS	VEI-LINGS	BOL-LOCKS	WAL-LOPER	IMP-LUNGE	DIS-MASTS
COW-LINGS	WAI-LINGS	BUL-LOCKS	CYC-LOPES	ANK-LUNGS	DUR-MASTS
CUL-LINGS	WAL-LINGS	CAR-LOCKS	WAR-LORDS	FAI-LURES	TOP-MASTS
CUR-LINGS	WAR-LINGS	DAG-LOCKS	DEP-LORES	SOI-LURES	ABO-MASUS
CYC-LINGS	WAU-LINGS	EAR-LOCKS	EXP-LORES	MOL-LUSKS	MIS-MATCH
DAR-LINGS	WAW-LINGS	ELF-LOCKS	FAH-LORES	EVO-LUTED	OUT-MATCH
DEA-LINGS	WEL-LINGS	FET-LOCKS	IMP-LORES	POL-LUTED	ANI-MATED
DEV-LINGS	WHA-LINGS	GEN-LOCKS	ENC-LOSED	POL-LUTER	CLI-MATED
DIL-LINGS	WIT-LINGS	GUN-LOCKS	INC-LOSED	EVO-LUTES	CRE-MATED
EAN-LINGS	YEL-LINGS	HEM-LOCKS	REC-LOSED	POL-LUTES	FOR-MATED
FAB-LINGS	YOW-LINGS	HIL-LOCKS	UNC-LOSED	AFF-LUXES	GEM-MATED
FAI-LINGS	DIS-LINKS	HOO-LOCKS	UPC-LOSED	EFF-LUXES	MIS-MATED
FAL-LINGS	BIR-LINNS	KIL-LOCKS	ENC-LOSER	INF-LUXES	PAL-MATED
FAT-LINGS	ANT-LIONS	LAY-LOCKS	INC-LOSER	REF-LUXES	SIG-MATED
FEE-LINGS	BIL-LIONS	MUL-LOCKS	CEL-LOSES	WIL-LYART	SUM-MATED
FIL-LINGS	BUL-LIONS	PAD-LOCKS	CYC-LOSES	APP-LYING	ANI-MATER
FOI-LINGS	CUL-LIONS	PEL-LOCKS	ENC-LOSES	BEL-LYING	ANI-MATES
FOO-LINGS	GIL-LIONS	PIL-LOCKS	INC-LOSES	BUL-LYING	BRO-MATES
FOP-LINGS	HAL-LIONS	POL-LOCKS	KYL-LOSES	COL-LYING	CLI-MATES
FOW-LINGS	HEL-LIONS	PUT-LOCKS	PEP-LOSES	CUL-LYING	CRE-MATES
GAD-LINGS	JIL-LIONS	ROL-LOCKS	PSI-LOSES	DAL-LYING	FOR-MATES
GOD-LINGS	MIL-LIONS	ROW-LOCKS	PTI-LOSES	DOL-LYING	GEM-MATES
GOS-LINGS	MUL-LIONS	RUL-LOCKS	REC-LOSES	DUP-LYING	IMA-MATES
HAL-LINGS	PIL-LIONS	SCH-LOCKS	THY-LOSES	FER-LYING	MIS-MATES
HAR-LINGS	RUL-LIONS	SIL-LOCKS	UNC-LOSES	FOL-LYING	PRI-MATES
HEA-LINGS	ZIL-LIONS	UNB-LOCKS	UPC-LOSES	GAL-LYING	SIG-MATES
HEE-LINGS	OBE-LISKS	WAR-LOCKS	EPU-LOTIC	GIL-LYING	SUM-MATES
HER-LINGS	ODA-LISKS	WED-LOCKS	PSI-LOTIC	GUL-LYING	HAE-MATIN
HID-LINGS	ANG-LISTS	EXP-LODES	FUR-LOUGH	IMP-LYING	CLI-MAXES
HIR-LINGS	BIB-LISTS	IMP-LODES	TUR-LOUGH	JEE-LYING	DIS-MAYED
HOW-LINGS	CEL-LISTS	DIS-LODGE	PAR-LOURS	JEL-LYING	UNA-MAZED
HUR-LINGS	CYC-LISTS	HAY-LOFTS	JEA-LOUSE	JOL-LYING	MIZ-MAZES
INK-LINGS	DIA-LISTS	TOP-LOFTY	GEA-LOUSY	OUT-LYING	NUT-MEALS
KEE-LINGS	DUA-LISTS	APO-LOGIA	JEA-LOUSY	RAL-LYING	OAT-MEALS
KID-LINGS	IDO-LISTS	ANA-LOGIC	FAL-LOUTS	REP-LYING	PER-MEASE
KIL-LINGS	OCU-LISTS	DIA-LOGIC	ROL-LOUTS	SAL-LYING	PIG-MEATS
KIT-LINGS	REA-LISTS	ECO-LOGIC	UNG-LOVED	SUL-LYING	PRE-MEDIC
LAL-LINGS	STY-LISTS	EPI-LOGIC	PUL-LOVER	TAL-LYING	DYS-MELIC
MAD-LINGS	UNA-LISTS	GEO-LOGIC	UNG-LOVES	WIL-LYING	VER-MELLS
MAI-LINGS	VIO-LISTS	NEO-LOGIC	BEL-LOWED	ANA-LYSED	TAG-MEMES
MAR-LINGS	WHO-LISTS	URO-LOGIC	BIL-LOWED	DIA-LYSED	COM-MENDS
MER-LINGS	HOP-LITES	KIL-LOGIE	FAL-LOWED	ANA-LYSES	REA-MENDS
MIL-LINGS	HYA-LITES	ANA-LOGON	FOL-LOWED	BIO-LYSES	STA-MENED
MOR-LINGS	MEL-LITES	AMY-LOIDS	GAL-LOWED	DIA-LYSES	SAR-MENTA
MOS-LINGS	PER-LITES	CHE-LOIDS	HAL-LOWED	ANA-LYSIS	SUB-MENTA
NAI-LINGS	SPI-LITES	COL-LOIDS	HOL-LOWED	BIO-LYSIS	TEG-MENTA
NUL-LINGS	STY-LITES	CYC-LOIDS	MEL-LOMED	DIA-LYSIS	TOR-MENTA
OAK-LINGS	THU-LITES	STY-LOIDS	PIL-LOWED	ACO-LYTES	GRA-MERCY
PEE-LINGS	TIL-LITES	TAB-LOIDS	REF-LOWED	GRI-MACED	HAM-MERED
PIG-LINGS	URA-LITES	PUR-LOINS	SAL-LOWED	GRI-MACES	MAM-MERED
PIL-LINGS	ZEO-LITES	SIR-LOINS	TAL-LOWED	CRO-MACKS	SIM-MERED
POL-LINGS	ZOO-LITES	SUR-LOINS	UNB-LOWED	PLU-MAGES	SUM-MERED
PUR-LINGS	NEO-LITHS	COU-LOIRS	UPF-LOWED	PRI-MAGES	YAM-MERED
RAI-LINGS	OTO-LITHS	RAC-LOIRS	WAL-LOWED	RUM-MAGES	DUM-MERER
RAT-LINGS	TAL-LITHS	LOB-LOLLY	WIL-LOWED	BAR-MAIDS	HAM-MERER
REE-LINGS	TRI-LITHS	DIP-LOMAS	YEL-LOWED	MER-MAIDS	CHI-MERES

COM-MERES	DER-MISES	VER-MOUTH	URA-NIDES	CAR-NYING	DEM-OLOGY
ISO-MERES	EXO-MISES	COM-MOVED	ALL-NIGHT	HIN-NYING	DOS-OLOGY
URO-MERES	ITE-MISES	OUT-MOVED	MID-NIGHT	NAN-NYING	DOX-OLOGY
COM-MERGE	KER-MISES	PRE-MOVED	OUT-NIGHT	PHO-NYING	ETH-OLOGY
SUB-MERGE	PRE-MISES	COM-MOVES	SEN-NIGHT	STO-NYING	ETI-OLOGY
SUB-MERSE	PRO-MISES	OUT-MOVES	UNK-NIGHT	UPR-OARED	GEM-OLOGY
COS-MESES	SUR-MISES	PRE-MOVES	ADE-NINES	ACC-OASTS	HOM-OLOGY
SIA-MESES	CHA-MISOS	SCH-MUCKS	ALA-NINES	DIS-OBEYS	HOR-OLOGY
GUN-METAL	ANI-MISTS	EAR-MUFFS	CYA-NINES	KIL-OBITS	IDE-OLOGY
PRO-METAL	ATO-MISTS	GEM-MULES	GUA-NINES	BAS-OCHES	KID-OLOGY
HEL-METED	CHE-MISTS	PLU-MULES	PEN-NINES	BRI-OCHES	MEN-OLOGY
DIA-METER	COS-MISTS	MUL-MULLS	QUI-NINES	BRO-OCHES	MIS-OLOGY
GEO-METER	GNO-MISTS	MUR-MURED	ACO-NITES	CAR-OCHES	MON-OLOGY
LUX-METER	PAL-MISTS	UNA-MUSED	ALU-NITES	GAL-OCHES	MYC-OLOGY
ODO-METER	PLU-MISTS	ANI-MUSES	AXI-NITES	KLO-OCHES	NOM-OLOGY
OHM-METER	RHY-MISTS	COR-MUSES	BAI-NITES	SMO-OCHES	NOS-OLOGY
OXI-METER	SUM-MISTS	HOU-MUSES	BOR-NITES	SOR-OCHES	OEC-OLOGY
TRI-METER	AZY-MITES	HUM-MUSES	CRI-NITES	SYN-ODALS	OEN-OLOGY
UDO-METER	ERE-MITES	LAC-MUSES	CYA-NITES	MEL-ODEON	ONC-OLOGY
VIA-METER	GUM-MITES	LIT-MUSES	DUN-NITES	MEL-ODIST	ONT-OLOGY
COS-METIC	MAR-MITES	PRI-MUSES	EBO-NITES	MON-ODIST	OPT-OLOGY
HER-METIC	TER-MITES	SHA-MUSES	ERI-NITES	PAR-ODIST	ORE-OLOGY
MIS-METRE	COM-MIXED	WAM-MUSES	FAI-NITES	ALL-ODIUM	OUR-OLOGY
SIA-MEZES	PRE-MIXED	BES-MUTCH	GAH-NITES	MAL-ODOUR	PED-OLOGY
GIM-MICKS	APO-MIXES	COM-MUTED	GRA-NITES	DYS-ODYLE	PEL-OLOGY
MIM-MICKS	COM-MIXES	PER-MUTED	ICH-NITES	CAC-ODYLS	PEN-OLOGY
GIM-MICKY	PRE-MIXES	COM-MUTER	KAI-NITES	KAK-ODYLS	POD-OLOGY
SAW-MILLS	BUM-MOCKS	PER-MUTES	KER-NITES	SHR-OFFED	POM-OLOGY
ALU-MINAS	GAM-MOCKS	GEO-MYOID	KYA-NITES	TOB-OGGIN	POS-OLOGY
STA-MINAS	HAM-MOCKS	COR-NACRE	LIG-NITES	SHO-OGLED	RHE-OLOGY
EXA-MINED	HOM-MOCKS	HOB-NAILS	MAN-NITES	SHO-OGLES	SER-OLOGY
FUL-MINED	HUM-MOCKS	TOE-NAILS	PYC-NITES	ASS-OILED	SEX-OLOGY
VER-MINED	MAM-MOCKS	TRE-NAILS	REU-NITES	BEM-OILED	SIT-OLOGY
EXA-MINER	MUM-MOCKS	MIS-NAMED	SYE-NITES	BET-OILED	THE-OLOGY
TER-MINER	SCH-MOCKS	OUT-NAMED	URA-NITES	EMB-OILED	TOC-OLOGY
BRO-MINES	ALA-MODES	SIR-NAMED	ZOO-NITES	ENT-OILED	TOK-OLOGY
CAR-MINES	COM-MODES	SUR-NAMED	CAR-NIVAL	REB-OILED	TOP-OLOGY
DES-MINES	OUT-MODES	MIS-NAMES	CHE-NIXES	REC-OILED	TYP-OLOGY
EXA-MINES	TUR-MOILS	OUT-NAMES	HOB-NOBBY	UNC-OILED	VIN-OLOGY
FLA-MINES	GRI-MOIRE	SIR-NAMES	BAN-NOCKS	UNS-OILED	VIR-OLOGY
FUL-MINES	WAG-MOIRE	SUR-NAMES	DUN-NOCKS	UPB-OILED	XYL-OLOGY
HAR-MINES	PRE-MOLAR	ORD-NANCE	FIN-NOCKS	UPC-OILED	ZYM-OLOGY
JAS-MINES	WAD-MOLLS	PER-NANCY	JAN-NOCKS	REC-OILER	STR-OMBUS
PRI-MINES	HOR-MONAL	LAG-NAPPE	MIN-NOCKS	ABJ-OINTS	THR-OMBUS
THY-MINES	CRE-MONAS	GUR-NARDS	PIN-NOCKS	ADJ-OINTS	ABD-OMENS
BEA-MINGS	COM-MONER	REY-NARDS	WIN-NOCKS	APP-OINTS	AGN-OMENS
BOO-MINGS	GAM-MONER	ENS-NARES	DIA-NODAL	INJ-OINTS	BLO-OMERS
BRI-MINGS	SER-MONER	INS-NARES	SPI-NODES	REP-OINTS	INC-OMERS
COA-MINGS	SUM-MONER	PRE-NASAL	ADE-NOMAS	UNJ-OINTS	ION-OMERS
FAR-MINGS	COM-MONEY	EPI-NASTY	COG-NOMEN	BEH-OLDEN	MON-OMERS
FOA-MINGS	OKI-MONOS	NEO-NATAL	BIO-NOMIC	EMB-OLDEN	ALM-ONERS
FOR-MINGS	BAL-MORAL	PRE-NATAL	ECO-NOMIC	BEH-OLDER	BAC-ONERS
FRA-MINGS	CRE-MORNE	COG-NATES	ISO-NOMIC	EMP-OLDER	BYW-ONERS
GUM-MINGS	CRO-MORNE	CYA-NATES	ZOO-NOMIC	IMP-OLDER	COR-ONERS
HUM-MINGS	OXY-MORON	EMA-NATES	HYP-NONES	INH-OLDER	CRO-ONERS
LAM-MINGS	BIO-MORPH	KHA-NATES	QUI-NONES	UNF-OLDER	INT-ONERS
LEM-MINGS	ISO-MORPH	MAG-NATES	CHI-NOOKS	UNS-OLDER	TEN-ONERS
MAI-MINGS	ZOO-MORPH	NEO-NATES	SCH-NOOKS	UPH-OLDER	WAG-ONERS
MUM-MINGS	PRE-MORSE	PHE-NATES	MID-NOONS	ACR-OLEIN	INH-OOPED
PRI-MINGS	COS-MOSES	PHO-NATES	SIG-NORIA	IND-OLENT	SCR-OOPED
RIM-MINGS	GUM-MOSES	PRO-NATES	CYA-NOSED	INS-OLENT	UNH-OOPED
ROA-MINGS	KOS-MOSES	RUI-NATES	STE-NOSED	RED-OLENT	CAB-OOSES
ROU-MINGS	MAR-MOSES	TAN-NATES	CYA-NOSES	VIN-OLENT	PAP-OOSES
SEE-MINGS	PHI-MOSES	URI-NATES	HYP-NOSES	LIN-OLEUM	SHM-OOSES
SOU-MINGS	HAR-MOSTS	BEK-NAVES	LIG-NOSES	ROS-OLIOS	UNL-OOSES
SUM-MINGS	MID-MOSTS	RED-NECKS	MAN-NOSES	COR-OLLAS	VAM-OOSES
TEA-MINGS	PRO-MOTED	UNS-NECKS	PYC-NOSES	AER-OLOGY	SHM-OOZED
WAR-MINGS	COM-MOTES	WRY-NECKS	STE-NOSES	AGR-OLOGY	SHM-OOZES
TRO-MINOS	PRO-MOTES	KER-NELLY	ZOO-NOSES	ALG-OLOGY	ATR-OPINE
CAT-MINTS	MAM-MOTHS	DIS-NESTS	PRO-NOTAL	ARC-OLOGY	BLO-OPING
VAR-MINTS	PRO-MOTOR	EAR-NESTS	CON-NOTED	ATM-OLOGY	DEL-OPING
TER-MINUS	DIS-MOUNT	COR-NETTS	KEY-NOTED	AUT-OLOGY	DRO-OPING
PIS-MIRES	SEA-MOUNT	WHE-NEVER	CON-NOTES	AXI-OLOGY	GAL-OPING
ATO-MISER	SUR-MOUNT	COR-NICHE	KEY-NOTES	BAT-OLOGY	GLO-OPING
PRO-MISER	DOR-MOUSE	DOR-NICKS	PRO-NOTUM	BRY-OLOGY	SCO-OPING
SUR-MISER	TIT-MOUSE	MIN-NICKS	PRO-NOUNS	CAC-OLOGY	SNO-OPING
ATO-MISES	BAD-MOUTH	PAN-NICKS	WIN-NOWED	CET-OLOGY	STO-OPING
CHA-MISES	BIG-MOUTH	CYA-NIDES	MAG-NOXES	CHA-OLOGY	SWO-OPING
CHE-MISES	DRY-MOUTH		TAN-NOYED	CYT-OLOGY	TRO-OPING

UNC-OPING	KOT-OWING	SUP-PAWNS	FOR-PINES	TIN-PLATE	TEM-PORAL
UNP-OPING	MIA-OWING	DIS-PEACE	PRO-PINES	VAM-PLATE	OOS-PORES
UNR-OPING	SHR-OWING	BES-PEAKS	BUM-PINGS	DIS-PLAYS	AIR-PORTS
WHO-OPING	STR-OWING	RES-PEAKS	CAP-PINGS	GUN-PLAYS	BES-PORTS
EUR-OPIUM	THR-OWING	UNS-PEAKS	CAR-PINGS	MIS-PLAYS	CAR-PORTS
AUT-OPTIC	WID-OWING	UPS-PEAKS	COM-PINGS	OUT-PLAYS	COM-PORTS
ENT-OPTIC	BEH-OWLED	COM-PEARS	CUP-PINGS	MIS-PLEAD	DIS-PORTS
HOL-OPTIC	SCR-OWLED	UPS-PEARS	DAM-PINGS	COM-PLEAT	GUN-PORTS
PAN-OPTIC	UNC-OWLED	HEN-PECKS	DIP-PINGS	COM-PLIED	OUT-PORTS
SYN-OPTIC	DIS-OWNED	RYE-PECKS	DOP-PINGS	SUP-PLIED	PUR-PORTS
CAP-ORALS	REN-OWNED	TRI-PEDAL	GAS-PINGS	TRI-PLIED	RAP-PORTS
CHL-ORALS	UNG-OWNED	OUT-PEEPS	HAR-PINGS	COM-PLIER	SEA-PORTS
COL-ORANT	DIS-OWNER	COM-PEERS	HEL-PINGS	DIM-PLIER	SUP-PORTS
IGN-ORANT	REN-OWNER	OUT-PEERS	HIP-PINGS	PIM-PLIER	COM-POSED
ROB-ORANT	UPT-OWNER	RES-PELLS	HOP-PINGS	POP-PLIER	DIS-POSED
SON-ORANT	MON-OXIDE	UNS-PELLS	KEE-PINGS	PUR-PLIER	PRE-POSED
CHL-ORATE	PER-OXIDE	DIS-PENCE	KEM-PINGS	RIP-PLIER	PRO-POSED
DEC-ORATE	SUB-OXIDE	FIP-PENCE	LAM-PINGS	SUP-PLIER	PUR-POSED
PEJ-ORATE	TRI-OXIDE	SIX-PENCE	LAP-PINGS	COM-PLIES	SUP-POSED
PER-ORATE	ANN-OYERS	SUS-PENCE	LIM-PINGS	SUP-PLIES	COM-POSER
PRI-ORATE	CAL-OYERS	TEN-PENCE	LIS-PINGS	TRI-PLIES	DIS-POSER
SOR-ORATE	ENJ-OYERS	TUP-PENCE	LOO-PINGS	CAM-PLING	PRO-POSER
ABS-ORBED	DIS-PACED	TWO-PENCE	LOP-PINGS	COU-PLING	SUP-POSER
ADS-ORBED	OUT-PACED	COM-PENDS	MAP-PINGS	DAP-PLING	COM-POSES
DES-ORBED	DIS-PACES	DIS-PENDS	RAM-PINGS	DIM-PLING	DIS-POSES
DIS-ORBED	OUT-PACES	PAR-PENDS	RAP-PINGS	DIS-PLING	PRE-POSES
RES-ORBED	CAL-PACKS	PER-PENDS	RAS-PINGS	DUM-PLING	PRO-POSES
RES-ORCIN	ICE-PACKS	PRO-PENDS	REP-PINGS	HIR-PLING	PUR-POSES
ACC-ORDER	MAN-PACKS	STI-PENDS	RIS-PINGS	HOP-PLING	SUP-POSES
DIS-ORDER	MUD-PACKS	SUS-PENDS	SHA-PINGS	NIP-PLING	TRI-POSES
EMB-ORDER	RAT-PACKS	DAM-PENED	SNI-PINGS	PEO-PLING	OVI-POSIT
IMB-ORDER	COM-PACTS	DEE-PENED	SOO-PINGS	POP-PLING	BED-POSTS
MIS-ORDER	COM-PADRE	HAP-PENED	SOP-PINGS	PUR-PLING	COM-POSTS
PRE-ORDER	NEO-PAGAN	LIP-PENED	STO-PINGS	RIP-PLING	DIS-POSTS
REC-ORDER	PRO-PAGED	REO-PENED	TAM-PINGS	RUM-PLING	OUT-POSTS
SUB-ORDER	RAM-PAGED	UNO-PENED	TAP-PINGS	SAM-PLING	WAY-POSTS
DEF-ORMER	COM-PAGES	PRO-PENES	TIP-PINGS	SAP-PLING	COM-POTES
INF-ORMER	KIP-PAGES	TER-PENES	TOP-PINGS	SIM-PLING	COM-POUND
REF-ORMER	PRO-PAGES	SIX-PENNY	VAM-PINGS	SIP-PLING	LIS-POUND
NOT-ORNIS	RAM-PAGES	TEN-PENNY	WAR-PINGS	SOU-PLING	PRO-POUND
CHO-OSIER	SEE-PAGES	TUP-PENNY	WEE-PINGS	STA-PLING	OUT-POURS
SMO-OTHER	DES-PAIRS	TWO-PENNY	YEL-PINGS	SUP-PLING	BES-POUTS
GAR-OTTER	PRO-PALED	PAR-PENTS	CAM-PIONS	TIP-PLING	DRO-POUTS
ARN-OTTOS	PRO-PALES	PER-PENTS	LAM-PIONS	TOP-PLING	EEL-POUTS
RID-OTTOS	OPO-PANAX	SER-PENTS	POM-PIONS	TRI-PLING	MAN-POWER
RIS-OTTOS	CRE-PANCE	COM-PERES	PUM-PIONS	WIM-PLING	OUT-POWER
BES-OUGHT	COM-PANDS	LAM-PERNS	RAM-PIONS	COM-PLOTS	COW-POXES
UNB-OUGHT	PAR-PANES	DIS-PERSE	TAM-PIONS	MAR-PLOTS	UPS-PRANG
UNF-OUGHT	PRO-PANES	SEX-PERTS	TOM-PIONS	SUB-PLOTS	STU-PRATE
UNS-OUGHT	TRE-PANGS	ANA-PESTS	BAG-PIPER	EAR-PLUGS	OUT-PRAYS
ANN-OUNCE	TYM-PANIC	TEM-PESTS	BAG-PIPES	DIS-PLUME	RES-PRAYS
DEN-OUNCE	JOG-PANTS	PRO-PHAGE	DES-PISES	TRI-PODAL	BES-PRENT
REN-OUNCE	FLY-PAPER	ANA-PHASE	JAS-PISES	SYM-PODIA	COM-PRESS
REC-OUPED	HIP-PARCH	PRO-PHASE	KAL-PISES	ACU-POINT	SUP-PRESS
CAR-OUSEL	JEO-PARDS	CAM-PHENE	FLY-PITCH	DEW-POINT	KOU-PREYS
RAG-OUTED	LEO-PARDS	DIA-PHONE	DIS-PLACE	GUN-POINT	LAM-PREYS
RER-OUTED	JEO-PARDY	EAR-PHONE	MIS-PLACE	MIS-POINT	OUT-PRICE
SPR-OUTED	COM-PARED	GEO-PHONE	OUT-PLACE	OUT-POINT	COM-PRINT
STR-OUTED	PRE-PARED	SUL-PHONE	CHA-PLAIN	PAR-POINT	MIS-PRINT
ACC-OUTER	UNS-PARED	TRI-PHONE	COM-PLAIN	PIN-POINT	OFF-PRINT
DEV-OUTER	PRE-PARER	GRY-PHONS	AIR-PLANE	POR-POISE	SUB-PRIOR
ACC-OUTRE	COM-PARES	SYM-PHONY	JET-PLANE	COW-POKES	COM-PRISE
REM-OVALS	PRE-PARES	SUB-PHYLA	SEA-PLANE	NON-POLAR	MES-PRISE
INN-OVATE	CAR-PARKS	EAR-PICKS	SPY-PLANE	SUB-POLAR	MIS-PRISE
REN-OVATE	DIS-PARKS	RAM-PICKS	TRI-PLANE	UNI-POLAR	SUR-PRISE
ROT-OVATE	CLI-PARTS	COD-PIECE	VOL-PLANE	MAY-POLES	DIS-PRIZE
SUB-OVATE	COM-PARTS	EAR-PIECE	WAR-PLANE	TAD-POLES	MES-PRIZE
EST-OVERS	DIS-PARTS	DRA-PIERS	DIS-PLANT	RED-POLLS	MIS-PRIZE
FLY-OVERS	OUT-PARTS	RIP-PIERS	SUP-PLANT	DES-PONDS	OUT-PRIZE
GRO-OVERS	RAM-PARTS	DES-PIGHT	SHI-PLAPS	RES-PONDS	DIS-PROOF
POP-OVERS	LAM-PASSE	GAR-PIKES	WHI-PLASH	DIS-PONES	RAT-PROOF
REC-OVERS	DES-PATCH	RAM-PIKES	AXO-PLASM	PRE-PONES	SUN-PROOF
REM-OVERS	DIS-PATCH	COM-PILED	BIO-PLASM	PRO-PONES	PIT-PROPS
UNC-OVERS	PAL-PATED	COM-PILER	EXO-PLASM	ARA-PONGA	MIS-PROUD
ALL-OWING	TOW-PATHS	COM-PILES	NEO-PLASM	KAM-PONGS	DIS-PROVE
ARR-OWING	WAR-PATHS	FOR-PINED	BIO-PLAST	HAR-POONS	PRE-PUCES
ELB-OWING	DIA-PAUSE	PRO-PINED	SYM-PLAST	LAM-POONS	SEP-PUKUS
EMB-OWING		ALE-PINES	OMO-PLATE	POM-POONS	SCA-PULAS
END-OWING		CHO-PINES	TEM-PLATE	COR-PORAL	SCO-PULAS

STI-PULED	LAI-RAGES	TER-RASES	EMB-READS	REP-RIEVE	IND-RISES
STI-PULES	MOO-RAGES	ENG-RASPS	MIS-READS	RET-RIEVE	LAI-RISES
COM-PULSE	OUT-RAGES	AGG-RATED	RET-READS	THU-RIFER	MOR-RISES
KEY-PUNCH	OUV-RAGES	DIS-RATED	UNT-READS	MID-RIFFS	NEB-RISES
ARA-PUNGA	OVE-RAGES	EPU-RATED	INB-REAKS	SHE-RIFFS	REA-RISES
TRA-PUNTO	PEE-RAGES	EVI-RATED	UPB-REAKS	AFF-RIGHT	REP-RISES
MUD-PUPPY	PIE-RAGES	HYD-RATED	INC-REATE	BED-RIGHT	SUN-RISES
COU-PURES	STO-RAGES	ITE-RATED	LAU-REATE	OUT-RIGHT	TSU-RISES
GUI-PURES	UMB-RAGES	LIB-RATED	OCH-REATE	FAV-RILES	ATT-RITES
PUR-PURES	VIT-RAGES	MIG-RATED	REC-REATE	NIT-RILES	AZU-RITES
PUR-PURIN	HOO-RAHED	MIS-RATED	UNC-REATE	MOO-RILLS	CUP-RITES
CUT-PURSE	HUR-RAHED	NAR-RATED	SUR-REBUT	BEG-RIMED	DIO-RITES
DIS-PURSE	EMB-RAIDS	NIT-RATED	REG-REDES	REP-RIMED	EUC-RITES
CAM-PUSES	UPB-RAIDS	OPE-RATED	SAC-REDLY	UNP-RIMED	FER-RITES
GAU-PUSES	ENG-RAILS	OUT-RATED	UNB-REECH	BEG-RIMES	GUE-RITES
GAW-PUSES	ENT-RAILS	PRO-RATED	INB-REEDS	REP-RIMES	NAC-RITES
HIP-PUSES	PED-RAILS	REG-RATED	SHE-REEFS	REG-RINDS	NEU-RITES
MAW-PUSES	DAR-RAINE	RET-RATED	TER-REENS	AZU-RINES	NIT-RITES
PAP-PUSES	MIG-RAINE	SER-RATED	REP-REEVE	CHO-RINES	PIC-RITES
RUM-PUSES	CLA-RAINS	SPI-RATED	OUT-REIGN	CIT-RINES	REW-RITES
WAM-PUSES	DAR-RAINS	TIT-RATED	MUR-RELET	DOU-RINES	THO-RITES
PRO-PYLON	DET-RAINS	UMB-RATED	SHA-REMAN	LAT-RINES	UNW-RITES
SEA-QUAKE	ENG-RAINS	UNC-RATED	SHI-REMAN	NEU-RINES	COR-RIVAL
ALI-QUANT	ENT-RAINS	VIB-RATED	SHO-REMAN	PEB-RINES	DEP-RIVAL
MUS-QUASH	ING-RAINS	REG-RATER	STO-REMAN	TAU-RINES	OUT-RIVAL
CUM-QUATS	MUR-RAINS	AGG-RATES	SHA-REMEN	TER-RINES	DEP-RIVED
KUM-QUATS	REF-RAINS	CAP-RATES	SHI-REMEN	VIT-RINES	REP-RIVED
COT-QUEAN	RET-RAINS	CED-RATES	SHO-REMEN	BAR-RINGS	RED-RIVEN
CON-QUEST	TER-RAINS	CIT-RATES	STO-REMEN	BEA-RINGS	UND-RIVEN
OPA-QUEST	UPT-RAINS	DIS-RATES	UPT-RENDS	EAR-RINGS	DEP-RIVES
UNI-QUEST	VIT-RAINS	EMI-RATES	CUR-RENTS	FAI-RINGS	RED-RIVES
LAC-QUEYS	APP-RAISE	EPU-RATES	MAN-RENTS	FEE-RINGS	REP-RIVES
DIS-QUIET	BEP-RAISE	EVI-RATES	TOR-RENTS	FIR-RINGS	APP-ROACH
BAS-QUINE	UNP-RAISE	FER-RATES	ENT-REPOT	FUR-RINGS	ENC-ROACH
MES-QUINE	EXT-RAITS	HYD-RATES	DIE-RESES	GEA-RINGS	REP-ROACH
VER-QUIRE	RET-RAITS	ING-RATES	DIU-RESES	HEA-RINGS	OUT-ROARS
MES-QUITE	SWA-RAJES	ITE-RATES	ENU-RESES	HER-RINGS	CAP-ROATE
MES-QUITS	BUN-RAKUS	LIB-RATES	IMP-RESES	INB-RINGS	DIS-ROBED
MIS-QUOTE	CHO-RALES	MIG-RATES	IMP-RESTS	JAR-RINGS	DIS-ROBES
AGG-RACED	CHO-RALLY	MIS-RATES	ACC-RETES	JEE-RINGS	MIC-ROBES
EMB-RACED	FLO-RALLY	NAR-RATES	EXC-RETES	LEE-RINGS	SAP-ROBES
ENG-RACED	NEU-RALLY	NIT-RATES	SEC-RETES	LOU-RINGS	BED-ROCKS
OUT-RACED	PLU-RALLY	OPE-RATES	MUR-RHINE	MOO-RINGS	DEF-ROCKS
REB-RACED	RET-RALLY	PIC-RATES	MYR-RHINE	PAI-RINGS	PAR-ROCKS
RET-RACED	SPI-RALLY	PRO-RATES	DEC-RIALS	POU-RINGS	SOU-ROCKS
TER-RACED	GOU-RAMIS	REG-RATES	GHA-RIALS	PUR-RINGS	TAR-ROCKS
UNB-RACED	MAC-RAMIS	RET-RATES	PAI-RIALS	ROA-RINGS	UNF-ROCKS
UNG-RACED	GUA-RANAS	SER-RATES	PAT-RIALS	SAC-RINGS	COR-RODED
UNT-RACED	AMO-RANCE	TIT-RATES	RET-RIALS	SCO-RINGS	COR-RODES
EMB-RACER	ENT-RANCE	UNC-RATES	HAU-RIANT	SEA-RINGS	TET-RODES
AGG-RACES	ITE-RANCE	VIB-RATES	UNP-RICED	SHA-RINGS	PRO-ROGUE
BAR-RACES	OUT-RANCE	SER-RATUS	ALT-RICES	SHO-RINGS	EMB-ROILS
EMB-RACES	OPE-RANDS	DEP-RAVED	AVA-RICES	SNA-RINGS	FIB-ROINS
ENG-RACES	WAR-RANDS	EMB-RAVED	CAP-RICES	SNO-RINGS	LIG-ROINS
OUT-RACES	CIT-RANGE	ENG-RAVED	IMB-RICES	SOA-RINGS	PYR-ROLES
REB-RACES	EST-RANGE	ENG-RAVEN	MAT-RICES	SOU-RINGS	SAF-ROLES
RET-RACES	GUA-RANIS	ENG-RAVER	MOR-RICES	STA-RINGS	ESC-ROLLS
TER-RACES	DIS-RANKS	DEP-RAVES	NOU-RICES	SUB-RINGS	PAY-ROLLS
THO-RACES	OUT-RANKS	EMB-RAVES	OPO-RICES	TAR-RINGS	FIB-ROMAS
UNB-RACES	AMA-RANTS	ENG-RAVES	TUT-RICES	TOU-RINGS	NEU-ROMAS
UNT-RACES	COU-RANTS	STO-RAXES	DER-RICKS	UPB-RINGS	PLE-ROMAS
AMT-RACKS	CUR-RANTS	STY-RAXES	HAY-RICKS	VEE-RINGS	LAD-RONES
BAR-RACKS	ENT-RANTS	THO-RAXES	PAT-RICKS	WEA-RINGS	MAD-RONES
CAR-RACKS	HYD-RANTS	AFF-RAYED	FLO-RIDER	CHA-RIOTS	MUC-RONES
HAT-RACKS	INT-RANTS	BET-RAYED	HOR-RIDER	PAT-RIOTS	NEU-RONES
OST-RACON	MIG-RANTS	BEW-RAYED	MAN-RIDER	CIR-RIPED	PAT-RONNE
PER-RADII	ODO-RANTS	DEF-RAYED	OUT-RIDER	REA-RISEN	AFF-RONTE
ENG-RAFFS	OPE-RANTS	EST-RAYED	PUT-RIDER	UNA-RISEN	AFF-RONTS
ENG-RAFTS	REG-RANTS	FOR-RAYED	TOR-RIDER	APP-RISER	APP-ROOFS
IND-RAFTS	SPI-RANTS	HOO-RAYED	CYP-RIDES	APP-RISES	REP-ROOFS
ING-RAFTS	VAG-RANTS	HUR-RAYED	DEB-RIDES	CER-RISES	SUN-ROOFS
RED-RAFTS	WAR-RANTS	UNP-RAYED	HAY-RIDES	CHO-RISES	BED-ROOMS
AVE-RAGED	UND-RAPED	WAR-RAYED	HYD-RIDES	DER-RISES	BOX-ROOMS
OUT-RAGED	IGA-RAPES	UNG-RAZED	NIT-RIDES	DIA-RISES	GUN-ROOMS
UMB-RAGED	CHA-RASES	OUT-REACH	OUT-RIDES	ECC-RISES	LEG-ROOMS
AVE-RAGES	MAD-RASES	UNP-REACH	EST-RIDGE	EMP-RISES	TAP-ROOMS
BAR-RAGES	NAR-RASES	BET-READS	POR-RIDGE	HUB-RISES	GAD-ROONS
BEE-RAGES	SUC-RASES		AGG-RIEVE	HYB-RISES	GOD-ROONS
COU-RAGES	TAR-RASES		ENG-RIEVE	IBE-RISES	PAT-ROONS

OUT-ROOPS	MAC-RURAL	CRE-SCENT	NUT-SHELL	CON-SIDER	KID-SKINS
CHE-ROOTS	CHO-RUSES	REA-SCENT	SEA-SHELL	OFF-SIDER	OIL-SKINS
DIS-ROOTS	CIT-RUSES	OUT-SCOLD	POT-SHERD	OUT-SIDER	PIG-SKINS
OUT-ROOTS	CYP-RUSES	BIO-SCOPE	BLU-SHETS	AIR-SIDES	RED-SKINS
RED-ROOTS	EST-RUSES	DIA-SCOPE	FRE-SHETS	BED-SIDES	NUM-SKULL
TAP-ROOTS	MIU-RUSES	EPI-SCOPE	PLA-SHETS	DEP-SIDES	FOR-SLACK
IMP-ROPER	OVE-RUSES	IRI-SCOPE	BLA-SHIER	OFF-SIDES	PUR-SLAIN
OUT-ROPER	WAL-RUSES	OTO-SCOPE	BOL-SHIER	OUT-SIDES	PUR-SLANE
UNP-ROPER	BUL-RUSHY	SIX-SCORE	BRA-SHIER	PRE-SIDES	BOB-SLEDS
OUT-ROPES	ENC-RUSTS	OUT-SCORN	BRU-SHIER	SEA-SIDES	DOG-SLEDS
TOW-ROPES	ENT-RUSTS	MUD-SCOWS	FLA-SHIER	SUB-SIDES	DOG-SLEEP
BEP-ROSED	INC-RUSTS	AIR-SCREW	FLE-SHIER	TOP-SIDES	OUT-SLEEP
FIB-ROSED	INT-RUSTS	SET-SCREW	FLU-SHIER	WAY-SIDES	OUT-SLEPT
NEC-ROSED	UNT-RUSTS	OFF-SCUMS	MAR-SHIER	DIS-SIGHT	PAI-SLEYS
BEP-ROSES	UNT-RUSTY	PRE-SCUTA	PLA-SHIER	EYE-SIGHT	PAR-SLEYS
FIB-ROSES	UNT-RUTHS	DEI-SEALS	PLU-SHIER	OUT-SIGHT	MUD-SLIDE
HID-ROSES	AMU-SABLE	DIS-SEATS	SLO-SHIER	CON-SIGNS	GRI-SLIER
NEC-ROSES	ERA-SABLE	DIS-SECTS	SLU-SHIER	MIS-SILES	MEA-SLIER
NEU-ROSES	KIS-SABLE	TRI-SECTS	SPO-SHIER	COO-SINED	BIR-SLING
PHA-ROSES	LAP-SABLE	ALL-SEEDS	SWA-SHIER	CUI-SINES	BRI-SLING
SUC-ROSES	LEA-SABLE	ANI-SEEDS	SWI-SHIER	PEP-SINES	ENI-SLING
CHA-ROSET	MIS-SABLE	HAY-SEEDS	TRA-SHIER	VER-SINES	FIS-SLING
NIG-ROSIN	PAS-SABLE	LIN-SEEDS	BOL-SHIES	BIA-SINGS	HAS-SLING
DEF-ROSTS	RAI-SABLE	MAW-SEEDS	QUA-SHIES	BUS-SINGS	HIR-SLING
GAR-ROTED	REU-SABLE	MIS-SEEMS	STA-SHIES	CEA-SINGS	HOU-SLING
PAR-ROTED	RIN-SABLE	MAH-SEERS	STI-SHIES	CHA-SINGS	INI-SLING
GAR-ROTES	UNU-SABLE	CON-SEILS	STU-SHIES	CLO-SINGS	MEA-SLING
THO-ROUGH	DAY-SACKS	DIS-SEISE	TUM-SHIES	CUR-SINGS	MOU-SLING
REG-ROUND	HOP-SACKS	PER-SEITY	MAN-SHIFT	GAS-SINGS	NOU-SLING
SUR-ROUND	RAN-SACKS	DIS-SEIZE	FLA-SHILY	GUI-SINGS	NUR-SLING
UNG-ROUND	CRU-SADES	BON-SELLA	TRA-SHILY	HIS-SINGS	QUI-SLING
ING-ROUPS	DIP-SADES	TES-SELLA	OUT-SHINE	HOU-SINGS	TOU-SLING
REG-ROUPS	PAS-SADES	VUL-SELLA	SUN-SHINE	LEA-SINGS	TUS-SLING
REA-ROUSE	TOR-SADES	MAM-SELLE	SUN-SHINY	MOU-SINGS	WAR-SLING
MIS-ROUTE	PRE-SAGER	NOU-SELLS	AIR-SHIPS	NUR-SINGS	COW-SLIPS
APP-ROVED	ABU-SAGES	OUT-SELLS	DOG-SHIPS	PAR-SINGS	PAY-SLIPS
IMP-ROVED	COR-SAGES	TAS-SELLS	DON-SHIPS	PAS-SINGS	FOR-SLOES
REP-ROVED	MAS-SAGES	WOO-SELLS	END-SHIPS	PAU-SINGS	FOR-SLOWS
UNP-ROVED	MES-SAGES	HOR-SEMEN	FOX-SHIPS	PRO-SINGS	OUT-SMART
APP-ROVER	PAS-SAGES	HOU-SEMEN	GOD-SHIPS	RAI-SINGS	MOU-SMEES
IMP-ROVER	PAY-SAGES	PRO-SEMEN	GUN-SHIPS	RIN-SINGS	GUN-SMITH
REP-ROVER	PLU-SAGES	GOD-SENDS	HER-SHIPS	SEN-SINGS	TIN-SMITH
APP-ROVES	PRE-SAGES	MIS-SENDS	KIN-SHIPS	SOS-SINGS	COR-SNEDS
IMP-ROVES	PRI-SAGES	NON-SENSE	LUD-SHIPS	SOU-SINGS	PIG-SNIES
REP-ROVES	SAU-SAGES	CON-SENTS	MID-SHIPS	TEA-SINGS	PAR-SNIPS
BOR-ROWED	SAP-SAGOS	DIS-SENTS	NUN-SHIPS	TOS-SINGS	TIN-SNIPS
BUR-ROWED	LUG-SAILS	PRE-SENTS	SIB-SHIPS	TOU-SINGS	OUT-SOARS
ESC-ROWED	OUT-SAILS	TES-SERAL	SON-SHIPS	VER-SINGS	BED-SOCKS
FAR-ROWED	SKY-SAILS	SUB-SERES	WAR-SHIPS	FIS-SIPED	CAS-SOCKS
FUR-ROWED	TOP-SAILS	SAN-SERIF	WOR-SHIPS	GOS-SIPED	HAS-SOCKS
HAR-ROWED	TRY-SAILS	KAI-SERIN	RED-SHIRE	TAR-SIPED	LAS-SOCKS
MAR-ROWED	VAS-SAILS	BER-SERKS	GOB-SHITE	CAS-SISES	TUS-SOCKS
NAR-ROWED	VES-SAILS	CON-SERVE	GUM-SHOED	MIS-SISES	EPI-SODIC
SOR-ROWED	WAS-SAILS	DIS-SERVE	GUM-SHOES	TUS-SISES	PRO-SODIC
TAR-ROWED	COR-SAIRS	PRE-SERVE	OUT-SHONE	BAS-SISTS	DEA-SOILS
BOR-ROWER	PRO-SAIST	SUB-SERVE	ATI-SHOOS	CON-SISTS	SUB-SOILS
NAR-ROWER	FOR-SAKES	WAD-SETTS	SAM-SHOOS	PER-SISTS	TOP-SOILS
SOR-ROWER	CAU-SALLY	DIS-SEVER	OFF-SHOOT	SEN-SISTS	SUB-SOLAR
ING-ROWTH	DOR-SALLY	WHO-SEVER	OUT-SHOOT	SUB-SISTS	CON-SOLED
REG-ROWTH	WEA-SANDS	PUR-SEWED	COP-SHOPS	AMO-SITES	CON-SOLER
UPG-ROWTH	LAP-SANGS	EYE-SHADE	GIN-SHOPS	FEL-SITES	CON-SOLES
SUR-ROYAL	LIN-SANGS	SUN-SHADE	POT-SHOPS	WEB-SITES	OUT-SOLES
CHE-RUBIN	PEA-SANTS	AIR-SHAFT	TOY-SHOPS	ZOI-SITES	RIS-SOLES
EXT-RUDER	VER-SANTS	CAM-SHAFT	OFF-SHORE	SUB-SIZAR	DIS-SOLVE
INT-RUDER	GUI-SARDS	RED-SHANK	SEA-SHORE	CAP-SIZED	CAS-SONES
OBT-RUDER	MAN-SARDS	DAR-SHANS	GEM-SHORN	OUT-SIZED	DAP-SONES
DET-RUDES	IRI-SATED	MIS-SHAPE	RED-SHORT	CAP-SIZES	SUB-SONGS
EXT-RUDES	PUL-SATED	POT-SHARD	BOW-SHOTS	OUT-SIZES	PAR-SONIC
INT-RUDES	IRI-SATES	JOB-SHARE	EAR-SHOTS	FRI-SKERS	SUB-SONIC
OBT-RUDES	PUL-SATES	POT-SHARE	GUN-SHOTS	WHI-SKERS	RAI-SONNE
ACC-RUING	SAK-SAULS	RED-SHARE	HOT-SHOTS	FLI-SKIER	FOR-SOOTH
EMB-RUING	PER-SAUNT	FOX-SHARK	MUG-SHOTS	FRI-SKIER	CEN-SORED
IMB-RUING	JIG-SAWED	SAW-SHARK	OUT-SHOTS	DRO-SKIES	BED-SORES
MIS-RULED	SEE-SAWED	CUM-SHAWS	SUB-SHRUB	PLI-SKIES	CUR-SORES
FER-RULES	SEA-SCAPE	TRI-SHAWS	PEI-SHWAS	WHI-SKIES	EYE-SORES
MIS-RULES	SKY-SCAPE	DEI-SHEAL	FOS-SICKS	CAT-SKINS	TUS-SORES
SPO-RULES	TWI-SCARS	COW-SHEDS	LOP-SIDED	DOG-SKINS	ALL-SORTS
ZEB-RULES	REA-SCEND	DRI-SHEEN	PRE-SIDED	GRI-SKINS	CON-SORTS
UNP-RUNED	ACE-SCENT	EGG-SHELL	SUB-SIDED		PAS-SOUTS

LEA-SOWED	WOR-STEDS	CAP-STONE	OUT-SWELL	POS-TALLY	PRO-TENSE
AIR-SPACE	CHA-STENS	FEL-STONE	PIG-SWILL	REC-TALLY	SUB-TENSE
OUT-SPANS	GLI-STENS	GEM-STONE	OUT-SWIMS	PAN-TALON	CON-TENTS
FEL-SPARS	GUE-STENS	GUN-STONE	BAT-SWING	TAN-TALUS	POR-TENTS
CRI-SPATE	MOI-STENS	ICE-STONE	BEE-SWING	ENS-TAMPS	DIP-TERAS
FOR-SPEAK	EXI-STENT	INK-STONE	OUT-SWING	CUR-TANAS	SES-TERCE
MIS-SPEAK	MIS-STEPS	KEY-STONE	FOR-SWINK	LAN-TANAS	HAL-TERES
NEW-SPEAK	OUT-STEPS	LAP-STONE	NEW-SWIRE	SUL-TANAS	MID-TERMS
OUT-SPEAK	TRI-STICH	MUD-STONE	CUS-SWORD	TAR-TANAS	MIS-TERMS
SEA-SPEAK	CAN-STICK	OIL-STONE	PAS-SWORD	VEN-TANAS	BIT-TERNS
KEN-SPECK	DIP-STICK	POT-STONE	FOR-SWORE	BOS-TANGI	CIS-TERNS
AIR-SPEED	GUN-STICK	RAG-STONE	OUT-SWORE	CON-TANGO	CIT-TERNS
GOD-SPEED	LIP-STICK	RIB-STONE	FOR-SWORN	MUS-TANGS	GIT-TERNS
MIS-SPELL	MAL-STICK	ROE-STONE	MAN-SWORN	PLA-TANNA	LAN-TERNS
MIS-SPELT	MAP-STICK	RUB-STONE	OUT-SWORN	MON-TANTO	LEC-TERNS
FOR-SPEND	MOP-STICK	SUN-STONE	ABA-TABLE	TAN-TARAS	LET-TERNS
MIS-SPEND	BEA-STIES	TIN-STONE	BEA-TABLE	TUA-TARAS	PAS-TERNS
OUT-SPEND	CRU-STIES	OUT-STOOD	BIS-TABLE	BAS-TARDY	PAT-TERNS
FOR-SPENT	PIG-STIES	AIR-STOPS	BOO-TABLE	DAS-TARDY	POS-TERNS
MIS-SPENT	TOA-STIES	HER-STORY	EVI-TABLE	MOR-TARED	SAL-TERNS
OUT-SPENT	TRU-STIES	BED-STRAW	GET-TABLE	NEC-TARED	TES-TERNS
EPI-SPERM	ADU-STING	AIR-STRIP	GUS-TABLE	UPS-TARED	WES-TERNS
ZOO-SPERM	AGI-STING	OUT-STRIP	IMI-TABLE	CEN-TARES	CON-TERNS
ALL-SPICE	BLA-STING	ANE-STRUM	INS-TABLE	HEC-TARES	PRE-TESTS
UNE-SPIED	BOA-STING	HUM-STRUM	LET-TABLE	LAE-TARES	PRO-TESTS
BON-SPIEL	BOO-STING	DYE-STUFF	LIF-TABLE	TAR-TARES	CON-TEXTS
CRI-SPINS	BRA-STING	FRU-STUMS	MOO-TABLE	UPS-TARES	MAR-TEXTS
ISO-SPINS	BRU-STING	MOI-STURE	PAN-TABLE	RES-TARTS	PRE-TEXTS
TOP-SPINS	BUI-STING	DIA-STYLE	PIN-TABLE	UPS-TARTS	SUB-TEXTS
CON-SPIRE	BUR-STING	EPI-STYLE	POR-TABLE	DIS-TASTE	URE-THANE
PER-SPIRE	CHE-STING	PRO-STYLE	QUO-TABLE	ACE-TATES	URE-THANS
CES-SPITS	COA-STING	SUB-STYLE	REN-TABLE	AGI-TATES	XAN-THANS
FOR-SPOKE	CRE-STING	URO-STYLE	SOR-TABLE	CAN-TATES	ANA-THEMA
MIS-SPOKE	CRU-STING	WAE-SUCKS	STA-TABLE	DIC-TATES	EPI-THEMA
OUT-SPOKE	EGE-STING	PUR-SUERS	SUI-TABLE	EVI-TATES	ERY-THEMA
CES-SPOOL	EXI-STING	PER-SUING	TAS-TABLE	GES-TATES	BUR-THENS
SES-SPOOL	FEA-STING	PUR-SUING	TES-TABLE	GUT-TATES	HEA-THENS
TEA-SPOON	FOI-STING	TIS-SUING	TIL-TABLE	IMI-TATES	ISO-THERE
DIA-SPORE	FRI-STING	CAT-SUITS	UNS-TABLE	INS-TATES	ISO-THERM
EPI-SPORE	FRO-STING	LAW-SUITS	WAS-TABLE	LAC-TATES	AES-THETE
EXO-SPORE	GHA-STING	MIS-SUITS	WRI-TABLE	NIC-TATES	FOO-THILL
ZOO-SPORE	GHO-STING	NON-SUITS	CAT-TABUS	RES-TATES	WAN-THILL
MAR-SPORT	GIU-STING	PUR-SUITS	COT-TABUS	SAL-TATES	IAN-THINE
OUT-SPORT	GUE-STING	SUN-SUITS	MUS-TACHE	UNS-TATES	XAN-THINE
PAS-SPORT	HEI-STING	CAE-SURAL	SOU-TACHE	SUR-TAXED	ANY-THING
INK-SPOTS	HOA-STING	MEN-SURAL	SUB-TACKS	CUR-TAXES	BEA-THING
SUN-SPOTS	HOI-STING	CAE-SURAS	TIE-TACKS	GEO-TAXES	BER-THING
TOS-SPOTS	JOI-STING	CEN-SURED	TIN-TACKS	SUR-TAXES	BIR-THING
BOW-SPRIT	JOU-STING	CLO-SURED	UNS-TACKS	SYN-TAXES	CLO-THING
OLD-SQUAW	MOI-STING	FIS-SURED	CON-TACTS	GEO-TAXIS	EAR-THING
HAY-STACK	MOU-STING	LEI-SURED	PEN-TACTS	MIS-TEACH	FAI-THING
PAL-STAFF	MUI-STING	MEA-SURED	SYN-TAGMA	BES-TEADS	FAR-THING
TIP-STAFF	PRE-STING	TON-SURED	BOB-TAILS	ONS-TEADS	FRO-THING
SUB-STAGE	QUE-STING	MEA-SURER	CUR-TAILS	LAC-TEALS	GIR-THING
EYE-STALK	REA-STING	BRI-SURES	FAN-TAILS	PRO-TEASE	LOA-THING
BOR-STALL	REE-STING	CEN-SURES	PIG-TAILS	ZAI-TECHS	MOU-THING
LAY-STALL	REI-STING	CLO-SURES	PIN-TAILS	MAN-TEELS	NAE-THING
HAT-STAND	ROA-STING	ERA-SURES	VEN-TAILS	UNS-TEELS	NOR-THING
INK-STAND	ROI-STING	FIS-SURES	WAG-TAILS	CAN-TEENS	QUE-THING
OUT-STAND	ROO-STING	FRI-SURES	MIS-TAKEN	FIF-TEENS	SCA-THING
CAM-STANE	ROU-STING	LEA-SURES	OUT-TAKEN	POS-TEENS	SCY-THING
PRI-STANE	ROY-STING	LEI-SURES	PAR-TAKEN	RAT-TEENS	SEE-THING
OUT-STARE	TOA-STING	MEA-SURES	PER-TAKEN	SIX-TEENS	SLO-THING
DAY-STARS	TRU-STING	MOR-SURES	PAR-TAKER	SUB-TEENS	SMI-THING
RED-START	TRY-STING	SEA-SURES	MIS-TAKES	DOG-TEETH	SOO-THING
APO-STATE	TWI-STING	SEY-SURES	OFF-TAKES	SAW-TEETH	SOU-THING
ARI-STATE	WHI-STING	TON-SURES	OUT-TAKES	MIS-TELLS	SOW-THING
CON-STATE	WOR-STING	BYS-SUSES	PAR-TAKES	OUT-TELLS	SWA-THING
CRI-STATE	WRA-STING	CEN-SUSES	PER-TAKES	SYS-TEMED	TEE-THING
CRU-STATE	WRE-STING	CIS-SUSES	CAN-TALAS	ERO-TEMES	TOO-THING
ECO-STATE	YEA-STING	MIS-SUSES	DAY-TALER	CON-TEMPT	TRO-THING
MIS-STATE	EGE-STIVE	PAS-SUSES	DAY-TALES	CON-TENDS	WOR-THING
PRO-STATE	FAT-STOCK	RHE-SUSES	SCY-TALES	DIS-TENDS	WRA-THING
SUB-STATE	GUN-STOCK	TAS-SWAGE	OUT-TALKS	POR-TENDS	WRE-THING
PAL-STAVE	LIN-STOCK	COX-SWAIN	BRU-TALLY	PRE-TENDS	WRI-THING
BOB-STAYS	PEN-STOCK	FOR-SWEAR	DIS-TALLY	PRO-TENDS	FOR-THINK
OUT-STAYS	ASY-STOLE	MEN-SWEAR	FES-TALLY	SUB-TENDS	MIS-THINK
BED-STEAD	DIA-STOLE	OUT-SWEAR	MEN-TALLY	PEN-TENES	OUT-THINK
OER-STEDS	CAM-STONE	PEE-SWEEP	MOR-TALLY	PRE-TENSE	XAN-THINS

BOL-THOLE	BED-TIMES	NUT-TINGS	SCO-TOMIA	BES-TOWER	DEX-TRINE
POR-THOLE	CEN-TIMES	PAN-TINGS	CAN-TONAL	COT-TOWNS	DOC-TRINE
SHI-THOLE	DAY-TIMES	PAR-TINGS	BUT-TONED	DOG-TOWNS	LUS-TRINE
SHO-THOLE	LAY-TIMES	PAS-TINGS	CAN-TONED	ECO-TOXIC	DEX-TRINS
HAW-THORN	MIS-TIMES	PEL-TINGS	CAR-TONED	EXO-TOXIC	GAS-TRINS
LAN-THORN	OFT-TIMES	PET-TINGS	COT-TONED	EXO-TOXIN	HIS-TRIOS
BOO-THOSE	PAS-TIMES	PIT-TINGS	DAN-TONED	NEO-TOXIN	CAN-TRIPS
SPA-THOSE	RAG-TIMES	PLA-TINGS	UNA-TONED	ZOO-TOXIN	UNS-TRIPS
APH-THOUS	SEP-TIMES	POS-TINGS	WAN-TONED	COA-TRACK	CEN-TRIST
XAN-THOUS	TEA-TIMES	POU-TINGS	WAN-TONER	ABS-TRACT	CON-TRIST
URE-THRAE	WAR-TIMES	PRA-TINGS	ACE-TONES	CON-TRACT	SUB-TRIST
COR-TICAL	DIS-TINCT	PUT-TINGS	CEN-TONES	DIS-TRACT	CON-TRITE
CRI-TICAL	INS-TINCT	RAN-TINGS	DUO-TONES	PRO-TRACT	EPI-TRITE
EME-TICAL	DES-TINED	RAT-TINGS	HIS-TONES	SUB-TRACT	CAR-TROAD
ERO-TICAL	BOT-TINES	RES-TINGS	ISO-TONES	CON-TRAIL	BES-TRODE
FIS-TICAL	CYS-TINES	RIO-TINGS	LAC-TONES	DIS-TRAIL	CEN-TRODE
HEC-TICAL	DEN-TINES	ROO-TINGS	OXY-TONES	DIS-TRAIN	UPS-TROKE
MYS-TICAL	DES-TINES	ROU-TINGS	PEP-TONES	QUA-TRAIN	CIS-TRONS
NAU-TICAL	DIE-TINES	RUS-TINGS	TRI-TONES	RES-TRAIN	ISO-TRONS
POE-TICAL	EME-TINES	RUT-TINGS	BIL-TONGS	DIS-TRAIT	KRY-TRONS
RUS-TICAL	ISA-TINES	SAL-TINGS	PAK-TONGS	POR-TRAIT	NEU-TRONS
STA-TICAL	PAN-TINES	SEA-TINGS	DIA-TONIC	MAN-TRAMS	ZOE-TROPE
TAC-TICAL	PEC-TINES	SET-TINGS	DYS-TONIC	CAL-TRAPS	ZOO-TROPE
THE-TICAL	ROU-TINES	SIF-TINGS	EPI-TONIC	FLY-TRAPS	DOG-TROTS
TRI-TICAL	SES-TINES	SIT-TINGS	ISO-TONIC	MAN-TRAPS	FOO-TROTS
VER-TICAL	TAR-TINES	SKA-TINGS	LEP-TONIC	SUN-TRAPS	FOX-TROTS
VOR-TICAL	TON-TINES	SLA-TINGS	PLA-TONIC	UNS-TRAPS	JOG-TROTS
LAT-TICED	BAI-TINGS	SOR-TINGS	PLU-TONIC	CON-TRATS	DES-TROYS
MOR-TICED	BAN-TINGS	SOT-TINGS	PRO-TONIC	POR-TRAYS	UNS-TRUCK
PEN-TICED	BAS-TINGS	SUI-TINGS	SUB-TONIC	MAL-TREAT	DIS-TRUST
COR-TICES	BAT-TINGS	TAS-TINGS	SYN-TONIC	MIS-TREAT	MIS-TRUST
FAC-TICES	BEA-TINGS	TAT-TINGS	TEC-TONIC	YES-TREEN	MIS-TRYST
FRU-TICES	BEL-TINGS	TEN-TINGS	BOU-TONNE	COW-TREES	MYO-TUBES
JUS-TICES	BET-TINGS	TES-TINGS	CRE-TONNE	BUT-TRESS	SCH-TUCKS
LAT-TICES	BOA-TINGS	TIL-TINGS	CAR-TOONS	DIS-TRESS	NOC-TULES
MOR-TICES	BOL-TINGS	TIN-TINGS	FES-TOONS	DOC-TRESS	PUS-TULES
PEN-TICES	BRU-TINGS	TOT-TINGS	PLA-TOONS	EDI-TRESS	SPA-TULES
STA-TICES	BUN-TINGS	TUF-TINGS	PON-TOONS	FOR-TRESS	CON-TUNDS
VER-TICES	BUS-TINGS	TUT-TINGS	PUL-TOONS	FOS-TRESS	DIS-TUNED
VOR-TICES	CAN-TINGS	UNI-TINGS	TES-TOONS	HUN-TRESS	FOR-TUNED
BED-TICKS	CAS-TINGS	VEN-TINGS	DOG-TOOTH	INS-TRESS	MIS-TUNED
BES-TICKS	COA-TINGS	VES-TINGS	SAW-TOOTH	LEC-TRESS	DIS-TUNES
SCH-TICKS	CUT-TINGS	WAF-TINGS	BIO-TOPES	MAT-TRESS	FOR-TUNES
UNS-TICKS	DOA-TINGS	WAI-TINGS	EPI-TOPES	MIS-TRESS	MIS-TUNES
SUB-TIDAL	EAS-TINGS	WAN-TINGS	ISO-TOPES	ORA-TRESS	LEC-TURNS
BAS-TIDES	FAS-TINGS	WAS-TINGS	ISO-TOPIC	POR-TRESS	NOC-TURNS
EBB-TIDES	FEL-TINGS	WES-TINGS	PHO-TOPIC	REC-TRESS	OUT-TURNS
PEP-TIDES	FIT-TINGS	WHI-TINGS	SCO-TOPIC	SUI-TRESS	VUL-TURNS
RIP-TIDES	FLU-TINGS	WIT-TINGS	PRO-TORES	VIC-TRESS	BEL-TWAYS
TRI-TIDES	FLY-TINGS	WRI-TINGS	RES-TORES	WAI-TRESS	CAR-TWAYS
BUS-TIERS	FOO-TINGS	SAL-TIRES	VIA-TORES	FOO-TREST	FLA-TWAYS
COT-TIERS	GET-TINGS	UNS-TITCH	HIS-TORIC	WHI-TRETS	FOO-TWAYS
EMP-TIERS	GRA-TINGS	AOR-TITIS	RHE-TORIC	BES-TREWS	GOA-TWEED
PUT-TIERS	HAL-TINGS	CYS-TITIS	SAR-TORII	MIS-TRIAL	GOU-TWEED
REN-TIERS	HAS-TINGS	MAS-TITIS	BIS-TORTS	DIA-TRIBE	KNO-TWEED
SAL-TIERS	HAT-TINGS	OUS-TITIS	CON-TORTS	SUB-TRIBE	WAR-TWEED
CAI-TIFFS	HEA-TINGS	REC-TITIS	DIS-TORTS	GEN-TRICE	PEE-TWEET
MAS-TIFFS	HOS-TINGS	WIS-TITIS	AMI-TOSES	PAI-TRICK	DIR-TYING
PON-TIFFS	HOT-TINGS	MIS-TITLE	CES-TOSES	BES-TRIDE	DIT-TYING
SCU-TIGES	HOU-TINGS	SUB-TITLE	KUR-TOSES	DES-TRIER	EMP-TYING
VEN-TIGES	HUN-TINGS	SUR-TITLE	LAC-TOSES	PAL-TRIER	HOG-TYING
VES-TIGES	HUS-TINGS	BIT-TOCKS	MAL-TOSES	SUL-TRIER	JET-TYING
AIR-TIGHT	HUT-TINGS	BUT-TOCKS	PEC-TOSES	WIN-TRIER	JUT-TYING
PAN-TILED	JES-TINGS	CAS-TOCKS	PEN-TOSES	CEN-TRIES	PAR-TYING
FER-TILER	JOT-TINGS	CUS-TOCKS	PHY-TOSES	FRA-TRIES	PUT-TYING
SUB-TILER	KAR-TINGS	FUT-TOCKS	SUB-TOTAL	GAN-TRIES	BIO-TYPES
GEN-TILES	LAS-TINGS	HAT-TOCKS	TEE-TOTAL	GEN-TRIES	ECO-TYPES
PAN-TILES	LET-TINGS	MAT-TOCKS	CAR-TOUCH	HOS-TRIES	ISO-TYPES
PON-TILES	LIS-TINGS	PUT-TOCKS	ACA-TOURS	PAN-TRIES	SUB-TYPES
REP-TILES	LOO-TINGS	RES-TOCKS	BIT-TOURS	PAS-TRIES	TIN-TYPES
SEX-TILES	MAL-TINGS	UNS-TOCKS	CON-TOURS	PEL-TRIES	ZOO-TYPES
TEX-TILES	MAT-TINGS	POR-TOISE	DOR-TOURS	POE-TRIES	ZOO-TYPIC
BAT-TILLS	MEE-TINGS	TOR-TOISE	FAI-TOURS	RIO-TRIES	MAR-TYRED
BES-TILLS	MEL-TINGS	PIS-TOLES	SAN-TOURS	SEN-TRIES	DEB-UGGED
DIS-TILLS	MIS-TINGS	SCA-TOLES	SUR-TOUTS	SMY-TRIES	SHR-UGGED
INS-TILLS	MOO-TINGS	SKA-TOLES	BES-TOWED	VES-TRIES	CUC-UMBER
MIS-TIMED	MUN-TINGS	SYS-TOLES	KOW-TOWED	VIN-TRIES	ENC-UMBER
RAG-TIMER	NES-TINGS	EPI-TOMES	TAT-TOWED	WAS-TRIES	REN-UMBER
AIR-TIMES	NET-TINGS	LEP-TOMES	UNS-TOWED	TES-TRILL	NEL-UMBOS

PEN-UMBRA	ACC-USERS	COU-VERTS	WIT-WALLS	WEB-WHEEL	LAP-WORKS
CHA-UNCES	ARO-USERS	CUL-VERTS	ELL-WANDS	ANY-WHERE	LEG-WORKS
ENO-UNCES	EXC-USERS	PER-VERTS	AIR-WARDS	ERE-WHILE	NET-WORKS
FLO-UNCES	GRO-USERS	SIE-VERTS	BED-WARDS	TAR-WHINE	OUT-WORKS
FRO-UNCES	INF-USERS	SUB-VERTS	FOR-WARDS	BLO-WHOLE	RAG-WORKS
PRA-UNCES	MIS-USERS	HAR-VESTS	FRO-WARDS	OUT-WICKS	RIB-WORKS
TRO-UNCES	PER-USERS	CON-VEXED	GOD-WARDS	OUT-WINDS	TUT-WORKS
CAR-UNCLE	REF-USERS	CON-VEXES	HAY-WARDS	ENT-WINED	WAX-WORKS
FUR-UNCLE	SCO-USERS	PLU-VIALS	HOG-WARDS	INT-WINED	BUD-WORMS
HOM-UNCLE	SMO-USERS	SER-VICED	LEE-WARDS	UNT-WINED	CAT-WORMS
PED-UNCLE	TRO-USERS	CRE-VICES	NAY-WARDS	ENT-WINES	CUT-WORMS
FLO-UNDER	ACC-USING	SER-VICES	NOR-WARDS	INT-WINES	EEL-WORMS
GAZ-UNDER	ARO-USING	CER-VICES	OUT-WARDS	LAU-WINES	LOB-WORMS
GRO-UNDER	BEM-USING	BRE-VIERS	SEA-WARDS	UNT-WINES	LUG-WORMS
REF-UNDER	BLO-USING	CLA-VIERS	SKY-WARDS	BRE-WINGS	RAG-WORMS
ROT-UNDER	CHO-USING	KLA-VIERS	STE-WARDS	DRA-WINGS	SEA-WORMS
DIS-UNION	DEF-USING	PRE-VIEWS	SUN-WARDS	GRO-WINGS	WEB-WORMS
AUT-UNITE	DIS-USING	PUR-VIEWS	SEA-WARES	INS-WINGS	OUT-WORTH
BRA-UNITE	EFF-USING	SUR-VIEWS	TIN-WARES	LAP-WINGS	TAM-WORTH
DIS-UNITE	EXC-USING	PUL-VILLI	UNA-WARES	OUT-WINGS	WAN-WORTH
REP-UNITS	FLO-USING	DRE-VILLS	WET-WARES	RED-WINGS	BLA-WORTS
SUB-UNITS	FOC-USING	PRO-VINED	BUL-WARKS	SHO-WINGS	BUG-WORTS
DIS-UNITY	GRO-USING	SPA-VINED	PRE-WARMS	SLO-WINGS	FEL-WORTS
IMM-UNITY	HOC-USING	FLA-VINES	UPS-WARMS	STE-WINGS	FIG-WORTS
IMP-UNITY	INC-USING	MAU-VINES	FOR-WARNS	STO-WINGS	MAD-WORTS
JEJ-UNITY	INF-USING	NER-VINES	PRE-WARNS	THA-WINGS	MUD-WORTS
TRI-UNITY	MIS-USING	OLI-VINES	BLE-WARTS	UPS-WINGS	MUG-WORTS
BEG-UNKED	PER-USING	PRO-VINES	TIS-WASES	VIE-WINGS	RAG-WORTS
DEB-UNKED	REC-USING	SYL-VINES	TIZ-WASES	WAX-WINGS	RIB-WORTS
DEC-UPLED	REF-USING	PRO-VIRAL	FOR-WASTE	CHE-WINKS	OUT-WOUND
OCT-UPLED	SMO-USING	SUB-VIRAL	RAD-WASTE	HAY-WIRES	POW-WOWED
SCR-UPLED	SPO-USING	POX-VIRUS	OUT-WATCH	WAY-WISER	EEL-WRACK
SHT-UPPED	AFL-UTTER	PRO-VIRUS	POM-WATER	BRE-WISES	OUT-WREST
TIT-UPPED	INP-UTTER	PRE-VISED	RED-WATER	ENT-WISTS	AVO-WRIES
ACC-URATE	REB-UTTER	CLE-VISES	SEA-WATER	INT-WISTS	CHO-WRIES
DEP-URATE	SPL-UTTER	PAR-VISES	AIR-WAVES	UNT-WISTS	SCO-WRIES
FIG-URATE	STR-UTTER	PEL-VISES	EAR-WAXES	MID-WIVED	MIS-WRITE
INA-URATE	PER-VADED	PRE-VISES	PAX-WAXES	ALE-WIVES	MIS-WROTE
IND-URATE	COU-VADES	TRA-VISES	UNS-WAYED	HUS-WIVES	BOW-YANGS
MAT-URATE	PER-VADES	TRE-VISES	UPS-WAYED	MID-WIVES	HAL-YARDS
OBD-URATE	PRE-VAILS	PRO-VISOR	LEG-WEARS	SEA-WIVES	INN-YARDS
OBT-URATE	TRA-VAILS	CUR-VITAL	OUT-WEARS	REA-WOKEN	LAN-YARDS
SAT-URATE	CHE-VALET	GRA-VITAS	UNS-WEARS	AIR-WOMAN	TAN-YARDS
CON-URBAN	DIS-VALUE	CON-VIVES	FOR-WEARY	BAT-WOMAN	BIC-YCLED
SUB-URBAN	OUT-VALUE	SUR-VIVES	OUT-WEARY	LAY-WOMAN	CAL-YCLED
EXP-URGED	TRI-VALVE	SUB-VOCAL	COB-WEBBY	MAD-WOMAN	REC-YCLED
RES-URGED	UNI-VALVE	UNI-VOCAL	BUR-WEEDS	PEN-WOMAN	EMP-YESES
SCO-URGED	DOG-VANES	OUT-VOICE	CUD-WEEDS	SEA-WOMAN	LAD-YLIKE
SPL-URGED	SER-VANTS	CON-VOLVE	HOG-WEEDS	TOY-WOMAN	DIS-YOKED
UNP-URGED	CAN-VASES	OUT-VOTED	MAT-WEEDS	AIR-WOMEN	MIS-YOKES
UPS-URGED	SIL-VATIC	OUT-VOTER	MAY-WEEDS	BAT-WOMEN	DIS-YOKES
SCO-URGER	SYL-VATIC	OUT-VOTES	OAR-WEEDS	LAY-WOMEN	MIS-YOKES
EXP-URGES	MAU-VEINS	DIS-VOUCH	ORE-WEEDS	MAD-WOMEN	GUA-YULES
RES-URGES	LOW-VELDS	UNA-VOWED	OUT-WEEDS	PEN-WOMEN	BEN-ZINES
SCO-URGES	KNE-VELLS	BIV-VYING	PIG-WEEDS	SEA-WOMEN	FAN-ZINES
SPL-URGES	PRO-VENDS	CHE-VYING	RAG-WEEDS	TOY-WOMEN	OXA-ZINES
UPS-URGES	SCA-VENGE	CHI-VYING	SEA-WEEDS	BAR-WOODS	RHI-ZINES
MAN-URIAL	OUT-VENOM	NAV-VYING	TAR-WEEDS	BOX-WOODS	BUZ-ZINGS
REB-URIAL	CON-VENTS	OUT-VYING	BET-WEENS	CAM-WOODS	FIZ-ZINGS
TEN-URIAL	PRE-VENTS	SAV-VYING	MIS-WEENS	DAG-WOODS	GLA-ZINGS
DAT-URINE	SOL-VENTS	ASS-WAGED	ENS-WEEPS	DOG-WOODS	GLO-ZINGS
FIG-URINE	PAR-VENUS	ASS-WAGES	OUT-WEEPS	ELM-WOODS	GRA-ZINGS
LEM-URINE	PRE-VERBS	BRE-WAGES	UPS-WEEPS	LOG-WOODS	SEI-ZINGS
SCI-URINE	PRO-VERBS	FLO-WAGES	OUT-WEIGH	NUT-WOODS	SUB-ZONAL
XEN-URINE	CON-VERGE	STO-WAGES	IND-WELLS	PLY-WOODS	TRI-ZONAL
LAZ-URITE	PER-VERSE	REA-WAKED	INK-WELLS	RED-WOODS	BLA-ZONED
ROB-URITE	REN-VERSE	REA-WAKEN	MAX-WELLS	SAP-WOODS	CAL-ZONES
RET-URNED	SUB-VERSE	REA-WAKES	OUT-WELLS	KEY-WORDS	SUB-ZONES
UNB-URNED	TRA-VERSE	GUN-WALES	UPS-WELLS	MIS-WORDS	TRI-ZONES
UNT-URNED	UNI-VERSE	QAW-WALIS	MIS-WELLS	NAY-WORDS	GAD-ZOOKS
UPT-URNED	REN-VERST	JAY-WALKS	BOB-WHEEL	WAN-WORDY	MAD-ZOONS
DIS-USAGE	SUB-VERST	OUT-WALKS	COG-WHEEL	ART-WORKS	MAT-ZOONS
MIS-USAGE	CON-VERTS	GAD-WALLS	FLY-WHEEL	CAT-WORKS	
SPO-USAGE		SET-WALLS	RAG-WHEEL	CUT-WORKS	

Section Three

Endings

Introduction

Although it may be easier to spot beginnings of words when looking for a play (perhaps there is a word beginning with BE- or DIS- or QU- or RE- or UN- ?) some of the common endings, such as -ED, -ER and -ING – not forgetting the humble -S – also come easily to mind. As you become more adept, however, you will start looking for other endings in the hope of discovering a bonus word.

In the following sets of lists the words are arranged according to their endings rather than their beginnings. The first set of lists covers useful suffixes, and the second set words ending in A, I, O or U.

Useful Suffixes

The following lists are of 7- and 8-letter words ending with these suffixes:

-ABLE	-FORM	-LAND	-SMEN
-AGE	-FUL	-LESS	-SOME
-ANCE	-GEN	-LET	-TIME
-ANCY	-GRAM	-LIKE	-TION
-ARCH	-HOLE	-LOGY	-URE
-BACK	-HOOD	-LY	-WARD
-BALL	-HORN	-MAN	-WARDS
-BAND	-IBLE	-MEN	-WAY
-BIRD	-IFY	-NESS	-WISE
-DOM	-INGS	-OID	-WOOD
-EAUX	-ISE	-OR	-WORK
-ENCE	-ISH	-OUS	-WORM
-ENCY	-ISM	-OUT	-WORT
-EST	-IST	-SET	-YARD
-ETTE	-ITY	-SHIP	
-EUR	-IUM	-SKIN	
-FISH	-KIN	-SMAN	

Words ending with -INGS, -LY and -EST should be especially useful, as Scrabble players often ponder questions such as:

'I know HOSTING is a word, but does it take an S?'

'I know SULTRY is all right, but what about SULTRILY?'

'I know the adjective OARY, but is the superlative OARIEST acceptable?'

Familiarity with the lists here should provide instant answers to these and similar questions.

In the case of the -EST words, where these are superlatives, it can be assumed that the corresponding comparatives ending in -ER, eg OARIER, are also acceptable.

Note that sometimes words qualify for more than one suffix list. For example, the -FISH words also appear in the -ISH list, the -SKIN words also appear in the -KIN list, and the -SMAN and -SMEN words also appear in the -MAN and -MEN lists respectively.

As it was felt that it would be helpful if all the lists were complete, words that coincidentally end in the suffix letters have been retained, even though the letters are not used as a suffix in them. Examples of such words are OUTDANCE and UNDEVOUT, which are shown in the -ANCE and -OUT lists respectively.

Chambers Back-Words, which lists all words according to alphabetical sequence of endings, can be used as a pointer to other endings, but note that it is *not* based on *Official Scrabble®️ Words*.

ENDINGS: Useful Suffixes

WORDS ENDING IN -ABLE

7-letter words -ABLE

ACCABLE	CITABLE	EATABLE	FRIABLE	MIRABLE	PARABLE	ROWABLE	SUEABLE	UNHABLE
ACTABLE	CURABLE	EFFABLE	HATABLE	MIXABLE	PAYABLE	RULABLE	TAKABLE	VATABLE
AFFABLE	DATABLE	EQUABLE	HIRABLE	MOVABLE	PLIABLE	SALABLE	TAMABLE	VOCABLE
AMIABLE	DISABLE	ERRABLE	LIKABLE	MUTABLE	POTABLE	SAVABLE	TAXABLE	VOLABLE
ASTABLE	DOWABLE	FADABLE	LIVABLE	NAMABLE	RATABLE	SAYABLE	TENABLE	
BATABLE	DUPABLE	FINABLE	LOSABLE	NOTABLE	RETABLE	SEEABLE	TOWABLE	
BUYABLE	DURABLE	FIXABLE	LOVABLE	PACABLE	RIDABLE	SIZABLE	TRIABLE	
CAPABLE	DYEABLE	FLYABLE	MAKABLE	PAPABLE	ROPABLE	SKIABLE	TUNABLE	

8-letter words -ABLE

ABATABLE	DAMNABLE	GAINABLE	KNOWABLE	OPENABLE	REUSABLE	SPARABLE	UNUSABLE
ADORABLE	DATEABLE	GETTABLE	LAPSABLE	OPERABLE	RIDEABLE	STATABLE	UNVIABLE
AMENABLE	DENIABLE	GRADABLE	LAUDABLE	OPINABLE	RINSABLE	STORABLE	VALUABLE
AMICABLE	DIGGABLE	GROWABLE	LEASABLE	PALPABLE	ROLLABLE	SUITABLE	VARIABLE
AMUSABLE	DISHABLE	GUIDABLE	LETTABLE	PANTABLE	ROPEABLE	SYLLABLE	VIEWABLE
ARGUABLE	DRAWABLE	GULLABLE	LEVIABLE	PASSABLE	RUINABLE	TAKEABLE	VIOLABLE
AVOWABLE	DRIVABLE	GUSTABLE	LIFTABLE	PECCABLE	RUNNABLE	TALKABLE	VITIABLE
BAILABLE	DUTIABLE	HANGABLE	LIKEABLE	PINTABLE	SAILABLE	TAMEABLE	VOIDABLE
BANKABLE	EDUCABLE	HATEABLE	LINKABLE	PITIABLE	SALEABLE	TANNABLE	WALKABLE
BEARABLE	ENVIABLE	HEALABLE	LIQUABLE	PLACABLE	SALVABLE	TAPEABLE	WARHABLE
BEATABLE	ERASABLE	HELPABLE	LIVEABLE	PLAYABLE	SATIABLE	TAPPABLE	WASHABLE
BEDDABLE	EVADABLE	HIREABLE	LOANABLE	PORTABLE	SCALABLE	TASTABLE	WASTABLE
BIDDABLE	EVITABLE	HUGGABLE	LOCKABLE	POSEABLE	SEIZABLE	TEARABLE	WEARABLE
BISTABLE	EVOCABLE	HUMMABLE	LOVEABLE	POURABLE	SELLABLE	TELLABLE	WELDABLE
BLAMABLE	EXORABLE	IMITABLE	LUGGABLE	PRIZABLE	SHAKABLE	TESTABLE	WILLABLE
BOOKABLE	EXPIABLE	INARABLE	MAILABLE	PROBABLE	SHAMABLE	TILLABLE	WINNABLE
BOOTABLE	FELLABLE	INSTABLE	MAKEABLE	PROVABLE	SHAPABLE	TILTABLE	WORKABLE
CHEWABLE	FILMABLE	INVIABLE	MISSABLE	QUOTABLE	SINGABLE	TIPPABLE	WRITABLE
CITEABLE	FISHABLE	ISOLABLE	MOCKABLE	RAISABLE	SIZEABLE	TITHABLE	
CLUBABLE	FOLDABLE	ISSUABLE	MOOTABLE	RATEABLE	SMOKABLE	TOLLABLE	
COOKABLE	FORDABLE	JUMPABLE	MOVEABLE	READABLE	SOCIABLE	TRADABLE	
CULPABLE	FORMABLE	KICKABLE	NAMEABLE	RELIABLE	SOLVABLE	TUNEABLE	
CURBABLE	FUNDABLE	KISSABLE	OATHABLE	RENTABLE	SORTABLE	UNSTABLE	

WORDS ENDING IN -AGE

7-letter words -AGE

ABUSAGE	BROCAGE	CRANAGE	HAULAGE	MILEAGE	PLUSAGE	SALVAGE	TANKAGE	VITRAGE
ACREAGE	BROKAGE	DISCAGE	HEADAGE	MINTAGE	PONDAGE	SAUSAGE	TANNAGE	VOLTAGE
AJUTAGE	BUOYAGE	DOCKAGE	HERBAGE	MOCKAGE	PONTAGE	SCAVAGE	TEENAGE	WAFTAGE
AMENAGE	BURGAGE	DRAYAGE	HIREAGE	MONTAGE	PORTAGE	SCUTAGE	TENTAGE	WAINAGE
APANAGE	CABBAGE	DUNNAGE	HOSTAGE	MOORAGE	POSTAGE	SEEPAGE	THANAGE	WANTAGE
ARRIAGE	CARNAGE	ESCUAGE	KEELAGE	MOULAGE	POTTAGE	SELVAGE	TILLAGE	WASTAGE
ASSUAGE	CARTAGE	ETALAGE	KIPPAGE	OUTRAGE	PRESAGE	SERFAGE	TOLLAGE	WATTAGE
ASSWAGE	CENTAGE	FALDAGE	LAIRAGE	OUVRAGE	PRIMAGE	SIGNAGE	TONNAGE	WEFTAGE
AULNAGE	COINAGE	FARDAGE	LASTAGE	OVERAGE	PRISAGE	SINKAGE	TRUCAGE	WINDAGE
AVERAGE	COLLAGE	FLOTAGE	LEAFAGE	PACKAGE	PROPAGE	SOAKAGE	TUNNAGE	WORDAGE
BAGGAGE	COMPAGE	FLOWAGE	LEAKAGE	PANNAGE	QUAYAGE	SOCCAGE	UMBRAGE	YARDAGE
BANDAGE	CORDAGE	FOGGAGE	LIGNAGE	PASSAGE	RAMPAGE	SOILAGE	UPSTAGE	
BARRAGE	CORKAGE	FOLIAGE	LINEAGE	PAYSAGE	REMUAGE	SONDAGE	VANTAGE	
BEERAGE	CORNAGE	FOOTAGE	LINKAGE	PEERAGE	RESTAGE	SPINAGE	VENDAGE	
BONDAGE	CORSAGE	FULLAGE	LOCKAGE	PEONAGE	RIBCAGE	STORAGE	VENTAGE	
BOSCAGE	COTTAGE	GARBAGE	LUGGAGE	PIERAGE	ROOTAGE	STOWAGE	VIDUAGE	
BOSKAGE	COURAGE	GUIDAGE	MASSAGE	PILLAGE	RUMMAGE	SULLAGE	VILLAGE	
BREWAGE	COWHAGE	GUNNAGE	MESSAGE	PLUMAGE	SACKAGE	TALLAGE	VINTAGE	

8-letter words -AGE

ACCORAGE	BLINDAGE	COZENAGE	FLOATAGE	HERITAGE	PILOTAGE	SPILLAGE	SUBSTAGE
ACIERAGE	BLOCKAGE	CRIBBAGE	FOOTPAGE	LANGRAGE	PLANTAGE	SPOILAGE	SUFFRAGE
ADJUTAGE	BREAKAGE	DIALLAGE	FRAUTAGE	LANGUAGE	PLUSSAGE	SPOUSAGE	TASSWAGE
AGIOTAGE	BROCKAGE	DISUSAGE	FRONDAGE	LEVERAGE	POUNDAGE	SQUIRAGE	THIRLAGE
ALIENAGE	CABOTAGE	DRAINAGE	FRONTAGE	MALAXAGE	PROPHAGE	STAFFAGE	TRACKAGE
ALTARAGE	CARRIAGE	DRESSAGE	FROTTAGE	MARITAGE	PUCELAGE	STALLAGE	TRUCKAGE
AMPERAGE	CARUCAGE	DRIFTAGE	FRUITAGE	MARRIAGE	PUPILAGE	STEARAGE	TRUQUAGE
APPANAGE	CHANTAGE	ENALLAGE	FUSELAGE	MESSUAGE	ROUGHAGE	STEERAGE	TUTELAGE
BADINAGE	CHUMMAGE	ENDAMAGE	GRAINAGE	METAYAGE	SABOTAGE	STERNAGE	TUTORAGE
BARONAGE	CLEARAGE	ENSILAGE	GRILLAGE	MISUSAGE	SEWERAGE	STILLAGE	UMPIRAGE
BERTHAGE	CLEAVAGE	ENVISAGE	GROUPAGE	MORTGAGE	SHORTAGE	STOPPAGE	VAULTAGE
BEVERAGE	CLOUDAGE	EQUIPAGE	GUARDAGE	MUCILAGE	SLIPPAGE	STREWAGE	VAUNTAGE
BIRDCAGE	COVERAGE	FERRIAGE	HELOTAGE	OVERPAGE	SMALLAGE	STUMPAGE	VERBIAGE

VICARAGE   VICINAGE   WAGONAGE   WATERAGE   WEIGHAGE   WHARFAGE   WRAPPAGE   WRECKAGE

WORDS ENDING IN -ANCE

7-letter words -ANCE

ADVANCE   ASKANCE   CREANCE   ENHANCE   JOYANCE   PENANCE   SONANCE   VACANCE
AIDANCE   BALANCE   DURANCE   FINANCE   NOYANCE   ROMANCE   SURANCE   VALANCE

8-letter words -ANCE

ABEYANCE   AMORANCE   DEVIANCE   GUIDANCE   NUISANCE   PASTANCE   RESIANCE   VALIANCE
ABIDANCE   BECHANCE   DISTANCE   INSTANCE   ORDNANCE   PITTANCE   RIDDANCE   VARIANCE
AFFIANCE   BUOYANCE   ELEGANCE   ISSUANCE   OUTDANCE   PORTANCE   SORTANCE   VOIDANCE
ALLIANCE   CREPANCE   ENTRANCE   ITERANCE   OUTRANCE   RADIANCE   TADVANCE
AMBIANCE   DEFIANCE   EXITANCE   LAITANCE   PARLANCE   RELIANCE   TENDANCE

WORDS ENDING IN -ANCY

7-letter words -ANCY

INFANCY   PLIANCY   SONANCY   TENANCY   TRUANCY   VACANCY

8-letter words -ANCY

ABEYANCY   DEVIANCY   GEOMANCY   MORDANCY   PERNANCY   RAMPANCY   VALIANCY   ZOOMANCY
BUOYANCY   DORMANCY   IMITANCY   MYOMANCY   PIQUANCY   UNCHANCY   VERDANCY
CLAMANCY   ELEGANCY   INSTANCY   PECCANCY   RADIANCY   VAGRANCY   VIBRANCY

WORDS ENDING IN -ARCH

7-letter words -ARCH

ENDARCH   HEXARCH   MESARCH   MONARCH   NAVARCH   NOMARCH   TOPARCH   TRIARCH   XERARCH

8-letter words -ARCH

ETHNARCH   HIERARCH   OLIGARCH   OVERARCH   PHYLARCH   RESEARCH   TETRARCH
HEPTARCH   HIPPARCH   OUTMARCH   PENTARCH   POLYARCH   TAXIARCH   UNSTARCH

WORDS ENDING IN -BACK

7-letter words -BACK

CUTBACK   FINBACK   LAYBACK   PAYBACK   RUNBACK   SOWBACK   WETBACK
DIEBACK   HOGBACK   OUTBACK   REDBACK   SETBACK   TIEBACK

8-letter words -BACK

BAREBACK   DRAWBACK   FULLBACK   KICKBACK   PICKBACK   SOFTBACK   TURNBACK
BLUEBACK   FASTBACK   HARDBACK   LIFTBACK   PLAYBACK   SWAYBACK
CLAWBACK   FEEDBACK   HOLDBACK   LOANBACK   SKEWBACK   TAILBACK
COMEBACK   FLATBACK   HUMPBACK   MOSSBACK   SLOWBACK   TALKBACK

WORDS ENDING IN -BALL

7-letter words -BALL

EYEBALL   ICEBALL   NETBALL   ODDBALL   PATBALL   PINBALL   PROBALL

8-letter words -BALL

BASEBALL   CORNBALL   FISHBALL   GOOFBALL   HIGHBALL   MEATBALL   PUFFBALL   WASHBALL
BLOWBALL   FASTBALL   FOOTBALL   HANDBALL   KICKBALL   MOTHBALL   SNOWBALL
COALBALL   FIREBALL   GOALBALL   HARDBALL   KORFBALL   PITHBALL   SOFTBALL

WORDS ENDING IN -BAND

7-letter words -BAND

ARMBAND   DISBAND   HATBAND   HAYBAND   HUSBAND   PROBAND   RIBBAND   SALBAND   TURBAND

8-letter words -BAND

BACKBAND	BROWBAND	HEADBAND	NOSEBAND	RAINBAND	SIDEBAND
BASEBAND	FAHLBAND	NECKBAND	PLATBAND	SARABAND	WAVEBAND

WORDS ENDING IN -BIRD

7-letter words -BIRD

ANTBIRD   AWLBIRD   CATBIRD   COWBIRD   REDBIRD   SEABIRD   SUNBIRD   WOSBIRD

8-letter words -BIRD

BLUEBIRD	COCKBIRD	HANGBIRD	LOVEBIRD	SNOWBIRD	SURFBIRD	YARDBIRD
CAGEBIRD	FERNBIRD	LADYBIRD	PUFFBIRD	SONGBIRD	WHIPBIRD

WORDS ENDING IN -DOM

7-letter words -DOM

BABUDOM	DOLLDOM	FIEFDOM	FREEDOM	HEIRDOM	POPEDOM	STARDOM
BOREDOM	DUKEDOM	FILMDOM	GURUDOM	HOBODOM	RHABDOM	TSARDOM
CZARDOM	EARLDOM	FOGYDOM	HALIDOM	KINGDOM	SERFDOM

8-letter words -DOM

BABELDOM	CLERKDOM	FOGEYDOM	LIEGEDOM	QUEENDOM	SHEIKDOM	UNSELDOM
BIRTHDOM	DEVILDOM	GYPSYDOM	NOVELDOM	QUEERDOM	SWELLDOM	UNWISDOM
BLOKEDOM	DUNCEDOM	HIPPYDOM	PAPPADOM	REBELDOM	THANEDOM	VILLADOM
CHIEFDOM	FAIRYDOM	LEECHDOM	PUPPYDOM	SAINTDOM	THRALDOM	WHOREDOM

WORDS ENDING IN -EAUX

7-letter words -EAUX

BATEAUX   BUREAUX   CADEAUX   COTEAUX   GATEAUX   RESEAUX

8-letter words -EAUX

BANDEAUX	CHAPEAUX	JAMBEAUX	MORCEAUX	PONCEAUX	ROULEAUX	TONNEAUX
BERCEAUX	CHATEAUX	MANTEAUX	PLATEAUX	RONDEAUX	TABLEAUX	TRUMEAUX

WORDS ENDING IN -ENCE

7-letter words -ENCE

ABSENCE	COGENCE	ESSENCE	FAYENCE	LATENCE	OFFENCE	REGENCE	SILENCE	VALENCE
CADENCE	DEFENCE	FAIENCE	FLUENCE	LICENCE	POTENCE	SCIENCE	URGENCE

8-letter words -ENCE

AMBIENCE	DISPENCE	FLORENCE	OPULENCE	PUNGENCE	SITHENCE	TUPPENCE
AUDIENCE	EMINENCE	LENIENCE	PATIENCE	SALIENCE	SIXPENCE	TWOPENCE
CLARENCE	EVIDENCE	MERGENCE	PRESENCE	SAPIENCE	SUSPENCE	VERGENCE
COMMENCE	EXIGENCE	NASCENCE	PRETENCE	SENTENCE	TENDENCE	VIOLENCE
CREDENCE	FIPPENCE	NOWHENCE	PRUDENCE	SEQUENCE	TENPENCE

WORDS ENDING IN -ENCY

7-letter words -ENCY

ARDENCY	COGENCY	FLUENCY	LUCENCY	PATENCY	PUDENCY	REGENCY	VALENCY
CADENCY	DECENCY	LATENCY	ORIENCY	POTENCY	RECENCY	URGENCY	VIVENCY

8-letter words -ENCY

CLEMENCY	EXIGENCY	LAMBENCY	PENDENCY	SALIENCY	TENDENCY
CURRENCY	FERVENCY	LENIENCY	PUNGENCY	SOLVENCY	VERGENCY
EMINENCY	FULGENCY	NASCENCY	REAGENCY	TANGENCY

WORDS ENDING IN -EST

7-letter words -EST

ACHIEST	CAMPEST	DOPIEST	FOZIEST	KEENEST	MIRIEST	PIPIEST	SAIDEST	TOWIEST
ACIDEST	CANIEST	DOTIEST	FULLEST	KINDEST	MIRKEST	POKIEST	SAIREST	TRITEST
ACQUEST	CANTEST	DOUCEST	FUMIEST	LACIEST	MITIEST	POOREST	SALTEST	TUNIEST
ACUTEST	CHICEST	DOUREST	FUNNEST	LAKIEST	MIXIEST	PORIEST	SAMIEST	UGLIEST
ADDREST	CLOSEST	DOVIEST	GABFEST	LANGEST	MOOTEST	POSHEST	SEAREST	UNBLEST
AERIEST	COKIEST	DOWIEST	GAINEST	LANKEST	MOPIEST	POSIEST	SEIKEST	VAGUEST
AGILEST	COLDEST	DOZIEST	GAMIEST	LARGEST	MOTIEST	POXIEST	SEXIEST	VAINEST
AIRIEST	CONFEST	DROLEST	GASHEST	LAZIEST	MURKEST	PRETEST	SICKEST	VASTEST
AMPLEST	CONGEST	DUFFEST	GAZIEST	LEANEST	NAIFEST	PRONEST	SIZIEST	VERIEST
ANAPEST	CONTEST	DULLEST	GLUIEST	LEFTEST	NAIVEST	PROTEST	SKEWEST	VINIEST
ARCHEST	COOLEST	DUMBEST	GOLDEST	LENGEST	NEAREST	PUIREST	SKYIEST	VOGIEST
ARIDEST	COSIEST	DUNNEST	GOOIEST	LEWDEST	NEATEST	PULIEST	SLOWEST	WALIEST
ARTIEST	COXIEST	DUSKEST	GORIEST	LIEFEST	NESHEST	PUNIEST	SNIDEST	WANIEST
ASHIEST	COZIEST	DYKIEST	GOWDEST	LIEVEST	NIGHEST	PUNKEST	SOFTEST	WANNEST
AULDEST	CRUDEST	EARNEST	GRAVEST	LIMIEST	NOBLEST	QUAREST	SOONEST	WARIEST
AVIDEST	CURTEST	EASIEST	GRAYEST	LIMPEST	NOSIEST	RACIEST	SOUREST	WARMEST
AWAREST	DAFTEST	EDGIEST	GREYEST	LINIEST	NUMBEST	RADDEST	SPAREST	WATTEST
AWNIEST	DAMPEST	EELIEST	HARDEST	LITHEST	OAKIEST	RADGEST	SPRYEST	WAVIEST
BABIEST	DANKEST	EERIEST	HARVEST	LOGIEST	OARIEST	RANKEST	STALEST	WAXIEST
BALDEST	DARKEST	EGGIEST	HAZIEST	LONGEST	OBESEST	RASHEST	STEYEST	WEAKEST
BARGEST	DEADEST	ELMIEST	HEPPEST	LOOSEST	OILIEST	RATHEST	SUAVEST	WEETEST
BASSEST	DEAFEST	EVENEST	HIGHEST	LOTHEST	ONLIEST	REALEST	SUGGEST	WETTEST
BEQUEST	DEAREST	FABBEST	HIPPEST	LOUDEST	OORIEST	REDDEST	TAKIEST	WHITEST
BIGGEST	DEEDEST	FADIEST	HOKIEST	LOWSEST	OOSIEST	REQUEST	TALLEST	WILDEST
BLATEST	DEEPEST	FAINEST	HOLIEST	LUSHEST	OOZIEST	RICHEST	TANNEST	WILIEST
BLUIEST	DEFFEST	FAIREST	HOMIEST	MADDEST	OPENEST	RICIEST	TARTEST	WILLEST
BOLDEST	DEFTEST	FALSEST	HOTTEST	MAINEST	ORBIEST	RILIEST	TAUTEST	WINIEST
BONIEST	DEIDEST	FASTEST	ICKIEST	MATIEST	OULDEST	RIMIEST	TAWIEST	WIRIEST
BOSSEST	DENSEST	FATTEST	IFFIEST	MAUVEST	OURIEST	ROKIEST	TEDIEST	WOTTEST
BOXIEST	DEWIEST	FELLEST	IMPREST	MAZIEST	OUTJEST	ROPIEST	TEMPEST	WOWFEST
BRAVEST	DICIEST	FIKIEST	INANEST	MEANEST	OWLIEST	RORIEST	TENSEST	YUKIEST
BRAWEST	DIKIEST	FIRMEST	INKIEST	MEEKEST	OWRIEST	ROSIEST	TERSEST	ZANIEST
BUMMEST	DIMMEST	FITTEST	INQUEST	MEETEST	PACIEST	RUBIEST	TIDIEST	
BUSIEST	DINKEST	FLUIEST	IRATEST	MIDDEST	PALIEST	RULIEST	TINIEST	
CAGIEST	DISGEST	FONDEST	JIMPEST	MILDEST	PERTEST	RUMMEST	TOEIEST	
CAKIEST	DISNEST	FOULEST	JOKIEST	MIMMEST	PINIEST	SADDEST	TONIEST	
CALMEST	DOMIEST	FOXIEST	JUSTEST	MINIEST	PINKEST	SAGIEST	TOOMEST	

8-letter words -EST

ACERBEST	BILGIEST	BRISKEST	CLAYIEST	DANDIEST	DROLLEST	FERNIEST	FUBBIEST
ACIDIEST	BIRKIEST	BROADEST	CLEANEST	DAUBIEST	DRONIEST	FETIDEST	FUBSIEST
ACRIDEST	BIRSIEST	BROWNEST	CLEAREST	DEBBIEST	DRUNKEST	FICKLEST	FUFFIEST
ADEPTEST	BITSIEST	BUDDIEST	COALIEST	DEEDIEST	DRUSIEST	FIERCEST	FUGGIEST
AFFOREST	BITTIEST	BUGGIEST	COARSEST	DEFOREST	DRUXIEST	FIERIEST	FUNKIEST
ALCAHEST	BLACKEST	BULGIEST	COBBIEST	DEMUREST	DUCKIEST	FILMIEST	FUNNIEST
ALERTEST	BLANDEST	BULKIEST	COCKIEST	DICKIEST	DUDDIEST	FINNIEST	FURRIEST
ALKAHEST	BLANKEST	BULLIEST	COMBIEST	DICTIEST	DULLIEST	FIRRIEST	FURTHEST
ANAPAEST	BLEAKEST	BUMPIEST	CONKIEST	DIDDIEST	DUMMIEST	FISHIEST	FURZIEST
ANGRIEST	BLEAREST	BUNTIEST	CONQUEST	DILLIEST	DUMPIEST	FISTIEST	FUSSIEST
ANTSIEST	BLINDEST	BURLIEST	COOMIEST	DINGIEST	DUNGIEST	FITLIEST	FUSTIEST
ARBALEST	BLITHEST	BURRIEST	COPSIEST	DINKIEST	DUNNIEST	FIZZIEST	FUTILEST
ARTSIEST	BLOKIEST	BUSHIEST	CORKIEST	DIPPIEST	DURGIEST	FLAKIEST	FUZZIEST
ASTUTEST	BLONDEST	BUSTIEST	CORNIEST	DIRTIEST	DUSKIEST	FLAMIEST	GABBIEST
BAGGIEST	BLOWIEST	BUTCHEST	COUTHEST	DISHIEST	DUSTIEST	FLARIEST	GAMMIEST
BALDIEST	BLUDIEST	BUXOMEST	CRAPIEST	DITSIEST	DWARFEST	FLASHEST	GAPPIEST
BALKIEST	BLUFFEST	BUZZIEST	CRASSEST	DITZIEST	EAGEREST	FLATTEST	GASPIEST
BALMIEST	BLUNTEST	CADGIEST	CRAZIEST	DIVINEST	EARLIEST	FLAWIEST	GASSIEST
BANALEST	BODGIEST	CALMIEST	CREPIEST	DIZZIEST	EMONGEST	FLAXIEST	GAUCHEST
BANDIEST	BOGGIEST	CAMPIEST	CRISPEST	DOCILEST	EMPTIEST	FLEETEST	GAUCIEST
BARDIEST	BONNIEST	CANNIEST	CRONKEST	DODDIEST	ENFOREST	FLIPPEST	GAUDIEST
BARGHEST	BOOKIEST	CANTIEST	CROOKEST	DODGIEST	EVILLEST	FLORIEST	GAUMIEST
BARKIEST	BOOKREST	CARNIEST	CROSSEST	DOGGIEST	EXACTEST	FLUKIEST	GAUNTEST
BARMIEST	BOOZIEST	CATTIEST	CRUMPEST	DOILTEST	FADDIEST	FLUSHEST	GAUZIEST
BASSIEST	BOSKIEST	CAULDEST	CURDIEST	DONSIEST	FAINTEST	FLUTIEST	GAWCIEST
BATTIEST	BOSSIEST	CHARIEST	CURLIEST	DOOMIEST	FANCIEST	FOAMIEST	GAWKIEST
BAWDIEST	BOUSIEST	CHASTEST	CURNIEST	DORKIEST	FARTHEST	FOGGIEST	GAWSIEST
BEADIEST	BRAIDEST	CHEAPEST	CURRIEST	DORTIEST	FATTIEST	FOOTIEST	GEEKIEST
BEAKIEST	BRAKIEST	CHEWIEST	CURVIEST	DOTTIEST	FEEBLEST	FOOTREST	GELIDEST
BEAMIEST	BRASHEST	CHIEFEST	CUSHIEST	DOTTLEST	FEINTEST	FORKIEST	GEMMIEST
BEEFIEST	BRENTEST	CHILLEST	CUTTIEST	DOWDIEST	FELTIEST	FRAILEST	GENTIEST
BEERIEST	BRIEFEST	CHOICEST	DAFFIEST	DOWNIEST	FENDIEST	FRANKEST	GENTLEST
BENDIEST	BRILLEST	CHOKIEST	DAGGIEST	DRABBEST	FENNIEST	FRESHEST	GIDDIEST
BENTIEST	BRINIEST	CISSIEST	DAMPIEST	DREAREST	FERLIEST	FROWIEST	GIMPIEST

GINNIEST	HUMANEST	LUSHIEST	NOOKIEST	RANGIEST	SHINIEST	SUDSIEST	UNHONEST
GIRNIEST	HUMBLEST	LUSTIEST	NOUNIEST	RAPIDEST	SHOALEST	SUETIEST	UNIQUEST
GLADDEST	HUMIDEST	MALTIEST	NUBBIEST	RASPIEST	SHORTEST	SULKIEST	UNPRIEST
GLADIEST	HUMPIEST	MANGIEST	NUTTIEST	RATTIEST	SHOWIEST	SUNNIEST	UNRIPEST
GLARIEST	HUNKIEST	MANIFEST	OBTUSEST	RAUCLEST	SILKIEST	SUPPLEST	UNSAFEST
GLAZIEST	HUSHIEST	MANKIEST	OFTENEST	READIEST	SILLIEST	SURFIEST	UNSUREST
GLEGGEST	HUSKIEST	MANLIEST	OPAQUEST	REAMIEST	SILTIEST	SURGIEST	UNTRUEST
GLIBBEST	IMMODEST	MARDIEST	ORANGEST	REARREST	SIMPLEST	SURLIEST	UNWISEST
GLIDDEST	IMPUREST	MARLIEST	ORNATEST	REDDIEST	SINKIEST	SVELTEST	URBANEST
GLUMMEST	INDIGEST	MASHIEST	OUTWREST	REEDIEST	SISSIEST	SWALIEST	UTTEREST
GOATIEST	INEPTEST	MASSIEST	OVERKEST	REEKIEST	SKIEYEST	SWANKEST	VAIRIEST
GODLIEST	INERTEST	MASTIEST	PALLIEST	REFOREST	SKINTEST	SWEETEST	VALIDEST
GOLDIEST	INSANEST	MATUREST	PALMIEST	REINVEST	SKIVIEST	SWELLEST	VAPIDEST
GOODIEST	INTEREST	MAWKIEST	PALSIEST	REMOTEST	SLACKEST	SWIFTEST	VASTIEST
GOOFIEST	IRONIEST	MEAGREST	PAPPIEST	RESTIEST	SLATIEST	SWIPIEST	VEALIEST
GOOPIEST	ITCHIEST	MEALIEST	PARKIEST	RIBBIEST	SLEEKEST	SWISHEST	VEILIEST
GOOSIEST	JAGGIEST	MEATIEST	PASTIEST	RICHTEST	SLICKEST	TACKIEST	VEINIEST
GORMIEST	JAMMIEST	MELTIEST	PAWKIEST	RIDGIEST	SLIMIEST	TAGGIEST	VIEWIEST
GORSIEST	JANTIEST	MERRIEST	PEAKIEST	RIFTIEST	SLIMMEST	TALCIEST	VIVIDEST
GOUTIEST	JAZZIEST	MESHIEST	PEARTEST	RIGHTEST	SLOPIEST	TALKFEST	VOGUIEST
GRANDEST	JEMMIEST	MESSIEST	PEATIEST	RIGIDEST	SLUGFEST	TALKIEST	VUGGIEST
GRAPIEST	JERKIEST	MIFFIEST	PEERIEST	RINDIEST	SMALLEST	TANGIEST	WACKIEST
GREATEST	JETTIEST	MIGHTEST	PEPPIEST	RISKIEST	SMARTEST	TARDIEST	WALLIEST
GREENEST	JIMPIEST	MILKIEST	PERKIEST	RITZIEST	SMOKIEST	TARRIEST	WALTIEST
GRIMIEST	JOLLIEST	MIMSIEST	PESKIEST	ROARIEST	SMUGGEST	TARTIEST	WANKIEST
GRIMMEST	JOLTIEST	MINGIEST	PETTIEST	ROCKIEST	SNAKIEST	TASTIEST	WARBIEST
GRITTEST	JOWLIEST	MINTIEST	PHATTEST	ROILIEST	SNARIEST	TATTIEST	WARTIEST
GRODIEST	JUICIEST	MINUTEST	PHONIEST	ROOFIEST	SNELLEST	TAWNIEST	WASHIEST
GROSSEST	JUMPIEST	MIRLIEST	PICKIEST	ROOKIEST	SNIPIEST	TAWTIEST	WASPIEST
GROUSEST	JUNKIEST	MISSIEST	PIGGIEST	ROOMIEST	SNODDEST	TEARIEST	WASPNEST
GRUFFEST	KEDGIEST	MISTIEST	PINKIEST	ROOPIEST	SNOWIEST	TECHIEST	WEARIEST
GRUMMEST	KIDGIEST	MOCHIEST	PIPPIEST	ROOTIEST	SNUGGEST	TEENIEST	WEBBIEST
GUCKIEST	KINKIEST	MOISTEST	PITHIEST	RORTIEST	SOAPIEST	TENTIEST	WEDGIEST
GULFIEST	KITTLEST	MOODIEST	PLAINEST	ROUGHEST	SOBEREST	TEPIDEST	WEEDIEST
GUMMIEST	KOOKIEST	MOONIEST	PLATIEST	ROUNDEST	SODDIEST	TESTIEST	WEENIEST
GUNGIEST	LAIGHEST	MOORIEST	PLUMIEST	ROUPIEST	SOGGIEST	TEUCHEST	WEEPIEST
GURLIEST	LAIRIEST	MOPPIEST	PLUMPEST	ROWDIEST	SOILIEST	TEUGHEST	WEIRDEST
GUSHIEST	LANKIEST	MOROSEST	PLUSHEST	RUDDIEST	SOLIDEST	THAWIEST	WENNIEST
GUSTIEST	LARDIEST	MOSSIEST	POCKIEST	RUGGIEST	SOMBREST	THEWIEST	WERSHEST
GUTSIEST	LARKIEST	MOTHIEST	PODDIEST	RUMMIEST	SONGFEST	THICKEST	WHEYIEST
GUTTIEST	LATHIEST	MOTLIEST	PODGIEST	RUNNIEST	SONSIEST	THINNEST	WHINIEST
HAILIEST	LAWNIEST	MOTTIEST	POLITEST	RUNTIEST	SOOTHEST	THYMIEST	WHITIEST
HAIRIEST	LEADIEST	MOUSIEST	PONCIEST	RUSHIEST	SOOTIEST	TICHIEST	WIMPIEST
HAMMIEST	LEAFIEST	MUCKIEST	PONGIEST	RUSTIEST	SOPPIEST	TIDDIEST	WINDIEST
HANDIEST	LEAKIEST	MUDDIEST	POOFIEST	RUTTIEST	SORRIEST	TIGHTEST	WINGIEST
HANGNEST	LEARIEST	MUGGIEST	POOVIEST	SAGGIEST	SOUNDEST	TILLIEST	WISPIEST
HAPPIEST	LEAVIEST	MUMSIEST	POPPIEST	SALTIEST	SOUPIEST	TIMIDEST	WITHIEST
HARDIEST	LEDGIEST	MURKIEST	PORKIEST	SANDIEST	SPACIEST	TINNIEST	WITTIEST
HARSHEST	LEERIEST	MURLIEST	PORTIEST	SAPPIEST	SPARSEST	TINTIEST	WONKIEST
HASHIEST	LEGGIEST	MUSHIEST	POTTIEST	SARKIEST	SPEWIEST	TIPPIEST	WOODIEST
HASTIEST	LEISHEST	MUSKIEST	POUTIEST	SASSIEST	SPICIEST	TIPSIEST	WOOFIEST
HEADIEST	LICHTEST	MUSSIEST	PRICIEST	SAUCIEST	SPICKEST	TIREDEST	WOOZIEST
HEADREST	LIGHTEST	MUSTIEST	PRIMMEST	SAVAGEST	SPIKIEST	TOFFIEST	WORDIEST
HEAPIEST	LINGIEST	MUZZIEST	PRIVIEST	SAVVIEST	SPINIEST	TOSHIEST	WORMIEST
HEAVIEST	LINTIEST	NAGGIEST	PROSIEST	SCALIEST	SPIRIEST	TOSSIEST	WRONGEST
HEDGIEST	LIPPIEST	NAKEDEST	PROUDEST	SCANTEST	SPRUCEST	TOTTIEST	YAPPIEST
HEFTIEST	LITTLEST	NAPPIEST	PUDGIEST	SCARCEST	SPUMIEST	TOUGHEST	YAWNIEST
HEMPIEST	LIVIDEST	NARKIEST	PUDSIEST	SCARIEST	SQUAREST	TOUSIEST	YOLKIEST
HENNIEST	LOAMIEST	NASTIEST	PUFFIEST	SEAMIEST	STABLEST	TOUTIEST	YOUNGEST
HERBIEST	LOATHEST	NATTIEST	PUGGIEST	SECUREST	STAGIEST	TOUZIEST	YUCKIEST
HILLIEST	LOFTIEST	NEEDIEST	PULPIEST	SEDATEST	STAIDEST	TOWNIEST	YUKKIEST
HIPPIEST	LOOBIEST	NERDIEST	PURPLEST	SEDGIEST	STARKEST	TOWSIEST	YUMMIEST
HOARIEST	LOONIEST	NERVIEST	PURSIEST	SEEDIEST	STEEPEST	TOWZIEST	ZAPPIEST
HOARSEST	LOOPIEST	NETTIEST	PURTIEST	SEELIEST	STEEVEST	TRIFFEST	ZESTIEST
HOOKIEST	LOSSIEST	NEWSIEST	PUSHIEST	SEEPIEST	STEWIEST	TRIGGEST	ZINCIEST
HOOLIEST	LOURIEST	NIFFIEST	QUAKIEST	SEMPLEST	STIEVEST	TRIMMEST	ZINGIEST
HOPPIEST	LOUSIEST	NIFTIEST	QUEEREST	SERENEST	STIFFEST	TRIPIEST	ZINKIEST
HORNIEST	LOWLIEST	NIMBLEST	QUICKEST	SEVEREST	STILLEST	TUBBIEST	ZIPPIEST
HORSIEST	LUCIDEST	NIPPIEST	QUIETEST	SHADIEST	STIVIEST	TUFTIEST	
HOUSIEST	LUCKIEST	NIRLIEST	RABIDEST	SHAKIEST	STONIEST	TUMPIEST	
HUFFIEST	LUMMIEST	NITTIEST	RAGGIEST	SHALIEST	STOUTEST	TURFIEST	
HULKIEST	LUMPIEST	NOBBIEST	RAINIEST	SHARPEST	SUBTLEST	TUSKIEST	
HULLIEST	LURIDEST	NOISIEST	RANDIEST	SHEEREST		TWINIEST	

WORDS ENDING IN -ETTE

7-letter words -ETTE

AILETTE	BURETTE	CUVETTE	GALETTE	LAYETTE	MOFETTE	OCTETTE	STRETTE
ARIETTE	BUVETTE	DINETTE	GAZETTE	LORETTE	MUSETTE	PALETTE	VEDETTE
AVIETTE	CUNETTE	FOUETTE	GENETTE	LUNETTE	NAVETTE	PIPETTE	VIDETTE
BLUETTE	CURETTE	FUMETTE	LADETTE	MINETTE	NONETTE	ROSETTE	

8-letter words -ETTE

AIGRETTE	BIMBETTE	DANCETTE	GRISETTE	NOISETTE	REINETTE	SEXTETTE	VIGNETTE
AMUSETTE	BRUNETTE	DISKETTE	HACKETTE	OMELETTE	ROOMETTE	SOCKETTE	
ANISETTE	CASSETTE	DRABETTE	JEANETTE	PALMETTE	ROQUETTE	SPINETTE	
BAGUETTE	COQUETTE	FAUVETTE	JOCKETTE	PIANETTE	ROULETTE	SUEDETTE	
BARBETTE	CORVETTE	FOSSETTE	MAQUETTE	POCHETTE	SEPTETTE	TOILETTE	
BARRETTE	CREVETTE	FRISETTE	MOQUETTE	RACLETTE	SESTETTE	UMBRETTE	

WORDS ENDING IN -EUR

7-letter words -EUR

AMATEUR	DOUCEUR	FLANEUR	HAUTEUR	MASSEUR	PRIMEUR	REMUEUR	SIGNEUR
DANSEUR	FARCEUR	FRISEUR	LIQUEUR	MINCEUR	PRONEUR	SABREUR	

8-letter words -EUR

BATELEUR	CISELEUR	ECRASEUR	FROTTEUR	LONGUEUR	SEIGNEUR	TAILLEUR	VOYAGEUR
BLAGUEUR	CLAQUEUR	FROIDEUR	GRANDEUR	MONSIEUR	SIFFLEUR	TROUVEUR	
CHASSEUR	COIFFEUR	FRONDEUR	JONGLEUR	SABOTEUR	SIGNIEUR	TRUQUEUR	

WORDS ENDING IN -FISH

7-letter words -FISH

BATFISH	COWFISH	GEMFISH	JEWFISH	MUFFISH	RAFFISH	SELFISH	TOFFISH
CATFISH	DOGFISH	HAGFISH	LUBFISH	PINFISH	REDFISH	SERFISH	TUBFISH
CODFISH	GARFISH	HUFFISH	MUDFISH	PUPFISH	SAWFISH	SUNFISH	WOLFISH

8-letter words -FISH

BAITFISH	CRAWFISH	DWARFISH	KINGFISH	PIPEFISH	SCARFISH	STIFFISH	WEAKFISH
BLOWFISH	CRAYFISH	FLATFISH	LUMPFISH	ROCKFISH	SCOMFISH	SURFFISH	
BLUEFISH	DEALFISH	GOATFISH	MILKFISH	ROSEFISH	SCUMFISH	TILEFISH	
BOARFISH	DRAFFISH	GOLDFISH	MONKFISH	SAILFISH	SPOFFISH	TOADFISH	
COALFISH	DRUMFISH	GRUFFISH	OVERFISH	SALTFISH	STARFISH	WALLFISH	

WORDS ENDING IN -FORM

7-letter words -FORM

ACIFORM	AVIFORM	DEIFORM	DISFORM	OVIFORM	PREFORM	UNIFORM
ALIFORM	CONFORM	DIFFORM	MISFORM	PERFORM	TRIFORM	ZOEFORM

8-letter words -FORM

AERIFORM	ENSIFORM	LANDFORM	NAPIFORM	PILIFORM	RANIFORM	SLIPFORM	WAVEFORM
AURIFORM	FILIFORM	LAVAFORM	NATIFORM	PISIFORM	REINFORM	TUBIFORM	
COLIFORM	FUSIFORM	LYRIFORM	NUBIFORM	PLATFORM	RENIFORM	UNCIFORM	
CONIFORM	GASIFORM	MANIFORM	OMNIFORM	PYRIFORM	RETIFORM	VARIFORM	
CUBIFORM	IODOFORM	MURIFORM	PALIFORM	RAMIFORM	SETIFORM	VASIFORM	

WORDS ENDING IN -FUL

7-letter words -FUL

BALEFUL	CROPFUL	DUREFUL	FORKFUL	GUTSFUL	HURTFUL	MASTFUL	PAILFUL	PLOTFUL
BANEFUL	DAREFUL	DUTIFUL	FRETFUL	HANDFUL	JESTFUL	MAZEFUL	PAINFUL	POKEFUL
BASHFUL	DEEDFUL	EASEFUL	GAINFUL	HARMFUL	LIFEFUL	MINDFUL	PALMFUL	PREYFUL
BODEFUL	DERNFUL	FATEFUL	GASHFUL	HATEFUL	LISTFUL	MISTFUL	PESTFUL	PUSHFUL
BOOKFUL	DIREFUL	FEARFUL	GAZEFUL	HEEDFUL	LOCKFUL	MOANFUL	PIPEFUL	RAGEFUL
BOWLFUL	DISHFUL	FISHFUL	GLADFUL	HELPFUL	LOOFFUL	MUSEFUL	PITHFUL	RESTFUL
BRIMFUL	DOLEFUL	FISTFUL	GLEEFUL	HOPEFUL	LUNGFUL	NEEDFUL	PITIFUL	RISKFUL
CAREFUL	DOOMFUL	FOODFUL	GUSTFUL	HORNFUL	LUSTFUL	NESTFUL	PLAYFUL	ROOMFUL

RUTHFUL	SIGHFUL	SONGFUL	TANKFUL	TOILFUL	VIALFUL	WILEFUL	WORKFUL
SACKFUL	SKEPFUL	SOULFUL	TEARFUL	TRAYFUL	WAILFUL	WILLFUL	ZEALFUL
SHIPFUL	SKILFUL	TACTFUL	TEEMFUL	TUBEFUL	WAKEFUL	WISHFUL	ZESTFUL
SHOPFUL	SKINFUL	TALEFUL	TENTFUL	TUNEFUL	WAMEFUL	WISTFUL	

8-letter words -FUL

APRONFUL	DREADFUL	GLOOMFUL	MOURNFUL	RIGHTFUL	SPITEFUL	TROUTFUL	WATCHFUL
AVAILFUL	DREAMFUL	GRACEFUL	MOUTHFUL	SCENTFUL	SPOILFUL	TRUNKFUL	WEARIFUL
BASINFUL	EVENTFUL	GRATEFUL	NIEVEFUL	SCOOPFUL	SPOONFUL	TRUSTFUL	WORTHFUL
BELLYFUL	FAITHFUL	GRIEFFUL	NOISEFUL	SCORNFUL	SPORTFUL	TRUTHFUL	WRACKFUL
BLAMEFUL	FANCIFUL	GROANFUL	PAUSEFUL	SENSEFUL	STARTFUL	UDDERFUL	WRATHFUL
BLISSFUL	FAULTFUL	GUILEFUL	PEACEFUL	SHAMEFUL	STICKFUL	UNARTFUL	WREAKFUL
BLUSHFUL	FEASTFUL	HOUSEFUL	PLAINFUL	SHELLFUL	STORMFUL	UNJOYFUL	WRECKFUL
BOASTFUL	FORCEFUL	LADLEFUL	PLATEFUL	SKILLFUL	SURGEFUL	UNLAWFUL	WRONGFUL
CHARMFUL	FOUNTFUL	LAUGHFUL	POUCHFUL	SLOTHFUL	TABLEFUL	UNUSEFUL	YOUTHFUL
CHEERFUL	FRAUDFUL	LIGHTFUL	POWERFUL	SMILEFUL	TASTEFUL	UNWILFUL	
CHESTFUL	FREAKFUL	LOATHFUL	PRANKFUL	SNOOTFUL	THANKFUL	VAUNTFUL	
CRIMEFUL	FRISKFUL	MENSEFUL	PRESSFUL	SOOTHFUL	TOOTHFUL	VENGEFUL	
DEARNFUL	FRUITFUL	MERCIFUL	PRIDEFUL	SPADEFUL	TRADEFUL	VOICEFUL	
DEATHFUL	GHASTFUL	MIGHTFUL	PROUDFUL	SPEEDFUL	TRISTFUL	WAGONFUL	
DOUBTFUL	GLASSFUL	MIRTHFUL	PURSEFUL	SPELLFUL	TROTHFUL	WASTEFUL	

WORDS ENDING IN -GEN

7-letter words -GEN

ACROGEN	CRYOGEN	HUMOGEN	LUCIGEN	MUTAGEN	RONTGEN	TWIGGEN
ANLAGEN	ENDOGEN	KEROGEN	MITOGEN	ONCOGEN	SMIDGEN	XYLOGEN
ANTIGEN	HALOGEN	LOXYGEN	MUCIGEN	PYROGEN	TRUDGEN	ZYMOGEN

8-letter words -GEN

ABORIGEN	COLLAGEN	DIPLOGEN	FLORIGEN	HYDROGEN	OSTEOGEN	ROENTGEN
ALLERGEN	CULTIGEN	ENLARGEN	GLYCOGEN	MISCEGEN	PATHOGEN	STARAGEN
ANDROGEN	CYANOGEN	ESTROGEN	HISTOGEN	NITROGEN	PHOTOGEN	

WORDS ENDING IN -GRAM

7-letter words -GRAM

ANAGRAM	EPIGRAM	ISOGRAM	PANGRAM	TANGRAM
DIAGRAM	GROGRAM	MYOGRAM	PROGRAM	TRIGRAM

8-letter words -GRAM

AEROGRAM	DECIGRAM	HEXAGRAM	KILOGRAM	LIPOGRAM	MARIGRAM	NOMOGRAM	SONOGRAM
BAROGRAM	ECHOGRAM	HOLOGRAM	KYMOGRAM	LOGOGRAM	MONOGRAM	PARAGRAM	TELEGRAM
DECAGRAM	ERGOGRAM	IDEOGRAM	LEXIGRAM	MAILGRAM	NANOGRAM	SKIAGRAM	TOMOGRAM

WORDS ENDING IN -HOLE

7-letter words -HOLE

AIRHOLE	ASSHOLE	CATHOLE	FOXHOLE	KEYHOLE	MANHOLE	PINHOLE	SPYHOLE
ARMHOLE	BOTHOLE	DOGHOLE	JAWHOLE	LUGHOLE	MUDHOLE	POTHOLE	

8-letter words -HOLE

ARSEHOLE	BOREHOLE	FUNKHOLE	LOOPHOLE	SHOTHOLE	WOODHOLE
BLOWHOLE	BUNGHOLE	KNEEHOLE	PORTHOLE	SINKHOLE	WORMHOLE
BOLTHOLE	DOWNHOLE	LAMPHOLE	SHITHOLE	WEEPHOLE	

WORDS ENDING IN -HOOD

7-letter words -HOOD

APEHOOD	BOYHOOD	CATHOOD	CUBHOOD	ELFHOOD	GODHOOD	HOGHOOD	MANHOOD	NUNHOOD

8-letter words -HOOD

BABYHOOD	GIRLHOOD	KINGHOOD	MAIDHOOD	MONKHOOD	POPEHOOD	SELFHOOD	WIFEHOOD
DOLLHOOD	IDLEHOOD	LADYHOOD	MISSHOOD	PAGEHOOD	PUMPHOOD	SERFHOOD	WIVEHOOD

WORDS ENDING IN -HORN

7-letter words -HORN

ALPHORN	BIGHORN	DISHORN	INKHORN	SAXHORN	UNSHORN
ALTHORN	COEHORN	FOGHORN	LEGHORN	TINHORN	

8-letter words -HORN

BUCKHORN	DEERHORN	HAWTHORN	LANTHORN	SHOEHORN	WALDHORN
CRUMHORN	GEMSHORN	KRUMHORN	LONGHORN	SLUGHORN	

WORDS ENDING IN -IBLE

7-letter words -IBLE

AUDIBLE	DELIBLE	DOCIBLE	FUSIBLE	LEGIBLE	PATIBLE	RIBIBLE	RISIBLE	VISIBLE

8-letter words -IBLE

CREDIBLE	ELUDIBLE	FALLIBLE	FORCIBLE	MANDIBLE	POSSIBLE	SUASIBLE	THURIBLE
CRUCIBLE	ERODIBLE	FEASIBLE	GULLIBLE	MISCIBLE	RINSIBLE	TANGIBLE	VENDIBLE
EDUCIBLE	EVASIBLE	FENCIBLE	HORRIBLE	PARTIBLE	RUNCIBLE	TENSIBLE	VINCIBLE
ELIGIBLE	EXIGIBLE	FLEXIBLE	INEDIBLE	PASSIBLE	SENSIBLE	TERRIBLE	

WORDS ENDING IN -IFY

7-letter words -IFY

ACETIFY	CARNIFY	DENSIFY	GLORIFY	MAGNIFY	NITRIFY	RECTIFY	TERRIFY	YUPPIFY
ACIDIFY	CERTIFY	DIGNIFY	GRATIFY	MERCIFY	NULLIFY	REUNIFY	TESTIFY	ZINCIFY
AMPLIFY	CHYLIFY	DULCIFY	HORRIFY	MOLLIFY	PETRIFY	SACRIFY	THURIFY	ZINKIFY
ANGLIFY	CHYMIFY	FALSIFY	ICONIFY	MORTIFY	PLEBIFY	SALSIFY	TIPSIFY	ZOMBIFY
BEATIFY	CLARIFY	FARCIFY	JELLIFY	MUMMIFY	PONTIFY	SCARIFY	UNDEIFY	
BRUTIFY	CRUCIFY	FISHIFY	JOLLIFY	MUNDIFY	PROSIFY	SCORIFY	VERBIFY	
CALCIFY	DAMNIFY	FORTIFY	JUSTIFY	MYSTIFY	PULPIFY	SIGNIFY	VERSIFY	
CAPRIFY	DANDIFY	FRUTIFY	LIGNIFY	NIGRIFY	QUALIFY	SPECIFY	VITRIFY	

8-letter words -IFY

ALKALIFY	DENAZIFY	ETHERIFY	GLASSIFY	MOISTIFY	REMODIFY	SANCTIFY	SOLIDIFY
BEAUTIFY	DETOXIFY	FLINTIFY	HUMIDIFY	PRETTIFY	REPURIFY	SANGUIFY	STELLIFY
BRONZIFY	DIVINIFY	FLUIDIFY	IDENTIFY	QUANTIFY	RESINIFY	SAPONIFY	STRATIFY
CLASSIFY	EMULSIFY	FRUCTIFY	KARSTIFY	QUIZZIFY	REVIVIFY	SILICIFY	STULTIFY
COCKNIFY	ESTERIFY	GENTRIFY	LAPIDIFY	REAEDIFY	RIGIDIFY	SIMPLIFY	ZINCKIFY

WORDS ENDING IN -INGS

7-letter words -INGS

ACHINGS	CAKINGS	DYEINGS	GIVINGS	LIKINGS	OGLINGS	RIDINGS	SPYINGS	UNKINGS
ACTINGS	CANINGS	EARINGS	GORINGS	LIMINGS	ONDINGS	RISINGS	STRINGS	UPPINGS
AGEINGS	CASINGS	EATINGS	HAVINGS	LININGS	OUTINGS	ROBINGS	TAKINGS	URGINGS
AIRINGS	CAVINGS	EDGINGS	HAYINGS	LIVINGS	PAGINGS	RODINGS	TAMINGS	URNINGS
ANTINGS	CAWINGS	ELDINGS	HAZINGS	LOBINGS	PALINGS	ROPINGS	TARINGS	VEXINGS
ARCINGS	CODINGS	ENDINGS	HEWINGS	LORINGS	PARINGS	ROVINGS	TAWINGS	VIKINGS
AWNINGS	COMINGS	ENRINGS	HEXINGS	LOSINGS	PAVINGS	ROWINGS	TAXINGS	WADINGS
BAAINGS	COOINGS	ERRINGS	HIDINGS	LOVINGS	PAYINGS	RUEINGS	TIDINGS	WAKINGS
BAKINGS	COPINGS	FACINGS	HIRINGS	LOWINGS	PILINGS	RULINGS	TILINGS	WANINGS
BESINGS	COVINGS	FADINGS	HOLINGS	LUGINGS	PIPINGS	SAVINGS	TIMINGS	WAVINGS
BIDINGS	CRYINGS	FILINGS	HOMINGS	LUTINGS	POLINGS	SAWINGS	TIRINGS	WAXINGS
BIKINGS	DARINGS	FININGS	INNINGS	MAKINGS	POSINGS	SAYINGS	TOLINGS	WIPINGS
BITINGS	DATINGS	FIRINGS	JAPINGS	MAYINGS	PRYINGS	SEEINGS	TONINGS	WIRINGS
BLUINGS	DICINGS	FIXINGS	JAWINGS	MININGS	PULINGS	SEWINGS	TOWINGS	WONINGS
BODINGS	DIVINGS	FLYINGS	KITINGS	MOWINGS	RACINGS	SIDINGS	TOYINGS	WOOINGS
BONINGS	DONINGS	FOXINGS	LACINGS	MUSINGS	RAGINGS	SIZINGS	TRYINGS	YOKINGS
BORINGS	DOPINGS	FRYINGS	LADINGS	NAMINGS	RAKINGS	SKIINGS	TUBINGS	ZONINGS
BOWINGS	DOTINGS	GAMINGS	LASINGS	NIDINGS	RATINGS	SOWINGS	TUNINGS	
BOXINGS	DOZINGS	GAPINGS	LAWINGS	NOSINGS	RAVINGS	SPAINGS	TYPINGS	
BUSINGS	DRYINGS	GATINGS	LAYINGS	OFFINGS	RAWINGS	SPRINGS	ULLINGS	

8-letter words -INGS

ABIDINGS	AMBLINGS	ARCKINGS	BACKINGS	BAITINGS	BALLINGS	BANGINGS	BANTINGS
AISLINGS	ANGLINGS	AWAKINGS	BAGGINGS	BALKINGS	BANDINGS	BANKINGS	BARRINGS

BASHINGS	DAFFINGS	GANGINGS	JIBBINGS	MISTINGS	RAISINGS	SIFTINGS	TITLINGS
BASTINGS	DAGGINGS	GASPINGS	JIGGINGS	MOBBINGS	RAMPINGS	SIGNINGS	TOILINGS
BATTINGS	DAMPINGS	GASSINGS	JOBBINGS	MOCKINGS	RANKINGS	SINDINGS	TOLLINGS
BAWLINGS	DANCINGS	GAUGINGS	JOGGINGS	MOORINGS	RANTINGS	SINGINGS	TOOLINGS
BEADINGS	DARLINGS	GEARINGS	JOININGS	MOOTINGS	RAPPINGS	SINKINGS	TOPPINGS
BEAMINGS	DARNINGS	GELDINGS	JOTTINGS	MORLINGS	RASPINGS	SITTINGS	TOSSINGS
BEARINGS	DAUBINGS	GETTINGS	JUGGINGS	MORNINGS	RATLINGS	SKATINGS	TOTTINGS
BEATINGS	DAWNINGS	GILDINGS	KARTINGS	MOSHINGS	RATTINGS	SKIVINGS	TOURINGS
BEDDINGS	DEALINGS	GIRDINGS	KAYOINGS	MOSLINGS	READINGS	SLATINGS	TOUSINGS
BEGGINGS	DECKINGS	GLAZINGS	KEELINGS	MOUSINGS	REDDINGS	SLICINGS	TRACINGS
BELTINGS	DEVLINGS	GLIDINGS	KEENINGS	MUGGINGS	REDWINGS	SLIDINGS	TRADINGS
BENDINGS	DIGGINGS	GLOVINGS	KEEPINGS	MUMMINGS	REEDINGS	SLOWINGS	TUBBINGS
BETTINGS	DILLINGS	GLOZINGS	KEMPINGS	MUNTINGS	REEFINGS	SMILINGS	TUFTINGS
BIASINGS	DIPPINGS	GODLINGS	KENNINGS	NAILINGS	REELINGS	SMOKINGS	TUGGINGS
BIDDINGS	DISHINGS	GOLFINGS	KERNINGS	NECKINGS	RENNINGS	SNARINGS	TUNNINGS
BILLINGS	DOATINGS	GOSLINGS	KIDLINGS	NESTINGS	REPPINGS	SNIPINGS	TURFINGS
BINDINGS	DOCKINGS	GRATINGS	KILLINGS	NETTINGS	RESTINGS	SNORINGS	TURNINGS
BIRDINGS	DODGINGS	GRAVINGS	KIRKINGS	NITHINGS	RIBBINGS	SOAKINGS	TUSKINGS
BIRLINGS	DOGGINGS	GRAZINGS	KITLINGS	NODDINGS	RIDGINGS	SOARINGS	TUTTINGS
BLUEINGS	DOPPINGS	GREYINGS	KNIFINGS	NOGGINGS	RIFLINGS	SOBBINGS	TWININGS
BOATINGS	DRAWINGS	GRICINGS	LAGGINGS	NOONINGS	RIGGINGS	SOGGINGS	UNBEINGS
BOILINGS	DROVINGS	GROWINGS	LALLINGS	NOTHINGS	RIGLINGS	SOILINGS	UNDOINGS
BOLTINGS	DUBBINGS	GUIDINGS	LAMMINGS	NULLINGS	RIMMINGS	SOOPINGS	UNITINGS
BONDINGS	DUCKINGS	GUISINGS	LAMPINGS	NURSINGS	RINGINGS	SOPPINGS	UNSLINGS
BOOKINGS	DUFFINGS	GUMMINGS	LANDINGS	NUTTINGS	RINSINGS	SORNINGS	UNTYINGS
BOOMINGS	DUNNINGS	GUNNINGS	LAPPINGS	OAKLINGS	RIOTINGS	SORTINGS	UPBRINGS
BOWLINGS	EANLINGS	HACKINGS	LAPWINGS	ONGOINGS	RISPINGS	SOSSINGS	UPGOINGS
BREWINGS	EARNINGS	HAININGS	LASHINGS	OPENINGS	ROADINGS	SOTTINGS	UPSWINGS
BRIMINGS	EARRINGS	HALLINGS	LASTINGS	OUTWINGS	ROAMINGS	SOUMINGS	VAMPINGS
BROKINGS	EASTINGS	HALTINGS	LATHINGS	PACKINGS	ROARINGS	SOURINGS	VANNINGS
BRUTINGS	EEVNINGS	HANGINGS	LEADINGS	PADDINGS	ROCKINGS	SOUSINGS	VARYINGS
BUCKINGS	EILDINGS	HARLINGS	LEANINGS	PAIRINGS	RODDINGS	SPACINGS	VEERINGS
BUDDINGS	ENVYINGS	HARPINGS	LEASINGS	PANNINGS	ROLFINGS	SPILINGS	VEILINGS
BUFFINGS	ETCHINGS	HASTINGS	LEAVINGS	PANTINGS	ROLLINGS	STAGINGS	VEININGS
BUGGINGS	EVENINGS	HATTINGS	LEERINGS	PARKINGS	ROOFINGS	STARINGS	VENTINGS
BULLINGS	FABLINGS	HAWKINGS	LEGGINGS	PARSINGS	ROOTINGS	STEWINGS	VERSINGS
BUMPINGS	FAGGINGS	HEADINGS	LEKKINGS	PARTINGS	ROUMINGS	STONINGS	VESTINGS
BUNTINGS	FAILINGS	HEALINGS	LEMMINGS	PASSINGS	ROUTINGS	STOPINGS	VIEWINGS
BURNINGS	FAIRINGS	HEARINGS	LENDINGS	PASTINGS	RUBBINGS	STOVINGS	VOGUINGS
BUSHINGS	FALLINGS	HEATINGS	LETTINGS	PAUSINGS	RUCHINGS	STOWINGS	VOICINGS
BUSKINGS	FANNINGS	HEAVINGS	LICKINGS	PECKINGS	RUGGINGS	SUBBINGS	VOIDINGS
BUSSINGS	FARCINGS	HEDGINGS	LIGGINGS	PEELINGS	RUININGS	SUBRINGS	WADDINGS
BUSTINGS	FARDINGS	HEELINGS	LIMPINGS	PEGGINGS	RUNNINGS	SUCKINGS	WAFTINGS
BUZZINGS	FARMINGS	HELPINGS	LISPINGS	PELTINGS	RUSTINGS	SUGGINGS	WAILINGS
CABLINGS	FASTINGS	HERLINGS	LISTINGS	PETTINGS	RUTTINGS	SUITINGS	WAITINGS
CALLINGS	FATLINGS	HERRINGS	LOADINGS	PICKINGS	SACKINGS	SUMMINGS	WALKINGS
CANTINGS	FAWNINGS	HIDLINGS	LOAFINGS	PIGGINGS	SACRINGS	SURFINGS	WALLINGS
CAPPINGS	FEEDINGS	HILDINGS	LOANINGS	PIGLINGS	SAGGINGS	SURGINGS	WANTINGS
CARLINGS	FEELINGS	HIPPINGS	LODGINGS	PILLINGS	SAILINGS	SWALINGS	WARDINGS
CARPINGS	FEERINGS	HIRLINGS	LOGGINGS	PINKINGS	SALTINGS	SWAYINGS	WARLINGS
CARVINGS	FELTINGS	HISSINGS	LONGINGS	PINNINGS	SALVINGS	SYNDINGS	WARMINGS
CASTINGS	FENCINGS	HOGGINGS	LOONINGS	PIONINGS	SANDINGS	TABLINGS	WARNINGS
CATLINGS	FERNINGS	HOLDINGS	LOOPINGS	PITTINGS	SAPLINGS	TACKINGS	WARPINGS
CEASINGS	FEUDINGS	HOPPINGS	LOOTINGS	PLACINGS	SARKINGS	TAGGINGS	WASHINGS
CEILINGS	FILLINGS	HORNINGS	LOPPINGS	PLATINGS	SCALINGS	TAILINGS	WASTINGS
CHASINGS	FINDINGS	HORSINGS	LORDINGS	POLLINGS	SCORINGS	TALKINGS	WAULINGS
CHIDINGS	FIRRINGS	HOSTINGS	LOURINGS	POSTINGS	SCRYINGS	TAMPINGS	WAWLINGS
CIELINGS	FISHINGS	HOTTINGS	LUGEINGS	POURINGS	SEALINGS	TANKINGS	WAXWINGS
CLOSINGS	FITTINGS	HOUSINGS	LURKINGS	POUTINGS	SEARINGS	TANLINGS	WEARINGS
COAMINGS	FIZZINGS	HOUTINGS	MADLINGS	PRATINGS	SEATINGS	TANNINGS	WEAVINGS
COATINGS	FLUTINGS	HOWLINGS	MAILINGS	PRAYINGS	SEEDINGS	TAPPINGS	WEBBINGS
CODLINGS	FLYTINGS	HUMMINGS	MAIMINGS	PRIMINGS	SEELINGS	TARRINGS	WEDDINGS
COGGINGS	FOAMINGS	HUNTINGS	MALTINGS	PROSINGS	SEEMINGS	TASKINGS	WEDGINGS
COININGS	FOILINGS	HURLINGS	MAPPINGS	PROVINGS	SEININGS	TASTINGS	WEEDINGS
COLLINGS	FOLDINGS	HUSKINGS	MARKINGS	PRUNINGS	SEIZINGS	TATTINGS	WEEPINGS
COMBINGS	FOOLINGS	HUSTINGS	MARLINGS	PUDDINGS	SELFINGS	TEAMINGS	WELDINGS
COMPINGS	FOOTINGS	HUTTINGS	MASHINGS	PUFFINGS	SENDINGS	TEASINGS	WELLINGS
CONNINGS	FOPLINGS	HYLDINGS	MATTINGS	PUGGINGS	SENSINGS	TELLINGS	WESTINGS
CORDINGS	FORGINGS	IMAGINGS	MEANINGS	PUNNINGS	SERVINGS	TENTINGS	WHALINGS
COWLINGS	FORMINGS	INBEINGS	MEETINGS	PURGINGS	SETTINGS	TESTINGS	WHININGS
CRAVINGS	FOWLINGS	INBRINGS	MELTINGS	PURLINGS	SHADINGS	THAWINGS	WHITINGS
CUBBINGS	FRAMINGS	INGOINGS	MENDINGS	PURRINGS	SHAKINGS	TICKINGS	WIGGINGS
CULLINGS	FRAYINGS	INKLINGS	MERLINGS	PUTTINGS	SHAPINGS	TIFFINGS	WILDINGS
CUNNINGS	FUCKINGS	INSWINGS	MESHINGS	PYONINGS	SHARINGS	TILLINGS	WINCINGS
CUPPINGS	FUNDINGS	IRONINGS	MICHINGS	QUAKINGS	SHAVINGS	TILTINGS	WINDINGS
CURLINGS	FURRINGS	JARRINGS	MILKINGS	QUEUINGS	SHOEINGS	TINNINGS	WINKINGS
CURSINGS	GADLINGS	JEERINGS	MILLINGS	RACKINGS	SHORINGS	TINTINGS	WINNINGS
CUTTINGS	GAFFINGS	JERKINGS	MINCINGS	RAGGINGS	SHOWINGS	TIPPINGS	WISHINGS
CYCLINGS	GAININGS	JESTINGS	MINDINGS	RAILINGS	SIBLINGS	TITHINGS	WITLINGS

```
WITTINGS    WOLVINGS    WORDINGS    WRITINGS    YELLINGS    YOWLINGS
WOLFINGS    WONNINGS    WORKINGS    YAWNINGS    YELPINGS
```

WORDS ENDING IN -ISE

7-letter words -ISE

```
ABSCISE   ATOMISE   COTTISE   ELEGISE   IRIDISE   MAPWISE   PENTISE   REARISE   SURMISE
ADONISE   AZOTISE   CYANISE   EMPRISE   IRONISE   MORTISE   PEPTISE   REPRISE   TRENISE
AGONISE   BAPTISE   DESPISE   ENDWISE   ITEMISE   MYTHISE   POETISE   RIOTISE   UNITISE
ANODISE   CHAMISE   DIARISE   FADAISE   KYANISE   OBELISE   PRECISE   SOUBISE   UPRAISE
ANYWISE   CHEMISE   DOCKISE   GALLISE   LAICISE   OXIDISE   PREMISE   STYLISE   UTILISE
APPRISE   COALISE   EBONISE   HEROISE   LAIRISE   OZONISE   PREVISE   SUCCISE
ARABISE   COGNISE   ECHOISE   ICONISE   LIONISE   PARVISE   PROMISE   SUNRISE
ATHEISE   CONCISE   EGOTISE   IDOLISE   MALAISE   PECTISE   REALISE   SUNWISE
```

8-letter words -ISE

```
ALBITISE   CIVILISE   EMPERISE   IDEALISE   MONETISE   POLEMISE   SATIRISE   THEORISE
ALKALISE   COLONISE   ENERGISE   IMMUNISE   MOONRISE   POLONISE   SIDEWISE   THUSWISE
AMORTISE   COMBWISE   EQUALISE   INFAMISE   MORALISE   PORPOISE   SIMILISE   TORTOISE
ANNALISE   COMPRISE   ERGOTISE   JUMBOISE   MOTORISE   PORTOISE   SINICISE   TOTALISE
APHETISE   COVETISE   ETERNISE   LEGALISE   NASALISE   PRACTISE   SIRENISE   TREATISE
APHORISE   CRABWISE   ETHERISE   LIKEWISE   NEBULISE   PTYALISE   SOBERISE   TUTORISE
APPETISE   CURARISE   ETHICISE   LOCALISE   NODALISE   PYRITISE   SODOMISE   UNIONISE
APPRAISE   CUTINISE   EULOGISE   LOGICISE   NOMADISE   QUANTISE   SOLARISE   UNPRAISE
ARCHAISE   DEMONISE   EUPHUISE   LONGWISE   NOTARISE   RACEMISE   SOLECISE   URBANISE
ARCHWISE   DEPUTISE   EXERCISE   MACARISE   NOVELISE   READVISE   SOMEWISE   VALORISE
ATHETISE   DIGITISE   EXORCISE   MADERISE   OPTIMISE   REGULISE   SORORISE   VAPORISE
BANALISE   DIMERISE   FABULISE   MARQUISE   ORGANISE   REREVISE   STEPWISE   VELARISE
BENDWISE   DISGUISE   FARADISE   MAUVAISE   OVERWISE   RESINISE   SUBERISE   VITALISE
BEPRAISE   DISSEISE   FEMINISE   MAXIMISE   PAGANISE   RIGIDISE   SUBITISE   VOCALISE
BOTANISE   DIVINISE   FINALISE   MELODISE   PAIRWISE   RINGWISE   SUCHWISE   VOLUMISE
BRANDISE   DROPWISE   FLATWISE   MEMORISE   PALEWISE   RIVALISE   SURPRISE   VOWELISE
CANALISE   DYNAMISE   FLUIDISE   MESPRISE   PAPALISE   ROBOTISE   TEAMWISE   WOMANISE
CANONISE   EBIONISE   FOCALISE   MINIMISE   PARADISE   ROYALISE   TELEVISE
CAPONISE   EDGEWISE   HEPATISE   MISPRISE   PENALISE   RURALISE   TENTWISE
CHASTISE   ELSEWISE   HUMANISE   MOBILISE   POLARISE   SANITISE   TETANISE
```

WORDS ENDING IN -ISH

7-letter words -ISH

```
ABOLISH   CATFISH   DRONISH   GARNISH   JEWFISH   MOORISH   POORISH   SADDISH   TOWNISH
ALUMISH   CATTISH   DULLISH   GEMFISH   JIGGISH   MOREISH   POPPISH   SALTISH   TUBBISH
ANGUISH   CHERISH   DUMPISH   GIRLISH   KERNISH   MUDFISH   PRUDISH   SAWFISH   TUBFISH
BABYISH   CLAYISH   DUNNISH   GNOMISH   KNAVISH   MUFFISH   PUBLISH   SELFISH   VAMPISH
BADDISH   CODFISH   DUSKISH   GOATISH   LADDISH   MUGGISH   PUCKISH   SERFISH   VARNISH
BALDISH   COLDISH   EVANISH   GOLDISH   LADYISH   MUMPISH   PUGGISH   SICKISH   VOGUISH
BATFISH   COLTISH   FADDISH   GOODISH   LARGISH   MURKISH   PUPFISH   SLAVISH   WAGGISH
BEAMISH   COOLISH   FAIRISH   GREYISH   LARKISH   NEBBISH   RAFFISH   SLOWISH   WAMPISH
BEARISH   COWFISH   FALSISH   GUARISH   LEFTISH   NICEISH   RAMMISH   SNAKISH   WANNISH
BEAUISH   CUBBISH   FASTISH   GULLISH   LOMPISH   NOURISH   RATTISH   SNOWISH   WARMISH
BIGGISH   CULTISH   FATTISH   HAGFISH   LONGISH   NUNNISH   REDDISH   SOFTISH   WASPISH
BLEMISH   CURRISH   FENNISH   HAGGISH   LOUDISH   OGREISH   REDFISH   SOTTISH   WEARISH
BOARISH   DAMPISH   FILMISH   HARDISH   LOUTISH   OOFTISH   RELLISH   SOURISH   WENNISH
BOBBISH   DANKISH   FINEISH   HASHISH   LUBFISH   PARKISH   RIGGISH   STYLISH   WETTISH
BOOKISH   DARKISH   FLEMISH   HAWKISH   LUMPISH   PECKISH   ROGUISH   SUNFISH   WHEYISH
BOORISH   DERVISH   FOGYISH   HELLISH   LUSKISH   PEEVISH   ROINISH   SWINISH   WHITISH
BRINISH   DIMMISH   FOOLISH   HIGHISH   MAIDISH   PETTISH   ROMPISH   TALLISH   WHORISH
BRUTISH   DOGFISH   FOPPISH   HIPPISH   MANNISH   PIEDISH   ROOKISH   TARNISH   WILDISH
BUCKISH   DOGGISH   FULLISH   HOBBISH   MAWKISH   PIGGISH   ROYNISH   TARTISH   WIMPISH
BULLISH   DOLLISH   FURBISH   HOGGISH   MISSISH   PINFISH   RUBBISH   TIGRISH   WOLFISH
BURNISH   DOLTISH   FURNISH   HORNISH   MOBBISH   PINKISH   RUMMISH   TITTISH   WOLVISH
CADDISH   DONNISH   GAMPISH   HOTTISH   MONKISH   PLANISH   RUNTISH   TOFFISH   WORDISH
CARLISH   DOVEISH   GARFISH   HUFFISH   MOONISH   PLENISH   RUTTISH   TONNISH   YOBBISH
```

8-letter words -ISH

```
ADMONISH   BLOCKISH   BRACKISH   BROWNISH   CLIQUISH   CRAWFISH   DIMINISH   DWARFISH
ASTONISH   BLOKEISH   BRAINISH   CAMELISH   CLODDISH   CRAYFISH   DOWDYISH   EMPERISH
BABELISH   BLOWFISH   BRANDISH   CHILDISH   CLOWNISH   CROSSISH   DRABBISH   ENRAVISH
BAITFISH   BLUEFISH   BRATTISH   CHURLISH   CLUBBISH   DANDYISH   DRAFFISH   ESSAYISH
BLACKISH   BLUNTISH   BRISKISH   CLANNISH   COALFISH   DEALFISH   DROLLISH   FAINTISH
BLANDISH   BOARFISH   BROADISH   CLAPDISH   COARSISH   DEMOLISH   DROOGISH   FEEBLISH
BLIMPISH   BOOBYISH   BROGUISH   CLERKISH   COMPLISH   DEVILISH   DRUMFISH   FEVERISH
```

FIENDISH	GREENISH	OVERFISH	RIGHTISH	SHREWISH	SPARKISH	SWELLISH	TRICKISH
FIFTYISH	GRUFFISH	PAGANISH	ROCKFISH	SKIRMISH	SPOFFISH	SYLPHISH	UNMODISH
FLATFISH	IDIOTISH	PIPEFISH	ROSEFISH	SKITTISH	SPOOKISH	THICKISH	UNPOLISH
FLATTISH	JINGOISH	PLAINISH	ROUGHISH	SLANGISH	SQUARISH	THIEVISH	VAGARISH
FLIRTISH	KINGFISH	PLUMPISH	ROUNDISH	SLIMMISH	STABLISH	THINNISH	VANQUISH
FLOURISH	KNACKISH	POKERISH	ROWDYISH	SLOBBISH	STANDISH	TICKLISH	VIGORISH
FOGEYISH	LANGUISH	PRANKISH	SAILFISH	SLUGGISH	STARFISH	TIGERISH	VIPERISH
FORTYISH	LIGHTISH	PRIGGISH	SAINTISH	SLUTTISH	STARTISH	TIGHTISH	VIXENISH
FRAILISH	LIVERISH	PROUDISH	SALTFISH	SMALLISH	STEEPISH	TILEFISH	WALLFISH
FREAKISH	LUMPFISH	PSEUDISH	SCAMPISH	SMARTISH	STIFFISH	TINGLISH	WATERISH
FRESHISH	MILKFISH	PUPPYISH	SCARFISH	SNAPPISH	STILTISH	TOADFISH	WEAKFISH
FRUMPISH	MONKFISH	PURPLISH	SCOMFISH	SNEAKISH	STOUTISH	TOADYISH	WOMANISH
GHOULISH	NANNYISH	QUALMISH	SCUMFISH	SNOBBISH	SUMPHISH	TOLLDISH	YOKELISH
GLUMPISH	NOHOWISH	QUEERISH	SHARPISH	SNUBBISH	SURFFISH	TOUGHISH	YOUNGISH
GOATFISH	NOVELISH	QUIPPISH	SHEEPISH	SOLIDISH	SWAINISH	TOVARISH	
GOLDFISH	NYMPHISH	QUIRKISH	SHORTISH	SORRYISH	SWEETISH	TRAMPISH	

WORDS ENDING IN -ISM

7-letter words -ISM

ABLEISM	BROMISM	CULTISM	EROTISM	HEROISM	LIONISM	PHAEISM	STATISM	YOBBISM
AMORISM	BRUXISM	CZARISM	ETACISM	HEURISM	LOOKISM	PHOBISM	TACHISM	ZANYISM
ANIMISM	CAMBISM	DIORISM	FADDISM	HOBOISM	MAIDISM	PHOTISM	TACTISM	
ASTEISM	CHARISM	DONNISM	FALSISM	IDOLISM	MYALISM	PIANISM	TOURISM	
ATAVISM	CHEMISM	DUALISM	FASCISM	IMAGISM	MYTHISM	PIETISM	TROPISM	
ATHEISM	CHORISM	ECHOISM	FATTISM	ITACISM	NEURISM	REALISM	TSARISM	
ATOMISM	CLADISM	EGOTISM	FIDEISM	KARAISM	ODYLISM	SELFISM	TYCHISM	
BABUISM	COPYISM	ELITISM	FOGYISM	LADYISM	ONANISM	SENSISM	URANISM	
BAPTISM	COSMISM	ENTRISM	FOODISM	LEFTISM	ORALISM	SIZEISM	UTOPISM	
BOGYISM	CRETISM	EPICISM	GURUISM	LEGGISM	PEONISM	SOPHISM	WHOLISM	

8-letter words -ISM

ACOSMISM	BULLYISM	DWARFISM	FOGEYISM	METOPISM	PAPALISM	RIGORISM	TERATISM
ACROTISM	CABALISM	DYNAMISM	FUTURISM	MINIMISM	PARTYISM	ROWDYISM	THUGGISM
ACTINISM	CAFFEISM	EBIONISM	GIANTISM	MODALISM	PELORISM	ROYALISM	TIGERISM
ACTIVISM	CENTRISM	EMBOLISM	GYPSYISM	MONADISM	PETALISM	RURALISM	TITANISM
ALARMISM	CHARTISM	ENDEMISM	HEDONISM	MORALISM	PEYOTISM	SAINTISM	TOADYISM
ALBINISM	CLASSISM	ENTRYISM	HELOTISM	NATIVISM	PHALLISM	SAPPHISM	TOKENISM
ALGORISM	CLIQUISM	ERETHISM	HOBBYISM	NATURISM	PHRENISM	SATANISM	TOTEMISM
ALIENISM	CLUBBISM	ERGOTISM	HUMANISM	NAVALISM	PLUMBISM	SAVAGISM	TRIALISM
ALPINISM	CRONYISM	ESCAPISM	HYLICISM	NEGROISM	POLONISM	SCIOLISM	TROILISM
ALTRUISM	CULLYISM	ETHERISM	IDEALISM	NEPOTISM	POPULISM	SCRIBISM	TUTORISM
ANEURISM	CYNICISM	ETHICISM	IDIOTISM	NIHILISM	PRIAPISM	SEISMISM	ULTRAISM
APHORISM	DANDYISM	EUGENISM	INCIVISM	NIMBYISM	PRIGGISM	SIMPLISM	UNDINISM
APTERISM	DEMONISM	EUMERISM	INTIMISM	NOMADISM	PROSAISM	SINAPISM	UNIONISM
ARCHAISM	DEVILISM	EUPHUISM	JINGOISM	NOVELISM	PSELLISM	SNOBBISM	UNTRUISM
ASTERISM	DIMERISM	EXORCISM	LACONISM	OBEAHISM	PSEPHISM	SOLARISM	VEGANISM
ATROPISM	DIOECISM	FAIRYISM	LEGALISM	OCKERISM	PSYCHISM	SOLECISM	VIRILISM
BABELISM	DIRIGISM	FAKIRISM	LOCALISM	OPIUMISM	PTYALISM	SOLIDISM	VITALISM
BATHMISM	DITHEISM	FAMILISM	LOGICISM	OPTIMISM	PUGILISM	SOMATISM	VOCALISM
BETACISM	DONATISM	FARADISM	LYRICISM	ORGANISM	PUPPYISM	STOICISM	VOLTAISM
BOGEYISM	DOWDYISM	FATALISM	MACARISM	PACIFISM	QUIETISM	STRABISM	ZOMBIISM
BOOBYISM	DRUDGISM	FEMINISM	MELANISM	PAGANISM	RACEMISM	SWINGISM	
BOTULISM	DRUIDISM	FINALISM	MERYCISM	PALUDISM	REGALISM	SYBOTISM	

WORDS ENDING IN -IST

7-letter words -IST

ABLEIST	CASUIST	CYCLIST	ELOGIST	FUGUIST	IVORIST	PIANIST	SIZEIST	UPHOIST
ACQUIST	CELLIST	CZARIST	ENTRIST	GAMBIST	JUDOIST	PIARIST	SOLOIST	UTOPIST
AGONIST	CHEKIST	DENTIST	ENTWIST	GNOMIST	LEFTIST	PIETIST	SOPHIST	VACUIST
AMORIST	CHEMIST	DIALIST	EPICIST	HARPIST	MAPPIST	PLENIST	STATIST	VIOLIST
ANGLIST	CHORIST	DIARIST	EXODIST	HERBIST	METRIST	PLUMIST	STYLIST	WHOLIST
ANIMIST	CHUTIST	DIETIST	FADDIST	HORNIST	MYTHIST	POLOIST	SUBSIST	
ATHEIST	CLADIST	DUALIST	FASCIST	HYLOIST	NAIVIST	PROTIST	SUMMIST	
ATOMIST	COEXIST	DUMAIST	FATTIST	HYMNIST	OCULIST	QUERIST	TACHIST	
ATTRIST	CONSIST	EBONIST	FAUNIST	IAMBIST	OLIGIST	REALIST	TOURIST	
BAPTIST	COPYIST	ECHOIST	FEUDIST	IDOLIST	ONANIST	RHYMIST	TROPIST	
BASSIST	CORNIST	EGOTIST	FIDEIST	IMAGIST	PALMIST	SACRIST	TSARIST	
BIBLIST	COSMIST	ELEGIST	FLORIST	INTWIST	PERSIST	SELFIST	UNALIST	
CAMBIST	CULTIST	ELITIST	FLUTIST	IRONIST	PHOBIST	SENSIST	UNTWIST	

8-letter words -IST

ACOSMIST	BOTANIST	DRUGGIST	FUTURIST	LOGICIST	NEPOTIST	RALLYIST	SUBTRIST
ACTIVIST	BURINIST	DUELLIST	GARAGIST	LOYALIST	NIELLIST	REGALIST	TANGOIST
ALARMIST	CABALIST	DUETTIST	GROUPIST	LUMINIST	NIHILIST	REVERIST	TENORIST
ALIENIST	CALORIST	DYNAMIST	HANDLIST	LUNARIST	NOVELIST	RIGHTIST	THEORIST
ALPINIST	CANOEIST	ENTRYIST	HEDONIST	LUTANIST	ODONTIST	RIGORIST	TOTEMIST
ALTRUIST	CANONIST	ERRORIST	HOBBYIST	LUTENIST	OOLOGIST	ROYALIST	TRIADIST
ANNALIST	CENTOIST	ESCAPIST	HOMILIST	LUXURIST	OPTIMIST	RURALIST	TRIALIST
APHORIST	CENTRIST	ESSAYIST	HUMANIST	LYRICIST	ORGANIST	SAFARIST	TROILIST
APIARIST	CERAMIST	ETHERIST	HUMORIST	MAXIMIST	PACIFIST	SAPPHIST	ULTRAIST
AQUARIST	CHARTIST	ETHICIST	HYLICIST	MEDALIST	PAPALIST	SATIRIST	UNIONIST
ARBALIST	CIVILIST	EUGENIST	HYPOCIST	MELODIST	PARODIST	SCIOLIST	UNSEXIST
ARBORIST	CLASSIST	EULOGIST	IDEALIST	METALIST	PEYOTIST	SHOOTIST	VISAGIST
ARCANIST	CLUBBIST	EUPHUIST	IDYLLIST	MINIMIST	POLEMIST	SILURIST	VITALIST
ARCHAIST	COLONIST	EXORCIST	INTIMIST	MODALIST	POPULIST	SIMONIST	VOCALIST
ARMORIST	CONTRIST	FABULIST	JINGOIST	MONODIST	PROSAIST	SIMPLIST	VOLUMIST
ARSONIST	CREOLIST	FATALIST	JUNGLIST	MORALIST	PSALMIST	SOLARIST	VOTARIST
AVIARIST	DEMONIST	FEMINIST	LEGALIST	MOTORIST	PSYCHIST	SOLECIST	
BACKLIST	DEMOTIST	FIGURIST	LINGUIST	MURALIST	PUCKFIST	SOLIDIST	
BANJOIST	DIGAMIST	FINALIST	LOBBYIST	NATIVIST	PUGILIST	SOMATIST	
BIGAMIST	DITHEIST	FLAUTIST	LOCALIST	NATURIST	QUIETIST	STOCKIST	

WORDS ENDING IN -ITY

7-letter words -ITY

ABILITY	AUREITY	DABBITY	EXILITY	JOLLITY	PANEITY	REALITY	TRINITY
ACIDITY	AVIDITY	DACOITY	FALSITY	LAICITY	PAUCITY	SICCITY	UNICITY
AGILITY	BREVITY	DENSITY	FATUITY	NULLITY	PRAVITY	SPIRITY	UTILITY
AMENITY	CHARITY	DIGNITY	FURMITY	OBESITY	PRIVITY	SUAVITY	VACUITY
ANILITY	CLARITY	DUALITY	GASEITY	OMNEITY	PROBITY	SURDITY	VARSITY
ANNUITY	CRUDITY	EDACITY	GRAVITY	OPACITY	QUALITY	TENSITY	VASTITY
ARIDITY	CURVITY	EGALITY	INANITY	ORALITY	RABBITY	TENUITY	VIDUITY

8-letter words -ITY

ACERBITY	CIRCUITY	FIDELITY	IMPURITY	MORALITY	QUANTITY	SEROSITY	VALIDITY
ACRIDITY	CIVILITY	FINALITY	INEQUITY	MOROSITY	QUEERITY	SEVERITY	VAPIDITY
ACTIVITY	CONCEITY	FLUIDITY	INFINITY	MOTILITY	QUIDDITY	SODALITY	VELLEITY
ADUNCITY	CUPIDITY	FORTUITY	INIQUITY	MOTIVITY	RABIDITY	SOLICITY	VELOCITY
AFFINITY	DEBILITY	FUGACITY	INSANITY	MUCOSITY	RAPACITY	SOLIDITY	VENALITY
ALACRITY	DICACITY	FUMOSITY	INTIMITY	MULTEITY	RAPIDITY	SONORITY	VENOSITY
ALGIDITY	DISUNITY	FURACITY	JEJUNITY	NASALITY	REGALITY	SORORITY	VERACITY
ALTERITY	DIVINITY	FUTILITY	JOCOSITY	NATALITY	RIGIDITY	SPARSITY	VICINITY
ASPERITY	DOCILITY	FUTURITY	LABILITY	NATIVITY	RIVALITY	TEMERITY	VINOSITY
ASTUCITY	DUMOSITY	GELIDITY	LEGALITY	NIHILITY	RUGOSITY	TENACITY	VIRIDITY
ATROCITY	ENORMITY	GRATUITY	LEGERITY	NOBILITY	RURALITY	TEPIDITY	VIRILITY
AUDACITY	EQUALITY	GULOSITY	LIVIDITY	NODALITY	SAGACITY	TIMIDITY	VITALITY
AXIALITY	EQUINITY	HEREDITY	LOCALITY	NODOSITY	SALACITY	TONALITY	VIVACITY
BANALITY	ETERNITY	HILARITY	LUCIDITY	NUBILITY	SALINITY	TONICITY	VIVIDITY
BASICITY	EXIGUITY	HUMANITY	MAJORITY	OBTUSITY	SANCTITY	TOTALITY	VOCALITY
BISCUITY	FACILITY	HUMIDITY	MATURITY	ORGANITY	SAPIDITY	TOXICITY	VORACITY
CADUCITY	FATALITY	HUMILITY	MEGACITY	OTIOSITY	SATANITY	TRIALITY	
CALAMITY	FELICITY	IDEALITY	MINACITY	PERSEITY	SCANTITY	TRIUNITY	
CALIDITY	FELINITY	IDENTITY	MINORITY	PILOSITY	SCARCITY	TUMIDITY	
CANINITY	FEMALITY	IMMANITY	MOBILITY	POLARITY	SECURITY	UBIQUITY	
CAPACITY	FEMINITY	IMMUNITY	MODALITY	POROSITY	SEDULITY	UNFIXITY	
CELERITY	FERACITY	IMPARITY	MOLALITY	PRIORITY	SENILITY	URBANITY	
CHASTITY	FEROCITY	IMPUNITY	MOLARITY	PUDICITY	SERENITY	VAGILITY	

WORDS ENDING IN -IUM

7-letter words -IUM

ALODIUM	CALCIUM	ERODIUM	HOLMIUM	NATRIUM	PLAGIUM	RHODIUM	TERBIUM	URANIUM
ALUMIUM	CAMBIUM	FERMIUM	IRIDIUM	NIOBIUM	PREMIUM	SPODIUM	THORIUM	UREDIUM
BALLIUM	CRANIUM	GALLIUM	ISCHIUM	ORARIUM	PROTIUM	STADIUM	THULIUM	YTTRIUM
CADMIUM	ELOGIUM	HAFNIUM	LITHIUM	OXONIUM	PYTHIUM	STIBIUM	TRITIUM	ZOARIUM
CAESIUM	ELUVIUM	HAHNIUM	MUONIUM	PALLIUM	RHENIUM	TAEDIUM	TRIVIUM	

8-letter words -IUM

ACHENIUM	ALLODIUM	APTERIUM	ASPIDIUM	BRACHIUM	CIBORIUM	CORONIUM	DELIRIUM
ACTINIUM	ALLUVIUM	AQUARIUM	BASIDIUM	CALADIUM	CONARIUM	CYATHIUM	DIDYMIUM
AECIDIUM	AMMONIUM	ASCIDIUM	BDELLIUM	CHROMIUM	CONIDIUM	CYMATIUM	DILUVIUM

DOMATIUM	GONIDIUM	INDUSIUM	NEBULIUM	PECULIUM	ROSARIUM	SOLARIUM	VANADIUM
EMPORIUM	GRAPHIUM	INGENIUM	NOBELIUM	PERIDIUM	RUBIDIUM	SOLATIUM	VELARIUM
ENCOMIUM	GYNECIUM	LIXIVIUM	ONCIDIUM	PHORMIUM	SAMARIUM	SOREDIUM	VENIDIUM
ERYNGIUM	HELENIUM	LUTECIUM	ONYCHIUM	POLONIUM	SCANDIUM	SPLENIUM	VIVARIUM
EULOGIUM	HYMENIUM	LUTETIUM	OOGONIUM	PUPARIUM	SCHOLIUM	SUDARIUM	ZOOECIUM
EUROPIUM	ILLINIUM	MASURIUM	OPSONIUM	PYGIDIUM	SELENIUM	SYCONIUM	
EXORDIUM	ILLUVIUM	MECONIUM	ORDALIUM	PYXIDIUM	SILICIUM	THALLIUM	
FRANCIUM	IMPERIUM	MOTORIUM	OSSARIUM	RANARIUM	SILPHIUM	TITANIUM	
GERANIUM	INDICIUM	MYCELIUM	PATAGIUM	REFUGIUM	SIMULIUM	TRILLIUM	

WORDS ENDING IN -KIN

7-letter words -KIN

BARMKIN	BUMPKIN	CUTIKIN	GHERKIN	LADYKIN	LUMPKIN	OILSKIN	RAMEKIN
BAWDKIN	CANAKIN	DOGSKIN	GRISKIN	LAMBKIN	MANAKIN	PIGSKIN	REDSKIN
BODIKIN	CANIKIN	DOITKIN	HUFFKIN	LIMPKIN	MANIKIN	PUMPKIN	SIMPKIN
BRODKIN	CATSKIN	FINIKIN	KIDSKIN	LORDKIN	MINIKIN	RAMAKIN	WOLFKIN

8-letter words -KIN

BAUDEKIN	BYRLAKIN	COONSKIN	DEVILKIN	LAMBSKIN	MUNCHKIN	SPILIKIN	WOODSKIN
BEARSKIN	CALFSKIN	COOTIKIN	DUNNAKIN	LARRIKIN	MUTCHKIN	SWANSKIN	
BOOTIKIN	CANNIKIN	CUITIKIN	FISHSKIN	MANNIKIN	PANNIKIN	TURNSKIN	
BRODEKIN	CAPESKIN	DAMASKIN	FORESKIN	MOLESKIN	PONYSKIN	WINESKIN	
BUCKSKIN	CIDERKIN	DEERSKIN	GOATSKIN	MOUSEKIN	SEALSKIN	WOLFSKIN	

WORDS ENDING IN -LAND

7-letter words -LAND

BOGLAND	ELFLAND	GARLAND	GOWLAND	LAWLAND	MIDLAND	OUTLAND
COTLAND	FENLAND	GOLLAND	HOLLAND	LOWLAND	NORLAND	WETLAND

8-letter words -LAND

BACKLAND	CROPLAND	FILMLAND	HEADLAND	LAKELAND	OVERLAND	SLOBLAND	WASHLAND
BOOKLAND	DOCKLAND	FOLKLAND	HIGHLAND	MAINLAND	PARKLAND	SOAPLAND	WILDLAND
CLUBLAND	DOWNLAND	FORELAND	HOMELAND	MOORLAND	PORTLAND	TIDELAND	WOODLAND
CORNLAND	EASTLAND	GANGLAND	LACKLAND	MOSSLAND	SHETLAND	TOWNLAND	YARDLAND

WORDS ENDING IN -LESS

7-letter words -LESS

AGELESS	AWNLESS	ENDLESS	HAPLESS	LAWLESS	RAYLESS	SINLESS	TOPLESS
AIDLESS	BITLESS	EYELESS	HATLESS	LEGLESS	RIBLESS	SONLESS	TOYLESS
AIMLESS	BRALESS	FINLESS	HUELESS	LIDLESS	RIMLESS	SUMLESS	UNBLESS
AIRLESS	BUDLESS	FOGLESS	JOBLESS	LIPLESS	RODLESS	SUNLESS	USELESS
ARMLESS	CUBLESS	GODLESS	JOYLESS	NAPLESS	SACLESS	TAXLESS	WAYLESS
ARTLESS	EARLESS	GUNLESS	KEYLESS	OARLESS	SAPLESS	TIELESS	WIGLESS
AWELESS	EBBLESS	GUTLESS	KINLESS	PIPLESS	SEXLESS	TOELESS	WITLESS

8-letter words -LESS

BARKLESS	COMBLESS	FEETLESS	HATELESS	LEAFLESS	NATHLESS	RESTLESS	SEAMLESS
BASELESS	CORDLESS	FINELESS	HEADLESS	LIFELESS	NEEDLESS	RIFTLESS	SEATLESS
BASHLESS	CORELESS	FIRELESS	HEEDLESS	LIMBLESS	NEWSLESS	RINDLESS	SEEDLESS
BATELESS	CURBLESS	FIRMLESS	HEIRLESS	LISTLESS	NOSELESS	RINGLESS	SEEMLESS
BEAMLESS	CURELESS	FLAWLESS	HELMLESS	LORDLESS	NOTELESS	RITELESS	SELFLESS
BODILESS	DATELESS	FOAMLESS	HELPLESS	LOVELESS	PAINLESS	RIVALESS	SHIPLESS
BONELESS	DEEDLESS	FOODLESS	HERBLESS	LUCKLESS	PANGLESS	ROADLESS	SHOELESS
BOOKLESS	DEVILESS	FOOTLESS	HIVELESS	LUSTLESS	PASSLESS	ROOFLESS	SHUNLESS
BOOTLESS	DISKLESS	FORMLESS	HOMELESS	MAIDLESS	PATHLESS	ROOTLESS	SIGNLESS
BRIMLESS	DUCTLESS	FUNDLESS	HOODLESS	MAKELESS	PEERLESS	ROSELESS	SKILLESS
BROWLESS	DUSTLESS	GAINLESS	HOOFLESS	MANELESS	PIPELESS	RULELESS	SKINLESS
CALFLESS	EASELESS	GATELESS	HOPELESS	MASTLESS	PITHLESS	RUMPLESS	SNOWLESS
CARELESS	ECHOLESS	GAUMLESS	HORNLESS	MATELESS	PITILESS	RUSTLESS	SOAPLESS
CASHLESS	EDGELESS	GEARLESS	HURTLESS	MEATLESS	PLANLESS	RUTHLESS	SOILLESS
CHAPLESS	FACELESS	GOALLESS	IDEALESS	MILKLESS	PLOTLESS	SACKLESS	SONGLESS
CHINLESS	FADELESS	GOLDLESS	KINDLESS	MINDLESS	RAILLESS	SAIKLESS	SOOTLESS
CLAWLESS	FAMELESS	GORMLESS	KINGLESS	MOONLESS	RAINLESS	SAILLESS	SOULLESS
CLOYLESS	FANGLESS	HAIRLESS	KNOTLESS	MOVELESS	RECKLESS	SALTLESS	SPANLESS
CLUELESS	FEARLESS	HANDLESS	LANDLESS	NAILLESS	REDELESS	SATELESS	SPOTLESS
COATLESS	FECKLESS	HARMLESS	LEADLESS	NAMELESS	REINLESS	SCARLESS	SPURLESS

STARLESS	TAMELESS	THAWLESS	TOILLESS	TUSKLESS	VOTELESS	WEETLESS	WONTLESS
STAYLESS	TAPELESS	THEWLESS	TOMBLESS	TYRELESS	WAGELESS	WELDLESS	WOODLESS
STEMLESS	TEARLESS	THOWLESS	TONELESS	VANELESS	WAKELESS	WIFELESS	WORDLESS
STIRLESS	TEEMLESS	TIDELESS	TOWNLESS	VEILLESS	WARELESS	WINDLESS	WORKLESS
STOPLESS	TENTLESS	TIMELESS	TREELESS	VERBLESS	WARTLESS	WINGLESS	ZEALLESS
TACTLESS	TERMLESS	TINTLESS	TUBELESS	VICELESS	WAVELESS	WIRELESS	ZONELESS
TAILLESS	TEXTLESS	TIRELESS	TUNELESS	VIEWLESS	WEEDLESS	WITELESS	

WORDS ENDING IN -LET

7-letter words -LET

ANNULET	CANTLET	DEERLET	FONTLET	JINGLET	MOONLET	RINGLET	SKILLET	TRIOLET
ARCHLET	CAPELET	DEVILET	FORTLET	KINGLET	NECKLET	RIPPLET	STARLET	TRIPLET
BEAMLET	CHAMLET	DOUBLET	FROGLET	LAKELET	NOTELET	RIVULET	STEMLET	VEINLET
BENDLET	CHAPLET	DOVELET	GANTLET	LEAFLET	OSSELET	ROOTLET	STERLET	WAVELET
BOMBLET	CIRCLET	DRIBLET	HACKLET	LOBELET	PARTLET	ROYALET	SWALLET	WINGLET
BOOKLET	CORSLET	DROPLET	HARSLET	MANTLET	PIKELET	RUNDLET	TARTLET	ZONULET
BOOMLET	COUPLET	EPAULET	HERBLET	MARTLET	PLAYLET	SCARLET	TEMPLET	
CACOLET	COVELET	FLATLET	HORNLET	MEDALET	QUILLET	SINGLET	TRIBLET	

8-letter words -LET

BANDELET	CHEVALET	DRIBBLET	GREENLET	NERVELET	PLUMELET	SPIKELET	VERSELET
BARRULET	CLOUDLET	DRUPELET	GROUPLET	NONUPLET	QUEENLET	SWIFTLET	WRISTLET
BRACELET	CORSELET	FLAMELET	HEARTLET	OCTUPLET	RECOLLET	TERCELET	
BRACTLET	COURTLET	FRONTLET	HERBELET	PAMPHLET	ROUNDLET	TRICKLET	
BROOKLET	COVERLET	FRUITLET	LANCELET	PISTOLET	SEXTOLET	TROUTLET	
CAPELLET	CROSSLET	GAUNTLET	MANTELET	PLANTLET	SPANGLET	UNDERLET	
CHAINLET	CROWNLET	GLOBULET	MURRELET	PLATELET	SPARKLET	VALVELET	

WORDS ENDING IN -LIKE

7-letter words -LIKE

CATLIKE	GODLIKE	MISLIKE	RIBLIKE	SACLIKE	SUNLIKE	UNALIKE	WIGLIKE
DISLIKE	LIPLIKE	NUTLIKE	RODLIKE	SICLIKE	TOYLIKE	WARLIKE	

8-letter words -LIKE

BIRDLIKE	HIVELIKE	LIFELIKE	PIPELIKE	RUSHLIKE	STARLIKE	TUBELIKE	WOMBLIKE
CRABLIKE	HOMELIKE	LIONLIKE	PITHLIKE	SEEDLIKE	SUCHLIKE	WARTLIKE	
DOVELIKE	LADYLIKE	MILKLIKE	ROOFLIKE	SERFLIKE	SWANLIKE	WAVELIKE	
HAIRLIKE	LATHLIKE	NESTLIKE	ROOTLIKE	SNOWLIKE	TAPELIKE	WHIPLIKE	
HAWKLIKE	LEAFLIKE	PARKLIKE	ROSELIKE	SONGLIKE	TRAPLIKE	WIFELIKE	

WORDS ENDING IN -LOGY

7-letter words -LOGY

ANALOGY	BIOLOGY	ECOLOGY	MYOLOGY	NOOLOGY	OTOLOGY	UFOLOGY	ZOOLOGY
APOLOGY	DYSLOGY	GEOLOGY	NEOLOGY	OROLOGY	TRILOGY	UROLOGY	

8-letter words -LOGY

AEROLOGY	BATOLOGY	DOSOLOGY	KIDOLOGY	OENOLOGY	PELOLOGY	SITOLOGY	XYLOLOGY
AGROLOGY	BRYOLOGY	DOXOLOGY	MENOLOGY	ONCOLOGY	PENOLOGY	THEOLOGY	ZYMOLOGY
ALGOLOGY	CACOLOGY	ETHOLOGY	MISOLOGY	ONTOLOGY	PODOLOGY	TOCOLOGY	
ANTILOGY	CETOLOGY	ETIOLOGY	MONOLOGY	OPTOLOGY	POMOLOGY	TOKOLOGY	
ARCOLOGY	CHAOLOGY	GEMOLOGY	MYCOLOGY	OREOLOGY	POSOLOGY	TOPOLOGY	
ATMOLOGY	CYTOLOGY	HOMOLOGY	NOMOLOGY	OUROLOGY	RHEOLOGY	TYPOLOGY	
AUTOLOGY	DEKALOGY	HOROLOGY	NOSOLOGY	PARALOGY	SEROLOGY	VINOLOGY	
AXIOLOGY	DEMOLOGY	IDEOLOGY	OECOLOGY	PEDOLOGY	SEXOLOGY	VIROLOGY	

WORDS ENDING IN -LY

7-letter words -LY

ACUTELY	AMIABLY	AUDIBLY	BANALLY	BLEAKLY	BOSSILY	BROADLY	CAVALLY	CLEANLY
ADEPTLY	ANGERLY	AURALLY	BAWDILY	BLINDLY	BRAMBLY	BUIRDLY	CHARILY	CLEARLY
AFFABLY	ANGRILY	AWFULLY	BEAMILY	BLOWFLY	BRAVELY	BULKILY	CHEAPLY	CLERKLY
AGILELY	ANOMALY	AXIALLY	BEASTLY	BLUFFLY	BRIEFLY	BUMPILY	CHEERLY	CLOSELY
ALERTLY	APETALY	BAGGILY	BLACKLY	BLUNTLY	BRISKLY	CANNILY	CHIEFLY	COCKILY
ALONELY	APHYLLY	BAIRNLY	BLANDLY	BONNILY	BRISTLY	CAPABLY	CHILDLY	CORNFLY
ALOOFLY	APISHLY	BALMILY	BLANKLY	BOOZILY	BRITTLY	CATTILY	CIVILLY	COURTLY

CRACKLY	FIFTHLY	GRIZZLY	LARGELY	MUSKILY	PROSILY	SHOOGLY	STERNLY	TWADDLY
CRASSLY	FINALLY	GROSSLY	LEGALLY	MUSTILY	PROUDLY	SHORTLY	STIFFLY	TWIDDLY
CRAZILY	FIREFLY	GRUFFLY	LEGIBLY	MUTABLY	PUFFILY	SHOWILY	STONILY	UNAPTLY
CRINKLY	FIRSTLY	GRUMBLY	LICHTLY	MUZZILY	PULPILY	SHRILLY	STOUTLY	UNFITLY
CRISPLY	FIXEDLY	GRYESLY	LICITLY	NAIVELY	QUEENLY	SIGHTLY	STUBBLY	UNGODLY
CROSSLY	FLEETLY	GRYSELY	LIGHTLY	NAKEDLY	QUEERLY	SILKILY	STUMBLY	UNMANLY
CRUDELY	FLESHLY	GYRALLY	LITHELY	NARGILY	QUICKLY	SILLILY	SUAVELY	UNTRULY
CRUELLY	FOAMILY	HAMMILY	LIVIDLY	NASALLY	QUIETLY	SIXTHLY	SULKILY	USUALLY
CRUMBLY	FOCALLY	HANDILY	LOATHLY	NASTILY	RABIDLY	SLACKLY	SUNNILY	UTTERLY
DANDILY	FOGGILY	HAPPILY	LOCALLY	NATTILY	RAPIDLY	SLANTLY	SURLILY	VAGUELY
DAZEDLY	FRAILLY	HARDILY	LOFTILY	NEEDILY	RATABLY	SLEEKLY	SWEETLY	VALIDLY
DEARNLY	FRANKLY	HARSHLY	LOOBILY	NERVILY	READILY	SLICKLY	SWIFTLY	VAPIDLY
DEATHLY	FRECKLY	HARTELY	LOOSELY	NIFTILY	REAPPLY	SLIMILY	TACITLY	VENALLY
DEEDILY	FRESHLY	HASTILY	LOUSILY	NIGHTLY	REGALLY	SMARTLY	TACKILY	VERMILY
DENSELY	FRIARLY	HAZELLY	LOVERLY	NINTHLY	RIGHTLY	SMICKLY	TARDILY	VEXEDLY
DIRTILY	FRITFLY	HEADILY	LOWLILY	NIPPILY	RIGIDLY	SMOKILY	TASTILY	VISIBLY
DISALLY	FRIZZLY	HEARTLY	LOYALLY	NOBBILY	RISKILY	SNAKILY	TATTILY	VITALLY
DIZZILY	FUGALLY	HEAVILY	LUCIDLY	NODALLY	ROCKILY	SNIDELY	TAXABLY	VIVIDLY
DOUCELY	FUNNILY	HEFTILY	LUCKILY	NOISILY	ROOMILY	SNOWILY	TECHILY	VIXENLY
DOWDILY	FUSSILY	HOARILY	LUMPILY	NOTABLY	ROUGHLY	SNUFFLY	TENSELY	VOCALLY
DREADLY	FUSTILY	HUFFILY	LURIDLY	NOTEDLY	ROUNDLY	SOAPILY	TENTHLY	VOLUBLY
DRIBBLY	FUZZILY	HUMANLY	LUSTILY	NUTTILY	ROWDILY	SOBERLY	TEPIDLY	VOWELLY
DRIZZLY	GALLFLY	HUMIDLY	LYINGLY	NYMPHLY	ROYALLY	SOGGILY	TERSELY	VYINGLY
DROPFLY	GAUDILY	HUSKILY	MASCULY	ORDERLY	RUDDILY	SOLIDLY	TESTILY	WEARILY
DUCALLY	GAUNTLY	IDEALLY	MEATILY	OVERFLY	RUMMILY	SOOTHLY	THICKLY	WEEVILY
DUOPOLY	GELIDLY	IGNOBLY	MERRILY	OVERPLY	RURALLY	SOOTILY	THIRDLY	WEIRDLY
DURABLY	GHASTLY	INANELY	MESALLY	OVERTLY	RUSTILY	SOPPILY	THISTLY	WHITELY
DUSKILY	GHOSTLY	INAPTLY	MESSILY	PANOPLY	SAINTLY	SORRILY	THRILLY	WIGHTLY
DUSTILY	GIANTLY	INEPTLY	METALLY	PAPALLY	SALABLY	SOUNDLY	TIGERLY	WINDILY
DYINGLY	GIDDILY	INERTLY	MIFFILY	PAWKILY	SALTILY	SPANGLY	TIGHTLY	WITTILY
EAGERLY	GODLILY	INJELLY	MILKILY	PEARTLY	SANDFLY	SPARELY	TIMIDLY	WOFULLY
EARTHLY	GOOFILY	IRATELY	MISALLY	PENALLY	SAUCILY	SPARKLY	TIPSILY	WOMANLY
ELDERLY	GOUTFLY	JADEDLY	MISERLY	PERKILY	SCANTLY	SPICILY	TIREDLY	WOOZILY
EMPTILY	GRADELY	JAZZILY	MISTILY	PESKILY	SCRAWLY	SPIKILY	TONALLY	WORDILY
EQUABLY	GRANDLY	JOINTLY	MIXEDLY	PETTILY	SEEDILY	SPINDLY	TOSSILY	WORLDLY
EQUALLY	GRAVELY	JOLLILY	MODALLY	PIOUSLY	SHADILY	SPRAWLY	TOTALLY	WRIGGLY
ERECTLY	GRAYFLY	JUMPILY	MOISTLY	PITHILY	SHAKILY	SQUALLY	TOUGHLY	WRINKLY
EXACTLY	GREATLY	JURALLY	MONTHLY	PLAINLY	SHAMBLY	STAGILY	TREACLY	WRONGLY
FADEDLY	GREENLY	KINKILY	MOODILY	PLIABLY	SHAPELY	STAIDLY	TREMBLY	YOUNGLY
FAINTLY	GREISLY	KNOBBLY	MORALLY	PLUMPLY	SHARPLY	STALELY	TRICKLY	YOUTHLY
FAIRILY	GRIESLY	KNUBBLY	MOVABLY	PRICKLY	SHEERLY	STARKLY	TRIFOLY	
FALSELY	GRIMILY	KNUCKLY	MUDDILY	PRIMELY	SHINGLY	STARTLY	TRITELY	
FATALLY	GRISELY	LADYFLY	MURKILY	PRIVILY	SHOGGLY	STATELY	TUMIDLY	
FIERILY	GRISTLY	LANKILY	MUSHILY	PRONELY	SHOOFLY	STEEPLY	TUNABLY	

8-letter words -LY

ABJECTLY	BEARABLY	CHIRPILY	DAMNABLY	EPICALLY	FORCEDLY	GRUMPILY	JAUNTILY
ABRUPTLY	BEASTILY	CHOICELY	DAPPERLY	ERRANTLY	FORCIBLY	GUILTILY	JEJUNELY
ABSENTLY	BEGGARLY	CHORALLY	DARINGLY	ERRINGLY	FORKEDLY	HEARTILY	JOCOSELY
ABSURDLY	BEHOVELY	CHURCHLY	DECENTLY	EVANGELY	FORMALLY	HEAVENLY	JOCUNDLY
ACHINGLY	BENIGNLY	CLAMMILY	DEMISSLY	EXPERTLY	FORMERLY	HECTORLY	JOKINGLY
ACTIVELY	BESEEMLY	CLEVERLY	DEMURELY	FACIALLY	FOURTHLY	HEROICLY	JOVIALLY
ACTUALLY	BITCHILY	CLONALLY	DENIABLY	FACILELY	FRIENDLY	HIDDENLY	JOYFULLY
ADORABLY	BITTERLY	CLOUDILY	DEUCEDLY	FALLIBLY	FRIGIDLY	HITCHILY	JOYOUSLY
ADROITLY	BLAMABLY	CLUMSILY	DEVOUTLY	FAMOUSLY	FRISKILY	HOARSELY	KERNELLY
AERIALLY	BLEARILY	COARSELY	DIRECTLY	FATHERLY	FROSTILY	HOLLOWLY	KINDLILY
AGUISHLY	BLITHELY	COGENTLY	DISAPPLY	FAULTILY	FROTHILY	HOMELILY	KNIGHTLY
AMAZEDLY	BLOODILY	COMMONLY	DISMALLY	FEASIBLY	FRUGALLY	HONESTLY	LABIALLY
AMENABLY	BORINGLY	CONVEXLY	DISTALLY	FELLOWLY	FUTILELY	HOPINGLY	LATENTLY
AMICABLY	BOUNCILY	COOINGLY	DIVERSLY	FERVIDLY	GAPINGLY	HORRIBLY	LATTERLY
AMUSEDLY	BOVINELY	COUSINLY	DIVINELY	FESTALLY	GARISHLY	HORRIDLY	LAUDABLY
ANIMALLY	BOYISHLY	COVERTLY	DOCTORLY	FEUDALLY	GENIALLY	HORSEFLY	LAVISHLY
ANNUALLY	BRASSILY	COWARDLY	DOGGEDLY	FIERCELY	GIBINGLY	HOUSEFLY	LAWFULLY
APICALLY	BRAZENLY	COYISHLY	DOOLALLY	FILIALLY	GIFTEDLY	HUMANELY	LAWYERLY
ARCANELY	BREEZILY	CRABBILY	DORSALLY	FILTHILY	GINGELLY	HUNGERLY	LEADENLY
ARDENTLY	BRIGHTLY	CRAFTILY	DOTINGLY	FINITELY	GINGERLY	HUNGRILY	LETHALLY
ARGUABLY	BROKENLY	CRANEFLY	DREAMILY	FISCALLY	GLASSILY	IMMANELY	LIMPIDLY
ARGUTELY	BRUTALLY	CRANKILY	DREARILY	FITFULLY	GLITZILY	IMPISHLY	LINEALLY
ARRANTLY	CANDIDLY	CRAVENLY	DROOPILY	FLABBILY	GLOBALLY	IMPURELY	LINEARLY
ARTFULLY	CARNALLY	CREAKILY	DROWSILY	FLASHILY	GLOOMILY	INFIRMLY	LIQUIDLY
ASSEMBLY	CASUALLY	CREDIBLY	EASTERLY	FLEXIBLY	GLOSSILY	INNATELY	LISSOMLY
ASTUTELY	CATCHFLY	CROAKILY	EFFETELY	FLIMSILY	GOLDENLY	INSANELY	LITHERLY
AUGUSTLY	CAUSALLY	CROUSELY	EIGHTHLY	FLINTILY	GRAITHLY	INTENTLY	LIVELILY
AVERSELY	CHASTELY	CRUSTILY	ELATEDLY	FLOPPILY	GRAVELLY	INWARDLY	LOBLOLLY
AVOWEDLY	CHEEKILY	CULPABLY	ELIGIBLY	FLORALLY	GREASILY	IREFULLY	LOSINGLY
BADGERLY	CHEERILY	CURSEDLY	ENTIRELY	FLORIDLY	GREEDILY	ISSUABLY	LOUCHELY
BANKERLY	CHILLILY	DAINTILY	ENVIABLY	FLUENTLY	GREENFLY	JAGGEDLY	LOVELILY

LOVINGLY	NATIVELY	PROBABLY	SALEABLY	SLOPPILY	STINGILY	TRASHILY	URGENTLY
LUBBERLY	NEURALLY	PROLIXLY	SAVAGELY	SLOVENLY	STOCKILY	TRENDILY	USEFULLY
LUMBERLY	NEWISHLY	PROMPTLY	SAVINGLY	SMALMILY	STODGILY	TREVALLY	UVULARLY
LUMPENLY	NOCENTLY	PROPERLY	SAVOURLY	SMARMILY	STOLIDLY	TRIBALLY	VACANTLY
MAIDENLY	NORMALLY	PROVABLY	SCANTILY	SMEARILY	STONEFLY	TRICKILY	VALUABLY
MALIGNLY	OBTUSELY	PRYINGLY	SCARCELY	SMOOTHLY	STORMILY	TRUSTILY	VARIABLY
MANFULLY	OCCULTLY	PUBLICLY	SCRAGGLY	SMUDGILY	STRAGGLY	TRYINGLY	VARIEDLY
MANNERLY	OCULARLY	PULINGLY	SCRIBBLY	SMUTTILY	STRAITLY	TUNBELLY	VENDIBLY
MANUALLY	ODIOUSLY	PUTRIDLY	SCRIGGLY	SNAPPILY	STRICTLY	TURBIDLY	VENIALLY
MARKEDLY	ONWARDLY	QUAINTLY	SCRIMPLY	SNEAKILY	STRONGLY	TURGIDLY	VERBALLY
MASTERLY	OPAQUELY	QUEASILY	SCURVILY	SNIFFILY	STUFFILY	UNCOMELY	VERNALLY
MATRONLY	ORNATELY	QUIRKILY	SEAMANLY	SNIVELLY	STUMPILY	UNCOSTLY	VEXINGLY
MATURELY	PALLIDLY	QUOTABLY	SECANTLY	SNOOTILY	STUPIDLY	UNEASILY	VIOLABLY
MEAGRELY	PALPABLY	RACIALLY	SECONDLY	SNOTTILY	STURDILY	UNEVENLY	VIRGINLY
MEDIALLY	PALTRILY	RADIALLY	SECRETLY	SOCIABLY	SUDDENLY	UNFAIRLY	VISUALLY
MELLOWLY	PANDERLY	RAGGEDLY	SECURELY	SOCIALLY	SUITABLY	UNGAINLY	VULGARLY
MENTALLY	PASSABLY	RAGINGLY	SEDATELY	SOLEMNLY	SULLENLY	UNGENTLY	WANTONLY
MESIALLY	PASSIBLY	RAKISHLY	SENILELY	SOMBRELY	SULTRILY	UNHOLILY	WEASELLY
MIGHTILY	PASTORLY	RANDOMLY	SENSIBLY	SORDIDLY	SUMMERLY	UNHOMELY	WEEVILLY
MINUTELY	PATCHILY	RASCALLY	SERENELY	SOUTERLY	SUPERBLY	UNIQUELY	WESTERLY
MISAPPLY	PATENTLY	RATEABLY	SERIALLY	SOVRANLY	SUPINELY	UNITEDLY	WHEEZILY
MODERNLY	PEDATELY	RAVINGLY	SEVERELY	SPARSELY	SUPPLELY	UNJUSTLY	WHIMSILY
MODESTLY	PETTEDLY	READABLY	SEXUALLY	SPEEDILY	SYMPHILY	UNKINDLY	WHITEFLY
MODISHLY	PITIABLY	RECENTLY	SHABBILY	SPIRALLY	TAKINGLY	UNKINGLY	WICKEDLY
MOLTENLY	PLACABLY	RECTALLY	SHAGGILY	SPONGILY	TANGIBLY	UNLIKELY	WILFULLY
MOMENTLY	PLACIDLY	REDBELLY	SHAUCHLY	SPOOKILY	TARNALLY	UNLIVELY	WINGEDLY
MONOPOLY	PLAGUILY	REFLEXLY	SHIFTILY	SPOONILY	TARTARLY	UNLORDLY	WINTERLY
MOPINGLY	PLIANTLY	RELIABLY	SHIRTILY	SPORTILY	TASSELLY	UNLOVELY	WITTOLLY
MOPISHLY	PLUCKILY	REMISSLY	SHODDILY	SPOTTILY	TAWDRILY	UNMEETLY	WIZARDLY
MORBIDLY	PLURALLY	REMOTELY	SHREWDLY	SPRITELY	TENDERLY	UNREALLY	WOEFULLY
MOROSELY	POLITELY	RETRALLY	SICKERLY	SPRUCELY	TERRIBLY	UNSAFELY	WOODENLY
MORTALLY	POPISHLY	RITUALLY	SICKLILY	SQUARELY	TETCHILY	UNSEEMLY	WOOINGLY
MOTHERLY	PORTERLY	ROBUSTLY	SIGNALLY	SQUIGGLY	THWARTLY	UNTIDILY	WORTHILY
MOVEABLY	POSINGLY	ROOTEDLY	SILENTLY	SQUIRELY	TIMOUSLY	UNTIMELY	WOUNDILY
MOVINGLY	POSSIBLY	ROTTENLY	SILVERLY	STANCHLY	TINSELLY	UNUSABLY	WRATHILY
MULISHLY	POSTALLY	ROTUNDLY	SINFULLY	STARRILY	TONISHLY	UNWARELY	WRITERLY
MULTIPLY	POTENTLY	ROVINGLY	SISTERLY	STATEDLY	TOOTHILY	UNWARILY	YEOMANLY
MUSINGLY	PREPPILY	RUEFULLY	SKIMPILY	STEADILY	TORPIDLY	UNWIFELY	YONDERLY
MUTUALLY	PRETTILY	RUGGEDLY	SLANGILY	STEAMILY	TORRIDLY	UNWISELY	YONGTHLY
NARGHILY	PRIESTLY	RUGOSELY	SLEAZILY	STEEVELY	TOUCHILY	UPPISHLY	ZOOPHILY
NARGILLY	PRIMALLY	SACREDLY	SLEEPILY	STICKILY	TOWARDLY	UPWARDLY	
NARROWLY	PRINCELY	SAILORLY	SLIGHTLY	STIEVELY	TOYISHLY	URBANELY	

WORDS ENDING IN -MAN

7-letter words -MAN

ARTSMAN	BYREMAN	FOREMAN	HERDMAN	LANDMAN	MOORMAN	POSTMAN	SIDEMAN	TURFMAN
BASEMAN	CASEMAN	FREEMAN	HIGHMAN	LENSMAN	MOOTMAN	RAFTMAN	SNOWMAN	UNHUMAN
BATSMAN	CAVEMAN	FROGMAN	HOODMAN	LINEMAN	NEWSMAN	RAILMAN	SOKEMAN	UNWOMAN
BEADMAN	CHAPMAN	GADSMAN	HOSEMAN	LINKMAN	OARSMAN	REELMAN	SONGMAN	WAKEMAN
BEDEMAN	CLUBMAN	GATEMAN	INHUMAN	LOCKMAN	ODDSMAN	REPOMAN	SPAEMAN	WIREMAN
BELLMAN	COALMAN	GLEEMAN	ISLEMAN	LOCOMAN	OTTOMAN	RINGMAN	SURFMAN	WOODMAN
BELTMAN	DAYSMAN	GOODMAN	JACKMAN	MAGSMAN	OVERMAN	ROADMAN	SWAGMAN	WOOLMAN
BILLMAN	DECUMAN	GOWNMAN	JARKMAN	MAILMAN	PACKMAN	RODSMAN	TAPSMAN	WORKMAN
BIRDMAN	DRAYMAN	GUDEMAN	JAZZMAN	MALTMAN	PASSMAN	SAGAMAN	TAXIMAN	YARDMAN
BOATMAN	DUSTMAN	HANGMAN	JUNKMAN	MARKMAN	PEATMAN	SANDMAN	TOLLMAN	YEGGMAN
BONDMAN	FACEMAN	HANUMAN	JURYMAN	MASHMAN	PIKEMAN	SHIPMAN	TOOLMAN	
BOOKMAN	FIREMAN	HEADMAN	KEELMAN	MOBSMAN	POLLMAN	SHOPMAN	TOPSMAN	
BUSHMAN	FOOTMAN	HELIMAN	KINSMAN		PORTMAN	SHOWMAN	TRUEMAN	

8-letter words -MAN

AIRWOMAN	BUTTYMAN	EARTHMAN	HELMSMAN	LOCKSMAN	PLACEMAN	ROADSMAN	SQUAWMAN
ALDERMAN	CHAINMAN	EVERYMAN	HENCHMAN	LODESMAN	PLAIDMAN	ROUTEMAN	STALLMAN
BAILSMAN	CHAIRMAN	FERRYMAN	HERDSMAN	MADWOMAN	PLATEMAN	SALESMAN	STEELMAN
BANDSMAN	CHESSMAN	FORGEMAN	HIELAMAN	MARCHMAN	PREHUMAN	SCENEMAN	STOCKMAN
BANDYMAN	CHOIRMAN	FREEDMAN	HOASTMAN	MARKSMAN	PRESSMAN	SEAWOMAN	STOREMAN
BANKSMAN	CLANSMAN	FRESHMAN	HOISTMAN	MERESMAN	PRIZEMAN	SEEDSMAN	STUNTMAN
BARGEMAN	CLASSMAN	FRONTMAN	HORSEMAN	MERRYMAN	PROSEMAN	SHAREMAN	SUBHUMAN
BATWOMAN	COACHMAN	FUGLEMAN	HOUSEMAN	MONEYMAN	PUNTSMAN	SHEARMAN	SUPERMAN
BEADSMAN	CRAGSMAN	GANGSMAN	HUNTSMAN	MOTORMAN	QUILLMAN	SHIREMAN	SWAGSMAN
BEDESMAN	DAIRYMAN	GAVELMAN	ISLESMAN	NOBLEMAN	RAFTSMAN	SHOREMAN	SWORDMAN
BONDSMAN	DALESMAN	GLASSMAN	LANDSMAN	OVERSMAN	RAMPSMAN	SIDESMAN	TACKSMAN
BOTHYMAN	DOOMSMAN	GOADSMAN	LAYWOMAN	PENWOMAN	RANCHMAN	SOUNDMAN	TALESMAN
BRAKEMAN	DOORSMAN	GOWNSMAN	LEADSMAN	PETERMAN	REINSMAN	SPACEMAN	TALISMAN
BRIDEMAN	DRAGOMAN	HANDYMAN	LIEGEMAN	PILOTMAN	RIFLEMAN	SPADEMAN	TALLYMAN
BRINKMAN	DRAGSMAN	HEADSMAN	LINESMAN	PITCHMAN	RIVERMAN	SPEARMAN	TIDESMAN

TOWNSMAN	TRASHMAN	TRUCKMAN	WATERMAN	WHEELMAN	WOODSMAN
TOYWOMAN	TREWSMAN	UNDERMAN	WEALSMAN	WIDOWMAN	YARRAMAN
TRACKMAN	TRUCHMAN	WATCHMAN	WHALEMAN	WINCHMAN	

WORDS ENDING IN -MEN

7-letter words -MEN

ABDOMEN	BONDMEN	DUSTMEN	HANGMEN	KEELMEN	MOBSMEN	POSTMEN	SHOWMEN	TRUEMEN
AGNOMEN	BOOKMEN	FACEMEN	HEADMEN	KINSMEN	MOLIMEN	PUTAMEN	SIDEMEN	TURFMEN
ALBUMEN	BUSHMEN	FIREMEN	HELIMEN	LANDMEN	MOORMEN	RAFTMEN	SNOWMEN	VELAMEN
ARTSMEN	BYREMEN	FOOTMEN	HERDMEN	LENSMEN	MOOTMEN	RAILMEN	SOKEMEN	WAKEMEN
BASEMEN	CACUMEN	FORAMEN	HIGHMEN	LINEMEN	NEWSMEN	REELMEN	SONGMEN	WIREMEN
BATSMEN	CASEMEN	FOREMEN	HILLMEN	LINKMEN	OARSMEN	REGIMEN	SPAEMEN	WOODMEN
BEADMEN	CAVEMEN	FREEMEN	HOODMEN	LOCKMEN	ODDSMEN	REPOMEN	SUDAMEN	WOOLMEN
BEDEMEN	CERUMEN	FROGMEN	HOSEMEN	LOCOMEN	OVERMEN	RINGMEN	SURFMEN	WORKMEN
BELLMEN	CHAPMEN	GADSMEN	ISLEMEN	MAGSMEN	PACKMEN	ROADMEN	SWAGMEN	YARDMEN
BELTMEN	CLUBMEN	GATEMEN	JACKMEN	MAILMEN	PASSMEN	RODSMEN	TAPSMEN	YEGGMEN
BILLMEN	COALMEN	GLEEMEN	JARKMEN	MALTMEN	PEATMEN	SAGAMEN	TAXIMEN	
BIRDMEN	DAYSMEN	GOODMEN	JAZZMEN	MARKMEN	PIKEMEN	SANDMEN	TOLLMEN	
BITUMEN	DRAYMEN	GOWNMEN	JUNKMEN	MASHMEN	POLLMEN	SHIPMEN	TOOLMEN	
BOATMEN	DURAMEN	GUDEMEN	JURYMEN	MILKMEN	PORTMEN	SHOPMEN	TOPSMEN	

8-letter words -MEN

AIRWOMEN	CHAIRMEN	FERRYMEN	HOASTMEN	MERRYMEN	RAFTSMEN	SOUNDMEN	TIDESMEN	
ALDERMEN	CHESSMEN	FORGEMEN	HOISTMEN	MONEYMEN	RAMPSMEN	SPACEMEN	TOWNSMEN	
BAILSMEN	CHOIRMEN	FREEDMEN	HORSEMEN	MOTORMEN	RANCHMEN	SPADEMEN	TOYWOMEN	
BANDSMEN	CLANSMEN	FRESHMEN	HOUSEMEN	NOBLEMEN	REINSMEN	SPEARMEN	TRACKMEN	
BANDYMEN	CLASSMEN	FRONTMEN	HUNTSMEN	OVERSMEN	RIFLEMEN	SPECIMEN	TRASHMEN	
BANKSMEN	CLINAMEN	FUGLEMEN	ISLESMEN	PENWOMEN	RIVERMEN	SQUAWMEN	TREWSMEN	
BARGEMEN	COACHMEN	GANGSMEN	LANDSMEN	PETERMEN	ROADSMEN	STALLMEN	TRUCHMEN	
BATWOMEN	COGNOMEN	GAVELMEN	LAYWOMEN	PILOTMEN	ROUTEMEN	STEELMEN	TRUCKMEN	
BEADSMEN	CRAGSMEN	GLASSMEN	LEADSMEN	PITCHMEN	SALESMEN	STOCKMEN	UNDERMEN	
BEDESMEN	CYCLAMEN	GOADSMEN	LIEGEMEN	PLACEMEN	SCENEMEN	STOREMEN	WATCHMEN	
BONDSMEN	DAIRYMEN	GOWNSMEN	LINESMEN	PLAIDMEN	SEAWOMEN	STUNTMEN	WATERMEN	
BOTHYMEN	DALESMEN	GRAVAMEN	LOCKSMEN	PLATEMEN	SEEDSMEN	SUPERMEN	WEALSMEN	
BRAKEMEN	DOOMSMEN	HANDYMEN	LODESMEN	PRESSMEN	SHAREMEN	SWAGSMEN	WHALEMEN	
BRIDEMEN	DOORSMEN	HEADSMEN	MADWOMEN	PRIZEMEN	SHEARMEN	SWORDMEN	WHEELMEN	
BRINKMEN	DRAGSMEN	HELMSMEN	MARCHMEN	PROSEMEN	SHIREMEN	TACKSMEN	WIDOWMEN	
BUTTYMEN	EARTHMEN	HENCHMEN	MARKSMEN	PUNTSMEN	SHOREMEN	TALESMEN	WINCHMEN	
CHAINMEN	EVERYMEN	HERDSMEN	MERESMEN	QUILLMEN	SIDESMEN	TALLYMEN	WOODSMEN	

WORDS ENDING IN -NESS

7-letter words -NESS

ALLNESS	DIMNESS	FEWNESS	HIPNESS	LIONESS	ODDNESS	RAWNESS	SHINESS	WANNESS
APTNESS	DRYNESS	FITNESS	HOTNESS	LOWNESS	OLDNESS	REDNESS	SHYNESS	WETNESS
BADNESS	DULNESS	FULNESS	ICINESS	MADNESS	ONENESS	RUMNESS	SLYNESS	WITNESS
BIGNESS	FARNESS	GAYNESS	ILLNESS	NEWNESS	OUTNESS	SADNESS	TWONESS	WRYNESS
COYNESS	FATNESS	HARNESS	LAXNESS	NOWNESS	PATNESS	SETNESS	WAENESS	

8-letter words -NESS

ACIDNESS	CALMNESS	DONENESS	FONDNESS	HAZINESS	LONENESS	NUDENESS	RICHNESS	
AGEDNESS	CAMPNESS	DOPINESS	FOULNESS	HERENESS	LONGNESS	NULLNESS	RIFENESS	
AIRINESS	CANONESS	DOURNESS	FOXINESS	HIGHNESS	LOUDNESS	NUMBNESS	RIPENESS	
ALBNESS	COLDNESS	DOWFNESS	FOZINESS	HOLINESS	LUSHNESS	OILINESS	ROPINESS	
ARCHNESS	COOLNESS	DOZINESS	FREENESS	HUGENESS	MATINESS	OOZINESS	ROSINESS	
ARIDNESS	COSINESS	DRABNESS	FULLNESS	IDLENESS	MAZINESS	OPENNESS	RUDENESS	
ARTINESS	COXINESS	DULLNESS	GAMENESS	IFFINESS	MEANNESS	PALENESS	SAFENESS	
AVIDNESS	CURTNESS	DUMBNESS	GAMINESS	INKINESS	MEEKNESS	PERTNESS	SAGENESS	
BALDNESS	CUTENESS	DUSKNESS	GAMYNESS	JIMPNESS	MEETNESS	PIEDNESS	SALTNESS	
BARENESS	DAFTNESS	EASINESS	GASTNESS	JUSTNESS	MILDNESS	PINKNESS	SAMENESS	
BARONESS	DAMPNESS	EDGINESS	GLADNESS	KEENNESS	MIRINESS	POORNESS	SANENESS	
BASENESS	DANKNESS	EERINESS	GLIBNESS	KINDNESS	MUCHNESS	PORINESS	SEARNESS	
BEINNESS	DARKNESS	EVENNESS	GLUMNESS	LAMENESS	MUTENESS	POSHNESS	SEEDNESS	
BLUENESS	DEADNESS	EVILNESS	GONENESS	LANKNESS	NAFFNESS	PRIMNESS	SELFNESS	
BOLDNESS	DEAFNESS	FAINNESS	GOODNESS	LATENESS	NEARNESS	PUNINESS	SEXINESS	
BONINESS	DEARNESS	FAIRNESS	GORINESS	LAZINESS	NEATNESS	PURENESS	SICKNESS	
BOXINESS	DEEPNESS	FASTNESS	GREYNESS	LEANNESS	NESHNESS	RACINESS	SIZINESS	
BUSINESS	DEFTNESS	FELLNESS	GRIMNESS	LEWDNESS	NEXTNESS	RANKNESS	SKEWNESS	
BUSYNESS	DEMONESS	FINENESS	GRUMNESS	LIKENESS	NICENESS	RARENESS	SLIMNESS	
CAGINESS	DEWINESS	FIRMNESS	HALENESS	LIMINESS	NIGHNESS	RASHNESS	SLOWNESS	
CAGYNESS	DIRENESS	FLATNESS	HARDNESS	LIMPNESS	NOSINESS	REALNESS	SMUGNESS	

SNUGNESS	SUCHNESS	THATNESS	TITANESS	VAINNESS	WARMNESS	WHATNESS	WOODNESS
SOFTNESS	SURENESS	THINNESS	TRIGNESS	VASTNESS	WASTNESS	WIDENESS	ZANINESS
SOLENESS	TALLNESS	THISNESS	TRIMNESS	VILDNESS	WAVINESS	WILDNESS	
SORENESS	TAMENESS	THUSNESS	TRUENESS	VILENESS	WAXINESS	WILINESS	
SOURNESS	TARTNESS	TIDINESS	TWEENESS	VOIDNESS	WEAKNESS	WIRINESS	
SPRYNESS	TAUTNESS	TININESS	UGLINESS	WARINESS	WELLNESS	WISENESS	

WORDS ENDING IN -OID

7-letter words -OID

ACAROID	BYSSOID	CRINOID	ERICOID	HISTOID	MUSCOID	PIGMOID	SPIROID	VESPOID
ADENOID	CESTOID	CTENOID	ETHMOID	HYALOID	MYELOID	PLACOID	STEROID	XIPHOID
AGAMOID	CHELOID	CYCLOID	FACTOID	HYDROID	NAEVOID	PYGMOID	STYLOID	ZEBROID
AMBROID	CHOROID	CYSTOID	FIBROID	HYPNOID	NEGROID	QUINOID	TABLOID	ZINCOID
AMYLOID	CIRSOID	DELTOID	FUNGOID	LABROID	OBOVOID	RHIZOID	TENIOID	
ANDROID	CISSOID	DENTOID	GLENOID	LENTOID	OCELOID	SARCOID	THEROID	
ANEROID	COCCOID	DERMOID	GLOBOID	LIANOID	OCHROID	SAUROID	THYROID	
ANTHOID	COLLOID	DESMOID	GOBIOID	LITHOID	OSTEOID	SIALOID	TIGROID	
ARCTOID	COTTOID	DIPLOID	HAPLOID	MASTOID	PERCOID	SIGMOID	TURDOID	
ASTROID	CRICOID	DISCOID	HELCOID	MATTOID	PHACOID	SPAROID	TYPHOID	

8-letter words -OID

ACTINOID	CANCROID	ECHINOID	HYRACOID	PARANOID	RESINOID	SOLENOID	THYREOID
ALKALOID	CARDIOID	EMBRYOID	KERATOID	PETALOID	RETINOID	SORICOID	THYRSOID
AMBEROID	CENTROID	EMULSOID	LAMBDOID	PEZIZOID	RHABDOID	SPHENOID	TRICHOID
AMMONOID	CERATOID	ERGATOID	LEMUROID	PHALLOID	RHOMBOID	SPHEROID	TRIPLOID
AMOEBOID	CHORIOID	GABBROID	LIGULOID	PHELLOID	SCAPHOID	SPONGOID	TROCHOID
ARILLOID	CICHLOID	GALENOID	LYMPHOID	PHYLLOID	SCHIZOID	SQUALOID	VOLUTOID
ASTEROID	CLUPEOID	GEOMYOID	MEDUSOID	PINACOID	SCINCOID	STURNOID	YPSILOID
ATHETOID	CONCHOID	HELICOID	MYTILOID	PINAKOID	SCIUROID	TAENIOID	
AUTACOID	CORACOID	HISTIOID	NEMATOID	PITYROID	SCLEROID	TAPIROID	
BLASTOID	CORONOID	HOMALOID	NEPHROID	POLYPOID	SEPALOID	TARSIOID	
BOTRYOID	COTYLOID	HOMINOID	ODONTOID	PRISMOID	SESAMOID	TERATOID	
CALYCOID	DENDROID	HUMANOID	OMOHYOID	PSYCHOID	SILUROID	TETANOID	
CAMELOID	DORIDOID	HYDATOID	ONISCOID	PYRENOID	SINUSOID	THALLOID	

WORDS ENDING IN -OR

7-letter words -OR

ABACTOR	BIOPHOR	DILATOR	EVERTOR	LANGUOR	OFFEROR	QUITTOR	SIGNIOR	VENATOR
ABETTOR	CAMPHOR	DILUTOR	EVICTOR	LAXATOR	OUTDOOR	REACTOR	SIMILOR	VISITOR
ABLATOR	CHADDOR	DIVISOR	EXACTOR	LEGATOR	PANDOOR	REALTOR	SPONSOR	WARRIOR
ADAPTOR	CHANTOR	DONATOR	EXCITOR	LEVATOR	PARADOR	RELATOR	SQUALOR	ZELATOR
ADVISOR	CHIKHOR	EDUCTOR	FEOFFOR	MACHZOR	PARITOR	REVISOR	STENTOR	
AERATOR	CLANGOR	EJECTOR	GENITOR	MAORMOR	PICADOR	REVIVOR	STRIDOR	
AGISTOR	CREATOR	ELECTOR	GRANTOR	MARKHOR	PLEDGOR	ROTATOR	TANDOOR	
ALIENOR	CURATOR	EMPEROR	HERITOR	MATADOR	PLESSOR	SCISSOR	TEMBLOR	
ATHANOR	DEBITOR	EMULSOR	HUMIDOR	MIRADOR	PRAETOR	SENATOR	TRACTOR	
AUDITOR	DECOLOR	ENACTOR	INCISOR	MONITOR	PRESSOR	SEPTUOR	TRAITOR	
AVIATOR	DELATOR	EQUATOR	ISOCHOR	MORMAOR	PROCTOR	SETTLOR	TWISTOR	
BELABOR	DEVISOR	ERECTOR	JANITOR	OBLIGOR	QUESTOR	SEXTUOR	UNVISOR	

8-letter words -OR

ABDUCTOR	BEHAVIOR	DETECTOR	EXPIATOR	INVESTOR	PLEDGEOR	RELEASOR	TOREADOR
ACCENTOR	BISECTOR	DEVIATOR	EXTENSOR	ISOLATOR	PREDATOR	REMITTOR	TRADITOR
ACCEPTOR	CANEPHOR	DICTATOR	EXTERIOR	KURVEYOR	PRODITOR	RESISTOR	TRAPDOOR
ACTUATOR	CHELATOR	DIRECTOR	GILLYVOR	LICENSOR	PROMISOR	RONCADOR	TRICOLOR
ADDUCTOR	COFACTOR	DISCOLOR	GOVERNOR	MAINDOOR	PROMOTOR	SCULPTOR	ULTERIOR
ADJUSTOR	COLLATOR	DISFAVOR	HELIODOR	MANDATOR	PRONATOR	SECTATOR	UNANCHOR
ADULATOR	CONCOLOR	DISHONOR	IDOLATOR	MEDIATOR	PROVEDOR	SEDUCTOR	UNICOLOR
AGITATOR	CONJUROR	EDUCATOR	IMITATOR	METAPHOR	PROVIDOR	SEIGNIOR	URINATOR
ANCESTOR	CONVENOR	EFFECTOR	IMPOSTOR	MIGRATOR	PROVISOR	SELECTOR	VALUATOR
ANIMATOR	CONVEYOR	ELEVATOR	INCENSOR	MISCOLOR	PULSATOR	SERVITOR	VARACTOR
ANTERIOR	CORRIDOR	ELICITOR	INCEPTOR	NARRATOR	PURVEYOR	SPLENDOR	VARISTOR
ARRESTOR	CREDITOR	EMBRASOR	INDUCTOR	NEIGHBOR	PURVEYOR	STRESSOR	VERDEROR
ASSENTOR	CREMATOR	EMULATOR	INFECTOR	NONJUROR	QUAESTOR	SUBFLOOR	VIBRATOR
ASSERTOR	CURSITOR	ENDEAVOR	INFERIOR	OBJECTOR	RADIATOR	SUBPRIOR	VIOLATOR
ASSESSOR	CUSPIDOR	EPILATOR	INFLATOR	OCCLUSOR	RECAPTOR	SUPERIOR	VITIATOR
ASSIGNOR	DEFECTOR	EVOCATOR	INJECTOR	OPERATOR	RECEPTOR	SURVEYOR	WHEREFOR
ATTESTOR	DEFLATOR	EXCEPTOR	INTERIOR	PATENTOR	REDACTOR	SURVIVOR	
BACHELOR	DEMEANOR	EXECUTOR	INVENTOR	PHOSPHOR	REGRATOR	TESTATOR	
BARRATOR	DEPICTOR	EXPANDOR	INVERTOR	PISCATOR	REJECTOR	THEREFOR	

WORDS ENDING IN -OUS

7-letter words -OUS

ACAJOUS	AZYGOUS	CONGOUS	FULVOUS	IGNEOUS	OBVIOUS	PLUMOUS	SINUOUS	VALGOUS
ACEROUS	AZYMOUS	COPIOUS	FUNGOUS	IMPIOUS	OCHROUS	POMPOUS	SOUKOUS	VARIOUS
ACETOUS	BADIOUS	CORIOUS	FURIOUS	INVIOUS	ODOROUS	PORTOUS	SPINOUS	VEINOUS
ACINOUS	BILIOUS	CORMOUS	FUSCOUS	JEALOUS	OMINOUS	PULPOUS	SPUMOUS	VICIOUS
AENEOUS	BIVIOUS	CUPROUS	GASEOUS	LENTOUS	ONEROUS	RAMEOUS	SUCCOUS	VIDUOUS
AGAMOUS	BRUMOUS	CURIOUS	GEALOUS	LEPROUS	ONYMOUS	RAUCOUS	TALCOUS	VILLOUS
AMADOUS	BULBOUS	DEVIOUS	GIBBOUS	LIMBOUS	OPACOUS	RHODOUS	TEDIOUS	VISCOUS
AMOROUS	BURNOUS	DUBIOUS	GLEBOUS	LUTEOUS	OSMIOUS	RIOTOUS	TENUOUS	VOUDOUS
ANUROUS	CACHOUS	DUTEOUS	GLOBOUS	NACROUS	OSSEOUS	ROUCOUS	TIMEOUS	ZEALOUS
ANXIOUS	CALLOUS	EMULOUS	GRUMOUS	NERVOUS	PAPPOUS	ROUTOUS	TYPHOUS	ZINCOUS
APODOUS	CARIOUS	ENVIOUS	GUMMOUS	NIMIOUS	PARLOUS	RUBIOUS	UBEROUS	
AQUEOUS	CASEOUS	ESTROUS	HEINOUS	NIOBOUS	PERLOUS	RUINOUS	UMBROUS	
ARDUOUS	CEREOUS	FATUOUS	HERBOUS	NITROUS	PETROUS	SANIOUS	URANOUS	
ATHEOUS	CHYMOUS	FEATOUS	HIDEOUS	NIVEOUS	PICEOUS	SARCOUS	URINOUS	
ATOKOUS	CIRROUS	FERROUS	HUGEOUS	NOCUOUS	PILEOUS	SERIOUS	USUROUS	
AZOTOUS	CITROUS	FIBROUS	HYDROUS	NOXIOUS	PITEOUS	SIMIOUS	VACUOUS	

8-letter words -OUS

ACARPOUS	CERNUOUS	EXIGUOUS	GRISEOUS	NIDOROUS	PRECIOUS	SONOROUS	ULCEROUS
ADUNCOUS	CHLOROUS	EXIMIOUS	GYPSEOUS	NODULOUS	PREVIOUS	SOPOROUS	UNCTUOUS
AMBEROUS	CITREOUS	FABULOUS	HALITOUS	NUBILOUS	PYRITOUS	SPACIOUS	UNDULOUS
ANOUROUS	CORNEOUS	FACTIOUS	HUMOROUS	NUMEROUS	PYRRHOUS	SPECIOUS	UNJOYOUS
ANTICOUS	COUSCOUS	FASHIOUS	ICHOROUS	NUMINOUS	RAMULOUS	SPERMOUS	USURIOUS
APHONOUS	COVETOUS	FASTUOUS	INCUBOUS	OCHEROUS	RAVENOUS	SPURIOUS	UXORIOUS
APHTHOUS	COVINOUS	FEATEOUS	INERMOUS	OCHREOUS	RESINOUS	SQUAMOUS	VALOROUS
APTEROUS	CRIBROUS	FEATUOUS	INFAMOUS	OESTROUS	RIGOROUS	STANNOUS	VANADOUS
ARACEOUS	CROCEOUS	FELONOUS	KOUSKOUS	OOGAMOUS	RUMOROUS	STOCIOUS	VAPOROUS
ARANEOUS	CROUPOUS	FERREOUS	LACTEOUS	ORAGIOUS	SABULOUS	STOTIOUS	VENOMOUS
ARBOROUS	CUMBROUS	FEVEROUS	LEAPROUS	ORDUROUS	SAPAJOUS	STRATOUS	VENTROUS
ASPEROUS	CUPREOUS	FIDDIOUS	LIBELOUS	ORGULOUS	SAPOROUS	STRUMOUS	VERTUOUS
ASTOMOUS	DARTROUS	FLATUOUS	LIGNEOUS	OVARIOUS	SAVOROUS	STUDIOUS	VIGOROUS
ATROPOUS	DECOROUS	FLEXUOUS	LUMINOUS	PABULOUS	SCABIOUS	SUBEROUS	VIPEROUS
BIBULOUS	DESIROUS	FRABJOUS	LUSCIOUS	PALUDOUS	SCABROUS	SUDOROUS	VIRTUOUS
BIGAMOUS	DEXTROUS	GEMINOUS	LUSTROUS	PAPULOUS	SCARIOUS	TEMEROUS	VITREOUS
BIMANOUS	DIDYMOUS	GEMMEOUS	MANITOUS	PATULOUS	SCIOLOUS	TENUIOUS	WAVEROUS
BIPAROUS	DIGAMOUS	GENEROUS	MARABOUS	PERILOUS	SCLEROUS	THALLOUS	WONDROUS
BIRAMOUS	DIGYNOUS	GLABROUS	MELANOUS	PERVIOUS	SCORIOUS	TIMOROUS	WRONGOUS
CADUCOUS	DIMEROUS	GLAREOUS	MIASMOUS	PETALOUS	SEDULOUS	TINAMOUS	XANTHOUS
CAESIOUS	DIPNOOUS	GLAUCOUS	MUTICOUS	PLUMBOUS	SELENOUS	TITANOUS	YTTRIOUS
CANOROUS	DITOKOUS	GLORIOUS	MUTINOUS	PLUVIOUS	SENSUOUS	TORTIOUS	
CAPTIOUS	DOLOROUS	GOITROUS	NACREOUS	POACEOUS	SEPALOUS	TORTUOUS	
CARIBOUS	EDACIOUS	GORGEOUS	NAUSEOUS	POLYPOUS	SETULOUS	TUBEROUS	
CARNEOUS	ENORMOUS	GRACIOUS	NEBULOUS	POPULOUS	SIBILOUS	TUBULOUS	
CAUTIOUS	EPIGEOUS	GRIEVOUS	NEMOROUS	PORTEOUS	SOMBROUS	TUMOROUS	

WORDS ENDING IN -OUT

7-letter words -OUT

ASPROUT	DROPOUT	HANDOUT	HOLDOUT	PASSOUT	SURTOUT	UNSHOUT	WITHOUT
BESPOUT	EELPOUT	HANGOUT	LOCKOUT	ROLLOUT	TAKEOUT	WASHOUT	
COOKOUT	FALLOUT	HIDEOUT	LOOKOUT	SPINOUT	TURNOUT	WIPEOUT	

8-letter words -OUT

BLACKOUT	FLAMEOUT	LAYABOUT	RACAHOUT	SPEAKOUT	THEREOUT
BROWNOUT	GADABOUT	MARABOUT	RUNABOUT	STANDOUT	UNDEVOUT
CHECKOUT	KNOCKOUT	PRINTOUT	SLEEPOUT	TACAHOUT	WHEREOUT

WORDS ENDING IN -SET

7-letter words -SET

BACKSET	BRASSET	CRESSET	HANDSET	HEADSET	MOONSET	SEAMSET	TYPESET
BONESET	CHIPSET	FILMSET	HAROSET	MINDSET	OVERSET	TWINSET	

8-letter words -SET

CHAROSET	MARMOSET	QUICKSET	SOMERSET	THICKSET	THORNSET	UNDERSET

WORDS ENDING IN -SHIP

7-letter words -SHIP

AIRSHIP	DONSHIP	FOXSHIP	GUNSHIP	KINSHIP	MIDSHIP	SIBSHIP	WARSHIP
DOGSHIP	ENDSHIP	GODSHIP	HERSHIP	LUDSHIP	NUNSHIP	SONSHIP	WORSHIP

8-letter words -SHIP

ANTISHIP	DEMYSHIP	FLAGSHIP	HEADSHIP	LADYSHIP	MATESHIP	RAJASHIP	TREESHIP
BARDSHIP	DOGESHIP	FORESHIP	HEIRSHIP	LONGSHIP	PEATSHIP	SERFSHIP	TWINSHIP
CLANSHIP	DUKESHIP	GURUSHIP	HEROSHIP	LORDSHIP	POETSHIP	TOWNSHIP	WARDSHIP
DEANSHIP	FIRESHIP	HARDSHIP	KINGSHIP	MAGESHIP	POPESHIP	TRANSHIP	WINDSHIP

WORDS ENDING IN -SKIN

7-letter words -SKIN

CATSKIN	DOGSKIN	GRISKIN	KIDSKIN	OILSKIN	PIGSKIN	REDSKIN

8-letter words -SKIN

BEARSKIN	CAPESKIN	DEERSKIN	GOATSKIN	PONYSKIN	TURNSKIN	WOODSKIN
BUCKSKIN	COONSKIN	FISHSKIN	LAMBSKIN	SEALSKIN	WINESKIN	
CALFSKIN	DAMASKIN	FORESKIN	MOLESKIN	SWANSKIN	WOLFSKIN	

WORDS ENDING IN -SMAN

7-letter words -SMAN

ARTSMAN	DAYSMAN	KINSMAN	MAGSMAN	NEWSMAN	ODDSMAN	RODSMAN	TOPSMAN
BATSMAN	GADSMAN	LENSMAN	MOBSMAN	OARSMAN	PASSMAN	TAPSMAN	

8-letter words -SMAN

BAILSMAN	CLANSMAN	GANGSMAN	HUNTSMAN	MARKSMAN	REINSMAN	TALESMAN
BANDSMAN	CLASSMAN	GLASSMAN	ISLESMAN	MERESMAN	ROADSMAN	TALISMAN
BANKSMAN	CRAGSMAN	GOADSMAN	LANDSMAN	OVERSMAN	SALESMAN	TIDESMAN
BEADSMAN	DALESMAN	GOWNSMAN	LEADSMAN	PRESSMAN	SEEDSMAN	TOWNSMAN
BEDESMAN	DOOMSMAN	HEADSMAN	LINESMAN	PUNTSMAN	SIDESMAN	TREWSMAN
BONDSMAN	DOORSMAN	HELMSMAN	LOCKSMAN	RAFTSMAN	SWAGSMAN	WEALSMAN
CHESSMAN	DRAGSMAN	HERDSMAN	LODESMAN	RAMPSMAN	TACKSMAN	WOODSMAN

WORDS ENDING IN -SMEN

7-letter words -SMEN

ARTSMEN	DAYSMEN	KINSMEN	MAGSMEN	NEWSMEN	ODDSMEN	RODSMEN	TOPSMEN
BATSMEN	GADSMEN	LENSMEN	MOBSMEN	OARSMEN	PASSMEN	TAPSMEN	

8-letter words -SMEN

BAILSMEN	CHESSMEN	DOORSMEN	HEADSMEN	LEADSMEN	OVERSMEN	ROADSMEN	TALESMEN
BANDSMEN	CLANSMEN	DRAGSMEN	HELMSMEN	LINESMEN	PRESSMEN	SALESMEN	TIDESMEN
BANKSMEN	CLASSMEN	GANGSMEN	HERDSMEN	LOCKSMEN	PUNTSMEN	SEEDSMEN	TOWNSMEN
BEADSMEN	CRAGSMEN	GLASSMEN	HUNTSMEN	LODESMEN	RAFTSMEN	SIDESMEN	TREWSMEN
BEDESMEN	DALESMEN	GOADSMEN	ISLESMEN	MARKSMEN	RAMPSMEN	SWAGSMEN	WEALSMEN
BONDSMEN	DOOMSMEN	GOWNSMEN	LANDSMEN	MERESMEN	REINSMEN	TACKSMEN	WOODSMEN

WORDS ENDING IN -SOME

7-letter words -SOME

AWESOME	EPISOME	GAYSOME	LISSOME	NOYSOME	TRISOME	TWOSOME	WAESOME	WOESOME
BEESOME	FULSOME	IRKSOME	NOISOME	TOYSOME	TWASOME	UROSOME	WINSOME	

8-letter words -SOME

ACROSOME	DOLESOME	GAMESOME	HEALSOME	LONESOME	MURKSOME	ROOMSOME	WORKSOME
AUTOSOME	DUELSOME	GLADSOME	HOLESOME	LONGSOME	PLAYSOME	TEDISOME	
CLOYSOME	FEARSOME	GLEESOME	JOKESOME	LOVESOME	POLYSOME	TIRESOME	
CYTOSOME	FLEASOME	GRUESOME	LIFESOME	LYSOSOME	PYROSOME	TOILSOME	
DARKSOME	FOURSOME	HANDSOME	LIPOSOME	MEROSOME	RIBOSOME	TWIGSOME	

WORDS ENDING IN -TIME

7-letter words -TIME

AIRTIME	BEDTIME	DAYTIME	MISTIME	RAGTIME	TEATIME
ANYTIME	CENTIME	LAYTIME	PASTIME	SEPTIME	WARTIME

8-letter words -TIME

DOWNTIME	GOODTIME	MARITIME	MEANTIME	OVERTIME	REALTIME	XENOTIME
FORETIME	LIFETIME	MEALTIME	NOONTIME	PLAYTIME	SOMETIME

WORDS ENDING IN -TION

7-letter words -TION

AMATION	CAPTION	DICTION	EMOTION	FICTION	MIXTION	PORTION	STATION	UNCTION
AUCTION	CAUTION	EDITION	EMPTION	LECTION	ORATION	RECTION	SUCTION	UNITION
BASTION	COCTION	ELATION	ENATION	MENTION	OVATION	RUCTION	TACTION	
CANTION	COITION	ELUTION	FACTION	MICTION	PACTION	SECTION	TUITION	

8-letter words -TION

ABLATION	COACTION	EJECTION	FRUITION	LEGATION	NIDATION	REACTION	TAXATION
ABLUTION	CONATION	ELECTION	FUNCTION	LENITION	NODATION	RELATION	TRACTION
ABORTION	CREATION	EMICTION	GELATION	LIBATION	NOLITION	REMOTION	VACATION
ADAPTION	DELATION	ENACTION	GUMPTION	LIGATION	NOTATION	ROGATION	VENATION
ADDITION	DELETION	EQUATION	GYRATION	LIMATION	NOVATION	ROTATION	VEXATION
ADNATION	DEMOTION	ERECTION	HALATION	LOBATION	NUDATION	SANCTION	VOCATION
ADOPTION	DERATION	ERUPTION	HIMATION	LOCATION	NUTATION	SCONTION	VOLITION
AERATION	DEVOTION	EVECTION	IDEATION	LOCUTION	OBLATION	SEDATION	VOLUTION
AGNATION	DILATION	EVICTION	IGNITION	LUNATION	PACATION	SEDITION	ZONATION
AMBITION	DILUTION	EXACTION	ILLATION	LUXATION	PETITION	SOLATION	
AUDITION	DONATION	EXERTION	INACTION	MONITION	POSITION	SOLUTION	
AVIATION	DOTATION	FIXATION	INUSTION	MUNITION	POTATION	SORPTION	
BIBATION	DURATION	FLECTION	JOBATION	MUTATION	PUNITION	STICTION	
CIBATION	EDUCTION	FRACTION	JUNCTION	NATATION	PUPATION	SUDATION	
CITATION	EGESTION	FRICTION	LAVATION	NEGATION	QUESTION	SWAPTION	

WORDS ENDING IN -URE

7-letter words -URE

ABATURE	COUPURE	FACTURE	GARBURE	MEASURE	OUTDURE	PROCURE	SEIZURE	VERDURE
BORDURE	COUTURE	FAILURE	GESTURE	MIXTURE	PARTURE	PULTURE	SEYSURE	VETTURE
BRISURE	CULTURE	FEATURE	GRAVURE	MONTURE	PASTURE	PURPURE	SOILURE	VOITURE
CAPTURE	DASYURE	FISSURE	GUIPURE	MORSURE	PERDURE	RAPTURE	STATURE	VULTURE
CENSURE	DENTURE	FIXTURE	HACHURE	MULTURE	PERJURE	RECOURE	TEXTURE	WAFTURE
CLOSURE	DISCURE	FLEXURE	LEASURE	NERVURE	PICTURE	RONDURE	TONSURE	
CLOTURE	EPICURE	FRISURE	LECTURE	NURTURE	PLEXURE	RUPTURE	TORTURE	
CONJURE	ERASURE	FRITURE	LEISURE	OBSCURE	POSTURE	SEASURE	VENTURE	

8-letter words -URE

ANNEXURE	CISELURE	DISCOURE	FRACTURE	LIGATURE	PLEASURE	ROUNDURE	TREASURE
APERTURE	COCKSURE	DISINURE	GENITURE	LINCTURE	PRESSURE	SCISSURE	TRESSURE
ARMATURE	COIFFURE	ENACTURE	IMMATURE	MANICURE	PUNCTURE	SCRIMURE	
AVENTURE	CREATURE	ENCOLURE	INCISURE	MOISTURE	REASSURE	SINECURE	
BROCHURE	CUBATURE	EXPOSURE	INSECURE	OVERTURE	REFIGURE	TAINTURE	
CEINTURE	CYNOSURE	FILATURE	JOINTURE	PAINTURE	REINSURE	TINCTURE	
CINCTURE	DENATURE	FIXATURE	JUNCTURE	PEDICURE	REPOSURE	TOURNURE	

WORDS ENDING IN -WARD

7-letter words -WARD

AIRWARD	FORWARD	HAYWARD	NAYWARD	SEAWARD	SUNWARD	WEYWARD
AWKWARD	FROWARD	HOGWARD	NORWARD	SKYWARD	VANWARD	
BEDWARD	GODWARD	LEEWARD	OUTWARD	STEWARD	WAYWARD	

8-letter words -WARD

BACKWARD	EASTWARD	HINDWARD	KIRKWARD	PARKWARD	SIDEWARD	WESTWARD	WOOLWARD
BEARWARD	FOREWARD	HIVEWARD	LANDWARD	REARWARD	THRAWARD	WINDWARD	
DOWNWARD	HELLWARD	HOMEWARD	LEFTWARD	REREWARD	UNTOWARD	WOODWARD	

WORDS ENDING IN -WARDS

7-letter words -WARDS

ADWARDS	COWARDS	INWARDS	ONWARDS	REWARDS	TOWARDS	UPWARDS	USWARDS	VAWARDS

8-letter words -WARDS

AIRWARDS	FORWARDS	GODWARDS	HOGWARDS	NAYWARDS	OUTWARDS	SKYWARDS	SUNWARDS
BEDWARDS	FROWARDS	HAYWARDS	LEEWARDS	NORWARDS	SEAWARDS	STEWARDS	

WORDS ENDING IN -WAY

7-letter words -WAY

ARCHWAY	CARTWAY	FLYAWAY	GATEWAY	HIGHWAY	PARKWAY	ROADWAY	SLIPWAY	TIDEWAY
AREAWAY	CUTAWAY	FOLKWAY	GETAWAY	LANEWAY	PATHWAY	RODEWAY	SOMEWAY	TRAMWAY
BELTWAY	DOORWAY	FOOTWAY	HALFWAY	LAYAWAY	RACEWAY	ROPEWAY	SPURWAY	WALKWAY
BIKEWAY	FAIRWAY	FREEWAY	HALLWAY	LICHWAY	RAILWAY	RUNAWAY	TAXIWAY	WELAWAY
CARAWAY	FARAWAY	GANGWAY	HEADWAY	PACKWAY	RINGWAY	SHIPWAY	THRUWAY	WIREWAY

8-letter words -WAY

ALLEYWAY	CAUSEWAY	EVERYWAY	HEREAWAY	MULLOWAY	SOAKAWAY	STAYAWAY	THATAWAY
BROADWAY	CLEARWAY	FLOODWAY	HOISTWAY	OVERSWAY	SOARAWAY	STERNWAY	TRACKWAY
CABLEWAY	CROSSWAY	FOLDAWAY	HORSEWAY	RIDGEWAY	SPEEDWAY	STOWAWAY	UNDERWAY
CARRAWAY	CYCLEWAY	GIVEAWAY	LOCKAWAY	RIVERWAY	SPILLWAY	TAKEAWAY	WATERWAY
CASTAWAY	DRIVEWAY	HATCHWAY	MOTORWAY	ROCKAWAY	STAIRWAY	TEARAWAY	WELLAWAY

WORDS ENDING IN -WISE

7-letter words -WISE

ANYWISE	ENDWISE	MAPWISE	SUNWISE

8-letter words -WISE

ARCHWISE	CRABWISE	ELSEWISE	LONGWISE	PALEWISE	SOMEWISE	TEAMWISE
BENDWISE	DROPWISE	FLATWISE	OVERWISE	RINGWISE	STEPWISE	TENTWISE
COMBWISE	EDGEWISE	LIKEWISE	PAIRWISE	SIDEWISE	SUCHWISE	THUSWISE

WORDS ENDING IN -WOOD

7-letter words -WOOD

BARWOOD	CAMWOOD	DOGWOOD	LOGWOOD	PLYWOOD	SAPWOOD
BOXWOOD	DAGWOOD	ELMWOOD	NUTWOOD	REDWOOD	

8-letter words -WOOD

BASSWOOD	CORDWOOD	GILTWOOD	IRONWOOD	OVENWOOD	ROSEWOOD	WORMWOOD
BENTWOOD	CORKWOOD	HARDWOOD	KINGWOOD	PINEWOOD	SOFTWOOD	
COLTWOOD	FIREWOOD	HAREWOOD	MILKWOOD	PULPWOOD	WILDWOOD	

WORDS ENDING IN -WORK

7-letter words -WORK

ARTWORK	LAPWORK	NETWORK	RAGWORK	TUTWORK
CUTWORK	LEGWORK	OUTWORK	RIBWORK	WAXWORK

8-letter words -WORK

BACKWORK	CASEWORK	FORMWORK	HORNWORK	OPENWORK	RACKWORK	STUDWORK
BODYWORK	CRIBWORK	FRETWORK	IRONWORK	OVERWORK	RINGWORK	TEAMWORK
BOOKWORK	FIREWORK	HANDWORK	KNOTWORK	PARTWORK	ROCKWORK	WIREWORK
CAGEWORK	FLUEWORK	HEADWORK	KOFTWORK	PILEWORK	ROPEWORK	WOODWORK
CAPEWORK	FOOTWORK	HOMEWORK	LINKWORK	PIPEWORK	SLOPWORK	WOOLWORK

WORDS ENDING IN -WORM

7-letter words -WORM

BUDWORM   CATWORM   CUTWORM   EELWORM   LOBWORM   LUGWORM   RAGWORM   SEAWORM   WEBWORM

8-letter words -WORM

BOOKWORM	FLATWORM	LINDWORM	PILLWORM	SHIPWORM	TAPEWORM	WOODWORM
CORNWORM	GAPEWORM	MALTWORM	RINGWORM	SILKWORM	WHIPWORM	
FIREWORM	HORNWORM	MEALWORM	SANDWORM	SLOWWORM	WIREWORM	

WORDS ENDING IN -WORT

7-letter words -WORT

BLAWORT   BUGWORT   FELWORT   FIGWORT   MADWORT   MUDWORT   MUGWORT   RAGWORT   RIBWORT

8-letter words -WORT

BELLWORT	GOUTWORT	LUNGWORT	MOONWORT	PIPEWORT	SOAPWORT	WARTWORT
COLEWORT	HONEWORT	MILKWORT	PILEWORT	SALTWORT	STARWORT	
FLEAWORT	HORNWORT	MODIWORT	PILLWORT	SANDWORT	WALLWORT	

WORDS ENDING IN -YARD

7-letter words -YARD

HALYARD   INNYARD   LANYARD   TANYARD

8-letter words -YARD

BACKYARD	DOCKYARD	KIRKYARD	RICKYARD	SHIPYARD	WHINYARD
BARNYARD	FARMYARD	MAINYARD	SALEYARD	SHOWYARD	WILLYARD
BONEYARD	KAILYARD	METEYARD	SAVOYARD	VINEYARD	WOODYARD

Unusual Vowel Endings

When Scrabble players think about the endings of words, they are likely to concentrate on words with the more obvious endings, for example -ATE, -ISE, -URE and -ENT, and the common extensions -ED, -ER and -S. Such words tend to end with a fairly restricted group of letters – usually D, E, R, S and T.

Words ending with unusual letters don't spring easily to mind. It takes some effort to start thinking about words ending in A, I, O and U, yet these four letters make up 30% of the tiles in a Scrabble set and they will frequently appear on your rack. Familiarity with everyday English does not encourage you to think of these letters at the end of words, but they can be very useful for linking on to other letters on the board, making 2-letter words which begin or end with A, I, O or U.

The following lists provide ammunition for correcting that rather limiting view of word endings. They are of all valid words of length two to eight letters which end with A, I, O or U.

WORDS ENDING IN -A

2-letter words ending in -A

AA	DA	FA	KA	MA	PA
BA	EA	HA	LA	NA	TA

3-letter words ending in -A

ABA	ANA	BRA	GOA	LEA	OCA	POA	SKA	UVA	ZOA
AGA	AVA	CHA	HOA	MAA	ODA	QUA	SMA	VIA	
AHA	AWA	ERA	ITA	MNA	OVA	RIA	SPA	WHA	
AIA	BAA	ETA	KEA	MOA	PEA	RYA	TEA	YEA	
ALA	BOA	FRA	KOA	OBA	PIA	SEA	TWA	ZEA	

4-letter words ending in -A

ABBA	BONA	EGMA	HUMA	LANA	MYNA	PEBA	ROMA	TAHA	VASA
ACTA	BORA	EKKA	IDEA	LAVA	NADA	PELA	ROTA	TAKA	VEGA
AGHA	BUBA	EMMA	ILEA	LEVA	NAGA	PICA	RUSA	TALA	VELA
AGMA	BUNA	EPHA	ILIA	LIMA	NALA	PIKA	SAGA	TANA	VENA
ALFA	CABA	ETNA	ILKA	LIRA	NANA	PILA	SAMA	TAPA	VINA
ALGA	CAPA	EYRA	INIA	LOMA	NAPA	PINA	SENA	TARA	VISA
ALMA	CASA	FETA	IOTA	LOTA	NIPA	PIPA	SERA	TAVA	VITA
AMLA	CECA	FLEA	IXIA	LUNA	NOMA	PITA	SETA	TAWA	VIVA
ANNA	COCA	FORA	JOTA	MAMA	NOTA	PLEA	SHEA	TAXA	VOLA
ANOA	CODA	GAGA	JUBA	MANA	NOVA	PROA	SHWA	TELA	WAKA
ANTA	COLA	GALA	JUGA	MARA	OBIA	PUJA	SIDA	TIKA	WEKA
AQUA	COMA	GENA	JURA	MASA	OCTA	PULA	SIKA	TOEA	WETA
ARBA	COXA	GETA	KAKA	MAYA	ODEA	PUMA	SIMA	TOGA	WHOA
AREA	CYMA	GIGA	KAMA	MEGA	OKRA	PUNA	SKUA	TOLA	YOGA
ARIA	DATA	GILA	KANA	MELA	OKTA	PUPA	SOCA	TOSA	YUCA
ARNA	DEVA	GLIA	KARA	MESA	OLLA	RACA	SODA	TUBA	YUGA
AULA	DIKA	GUGA	KATA	MICA	ORCA	RAGA	SOFA	TUFA	ZETA
AURA	DISA	GULA	KAVA	MINA	ORRA	RAJA	SOJA	TUNA	ZILA
BABA	DITA	HAKA	KETA	MOLA	OSSA	RANA	SOLA	ULNA	ZOEA
BEMA	DIVA	HILA	KINA	MONA	PACA	RATA	SOMA	ULVA	ZONA
BETA	DONA	HIYA	KIVA	MORA	PAPA	RHEA	SORA	UREA	ZUPA
BIGA	DOPA	HOYA	KOLA	MOWA	PARA	RIMA	SOYA	URVA	ZYGA
BOBA	DUMA	HUIA	KORA	MOXA	PAUA	RIVA	STOA	UVEA	
BOMA	DURA	HULA	LAMA	MOYA	PAWA	RIZA	SURA	VARA	

5-letter words ending in -A

ABACA	ABUNA	AECIA	AGILA	ALAPA	ALIYA	ALPHA	AMEBA	ANANA	ANTRA
ABAYA	ADYTA	AFARA	AGORA	ALDEA	ALOHA	ALULA	AMNIA	ANIMA	AORTA

PANOCHA	PIRAGUA	PUPUNHA	ROMNEYA	SCHOLIA	SPATULA	TAMBURA	TREHALA	VIHUELA
PAPILLA	PIRANHA	PURPURA	ROSACEA	SCOPULA	SPECTRA	TANAGRA	TRISULA	VINCULA
PAPRIKA	PISCINA	PYAEMIA	ROSALIA	SCOTOMA	SPECULA	TANIWHA	TSARINA	VIRANDA
PARATHA	PITUITA	PYGIDIA	ROSELLA	SCYBALA	SPICULA	TANTARA	TUATARA	VISCERA
PARAZOA	PLACITA	PYREXIA	ROSEOLA	SECRETA	SPIRAEA	TAPIOCA	TUTANIA	VIVARIA
PAREIRA	PLANULA	PYXIDIA	ROTUNDA	SEDILIA	SPLENIA	TARTANA	TYMPANA	VIVERRA
PARELLA	PLATINA	QUASSIA	RUBELLA	SEQUELA	SQUILLA	TAVERNA	ULNARIA	VOLUSPA
PARERGA	PLECTRA	RABANNA	RUBEOLA	SEQUOIA	SRADDHA	TEDESCA	URAEMIA	WALLABA
PARGANA	PLEROMA	RADIATA	RUELLIA	SERIEMA	STAMINA	TEGMINA	URETHRA	WEIGELA
PARTITA	PLUMULA	RAMENTA	RUFIYAA	SERINGA	STASIMA	TEMPERA	VALONEA	WOODSIA
PASSATA	PODAGRA	RAOULIA	RUSALKA	SERPULA	STOMATA	TEMPURA	VALONIA	WOOMERA
PATAGIA	PODESTA	RATAFIA	SABELLA	SESTINA	STRETTA	TEQUILA	VALVULA	WOORARA
PATELLA	POLACCA	REFUGIA	SABURRA	SEVRUGA	STRIATA	TEREBRA	VANESSA	XERASIA
PAVLOVA	POLENTA	REGALIA	SACELLA	SHASTRA	SUBAQUA	TESSERA	VANILLA	YAMULKA
PAXIUBA	POLYNIA	REGATTA	SAGITTA	SHEHITA	SUBAREA	THEMATA	VARIOLA	YESHIVA
PECULIA	POLYNYA	REGMATA	SAMBUCA	SHEIKHA	SUCCUBA	THRIMSA	VASCULA	ZAKUSKA
PEISHWA	POLYOMA	REPLICA	SAMSARA	SHICKSA	SUDARIA	THRYMSA	VEDALIA	ZAMARRA
PELORIA	POLYZOA	RESIDUA	SANGOMA	SIGNORA	SULTANA	TILAPIA	VELARIA	ZANELLA
PENTHIA	POTASSA	RETSINA	SANGRIA	SILESIA	SUMATRA	TOCCATA	VENTANA	ZAREEBA
PEREIRA	PRECAVA	RHODORA	SAPHENA	SILIQUA	SYCONIA	TOHEROA	VERANDA	ZEBRINA
PERGOLA	PRIMULA	RHYTINA	SARCOMA	SILPHIA	SYNOVIA	TOHUNGA	VERBENA	ZEBRULA
PERIDIA	PRONOTA	RICKSHA	SARDANA	SINOPIA	SYRINGA	TOMBOLA	VERRUCA	ZEMSTVA
PERINEA	PROPYLA	RICOTTA	SATSUMA	SKIMMIA	TAFFETA	TOMENTA	VERRUGA	ZIGANKA
PERSONA	PTERYLA	RIVIERA	SAVANNA	SOKAIYA	TAGMATA	TORMINA	VETTURA	ZIMOCCA
PESSIMA	PUDENDA	ROBINIA	SCAGLIA	SOLARIA	TALARIA	TOSTADA	VEXILLA	ZIZANIA
PETUNIA	PUNALUA	ROBUSTA	SCAPULA	SOLATIA	TALOOKA	TOXEMIA	VIATICA	ZOOECIA
PINNULA	PUPARIA	ROMAIKA	SCHISMA	SOREDIA	TAMASHA	TRACHEA	VIDENDA	

8-letter words ending in -A

ABDOMINA	AYURVEDA	CARNAUBA	CYMBIDIA	FANTASIA	HETAIRIA	MANTISSA	PARABEMA
ABSCISSA	AZOTURIA	CASTELLA	CZAREVNA	FASCIOLA	HIRAGANA	MANUBRIA	PARABOLA
ACADEMIA	BABIRUSA	CATHEDRA	CZARITSA	FASCISTA	HORDEOLA	MANYATTA	PARANOEA
ACHAENIA	BABUSHKA	CATHISMA	DECENNIA	FENESTRA	HOSPITIA	MARCELLA	PARANOIA
ADESPOTA	BACTERIA	CATTLEYA	DEMENTIA	FIBRILLA	HYDREMIA	MARCHESA	PARHELIA
ADULARIA	BALLISTA	CAVATINA	DEMERARA	FISTIANA	HYDROZOA	MARINERA	PAROEMIA
ADYNAMIA	BANDANNA	CECROPIA	DENTALIA	FLABELLA	HYPALGIA	MARIPOSA	PAROUSIA
AGNOMINA	BARATHEA	CERCARIA	DENTARIA	FLAGELLA	HYPOGAEA	MARSUPIA	PASHMINA
AGRAPHIA	BARRANCA	CHALAZIA	DIARRHEA	FLOTILLA	HYSTERIA	MARTYRIA	PELLAGRA
AKINESIA	BASILICA	CHARISMA	DIASPORA	FOCACCIA	IMPLUVIA	MASSOOLA	PENUMBRA
ALGAROBA	BATTALIA	CHICKPEA	DIASTEMA	FORAMINA	INSIGNIA	MATADORA	PERFECTA
ALIGARTA	BAUHINIA	CHILLADA	DICENTRA	FUGHETTA	INSOMNIA	MATAMATA	PERIAGUA
ALLELUIA	BERGENIA	CHIMAERA	DICHASIA	GALLABEA	INTARSIA	MBAQANGA	PETECHIA
ALOPECIA	BERYLLIA	CHINAMPA	DIELYTRA	GALLABIA	INTIFADA	MELANOMA	PHACELIA
AMBROSIA	BETHESDA	CHINKARA	DIPLEGIA	GALLERIA	ISABELLA	MELODICA	PHOTINIA
AMYGDALA	BIGNONIA	CHIRAGRA	DIPLOPIA	GALTONIA	ISCHEMIA	MENSTRUA	PHOTOPIA
ANACONDA	BISCACHA	CHLOASMA	DIPLOZOA	GAMBETTA	ISCHURIA	MESHUGGA	PHYSALIA
ANALECTA	BIZCACHA	CHOLEMIA	DJELLABA	GAMMADIA	IZVESTIA	METANOIA	PIASSABA
ANALEMMA	BLASTEMA	CHURINGA	DULCIANA	GAMMATIA	JAPONICA	MIASMATA	PIASSAVA
ANAPHORA	BLASTULA	CHYLURIA	DYSCHROA	GARCINIA	JARARACA	MILIARIA	PIZZERIA
ANASARCA	BONSELLA	CIABATTA	DYSLEXIA	GARDENIA	JARARAKA	MILTONIA	PLACENTA
ANATHEMA	BRANCHIA	CINCHONA	DYSMELIA	GASTRAEA	KALYPTRA	MINNEOLA	PLANURIA
ANGELICA	BRASSICA	CISTERNA	DYSPNOEA	GASTRULA	KARATEKA	MONSTERA	PLATANNA
ANOESTRA	BREGMATA	CLAUSTRA	DYSTOCIA	GEMATRIA	KATAKANA	MONTARIA	PLATYSMA
ANOREXIA	BRITZSKA	CLAUSULA	DYSTONIA	GEROPIGA	KAZATZKA	MOUSSAKA	PLETHORA
ANTEFIXA	BROMELIA	CLITELLA	DYSTOPIA	GESNERIA	KHANSAMA	MOZZETTA	POLLINIA
ANTHELIA	BRONCHIA	COCCIDIA	ECCLESIA	GLABELLA	KINAKINA	MRIDANGA	POLYGALA
ANTHEMIA	BROUHAHA	COENOBIA	EFFLUVIA	GLAUCOMA	KRAMERIA	MYCETOMA	POLYURIA
ANTISERA	BUDDLEIA	COLCHICA	EGOMANIA	GLIOMATA	LAVATERA	MYOTONIA	POSTCAVA
APOLOGIA	BURLETTA	COLLEGIA	ENCAENIA	GLORIOSA	LECANORA	MYXEDEMA	PRAECAVA
APOSITIA	CAATINGA	COLLYRIA	ENDOSTEA	GLOSSINA	LEUKEMIA	MYXOMATA	PREDELLA
APYREXIA	CABRETTA	COLOBOMA	ENGRAMMA	GLOXINIA	LIPOMATA	NAVICULA	PRESCUTA
ARAPAIMA	CACHEXIA	CONFERVA	EPHEMERA	GLYCERIA	LISTERIA	NUBECULA	PRESIDIA
ARAPONGA	CACHUCHA	CONSULTA	EPICEDIA	GOLFIANA	LODICULA	NYMPHAEA	PROFORMA
ARAPUNGA	CACUMINA	CONTAGIA	EPIFAUNA	GUERILLA	LONICERA	ODONTOMA	PROGERIA
ARBORETA	CALATHEA	CONTESSA	EPITHEMA	GURDWARA	LYMPHOMA	OEDEMATA	PROTOZOA
ASPHYXIA	CALCANEA	CONTINUA	EPOPOEIA	GYMKHANA	MACAHUBA	OITICICA	PRUNELLA
ASTHENIA	CALCARIA	CONURBIA	EQUISETA	GYMNASIA	MADRASSA	OLIGURIA	PRYTANEA
ASTIGMIA	CALDARIA	COPROSMA	ERYTHEMA	GYNAECIA	MAGNESIA	OMBRELLA	PTERYGIA
ATARAXIA	CALISAYA	COQUILLA	ESTANCIA	GYNOECIA	MAGNOLIA	OPERCULA	PUTAMINA
ATHEROMA	CALVARIA	CORMIDIA	ESTHESIA	HABANERA	MAHARAJA	OPERETTA	PYCNIDIA
AUBRETIA	CALYPTRA	COXALGIA	ETCETERA	HACIENDA	MAIOLICA	OPUSCULA	QUADRIGA
AUBRIETA	CAMELLIA	CREDENDA	EUPEPSIA	HAMARTIA	MAJOLICA	ORCHELLA	QUINELLA
AURICULA	CAMPAGNA	CREDENZA	EUPHOBIA	MALVASIA	MANDIOCA	ORCHILLA	RACHILLA
AUTOMATA	CAPOEIRA	CRIBELLA	EUPHONIA	HEARTPEA	MAMMILLA	PALESTRA	RADIALIA
AUTOPSIA	CAPYBARA	CRITERIA	EUPHORIA	HEMIOLIA	MANDIOCA	PANDEMIA	RAKSHASA
AVIFAUNA	CARACARA	CROMORNA	EXCERPTA	HEMIOPIA	MANDORLA	PANMIXIA	RAPHANIA
		CUNABULA	FALDETTA	HERBARIA	MANTILLA	PANORAMA	REDDENDA

RENDZINA	SCOTOPIA	SINFONIA	SUBPHYLA	TAPADERA	TRAUMATA	VELATURA	YARMULKA
RESINATA	SCROFULA	SONATINA	SUBPOENA	TAQUERIA	TRICHINA	VENDETTA	YERSINIA
RESPONSA	SCUTELLA	SORBARIA	SUBTOPIA	TEGMENTA	TRIDACNA	VERONICA	YOKOZUNA
RETINULA	SEMANTRA	SPIRILLA	SUBUCULA	TENACULA	TRIFECTA	VERTEBRA	YTTERBIA
REWAREWA	SEMICOMA	SPORIDIA	SUBURBIA	TENTORIA	TRIFORIA	VESICULA	ZAMBOMBA
RHIZOBIA	SEMOLINA	SQUAMULA	SUDAMINA	TEQUILLA	TRILEMMA	VESTIGIA	ZAMPOGNA
RUTABAGA	SEMUNCIA	STAPELIA	SVASTIKA	TERATOMA	TRIPUDIA	VIBRISSA	ZARZUELA
SACRARIA	SENSILLA	STAROSTA	SWASTIKA	TERRARIA	TRITONIA	VICTORIA	ZASTRUGA
SALICETA	SENSORIA	STEATOMA	SWEETPEA	TERRELLA	TROCHLEA	VIEWDATA	ZIRCONIA
SAPUCAIA	SEPARATA	STEMMATA	SYMPODIA	TERZETTA	TROPARIA	VIRAEMIA	ZOIATRIA
SARMENTA	SEPTARIA	STERIGMA	SYMPOSIA	TESSELLA	TSAREVNA	VIRTUOSA	ZOOCYTIA
SASARARA	SEPTLEVA	STICHERA	SYNANGIA	TETRAPLA	TSARITSA	VISCACHA	ZOOGLOEA
SASTRUGA	SERENATA	STIGMATA	SYNAPHEA	THERIACA	ULTIMATA	VITICETA	ZOONOMIA
SAYONARA	SHAMIANA	STOCCATA	SYNCYTIA	THIOUREA	UMBRELLA	VIZCACHA	ZUCHETTA
SCHAPSKA	SHECHITA	STOMODEA	SYNECHIA	TOQUILLA	UNDERSEA	VIZCACHA	ZYGANTRA
SCHEMATA	SHIGELLA	STOTINKA	SYNEDRIA	TORMENTA	UREDINIA	WISTARIA	ZYGOMATA
SCIATICA	SHRADDHA	STROBILA	SYNTAGMA	TORTILLA	UROPYGIA	WISTERIA	
SCLEREMA	SIDALCEA	STROMATA	SYSSITIA	TOXAEMIA	VACCINIA	XANTHOMA	
SCLEROMA	SIGNORIA	STRONTIA	TAKAMAKA	TOXOCARA	VAGINULA	XENOPHYA	
SCOLIOMA	SILICULA	SUBCOSTA	TAMANDUA	TRACHOMA	VALLONIA	XEROMATA	
SCOTOMIA	SIMARUBA	SUBMENTA	TAMBOURA	TRAPEZIA	VELAMINA	XYLOMATA	

WORDS ENDING IN -I

2-letter words ending in -I

AI	DI	HI	MI	PI	SI	XI
BI	GI	LI	OI	QI	TI	

3-letter words ending in -I

AMI	DEI	HUI	LEI	PHI	RAI	SKI	TUI
ANI	GHI	KAI	MOI	POI	SAI	SUI	UNI
CHI	HOI	KOI	OBI	PSI	SEI	TAI	

4-letter words ending in -I

ANTI	DELI	GLEI	KAMI	MANI	NAOI	PURI	SARI	TAXI	WADI
ASCI	DIVI	GYRI	KATI	MAXI	NEVI	QADI	SATI	TIKI	WALI
BANI	DIXI	HAJI	KAZI	MERI	NIDI	RABI	SEMI	TIPI	WILI
BENI	ETUI	HILI	KEPI	MIDI	NISI	RAGI	SIMI	TITI	YETI
CADI	EUOI	HOKI	KIWI	MINI	NODI	RAKI	SIRI	TOPI	YOGI
CAPI	FENI	IMPI	KURI	MIRI	NORI	RAMI	SOLI	TORI	YONI
CEDI	FINI	INTI	LOBI	MODI	PENI	RANI	SORI	UNCI	ZATI
CHAI	FOCI	KADI	LOCI	MOKI	PERI	ROJI	TABI	VAGI	ZITI
DALI	FUCI	KAKI	MAGI	MOOI	PILI	ROTI	TAKI	VALI	ZORI
DARI	GADI	KALI	MALI	MUTI	PIPI	SAKI	TALI	VLEI	

5-letter words ending in -I

ABACI	BLINI	COMBI	FERMI	ISSEI	LUNGI	OVOLI	RECTI	SULCI	TRAGI
ACARI	BRAVI	CORGI	FRATI	JINNI	LURGI	OZEKI	REIKI	SUSHI	TUTTI
ACINI	BUFFI	CORNI	FUNDI	KANJI	MAQUI	PAGRI	RISHI	SWAMI	URAEI
AGAMI	BWAZI	CURSI	FUNGI	KARRI	MEDII	PALKI	RUBAI	TAKHI	URALI
AGGRI	BYSSI	DARZI	GARNI	KATTI	MODII	PALPI	SALMI	TANGI	URARI
AGUTI	CACTI	DHOBI	GENII	KAURI	MOOLI	PAOLI	SAMPI	TANTI	UTERI
AIDOI	CARDI	DHOTI	GHAZI	KHADI	MUFTI	PARDI	SCAPI	TARSI	VILLI
AIOLI	CARPI	DILLI	GOBBI	KHAKI	MYTHI	PARKI	SCUDI	TEMPI	WONGI
ALIBI	CEILI	DUOMI	GUSLI	KIKOI	NAEVI	PARTI	SERAI	TERAI	XYSTI
APPUI	CERCI	ELCHI	HADJI	KIRRI	NIMBI	PERAI	SHCHI	THAGI	ZIMBI
ARDRI	CESTI	ELEMI	HAJJI	KOORI	NISEI	PILEI	SHOGI	THOLI	ZOMBI
ASSAI	CHILI	ENNUI	HONGI	KUKRI	NOMOI	PIRAI	SHOJI	THYMI	
AULOI	CHOLI	ENOKI	HOURI	LASSI	OBELI	POORI	SOLDI	TONDI	
AUREI	CIPPI	ENVOI	IAMBI	LATHI	OBOLI	PUTTI	SPAHI	TOPHI	
BAJRI	CIRRI	FARCI	IMARI	LAZZI	OCULI	QUASI	STOAI	TOPOI	
BASSI	COATI	FASCI	IMSHI	LENTI	OKAPI	RABBI	STYLI	TORII	
BENNI	COCCI	FASTI	INDRI	LICHI	ORIBI	RADII	SUCCI	TORSI	

6-letter words ending in -I

ACULEI	ARGALI	BAILLI	BINGHI	CALAMI	CHILLI	CUMULI	DHOOTI	EMBOLI	GEMINI
AGOUTI	ARGULI	BANZAI	BOLETI	CANTHI	CHOKRI	CURARI	DJINNI	EPHEBI	GHARRI
ALKALI	ARILLI	BHAKTI	BONSAI	CAROLI	CHOWRI	CYATHI	DROMOI	EURIPI	GILGAI
ALUMNI	ARIOSI	BHINDI	BORZOI	CESTUI	CLYPEI	CYTISI	DUETTI	FLOCCI	GLUTEI
ANNULI	ASKARI	BHISTI	BUKSHI	CHATTI	COLOBI	DECANI	ECHINI	GARDAI	GOMUTI
ARCHEI	AVANTI	BIKINI	BURITI	CHICHI	CONGII	DEWANI	ELTCHI	GELATI	GRIGRI

GURAMI	KABUKI	MAULVI	NEROLI	PAPYRI	SACCOI	SCAMPI	SOUARI	TOITOI	YANQUI
HAIKAI	KAIKAI	MAZHBI	NIELLI	PERITI	SAFARI	SCYPHI	STRATI	TORULI	YOGINI
HAMULI	KIMCHI	MEISHI	NILGAI	PHALLI	SAIKEI	SESELI	SUNDRI	TROCHI	ZUFOLI
HUMERI	KOUROI	MILADI	NOSTOI	PITHOI	SAKKOI	SHALLI	TAHINI	TROPHI	
ILLUPI	KOWHAI	MIRITI	NUCLEI	PITURI	SALAMI	SHTCHI	TAMARI	TSOTSI	
INCAVI	KUMARI	MISHMI	OCELLI	POLYPI	SALUKI	SHUFTI	TAPETI	TUMULI	
INCUBI	LIMULI	MODULI	OCTOPI	PUTELI	SAMITI	SIDDHI	TATAMI	UAKARI	
JAWARI	LITCHI	MOPANI	OCTROI	RAGINI	SANCAI	SILENI	THALLI	UNCINI	
JOWARI	LOBULI	MUESLI	OURALI	RAMULI	SANDHI	SIMPAI	THOLOI	URACHI	
JUDOGI	LOCULI	MUNSHI	OURARI	RENVOI	SANSEI	SMALTI	THYRSI	WAKIKI	
JUNGLI	MALLEI	MYTHOI	OUREBI	RHOMBI	SATORI	SOLIDI	TIFOSI	WAPITI	
JUPATI	MANATI	NAGARI	PALAGI	RUBATI	SBIRRI	SONERI	TITOKI	XYSTOI	

7-letter words ending in -I

ABOMASI	BOUILLI	COLOSSI	FORZATI	KAMICHI	ORIGAMI	RHOMBOI	SIGNORI	TSUNAMI
ACOUCHI	BRONCHI	CORTILI	FUMETTI	LAMPUKI	OUAKARI	RHONCHI	SONDELI	TYMPANI
ALFAQUI	CADUCEI	CRIMINI	FUSILLI	LAPILLI	OUSTITI	RHYTHMI	SOPRANI	URCEOLI
ALIZARI	CALATHI	DAKOITI	GHILGAI	LECYTHI	PACHISI	RIKISHI	SORDINI	VENTURI
ALVEOLI	CALCULI	DAQUIRI	GINGILI	MACRAMI	PADRONI	RILIEVI	SPLENII	VITELLI
AMORINI	CALZONI	DASHEKI	GLUTAEI	MAESTRI	PALAZZI	RIPIENI	STAMNOI	VOLVULI
ANESTRI	CANZONI	DASHIKI	GNOCCHI	MAFIOSI	PECCAVI	SACCULI	STICHOI	WISTITI
ANZIANI	CAVETTI	DEMENTI	GOURAMI	MARCONI	PENUCHI	SAIMIRI	STIMULI	WOORALI
APPALTI	CEMBALI	DENARII	GRADINI	MARTINI	PINDARI	SAMADHI	STRETTI	WOURALI
ARCHAEI	CHAPATI	DIDAKAI	GUARANI	MATSURI	PRELUDI	SAMURAI	SUCCUBI	ZAKUSKI
ASSAGAI	CHARQUI	DIDAKEI	HALLALI	MENISCI	PRONAOI	SAOUARI	SUNDARI	ZAMPONI
ASSEGAI	CHIASMI	DIDICOI	HIBACHI	MODELLI	PULVINI	SARANGI	SURCULI	ZUFFOLI
ASTATKI	CHILIOI	DOCHMII	JACUZZI	MODIOLI	QAWWALI	SASHIMI	SYLLABI	
BACCHII	CHONDRI	EFFENDI	JAMDANI	MOLOSSI	QUILLAI	SCALENI	TERMINI	
BACILLI	CHORAGI	ELENCHI	JAMPANI	NAUPLII	RABBONI	SCHERZI	THALAMI	
BAMBINI	CHOREGI	EMERITI	JINJILI	NAUTILI	RANGOLI	SECONDI	THROMBI	
BASENJI	CHUPATI	EPIGONI	JUKSKEI	NONETTI	RAVIOLI	SENARII	TIMPANI	
BAZOUKI	CLARINI	ETOURDI	KABADDI	NUCELLI	REMBLAI	SERKALI	TONDINI	
BILIMBI	COENURI	FAGOTTI	KACHERI	NURAGHI	REVERSI	SERRATI	TORTONI	
BIRYANI	COLIBRI	FLOKATI	KAHAWAI	OMPHALI	RHIZOPI	SHIKARI	TRIPOLI	

8-letter words ending in -I

ACOEMETI	CALCANEI	CROSTINI	FUNICULI	MAHARANI	PEDICULI	SCALDINI	TERAKIHI
ALBERGHI	CALYCULI	CUNJEVOI	GINGLYMI	MALLEOLI	PEPERONI	SFORZATI	TERIYAKI
AMORETTI	CANCELLI	DAIQUIRI	GLADIOLI	MARAVEDI	PERFECTI	SHANGHAI	TERZETTI
ANOESTRI	CANTHARI	DECUBITI	GRAFFITI	MARCHESI	PERIBOLI	SHERWANI	THESAURI
ANTENATI	CAPITANI	DIADOCHI	HAEREMAI	MARIACHI	PERRADII	SIGISBEI	TRAPEZII
ASSEGAAI	CAPRICCI	DIPTEROI	HALLOUMI	MENOMINI	PIROSHKI	SOFFIONI	TZATZIKI
BANDITTI	CASTRATI	DIVIDIVI	HETAIRAI	MONOKINI	PIROZHKI	SOLFEGGI	UMBILICI
BERIBERI	CHAPATTI	DRACHMAI	HYDROSKI	MORBILLI	POSTNATI	SOUVLAKI	URANISCI
BIMBASHI	CHUPATTI	DUPONDII	KACHAHRI	NANNYGAI	PRODROMI	STAPEDII	UTRICULI
BIRIYANI	CICERONI	DURUKULI	KOFTGARI	NARCISSI	PULVILLI	STOTINKI	VIRTUOSI
BONAMANI	CICISBEI	DUUMVIRI	KOHLRABI	NENNIGAI	RENMINBI	STROBILI	YAKITORI
BOSTANGI	CONCEPTI	ESOPHAGI	KOMITAJI	NIRAMIAI	RETIARII	SUKIYAKI	ZASTRUGI
BOUZOUKI	CONCERTI	FASCISMI	LEKYTHOI	NUCLEOLI	RIGATONI	SUMOTORI	ZECCHINI
BOZZETTI	CONCETTI	FASCISTI	LIBRETTI	OBLIGATI	RISPETTI	TAGLIONI	ZOOPHORI
BRINDISI	CONDUCTI	FEDELINI	LINGUINI	OUISTITI	RYOTWARI	TANDOORI	ZUCCHINI
BROCCOLI	CONFETTI	FLOCCULI	LITERATI	PARCHESI	SANNYASI	TARAKIHI	
BUMALOTI	CORNETTI	FORZANDI	LUMBRICI	PASTICCI	SARTORII	TEDESCHI	
CALAMARI	COTHURNI	FRASCATI	MACARONI	PASTRAMI	SASTRUGI	TEOCALLI	

WORDS ENDING IN -O

2-letter words ending in -O

BO	GO	IO	KO	MO	OO	SO	WO	ZO
DO	HO	JO	LO	NO	PO	TO	YO	

3-letter words ending in -O

ADO	BRO	DUO	GEO	ISO	OBO	PRO	TOO	WHO	ZOO
AGO	COO	DZO	GIO	LOO	OHO	RHO	TWO	WOO	
BIO	DOO	EGO	GOO	MHO	PHO	ROO	UDO	YGO	
BOO	DSO	FRO	HOO	MOO	POO	THO	UFO	ZHO	

4-letter words ending in -O

AERO	ALSO	AMMO	ARVO	BITO	BOYO	BROO	BUFO	CITO	DADO
AFRO	ALTO	ANNO	AUTO	BOKO	BOZO	BUBO	CAPO	COCO	DAGO
AGIO	AMBO	ARCO	BEGO	BOLO	BRIO	BUDO	CIAO	COHO	DECO

DEMO	FADO	HARO	JOMO	LIMO	MISO	PACO	SECO	TARO	UPGO
DIDO	FARO	HERO	JUDO	LINO	MOJO	PEPO	SEGO	THRO	URAO
DINO	FICO	HOBO	KAGO	LOBO	MOKO	PESO	SHMO	TIRO	VETO
DODO	FIGO	HOMO	KAYO	LOCO	MONO	POCO	SHOO	TOCO	VINO
DOJO	FILO	HUSO	KENO	LOGO	MUSO	POGO	SIJO	TOHO	VIVO
DURO	FINO	HYPO	KILO	LOTO	ODSO	POLO	SILO	TOKO	WINO
DZHO	GAJO	INFO	KINO	LUDO	OLEO	PROO	SKEO	TRIO	YUKO
ECCO	GAPO	INGO	KOLO	MAKO	OLIO	PYRO	SKIO	TYPO	ZERO
ECHO	GIRO	INRO	KOTO	MANO	ONTO	REDO	SOHO	TYRO	ZOBO
EDDO	GOBO	INTO	LAZO	MEMO	OPPO	REGO	SOLO	UMBO	
ERGO	GOGO	JATO	LENO	MICO	ORZO	REPO	SUMO	UNCO	
EURO	GYRO	JIAO	LIDO	MILO	OTTO	RIVO	SYBO	UNDO	
EXPO	HALO	JOCO	LILO	MINO	OUZO	SAGO	TACO	UNTO	

5-letter words ending in -O

ADDIO	BUNCO	CONTO	FATSO	HELLO	LAZZO	MOTTO	PORNO	SALTO	TORSO
AGGRO	BUNKO	CONVO	FIBRO	HILLO	LENTO	MUCRO	POTOO	SALVO	TURBO
AMIGO	BUROO	CORNO	FOLIO	HIMBO	LESBO	MUNGO	POTTO	SAMBO	TYPTO
AMNIO	BURRO	CORSO	FORDO	HIPPO	LIMBO	NACHO	PRIMO	SANKO	UREDO
AUDIO	CACAO	CREDO	FORGO	HOLLO	LINGO	NAPOO	PROMO	SARGO	VERSO
AVISO	CAMEO	CUFFO	FUERO	HOWSO	LITHO	NARCO	PROSO	SCHMO	VIDEO
AWETO	CAMPO	CURIO	GADSO	HULLO	LLANO	NEGRO	PULMO	SCUDO	VIREO
BABOO	CANTO	CUTTO	GAMBO	HYDRO	LOTTO	NGAIO	PUNTO	SECCO	VISTO
BACCO	CARGO	CYCLO	GARBO	IGAPO	MACHO	ORTHO	PUTTO	SEGNO	VULGO
BALOO	CASCO	DANIO	GAZOO	IGLOO	MACRO	OUTDO	QUIPO	SERVO	WACKO
BANCO	CELLO	DECKO	GECKO	IMAGO	MAIKO	OUTGO	RADIO	SHAKO	WAHOO
BANJO	CENTO	DEKKO	GESSO	INTRO	MAMBO	OVOLO	RATIO	SICKO	WHOSO
BARDO	CHACO	DIAZO	GIPPO	IROKO	MANGO	PANTO	RATOO	SMOKO	YAHOO
BASHO	CHIAO	DILDO	GISMO	JAMBO	MANTO	PAOLO	RAZOO	SOCKO	YARTO
BASSO	CHICO	DINGO	GIZMO	JELLO	MATLO	PAREO	REALO	SOLDO	YOBBO
BASTO	CHIMO	DIPSO	GOBBO	JINGO	MATZO	PASEO	RECCO	SORDO	ZAMBO
BEANO	CHINO	DISCO	GODSO	JOCKO	MENTO	PATIO	RECTO	SORGO	ZHOMO
BILBO	CHOCO	DITTO	GOMBO	JUMBO	MESTO	PEDRO	REFFO	SPADO	ZINCO
BIMBO	CHOKO	DOGGO	GONZO	JUNCO	METRO	PESTO	REGGO	STYLO	ZIPPO
BINGO	CISCO	DOHYO	GREGO	JUNTO	MEZZO	PHOTO	REPRO	TABOO	ZOCCO
BOMBO	CLARO	DSOBO	GUACO	KAZOO	MICRO	PIANO	RETRO	TACHO	ZOPPO
BONGO	COCCO	DSOMO	GUANO	KEMBO	MILKO	PIEZO	RHINO	TANGO	ZORRO
BORGO	COMBO	DUMBO	GUIRO	KENDO	MISDO	PINGO	RODEO	TANTO	
BRAVO	COMMO	DUNNO	GUMBO	KIDDO	MISGO	PINKO	RONDO	TEMPO	
BUCKO	COMPO	DUOMO	GUSTO	KIMBO	MOLTO	PINTO	RONEO	TENNO	
BUFFO	CONDO	ESTRO	GYPPO	LARGO	MONDO	POLIO	RUMBO	TIMBO	
BUMBO	CONGO	FANGO	HALLO	LASSO	MORRO	PONGO	SADDO	TONDO	

6-letter words ending in -O

ABRAZO	BOLERO	CUCKOO	FUGATO	HAIRDO	LUCUMO	PEDALO	RIGHTO	SPINTO	TURACO
ADAGIO	BONITO	DAIMIO	FUMADO	HALLOO	MACACO	PEPINO	ROBALO	STALKO	TUXEDO
AIKIDO	BOOBOO	DAYGLO	GABBRO	HERETO	MANITO	PHYLLO	ROCOCO	STANZO	ULTIMO
AKIMBO	BRONCO	DOMINO	GALAGO	HETERO	MANOAO	PHYSIO	ROTOLO	STEREO	VAUDOO
ALBEDO	BUMALO	DORADO	GAUCHO	HONCHO	MATICO	POMATO	RUBATO	STINGO	VIBRIO
ALBINO	BURGOO	DRONGO	GAZEBO	HOODOO	MEDICO	POMELO	SAMFOO	STINKO	VIGORO
ALBUGO	CALICO	DUELLO	GELATO	HOOROO	MELANO	PONCHO	SANCHO	STUCCO	VIRAGO
ANATTO	CALIGO	DUETTO	GENTOO	IGNARO	MERINO	POTATO	SAPEGO	STUDIO	VIRINO
ANGICO	CAMSHO	DYNAMO	GHERAO	INCAVO	MIKADO	PRESTO	SBIRRO	SUBITO	VOMITO
APOLLO	CASINO	EMBRYO	GHETTO	INDIGO	MIOMBO	PRONTO	SCHIZO	TATTOO	VOODOO
ARIOSO	CATALO	ENDURO	GIGOLO	JOURNO	MODULO	PSEUDO	SCRUTO	TECHNO	VORAGO
ARISTO	CHEAPO	ENHALO	GINGKO	KAKAPO	MORPHO	PSYCHO	SHACKO	TENUTO	WANDOO
ARROYO	CHOCHO	ERINGO	GINKGO	KATIPO	NANDOO	PUEBLO	SHEEPO	TERCIO	WEIRDO
BABACO	CHOCKO	ERYNGO	GITANO	KIMONO	NARDOO	PUKEKO	SHIPPO	TEREDO	WHACKO
BAGNIO	CHROMO	ESCUDO	GIUSTO	KOODOO	NIELLO	PUMELO	SHIVOO	THICKO	WHAMMO
BAGUIO	CICERO	FASCIO	GOMBRO	KORERO	NUNCIO	PUNCTO	SISSOO	THUGGO	WHATSO
BAMBOO	COLUGO	FIASCO	GOMUTO	LANUGO	NYMPHO	QUANGO	SKIDOO	TIFOSO	ZELOSO
BARRIO	COMEDO	FINSKO	GOOROO	LAVABO	OCTAVO	QUARTO	SMALTO	TOMATO	ZOOZOO
BASUCO	COMODO	FOREGO	GORGIO	LEGATO	OVERDO	RABATO	SOLANO	TORERO	ZORINO
BISTRO	COROZO	FORHOO	GRINGO	LIBERO	OVERGO	RANCHO	SOLITO	TRILLO	ZUFOLO
BLANCO	CRAMBO	FRANCO	GROTTO	LIBIDO	PALOLO	REBATO	SORGHO	TROPPO	ZYDECO
BLOTTO	CRYPTO	FRESCO	GUANGO	LOLIGO	PARAMO	REGULO	SPEEDO	TUPELO	

7-letter words ending in -O

AGITATO	ANNATTO	AVOCADO	BEEFALO	BUDGERO	CALANDO	CAVETTO	CHICANO	CORANTO
AILANTO	APPALTO	AZULEJO	BOTARGO	BUFFALO	CALYPSO	CEMBALO	CHORIZO	CORNUTO
ALBERGO	ARNOTTO	BAMBINO	BRACCIO	BUGABOO	CANTICO	CENTAVO	CLARINO	CRIOLLO
ALLEGRO	ARRIERO	BAROCCO	BRASERO	BUMMALO	CARABAO	CENTIMO	COMMODO	CRUSADO
AMORINO	ASINICO	BARRICO	BRAVADO	BURRITO	CASSINO	CHAMISO	CONCEDO	CRUZADO
AMOROSO	ATISHOO	BATTERO	BRONCHO	BUSHIDO	CATTALO	CHEERIO	COQUITO	CURACAO

CYMBALO	GRADINO	MEMENTO	OKIMONO	PINTADO	RIDOTTO	SHAKUDO	THERETO	VIBRATO
DIABOLO	GUANACO	MESTIZO	OLOROSO	PLACEBO	RILIEVO	SHAMPOO	TIMPANO	VILIACO
EIGHTVO	HIDALGO	MISTICO	OREGANO	PLENIPO	RIPIENO	SIROCCO	TOBACCO	VILIAGO
ELECTRO	HISTRIO	MOCKADO	PAISANO	POINADO	RISOTTO	SOLDADO	TOMBOLO	VIRANDO
EMBARGO	HORNITO	MODELLO	PAKAPOO	POMPANO	RONDINO	SOPRANO	TONDINO	VOLCANO
ESPARTO	HUANACO	MONTERO	PALAZZO	POMPELO	ROSOLIO	SORDINO	TORNADO	VOLPINO
ETAERIO	IMPASTO	MORELLO	PAMPERO	PORRIGO	SAGUARO	SQUACCO	TORPEDO	WENDIGO
FAGOTTO	INFERNO	MORENDO	PAPILIO	PORTICO	SALTATO	STRETTO	TOURACO	WHERESO
FARRAGO	LENTIGO	MORISCO	PASSADO	POTOROO	SAMSHOO	SUBZERO	TREMOLO	WHERETO
FERRUGO	LLANERO	MOROCCO	PATRICO	PRIMERO	SAPSAGO	SUPREMO	TROMINO	WINDIGO
FINNSKO	LUMBAGO	MULATTO	PEDRERO	PRIVADO	SCALADO	SYNCHRO	TWIGLOO	ZAMARRO
FORZATO	MADRONO	NATHEMO	PEEKABO	PROVISO	SCHERZO	TAMARAO	TYMPANO	ZANJERO
FUMETTO	MAESTRO	NAVARHO	PERSICO	PROXIMO	SCIOLTO	TANGELO	UNDERDO	ZEMSTVO
FURIOSO	MAFIOSO	NELUMBO	PIANINO	PRURIGO	SECONDO	TEDESCO	UNDERGO	ZOCCOLO
GAMBADO	MAGNETO	NITROSO	PICCOLO	REJONEO	SENECIO	TENTIGO	VAQUERO	ZORILLO
GESTAPO	MALICHO	NONETTO	PIFFERO	RELIEVO	SERPIGO	TESTUDO	VERISMO	ZUFFOLO
GIOCOSO	MARCATO	NORTENO	PIMENTO	REVERSO	SFUMATO	THEORBO	VERTIGO	

8-letter words ending in -O

ALFRESCO	CASTRATO	ESPRESSO	HUAQUERO	MAMELUCO	PEPERINO	SEICENTO	TENEBRIO
AMARETTO	CAUDILLO	ESPUMOSO	HUBBUBOO	MANCANDO	PERDENDO	SERAGLIO	TERRAZZO
AMORETTO	CHARANGO	EXPRESSO	IMPETIGO	MANZELLO	PERFECTO	SESTETTO	TERZETTO
ARMIGERO	CHARNECO	FALSETTO	INNUENDO	MARTELLO	PIMIENTO	SFORZATO	TRAPUNTO
ARPEGGIO	CHECHAKO	FANDANGO	INTAGLIO	MODERATO	PLUMBAGO	SIGISBEO	TRECENTO
ASSIENTO	CICISBEO	FASCISMO	INTONACO	MONTANTO	POIGNADO	SMORZATO	TUCOTUCO
AUTOGIRO	CILANTRO	FELLATIO	JACKAROO	MOSQUITO	POLITICO	SOLIDAGO	TUCUTUCO
AUTOGYRO	COCKATOO	FINNESKO	JACKEROO	NEUTRINO	PRELUDIO	SOMBRERO	TWELVEMO
BALLYHOO	COMMANDO	FINOCHIO	JALAPENO	NOCTILIO	PRESIDIO	SPADILLO	UMBRELLO
BARBASCO	CONCERTO	FLAMENCO	JILLAROO	OBLIGATO	PRUNELLO	SPICCATO	VARGUENO
BARGELLO	CONCETTO	FLAMINGO	JORDELOO	OCOTILLO	PULVILIO	STACCATO	VARLETTO
BARRANCO	CONTANGO	FORZANDO	JUNKANOO	ORATORIO	RANCHERO	STAMPEDO	VERDELHO
BESOGNIO	CONTINUO	GALAPAGO	KAKEMONO	OSTINATO	REDDENDO	STICCADO	VILLAGIO
BONAMANO	CONTORNO	GARBANZO	KANGAROO	OTTAVINO	RENEGADO	STICCATO	VILLIAGO
BORACHIO	CORAGGIO	GARDYLOO	LENTANDO	PACHINKO	RISOLUTO	STILETTO	VINDALOO
BORDELLO	CORNETTO	GAZPACHO	LIBECCIO	PADERERO	RISPETTO	STOCCADO	VIRTUOSO
BOZZETTO	COROCORO	GILLAROO	LIBRETTO	PALAMINO	RITENUTO	STOCCATO	VITILIGO
BUCKAROO	CRUZEIRO	GRACIOSO	LOCOFOCO	PALISADO	ROSOGLIO	SUBAUDIO	WALLAROO
BUCKAYRO	CURCULIO	GRAFFITO	MACHISMO	PALMETTO	SALTANDO	SUPEREGO	WANDEROO
CACAFOGO	DOLOROSO	GRAZIOSO	MAESTOSO	PALOMINO	SARGASSO	SUPERLOO	YAKIMONO
CAMISADO	DUETTINO	GUACHARO	MAKIMONO	PARLANDO	SCALDINO	SUPPEAGO	ZECCHINO
CAPITANO	ENCIERRO	HALLALOO	MALGRADO	PATERERO	SCENARIO	TAPACOLO	ZUCHETTO
CAPUCCIO	ESCALADO	HEREUNTO	MALLECHO	PEEKABOO	SCIROCCO	TAPACULO	
		HITHERTO			SCORDATO	TAPADERO	

WORDS ENDING IN -U

2-letter words ending in -U

GU	MU	NU	OU	XU	YU

3-letter words ending in -U

AYU	ECU	FLU	GJU	KYU	MOU	TAU	YOU
CRU	EMU	FOU	GNU	LEU	PIU	UTU	
EAU	FEU	GAU	JEU	MEU	SOU	VAU	

4-letter words ending in -U

AITU	BEAU	FRAU	KUKU	LULU	PRAU	RATU	TAPU	TOFU	ZEBU
BABU	CHOU	GENU	KURU	MASU	PUDU	RIMU	TATU	TOLU	ZOBU
BAJU	CLOU	GURU	KUZU	MENU	PUKU	RURU	TEGU	TUTU	ZULU
BALU	ECRU	JUJU	LIEU	MOTU	PULU	SULU	THOU	UNAU	
BAPU	EMEU	KUDU	LUAU	OMBU	RAKU	TABU	THRU	VATU	

5-letter words ending in -U

ADIEU	BUCHU	COYPU	KANZU	NANDU	PERDU	SADHU	TATOU	VOULU
BANTU	BUCKU	FICHU	KOMBU	NIKAU	PILAU	SAJOU	UHURU	WUSHU
BAYOU	BUNDU	HAIKU	KUDZU	NOYAU	POILU	SAMFU	URUBU	
BIJOU	BUSSU	HOKKU	LASSU	OTAKU	PRAHU	SHOYU	VERTU	
BOYAU	CORNU	JAMBU	MUNTU	PAREU	QUIPU	SNAFU	VIRTU	

6-letter words ending in -U

ABATTU	BATEAU	CONGOU	GAGAKU	JABIRU	MZUNGU	ORMOLU	ROUCOU	TAMANU
ACAJOU	BUREAU	COTEAU	GATEAU	KIKUYU	NHANDU	PILLAU	SADDHU	TELEDU
AMADOU	CACHOU	DETENU	GOMOKU	LANDAU	NILGAU	PIUPIU	SAMSHU	VOUDOU
APERCU	CADEAU	EPERDU	INGENU	MILIEU	NOGAKU	RESEAU	SUBFEU	YNAMBU

7-letter words ending in -U

BABASSU	CAMAIEU	CHANOYU	INCONNU	MOINEAU	PLATEAU	ROULEAU	TABLEAU	TONNEAU
BANDEAU	CARDECU	CHAPEAU	JAMBEAU	MORCEAU	PONCEAU	SAPAJOU	TAMANDU	TRUMEAU
BEBEERU	CARIBOU	CHATEAU	MANITOU	NOUVEAU	PURLIEU	SEPPUKU	TAMARAU	
BERCEAU	CATECHU	CORBEAU	MANTEAU	NYLGHAU	ROKKAKU	SHIATSU	TIMARAU	
BUNRAKU	CATTABU	FABLIAU	MARABOU	PARVENU	RONDEAU	SHIATZU	TINAMOU	

8-letter words ending in -U

ABOIDEAU	CARIACOU	FLAMBEAU	KINKAJOU	NINJUTSU	PYENGADU	THANKYOU
ABOITEAU	CARJACOU	HAUSFRAU	MINSHUKU	NUNCHAKU	SUCURUJU	TIRAMISU
CARCAJOU	FELDGRAU	KABELJOU	NINJITSU	PIRARUCU	SURUCUCU	TSUTSUMU

Section Four

Variants

Introduction

Can't remember if the correct spelling is KEIR or KIER or both? And what about those American spellings? Can you have VIGOR as well as VIGOUR, and are PALLOR and PALLOUR both right? And then there is the confusing array of words that end with -EY, -IE and -Y? Can you remember which is which?

The lists in this section show you variant spellings, all of which – there may be two or even three variants – are valid words. Sometimes they are of completely different words which just look similar (as MEIN and MIEN); often they are just different spellings of the same word (as KEIR and KIER).

The words shown in the lists are of various lengths; only the most useful lengths, judged by practical use, are included here. Brief descriptions of the lists are:

Lists 1 and 2

Words spelled with either AE or E (such as AESTIVAL and ESTIVAL), and those spelled with either OE or E (such as OESTRAL and ESTRAL).

List 3

Words with either EI or IE (such as MEIN and MIEN).

Lists 4 to 6

Words spelled with either ER or RE endings (such as CENTER and CENTRE), those with either ER or OR endings (such as ADVISER and ADVISOR), and those with either OUR or OR endings (such as HARBOUR and HARBOR).

Lists 7 and 8

Words spelled with either ABLE or IBLE endings (such as IGNITABLE and IGNITIBLE) and those with either SMAN or MAN endings (such as WOODSMAN and WOODMAN).

List 9

Words spelled with either EN or IN beginnings (such as ENCLOSE and INCLOSE).

Lists 10, 11 and 12

Words having forms spelled with either one or two L's (such as PEDALLED/PEDALED, PEDALLING/PEDALING, and LIBELLER/LIBELER.

Lists 13 to 16

Words spelled with various combinations of the EY, IE and Y endings (such as BLIMEY/BLIMY, SARNEY/SARNIE, BOLSHIE/BOLSHY and the 3-way DICKEY/DICKIE/DICKY).

List 1: VARIANTS AE/E

6/5-letter words

AEDILE - EDILE	COSTAE - COSTE	HAEMAL - HEMAL	PENNAE - PENNE	TAENIA - TENIA
AEMULE - EMULE	CURIAE - CURIE	HYAENA - HYENA	PHYLAE - PHYLE	TESTAE - TESTE
AETHER - ETHER	DAEDAL - DEDAL	LAERED - LERED	SCALAE - SCALE	TOGAED - TOGED
AGAPAE - AGAPE	DAEMON - DEMON	MARAES - MARES	SCOPAE - SCOPE	UMBRAE - UMBRE
BLAEST - BLEST	FAECAL - FECAL	NAEVES - NEVES	SELLAE - SELLE	VISAED - VISED
BURSAE - BURSE	FAECES - FECES	NAEVUS - NEVUS	SERRAE - SERRE	
CAECAL - CECAL	FOSSAE - FOSSE	PAEANS - PEANS	SPICAE - SPICE	
CAECUM - CECUM	FRAENA - FRENA	PAEONS - PEONS	SPINAE - SPINE	
CAUSAE - CAUSE	GNOMAE - GNOME	PAEONY - PEONY	STELAE - STELE	

7/6-letter words

AEDILES - EDILES	CAESTUS - CESTUS	LAERING - LERING	SCAPAED - SCAPED
AEGISES - EGISES	CAESURA - CESURA	LIGULAE - LIGULE	SPHAERE - SPHERE
AEMULED - EMULED	CESURAE - CESURE	LUNULAE - LUNULE	SPIRAEA - SPIREA
AEMULES - EMULES	CONCHAE - CONCHE	MACULAE - MACULE	SQUAMAE - SQUAME
AETHERS - ETHERS	CONGAED - CONGED	METOPAE - METOPE	TAEDIUM - TEDIUM
ALTHAEA - ALTHEA	COTYLAE - COTYLE	MURAENA - MURENA	TAENIAE - TENIAE
ANAEMIA - ANEMIA	DAEMONS - DEMONS	NATURAE - NATURE	TAENIAS - TENIAS
ANAEMIC - ANEMIC	FRAENUM - FRENUM	NEBULAE - NEBULE	URAEMIA - UREMIA
ARCHAEI - ARCHEI	GLUTAEI - GLUTEI	PAPULAE - PAPULE	URAEMIC - UREMIC
AREOLAE - AREOLE	HENNAED - HENNED	PRAESES - PRESES	ZONULAE - ZONULE
CAERULE - CERULE	HYAENAS - HYENAS	PRAETOR - PRETOR	
CAESIUM - CESIUM	INTIMAE - INTIME	PYAEMIA - PYEMIA	

8/7-letter words

ACHAENIA - ACHENIA	CHIMAERA - CHIMERA	MURAENAS - MURENAS	SAECULUM - SECULUM
AEMULING - EMULING	DAEMONIC - DEMONIC	NOVELLAE - NOVELLE	SCARPAED - SCARPED
AESTHETE - ESTHETE	EPIGAEAL - EPIGAEL	PAEONIES - PEONIES	SPELAEAN - SPELEAN
AESTIVAL - ESTIVAL	EPIGAEAN - EPIGEAN	PIGMAEAN - PIGMEAN	SPHAERES - SPHERES
ALTHAEAS - ALTHEAS	FOVEOLAE - FOVEOLE	PISCINAE - PISCINE	SPICULAE - SPICULE
ANAEMIAS - ANEMIAS	GLUTAEAL - GLUTEAL	PLUMULAE - PLUMULE	SPIRAEAS - SPIREAS
ANAPAEST - ANAPEST	GLUTAEUS - GLUTEUS	PRAECAVA - PRECAVA	TAEDIUMS - TEDIUMS
ARCHAEUS - ARCHEUS	GYNAECIA - GYNECIA	PRAEDIAL - PREDIAL	TAENIOID - TENIOID
CAECITIS - CECITIS	HALLOAED - HALLOED	PRAEFECT - PREFECT	TOXAEMIA - TOXEMIA
CAESIUMS - CESIUMS	HOLLOAED - HOLLOED	PRAETORS - PRETORS	TOXAEMIC - TOXEMIC
CAESURAE - CESURAE	HYPOGAEA - HYPOGEA	PYAEMIAS - PYEMIAS	URAEMIAS - UREMIAS
CAESURAL - CESURAL	LERNAEAN - LERNEAN	PYGMAEAN - PYGMEAN	VALVULAE - VALVULE
CAESURAS - CESURAS	MICELLAE - MICELLE	QUAESTOR - QUESTOR	

9/8-letter words

ABSCISSAE - ABSCISSE	HYDRAEMIA - HYDREMIA	PALAESTRA - PALESTRA
ACHAENIUM - ACHENIUM	HYMENAEAL - HYMENEAL	PERINAEUM - PERINEUM
AEOLIPILE - EOLIPILE	HYMENAEAN - HYMENEAN	PHAENOGAM - PHENOGAM
AESTHESIA - ESTHESIA	HYPOGAEAL - HYPOGEAL	PRAEAMBLE - PREAMBLE
AESTHETES - ESTHETES	HYPOGAEAN - HYPOGEAN	PRAECAVAE - PRECAVAE
AESTIVATE - ESTIVATE	HYPOGAEUM - HYPOGEUM	PRAEDIALS - PREDIALS
AETIOLOGY - ETIOLOGY	ISCHAEMIA - ISCHEMIA	PRAEFECTS - PREFECTS
ANAPAESTS - ANAPESTS	ISCHAEMIC - ISCHEMIC	PRAESIDIA - PRESIDIA
CAERULEAN - CERULEAN	LAEVIGATE - LEVIGATE	PRIMAEVAL - PRIMEVAL
CHIMAERAS - CHIMERAS	LAEVULOSE - LEVULOSE	QUAESTORS - QUESTORS
CHOLAEMIA - CHOLEMIA	LAVOLTAED - LAVOLTED	SAECULUMS - SECULUMS
DAEDALIAN - DEDALIAN	LEUKAEMIA - LEUKEMIA	STOMODAEA - STOMODEA
DEFAECATE - DEFECATE	LODICULAE - LODICULE	STROBILAE - STROBILE
DIAERESES - DIERESES	LONGAEVAL - LONGEVAL	TOXAEMIAS - TOXEMIAS
DIAERESIS - DIERESIS	MEDIAEVAL - MEDIEVAL	VAGINULAE - VAGINULE
EPIGAEOUS - EPIGEOUS	PAEDERAST - PEDERAST	
GYNAECIUM - GYNECIUM	PAEDOLOGY - PEDOLOGY	

List 2: VARIANTS OE/E

6/5-letter words

AMOEBA - AMEBA	ECHOES - ECHES	HALOES - HALES	REDOES - REDES	TIROES - TIRES
APNOEA - APNEA	FOETAL - FETAL	KYLOES - KYLES	SHOOED - SHOED	TYROES - TYRES
CANOED - CANED	FOETID - FETID	LAZOED - LAZED	SILOED - SILED	UNDOER - UNDER
CANOES - CANES	FOETOR - FETOR	LAZOES - LAZES	SOEVER - SEVER	ZOOEAE - ZOEAE
COELOM - CELOM	FOETUS - FETUS	OEDEMA - EDEMA	SOLOED - SOLED	ZOOEAL - ZOEAL
ECHOED - ECHED	HALOED - HALED	PEKOES - PEKES	STOEPS - STEPS	ZOOEAS - ZOEAS

7/6-letter words

AMOEBAE - AMEBAE	COELIAC - CELIAC	HILLOED - HILLED	OESTRUM - ESTRUM
AMOEBAS - AMEBAS	COELOMS - CELOMS	HULLOED - HULLED	OESTRUS - ESTRUS
AMOEBIC - AMEBIC	DECKOED - DECKED	IMAGOES - IMAGES	PINNOED - PINNED
ANOETIC - ANETIC	DINGOES - DINGES	KEMBOED - KEMBED	SALTOED - SALTED
APNOEAS - APNEAS	DISCOED - DISCED	LASSOES - LASSES	SALVOES - SALVES
BRAVOES - BRAVES	DITTOED - DITTED	LOESSES - LESSES	SHAKOES - SHAKES
BUNCOED - BUNCED	FOETORS - FETORS	MANGOES - MANGES	SPADOES - SPADES
BUNKOED - BUNKED	FORGOES - FORGES	MOTTOES - MOTTES	TANGOED - TANGED
CHACOES - CHACES	GESSOES - GESSES	OEDEMAS - EDEMAS	TOENAIL - TENAIL
CHOENIX - CHENIX	HELLOED - HELLED	OESTRAL - ESTRAL	UNSHOED - UNSHED

8/7-letter words

ANOESTRA - ANESTRA	FOEDARIE - FEDARIE	OECOLOGY - ECOLOGY	STANZOES - STANZES
ANOESTRI - ANESTRI	FOETIDER - FETIDER	OEDEMATA - EDEMATA	TOENAILS - TENAILS
CALICOES - CALICES	FOETUSES - FETUSES	OESTROUS - ESTROUS	
COELIACS - CELIACS	GYNOECIA - GYNECIA	OESTRUMS - ESTRUMS	
DYSPNOEA - DYSPNEA	HALLOOED - HALLOED	REBATOES - REBATES	

9/8-letter words

ANOESTRUM - ANESTRUM	FOETICIDE - FETICIDE	OECUMENIC - ECUMENIC
ANOESTRUS - ANESTRUS	FOETIDEST - FETIDEST	OESOPHAGI - ESOPHAGI
CHOENIXES - CHENIXES	GOLOSHOES - GOLOSHES	OESTROGEN - ESTROGEN
COENOBITE - CENOBITE	GYNOECIUM - GYNECIUM	OESTRUSES - ESTRUSES
DIARRHOEA - DIARRHEA	HOMOEOBOX - HOMEOBOX	PASSADOES - PASSADES
DIOESTRUS - DIESTRUS	HOMOEOSES - HOMEOSES	POENOLOGY - PENOLOGY
DYSPNOEAL - DYSPNEAL	HOMOEOSIS - HOMEOSIS	TORNADOES - TORNADES
DYSPNOEAS - DYSPNEAS	HOMOEOTIC - HOMEOTIC	WHOSOEVER - WHOSEVER
DYSPNOEIC - DYSPNEIC	IMPASTOED - IMPASTED	
FOEDARIES - FEDARIES	MYXOEDEMA - MYXEDEMA	

List 3: VARIANTS EI/IE

4-letter words

BEIN - BIEN	DEID - DIED	KEIR - KIER	LEIS - LIES	NEIF - NIEF
CEIL - CIEL	HEID - HIED	LEIR - LIER	MEIN - MIEN	WEIL - WIEL

5-letter words

CEILS - CIELS	LEIRS - LIERS	NEIVE - NIEVE	VLEIS - VLIES
FEINT - FIENT	MEINS - MIENS	PREIF - PRIEF	WEILS - WIELS
KEIRS - KIERS	NEIFS - NIEFS	REIVE - RIEVE	

6-letter words

CEILED - CIELED	NEIVES - NIEVES	REIVER - RIEVER
FEINTS - FIENTS	PREIFE - PRIEFE	REIVES - RIEVES
LEIGER - LIEGER	PREIFS - PRIEFS	SHREIK - SHRIEK

7-letter words

CEILING - CIELING	OMNEITY - OMNIETY	REIVING - RIEVING	SIZEIST - SIZIEST
GREISLY - GRIESLY	PREIFES - PRIEFES	SCREICH - SCRIECH	SKREIGH - SKRIEGH
LEIGERS - LIEGERS	REIVERS - RIEVERS	SHREIKS - SHRIEKS	

8-letter words

CEILINGS - CIELINGS	SHEILING - SHIELING	SKREIGHS - SKRIEGHS
SCREICHS - SCRIECHS	SHREIKED - SHRIEKED	

9-letter words

OMNEITIES - OMNIETIES	SHEILINGS - SHIELINGS	SKREIGHED - SKRIEGHED
SCREICHED - SCRIECHED	SHREIKING - SHRIEKING	

List 4: VARIANTS -RE/-ER endings

5-letter words

BARRE - BARER	FAYRE - FAYER	MITRE - MITER	SABRE - SABER	SPARE - SPAER
BLARE - BLAER	FIBRE - FIBER	NITRE - NITER	SERRE - SERER	STERE - STEER
BRERE - BREER	FRERE - FREER	OCHRE - OCHER	SHERE - SHEER	TITRE - TITER
CABRE - CABER	LITRE - LITER	OUTRE - OUTER	SHIRE - SHIER	TWIRE - TWIER
CHERE - CHEER	LIVRE - LIVER	PETRE - PETER	SHORE - SHOER	UMBRE - UMBER
EAGRE - EAGER	METRE - METER	POWRE - POWER	SKYRE - SKYER	

6-letter words

BISTRE - BISTER	LETTRE - LETTER	SEMPRE - SEMPER	TENDRE - TENDER
CENTRE - CENTER	LOUVRE - LOUVER	SOMBRE - SOMBER	TIMBRE - TIMBER
DARTRE - DARTER	LUSTRE - LUSTER	SPARRE - SPARER	VENTRE - VENTER
FOUTRE - FOUTER	ONEYRE - ONEYER	SQUIRE - SQUIER	ZAFFRE - ZAFFER
GAUFRE - GAUFER	POUDRE - POUDER	STAYRE - STAYER	
GOITRE - GOITER	SCARRE - SCARER	STOWRE - STOWER	

7-letter words

CALIBRE - CALIBER	COMPERE - COMPEER	POULDRE - POULDER	SPECTRE - SPECTER
CHAMBRE - CHAMBER	DIOPTRE - DIOPTER	SALTIRE - SALTIER	THEATRE - THEATER
CHANCRE - CHANCER	PHILTRE - PHILTER	SCEPTRE - SCEPTER	

8-letter words

ACCOUTRE - ACCOUTER   RECENTRE - RECENTER

9-letter words

CONCENTRE - CONCENTER	DECIMETRE - DECIMETER	SALTPETRE - SALTPETER
DECILITRE - DECILITER	EPICENTRE - EPICENTER	SEPULCHRE - SEPULCHER

List 5: VARIANTS -ER/-OR endings

5-letter words

FAVER - FAVOR	LIVER - LIVOR	MINER - MINOR	SAVER - SAVOR	TRIER - TRIOR
HONER - HONOR	MILER - MILOR	PRIER - PRIOR	TAXER - TAXOR	

6-letter words

BAILER - BAILOR	CONDER - CONDOR	MAINER - MAINOR	STATER - STATOR
BETTER - BETTOR	CURSER - CURSOR	PASTER - PASTOR	TENSER - TENSOR
BITTER - BITTOR	GIMMER - GIMMOR	RIZZER - RIZZOR	TERMER - TERMOR
CANTER - CANTOR	JAILER - JAILOR	SAILER - SAILOR	VENDER - VENDOR
CASTER - CASTOR	KRONER - KRONOR	SALVER - SALVOR	WELDER - WELDOR
CENSER - CENSOR	LESSER - LESSOR	SIGNER - SIGNOR	

7-letter words

ABETTER - ABETTOR	DILATER - DILATOR	HUMIDER - HUMIDOR	REVISER - REVISOR
ADAPTER - ADAPTOR	DILUTER - DILUTOR	OFFERER - OFFEROR	REVIVER - REVIVOR
ADVISER - ADVISOR	ERECTER - ERECTOR	PLEDGER - PLEDGOR	SETTLER - SETTLOR
AGISTER - AGISTOR	EXACTER - EXACTOR	PRESSER - PRESSOR	TWISTER - TWISTOR
CHANTER - CHANTOR	EXCITER - EXCITOR	QUESTER - QUESTOR	VISITER - VISITOR
CLANGER - CLANGOR	FEOFFER - FEOFFOR	QUITTER - QUITTOR	
DEVISER - DEVISOR	GRANTER - GRANTOR	RELATER - RELATOR	

8-letter words

ACCEPTER - ACCEPTOR	DEFLATER - DEFLATOR	LICENSER - LICENSOR
ADJUSTER - ADJUSTOR	DEPICTER - DEPICTOR	PROMISER - PROMISOR
ANIMATER - ANIMATOR	DIRECTER - DIRECTOR	PROMOTER - PROMOTOR
ARRESTER - ARRESTOR	EFFECTER - EFFECTOR	PROVIDER - PROVIDOR
ASSENTER - ASSENTOR	EXECUTER - EXECUTOR	REGRATER - REGRATOR
ASSERTER - ASSERTOR	EXPANDER - EXPANDOR	REJECTER - REJECTOR
ATTESTER - ATTESTOR	IDOLATER - IDOLATOR	RELEASER - RELEASOR
CONJURER - CONJUROR	IMPOSTER - IMPOSTOR	REMITTER - REMITTOR
CONVENER - CONVENOR	INCENSER - INCENSOR	VERDERER - VERDEROR
CONVEYER - CONVEYOR	INVERTER - INVERTOR	VIOLATER - VIOLATOR

9-letter words

ADDRESSER - ADDRESSOR
AUGMENTER - AUGMENTOR
COMMENTER - COMMENTOR
COMPACTER - COMPACTOR
COMPANDER - COMPANDOR
CONCOCTER - CONCOCTOR
CONFIRMER - CONFIRMOR
CONNECTER - CONNECTOR
CONSIGNER - CONSIGNOR
CONSULTER - CONSULTOR
CONTEMNER - CONTEMNOR

CONVERTER - CONVERTOR
CORRECTER - CORRECTOR
DESOLATER - DESOLATOR
DISRUPTER - DISRUPTOR
EXHIBITER - EXHIBITOR
EXPEDITER - EXPEDITOR
HUNDREDER - HUNDREDOR
INFLICTER - INFLICTOR
INHABITER - INHABITOR
INHIBITER - INHIBITOR
MORTGAGER - MORTGAGOR

PERFECTER - PERFECTOR
PREDICTER - PREDICTOR
PROTESTER - PROTESTOR
RECOVERER - RECOVEROR
REFLECTER - REFLECTOR
RESPONSER - RESPONSOR
SUSPENSER - SUSPENSOR
TELEVISER - TELEVISOR
TORMENTER - TORMENTOR
WARRANTER - WARRANTOR

List 6: VARIANTS -OUR/-OR endings

5/4-letter words

FLOUR - FLOR   ODOUR - ODOR

6/5-letter words

ARBOUR - ARBOR
ARDOUR - ARDOR
ARMOUR - ARMOR
COLOUR - COLOR

DOLOUR - DOLOR
FAVOUR - FAVOR
HONOUR - HONOR
HUMOUR - HUMOR

LABOUR - LABOR
RIGOUR - RIGOR
RUMOUR - RUMOR
SAVOUR - SAVOR

TABOUR - TABOR
TENOUR - TENOR
TUMOUR - TUMOR
VALOUR - VALOR

VAPOUR - VAPOR
VIGOUR - VIGOR

7/6-letter words

BITTOUR - BITTOR
CANDOUR - CANDOR
CLAMOUR - CLAMOR
ENAMOUR - ENAMOR

FAITOUR - FAITOR
FLAVOUR - FLAVOR
FULGOUR - FULGOR
GLAMOUR - GLAMOR

HARBOUR - HARBOR
MAINOUR - MAINOR
PARLOUR - PARLOR
PAVIOUR - PAVIOR

RANCOUR - RANCOR
SUCCOUR - SUCCOR

8/7-letter words

BELABOUR - BELABOR   CLANGOUR - CLANGOR   DECOLOUR - DECOLOR   STENTOUR - STENTOR

9/8-letter words

BEHAVIOUR - BEHAVIOR
DEMEANOUR - DEMEANOR
DISCOLOUR - DISCOLOR
DISFAVOUR - DISFAVOR

DISHONOUR - DISHONOR
ENDEAVOUR - ENDEAVOR
MISCOLOUR - MISCOLOR
NEIGHBOUR - NEIGHBOR

SPLENDOUR - SPLENDOR
TRICOLOUR - TRICOLOR
UNICOLOUR - UNICOLOR

List 7: VARIANTS -ABLE/-IBLE endings

8-letter words

EDUCABLE - EDUCIBLE
GULLABLE - GULLIBLE

PASSABLE - PASSIBLE
RINSABLE - RINSIBLE

9-letter words

AVERTABLE - AVERTIBLE
CLASSABLE - CLASSIBLE

COMPTABLE - COMPTIBLE
IGNITABLE - IGNITIBLE

INTENABLE - INTENIBLE

List 8: VARIANTS -SMAN/-MAN endings

7/6-letter words

BATSMAN - BATMAN   RODSMAN - RODMAN   TOPSMAN - TOPMAN

8/7-letter words

BEADSMAN - BEADMAN
BEDESMAN - BEDEMAN
BONDSMAN - BONDMAN
GOWNSMAN - GOWNMAN
HEADSMAN - HEADMAN

HERDSMAN - HERDMAN
ISLESMAN - ISLEMAN
LANDSMAN - LANDMAN
LINESMAN - LINEMAN
LOCKSMAN - LOCKMAN

MARKSMAN - MARKMAN
OVERSMAN - OVERMAN
RAFTSMAN - RAFTMAN
ROADSMAN - ROADMAN
SIDESMAN - SIDEMAN

SWAGSMAN - SWAGMAN
WOODSMAN - WOODMAN

9/8-letter words

BRIDESMAN - BRIDEMAN	SHORESMAN - SHOREMAN	SWORDSMAN - SWORDMAN
SHARESMAN - SHAREMAN	SPADESMAN - SPADEMAN	

List 9: VARIANTS EN-/IN- beginnings

7-letter words

ENARMED - INARMED	ENDORSE - INDORSE	ENGULPH - INGULPH	ENTHRAL - INTHRAL
ENCAGED - INCAGED	ENDUING - INDUING	ENISLED - INISLED	ENTOMBS - INTOMBS
ENCAGES - INCAGES	ENFANTS - INFANTS	ENISLES - INISLES	ENTRANT - INTRANT
ENCASED - INCASED	ENFIXED - INFIXED	ENLACED - INLACED	ENTREAT - INTREAT
ENCASES - INCASES	ENFIXES - INFIXES	ENLACES - INLACES	ENTROLD - INTROLD
ENCAVED - INCAVED	ENFLAME - INFLAME	ENLOCKS - INLOCKS	ENTRUST - INTRUST
ENCAVES - INCAVES	ENFOLDS - INFOLDS	ENQUIRE - INQUIRE	ENTWINE - INTWINE
ENCHASE - INCHASE	ENFORCE - INFORCE	ENQUIRY - INQUIRY	ENTWIST - INTWIST
ENCLASP - INCLASP	ENFORMS - INFORMS	ENSEAMS - INSEAMS	ENURING - INURING
ENCLOSE - INCLOSE	ENGINES - INGINES	ENSHELL - INSHELL	ENVIOUS - INVIOUS
ENCRUST - INCRUST	ENGLOBE - INGLOBE	ENSNARE - INSNARE	ENWALLS - INWALLS
ENDARTS - INDARTS	ENGRAFT - INGRAFT	ENSOULS - INSOULS	ENWINDS - INWINDS
ENDEWED - INDEWED	ENGRAIN - INGRAIN	ENSURED - INSURED	ENWOUND - INWOUND
ENDITED - INDITED	ENGROSS - INGROSS	ENSURER - INSURER	ENWRAPS - INWRAPS
ENDITES - INDITES	ENGULFS - INGULFS	ENSURES - INSURES	

8-letter words

ENACTION - INACTION	ENFLAMES - INFLAMES	ENSHRINE - INSHRINE
ENACTIVE - INACTIVE	ENFOLDED - INFOLDED	ENSNARED - INSNARED
ENARCHED - INARCHED	ENFORCED - INFORCED	ENSNARES - INSNARES
ENARCHES - INARCHES	ENFORCES - INFORCES	ENSOULED - INSOULED
ENARMING - INARMING	ENFORMED - INFORMED	ENSPHERE - INSPHERE
ENCAGING - INCAGING	ENGLOBED - INGLOBED	ENSURERS - INSURERS
ENCASING - INCASING	ENGLOBES - INGLOBES	ENSURING - INSURING
ENCAVING - INCAVING	ENGRAFTS - INGRAFTS	ENSWATHE - INSWATHE
ENCHASED - INCHASED	ENGRAINS - INGRAINS	ENTENDER - INTENDER
ENCHASES - INCHASES	ENGROOVE - INGROOVE	ENTHRALL - INTHRALL
ENCLASPS - INCLASPS	ENGULFED - INGULFED	ENTHRALS - INTHRALS
ENCLOSED - INCLOSED	ENGULPHS - INGULPHS	ENTOMBED - INTOMBED
ENCLOSER - INCLOSER	ENHEARSE - INHEARSE	ENTRANTS - INTRANTS
ENCLOSES - INCLOSES	ENISLING - INISLING	ENTREATS - INTREATS
ENCREASE - INCREASE	ENLACING - INLACING	ENTRENCH - INTRENCH
ENCRUSTS - INCRUSTS	ENLOCKED - INLOCKED	ENTRUSTS - INTRUSTS
ENDARTED - INDARTED	ENMESHED - INMESHED	ENTWINED - INTWINED
ENDEWING - INDEWING	ENMESHES - INMESHES	ENTWINES - INTWINES
ENDITING - INDITING	ENQUIRED - INQUIRED	ENTWISTS - INTWISTS
ENDORSED - INDORSED	ENQUIRER - INQUIRER	ENVEIGLE - INVEIGLE
ENDORSES - INDORSES	ENQUIRES - INQUIRES	ENVIABLE - INVIABLE
ENFESTED - INFESTED	ENSCONCE - INSCONCE	ENWALLED - INWALLED
ENFIXING - INFIXING	ENSEAMED - INSEAMED	
ENFLAMED - INFLAMED	ENSHELLS - INSHELLS	

9-letter words

ENACTIONS - INACTIONS	ENGROOVES - INGROOVES	ENSNARING - INSNARING
ENARCHING - INARCHING	ENGROSSED - INGROSSED	ENSOULING - INSOULING
ENCHASING - INCHASING	ENGROSSES - INGROSSES	ENSPHERED - INSPHERED
ENCLASPED - INCLASPED	ENGULFING - INGULFING	ENSPHERES - INSPHERES
ENCLOSERS - INCLOSERS	ENGULPHED - INGULPHED	ENSWATHED - INSWATHED
ENCLOSING - INCLOSING	ENHEARSED - INHEARSED	ENSWATHES - INSWATHES
ENCLOSURE - INCLOSURE	ENHEARSES - INHEARSES	ENTENDERS - INTENDERS
ENCREASED - INCREASED	ENLOCKING - INLOCKING	ENTHRALLS - INTHRALLS
ENCREASES - INCREASES	ENMESHING - INMESHING	ENTOMBING - INTOMBING
ENCRUSTED - INCRUSTED	ENQUIRERS - INQUIRERS	ENTREATED - INTREATED
ENDARTING - INDARTING	ENQUIRIES - INQUIRIES	ENTRUSTED - INTRUSTED
ENDORSING - INDORSING	ENQUIRING - INQUIRING	ENTWINING - INTWINING
ENFLAMING - INFLAMING	ENSCONCED - INSCONCED	ENTWISTED - INTWISTED
ENFOLDING - INFOLDING	ENSCONCES - INSCONCES	ENUREMENT - INUREMENT
ENFORCING - INFORCING	ENSEAMING - INSEAMING	ENVEIGLED - INVEIGLED
ENFORMING - INFORMING	ENSHEATHE - INSHEATHE	ENVEIGLES - INVEIGLES
ENGLOBING - INGLOBING	ENSHELLED - INSHELLED	ENWALLING - INWALLING
ENGRAFTED - INGRAFTED	ENSHELTER - INSHELTER	ENWINDING - INWINDING
ENGRAINED - INGRAINED	ENSHRINED - INSHRINED	ENWRAPPED - INWRAPPED
ENGROOVED - INGROOVED	ENSHRINES - INSHRINES	ENWREATHE - INWREATHE

List 10: VARIANTS -LLED/-LED endings

7/6-letter words

DIALLED - DIALED   SCALLED - SCALED   STALLED - STALED
PROLLED - PROLED   SPILLED - SPILED   STILLED - STILED

8/7-letter words

CUPELLED - CUPELED   HOVELLED - HOVELED   METALLED - METALED   TOWELLED - TOWELED
DEVILLED - DEVILED   LIBELLED - LIBELED   MODELLED - MODELED   UNFILLED - UNFILED
EMBALLED - EMBALED   MEDALLED - MEDALED   PEDALLED - PEDALED   UNTILLED - UNTILED

9/8-letter words

BATTELLED - BATTELED   SIGNALLED - SIGNALED   TRAVELLED - TRAVELED
CORBELLED - CORBELED   TASSELLED - TASSELED   TUNNELLED - TUNNELED
GROVELLED - GROVELED   TEASELLED - TEASELED   WEASELLED - WEASELED
NICKELLED - NICKELED   TEAZELLED - TEAZELED   WEEVILLED - WEEVILED
REDIALLED - REDIALED   TINSELLED - TINSELED

List 11: VARIANTS -LLING/-LING endings

8/7-letter words

DIALLING - DIALING   SPILLING - SPILING   STILLING - STILING
PROLLING - PROLING   STALLING - STALING

9/8-letter words

CUPELLING - CUPELING   HOVELLING - HOVELING   MODELLING - MODELING
DEVILLING - DEVILING   LIBELLING - LIBELING   PEDALLING - PEDALING
EMBALLING - EMBALING   MEDALLING - MEDALING   TOWELLING - TOWELING
GRUELLING - GRUELING   METALLING - METALING

List 12: VARIANTS -LLER/-LER endings

7/6-letter words

DROLLER - DROLER   PROLLER - PROLER

8/7-letter words

LIBELLER - LIBELER   MODELLER - MODELER

9/8-letter words

GROVELLER - GROVELER   SIGNALLER - SIGNALER   TUNNELLER - TUNNELER
HOSTELLER - HOSTELER   TEASELLER - TEASELER   WEASELLER - WEASELER
SHOVELLER - SHOVELER   TRAVELLER - TRAVELER

VARIANTS -EY/-IE/-Y endings

List 13: -EY/-Y endings only

5/4-letter words

ALLEY - ALLY   GAMEY - GAMY   LINEY - LINY   POKEY - POKY   TONEY - TONY
CAGEY - CAGY   HOLEY - HOLY   MATEY - MATY   POLEY - POLY   UPSEY - UPSY
CAKEY - CAKY   HOMEY - HOMY   MONEY - MONY   PONEY - PONY   WANEY - WANY
CONEY - CONY   JASEY - JASY   MOPEY - MOPY   POSEY - POSY   WAVEY - WAVY
COREY - CORY   JOKEY - JOKY   NOSEY - NOSY   RENEY - RENY   WINEY - WINY
DOPEY - DOPY   LACEY - LACY   PACEY - PACY   RICEY - RICY   YAWEY - YAWY
FOGEY - FOGY   LIMEY - LIMY   PINEY - PINY   ROPEY - ROPY

6/5-letter words

BLIMEY - BLIMY   DINGEY - DINGY   GULLEY - GULLY   KARSEY - KARSY   PARLEY - PARLY
BOOZEY - BOOZY   DOYLEY - DOYLY   GYNNEY - GYNNY   LINNEY - LINNY   PEAVEY - PEAVY
BURLEY - BURLY   FLUKEY - FLUKY   HOOKEY - HOOKY   MANGEY - MANGY   PHONEY - PHONY
CARNEY - CARNY   GALLEY - GALLY   HOOLEY - HOOLY   MICKEY - MICKY   PIONEY - PIONY
CHOKEY - CHOKY   GILPEY - GILPY   HORSEY - HORSY   MIMSEY - MIMSY   PONCEY - PONCY
CREPEY - CREPY   GOOSEY - GOOSY   HURLEY - HURLY   MURREY - MURRY   PRICEY - PRICY
CURNEY - CURNY   GRAPEY - GRAPY   JOLLEY - JOLLY   OCHREY - OCHRY   PUDSEY - PUDSY

SAVVEY - SAVVY	SPACEY - SPACY	STOREY - STORY	TICKEY - TICKY	VERREY - VERRY
SCAREY - SCARY	STAGEY - STAGY	TAWNEY - TAWNY	TRIPEY - TRIPY	WHITEY - WHITY

7/6-letter words

CHANCEY - CHANCY	FIDDLEY - FIDDLY	SPINNEY - SPINNY	TIDDLEY - TIDDLY
CHOOSEY - CHOOSY	FLUNKEY - FLUNKY	SPOONEY - SPOONY	TROLLEY - TROLLY
CLIQUEY - CLIQUY	PLAGUEY - PLAGUY	SPURREY - SPURRY	WHIMSEY - WHIMSY
CRICKEY - CRICKY	SHANTEY - SHANTY	STRIPEY - STRIPY	WHISKEY - WHISKY
CURTSEY - CURTSY	SHIMMEY - SHIMMY	SWEENEY - SWEENY	

8/7-letter words

MALARKEY - MALARKY

List 14: -EY/-IE endings only

5-letter words

CUTEY - CUTIE

6-letter words

BAILEY - BAILIE	HAWKEY - HAWKIE	JARVEY - JARVIE	SARNEY - SARNIE

7-letter words

CHARLEY - CHARLIE	SHAWLEY - SHAWLIE

List 15: -IE/-Y endings only

5/4-letter words

AERIE - AERY	DIXIE - DIXY	GYNIE - GYNY	PIXIE - PIXY
ALKIE - ALKY	DOGIE - DOGY	LOGIE - LOGY	PUMIE - PUMY
BONIE - BONY	EERIE - EERY	NIXIE - NIXY	RELIE - RELY
CAVIE - CAVY	EYRIE - EYRY	OLDIE - OLDY	RORIE - RORY

6/5-letter words

ANOMIE - ANOMY	CUDDIE - CUDDY	KELPIE - KELPY	PEERIE - PEERY	SURFIE - SURFY
AUNTIE - AUNTY	CURRIE - CURRY	KELTIE - KELTY	PERDIE - PERDY	TALKIE - TALKY
AWMRIE - AWMRY	DEARIE - DEARY	KILTIE - KILTY	PIGGIE - PIGGY	TANGIE - TANGY
BADDIE - BADDY	DEAWIE - DEAWY	KOOKIE - KOOKY	PINKIE - PINKY	TATTIE - TATTY
BIGGIE - BIGGY	DOBBIE - DOBBY	LALDIE - LALDY	PINNIE - PINNY	TECHIE - TECHY
BILLIE - BILLY	DOGGIE - DOGGY	LAMMIE - LAMMY	PONTIE - PONTY	TEDDIE - TEDDY
BITTIE - BITTY	DORMIE - DORMY	LEFTIE - LEFTY	PORGIE - PORGY	TENTIE - TENTY
BLOWIE - BLOWY	DUDDIE - DUDDY	LINTIE - LINTY	PRATIE - PRATY	TINNIE - TINNY
BLUDIE - BLUDY	FAERIE - FAERY	LIPPIE - LIPPY	PREMIE - PREMY	TOTTIE - TOTTY
BONNIE - BONNY	FOODIE - FOODY	LOONIE - LOONY	PUGGIE - PUGGY	TOWNIE - TOWNY
BOODIE - BOODY	FOOTIE - FOOTY	LUCKIE - LUCKY	PURPIE - PURPY	TUSHIE - TUSHY
BOOKIE - BOOKY	FROWIE - FROWY	LUVVIE - LUVVY	PUTTIE - PUTTY	WADDIE - WADDY
BOTHIE - BOTHY	FUNDIE - FUNDY	MASHIE - MASHY	RANDIE - RANDY	WALLIE - WALLY
BUNJIE - BUNJY	GAUCIE - GAUCY	MEALIE - MEALY	REEKIE - REEKY	WASPIE - WASPY
CABBIE - CABBY	GILLIE - GILLY	MEANIE - MEANY	RHODIE - RHODY	WEDGIE - WEDGY
CADDIE - CADDY	GIRLIE - GIRLY	MOBBIE - MOBBY	ROARIE - ROARY	WEEPIE - WEEPY
CANDIE - CANDY	GUSTIE - GUSTY	MOCHIE - MOCHY	ROOKIE - ROOKY	WELLIE - WELLY
CHEWIE - CHEWY	GYPPIE - GYPPY	MOGGIE - MOGGY	ROOMIE - ROOMY	WOODIE - WOODY
CIGGIE - CIGGY	HANKIE - HANKY	MOLLIE - MOLLY	SILKIE - SILKY	YABBIE - YABBY
COLLIE - COLLY	HIPPIE - HIPPY	MOSSIE - MOSSY	SKIVIE - SKIVY	YAPPIE - YAPPY
COMMIE - COMMY	HONKIE - HONKY	NIRLIE - NIRLY	SOAPIE - SOAPY	YUPPIE - YUPPY
COOKIE - COOKY	HOWDIE - HOWDY	NOOKIE - NOOKY	SOFTIE - SOFTY	
COOLIE - COOLY	JEELIE - JEELY	PALMIE - PALMY	SONSIE - SONSY	
COWRIE - COWRY	JUMBIE - JUMBY	PARDIE - PARDY	STIMIE - STIMY	
CRUSIE - CRUSY	JUNKIE - JUNKY	PARKIE - PARKY	SUBBIE - SUBBY	

7/6-letter words

BOLSHIE - BOLSHY	CHAPPIE - CHAPPY	COUTHIE - COUTHY	GRANNIE - GRANNY
BOOKSIE - BOOKSY	CHEAPIE - CHEAPY	CREEPIE - CREEPY	GREENIE - GREENY
BRASSIE - BRASSY	CHINKIE - CHINKY	DRAPPIE - DRAPPY	GRIESIE - GRIESY
BRICKIE - BRICKY	CHIPPIE - CHIPPY	DRUGGIE - DRUGGY	GROUPIE - GROUPY
BROWNIE - BROWNY	CONCHIE - CONCHY	FLOOSIE - FLOOSY	INCONIE - INCONY
CALORIE - CALORY	COONTIE - COONTY	FLOOZIE - FLOOZY	JACKSIE - JACKSY

JAUNTIE - JAUNTY	QUEENIE - QUEENY	SKELLIE - SKELLY	SWEETIE - SWEETY
JOHNNIE - JOHNNY	REALLIE - REALLY	SKOLLIE - SKOLLY	TOASTIE - TOASTY
NIGHTIE - NIGHTY	REALTIE - REALTY	SMARTIE - SMARTY	TOOTSIE - TOOTSY
NITERIE - NITERY	REECHIE - REECHY	SNOTTIE - SNOTTY	TRANNIE - TRANNY
OVERLIE - OVERLY	REVERIE - REVERY	SPARKIE - SPARKY	TROELIE - TROELY
PLOTTIE - PLOTTY	ROUGHIE - ROUGHY	SPUNKIE - SPUNKY	UNWARIE - UNWARY
PLUMPIE - PLUMPY	SHELTIE - SHELTY	STEAMIE - STEAMY	WHEELIE - WHEELY
POLONIE - POLONY	SHORTIE - SHORTY	STIFFIE - STIFFY	

8/7-letter words

BATTERIE - BATTERY	CHRISTIE - CHRISTY	POLLICIE - POLLICY	SQUADDIE - SQUADDY
BHEESTIE - BHEESTY	OBSEQUIE - OBSEQUY	SCROGGIE - SCROGGY	VISNOMIE - VISNOMY

List 16: -EY/-IE/-Y endings

5/5/4-letter words

BOGEY - BOGIE - BOGY

6/6/5-letter words

BUNGEY - BUNGIE - BUNGY	GOOLEY - GOOLIE - GOOLY	POWNEY - POWNIE - POUNY
DARKEY - DARKIE - DARKY	MEINEY - MEINIE - MEINY	STOGEY - STOGIE - STOGY
DICKEY - DICKIE - DICKY	MOUSEY - MOUSIE - MOUSY	WILLEY - WILLIE - WILLY

7/7/6-letter words

CHANTEY - CHANTIE - CHANTY	PIGSNEY - PIGSNIE - PIGSNY	SWANKEY - SWANKIE - SWANKY

———— **Section Five** ————

Bonus Word Lists

Introduction

As there is a 50-point bonus for playing all seven tiles in one turn, 7-letter words are an essential part of the Scrabble player's vocabulary. Seven tiles can of course also be played around an existing letter on the board, so 8-letter words too are a key part of the Scrabble player's word knowledge.

Any words which use all seven of the letters on your rack are called bonus words, or just plain bonuses. Bonuses usually have seven or eight letters, but very occasionally can have more if played around several letters on the board. In the USA and some other parts of the world, words which score a 50-point bonus are called 'bingos'.

6-plus-1 sets

Some 7-letter words are more useful than others, simply because they are more likely to occur, given the distribution of letters in the Scrabble set. For this reason, it is an unnecessary task (and a painstakingly lengthy one!) to attempt to learn all of the 7-letter words. There are over 26,000 of these, and it is much more worthwhile (and a lot easier!) to concentrate on some of the 20% or so that are going to be the most useful to you.

Such 7-letter words can be arranged conveniently according to common 6-letter groups of letters (stems). Each stem yields a set of 7-letter words that can be made by the addition of a single seventh letter. These are the '6-plus-1 sets' – six letters plus another one letter to make a variety of 7-letter words. The more different letters of the alphabet that can be added to a stem, the more useful it is to the Scrabble player.

7-plus-1 sets

Perhaps your seven letters do not make a bonus word by themselves. Even if they do, perhaps the bonus word won't fit in on the board anywhere. These are the occasions when you may need to think bigger – 8-letter words! Of course, it is possible that the 7-letter word on your rack could go down on the board, but the 8-letter word might score quite a few more points. Sometimes an 8-letter word will score a lot more points, if it covers two triple-word-score squares – this is the 'nine-timer' that Scrabble players strive for.

As with the 6-plus-1 sets, some stems are more useful than others and the lists given here are based on these.

The 6-letter stems

The 250 6-letter stems used as the basis for the 6-plus-1 sets represent the 250 most likely and most fruitful stems, based on an algorithm of the probability of the six letters occurring and the probability of picking up letters that combine with the stem.

A list of these stems is shown before the 6-plus-1 sets. The letters in the stems are in alphabetical order and, in turn, the stems are listed in alphabetical order. Alongside each stem is shown its ranking in the top 250, as well as a mnemonic keyword of the stem and a suggested mnemonic phrase for the combining letter as an aide-mémoire.

The mnemonic phrase in each case contains only the combining letters for the stem and so can help you remember whether a particular stem does or does not make a bonus word with the seventh letter. For example, AEINRT has a ranking of 1 (the top ranking), mnemonic keyword RETAIN and mnemonic phrase 'double imperfection outweighs joke'. The phrase does not contain an A, which tells you that RETAIN plus an A does not yield a 7-letter word. Similarly, AAEMNT has a ranking of 229, mnemonic keyword (MAN ATE) and mnemonic phrase 'slurping dinner'.

Note that not all the mnemonic keywords are real words or words that are valid for Scrabble. In either of these cases the keyword is shown in brackets, as at MAN ATE above. Where possible, as with (MAN ATE) and 'slurping dinner', keywords are specifically chosen to give an association with the mnemonic phrase.

These 6-letter stems make learning easier and should help recollection during an actual game. If the concept is new to you, then just concentrate on two or three of the most fertile stems, such as AEINRT, AENRST and EGINRS. You might also have fun dreaming up your own mnemonic phrases for your favourite stems.

The 7-letter stems

The 250 7-letter stems used as the basis for the 7-plus-1 sets represent the 250 most likely and most fruitful stems, based on an algorithm of the probability of the seven letters occurring and the probability of an eighth letter combining with the stem. As with the 6-letter stems, a list of the stems, their ranking, mnemonic keyword and (where possible) suggested mnemonic phrase are supplied before the bonus lists.

Alphabetic lists of all the words in the bonus sets

Following the 6-plus-1 sets is a straightforward alphabetical listing of all the 7-letter words appearing in the 6-plus-1 sets. Duplicates have been removed. Similarly, an alphabetic list of the 8-letter words follows the 7-plus-1 sets.

Additional bonus sets

Section Five also contains:

☆ additional high probability bonus words

☆ AEIO bonus words

☆ 6-letter stems combining with each vowel

More about all of these later on.

SUMMARY OF 6-LETTER STEMS
in alphabetical order with ranking, keywords, combining letters and mnemonics

Stem	Rank	Keyword	Combining Letters	Mnemonic
AAEMNT	229	(MAN ATE)	DEGILNPRSU	slurping dinner
ABDEIR	134	(ABRIDE)	CDEGLMNRSTUW	clustered new gem
ABEILS	188	ISABEL	ADEFIKMNRSTWYZ	zesty fair maiden wakes
ABELRT	207	ALBERT	AEHIMNOSTW	showiest man
ABEORS	144	(A SOBER)	BEGIJLNPRTUVWXYZ	JP vexing blitz jury
ABERST	122	BREAST	ABDEGHILMNORSTUVWXY	why even buxom girls date
ACDERS	240	SACRED	ABEFGHIKLNOPRTU	holier, but liar kept fibbing
ACEILR	121	ECLAIR	BDFGHMNOPRSTUVY	thumbs up for no groovy food
ACEINR	65	CANIER	ABDEFGLMNPRST	feeble degenerate MPs
ACEINS	119	INCASE	DFGHLMNOPRSTUVY	sporty thugs found mouldy TV
ACELST	243	CASTLE	ABDEHIKLMNOPRSUY	an absurdly pink home
ACENRS	175	(CANERS)	CDEHIKLNOPSTUVYZ	cheeky novelists zipped up
ACENRT	96	NECTAR	ADEFHILOSTUY	hideously fat
ACENST	149	STANCE	ACDEHIKLNOPRSTU	postured in chalk
ACEORS	103	COARSE	ADEGHILMNRSTUX	light sand mixture
ACEOST	146	(EATSOC)	DEILMNPRTUV	inverted lump
ACERST	141	CATERS	ADEHIKLMNOPRSTUY	desperately link mouths
ACIRST	245	ARTICS	ABCDEGIKMRSTUWYZ	wizard struck by ice gem
ADEERS	70	SEARED	BCDGHIKLMNOPRSTVW	shocking! MTV drops bowls
ADEEST	85	SEATED	BCDFHILMNRSTUWY	truly finds bum twitchy
ADEGLN	197	DANGLE	BCDEFIJMNRSTUW	if it's December, it's just mid-winter
ADEGNR	126	DANGER	EILOPRSTU	too perilous
ADEGRS	221	GRADES	BCDEFGILNPRSTU	bungled specific results
ADEILR	19	DERAIL	ABCDEGILOPRSTVY	gravity disables cop
ADEILS	33	LADIES	BCDEFGHIKLMNOPRSTUVY	sickly blondes hug TV performer
ADEINR	4	RAINED	ABCDFGHIMOPRSTUV	Cuba might drop favours
ADEINS	22	(SANDIE)	ABCDEGKLMOPRSTUV	swamp track above glade
ADEIRS	12	RAISED	ABCEFGHIKLMNOPRTUV	levitating brick for chump
ADEIST	26	(IDATES)	BCDEFGLMNORSUVW	November wolf cudgels
ADELNR	79	LANDER	ABDEGHKLMOSUY	hooked balmy gulls
ADELNS	137	(SANDLE)	CDEGHIKORSTU	dig truck shoe
ADELRS	88	ALDERS	BCDEFGHIKMNOPRSTUWZ	computer whizz kid finds bug
ADELST	110	SALTED	BCDEIKLNOPRSTU	pickled Burtons
ADEMNS	246	AMENDS	ADEGINOPRSTUY	designs your patio
ADENRS	62	SANDER	CDEFGHIKLMPRSTUWZ	scum wrecked prize flight
ADENRU	64	UNREAD	BCDEGHIKLMOPSTY	policed mighty books
ADENST	36	STANED	ACEGHIKLMNOPRTUVY	having mucky petrol
ADEORS	48	ADORES	CDEFILMRTUVW	multi-curved wife
ADEPRT	228	PARTED	AEIMOPSTU	semi-utopia
ADERRS	235	(DARERS)	ACEGILNOPTW	go lie on cowpat
ADERST	49	STARED	BCDEFGHIKLMNOPRTVWY	women looked fetching by the privy
ADGINR	135	DARING	BCEFGILMNOPRSTUWY	stop ferociously big women
ADINRS	105	DRAINS	ABEFGKLMNOQTUW	baulk monumental quag flow
AEELRS	72	LEASER	CDEGHIKMOPSTUVXY	pick the sexy movie guide
AEEMRS	238	SEAMER	BCDGHIKLNPRSTU	thugs drink in public
AEEPRT	142	REPEAT	ADHIKLMORSUYZ	ask him you lizard
AEERRS	162	ERASER	BCDGHIMNOPRSTUVW	chimp rubbing out VW doors
AEERST	20	EATERS	ABCDFGHIKLMNOPRSTUW	humpback flings out word
AEGILN	55	(EALING)	CDEFGHKLMNRPSTUVY	kung fu speed, clever myth
AEGINR	15	REGAIN	BCDEFGHKLMNOPRSTVW	Government blocked show flop
AEGLNR	91	ANGLER	ABCDEGIJLMPSTUWY	Jimmy gutted best wet plaice
AEGLNS	170	GLEANS	ABCDFGIJLMOPRSTUWY	joyful impact from wordbags
AEGLNT	118	TANGLE	DEHIORSTUW	twisted hour
AEGLRS	167	LAGERS	ABDEFGIKMNOPSTVYZ	vat stopped making fizzy booze
AEGLST	187	(ALGETS)	ABEHILNORTW	brother-in-law
AEGNRS	86	ANGERS	BDEGHILMOPRSTUW	grumped whilst bored
AEGNRT	54	GARNET	ADEFILMNPRSU	super-inflamed
AEGNST	115	AGENTS	ADEHILMNRT	thrilled man
AEGRST	80	GREATS	ABDEGHILNOPRSTVY	very old thespians brag
AEHLRT	212	LATHER	ABCEFIMNOSY	foamy ambiences
AEHRST	169	HATERS	BCDEFGHILMNOPSTVW	hostile VIP's wife coming to bed
AEILMN	133	MENIAL	ACFGHLMNOPRST	half rags can't mop
AEILNT	11	ENTAIL	AEFGMOPRSUV	Pam favours egg
AEILRS	16	SAILER	ABCDEGHIJKLMNPRSTVW	jackman viewing the pirate's blade
AEILRT	10	RETAIL	BCDEHKLMNPRSTUWY	spend the weekly crumbs

AEILSS	248	LASSIE	ABCDFGHIKLMNPRSUVW	having a nap as film runs backwards
AEILST	24	(SALTIE)	BCDGHIKLNOPRUVWYZ	providing boozy working lunch
AEIMNR	61	REMAIN	BCDEFGHKLORSTVW	fevered dog left chewed books
AEIMNS	98	MANIES	ACDEFGHJKLMORST	lots of jagged thermal rocks
AEIMNT	53	INMATE	ABCDEGILNRSXY	exercising badly in cell
AEIMRS	112	ARMIES	BDEFGHLMNPRSTUW	helmeted grunts spew beef
AEIMST	95	(MISEAT)	CDEGHIKMNOPRSTZ	choking on imported zos
AEINRS	6	SARNIE	CDFGHIJKLMNOPRSTV	giving Josh mild pork flitch
AEINRT	1	RETAIN	BCDEFGHIJKLMNOPRSTUW	double imperfection outweighs joke
AEINST	2	(SATINE)	ABCDEFGIJKLMNOPRSTUVWZ	a perfect bemused jovial twinkling gaze
AEIPRS	75	PRAISE	ACDEGHKLMNOPRSTUVW	acknowledge mother's veg and pud
AEIRST	3	SATIRE	ABCDEFGHIKLMNOPRSTVW	keep waking as vampires fetch blood
AEIRTT	29	ATTIRE	ABCDEFLNPRSTVWX	vest, belt, scarf and waxed cap
AEISTT	83	(TASTIE)	ABCFHKMNOPRTUVWY	buy watch from TV punk
AELMNT	211	LAMENT	ABDEIMOSTU	mutated bodies
AELNRS	63	LEARNS	ABCDFGIKNOPRSTZ	if boozing pack darts
AELNRT	28	ANTLER	BCEGHILNPSTUV	visit huge public tine
AELNST	34	LATENS	ACDEGHIKMNOPRTUVYZ	making chap tardy, overdue and dazed
AELORS	42	(ALOSER)	BCDEFGHLMNOPST	MP closes off the gold bonds
AELOST	46	(SOLATE)	BCDEFGHIKMNPRVZ	give beekeeping chief mid-prize
AELPRS	231	(PALERS)	ACDEFGHIKMNOPRTUWY	dye my face pink and throw gunk
AELPRT	206	PLATER	ACEIMNOSTY	non-systematic
AELRST	38	ALERTS	BCDEFGHIKLMNOPSTUVWY	give up! I knew botulism is in cheesy food
AEMNST	168	STAMEN	ABDEGHILOPRSUY	spoiled large shrubbery
AEMRST	124	MATERS	ABCDEHIJKLMNOPRSTUWY	plucky mothers sunbathed with joy
AENNST	152	(ANNETS)	ACDEFGIKLRTW	wild cricket flag
AENPST	185	PATENS	ACDEHILMRSTUWYZ	the clumsy wizard
AENRRT	87	ERRANT	AEGIOPSTY	gay postie
AENRSS	223	SNARES	ACDEFGHIKLORSTWY	God catches wicker fly
AENRST	9	ASTERN	ABCDEGHIKLMNOPRSTUVWY	moved ship light back to runway
AENRTT	71	NATTER	ACDEILNPRSUY	discuss and parley
AENSTT	116	(ATTENS)	BCDEFGILNOPRTUX	flexed copper tubing
AEORST	13	ORATES	BCDEGHILMNPRT	PM belched greeting
AEPRST	129	PATERS	ACDEGHILMNOPRSTUYZ	long-standing much-prized daddy
AERRST	138	RATERS	BCDEFGIKMNOPSTY	good pick - it's to my benefit
AERSST	220	ASSERT	ABCEFGHIKLMNPRSTVWY	I'm clever by fighting newspeak
AERSTT	97	TASTER	BCDEGHILMNOPRSTUVWYZ	zombie's rhyming couplets with video
AERSTW	194	WATERS	ABDEFHILMNSTY	lamented by fish
AGILNR	199	(RALING)	BCDEFGHIKMNOPTWY	mighty bone picked by bitchy wife
AGILNS	219	SIGNAL	ABCDEFGHIJKMNPSTUVWY	defying Jack waved thumbs-up
AGILNT	174	(LATING)	BCEFHIKMNOPRSY	bishop's hymnbook on fire shook choir
AGINRS	123	GRAINS	ABCDEFGHIKMNOPTVWY	feed the pack by moving wheat
AGINRT	69	RATING	ACDEFGIKLMNOPRSTY	I get sick and tired of playing if mine is not top
AGINST	108	SATING	ABCDEFGHKLMNOPRTUVWXY	why do you vengefully mock the bad expert?
AINRST	40	TRAINS	ADEGHLMOPQSTU	glum Thomas had to queue up
AINSTT	213	TAINTS	ADEGIMNORS	odd smearings
ANORST	60	(STAR ON)	ABCEILMNOPTUY	yet public moan
BDEIRS	242	BRIDES	ABCDEGIKLNORTUV	begun divorce talk
BEILRS	205	LIBERS	ABDEGIJKMNORST	designs on job market
BEIRST	184	TRIBES	ADEFHIKLMOSTU	folk must all hide
BEORST	225	STROBE	ADHILMNOPSTUV	all lumps and dots vanish
CEINOS	109	COSINE	ABCDEGILMNRSTV	made big vertical angles
CEINRS	183	(NICERS)	ADEGHIKMOPSTVW	give vodka to the wimps
CEINST	196	INSECT	AEFHIJKLOPRSY	apish horsefly jokes
CEIORS	156	COSIER	ABCDHLNPRSTUVWZ	Tarzan vaults, a bad crash and traps walnuts
CEIRST	166	CITERS	ACDEHIKLMNOPTUW	liked to chant well on podium
CENORS	172	(CONERS)	ADEFGIKLNOPRSTU	disrupted King Kong falls
CENOST	224	CENTOS	ADEFGHIKNRTUV	taking five hundred
CEORST	234	ESCORT	AHIKLNOPRSTUV	punkish violator
DEEINR	43	DENIER	BCEFGHLMOPRSUWX	superb legs welcome hose for exposure
DEEIRS	58	DESIRE	ABCDEFGLMNOPRSTUV	observed a peaceful megaton bomb
DEELNS	239	(ENDLES)	ABDEFGILRSTWY	wild grey beards grew fast
DEENRS	92	(ENDERS)	ABCDEFGHILMOPRSTUVZ	I gazed at Chambers for plural of LEV
DEENST	111	NESTED	ACDEILMNORSTUX	is column x-rated?

DEERST	151	RESTED	ACDEINOPSVWXY	Picasso views sine wave on X and Y axis
DEGILN	164	DINGLE	ABEGHIJMNOPSTUVW	a bungee jumping woman has negative view
DEGINR	82	RINGED	ABCDEFHINORSUWY	we are surrounded by fire chiefs
DEGINS	154	SIGNED	AEGILMNORSTUWY	wrote amusingly
DEGIRS	210	DIRGES	ABEFGILNRSU	big funerals
DEILNS	120	(INDLES)	ADEGIKMNOPTWY	a wonky pig mated
DEILRT	73	(TRIDLE)	ABDEFHKLNOPUWY	helped boy on fun walk
DEINOS	41	ONSIDE	ACDGHILMNPRST	car dips main lights
DEINRS	51	DINERS	ABCEFGHIKMNOPTUVW	weeping into a bucket of vintage champagne
DEINRU	52	RUINED	ACDEFGHIJMNOSTW	James is good at fetching wood
DEINST	32	(SINTED)	ABDEFGIKLMNOPRSTUY	king buys platformed boots
DEIORS	27	(ORIDES)	ABCDEHLMNOPSTVWZ	twelve amazed blond chaps
DEIOST	35	(ODSITE)	ACDFHJMNOPRTUVWXZ	coax vacant farm cow to jump hazard
DEIPRT	215	(TRIPED)	ACEILMNOPS	a noise clamp
DEIRST	57	STRIDE	ABCEFHIKNOPRSUV	car runs over fake bishop
DEIRSU	143	(URDIES)	ABCDEGHKNPQRST	eats qat and gets back near garden path
DELNOS	181	OLDENS	ABDFGIMORSUWZ	biogs of famous wizards
DELORS	145	(OLDERS)	ABCEFGHIMNPSTWY	bigwig faces nymphet
DELORT	100	(DOLTER)	ADILNOPSTU	so dull and stupid
DENORU	99	UNDOER	ABDFGILMNPRSW	windbags limp far
DENOST	74	STONED	ABCEFIMNORTU	I am a fat bouncer
DENRSU	179	(UNDERS)	ABDEFGHIKLNOPSTU	a daft bloke pushing a bike
DENSTU	217	(STUNED)	ABDEHIMNORT	hit the board men
DEORST	50	STORED	ABEFGHIKLMNOPRTUWY	rifleman put away the rogue blank
DEOSTU	180	OUSTED	CGHIJLMNOPRTUX	hint - joining or mixing lip colour
DERSTU	244	RUSTED	BCGILNOPRSTU	sporting club
DGINOR	209	(ORDING)	ACDEFHLNRSTVW	we searched twelve fans
EEFIRS	241	(FERIES)	ADEFHILNPRSZ	he fell in a dazed spiral spin
EEGNRS	237	GREENS	ADEIMOSTV	avoids meat
EEILRS	90	RELIES	ABDEFGHLNPRSTUV	pub gave all left-handers a free beer
EEILRV	232	RELIVE	ADEGILMNORS	see again milord?
EEILST	89	ELITES	CEFGHKLMNOPRSVX	frogs expel venom from cheeks
EEIMNS	192	(EMINES)	ADEGILMORSTWY	wild mister dayglo
EEIMRS	202	MISERE	ABCDEGHMNOPRSTX	grass expected amongst herbs
EEINRT	8	ENTIRE	ABCEFGHIKNPRSTU	backing super fight
EEIRRS	182	(ERRIES)	ABDFHJLMNOPSTVW	bloodshot fan of vamp holds jaw
EEIRST	31	(ESTIER)	ABCDEHKLMNPRTUVWZ	dazed humpback whale ducked the water event
EEIRSV	222	REVISE	CDEGHLNOPRSTVW	prevented clog show
EELNST	161	NESTLE	ADEGILPRSTUY	guilty spread
EELRST	157	(ELTERS)	ABCFGHIKLMNPSTVWYZ	lazy fish gawps at bikini victim
EENRST	56	ENTERS	ACDEGHILNPRSTUVWXY	why nag vexed culprits
EEORSV	247	(OVERSE)	ABCEIKLMRTUW	writable muck
EERRST	236	RESTER	ABEFGIMNOSTUVW	moves few wings about
EERSTT	200	STREET	ABCEFGHILNOPRSTUY	police chief is busy patrolling
EFIRST	191	STRIFE	ABDFHIKLMNOSTUW	I found him on walkabouts
EGHINT	250	(ETHING)	ABCDEFILMNRST	bald man finds Scrabble a test
EGILNR	125	LINGER	ACEFGHIJMPSTY	this pig eats at the majesty cafe
EGILNS	117	SINGLE	ABDEFGHIJKLMNOPRSTUWZ	howzat! fumbling fielder jumps keeper
EGILNT	66	TINGLE	ABDEFHIJKLMOPRSTUW	dim halfwit jumps off kerb
EGILOS	132	LOGIES	ABELNOPRSTU	unsupportable
EGILRS	159	(GIRLES)	ABDEGIKLNOSTUY	studying a bloke
EGILST	190	LEGIST	ABEGHLMNOPRSUZ	zebra pulls a ploughman
EGINNR	178	GINNER	ACDEFGIKMNRSTUVY	fed my starving ducks
EGINOS	78	INGOES	ABCDEHJLMPRUWY	jumbled up archway
EGINRS	68	SINGER	ABCDEFGLMNOPRSTUVWYZ	crazy fangs loved wet bump
EGINRT	39	(TINGER)	AEHILMNOSTUVY	evil human toys
EGINST	107	(ESTING)	ABDHIJKLMNRSTUVWZ	wizard's junk habit - valium!
EGNORS	155	(SONGER)	ACEIMOPSUVY	my voice pauses
EHINRS	227	SHRINE	ACDEIKMOSVW	wicked sad moves
EHIRST	153	(ITHERS)	ABCDEFGHILMOPTUVWZ	cow fight at medieval booze-up
EHORST	189	OTHERS	ABCDEFILMNOPRSTUWX	mixed up fan bets on World Cup
EIILST	139	(TILIES)	ACIKLMNOPRTU	column paintwork
EIINRT	30	INTIRE	ACDEFGHLMNTVW	fame changed twelve men
EILNOS	47	(OLINES)	CDFGILMOPRSTU	PC Plod forgot music
EILNRS	77	LINERS	ABEGIKMOPTV	make a boat pivot at gap
EILNST	45	SILENT	ACDEGIKLNOPRSUVW	uncle avoids speaking words
EILORS	37	OILERS	BCDGIMNOPRSTUV	doping sunburn victim
EILORT	18	TOILER	BCDEFJMNOPSTU	competed on fun jobs
EILOST	21	(ELIOTS)	ABCEGHILMNOPRTUVW	poet begun which marvel?

EILRST	44	LITERS	ABCEFGHIKLMNOPSTU	spaceman flight out to black hole
EILSTU	136	(UTILES)	ABDFGILNOPRT	forbid planting
EIMNOS	131	MONIES	ACDEGLOPRSTW	word gets placed
EIMNRS	177	MINERS	ACDEGHKLMOTUV	hated coal glove muck
EIMNST	201	(MINEST)	ADEGIKOPRSTUW	I worked upstage
EIMOST	150	SOMITE	ADFGHLMNPRSTUVZ	mad vandals turn up gas, flash zap!
EIMRST	140	MITRES	ABCEFHIKLMNOPRSTUY	scornfully mock the bishop's hat
EINNST	113	SINNET	ADEGILOPRSTUV	I upstaged lover
EINOPS	130	PONIES	DEGHIKLMNPRSTWY	temptingly whiskered
EINORS	7	SENIOR	ACDGHIJLMOPRSTUVW	jovial chap would jump at guitar music
EINOSS	204	SONSIE	ABCDIKLMNPRSTU	public drink mats
EINOST	14	TONIES	ABCDHJLMNOPRSTW	bad actors plan major award show
EINPRS	158	SNIPER	ACDEGIKLNOPSTU	picks out distant leg
EINPST	148	INSTEP	ACDEIKLMNOPRSTU	includes postmark
EINRSS	249	RESINS	ACEGHKNOPRTUV	over tough pancake
EINRST	17	INTERS	ACDEFGKLMNOPSTUVWY	faulty packages moved down
EINRSV	226	VINERS	ACDEGHLMOSTW	matches glowed
EINRTT	76	TINTER	ABCDEGIKOSUW	abused wicked ego
EINRTU	25	UNITER	ABDEGMOPRSTVW	wordgames proved to be better
EINSST	218	INSETS	ACDEFGHLMNOPRSUVWY	could you add very many pages when full?
EINSTT	160	(INTEST)	ADGIKMNOPRUWY	making up a wordy pun
EINSTU	81	UNITES	ADGILMNPQRST	qanat plans and diagrams
EIOPST	101	POSTIE	ACDEHKLMNORSTUXY	X-rays unlocked them letter secrets
EIORSS	214	(SORIES)	BCDEFHLMNPRTUVX	deluxe chef held bumper event
EIORST	5	(TORIES)	ABCDFGHIKLMNOPSTUVW	if voting slumps, this is a drawback
EIORSV	127	VIROSE	ACDEILMNRST	terminal disease scare
EIOSTT	93	(OTTIES)	ABCDEGHLMNOPRTUW	placed wrong thumb on button
EIPRST	147	PRIEST	ACDEHILMNOPSTUVXY	such expletives at mass on Sunday
EIRRST	165	TRIERS	ADEKMORSTUVW	vet us mad workers
EIRSTT	104	SITTER	ABCEFHJKLMNOPRSTUVW	just watch known volume pour from burette
EIRSTV	163	RIVETS	ADEGHINOPRSTU	are tapped in on tough heads
ELNSTU	216	(LETSUN)	ABEFGINOPRT	print bingo on front page
ELORST	67	(TOLERS)	ABCDFHIJLNOPSTUVW	not flush, low-paid vacation job
ELOSTU	173	TOUSLE	BDFILNOPRSTUVZ	provision for doubtful zoo
ELRSTU	208	ULSTER	ABCDFGHINOPRSTY	coat for body shaping
EMNORS	230	SERMON	ADEFGILOST	sit deaf to false god
EMNOST	186	(MONETS)	ABDEFGHILMOPRSUY	buyer of gold has mishap
EMORST	198	(MOTERS)	ABDEGHINOPRSU	boring rude phrases
ENOPRS	203	PERSON	ACDEGHIORSTUY	sues dog charity
ENORST	23	STONER	ABCDHIKLMNOPRSTUY	shuts door on pyramid block
ENOSTT	195	(ONTEST)	ACDHIJLOPRSU	rich judo pals
ENOSTU	94	(O TUNES)	ACDGLMNORSTU	damn cultural songs
ENRSTU	84	TUNERS	ABCDEFGHILMNOPRST	old pianofortes become all right
EOPRST	193	REPOTS	ABCDFHILMNOPRSTUWX	mix a bunch of dwarf bulbs in a pot
EORRST	106	SORTER	ACDEGHIKMNOPRSTUVWY	dynamic worker puts vague chaos into order
EORSTT	114	OTTERS	ABCDEHIJLNOPRTUWXY	why include an expert on the job?
GIINRT	233	TIRING	ABCDEFGLMNORSTW	common words are forgettable
GILNOT	171	TOLING	ABCEFHIJLMOPSTUW	it's a whale! jump off beach towel
GINORS	128	SIGNOR	ABCDEGHILMNOPSTUVWY	he loves watching and spying bums
GINORT	102	ROTING	ADEFIKOPRSTUW	task for proud wife
GINOST	176	(TO SING)	ACDFHKLMNOPRSTUVWY	top hymns favour duckwalk
INORST	59	(TRIONS)	ABCEFGHILNOTU	a touching fable

7-LETTER SETS
from the top 250 6-letter stems

AAEMNT 229
(MAN ATE)
D MANDATE
E EMANATE
  ENEMATA
  MANATEE
G GATEMAN
  MAGENTA
  MAGNATE
I AMENTIA
  ANIMATE
L AMENTAL
N EMANANT
P PEATMAN
R RAMENTA
S NAMASTE
U MANTEAU

ABDEIR 134
(ABRIDE)
C CARBIDE
D BRAIDED
E BEADIER
  BEARDIE
G ABRIDGE
  BRIGADE
L BALDIER
  BRAILED
  RAILBED
  RIDABLE
M EMBRAID
N BANDIER
  BRAINED
R BARDIER
  BRAIDER
  BRIARED
  RABIDER
S BRAISED
  DARBIES
  SEABIRD
  SIDEBAR
T TRIBADE
U DAUBIER
W BAWDIER

ABEILS 188
ISABEL
A ABELIAS
D BALDIES
  DIABLES
  DISABLE
E BAILEES
F FAIBLES
I BAILIES
K SKIABLE
M ABLEISM
  EMBAILS
  LAMBIES
N LESBIAN
R BAILERS
S ABSEILS
  ISABELS
  LABISES
T ABLEIST
  ALBITES
  ASTILBE
  BESTIAL
  LIBATES
  STABILE
W BEWAILS
Y BAILEYS
Z SIZABLE

ABELRT 207
ALBERT
A RATABLE
E BLEATER
  RETABLE
H BLATHER
  HALBERT
I LIBRATE
  TABLIER
  TRIABLE
M LAMBERT
N BRANTLE
O BLOATER
S ALBERTS
  BATLERS
  BLASTER
  LABRETS
  STABLER
T BATTLER
  BLATTER
  BRATTLE
W BLEWART

ABEORS 144
(A SOBER)
B EARBOBS
E AEROBES
G BORAGES
I ISOBARE
J JERBOAS
L LABROSE
N BORANES
P SAPROBE
R ARBORES
  BRASERO
T BOASTER
  BOATERS
  BORATES
  SORBATE
U AEROBUS
V BRAVOES
X BORAXES
Y ROSEBAY
Z BEZOARS

ABERST 122
BREAST
A ABREAST
B BARBETS
  RABBETS
  STABBER
D DABSTER
  TABERDS
E BEATERS
  BERATES
  REBATES
G BARGEST
H BATHERS
  BERTHAS
  BREATHS
I BAITERS
  BARITES
L ALBERTS
  BATLERS
  BLASTER
  LABRETS
  STABLER
M TAMBERS
N BANTERS
O BOASTER
  BOATERS
  BORATES
  SORBATE
R BARRETS
  BARTERS
S BASTERS
  BESTARS
  BRASSET
  BREASTS
T BATTERS
  TABRETS
U ARBUTES
  SURBATE
V BRAVEST
W BRAWEST
  WABSTER
X BAXTERS
Y BARYTES
  BETRAYS

ACDERS 240
SACRED
A ARCADES
B DECARBS
E CREASED
  DECARES
  SEARCED
F SCARFED
G CADGERS
H CRASHED
I CARDIES
  DARCIES
  RADICES
  SIDECAR
K DACKERS
L CRADLES
  SCALDER
N DANCERS
O SARCODE
P REDCAPS
  SCARPED
  SCRAPED
R CARDERS
  SCARRED
T REDACTS
  SCARTED
U CRUSADE
  SCAURED

ACEILR 121
ECLAIR
B CALIBER
  CALIBRE
D DECRIAL
  RADICEL
  RADICLE
F FILACER
G GLACIER
  GRACILE
H CHARLIE
M CALMIER
  CLAIMER
  MIRACLE
  RECLAIM
N CARLINE
O CALORIE
  CARIOLE
  COALIER
  LORICAE
P CALIPER
  REPLICA
R CERRIAL
S CLARIES
  ECLAIRS
  SCALIER
T ARTICLE
  RECITAL
  TALCIER
U AURICLE
V CALIVER
  CLAVIER
  VELARIC
Y CLAYIER

ACEINR 65
CANIER
A ACARINE
  CARINAE
B CARBINE
D CAIRNED
  CARNIED
E CINEREA
F FANCIER
G GRECIAN
L CARLINE
M CARMINE
N CANNIER
P CAPRINE
R CARNIER
S ARSENIC
  CARNIES
  CERASIN
T CANTIER
  CERTAIN
  CREATIN
  CRINATE
  NACRITE

ACEINS 119
INCASE
D CANDIES
  INCASED
F FANCIES
  FASCINE
  FIANCES
G CEASING
  INCAGES
H CHAINES
  INCHASE
L INLACES
  SANICLE
  SCALENI
M AMNESIC
  CINEMAS
N CANINES
  NANCIES
O ACINOSE
P INSCAPE
  PINCASE
R ARSENIC
  CARNIES
  CERASIN
S CASEINS
  INCASES
T CANIEST
  CINEAST
U EUCAINS
V INCAVES
Y CYANISE

ACELST 243
CASTLE
A ACETALS
  LACTASE
B CABLETS
D CASTLED
  SCLATED
E CELESTA
H CHALETS
  LATCHES
  SATCHEL
I ASTELIC
  ELASTIC
  LACIEST
  LATICES
  SALICET
K TACKLES
L CALLETS
M CALMEST
  CAMLETS
N CANTLES
  CENTALS
  LANCETS
  SCANTLE
O ALECOST
  LACTOSE
  LOCATES
  SCATOLE
  TALCOSE
P CAPLETS
  PLACETS
R CARTELS
  CLARETS
  SCARLET
  TARCELS
S CASTLES
  SCLATES
U CAUTELS
  SULCATE
Y ACETYLS
  SCYTALE

ACENRS 175
(CANERS)
C CANCERS
D DANCERS
E CAREENS
  CASERNE
  ENRACES
H CHENARS
  RANCHES
I ARSENIC
  CARNIES
  CERASIN
K CANKERS
L LANCERS
  RANCELS
N CANNERS
  SCANNER
O CARNOSE
  COARSEN
  CORNEAS
  EARCONS
P PRANCES
S ANCRESS
  CASERNS
T CANTERS
  CARNETS
  NECTARS
  RECANTS
  SCANTER
  TANRECS
  TRANCES
U SURANCE
V CAVERNS
  CRAVENS
Y CARNEYS
  SCENARY

Z ZARNECS

ACENRT 96
NECTAR
A CATERAN
D CANTRED
  TRANCED
E CENTARE
  CRENATE
F CANTREF
H CHANTER
  TRANCHE
I CANTIER
  CERTAIN
  CREATIN
  CRINATE
  NACRITE
L CENTRAL
O ENACTOR
S CANTERS
  CARNETS
  NECTARS
  RECANTS
  SCANTER
  TANRECS
  TRANCES
T TRANECT
U CENTAUR
  UNCRATE
  UNTRACE
Y ENCRATY
  NECTARY

ACENST 149
STANCE
A CATENAS
C ACCENTS
D DECANTS
  DESCANT
  SCANTED
E CETANES
  TENACES
H CHASTEN
  NATCHES
I CANIEST
  CINEAST
K NACKETS
L CANTLES
  CENTALS
  LANCETS
  SCANTLE
N NASCENT
O COSTEAN
  OCTANES
P CATNEPS
R CANTERS
  CARNETS
  NECTARS
  RECANTS
  SCANTER
  TANRECS
  TRANCES
S ASCENTS
  SECANTS
  STANCES
T CANTEST
U NUTCASE

ACEORS 103
COARSE
A ROSACEA
D SARCODE

E ACEROSE	SCANTER	REASTED	GRADINE	LADDIES	SDAINED
G CARGOES	TANRECS	REDATES	GRAINED	E AEDILES	E ANISEED
CORSAGE	TRANCES	SEDATER	READING	DEISEAL	G AGNISED
SOCAGER	O COASTER	STEARED	L DANGLER	F DISLEAF	K KANDIES
H CHOREAS	COATERS	TASERED	GNARLED	G SILAGED	L DENIALS
ORACHES	P CARPETS	V ADVERSE	O GROANED	H HALIDES	SNAILED
ROACHES	PRECAST	EVADERS	P PRANGED	I DAILIES	M DEMAINS
I ORACIES	SPECTRA	W DRAWEES	R GNARRED	LIAISED	MAIDENS
SCORIAE	R CARTERS		GRANDER	SEDILIA	MEDIANS
L CLAROES	CRATERS	**ADEEST 85**	S DANGERS	K SKAILED	MEDINAS
COALERS	TRACERS	SEATED	GANDERS	L DALLIES	SIDEMAN
ESCOLAR	S ACTRESS	B BESTEAD	GARDENS	DISLEAL	O ADONISE
ORACLES	CASTERS	DEBATES	T DRAGNET	LALDIES	ANODISE
M AMORCES	RECASTS	C TEDESCA	GRANTED	SALLIED	SODAINE
N CARNOSE	T SCATTER	D DEADEST	U ENGUARD	M MAELIDS	P PANDIES
COARSEN	U ACTURES	SEDATED	RAUNGED	MEDIALS	PANSIED
CORNEAS	CAUTERS	STEADED		MISDEAL	SPAINED
EARCONS	CRUSTAE	F DEAFEST	**ADEGRS 221**	MISLEAD	R RANDIES
R COARSER	CURATES	DEFASTE	GRADES	N DENIALS	SANDIER
S ROSACES	Y SECTARY	DEFEATS	B BADGERS	SNAILED	SARDINE
T COASTER		FEASTED	C CADGERS	O DEASOIL	S SDAINES
COATERS	**ACIRST 245**	H HEADSET	D GADDERS	P ALIPEDS	T DETAINS
U ACEROUS	ARTICS	I IDEATES	E DRAGEES	PAIDLES	INSTEAD
CAROUSE	A CARITAS	L DELATES	GREASED	PALSIED	SAINTED
X COAXERS	B CABRITS	STEALED	F DEFRAGS	R DERAILS	SATINED
	C ARCTICS	M STEAMED	G DAGGERS	REDIALS	STAINED
ACEOST 146	D DRASTIC	N STANDEE	I AGRISED	SIDERAL	V INVADES
(EATSOC)	E CRISTAE	STEANED	L DARGLES	S AIDLESS	W DEWANIS
D COASTED	RACIEST	R DEAREST	N DANGERS	DEASILS	
E ACETOSE	STEARIC	DERATES	GANDERS	T DETAILS	**ADEIRS 12**
COATEES	G GASTRIC	ESTRADE	GARDENS	DILATES	RAISED
I SOCIATE	I SATIRIC	REASTED	P GRASPED	U AUDILES	A ARAISED
L ALECOST	K KARSTIC	REDATES	SPADGER	DEASIUL	B BRAISED
LACTOSE	M MATRICS	SEDATER	SPARGED	V DEVISAL	DARBIES
LOCATES	R TRICARS	STEARED	R GRADERS	Y DIALYSE	SEABIRD
SCATOLE	S RACISTS	TASERED	REGARDS	EYLIADS	SIDEBAR
TALCOSE	SACRIST	S SEDATES	S GRASSED		C CARDIES
M CAMOTES	T ASTRICT	T ESTATED	T RADGEST	**ADEINR 4**	DARCIES
COMATES	U URTICAS	U SAUTEED	U SUGARED	RAINED	RADICES
N COSTEAN	W TWISCAR	W SWEATED		A ARANEID	E DEARIES
OCTANES	Y SATYRIC	Y YEASTED	**ADEILR 19**	B BANDIER	READIES
P CAPOTES	Z CZARIST		DERAIL	BRAINED	F FRAISED
SCOPATE		**ADEGLN 197**	A RADIALE	C CAIRNED	G AGRISED
TOECAPS	**ADEERS 70**	DANGLE	B BALDIER	CARNIED	H SHADIER
R COASTER	SEARED	B BANGLED	BRAILED	D DANDIER	I AIRSIDE
COATERS	B DEBASER	C CANGLED	RAILBED	DRAINED	DAIRIES
T COSTATE	SABERED	CLANGED	RIDABLE	F FRIANDE	DIARIES
U ACETOUS	C CREASED	GLANCED	C DECRIAL	G AREDING	DIARISE
V AVOCETS	DECARES	D DANGLED	RADICEL	DEARING	K DAIKERS
OCTAVES	SEARCED	GLADDEN	RADICLE	DERAIGN	DARKIES
	D DEADERS	E GLEANED	D DIEDRAL	EARDING	L DERAILS
ACERST 141	G DRAGEES	F FANGLED	DRAILED	GRADINE	REDIALS
CATERS	GREASED	FLANGED	E LEADIER	GRAINED	SIDERAL
A ACATERS	H ADHERES	I ALIGNED	G GLADIER	READING	M ADMIRES
D REDACTS	HEADERS	DEALING	GLAIRED	H HANDIER	MARDIES
SCARTED	HEARSED	LEADING	I DELIRIA	I DENARII	MISREAD
E CERATES	SHEARED	J JANGLED	IRIDEAL	M ADERMIN	SIDEARM
CREATES	I DEARIES	M MANGLED	L DALLIER	INARMED	N RANDIES
ECARTES	READIES	N ENDLANG	DIALLER	O ANEROID	SANDIER
SECRETA	K SKEARED	R DANGLER	RALLIED	P PARDINE	SARDINE
H ARCHEST	L DEALERS	GNARLED	O DARIOLE	R DRAINER	O ROADIES
CHARETS	LEADERS	S DANGLES	P PEDRAIL	RANDIER	SOREDIA
CHASTER	REDEALS	GLANDES	PREDIAL	S RANDIES	P ASPIRED
RATCHES	M REMADES	SLANGED	R LARDIER	SANDIER	DESPAIR
I CRISTAE	REMEADS	T TANGLED	S DERAILS	SARDINE	DIAPERS
RACIEST	SMEARED	U LANGUED	REDIALS	T DETRAIN	PRAISED
STEARIC	N DEANERS	W WANGLED	SIDERAL	TRAINED	R ARRIDES
K RACKETS	ENDEARS		T DILATER	U UNAIRED	RAIDERS
STACKER	O OREADES	**ADEGNR 126**	TRAILED	URANIDE	T ARIDEST
TACKERS	P PREASED	DANGER	V VALIDER	V INVADER	ASTERID
L CARTELS	R DREARES	E ANGERED	Y READILY	RAVINED	ASTRIDE
CLARETS	READERS	DERANGE			DIASTER
SCARLET	REDSEAR	ENRAGED	**ADEILS 33**	**ADEINS 22**	DISRATE
TARCELS	REREADS	GRANDEE	LADIES	(SANDIE)	STAIDER
M MERCATS	S RESEDAS	GRENADE	B BALDIES	A NAIADES	STAIRED
N CANTERS	T DEAREST	I AREDING	DIABLES	B BANDIES	TARDIES
CARNETS	DERATES	DEARING	DISABLE	C CANDIES	TIRADES
NECTARS	ESTRADE	DERAIGN	C SCAILED	INCASED	U RESIDUA
RECANTS		EARDING	D DAIDLES	D DANDIES	

Column 1

V ADVISER
  VARDIES

ADEIST 26
(IDATES)
B BASTIDE
C ACIDEST
  DACITES
D TADDIES
E IDEATES
F DAFTIES
  FADIEST
G AGISTED
L DETAILS
  DILATES
M MISDATE
N DETAINS
  INSTEAD
  SAINTED
  SATINED
  STAINED
O IODATES
  TOADIES
R ARIDEST
  ASTERID
  ASTRIDE
  DIASTER
  DISRATE
  STAIDER
  STAIRED
  TARDIES
  TIRADES
S DISSEAT
  SAIDEST
U DAUTIES
V AVIDEST
  DATIVES
  VISTAED
W DAWTIES
  WAISTED

ADELNR 79
LANDER
A ADRENAL
B BLANDER
D DANDLER
E LEARNED
G DANGLER
  GNARLED
H HANDLER
K RANKLED
L LANDLER
M MANDREL
O LADRONE
S DARNELS
  ENLARDS
  LANDERS
  SLANDER
  SNARLED
U LAUNDER
  LURDANE
  RUNDALE
Y DEARNLY

ADELNS 137
(SANDLE)
C CALENDS
  CANDLES
D DANDLES
E LEADENS
G DANGLES
  GLANDES
  SLANGED
H HANDLES
  HANDSEL
I DENIALS
  SNAILED
K KALENDS
O LOADENS

Column 2

R DARNELS
  ENLARDS
  LANDERS
  SLANDER
  SNARLED
S SENDALS
T DENTALS
  SLANTED
U UNLADES
  UNLEADS

ADELRS 88
ALDERS
B BEDRALS
C CRADLES
  SCALDER
D LADDERS
  RADDLES
  SADDLER
E DEALERS
  LEADERS
  REDEALS
F FARDELS
G DARGLES
H HARELDS
  HERALDS
I DERAILS
  REDIALS
  SIDERAL
K DARKLES
M MEDLARS
N DARNELS
  ENLARDS
  LANDERS
  SLANDER
  SNARLED
O LOADERS
  ORDEALS
  RELOADS
P PEDLARS
R LARDERS
S SARDELS
T DARTLES
U LAUDERS
W WARSLED
Z DRAZELS

ADELST 110
SALTED
B BALDEST
  BLASTED
  STABLED
C CASTLED
  SCLATED
D STADDLE
E DELATES
  STEALED
I DETAILS
  DILATES
K SKLATED
  STALKED
L STALLED
N DENTALS
  SLANTED
O SALTOED
P SPALTED
  STAPLED
R DARTLES
S DESALTS
T SLATTED
U AULDEST
  SALUTED

ADEMNS 246
AMENDS
A ANADEMS
  MAENADS
D DEMANDS
  MADDENS

Column 3

E AMENDES
  DEMEANS
G GADSMEN
I DEMAINS
  MAIDENS
  MEDIANS
  MEDINAS
  SIDEMAN
N SANDMEN
O DAEMONS
  MASONED
  MODENAS
  MONADES
  NOMADES
P DAMPENS
R MANREDS
  RANDEMS
  REMANDS
S DESMANS
  MADNESS
T TANDEMS
U MEDUSAN
  SUDAMEN
Y DAYSMEN

ADENRS 62
SANDER
C DANCERS
D DANDERS
E DEANERS
  ENDEARS
F FARDENS
G DANGERS
  GANDERS
  GARDENS
H HANDERS
  HARDENS
I RANDIES
  SANDIER
  SARDINE
K DARKENS
L DARNELS
  ENLARDS
  LANDERS
  SLANDER
  SNARLED
M MANREDS
  RANDEMS
  REMANDS
P PANDERS
R DARNERS
  ERRANDS
  SNARRED
S SANDERS
  SARSDEN
T ENDARTS
  STANDER
  STARNED
U ASUNDER
  DANSEUR
  DAUNERS
W DAWNERS
  WANDERS
  WARDENS
Z ZANDERS

ADENRU 64
UNREAD
B UNBARED
C DURANCE
  UNRACED
D DAUNDER
E UNEARED
G ENGUARD
  RAUNGED
H UNHEARD
I UNAIRED
  URANIDE
K UNRAKED

Column 4

L LAUNDER
  LURDANE
  RUNDALE
M DURAMEN
  MANURED
  MAUNDER
  UNARMED
O RONDEAU
P UNPARED
S ASUNDER
  DANSEUR
  DAUNERS
T DAUNTER
  NATURED
  UNRATED
  UNTREAD
Y UNREADY

ADENST 36
STANED
A ANSATED
C DECANTS
  DESCANT
  SCANTED
E STANDEE
  STEANED
G STANGED
H HANDSET
I DETAINS
  INSTEAD
  SAINTED
  SATINED
  STAINED
K DANKEST
L DENTALS
  SLANTED
M TANDEMS
N STANDEN
O ASTONED
  DONATES
  ONSTEAD
P PEDANTS
  PENTADS
R ENDARTS
  STANDER
  STARNED
T ATTENDS
U SAUNTED
  UNSATED
V ADVENTS
Y STAYNED

ADEORS 48
ADORES
C SARCODE
D DEODARS
E OREADES
F FEDORAS
I ROADIES
  SOREDIA
L LOADERS
  ORDEALS
  RELOADS
M RADOMES
R ADORERS
  DROSERA
T DOATERS
  ROASTED
  TORSADE
  TROADES
U AROUSED
V SAVORED
W REDOWAS

ADEPRT 228
PARTED
A ADAPTER
  READAPT
E ADEPTER

Column 5

  PREDATE
  TAPERED
I DIPTERA
  PARTIED
  PIRATED
M TRAMPED
O ADOPTER
  READOPT
P TRAPPED
S DEPARTS
  DRAPETS
  PETARDS
T PRATTED
U UPRATED

ADERRS 235
(DARERS)
A ARRASED
C CARDERS
  SCARRED
E DREARES
  READERS
  REDSEAR
  REREADS
G GRADERS
  REGARDS
I ARRIDES
  RAIDERS
L LARDERS
N DARNERS
  ERRANDS
  SNARRED
O ADORERS
  DROSERA
P DRAPERS
  SPARRED
T DARTERS
  DARTRES
  RETARDS
  STARRED
  TRADERS
W DRAWERS
  REDRAWS
  REWARDS
  WARDERS

ADERST 49
STARED
B DABSTER
  TABERDS
C REDACTS
  SCARTED
D ADDREST
  RADDEST
E DEAREST
  DERATES
  ESTRADE
  REASTED
  REDATES
  SEDATER
  STEARED
  TASERED
F STRAFED
G RADGEST
H DEARTHS
  HARDEST
  HATREDS
  THREADS
  TRASHED
I ARIDEST
  ASTERID
  ASTRIDE
  DIASTER
  DISRATE
  STAIDER
  STAIRED
  TARDIES
  TIRADES
K DARKEST

Column 6

  STARKED
L DARTLES
M SMARTED
N ENDARTS
  STANDER
  STARNED
O DOATERS
  ROASTED
  TORSADE
  TROADES
P DEPARTS
  DRAPETS
  PETARDS
R DARTERS
  DARTRES
  RETARDS
  STARRED
  TRADERS
T STARTED
  TETRADS
V ADVERTS
  STARVED
W STEWARD
  STRAWED
  WRASTED
Y STRAYED

ADGINR 135
DARING
B BARDING
  BRIGAND
C CARDING
E AREDING
  DEARING
  DERAIGN
  EARDING
  GRADINE
  GRAINED
  READING
F FARDING
G GRADING
  NIGGARD
I GRADINI
  RAIDING
L DARLING
  LARDING
M MRIDANG
N DARNING
  NARDING
  RANDING
O ADORING
  GRADINO
  ROADING
P DRAPING
R DARRING
S DARINGS
  GRADINS
T DARTING
  TRADING
U DAURING
W DRAWING
  WARDING
Y YARDING

ADINRS 105
DRAINS
A RADIANS
B RIBANDS
E RANDIES
  SANDIER
  SARDINE
F FRIANDS
G DARINGS
  GRADINS
K DISRANK
L ALDRINS
M MANDIRS
N INNARDS
O INROADS

ORDAINS
SADIRON
Q QINDARS
T INDARTS
U DURIANS
SUNDARI
W INWARDS

AEELRS 72
LEASER
C ALERCES
CEREALS
RESCALE
D DEALERS
LEADERS
REDEALS
E RELEASE
G GALERES
REGALES
H HEALERS
I EARLIES
REALISE
K LEAKERS
M MEALERS
O AREOLES
P LEAPERS
PLEASER
RELAPSE
REPEALS
S EARLESS
LEASERS
RESALES
RESEALS
SEALERS
T ELATERS
REALEST
RELATES
STEALER
U LEASURE
V LAVEERS
LEAVERS
REVEALS
SEVERAL
VEALERS
X RELAXES
Y SEALERY

AEEMRS 238
SEAMER
B BEAMERS
BESMEAR
C AMERCES
CAREMES
RACEMES
D REMADES
REMEADS
SMEARED
G MEAGRES
H HAREEMS
MAHSEER
I SEAMIER
SERIEMA
K REMAKES
L MEALERS
N RENAMES
P AMPERES
EMPARES
R REAMERS
S SEAMERS
T STEAMER
TEAMERS
U MEASURE

AEEPRT 142
REPEAT
A PATERAE
D ADEPTER
PREDATE
TAPERED

H PREHEAT
I PEATIER
K PERTAKE
L PLEATER
PRELATE
M TEMPERA
O OPERATE
R PEARTER
TAPERER
S REPEATS
U EPURATE
Y PEATERY
Z TRAPEZE

AEERRS 162
ERASER
B BEARERS
BREARES
C CAREERS
CREASER
D DREARES
READERS
REDSEAR
REREADS
G GREASER
H HEARERS
REHEARS
SHEARER
I REARISE
M REAMERS
N EARNERS
O REAROSE
P REAPERS
R REARERS
S ERASERS
T SERRATE
TEARERS
U ERASURE
V REAVERS
W SWEARER
WEARERS

AEERST 20
EATERS
A AERATES
B BEATERS
BERATES
REBATES
C CERATES
CREATES
ECARTES
SECRETA
D DEAREST
DERATES
ESTRADE
REASTED
REDATES
SEDATER
STEARED
TASERED
F AFREETS
FEASTER
G ERGATES
RESTAGE
H AETHERS
HEATERS
REHEATS
I AERIEST
SERIATE
K RETAKES
SAKERET
L ELATERS
REALEST
RELATES
STEALER
M STEAMER
TEAMERS
N EARNEST
EASTERN

NEAREST
O ROSEATE
P REPEATS
R SERRATE
TEARERS
S RESEATS
SAETERS
SEAREST
SEATERS
STEARES
TEASERS
TESSERA
T ESTREAT
RESTATE
U AUSTERE
W SWEATER

AEGILN 55
(EALING)
C ANGELIC
ANGLICE
D ALIGNED
DEALING
LEADING
E LINEAGE
F FEALING
FINAGLE
LEAFING
G GEALING
LIGNAGE
H HEALING
K LEAKING
LINKAGE
L NIGELLA
M LEAMING
MEALING
N ANELING
EANLING
LEANING
NEALING
P LEAPING
PEALING
PLEAING
R ENGRAIL
LAERING
LEARING
NARGILE
REALIGN
REGINAL
S LEASING
LINAGES
SEALING
T ATINGLE
ELATING
GELATIN
GENITAL
U LINGUAE
V LEAVING
Y ALEYING

AEGINR 15
REGAIN
B BEARING
C GRECIAN
D AREDING
DEARING
DERAIGN
EARDING
GRADINE
GRAINED
READING
E REGINAE
F FEARING
G GEARING
NAGGIER
H HEARING
K REAKING
L ENGRAIL
LAERING

LEARING
NARGILE
REALIGN
REGINAL
M GERMAIN
MANGIER
MEARING
REAMING
N AGINNER
EARNING
ENGRAIN
GRANNIE
NEARING
O ORIGANE
P REAPING
R ANGRIER
EARRING
GRAINER
RANGIER
REARING
S ANGRIES
EARINGS
ERASING
GAINERS
GRAINES
REGAINS
REGINAS
SEARING
SERINGA
T GRANITE
GRATINE
INGRATE
TANGIER
TEARING
V REAVING
VINEGAR
W WEARING

AEGLNR 91
ANGLER
A ALNAGER
B BRANGLE
C CLANGER
D DANGLER
GNARLED
E ENLARGE
GENERAL
GLEANER
G GANGREL
I ENGRAIL
LAERING
LEARING
NARGILE
REALIGN
REGINAL
J JANGLER
L LANGREL
M MANGLER
P GRAPNEL
S ANGLERS
LARGENS
SLANGER
T TANGLER
TRANGLE
U GRANULE
W WANGLER
WRANGLE
Y ANGERLY

AEGLNS 170
GLEANS
A ALNAGES
ANLAGES
GALENAS
LAGENAS
LASAGNE
B BANGLES
C CANGLES
GLANCES

D DANGLES
GLANDES
SLANGED
F FANGLES
FLANGES
G LAGGENS
I LEASING
LINAGES
SEALING
J JANGLES
L LEGLANS
M MANGELS
MANGLES
O ENGAOLS
P SPANGLE
R ANGLERS
LARGENS
SLANGER
S GLASSEN
T LANGEST
TANGLES
U ANGELUS
LAGUNES
LANGUES
W WANGLES
Y LYNAGES

AEGLNT 118
TANGLE
D TANGLED
E ELEGANT
H ALENGTH
I ATINGLE
ELATING
GELATIN
GENITAL
O TANGELO
R TANGLER
TRANGLE
S LANGEST
TANGLES
T GANTLET
U LANGUET
W TWANGLE

AEGLRS 167
LAGERS
A ALEGARS
LAAGERS
B GARBLES
D DARGLES
E GALERES
REGALES
F REFLAGS
G GARGLES
LAGGERS
RAGGLES
I GRAILES
K GRAKLES
M MALGRES
N ANGLERS
LARGENS
SLANGER
O GAOLERS
P GRAPLES
S LARGESS
T LARGEST
V GRAVELS
VERGLAS
Y ARGYLES
GRAYLES
Z GLAZERS

AEGLST 187
(ALGETS)
A AGELAST
ALGATES
LASTAGE
B GABLETS

E EAGLETS
LEGATES
TEAGLES
TELEGAS
H HAGLETS
I AGILEST
AIGLETS
LIGATES
TAIGLES
L GALLETS
N LANGEST
TANGLES
O LEGATOS
R LARGEST
T GESTALT
W TALWEGS

AEGNRS 86
ANGERS
B BANGERS
GRABENS
D DANGERS
GANDERS
GARDENS
E ENRAGES
G GANGERS
GRANGES
NAGGERS
H GNASHER
HANGERS
REHANGS
I ANGRIES
EARINGS
ERASING
GAINERS
GRAINES
REGAINS
REGINAS
SEARING
SERINGA
L ANGLERS
LARGENS
SLANGER
M ENGRAMS
GERMANS
MANGERS
O ONAGERS
ORANGES
P ENGRASP
R GARNERS
RANGERS
S SERANGS
T ARGENTS
GARNETS
STRANGE
U RAUNGES
UNGEARS
W GNAWERS

AEGNRT 54
GARNET
A TANAGER
D DRAGNET
GRANTED
E GRANTEE
GREATEN
REAGENT
F ENGRAFT
I GRANITE
GRATINE
INGRATE
TANGIER
TEARING
L TANGLER
TRANGLE
M GARMENT
MARGENT
RAGMENT
N REGNANT

P TREPANG
R GRANTER
  REGRANT
S ARGENTS
  GARNETS
  STRANGE
U GAUNTER

AEGNST 115
AGENTS
A AGNATES
D STANGED
E NEGATES
H STENGAH
I EASTING
  EATINGS
  GAINEST
  GENISTA
  INGATES
  INGESTA
  SEATING
  TANGIES
  TEASING
  TSIGANE
L LANGEST
  TANGLES
M MAGNETS
N GANNETS
R ARGENTS
  GARNETS
  STRANGE
T GESTANT

AEGRST 80
GREATS
A AGRASTE
B BARGEST
D RADGEST
E ERGATES
  RESTAGE
G GAGSTER
  GARGETS
  STAGGER
  TAGGERS
H GATHERS
I AGISTER
  GAITERS
  STAGIER
  STRIGAE
  TRIAGES
L LARGEST
N ARGENTS
  GARNETS
  STRANGE
O ORGEATS
  STORAGE
  TOERAGS
P PARGETS
R GARRETS
  GARTERS
  GRATERS
S GASTERS
  STAGERS
T TARGETS
V GRAVEST
Y GRAYEST
  GYRATES
  STAGERY

AEHLRT 212
LATHER
A TREHALA
B BLATHER
  HALBERT
C ARCHLET
E LEATHER
F FARTHEL
I LATHIER
M THERMAL

N ENTHRAL
O LOATHER
S HALTERS
  HARSLET
  LATHERS
  SLATHER
  THALERS
Y EARTHLY
  HARTELY
  HEARTLY
  LATHERY

AEHRST 169
HATERS
B BATHERS
  BERTHAS
  BREATHS
C ARCHEST
  CHARETS
  CHASTER
  RATCHES
D DEARTHS
  HARDEST
  HATREDS
  THREADS
  TRASHED
E AETHERS
  HEATERS
  REHEATS
F FATHERS
  SHAFTER
G GATHERS
H HEARTHS
I HASTIER
  SHERIAT
L HALTERS
  HARSLET
  LATHERS
  SLATHER
  THALERS
M HAMSTER
N ANTHERS
  HARTENS
  THENARS
O ASTHORE
  EARSHOT
  HAROSET
P SPARTHE
  TEPHRAS
  THREAPS
S RASHEST
  SHASTER
  TRASHES
T HATTERS
  RATHEST
  SHATTER
  THREATS
V HARVEST
  THRAVES
W THAWERS
  WREATHS

AEILMN 133
MENIAL
A LAMINAE
C CNEMIAL
  MELANIC
F FEMINAL
  INFLAME
G LEAMING
  MEALING
H HELIMAN
L MANILLE
M MAILMEN
N LINEMAN
  MELANIN
O MINEOLA
P IMPANEL
  MANIPLE

R MANLIER
  MARLINE
  MINERAL
  RAILMEN
S ISLEMAN
  MENIALS
  SEMINAL
T AILMENT
  ALIMENT

AEILNT 11
ENTAIL
A ANTLIAE
E LINEATE
F INFLATE
G ATINGLE
  ELATING
  GELATIN
  GENITAL
M AILMENT
  ALIMENT
O ELATION
  TOENAIL
P PANTILE
R ENTRAIL
  LATRINE
  RATLINE
  RETINAL
  TRENAIL
S EASTLIN
  ELASTIN
  ENTAILS
  SALIENT
  SLAINTE
  STANIEL
  TENAILS
U ALUNITE
V VENTAIL

AEILRS 16
SAILER
A AERIALS
B BAILERS
C CLARIES
  ECLAIRS
  SCALIER
D DERAILS
  REDIALS
  SIDERAL
E EARLIES
  REALISE
G GRAILES
H HAILERS
  SHALIER
I LAIRISE
J JAILERS
K LAIKERS
  SERKALI
L RALLIES
M MAILERS
  REALISM
N NAILERS
P PALSIER
  PARLIES
R RAILERS
  RERAILS
S AIRLESS
  SAILERS
  SERAILS
  SERIALS
T REALIST
  RETAILS
  SALTIER
  SALTIRE
  SLATIER
V REVISAL
W SWALIER
  WAILERS

AEILRT 10
RETAIL
B LIBRATE
  TABLIER
  TRIABLE
C ARTICLE
  RECITAL
  TALCIER
D DILATER
  TRAILED
E ATELIER
  REALTIE
H LATHIER
K TALKIER
L LITERAL
  TALLIER
M LAMITER
  MALTIER
N ENTRAIL
  LATRINE
  RATLINE
  RELIANT
  RETINAL
  TRENAIL
P PLAITER
  PLATIER
R RETIRAL
  RETRIAL
  TRAILER
S REALIST
  RETAILS
  SALTIER
  SALTIRE
  SLATIER
T TERTIAL
U URALITE
W WALTIER
Y IRATELY
  REALITY

AEILSS 248
LASSIE
A ALIASES
B ABSEILS
  ISABELS
  LABISES
C SALICES
D AIDLESS
  DEASILS
F FALSIES
  FILASSE
G ALGESIS
  LIGASES
  SILAGES
H SHEILAS
I LIAISES
  SILESIA
K ALSIKES
L ALLISES
  SALLIES
M AIMLESS
  MESAILS
  SAMIELS
  SEISMAL
N SALINES
  SILANES
P ESPIALS
  LAPISES
  LIPASES
  PALSIES
R AIRLESS
  SAILERS
  SERAILS
  SERIALS
S LAISSES
  LASSIES
U SAULIES
V VALISES
  VESSAIL

W WALISES

AEILST 24
(SALTIE)
B ABLEIST
  ALBITES
  ASTILBE
  BESTIAL
  LIBATES
  STABILE
C ASTELIC
  ELASTIC
  LACIEST
  LATICES
  SALICET
D DETAILS
  DILATES
G AGILEST
  AIGLETS
  LIGATES
  TAIGLES
H HALITES
I LAITIES
K LAKIEST
  TALKIES
L TAILLES
  TALLIES
N EASTLIN
  ELASTIN
  ENTAILS
  SALIENT
  SLAINTE
  STANIEL
  TENAILS
O ISOLATE
P APLITES
  PALIEST
  TALIPES
R REALIST
  RETAILS
  SALTIER
  SALTIRE
  SLATIER
U SITULAE
V ESTIVAL
W WALIEST
Y TAILYES
Z LAZIEST

AEIMNR 61
REMAIN
B MIRBANE
C CARMINE
D ADERMIN
  INARMED
E REMANIE
F FIREMAN
G GERMAIN
  MANGIER
  MEARING
  REAMING
H HARMINE
K MANKIER
  RAMEKIN
L MANLIER
  MARLINE
  MINERAL
  RAILMEN
O MORAINE
R MARINER
S MARINES
  REMAINS
  SEMINAR
  SIRNAME
T MINARET
  RAIMENT
V VERMIAN
W WIREMAN

AEIMNS 98
MANIES
A AMNESIA
  ANEMIAS
C AMNESIC
  CINEMAS
D DEMAINS
  MAIDENS
  MEDIANS
  MEDINAS
  SIDEMAN
E MEANIES
  NEMESIA
F FAMINES
  INFAMES
G ENIGMAS
  GAMINES
  MEASING
  SEAMING
H HAEMINS
  HEMINAS
J JASMINE
K KINEMAS
L ISLEMAN
  MENIALS
  SEMINAL
M MISNAME
O ANOMIES
R MARINES
  REMAINS
  SEMINAR
  SIRNAME
S INSEAMS
  SAMISEN
T INMATES
  MAINEST
  MANTIES
  TAMINES

AEIMNT 53
INMATE
A AMENTIA
  ANIMATE
B AMBIENT
C EMICANT
  NEMATIC
D MEDIANT
E MATINEE
G MINTAGE
  TEAMING
  TEGMINA
I INTIMAE
  MINIATE
L AILMENT
  ALIMENT
N MANNITE
R MINARET
  RAIMENT
S INMATES
  MAINEST
  MANTIES
  TAMINES
X TAXIMEN
Y AMENITY
  ANYTIME

AEIMRS 112
ARMIES
B AMBRIES
D ADMIRES
  MARDIES
  MISREAD
  SIDEARM
E SEAMIER
  SERIEMA
F MISFARE
G GISARME
  MAIGRES
  MIRAGES

H MASHIER
  MISHEAR
L MAILERS
  REALISM
M RAMMIES
N MARINES
  REMAINS
  SEMINAR
  SIRNAME
P IMPRESA
  SAMPIRE
R MARRIES
  SIMARRE
S MASSIER
T IMARETS
  MAESTRI
  MAISTER
  MASTIER
  MISRATE
  SEMITAR
  SMARTIE
U UREMIAS
W AWMRIES

AEIMST 95
(MISEAT)
C ACMITES
  ETACISM
  MICATES
  SEMATIC
D MISDATE
E STEAMIE
G GAMIEST
  SIGMATE
H ATHEISM
I AMITIES
  ATIMIES
K MISTAKE
M MISMATE
  TAMMIES
N INMATES
  MAINEST
  MANTIES
  TAMINES
O AMOSITE
  ATOMIES
  ATOMISE
  OSMIATE
P IMPASTE
  PASTIME
R IMARETS
  MAESTRI
  MAISTER
  MASTIER
  MISRATE
  SEMITAR
  SMARTIE
S ASTEISM
  SAMIEST
  SAMITES
  TAMISES
T MATIEST
  MATTIES
Z MAZIEST
  MESTIZA

AEINRS 6
SARNIE
C ARSENIC
  CARNIES
  CERASIN
D RANDIES
  SANDIER
  SARDINE
F INFARES
  SERAFIN
G ANGRIES
  EARINGS
  ERASING

GAINERS
GRAINES
REGAINS
REGINAS
SEARING
SERINGA
H ARSHINE
  HERNIAS
I SENARII
J INJERAS
K SNAKIER
L NAILERS
M MARINES
  REMAINS
  SEMINAR
  SIRNAME
N INSANER
  INSNARE
O ERASION
P RAPINES
R SIERRAN
  SNARIER
S ARSINES
  SARNIES
T ANESTRI
  ANTSIER
  NASTIER
  RATINES
  RESIANT
  RETAINS
  RETINAS
  RETSINA
  STAINER
  STARNIE
  STEARIN
V AVENIRS
  RAVINES

AEINRT 1
RETAIN
B ATEBRIN
C CANTIER
  CERTAIN
  CREATIN
  CRINATE
  NACRITE
D DETRAIN
  TRAINED
E RETINAE
  TRAINEE
F FAINTER
  FENITAR
G GRANITE
  GRATINE
  INGRATE
  TANGIER
  TEARING
H HAIRNET
  INEARTH
  THERIAN
I INERTIA
J JANTIER
  NARTJIE
K KERATIN
L ENTRAIL
  LATRINE
  RATLINE
  RELIANT
  RETINAL
  TRENAIL
M MINARET
  RAIMENT
N ENTRAIN
  TRANNIE
O OTARINE
P PAINTER
  PERTAIN
  REPAINT
R RETRAIN

TERRAIN
TRAINER
S ANESTRI
  ANTSIER
  NASTIER
  RATINES
  RESIANT
  RETAINS
  RETINAS
  RETSINA
  STAINER
  STARNIE
  STEARIN
T INTREAT
  ITERANT
  NATTIER
  NITRATE
  TARTINE
  TERTIAN
U RUINATE
  TAURINE
  URANITE
  URINATE
W TAWNIER
  TINWARE

AEINST 2
(SATINE)
A TAENIAS
B BASINET
  BESAINT
  BESTAIN
C CANIEST
  CINEAST
D DETAINS
  INSTEAD
  SAINTED
  SATINED
  STAINED
E ETESIAN
F FAINEST
  NAIFEST
G EASTING
  EATINGS
  GAINEST
  GENISTA
  INGATES
  INGESTA
  SEATING
  TANGIES
  TEASING
  TSIGANE
I ISATINE
J JANTIES
  TAJINES
K INTAKES
  KENTIAS
  TANKIES
L EASTLIN
  ELASTIN
  ENTAILS
  SALIENT
  SLAINTE
  STANIEL
  TENAILS
M INMATES
  MAINEST
  MANTIES
  TAMINES
N INANEST
O ATONIES
P PANTIES
  PATINES
  SAPIENT
  SPINATE
R ANESTRI
  ANTSIER
  NASTIER
  RATINES

RESIANT
RETAINS
RETINAS
RETSINA
STAINER
STARNIE
STEARIN
S ENTASIS
  NASTIES
  SESTINA
  TANSIES
  TISANES
T INSTATE
  SATINET
U AUNTIES
  SINUATE
V NAIVEST
  NATIVES
  VAINEST
W AWNIEST
  TAWNIES
  WANIEST
  WANTIES
Z ZANIEST

AEIPRS 75
PRAISE
A SPIRAEA
C EPACRIS
  SCRAPIE
  SPACIER
D ASPIRED
  DESPAIR
  DIAPERS
  PRAISED
E APERIES
  EPEIRAS
G GASPIER
  PRISAGE
  SPAIRGE
H HARPIES
  SHARPIE
K PARKIES
  SPARKIE
L PALSIER
  PARLIES
M IMPRESA
  SAMPIRE
N RAPINES
O SOAPIER
P APPRISE
  SAPPIER
R PARRIES
  PRAISER
  RAPIERS
  RASPIER
  REPAIRS
S ASPIRES
  PARESIS
  PRAISES
  SPIREAS
T PARTIES
  PASTIER
  PIASTRE
  PIRATES
  PRATIES
  TRAIPSE
U SPURIAE
  UPRAISE
V PARVISE
W WASPIER

AEIRST 3
SATIRE
A ARISTAE
  ASTERIA
  ATRESIA
B BAITERS
  BARITES

C CRISTAE
  RACIEST
  STEARIC
D ARIDEST
  ASTERID
  ASTRIDE
  DIASTER
  DISRATE
  STAIDER
  STAIRED
  TARDIES
  TIRADES
E AERIEST
  SERIATE
F FAIREST
G AGISTER
  GAITERS
  STAGIER
  STRIGAE
  TRIAGES
H HASTIER
  SHERIAT
I AIRIEST
  IRISATE
K ARKITES
  KARITES
L REALIST
  RETAILS
  SALTIER
  SALTIRE
  SLATIER
M IMARETS
  MAESTRI
  MAISTER
  MASTIER
  MISRATE
  SEMITAR
  SMARTIE
N ANESTRI
  ANTSIER
  NASTIER
  RATINES
  RESIANT
  RETAINS
  RETINAS
  RETSINA
  STAINER
  STARNIE
  STEARIN
O OARIEST
  OTARIES
P PARTIES
  PASTIER
  PIASTRE
  PIRATES
  PRATIES
  TRAIPSE
R ARTSIER
  SERRATI
  TARRIES
  TARSIER
S ARTSIES
  SAIREST
  SATIRES
  TIRASSE
T ARTIEST
  ARTISTE
  ATTIRES
  IRATEST
  STRIATE
  TASTIER
  TERTIAS
V TAIVERS
  VASTIER
W WAISTER
  WAITERS
  WARIEST

AEIRTT 29
ATTIRE
A ARIETTA
B BATTIER
  BIRETTA
C CATTIER
  CITRATE
D ATTIRED
E ARIETTE
  ITERATE
F FATTIER
L TERTIAL
N INTREAT
  ITERANT
  NATTIER
  NITRATE
  TARTINE
  TERTIAN
P PARTITE
R RATTIER
  RETRAIT
S ARTIEST
  ARTISTE
  ATTIRES
  IRATEST
  STRIATE
  TASTIER
  TERTIAS
T ATTRITE
  TATTIER
  TITRATE
V TAIVERT
W TAWTIER
X EXTRAIT

AEISTT 83
(TASTIE)
A SATIATE
B BATISTE
C CATTIES
  STATICE
  TIETACS
F FATTIES
H ATHEIST
  STAITHE
K TAKIEST
M MATIEST
  MATTIES
N INSTATE
  SATINET
O OSTIATE
  TOASTIE
P PATTIES
  TAPETIS
R ARTIEST
  ARTISTE
  ATTIRES
  IRATEST
  STRIATE
  TASTIER
  TERTIAS
T TATTIES
U SITUATE
V STATIVE
W TAWIEST
  TWAITES
Y SATIETY

AELMNT 211
LAMENT
A AMENTAL
B BELTMAN
  LAMBENT
D MANTLED
E MANTEEL
I AILMENT
  ALIMENT
M MALTMEN

Column 1

```
O LOMENTA
  OMENTAL
  TELAMON
S LAMENTS
  MANTELS
  MANTLES
T MANTLET
U NUTMEAL

AELNRS 63
LEARNS
A ARSENAL
B BRANLES
  BRANSLE
C LANCERS
  RANCELS
D DARNELS
  ENLARDS
  LANDERS
  SLANDER
  SNARLED
F SALFERN
G ANGLERS
  LARGENS
  SLANGER
I NAILERS
K RANKLES
N ENSNARL
  LANNERS
O ORLEANS
P PLANERS
  REPLANS
R SNARLER
S RANSELS
T ANTLERS
  RENTALS
  SALTERN
  STERNAL
Z RANZELS

AELNRT 28
ANTLER
B BRANTLE
C CENTRAL
E ALTERNE
  ENTERAL
  ETERNAL
G TANGLER
  TRANGLE
H ENTHRAL
I ENTRAIL
  LATRINE
  RATLINE
  RELIANT
  RETINAL
  TRENAIL
L ENTRALL
N LANTERN
P PANTLER
  PLANTER
  REPLANT
S ANTLERS
  RENTALS
  SALTERN
  STERNAL
T TRENTAL
U NEUTRAL
V VENTRAL

AELNST 34
LATENS
A SEALANT
C CANTLES
  CENTALS
  LANCETS
  SCANTLE
D DENTALS
  SLANTED
E ELANETS
```

Column 2

```
  LATEENS
  LEANEST
G LANGEST
  TANGLES
H HANTLES
I EASTLIN
  ELASTIN
  ENTAILS
  SALIENT
  SLAINTE
  STANIEL
  TENAILS
K ANKLETS
  ASKLENT
  LANKEST
M LAMENTS
  MANTELS
  MANTLES
N STANNEL
O ETALONS
P PLANETS
  PLATENS
R ANTLERS
  RENTALS
  SALTERN
  STERNAL
T LATTENS
  TALENTS
U ELUANTS
  UNLASTE
V LEVANTS
Y STANYEL
Z ZELANTS

AELORS 42
(ALOSER)
B LABROSE
C CLAROES
  COALERS
  ESCOLAR
  ORACLES
D LOADERS
  ORDEALS
  RELOADS
E AREOLES
F LOAFERS
  SAFROLE
G GAOLERS
H SHOALER
L ROSELLA
M MORALES
N ORLEANS
O AEROSOL
  ROSEOLA
P REPOSAL
  REPOSAL
S OARLESS
  SOLERAS
T OESTRAL

AELOST 46
(SOLATE)
B BOATELS
  OBLATES
C ALECOST
  LACTOSE
  LOCATES
  SCATOLE
  TALCOSE
D SALTOED
E OLEATES
F FOLATES
G LEGATOS
H LOATHES
I ISOLATE
K SKATOLE
M MALTOSE
N ETALONS
P APOSTLE
```

Column 3

```
  PELOTAS
R OESTRAL
V SOLVATE
Z ZEALOTS

AELPRS 231
(PALERS)
A EARLAPS
C CARPELS
  CLASPER
  CRAPLES
  PARCELS
  PLACERS
  SCALPER
D PEDLARS
E LEAPERS
  PLEASER
  RELAPSE
  REPEALS
F FELSPAR
G GRAPLES
H SPHERAL
I PALSIER
  PARLIES
K SPARKLE
M EMPARLS
  LAMPERS
  PALMERS
  SAMPLER
N PLANERS
  REPLANS
O PAROLES
  REPOSAL
P LAPPERS
  RAPPELS
  SLAPPER
R PARRELS
T PALTERS
  PLASTER
  PLATERS
  PSALTER
  STAPLER
U PERUSAL
  SERPULA
W PRAWLES
Y PARLEYS
  PARSLEY
  PLAYERS
  REPLAYS
  SPARELY

AELPRT 206
PLATER
A APTERAL
C PLECTRA
E PLEATER
  PRELATE
I PLAITER
  PLATIER
M TRAMPLE
N PANTLER
  PLANTER
  REPLANT
O PROLATE
S PALTERS
  PLASTER
  PLATERS
  PSALTER
  STAPLER
T PARTLET
  PLATTER
  PRATTLE
Y PEARTLY
  PRELATY
  PTERYLA
```

Column 4

```
AELRST 38
ALERTS
B ALBERTS
  BATLERS
  BLASTER
  LABRETS
  STABLER
C CARTELS
  CLARETS
  SCARLET
  TARCELS
D DARTLES
E ELATERS
  REALEST
  RELATES
  STEALER
F FALTERS
G LARGEST
H HALTERS
  HARSLET
  LATHERS
  SLATHER
I REALIST
  RETAILS
  SALTIER
  SALTIRE
  SLATIER
K STALKER
  TALKERS
L STELLAR
  TELLARS
M ARMLETS
  MARTELS
N ANTLERS
  RENTALS
  SALTERN
  STERNAL
O OESTRAL
P PALTERS
  PLASTER
  PLATERS
  PSALTER
  STAPLER
S ARTLESS
  LASTERS
  SALTERS
  SLATERS
  TARSELS
T RATTLES
  SLATTER
  STARLET
  STARTLE
  TATLERS
U SALUTER
V TRAVELS
  VARLETS
  VESTRAL
W WASTREL
Y RAYLETS

AEMNST 168
STAMEN
A NAMASTE
B BATSMEN
D TANDEMS
E ENTAMES
  MEANEST
G MAGNETS
H ANTHEMS
  HETMANS
I INMATES
  MAINEST
  MANTIES
  TAMINES
L LAMENTS
  MANTELS
  MANTLES
O MANTOES
```

Column 5

```
P ENSTAMP
  TAPSMEN
R ARTSMEN
  MARTENS
  SARMENT
  SMARTEN
S STAMENS
U UNTAMES
  UNTEAMS
Y AMNESTY

AEMRST 124
MATERS
A AMEARST
  RETAMAS
B TAMBERS
C MERCATS
D SMARTED
E STEAMER
  TEAMERS
H HAMSTER
I IMARETS
  MAESTRI
  MAISTER
  MASTIER
  MISRATE
  SEMITAR
  SMARTIE
J RAMJETS
K MARKETS
L ARMLETS
  MARTELS
M STAMMER
N ARTSMEN
  MARTENS
  SARMENT
  SMARTEN
O AMORETS
  MAESTRO
  OMERTAS
P EMPARTS
  STAMPER
  TAMPERS
R SMARTER
S MASTERS
  STREAMS
T MATTERS
  SMATTER
U MATURES
  STRUMAE
W WARMEST
Y MASTERY
  MAYSTER
  STREAMY

AENNST 152
(ANNETS)
A ANNATES
C NASCENT
D STANDEN
E NEATENS
F ENFANTS
G GANNETS
I INANEST
K KANTENS
L STANNEL
R TANNERS
T TANNEST
  TENANTS
W WANNEST

AENPST 185
PATENS
A ANAPEST
  PEASANT
C CATNEPS
D PEDANTS
  PENTADS
E NEPETAS
```

Column 6

```
  PENATES
  PESANTE
H HAPTENS
I PANTIES
  PATINES
  SAPIENT
  SPINATE
L PLANETS
  PLATENS
M ENSTAMP
  TAPSMEN
R ARPENTS
  ENTRAPS
  PANTERS
  PARENTS
  PASTERN
  PERSANT
  TREPANS
S APTNESS
  PATNESS
  PESANTS
T PATENTS
  PATTENS
U PEANUTS
  PESAUNT
W STEWPAN
Y SYNAPTE
Z PEZANTS

AENRRT 87
ERRANT
A NARRATE
E TERRANE
G GRANTER
  REGRANT
I RETRAIN
  TERRAIN
  TRAINER
O ORNATER
P PARTNER
S ERRANTS
  RANTERS
T TRANTER
Y TERNARY

AENRSS 223
SNARES
A NARASES
C ANCRESS
  CASERNS
D SANDERS
  SARSDEN
E ENSEARS
F FARNESS
G SERANGS
H HARNESS
I ARSINES
  SARNIES
K KRANSES
L RANSELS
O REASONS
R SERRANS
  SNARERS
S SARSENS
T SARSNET
  TRANSES
W ANSWERS
  RAWNESS
Y SARNEYS

AENRST 9
ASTERN
A ANESTRA
B BANTERS
C CANTERS
  CARNETS
  NECTARS
  RECANTS
  SCANTER
```

TANRECS
TRANCES
D ENDARTS
STANDER
STARNED
E EARNEST
EASTERN
NEAREST
G ARGENTS
GARNETS
STRANGE
H ANTHERS
HARTENS
THENARS
I ANESTRI
ANTSIER
NASTIER
RATINES
RESIANT
RETAINS
RETINAS
RETSINA
STAINER
STARNIE
STEARIN
K RANKEST
STARKEN
TANKERS
L ANTLERS
RENTALS
SALTERN
STERNAL
M ARTSMEN
MARTENS
SARMENT
SMARTEN
N TANNERS
O ATONERS
SENATOR
TREASON
P ARPENTS
ENTRAPS
PANTERS
PARENTS
PASTERN
PERSANT
TREPANS
R ERRANTS
RANTERS
S SARSNET
TRANSES
T NATTERS
RATTENS
U AUNTERS
NATURES
SAUNTER
V SERVANT
TAVERNS
VERSANT
W STRAWEN
WANTERS
Y TRAYNES

AENRTT 71
NATTER
A TARTANE
C TRANECT
D TRANTED
E ENTREAT
RATTEEN
TERNATE
I INTREAT
ITERANT
NATTIER
NITRATE
TARTINE
TERTIAN
L TRENTAL
N ENTRANT

P PATTERN
REPTANT
R TRANTER
S NATTERS
RATTENS
U TAUNTER
Y NATTERY

AENSTT 116
(ATTENS)
B BATTENS
C CANTEST
D ATTENDS
E NEATEST
F FATTENS
G GESTANT
I INSTATE
SATINET
L LATTENS
TALENTS
N TANNEST
TENANTS
O ATTONES
NOTATES
P PATENTS
PATTENS
R NATTERS
RATTENS
T ATTENTS
U ATTUNES
NUTATES
TAUTENS
TETANUS
UNSTATE
X SEXTANT

AEORST 13
ORATES
B BOASTER
BOATERS
BORATES
SORBATE
C COASTER
COATERS
D DOATERS
ROASTED
TORSADE
TROADES
E ROSEATE
G ORGEATS
STORAGE
TOERAGS
H ASTHORE
EARSHOT
HAROSET
I OARIEST
OTARIES
L OESTRAL
M AMORETS
MAESTRO
OMERTAS
N ATONERS
SENATOR
TREASON
P ESPARTO
PROTEAS
SEAPORT
R ROASTER
T ROTATES
TOASTER

AEPRST 129
PATERS
A PETARAS
C CARPETS
PRECAST
SPECTRA
D DEPARTS
DRAPETS

PETARDS
E REPEATS
G PARGETS
H SPARTHE
TEPHRAS
THREAPS
I PARTIES
PASTIER
PIASTRE
PIRATES
PRATIES
TRAIPSE
L PALTERS
PLASTER
PLATERS
PSALTER
STAPLER
M EMPARTS
STAMPER
TAMPERS
N ARPENTS
ENTRAPS
PANTERS
PARENTS
PASTERN
PERSANT
TREPANS
O ESPARTO
PROTEAS
SEAPORT
P TAPPERS
R PARTERS
PRATERS
S PASTERS
REPASTS
SPAREST
T PATTERS
SPATTER
TAPSTER
U PASTURE
UPRATES
UPSTARE
UPTEARS
Y YAPSTER
Z PATZERS

AERRST 138
RATERS
B BARRETS
BARTERS
C CARTERS
CRATERS
TRACERS
D DARTERS
DARTRES
RETARDS
STARRED
TRADERS
E SERRATE
TEARERS
F FRATERS
RAFTERS
G GARRETS
GARTERS
GRATERS
I ARTSIER
SERRATI
TARRIES
TARSIER
K KARTERS
KRATERS
STARKER
M SMARTER
N ERRANTS
RANTERS
O ROASTER
P PARTERS
PRATERS
S ARRESTS

RASTERS
STARERS
T RATTERS
RESTART
STARTER
Y STRAYER

AERSST 220
ASSERT
A SEARATS
B BASTERS
BESTARS
BRASSET
BREASTS
C ACTRESS
CASTERS
RECASTS
E RESEATS
SAETERS
SEAREST
SEATERS
STEARES
TEASERS
TESSERA
F FASTERS
STRAFES
G GASTERS
STAGERS
H RASHEST
SHASTER
TRASHES
I ARTSIES
SAIREST
SATIRES
TIRASSE
K SKATERS
STRAKES
STREAKS
TASKERS
L ARTLESS
LASTERS
SALTERS
SLATERS
TARSELS
M MASTERS
STREAMS
N SARSNET
TRANSES
P PASTERS
REPASTS
SPAREST
R ARRESTS
RASTERS
STARERS
S ASSERTS
TRASSES
T ASTERTS
STARETS
STATERS
TASTERS
V STARVES
W WASTERS
Y ESTRAYS
STAYERS
STAYRES

AERSTT 97
TASTER
B BATTERS
TABRETS
C SCATTER
D STARTED
TETRADS
E ESTREAT
RESTATE
G TARGETS
H HATTERS
RATHEST
SHATTER

THREATS
I ARTIEST
ARTISTE
ATTIRES
IRATEST
STRIATE
TASTIER
TERTIAS
L RATTLES
SLATTER
STARLET
STARTLE
TATLERS
M MATTERS
SMATTER
N NATTERS
RATTENS
O ROTATES
TOASTER
P PATTERS
SPATTER
TAPSTER
R RATTERS
RESTART
STARTER
S ASTERTS
STARETS
STATERS
TASTERS
T STRETTA
TARTEST
TATTERS
U ASTUTER
STATURE
V VATTERS
W SWATTER
TEWARTS
Y YATTERS
Z STARETZ

AERSTW 194
WATERS
A AWAREST
B BRAWEST
WABSTER
D STEWARD
STRAWED
E SWEATER
F FRETSAW
WAFTERS
H THAWERS
WREATHS
I WAISTER
WAITERS
WARIEST
L WASTREL
M WARMEST
N STRAWEN
WANTERS
S WASTERS
T SWATTER
TEWARTS
Y WASTERY

AGILNR 199
(RALING)
B BLARING
C CARLING
D DARLING
LARDING
E ENGRAIL
LAERING
LEARING
NARGILE
REALIGN
REGINAL
F FLARING
G GLARING

H HARLING
I GLAIRIN
LAIRING
RAILING
K LARKING
M MARLING
N LARNING
O RANGOLI
P PARLING
T RATLING
W WARLING
Y ANGRILY
NARGILY
RAYLING

AGILNS 219
SIGNAL
A AGNAILS
B SABLING
C LACINGS
SCALING
D LADINGS
LIGANDS
E LEASING
LINAGES
SEALING
F FALSING
G GINGALS
LAGGINS
H HALSING
LASHING
SHALING
I AISLING
NILGAIS
SAILING
J JINGALS
K SLAKING
M LINGAMS
MALIGNS
N LINSANG
P LAPSING
PALINGS
SAPLING
S LASINGS
SIGNALS
T ANGLIST
LASTING
SALTING
SLATING
STALING
U LINGUAS
NILGAUS
SALUING
V SALVING
SLAVING
VALSING
W LAWINGS
SWALING
Y LAYINGS
SLAYING

AGILNT 174
(LATING)
B TABLING
C CATLING
TALCING
E ATINGLE
ELATING
GELATIN
GENITAL
F FATLING
H HALTING
LATHING
I TAILING
K TALKING
M MALTING
N TANLING
O ANTILOG
P PLATING

R RATLING
S ANGLIST
  LASTING
  SALTING
  SLATING
  STALING
Y GIANTLY

AGINRS 123
GRAINS
A NAGARIS
  SANGRIA
  SARANGI
B SABRING
C ARCINGS
  RACINGS
  SACRING
  SCARING
D DARINGS
  GRADINS
E ANGRIES
  EARINGS
  ERASING
  GAINERS
  GRAINES
  REGAINS
  REGINAS
  SEARING
  SERINGA
F FARSING
G RAGINGS
  SIRGANG
H GARNISH
  RASHING
  SHARING
I AIRINGS
  ARISING
  RAGINIS
  RAISING
  SAIRING
K RAKINGS
  SARKING
M MARGINS
N SNARING
O IGNAROS
  ORIGANS
  SIGNORA
  SOARING
P PARINGS
  PARSING
  RASPING
  SPARING
T GASTRIN
  GRATINS
  RATINGS
  STARING
  TARINGS
V RAVINGS
W RAWINGS
Y SIGNARY
  SYRINGA

AGINRT 69
RATING
A GRANITA
C CARTING
  CRATING
  TRACING
D DARTING
  TRADING
E GRANITE
  GRATINE
  INGRATE
  TANGIER
  TEARING
F FARTING
  INGRAFT
  RAFTING
G GRATING

  TARGING
I AIRTING
  RAITING
K KARTING
L RATLING
M MARTING
  MIGRANT
N RANTING
O ORATING
  ROATING
P PARTING
  PRATING
  TRAPING
R TARRING
S GASTRIN
  GRATINS
  RATINGS
  STARING
  TARINGS
T RATTING
Y GIANTRY

AGINST 108
SATING
A AGAINST
  GITANAS
B BASTING
C ACTINGS
  CASTING
D DATINGS
E EASTING
  EATINGS
  GAINEST
  GENISTA
  INGATES
  INGESTA
  SEATING
  TANGIES
  TEASING
  TSIGANE
F FASTING
G GASTING
  GATINGS
  STAGING
H HASTING
  TASHING
K SKATING
  STAKING
  TAKINGS
  TASKING
L ANGLIST
  LASTING
  SALTING
  SLATING
  STALING
M MASTING
N ANTINGS
  STANING
O AGONIST
  GITANOS
P PASTING
R GASTRIN
  GRATINS
  RATINGS
  STARING
  TARINGS
T STATING
  TASTING
U SAUTING
V STAVING
W STAWING
  TAWINGS
  WASTING
X TAXINGS
Y STAYING

AINRST 40
TRAINS
A ANTIARS
  ARTISAN
  TSARINA
D INDARTS
E ANESTRI
  ANTSIER
  NASTIER
  RATINES
  RESIANT
  RETAINS
  RETINAS
  RETSINA
  STAINER
  STARNIE
  STEARIN
G GASTRIN
  GRATINS
  STARING
  TARINGS
H TARNISH
L RATLINS
M MARTINS
O AROINTS
  RATIONS
P SPIRANT
  SPRAINT
Q QINTARS
S INSTARS
  SANTIRS
  STRAINS
T STRAINT
  TRANSIT
U NUTRIAS

AINSTT 213
TAINTS
A ATTAINS
D DISTANT
E INSTATE
  SATINET
G STATING
  TASTING
I TITANIS
  TITIANS
M MATTINS
N INSTANT
O STATION
R STRAINT
  TRANSIT
S TANISTS

ANORST 60
(STAR ON)
A TORANAS
B BARTONS
C CANTORS
  CARTONS
  CONTRAS
  CRATONS
E ATONERS
  SENATOR
  TREASON
I AROINTS
  RATIONS
L LATRONS
M MATRONS
  TRANSOM
N NATRONS
O RATOONS
P PARTONS
  PATRONS
  TARPONS
T ATTORNS
  RATTONS
  ROTTANS
U ROUSANT

  SANTOUR
Y AROYNTS

BDEIRS 242
BRIDES
A BRAISED
  DARBIES
  SEABIRD
  SIDEBAR
B DIBBERS
C SCRIBED
D BIDDERS
E DERBIES
G BEGIRDS
  BRIDGES
I BIRDIES
  BRIDIES
K BRISKED
L BIRSLED
  BRIDLES
N BINDERS
  REBINDS
O BORIDES
  DISROBE
R BIRDERS
T BESTRID
  BISTRED
U BRUISED
  BURDIES
V VERBIDS

BEILRS 205
LIBERS
A BAILERS
B LIBBERS
D BIRSLED
  BRIDLES
E BELIERS
G GERBILS
I RISIBLE
J JERBILS
  JIRBLES
K BILKERS
M LIMBERS
N BERLINS
O BOILERS
  LIBEROS
  REBOILS
R BIRLERS
S BIRSLES
  RIBLESS
T BLISTER
  BRISTLE
  RIBLETS

BEIRST 184
TRIBES
A BAITERS
  BARITES
D BESTRID
  BISTRED
E REBITES
F FIBSTER
H HERBIST
I BITSIER
K BRISKET
L BLISTER
  BRISTLE
  RIBLETS
M BETRIMS
  TIMBERS
  TIMBRES
O ORBIEST
  SORBITE
S BESTIRS
  BISTERS
  BISTRES
T BITTERS
U BUSTIER

  RUBIEST

BEORST 225
STROBE
A BOASTER
  BOATERS
  BORATES
  SORBATE
D DEBTORS
  STROBED
H BOSHTER
  BOTHERS
I ORBIEST
  SORBITE
L BOLSTER
  BOLTERS
  LOBSTER
M BESTORM
  MOBSTER
N BRETONS
  SORBENT
O BOOSTER
  REBOOTS
P BESPORT
S BESORTS
  SORBETS
  STROBES
T BETTORS
U OBTUSER
V OBVERTS

CEINOS 109
COSINE
A ACINOSE
B EBONICS
C CONCISE
D CONDIES
  SECONDI
E SENECIO
G COGNISE
  COIGNES
I ICONISE
  CINEOLS
L CONSEIL
  INCLOSE
M INCOMES
  MESONIC
N CONINES
R COINERS
  CRINOSE
  CRONIES
  ORCEINS
  ORCINES
  RECOINS
  SERICON
S CESSION
  COSINES
T NOTICES
  SECTION
V NOVICES

CEINRS 183
(NICERS)
A ARSENIC
  CARNIES
  CERASIN
D CINDERS
  DISCERN
  RESCIND
E CERESIN
  SCRIENE
  SINCERE
G CRINGES
H NICHERS
  RICHENS
I IRENICS
  SERICIN
  SIRENIC
K NICKERS

  SNICKER
M CREMSIN
  MINCERS
O COINERS
  CRINOSE
  CRONIES
  ORCEINS
  ORCINES
  RECOINS
  SERICON
P PINCERS
  PRINCES
S SCRINES
T CISTERN
  CRETINS
V CRIVENS
W WINCERS

CEINST 196
INSECT
A CANIEST
  CINEAST
E ENTICES
F INFECTS
H ETHNICS
  STHENIC
I INCITES
J INJECTS
K SNICKET
  TICKENS
L CLIENTS
  LECTINS
  STENCIL
O NOTICES
  SECTION
P INCEPTS
  INSPECT
  PECTINS
  PEINCTS
R CISTERN
  CRETINS
S INCESTS
  INSECTS
Y CYSTINE

CEIORS 156
COSIER
A ORACIES
  SCORIAE
B CORBIES
C CICEROS
D DISCOER
H COHEIRS
  HEROICS
L RECOILS
N COINERS
  CRINOSE
  CRONIES
  ORCEINS
  ORCINES
  RECOINS
  SERICON
P COPIERS
  COPSIER
  PERSICO
R CIRROSE
  CORRIES
  CROSIER
S COSIERS
T EROTICS
  TERCIOS
U SCOURIE
V CORSIVE
  VOICERS
W COWRIES
  SCOWRIE
Z COZIERS

CEIRST 166
CITERS
A CRISTAE
  RACIEST
  STEARIC
C CRETICS
D CREDITS
  DIRECTS
E CERITES
  RECITES
  TIERCES
H CITHERS
  ESTRICH
  RICHEST
I ERISTIC
  RICIEST
K RICKETS
  STICKER
  TICKERS
L RELICTS
M CRETISM
  METRICS
N CISTERN
  CRETINS
O EROTICS
  TERCIOS
P TRICEPS
T TRISECT
U CUITERS
  CURITES
  ICTERUS
W TWICERS

CENORS 172
(CONERS)
A CARNOSE
  COARSEN
  CORNEAS
  EARCONS
D CONDERS
  CORSNED
  SCORNED
E ENCORES
  NECROSE
F CONFERS
G CONGERS
I COINERS
  CRINOSE
  CRONIES
  ORCEINS
  ORCINES
  RECOINS
  SERICON
K CONKERS
  RECKONS
L CORNELS
N CONNERS
O CEROONS
P CREPONS
R CORNERS
  SCORNER
S CENSORS
T CONSTER
  CORNETS
  CRESTON
  CRONETS
U CONURES
  ROUNCES

CENOST 224
CENTOS
A COSTEAN
  OCTANES
D DOCENTS
E CENOTES
F CONFEST
G CONGEST
H NOTCHES
  TECHNOS

I NOTICES
  SECTION
K NOCKETS
N CONSENT
  NOCENTS
R CONSTER
  CORNETS
  CRESTON
  CRONETS
T CONTEST
U CONTUSE
  ECONUTS
V COVENTS

CEORST 234
ESCORT
A COASTER
  COATERS
H HECTORS
  ROCHETS
  ROTCHES
  TOCHERS
  TORCHES
  TROCHES
I EROTICS
  TERCIOS
K RESTOCK
  ROCKETS
  STOCKER
L COLTERS
  CORSLET
  COSTREL
  LECTORS
N CONSTER
  CORNETS
  CRESTON
  CRONETS
O SCOOTER
P COPTERS
R RECTORS
S CORSETS
  COSTERS
  ESCORTS
  SCOTERS
  SECTORS
T COTTERS
U COUTERS
  CROUTES
  SCOUTER
V CORVETS
  COVERTS
  VECTORS

DEEINR 43
DENIER
B BENDIER
  INBREED
C CEDRINE
E NEEDIER
F DEFINER
  ENFIRED
  FENDIER
  REFINED
G DREEING
  ENERGID
  GREINED
  REEDING
  REIGNED
H INHERED
L RELINED
M ERMINED
O ORDINEE
P REPINED
  RIPENED
R DERNIER
  NERDIER
S DENIERS
  NEREIDS
  RESINED

U UREDINE
W WIDENER
X INDEXER

DEEIRS 58
DESIRE
A DEARIES
  READIES
B DERBIES
C DECRIES
D DERIDES
  DESIRED
  DIEDRES
  RESIDED
E SEEDIER
F DEFIERS
G SEDGIER
L RESILED
M REMEIDS
  REMISED
N DENIERS
  NEREIDS
  RESINED
O OREIDES
  OSIERED
P PREDIES
  PRESIDE
  SPEIRED
R DERRIES
  DESIRER
  RESIDER
  SERRIED
S DESIRES
  RESIDES
T DIETERS
  REISTED
U RESIDUE
  UREIDES
V DERIVES
  DEVISER
  DIVERSE
  REVISED

DEELNS 239
(ENDLES)
A LEADENS
B BLENDES
D LEDDENS
E NEEDLES
F FLENSED
G LEGENDS
I ENISLED
  ENSILED
  LINSEED
L SNELLED
R LENDERS
  SLENDER
S ENDLESS
T DENTELS
  NESTLED
W WEDELNS
Y DENSELY

DEENRS 92
(ENDERS)
A DEANERS
  ENDEARS
B BENDERS
C DECERNS
  SCERNED
D REDDENS
E NEEDERS
  SERENED
  SNEERED
F FENDERS
G GENDERS
H HERDENS
I DENIERS
  NEREIDS

  RESINED
L LENDERS
  SLENDER
M MENDERS
O ENDORSE
P SPENDER
R RENDERS
S REDNESS
  SENDERS
T STERNED
  TENDERS
  TENDRES
U ENDURES
  ENSURED
V VENDERS
Z DZERENS

DEENST 111
NESTED
A STANDEE
  STEANED
C DESCENT
  SCENTED
D STENDED
E STEENED
I DESTINE
  ENDITES
  STEINED
L DENTELS
  NESTLED
M DEMENTS
N DENNETS
  STENNED
O DENOTES
R STERNED
  TENDERS
  TENDRES
S DENSEST
T DETENTS
  STENTED
U DETENUS
  DETUNES
X EXTENDS

DEERST 151
RESTED
A DEAREST
  DERATES
  ESTRADE
  REASTED
  REDATES
  SEDATER
  STEARED
  TASERED
C CRESTED
D REDDEST
  TEDDERS
E REESTED
  STEERED
I DIETERS
  REISTED
N STERNED
  TENDERS
  TENDRES
O OERSTED
  ROSETED
  TEREDOS
P PRESTED
S DESERTS
  DESSERT
  TRESSED
V STERVED
  VERDETS
W STREWED
  WRESTED
X DEXTERS
Y DYESTER

DEGILN 164
DINGLE
A ALIGNED
  DEALING
  LEADING
B BINGLED
E DELEING
G GELDING
  NIGGLED
H HINDLEG
I EILDING
  ELIDING
J JINGLED
M MEDLING
  MELDING
  MINGLED
N LENDING
O GLENOID
P PINGLED
S DINGLES
  ELDINGS
  ENGILDS
  SINGLED
T GLINTED
  TINGLED
U ELUDING
  INDULGE
V DELVING
  DEVLING
W WELDING

DEGINR 82
RINGED
A AREDING
  DEARING
  DERAIGN
  EARDING
  GRADINE
  GRAINED
  READING
B BREDING
C CRINGED
D GRINDED
  REDDING
E DREEING
  ENERGID
  GREINED
  REEDING
  REIGNED
F FRINGED
H HERDING
I DINGIER
N GRINNED
  RENDING
O ERODING
  GROINED
  IGNORED
  NEGROID
  REDOING
R GRINDER
  REGRIND
S DINGERS
  ENGIRDS
U DUNGIER
W REDWING
  WRINGED
Y YERDING

DEGINS 154
SIGNED
A AGNISED
E SDEIGNE
  SEEDING
G EDGINGS
  SNIGGED
I DINGIES
L ELDINGS
  ENGILDS

  SINGLED
M SMIDGEN
N ENDINGS
  SENDING
O DINGOES
R DINGERS
  ENGIRDS
S DESIGNS
  SDEIGNS
T NIDGETS
  STEDING
  STINGED
U GUNDIES
  SUEDING
W SWINDGE
  SWINGED
Y DINGEYS
  DYEINGS

DEGIRS 210
DIRGES
A AGRISED
B BEGIRDS
  BRIDGES
E SEDGIER
F FRIDGES
G DIGGERS
I DIRIGES
L GILDERS
  GIRDLES
  GLIDERS
  GRISLED
  LIDGERS
  RIDGELS
N DINGERS
  ENGIRDS
R GIRDERS
  RIDGERS
S DIGRESS
U GUIDERS

DEILNS 120
(INDLES)
A DENIALS
  SNAILED
D DINDLES
  SLIDDEN
E ENISLED
  ENSILED
  LINSEED
G DINGLES
  ELDINGS
  ENGILDS
  SINGLED
I INISLED
K KINDLES
M MILDENS
N DINNLES
  LINDENS
O DOLINES
  INDOLES
  SONDELI
P SPELDIN
  SPINDLE
  SPLINED
T DENTILS
W SWINDLE
  WINDLES
Y SNIDELY

DEILRT 73
(TRIDLE)
A DILATER
  TRAILED
B DRIBLET
D TIDDLER
E RETILED
F FLIRTED
  TRIFLED

H THIRLED
K KIRTLED
L TRILLED
N TENDRIL
  TRINDLE
O DOILTER
P TRIPLED
U DILUTER
W TWIRLED
Y TIREDLY

DEINOS 41
ONSIDE
A ADONISE
  ANODISE
  SODAINE
C CONDIES
  SECONDI
D NODDIES
G DINGOES
H HOIDENS
I IODINES
  IONISED
L DOLINES
  INDOLES
  SONDELI
M MISDONE
N ONDINES
P DISPONE
  SPINODE
R DONSIER
  INDORSE
  ROSINED
S ONSIDES
T DITONES
  STONIED

DEINRS 51
DINERS
A RANDIES
  SANDIER
  SARDINE
B BINDERS
  REBINDS
C CINDERS
  DISCERN
  RESCIND
E DENIERS
  NEREIDS
  RESINED
F FINDERS
  FRIENDS
G DINGERS
  ENGIRDS
H HINDERS
  SHRINED
I INSIDER
K KINDERS
  KINREDS
  REDSKIN
M MINDERS
  REMINDS
N DINNERS
O DONSIER
  INDORSE
  ROSINED
P PINDERS
T TINDERS
U INSURED
V VERDINS
W REWINDS
  WINDERS

DEINRU 52
RUINED
A UNAIRED
  URANIDE
C INDUCER
D UNDRIED

E UREDINE
F UNFIRED
G DUNGIER
H UNHIRED
I URIDINE
J INJURED
M UNRIMED
N DUNNIER
  INURNED
O DOURINE
S INSURED
T INTRUDE
  TURDINE
  UNTIRED
  UNTRIDE
  UNTRIED
W UNWIRED

DEINST 32
(SINTED)
A DETAINS
  INSTEAD
  SAINTED
  SATINED
  STAINED
B BIDENTS
D DISTEND
E DESTINE
  ENDITES
  STEINED
F SNIFTED
G NIDGETS
  STEDING
  STINGED
I INDITES
  TINEIDS
K DINKEST
  KINDEST
L DENTILS
M MINDSET
N DENTINS
  INDENTS
  INTENDS
O DITONES
  STONIED
P STIPEND
R TINDERS
S DISNEST
  DISSENT
  SNIDEST
T DENTIST
  DISTENT
  STINTED
U DISTUNE
  DUNITES
Y DENSITY
  DESTINY

DEIORS 27
(ORIDES)
A ROADIES
  SOREDIA
B BORIDES
  DISROBE
C DISCOER
D DORISED
  SODDIER
E OREIDES
  OSIERED
H RHODIES
L SOLDIER
  SOLIDER
M MISDOER
  MOIDERS
N DONSIER
  INDORSE
  ROSINED
O OROIDES
P PERIODS

S DORISES
  DOSSIER
T EDITORS
  ROISTED
  ROSITED
  SORTIED
  STEROID
  STORIED
  TIERODS
  TRIODES
V DEVISOR
  DEVOIRS
  VISORED
  VOIDERS
W DOWRIES
  ROWDIES
  WEIRDOS
Z DORIZES

DEIOST 35
(ODSITE)
A IODATES
  TOADIES
C CESTOID
  COTISED
D TODDIES
F FOISTED
H HOISTED
J JOISTED
M DOMIEST
  MODISTE
  MOISTED
N DITONES
  STONIED
O OSTEOID
P DEPOSIT
  DOPIEST
  PODITES
  POSITED
  SOPITED
  TOPSIDE
R EDITORS
  ROISTED
  ROSITED
  SORTIED
  STEROID
  STORIED
  TIERODS
  TRIODES
T DOTIEST
  STOITED
U OUTSIDE
  TEDIOUS
V DOVIEST
W DOWIEST
X EXODIST
Z DOZIEST

DEIPRT 215
(TRIPED)
A DIPTERA
  PARTIED
  PIRATED
C PREDICT
E TEPIDER
I RIPTIDE
L TRIPLED
M DIREMPT
N PRINTED
O DIOPTER
  DIOPTRE
  PERIDOT
  PROTEID
P TRIPPED
S SPIRTED
  STRIPED

DEIRST 57
STRIDE
A ARIDEST
  ASTERID
  ASTRIDE
  DIASTER
  DISRATE
  STAIDER
  STAIRED
  TARDIES
  TIRADES
B BESTRID
  BISTRED
C CREDITS
  DIRECTS
E DIETERS
  REISTED
F FRISTED
H DITHERS
  SHIRTED
I DIRTIES
  DITSIER
K SKIRTED
N TINDERS
O EDITORS
  ROISTED
  ROSITED
  SORTIED
  STEROID
  STORIED
  TIERODS
  TRIODES
P SPIRTED
  STRIPED
R STIRRED
S DISSERT
  STRIDES
U DUSTIER
  REDUITS
  STUDIER
V DIVERTS
  STRIVED
  VERDITS

DEIRSU 143
(URDIES)
A RESIDUA
B BRUISED
  BURDIES
C CRUISED
  DISCURE
D RUDDIES
E RESIDUE
  UREIDES
G GUIDERS
H HURDIES
K DUIKERS
  DUSKIER
N INSURED
P PUDSIER
  SIRUPED
Q SQUIRED
R DRUSIER
  DURRIES
S DISEURS
  SUDSIER
T DUSTIER
  REDUITS
  STUDIER

DELNOS 181
OLDENS
A LOADENS
B BLONDES
  BOLDENS
D NODDLES
F ENFOLDS
  FONDLES
G DONGLES

  GOLDENS
I DOLINES
  INDOLES
  SONDELI
M DOLMENS
O NOODLES
  SNOOLED
R RONDELS
S OLDNESS
U LOUDENS
  NODULES
  NOUSLED
W DOWLNES
Z DONZELS

DELORS 145
(OLDERS)
A LOADERS
  ORDEALS
  RELOADS
B BORDELS
C SCOLDER
E RESOLED
F FOLDERS
G LODGERS
H HOLDERS
I SOLDIER
  SOLIDER
M SMOLDER
N RONDELS
P POLDERS
S DORSELS
  RODLESS
  SOLDERS
T DROLEST
  OLDSTER
  STRODLE
W WELDORS
Y YODLERS

DELORT 100
(DOLTER)
A DELATOR
  LEOTARD
D TODDLER
I DOILTER
L TROLLED
N ENTROLD
O ROOTLED
P DROPLET
S DROLEST
  OLDSTER
  STRODLE
T DOTTLER
  DOTTREL
U TROULED

DENORU 99
UNDOER
A RONDEAU
B BOUNDER
  REBOUND
  UNROBED
D REDOUND
  ROUNDED
  UNDERDO
F FOUNDER
  REFOUND
G GUERDON
  UNDERGO
  UNGORED
I DOURINE
L LOUNDER
  ROUNDEL
  ROUNDLE
M MOURNED
N ENROUND
P POUNDER
  UNROPED

R RONDURE
  ROUNDER
  UNORDER
S ENDUROS
  RESOUND
  SOUNDER
  UNDOERS
W REWOUND
  WOUNDER

DENOST 74
STONED
A ASTONED
  DONATES
  ONSTEAD
B OBTENDS
C DOCENTS
E DENOTES
F FONDEST
I DITONES
  STONIED
M ENDMOST
N STONNED
  TENDONS
O SNOOTED
  STOODEN
R RODENTS
  SNORTED
T SNOTTED
U DEUTONS
  SNOUTED

DENRSU 179
(UNDERS)
A ASUNDER
  DANSEUR
  DAUNERS
B BURDENS
D DUNDERS
E ENDURES
  ENSURED
F FUNDERS
  REFUNDS
G GERUNDS
  NUDGERS
H HURDENS
I INSURED
K DUNKERS
L LURDENS
  NURDLES
  NURSLED
  RUNDLES
N UNDERNS
O ENDUROS
  RESOUND
  SOUNDER
  UNDOERS
P SPURNED
S SUNDERS
  UNDRESS
T RETUNDS
U UNSURED

DENSTU 217
(STUNED)
A SAUNTED
  UNSATED
B SUBTEND
D STUDDEN
E DETENUS
  DETUNES
H SHUNTED
I DISTUNE
  DUNITES
M DUSTMEN
N DUNNEST
  STUNNED
O DEUTONS
  SNOUTED

Column 1

```
R RETUNDS
T STUDENT
  STUNTED

DEORST 50
STORED
A DOATERS
  ROASTED
  TORSADE
  TROADES
B DEBTORS
  STROBED
E OERSTED
  ROSETED
  TEREDOS
F DEFROST
  FROSTED
G STODGER
H DEHORTS
  SHORTED
I EDITORS
  ROISTED
  ROSITED
  SORTIED
  STEROID
  STORIED
  TIERODS
  TRIODES
K STROKED
L DROLEST
  OLDSTER
  STRODLE
M STORMED
N RODENTS
  SNORTED
O ROOSTED
P DEPORTS
  REDTOPS
  SPORTED
R DORTERS
  RODSTER
T DETORTS
U DETOURS
  DOUREST
  DOUTERS
  OUTREDS
  ROUSTED
W STROWED
  WORSTED
Y DESTROY
  ROYSTED
  STROYED

DEOSTU 180
OUSTED
C CUSTODE
  DOUCEST
  DOUCETS
  SCOUTED
G DEGOUTS
H SHOUTED
  SOUTHED
I OUTSIDE
  TEDIOUS
J JOUSTED
L LOUDEST
  OULDEST
  TOUSLED
M MOUSTED
  SMOUTED
N DEUTONS
  SNOUTED
O OUTDOES
P SPOUTED
R DETOURS
  DOUREST
  DOUTERS
  OUTREDS
  ROUSTED
```

Column 2

```
T DUETTOS
  TESTUDO
U DUTEOUS
X TUXEDOS

DERSTU 244
RUSTED
B BURSTED
C CRUDEST
  CRUSTED
G TRUDGES
I DUSTIER
  REDUITS
  STUDIER
L LUSTRED
  RUSTLED
  STRUDEL
N RETUNDS
O DETOURS
  DOUREST
  DOUTERS
  OUTREDS
  ROUSTED
P SPURTED
R RUSTRED
S DUSTERS
  TRUSSED
T STURTED
  TRUSTED
U SUTURED

DGINOR 209
(ORDING)
A ADORING
  GRADINO
  ROADING
C CORDING
D RODDING
E ERODING
  GROINED
  IGNORED
  NEGROID
  REDOING
F FORDING
H HORDING
L GIRLOND
  LORDING
N DRONING
R DORRING
S RODINGS
T DORTING
V DROVING
W WORDING
```

Column 3

```
D GENDERS
E RENEGES
I GREISEN
M GERMENS
O ENGORES
  NEGROES
S NEGRESS
T GERENTS
  REGENTS
V VENGERS

EEILRS 90
RELIES
A EARLIES
  REALISE
B BELIERS
D RESILED
E SEELIER
F FERLIES
  RELIEFS
G LEIGERS
  LIEGERS
H LEISHER
L LEISLER
N LIERNES
  RELINES
P REPLIES
  SPIELER
R RELIERS
S RESILES
T LEISTER
  RETILES
  STERILE
U LEISURE
V RELIVES
  REVILES
  SERVILE

EEILRV 232
RELIVE
A LEAVIER
  VEALIER
D DELIVER
  RELIVED
  REVILED
E RELIEVE
G VELIGER
I VEILIER
L EVILLER
M VERMEIL
N LIVENER
O OVERLIE
  RELIEVO
R RELIVER
  REVILER
S RELIVES
  REVILES
  SERVILE

EEILST 89
ELITES
C SECTILE
E EELIEST
F FELSITE
  LEFTIES
  LIEFEST
G ELEGIST
  ELEGITS
H SHELTIE
K KELTIES
  SLEEKIT
L TELLIES
M ELMIEST
N SETLINE
  TENSILE
O ESTOILE
  ETOILES
P EPISTLE
  PELITES
```

Column 4

```
R LEISTER
  RETILES
  STERILE
S TELESIS
  TIELESS
V LEVITES
  LIEVEST
X SEXTILE

EEIMNS 192
(EMINES)
A MEANIES
  NEMESIA
D DESMINE
  SIDEMEN
E ENEMIES
G SEEMING
I MEINIES
L ISLEMEN
M IMMENSE
O SEMEION
R ERMINES
S INSEEMS
  MISSEEN
  NEMESIS
  SIEMENS
T EMETINS
W MISWEEN
Y MEINEYS
  MENYIES

EEIMRS 202
MISERE
A SEAMIER
  SERIEMA
B BEMIRES
  BIREMES
C MERCIES
D REMEIDS
  REMISED
E EMERIES
G EMIGRES
  REGIMES
  REMIGES
H MESHIER
M IMMERSE
N ERMINES
O ISOMERE
P EMPIRES
  EMPRISE
  EPIMERS
  IMPRESE
  PREMIES
  PREMISE
  SPIREME
R MERRIES
S MESSIER
  MISERES
  REMISES
T MEISTER
  METIERS
  RETIMES
  TREMIES
  TRISEME
X REMIXES

EEINRT 8
ENTIRE
A RETINAE
  TRAINEE
B BENTIER
C ENTERIC
  ENTICER
E TEENIER
F FEINTER
G GENTIER
  INTEGER
  TEERING
  TREEING
```

Column 5

```
H NEITHER
  THEREIN
I ERINITE
  NITERIE
K KERNITE
N INTERNE
P INEPTER
R INERTER
  REINTER
  RENTIER
  TERRINE
S ENTIRES
  ENTRIES
  NERITES
  TRENISE
T NETTIER
  TENTIER
U NEURITE
  RETINUE
  REUNITE
  UTERINE

EEIRRS 182
(ERRIES)
A REARISE
B BERRIES
D DERRIES
  DESIRER
  RESIDER
  SERRIED
F FERRIES
H HERRIES
J JERRIES
L RELIERS
M MERRIES
N RESINER
O ROSIERE
P PERRIES
  REPRISE
  RESPIRE
S SERRIES
  SIRREES
T ETRIERS
  REITERS
  RESTIER
  RETIRES
  RETRIES
  TERRIES
V REIVERS
  REVERSI
  REVISER
  RIEVERS
W REWIRES

EEIRST 31
(ESTIER)
A AERIEST
  SERIATE
B REBITES
C CERITES
  RECITES
  TIERCES
D DIETERS
  REISTED
E EERIEST
H HEISTER
K KEISTER
L LEISTER
  RETILES
  STERILE
M MEISTER
  METIERS
  RETIMES
  TREMIES
  TRISEME
N ENTIRES
  ENTRIES
  NERITES
  TRENISE
```

Column 6

```
P RESPITE
R ETRIERS
  REITERS
  RESTIER
  RETIRES
  RETRIES
  TERRIES
T TESTIER
U SUETIER
V RESTIVE
  SIEVERT
  STIEVER
  VERIEST
W STEWIER
Z ZESTIER

EEIRSV 222
REVISE
C SCRIEVE
  SERVICE
D DERIVES
  DEVISER
  DIVERSE
  REVISED
E VEERIES
G GRIEVES
  REGIVES
H SHRIEVE
L RELIVES
  REVILES
  SERVILE
N ENVIERS
  INVERSE
  VENIRES
  VERSINE
O EROSIVE
P PREVISE
  PRIEVES
R REIVERS
  REVERSI
  REVISER
  RIEVERS
S IVRESSE
  REVISES
T RESTIVE
  SIEVERT
  STIEVER
  VERIEST
V REVIVES
W REVIEWS
  VIEWERS

EELNST 161
NESTLE
A ELANETS
  LATEENS
  LEANEST
D DENTELS
  NESTLED
E STELENE
G GENTLES
  LENGEST
I SETLINE
  TENSILE
L TELLENS
P PENTELS
R RELENTS
  SLENTER
S NESTLES
T NETTLES
  TELNETS
U UNSTEEL
Y ENSTYLE
  TENSELY

EELRST 157
(ELTERS)
A ELATERS
```

REALEST
RELATES
STEALER
B BELTERS
  TREBLES
C TERCELS
F FELTERS
  REFLETS
  TELFERS
G REGLETS
H SHELTER
I LEISTER
  RETILES
  STERILE
K KELTERS
  KESTREL
  SKELTER
L RETELLS
  TELLERS
M SMELTER
N RELENTS
  SLENTER
P PELTERS
  PETRELS
  RESPELT
  SPELTER
S STREELS
  TRESSEL
T LETTERS
  LETTRES
  SETTLER
  STERLET
  TRESTLE
V SVELTER
W SWELTER
  WELTERS
  WRESTLE
Y RESTYLE
  TERSELY
Z SELTZER

EENRST 56
ENTERS
A EARNEST
  EASTERN
  NEAREST
C CENTERS
  CENTRES
  TENRECS
D STERNED
  TENDERS
  TENDRES
E ENTREES
  RETENES
G GERENTS
  REGENTS
H THRENES
I ENTIRES
  ENTRIES
  NERITES
  TRENISE
L RELENTS
  SLENTER
N RENNETS
  TENNERS
P PRESENT
. REPENTS
  SERPENT
R RENTERS
  STERNER
S NESTERS
  RESENTS
  STRENES
T TENTERS
  TESTERN
U NEUTERS
  RETUNES
  TENURES
  TUREENS

V VENTERS
  VENTRES
W WESTERN
X EXTERNS
Y STYRENE
  YESTERN

EEORSV 247
(OVERSE)
A OVERSEA
B OBSERVE
  OBVERSE
  VERBOSE
C CORVEES
E OVERSEE
I EROSIVE
K EVOKERS
  REVOKES
L RESOLVE
M REMOVES
R REVERSO
T ESTOVER
  OVERSET
U OEUVRES
  OVERUSE
W OVERSEW

EERRST 236
RESTER
A SERRATE
  TEARERS
B BERRETS
E RETREES
  STEERER
F FERRETS
G REGRETS
I ETRIERS
  REITERS
  RESTIER
  RETIRES
  RETRIES
M TERMERS
N RENTERS
  STERNER
O RESTORE
S RESTERS
T TERRETS
U URETERS
V REVERTS
W STREWER
  WRESTER

EERSTT 200
STREET
A ESTREAT
  RESTATE
B BETTERS
C TERCETS
E TEETERS
  TERETES
F FETTERS
G GETTERS
H TETHERS
I TESTIER
L LETTERS
  LETTRES
  SETTLER
  STERLET
  TRESTLE
N TENTERS
  TESTERN
O ROSETTE
P PERTEST
  PETTERS
  PRETEST
R TERRETS
S SETTERS
  STREETS

TERSEST
TESTERS
T STRETTE
  TETTERS
U TRUSTEE
Y STREETY

EFIRST 191
STRIFE
A FAIREST
B FIBSTER
D FRISTED
F RESTIFF
  STIFFER
H SHIFTER
I FISTIER
K FRISKET
L FILTERS
  LIFTERS
  STIFLER
  TRIFLES
M FIRMEST
  FREMITS
N SNIFTER
O FOISTER
  FORTIES
S SIFTERS
  STRIFES
T FITTERS
  TITFERS
U FUSTIER
  SURFEIT
W SWIFTER

EGHINT 250
(ETHING)
A GAHNITE
  HEATING
B BENIGHT
C ETCHING
D NIGHTED
E THEEING
F HEFTING
I NIGHTIE
L ENLIGHT
  LIGHTEN
M THEMING
N HENTING
R RIGHTEN
S NIGHEST
T TIGHTEN

EGILNR 125
LINGER
A ENGRAIL
  LAERING
  LEARING
  NARGILE
  REALIGN
  REGINAL
C CLINGER
  CRINGLE
E LEERING
  REELING
F FLINGER
G NIGGLER
H HERLING
I LEIRING
  LINGIER
J JINGLER
M GREMLIN
  MERLING
  MINGLER
P PINGLER
S GIRNELS
  LINGERS
  SLINGER
T RINGLET
  TINGLER

TRINGLE
Y RELYING

EGILNS 117
SINGLE
A LEASING
  LINAGES
  SEALING
B BINGLES
D DINGLES
  ELDINGS
  ENGILDS
  SINGLED
E LEESING
  SEELING
F SELFING
G GINGLES
  NIGGLES
  SNIGGLE
H SHINGLE
I SEILING
J JINGLES
K KINGLES
L LEGLINS
  LINGELS
  LINGLES
  SELLING
M MINGLES
N GINNELS
O ELOIGNS
  LEGIONS
  LIGNOSE
  LINGOES
P PINGLES
  SPIGNEL
R GIRNELS
  LINGERS
  SLINGER
S SINGLES
T GLISTEN
  LESTING
  SINGLET
  TINGLES
U LUNGIES
  SLUEING
W SLEWING
  SWINGLE
Z ZINGELS

EGILNT 66
TINGLE
A ATINGLE
  ELATING
  GELATIN
  GENITAL
B BELTING
D GLINTED
  TINGLED
E GENTILE
F FELTING
H ENLIGHT
  LIGHTEN
I IGNITE
J JINGLET
K KINGLET
L TELLING
M MELTING
O LENTIGO
P PELTING
R RINGLET
  TINGLER
  TRINGLE
S GLISTEN
  LESTING
  SINGLET
  TINGLES
T ETTLING
  LETTING
U ELUTING

W WELTING
  WINGLET
Y RELYING

EGILOS 132
LOGIES
A GOALIES
  SOILAGE
B OBLIGES
E ELOGIES
L GOLLIES
N ELOIGNS
  LEGIONS
  LIGNOSE
  LINGOES
O GOOLIES
  OLOGIES
P EPILOGS
R GLOIRES
  GLORIES
S GLIOSES
T ELOGIST
  LOGIEST
U OUGLIES

EGILRS 159
(GIRLES)
A GRAILES
B GERBILS
D GILDERS
  GIRDLES
  GLIDERS
  GRISLED
  LIDGERS
E LEIGERS
  LIEGERS
G LIGGERS
I GIRLIES
K KILERGS
L GRILLES
N GIRNELS
  LINGERS
  SLINGER
O GLOIRES
  GLORIES
S GRILSES
T GLISTER
  GRISTLE
U GUILERS
  LIGURES
  LURGIES
Y GREISLY
  GRIESLY
  GRISELY

EGILST 190
LEGIST
A AGILEST
  AIGLETS
  LIGATES
  TAIGLES
B GIBLETS
E ELEGIST
  ELEGITS
G GIGLETS
H SLEIGHT
L GILLETS
M GIMLETS
N GLISTEN
  LESTING
  SINGLET
  TINGLES
O ELOGIST
  LOGIEST
P PIGLETS
R GLISTER
  GRISTLE
S LEGISTS
U GLUIEST

UGLIEST
Z GLITZES

EGINNR 178
GINNER
A AGINNER
  EARNING
  ENGRAIN
  GRANNIE
  NEARING
C CERNING
D GRINNED
  RENDING
E ENGINER
  INGENER
F FERNING
G GERNING
I GINNIER
  REINING
K KERNING
M RINGMEN
N RENNING
R GRINNER
S ENRINGS
  GINNERS
T RENTING
  RINGENT
  TERNING
U ENURING
V NERVING
Y GINNERY
  RENYING

EGINOS 78
INGOES
A AGONIES
  AGONISE
B BIOGENS
C COGNISE
  COIGNES
D DINGOES
E SOIGNEE
H SHOEING
J JINGOES
L ELOIGNS
  LEGIONS
  LIGNOSE
  LINGOES
M MISGONE
P EPIGONS
  PIGEONS
  PINGOES
R ERINGOS
  IGNORES
  REGIONS
  SIGNORE
U IGNEOUS
W WIGEONS
Y ISOGENY

EGINRS 68
SINGER
A ANGRIES
  EARINGS
  ERASING
  GAINERS
  GRAINES
  REGAINS
  REGINAS
  SEARING
  SERINGA
B BINGERS
C CRINGES
D DINGERS
  ENGIRDS
E GREISEN
F FINGERS
  FRINGES
G GINGERS

NIGGERS
SNIGGER
L GIRNELS
  LINGERS
  SLINGER
M GERMINS
N ENRINGS
  GINNERS
O ERINGOS
  IGNORES
  REGIONS
  SIGNORE
P PERSING
  PINGERS
  SPRINGE
R ERRINGS
  GIRNERS
  RINGERS
  SERRING
S INGRESS
  RESIGNS
  SIGNERS
  SINGERS
T RESTING
  STINGER
U REUSING
  RUEINGS
  SIGNEUR
V SERVING
  VERSING
W SWINGER
  WINGERS
Y SYRINGE
Z ZINGERS

EGINRT 39
(TINGER)
A GRANITE
  GRATINE
  INGRATE
  TANGIER
  TEARING
E GENTIER
  INTEGER
  TEERING
  TREEING
H RIGHTEN
I IGNITER
  TIERING
  TIGRINE
L RINGLET
  TINGLER
  TRINGLE
M METRING
  TERMING
N RENTING
  RINGENT
  TERNING
O GENITOR
S RESTING
  STINGER
T GITTERN
  RETTING
U TRUEING
V VERTING
Y RETYING

EGINST 107
(ESTING)
A EASTING
  EATINGS
  GAINEST
  GENISTA
  INGATES
  INGESTA
  SEATING
  TANGIES
  TEASING
  TSIGANE

B BESTING
D NIDGETS
  STEDING
  STINGED
H NIGHEST
I IGNITES
J JESTING
K KESTING
L GLISTEN
  LESTING
  SINGLET
  TINGLES
M STEMING
  TEMSING
N NESTING
  SENTING
  TENSING
R RESTING
  STINGER
S INGESTS
  SIGNETS
T SETTING
  TESTING
U GUNITES
V VESTING
W STEWING
  TWINGES
Z ZESTING

EGNORS 155
(SONGER)
A ONAGERS
  ORANGES
C CONGERS
E ENGORES
  NEGROES
I ERINGOS
  IGNORES
  REGIONS
  SIGNORE
M MONGERS
  MORGENS
O ORGONES
  OROGENS
P SPONGER
S ENGROSS
U SURGEON
V GOVERNS
Y ERYNGOS
  GROYNES

EHINRS 227
SHRINE
A ARSHINE
  HERNIAS
C NICHERS
  RICHENS
D HINDERS
  SHRINED
E HENRIES
  INHERES
I SHINIER
K KERNISH
M MENHIRS
O HEROINS
  INSHORE
S SHINERS
  SHRINES
V SHRIVEN
W WHINERS

EHIRST 153
(ITHERS)
A HASTIER
  SHERIAT
B HERBIST
C CITHERS
  ESTRICH

RICHEST
D DITHERS
  SHIRTED
E HEISTER
F SHIFTER
G SIGHTER
H HITHERS
I HIRSTIE
L SLITHER
M HERMITS
  MITHERS
O HERIOTS
  HOISTER
  SHORTIE
  TOSHIER
P HIPSTER
T HITTERS
  TITHERS
U HIRSUTE
V THRIVES
W SWITHER
  WITHERS
  WRITHES
Z ZITHERS

EHORST 189
OTHERS
A ASTHORE
  EARSHOT
  HAROSET
B BOSHTER
  BOTHERS
C HECTORS
  ROCHETS
  ROTCHES
  TOCHERS
  TORCHES
  TROCHES
D DEHORTS
  SHORTED
E HETEROS
F FOTHERS
I HERIOTS
  HOISTER
  SHORTIE
  TOSHIER
L HOLSTER
  HOSTLER
M MOTHERS
  SMOTHER
N HORNETS
  SHORTEN
  THRENOS
  THRONES
O HOOTERS
  SHOOTER
  SOOTHER
P POTHERS
  STROPHE
  THORPES
R RHETORS
  ROTHERS
  SHORTER
S TOSHERS
T HOTTERS
U SHOUTER
  SOUTHER
W THROWES
X EXHORTS

EIILST 139
(TILIES)
A LAITIES
C ELICITS
I ILEITIS
K KILTIES
L ILLITES
M ELITISM
  LIMIEST

LIMITES
N LINIEST
  LINTIES
O IOLITES
  OILIEST
P SPILITE
R RILIEST
  SILTIER
T ELITIST
U UTILISE
W WILIEST

EIINRT 30
INTIRE
A INERTIA
C CITRINE
  CRINITE
  INCITER
  NERITIC
D INDITER
  NITRIDE
E ERINITE
  NITERIE
F NIFTIER
G IGNITER
  TIERING
  TIGRINE
H INHERIT
L LINTIER
  NITRILE
M INTERIM
  MINTIER
  TERMINI
N TINNIER
T NITRITE
  NITTIER
  TINTIER
V INVITER
  VITRINE
W TWINIER

EILNOS 47
(OLINES)
C CINEOLS
  CONSEIL
  INCLOSE
D DOLINES
  INDOLES
  SONDELI
F OLEFINS
G ELOIGNS
  LEGIONS
  LIGNOSE
  LINGOES
I ELISION
  ISOLINE
  LIONISE
L LIONELS
  NIELLOS
M MOLINES
O LOONIES
P EPSILON
  PINOLES
R NEROLIS
S ESLOINS
  INSOLES
  LESIONS
  LIONESS
T ENTOILS
  LIONETS
  ONLIEST
U ELUSION

EILNRS 77
LINERS
A NAILERS
B BERLINS
E LIERNES
  RELINES

G GIRNELS
  LINGERS
  SLINGER
I INLIERS
K LINKERS
  SLINKER
M LIMNERS
  MERLINS
O NEROLIS
P PILSNER
T LINTERS
  SLINTER
  SNIRTLE
V SILVERN

EILNST 45
SILENT
A EASTLIN
  ELASTIN
  ENTAILS
  SALIENT
  SLAINTE
  STANIEL
  TENAILS
C CLIENTS
  LECTINS
  STENCIL
D DENTILS
E SETLINE
  TENSILE
G GLISTEN
  LESTING
  SINGLET
  TINGLES
I LINIEST
  LINTIES
K LENTISK
  TINKLES
L LENTILS
  LINTELS
  TELLINS
N LINNETS
O ENTOILS
  LIONETS
  ONLIEST
P PINTLES
  PLENIST
R LINTERS
  SLINTER
  SNIRTLE
S ENLISTS
  LISTENS
  SILENTS
  TINSELS
U LUTEINS
  UNTILES
  UTENSIL
V VENTILS
W WESTLIN
  WINTLES

EILORS 37
OILERS
B BOILERS
  LIBEROS
  REBOILS
C RECOILS
D SOLDIER
  SOLIDER
G GLOIRES
  GLORIES
I SOILIER
M MOILERS
N NEROLIS
O ORIOLES
P SLOPIER
  SPOILER
R LORRIES
S LORISES

LOSSIER
  RISSOLE
T LOITERS
  TOILERS
U LOUSIER
  SOILURE
V OLIVERS
  VIOLERS

EILORT 18
TOILER
B TRILOBE
C CORTILE
D DOILTER
E TROELIE
F LOFTIER
  TREFOIL
J JOLTIER
M MOTLIER
N RETINOL
O TROOLIE
P POITREL
  POLITER
S LOITERS
  TOILERS
T TORTILE
  TRIOLET
U OUTLIER

EILOST 21
(ELIOTS)
A ISOLATE
B BETOILS
C CITOLES
E ESTOILE
  ETOILES
G ELOGIST
  LOGIEST
H EOLITHS
  HOLIEST
  HOSTILE
I IOLITES
  OILIEST
L OILLETS
M MOTILES
N ENTOILS
  LIONETS
  ONLIEST
O OOLITES
  OSTIOLE
  STOOLIE
P PIOLETS
  PISTOLE
R LOITERS
  TOILERS
T LITOTES
  TOILETS
U OUTLIES
V OLIVETS
  VIOLETS
W OWLIEST

EILRST 44
LITERS
A REALIST
  RETAILS
  SALTIER
  SALTIRE
  SLATIER
B BLISTER
  BRISTLE
  RIBLETS
C RELICTS
E LEISTER
  RETILES
  STERILE
F FILTERS
  LIFTERS
  STIFLER

TRIFLES
G GLISTER
GRISTLE
H SLITHER
I RILIEST
SILTIER
K KILTERS
KIRTLES
L RILLETS
STILLER
TILLERS
TRELLIS
M MILTERS
N LINTERS
SLINTER
SNIRTLE
O LOITERS
TOILERS
P SPIRTLE
TRIPLES
S LISTERS
T LITTERS
SLITTER
STILTER
TESTRIL
TILTERS
TITLERS
U LUSTIER
RULIEST
RUTILES

EILSTU 136
(UTILES)
A SITULAE
B BLUIEST
SUBTILE
D DILUTES
F FLUIEST
SULFITE
G GLUIEST
UGLIEST
I UTILISE
L TUILLES
N LUTEINS
UNTILES
UTENSIL
O OUTLIES
P PULIEST
PUTELIS
STIPULE
R LUSTIER
RULIEST
RUTILES
T TITULES

EIMNOS 131
MONIES
A ANOMIES
C INCOMES
MESONIC
D MISDONE
E SEMEION
G MISGONE
L MOLINES
O MOONIES
NOISOME
P IMPONES
PEONISM
R MERINOS
MERSION
S EONISMS
T MOISTEN
MONTIES
W WINSOME

EIMNRS 177
MINERS
A MARINES
REMAINS

SEMINAR
SIRNAME
C CREMSIN
MINCERS
D MINDERS
REMINDS
E ERMINES
G GERMINS
H MENHIRS
K MERKINS
L LIMNERS
MERLINS
M NIMMERS
O MERINOS
MERSION
T ENTRISM
MINSTER
MINTERS
REMINTS
U MURINES
NEURISM
V VERMINS

EIMNST 201
(MINEST)
A INMATES
MAINEST
D MINDSET
E EMETINS
G STEMING
TEMSING
I MINIEST
K MISKENT
O MOISTEN
MONTIES
P PIMENTS
R ENTRISM
MINSTER
MINTERS
REMINTS
S MISSENT
T MITTENS
SMITTEN
U MINUETS
MINUTES
MISTUNE
MUNITES
MUTINES
W MISWENT

EIMOST 150
SOMITE
A AMOSITE
ATOMIES
ATOMISE
OSMIATE
D DOMIEST
MODISTE
MOISTED
F FOMITES
G EGOTISM
H HOMIEST
L MOTILES
M TOMMIES
N MOISTEN
MONTIES
P MOPIEST
OPTIMES
R EROTISM
MOISTER
MORTISE
TRISOME
S MITOSES
SOMITES
T MOTIEST
TITMOSE
U TIMEOUS

V MOTIVES
Z MESTIZO

EIMRST 140
MITRES
A IMARETS
MAESTRI
MAISTER
MASTIER
MISRATE
SEMITAR
SMARTIE
B BETRIMS
TIMBERS
TIMBRES
C CRETISM
METRICS
E MEISTER
METIERS
RETIMES
TREMIES
TRISEME
F FIRMEST
FREMITS
H HERMITS
MITHERS
I MIRIEST
MISTIER
RIMIEST
K MIRKEST
L MILTERS
M MISTERM
N ENTRISM
MINSTER
MINTERS
REMINTS
O EROTISM
MOISTER
MORTISE
TRISOME
P IMPREST
PERMITS
R RETRIMS
TRIMERS
S MISTERS
SMITERS
T METRIST
U MUSTIER
Y MISTERY
SMYTRIE

EINNST 113
SINNET
A INANEST
D DENTINS
INDENTS
INTENDS
E INTENSE
TENNIES
G NESTING
SENTING
TENSING
I INTINES
TINNIES
L LINNETS
O INTONES
TENSION
P PINNETS
SPINNET
TENPINS
R INTERNS
TINNERS
S SENNITS
SINNETS
T INTENTS
TUNNIES
V INVENTS

EINOPS 130
PONIES
D DISPONE
SPINODE
E PEONIES
G EPIGONS
PIGEONS
PINGOES
H PHONIES
I PIONIES
K PINKOES
L EPSILON
PINOLES
M IMPONES
PEONISM
N PENSION
P PEPINOS
R ORPINES
PIONERS
PROINES
S SPINOSE
T POINTES
PONTIES
W POWNIES
Y PIONEYS

EINORS 7
SENIOR
A ERASION
C COINERS
CRINOSE
CRONIES
ORCEINS
ORCINES
RECOINS
SERICON
D DONSIER
INDORSE
ROSINED
G ERINGOS
IGNORES
REGIONS
SIGNORE
H HEROINS
INSHORE
I IONISER
IRONIES
IRONISE
NOISIER
J JOINERS
REJOINS
L NEROLIS
M MERINOS
MERSION
O EROSION
P ORPINES
PIONERS
PROINES
R IRONERS
S ORNISES
SENIORS
SONERIS
SONSIER
T NORITES
ORIENTS
STONIER
TERSION
TRIONES
U URINOSE
V RENVOIS
VERSION
W SNOWIER

EINOSS 204
SONSIE
A ANOESIS
B BESOINS
C CESSION
COSINES

D ONSIDES
I IONISES
K KENOSIS
L ESLOINS
INSOLES
LESIONS
LIONESS
M EONISMS
N SONNIES
P SPINOSE
R ORNISES
SENIORS
SONERIS
SONSIER
S ESSOINS
OSSEINS
SESSION
T NOSIEST
SONTIES
STONIES
U SINUOSE

EINOST 14
TONIES
A ATONIES
B BONIEST
EBONIST
C NOTICES
SECTION
D DITONES
STONIED
H HISTONE
J JONTIES
L ENTOILS
LIONETS
ONLIEST
M MOISTEN
MONTIES
N INTONES
TENSION
O ISOTONE
P POINTES
PONTIES
R NORITES
ORIENTS
STONIER
TERSION
TRIONES
S NOSIEST
SONTIES
STONIES
T SNOTTIE
TONIEST
TONITES
TONITES
W TOWNIES

EINPRS 158
SNIPER
A RAPINES
C PINCERS
PRINCES
D PINDERS
E EREPSIN
REPINES
G PERSING
PINGERS
SPRINGE
I INSPIRE
PIRNIES
SNIPIER
SPINIER
K PERKINS
L PILSNER
N PINNERS
SPINNER
O ORPINES
PIONERS
PROINES
P NIPPERS

SNIPPER
S SNIPERS
T NIPTERS
PTERINS
U PRUINES
PURINES
UPRISEN

EINPST 148
INSTEP
A PANTIES
PATINES
SAPIENT
SPINATE
C INCEPTS
INSPECT
PECTINS
PEINCTS
D STIPEND
E PENTISE
I PINIEST
PINITES
TIEPINS
K PINKEST
L PINTLES
PLENIST
M PIMENTS
N PINNETS
SPINNET
TENPINS
O POINTES
PONTIES
P SNIPPET
R NIPTERS
PTERINS
S INSTEPS
SPINETS
T SPITTEN
U PUNIEST
PUNTIES

EINRSS 249
RESINS
A ARSINES
SARNIES
C SCRINES
E SEINERS
SEREINS
SERINES
G INGRESS
RESIGNS
SIGNERS
SINGERS
H SHINERS
SHRINES
K SINKERS
N SINNERS
O ORNISES
SENIORS
SONERIS
SONSIER
P SNIPERS
R RINSERS
T INSERTS
SINTERS
U INSURES
SUNRISE
V VERSINS

EINRST 17
INTERS
A ANESTRI
ANTSIER
NASTIER
RATINES
RESIANT
RETAINS
RETINAS
RETSINA

STAINER
STARNIE
STEARIN
C CISTERN
CRETINS
D TINDERS
E ENTIRES
ENTRIES
NERITES
TRENISE
F SNIFTER
G RESTING
STINGER
K SKINTER
STINKER
TINKERS
L LINTERS
SLINTER
SNIRTLE
M ENTRISM
MINSTER
MINTERS
REMINTS
N INTERNS
TINNERS
O NORITES
ORIENTS
STONIER
TERSION
TRIONES
P NIPTERS
PTERINS
S INSERTS
SINTERS
T ENTRIST
STINTER
TINTERS
U TRIUNES
UNITERS
V INVERTS
STRIVEN
W TWINERS
WINTERS
Y SINTERY

EINRSV 226
VINERS
A AVENIRS
RAVINES
C CRIVENS
D VERDINS
E ENVIERS
INVERSE
VENIRES
VERSINE
G SERVING
VERSING
H SHRIVEN
L SILVERN
M VERMINS
O RENVOIS
VERSION
S VERSINS
T INVERTS
STRIVEN
W WIVERNS

EINRTT 76
TINTER
A INTREAT
ITERANT
NATTIER
NITRATE
TARTINE
TERTIAN
B BITTERN
C CITTERN
D TRIDENT
E NETTIER

TENTIER
G GITTERN
RETTING
I NITRITE
NITTIER
TINTIER
K KNITTER
TRINKET
O TRITONE
S ENTRIST
STINTER
TINTERS
U NUTTIER
W TWINTER
WRITTEN

EINRTU 25
UNITER
A RUINATE
TAURINE
URANITE
URINATE
B BUNTIER
TRIBUNE
TURBINE
D INTRUDE
TURDINE
UNTIRED
UNTRIDE
UNTRIED
E NEURITE
RETINUE
REUNITE
UTERINE
G TRUEING
M MINUTER
O ROUTINE
P REPUNIT
R RUNTIER
S TRIUNES
UNITERS
T NUTTIER
V UNRIVET
VENTURI
W UNWRITE

EINSST 218
INSETS
A ENTASIS
NASTIES
SESTINA
TANSIES
TISANES
C INCESTS
INSECTS
D DISNEST
DISSENT
SNIDEST
E SEITENS
SESTINE
F FITNESS
INFESTS
G INGESTS
SIGNETS
H SITHENS
L ENLISTS
LISTENS
SILENTS
TINSELS
M MISSENT
N SENNITS
SINNETS
O NOSIEST
SONTIES
STONIES
P INSTEPS
SPINETS
R INSERTS
SINTERS

S SENSIST
U INTUSES
V INVESTS
W WISENTS
WITNESS
Y TINSEYS

EINSTT 160
(INTEST)
A INSTATE
SATINET
D DENTIST
DISTENT
STINTED
G SETTING
TESTING
I SITTINE
TINIEST
K KITTENS
M MITTENS
SMITTEN
N INTENTS
O SNOTTIE
TONIEST
TONITES
P SPITTEN
R ENTRIST
STINTER
TINTERS
U TUNIEST
W ENTWIST
TWINSET
Y TENSITY

EINSTU 81
UNITES
A AUNTIES
SINUATE
D DISTUNE
DUNITES
G GUNITES
I UNITIES
UNITISE
L LUTEINS
UNTILES
UTENSIL
M MINUETS
MINUTES
MISTUNE
MUNITES
MUTINES
N TUNNIES
P PUNIEST
PUNTIES
Q INQUEST
QUINTES
R TRIUNES
UNITERS
S INTUSES
T TUNIEST

EIOPST 101
POSTIE
A ATOPIES
OPIATES
C POETICS
D DEPOSIT
DOPIEST
POSITED
SOPITED
TOPSIDE
E POETISE
H ETHIOPS
OPHITES
K POKIEST
L PIOLETS
PISTOLE
M MOPIEST

OPTIMES
N POINTES
PONTIES
O ISOTOPE
R PERIOST
REPOSIT
RIPOSTE
ROPIEST
S POSIEST
POSTIES
SEPIOST
SOPITES
T POTTIES
TIPTOES
U PITEOUS
X POXIEST
Y ISOTYPE

EIORSS 214
(SORIES)
B BOSSIER
RIBOSES
C COSIERS
D DORISES
DOSSIER
E SOIREES
F FROISES
H HOSIERS
L LORISES
LOSSIER
RISSOLE
M ISOMERS
MOISERS
MOSSIER
N ORNISES
SONERIS
SONSIER
P POISERS
R ORRISES
ROSIERS
T ROSIEST
SORITES
SORTIES
STORIES
TOSSIER
U SERIOUS
V VIROSES
X XEROSIS

EIORST 5
(TORIES)
A OARIEST
OTARIES
B ORBIEST
SORBITE
C EROTICS
TERCIOS
D EDITORS
ROISTED
ROSITED
SORTIED
STEROID
STORIED
TIERODS
TRIODES
F FOISTER
FORTIES
G GOITERS
GOITRES
GORIEST
H HERIOTS
HOISTER
SHORTIE
TOSHIER
I RIOTISE
K ROKIEST
L LOITERS

TOILERS
M EROTISM
MOISTER
MORTISE
TRISOME
N NORITES
ORIENTS
STONIER
TERSION
TRIONES
O OORIEST
ROOTIES
SOOTIER
TOORIES
P PERIOST
PORIEST
REPOSIT
RIPOSTE
ROPIEST
R RIOTERS
ROISTER
RORIEST
S ROSIEST
SORITES
SORTIES
STORIES
TOSSIER
T STOITER
U OURIEST
TOURIES
TOUSIER
V TORSIVE
W OWRIEST
TOWSIER

EIORSV 127
VIROSE
A OVARIES
C CORSIVE
VOICERS
D DEVISOR
DEVOIRS
VISORED
VOIDERS
E EROSIVE
I IVORIES
L OLIVERS
VIOLERS
M VERISMO
N RENVOIS
VERSION
R REVISOR
S VIROSES
T TORSIVE

EIOSTT 93
(OTTIES)
A OSTIATE
TOASTIE
B BOTTIES
C COTTISE
D DOTIEST
STOITED
E TOEIEST
G EGOTIST
H HOTTIES
L LITOTES
TOILETS
M MOTIEST
TITMOSE
N SNOTTIE
TONIEST
TONITES
O TOOTSIE
P POTTIES
TIPTOES
R STOITER
T TOTTIES
U TOUSTIE

W TOWIEST

EIPRST 147
PRIEST
A PARTIES
PASTIER
PIASTRE
PIRATES
PRATIES
TRAIPSE
C TRICEPS
D SPIRTED
STRIPED
E RESPITE
H HIPSTER
I PITIERS
TIPSIER
L SPIRTLE
TRIPLES
M IMPREST
PERMITS
N NIPTERS
PTERINS
O PERIOST
PORIEST
REPOSIT
RIPOSTE
ROPIEST
P TIPPERS
S ESPRITS
PERSIST
PRIESTS
SITREPS
SPRITES
STIRPES
STRIPES
TRIPSES
T PITTERS
SPITTER
TIPSTER
U PERITUS
PUIREST
V PRIVETS
X EXTIRPS
Y PYRITES
STRIPEY

EIRRST 165
TRIERS
A ARTSIER
SERRATI
TARRIES
TARSIER
D STIRRED
E ETRIERS
REITERS
RESTIER
RETIRES
RETRIES
TERRIES
K SKIRRET
SKIRTER
STRIKER
M RETRIMS
TRIMERS
O RIOTERS
ROISTER
RORIEST
R STIRRER
S STIRRES
T RITTERS
TERRITS
U RUSTIER
V STRIVER
W WRITERS

EIRSTT 104
SITTER
A ARTIEST

ARTISTE
ATTIRES
IRATEST
STRIATE
TASTIER
TERTIAS
B BITTERS
C TRISECT
E TESTIER
F FITTERS
TITFERS
H HITTERS
TITHERS
J JITTERS
K SKITTER
L LITTERS
SLITTER
STILTER
TESTRIL
TILTERS
TITLERS
M METRIST
N ENTRIST
STINTER
TINTERS
O STOITER
P PITTERS
SPITTER
TIPSTER
R RITTERS
TERRITS
S SITTERS
T STRETTI
TITTERS
TRITEST
U TERTIUS
V TRIVETS
W TWISTER
WITTERS

EIRSTV 163
RIVETS
A TAIVERS
VASTIER
D DIVERTS
STRIVED
VERDITS
E RESTIVE
SIEVERT
STIEVER
VERIEST
G GRIVETS
H THRIVES
I REVISIT
STIVIER
VISITER
N INVERTS
STRIVEN
O TORSIVE
P PRIVETS
R STRIVER
S STIVERS
STRIVES
TREVISS
VERISTS
T TRIVETS
U VIRTUES

ELNSTU 216
(LETSUN)
A ELUANTS
UNLASTE
B SUNBELT
UNBELTS
UNBLEST
E ELUENTS
UNSTEEL
F FLUENTS
NESTFUL

NETFULS
G ENGLUTS
GLUTENS
I LUTEINS
N TUNNELS
O LENTOUS
P PENULTS
R RUNLETS
T NUTLETS

ELORST 67
(TOLERS)
A OESTRAL
B BOLSTER
BOLTERS
LOBSTER
C COLTERS
CORSLET
COSTREL
LECTORS
D DROLEST
OLDSTER
STRODLE
F FLORETS
LOFTERS
H HOLSTER
HOSTLER
I LOITERS
TOILERS
J JOLTERS
L TOLLERS
N LENTORS
O LOOTERS
RETOOLS
ROOTLES
TOOLERS
P PETROLS
S OSTLERS
STEROLS
TORSELS
T SETTLOR
SLOTTER
TOLTERS
U ELUTORS
OUTLERS
TROULES
V REVOLTS
W TROWELS
WORTLES

ELOSTU 173
TOUSLE
B BOLETUS
D LOUDEST
OULDEST
TOUSLED
F FOULEST
I OUTLIES
L OUTSELL
N LENTOUS
O OUTSOLE
P TUPELOS
R ELUTORS
OUTLERS
TROULES
S LOTUSES
SOLUTES
TOUSLES
T OUTLETS
U LUTEOUS
V VOLUTES
Z TOUZLES

ELRSTU 208
ULSTER
A SALUTER
B BLUSTER

BUSTLER
BUTLERS
SUBTLER
C CLUSTER
CULTERS
CUSTREL
CUTLERS
RELUCTS
D LUSTRED
RUSTLED
STRUDEL
F FLUSTER
FLUTERS
RESTFUL
G GURLETS
H HURTLES
HUSTLER
I LUSTIER
RULIEST
RUTILES
N RUNLETS
O ELUTORS
OUTLERS
TROULES
P SPURTLE
R RUSTLER
S LUSTERS
LUSTRES
RESULTS
RUSTLES
SUTLERS
ULSTERS
T TURTLES
Y SUTLERY

EMNORS 230
SERMON
A ENAMORS
MOANERS
OARSMEN
D MODERNS
RODSMEN
E MOREENS
F ENFORMS
G MONGERS
MORGENS
I MERINOS
MERSION
L MERLONS
O MOONERS
S SERMONS
T MENTORS
MONSTER
MONTRES

EMNOST 186
(MONETS)
A MANTOES
B ENTOMBS
D ENDMOST
E TEMENOS
TENEMES
F FOMENTS
G EMONGST
H MONETHS
I MOISTEN
MONTIES
L LOMENTS
MELTONS
M MOMENTS
MONTEMS
O MOONSET
P POSTMEN
TOPSMEN
R MENTORS
MONSTER
MONTRES
S STEMSON
U UNSMOTE

Y ETYMONS

EMORST 198
(MOTERS)
A AMORETS
MAESTRO
OMERTAS
B BESTORM
MOBSTER
D STORMED
E METEORS
REMOTES
G GROMETS
H MOTHERS
SMOTHER
I EROTISM
MOISTER
MORTISE
TRISOME
N MENTORS
MONSTER
MONTRES
O MOOTERS
P STOMPER
TROMPES
R TERMORS
TREMORS
S MOTSERS
U MOUTERS
OESTRUM

ENOPRS 203
PERSON
A PERSONA
C CREPONS
D PONDERS
RESPOND
E OPENERS
PERONES
REOPENS
REPONES
G SPONGER
H PHONERS
I ORPINES
PIONERS
PROINES
O OPERONS
SNOOPER
R PERRONS
S PERSONS
T POSTERN
PRONEST
U UNROPES
Y PROYNES
PYONERS

ENORST 23
STONER
A ATONERS
SENATOR
TREASON
B BRETONS
SORBENT
C CONSTER
CORNETS
CRESTON
CRONETS
D RODENTS
SNORTED
H HORNETS
SHORTEN
THRENOS
THRONES
I NORITES
ORIENTS
STONIER
TERSION
TRIONES
K STONKER

STROKEN
TONKERS
L LENTORS
M MENTORS
MONSTER
MONTRES
N STONERN
O ENROOTS
P POSTERN
PRONEST
R SNORTER
S STONERS
TENSORS
T ROTTENS
SNOTTER
STENTOR
U TENOURS
TONSURE
Y TYRONES

ENOSTT 195
(ONTEST)
A ATTONES
NOTATES
C CONTEST
D SNOTTED
H SHOTTEN
I SNOTTIE
TONIEST
TONITES
J JETTONS
L TONLETS
O TESTOON
P POTENTS
R ROTTENS
SNOTTER
STENTOR
S OSTENTS
TESTONS
U STOUTEN
TENUTOS

ENOSTU 94
(O TUNES)
A SOUTANE
C CONTUSE
ECONUTS
D DEUTONS
SNOUTED
G TONGUES
L LENTOUS
M UNSMOTE
N NEUSTON
O UNSOOTE
R TENOURS
TONSURE
S OUTNESS
TONUSES
T STOUTEN
TENUTOS
U TENUOUS

ENRSTU 84
TUNERS
A AUNTERS
NATURES
SAUNTER
B BRUNETS
BUNTERS
BURNETS
BURSTEN
C ENCRUST
D RETUNDS
E NEUTERS
RETUNES
TENURES
TUREENS
F FUNSTER
G GUNTERS

GURNETS
SURGENT
H HUNTERS
SHUNTER
UNHERST
I TRIUNES
UNITERS
L RUNLETS
M MUNSTER
STERNUM
N RUNNETS
O TENOURS
TONSURE
P PUNSTER
PUNTERS
R RETURNS
TURNERS
S UNRESTS
T ENTRUST
NUTTERS

EOPRST 193
REPOTS
A ESPARTO
PROTEAS
SEAPORT
B BESPORT
C COPTERS
D DEPORTS
REDTOPS
SPORTED
F FORPETS
H POTHERS
STROPHE
THORPES
I PERIOST
PORIEST
REPOSIT
RIPOSTE
ROPIEST
L PETROLS
M STOMPER
TROMPES
N POSTERN
PRONEST
O POOREST
POOTERS
STOOPER
P STOPPER
TOPPERS
R PORTERS
PRETORS
REPORTS
SPORTER
S PORTESS
POSTERS
PRESTOS
REPOSTS
T POTTERS
PROTEST
SPOTTER
U PETROUS
POSTURE
POUTERS
PROTEUS
SEPTUOR
SPOUTER
TROUPES
W POWTERS
X EXPORTS

EORRST 106
SORTER
A ROASTER
C RECTORS
D DORTERS
RODSTER
E RESTORE

G	GROSERT	D	DETORTS	N	TRINING	D	RODINGS	I	RIOTING	T SOTTING
H	RHETORS	E	ROSETTE	O	RIOTING	E	ERINGOS	K	TROKING	U OUSTING
	ROTHERS	H	HOTTERS	R	TIRRING		IGNORES	O	ROOTING	OUTINGS
	SHORTER	I	STOITER	S	STIRING		REGIONS	P	PORTING	TOUSING
I	RIOTERS	J	JOTTERS		TIRINGS		SIGNORE		TROPING	V STOVING
	ROISTER	L	SETTLOR	T	RITTING	G	GORINGS	R	RORTING	W STOWING
	RORIEST		SLOTTER	W	TWIRING		GRINGOS	S	ROSTING	TOWINGS
K	STROKER		TOLTERS		WRITING	H	HORSING		SORTING	TOWSING
M	TERMORS	N	ROTTENS				SHORING		STORING	Y TOYINGS
	TREMORS		SNOTTER	**GILNOT 171**		I	ORIGINS		TRIGONS	
N	SNORTER		STENTOR	TOLING			SIGNIOR	T	ROTTING	**INORST 59**
O	ROOSTER	O	TOOTERS	A	ANTILOG		SIGNORI	U	ROUTING	(TRIONS)
	ROOTERS	P	POTTERS	B	BILTONG	L	LORINGS		TOURING	A AROINTS
	TOREROS		PROTEST		BOLTING	M	SMORING	W	ROWTING	RATIONS
P	PORTERS		SPOTTER	C	COLTING	N	SNORING		TROWING	B RIBSTON
	PRETORS	R	RETORTS	E	LENTIGO		SORNING			C CISTRON
	REPORTS		ROTTERS	F	LOFTING	O	ROOSING	**GINOST 176**		CITRONS
	SPORTER		TORRETS	H	THOLING	P	PROIGNS	(TO SING)		CORNIST
R	RORTERS	T	STOTTER	I	TOILING		PROSING	A	AGONIST	E NORITES
	TERRORS		STRETTO	J	JOLTING		ROPINGS		GITANOS	ORIENTS
S	RESORTS		TOTTERS	L	TOLLING	S	GRISONS	C	COSTING	STONIER
	ROSTERS	U	STOUTER	M	MOLTING		INGROSS		GNOSTIC	TERSION
	SORTERS		TOUTERS	O	LOOTING		SIGNORS	D	DOTINGS	TRIONES
	STORERS	W	SWOTTER		TOOLING	T	ROSTING	F	SOFTING	F FORINTS
T	RETORTS	X	EXTORTS	P	POLTING		SORTING	H	HOSTING	G ROSTING
	ROTTERS	Y	ROSETTY	S	LINGOTS		STORING		TOSHING	SORTING
	TORRETS				TIGLONS		TRIGONS	K	STOKING	STORING
U	RETOURS	**GIINRT 233**			TOLINGS	U	ROUSING	L	LINGOTS	TRIGONS
	ROUSTER	TIRING		T	LOTTING		SOURING		TIGLONS	H HORNIST
	ROUTERS	A	AIRTING	U	LOUTING	V	ROVINGS		TOLINGS	I IRONIST
	TOURERS		RAITING	W	LOWTING	W	ROWINGS	M	GNOMIST	L NOSTRIL
	TROUSER	B	RINGBIT				WORSING	N	STONING	N INTRONS
V	TROVERS	C	TRICING	**GINORS 128**		Y	ROSYING		TONINGS	O ISOTRON
W	STROWER	D	DIRTING	SIGNOR			SIGNORY	O	SOOTING	NITROSO
Y	ROYSTER	E	IGNITER	A	IGNAROS			P	POSTING	TORSION
			TIERING		ORIGANS	**GINORT 102**			STOPING	T TRITONS
EORSTT 114			TIGRINE		SIGNORA	ROTING		R	ROSTING	U NITROUS
OTTERS		F	RIFTING		SOARING	A	ORATING		SORTING	TURIONS
A	ROTATES	G	GIRTING	B	BORINGS		ROATING		STORING	
	TOASTER		RINGGIT		ROBINGS	D	DORTING		TRIGONS	
B	BETTORS	L	TIRLING		SORBING	E	GENITOR	S	STINGOS	
C	COTTERS	M	MITRING	C	SCORING	F	FORTING		TOSSING	

7-LETTER SETS LIST
alphabetical list of all words appearing in 7-letter sets

ABELIAS	ALECOST	APOSTLE	ATRESIA	BEMIRES	BOLSTER	CAMOTES	CENTAUR	CONFERS
ABLEISM	ALEGARS	APPRISE	ATTAINS	BENDERS	BOLTERS	CANCERS	CENTERS	CONFEST
ABLEIST	ALENGTH	APTERAL	ATTENDS	BENDIER	BOLTING	CANDIES	CENTRAL	CONGERS
ABREAST	ALERCES	APTNESS	ATTENTS	BENIGHT	BONIEST	CANDLES	CENTRES	CONGEST
ABRIDGE	ALEYING	ARAISED	ATTIRED	BENTIER	BOOSTER	CANGLED	CERASIN	CONINES
ABSEILS	ALGATES	ARANEID	ATTIRES	BERATES	BORAGES	CANGLES	CERATES	CONKERS
ACARINE	ALGESIS	ARBORES	ATTONES	BERLINS	BORANES	CANIEST	CEREALS	CONNERS
ACATERS	ALIASES	ARBUTES	ATTORNS	BERRETS	BORATES	CANINES	CERESIN	CONSEIL
ACCENTS	ALIGNED	ARCADES	ATTRITE	BERRIES	BORAXES	CANKERS	CERITES	CONSENT
ACEROSE	ALIMENT	ARCHEST	ATTUNES	BERTHAS	BORDELS	CANNERS	CERNING	CONSTER
ACEROUS	ALIPEDS	ARCHLET	AUDILES	BESAINT	BORIDES	CANNIER	CERRIAL	CONTEST
ACETALS	ALLISES	ARCINGS	AULDEST	BESMEAR	BORINGS	CANTERS	CERTAIN	CONTRAS
ACETOSE	ALNAGER	ARCTICS	AUNTERS	BESOINS	BOSHTER	CANTEST	CESSION	CONTUSE
ACETOUS	ALNAGES	AREDING	AUNTIES	BESORTS	BOSSIER	CANTIER	CESTOID	CONURES
ACETYLS	ALSIKES	AREFIES	AURICLE	BESPORT	BOTHERS	CANTLES	CETANES	COPIERS
ACIDEST	ALTERNE	AREOLES	AUSTERE	BESTAIN	BOTTIES	CANTORS	CHAINES	COPSIER
ACINOSE	ALUNITE	ARGENTS	AVENIRS	BESTARS	BOUNDER	CANTRED	CHALETS	COPTERS
ACMITES	AMBIENT	ARGYLES	AVIDEST	BESTEAD	BRAIDED	CANTREF	CHANTER	CORBIES
ACTINGS	AMBRIES	ARIDEST	AVOCETS	BESTIAL	BRAIDER	CAPLETS	CHARETS	CORDING
ACTRESS	AMEARST	ARIETTA	AWAREST	BESTING	BRAILED	CAPOTES	CHARLIE	CORNEAS
ACTURES	AMENDES	ARIETTE	AWMRIES	BESTIRS	BRAINED	CAPRINE	CHASTEN	CORNELS
ADAPTER	AMENITY	ARISING	AWNIEST	BESTORM	BRAISED	CARBIDE	CHASTER	CORNERS
ADDREST	AMENTAL	ARISTAE	BADGERS	BESTRID	BRANGLE	CARBINE	CHENARS	CORNETS
ADEPTER	AMENTIA	ARKITES	BAILEES	BETOILS	BRANLES	CARDERS	CHOREAS	CORNIST
ADERMIN	AMERCES	ARMLETS	BAILERS	BETRAYS	BRANSLE	CARDIES	CICEROS	CORRIES
ADHERES	AMITIES	AROINTS	BAILEYS	BETRIMS	BRANTLE	CARDING	CINDERS	CORSAGE
ADMIRES	AMNESIA	AROUSED	BAILIES	BETTERS	BRASERO	CAREENS	CINEAST	CORSETS
ADONISE	AMNESIC	AROYNTS	BAITERS	BETTORS	BRASSET	CAREERS	CINEMAS	CORSIVE
ADOPTER	AMNESTY	ARPENTS	BALDEST	BEWAILS	BRATTLE	CAREMES	CINEOLS	CORSLET
ADORERS	AMORCES	ARRASED	BALDIER	BEZOARS	BRAVEST	CARGOES	CINEREA	CORSNED
ADORING	AMORETS	ARRESTS	BALDIES	BIDDERS	BRAVOES	CARINAE	CIRROSE	CORTILE
ADRENAL	AMOSITE	ARRIDES	BANDIER	BIDENTS	BRAWEST	CARIOLE	CISTERN	CORVEES
ADVENTS	AMPERES	ARSENAL	BANDIES	BILKERS	BREARES	CARITAS	CISTRON	CORVETS
ADVERSE	ANADEMS	ARSENIC	BANGERS	BILTONG	BREASTS	CARLINE	CITHERS	COSIERS
ADVERTS	ANAPEST	ARSHINE	BANGLED	BINDERS	BREATHS	CARLING	CITOLES	COSINES
ADVISER	ANCRESS	ARSINES	BANGLES	BINGERS	BREDING	CARMINE	CITRATE	COSTATE
AEDILES	ANELING	ARTICLE	BANTERS	BINGLED	BRETONS	CARNETS	CITRINE	COSTEAN
AERATES	ANEMIAS	ARTIEST	BARBETS	BINGLES	BRIARED	CARNEYS	CITRONS	COSTERS
AERIALS	ANEROID	ARTISAN	BARDIER	BIOGENS	BRIDGES	CARNIED	CITTERN	COSTING
AERIEST	ANESTRA	ARTISTE	BARDING	BIRDERS	BRIDIES	CARNIER	CLAIMER	COSTREL
AEROBES	ANESTRI	ARTLESS	BARGEST	BIRDIES	BRIDLES	CARNIES	CLANGED	COTISED
AEROBUS	ANGELIC	ARTSIER	BARITES	BIREMES	BRIGADE	CARNOSE	CLANGER	COTTERS
AEROSOL	ANGELUS	ARTSIES	BARRETS	BIRETTA	BRIGAND	CAROUSE	CLARETS	COTTISE
AETHERS	ANGERED	ARTSMEN	BARTERS	BIRLERS	BRISKED	CARPELS	CLARIES	COUTERS
AFREETS	ANGERLY	ASCENTS	BARTONS	BIRSLED	BRISKET	CARPETS	CLAROES	COVENTS
AGAINST	ANGLERS	ASKLENT	BARYTES	BIRSLES	BRISTLE	CARTELS	CLASPER	COVERTS
AGELAST	ANGLICE	ASPIRED	BASINET	BISTERS	BRUISED	CARTERS	CLAVIER	COWRIES
AGILEST	ANGLIST	ASPIRES	BASTERS	BISTRED	BRUNETS	CARTING	CLAYIER	COZIERS
AGINNER	ANGRIER	ASSERTS	BASTIDE	BISTRES	BUNTERS	CARTONS	CLIENTS	CRADLES
AGISTED	ANGRIES	ASTEISM	BASTING	BITSIER	BUNTIER	CASEINS	CLINGER	CRAPLES
AGISTER	ANGRILY	ASTELIC	BATHERS	BITTERN	BURDENS	CASERNE	CLUSTER	CRASHED
AGNAILS	ANIMATE	ASTERIA	BATISTE	BITTERS	BURDIES	CASERNS	CNEMIAL	CRATERS
AGNATES	ANISEED	ASTERID	BATLERS	BLANDER	BURNETS	CASTERS	COALERS	CRATING
AGNISED	ANKLETS	ASTERTS	BATSMEN	BLARING	BURSTED	CASTING	COALIER	CRATONS
AGONIES	ANLAGES	ASTHORE	BATTENS	BLASTED	BURSTEN	CASTLED	COARSEN	CRAVENS
AGONISE	ANNATES	ASTILBE	BATTERS	BLASTER	BUSTIER	CASTLES	COARSER	CREASED
AGONIST	ANODISE	ASTONED	BATTIER	BLATHER	BUSTLER	CATENAS	COASTED	CREASER
AGRASTE	ANOESIS	ASTRICT	BATTLER	BLATTER	BUTLERS	CATERAN	COASTER	CREATES
AGRISED	ANOMIES	ASTRIDE	BAWDIER	BLEATER	CABLETS	CATLING	COATEES	CREATIN
AIDLESS	ANSATED	ASTUTER	BAXTERS	BLENDES	CABRITS	CATNEPS	COATERS	CREDITS
AIGLETS	ANSWERS	ASUNDER	BEADIER	BLEWART	CADGERS	CATTIER	COAXERS	CREMSIN
AILMENT	ANTHEMS	ATEBRIN	BEAMERS	BLISTER	CAIRNED	CATTIES	COGNISE	CREPONS
AIMLESS	ANTHERS	ATELIER	BEARDIE	BLOATER	CALENDS	CAUTELS	COHEIRS	CRESTED
AIRIEST	ANTIARS	ATHEISM	BEARERS	BLONDES	CALIBER	CAUTERS	COIGNES	CRESTON
AIRINGS	ANTILOG	ATHEIST	BEARING	BLUIEST	CALIBRE	CAVERNS	COINERS	CRETICS
AIRLESS	ANTINGS	ATIMIES	BEATERS	BLUSTER	CALIPER	CEASING	COLTERS	CRETINS
AIRSIDE	ANTLERS	ATINGLE	BEDRALS	BOASTER	CALIVER	CEDRINE	COLTING	CRETISM
AIRTING	ANTLIAE	ATOMIES	BEGIRDS	BOATELS	CALLETS	CELESTA	COMATES	CRINATE
AISLING	ANTSIER	ATOMISE	BELIERS	BOATERS	CALMEST	CENOTES	CONCISE	CRINGED
ALBERTS	ANYTIME	ATONERS	BELTERS	BOILERS	CALMIER	CENSORS	CONDERS	CRINGES
ALBITES	APERIES	ATONIES	BELTING	BOLDENS	CALORIE	CENTALS	CONDIES	CRINGLE
ALDRINS	APLITES	ATOPIES	BELTMAN	BOLETUS	CAMLETS	CENTARE		

CRINITE	DEAFEST	DESTINY	DOILTER	EARLAPS	ENDUROS	ERASURE	FASTING	FRINGES
CRINOSE	DEALERS	DESTROY	DOLINES	EARLESS	ENEMATA	EREPSIN	FATHERS	FRISEES
CRISTAE	DEALING	DETAILS	DOLMENS	EARLIES	ENEMIES	ERGATES	FATLING	FRISKET
CRIVENS	DEANERS	DETAINS	DOMIEST	EARNERS	ENERGID	ERINGOS	FATTENS	FRISTED
CRONETS	DEAREST	DETENTS	DONATES	EARNEST	ENFANTS	ERINITE	FATTIER	FROISES
CRONIES	DEARIES	DETENUS	DONGLES	EARNING	ENFIRED	ERISTIC	FATTIES	FROSTED
CROSIER	DEARING	DETORTS	DONSIER	EARRING	ENFIRES	ERMINED	FEALING	FUNDERS
CROUTES	DEARNLY	DETOURS	DONZELS	EARSHOT	ENFOLDS	ERMINES	FEARING	FUNSTER
CRUDEST	DEARTHS	DETRAIN	DOPIEST	EARTHLY	ENFORMS	ERODING	FEASTED	FUSTIER
CRUISED	DEASILS	DETUNES	DORISED	EASTERN	ENGAOLS	EROSION	FEASTER	GABLETS
CRUSADE	DEASIUL	DEUTONS	DORISES	EASTING	ENGILDS	EROSIVE	FEDORAS	GADDERS
CRUSTAE	DEASOIL	DEVISAL	DORIZES	EASTLIN	ENGINER	EROTICS	FEERIES	GADSMEN
CRUSTED	DEBASER	DEVISER	DORRING	EATINGS	ENGIRDS	EROTISM	FEERINS	GAGSTER
CUITERS	DEBATES	DEVISOR	DORSELS	EBONICS	ENGLUTS	ERRANDS	FEINTER	GAHNITE
CULTERS	DEBTORS	DEVLING	DORTERS	EBONIST	ENGORES	ERRANTS	FELSITE	GAINERS
CURATES	DECANTS	DEVOIRS	DORTING	ECARTES	ENGRAFT	ERRINGS	FELSPAR	GAINEST
CURIETS	DECARBS	DEWANIS	DOSSIER	ECLAIRS	ENGRAIL	ERYNGOS	FELTERS	GAITERS
CUSTODE	DECARES	DEXTERS	DOTIEST	ECONUTS	ENGRAIN	ESCOLAR	FELTING	GALENAS
CUSTREL	DECERNS	DIABLES	DOTINGS	EDGINGS	ENGRAMS	ESCORTS	FEMINAL	GALERES
CUTLERS	DECRIAL	DIALLER	DOTTLER	EDITORS	ENGRASP	ESLOINS	FENDERS	GALLETS
CYANISE	DECRIES	DIALYSE	DOTTREL	EELIEST	ENGROSS	ESPARTO	FENDIER	GAMIEST
CYSTINE	DEFASTE	DIAPERS	DOUCEST	EERIEST	ENGUARD	ESPIALS	FENITAR	GAMINES
CZARIST	DEFEATS	DIARIES	DOUCETS	EFFEIRS	ENIGMAS	ESPRITS	FERLIES	GANDERS
DABSTER	DEFIERS	DIARISE	DOUREST	EGOTISM	ENISLED	ESSOINS	FERNING	GANGERS
DACITES	DEFINER	DIASTER	DOURINE	EGOTIST	ENLARDS	ESTATED	FERRETS	GANGREL
DACKERS	DEFRAGS	DIBBERS	DOUTERS	EILDING	ENLARGE	ESTIVAL	FERRIES	GANNETS
DAEMONS	DEFROST	DIEDRAL	DOVIEST	ELANETS	ENLIGHT	ESTOILE	FETTERS	GANTLET
DAFTIES	DEGOUTS	DIEDRES	DOWIEST	ELASTIC	ENLISTS	ESTOVER	FIANCES	GAOLERS
DAGGERS	DEHORTS	DIETERS	DOWLNES	ELASTIN	ENRACES	ESTRADE	FIBSTER	GARBLES
DAIDLES	DEISEAL	DIGGERS	DOWRIES	ELATERS	ENRAGED	ESTRAYS	FILACER	GARDENS
DAIKERS	DELATES	DIGRESS	DOZIEST	ELATING	ENRAGES	ESTREAT	FILASSE	GARGETS
DAILIES	DELATOR	DILATER	DRAGEES	ELATION	ENRINGS	ESTRICH	FILTERS	GARGLES
DAIRIES	DELEING	DILATES	DRAGNET	ELDINGS	ENROOTS	ETACISM	FINAGLE	GARMENT
DALLIER	DELIRIA	DILUTER	DRAILED	ELEGANT	ENROUND	ETALONS	FINDERS	GARNERS
DALLIES	DELIVER	DILUTES	DRAINED	ELEGIST	ENSEARS	ETCHING	FINEERS	GARNETS
DAMPENS	DELVING	DINDLES	DRAINER	ELEGITS	ENSILED	ETERNAL	FINGERS	GARNISH
DANCERS	DEMAINS	DINGERS	DRAPERS	ELICITS	ENSNARL	ETESIAN	FIREMAN	GARRETS
DANDERS	DEMANDS	DINGEYS	DRAPETS	ELIDING	ENSTAMP	ETHIOPS	FIRMEST	GARTERS
DANDIER	DEMEANS	DINGIER	DRAPING	ELISION	ENSTYLE	ETHNICS	FISTIER	GASPIER
DANDIES	DEMENTS	DINGIES	DRASTIC	ELITISM	ENSURED	ETTLING	FITNESS	GASTERS
DANDLER	DENARII	DINGLES	DRAWEES	ELITIST	ENTAILS	ETYMONS	FITTERS	GASTING
DANDLES	DENIALS	DINGOES	DRAWERS	ELMIEST	ENTAMES	EUCAINS	FLANGED	GASTRIC
DANGERS	DENIERS	DINKEST	DRAWING	ELOGIES	ENTASIS	EVADERS	FLANGES	GASTRIN
DANGLED	DENNETS	DINNERS	DRAZELS	ELOGIST	ENTERAL	EVILLER	FLARING	GATEMAN
DANGLER	DENOTES	DINNLES	DREARES	ELOIGNS	ENTERIC	EVOKERS	FLENSED	GATINGS
DANGLES	DENSELY	DIOPTER	DREEING	ELUANTS	ENTHRAL	EXHORTS	FLINGER	GAUNTER
DANKEST	DENSEST	DIOPTRE	DRIBLET	ELUENTS	ENTICER	EXODIST	FLIRTED	GEALING
DANSEUR	DENSITY	DIPTERA	DROLEST	ELUDING	ENTICES	EXPORTS	FLORETS	GEARING
DARBIES	DENTALS	DIRECTS	DRONING	ELUSION	ENTIRES	EXTENDS	FLUENTS	GELATIN
DARCIES	DENTELS	DIREMPT	DROPLET	ELUTING	ENTOILS	EXTERNS	FLUIEST	GELDING
DARGLES	DENTILS	DIRIGES	DROSERA	ELUTORS	ENTOMBS	EXTIRPS	FLUSTER	GENDERS
DARINGS	DENTINS	DIRTIES	DROVING	EMANANT	ENTRAIL	EXTORTS	FLUTERS	GENERAL
DARIOLE	DENTIST	DIRTING	DRUSIER	EMANATE	ENTRAIN	EXTRAIT	FOISTED	GENISTA
DARKENS	DEODARS	DISABLE	DUETTOS	EMBAILS	ENTRALL	EYLIADS	FOISTER	GENITAL
DARKEST	DEPARTS	DISCERN	DUIKERS	EMBRAID	ENTRANT	FADIEST	FOLATES	GENITOR
DARKIES	DEPORTS	DISCOER	DUNDERS	EMERIES	ENTRAPS	FAERIES	FOLDERS	GENTIER
DARKLES	DEPOSIT	DISCURE	DUNGIER	EMETINS	ENTREAT	FAIBLES	FOMENTS	GENTILE
DARLING	DERAIGN	DISEURS	DUNITES	EMICANT	ENTREES	FAINEST	FOMITES	GENTLES
DARNELS	DERAILS	DISLEAF	DUNKERS	EMIGRES	ENTRIES	FAINTER	FONDEST	GERBILS
DARNERS	DERANGE	DISLEAL	DUNNEST	EMONGST	ENTRISM	FAIREST	FONDLES	GERENTS
DARNING	DERATES	DISNEST	DUNNIER	EMPARES	ENTRIST	FALSIES	FORDING	GERMAIN
DARRING	DERBIES	DISPONE	DURAMEN	EMPARLS	ENTRUST	FALSING	FORINTS	GERMANS
DARTERS	DERIDES	DISRANK	DURANCE	EMPARTS	ENTWIST	FALTERS	FORPETS	GERMENS
DARTING	DERIVES	DISRATE	DURIANS	EMPIRES	ENURING	FAMINES	FORTIES	GERMINS
DARTLES	DERNIER	DISROBE	DURRIES	EMPRISE	ENVIERS	FANCIER	FORTING	GERNING
DARTRES	DERRIES	DISSEAT	DUSKIER	ENACTOR	EOLITHS	FANCIES	FOTHERS	GERUNDS
DATINGS	DESALTS	DISSENT	DUSTERS	ENAMORS	EONISMS	FANGLED	FOULEST	GESTALT
DATIVES	DESCANT	DISSERT	DUSTIER	ENCORES	EPACRIS	FANGLES	FOUNDER	GESTANT
DAUBIER	DESCENT	DISTANT	DUSTMEN	ENCRATY	EPEIRAS	FARDELS	FRAISED	GETTERS
DAUNDER	DESERTS	DISTEND	DUTEOUS	ENCRUST	EPIGONS	FARDENS	FRATERS	GIANTLY
DAUNERS	DESIGNS	DISTENT	DYEINGS	ENDARTS	EPILOGS	FARDING	FREESIA	GIANTRY
DAUNTER	DESIRED	DISTUNE	DYESTER	ENDEARS	EPIMERS	FARNESS	FREMITS	GIBLETS
DAURING	DESIRER	DITHERS	DZERENS	ENDINGS	EPISTLE	FARSING	FRETSAW	GIGLETS
DAUTIES	DESIRES	DITONES	EAGLETS	ENDITES	EPSILON	FARTHEL	FRIANDE	GILDERS
DAWNERS	DESMANS	DITSIER	EANLING	ENDLANG	EPURATE	FARTING	FRIANDS	GILLETS
DAWTIES	DESMINE	DIVERSE	EARBOBS	ENDLESS	ERASERS	FASCINE	FRIDGES	GIMLETS
DAYSMEN	DESPAIR	DIVERTS	EARCONS	ENDMOST	ERASING	FASTERS	FRIEZES	GINGALS
DEADERS	DESSERT	DOATERS	EARDING	ENDORSE	ERASION		FRINGED	GINGERS
DEADEST	DESTINE	DOCENTS	EARINGS	ENDURES				

GINGLES	GRAPNEL	HARTENS	ILLITES	INSTEAD	JIRBLES	LANDLER	LEISHER	LITTERS
GINNELS	GRASPED	HARVEST	IMARETS	INSTEPS	JITTERS	LANGEST	LEISLER	LIVENER
GINNERS	GRASSED	HASTIER	IMMENSE	INSURED	JOINERS	LANGREL	LEISTER	LOADENS
GINNERY	GRATERS	HASTING	IMMERSE	INSURES	JOISTED	LANGUED	LEISURE	LOADERS
GINNIER	GRATINE	HATREDS	IMPANEL	INTAKES	JOLTERS	LANGUES	LENDERS	LOAFERS
GIRDERS	GRATING	HATTERS	IMPASTE	INTEGER	JOLTIER	LANGUET	LENDING	LOATHER
GIRDLES	GRATINS	HEADERS	IMPONES	INTENDS	JOLTING	LANKEST	LENGEST	LOATHES
GIRLIES	GRAVELS	HEADSET	IMPRESA	INTENSE	JONTIES	LANNERS	LENTIGO	LOBSTER
GIRLOND	GRAVEST	HEALERS	IMPRESE	INTENTS	JOTTERS	LANTERN	LENTILS	LOCATES
GIRNELS	GRAYEST	HEALING	IMPREST	INTERIM	JOUSTED	LAPISES	LENTISK	LODGERS
GIRNERS	GRAYLES	HEARERS	INANEST	INTERNE	KALENDS	LAPPERS	LENTORS	LOFTERS
GIRTING	GREASED	HEARING	INARMED	INTERNS	KANDIES	LAPSING	LENTOUS	LOFTIER
GISARME	GREASER	HEARSED	INBREED	INTIMAE	KANTENS	LARDERS	LEOTARD	LOFTING
GITANAS	GREATEN	HEARTHS	INCAGES	INTINES	KARITES	LARDIER	LESBIAN	LOGIEST
GITANOS	GRECIAN	HEARTLY	INCASED	INTONES	KARSTIC	LARDING	LESIONS	LOITERS
GITTERN	GREINED	HEATERS	INCASES	INTREAT	KARTERS	LARGENS	LESTING	LOMENTA
GLACIER	GREISEN	HEATING	INCAVES	INTRONS	KARTING	LARGESS	LETTERS	LOMENTS
GLADDEN	GREISLY	HECTORS	INCEPTS	INTRUDE	KEISTER	LARGEST	LETTING	LOONIES
GLADIER	GREMLIN	HEFTING	INCESTS	INTUSES	KELTERS	LARKING	LETTRES	LOOTERS
GLAIRED	GRENADE	HEIFERS	INCHASE	INURNED	KELTIES	LARNING	LEVANTS	LOOTING
GLAIRIN	GRIESLY	HEISTER	INCITER	INVADER	KENOSIS	LASAGNE	LEVITES	LORDING
GLANCED	GRIEVES	HELIMAN	INCITES	INVADES	KENTIAS	LASINGS	LIAISED	LORICAE
GLANCES	GRILLES	HEMINAS	INCLOSE	INVENTS	KERATIN	LASSIES	LIAISES	LORINGS
GLANDES	GRILSES	HENRIES	INCOMES	INVERSE	KERNING	LASTAGE	LIBATES	LORISES
GLARING	GRINDED	HENTING	INDARTS	INVERTS	KERNISH	LASTERS	LIBBERS	LORRIES
GLASSEN	GRINDER	HERALDS	INDENTS	INVESTS	KERNITE	LASTING	LIBEROS	LOSSIER
GLAZERS	GRINGOS	HERBIST	INDITER	INVITER	KESTING	LATCHES	LIBRATE	LOTTING
GLEANED	GRINNED	HERDENS	INDITES	INWARDS	KESTREL	LATEENS	LIDGERS	LOTUSES
GLEANER	GRINNER	HERDING	INDOLES	IODATES	KILERGS	LATHERS	LIEFEST	LOUDENS
GLENOID	GRISELY	HERIOTS	INDORSE	IODINES	KILTERS	LATHERY	LIEGERS	LOUDEST
GLIDERS	GRISLED	HERLING	INDUCER	IOLITES	KILTIES	LATHIER	LIERNES	LOUNDER
GLINTED	GRISONS	HERMITS	INDULGE	IONISED	KINDERS	LATHING	LIEVEST	LOUSIER
GLIOSES	GRISTLE	HERNIAS	INEARTH	IONISER	KINDEST	LATICES	LIFTERS	LOUTING
GLISTEN	GRIVETS	HEROICS	INEPTER	IONISES	KINDLES	LATRINE	LIGANDS	LOWTING
GLISTER	GROANED	HEROINS	INERTER	IRATELY	KINEMAS	LATRONS	LIGASES	LUNGIES
GLITZES	GROINED	HETEROS	INERTIA	IRATEST	KINGLES	LATTENS	LIGATES	LURDANE
GLOIRES	GROMETS	HETMANS	INFAMES	IRENICS	KINGLET	LAUDERS	LIGGERS	LURDENS
GLORIES	GROSERT	HINDERS	INFARES	IRIDEAL	KINREDS	LAUNDER	LIGHTEN	LURGIES
GLUIEST	GROYNES	HINDLEG	INFECTS	IRISATE	KIRTLED	LAVEERS	LIGNAGE	LUSTERS
GLUTENS	GUERDON	HIPSTER	INFESTS	IRONERS	KIRTLES	LAWINGS	LIGNITE	LUSTIER
GNARLED	GUIDERS	HIRSTIE	INFLAME	IRONIES	KITTENS	LAYINGS	LIGNOSE	LUSTRED
GNARRED	GUILERS	HIRSUTE	INFLATE	IRONISE	KNITTER	LAZIEST	LIGURES	LUSTRES
GNASHER	GUNDIES	HISTONE	INGATES	IRONIST	KRANSES	LEADENS	LIMBERS	LUTEINS
GNAWERS	GUNITES	HITHERS	INGENER	ISABELS	KRATERS	LEADERS	LIMIEST	LUTEOUS
GNOMIST	GUNTERS	HOIDENS	INGESTA	ISATINE	LAAGERS	LEADIER	LIMITES	LYNAGES
GNOSTIC	GURLETS	HOISTED	INGESTS	ISLEMAN	LABISES	LEADING	LIMNERS	MADDENS
GOALIES	GURNETS	HOISTER	INGRAFT	ISLEMEN	LABRETS	LEAFING	LINAGES	MADNESS
GOITERS	GYRATES	HOLDERS	INGRATE	ISOBARE	LABROSE	LEAKERS	LINDENS	MAELIDS
GOITRES	HAEMINS	HOLIEST	INGRESS	ISOGENY	LACIEST	LEAKING	LINEAGE	MAENADS
GOLDENS	HAGLETS	HOLSTER	INGROSS	ISOLATE	LACINGS	LEAMING	LINEATE	MAESTRI
GOLLIES	HAILERS	HOMIEST	INHERED	ISOLINE	LACTASE	LEANEST	LINEMAN	MAESTRO
GOOLIES	HAIRNET	HOOTERS	INHERES	ISOMERE	LACTOSE	LEANING	LINGAMS	MAGENTA
GORIEST	HALBERT	HORDING	INHERIT	ISOMERS	LADDERS	LEAPERS	LINGELS	MAGNATE
GORINGS	HALIDES	HORNETS	INISLED	ISOTONE	LADDIES	LEAPING	LINGERS	MAGNETS
GOVERNS	HALITES	HORNIST	INJECTS	ISOTOPE	LADINGS	LEARING	LINGIER	MAHSEER
GRABENS	HALSING	HORSING	INJERAS	ISOTRON	LADRONE	LEARNED	LINGLES	MAIDENS
GRACILE	HALTERS	HOSIERS	INJURED	ISOTYPE	LAERING	LEASERS	LINGOES	MAIGRES
GRADERS	HALTING	HOSTILE	INLACES	ITERANT	LAGENAS	LEASING	LINGOTS	MAILERS
GRADINE	HAMSTER	HOSTING	INLIERS	ITERATE	LAGGENS	LEASURE	LINGUAE	MAILMEN
GRADING	HANDERS	HOSTLER	INMATES	IVORIES	LAGGERS	LEATHER	LINGUAS	MAINEST
GRADINI	HANDIER	HOTTERS	INNARDS	IVRESSE	LAGGINS	LECTINS	LINIEST	MAISTER
GRADINO	HANDLER	HOTTIES	INQUEST	JAILERS	LAGUNES	LECTORS	LINKAGE	MALGRES
GRADINS	HANDLES	HUNTERS	INROADS	JANGLED	LAIKERS	LEDDENS	LINKERS	MALIGNS
GRAILES	HANDSEL	HURDENS	INSANER	JANGLER	LAIRING	LEERING	LINNETS	MALTIER
GRAINED	HANDSET	HURDIES	INSCAPE	JANGLES	LAIRISE	LEFTIES	LINSANG	MALTING
GRAINER	HANGERS	HURTLES	INSEAMS	JANTIER	LAISSES	LEGATES	LINSEED	MALTMEN
GRAINES	HANTLES	HUSTLER	INSECTS	JANTIES	LAITIES	LEGATOS	LINTELS	MALTOSE
GRAKLES	HAPTENS	ICONISE	INSEEMS	JASMINE	LAKIEST	LEGENDS	LINTERS	MANATEE
GRANDEE	HARDENS	ICTERUS	INSERTS	JERBILS	LALDIES	LEGISTS	LINTIER	MANDATE
GRANDER	HARDEST	IDEATES	INSHORE	JERBOAS	LAMBENT	LEGLANS	LINTIES	MANDIRS
GRANGES	HAREEMS	IGNAROS	INSIDER	JERRIES	LAMBERT	LEGLINS	LIONELS	MANDREL
GRANITA	HARELDS	IGNEOUS	INSNARE	JESTING	LAMBIES	LEIGERS	LIONESS	MANGELS
GRANITE	HARLING	IGNITER	INSOLES	JETTONS	LAMENTS	LEIRING	LIONETS	MANGERS
GRANNIE	HARMINE	IGNITES	INSPECT	JINGALS	LAMINAE	LIONISE	MANGIER
GRANTED	HARNESS	IGNORED	INSPIRE	JINGLED	LAMITER	LIPASES	MANGLED
GRANTEE	HAROSET	IGNORES	INSTANT	JINGLER	LAMPERS	LISTENS	MANGLER
GRANTER	HARPIES	ILEITIS	INSTARS	JINGLES	LANCERS	LISTERS	MANGLES
GRANULE	HARSLET		INSTATE	JINGLET	LANCETS	LITERAL	MANILLE
GRAPLES	HARTELY			JINGOES	LANDERS	LITOTES	MANIPLE

MANKIER	MERRIES	MOLINES	NEITHER	OARLESS	OUSTING	PEARTER	PIONIES	PREIFES
MANLIER	MERSION	MOLTING	NEMATIC	OARSMEN	OUTDOES	PEARTLY	PIRATED	PRELATE
MANNITE	MESAILS	MOMENTS	NEMESIA	OBLATES	OUTINGS	PEASANT	PIRATES	PRELATY
MANREDS	MESHIER	MONADES	NEMESIS	OBLIGES	OUTLERS	PEATERY	PIRNIES	PREMIES
MANTEAU	MESONIC	MONETHS	NEPETAS	OBSERVE	OUTLETS	PEATIER	PISTOLE	PREMISE
MANTEEL	MESSIER	MONGERS	NERDIER	OBTENDS	OUTLIER	PEATMAN	PITEOUS	PRESENT
MANTELS	MESTIZA	MONSTER	NEREIDS	OBTUSER	OUTLIES	PECTINS	PITIERS	PRESIDE
MANTIES	MESTIZO	MONTEMS	NERITES	OBVERSE	OUTNESS	PEDANTS	PITTERS	PRESTED
MANTLED	METEORS	MONTIES	NEROLIS	OBVERTS	OUTREDS	PEDLARS	PLACERS	PRESTOS
MANTLES	METIERS	MONTRES	NERVING	OCTANES	OUTSELL	PEDRAIL	PLACETS	PRETEST
MANTLET	METRICS	MOONERS	NESTERS	OCTAVES	OUTSIDE	PEINCTS	PLAITER	PRETORS
MANTOES	METRING	MOONIES	NESTFUL	OERSTED	OUTSOLE	PELITES	PLANERS	PREVISE
MANURED	METRIST	MOONSET	NESTING	OESTRAL	OVARIES	PELOTAS	PLANETS	PRIEFES
MARDIES	MICATES	MOOTERS	NESTLED	OESTRUM	OVERLIE	PELTERS	PLANTER	PRIESTS
MARGENT	MIGRANT	MOPIEST	NESTLES	OEUVRES	OVERSEA	PELTING	PLASTER	PRIEVES
MARGINS	MILDENS	MORAINE	NETFULS	OILIEST	OVERSEE	PENATES	PLATENS	PRINCES
MARINER	MILTERS	MORALES	NETTIER	OILLETS	OVERSET	PENSION	PLATERS	PRINTED
MARINES	MINARET	MOREENS	NETTLES	OLDNESS	OVERSEW	PENTADS	PLATIER	PRISAGE
MARKETS	MINCERS	MORGENS	NEURISM	OLDSTER	OVERUSE	PENTELS	PLATING	PRIVETS
MARLINE	MINDERS	MORTISE	NEURITE	OLEATES	OWLIEST	PENTISE	PLATTER	PROGINS
MARLING	MINDSET	MOSSIER	NEUSTON	OLEFINS	OWRIEST	PENULTS	PLAYERS	PROINES
MARRIES	MINEOLA	MOTHERS	NEUTERS	OLIVERS	PAIDLES	PEONIES	PLEAING	PROLATE
MARTELS	MINERAL	MOTIEST	NEUTRAL	OLIVETS	PAINTER	PEONISM	PLEASER	PRONEST
MARTENS	MINGLED	MOTILES	NICHERS	OLOGIES	PALIEST	PEPINOS	PLEATER	PROSING
MARTING	MINGLER	MOTIVES	NICKERS	OMENTAL	PALINGS	PERIDOT	PLECTRA	PROTEAS
MARTINS	MINGLES	MOTLIER	NIDGETS	OMERTAS	PALMERS	PERIODS	PLENIST	PROTEID
MASHIER	MINIATE	MOTSERS	NIELLOS	ONAGERS	PALSIED	PERIOST	PODITES	PROTEST
MASONED	MINIEST	MOURNED	NIFTIER	ONDINES	PALSIER	PERITUS	POETICS	PROTEUS
MASSIER	MINSTER	MOUSTED	NIGELLA	ONLIEST	PALSIES	PERKINS	POETISE	PROYNES
MASTERS	MINTAGE	MOUTERS	NIGGARD	ONSIDES	PALTERS	PERMITS	POINTES	PRUINES
MASTERY	MINTERS	MRIDANG	NIGGERS	ONSTEAD	PANDERS	PERONES	POISERS	PSALTER
MASTIER	MINTIER	MUNITES	NIGGLED	OOLITES	PANDIES	PERRIES	POITREL	PTERINS
MASTING	MINUETS	MUNSTER	NIGGLER	OORIEST	PANSIED	PERRONS	POKIEST	PTERYLA
MATIEST	MINUTER	MURINES	NIGGLES	OPENERS	PANTERS	PERSANT	POLDERS	PUDSIER
MATINEE	MINUTES	MUSTIER	NIGHEST	OPERATE	PANTIES	PERSICO	POLITER	PUIREST
MATRICS	MIRACLE	MUTINES	NIGHTED	OPERONS	PANTILE	PERSING	POLTING	PULIEST
MATRONS	MIRAGES	NACKETS	NIGHTIE	OPHITES	PANTLER	PERSIST	PONDERS	PUNIEST
MATTERS	MIRBANE	NACRITE	NILGAIS	OPIATES	PARCELS	PERSONA	PONTIES	PUNSTER
MATTIES	MIRIEST	NAGARIS	NILGAUS	OPTIMES	PARDINE	PERSONS	POOREST	PUNTERS
MATTINS	MIRKEST	NAGGERS	NIMMERS	ORACHES	PARENTS	PERTAIN	POOTERS	PUNTIES
MATURES	MISDATE	NAGGIER	NIPPERS	ORACIES	PARESIS	PERTAKE	PORIEST	PURINES
MAUNDER	MISDEAL	NAIADES	NIPTERS	ORACLES	PARGETS	PERTEST	PORTERS	PUTELIS
MAYSTER	MISDOER	NAIFEST	NITERIE	ORANGES	PARINGS	PERUSAL	PORTESS	PYONERS
MAZIEST	MISDONE	NAILERS	NITRATE	ORATING	PARKIES	PESANTE	PORTING	PYRITES
MEAGRES	MISERES	NAIVEST	NITRIDE	ORBIEST	PARLEYS	PESANTS	POSIEST	QINDARS
MEALERS	MISFARE	NAMASTE	NITRILE	ORCEINS	PARLIES	PESAUNT	POSITED	QINTARS
MEALING	MISGONE	NANCIES	NITRITE	ORCINES	PARLING	PETARAS	POSTERN	QUINTES
MEANEST	MISHEAR	NARASES	NITROSO	ORDAINS	PAROLES	PETARDS	POSTERS	RABBETS
MEANIES	MISKENT	NARDING	NITROUS	ORDEALS	PARRELS	PETRELS	POSTIES	RABIDER
MEARING	MISLEAD	NARGILE	NITTIER	ORDINEE	PARRIES	PETROLS	POSTING	RACEMES
MEASING	MISMATE	NARGILY	NOCENTS	OREADES	PARSING	PETROUS	POSTMEN	RACIEST
MEASURE	MISNAME	NARRATE	NOCKETS	OREIDES	PARTERS	PETTERS	POSTURE	RACINGS
MEDIALS	MISRATE	NARTJIE	NODDIES	ORGEATS	PARTIED	PEZANTS	POTENTS	RACISTS
MEDIANS	MISREAD	NASCENT	NODDLES	ORGONES	PARTIES	PHONERS	POTHERS	RACKETS
MEDIANT	MISSEEN	NASTIER	NODULES	ORIENTS	PARTING	PHONIES	POTTERS	RADDEST
MEDINAS	MISSENT	NASTIES	NOISIER	ORIGANE	PARTITE	PIASTRE	POTTIES	RADDLES
MEDLARS	MISTAKE	NATCHES	NOISOME	ORIGANS	PARTLET	PIGEONS	POUNDER	RADGEST
MEDLING	MISTERM	NATIVES	NOMADES	ORIGINS	PARTNER	PIGLETS	POUTERS	RADIALE
MEDUSAN	MISTERS	NATRONS	NOODLES	ORIOLES	PARVISE	PILSNER	POWNIES	RADIANS
MEINEYS	MISTERY	NATTERS	NORITES	ORNATER	PASTERN	PIMENTS	POWTERS	RADICEL
MEINIES	MISTIER	NATTERY	NOSIEST	OROGENS	PASTERS	PINCASE	POXIEST	RADICES
MEISTER	MISTUNE	NATTIER	NOSTRIL	OROIDES	PASTIER	PINCERS	PRAISED	RADICLE
MELANIC	MISWEEN	NATURED	NOTATES	ORPINES	PASTIME	PINDERS	PRAISER	RADOMES
MELANIN	MISWENT	NATURES	NOTCHES	ORRISES	PASTING	PINGERS	PRAISES	RAFTERS
MELDING	MITHERS	NEALING	NOTICES	OSIERED	PASTURE	PINGLED	PRANCES	RAFTING
MELTING	MITOSES	NEAREST	NOUSLED	OSMIATE	PATENTS	PINGLER	PRANGED	RAGGLES
MELTONS	MITRING	NEARING	NOVICES	OSSEINS	PATERAE	PINGLES	PRATERS	RAGINGS
MENDERS	MITTENS	NEATENS	NUDGERS	OSTENTS	PATINES	PINGOES	PRATIES	RAGINIS
MENHIRS	MOANERS	NEATEST	NURDLES	OSTEOID	PATNESS	PINIEST	PRATING	RAGMENT
MENIALS	MOBSTER	NECROSE	NURSLED	OSTIATE	PATRONS	PINITES	PRATTED	RAIDERS
MENTORS	MODENAS	NECTARS	NUTATES	OSTIOLE	PATTENS	PINKEST	PRATTLE	RAIDING
MENYIES	MODERNS	NECTARY	NUTCASE	OSTLERS	PATTERN	PINKOES	PRAWLES	RAILBED
MERCATS	MODISTE	NEEDERS	NUTLETS	OTARIES	PATTERS	PINNERS	PREASED	RAILERS
MERCIES	MOIDERS	NEEDIER	NUTMEAL	OTARINE	PATTIES	PINNETS	PRECAST	RAILING
MERINOS	MOILERS	NEEDLES	NUTRIAS	OUGLIES	PATZERS	PINOLES	PREDATE	RAILMEN
MERKINS	MOISERS	NEGATES	NUTTERS	OULDEST	PEALING	PINTLES	PREDICT	RAIMENT
MERLING	MOISTED	NEGRESS	NUTTIER	OURIEST	PEANUTS	PIOLETS	PREDIAL	RAISING
MERLINS	MOISTEN	NEGROES	OARIEST	OURIEST	PEANUTS	PIONERS	PREDIES	RAITING
MERLONS	MOISTER	NEGROID	OARIEST	OURIEST	PEANUTS	PIONEYS	PREHEAT	RAKINGS

RALLIED	REASONS	RELIEFS	RESINED	RHETORS	ROSETTY	SALUING	SCOUTED	SERIEMA
RALLIES	REASTED	RELIERS	RESINER	RHODIES	ROSIERE	SALUTED	SCOUTER	SERINES
RAMEKIN	REAVERS	RELIEVE	RESOLED	RIBANDS	ROSIERS	SALUTER	SCOWRIE	SERINGA
RAMENTA	REAVING	RELIEVO	RESOLVE	RIBLESS	ROSIEST	SALVING	SCRAPED	SERIOUS
RAMJETS	REBATES	RELINED	RESORTS	RIBLETS	ROSINED	SAMIELS	SCRAPIE	SERKALI
RAMMIES	REBINDS	RELINES	RESOUND	RIBOSES	ROSITED	SAMIEST	SCRIBED	SERMONS
RANCELS	REBITES	RELIVED	RESPELT	RIBSTON	ROSTERS	SAMISEN	SCRIENE	SERPENT
RANCHES	REBOILS	RELIVER	RESPIRE	RICHENS	ROSTING	SAMITES	SCRIEVE	SERPULA
RANDEMS	REBOOTS	RELIVES	RESPITE	RICHEST	ROSYING	SAMPIRE	SCRINES	SERRANS
RANDIER	REBOUND	RELOADS	RESPOND	RICIEST	ROTATES	SAMPLER	SCYTALE	SERRATE
RANDIES	RECANTS	RELUCTS	RESTAGE	RICKETS	ROTCHES	SANDERS	SDAINED	SERRATI
RANDING	RECASTS	RELYING	RESTART	RIDABLE	ROTHERS	SANDIER	SDAINES	SERRIED
RANGERS	RECITAL	REMADES	RESTATE	RIDGELS	ROTTANS	SANDMEN	SDEIGNE	SERRIES
RANGIER	RECITES	REMAINS	RESTERS	RIDGERS	ROTTENS	SANGRIA	SDEIGNS	SERRING
RANGOLI	RECKONS	REMAKES	RESTFUL	RIEVERS	ROTTERS	SANICLE	SEABIRD	SERVANT
RANKEST	RECLAIM	REMANDS	RESTIER	RIFTING	ROTTING	SANTIRS	SEALANT	SERVICE
RANKLED	RECOILS	REMANIE	RESTIFF	RIGHTEN	ROUNCES	SANTOUR	SEALERS	SERVILE
RANKLES	RECOINS	REMEADS	RESTING	RILIEST	ROUNDED	SAPIENT	SEALERY	SERVING
RANSELS	RECTORS	REMEIDS	RESTIVE	RILLETS	ROUNDEL	SAPLING	SEALING	SESSION
RANTERS	REDACTS	REMIGES	RESTOCK	RIMIEST	ROUNDER	SAPPIER	SEAMERS	SESTINA
RANTING	REDATES	REMINDS	RESTORE	RINGBIT	ROUNDLE	SAPROBE	SEAMIER	SESTINE
RAPIERS	REDCAPS	REMINTS	RESTYLE	RINGENT	ROUSANT	SARANGI	SEAMING	SETLINE
RAPINES	REDDENS	REMISED	RESULTS	RINGERS	ROUSING	SARCODE	SEAPORT	SETTERS
RAPPELS	REDDEST	REMISES	RETABLE	RINGGIT	ROUSTED	SARDELS	SEARATS	SETTING
RASHEST	REDDING	REMIXES	RETAILS	RINGLET	ROUSTER	SARDINE	SEARCED	SETTLER
RASHING	REDEALS	REMOTES	RETAINS	RINGMEN	ROUTERS	SARKING	SEAREST	SETTLOR
RASPIER	REDIALS	REMOVES	RETAKES	RINSERS	ROUTINE	SARMENT	SEARING	SEVERAL
RASPING	REDNESS	RENAMES	RETAMAS	RIOTERS	ROUTING	SARNEYS	SEATERS	SEXTANT
RASTERS	REDOING	RENDERS	RETARDS	RIOTING	ROVINGS	SARNIES	SEATING	SEXTILE
RATABLE	REDOUND	RENDING	RETELLS	RIOTISE	ROWDIES	SARSDEN	SECANTS	SHADIER
RATCHES	REDOWAS	RENEGES	RETENES	RIPENED	ROWINGS	SARSENS	SECONDI	SHAFTER
RATHEST	REDRAWS	RENNETS	RETILED	RIPOSTE	ROWTING	SARSNET	SECRETA	SHALIER
RATINES	REDSEAR	RENNING	RETILES	RIPTIDE	ROYSTED	SATCHEL	SECTARY	SHALING
RATINGS	REDSKIN	RENTALS	RETIMES	RISIBLE	ROYSTER	SATIATE	SECTILE	SHARING
RATIONS	REDTOPS	RENTERS	RETINAE	RISSOLE	RUBIEST	SATIETY	SECTION	SHARPIE
RATLINE	REDUITS	RENTIER	RETINAL	RITTERS	RUDDIES	SATINED	SECTORS	SHASTER
RATLING	REDWING	RENTING	RETINAS	RITTING	RUEINGS	SATINET	SEDATED	SHATTER
RATLINS	REEDING	RENVOIS	RETINOL	ROACHES	RUINATE	SATIRES	SEDATER	SHEARED
RATOONS	REELING	RENYING	RETINUE	ROADIES	RULIEST	SATIRIC	SEDATES	SHEARER
RATTEEN	REESTED	REOPENS	RETIRAL	ROADING	RUNDALE	SATYRIC	SEDGIER	SHEILAS
RATTENS	REFINED	REPAINT	RETIRES	ROASTED	RUNDLES	SAULIES	SEDILIA	SHELTER
RATTERS	REFINES	REPAIRS	RETOOLS	ROASTER	RUNLETS	SAUNTED	SEEDIER	SHELTIE
RATTIER	REFLAGS	REPASTS	RETORTS	ROATING	RUNNETS	SAUNTER	SEEDING	SHERIAT
RATTING	REFLETS	REPEALS	RETOURS	ROBINGS	RUNTIER	SAUTEED	SEELIER	SHIFTER
RATTLES	REFOUND	REPEATS	RETRAIN	ROCHETS	RUSTIER	SAUTING	SEELING	SHINERS
RATTONS	REFUNDS	REPENTS	RETRAIT	ROCKETS	RUSTLED	SAVORED	SEEMING	SHINGLE
RAUNGED	REGAINS	REPINED	RETREES	RODDING	RUSTLER	SCAILED	SEILING	SHINIER
RAUNGES	REGALES	REPINES	RETRIAL	RODENTS	RUSTLES	SCALDER	SEINERS	SHIRTED
RAVINED	REGARDS	REPLANS	RETRIES	RODINGS	RUSTRED	SCALENI	SEISMAL	SHOALER
RAVINES	REGENTS	REPLANT	RETRIMS	RODLESS	RUTILES	SCALIER	SEITENS	SHOEING
RAVINGS	REGIMES	REPLAYS	RETSINA	RODMEN	SABERED	SCALING	SELFING	SHOOTER
RAWINGS	REGINAE	REPLICA	RETTING	RODSTER	SABLING	SCALPER	SELLING	SHORING
RAWNESS	REGINAL	REPLIES	RETUNDS	ROISTED	SABRING	SCANNER	SELTZER	SHORTED
RAYLETS	REGINAS	REPONES	RETUNES	ROISTER	SACRING	SCANTED	SEMATIC	SHORTEN
RAYLING	REGIONS	REPORTS	RETURNS	ROKIEST	SACRIST	SCANTER	SEMEION	SHORTER
READAPT	REGLETS	REPOSAL	REUNITE	RONDEAU	SADDLER	SCANTLE	SEMINAL	SHORTIE
READERS	REGNANT	REPOSIT	REUSING	RONDELS	SADIRON	SCARFED	SEMINAR	SHOTTEN
READIES	REGRANT	REPOSTS	REVEALS	RONDURE	SAETERS	SCARING	SEMITAR	SHOUTED
READILY	REGRETS	REPRISE	REVERSI	ROOSING	SAFROLE	SCARLET	SENARII	SHOUTER
READING	REGRIND	REPUNIT	REVERSO	ROOSTED	SAIDEST	SCARPED	SENATOR	SHRIEVE
READOPT	REHANGS	RERAILS	REVERTS	ROOSTER	SAILERS	SCARRED	SENDALS	SHRINED
REAGENT	REHEARS	REREADS	REVIEWS	ROOTIES	SAILING	SCARTED	SENDERS	SHRINES
REAKING	REHEATS	RESALES	REVILED	ROOTING	SAINTED	SCATOLE	SENDING	SHRIVEN
REALEST	REIFIES	RESCALE	REVILER	ROOTLED	SAIREST	SCATTER	SENECIO	SHUNTED
REALIGN	REIGNED	RESCIND	REVILES	ROOTLES	SAIRING	SCENARY	SENIORS	SHUNTER
REALISE	REINING	RESEALS	REVISAL	ROPIEST	SAKERET	SCENTED	SENNITS	SIDEARM
REALISM	REINTER	RESEATS	REVISED	ROPINGS	SALFERN	SCERNED	SENSIST	SIDEBAR
REALIST	REISTED	RESEDAS	REVISER	RORIEST	SALICES	SCLATED	SENTING	SIDECAR
REALITY	REITERS	RESENTS	REVISES	RORTERS	SALICET	SCLATES	SEPIOST	SIDEMAN
REALTIE	REIVERS	RESIANT	REVISIT	RORTING	SALIENT	SCOLDER	SEPTUOR	SIDEMEN
REAMERS	REJOINS	RESIDED	REVISOR	ROSACEA	SALINES	SCOOTER	SERAFIN	SIDERAL
REAMING	RELAPSE	RESIDER	REVIVES	ROSACES	SALLIED	SCOPATE	SERANGS	SIEMENS
REAPERS	RELATES	RESIDES	REVOKES	ROSEATE	SALLIES	SCORIAE	SEREINS	SIERRAN
REAPING	RELAXES	RESIDUA	REVOLTS	ROSEBAY	SALTERN	SCORING	SERENED	SIEVERT
REARERS	RELEASE	RESIDUE	REWARDS	ROSELLA	SALTERS	SCORNED	SERIALS	SIFTERS
REARING	RELENTS	RESIGNS	REWINDS	ROSEOLA	SALTIER	SCORNER	SERIATE	SIGHTER
REARISE	RELIANT	RESILED	REWIRES	ROSETED	SALTING	SCOTERS	SERICIN	SIGMATE
REAROSE	RELICTS	RESILES	REWOUND	ROSETTE	SALTOED	SCOURIE	SERICON	SIGNALS
								SIGNARY

SIGNERS	SLITTER	SOOTIER	STABBER	STELENE	STRAKES	SWEATER	TARRING	TENUOUS
SIGNETS	SLOPIER	SOOTING	STABILE	STELLAR	STRANGE	SWELTER	TARSELS	TENURES
SIGNEUR	SLOTTER	SOPITED	STABLED	STEMING	STRAWED	SWIFTER	TARSIER	TENUTOS
SIGNIOR	SLUEING	SOPITES	STABLER	STEMSON	STRAWEN	SWINDGE	TARTANE	TEPHRAS
SIGNORA	SMARTED	SORBATE	STACKER	STENCIL	STRAYED	SWINDLE	TARTEST	TEPIDER
SIGNORE	SMARTEN	SORBENT	STADDLE	STENDED	STRAYER	SWINGED	TARTIER	TERCELS
SIGNORI	SMARTER	SORBETS	STAGERS	STENGAH	STREAKS	SWINGER	TARTINE	TERCETS
SIGNORS	SMARTIE	SORBING	STAGERY	STENNED	STREAMS	SWINGLE	TASERED	TERCIOS
SIGNORY	SMATTER	SORBITE	STAGGER	STENTED	STREAMY	SWITHER	TASHING	TEREDOS
SILAGED	SMEARED	SOREDIA	STAGIER	STENTOR	STREELS	SWOTTER	TASKERS	TERETES
SILAGES	SMELTER	SORITES	STAGING	STERILE	STREETS	SYNAPTE	TASKING	TERMERS
SILANES	SMIDGEN	SORNING	STAIDER	STERLET	STREETY	SYRINGA	TASTERS	TERMING
SILENTS	SMITERS	SORTERS	STAINED	STERNAL	STRENES	SYRINGE	TASTIER	TERMINI
SILESIA	SMITTEN	SORTIED	STAINER	STERNED	STRETTA	TABERDS	TASTING	TERMORS
SILTIER	SMOLDER	SORTIES	STAIRED	STERNER	STRETTE	TABLIER	TATLERS	TERNARY
SILVERN	SMORING	SORTING	STAITHE	STERNUM	STRETTI	TABLING	TATTERS	TERNATE
SIMARRE	SMOTHER	SOTTING	STAKING	STEROID	STRETTO	TABRETS	TATTIER	TERNING
SINCERE	SMOUTED	SOUNDER	STALING	STEROLS	STREWED	TACKERS	TATTIES	TERRAIN
SINGERS	SMYTRIE	SOURING	STALKED	STERVED	STREWER	TACKLES	TAUNTER	TERRANE
SINGLED	SNAILED	SOUTANE	STALKER	STEWARD	STRIATE	TADDIES	TAURINE	TERRETS
SINGLES	SNAKIER	SOUTHED	STALLED	STEWIER	STRIDES	TAENIAS	TAUTENS	TERRIES
SINGLET	SNARERS	SOUTHER	STAMENS	STEWING	STRIFES	TAGGERS	TAVERNS	TERRINE
SINKERS	SNARIER	SPACIER	STAMMER	STHENIC	STRIGAE	TAIGLES	TAWIEST	TERRITS
SINNERS	SNARING	SPADGER	STAMPER	STICKER	STRIKER	TAILING	TAWINGS	TERRORS
SINNETS	SNARLED	SPAINED	STANCES	STIEVER	STRIPED	TAILLES	TAWNIER	TERSELY
SINTERS	SNARLER	SPAIRGE	STANDEE	STIEVER	STRIPES	TAILYES	TAWNIES	TERSEST
SINTERY	SNARRED	SPALTED	STANDEN	STIFFER	STRIPEY	TAIVERS	TAWTIER	TERSION
SINUATE	SNEERED	SPANGLE	STANDER	STIFLER	STRIVED	TAIVERT	TAXIMEN	TERTIAL
SINUOSE	SNELLED	SPARELY	STANGED	STILLER	STRIVEN	TAJINES	TAXINGS	TERTIAN
SIRENIC	SNICKER	SPAREST	STANIEL	STILTER	STRIVER	TAKIEST	TAXINGS	TERTIAS
SIRGANG	SNICKET	SPARGED	STANING	STINGED	STRIVES	TAKINGS	TEAGLES	TERTIUS
SIRNAME	SNIDELY	SPARING	STANNEL	STINGER	STROBED	TALCIER	TEAMERS	TESSERA
SIRREES	SNIDEST	SPARKIE	STANYEL	STINGOS	STROBES	TALCING	TEAMING	TESTERN
SIRUPED	SNIFTED	SPARKLE	STAPLED	STINKER	STRODLE	TALCOSE	TEARERS	TESTERS
SITHENS	SNIFTER	SPARRED	STAPLER	STINTED	STROKED	TALENTS	TEARING	TESTIER
SITREPS	SNIGGED	SPARTHE	STARERS	STINTER	STROKEN	TALIPES	TEASELS	TESTING
SITTERS	SNIGGER	SPATTER	STARETS	STIPEND	STROKER	TALKERS	TEASERS	TESTONS
SITTINE	SNIGGLE	SPEARED	STARETZ	STIPULE	STROPHE	TALKIER	TEASING	TESTOON
SITUATE	SNIPERS	SPECTRA	STARING	STIRING	STROWED	TALKIES	TECHNOS	TESTRIL
SITULAE	SNIPIER	SPEIRED	STARKED	STIRPES	STROWER	TALKING	TEDDERS	TESTUDO
SIZABLE	SNIPPER	SPELDIN	STARKEN	STIRRED	STROYED	TALLIER	TEDESCA	TETANUS
SKAILED	SNIPPET	SPELTER	STARKER	STIRRER	STRUDEL	TALLIES	TEENIER	TETHERS
SKATERS	SNIRTLE	SPENDER	STARLET	STIRRES	STRUMAE	TALWEGS	TEERING	TETRADS
SKATING	SNOOLED	SPHERAL	STARNED	STIVERS	STUDDEN	TAMBERS	TEETERS	TETTERS
SKATOLE	SNOOPER	SPIELER	STARNIE	STIVIER	STUDENT	TAMINES	TEGMINA	TEWARTS
SKEARED	SNOOTED	SPIGNEL	STARRED	STOCKER	STUDIER	TAMINGS	TELAMON	THALERS
SKELTER	SNORING	SPILITE	STARTED	STODGER	STUNNED	TAMISES	TELEGAS	THAWERS
SKIABLE	SNORTED	SPINATE	STARTER	STOITED	STUNNER	TAMMIES	TELESIS	THEEING
SKINTER	SNORTER	SPINDLE	STARTLE	STOITER	STUNTED	TAMPERS	TELFERS	THEMING
SKIRRET	SNOTTED	SPINETS	STARVED	STOKING	STURTED	TANAGER	TELLARS	THENARS
SKIRTED	SNOTTER	SPINIER	STARVES	STOMPER	STYRENE	TANDEMS	TELLENS	THEREIN
SKIRTER	SNOTTIE	SPINNER	STATERS	STONERN	SUBTEND	TANGELO	TELLIES	THERIAN
SKITTER	SNOUTED	SPINNET	STATICE	STONERS	SUBTILE	TANGIER	TELLING	THERMAL
SKLATED	SNOWIER	SPINODE	STATING	STONIED	SUBTLER	TANGIES	TELLINS	THIRLED
SLAINTE	SOAPIER	SPINOSE	STATION	STONIER	SUDAMEN	TANGLED	TEMENOS	THOLING
SLAKING	SOARING	SPIRAEA	STATIVE	STONIES	SUDSIER	TANGLER	TEMPERA	THORPES
SLANDER	SOCAGER	SPIRANT	STATURE	STONING	SUEDING	TANGLES	TEMPLAR	THRAVES
SLANGED	SOCIATE	SPIREAS	STAVING	STONKER	SUETIER	TANISTS	TEMSING	THREADS
SLANGER	SODAINE	SPIREME	STAWING	STONNED	SUGARED	TANKERS	TENACES	THREAPS
SLANTED	SODDIER	SPIRTED	STAYERS	STOODEN	SULCATE	TANKIES	TENACES	THREATS
SLAPPER	SOFTING	SPIRTLE	STAYING	STOOLIE	SULFITE	TANLING	TENAILS	THRENES
SLATERS	SOIGNEE	SPITTEN	STAYNED	STOOPER	SUNBELT	TANNERS	TENANTS	THRENOS
SLATHER	SOILAGE	SPITTER	STAYRES	STOPING	SUNDARI	TANNEST	TENDERS	THRIVES
SLATIER	SOILIER	SPLINED	STEADED	STOPPER	SUNDERS	TANRECS	TENDONS	THRONES
SLATING	SOILURE	SPOILER	STEALED	STORAGE	SUNRISE	TANSIES	TENDRES	THROWES
SLATTED	SOIREES	SPONGER	STEALER	STORERS	SURANCE	TAPERED	TENDRIL	TICKENS
SLATTER	SOLDERS	SPORTED	STEAMED	STORIED	SURBATE	TAPERER	TENNERS	TICKERS
SLAVING	SOLDIER	SPORTER	STEAMER	STORIES	SURFEIT	TAPETIS	TENNIES	TIDDLER
SLAYING	SOLERAS	SPOTTER	STEAMIE	STORING	SURGENT	TAPPERS	TENOURS	TIELESS
SLEEKIT	SOLIDER	SPOUTED	STEANED	STORMED	SURGEON	TAPSMEN	TENPINS	TIEPINS
SLEIGHT	SOLUTES	SPOUTER	STEARED	STOTTER	SUTLERS	TAPSTER	TENRECS	TIERCES
SLENDER	SOLVATE	SPRAINT	STEARES	STOUTEN	SUTLERY	TARCELS	TENSELY	TIERING
SLENTER	SOMITES	SPRINGE	STEARIC	STOUTER	SUTURED	TARDIES	TENSILE	TIERODS
SLEWING	SONDELI	SPRITES	STEARIN	STOVING	SVELTER	TARGETS	TENSING	TIETACS
SLIDDEN	SONERIS	SPURIAE	STEDING	STOWING	SWALIER	TARGING	TENSION	TIGHTEN
SLINGER	SONNIES	SPURNED	STEENED	STRAFED	SWALING	TARINGS	TENSITY	TIGLONS
SLINKER	SONSIER	SPURTED	STEERED	STRAFES	SWATTER	TARNISH	TENSORS	TIGRINE
SLINTER	SONTIES	SPURTLE	STEERER	STRAINS	SWEARER	TARPONS	TENTERS	TILLERS
SLITHER	SOOTHER	SQUIRED	STEINED	STRAINT	SWEATED	TARRIES	TENTIER	TILTERS

TIMBERS	TOILING	TOWNIES	TREVISS	TRUSSED	UNITERS	UTENSIL	VIOLETS	WIDENER
TIMBRES	TOLINGS	TOWSIER	TRIABLE	TRUSTED	UNITIES	UTERINE	VIROSES	WIGEONS
TIMEOUS	TOLLERS	TOWSING	TRIAGES	TRUSTEE	UNITISE	UTILISE	VIRTUES	WILIEST
TINDERS	TOLLING	TOYINGS	TRIBADE	TSARINA	UNLADES	VAINEST	VISITER	WINCERS
TINEIDS	TOLTERS	TRACERS	TRIBUNE	TSIGANE	UNLASTE	VALIDER	VISORED	WINDERS
TINGLED	TOMMIES	TRACING	TRICARS	TUILLES	UNLEADS	VALISES	VISTAED	WINDLES
TINGLER	TONEMES	TRADERS	TRICEPS	TUNIEST	UNORDER	VALSING	VITRINE	WINGERS
TINGLES	TONGUES	TRADING	TRICING	TUNNELS	UNPARED	VARDIES	VOICERS	WINGLET
TINIEST	TONIEST	TRAILED	TRIDENT	TUNNIES	UNRACED	VARLETS	VOIDERS	WINSOME
TINKERS	TONINGS	TRAILER	TRIFLED	TUPELOS	UNRAKED	VASTIER	VOLUTES	WINTERS
TINKLES	TONITES	TRAINED	TRIFLES	TURBINE	UNRATED	VATTERS	WABSTER	WINTLES
TINNERS	TONKERS	TRAINEE	TRIGONS	TURDINE	UNREADY	VEALERS	WAFTERS	WIREMAN
TINNIER	TONLETS	TRAINER	TRILLED	TUREENS	UNRESTS	VEALIER	WAILERS	WISENTS
TINNIES	TONSURE	TRAIPSE	TRILOBE	TURIONS	UNRIMED	VECTORS	WAISTED	WITHERS
TINSELS	TONUSES	TRAMPED	TRIMERS	TURNERS	UNRIVET	VEERIES	WAISTER	WITNESS
TINSEYS	TOOLERS	TRAMPLE	TRINDLE	TURTLES	UNROBED	VEILIER	WAITERS	WITTERS
TINTERS	TOOLING	TRANCED	TRINGLE	TUXEDOS	UNROPED	VELARIC	WALIEST	WIVERNS
TINTIER	TOORIES	TRANCES	TRINING	TWAITES	UNROPES	VELIGER	WALISES	WORDING
TINWARE	TOOTERS	TRANCHE	TRINKET	TWANGLE	UNSATED	VENDERS	WALTIER	WORSING
TIPPERS	TOOTSIE	TRANECT	TRIODES	TWICERS	UNSMOTE	VENGERS	WANDERS	WORSTED
TIPSIER	TOPPERS	TRANGLE	TRIOLET	TWINERS	UNSOOTE	VENIRES	WANGLED	WORTLES
TIPSTER	TOPSIDE	TRANNIE	TRIONES	TWINGES	UNSTATE	VENTAIL	WANGLER	WOUNDER
TIPTOES	TOPSMEN	TRANSES	TRIPLED	TWINIER	UNSTEEL	VENTERS	WANGLES	WRANGLE
TIRADES	TORANAS	TRANSIT	TRIPLES	TWINSET	UNSURED	VENTILS	WANIEST	WRASTED
TIRASSE	TORCHES	TRANSOM	TRIPPED	TWINTER	UNTAMES	VENTRAL	WANNEST	WREATHS
TIREDLY	TOREROS	TRANTED	TRIPSES	TWIRING	UNTEAMS	VENTRES	WANTERS	WRESTED
TIRINGS	TORRETS	TRANTER	TRISECT	TWIRLED	UNTILES	VENTURI	WANTIES	WRESTER
TIRLING	TORSADE	TRAPEZE	TRISEME	TWISCAR	UNTIRED	VERBIDS	WARDENS	WRESTLE
TIRRING	TORSELS	TRAPING	TRISOME	TWISTER	UNTRACE	VERBOSE	WARDERS	WRINGED
TISANES	TORSION	TRAPPED	TRITEST	TYRONES	UNTREAD	VERDETS	WARDING	WRITERS
TITANIS	TORSIVE	TRASHED	TRITONE	UGLIEST	UNTRIDE	VERDINS	WARIEST	WRITHES
TITFERS	TORTILE	TRASHES	TRITONS	ULSTERS	UNTRIED	VERDITS	WARLING	WRITING
TITHERS	TOSHERS	TRASSES	TRIUNES	UNAIRED	UNWIRED	VERGLAS	WARMEST	WRITTEN
TITIANS	TOSHIER	TRAVELS	TRIVETS	UNARMED	UNWRITE	VERIEST	WARSLED	XEROSIS
TITLERS	TOSHING	TRAYNES	TROADES	UNBARED	UPRAISE	VERISMO	WASPIER	YAPSTER
TITMOSE	TOSSIER	TREASON	TROCHES	UNBELTS	UPRATED	VERISTS	WASTERS	YARDING
TITRATE	TOSSING	TREBLES	TROELIE	UNBLEST	UPRATES	VERMEIL	WASTERY	YATTERS
TITTERS	TOTTERS	TREEING	TROKING	UNCRATE	UPRISEN	VERMIAN	WASTING	YEASTED
TITULES	TOTTIES	TREFOIL	TROLLED	UNDERDO	UPSTARE	VERMINS	WASTREL	YERDING
TOADIES	TOURERS	TREHALA	TROMPES	UNDERGO	UPTEARS	VERSANT	WEARERS	YESTERN
TOASTER	TOURIES	TRELLIS	TROOLIE	UNDERNS	URALITE	VERSINE	WEARING	YODLERS
TOASTIE	TOURING	TREMIES	TROOPING	UNDOERS	URANIDE	VERSING	WEDELNS	ZANDERS
TOCHERS	TOUSIER	TREMORS	TROPING	UNDRESS	URANITE	VERSINS	WEIRDOS	ZANIEST
TODDIES	TOUSING	TRENAIL	TROULED	UNDRIED	UREDINE	VERSION	WELDING	ZARNECS
TODDLER	TOUSLED	TRENISE	TROULES	UNEARED	UREIDES	VERTING	WELDORS	ZEALOTS
TOECAPS	TOUSLES	TRENTAL	TROUPES	UNFIRED	UREMIAS	VESSAIL	WELTERS	ZELANTS
TOEIEST	TOUSTIE	TREPANG	TROUSER	UNGEARS	URETERS	VESTING	WELTING	ZESTIER
TOENAIL	TOUTERS	TREPANS	TROWELS	UNGORED	URIDINE	VESTRAL	WESTERN	ZESTING
TOERAGS	TOUZLES	TRESSED	TROWING	UNHEARD	URINATE	VIEWERS	WESTING	ZINGELS
TOILERS	TOWIEST	TRESSEL	TRUDGES	UNHERST	URINOSE	VINEGAR	WESTLIN	ZINGERS
TOILETS	TOWINGS	TRESTLE	TRUEING	UNHIRED	URTICAS	VIOLERS	WHINERS	ZITHERS

SUMMARY OF 7-LETTER STEMS
in alphabetical order with ranking, keywords, combining letters and mnemonics

Stem	Rank	Keyword	Combining Letters	Mnemonic
AADEIRT	157	RADIATE	CDENSV	send CVs
AAEGINR	240	REGINAE	BCDFGLNST	—
AAEILNT	113	ANTLIAE	CDEGHMPTV	met pegged vetch
AAEINRT	35	(ARANITE)	BCDGMOSTUZ	buzz custom dog
AAEINST	221	TAENIAS	BCGHMRTV	—
AAEINTT	231	(A NATTIE)	DELNRST	slenderest
AAEIRST	222	ASTERIA	DHNPSTV	—
AAENRST	112	ANESTRA	BCEGIJMORTV	reject big move
ABEINST	100	BESTAIN	ACDEGHIKLMOPRST	slight pock-marked
ABEORST	151	BOASTER	ADEHILMNPRSTU	is a lame turnip-head
ACDEINR	227	CAIRNED	ADEHINRT	heard the rain
ACEILRT	212	ARTICLE	ADKMNOPRSTVY	monks vodka party
ACEINOT	147	ACONITE	DHNRSTVX	—
ACEINRS	116	ARSENIC	ABEFGHIKLMNOST	something to kill off bats
ACEINRT	76	CERTAIN	ADEGLOSTVX	gold vase tax
ACEINST	99	CANIEST	ABDEFHIMNORSTVY	never eat dirty fresh bamboo
ACENORT	115	(CORN TEA)	CDEHIOPSTU	hideous cup diet
ACEORST	232	COASTER	CDEFGHLNRSTUVX	excludes fervent hug
ACINORT	213	(CORTINA)	ACDEFHLMRST	fleet car that's made
ADEEGNR	176	ANGERED	CDEILMNORSUV	red verminous clod
ADEEILR	192	LEADIER	BDLMPRSTZ	—
ADEEILS	217	AEDILES	BHIKMNRSTVY	vibist shrinks hymns
ADEEILT	248	(DIALTEE)	BCDNPRS	—
ADEEINR	150	(DINEEAR)	CFGMPST	—
ADEEINS	230	ANISEED	LMNRST	—
ADEEINT	58	(NITE ADE)	DELMPRS	redeems sleep
ADEEIRS	141	READIES	BCFGJLMNPTV	—
ADEEIRT	42	(DIERATE)	ABHLMNSTV	shall blast vatman
ADEEIST	153	IDEATES	BDHJLMNRSV	—
ADEELRT	216	RELATED	CDFHILNPRSV	VIP's inch-frill dirndl
ADEENRS	137	ENDEARS	CEGIKMNOSUW	we use smocking
ADEENRT	119	(END TEAR)	BCDHILPTUV	pitbull bit livid child
ADEERST	102	DERATES	BCEFGHIKLMPRSTWY	pricy big milky wet fish
ADEGINR	43	READING	ABDEHKLMNORSTY	storybook had lament
ADEGINT	194	(DIEGNAT)	ABILRSV	viral labs
ADEGNOR	228	GROANED	BEFIJNT	benefit jibe
ADEGORT	132	(DOGTEAR)	EHINRSTU	hirsuteness
ADEIINT	201	(DAINTIE)	CGMORS	cog rooms
ADEILNS	160	DENIALS	DEGNORUV	no, never dug
ADEILNT	51	(LENT AID)	ABDEFGOPUV	gave up pub food
ADEILOR	223	DARIOLE	FLSTVX	—
ADEILOS	134	DEASOIL	CGMNPRSTU	strung up scum
ADEILOT	86	(ADOLITE)	FNPRSTV	—
ADEILRT	68	TRAILED	BCELOPSTY	by telescope
ADEILST	123	DILATES	BCEGIMOPRVY	my iceberg movie epic
ADEINOR	33	ANEROID	BDGRSTU	turd bugs
ADEINOS	54	ANODISE	CDGHLMRSTXZ	—
ADEINOT	7	(ON A DIET)	BCILMNPRSTV	slim in BBC TV script
ADEINRS	11	RANDIES	ABEFGILMNOPRSTUVY	film about spying perv
ADEINRT	6	TRAINED	ACDEGIOPSTU	educate pig to sit
ADEINRU	103	UNAIRED	FHIOPSTV	I stop VHF
ADEINST	18	INSTEAD	BCDEGHIMOPRSTUVY	Tom Thumb discovers pigmy
ADEIORS	111	ROADIES	CDFLNPT	—
ADEIORT	16	(TOADIER)	CGKLMNRSTV	—
ADEIOST	110	TOADIES	GLMNPRXZ	—
ADEIPRS	208	DESPAIR	ACDEGHILNOPRSTU	poor English education
ADEIRST	15	TARDIES	ABCDEHIKLMNOPSTW	slowcoach kept behind men
ADEIRTT	218	ATTIRED	CELNOST	cool stone
ADELIRS	49	DERAILS	ABCDEGILNOPTUY	delay public outing
ADELNOR	191	LADRONE	BCEFPSUV	Eve's beef cup
ADENORS	108	(DARES ON)	BCEILMPT	implicit bet
ADENORT	48	TORNADE	CGIOPSTY	cosy pigsty
ADENRST	238	STANDER	BCDGIOSUX	six big cuboids
ADENRTU	130	(RUDE ANT)	BCDEHIMPRST	spider bit chimp
ADEORST	72	ROASTED	BCGILMNPRSUX	spring club mix
ADINORS	106	(ROAD SIN)	CDEGLNPRSTUV	reversed up green culvert
ADINORT	104	(ROAD NIT)	CENOSU	no success
ADINRST	179	INDARTS	ABEFGIKORU	broke a figure

ADIORST	143	ASTROID	EILNPSTU	puts line
AEEGINR	62	REGINAE	BDGILMPRSTZ	prim bird's glitz
AEEGIRT	190	(IEGREAT)	HIMNTV	nth vim
AEEGNRS	245	ENRAGES	ACDGHILMNTUV	living Dutchman
AEEGNRT	173	REAGENT	EIMNRSU	ruins me
AEEGRST	236	RESTAGE	ABDEMNRSTUW	bans water and mud
AEEILNS	178	SEALINE	CDEGNPS	pence edges
AEEILNT	63	(ELATINE)	ADGLMPRV	damp lava rag
AEEILRS	91	(SEALIER)	CDFGHLMPRSTVYZ	—
AEEILRT	20	ATELIER	BDFHMNOPRSTV	posh Bond from TV
AEEILST	118	(EALIEST)	BDFGKLMPRSTV	—
AEEINRS	34	(ENRAISE)	CDGHKMNPRSTU	struck dung hump
AEEINRT	29	TRAINEE	CDGHKLPRS	—
AEEINST	90	ETESIAN	BCDGMRTV	—
AEEIRST	9	SERIATE	DEHLMNOPRSTVWY	world symphony event
AEELNRT	177	ETERNAL	BDHINSVX	six bhindi vids
AEELORT	67	(ORELATE)	ACISTVW	awaits CV
AEELRST	47	STEALER	ABCDEFHIMNOPRSTUY	thief raids bus company
AEENORS	171	(EREASON)	BDPRST	—
AEENRST	21	EASTERN	ACEFGHIJLMORSTV	chose flight from Java
AEENRTT	247	ENTREAT	ADEFHRSVXY	read heavy faxes
AEENRTV	237	VETERAN	DELMNORSTU	tremendous lot
AEEORST	83	ROSEATE	BCIKLMNPV	civil MP in bikini
AEERRST	193	TEARERS	BCDEFGIKLMNPRSTUVW	but we like fingerlicking virus dump!
AEGILNR	27	REALIGN	ABCDEGHIJMNOPRSTXY	straightened spicy jam box
AEGILNS	126	SEALING	BDEFGHKLMNOPRSTVW	the stopper prevents knowledge of bomb
AEGILNT	45	GENITAL	ABCDEGHMNOPRSVXZ	sex-change perv amazed Bob
AEGILRS	167	GRAILES	ACDEGMNOSTYZ	stones got coated enzymes
AEGINOR	136	ORIGANE	BDLRSZ	—
AEGINOS	168	AGONIES	BCDLNRSZ	—
AEGINRS	31	REGAINS	ABCDEGHKLMNOPRSTVWY	very happy lord gets back women
AEGINRT	26	TEARING	ABCDEHKLMPSTVW	wept at smashed black vase
AEGINST	39	TEASING	ABDEFGHLMNNRSTUVWY	very naughty bawdy females
AEGNRST	127	STRANGE	ABDEFGILMOPRU	odd flip-up boardgame
AEGORST	142	TOERAGS	CDHLNOPRSTU	Hotspurs couldn't shoot
AEHIRST	128	HASTIER	ACDEINORSUWY	runs on causeway side
AEIINRS	146	SENARII	BCDKLNSTY	—
AEIINST	120	ISATINE	BCDFKLMPRSVXZ	—
AEIIRST	97	AIRIEST	DFHLMNPRSVWZ	—
AEILNOR	55	ALIENOR	CFGLSTV	—
AEILNOS	69	(SEALION)	DGKMNPRT	—
AEILNOT	36	ELATION	DFGPRST	—
AEILNPT	180	PANTILE	ABCDEGORST	gets a scoreboard
AEILNRS	28	NAILERS	BCDGHIMOPRSTUVXY	MD's itchy poxvirus bug
AEILNRT	5	ENTRAIL	CEGIMNOPSTUVY	veggy consumption
AEILNRU	184	(LUNAIRE)	ABFHMST	fab maths
AEILNST	50	ENTAILS	BFGIKMOPRSUVW	survivor of mugwump book
AEILORS	22	(ORALISE)	ACDFGHMNPSTVYZ	vast zany champ had fag
AEILORT	8	(ORALITE)	CDEFHNPSTV	chef's speed event
AEILOST	37	ISOLATE	CDFGKMNPRSTV	—
AEILOTT	154	(ATOILET)	DENRSVZ	severed sneeze
AEILPRT	139	PLAITER	ABCDEIKNORS	broken sidecar
AEILRST	13	RETAILS	BCDEFGIKLMNOPRSTU	kept selling record bumf
AEILRSU	188	(USALIER)	ACDFHLNQRT	talaq handcraft
AEILRTT	93	TERTIAL	CDEFGIMNORSY	reinforced my scoring
AEIMNOT	200	(OMINATE)	ADMNPSZ	zaps sandman
AEIMNRS	131	SEMINAR	BCDEGHKLNORSTUY	lecture on chunky bodgers
AEIMNRT	225	MINARET	AGLSTUWY	gutsy law
AEIMNST	109	INMATES	ABCDEFGIKLNORS	assigned far cell-block
AEIMRST	105	SMARTIE	BCDEGILMNOPSTUWXY	sweety compound in long box
AEINNOT	98	ENATION	CDGMRSTV	—
AEINNRS	101	INSNARE	CDEGIMOPSTUW	cop misguided twit
AEINORS	14	ERASION	BCDFGLMNSTV	—
AEINORT	2	OTARINE	ABCDLNPRSTZ	abstract plaza band
AEINOST	17	ATONIES	BCDLMNPRSVX	—
AEINOTT	84	(ATONITE)	CDILNR	CID in drill
AEINPRS	185	RAPINES	ADEFGHLNPTUW	laughed and wept at fun
AEINPRT	53	PAINTER	DEGHILORSTUX	his gold texture
AEINPST	169	SPINATE	BDHILNOPRSTUY	thy truly spiny body
AEINRRT	125	TRAINER	ENOPSVW	swop new vows
AEINRSS	224	SARNIES	CDEFGHILMNOTUWX	welcome to foxhunting mud
AEINRST	1	RETAINS	ABCDEFGHIJKLMNOPRSTUW	stopped wrongful hijack mob
AEINRSU	60	(UNRAISE)	BDELMNPSTVZ	zz - embedded sleep event
AEINRTT	57	(TAINTER)	ACDGLMNOPSU	goldman's cup
AEINRTU	30	RUINATE	ABDHJLMPQSTV	vamp had last qat jab
AEINSTT	80	INSTATE	ABCDEFGHJNPRSTVW	Javan dwarf sheep can't beg

AEINSTU	244	AUNTIES	DGJLPQRV	—
AEINSTV	148	NATIVES	ACDEGIKLOTU	tackled dialogue
AEIORST	10	OTARIES	BDEHJLMNRV	never be helm DJ
AEIPRST	138	PARTIES	ACDEGIKLMNPSVWY	wicked vamps playing
AEIRRST	81	TARRIES	BCEFHILNORSTW	belch frontwise
AEIRSST	189	SATIRES	ACDEGHIKLMNPRSTVW	watching skimpier devil
AEIRSTT	92	ATTIRES	ABCDEGLMNRSTWX	beeswax clad garments
AEIRSTV	235	VASTIER	ABEGIOPSY	big pageboys
AEIRSTW	187	WAITERS	BDEFHIMNPRST	fresh herbs tempted diner
AELNORS	204	ORLEANS	DFILMPUV	film-vid pupil
AELNRST	122	RENTALS	BEGHINPSTUV	begun shipping TVs
AELORST	38	OESTRAL	BCDEFGHILMPRUVYZ	verify much puzzled bug
AELORSU	135	(OURSEAL)	ABCDEFGMNPTU	defunct pub game
AELRSTU	214	SALUTER	BCEFGINOPSTV	Bob gets fivepence
AENORST	4	SENATOR	ABCDEFGIMNPRSTVW	big fat American VIP weds
AENORTT	145	(RATNOTE)	BCDGILMPSXY	digs pixy climb
AENRSTT	196	NATTERS	ACEILNOPRSU	peculiar son
AENRSTU	159	SAUNTER	BCDGHILMPSTVW	wimps blight dim victim
AEOPRST	233	ESPARTO	BDEFGHLNRSTUV	the seven fudge rebels
AEORRST	107	ROASTER	ABCDGILMNOPRST	blaming cold pot-roast
AEORSTT	250	TOASTER	ABCGHNPRSTU	punchbag star
AGILNOT	186	ANTILOG	ABCEFGHIPRSY	brag, speechify
AGINORS	202	SOARING	DEILMRSTUV	evil red smut
AGINORT	144	ORATING	BILNOSTVY	vinyl bolts
AGINRST	156	STARING	ABCDEFGHKLMNOPRSTVWY	vagrant watchmaker's body flops
AILNORT	121	(TRIONAL)	ACEFGHMZ	amaze egg chef
AILNOST	199	(SIN A LOT)	AEGLNO	engaol
AILORST	197	TAILORS	BCDEMOSUY	my bus code
AINORST	40	RATIONS	BCDEGHJKOPSTUX	expect the budget jokes
BEINOST	243	BONIEST	ABEINRSTU	auntie's bra
CEEINRT	246	ENTICER	AFGINOPSTU	stuffing a pot
CEINORS	181	COINERS	ABCDFHILMNPRSTU	plain mad bushcraft
CEINORT	73	RECTION	ACDEFGHJMPRSTUV	chef judged Spam advert
CEINOST	165	NOTICES	ACDEKLMOPRSTUXY	sees exclamatory loudspeaker
DEEINRS	96	RESINED	ABEFGHKNOSTUWX	about the known sex gaff
DEEINRT	59	(DIRTEEN)	ADKMNORSUVWX	wax marks on VDU
DEEINST	41	DESTINE	ABDEFGHILMNOPRSTUV	disproving humble fate
DEEIRST	61	DIETERS	ABCDEGIMNPRSTUVW	reducing vast wide bumps
DEENORS	133	ENDORSE	ACDEIMNRSTW	wartime dances
DEENORT	162	(RENOTED)	CHILMOSU	scholium
DEENRTU	219	DENTURE	ADEILNORSV	island lover
DEIINRT	210	NITRIDE	ACDGMOPSU	Scamp's a pup dog
DEIIRST	242	(TIDIERS)	ACEGHLNOPT	change the plot
DEILNOS	129	(SLID EON)	ACEGIORSU	curious age
DEILORS	195	SOLDIER	ACILNSTUY	sly lunatic
DEINORS	23	INDORSE	ACDEGHIJLNPSTUW	upheld sign and cut jaw
DEINORT	32	(IRODENT)	ACEIMST	cats eat mice
DEINOST	65	DITONES	ACEHIMRSW	wise charm
DEINRST	71	TINDERS	ADEGILOPTUX	poll-tax guide
DEINRTU	124	UNTRIED	ABDEIMPRSW	swamp bride
DEINSTU	175	DUNITES	ADEFGILMNQRSU	minerals in quaggier fields
DEIORST	44	EDITORS	ABCGIKLMNPSTUW	masking public wit
DEIORTU	241	OUTRIDE	CEHRSV	serve cheese
DEIRSTU	226	DUSTIER	CDEGLNOPQRSTX	QPR's good, excellent
DENORST	205	SNORTED	AEIMNPU	emu pain
DENORTU	152	(NOTRUDE)	CDEFGLORSTW	good flowers cost lots
EEGINRS	89	GREISEN	ABCDEFGHJKLMNOPRSTUVW	hoped job takeover gamble was unsuccessful
EEGINRT	220	INTEGER	ACGMNPSUVWX	Xmas vacs swung up
EEGINST	149	(GETSINE)	ABCDGHKLMNOPRTUVWX	black VW on orthodox campground
EEILNST	85	TENSILE	BDEGIKNOPRSTV	over-strong bike speedo
EEILORS	182	(LIESORE)	FIKLNPTVW	if VIP will knit kilt, I'll lift it
EEILORT	114	TROELIE	ADHKMRS	shark mad
EEILRST	79	STERILE	ACEFIKLMNOPST	keeps me clean of infection
EEINORS	95	(EROSINE)	DGHKLMPSTV	—
EEINORT	19	(TRIE ONE)	BCDHIMRSTX	six timid rich birds
EEINOST	75	(ETONIES)	BCDGLMRST	—
EEINRST	12	ENTRIES	ACDEFGIKLNORSTUVXY	take index of curvy girls
EEINRSU	172	(USEREIN)	ACDFGNPQRSTV	qat pangs and fast caravan
EEINRTT	170	TENTIER	BCEHILNOSY	chinless boy
EEINSTT	163	(SITETEN)	ABDEFGILMNOPRTWX	rainbow got exemplified
EEIORST	64	(OTERIES)	ACGHLMNPS	slang champ
EELORST	155	(LETSORE)	ACEHILMNTU	cult machine
EENORST	46	(ENSTORE)	ADFGHILMNOPTVX	avoid fixing hot lamp
EGILNOR	198	(LONERIG)	ABEFISW	Web is fab
EGINORS	70	IGNORES	ABDEILMPRSTY	depart miserably
EGINORT	183	GENITOR	CHNSTUWXZ	Wushu cuz hunts xu

Stem	No.	Word	Letters	Clue
EGINRST	88	RESTING	ACDEHILNOPRSTVW	recover in hospital ward
EGIORST	209	GORIEST	DEHMNSUVYZ	seven mushed enzymes
EGNORST	215	(ESTRONG)	AEGINRSTUW	new guitars
EHIORST	206	HOISTER	ACEGMNPRSTUVW	water games can upset vac
EIILRST	207	SILTIER	ABDELMNOPTU	unpolluted lamb
EIINORT	78	(IRONITE)	DEFPRS	feed press
EIINRST	56	(TINIERS)	ABCDEFGHLMOPSTUV	shaved goosebumps - tactful
EILNORS	77	NEROLIS	ACDEGPRT	caged pet rat
EILNORT	87	RETINOL	APRSTW	past war
EILNOST	24	ENTOILS	ACEHILMNOPRUVW	win lamp voucher
EILNRST	74	SNIRTLE	ADEGIKMOPSUY	amused podgy kid
EILORST	25	LOITERS	ABCDEFILNOPTU	find out about place
EILRSTU	164	LUSTIER	ABCDGHIMNOQRSTV	qanat - Arabic irrigation having no dams
EIMNOST	234	MOISTEN	ACDEGHKLNOPS	chalk and sponge
EIMORST	158	MOISTER	ACDEFGHOPRSTUWY	wet cad grows up hefty
EINOPRS	166	ORPINES	CDEFGILOPRSTUV	golf is productive
EINOPRT	239	POINTER	ACHILMSU	musical hum
EINORRT	82	(TORRINE)	ACEFHILSV	safe vehicle
EINORST	3	(IN-STORE)	ABCDEGHIJLNOPRSTUVYZ	crazy juveniles shopped by night
EINORSU	203	URINOSE	CDFMNPSTV	–
EINORTT	66	TRITONE	ACDEGKLNSU	sang and clucked
EINORTU	140	ROUTINE	CGJNPST	–
EINOSTT	249	TONIEST	BCEGJNPRSTW	twerp gets secret benj
EINRSTT	211	TINTERS	ABCDEGIKOSUWY	causeway guidebook
EINRSTU	52	UNITERS	ABCDEILMNOPQTVW	cabmen to develop low IQ
EIOPRST	174	ROPIEST	CDEFHKLMNORSTUV	thunder struck lover for me
EIORRST	117	RIOTERS	ABFHIMNOPRSTUV	ambush pub via front
EIORSTT	229	STOITER	CDHLMNOPRSUV	voodoo sulphur columns
EIORSTU	94	TOUSIER	CDFGHLMNPQRTV	–
ENORSTU	161	(NOT SURE)	BCDFGHILMNSTVY	midnight visibility is filmic

8-LETTER SETS
from the top 250 7-letter stems

AADEIRT 157
RADIATE
C RADICATE
D RADIATED
E ERADIATE
N DENTARIA
 RAINDATE
S DATARIES
 RADIATES
V VARIATED

AAEGINR 240
REGINAE
B ABEARING
C CANAIGRE
D AREADING
 DRAINAGE
 GARDENIA
F AFEARING
G GRAINAGE
L REGALIAN
N ANEARING
S ANGARIES
T AERATING

AAEILNT 113
ANTLIAE
C ANALCITE
 LAITANCE
D DENTALIA
E ALIENATE
G AGENTIAL
 ALGINATE
H ANTHELIA
M ALAIMENT
 LAMINATE
P PALATINE
T ANTLIATE
V AVENTAIL

AAEINRT 35
(ARANITE)
B RABATINE
C CARINATE
D DENTARIA
 RAINDATE
G AERATING
M ANIMATER
 MARINATE
O AERATION
S ANTISERA
 ARTESIAN
 RESINATA
T REATTAIN
U INAURATE
Z ATRAZINE

AAEINST 221
TAENIAS
B BASANITE
C ESTANCIA
G SAGINATE
H ASTHENIA
M AMENTIAS
 ANIMATES
R ANTISERA
 ARTESIAN
 RESINATA
T ASTATINE
 SANITATE
 TANAISTE
V SANATIVE

AAEINTT 231
(A NATTIE)
D ATTAINED
E TAENIATE
L ANTLIATE
N ANTENATI
R REATTAIN
S ASTATINE
 SANITATE
 TANAISTE
T TITANATE

AAEIRST 222
ASTERIA
D DATARIES
 RADIATES
H HETAIRAS
N ANTISERA
 ARTESIAN
 RESINATA
P ASPIRATE
 PARASITE
 SEPTARIA
S ASTERIAS
 ATRESIAS
T ARIETTAS
 ARISTATE
V VARIATES

AAENRST 112
ANESTRA
B ANTBEARS
 RATSBANE
C CANASTER
 CATERANS
E ARSENATE
 SERENATA
G STARAGEN
 TANAGERS
I ANTISERA
 RESINATA
 ARTESIAN
J NAARTJES
M SARMENTA
 SEMANTRA
O ANOESTRA
R NARRATES
T TARTANES
V TAVERNAS
 TSAREVNA

ABEINST 100
BESTAIN
A BASANITE
C CABINETS
D BANDIEST
E BETAINES
G BEATINGS
H ABSINTHE
I BAINITES
K BEATNIKS
L INSTABLE
M AMBIENTS
O BOTANIES
 BOTANISE
 NIOBATES
 OBEISANT
P BEPAINTS
R ATEBRINS
 BANISTER
S BASINETS
 BASSINET

 BESAINTS
 BESTAINS
T TABINETS

ABEORST 151
BOASTER
A RABATOES
D BROADEST
E ABORTEES
 REBATOES
H BATHORSE
I SABOTIER
L BLOATERS
 SORTABLE
 STORABLE
M BROMATES
N BARONETS
P PROBATES
R ARBORETS
 TABORERS
S BOASTERS
 SORBATES
T ABETTORS
 BATTEROS
 TABORETS
U SABOTEUR

ACDEINR 227
CAIRNED
A CANARIED
 RADIANCE
D CANDIDER
 RIDDANCE
E DERACINE
H INARCHED
I ACRIDINE
N CRANNIED
R RANCIDER
T CRINATED
 DICENTRA

ACEILRT 212
ARTICLE
A TAILRACE
D ARTICLED
K TALCKIER
M METRICAL
N CLARINET
O EROTICAL
 LORICATE
P PARTICLE
 PRELATIC
R CLARTIER
S ALTRICES
 ARTICLES
 RECITALS
 SELICTAR
T TRACTILE
V VERTICAL
Y LITERACY

ACEINOT 147
ACONITE
D ACTIONED
H INCHOATE
N ENACTION
R ACTIONER
 ANORETIC
 CREATION
 REACTION
S ACONITES
 CANOEIST

T TACONITE
V CONATIVE
X EXACTION

ACEINRS 116
ARSENIC
A CANARIES
B CARBINES
E CINEREAS
 INCREASE
 RESIANCE
F FANCIERS
G CREASING
 GRECIANS
 SEARCING
H INARCHES
I RIANCIES
K SKINCARE
L CARLINES
M CARMINES
N CRANNIES
O SCENARIO
S ARSENICS
 CERASINS
 RACINESS
T CANISTER
 CARNIEST
 CISTERNA
 CREATINS
 NACRITES
 SCANTIER

ACEINRT 76
CERTAIN
A CARINATE
D CRINATED
 DICENTRA
E CENTIARE
 CREATINE
 INCREATE
 ITERANCE
G CATERING
 CITRANGE
 CREATING
 REACTING
L CLARINET
O ACTIONER
 ANORETIC
 CREATION
 REACTION
S CANISTER
 CARNIEST
 CISTERNA
 CREATINS
 NACRITES
 SCANTIER
T INTERACT
V NAVICERT
X XERANTIC

ACEINST 99
CANIEST
A ESTANCIA
B CABINETS
D DISTANCE
E CINEASTE
F FANCIEST
H ASTHENIC
 CHANTIES
I CANITIES
M SEMANTIC
N ANCIENTS

 CANNIEST
 INSTANCE
O ACONITES
 CANOEIST
R CANISTER
 CARNIEST
 CISTERNA
 CREATINS
 NACRITES
 SCANTIER
S CINEASTS
 SCANTIES
T CANTIEST
 NICTATES
 TETANICS
V CISTVAEN
 VESICANT
Y CYANITES

ACENORT 115
(CORN TEA)
C ACCENTOR
D CARTONED
E CAROTENE
H ANCHORET
I ACTIONER
 ANORETIC
 CREATION
 REACTION
O CORONATE
P PORTANCE
S ANCESTOR
 ENACTORS
 SARCONET
 SORTANCE
T CONTRATE
U COURANTE
 OUTRANCE

ACEORST 232
COASTER
C ECTOSARC
D REDCOATS
E CREASOTE
F FORECAST
G ESCARGOT
H CHAROSET
 THORACES
L SECTORAL
N ANCESTOR
 ENACTORS
 SARCONET
 SORTANCE
R ACROTERS
 CREATORS
 REACTORS
S COARSEST
 COASTERS
T SECTATOR
U OUTRACES
V OVERACTS
 OVERCAST
X EXACTORS

ACINORT 213
(CORTINA)
A RAINCOAT
C NARCOTIC
D TORNADIC
E ACTIONER
 ANORETIC
 CREATION

 REACTION
F FRACTION
H ANORTHIC
L CILANTRO
 CONTRAIL
M ROMANTIC
R CONTRAIR
S CANTORIS
 CAROTINS
T TRACTION

ADEEGNR 176
ANGERED
C ENGRACED
D DANGERED
 DERANGED
 GARDENED
E RENEGADE
I REGAINED
L ENLARGED
 LARGENED
M GENDARME
N ENDANGER
 ENRANGED
O RENEGADO
R GARDENER
 GARNERED
S DERANGES
 GRANDEES
 GRENADES
U DUNGAREE
 RENAGUED
 UNGEARED
V ENGRAVED

ADEEILR 192
LEADIER
B RIDEABLE
D DEADLIER
 REDIALED
L REALLIED
M REMEDIAL
P PEDALIER
R DERAILER
 RERAILED
S REALISED
 SIDEREAL
T RETAILED
Z REALIZED

ADEEILS 217
AEDILES
B ABSEILED
H DEISHEAL
I IDEALISE
K LAKESIDE
M LIMEADES
N DELAINES
R REALISED
 SIDEREAL
S DEISEALS
 IDEALESS
T LEADIEST
V DISLEAVE
Y EYELIADS

ADEEILT 248
(DIALTEE)
B DELIBATE
C DELICATE
D DETAILED

N ENTAILED
LINEATED
P DEPILATE
EPILATED
PILEATED
R RETAILED
S LEADIEST

ADEEINR 150
(DINEEAR)
C DERACINE
F FREDAINE
G REGAINED
M REMAINED
P PINDAREE
S ARSENIDE
DENARIES
DRAISENE
NEARSIDE
T DETAINER
RETAINED

ADEEINS 230
ANISEED
L DELAINES
M DEMAINES
INSEAMED
N ADENINES
ANDESINE
R ARSENIDE
DENARIES
DRAISENE
NEARSIDE
S ANISEEDS
T ANDESITE

ADEEINT 58
(NITE ADE)
D DETAINED
E DETAINEE
L ENTAILED
LINEATED
M DEMENTIA
P DIAPENTE
R DETAINER
RETAINED
S ANDESITE

ADEEIRS 141
READIES
B BEARDIES
C DECIARES
F FEDARIES
G DISAGREE
J JADERIES
L REALISED
SIDEREAL
M MADERISE
N ARSENIDE
DENARIES
DRAISENE
NEARSIDE
P AIRSPEED
T READIEST
SERIATED
SIDERATE
STEADIER
V READVISE

ADEEIRT 42
(DIERATE)
A ERADIATE
B EBRIATED
H DEATHIER
L RETAILED
M DIAMETER
REMEDIAT
N DETAINER
RETAINED

S READIEST
SERIATED
SIDERATE
STEADIER
T ITERATED
V DERIVATE
EVIRATED
TAIVERED

ADEEIST 153
IDEATES
B BEADIEST
DIABETES
D STEADIED
H ATHEISED
HEADIEST
J JADEITES
L LEADIEST
M MEDIATES
N ANDESITE
R READIEST
SERIATED
SIDERATE
STEADIER
S STEADIES
V DEVIATES
SEDATIVE

ADEELRT 216
RELATED
C CLARETED
DECRETAL
TREACLED
D TREADLED
F DEFLATER
FALTERED
REFLATED
H HALTERED
LATHERED
I RETAILED
L TELLARED
N ANTLERED
P PALTERED
R TREADLER
S TREADLES
V TRAVELED

ADEENRS 137
ENDEARS
C ASCENDER
REASCEND
E ENSEARED
SERENADE
G DERANGES
GRANDEES
GRENADES
I ARSENIDE
DENARIES
DRAISENE
NEARSIDE
K KNEADERS
M AMENDERS
MEANDERS
REAMENDS
N ENSNARED
O REASONED
S DEARNESS
U UNDERSEA
W ANSWERED

ADEENRT 119
(END TEAR)
B BANTERED
C CANTERED
CRENATED
DECANTER
NECTARED
RECANTED
D ENDARTED

H ADHERENT
HARTENED
THREADEN
I DETAINER
RETAINED
L ANTLERED
P PARENTED
T ATTENDER
NATTERED
RATTENED
U DENATURE
V AVENTRED

ADEERST 102
DERATES
B BETREADS
BREASTED
DEBATERS
C CEDRATES
E RESEATED
F DRAFTEES
G RESTAGED
H HEADREST
I READIEST
SERIATED
SIDERATE
STEADIER
K STREAKED
L TREADLES
M MASTERED
STREAMED
P PEDERAST
PREDATES
REPASTED
TRAPESED
R ARRESTED
DREAREST
RETREADS
SERRATED
TREADERS
S ASSERTED
ESTRADES
T ASTERTED
RESTATED
W DEWATERS
TARWEEDS
WASTERED
Y ESTRAYED

ADEGINR 43
READING
A AREADING
DRAINAGE
GARDENIA
B BEARDING
BREADING
D DREADING
E REGAINED
H ADHERING
HEADRING
K DAKERING
L DANGLIER
DEARLING
DRAGLINE
M DREAMING
MARGINED
N GRANNIED
O ORGANDIE
R DREARING
S DERAIGNS
GRADINES
READINGS
T DERATING
GRADIENT
REDATING
TREADING
Y DERAYING
READYING
YEARDING

ADEGINT 194
(DIEGNAT)
A INDAGATE
B DEBATING
I IDEATING
L DELATING
R DERATING
GRADIENT
REDATING
TREADING
S SEDATING
STEADING
V VINTAGED

ADEGNOR 228
GROANED
B BONDAGER
E RENEGADO
F FRONDAGE
I ORGANDIE
J JARGONED
N ANDROGEN
DRAGONNE
T DRAGONET

ADEGORT 132
(DOGTEAR)
E DEROGATE
H GOATHERD
I ERGATOID
N DRAGONET
R GARROTED
S GOADSTER
T GAROTTED
U OUTRAGED
RAGOUTED

ADEIINT 201
(DAINTIE)
C ACTINIDE
DIACTINE
INDICATE
G IDEATING
M MINIATED
O IDEATION
TAENIOID
R DAINTIER
S ADENITIS
DAINTIES

ADEILNS 160
DENIALS
D ISLANDED
LANDSIDE
E DELAINES
G DEALINGS
LEADINGS
SIGNALED
N ANNELIDS
LINDANES
O NODALISE
R ISLANDER
U UNSAILED
V ANDVILES

ADEILNT 51
(LENT AID)
A DENTALIA
B BIDENTAL
D TIDELAND
E ENTAILED
LINEATED
F INFLATED
G DELATING
O DELATION
P PANTILED
U UNTAILED
V DIVALENT

ADEILOR 223
DARIOLE
F FORELAID
L ARILLODE
S DARIOLES
SOLIDARE
SOREDIAL
T IDOLATER
TAILORED
V OVERLAID
X EXORDIAL

ADEILOS 134
DEASOIL
C COALISED
G GOLIASED
M DAMOISEL
N NODALISE
P EPISODAL
OPALISED
SEPALOID
R DARIOLES
SOLIDARE
SOREDIAL
S ASSOILED
DEASOILS
T DIASTOLE
ISOLATED
SODALITE
U DOULEIAS

ADEILOT 86
(ADOLITE)
F FOLIATED
N DELATION
P PETALOID
R IDOLATER
TAILORED
S DIASTOLE
ISOLATED
SODALITE
SOLIDATE
T DATOLITE
V DOVETAIL
VIOLATED

ADEILRT 68
TRAILED
B LIBRATED
C ARTICLED
E RETAILED
L TRIALLED
O IDOLATER
TAILORED
P DIPTERAL
TRIPEDAL
S DILATERS
LARDIEST
T DETRITAL
Y DIELYTRA

ADEILST 123
DILATES
B BALDIEST
C CITADELS
DIALECTS
E LEADIEST
G GLADIEST
I IDEALIST
M MEDALIST
MISDEALT
O DIASTOLE
ISOLATED
SODALITE
SOLIDATE
P TALIPEDS
R DILATERS
LARDIEST

V VALIDEST
Y DIASTYLE
STEADILY

ADEINOR 33
ANEROID
B DEBONAIR
D ORDAINED
G ORGANDIE
R ORDAINER
REORDAIN
S ANEROIDS
DONARIES
T AROINTED
DERATION
ORDINATE
RATIONED
U DOUANIER

ADEINOS 54
ANODISE
C DIOCESAN
OCEANIDS
D ADENOIDS
ADONISED
ANODISED
G AGONISED
DIAGNOSE
H ADHESION
L NODALISE
M NOMADIES
NOMADISE
R ANEROIDS
DONARIES
S ADONISES
ANODISES
T ASTONIED
SEDATION
X DIOXANES
Z ADONIZES
ANODIZES

ADEINOT 7
(ON A DIET)
B OBTAINED
C ACTIONED
I IDEATION
TAENIOID
L DELATION
M DOMINATE
NEMATOID
N ANOINTED
ANTINODE
P ANTIPODE
R AROINTED
DERATION
ORDINATE
RATIONED
S ASTONIED
SEDATION
T ANTIDOTE
TETANOID
V DONATIVE

ADEINRS 11
RANDIES
A ARANEIDS
B BRANDIES
BRANDISE
E ARSENIDE
DENARIES
DRAISENE
NEARSIDE
F FRIANDES
G DERAIGNS
GRADINES
READINGS
I DRAISINE
L ISLANDER

M ADERMINS
SIRNAMED
N INSNARED
O ANEROIDS
DONARIES
P SPRAINED
R DRAINERS
SERRANID
S ARIDNESS
SARDINES
T DETRAINS
RANDIEST
STRAINED
U DENARIUS
UNRAISED
URANIDES
V INVADERS
SANDIVER
Y SYNEDRIA

ADEINRT 6
TRAINED
A DENTARIA
RAINDATE
C CRINATED
DICENTRA
D INDARTED
E DETAINER
RETAINED
G DERATING
GRADIENT
REDATING
TREADING
I DAINTIER
O AROINTED
DERATION
ORDINATE
RATIONED
P DIPTERAN
S DETRAINS
RANDIEST
STRAINED
T NITRATED
U DATURINE
INDURATE
RUINATED
URINATED

ADEINRU 103
UNAIRED
F UNFAIRED
H UNHAIRED
I UREDINIA
O DOUANIER
P UNPAIRED
UNREPAID
S DENARIUS
UNRAISED
URANIDES
T DATURINE
INDURATE
RUINATED
URINATED
V UNVARIED

ADEINST 18
INSTEAD
B BANDIEST
C DISTANCE
D DANDIEST
E ANDESITE
G SEDATING
STEADING
H HANDIEST
I ADENITIS
DAINTIES
M MEDIANTS
TIDESMAN
O ASTONIED

SEDATION
P DEPAINTS
R DETRAINS
RANDIEST
STRAINED
S SANDIEST
T INSTATED
U AUDIENTS
SINUATED
V DEVIANTS
Y DESYATIN

ADEIORS 111
ROADIES
C IDOCRASE
D ROADSIDE
SIDEROAD
F FORESAID
L DARIOLES
SOLIDARE
SOREDIAL
N ANEROIDS
DONARIES
P DIASPORE
PARODIES
T ASTEROID

ADEIORT 16
(TOADIER)
C CERATOID
G ERGATOID
K KERATOID
L IDOLATER
TAILORED
M MEDIATOR
N AROINTED
DERATION
ORDINATE
RATIONED
R ADROITER
S ASTEROID
T TERATOID
V DEVIATOR

ADEIOST 110
TOADIES
G GODETIAS
L DIASTOLE
ISOLATED
SODALITE
SOLIDATE
M ATOMISED
N ASTONIED
SEDATION
P DIOPTASE
R ASTEROID
X OXIDATES
Z AZOTISED

ADEIPRS 208
DESPAIR
A PARADISE
C EPACRIDS
D DISPREAD
E AIRSPEED
G SPAIRGED
H RAPHIDES
I PRESIDIA
L PEDRAILS
PREDIALS
N SPRAINED
O DIASPORE
PARODIES
P APPRISED
DRAPPIES
R DRAPIERS
S DESPAIRS
T DIPTERAS
RAPIDEST

SPIRATED
TARSIPED
TRAIPSED
U UPRAISED

ADEIRST 15
TARDIES
A DATARIES
RADIATES
B BARDIEST
BRAIDEST
RABIDEST
TRIBADES
C ACRIDEST
D DISRATED
E READIEST
SERIATED
SIDERATE
STEADIER
H HAIRSTED
HARDIEST
I IRISATED
K STRAIKED
L DILATERS
LARDIEST
M MARDIEST
MISRATED
READMITS
N DETRAINS
RANDIEST
STRAINED
O ASTEROID
P DIPTERAS
RAPIDEST
SPIRATED
TARSIPED
TRAIPSED
S ASTERIDS
DIASTERS
DISASTER
DISRATES
T STRAITED
STRIATED
TARDIEST
W TAWDRIES

ADEIRTT 218
ATTIRED
C TETRACID
TETRADIC
E ITERATED
L DETRITAL
N NITRATED
O TERATOID
S STRAITED
STRIATED
TARDIEST
T ATTRITED
TITRATED

ADELIRS 49
DERAILS
A SALARIED
B RAILBEDS
C DECRIALS
RADICELS
RADICLES
D DIEDRALS
E REALISED
SIDEREAL
G SLAIRGED
I LAIRISED
L DALLIERS
DIALLERS
N ISLANDER
O DARIOLES
SOLIDARE
SOREDIAL
P PEDRAILS

PREDIALS
T DILATERS
LARDIEST
U RESIDUAL
Y DIALYSER

ADELNOR 191
LADRONE
B BANDEROL
C COLANDER
E OLEANDER
F FORELAND
P PONDERAL
S LADRONES
SOLANDER
U UNLOADER
URODELAN
V OVERLAND
RONDAVEL

ADENORS 108
(DARES ON)
B BANDORES
BROADENS
C DRACONES
ENDOSARC
E REASONED
I ANEROIDS
DONARIES
L LADRONES
SOLANDER
M MADRONES
RANSOMED
ROADSMEN
P OPERANDS
PANDORES
T TORNADES

ADENORT 48
TORNADE
C CARTONED
G DRAGONET
I AROINTED
DERATION
ORDINATE
RATIONED
O RATOONED
P PRONATED
S TORNADES
T ATTORNED
Y AROYNTED

ADENRST 238
STANDER
B BANDSTER
C CANTREDS
D STRANDED
G DRAGNETS
GRANDEST
I DETRAINS
RANDIEST
STRAINED
O TORNADES
S STANDERS
U DAUNTERS
TRANSUDE
UNTREADS
X DEXTRANS

ADENRTU 130
(RUDE ANT)
B BREADNUT
TURBANED
C UNCARTED
UNCRATED
UNDERACT
UNTRACED
D DRAUNTED
UNTRADED

E DENATURE
H UNTHREAD
I DATURINE
INDURATE
RUINATED
URINATED
M UNDREAMT
P DEPURANT
R UNTARRED
S DAUNTERS
TRANSUDE
UNTREADS
T TRUANTED

ADEORST 72
ROASTED
B BROADEST
C REDCOATS
G GOADSTER
I ASTEROID
L DELATORS
LEOTARDS
LODESTAR
M STROAMED
N TORNADES
P ADOPTERS
ASPORTED
READOPTS
R ROADSTER
S ASSORTED
TORSADES
U OUTDARES
X EXTRADOS

ADINORS 106
(ROAD SIN)
C SARDONIC
D ANDROIDS
DISADORN
E ANEROIDS
DONARIES
G ROADINGS
L ORDINALS
N ANDIRONS
P PONIARDS
R ORDINARS
S SADIRONS
T INTRADOS
U DINOSAUR
V VIRANDOS

ADINORT 104
(ROAD NIT)
C TORNADIC
E AROINTED
DERATION
ORDINATE
RATIONED
N ORDINANT
O TANDOORI
S INTRADOS
U DURATION

ADINRST 179
INDARTS
A INTRADAS
RADIANTS
B ANTBIRDS
E DETRAINS
RANDIEST
STRAINED
F INDRAFTS
G TRADINGS
I DISTRAIN
K STINKARD
O INTRADOS
R TRIDARNS
U UNITARDS

ADIORST 143
ASTROID
E ASTEROID
I TARSIOID
L DILATORS
N INTRADOS
P PARODIST
PAROTIDS
S ASTROIDS
T STRADIOT
U AUDITORS

AEEGINR 62
REGINAE
B BAREGINE
BERGENIA
D REGAINED
G AGREEING
I AEGIRINE
L ALGERINE
M GERMAINE
P PERIGEAN
R REGAINER
S GESNERIA
T GRATINEE
Z RAZEEING

AEEGIRT 190
(IEGREAT)
H HERITAGE
I AEGIRITE
M EMIGRATE
REMIGATE
N GRATINEE
T AIGRETTE
V ERGATIVE

AEEGNRS 245
ENRAGES
A SANGAREE
C ENGRACES
D DERANGES
GRANDEES
GRENADES
G ENGAGERS
H SHAGREEN
I GESNERIA
L ENLARGES
GENERALS
GLEANERS
M AGREMENS
N ENRANGES
T ESTRANGE
GRANTEES
GREATENS
REAGENTS
SEGREANT
SERGEANT
STERNAGE
U RENAGUES
V AVENGERS
ENGRAVES

AEEGNRT 173
REAGENT
E GENERATE
RENEGATE
TEENAGER
I GRATINEE
M AGREMENT
N GENERANT
R ETRANGER
S ESTRANGE
GRANTEES
GREATENS
REAGENTS
SEGREANT
SERGEANT
STERNAGE

U GAUNTREE

AEEGRST 236
RESTAGE
A STEARAGE
B ABSTERGE
D RESTAGED
E EAGEREST
  ETAGERES
  STEERAGE
M GAMESTER
  MEAGREST
N ESTRANGE
  GRANTEES
  GREATENS
  REAGENTS
  SEGREANT
  SERGEANT
  STERNAGE
R REGRATES
S RESTAGES
T GREATEST
U TREAGUES
W STREWAGE

AEEILNS 178
SEALINE
C SALIENCE
D DELAINES
E ALIENEES
G ENSILAGE
  LINEAGES
N SELENIAN
P ALEPINES
  PENALISE
  SEPALINE
S SEALINES

AEEILNT 63
(ELATINE)
A ALIENATE
D ENTAILED
  LINEATED
G GALENITE
  GELATINE
  LEGATINE
L TENAILLE
M MELANITE
P PETALINE
  TAPELINE
R ELATERIN
  ENTAILER
  TREENAIL
V ELVANITE
  VENTAILE

AEEILRS 91
(SEALIER)
C ESCALIER
D REALISED
  SIDEREAL
F SERAFILE
G GASELIER
H SHIRALEE
L REALLIES
M ALMERIES
  MEASLIER
P ESPALIER
  PEARLIES
R REALISER
S REALISES
T ATELIERS
  EARLIEST
  LEARIEST
  REALTIES
V VELARISE
Y YEARLIES
Z REALIZES
  SLEAZIER

AEEILRT 20
ATELIER
L ELATERIN
B LIBERATE
D RETAILED
F FRAILTEE
H ETHERIAL
M EREMITAL
  MATERIEL
  REALTIME
N ELATERIN
  ENTAILER
  TREENAIL
O AEROLITE
P PEARLITE
R RETAILER
S ATELIERS
  EARLIEST
  LEARIEST
  REALTIES
T LATERITE
  LITERATE
V LEVIRATE
  RELATIVE

AEEILST 118
(EALIEST)
B SEABLITE
D LEADIEST
F FEALTIES
  LEAFIEST
G ELEGIAST
K LEAKIEST
L LEALTIES
M MEALIEST
P EPILATES
R ATELIERS
  EARLIEST
  LEARIEST
  REALTIES
S ASTELIES
T AILETTES
V ELATIVES
  LEAVIEST
  VEALIEST

AEEINRS 34
(ENRAISE)
C CINEREAS
  INCREASE
  RESIANCE
D ARSENIDE
  DENARIES
  DRAISENE
  NEARSIDE
G GESNERIA
H INHEARSE
K SNEAKIER
M REMANIES
N ANSERINE
P NAPERIES
R REARISEN
S SENARIES
T ARSENITE
  RESINATE
  STEARINE
  TRAINEES
U UNEASIER

AEEINRT 29
TRAINEE
C CENTIARE
  CREATINE
  INCREATE
  ITERANCE
D DETAINER
  RETAINED
G GRATINEE
H ATHERINE
K ANKERITE

KREATINE
L ELATERIN
  ENTAILER
  TREENAIL
P APERIENT
R RETAINER
S ARSENITE
  RESINATE
  STEARINE
  TRAINEES

AEEINST 90
ETESIAN
B BETAINES
C CINEASTE
D ANDESITE
G SAGENITE
M MATINEES
  SEMINATE
R ARSENITE
  RESINATE
  STEARINE
  TRAINEES
T ANISETTE
  TETANIES
  TETANISE
V NAIVETES

AEEIRST 9
SERIATE
D READIEST
  SERIATED
  SIDERATE
  STEADIER
E EATERIES
H HEARTIES
L ATELIERS
  EARLIEST
  LEARIEST
  REALTIES
M EMIRATES
  REAMIEST
  STEAMIER
N ARSENITE
  RESINATE
  STEARINE
  TRAINEES
O ETAERIOS
P PETARIES
R ARTERIES
  REASTIER
S SERIATES
T ARIETTES
  ITERATES
  TEARIEST
  TREATIES
  TREATISE
V EVIRATES
W SWEATIER
  TAWERIES
  WEARIEST
Y YEASTIER

AEELNRT 177
ETERNAL
B RENTABLE
D ANTLERED
H LEATHERN
I ELATERIN
  ENTAILER
  TREENAIL
N LANNERET
S ALTERNES
V LEVANTER
  RELEVANT
X EXTERNAL

AEELORT 67
(ORELATE)
A AREOLATE
C RELOCATE
I AEROLITE
S OLEASTER
T TOLERATE
V ELEVATOR
W TOLEWARE

AEELRST 47
STEALER
A LAETARES
B BLEAREST
  BLEATERS
  RETABLES
C CLEAREST
  SCELERAT
  TREACLES
D TREADLES
E TEASELER
F REFLATES
H HALTERES
  LEATHERS
I ATELIERS
  EARLIEST
  LEARIEST
  REALTIES
M LAMETERS
N ALTERNES
O OLEASTER
P PLEATERS
  PRELATES
R RELATERS
S STEALERS
  TEARLESS
  TESSERAL
T ALERTEST
U RESALUTE
Y EASTERLY

AEENORS 171
(EREASON)
B SEABORNE
D REASONED
P PERAEONS
  PERSONAE
R REASONER
S SEASONER
T RESONATE

AEENRST 21
EASTERN
A ARSENATE
  SERENATA
C CENTARES
  REASCENT
  SARCENET
E SERENATE
F FASTENER
  FENESTRA
G ESTRANGE
  GRANTEES
  GREATENS
  REAGENTS
  SEGREANT
  SERGEANT
  STERNAGE
H HASTENER
  HEARTENS
I ARSENITE
  RESINATE
  STEARINE
  TRAINEES
J SERJEANT
L ALTERNES
M REMANENTS
O RESONATE
R TERRANES

S ASSENTER
  EARNESTS
  SARSENET
T ENTREATS
  RATTEENS
V AVENTRES
  VETERANS

AEENRTT 247
ENTREAT
A ANTEATER
D ATTENDER
  NATTERED
  RATTENED
E ENTERATE
F FATTENER
H HATERENT
  THREATEN
R NATTERER
S ENTREATS
  RATTEENS
V ANTEVERT
X EXTERNAT
  EXTRANET
Y ENTREATY

AEENRTV 237
VETERAN
D AVENTRED
E ENERVATE
  VENERATE
L LEVANTER
  RELEVANT
M AVERMENT
N REVENANT
O OVERNEAT
  RENOVATE
R TAVERNER
S AVENTRES
  VETERANS
T ANTEVERT
U AVENTURE

AEEORST 83
ROSEATE
B ABORTEES
  REBATOES
C CREASOTE
I ETAERIOS
K KERATOSE
  KREASOTE
L OLEASTER
M EROTEASE
N RESONATE
P OPERATES
  PROTEASE
V OVEREATS

AEERRST 193
TEARERS
B REBATERS
  TABRERES
  TEREBRAS
C CATERERS
  RETRACES
  TERRACES
D ARRESTED
  DREAREST
  RETREADS
  SERRATED
  TREADERS
E ARRESTEE
F FERRATES
G REGRATES
I ARTERIES
  REASTIER
K RETAKERS
  STREAKER
L RELATERS

M REMASTER
  STREAMER
N TERRANES
P TAPERERS
R ARRESTER
  REARREST
S ASSERTER
  REASSERT
  SERRATES
  TERRASSES
T RETRATES
  RETREATS
  TREATERS
U AUSTERER
  TREASURE
V TRAVERSE
W WATERERS

AEGILNR 27
REALIGN
A REGALIAN
B BLEARING
C CLEARING
D DANGLIER
  DEARLING
  DRAGLINE
E ALGERINE
G GANGLIER
H NARGHILE
  NARGILEH
I GAINLIER
J JANGLIER
M GERMINAL
  MALIGNER
  MALINGER
N LEARNING
O GERANIOL
  REGIONAL
P PEARLING
R GNARLIER
S ENGRAILS
  NARGILES
  REALIGNS
  SALERING
  SANGLIER
  SIGNALER
  SLANGIER
T ALERTING
  ALTERING
  INTEGRAL
  RELATING
  TANGLIER
  TRIANGLE
X RELAXING
Y LAYERING
  RELAYING
  YEARLING

AEGILNS 126
SEALING
B SINGABLE
D DEALINGS
  LEADINGS
  SIGNALED
E ENSILAGE
  LINEAGES
F FINAGLES
G LIGNAGES
H HEALINGS
  LEASHING
  SHEALING
K LINKAGES
L NIGELLAS
M MEASLING
N EANLINGS
  LEANINGS
O GASOLINE
P ELAPSING

PLEASING
R ENGRAILS
NARGILES
REALIGNS
SALERING
SANGLIER
SIGNALER
SLANGIER
S GAINLESS
GLASSINE
LEASINGS
SEALINGS
T EASTLING
GELATINS
GENITALS
STEALING
V LEAVINGS
SLEAVING
W SWEALING

AEGILNT 45
GENITAL
A AGENTIAL
ALGINATE
B BELATING
BLEATING
TANGIBLE
C CLEATING
D DELATING
E GALENITE
GELATINE
LEGATINE
G TEAGLING
H ATHELING
M LIGAMENT
METALING
N GANTLINE
LATENING
O GELATION
LEGATION
P PLEATING
R ALERTING
ALTERING
INTEGRAL
RELATING
TANGLIER
TRIANGLE
S EASTLING
GELATINS
GENITALS
STEALING
V VALETING
X EXALTING
Z TEAZLING

AEGILRS 167
GRAILES
A GASALIER
LAIRAGES
REGALIAS
C GLACIERS
D SLAIRGED
E GASELIER
G SLAGGIER
M GREMIALS
LAMIGERS
REGALISM
N ENGRAILS
NARGILES
REALIGNS
SALERING
SANGLIER
SIGNALER
SLANGIER
O GASOLIER
GIRASOLE
SERAGLIO
S GLASSIER
T GLARIEST

REGALIST
Y GREASILY
Z GLAZIERS

AEGINOR 136
ORIGANE
B ABORIGEN
D ORGANDIE
L GERANIOL
REGIONAL
R ORANGIER
S IGNAROES
ORGANISE
ORIGANES
Z ORGANIZE

AEGINOS 168
AGONIES
B BEGONIAS
C COINAGES
D AGONISED
DIAGNOSE
L GASOLINE
N GANOINES
R IGNAROES
ORGANISE
ORIGANES
S AGONISES
Z AGONIZES

AEGINRS 31
REGAINS
A ANGARIES
B BEARINGS
SABERING
C CREASING
GRECIANS
SEARCING
D DERAIGNS
GRADINES
READINGS
E GESNERIA
G GEARINGS
GREASING
SNAGGIER
H HEARINGS
HEARSING
SHEARING
K SKEARING
L ENGRAILS
NARGILES
REALIGNS
SALERING
SANGLIER
SIGNALER
SLANGIER
M GERMAINS
SMEARING
N AGINNERS
EARNINGS
ENGRAINS
GRANNIES
O IGNAROES
ORGANISE
ORIGANES
P PREASING
SPEARING
R EARRINGS
GRAINERS
S REASSIGN
SEARINGS
SERINGAS
T ANGRIEST
ASTRINGE
GANISTER
GANTRIES
GRANITES
INGRATES
RANGIEST

REASTING
STEARING
TASERING
V VINEGARS
W SWEARING
WEARINGS
Y RESAYING

AEGINRT 26
TEARING
A AERATING
B BERATING
REBATING
C CATERING
CITRANGE
CREATING
REACTING
D DERATING
GRADIENT
REDATING
TREADING
E GRATINEE
H EARTHING
HEARTING
INGATHER
K RETAKING
L ALERTING
ALTERING
INTEGRAL
RELATING
TANGLIER
TRIANGLE
M EMIGRANT
P TAPERING
S ANGRIEST
ASTRINGE
GANISTER
GANTRIES
GRANITES
INGRATES
RANGIEST
REASTING
STEARING
TASERING
T ARETTING
TREATING
V AVERTING
TAVERING
VINTAGER
W TWANGIER
WATERING

AEGINST 39
TEASING
A SAGINATE
B BEATINGS
D SEDATING
STEADING
E SAGENITE
F FEASTING
G NAGGIEST
H GAHNITES
HEATINGS
L EASTLING
GELATINS
GENITALS
STEALING
M MANGIEST
MINTAGES
STEAMING
TEAMINGS
N ANTIGENS
GENTIANS
STEANING
R ANGRIEST
ASTRINGE
GANISTER
GANTRIES
GRANITES

INGRATES
RANGIEST
REASTING
STEARING
TASERING
S EASTINGS
GENISTAS
GIANTESS
SEATINGS
TEASINGS
TSIGANES
T ESTATING
TANGIEST
U SAUTEING
V VINTAGES
W SWEATING
Y YEASTING

AEGNRST 127
STRANGE
A STARAGEN
TANAGERS
B BANGSTER
D DRAGNETS
GRANDEST
E ESTRANGE
GRANTEES
GREATENS
REAGENTS
SEGREANT
SERGEANT
STERNAGE
F ENGRAFTS
G GANGSTER
I ANGRIEST
ASTRINGE
GANISTER
GANTRIES
GRANITES
INGRATES
RANGIEST
REASTING
STEARING
TASERING
L STRANGLE
TANGLERS
TRANGLES
M GARMENTS
MARGENTS
RAGMENTS
O ORANGEST
RAGSTONE
STONERAG
P TREPANGS
R GRANTERS
REGRANTS
STRANGER
U STRAUNGE

AEGORST 142
TOERAGS
C ESCARGOT
D GOADSTER
H SHORTAGE
L GLOATERS
LEGATORS
N ORANGEST
RAGSTONE
STONERAG
O ROOTAGES
P PORTAGES
POTAGERS
R GARROTES
S STORAGES
T GAROTTES
U OUTRAGES

AEHIRST 128
HASTIER
A HETAIRAS
C CHARIEST
STICHERA
THERIACS
D HAIRSTED
HARDIEST
E HEARTIES
I HAIRIEST
N HAIRNETS
INEARTHS
THERIANS
O HOARIEST
R TRASHIER
S SHERIATS
U THESAURI
W SWATHIER
WATERISH
Y HYSTERIA

AEIINRS 146
SENARII
B BINARIES
C RIANCIES
D DRAISINE
K KAISERIN
L AIRLINES
SNAILIER
N SIRENIAN
S AIRINESS
T INERTIAS
RAINIEST
Y YERSINIA

AEIINST 120
ISATINE
B BAINITES
C CANITIES
D ADENITIS
DAINTIES
F FAINITES
K KAINITES
L ALIENIST
LITANIES
M MINIATES
P PIANISTE
R INERTIAS
RAINIEST
S ISATINES
SANITIES
SANITISE
V VANITIES
X AXINITES
Z SANITIZE

AEIIRST 97
AIRIEST
D IRISATED
F RATIFIES
H HAIRIEST
L LAIRIEST
LISTERIA
M AIRTIMES
SERIATIM
N INERTIAS
RAINIEST
P PARITIES
R RARITIES
S IRISATES
SATIRISE
V VAIRIEST
W WISTERIA
Z SATIRIZE

AEILNOR 55
ALIENOR
C ACROLEIN
CREOLIAN

LONICERA
F FORELAIN
G GERANIOL
REGIONAL
L ALLERION
S AILERONS
ALERIONS
ALIENORS
T ORIENTAL
RELATION
TAILERON
V OVERLAIN

AEILNOS 69
(SEALION)
D NODALISE
G GASOLINE
K KAOLINES
M LAMINOSE
MINEOLAS
SEMOLINA
N SOLANINE
P OPALINES
R AILERONS
ALERIONS
ALIENORS
T ELATIONS
INSOLATE
TOENAILS

AEILNOT 36
ELATION
D DELATION
F OLEFIANT
G GELATION
LEGATION
P ANTIPOLE
R ORIENTAL
RELATION
TAILERON
S ELATIONS
INSOLATE
TOENAILS
T TONALITE

AEILNPT 180
PANTILE
A PALATINE
B PINTABLE
C PECTINAL
PLANETIC
D PANTILED
E PETALINE
TAPELINE
G PLEATING
O ANTIPOLE
R TRIPLANE
S PANTILES
PLAINEST
T TINPLATE

AEILNRS 28
NAILERS
B RINSABLE
C CARLINES
D ISLANDER
G ENGRAILS
NARGILES
REALIGNS
SALERING
SANGLIER
SIGNALER
SLANGIER
H INHALERS
I AIRLINES
SNAILIER
M MARLINES
MINERALS
O AILERONS

```
    ALERIONS
    ALIENORS
P   PEARLINS
    PRALINES
S   RAINLESS
T   ENTRAILS
    LATRINES
    RATLINES
    TRENAILS
U   LUNARIES
V   RAVELINS
X   RELAXINS
Y   INLAYERS
    SNAILERY
```

AEILNRT 5
```
    ENTRAIL
C   CLARINET
E   ELATERIN
    ENTAILER
    TREENAIL
G   ALERTING
    ALTERING
    INTEGRAL
    RELATING
    TANGLIER
    TRIANGLE
I   INERTIAL
M   TERMINAL
    TRAMLINE
N   INTERNAL
O   ORIENTAL
    RELATION
    TAILERON
P   TRIPLANE
S   ENTRAILS
    LATRINES
    RATLINES
    TRENAILS
T   RATTLINE
U   AUNTLIER
    RETINULA
    TENURIAL
V   INTERVAL
Y   INTERLAY
```

AEILNRU 184
```
   (LUNAIRE)
A   AURELIAN
B   RUINABLE
F   FRAULEIN
H   INHAULER
M   LEMURIAN
S   LUNARIES
T   AUNTLIER
    RETINULA
    TENURIAL
```

AEILNST 50
```
    ENTAILS
B   INSTABLE
F   INFLATES
G   EASTLING
    GELATINS
    GENITALS
    STEALING
I   ALIENIST
    LITANIES
K   LANKIEST
M   AILMENTS
    ALIMENTS
    MANLIEST
O   ELATIONS
    INSOLATE
    TOENAILS
P   PANTILES
    PLAINEST
R   ENTRAILS
    LATRINES
    RATLINES
    TRENAILS
S   EASTLINS
    ELASTINS
    SALIENTS
    STANIELS
U   ALUNITES
    INSULATE
V   VENTAILS
W   LAWNIEST
```

AEILORS 22
```
   (ORALISE)
A   OLEARIAS
C   CALORIES
    CARIOLES
D   DARIOLES
    SOLIDARE
    SOREDIAL
F   FORESAIL
G   GASOLIER
    GIRASOLE
    SERAGLIO
H   AIRHOLES
    SHOALIER
M   MORALISE
N   AILERONS
    ALERIONS
    ALIENORS
P   PELORIAS
    POLARISE
S   SOLARISE
T   SOTERIAL
V   OVERSAIL
    VALORISE
    VARIOLES
    VOLARIES
Y   ROYALISE
Z   SOLARIZE
```

AEILORT 8
```
   (ORALITE)
C   EROTICAL
    LORICATE
D   IDOLATER
    TAILORED
E   AEROLITE
F   FLOATIER
H   AEROLITH
N   ORIENTAL
    RELATION
    TAILERON
P   EPILATOR
    PETIOLAR
S   SOTERIAL
T   LITERATO
V   VIOLATER
```

AEILOST 37
```
    ISOLATE
C   ALOETICS
    COALIEST
    SOCIETAL
D   DIASTOLE
    ISOLATED
    SODALITE
    SOLIDATE
F   FOLIATES
G   OTALGIES
K   KEITLOAS
M   LOAMIEST
N   ELATIONS
    INSOLATE
    TOENAILS
P   SPOLIATE
R   SOTERIAL
S   ISOLATES
T   TOTALISE
V   VIOLATES
```

AEILOTT 154
```
   (ATOILET)
D   DATOLITE
E   ETIOLATE
N   TONALITE
R   LITERATO
S   TOTALISE
V   VOLITATE
Z   TOTALIZE
```

AEILPRT 139
```
    PLAITER
A   PARIETAL
B   PARTIBLE
C   PARTICLE
    PRELATIC
D   DIPTERAL
    TRIPEDAL
E   PEARLITE
I   LIPARITE
K   TRAPLIKE
N   TRIPLANE
O   EPILATOR
    PETIOLAR
R   PALTRIER
S   PILASTER
    PLAISTER
    PLAITERS
```

AEILRST 13
```
    RETAILS
B   LIBRATES
    TABLIERS
C   ALTRICES
    ARTICLES
    RECITALS
    SELICTAR
D   DILATERS
    LARDIEST
E   ATELIERS
    EARLIEST
    LEARIEST
    REALTIES
F   FLARIEST
    FRAILEST
G   GLARIEST
    REGALIST
I   LAIRIEST
    LISTERIA
K   LARKIEST
    STALKIER
    STARLIKE
L   LITERALS
    TALLIERS
M   MALTIERS
    MARLIEST
N   ENTRAILS
    LATRINES
    RATLINES
    TRENAILS
O   SOTERIAL
P   PILASTER
    PLAISTER
    PLAITERS
R   RETIRALS
    RETRIALS
    TRAILERS
S   REALISTS
    SALTIERS
    SALTIRES
    SLAISTER
T   TERTIALS
U   URALITES
```

AEILRSU 188
```
   (USALIER)
A   AURELIAS
C   AURICLES
D   RESIDUAL
F   FAILURES
H   HAULIERS
L   RUELLIAS
N   LUNARIES
Q   SQUAILER
R   RURALISE
T   URALITES
```

AEILRTT 93
```
    TERTIAL
C   TRACTILE
D   DETRITAL
E   LATERITE
    LITERATE
F   FILTRATE
G   AGLITTER
I   LITERATI
M   REMITTAL
N   RATTLINE
O   LITERATO
R   RATTLIER
S   TERTIALS
Y   ALTERITY
```

AEIMNOT 200
```
   (OMINATE)
A   METANOIA
D   DOMINATE
    NEMATOID
M   AMMONITE
N   NOMINATE
P   PTOMAINE
S   SOMNIATE
Z   MONAZITE
```

AEIMNRS 131
```
    SEMINAR
B   MIRBANES
C   CARMINES
D   ADERMINS
    SIRNAMED
E   REMANIES
G   GERMAINS
    SMEARING
H   HARMINES
    SHIREMAN
K   RAMEKINS
L   MARLINES
    MINERALS
N   REINSMAN
O   MORAINES
R   MARINERS
S   SEMINARS
    SIRNAMES
T   MINARETS
    RAIMENTS
U   ANEURISM
Y   SEMINARY
```

AEIMNRT 225
```
    MINARET
A   ANIMATER
    MARINATE
G   EMIGRANT
L   TERMINAL
    TRAMLINE
S   MINARETS
    RAIMENTS
T   MARTINET
U   RUMINATE
W   WARIMENT
Y   TYRAMINE
```

AEIMNST 109
```
    INMATES
A   AMENTIAS
    ANIMATES
B   AMBIENTS
C   SEMANTIC
D   MEDIANTS
    TIDESMAN
E   MATINEES
    SEMINATE
F   MANIFEST
G   MANGIEST
    MINTAGES
    STEAMING
    TEAMINGS
I   MINIATES
K   MANKIEST
    MISTAKEN
L   AILMENTS
    ALIMENTS
    MANLIEST
N   MANNITES
O   SOMNIATE
R   MINARETS
    RAIMENTS
S   MANTISES
    MATINESS
```

AEIMRST 105
```
    SMARTIE
B   BARMIEST
C   CERAMIST
    MATRICES
D   MARDIEST
    MISRATED
    READMITS
E   EMIRATES
    REAMIEST
    STEAMIER
G   MAGISTER
    MIGRATES
    RAGTIMES
    STERIGMA
I   AIRTIMES
    SERIATIM
L   MALTIERS
    MARLIEST
M   MARMITES
N   MINARETS
    RAIMENTS
O   AMORTISE
    ATOMISER
P   APTERISM
    PRIMATES
S   ASTERISM
    MAISTERS
    MISRATES
    SEMITARS
    SMARTIES
T   MISTREAT
    TERATISM
U   MURIATES
    SEMITAUR
W   WARTIMES
X   MATRIXES
Y   SYMITARE
```

AEINNOT 98
```
    ENATION
C   ENACTION
D   ANOINTED
    ANTINODE
G   NEGATION
M   NOMINATE
R   ANOINTER
    INORNATE
S   ENATIONS
T   INTONATE
V   INNOVATE
    VENATION
```

AEINNRS 101
```
    INSNARE
C   CRANNIES
D   INSNARED
E   ANSERINE
G   AGINNERS
    EARNINGS
    ENGRAINS
    GRANNIES
I   SIRENIAN
M   REINSMAN
O   RAISONNE
P   PANNIERS
S   INSNARES
T   ENTRAINS
    TRANNIES
U   ANEURINS
    UNARISEN
W   SWANNIER
```

AEINORS 14
```
    ERASION
B   BARONIES
C   SCENARIO
D   ANEROIDS
    DONARIES
F   FARINOSE
G   IGNAROES
    ORGANISE
    ORIGANES
L   AILERONS
    ALERIONS
    ALIENORS
M   MORAINES
N   RAISONNE
S   ERASIONS
    SENSORIA
T   ANOESTRI
    ARSONITE
    NOTARIES
    NOTARISE
    ROSINATE
V   AVERSION
```

AEINORT 2
```
    OTARINE
A   AERATION
B   BARITONE
    OBTAINER
C   ACTIONER
    ANORETIC
    CREATION
    REACTION
D   AROINTED
    DERATION
    ORDINATE
    RATIONED
L   ORIENTAL
    RELATION
    TAILERON
N   ANOINTER
    INORNATE
P   ATROPINE
R   ANTERIOR
S   ANOESTRI
    ARSONITE
    NOTARIES
    NOTARISE
    ROSINATE
T   TENTORIA
Z   NOTARIZE
```

AEINOST 17
```
    ATONIES
B   BOTANIES
    BOTANISE
    NIOBATES
    OBEISANT
C   ACONITES
```

CANOEIST
D ASTONIED
 SEDATION
L ELATIONS
 INSOLATE
 TOENAILS
M SOMNIATE
N ENATIONS
P SAPONITE
R ANOESTRI
 ARSONITE
 NOTARIES
 NOTARISE
 ROSINATE
S ASSIENTO
 ASTONIES
V STOVAINE
X SAXONITE

AEINOTT 84
(ATONITE)
C TACONITE
D ANTIDOTE
 TETANOID
I NOTITIAE
L TONALITE
N INTONATE
R TENTORIA

AEINPRS 185
RAPINES
A PANARIES
D SPRAINED
E NAPERIES
F FIREPANS
G PREASING
 SPEARING
H HEPARINS
 PARISHEN
 SERAPHIN
L PEARLINS
 PRALINES
N PANNIERS
P SNAPPIER
T PAINTERS
 PANTRIES
 PERTAINS
 PINASTER
 PRISTANE
 REPAINTS
U UNPRAISE
W SPAWNIER

AEINPRT 53
PAINTER
D DIPTERAN
E APERIENT
G TAPERING
H PERIANTH
I PAINTIER
L TRIPLANE
O ATROPINE
R TERRAPIN
S PAINTERS
 PANTRIES
 PERTAINS
 PINASTER
 PRISTANE
 REPAINTS
T TRIPTANE
U PAINTURE
X EXPIRANT

AEINPST 169
SPINATE
B BEPAINTS
D DEPAINTS
H PENTHIAS
 THESPIAN

I PIANISTE
L PANTILES
 PLAINEST
N PANTINES
O SAPONITE
P NAPPIEST
R PAINTERS
 PANTRIES
 PERTAINS
 PINASTER
 PRISTANE
 REPAINTS
S STEAPSIN
T PATIENTS
U PETUNIAS
 SUPINATE
Y EPINASTY

AEINRRT 125
TRAINER
E RETAINER
N INERRANT
O ANTERIOR
P TERRAPIN
S RESTRAIN
 RETRAINS
 STRAINER
 TERRAINS
 TRAINERS
 TRANSIRE
V VERATRIN
W INTERWAR

AEINRSS 224
SARNIES
C ARSENICS
 CERASINS
 RACINESS
D ARIDNESS
 SARDINES
E SENARIES
F FAIRNESS
 SANSERIF
 SERAFINS
G REASSIGN
 SEARINGS
 SERINGAS
H ARSHINES
I AIRINESS
L RAINLESS
M SEMINARS
 SIRNAMES
N INSNARES
O ERASIONS
 SENSORIA
T ARTINESS
 RESIANTS
 RETSINAS
 SNARIEST
 STAINERS
 STARNIES
 STEARINS
U SENARIUS
W WARINESS
X XERANSIS

AEINRST 1
RETAINS
A ANTISERA
 ARTESIAN
 RESINATA
B ATEBRINS
 BANISTER
C CANISTER
 CARNIEST
 CISTERNA
 CREATINS
 NACRITES
 SCANTIER

D DETRAINS
 RANDIEST
 STRAINED
E ARSENITE
 RESINATE
 STEARINE
 TRAINEES
F FENITARS
G ANGRIEST
 ASTRINGE
 GANISTER
 GANTRIES
 GRANITES
 INGRATES
 RANGIEST
 REASTING
 STEARING
 TASERING
H HAIRNETS
 INEARTHS
 THERIANS
I INERTIAS
 RAINIEST
J NARTJIES
K KERATINS
 NARKIEST
L ENTRAILS
 LATRINES
 RATLINES
 TRENAILS
M MINARETS
 RAIMENTS
N ENTRAINS
 TRANNIES
O ANOESTRI
 ARSONITE
 NOTARIES
 NOTARISE
 ROSINATE
P PAINTERS
 PANTRIES
 PERTAINS
 PINASTER
 PRISTANE
 REPAINTS
R RESTRAIN
 RETRAINS
 STRAINER
 TERRAINS
 TRAINERS
 TRANSIRE
S ARTINESS
 RESIANTS
 RETSINAS
 SNARIEST
 STAINERS
 STARNIES
 STEARINS
T INTREATS
 NITRATES
 STRAITEN
 TARTINES
 TERTIANS
U RUINATES
 TAURINES
 URANITES
 URINATES
W TINWARES

AEINRSU 60
(UNRAISE)
B ANBURIES
 URBANISE
D DENARIUS
 UNRAISED
 URANIDES
E UNEASIER
L LUNARIES
M ANEURISM

N ANEURINS
 UNARISEN
P UNPRAISE
S SENARIUS
T RUINATES
 TAURINES
 URANITES
 URINATES
V VAURIENS
Z AZURINES
 SUZERAIN

AEINRTT 57
(TAINTER)
A REATTAIN
C INTERACT
D NITRATED
G ARETTING
 TREATING
L RATTLING
M MARTINET
N INTRANET
O TENTORIA
P TRIPTANE
S INTREATS
 NITRATES
 STRAITEN
 TARTINES
 TERTIANS
U TAINTURE

AEINRTU 30
RUINATE
A INAURATE
B BRAUNITE
 URBANITE
D DATURINE
 INDURATE
 RUINATED
 URINATED
H HAURIENT
J JAUNTIER
L AUNTLIER
 RETINULA
 TENURIAL
M RUMINATE
P PAINTURE
Q QUAINTER
S RUINATES
 TAURINES
 URANITES
 URINATES
T TAINTURE
V VAUNTIER

AEINSTT 80
INSTATE
A ASTATINE
 SANITATE
 TANAISTE
B TABINETS
C CANTIEST
 NICTATES
 TETANICS
D INSTATED
E ANISETTE
 TETANIES
 TETANISE
F FAINTEST
G ESTATING
 TANGIEST
H HESITANT
J JANTIEST
N ANTIENTS
 STANNITE
P PATIENTS
R INTREATS
 NITRATES
 STRAITEN

 TARTINES
 TERTIANS
S ANTSIEST
 INSTATES
 NASTIEST
 SATINETS
 TITANESS
T NATTIEST
V TASTEVIN
W TAWNIEST

AEINSTU 244
AUNTIES
D AUDIENTS
 SINUATED
G SAUTEING
J JAUNTIES
L ALUNITES
 INSULATE
P PETUNIAS
 SUPINATE
Q ANTIQUES
 QUANTISE
R RUINATES
 TAURINES
 URANITES
 URINATES
V SUIVANTE

AEINSTV 148
NATIVES
A SANATIVE
C CISTVAEN
 VESICANT
D DEVIANTS
E NAIVETES
G VINTAGES
I VANITIES
K KISTVAEN
L VENTAILS
O STOVAINE
T TASTEVIN
U SUIVANTE

AEIORST 10
OTARIES
B SABOTIER
D ASTEROID
E ETAERIOS
H HOARIEST
J JAROSITE
L SOTERIAL
M AMORTISE
 ATOMISER
N ANOESTRI
 ARSONITE
 NOTARIES
 NOTARISE
 ROSINATE
R ROARIEST
 ROTARIES
V VIATORES
 VOTARIES

AEIPRST 138
PARTIES
A ASPIRATE
 PARASITE
 SEPTARIA
C CRAPIEST
 CRISPATE
 PICRATES
 PRACTISE
D DIPTERAS
 RAPIDEST
 SPIRATED
 TARSIPED
 TRAIPSED
E PETARIES

 TARTINES
 TERTIANS
S ANTSIEST
 INSTATES
 NASTIEST
 SATINETS
 TITANESS
T NATTIEST
V TASTEVIN
W TAWNIEST

AEINSTU 244
AUNTIES
D AUDIENTS
 SINUATED
G SAUTEING
J JAUNTIES
L ALUNITES
 INSULATE
P PETUNIAS
 SUPINATE
Q ANTIQUES
 QUANTISE
R RUINATES
 TAURINES
 URANITES
 URINATES
V SUIVANTE

AEIRRST 81
TARRIES
B ARBITERS
 RAREBITS
C ERRATICS
E ARTERIES
 REASTIER
F FRATRIES
H THRASHER
I RARITIES
L RETIRALS
 RETRIALS
 TRAILERS
N RESTRAIN
 RETRAINS
 STRAINER
 TERRAINS
 TRAINERS
 TRANSIRE
O ROARIEST
 ROTARIES
R STARRIER
 TARRIERS
S TARSIERS
T RETRAITS
 STRAITER
 TARRIEST
W STRAWIER

AEIRSST 189
SATIRES
A ASTERIAS
 ATRESIAS
C SCARIEST
D ASTERIDS
 DIASTERS
 DISASTER
 DISRATES
E SERIATES
G AGISTERS
H SHERIATS
I IRISATES
 SATIRISE
K ASTERISK
 SARKIEST
L REALISTS
 SALTIERS
 SALTIRES
 SLAISTER
M ASTERISM
 MAISTERS
 MISRATES
 SEMITARS
 SMARTIES
N ARTINESS
 RESIANTS

G GRAPIEST
I PARITIES
K PARKIEST
L PILASTER
 PLAISTER
 PLAITERS
M APTERISM
 PRIMATES
N PAINTERS
 PANTRIES
 PERTAINS
 PINASTER
 PRISTANE
 REPAINTS
P PERIAPTS
S PASTRIES
 PIASTRES
 RASPIEST
 TRAIPSES
V PRIVATES
W WIRETAPS
Y ASPERITY

```
RETSINAS
SNARIEST
STAINERS
STARNIES
STEARINS
P PASTRIES
  PIASTRES
  RASPIEST
  TRAIPSES
R TARSIERS
S TIRASSES
T ARTISTES
  ARTSIEST
  STRIATES
V TRAVISES
W WAISTERS
  WAITRESS
  WASTRIES

AEIRSTT  92
ATTIRES
A ARIETTAS
  ARISTATE
B BIRETTAS
C CITRATES
  CRISTATE
  SCATTIER
D STRAITED
  STRIATED
  TARDIEST
E ARIETTES
  ITERATES
  TEARIEST
  TREATIES
  TREATISE
G STRIGATE
L TERTIALS
M MISTREAT
  TERATISM
N INTREATS
  NITRATES
  STRAITEN
  TARTINES
  TERTIANS
R RETRAITS
  STRAITER
  TARRIEST
S ARTISTES
  ARTSIEST
  STRIATES
T ATTRITES
  RATTIEST
  TARTIEST
  TITRATES
W WARTIEST
X EXTRAITS

AEIRSTV 235
VASTIER
A VARIATES
B VIBRATES
E EVIRATES
G VIRGATES
  VITRAGES
I VAIRIEST
O VIATORES
  VOTARIES
P PRIVATES
S TRAVISES
Y VESTIARY

AEIRSTW 187
WAITERS
B WARBIEST
D TAWDRIES
E SWEATIER
  TAWERIES
  WEARIEST
F WASTRIFE
```

```
H SWATHIER
  WATERISH
I WISTERIA
M WARTIMES
N TINWARES
P WIRETAPS
R STRAWIER
S WAISTERS
  WAITRESS
  WASTRIES
T WARTIEST

AELNORS 204
ORLEANS
D LADRONES
  SOLANDER
F FARNESOL
I AILERONS
  ALERIONS
  ALIENORS
L LLANEROS
M ALMONERS
P PERSONAL
  PSORALEN
U ALEURONS
V VERONALS

AELNRST 122
RENTALS
B BRANTLES
E ALTERNES
G STRANGLE
  TANGLERS
  TRANGLES
H ENTHRALS
I ENTRAILS
  LATRINES
  RATLINES
  TRENAILS
N LANTERNS
P PANTLERS
  PLANTERS
  REPLANTS
S SALTERNS
T SLATTERN
  TRENTALS
U NEUTRALS
V VENTRALS

AELORST  38
OESTRAL
B BLOATERS
  SORTABLE
  STORABLE
C SECTORAL
D DELATORS
  LEOTARDS
  LODESTAR
E OLEASTER
F FLOATERS
  FORESTAL
  REFLOATS
G GLOATERS
  LEGATORS
H LOATHERS
I SOTERIAL
L REALLOTS
M MOLERATS
P PETROSAL
  PROLATES
R REALTORS
  RELATORS
U ROSULATE
V LEVATORS
Y ROYALETS
Z ZELATORS
```

```
AELORSU 135
(OURSEAL)
A AUREOLAS
B RUBEOLAS
C CAROUSEL
D ROULADES
E AUREOLES
F FUSAROLE
G GLAREOUS
M RAMULOSE
N ALEURONS
P LEAPROUS
T ROSULATE
U ROULEAUS

AELRSTU 214
SALUTER
B BALUSTER
C RAUCLEST
E RESALUTE
F REFUTALS
G GAULTERS
  GESTURAL
  TRAGULES
I URALITES
N NEUTRALS
O ROSULATE
P APLUSTRE
S SALUTERS
T LUSTRATE
  TUTELARS
V VAULTERS
  VESTURAL

AENORST   4
SENATOR
A ANOESTRA
B BARONETS
C ANCESTOR
  ENACTORS
  SARCONET
  SORTANCE
D TORNADES
E RESONATE
F SEAFRONT
G ORANGEST
  RAGSTONE
  STONERAG
I ANOESTRI
  ARSONITE
  NOTARIES
  NOTARISE
  ROSINATE
M MONSTERA
  STOREMAN
N NORTENAS
  RESONANT
P OPERANTS
  PRONATES
R ANTRORSE
S ASSENTOR
  SENATORS
  TREASONS
T ORNATEST
V VENATORS
W STONERAW

AENORTT 145
(RATNOTE)
B BETATRON
C CONTRATE
D ATTORNED
G TETRAGON
I TENTORIA
L TETRONAL
  TOLERANT
M TORMENTA
P PATENTOR
S ORNATEST
```

```
X TETRAXON
Y ATTORNEY

AENRSTT 196
NATTERS
A TARTANES
C TRANECTS
  TRANSECT
E ENTREATS
  RATTEENS
I INTREATS
  NITRATES
  STRAITEN
  TARTINES
  TERTIANS
L SLATTERN
  TRENTALS
N ENTRANTS
O ORNATEST
P PATTERNS
  TRANSEPT
R TRANTERS
S TARTNESS
U TAUNTERS

AENRSTU 159
SAUNTER
B UNBRASTE
  URBANEST
C CENTAURS
  RECUSANT
  UNCRATES
  UNTRACES
D DAUNTERS
  TRANSUDE
  UNTREADS
G STRAUNGE
H HAUNTERS
  UNEARTHS
  UNHEARTS
  URETHANS
I RUINATES
  TAURINES
  URANITES
  URINATES
L NEUTRALS
M ANESTRUM
  MENSTRUA
  TRANSUME
P PERSAUNT
S ANESTRUS
  SAUNTERS
T TAUNTERS
V VAUNTERS
W UNWATERS

AEOPRST 233
ESPARTO
B PROBATES
D ADOPTERS
  ASPORTED
  READOPTS
E OPERATES
  PROTEASE
F FOREPAST
G PORTAGES
  POTAGERS
H POTSHARE
L PETROSAL
  PROLATES
N OPERANTS
  PRONATES
R PRAETORS
  PRORATES
S ESPARTOS
  PORTASES
  PROTASES
  SEAPORTS
T PROSTATE
```

```
U APTEROUS
V OVERPAST

AEORRST 107
ROASTER
A AERATORS
B ARBORETS
  TABORERS
C ACROTERS
  CREATORS
  REACTORS
D ROADSTER
G GARROTES
I ROARIEST
  ROTARIES
L REALTORS
  RELATORS
M REARMOST
N ANTRORSE
O SORORATE
P PRAETORS
  PRORATES
R ARRESTOR
S ASSERTOR
  ASSORTER
  ORATRESS
  ROASTERS
T ROSTRATE

AEORSTT 250
TOASTER
A AEROSTAT
B ABETTORS
  BATTEROS
  TABORETS
C SECTATOR
G GAROTTES
H RHEOSTAT
N ORNATEST
P PROSTATE
R ROSTRATE
S STRATOSE
  TOASTERS
T ATTESTOR
  TESTATOR
U OUTRATES
  OUTSTARE

AGILNOT 186
ANTILOG
A GALTONIA
B BLOATING
  OBLIGANT
C LOCATING
E GELATION
  LEGATION
F FLOATING
G GLOATING
  GOATLING
H LOATHING
I INTAGLIO
  LIGATION
  TAGLIONI
P PLOATING
R TRIGONAL
S ANTILOGS
  SALTOING
Y ANTILOGY

AGINORS 202
SOARING
D ROADINGS
E IGNAROES
  ORGANISE
  ORIGANES
I SIGNORIA
L SIGNORAL
M ORGANISM
  ROAMINGS
```

```
R GARRISON
  ROARINGS
S ASSIGNOR
  SOARINGS
T ORGANIST
  ROASTING
U AROUSING
V SAVORING

AGINORT 144
ORATING
B ABORTING
  TABORING
I RIGATONI
L TRIGONAL
N IGNORANT
O ROGATION
S ORGANIST
  ROASTING
T ROTATING
  TROATING
V GRAVITON
Y GYRATION
  ORGANITY

AGINRST 156
STARING
A GRANITAS
B BRASTING
C SCARTING
  TRACINGS
D TRADINGS
E ANGRIEST
  ASTRINGE
  GANISTER
  GANTRIES
  GRANITES
  INGRATES
  RANGIEST
  REASTING
  STEARING
  TASERING
F INGRAFTS
  STRAFING
G GRATINGS
H TRASHING
K KARTINGS
  STARKING
L RATLINGS
  STARLING
M MIGRANTS
  SMARTING
N RANTINGS
  STARNING
O ORGANIST
  ROASTING
P PARTINGS
  PRATINGS
R STARRING
  TARRINGS
S GASTRINS
  STARINGS
T RATTINGS
  STARTING
V STARVING
W STRAWING
  WRASTING
Y STRAYING
```

```
R GARRISON
  ROARINGS
S ASSIGNOR
  SOARINGS
T ORGANIST
  ROASTING
U AROUSING
V SAVORING

AGINORT 144
ORATING
B ABORTING
  TABORING
I RIGATONI
L TRIGONAL
N IGNORANT
O ROGATION
S ORGANIST
  ROASTING
T ROTATING
  TROATING
V GRAVITON
Y GYRATION
  ORGANITY

AGINRST 156
STARING
A GRANITAS
B BRASTING
C SCARTING
  TRACINGS
D TRADINGS
E ANGRIEST
  ASTRINGE
  GANISTER
  GANTRIES
  GRANITES
  INGRATES
  RANGIEST
  REASTING
  STEARING
  TASERING
F INGRAFTS
  STRAFING
G GRATINGS
H TRASHING
K KARTINGS
  STARKING
L RATLINGS
  STARLING
M MIGRANTS
  SMARTING
N RANTINGS
  STARNING
O ORGANIST
  ROASTING
P PARTINGS
  PRATINGS
R STARRING
  TARRINGS
S GASTRINS
  STARINGS
T RATTINGS
  STARTING
V STARVING
W STRAWING
  WRASTING
Y STRAYING

AILNORT 121
(TRIONAL)
A NOTARIAL
  RATIONAL
C CILANTRO
  CONTRAIL
E ORIENTAL
  RELATION
  TAILERON
F FLATIRON
```

BONUS WORD LISTS: 8-Letter Sets 172

```
    INFLATOR     G ERECTING     C CONCEITS       STEEDING     DEENORT 162    DEILORS 195
G TRIGONAL         GENTRICE     D DEONTICS     H DISTHENE     (RENOTED)      SOLDIER
H HORNTAIL       I ICTERINE     E ICESTONE     I DIETINES     C CENTRODE     A DARIOLES
M TORMINAL       N INCENTRE       SEICENTO     L ENLISTED     H DETHRONE       SOLIDARE
Z TRIZONAL       O ERECTION     K CONKIEST       LINTSEED       THRENODE       SOREDIAL
                   NEOTERIC     L LECTIONS       LISTENED     I ORIENTED     C SCLEROID
AILNOST 199      P PRENTICE     M CENTIMOS       TINSELED     L REDOLENT     I IDOLISER
(SIN A LOT)      S CENTRIES     O COONTIES     M DEMENTIS     M ENTODERM     L DOLLIERS
A AILANTOS         ENTERICS     P PONCIEST       SEDIMENT     O ENROOTED     N DISENROL
E ELATIONS         ENTICERS     R CORNIEST       TIDESMEN     S ERODENTS     S SOLDIERS
  INSOLATE         SCIENTER       RECTIONS     N DENTINES     U DEUTERON     T STOLIDER
  TOENAILS         SECRETIN     S SECTIONS       DESINENT                    U SOULDIER
G ANTILOGS       T RETICENT     T CENTOIST     O SIDENOTE     DEENRTU 219    Y SOLDIERY
  SALTOING       U CEINTURE       STENOTIC     P PENTISED     DENTURE
L STALLION         ENURETIC     U COUNTIES     R INSERTED     A DENATURE     DEINORS 23
N ANTLIONS                      X EXCITONS       NERDIEST     D RETUNDED     INDORSE
O SOLATION       CEINORS 181    Y CYTOSINE       RESIDENT     E NEUTERED     A ANEROIDS
                 COINERS                         SINTERED     I REUNITED       DONARIES
AILORST 197      A SCENARIO     DEEINRS 96       TRENDIES     L UNDERLET     C CONSIDER
TAILORS          B BICORNES     RESINED        S DESTINES     N UNTENDER     D INDORSED
B ORBITALS       C CONCISER     A ARSENIDE     T DINETTES     O DEUTERON     E ORDINEES
  STROBILA         CORNICES       DENARIES     U DETINUES     R RETURNED     G NEGROIDS
C CALORIST         CROCEINS       DRAISENE     V EVIDENTS     S DENTURES     H HORDEINS
D DILATORS       D CONSIDER       NEARSIDE       INVESTED       SEDERUNT     I DERISION
E SOTERIAL       F CONIFERS     B INBREEDS                      UNDERSET       IRONISED
M MORALIST         FORENSIC     E NEREIDES     DEEIRST 61       UNDESERT       RESINOID
O ISOLATOR         FORINSEC     F DEFINERS     DIETERS        V VENTURED     J JOINDERS
S SOLARIST         FORNICES     G DESIGNER     A READIEST                    L DISENROL
U SUTORIAL         INFORCES       ENERGIDS       SERIATED     DEIINRT 210    N ENDIRONS
Y ROYALIST       H CHORINES       REDESIGN       SIDERATE     NITRIDE        P DISPONER
  SOLITARY       I RECISION       READINGS       STEADIER     A DAINTIER       POINDERS
                   SORICINE       RESIGNED     B BESTRIDE     C INDIRECT       PRISONED
AINORST 40       L INCLOSER     H DRISHEEN     C DISCREET     D NITRIDED     S INDORSES
RATIONS            LICENSOR     K DEERSKIN       DISCRETE     G DIRIGENT     T DRONIEST
B TABORINS       M CREMOSIN     N SINNERED     D REDDIEST     M DIRIMENT     U DOURINES
C CANTORIS         INCOMERS     O ORDINEES     E REEDIEST     O RETINOID       SOURDINE
  CAROTINS         SERMONIC     S DIRENESS     G DIGESTER     P INTREPID     W DISOWNER
D INTRADOS       N INCENSOR     T INSERTED       ESTRIDGE     S DISINTER       WINDORES
E ANOESTRI       P CONSPIRE       NERDIEST     I SIDERITE       INDITERS       WINDROSE
  ARSONITE         INCORPSE       RESIDENT     M DEMERITS       NITRIDES
  NOTARIES       S NECROSIS       SINTERED       DEMISTER       RINDIEST     DEINORT 32
  NOTARISE         SERICONS       TRENDIES       DIMETERS     U UNTIDIER     (IRODENT)
  ROSINATE       T CORNIEST     U UREDINES       MISTERED                    A AROINTED
G ORGANIST         RECTIONS     W WIDENERS     N INSERTED     DEIIRST 242      DERATION
  ROASTING       U NOURICES     X INDEXERS       NERDIEST     (TIDIERS)        ORDINATE
H TRAHISON         ROUNCIES                      RESIDENT     A IRISATED       RATIONED
J JANITORS                      DEEINRT 59       SINTERED     C ICTERIDS     C CENTROID
K SKIATRON       CEINORT 73     (DIRTEEN)        TRENDIES     E SIDERITE       DOCTRINE
O ORATIONS       RECTION        A DETAINER     P PRIESTED     G RIDGIEST     E ORIENTED
P ATROPINS       A ACTIONER       RETAINED       RESPITED       RIGIDEST     I RETINOID
S ARSONIST         ANORETIC     D DENDRITE     R DESTRIER     H DISHERIT     M DORMIENT
T STRONTIA         CREATION     K TINKERED     S EDITRESS     L REDISTIL     S DRONIEST
U SUTORIAN         REACTION     M REMINTED       RESISTED     N DISINTER     T INTORTED
X TRIAXONS       C CONCERTI     N INDENTER       SISTERED       INDITERS
                   NECROTIC       INTENDER     T TIREDEST       NITRIDES     DEINOST 65
BEINOST 243      D CENTROID       INTERNED     U ERUDITES       RINDIEST     DITONES
BONIEST            DOCTRINE     O ORIENTED       SURETIED     O DIORITES     A ASTONIED
A BOTANIES       E ERECTION     R INTERRED     V VERDITES     P RIPTIDES       SEDATION
  BOTANISE         NEOTERIC       TRENDIER     W WEIRDEST       SPIRITED     C DEONTICS
  NIOBATES       F INFECTOR     S INSERTED                    T DIRTIEST     E SIDENOTE
  OBEISANT       G GERONTIC       NERDIEST     DEENORS 133      TRITIDES     H HEDONIST
B NOBBIEST       H NOTCHIER       RESIDENT     ENDORSE                       I EDITIONS
E BETONIES       J INJECTOR       SINTERED     A REASONED     DEILNOS 129      SEDITION
  EBONITES       M INTERCOM       TRENDIES     C CENSORED     (SLID EON)     M DEMONIST
I NIOBITES       P ENTROPIC     U REUNITED       NECROSED     A NODALISE     R DRONIEST
N BONNIEST         INCEPTOR     V INVERTED       SECONDER     C INCLOSED     S DONSIEST
R BORNITES       R TRICORNE     W WINTERED     D ENDORSED     E ESLOINED     W DOWNIEST
  RIBSTONE       S CORNIEST     X DEXTRINE     E ENDORSEE     G GLENOIDS
S EBONISTS         RECTIONS                    I ORDINEES       SIDELONG     DEINRST 71
T BOTTINES       T CONTRITE     DEEINST 41     M SERMONED     I LIONISED     TINDERS
U BOUNTIES         CORNETTI     DESTINE        N ENDERONS     O SOLENOID     A DETRAINS
                 U NEUROTIC     A ANDESITE     R ENDORSER     R DISENROL       RANDIEST
CEEINRT 246      V CONTRIVE     B BENDIEST     S ENDORSES     S SONDELIS       STRAINED
ENTICER                        D DESTINED     T ERODENTS     U DELUSION     D STRIDDEN
A CENTIARE       CEINOST 165    E NEEDIEST     W ENDOWERS       INSOULED     E INSERTED
  CREATINE       NOTICES        F FENDIEST       WORSENED       UNSOILED       NERDIEST
  INCREASE       A ACONITES       INFESTED                                     RESIDENT
  ITERANCE         CANOEIST     G INGESTED                                     SINTERED
F FRENETIC                        SIGNETED                                     TRENDIES
```

G STRINGED
I DISINTER
  INDITERS
  NITRIDES
  RINDIEST
L SNIRTLED
  TENDRILS
  TRINDLES
O DRONIEST
P SPRINTED
T STRIDENT
  TRIDENTS
U INTRUDES
X DEXTRINS

DEINRTU 124
UNTRIED
A DATURINE
  INDURATE
  RUINATED
  URINATED
B TURBINED
  UNDERBIT
D INTRUDED
E REUNITED
I UNTIDIER
M RUDIMENT
P TURNIPED
R INTRUDER
S INTRUDES
W UNDERWIT

DEINSTU 175
DUNITES
A AUDIENTS
  SINUATED
D DISTUNED
E DETINUES
F UNSIFTED
G DUNGIEST
I DISUNITE
  NUDITIES
  UNITISED
  UNTIDIES
L DILUENTS
  INSULTED
  UNLISTED
M MISTUNED
N DUNNIEST
  DUNNITES
Q SQUINTED
R INTRUDES
S DISTUNES
U UNSUITED

DEIORST 44
EDITORS
A ASTEROID
B DEBITORS
C CORDITES
G GRODIEST
  STODGIER
I DIORITES
K DORKIEST
L STOLIDER
M MORTISED
N DRONIEST
P DIOPTERS
  DIOPTRES
  DIPTEROS
  PERIDOTS
  PROTEIDS
  RIPOSTED
S STEROIDS
T DORTIEST
U IODURETS
  OUTRIDES
  OUTSIDER
  SUITORED

W ROWDIEST
  WORDIEST

DEIORTU 241
OUTRIDE
C OUTCRIED
E ETOURDIE
H OUTHIRED
R OUTRIDER
S IODURETS
  OUTRIDES
  OUTSIDER
V OUTDRIVE

DEIRSTU 226
DUSTIER
C CRUDITES
  CURDIEST
  CURTSIED
D RUDDIEST
  STURDIED
E ERUDITES
  SURETIED
G DURGIEST
L DILUTERS
  LURIDEST
N INTRUDES
O IODURETS
  OUTRIDES
  OUTSIDER
  SUITORED
P DISPUTER
  STUPIDER
Q SQUIRTED
R STURDIER
S DIESTRUS
  DRUSIEST
  STUDIERS
  STURDIES
T DETRITUS
X DRUXIEST

DENORST 205
SNORTED
A TORNADES
E ERODENTS
I DRONIEST
M MORDENTS
N TENDRONS
P PORTENDS
  PROTENDS
U ROUNDEST
  TONSURED
  UNSORTED

DENORTU 152
(NOTRUDE)
C CORNUTED
  TROUNCED
D ROTUNDED
E DEUTERON
F FORTUNED
G TRUDGEON
L ROUNDLET
O UNROOTED
R ROTUNDER
S ROUNDEST
  TONSURED
  UNSORTED
T UNROTTED
W UNDERTOW

EEGINRS 89
GREISEN
A GESNERIA
B BIGENERS
C CREESING
  GENERICS

D DESIGNER
  ENERGIDS
  REDESIGN
  REEDINGS
  RESIGNED
E ENERGIES
  ENERGISE
F FEERINGS
  REEFINGS
G GREESING
H GREENISH
  SHEERING
J JEERINGS
K KREESING
  SKEERING
L LEERINGS
  REELINGS
M REGIMENS
N ENGINERS
  INGENERS
  SERENING
  SNEERING
O ERINGOES
P SPEERING
  SPREEING
R RESIGNER
S GREISENS
T GENTRIES
  INTEGERS
  REESTING
  STEERING
  STREIGNE
U SEIGNEUR
V SEVERING
  VEERINGS
W SEWERING

EEGINRT 220
INTEGER
A GRATINEE
C ERECTING
  GENTRICE
G GREETING
M METERING
  REGIMENT
N ENTERING
P PETERING
S GENTRIES
  INTEGERS
  REESTING
  STEERING
  STREIGNE
U GENITURE
V EVERTING
W TWEERING
X EXERTING
  GENETRIX

EEGINST 149
(GETSINE)
A SAGENITE
B BEIGNETS
C GENETICS
D INGESTED
  SIGNETED
  STEEDING
G EGESTING
H SEETHING
  SHEETING
K KITENGES
  STEEKING
L GENTILES
  SLEETING
  STEELING
M MEETINGS
  STEEMING
N STEENING
O EGESTION

P STEEPING
R GENTRIES
  INTEGERS
  REESTING
  STEERING
  STREIGNE
T GENTIEST
U EUGENIST
V STEEVING
  VENTIGES
W SWEETING
X EXIGENTS

EEILNST 85
TENSILE
B STILBENE
  TENSIBLE
D ENLISTED
  LINTSEED
  LISTENED
  TINSELED
E SELENITE
G GENTILES
  SLEETING
  STEELING
I LENITIES
K NESTLIKE
N LENIENTS
  SENTINEL
O NOSELITE
P PLENTIES
R LISTENER
  SILENTER
S SETLINES
T ENTITLES
V VEINLETS

EEILORS 182
(LIESORE)
F FORELIES
I OILERIES
K ROSELIKE
L ORSEILLE
N ELOINERS
P PELORIES
T LITEROSE
  TROELIES
V OVERLIES
  RELIEVOS
  VOLERIES
W OWLERIES

EEILORT 114
TROELIE
A AEROLITE
D DOLERITE
  LOITERED
H HOTELIER
K LORIKEET
M MOTELIER
R LOITERER
S LITEROSE
  TROELIES

EEILRST 79
STERILE
A ATELIERS
  EARLIEST
  LEARIEST
  REALTIES
C RETICLES
  SCLERITE
  TIERCELS
E LEERIEST
  SLEETIER
  STEELIER
F FERLIEST
I TILERIES
K TRISKELE

L TREILLES
M TERMLIES
N LISTENER
  SILENTER
O LITEROSE
  TROELIES
P EPISTLER
  PELTRIES
  PERLITES
  REPTILES
S LEISTERS
  RITELESS
  TIRELESS
T RETILES

EEINORS 95
(EROSINE)
D ORDINEES
G ERINGOES
H HEROINES
K KEROSINE
L ELOINERS
M EMERSION
P ISOPRENE
  PIONEERS
S ESSOINER
T SEROTINE
V EVERSION

EEINORT 19
(TRIE ONE)
B TENEBRIO
C ERECTION
  NEOTERIC
D ORIENTED
H ETHERION
I ERIONITE
M TIMONEER
R REORIENT
S SEROTINE
T TENORITE
X EXERTION

EEINOST 75
(ETONIES)
B BETONIES
  EBONITES
C ICESTONE
  SEICENTO
D SIDENOTE
G EGESTION
L NOSELITE
M MONETISE
  SEMITONE
R SEROTINE
S ESSONITE
T NOISETTE
  TEOSINTE

EEINRST 12
ENTRIES
A ARSENITE
  RESINATE
  STEARINE
  TRAINEES
C CENTRIES
  ENTERICS
  ENTICERS
  SCIENTER
  SECRETIN
D INSERTED
  NERDIEST
  RESIDENT
  SINTERED
  TRENDIES
E ETERNISE
  TEENSIER
F FERNIEST
G GENTRIES

  INTEGERS
  REESTING
  STEERING
  STREIGNE
I ERINITES
  NITERIES
K KERNITES
L LISTENER
  SILENTER
N INTENSER
  INTERNES
O SEROTINE
R INSERTER
  REINSERT
  REINTERS
  RENTIERS
  TERRINES
S INTERESS
  SENTRIES
  TRENISES
T INERTEST
  INTEREST
  STERNITE
U ESURIENT
  NEURITES
  RETINUES
  REUNITES
V NERVIEST
  REINVEST
  SERVIENT
  SIRVENTE
X INTERSEX
Y SERENITY

EEINRSU 172
(USEREIN)
A UNEASIER
C INSECURE
  SINECURE
D UREDINES
F REINFUSE
G SEIGNEUR
N NEURINES
P PENURIES
  RESUPINE
Q ENQUIRES
  INQUERES
  SQUIREEN
R REINSURE
S ENURESIS
T ESURIENT
  NEURITES
  RETINUES
  REUNITES
V UNIVERSE

EEINRTT 170
TENTIER
B REBITTEN
C RETICENT
E REINETTE
  TEENTIER
H THIRTEEN
I INTERTIE
  RETINITE
L NETTLIER
N RENITENT
O TENORITE
S INERTEST
  INTEREST
  STERNITE
Y ENTIRETY
  ETERNITY

EEINSTT 163
(SITETEN)
A ANISETTE
  TETANIES
  TETANISE

B BENTIEST
D DINETTES
E TEENIEST
F FEINTEST
G GENTIEST
I ENTITIES
L ENTITLES
M MINETTES
N SENTIENT
O NOISETTE
　TEOSINTE
P INEPTEST
　SPINETTE
R INERTEST
　INTEREST
　STERNITE
T NETTIEST
　TENTIEST
W TENTWISE
　TWENTIES
X EXISTENT

EEIORST 64
(OTERIES)
A ETAERIOS
C COTERIES
　ESOTERIC
G ERGOTISE
H ISOTHERE
　THEORIES
　THEORISE
L LITEROSE
　TROELIES
M TIRESOME
N SEROTINE
P POETRIES
S EROTESIS

EELORST 155
(LETSORE)
A OLEASTER
C CORSELET
　ELECTORS
　ELECTROS
　SELECTOR
E SLOETREE
H HOSTELER
I LITEROSE
　TROELIES
L SOLLERET
M MOLESTER
N ENTRESOL
T LORETTES
U RESOLUTE

EENORST 46
(ENSTORE)
A RESONATE
D ERODENTS
F ENFOREST
　SOFTENER
G ESTROGEN
H HONESTER
I SEROTINE
L ENTRESOL
M SERMONET
　STOREMEN
N TENONERS
O ROESTONE
P PROTENSE
T ONSETTER
V OVERNETS
X EXTENSOR

EGILNOR 198
(LONERIG)
A GERANIOL
　REGIONAL
B IGNOBLER

E ELOIGNER
F FLORIGEN
I RELIGION
S RESOLING
W LOWERING

EGINRS 70
IGNORES
A IGNAROES
　ORGANISE
　ORIGANES
B SOBERING
D NEGROIDS
E ERINGOES
I SEIGNIOR
L RESOLING
M NEGROISM
P PERIGONS
　REPOSING
　SPONGIER
R IGNORERS
S GORINESS
　SIGNORES
T GENITORS
　ROSETING
Y SEIGNORY

EGINORT 183
GENITOR
C GERONTIC
H THROEING
N NITROGEN
S GENITORS
　ROSETING
T OTTERING
U OUTREIGN
　ROUTEING
W TOWERING
X OXTERING
Z ROZETING

EGINRST 88
RESTING
A ANGRIEST
　ASTRINGE
　GANISTER
　GANTRIES
　GRANITES
　INGRATES
　RANGIEST
　REASTING
　STEARING
　TASERING
C CRESTING
D STRINGED
E GENTRIES
　INTEGERS
　REESTING
　STEERING
　STREIGNE
H RIGHTENS
I GIRNIEST
　IGNITERS
　REISTING
　STINGIER
　STRIGINE
L LINGSTER
　RINGLETS
　STERLING
　TINGLERS
　TRINGLES
N STERNING
O GENITORS
　ROSETING
P PRESTING
R RESTRING
　RINGSTER
　STRINGER
S RESTINGS

STINGERS
TRESSING
TRIGNESS
T GITTERNS
V STERVING
W STREWING
　WRESTING

EGIORST 209
GORIEST
D GRODIEST
　STODGIER
E ERGOTISE
H GHOSTIER
M ERGOTISM
　GORMIEST
N GENITORS
　ROSETING
S GORSIEST
　STRIGOSE
U GOUSTIER
V VERTIGOS
Y OYSTRIGE
Z ZORGITES

EGNORST 215
(ESTRONG)
A ORANGEST
　RAGSTONE
　STONERAG
E ESTROGEN
G GONGSTER
I GENITORS
　ROSETING
N RONTGENS
R STRONGER
S SONGSTER
T TONGSTER
U STURGEON
W WRONGEST

EHIORST 206
HOISTER
A HOARIEST
C ROTCHIES
　THEORICS
E ISOTHERE
　THEORIES
　THEORISE
G GHOSTIER
M ISOTHERM
　MOITHERS
N HORNIEST
P TROPHIES
R HERITORS
S HOISTERS
　HORSIEST
　HOSTRIES
　SHORTIES
T THEORIST
　THORITES
U OUTHIRES
V OVERHITS
W WORTHIES

EIILRST 207
SILTIER
A LAIRIEST
　LISTERIA
B TRILBIES
D REDISTIL
E TILERIES
L STILLIER
M LIMITERS
　MIRLIEST
N NIRLIEST
　NITRILES
P TRIPLIES

T STILTIER
U UTILISER

EIINORT 78
(IRONITE)
D RETINOID
E IRONITE
F NOTIFIER
P POINTIER
R INTERIOR
S IRONIEST

EIINRST 56
(TINIERS)
A INERTIAS
　RAINIEST
B BRINIEST
C CITRINES
　CRINITES
　INCITERS
D DISINTER
　INDITERS
　NITRIDES
　RINDIEST
E ERINITES
　NITERIES
F SNIFTIER
G GIRNIEST
　IGNITERS
　REISTING
　STINGIER
　STRIGINE
H INHERITS
L NIRLIEST
　NITRILES
M INTERIMS
　MINISTER
O IRONIEST
P PRISTINE
S SINISTER
T NITRITES
　STINTIER
U NEURITIS
V INVITERS
　VINTRIES
　VITRINES

EILNORS 77
NEROLIS
A AILERONS
　ALERIONS
　ALIENORS
C INCLOSER
　LICENSOR
D DISENROL
E ELOINERS
G RESOLING
P PROLINES
R LORINERS
T RETINOLS

EILNORT 87
RETINOL
A ORIENTAL
　RELATION
　TAILERON
P TOPLINER
R RITORNEL
S RETINOLS
T TROTLINE
W TOWNLIER

EILNOST 24
ENTOILS
A ELATIONS
　INSOLATE
　TOENAILS
C LECTIONS
E NOSELITE

H HOTLINES
　NEOLITHS
I ETIOLINS
L STELLION
M MOLINETS
N INSOLENT
O LOONIEST
　OILSTONE
P POINTELS
　PONTILES
　TOPLINES
R RETINOLS
U ELUTIONS
　OUTLINES
V NOVELIST
　VIOLENTS
W TOWLINES

EILNRST 74
SNIRTLE
A ENTRAILS
　LATRINES
　RATLINES
　TRENAILS
D SNIRTLED
　TENDRILS
　TRINDLES
E LISTENER
　SILENTER
G LINGSTER
　RINGLETS
　STERLING
　TINGLERS
　TRINGLES
I NIRLIEST
　NITRILES
K LINKSTER
　STRINKLE
M MINSTREL
O RETINOLS
P SPLINTER
S SLINTERS
　SNIRTLES
U INSULTER
　LUSTRINE
Y TINSELRY

EILORST 25
LOITERS
A SOTERIAL
B STROBILE
　TRILOBES
C CLOISTER
　COISTREL
　COSTLIER
　CREOLIST
D STOLIDER
E LITEROSE
　TROELIES
F FLORIEST
I ROILIEST
L TRILLOES
　TROLLIES
N RETINOLS
O TROOLIES
P POITRELS
T TRIOLETS
U LOURIEST
　OUTLIERS

EILRSTU 164
LUSTIER
A URALITES
B BURLIEST
　SUBTILER
C CURLIEST
　UTRICLES

D DILUTERS
　LURIDEST
G GURLIEST
H LUTHIERS
I UTILISER
M MURLIEST
N INSULTER
　LUSTRINE
O LOURIEST
　OUTLIERS
Q QUILTERS
R SULTRIER
S SURLIEST
T SURTITLE
V RIVULETS

EIMNOST 234
MOISTEN
A SOMNIATE
C CENTIMOS
D DEMONIST
E MONETISE
　SEMITONE
G MITOGENS
H HOISTMEN
K TOKENISM
L MOLINETS
N MENTIONS
O EMOTIONS
　MOONIEST
P EMPTIONS
　NEPOTISM
　PIMENTOS
S MOISTENS

EIMORST 158
MOISTER
A AMORTISE
　ATOMISER
C MORTICES
D MORTISED
E TIRESOME
F SETIFORM
G ERGOTISM
　GORMIEST
H ISOTHERM
　MOITHERS
O MOORIEST
　MOTORISE
　ROOMIEST
P IMPOSTER
R MORTISER
　STORMIER
S EROTISMS
　MORTISES
　TRISOMES
T OMITTERS
U MISROUTE
　MOISTURE
W MISWROTE
　WORMIEST
Y ISOMETRY

EINOPRS 166
ORPINES
C CONSPIRE
　INCORPSE
D DISPONER
　POINDERS
　PRISONED
E ISOPRENE
　PIONEERS
F FORPINES
G PERIGONS
　REPOSING
　SPONGIER
I PIENIPOS
L PROLINES
O POISONER

```
        SNOOPIER      H HORNIEST     EINORTU 140    U RUNTIEST     S PERIOSTS      V VIRETOTS
        SPOONIER      I IRONIEST     ROUTINE        W TWINTERS       PROSIEST
P POPERINS      J JOINTERS     C NEUROTIC     Y ENTRYIST       REPOSITS     EIORSTU 94
  PROPINES      L RETINOLS     G OUTREIGN                      RIPOSTES     TOUSIER
R PRISONER      N INTONERS       ROUTEING     EINRSTU 52       TRIPOSES   C CITREOUS
S PORINESS        TERNIONS     J JOINTURE     UNITERS        T PORTIEST     OUTCRIES
  PRESSION      O SNOOTIER     N NEUTRINO   A RUINATES         RISPETTO   D IODURETS
  ROPINESS      P POINTERS     P ERUPTION     TAURINES         SPOTTIER     OUTRIDES
T POINTERS        PROTEINS     S ROUTINES     URANITES       U ROUPIEST     OUTSIDER
  PROTEINS        REPOINTS       SNOUTIER     URINATES         SPOUTIER     SUITORED
  REPOINTS      R INTRORSE     T RITENUTO   B TRIBUNES       V PIVOTERS   F FOUSTIER
U PRUINOSE        SNORTIER                     TURBINES         SPORTIVE   G GOUSTIER
V OVERSPIN      S TERSIONS     EINOSTT 249  C CURNIEST                    H OUTHIRES
  PROVINES      T SNOTTIER     TONIEST      D INTRUDES       EIORRST 117  L LOURIEST
                  TENORIST     B BOTTINES   E ESURIENT       RIOTERS        OUTLIERS
EINOPRT 239       TRITONES     C CENTOIST     NEURITES     A ROARIEST     M MISROUTE
POINTER         U ROUTINES       STENOTIC     RETINUES       ROTARIES       MOISTURE
A ATROPINE        SNOUTIER     E NOISETTE     REUNITES     B ORBITERS     N ROUTINES
C ENTROPIC      V INVESTOR       TEOSINTE   I NEURITIS     F FROSTIER       SNOUTIER
  INCEPTOR      Y TYROSINE     G TENTIGOS   L INSULTER       ROTIFERS     P ROUPIEST
H TRIPHONE      Z TRIZONES     J JETTISON     LUSTRINE     H HERITORS       SPOUTIER
I POINTIER                     N TINSTONE   M TERMINUS     I RIOTRIES     Q QUOITERS
L TOPLINER      EINORSU 203      TONTINES   N RUNNIEST     M MORTISER     R STOURIER
M ORPIMENT      URINOSE        P NEPOTIST     STURNINE       STORMIER     T TOUSTIER
S POINTERS      C NOURICES     R SNOTTIER   O ROUTINES     N INTRORSE       TUTORISE
  PROTEINS        ROUNCIES       TENORIST     SNOUTIER       SNORTIER     V VIRTUOSE
  REPOINTS      D DOURINES       TRITONES   P REPUNITS     O ROOTSIER       VITREOUS
U ERUPTION        SOURDINE     S SNOTTIES     UNPRIEST     P PIERROTS       VOITURES
                F REFUSION       STONIEST     UNRIPEST       SPORTIER
EINORRT 82      M INERMOUS     T TOTIENTS   Q SQUINTER     R ERRORIST     ENORSTU 161
(TORRINE)         MONSIEUR     W TOWNIEST   T RUNTIEST     S RESISTOR     (NOT SURE)
A ANTERIOR      N REUNIONS                  V UNRIVETS       ROISTERS     B RUBSTONE
C TRICORNE      P PRUINOSE     EINRSTT 211    VENTURIS       SORRIEST     C CONSTRUE
E REORIENT      S NEUROSIS     TINTERS      W UNWRITES     T RORTIEST       CORNUTES
F FRONTIER        RESINOUS     A INTREATS                  U STOURIER       COUNTERS
H THORNIER      T ROUTINES       NITRATES   EIOPRST 174    V SERVITOR       RECOUNTS
I INTERIOR        SNOUTIER       STRAITEN   ROPIEST                         TROUNCES
L RITORNEL      V SOUVENIR       TARTINES   C PERSICOT     EIORSTT 229    D ROUNDEST
S INTRORSE                       TERTIANS   D DIOPTERS     STOITER          TONSURED
  SNORTIER      EINORTT 66     B BITTERNS     DIOPTRES     C COTTIERS       UNSORTED
V INVERTOR      TRITONE        C CENTRIST     DIPTEROS     D DORTIEST     F FORTUNES
                A TENTORIA       CITTERNS     PERIDOTS     H THEORIST     G STURGEON
EINORST 3       C CONTRITE     D STRIDENT     PROTEIDS       THORITES     H SOUTHERN
(IN-STORE)        CORNETTI       TRIDENTS     RIPOSTED     L TRIOLETS     I ROUTINES
A ANOESTRI      D INTORTED     E INERTEST   E POETRIES     M OMITTERS       SNOUTIER
  ARSONITE      E TENORITE       INTEREST   F FIREPOTS     N SNOTTIER     L TURNSOLE
  NOTARIES      G OTTERING       STERNITE   H TROPHIES       TENORIST     M MONTURES
  NOTARISE      K KNOTTIER     G GITTERNS   K PORKIEST       TRITONES       MOUNTERS
  ROSINATE      L TROTLINE     I NITRITES   L POITRELS     O ROOTIEST       REMOUNTS
B BORNITES      N TONTINER       STINTIER   M IMPOSTER       TORTOISE     N NEUTRONS
  RIBSTONE      S SNOTTIER     K KNITTERS   N POINTERS     P PORTIEST     S TONSURES
C CORNIEST        TENORIST       TRINKETS     PROTEINS       RISPETTO     T STENTOUR
  RECTIONS        TRITONES     O SNOTTIER     REPOINTS       SPOTTIER     V VENTROUS
D DRONIEST      U RITENUTO       TENORIST   O PORTOISE     R RORTIEST     Y TOURNEYS
E SEROTINE                       TRITONES     ROOPIEST     S STOITERS
G GENITORS                     S ENTRISTS   R PIERROTS     U TOUSTIER
  ROSETING                       STINTERS     SPORTIER       TUTORISE
```

8-LETTER SETS LIST

alphabetical list of all words appearing in 8-letter sets

ABEARING	ALMERIES	APLUSTRE	ATRESIAS	BICORNES	CENTRIST	CREATINS	DENTINES
ABETTORS	ALMONERS	APPRISED	ATROPINE	BIDENTAL	CENTRODE	CREATION	DENTURES
ABORIGEN	ALOETICS	APTERISM	ATROPINS	BIGENERS	CENTROID	CREATORS	DEONTICS
ABORTEES	ALTERING	APTEROUS	ATTAINED	BINARIES	CERAMIST	CREESING	DEPAINTS
ABORTING	ALTERITY	ARANEIDS	ATTENDER	BIRETTAS	CERASINS	CREMOSIN	DEPILATE
ABSEILED	ALTERNES	ARBITERS	ATTESTOR	BITTERNS	CERATOID	CRENATED	DERACINE
ABSINTHE	ALTRICES	ARBORETS	ATTORNED	BLEAREST	CHANTIES	CRINATED	DERAIGNS
ABSTERGE	ALUNITES	AREADING	ATTORNEY	BLEARING	CHARIEST	CRINITES	DERAILED
ACCENTOR	AMBIENTS	AREOLATE	ATTRITED	BLEATERS	CHAROSET	CRISPATE	DERAILER
ACONITES	AMENDERS	ARETTING	ATTRITES	BLEATING	CHORINES	CRISTATE	DERANGED
ACRIDEST	AMENTIAS	ARIDNESS	AUDIENTS	BLOATERS	CILANTRO	CROCEINS	DERANGES
ACRIDINE	AMMONITE	ARIETTAS	AUDITORS	BLOATING	CINEASTE	CRUDITES	DERATING
ACROLEIN	AMORTISE	ARIETTES	AUNTLIER	BOASTERS	CINEASTS	CURDIEST	DERATION
ACROTERS	ANALCITE	ARILLODE	AURELIAN	BONDAGER	CINEREAS	CURLIEST	DERAYING
ACTINIDE	ANBURIES	ARISTATE	AURELIAS	BONNIEST	CISTERNA	CURNIEST	DERISION
ACTIONED	ANCESTOR	AROINTED	AUREOLAS	BORNITES	CISTVAEN	CURTSIED	DERIVATE
ACTIONER	ANCHORET	AROUSING	AUREOLES	BOTANIES	CITADELS	CYANITES	DEROGATE
ADENINES	ANCIENTS	AROYNTED	AURICLES	BOTANISE	CITRANGE	CYTOSINE	DESIGNER
ADENITIS	ANDESINE	ARRESTED	AUSTERER	BOTTINES	CITRATES	DAINTIER	DESINENT
ADENOIDS	ANDESITE	ARRESTEE	AVENGERS	BOUNTIES	CITREOUS	DAINTIES	DESPAIRS
ADERMINS	ANDIRONS	ARRESTER	AVENTAIL	BRAIDEST	CITRINES	DAKERING	DESTINED
ADHERENT	ANDROGEN	ARRESTOR	AVENTRED	BRANDIES	CITTERNS	DALLIERS	DESTINES
ADHERING	ANDROIDS	ARSENATE	AVENTRES	BRANDISE	CLARETED	DAMOISEL	DESTRIER
ADHESION	ANDVILES	ARSENICS	AVENTURE	BRANTLES	CLARINET	DANDIEST	DESYATIN
ADONISED	ANEARING	ARSENIDE	AVERMENT	BRASTING	CLARTIER	DANGERED	DETAILED
ADONISES	ANEROIDS	ARSENITE	AVERSION	BRAUNITE	CLEAREST	DANGLIER	DETAINED
ADONIZES	ANESTRUM	ARSHINES	AVERTING	BREADING	CLEARING	DARIOLES	DETAINEE
ADOPTERS	ANESTRUS	ARSONIST	AXINITES	BREADNUT	CLEATING	DATARIES	DETAINER
ADROITER	ANEURINS	ARSONITE	AZOTISED	BREASTED	CLOISTER	DATOLITE	DETHRONE
AEGIRINE	ANEURISM	ARTERIES	AZURINES	BRINIEST	COALIEST	DATURINE	DETINUES
AEGIRITE	ANGARIES	ARTESIAN	BAINITES	BROADENS	COALISED	DAUNTERS	DETRAINS
AERATING	ANGRIEST	ARTICLED	BALDIEST	BROADEST	COARSEST	DEADLIER	DETRITAL
AERATION	ANIMATER	ARTICLES	BALUSTER	BROMATES	COASTERS	DEALINGS	DETRITUS
AERATORS	ANIMATES	ARTINESS	BANDEROL	BURLIEST	COINAGES	DEARLING	DEUTERON
AEROLITE	ANISEEDS	ARTISTES	BANDIEST	CABINETS	COISTREL	DEARNESS	DEVIANTS
AEROLITH	ANISETTE	ARTSIEST	BANDORES	CALORIES	COLANDER	DEASOILS	DEVIATES
AEROSTAT	ANKERITE	ASCENDER	BANDSTER	CALORIST	CONATIVE	DEATHIER	DEVIATOR
AFEARING	ANNELIDS	ASPERITY	BANGSTER	CANAIGRE	CONCEITS	DEBATERS	DEWATERS
AGENTIAL	ANODISED	ASPIRATE	BANISTER	CANARIED	CONCERTI	DEBATING	DEXTRANS
AGINNERS	ANODISES	ASPORTED	BANTERED	CANARIES	CONCISER	DEBITORS	DEXTRINE
AGISTERS	ANODIZES	ASSENTER	BARDIEST	CANASTER	CONIFERS	DEBONAIR	DEXTRINS
AGLITTER	ANOESTRA	ASSENTOR	BAREGINE	CANDIDER	CONKIEST	DECANTER	DIABETES
AGONISED	ANOESTRI	ASSERTED	BARITONE	CANISTER	CONSIDER	DECIARES	DIACTINE
AGONISES	ANOINTED	ASSERTER	BARMIEST	CANITIES	CONSPIRE	DECRETAL	DIAGNOSE
AGONIZES	ANOINTER	ASSERTOR	BARONETS	CANNIEST	CONSTRUE	DECRIALS	DIALECTS
AGREEING	ANORETIC	ASSIENTO	BARONIES	CANOEIST	CONTRAIL	DEERSKIN	DIALLERS
AGREMENS	ANORTHIC	ASSIGNOR	BASANITE	CANTERED	CONTRAIR	DEFINERS	DIALYSER
AGREMENT	ANSERINE	ASSOILED	BASINETS	CANTIEST	CONTRATE	DEFLATER	DIAMETER
AIGRETTE	ANSWERED	ASSORTED	BASSINET	CANTORIS	CONTRITE	DEISEALS	DIAPENTE
AILANTOS	ANTBEARS	ASSORTER	BATHORSE	CANTREDS	CONTRIVE	DEISHEAL	DIASPORE
AILERONS	ANTBIRDS	ASTATINE	BATTEROS	CARBINES	COONTIES	DELAINES	DIASTERS
AILETTES	ANTEATER	ASTELIES	BEADIEST	CARINATE	CORDITES	DELATING	DIASTOLE
AILMENTS	ANTENATI	ASTERIAS	BEARDIES	CARIOLES	CORNETTI	DELATION	DIASTYLE
AIRHOLES	ANTERIOR	ASTERIDS	BEARDING	CARLINES	CORNICES	DELATORS	DICENTRA
AIRINESS	ANTEVERT	ASTERISK	BEARINGS	CARMINES	CORNIEST	DELIBATE	DIEDRALS
AIRLINES	ANTHELIA	ASTERISM	BEATINGS	CARNIEST	CORNUTED	DELICATE	DIELYTRA
AIRSPEED	ANTIDOTE	ASTEROID	BEATNIKS	CAROTENE	CORNUTES	DELUSION	DIESTRUS
AIRTIMES	ANTIENTS	ASTERTED	BEGONIAS	CAROTINS	CORONATE	DEMAINES	DIETINES
ALAIMENT	ANTIGENS	ASTHENIA	BEIGNETS	CAROUSEL	CORSELET	DEMENTIA	DIGESTER
ALEPINES	ANTILOGS	ASTHENIC	BELATING	CARTONED	COSTLIER	DEMENTIS	DILATERS
ALERIONS	ANTILOGY	ASTONIED	BENDIEST	CATERANS	COTERIES	DEMERITS	DILATORS
ALERTEST	ANTINODE	ASTONIES	BENTIEST	CATERERS	COTTIERS	DEMISTER	DILUENTS
ALERTING	ANTIPODE	ASTRINGE	BEPAINTS	CATERING	COUNTERS	DEMONIST	DILUTERS
ALEURONS	ANTIPOLE	ASTROIDS	BERATING	CEDRATES	COUNTIES	DENARIES	DIMETERS
ALGERINE	ANTIQUES	ATEBRINS	BERGENIA	CEINTURE	COURANTE	DENARIUS	DINETTES
ALGINATE	ANTISERA	ATELIERS	BESAINTS	CENSORED	CRANNIED	DENATURE	DINOSAUR
ALIENATE	ANTLERED	ATHEISED	BESTAINS	CENTARES	CRANNIES	DENDRITE	DIOCESAN
ALIENEES	ANTLIATE	ATHELING	BESTRIDE	CENTAURS	CRAPIEST	DENTALIA	DIOPTASE
ALIENIST	ANTLIONS	ATHERINE	BETAINES	CENTIARE	CREASING	DENTARIA	DIOPTERS
ALIENORS	ANTRORSE	ATOMISED	BETATRON	CENTIMOS	CREASOTE		DIOPTRES
ALIMENTS	ANTSIEST	ATOMISER	BETONIES	CENTOIST	CREATINE		DIORITES
ALLERION	APERIENT	ATRAZINE	BETREADS	CENTRIES	CREATING		

DIOXANES	EARTHING	ENTITLES	EXIGENTS	GAMESTER	GRADINES	IDEALIST	INSULTED
DIPTERAL	EASTERLY	ENTODERM	EXISTENT	GANGLIER	GRAINAGE	IDEATING	INSULTER
DIPTERAN	EASTINGS	ENTRAILS	EXORDIAL	GANGSTER	GRAINERS	IDEATION	INTAGLIO
DIPTERAS	EASTLING	ENTRAINS	EXPIRANT	GANISTER	GRANDEES	IDOCRASE	INTEGERS
DIPTEROS	EASTLINS	ENTRANTS	EXTENSOR	GANOINES	GRANDEST	IDOLATER	INTEGRAL
DIRENESS	EATERIES	ENTREATS	EXTERNAL	GANTLINE	GRANITAS	IDOLISER	INTENDER
DIRIGENT	EBONISTS	ENTREATY	EXTERNAT	GANTRIES	GRANITES	IGNAROES	INTENSER
DIRIMENT	EBONITES	ENTRESOL	EXTRADOS	GARDENED	GRANNIED	IGNITERS	INTERACT
DIRTIEST	EBRIATED	ENTRISTS	EXTRAITS	GARDENER	GRANNIES	IGNOBLER	INTERCOM
DISADORN	ECTOSARC	ENTROPIC	EXTRANET	GARDENIA	GRANTEES	IGNORANT	INTERESS
DISAGREE	EDITIONS	ENTRYIST	EYELIADS	GARMENTS	GRANTERS	IGNORERS	INTEREST
DISASTER	EDITRESS	ENURESIS	FAILURES	GARNERED	GRAPIEST	IMPOSTER	INTERIMS
DISCREET	EGESTING	ENURETIC	FAINITES	GAROTTED	GRATINEE	INARCHED	INTERIOR
DISCRETE	EGESTION	EPACRIDS	FAINTEST	GAROTTES	GRATINGS	INARCHES	INTERLAY
DISENROL	ELAPSING	EPILATED	FAIRNESS	GARRISON	GRAVITON	INAURATE	INTERNAL
DISHERIT	ELASTINS	EPILATES	FALTERED	GARROTED	GREASILY	INBREEDS	INTERNED
DISINTER	ELATERIN	EPILATOR	FANCIERS	GARROTES	GREASING	INCENSOR	INTERNES
DISLEAVE	ELATIONS	EPINASTY	FANCIEST	GASALIER	GREATENS	INCENTRE	INTERRED
DISOWNER	ELATIVES	EPISODAL	FARINOSE	GASELIER	GREATEST	INCEPTOR	INTERSEX
DISPONER	ELECTORS	EPISTLER	FARNESOL	GASOLIER	GRECIANS	INCHOATE	INTERTIE
DISPREAD	ELECTROS	ERADIATE	FASTENER	GASOLINE	GREENIES	INCITERS	INTERVAL
DISPUTER	ELEGIAST	ERASIONS	FATTENER	GASTRINS	GREENISH	INCLOSED	INTERWAR
DISRATED	ELEVATOR	ERECTING	FEALTIES	GAULTERS	GREESING	INCLOSER	INTONATE
DISRATES	ELOIGNER	ERECTION	FEASTING	GAUNTREE	GREETING	INCOMERS	INTONERS
DISTANCE	ELOINERS	EREMITAL	FEDARIES	GEARINGS	GREISENS	INCORPSE	INTORTED
DISTHENE	ELUTIONS	ERGATIVE	FEERINGS	GELATINE	GREMIALS	INCREASE	INTRADAS
DISTRAIN	ELVANITE	ERGATOID	FEINTEST	GELATINS	GRENADES	INCREATE	INTRADOS
DISTUNED	EMERSION	ERGOTISE	FENDIEST	GELATION	GRODIEST	INDAGATE	INTRANET
DISTUNES	EMIGRANT	ERGOTISM	FENESTRA	GENDARME	GURLIEST	INDARTED	INTREATS
DISUNITE	EMIGRATE	ERINGOES	FENITARS	GENERALS	GYRATION	INDENTER	INTREPID
DIVALENT	EMIRATES	ERINITES	FERLIEST	GENERANT	HAIRIEST	INDEXERS	INTRORSE
DOCTRINE	EMOTIONS	ERIONITE	FERNIEST	GENERATE	HAIRNETS	INDICATE	INTRUDED
DOLERITE	EMPTIONS	ERODENTS	FERRATES	GENERICS	HAIRSTED	INDIRECT	INTRUDER
DOLLIERS	ENACTION	EROTEMAS	FILTRATE	GENETICS	HALTERED	INDITERS	INTRUDES
DOMINATE	ENACTORS	EROTESIS	FINAGLES	GENETRIX	HALTERES	INDORSED	INVADERS
DONARIES	ENATIONS	EROTICAL	FIREPANS	GENISTAS	HANDIEST	INDORSES	INVERTED
DONATIVE	ENDANGER	EROTISMS	FIREPOTS	GENITALS	HARDIEST	INDRAFTS	INVERTOR
DONSIEST	ENDARTED	ERRATICS	FLARIEST	GENITORS	HARMINES	INDURATE	INVESTED
DORKIEST	ENDERONS	ERRORIST	FLATIRON	GENITURE	HARTENED	INEARTHS	INVESTOR
DORMIENT	ENDIRONS	ERUDITES	FLOATERS	GENTIANS	HASTENER	INEPTEST	INVITERS
DORTIEST	ENDORSED	ERUPTION	FLOATIER	GENTIEST	HATERENT	INERMOUS	IODURETS
DOUANIER	ENDORSEE	ESCALIER	FLOATING	GENTILES	HAULIERS	INERRANT	IRISATED
DOULEIAS	ENDORSER	ESCARGOT	FLORIEST	GENTRICE	HAUNTERS	INERTEST	IRISATES
DOURINES	ENDORSES	ESLOINED	FLORIGEN	GENTRIES	HAURIENT	INERTIAL	IRONIEST
DOVETAIL	ENDOSARC	ESOTERIC	FOLIATED	GERANIOL	HEADIEST	INERTIAS	IRONISED
DOWNIEST	ENDOWERS	ESPALIER	FOLIATES	GERMAINE	HEADREST	INFECTOR	ISATINES
DRACONES	ENERGIDS	ESPARTOS	FORECAST	GERMAINS	HEADRING	INFESTED	ISLANDED
DRAFTEES	ENERGIES	ESSOINER	FORELAID	GERMINAL	HEALINGS	INFLATED	ISLANDER
DRAGLINE	ENERGISE	ESSONITE	FORELAIN	GERONTIC	HEARINGS	INFLATES	ISOLATED
DRAGNETS	ENERVATE	ESTANCIA	FORELAND	GESNERIA	HEARSING	INFLATOR	ISOLATES
DRAGONET	ENFOREST	ESTATING	FORELIES	GESTURAL	HEARTENS	INFORCES	ISOLATOR
DRAGONNE	ENGAGERS	ESTRADES	FORENSIC	GHOSTIER	HEARTIES	INGATHER	ISOMETRY
DRAINAGE	ENGINERS	ESTRANGE	FOREPAST	GIANTESS	HEARTING	INGENERS	ISOPRENE
DRAINERS	ENGRACED	ESTRAYED	FORESAID	GIRASOLE	HEATINGS	INGESTED	ISOTHERE
DRAISENE	ENGRACES	ESTRIDGE	FORESAIL	GIRNIEST	HEDONIST	INGRAFTS	ISOTHERM
DRAISINE	ENGRAFTS	ESTROGEN	FORESTAL	GITTERNS	HEPARINS	INGRATES	ITERANCE
DRAPIERS	ENGRAILS	ESURIENT	FORINSEC	GLACIERS	HERITAGE	INHALERS	ITERATED
DRAPPIES	ENGRAINS	ETAERIOS	FORNICES	GLADIEST	HERITORS	INHALER	ITERATES
DRAUNTED	ENGRAVED	ETAGERES	FORPINES	GLAREOUS	HEROINES	INHEARSE	JADEITES
DREADING	ENGRAVES	ETERNISE	FORTUNED	GLARIEST	HESITANT	INHERITS	JADERIES
DREAMING	ENLARGED	ETERNITY	FORTUNES	GLASSIER	HETAIRAS	INJECTOR	JANGLIER
DREAREST	ENLARGES	ETHERIAL	FOUSTIER	GLASSINE	HOARIEST	INLAYERS	JANITORS
DREARING	ENLISTED	ETHERION	FRACTION	GLAZIERS	HOISTERS	INNOVATE	JANTIEST
DRISHEEN	ENQUIRES	ETIOLATE	FRAILEST	GLEANERS	HOISTMEN	INORNATE	JARGONED
DRONIEST	ENRANGED	ETIOLINS	FRAILTEE	GLENOIDS	HONESTER	INQUERES	JAROSITE
DRUSIEST	ENRANGES	ETOURDIE	FRATRIES	GLOATERS	HORDEINS	INSEAMED	JAUNTIER
DRUXIEST	ENROOTED	ETRANGER	FRAULEIN	GLOATING	HORNIEST	INSECURE	JAUNTIES
DUNGAREE	ENSEARED	EUGENIST	FREDAINE	GNARLIER	HORNTAIL	INSERTED	JEERINGS
DUNGIEST	ENSILAGE	EVERSION	FRENETIC	GOADSTER	HORSIEST	INSERTER	JETTISON
DUNNIEST	ENSNARED	EVERTING	FRIANDES	GOATHERD	HOSTELER	INSNARED	JOINDERS
DUNNITES	ENSNARES	EVIDENTS	FRONDAGE	GOATLING	HOSTRIES	INSNARES	JOINTERS
DURATION	ENTAILED	EVIRATED	FRONTIER	GODETIAS	HOTELIER	INSOLATE	JOINTURE
DURGIEST	ENTAILER	EVIRATES	FROSTIER	GOLIASED	HOTLINES	INSOLENT	KAINITES
EAGEREST	ENTERATE	EXACTION	FUSAROLE	GONGSTER	HYSTERIA	INSOULED	KAISERIN
EANLINGS	ENTERICS	EXACTORS	GAHNITES	GORINESS	ICESTONE	INSTABLE	KAOLINES
EARLIEST	ENTERING	EXALTING	GAINLESS	GORMIEST	ICTERIDS	INSTANCE	KARTINGS
EARNESTS	ENTHRALS	EXCITONS	GAINLIER	GORSIEST	ICTERINE	INSTATED	KEITLOAS
EARNINGS	ENTICERS	EXERTING	GALENITE	GOUSTIER	IDEALESS	INSTATES	KERATINS
EARRINGS	ENTITIES	EXERTION	GALTONIA	GRADIENT	IDEALISE	INSULATE	KERATOID

KERATOSE	LINKSTER	MIGRANTS	NEPOTISM	ORGANDIE	PATTERNS	POTAGERS	RASPIEST
KERNITES	LINTSEED	MIGRATES	NEPOTIST	ORGANISE	PEARLIES	POTSHARE	RATIFIES
KEROSINE	LIONISED	MINARETS	NERDIEST	ORGANISM	PEARLING	PRACTISE	RATIONAL
KISTVAEN	LIPARITE	MINEOLAS	NEREIDES	ORGANIST	PEARLINS	PRAETORS	RATIONED
KITENGES	LISTENED	MINERALS	NERVIEST	ORGANITY	PEARLITE	PRALINES	RATLINES
KNEADERS	LISTENER	MINETTES	NESTLIKE	ORGANIZE	PECTINAL	PRATINGS	RATLINGS
KNITTERS	LISTERIA	MINIATED	NETTIEST	ORIENTAL	PEDALIER	PREASING	RATOONED
KNOTTIER	LITANIES	MINIATES	NETTLIER	ORIENTED	PEDERAST	PREDATES	RATSBANE
KREASOTE	LITERACY	MINISTER	NEURINES	ORIGANES	PEDRAILS	PREDIALS	RATTEENS
KREATINE	LITERALS	MINSTREL	NEURITES	ORNATEST	PELORIAS	PRELATES	RATTENED
KREESING	LITERATE	MINTAGES	NEURITIS	ORPIMENT	PELORIES	PRELATIC	RATTIEST
LADRONES	LITERATI	MIRBANES	NEUROSIS	ORSEILLE	PELTRIES	PRENTICE	RATTINGS
LAETARES	LITERATO	MIRLIEST	NEUROTIC	OTALGIES	PENALISE	PRESIDIA	RATTLIER
LAIRAGES	LITEROSE	MISDEALT	NEUTERED	OTTERING	PENTHIAS	PRESSION	RATTLINE
LAIRIEST	LLANEROS	MISRATED	NEUTRALS	OUTCRIED	PENTISED	PRESTING	RAUCLEST
LAIRISED	LOAMIEST	MISRATES	NEUTRINO	OUTCRIES	PENURIES	PRIESTED	RAVELINS
LAITANCE	LOATHERS	MISROUTE	NEUTRONS	OUTDARES	PERAEONS	PRIMATES	RAZEEING
LAKESIDE	LOATHING	MISTAKEN	NICTATES	OUTDRIVE	PERIANTH	PRISONED	REACTING
LAMETERS	LOCATING	MISTERED	NIGELLAS	OUTHIRED	PERIAPTS	PRISONER	REACTION
LAMIGERS	LODESTAR	MISTREAT	NIOBATES	OUTHIRES	PERIDOTS	PRISTANE	REACTORS
LAMINATE	LOITERED	MISTUNED	NIOBITES	OUTLIERS	PERIGEAN	PRISTINE	READIEST
LAMINOSE	LOITERER	MISWROTE	NIRLIEST	OUTLINES	PERIGONS	PRIVATES	READINGS
LAMITERS	LONICERA	MITOGENS	NITERIES	OUTRACES	PERIOSTS	PROBATES	READMITS
LANDSIDE	LOONIEST	MOISTENS	NITRATED	OUTRAGED	PERLITES	PROLATES	READOPTS
LANKIEST	LORETTES	MOISTURE	NITRATES	OUTRAGES	PERSAUNT	PROLINES	READVISE
LANNERET	LORICATE	MOITHERS	NITRIDED	OUTRANCE	PERSICOT	PRONATED	READYING
LANTERNS	LORIKEET	MOLERATS	NITRIDES	OUTRATES	PERSONAE	PRONATES	REAGENTS
LARDIEST	LORINERS	MOLESTER	NITRILES	OUTREIGN	PERSONAL	PROPINES	REALIGNS
LARGENED	LOURIEST	MOLINETS	NITRITES	OUTRIDER	PERTAINS	PRORATES	REALISED
LARKIEST	LOWERING	MONAZITE	NITROGEN	OUTRIDES	PETALINE	PROSIEST	REALISER
LATENING	LUNARIES	MONETISE	NOBBIEST	OUTSIDER	PETALOID	PROSTATE	REALISES
LATERITE	LURIDEST	MONSIEUR	NODALISE	OUTSTARE	PETARIES	PROTASES	REALISTS
LATHERED	LUSTRATE	MONSTERA	NOISETTE	OVERACTS	PETERING	PROTEASE	REALIZED
LATRINES	LUSTRINE	MONTURES	NOMADIES	OVERCAST	PETIOLAR	PROTEIDS	REALIZES
LAWNIEST	LUTHIERS	MOONIEST	NOMADISE	OVEREATS	PETROSAL	PROTEINS	REALLIED
LAYERING	MADERISE	MOORIEST	NOMINATE	OVERHITS	PETUNIAS	PROTENDS	REALLIES
LEADIEST	MADRONES	MORAINES	NORTENAS	OVERLAID	PIANISTE	PROTENSE	REALLOTS
LEADINGS	MAGISTER	MORALISE	NOSELITE	OVERLAIN	PIASTRES	PROVINES	REALTIES
LEAFIEST	MAISTERS	MORALIST	NOTARIAL	OVERLAND	PICRATES	PRUINOSE	REALTIME
LEAKIEST	MALIGNER	MORDENTS	NOTARIES	OVERLIES	PIERROTS	PSORALEN	REALTORS
LEALTIES	MALINGER	MORTICES	NOTARISE	OVERNEAT	PILASTER	PTOMAINE	REAMENDS
LEANINGS	MANGIEST	MORTISED	NOTARIZE	OVERNETS	PILEATED	QUAINTER	REAMIEST
LEAPROUS	MANIFEST	MORTISER	NOTCHIER	OVERPAST	PIMENTOS	QUANTISE	REARISEN
LEARIEST	MANKIEST	MORTISES	NOTIFIER	OVERSAIL	PINASTER	QUANTIZE	REARMOST
LEARNING	MANLIEST	MOTELIER	NOTITIAE	OVERSPIN	PINDAREE	QUILTERS	REARREST
LEASHING	MANNITES	MOTORISE	NOURICES	OWLERIES	PINTABLE	QUOITERS	REASCEND
LEASINGS	MANTISES	MOUNTERS	NOVELIST	OXIDATES	PIONEERS	RABATINE	REASCENT
LEATHERN	MARDIEST	MURIATES	NUDITIES	OXTERING	PIVOTERS	RABATOES	REASONED
LEATHERS	MARGENTS	MURLIEST	OBEISANT	OYSTRIGE	PLAINEST	RABIDEST	REASONER
LEAVIEST	MARGINED	NAARTJES	OBLIGANT	PAINTERS	PLAISTER	RACINESS	REASSERT
LEAVINGS	MARINATE	NACRITES	OBTAINED	PAINTIER	PLAITERS	RADIANCE	REASSIGN
LECTIONS	MARINERS	NAGGIEST	OBTAINER	PAINTURE	PLANETIC	RADIANTS	REASTIER
LEERIEST	MARLIEST	NAIVETES	OCEANIDS	PALATINE	PLANTERS	RADIATED	REASTING
LEERINGS	MARLINES	NAPERIES	OILERIES	PALTERED	PLEASING	RADIATES	REATTAIN
LEGATINE	MARMITES	NAPPIEST	OILSTONE	PALTRIER	PLEATERS	RADICATE	REBATERS
LEGATION	MARTINET	NARCOTIC	OLEANDER	PANARIES	PLEATING	RADICELS	REBATING
LEGATORS	MASTERED	NARGHILE	OLEARIAS	PANDORES	PLENTIES	RADICLES	REBATOES
LEISTERS	MATERIEL	NARGILEH	OLEASTER	PANNIERS	PLOATING	RAGMENTS	REBITTEN
LEMURIAN	MATINEES	NARGILES	OLEFIANT	PANTILED	POETRIES	RAGOUTED	RECANTED
LENIENTS	MATINESS	NARKIEST	OMITTERS	PANTILES	POINDERS	RAGSTONE	RECISION
LENITIES	MATRICES	NARRATES	ONSETTER	PANTINES	POINTELS	RAILBEDS	RECITALS
LEOTARDS	MATRIXES	NARTJIES	OPALINES	PANTLERS	POINTERS	RAIMENTS	RECOUNTS
LEVANTER	MEAGREST	NASTIEST	OPALISED	PANTRIES	POINTIER	RAINCOAT	RECTIONS
LEVATORS	MEALIEST	NATTERED	OPERANDS	PARADISE	POISONER	RAINDATE	RECUSANT
LEVIRATE	MEANDERS	NATTERER	OPERANTS	PARASITE	POITRELS	RAINIEST	REDATING
LIBERATE	MEASLIER	NATTIEST	OPERATES	PARENTED	POLARISE	RAINLESS	REDCOATS
LIBRATED	MEASLING	NAVICERT	ORANGEST	PARIETAL	PONCIEST	RAISONNE	REDDIEST
LIBRATES	MEDALIST	NEARSIDE	ORANGIER	PARISHEN	PONDERAL	RAMEKINS	REDESIGN
LICENSOR	MEDIANTS	NECROSED	ORATIONS	PARITIES	PONIARDS	RAMULOSE	REDIALED
LIGAMENT	MEDIATES	NECROSIS	ORATRESS	PARKIEST	PONTILES	RANCIDER	REDISTIL
LIGATION	MEDIATOR	NECROTIC	ORBITALS	PARODIES	POPERINS	RANDIEST	REDOLENT
LIGNAGES	MEETINGS	NECTARED	ORBITERS	PARODIST	PORINESS	RANGIEST	REEDIEST
LIMEADES	MELANITE	NEEDIEST	ORDAINED	PAROTIDS	PORKIEST	RANGOLIS	REEDINGS
LIMITERS	MENSTRUA	NEGATION	ORDAINER	PARTIBLE	PORTAGES	RANSOMED	REEFINGS
LINDANES	MENTIONS	NEGROIDS	ORDINALS	PARTICLE	PORTANCE	RANTINGS	REELINGS
LINEAGES	METALING	NEGROISM	ORDINANT	PARTINGS	PORTASES	RAPHIDES	REESTING
LINEATED	METANOIA	NEMATOID	ORDINARS	PASTRIES	PORTENDS	RAPIDEST	REFLATED
LINGSTER	METERING	NEOLITHS	ORDINATE	PATENTOR	PORTIEST	RAREBITS	REFLATES
LINKAGES	METRICAL	NEOTERIC	ORDINEES	PATIENTS	PORTOISE	RARITIES	REFLOATS

REFUSION	RESOLING	ROMANTIC	SATINETS	SERIATIM	SNIRTLES	STARVING	STREWAGE
REFUTALS	RESOLUTE	RONDAVEL	SATIRISE	SERICONS	SNOOPIER	STEADIED	STREWING
REGAINED	RESONANT	RONTGENS	SATIRIZE	SERINGAS	SNOOTIER	STEADIER	STRIATED
REGAINER	RESONATE	ROOMIEST	SAUNTERS	SERJEANT	SNORTIER	STEADIES	STRIATES
REGALIAN	RESORCIN	ROOPIEST	SAUTEING	SERMONED	SNOTTIER	STEADILY	STRIDDEN
REGALIAS	RESPITED	ROOTAGES	SAVORING	SERMONET	SNOTTIES	STEADING	STRIDENT
REGALING	RESTAGED	ROOTIEST	SAXONITE	SERMONIC	SNOUTIER	STEALERS	STRIGATE
REGALISM	RESTAGES	ROOTSIER	SCANTIER	SEROTINE	SOARINGS	STEALING	STRIGINE
REGALIST	RESTATED	ROPINESS	SCANTIES	SERRANID	SOBERING	STEAMIER	STRIGOSE
REGIMENS	RESTINGS	RORTIEST	SCARIEST	SERRATED	SOCIETAL	STEAMING	STRINGED
REGIMENT	RESTRAIN	ROSELIKE	SCARTING	SERRATES	SODALITE	STEANING	STRINGER
REGIONAL	RESTRING	ROSETING	SCATTIER	SERVIENT	SOFTENER	STEAPSIN	STRINKLE
REGRANTS	RESUPINE	ROSINATE	SCELERAT	SERVITOR	SOLANDER	STEARAGE	STROAMED
REGRATES	RETABLES	ROSTRATE	SCENARIO	SETIFORM	SOLANINE	STEARINE	STROBILA
REINETTE	RETAILED	ROSULATE	SCIENTER	SETLINES	SOLARISE	STEARING	STROBILE
REINFUSE	RETAILER	ROTARIES	SCLERITE	SEVERING	SOLARIST	STEARINS	STRONGER
REINSERT	RETAINED	ROTATING	SCLEROID	SEWERING	SOLARIZE	STEEDING	STRONTIA
REINSMAN	RETAINER	ROTCHIES	SEABLITE	SHAGREEN	SOLATION	STEEKING	STUDIERS
REINSURE	RETAKERS	ROTIFERS	SEABORNE	SHEALING	SOLDIERS	STEELIER	STUPIDER
REINTERS	RETAKING	ROTUNDED	SEAFRONT	SHEARING	SOLDIERY	STEELING	STURDIED
REINVEST	RETICENT	ROTUNDER	SEALINES	SHEERING	SOLENOID	STEEMING	STURDIER
REISTING	RETICLES	ROULADES	SEALINGS	SHEETING	SOLIDARE	STEENING	STURDIES
RELATERS	RETINITE	ROULEAUS	SEAPORTS	SHERIATS	SOLIDATE	STEEPING	STURGEON
RELATING	RETINOID	ROUNCIES	SEARCING	SHIRALEE	SOLITARY	STEERAGE	STURNINE
RELATION	RETINOLS	ROUNDEST	SEARINGS	SHIREMAN	SOLLERET	STEERING	SUBTILER
RELATIVE	RETINUES	ROUNDLET	SEASONER	SHOALIER	SOMNIATE	STEEVING	SUITORED
RELATORS	RETINULA	ROUPIEST	SEATINGS	SHORTAGE	SONDELIS	STELLION	SUIVANTE
RELAXING	RETIRALS	ROUTEING	SECONDER	SHORTIES	SONGSTER	STENOTIC	SULTRIER
RELAXINS	RETITLES	ROUTINES	SECRETIN	SIDELONG	SORBATES	STENTOUR	SUPINATE
RELAYING	RETRACES	ROWDIEST	SECTATOR	SIDENOTE	SOREDIAL	STERIGMA	SURETIED
RELEVANT	RETRAINS	ROYALETS	SECTIONS	SIDERATE	SORICINE	STERLING	SURLIEST
RELIEVOS	RETRAITS	ROYALISE	SECTORAL	SIDEREAL	SORORATE	STERNAGE	SURTITLE
RELIGION	RETRATES	ROYALIST	SEDATING	SIDERITE	SORRIEST	STERNING	SUTORIAL
RELOCATE	RETREADS	ROZETING	SEDATION	SIDEROAD	SORTABLE	STERNITE	SUTORIAN
REMAINED	RETREATS	RUBEOLAS	SEDATIVE	SIGNALED	SORTANCE	STEROIDS	SUZERAIN
REMANETS	RETRIALS	RUBSTONE	SEDERUNT	SIGNALER	SOTERIAL	STERVING	SWANNIER
REMANIES	RETSINAS	RUDDIEST	SEDIMENT	SIGNETED	SOULDIER	STICHERA	SWATHIER
REMASTER	RETUNDED	RUDIMENT	SEDITION	SIGNORES	SOURDINE	STILBENE	SWEALING
REMEDIAL	RETURNED	RUELLIAS	SEETHING	SIGNORIA	SOUTHERN	STILLIER	SWEARING
REMEDIAT	REUNIONS	RUINABLE	SEGREANT	SILENTER	SOUVENIR	STILTIER	SWEATIER
REMIGATE	REUNITED	RUINATED	SEICENTO	SINECURE	SPAIRGED	STINGERS	SWEATING
REMINTED	REUNITES	RUINATES	SEIGNEUR	SINGABLE	SPAWNIER	STINGIER	SWEETING
REMITTAL	REVENANT	RUMINATE	SEIGNIOR	SINISTER	SPEARING	STINKARD	SYMITARE
REMOUNTS	RHEOSTAT	RUNNIEST	SEIGNORY	SINNERED	SPEERING	STINTERS	SYNEDRIA
RENAGUED	RIANCIES	RUNTIEST	SELECTOR	SINTERED	SPINETTE	STINTIER	TABINETS
RENAGUES	RIBSTONE	RURALISE	SELENIAN	SINUATED	SPIRATED	STODGIER	TABLIERS
RENEGADE	RIDDANCE	SABERING	SELENITE	SIRENIAN	SPIRITED	STOITERS	TABORERS
RENEGADO	RIDEABLE	SABOTEUR	SELICTAR	SIRNAMED	SPLINTER	STOLIDER	TABORETS
RENEGATE	RIDGIEST	SABOTIER	SEMANTIC	SIRNAMES	SPOLIATE	STONERAG	TABORING
RENITENT	RIGATONI	SAGENITE	SEMANTRA	SIRVENTE	SPONGIER	STONERAW	TABORINS
RENOVATE	RIGHTENS	SAGINATE	SEMINARS	SISTERED	SPOONIER	STONIEST	TABRERES
RENTABLE	RIGIDEST	SALARIED	SEMINARY	SKEARING	SPORTIER	STORABLE	TACONITE
RENTIERS	RINDIEST	SALERING	SEMINATE	SKEERING	SPORTIVE	STORAGES	TAENIATE
REORDAIN	RINGLETS	SALIENCE	SEMITARS	SKIATRON	SPOTTIER	STOREMAN	TAENIOID
REORIENT	RINGSTER	SALIENTS	SEMITAUR	SKINCARE	SPOUTIER	STOREMEN	TAGLIONI
REPAINTS	RINSABLE	SALTERNS	SEMITONE	SLAGGIER	SPRAINED	STORMIER	TAILERON
REPASTED	RIOTRIES	SALTIERS	SEMOLINA	SLAIRGED	SPREEING	STOURIER	TAILORED
REPLANTS	RIPIENOS	SALTIRES	SENARIES	SLAISTER	SPRINTED	STOVAINE	TAILRACE
REPOINTS	RIPOSTED	SALTOING	SENARIUS	SLANGIER	SQUAILER	STRADIOT	TAINTURE
REPOSING	RIPOSTES	SALUTERS	SENATORS	SLATTERN	SQUINTED	STRAFING	TAIVERED
REPOSITS	RIPTIDES	SANATIVE	SENSORIA	SLEAVING	SQUINTER	STRAIKED	TALCKIER
REPTILES	RISPETTO	SANDIEST	SENTIENT	SLEAZIER	SQUIREEN	STRAINED	TALIPEDS
REPUNITS	RITELESS	SANDIVER	SENTINEL	SLEETIER	SQUIRTED	STRAINER	TALLIERS
RERAILED	RITENUTO	SANGAREE	SENTRIES	SLEETING	STAINERS	STRAITED	TANAGERS
RESALUTE	RITORNEL	SANGLIER	SEPALINE	SLINTERS	STALKIER	STRAITEN	TANAISTE
RESAYING	RIVULETS	SANITATE	SEPALOID	SLOETREE	STALLION	STRAITER	TANDOORI
RESEATED	ROADINGS	SANITIES	SEPTARIA	SMARTIES	STANDERS	STRANDED	TANGIBLE
RESIANCE	ROADSIDE	SANITISE	SERAFILE	SMARTING	STANIELS	STRANGER	TANGIEST
RESIANTS	ROADSMEN	SANITIZE	SERAFINS	SMEARING	STANNITE	STRANGLE	TANGLERS
RESIDENT	ROADSTER	SANSERIF	SERAGLIO	SNAGGIER	STARAGEN	STRATOSE	TANGLIER
RESIDUAL	ROAMINGS	SAPONITE	SERAPHIN	SNAILERY	STARINGS	STRAUNGE	TAPELINE
RESIGNED	ROARIEST	SARCENET	SERENADE	SNAILIER	STARKING	STRAWIER	TAPERERS
RESIGNER	ROARINGS	SARCONET	SERENATA	SNAPPIER	STARLIKE	STRAWING	TAPERING
RESINATA	ROASTERS	SARDINES	SERENATE	SNARIEST	STARLING	STRAYING	TARDIEST
RESINATE	ROASTING	SARDONIC	SERENING	SNARLIER	STARNIES	STREAKED	TARRIERS
RESINOID	ROESTONE	SARKIEST	SERENITY	SNEAKIER	STARNING	STREAKER	TARRIEST
RESINOUS	ROGATION	SARMENTA	SERGEANT	SNEERING	STARRIER	STREAMED	TARRINGS
RESISTED	ROILIEST	SARSENET	SERIATED	SNIFTIER	STARRING	STREAMER	TARSIERS
RESISTOR	ROISTERS		SERIATES	SNIRTLED	STARTING	STREIGNE	TARSIOID

TARSIPED	TERRANES	TIRESOME	TRANSIRE	TRIOLETS	UNDREAMT	URODELAN	VIRGATES
TARTANES	TERRAPIN	TITANATE	TRANSUDE	TRIPEDAL	UNEARTHS	UTILISER	VIRTUOSE
TARTIEST	TERRASES	TITANESS	TRANSUME	TRIPHONE	UNEASIER	UTRICLES	VITRAGES
TARTINES	TERRINES	TITRATED	TRANTERS	TRIPLANE	UNFAIRED	VAIRIEST	VITREOUS
TARTNESS	TERSIONS	TITRATES	TRAPESED	TRIPLIES	UNGEARED	VALETING	VITRINES
TARWEEDS	TERTIALS	TOASTERS	TRAPLIKE	TRIPOSES	UNHAIRED	VALIDEST	VOITURES
TASERING	TERTIANS	TOENAILS	TRASHIER	TRIPTANE	UNHEARTS	VALORISE	VOLARIES
TASTEVIN	TESSERAL	TOKENISM	TRASHING	TRISKELE	UNITARDS	VANITIES	VOLERIES
TAUNTERS	TESTATOR	TOLERANT	TRAVELED	TRISOMES	UNITISED	VARIATED	VOLITATE
TAURINES	TETANICS	TOLERATE	TRAVERSE	TRITIDES	UNIVERSE	VARIATES	VOTARIES
TAVERING	TETANIES	TOLEWARE	TRAVISES	TRITONES	UNLISTED	VARIOLES	WAISTERS
TAVERNAS	TETANISE	TONALITE	TREACLED	TRIZONAL	UNLOADER	VAULTERS	WAITRESS
TAVERNER	TETANOID	TONGSTER	TREACLES	TRIZONES	UNPAIRED	VAUNTERS	WARBIEST
TAWDRIES	TETRACID	TONSURED	TREADERS	TROATING	UNPRAISE	VAUNTIER	WARIMENT
TAWERIES	TETRADIC	TONSURES	TREADING	TROELIES	UNPRIEST	VAURIENS	WARINESS
TAWNIEST	TETRAGON	TONTINER	TREADLED	TROLLIES	UNRAISED	VEALIEST	WARTIEST
TEAGLING	TETRAXON	TONTINES	TREADLER	TROOLIES	UNREPAID	VEERINGS	WARTIMES
TEAMINGS	TETRONAL	TOPLINER	TREADLES	TROPHIES	UNRIPEST	VEINLETS	WASTERED
TEARIEST	THEORICS	TOPLINES	TREAGUES	TROTLINE	UNRIVETS	VELARISE	WASTRIES
TEARLESS	THEORIES	TORMENTA	TREASONS	TROUNCED	UNROOTED	VELARISE	WASTRIFE
TEASELER	THEORISE	TORMINAL	TREASURE	TROUNCES	UNROTTED	VENATION	WATERERS
TEASINGS	THEORIST	TORNADES	TREATERS	TRUANTED	UNSAILED	VENATORS	WATERING
TEAZLING	THERIACS	TORNADIC	TREATIES	TRUDGEON	UNSIFTED	VENERATE	WATERISH
TEENAGER	THERIANS	TORSADES	TREATING	TSAREVNA	UNSOILED	VENTAILE	WEARIEST
TEENIEST	THESAURI	TORTOISE	TREATISE	TSIGANES	UNSORTED	VENTAILS	WEARINGS
TEENSIER	THESPIAN	TOTALISE	TREENAIL	TURBANED	UNSUITED	VENTIGES	WEIRDEST
TEENTIER	THIRTEEN	TOTALIZE	TREFOILS	TURBINED	UNTAILED	VENTRALS	WIDENERS
TELLARED	THORACES	TOTIENTS	TREILLES	TURBINES	UNTARRED	VENTROUS	WINDORES
TENAILLE	THORITES	TOURNEYS	TRENAILS	TURNIPED	UNTENDER	VENTURED	WINDROSE
TENDRILS	THORNIER	TOUSTIER	TRENDIER	TURNSOLE	UNTHREAD	VENTURIS	WINTERED
TENDRONS	THREADEN	TOWERING	TRENDIES	TUTELARS	UNTIDIER	VERATRIN	WIRETAPS
TENEBRIO	THREATEN	TOWLINES	TRENISES	TUTORISE	UNTIDIES	VERDITES	WISTERIA
TENONERS	THRENODE	TOWNIEST	TRENTALS	TWANGIER	UNTRACED	VERONALS	WORDIEST
TENORIST	THROEING	TOWNLIER	TREPANGS	TWEERING	UNTRACES	VERTICAL	WORMIEST
TENORITE	TIDELAND	TRACINGS	TRESSING	TWENTIES	UNTRADED	VERTIGOS	WORSENED
TENSIBLE	TIDESMAN	TRACTILE	TRIALLED	TWINTERS	UNTREADS	VESICANT	WORTHIES
TENTIEST	TIDESMEN	TRACTION	TRIANGLE	TYRAMINE	UNVARIED	VESTIARY	WRASTING
TENTIGOS	TIERCELS	TRADINGS	TRIAXONS	TYROSINE	UNWATERS	VESTURAL	WRESTING
TENTORIA	TILERIES	TRAGULES	TRIBADES	UNARISEN	UNWRITES	VETERANS	WRONGEST
TENTWISE	TIMONEER	TRAHISON	TRIBUNES	UNBRASTE	UPRAISED	VIATORES	XERANSIS
TENURIAL	TINGLERS	TRAILERS	TRICORNE	UNCARTED	URALITES	VIBRATES	XERANTIC
TEOSINTE	TINKERED	TRAINEES	TRIDARNS	UNCRATED	URANIDES	VINEGARS	YEARDING
TERATISM	TINKLERS	TRAINERS	TRIDENTS	UNCRATES	URANITES	VINTAGED	YEARLIES
TERATOID	TINPLATE	TRAIPSED	TRIGNESS	UNDERACT	URBANEST	VINTAGER	YEARLING
TEREBRAS	TINSELED	TRAIPSES	TRIGONAL	UNDERBIT	URBANISE	VINTAGES	YEASTIER
TERMINAL	TINSELRY	TRAMLINE	TRILBIES	UNDERLET	URBANITE	VINTRIES	YEASTING
TERMINUS	TINSTONE	TRANECTS	TRILLOES	UNDERSEA	UREDINES	VIOLATED	YERSINIA
TERMLIES	TINWARES	TRANGLES	TRILOBES	UNDERSET	UREDINIA	VIOLATER	ZELATORS
TERNIONS	TIRASSES	TRANNIES	TRINDLES	UNDERTOW	URETHANS	VIOLATES	ZORGITES
TERRACES	TIREDEST	TRANSECT	TRINGLES	UNDERWIT	URINATED	VIOLENTS	
TERRAINS	TIRELESS	TRANSEPT	TRINKETS	UNDESERT	URINATES	VIRANDOS	
						VIRETOTS	

Additional High Probability Words

There are many 7- and 8-letter words that use likely combinations of letters but which don't appear in the 6-plus-1 and 7-plus-1 bonus sets. These are listed under the headings shown below, along with their criteria for inclusion.

Additional words – 1- and 2-point tiles

This section contains two alphabetical listings, one of 7-letter words and one of 8-letter words. Criteria for inclusion are that the words:

☆ are not included in the 6-plus-1 and 7-plus-1 bonus sets

☆ contain only the 1- and 2-point tiles ADEGILNORSTU

☆ contain no duplicates, except for A (up to 2 allowed), E (up to 3), I (up to 2) and O (up to 2). Note that multiple duplicate letters are allowed, as in DEITIES (2 E's and 2 I's) and GAINSAID (2 A's and 2 I's).

Additional words – 3- and 4-point tiles

This section contains two alphabetical listings, one of 7-letter words and one of 8-letter words. Criteria for inclusion are that the words:

☆ are not included in the 6-plus-1 and 7-plus-1 bonus sets

☆ contain any one of the 3- and 4-point tiles BCFHMPVWY. For ease of learning, the words containing any one of the tiles BCFHMPVWY have been grouped according to the tile contained – that is, all the B words are grouped together, then the C words, and so on

☆ otherwise contain only the 1- and 2-point tiles ADEGILNORSTU

☆ contain no duplicates, except for A (up to 2 allowed), E (up to 3), I (up to 2), O (up to 2). Note that multiple duplicate letters are allowed, as in ABIGAIL (2 A's and 2 I's) and ABNEGATE (2 A's and 2 E's).

ADDITIONAL BONUS WORDS (1 and 2 point tiles only)

7-letter words (1 and 2 point tiles only)

ADAGIOS	DAUTING	DUOTONE	GENTOOS	GUESTED	LIGROIN	OUTGOES	SAUROID	TEGULAR
ADULATE	DEERLET	DURANTS	GEOIDAL	GUESTEN	LISTING	OUTGONE	SAUTOIR	TELEDUS
AENEOUS	DEGREES	DURGANS	GESTURE	GUIDONS	LOADING	OUTLAID	SEALINE	TENIOID
AEOLIAN	DEITIES	DURIONS	GIAOURS	GUILDER	LOGANIA	OUTLAIN	SETUALE	TENURED
AERATED	DELAINE	DUSTING	GIRASOL	GUINEAS	LOGOUTS	OUTLAND	SIALOID	TIARAED
AGENDAS	DELETES	EATAGES	GIROSOL	GUISARD	LOIDING	OUTLIED	SIDLING	TIDINGS
AGENTED	DELOUSE	EDENTAL	GIUSTED	GUITARS	LONGEST	OUTLINE	SILOING	TIGROID
AGISTOR	DELUGES	EDGIEST	GLADIUS	GULDENS	LOONIER	OUTRAGE	SILTING	TILINGS
AGNOSIA	DENGUES	EDITING	GLEETED	GUSTIER	LOOSING	OUTRIDE	SILURID	TINDALS
AGOUTAS	DENTURE	EDITION	GLENTED	GUTSIER	LORIOTS	OUTRODE	SINGULT	TOLUENE
AGOUTIS	DETENUE	EGESTED	GLIADIN	IDOLISE	LOTIONS	OUTSAIL	SIRLOIN	TONGUED
AGROUND	DETERGE	EGOTISE	GLOATED	IDOLIST	LOUNGED	OUTSOAR	SLADANG	TORDION
AGUISED	DETINUE	EIDOLON	GLOATER	IGNITED	LOUNGER	OUTSOLD	SLEDGER	TORNADE
AIERIES	DIALING	ELEGIES	GLORIAS	IGUANAS	LOUNGES	RADIALS	SLEETED	TORNADO
AILANTO	DIALIST	ELEGISE	GLORIED	IGUANID	LOURING	RADIANT	SLIDING	TOROIDS
AILERON	DIALOGS	ELOINED	GLOUTED	INDIGOS	LOUSING	RADIATE	SOILING	TORULAE
AIRLINE	DIARIAL	ELOINER	GLUTAEI	INDOORS	LUNATED	RADULAE	SOLARIA	TORULIN
ALERION	DIARIAN	ELUATES	GOATEED	INDULTS	LURDANS	RAGLANS	SOLATIA	TRAGULE
ALERTED	DIARIST	ELUDERS	GOATEES	INDUSIA	LUSTING	RAGOUTS	SOLITON	TREADLE
ALEURON	DIETINE	ELUTION	GOATIER	INSULAE	LUTINGS	RAGULED	SOLOING	TREAGUE
ALGESIA	DIETING	ENGORED	GODETIA	INSULAR	NARDOOS	RANULAS	SONDAGE	TRIDUAN
ALIENED	DIGITAL	ENTERED	GODLIER	INTRADA	NATURAE	RAOULIA	SOOGEED	TRISULA
ALIENEE	DIGLOTS	ERELONG	GOETIES	INTROLD	NATURAL	REDEALT	SOOGIED	TROGONS
ALIENOR	DIGONAL	ERODENT	GOITRED	INULASE	NAUTILI	REDLEGS	SOOLING	TRUDGEN
ALIUNDE	DILATOR	ERUDITE	GOLDARN	IODURET	NEEDLER	REGALED	SORDINI	TRUNDLE
ALOGIAS	DILUENT	ETAERIO	GOLDEST	ISODONT	NEGATED	REGALIA	SORDINO	TUNDRAS
ALONGST	DILUTEE	ETAGERE	GOLDIER	LAETARE	NODULAR	REGULAE	SOULDAN	TURDION
ALSOONE	DILUTOR	ETALAGE	GOLIARD	LAGOONS	NOUGATS	REGULOS	STADIAL	ULNARIA
ALTERED	DIORITE	ETIOLIN	GONADAL	LAIDING	NOURSLE	RELATED	STEELED	ULTIONS
ANALOGS	DIRLING	ETOURDI	GONDOLA	LAIRAGE	OARAGES	RENAGUE	STILING	UNALIST
ANEARED	DISROOT	EUGENIA	GONIDIA	LANDAUS	ODORANT	RENEGED	STOOGED	UNDEALT
ANGORAS	DISTAIN	EUGENOL	GOODIER	LANGUID	ODORATE	RENEGUE	STOOLED	UNEDGES
ANGULAR	DIURNAL	EULOGIA	GOODIES	LANGUOR	OILNUTS	RETUNED	STRIGIL	UNGILDS
ANURIAS	DOATING	GADROON	GOOIEST	LANGURS	OLEARIA	RIDGILS	SUDARIA	UNGIRDS
AREOLAE	DOGATES	GALEATE	GOONDAS	LANIARD	OLIGIST	RIDINGS	SUDORAL	UNIDEAL
ARGALIS	DOGEATE	GALIOTS	GOOSIER	LANUGOS	ONDATRA	RIGLINS	SUIDIAN	UNITARD
ARGANDS	DOILIES	GALOOTS	GOURDES	LARDONS	ONEROUS	RIOTOUS	SUITING	UNLOADS
AROUSAL	DOLINAS	GANOIDS	GOUTIER	LARDOON	OODLINS	RITUALS	SULTANA	UNLOOSE
ASTOUND	DOLOURS	GARDANT	GRADATE	LARIATS	OORIALS	ROILING	SUNDIAL	UNLORDS
ASTRAND	DOOLIES	GARIALS	GRADUAL	LATENED	ORATION	RONEOED	SURLOIN	UNOILED
ASTROID	DOTAGES	GARLAND	GRANOLA	LATRIAS	ORDINAL	ROOTAGE	TAENIAE	UNREELS
AUDIENT	DOUANES	GARUDAS	GREENED	LAUDING	OREGANO	ROSALIA	TAGUANS	UNROOST
AUDITOR	DOULEIA	GATEAUS	GREENIE	LEAGUED	ORGIAST	ROTULAS	TAIGLED	UNROOTS
AUGITES	DOUSING	GAUDIER	GREETED	LEAGUER	OROTUND	ROTUNDA	TAILARD	UNSOLID
AULNAGE	DOUTING	GAUDIES	GREETES	LEAGUES	ORTOLAN	ROTUNDS	TAILORS	UNSTAID
AURATED	DRAGONS	GAULTER	GRIESIE	LEDGERS	OTALGIA	ROULADE	TALIONS	UNTILED
AURATES	DRAGOON	GAUNTED	GROUNDS	LEDGIER	OUGLIED	RULINGS	TALONED	URINALS
AUREATE	DRAUNTS	GEALOUS	GROUSED	LEGATEE	OULONGS	RUNDLET	TANDOOR	URODELE
AURELIA	DROGUES	GELADAS	GROUTED	LEGATOR	OURALIS	RUSTING	TANGOED	
AUREOLA	DROGUET	GELDERS	GRUNTED	LEIDGER	OUTAGES	SAGOUIN	TARANDS	
AUREOLE	DRONGOS	GELIDER	GRUNTLE	LENTOID	OUTDARE	SAGUARO	TAUREAN	
AUSTRAL	DUALINS	GENTEEL	GUARANI	LIAISON	OUTDONE	SALIGOT	TEAGLED	
DALTONS	DUALIST	GENTLED	GUARDEE	LIANOID	OUTEDGE	SAOUARI	TEENAGE	
DATURAS		GENTLER	GUERITE	LIGATED	OUTGOER	SAURIAN	TEGULAE	

8-letter words (1 and 2 point tiles only)

ADRENALS	AUDITION	DIAGONAL	DOORNAIL	ENGAOLED	GARDANTS	GLORIOUS	GREENLET
ADULATES	AULNAGER	DIALOGUE	DORISING	ENGIRDLE	GARLANDS	GODLIEST	GRIDELIN
ADULATOR	AULNAGES	DIGITALS	DRAGOONS	ENGOULED	GASOLENE	GOITROUS	GRUNTLED
ADUSTING	AUREOLED	DILATING	DRAILING	ENGUARDS	GASTRULA	GOLDENER	GRUNTLES
AERONAUT	AUTOGIRO	DILATION	DROGUETS	ENSEALED	GAUDIEST	GOLDIEST	GUARANIS
AEROTONE	DANEGELT	DILIGENT	DROILING	ENSOULED	GELIDEST	GOLIARDS	GUARDANT
AGOUTIES	DANGLERS	DILUTEES	DRONGOES	ENTOILED	GENERALE	GONADIAL	GUARDEES
AGRESTAL	DARLINGS	DILUTORS	EASTLAND	ETALAGES	GENEROUS	GONDOLAS	GUARDIAN
ALEURONE	DARTLING	DINGIEST	EGLATERE	EUGENIAS	GESTURED	GONIDIAL	GUDESIRE
ALIASING	DEERLETS	DISINURE	EGOITIES	EUGENOLS	GIRLONDS	GOODIEST	GUERDONS
ALIENAGE	DEGREASE	DISLOIGN	EGOTISED	EULOGIES	GIRTLINE	GOODLIER	GUERIDON
ALNAGERS	DELEGATE	DISTRAIL	EILDINGS	EULOGISE	GLADIATE	GOODSIRE	GUERITES
ANALOGUE	DELETING	DIURNALS	ELEGISED	EULOGIST	GLAIRINS	GRADATES	GUILDERS
ANGULATE	DELETION	DOATINGS	ELOIGNED	GADROONS	GLANDERS	GRADUALS	GUILTIER
ARAISING	DESIRING	DOGEATES	ELONGATE	GAIETIES	GLEETIER	GRANOLAS	IDOLATOR
ARANEOUS	DESOLATE	DONATORS	ENDOSTEA	GAINSAID	GLIADINE	GRANULES	IGUANIDS
ARGONAUT	DETENUES			GALEATED	GLIADINS	GRANULES	INDIGEST
AUDITING	DETERGES			GALENOID	GLORIOSA	GREENEST	INDIGOES

INDULGER	LIGNEOUS	NAUSEATE	OUTLEARN	RETOOLED	SALUTING	TAILARDS	TURDIONS
INDULGES	LIGNITES	NEEDLERS	OUTLINED	RIGADOON	SEEDLING	TAILINGS	ULSTERED
INDUSIAL	LIGROINS	NEEDLIER	RADIOING	RINGSIDE	SEGOLATE	TANDOORS	UNDERLIE
INOSITOL	LINGERED	NIDOROUS	RADULATE	RINGTAIL	SELADANG	TANGELOS	UNELATED
INTARSIA	LINGERIE	NODULOSE	RAILINGS	RIOTINGS	SELENATE	TEASELED	UNLEASED
INTRIGUE	LINGIEST	NOURSLED	RAOULIAS	RISOLUTO	SELENIDE	TEENAGED	UNLOOSED
ISOGONAL	LINGUIST	ODORANTS	REEDLING	ROISTING	SIDELINE	TINGLIER	UNREELED
ISOLOGUE	LOADINGS	OLIGURIA	REGELATE	ROOSTING	SIDELING	TIRELING	UNSALTED
LAAGERED	LOADSTAR	ONDATRAS	REGULATE	ROOTINGS	SIGNIEUR	TOILINGS	UNSEALED
LANGUETS	LOGANIAS	OOGENIES	REGULINE	ROOTLING	SILUROID	TOLUENES	UNSEATED
LANGUORS	LOOSENED	ORAGIOUS	REGULISE	ROSITING	SINGULAR	TOOLINGS	UNSEELED
LANIARDS	LOOSENER	ORDALIAN	RELEASED	ROTUNDAS	SLUDGIER	TORDIONS	UNSOLDER
LARDOONS	LOOTINGS	OREGANOS	RELEGATE	ROUNDELS	SOLIDAGO	TORNADOS	URIDINES
LAUNDERS	LORDINGS	ORIGINAL	RELENTED	ROUNDLES	SOLITUDE	TOROIDAL	URODELES
LAUREATE	LOUNDERS	ORTOLANS	RENEGUED	ROUSTING	SOLUTION	TORULINS	UROSTEGE
LEAGUERS	LOUNGERS	OSTEOGEN	RENEGUES	ROUTINGS	STEGODON	TORULOSE	UTILISED
LEDGIEST	LOURINGS	OTALGIAS	RESEALED	RUNAGATE	STOOLING	TOURINGS	
LEGATEES	LUNARIST	OUTDOING	RESENTED	RUNDALES	STREELED	TOUSLING	
LEGIONED	LURDANES	OUTEDGES	RESIDING	RUNDLETS	STRIDING	TRAILING	
LEIDGERS	LUSTERED	OUTGLARE	RESILING	RUSTLING	STURNOID	TROULING	
LEISURED	LUSTRING	OUTGOERS	RESULTED	SALADING	SUDATING	TRUDGENS	
LIGATURE	NATURALS	OUTLANDS	RETILING	SALTANDO	SUDATION	TRUNDLES	

ADDITIONAL BONUS WORDS (with one 3 or 4 point tile)

7-letter words with one B and six 1-2 point tiles

ABALONE	BAILING	BEETLED	BLUDGER	BOTARGO	BURGLED	ENROBED	OBITUAL	SUBADAR
ABASING	BAILORS	BEETLES	BLUDGES	BOUDOIR	BURGLES	ENROBES	OBLIGED	SUBAREA
ABATING	BAINITE	BEGILDS	BLUDIER	BOUGETS	BURGOOS	GABIONS	OBLIGEE	SUBARID
ABATORS	BAITING	BEGONIA	BLUEING	BOUGIES	BURIALS	GARBLED	OBLIGOR	SUBDEAN
ABATURE	BALADIN	BEGORED	BLUINGS	BOULDER	BURITIS	GARBOIL	OBLONGS	SUBEDAR
ABIDING	BALDING	BEGUILE	BLUNDER	BOULTED	BURLING	GILBERT	OBTAINS	SUBEDIT
ABIGAIL	BALEENS	BEGUINE	BLUNGED	BOULTER	BURTONS	GLEBOUS	OBTRUDE	SUBERIN
ABLATED	BALISTA	BEGUINS	BLUNGER	BOURDON	BUSGIRL	GLOBATE	OBTUNDS	SUBGOAL
ABLATES	BANALER	BEIGELS	BLUNGES	BOURNES	BUSTARD	GLOBINS	ONBOARD	SUBLATE
ABLATOR	BANDAGE	BEIGNET	BLUNTED	BOUSIER	BUSTING	GLOBOID	ORBITAL	SUBRING
ABLAUTS	BANDARS	BELATED	BLUNTER	BOUSING	BUSTLED	GLOBOSE	ORBITAS	SUBTEEN
ABODING	BANDEAU	BELATES	BLURTED	BOUTADE	BUTANES	GLOBOUS	ORBITED	SUEABLE
ABORTED	BANDITS	BELAUDS	BOASTED	BOUTONS	BUTANOL	GOBIIDS	OUABAIN	SUNBEAT
ABORTEE	BANDOGS	BELGARD	BOATIES	BRIDALS	BUTENES	GOBIOID	OUREBIS	SUNBIRD
ABOULIA	BANDORE	BELONGS	BOATING	BRIDING	DAGOBAS	GOBLETS	OUTBARS	TABANID
ABOUNDS	BANDROL	BELUGAS	BODEGAS	BRIDOON	DATABLE	GOBLINS	OUTBIDS	TABARDS
ABRADES	BANDURA	BENDLET	BODGERS	BRIGUED	DATABUS	GOOBERS	OUTBRAG	TABLEAU
ABRAIDS	BAREGES	BERATED	BODGIER	BRIGUES	DAUBERS	GUNBOAT	OUTBRED	TABLOID
ABREGES	BARGAIN	BERLINE	BODGIES	BRINDLE	DAUBING	IGNOBLE	RAGBOLT	TABOOED
ABROADS	BARGEES	BESIEGE	BODINGS	BROADEN	DEBATER	INBOARD	RAILBUS	TABORED
ABSTAIN	BARONET	BETAINE	BODRAGS	BROGANS	DEBITOR	INBURST	RATBAGS	TABORIN
ABULIAS	BARONGS	BETIDES	BOGLAND	BROGUES	DEBTEES	INDABAS	REBADGE	TABOURS
ABUSAGE	BASIDIA	BETREAD	BOILING	BROILED	DIABASE	INGLOBE	REBATED	TABUING
ABUSING	BASILAR	BIASING	BOINGED	BROLGAS	DIABOLO	INORBED	REBOANT	TABULAE
ABUSION	BASTARD	BIDINGS	BOLDEST	BRUITED	DINGBAT	LABIATE	REBUILD	TABULAR
AIBLINS	BASTION	BIGENER	BOLEROS	BRUNTED	DISTURB	LABORED	REBUILT	TENABLE
AIRBASE	BATONED	BIGOTED	BOLIDES	BRUTING	DOGBANE	LABOURS	REDOUBT	TOOLBAG
ALBEDOS	BATOONS	BILGIER	BONDAGE	BUDGERO	DOGBOLT	LABRIDS	RIBALDS	TOOLBAR
ALBERGO	BAUERAS	BILIANS	BONDERS	BUDGERS	DOUBLER	LABROID	RIBAUDS	TREBLED
ALBINOS	BAUSOND	BILIOUS	BONESET	BUDGETS	DOUBLES	LIBATED	ROBALOS	TROUBLE
ALBUGOS	BEADING	BINGIES	BONITOS	BUDGIES	DOUBLET	LIBIDOS	ROBINIA	TUBAGES
ALGEBRA	BEADLES	BIODATA	BONSOIR	BUGLERS	DOUBTER	LOBINGS	ROBUSTA	TUBINGS
ANTBEAR	BEAGLED	BIOTINS	BOODIES	BUGLETS	DURABLE	LOOBIER	ROSEBUD	TULBANS
ANTBIRD	BEAGLER	BIRDING	BOODLES	BUILDER	DUSTBIN	LOOBIES	ROUBLES	TUNABLE
ARABINS	BEAGLES	BIRLING	BOOGIED	BUISTED	EARLOBE	NEBULAE	RUBATOS	TURBAND
ARABISE	BEANIES	BITINGS	BOOGIES	BULGERS	EATABLE	NEBULAR	RUBEOLA	TURBANS
ARBLAST	BEASTIE	BITONAL	BOOSING	BULGIER	EBONIES	NEBULAS	RUBINES	TURBOND
ASTABLE	BEATING	BLAGUES	BOOSTED	BULGINE	EBONISE	NEBULES	RUGBIES	UNBARES
ATABEGS	BEDERAL	BLEARED	BOOTEES	BUNDLES	EBONITE	NIOBATE	SABATON	UNBATED
ATABRIN	BEDOUIN	BLEATED	BOOTIES	BUNGEES	EBRIATE	NIOBITE	SALBAND	UNBEARS
AUBADES	BEDSORE	BLEEDER	BOOTING	BUNGIES	EBRIOSE	NIOBOUS	SANDBAG	UNBEGET
AUBERGE	BEDUINS	BLENDER	BOOTLEG	BUNGLED	EDIBLES	NOBLEST	SEEABLE	UNBEGOT
AUDIBLE	BEDUNGS	BLINDER	BOREENS	BUNGLER	ENABLED	NOSEBAG	SIBLING	UNBOLTS
BAAINGS	BEELINE	BLOATED	BORNITE	BUNGLES	ENABLER	NOTABLE	SOBERED	UNBOOTS
BADIOUS	BEERAGE	BLONDER	BORONIA	BUNTALS	ENABLES	OBDURES	SOROBAN	UNROBES
BAGNIOS	BEETING	BLOUSED	BORSTAL	BURGEES	ENGLOBE	OBELION	STIBIAL	
BAGUIOS		BLOUSON		BURGEON	ENGOBES	OBELISE	STIBINE	

7-letter words with one C and six 1-2 point tiles

ACARIDS	CANTLED	CLEANER	COOLEST	CRUSTAL	EDUCATE	INCUSED	ORACLED	SEDUCER
ACAROID	CANULAE	CLEANSE	COOLIES	CTENOID	EDUCING	INDICES	ORCINOL	SELENIC
ACATOUR	CANULAS	CLEARED	COOLING	CUDGELS	EDUCTOR	INDICTS	ORGANIC	SILENCE
ACEDIAS	CARDOON	CLEATED	COONTIE	CUISINE	EGENCES	INDUCES	OSCULAR	SILICON
ACERATE	CARGOED	CLOISON	COOTIES	CUNDIES	EIDETIC	INDUCTS	OSTRACA	SINICAL
ACETONE	CARINAS	CLOSING	CORANTO	CUNEATE	EIRENIC	INLACED	OUTRACE	SLICING
ACIDIER	CARIOUS	CLOSURE	CORDAGE	CURATED	ELANCED	INOCULA	RACOONS	SLUICED
ACINOUS	CARLOAD	CLOTURE	CORDATE	CURDING	ELANCES	IRACUND	RADICAL	SOLACED
ACONITE	CARLOTS	CLOURED	CORDIAL	CURDLES	ELECTED	ISODICA	REACTED	SOLICIT
ACORNED	CARNAGE	CLOUTED	CORDITE	CURIOSA	ELECTOR	ITALICS	RECEDES	SORITIC
ACREAGE	CARNALS	CLOUTER	CORDONS	CURLING	ELECTRO	LACINIA	RECENSE	SOUCING
ACRIDIN	CAROLUS	CLUDGIE	CORIOUS	CURSING	ELEGIAC	LACTONE	RECITED	SOURCED
ACROGEN	CAROTID	CLUEING	CORNAGE	CURTAIL	ELOCUTE	LACUNAE	RECLINE	STOICAL
ACTINAL	CAROTIN	COAGULA	CORNEAL	CURTAIN	ENACTED	LACUNAR	RECLOSE	SUCTION
ACTINIA	CARTAGE	COAITAS	CORNUAL	CURTALS	ENCAGED	LAICISE	RECLUSE	SUICIDE
ACTIONS	CARTOON	COALING	CORNUTE	CURTANA	ENCAGES	LATENCE	RECODES	SURCOAT
AECIDIA	CASTRAL	COALISE	CORNUTO	CUSTARD	ENCASED	LAUNCED	RECOUNT	TALCOUS
AGARICS	CATALOG	COALTAR	CORONAE	CUTLINE	ENCLOSE	LAUNCES	RECTION	TEDESCO
AGNATIC	CATALOS	COASTAL	CORONAL	DACOITS	ENCLOUD	LECTERN	RECUILE	TIERCED
AIDANCE	CATELOG	COATING	CORONAS	DEACONS	ENCODES	LECTION	RECULED	TIERCEL
ALCAIDE	CATENAE	CODEINE	CORONET	DECAGON	ENCORED	LECTURE	RECULES	TINCALS
ALGINIC	CATERED	CODGERS	CORONIS	DECANAL	ENERGIC	LECTURN	RECUSED	TOUCANS
ALICANT	CATIONS	CODINGS	CORTEGE	DECANES	ENGRACE	LEUCINE	REDCOAT	TOURACO
ALOETIC	CAUDATE	CODLING	CORTILI	DECEASE	ENLACED	LEUCINS	REDUCES	TRADUCE
ANCILIA	CAUDLES	CODLINS	COSTARD	DECEITS	ENLACES	LEUCITE	REGENCE	TREACLE
ANELACE	CAUDRON	COENURI	COTERIE	DECIARE	ENRACED	LICENSE	RESCUED	TRIACID
ANGICOS	CAULDER	COGENER	COTIDAL	DECLARE	ENTICED	LICTORS	RETICLE	TRIADIC
ANICUTS	CAULINE	COGNATE	COTINGA	DECLINE	ERECTED	LINCTUS	RUCOLAS	TROUNCE
ANLACES	CAUSING	COIGNED	COTLAND	DECOLOR	ERGODIC	LINOCUT	RUCTION	TRUCAGE
ANOETIC	CAUTION	COILING	COUGARS	DECREES	ERICOID	LOCATED	SACATON	TRUCIAL
ANTACID	CEDRATE	COINAGE	COULEES	DECREET	EROTICA	LOCUSTA	SALICIN	TRUNCAL
ARCTANS	CEDULAS	COITION	COULOIR	DECURIA	ERUCTED	LUCARNE	SARCOID	TUNICLE
ARCTIID	CEILING	COLDEST	COULTER	DEISTIC	ESCUAGE	LUCERNE	SARONIC	TURACIN
ARCTOID	CELADON	COLITIS	COUNSEL	DELICES	EUCAINE	LUCERNS	SATANIC	TURACOS
ARCUATE	CELESTE	COLOGNE	COUNTED	DELICTS	EUCLASE	LUCIDER	SAUCIER	ULCERED
ARNICAS	CENSUAL	COLONES	COUNTER	DELTAIC	EUCRITE	LUCIGEN	SAUCING	ULICONS
ASCARID	CENSURE	COLORED	COURAGE	DEONTIC	EUGENIC	LUNATIC	SCAGLIA	UNACTED
ASCAUNT	CENTAGE	COLOURS	COURANT	DESCALE	GARCONS	NACROUS	SCALADE	UNCAGED
ASCIDIA	CENTRED	COLUGOS	COURING	DIALECT	GARLICS	NAUTICS	SCALADO	UNCAGES
ASINICO	CERATED	COLURES	COURLAN	DICIEST	GAUCIER	NEGLECT	SCALENE	UNCARTS
ASOCIAL	CEREOUS	CONARIA	COURSED	DICINGS	GENERIC	NOCTUAS	SCANDAL	UNCASED
ATOCIAS	CESTODE	CONATUS	COURTED	DICTIER	GENETIC	NOCTUID	SCEDULE	UNCIALS
AUCTION	CESURAE	CONDOLE	COUTILS	DICTING	GIRONIC	NOCTULE	SCIARID	UNCITED
AUGITIC	CESURAL	CONDORS	CRANAGE	DICTION	GLACEED	NODICAL	SCIOLTO	UNCLEAR
AUTOCAR	CIDARIS	CONDUIT	CRANIAL	DIOCESE	GLUCINA	NOTICED	SCOLION	UNCLOGS
CADGIER	CIELING	CONGAED	CREATED	DISCAGE	GLUCOSE	NOURICE	SCOOGED	UNCLOSE
CADRANS	CIERGES	CONGEAL	CREDENT	DISCANT	GONADIC	NUCLEAR	SCOOTED	UNCOILS
CAERULE	CILIATE	CONGEED	CREEDAL	DISCING	GONIDIC	NUCLIDE	SCOUGED	UNCOLTS
CAESURA	CINEOLE	CONGEES	CREEING	DOCILER	GREECES	OCARINA	SCOURED	UNCORDS
CAGIEST	CINGULA	CONGIUS	CREESED	DOCTORS	GRIECED	OCEANID	SCOURGE	UNLACED
CAGOULE	CIRSOID	CONGOUS	CRENELS	DOGCART	GRIECES	OCELOID	SCROOGE	UNLACES
CAGOULS	CITADEL	CONGREE	CREOLES	DOUCINE	GUANACO	OCELOTS	SCROTAL	UNSCALE
CALANDO	CITRINS	CONGRUE	CREOSOL	DRACONE	ICTERID	OCREATE	SCROUGE	URACILS
CALDERA	CITROUS	CONIDIA	CRINOID	DUCTILE	IDENTIC	OCTAGON	SCUDLER	URCEOLI
CALDRON	CLADIST	CONOIDS	CROODLE	DUCTING	ILIACUS	OCTROIS	SCUNGED	URGENCE
CALIGOS	CLANGOR	CONSOLE	CROONED	DULCIAN	INCAGED	OCTUORS	SCUTAGE	URICASE
CANARDS	CLARAIN	CONSORT	CROTALA	DULCITE	INCEDES	OCULARS	SECEDER	UTRICLE
CANDELA	CLARINI	CONSULT	CROTALS	DULCOSE	INCISED	OCULATE	SECLUDE	
CANDORS	CLARINO	CONTOUR	CROTONS	DULOTIC	INCISOR	OCULIST	SECONDE	
CANDOUR	CLARION	CONTROL	CROUTON	ECLOGUE	INCITED	ODONTIC	SECONDO	
CANGUES	CLARTED	COOINGS	CRUISIE	ECLOSED	INCLUDE	OILCANS	SECRETE	
CANTARS	CLAUTED	COOLANT	CRUSADO	ECURIES	INCRUST	ONEIRIC	SECULAR	
CANTDOG	CLEANED	COOLERS	CRUSIAN	EDICTAL	INCUDES	OOLITIC	SECURED	

7-letter words with one F and six 1-2 point tiles

AEFAULD	DEFILER	EARFULS	FADINGS	FANTAIL	FEATING	FEESING	FEUDING	FIGURES
AFEARED	DEFILES	EASEFUL	FAGOTED	FANTEEG	FEATOUS	FEIGNED	FEUDIST	FILARIA
AIRFOIL	DEFINES	EDIFIER	FAILING	FANTODS	FEATURE	FEINTED	FEUTRED	FILIATE
AIRLIFT	DEFLATE	EDIFIES	FAILURE	FARDAGE	FEDARIE	FELINES	FEUTRES	FILINGS
AREFIED	DEFOULS	EELFARE	FAINTED	FARINAS	FEDERAL	FELTIER	FIATING	FINALES
DAFTARS	DEIFIER	ENFILED	FAIRIES	FATIGUE	FEEDERS	FERLIED	FIDEIST	FINIALS
DAREFUL	DEIFIES	ENFREED	FAIRING	FAULTED	FEEDING	FERTILE	FIDGETS	FIORINS
DEAFENS	DERNFUL	ENFREES	FAITORS	FAUNIST	FEEDLOT	FERULAS	FIDGIER	FIREDOG
DEFAULT	DIREFUL	ENGULFS	FAITOUR	FAUTORS	FEELERS	FERULES	FIELDER	FIRINGS
DEFENSE	DOOFERS	FADAISE	FALDAGE	FEAGUED	FEELING	FESTOON	FIGURAL	FIRLOTS
DEFIANT	DRAFTEE	FADEURS	FANTADS	FEAGUES	FEERING	FETIDER	FIGURED	FISTING

FISTULA	FLORIST	FOOLING	FORLANA	FRIGATE	FUTILER	LEAFIER	REFUSED	TENFOLD
FITLIER	FLORUIT	FOOTAGE	FORLEND	FRIGOTS	GAINFUL	LIFTING	REFUTAL	TINFOIL
FLAGONS	FLOTAGE	FOOTERS	FORLENT	FROGLET	GAUFERS	LOAFING	REFUTED	TINFULS
FLANEUR	FLOURED	FOOTIER	FORLESE	FRONTAL	GAUFRES	NEEDFUL	REFUTES	TURFING
FLAUNES	FLOUSED	FOOTIES	FORSAID	FRONTED	GOLFERS	OFTENER	REIFIED	UNDEAFS
FLAUNTS	FLOUTED	FOOTING	FORSLOE	FRUITED	GOOFIER	OLEFINE	RIFLING	UNFAIRS
FLEDGES	FLUATES	FOOTLED	FORTUNE	FUGATOS	GRAFTED	ONEFOLD	ROLFING	UNFILDE
FLEEING	FLUTIER	FOOTLES	FOUDRIE	FULGENT	GRIFTED	ONESELF	ROOFING	UNFILED
FLEERED	FLUTINA	FOOTRAS	FOUGADE	FULGORS	GRUFTED	OURSELF	RUNFLAT	UNFOLDS
FLEETED	FLUTING	FORAGED	FOULARD	FUNDIES	GULFIER	RAFALES	SEAFOOD	UNFOOLS
FLEETER	FOALING	FORAGES	FOULDER	FUNERAL	GUNFIRE	RAGEFUL	SERFAGE	UNFREED
FLEURET	FOETORS	FORDOES	FOULING	FUNGOID	INDRAFT	REEFING	SIFTING	UNIFIED
FLEURON	FOILING	FORDONE	FOURGON	FURANES	INFAUST	REFLATE	SOLFEGE	UNIFIER
FLINDER	FOLDING	FOREGUT	FOUTERS	FURIOSO	INFIDEL	REFLOAT	SONGFUL	UNIFIES
FLITING	FOLIAGE	FOREIGN	FOUTRAS	FURLANA	INFIELD	REFOOTS	STIFLED	UNROOFS
FLOATED	FOLIATE	FORELEG	FOUTRED	FURLING	INFOLDS	REFUELS	SULFATE	UNSAFER
FLOATER	FOLIOED	FORELIE	FOUTRES	FURLONG	INFULAE	REFUGED	SULFIDE	
FLOORED	FOLIOSE	FORESEE	FRAGILE	FUROLES	INFUSED	REFUGEE	SULFONE	
FLOOSIE	FONDLER	FORGETS	FREEING	FUSAROL	INFUSER	REFUGES	SUNROOF	
FLOREAT	FONDUES	FORGOES	FRENULA	FUSTIAN	INGULFS	REFUGIA	SURFING	
FLORINS	FOODIES	FORGONE	FRESNEL	FUSTING	LEAFAGE	REFUSAL	TEARFUL	

7-letter words with one H and six 1-2 point tiles

AIRHEAD	EARTHED	HAIRDOS	HEISTED	HOLDOUT	LARGISH	ONSHORE	SHOOGLE	TOHUNGA
AIRHOLE	EARTHEN	HAIRING	HERNIAE	HOLINGS	LATHEES	ORTHIAN	SHOOING	TOUGHEN
ALIGHTS	ENHALOS	HALITUS	HERNIAL	HONORED	LAUGHED	OUTHIRE	SHOOLED	TOUGHER
ALRIGHT	ENOUGHS	HALOGEN	HEROINE	HONOURS	LAUGHER	OUTLASH	SHOTGUN	TOUGHIE
ALTHEAS	ENROUGH	HALOIDS	HEROISE	HOODIES	LEASHED	RAGHEAD	SHRINAL	TROUGHS
ALTHORN	ENTHUSE	HALOING	HEROONS	HOODING	LEGHORN	REHEELS	SHULING	TUGHRAS
ANGUISH	ETHANES	HANDOUT	HETAERA	HOOLIER	LENGTHS	REHOUSE	SIGHTED	TUSHING
ANOTHER	ETHANOL	HANGARS	HETAIRA	HOOTING	LETHEAN	RELIGHT	SITHING	UNDIGHT
ANTHOID	ETHENES	HANGOUT	HIDAGES	HORDEIN	LETHEES	RHODOUS	SLOTHED	UNEARTH
ARGHANS	GALUTHS	HARLOTS	HIDALGA	HORNITO	LETHIED	RIGHTED	SOOTHED	UNGIRTH
ARSHEEN	GASAHOL	HARTALS	HIDALGO	HORNLET	LEUGHEN	RIGHTOS	SOREHON	UNHAIRS
ATHANOR	GASOHOL	HAUDING	HIDEOUS	HOSTAGE	LIGHTED	ROGUISH	SOUGHED	UNHEADS
ATHEISE	GHARIAL	HAULAGE	HIDEOUT	HOTLINE	LIGHTER	ROINISH	SOUGHED	UNHEALS
ATHEOUS	GHASTED	HAULERS	HIDINGS	HOUDANS	LITHIAS	ROUGHED	TAHINAS	UNHEART
ATISHOO	GHERAOS	HAULIER	HIDLING	HOUSIER	LITHING	ROUGHEN	TAHINIS	UNHELED
AUTHORS	GHOSTED	HAULING	HIDLINS	HOUSING	LITHOID	ROUGHIE	TEUGHER	UNHELES
DAHLIAS	GIRLISH	HAUNTED	HILDING	HOUTING	LOATHED	ROUTHIE	THANAGE	UNHOARD
DARSHAN	GIRTHED	HAUNTER	HILTING	HUNGERS	LONGISH	RUNTISH	THANAGE	UNHOODS
DASHEEN	GNASHED	HAUSING	HIRAGES	HURDLES	LOUDISH	RUSHING	THEINES	UNHOODS
DASHING	GNATHAL	HEADAGE	HIREAGE	HURLIES	LOUTISH	SEETHED	THEROID	UNHORSE
DEHORNS	GOATISH	HEADIER	HIRINGS	HURLING	LUSHIER	SEETHER	THEROID	UNLEASH
DELIGHT	GOLDISH	HEADING	HIRLING	HURTING	LUSHING	SHADING	THONDER	UNRIGHT
DHARNAS	GOODISH	HEADRIG	HIRSLED	HURTLED	LUTHERN	SHAITAN	THONGED	UNSHALE
DHOOTIS	GOULASH	HEARTED	HIRUDIN	HUSTLED	LUTHIER	SHARIAT	THORIAS	UNSHOED
DISHIER	GRAITHS	HEARTEN	HISTING	INHALED	NAUGHTS	SHEALED	THORNED	UNSHOOT
DISHING	GREENTH	HEDERAL	HISTOID	INHALER	NEIGHED	SHEELED	THORONS	UNSIGHT
DISHORN	GUARISH	HEDGERS	HISTRIO	INHALES	NEOLITH	SHEENED	THRANGS	URETHAN
DOGHOLE	GUNSHOT	HEDGIER	HOARING	INHAULS	NORTHED	SHEERED	THRONED	UROLITH
DOLTISH	GUSHIER	HEEDING	HOARSEN	INHAUST	NOUGHTS	SHEETED	THRONGS	USHERED
DRAUGHT	HADRONS	HEELERS	HOASTED	INSIGHT	NOURISH	SHIELED	THULIAS	
DRONISH	HAGDENS	HEELING	HOGTIED	INSOOTH	NURAGHE	SHINDIG	THUNDER	
DROUGHT	HAGDONS	HEGIRAS	HOGTIES	INTHRAL	NURAGHI	SHITING	TIGRISH	
DROUTHS	HAILIER	HEINOUS	HOISING	LAIGHER	NURHAGS	SHOALED	TOEHOLD	
DUSHING	HAILING	HEIRING	HOLDING		OGREISH	SHOOGIE	TOHEROA	

7-letter words with one M and six 1-2 point tiles

ADENOMA	ALODIUM	AMOROUS	DELIMIT	DOMAINS	ELEMENT	EMULGES	GADSMAN	GOMERIL
ADMIRAL	ALUMINA	AMOUNTS	DEMAINE	DOMATIA	ELOGIUM	EMULING	GAMELAN	GOMUTIS
AEMULED	ALUMNAE	AMRITAS	DEMEANE	DOMINEE	EMAILED	EMULSIN	GAMETAL	GOMUTOS
AEMULES	AMADOUS	AMULETS	DEMENTI	DOMINIE	EMERALD	EMULSOR	GAMETES	GOODMAN
AGAMIDS	AMATEUR	AMUSING	DEMERGE	DOMINOS	EMERGED	EMUNGED	GATEMEN	GOODMEN
AGAMOID	AMATING	ANGIOMA	DEMERIT	DOOMIER	EMERGES	EMUNGES	GAUMIER	GORMAND
AGAMOUS	AMATION	ANIMALS	DEMERSE	DOOMING	EMERIED	EMURING	GENOMES	GOURAMI
AGNAMED	AMATOLS	ANIMIST	DEMESNE	DOORMAT	EMERITI	ENAMELS	GEOMANT	GOURMET
AGNAMES	AMELIAS	ANOSMIA	DEMOTES	DORMANT	EMERODS	ENAMOUR	GERMANE	GRANDAM
AIRMAIL	AMENAGE	ARTSMAN	DEMOUNT	DROMONS	EMERSED	ENARMED	GLAMORS	GRANDMA
AIRTIME	AMENDER	ATRIUMS	DEMURES	DROOMES	EMETINE	ENDGAME	GLAMOUR	GREMIAL
ALAMODE	AMILDAR	AUGMENT	DIAGRAM	DRUMLIN	EMEUTES	ENGLOOM	GLAUMED	GROOMED
ALAMORT	AMONGST	AUMAILS	DIATOMS	DUALISM	EMICATE	ENTAMED	GLEAMED	GRUMOSE
ALARMED	AMORANT	DAIMIOS	DIMETER	DUMAIST	EMONGES	EREMITE	GLEEMAN	GUDEMAN
ALARUMS	AMORINI	DAIMONS	DIORAMA	DURMAST	EMOTING	ERMELIN	GLEEMEN	GUDEMEN
ALMAINS	AMORINO	DAMAGES	DIORISM	DUSTMAN	EMOTION	ERODIUM	GLIOMAS	GUNROOM
ALMONDS	AMORIST	DAMOSEL	DISLIMN	EARLDOM	EMULATE	EROTEMA	GLOOMED	GURAMIS
ALMONER	AMOROSA	DEEMING	DOLMANS	EDEMATA	EMULGED	EROTEME	GOMERAL	IDOLISM

IMAGINE	MAINOUR	MATSURI	MILADIS	MONILIA	MURAENA	RAGTIME	SIMILOR	TEDIUMS
IMAGIST	MALAISE	MATURED	MILAGES	MONITOR	MURAGES	RAILMAN	SIMITAR	TEEMERS
IMAGOES	MALATES	MAUDLIN	MILDEST	MONTAGE	MURENAS	RAMEOUS	SIMULAR	TEEMING
INDIUMS	MALEATE	MAUGRED	MILEAGE	MONTERO	MURGEON	RANDOMS	SLIMIER	TIMARAU
IONIUMS	MALGRED	MAUGRES	MILIEUS	MONTURE	MURIATE	READMIT	SLIMING	TIMIDER
IONOMER	MALISON	MAULERS	MILITAR	MOODIER	MURLAIN	REAMEND	SLOOMED	TIMINGS
ISODOMA	MALTASE	MAULGRE	MILORDS	MOODIES	MURLANS	REDEEMS	SMARAGD	TINAMOU
ISOGRAM	MANAGED	MAULING	MILREIS	MOOLIES	MURLING	REELMAN	SMELTED	TOOLMAN
ITEMING	MANAGER	MEALIER	MILTING	MOOLING	MURLINS	REELMEN	SMIDGIN	TOOLMEN
ITEMISE	MANAGES	MEALIES	MINGIER	MOONIER	MUSTANG	REGIMEN	SMILING	TOOMING
LADANUM	MANATIS	MEANDER	MINORED	MOONLET	MUSTARD	REGMATA	SMITING	TORMINA
LAMETER	MANDIRA	MEASLED	MINUTED	MOONLIT	MUSTING	RELUMED	SMOILED	TOURISM
LAMIGER	MANDOLA	MEATIER	MINUTIA	MOORAGE	MUTAGEN	RELUMES	SMOORED	TRANGAM
LAMINAR	MANDORA	MEDALET	MISDIAL	MOORING	MUTANDA	REMANET	SMOOTED	TRAUMAS
LEGITIM	MANDRIL	MEDIATE	MISDIET	MOOTING	MUTINED	REMEDES	SOLANUM	TREMOLO
LEGROOM	MANEGED	MEDUSAE	MISLAID	MORDANT	NATRIUM	REMODEL	SOLIDUM	TROMINO
LEGUMES	MANEGES	MEERING	MISRULE	MORDENT	NEMORAL	REMOULD	SOMEONE	TRUEMAN
LEGUMIN	MANGALS	MEETING	MISTING	MORENDO	NEUROMA	REMOUNT	SOMITAL	TRUEMEN
LEMONED	MANGELS	MEGARAD	MISTLED	MORGUES	NIMIOUS	REMUAGE	SOMNIAL	TSARDOM
LEMURES	MANGOLD	MEGARON	MISTOLD	MORIONS	NORMALS	REMUDAS	SOOMING	TSUNAMI
LIGNUMS	MANILAS	MEGATON	MISTRAL	MORLING	NOSTRUM	RENAMED	SOUMING	TURMOIL
LIMEADE	MANITOS	MELANGE	MITERED	MORTALS	NOTAEUM	RENAMES	STADIUM	UNAIMED
LIMINGS	MANITOU	MELANOS	MITOGEN	MORULAE	NUMERAL	RETIMED	STAMINA	UNLIMED
LIMITED	MANOAOS	MELDERS	MOATING	MOTIONS	NUTMEGS	ROADMAN	STAMNOI	UNLIMES
LIMITER	MANSARD	MELTIER	MODELER	MOTORED	OARSMAN	ROADMEN	STAMNOI	UNLIMES
LIONISM	MANTIDS	MENAGED	MODIOLI	MOULAGE	OATMEAL	ROAMING	STARDOM	UNMATED
LOAMIER	MANTRAS	MENAGES	MODULAR	MOULDER	OEDEMAS	RODSMAN	STEEMED	UNMETED
LOAMING	MANTUAS	MENEERS	MODULES	MOULINS	OENOMEL	ROMAGES	STIMIED	UNMOORS
LOOMING	MANUALS	MENSUAL	MOGULED	MOULTED	OMELETS	ROMAUNT	STIMING	UNMORAL
LUMINED	MANURES	MENTEES	MOIDORE	MOULTEN	OMINOUS	ROOMIES	STIMULI	UNSMART
LUMINES	MARAUDS	MERITED	MOILING	MOUNTED	ORALISM	ROOMING	SUMATRA	UNTAMED
MADLING	MARGOSA	MESELED	MOINEAU	MOUNTER	ORGANUM	ROUMING	SURAMIN	UNTRIMS
MADRONA	MARINAS	METAGES	MOLDING	MOUSIER	ORIGAMI	SAGAMEN	SURNAME	URAEMIA
MADRONE	MARITAL	METALED	MOLERAT	MOUSING	ORMOLUS	SALAMON	TAEDIUM	URANISM
MADRONO	MARLINS	METERED	MOLINET	MOUSLED	OSMUNDA	SAMURAI	TALMUDS	UROSOME
MAGIANS	MAROONS	MEUSING	MONARDA	MOUTANS	OSTEOMA	SANGOMA	TAMALES	
MAGNETO	MARTIAL	MIAULED	MONAULS	MOUTONS	OUTMANS	SEAMAID	TAMANDU	
MAIDANS	MARTINI	MIDAIRS	MONDIAL	MUDGERS	OUTMODE	SEGMENT	TAMANUS	
MAIDING	MASTOID	MIDGETS	MONGOLS	MUDIRIA	OUTNAME	SIAMANG	TAMARIN	
MAILING	MATADOR	MIDIRON	MONGREL	MUISTED	RADIUMS	SIGMOID	TAMARIS	
MAINORS	MATINAL	MIGRATE	MONIALS	MUNITED	RAGMANS	SIMILAR	TANGRAM	

7-letter words with one P and six 1-2 point tiles

ADAPTOR	DEPONES	EPIDOTE	LEPROUS	PAGODAS	PARTIAL	PERIGEE	PIROGUE	PLUNGED
ADIPOSE	DEPOSAL	EPIGEAL	LEPTONS	PAGURID	PARULIS	PERIGON	PITARAS	PLUNGER
ADOPTEE	DEPOSER	EPIGEAN	LIPIDES	PAIGLES	PATINAS	PERINEA	PITURIS	PLUNGES
AIRGAPS	DEPUTES	EPIGENE	LIPOIDS	PAINTED	PATINED	PERLITE	PLAGUED	PLUSAGE
AIRSTOP	DESPISE	EPIGONE	LISPING	PAIRIAL	PATRIAL	PERLOUS	PLAGUES	PLUSING
ALEPINE	DESPOIL	EPIGONI	LISPUND	PAIRING	PATROLS	PERSUED	PLAINED	PLUTONS
ALPEENS	DESPOIL	EPILATE	LOOPERS	PAISANO	PATROON	PERTUSE	PLAINER	PODAGRA
ALPINES	DIAPASE	EPISODE	LOOPIER	PALADIN	PATULIN	PERUSED	PLAINTS	PODESTA
APNOEAS	DIAPIRS	EPUISEE	LOOPING	PALAGIS	PAUSING	PESTLED	PLAITED	PODGIER
APODOUS	DIPLOES	ERUPTED	LOUPING	PALATED	PEARLED	PETERED	PLANTAR	POESIED
APOGEAL	DIPLONS	ESTREPE	LUPINES	PALATES	PEARLIN	PETIOLE	PLANTAS	POINADO
APOGEAN	DIPLONT	GALIPOT	NAGAPIE	PANDARS	PEASING	PETUNIA	PLANTED	POINDER
APOGEES	DIPOLAR	GALOPED	NAPOOED	PANDITS	PEDALOS	PIANIST	PLASTID	POINTED
APORIAS	DISPART	GALOPIN	NAUPLII	PANDOOR	PEELERS	PIARIST	PLATANE	POINTEL
APOSTIL	DISPORT	GAUPERS	NUPTIAL	PANDORA	PEELING	PIDGEON	PLATANS	POINTER
APRONED	DISPUTE	GESTAPO	OPALINE	PANDORE	PEENGED	PIDGINS	PLATEAU	POISING
APSIDAL	DISRUPT	GILPIES	OPENEST	PANDOUR	PEENGES	PIERAGE	PLATINA	POLARON
APTERIA	DOPANTS	GIPSIED	OPERAND	PANDURA	PEERAGE	PIERIDS	PLATOON	POLENTA
ASPERGE	DOPINGS	GLOOPED	OPERANT	PARADES	PEERIES	PIETIES	PLAUDIT	POLINGS
ASPIDIA	DROPOUT	GOOPIER	OPEROSE	PARADOS	PEERING	PILEATE	PLEADER	POLOIST
ASPIRIN	DRUPELS	GOPURAS	OPIATED	PARAGES	PEISING	PIGNUTS	PLEASED	POLONIE
ASPREAD	DUPIONS	GRANDPA	OPTIONS	PARAGON	PELAGES	PIGSNIE	PLEASER	PONDAGE
ASPROUT	DUPLETS	GRAUPEL	OPULENT	PARANGS	PELOIDS	PIGTAIL	PLEATED	PONGEES
ATROPIA	DUPLIES	GROUPED	OPUNTIA	PARASOL	PELORIA	PILEOUS	PLEDGED	PONGIDS
ATROPIN	EARPLUG	GROUPIE	OROPESA	PARDALE	PELORUS	PILINGS	PLEDGER	PONGIER
DAPSONE	EELPOUT	GULPERS	OUTLEAP	PARDALS	PENSILE	PILOTED	PLEDGES	PONGOES
DEEPENS	ELAPSED	GUNPORT	OUTPEER	PARDONS	PENTODE	PILOTIS	PLEDGET	PONIARD
DEEPEST	ELOPERS	IGARAPE	OUTROPE	PARIALS	PENTOSE	PINATAS	PLEDGOR	PONTAGE
DEEPIES	ELOPING	INGROUP	OUTSPAN	PARISON	PEONAGE	PINDARI	PLEURAE	PONTILE
DELAPSE	ENSTEEP	LAPDOGS	PADANGS	PARLOUS	PERAEON	PINGUID	PLEURON	PONTILS
DELOPES	EPAULES	LAPSANG	PADRONE	PAROLED	PERDUES	PINTADO	PLOATED	POODLES
DEPAINT	EPAULET	LEEPING	PADRONI	PAROLEE	PEREGAL	PINTAIL	PLONGED	POOLING
DEPLANE	EPEIRID	LEIPOAS	PAENULA	PAROTID	PEREION	PIONEER	PLONGES	POOTING
DEPLETE	EPERDUE	LEOPARD	PAGEANT	PAROTIS	PERGOLA	PIRAGUA	PLOUTER	PORGIES
DEPLORE	EPERGNE	LEPROSE	PAGINAL	PARTANS	PERIDIA	PIRANAS	PLUNDER	PORTAGE

PORTALS	POUTING	PROTEGE	PURLING	SANDPIT	SPAROID	SPLURGE	TERPENE	UNSPILT
PORTEND	PRALINE	PROTEIN	PURLINS	SEEDLIP	SPARTAN	SPOILED	TILAPIA	UNSTRAP
PORTION	PREEING	PROTEND	PURLOIN	SEEPAGE	SPATIAL	SPONDEE	TIPULAS	UNSTRIP
PORTOUS	PREENED	PROTONS	PURSING	SEEPIER	SPATULA	SPONGED	TONEPAD	UPDATES
POSAUNE	PRELUDE	PROULED	PUSLING	SEEPING	SPATULE	SPOOLED	TOPLINE	UPDRAGS
POSITON	PRELUDI	PRUDENT	PUTEALS	SERPIGO	SPEANED	SPOOLER	TOPSAIL	UPGRADE
POSTAGE	PRENTED	PRUINAS	PUTLOGS	SINOPIA	SPEEDER	SPOONED	TOPSOIL	UPLANDS
POSTEEN	PRESAGE	PRUNTED	RAGTOPS	SLEEPER	SPEELED	SPOORED	TORPEDO	UPLEADS
POTAGER	PRETEND	PTERION	REPLETE	SLOPING	SPEELER	SPORULE	TORPIDS	UPLEANS
POTAGES	PRIDIAN	PUDGIER	REPLIED	SLURPED	SPEERED	SPUEING	TOUPEES	UPLEANT
POTEENS	PRIDING	PUERILE	REPOINT	SNEAPED	SPELDER	STEEPED	TRAPANS	UPLOADS
POTGUNS	PRISING	PUERING	REPONED	SNOOPED	SPELEAN	STEEPEN	TRIPODS	UPRISAL
POTIONS	PROINED	PULDRON	REPOSED	SOAPING	SPELIED	STEEPER	TRIPOLI	UPROOTS
POUDERS	PROLEGS	PULINGS	REPTILE	SOLIPED	SPILING	STEEPLE	TROOPED	UPSILON
POUDRES	PROLINE	PULSATE	REPUGNS	SOOPING	SPINAGE	STOOPED	TROUPED	UPSTAGE
POULARD	PROLING	PULSING	REPULSE	SOPRANI	SPINOUT	STUPING	TURNIPS	UPSTAIR
POULDER	PROLONG	PULTANS	REPUTED	SOPRANO	SPINULE	SUNTRAP	UNIPEDS	UPSTAND
POULDRE	PRONAOI	PULTONS	REPUTES	SOUPIER	SPIRING	TADPOLE	UNIPODS	UPSTOOD
POULTER	PRONAOS	PULTOON	RIPIENO	SOUPLED	SPIROID	TAIPANS	UNPAGED	UPTRAIN
POUNDAL	PRONATE	PUNDITS	RISPING	SPADING	SPITING	TALIPED	UNPLAIT	UPTREND
POURIES	PRONGED	PUNTEES	ROOPING	SPAEING	SPLENIA	TAPUING	UNPOSED	UROPODS
POURING	PRONOTA	PURITAN	ROUPING	SPANGED	SPLENII	TARPANS	UNSPIDE	UTOPIAN
POUTIER	PROTEAN	PURLINE	SALPIAN	SPANIEL	SPLODGE	TAUPIES	UNSPIED	UTOPIAS

7-letter words with one V and six 1-2 point tiles

ADVENES	DILUVIA	EVULSED	LOVAGES	RAVELIN	TAVERED	VALONEA	VELURES	VIOLONE
ADVISOR	DIVERGE	GARVIES	LOVERED	RAVENED	TAVERNA	VALONIA	VENATOR	VIRAGOS
ALEVINS	DIVINER	GAVIALS	LOVINGS	RAVIOLI	TENSIVE	VALOURS	VENDAGE	VIRANDA
ANDVILE	DIVINES	GENEVAS	NAEVOID	REEVING	TRAVAIL	VALUATE	VENDEES	VIRANDO
AVAILED	DIVINGS	GLAIVED	NAIVETE	REGIVEN	TRAVOIS	VALUERS	VENDORS	VIRGATE
AVAILES	DIVISOR	GLAIVES	NAIVIST	REIVING	TRIVIAL	VALUING	VENDUES	VIRGINS
AVALING	DIVULGE	GLEAVES	NAVAIDS	REVALUE	UNALIVE	VALUTAS	VENEERS	VIRGULE
AVAUNTS	DOGVANE	GLOVERS	NERVATE	REVENGE	UNGLOVE	VANDALS	VENITES	VIRINOS
AVENGED	DOVELET	GRAVIES	NERVOUS	REVENUE	UNITIVE	VANITAS	VENTAGE	VIRIONS
AVENGER	DRIVELS	GREAVED	NERVULE	REVEUSE	UNLIVED	VANTAGE	VENTIGE	VIROIDS
AVENGES	DRIVING	GREAVES	NIVEOUS	RIEVING	UNLIVES	VAREUSE	VENTOSE	VIRTUAL
AVENTRE	ELATIVE	GRIEVED	NOVALIA	RILIEVO	UNLOVED	VARIANT	VENTRED	VISAGED
AVENUES	ELEVATE	GROOVED	OLIVINE	RIVAGES	UNLOVES	VARIATE	VENTURE	VISAING
AVERAGE	ELEVENS	GROOVES	OUTGAVE	RIVETED	UNRAVEL	VARIOLA	VENULES	VISEING
AVERTED	ELEVONS	GROVELS	OUTGIVE	RIVLINS	UNREAVE	VARIOLE	VERANDA	VISITED
AVIATED	ELUSIVE	GROVETS	OUTLIVE	RIVULET	UNREEVE	VARIOUS	VERDANT	VISITEE
AVIATES	ENDIVES	INVALID	OUTVIED	SALVAGE	UNSAVED	VAUDOOS	VERDITE	VISITOR
AVIATOR	ENERVED	INVIOUS	OUTVIES	SALVETE	UNVAILE	VAULTED	VERONAL	VITRAGE
AVIDINS	ENERVES	INVITED	OUVERTE	SAVAGED	UNVAILS	VAULTER	VERSUTE	VITRAIL
AVISING	ENGRAVE	INVITEE	OUVRAGE	SAVAGER	UNVEILS	VAUNTED	VERTIGO	VITRAIN
AVOURES	ENSLAVE	INVITES	OVARIAN	SAVARIN	UNVISOR	VAUNTER	VERTUES	VITRIOL
AVULSED	ENVAULT	IVORIED	OVATING	SAVIOUR	UNVITAL	VAURIEN	VESTIGE	VITULAR
DATIVAL	ENVIOUS	IVORIST	OVATORS	SELVAGE	UVEITIS	VAUTING	VESTURE	VOGIEST
DEAVING	EVADING	LARVATE	OVERAGE	SEVERED	VAGINAE	VEDALIA	VETERAN	VOGUERS
DEEVING	EVANGEL	LAVAGES	OVERATE	SEVRUGA	VAGINAL	VEERING	VETOING	VOGUIER
DELVERS	EVASION	LEAVENS	OVERDUE	SIEVING	VAGINAS	VEGETAL	VIATORS	VOIDEES
DESERVE	EVENERS	LEVATOR	OVEREAT	SLEAVED	VAGITUS	VEILING	VIDUAGE	VOIDING
DEVALUE	EVENEST	LEVERED	OVERGET	SLEEVED	VAGRANT	VEINIER	VIGOROS	VOITURE
DEVIANT	EVENTED	LEVERET	OVERGOT	SLEEVER	VAGUEST	VEINLET	VIGOURS	VOLANTE
DEVIATE	EVENTER	LIVENED	OVERING	SLIVING	VAILING	VELARIA	VINIEST	VOLTAGE
DEVILET	EVERTED	LIVIDER	OVERNET	SOLVENT	VALETAS	VELATED	VINTAGE	VOLUTED
DEVIOUS	EVIDENT	LIVINGS	OVOIDAL	SOLVING	VALETED	VELATES	VIOLATE	VOLUTIN
DEVISEE	EVIRATE	LOAVING	OVULATE	STEEVED	VALETES	VELETAS	VIOLENT	VOTEENS
DEVOTEE	EVITING	LOUVERS	RAVAGED	STEEVER	VALGOUS	VELOUTE	VIOLINS	VOULGES
DEVOTES	EVOLUES	LOUVRED	RAVAGES	STIVING	VALIANT	VELURED	VIOLIST	VULGARS
DEVOURS	EVOLUTE	LOUVRES		TARDIVE	VALINES			VULGATE

7-letter words with one W and six 1-2 point tiles

ADAWING	DOWSING	GUNWALE	NEWSIER	OUTWORE	STOWAGE	SWOUNED	TWEERED	UNWEALS
AIRGLOW	EARWIGS	GWINIAD	NUTWOOD	OUTWORN	SUNGLOW	TARWEED	TWIGLOO	UNWIRES
ANTIWAR	ENDOWER	INDWELT	OARWEED	RAGWEED	SUNWARD	TOWAGES	TWINGED	UNWISER
AWAITED	ENDWISE	LAUWINE	ONWARDS	RENEWAL	SWEALED	TOWARDS	TWINNED	UNWOODED
AWARNED	ENSEWED	LAWNIER	OREWEED	RENEWED	SWEEING	TOWELED	UNDRAWS	UNWROTE
DANELAW	GAWSIER	LAWSUIT	OUTGREW	SEAWARD	SWEELED	TOWERED	UNLAWED	WADINGS
DAWTING	GLOWERS	LEASOWE	OUTGROW	SEAWARE	SWEERED	TOWLINE	UNSEWED	WAGERED
DEWATER	GODOWNS	LEEWARD	OUTLAWS	SEAWEED	SWEETED	TOWNEES	UNSWEAR	WAGONED
DEWIEST	GODWITS	LEGWEAR	OUTWARD	SEEWING	SWEETEN	TOWNIER	UNSWORE	WAGONER
DISGOWN	GOWANED	LEWDEST	OUTWEAR	SERUEWE	SWEETER	TRAWLED	UNWAGED	WAGTAIL
DOGTOWN	GOWDEST	LEWISIA	OUTWEED	SEWERED	SWEETIE	TULWARS	UNWAGES	WAILING
DOWAGER	GOWLAND	LOWERED	OUTWIND	SINEWED	SWELTED	TWANGED	UNWARES	WAINAGE
DOWNERS	GOWLANS	LOWINGS	OUTWING	SLOWING	SWIRLED	TWEEDLE	UNWARIE	WAITING
DOWNIER	GROWLED	LOWSING	OUTWINS	SOWLING	SWOONED	TWEELED	UNWATER	WALNUTS

WANDOOS	WEANELS	WEEDIER	WEISING	WIELDER	WINDIGO	WITLING	WOOLDER	WURLIES
WANTAGE	WEANERS	WEEDING	WELDERS	WIENIES	WINDORE	WONDERS	WOOLENS	
WARDOGS	WEARIED	WEENIER	WENDIGO	WILDERS	WINGIER	WONGIED	WOORALI	
WARISON	WEARIES	WEENIES	WERGILD	WILDEST	WINIEST	WOODIER	WORDAGE	
WASTAGE	WEASAND	WEETING	WETLAND	WILDING	WINTLED	WOODIES	WOULDST	
WATERED	WEDGIER	WEIGELA	WIDGEON	WILTING	WIRIEST	WOODING	WOURALI	
WAULING	WEDGIES	WEIRDIE	WIDGETS	WINDAGE	WIRINGS	WOODSIA	WRONGED	
WAURING	WEEDERS	WEIRING	WIDGIES	WINDIER	WISTING	WOOINGS	WROOTED	

7-letter words with one Y and six 1-2 point tiles

AGILITY	DEANERY	ELYTRON	GEODESY	INYALAS	NOYADES	SAINTLY	TANYARD	UNROYAL
ALAYING	DELAYER	ENTAYLE	GOLDEYE	LANIARY	OLITORY	SATYRAL	TARDILY	URANYLS
ALREADY	DENTARY	ESLOYNE	GOOLEYS	LANYARD	ONEYERS	SATYRID	TELERGY	UROLOGY
ANALOGY	DIETARY	ESOTERY	GOONEYS	LAUNDRY	ONEYRES	SEEDILY	TIDYING	YAOURTS
ANALYSE	DIGNITY	ESTUARY	GOOSERY	LAYERED	ORALITY	SOOTILY	TIGERLY	YARDAGE
ANALYST	DIRTILY	EUSTYLE	GRADELY	LAYOUTS	ORANGEY	SOUNDLY	TINDERY	YARDANG
ANILITY	DISTYLE	EYALETS	GRANDLY	LITURGY	OROGENY	STAGILY	TOURNEY	YEADING
ANTIGAY	DOYLIES	EYELETS	GREATLY	LUNYIES	OSTIARY	STAIDLY	TRAGEDY	YEALDON
ANYROAD	DRAYAGE	EYELIAD	GREENLY	LYRATED	OUTLAYS	STERNLY	TRAYNED	YEARNED
ARAYSED	DRYINGS	EYELIDS	GREYEST	NAILERY	RAIYATS	STONILY	TRILOGY	YEEDING
ARIDITY	DUALITY	EYESORE	GRISTLY	NASTILY	RELAYED	STRINGY	TRYINGS	YIELDER
ASTYLAR	DUSTILY	GAINSAY	GUILDRY	NEEDILY	RENAYED	STYLING	TRYSAIL	YIRDING
AUREITY	DYELINE	GASEITY	GURNEYS	NEOLOGY	RENEYED	STYLOID	TUILYIE	YODLING
DASYURE	DYSURIA	GAUDERY	GUYLERS	NITRYLS	RIGIDLY	STYRING	TUYERES	YOGINIS
DAYLONG	EAGERLY	GAUDILY	GYRATED	NOISILY	ROUNDLY	SURDITY	TYRANED	YOGURTS
DAYSTAR	EGALITY	GAUNTLY	INERTLY	NOSEGAY	ROYALET	SYENITE	UNGODLY	YONDERS
DAYTALE	ELUSORY	GAUNTRY	INLAYER	NOTEDLY	RUSTILY	SYNODAL	UNITARY	YOUNGER

8-letter words with one B and seven 1-2 point tiles

ABALONES	BANDORAS	BESOULED	BOATINGS	BUILDING	ERODIBLE	OBSOLETE	SUITABLE
ABATURES	BANDROLS	BESTRODE	BODGIEST	BUISTING	GABIONED	OBTRUDES	SURBATED
ABIDINGS	BANDURAS	BESUITED	BOGLANDS	BULGIEST	GADABOUT	ORBITIES	TABANIDS
ABIGAILS	BANLIEUE	BETIDING	BOILINGS	BULGINES	GAINABLE	ORBITING	TABLINGS
ABLATING	BARDLING	BETOILED	BOLTINGS	BUNGLERS	GARBOILS	OSNABURG	TABLOIDS
ABLATION	BARGAINS	BIELDIER	BONDAGES	BURGANET	GILBERTS	OUABAINS	TABOOING
ABLATORS	BARGEESE	BIELDING	BOOSTING	BURGEONS	GLABRATE	OUTBOARD	TABOURED
ABLUTION	BARGOOSE	BIGARADE	BOOTLEGS	BURGONET	GLABROUS	OUTBRAGS	TABOURIN
ABNEGATE	BARONAGE	BILANDER	BORONIAS	BURINIST	GLOBATED	OUTBREED	TEABOARD
ABOIDEAU	BARONIAL	BILGIEST	BOSTANGI	BURNSIDE	GLOBOIDS	RAGBOLTS	TEARABLE
ABOITEAU	BARTISAN	BILTONGS	BOTARGOS	BURSTING	GRADABLE	RAISABLE	TENEBRAE
ABORDING	BASELARD	BINAURAL	BOUDERIE	BUSTLING	GUIDABLE	RATEABLE	TOOLBAGS
ABORIGIN	BASIDIAL	BIRDINGS	BOUDOIRS	BUTANOLS	GUNBOATS	READABLE	TOOLBARS
ABORTION	BATELEUR	BIRDSONG	BOULDERS	BUTLERED	GUSTABLE	REBADGES	TRADABLE
ABOULIAS	BATOONED	BIRLINGS	BOULTERS	DATEABLE	INARABLE	REBITING	TREBLING
ABRADING	BAUDRONS	BIRSLING	BOULTING	DAUBIEST	INEDIBLE	REBOILED	TRIBUNAL
ABRASION	BEADINGS	BISERIAL	BOUNDERS	DAUBINGS	INGLOBED	REBOOTED	TRILOBED
ABRIDGES	BEAGLERS	BLANDEST	BOUNTREE	DEALBATE	INGLOBES	REBOUNDS	TROUBLED
ABROGATE	BEAUTIED	BLASTING	BOURDONS	DEBASING	ISOBRONT	REBUILDS	TROUBLES
ABSENTED	BEAUTIES	BLASTOID	BOURGEON	DEBITING	LABIATES	REDOUBLE	TUBENOSE
ABSENTEE	BEDEGUAR	BLAUDING	BOUTADES	DEBUTING	LABORING	REDOUBTS	TUBEROSE
ABSOLUTE	BEDERALS	BLEEDERS	BRAIDING	DENIABLE	LABOURED	REUSABLE	TUNEABLE
ABUTILON	BEDOUINS	BLEEDING	BRAILING	DIABOLOS	LABROIDS	RINGBITS	TURBANDS
ADORABLE	BEELINES	BLENDERS	BRAISING	DIATRIBE	LIBATING	RINSIBLE	TURBINAL
ALBITISE	BEERAGES	BLEUATRE	BRANGLED	DINGBATS	LIBATION	ROBINIAS	TURBONDS
ALGEBRAS	BEERIEST	BLINDAGE	BRANGLES	DOGBANES	LOBATION	ROBOTISE	UBERTIES
ANAEROBE	BEETLING	BLINDERS	BRATLING	DOGBOLTS	LOGBOARD	SABOTAGE	UBIETIES
ARABISED	BEGUILED	BLINDEST	BREEDING	DOUBLERS	LONGBOAT	SABULINE	UNABATED
ARBALEST	BEGUILER	BLONDEST	BRIDLING	DOUBLETS	LOOBIEST	SAIBLING	UNBAITED
ARBALIST	BEGUILES	BLOODIER	BRIDOONS	DOUBLING	NEBULISE	SATIABLE	UNBEGETS
ARGUABLE	BEGUINES	BLOODIES	BRIGADES	DOUBTERS	NEOBLAST	SEABOARD	UNBELTED
ATABRINS	BELEEING	BLOODING	BRIGANDS	DOUBTING	NOBODIES	SIBILANT	UNBIASED
AUBERGES	BELGARDS	BLOUSING	BRINDLES	DRIBLETS	NOTABLES	SIBILATE	UNBOLTED
AUBRETIA	BELONGED	BLUDGEON	BRIONIES	DURABLES	OBDURATE	SONGBIRD	UNBOOTED
AUBRIETA	BELONGER	BLUDGERS	BRISLING	DUTIABLE	OBDURING	SORBITOL	UNBRIDLE
AUDIBLES	BELTINGS	BLUDIEST	BRISTLED	EARLOBES	OBEDIENT	STABLING	UNILOBAR
BADINAGE	BENDLETS	BLUEINGS	BROILING	EATABLES	OBELISED	STROBILI	UNILOBED
BAITINGS	BENISEED	BLUENOSE	BROODING	EBENISTE	OBLATION	STROBING	UNSTABLE
BALADINE	BENITIER	BLUESIER	BRUISING	EBIONISE	OBLIGATE	SUBAGENT	
BALADINS	BERLINES	BLUIDIER	BRUITING	EBONISED	OBLIGATI	SUBERATE	
BALISTAE	BESEEING	BLUNDERS	BRUSTING	EDGEBONE	OBLIGATO	SUBGENRE	
BANALEST	BESIEGED	BLUNGERS	BRUTINGS	ENABLERS	OBLIGEES	SUBGRADE	
BANALISE	BESIEGER	BLURTING	BUDGEREE	ENGLOBED	OBLIGORS	SUBLATED	
BANDAGES	BESOGNIO	BOARDING	BUDGEROS	ENGLOBES	OBSIDIAN	SUBORNED	
BANDELET	BESORTED	BOASTING	BUILDERS	ERASABLE	OBSIGNED	SUBTIDAL	

8-letter words with one C and seven 1-2 point tiles

ACATOURS	CARDITIS	CLOUDING	COTLANDS	DURANCES	INDUCTEE	OCTAGONS	SCREENED
ACAULINE	CARDOONS	CLOURING	COULOIRS	ECAUDATE	INDUCTOR	OCULATED	SCROOGED
ACAULOSE	CAREENED	CLOUTERS	COULTERS	ECLOGITE	IRENICAL	ONISCOID	SCROOGES
ACETONES	CARGEESE	CLOUTING	COUNTROL	ECLOGUES	IRONICAL	ORACLING	SCROUNGE
ACIDIEST	CARGOOSE	CLUDGIES	COURAGES	EDACIOUS	ISOCLINE	ORCINOLS	SCUNGIER
ACIERAGE	CARLINGS	COALTARS	COURANTS	ECLOSING	ISODICON	ORGASTIC	SCUTIGER
ACIERATE	CARLOADS	COASTING	COURLANS	ECLOSION	ISOGONIC	OROGENIC	SECEDING
ACREAGES	CARNAGES	COATINGS	COURSING	EDUCATES	ISOTONIC	OSCULANT	SECERNED
ACRIDINS	CARNEOUS	CODEINES	COURTING	EDUCATOR	LACERANT	OSCULATE	SECODONT
ACROGENS	CAROUSAL	CODLINGS	CRADLING	EDUCTION	LACERATE	OSTRACOD	SECONDEE
ACTINIAE	CAROUSED	COGENERS	CRANAGES	EDUCTORS	LACINIAE	OSTRACON	SECRETED
ACTINIAS	CARTAGES	COGNATES	CREODONT	EGENCIES	LACTEOUS	OUTDANCE	SECTORED
ACTINOID	CARTLOAD	COGNISED	CREOSOTE	EGOISTIC	LACTONES	OUTRACED	SECURING
ACUITIES	CARTOONS	COISTRIL	CRINGLES	EIDETICS	LACUNARS	OUTSCOLD	SEDUCING
ACULEATE	CASTLING	COITIONS	CRINOIDS	ELECTING	LACUNATE	OUTSCORN	SEDUCTOR
ADUNCATE	CATALOES	COLESEED	CROODLES	ELECTION	LACUNOSE	RADICALS	SELECTED
AESCULIN	CATALOGS	COLOGNES	CROSTINI	ELECTRON	LAICISED	RADICANT	SERICITE
AGACERIE	CATELOGS	COLONIES	CROUTONS	ELEGANCE	LANCETED	RADICULE	SIDALCEA
AGENCIES	CATLINGS	COLONISE	CRUISING	ELEGIACS	LANDRACE	RECEDING	SILENCED
AGNOSTIC	CAUDLING	COLONIST	CRUSTING	ELICITED	LATENCES	RECENSED	SILENCER
AGRESTIC	CAUDRONS	COLORANT	CUITERED	ELICITOR	LECANORA	RECITING	SILICATE
AIDANCES	CAULDEST	COLORING	CULTIGEN	ELOCUTED	LECTERNS	RECLINED	SILICONE
ALCAIDES	CAULDRON	COLOURED	CURATING	ELOCUTES	LECTURED	RECLINES	SLUICIER
ALGICIDE	CAUSERIE	CONARIAL	CURDLING	ENACTURE	LECTURES	RECLOSED	SLUICING
ALICANTS	CAUTIONS	CONDOLES	CURLINGS	ENCLOSED	LECTURNS	RECODING	SOLACING
ANALECTS	CEILINGS	CONDUITS	CURTAILS	ENCLOSER	LEGACIES	RECOILED	SORICOID
ANALOGIC	CELADONS	CONGEALS	CURTAINS	ENCLOUDS	LEUCINES	RECOINED	SOURCING
ANECDOTE	CELERIES	CONGRATS	CURTANAS	ENCOLOUR	LEUCITES	RECUILED	SUICIDAL
ANELACES	CENSURED	CONGREED	CUTESIER	ENCOLURE	LEUCOSIN	RECUILES	SULCATED
ANGELICA	CENTAGES	CONGREES	CUTINISE	ENCRADLE	LICENSED	RECULING	SULTANIC
ANTACIDS	CENTERED	CONGREET	DECAGONS	ENCREASE	LICENSEE	RECUSING	SURGICAL
ANTECEDE	CERESINE	CONGRUED	DECENTER	ERECTILE	LICENSER	REDUCING	SURICATE
ANTICOUS	CERULEAN	CONGRUES	DECISION	EROGENIC	LINCTURE	REGENCES	TALIONIC
AORISTIC	CERULEIN	CONIDIAL	DECLARES	ERUCTING	LINOCUTS	REGICIDE	TELECINE
ARACEOUS	CERUSITE	CONOIDAL	DECLINES	ESCALADE	LITURGIC	RELIANCE	TELERGIC
ARCADING	CIELINGS	CONSOLED	DECOLORS	ESCALADO	LOCATION	RELUCENT	TENACULA
ARCANIST	CILIATES	CONSOLER	DECOLOUR	ESCALATE	LOCUSTAE	RELUCTED	TOURACOS
ARCTIIDS	CINEOLES	CONSULAR	DECORATE	ESCAROLE	LOCUSTED	RESCALED	TRADUCES
ARCUATED	CINEREAL	CONSULTA	DECOROUS	ESCORTED	LOCUTION	RESCUING	TRAGICAL
ASCIDIAN	CISELEUR	CONTAGIA	DECREASE	ESCULENT	LOGICIAN	RESECTED	TRIDACNA
AUCTIONS	CISELURE	CONTOURS	DECREETS	ESTACADE	LOGICISE	RESELECT	TRIGONIC
AUDIENCE	CISLUNAR	CONTROLE	DECURIAS	EUCAINES	LOGICIST	RETICULE	TRUCAGES
AURICLED	CLANGERS	CONTROLS	DECURIES	EUCRITES	LOGISTIC	RIDICULE	TUNICLES
AUTACOID	CLANGORS	CONTROUL	DECURION	EUGENICS	LORDOTIC	RUCTIONS	TURACINS
AUTOCADE	CLANGOUR	CONTUSED	DENTICLE	GARCINIA	LUCARNES	RUSTICAL	TURACOUS
AUTOCARS	CLARAINS	COOEEING	DERELICT	GAUCIEST	LUCERNES	SALICETA	ULCERATE
CADASTRE	CLARINOS	COOLANTS	DESELECT	GELASTIC	LUCIDEST	SALICINE	ULCERING
CADGIEST	CLARIONS	COOSENED	DIACONAL	GENOCIDE	LUCIGENS	SATURNIC	UNCLOSED
CAESURAE	CLARTING	COOSINED	DIALOGIC	GENTILIC	LUNACIES	SCAILING	UNCOATED
CAESURAL	CLAUSTRA	CORANTOS	DIATONIC	GEODESIC	LUNATICS	SCALDING	UNCOILED
CAGOULES	CLAUTING	CORDAGES	DICTIONS	GEODETIC	NACREOUS	SCALDINO	UNCOLTED
CALDERAS	CLEANERS	CORDIALS	DISCOING	GLACIATE	NAUTICAL	SCALDINI	UNCREATE
CALDRONS	CLEANEST	CORDINGS	DISCOLOR	GLUCINAS	NEGLECTS	SCANTLED	UNGRACED
CALENDAR	CLEANSED	COREGENT	DISCOUNT	GRACIOSO	NEOLOGIC	SCAUDING	UNICOLOR
CALENDER	CLEANSER	CORNAGES	DISCOURE	GRACIOUS	NEURITIC	SCAURING	UNSCALED
CALIGOES	CLEARAGE	CORNEOUS	DISGRACE	GRANITIC	NICETIES	SCIAENID	UNSECRET
CALUTRON	CLERGIES	CORNUTOS	DIURETIC	GUANACOS	NOCTILIO	SCIURINE	UNSLICED
CANALISE	CLINGERS	CORODIES	DOCILEST	GUIDANCE	NOCTUIDS	SCIUROID	UNSOCIAL
CANDELAS	CLINGIER	CORONALS	DOCTORAL	ICONISED	NOCTULES	SCLATING	URALITIC
CANDOURS	CLITORIS	CORONETS	DOGCARTS	IDIOLECT	NOTECASE	SCLEREID	URANISCI
CANOODLE	CLOSETED	CORSETED	DOUCINES	INCISURE	NUCLEASE	SCOLDING	URANITIC
CANOROUS	CLOSURED	CORTEGES	DUCATOON	INCLUDES	NUCLEATE	SCOOTING	URGENCES
CANTDOGS	CLOTURED	CORTISOL	DULCIANA	INDICTEE	NUCLEIDE	SCORDATO	UROLOGIC
CARANGID	CLOTURES	COTELINE	DULCIANS	INDOCILE	NUCLIDES	SCOURGED	
CARDIGAN	CLOUDAGE	COTINGAS	DULCITES	INDUCERS	OCARINAS	SCOURING	
CARDINAL	CLOUDIER	COTISING		INDUCIAE	OCEANAUT	SCOUTING	

8-letter words with one F and seven 1-2 point tiles

AEROFOIL	DEARNFUL	DEFLUENT	EELFARES	FALDAGES	FATIGUED	FEATURES	FEGARIES
AIRFIELD	DEFAULTS	DEFOREST	ENFESTED	FANTAILS	FATIGUES	FEDELINI	FEISTIER
AIRFOILS	DEFERENT	DEFUSING	ENFILADE	FANTEEGS	FATLINGS	FEDERALS	FELDGRAU
AIRLIFTS	DEFILERS	DEIFIERS	ENGULFED	FANTIGUE	FAULTIER	FEDERATE	FELONIES
ARGUFIED	DEFILING	DRAFTING	FAILINGS	FARADISE	FAULTING	FEEDINGS	FELONOUS
ARGUFIES	DEFINITE	DRIFTAGE	FAINTIER	FARDAGES	FAUSTIAN	FEEDLOTS	FELSTONE
AURIFIED	DEFLATES	DRIFTING	FAIRINGS	FARDINGS	FEATEOUS	FEELGOOD	FELTERED
AURIFIES	DEFLATOR	EDIFIERS	FAITOURS	FASTENED	FEATURED	FEELINGS	FELTINGS

FERITIES	FINGERED	FLOTAGES	FOOTRULE	FOUTRING	GATEFOLD	OUTFLING	TRADEFUL
FESTERED	FINITUDE	FLOUNDER	FORDOING	FRAISING	GOLFIANA	RATIFIED	TRIFLING
FEUDINGS	FIREDOGS	FLOURING	FOREDATE	FRAUTAGE	GOOFIEST	REDEFINE	TURFINGS
FEUTRING	FIRESIDE	FLOUSING	FOREGOES	FREELOAD	GRATEFUL	REFLUENT	UGLIFIED
FIELDERS	FISTIANA	FLOUTING	FOREGONE	FRIGATES	GROANFUL	REFOOTED	UGLIFIES
FIELDING	FISTULAE	FLUIDISE	FOREGUTS	FRISTING	GULFIEST	REFOUNDS	UNAFRAID
FIERIEST	FISTULAR	FLUORIDE	FORELEGS	FROGLETS	GUNFIRES	REFUGEES	UNFEARED
FIGULINE	FLAGRANT	FLUORINE	FORELEND	FRONDOSE	INFERIAE	REFUSING	UNFOLDER
FIGURANT	FLANERIE	FLUORITE	FORELENT	FRONTAGE	INFIDELS	REFUTING	UNFOOLED
FIGURATE	FLANEURS	FLUTINAS	FORESEEN	FRONTALS	INFIELDS	RIFLINGS	UNFOOTED
FIGURINE	FLAUNTED	FLUTINGS	FORESIDE	FROSTING	INFLATUS	ROLFINGS	UNFORGED
FIGURIST	FLAUNTER	FOEDARIE	FORESTED	FRUITAGE	INGULFED	ROOFIEST	UNFORGOT
FILAGREE	FLEDGIER	FOETIDER	FORETOLD	FRUITING	INTIFADA	ROOFINGS	UNGIFTED
FILANDER	FLEERING	FOILINGS	FORLANAS	FRUITION	LADIFIES	SAFARIED	UNIFIERS
FILARIAS	FLEETING	FOISTING	FORLENDS	FUNERALS	LEAFAGES	SAFRONAL	UNIFILAR
FILATURE	FLEURETS	FOLDINGS	FORSLOED	FUNEREAL	LENIFIED	SALIFIED	UNRIFLED
FILIATED	FLEURONS	FOLIAGED	FOSTERED	FURLANAS	LENIFIES	SANIFIED	UNROOFED
FILIATES	FLINDERS	FOLIAGES	FOUDRIES	FURLONGS	LOAFINGS	SAUFGARD	UNSELFED
FILIGREE	FLINGERS	FOLIOING	FOUGADES	FUSELAGE	NEEDFIRE	SNOOTFUL	URNFIELD
FILTERED	FLINTIER	FONDLERS	FOULARDS	FUSILEER	NOISEFUL	SOFTENED	
FINAGLED	FLIRTING	FOOLINGS	FOULDERS	FUSILIER	NOTIFIED	SOFTLING	
FINALISE	FLOATAGE	FOOTAGES	FOUNDERS	GADFLIES	NOTIFIES	STIFLING	
FINALIST	FLOODING	FOOTGEAR	FOURGONS	GASFIELD	OLEFINES	SULFATED	
FINEERED	FLOORING	FOOTINGS	FOURTEEN	GASIFIED	OUTFIELD	TELFERED	
FINERIES	FLORUITS	FOOTLING	FOUTERED	GASIFIER	OUTFLIES	TINFOILS	

8-letter words with one H and seven 1-2 point tiles

AIRHEADS	ENSHROUD	HARIGALS	HIDLINGS	HURTLING	RELISHED	SHORTING	TOADRUSH
ALIGHTED	ENTHUSED	HARLINGS	HILDINGS	HUSTLING	RHAGADES	SHOULDER	TOEHOLDS
ALTHORNS	ETHANOLS	HASTENED	HINDLEGS	INHOLDER	RINGHALS	SHOUTING	TOHEROAS
ANHEDRAL	ETHEREAL	HATGUARD	HIREAGES	INTHRALS	ROUGHENS	SLEIGHED	TOHUNGAS
ARSEHOLE	ETHERISE	HAULAGES	HIRELING	LAIGHEST	ROUGHEST	SLEIGHER	TOUGHENS
ASHLARED	GALOSHED	HAURIANT	HIRLINGS	LANGUISH	ROUGHIES	SLEUTHED	TOUGHIES
ASHLERED	GARISHED	HEADAGES	HIRSLING	LATHINGS	ROUNDISH	SLIGHTED	TREHALAS
ATHANORS	GATHERED	HEADGEAR	HIRUDINS	LAUGHERS	SEAHOUND	SLIGHTER	UNDIGHTS
AUTHORED	GHARIALS	HEADINGS	HISTOGEN	LAUGHIER	SHAGROON	SLOTHING	UNEATHES
DANELAGH	GHERAOED	HEADLINE	HISTRION	LAUGHTER	SHEADING	SLOUGHED	UNGIRTHS
DAUGHTER	GINHOUSE	HEADNOTE	HOARDING	LEGHORNS	SHEARLEG	SLUGHORN	UNHAILED
DELIGHTS	GIRLHOOD	HEADRAIL	HOASTING	LIGHTENS	SHEELING	SOOTHING	UNHALSED
DHOOLIES	GOLOSHED	HEADRIGS	HOISTING	LIGHTERS	SHEENIER	SOREHEAD	UNHEALED
DIANTHUS	GRAITHED	HEALDING	HOLDINGS	LINISHED	SHEERLEG	SOUTHING	UNHEARSE
DINGHIES	GREENTHS	HEDGIEST	HONOURED	LINISHER	SHEETIER	SOUTHRON	UNHEATED
DISHONOR	HAILIEST	HEELINGS	HOOLIEST	LITHARGE	SHEILING	SUNLIGHT	UNHOARDS
DOGHOLES	HAIRLINE	HEISTING	HOOLIGAN	LUTHERNS	SHETLAND	THANAGES	UNHOLIER
DOUGHIER	HALATION	HELIODOR	HORDEOLA	NIGHTIES	SHIELDER	THINGIER	UNHORSED
DRAUGHTS	HALIOTIS	HELOTAGE	HORNGELD	OUGHLIED	SHIELING	THINGIES	UNLASHED
DROOGISH	HALOGENS	HEREUNTO	HORNITOS	OUGHLIES	SHINGLED	THIOUREA	UNRIGHTS
DROUGHTS	HALTINGS	HERLINGS	HORNLETS	OUTSHINE	SHINGLER	THIRDING	UNSHALED
EIGHTEEN	HANDLERS	HEROISED	HOURLONG	OUTSHONE	SHIRTING	THIRLAGE	UNSHARED
EIGHTIES	HANDLIST	HETAERAE	HOUSLING	RAGHEADS	SHOALING	THIRLING	URETHANE
ENHALOED	HANDOUTS	HETAIRAI	HOUTINGS	RAILHEAD	SHOETREE	THOUSAND	UROLITHS
ENHALOES	HANDRAIL	HETAIRIA	HUITAINS	REGOLITH	SHOGUNAL	THRANGED	USHERING
ENHEARSE	HANGOUTS	HIDALGAS	HUNGERED	REHANDLE	SHOOGIED	THRONGED	
ENLIGHTS	HARANGUE	HIDALGOS	HURDLING	REHEATED	SHOOGLED	THUNDERS	
ENROUGHS	HARDLINE	HIDEOUTS	HURLINGS	REHOUSED	SHOOLING	TIGERISH	
ENSHIELD				RELIGHTS	SHOOTING	TINGLISH	

8-letter words with one M and seven 1-2 point tiles

ADEEMING	ALUMINAS	AUTOSOME	DIAMANTE	DOOMSTER	EMANATED	ENDEMIAL	GEMSTONE
ADENOMAS	AMATEURS	DALESMAN	DIASTEMA	DOORMATS	EMANATES	ENDGAMES	GEOMANTS
ADMIRALS	AMATIONS	DALESMEN	DIGAMIES	DOORSMAN	EMENDALS	ENGLOOMS	GEOMETER
ADMIRING	AMENAGED	DEEMSTER	DIGAMIST	DOORSMEN	EMENDATE	ENMITIES	GERANIUM
AEMULING	AMENAGES	DELIMITS	DIGAMOUS	DORMANTS	EMERALDS	ENORMOUS	GIANTISM
AGAMOIDS	AMIANTUS	DELIRIUM	DIMERISE	DORMOUSE	EMERAUDE	ENSEAMED	GIMLETED
AGERATUM	AMILDARS	DEMEANES	DIMEROUS	DRAGOMAN	EMERGENT	ENTREMES	GLADSOME
AIRMAILS	AMOUNTED	DEMEANOR	DIORAMAS	DRAGSMAN	EMERITUS	EREMITES	GLAMORED
ALAMODES	ANGIOMAS	DEMERGES	DISMOUNT	DRAGSMEN	EMETINES	ERMELINS	GLAMOURS
ALARMING	ANGSTROM	DEMERSAL	DOLESOME	DRUMLINS	EMONGEST	ERODIUMS	GLEAMIER
ALARMIST	ANIMATED	DEMISING	DOLOMITE	DUELSOME	EMULATED	EROTEMES	GLEESOME
ALARUMED	ANIMATOR	DEMIURGE	DOMAINAL	DUNGMERE	EMULATES	EUGENISM	GLIOMATA
ALASTRIM	ANTEROOM	DEMONISE	DOMANIAL	DURAMENS	EMULATOR	GAMELANS	GLOOMIER
ALDERMAN	ARGEMONE	DEMOTING	DOMINEER	EARLDOMS	EMULGENT	GAMESIER	GOADSMAN
ALDERMEN	ARGUMENT	DEMOTION	DOMINEES	EGOMANIA	EMULSION	GAUMIEST	GOADSMEN
ALGORISM	ARMGAUNT	DEMOUNTS	DOMINIES	ELEMENTS	EMULSOID	GEMATRIA	GOMERALS
ALIENISM	ASTIGMIA	DEMUREST	DOMINOES	ELOGIUMS	ENAMORED	GEMINATE	GOMERILS
ALODIUMS	AUGMENTS	DEMURING	DONATISM	EMAILING	ENAMOURS	GEMINIES	GONIDIUM
ALTRUISM	AUMAILED	DIAGRAMS	DOOMIEST	EMANATED	ENDAMAGE	GEMINOUS	GOODTIME

GORAMIES	LODGMENT	MARGINAL	MESOLITE	MONORAIL	MURIATED	ROUMINGS	SUDAMINA
GORMANDS	LONESOME	MARIGOLD	MESOTRON	MONTAGED	MURLAINS	ROUTEMAN	SUMOTORI
GOURAMIS	LONGSOME	MARINADE	METAIRIE	MONTAGES	MUSLINED	ROUTEMEN	SURNAMED
GOURMAND	LUMINIST	MARITAGE	MEUNIERE	MONTARIA	MUSLINET	SAGAMORE	TAEDIUMS
GOURMETS	MADLINGS	MARLINGS	MIAULING	MONTEROS	MUSTERED	SAILROOM	TALESMAN
GRADATIM	MADRIGAL	MAROONED	MIDIRONS	MOODIEST	MUTAGENS	SAINTDOM	TALESMEN
GRANDAMS	MADRONAS	MARTAGON	MIGRAINE	MOONLETS	MUTINEER	SALEROOM	TALISMAN
GRANDMAS	MADRONOS	MARTINIS	MIGRATED	MOONRISE	MUTINIED	SALMONET	TAMANDUS
GREMLINS	MAGDALEN	MASTODON	MILADIES	MOONSAIL	MUTINIES	SALMONID	TAMANOIR
GRIMIEST	MAGENTAS	MATADORE	MILEAGES	MOONSEED	NATRIUMS	SEADROME	TAMARIND
GRUESOME	MAGNATES	MATADORS	MILTONIA	MOORAGES	NATURISM	SEAMOUNT	TAMARINS
GUNMETAL	MAGNESIA	MATERIAL	MINGIEST	MOORINGS	NEMATODE	SEEMLIER	TANGRAMS
GUNROOMS	MAGNETOS	MATERNAL	MINGLERS	MOORLAND	NEMOROUS	SELENIUM	TEDISOME
IDEALISM	MAGNOLIA	MATRONAL	MINUTIAE	MOOTINGS	NEUROMAS	SEMILUNE	TELEGRAM
IDEOGRAM	MAILINGS	MATURING	MIRLITON	MORAINAL	NOTAEUMS	SIGMATED	TELOMERE
IGNOMIES	MAINDOOR	MAULGRED	MISALIGN	MORDANTS	NUMERALS	SIMULANT	TEMEROUS
ILMENITE	MAINOURS	MAULGRES	MISDOING	MORLINGS	NUMERATE	SIMULATE	TIGERISM
IMAGINAL	MAINSAIL	MAUNDERS	MISGUIDE	MORTLING	NUTMEALS	SLOOMIER	TIMARAUS
IMAGINED	MALADIES	MAUNDIES	MISLETOE	MOTIONAL	OATMEALS	SLOOMING	TIMELIER
IMAGINER	MALANDER	MAUNGIER	MISRULED	MOTIONED	ODOMETER	SMELTING	TIMELINE
IMAGINES	MALEATES	MEASURED	MISTLING	MOTORAIL	OEDEMATA	SMIDGEON	TIMOROUS
INSEEMED	MALGRADO	MEDALETS	MISTRIAL	MOTORIAL	OENOMELS	SMILODON	TINAMOUS
IONOMERS	MALIGNED	MEDALING	MITERING	MOTORING	OOGAMIES	SMOILING	TIRAMISU
ITEMISED	MALODOUR	MEGADOSE	MODALIST	MOULAGES	ORDALIUM	SMOORING	TOILSOME
LADANUMS	MALONATE	MEGARADS	MODELERS	MOULDERS	ORGASMED	SMOOTING	TRANGAMS
LAMENTED	MALTINGS	MEGARONS	MODELING	MOULDIER	ORIGAMIS	SMOULDER	TREMOLOS
LEADSMAN	MANAGERS	MEGASTAR	MODERATE	MOULDING	ORIGANUM	SMOUTING	TRIALISM
LEADSMEN	MANATEES	MEGATONS	MODERATO	MOULINET	OUTMODES	SMUDGIER	TROILISM
LEGITIMS	MANDATES	MEIONITE	MODESTER	MOULTING	OUTNAMED	SODOMITE	TROMINOS
LEGROOMS	MANDATOR	MELANGES	MODIOLAR	MOUNSEER	OUTNAMES	SOLARIUM	TURMOILS
LEGUMINS	MANDIRAS	MELANOUS	MODIOLUS	MOUSLING	RELUMINE	SOLATIUM	UDOMETER
LEMONADE	MANDOLAS	MELINITE	MODULATE	MOUSTING	RELUMING	SOLEMNER	ULTRAISM
LEMONIER	MANDORAS	MELODEON	MOIDORES	MOUTERED	REMEDIES	SOMEDEAL	UNMAILED
LEMURINE	MANDORLA	MELODIES	MOIETIES	MRIDANGA	REMEDING	SOMEDELE	UNMELTED
LEMUROID	MANDRELS	MELODION	MOINEAUS	MRIDANGS	REMIGIAL	SOMEGATE	UNMOORED
LIEGEDOM	MANDRILS	MELODISE	MOISTING	MUDIRIAS	REMISING	SONOGRAM	UNSEAMED
LIEGEMAN	MANGLERS	MELODIST	MOLESTED	MUDSTONE	REMODELS	SOREDIUM	UNSELDOM
LIEGEMEN	MANGOLDS	MELTINGS	MONARDAS	MUENSTER	REMOTION	STAMENED	UNTEAMED
LIMATION	MANITOUS	MENSURAL	MONAURAL	MUISTING	REMUAGES	STAMINAL	URAEMIAS
LIMITEDS	MANORIAL	MERENGUE	MONGRELS	MULETEER	RESUMING	STEELMAN	
LIMNAEID	MANSUETE	MERIDIAN	MONILIAS	MUNGOOSE	RETIMING	STEELMEN	
LIMONITE	MANTEAUS	MERINGUE	MONITORS	MURAENAS	ROADSMAN	STEREOME	
LODESMAN	MANTEELS	MERITING	MONODIES	MURALIST	ROMAUNTS	STOMODEA	
LODESMEN	MANURIAL	MERLINGS	MONODIST	MURGEONS		STORMING	

8-letter words with one P and seven 1-2 point tiles

ADAPTERS	DEPUTING	EPIGEOUS	LEOPARDS	PALISADE	PEDALING	PESTERED	PLATOONS
ADAPTING	DEPUTISE	EPIGONES	LEPIDOTE	PALISADO	PEDALOES	PESTLING	PLAUDITE
ADAPTION	DIAPASON	EPILOGUE	LEPORINE	PALUDINE	PEDESTAL	PETALOUS	PLAUDITS
ADAPTORS	DIAPAUSE	EPISTLED	LISPOUND	PALUDOSE	PEDIGREE	PETIOLED	PLEADERS
ADESPOTA	DIASPORA	EPULIDES	LOOPIEST	PANDOORS	PEELINGS	PETIOLES	PLEADING
ADOPTEES	DIPLEGIA	EPURATED	LOOPINGS	PANDORAS	PEERAGES	PETRONEL	PLEASANT
ADOPTING	DIPLOGEN	EPURATES	NAGAPIES	PANDOURS	PEERIEST	PIDGEONS	PLEASURE
ADOPTION	DIPLONTS	ERUPTING	NEUROPIL	PANDURAS	PEIGNOIR	PIERAGES	PLEDGEES
AIRPLANE	DIPNOOUS	ESPIEGLE	NUPTIALS	PARADING	PELAGIAN	PIGEONED	PLEDGEOR
ALPINIST	DIPTEROI	ESTREPED	OPERATED	PARAGONS	PELERINE	PIGTAILS	PLEDGERS
ANGUIPED	DISPLANT	EUPATRID	OPIATING	PARANETE	PELTERED	PILOTAGE	PLEDGETS
ANTELOPE	DISPLING	GALIPOTS	OPTIONAL	PARANOID	PELTINGS	PILOTING	PLEDGORS
APIARIES	DISPONEE	GALOPINS	OPUNTIAS	PARDALES	PENDULAR	PILSENER	PLEONAST
APIARIST	DISPONGE	GANTLOPE	OUTLEAPS	PARDALIS	PENTODES	PINDARIS	PLIOSAUR
APOLOGIA	DISPUNGE	GAPESEED	OUTPEERS	PARENTAL	PEONAGES	PINERIES	PLOIDIES
APOLOGUE	DOGSLEEP	GLOOPIER	OUTROPES	PARGETED	PEREGALS	PINGLERS	PLOUTERS
APOSITIA	DOORSTEP	GOALPOST	OUTSLEEP	PARLANDO	PERGOLAS	PINTADOS	PLUNDERS
ASPERATE	DROOPING	GOOPIEST	OUTSPEND	PAROLEES	PERIAGUA	PINTAILS	PLUNGERS
ASPERGED	DROPLETS	GOSPODAR	PAENULAE	PAROLING	PERIDIAL	PIRAGUAS	PLURISIE
ASPIRANT	DROPOUTS	GRANDPAS	PAENULAS	PAROUSIA	PERIDOTE	PIRATING	PODAGRAL
ASPIRING	DRUPELET	GRAPNELS	PAEONIES	PARTIALS	PERIGEAL	PIROGUES	PODAGRAS
ATROPIAS	DUPERIES	GRAUPELS	PAGANISE	PARTISAN	PERIGEES	PISOLITE	PODARGUS
ATROPOUS	EARPLUGS	GROUPIES	PAGEANTS	PASEARED	PERIGONE	PLAGUIER	PODGIEST
AUTOPSIA	EELPOUTS	GROUPIST	PAGINATE	PASTORAL	PERILOUS	PLAIDING	POETISED
DELOPING	EPANODOS	GROUPLET	PAGURIAN	PASTURAL	PERILUNE	PLAITING	POIGNADO
DEPLANES	EPAULETS	GUNPORTS	PAGURIDS	PASTURED	PERINEAL	PLANTAGE	POISONED
DEPLETES	EPEIRIDS	IGARAPES	PAIRIALS	PATERNAL	PERONEAL	PLANURIA	POLARONS
DEPLORES	EPERGNES	INGROUPS	PAIRINGS	PATRIALS	PERONEUS	PLASTRON	POLENTAS
DEPORTEE	EPIDOTES	INSPIRED	PALADINS	PATRONAL	PERSUADE	PLATANES	POLITIES
DEPOSING	EPIDURAL	ISOPODAN	PALATING	PATROONS	PERSUING	PLATEAUS	POLONIES
DEPURATE	EPIGAEAL	LAPIDATE	PALESTRA	PATULINS	PERTUSED	PLATINAS	POLONISE
DEPUTIES	EPIGAEAN	LAPSTONE	PALINODE	PAULDRON	PERUSING	PLATINGS	PONDAGES

PONGIEST	POUNDERS	PROUDEST	REPLETED	SPANDRIL	SPORTING	TAPADERO	UNPEERED
PONTAGES	POURINGS	PROULING	REPLETES	SPANGLED	SPOUTING	TAPENADE	UNPITIED
POOLSIDE	POUTINGS	PUDGIEST	REPOSTED	SPANGLER	SPRANGLE	TAPIROID	UNPLAITS
PORTAGUE	PRAEDIAL	PUGILIST	REPUGNED	SPANGLET	SPRINGAL	TEASPOON	UNPOISED
PORTEOUS	PRAISING	PULDRONS	REPULSED	SPARLING	SPRINGED	TERPENES	UNPOLITE
PORTIGUE	PRANDIAL	PULSATED	REPUTING	SPATULAR	SPRINGLE	TILAPIAS	UNPOSTED
PORTIONS	PRELUDES	PULSATOR	RESPLEND	SPEEDIER	SPROUTED	TONEPADS	UNREAPED
PORTLAND	PRELUDIO	PULSIDGE	SALOPIAN	SPEEDING	SPURLING	TOPLINED	UNSOAPED
PORTOLAN	PRENASAL	PULTOONS	SAUROPOD	SPEELING	SPURTING	TORPEDOS	UNSPARED
PORTULAN	PRENATAL	PUREEING	SEAPLANE	SPEIRING	STAPEDII	TRAGOPAN	UNSPOILT
POSITING	PRESAGED	PURITANS	SEPARATE	SPELAEAN	STAPELIA	TRIAPSAL	UPDATING
POSITION	PRESIDIO	PURITIES	SERPULAE	SPELDING	STAPLING	TRIPLIED	UPGRADES
POSITRON	PRESTIGE	PURLINES	SINOPITE	SPELDRIN	STEEPIER	TRIPLING	UPLANDER
POSTERED	PRETENDS	PURLINGS	SIRUPING	SPERLING	STEEPLED	TRIPLOID	UPLEANED
POSTLUDE	PRETENSE	PURLOINS	SLEEPIER	SPIELING	STIPULAR	TRIPODAL	UPRATING
POSTORAL	PRODIGAL	PURSLAIN	SLEEPING	SPIRLING	STIPULED	TRIPOLIS	UPRISING
POSTURAL	PRODNOSE	PURSLANE	SLEEPOUT	SPIRTING	STOOPING	TRIPUDIA	UPROOTAL
POSTURED	PROIGNED	RAPESEED	SLURPING	SPLENDOR	STRIPING	TROOPIAL	UPROOTED
POULAINE	PROLATED	READAPTS	SOAPLAND	SPLINTED	STROUPAN	TROOPING	UPSTAGED
POULARDS	PROLOGUE	REEDSTOP	SOLPUGID	SPLURGED	SUPERATE	TROUPIAL	UPSTARED
POULDERS	PROLONGE	RELAPSED	SOPITING	SPOILAGE	SUPEREGO	TROUPING	UPTRAINS
POULDRES	PROLONGS	REOPENED	SORPTION	SPOILING	SUPERLOO	UNDERLAP	UPTRENDS
POULDRON	PRONOTAL	REPEALED	SOUPLING	SPONGOID	SUPERNAL	UNDERLIP	UTOPIANS
POULTERS	PROTEGEE	REPEATED	SPADROON	SPOOLING	TADPOLES	UNESPIED	
POUNDAGE	PROTEGES	REPENTED	SPALTING	SPOORING	TAILSPIN	UNIPOLAR	
POUNDALS	PROTEOSE	REPETEND	SPANDREL	SPORIDIA	TALAPOIN	UNPEELED	

8-letter words with one V and seven 1-2 point tiles

AASVOGEL	DILUVION	GRAVITAS	NOVELISE	OVULATES	STRIVING	VARIANTS	VIOLONES
ADVISING	DISGAVEL	GRIEVOUS	NOVITIES	RAVENOUS	TELEVISE	VARIETAL	VIRAGOES
AESTIVAL	DISVALUE	GROVELED	OLIVINES	RAVIOLIS	TRAVAILS	VARIOLAS	VIRANDAS
AGENTIVE	DIVAGATE	IDEATIVE	OUTDROVE	RELIEVED	TRAVELOG	VAULTAGE	VIRGINAL
ALVEATED	DIVERGES	INDUVIAE	OUTGIVEN	RELIEVES	UNGLOVED	VAULTING	VIRGINED
AUDITIVE	DIVINERS	INDUVIAL	OUTGIVES	RELIVING	UNGLOVES	VAUNTAGE	VIRGULES
AVAILING	DIVINEST	INGROOVE	OUTLIVED	RESOLVED	UNRAVELS	VEDALIAS	VIROGENE
AVAUNTED	DIVULGES	INVALIDS	OUTLIVES	REVALUED	UNREAVED	VEGELATE	VIRTUOSA
AVERAGED	DOGVANES	INVEAGLE	OUTRIVAL	REVALUES	UNREAVES	VEGETALS	VIRTUOSO
AVERAGES	DOVERING	INVEIGLE	OUVRAGES	REVEALED	UNREEVED	VEILIEST	VIRULENT
AVIARIES	DOVELETS	INVITEES	OVARIOLE	REVENGED	UNREEVES	VEILINGS	VISIONAL
AVIARIST	DROVINGS	INVOLUTE	OVARIOUS	REVENGES	UNSOLVED	VEINIEST	VISIONED
AVIATING	DUVETINE	LARVATED	OVARITIS	REVENUED	UNVAILED	VELATURA	VISIONER
AVIATION	EGESTIVE	LAVATION	OVATIONS	REVENUES	UNVAILES	VELIGERS	VISORING
AVIATORS	ELEVATED	LAVEERED	OVERAGES	REVESTED	UNVEILED	VELOUTES	VISTAING
AVOIDING	ELEVATES	LAVENDER	OVERDOES	REVILING	UNVEILER	VELURING	VITALISE
AVOISION	ENDEAVOR	LEAVENED	OVERDONE	REVISING	UNVERSED	VENDAGES	VITRAINS
AVULSING	ENGRIEVE	LENITIVE	OVERDOSE	REVISION	VAGARIES	VENDEUSE	VITRIOLS
AVULSION	ENGROOVE	LEVANTED	OVERDUST	REVOLTED	VAGINATE	VENEREAL	VITULINE
DELETIVE	ENSLAVED	LEVEEING	OVERGETS	REVOLUTE	VAGINULA	VENERIES	VOGUIEST
DELIVERS	ENSLAVER	LEVERAGE	OVERGOES	RIVALISE	VAGINULE	VENTAGES	VOIDINGS
DELUSIVE	ENVAULTS	LEVERETS	OVERGONE	RIVETING	VAGRANTS	VENTURES	VOLANTES
DERISIVE	ENVEIGLE	LEVERING	OVERLADE	SALIVATE	VALERIAN	VERANDAS	VOLITION
DERIVING	ENVISAGE	LEVIGATE	OVERLEND	SALVAGED	VALIANTS	VERITIES	VOLTAGES
DESILVER	EVALUATE	LEVITIES	OVERLENT	SAVEGARD	VALIDATE	VERLIGTE	VOLUTINS
DEVALUES	EVANGELS	LIVENERS	OVERLOAD	SAVOURED	VALONEAS	VERSELET	VOLUTION
DEVILETS	EVENTERS	LIVERIED	OVERLONG	SELVAGED	VALONIAS	VESTIGIA	VOLUTOID
DEVILING	EVENTIDE	LIVERIES	OVERLOUD	SELVAGEE	VALOROUS	VESTURED	VORAGOES
DEVISING	EVENTUAL	LIVIDEST	OVERSEEN	SELVEDGE	VALUATED	VIDEOING	VULGATES
DEVLINGS	EVOLUTED	LOUVERED	OVERSIDE	SILVERED	VALUATES	VIDUAGES	
DEVOTEES	EVOLUTES	NAVIGATE	OVERSOLD	SLAVERED	VALUATOR	VIGILANT	
DEVOTING	EVULGATE	NEGATIVE	OVERSOUL	SLEEVING	VANADOUS	VIGOROUS	
DEVOTION	EVULSING	NERVELET	OVERTOIL	SLIVERED	VANGUARD	VILIAGOS	
DEVOUTER	EVULSION	NERVULES	OVERTONE	SOLUTIVE	VANTAGED	VINDALOO	
DILATIVE	GENITIVE	NOSEDIVE	OVERUSED	SOLVATED	VANTAGES	VINERIES	
DILUVIAN	GOVERNED	NOVELESE	OVULATED	STRAVAIG	VARGUENO	VIOLATOR	

8-letter words with one W and seven 1-2 point tiles

AIRGLOWS	EASTWARD	LEEWARDS	OUTGROWN	OUTWINGS	SINEWIER	TRAWLING	UNSTOWED
AWAITING	EDGEWISE	LEGWEARS	OUTGROWS	OWELTIES	STROWING	TWANGLED	UNTOWARD
AWARDING	GILTWOOD	LEWDSTER	OUTLAWED	RADWASTE	SWARDING	TWANGLES	UNWASTED
AWEARIED	GLOWERED	LEWISITE	OUTSWEAR	RAGWEEDS	SWEELING	TWEEDIER	WAGONERS
DANELAWS	GOATWEED	LONGWISE	OUTSWING	REDWINGS	SWELTING	TWEEDLER	WAGTAILS
DOGTOWNS	GOUTWEED	LUNGWORT	OUTSWORE	RENEWALS	SWINDLER	TWEEDLES	WAILINGS
DOWAGERS	GOWLANDS	NEWSGIRL	OUTSWORN	RINGWISE	SWINGIER	TWEELING	WAINAGES
DOWERING	GUNWALES	NEWSREEL	OUTWARDS	SANDWORT	SWINGLED	TWEENIES	WAITINGS
DRAWINGS	GWINIADS	NUTWOODS	OUTWEARS	SEAWATER	SWIRLING	TWIGLOOS	WANDEROO
DRAWLING	LAUWINES	OARWEEDS	OUTWEEDS	SERUEWED	SWORDING	TWIRLING	WANGLERS
DROWSING	LEASOWED	OREWEEDS	OUTWINDS	SEWERAGE	TOWELING	UNAWARES	WANTAGES

WARDINGS	WEASELER	WEIRDING	WETLANDS	WINDIEST	WISTARIA	WOOLDING	WRANGLED
WARLINGS	WEDGIEST	WELDINGS	WIDGEONS	WINDIGOS	WITLINGS	WOORALIS	WRANGLES
WARSLING	WEEDIEST	WELTERED	WIELDERS	WINDSAIL	WONDROUS	WORDAGES	WRESTLED
WATERAGE	WEEDINGS	WENDIGOS	WIELDIER	WINERIES	WOODENER	WORDINGS	WRITINGS
WATERLOG	WEENIEST	WEREGILD	WIELDING	WINGIEST	WOODIEST	WORSTING	WRONGOUS
WAULINGS	WEIGELAS	WERGILDS	WILDINGS	WINGLETS	WOODSIER	WOUNDERS	WROOTING
WEASELED	WEIRDIES	WESTERED	WINDAGES	WISELING	WOOLDERS	WOURALIS	

8-letter words with one Y and seven 1-2 point tiles

ADROITLY	DARINGLY	ENTAYLES	GYROIDAL	ODIOUSLY	SEROLOGY	SYRINGED	YARDAGES
ADULTERY	DAYTALER	ENTIRELY	GYROLITE	ORNATELY	SITOLOGY	TANYARDS	YARDANGS
AERODYNE	DAYTALES	ERYNGOES	IDEALITY	OUTLYING	SNOOTILY	TARDYING	YEALDONS
AEROLOGY	DELAYERS	ESLOYNED	IDEOLOGY	REGALITY	SODALITY	TELEGONY	YEARLONG
ALEATORY	DELAYING	ETIOLOGY	IDOLATRY	RESTYLED	SOLIDARY	TENDERLY	YELDRING
ALGIDITY	DELETORY	EYELINER	INDUSTRY	ROOTEDLY	SOLIDITY	TOADYING	YESTREEN
ANALYSED	DELUSORY	GARDYLOO	IODYRITE	ROTUNDLY	SONORITY	TRENDILY	YGLAUNST
ANALYSER	DIGYNOUS	GEALOUSY	LANYARDS	ROYSTING	SOUTERLY	TUILYIED	YIELDERS
ARAYSING	DILATORY	GELIDITY	LARYNGES	RUGOSELY	STINGILY	TUILYIES	YIELDING
ARDENTLY	DIRTYING	GEOLATRY	LEGATARY	RUGOSITY	STODGILY	TURGIDLY	YOLDRING
ARGUTELY	DISUNITY	GOLDEYES	LEGENDRY	SALEYARD	STOREYED	UNDERLAY	YOUNGEST
AUDITORY	DONATARY	GOLIARDY	LEGERITY	SALINITY	STORYING	UNDERSAY	YULETIDE
AUTODYNE	DONATORY	GONDELAY	LIENTERY	SALUTARY	STRONGLY	UNEASILY	
AUTOGENY	DOTINGLY	GOODYEAR	NASALITY	SANATORY	STRONGYL	UNITEDLY	
AUTOGYRO	DRAYAGES	GREEDILY	NEGATORY	SANITARY	STROYING	UNSTAYED	
AUTOLOGY	DYELINES	GUARANTY	NITROSYL	SEDATELY	STUDYING	UNSTEADY	
AUTOLYSE	DYSTONIA	GUERNSEY	NODALITY	SEDULITY	STURDILY	UNTIDILY	
DAINTILY	ENSTYLED	GULOSITY	NODOSITY	SENILITY	SUDATORY	URGENTLY	
DAIRYING	ENTAYLED	GUNLAYER	NUGATORY	SERENELY	SYNERGID	UROSTYLE	

———————— AEIO Bonus Words ————————

All 7- and 8-letter words which contain one each of the four vowels AEIO are given in the following lists. These lists may repeat words in the 6-plus-1 and 7-plus-1 bonus sets.

To make them easier to learn, the words are grouped according to the sequence of the four vowels – for example, AVOIDED, AGONISE and CALORIE all appear in the AOIE portion of the 7-letter list. The vowel groupings (such as AOIE) are listed alphabetically.

Within a vowel grouping, the words are listed in alphabetical order of the last three letters. Thus, in the AOIE portion of the 7-letter list, AVOIDED occurs before AGONISE, as the sequence -DED alphabetically precedes -ISE.

Where there are several words with the same last three letters, they are listed alphabetically by the first four letters. Thus, ADONISE precedes AGONISE.

AEIO bonus words containing only these vowels are listed first, followed by lists of the few that also contain a U.

AEIO BONUS WORDS (no U)

7-letter AEIO words (no U)

AEIO ALERION	AOEI AMOEBIC	AGONIZE	EMPORIA	ROARIER	COELIAC
AEOI AEROBIC	ANOESIS	ANODIZE	PELORIA	SOAPIER	LOBELIA
PAEONIC	ALOETIC	ATOMIZE	IAOE DIAZOES	BOATIES	TOXEMIA
ADENOID	ANOETIC	AZOTIZE	IMAGOES	GOALIES	GODETIA
ANEROID	AOIE AVOIDED	CALORIE	ISAGOGE	ORACIES	OIAE COINAGE
NAEVOID	CAMOGIE	EAIO ELATION	MIAOWED	OTARIES	FOLIAGE
ALVEOLI	ACCOIED	ENATION	IEOA ICEBOAT	OVARIES	SOILAGE
AIEO ARRIERO	AGONIES	ERASION	MINEOLA	ROADIES	ORIGANE
ALIENOR	ANOMIES	EVASION	IOAE DIOXANE	SOAPIES	OXIDASE
AILERON	ATOMIES	EAOI DEASOIL	ISOBARE	TOADIES	FOLIATE
AIOE PAIOCKE	ATONIES	EIOA KEITLOA	ISOBASE	COCAINE	OBVIATE
AZIONES	ATOPIES	EPIZOAN	ISOLATE	MORAINE	OSMIATE
VAIVODE	GANOINE	FEIJOAS	NIOBATE	OPALINE	OSTIATE
WAIVODE	KAOLINE	LEIPOAS	VIOLATE	OTARINE	OXIDATE
WAIWODE	ARMOIRE	HEMIOLA	IODATES	OXAZINE	SOCIATE
RADIOED	ADONISE	EOAI JEOFAIL	OAIE OAKIEST	SODAINE	LORICAE
AIRHOLE	AGONISE	EOIA GEOIDAL	OARIEST	COALISE	VOMICAE
CARIOLE	ANODISE	EXORDIA	TOADIED	COALIZE	SCORIAE
DARIOLE	ATOMISE	EROTICA	COALIER	TOASTIE	OPIATED
VARIOLE	AZOTISE	EXOTICA	FOAMIER	OEAI TOENAIL	OPIATES
ACINOSE	ACONITE	ENCOMIA	GOATIER	OCEANIC	
ADIPOSE	AMOSITE	BEGONIA	HOARIER	OCEANID	
ABIOSES	ADONIZE	ECTOPIA	LOAMIER	OEIA SOREDIA	

8-letter AEIO words (no U)

AEIO ARPEGGIO	ANTIPOLE	SAVORIES	AZOTISES	SEPALOID
ADHESION	ARVICOLE	SAXONIES	ANOINTED	SESAMOID
ALLERION	CABRIOLE	CAMOMILE	AROINTED	TERATOID
ANNEXION	CAMISOLE	APOCRINE	ADROITER	TETANOID
APHELION	CAPRIOLE	ARMOZINE	ANOINTER	HEXAFOIL
AVERSION	CARRIOLE	ATROPINE	ACONITES	EIAO DEVIATOR
ANTERIOR	FASCIOLE	GASOLINE	AMOSITES	EPILATOR
ALERIONS	GLADIOLE	LANOLINE	APOMIXES	EXPIATOR
AERIFORM	AIRDROME	PAVONINE	ADONIZED	MEDIATOR
AEOI AEROBICS	BARITONE	WAGMOIRE	AGONIZED	EIOA EPIZOANS
PAEONICS	ANTIPOPE	AMORTISE	ATOMIZED	EPIFOCAL
ADENOIDS	CALLIOPE	APHORISE	ANODIZED	EPISODAL
ANEROIDS	ALBICORE	CANONISE	AZOTIZED	PETIOLAR
AEROLITH	HALICORE	CAPONISE	ATOMIZER	HEMIOLAS
DAEMONIC	FARINOSE	VALORISE	ADONIZES	REGIONAL
ANECHOIC	LAMINOSE	VAPORISE	AGONIZES	KEITLOAS
AMBEROID	VARICOSE	AMMONITE	ANODIZES	SEMICOMA
ASTEROID	ANTIDOTE	APPOSITE	ATOMIZES	EOAI ESOPHAGI
ATHETOID	HALIMOTE	ARSONITE	AZOTIZES	REORDAIN
CAMELOID	TAILORED	DATOLITE	EAIO GERANIOL	JEOFAILS
GALENOID	AIRBORNE	FAVORITE	CREATION	TEOCALLI
MALLEOLI	ACIDOSES	JAROSITE	DELATION	EXOGAMIC
AIEO ARMIGERO	AMITOSES	SAPONITE	DERATION	GEOTAXIS
KAKIEMON	AOEI ACROLEIN	SAXONITE	ENACTION	EOIA EROTICAL
ASSIENTO	ALOETICS	TACONITE	EXACTION	HEROICAL
AILERONS	CANOEING	ABORTIVE	GELATION	KELOIDAL
ALIENORS	CANOEIST	ADOPTIVE	LEGATION	DEMONIAC
TAILERON	ANORETIC	AMORTIZE	NEGATION	EXORDIAL
ARRIEROS	ANOESTRI	APHORIZE	REACTION	MEMORIAL
AIOE VAIVODES	AMORETTI	CANONIZE	RELATION	BESONIAN
WAIVODES	ANOREXIC	CAPONIZE	SEDATION	BEZONIAN
WAIWODES	AOIE ABORIGEN	VALORIZE	VENATION	CREOLIAN
PAIOCKES	ASTONIED	VAPORIZE	VEXATION	DEMONIAN
AIRHOLES	CANOPIED	ASSOILED	BEHAVIOR	BEGONIAS
CARIOLES	PARODIED	ADJOINED	SERAGLIO	ECTOPIAS
DARIOLES	CAPONIER	GANOINES	ELATIONS	PELORIAS
VARIOLES	GASOLIER	KAOLINES	ENATIONS	MELODICA
AIRWOMEN	SABOTIER	ARMOIRES	ERASIONS	VERONICA
ACTIONED	APHONIES	ADONISED	EVASIONS	GEROPIGA
GABIONED	ARGOSIES	AGONISED	SCENARIO	SEMOLINA
RATIONED	ARMORIES	ANODISED	FELLATIO	CECROPIA
ACTIONER	ASTONIES	ATOMISED	EAOI EPAGOGIC	SENSORIA
RAISONNE	AVOWRIES	AZOTISED	DEASOILS	TENTORIA
ANTINODE	BARONIES	DAMOISEL	METAZOIC	IAOE DIALOGED
ANTIPODE	CALORIES	ATOMISER	CERATOID	ISAGOGES
ARILLODE	CAMOGIES	ADONISES	ERGATOID	FIASCOES
PALINODE	CANOPIES	AGONISES	KERATOID	IGNAROES
CALICOES	JALOPIES	ANODISES	NEMATOID	VIRAGOES
CALIGOES	PARODIES	ATOMISES	PETALOID	

DIASTOLE	COALIEST	MORALISE	OPALINES	SOLIDARE
GIRASOLE	FOAMIEST	NODALISE	OXAZINES	COGITATE
DIAPHONE	GOATIEST	NOMADISE	COALISED	DOMINATE
DIASCOPE	HOARIEST	NOTARISE	OPALISED	FORMIATE
DIASPORE	LOAMIEST	ORGANISE	COALISES	LORICATE
PINAFORE	ROARIEST	POLARISE	OXALISES	MOTIVATE
DIAGNOSE	SOAPIEST	ROYALISE	COALIZED	NOMINATE
VIATORES	ROADSIDE	SOLARISE	OPALIZED	OBLIGATE
IEAO LITERATO	SODAMIDE	TOTALISE	COALIZES	OPPILATE
IEOA ICEBOATS	COVARIED	VOCALISE	OEAI FORELAID	OPTIMATE
MINEOLAS	CROAKIER	WOMANISE	FORESAID	ORDINATE
SIDEROAD	FLOATIER	BORACITE	OVERLAID	OSCITATE
LIFEBOAT	ORANGIER	MONAZITE	OVERPAID	ROSINATE
MINNEOLA	POACHIER	SODALITE	DOVETAIL	SOLIDATE
IDEOGRAM	SHOALIER	TONALITE	FORESAIL	SOMNIATE
IOAE PILOTAGE	BOTANIES	COACTIVE	OVERSAIL	SPOLIATE
IRONWARE	COACHIES	CONATIVE	FORELAIN	VOLITATE
DIOPTASE	COVARIES	DONATIVE	OVERLAIN	OPINABLE
IDOCRASE	DONARIES	LOCATIVE	OVERHAIR	SOCIABLE
BILOBATE	GORAMIES	OPTATIVE	OCEANIDS	VOIDABLE
IMMOLATE	NOMADIES	ROTATIVE	TOENAILS	FOLIAGED
INCHOATE	NOTARIES	VOCATIVE	OBEAHING	COINAGES
INNOVATE	OCCAMIES	BOTANIZE	OBEAHISM	FOLIAGES
INORNATE	OTALGIES	FOCALIZE	OPERATIC	SOILAGES
INSOLATE	ROSARIES	LOCALIZE	POEMATIC	VOIDANCE
INTONATE	ROTARIES	MORALIZE	OEIA COELIACS	ORIGANES
PRIORATE	TOASTIES	NODALIZE	OBEISANT	GOLIASED
ISOLABLE	VOLARIES	NOMADIZE	OLEFIANT	GOLIASES
VIOLABLE	VOTARIES	NOTARIZE	POETICAL	OXIDASES
DIOXANES	FORHAILE	ORGANIZE	GYNOECIA	FOLIATED
ISOBARES	VOLATILE	POLARIZE	COLLEGIA	OBVIATED
BIOGASES	COALMINE	ROYALIZE	PROEMIAL	OXIDATED
ISOBASES	CORAMINE	SOLARIZE	SOREDIAL	FOLIATES
ISOLATED	DOPAMINE	TOTALIZE	SOTERIAL	OBVIATES
VIOLATED	MONDAINE	VOCALIZE	COMEDIAN	OSMIATES
IDOLATER	PROCAINE	WOMANIZE	GODETIAS	OXIDATES
VIOLATER	PTOMAINE	ROCAILLE	LOBELIAS	SOCIATES
ISOLATES	SOLANINE	OBTAINED	TOXEMIAS	OIEA TOISEACH
NIOBATES	STOVAINE	ORDAINED	BROMELIA	LONICERA
VIOLATES	TOPAZINE	OBTAINER	CHOLEMIA	ORIENTAL
IOEA DIOCESAN	BOTANISE	ORDAINER	PROGERIA	SOCIETAL
OAEI TOXAEMIC	FOCALISE	COCAINES	OIAE BONIFACE	
OAIE ORGANDIE	LOCALISE	MORAINES	SPOILAGE	

AEIO BONUS WORDS (with U)

7-letter AEIO words (with U)

EOIA EULOGIA	OEIA DOULEIA
SEQUOIA	OIEA MOINEAU

8-letter AEIO words (with U)

AEIO CAESIOUS	EDACIOUS	EUPHORIA	POULAINE
AOIE AGOUTIES	EOIA EUPHOBIA	IAOE DIALOGUE	ODALIQUE
JALOUSIE	SEQUOIAS	IOEA THIOUREA	OEIA DOULEIAS
EAIO EQUATION	EUPHONIA	OAIE DOUANIER	OIEA MOINEAUS

Further Bonus Sets

6-letter stems that combine with each vowel

All the bonus sets shown earlier are worth knowing because the words are likely to appear on your rack and, in the case of 8-letter words, be playable through a letter already on the board. This additional category of bonus word sets focuses on those 6-letter stems that are of particular interest because they combine with each of the five vowels.

The vowels make up some 40% of the letter pool at the start of a game, with the chances of picking a vowel from the bag varying as the game progresses. Often the chance of picking any vowel may rise to 50% or more towards the end of a game and it may be a good idea to play off one awkward consonant to 'fish' for a vowel in the hope of a late winning bonus play.

Many of the 6-letter stems are memorable, forming everyday keywords such as CANDLE and PARDON, making it easier for you to spot the 7-letter bonuses whenever and however the letters arrive on your rack. When the keywords are not real words or are not allowable for Scrabble, they are shown in brackets.

Not every 6-letter stem combining with each of the vowels is listed here. We have excluded some where the 6-letter stem itself is less likely or less memorable. Also excluded from these lists are the 63 stems already shown in the top 250 6-letter bonus stems, but for convenience these have been listed at the end of this introduction.

There are four categories selected as follows:

☆ 6-letter stems that have two vowels and no S

☆ 6-letter stems that have two vowels and just one S

☆ 6-letter stems that combine with AEIOU and Y only

☆ 6-letter stems that combine with AEIOU only

There are a few stems that meet two or more criteria. In such cases the stems are included in all of the relevant categories for completeness.

The following are stems in the top 250 6-letter bonus stems that combine with each vowel and which are excluded from the Further Bonus Sets:

ABERST	AENRST	DENRSU	EINNST
ACDERS	AEPRST	DEORST	EINPRS
ACELST	ANORST	EERRST	EINPST
ACENRT	BDEIRS	EERSTT	EINRTT
ACENST	BEIRST	EGILNS	EIPRST
ACERST	CEIRST	EGILNT	EIRSTV
ADEIRS	CENORS	EGILRS	EMNOST
ADEMNS	DEENRS	EGINRT	EMORST
ADENST	DEENST	EGNORS	ENOPRS
ADEPRT	DEGILN	EHIRST	EORRST
AEINST	DEGINR	EHORST	EORSTT
AELMNT	DEGINS	EILNST	GILNOT
AELNST	DEINRS	EILOST	GINORS
AELPRS	DEINST	EILRST	GINORT
AEMNST	DEIRST	EIMNST	INORST
AEMRST	DENOST	EIMRST	

6-LETTER STEMS – 2 VOWELS, NO S

ABERTT
BATTER
A RABATTE
　TABARET
E ABETTER
I BATTIER
　BIRETTA
L BATTLER
　BLATTER
　BRATTLE
O ABETTOR
　BATTERO
　TABORET
S BATTERS
　TABRETS
U ABUTTER
Y BATTERY

ABGINT
BATING
A ABATING
B TABBING
D DINGBAT
E BEATING
H BATHING
I BAITING
L TABLING
N BANTING
O BOATING
S BASTING
T BATTING
U TABUING
Y BAYTING

ACDELN
CANDLE
A CANDELA
　DECANAL
D CANDLED

E CLEANED
　ELANCED
　ENLACED
G CANGLED
　CLANGED
　GLANCED
H LANCHED
I INLACED
K CLANKED
O CELADON
S CALENDS
　CANDLES
T CANTLED
U LAUNCED
　UNLACED

ACDELR
CRADLE
A CALDERA
D CLADDER
　CRADLED
E CLEARED
　CREEDAL
　DECLARE
H CHALDER
I DECRIAL
　RADICEL
　RADICLE
O ORACLED
S CRADLES
　SCALDER
T CLARTED
U CAULDER
W CRAWLED

ADNOPR
PARDON
A PANDORA
B PROBAND

E APRONED
　OPERAND
　PADRONE
　PANDORE
I PADRONI
　PONIARD
O PANDOOR
S PARDONS
U PANDOUR
V PROVAND

AEGMNT
MAGNET
A GATEMAN
　MAGENTA
　MAGNATE
E GATEMEN
I MINTAGE
　TEAMING
　TEGMINA
O GEOMANT
　MAGNETO
　MEGATON
　MONTAGE
R GARMENT
　MARGENT
　RAGMENT
S MAGNETS
U AUGMENT
　MUTAGEN

AGILNV
(VALING)
A AVALING
　VAGINAL
C CALVING
E LEAVING
H HALVING
I VAILING

O LOAVING
S SALVING
　SLAVING
　VALSING
U VALUING
V VALVING

AIMNRT
MARTIN
A TAMARIN
E MINARET
　RAIMENT
G MARTING
　MIGRANT
I MARTINI
O TORMINA
S MARTINS
U NATRIUM
V VARMINT

BDEORR
BORDER
A BOARDER
　BROADER
E REBORED
I BROIDER
O BROODER
S BORDERS
U BORDURE
　BOURDER

CDDEER
(CEDDER)
A CEDARED
E DECREED
　RECEDED
I DECIDER
・ DECRIED
O DECODER

RECODED
U REDUCED

CEEGNR
(CRENGE)
A ENGRACE
E REGENCE
I CREEING
　ENERGIC
　GENERIC
O COGENER
　CONGREE
U URGENCE
Y REGENCY

DEERRV
(VERRED)
A AVERRED
E REVERED
I REDRIVE
　RIVERED
O OVERRED
　REDROVE
U VERDURE

DEHLLO
(HOLLED)
A HALLOED
E HELLOED
I HILLOED
O HOLLOED
U HULLOED

EENRRV
NERVER
A RAVENER
E VENERER
I NERVIER
　VERNIER

O OVERREN
S NERVERS
U NERVURE

EGINNP
PENING
A NEAPING
　PEANING
D PENDING
E PEENING
F PFENNIG
I PEINING
N PENNING
O OPENING
U PENGUIN

ENNORT
(TONNER)
A NORTENA
D DONNERT
　TENDRON
E ENTERON
　TENONER
F FORNENT
G RONTGEN
I INTONER
　TERNION
O NORTENO
S STONERN
U NEUTRON

6-LETTER STEMS – 2 VOWELS, ONE S

AACNST
(SCANTA)
A CANASTA
E CATENAS
F CAFTANS
H ACANTHS
I SATANIC
O SACATON
P CAPSTAN
　CAPTANS
　CATNAPS
R ARCTANS
　CANTARS
U ASCAUNT

ABELST
TABLES
A ABLATES
　ASTABLE
C CABLETS
D BALDEST
　BLASTED
　STABLED
E BELATES
G GABLETS
I ABLEIST
　ALBITES
　ASTILBE
　BESTIAL
　LIBATES
　STABILE
L BALLETS
O BOATELS

OBLATES
R ALBERTS
　BATLERS
　BLASTER
　LABRETS
　STABLER
S BASTLES
　STABLES
T BATLETS
　BATTELS
　BATTLES
　BLATEST
　TABLETS
U SUBLATE
Y BAETYLS
　BEASTLY

ACDELS
SCALED
A SCALADE
D SCALDED
E DESCALE
H CLASHED
I SCAILED
K SLACKED
L SCALLED
M MASCLED
N CALENDS
　CANDLES
O SOLACED
P CLASPED
　SCALPED
R CRADLES

SCALDER
S CLASSED
　DECLASS
T CASTLED
　SCLATED
U CAUDLES
　CEDULAS

ACDEPS
SPACED
A SCAPAED
E ESCAPED
I DISPACE
L CLASPED
　SCALPED
M DECAMPS
　SCAMPED
O PEACODS
　PEASCOD
R REDCAPS
　SCARPED
　SCRAPED
U SCAUPED

ACEMNS
(MANCES)
A CASEMAN
E CASEMEN
　MENACES
H MANCHES
I AMNESIC
　CINEMAS
L ENCALMS

O ANCOMES
P ENCAMPS
U ACUMENS

AEPPRS
SAPPER
A APPEARS
C CAPPERS
D DAPPERS
E RAPPEES
F FRAPPES
H PERHAPS
I APPRISE
　SAPPIER
L LAPPERS
　RAPPELS
　SLAPPER
M MAPPERS
　PAMPERS
　PREAMPS
N NAPPERS
　PARPENS
　PARSNEP
　SNAPPER
O APPOSER
R RAPPERS
S APPRESS
　SAPPERS
T TAPPERS
U PAUPERS
　UPSPEAR
W SWAPPER
　WAPPERS

Y PREPAYS
　YAPPERS
Z ZAPPERS

AIMNST
MATINS
A MANATIS
　STAMINA
D MANTIDS
E INMATES
　MAINEST
　MANTIES
　TAMINES
G MASTING
　TAMINGS
I ANIMIST
O MANITOS
　STAMNOI
R MARTINS
T MATTINS
U TSUNAMI

AIMRST
(ARMIST)
A AMRITAS
　TAMARIS
B IMBRAST
C MATRICS
E IMARETS
　MAESTRI
　MAISTER
　MASTIER
　MISRATE

SEMITAR
　SMARTIE
H THAIRMS
　THIRAMS
　THRIMSA
I SIMITAR
L MISTRAL
N MARTINS
O AMORIST
P ARMPITS
　IMPARTS
S TSARISM
U ATRIUMS
　MATSURI
Y MAISTRY
　SYMITAR

AINPRS
SPRAIN
A PIRANAS
E RAPINES
G PARINGS
　PARSING
　RASPING
　SPARING
I ASPIRIN
K KIRPANS
　PARKINS
O PARISON
　SOPRANI
P PARSNIP
S SPINARS
　SPRAINS

T SPIRANT	**CDDEIS**	F FENCERS	W SCROWLE	SPEARED	PEDALOS
SPRAINT	DISCED	I CERESIN	Y SCROYLE	D PEDDERS	E DELOPES
U PRUINAS	A CADDIES	SCRIENE		SPREDDE	G SPLODGE
W INWRAPS	E DECIDES	SINCERE	**CILNOS**	E SPEEDER	I DESPOIL
	I DISCIDE	L CRENELS	COLINS	SPEERED	DIPLOES
AIPRST	O DISCOED	O ENCORES	A OILCANS	H SPHERED	DIPOLES
RAPIST	U CUDDIES	NECROSE	D CODLINS	I PREDIES	PELOIDS
A PITARAS		P SPENCER	E CINEOLS	PRESIDE	SOLIPED
D DISPART	**CDEERS**	S CENSERS	CONSEIL	SPEIRED	SPOILED
E PARTIES	SCREED	SCERNES	INCLOSE	L SPELDER	O POODLES
PASTIER	A CREASED	SCREENS	G CLOSING	M PREMEDS	SPOOLED
PIASTRE	DECARES	SECERNS	I SILICON	N SPENDER	P SLOPPED
PIRATES	SEARCED	T CENTERS	K INLOCKS	O DEPOSER	R POLDERS
PRATIES	E CREESED	CENTRES	L COLLINS	REPOSED	U SOUPLED
TRAIPSE	DECREES	TENRECS	O CLOISON	R SPERRED	Y DEPLOYS
H HARPIST	RECEDES	U CENSURE	SCOLION	S DEPRESS	PODLEYS
I PIARIST	SECEDER	Y SCENERY	U ULICONS	PRESSED	
M ARMPITS	I DECRIES		UNCOILS	SPERSED	**DENOPS**
IMPARTS	K DECKERS	**CEHORS**		T PRESTED	(SPONED)
N SPIRANT	N DECERNS	OCHERS	**CILOST**	U PERDUES	A DAPSONE
SPRAINT	SCERNED	A CHOREAS	(STOLIC)	PERSUED	D DESPOND
O AIRSTOP	O RECODES	ORACHES	A STOICAL	PERUSED	E DEPONES
PAROTIS	S SCREEDS	ROACHES	C CITOLES		SPONDEE
S RAPISTS	T CRESTED	B BROCHES	H COLTISH	**DEILPS**	G SPONGED
U UPSTAIR	U RECUSED	C CROCHES	I COLITIS	DISPEL	I DISPONE
	REDUCES	E CHOREES	SOLICIT	A ALIPEDS	SPINODE
ALRSTU	RESCUED	COHERES	O SCIOLTO	PAIDLES	O SNOOPED
ULTRAS	SECURED	ECHOERS	R LICTORS	PALSIED	SPOONED
A AUSTRAL	SEDUCER	I COHEIRS	U COUTILS	C SPLICED	R PONDERS
C CRUSTAL	W DECREWS	HEROICS	OCULIST	D DISPLED	RESPOND
CURTALS	SCREWED	K CHOKERS		PIDDLES	U UNPOSED
E SALUTER		HOCKERS	**DDEIMS**	E SEEDLIP	
I RITUALS	**CDEINS**	SHOCKER	DESMID	SPIELED	**DINORS**
TRISULA	(DINCES)	L CHOLERS	A DIADEMS	I LIPIDES	(INDORS)
L LUSTRAL	A CANDIES	ORCHELS	E DEMISED	L SPILLED	A INROADS
O ROTULAS	INCASED	M CHROMES	MISDEED	M DIMPLES	ORDAINS
SUTURAL	E INCEDES	O CHOOSER	I MIDDIES	MISPLED	SADIRON
W TULWARS	I INCISED	SOROCHE	L MIDDLES	SIMPLED	E DONSIER
	INDICES	P PORCHES	N MIDDENS	N SPELDIN	INDORSE
AMNSTU	K DICKENS	S COSHERS	O DESMOID	SPINDLE	ROSINED
(UNMATS)	SNICKED	T HECTORS	S DESMIDS	SPLINED	G RODINGS
A MANTUAS	O CONDIES	ROCHETS	T MIDDEST	O DESPOIL	H DISHORN
TAMANUS	SECONDI	ROTCHES	U DEDIMUS	DIPLOES	DRONISH
B NUMBATS	R CINDERS	TOCHERS	MUDDIES	DIPOLES	I SORDINI
C SANCTUM	DISCERN	TORCHES		PELOIDS	O INDOORS
D DUSTMAN	RESCIND	TROCHES	**DDEIST**	SOLIPED	SORDINO
E UNTAMES	U CUNDIES	U CHOREUS	(EDDITS)	SPOILED	U DURIONS
UNTEAMS	INCUDES	Y COSHERY	A TADDIES	P SIPPLED	
G MUSTANG	INCUSED	Z SCHERZO	E DEIDEST	SLIPPED	**EEKPRS**
I TSUNAMI	INDUCES		TEDDIES	S DISPELS	(KREEPS)
O AMOUNTS	X EXSCIND	**CELORS**	I STIDDIE	DISPLES	A PARKEES
MOUTANS		CLOSER	TIDDIES	U DUPLIES	RESPEAK
OUTMANS	**CDEOST**	A CLAROES	L TIDDLES		SPEAKER
R UNSMART	COSTED	COALERS	M MIDDEST	**DEIPRS**	C PECKERS
T MUTANTS	A COASTED	ESCOLAR	N DISTEND	PRISED	E KEEPERS
U AUTUMNS	C DECOCTS	ORACLES	O TODDIES	A ASPIRED	I PESKIER
	E CESTODE	B CORBELS	U STUDIED	DESPAIR	L KELPERS
BEISTT	TEDESCO	D SCOLDER		DIAPERS	M KEMPERS
(BITTES)	I CESTOID	E CREOLES	**DEEMRS**	PRAISED	O RESPOKE
A BATISTE	COTISED	RECLOSE	(MERSED)	C CRISPED	U PERUKES
E BETTIES	K DOCKETS	H CHOLERS	A REMADES	DISCERP	
H THIBETS	STOCKED	ORCHELS	REMEADS	D DISPRED	**EELPRS**
I BITTIES	L COLDEST	I RECOILS	SMEARED	E PREDIES	LEPERS
O BOTTIES	N DOCENTS	K LOCKERS	E DEMERSE	PRESIDE	A LEAPERS
R BITTERS	O SCOOTED	L ESCROLL	EMERSED	SPEIRED	PLEASER
U BUTTIES	U CUSTODE	M CORMELS	REDEEMS	I PIERIDS	RELAPSE
	DOUCEST	N CORNELS	REMEDES	N PINDERS	REPEALS
CDDEES	DOUCETS	O COOLERS	I REMEIDS	O PERIODS	D SPELDER
(DESCED)	SCOUTED	CREOSOL	REMISED	P DIPPERS	E PEELERS
A DECADES	Y CYTODES	S CLOSERS	L MELDERS	S SPIDERS	SLEEPER
E SECEDED		CRESOLS	N MENDERS	T SPIRTED	SPEELER
I DECIDES	**CEENRS**	ESCROLS	O EMERODS	STRIPED	H HELPERS
N DESCEND	SCREEN	T COLTERS	P PREMEDS	U PUDSIER	I REPLIES
SCENDED	A CAREENS	CORSLET	U DEMURES	SIRUPED	SPIELER
O DECODES	CASERNE	COSTREL	RESUMED	Y SPIDERY	K KELPERS
U DEDUCES	ENRACES	LECTORS			L RESPELL
SEDUCED	D DECERNS	U CLOSURE	**DEEPRS**	**DELOPS**	SPELLER
	SCERNED	COLURES	SPREED	(PLODES)	M SEMPLER
	E RECENSE	V CLOVERS	A PREASED	A DEPOSAL	O ELOPERS

LEPROSE
T PELTERS
PETRELS
RESPELT
SPELTER
U REPULSE
Y SLEEPRY
YELPERS

EELRSV
LEVERS
A LAVEERS
LEAVERS
REVEALS
SEVERAL
VEALERS
D DELVERS
E SLEEVER
I RELIVES
REVILES
SERVILE
O RESOLVE
R VERRELS
T SVELTER
U VELURES
V VERVELS

EENPST
(ENSTEP)
A NEPETAS
PENATES
PESANTE
E ENSTEEP
STEEPEN
I PENTISE
L PENTELS
O OPENEST
PENTOSE
POSTEEN
POTEENS
R PRESENT
REPENTS
SERPENT
U PUNTEES
W ENSWEPT
Y STEPNEY

EERRSV
SERVER
A REAVERS
B REVERBS
E RESERVE
REVERES
REVERSE
SEVERER
G VERGERS
I REIVERS
REVERSI
REVISER
RIEVERS
L VERRELS
N NERVERS
O REVERSO
S SERVERS
VERSERS
T REVERTS
U REVEURS
W SWERVER
Y SERVERY

EERSVW
SWERVE
A WEAVERS
D SWERVED
E SERVEWE

WEEVERS
I REVIEWS
VIEWERS
O OVERSEW
R SWERVER
S SWERVES
U SURVEWE

EGILLS
(GILLES)
A GALLIES
GALLISE
E GELLIES
I GILLIES
N LEGLINS
LINGELS
LINGLES
SELLING
O GOLLIES
R GRILLES
T GILLETS
U GULLIES
LIGULES

EGINPS
(SPINGE)
A PEASING
SPAEING
SPINAGE
E SEEPING
H HESPING
PHESING
I PEISING
PIGSNIE
L PINGLES
SPIGNEL
O EPIGONS
PIGEONS
PINGOES
P PIGPENS
R PERSING
PINGERS
SPRINGE
S GIPSENS
U SPUEING
W SPEWING
Y ESPYING
PEYSING
PIGSNEY

EILLPS
(SPILLE)
A ILLAPSE
D SPILLED
E ELLIPSE
I ILLIPES
O POLLIES
R SPILLER
S LIPLESS
U PILULES

EILLST
(ILLEST)
A TAILLES
TALLIES
B BESTILL
BILLETS
C CELLIST
D STILLED
E TELLIES
F FILLETS
G GILLETS
I ILLITES
J JILLETS
K SKILLET

M MILLETS
MISTELL
N LENTILS
LINTELS
TELLINS
O OILLETS
R RILLETS
STILLER
TILLERS
TRELLIS
S LISTELS
T LITTLES
U TUILLES
W WILLEST
WILLETS

EILNPS
SPLINE
A ALPINES
SPANIEL
SPLENIA
C PENCILS
SPLENIC
D SPELDIN
SPINDLE
SPLINED
E PENSILE
G PINGLES
SPIGNEL
H PLENISH
I SPLENII
O EPSILON
PINOLES
P LIPPENS
NIPPLES
R PILSNER
S PENSILS
SPINELS
SPLINES
T PINTLES
PLENIST
U LUPINES
SPINULE

EILPST
STIPEL
A APLITES
PALIEST
TALIPES
E EPISTLE
PELITES
G PIGLETS
I SPILITE
M LIMPEST
LIMPETS
N PINTLES
PLENIST
O PIOLETS
PISTOLE
P STIPPLE
TIPPLES
R SPIRTLE
TRIPLES
S STIPELS
T SPITTLE
U PULIEST
PUTELIS
STIPULE

EIMMRS
MIMERS
A RAMMIES
D DIMMERS
E IMMERSE
G GIMMERS

MEGRIMS
H SHIMMER
I MIMSIER
K KIMMERS
SKIMMER
L LIMMERS
SLIMMER
N NIMMERS
O MEMOIRS
S MERISMS
SIMMERS
T MISTERM
U IMMURES
MUMSIER
RUMMIES
W SWIMMER
Z ZIMMERS

EIMPRS
SIMPER
A IMPRESA
SAMPIRE
C SPERMIC
E EMPIRES
EMPRISE
EPIMERS
IMPRESE
PREMIES
PREMISE
SPIREME
I PISMIRE
PRIMSIE
L PRELIMS
SIMPLER
O IMPOSER
PROMISE
R PRIMERS
S IMPRESS
PREMISS
SIMPERS
T IMPREST
PERMITS
U RUMPIES
SPUMIER
UMPIRES

EIMPST
(IMPETS)
A IMPASTE
PASTIME
E EMPTIES
SEPTIME
I PIETISM
J JIMPEST
L LIMPEST
LIMPETS
N PIMENTS
O MOPIEST
OPTIMES
R IMPREST
PERMITS
S MISSTEP
U IMPETUS
IMPUTES

EIPRRS
PRISER
A PARRIES
PRAISER
RAPIERS
RASPIER
REPAIRS
C CRISPER
PRICERS
E PERRIES

REPRISE
RESPIRE
G GRIPERS
I SPIRIER
M PRIMERS
O PROSIER
P RIPPERS
S PRISERS
U PURSIER
Z PRIZERS

EIPSTT
(PITTES)
A PATTIES
TAPETIS
D SPITTED
E PETTIES
H PETTISH
I PIETIST
L SPITTLE
N SPITTEN
O POTTIES
TIPTOES
P TIPPETS
R PITTERS
SPITTER
TIPSTER
U PUTTIES

ELOPRS
SPLORE
A PAROLES
REPOSAL
D POLDERS
E ELOPERS
LEPROSE
G PROLEGS
I SLOPIER
SPOILER
L POLLERS
O LOOPERS
SPOOLER
P LOPPERS
PROPELS
R PROLERS
S PLESSOR
SPLORES
T PETROLS
U LEPROUS
PELOROUS
PERLOUS
SPORULE
V PLOVERS
X PLEXORS
Y LEPROSY

EOPPRS
(SOPPER)
A APPOSER
B BOPPERS
C COPPERS
D DOPPERS
E PREPOSE
H HOPPERS
SHOPPER
I SOPPIER
L LOPPERS
PROPELS
M MOPPERS
O OPPOSER
PROPOSE
P POPPERS
R PROPERS
PROSPER
S OPPRESS

PORPESS
T STOPPER
TOPPERS
U PURPOSE
W SWOPPER
Y PYROPES
YOPPERS

EPRRSU
PURSER
A PARURES
UPREARS
C SPRUCER
D SPURRED
E PERUSER
REPURES
G PURGERS
I PURSIER
L PURLERS
SLURPER
N PRUNERS
SPURNER
O POURERS
R SPURRER
S PURSERS
U PURSUER
USURPER
Y SPURREY

EPRSTU
UPREST
A PASTURE
UPRATES
UPSTARE
UPTEARS
C PRECUTS
D SPURTED
E PERTUSE
REPUTES
I PERITUS
PUIREST
L SPURTLE
M STUMPER
SUMPTER
N PUNSTER
PUNTERS
O PETROUS
POSTURE
POUTERS
PROTEUS
SEPTUOR
SPOUTER
TROUPES
S UPRESTS
T PUTTERS
SPUTTER
U PUTURES

NORSTU
(UNROTS)
A ROUSANT
SANTOUR
B BURTONS
D ROTUNDS
E TENOURS
TONSURE
I NITROUS
TURIONS
M NOSTRUM
O UNROOST
UNROOTS
U OUTRUNS

FURTHER BONUS SETS

6-LETTER STEMS THAT COMBINE WITH AEIOU AND Y ONLY

ANRSTT
A RATTANS, TANTRAS, TARTANS
E NATTERS, RATTENS
I STRAINT, TRANSIT
O ATTORNS, RATTONS, ROTTANS
U TRUANTS
Y TYRANTS

BELMRT
A LAMBERT
E TREMBLE
I TIMBREL
O TEMBLOR
U TUMBLER, TUMBREL
Y TREMBLY

CEEGNR
A ENGRACE
E REGENCE
I CREEING, ENERGIC, GENERIC
O COGENER, CONGREE
U URGENCE
Y REGENCY

CEHPRS
A EPARCHS, PARCHES
E PERCHES
I CERIPHS, CIPHERS, SPHERIC
O PORCHES
U CHERUPS
Y CHYPRES, CYPHERS

CELRST
A CARTELS, CLARETS, SCARLET, TARCELS
E TERCELS
I RELICTS
O COLTERS, CORSLET, COSTREL, LECTORS
U CLUSTER, CULTERS, CUSTREL, CUTLERS, RELUCTS
Y CLYSTER

CEPRSS
A ESCARPS, PARSECS, SCRAPES, SPACERS
E PRECESS
I SPICERS
O CORPSES, PROCESS
U PERCUSS, SPRUCES
Y CYPRESS

CEPRST
A CARPETS, PRECAST, SPECTRA
E RECEPTS, RESPECT, SCEPTER, SCEPTRE, SPECTER, SPECTRE
I TRICEPS
O COPTERS
U PRECUTS
Y SCEPTRY

DGINRS
A DARINGS, GRADINS
E DINGERS, ENGIRDS
I RIDINGS
O RODINGS
U UNGIRDS
Y DRYINGS

ELNRST
A ANTLERS, RENTALS, SALTERN, STERNAL
E RELENTS, SLENTER
I LINTERS, SLINTER, SNIRTLE
O LENTORS
U RUNLETS
Y STERNLY

ELRSTT
A RATTLES, SLATTER, STARLET, STARTLE, TATLERS
E LETTERS, LETTRES, SETTLER, STERLET, TRESTLE
I LITTERS, SLITTER, STILTER, TESTRIL, TILTERS, TITLERS
O SETTLOR, SLOTTER, TOLTERS
U TURTLES
Y TETRYLS

EPRSST
A PASTERS, REPASTS, SPAREST
E PESTERS, PRESETS
I ESPRITS, PERSIST, PRIESTS, SITREPS, SPRITES, STIRPES, STRIPES, TRIPSES
O PORTESS, POSTERS, PRESTOS, REPOSTS
U UPRESTS
Y SPRYEST

ERRSTT
A RATTERS, RESTART, STARTER
E TERRETS
I RITTERS, TERRITS
O RETORTS, ROTTERS, TORRETS
U RUTTERS, TRUSTER, TURRETS
Y TRYSTER

FGILNT
A FATLING
E FELTING
I FLITING, LIFTING
O LOFTING
U FLUTING
Y FLYTING

GHINTT
A HATTING, TATHING
E TIGHTEN
I HITTING, TITHING
O HOTTING, TONIGHT
U HUTTING
Y TYTHING

GILNST
A ANGLIST, LASTING, SALTING, SLATING, STALING
E GLISTEN, LESTING, SINGLET, TINGLES
I LISTING, SILTING, STILING, TILINGS
O LINGOTS, TIGLONS, TOLINGS
U LUSTING, LUTINGS, SINGULT
Y STYLING

GIMNST
A MASTING, TAMINGS
E STEMING, TEMSING
I MISTING, SMITING, STIMING, TIMINGS
O GNOMIST
U MUSTING
Y STYMING

GINSTT
A STATING, TASTING
E SETTING, TESTING
I SITTING
O SOTTING
U TUTSING
Y STYTING

6-LETTER STEMS THAT COMBINE WITH AEIOU ONLY

ACHKRS
A CHAKRAS, CHARKAS
E HACKERS
I RICKSHA
O CHOKRAS
U CHUKARS

ACRRST
A CARRATS
E CARTERS, CRATERS, TRACERS
I TRICARS
O CARROTS, TROCARS
U CRATURS

ADGNRS
A ARGANDS
E DANGERS, GANDERS, GARDENS
I DARINGS, GRADINS
O DRAGONS
U DURGANS

AMNRST
A ARTSMAN, MANTRAS
E ARTSMEN, MARTENS, SARMENT, SMARTEN
I MARTINS
O MATRONS, TRANSOM
U UNSMART

ANPRST
A PARTANS, SPARTAN, TARPANS, TRAPANS
E ARPENTS, ENTRAPS, PANTERS, PARENTS, PASTERN, PERSANT, TREPANS
I SPIRANT, SPRAINT
O PARTONS, PATRONS, TARPONS
U SUNTRAP, UNSTRAP

BDELNR
A BLANDER
E BLENDER
I BLINDER, BRINDLE
O BLONDER
U BLUNDER

BDGINN
A BANDING
E BENDING
I BINDING
O BONDING
U BUNDING

BELRST
A ALBERTS, BATLERS, BLASTER, LABRETS, STABLER
E BELTERS, TREBLES
I BLISTER, BRISTLE, RIBLETS
O BOLSTER, BOLTERS, LOBSTER
U BLUSTER, BUSTLER, BUTLERS, SUBTLER

BERSTT
A BATTERS, TABRETS
E BETTERS
I BITTERS
O BETTORS
U BUTTERS

BGGGIN
A BAGGING
E BEGGING
I BIGGING
O BOGGING
U BUGGING

BGILLN
A BALLING
E BELLING
I BILLING
O BOLLING
U BULLING

BGILNS
A SABLING
E BINGLES
I SIBLING
O GLOBINS, GOBLINS, LOBINGS
U BLUINGS

BGINTT
A BATTING
E BETTING
I BITTING
O BOTTING
U BUTTING

CCDEKL
A CACKLED, CLACKED
E CLECKED
I CLICKED
O CLOCKED, COCKLED
U CLUCKED

CCEHRS
A CREACHS
E CRECHES, SCREECH
I SCREICH, SCRIECH
O CROCHES
U CURCHES

CDDEER
A CEDARED
E DECREED, RECEDED
I DECIDER, DECRIED
O DECODER, RECODED
U REDUCED

CDDEIS
A CADDIES
E DECIDES
I DISCIDE
O DISCOED
U CUDDIES

CDEKNS
A SNACKED
E SNECKED
I DICKENS, SNICKED
O DOCKENS
U SUNDECK, UNDECKS

CDEKRS
A DACKERS
E DECKERS
I DICKERS, SCRIKED
O DOCKERS
U DUCKERS

CDEKRT
A TRACKED
E TRECKED
I TRICKED
O TROCKED
U TRUCKED

CENRST	**DEHNRS**	**DFGINN**	O GROSETS	**EMPRST**	TINTERS
A CANTERS	A HANDERS	A FANDING	STORGES	A EMPARTS	O ROTTENS
CARNETS	HARDENS	E FENDING	U GUTSERS	STAMPER	SNOTTER
NECTARS	E HERDENS	I FINDING		TAMPERS	STENTOR
RECANTS	I HINDERS	O FONDING	**EHKRSS**	E TEMPERS	U ENTRUST
SCANTER	SHRINED	U FUNDING	A SHAKERS	I IMPREST	NUTTERS
TANRECS	O DEHORNS		E SHREEKS	PERMITS	
TRANCES	U HURDENS	**DGINNW**	I SHREIKS	O STOMPER	**ENSSST**
E CENTERS		A DAWNING	SHRIEKS	TROMPES	A ASSENTS
CENTRES	**DELSTT**	E WENDING	SHRIKES	U STUMPER	SNASTES
TENRECS	A SLATTED	I DWINING	O KOSHERS	SUMPTER	E SETNESS
I CISTERN	E SETTLED	WINDING	U HUSKERS		I SENSIST
CRETINS	I STILTED	O DOWNING		**EMRRST**	O SESTONS
O CONSTER	O DOTTLES	U WINDGUN	**EHLRST**	A SMARTER	U SUNSETS
CORNETS	SLOTTED		A HALTERS	E TERMERS	
CRESTON	U SUTTLED	**DGINST**	HARSLET	I RETRIMS	**EPRRSS**
CRONETS		A DATINGS	LATHERS	TRIMERS	A PARSERS
U ENCRUST	**DEMNST**	E NIDGETS	SLATHER	O TERMORS	RASPERS
	A TANDEMS	STEDING	THALERS	TREMORS	SPARERS
CGIKNR	E DEMENTS	STINGED	E SHELTER	U STURMER	SPARRES
A ARCKING	I MINDSET	I TIDINGS	I SLITHER		SPARSER
CARKING	O ENDMOST	O DOTINGS	O HOLSTER	**EMRSST**	E PRESSER
CRAKING	U DUSTMEN	U DUSTING	HOSTLER	A MASTERS	REPRESS
RACKING			U HURTLES	STREAMS	SPERRES
E RECKING	**DENNST**	**EFHLSS**	HUSTLER	E RESTEMS	I PRISERS
I RICKING	A STANDEN	A FLASHES		I MISTERS	O PRESSOR
O CORKING	E DENNETS	E FLESHES	**EKLNRS**	SMITERS	PROSERS
ROCKING	STENNED	I SELFISH	A RANKLES	O MOTSERS	U PURSERS
U RUCKING	I DENTINS	O FLOSHES	E KERNELS	U ESTRUMS	
	INDENTS	U FLUSHES	I LINKERS	MUSTERS	**EPRSTT**
CHILST	O STONNED		SLINKER	STUMERS	A PATTERS
A CHITALS	TENDONS	**EFLRST**	O SNORKEL		SPATTER
E ELTCHIS	U DUNNEST	A FALTERS	U LUNKERS	**ENNRST**	TAPSTER
I LITCHIS	STUNNED	E FELTERS	RUNKLES	A TANNERS	E PERTEST
O COLTISH		REFLETS		E RENNETS	PETTERS
U CULTISH	**DENPRS**	TELFERS	**EKRSST**	TENNERS	PRETEST
	A PANDERS	I FILTERS	A SKATERS	I INTERNS	I PITTERS
DDDELP	E SPENDER	LIFTERS	STRAKES	TINNERS	SPITTER
A PADDLED	I PINDERS	STIFLER	STREAKS	O STONERN	TIPSTER
E PEDDLED	O PONDERS	TRIFLES	TASKERS	U RUNNETS	O POTTERS
I PIDDLED	RESPOND	O FLORETS	E STREEKS	STUNNER	PROTEST
O PLODDED	U SPURNED	LOFTERS	I STRIKES		SPOTTER
U PUDDLED		U FLUSTER	O STOKERS	**ENPRST**	U PUTTERS
	DENRST	FLUTERS	STROKES	A ARPENTS	SPUTTER
DDELPR	A ENDARTS	RESTFUL	U TUSKERS	ENTRAPS	
A PADDLER	STANDER			PANTERS	**ERRSST**
E PEDDLER	STARNED	**EFLRTT**	**ELPRST**	PARENTS	A ARRESTS
I PIDDLER	E STERNED	A FLATTER	A PALTERS	PASTERN	RASTERS
O PLODDER	TENDERS	E FETTLER	PLASTER	PERSANT	STARERS
U PUDDLER	TENDRES	I FLITTER	PLATERS	TREPANS	E RESTERS
	I TINDERS	O FORTLET	PSALTER	E PRESENT	I STIRRES
DEERRV	O RODENTS	U FLUTTER	STAPLER	REPENTS	O RESORTS
A AVERRED	SNORTED		E PELTERS	SERPENT	ROSTERS
E REVERED	U RETUNDS	**EGGLRS**	PETRELS	I NIPTERS	SORTERS
I REDRIVE		A GARGLES	RESPELT	PTERINS	STORERS
RIVERED	**DENSTT**	LAGGERS	SPELTER	O POSTERN	U RUSTRES
O OVERRED	A ATTENDS	RAGGLES	I SPIRTLE	PRONEST	TRUSSER
REDROVE	E DETENTS	E EGGLERS	TRIPLES	U PUNSTER	
U VERDURE	STENTED	LEGGERS	O PETROLS	PUNTERS	**ERSSST**
	I DENTIST	I LIGGERS	U SPURTLE		A ASSERTS
DEGLNS	DISTENT	O LOGGERS		**ENRSST**	TRASSES
A DANGLES	STINTED	SLOGGER	**ELRSST**	A SARSNET	E TRESSES
GLANDES	O SNOTTED	U GURGLES	A ARTLESS	TRANSES	I RESISTS
SLANGED	U STUDENT	LUGGERS	LASTERS	E NESTERS	SISTERS
E LEGENDS	STUNTED	SLUGGER	SALTERS	RESENTS	O TOSSERS
I DINGLES			SLATERS	STRENES	U RUSSETS
ELDINGS	**DEPRST**	**EGMNST**	TARSELS	I INSERTS	TRUSSES
ENGILDS	A DEPARTS	A MAGNETS	E STREELS	SINTERS	TUSSERS
SINGLED	DRAPETS	E SEGMENT	TRESSEL	O STONERS	
O DONGLES	PETARDS	I STEMING	I LISTERS	TENSORS	**ERSTTT**
GOLDENS	E PRESTED	TEMSING	O OSTLERS	U UNRESTS	A STRETTA
U GULDENS	I SPIRTED	O EMONGST	STEROLS		TARTEST
	STRIPED	U NUTMEGS	TORSELS	**ENRSTT**	TATTERS
DEHLLO	O DEPORTS		U LUSTERS	A NATTERS	E STRETTE
A HALLOED	REDTOPS	**EGRSST**	LUSTRES	RATTENS	TETTERS
E HELLOED	SPORTED	A GASTERS	RESULTS	E TENTERS	I STRETTI
I HILLOED	U SPURTED	STAGERS	RUSTLES	TESTERN	TITTERS
O HOLLOED		E REGESTS	SUTLERS	I ENTRIST	TRITEST
U HULLOED		I TIGRESS	ULSTERS	STINTER	O STOTTER

	STRETTO
	TOTTERS
U	STUTTER

FGILNR
A	FLARING
E	FLINGER
I	RIFLING
O	ROLFING
U	FURLING

GGGILN
A	LAGGING
E	LEGGING
I	LIGGING
O	LOGGING
U	LUGGING

GGINNR
A	RANGING
E	GERNING
I	GIRNING
	RINGING
O	GRONING
U	GURNING

GGINRS
A	RAGINGS
	SIRGANG
E	GINGERS
	NIGGERS
	SNIGGER
I	GRISING
O	GORINGS
	GRINGOS
U	SURGING
	URGINGS

GHINNT
A	TANGHIN
E	HENTING
I	HINTING
	NITHING
O	NOTHING
U	HUNTING

GHINPS
A	HASPING
	PASHING
	PHASING
	SHAPING

E	HESPING
	PHESING
I	PISHING
O	GINSHOP
	POSHING
U	GUNSHIP
	PUSHING

GILNPP
A	LAPPING
	PALPING
E	LEPPING
I	LIPPING
O	LOPPING
U	PULPING

GILNPS
A	LAPSING
	PALINGS
	SAPLING
E	PINGLES
	SPIGNEL
I	LISPING
	PILINGS
	SPILING

O	POLINGS
	SLOPING
U	PLUSING
	PULINGS
	PULSING
	PUSLING

GIMNPR
A	RAMPING
E	IMPREGN
	PERMING
I	PRIMING
O	ROMPING
U	RUMPING

GIMNSS
A	MASSING
E	MESSING
I	MISSING
O	MOSSING
U	MUSINGS
	MUSSING

GINNRS
A	SNARING
E	ENRINGS
	GINNERS
I	RINSING
O	SNORING
	SORNING
U	NURSING
	URNINGS

GINPPP
A	PAPPING
E	PEPPING
I	PIPPING
O	POPPING
U	PUPPING

GINPPS
A	SAPPING
E	PIGPENS
I	PIPINGS
	SIPPING
O	SOPPING
U	SUPPING
	UPPINGS

GINPTT
A	PATTING
E	PETTING
I	PITTING
O	POTTING
U	PUTTING

GINRTT
A	RATTING
E	GITTERN
	ETTING
I	RITTING
O	ROTTING
U	RUTTING

LNPSTU
A	PULTANS
E	PENULTS
I	UNSPILT
O	PLUTONS
	PULTONS
U	PULTUNS

Section Six

Hooks and Blockers

Introduction

Which 2-letter words can be transformed into which 3-letter words by adding a single letter at either the beginning or the end? An example is HI, which by the addition of a letter at the front becomes CHI, GHI and PHI and by the addition of a letter at the back becomes HIC, HID, HIE, HIM, HIN, HIP, HIS and HIT. Such words, which can add a letter at the front or back, are called hooks, as they provide places for other words to hook on to.

Conversely, words which cannot have a letter added at the front or back are called blockers.

Hooks

The hooks have been arranged in two parts. In the first part, all the 2- and 3-letter root words are arranged in alphabetical order, with all the possible front and back hooks listed immediately after each root word. This is a useful arrangement for learning the hooks of words that occur most often in games. This list also contains words that have no hooks. These are of course blockers, but we felt that it would be helpful to show these here, as well as in the Blockers section.

The second part lists all words of length two to eight letters which can have a hook, arranged by hook letter. All the possible front and back A hooks are shown first, then the B hooks, then the C hooks, and so on.

In actual play, it can be very useful to play a 3-letter word (NIP, say) which has an unusual extension to four letters (in this case, NIPA). The chances are that your opponent won't know NIPA, and if the S's and blanks have already been played the opening is likely to be safe until you want to put your A on the end of NIP. You will find all the hooks to NIP (SNIP, NIPA, NIPS) following NIP in the first part. NIPA and other interesting A hooks are all listed together under the A Hook lists in the second part.

For 8-letter word -S hooks, only a specific subset of the possible hooks is shown. We have omitted all 9-letter words which are -S inflections of 8-letter words as they are of little practical value. For example, the hook AARDVARK-S is not listed. However, where 9-letter words are *non-plural* -S hooks of 8-letter words already ending in -S and are therefore of special interest (for example, NERVINES-S and TYRANNES-S), we have retained them.

HOOKS – by root word

2-LETTER WORD HOOKS: including all root words

AA	AMP	KAT	BAR	DIP	ELF	FAW	HID	GIO	LAG
BAA	**AN**	LAT	BAS	DIT	ELK	FAX	HIE	ION	LAH
MAA	BAN	MAT	BAT	DIV	ELL	FAY	HIM	IOS	LAM
AAS	CAN	NAT	BAY	**DO**	ELM	**FY**	HIN	**IS**	LAP
AD	DAN	OAT	**BE**	ADO	ELS	**GI**	HIP	AIS	LAR
BAD	EAN	PAT	BED	UDO	ELT	GIB	HIS	BIS	LAS
CAD	FAN	QAT	BEE	DOB	**EM**	GID	HIT	GIS	LAT
DAD	GAN	RAT	BEG	DOC	GEM	GIE	**HO**	GIS	LAV
FAD	HAN	SAT	BEL	DOD	HEM	GIF	MHO	HIS	LAW
GAD	MAN	TAT	BEN	DOE	REM	GIG	OHO	HIS	LAX
HAD	NAN	VAT	BET	DOG	WEM	GIN	PHO	LIS	LAY
LAD	PAN	WAT	BEY	DOH	EME	GIO	RHO	MIS	**LI**
MAD	RAN	ATE	BEZ	DON	EMS	GIP	THO	NIS	LIB
PAD	SAN	**AW**	**BI**	DOO	EMU	GIS	WHO	PIS	LID
RAD	TAN	CAW	OBI	DOP	**EN**	GIT	ZHO	QIS	LIE
SAD	WAN	DAW	BIB	DOR	BEN	**GO**	HOA	SIS	LIG
TAD	ANA	FAW	BID	DOS	DEN	AGO	HOB	VIS	LIN
WAD	AND	HAW	BIG	DOT	EEN	EGO	HOC	WIS	LIP
ADD	ANE	JAW	BIN	DOW	FEN	YGO	HOD	XIS	LIS
ADO	ANI	KAW	BIO	**EA**	GEN	GOA	HOE	ISH	LIT
ADS	ANN	LAW	BIS	KEA	HEN	GOB	HOG	ISM	**LO**
ADZ	ANT	MAW	BIT	LEA	KEN	GOD	HOH	ISO	LOB
AE	ANY	PAW	BIZ	PEA	MEN	GOE	HOI	**IT**	LOD
DAE	**AR**	RAW	**BO**	SEA	PEN	GON	HON	AIT	LOG
GAE	BAR	SAW	OBO	TEA	REN	GOO	HOO	BIT	LOO
HAE	CAR	TAW	BOA	YEA	SEN	GOS	HOP	CIT	LOP
KAE	EAR	WAW	BOB	ZEA	TEN	GOT	HOS	DIT	LOR
MAE	FAR	YAW	BOD	EAN	WEN	GOV	HOT	FIT	LOS
NAE	GAR	AWA	BOG	EAR	YEN	GOY	HOW	GIT	LOT
SAE	JAR	AWE	BOH	EAS	END	**GU**	HOX	HIT	LOW
TAE	LAR	AWL	BOK	EAT	ENE	GUB	HOY	KIT	LOX
VAE	MAR	AWN	BON	EAU	ENG	GUE	**ID**	LIT	LOY
WAE	OAR	**AX**	BOO	**EE**	ENS	GUM	AID	NIT	**MA**
AH	PAR	FAX	BOP	BEE	**ER**	GUN	BID	PIT	SMA
BAH	SAR	LAX	BOR	CEE	HER	GUP	CID	RIT	MAA
DAH	TAR	MAX	BOS	DEE	PER	GUR	DID	SIT	MAC
FAH	WAR	PAX	BOT	FEE	ERA	GUS	FID	TIT	MAD
HAH	ARB	RAX	BOW	GEE	ERE	GUT	GID	WIT	MAE
LAH	ARC	SAX	BOX	JEE	ERF	GUV	HID	ZIT	MAG
PAH	ARD	TAX	BOY	LEE	ERG	GUY	KID	ITA	MAK
RAH	ARE	WAX	**BY**	NEE	ERK	**HA**	LID	ITS	MAL
YAH	ARK	ZAX	ABY	PEE	ERN	AHA	MID	**JO**	MAM
AHA	ARM	AXE	BYE	REE	ERR	CHA	NID	JOB	MAN
AHS	ARS	**AY**	BYS	SEE	ERS	WHA	RID	JOE	MAP
AI	ART	BAY	**CH**	TEE	**ES**	HAD	TID	JOG	MAR
KAI	ARY	CAY	ACH	VEE	HES	HAE	VID	JOR	MAS
RAI	**AS**	DAY	ECH	WEE	LES	HAG	IDE	JOT	MAT
SAI	AAS	FAY	ICH	ZEE	MES	HAH	IDS	JOW	MAW
TAI	BAS	GAY	OCH	EEK	OES	HAJ	**IF**	JOY	MAX
AIA	DAS	HAY	CHA	EEL	RES	HAM	GIF	**KA**	MAY
AID	EAS	JAY	CHE	EEN	TES	HAN	KIF	SKA	**ME**
AIL	FAS	KAY	CHI	**EF**	YES	HAP	IFF	KAE	EME
AIM	GAS	LAY	**DA**	DEF	ESS	HAS	IFS	KAI	MEG
AIN	HAS	MAY	ODA	KEF	EST	HAT	**IN**	KAM	MEL
AIR	KAS	NAY	DAB	NEF	**EX**	HAW	AIN	KAS	MEN
AIS	LAS	PAY	DAD	REF	HEX	HAY	BIN	KAT	MES
AIT	MAS	RAY	DAE	TEF	KEX	**HE**	DIN	KAW	MET
AM	NAS	SAY	DAG	EFF	LEX	CHE	FIN	KAY	MEU
BAM	PAS	TAY	DAH	EFS	REX	SHE	GIN	**KO**	MEW
CAM	RAS	WAY	DAK	EFT	SEX	THE	HIN	KOA	**MI**
DAM	VAS	AYE	DAL	**EH**	VEX	HEM	KIN	KOB	AMI
GAM	WAS	AYS	DAM	REH	WEX	HEN	LIN	KOI	MID
HAM	ASH	AYU	DAN	EHS	YEX	HEP	PIN	KON	MIL
JAM	ASK	**BA**	DAP	**EL**	ZEX	HER	RIN	KOP	MIM
KAM	ASP	ABA	DAS	BEL	**FA**	HES	SIN	KOS	MIR
LAM	ASS	OBA	DAW	CEL	FAB	HET	TIN	KOW	MIS
MAM	**AT**	BAA	DAY	DEL	FAD	HEW	VIN	**KY**	MIX
NAM	BAT	BAC	**DI**	EEL	FAG	HEX	WIN	SKY	MIZ
PAM	CAT	BAD	DIB	GEL	FAH	HEY	YIN	KYE	**MO**
RAM	EAT	BAG	DID	MEL	FAN	**HI**	INK	KYU	MOA
SAM	FAT	BAH	DIE	SEL	FAP	CHI	INN	**LA**	MOB
TAM	GAT	BAM	DIG	TEL	FAR	GHI	INS	ALA	MOD
YAM	HAT	BAN	DIM	ZEL	FAS	PHI	**IO**	LAB	MOE
AMI		BAP	DIN	ELD	FAT	HIC	BIO	LAC	MOG

MOI	**NY**	OOH	HOP	LOW	PIR	SOH	TOP	PUR	LYE
MOM	ANY	POH	KOP	MOW	PIS	SOL	TOR	SUR	NYE
MON	SNY	SOH	LOP	NOW	PIT	SON	TOT	URD	OYE
MOO	NYE	OHM	MOP	POW	PIU	SOP	TOW	URE	PYE
MOP	NYS	OHO	OOP	ROW	PIX	SOS	TOY	URN	RYE
MOR	**OB**	**OI**	POP	SOW	**PO**	SOT	**UG**	**US**	SYE
MOT	BOB	HOI	SOP	TOW	POA	SOU	BUG	BUS	TYE
MOU	COB	KOI	TOP	VOW	POD	SOV	DUG	GUS	WYE
MOW	DOB	MOI	WOP	WOW	POH	SOW	FUG	JUS	YEA
MOY	FOB	POI	OPE	YOW	POI	SOX	HUG	MUS	YEN
MOZ	GOB	OIK	OPS	OWE	POM	SOY	JUG	NUS	YEP
MU	HOB	OIL	OPT	OWL	POO	**ST**	LUG	PUS	YES
EMU	JOB	OM	**OR**	OWN	POP	EST	MUG	SUS	YET
MUD	KOB	MOM	BOR	OWT	POS	PST	PUG	WUS	YEW
MUG	LOB	NOM	COR	**OX**	POT	STY	RUG	YUS	YEX
MUM	MOB	OOM	DOR	BOX	POW	**TA**	TUG	USE	**YO**
MUN	NOB	POM	FOR	COX	POX	ETA	VUG	**UT**	YOB
MUS	ROB	ROM	JOR	FOX	POZ	ITA	YUG	BUT	YOD
MUX	SOB	TOM	LOR	HOX	**QI**	TAB	UGH	CUT	YOK
MY	YOB	OMS	MOR	LOX	QIS	TAD	UGS	GUT	YON
NA	OBA	**ON**	NOR	NOX	**RE**	TAE	**UM**	HUT	YOS
ANA	OBI	BON	OOR	POX	ARE	TAG	BUM	JUT	YOU
MNA	OBO	CON	TOR	SOX	ERE	TAI	CUM	NUT	YOW
NAB	OBS	DON	VOR	VOX	IRE	TAJ	FUM	OUT	**YU**
NAE	**OD**	EON	ORB	WOX	ORE	TAK	GUM	PUT	AYU
NAG	BOD	FON	ORC	**OY**	PRE	TAM	HUM	RUT	KYU
NAM	COD	GON	ORD	BOY	URE	TAN	LUM	TUT	YUG
NAN	DOD	HON	ORE	COY	REC	TAP	MUM	UTE	YUK
NAP	GOD	ION	ORF	FOY	RED	TAR	RUM	UTS	YUP
NAS	HOD	KON	ORS	GOY	REE	TAT	SUM	UTU	YUS
NAT	LOD	MON	ORT	HOY	REF	TAU	TUM	**WE**	**ZO**
NAY	MOD	NON	**OS**	JOY	REH	TAW	VUM	AWE	DZO
NE	NOD	OON	BOS	LOY	REM	TAX	**UN**	EWE	ZOA
ANE	POD	SON	COS	MOY	REN	TAY	BUN	OWE	ZOO
ENE	ROD	TON	DOS	NOY	REP	**TE**	DUN	WEB	ZOS
ONE	SOD	WON	GOS	SOY	RES	ATE	FUN	WED	
NEB	TOD	YON	HOS	TOY	RET	UTE	GUN	WEE	
NED	YOD	ONE	IOS	OYE	REV	TEA	MUN	WEM	
NEE	ODA	ONS	KOS	OYS	REW	TED	NUN	WEN	
NEF	ODD	**OO**	LOS	**PA**	REX	TEE	PUN	WET	
NEK	ODE	BOO	NOS	SPA	REZ	TEF	RUN	WEX	
NEP	ODS	COO	OOS	PAD	**SH**	TEG	SUN	WEY	
NET	**OE**	DOO	POS	PAH	ASH	TEL	TUN	**WO**	
NEW	DOE	GOO	SOS	PAL	ISH	TEN	UNI	TWO	
NO	FOE	HOO	WOS	PAM	SHE	TES	UNS	WOE	
NOB	GOE	LOO	YOS	PAN	SHY	TEW	**UP**	WOG	
NOD	HOE	MOO	ZOS	PAP	**SI**	**TI**	CUP	WOK	
NOG	JOE	POO	**OU**	PAR	PSI	TIC	DUP	WON	
NOH	MOE	ROO	FOU	PAS	SIB	TID	GUP	WOO	
NOM	ROE	TOO	MOU	PAT	SIC	TIE	HUP	WOP	
NON	TOE	WOO	SOU	PAW	SIM	TIG	OUP	WOS	
NOR	VOE	ZOO	YOU	PAX	SIN	TIL	PUP	WOT	
NOS	WOE	OOF	OUD	PAY	SIP	TIN	SUP	WOW	
NOT	OES	OOH	OUK	**PH**	SIR	TIP	TUP	WOX	
NOW	**OF**	OOM	OUP	PHI	SIS	TIS	YUP	**XI**	
NOX	OOF	OON	OUR	PHO	SIT	TIT	UPS	XIS	
NOY	OFF	OOP	OUT	PHS	SIX	**TO**	**UR**	**XU**	
NU	OFT	OOR	**OW**	**PI**	**SO**	TOC	BUR	**YE**	
GNU	**OH**	OOS	BOW	PIA	DSO	TOD	CUR	AYE	
NUB	BOH	**OP**	COW	PIC	ISO	TOE	FUR	BYE	
NUN	DOH	BOP	DOW	PIE	SOB	TOG	GUR	DYE	
NUR	FOH	COP	HOW	PIG	SOC	TOM	LUR	EYE	
NUS	HOH	DOP	JOW	PIN	SOD	TON	NUR	HYE	
NUT	NOH	FOP	KOW	PIP	SOG	TOO	OUR	KYE	

3-LETTER WORD HOOKS: including all root words

AAS	**AGE**	FAIR	GALL	VANE	ARDS	VARY	NAVE	**BAND**	**ABID**
BAAS	CAGE	GAIR	HALL	WANE	**ARE**	WARY	PAVE	BANE	BIDE
MAAS	GAGE	HAIR	MALL	ANES	BARE	ARYL	RAVE	BANG	BIDS
ABA	MAGE	LAIR	PALL	ANEW	CARE	**ASH**	SAVE	BANI	**BIG**
BABA	PAGE	MAIR	TALL	**ANI**	DARE	BASH	WAVE	BANK	BIGA
CABA	RAGE	PAIR	WALL	BANI	FARE	CASH	AVER	BANS	BIGG
ABAC	SAGE	SAIR	ALLS	MANI	GARE	DASH	AVES	BANT	BIGS
ABAS	WAGE	VAIR	ALLY	RANI	HARE	FASH	**AWA**	**BAP**	**BIN**
ABB	AGED	AIRN	**ALP**	ANIL	LARE	GASH	PAWA	BAPS	BIND
ABBA	AGEE	AIRS	CALP	ANIS	MARE	HASH	TAWA	BAPU	BINE
ABBE	AGEN	AIRT	PALP	**ANN**	NARE	LASH	AWAY	**BAR**	BING
ABBS	AGES	AIRY	SALP	CANN	PARE	MASH	**AWE**	BARB	BINK
ABY	**AGO**	**AIS**	ALPS	JANN	RARE	PASH	WAWE	BARD	BINS
BABY	DAGO	DAIS	**ALS**	ANNA	TARE	RASH	AWED	BARE	BINT
GABY	KAGO	KAIS	DALS	ANNO	VARE	SASH	AWES	BARF	**BIO**
ABYE	SAGO	PAIS	GALS	ANNS	WARE	TASH	**AWL**	BARK	BIOG
ACE	AGOG	RAIS	MALS	**ANT**	YARE	WASH	BAWL	BARM	BIOS
DACE	AGON	SAIS	PALS	BANT	AREA	ASHY	BAWN	BARN	**BIS**
FACE	**AHA**	TAIS	SALS	CANT	ARED	**ASK**	DAWN	BARP	IBIS
LACE	TAHA	**AIT**	ALSO	DANT	AREG	BASK	FAWN	BARS	OBIS
MACE	**AHS**	BAIT	**ALT**	GANT	ARES	CASK	LAWN	**BAS**	BISE
PACE	DAHS	GAIT	DALT	KANT	ARET	HASK	PAWN	ABAS	BISH
RACE	FAHS	RAIT	HALT	LANT	AREW	MASK	RAWN	OBAS	BISK
TACE	LAHS	TAIT	MALT	PANT	**ARK**	TASK	SAWN	BASE	**BIT**
ACED	PAHS	WAIT	SALT	RANT	BARK	ASKS	YAWN	BASH	OBIT
ACER	RAHS	AITS	ALTO	SANT	CARK	**ASP**	AWNS	BASK	BITE
ACES	YAHS	AITU	ALTS	VANT	DARK	GASP	AWNY	BASS	BITO
ACH	**AIA**	**AKE**	**AMI**	WANT	HARK	HASP	**AXE**	BAST	BITS
BACH	AIAS	BAKE	KAMI	ANTA	JARK	JASP	AXED	**BAT**	BITT
EACH	**AID**	CAKE	RAMI	ANTE	KARK	RASP	AXEL	BATE	**BIZ**
NACH	GAID	FAKE	AMID	ANTI	LARK	WASP	AXES	BATH	**BOA**
RACH	KAID	HAKE	AMIE	ANTS	MARK	ASPS	**AYE**	BATS	BOAK
TACH	LAID	JAKE	AMIR	**ANY**	NARK	**ASS**	BAYE	BATT	BOAR
ACHE	MAID	LAKE	AMIS	CANY	PARK	BASS	AYES	**BAY**	BOAS
ACHY	PAID	MAKE	**AMP**	MANY	SARK	JASS	**AYS**	BAYE	BOAT
ACT	RAID	RAKE	CAMP	WANY	WARK	LASS	BAYS	BAYS	**BOB**
FACT	SAID	SAKE	DAMP	ZANY	ARKS	MASS	CAYS	BAYT	BOBA
PACT	WAID	TAKE	GAMP	**APE**	**ARM**	PASS	DAYS	**BED**	BOBS
TACT	AIDE	WAKE	LAMP	CAPE	BARM	SASS	FAYS	ABED	**BOD**
ACTA	AIDS	AKED	RAMP	GAPE	FARM	TASS	GAYS	BEDE	BODE
ACTS	**AIL**	AKEE	SAMP	JAPE	HARM	**ATE**	HAYS	BEDS	BODS
ADD	BAIL	AKES	TAMP	NAPE	MARM	BATE	JAYS	**BEE**	BODY
WADD	FAIL	**ALA**	VAMP	PAPE	WARM	CATE	KAYS	BEEF	**BOG**
ADDS	HAIL	ALAE	AMPS	RAPE	ARMS	DATE	LAYS	BEEN	BOGS
ADO	JAIL	ALAP	**ANA**	TAPE	ARMY	FATE	MAYS	BEEP	BOGY
DADO	KAIL	ALAR	KANA	APED	**ARS**	GATE	NAYS	BEER	**BOH**
FADO	MAIL	ALAS	LANA	APES	BARS	HATE	PAYS	BEES	BOHS
ADOS	NAIL	ALAY	MANA	APEX	CARS	LATE	RAYS	BEET	**BOK**
ADS	PAIL	**ALB**	NANA	**APT**	EARS	MATE	SAYS	**BEG**	BOKE
BADS	RAIL	ALBE	RANA	RAPT	GARS	PATE	TAYS	BEGO	BOKO
CADS	SAIL	ALBS	TANA	APTS	JARS	RATE	WAYS	BEGS	BOKS
DADS	TAIL	**ALE**	ANAL	**ARB**	MARS	SATE	**AYU**	**BEL**	**BON**
FADS	VAIL	BALE	ANAN	BARB	OARS	TATE	AYUS	BELL	EBON
HADS	WAIL	DALE	ANAS	CARB	PARS	WATE	**BAA**	BELS	BONA
LADS	AILS	EALE	**AND**	GARB	SARS	YATE	BAAS	BELT	BOND
MADS	**AIM**	GALE	BAND	ARBA	TARS	**AUF**	**BAC**	**BEN**	BONE
PADS	KAIM	HALE	FAND	ARBS	WARS	CAUF	ABAC	BEND	BONG
RADS	MAIM	KALE	HAND	**ARC**	ARSE	LAUF	BACH	BENE	BONK
TADS	SAIM	MALE	LAND	MARC	**ART**	AUFS	BACK	BENI	BONY
WADS	AIMS	PALE	MAND	NARC	CART	**AUK**	BACS	BENJ	**BOO**
ADZ	**AIN**	RALE	PAND	ARCH	DART	BAUK	**BAD**	BENS	BOOB
ADZE	CAIN	SALE	RAND	ARCO	FART	CAUK	BADE	BENT	BOOH
AFT	FAIN	TALE	SAND	ARCS	GART	WAUK	BADS	**BET**	BOOK
BAFT	GAIN	VALE	WAND	**ARD**	HART	AUKS	**BAG**	ABET	BOOL
DAFT	HAIN	WALE	ANDS	BARD	KART	**AVA**	BAGS	BETA	BOOM
HAFT	KAIN	YALE	**ANE**	CARD	MART	KAVA	**BAH**	BETE	BOON
RAFT	LAIN	ALEE	BANE	EARD	PART	LAVA	BAHT	BETH	BOOR
WAFT	MAIN	ALES	CANE	FARD	TART	TAVA	**BAM**	BETS	BOOS
AGA	NAIN	ALEW	FANE	HARD	WART	AVAL	BAMS	**BEY**	BOOT
GAGA	PAIN	**ALL**	GANE	LARD	ARTS	AVAS	**BAN**	OBEY	**BOP**
NAGA	RAIN	BALL	JANE	MARD	ARTY	**AVE**	BANC	BEYS	BOPS
RAGA	SAIN	CALL	LANE	NARD	**ARY**	CAVE		**BEZ**	**BOR**
SAGA	VAIN	FALL	MANE	PARD	MARY	FAVE		**BIB**	BORA
AGAR	WAIN		PANE	SARD	NARY	GAVE		BIBS	BORD
AGAS	AINE		SANE	WARD	OARY	HAVE		**BID**	BORE
	AIR		TANE	YARD		LAVE			BORN

BORS	**BYE**	CHEW	COSY	**DALT**	**DINO**	DOWP	**EAST**	LEFT	**CELT**
BORT	ABYE	CHEZ	**COT**	**DAM**	DINS	DOWS	EASY	REFT	DELT
BOS	BYES	**CHI**	SCOT	DAME	DINT	DOWT	**EAT**	WEFT	FELT
OBOS	**BYS**	CHIC	COTE	DAMN	**DIP**	**DRY**	BEAT	EFTS	GELT
BOSH	**CAB**	CHID	COTH	DAMP	DIPS	**DSO**	FEAT	**EGG**	KELT
BOSK	CABA	CHIK	COTS	DAMS	ADRY	ODSO	GEAT	TEGG	MELT
BOSS	CABS	CHIN	COTT	**DAN**	**DIT**	DSOS	HEAT	YEGG	PELT
BOT	**CAD**	CHIP	**COW**	DANG	ADIT	**DUB**	JEAT	EGGS	TELT
BOTH	ECAD	CHIS	SCOW	DANK	EDIT	DUBS	LEAT	EGGY	WELT
BOTS	SCAD	CHIT	COWL	DANS	**DITA**	**DUD**	MEAT	**EGO**	YELT
BOTT	CADE	CHIV	COWP	DANT	DITE	DUDE	NEAT	BEGO	ELTS
BOW	CADI	CHIZ	COWS	**DAP**	DITS	DUDS	PEAT	REGO	**EME**
BOWL	CADS	**CID**	**COX**	DAPS	DITT	**DUE**	SEAT	SEGO	DEME
BOWR	**CAM**	CIDE	COXA	**DAS**	**DIV**	DUED	TEAT	EGOS	FEME
BOWS	SCAM	CIDS	COXY	DASH	DIVA	DUEL	**EATH**	**EHS**	HEME
BOX	CAME	**CIG**	**COY**	**DAW**	DIVI	DUES	EATS	REHS	LEME
BOXY	CAMP	CIGS	COZ	ADAW	DIVS	DUET	**EAU**	**EIK**	MEME
BOY	CAMS	**CIT**	COZE	DAWD	**DOB**	**DUG**	BEAU	REIK	SEME
BOYG	**CAN**	CITE	COZY	DAWK	DOBS	DUGS	EAUS	SEIK	TEME
BOYO	SCAN	CITO	**CRU**	DAWN	**DOC**	**DUN**	EAUX	EIKS	EMES
BOYS	CANE	CITS	ECRU	DAWS	DOCK	DUNE	**EBB**	**EKE**	EMEU
BRA	CANG	CITY	CRUD	DAWT	DOCS	DUNG	EBBS	LEKE	**EMS**
BRAD	CANN	**CLY**	CRUE	**DAY**	**DOD**	DUNK	**ECH**	PEKE	GEMS
BRAE	CANS	**COB**	CRUS	DAYS	DODO	DUNS	EECH	REKE	HEMS
BRAG	CANT	COBB	CRUX	**DEB**	DODS	DUNT	HECH	EKED	REMS
BRAN	CANY	COBS	**CRY**	DEBS	**DOE**	**DUO**	LECH	EKES	TEMS
BRAS	**CAP**	**COD**	SCRY	DEBT	DOEK	DUOS	PECH	**ELD**	WEMS
BRAT	CAPA	CODA	**CUB**	**DEE**	DOEN	**DUP**	TECH	GELD	**EMU**
BRAW	CAPE	CODE	CUBE	IDEE	DOER	DUPE	YECH	HELD	EMUS
BRAY	CAPI	CODS	CUBS	DEED	DOES	DUPS	**ECHE**	MELD	**END**
BRO	CAPO	**COG**	**CUD**	DEEK	**DOG**	**DUX**	ECHO	SELD	BEND
BROD	CAPS	COGS	SCUD	DEEM	DOGE	**DYE**	ECHT	TELD	FEND
BROG	**CAR**	**COL**	CUDS	DEEN	DOGS	DYED	**ECU**	VELD	HEND
BROO	SCAR	COLA	**CUE**	DEEP	DOGY	DYER	ECUS	WELD	LEND
BROS	CARB	COLD	CUED	DEER	**DOH**	DYES	**EDH**	YELD	MEND
BROW	CARD	COLE	CUES	DEES	DOHS	**DZO**	EDHS	ELDS	PEND
BUB	CARE	COLL	**CUM**	DEEV	**DON**	DZOS	**EEK**	**ELF**	REND
BUBA	CARK	COLS	SCUM	**DEF**	DONA	**EAN**	DEEK	DELF	SEND
BUBO	CARL	COLT	**CUP**	DEFT	DONE	BEAN	GEEK	PELF	TEND
BUBS	CARP	**CON**	SCUP	DEFY	DONG	DEAN	KEEK	SELF	VEND
BUD	CARR	ICON	CUPS	**DEI**	DONS	GEAN	LEEK	ELFS	WEND
BUDO	CARS	COND	**CUR**	DEID	**DOP**	JEAN	MEEK	**ELK**	ENDS
BUDS	CART	CONE	SCUR	DEIL	DOPA	LEAN	PEEK	WELK	**ENE**
BUG	**CAT**	CONF	CURB	**DEL**	DOPE	MEAN	REEK	YELK	BENE
BUGS	SCAT	CONK	CURD	DELE	DOPS	PEAN	SEEK	ELKS	DENE
BUM	CATE	CONN	CURE	DELF	DOPY	REAN	WEEK	**ELL**	GENE
BUMF	CATS	CONS	CURL	DELI	**DOR**	SEAN	**EEL**	BELL	MENE
BUMP	**CAW**	CONY	CURN	DELL	DORK	WEAN	FEEL	CELL	NENE
BUMS	SCAW	**COO**	CURR	DELS	DORP	YEAN	HEEL	DELL	PENE
BUN	CAWK	COOF	CURS	DELT	DORR	**EAR**	JEEL	FELL	TENE
BUNA	CAWS	COOK	CURT	**DEN**	DORS	BEAR	KEEL	HELL	ENES
BUND	**CAY**	COOL	**CUT**	DENE	DORT	DEAR	PEEL	JELL	ENEW
BUNG	CAYS	COOM	SCUT	DENS	DORY	FEAR	REEL	KELL	**ENG**
BUNK	**CEE**	COON	CUTE	DENT	**DOS**	GEAR	SEEL	MELL	LENG
BUNS	CEES	COOP	CUTS	DENY	ADOS	HEAR	TEEL	PELL	MENG
BUNT	**CEL**	COOS	**CUZ**	**DEW**	UDOS	LEAR	WEEL	SELL	ENGS
BUR	CELL	COOT	**CWM**	DEWS	DOSE	NEAR	EELS	TELL	**ENS**
BURD	CELS	**COP**	CWMS	DEWY	DOSH	PEAR	EELY	VELL	BENS
BURG	CELT	SCOP	**DAB**	**DEY**	DOSS	REAR	**EEN**	WELL	CENS
BURK	**CEP**	COPE	DABS	DEYS	DOST	SEAR	BEEN	YELL	DENS
BURL	CEPS	COPS	**DAD**	**DIB**	**DOT**	TEAR	DEEN	ELLS	FENS
BURN	**CHA**	COPY	DADO	DIBS	DOTE	WEAR	KEEN	**ELM**	GENS
BURP	CHAD	**COR**	DADS	**DID**	DOTH	YEAR	PEEN	HELM	HENS
BURR	CHAI	CORD	**DAE**	DIDO	DOTS	EARD	REEN	YELM	KENS
BURS	CHAL	CORE	DAES	**DIE**	DOTY	EARL	SEEN	ELMY	LENS
BURY	CHAM	CORF	**DAG**	DIEB	**DOW**	EARN	TEEN	ELMS	PENS
BUS	CHAP	CORK	DAGO	DIED	DOWD	EARS	WEEN	**ELS**	RENS
BUSH	CHAR	CORM	DAGS	DIES	DOWF	**EAS**	**EFF**	BELS	SENS
BUSK	CHAS	CORN	**DAH**	DIET	DOWL	CEAS	JEFF	CELS	TENS
BUSS	CHAT	CORS	DAHL	**DIG**	DOWN	KEAS	TEFF	DELS	WENS
BUST	CHAW	CORY	DAHS	DIGS		LEAS	EFFS	EELS	YENS
BUSY	CHAY	**COS**	**DAK**	**DIM**		PEAS	**EFT**	GELS	**EON**
BUT	**CHE**	COSE	DAKS	DIME		SEAS	DEFT	MELS	AEON
ABUT	ACHE	COSH	**DAL**	DIMS		TEAS	HEFT	SELS	NEON
BUTE	ECHE	COSS	ODAL	**DIN**		YEAS		TELS	PEON
BUTS	OCHE	COST	UDAL	DINE		ZEAS		ZELS	EONS
BUTT	**CHEF**		DALE	DING		EASE		**ELSE**	**ERA**
BUY	CHER		DALI	DINK				**ELT**	SERA
BUYS			DALS					BELT	ERAS

ERE	WETA	**FEN**	FORD	GANG	GINN	GUST	HEME	HISN	WHOW
BERE	ZETA	FEND	FORE	GANT	GINS	**GUT**	HEMP	HISS	HOWE
CERE	ETAS	FENI	FORK	**GAP**	**GIO**	GUTS	HEMS	HIST	HOWF
DERE	ETAT	FENS	FORM	GAPE	AGIO	**GUV**	**HEN**	**HIT**	HOWK
FERE	**ETH**	FENT	FORT	GAPO	GIOS	GUVS	THEN	CHIT	HOWL
GERE	BETH	**FET**	**FOU**	GAPS	**GIP**	**GUY**	WHEN	SHIT	HOWS
HERE	ETHE	FETA	FOUD	**GAR**	GIPS	GUYS	HEND	WHIT	**HOX**
LERE	ETHS	FETE	FOUL	AGAR	**GIS**	**GYM**	HENS	HITS	**HOY**
MERE	**EUK**	FETS	FOUR	GARB	EGIS	GYMP	HENT	**HOA**	AHOY
PERE	NEUK	FETT	FOUS	GARE	GISM	GYMS	**HEP**	WHOA	HOYA
SERE	YEUK	**FEU**	**FOX**	GARS	GIST	**GYP**	HEPS	HOAR	HOYS
WERE	EUKS	FEUD	FOXY	GART	**GIT**	GYPS	HEPT	HOAS	**HUB**
ERED	**EVE**	FEUS	**FOY**	**GAS**	GITE	**HAD**	**HER**	HOAX	CHUB
ERES	LEVE	**FEW**	FOYS	AGAS	GITS	CHAD	CHER	**HOB**	HUBS
ERF	MEVE	**FEY**	**FRA**	GASH	**GOA**	SHAD	HERB	HOBO	**HUE**
KERF	NEVE	FEYS	FRAB	GASP	GOAD	HADE	HERD	HOBS	HUED
SERF	YEVE	**FEZ**	FRAE	GAST	GOAF	HADJ	HERE	**HOC**	HUER
TERF	EVEN	**FIB**	FRAG	**GAT**	GOAL	HADS	HERL	CHOC	HUES
ERG	EVER	FIBS	FRAP	GATE	GOAS	**HAE**	HERM	HOCK	**HUG**
BERG	EVES	**FID**	FRAS	GATH	GOAT	THAE	HERN	**HOD**	CHUG
ERGO	EVET	FIDS	FRAU	GATS	**GOB**	HAEM	HERO	SHOD	THUG
ERGS	**EWE**	**FIE**	FRAY	**GAU**	GOBO	HAET	HERS	HODS	HUGE
ERK	EWER	FIEF	**FRO**	GAUD	GOBS	**HAG**	HERY	**HOE**	HUGS
BERK	EWES	FIER	AFRO	GAUM	GOBY	HAGG	**HES**	SHOE	HUGY
JERK	**EWK**	**FIG**	FROG	GAUN	**GOD**	HAGS	SHES	HOED	**HUH**
MERK	EWKS	FIGO	FROM	GAUP	GODS	**HAH**	HESP	HOER	CHUM
NERK	**EWT**	FIGS	FROW	GAUR	**GOE**	SHAH	HEST	HOES	**HUI**
PERK	NEWT	**FIL**	**FRY**	GAUS	YGOE	**HAJ**	**HET**	**HOG**	HUIA
SERK	EWTS	FILE	**FUB**	**GAY**	GOEL	HAJI	WHET	SHOG	HUIS
YERK	**EYE**	FILL	FUBS	GAYS	GOER	HAJJ	HETE	HOGG	**HUM**
ERKS	EYED	FILO	**FUD**	**GED**	GOES	**HAM**	HETS	HOGH	HUMA
ERN	EYES	FILS	FUDS	GEDS	GOEY	CHAM	**HEW**	HOGS	HUMF
DERN	**FAB**	**FIN**	**FUG**	**GEE**	**GON**	SHAM	CHEW	**HOH**	HUMP
FERN	**FAD**	FIND	FUGS	AGEE	AGON	WHAM	PHEW	PHOH	HUMS
HERN	FADE	FINE	**FUM**	GEED	GONE	HAME	SHEW	HOHS	**HUP**
KERN	FADO	FINI	FUME	GEEK	GONG	HAMS	THEW	**HOI**	HUPS
PERN	FADS	FINK	FUMS	GEEP	GONK	**HAN**	WHEW	HOIK	**HUT**
TERN	FADY	FINO	FUMY	GEES	GONS	KHAN	HEWN	**HON**	CHUT
ERNE	**FAG**	FINS	**FUN**	**GEL**	**GOO**	SHAN	HEWS	CHON	PHUT
ERNS	FAGS	**FIR**	FUND	GELD	GOOD	THAN	**HEX**	PHON	SHUT
ERR	**FAH**	FIRE	FUNG	GELS	GOOF	HAND	**HEY**	THON	HUTS
SERR	FAHS	FIRK	FUNK	GELT	GOOK	HANG	THEY	HOND	**HYE**
ERRS	**FAN**	FIRM	FUNS	**GEM**	GOOL	HANK	WHEY	HONE	HYED
ERS	FAND	FIRN	**FUR**	GEMS	GOON	**HAP**	HEYS	HONG	HYEN
HERS	FANE	FIRS	FURL	**GEN**	GOOP	CHAP	**HIC**	HONK	HYES
VERS	FANG	**FIT**	FURR	AGEN	GOOR	WHAP	CHIC	HONS	**HYP**
ERST	FANK	FITS	FURS	GENA	GOOS	HAPS	HICK	**HOO**	HYPE
ESS	FANS	FITT	FURY	GENE	**GOS**	**HAS**	**HID**	SHOO	HYPO
CESS	**FAP**	**FIX**	**GAB**	GENS	EGOS	CHAS	CHID	HOOD	HYPS
FESS	**FAR**	**FIZ**	GABS	GENT	GOSH	HASH	WHID	HOOK	**ICE**
JESS	FARD	FIZZ	GABY	GENU	**GOT**	HASK	HIDE	HOON	BICE
LESS	FARE	**FLU**	**GAD**	**GEO**	**GOV**	HASP	**HIE**	HOOP	DICE
MESS	FARL	FLUB	EGAD	GEOS	GOVS	HAST	HIED	HOOT	LICE
NESS	FARM	FLUE	IGAD	**GET**	**GOY**	**HAT**	HIES	**HOS**	MICE
SESS	FARO	FLUS	GADE	GETA	GOYS	CHAT	**HIM**	MHOS	NICE
ESSE	FARS	FLUX	GADI	GETS	**GUB**	GHAT	SHIM	OHOS	PICE
EST	FART	**FLY**	GADS	**GEY**	GUBS	KHAT	WHIM	PHOS	RICE
BEST	**FAS**	**FOB**	**GAE**	**GHI**	**GUE**	PHAT	**HIN**	RHOS	SICE
FEST	FASH	FOBS	GAED	GHIS	AGUE	SHAT	CHIN	ZHOS	TICE
GEST	FAST	**FOE**	GAES	**GIB**	GUES	THAT	SHIN	HOSE	VICE
HEST	**FAT**	FOEN	**GAG**	GIBE	**GUM**	WHAT	WHIN	HOSS	WICE
JEST	FATE	FOES	GAGA	GIBS	GUMP	HATE	HIND	HOST	ICED
KEST	FATS	**FOG**	GAGE	**GID**	GUMS	HATH	HING	**HOT**	ICER
LEST	**FAW**	FOGS	GAGS	GIDS	**GUN**	HATS	HINS	PHOT	ICES
NEST	FAWN	FOGY	**GAL**	**GIE**	GUNK	**HAW**	HINT	WHOT	**ICH**
PEST	FAWS	**FOH**	EGAL	GIED	GUNS	CHAW	**HIP**	HOTE	DICH
REST	**FAX**	FOHN	GALA	GIEN	**GUP**	SHAW	CHIP	HOTS	LICH
TEST	**FAY**	FOHS	GALE	GIES	GUPS	THAW	SHIP	**HOW**	RICH
VEST	FAYS	**FON**	GALL	**GIF**	**GUR**	HAWK	WHIP	CHOW	SICH
WEST	**FED**	FOND	GALS	GIFT	GURL	HAWM	HIPS	DHOW	TICH
YEST	FEDS	FONE	**GAM**	**GIG**	GURN	HAWS	HIPT	SHOW	WICH
ZEST	**FEE**	FONS	OGAM	GIGA	GURS	**HAY**	**HIS**		**ICY**
ESTS	FEED	FONT	GAMB	GIGS	GURU	CHAY	CHIS		RICY
ETA	FEEL	**FOP**	GAME	**GIN**	**GUS**	SHAY	GHIS		**IDE**
BETA	FEER	FOPS	GAMP	AGIN	GUSH	HAYS	HISH		AIDE
FETA	FEES	**FOR**	GAMS	GING		**HEM**			BIDE
GETA	FEET	FORA	GAMY	GINK		AHEM			CIDE
KETA		FORB	**GAN**			THEM			HIDE
SETA			GANE						NIDE

RIDE	PINK	BITS	JUG	KINK	SLAP	GLEG	LIPS	SLOW	MANI
SIDE	RINK	CITS	JUGA	KINO	LAPS	LEGS	LIS	LOWE	MANO
TIDE	SINK	DITS	JUGS	KINS	LAR	LEI	LISK	LOWN	MANS
VIDE	TINK	FITS	JUS	KIP	ALAR	GLEI	LISP	LOWS	MANY
WIDE	WINK	GITS	GJUS	SKIP	LARD	VLEI	LIT	LOWT	MAP
IDEA	INKS	HITS	JUST	KIPE	LARE	LEIR	ALIT	LOX	MAPS
IDEE	INKY	KITS	JUT	KIPP	LARK	LEIS	FLIT	LOY	MAR
IDEM	INN	NITS	JUTE	KIPS	LARN	LEK	GLIT	CLOY	MARA
IDES	GINN	PITS	JUTS	KIR	LAS	LEKE	SLIT	PLOY	MARC
IDS	JINN	RITS	KAE	KIRK	ALAS	LEKS	LITE	LOYS	MARD
AIDS	LINN	SITS	KAED	KIRN	LASE	LEP	LITH	LUD	MARE
BIDS	WINN	TITS	KAES	KIRS	LASH	LEPS	LOB	LUDO	MARG
CIDS	INNS	WITS	KAI	KIT	LASS	LES	BLOB	LUDS	MARK
FIDS	INS	ZITS	KAID	SKIT	LAST	ALES	GLOB	LUG	MARL
GIDS	BINS	IVY	KAIE	KITE	LAT	ULES	SLOB	LUGE	MARM
KIDS	DINS	JAB	KAIF	KITH	BLAT	LESS	LOBI	LUGS	MARS
LIDS	FINS	JABS	KAIL	KITS	FLAT	LEST	LOBE	LUM	MART
MIDS	GINS	JAG	KAIM	KOA	PLAT	LET	LOBO	ALUM	MARY
NIDS	HINS	JAGS	KAIN	KOAN	SLAT	LETS	LOBS	GLUM	MAS
RIDS	KINS	JAK	KAIS	KOAS	LATE	LEU	LOD	PLUM	MASA
TIDS	LINS	JAKE	KAM	KOB	LATH	LEV	ALOD	SLUM	MASE
VIDS	PINS	JAKS	KAMA	KOBS	LATS	LEVA	CLOD	LUMP	MASH
IFF	RINS	JAM	KAME	KOI	LAV	LEVE	PLOD	LUMS	MASK
BIFF	SINS	JAMB	KAMI	KON	LAVA	LEVY	LODE	LUR	MASS
JIFF	TINS	JAMS	KAS	IKON	LAVE	LEW	LODS	BLUR	MAST
MIFF	VINS	JAP	SKAS	KOND	LAVS	ALEW	LOG	LURE	MASU
NIFF	WINS	JAPE	KAT	KONK	LAW	BLEW	CLOG	LURK	MAT
RIFF	YINS	JAPS	IKAT	KONS	CLAW	CLEW	FLOG	LURS	MATE
TIFF	ION	JAR	SKAT	KOP	FLAW	FLEW	SLOG	SLUR	MATH
ZIFF	CION	AJAR	KATA	KOPH	SLAW	SLEW	LOGE	LUV	MATS
IFFY	LION	JARK	KATI	KOPS	LAWK	LEWD	LOGO	LUVS	MATY
IFS	PION	JARL	KATS	KOS	LAWN	LEX	LOGS	LUX	MAW
KIFS	IONS	JARS	KAW	KOSS	LAWS	FLEX	LOGY	LUXE	MAWK
ILK	IOS	JAW	SKAW	KOW	LAX	ILEX	LOO	FLUX	MAWR
BILK	IRE	JAWS	KAWS	KOWS	FLAX	ULEX	LOOF	LUZ	MAWS
MILK	CIRE	JAY	KAY	KYE	LAY	LEY	LOOK	LYE	MAX
SILK	DIRE	JAYS	KAYO	KYU	ALAY	ALEY	LOOM	LYES	MAXI
ILKA	FIRE	JEE	KAYS	KYUS	BLAY	BLEY	LOON	LYM	MAY
ILKS	HIRE	AJEE	OKAY	LAB	CLAY	CLEY	LOOP	LYME	MAYA
ILL	LIRE	JEED	KEA	BLAB	FLAY	FLEY	LOOR	LYMS	MAYS
BILL	MIRE	JEEL	KEAS	FLAB	PLAY	GLEY	LOOS	MAA	MEG
CILL	SIRE	JEER	KEB	SLAB	SLAY	SLEY	LOOT	MAAR	MEGA
DILL	TIRE	JEES	KEBS	LABS	LAYS	LEYS	LOP	MAAS	MEGS
FILL	VIRE	JET	KED	LAC	LEA	LEZ	CLOP	MAC	MEL
GILL	WIRE	JETE	AKED	LACE	FLEA	LEZZ	FLOP	MACE	MELA
HILL	IRES	JETS	EKED	LACK	ILEA	LIB	GLOP	MACK	MELD
JILL	IRK	JEU	KEDS	LACS	PLEA	GLIB	PLOP	MACS	MELL
KILL	BIRK	JEUX	KEF	LACY	LEAD	LIBS	SLOP	MAD	MELS
LILL	DIRK	JEW	KEFS	LAD	LEAF	LID	LOPE	MADE	MELT
MILL	FIRK	JEWS	KEG	BLAD	LEAK	SLID	LOPS	MADS	MEN
NILL	KIRK	JIB	KEGS	CLAD	LEAL	LIDO	LOR	MAE	AMEN
PILL	LIRK	JIBE	SKEG	GLAD	LEAM	LIDS	FLOR	MAG	OMEN
RILL	MIRK	JIBS	KEN	LADE	LEAN	LIE	LORD	MAGE	MEND
SILL	YIRK	JIG	KENO	LADS	LEAP	PLIE	LORE	MAGG	MENE
TILL	IRKS	JIGS	KENS	LADY	LEAR	LIED	LORN	MAGI	MENG
VILL	ISH	JIZ	KENT	LAG	LEAS	LIEF	LORY	MAGS	MENT
WILL	BISH	JIZZ	KEP	BLAG	LEAT	LIEN	LOS	MAK	MENU
YILL	DISH	JOB	SKEP	CLAG	LED	LIER	LOSE	MAKE	MES
ILLS	FISH	JOBE	KEPI	FLAG	BLED	LIES	LOSH	MAKO	EMES
ILLY	HISH	JOBS	KEPS	SLAG	FLED	LIEU	LOSS	MAKS	MESA
IMP	KISH	JOE	KEPT	LAGS	GLED	LIG	LOST	MAL	MESE
GIMP	PISH	JOES	KET	LAH	PLED	LIGS	LOT	MALE	MESH
JIMP	WISH	JOEY	KETA	BLAH	SLED	LIN	BLOT	MALI	MESS
LIMP	ISM	JOG	KETS	LAHS	LEE	BLIN	CLOT	MALL	MET
PIMP	GISM	JOGS	KEX	LAM	ALEE	LIND	PLOT	MALM	METE
SIMP	JISM	JOR	KEY	CLAM	BLEE	LINE	SLOT	MALS	METS
WIMP	ISMS	JORS	KEYS	FLAM	FLEE	LING	LOTA	MALT	MEU
IMPI	ISO	JOT	KID	GLAM	GLEE	LINK	LOTE	MAM	EMEU
IMPS	MISO	JOTA	SKID	SLAM	SLEE	LINN	LOTH	IMAM	MEUS
INK	ISOS	JOTS	KIDS	LAMA	LEED	LINO	LOTO	MAMA	MEW
BINK	ITA	JOW	KIF	LAMB	LEEK	LINS	LOTS	MAMS	MEWL
DINK	DITA	JOWL	KIFS	LAME	LEEP	LINT	LOW	MAN	MEWS
FINK	PITA	JOWS	KIN	LAMP	LEER	LINY	ALOW	MANA	SMEW
GINK	VITA	JOY	AKIN	LAMS	LEES	LIP	BLOW	MAND	MHO
JINK	ITAS	JOYS	SKIN	LAP	LEET	BLIP	CLOW	MANE	MHOS
KINK	ITS	JUD	KINA	CLAP	LEG	CLIP	FLOW	MANG	MID
LINK	AITS	JUDO	KIND	FLAP	CLEG	FLIP	GLOW		AMID
MINK		JUDS	KINE	PLAP	FLEG	SLIP	PLOW		MIDI
OINK		JUDY	KING						

HOOKS BY ROOT WORD: 3-Letter Words

MIDS	MORS	NEDS	NORI	**OBI**	VOES	HOLM	OONT	**ORE**	DOUT
MIL	MORT	**NEE**	NORK	LOBI	WOES	OLMS	**OOP**	BORE	GOUT
MILD	**MOT**	KNEE	NORM	OBIA	**OFF**	**OMS**	COOP	CORE	HOUT
MILE	MOTE	SNEE	**NOS**	OBIS	BOFF	COMS	GOOP	FORE	LOUT
MILK	MOTH	NEED	NOSE	OBIT	COFF	MOMS	HOOP	GORE	NOUT
MILL	MOTS	NEEM	NOSH	**OBO**	DOFF	NOMS	LOOP	HORE	POUT
MILO	MOTT	NEEP	NOSY	GOBO	GOFF	POMS	MOOP	KORE	ROUT
MILS	MOTU	**NEF**	**NOT**	HOBO	KOFF	TOMS	NOOP	LORE	SOUT
MILT	**MOU**	NEFS	KNOT	LOBO	TOFF	**ONE**	POOP	MORE	TOUT
MIM	MOUE	**NEK**	SNOT	ZOBO	OFFS	BONE	ROOP	PORE	OUTS
MIME	MOUP	NEKS	NOTA	OBOE	**OFT**	CONE	SOOP	RORE	**OVA**
MIR	MOUS	**NEP**	NOTE	OBOL	COFT	DONE	YOOP	SORE	NOVA
AMIR	**MOW**	NEPS	NOTT	OBOS	LOFT	FONE	OOPS	TORE	OVAL
EMIR	MOWA	**NET**	**NOW**	**OBS**	SOFT	GONE	**OOR**	WORE	**OWE**
SMIR	MOWN	NETE	ANOW	BOBS	TOFT	HONE	BOOR	YORE	HOWE
MIRE	MOWS	NETS	ENOW	COBS	**OHM**	LONE	DOOR	ORES	LOWE
MIRI	**MOY**	NETT	KNOW	DOBS	OHMS	NONE	GOOR	**ORF**	YOWE
MIRK	MOYA	**NEW**	SNOW	FOBS	**OHO**	PONE	LOOR	CORF	OWED
MIRS	MOYL	ANEW	NOWL	GOBS	COHO	RONE	MOOR	ORFE	OWER
MIRV	MOYS	ENEW	NOWN	HOBS	SOHO	SONE	POOR	ORFS	OWES
MIRY	**MOZ**	KNEW	NOWS	JOBS	TOHO	TONE	**OOS**	**ORS**	**OWL**
MIS	MOZE	NEWS	NOWT	KOBS	OHOS	ZONE	BOOS	BORS	BOWL
AMIS	MOZZ	NEWT	NOWY	LOBS	**OIK**	ONER	COOS	CORS	COWL
MISE	**MUD**	**NIB**	**NOX**	MOBS	HOIK	ONES	GOOS	DORS	DOWL
MISO	MUDS	SNIB	**NOY**	NOBS	OIKS	**ONS**	LOOS	HORS	FOWL
MISS	**MUG**	**NID**	NOYS	ROBS	**OIL**	CONS	MOOS	JORS	GOWL
MIST	MUGS	NIDE	**NTH**	SOBS	BOIL	DONS	POOS	MORS	HOWL
MIX	**MUM**	NIDI	**NUB**	YOBS	COIL	EONS	ROOS	TORS	JOWL
MIXT	MUMM	NIDS	KNUB	**OCA**	FOIL	FONS	WOOS	VORS	NOWL
MIXY	MUMP	**NIE**	SNUB	COCA	MOIL	GONS	ZOOS	**ORT**	SOWL
MIZ	MUMS	NIED	NUBS	SOCA	NOIL	HONS	OOSE	BORT	YOWL
MIZZ	**MUN**	NIEF	**NUN**	OCAS	ROIL	IONS	OOSY	DORT	OWLS
MNA	MUNT	NIES	NUNS	**OCH**	SOIL	KONS	**OPE**	FORT	OWLY
MNAS	**MUS**	**NIL**	**NUR**	COCH	TOIL	OONS	COPE	MORT	**OWN**
MOA	EMUS	ANIL	KNUR	LOCH	OILS	PONS	DOPE	PORT	DOWN
MOAN	MUSE	NILL	NURD	MOCH	OILY	SONS	HOPE	RORT	GOWN
MOAS	MUSH	NILS	NURL	ROCH	**OKE**	TONS	LOPE	SORT	LOWN
MOAT	MUSK	**NIM**	NURR	OCHE	BOKE	WONS	MOPE	TORT	MOWN
MOB	MUSO	NIMB	NURS	**ODA**	COKE	ONST	NOPE	WORT	NOWN
MOBS	MUSS	NIMS	**NUS**	CODA	HOKE	**OOF**	POPE	ORTS	POWN
MOD	MUST	**NIP**	GNUS	SODA	JOKE	COOF	ROPE	**OUD**	SOWN
MODE	**MUX**	SNIP	ONUS	ODAL	LOKE	GOOF	TOPE	FOUD	TOWN
MODI	**NAB**	**NIS**	KNUT	ODAS	MOKE	HOOF	OPED	LOUD	OWNS
MODS	SNAB	ANIS	NUTS	**ODD**	POKE	LOOF	OPEN	OUDS	**OWT**
MOE	NABK	UNIS	**NYE**	ODDS	ROKE	POOF	OPES	**OUK**	DOWT
MOES	NABS	NISI	SNYE	**ODE**	SOKE	ROOF	**OPS**	BOUK	LOWT
MOG	**NAE**	**NIT**	NYED	BODE	TOKE	WOOF	BOPS	GOUK	NOWT
SMOG	**NAG**	KNIT	NYES	CODE	WOKE	YOOF	COPS	JOUK	ROWT
MOGS	KNAG	UNIT	**NYS**	LODE	YOKE	OOFS	DOPS	POUK	TOWT
MOI	SNAG	NITE	**OAF**	MODE	OKES	**OOH**	FOPS	SOUK	OWTS
MOIL	NAGA	NITS	GOAF	NODE	**OLD**	BOOH	HOPS	TOUK	**OYE**
MOIT	NAGS	**NIX**	LOAF	RODE	BOLD	POOH	KOPS	YOUK	OYER
MOM	**NAM**	NIXY	OAFS	YODE	COLD	OOHS	LOPS	ZOUK	OYES
MOME	NAME	**NOB**	**OAK**	ODEA	FOLD	**OOM**	MOPS	OUKS	OYEZ
MOMS	NAMS	KNOB	BOAK	ODES	GOLD	BOOM	OOPS	**OUP**	**OYS**
MON	**NAN**	SNOB	SOAK	**ODS**	HOLD	COOM	POPS	COUP	BOYS
MONA	ANAN	NOBS	OAKS	BODS	MOLD	DOOM	SOPS	DOUP	FOYS
MONG	NANA	**NOD**	OAKY	CODS	SOLD	LOOM	TOPS	LOUP	GOYS
MONK	NANS	SNOD	**OAR**	DODS	TOLD	ROOM	WOPS	MOUP	HOYS
MONO	**NAP**	NODE	BOAR	GODS	WOLD	SOOM	**OPT**	NOUP	JOYS
MONY	KNAP	NODI	HOAR	HODS	YOLD	TOOM	OPTS	ROUP	LOYS
MOO	SNAP	NODS	ROAR	LODS	OLDS	ZOOM	**ORB**	SOUP	MOYS
MOOD	NAPA	**NOG**	SOAR	MODS	OLDY	OOMS	FORB	OUPH	NOYS
MOOI	NAPE	SNOG	VOAR	NODS	**OLE**	**OON**	SORB	OUPS	SOYS
MOOK	NAPS	NOGG	**OAT**	PODS	BOLE	BOON	ORBS	**OUR**	TOYS
MOOL	**NAS**	NOGS	BOAT	RODS	COLE	COON	ORBY	COUR	**PAD**
MOON	ANAS	**NOH**	COAT	SODS	DOLE	GOON	**ORC**	DOUR	PADS
MOOP	MNAS	**NOM**	DOAT	TODS	GOLE	HOON	TORC	FOUR	**PAH**
MOOR	**NAT**	NOMA	GOAT	ODSO	HOLE	LOON	ORCA	HOUR	OPAH
MOOS	NATS	NOME	MOAT	**OES**	JOLE	MOON	ORCS	JOUR	PAHS
MOOT	**NAY**	NOMS	OATH	DOES	MOLE	NOON	**ORD**	LOUR	**PAL**
MOP	NAYS	**NON**	OATS	FOES	NOLE	POON	BORD	POUR	OPAL
MOPE	**NEB**	ANON	**OBA**	GOES	POLE	ROON	CORD	SOUR	PALE
MOPS	SNEB	NONE	BOBA	HOES	ROLE	SOON	FORD	TOUR	PALL
MOPY	NEBS	NONG	OBAS	JOES	SOLE	TOON	LORD	YOUR	PALM
MOR	**NED**	**NOR**		MOES	TOLE	WOON	SORD	OURN	PALP
MORA	SNED			NOES	VOLE	ZOON	WORD	OURS	PALS
MORE				ROES	OLEO	OONS	ORDS	**OUT**	PALY
MORN				TOES	**OLM**			BOUT	**PAM**

SPAM	PENE	**PIX**	**PUH**	**RAN**	**REF**	TRIM	ROTS	SAIN	SENS
PAMS	PENI	PIXY	**PUN**	BRAN	TREF	RIMA	**ROW**	SAIR	SENT
PAN	PENK	**PLY**	SPUN	CRAN	REFS	RIME	AROW	SAIS	**SET**
SPAN	PENS	**POA**	PUNA	GRAN	REFT	RIMS	BROW	**SAL**	SETA
PAND	PENT	POAS	PUNK	RANA	**REH**	RIMU	CROW	SALE	SETS
PANE	**PEP**	**POD**	PUNS	RAND	REHS	RIMY	DROW	SALP	SETT
PANG	PEPO	APOD	PUNT	RANG	**REM**	**RIN**	FROW	SALS	**SEW**
PANS	PEPS	PODS	PUNY	RANI	REMS	GRIN	GROW	SALT	SEWN
PANT	**PER**	**POH**	**PUP**	RANK	**REN**	TRIN	PROW	**SAM**	SEWS
PAP	PERE	**POI**	PUPA	RANT	BREN	RIND	VROW	SAMA	**SEX**
PAPA	PERI	POIS	PUPS	**RAP**	GREN	RINE	ROWS	SAME	SEXT
PAPE	PERK	**POM**	**PUR**	CRAP	WREN	RING	ROWT	SAMP	SEXY
PAPS	PERM	POME	SPUR	DRAP	REND	RINK	**RUB**	**SAN**	**SEY**
PAR	PERN	POMP	PURE	FRAP	RENS	RINS	DRUB	SAND	SEYS
SPAR	PERT	POMS	PURI	TRAP	RENT	**RIP**	GRUB	SANE	**SEZ**
PARA	PERV	**POO**	PURL	WRAP	RENY	DRIP	RUBE	SANG	**SHE**
PARD	**PET**	POOD	PURR	RAPE	**REP**	GRIP	RUBS	SANK	SHEA
PARE	SPET	POOF	PURS	RAPS	PREP	TRIP	RUBY	SANS	SHED
PARK	PETS	POOH	**PUS**	RAPT	REPO	RIPE	**RUC**	SANT	SHES
PARP	**PEW**	POOK	PUSH	**RAS**	REPP	RIPP	RUCK	**SAP**	SHET
PARR	SPEW	POOL	PUSS	BRAS	REPS	RIPS	RUCS	SAPS	SHEW
PARS	PEWS	POON	**PUT**	ERAS	**RES**	RIPT	**RUD**	**SAR**	**SHY**
PART	**PHI**	POOP	PUTS	FRAS	ARES	**RIT**	CRUD	SARD	ASHY
PAS	PHIS	POOR	PUTT	RASE	ERES	BRIT	RUDD	SARI	**SIB**
SPAS	PHIZ	POOS	PUTZ	RASH	IRES	CRIT	RUDE	SARK	SIBB
UPAS	**PHO**	POOT	**PUY**	RASP	ORES	FRIT	RUDS	SARS	SIBS
PASH	PHOH	**POP**	PUYS	RAST	TRES	GRIT	**RUE**	**SAT**	**SIC**
PASS	PHON	POPE	**PYE**	**RAT**	URES	WRIT	CRUE	SATE	SICE
PAST	PHOS	POPS	PYES	BRAT	REST	RITE	GRUE	SATI	SICH
PAT	PHOT	**POS**	PYET	DRAT	**RET**	RITS	TRUE	**SAW**	SICK
SPAT	**PHS**	EPOS	**PYX**	GRAT	ARET	RITT	RUED	SAWN	SICS
PATE	**PIA**	POSE	**QAT**	PRAT	RETE	**RIZ**	RUES	SAWS	**SIM**
PATH	PIAS	POSH	QATS	TRAT	RETS	FRIZ	**RUG**	**SAX**	SIMA
PATS	**PIC**	POSS	**QIS**	RATA	**REV**	RIZA	DRUG	**SAY**	SIMI
PAW	EPIC	POST	**QUA**	RATE	REVS	**ROB**	TRUG	SAYS	SIMP
SPAW	SPIC	POSY	AQUA	RATH	**REW**	PROB	RUGS	**SAZ**	SIMS
PAWA	PICA	**POT**	QUAD	RATS	AREW	ROBE	**RUM**	**SEA**	**SIN**
PAWK	PICE	SPOT	QUAG	RATU	BREW	ROBS	ARUM	SEAL	SIND
PAWL	PICK	POTE	QUAT	**RAW**	CREW	**ROC**	DRUM	SEAM	SINE
PAWN	PICS	POTS	QUAY	BRAW	DREW	CROC	GRUM	SEAN	SING
PAWS	**PIE**	POTT	**RAD**	CRAW	GREW	ROCH	RUME	SEAR	SINK
PAX	SPIE	**POW**	BRAD	DRAW	TREW	ROCK	RUMP	SEAS	SINS
PAY	PIED	SPOW	DRAD	RAWN	REWS	ROCS	RUMS	SEAT	**SIP**
APAY	PIER	POWN	GRAD	RAWS	**REX**	**ROD**	**RUN**	**SEC**	SIPE
SPAY	PIES	POWS	PRAD	**RAX**	PREX	BROD	RUND	SECO	SIPS
PAYS	PIET	**POX**	TRAD	**RAY**	**REZ**	PROD	RUNE	SECS	**SIR**
PEA	**PIG**	POXY	RADE	BRAY	TREZ	RODE	RUNG	SECT	SIRE
PEAG	PIGS	**POZ**	RADS	DRAY	**RHO**	RODS	RUNS	**SED**	SIRI
PEAK	**PIN**	POZZ	**RAG**	FRAY	RHOS	**ROE**	RUNT	USED	SIRS
PEAL	SPIN	**PRE**	BRAG	GRAY	**RHY**	ROED	**RUT**	**SEE**	**SIS**
PEAN	PINA	PREE	CRAG	PRAY	**RIA**	ROES	RUTH	SEED	PSIS
PEAR	PINE	PREP	DRAG	TRAY	ARIA	BRUT	RUTS	SEEK	SISS
PEAS	PING	PREX	FRAG	RAYS	RIAL	**ROK**	**RYA**	SEEL	SIST
PEAT	PINK	PREY	RAGA	**REC**	RIAS	ROKE	RYAL	SEEM	**SIT**
PEC	PINS	**PRO**	RAGE	RECK	**RIB**	ROKS	RYAS	SEEN	SITE
SPEC	PINT	PROA	RAGG	RECS	CRIB	ROKY	**RYE**	SEEP	SITH
PECH	PINY	PROB	RAGI	**RED**	DRIB	**ROM**	TRYE	SEER	SITS
PECK	**PIP**	PROD	RAGS	ARED	RIBS	FROM	RYES	SEES	**SIX**
PECS	PIPA	PROF	**RAH**	BRED	**RID**	PROM	**SAB**	**SEG**	**SKA**
PED	PIPE	PROG	RAHS	CRED	ARID	ROMA	SABS	SEGO	SKAG
APED	PIPI	PROM	**RAI**	ERED	GRID	ROMP	**SAC**	SEGS	SKAS
OPED	PIPS	PROO	RAID	REDD	IRID	**ROO**	SACK	**SEI**	SKAT
SPED	PIPY	PROP	RAIK	REDE	RIDE	BROO	SACS	SEIF	SKAW
PEDS	**PIR**	PROS	RAIL	REDO	RIDS	PROO	**SAD**	SEIK	**SKI**
PEE	PIRL	PROW	RAIN	REDS	**RIG**	ROOD	SADE	SEIL	SKID
EPEE	PIRN	**PRY**	RAIS	**REE**	BRIG	ROOF	**SAE**	SEIR	SKIM
PEED	PIRS	SPRY	RAIT	BREE	FRIG	ROOK	**SAG**	SEIS	SKIN
PEEK	**PIS**	PRYS	**RAJ**	CREE	GRIG	ROOM	SAGA	**SEL**	SKIO
PEEL	PISE	**PSI**	RAJA	DREE	PRIG	ROON	SAGE	SELD	SKIP
PEEN	PISH	PSIS	**RAM**	FREE	TRIG	ROOP	SAGO	SELE	SKIS
PEEP	PISS	**PST**	CRAM	GREE	RIGG	ROOS	SAGS	SELF	SKIT
PEER	**PIT**	**PUB**	DRAM	PREE	RIGS	ROOT	SAGY	SELL	**SKY**
PEES	SPIT	PUBS	GRAM	TREE	**RIM**	**ROT**	**SAI**	SELS	ESKY
PEG	PITA	**PUD**	PRAM	REED	BRIM	GROT	SAIC	**SEN**	SKYR
PEGH	PITH	PUDS	TRAM	REEF	CRIM	TROT	SAID	SENA	**SLY**
PEGS	PITS	PUDU	RAMI	REEK	GRIM	ROTA	SAIL	SEND	**SMA**
PEN	PITY	**PUG**	RAMP	REEL	PRIM	ROTE	SAIM		**SNY**
OPEN	**PIU**	PUGH	RAMS	REEN		ROTI			SNYE
PEND	PIUM	PUGS		REES		ROTL			**SOB**

SOBS	SUID	TARO	THOU	STOP	JUDS	SURD	VEER	WANY	WHOT
SOC	SUIT	TARP	THY	TOPE	LUDS	TURD	VEES	WAP	WHOW
SOCA	SUK	TARS	TIC	TOPI	MUDS	URDE	VEG	SWAP	WHY
SOCK	SUKH	TART	OTIC	TOPS	OUDS	URDS	VEGA	WAPS	WIG
SOCS	SUKS	TAT	TICE	TOR	PUDS	URDY	VET	WAR	SWIG
SOD	SUM	ETAT	TICH	TORC	RUDS	URE	VETO	WARD	TWIG
SODA	SUMO	TATE	TICK	TORE	SUDS	CURE	VETS	WARE	WIGS
SODS	SUMP	TATH	TICS	TORI	WUDS	DURE	VEX	WARK	WIN
SOG	SUMS	TATS	TID	TORN	UEY	IURE	VEXT	WARM	TWIN
SOGS	SUN	TATT	TIDE	TORR	QUEY	JURE	EVET	WARN	WIND
SOH	SUNG	TATU	TIDS	TORS	UEYS	LURE	VIA	WARP	WINE
SOHO	SUNK	TAU	TIDY	TORT	UFO	MURE	VIAE	WARS	WING
SOHS	SUNN	TAUS	TIE	STOT	BUFO	PURE	VIAL	WART	WINK
SOL	SUNS	TAUT	TIED	TOT	UFOS	SURE	VIAS	WARY	WINN
SOLA	SUP	STIE	TIER	TOTE	UGH	URES	VID	WAS	WINO
SOLD	SUPE	TAW	TIES	TOTS	EUGH	URN	AVID	TWAS	WINS
SOLE	SUPS	STAW	TIG	TOW	PUGH	BURN	VIDE	WASE	WINY
SOLI	SUQ	TAWA	TIGE	STOW	UGHS	CURN	VIDS	WASH	WIS
SOLO	SUQS	TAWS	TIGS	TOWN	UGS	DURN	VIE	WASM	IWIS
SOLS	SUR	TAWT	TIL	TOWS	BUGS	GURN	VIED	WASP	YWIS
SON	SURA	TAX	TILE	TOWT	DUGS	OURN	VIER	WAST	WISE
SONE	SURD	TAXA	TILL	TOWY	FUGS	TURN	VIES	WAT	WISH
SONG	SURE	TAXI	TILS	TOY	HUGS	URNS	VIEW	SWAT	WISP
SONS	SURF	TAY	TILT	TOYS	JUGS	USE	VIM	WATE	WIST
SOP	SUS	TAYS	TIN	TRY	LUGS	FUSE	VIMS	WATS	WIT
SOPH	SUSS	TEA	TIND	TRYE	MUGS	MUSE	VIN	WATT	TWIT
SOPS	SWY	TEAD	TINE	TRYP	PUGS	RUSE	VINA	WAW	WITE
SOS	SYE	TEAK	TING	TUB	RUGS	USED	VINE	WAWE	WITH
DSOS	SYED	TEAL	TINK	TUBA	TUGS	USER	VINO	WAWL	WITS
ISOS	SYEN	TEAM	TINS	TUBE	VUGS	USES	VINS	WAWS	WOE
SOSS	YES	TEAR	TINT	TUBS	YUGS	UTE	VINT	WAX	WOES
SOT	TAB	TEAS	TINY	TUG	UKE	BUTE	VINY	WAXY	WOG
SOTS	STAB	TEAT	TIP	TUGS	BUKE	CUTE	VIS	WAY	WOGS
SOU	TABI	TED	TIPI	TUI	DUKE	JUTE	VISA	AWAY	WOK
SOUK	TABS	TEDS	TIPS	ETUI	JUKE	LUTE	VISE	SWAY	WOKE
SOUL	TABU	STED	TIPT	TUIS	LUKE	MUTE	VLY	WAYS	WOKS
SOUM	TAD	TEDY	TIS	TUM	NUKE	UTES	VOE	WEB	WON
SOUP	TADS	TEE	UTIS	STUM	PUKE	UTS	EVOE	WEBS	WONK
SOUR	TAE	TEED	TIT	TUMP	YUKE	BUTS	VOES	WED	WONS
SOUS	TAED	TEEL	TITI	TUMS	UKES	CUTS	VOL	AWED	WONT
SOUT	TAEL	TEEM	TITS	TUN	ULE	GUTS	VOLA	OWED	WOO
SOV	TAES	TEEN	TOC	TUND	DULE	HUTS	VOLE	WEDS	WOOD
SOVS	TAG	TEER	ATOC	TUNE	GULE	JUTS	VOLK	WEE	WOOF
SOW	STAG	TEES	TOCK	TUNS	HULE	NUTS	VOLS	SWEE	WOOL
SOWF	TAGS	TEF	TOCO	TUNY	MULE	OUTS	VOLT	TWEE	WOON
SOWL	TAI	TEFF	TOCS	TUP	PULE	PUTS	VOR	WEED	WOOS
SOWM	TAIL	TEFS	TOD	TUPS	RULE	RUTS	VORS	WEEK	WOOT
SOWN	TAIS	TEG	TODS	TUT	TULE	TUTS	VOW	WEEL	WOP
SOWP	TAIT	TEGG	TODY	TUTS	YULE	UTUS	AVOW	WEEM	SWOP
SOWS	TAJ	TEGS	TOE	TUTU	ULES	UTU	VOWS	WEEN	WOPS
SOX	TAK	TEGU	TOEA	TUX	UNI	TUTU	VOX	WEEP	WOS
SOY	TAKA	TEL	TOED	TWA	UNIS	UVA	VUG	WEER	WOST
SOYA	TAKE	TELA	TOES	TWAE	UNIT	UVAE	VUGS	WEES	WOT
SOYS	TAKI	TELD	TOEY	TWAL	UNS	UVAS	VUM	WEET	SWOT
SPA	TAKS	TELS	TOG	TWAS	BUNS	VAC	OVUM	WEM	WOTS
SPAE	TAKY	TELT	TOGA	TWAT	DUNS	VACS	VUMS	WEMB	WOW
SPAG	TAM	TEN	TOGE	TWAY	FUNS	VAE	WAD	WEMS	WOWF
SPAM	TAME	ETEN	TOGS	TWO	GUNS	UVAE	SWAD	WEN	WOWS
SPAN	TAMP	STEN	TOM	TWOS	NUNS	VAES	WADD	WEND	WOX
SPAR	TAMS	TEND	TOMB	TWP	PUNS	VAN	WADE	WENS	WRY
SPAS	TAN	TENE	TOME	TYE	RUNS	VANE	WADI	WENT	AWRY
SPAT	TANA	TENS	TOMS	STYE	SUNS	VANG	WADS	WET	WUD
SPAW	TANE	TENT	TON	TYED	TUNS	VANS	WADT	WETA	WUDS
SPAY	TANG	TES	TONE	TYES	UPS	VANT	WADY	WETS	WUS
SPY	TANH	UTES	TONG	TYG	CUPS	VAS	WAE	WEX	WUSS
ESPY	TANK	TEST	TONK	YGS	DUPS	VASA	TWAE	WEXE	WYE
STY	TANS	TEW	TONS	UDO	GUPS	VASE	WAES	WEY	WYES
STYE	TAP	STEW	TONY	BUDO	HUPS	VAST	WAG	SWEY	WYN
SUB	ATAP	TEWS	TOO	JUDO	OUPS	VAT	SWAG	WEYS	WYND
SUBS	STAP	THE	TOOK	LUDO	PUPS	VATS	WAGS	WHA	WYNN
SUD	TAPA	ETHE	TOOL	UDOS	SUPS	VATU	WAN	WHAM	WYNS
SUDD	TAPE	THEE	TOOM	UDS	TUPS	VAU	SWAN	WHAP	XIS
SUDS	TAPS	THEM	TOON	BUDS	YUPS	VAUS	WAND	WHAT	AXIS
SUE	TAPU	THEN	TOOT	CUDS	UPSY	VAUT	WANE	WHO	YAH
SUED	TAR	THEW	TOP	DUDS	URD	VEE	WANG	WHOA	AYAH
SUER	TARA	THEY	ATOP	FUDS	BURD	VEEP	WANK	WHOM	YAHS
SUES	STAR	THO			CURD		WANS	WHOP	YAK
SUET	TARE	THON			NURD		WANT		YAKS
SUI	TARN								

YAM	YEAD	BYES	YEST	YIPS	**YOU**	YUKS	ZEAL	DZHO	**ZOO**
LYAM	YEAH	DYES	**YET**	**YOB**	YOUK	YUKY	ZEAS	ZHOS	**ZOOM**
YAMS	YEAN	EYES	PYET	YOBS	YOUR	YUP	**ZED**	**ZIG**	**ZOON**
YAP	YEAR	HYES	YETI	**YOD**	**YOW**	UPS	ZEDS	ZIGS	**ZOOS**
YAPP	YEAS	LYES	YETT	YODE	YOWE	**YUS**	ZEE	**ZIP**	**ZOS**
YAPS	**YEN**	NYES	**YEW**	**YOK**	YOWL	AYUS	MZEE	ZIPS	DZOS
YAW	HYEN	OYES	YEWS	YOKE	YOWS	KYUS	ZEES	**ZIT**	**ZUZ**
YAWL	SYEN	PYES	**YEX**	YOKS	**YUG**	**ZAG**	**ZEK**	ZITE	
YAWN	YENS	RYES	YGO	**YON**	YUGA	ZAGS	ZEKS	ZITI	
YAWP	**YEP**	SYES	YGOE	YOND	YUGS	**ZAP**	**ZEL**	ZITS	
YAWS	YEPS	TYES	YIN	YONI	**YUK**	ZAPS	ZELS	**ZIZ**	
YAWY	**YES**	WYES	YINS	YONT	YUKE	**ZAX**	**ZEX**	ZIZZ	
YEA	AYES	YESK	YIP	**YOS**	YUKO	**ZEA**	**ZHO**	**ZOA**	

HOOKS – by hook letter

2→3

A-AS	A-CH	A-HA	A-IS	A-MI	A-NY	A-TE	A-YU
A-BA	A-DO	A-ID	A-IT	A-NA	A-RE	A-WE	
A-BY	A-GO	A-IN	A-LA	A-NE	A-SH	A-YE	

3→4

A-BAC	A-DAW	A-GED	A-IDE	A-LAS	A-MEN	A-NON	A-RET	A-TOC	A-XIS
A-BAS	A-DIT	A-GEE	A-IDS	A-LAY	A-MID	A-NOW	A-REW	A-TOM	A-YAH
A-BED	A-DOS	A-GEN	A-ITS	A-LEE	A-MIR	A-NUS	A-RIA	A-TOP	A-YES
A-BET	A-DRY	A-GIN	A-JAR	A-LES	A-MIS	A-PAY	A-RID	A-VAS	A-YUS
A-BID	A-EON	A-GIO	A-JEE	A-LEW	A-NAN	A-PED	A-ROW	A-VID	
A-BUT	A-FAR	A-GON	A-KED	A-LIT	A-NAS	A-POD	A-RUM	A-VOW	
A-BYE	A-FRO	A-GUE	A-KIN	A-LOD	A-NEW	A-QUA	A-SAR	A-WAY	
A-CHE	A-GAR	A-HEM	A-LAP	A-LOW	A-NIL	A-RED	A-SHY	A-WED	
A-CID	A-GAS	A-HOY	A-LAR	A-LUM	A-NIS	A-RES	A-TAP	A-WRY	

4→5

A-BACK	A-BODE	A-CORN	A-FORE	A-GIST	A-HING	A-LIEN	A-MATE	A-MUSE
A-BACS	A-BOIL	A-CRED	A-FOUL	A-GLEE	A-HINT	A-LIKE	A-MAZE	A-NANA
A-BAFT	A-BORD	A-CUTE	A-FRIT	A-GLEY	A-HOLD	A-LINE	A-MEER	A-NEAR
A-BAND	A-BORE	A-DAWS	A-GAIN	A-GLOW	A-HULL	A-LIVE	A-MEND	A-NIGH
A-BASE	A-BORT	A-DAYS	A-GAPE	A-GONE	A-IDES	A-LODS	A-MENE	A-NILS
A-BASH	A-BOUT	A-DEEM	A-GARS	A-GONS	A-ISLE	A-LOFT	A-MENT	A-NODE
A-BASK	A-BRAY	A-DITS	A-GAST	A-GOOD	A-ITCH	A-LONE	A-MICE	A-PACE
A-BATE	A-BRIM	A-DOWN	A-GATE	A-GREE	A-KING	A-LONG	A-MINE	A-PAGE
A-BEAM	A-BUNA	A-DRAD	A-GAVE	A-GRIN	A-LACK	A-LOOF	A-MIRS	A-PAID
A-BEAR	A-BUTS	A-DUST	A-GAZE	A-GUES	A-LAND	A-LOUD	A-MISS	A-PART
A-BETS	A-BUZZ	A-EGIS	A-GENE	A-HEAD	A-LANG	A-LOWE	A-MITY	A-PAYS
A-BIDE	A-BYES	A-EONS	A-GENT	A-HEAP	A-LAPS	A-LUMS	A-MONG	A-PEAK
A-BLED	A-CIDS	A-FEAR	A-GILA	A-HENT	A-LATE	A-LURE	A-MORT	A-PEEK
A-BLET	A-COCK	A-FIRE	A-GING	A-HIGH	A-LAYS	A-MAIN	A-MOVE	A-PERT
A-BLOW	A-COLD	A-FOOT	A-GIOS	A-HIND	A-LEFT	A-MASS	A-MUCK	A-PHIS

A-PING	A-REAR	A-RISE	A-SKER	A-TILT	A-URIC	A-VISE	A-WASH	A-YELP
A-PISH	A-REDD	A-ROMA	A-SKEW	A-TOCS	A-VAIL	A-VOID	A-WAVE	A-YONT
A-PODS	A-REDE	A-ROSE	A-SPIC	A-TOKE	A-VALE	A-VOWS	A-WAYS	A-ZINE
A-POOP	A-RETE	A-RUMS	A-STIR	A-TOLL	A-VANT	A-WAIT	A-WEEL	A-ZOIC
A-PORT	A-RETS	A-SCOT	A-STUN	A-TOMS	A-VAST	A-WAKE	A-WING	A-ZYME
A-PSIS	A-RIAS	A-SHES	A-SWAY	A-TONE	A-VERS	A-WARD	A-WOKE	
A-READ	A-RIEL	A-SHET	A-SWIM	A-TONY	A-VERT	A-WARE	A-WORK	
A-REAL	A-RIOT	A-SIDE	A-TAPS	A-TRIP	A-VINE	A-WARN	A-YAHS	

5→6

A-BANDS	A-BUSED	A-FRONT	A-LEVIN	A-NEATH	A-SHAME	A-SWARM	A-VOIDS
A-BASED	A-BUSES	A-GAMIC	A-LIENS	A-NIGHT	A-SHETS	A-SWING	A-VOUCH
A-BASES	A-CATER	A-GATES	A-LIGHT	A-NODAL	A-SHIER	A-SWIRL	A-VOWED
A-BATED	A-CATES	A-GAZED	A-LINED	A-NODES	A-SHINE	A-SWOON	A-VOWER
A-BATES	A-CETYL	A-GEIST	A-LINES	A-NOINT	A-SHORE	A-THROB	A-WAITS
A-BEARS	A-CIDER	A-GENES	A-LOGIA	A-NOMIC	A-SIDES	A-TOKES	A-WAKED
A-BIDED	A-CORNS	A-GENTS	A-LURES	A-PHONY	A-SKERS	A-TOLLS	A-WAKEN
A-BIDES	A-CRAWL	A-GHAST	A-MATED	A-PIECE	A-SLAKE	A-TONAL	A-WAKES
A-BLATE	A-CROSS	A-GILAS	A-MATES	A-PODAL	A-SLANT	A-TONED	A-WARDS
A-BLAZE	A-CUTER	A-GINGS	A-MAZED	A-RABIS	A-SLEEP	A-TONER	A-WARNS
A-BLEST	A-CUTES	A-GISTS	A-MAZES	A-RAISE	A-SLOPE	A-TONES	A-WATCH
A-BLETS	A-DAWED	A-GLEAM	A-MEERS	A-REACH	A-SMEAR	A-TONIC	A-WEARY
A-BLINS	A-DEEMS	A-GOING	A-MENDS	A-READS	A-SPICK	A-TOPIC	A-WEIGH
A-BLOOM	A-DOORS	A-GOUTY	A-MENED	A-REDES	A-SPICS	A-TRIAL	A-WHEEL
A-BLUSH	A-DREAD	A-GREED	A-MENTA	A-RETES	A-SPINE	A-TWAIN	A-WHILE
A-BOARD	A-DRIFT	A-GREES	A-MIDST	A-RIDER	A-SPIRE	A-TWEEL	A-WOKEN
A-BODED	A-DROIT	A-GREGE	A-MINES	A-RIELS	A-SPORT	A-UNTIE	A-WRACK
A-BODES	A-DUSTS	A-GRISE	A-MISES	A-RIGHT	A-SPOUT	A-URATE	A-WRONG
A-BORDS	A-EDILE	A-GRIZE	A-MOOVE	A-RISEN	A-SQUAT	A-VAILS	A-ZINES
A-BORNE	A-EMULE	A-GUISE	A-MORAL	A-RISES	A-STARE	A-VALES	A-ZONAL
A-BORTS	A-ETHER	A-HORSE	A-MOUNT	A-ROMAS	A-START	A-VAUNT	A-ZYMES
A-BOUND	A-FEARS	A-IDANT	A-MOVED	A-ROUND	A-STERN	A-VENGE	
A-BOUTS	A-FIELD	A-ISLED	A-MOVES	A-ROUSE	A-STONE	A-VENUE	
A-BRAID	A-FLAME	A-ISLES	A-MUSED	A-SCEND	A-STONY	A-VERSE	
A-BRAYS	A-FLOAT	A-KIMBO	A-MUSER	A-SCENT	A-STOOP	A-VERTS	
A-BROAD	A-FREET	A-LARUM	A-MUSES	A-SCOTS	A-STRAY	A-VISED	
A-BUNAS	A-FRESH	A-LATED	A-NANAS	A-SEITY	A-STRUT	A-VISES	
A-BURST	A-FRITS	A-LEGGE	A-NEARS	A-SHAKE	A-STUNS	A-VITAL	

6→7

A-BANDED	A-BYSSAL	A-GEISTS	A-MASSED	A-PAYING	A-SEPSES	A-STARTS	A-UNTIES
A-BASHED	A-CATERS	A-GINNER	A-MASSES	A-PHASIC	A-SEPSIS	A-STATIC	A-URATES
A-BASHES	A-CAUDAL	A-GRASTE	A-MATING	A-PHESES	A-SEPTIC	A-STONED	A-VAILED
A-BASING	A-CERATE	A-GRISED	A-MAZING	A-PHONIC	A-SEXUAL	A-STONES	A-VAUNTS
A-BATING	A-CEROUS	A-GRISES	A-MENAGE	A-PHOTIC	A-SHAMED	A-STOUND	A-VENGED
A-BETTED	A-CETYLS	A-GRIZES	A-MENDED	A-PLENTY	A-SHAMES	A-STRAND	A-VENGER
A-BETTER	A-CLINIC	A-GROUND	A-MENDER	A-POSTIL	A-SHIEST	A-STRICT	A-VENGES
A-BETTOR	A-CORNED	A-GUISED	A-MENING	A-PTERIA	A-SHIVER	A-STRIDE	A-VENTRE
A-BIDDEN	A-CUTELY	A-GUISES	A-MENTAL	A-QUIVER	A-SKLENT	A-STYLAR	A-VENUES
A-BIDING	A-CUTEST	A-HEIGHT	A-MENTUM	A-RACHIS	A-SLAKED	A-SUDDEN	A-VERTED
A-BIOTIC	A-CYCLIC	A-HUNGRY	A-MISSES	A-RAISED	A-SLAKES	A-SUNDER	A-VIATOR
A-BODING	A-DAWING	A-ISLING	A-MOOVED	A-RAISES	A-SOCIAL	A-TACTIC	A-VISING
A-BOUGHT	A-DEEMED	A-ITCHES	A-MOOVES	A-REDING	A-SPERSE	A-TAXIES	A-VOIDED
A-BOUNDS	A-DHARMA	A-LARUMS	A-MOUNTS	A-RETTED	A-SPICKS	A-THEISM	A-VOWERS
A-BRAIDS	A-DREADS	A-LAYING	A-MOVING	A-RIPPLE	A-SPINES	A-THEIST	A-VOWING
A-BRAYED	A-DUSTED	A-LEGGED	A-MUSERS	A-RISING	A-SPIRED	A-THIRST	A-WAITED
A-BREAST	A-EDILES	A-LEGGES	A-MUSING	A-ROUSED	A-SPIRES	A-THRILL	A-WAKENS
A-BRIDGE	A-EGISES	A-LENGTH	A-MUSIVE	A-ROUSER	A-SPORTS	A-THWART	A-WAKING
A-BROACH	A-EMULED	A-LEVINS	A-NEARED	A-ROUSES	A-SPRAWL	A-TINGLE	A-WARDED
A-BROADS	A-EMULES	A-LIGHTS	A-NOESES	A-SCENDS	A-SPREAD	A-TONERS	A-WARNED
A-BUSING	A-ETHERS	A-LINING	A-NOESIS	A-SCENTS	A-SPROUT	A-TONIES	A-WHEELS
A-BUTTED	A-FEARED	A-LONELY	A-NOETIC	A-SCONCE	A-SQUINT	A-TONING	A-ZYMITE
A-BUTTER	A-FREETS	A-LUMINA	A-NOINTS	A-SCRIBE	A-STABLE	A-TROPHY	

7→8

A-BANDING	A-BRAYING	A-COSMISM	A-FEARING	A-KINESES	A-MENDERS	A-MUSETTE
A-BASHING	A-BRIDGED	A-COSMIST	A-FLUTTER	A-KINESIS	A-MENDING	A-NEARING
A-BATABLE	A-BRIDGES	A-DEEMING	A-GINNERS	A-LEGGING	A-MIDMOST	A-NEURISM
A-BEARING	A-BROOKED	A-DHARMAS	A-GLIMMER	A-LIGHTED	A-MISSING	A-NOINTED
A-BETTERS	A-BUTMENT	A-DREADED	A-GLITTER	A-LOGICAL	A-MITOSES	A-PHONIES
A-BETTING	A-BUTTERS	A-DUSTING	A-GNOSTIC	A-MASSING	A-MITOSIS	A-PIARIST
A-BETTORS	A-BUTTING	A-DYNAMIC	A-GRAPHIC	A-MEIOSES	A-MITOTIC	A-PLASTIC
A-BIDINGS	A-CANTHUS	A-EMULING	A-GREEING	A-MEIOSIS	A-MOOVING	A-POSTILS
A-BOUNDED	A-CAUDATE	A-ESTHETE	A-GRISING	A-MENAGED	A-MORTISE	A-PYRETIC
A-BRAIDED	A-CAULINE	A-ESTIVAL	A-GUISING	A-MENAGES	A-MOUNTED	A-PYREXIA

A-RAISING　A-SCRIBES　A-SPIRANT　A-STOUNDS　A-TYPICAL　A-VENTURE　A-WAKINGS
A-REACHED　A-SEISMIC　A-SPIRING　A-STUNNED　A-VAILING　A-VERSION　A-WANTING
A-REACHES　A-SEITIES　A-SPORTED　A-SYNERGY　A-VARICES　A-VERTING　A-WARDING
A-READING　A-SEPTATE　A-STARTED　A-SYSTOLE　A-VAUNTED　A-VIATORS　A-WARNING
A-RETTING　A-SHAMING　A-STEROID　A-THEISMS　A-VENGERS　A-VOIDING　A-WEARIED
A-ROUSERS　A-SLAKING　A-STHENIC　A-THEISTS　A-VENGING　A-VOUCHED　A-ZYGOSES
A-ROUSING　A-SPERSED　A-STONIED　A-TREMBLE　A-VENTAIL　A-VOUCHES　A-ZYMITES
A-SCENDED　A-SPERSES　A-STONIES　A-TROPISM　A-VENTRED　A-WAITING
A-SCRIBED　A-SPHERIC　A-STONING　A-TWITTER　A-VENTRES　A-WAKENED

8→9

A-BASEMENT　A-ESTHETES　A-MORALISM　A-PIARISTS　A-STARTING　A-TROPHIED
A-BASHLESS　A-ESTIVATE　A-MORALIST　A-PRIORITY　A-STEROIDS　A-TROPHIES
A-BATEMENT　A-ETIOLOGY　A-MORNINGS　A-PYREXIAS　A-STONYING　A-TROPISMS
A-BODEMENT　A-FOREHAND　A-MOROSITY　A-RACHISES　A-STOUNDED　A-VASCULAR
A-BOUNDING　A-FORESAID　A-MORTISED　A-REACHING　A-STRADDLE　A-VAUNTING
A-BRAIDING　A-FORETIME　A-MORTISES　A-RHYTHMIC　A-STRINGED　A-VENGEFUL
A-BRIDGING　A-GELASTIC　A-MOUNTING　A-SCENDING　A-STRINGER　A-VENTAILE
A-BROOKING　A-HUNGERED　A-MUSETTES　A-SCRIBING　A-STUNNING　A-VENTAILS
A-BUTMENTS　A-LIGHTING　A-MUSINGLY　A-SEPALOUS　A-SYMMETRY　A-VENTRING
A-CELLULAR　A-LITERACY　A-NEURISMS　A-SEXUALLY　A-SYNDETIC　A-VENTURES
A-COSMISMS　A-LITERATE　A-NOINTING　A-SMOULDER　A-SYSTOLES　A-VERSIONS
A-COSMISTS　A-LONENESS　A-NUCLEATE　A-SPERSING　A-THEISTIC　A-VOCATION
A-CUTENESS　A-LUMINOUS　A-PATHETIC　A-SPIRANTS　A-THEMATIC　A-VOIDABLE
A-DREADING　A-MAZEMENT　A-PERIODIC　A-SPIRATED　A-THEOLOGY　A-VOIDANCE
A-EOLIPILE　A-MENAGING　A-PERTNESS　A-SPLENIUM　A-TONALITY　A-VOUCHING
A-ESTHESIA　A-MIDSHIPS　A-PETALOUS　A-SPORTING　A-TONICITY　A-WAKENING

2→3

AH-A　AW-A　CH-A　HO-A　MA-A　OD-A　TE-A
AI-A　BA-A　ER-A　IT-A　MO-A　PI-A　YE-A
AN-A　BO-A　GO-A　KO-A　OB-A　PO-A　ZO-A

3→4

ABB-A　BUN-A　GAG-A　KAM-A　MAY-A　NOM-A　PRO-A　SAM-A　TAP-A　VIN-A
ACT-A　CAB-A　GAL-A　KAT-A　MEG-A　NOT-A　PUN-A　SEN-A　TAR-A　VIS-A
ANN-A　CAP-A　GEN-A　KET-A　MEL-A　OBI-A　PUP-A　SET-A　TAW-A　VOL-A
ANT-A　COD-A　GET-A　KIN-A　MES-A　ODE-A　RAG-A　SHE-A　TAX-A　WET-A
ARB-A　COL-A　GIG-A　LAM-A　MON-A　ORC-A　RAJ-A　SIM-A　TEL-A　WHO-A
ARE-A　COX-A　HOY-A　LAV-A　MOR-A　PAP-A　RAN-A　SOC-A　TOE-A　YUG-A
BET-A　DIT-A　HUI-A　LEV-A　MOW-A　PAR-A　RAT-A　SOD-A　TOG-A
BIG-A　DIV-A　HUM-A　LOT-A　MOY-A　PAW-A　RIM-A　SOL-A　TUB-A
BOB-A　DON-A　IDE-A　MAM-A　NAG-A　PIC-A　RIZ-A　SOY-A　TUN-A
BON-A　DOP-A　ILK-A　MAN-A　NAN-A　PIN-A　ROM-A　SUR-A　URE-A
BOR-A　FET-A　JOT-A　MAR-A　NAP-A　PIP-A　ROT-A　TAK-A　VAS-A
BUB-A　FOR-A　JUG-A　MAS-A　NIP-A　PIT-A　SAG-A　TAN-A　VEG-A

4→5

ABAC-A　CART-A　DOUR-A　HALF-A　LUFF-A　PAIS-A　POOK-A　SCOP-A　TANK-A
AFAR-A　CELL-A　DOWN-A　HALM-A　MANG-A　PALE-A　PORT-A　SCUT-A　TEST-A
ALAP-A　CHAR-A　DRAM-A　HAST-A　MANI-A　PALL-A　PRIM-A　SELL-A　THAN-A
ANAN-A　CHAY-A　ERIC-A　HERM-A　MASS-A　PAND-A　PUCK-A　SENS-A　THEM-A
BAND-A　CHIC-A　FAUN-A　HOOK-A　MENT-A　PANG-A　PULK-A　SEPT-A　TIAR-A
BANI-A　CHIN-A　FELL-A　HOST-A　MISS-A　PARK-A　PUNK-A　SERR-A　TINE-A
BAST-A　COCO-A　FEST-A　HYEN-A　MOCH-A　PASH-A　QUIN-A　SESS-A　TONG-A
BATT-A　COST-A　FETT-A　IDOL-A　MOLL-A　PAST-A　RAGG-A　SHAM-A　TREF-A
BUFF-A　COTT-A　FLOR-A　KANG-A　MOOL-A　PELT-A　RAIT-A　SHAY-A　TRON-A
BULL-A　DARG-A　FOND-A　KIND-A　MUSH-A　PIET-A　RAST-A　SOFT-A　VEST-A
BURK-A　DELT-A　FOSS-A　KIPP-A　NERK-A　PILE-A　ROOS-A　SORD-A　VILL-A
BURS-A　DERM-A　GALE-A　LAIK-A　NORI-A　PINT-A　SAKI-A　SPIC-A　VIOL-A
CALL-A　DICT-A　GAMB-A　LING-A　NORM-A　PLAY-A　SALP-A　SPIN-A　VOLT-A
CALP-A　DONG-A　GRAM-A　LONG-A　NULL-A　POLK-A　SALS-A　TALE-A　WALL-A
CANN-A　DORS-A　GUAN-A　LOOF-A　PACT-A　PONG-A　SANS-A　TANG-A　WINN-A

5→6

AMENT-A　CHICH-A　EGEST-A　FRUST-A　MINIM-A　PATIN-A　SAHIB-A　STRUM-A
AMRIT-A　CHORD-A　EJECT-A　GLOSS-A　MONER-A　PETAR-A　SATYR-A　TALUK-A
ANTAR-A　CHORE-A　ENTER-A　HALLO-A　OBELI-A　PLANT-A　SCARP-A　TAPET-A
ARGAL-A　CONCH-A　EPOCH-A　HOLLO-A　OCHRE-A　PLASM-A　SHIRR-A　TARSI-A
BERTH-A　CORNU-A　FASCI-A　KUTCH-A　ORBIT-A　QUANT-A　SOLER-A　TORAN-A
CABAL-A　CRUST-A　FAVEL-A　LORIC-A　ORGAN-A　QUINT-A　SPIRE-A　VALET-A
CHARK-A　CUBIC-A　FIEST-A　MAXIM-A　PAGOD-A　QUOTH-A　STERN-A　YOJAN-A
CHART-A　CUTCH-A　FRISK-A　MIASM-A　PATER-A　RHUMB-A　STRIG-A

6→7

ACANTH-A	CHIASM-A	DEJECT-A	INGEST-A	MARKKA-A	ROBUST-A	SHEIKH-A	TRISUL-A
ADDEND-A	CHIMER-A	DRACHM-A	KHALIF-A	MOMENT-A	ROSACE-A	SIGNOR-A	TYMPAN-A
ANALOG-A	CHOLER-A	EMBLEM-A	LAVOLT-A	OSMUND-A	ROTUND-A	SQUILL-A	
ANONYM-A	COTING-A	EROTIC-A	LOCUST-A	PERSON-A	SCHISM-A	SULTAN-A	
ASHRAM-A	CROTAL-A	EXOTIC-A	LOMENT-A	PLACIT-A	SECRET-A	TARTAN-A	
CANDID-A	CURIOS-A	GUNNER-A	MADRAS-A	POTASS-A	SEQUEL-A	TAVERN-A	
CEMENT-A	CYATHI-A	INFANT-A	MANDIR-A	PROPYL-A	SERING-A	TEMPER-A	

7→8

ABSCISS-A	AUTOMAT-A	DEMENTI-A	MANDIOC-A	MONSTER-A	SALICET-A	TAMANDU-A
AMYGDAL-A	BRONCHI-A	DULCIAN-A	MARCHES-A	MRIDANG-A	SARMENT-A	TAMBOUR-A
ANGELIC-A	CHARISM-A	EPITHEM-A	MARINER-A	NYMPHAE-A	SCIATIC-A	THERIAC-A
ANTEFIX-A	CISTERN-A	EXCERPT-A	MATADOR-A	PERFECT-A	SIGNORI-A	TORMENT-A
ARBORET-A	CONSULT-A	FASCIST-A	MELODIC-A	RAKSHAS-A	SYNTAGM-A	

8→9

AQUATINT-A	DIDRACHM-A	FANFARON-A	HYPODERM-A	NICOTIAN-A	SOUVLAKI-A
ARGUMENT-A	ESOTERIC-A	HARMONIC-A	JAMBOLAN-A	PHANTASM-A	
CANEPHOR-A	EXANTHEM-A	HIERATIC-A	MATACHIN-A	SLIVOVIC-A	

2→3

B-AA	B-AN	B-AY	B-ID	B-IT	B-ON	B-OS	B-UG	B-US
B-AD	B-AR	B-EE	B-IN	B-OB	B-OO	B-OW	B-UM	B-UT
B-AH	B-AS	B-EL	B-IO	B-OD	B-OP	B-OX	B-UN	B-YE
B-AM	B-AT	B-EN	B-IS	B-OH	B-OR	B-OY	B-UR	

3→4

B-AAS	B-ANT	B-AYE	B-ERE	B-IOS	B-LEY	B-OFF	B-ORS	B-REE	B-UKE
B-ABA	B-ARB	B-AYS	B-ERG	B-IRK	B-LIN	B-OIL	B-ORT	B-REN	B-UNS
B-ABY	B-ARD	B-EAN	B-ERK	B-ISH	B-LIP	B-OKE	B-OUK	B-REW	B-URD
B-ACH	B-ARE	B-EAR	B-EST	B-ITS	B-LOB	B-OLD	B-OUT	B-RIG	B-URN
B-ADS	B-ARK	B-EAT	B-ETA	B-LAB	B-LOT	B-OLE	B-OWL	B-RIM	B-UTE
B-AFT	B-ARM	B-EAU	B-ETH	B-LAD	B-LOW	B-ONE	B-OYS	B-RIT	B-UTS
B-AIL	B-ARS	B-EEN	B-ICE	B-LAG	B-LUR	B-OOH	B-RAD	B-ROD	B-YES
B-AIT	B-ASH	B-EGO	B-IDE	B-LAH	B-OAK	B-OOM	B-RAG	B-ROO	
B-AKE	B-ASK	B-ELL	B-IDS	B-LAT	B-OAR	B-OON	B-RAN	B-ROW	
B-ALE	B-ASS	B-ELS	B-IFF	B-LAY	B-OAT	B-OOR	B-RAS	B-RUT	
B-ALL	B-ATE	B-ELT	B-ILK	B-LED	B-OBA	B-OOS	B-RAT	B-UDO	
B-AND	B-AUK	B-END	B-ILL	B-LEE	B-OBS	B-OPS	B-RAW	B-UDS	
B-ANE	B-AWL	B-ENE	B-INK	B-LET	B-ODE	B-ORD	B-RAY	B-UFO	
B-ANI	B-AWN	B-ENS	B-INS	B-LEW	B-ODS	B-ORE	B-RED	B-UGS	

4→5

B-ABAS	B-ASKS	B-ETHS	B-LASE	B-LIPS	B-OFFS	B-OWLS	B-REDE	B-ROOM
B-AFFY	B-AUKS	B-EVER	B-LASH	B-LIST	B-OGLE	B-OXEN	B-REED	B-ROOS
B-AILS	B-AWLS	B-HANG	B-LAST	B-LITE	B-OILS	B-OXER	B-REES	B-ROSE
B-AIRN	B-AWNS	B-ICES	B-LATE	B-LIVE	B-OINK	B-RACE	B-RENS	B-ROWS
B-AITS	B-AYES	B-IDES	B-LATS	B-LOBS	B-OKES	B-RACH	B-RENT	B-RULE
B-AKED	B-EACH	B-ILKS	B-LAUD	B-LOCK	B-OLDS	B-RACK	B-REWS	B-RUME
B-AKES	B-EANS	B-ILLS	B-LAYS	B-LOKE	B-ONCE	B-RADS	B-RICK	B-RUNT
B-ALAS	B-EARD	B-ILLY	B-LAZE	B-LOOM	B-ONER	B-RAGS	B-RIDE	B-RUSH
B-ALES	B-EARS	B-INGO	B-LEAK	B-LOOP	B-ONES	B-RAID	B-RIGS	B-RUST
B-ALKY	B-EAST	B-INKS	B-LEAR	B-LORE	B-OOHS	B-RAIL	B-RILL	B-UDOS
B-ALLS	B-EATH	B-IOTA	B-LEAT	B-LOTS	B-OOMS	B-RAIN	B-RIMS	B-UFOS
B-ALLY	B-EATS	B-IRKS	B-LEED	B-LOWN	B-OONS	B-RAKE	B-RINE	B-UKES
B-ALMS	B-EAUX	B-ITCH	B-LEEP	B-LOWS	B-OOSE	B-RAND	B-RING	B-UMBO
B-ANAL	B-EECH	B-LABS	B-LEES	B-LUES	B-OOZE	B-RANK	B-RINK	B-UMPH
B-ANDS	B-EERY	B-LACK	B-LEND	B-LUFF	B-OOZY	B-RASH	B-RISE	B-UNCE
B-ANES	B-EGAD	B-LADE	B-LENT	B-LUNT	B-ORDS	B-RAST	B-RISK	B-UNCO
B-ANNS	B-ELLS	B-LADS	B-LESS	B-LURS	B-ORES	B-RATS	B-RITS	B-URDS
B-ANTS	B-ELTS	B-LAER	B-LEST	B-LUSH	B-ORTS	B-RAVE	B-ROAD	B-URNS
B-ARBS	B-ENDS	B-LAGS	B-LETS	B-LEYS	B-OAKS	B-RAWN	B-ROCH	B-USED
B-ARDS	B-ENES	B-LAHS	B-LEYS	B-OARS	B-OUKS	B-RAWS	B-ROCK	B-USES
B-ARED	B-ERES	B-LAIN	B-LIMP	B-OAST	B-OURN	B-RAYS	B-RODS	B-UTES
B-ARES	B-ERGS	B-LAME	B-LIMY	B-OATS	B-OUTS	B-RAZE	B-ROIL	
B-ARKS	B-ERKS	B-LAND	B-LIND	B-OBAS	B-OWED	B-READ	B-ROKE	
B-ARMS	B-ESTS	B-LANK	B-LINK	B-OCHE	B-OWER	B-REAK	B-ROOD	
B-ARMY	B-ETAS	B-LARE	B-LINS	B-ODES	B-OWES	B-REAM	B-ROOK	

5→6

B-ABIES	B-ATMAN	B-LANCH	B-LOCKS	B-OOHED	B-RAISE	B-REEDS	B-ROOKS
B-ACHED	B-EAGLE	B-LANDS	B-LOKES	B-OOSES	B-RAKED	B-REEKS	B-ROOMS
B-ACHES	B-EANED	B-LANKS	B-LOOMS	B-OOZED	B-RAKES	B-REGMA	B-ROOMY
B-ADMAN	B-EARDS	B-LANKY	B-LOOPS	B-OOZES	B-RANCH	B-RENNE	B-ROOSE
B-ADMEN	B-EARED	B-LARES	B-LORES	B-ORATE	B-RANDS	B-REVET	B-ROSES
B-AILED	B-EASTS	B-LASTS	B-LOTTO	B-ORDER	B-RANDY	B-RICKS	B-ROUGH
B-AIRNS	B-EATEN	B-LATER	B-LOUSE	B-OTHER	B-RANKS	B-RIDES	B-RUMAL
B-AKING	B-EATER	B-LAUDS	B-LOWED	B-OUGHT	B-RASES	B-RIDGE	B-RUMES
B-ALDER	B-EGGAR	B-LAZED	B-LOWER	B-OUNCE	B-RATTY	B-RIGHT	B-RUNCH
B-ALLOT	B-EGGED	B-LAZES	B-LOWSE	B-OVATE	B-RAVED	B-RILLS	B-RUNTS
B-ALLOW	B-ELATE	B-LEACH	B-LUFFS	B-OVINE	B-RAVER	B-RINES	B-RUSHY
B-ANANA	B-ENDED	B-LEAKS	B-LUNGE	B-OWING	B-RAVES	B-RINGS	B-RUSTS
B-ANGER	B-HANGS	B-LEAKY	B-LUNTS	B-OWLED	B-RAWER	B-RINKS	B-UGGED
B-ANGLE	B-ICKER	B-LEARS	B-OASTS	B-OWLER	B-RAWLY	B-RISES	B-UMBOS
B-ANKER	B-INGLE	B-LEARY	B-OATER	B-OWNED	B-RAWNS	B-RISKS	B-UNCES
B-ANTED	B-INNED	B-LEATS	B-OCHES	B-OXERS	B-RAYED	B-RISKY	B-UNCOS
B-ARISH	B-IONIC	B-LEEPS	B-OFFED	B-RACED	B-RAZED	B-ROACH	B-UNION
B-ARKED	B-IOTAS	B-LENDS	B-OGLES	B-RACER	B-RAZES	B-ROADS	B-UNKED
B-ARRET	B-ISHES	B-LIGHT	B-OILED	B-RACES	B-REACH	B-ROCKS	B-URGER
B-ARROW	B-ITCHY	B-LIMEY	B-OILER	B-RACKS	B-READS	B-ROGUE	B-URIAL
B-ASHES	B-LACKS	B-LIMPS	B-OINKS	B-RAIDS	B-REAKS	B-ROILS	B-URNED
B-ASKED	B-LADED	B-LINDS	B-OLDEN	B-RAILS	B-REAMS	B-ROKED	B-USING
B-ASSES	B-LADES	B-LINKS	B-OLDER	B-RAINS	B-REAST	B-ROKER	B-UTTER
B-ASSET	B-LAMED	B-LITES	B-ONCES	B-RAINY	B-REDES	B-ROKES	
B-ASTER	B-LAMES	B-LITHE	B-ONERS	B-RAIRD	B-REECH	B-ROODS	

6→7

B-ABYING	B-EAGLES	B-LANKED	B-LOBBED	B-OILERY	B-RACERS	B-RAZING	B-ROKERS
B-ACHING	B-EANING	B-LANKER	B-LOCKED	B-OILING	B-RACHES	B-REAMED	B-ROKING
B-ACKERS	B-EARDED	B-LANKLY	B-LOCKER	B-OINKED	B-RACING	B-REASTS	B-ROOKED
B-AFFIES	B-EARING	B-LASHES	B-LOOMED	B-OLDENS	B-RACKET	B-REDING	B-ROOMED
B-AILING	B-EATERS	B-LASTED	B-LOOPED	B-OLDEST	B-RAGGED	B-REEDER	B-ROOSES
B-ALLIUM	B-EATING	B-LASTER	B-LOOPER	B-ONDING	B-RAIDED	B-RENNES	B-ROTHER
B-ALLONS	B-EECHES	B-LATEST	B-LOTTED	B-ONUSES	B-RAIDER	B-RENTER	B-ROUGHS
B-ALLOTS	B-EERIER	B-LATHER	B-LOUSED	B-OODLES	B-RAILED	B-REVETS	B-ROUGHT
B-ALLOWS	B-EGGARS	B-LATTER	B-LOUSES	B-OOHING	B-RAINED	B-RICKED	B-RUCKLE
B-ANALLY	B-EGGING	B-LAUDED	B-LOWERS	B-OOZIER	B-RAIRDS	B-RICKLE	B-RUMMER
B-ANANAS	B-ELATED	B-LAZING	B-LOWING	B-OOZILY	B-RAISED	B-RIDGED	B-RUNTED
B-ANGERS	B-ELATES	B-LEAKER	B-LOWSES	B-OOZING	B-RAISES	B-RIDGES	B-RUSHED
B-ANGLED	B-ENDING	B-LEARED	B-LUBBER	B-ORATES	B-RAKING	B-RIDING	B-RUSHER
B-ANGLES	B-ICKERS	B-LEEPED	B-LUFFED	B-ORDERS	B-RAMBLE	B-RIMING	B-RUSHES
B-ANKERS	B-INGLES	B-LENDER	B-LUNGED	B-ORDURE	B-RANDED	B-RIMMED	B-UCKERS
B-ANTING	B-INNING	B-LESSES	B-LUNGES	B-OTHERS	B-RANKED	B-RINDED	B-UGGING
B-ARKING	B-ITCHED	B-LETTED	B-LUNKER	B-OUCHES	B-RASHED	B-RINGER	B-ULLING
B-ARRACK	B-ITCHES	B-LIGHTS	B-LUNTED	B-OUGHTS	B-RASHER	B-RISKED	B-UMBLES
B-ARRETS	B-LACKED	B-LINKED	B-LUSHED	B-OULDER	B-RASHES	B-RISKER	B-UNIONS
B-ARROWS	B-LACKER	B-LINKER	B-LUSHER	B-OUNCES	B-RASSES	B-ROCHES	B-UNKING
B-ASKING	B-LADDER	B-LINNED	B-LUSHES	B-OVATES	B-RATTLE	B-ROCKED	B-URGERS
B-ASSETS	B-LAGGED	B-LIPPED	B-LUSTER	B-OWLERS	B-RAUNCH	B-ROCKET	B-URIALS
B-ASSIST	B-LAGGER	B-LISSES	B-OATERS	B-OWLING	B-RAVING	B-RODDED	B-URNING
B-ASTERS	B-LAMING	B-LISTER	B-OFFING	B-OWNING	B-RAWEST	B-ROGUES	B-UTTERS
B-ATONED	B-LANDER	B-LITHER	B-OILERS	B-RABBLE	B-RAYING	B-ROILED	

7→8

B-ADLANDS	B-LADDERY	B-LIMBING	B-LUNTING	B-RAISING	B-REAKING	B-ROADWAY
B-AILMENT	B-LAGGERS	B-LINKERS	B-LUSHERS	B-RAMBLED	B-REAMING	B-ROCKETS
B-ALLIUMS	B-LAGGING	B-LINKING	B-LUSHING	B-RAMBLES	B-REASTED	B-RODDING
B-ANTINGS	B-LANCHED	B-LINNING	B-LUSTERS	B-RANCHED	B-REECHED	B-ROGUISH
B-ARRACKS	B-LANCHES	B-LIPPING	B-OINKING	B-RANCHER	B-REECHES	B-ROILING
B-ARTISAN	B-LANKEST	B-LISTERS	B-OLDENED	B-RANCHES	B-REEDERS	B-ROOKING
B-ASSISTS	B-LANKING	B-LITHELY	B-OLDNESS	B-RANDIES	B-REEDING	B-ROOMIER
B-ATONING	B-LASTERS	B-LITHEST	B-ONDINGS	B-RANDING	B-REGMATA	B-ROOMING
B-EARDING	B-LASTING	B-LOBBING	B-OOZIEST	B-RANKING	B-RENNING	B-ROTHERS
B-EARINGS	B-LATHERS	B-LOCKAGE	B-ORDERED	B-RASHEST	B-RICKING	B-RUMMERS
B-EATABLE	B-LAUDING	B-LOCKERS	B-ORDERER	B-RASHING	B-RIDGING	B-RUNCHES
B-EATINGS	B-LEACHED	B-LOCKING	B-ORDURES	B-RATCHET	B-RIGHTEN	B-RUSHERS
B-EERIEST	B-LEACHES	B-LOOMING	B-RABBLED	B-RATLING	B-RIGHTER	B-RUSHIER
B-ELATING	B-LEARIER	B-LOOPERS	B-RABBLES	B-RATPACK	B-RIGHTLY	B-RUSHING
B-ENDINGS	B-LEARING	B-LOOPING	B-RACHIAL	B-RATTIER	B-RIMLESS	B-RUSTING
B-ENDWISE	B-LEEPING	B-LOTTING	B-RACKETS	B-RATTISH	B-RIMMING	B-ULLINGS
B-ETACISM	B-LENDERS	B-LOUSING	B-RAGGING	B-RATTLED	B-RINGERS	B-URNINGS
B-ITCHIER	B-LENDING	B-LUBBERS	B-RAIDING	B-RATTLES	B-RINGING	B-UTTERED
B-ITCHING	B-LETTING	B-LUFFING	B-RAILING	B-REACHED	B-RISKING	
B-LACKING	B-LIGHTED	B-LUNGING	B-RAINIER	B-REACHES	B-ROACHED	
B-LADDERS	B-LIGHTER	B-LUNKERS	B-RAINING	B-READING	B-ROACHES	

8→9

B-AILMENTS	B-LASTINGS	B-LUSTROUS	B-RAMBLING	B-REASTING	B-ROADSIDE
B-ARTISANS	B-LATHERED	B-OILERIES	B-RANCHERS	B-REECHING	B-ROADWAYS
B-EASTINGS	B-LEACHING	B-OLDENING	B-RANCHING	B-REEDINGS	B-ROOMIEST
B-EERINESS	B-LEARIEST	B-OOZINESS	B-RATCHETS	B-REVETTED	B-RUSHIEST
B-ELATEDLY	B-LENDINGS	B-ORDERERS	B-RATLINGS	B-RICKYARD	B-UTTERING
B-ETACISMS	B-LIGHTERS	B-ORDERING	B-RATTIEST	B-RIDGINGS	
B-ITCHIEST	B-LIGHTING	B-RABBLING	B-RATTLING	B-RIGHTENS	
B-LADDERED	B-LINDWORM	B-RACKETED	B-RAUNCHED	B-RIGHTEST	
B-LANCHING	B-LOCKAGES	B-RAINIEST	B-RAUNCHES	B-RINGINGS	
B-LANKNESS	B-LUSTERED	B-RAINLESS	B-REACHING	B-ROACHING	

2→3

AR-B	DA-B	FA-B	GU-B	KO-B	LO-B	NE-B	OR-B	TA-B
BI-B	DI-B	GI-B	HO-B	LA-B	MO-B	NO-B	SI-B	WE-B
BO-B	DO-B	GO-B	JO-B	LI-B	NA-B	NU-B	SO-B	YO-B

3→4

BAR-B	CAR-B	CUR-B	DOO-B	FOR-B	GAM-B	HER-B	LAM-B	PRO-B	TOM-B
BOO-B	COB-B	DIE-B	FLU-B	FRA-B	GAR-B	JAM-B	NIM-B	SIB-B	WEM-B

4→5

ACER-B	COOM-B	CUBE-B	NEEM-B	SLUB-B	THRO-B	ZINE-B
BLUR-B	COUR-B	DEMO-B	PLUM-B	SLUR-B	ZEBU-B	

5→6

SCRAM-B   SUPER-B

6→7

PROVER-B

2→3

C-AD	C-AR	C-AY	C-HA	C-ID	C-OD	C-OP	C-OW	C-UM	C-UT
C-AM	C-AT	C-EE	C-HE	C-IT	C-ON	C-OR	C-OX	C-UP	
C-AN	C-AW	C-EL	C-HI	C-OB	C-OO	C-OS	C-OY	C-UR	

3→4

C-ABA	C-ARD	C-ELS	C-HIC	C-IDE	C-LEW	C-ODS	C-OOP	C-RAP	C-URD
C-ADS	C-ARE	C-ELT	C-HID	C-IDS	C-LIP	C-OFF	C-OOS	C-RAW	C-URE
C-AGE	C-ARK	C-ENS	C-HIN	C-ILL	C-LOD	C-OFT	C-OPE	C-RED	C-URN
C-AIN	C-ARS	C-ERE	C-HIP	C-ION	C-LOG	C-OHO	C-OPS	C-REE	C-UTE
C-AKE	C-ART	C-ESS	C-HIS	C-IRE	C-LOP	C-OIL	C-ORD	C-REW	C-UTS
C-ALL	C-ASH	C-HAD	C-HIT	C-ITS	C-LOT	C-OKE	C-ORE	C-RIB	
C-ALP	C-ASK	C-HAM	C-HOC	C-LAD	C-LOW	C-OLD	C-ORF	C-RIM	
C-AMP	C-ATE	C-HAP	C-HON	C-LAG	C-LOY	C-OLE	C-ORS	C-RIT	
C-ANE	C-AUF	C-HAS	C-HOP	C-LAM	C-OAT	C-OMS	C-OUP	C-ROC	
C-ANN	C-AUK	C-HAT	C-HOW	C-LAP	C-OBS	C-ONE	C-OUR	C-ROW	
C-ANT	C-AVE	C-HAW	C-HUB	C-LAT	C-OCA	C-ONS	C-OWL	C-RUD	
C-ANY	C-AYS	C-HAY	C-HUG	C-LAW	C-OCH	C-OOF	C-RAG	C-RUE	
C-APE	C-EAS	C-HER	C-HUM	C-LAY	C-ODA	C-OOM	C-RAM	C-UDS	
C-ARB	C-ELL	C-HEW	C-HUT	C-LEG	C-ODE	C-OON	C-RAN	C-UPS	

4→5

C-ABAS	C-ANNS	C-AVER	C-HAFT	C-HEAT	C-HOKE	C-HURL	C-LANK	C-LICK
C-ABLE	C-ANON	C-AVES	C-HAIN	C-HECK	C-HONS	C-HYLE	C-LAPS	C-LIED
C-ACHE	C-ANTS	C-AWED	C-HAIR	C-HERE	C-HOOF	C-IDES	C-LASH	C-LIES
C-AGED	C-APED	C-AXON	C-HAMS	C-HEST	C-HOOK	C-ILIA	C-LASS	C-LIFT
C-AGES	C-APES	C-EASE	C-HANK	C-HEWS	C-HOPS	C-ILLS	C-LATS	C-LIMB
C-AIRN	C-ARBS	C-ELLS	C-HAPS	C-HICK	C-HORE	C-INCH	C-LAVE	C-LIME
C-AKED	C-ARDS	C-ELTS	C-HARD	C-HIDE	C-HOSE	C-IONS	C-LAWS	C-LINE
C-AKES	C-ARED	C-EORL	C-HARE	C-HILD	C-HOUT	C-IRES	C-LAYS	C-LING
C-ALLS	C-ARES	C-ERED	C-HARK	C-HILI	C-HOWS	C-LACK	C-LEAN	C-LINK
C-ALMS	C-ARET	C-ERES	C-HARM	C-HILL	C-HUBS	C-LADE	C-LEAR	C-LINT
C-ALPS	C-ARKS	C-ERIC	C-HART	C-HINS	C-HUCK	C-LADS	C-LEAT	C-LIPS
C-AMIS	C-ARSE	C-ERNE	C-HATS	C-HIPS	C-HUFF	C-LAGS	C-LEEK	C-LOAM
C-AMPS	C-ARTS	C-ESSE	C-HAVE	C-HITS	C-HUGS	C-LAME	C-LEEP	C-LOCK
C-ANAL	C-ASKS	C-HACK	C-HAWS	C-HIVE	C-HUMP	C-LAMP	C-LEFT	C-LODS
C-ANES	C-AUKS	C-HADS	C-HAYS	C-HIZZ	C-HUMS	C-LAMS	C-LEGS	C-LOGS
C-ANNA	C-AULD	C-HAFF	C-HEAP	C-HOCK	C-HUNK	C-LANG	C-LEVE	C-LOKE

C-LONE	C-LOWS	C-OHOS	C-OPES	C-OYER	C-RAVE	C-RIBS	C-RORE	C-TENE
C-LOOP	C-LOYS	C-OILS	C-ORAL	C-RACK	C-RAWS	C-RICK	C-ROST	C-ULEX
C-LOOT	C-LUCK	C-OKES	C-ORDS	C-RAFT	C-RAZE	C-RIME	C-ROUP	C-URDS
C-LOPS	C-LUES	C-OLDS	C-ORES	C-RAGS	C-REAK	C-RIMS	C-ROUT	C-URDY
C-LOSE	C-LUMP	C-OMER	C-OUCH	C-RAKE	C-REAM	C-RINE	C-ROWS	C-URES
C-LOTE	C-LUNG	C-ONES	C-OULD	C-RAMP	C-REDO	C-RISE	C-RUCK	C-URNS
C-LOTH	C-OAST	C-ONTO	C-OUPS	C-RAMS	C-REDS	C-RISP	C-RUDE	C-UTES
C-LOTS	C-OATS	C-OOFS	C-OURS	C-RANK	C-REED	C-RITS	C-RUDS	C-UTIS
C-LOUD	C-OBIA	C-OOMS	C-OVEN	C-RAPE	C-REEK	C-ROCK	C-RUES	
C-LOUR	C-OCAS	C-OONS	C-OVER	C-RAPS	C-REEL	C-ROCS	C-RUMP	
C-LOUT	C-ODAS	C-OOPS	C-OWED	C-RARE	C-REES	C-RONE	C-RUSE	
C-LOVE	C-ODES	C-OPAL	C-OWER	C-RASH	C-REST	C-ROOK	C-RUSH	
C-LOWN	C-OFFS	C-OPED	C-OWLS	C-RATE	C-REWS	C-ROON	C-RUST	

5→6

C-ABLED	C-ENTRY	C-HEWER	C-LACKS	C-LOAMS	C-ONNED	C-RATES	C-ROTAL
C-ABLES	C-EORLS	C-HICKS	C-LADES	C-LOCKS	C-OOPED	C-RAVED	C-ROTCH
C-ABLET	C-ERING	C-HIDED	C-LAMES	C-LOKES	C-OPALS	C-RAVEN	C-ROUPS
C-ACHED	C-ERNED	C-HIDER	C-LAMMY	C-LOOPS	C-OPING	C-RAVER	C-ROUPY
C-ACHES	C-ERNES	C-HIDES	C-LAMPS	C-LOOTS	C-OPTER	C-RAVES	C-ROUSE
C-AGING	C-ESSES	C-HILLS	C-LANKS	C-LOSED	C-ORALS	C-RAWLY	C-ROUTE
C-AIRNS	C-HACKS	C-HILLY	C-LASTS	C-LOSER	C-OSIER	C-RAYON	C-ROUTS
C-AKING	C-HAFFS	C-HIPPY	C-LATCH	C-LOSES	C-OSMIC	C-RAZED	C-ROWED
C-ALLOW	C-HAFTS	C-HIVED	C-LAVER	C-LOTES	C-OTTAR	C-RAZES	C-RUCKS
C-AMASS	C-HAINS	C-HIVES	C-LAVES	C-LOUGH	C-OTTER	C-REACH	C-RUDDY
C-AMBER	C-HAIRS	C-HOCKS	C-LAWED	C-LOURS	C-OUPED	C-REAKS	C-RUDER
C-AMPLE	C-HAMMY	C-HOKED	C-LEANS	C-LOUTS	C-OUTER	C-REAMS	C-RUDES
C-AMPLY	C-HANCE	C-HOKES	C-LEARS	C-LOVER	C-OVARY	C-REAMY	C-RUMEN
C-ANGLE	C-HANKS	C-HOKEY	C-LEATS	C-LOVES	C-OVENS	C-REATE	C-RUMMY
C-ANKER	C-HAPPY	C-HOOFS	C-LEAVE	C-LOWNS	C-OVERS	C-REDOS	C-RUMPS
C-ANNAS	C-HARDS	C-HOOKS	C-LEEKS	C-LUCKS	C-OVERT	C-REEDS	C-RUMPY
C-ANTAR	C-HARED	C-HOPPY	C-LEEPS	C-LUCKY	C-OWING	C-REEKS	C-RUNCH
C-ANTED	C-HARES	C-HORAL	C-LEFTS	C-LUMPS	C-OWLED	C-REEKY	C-RURAL
C-APING	C-HARKS	C-HOSEN	C-LEUCH	C-LUMPY	C-OWRIE	C-REELS	C-RUSES
C-ARETS	C-HARMS	C-HOSES	C-LEUGH	C-LUNCH	C-RACKS	C-RESTS	C-RUSTS
C-ARKED	C-HARRY	C-HOUGH	C-LEVER	C-LYING	C-RAFTS	C-RIANT	C-RUSTY
C-ARSES	C-HARTS	C-HOUSE	C-LEVIS	C-OASTS	C-RAGGY	C-RICKS	C-TENES
C-ARTEL	C-HASTE	C-HOUTS	C-LICKS	C-OATER	C-RAKED	C-RIMED	C-UMBER
C-ASHES	C-HAUNT	C-HUBBY	C-LIFTS	C-OBIAS	C-RAKES	C-RIMES	C-UPPED
C-ASKED	C-HAWED	C-HUCKS	C-LIMAX	C-OCHES	C-RAMPS	C-RINES	C-UPPER
C-ASTER	C-HAZAN	C-HUFFS	C-LIMBS	C-OCKER	C-RANCH	C-RIPES	C-URARI
C-AUGHT	C-HEAPS	C-HUFFY	C-LIMES	C-ODDER	C-RANKS	C-RISES	C-URATE
C-AVERS	C-HEAPY	C-HUMPS	C-LINCH	C-ODIST	C-RANTS	C-RISPS	C-UTTER
C-AWING	C-HEATS	C-HUNKS	C-LINES	C-OFFED	C-RAPES	C-ROCKS	C-YCLED
C-AXONS	C-HECKS	C-HUNKY	C-LINGS	C-OFFER	C-RASES	C-RONES	C-YESES
C-EASED	C-HERRY	C-HURLS	C-LINGY	C-OILED	C-RATCH	C-ROOKS	
C-EASES	C-HESTS	C-HYLES	C-LINKS	C-OLDER	C-RATED	C-ROONS	
C-ENTER	C-HEWED	C-ILIUM	C-LINTS	C-OMERS	C-RATER	C-RORES	

6→7

C-ABLETS	C-EASING	C-HIDDEN	C-HUPPAH	C-LEANLY	C-LOTTED	C-OUCHES	C-RAVERS
C-ABLING	C-ENSURE	C-HIDERS	C-ILICES	C-LEARED	C-LOUGHS	C-OUPING	C-RAVING
C-ACHING	C-ENTERS	C-HIDING	C-INCHED	C-LEAVED	C-LOURED	C-OURIER	C-RAYONS
C-ACUMEN	C-ERNING	C-HILLED	C-INCHES	C-LEAVER	C-LOUTED	C-OUTERS	C-RAZING
C-AIRNED	C-HACKED	C-HIPPED	C-LACKED	C-LEAVES	C-LOVERS	C-OUTHER	C-REAKED
C-ALLOWS	C-HAINED	C-HIPPER	C-LACKER	C-LEEPED	C-LOWNED	C-OUVERT	C-REAMED
C-AMBERS	C-HAIRED	C-HIPPIE	C-LADDER	C-LICHES	C-LUBBER	C-OVERED	C-REAMER
C-AMISES	C-HALLAN	C-HITTER	C-LAGGED	C-LICKED	C-LUMBER	C-OWLING	C-REATES
C-AMUSES	C-HAMLET	C-HIVING	C-LAMBER	C-LICKER	C-LUMPED	C-RACKED	C-RESTED
C-ANGLED	C-HANCES	C-HIZZED	C-LAMMED	C-LIFTED	C-LUMPER	C-RACKER	C-RIBBED
C-ANGLES	C-HANGED	C-HIZZES	C-LAMPED	C-LIMBED	C-LUSTER	C-RAFTED	C-RICKED
C-ANKERS	C-HANGER	C-HOCKED	C-LANGER	C-LIMBER	C-OATERS	C-RAGGED	C-RIMING
C-ANTARS	C-HAPPED	C-HOCKER	C-LANKED	C-LINGER	C-OCKERS	C-RAKING	C-RINGED
C-ANTING	C-HARING	C-HOKIER	C-LAPPED	C-LINKED	C-ODISTS	C-RAMMED	C-RINGER
C-ARABIN	C-HARKED	C-HOKING	C-LAPPER	C-LINKER	C-OFFERS	C-RAMMER	C-RIPPLE
C-ARKING	C-HARMED	C-HOOFED	C-LASHED	C-LIPPED	C-OFFING	C-RAMPED	C-RISPED
C-ARLING	C-HASTEN	C-HOPPED	C-LASHER	C-LIPPIE	C-OILING	C-RANKED	C-RITTER
C-AROUSE	C-HATTED	C-HOPPER	C-LASHES	C-LITTER	C-OLDEST	C-RANKLE	C-ROCHES
C-ARRACK	C-HATTER	C-HOUGHS	C-LASSES	C-LIVERS	C-OLDISH	C-RAPIER	C-ROCHET
C-ARRECT	C-HAUNTS	C-HOUSED	C-LASSIS	C-LOCKED	C-ONNING	C-RAPPED	C-ROCKED
C-ARTELS	C-HAWING	C-HOUSES	C-LATTER	C-LOCKER	C-OOPING	C-RASHED	C-ROCKET
C-ASHIER	C-HAZANS	C-HUCKLE	C-LAVERS	C-LOCKER	C-OPTERS	C-RASHES	C-ROOKED
C-ASKING	C-HEATED	C-HUFFED	C-LAWING	C-LOGGED	C-ORACLE	C-RATERS	C-ROQUET
C-ASTERS	C-HEATER	C-HUGGED	C-LAYING	C-LOGGER	C-OSIERS	C-RATING	C-ROSIER
C-ASTRAL	C-HEWERS	C-HUMMED	C-LEANED	C-LOPPED	C-OTTARS	C-RAUNCH	C-ROSSER
C-AULDER	C-HEWING	C-HUNTER	C-LEANER	C-LOSING	C-OTTERS	C-RAVENS	C-ROUPED

C-ROUTES	C-RUDDLE	C-RUMBLE	C-RUMPLE	C-RUSHER	C-ULLING	C-UPPERS	C-URATES
C-ROWING	C-RUDELY	C-RUMBLY	C-RUNKLE	C-RUSHES	C-UMBERS	C-UPPING	C-UTISES
C-RUDDED	C-RUDEST	C-RUMPED	C-RUSHED	C-RUSTED	C-UNDIES	C-URARIS	C-UTTERS

7→8

C-AMASSES	C-HAPPIES	C-HOKIEST	C-LASHERS	C-LOTTING	C-RANCHES	C-ROQUETS
C-AMBERED	C-HAPPING	C-HOOFING	C-LASHING	C-LOURING	C-RANKING	C-ROSIERS
C-ANGLING	C-HARKING	C-HOOKIES	C-LATCHED	C-LOUTING	C-RANKLED	C-ROTCHES
C-ANNULAR	C-HARMFUL	C-HOPPERS	C-LATCHES	C-LOVERED	C-RANKLES	C-ROUPIER
C-ANTINGS	C-HARMING	C-HOPPIER	C-LAWLESS	C-LOWNING	C-RAPPING	C-ROUPING
C-ARABINS	C-HAROSET	C-HOPPING	C-LEANEST	C-LUBBERS	C-RASHING	C-ROWDIES
C-AROUSAL	C-HARPIES	C-HORDING	C-LEANING	C-LUCKIER	C-RATCHES	C-RUDDIER
C-AROUSED	C-HARRIER	C-HOUSING	C-LEARING	C-LUMBERS	C-RAVENED	C-RUDDING
C-AROUSER	C-HASTENS	C-HUCKLES	C-LEAVERS	C-LUMPERS	C-RAVINGS	C-RUDDLED
C-AROUSES	C-HATTERS	C-HUFFIER	C-LEAVING	C-LUMPIER	C-REAKING	C-RUDDLES
C-ARRACKS	C-HATTING	C-HUFFING	C-LEEPING	C-LUMPING	C-REAMERS	C-RUMBLED
C-ARRIAGE	C-HAUNTED	C-HUGGING	C-LEMMING	C-LUNCHES	C-REAMIER	C-RUMBLES
C-AULDEST	C-HAUNTER	C-HUMMING	C-LICKERS	C-LUSTERS	C-REAMING	C-RUMMIER
C-ENSURED	C-HAZANIM	C-HUMPING	C-LICKING	C-OFFERED	C-REEKIER	C-RUMMIES
C-ENSURES	C-HEATERS	C-HUNKIER	C-LIMBERS	C-OLDNESS	C-RESTING	C-RUMPING
C-ENTERED	C-HEATING	C-HUNTERS	C-LIMBING	C-ORACLES	C-RIBBING	C-RUMPLED
C-ENTRIES	C-HERRIED	C-HUPPAHS	C-LINCHES	C-OSMOSES	C-RIBWORK	C-RUMPLES
C-ENTRISM	C-HERRIES	C-HUTZPAH	C-LINGERS	C-OVARIES	C-RICKETS	C-RUNCHES
C-ENTRIST	C-HIDINGS	C-INCHING	C-LINGIER	C-OVERAGE	C-RICKING	C-RUNKLED
C-HACKING	C-HILDING	C-LACKERS	C-LINKERS	C-OVERALL	C-RINGERS	C-RUNKLES
C-HAINING	C-HILLIER	C-LACKING	C-LINKING	C-OVERING	C-RINGING	C-RUSHERS
C-HAIRING	C-HILLING	C-LADDERS	C-LIPPIES	C-OVERTLY	C-RIPPLED	C-RUSHING
C-HALLANS	C-HIPPIER	C-LAGGING	C-LIPPING	C-RACKERS	C-RIPPLES	C-RUSTIER
C-HAMLETS	C-HIPPIES	C-LAMBERS	C-LITTERS	C-RACKING	C-RISPING	C-RUSTILY
C-HAMPERS	C-HIPPING	C-LAMMING	C-LOCKERS	C-RAFTING	C-RITTERS	C-RUSTING
C-HANDLER	C-HIRLING	C-LAMPERS	C-LOCKING	C-RAGGIER	C-ROCHETS	C-ULLINGS
C-HANGERS	C-HITTERS	C-LAMPING	C-LOGGERS	C-RAMMERS	C-ROCKERY	C-UMBERED
C-HANGING	C-HITTING	C-LANKING	C-LOGGING	C-RAMMING	C-ROCKETS	C-UMBROUS
C-HAPLESS	C-HIZZING	C-LAPPERS	C-LOPPING	C-RAMPING	C-ROCKING	C-UPPINGS
C-HAPPIER	C-HOCKING	C-LAPPING	C-LOSINGS	C-RANCHED	C-ROOKING	

8→9

C-AMPHORIC	C-HARMLESS	C-HOPPIEST	C-LICKINGS	C-RANCHING	C-ROQUETED
C-ANNULATE	C-HAROSETH	C-HOPPINGS	C-LINGIEST	C-RANKLING	C-ROQUETTE
C-AROUSALS	C-HAROSETS	C-HOROLOGY	C-LITTERED	C-RANKNESS	C-ROUPIEST
C-AROUSERS	C-HASTENED	C-HUFFIEST	C-LUCKIEST	C-RAUNCHED	C-RUDDIEST
C-AROUSING	C-HASTENER	C-HUNKIEST	C-LUMPIEST	C-RAUNCHES	C-RUDDLING
C-ARRIAGES	C-HATTERED	C-LAPPERED	C-LUSTERED	C-RAVENING	C-RUDENESS
C-AVIARIES	C-HAUNTERS	C-LAPPINGS	C-OFFERING	C-REAMIEST	C-RUMBLIER
C-EASELESS	C-HAUNTING	C-LASHINGS	C-OVERAGES	C-REEKIEST	C-RUMBLING
C-ENSURING	C-HEATINGS	C-LATCHING	C-OVERALLS	C-REMASTER	C-RUMMIEST
C-ENTERING	C-HERRYING	C-LAVATION	C-OVERSLIP	C-RESTLESS	C-RUMPLING
C-ENTRISMS	C-HIDLINGS	C-LEANINGS	C-OVERTURE	C-RETINOID	C-RUNKLING
C-ENTRISTS	C-HILLIEST	C-LEANNESS	C-RAFTSMAN	C-RIBWORKS	C-RUSTIEST
C-HANDLERS	C-HIPPIEST	C-LEAVINGS	C-RAFTSMEN	C-RINGINGS	C-RUSTLESS
C-HAPPIEST	C-HIPPINGS		C-RAGGIEST	C-RIPPLING	C-UMBERING

2→3

AR-C	DO-C	HO-C	MA-C	PI-C	SI-C	TI-C
BA-C	HI-C	LA-C	OR-C	RE-C	SO-C	TO-C

3→4

ABA-C	CHI-C	SAI-C
BAN-C	MAR-C	TOR-C

4→5

ANTI-C	COSE-C	ILEA-C	MAGI-C	MANI-C	SERA-C	TOPI-C	TRON-C	YOGI-C
BOBA-C	DARI-C	ILIA-C	MALI-C	RABI-C	TARO-C	TORI-C	VARE-C	

5→6

AGAMI-C	CHOLI-C	LENTI-C	MYTHI-C	THYMI-C
CALPA-C	IAMBI-C	MANIA-C	PARSE-C	TRAGI-C

6→7

EMBOLI-C	EPHEBI-C	PHALLI-C	RHOMBI-C	SCORIA-C	THALLI-C	TROPHI-C

7→8

AMMONIA-C	APHASIA-C	CHOREGI-C	OMPHALI-C	SYLLABI-C	TYMPANI-C
AMNESIA-C	CHORAGI-C	NURAGHI-C	RHYTHMI-C	THALAMI-C	

8→9

EGOMANIA-C	INSOMNIA-C	PARANOIA-C	PRODROMI-C	VIRTUOSI-C
FASCISTI-C	MACARONI-C	PAROEMIA-C	SYMPOSIA-C	ZOOPHORI-C

2→3

D-AD	D-AN	D-EE	D-ID	D-OD	D-OO	D-OW	D-UP
D-AE	D-AS	D-EF	D-IN	D-OE	D-OP	D-SO	D-YE
D-AH	D-AW	D-EL	D-IT	D-OH	D-OR	D-UG	D-ZO
D-AM	D-AY	D-EN	D-OB	D-ON	D-OS	D-UN	

3→4

D-ACE	D-AMP	D-EAR	D-ENS	D-IRK	D-ONE	D-OUR	D-RAW	D-SOS	D-ZHO
D-ADO	D-ANT	D-EEK	D-ERE	D-ISH	D-ONS	D-OUT	D-RAY	D-UDS	D-ZOS
D-ADS	D-ARE	D-EEN	D-ERN	D-ITA	D-OOM	D-OWL	D-REE	D-UGS	
D-AFT	D-ARK	D-EFT	D-HOW	D-ITS	D-OOR	D-OWN	D-REW	D-UKE	
D-AGO	D-ART	D-ELF	D-ICE	D-OAT	D-OOS	D-OWT	D-RIB	D-ULE	
D-AHS	D-ASH	D-ELL	D-ICH	D-OBS	D-OPE	D-RAD	D-RIP	D-UNS	
D-AIS	D-ATE	D-ELS	D-ILL	D-ODS	D-OPS	D-RAG	D-ROW	D-UPS	
D-ALE	D-AWN	D-ELT	D-INK	D-OES	D-ORS	D-RAM	D-RUB	D-URE	
D-ALS	D-AYS	D-EME	D-INS	D-OFF	D-ORT	D-RAP	D-RUG	D-URN	
D-ALT	D-EAN	D-ENE	D-IRE	D-OLE	D-OUP	D-RAT	D-RUM	D-YES	

4→5

D-ACES	D-ARKS	D-EMIT	D-ILLS	D-OPED	D-RAIL	D-REAR	D-ROLE	D-UNCE
D-ADOS	D-ARTS	D-ENES	D-ILLY	D-OPES	D-RAIN	D-RECK	D-ROLL	D-URES
D-AFFY	D-AUNT	D-ERED	D-INGO	D-ORTS	D-RAKE	D-REED	D-RONE	D-URNS
D-AINE	D-AWED	D-ERES	D-INKS	D-OUPS	D-RAMS	D-REES	D-ROOK	D-WALE
D-AIRY	D-AWNS	D-ERNS	D-INKY	D-OUTS	D-RANK	D-RENT	D-ROOP	D-WANG
D-ALES	D-EANS	D-ESSE	D-IOTA	D-OVER	D-RANT	D-REST	D-ROVE	D-WELL
D-ALLY	D-EARN	D-EVIL	D-IRKS	D-OWED	D-RAPE	D-RIBS	D-ROWS	D-WELT
D-ALTS	D-EARS	D-HOLE	D-ITAS	D-OWER	D-RAPS	D-RICE	D-RUBS	D-WILE
D-AMPS	D-EATH	D-HOLS	D-ITCH	D-OWLS	D-RAVE	D-RIFT	D-RUGS	D-WINE
D-ANCE	D-ECAD	D-HOWS	D-JINN	D-OWNS	D-RAWN	D-RILL	D-RUMS	D-ZHOS
D-ANTS	D-ELFS	D-ICED	D-OATS	D-OWTS	D-RAWS	D-RINK	D-RUSE	
D-ARED	D-ELLS	D-ICER	D-OFFS	D-RAFF	D-RAYS	D-RIPS	D-UKES	
D-ARES	D-ELTS	D-ICES	D-OILY	D-RAFT	D-READ	D-RIVE	D-ULES	
D-ARIS	D-EMES	D-ICKY	D-OOMS	D-RAGS	D-REAM	D-ROIL	D-UMBO	

5→6

D-ADDED	D-EARED	D-EMOTE	D-INNED	D-ORMER	D-RAPED	D-RIVER	D-RUSES
D-ADDLE	D-EARLY	D-EMURE	D-INNER	D-OUGHT	D-RAPER	D-RIVES	D-UDDER
D-AFTER	D-EARNS	D-ERING	D-IOTAS	D-OUTED	D-RAPES	D-ROGER	D-UMBER
D-AGGER	D-EARTH	D-ESSES	D-IRKED	D-OUTER	D-RAWER	D-ROGUE	D-UMBOS
D-AMPLY	D-EAVES	D-EVILS	D-ISHES	D-OVERS	D-READS	D-ROILS	D-UNCES
D-ANGER	D-ECADS	D-HOLES	D-JEBEL	D-OWING	D-REAMS	D-ROLES	D-UNDER
D-ANGLE	D-EDUCE	D-HOOLY	D-JINNI	D-OWNED	D-REAMY	D-ROLLS	D-UNITE
D-ANKER	D-EDUCT	D-HURRA	D-OATER	D-OWNER	D-REARS	D-RONES	D-UNKED
D-ANTED	D-EIDER	D-ICERS	D-OCKER	D-RAFFS	D-RECKS	D-ROOKS	D-UPPED
D-APPLE	D-EJECT	D-ICIER	D-ODDER	D-RAFTS	D-RICES	D-ROOPS	D-WALES
D-ASHES	D-ELATE	D-ICING	D-OFFED	D-RAGEE	D-RIFTS	D-ROOPY	D-WANGS
D-AUNTS	D-ELOPE	D-ICKER	D-OFFER	D-RAGGY	D-RIFTY	D-ROUTH	D-WELLS
D-AVENS	D-ELUDE	D-IMPLY	D-OILED	D-RAILS	D-RILLS	D-ROVER	D-WILES
D-AWING	D-ELVER	D-INGLE	D-OLENT	D-RAINS	D-RINKS	D-ROVES	D-WINED
D-AWNED	D-ELVES	D-INKED	D-ONNED	D-RAKES	D-RIVEL	D-RUGGY	D-WINES
D-AWNER	D-EMITS	D-INKER	D-OPING	D-RANTS	D-RIVEN	D-RUMLY	

6→7

D-ACKERS	D-ANGLER	D-EATHLY	D-ELOPED	D-EMURES	D-INKIER	D-JIBBAH	D-OUTING
D-ADDING	D-ANGLES	D-EDUCED	D-ELOPES	D-EPOSES	D-INKING	D-OATERS	D-OVERED
D-ADDLED	D-ANTING	D-EDUCES	D-ELUDED	D-EVOLVE	D-INNERS	D-OCKERS	D-OWNERS
D-ADDLES	D-APPLES	D-EDUCTS	D-ELUDER	D-HURRAS	D-INNING	D-OFFERS	D-OWNING
D-AFFIES	D-ARLING	D-EFTEST	D-ELUDES	D-ICIEST	D-IREFUL	D-OFFING	D-RABBET
D-AGGERS	D-AUNTER	D-EJECTA	D-ELVERS	D-ICINGS	D-IRKING	D-ONNING	D-RABBLE
D-ALLIED	D-AWNERS	D-EJECTS	D-EMERGE	D-ICKERS	D-ITCHED	D-OODLES	D-RAFTED
D-ALLIES	D-AWNING	D-ELAPSE	D-EMOTED	D-ICKIER	D-ITCHES	D-ORMERS	D-RAFTER
D-ANGERS	D-EARING	D-ELATED	D-EMOTES	D-INGLES	D-IZZARD	D-OUCHES	D-RAGEES
D-ANGLED	D-EARTHS	D-ELATES	D-EMURED	D-INGOES	D-JEBELS	D-OUTERS	D-RAGGED

D-RAGGLE	D-RAPING	D-REAMER	D-RIVELS	D-ROLLER	D-RUBBED	D-UDDERS	D-UNSHED
D-RAILED	D-RAPPED	D-REARER	D-RIVERS	D-ROOKED	D-RUGGED	D-ULLING	D-UPPING
D-RAINED	D-RATTED	D-RIBBED	D-RIVING	D-ROOPED	D-RUGGER	D-ULOSES	D-WELLED
D-RAMMED	D-RAUGHT	D-RIBLET	D-ROGERS	D-ROUGHT	D-RUMBLE	D-ULOSIS	D-WINDLE
D-RANTED	D-RAWING	D-RIFTED	D-ROGUES	D-ROUTHS	D-RUMMER	D-UNITES	D-WINING
D-RAPERS	D-READER	D-RILLED	D-ROILED	D-ROVERS	D-UBIETY	D-UNKING	D-YESTER
D-RAPIER	D-REAMED	D-RIPPED	D-ROLLED	D-ROVING	D-UCKERS	D-UNNEST	

7→8

D-ADDLING	D-ELATION	D-ENOUNCE	D-ONENESS	D-RAINING	D-RIFTIER	D-RUGGERS
D-ALLYING	D-ELOPING	D-EPILATE	D-OVERING	D-RAMMING	D-RIFTING	D-RUGGIER
D-ANGERED	D-ELUDERS	D-EPURATE	D-RABBETS	D-RANTING	D-RILLING	D-RUGGING
D-ANGLERS	D-ELUDING	D-ESCRIBE	D-RABBLED	D-RAPIERS	D-RINKING	D-RUMBLED
D-ANGLING	D-ELUSION	D-EVOLVED	D-RABBLER	D-RAPPING	D-RIPPIER	D-RUMBLES
D-ARRAIGN	D-ELUSIVE	D-EVOLVES	D-RABBLES	D-RAWINGS	D-RIPPING	D-RUMMERS
D-AUNTERS	D-ELUSORY	D-HURRIES	D-RAFFISH	D-READERS	D-ROILING	D-UPLYING
D-AWNINGS	D-EMERGED	D-ICKIEST	D-RAFTERS	D-READING	D-ROLLING	D-WELLING
D-ECURIES	D-EMERGES	D-INKIEST	D-RAFTING	D-REAMERS	D-ROOKING	D-WINDLES
D-EDUCING	D-EMERSED	D-ITCHING	D-RAGGIER	D-REAMIER	D-ROOPIER	
D-EJECTED	D-EMITTED	D-IZZARDS	D-RAGGING	D-REAMING	D-ROOPING	
D-ELAPSED	D-EMOTING	D-JELLABA	D-RAGGLED	D-REARING	D-ROVINGS	
D-ELAPSES	D-EMOTION	D-JIBBAHS	D-RAGGLES	D-RIBBING	D-ROWNDED	
D-ELATING	D-EMURING	D-OLOROSO	D-RAILING	D-RIBLETS	D-RUBBING	

8→9

D-ALLIANCE	D-EJECTION	D-EMOTIONS	D-ESCRIBED	D-RAFTSMAN	D-ROOPIEST
D-ANGERING	D-ELAPSING	D-EMULSIFY	D-ESCRIBES	D-RAFTSMEN	D-ROUTHIER
D-ANGLINGS	D-ELATIONS	D-ENOUNCED	D-EVALUATE	D-RAGGIEST	D-RUBBINGS
D-ARRAIGNS	D-ELUSIONS	D-ENOUNCES	D-EVOLVING	D-RAGGLING	D-RUGGIEST
D-EBAUCHES	D-EMERGING	D-EPILATED	D-EXTRORSE	D-REAMIEST	D-RUMBLING
D-ECAUDATE	D-EMERSION	D-EPILATES	D-IREFULLY	D-RIFTIEST	D-UBIETIES
D-EDUCIBLE	D-EMISSION	D-EPILATOR	D-JELLABAS	D-RIFTLESS	D-WELLINGS
D-EDUCTION	D-EMISSIVE	D-EPURATED	D-RABBLERS	D-RIVELLED	
D-EJECTING	D-EMITTING	D-EPURATES	D-RABBLING	D-ROLLINGS	

2→3

AD-D	BE-D	DO-D	GO-D	LI-D	MU-D	OU-D	TA-D	WE-D
AI-D	BI-D	EL-D	HA-D	LO-D	NE-D	PA-D	TE-D	YO-D
AN-D	BO-D	EN-D	HI-D	MA-D	NO-D	PO-D	TI-D	
AR-D	DA-D	FA-D	HO-D	MI-D	OD-D	RE-D	TO-D	
BA-D	DI-D	GI-D	LA-D	MO-D	OR-D	SO-D	UR-D	

3→4

ACE-D	BRO-D	DIE-D	FOR-D	HOE-D	LIE-D	PAN-D	ROO-D	SUE-D	VIE-D
AGE-D	BUN-D	DOW-D	FOU-D	HON-D	LIN-D	PAR-D	RUD-D	SUI-D	WAD-D
AKE-D	BUR-D	DUE-D	FUN-D	HOO-D	LOR-D	PEE-D	RUE-D	SUR-D	WAN-D
AMI-D	CAR-D	DYE-D	GAE-D	HUE-D	MAN-D	PEN-D	RUN-D	SYE-D	WAR-D
APE-D	CHA-D	EAR-D	GAU-D	HYE-D	MAR-D	PIE-D	SAI-D	TAE-D	WEE-D
ARE-D	CHI-D	EKE-D	GEE-D	ICE-D	MEL-D	POO-D	SAN-D	TEA-D	WEN-D
AWE-D	COL-D	ERE-D	GEL-D	JEE-D	MEN-D	PRO-D	SAR-D	TEE-D	WIN-D
AXE-D	CON-D	EYE-D	GIE-D	KAE-D	MIL-D	QUA-D	SEE-D	TEL-D	WOO-D
BAN-D	COR-D	FAN-D	GOA-D	KAI-D	MOO-D	RAI-D	SEL-D	TEN-D	WYN-D
BAR-D	CRU-D	FAR-D	GOO-D	KIN-D	NEE-D	RAN-D	SEN-D	TIE-D	YEA-D
BEN-D	CUE-D	FEE-D	HAN-D	KON-D	NIE-D	RED-D	SHE-D	TIN-D	YON-D
BIN-D	CUR-D	FEN-D	HEN-D	LAR-D	NUR-D	REE-D	SIN-D	TOE-D	
BON-D	DAW-D	FEU-D	HER-D	LEA-D	NYE-D	REN-D	SKI-D	TUN-D	
BOR-D	DEE-D	FIN-D	HIE-D	LEE-D	OPE-D	RIN-D	SOL-D	TYE-D	
BRA-D	DEI-D	FON-D	HIN-D	LEW-D	OWE-D	ROE-D	SUD-D	USE-D	

4→5

ABLE-D	BAKE-D	BLIN-D	CAGE-D	CLOU-D	CROW-D	DOLE-D	ECHE-D	FIKE-D
ACHE-D	BALE-D	BLUE-D	CAKE-D	CLUE-D	CUBE-D	DOME-D	EDGE-D	FILE-D
ACRE-D	BANE-D	BOAR-D	CANE-D	CODE-D	CURE-D	DOPE-D	ELAN-D	FINE-D
AGUE-D	BARE-D	BODE-D	CAPE-D	COKE-D	DARE-D	DOSE-D	ERNE-D	FIRE-D
AIDE-D	BASE-D	BOKE-D	CARE-D	CONE-D	DATE-D	DOTE-D	FACE-D	FRAU-D
ALKY-D	BATE-D	BONE-D	CASE-D	COPE-D	DAZE-D	DOVE-D	FADE-D	FREE-D
ALOE-D	BAYE-D	BOOR-D	CAUL-D	CORE-D	DELE-D	DOZE-D	FAKE-D	FUME-D
AMEN-D	BEAR-D	BORE-D	CAVE-D	COSE-D	DERE-D	DREE-D	FAME-D	FUSE-D
ANTE-D	BEMA-D	BOUN-D	CEDE-D	COTE-D	DICE-D	DUKE-D	FARE-D	FYKE-D
APAY-D	BETE-D	BRAN-D	CERE-D	COUR-D	DIKE-D	DUPE-D	FATE-D	GAGE-D
AREA-D	BIDE-D	BREE-D	CHAR-D	COVE-D	DINE-D	DURE-D	FAZE-D	GAME-D
ARED-D	BIKE-D	BROO-D	CIDE-D	COZE-D	DITE-D	DYKE-D	FETE-D	GAPE-D
ARLE-D	BLEE-D	BYKE-D	CITE-D	CREE-D	DIVE-D	EASE-D	FIFE-D	GATE-D

GAZE-D	HOKE-D	LERE-D	MEVE-D	PENE-D	RILE-D	SNEE-D	TINE-D	VOTE-D
GIBE-D	HOLE-D	LIAR-D	MIME-D	PIKE-D	RIME-D	SOLE-D	TIRE-D	WADE-D
GIVE-D	HOME-D	LIKE-D	MINE-D	PILE-D	RIPE-D	SOLI-D	TOGE-D	WAGE-D
GLEE-D	HONE-D	LIME-D	MIRE-D	PINE-D	RIVE-D	SORE-D	TOKE-D	WAKE-D
GLUE-D	HOPE-D	LINE-D	MONA-D	PIPE-D	ROBE-D	SOWN-D	TOLE-D	WALE-D
GOOL-D	HOSE-D	LITE-D	MOPE-D	PLEA-D	RODE-D	SPAE-D	TONE-D	WAME-D
GORE-D	HOVE-D	LIVE-D	MOSE-D	PLIE-D	ROKE-D	SPAR-D	TOPE-D	WANE-D
GRAN-D	HYPE-D	LOBE-D	MOTE-D	POKE-D	ROPE-D	SPAY-D	TOSE-D	WARE-D
GREE-D	IDLE-D	LOME-D	MOVE-D	POLE-D	ROSE-D	SPIE-D	TOTE-D	WAVE-D
GRIN-D	ISLE-D	LOOR-D	MOZE-D	PORE-D	ROTE-D	SPUE-D	TOZE-D	WEAL-D
GRUE-D	JADE-D	LOPE-D	MURE-D	POSE-D	ROVE-D	STED-D	TREE-D	WEIR-D
GUAR-D	JAPE-D	LOSE-D	MUSE-D	POTE-D	RULE-D	STEN-D	TRIE-D	WEXE-D
GYBE-D	JIBE-D	LOUN-D	MUTE-D	POWN-D	RUNE-D	STIE-D	TRUE-D	WIEL-D
GYRE-D	JIVE-D	LOVE-D	NAME-D	PREE-D	RYKE-D	STYE-D	TUBE-D	WILE-D
GYVE-D	JOBE-D	LOWE-D	NOMA-D	PUKE-D	SAFE-D	SURE-D	TUNE-D	WINE-D
HADE-D	JOKE-D	LOWN-D	NOSE-D	PULE-D	SATE-D	SWEE-D	TYNE-D	WIPE-D
HALE-D	JOLE-D	LUGE-D	NOTE-D	PURE-D	SAVE-D	SYNE-D	TYPE-D	WIRE-D
HAME-D	JUKE-D	LURE-D	NOUL-D	PYNE-D	SCAN-D	SYPE-D	TYRE-D	WISE-D
HARE-D	KITE-D	LUTE-D	NUKE-D	QUAY-D	SEEL-D	TABI-D	UNBE-D	WITE-D
HATE-D	KNEE-D	LYSE-D	OCTA-D	RABI-D	SERE-D	TAME-D	URGE-D	WIVE-D
HAUL-D	LACE-D	LYTE-D	OGLE-D	RACE-D	SHAN-D	TARE-D	VADE-D	WOOL-D
HAZE-D	LADE-D	MACE-D	OOZE-D	RAGE-D	SHOE-D	TEEN-D	VALI-D	WYTE-D
HEAL-D	LAIR-D	MANE-D	PACE-D	RAKE-D	SIDE-D	TEME-D	VANE-D	YEAR-D
HEAR-D	LAKE-D	MASE-D	PAGE-D	RAPE-D	SILE-D	THEE-D	VICE-D	YOKE-D
HELE-D	LAME-D	MATE-D	PALE-D	RASE-D	SINE-D	THIR-D	VINE-D	YUKE-D
HIDE-D	LASE-D	MAUN-D	PANE-D	RATE-D	SIPE-D	TICE-D	VIOL-D	ZONE-D
HIKE-D	LATE-D	MAZE-D	PARE-D	RAVE-D	SIRE-D	TIDE-D	VIRE-D	
HIRE-D	LAVE-D	MENE-D	PATE-D	RAZE-D	SIZE-D	TILE-D	VISE-D	
HIVE-D	LAZE-D	MERE-D	PAVE-D	REKE-D	SLUE-D	TIME-D	VISE-D	
HOAR-D	LEME-D	METE-D	PAYS-D	RICE-D	SLUE-D	TIME-D	VOLE-D	

5→6

ABASE-D	BELEE-D	CAUSE-D	DAINE-D	FADGE-D	GLIDE-D	INKLE-D	MENGE-D
ABATE-D	BELIE-D	CEASE-D	DAMME-D	FAINE-D	GLOBE-D	INURE-D	MENSE-D
ABIDE-D	BELLE-D	CEAZE-D	DANCE-D	FALSE-D	GLOVE-D	ISSUE-D	MERGE-D
ABODE-D	BILGE-D	CENSE-D	DARRE-D	FARCE-D	GLOZE-D	JOULE-D	METRE-D
ABUSE-D	BINGE-D	CERNE-D	DAUBE-D	FARSE-D	GOOSE-D	JUDGE-D	MEUSE-D
ACARI-D	BIRLE-D	CESSE-D	DEARE-D	FAYNE-D	GORGE-D	JUICE-D	MICHE-D
ADDLE-D	BITTE-D	CHACE-D	DEAVE-D	FEARE-D	GOUGE-D	KEDGE-D	MIEVE-D
ADORE-D	BLADE-D	CHAFE-D	DEEVE-D	FEESE-D	GRACE-D	KERNE-D	MILLE-D
AFEAR-D	BLAME-D	CHARE-D	DELVE-D	FEEZE-D	GRADE-D	KERVE-D	MILOR-D
AGAMI-D	BLARE-D	CHASE-D	DEMAN-D	FENCE-D	GRAPE-D	KITHE-D	MINCE-D
AGAZE-D	BLAZE-D	CHIDE-D	DEUCE-D	FESSE-D	GRATE-D	KNIFE-D	MINGE-D
AGREE-D	BODGE-D	CHIEL-D	DINGE-D	FIBRE-D	GRAVE-D	KNIVE-D	MITRE-D
AISLE-D	BOMBE-D	CHIME-D	DIRKE-D	FIDGE-D	GRAZE-D	KYNDE-D	MOBLE-D
ALATE-D	BOOSE-D	CHINE-D	DODGE-D	FILLE-D	GRIDE-D	KYTHE-D	MOOVE-D
ALEYE-D	BOOZE-D	CHIVE-D	DONNE-D	FITTE-D	GRIME-D	LADLE-D	MORNE-D
ALINE-D	BOTTE-D	CHOKE-D	DOUSE-D	FLAKE-D	GRIPE-D	LANCE-D	MOUSE-D
AMATE-D	BOUGE-D	CLEPE-D	DOWSE-D	FLAME-D	GRISE-D	LANDE-D	MOYLE-D
AMAZE-D	BOUSE-D	CLIPE-D	DRAPE-D	FLARE-D	GRONE-D	LAPSE-D	MUDGE-D
AMBLE-D	BOWNE-D	CLOKE-D	DRONE-D	FLITE-D	GROPE-D	LATHE-D	MUSSE-D
AMENE-D	BOWSE-D	CLONE-D	DWINE-D	FLUKE-D	GRYDE-D	LEARE-D	NACRE-D
AMOVE-D	BRACE-D	CLOSE-D	EDUCE-D	FLUTE-D	GUIDE-D	LEASE-D	NAPPE-D
AMUSE-D	BRAKE-D	CLOYE-D	ELATE-D	FLYPE-D	GUILE-D	LEAVE-D	NEESE-D
ANELE-D	BRAVE-D	CLYPE-D	ELIDE-D	FLYTE-D	GUISE-D	LEGGE-D	NEEZE-D
ANGLE-D	BRAZE-D	COATE-D	ELOPE-D	FORCE-D	GUYLE-D	LEVEE-D	NERVE-D
ANKLE-D	BREDE-D	COCCI-D	ELUDE-D	FORGE-D	HALSE-D	LIGAN-D	NICHE-D
APPAY-D	BRIBE-D	COMBE-D	ELUTE-D	FORME-D	HALVE-D	LIGGE-D	NOISE-D
ARGAN-D	BRIDE-D	CONGE-D	EMCEE-D	FORTE-D	HASTE-D	LITHE-D	NOOSE-D
ARGUE-D	BRINE-D	CONNE-D	EMOTE-D	FOSSE-D	HAUSE-D	LOAVE-D	NUDGE-D
ATONE-D	BROKE-D	COOEE-D	EMOVE-D	FOULE-D	HAWSE-D	LODGE-D	NURSE-D
AVALE-D	BRUTE-D	COPSE-D	EMULE-D	FOYLE-D	HEAVE-D	LONGE-D	OCHRE-D
AVISE-D	BUDGE-D	COSTE-D	EMURE-D	FOYNE-D	HEDGE-D	LOOSE-D	OPINE-D
AVIZE-D	BUFFE-D	COUPE-D	ENDUE-D	FRAME-D	HEEZE-D	LOUPE-D	ORATE-D
AVYZE-D	BUGLE-D	COURE-D	ENSUE-D	FUDGE-D	HEFTE-D	LOURE-D	OUTRE-D
AWAKE-D	BULGE-D	CRAKE-D	ENURE-D	FUGLE-D	HELVE-D	LOUSE-D	OVATE-D
BADGE-D	BUNCE-D	CRANE-D	ERASE-D	GABLE-D	HERSE-D	LOWNE-D	PAIRE-D
BAIZE-D	BURKE-D	CRATE-D	ERODE-D	GAFFE-D	HERYE-D	LUNGE-D	PANNE-D
BARBE-D	BUTTE-D	CRAVE-D	ETTLE-D	GAMME-D	HINGE-D	MACLE-D	PARGE-D
BARGE-D	CABLE-D	CRAZE-D	EVADE-D	GARBE-D	HOISE-D	MAILE-D	PARLE-D
BARRE-D	CACHE-D	CREWE-D	EVITE-D	GARRE-D	HOOVE-D	MANGE-D	PARSE-D
BASSE-D	CADGE-D	CRIME-D	EVOKE-D	GAUGE-D	HORDE-D	MARLE-D	PASSE-D
BASTE-D	CALVE-D	CRINE-D	EXEME-D	GEARE-D	HORSE-D	MASSE-D	PASTE-D
BATHE-D	CANOE-D	CROME-D	EXILE-D	GERNE-D	HOUSE-D	MATTE-D	PATTE-D
BEARE-D	CARTE-D	CURSE-D	EXTOL-D	GESSE-D	IMAGE-D	MEANE-D	PAUSE-D
BECKE-D	CARVE-D	CURVE-D	EXUDE-D	GLARE-D	IMBUE-D	MEASE-D	PEACE-D
BEDYE-D	CASTE-D	CYCLE-D	FABLE-D	GLAZE-D	INDUE-D	MEDLE-D	PEASE-D

PEAZE-D	PROSE-D	RHYME-D	SEINE-D	SLIVE-D	STARE-D	TEAZE-D	VALUE-D
PECKE-D	PROVE-D	RIDGE-D	SEISE-D	SLOPE-D	STATE-D	TEENE-D	VALVE-D
PEEPE-D	PRUNE-D	RIFLE-D	SEIZE-D	SMILE-D	STAVE-D	TEMSE-D	VARVE-D
PEEVE-D	PRYSE-D	RIFTE-D	SEMEE-D	SMOKE-D	STEAR-D	TENSE-D	VAUTE-D
PEISE-D	PULSE-D	RILLE-D	SENSE-D	SMORE-D	STEDE-D	TERNE-D	VAWTE-D
PEIZE-D	PUNCE-D	RINSE-D	SERRE-D	SNAKE-D	STEEL-D	TESTE-D	VENGE-D
PENNE-D	PUREE-D	ROATE-D	SERVE-D	SNARE-D	STEME-D	TETRA-D	VERGE-D
PERCE-D	PURGE-D	ROGUE-D	SHADE-D	SNIPE-D	STILE-D	THEME-D	VERSE-D
PERVE-D	PURSE-D	ROOSE-D	SHAKE-D	SNOKE-D	STIME-D	THOLE-D	VISIE-D
PETAR-D	PUSLE-D	ROUGE-D	SHALE-D	SNORE-D	STIRE-D	THROE-D	VOGUE-D
PEYSE-D	QUAKE-D	ROUSE-D	SHAME-D	SOARE-D	STIVE-D	TINGE-D	VOICE-D
PHASE-D	QUEME-D	ROUTE-D	SHAPE-D	SOLVE-D	STOKE-D	TITHE-D	VOLVE-D
PHESE-D	QUEUE-D	ROYNE-D	SHARE-D	SOOLE-D	STOLE-D	TITLE-D	WAITE-D
PHONE-D	QUIRE-D	RUCHE-D	SHAVE-D	SOOTE-D	STONE-D	TOAZE-D	WAIVE-D
PIECE-D	QUITE-D	RUFFE-D	SHIEL-D	SOUCE-D	STOPE-D	TODDE-D	WANZE-D
PIQUE-D	QUOTE-D	RYMME-D	SHINE-D	SOUSE-D	STORE-D	TOILE-D	WARRE-D
PLACE-D	QUYTE-D	SABLE-D	SHITE-D	SOWCE-D	STOUN-D	TOUSE-D	WASTE-D
PLANE-D	RAILE-D	SABRE-D	SHORE-D	SOWLE-D	STOVE-D	TOUZE-D	WEAVE-D
PLATE-D	RAINE-D	SAINE-D	SHOVE-D	SOWSE-D	STOWN-D	TOWSE-D	WEDGE-D
PLONG-D	RAISE-D	SALUE-D	SHREW-D	SPACE-D	STUPE-D	TOWZE-D	WEETE-D
PLUME-D	RANCE-D	SALVE-D	SHROW-D	SPADE-D	STYLE-D	TRACE-D	WEFTE-D
POISE-D	RANGE-D	SASSE-D	SHULE-D	SPANE-D	STYME-D	TRADE-D	WEISE-D
PONCE-D	RANKE-D	SAUCE-D	SIDLE-D	SPARE-D	STYRE-D	TRAPE-D	WEIZE-D
PORGE-D	RAYLE-D	SAUTE-D	SIEGE-D	SPAUL-D	STYTE-D	TRICE-D	WELKE-D
POSSE-D	RAZEE-D	SCALE-D	SIEVE-D	SPICE-D	SUEDE-D	TRINE-D	WHALE-D
POUPE-D	REAME-D	SCAPE-D	SINGE-D	SPIKE-D	SUITE-D	TROKE-D	WHILE-D
POWRE-D	RECCE-D	SCARE-D	SITHE-D	SPILE-D	SURGE-D	TROPE-D	WHINE-D
POYSE-D	REEDE-D	SCENE-D	SKATE-D	SPINE-D	SWAGE-D	TWINE-D	WHITE-D
PRATE-D	REEVE-D	SCOPE-D	SKIVE-D	SPIRE-D	SWALE-D	TWIRE-D	WHORE-D
PREVE-D	REGAR-D	SCORE-D	SKITE-D	SPITE-D	SWEAR-D	TYTHE-D	WINCE-D
PRICE-D	RELIE-D	SCREE-D	SKYRE-D	SPOKE-D	SWIPE-D	UNCLE-D	WINGE-D
PRIDE-D	REMAN-D	SCUSE-D	SKYTE-D	SPRED-D	SWIVE-D	UNITE-D	WITHE-D
PRIME-D	RENNE-D	SEAME-D	SLAKE-D	SPREE-D	SWOUN-D	UNTIE-D	WOLVE-D
PRISE-D	RENTE-D	SEARE-D	SLATE-D	SPUME-D	TABLE-D	UPTIE-D	WORSE-D
PRIZE-D	RETIE-D	SEASE-D	SLAVE-D	STAGE-D	TARGE-D	URINE-D	YODLE-D
PROBE-D	RETRO-D	SEAZE-D	SLICE-D	STAKE-D	TARRE-D	USURE-D	ZINKE-D
PROKE-D	REUSE-D	SEDGE-D	SLIDE-D	STALE-D	TASTE-D	VAGUE-D	
PROLE-D	REVIE-D	SEGUE-D	SLIME-D	STANE-D	TEASE-D	VALSE-D	

6→7

ABDUCE-D	ARAYSE-D	BENAME-D	BUMMLE-D	COGGLE-D	DAWDLE-D	DEVISE-D
ABJURE-D	ARCADE-D	BERATE-D	BUNDLE-D	COHERE-D	DAZZLE-D	DEVOTE-D
ABLATE-D	AROUSE-D	BERTHE-D	BUNGLE-D	COIGNE-D	DEBASE-D	DIBBLE-D
ABRADE-D	ARRIDE-D	BETIDE-D	BURBLE-D	COLLAR-D	DEBATE-D	DIDDLE-D
ACCEDE-D	ARRIVE-D	BETIME-D	BURGLE-D	COLLIE-D	DECIDE-D	DILATE-D
ACCITE-D	ASHAME-D	BEWARE-D	BUSTLE-D	COLOBI-D	DECKLE-D	DILUTE-D
ACCRUE-D	ASLAKE-D	BEZZLE-D	BUTTLE-D	CONCHE-D	DECODE-D	DIMPLE-D
ACCUSE-D	ASPIRE-D	BINGLE-D	CACKLE-D	CONGEE-D	DECOKE-D	DINDLE-D
ADDUCE-D	ASSIZE-D	BIRDIE-D	CADDIE-D	CONJEE-D	DECREE-D	DINNLE-D
ADHERE-D	ASSUME-D	BIRSLE-D	CAJOLE-D	CORPSE-D	DEDUCE-D	DISMAY-D
ADJURE-D	ASSURE-D	BISTRE-D	CALQUE-D	COTISE-D	DEFACE-D	DISPLE-D
ADMIRE-D	ASTONE-D	BLENDE-D	CAMPLE-D	COUCHE-D	DEFAME-D	DISUSE-D
ADVENE-D	ATTIRE-D	BLOUSE-D	CANDIE-D	COUPLE-D	DEFILE-D	DIVIDE-D
ADVISE-D	ATTUNE-D	BLOWSE-D	CANDLE-D	COURSE-D	DEFINE-D	DIVINE-D
AEMULE-D	AURATE-D	BLOWZE-D	CANGLE-D	CRADLE-D	DEFUSE-D	DONATE-D
AERATE-D	AVAILE-D	BLUDGE-D	CANTLE-D	CREASE-D	DEFUZE-D	DOODLE-D
AFFEAR-D	AVENGE-D	BLUNGE-D	CASTLE-D	CREATE-D	DELATE-D	DORISE-D
AFFINE-D	AVIATE-D	BOBBLE-D	CAUDLE-D	CREESE-D	DELETE-D	DORIZE-D
AGNAME-D	AVULSE-D	BOGGLE-D	CENTRE-D	CRINGE-D	DELOPE-D	DOTTLE-D
AGNISE-D	AWHAPE-D	BOODIE-D	CERATE-D	CROSSE-D	DELUDE-D	DOUBLE-D
AGNIZE-D	BABBLE-D	BOOGIE-D	CHAINE-D	CROUPE-D	DELUGE-D	DOUCHE-D
AGRISE-D	BAFFLE-D	BOTTLE-D	CHANCE-D	CRUISE-D	DEMISE-D	DREDGE-D
AGRIZE-D	BANGLE-D	BOUNCE-D	CHANGE-D	CUDDLE-D	DEMODE-D	DROMON-D
AGRYZE-D	BASQUE-D	BRAIDE-D	CHARGE-D	CUFFLE-D	DEMOTE-D	DROWSE-D
AGUISE-D	BATTLE-D	BRAISE-D	CHAUFE-D	CURATE-D	DEMURE-D	DRUDGE-D
AGUIZE-D	BEAGLE-D	BREEZE-D	CHEESE-D	CURDLE-D	DENOTE-D	DUMPLE-D
ALEGGE-D	BEDAZE-D	BRIDGE-D	CHILDE-D	CURRIE-D	DENUDE-D	ECLOSE-D
ALLEGE-D	BEETLE-D	BRIDLE-D	CHIRRE-D	DABBLE-D	DEPONE-D	EFFACE-D
ALLUDE-D	BEHAVE-D	BRIGUE-D	CHOUSE-D	DADDLE-D	DEPOSE-D	EFFERE-D
ALLURE-D	BEHOVE-D	BROCHE-D	CHROME-D	DAGGLE-D	DEPUTE-D	EFFUSE-D
AMENDE-D	BEJADE-D	BRONZE-D	CIRCLE-D	DAIDLE-D	DERATE-D	ELANCE-D
AMERCE-D	BELACE-D	BROWSE-D	CLEAVE-D	DAMAGE-D	DERIDE-D	ELAPSE-D
AMOOVE-D	BELATE-D	BRUISE-D	CLOTHE-D	DANDLE-D	DERIVE-D	EMBALE-D
ANNEXE-D	BELOVE-D	BUBBLE-D	COBBLE-D	DANGLE-D	DESINE-D	EMBASE-D
ANSATE-D	BEMETE-D	BUCKLE-D	COCKLE-D	DAPPLE-D	DESIRE-D	EMBRUE-D
APPOSE-D	BEMIRE-D	BUDDLE-D	CODDLE-D	DARKLE-D	DESYNE-D	EMERGE-D
ARAISE-D	BEMUSE-D	BUMBLE-D	COERCE-D	DARTLE-D	DETUNE-D	EMMOVE-D

EMPALE-D	GABBLE-D	INCITE-D	MINUTE-D	PLAGUE-D	REPUTE-D	SIPPLE-D	SWINGE-D
EMPARE-D	GAGGLE-D	INCUSE-D	MISCUE-D	PLEASE-D	RESCUE-D	SIZZLE-D	SWOUNE-D
EMULGE-D	GAMBLE-D	INDITE-D	MISTLE-D	PLEDGE-D	RESIDE-D	SKLATE-D	TACKLE-D
EMUNGE-D	GARAGE-D	INDUCE-D	MISUSE-D	PLONGE-D	RESILE-D	SLEAVE-D	TAIGLE-D
ENABLE-D	GARBLE-D	INFAME-D	MIZZLE-D	PLUNGE-D	RESKUE-D	SLEDGE-D	TANGLE-D
ENCAGE-D	GARGLE-D	INFUSE-D	MOBBLE-D	POINTE-D	RESOLE-D	SLEEVE-D	TATTLE-D
ENCASE-D	GENTLE-D	INHALE-D	MOTIVE-D	POLICE-D	RESUME-D	SLUICE-D	TEAGLE-D
ENCAVE-D	GHESSE-D	INHERE-D	MOTTLE-D	POMADE-D	RETILE-D	SMOILE-D	TEAZLE-D
ENCODE-D	GIGGLE-D	INHUME-D	MOUSLE-D	POPPLE-D	RETIME-D	SMOUSE-D	TEETHE-D
ENCORE-D	GILLIE-D	INISLE-D	MUDDLE-D	POTCHE-D	RETIRE-D	SMOYLE-D	TEMPLE-D
ENDITE-D	GIRDLE-D	INJURE-D	MUFFLE-D	POUFFE-D	RETUNE-D	SMUDGE-D	TENURE-D
ENDURE-D	GLAIVE-D	INLACE-D	MUMBLE-D	POUNCE-D	REURGE-D	SNEBBE-D	THIEVE-D
ENERVE-D	GLANCE-D	INSURE-D	MUNITE-D	PRAISE-D	REVERE-D	SNEEZE-D	THRIVE-D
ENFACE-D	GLEDGE-D	INTONE-D	MUSCLE-D	PRANCE-D	REVILE-D	SNOOZE-D	THRONE-D
ENFIRE-D	GOATEE-D	INVADE-D	MUTATE-D	PREACE-D	REVISE-D	SNUBBE-D	TICKLE-D
ENFREE-D	GOBBLE-D	INVITE-D	MUTINE-D	PREASE-D	REVIVE-D	SNUDGE-D	TIDDLE-D
ENGAGE-D	GOGGLE-D	INVOKE-D	MUZZLE-D	PREEVE-D	REVOKE-D	SOLACE-D	TIERCE-D
ENGINE-D	GOITRE-D	IODISE-D	NATURE-D	PREVUE-D	REWIRE-D	SOMBRE-D	TINGLE-D
ENGORE-D	GOLLAN-D	IODIZE-D	NEEDLE-D	PRIEVE-D	REZONE-D	SOOGEE-D	TINKLE-D
ENISLE-D	GOOGLE-D	IONISE-D	NEGATE-D	PRINCE-D	RIDDLE-D	SOOGIE-D	TIPPLE-D
ENLACE-D	GOWLAN-D	IONIZE-D	NESTLE-D	PROINE-D	RIFFLE-D	SOOTHE-D	TIPTOE-D
ENMOVE-D	GRAINE-D	JABBLE-D	NETTLE-D	PROVEN-D	RIPPLE-D	SOPITE-D	TISSUE-D
ENNUYE-D	GREASE-D	JANGLE-D	NIBBLE-D	PROYNE-D	ROOTLE-D	SORTIE-D	TITTLE-D
ENRACE-D	GREAVE-D	JAUNCE-D	NIGGLE-D	PSYCHE-D	ROTATE-D	SOUPLE-D	TITULE-D
ENRAGE-D	GREETE-D	JAUNSE-D	NIPPLE-D	PUDDLE-D	RUCKLE-D	SOURCE-D	TODDLE-D
ENROBE-D	GRIECE-D	JEELIE-D	NOBBLE-D	PUGGLE-D	RUDDLE-D	SOWSSE-D	TOGATE-D
ENSILE-D	GRIEVE-D	JERQUE-D	NODDLE-D	PUMICE-D	RUFFLE-D	SOZZLE-D	TOGGLE-D
ENSURE-D	GRILLE-D	JIGGLE-D	NODULE-D	PUPATE-D	RUMBLE-D	SPALLE-D	TONGUE-D
ENTAME-D	GRIPPE-D	JINGLE-D	NONAGE-D	PURFLE-D	RUMPLE-D	SPARGE-D	TOOTLE-D
ENTICE-D	GROOVE-D	JIRBLE-D	NOODLE-D	PURPLE-D	RUNDLE-D	SPARKE-D	TOPPLE-D
ENZONE-D	GROUSE-D	JOGGLE-D	NOTATE-D	PURSUE-D	RUNKLE-D	SPARRE-D	TORQUE-D
EQUATE-D	GRUDGE-D	JOSTLE-D	NOTICE-D	PUTTIE-D	RUSTLE-D	SPATHE-D	TOUCHE-D
ERMINE-D	GUDDLE-D	JOUNCE-D	NOUSLE-D	PUZZLE-D	RUSTRE-D	SPERRE-D	TOUSLE-D
ESCAPE-D	GUGGLE-D	JUGGLE-D	NUANCE-D	QUAERE-D	SADDLE-D	SPERSE-D	TOUZLE-D
ESTATE-D	GURGLE-D	JUMBLE-D	NUBBLE-D	QUICHE-D	SAGGAR-D	SPHERE-D	TOWMON-D
EUCHRE-D	GUTTLE-D	JUSTLE-D	NURDLE-D	RABBLE-D	SALUTE-D	SPLICE-D	TRANCE-D
EVINCE-D	GUZZLE-D	KECKLE-D	NURSLE-D	RACEME-D	SAMPLE-D	SPLINE-D	TRAYNE-D
EVOLVE-D	GYRATE-D	KIBBLE-D	NUTATE-D	RADDLE-D	SAPPLE-D	SPONGE-D	TREBLE-D
EVULSE-D	HACKLE-D	KINDLE-D	NUZZLE-D	RAFFLE-D	SAVAGE-D	SPOUSE-D	TRIFLE-D
EXCIDE-D	HAGGLE-D	KIRTLE-D	OBDURE-D	RAGGLE-D	SCARRE-D	SPRUCE-D	TRIPLE-D
EXCISE-D	HAMBLE-D	KITTLE-D	OBJURE-D	RAMBLE-D	SCATHE-D	SPULYE-D	TROMPE-D
EXCITE-D	HANDLE-D	KREESE-D	OBLIGE-D	RANKLE-D	SCERNE-D	SPURNE-D	TROULE-D
EXCUSE-D	HASSLE-D	LANGUE-D	OPAQUE-D	RATTLE-D	SCHEME-D	SQUARE-D	TROUPE-D
EXHALE-D	HEARSE-D	LAUNCE-D	OPIATE-D	RAUNGE-D	SCLATE-D	SQUIRE-D	TRUDGE-D
EXHUME-D	HECKLE-D	LEAGUE-D	OPPOSE-D	RAVAGE-D	SCONCE-D	STABLE-D	TUMBLE-D
EXPIRE-D	HEDDLE-D	LIAISE-D	ORACLE-D	RAVINE-D	SCORSE-D	STAPLE-D	TURBAN-D
EXPOSE-D	HIGGLE-D	LIBATE-D	OSMOSE-D	REBATE-D	SCRAPE-D	STARVE-D	TURTLE-D
FACETE-D	HIRPLE-D	LIGATE-D	OUGLIE-D	REBORE-D	SCRIBE-D	STATUE-D	TUSSLE-D
FADDLE-D	HIRSLE-D	LOATHE-D	OUTLIE-D	REBUKE-D	SCRIKE-D	STAYNE-D	TWEEZE-D
FANGLE-D	HOBBLE-D	LOCATE-D	OUTVIE-D	RECEDE-D	SCRIVE-D	STEALE-D	TWINGE-D
FANKLE-D	HODDLE-D	LOUNGE-D	OUTWIN-D	RECITE-D	SCRUZE-D	STEANE-D	ULLAGE-D
FEAGUE-D	HOGTIE-D	LOUVRE-D	PADDLE-D	RECODE-D	SCULLE-D	STEARE-D	UMPIRE-D
FEEBLE-D	HOMAGE-D	LUMINE-D	PALATE-D	RECULE-D	SCUNGE-D	STEDDE-D	UNBARE-D
FETTLE-D	HOPPLE-D	LUNATE-D	PARADE-D	RECURE-D	SCYTHE-D	STEEVE-D	UNBONE-D
FEUTRE-D	HUDDLE-D	LUSTRE-D	PAROLE-D	RECUSE-D	SDAINE-D	STEMME-D	UNCAGE-D
FICKLE-D	HUMBLE-D	LUXATE-D	PARPEN-D	REDATE-D	SEARCE-D	STEPPE-D	UNCAPE-D
FIDDLE-D	HURDLE-D	LYRATE-D	PATINE-D	REDDLE-D	SECEDE-D	STERVE-D	UNCASE-D
FIGURE-D	HURTLE-D	MACKLE-D	PEARCE-D	REDUCE-D	SECURE-D	STIFLE-D	UNCOPE-D
FISSLE-D	HUSTLE-D	MADAME-D	PEBBLE-D	REFACE-D	SEDATE-D	STIMIE-D	UNDATE-D
FIXATE-D	IDEATE-D	MALGRE-D	PEDDLE-D	REFINE-D	SEDUCE-D	STIRRE-D	UNEDGE-D
FIZZLE-D	IGNITE-D	MALICE-D	PEENGE-D	REFUGE-D	SEETHE-D	STODGE-D	UNFREE-D
FLANGE-D	IGNORE-D	MANAGE-D	PEOPLE-D	REFUSE-D	SEMBLE-D	STONNE-D	UNGLUE-D
FLEDGE-D	ILLUDE-D	MANEGE-D	PERSUE-D	REFUTE-D	SERENE-D	STOOGE-D	UNGYVE-D
FLEECE-D	ILLUME-D	MANGLE-D	PERUKE-D	REGALE-D	SETTLE-D	STOOPE-D	UNHELE-D
FLENSE-D	IMBASE-D	MANTLE-D	PERUSE-D	REHEAR-D	SEVERE-D	STRAFE-D	UNHIVE-D
FLOUSE-D	IMBIBE-D	MANURE-D	PESTLE-D	RELATE-D	SHEAVE-D	STRIPE-D	UNLACE-D
FONDLE-D	IMBRUE-D	MARBLE-D	PETTLE-D	RELINE-D	SHELVE-D	STRIVE-D	UNLADE-D
FOOTLE-D	IMMURE-D	MASCLE-D	PHEESE-D	RELIVE-D	SHINNE-D	STROBE-D	UNLIME-D
FOOZLE-D	IMPALE-D	MATURE-D	PHEEZE-D	RELUME-D	SHOOLE-D	STROKE-D	UNLINE-D
FORAGE-D	IMPAVE-D	MAUGRE-D	PHRASE-D	REMBLE-D	SHOTTE-D	STYMIE-D	UNLIVE-D
FOUTRE-D	IMPEDE-D	MEASLE-D	PIAFFE-D	REMEDE-D	SHRIKE-D	SUBDUE-D	UNLOVE-D
FRAISE-D	IMPONE-D	MEDDLE-D	PICKLE-D	REMISE-D	SHRINE-D	SUCKLE-D	UNPOPE-D
FRAPPE-D	IMPOSE-D	MEGARA-D	PICOTE-D	REMOVE-D	SHRIVE-D	SUDATE-D	UNRAKE-D
FRIDGE-D	IMPUTE-D	MENACE-D	PIDDLE-D	RENAME-D	SHROVE-D	SUPPLE-D	UNROBE-D
FRIEZE-D	INCAGE-D	MENAGE-D	PIERCE-D	RENEGE-D	SICKLE-D	SUTTLE-D	UNROPE-D
FRINGE-D	INCASE-D	METTLE-D	PIFFLE-D	REPINE-D	SIFFLE-D	SUTURE-D	UNRULE-D
FUDDLE-D	INCAVE-D	MICATE-D	PIMPLE-D	REPONE-D	SILAGE-D	SWARVE-D	UNSHOE-D
FUMBLE-D	INCEDE-D	MIDDLE-D	PINGLE-D	REPOSE-D	SIMPLE-D	SWATHE-D	UNSURE-D
FUZZLE-D	INCISE-D	MINGLE-D	PIRATE-D	REPURE-D	SINGLE-D	SWERVE-D	UNTAME-D

UNTILE-D	UPGAZE-D	VELATE-D	VOLUME-D	WAFFLE-D	WARSLE-D	WILLIE-D	WRAXLE-D
UNTUNE-D	UPRATE-D	VELURE-D	VOLUTE-D	WAGGLE-D	WATTLE-D	WIMBLE-D	WRETHE-D
UNWIRE-D	VACATE-D	VENTRE-D	VOYAGE-D	WAMBLE-D	WHEEZE-D	WIMPLE-D	WRITHE-D
UNWIVE-D	VALETE-D	VISAGE-D	WABBLE-D	WANGLE-D	WHINGE-D	WINKLE-D	WUZZLE-D
UNYOKE-D	VAMOSE-D	VISITE-D	WADDIE-D	WARBLE-D	WIDDLE-D	WINTLE-D	ZONATE-D
UPDATE-D	VAUNCE-D	VIZZIE-D	WADDLE-D	WARRAN-D	WIGGLE-D	WOBBLE-D	

7→8

ABRIDGE-D	BARBATE-D	COMPETE-D	DEHISCE-D	EGOTISE-D	EXPUNGE-D	IMITATE-D
ABROOKE-D	BAUCHLE-D	COMPILE-D	DELAPSE-D	EGOTIZE-D	EXPURGE-D	IMMERGE-D
ABSCISE-D	BEGRIME-D	COMPOSE-D	DELOUSE-D	ELEGISE-D	EXTRUDE-D	IMMERSE-D
ABSOLVE-D	BEGUILE-D	COMPUTE-D	DEMEANE-D	ELEGIZE-D	FALCATE-D	IMPASTE-D
ACCINGE-D	BEHOOVE-D	CONACRE-D	DEMERGE-D	ELEVATE-D	FANFARE-D	IMPINGE-D
ACCRETE-D	BEKNAVE-D	CONCAVE-D	DEMERSE-D	ELOCUTE-D	FATIGUE-D	IMPLATE-D
ACCURSE-D	BELIEVE-D	CONCEDE-D	DENTATE-D	EMANATE-D	FEATURE-D	IMPLETE-D
ACHIEVE-D	BEPROSE-D	CONCISE-D	DEPLANE-D	EMBATHE-D	FELLATE-D	IMPLODE-D
ACQUIRE-D	BEREAVE-D	CONDOLE-D	DEPLETE-D	EMBLAZE-D	FIBROSE-D	IMPLORE-D
ACTUATE-D	BESHAME-D	CONDONE-D	DEPLORE-D	EMBOGUE-D	FILIATE-D	IMPROVE-D
ADJUDGE-D	BESIEGE-D	CONDUCE-D	DEPLUME-D	EMBRACE-D	FINAGLE-D	IMPULSE-D
ADONISE-D	BESLAVE-D	CONFIDE-D	DEPRAVE-D	EMBRAVE-D	FINANCE-D	INCENSE-D
ADONIZE-D	BESPICE-D	CONFINE-D	DEPRIVE-D	EMBREWE-D	FINESSE-D	INCHASE-D
ADULATE-D	BETEEME-D	CONFUSE-D	DERANGE-D	EMBRUTE-D	FISSURE-D	INCLINE-D
ADVANCE-D	BETITLE-D	CONFUTE-D	DESCALE-D	EMICATE-D	FLOUNCE-D	INCLOSE-D
AFFEARE-D	BEWHORE-D	CONGREE-D	DESERVE-D	EMPAIRE-D	FOLIAGE-D	INCLUDE-D
AFFORCE-D	BICYCLE-D	CONGRUE-D	DESPISE-D	EMPAYRE-D	FOLIATE-D	INCURVE-D
AGGRACE-D	BLOOSME-D	CONJURE-D	DESTINE-D	EMPERCE-D	FORMATE-D	INDORSE-D
AGGRADE-D	BRABBLE-D	CONNIVE-D	DETERGE-D	EMPLACE-D	FORPINE-D	INDULGE-D
AGGRATE-D	BRAMBLE-D	CONNOTE-D	DETRUDE-D	EMPLANE-D	FORSLOE-D	INFLAME-D
AGITATE-D	BRANGLE-D	CONSOLE-D	DEVALUE-D	EMPLUME-D	FORTUNE-D	INFLATE-D
AGONISE-D	BRATTLE-D	CONSUME-D	DEVIATE-D	EMULATE-D	FRAZZLE-D	INFORCE-D
AGONIZE-D	BREATHE-D	CONTUSE-D	DEVOICE-D	ENCHAFE-D	FRECKLE-D	INGLOBE-D
ALLEDGE-D	BREVETE-D	CONVENE-D	DEVOLVE-D	ENCHASE-D	FRIBBLE-D	INHERCE-D
ALLEGGE-D	BRIGADE-D	CONVIVE-D	DIALYSE-D	ENCLAVE-D	FRIZZLE-D	INNERVE-D
AMENAGE-D	BRINDLE-D	CONVOKE-D	DIALYZE-D	ENCLOSE-D	FROUNCE-D	INQUERE-D
ANALYSE-D	BRISTLE-D	COPPICE-D	DIARISE-D	ENDORSE-D	FRUMPLE-D	INQUIRE-D
ANALYZE-D	BROCADE-D	CORNICE-D	DIARIZE-D	ENFLAME-D	FULMINE-D	INSNARE-D
ANIMATE-D	BUMBAZE-D	CORNUTE-D	DICTATE-D	ENFORCE-D	FURCATE-D	INSPIRE-D
ANODISE-D	CABBAGE-D	CORRADE-D	DIFFUSE-D	ENFRAME-D	FURNACE-D	INSTATE-D
ANODIZE-D	CADENCE-D	CORRODE-D	DISABLE-D	ENGLOBE-D	GALEATE-D	INTERNE-D
ANTICKE-D	CALCINE-D	COSTATE-D	DISCAGE-D	ENGORGE-D	GALLISE-D	INTRUDE-D
ANTIQUE-D	CALIBRE-D	COSTUME-D	DISCASE-D	ENGRACE-D	GALLIZE-D	INTWINE-D
APANAGE-D	CALYCLE-D	COTTAGE-D	DISCIDE-D	ENGRAVE-D	GALOCHE-D	INVOICE-D
APPEASE-D	CAPSIZE-D	COTTISE-D	DISCURE-D	ENHANCE-D	GAROTTE-D	INVOLVE-D
APPRISE-D	CAPTIVE-D	COWHIDE-D	DISEASE-D	ENLARGE-D	GARROTE-D	IRIDISE-D
APPRIZE-D	CAPTURE-D	CRACKLE-D	DISEDGE-D	ENNOBLE-D	GAZETTE-D	IRIDIZE-D
APPROVE-D	CARCASE-D	CRANKLE-D	DISHOME-D	ENOUNCE-D	GEMMATE-D	IRISATE-D
ARABISE-D	CAROUSE-D	CREMATE-D	DISLIKE-D	ENPLANE-D	GESTATE-D	IRONISE-D
ARABIZE-D	CASCADE-D	CRENATE-D	DISPACE-D	ENQUIRE-D	GESTURE-D	IRONIZE-D
ARCHIVE-D	CAUDATE-D	CRIBBLE-D	DISPONE-D	ENRANGE-D	GHILLIE-D	ISOLATE-D
ARCUATE-D	CAYENNE-D	CRIMPLE-D	DISPOSE-D	ENSLAVE-D	GLIMPSE-D	ITEMISE-D
ARRANGE-D	CENSURE-D	CRINATE-D	DISPUTE-D	ENSNARE-D	GLOBATE-D	ITEMIZE-D
ARTICLE-D	CHALICE-D	CRINKLE-D	DISRATE-D	ENSTYLE-D	GRABBLE-D	ITERATE-D
ASCRIBE-D	CHAUNCE-D	CRIPPLE-D	DISROBE-D	ENTAYLE-D	GRADATE-D	JALOUSE-D
ASKANCE-D	CHAUNGE-D	CROODLE-D	DISTUNE-D	ENTHUSE-D	GRANNIE-D	JAWBONE-D
ASPERGE-D	CHELATE-D	CRUDDLE-D	DISYOKE-D	ENTITLE-D	GRAPPLE-D	KEYNOTE-D
ASPERSE-D	CHICANE-D	CRUMBLE-D	DIVERGE-D	ENTWINE-D	GRIMACE-D	KNAPPLE-D
ASSIEGE-D	CHORTLE-D	CRUMPLE-D	DIVERSE-D	EPILATE-D	GRIZZLE-D	KNOBBLE-D
ASSUAGE-D	CHUCKLE-D	CRUNKLE-D	DIVORCE-D	EPISTLE-D	GRUBBLE-D	KNUBBLE-D
ASSWAGE-D	CLAVATE-D	CRUSADE-D	DIVULGE-D	EPURATE-D	GRUMBLE-D	KNUCKLE-D
ATHEISE-D	CLEANSE-D	CUITTLE-D	DOCKISE-D	ESCRIBE-D	GRUNTLE-D	KYANISE-D
ATHEIZE-D	CLIMATE-D	CULTURE-D	DOCKIZE-D	ESLOYNE-D	GUMSHOE-D	KYANIZE-D
ATOMISE-D	CLOSURE-D	CURETTE-D	DOGGONE-D	ESPOUSE-D	GUTTATE-D	LACTATE-D
ATOMIZE-D	CLOTURE-D	CURVATE-D	DRABBLE-D	ESTREPE-D	HACHURE-D	LAICISE-D
ATTACHE-D	COALISE-D	CYANIDE-D	DRAGGLE-D	EVIRATE-D	HASTATE-D	LAICIZE-D
ATTRITE-D	COALIZE-D	CYANISE-D	DRIBBLE-D	EVITATE-D	HERBAGE-D	LAIRISE-D
ATTUITE-D	COCKEYE-D	CYANIZE-D	DRIZZLE-D	EVOCATE-D	HEROISE-D	LAIRIZE-D
AUREOLE-D	COGNISE-D	DEBRIDE-D	DRUMBLE-D	EVOLUTE-D	HEROIZE-D	LARVATE-D
AURICLE-D	COGNIZE-D	DECEASE-D	DWINDLE-D	EXAMINE-D	HYDRATE-D	LATTICE-D
AVENTRE-D	COLLATE-D	DECEIVE-D	EBONISE-D	EXAMPLE-D	ICONISE-D	LEASOWE-D
AVERAGE-D	COLLIDE-D	DECLARE-D	EBONIZE-D	EXCLUDE-D	ICONIZE-D	LECTURE-D
AZOTISE-D	COLLUDE-D	DECLINE-D	EBRIATE-D	EXCRETE-D	IDOLISE-D	LEISURE-D
AZOTIZE-D	COMBINE-D	DECUPLE-D	ECHOISE-D	EXCURSE-D	IDOLIZE-D	LIBRATE-D
BALANCE-D	COMMOVE-D	DECURVE-D	ECHOIZE-D	EXECUTE-D	ILLAPSE-D	LICENCE-D
BALLADE-D	COMMUNE-D	DEFENCE-D	ECLIPSE-D	EXPIATE-D	IMAGINE-D	LICENSE-D
BANDAGE-D	COMMUTE-D	DEFLATE-D	EDUCATE-D	EXPLODE-D	IMBATHE-D	LINEATE-D
BAPTISE-D	COMPARE-D	DEFORCE-D	EFFORCE-D	EXPLORE-D	IMBRUTE-D	LIONISE-D
BAPTIZE-D	COMPERE-D	DEGRADE-D	EFFULGE-D	EXPULSE-D	IMBURSE-D	LIONIZE-D

LIQUATE-D	OVERAWE-D	PREVISE-D	REPRIZE-D	SERVICE-D	SULFATE-D	UNLOOSE-D
LOZENGE-D	OVERDYE-D	PRICKLE-D	REPROVE-D	SHACKLE-D	SUMMATE-D	UNNERVE-D
MACHINE-D	OVEREYE-D	PROBATE-D	REPRYVE-D	SHAMBLE-D	SUNBAKE-D	UNNOBLE-D
MANACLE-D	OVERUSE-D	PROCURE-D	REPULSE-D	SHEATHE-D	SUPPOSE-D	UNPLACE-D
MANDATE-D	OVULATE-D	PRODUCE-D	REQUERE-D	SHINGLE-D	SURBASE-D	UNPLUME-D
MASSAGE-D	OXIDATE-D	PROFANE-D	REQUIRE-D	SHMOOSE-D	SURBATE-D	UNPURSE-D
MAULGRE-D	OXIDISE-D	PROFILE-D	REQUITE-D	SHMOOZE-D	SURFACE-D	UNQUOTE-D
MEASURE-D	OXIDIZE-D	PROLATE-D	REQUOTE-D	SHOGGLE-D	SURMISE-D	UNREAVE-D
MEDIATE-D	OZONISE-D	PROMISE-D	REROUTE-D	SHOOGIE-D	SURNAME-D	UNREEVE-D
MESSAGE-D	OZONIZE-D	PROMOTE-D	RESCALE-D	SHOOGLE-D	SURVEWE-D	UNSCALE-D
MIDWIFE-D	PACKAGE-D	PRONATE-D	RESCORE-D	SHRIEVE-D	SURVIVE-D	UNSENSE-D
MIDWIVE-D	PALMATE-D	PROPAGE-D	RESEIZE-D	SHUTTLE-D	SUSPIRE-D	UNSHALE-D
MIGRATE-D	PALPATE-D	PROPALE-D	RESERVE-D	SIAMESE-D	SWADDLE-D	UNSHAPE-D
MINIATE-D	PANCAKE-D	PROPINE-D	RESHAPE-D	SIAMEZE-D	SWINDGE-D	UNSTATE-D
MISDATE-D	PANICLE-D	PROPONE-D	RESOLVE-D	SIGMATE-D	SWINDLE-D	UNTRACE-D
MISFARE-D	PANTILE-D	PROPOSE-D	RESPIRE-D	SILENCE-D	SWINGLE-D	UNTWINE-D
MISFILE-D	PARABLE-D	PRORATE-D	RESPITE-D	SINUATE-D	SWIZZLE-D	UNVAILE-D
MISFIRE-D	PASSAGE-D	PROVIDE-D	RESTAGE-D	SIRNAME-D	SYRINGE-D	UNVOICE-D
MISHEAR-D	PASTURE-D	PROVINE-D	RESTATE-D	SITUATE-D	TALLAGE-D	UPCLOSE-D
MISLIKE-D	PECTISE-D	PROVOKE-D	RESTORE-D	SKELLIE-D	TAMARIN-D	UPGRADE-D
MISLIVE-D	PECTIZE-D	PULSATE-D	RESTYLE-D	SKITTLE-D	TAPPICE-D	UPHEAVE-D
MISMATE-D	PEDICLE-D	PURPOSE-D	RESURGE-D	SKUTTLE-D	TARTANE-D	UPRAISE-D
MISNAME-D	PENANCE-D	QUACKLE-D	RETITLE-D	SMUGGLE-D	TEENAGE-D	UPROUSE-D
MISRATE-D	PENTICE-D	QUIBBLE-D	RETRACE-D	SNABBLE-D	TERRACE-D	UPSTAGE-D
MISRULE-D	PENTISE-D	QUIDDLE-D	RETRATE-D	SNAFFLE-D	TEXTURE-D	UPSTARE-D
MISTIME-D	PEPTISE-D	QUIESCE-D	REUNITE-D	SNIFFLE-D	THIMBLE-D	UPSURGE-D
MISTUNE-D	PEPTIZE-D	QUINCHE-D	REVALUE-D	SNIGGLE-D	TITRATE-D	UPVALUE-D
MISYOKE-D	PERDURE-D	RABATTE-D	REVENGE-D	SNIRTLE-D	TONSURE-D	URINATE-D
MONOCLE-D	PERFUME-D	RADIATE-D	REVENUE-D	SNOOZLE-D	TOPLINE-D	UTILISE-D
MONTAGE-D	PERFUSE-D	RAMPAGE-D	REVERSE-D	SNUFFLE-D	TORTURE-D	UTILIZE-D
MORTICE-D	PERJURE-D	RAMPIRE-D	REVOLVE-D	SNUGGLE-D	TRADUCE-D	VACUATE-D
MORTISE-D	PERMUTE-D	RAPTURE-D	RHOMBOI-D	SNUZZLE-D	TRAIPSE-D	VALANCE-D
MULTURE-D	PERTUSE-D	RAWBONE-D	RIPOSTE-D	SOLVATE-D	TRAMPLE-D	VALUATE-D
MURIATE-D	PERVADE-D	REALISE-D	ROMANCE-D	SPAIRGE-D	TRAPEZE-D	VAMOOSE-D
MYTHISE-D	PETIOLE-D	REALIZE-D	ROSETTE-D	SPANGLE-D	TREACLE-D	VAMPIRE-D
MYTHIZE-D	PHONATE-D	REALLIE-D	RUINATE-D	SPARKLE-D	TREADLE-D	VANDYKE-D
NARRATE-D	PICTURE-D	REAWAKE-D	RUMMAGE-D	SPECKLE-D	TREDDLE-D	VANTAGE-D
NECROSE-D	PILEATE-D	REBADGE-D	RUPTURE-D	SPICATE-D	TREMBLE-D	VARIATE-D
NICTATE-D	PILLAGE-D	REBRACE-D	SALTATE-D	SPINDLE-D	TRICKLE-D	VENTURE-D
NITRATE-D	PINNATE-D	RECEIVE-D	SALVAGE-D	SPLODGE-D	TRILOBE-D	VERDURE-D
NITRIDE-D	PIPETTE-D	RECENSE-D	SATIATE-D	SPLURGE-D	TRINDLE-D	VESTURE-D
NOURSLE-D	PLACATE-D	RECLINE-D	SCABBLE-D	SPREAZE-D	TRIPPLE-D	VIBRATE-D
NURTURE-D	PLICATE-D	RECLOSE-D	SCAMBLE-D	SPREEZE-D	TROUBLE-D	VICIATE-D
OBELISE-D	PLUMAGE-D	RECOURE-D	SCANTLE-D	SPRINGE-D	TROUNCE-D	VINTAGE-D
OBELIZE-D	POETISE-D	RECOYLE-D	SCAPPLE-D	SPULYIE-D	TRUCKLE-D	VIOLATE-D
OBLIQUE-D	POETIZE-D	RECUILE-D	SCEDULE-D	SPULZIE-D	TRUFFLE-D	VITIATE-D
OBSCURE-D	POLLUTE-D	RECURVE-D	SCEPTRE-D	SQUEEZE-D	TUILYIE-D	WARFARE-D
OBSERVE-D	POSTURE-D	RECYCLE-D	SCHAPPE-D	SQUIDGE-D	TUILZIE-D	WAYFARE-D
OBTRUDE-D	POTHOLE-D	REFEREE-D	SCHOOLE-D	STARTLE-D	TUMESCE-D	WELCOME-D
OBVIATE-D	POURSUE-D	REFLATE-D	SCIENCE-D	STATURE-D	TURBINE-D	WHAISLE-D
OCCLUDE-D	PRAIRIE-D	REFRAME-D	SCOURGE-D	STEEPLE-D	TWADDLE-D	WHAIZLE-D
OCTUPLE-D	PRANCKE-D	REGORGE-D	SCOURSE-D	STICKLE-D	TWANGLE-D	WHEEDLE-D
OCULATE-D	PRANKLE-D	REGRADE-D	SCREEVE-D	STIDDIE-D	TWATTLE-D	WHEENGE-D
OPERATE-D	PRATTLE-D	REGRATE-D	SCRIEVE-D	STIPPLE-D	TWEEDLE-D	WHEEPLE-D
OUTDARE-D	PRAUNCE-D	REGREDE-D	SCROOGE-D	STIPULE-D	TWIDDLE-D	WHEEZLE-D
OUTDATE-D	PREASSE-D	REHOUSE-D	SCROUGE-D	STOPPLE-D	TWINKLE-D	WHEMMLE-D
OUTDURE-D	PRECEDE-D	REISSUE-D	SCROWLE-D	STRIATE-D	TWIZZLE-D	WHIFFLE-D
OUTFACE-D	PRECISE-D	REJOICE-D	SCRUPLE-D	STRODLE-D	TYRANNE-D	WHIMPLE-D
OUTHIRE-D	PREDATE-D	REJUDGE-D	SCUDDLE-D	STUBBLE-D	ULULATE-D	WHISTLE-D
OUTHYRE-D	PREFACE-D	RELAPSE-D	SCUFFLE-D	STUMBLE-D	UMBRAGE-D	WHITTLE-D
OUTLINE-D	PREFADE-D	RELEASE-D	SCUMBLE-D	STYLISE-D	UNBRACE-D	WHOMBLE-D
OUTLIVE-D	PRELUDE-D	RELIEVE-D	SCUTTLE-D	STYLIZE-D	UNCLOSE-D	WHOMMLE-D
OUTMODE-D	PREMISE-D	REMERGE-D	SDEIGNE-D	SUBDUCE-D	UNCRATE-D	WHUMMLE-D
OUTMOVE-D	PREMOVE-D	RENAGUE-D	SECLUDE-D	SUBLATE-D	UNCURSE-D	WRANGLE-D
OUTNAME-D	PREPARE-D	RENEGUE-D	SECONDE-D	SUBLIME-D	UNGLOVE-D	WREATHE-D
OUTPACE-D	PREPONE-D	REPIQUE-D	SECRETE-D	SUBSIDE-D	UNHINGE-D	WRESTLE-D
OUTRACE-D	PREPOSE-D	REPLACE-D	SELVAGE-D	SUBSUME-D	UNHORSE-D	WRIGGLE-D
OUTRAGE-D	PRESAGE-D	REPLETE-D	SERIATE-D	SUFFICE-D	UNHOUSE-D	WRINKLE-D
OUTRATE-D	PRESIDE-D	REPRIME-D	SERRATE-D	SUFFUSE-D	UNITISE-D	YCLEEPE-D
OUTSIZE-D	PRESUME-D	REPRISE-D	SERUEWE-D	SULCATE-D	UNITIZE-D	
OUTVOTE-D	PREVENE-D	REPRIVE-D	SERVEWE-D			

8→9

ABDICATE-D	ABSTERGE-D	ACIERATE-D	ADVOCATE-D	AGGRIEVE-D	ALKALISE-D
ABERRATE-D	ACCORAGE-D	ACTIVATE-D	AFFIANCE-D	ALBITISE-D	ALKALIZE-D
ABNEGATE-D	ACCOUTRE-D	ACULEATE-D	AFFRONTE-D	ALBITIZE-D	ALLIGATE-D
ABROGATE-D	ACERBATE-D	ADUNCATE-D	AFTEREYE-D	ALIENATE-D	ALLOCATE-D

AMBULATE-D	CARACOLE-D	DELIBATE-D	EMENDATE-D	FABULISE-D	INTIMATE-D
AMORTISE-D	CASEMATE-D	DEMONISE-D	EMIGRATE-D	FABULIZE-D	INTITULE-D
AMORTIZE-D	CASTRATE-D	DEMONIZE-D	EMMARBLE-D	FARADISE-D	INTONATE-D
AMPUTATE-D	CATALYSE-D	DENATURE-D	EMPEOPLE-D	FARADIZE-D	INTRIGUE-D
ANGULATE-D	CATALYZE-D	DENOTATE-D	EMPERISE-D	FASCIATE-D	INTUBATE-D
ANKYLOSE-D	CATENATE-D	DENOUNCE-D	EMPERIZE-D	FASCICLE-D	INVEAGLE-D
ANNALISE-D	CAVITATE-D	DENUDATE-D	EMPIERCE-D	FATIGATE-D	INVEIGLE-D
ANNALIZE-D	CENTUPLE-D	DEPILATE-D	EMPLONGE-D	FEDERATE-D	INVOLUTE-D
ANNOTATE-D	CHASTISE-D	DEPURATE-D	EMPURPLE-D	FEMINISE-D	IRRIGATE-D
ANNOUNCE-D	CICERONE-D	DEPUTISE-D	ENCHARGE-D	FEMINIZE-D	IRRITATE-D
ANNULATE-D	CINCTURE-D	DEPUTIZE-D	ENCIRCLE-D	FILIGREE-D	JACULATE-D
ANTECEDE-D	CIVILISE-D	DEROGATE-D	ENCLOTHE-D	FILTRATE-D	JALOUSIE-D
ANTEDATE-D	CIVILIZE-D	DESCRIBE-D	ENCRADLE-D	FINALISE-D	JAUNDICE-D
ANTICIZE-D	CLODPATE-D	DESCRIVE-D	ENCREASE-D	FINALIZE-D	JEALOUSE-D
APHETISE-D	COALESCE-D	DESOLATE-D	ENDAMAGE-D	FLUIDISE-D	JOINTURE-D
APHETIZE-D	COGITATE-D	DETHRONE-D	ENERGISE-D	FLUIDIZE-D	JUBILATE-D
APHORISE-D	COGNOSCE-D	DETONATE-D	ENERGIZE-D	FOCALISE-D	JUGULATE-D
APHORIZE-D	COHOBATE-D	DEVELOPE-D	ENERVATE-D	FOCALIZE-D	JULIENNE-D
APPANAGE-D	COIFFURE-D	DIAGNOSE-D	ENFEEBLE-D	FOREBODE-D	JUMBOISE-D
APPETISE-D	COINCIDE-D	DIALOGUE-D	ENFIERCE-D	FOREDATE-D	JUMBOIZE-D
APPETIZE-D	COINHERE-D	DIGITATE-D	ENFILADE-D	FORENAME-D	KEFUFFLE-D
APPRAISE-D	COLLAPSE-D	DIGITISE-D	ENGIRDLE-D	FORHAILE-D	KEYSTONE-D
APRICATE-D	COLLOGUE-D	DIGITIZE-D	ENGRIEVE-D	FORHOOIE-D	KLONDIKE-D
ARCHAISE-D	COLLOQUE-D	DIMERISE-D	ENGROOVE-D	FORJUDGE-D	KLONDYKE-D
ARCHAIZE-D	COLONISE-D	DIMERIZE-D	ENHEARSE-D	FORWASTE-D	KREASOTE-D
AREOLATE-D	COLONIZE-D	DISABUSE-D	ENKINDLE-D	FRACTURE-D	KREOSOTE-D
ARILLATE-D	COMEDDLE-D	DISAGREE-D	ENLUMINE-D	FREEBASE-D	LACERATE-D
ARROGATE-D	COMMENCE-D	DISBURSE-D	ENRAUNGE-D	FUMIGATE-D	LAMBASTE-D
ASPERATE-D	COMMERCE-D	DISCIPLE-D	ENSAMPLE-D	GANGRENE-D	LAMINATE-D
ASPIRATE-D	COMMERGE-D	DISCLOSE-D	ENSCONCE-D	GARROTTE-D	LANGUAGE-D
ASSEMBLE-D	COMPESCE-D	DISCOURE-D	ENSHRINE-D	GEFUFFLE-D	LAPIDATE-D
ASSONATE-D	COMPLETE-D	DISGORGE-D	ENSILAGE-D	GEMINATE-D	LAUREATE-D
ASTRINGE-D	COMPRISE-D	DISGRACE-D	ENSPHERE-D	GENERATE-D	LEGALISE-D
ATCHIEVE-D	COMPULSE-D	DISGRADE-D	ENSWATHE-D	GLACIATE-D	LEGALIZE-D
ATHETISE-D	CONCEIVE-D	DISGUISE-D	ENTANGLE-D	GLISSADE-D	LEVERAGE-D
ATHETIZE-D	CONCLUDE-D	DISHABLE-D	ENTHRONE-D	GRADUATE-D	LEVIGATE-D
ATMOLYSE-D	CONCRETE-D	DISHORSE-D	ENTRANCE-D	HARANGUE-D	LEVITATE-D
ATMOLYZE-D	CONDENSE-D	DISHOUSE-D	ENVEIGLE-D	HEADLINE-D	LIBERATE-D
AUTOLYSE-D	CONFLATE-D	DISINURE-D	ENVELOPE-D	HEBETATE-D	LIGATURE-D
AUTOLYZE-D	CONGLOBE-D	DISLEAVE-D	ENVISAGE-D	HEPATISE-D	LIQUESCE-D
AUTOMATE-D	CONSERVE-D	DISLODGE-D	EQUALISE-D	HEPATIZE-D	LITIGATE-D
AUTOTYPE-D	CONSPIRE-D	DISPENCE-D	EQUALIZE-D	HESITATE-D	LOBULATE-D
BACKBONE-D	CONSTATE-D	DISPENSE-D	EQUIPAGE-D	HUMANISE-D	LOCALISE-D
BACKFIRE-D	CONSTRUE-D	DISPERSE-D	ERADIATE-D	HUMANIZE-D	LOCALIZE-D
BALDPATE-D	CONTINUE-D	DISPLACE-D	ERGOTISE-D	IDEALISE-D	LOCOMOTE-D
BANALISE-D	CONTRIVE-D	DISPLODE-D	ERGOTIZE-D	IDEALIZE-D	LOGICISE-D
BANALIZE-D	CONVERGE-D	DISPLUME-D	ERUCTATE-D	ILLUMINE-D	LOGICIZE-D
BARBECUE-D	CONVERSE-D	DISPONGE-D	ESCALADE-D	IMMANTLE-D	LOOPHOLE-D
BARBEQUE-D	CONVINCE-D	DISPRIZE-D	ESCALATE-D	IMMINGLE-D	LORICATE-D
BARNACLE-D	CONVOLVE-D	DISPROVE-D	ESCALOPE-D	IMMOLATE-D	LUNULATE-D
BECHANCE-D	CONVULSE-D	DISPUNGE-D	ESTIMATE-D	IMMUNISE-D	LUSTRATE-D
BEDABBLE-D	COPULATE-D	DISPURSE-D	ESTIVATE-D	IMMUNIZE-D	MACARISE-D
BEDAGGLE-D	COQUETTE-D	DISSEISE-D	ESTRANGE-D	IMPLEDGE-D	MACARIZE-D
BEDAZZLE-D	CORONATE-D	DISSEIZE-D	ETERNISE-D	IMPLUNGE-D	MACERATE-D
BEFRINGE-D	CORVETTE-D	DISSERVE-D	ETERNIZE-D	IMPRESSE-D	MACULATE-D
BEFUDDLE-D	CREASOTE-D	DISSOLVE-D	ETHERISE-D	IMPURPLE-D	MADERISE-D
BEGRUDGE-D	CRENELLE-D	DISSUADE-D	ETHERIZE-D	INCHOATE-D	MADERIZE-D
BELITTLE-D	CREOSOTE-D	DISTANCE-D	ETHICISE-D	INCORPSE-D	MAINLINE-D
BEMUDDLE-D	CREVASSE-D	DISTASTE-D	ETHICIZE-D	INCREASE-D	MALAXATE-D
BEMUFFLE-D	CRITIQUE-D	DISUNITE-D	ETHYLATE-D	INCUBATE-D	MALLEATE-D
BENEFICE-D	CRUSTATE-D	DISVALUE-D	ETIOLATE-D	INDAGATE-D	MANICURE-D
BEPRAISE-D	CULTRATE-D	DIVAGATE-D	EULOGISE-D	INDICATE-D	MARINADE-D
BLOCKADE-D	CUMULATE-D	DIVINISE-D	EULOGIZE-D	INDURATE-D	MARINATE-D
BOTANISE-D	CURARISE-D	DIVINIZE-D	EUPHUISE-D	INFAMISE-D	MASSACRE-D
BOTANIZE-D	CURARIZE-D	DOMICILE-D	EUPHUIZE-D	INFAMIZE-D	MATURATE-D
BRATTICE-D	CUTINISE-D	DOMINATE-D	EVACUATE-D	INFRINGE-D	MAXIMISE-D
BRETTICE-D	CUTINIZE-D	DOWNSIZE-D	EVALUATE-D	INGROOVE-D	MAXIMIZE-D
BROMELIA-D	DARRAINE-D	DUBITATE-D	EVANESCE-D	INHEARSE-D	MEDICATE-D
BULLDOZE-D	DEBOUCHE-D	DYNAMISE-D	EVIDENCE-D	INHUMATE-D	MEDICINE-D
CALCEATE-D	DECIMATE-D	DYNAMITE-D	EVULGATE-D	INITIATE-D	MEDITATE-D
CANALISE-D	DECLASSE-D	DYNAMIZE-D	EXCAVATE-D	INNOVATE-D	MELODISE-D
CANALIZE-D	DECORATE-D	EBIONISE-D	EXCHANGE-D	INSCONCE-D	MELODIZE-D
CANONISE-D	DECOUPLE-D	EBIONIZE-D	EXECRATE-D	INSCRIBE-D	MEMORISE-D
CANONIZE-D	DECREASE-D	ECHINATE-D	EXERCISE-D	INSHRINE-D	MEMORIZE-D
CANOODLE-D	DEDICATE-D	EFFIERCE-D	EXHUMATE-D	INSOLATE-D	METALIZE-D
CANTHARI-D	DEFILADE-D	ELONGATE-D	EXORCISE-D	INSPHERE-D	MICROCAR-D
CAPONISE-D	DEGREASE-D	EMACIATE-D	EXORCIZE-D	INSTANCE-D	MILITATE-D
CAPONIZE-D	DELEGATE-D	EMBATTLE-D	EXPEDITE-D	INSULATE-D	MINIMISE-D
CAPRIOLE-D		EMBEZZLE-D	EXUVIATE-D	INSWATHE-D	

MINIMIZE-D	OVERCROW-D	PROTRUDE-D	RIVALISE-D	SPREETHE-D	TRITIATE-D
MISGUIDE-D	OVERDOSE-D	PTYALISE-D	RIVALIZE-D	SPRINGAL-D	TRIVALVE-D
MISJUDGE-D	OVERHALE-D	PTYALIZE-D	ROBOTISE-D	SPRINKLE-D	TRUNCATE-D
MISLEEKE-D	OVERHEAR-D	PULVILLE-D	ROBOTIZE-D	SPUILZIE-D	TUBERCLE-D
MISMETRE-D	OVERHYPE-D	PUMICATE-D	ROSTRATE-D	SQUABBLE-D	TUBULATE-D
MISPLACE-D	OVERLADE-D	PUNCTATE-D	ROTAVATE-D	SQUATTLE-D	TUNICATE-D
MISPRISE-D	OVERLIVE-D	PUNCTURE-D	ROTOVATE-D	SQUEEGEE-D	TUTORISE-D
MISPRIZE-D	OVERNAME-D	PURCHASE-D	ROYALISE-D	SQUIGGLE-D	TUTORIZE-D
MISQUOTE-D	OVERRAKE-D	PURLICUE-D	ROYALIZE-D	SQUILGEE-D	ULCERATE-D
MISROUTE-D	OVERRATE-D	PYRITISE-D	RUMINATE-D	STAGNATE-D	UNBRIDLE-D
MISSHAPE-D	OVERRULE-D	PYRITIZE-D	RURALISE-D	STAMPEDE-D	UNBUCKLE-D
MISSTATE-D	OVERSIZE-D	PYROLYSE-D	RURALIZE-D	STELLATE-D	UNBUNDLE-D
MISTITLE-D	OVERTIME-D	PYROLYZE-D	SABOTAGE-D	STOCKADE-D	UNCHARGE-D
MITIGATE-D	OVERTIRE-D	QUADRATE-D	SAGINATE-D	STRADDLE-D	UNCINATE-D
MOBILISE-D	OVERTURE-D	QUAGMIRE-D	SALIVATE-D	STRAGGLE-D	UNCLOTHE-D
MOBILIZE-D	OVERTYPE-D	QUANTISE-D	SANGUINE-D	STRANGLE-D	UNCOUPLE-D
MODERATE-D	PAGANISE-D	QUANTIZE-D	SANITATE-D	STREIGNE-D	UNCREATE-D
MODULATE-D	PAGANIZE-D	RACEMISE-D	SANITISE-D	STRICKLE-D	UNDAZZLE-D
MONETISE-D	PAGINATE-D	RACEMIZE-D	SANITIZE-D	STRIDDLE-D	UNDERUSE-D
MONETIZE-D	PALISADE-D	RADICATE-D	SAPPHIRE-D	STRINKLE-D	UNDOUBLE-D
MONOTONE-D	PALLIATE-D	RAMPAUGE-D	SATIRISE-D	STRODDLE-D	UNDULATE-D
MORALISE-D	PAPALISE-D	READVISE-D	SATIRIZE-D	STRUGGLE-D	UNHEARSE-D
MORALIZE-D	PAPALIZE-D	REAROUSE-D	SATURATE-D	STUPRATE-D	UNIONISE-D
MORTGAGE-D	PARALYSE-D	REASSUME-D	SCAVENGE-D	SUBERISE-D	UNIONIZE-D
MOTIVATE-D	PARALYZE-D	REASSURE-D	SCHEDULE-D	SUBERIZE-D	UNMANTLE-D
MOTORISE-D	PATRIATE-D	RECENTRE-D	SCHMOOZE-D	SUBITISE-D	UNMUFFLE-D
MOTORIZE-D	PECULATE-D	RECHARGE-D	SCLEROSE-D	SUBITIZE-D	UNMUZZLE-D
MURICATE-D	PEDICURE-D	RECLOTHE-D	SCRABBLE-D	SUBLEASE-D	UNPEOPLE-D
MUTILATE-D	PEDIGREE-D	RECOURSE-D	SCRAMBLE-D	SUBMERGE-D	UNPRAISE-D
NASALISE-D	PEJORATE-D	RECREATE-D	SCRATTLE-D	SUBMERSE-D	UNRIDDLE-D
NASALIZE-D	PENALISE-D	REDARGUE-D	SCRIBBLE-D	SUBSERVE-D	UNRUFFLE-D
NAUSEATE-D	PENALIZE-D	REDEFINE-D	SCRIGGLE-D	SUBTITLE-D	UNSADDLE-D
NAVIGATE-D	PERCEIVE-D	REDIVIDE-D	SCROUNGE-D	SUBTRUDE-D	UNSETTLE-D
NEBULISE-D	PERMEATE-D	REDOUBLE-D	SCROWDGE-D	SUBVERSE-D	UNSLUICE-D
NEBULIZE-D	PERORATE-D	REFIGURE-D	SELVEDGE-D	SUFFLATE-D	UNSPHERE-D
NECKLACE-D	PEROXIDE-D	REFRINGE-D	SEMINATE-D	SULPHATE-D	UNSWATHE-D
NEGATIVE-D	PERSPIRE-D	REGELATE-D	SENTENCE-D	SUNBATHE-D	UNTACKLE-D
NICKNAME-D	PERSUADE-D	REGULATE-D	SEPARATE-D	SUPERATE-D	UNTANGLE-D
NICOTINE-D	PERSWADE-D	REGULISE-D	SEPTUPLE-D	SUPINATE-D	UNTHRONE-D
NODALISE-D	PERVIATE-D	REGULIZE-D	SEQUENCE-D	SURCEASE-D	URBANISE-D
NODALIZE-D	PINAFORE-D	REHANDLE-D	SERENADE-D	SURPLICE-D	URBANIZE-D
NOMADISE-D	PINNACLE-D	REHEARSE-D	SEROTYPE-D	SURPRISE-D	URTICATE-D
NOMADIZE-D	PIRLICUE-D	REILLUME-D	SEXTUPLE-D	SYLLABLE-D	VAGINATE-D
NOMINATE-D	PLEASURE-D	REIMPOSE-D	SHAUCHLE-D	TABULATE-D	VALIDATE-D
NOSEDIVE-D	POLARISE-D	REINFUSE-D	SHOWCASE-D	TAILGATE-D	VALORISE-D
NOTARISE-D	POLARIZE-D	REINSURE-D	SIBILATE-D	TAILPIPE-D	VALORIZE-D
NOTARIZE-D	POLEMISE-D	REKINDLE-D	SIDELINE-D	TALLIATE-D	VAMBRACE-D
NOVELISE-D	POLEMIZE-D	RELEGATE-D	SIDERATE-D	TELEVISE-D	VAPORISE-D
NOVELIZE-D	POLONISE-D	RELOCATE-D	SILICATE-D	TENTACLE-D	VAPORIZE-D
NUCLEATE-D	POLONIZE-D	RELUMINE-D	SIMILISE-D	TETANISE-D	VAPULATE-D
NUMERATE-D	POPULATE-D	REMARQUE-D	SIMILIZE-D	TETANIZE-D	VEGETATE-D
OBDURATE-D	PORPOISE-D	REMIGATE-D	SIMULATE-D	THEORISE-D	VELARISE-D
OBLIGATE-D	POSTCODE-D	RENEGADE-D	SINICISE-D	THEORIZE-D	VELARIZE-D
OBTURATE-D	POSTDATE-D	RENFORCE-D	SINICIZE-D	THRAPPLE-D	VENERATE-D
OBVOLUTE-D	POSTPONE-D	RENOUNCE-D	SIRENISE-D	THROPPLE-D	VERJUICE-D
OCCUPATE-D	POSTPOSE-D	RENOVATE-D	SIRENIZE-D	THROTTLE-D	VESICATE-D
OCELLATE-D	POULTICE-D	RENVERSE-D	SNOWSHOE-D	TIDIVATE-D	VIGNETTE-D
OPPILATE-D	POURTRAY-D	REPARTEE-D	SOBERISE-D	TINCTURE-D	VITALISE-D
OPTIMISE-D	PRACTICE-D	REPEOPLE-D	SOBERIZE-D	TINPLATE-D	VITALIZE-D
OPTIMIZE-D	PRACTISE-D	REPERUSE-D	SODOMISE-D	TITIVATE-D	VOCALISE-D
ORDINATE-D	PREAMBLE-D	REPHRASE-D	SODOMIZE-D	TITUBATE-D	VOCALIZE-D
ORECROWE-D	PRECLUDE-D	REPREEVE-D	SOLARISE-D	TOLERATE-D	VOLITATE-D
ORGANISE-D	PREJUDGE-D	REPRIEVE-D	SOLARIZE-D	TORQUATE-D	VOLPLANE-D
ORGANIZE-D	PREMIERE-D	REQUOYLE-D	SOLECISE-D	TOTALISE-D	VOLUMISE-D
OSCITATE-D	PRENTICE-D	REREVISE-D	SOLECIZE-D	TOTALIZE-D	VOLUMIZE-D
OSCULATE-D	PREPENSE-D	RESALUTE-D	SOLIDATE-D	TRABEATE-D	VOUTSAFE-D
OUTBRAVE-D	PRESERVE-D	RESEMBLE-D	SOMNIATE-D	TRAMLINE-D	VOWELISE-D
OUTCASTE-D	PRESSURE-D	RESETTLE-D	SORORISE-D	TRANSUDE-D	VOWELIZE-D
OUTDANCE-D	PRIMROSE-D	RESINISE-D	SORORIZE-D	TRANSUME-D	WOMANISE-D
OUTGLARE-D	PRODNOSE-D	RESINIZE-D	SPECIATE-D	TRAUCHLE-D	WOMANIZE-D
OUTPLACE-D	PROGRADE-D	RESONATE-D	SPECTATE-D	TRAVERSE-D	WORMHOLE-D
OUTPRICE-D	PROLAPSE-D	RESOURCE-D	SPOLIATE-D	TREASURE-D	
OUTPRIZE-D	PROLOGUE-D	RETRIEVE-D	SPRACKLE-D	TREPHINE-D	
OUTSTARE-D	PROLONGE-D	RIDICULE-D	SPRANGLE-D	TRESSURE-D	
OUTVALUE-D	PROMULGE-D	RIGIDISE-D	SPRATTLE-D	TRIANGLE-D	
OUTVOICE-D	PROROGUE-D	RIGIDIZE-D	SPREATHE-D	TRICYCLE-D	

2→3

E-AN	E-AS	E-CH	E-EN	E-ME	E-NE	E-RE	E-TA	E-YE
E-AR	E-AT	E-EL	E-GO	E-MU	E-ON	E-ST	E-WE	

3→4

E-ACH	E-BON	E-CRU	E-GAD	E-KED	E-MUS	E-PEE	E-RED	E-TAT	E-UGH
E-ALE	E-CAD	E-DIT	E-GAL	E-MES	E-NEW	E-PIC	E-RES	E-TEN	E-VET
E-ARD	E-CHE	E-ECH	E-GIS	E-MEU	E-NOW	E-POS	E-SKY	E-THE	E-VOE
E-ARS	E-COD	E-ELS	E-GOS	E-MIR	E-ONS	E-RAS	E-SPY	E-TUI	E-YES

4→5

E-ALES	E-DICT	E-KING	E-LOPS	E-MOTE	E-PICS	E-RODE	E-TENS	E-VETS
E-ARDS	E-DITS	E-LAND	E-LUTE	E-MOVE	E-POXY	E-ROSE	E-TUIS	E-VITE
E-ARED	E-DUCE	E-LATE	E-MAIL	E-MULE	E-PROM	E-SCOT	E-TWEE	E-WEST
E-AVES	E-DUCT	E-LITE	E-MEER	E-MURE	E-QUID	E-SILE	E-UGHS	E-WHOW
E-BONY	E-EVEN	E-LOGE	E-MEND	E-NEWS	E-QUIP	E-SKER	E-VADE	
E-CADS	E-GEST	E-LOGY	E-MEUS	E-NORM	E-RASE	E-STOP	E-VENT	
E-CLAT	E-HING	E-LOIN	E-MIRS	E-PACT	E-RICK	E-TAPE	E-VERT	
E-CRUS	E-IKON	E-LOPE	E-MONG	E-PEES	E-RING	E-TATS	E-VERY	

5→6

E-AGLET	E-EVENS	E-LITES	E-MESES	E-NOSES	E-RASES	E-SPIAL	E-THANE
E-ASTER	E-GALLY	E-LOGES	E-METIC	E-PACTS	E-RICKS	E-SPIED	E-TOILE
E-CARTE	E-GESTS	E-LOINS	E-MOTED	E-PARCH	E-RODED	E-SPIES	E-TRIER
E-CLATS	E-IDOLA	E-LOPED	E-MOTES	E-PERDU	E-RODES	E-SPRIT	E-TYPIC
E-CLOSE	E-IKONS	E-LOPER	E-MOVED	E-POSES	E-SCAPE	E-STATE	E-VADED
E-CURIE	E-LANCE	E-LOPES	E-MOVES	E-PRISE	E-SCARP	E-STEEM	E-VADES
E-DICTS	E-LANDS	E-LUTED	E-MULES	E-PROMS	E-SCOTS	E-STOPS	E-VENTS
E-DITED	E-LAPSE	E-LUTES	E-MURED	E-QUANT	E-SCROW	E-STRAY	E-VERTS
E-DUCES	E-LATED	E-MAILS	E-MURES	E-QUIDS	E-SCUDO	E-STRUM	E-VOLVE
E-DUCTS	E-LATER	E-MEERS	E-NERVE	E-QUINE	E-SILES	E-TALON	
E-ECHED	E-LEGIT	E-MENDS	E-NEWED	E-QUIPS	E-SKERS	E-TAPES	
E-ECHES	E-LICIT	E-MERGE	E-NODAL	E-RASED	E-SKIES	E-TERNE	

6→7

E-AGLETS	E-IRENIC	E-LUTING	E-MURING	E-RECTOR	E-SPOUSE	E-STRUMS	E-VENTER
E-ASTERN	E-LANCED	E-MAILED	E-NATION	E-RODENT	E-SPRITS	E-TALONS	E-VERTED
E-BONIST	E-LANCES	E-MENDED	E-NERVED	E-RODING	E-SPYING	E-TERNAL	E-VICTOR
E-CARTES	E-LAPSED	E-MERGED	E-NERVES	E-SCAPED	E-SQUIRE	E-THANES	E-VOLUTE
E-CLOSED	E-LECTOR	E-MERGES	E-NEWING	E-SCAPES	E-STATED	E-TOILES	E-VOLVED
E-CLOSES	E-LEGIST	E-METICS	E-PERDUE	E-SCARPS	E-STATES	E-TRIERS	E-VOLVES
E-CURIES	E-LOGIES	E-MICATE	E-PICENE	E-SCRIBE	E-STEEMS	E-UPHROE	
E-DENTAL	E-LOPERS	E-MOTION	E-QUANTS	E-SCROLL	E-STOVER	E-VADING	
E-DITING	E-LOPING	E-MOTIVE	E-RASING	E-SCROWS	E-STRAYS	E-VANISH	
E-ECHING		E-MOVING	E-RASURE	E-SPIALS	E-STRICH	E-VENTED	

7→8

E-BONISTS	E-LEVATOR	E-MIGRATE	E-QUIPPED	E-SCAPING	E-STATING	E-VENTERS
E-CAUDATE	E-MAILING	E-MISSILE	E-RADIATE	E-SCARPED	E-STEEMED	E-VENTING
E-CLOSING	E-MENDING	E-MISSION	E-RASURES	E-SCRIBED	E-STOPPED	E-VERSION
E-COSTATE	E-MERGING	E-MISSIVE	E-RECTION	E-SCRIBES	E-STOVERS	E-VERTING
E-DENTATE	E-MERSION	E-MOTIONS	E-RECTORS	E-SCROLLS	E-STRANGE	E-VICTORS
E-LANCING	E-METICAL	E-NATIONS	E-RODENTS	E-SPECIAL	E-STRAYED	E-VOCABLE
E-LAPSING	E-MICATED	E-NERVATE	E-SCALADE	E-SPOUSAL	E-TYPICAL	E-VOLUTED
E-LECTION	E-MICATES	E-NERVING	E-SCALADO	E-SPOUSED	E-UPHROES	E-VOLUTES
E-LECTORS	E-MICTION	E-PICENES	E-SCALIER	E-SPOUSES	E-VACUATE	E-VOLVING
E-LEGISTS	E-MIGRANT	E-QUALITY	E-SCALLOP	E-SQUIRES	E-VALUATE	E-VULGATE

8→9

E-IRENICON	E-MERSIONS	E-NUMERATE	E-SCALLOPS	E-STOPPING	E-VANISHED
E-JACULATE	E-MICATING	E-PISTOLET	E-SCARPING	E-STRANGER	E-VANISHES
E-LATERITE	E-MICTIONS	E-QUIPPING	E-SCRIBING	E-STRAYING	E-VENTINGS
E-LECTIONS	E-MIGRANTS	E-RADIATED	E-SPOUSALS	E-STRICHES	E-VERSIONS
E-LECTRESS	E-MIGRATED	E-RADIATES	E-SPOUSING	E-VACUATED	E-VINCIBLE
E-LEVATORS	E-MIGRATES	E-RADICATE	E-SQUIRESS	E-VACUATES	E-VOCATION
E-LOCUTION	E-MISSIONS	E-RECTIONS	E-STABLISH	E-VAGINATE	E-VOCATIVE
E-LOCUTORY	E-MOTIONAL	E-ROSTRATE	E-STEEMING	E-VALUATED	E-VOLUTION
E-MERGENCE	E-NUCLEATE	E-SCALADES	E-STOPPAGE	E-VALUATES	E-VULGATES

2→3

AN-E	AY-E	DI-E	GI-E	HO-E	LI-E	NY-E	OW-E	TA-E	US-E
AR-E	BE-E	DO-E	GO-E	ID-E	MA-E	OD-E	OY-E	TE-E	UT-E
AT-E	BY-E	EM-E	GU-E	JO-E	MO-E	ON-E	PI-E	TI-E	WE-E
AW-E	CH-E	EN-E	HA-E	KA-E	NA-E	OP-E	RE-E	TO-E	WO-E
AX-E	DA-E	ER-E	HI-E	KY-E	NE-E	OR-E	SH-E	UR-E	

3→4

ABB-E	BOR-E	DIV-E	GAL-E	JUT-E	MAD-E	NON-E	RET-E	STY-E	VAS-E
ABY-E	BRA-E	DOG-E	GAM-E	KAI-E	MAG-E	NOS-E	RID-E	SUP-E	VIA-E
ACH-E	BUT-E	DON-E	GAN-E	KAM-E	MAK-E	NOT-E	RIM-E	SUR-E	VID-E
ADZ-E	CAD-E	DOP-E	GAP-E	KIN-E	MAL-E	OBO-E	RIN-E	TAK-E	VIN-E
AGE-E	CAM-E	DOS-E	GAR-E	KIP-E	MAN-E	OCH-E	RIP-E	TAM-E	VIS-E
AID-E	CAN-E	DOT-E	GAT-E	KIT-E	MAR-E	OOS-E	RIT-E	TAN-E	VOL-E
AIN-E	CAP-E	DUD-E	GEN-E	LAC-E	MAS-E	ORF-E	ROB-E	TAP-E	WAD-E
AKE-E	CAR-E	DUN-E	GIB-E	LAD-E	MAT-E	PAL-E	ROD-E	TAR-E	WAG-E
ALA-E	CAT-E	DUP-E	GIT-E	LAM-E	MEN-E	PAN-E	ROK-E	TAT-E	WAN-E
ALB-E	CID-E	EAS-E	GON-E	LAR-E	MES-E	PAP-E	ROT-E	TEN-E	WAR-E
ALE-E	CIT-E	ECH-E	HAD-E	LAS-E	MET-E	PAR-E	RUB-E	THE-E	WAS-E
AMI-E	COD-E	ELS-E	HAM-E	LAT-E	MIL-E	PAT-E	RUD-E	TIC-E	WAT-E
ANT-E	COL-E	ERN-E	HAT-E	LAV-E	MIM-E	PEN-E	RUM-E	TID-E	WAW-E
ARS-E	CON-E	ESS-E	HEM-E	LEK-E	MIR-E	PER-E	RUN-E	TIG-E	WEX-E
BAD-E	COP-E	ETH-E	HER-E	LEV-E	MIS-E	PIC-E	SAD-E	TIL-E	WIN-E
BAN-E	COR-E	FAD-E	HET-E	LIN-E	MOD-E	PIN-E	SAG-E	TIN-E	WIS-E
BAR-E	COS-E	FAN-E	HID-E	LIT-E	MOM-E	PIP-E	SAL-E	TIT-E	WIT-E
BAS-E	COT-E	FAR-E	HON-E	LOB-E	MOP-E	PIS-E	SAM-E	TOG-E	WOK-E
BAT-E	COZ-E	FAT-E	HOP-E	LOD-E	MOR-E	POM-E	SAN-E	TOM-E	YGO-E
BAY-E	CRU-E	FET-E	HOS-E	LOG-E	MOT-E	POP-E	SAT-E	TON-E	YOD-E
BED-E	CUB-E	FIL-E	HOT-E	LOP-E	MOU-E	POS-E	SEL-E	TOP-E	YOK-E
BEN-E	CUR-E	FIN-E	HOW-E	LOR-E	MOZ-E	POT-E	SIC-E	TOR-E	YOW-E
BET-E	CUT-E	FIR-E	HUG-E	LOS-E	MUS-E	PRE-E	SIN-E	TOT-E	YUK-E
BID-E	DAL-E	FLU-E	HYP-E	LOT-E	NAM-E	PUR-E	SIP-E	TRY-E	ZIT-E
BIN-E	DAM-E	FON-E	IDE-E	LOW-E	NAP-E	RAD-E	SIR-E	TUB-E	
BIS-E	DEL-E	FOR-E	JAK-E	LUG-E	NET-E	RAG-E	SIT-E	TUN-E	
BIT-E	DEN-E	FRA-E	JAP-E	LUR-E	NID-E	RAP-E	SNY-E	TWA-E	
BOD-E	DIM-E	FUM-E	JET-E	LUX-E	NIT-E	RAS-E	SOL-E	URD-E	
BOK-E	DIN-E	GAD-E	JIB-E	LYM-E	NOD-E	RAT-E	SON-E	UVA-E	
BON-E	DIT-E	GAG-E	JOB-E	MAC-E	NOM-E	RED-E	SPA-E	VAN-E	

4→5

ABAS-E	BLAT-E	CLOY-E	EATH-E	GRAT-E	LOUP-E	PAIR-E	RANG-E	SHIN-E
ABID-E	BOMB-E	COAT-E	ERAS-E	GRID-E	LOUR-E	PAIS-E	RANK-E	SHIR-E
AGEN-E	BOOS-E	COHO-E	FAIN-E	GRIM-E	LOWN-E	PARS-E	RATH-E	SHIT-E
AGOG-E	BORD-E	COMA-E	FARL-E	GRIP-E	LOWS-E	PASS-E	RAZE-E	SHIV-E
AGON-E	BORE-E	COMB-E	FARS-E	GRIS-E	LUNG-E	PAST-E	REAM-E	SHOP-E
AINE-E	BORN-E	CONN-E	FEAR-E	GRUM-E	MAIL-E	PEAR-E	REED-E	SHOT-E
ALBE-E	BOTT-E	COPS-E	FEES-E	GUID-E	MAIR-E	PEAS-E	RENT-E	SHUL-E
ALGA-E	BOWS-E	CORS-E	FEHM-E	GUYS-E	MANG-E	PECK-E	RIFT-E	SHUT-E
ALOW-E	BRED-E	COST-E	FESS-E	HAST-E	MANS-E	PEEP-E	RILL-E	SING-E
AMEN-E	BRER-E	COUP-E	FIER-E	HAUT-E	MARA-E	PENI-E	RIMA-E	SITH-E
AMID-E	BROS-E	COUR-E	FILL-E	HAWS-E	MARG-E	PERV-E	RINS-E	SKAT-E
ANIL-E	BRUT-E	COXA-E	FITT-E	HEAR-E	MARL-E	PHON-E	RONT-E	SKIT-E
ANIS-E	BUFF-E	CRAM-E	FLAK-E	HEFT-E	MASS-E	PIOY-E	ROOS-E	SKYR-E
ANTA-E	BURK-E	CRAN-E	FLAM-E	HERO-E	MATT-E	PLAN-E	ROUL-E	SLAT-E
APOD-E	BURS-E	CRAP-E	FLIT-E	HERS-E	MEAN-E	PLAT-E	ROUT-E	SLID-E
AQUA-E	BUTT-E	CREW-E	FORM-E	HERY-E	MENG-E	PLUM-E	RUFF-E	SLIM-E
ARED-E	CADE-E	CRIM-E	FORT-E	HING-E	MERL-E	POIS-E	SAIC-E	SLIP-E
ARET-E	CADI-E	CRUD-E	FOSS-E	HORS-E	MEUS-E	POSS-E	SAIN-E	SLOP-E
ARIS-E	CARS-E	CRUS-E	FOUL-E	INBY-E	MILL-E	POUK-E	SALS-E	SMIT-E
ATOK-E	CART-E	CURS-E	FRIZ-E	JAMB-E	MINA-E	PRAT-E	SAUT-E	SNAR-E
AURA-E	CAST-E	DAUB-E	FUSE-E	JASP-E	MING-E	PRIM-E	SCAR-E	SNIP-E
AVAL-E	CEAS-E	DEAR-E	FUZE-E	KERN-E	MINK-E	PROB-E	SCOP-E	SOAR-E
AXIL-E	CENS-E	DEER-E	GAFF-E	KITH-E	MOOS-E	PROS-E	SCUT-E	SOLD-E
AZYM-E	CESS-E	DEEV-E	GARB-E	KNOW-E	MORN-E	PRYS-E	SEAM-E	SONS-E
BARB-E	CHAP-E	DENS-E	GEAR-E	KYND-E	MORS-E	PUPA-E	SEAR-E	SOOT-E
BASS-E	CHAR-E	DHOL-E	GEES-E	LAND-E	MOTT-E	PURE-E	SEAS-E	SORE-E
BAST-E	CHAS-E	DING-E	GEST-E	LAPS-E	MOUS-E	PURS-E	SEIS-E	SOUS-E
BATH-E	CHER-E	DIRK-E	GLAD-E	LATH-E	MOYL-E	QUIN-E	SELL-E	SOWL-E
BEAR-E	CHID-E	DIXI-E	GLED-E	LEAR-E	MUSS-E	QUIT-E	SEME-E	SOWN-E
BECK-E	CHIN-E	DONE-E	GLID-E	LEAS-E	NACH-E	RACH-E	SEMI-E	SOWS-E
BELL-E	CHIV-E	DOOL-E	GLOB-E	LEES-E	NEUM-E	RAGE-E	SENS-E	SPAN-E
BIGA-E	CHUT-E	DORS-E	GLUM-E	LEFT-E	NOUL-E	RAIL-E	SERR-E	SPAR-E
BING-E	CLAD-E	DOUC-E	GOLP-E	LEVE-E	NOVA-E	RAIN-E	SETA-E	SPAT-E
BIRL-E	CLAM-E	DOWL-E	GOOS-E	LITH-E	NURS-E	RAIS-E	SHAD-E	SPIC-E
BITT-E	CLIP-E	DOWS-E	GRAD-E	LONG-E	ODYL-E	RAKE-E	SHAM-E	SPIK-E
BLAD-E	CLOT-E	DRAP-E	GRAM-E	LOOS-E	OUPH-E	RAMI-E	SHAW-E	SPIN-E

SPIT-E	SUIT-E	TEEN-E	THIN-E	TRAP-E	TWIT-E	VEAL-E	WAID-E	WING-E
STAG-E	SWAG-E	TELA-E	THRO-E	TRIN-E	TYND-E	VEHM-E	WAIT-E	WITH-E
STAR-E	SYBO-E	TEMS-E	TING-E	TRIP-E	ULNA-E	VENA-E	WAST-E	WRIT-E
STED-E	SYCE-E	TENS-E	TOIL-E	TROD-E	UNDE-E	VERS-E	WEEK-E	ZOEA-E
STEM-E	TACH-E	TERF-E	TOPE-E	TRON-E	UNIT-E	VILD-E	WEET-E	ZONA-E
STIR-E	TASS-E	TERN-E	TORS-E	TUBA-E	UPBY-E	VITA-E	WEFT-E	
STOA-E	TAWS-E	TEST-E	TORT-E	TUFF-E	URDE-E	VOLA-E	WELK-E	
STOP-E	TEAD-E	THAN-E	TOWS-E	TURM-E	VAIR-E	VOLT-E	WHIN-E	
SUED-E	TEAS-E	THEM-E	TRAD-E	TWIN-E	VAUT-E	WACK-E	WHIT-E	

5→6

ALLEL-E	CHILD-E	FAUNA-E	IMPED-E	ORCIN-E	PURIN-E	SILVA-E	TESTE-E
ALULA-E	CHIRR-E	FEMAL-E	INCUS-E	ORPIN-E	PUTTI-E	SNATH-E	THECA-E
AMEBA-E	CHORE-E	FILOS-E	INDOL-E	OUTBY-E	QUART-E	SOOTH-E	THORP-E
AMEND-E	CLOTH-E	FINAL-E	INFER-E	PALEA-E	QUICH-E	SOURS-E	THROW-E
AMPUL-E	CNIDA-E	FITCH-E	JAMBE-E	PALLA-E	QUINT-E	SPALL-E	TIBIA-E
ANNEX-E	COATE-E	FLORA-E	KARAT-E	PARDI-E	RALLY-E	SPARK-E	TOUCH-E
AORTA-E	COIGN-E	FORBY-E	KINAS-E	PARKI-E	RAVIN-E	SPARS-E	TRIST-E
AVAIL-E	COMIC-E	FOSSA-E	LAMIA-E	PAROL-E	REBIT-E	SPICA-E	TROAD-E
AVERS-E	CONCH-E	FOVEA-E	LARVA-E	PASSE-E	RECIT-E	SPINA-E	TROMP-E
BACCA-E	CONGE-E	FRORN-E	LASSI-E	PATIN-E	REDIA-E	SPRIT-E	TWYER-E
BARGE-E	CONIN-E	FUNDI-E	LATHE-E	PATTE-E	REGAL-E	SPURN-E	ULNAR-E
BERTH-E	COOMB-E	FURAN-E	LIBRA-E	PAVAN-E	REPOS-E	STEAL-E	UMBRA-E
BETID-E	CORPS-E	FUROL-E	LIPID-E	PAVIS-E	ROTCH-E	STEAN-E	UNBAR-E
BLEND-E	COSTA-E	FUROR-E	LOATH-E	PELTA-E	RUBIN-E	STEAR-E	UNCAP-E
BLOND-E	COUCH-E	FUSIL-E	LOBOS-E	PENNA-E	SAITH-E	STEDD-E	UNRIP-E
BLOWS-E	COUPE-E	GALEA-E	LOCAL-E	PERDU-E	SALAD-E	STELA-E	UNTIL-E
BOORD-E	COURS-E	GAMIN-E	LUNGI-E	PETIT-E	SALLE-E	STONN-E	UPTAK-E
BOURN-E	CREES-E	GEMMA-E	LUPIN-E	PHEER-E	SALPA-E	STOOP-E	URBAN-E
BRAID-E	CROSS-E	GENOM-E	LYSIN-E	PHOCA-E	SASIN-E	STRIA-E	UVULA-E
BREES-E	CROUP-E	GOURD-E	LYTTA-E	PHYLA-E	SAVIN-E	STRIP-E	VALET-E
BROCH-E	CROUT-E	GRAIL-E	MADAM-E	PICOT-E	SCALA-E	SUMMA-E	VALIS-E
BROOS-E	CURAT-E	GRAIN-E	MALIC-E	PINNA-E	SCATH-E	SWATH-E	VERTU-E
BROWS-E	CURIA-E	GRAND-E	MAMMA-E	PLAST-E	SCHMO-E	SWING-E	VIRTU-E
BULLA-E	CUTTO-E	GREES-E	MEATH-E	PLEAS-E	SCOPA-E	SWOUN-E	VISIT-E
BUNJE-E	DECAD-E	GREET-E	MEDIA-E	PLICA-E	SCRAP-E	SYLVA-E	VITTA-E
BURSA-E	DEMUR-E	GRIFF-E	MISER-E	PLONG-E	SCRAY-E	TALEA-E	VULVA-E
CAMES-E	DEVOT-E	GRILL-E	MISSA-E	POINT-E	SCULL-E	TALPA-E	WALIS-E
CAMIS-E	DILDO-E	GUTTA-E	MORAL-E	POLYP-E	SELLA-E	TAMAL-E	WHEAR-E
CANNA-E	DONNE-E	GYROS-E	NOMAD-E	POTCH-E	SERIN-E	TAMIN-E	ZOMBI-E
CAPOT-E	DREAR-E	HEARS-E	NOULD-E	POULP-E	SERRA-E	TAMIS-E	ZOOEA-E
CAUSA-E	DROWS-E	HEAST-E	NUCHA-E	PREIF-E	SEVER-E	TANGI-E	
CELLA-E	EPRIS-E	HERMA-E	OCREA-E	PRIEF-E	SHOOL-E	TEETH-E	
CHAIN-E	EQUIP-E	HOARS-E	OPPOS-E	PROIN-E	SHOTT-E	TENIA-E	
CHAIS-E	EXPOS-E	HUMAN-E	ORACH-E	PROYN-E	SILEN-E	TERRA-E	
CHELA-E	FACET-E	HYPHA-E	ORANG-E	PSYCH-E		TESTA-E	

6→7

ABOLLA-E	BERLIN-E	CLEANS-E	EPERDU-E	HARMIN-E	LORICA-E	PANGEN-E	RETINA-E
ACQUIT-E	BESPAT-E	CLOACA-E	EPIGON-E	HERNIA-E	LUCERN-E	PAPULA-E	RETIRE-E
AFFAIR-E	BETEEM-E	COELOM-E	EPUISE-E	HEROIN-E	LUNULA-E	PARDAL-E	REVERS-E
AFFEAR-E	BICORN-E	COMMER-E	ESCAPE-E	HYDRIA-E	LURDAN-E	PAROLE-E	ROSIER-E
ALIDAD-E	BLINTZ-E	COMMOT-E	EUCAIN-E	IMPING-E	MACULA-E	PATERA-E	SCHOOL-E
ALSOON-E	BOUCHE-E	COMPER-E	EXEDRA-E	IMPROV-E	MARLIN-E	PENSIL-E	SCORIA-E
ALTERN-E	BREATH-E	COMPOS-E	EXTERN-E	INFANT-E	MARQUE-E	PEPSIN-E	SCOURS-E
ALUMNA-E	BREVET-E	COMPOT-E	FACULA-E	INFULA-E	MATRIC-E	PESANT-E	SCROWL-E
AMOEBA-E	BUGGAN-E	CONCHA-E	FETICH-E	INGENU-E	MAUVIN-E	PICOTE-E	SDEIGN-E
ANTICK-E	CAGOUL-E	CORONA-E	FIANCE-E	INSULA-E	MEDUSA-E	PISTOL-E	SECOND-E
ANTLIA-E	CAMERA-E	COUCHE-E	FIBROS-E	INTERN-E	MEGASS-E	PLATAN-E	SECRET-E
APHTHA-E	CANULA-E	CRISTA-E	FIBULA-E	INTIMA-E	MODIST-E	PLEDGE-E	SEROSA-E
ARABIS-E	CAPRIC-E	CRUSTA-E	FITCHE-E	INULAS-E	MORULA-E	PLEURA-E	SHEATH-E
AREOLA-E	CARINA-E	CYANIN-E	FLAVIN-E	INVITE-E	MOUSME-E	POMMEL-E	SIGNOR-E
ARISTA-E	CASERN-E	DEFAST-E	FOLIOS-E	ISATIN-E	MUCOSA-E	PONTIL-E	SITULA-E
ARSHIN-E	CATENA-E	DEMAIN-E	FORBAD-E	ISOBAR-E	MURRIN-E	POOGYE-E	SIXAIN-E
ARTIST-E	CAVIAR-E	DEMEAN-E	FORMAT-E	ISOMER-E	NATURA-E	PRANCK-E	SODAIN-E
ASPERS-E	CELLOS-E	DENTIN-E	FRAPPE-E	JAGHIR-E	NEBULA-E	PRECIS-E	SOIGNE-E
ATTACH-E	CESURA-E	DETENT-E	FRIAND-E	KAGOUL-E	NEURON-E	PROTYL-E	SPARTH-E
ATTRIT-E	CHAETA-E	DETENU-E	FRIJOL-E	KAOLIN-E	OBLIGE-E	PSHAER-E	SPHAER-E
AUGUST-E	CHIMER-E	DEVISE-E	GANOIN-E	LACUNA-E	OCHREA-E	PURLIN-E	SPHEAR-E
AURORA-E	CHINES-E	DEVOTE-E	GARROT-E	LAMINA-E	OCTETT-E	RADIAL-E	SPREDD-E
AXILLA-E	CHOANA-E	DILUTE-E	GERMAN-E	LEASOW-E	OLEFIN-E	RADULA-E	SPRING-E
BAILLI-E	CHOPIN-E	DIOXAN-E	GLOSSA-E	LEGATE-E	ORIGAN-E	RATLIN-E	SQUAMA-E
BALLAD-E	CHORAL-E	DIVERS-E	GLYCIN-E	LEUCIN-E	OUVERT-E	REFUGE-E	STAITH-E
BEGUIN-E	CHORDA-E	DURESS-E	GRADIN-E	LIGULA-E	PAIOCK-E	REGINA-E	STATIC-E
BELDAM-E	CINEOL-E	EMETIN-E	GRANDE-E	LINGUA-E	PAJOCK-E	REGULA-E	STRIGA-E
BENZOL-E	CITRIN-E	ENTETE-E	GRATIN-E	LISSOM-E	PALAMA-E	REQUIT-E	STROOK-E

STRUMA-E	SURVEW-E	TARTAN-E	TONNAG-E	UNBORN-E	VAGINA-E	VISITE-E	ZONULA-E
SUBTIL-E	SYMBOL-E	TARTAR-E	TORULA-E	UNGULA-E	VERDIT-E	VOLANT-E	
SUCCOS-E	TABULA-E	TEGULA-E	TRITON-E	UNLAST-E	VERSIN-E	VOMICA-E	
SUMMAT-E	TAENIA-E	TIMBAL-E	TROCHE-E	UNVAIL-E	VESICA-E	WREATH-E	

7→8

ABSCISS-E	CANNULA-E	DUCHESS-E	IMPRESS-E	MESQUIT-E	PORTESS-E	SPICULA-E
ABSINTH-E	CAPELIN-E	DUVETYN-E	INCONNU-E	METAMER-E	PORTIER-E	STAMPED-E
ACALEPH-E	CARABIN-E	DYSODIL-E	INDULIN-E	MICELLA-E	PRACTIC-E	STEARIN-E
ACKNOWN-E	CARACOL-E	EMPRESS-E	INFAUNA-E	MINUTIA-E	PRECAVA-E	SUCCUBA-E
ACRIDIN-E	CARDECU-E	ENDORSE-E	INHUMAN-E	MONDAIN-E	PREMIER-E	SUNBATH-E
ACTINIA-E	CERESIN-E	ENVELOP-E	INTERNE-E	MONOPOD-E	PROLONG-E	SUSPENS-E
AFFRONT-E	CHALAZA-E	ESCALOP-E	ISOCHOR-E	MUSICAL-E	PROMISE-E	SYLPHID-E
AGACANT-E	CHLORIN-E	ETOURDI-E	JEALOUS-E	NEBBISH-E	PROTEAS-E	SYMITAR-E
ALEURON-E	CINEAST-E	EXAMINE-E	LACINIA-E	NEGLIGE-E	PROTEGE-E	TACHISM-E
ALKALIS-E	COCHLEA-E	EXCLUDE-E	LAMBAST-E	NOCTURN-E	PROTHYL-E	TACHIST-E
AMPHORA-E	COMPLIN-E	EXHEDRA-E	LAMELLA-E	NOTITIA-E	PTERYLA-E	TEREBRA-E
AMPULLA-E	CONTRAT-E	FIMBRIA-E	LANOLIN-E	NOVELLA-E	QUADRAT-E	TESSERA-E
AMYGDAL-E	CONTROL-E	FISTULA-E	LARGESS-E	ONCOGEN-E	RATTLIN-E	THIAMIN-E
ANTENNA-E	CORYPHE-E	FORMULA-E	LICENSE-E	OUVRIER-E	REHEARS-E	TORCHER-E
ARMILLA-E	COURANT-E	FOSSULA-E	LINGULA-E	OUTCAST-E	RELEASE-E	TRACHEA-E
ATROPIN-E	CREATIN-E	FOVEOLA-E	LOCUSTA-E	PAENULA-E	RETRAIT-E	TRICORN-E
AUTOMAT-E	CURARIS-E	FURCULA-E	LUPULIN-E	PAPILLA-E	RIBSTON-E	URETHAN-E
BACKBIT-E	CYPSELA-E	FUSAROL-E	LYOPHIL-E	PATELLA-E	SALICIN-E	URETHRA-E
BALADIN-E	DARRAIN-E	GELATIN-E	MALEFIC-E	PERIDOT-E	SCAPULA-E	VALVULA-E
BALISTA-E	DAUPHIN-E	GENERAL-E	MAMILLA-E	PERIGON-E	SCHMOOZ-E	VENTAIL-E
BARCHAN-E	DEBOUCH-E	GERMAIN-E	MARCHES-E	PERSONA-E	SCISSIL-E	VERRUCA-E
BARGEES-E	DECIDUA-E	GIRASOL-E	MARQUIS-E	PFENNIG-E	SCURRIL-E	VITAMIN-E
BARYTON-E	DECLASS-E	GLIADIN-E	MATADOR-E	PIANIST-E	SECONDE-E	WANNABE-E
BENEFIC-E	DEVELOP-E	GRAMARY-E	MATELOT-E	PISCINA-E	SELVAGE-E	XANTHIN-E
BESTRID-E	DEXTRIN-E	GRATINE-E	MAUVAIS-E	PLACCAT-E	SEQUELA-E	
BIOPHOR-E	DISPONE-E	HALIMOT-E	MAUVEIN-E	PLANULA-E	SERPULA-E	
BURNOUS-E	DIVORCE-E	HETAERA-E	MAXILLA-E	PLAUDIT-E	SESTETT-E	
CAESURA-E	DOMICIL-E	HOLESOM-E	MEDULLA-E	PLUMULA-E	SEXTETT-E	
CAFFEIN-E	DRACHMA-E	HOLYDAM-E	MESQUIN-E	PORPESS-E	SILICON-E	

8→9

ABORIGIN-E	CIRRIPED-E	EPIFAUNA-E	MANDOLIN-E	PRAECAVA-E	SYNOPSIS-E
ABSCISSA-E	CISTERNA-E	ETRANGER-E	MARGARIN-E	PRETERIT-E	SYPHILIS-E
ACANTHIN-E	CLAUSULA-E	EUCARYOT-E	METHADON-E	PRINCESS-E	TESSELLA-E
AFFRONTE-E	COCHLEAR-E	EUKARYOT-E	MILLEPED-E	PROLAMIN-E	THEREFOR-E
ALIZARIN-E	CONCOURS-E	EXIGEANT-E	MILLIPED-E	PROVEDOR-E	THIOPHEN-E
ALTERNAT-E	CONFERVA-E	FIBRILLA-E	MISCEGEN-E	QUADRIGA-E	THYROXIN-E
ANGUIPED-E	CONFRONT-E	FIGURANT-E	MORTGAGE-E	QUARTETT-E	TORCHIER-E
APPRAISE-E	CROSSBIT-E	FISSIPED-E	MULTIPED-E	QUINTETT-E	TRACHEID-E
AVENTAIL-E	CURCUMIN-E	FROSTBIT-E	MUSCADIN-E	RATIONAL-E	TRICHINA-E
AVIFAUNA-E	CURTALAX-E	FURFUROL-E	NIGROSIN-E	READEIFY-E	TRITICAL-E
BACCHANT-E	CUSPIDOR-E	GAILLARD-E	NUBECULA-E	REMEDIAT-E	TYRANNIS-E
BACKSLID-E	DANCETTE-E	GARAGIST-E	OENOPHIL-E	RESTRING-E	UNDERBIT-E
BALLADIN-E	DARRAIGN-E	GASTNESS-E	PALESTRA-E	RETINULA-E	UNDERSAY-E
BALLISTA-E	DEBUTANT-E	GASTRULA-E	PALMIPED-E	RICERCAR-E	VAGINULA-E
BANDEROL-E	DECLASSE-E	GLABELLA-E	PARAFFIN-E	SAFRANIN-E	VERATRIN-E
BAUDRICK-E	DEDICATE-E	GLYCERIN-E	PAROCHIN-E	SARABAND-E	VERTEBRA-E
BLASTULA-E	DESPOTAT-E	HARMALIN-E	PASTORAL-E	SCELERAT-E	VESICULA-E
BOUTONNE-E	DETRAQUE-E	HOSPITAL-E	PENTOSAN-E	SCLEREID-E	VIBRISSA-E
BRANCHIA-E	DIPLOMAT-E	INTERESS-E	PETECHIA-E	SEMUNCIA-E	VIGILANT-E
BRASSIER-E	DIRIGISM-E	INTERVAL-E	PHOTOGEN-E	SERAPHIN-E	VISAGIST-E
CANEPHOR-E	DISTRAIT-E	INTIMIST-E	PINNIPED-E	SIMPLIST-E	VITELLIN-E
CAPONIER-E	ECCLESIA-E	KHALIFAT-E	PLACENTA-E	SLUGHORN-E	VULSELLA-E
CARTOUCH-E	ECSTASIS-E	LODICULA-E	PLEONAST-E	SQUADRON-E	WHEREFOR-E
CERCARIA-E	EMPHASIS-E	MAGDALEN-E	POLYPHON-E	STROBILA-E	XYLOIDIN-E
CHAPERON-E	ENSHEATH-E	MAMMILLA-E	PONTIFIC-E	STRONGYL-E	YERSINIA-E
CHLORDAN-E	EPHEMERA-E	MANDARIN-E	POSTCAVA-E	SUBCOSTA-E	ZOOGLOEA-E

2→3

F-AD	F-AR	F-AW	F-EE	F-IN	F-OE	F-OP	F-OX	F-UM
F-AH	F-AS	F-AX	F-EN	F-IT	F-OH	F-OR	F-OY	F-UN
F-AN	F-AT	F-AY	F-ID	F-OB	F-ON	F-OU	F-UG	F-UR

3→4

F-ACE	F-AHS	F-AKE	F-ARD	F-ART	F-AWN	F-EEL	F-END	F-ESS	F-ILL
F-ACT	F-AIL	F-ALL	F-ARE	F-ASH	F-AYS	F-ELL	F-ENS	F-EST	F-INK
F-ADO	F-AIN	F-AND	F-ARM	F-ATE	F-EAR	F-ELT	F-ERE	F-ETA	F-INS
F-ADS	F-AIR	F-ANE	F-ARS	F-AVE	F-EAT	F-EME	F-ERN	F-IDS	F-IRE

F-IRK	F-LAP	F-LED	F-LIP	F-LUX	F-ONS	F-OUD	F-RAS	F-RIZ	F-USE
F-ISH	F-LAT	F-LEE	F-LIT	F-OBS	F-OPS	F-OUR	F-RAY	F-ROM	
F-ITS	F-LAW	F-LEG	F-LOG	F-OES	F-ORB	F-OWL	F-REE	F-ROW	
F-LAB	F-LAX	F-LEW	F-LOP	F-OIL	F-ORD	F-OYS	F-RET	F-UDS	
F-LAG	F-LAY	F-LEX	F-LOR	F-OLD	F-ORE	F-RAG	F-RIG	F-UGS	
F-LAM	F-LEA	F-LEY	F-LOW	F-ONE	F-ORT	F-RAP	F-RIT	F-UNS	

4→5

F-ABLE	F-ANON	F-ECHT	F-INCH	F-LATS	F-LINT	F-LOWS	F-ORES	F-RETS
F-ACED	F-ARDS	F-EELS	F-INKS	F-LAWN	F-LIPS	F-LUES	F-ORTS	F-RIGS
F-ACER	F-ARED	F-ELLS	F-IRES	F-LAWS	F-LISK	F-LUFF	F-OSSA	F-RILL
F-ACES	F-ARES	F-ELTS	F-IRKS	F-LAYS	F-LITE	F-LUKE	F-OUDS	F-RISK
F-ACTS	F-ARLE	F-EMES	F-ITCH	F-LEAM	F-LOCK	F-LUMP	F-OURS	F-RITS
F-ADOS	F-ARMS	F-ENDS	F-LABS	F-LEAS	F-LOGS	F-LUNG	F-OWLS	F-ROCK
F-AERY	F-ARSE	F-ERES	F-LACK	F-LEER	F-LONG	F-LUSH	F-OYER	F-RONT
F-AILS	F-ARTS	F-ERNS	F-LAGS	F-LEES	F-LOOR	F-LUTE	F-RACK	F-RORE
F-AINE	F-ASCI	F-ESSE	F-LAIR	F-LEET	F-LOPS	F-LYTE	F-RAGS	F-RORY
F-AIRS	F-AVER	F-ESTS	F-LAKE	F-LEGS	F-LORY	F-OGLE	F-RAIL	F-ROST
F-AIRY	F-AWNS	F-ETAS	F-LAKY	F-LEME	F-LOSH	F-OILS	F-RANK	F-ROWS
F-AKED	F-AXED	F-ETCH	F-LAME	F-LEYS	F-LOSS	F-OLDS	F-RAPS	F-RUMP
F-AKES	F-AXES	F-EVER	F-LAMS	F-LICK	F-LOTA	F-OLIO	F-RATE	F-RUSH
F-ALLS	F-AYRE	F-EWER	F-LANK	F-LIER	F-LOTE	F-ONLY	F-RAYS	F-RUST
F-ANAL	F-EARS	F-EYED	F-LAPS	F-LIES	F-LOUR	F-ORBS	F-REAK	F-USED
F-ANDS	F-EAST	F-ILLS	F-LARE	F-LIMP	F-LOUT	F-ORBY	F-REED	F-USES
F-ANES	F-EATS	F-ILLY	F-LASH	F-LING	F-LOWN	F-ORDS	F-REES	

5→6

F-ABLED	F-ARLES	F-ICHES	F-LAWNS	F-LINTY	F-LUSHY	F-OWLED	F-RISKS
F-ABLER	F-ARMED	F-INGAN	F-LAXES	F-LISKS	F-LUTED	F-OWLER	F-RISKY
F-ABLES	F-ARROW	F-INKED	F-LAYER	F-LITED	F-LUTER	F-OYERS	F-ROCKS
F-ACERS	F-ARSES	F-INNED	F-LEAMS	F-LITES	F-LUTES	F-RAILS	F-RONTS
F-ACING	F-ASHES	F-INNER	F-LEDGE	F-LOCKS	F-LUXES	F-RAISE	F-ROSTS
F-ACTOR	F-ASTER	F-IRKED	F-LEDGY	F-LONGS	F-LYING	F-RANKS	F-RUMPS
F-ADDLE	F-AWNED	F-ISHES	F-LEECH	F-LORAL	F-LYTED	F-RATCH	F-RUMPY
F-AERIE	F-AWNER	F-ITCHY	F-LEERS	F-LOSSY	F-LYTES	F-RATER	F-RUSTS
F-AILED	F-AXING	F-LACKS	F-LEETS	F-LOTAS	F-ODDER	F-RAYED	F-UGGED
F-AIRED	F-AYRES	F-LAIRS	F-LEMES	F-LOTES	F-OGLES	F-REAKS	F-UNDER
F-AIRER	F-EARED	F-LAKED	F-LETCH	F-LOURS	F-OILED	F-REEST	F-UNKED
F-AKING	F-EASTS	F-LAKES	F-LEXES	F-LOURY	F-OLDER	F-REMIT	F-USING
F-ALLOW	F-EERIE	F-LAMED	F-LICKS	F-LOUSE	F-OLIOS	F-RENNE	F-UTILE
F-ALTER	F-ENDED	F-LAMES	F-LIERS	F-LOUTS	F-ONNED	F-RICHT	
F-AMINE	F-ESSES	F-LANCH	F-LIGHT	F-LOWED	F-ORMER	F-RIDGE	
F-ANGLE	F-ESTER	F-LANKS	F-LIMPS	F-LOWER	F-OTHER	F-RIGHT	
F-ANION	F-ETTLE	F-LARES	F-LINCH	F-LUFFS	F-OUGHT	F-RIGID	
F-ANKLE	F-EWEST	F-LASER	F-LINGS	F-LUMPS	F-OUTER	F-RILLS	
F-ARCED	F-EYING	F-LAWED	F-LINTS	F-LURRY	F-OUTRE	F-RISES	

6→7

F-ABLING	F-ARMING	F-INGANS	F-LAUNCH	F-LOSSES	F-ONNING	F-RATERS	F-ROUGHY
F-ACTION	F-ARRANT	F-INKING	F-LAWING	F-LOURED	F-ORGONE	F-RAUGHT	F-ROUNCE
F-ACTIVE	F-ARROWS	F-INNERS	F-LAYERS	F-LOUSED	F-ORMERS	F-RAYING	F-RUMPED
F-ACTORS	F-ASHERY	F-IRKING	F-LAYING	F-LOUSES	F-ORPINE	F-RAZZLE	F-RUMPLE
F-ACTUAL	F-ASTERS	F-ITCHES	F-LECHES	F-LOUTED	F-OTHERS	F-REAKED	F-RUSHED
F-ACTURE	F-ATTEST	F-LACKER	F-LEDGES	F-LOWERS	F-OULDER	F-REMITS	F-RUSHES
F-ADDLED	F-AWNERS	F-LAGGED	F-LEEING	F-LOWERY	F-OULERS	F-RETTED	F-UCKERS
F-ADDLES	F-AWNING	F-LAKIER	F-LEERED	F-LOWING	F-OUTRED	F-RICHTS	F-UGGING
F-AERIES	F-EARFUL	F-LAKING	F-LEGGED	F-LUFFED	F-OWLERS	F-RIDGED	F-ULLAGE
F-AILING	F-EARING	F-LAMING	F-LEMING	F-LUMMOX	F-OWLING	F-RIDGES	F-ULLING
F-AIRILY	F-EASTED	F-LAMMED	F-LENSES	F-LUMPED	F-RABBIT	F-RIGGED	F-UMBLES
F-AIRING	F-EASTER	F-LANKED	F-LICKED	F-LUSHED	F-RAGGED	F-RIGGER	F-UNDIES
F-AIRWAY	F-EATING	F-LANKER	F-LICKER	F-LUSHER	F-RAILER	F-RIGHTS	F-UNFAIR
F-ALLOWS	F-ENDING	F-LAPPED	F-LIGHTS	F-LUSHES	F-RAILLY	F-RILLED	F-UNKING
F-ALTERS	F-ERNING	F-LAPPER	F-LIMPED	F-LUSTER	F-RAISED	F-RINGED	F-UNNEST
F-AMINES	F-ESTERS	F-LASERS	F-LINGER	F-LUTERS	F-RAISES	F-RIPPER	
F-ANGLED	F-ETCHED	F-LASHED	F-LIPPED	F-LUTING	F-RANKED	F-RISKED	
F-ANGLES	F-ETCHES	F-LASHER	F-LITING	F-LUTIST	F-RANKER	F-RISKER	
F-ANIONS	F-ETTLED	F-LASHES	F-LITTER	F-LYINGS	F-RANKLY	F-RITTED	
F-ANKLED	F-ETTLES	F-LASKET	F-LOCKED	F-LYTING	F-RAPPED	F-RITTER	
F-ANKLES	F-INCHED	F-LATTEN	F-LOGGED	F-OILING	F-RAPPEE	F-ROCKED	
F-ARCING	F-INCHES	F-LATTER	F-LOPPED	F-ONDING	F-RASSES	F-ROSTED	

7→8

F-ACTIONS	F-ADDLING	F-AIRWAYS	F-ALTERED	F-ARCINGS	F-AWNINGS	F-EASTING
F-ACTURES	F-AIRINGS	F-ALLOWED	F-ANGLING	F-ARROWED	F-EARLESS	F-ESTIVAL

F-ETCHING	F-LASKETS	F-LIGHTED	F-LOUSING	F-RACKING	F-RIGGING	F-RITTING
F-ETTLING	F-LATTENS	F-LIMPING	F-LOUTING	F-RAGGING	F-RIGHTED	F-ROCKING
F-LABELLA	F-LAWLESS	F-LINCHES	F-LOWERED	F-RAGMENT	F-RIGHTEN	F-ROSTING
F-LACKERS	F-LECTION	F-LINGERS	F-LUFFING	F-RAISING	F-RIGIDER	F-ROUNCES
F-LAGGING	F-LEDGIER	F-LINTIER	F-LUMPING	F-RANKEST	F-RIGIDLY	F-RUMPING
F-LAKIEST	F-LEECHED	F-LIPPING	F-LURRIES	F-RANKING	F-RILLING	F-RUMPLED
F-LAMMING	F-LEECHES	F-LITTERS	F-LUSHERS	F-RAPPING	F-RINGING	F-RUMPLES
F-LANCHED	F-LEERING	F-LOCKING	F-LUSHEST	F-RATCHES	F-RIPPERS	F-RUSHING
F-LANCHES	F-LEGGING	F-LOGGING	F-LUSHIER	F-RAZZLES	F-RISKERS	F-ULLAGES
F-LANKING	F-LETCHED	F-LOPPING	F-LUSHING	F-REAKING	F-RISKFUL	F-UNCTION
F-LAPPERS	F-LETCHES	F-LOSSIER	F-LUSTERS	F-RETTING	F-RISKIER	F-UNFAIRS
F-LAPPING	F-LICHTER	F-LOUNDER	F-LUTINGS	F-RICHTED	F-RISKILY	F-UTILITY
F-LASHERS	F-LICKERS	F-LOURIER	F-LUTISTS	F-RIDGING	F-RISKING	
F-LASHING	F-LICKING	F-LOURING	F-ORPINES	F-RIGGERS	F-RITTERS	

8→9

F-ALLOWING	F-LAPPINGS	F-LETCHING	F-LOWERING	F-RATCHING	F-RISKIEST
F-ALTERING	F-LASHINGS	F-LIGHTING	F-LUMMOXES	F-RECKLING	F-ROCKINGS
F-ARROWING	F-LAUGHTER	F-LINTIEST	F-LUSHIEST	F-RICHTING	F-RUMPLING
F-ASHERIES	F-LAUNCHED	F-LITTERED	F-LUSHNESS	F-RIGGINGS	F-UNCTIONS
F-EASTINGS	F-LAUNCHES	F-LOGGINGS	F-LUSTERED	F-RIGHTENS	
F-LABELLUM	F-LECTIONS	F-LOSSIEST	F-LUSTRATE	F-RIGHTFUL	
F-LACKERED	F-LEDGIEST	F-LOUNDERS	F-RACKINGS	F-RIGHTING	
F-LAGGINGS	F-LEECHING	F-LOURIEST	F-RAGMENTS	F-RIGIDEST	
F-LANCHING	F-LEERINGS	F-LOWERIER	F-RANKNESS	F-RIGIDITY	

2→3

EF-F	ER-F	IF-F	OF-F	OR-F	TE-F
EL-F	GI-F	NE-F	OO-F	RE-F	

3→4

BAR-F	CON-F	DOW-F	HOO-F	LEA-F	POO-F	SEI-F	TEF-F
BEE-F	COO-F	FIE-F	HOW-F	LIE-F	PRO-F	SEL-F	WOO-F
BUM-F	COR-F	GOA-F	HUM-F	LOO-F	REE-F	SOW-F	WOW-F
CHE-F	DEL-F	GOO-F	KAI-F	NIE-F	ROO-F	SUR-F	

4→5

HOUF-F	HOWF-F	KALI-F	PROO-F	SCAR-F	SCUR-F	SHEA-F	SOWF-F

5→6

BELIE-F   RELIE-F

6→7

SHERIF-F

2→3

G-AD	G-AR	G-EE	G-HI	G-IO	G-OB	G-OO	G-UN	G-UT
G-AE	G-AS	G-EL	G-ID	G-IS	G-OD	G-OS	G-UP	
G-AM	G-AT	G-EM	G-IF	G-IT	G-OE	G-OY	G-UR	
G-AN	G-AY	G-EN	G-IN	G-NU	G-ON	G-UM	G-US	

3→4

G-ABY	G-AMP	G-AYS	G-EST	G-ITS	G-LOB	G-OES	G-OUK	G-REW	G-ULE
G-ADS	G-ANE	G-EAN	G-ETA	G-JUS	G-LOP	G-OFF	G-OUT	G-RID	G-UNS
G-AGA	G-ANT	G-EAR	G-HAT	G-LAD	G-LOW	G-OLD	G-OWL	G-RIG	G-UPS
G-AGE	G-APE	G-EAT	G-HIS	G-LAM	G-LUG	G-OLE	G-OWN	G-RIM	G-URN
G-AID	G-ARB	G-EEK	G-IDS	G-LED	G-LUM	G-ONE	G-OYS	G-RIN	G-UTS
G-AIN	G-ARE	G-ELD	G-ILL	G-LEE	G-NAT	G-ONS	G-RAD	G-RIP	
G-AIR	G-ARS	G-ELS	G-IMP	G-LEG	G-NUS	G-OOF	G-RAM	G-RIT	
G-AIT	G-ART	G-ELT	G-INK	G-LEI	G-OAF	G-OON	G-RAN	G-ROT	
G-ALA	G-ASH	G-EMS	G-INN	G-LEY	G-OAT	G-OOP	G-RAT	G-ROW	
G-ALE	G-ASP	G-ENE	G-INS	G-LIB	G-OBO	G-OOR	G-RAY	G-RUB	
G-ALL	G-ATE	G-ENS	G-IOS	G-LID	G-OBS	G-OOS	G-REE	G-RUE	
G-ALS	G-AVE	G-ERE	G-ISM	G-LIT	G-ODS	G-ORE	G-REN	G-RUM	

4→5

G-ABLE	G-AGES	G-AIRS	G-ALAS	G-ALLS	G-AMBO	G-ANTS	G-APES	G-ARUM
G-AGED	G-AIDS	G-AITS	G-ALES	G-ALLY	G-AMPS	G-APED	G-ARBS	G-ASPS

G-AUNT	G-HOST	G-LAZE	G-LOBE	G-OATS	G-OWLS	G-RAZE	G-RIND	G-ROVE
G-EANS	G-ILLS	G-LAZY	G-LOBS	G-OBOS	G-OWNS	G-REED	G-RINS	G-ROWS
G-EARS	G-ILLY	G-LEAM	G-LODE	G-ODSO	G-RACE	G-REEN	G-RIOT	G-RUBS
G-EATS	G-IMPS	G-LEAN	G-LOOM	G-OFFS	G-RADE	G-REES	G-RIPE	G-RUED
G-ELDS	G-INKS	G-LEED	G-LOOP	G-OLDS	G-RADS	G-REGO	G-RIPS	G-RUES
G-ELTS	G-IRON	G-LEEK	G-LOPS	G-OLDY	G-RAFF	G-REIN	G-RISE	G-RUFF
G-EMMA	G-ISMS	G-LEES	G-LORY	G-OLPE	G-RAFT	G-RENS	G-RITS	G-RUME
G-ENES	G-LACE	G-LEET	G-LOSS	G-ONER	G-RAIL	G-REWS	G-ROAN	G-RUMP
G-ERES	G-LADE	G-LEIS	G-LOUT	G-OOFS	G-RAIN	G-RICE	G-ROIN	G-RUNT
G-ERNE	G-LADS	G-LENS	G-LOVE	G-OONS	G-RAMS	G-RIDE	G-ROMA	G-RYKE
G-ESSE	G-LADY	G-LENT	G-LOWS	G-OOPS	G-RAND	G-RIDS	G-RONE	G-RYPE
G-ESTS	G-LAIK	G-LEYS	G-LUES	G-OOSE	G-RANT	G-RIFF	G-ROOF	G-ULES
G-ETAS	G-LAIR	G-LIBS	G-LUGS	G-OOSY	G-RAPE	G-RIFT	G-ROOM	G-UMBO
G-HAST	G-LAMS	G-LIFT	G-NATS	G-ORAL	G-RASP	G-RIGS	G-ROPE	G-URGE
G-HATS	G-LAND	G-LIKE	G-NOME	G-ORES	G-RATE	G-RILL	G-ROTS	G-URNS
G-HAUT	G-LARE	G-LINT	G-OAFS	G-OUKS	G-RAVE	G-RIME	G-ROUP	G-URUS
G-HEST	G-LASS	G-LISK	G-OARY	G-OUTS	G-RAYS	G-RIMY	G-ROUT	G-YELD

5→6

G-ABIES	G-ASSES	G-LANCE	G-LOVED	G-OWLED	G-RAVER	G-RINDS	G-ROVES
G-ABLED	G-ASTER	G-LANDS	G-LOVER	G-OWNED	G-RAVES	G-RIOTS	G-ROWER
G-ABLES	G-AUGER	G-LARES	G-LOVES	G-RACED	G-RAYED	G-RIPED	G-ROWTH
G-ABLET	G-AUNTS	G-LAZED	G-LOWED	G-RACES	G-RAYLE	G-RIPER	G-ROYNE
G-ADDED	G-EARED	G-LAZES	G-LOWER	G-RAFFS	G-RAZED	G-RIPES	G-RUING
G-ADDER	G-ELDER	G-LEAMS	G-LUMPS	G-RAFTS	G-RAZES	G-RISES	G-RUMES
G-AGGER	G-ENTRY	G-LEANS	G-LUMPY	G-RAILE	G-REAVE	G-RIVET	G-RUMLY
G-AGING	G-ERNED	G-LEAVE	G-NOMES	G-RAILS	G-REEDS	G-ROANS	G-RUMPS
G-ALLEY	G-ERNES	G-LEDGE	G-NOMIC	G-RAINE	G-REEDY	G-ROINS	G-RUMPY
G-ALLOW	G-EEKS	G-LEEKS	G-NOSES	G-RAINS	G-REENS	G-ROMAS	G-RUNTS
G-AMBIT	G-HARRY	G-LEETS	G-OBANG	G-RAINY	G-REGOS	G-RONES	G-RYKES
G-AMBLE	G-HAZEL	G-LIFTS	G-OBOES	G-RANDS	G-REINS	G-ROOFS	G-UMBOS
G-AMBOS	G-HOSTS	G-LIKES	G-ODSOS	G-RANGE	G-RESES	G-ROOMS	G-UNITE
G-AMINE	G-IMPED	G-LINTS	G-OFFED	G-RANTS	G-RICER	G-ROPED	G-UNMAN
G-AMMON	G-INGLE	G-LISKS	G-OFFER	G-RAPED	G-RICES	G-ROPER	G-URGES
G-ANGER	G-INNED	G-LOBBY	G-OLDEN	G-RAPES	G-RIDES	G-ROPES	G-URNED
G-ANTED	G-INNER	G-LOBED	G-OLDER	G-RASPS	G-RIEVE	G-ROSET	G-USHER
G-APING	G-IRONS	G-LOBES	G-OLPES	G-RATED	G-RIFFS	G-ROUGH	G-UTTER
G-ARISH	G-LACES	G-LOOMS	G-ONERS	G-RATER	G-RIFTS	G-ROUND	
G-ARRET	G-LADES	G-LOOPS	G-ONION	G-RATES	G-RILLE	G-ROUPS	
G-ARUMS	G-LAIKS	G-LOOPY	G-OOSES	G-RAVED	G-RILLS	G-ROUPY	
G-ASHES	G-LAIRS	G-LOSSY	G-ORALS	G-RAVEL	G-RIMED	G-ROUSE	
G-ASPER	G-LAIRY	G-LOUTS	G-ORGIA	G-RAVEN	G-RIMES	G-ROUTS	

6→7

G-ABLETS	G-AUNTER	G-LANDES	G-LORIES	G-RAFTER	G-RAZING	G-RIPPLE	G-RUBBED
G-ADDERS	G-AUNTLY	G-LASSES	G-LOSSES	G-RAILES	G-REAVES	G-RISING	G-RUBBER
G-ADDING	G-EARING	G-LAZIER	G-LOUTED	G-RAINED	G-REGALE	G-RITTED	G-RUBBLE
G-AGGERS	G-ELDERS	G-LAZING	G-LOVERS	G-RAINES	G-REINED	G-RITTER	G-RUEING
G-ALLEYS	G-ELDING	G-LEAMED	G-LOVING	G-RANGER	G-RENNED	G-RIVETS	G-RUMBLE
G-ALLIED	G-ENLOCK	G-LEANED	G-LOWERS	G-RANGES	G-RICERS	G-ROINED	G-RUMBLY
G-ALLIES	G-ELDING	G-LEANER	G-LOWING	G-RANTED	G-RICING	G-ROOMED	G-RUMMER
G-ALLIUM	G-ESTATE	G-LEAVES	G-LUGGED	G-RANTER	G-RIDDER	G-ROPERS	G-RUMPED
G-ALLONS	G-HASTED	G-LEDGES	G-LUTEAL	G-RAPIER	G-RIDDLE	G-ROPING	G-RUNTED
G-ALLOWS	G-HAZELS	G-LEEING	G-OBANGS	G-RAPING	G-RIDING	G-ROSETS	G-ULLING
G-AMBITS	G-HOSTED	G-LEGGER	G-OFFERS	G-RASPED	G-RIEVER	G-ROSSER	G-UNDIES
G-AMBLED	G-IMPING	G-LIBBED	G-OFFING	G-RASPER	G-RIEVES	G-ROUGHS	G-UNITES
G-AMBLER	G-INGLES	G-LIBBER	G-OLDENS	G-RASSES	G-RIFTED	G-ROUNDS	G-UNLESS
G-AMBLES	G-INNERS	G-LIMMER	G-OLDEST	G-RATERS	G-RIGGED	G-ROUPED	G-UNLOCK
G-AMINES	G-INNING	G-LISTEN	G-OLDISH	G-RATIFY	G-RILLED	G-ROUSED	G-UNSHIP
G-AMMONS	G-IRONIC	G-LISTER	G-OOSIER	G-RATINE	G-RILLES	G-ROUSER	G-UNSHOT
G-ANGERS	G-IZZARD	G-LITTER	G-ORGIAS	G-RATING	G-RIMIER	G-ROUSES	G-URNING
G-ANTING	G-LACIER	G-LOBATE	G-OUTFLY	G-RAUNCH	G-RIMING	G-ROUTED	G-USHERS
G-ARRETS	G-LADDER	G-LOBING	G-OWLING	G-RAVELS	G-RINDED	G-ROUTER	G-UTTERS
G-ASEITY	G-LADDIE	G-LOBOSE	G-OWNING	G-RAVERS	G-RIPERS	G-ROWERS	G-YMPING
G-ASPERS	G-LAIRED	G-LOBULE	G-RABBLE	G-RAVING	G-RIPING	G-ROWING	
G-ASTERS	G-LANCED	G-LOOMED	G-RACING	G-RAYING	G-RIPPED	G-ROWTHS	
G-AUGERS	G-LANCES	G-LOOPED	G-RAFTED	G-RAYLES	G-RIPPER	G-ROYNES	

7→8

G-ALLISES	G-ANGLING	G-ELDINGS	G-HASTING	G-LAIRING	G-LIBBING	G-LOAMING
G-ALLIUMS	G-ARISHES	G-ENLOCKS	G-HOSTING	G-LANCING	G-LIMMERS	G-LOBULAR
G-ALLOWED	G-EARINGS	G-ENTRIES	G-IZZARDS	G-LANDERS	G-LISTENS	G-LOBULES
G-ALLYING	G-EARLESS	G-ESTATED	G-LABELLA	G-LAZIEST	G-LISTERS	G-LOOMING
G-AMBLERS	G-ELASTIC	G-ESTATES	G-LADDIES	G-LEAMING	G-LITTERS	G-LOOPIER
G-AMBLING	G-ELATION	G-HARRIES	G-LAIRIER	G-LEANING	G-LITTERY	G-LOOPING

```
G-LOSSIER    G-OUTWEED    G-RASPERS    G-RIDDERS    G-RIPPIER    G-ROUSING    G-RUMMEST
G-LOUTING    G-RABBLED    G-RASPING    G-RIDDLES    G-RIPPING    G-ROUTERS    G-RUMNESS
G-LOVINGS    G-RABBLER    G-RATINGS    G-RIEVERS    G-RIPPLES    G-ROUTING    G-RUMPING
G-LOWERED    G-RABBLES    G-RAVINGS    G-RIEVING    G-RITTERS    G-ROWABLE    G-UNHOUSE
G-LUGGING    G-RAFTERS    G-RAYLING    G-RIFTING    G-RITTING    G-ROWINGS    G-UNLOCKS
G-LUMPIER    G-RAFTING    G-REAVING    G-RIGGING    G-ROINING    G-RUBBERS    G-UNSHIPS
G-LUMPISH    G-RAINIER    G-REEDIER    G-RILLING    G-ROOMING    G-RUBBING    G-UNSTICK
G-OFFERED    G-RAINING    G-REEKING    G-RIMIEST    G-ROUNDED    G-RUBBLES    G-UNSTOCK
G-OLDENED    G-RANGERS    G-REGALES    G-RINDING    G-ROUNDER    G-RUMBLED    G-UTTERED
G-ONENESS    G-RANTERS    G-REINING    G-RINNING    G-ROUPING    G-RUMBLER
G-OOSIEST    G-RANTING    G-RENNING    G-RIPPERS    G-ROUSERS    G-RUMBLES
```

8→9

```
G-ALLOWING   G-LEANINGS    G-MELINITE    G-RAINIEST    G-RAVELLED    G-RUMBLING
G-AMBLINGS   G-LISTENED    G-OFFERING    G-RAPESEED    G-REEDIEST    G-UNFOUGHT
G-ASEITIES   G-LITTERED    G-OLDENING    G-RATIFIED    G-ROUNDERS    G-UNHOUSES
G-ELATIONS   G-LOOPIEST    G-OUTFLIES    G-RATIFIER    G-ROUNDING    G-UNSTICKS
G-ESTATING   G-LOSSIEST    G-OUTWEEDS    G-RATIFIES    G-ROUTINGS    G-UNSTOCKS
G-HOSTINGS   G-LOWERING    G-RABBLERS    G-RAUNCHED    G-RUMBLERS    G-UTTERING
G-LAIRIEST   G-LUMPIEST    G-RABBLING    G-RAUNCHES    G-RUMBLIER
```

2→3

```
BA-G    DA-G    ER-G    HO-G    LO-G    MU-G    SO-G    TO-G
BE-G    DI-G    FA-G    JO-G    MA-G    NA-G    TA-G    WO-G
BI-G    DO-G    GI-G    LA-G    ME-G    NO-G    TE-G    YU-G
BO-G    EN-G    HA-G    LI-G    MO-G    PI-G    TI-G
```

3→4

```
AGO-G    BOY-G    DIN-G    GAN-G    HON-G    MON-G    QUA-G    SIN-G    TIN-G
ARE-G    BRA-G    DON-G    GIN-G    KIN-G    NOG-G    RAG-G    SKA-G    TON-G
BAN-G    BRO-G    DUN-G    GON-G    LIN-G    NON-G    RAN-G    SON-G    VAN-G
BIG-G    BUN-G    FAN-G    HAG-G    MAG-G    PAN-G    RIG-G    SPA-G    WAN-G
BIN-G    BUR-G    FRA-G    HAN-G    MAN-G    PEA-G    RIN-G    SUN-G    WIN-G
BIO-G    CAN-G    FRO-G    HIN-G    MAR-G    PIN-G    RUN-G    TAN-G
BON-G    DAN-G    FUN-G    HOG-G    MEN-G    PRO-G    SAN-G    TEG-G
```

4→5

```
AGIN-G    BEIN-G    CLAN-G    GULA-G    KAIN-G    SKEG-G    STUN-G    THIN-G
AKIN-G    BOON-G    COHO-G    HYLE-G    RUIN-G    SPAN-G    SWAN-G    THON-G
```

5→6

```
ACTIN-G    ELDIN-G    LAWIN-G    MIRIN-G    RAVIN-G    SATIN-G    TAKIN-G
BARON-G    ELFIN-G    LIKIN-G    PAVIN-G    RICIN-G    SAVIN-G    TAMIN-G
BASIN-G    GAMIN-G    LININ-G    POTIN-G    ROBIN-G    SERIN-G    ZAMAN-G
CONIN-G    KOBAN-G    LYSIN-G    PROLE-G    ROSIN-G    SEWIN-G
COVIN-G    LAKIN-G    MATIN-G    PURIN-G    SARIN-G    SPAIN-G
```

6→7

```
BIFFIN-G    CODLIN-G    FEERIN-G    HIPPIN-G    MUFFIN-G    PIGGIN-G    RUFFIN-G    WELKIN-G
BIGGIN-G    COFFIN-G    FIRKIN-G    HOGGIN-G    MUNTIN-G    PIPPIN-G    SEISIN-G    WITHIN-G
BOBBIN-G    COPPIN-G    GERMIN-G    JERKIN-G    MURLIN-G    PUFFIN-G    SEIZIN-G
BOFFIN-G    CUFFIN-G    GLOBIN-G    LAGGIN-G    NOGGIN-G    PURLIN-G    TANNIN-G
BUGGIN-G    DENTIN-G    GRADIN-G    MARLIN-G    NUBBIN-G    RAISIN-G    TELLIN-G
BUSKIN-G    DOBBIN-G    GRATIN-G    MARTIN-G    OUTWIN-G    RATLIN-G    TIFFIN-G
CALKIN-G    DUBBIN-G    HARMIN-G    MERLIN-G    PARKIN-G    RENNIN-G    TREPAN-G
CATALO-G    FARCIN-G    HENNIN-G    MINGIN-G    PERKIN-G    RIGLIN-G    VERSIN-G
```

7→8

```
ASPIRIN-G    EASTLIN-G    HALFLIN-G    PEARLIN-G    SCULPIN-G    STEARIN-G
CREATIN-G    GALOPIN-G    LITTLIN-G    RATTLIN-G    SPELDIN-G    TABORIN-G
CRISPIN-G    GLAIRIN-G    MAFFLIN-G    RELAXIN-G    SPONGIN-G    UNDERDO-G
```

8→9

```
ABSCISIN-G    DAMASKIN-G    SECRETIN-G    SPELDRIN-G    WARFARIN-G
BALLADIN-G    INVERTIN-G    SNEESHIN-G    TABOURIN-G
```

2→3

```
H-AD    H-AE    H-AH    H-AM    H-AN    H-AS    H-AT    H-AW    H-AY    H-EM
```

H-EN	H-EX	H-IS	H-OD	H-OI	H-OP	H-OX	H-UM	H-YE
H-ER	H-ID	H-IT	H-OE	H-ON	H-OS	H-OY	H-UP	
H-ES	H-IN	H-OB	H-OH	H-OO	H-OW	H-UG	H-UT	

3→4

H-ADS	H-ALT	H-ASK	H-EEL	H-ENS	H-IRE	H-OIK	H-OON	H-OWE	H-YES
H-AFT	H-AND	H-ASP	H-EFT	H-ERE	H-ISH	H-OKE	H-OOP	H-OWL	
H-AIL	H-ARD	H-ATE	H-ELD	H-ERN	H-ITS	H-OLD	H-OPE	H-OYS	
H-AIN	H-ARE	H-AVE	H-ELL	H-ERS	H-OAR	H-OLE	H-OPS	H-UGS	
H-AIR	H-ARK	H-AYS	H-ELM	H-EST	H-OBO	H-OLM	H-ORE	H-ULE	
H-AKE	H-ARM	H-EAR	H-EME	H-IDE	H-OBS	H-ONE	H-ORS	H-UPS	
H-ALE	H-ART	H-EAT	H-EMS	H-ILL	H-ODS	H-ONS	H-OUR	H-UTS	
H-ALL	H-ASH	H-ECH	H-END	H-INS	H-OES	H-OOF	H-OUT	H-YEN	

4→5

H-ABLE	H-ALTS	H-ASKS	H-EAST	H-EMES	H-ILLY	H-OLLA	H-ORAL	H-URDS
H-AILS	H-ANCE	H-ASPS	H-EATH	H-ENDS	H-IRES	H-OLMS	H-OURS	H-YENS
H-AIRS	H-ANDS	H-AULD	H-EATS	H-ERNS	H-ITCH	H-OMER	H-OUTS	
H-AIRY	H-ARDS	H-AUNT	H-ECHT	H-ESTS	H-OARS	H-ONER	H-OVEN	
H-AKES	H-ARED	H-AVER	H-EDGE	H-EUGH	H-OARY	H-ONES	H-OVER	
H-ALES	H-ARES	H-AVES	H-EDGY	H-EWER	H-OAST	H-OOFS	H-OWES	
H-ALFA	H-ARKS	H-AWED	H-EELS	H-EXES	H-OBOS	H-OONS	H-OWLS	
H-ALLS	H-ARMS	H-AZAN	H-EFTS	H-EYED	H-OIKS	H-OOPS	H-OWRE	
H-ALMA	H-ARTS	H-EARD	H-ELLS	H-IDES	H-OKES	H-OPED	H-ULES	
H-ALMS	H-ASHY	H-EARS	H-ELMS	H-ILLS	H-OLDS	H-OPES	H-UMPH	

5→6

H-ACKEE	H-AMATE	H-ARTAL	H-EASTS	H-ETHER	H-OCKER	H-OSIER	H-UMPTY
H-AGLET	H-AMBLE	H-ASHES	H-EATER	H-EUGHS	H-OGGIN	H-OTTER	H-UPPED
H-AILED	H-ANGER	H-AUGHT	H-EAVES	H-EWERS	H-OLDEN	H-OUSEL	H-USHER
H-AIRED	H-ANKER	H-AUNTS	H-EDGED	H-EXACT	H-OLDER	H-OUTED	
H-ALFAS	H-ARBOR	H-AVENS	H-EDGER	H-EYING	H-OLLAS	H-OVERS	
H-ALLOW	H-ARISH	H-AVERS	H-EDGES	H-ISHES	H-OMBRE	H-OWLED	
H-ALMAS	H-ARKED	H-AWING	H-EIGHT	H-ITCHY	H-OMERS	H-OWLER	
H-ALOED	H-ARLED	H-AZANS	H-ELVES	H-OARED	H-ONERS	H-OWLET	
H-ALOES	H-ARMED	H-EARDS	H-ENDED	H-OASTS	H-OOPED	H-OWRES	
H-ALTER	H-ARROW	H-EARTH	H-ERSES	H-OBOES	H-OPING	H-UGGED	

6→7

H-ABDABS	H-ALLOWS	H-ARLING	H-EATERS	H-EXACTS	H-OMBRES	H-OWLERS
H-ACKEES	H-ALTERS	H-ARMFUL	H-EATING	H-EXARCH	H-OOPING	H-OWLETS
H-ACKERS	H-AMBLED	H-ARMING	H-EDGERS	H-IDLING	H-OSIERS	H-OWLING
H-ADDING	H-AMBLES	H-ARROWS	H-EDGIER	H-ITCHED	H-OSIERY	H-UGGING
H-AGLETS	H-ANGERS	H-ASHIER	H-EDGING	H-ITCHES	H-OSTLER	H-ULLING
H-AILING	H-ANKERS	H-AUNTER	H-EIGHTS	H-OARIER	H-OTTERS	H-UMBLES
H-AIRIER	H-ARBORS	H-AUTEUR	H-ENDING	H-OARING	H-OUSELS	H-UPPING
H-AIRING	H-ARBOUR	H-EARING	H-ERRING	H-OCKERS	H-OUTING	H-USHERS
H-ALBERT	H-ARKING	H-EARTHS	H-EUREKA	H-OGGINS	H-OVERED	

7→8

H-AIRIEST	H-ALLOWED	H-ARMLESS	H-AUTEURS	H-EDGINGS	H-ITCHING	H-OTTERED
H-AIRLESS	H-ALTERED	H-ARROWED	H-EARINGS	H-ERRINGS	H-OARIEST	H-OUTINGS
H-AIRLINE	H-AMBLING	H-ASHIEST	H-EATINGS	H-EUREKAS	H-OROLOGY	H-OVERING
H-ALBERTS	H-ARBOURS	H-AUNTERS	H-EDGIEST	H-ITCHIER	H-OSTLERS	H-USHERED

8→9

H-AIRINESS	H-ALTERING	H-ARROWING	H-ODOGRAPH	H-OSIERIES
H-AIRLINES	H-ARBOURED	H-ESSONITE	H-ODOMETER	H-OTTERING
H-ALLOWING	H-ARQUEBUS	H-ITCHIEST	H-ODOMETRY	H-USHERING

2→3

AS-H	BO-H	DO-H	HA-H	IS-H	NO-H	PA-H	RE-H	UG-H
BA-H	DA-H	FA-H	HO-H	LA-H	OO-H	PO-H	SO-H	

3→4

ARC-H	BET-H	BOT-H	DAS-H	FAS-H	GUS-H	HOG-H	LAT-H	MAS-H	MUS-H
BAC-H	BIS-H	BUS-H	DOS-H	GAS-H	HAS-H	KIT-H	LIT-H	MAT-H	NOS-H
BAS-H	BOO-H	COS-H	DOT-H	GAT-H	HAT-H	KOP-H	LOS-H	MES-H	OAT-H
BAT-H	BOS-H	COT-H	EAT-H	GOS-H	HIS-H	LAS-H	LOT-H	MOT-H	OUP-H

```
PAS-H    PEG-H    PIT-H    PUG-H    RAT-H    SIC-H    SUK-H    TIC-H    WIT-H
PAT-H    PHO-H    POO-H    PUS-H    ROC-H    SIT-H    TAN-H    WAS-H    YEA-H
PEC-H    PIS-H    POS-H    RAS-H    RUT-H    SOP-H    TAT-H    WIS-H
```

4→5
```
ABAS-H    BUMP-H    DOSE-H    GIRT-H    MANE-H    PLUS-H    SOLA-H    TAIS-H    WOOS-H
ALMA-H    BURG-H    DUNS-H    GRIT-H    MARA-H    RAJA-H    SOOT-H    TAVA-H    WORT-H
ALME-H    CANE-H    EPHA-H    GULP-H    MARC-H    ROUT-H    SOUT-H    TENT-H
ARIS-H    CHIC-H    FLUS-H    HEAT-H    MARS-H    ROWT-H    STAP-H    THIG-H
BEAT-H    CLOT-H    FORT-H    HUMP-H    MEAT-H    SCAT-H    SUMP-H    TILT-H
BOOT-H    CRIT-H    FRIT-H    LEAS-H    MUST-H    SIRI-H    SURA-H    TOOT-H
BRAS-H    CRUS-H    GALA-H    LEIS-H    MYNA-H    SLOT-H    SWAT-H    TORC-H
BROG-H    DONA-H    GART-H    LOTA-H    NEAT-H    SMIT-H    SYNC-H    TROT-H
```

5→6
```
ALIYA-H    FELLA-H    HIGHT-H    MATZA-H    PALLA-H    SCART-H    SPILT-H    WALLA-H
ARRIS-H    FINIS-H    HIJRA-H    MATZO-H    PERIS-H    SCOUT-H    STOUT-H
CAMAS-H    GALUT-H    HOOKA-H    MINIS-H    POOJA-H    SHEIK-H    SUMAC-H
COSEC-H    GRUMP-H    HURRA-H    MOLLA-H    PUNKA-H    SKART-H    SWART-H
CREES-H    HALVA-H    IMPIS-H    MOOLA-H    RAKIS-H    SMOOT-H    TANNA-H
EIGHT-H    HAMZA-H    INWIT-H    NALLA-H    RUPIA-H    SNEES-H    THANA-H
FATWA-H    HEART-H    LOOFA-H    NULLA-H    SCARP-H    SPART-H    VAREC-H
```

6→7
```
ALIYOT-H    GRAMAS-H    MATZOT-H    OUTWIT-H    POORIS-H    SIMURG-H    SUCCOT-H    THANNA-H
BABOOS-H    HAGGIS-H    MEZUZA-H    PARKIS-H    SABKHA-H    STEALT-H    SUKKOT-H    TURBIT-H
CADDIS-H    MASTIC-H    MISSIS-H    PITARA-H    SAHIBA-H    STIRRA-H    TEREFA-H    UNGIRT-H
```

7→8
```
AMARANT-H    GALABIA-H    JAMBIYA-H    KHALIFA-H    OCTOPUS-H    SCAMPIS-H    YESHIVA-H
BEGORRA-H    HAROSET-H    KABBALA-H    MADRASA-H    PEISHWA-H    SHEHITA-H
GALABEA-H    HYDRANT-H    KASHRUT-H    NARGILE-H    SAVANNA-H    VERANDA-H
```

8→9
```
ALLELUIA-H    GALLABEA-H    MADRASSA-H    SHAMIANA-H    YESHIVOT-H
CHAROSET-H    GALLABIA-H    MAHARAJA-H    SHECHITA-H
DJELLABA-H    KHANSAMA-H    SANDARAC-H    TELESTIC-H
```

2→3
```
I-CH    I-ON    I-OS    I-RE    I-SH    I-SO    I-TA
```

3→4
```
I-BIS    I-DEE    I-KAT    I-LEA    I-MAM    I-RES    I-SOS    I-WIS
I-CON    I-GAD    I-KON    I-LEX    I-ONS    I-RID    I-URE
```

4→5
```
I-CONS    I-DEES    I-KONS    I-MINE    I-RATE    I-SLED    I-VIES
I-DANT    I-GAPO    I-MAGE    I-ODIC    I-RIDS    I-TEMS
I-DEAL    I-KATS    I-MAMS    I-RADE    I-SHES    I-VIED
```

5→6
```
I-BICES    I-DANTS    I-GUANA    I-MINES    I-RATER    I-SATIN
I-BISES    I-DEALS    I-LEXES    I-NYALA    I-RIDES    I-SLING
I-CONIC    I-GAPOS    I-MAGES    I-ODISM    I-RISES    I-TEMED
```

6→7
```
I-GUANAS    I-MAGISM    I-NYALAS    I-ODISMS    I-SATINS
```

7→8
```
I-MAGISMS    I-SABELLA    I-SLANDER
```

8→9
```
I-SABELLAS    I-SLANDERS    I-SOLATION
```

2→3
AM-I	CH-I	KA-I	MO-I	PH-I	TA-I
AN-I	HO-I	KO-I	OB-I	PO-I	UN-I

3→4
ANT-I	DAL-I	HAJ-I	MAG-I	MOD-I	PEN-I	RAN-I	SOL-I	TOP-I
BAN-I	DEL-I	IMP-I	MAL-I	MOO-I	PER-I	ROT-I	TAB-I	TOR-I
BEN-I	DIV-I	KAM-I	MAN-I	NID-I	PIP-I	SAR-I	TAK-I	WAD-I
CAD-I	FEN-I	KAT-I	MAX-I	NIS-I	PUR-I	SAT-I	TAX-I	YET-I
CAP-I	FIN-I	KEP-I	MID-I	NOD-I	RAG-I	SIM-I	TIP-I	YON-I
CHA-I	GAD-I	LOB-I	MIR-I	NOR-I	RAM-I	SIR-I	TIT-I	ZIT-I

4→5
ABAC-I	COAT-I	FUND-I	JINN-I	MOOL-I	PART-I	SERA-I	TEMP-I
BASS-I	COMB-I	FUNG-I	LASS-I	MYTH-I	PILE-I	SHOG-I	TORI-I
BLIN-I	CORN-I	HADJ-I	LATH-I	NIMB-I	POOR-I	SOLD-I	TORS-I
BUFF-I	CURS-I	HAJJ-I	LENT-I	OBOL-I	PUTT-I	STOA-I	VILL-I
CARD-I	DILL-I	HONG-I	LICH-I	PALP-I	REIK-I	SWAM-I	XYST-I
CARP-I	FAST-I	HOUR-I	LUNG-I	PARD-I	SAMP-I	TANG-I	ZIMB-I
CEIL-I	FERM-I	IAMB-I	MODI-I	PARK-I	SCUD-I	TARS-I	

5→6
ANNUL-I	CAROL-I	CLYPE-I	DUETT-I	POLYP-I	SHALL-I	SOLID-I
ARGAL-I	CHICH-I	DEWAN-I	GARDA-I	RHOMB-I	SILEN-I	TAPET-I
AVANT-I	CHILL-I	DJINN-I	JOWAR-I	SCAMP-I	SMALT-I	YOGIN-I

6→7
CHIASM-I	DEMENT-I	EPIGON-I	HALLAL-I	MARTIN-I	REVERS-I	SECOND-I	SIGNOR-I
DAKOIT-I	ELENCH-I	GRADIN-I	JAMPAN-I	QAWWAL-I	RHYTHM-I	SHIKAR-I	TYMPAN-I

7→8
CAPITAN-I	CONDUCT-I	DRACHMA-I	FASCIST-I	MARCHES-I	TANDOOR-I
CONCEPT-I	CORNETT-I	DUUMVIR-I	HETAIRA-I	PARCHES-I	
CONCERT-I	COTHURN-I	FASCISM-I	KOFTGAR-I	PERFECT-I	

8→9
ASTRAGAL-I	EUCALYPT-I	PEDIPALP-I	QUINTETT-I	ZAMINDAR-I
CHORIAMB-I	MATACHIN-I	PORTOLAN-I	STRELITZ-I	ZEMINDAR-I
DECEMVIR-I	PASTORAL-I	QUARTETT-I	TRIUMVIR-I	

2→3
J-AM	J-AW	J-EE	J-OE	J-OW	J-UG	J-UT
J-AR	J-AY	J-OB	J-OR	J-OY	J-US	

3→4
J-AIL	J-APE	J-ASS	J-EEL	J-ESS	J-IMP	J-OBS	J-ORS	J-OYS	J-UKE
J-AKE	J-ARK	J-AYS	J-EFF	J-EST	J-INK	J-OES	J-OUK	J-UDO	J-URE
J-ANE	J-ARS	J-EAN	J-ELL	J-IFF	J-INN	J-OKE	J-OUR	J-UDS	J-UTE
J-ANN	J-ASP	J-EAT	J-ERK	J-ILL	J-ISM	J-OLE	J-OWL	J-UGS	J-UTS

4→5
J-AILS	J-ANNS	J-AUNT	J-EELY	J-IFFY	J-ISMS	J-OURS	J-UDOS	J-UPON
J-AKES	J-APED	J-AWED	J-EFFS	J-ILLS	J-NANA	J-OUST	J-UKES	J-UTES
J-ALAP	J-APES	J-EANS	J-ELLS	J-INGO	J-OINT	J-OWED	J-UMBO	
J-AMBO	J-ARKS	J-EATS	J-ERKS	J-INKS	J-OKES	J-OWLS	J-UNCO	
J-ANES	J-ASPS	J-EELS	J-ESTS	J-INNS	J-OUKS	J-OWLY	J-UNTO	

5→6
J-AGGER	J-ANGLE	J-ASPER	J-EFFED	J-INKED	J-OUNCE	J-UDDER	J-UNKED
J-AILED	J-ANKER	J-ASSES	J-ESSES	J-INKER	J-OUSTS	J-UGGED	J-UNKET
J-ALAPS	J-APING	J-AUNTS	J-ESTER	J-NANAS	J-OWING	J-UMBOS	
J-AMBER	J-ARGON	J-AUNTY	J-IMPLY	J-OINTS	J-OWLED	J-UNCOS	
J-AMBOS	J-ARRAH	J-AWING	J-INGLE	J-OTTER	J-OWLER	J-UNCUS	

6→7
J-AGGERS	J-AILING	J-AMBERS	J-ANGLED	J-ANGLER	J-ANGLES	J-ANKERS	J-ARGONS

J-ASPERS	J-ESTERS	J-INKERS	J-OINTED	J-OUSTED	J-OWLIER	J-UGGING	J-UNKING
J-AUNTIE	J-INGLES	J-INKING	J-OTTERS	J-OUSTER	J-OWLING	J-UMBLES	
J-EFFING	J-INGOES	J-OCULAR	J-OUNCES	J-OWLERS	J-UDDERS	J-UNCATE	

7→8

J-AMBONES	J-ANGLING	J-OINTING	J-OUSTING	J-UDDERED
J-ANGLERS	J-AUNTIES	J-OUSTERS	J-OWLIEST	J-UNCTION

8→9

J-ANGLINGS   J-ASPEROUS   J-OCULARLY   J-UNCTIONS

2→3

HA-J   TA-J

3→4

BEN-J   HAD-J   HAJ-J

2→3

K-AE	K-AS	K-AY	K-EN	K-IF	K-OB	K-OP	K-YE
K-AI	K-AT	K-EA	K-EX	K-IN	K-OI	K-OS	K-YU
K-AM	K-AW	K-EF	K-ID	K-IT	K-ON	K-OW	

3→4

K-AGO	K-ALE	K-AVA	K-EFS	K-EST	K-ILL	K-NAG	K-NOT	K-OFF
K-AID	K-AMI	K-AYS	K-ELL	K-ETA	K-INK	K-NAP	K-NOW	K-ONS
K-AIL	K-ANA	K-EAS	K-ELT	K-HAN	K-INS	K-NEE	K-NUB	K-OPS
K-AIM	K-ANT	K-EEK	K-ENS	K-HAT	K-IRK	K-NEW	K-NUR	K-ORE
K-AIN	K-ARK	K-EEL	K-ERF	K-IDS	K-ISH	K-NIT	K-NUT	K-SAR
K-AIS	K-ART	K-EEN	K-ERN	K-IFS	K-ITS	K-NOB	K-OBS	K-YUS

4→5

K-AIDS	K-ARTS	K-ELTS	K-HATS	K-LOOF	K-NOBS	K-NURR	K-RAIT
K-AILS	K-AVAS	K-ERNE	K-HORS	K-LUTZ	K-NOCK	K-NURS	K-RANG
K-AIMS	K-AWED	K-ERNS	K-ILLS	K-NAGS	K-NOLL	K-NUTS	K-RILL
K-ALES	K-EDGE	K-ESTS	K-INKS	K-NAPS	K-NOUT	K-OFFS	K-RONE
K-AMIS	K-EDGY	K-ETAS	K-INKY	K-NAVE	K-NOWN	K-OKRA	K-SARS
K-ANAS	K-EECH	K-ETCH	K-IRKS	K-NEED	K-NOWS	K-OMBU	K-UDOS
K-ANTS	K-EELS	K-EXES	K-IWIS	K-NIFE	K-NUBS	K-ORES	K-URUS
K-ARKS	K-ELLS	K-EYED	K-LANG	K-NITS	K-NURL	K-RAFT	K-YANG

5→6

K-ABAYA	K-AWING	K-ENTIA	K-INGLE	K-NAGGY	K-NOLLS	K-RAFTS
K-ABELE	K-EBBED	K-ERNED	K-INKED	K-NAVES	K-NUBBY	K-RAITS
K-ALONG	K-EDGED	K-ERNES	K-INKLE	K-NICKS	K-NURLS	K-RATER
K-ANTAR	K-EDGER	K-ETTLE	K-IRKED	K-NIFES	K-NURRS	K-RILLS
K-ANTED	K-EDGES	K-EYING	K-ISHES	K-NIGHT	K-OBANG	K-RISES
K-ARKED	K-EIGHT	K-HODJA	K-LATCH	K-NOBBY	K-OKRAS	K-VETCH
K-ARRIS	K-EMBED	K-ICKER	K-LOOFS	K-NOCKS	K-OMBUS	K-YANGS

6→7

K-ABAYAS	K-EBBING	K-ENOSIS	K-ICKERS	K-INKLES	K-NAPPER	K-NUBBLY
K-ABELES	K-EDGERS	K-ERNING	K-IDLING	K-INSHIP	K-NICKER	K-NURLED
K-AMISES	K-EDGIER	K-ETCHES	K-INDIES	K-IRKING	K-NIGHTS	K-OBANGS
K-ANTARS	K-EDGING	K-ETTLES	K-INGLES	K-LINKER	K-NOBBLE	K-ONNING
K-ANTING	K-EECHES	K-HANJAR	K-INKIER	K-LUTZES	K-NOCKED	K-RATERS
K-ARKING	K-ENOSES	K-HODJAS	K-INKING	K-NAPPED	K-NUBBLE	K-RISING

7→8

K-EDGIEST	K-INSHIPS	K-NAPPERS	K-NIGHTLY	K-NOCKING	K-NURLING
K-ETCHING	K-LATCHES	K-NAPPING	K-NOBBIER	K-NUBBIER	K-OSMOSES
K-HANJARS	K-LINKERS	K-NICKERS	K-NOBBLED	K-NUBBLED	K-VETCHES
K-INKIEST	K-NAGGIER	K-NIGHTED	K-NOBBLES	K-NUBBLES	

8→9

K-NAGGIEST	K-NICKERED	K-NOBBLING	K-NUBBLIER
K-NEVELLED	K-NOBBIEST	K-NUBBIEST	K-NUBBLING

2→3

AR-K	BO-K	EE-K	ER-K	MA-K	OI-K	TA-K	YO-K
AS-K	DA-K	EL-K	IN-K	NE-K	OU-K	WO-K	YU-K

3→4

BAC-K	BUS-K	DOE-K	GOO-K	KIN-K	MAC-K	PAW-K	REC-K	SIN-K	WAN-K
BAN-K	CAR-K	DOO-K	GUN-K	KIR-K	MAR-K	PEA-K	REE-K	SOC-K	WAR-K
BAR-K	CAW-K	DOR-K	HAN-K	KON-K	MAS-K	PEC-K	RIN-K	SOU-K	WEE-K
BAS-K	CHI-K	DUN-K	HAS-K	LAC-K	MAW-K	PEE-K	ROC-K	SUN-K	WIN-K
BIN-K	CON-K	FAN-K	HAW-K	LAR-K	MIL-K	PEN-K	ROO-K	TAN-K	WON-K
BIS-K	COO-K	FIN-K	HIC-K	LAW-K	MIR-K	PER-K	RUC-K	TEA-K	YES-K
BOA-K	COR-K	FIR-K	HOC-K	LEA-K	MON-K	PIC-K	SAC-K	TIC-K	YOU-K
BON-K	DAN-K	FOR-K	HOI-K	LEE-K	MOO-K	PIN-K	SAN-K	TIN-K	
BOO-K	DAW-K	FUN-K	HON-K	LIN-K	MUS-K	POO-K	SAR-K	TOC-K	
BOS-K	DEE-K	GEE-K	HOO-K	LIS-K	NAB-K	PUN-K	SEE-K	TON-K	
BUN-K	DIN-K	GIN-K	HOW-K	LOO-K	NOR-K	RAI-K	SEI-K	TOO-K	
BUR-K	DOC-K	GON-K	JAR-K	LUR-K	PAR-K	RAN-K	SIC-K	VOL-K	

4→5

ABAC-K	BROO-K	CLAN-K	FRIS-K	SHAN-K	SNAR-K	SPUN-K	THAN-K
ABAS-K	CAUL-K	CRAN-K	GLEE-K	SHIR-K	SNOW-K	STAR-K	THEE-K
BLIN-K	CHAL-K	CREE-K	KAMI-K	SHOO-K	SPAN-K	STIR-K	THIN-K
BLOC-K	CHAR-K	CROC-K	MALI-K	SKIN-K	SPAR-K	STUN-K	TOPE-K
BOBA-K	CHIC-K	ERIC-K	PLAN-K	SLEE-K	SPEC-K	SWAN-K	TORS-K
BORA-K	CHIN-K	FLAN-K	SAIC-K	SMEE-K	SPIC-K	TALA-K	TWIN-K
BRAN-K	CHOC-K	FLIC-K	SCUL-K	SMIR-K	SPIN-K	TARO-K	WAUL-K

5→6

ANTIC-K	BEGUN-K	EMBAR-K	JAMBO-K	MEDIC-K	PANIC-K	SQUAW-K	ZEBEC-K
ASPIC-K	DEBAR-K	IMBAR-K	KALPA-K	PACHA-K	REBEC-K	UNBAR-K	

6→7

BOOBOO-K	CALPAC-K	DISBAR-K	FINNAC-K	LIMBEC-K	OOMIAC-K	OUTRAN-K	TIETAC-K

7→8

BALDRIC-K	BAUDRIC-K	OVERRAN-K	POLITIC-K	PRACTIC-K	TAMARIS-K

8→9

BERGAMAS-K

2→3

L-AD	L-AR	L-AW	L-EA	L-EX	L-IS	L-OD	L-OR	L-OX	L-UM
L-AH	L-AS	L-AX	L-EE	L-ID	L-IT	L-OO	L-OS	L-OY	L-UR
L-AM	L-AT	L-AY	L-ES	L-IN	L-OB	L-OP	L-OW	L-UG	L-YE

3→4

L-ACE	L-AND	L-AUF	L-ECH	L-ESS	L-INN	L-OCH	L-OOP	L-OUR	L-UKE
L-ADS	L-ANE	L-AVA	L-EEK	L-EST	L-INS	L-ODE	L-OOR	L-OUT	L-URE
L-AHS	L-ANT	L-AVE	L-EFT	L-EVE	L-ION	L-ODS	L-OOS	L-OWE	L-UTE
L-AID	L-ARD	L-AWN	L-EKE	L-ICE	L-IRE	L-OFT	L-OPE	L-OWN	L-YAM
L-AIN	L-ARE	L-AYS	L-EME	L-ICH	L-IRK	L-OKE	L-OPS	L-OWT	L-YES
L-AIR	L-ARK	L-EAN	L-END	L-IDS	L-OAF	L-ONE	L-ORD	L-OYS	
L-AKE	L-ASH	L-EAR	L-ENG	L-ILL	L-OBI	L-OOF	L-ORE	L-UDO	
L-AMP	L-ASS	L-EAS	L-ENS	L-IMP	L-OBO	L-OOM	L-OUD	L-UDS	
L-ANA	L-ATE	L-EAT	L-ERE	L-INK	L-OBS	L-OON	L-OUP	L-UGS	

4→5

L-ACED	L-ANDS	L-AVAS	L-EASE	L-EMES	L-EXES	L-OAFS	L-OOSE	L-OVER
L-ACES	L-ANES	L-AVER	L-EAST	L-EMMA	L-ILLS	L-OAST	L-OPED	L-OWED
L-AIDS	L-ANTS	L-AVES	L-EATS	L-ENDS	L-IMPS	L-OATH	L-OPES	L-OWER
L-AIRS	L-APSE	L-AWED	L-EDGE	L-ENES	L-INCH	L-OBOS	L-ORAL	L-OWES
L-AIRY	L-ARCH	L-AWNS	L-EDGY	L-ENGS	L-INGO	L-ODES	L-ORDS	L-OWLY
L-AKED	L-ARDS	L-AWNY	L-EECH	L-ERED	L-INKS	L-OKES	L-ORES	L-OWNS
L-AKES	L-ARES	L-AXES	L-EERY	L-ERES	L-INNS	L-ONER	L-OTIC	L-OWTS
L-AKIN	L-ARKS	L-EACH	L-EFTS	L-ESTS	L-IONS	L-OOFS	L-OTTO	L-UDOS
L-AMPS	L-ARUM	L-EANS	L-EGAL	L-ETCH	L-IRKS	L-OOMS	L-OUPS	L-URES
L-ANAS	L-AUFS	L-EARN	L-EGER	L-EUGH	L-ISLE	L-OONS	L-OURS	L-UTES
L-ANCE	L-AURA	L-EARS	L-EGGY	L-EVER	L-LAMA	L-OOPS	L-OUTS	L-YAMS

5→6

L-ACHES	L-ANKER	L-AURAS	L-ECHED	L-ETHAL	L-INKER	L-ONERS	L-OWNED
L-ACING	L-APPEL	L-AVERS	L-ECHES	L-EVITE	L-INNED	L-OOPED	L-UGGED
L-ADDER	L-APSES	L-AWFUL	L-EDGER	L-EXEME	L-INTER	L-OOSES	L-UMBER
L-AGGER	L-ARKED	L-AWING	L-EDGES	L-ICHES	L-IRKED	L-OPING	L-USHER
L-AIDED	L-AROID	L-EANED	L-EGERS	L-ICKER	L-ISLES	L-ORATE	
L-AIRED	L-ARUMS	L-EARED	L-EGGED	L-IMBED	L-IZARD	L-OTHER	
L-AKING	L-ARVAL	L-EARNS	L-EGGER	L-IMPED	L-LAMAS	L-OTTOS	
L-ALANG	L-ASHES	L-EASED	L-EMMAS	L-IMPLY	L-OAVES	L-OUPED	
L-AMBER	L-ASSES	L-EASES	L-ENVOY	L-INGLE	L-OCKER	L-OUTED	
L-AMENT	L-ASTER	L-EASTS	L-ERING	L-INGOT	L-OCULI	L-OVERS	
L-ANGER	L-ATRIA	L-EAVES	L-ESSES	L-INKED	L-ONELY	L-OWING	

6→7

L-ACKERS	L-APPELS	L-EASING	L-EGGERS	L-EVITES	L-INKERS	L-OCKERS	L-OVERLY
L-ADDERS	L-ARCHES	L-ECHING	L-EGGIER	L-EXEMES	L-INKING	L-OCULAR	L-OWLIER
L-AGGERS	L-ARKING	L-EDGERS	L-EGGING	L-ICKERS	L-INNING	L-OCULUS	L-OWNING
L-AIDING	L-ASTERS	L-EDGIER	L-EMURES	L-IGNITE	L-INTERS	L-OMENTA	L-OXYGEN
L-AIRIER	L-AWNIER	L-EECHED	L-ENDING	L-IMPING	L-IONISE	L-OOPING	L-UGGING
L-AIRING	L-EANING	L-EECHES	L-ENVOYS	L-INCHES	L-IONIZE	L-OUPING	L-ULLING
L-ALANGS	L-EARING	L-EERIER	L-ETCHED	L-INGLES	L-IRKING	L-OURIER	L-UMBERS
L-AMBERS	L-EARNED	L-EFTEST	L-ETCHES	L-INGOES	L-IZARDS	L-OUTING	L-USHERS
L-AMENTS	L-EARNER	L-EGALLY	L-EUGHEN	L-INGOTS	L-OBELIA	L-OVERED	

7→8

L-ABILITY	L-AWFULLY	L-EECHING	L-ETCHING	L-IONISED	L-OMENTUM
L-ACERATE	L-AWNIEST	L-EERIEST	L-EVIRATE	L-IONISES	L-ONENESS
L-AIRIEST	L-AZURITE	L-EGALITY	L-EVITATE	L-IONIZED	L-OURIEST
L-AMBLING	L-EARNERS	L-EGGIEST	L-IGNEOUS	L-IONIZES	L-OWLIEST
L-ANGUISH	L-EARNING	L-ENDINGS	L-IGNITES	L-ITERATE	L-OXYGENS
L-AUREATE	L-EDGIEST	L-EPIDOTE	L-INCHPIN	L-OCULATE	L-UMBERED

8→9

L-AMBLINGS	L-ETCHINGS	L-EVITATES	L-IONISING	L-OCELLATE
L-AZURITES	L-EVIRATES	L-IMITABLE	L-IONIZING	L-UMBERING
L-EARNINGS	L-EVITATED	L-INCHPINS	L-ITERATES	

2→3

AI-L	BE-L	EE-L	MA-L	MI-L	OW-L	SO-L	TI-L
AW-L	DA-L	EL-L	ME-L	OI-L	PA-L	TE-L	

3→4

ANA-L	CAR-L	DEL-L	FUR-L	JEE-L	MOI-L	PAL-L	RIA-L	SOW-L	VIA-L
ANI-L	CEL-L	DOO-L	GAL-L	JOW-L	MOO-L	PAW-L	ROT-L	TAE-L	WAW-L
ARY-L	CHA-L	DOW-L	GOA-L	KAI-L	MOY-L	PEA-L	RYA-L	TAI-L	WEE-L
AVA-L	COL-L	DUE-L	GOE-L	LEA-L	NIL-L	PEE-L	SAI-L	TEA-L	WOO-L
AXE-L	COO-L	EAR-L	GOO-L	MAL-L	NOW-L	PIR-L	SEA-L	TEE-L	YAW-L
BEL-L	COW-L	FAR-L	GUR-L	MAR-L	NUR-L	POO-L	SEE-L	TEL-L	YOW-L
BOO-L	CUR-L	FEE-L	HER-L	MEL-L	OBO-L	PUR-L	SEI-L	TIL-L	ZEA-L
BOW-L	DAH-L	FIL-L	HOW-L	MEW-L	ODA-L	RAI-L	SEL-L	TOO-L	
BUR-L	DEI-L	FOU-L	JAR-L	MIL-L	OVA-L	REE-L	SOU-L	TWA-L	

4→5

ALGA-L	BUBA-L	DRAW-L	HAZE-L	LORE-L	NAVE-L	RIVA-L	SNAR-L	VASA-L
ALKY-L	CABA-L	DURA-L	HOTE-L	LOSE-L	NEVE-L	RIVE-L	SORA-L	VENA-L
ALLY-L	CAME-L	EASE-L	HOVE-L	MERE-L	NOTA-L	ROMA-L	SORE-L	VINA-L
ANNA-L	CAVE-L	FAVE-L	IDEA-L	MERI-L	OCTA-L	ROTA-L	SPAW-L	VINY-L
AREA-L	CECA-L	FETA-L	IDYL-L	MESA-L	PANE-L	SAME-L	SPIE-L	WHEE-L
AURA-L	COMA-L	FORE-L	INTI-L	MESE-L	PAPA-L	SCOW-L	SURA-L	WHIR-L
BABE-L	COXA-L	GAVE-L	JUGA-L	MODE-L	PEAR-L	SCUL-L	SWAY-L	YODE-L
BABU-L	CRAW-L	GENA-L	JURA-L	MOLA-L	PERI-L	SEGO-L	SWEE-L	YOKE-L
BEDE-L	CREE-L	GIBE-L	KNAR-L	MONA-L	PIPA-L	SERA-L	THIR-L	ZOEA-L
BETE-L	CRUE-L	GLIA-L	KNEE-L	MORA-L	PROW-L	SHAW-L	TUBA-L	ZONA-L
BORE-L	DATA-L	GNAR-L	KNUR-L	MORE-L	PUPA-L	SHEA-L	TWEE-L	ZORI-L
BRAW-L	DHOL-L	GROW-L	LEME-L	MOTE-L	RATE-L	SHOO-L	UREA-L	ZYGA-L
BROO-L	DITA-L	GRUE-L	LEVE-L	MYAL-L	RAVE-L	SIZE-L	UVEA-L	

5→6

ANIMA-L	ATRIA-L	BEDEL-L	BURSA-L	CARVE-L	CORBE-L	DERMA-L	DRIVE-L
AORTA-L	BARBE-L	BEIGE-L	CAECA-L	CAUSA-L	COSTA-L	DORSA-L	DRUPE-L
ASSAI-L	BARRE-L	BORDE-L	CARTE-L	CHAPE-L	CREWE-L	DORSE-L	EISEL-L

ENROL-L	HOUSE-L	MENTA-L	OSTIA-L	RECTA-L	SERAI-L	TELIA-L	VARVE-L
FACIA-L	HYPHA-L	MEREL-L	PASTE-L	REDIA-L	SHOVE-L	TERCE-L	VERVE-L
FAUNA-L	JAMBU-L	MISSA-L	PENCE-L	RIDGE-L	SOREL-L	TERGA-L	VESTA-L
FAVEL-L	KERNE-L	MORAL-L	PENNA-L	RIGOL-L	SPINA-L	THECA-L	VISTA-L
FESTA-L	LABIA-L	MORSE-L	PETRE-L	RONDE-L	SPINE-L	TIBIA-L	VULVA-L
FLORA-L	LARVA-L	MUSSE-L	PLICA-L	SACRA-L	STIPE-L	TINEA-L	WASTE-L
FLOTE-L	LENTI-L	NEWEL-L	PODIA-L	SAMBA-L	STOMA-L	TOMIA-L	XENIA-L
FOVEA-L	MAMMA-L	NITRY-L	PORTA-L	SCRAW-L	SWIVE-L	TORSE-L	ZOOEA-L
GAMBO-L	MANGA-L	NORMA-L	PRIMA-L	SCROW-L	TASSE-L	TRAVE-L	
GRAVE-L	MANGE-L	NUCHA-L	RANCE-L	SCUTA-L	TEASE-L	UMBRA-L	
GROVE-L	MEDIA-L	OMASA-L	RECAL-L	SEPTA-L	TEAZE-L	UMBRE-L	

6→7

AMENTA-L	CHANCE-L	CUBICA-L	FULFIL-L	LUMINA-L	ORBITA-L	SCLERA-L	VAGINA-L
ANGINA-L	CHORDA-L	DISMAY-L	GENERA-L	LUSTRA-L	PALLIA-L	SCROTA-L	VESICA-L
AURORA-L	CHORIA-L	DISTIL-L	GINGAL-L	MAXIMA-L	PLEURA-L	SHRIVE-L	WADMOL-L
BORREL-L	CHROME-L	ELUVIA-L	GLOSSA-L	MIASMA-L	POINTE-L	STADIA-L	WOOSEL-L
BURREL-L	CLOACA-L	ELYTRA-L	HERNIA-L	MINIMA-L	QUANTA-L	STERNA-L	
CAMBIA-L	CONCHA-L	ENTERA-L	INSTAL-L	MUCHEL-L	QUINTA-L	TAPETA-L	
CAMERA-L	CORNEA-L	EPOCHA-L	INSTIL-L	MULMUL-L	REGINA-L	TASSEL-L	
CAPITA-L	CORNUA-L	ESCROL-L	ISCHIA-L	NATURA-L	RETINA-L	TERTIA-L	
CARREL-L	CORONA-L	FANNEL-L	LACUNA-L	NOMINA-L	ROSTRA-L	TIERCE-L	
CENTRA-L	CRANIA-L	FASCIA-L	LINGUA-L	OMENTA-L	SALIVA-L	TIMBRE-L	
CESURA-L	CRUSTA-L	FEMORA-L	LOCHIA-L	OPTIMA-L	SATYRA-L	TRIVIA-L	

7→8

ABOMASA-L	CEREBRA-L	DYSPNEA-L	ILLUVIA-L	NOUMENA-L	PYREXIA-L	TESTRIL-L
ACHENIA-L	CINEREA-L	ENTHRAL-L	IMPERIA-L	OOGONIA-L	REPOSAL-L	TORMINA-L
ACROMIA-L	CONARIA-L	ENTOZOA-L	INDICIA-L	PATAGIA-L	RESIDUA-L	TRACHEA-L
ALLUVIA-L	CONIDIA-L	EROTICA-L	INDUSIA-L	PERIDIA-L	SABURRA-L	TYMPANA-L
ANTENNA-L	CORPORA-L	EXCRETA-L	INERTIA-L	PERINEA-L	SAGITTA-L	URETHRA-L
APPERIL-L	CRIMINA-L	EXORDIA-L	INFAUNA-L	PERSONA-L	SOREDIA-L	VISCERA-L
BASIDIA-L	CROPFUL-L	FILARIA-L	INTHRAL-L	PESSIMA-L	SPECTRA-L	
BORSTAL-L	DECIDUA-L	GALANGA-L	KHEDIVA-L	PODAGRA-L	SPLENIA-L	
BRACHIA-L	DIHEDRA-L	GONIDIA-L	LIXIVIA-L	PRONOTA-L	STAMINA-L	
CAESURA-L	DILUVIA-L	HYDROXY-L	MALARIA-L	PUDENDA-L	STOMATA-L	
CANDIDA-L	DIPTERA-L	HYMENIA-L	MANDRIL-L	PUPARIA-L	SYNOVIA-L	
CAROUSE-L	DUODENA-L	HYPOGEA-L	MYCELIA-L	PYGIDIA-L	TESSERA-L	

8→9

ABDOMINA-L	CATHEDRA-L	ENDOSTEA-L	MENSTRUA-L	SENSORIA-L	THERIACA-L
AGNOMINA-L	CENTINEL-L	EPHEMERA-L	PANNIKEL-L	SIGNORIA-L	TRAPEZIA-L
AMBROSIA-L	CENTONEL-L	EPICEDIA-L	PAROEMIA-L	SPORIDIA-L	UNDERSEA-L
ANGELICA-L	CLAUSTRA-L	ERYTHEMA-L	PENUMBRA-L	SUBCOSTA-L	UREDINIA-L
ANTEFIXA-L	COLLEGIA-L	FENESTRA-L	PETECHIA-L	SUBMENTA-L	UROPYGIA-L
ASPHYXIA-L	CONTINUA-L	FORAMINA-L	PLACENTA-L	SUDAMINA-L	VACCINIA-L
BACTERIA-L	DECENNIA-L	FORESTAL-L	PRESIDIA-L	SYMPODIA-L	VERTEBRA-L
BASILICA-L	DIARRHEA-L	GHASTFUL-L	PROTOZOA-L	SYMPOSIA-L	VESTIGIA-L
BRANCHIA-L	DICHASIA-L	GYMNASIA-L	PTERYGIA-L	SYNCYTIA-L	
BRONCHIA-L	DYSPNOEA-L	HYPOGAEA-L	RITORNEL-L	SYNEDRIA-L	
CACUMINA-L	ECCLESIA-L	MANUBRIA-L	SCIATICA-L	TEGMENTA-L	
CALCANEA-L	EFFLUVIA-L	MARSUPIA-L	SEMUNCIA-L	TENTORIA-L	

2→3

M-AA	M-AN	M-AW	M-EN	M-IS	M-OE	M-OO	M-OW	M-UN
M-AD	M-AR	M-AX	M-ES	M-NA	M-OI	M-OP	M-OY	M-US
M-AE	M-AS	M-AY	M-HO	M-OB	M-OM	M-OR	M-UG	
M-AM	M-AT	M-EL	M-ID	M-OD	M-ON	M-OU	M-UM	

3→4

M-AAS	M-AKE	M-ANY	M-ASH	M-ELL	M-ESS	M-IRE	M-OES	M-OOS	M-UDS
M-ACE	M-ALE	M-ARC	M-ASK	M-ELS	M-EVE	M-IRK	M-OIL	M-OPE	M-UGS
M-ADS	M-ALL	M-ARD	M-ASS	M-ELT	M-HOS	M-ISO	M-OKE	M-OPS	M-ULE
M-AGE	M-ALS	M-ARE	M-ATE	M-EME	M-ICE	M-NAS	M-OLD	M-ORE	M-URE
M-AID	M-ALT	M-ARK	M-AYS	M-END	M-IDS	M-OAT	M-OLE	M-ORS	M-USE
M-AIL	M-ANA	M-ARM	M-EAN	M-ENE	M-IFF	M-OBS	M-OMS	M-ORT	M-UTE
M-AIM	M-AND	M-ARS	M-EAT	M-ENG	M-ILK	M-OCH	M-OON	M-OUP	M-ZEE
M-AIN	M-ANE	M-ART	M-EEK	M-ERE	M-ILL	M-ODE	M-OOP	M-OWN	
M-AIR	M-ANI	M-ARY	M-ELD	M-ERK	M-INK	M-ODS	M-OOR	M-OYS	

4→5

M-ACED	M-ACER	M-ACES	M-AGES	M-AGMA	M-AIDS	M-AILS	M-AIMS	M-AIRS

```
M-AKES   M-ANNA   M-ARMS   M-ELDS   M-ESNE   M-ISOS   M-OONS   M-OTTO   M-URES
M-ALAR   M-ANTA   M-ARTS   M-ELLS   M-ETHS   M-ITCH   M-OOPS   M-OUCH   M-URVA
M-ALES   M-ANUS   M-ASHY   M-ELTS   M-EVES   M-OATS   M-OOSE   M-OULD   M-USED
M-ALLS   M-ARCH   M-ASKS   M-EMES   M-ICKY   M-ODAL   M-OPED   M-OUPS   M-USER
M-ALMS   M-ARCS   M-AXES   M-ENDS   M-IFFY   M-ODES   M-OPES   M-OURN   M-USES
M-ALTS   M-ARES   M-AXIS   M-ENES   M-ILKS   M-OILS   M-OPUS   M-OUST   M-UTES
M-AMBO   M-ARIA   M-EANS   M-ENGS   M-ILLS   M-OKES   M-ORAL   M-OVER   M-UTIS
M-ANAS   M-ARID   M-EASE   M-ERED   M-INKS   M-OLDS   M-ORRA   M-OWED   M-ZEES
M-ANES   M-ARKS   M-EATH   M-ERES   M-IRES   M-OLLA            M-OWER
M-ANIS   M-ARLE   M-EATS   M-ERKS   M-IRKS   M-ONER   M-ORTS   M-ULES
```

5→6

```
M-ACERS   M-ALIGN   M-ANTIC   M-ASKER   M-EMBER   M-INION   M-ORALS   M-UNIFY
M-ACING   M-ALLEE   M-ANTIS   M-ASSES   M-ENDED   M-INTER   M-ORGUE   M-UNITE
M-ADDED   M-ALLOW   M-ANTRA   M-ASTER   M-ERING   M-ISLED   M-ORRIS   M-UNTIN
M-ADDER   M-AMBOS   M-ARISH   M-ATOKE   M-ERSES   M-ISTLE   M-OTHER   M-URENA
M-ADMAN   M-AMMON   M-ARKED   M-AVENS   M-ESSES   M-OCKER   M-OUGHT   M-URINE
M-ADMEN   M-ANANA   M-ARLED   M-EAGRE   M-ETAGE   M-ODALS   M-OUPED   M-URVAS
M-AGMAS   M-ANENT   M-ARLES   M-EANED   M-ETHYL   M-ODIST   M-OUSTS   M-USERS
M-AIDED   M-ANGEL   M-ARROW   M-EASED   M-ETTLE   M-OILED   M-OUTER   M-USHER
M-AILED   M-ANGER   M-ARTEL   M-EASES   M-ICHED   M-OILER   M-OVERS   M-USING
M-AIMED   M-ANGLE   M-ASCOT   M-EASLE   M-ICHES   M-OLLAS   M-OWING   M-UTTER
M-AKING   M-ANNAS   M-ASHES   M-EATHE   M-IMBAR   M-OOPED   M-UDDER
M-ALATE   M-ANTAS   M-ASKED   M-ELDER   M-INGLE   M-OPING   M-UGGED
```

6→7

```
M-ADDERS   M-ANGELS   M-ARROWS   M-EAGRES   M-ETHYLS   M-ITCHES   M-ORGUES   M-ULLING
M-ADDING   M-ANGERS   M-ARROWY   M-EANING   M-ETTLED   M-OCKERS   M-OTHERS   M-UMBLES
M-AGNATE   M-ANGLED   M-ARTELS   M-EARING   M-ETTLES   M-ODISTS   M-OUCHES   M-UNITED
M-AIDING   M-ANGLER   M-ASCOTS   M-EASING   M-ICHING   M-OILERS   M-OULDER   M-UNITES
M-AILING   M-ANGLES   M-ASHIER   M-EASLES   M-IFFIER   M-OILING   M-OUPING   M-UNTINS
M-AIMING   M-ARCHED   M-ASKERS   M-ELDERS   M-IMBARS   M-OMENTA   M-OUSTED   M-URENAS
M-ALIGNS   M-ARCHER   M-ASKING   M-ELDING   M-INGLES   M-ONEYER   M-OUTERS   M-URINES
M-ALLEES   M-ARCHES   M-ASTERS   M-EMBERS   M-INTERS   M-OOPING   M-OUTHER   M-USEFUL
M-ALLOWS   M-ARGENT   M-ATOKES   M-ENDING   M-IRITIS   M-OORIER   M-UCKERS   M-USHERS
M-AMMONS   M-ARKING   M-AVISES   M-ETAGES   M-ISTLES   M-OPUSES   M-UDDERS   M-UTTERS
M-ANANAS   M-ARLING   M-AXILLA   M-ETHANE   M-ITCHED   M-ORALLY   M-UGGING
```

7→8

```
M-ACERATE   M-ANGLING   M-ARROWED   M-ETHANOL   M-OORIEST   M-UNIFIED
M-AGISTER   M-ARCHERS   M-ASHIEST   M-IFFIEST   M-ORALISM   M-UNIFIES
M-AGNATES   M-ARCHING   M-AXILLAE   M-ISOGAMY   M-ORALITY   M-UNITING
M-AIDLESS   M-ARGENTS   M-ENDINGS   M-ITCHING   M-ORATORY   M-UNITION
M-ALIGNED   M-ARISHES   M-ERISTIC   M-OMENTUM   M-ORRISES   M-UTTERED
M-ANGLERS   M-ARRIAGE   M-ETHANES   M-ONEYERS   M-OUSTING   M-UTTERER
```

8→9

```
M-AGISTERS   M-ARRIAGES   M-ENARCHES   M-ETHYLENE   M-UNIFYING   M-UTTERERS
M-ALIGNING   M-ARROWING   M-ETHANOLS   M-IFFINESS   M-UNITIONS   M-UTTERING
M-AMMONITE   M-AXILLARY   M-ETHYLATE   M-ORALISMS   M-USEFULLY
```

2→3

```
AI-M   DA-M   GU-M   HI-M   LA-M   MO-M   NO-M   PA-M   SI-M   WE-M
AR-M   DI-M   HA-M   IS-M   MA-M   MU-M   OH-M   PO-M   TA-M
BA-M   EL-M   HE-M   KA-M   MI-M   NA-M   OO-M   RE-M   TO-M
```

3→4

```
BAR-M   DEE-M   FIR-M   HAE-M   LEA-M   NEE-M   PRO-M   SKI-M   TEE-M   WEE-M
BOO-M   DOO-M   FOR-M   HAW-M   LOO-M   NOR-M   ROO-M   SOU-M   THE-M   WHA-M
CHA-M   DOR-M   FRO-M   HER-M   MAL-M   PAL-M   SAI-M   SOW-M   TOO-M   WHO-M
COO-M   FAR-M   GAU-M   IDE-M   MAR-M   PER-M   SEA-M   SPA-M   WAR-M   ZOO-M
COR-M   FIL-M   GIS-M   KAI-M   MUM-M   PIU-M   SEE-M   TEA-M   WAS-M
```

4→5

```
ALAR-M   CHAR-M   FLEA-M   HARE-M   MINI-M   PURI-M   SEIS-M   STUM-M   TUIS-M
BREE-M   CHAS-M   GOLE-M   HAUL-M   MODE-M   REAL-M   SHAW-M   THRU-M
BROO-M   FLAM-M   HAKA-M   MAXI-M   PASH-M   REAR-M   SPAS-M   TOTE-M
```

5→6

BALSA-M	CONDO-M	MALIS-M	MONTE-M	MUTIS-M	PURIS-M	SHTUM-M
BESEE-M	LINGA-M	MERIS-M	MURRA-M	PARTI-M	SCRAW-M	YOGIS-M

6→7

BUCKRA-M GOPURA-M MANTRA-M MISSEE-M MISTER-M

7→8

CLASSIS-M TITANIS-M

8→9

LITERATI-M MEPHITIS-M MRIDANGA-M

2→3

N-AE	N-AS	N-EE	N-IS	N-OD	N-ON	N-OW	N-UN	N-UT
N-AM	N-AT	N-EF	N-IT	N-OH	N-OR	N-OX	N-UR	N-YE
N-AN	N-AY	N-ID	N-OB	N-OM	N-OS	N-OY	N-US	

3→4

N-ACH	N-APE	N-AVE	N-EON	N-EWT	N-ITS	N-OLE	N-OUP	N-OYS
N-AGA	N-ARC	N-AYS	N-ERK	N-ICE	N-OBS	N-OMS	N-OUT	N-UKE
N-AIL	N-ARD	N-EAR	N-ESS	N-IDE	N-ODE	N-ONE	N-OVA	N-UNS
N-AIN	N-ARE	N-EAT	N-EST	N-IDS	N-ODS	N-OON	N-OWL	N-URD
N-ALA	N-ARK	N-EFS	N-EUK	N-IFF	N-OES	N-OOP	N-OWN	N-UTS
N-ANA	N-ARY	N-ENE	N-EVE	N-ILL	N-OIL	N-OPE	N-OWT	N-YES

4→5

N-ACHE	N-ANCE	N-ARKS	N-ENES	N-EWER	N-ODES	N-OOPS	N-OWLS
N-ACRE	N-ANNA	N-AUNT	N-EONS	N-EWTS	N-OILS	N-OOSE	N-OWTS
N-AGAS	N-APES	N-AVAL	N-ERKS	N-ICER	N-OINT	N-OPAL	N-OYES
N-AILS	N-ARCO	N-AVES	N-ESTS	N-IDES	N-OMEN	N-OULD	N-UKES
N-AKED	N-ARCS	N-EARS	N-EUKS	N-IFFY	N-ONCE	N-OUPS	N-URDS
N-ALAS	N-ARDS	N-EATH	N-EVER	N-ILLS	N-ONES	N-OVUM	N-YAFF
N-ANAS	N-ARES	N-EDDY	N-EVES	N-ODAL	N-OONS	N-OWED	

5→6

N-ACHED	N-APERY	N-AUNTS	N-ESSES	N-ICHES	N-ONCES	N-UMBER
N-ACRED	N-APRON	N-EARED	N-ESTER	N-ICKER	N-OOSES	N-UMPTY
N-ACRES	N-ARKED	N-EARLY	N-ETHER	N-IMBED	N-OPALS	N-UNCLE
N-AGGER	N-ARRAS	N-EATEN	N-ETTLE	N-ODDER	N-OSIER	N-UTTER
N-AILED	N-ARROW	N-EATER	N-EWEST	N-OGGIN	N-OTARY	N-YAFFS
N-ANNAS	N-AUGHT	N-EBBED	N-ICHED	N-OINTS	N-OUGHT	

6→7

N-AGGERS	N-ARROWS	N-EARING	N-EMESES	N-ETTLES	N-OINTED	N-ULLING	N-UNHOOD
N-AILING	N-ASCENT	N-EBBING	N-EMESIS	N-ICHING	N-OODLES	N-UMBERS	N-UNSHIP
N-APHTHA	N-ATRIUM	N-EDDIES	N-EOLITH	N-ICKERS	N-OOLOGY	N-UMBLES	N-UTTERS
N-APRONS	N-AUGHTS	N-EGRESS	N-ESTERS	N-IFFIER	N-OUGHTS	N-UNCLES	N-YAFFED
N-ARKING	N-AYWORD	N-EITHER	N-ETTLED	N-OGGINS	N-OYESES	N-UNDINE	

7→8

N-APERIES	N-ATRIUMS	N-ETTLING	N-OTARIES	N-UMBERED	N-UNSHIPS
N-ARRASES	N-AYWORDS	N-IFFIEST	N-OVATION	N-UNDINES	N-YAFFING
N-ARROWED	N-EOLITHS	N-OINTING	N-ULLINGS	N-UNHOODS	

8→9

N-ARROWING	N-EVERMORE	N-OOSPHERE	N-UMBERING
N-EGRESSES	N-OOLOGIES	N-OVATIONS	

2→3

AI-N	BI-N	EA-N	GO-N	HO-N	MA-N	NO-N	PI-N	TE-N	WO-N
AN-N	BO-N	EE-N	GU-N	IN-N	ME-N	NU-N	RE-N	TI-N	YE-N
AW-N	DA-N	ER-N	HA-N	IO-N	MO-N	OO-N	SI-N	TO-N	YO-N
BA-N	DI-N	FA-N	HE-N	KO-N	MU-N	OW-N	SO-N	UR-N	
BE-N	DO-N	GI-N	HI-N	LI-N	NA-N	PA-N	TA-N	WE-N	

3→4

AGE-N	CAN-N	DOW-N	GOO-N	LAR-N	MOR-N	PIR-N	SEE-N	THO-N	YEA-N
AGO-N	CHI-N	EAR-N	GUR-N	LAW-N	MOW-N	POO-N	SEW-N	TOO-N	ZOO-N
AIR-N	CON-N	EVE-N	HER-N	LEA-N	NOW-N	POW-N	SKI-N	TOR-N	
ANA-N	COO-N	FAW-N	HEW-N	LIE-N	OPE-N	RAI-N	SOW-N	TOW-N	
BAR-N	COR-N	FIR-N	HIS-N	LIN-N	OUR-N	RAW-N	SPA-N	WAR-N	
BEE-N	CUR-N	FOE-N	HOO-N	LOO-N	PAW-N	REE-N	SUN-N	WEE-N	
BOO-N	DAM-N	FOH-N	HYE-N	LOR-N	PEA-N	ROO-N	SYE-N	WIN-N	
BOR-N	DAW-N	GAU-N	KAI-N	LOW-N	PEE-N	SAI-N	TAR-N	WOO-N	
BRA-N	DEE-N	GIE-N	KIR-N	MOA-N	PER-N	SAW-N	TEE-N	WYN-N	
BUR-N	DOE-N	GIN-N	KOA-N	MOO-N	PHO-N	SEA-N	THE-N	YAW-N	

4→5

AMMO-N	DEAR-N	GIRO-N	HOTE-N	LODE-N	RAMI-N	SATI-N	SPAW-N	VEGA-N
BAKE-N	DEMO-N	GIVE-N	HOVE-N	LOGO-N	RATA-N	SEME-N	SPUR-N	WAKE-N
BLOW-N	DIVA-N	GNAW-N	HUMA-N	LOSE-N	RAVE-N	SHEW-N	STAR-N	WHEE-N
BRAW-N	DOOR-N	GREE-N	KNOW-N	MIRI-N	RIPE-N	SHOO-N	STOW-N	WIDE-N
BROW-N	DOZE-N	GROW-N	LADE-N	MOTE-N	RISE-N	SHOW-N	TABU-N	WOKE-N
CAPO-N	DRAW-N	GYRO-N	LATE-N	NOME-N	RIVE-N	SHUL-N	TAKE-N	WOVE-N
CHAI-N	DROW-N	HALO-N	LEAR-N	PATE-N	ROMA-N	SILE-N	TAKI-N	YEAR-N
CLOW-N	ERGO-N	HAVE-N	LIKE-N	PAVE-N	RUME-N	SIRE-N	TAPE-N	YEVE-N
COVE-N	FLAW-N	HEBE-N	LIME-N	PREE-N	SAMA-N	SOKE-N	TOKE-N	YOGI-N
COZE-N	FLOW-N	HERO-N	LINE-N	PURI-N	SAME-N	SOLA-N	TREE-N	YOUR-N
CROW-N	FROW-N	HOSE-N	LIVE-N	QUEY-N	SARI-N	SOMA-N	VARA-N	ZUPA-N

5→6

ALDER-N	BROKE-N	DRIVE-N	INTRO-N	MODER-N	RATOO-N	SPOKE-N	VILLA-N
ALTER-N	CALLA-N	FARCI-N	JOTUN-N	MURRE-N	REEDE-N	STOLE-N	WARRE-N
AMNIO-N	CANTO-N	FLAME-N	KRONE-N	NORMA-N	REPLA-N	STONE-N	WEETE-N
ARISE-N	CARVE-N	FRORE-N	LARGE-N	PANTO-N	SCREE-N	STRAW-N	WHITE-N
ASTER-N	CAUSE-N	FROZE-N	LATHE-N	PARKI-N	SEAME-N	STREW-N	WICCA-N
AWAKE-N	CAVER-N	GAZOO-N	LEAVE-N	PATTE-N	SERRA-N	STROW-N	WORSE-N
AWOKE-N	CEDAR-N	GEMMA-N	LIGGE-N	PERCE-N	SHAKE-N	SYLVA-N	WROKE-N
BABOO-N	CHICO-N	GLAZE-N	LOIPE-N	PHOTO-N	SHAMA-N	TAVER-N	
BANIA-N	CHOSE-N	GODSO-N	LONGA-N	PIECE-N	SHAPE-N	THRAW-N	
BARRE-N	CLOVE-N	GRAVE-N	LOOSE-N	PLATE-N	SHAVE-N	THROW-N	
BESEE-N	COMMO-N	HASTE-N	LOUPE-N	POLEY-N	SILVA-N	TORTE-N	
BITTE-N	CRAVE-N	HEAVE-N	MACRO-N	PROVE-N	SITHE-N	UNDER-N	
BOREE-N	CRIME-N	HOOVE-N	MEDIA-N	RABBI-N	SLIVE-N	UNSEW-N	
BRAZE-N	DOLMA-N	INTER-N	MICRO-N	RATIO-N	SLOVE-N	VERVE-N	

6→7

ACKNOW-N	COARSE-N	HOMELY-N	PATTER-N	RETAKE-N	STONER-N	TRUDGE-N	UPTAKE-N
ANLAGE-N	CRYPTO-N	INWOVE-N	PHALLI-N	SALTER-N	STRIVE-N	UNDRAW-N	UTOPIA-N
BETAKE-N	EASTER-N	LETTER-N	POSTER-N	SHIPPO-N	STROKE-N	UNLADE-N	WESTER-N
BITTER-N	EMBRYO-N	MEDUSA-N	PROTEA-N	SHOTTE-N	TAMARI-N	UNWOVE-N	WRITHE-N
BRONZE-N	EPIZOA-N	MISSEE-N	QUINTA-N	SHRIVE-N	TERTIA-N	UPBLOW-N	YESTER-N
CAPITA-N	GELATI-N	NUCLEI-N	REDRAW-N	SIERRA-N	TESTER-N	UPDRAW-N	ZITHER-N
CHASTE-N	GODDAM-N	ORARIA-N	REGIME-N	SILVER-N	THRIVE-N	UPGROW-N	
CITHER-N	HOARSE-N	PASTER-N	REGIVE-N	SOLITO-N	TORULI-N	UPRISE-N	

7→8

ACTINIA-N	DEFROZE-N	FORESEE-N	MISGIVE-N	OVERSOW-N	REDRIVE-N	UNFROZE-N
ALIZARI-N	DILUVIA-N	FORFAIR-N	MISKNOW-N	PANACEA-N	REFROZE-N	UNLOOSE-N
APHELIA-N	DIPTERA-N	FORGIVE-N	MISTAKE-N	PARAZOA-N	REGALIA-N	UNSHAPE-N
AQUARIA-N	DISLIKE-N	FORSAKE-N	NORTHER-N	PARTAKE-N	RESPOKE-N	UNSPOKE-N
ASCIDIA-N	ECTOZOA-N	HISTRIO-N	OPHIURA-N	PERTAKE-N	RUBELLA-N	UPBROKE-N
AURELIA-N	ELECTRO-N	HYPOGEA-N	OUTFLOW-N	POLYZOA-N	SLATTER-N	UPSPOKE-N
BEREAVE-N	ENFROZE-N	LEATHER-N	OUTGIVE-N	PUNALUA-N	SOUTHER-N	UPTHROW-N
BESPOKE-N	ENGRAVE-N	MAGNETO-N	OUTGROW-N	QUARTER-N	SPREDDE-N	VITELLI-N
BESTREW-N	ENLARGE-N	MALARIA-N	OUTTAKE-N	REARISE-N	STROOKE-N	WREATHE-N
CHONDRI-N	FEDAYEE-N	METAZOA-N	OVERSEE-N	REAWAKE-N	THROMBI-N	
COLLAGE-N	FLITTER-N	MISDRAW-N	OVERSEW-N	REAWOKE-N	UNBROKE-N	

8→9

AMBROSIA-N	DISPROVE-N	HERBARIA-N	OUTSPOKE-N	OVERTAKE-N	STRONTIA-N
BACTERIA-N	DYSTOPIA-N	HYDROZOA-N	OVERBLOW-N	PANDEMIA-N	SUBTOPIA-N
BASILICA-N	EPICEDIA-N	HYPOGAEA-N	OVERDRAW-N	PROTOZOA-N	WINDBLOW-N
CALCANEA-N	FELLATIO-N	MAGNESIA-N	OVERFLOW-N	SANNYASI-N	WIREDRAW-N
CARETAKE-N	FOREKNOW-N	MISSHAPE-N	OVERGIVE-N	SCHNECKE-N	WITHDRAW-N
CASTELLA-N	FORESHEW-N	MISSPOKE-N	OVERGROW-N	SEPTARIA-N	
CERCARIA-N	FORESHOW-N	OUTBROKE-N	OVERLADE-N	SIGHTSEE-N	
COLLEGIA-N	FORSPOKE-N	OUTDRIVE-N	OVERRIPE-N	SPATLESE-N	

2→3

O-AR	O-BI	O-DA	O-NE	O-OM	O-OR	O-UP	O-WE
O-AT	O-BO	O-ES	O-OF	O-ON	O-OS	O-UR	O-YE
O-BA	O-CH	O-HO	O-OH	O-OP	O-RE	O-UT	

3→4

O-ARS	O-BIS	O-DAL	O-FAY	O-INK	O-NUS	O-PAH	O-PUS	O-UPS	O-WED
O-ARY	O-BIT	O-DAS	O-GAM	O-KAY	O-OMS	O-PAL	O-RES	O-URN	O-YES
O-BAS	O-BOS	O-DOR	O-GEE	O-LID	O-ONS	O-PED	O-TIC	O-UTS	
O-BEY	O-CHE	O-DSO	O-HOS	O-MEN	O-OPS	O-PEN	O-UDS	O-VUM	

4→5

O-ARED	O-CHER	O-FLAG	O-INKS	O-MEGA	O-PINE	O-RANT	O-VERS
O-AVES	O-DALS	O-GAMS	O-KAYS	O-OBIT	O-PING	O-RATE	O-VERT
O-BANG	O-DORS	O-GEES	O-LENT	O-OPED	O-PIUM	O-READ	O-VINE
O-BEYS	O-DOUR	O-GIVE	O-LIVE	O-PAHS	O-RACH	O-RIEL	O-VOID
O-BIAS	O-DSOS	O-GLED	O-LOGY	O-PALS	O-RACY	O-UNCE	O-WING
O-BITS	O-FAYS	O-HONE	O-MASA	O-PENS	O-RANG	O-VARY	O-ZONE

5→6

O-BANGS	O-FLAGS	O-MENED	O-PALED	O-PUSES	O-RATES	O-UNCES	O-ZONES
O-BITER	O-GAMIC	O-MENTA	O-PENED	O-RACHE	O-READS	O-URALI	
O-BLAST	O-GIVES	O-OBITS	O-PINED	O-RALLY	O-RIELS	O-URARI	
O-BLATE	O-INKED	O-OLOGY	O-PINES	O-RANGE	O-STEAL	O-VOIDS	
O-BOLUS	O-LIVER	O-OPING	O-PIUMS	O-RANTS	O-STENT	O-WRIER	
O-EDEMA	O-LIVES	O-OSIER	O-PULUS	O-RATED	O-TITIS	O-YESES	

6→7

O-BLASTS	O-EDEMAS	O-KIMONO	O-MENTUM	O-PINION	O-RATING	O-UAKARI	O-UTMOST
O-BOVATE	O-ESTRAL	O-LIVERS	O-MICRON	O-POSSUM	O-RATION	O-UGLIED	O-VARIES
O-CARINA	O-ESTRUM	O-LOGIES	O-NANISM	O-RACHES	O-ROTUND	O-UGLIES	O-VERBID
O-CELLAR	O-ESTRUS	O-MENING	O-PENING	O-RANGER	O-STENTS	O-URALIS	O-VERSET
O-CREATE	O-INKING	O-MENTAL	O-PINING	O-RANGES	O-STRICH	O-URARIS	O-WRIEST

7→8

O-CARINAS	O-ESTROUS	O-MICRONS	O-NANISMS	O-POSSUMS	O-UAKARIS	O-VARIOUS
O-ECOLOGY	O-ESTRUMS	O-MISSION	O-OLOGIES	O-RANGIER	O-UROLOGY	O-VERBIDS
O-EDEMATA	O-KIMONOS	O-MISSIVE	O-PINIONS	O-RATIONS	O-VARIOLE	O-VERSETS

8→9

O-ECUMENIC	O-ESTROGEN	O-MISSIONS	O-RANGIEST	O-UROSCOPY	O-ZONATION
O-ESOPHAGI	O-ESTRUSES	O-PINIONED	O-STRICHES	O-VARIOLES	

2→3

AD-O	BO-O	GI-O	HO-O	LO-O	OB-O	PH-O	TO-O	ZO-O
BI-O	DO-O	GO-O	IS-O	MO-O	OH-O	PO-O	WO-O	

3→4

ALS-O	BRO-O	DIN-O	FIN-O	KEN-O	MAK-O	PEP-O	SOH-O	YUK-O
ALT-O	BUB-O	DOD-O	GAP-O	KIN-O	MAN-O	PRO-O	SOL-O	
ANN-O	BUD-O	ECH-O	GOB-O	LID-O	MIL-O	RED-O	SUM-O	
ARC-O	CAP-O	ERG-O	HER-O	LIN-O	MIS-O	REP-O	TAR-O	
BEG-O	CIT-O	FAD-O	HOB-O	LOB-O	MON-O	SAG-O	TOC-O	
BIT-O	DAD-O	FAR-O	HYP-O	LOG-O	MUS-O	SEC-O	VET-O	
BOK-O	DAG-O	FIG-O	JUD-O	LOT-O	ODS-O	SEG-O	VIN-O	
BOY-O	DID-O	FIL-O	KAY-O	LUD-O	OLE-O	SKI-O	WIN-O	

4→5

BANC-O	BUFF-O	CHOC-O	DIPS-O	GECK-O	JAMB-O	MANG-O	PHOT-O	PUNT-O
BARD-O	BUNK-O	COMB-O	DISC-O	GISM-O	JELL-O	MENT-O	PING-O	PUTT-O
BASH-O	BURR-O	COMP-O	DITT-O	GODS-O	JOCK-O	MILK-O	PINK-O	QUIP-O
BASS-O	CAME-O	COND-O	DUMB-O	GUAN-O	KEMB-O	MOLT-O	PINT-O	REAL-O
BAST-O	CAMP-O	CORN-O	FANG-O	GUST-O	LASS-O	MOTT-O	PONG-O	RODE-O
BEAN-O	CANT-O	CORS-O	FATS-O	HALL-O	LENT-O	NACH-O	PORN-O	RONE-O
BING-O	CELL-O	CRED-O	FORD-O	HELL-O	LIMB-O	NARC-O	POTT-O	SALT-O
BOMB-O	CENT-O	CUFF-O	GADS-O	HILL-O	LING-O	PANT-O	PRIM-O	SANK-O
BONG-O	CHIC-O	DECK-O	GAMB-O	HOWS-O	LITH-O	PARE-O	PROM-O	SCUD-O
BUCK-O	CHIN-O	DING-O	GARB-O	HULL-O	MAIK-O	PEST-O	PROS-O	SICK-O

```
SOCK-O   SORD-O   TANG-O   TORS-O   VIDE-O   WACK-O
SOLD-O   TACH-O   TEMP-O   VERS-O   VIRE-O   ZINC-O
```

5→6

```
CHEAP-O   ERING-O   LIBER-O   PREST-O   RANCH-O   SOLAN-O   STINK-O   WEIRD-O
CHOCK-O   FASCI-O   MEDIC-O   PSEUD-O   RIGHT-O   SPEED-O   THICK-O   WHACK-O
CRYPT-O   FRANC-O   MORPH-O   PSYCH-O   SHACK-O   STALK-O   TRILL-O   WHATS-O
DORAD-O   GIUST-O   NYMPH-O   QUART-O   SHEEP-O   STERE-O   VIGOR-O
DUETT-O   HALLO-O   PEDAL-O   RABAT-O   SMALT-O   STING-O   VOMIT-O
```

6→7

```
BATTER-O   CYMBAL-O   MAGNET-O   PIMENT-O   REVERS-O   TAMARA-O   VERISM-O
BUDGER-O   GRADIN-O   PAMPER-O   PRIMER-O   SECOND-O   TYMPAN-O   WHERES-O
```

7→8

```
ARMIGER-O   CONCERT-O   FASCISM-O   PEEKABO-O   PRELUDI-O   SOMBRER-O
CAPITAN-O   CORNETT-O   FLAMING-O   PERFECT-O   RANCHER-O   STAMPED-O
COMMAND-O   EXPRESS-O   MONTANT-O   POLITIC-O   SESTETT-O
```

8→9

```
CABALLER-O   MAGNIFIC-O   PASTICCI-O   PULVILLI-O   QUINTETT-O
CAPRICCI-O   MANIFEST-O   PORTOLAN-O   QUARTETT-O   SOLFEGGI-O
```

2→3

```
P-AD   P-AR   P-AX   P-EN   P-IN   P-OH   P-OP   P-RE   P-UN   P-UT
P-AH   P-AS   P-AY   P-ER   P-IS   P-OI   P-OS   P-SI   P-UP   P-YE
P-AM   P-AT   P-EA   P-HI   P-IT   P-OM   P-OW   P-ST   P-UR
P-AN   P-AW   P-EE   P-HO   P-OD   P-OO   P-OX   P-UG   P-US
```

3→4

```
P-ACE   P-ALS   P-AVE   P-EKE   P-HEW   P-ISH   P-LOY   P-OOR   P-RAY   P-UGH
P-ACT   P-AND   P-AWA   P-ELF   P-HIS   P-ITA   P-LUG   P-OOS   P-REE   P-UGS
P-ADS   P-ANE   P-AWL   P-ELL   P-HOH   P-ITS   P-LUM   P-OPE   P-REP   P-UKE
P-AGE   P-ANT   P-AWN   P-ELT   P-HON   P-LAP   P-ODS   P-OPS   P-REX   P-ULE
P-AHS   P-APE   P-AYS   P-END   P-HOS   P-LAT   P-OKE   P-ORE   P-RIG   P-UNS
P-AID   P-ARD   P-EAN   P-ENE   P-HOT   P-LAY   P-OLE   P-ORT   P-RIM   P-UPS
P-AIL   P-ARE   P-EAR   P-ENS   P-HUT   P-LEA   P-OMS   P-OUK   P-ROB   P-URE
P-AIN   P-ARK   P-EAS   P-EON   P-ICE   P-LED   P-ONE   P-OUR   P-ROD   P-UTS
P-AIR   P-ARS   P-EAT   P-ERE   P-ILL   P-LIE   P-ONS   P-OUT   P-ROM   P-YES
P-AIS   P-ART   P-ECH   P-ERK   P-IMP   P-LOD   P-OOF   P-OWN   P-ROO   P-YET
P-ALE   P-ASH   P-EEK   P-ERN   P-INK   P-LOP   P-OOH   P-RAD   P-ROW
P-ALL   P-ASS   P-EEL   P-EST   P-INS   P-LOT   P-OON   P-RAM   P-SIS
P-ALP   P-ATE   P-EEN   P-HAT   P-ION   P-LOW   P-OOP   P-RAT   P-UDS
```

4→5

```
P-ACED   P-ARCH   P-EELS   P-HOTS   P-LAPS   P-LUFF   P-OURS   P-RIAL   P-ROOF
P-ACER   P-ARDS   P-EERY   P-HUTS   P-LASH   P-LUGS   P-OUTS   P-RICE   P-RORE
P-ACES   P-ARED   P-EGGY   P-HYLE   P-LAST   P-LUMP   P-OWER   P-RICK   P-ROSE
P-ACTA   P-ARES   P-EKES   P-ICKY   P-LATE   P-LUMS   P-OWNS   P-RICY   P-ROSY
P-ACTS   P-ARKS   P-ELFS   P-ILEA   P-LATS   P-LUSH   P-OWRE   P-RIDE   P-ROUL
P-AEON   P-ARLE   P-ELLS   P-ILLS   P-LAYS   P-ODAL   P-RADS   P-RIGS   P-ROVE
P-AGED   P-ARSE   P-ELTS   P-IMPS   P-LEAD   P-OINT   P-RAMS   P-RIMA   P-ROWS
P-AGES   P-ARTS   P-ENDS   P-INCH   P-LEAS   P-OKES   P-RANA   P-RIME   P-RUDE
P-AILS   P-ARTY   P-ENES   P-INGO   P-LEAT   P-OLIO   P-RANG   P-RIMS   P-RUNE
P-AIRS   P-AVER   P-EONS   P-INKS   P-LIED   P-ONCE   P-RANK   P-RIMY   P-RUNT
P-ALAS   P-AVES   P-EPOS   P-INKY   P-LIER   P-ONES   P-RASE   P-RINK   P-SHAW
P-ALAY   P-AVID   P-ERES   P-INTO   P-LIES   P-OOFS   P-RATE   P-RISE   P-SORA
P-ALES   P-AWED   P-ERKS   P-IONS   P-LING   P-OONS   P-RATS   P-ROBE   P-UKES
P-ALLS   P-AWLS   P-ERNS   P-ITAS   P-LINK   P-OOPS   P-RAWN   P-ROBS   P-ULES
P-ALLY   P-AWNS   P-ERST   P-ITCH   P-LODS   P-OPES   P-RAYS   P-RODS   P-UNCE
P-ALMS   P-AXES   P-ESKY   P-LACE   P-LONG   P-ORAL   P-REED   P-ROIN   P-UNTO
P-ALPS   P-EACH   P-ESTS   P-LACK   P-LOOK   P-ORES   P-REEN   P-ROKE   P-UPAS
P-ANCE   P-EANS   P-HANG   P-LAID   P-LOPS   P-ORGY   P-REES   P-ROLE   P-URES
P-ANDS   P-EARL   P-HARE   P-LAIN   P-LOTS   P-ORTS   P-REIF   P-ROLL   P-URGE
P-ANES   P-EARS   P-HOHS   P-LANE   P-LOWS   P-OTTO   P-RENT   P-RONE   P-USES
P-ANTS   P-EASE   P-HONE   P-LANK   P-LOYS   P-OUCH   P-REPS   P-RONE
P-APES   P-EATS   P-HONS   P-LANT   P-LUCK   P-OUKS   P-REST   P-RONG
```

5→6

P-ACERS	P-AVISE	P-HONES	P-LANTS	P-LUMPS	P-RATED	P-RILLS	P-ROVER
P-ACING	P-AWING	P-HONEY	P-LATED	P-LUMPY	P-RATER	P-RIMED	P-ROVES
P-ADDED	P-AWNED	P-HOOEY	P-LATEN	P-LUNGE	P-RATES	P-RIMER	P-ROYNE
P-ADDER	P-AWNER	P-ICKER	P-LATER	P-LUSHY	P-RAWNS	P-RIMES	P-RUDES
P-ADDLE	P-EANED	P-ILEUM	P-LAYER	P-LYING	P-RAXES	P-RIMUS	P-RUNED
P-AEONS	P-EARLS	P-ILEUS	P-LEACH	P-ODIUM	P-RAYED	P-RINKS	P-RUNES
P-AGING	P-EARLY	P-IMPED	P-LEADS	P-OINTS	P-REACH	P-RISER	P-RUNTS
P-AIRED	P-EARST	P-IMPLY	P-LEASE	P-OLDER	P-REENS	P-RISES	P-SHAWS
P-ALATE	P-EASED	P-INGLE	P-LEATS	P-OLIOS	P-REEVE	P-RIVET	P-SORAS
P-ALAYS	P-EASES	P-INION	P-LEDGE	P-ONCES	P-REFER	P-ROBED	P-TOSES
P-ALTER	P-ECHED	P-INKED	P-LEUCH	P-OOPED	P-REIFS	P-ROBES	P-UDDER
P-ANTED	P-EERIE	P-INKER	P-LEUGH	P-OSIER	P-REMIX	P-ROINS	P-UGGED
P-APERY	P-EGGED	P-INNED	P-LIERS	P-OTHER	P-RENTS	P-ROKED	P-UNCES
P-APISH	P-ELITE	P-INNER	P-LIGHT	P-OTTER	P-REPAY	P-ROKER	P-UPPED
P-APISM	P-ELVES	P-IONIC	P-LINGS	P-OTTOS	P-RESES	P-ROKES	P-URGED
P-ARISH	P-ENDED	P-IRATE	P-LINKS	P-OUNCE	P-RESET	P-ROLES	P-URGER
P-ARKED	P-ERSES	P-ISHES	P-LONGE	P-OUPED	P-RESTS	P-ROLLS	P-URGES
P-ARLED	P-ESTER	P-LACED	P-LONGS	P-OURIE	P-REVUE	P-RONES	P-URINE
P-ARLES	P-ETHER	P-LACES	P-LOOKS	P-OUTED	P-RIALS	P-ROPER	P-USHER
P-ARSES	P-ETTLE	P-LACET	P-LOUGH	P-OUTER	P-RICED	P-RORES	P-UTTER
P-ARSON	P-HANGS	P-LACKS	P-LOVER	P-OWRES	P-RICER	P-ROSED	
P-ASHES	P-HARES	P-LAIDS	P-LOWED	P-RAISE	P-RICES	P-ROSES	
P-ASSES	P-HAROS	P-LANCH	P-LUCKS	P-RANAS	P-RICEY	P-ROSIT	
P-ASTER	P-HEEZE	P-LANES	P-LUCKY	P-RANCE	P-RICKS	P-ROULS	
P-AVENS	P-HONED	P-LANKS	P-LUFFS	P-RANKS	P-RIDES	P-ROVED	
P-AVERS	P-HONER		P-LUMMY	P-RASES	P-RIEVE		

6→7

P-ACKERS	P-AWNING	P-IMPING	P-LEASED	P-OINTED	P-RAYING	P-RESTED	P-ROKING
P-ACTION	P-EANING	P-INCASE	P-LEASER	P-ONDING	P-REBORN	P-RESUME	P-ROLLED
P-ADDERS	P-EASING	P-INCHED	P-LEASES	P-OODLES	P-RECAST	P-REVERB	P-ROLLER
P-ADDING	P-EATERY	P-INCHES	P-LEDGER	P-OOPING	P-RECEDE	P-REVIEW	P-ROOFED
P-ADDLED	P-ECHING	P-INFOLD	P-LEDGES	P-ORCINE	P-RECEPT	P-REVISE	P-ROPERS
P-ADDLES	P-EERIER	P-INGLES	P-LESSOR	P-ORGIES	P-RECESS	P-REVUES	P-ROSIER
P-AGINGS	P-EGGING	P-INGOES	P-LIABLE	P-ORTHOS	P-REDATE	P-RICERS	P-ROSILY
P-AIRING	P-ELITES	P-INKIER	P-LIGHTS	P-OTHERS	P-REDIAL	P-RICIER	P-ROSING
P-ALATED	P-ENDING	P-INKING	P-LINKED	P-OTTERS	P-REEVED	P-RICING	P-ROVERS
P-ALLIUM	P-ENFOLD	P-INNATE	P-LONGED	P-OUCHES	P-REEVES	P-RICKED	P-ROVING
P-ALTERS	P-ENSILE	P-INNERS	P-LONGES	P-OULDER	P-REFACE	P-RICKER	P-ROYNED
P-ANTHER	P-ENTICE	P-INNING	P-LOPPED	P-OUNCES	P-REFECT	P-RICKLE	P-ROYNES
P-ANTING	P-EONISM	P-ITCHED	P-LOTTED	P-OUPING	P-REFERS	P-RICKLY	P-RUDERY
P-ANTLER	P-ESTERS	P-ITCHES	P-LOUGHS	P-OUTERS	P-REFORM	P-RIDING	P-RUDISH
P-APISMS	P-ETHERS	P-LACETS	P-LOVERS	P-OUTHER	P-REHEAT	P-RIEVES	P-RUNTED
P-APPOSE	P-ETTLED	P-LACING	P-LOWING	P-OUTING	P-RELATE	P-RIGGED	P-SALTER
P-ARABLE	P-ETTLES	P-LAIDED	P-LUFFED	P-RABBLE	P-REMISE	P-RIGGER	P-UBERTY
P-ARCHED	P-HANGED	P-LANKED	P-LUGGED	P-RAISED	P-REMISS	P-RIMERS	P-UCKERS
P-ARCHES	P-HATTER	P-LANNER	P-LUGGER	P-RAISER	P-REMOVE	P-RIMING	P-UDDERS
P-ARKING	P-HEEZED	P-LAPPED	P-LUMBER	P-RAISES	P-RENTED	P-RIMMED	P-UGGING
P-ARLING	P-HEEZES	P-LASHED	P-LUMPED	P-RANCED	P-REPACK	P-RINKED	P-ULLING
P-ARPENT	P-HIZZES	P-LASHES	P-LUMPEN	P-RANCES	P-REPAID	P-RISERS	P-UNTIES
P-ARSONS	P-HONERS	P-LASTER	P-LUMPER	P-RANGED	P-REPAYS	P-RISING	P-UPPING
P-ARTIES	P-HONEYS	P-LATENS	P-LUNGED	P-RANKED	P-REPONE	P-RIVETS	P-URGERS
P-ASTERN	P-HONIED	P-LATTER	P-LUNGES	P-RANKLE	P-REPOSE	P-ROBING	P-URGING
P-ASTERS	P-HONING	P-LAYERS	P-LUNKER	P-RATERS	P-REPPED	P-RODDED	P-URINES
P-ATRIAL	P-HUTTED	P-LAYING	P-LUSHER	P-RATING	P-RESENT	P-ROINED	P-USHERS
P-AVISES	P-ICKERS	P-LEADED	P-LUSHES	P-RATTED	P-RESETS	P-ROKERS	P-UTTERS
P-AWNERS	P-ICKIER	P-LEADER	P-LUTEAL	P-RATTLE	P-RESIDE		

7→8

P-ACTIONS	P-EARLIES	P-INCHING	P-LAYTIME	P-LUCKIER	P-OINTING	P-RATTLES
P-ADDLING	P-EERIEST	P-INFOLDS	P-LEACHED	P-LUCKILY	P-ORTOLAN	P-REACHED
P-AIRINGS	P-ENCHANT	P-INKIEST	P-LEACHES	P-LUFFING	P-OTTERED	P-REACHER
P-ALIFORM	P-ENFOLDS	P-INNINGS	P-LEADERS	P-LUGGERS	P-OUTINGS	P-REACHES
P-ALIMONY	P-ENLIGHT	P-ITCHIER	P-LEADING	P-LUGGING	P-RABBLES	P-RECEDED
P-ALTERED	P-ENTICED	P-ITCHING	P-LEASERS	P-LUMBAGO	P-RAISERS	P-RECEDES
P-ANTHERS	P-ENTICES	P-LACINGS	P-LEASING	P-LUMBERS	P-RAISING	P-RECEPTS
P-ANTINGS	P-ENTOMIC	P-LAIDING	P-LEASURE	P-LUMMIER	P-RANCING	P-REDATED
P-ANTLERS	P-EONISMS	P-LANCHED	P-LEDGERS	P-LUMPERS	P-RANGING	P-REDATES
P-ARCHING	P-ETTLING	P-LANCHES	P-LESSORS	P-LUMPIER	P-RANKING	P-REDIALS
P-ARISHES	P-HANGING	P-LANKING	P-LIGHTED	P-LUMPISH	P-RANKLED	P-REEVING
P-ARPENTS	P-HEEZING	P-LANNERS	P-LIGHTER	P-LUNGING	P-RANKLES	P-REFACED
P-ARTICLE	P-HONEYED	P-LAPPING	P-LINKING	P-LUNKERS	P-RATINGS	P-REFACES
P-ARTISAN	P-HUTTING	P-LASHING	P-LONGING	P-LUSHEST	P-RATTING	P-REFECTS
P-ARTWORK	P-ICKIEST	P-LASTERS	P-LOPPING	P-LUSHIER	P-RATTLED	P-REFORMS
P-EARLIER	P-INCASES	P-LAYBACK	P-LOTTING	P-LUSHIER	P-RATTLER	P-REGNANT

P-REHEATS	P-REMOVED	P-REPOSES	P-RESUMED	P-RICKETS	P-RIMMING	P-ROVINGS
P-REJUDGE	P-REMOVES	P-REPPING	P-RESUMES	P-RICKING	P-RINKING	P-ROYNING
P-RELATES	P-RENTING	P-RESCIND	P-REVERBS	P-RICKLES	P-RODDING	P-SALTERS
P-REMISED	P-REORDER	P-RESENTS	P-REVIEWS	P-RIEVING	P-ROINING	P-UDDERED
P-REMISES	P-REPACKS	P-RESERVE	P-REVISED	P-RIGGERS	P-ROLLERS	P-UNITION
P-REMIXED	P-REPONED	P-RESIDED	P-REVISES	P-RIGGING	P-ROLLING	P-UNITIVE
P-REMIXES	P-REPONES	P-RESIDES	P-RICIEST	P-RIGGISH	P-ROOFING	P-URGINGS
P-REMORSE	P-REPOSED	P-RESTING	P-RICKERS	P-RILLING	P-ROSIEST	P-UTTERED

8→9

P-ACTIONED	P-ITCHIEST	P-LUMPIEST	P-RECESSES	P-REMOVING	P-RESIDING
P-ALTERING	P-LANCHING	P-LUSHIEST	P-RECISION	P-REOCCUPY	P-RESUMING
P-ARTICLES	P-LASHINGS	P-OENOLOGY	P-REDATING	P-REORDAIN	P-REVIEWED
P-ARTISANS	P-LATITUDE	P-ORTHOSES	P-REDEFINE	P-REORDERS	P-REVISING
P-ARTWORKS	P-LAYBACKS	P-ORTOLANS	P-REDESIGN	P-REPACKED	P-REVISION
P-EARLIEST	P-LAYTIMES	P-OTTERING	P-REFACING	P-REPAYING	P-RIGGINGS
P-EATERIES	P-LEACHING	P-RAISINGS	P-REFERRED	P-REPONING	P-ROOFINGS
P-ENCHANTS	P-LEADINGS	P-RANKINGS	P-REFIGURE	P-REPOSING	P-ROOFLESS
P-ENLIGHTS	P-LEASINGS	P-RANKLING	P-REFORMED	P-RESCINDS	P-ROSINESS
P-ENTANGLE	P-LEASURES	P-RATTLERS	P-REHEATED	P-RESCRIPT	P-ROSTRATE
P-ENTICING	P-LIGHTERS	P-RATTLING	P-REJUDGED	P-RESELECT	P-RUDERIES
P-ETIOLATE	P-LIGHTFUL	P-REACHERS	P-REJUDGES	P-RESENTED	P-UBERTIES
P-HONEYING	P-LIGHTING	P-REACHING	P-RELATION	P-RESENTER	P-UNGENTLY
P-INFOLDED	P-LUCKIEST	P-RECEDING	P-REMISING	P-RESERVED	P-UNITIONS
P-INKINESS	P-LUMBAGOS	P-RECEPTOR	P-REMIXING	P-RESERVES	P-UTTERING
P-INNATELY	P-LUMMIEST	P-RECESSED	P-REMOTION	P-RESIDENT	

2→3

AM-P	DA-P	GI-P	HI-P	LI-P	NA-P	PA-P	SI-P	TO-P
AS-P	DI-P	GU-P	HO-P	LO-P	NE-P	PI-P	SO-P	WO-P
BA-P	DO-P	HA-P	KO-P	MA-P	OO-P	PO-P	TA-P	YE-P
BO-P	FA-P	HE-P	LA-P	MO-P	OU-P	RE-P	TI-P	YU-P

3→4

ALA-P	CHI-P	GAM-P	HEM-P	LIS-P	PAR-P	REP-P	SIM-P	TUM-P	YAP-P
BAR-P	COO-P	GAS-P	HES-P	LOO-P	PEE-P	RIP-P	SKI-P	VEE-P	YAW-P
BEE-P	COW-P	GAU-P	HOO-P	LUM-P	POM-P	ROM-P	SOU-P	WAR-P	
BUM-P	DAM-P	GEE-P	HUM-P	MOO-P	POO-P	ROO-P	SOW-P	WAS-P	
BUR-P	DEE-P	GOO-P	KIP-P	MOU-P	PRE-P	RUM-P	SUM-P	WEE-P	
CAM-P	DOR-P	GUM-P	LAM-P	MUM-P	PRO-P	SAL-P	TAM-P	WHA-P	
CAR-P	DOW-P	GYM-P	LEA-P	NEE-P	RAM-P	SAM-P	TAR-P	WHO-P	
CHA-P	FRA-P	HAS-P	LEE-P	PAL-P	RAS-P	SEE-P	TRY-P	WIS-P	

4→5

BLEE-P	CLAM-P	CRIM-P	POLY-P	SCAM-P	SCUL-P	SLUM-P	STUM-P	TRAM-P
CHAM-P	CRAM-P	GRUM-P	PRIM-P	SCAR-P	SKIM-P	SLUR-P	SWAM-P	
CHUM-P	CREE-P	PLUM-P	SALE-P	SCOW-P	SLEE-P	STIR-P	SWEE-P	

5→6

SCRIM-P   SCRUM-P   THREE-P

6→7

MANTRA-P   SCHLEP-P

7→8

AUTOCAR-P

2→3

Q-AT   Q-IS

3→4

Q-UEY

4→5

Q-UEYS   TALA-Q

2→3

R-AD	R-AN	R-AX	R-EH	R-EX	R-IT	R-OM	R-UM
R-AH	R-AS	R-AY	R-EM	R-HO	R-OB	R-OO	R-UN
R-AI	R-AT	R-EE	R-EN	R-ID	R-OD	R-OW	R-UT
R-AM	R-AW	R-EF	R-ES	R-IN	R-OE	R-UG	R-YE

3→4

R-ACE	R-AIN	R-ANI	R-AWN	R-EGO	R-ICE	R-ITS	R-OLE	R-ORT	R-UTS
R-ACH	R-AIS	R-ANT	R-AYS	R-EHS	R-ICH	R-OAR	R-ONE	R-OUP	R-YES
R-ADS	R-AIT	R-APE	R-EAN	R-EIK	R-ICY	R-OBS	R-OOF	R-OUT	
R-AFT	R-AKE	R-APT	R-EAR	R-EKE	R-IDE	R-OCH	R-OOM	R-OWT	
R-AGA	R-ALE	R-ARE	R-EEK	R-EMS	R-IDS	R-ODE	R-OON	R-UDS	
R-AGE	R-AMI	R-ASH	R-EEL	R-END	R-IFF	R-ODS	R-OOP	R-UGS	
R-AHS	R-AMP	R-ASP	R-EEN	R-ENS	R-ILL	R-OES	R-OOS	R-ULE	
R-AID	R-ANA	R-ATE	R-EFS	R-EST	R-INK	R-OIL	R-OPE	R-UNS	
R-AIL	R-AND	R-AVE	R-EFT	R-HOS	R-INS	R-OKE	R-ORE	R-USE	

4→5

R-ABID	R-AILS	R-AMPS	R-AWNS	R-EECH	R-EPOS	R-INKS	R-OONS	R-OVER
R-ACED	R-AINE	R-ANAS	R-AXED	R-EELS	R-ESTS	R-OARS	R-OOPS	R-OWED
R-ACER	R-AITS	R-ANCE	R-AXES	R-EGAL	R-ETCH	R-OARY	R-OOSE	R-OWER
R-ACES	R-AKED	R-ANDS	R-AYAH	R-EGMA	R-EVET	R-OAST	R-OPED	R-OWTS
R-ACHE	R-AKEE	R-ANIS	R-EACH	R-EGOS	R-HIES	R-ODES	R-OPES	R-ULES
R-AGAS	R-AKES	R-ANTS	R-EANS	R-EIKS	R-HONE	R-OILS	R-ORAL	R-UMBO
R-AGED	R-ALES	R-APED	R-EARS	R-EKED	R-ICED	R-OILY	R-ORES	R-URUS
R-AGEE	R-ALLY	R-APES	R-EAST	R-EKES	R-ICER	R-OKES	R-ORTS	R-USES
R-AGES	R-AMEN	R-ASPS	R-ECCE	R-EMIT	R-ICES	R-ONES	R-OUPS	
R-AHED	R-AMIE	R-AVER	R-ECCO	R-ENDS	R-IDES	R-OOFS	R-OUST	
R-AIDS	R-AMIS	R-AVES	R-EDDY	R-ENEW	R-ILLS	R-OOMS	R-OUTS	

5→6

R-ABIES	R-AKING	R-ASHES	R-EASTS	R-ENTER	R-ICIER	R-OPING	R-UGGED
R-ACERS	R-AMATE	R-ASPER	R-EAVES	R-ENVOI	R-ICING	R-OSIER	R-UMBOS
R-ACHES	R-AMBLE	R-ASSES	R-EDUCE	R-ENVOY	R-ICKER	R-OTARY	R-UNLET
R-ACING	R-AMENS	R-ASTER	R-EFFED	R-ESILE	R-ICTAL	R-OTHER	R-UNRIG
R-ADDER	R-AMIES	R-AUGHT	R-EGEST	R-ESTER	R-ICTUS	R-OTTER	R-USHER
R-ADDLE	R-ANGER	R-AVENS	R-EGRET	R-EVERT	R-INKED	R-OUGHT	R-UTILE
R-ADIOS	R-ANKER	R-AVERS	R-EJECT	R-EVERY	R-IZARD	R-OUNCE	R-UTTER
R-AFTER	R-ANKLE	R-AVINE	R-EKING	R-EVETS	R-OARED	R-OUPED	
R-AGING	R-ANTED	R-AWING	R-ELATE	R-EVOKE	R-OASTS	R-OUSTS	
R-AHING	R-APHIS	R-AXING	R-ELIDE	R-HEXES	R-OCHES	R-OUTED	
R-AIDED	R-APING	R-AYAHS	R-EMITS	R-HONES	R-OCKER	R-OUTER	
R-AIDER	R-APPEL	R-AZURE	R-EMOTE	R-ICERS	R-OILED	R-OVERS	
R-AILED	R-APTLY	R-EARED	R-EMOVE	R-ICHED	R-OOPED	R-OWING	
R-AKEES	R-AREFY	R-EARLY	R-ENEWS	R-ICHES	R-OOSES	R-UDDER	

6→7

R-ACKERS	R-AMBLES	R-EARING	R-EGESTS	R-ENDING	R-EVERTS	R-OARING	R-OUSTED
R-ADDLED	R-AMENTA	R-EASTED	R-EGRESS	R-ENEWED	R-EVOKED	R-OCKERS	R-OUSTER
R-ADDLES	R-ANGERS	R-ECLOSE	R-EGRETS	R-ENTERS	R-EVOKES	R-OILIER	R-OUTERS
R-AFTERS	R-ANKERS	R-EDDISH	R-EJECTS	R-ENVOIS	R-EVOLVE	R-OILING	R-OUTING
R-AGINGS	R-ANKLED	R-EDUCED	R-ELAPSE	R-ENVOYS	R-HACHIS	R-ONNING	R-OYSTER
R-AIDERS	R-ANKLES	R-EDUCES	R-ELATED	R-EPOSES	R-ICHING	R-OOPING	R-UDDERS
R-AIDING	R-ANTING	R-EECHED	R-ELATER	R-EPRISE	R-ICIEST	R-OSIERS	R-UGGING
R-AILING	R-APPELS	R-EECHES	R-ELATES	R-ESILES	R-ICKERS	R-OTHERS	R-UMBLES
R-ALLIED	R-APPORT	R-EFFING	R-EMERGE	R-ESTATE	R-INKING	R-OTTERS	R-UNRIGS
R-ALLIES	R-ASPERS	R-EGALLY	R-EMOTES	R-ESTERS	R-INNING	R-OUGHLY	R-USHERS
R-AMBLED	R-ASTERS	R-EGENCE	R-EMOVED	R-ETCHED	R-IZARDS	R-OUNCES	R-UTTERS
R-AMBLER	R-AZURES	R-EGENCY	R-EMOVES	R-ETCHES	R-OARIER	R-OUPING	

7→8

R-ADDLING	R-APPORTS	R-EGALITY	R-ELATION	R-ENEWING	R-EVOLUTE	R-OUSTERS
R-ADULATE	R-AREFIED	R-EGENCES	R-ELATIVE	R-ENFORCE	R-EVOLVED	R-OUSTING
R-ALLYING	R-AREFIES	R-EJECTED	R-EMERGED	R-ENOUNCE	R-EVOLVER	R-OUTINGS
R-AMBLERS	R-EASTING	R-EJECTOR	R-EMERGES	R-ENOUNCE	R-EVOLVES	R-OYSTERS
R-AMBLING	R-ECLOSED	R-ELAPSED	R-EMITTED	R-ESTATED	R-ICTUSES	
R-AMENTUM	R-ECLOSES	R-ELAPSES	R-EMITTER	R-ESTATES	R-OARIEST	
R-ANTINGS	R-EDUCING	R-ELATERS	R-EMOTION	R-ETCHING	R-OILIEST	
R-APHIDES	R-EECHING	R-ELATING	R-EMOVING	R-EVOKING	R-OTARIES	

8→9

R-AMBLINGS	R-EGENCIES	R-ELAPSING	R-EMISSIVE	R-ENOUNCED	R-EVOCABLE
R-ANTIPOLE	R-EGRESSES	R-ELATIONS	R-EMITTERS	R-ENOUNCES	R-EVOLVERS
R-AREFYING	R-EJECTING	R-ELATIVES	R-EMITTING	R-ERADIATE	R-EVOLVING
R-ECLOSING	R-EJECTION	R-EMERGING	R-EMOTIONS	R-ESTATING	R-EVULSION
R-EDUCIBLE	R-EJECTIVE	R-EMIGRATE	R-ENFORCED	R-EVERSION	R-UNCINATE
R-EDUCTION	R-EJECTORS	R-EMISSION	R-ENFORCES	R-EVERTING	

2→3

AI-R	DO-R	FA-R	JO-R	MA-R	NO-R	OU-R	SI-R
BA-R	EA-R	GU-R	LA-R	MI-R	NU-R	PA-R	TA-R
BO-R	ER-R	HE-R	LO-R	MO-R	OO-R	PI-R	TO-R

3→4

ACE-R	BOO-R	DEE-R	FEE-R	HOA-R	LEI-R	ONE-R	POO-R	SOU-R	USE-R
AGA-R	BOW-R	DOE-R	FIE-R	HOE-R	LIE-R	OWE-R	PUR-R	SPA-R	VEE-R
ALA-R	BUR-R	DOO-R	FOU-R	HUE-R	LOO-R	OYE-R	SAI-R	SUE-R	VIE-R
AMI-R	CAR-R	DOR-R	FUR-R	ICE-R	MAA-R	PAR-R	SEA-R	TEA-R	WEE-R
AVE-R	CHA-R	DYE-R	GAU-R	JEE-R	MAW-R	PEA-R	SEE-R	TEE-R	YEA-R
BEE-R	CHE-R	EVE-R	GOE-R	LEA-R	MOO-R	PEE-R	SEI-R	TIE-R	YOU-R
BOA-R	CUR-R	EWE-R	GOO-R	LEE-R	NUR-R	PIE-R	SKY-R	TOR-R	

4→5

ABLE-R	COVE-R	FIRE-R	IDLE-R	MASE-R	ONCE-R	RIDE-R	SOFA-R	TUNE-R
AIDE-R	CURE-R	FIVE-R	JAPE-R	MATE-R	PACE-R	RIFE-R	SOLA-R	TWEE-R
ANTA-R	CUTE-R	FLEE-R	JIBE-R	MAZE-R	PAGE-R	RIME-R	SOLE-R	ULNA-R
AREA-R	CYMA-R	FREE-R	JIVE-R	MERE-R	PALE-R	RIPE-R	SORE-R	UNDE-R
BAKE-R	DATE-R	GAME-R	JOKE-R	METE-R	PAPE-R	RISE-R	SPAE-R	URGE-R
BALE-R	DAZE-R	GAPE-R	KNUR-R	MILE-R	PARE-R	ROKE-R	STAR-R	VELA-R
BARE-R	DECO-R	GAZE-R	LAKE-R	MILO-R	PATE-R	ROPE-R	SUPE-R	VILE-R
BASE-R	DICE-R	GIBE-R	LAME-R	MIME-R	PAVE-R	ROVE-R	SURE-R	VINE-R
BIKE-R	DIKE-R	GIVE-R	LASE-R	MINA-R	PIKE-R	RUDE-R	SWEE-R	VIVE-R
BITE-R	DIME-R	GLUE-R	LATE-R	MINE-R	PILE-R	RULE-R	SYKE-R	VOLA-R
BLAE-R	DINE-R	GNAR-R	LAVE-R	MINO-R	PIPE-R	RYPE-R	TALA-R	VOTE-R
BLUE-R	DIRE-R	GONE-R	LEVE-R	MISE-R	PLIE-R	SAFE-R	TALE-R	WADE-R
BONE-R	DIVE-R	GULA-R	LIFE-R	MITE-R	POKE-R	SAGE-R	TAME-R	WAGE-R
BORE-R	DOPE-R	HALE-R	LIKE-R	MODE-R	POLE-R	SAKE-R	TAPE-R	WAKE-R
BREE-R	DOTE-R	HATE-R	LINE-R	MOLA-R	PORE-R	SANE-R	TATE-R	WALE-R
CAPE-R	DOVE-R	HAVE-R	LITE-R	MOPE-R	POSE-R	SAVE-R	TIGE-R	WATE-R
CARE-R	DOZE-R	HAZE-R	LIVE-R	MOVE-R	PUCE-R	SERE-R	TILE-R	WAVE-R
CATE-R	DUPE-R	HIDE-R	LONE-R	MUSE-R	PUKE-R	SHEA-R	TIME-R	WHIR-R
CAVE-R	EDGE-R	HIKE-R	LOPE-R	MUTE-R	PULE-R	SHIR-R	TITE-R	WIDE-R
CHAI-R	ETHE-R	HILA-R	LOSE-R	NAME-R	PURE-R	SHOE-R	TONE-R	WIPE-R
CHAR-R	FACE-R	HIRE-R	LOVE-R	NEVE-R	RACE-R	SIDE-R	TOPE-R	WIRE-R
CIDE-R	FADE-R	HIVE-R	LOWE-R	NICE-R	RAGE-R	SILE-R	TRIE-R	WISE-R
CITE-R	FAKE-R	HOME-R	LUGE-R	NITE-R	RAKE-R	SIMA-R	TRIO-R	YARE-R
CLOU-R	FAVE-R	HONE-R	LUNA-R	NOSE-R	RAPE-R	SIZE-R	TRUE-R	
CODE-R	FERE-R	HOPE-R	LUTE-R	NOTE-R	RARE-R	SLEE-R	TRYE-R	
COME-R	FIFE-R	HOVE-R	MACE-R	NUDE-R	RATE-R	SMIR-R	TUBA-R	
COPE-R	FILE-R	HUGE-R	MAKE-R	OCHE-R	RAVE-R	SNEE-R	TUBE-R	
CORE-R	FINE-R	HYPE-R	MANO-R	OGLE-R	RICE-R			

5→6

ABUSE-R	BIRLE-R	BUTTE-R	CLOSE-R	DINGE-R	FALSE-R	GRAVE-R	JAMBE-R
ACUTE-R	BITTE-R	CADGE-R	CLOVE-R	DODGE-R	FENCE-R	GRAZE-R	JASPE-R
ADORE-R	BLATE-R	CALVE-R	COATE-R	DORSE-R	FILLE-R	GRICE-R	JUICE-R
AERIE-R	BLAZE-R	CANTO-R	COMBE-R	DOUCE-R	FITTE-R	GRIPE-R	KEDGE-R
AGILE-R	BODGE-R	CARTE-R	CONDO-R	DOUSE-R	FLUTE-R	GROPE-R	KNOWE-R
AMBLE-R	BOMBE-R	CARVE-R	CONGE-R	DOVIE-R	FOLIA-R	GUIDE-R	KRONE-R
AMPLE-R	BONIE-R	CASTE-R	CONNE-R	DOWIE-R	FORCE-R	GUILE-R	LANCE-R
AMUSE-R	BONZE-R	CAUSE-R	COSTE-R	DOWSE-R	FORGE-R	GUISE-R	LANDE-R
ANGLE-R	BOOZE-R	CAVIE-R	COTTA-R	DRAPE-R	FORME-R	GUSLA-R	LARGE-R
ARGUE-R	BORDE-R	CELLA-R	COUPE-R	DRIVE-R	FOULE-R	GUYLE-R	LATHE-R
ATONE-R	BOWSE-R	CENSE-R	CRATE-R	DROLE-R	FRAME-R	HALSE-R	LEASE-R
AWARE-R	BRACE-R	CESSE-R	CRAVE-R	DROVE-R	FRATE-R	HALVE-R	LEAVE-R
BADGE-R	BRAVE-R	CHAFE-R	CRUDE-R	EERIE-R	GAFFE-R	HAWSE-R	LEDGE-R
BANDA-R	BRIBE-R	CHASE-R	CURSE-R	ELATE-R	GAMME-R	HEARE-R	LEFTE-R
BARBE-R	BROKE-R	CHIDE-R	CYCLE-R	ELOPE-R	GAUGE-R	HEAVE-R	LEGGE-R
BASSE-R	BRUTE-R	CHIME-R	DAMME-R	ELUDE-R	GIMME-R	HEDGE-R	LENTO-R
BASTE-R	BUDGE-R	CHINA-R	DANCE-R	ERASE-R	GLAZE-R	HITHE-R	LIEGE-R
BATHE-R	BUFFE-R	CHOKE-R	DAUBE-R	EVADE-R	GLIDE-R	HOOVE-R	LIEVE-R
BEARE-R	BUGLE-R	CIRCA-R	DEARE-R	EVOKE-R	GLOVE-R	INANE-R	LIGGE-R
BELIE-R	BULGE-R	CLAVE-R	DELVE-R	FABLE-R	GRADE-R	IRATE-R	LITHE-R
BINGE-R	BURSA-R	CLEVE-R	DENSE-R	FAINE-R	GRATE-R	ISSUE-R	LODGE-R

LOGIE-R	OORIE-R	PROBE-R	RHYME-R	SHARE-R	SPACE-R	TESTE-R	VOGUE-R
LONGE-R	OURIE-R	PROKE-R	RIDGE-R	SHAVE-R	SPADE-R	TITHE-R	VOICE-R
LOOSE-R	OWRIE-R	PROLE-R	RIEVE-R	SHINE-R	SPARE-R	TITLE-R	VULVA-R
LOWSE-R	PANDA-R	PRONE-R	RIFLE-R	SHIVE-R	SPICE-R	TOILE-R	WACKE-R
MAILE-R	PARSE-R	PROSE-R	RINSE-R	SHORE-R	SPIDE-R	TOUSE-R	WAITE-R
MANGE-R	PASSE-R	PROVE-R	RORIE-R	SHOVE-R	SPINA-R	TOWSE-R	WAIVE-R
MATTE-R	PASTE-R	PRUNE-R	ROUSE-R	SIEGE-R	STAGE-R	TRACE-R	WASTE-R
MAUVE-R	PATTE-R	PURGE-R	ROUTE-R	SINGE-R	STALE-R	TRADE-R	WEAVE-R
MEANE-R	PAUSE-R	PURSE-R	SALVE-R	SKATE-R	STARE-R	TRITE-R	WEETE-R
MENTO-R	PECKE-R	QUAKE-R	SALVO-R	SKIVE-R	STATE-R	TWICE-R	WHALE-R
MERGE-R	PEEPE-R	QUARE-R	SAMBA-R	SLATE-R	STELA-R	TWINE-R	WHINE-R
MICHE-R	PEEVE-R	QUOTE-R	SAUCE-R	SLAVE-R	STIVE-R	UNITE-R	WHITE-R
MILLE-R	PENNE-R	RADGE-R	SCALA-R	SLICE-R	STOKE-R	USAGE-R	WINCE-R
MINCE-R	PHONE-R	RAILE-R	SCALE-R	SLIDE-R	STONE-R	USURE-R	WINGE-R
MOUSE-R	PIECE-R	RAISE-R	SCARE-R	SLIVE-R	STORE-R	UVULA-R	WITHE-R
MUDGE-R	PLACE-R	RANGE-R	SCORE-R	SMILE-R	STOVE-R	VAGUE-R	WOLVE-R
NAIVE-R	PLANE-R	RANKE-R	SEAME-R	SMITE-R	SUAVE-R	VALUE-R	WORSE-R
NAPPE-R	PLATE-R	RATHE-R	SEARE-R	SMOKE-R	SUMMA-R	VEALE-R	WRITE-R
NERVE-R	POISE-R	REAME-R	SEINE-R	SNARE-R	SWIPE-R	VENGE-R	YODLE-R
NICHE-R	POSSE-R	REAVE-R	SEIZE-R	SNIDE-R	TASTE-R	VERGE-R	
NOBLE-R	PRATE-R	RECTO-R	SELLE-R	SNIPE-R	TAWIE-R	VERSE-R	
NUDGE-R	PRICE-R	REEDE-R	SERVE-R	SNORE-R	TEASE-R	VILLA-R	
NURSE-R	PRIME-R	REIVE-R	SHAKE-R	SOARE-R	TENNE-R	VIRGE-R	
OBESE-R	PRISE-R	RELIE-R	SHAME-R	SOLDE-R	TENSE-R	VISIE-R	
OLIVE-R	PRIZE-R	RENTE-R	SHAPE-R	SOLVE-R	TERSE-R	VOGIE-R	

6→7

ABJURE-R	CHANCE-R	DILATE-R	GIRDLE-R	IONISE-R	NEBULA-R	PUZZLE-R	SCRAPE-R
ACCEDE-R	CHANGE-R	DILUTE-R	GIRNIE-R	IONIZE-R	NEEDLE-R	QUARTE-R	SCRIBE-R
ACCUSE-R	CHARGE-R	DIVIDE-R	GOBBLE-R	JANGLE-R	NIBBLE-R	RABBLE-R	SCULLE-R
ADDUCE-R	CHASTE-R	DIVINE-R	GOGGLE-R	JERQUE-R	NIGGLE-R	RADULA-R	SCYTHE-R
ADHERE-R	CHAUFE-R	DOCILE-R	GRAINE-R	JINGLE-R	NIMBLE-R	RAFFLE-R	SECEDE-R
ADMIRE-R	CHEQUE-R	DOGGIE-R	GRAMMA-R	JUGGLE-R	NIRLIE-R	RAMBLE-R	SECURE-R
ADVISE-R	CHEWIE-R	DONSIE-R	GRANDE-R	JUMBLE-R	NOBBLE-R	RANDIE-R	SEDATE-R
ALLEGE-R	CHILDE-R	DOODLE-R	GRANGE-R	JUNKIE-R	NOOKIE-R	RATTLE-R	SEDUCE-R
ALNAGE-R	CHOICE-R	DOTTLE-R	GREASE-R	KIDGIE-R	OBTUSE-R	RAUCLE-R	SEETHE-R
AMENDE-R	CHOOSE-R	DREARE-R	GREETE-R	KINDLE-R	OFFICE-R	RAVAGE-R	SEMPLE-R
APPOSE-R	CIRCLE-R	DREDGE-R	GRIEVE-R	KITTLE-R	OPAQUE-R	REBATE-R	SERENE-R
AREOLA-R	CLAMBE-R	DRUDGE-R	GRIPPE-R	KOOKIE-R	OPPOSE-R	REBUKE-R	SETTLE-R
AROUSE-R	CLAVIE-R	DUDDIE-R	GROOVE-R	LACUNA-R	ORANGE-R	RECITE-R	SEVERE-R
ASSIZE-R	CLEAVE-R	ENABLE-R	GROUSE-R	LAMINA-R	ORNATE-R	REDUCE-R	SHRIVE-R
ASSURE-R	COARSE-R	ENDURE-R	GUSTIE-R	LEAGUE-R	OSCULA-R	REEKIE-R	SILKIE-R
ASTUTE-R	COBBLE-R	ENGAGE-R	GUZZLE-R	LEGATO-R	OUTLIE-R	REFINE-R	SIMPLE-R
AVENGE-R	COHERE-R	ENGINE-R	HACKLE-R	LIGULA-R	PADDLE-R	REFUSE-R	SIZZLE-R
AXILLA-R	COLLIE-R	ENSURE-R	HAGGLE-R	LINTIE-R	PALMIE-R	REFUTE-R	SKIVIE-R
BABBLE-R	COPULA-R	ENTICE-R	HANDLE-R	LIPPIE-R	PAPULA-R	REGULA-R	SLEDGE-R
BAFFLE-R	COUPLE-R	ESCAPE-R	HECKLE-R	LITTLE-R	PARKIE-R	RELATE-R	SLEEVE-R
BATTLE-R	COURSE-R	EVOLVE-R	HIGGLE-R	LOATHE-R	PEDDLE-R	RELIVE-R	SMOUSE-R
BEAGLE-R	CREASE-R	EXCITE-R	HIPPIE-R	LOONIE-R	PEERIE-R	REMOTE-R	SMUDGE-R
BIRKIE-R	CRINGE-R	EXCUSE-R	HOARSE-R	LOUNGE-R	PERUSE-R	REMOVE-R	SNEEZE-R
BITTIE-R	CROSSE-R	EXHUME-R	HOBBLE-R	LUCKIE-R	PHRASE-R	RENEGE-R	SNOOZE-R
BLENDE-R	CROUPE-R	EXPOSE-R	HOMAGE-R	LUNULA-R	PIAFFE-R	RENINE-R	SNUBBE-R
BLITHE-R	CRUISE-R	FACULA-R	HUMANE-R	MACULA-R	PICKLE-R	REPINE-R	SOAPIE-R
BLONDE-R	CUISSE-R	FEEBLE-R	HUMBLE-R	MANAGE-R	PIDDLE-R	RESCUE-R	SOCAGE-R
BLOWIE-R	CUPOLA-R	FETTLE-R	HURDLE-R	MANGLE-R	PIERCE-R	RESIDE-R	SOMBRE-R
BLUDGE-R	CURRIE-R	FIBULA-R	HUSTLE-R	MANURE-R	PIFFLE-R	RETAKE-R	SONSIE-R
BLUDIE-R	DABBLE-R	FICKLE-R	IGNITE-R	MARBLE-R	PIGGIE-R	RETIRE-R	SOOTHE-R
BLUNGE-R	DANDLE-R	FIDDLE-R	IGNORE-R	MARINE-R	PILULA-R	REVERE-R	SPARGE-R
BODGIE-R	DANGLE-R	FIERCE-R	IMBIBE-R	MASHIE-R	PINGLE-R	REVISE-R	SPARRE-R
BOGGLE-R	DAWDLE-R	FLEECE-R	IMPOSE-R	MASQUE-R	PINKIE-R	REVIVE-R	SPARSE-R
BONNIE-R	DAZZLE-R	FONDLE-R	IMPURE-R	MATURE-R	PLANTA-R	RIDDLE-R	SPENCE-R
BOOKIE-R	DEBASE-R	FOOTIE-R	IMPUTE-R	MEAGRE-R	PLASTE-R	RIFFLE-R	SPLICE-R
BOTTLE-R	DEBATE-R	FOOZLE-R	INCITE-R	MEALIE-R	PLEASE-R	RIPPLE-R	SPONGE-R
BOUNCE-R	DECIDE-R	FORAGE-R	INCOME-R	MEDDLE-R	PLEDGE-R	ROARIE-R	SPRUCE-R
BRAIDE-R	DECODE-R	FREEZE-R	INDITE-R	MENACE-R	PLUNGE-R	ROOKIE-R	SPURNE-R
BRIDLE-R	DEFACE-R	FROWIE-R	INDUCE-R	MINGLE-R	POINTE-R	ROOMIE-R	SQUARE-R
BRONZE-R	DEFILE-R	FUDDLE-R	INFUSE-R	MINUTE-R	POLITE-R	RUFFLE-R	STABLE-R
BROWSE-R	DEFINE-R	FUMBLE-R	INHALE-R	MISUSE-R	POTAGE-R	RUMBLE-R	STAPLE-R
BRUISE-R	DELUDE-R	FUTILE-R	INHUME-R	MOCHIE-R	POTCHE-R	RUSTLE-R	STEALE-R
BUCKLE-R	DEMURE-R	GABBLE-R	INJURE-R	MOROSE-R	PRAISE-R	SADDLE-R	STEEVE-R
BUMBLE-R	DEPOSE-R	GAMBLE-R	INSANE-R	MORULA-R	PRANCE-R	SALUTE-R	STEMME-R
BUNGLE-R	DERIDE-R	GARBLE-R	INSIDE-R	MOSSIE-R	PREMIE-R	SAMPLE-R	STEPPE-R
BURBLE-R	DESIRE-R	GAUCHE-R	INSULA-R	MOUSIE-R	PUDDLE-R	SAVAGE-R	STIEVE-R
BUSTLE-R	DEVISE-R	GAUCIE-R	INSURE-R	MUDDLE-R	PUGGIE-R	SCARCE-R	STIFLE-R
CACKLE-R	DIBBLE-R	GENTLE-R	INTONE-R	MUFFLE-R	PURPLE-R	SCHEME-R	STIRRE-R
CAJOLE-R	DICKIE-R	GIGGLE-R	INVADE-R	MUMBLE-R	PURSUE-R	SCORSE-R	STODGE-R
	DIDDLE-R		INVITE-R	MUZZLE-R	PUTTIE-R	SCOUSE-R	STOOPE-R

STRIKE-R	SWERVE-R	TAWTIE-R	TINKLE-R	TROUPE-R	UNTRUE-R	WALLIE-R	WOBBLE-R
STRIVE-R	SWINGE-R	TECHIE-R	TINNIE-R	TROUSE-R	UNWISE-R	WANGLE-R	WOODIE-R
STROKE-R	TABULA-R	TEGULA-R	TIPPLE-R	TRUDGE-R	UPMAKE-R	WARBLE-R	YAPPIE-R
SUBDUE-R	TACKLE-R	TENTIE-R	TODDLE-R	TUMBLE-R	URBANE-R	WASPIE-R	ZONULA-R
SUBTLE-R	TALKIE-R	THRIVE-R	TOTTIE-R	TURTLE-R	VISITE-R	WEDGIE-R	
SUCKLE-R	TANGIE-R	THROWE-R	TOUCHE-R	UNIQUE-R	VOYAGE-R	WEEPIE-R	
SUPPLE-R	TANGLE-R	TICKLE-R	TOUTIE-R	UNRIPE-R	WABBLE-R	WHINGE-R	
SURFIE-R	TATTIE-R	TIDDLE-R	TOWNIE-R	UNSAFE-R	WADDLE-R	WIGGLE-R	
SVELTE-R	TATTLE-R	TINGLE-R	TRIFLE-R	UNSURE-R	WAFFLE-R	WINKLE-R	

7→8

ABRIDGE-R	COLLIDE-R	ENQUIRE-R	KILLDEE-R	POSTURE-R	SCAMBLE-R	TONTINE-R
ABSOLVE-R	COLLUDE-R	ENSLAVE-R	LAMELLA-R	POTHOLE-R	SCAPULA-R	TOPLINE-R
ACHIEVE-R	COMMUTE-R	EPISTLE-R	LECTURE-R	PRATTLE-R	SCAVAGE-R	TORTURE-R
ADVERSE-R	COMPILE-R	ESPOUSE-R	LICENSE-R	PRECISE-R	SCOURGE-R	TOUSTIE-R
AGITATO-R	COMPOSE-R	EXAMINE-R	LINGULA-R	PREPARE-R	SCREEVE-R	TRADUCE-R
AIRLINE-R	COMPUTE-R	EXCLUDE-R	MAMILLA-R	PRESAGE-R	SCROUGE-R	TRAMPLE-R
ANALYSE-R	CONCEDE-R	EXCRETE-R	MEASURE-R	PRESUME-R	SCRUPLE-R	TREADLE-R
ANALYZE-R	CONCISE-R	EXECUTE-R	MEDULLA-R	PRIMSIE-R	SCUFFLE-R	TREMBLE-R
ANIMATE-R	CONFIDE-R	EXEMPLA-R	MICELLA-R	PRIVATE-R	SCUTTLE-R	TRIBUTE-R
APPEASE-R	CONFINE-R	EXPLODE-R	MISLIKE-R	PROCURE-R	SECONDE-R	TRIPPLE-R
APPRISE-R	CONJURE-R	EXPLORE-R	MORTICE-R	PRODUCE-R	SHINGLE-R	TROUBLE-R
APPRIZE-R	CONNIVE-R	EXPUNGE-R	MORTISE-R	PROFANE-R	SHUFFLE-R	TROUNCE-R
APPROVE-R	CONSOLE-R	EXTREME-R	MULTURE-R	PROFILE-R	SILENCE-R	TRUCKLE-R
ARRANGE-R	CONSUME-R	EXTRUDE-R	MUNDANE-R	PROFUSE-R	SINCERE-R	TRUNDLE-R
ASPERGE-R	CONVENE-R	FERTILE-R	NEWCOME-R	PROMISE-R	SKELLIE-R	TWADDLE-R
ATOMISE-R	COSTUME-R	FINESSE-R	NURTURE-R	PROMOTE-R	SMUGGLE-R	TWATTLE-R
ATOMIZE-R	COTTAGE-R	FISTULA-R	OBLIQUE-R	PROPOSE-R	SNIFFLE-R	TWEEDLE-R
AUGUSTE-R	COUTHIE-R	FORMULA-R	OBSCENE-R	PROVIDE-R	SNIGGLE-R	TWIDDLE-R
AULNAGE-R	CREEPIE-R	FRAGILE-R	OBSCURE-R	PROVISO-R	SNOTTIE-R	TWINKLE-R
AUSTERE-R	CRUSADE-R	FRIBBLE-R	OBSERVE-R	PROVOKE-R	SNUFFLE-R	UNWARIE-R
BAGPIPE-R	DAYTALE-R	FULSOME-R	OBTRUDE-R	QUEENIE-R	SPANGLE-R	UPGRADE-R
BALANCE-R	DECEIVE-R	FURCULA-R	OCCLUDE-R	QUIBBLE-R	SPARKIE-R	UTILISE-R
BEGINNE-R	DECLARE-R	GABELLE-R	OFFSIDE-R	QUIDDLE-R	SPARKLE-R	UTILIZE-R
BEGUILE-R	DEFLATE-R	GANGLIA-R	OUTRIDE-R	RAGTIME-R	SPATULA-R	VALVULA-R
BELIEVE-R	DEJEUNE-R	GAROTTE-R	OUTROPE-R	REALISE-R	SPECULA-R	VARIOLA-R
BESIEGE-R	DEMERGE-R	GRABBLE-R	OUTSIDE-R	REALIZE-R	SPICULA-R	VASCULA-R
BESLAVE-R	DESERVE-R	GREENIE-R	OUTVOTE-R	RECEIVE-R	SPRINGE-R	VENTURE-R
BOLSHIE-R	DESPISE-R	GRIZZLE-R	OVERLIE-R	RECLINE-R	SPUNKIE-R	VERBOSE-R
BONDAGE-R	DIALYSE-R	GRUMBLE-R	OVERSEE-R	REECHIE-R	SQUEEZE-R	VERDITE-R
BOOKSIE-R	DIALYZE-R	HEXAPLA-R	OXIDISE-R	REGRATE-R	STARTLE-R	VESTURE-R
BRASSIE-R	DIFFUSE-R	IDOLISE-R	OXIDIZE-R	REJOICE-R	STEAMIE-R	VIBRATO-R
BREATHE-R	DISPONE-R	IDOLIZE-R	OZONISE-R	RELAPSE-R	STIBBLE-R	VILLAGE-R
BRICKIE-R	DISPOSE-R	IGNOBLE-R	OZONIZE-R	RELEASE-R	STICKLE-R	VINTAGE-R
BRITTLE-R	DISPUTE-R	IMAGINE-R	PACKAGE-R	RELIEVE-R	STIPPLE-R	VIOLATE-R
BROWNIE-R	DIVORCE-R	IMMENSE-R	PAPILLA-R	RENEGUE-R	STRANGE-R	WARFARE-R
BRUSQUE-R	DOGGONE-R	IMPLORE-R	PARTAKE-R	REPLACE-R	STUMBLE-R	WAYFARE-R
CANNULA-R	DOMINEE-R	IMPROVE-R	PATELLA-R	REPROVE-R	SUBLIME-R	WELCOME-R
CAPABLE-R	DRABBLE-R	INCENSE-R	PECULIA-R	REQUIRE-R	SUBTILE-R	WHEEDLE-R
CAPTURE-R	DRIBBLE-R	INCLOSE-R	PERFUME-R	REQUITE-R	SUFFICE-R	WHEELIE-R
CAROUSE-R	DRUGGIE-R	INDULGE-R	PERJURE-R	RESOLVE-R	SUPPOSE-R	WHIFFLE-R
CHAPPIE-R	EMBRACE-R	INFLAME-R	PILLAGE-R	RESTORE-R	SUPREME-R	WHISTLE-R
CHICANE-R	ENCLOSE-R	INQUIRE-R	PLANULA-R	REVENGE-R	SURFACE-R	WHITTLE-R
CHINKIE-R	ENDORSE-R	INSPIRE-R	PLOOKIE-R	REVERSE-R	SURMISE-R	WINSOME-R
CHIPPIE-R	ENFORCE-R	INTENSE-R	PLOUKIE-R	REVOLVE-R	SWADDLE-R	WRANGLE-R
CLEANSE-R	ENGRAVE-R	INTRUDE-R	PLUMPIE-R	ROMANCE-R	SWANKIE-R	WREATHE-R
COCHLEA-R	ENHANCE-R	JAUNTIE-R	PLUMULA-R	ROUTHIE-R	SWINDLE-R	WRESTLE-R
COLLEGE-R	ENLARGE-R	JUSTICE-R	POLLUTE-R	RUMMAGE-R	TEENAGE-R	WRIGGLE-R

8→9

ABSOLUTE-R	BLASTULA-R	CONSTRUE-R	DISSUADE-R	FRONTAGE-R	INVEIGLE-R
ABSTRUSE-R	BULLDOZE-R	CONTINUE-R	DRICKSIE-R	GARROTTE-R	KLONDIKE-R
ANNOUNCE-R	CAPITULA-R	CONTRIVE-R	DYNAMITE-R	GLABELLA-R	KLONDYKE-R
APHORISE-R	CARABINE-R	CRIBELLA-R	EMBEZZLE-R	GRUESOME-R	LITERATO-R
APHORIZE-R	CARETAKE-R	DENOUNCE-R	ENERGISE-R	HANDSOME-R	LOCALISE-R
APPETISE-R	CATALYSE-R	DESCRIBE-R	ENERGIZE-R	HARANGUE-R	LOCALIZE-R
APPETIZE-R	CATALYZE-R	DESOLATE-R	EQUALISE-R	HARDLINE-R	MAINLINE-R
APPRAISE-R	CIVILISE-R	DETHRONE-R	EQUALIZE-R	HEADLINE-R	MEDICINE-R
ARCHAISE-R	CIVILIZE-R	DEVELOPE-R	ESTRANGE-R	HOROLOGE-R	MISGUIDE-R
ARCHAIZE-R	CLAUSULA-R	DIGITISE-R	EXCHANGE-R	IDEALISE-R	MOBILISE-R
ARTIFICE-R	CLITELLA-R	DIGITIZE-R	EXERCISE-R	IDEALIZE-R	MOBILIZE-R
ASSEMBLE-R	COALMINE-R	DISCRETE-R	EXORCISE-R	ILLUMINE-R	MODERATO-R
ASTRINGE-R	COMPLETE-R	DISGRACE-R	EXORCIZE-R	IMPOLITE-R	MORALISE-R
AURICULA-R	CONDENSE-R	DISGUISE-R	EXPEDITE-R	INCREASE-R	MORALIZE-R
BACKBITE-R	CONSERVE-R	DISPENSE-R	FIBRILLA-R	INSCRIBE-R	MORTGAGE-R
BARRETTE-R	CONSPIRE-R	DISPERSE-R	FOREBODE-R	INTRIGUE-R	NAVICULA-R

NEBBISHE-R	PENDICLE-R	PURCHASE-R	SCRIBBLE-R	SUNBATHE-R	TROCHLEA-R
NEBULISE-R	PERCEIVE-R	REASSURE-R	SCROGGIE-R	SURPRISE-R	UNBUNDLE-R
NEBULIZE-R	PERFECTO-R	REHEARSE-R	SCROUNGE-R	SUSPENSE-R	UNRIDDLE-R
NOVELISE-R	PERSUADE-R	REINSURE-R	SCUTELLA-R	TAILGATE-R	UNSTABLE-R
NOVELIZE-R	PERVERSE-R	RENOUNCE-R	SENSIBLE-R	TELEVISE-R	VAPORISE-R
NUISANCE-R	PHALANGE-R	RESEMBLE-R	SENTENCE-R	TESSELLA-R	VAPORIZE-R
OPERCULA-R	PLEASURE-R	RESPONSE-R	SEQUENCE-R	THEORISE-R	VESICULA-R
ORGANISE-R	POLARISE-R	RETINULA-R	SERENADE-R	THEORIZE-R	VIGNETTE-R
ORGANIZE-R	POLARIZE-R	RETRIEVE-R	SIGHTSEE-R	THROTTLE-R	VITALISE-R
OUTPLACE-R	POSTPONE-R	RIDICULE-R	SPIRILLA-R	TOTALISE-R	VITALIZE-R
OVERRIDE-R	PRACTISE-R	RINGSIDE-R	SPRINKLE-R	TOTALIZE-R	VOCALISE-R
OVERRULE-R	PRESBYTE-R	SCAVENGE-R	SQUABBLE-R	TRAVERSE-R	VOCALIZE-R
OVERTIME-R	PRESERVE-R	SCHEDULE-R	STRAGGLE-R	TREASURE-R	WARDROBE-R
PARALYSE-R	PROLONGE-R	SCRABBLE-R	STRANGLE-R	TREPHINE-R	WOMANISE-R
PARALYZE-R	PUNCTURE-R	SCRAMBLE-R	STRUGGLE-R	TRICYCLE-R	WOMANIZE-R

2→3

S-AD	S-AN	S-AX	S-EL	S-IN	S-KY	S-OD	S-OS	S-OY	S-UP
S-AE	S-AR	S-AY	S-EN	S-IS	S-MA	S-OH	S-OU	S-PA	S-UR
S-AI	S-AT	S-EA	S-EX	S-IT	S-NY	S-ON	S-OW	S-UM	S-US
S-AM	S-AW	S-EE	S-HE	S-KA	S-OB	S-OP	S-OX	S-UN	S-YE

3→4

S-AGA	S-AVE	S-EEK	S-HAT	S-INK	S-LID	S-NOD	S-ORB	S-PIN	S-UDS
S-AGE	S-AWN	S-EEL	S-HAW	S-INS	S-LIP	S-NOG	S-ORD	S-PIT	S-UNS
S-AGO	S-AYS	S-EEN	S-HAY	S-IRE	S-LIT	S-NOT	S-ORE	S-POT	S-UPS
S-AID	S-CAB	S-EGO	S-HES	S-ITS	S-LOB	S-NOW	S-ORT	S-PRY	S-URD
S-AIL	S-CAD	S-EIK	S-HET	S-KAS	S-LOG	S-NUB	S-OUK	S-PUD	S-URE
S-AIM	S-CAM	S-ELD	S-HEW	S-KAT	S-LOP	S-NYE	S-OUP	S-PUN	S-WAD
S-AIN	S-CAN	S-ELF	S-HIM	S-KAW	S-LOT	S-OAK	S-OUR	S-PUR	S-WAG
S-AIR	S-CAR	S-ELL	S-HIN	S-KEG	S-LOW	S-OAR	S-OUT	S-TAB	S-WAN
S-AIS	S-CAT	S-ELS	S-HIP	S-KEP	S-LUG	S-OBS	S-OWL	S-TAG	S-WAP
S-AKE	S-CAW	S-EME	S-HIT	S-KID	S-LUM	S-OCA	S-OWN	S-TAP	S-WAT
S-ALE	S-COG	S-END	S-HOD	S-KIN	S-LUR	S-ODA	S-OYS	S-TAR	S-WAY
S-ALP	S-COP	S-ENS	S-HOE	S-KIP	S-MEW	S-ODS	S-PAM	S-TAW	S-WEE
S-ALS	S-COT	S-ERA	S-HOG	S-KIT	S-MIR	S-OFT	S-PAN	S-TAY	S-WEY
S-ALT	S-COW	S-ERE	S-HOO	S-LAB	S-MOG	S-OHO	S-PAR	S-TED	S-WIG
S-AMP	S-CRY	S-ERF	S-HOP	S-LAG	S-MUG	S-OIL	S-PAS	S-TEN	S-WOP
S-AND	S-CUD	S-ERK	S-HOT	S-LAM	S-NAB	S-OKE	S-PAT	S-TEW	S-WOT
S-ANE	S-CUM	S-ERR	S-HOW	S-LAP	S-NAG	S-OLD	S-PAW	S-TIE	S-YEN
S-ANT	S-CUP	S-ESS	S-HUT	S-LAT	S-NAP	S-OLE	S-PAY	S-TOP	S-YES
S-ARD	S-CUR	S-ETA	S-ICE	S-LAW	S-NEB	S-ONE	S-PEC	S-TOT	
S-ARK	S-CUT	S-HAD	S-ICH	S-LAY	S-NED	S-ONS	S-PED	S-TOW	
S-ARS	S-EAN	S-HAG	S-IDE	S-LED	S-NEE	S-OOM	S-PET	S-TUB	
S-ASH	S-EAR	S-HAH	S-ILK	S-LEE	S-NIB	S-OON	S-PEW	S-TUM	
S-ASS	S-EAS	S-HAM	S-ILL	S-LEW	S-NIP	S-OOP	S-PIC	S-TUN	
S-ATE	S-EAT	S-HAN	S-IMP	S-LEY	S-NOB	S-OPS	S-PIE	S-TYE	

4→5

S-ABLE	S-AWED	S-CONE	S-CURS	S-EXES	S-HEAL	S-HOON	S-IRES	S-LAKE
S-AGAS	S-AXES	S-COOP	S-CUTE	S-HACK	S-HEAR	S-HOOT	S-IRIS	S-LAMS
S-AGES	S-CABS	S-COOT	S-CUTS	S-HADE	S-HEEL	S-HOPE	S-KAIL	S-LANE
S-AIDS	S-CADS	S-COPE	S-EANS	S-HADS	S-HELL	S-HOPS	S-KART	S-LANG
S-AILS	S-CAFF	S-CORE	S-EARS	S-HAFT	S-HEND	S-HORE	S-KATS	S-LANT
S-AIMS	S-CALL	S-CORN	S-EASE	S-HAGS	S-HENT	S-HORN	S-KAWS	S-LAPS
S-AINE	S-CALP	S-COTS	S-EATS	S-HAKE	S-HERD	S-HOTE	S-KEGS	S-LASH
S-AIRS	S-CAMP	S-COUP	S-ECCO	S-HALE	S-HERE	S-HOTS	S-KELL	S-LATE
S-AKES	S-CAMS	S-COUR	S-EDGE	S-HALL	S-HETS	S-HOUT	S-KEPS	S-LATS
S-ALES	S-CANS	S-COWL	S-EDGY	S-HALM	S-HEWN	S-HOVE	S-KIDS	S-LAVE
S-ALLY	S-CANT	S-COWP	S-EELS	S-HALT	S-HEWS	S-HOWS	S-KIER	S-LAWS
S-ALPS	S-CAPA	S-COWS	S-EELY	S-HAME	S-HIED	S-HUCK	S-KILL	S-LAYS
S-ALTO	S-CAPE	S-CRAB	S-EGOS	S-HAMS	S-HIES	S-HULE	S-KINK	S-LEEK
S-ALTS	S-CAPI	S-CRAG	S-EINE	S-HAND	S-HILL	S-HUNT	S-KINS	S-LEEP
S-AMBO	S-CARE	S-CRAM	S-ELFS	S-HANK	S-HINS	S-HUSH	S-KIPS	S-LEER
S-AMEN	S-CARP	S-CRAN	S-ELLS	S-HAPS	S-HIPS	S-HUTS	S-KITE	S-LEET
S-AMPS	S-CARS	S-CRAP	S-ENDS	S-HARD	S-HIRE	S-ICES	S-KITS	S-LEYS
S-ANDS	S-CART	S-CRAW	S-ENVY	S-HARE	S-HITS	S-IDES	S-KOFF	S-LICE
S-ANTS	S-CATS	S-CREE	S-ERED	S-HARK	S-HIVE	S-IDLE	S-KYTE	S-LICK
S-ARDS	S-CAUP	S-CREW	S-ERES	S-HARN	S-HOCK	S-ILEX	S-LABS	S-LIER
S-ARED	S-CAWS	S-CRIM	S-ERIC	S-HARP	S-HOED	S-ILKS	S-LACK	S-LILY
S-ARIS	S-CENT	S-CROW	S-ERKS	S-HASH	S-HOER	S-ILLS	S-LADE	S-LIME
S-ARKS	S-CION	S-CUDS	S-ERRS	S-HAVE	S-HOES	S-ILLY	S-LAGS	S-LIMY
S-AUNT	S-COFF	S-CUFF	S-EVEN	S-HAWM	S-HOGS	S-IMPS	S-LAID	S-LING
S-AVER	S-COGS	S-CULL	S-EVER	S-HAWS	S-HONE	S-INKS	S-LAIN	S-LINK
S-AVES	S-COLD	S-CUPS	S-EWER	S-HAYS	S-HOOK	S-INKY	S-LAIN	S-LIPS

S-LIVE	S-MITE	S-NUFF	S-PARD	S-PINA	S-TABS	S-TENT	S-TREW	S-WEAL
S-LOAN	S-MOCK	S-NYES	S-PARE	S-PINE	S-TACK	S-TERN	S-TRIG	S-WEAR
S-LOBS	S-MOGS	S-OAKS	S-PARK	S-PINK	S-TAGS	S-TEWS	S-TRIP	S-WEED
S-LOGS	S-MOKE	S-OARS	S-PARS	S-PINS	S-TAKE	S-TICH	S-TROW	S-WEEL
S-LOID	S-MOKO	S-OCAS	S-PART	S-PINY	S-TALE	S-TICK	S-TROY	S-WEEP
S-LOOM	S-MOLT	S-ODAS	S-PATE	S-PITS	S-TALK	S-TIED	S-TUBS	S-WEER
S-LOOP	S-MOOR	S-ODIC	S-PATS	S-PLAT	S-TALL	S-TIES	S-TUCK	S-WEES
S-LOOT	S-MOOT	S-OILS	S-PAUL	S-PLAY	S-TAMP	S-TIFF	S-TUFF	S-WEET
S-LOPE	S-MORE	S-OILY	S-PAWL	S-POKE	S-TANE	S-TILE	S-TUMP	S-WEIR
S-LOPS	S-MOTE	S-OKES	S-PAWN	S-POOF	S-TANG	S-TILL	S-TUMS	S-WELL
S-LOSH	S-MUGS	S-OLDS	S-PAWS	S-POOK	S-TANK	S-TILT	S-TUNS	S-WELT
S-LOTH	S-NABS	S-OLID	S-PAYS	S-POOL	S-TAPS	S-TIME	S-TYED	S-WEPT
S-LOTS	S-NAGS	S-ONCE	S-PEAK	S-POON	S-TARE	S-TING	S-TYES	S-WEYS
S-LOVE	S-NAIL	S-ONES	S-PEAL	S-POOR	S-TARN	S-TINK	S-TYRE	S-WIGS
S-LOWS	S-NAPS	S-OOMS	S-PEAN	S-POOT	S-TARS	S-TINT	S-TYTE	S-WILL
S-LUES	S-NARE	S-OOPS	S-PEAR	S-PORE	S-TART	S-TIRE	S-UMPH	S-WINE
S-LUGS	S-NARK	S-ORAL	S-PEAT	S-PORT	S-TASH	S-TOCK	S-URDS	S-WING
S-LUIT	S-NARY	S-ORBS	S-PECK	S-POSH	S-TATE	S-TOKE	S-URES	S-WINK
S-LUMP	S-NEAP	S-ORDS	S-PECS	S-POTS	S-TAWS	S-TOLE	S-URGE	S-WIPE
S-LUMS	S-NEBS	S-ORES	S-PEED	S-POUT	S-TAYS	S-TONE	S-USES	S-WIRE
S-LUNG	S-NECK	S-ORRA	S-PEEL	S-PRAD	S-TEAD	S-TONG	S-WACK	S-WISH
S-LURS	S-NEDS	S-ORTS	S-PEER	S-PRAT	S-TEAK	S-TONK	S-WADS	S-WITH
S-LUSH	S-NEED	S-OUKS	S-PELL	S-PRAY	S-TEAL	S-TONY	S-WAGE	S-WITS
S-MACK	S-NIBS	S-OUPS	S-PELT	S-PREE	S-TEAM	S-TOOK	S-WAGS	S-WIVE
S-MAIK	S-NICK	S-OURS	S-PEND	S-PRIG	S-TEAR	S-TOOL	S-WAIN	S-WOON
S-MALL	S-NIDE	S-OUTS	S-PENT	S-PROD	S-TEDS	S-TOPE	S-WALE	S-WOPS
S-MALM	S-NIES	S-OWED	S-PERM	S-PROG	S-TEED	S-TOPS	S-WALY	S-WORD
S-MALT	S-NIFF	S-OWER	S-PETS	S-PUDS	S-TEEL	S-TORE	S-WANG	S-WORE
S-MARM	S-NIPS	S-OWLS	S-PEWS	S-PULE	S-TEEM	S-TOSS	S-WANK	S-WORN
S-MART	S-NOBS	S-PACE	S-PICA	S-PUMY	S-TEEN	S-TOTS	S-WANS	S-WOTS
S-MASH	S-NODS	S-PACY	S-PICE	S-PUNK	S-TEER	S-TOUN	S-WAPS	S-YENS
S-MEEK	S-NOGS	S-PAIN	S-PICK	S-PURS	S-TEIL	S-TOUR	S-WARD	
S-MELL	S-NOOK	S-PALE	S-PICS	S-PYRE	S-TELA	S-TOUT	S-WARE	
S-MELT	S-NOOP	S-PALL	S-PIED	S-QUAD	S-TELL	S-TOWN	S-WARM	
S-MEWS	S-NOUT	S-PAMS	S-PIES	S-QUAT	S-TEME	S-TOWS	S-WART	
S-MILE	S-NOWS	S-PANE	S-PIKE	S-QUID	S-TEMS	S-TRAD	S-WASH	
S-MIRK	S-NOWY	S-PANG	S-PILE	S-QUIT	S-TEND	S-TRAP	S-WATS	
S-MIRS	S-NUBS	S-PANS	S-PILL	S-QUIZ	S-TENS	S-TRAY	S-WAYS	

5→6

S-ABLED	S-CAPED	S-CRAMS	S-ELFED	S-HEALS	S-IDLES	S-LEECH	S-MALTS
S-ABLES	S-CAPES	S-CRANS	S-ELVES	S-HEARS	S-IMPLY	S-LEEKS	S-MARMS
S-ACRED	S-CARED	S-CRAPE	S-ENATE	S-HEATH	S-INGLE	S-LEEPS	S-MARTS
S-ADDER	S-CARER	S-CRAPS	S-ENDED	S-HEAVE	S-INKER	S-LEETS	S-MATCH
S-ADDLE	S-CARES	S-CRAWL	S-ENTRY	S-HEELS	S-INNED	S-LICKS	S-MEATH
S-AGENE	S-CARPS	S-CRAWS	S-ERING	S-HELLS	S-INNER	S-LIGHT	S-MELLS
S-AGGER	S-CARRY	S-CREAK	S-ERRED	S-HELVE	S-INTER	S-LIMED	S-MELTS
S-AILED	S-CARTS	S-CREAM	S-ESSES	S-HENDS	S-KAILS	S-LIMES	S-MEUSE
S-AIRED	S-CATCH	S-CREED	S-ETTLE	S-HERDS	S-KARTS	S-LINGS	S-MIDDY
S-AIRER	S-CATTY	S-CREES	S-EVENS	S-HERRY	S-KELLS	S-LINKS	S-MIGHT
S-ALARY	S-CAUPS	S-CREWS	S-EVERY	S-HEUCH	S-KELLY	S-LIPPY	S-MILER
S-ALINE	S-CENTS	S-CRIED	S-EWERS	S-HEUGH	S-KELPS	S-LIVED	S-MILES
S-ALLEE	S-CERNE	S-CRIES	S-EXIST	S-HEWED	S-KETCH	S-LIVEN	S-MIRKS
S-ALLOW	S-CHOUT	S-CRIMP	S-HACKS	S-HEWER	S-KIERS	S-LIVER	S-MITER
S-ALTER	S-CIONS	S-CRIMS	S-HADED	S-HILLS	S-KILLS	S-LIVES	S-MITES
S-ALTOS	S-CLAVE	S-CRINE	S-HADES	S-HINNY	S-KINKS	S-LOANS	S-MOCKS
S-AMBOS	S-CLIFF	S-CROWS	S-HAFTS	S-HIPPO	S-KITED	S-LOBBY	S-MOGGY
S-AMPLE	S-COFFS	S-CRUMP	S-HAKES	S-HIRES	S-KITES	S-LOGAN	S-MOKES
S-APPLE	S-COLDS	S-CUFFS	S-HALED	S-HIVER	S-KOFFS	S-LOIDS	S-MOKOS
S-ARGUS	S-CONES	S-CULLS	S-HALES	S-HIVES	S-KRANS	S-LOOMS	S-MOLTS
S-ASHES	S-COOPS	S-CURRY	S-HALMS	S-HOCKS	S-KYTES	S-LOOPS	S-MOOCH
S-ASSES	S-COOTS	S-CURVY	S-HAMED	S-HOERS	S-LACKS	S-LOOTS	S-MOORS
S-AUGER	S-COPED	S-CUTCH	S-HAMES	S-HONKY	S-LADES	S-LOPED	S-MOOTS
S-AUNTS	S-COPES	S-CUTES	S-HAMMY	S-HOOKS	S-LAKED	S-LOPES	S-MORES
S-AVANT	S-CORED	S-DAINE	S-HANDS	S-HOOTS	S-LAKES	S-LOUGH	S-MOUCH
S-AVERS	S-CORER	S-DEIGN	S-HANDY	S-HOPPY	S-LANES	S-LOWED	S-MOUSE
S-AVINE	S-CORES	S-EANED	S-HANKS	S-HOUGH	S-LANTS	S-LOWER	S-MOYLE
S-AWING	S-CORIA	S-EARED	S-HARDS	S-HOUTS	S-LATCH	S-LOWLY	S-MUDGE
S-CABBY	S-CORNS	S-EASED	S-HARED	S-HOVED	S-LATED	S-LUMMY	S-MURRY
S-CAFFS	S-CORSE	S-EASES	S-HARES	S-HOVEL	S-LATER	S-LUMPS	S-MUTCH
S-CALLS	S-COUPS	S-EATER	S-HARKS	S-HOVER	S-LAVED	S-LUMPY	S-NAGGY
S-CALPS	S-COURS	S-EDGED	S-HARNS	S-HOVES	S-LAVER	S-LURRY	S-NAILS
S-CAMEL	S-COUTH	S-EDGES	S-HARPS	S-HUCKS	S-LAVES	S-LUSHY	S-NAKED
S-CAMPS	S-COWLS	S-EDILE	S-HAVEN	S-HULES	S-LAYER	S-MACKS	S-NAPPY
S-CANTS	S-COWPS	S-EDUCE	S-HAVER	S-HUNTS	S-LEAVE	S-MAIKS	S-NARES
S-CANTY	S-CRABS	S-EGGAR	S-HAVES	S-HYING	S-LEAZE	S-MALLS	S-NARKS
S-CAPAS	S-CRAGS	S-ELECT	S-HAWMS	S-ICKER	S-LEDGE	S-MALMS	S-NATCH
				S-IDLED			

S-NEAPS	S-PACES	S-PERST	S-PREES	S-TARES	S-TIMED	S-TREWS	S-WAINS
S-NEATH	S-PACEY	S-PHENE	S-PRENT	S-TARNS	S-TIMES	S-TRIDE	S-WALED
S-NECKS	S-PAINS	S-PICAS	S-PRIGS	S-TARRY	S-TINGS	S-TRIGS	S-WALES
S-NEEZE	S-PALES	S-PICKS	S-PRINT	S-TARTS	S-TINKS	S-TRIKE	S-WANKS
S-NELLY	S-PALLS	S-PIGHT	S-PRODS	S-TATER	S-TINTS	S-TRIPE	S-WANKY
S-NICKS	S-PANED	S-PIKED	S-PROGS	S-TATES	S-TINTY	S-TRIPS	S-WARDS
S-NIDES	S-PANES	S-PIKES	S-PRONG	S-TATUS	S-TIRED	S-TRIPY	S-WARMS
S-NIFFS	S-PANGS	S-PILED	S-PRYER	S-TAWED	S-TIRES	S-TRODE	S-WARTY
S-NIFFY	S-PARED	S-PILES	S-PUDDY	S-TEADS	S-TITCH	S-TROKE	S-WASHY
S-NIFTY	S-PARER	S-PILLS	S-PULES	S-TEAKS	S-TOCKS	S-TROLL	S-WATCH
S-NIPPY	S-PARES	S-PINAS	S-PUNKS	S-TEALS	S-TOKED	S-TROUT	S-WAYED
S-NOBBY	S-PARGE	S-PINED	S-PURGE	S-TEAMS	S-TOKES	S-TROWS	S-WEALS
S-NOOKS	S-PARKS	S-PINES	S-PYRES	S-TEARS	S-TOLED	S-TROYS	S-WEARS
S-NOOPS	S-PARKY	S-PINKS	S-QUADS	S-TEDDY	S-TOLES	S-TRUCK	S-WEELS
S-NOWED	S-PARRY	S-PINNY	S-QUAIL	S-TEELS	S-TONED	S-TUBBY	S-WEENY
S-NUBBY	S-PARSE	S-PINTO	S-QUARE	S-TEEMS	S-TONER	S-TUCKS	S-WEEPS
S-NUDGE	S-PARTS	S-PLASH	S-QUASH	S-TEENS	S-TONES	S-TUFFS	S-WEEPY
S-NUFFS	S-PATES	S-PLATS	S-QUATS	S-TEERS	S-TONKS	S-TUMPS	S-WEETS
S-OAKEN	S-PAULS	S-PLAYS	S-QUIDS	S-TEILS	S-TONNE	S-TUMPY	S-WELLS
S-OAKER	S-PAVIN	S-POKED	S-QUIFF	S-TELAE	S-TOOLS	S-TYING	S-WELTS
S-OARED	S-PAWLS	S-POKES	S-QUILL	S-TELLS	S-TOPED	S-TYRED	S-WILLS
S-ODIUM	S-PAWNS	S-PONGY	S-QUINT	S-TEMED	S-TOPES	S-TYRES	S-WINGE
S-OFTEN	S-PAYED	S-POOFS	S-QUIRE	S-TEMES	S-TORES	S-UDDER	S-WINGS
S-OILED	S-PEAKS	S-POOKS	S-QUIRT	S-TENCH	S-TOUNS	S-UNBED	S-WINGY
S-OLDER	S-PEALS	S-POOLS	S-QUITS	S-TENDS	S-TOURS	S-UNDER	S-WINKS
S-OLEIN	S-PEANS	S-POONS	S-TABLE	S-TENTS	S-TOUTS	S-UNHAT	S-WIPED
S-OLIVE	S-PEARS	S-POOTS	S-TACKS	S-TERES	S-TOWED	S-UNKET	S-WIPER
S-OMBRE	S-PEATS	S-PORES	S-TAKES	S-TERNS	S-TOWER	S-UNLIT	S-WIPES
S-ONCES	S-PECKS	S-PORTS	S-TALER	S-TEWED	S-TRADS	S-UNSET	S-WIRES
S-OOPED	S-PEELS	S-PORTY	S-TALES	S-TICKS	S-TRAIK	S-UPPED	S-WITCH
S-ORBED	S-PEERS	S-POTTY	S-TALKS	S-TICKY	S-TRAIN	S-UPPER	S-WIVED
S-OUGHT	S-PELLS	S-POUTS	S-TALKY	S-TIFFS	S-TRAIT	S-URGED	S-WIVES
S-OUTER	S-PELTS	S-POUTY	S-TAMPS	S-TILED	S-TRAMP	S-URGES	S-WOONS
S-OWING	S-PENCE	S-PRANG	S-TANGS	S-TILES	S-TRAPS	S-UTILE	S-WOOSH
S-OWLED	S-PENDS	S-PRATS	S-TANKS	S-TILLS	S-TRASS	S-WADDY	S-WORDS
S-PACED	S-PERMS	S-PRAYS	S-TAPES	S-TILLY	S-TRAYS	S-WAGED	S-WOUND
S-PACER	S-PERSE	S-PREED	S-TARED	S-TILTS	S-TRESS	S-WAGES	

6→7

S-ABLING	S-CERNED	S-CREWED	S-ELFISH	S-HELLED	S-INKING	S-LEAZES	S-MASHED
S-ACKERS	S-CERNES	S-CRIMPS	S-ENDING	S-HELLER	S-INNERS	S-LEDGER	S-MASHER
S-ADDLED	S-CHOUTS	S-CRIMPY	S-ENSATE	S-HELVED	S-INNING	S-LEDGES	S-MASHES
S-ADDLES	S-CLAVES	S-CRINES	S-ENSILE	S-HELVES	S-INTERS	S-LENDER	S-MATTER
S-AGENES	S-CLIFFS	S-CRUMMY	S-ENVIES	S-HEUCHS	S-IRENIC	S-LICKED	S-MEATHS
S-AGGERS	S-COFFED	S-CRUMPS	S-ERRING	S-HEUGHS	S-JAMBOK	S-LICKER	S-MELLED
S-AILING	S-COFFER	S-CRUMPY	S-ETTLED	S-HEWING	S-KELTER	S-LIGHTS	S-MELTED
S-AIRING	S-COGGED	S-CRUNCH	S-ETTLES	S-HIDDER	S-KIDDED	S-LIMIER	S-MEUSES
S-ALINES	S-COLDER	S-CRYING	S-EXISTS	S-HILLED	S-KIDDER	S-LIMING	S-MIGHTS
S-ALLEES	S-COLLOP	S-CUDDLE	S-EXPERT	S-HIPPED	S-KILLED	S-LIMMER	S-MILERS
S-ALLIED	S-COOPED	S-CUFFED	S-EXTANT	S-HIPPEN	S-KIMMER	S-LINGER	S-MITERS
S-ALLIES	S-COOPER	S-CUFFLE	S-HACKLE	S-HIPPER	S-KINKED	S-LINKER	S-MITTEN
S-ALLOWS	S-COPING	S-CULLED	S-HADING	S-HIPPOS	S-KIPPED	S-LINTER	S-MOCKED
S-ALTERN	S-COPULA	S-CULLER	S-HAFTED	S-HIVERS	S-KIPPER	S-LIPPED	S-MOILED
S-ALTERS	S-CORERS	S-CUMBER	S-HAGGED	S-HOCKED	S-KITING	S-LITHER	S-MOORED
S-AMPLER	S-CORING	S-CUMMER	S-HALING	S-HOCKER	S-KITTLE	S-LITTER	S-MOOTED
S-APPLES	S-CORNED	S-CUNNER	S-HALLOW	S-HOEING	S-LACKED	S-LIVERS	S-MOTHER
S-ARKING	S-CORNER	S-CUPPER	S-HAMBLE	S-HOGGED	S-LACKER	S-LIVING	S-MOUSED
S-AUGERS	S-CORSES	S-CURRED	S-HAMING	S-HOOTER	S-LAGGED	S-LOGANS	S-MOUSER
S-AUNTER	S-COUPED	S-CUTTER	S-HAMMED	S-HOPPED	S-LAKING	S-LOGGED	S-MOUSES
S-CALLED	S-COURED	S-CUTTLE	S-HAMMER	S-HOPPER	S-LAMMED	S-LOGGER	S-MOYLED
S-CAMELS	S-COURSE	S-CUZZES	S-HANKED	S-HOTTED	S-LAMMER	S-LOOMED	S-MOYLES
S-CAMMED	S-COUTER	S-DAINED	S-HARING	S-HOUGHS	S-LANDER	S-LOPING	S-MUDGED
S-CAMPED	S-COWLED	S-DAINES	S-HARKED	S-HOUTED	S-LANGER	S-LOPPED	S-MUDGER
S-CAMPER	S-COWPED	S-DEIGNS	S-HARPED	S-HOVELS	S-LAPPED	S-LOTTED	S-MUDGES
S-CANNED	S-COWRIE	S-EANING	S-HARPER	S-HOVERS	S-LAPPER	S-LOUGHS	S-MUGGED
S-CANNER	S-CRAGGY	S-EARING	S-HASHED	S-HOVING	S-LASHED	S-LOWEST	S-MUGGER
S-CANTED	S-CRANCH	S-EASING	S-HASHES	S-HUNTED	S-LASHER	S-LOWING	S-NAGGED
S-CANTER	S-CRANNY	S-EATERS	S-HATTER	S-HUNTER	S-LASHES	S-LUBBER	S-NAILED
S-CANTLE	S-CRAPES	S-EATING	S-HAVERS	S-HUSHED	S-LATHER	S-LUGGED	S-NAPPED
S-CAPING	S-CRAPPY	S-EDGIER	S-HAVING	S-HUSHES	S-LATTER	S-LUGGER	S-NAPPER
S-CARERS	S-CRATCH	S-EDUCED	S-HEALED	S-IDLING	S-LAVERS	S-LUMBER	S-NEAPED
S-CARING	S-CRAWLS	S-EDUCES	S-HEARER	S-IGNORE	S-LAVING	S-LUMPED	S-NEBBED
S-CARPED	S-CRAWLY	S-EELIER	S-HEATHS	S-ILEXES	S-LAVISH	S-LUSHED	S-NECKED
S-CARPER	S-CREAKS	S-EGGARS	S-HEATHY	S-IMPLEX	S-LAYERS	S-LUSHES	S-NEEZED
S-CARTED	S-CREAKY	S-ELECTS	S-HEAVED	S-INGLES	S-LAYING	S-MALLED	S-NEEZES
S-CARVES	S-CREAMS	S-ELFING	S-HEAVES	S-INKERS	S-LEAVED	S-MARTED	S-NIBBED
S-CATTED	S-CREEDS		S-HEELED	S-INKIER	S-LEAVES	S-MARTEN	S-NICKED

S-NICKER	S-PANNED	S-PILLED	S-QUIRTS	S-TELLAR	S-TOOLED	S-ULLAGE	S-WATTER
S-NIFFED	S-PARERS	S-PINIER	S-QUITCH	S-TEMPLE	S-TOPING	S-UNBEDS	S-WAYING
S-NIFFER	S-PARGED	S-PINNER	S-TABBED	S-TENDED	S-TOPPED	S-UNBELT	S-WEARER
S-NIGGER	S-PARGES	S-PINNET	S-TABLED	S-TENTED	S-TOPPER	S-UNDECK	S-WEEING
S-NIGGLE	S-PARING	S-PITTED	S-TABLES	S-TERNAL	S-TOPPLE	S-UNHATS	S-WEEPER
S-NIPPED	S-PARKED	S-PITTEN	S-TACKED	S-TERNED	S-TOSSES	S-UNLESS	S-WEETED
S-NIPPER	S-PARKIE	S-PITTER	S-TACKER	S-TEWING	S-TOTTED	S-UNLIKE	S-WEETEN
S-NODDED	S-PARKLY	S-PLASHY	S-TACKET	S-TIBIAL	S-TOTTER	S-UNROOF	S-WEETER
S-NODDER	S-PARSER	S-PLAYED	S-TAGGED	S-TICKED	S-TOUTER	S-UNSETS	S-WELLED
S-NOGGED	S-PARTAN	S-PODIUM	S-TAGGER	S-TICKER	S-TOWAGE	S-UNSUIT	S-WELTED
S-NUBBED	S-PATHED	S-PONGED	S-TAKING	S-TICKLE	S-TOWERS	S-UNWISE	S-WELTER
S-NUDGED	S-PATHIC	S-POOLED	S-TALKED	S-TIFFED	S-TOWING	S-UPPERS	S-WIGGED
S-NUDGES	S-PATTED	S-POORER	S-TALKER	S-TILING	S-TRAIKS	S-UPPING	S-WILLED
S-NUZZLE	S-PATTEE	S-PORTED	S-TAMPED	S-TILLED	S-TRAINS	S-URGENT	S-WILLER
S-OAKERS	S-PATTER	S-PORTER	S-TAMPER	S-TILLER	S-TRAITS	S-URGING	S-WINDLE
S-OARING	S-PAVINS	S-POSHES	S-TANGED	S-TILTED	S-TRAMPS	S-WADDLE	S-WINERY
S-ODIUMS	S-PAWNED	S-POTTED	S-TANNIC	S-TILTER	S-TRAPPY	S-WAGGED	S-WINGED
S-OILIER	S-PAWNER	S-POTTER	S-TAPPED	S-TIMING	S-TRIKES	S-WAGING	S-WINGER
S-OILING	S-PAYING	S-POUTED	S-TARING	S-TINGED	S-TRIPES	S-WALIER	S-WINGES
S-OLIVES	S-PEANED	S-POUTER	S-TARRED	S-TINKER	S-TRIPEY	S-WALING	S-WINKED
S-OMBRES	S-PECKED	S-PRAYED	S-TARTER	S-TINTED	S-TROKED	S-WALLET	S-WIPERS
S-OOPING	S-PEELED	S-PRAYER	S-TARTLY	S-TINTER	S-TROKES	S-WALLOW	S-WIPING
S-ORBING	S-PEELER	S-PRINTS	S-TASHED	S-TIPPLE	S-TROLLS	S-WANKED	S-WISHED
S-OUTERS	S-PEERED	S-PURGES	S-TASHES	S-TIRING	S-TROUTS	S-WANKER	S-WISHER
S-OUTHER	S-PELTER	S-PURRED	S-TATERS	S-TIRRED	S-TROWED	S-WANNED	S-WISHES
S-OWLING	S-PENCES	S-PUTTER	S-TATUED	S-TOCKED	S-TUBBED	S-WAPPED	S-WITCHY
S-PACERS	S-PERSES	S-QUAILS	S-TAWING	S-TOKING	S-TUMBLE	S-WAPPER	S-WITHER
S-PACIER	S-PHENES	S-QUARER	S-TEAMED	S-TONERS	S-TUMPED	S-WARDED	S-WIVING
S-PACING	S-PHENIC	S-QUELCH	S-TEAMER	S-TONIER	S-TUNNED	S-WARMED	S-WOONED
S-PAINED	S-PICKER	S-QUILLS	S-TEDDED	S-TONIES	S-TUSHIE	S-WARMER	S-WOPPED
S-PALLED	S-PIGHTS	S-QUINTS	S-TEEMED	S-TONING	S-UCKERS	S-WASHED	S-WORDED
S-PANGED	S-PIKING	S-QUIRED	S-TEENED	S-TONKER	S-UDDERS	S-WASHER	S-WOTTED
S-PANING	S-PILING	S-QUIRES	S-TEERED	S-TONNES	S-UGGING	S-WASHES	S-WOUNDS

7→8

S-ADDLING	S-COURSES	S-DEIGNED	S-HELLIER	S-KITTLES	S-LUMMIER	S-NAPPIER
S-ALLOWED	S-COUTERS	S-EARINGS	S-HELLING	S-LACKERS	S-LUMPIER	S-NAPPING
S-ALLYING	S-COUTHER	S-EATINGS	S-HELVING	S-LACKING	S-LUMPING	S-NATCHES
S-ANGUINE	S-COWLING	S-EDGIEST	S-HENDING	S-LAGGING	S-LURRIES	S-NEAPING
S-ARGUSES	S-COWPING	S-EDITION	S-HERRIES	S-LAMMERS	S-LUSHIER	S-NEBBING
S-AUNTERS	S-COWRIES	S-EDUCING	S-HIDDERS	S-LAMMING	S-LUSHING	S-NECKING
S-CAMMING	S-CRABBED	S-EDUCTOR	S-HILLING	S-LANDERS	S-MALLING	S-NEEZING
S-CAMPERS	S-CRAGGED	S-EELIEST	S-HINNIED	S-LAPPERS	S-MARTENS	S-NIBBING
S-CAMPING	S-CRAMMED	S-ELECTED	S-HINNIES	S-LAPPING	S-MARTING	S-NICKERS
S-CANDENT	S-CRAPPED	S-ELECTOR	S-HIPPENS	S-LASHERS	S-MASHERS	S-NICKING
S-CANNERS	S-CRAWLED	S-ELFHOOD	S-HIPPING	S-LASHING	S-MASHING	S-NIFFERS
S-CANNING	S-CRAWLER	S-ENDINGS	S-HITTING	S-LATCHES	S-MATCHED	S-NIFFIER
S-CANTEST	S-CREAKED	S-ENTRIES	S-HOCKERS	S-LATHERS	S-MATCHES	S-NIFFING
S-CANTIER	S-CREAMED	S-ETTLING	S-HOCKING	S-LEAVING	S-MATTERS	S-NIFTIER
S-CANTING	S-CREAMER	S-EXPERTS	S-HOGGING	S-LEDGERS	S-MEARING	S-NIGGERS
S-CANTLED	S-CREWING	S-FORZATI	S-HOOTERS	S-LEECHES	S-MELLING	S-NIGGLED
S-CANTLES	S-CRIBBLE	S-FORZATO	S-HOOTING	S-LEEPING	S-MELTING	S-NIGGLER
S-CARIOUS	S-CRIMPED	S-HACKLED	S-HOPPERS	S-LICKERS	S-MIDDIES	S-NIGGLES
S-CARPERS	S-CRUMPED	S-HACKLES	S-HOPPIER	S-LICKING	S-MITHERS	S-NIPPERS
S-CARPING	S-CRUNCHY	S-HADDOCK	S-HOPPING	S-LIGHTED	S-MOCKING	S-NIPPIER
S-CARRIER	S-CRYINGS	S-HAFTING	S-HOTTING	S-LIGHTER	S-MOILING	S-NIPPING
S-CARTING	S-CUDDLED	S-HAGGING	S-HOUTING	S-LIGHTLY	S-MOOCHED	S-NOBBIER
S-CATCHES	S-CUDDLES	S-HALLOWS	S-HUNTERS	S-LIMIEST	S-MOOCHES	S-NODDING
S-CATTERY	S-CUFFING	S-HAMBLED	S-HUNTING	S-LIMMERS	S-MOORING	S-NOGGING
S-CATTIER	S-CUFFLED	S-HAMBLES	S-HUSHING	S-LINGERS	S-MOOTING	S-NUBBIER
S-CATTING	S-CUFFLES	S-HAMMERS	S-HUTTING	S-LINKERS	S-MOTHERS	S-NUBBING
S-CERNING	S-CULLERS	S-HAMMING	S-IGNORES	S-LINKING	S-MOTHERY	S-NUDGING
S-CHAPPED	S-CULLING	S-HANKING	S-INKIEST	S-LINTERS	S-MOUCHED	S-NUZZLED
S-CHILLER	S-CULLION	S-HARKING	S-JAMBOKS	S-LIPPIER	S-MOUCHES	S-NUZZLES
S-COFFERS	S-CUMBERS	S-HARPERS	S-KELLIES	S-LIPPING	S-MOULDER	S-OFTENER
S-COFFING	S-CUMMERS	S-HARPIES	S-KELTERS	S-LITTERS	S-MOUSERS	S-OILIEST
S-COGGING	S-CUNNERS	S-HARPING	S-KEPPING	S-LOGGERS	S-MOUSING	S-OMNIFIC
S-COLLOPS	S-CUPPERS	S-HASHING	S-KETCHES	S-LOGGING	S-MOYLING	S-PACIEST
S-COOPERS	S-CURRIED	S-HATTERS	S-KIDDERS	S-LOOMING	S-MUDGERS	S-PAINING
S-COOPING	S-CURRIER	S-HAVINGS	S-KIDDING	S-LOPPING	S-MUDGING	S-PALLING
S-COPULAS	S-CURRIES	S-HEADING	S-KILLING	S-LOTTING	S-MUGGING	S-PANGING
S-CORIOUS	S-CURRING	S-HEALING	S-KIMMERS	S-LOWINGS	S-MUTCHES	S-PANNING
S-CORNERS	S-CURVIER	S-HEARERS	S-KINKING	S-LOWNESS	S-NAGGIER	S-PARABLE
S-CORNING	S-CUTCHES	S-HEARING	S-KINLESS	S-LUBBERS	S-NAGGING	S-PARGING
S-COUPING	S-CUTTERS	S-HEAVING	S-KIPPERS	S-LUGGERS	S-NAILERY	S-PARKIER
S-COURING	S-CUTTLES	S-HEELING	S-KIPPING	S-LUGGING	S-NAILING	S-PARKIES
S-COURSED	S-DAINING	S-HELLERS	S-KITTLED	S-LUMBERS	S-NAPPERS	S-PARKING

S-PARKISH	S-PLAYING	S-TABLING	S-TICKIES	S-TOPPLES	S-TUNNING	S-WATCHES
S-PARLING	S-PONGIER	S-TACKERS	S-TICKING	S-TOTTERS	S-TUSHIES	S-WEARERS
S-PARTANS	S-PONGING	S-TACKETS	S-TICKLED	S-TOTTING	S-UBEROUS	S-WEARING
S-PATTERS	S-PONTOON	S-TACKING	S-TICKLER	S-TOWAGES	S-ULLAGES	S-WEENIES
S-PATTING	S-POOKING	S-TAGGERS	S-TICKLES	S-TOWINGS	S-UNBAKED	S-WEEPERS
S-PAWNERS	S-POOLING	S-TAGGING	S-TIDDIES	S-TRAIKED	S-UNBELTS	S-WEEPIER
S-PAWNING	S-PORTERS	S-TALKERS	S-TIFFING	S-TRAINED	S-UNBLIND	S-WEEPING
S-PEAKING	S-PORTIER	S-TALKIER	S-TILLAGE	S-TRAINER	S-UNBLOCK	S-WEETEST
S-PEANING	S-PORTING	S-TALKING	S-TILLERS	S-TRAMMEL	S-UNBURNT	S-WEETING
S-PECKING	S-POTTERS	S-TALLAGE	S-TILLIER	S-TRAMPED	S-UNDECKS	S-WELLING
S-PEELERS	S-POTTIER	S-TAMPERS	S-TILLING	S-TRANGLE	S-UNDRESS	S-WELTERS
S-PEELING	S-POTTING	S-TAMPING	S-TILTERS	S-TRAPPED	S-UNROOFS	S-WELTING
S-PEERING	S-POUTERS	S-TANGING	S-TILTING	S-TRAPPER	S-UNSUITS	S-WIGGING
S-PELTERS	S-POUTIER	S-TANNATE	S-TINGING	S-TRASSES	S-URGINGS	S-WILLERS
S-PENDING	S-POUTING	S-TAPPING	S-TINKERS	S-TRESSED	S-WADDIES	S-WILLING
S-PERSING	S-PRATTLE	S-TARINGS	S-TINKING	S-TRESSES	S-WADDLED	S-WINDLES
S-PETTING	S-PRAYERS	S-TARRIER	S-TINTERS	S-TRICKLE	S-WADDLER	S-WINGERS
S-PIGHTED	S-PRAYING	S-TARRING	S-TINTIER	S-TRIDENT	S-WADDLES	S-WINGIER
S-PIKELET	S-PREEING	S-TARTISH	S-TINTING	S-TRIGGED	S-WAGGING	S-WINGING
S-PILINGS	S-PRIGGED	S-TASHING	S-TIPPLED	S-TRIPIER	S-WAINING	S-WINKING
S-PILLAGE	S-PRINTED	S-TEAMERS	S-TIPPLER	S-TRIPPED	S-WALIEST	S-WISHERS
S-PILLING	S-PRINTER	S-TEAMING	S-TIPPLES	S-TRIPPER	S-WALLETS	S-WISHING
S-PINIEST	S-PUDDING	S-TEARING	S-TIRRING	S-TROKING	S-WALLOWS	S-WISSING
S-PINNERS	S-PURLING	S-TEDDIES	S-TITCHES	S-TROLLED	S-WANKERS	S-WITCHED
S-PINNETS	S-PURRING	S-TEDDING	S-TOCCATA	S-TROLLER	S-WANKIER	S-WITCHES
S-PINNIES	S-PUTTERS	S-TEEMING	S-TOCKING	S-TROPHIC	S-WANKING	S-WITHERS
S-PINNING	S-QUAILED	S-TEENING	S-TONIEST	S-TROWING	S-WANNING	S-WOONING
S-PIRATED	S-QUAREST	S-TEERING	S-TONINGS	S-TRUMPET	S-WAPPERS	S-WOOSHED
S-PITCHER	S-QUASHED	S-TELLING	S-TONKERS	S-TUBBIER	S-WAPPING	S-WOOSHES
S-PITTERS	S-QUASHES	S-TEMPLES	S-TONKING	S-TUBBING	S-WARDING	S-WOPPING
S-PITTING	S-QUINIES	S-TENCHES	S-TOOLING	S-TUMBLED	S-WARMERS	S-WORDING
S-PLASHED	S-QUIRING	S-TENDING	S-TOPLESS	S-TUMBLER	S-WARMING	S-WOTTING
S-PLASHES	S-QUIRTED	S-TENTING	S-TOPPERS	S-TUMBLES	S-WASHERS	S-WOUNDED
S-PLATTED	S-QUIZZES	S-TERNING	S-TOPPING	S-TUMPIER	S-WASHIER	
S-PLATTER	S-TABBING	S-TICKERS	S-TOPPLED	S-TUMPING	S-WASHING	

8→9

S-ALLOWING	S-CURVIEST	S-LATHERED	S-PIGHTING	S-TANNATES	S-TROUTING
S-ARCOLOGY	S-DEIGNING	S-LAUGHTER	S-PIKELETS	S-TARRIEST	S-TRUMPETS
S-CANTIEST	S-EDITIONS	S-LAVISHLY	S-PILLAGES	S-TARRINGS	S-TUBBIEST
S-CANTLING	S-EDUCTION	S-LICKINGS	S-PILLINGS	S-TEAMINGS	S-TUMBLERS
S-CARPINGS	S-EDUCTORS	S-LIGHTEST	S-PINNINGS	S-TICKINGS	S-TUMBLING
S-CATTIEST	S-ELECTING	S-LIGHTING	S-PITTINGS	S-TICKLERS	S-TUMPIEST
S-CHILLERS	S-ELECTION	S-LIGHTISH	S-PLASHIER	S-TICKLING	S-TUNNINGS
S-CHILLING	S-ELECTIVE	S-LIMINESS	S-PLASHING	S-TILLAGES	S-UNBATHED
S-COPULATE	S-ELECTORS	S-LIPPIEST	S-PLATTERS	S-TILLIEST	S-UNBEATEN
S-COURSING	S-ELFHOODS	S-LUMBERED	S-PLATTING	S-TILLINGS	S-UNBLINDS
S-CRABBING	S-FORZANDI	S-LUMBERER	S-PONGIEST	S-TILTINGS	S-UNBLOCKS
S-CRAGGIER	S-FORZANDO	S-LUMMIEST	S-PONTOONS	S-TINTIEST	S-UNBURNED
S-CRAMMING	S-FORZATOS	S-LUMPIEST	S-PORTABLE	S-TINTINGS	S-UNSTRUCK
S-CRANCHED	S-GRAFFITI	S-LUSHINGS	S-PORTANCE	S-TINTLESS	S-UNTANNED
S-CRANCHES	S-GRAFFITO	S-MASHINGS	S-PORTIEST	S-TIPPLERS	S-WADDLERS
S-CRAPPIER	S-HACKLING	S-MATCHING	S-POTTIEST	S-TIPPLING	S-WADDLING
S-CRAPPING	S-HADDOCKS	S-MATTERED	S-POUTIEST	S-TOCCATAS	S-WALLOWED
S-CRATCHES	S-HALLOWED	S-MELTINGS	S-POUTINGS	S-TONELESS	S-WALLOWER
S-CRAWLERS	S-HAMBLING	S-MOCKINGS	S-PRATTLED	S-TOPPINGS	S-WANKIEST
S-CRAWLIER	S-HARPINGS	S-MOOCHING	S-PRATTLES	S-TOPPLING	S-WARMINGS
S-CRAWLING	S-HATTERED	S-MOTHERED	S-PRIGGING	S-TRAIKING	S-WASHIEST
S-CREAKIER	S-HEADINGS	S-MOUCHING	S-PRINTERS	S-TRAINERS	S-WASHINGS
S-CREAKING	S-HEALINGS	S-MOULDERS	S-PRINTING	S-TRAINING	S-WEARINGS
S-CREAMERS	S-HEARINGS	S-NAGGIEST	S-PUDDINGS	S-TRAMMELS	S-WEEPIEST
S-CREAMING	S-HEATHIER	S-NAPPIEST	S-PURLINGS	S-TRAMPING	S-WEEPINGS
S-CRIBBLED	S-HELLFIRE	S-NICKERED	S-PURRINGS	S-TRANGLES	S-WELLINGS
S-CRIBBLES	S-HINNYING	S-NIFFIEST	S-PUTTERED	S-TRAPPERS	S-WELTERED
S-CRIMPIER	S-HIPPINGS	S-NIFTIEST	S-QUAILING	S-TRAPPIER	S-WINERIES
S-CRIMPING	S-HOPPIEST	S-NIGGERED	S-QUASHING	S-TRAPPING	S-WINGBEAT
S-CRUMMIER	S-HOPPINGS	S-NIGGLERS	S-QUELCHED	S-TRESSING	S-WINGEING
S-CRUMPING	S-HOUTINGS	S-NIGGLING	S-QUELCHES	S-TRICKLED	S-WINGIEST
S-CRUNCHED	S-HOVELLED	S-NIPPIEST	S-QUINCHES	S-TRICKLES	S-WISHINGS
S-CRUNCHES	S-HOVELLER	S-NOBBIEST	S-QUIRTING	S-TRIGGING	S-WITCHIER
S-CUDDLING	S-HUNTINGS	S-NUBBIEST	S-QUITCHES	S-TRIPIEST	S-WITCHING
S-CUFFLING	S-KETCHING	S-NUZZLING	S-TABLINGS	S-TRIPLING	S-WITHERED
S-CULLINGS	S-KILLINGS	S-OILINESS	S-TACKINGS	S-TRIPPERS	S-WOOSHING
S-CULLIONS	S-KIPPERED	S-PARABLES	S-TALKIEST	S-TRIPPING	S-WORDLESS
S-CUMBERED	S-KITTLING	S-PARKIEST	S-TALKINGS	S-TROLLERS	S-WORDPLAY
S-CURRIERS	S-LAMMINGS	S-PATTERED	S-TALLAGES	S-TROLLING	S-WOUNDING
S-CURRYING	S-LASHINGS	S-PECULATE	S-TAMPINGS	S-TROSSERS	

2→3

AA-S	BI-S	EL-S	GU-S	IO-S	ME-S	OD-S	PA-S	TE-S	YE-S
AD-S	BO-S	EM-S	HA-S	IT-S	MI-S	OE-S	PH-S	TI-S	YO-S
AH-S	BY-S	EN-S	HE-S	KA-S	MU-S	OM-S	PI-S	UG-S	YU-S
AI-S	DA-S	ER-S	HI-S	KO-S	NA-S	ON-S	PO-S	UN-S	ZO-S
AR-S	DO-S	ES-S	HO-S	LA-S	NO-S	OO-S	QI-S	UP-S	
AS-S	EA-S	FA-S	ID-S	LI-S	NU-S	OP-S	RE-S	UT-S	
AY-S	EF-S	GI-S	IF-S	LO-S	NY-S	OR-S	SI-S	WO-S	
BA-S	EH-S	GO-S	IN-S	MA-S	OB-S	OY-S	SO-S	XI-S	

3→4

ABA-S	BET-S	CUR-S	ELD-S	GAE-S	HOB-S	KEN-S	MAM-S	NUR-S	PHI-S
ABB-S	BEY-S	CUT-S	ELF-S	GAG-S	HOD-S	KEP-S	MAN-S	NUT-S	PHO-S
ACE-S	BIB-S	CWM-S	ELK-S	GAL-S	HOE-S	KET-S	MAP-S	NYE-S	PIA-S
ACT-S	BID-S	DAB-S	ELL-S	GAM-S	HOG-S	KEY-S	MAR-S	OAF-S	PIC-S
ADD-S	BIG-S	DAD-S	ELM-S	GAP-S	HOH-S	KID-S	MAS-S	OAK-S	PIE-S
ADO-S	BIN-S	DAE-S	ELT-S	GAR-S	HON-S	KIF-S	MAT-S	OAR-S	PIG-S
AGA-S	BIO-S	DAG-S	EME-S	GAT-S	HOP-S	KIN-S	MAW-S	OAT-S	PIN-S
AGE-S	BIT-S	DAH-S	EMU-S	GAU-S	HOS-S	KIP-S	MAY-S	OBA-S	PIP-S
AIA-S	BOA-S	DAK-S	END-S	GAY-S	HOT-S	KIR-S	MEG-S	OBI-S	PIR-S
AID-S	BOB-S	DAL-S	ENE-S	GED-S	HOW-S	KIT-S	MEL-S	OBO-S	PIS-S
AIL-S	BOD-S	DAM-S	ENG-S	GEE-S	HOY-S	KOA-S	MES-S	OCA-S	PIT-S
AIM-S	BOG-S	DAN-S	EON-S	GEL-S	HUB-S	KOB-S	MET-S	ODA-S	POA-S
AIR-S	BOH-S	DAP-S	ERA-S	GEM-S	HUE-S	KON-S	MEU-S	ODD-S	POD-S
AIT-S	BOK-S	DAW-S	ERE-S	GEN-S	HUG-S	KOP-S	MEW-S	ODE-S	POI-S
AKE-S	BOO-S	DAY-S	ERG-S	GEO-S	HUI-S	KOS-S	MHO-S	OFF-S	POM-S
ALA-S	BOP-S	DEB-S	ERK-S	GET-S	HUM-S	KOW-S	MID-S	OHM-S	POO-S
ALB-S	BOR-S	DEE-S	ERN-S	GHI-S	HUP-S	KYU-S	MIL-S	OHO-S	POP-S
ALE-S	BOS-S	DEL-S	ERR-S	GIB-S	HUT-S	LAB-S	MIR-S	OIK-S	POS-S
ALL-S	BOT-S	DEN-S	EST-S	GID-S	HYE-S	LAC-S	MIS-S	OIL-S	POT-S
ALP-S	BOW-S	DEW-S	ETA-S	GIE-S	HYP-S	LAD-S	MNA-S	OKE-S	POW-S
ALT-S	BOY-S	DEY-S	ETH-S	GIG-S	ICE-S	LAG-S	MOA-S	OLD-S	PRO-S
AMI-S	BRA-S	DIB-S	EUK-S	GIN-S	IDE-S	LAH-S	MOB-S	OLM-S	PRY-S
AMP-S	BRO-S	DIE-S	EVE-S	GIO-S	ILK-S	LAM-S	MOD-S	ONE-S	PSI-S
ANA-S	BUB-S	DIG-S	EWE-S	GIP-S	ILL-S	LAP-S	MOE-S	OOF-S	PUB-S
AND-S	BUD-S	DIM-S	EWK-S	GIT-S	IMP-S	LAS-S	MOG-S	OOH-S	PUD-S
ANE-S	BUG-S	DIN-S	EWT-S	GJU-S	INK-S	LAT-S	MOM-S	OOM-S	PUG-S
ANI-S	BUM-S	DIP-S	EYE-S	GNU-S	INN-S	LAV-S	MOO-S	OON-S	PUN-S
ANN-S	BUN-S	DIT-S	FAD-S	GOA-S	ION-S	LAW-S	MOP-S	OOP-S	PUP-S
ANT-S	BUR-S	DIV-S	FAG-S	GOB-S	IRE-S	LAY-S	MOR-S	OPE-S	PUR-S
APE-S	BUS-S	DOB-S	FAH-S	GOD-S	IRK-S	LEA-S	MOT-S	OPT-S	PUS-S
APT-S	BUT-S	DOC-S	FAN-S	GOE-S	ISM-S	LEE-S	MOU-S	ORB-S	PUT-S
ARB-S	BUY-S	DOD-S	FAR-S	GON-S	ISO-S	LEG-S	MOW-S	ORC-S	PUY-S
ARC-S	BYE-S	DOE-S	FAT-S	GOO-S	ITA-S	LEI-S	MOY-S	ORD-S	PYE-S
ARD-S	CAB-S	DOG-S	FAW-S	GOV-S	JAB-S	LEK-S	MUD-S	ORE-S	QAT-S
ARE-S	CAD-S	DOH-S	FAY-S	GOY-S	JAG-S	LEP-S	MUG-S	ORF-S	RAD-S
ARK-S	CAM-S	DON-S	FED-S	GUB-S	JAK-S	LES-S	MUM-S	ORT-S	RAG-S
ARM-S	CAN-S	DOO-S	FEE-S	GUE-S	JAM-S	LET-S	MUS-S	OUD-S	RAH-S
ART-S	CAP-S	DOP-S	FEN-S	GUM-S	JAP-S	LEY-S	NAB-S	OUP-S	RAI-S
ASK-S	CAR-S	DOR-S	FET-S	GUN-S	JAR-S	LIB-S	NAG-S	OUR-S	RAM-S
ASP-S	CAT-S	DOS-S	FEU-S	GUP-S	JAW-S	LID-S	NAM-S	OUT-S	RAP-S
AUF-S	CAW-S	DOT-S	FEY-S	GUR-S	JAY-S	LIE-S	NAN-S	OWE-S	RAT-S
AUK-S	CAY-S	DOW-S	FIB-S	GUT-S	JEE-S	LIG-S	NAP-S	OWL-S	RAW-S
AVA-S	CEE-S	DSO-S	FID-S	GUV-S	JET-S	LIN-S	NAT-S	OWN-S	RAY-S
AVE-S	CEL-S	DUB-S	FIG-S	GUY-S	JEW-S	LIP-S	NAY-S	OWT-S	REC-S
AWE-S	CEP-S	DUD-S	FIL-S	GYM-S	JIB-S	LOB-S	NEB-S	OYE-S	RED-S
AWL-S	CHA-S	DUE-S	FIN-S	GYP-S	JIG-S	LOD-S	NED-S	PAD-S	REE-S
AWN-S	CHI-S	DUG-S	FIR-S	HAD-S	JOB-S	LOG-S	NEF-S	PAH-S	REF-S
AXE-S	CID-S	DUN-S	FIT-S	HAG-S	JOE-S	LOO-S	NEK-S	PAL-S	REH-S
AYE-S	CIG-S	DUO-S	FLU-S	HAM-S	JOG-S	LOP-S	NEP-S	PAM-S	REM-S
AYU-S	CIT-S	DUP-S	FOB-S	HAP-S	JOR-S	LOS-S	NET-S	PAN-S	REN-S
BAA-S	COB-S	DYE-S	FOE-S	HAT-S	JOT-S	LOT-S	NEW-S	PAP-S	REP-S
BAC-S	COD-S	DZO-S	FOG-S	HAW-S	JOW-S	LOW-S	NIB-S	PAR-S	RET-S
BAD-S	COG-S	EAN-S	FOH-S	HAY-S	JOY-S	LOY-S	NID-S	PAS-S	REV-S
BAG-S	COL-S	EAR-S	FON-S	HEM-S	JUD-S	LUD-S	NIE-S	PAT-S	REW-S
BAM-S	CON-S	EAT-S	FOP-S	HEN-S	JUG-S	LUG-S	NIL-S	PAW-S	RHO-S
BAN-S	COO-S	EAU-S	FOY-S	HEP-S	JUT-S	LUM-S	NIM-S	PAY-S	RIA-S
BAP-S	COP-S	EBB-S	FRA-S	HER-S	KAE-S	LUR-S	NIP-S	PEA-S	RIB-S
BAR-S	COR-S	ECU-S	FUB-S	HET-S	KAI-S	LUV-S	NIT-S	PEC-S	RID-S
BAS-S	COS-S	EDH-S	FUD-S	HEW-S	KAT-S	LYE-S	NOB-S	PED-S	RIG-S
BAT-S	COT-S	EEL-S	FUG-S	HEY-S	KAW-S	LYM-S	NOD-S	PEE-S	RIM-S
BAY-S	COW-S	EFF-S	FUM-S	HIE-S	KAY-S	MAA-S	NOG-S	PEG-S	RIN-S
BED-S	CRU-S	EFT-S	FUN-S	HIN-S	KEA-S	MAC-S	NOM-S	PEH-S	RIP-S
BEE-S	CUB-S	EGG-S	FUR-S	HIP-S	KEB-S	MAD-S	NOW-S	PEN-S	RIT-S
BEG-S	CUD-S	EGO-S	GAB-S	HIS-S	KED-S	MAG-S	NOY-S	PEP-S	ROB-S
BEL-S	CUE-S	EIK-S	GAD-S	HIT-S	KEF-S	MAK-S	NUB-S	PET-S	ROC-S
BEN-S	CUP-S	EKE-S		HOA-S	KEG-S	MAL-S	NUN-S	PEW-S	ROD-S

ROE-S	SAR-S	SKA-S	SUN-S	TEF-S	TOW-S	URN-S	VUM-S	WOK-S	YOK-S
ROK-S	SAW-S	SKI-S	SUP-S	TEG-S	TOY-S	USE-S	WAD-S	WON-S	YOW-S
ROO-S	SAY-S	SOB-S	SUQ-S	TEL-S	TUB-S	UTE-S	WAE-S	WOO-S	YUG-S
ROT-S	SEA-S	SOC-S	SUS-S	TEN-S	TUG-S	UTU-S	WAG-S	WOP-S	YUK-S
ROW-S	SEC-S	SOD-S	SYE-S	TEW-S	TUI-S	UVA-S	WAN-S	WOT-S	YUP-S
RUB-S	SEE-S	SOG-S	TAB-S	TIC-S	TUM-S	VAC-S	WAP-S	WOW-S	ZAG-S
RUC-S	SEG-S	SOH-S	TAD-S	TID-S	TUN-S	VAE-S	WAR-S	WUD-S	ZAP-S
RUD-S	SEI-S	SOL-S	TAE-S	TIE-S	TUP-S	VAN-S	WAT-S	WUS-S	ZEA-S
RUE-S	SEL-S	SON-S	TAG-S	TIG-S	TUT-S	VAT-S	WAW-S	WYE-S	ZED-S
RUG-S	SEN-S	SOP-S	TAI-S	TIL-S	TWA-S	VAU-S	WAY-S	WYN-S	ZEE-S
RUM-S	SET-S	SOS-S	TAK-S	TIN-S	TWO-S	VEE-S	WEB-S	YAH-S	ZEK-S
RUN-S	SEW-S	SOT-S	TAM-S	TIP-S	TYE-S	VET-S	WED-S	YAK-S	ZEL-S
RUT-S	SEY-S	SOU-S	TAN-S	TIT-S	TYG-S	VIA-S	WEE-S	YAM-S	ZHO-S
RYA-S	SHE-S	SOV-S	TAP-S	TOC-S	UDO-S	VID-S	WEM-S	YAP-S	ZIG-S
RYE-S	SIB-S	SOW-S	TAR-S	TOD-S	UEY-S	VIE-S	WEN-S	YAW-S	ZIP-S
SAB-S	SIC-S	SOY-S	TAT-S	TOE-S	UFO-S	VIM-S	WET-S	YEA-S	ZIT-S
SAC-S	SIM-S	SPA-S	TAU-S	TOG-S	UGH-S	VIN-S	WEY-S	YEN-S	ZOO-S
SAG-S	SIN-S	SUB-S	TAW-S	TOM-S	UKE-S	VOE-S	WIG-S	YEP-S	
SAI-S	SIP-S	SUD-S	TAY-S	TON-S	ULE-S	VOL-S	WIN-S	YEW-S	
SAL-S	SIR-S	SUE-S	TEA-S	TOP-S	UNI-S	VOR-S	WIT-S	YIN-S	
SAN-S	SIS-S	SUK-S	TED-S	TOR-S	URD-S	VOW-S	WOE-S	YIP-S	
SAP-S	SIT-S	SUM-S	TEE-S	TOT-S	URE-S	VUG-S	WOG-S	YOB-S	

4→5

ABAC-S	ANOA-S	BAJU-S	BENE-S	BLUB-S	BRAY-S	CAIN-S	CHEF-S	CODA-S
ABBA-S	ANTA-S	BAKE-S	BENI-S	BLUE-S	BREE-S	CAKE-S	CHEW-S	CODE-S
ABBE-S	ANTE-S	BALE-S	BENT-S	BLUR-S	BREN-S	CALF-S	CHIC-S	COED-S
ABET-S	ANTI-S	BALK-S	BERE-S	BOAK-S	BRER-S	CALK-S	CHIK-S	COFF-S
ABLE-S	APAY-S	BALL-S	BERG-S	BOAR-S	BREW-S	CALL-S	CHIN-S	COHO-S
ABUT-S	APOD-S	BALM-S	BERK-S	BOAT-S	BRIG-S	CALM-S	CHIP-S	COIF-S
ABYE-S	APSE-S	BALU-S	BERM-S	BOBA-S	BRIM-S	CALP-S	CHIT-S	COIL-S
ACER-S	AQUA-S	BANC-S	BEST-S	BOCK-S	BRIO-S	CAME-S	CHIV-S	COIN-S
ACHE-S	ARAK-S	BAND-S	BETA-S	BODE-S	BRIT-S	CAMP-S	CHOC-S	COIR-S
ACID-S	ARAR-S	BANE-S	BETE-S	BOFF-S	BROD-S	CANE-S	CHON-S	COIT-S
ACME-S	ARBA-S	BANG-S	BETH-S	BOIL-S	BROG-S	CANG-S	CHOP-S	COKE-S
ACNE-S	AREA-S	BANK-S	BHEL-S	BOKE-S	BROO-S	CANN-S	CHOW-S	COLA-S
ACRE-S	ARET-S	BANT-S	BICE-S	BOKO-S	BROW-S	CANT-S	CHUB-S	COLD-S
ACYL-S	ARIA-S	BAPU-S	BIDE-S	BOLD-S	BUAT-S	CAPA-S	CHUG-S	COLE-S
ADAW-S	ARIL-S	BARB-S	BIER-S	BOLE-S	BUBA-S	CAPE-S	CHUM-S	COLL-S
ADIT-S	ARLE-S	BARD-S	BIFF-S	BOLL-S	BUCK-S	CAPO-S	CIAO-S	COLT-S
ADZE-S	ARNA-S	BARE-S	BIGG-S	BOLO-S	BUDO-S	CARB-S	CIDE-S	COMA-S
AEON-S	ARSE-S	BARF-S	BIKE-S	BOLT-S	BUFF-S	CARD-S	CIEL-S	COMB-S
AERO-S	ARUM-S	BARK-S	BILE-S	BOMA-S	BUFO-S	CARE-S	CILL-S	COME-S
AFRO-S	ARVO-S	BARM-S	BILK-S	BOMB-S	BUHL-S	CARK-S	CION-S	COMP-S
AGAR-S	ARYL-S	BARN-S	BILL-S	BOND-S	BUIK-S	CARL-S	CIRE-S	CONE-S
AGHA-S	ATAP-S	BARP-S	BIND-S	BONE-S	BUKE-S	CARP-S	CIRL-S	CONF-S
AGIO-S	ATOC-S	BASE-S	BINE-S	BONG-S	BULB-S	CARR-S	CIST-S	CONK-S
AGMA-S	ATOK-S	BASK-S	BING-S	BONK-S	BULK-S	CART-S	CITE-S	CONN-S
AGON-S	ATOM-S	BAST-S	BINK-S	BOOB-S	BULL-S	CASA-S	CIVE-S	COOF-S
AGUE-S	AULA-S	BATE-S	BINT-S	BOOH-S	BUMF-S	CASE-S	CLAD-S	COOK-S
AIDE-S	AUNE-S	BATH-S	BIOG-S	BOOK-S	BUMP-S	CASK-S	CLAG-S	COOL-S
AIRN-S	AUNT-S	BATT-S	BIRD-S	BOOL-S	BUNA-S	CAST-S	CLAM-S	COOM-S
AIRT-S	AURA-S	BAUD-S	BIRK-S	BOOM-S	BUND-S	CATE-S	CLAN-S	COON-S
AITU-S	AUTO-S	BAUK-S	BIRL-S	BOON-S	BUNG-S	CAUK-S	CLAP-S	COOP-S
AKEE-S	AVER-S	BAUR-S	BIRR-S	BOOR-S	BUNK-S	CAUL-S	CLAT-S	COOT-S
ALAP-S	AVOW-S	BAWD-S	BISE-S	BOOT-S	BUNT-S	CAUM-S	CLAW-S	COPE-S
ALAY-S	AWAY-S	BAWL-S	BISK-S	BORA-S	BUOY-S	CAUP-S	CLAY-S	CORD-S
ALEW-S	AWDL-S	BAWN-S	BITE-S	BORD-S	BURD-S	CAVE-S	CLEF-S	CORE-S
ALFA-S	AXEL-S	BAWR-S	BITO-S	BORE-S	BURG-S	CAWK-S	CLEG-S	CORK-S
ALMA-S	AXIL-S	BAYE-S	BITT-S	BORT-S	BURK-S	CEDE-S	CLEM-S	CORM-S
ALME-S	AXLE-S	BAYT-S	BLAB-S	BOSK-S	BURL-S	CEDI-S	CLEW-S	CORN-S
ALOD-S	AXON-S	BEAD-S	BLAD-S	BOTT-S	BURN-S	CEIL-S	CLIP-S	COSE-S
ALOE-S	AYAH-S	BEAK-S	BLAE-S	BOUK-S	BURP-S	CELL-S	CLOD-S	COST-S
ALTO-S	AYRE-S	BEAM-S	BLAG-S	BOUN-S	BURR-S	CELT-S	CLOG-S	COTE-S
ALUM-S	AZAN-S	BEAN-S	BLAH-S	BOUT-S	BUSK-S	CENT-S	CLOP-S	COTH-S
AMAH-S	AZYM-S	BEAR-S	BLAT-S	BOWL-S	BUST-S	CERE-S	CLOU-S	COTT-S
AMBO-S	BABA-S	BEAT-S	BLAY-S	BOWR-S	BUTE-S	CERT-S	CLOW-S	COUP-S
AMEN-S	BABE-S	BECK-S	BLEB-S	BOYG-S	BUTT-S	CETE-S	CLOY-S	COUR-S
AMIE-S	BABU-S	BEDE-S	BLEE-S	BOYO-S	BYKE-S	CHAD-S	CLUB-S	COVE-S
AMIR-S	BACH-S	BEEF-S	BLET-S	BOZO-S	BYRE-S	CHAI-S	CLUE-S	COWL-S
AMIS-S	BACK-S	BEEP-S	BLEY-S	BRAD-S	BYTE-S	CHAL-S	COAL-S	COWP-S
AMLA-S	BAEL-S	BEER-S	BLIN-S	BRAE-S	CABA-S	CHAM-S	COAT-S	COZE-S
AMMO-S	BAFF-S	BEET-S	BLIP-S	BRAG-S	CADE-S	CHAP-S	COBB-S	CRAB-S
AMYL-S	BAFT-S	BELL-S	BLOB-S	BRAN-S	CADI-S	CHAR-S	COCA-S	CRAG-S
ANIL-S	BAHT-S	BELT-S	BLOC-S	BRAS-S	CAFE-S	CHAT-S	COCK-S	CRAM-S
ANKH-S	BAIL-S	BEMA-S	BLOT-S	BRAT-S	CAFF-S	CHAW-S	COCO-S	CRAN-S
ANNA-S	BAIT-S	BEND-S	BLOW-S	BRAW-S	CAGE-S	CHAY-S		CRAP-S

CRAW-S	DELE-S	DOUT-S	EMIT-S	FIAT-S	FRIG-S	GILD-S	GRIN-S	HEAL-S
CRED-S	DELF-S	DOVE-S	EMMA-S	FICO-S	FRIT-S	GILL-S	GRIP-S	HEAP-S
CREE-S	DELI-S	DOWD-S	ENEW-S	FIEF-S	FROG-S	GILT-S	GRIT-S	HEAR-S
CREW-S	DELL-S	DOWL-S	EORL-S	FIFE-S	FROW-S	GIMP-S	GROG-S	HEAT-S
CRIB-S	DELT-S	DOWN-S	EPEE-S	FIGO-S	FUCK-S	GING-S	GROT-S	HEBE-S
CRIM-S	DEME-S	DOWP-S	EPHA-S	FIKE-S	FUEL-S	GINK-S	GROW-S	HECK-S
CRIT-S	DEMO-S	DOWT-S	EPIC-S	FILE-S	FUFF-S	GIRD-S	GRUB-S	HEED-S
CROC-S	DENE-S	DOZE-S	ERIC-S	FILL-S	FULL-S	GIRL-S	GRUE-S	HEEL-S
CROP-S	DENT-S	DRAB-S	ERNE-S	FILM-S	FUME-S	GIRN-S	GUAN-S	HEFT-S
CROW-S	DERE-S	DRAG-S	ESNE-S	FILO-S	FUND-S	GIRO-S	GUAR-S	HEID-S
CRUD-S	DERM-S	DRAM-S	ESSE-S	FIND-S	FUNG-S	GIRR-S	GUCK-S	HEIR-S
CRUE-S	DERN-S	DRAP-S	ETAT-S	FINE-S	FUNK-S	GIRT-S	GUDE-S	HELE-S
CUBE-S	DERV-S	DRAW-S	ETEN-S	FINI-S	FURL-S	GISM-S	GUES-S	HELL-S
CUFF-S	DESK-S	DRAY-S	ETNA-S	FINK-S	FURR-S	GIST-S	GUFF-S	HELM-S
CUIF-S	DEVA-S	DREE-S	ETUI-S	FINO-S	FUSE-S	GITE-S	GUGA-S	HELP-S
CUIT-S	DHAK-S	DREG-S	EUGH-S	FIRE-S	FUST-S	GIVE-S	GUID-S	HEME-S
CULL-S	DHAL-S	DREK-S	EURO-S	FIRK-S	FUZE-S	GLAD-S	GULA-S	HEMP-S
CULM-S	DHOL-S	DREY-S	EVEN-S	FIRM-S	FYKE-S	GLAM-S	GULE-S	HEND-S
CULT-S	DHOW-S	DRIB-S	EVET-S	FIRN-S	FYLE-S	GLED-S	GULF-S	HENT-S
CUNT-S	DIAL-S	DRIP-S	EVIL-S	FISC-S	FYRD-S	GLEE-S	GULL-S	HERB-S
CURB-S	DICE-S	DROP-S	EWER-S	FISK-S	GADE-S	GLEI-S	GULP-S	HERD-S
CURD-S	DICK-S	DROW-S	EXAM-S	FIST-S	GADI-S	GLEN-S	GUMP-S	HERL-S
CURE-S	DICT-S	DRUB-S	EXIT-S	FITT-S	GAFF-S	GLEY-S	GUNK-S	HERM-S
CURL-S	DIDO-S	DRUG-S	EXON-S	FIVE-S	GAGE-S	GLIA-S	GURL-S	HERN-S
CURN-S	DIEB-S	DRUM-S	EXPO-S	FLAB-S	GAID-S	GLIB-S	GURN-S	HESP-S
CURR-S	DIET-S	DUAD-S	EXUL-S	FLAG-S	GAIN-S	GLIM-S	GURU-S	HEST-S
CUSK-S	DIKA-S	DUAL-S	EYOT-S	FLAK-S	GAIR-S	GLIT-S	GUST-S	HETE-S
CUSP-S	DIKE-S	DUAN-S	EYRA-S	FLAM-S	GAIT-S	GLOB-S	GYAL-S	HICK-S
CUTE-S	DILL-S	DUAR-S	EYRE-S	FLAN-S	GAJO-S	GLOM-S	GYBE-S	HIDE-S
CYAN-S	DIME-S	DUCE-S	FACE-S	FLAP-S	GALA-S	GLOP-S	GYMP-S	HIGH-S
CYMA-S	DINE-S	DUCK-S	FACT-S	FLAT-S	GALE-S	GLOW-S	GYRE-S	HIKE-S
CYME-S	DING-S	DUCT-S	FADE-S	FLAW-S	GALL-S	GLUE-S	GYRO-S	HILL-S
CYST-S	DINK-S	DUDE-S	FADO-S	FLAY-S	GAMB-S	GLUG-S	GYTE-S	HILT-S
CYTE-S	DINO-S	DUEL-S	FAFF-S	FLEA-S	GAME-S	GLUT-S	GYVE-S	HIND-S
CZAR-S	DINT-S	DUET-S	FAIK-S	FLEE-S	GAMP-S	GNAR-S	HAAF-S	HING-S
DACE-S	DIRK-S	DUFF-S	FAIL-S	FLEG-S	GANG-S	GNAT-S	HAAR-S	HINT-S
DADO-S	DIRL-S	DUKE-S	FAIN-S	FLEW-S	GANT-S	GNAW-S	HACK-S	HIRE-S
DAFF-S	DIRT-S	DULE-S	FAIR-S	FLEY-S	GAOL-S	GOAD-S	HADE-S	HIST-S
DAGO-S	DISA-S	DULL-S	FAKE-S	FLIC-S	GAPE-S	GOAF-S	HAEM-S	HIVE-S
DAHL-S	DISC-S	DUMA-S	FALL-S	FLIP-S	GAPO-S	GOAL-S	HAET-S	HOAR-S
DALE-S	DISK-S	DUMB-S	FAME-S	FLIT-S	GARB-S	GOAT-S	HAFF-S	HOBO-S
DALI-S	DITA-S	DUMP-S	FAND-S	FLOE-S	GASP-S	GOBO-S	HAFT-S	HOCK-S
DALT-S	DITE-S	DUNE-S	FANE-S	FLOG-S	GAST-S	GOEL-S	HAGG-S	HOER-S
DAME-S	DITT-S	DUNG-S	FANG-S	FLOP-S	GATE-S	GOER-S	HAIK-S	HOGG-S
DAMN-S	DIVA-S	DUNK-S	FANK-S	FLOR-S	GATH-S	GOFF-S	HAIL-S	HOGH-S
DAMP-S	DIVE-S	DUNT-S	FARD-S	FLOW-S	GAUD-S	GOLD-S	HAIN-S	HOIK-S
DANG-S	DIVI-S	DUPE-S	FARE-S	FLUB-S	GAUM-S	GOLE-S	HAIR-S	HOKE-S
DANK-S	DOAB-S	DURA-S	FARL-S	FLUE-S	GAUP-S	GOLF-S	HAJI-S	HOKI-S
DANT-S	DOAT-S	DURE-S	FARM-S	FOAL-S	GAUR-S	GOLP-S	HAKA-S	HOLD-S
DARE-S	DOCK-S	DURN-S	FARO-S	FOAM-S	GAUS-S	GONG-S	HAKE-S	HOLE-S
DARG-S	DODO-S	DURO-S	FART-S	FOHN-S	GAWD-S	GONK-S	HALE-S	HOLM-S
DARI-S	DOEK-S	DUSK-S	FAST-S	FOID-S	GAWK-S	GOOD-S	HALF-S	HOLT-S
DARK-S	DOER-S	DUST-S	FATE-S	FOIL-S	GAWP-S	GOOF-S	HALL-S	HOME-S
DARN-S	DOFF-S	DWAM-S	FAUN-S	FOIN-S	GAZE-S	GOOK-S	HALM-S	HOMO-S
DART-S	DOGE-S	DYAD-S	FAWN-S	FOLD-S	GEAL-S	GOOL-S	HALO-S	HOND-S
DATE-S	DOIT-S	DYER-S	FAZE-S	FOLK-S	GEAN-S	GOON-S	HALT-S	HONE-S
DAUB-S	DOJO-S	DYKE-S	FEAL-S	FOND-S	GEAR-S	GOOP-S	HAME-S	HONG-S
DAUD-S	DOLE-S	DYNE-S	FEAR-S	FONT-S	GEAT-S	GOOR-S	HAND-S	HONK-S
DAUR-S	DOLL-S	DZHO-S	FEAT-S	FOOD-S	GECK-S	GORE-S	HANG-S	HOOD-S
DAUT-S	DOLT-S	EALE-S	FECK-S	FOOL-S	GEEK-S	GORM-S	HANK-S	HOOF-S
DAWD-S	DOME-S	EARD-S	FEED-S	FOOT-S	GEEP-S	GORP-S	HARD-S	HOOK-S
DAWK-S	DONA-S	EARL-S	FEEL-S	FORB-S	GEIT-S	GOUK-S	HARE-S	HOON-S
DAWN-S	DONG-S	EARN-S	FEER-S	FORD-S	GELD-S	GOUT-S	HARK-S	HOOP-S
DAWT-S	DOOB-S	EASE-S	FELL-S	FORE-S	GELT-S	GOWD-S	HARL-S	HOOT-S
DAZE-S	DOOK-S	EAST-S	FELT-S	FORK-S	GENA-S	GOWF-S	HARM-S	HOPE-S
DEAD-S	DOOL-S	EBON-S	FEME-S	FORM-S	GENE-S	GOWK-S	HARN-S	HORN-S
DEAL-S	DOOM-S	ECAD-S	FEND-S	FORT-S	GENT-S	GOWL-S	HARO-S	HOSE-S
DEAN-S	DOOR-S	ECHE-S	FENI-S	FOUD-S	GENU-S	GOWN-S	HARP-S	HOST-S
DEAR-S	DOPA-S	ECRU-S	FENT-S	FOUL-S	GERE-S	GRAB-S	HART-S	HOUF-S
DEAW-S	DOPE-S	EDGE-S	FEOD-S	FOUR-S	GERM-S	GRAD-S	HASK-S	HOUR-S
DEBT-S	DORK-S	EDIT-S	FERE-S	FOWL-S	GEST-S	GRAM-S	HASP-S	HOUT-S
DECK-S	DORM-S	EEVN-S	FERM-S	FRAB-S	GETA-S	GRAN-S	HATE-S	HOVE-S
DEED-S	DORP-S	EGER-S	FERN-S	FRAG-S	GEUM-S	GRAY-S	HAUD-S	HOWE-S
DEEM-S	DORR-S	EGMA-S	FEST-S	FRAP-S	GHAT-S	GREE-S	HAUL-S	HOWF-S
DEEN-S	DORT-S	EILD-S	FETA-S	FRAS-S	GHEE-S	GREN-S	HAVE-S	HOWK-S
DEEP-S	DOSE-S	EKKA-S	FETE-S	FRAU-S	GIBE-S	GREW-S	HAWK-S	HOWL-S
DEEV-S	DOTE-S	ELAN-S	FETT-S	FRAY-S	GIFT-S	GREY-S	HAWM-S	HOYA-S
DEID-S	DOUC-S	EMEU-S	FEUD-S	FREE-S	GIGA-S	GRID-S	HAZE-S	HUCK-S
DEIL-S	DOUP-S	EMIR-S	FIAR-S	FRET-S	GILA-S	GRIG-S	HEAD-S	HUER-S

HUFF-S	JOKE-S	KILT-S	LAWK-S	LOME-S	MART-S	MODE-S	NAPA-S	OBOE-S
HUIA-S	JOLE-S	KINA-S	LAWN-S	LONG-S	MASA-S	MOHR-S	NAPE-S	OBOL-S
HULA-S	JOLL-S	KIND-S	LAZE-S	LOOF-S	MASE-S	MOIL-S	NARC-S	OCHE-S
HULE-S	JOLT-S	KING-S	LAZO-S	LOOK-S	MASK-S	MOIT-S	NARD-S	OCTA-S
HULK-S	JOMO-S	KINK-S	LEAD-S	LOOM-S	MAST-S	MOJO-S	NARE-S	ODAL-S
HULL-S	JOOK-S	KINO-S	LEAF-S	LOON-S	MASU-S	MOKE-S	NARK-S	ODSO-S
HUMA-S	JOTA-S	KIPE-S	LEAK-S	LOOP-S	MATE-S	MOKI-S	NAVE-S	ODYL-S
HUMF-S	JOUK-S	KIPP-S	LEAM-S	LOOT-S	MATH-S	MOKO-S	NAZE-S	OFAY-S
HUMP-S	JOUR-S	KIRK-S	LEAN-S	LOPE-S	MAUD-S	MOLA-S	NEAL-S	OGAM-S
HUNK-S	JOWL-S	KIRN-S	LEAP-S	LORD-S	MAUL-S	MOLD-S	NEAP-S	OGEE-S
HUNT-S	JUBA-S	KIST-S	LEAR-S	LORE-S	MAWK-S	MOLE-S	NEAR-S	OGLE-S
HURL-S	JUBE-S	KITE-S	LEAT-S	LOSE-S	MAWR-S	MOLL-S	NECK-S	OGRE-S
HURT-S	JUDO-S	KITH-S	LEEK-S	LOTA-S	MAXI-S	MOLT-S	NEED-S	OINK-S
HUSK-S	JUJU-S	KIVA-S	LEEP-S	LOTE-S	MAYA-S	MOME-S	NEEM-S	OINT-S
HUSO-S	JUKE-S	KIWI-S	LEER-S	LOTO-S	MAZE-S	MONA-S	NEEP-S	OKAY-S
HWYL-S	JUMP-S	KNAG-S	LEET-S	LOUN-S	MEAD-S	MONG-S	NEIF-S	OKRA-S
HYEN-S	JUNK-S	KNAP-S	LEFT-S	LOUP-S	MEAL-S	MONK-S	NEMN-S	OKTA-S
HYKE-S	JUST-S	KNAR-S	LEHR-S	LOUR-S	MEAN-S	MONO-S	NENE-S	OLEO-S
HYLE-S	JUTE-S	KNEE-S	LEIR-S	LOUT-S	MEAT-S	MOOD-S	NEON-S	OLIO-S
HYMN-S	JUVE-S	KNIT-S	LEME-S	LOVE-S	MEED-S	MOOK-S	NERD-S	OLLA-S
HYPE-S	KADE-S	KNOB-S	LEND-S	LOWE-S	MEER-S	MOOL-S	NERK-S	OLPE-S
HYPO-S	KADI-S	KNOP-S	LENG-S	LOWN-S	MEET-S	MOON-S	NEST-S	OMBU-S
IAMB-S	KAGO-S	KNOT-S	LENO-S	LOWT-S	MEIN-S	MOOP-S	NETE-S	OMEN-S
ICER-S	KAID-S	KNOW-S	LERE-S	LUAU-S	MELA-S	MOOR-S	NETT-S	OMER-S
ICON-S	KAIE-S	KNUB-S	LERP-S	LUCE-S	MELD-S	MOOT-S	NEUK-S	OMIT-S
IDEA-S	KAIF-S	KNUR-S	LEST-S	LUCK-S	MELL-S	MOPE-S	NEUM-S	ONCE-S
IDEE-S	KAIL-S	KNUT-S	LIAR-S	LUDO-S	MELT-S	MORA-S	NEVE-S	ONER-S
IDLE-S	KAIM-S	KOAN-S	LICK-S	LUFF-S	MEME-S	MORE-S	NEWT-S	OONT-S
IDOL-S	KAIN-S	KOFF-S	LIDO-S	LUGE-S	MEMO-S	MORN-S	NEXT-S	OOSE-S
IDYL-S	KAKA-S	KOHL-S	LIEF-S	LULL-S	MEND-S	MORT-S	NICK-S	OOZE-S
IKAT-S	KAKI-S	KOLA-S	LIEN-S	LULU-S	MENE-S	MOSE-S	NIDE-S	OPAH-S
IKON-S	KALE-S	KOLO-S	LIER-S	LUMP-S	MENG-S	MOST-S	NIEF-S	OPAL-S
IMAM-S	KALI-S	KONK-S	LIEU-S	LUNA-S	MENU-S	MOTE-S	NIFE-S	OPEN-S
IMPI-S	KAMA-S	KOOK-S	LIFT-S	LUNE-S	MEOW-S	MOTH-S	NIFF-S	OPPO-S
INFO-S	KAME-S	KOPH-S	LIKE-S	LUNG-S	MERC-S	MOTT-S	NIGH-S	ORAL-S
INTI-S	KAMI-S	KORA-S	LILL-S	LUNT-S	MERE-S	MOTU-S	NILL-S	ORCA-S
IOTA-S	KANA-S	KORE-S	LILO-S	LURE-S	MERI-S	MOUE-S	NIMB-S	ORFE-S
IRID-S	KANG-S	KOTO-S	LILT-S	LURK-S	MERK-S	MOUP-S	NINE-S	ORLE-S
IRON-S	KANT-S	KRAB-S	LIMA-S	LUSK-S	MERL-S	MOVE-S	NIPA-S	ORZO-S
ISLE-S	KAON-S	KSAR-S	LIMB-S	LUST-S	MESA-S	MOYL-S	NIRL-S	OTTO-S
ITEM-S	KARA-S	KUDU-S	LIME-S	LUTE-S	MESE-S	MOZE-S	NITE-S	OULK-S
IXIA-S	KARK-S	KUKU-S	LIMN-S	LUXE-S	METE-S	MUCK-S	NOCK-S	OUPH-S
JACK-S	KART-S	KURI-S	LIMO-S	LYAM-S	MEVE-S	MUFF-S	NODE-S	OUST-S
JADE-S	KATA-S	KURU-S	LIMP-S	LYME-S	MEWL-S	MUID-S	NOEL-S	OUZO-S
JAIL-S	KATI-S	KUZU-S	LIND-S	LYNE-S	MEZE-S	MUIL-S	NOGG-S	OVAL-S
JAKE-S	KAVA-S	KYLE-S	LINE-S	LYRE-S	MICA-S	MUIR-S	NOIL-S	OVEN-S
JAMB-S	KAYO-S	KYND-S	LING-S	LYSE-S	MICK-S	MULE-S	NOLE-S	OVER-S
JANE-S	KAZI-S	KYTE-S	LINK-S	LYTE-S	MICO-S	MULL-S	NOLL-S	OWRE-S
JANN-S	KECK-S	LACE-S	LINN-S	MAAR-S	MIDI-S	MUMM-S	NOMA-S	OXER-S
JAPE-S	KEEK-S	LACK-S	LINO-S	MACE-S	MIEN-S	MUMP-S	NOME-S	OYER-S
JARK-S	KEEL-S	LADE-S	LINT-S	MACK-S	MIFF-S	MUNT-S	NONE-S	PACA-S
JARL-S	KEEN-S	LAER-S	LION-S	MAGE-S	MIKE-S	MUON-S	NONG-S	PACE-S
JASP-S	KEEP-S	LAIC-S	LIRA-S	MAGG-S	MILD-S	MURE-S	NOOK-S	PACK-S
JATO-S	KEET-S	LAID-S	LIRK-S	MAID-S	MILE-S	MURK-S	NOON-S	PACO-S
JAUP-S	KEIR-S	LAIK-S	LISK-S	MAIK-S	MILK-S	MURL-S	NOOP-S	PACT-S
JEAN-S	KELL-S	LAIR-S	LISP-S	MAIL-S	MILL-S	MUSE-S	NORI-S	PAGE-S
JEAT-S	KELP-S	LAKE-S	LIST-S	MAIM-S	MILO-S	MUSK-S	NORK-S	PAIK-S
JEEL-S	KEMB-S	LAKH-S	LITE-S	MAIN-S	MILT-S	MUSO-S	NORM-S	PAIL-S
JEER-S	KEMP-S	LAMA-S	LITH-S	MAIR-S	MIME-S	MUST-S	NOSE-S	PAIN-S
JEFF-S	KENO-S	LAMB-S	LIVE-S	MAKE-S	MINA-S	MUTE-S	NOTE-S	PAIR-S
JELL-S	KENT-S	LAME-S	LOAD-S	MAKO-S	MINE-S	MUTI-S	NOUL-S	PALE-S
JERK-S	KEPI-S	LAMP-S	LOAF-S	MALE-S	MING-S	MUTT-S	NOUN-S	PALL-S
JEST-S	KERB-S	LANA-S	LOAM-S	MALI-S	MINI-S	MYNA-S	NOUP-S	PALM-S
JETE-S	KERF-S	LAND-S	LOAN-S	MALL-S	MINK-S	MYTH-S	NOVA-S	PALP-S
JIAO-S	KERN-S	LANE-S	LOBE-S	MALM-S	MINO-S	MZEE-S	NOWL-S	PAND-S
JIBE-S	KEST-S	LANK-S	LOBO-S	MALT-S	MINT-S	NAAM-S	NOWT-S	PANE-S
JIFF-S	KETA-S	LANT-S	LOCH-S	MAMA-S	MIRE-S	NAAN-S	NUDE-S	PANG-S
JILL-S	KHAN-S	LARD-S	LOCK-S	MANA-S	MIRK-S	NABK-S	NUFF-S	PANT-S
JILT-S	KHAT-S	LARE-S	LOCO-S	MANE-S	MIRV-S	NADA-S	NUKE-S	PAPA-S
JINK-S	KHOR-S	LARK-S	LODE-S	MANG-S	MISE-S	NAFF-S	NULL-S	PAPE-S
JINN-S	KHUD-S	LARN-S	LOFT-S	MANI-S	MISO-S	NAGA-S	NUMB-S	PARA-S
JIRD-S	KIBE-S	LASE-S	LOGE-S	MANO-S	MIST-S	NAIK-S	NURD-S	PARD-S
JISM-S	KICK-S	LAST-S	LOGO-S	MARA-S	MITE-S	NAIL-S	NURL-S	PARE-S
JIVE-S	KIER-S	LATH-S	LOID-S	MARC-S	MITT-S	NALA-S	NURR-S	PARK-S
JOBE-S	KIKE-S	LAUD-S	LOIN-S	MARE-S	MOAN-S	NAME-S	OAST-S	PARP-S
JOCK-S	KILL-S	LAUF-S	LOIR-S	MARG-S	MOAT-S	NANA-S	OATH-S	PARR-S
JOEY-S	KILN-S	LAVA-S	LOKE-S	MARK-S	MOCH-S		OBEY-S	PART-S
JOHN-S	KILO-S	LAVE-S	LOLL-S	MARL-S	MOCK-S		OBIA-S	PAST-S
JOIN-S	KILP-S		LOMA-S	MARM-S			OBIT-S	

PATE-S	PLAP-S	PULA-S	REAP-S	ROSE-S	SCOW-S	SIKE-S	SNIG-S	STEM-S
PATH-S	PLAT-S	PULE-S	REAR-S	ROST-S	SCUD-S	SILD-S	SNIP-S	STEN-S
PAUA-S	PLAY-S	PULK-S	RECK-S	ROTA-S	SCUG-S	SILE-S	SNOB-S	STEP-S
PAUL-S	PLEA-S	PULL-S	REDD-S	ROTE-S	SCUL-S	SILK-S	SNOD-S	STET-S
PAVE-S	PLEB-S	PULP-S	REDE-S	ROTI-S	SCUM-S	SILL-S	SNOG-S	STEW-S
PAWA-S	PLIE-S	PULU-S	REDO-S	ROTL-S	SCUP-S	SILO-S	SNOT-S	STIE-S
PAWK-S	PLIM-S	PUMA-S	REED-S	ROUE-S	SCUR-S	SILT-S	SNOW-S	STIR-S
PAWL-S	PLOD-S	PUMP-S	REEF-S	ROUL-S	SCUT-S	SIMA-S	SNUB-S	STOA-S
PAWN-S	PLOP-S	PUNA-S	REEK-S	ROUM-S	SCYE-S	SIMI-S	SNUG-S	STOB-S
PEAG-S	PLOT-S	PUNK-S	REEL-S	ROUP-S	SEAL-S	SIMP-S	SNYE-S	STOP-S
PEAK-S	PLOW-S	PUPA-S	REEN-S	ROUT-S	SEAM-S	SIND-S	SOAK-S	STOT-S
PEAL-S	PLOY-S	PURE-S	REGO-S	ROVE-S	SEAN-S	SINE-S	SOAP-S	STOW-S
PEAN-S	PLUG-S	PURI-S	REIF-S	ROWT-S	SEAR-S	SING-S	SOAR-S	STUB-S
PEAR-S	PLUM-S	PURL-S	REIK-S	RUBE-S	SEAT-S	SINK-S	SOCA-S	STUD-S
PEAT-S	POCK-S	PURR-S	REIN-S	RUCK-S	SECT-S	SIPE-S	SOCK-S	STUM-S
PEBA-S	POEM-S	PUTT-S	REKE-S	RUDD-S	SEED-S	SIRE-S	SODA-S	STUN-S
PECH-S	POET-S	PYAT-S	REND-S	RUDE-S	SEEK-S	SIRI-S	SOFA-S	STYE-S
PECK-S	POGO-S	PYET-S	RENT-S	RUFF-S	SEEL-S	SIST-S	SOFT-S	SUCK-S
PEEK-S	POKE-S	PYNE-S	REPO-S	RUIN-S	SEEM-S	SITE-S	SOIL-S	SUDD-S
PEEL-S	POLE-S	PYOT-S	REPP-S	RUKH-S	SEEP-S	SIZE-S	SOJA-S	SUER-S
PEEN-S	POLK-S	PYRE-S	REST-S	RULE-S	SEER-S	SKAG-S	SOKE-S	SUET-S
PEEP-S	POLL-S	PYRO-S	RETE-S	RUME-S	SEGO-S	SKAT-S	SOLA-S	SUID-S
PEER-S	POLO-S	QADI-S	RHEA-S	RUMP-S	SEIF-S	SKAW-S	SOLD-S	SUIT-S
PEGH-S	POLT-S	QOPH-S	RIAL-S	RUND-S	SEIL-S	SKEG-S	SOLE-S	SUKH-S
PEIN-S	POLY-S	QUAD-S	RICE-S	RUNE-S	SEIR-S	SKEO-S	SOLO-S	SULK-S
PEKE-S	POME-S	QUAG-S	RICK-S	RUNG-S	SEKT-S	SKEP-S	SOMA-S	SULU-S
PELA-S	POMP-S	QUAT-S	RIDE-S	RUNT-S	SELE-S	SKER-S	SONE-S	SUMP-S
PELE-S	POND-S	QUAY-S	RIEL-S	RURP-S	SELF-S	SKEW-S	SONG-S	SUNK-S
PELF-S	PONE-S	QUEY-S	RIEM-S	RURU-S	SELL-S	SKID-S	SOOK-S	SUNN-S
PELL-S	PONG-S	QUID-S	RIFF-S	RUSA-S	SEMI-S	SKIM-S	SOOM-S	SUPE-S
PELT-S	PONK-S	QUIM-S	RIFT-S	RUSE-S	SENA-S	SKIN-S	SOOP-S	SURA-S
PEND-S	PONT-S	QUIN-S	RIGG-S	RUSK-S	SEND-S	SKIO-S	SOOT-S	SURD-S
PENE-S	POOD-S	QUIP-S	RILE-S	RUST-S	SENT-S	SKIP-S	SOPH-S	SURE-S
PENI-S	POOF-S	QUIT-S	RILL-S	RUTH-S	SEPT-S	SKIT-S	SORA-S	SURF-S
PENK-S	POOL-S	QUOD-S	RIME-S	RYAL-S	SERE-S	SKUA-S	SORB-S	SWAB-S
PENT-S	POON-S	QUOP-S	RIMU-S	RYKE-S	SERF-S	SKUG-S	SORD-S	SWAD-S
PEON-S	POOP-S	RABI-S	RIND-S	RYND-S	SERK-S	SKYR-S	SORE-S	SWAG-S
PEPO-S	POOT-S	RACE-S	RINE-S	RYOT-S	SERR-S	SLAB-S	SORN-S	SWAN-S
PERE-S	POPE-S	RACK-S	RING-S	SACK-S	SETT-S	SLAE-S	SORT-S	SWAP-S
PERI-S	PORE-S	RAFF-S	RINK-S	SADE-S	SEXT-S	SLAG-S	SOUK-S	SWAT-S
PERK-S	PORK-S	RAFT-S	RIOT-S	SAFE-S	SHAD-S	SLAM-S	SOUL-S	SWAY-S
PERM-S	PORN-S	RAGA-S	RIPE-S	SAGA-S	SHAG-S	SLAP-S	SOUM-S	SWEE-S
PERN-S	PORT-S	RAGE-S	RIPP-S	SAGE-S	SHAH-S	SLAT-S	SOUP-S	SWEY-S
PERT-S	POSE-S	RAGG-S	RISE-S	SAGO-S	SHAM-S	SLAW-S	SOUR-S	SWIG-S
PERV-S	POST-S	RAGI-S	RISK-S	SAIC-S	SHAN-S	SLAY-S	SOUT-S	SWIM-S
PESO-S	POTE-S	RAID-S	RISP-S	SAID-S	SHAW-S	SLED-S	SOWF-S	SWOB-S
PEST-S	POTT-S	RAIK-S	RITE-S	SAIL-S	SHAY-S	SLEW-S	SOWL-S	SWOP-S
PHOH-S	POUF-S	RAIL-S	RITT-S	SAIM-S	SHEA-S	SLEY-S	SOWM-S	SWOT-S
PHON-S	POUK-S	RAIN-S	RIVA-S	SAIN-S	SHED-S	SLIM-S	SOWP-S	SYCE-S
PHOT-S	POUR-S	RAIT-S	RIVE-S	SAIR-S	SHET-S	SLIP-S	SOYA-S	SYEN-S
PHUT-S	POUT-S	RAJA-S	RIVO-S	SAKE-S	SHEW-S	SLIT-S	SPAE-S	SYKE-S
PICA-S	POWN-S	RAKE-S	RIZA-S	SAKI-S	SHIM-S	SLOB-S	SPAG-S	SYNC-S
PICK-S	PRAD-S	RAKI-S	ROAD-S	SALE-S	SHIN-S	SLOE-S	SPAM-S	SYND-S
PIER-S	PRAM-S	RAKU-S	ROAN-S	SALP-S	SHIP-S	SLOG-S	SPAR-S	SYNE-S
PIET-S	PRAT-S	RALE-S	ROAR-S	SALT-S	SHIR-S	SLOP-S	SPAT-S	SYPE-S
PIKA-S	PRAU-S	RAMI-S	ROBE-S	SAMA-S	SHIT-S	SLOT-S	SPAW-S	TABI-S
PIKE-S	PRAY-S	RAMP-S	ROCK-S	SAME-S	SHIV-S	SLOW-S	SPAY-S	TABU-S
PILE-S	PREE-S	RANA-S	RODE-S	SAMP-S	SHOE-S	SLUB-S	SPEC-S	TACE-S
PILI-S	PREP-S	RAND-S	ROIL-S	SAND-S	SHOG-S	SLUE-S	SPEK-S	TACK-S
PILL-S	PREY-S	RANI-S	ROIN-S	SANG-S	SHOO-S	SLUG-S	SPET-S	TACO-S
PIMP-S	PRIG-S	RANK-S	ROJI-S	SANT-S	SHOP-S	SLUM-S	SPEW-S	TACT-S
PINA-S	PRIM-S	RANT-S	ROKE-S	SARD-S	SHOT-S	SLUR-S	SPIC-S	TAEL-S
PINE-S	PROA-S	RAPE-S	ROLE-S	SARI-S	SHOW-S	SLUT-S	SPIE-S	TAHA-S
PING-S	PROB-S	RASE-S	ROLL-S	SARK-S	SHUL-S	SMEE-S	SPIK-S	TAHR-S
PINK-S	PROD-S	RASP-S	ROMA-S	SATE-S	SHUN-S	SMEW-S	SPIN-S	TAIL-S
PINT-S	PROF-S	RATA-S	ROMP-S	SATI-S	SHUT-S	SMIR-S	SPIT-S	TAIT-S
PION-S	PROG-S	RATE-S	RONE-S	SAUL-S	SHWA-S	SMIT-S	SPIV-S	TAKA-S
PIOY-S	PROM-S	RATH-S	RONT-S	SAUT-S	SIAL-S	SMOG-S	SPOT-S	TAKE-S
PIPA-S	PROP-S	RATU-S	ROOD-S	SAVE-S	SIBB-S	SMUG-S	SPUD-S	TAKI-S
PIPE-S	PROW-S	RAUN-S	ROOF-S	SCAB-S	SICE-S	SMUR-S	SPUE-S	TALA-S
PIPI-S	PUCE-S	RAVE-S	ROOK-S	SCAD-S	SICK-S	SMUT-S	SPUR-S	TALC-S
PIRL-S	PUCK-S	RAWN-S	ROOM-S	SCAG-S	SIDA-S	SNAB-S	STAB-S	TALE-S
PIRN-S	PUDU-S	RAZE-S	ROON-S	SCAM-S	SIDE-S	SNAG-S	STAG-S	TALK-S
PISE-S	PUER-S	READ-S	ROOP-S	SCAN-S	SIEN-S	SNAP-S	STAP-S	TAME-S
PITA-S	PUFF-S	REAK-S	ROOT-S	SCAR-S	SIFT-S	SNAR-S	STAR-S	TAMP-S
PITH-S	PUJA-S	REAL-S	ROPE-S	SCAT-S	SIGH-S	SNEB-S	STAW-S	TANA-S
PIUM-S	PUKE-S	REAM-S	RORE-S	SCAW-S	SIGN-S	SNED-S	STAY-S	TANG-S
PIZE-S	PUKU-S	REAN-S	RORT-S	SCOG-S	SIJO-S	SNEE-S	STED-S	TANH-S
PLAN-S				SCOT-S	SIKA-S	SNIB-S		

TANK-S	THIG-S	TOOL-S	TULE-S	VEAL-S	WAKA-S	WENT-S	WORK-S	YOGH-S
TAPA-S	THIN-S	TOOM-S	TUMP-S	VEEP-S	WAKE-S	WEST-S	WORM-S	YOGI-S
TAPE-S	THOU-S	TOON-S	TUNA-S	VEER-S	WAKF-S	WETA-S	WORT-S	YOKE-S
TAPU-S	THUD-S	TOOT-S	TUND-S	VEGA-S	WALD-S	WEXE-S	WRAP-S	YOLK-S
TARA-S	THUG-S	TOPE-S	TUNE-S	VEIL-S	WALE-S	WHAM-S	WREN-S	YOMP-S
TARE-S	TIAR-S	TOPI-S	TURD-S	VEIN-S	WALI-S	WHAP-S	WRIT-S	YONI-S
TARN-S	TICE-S	TORC-S	TURF-S	VELD-S	WALK-S	WHAT-S	WULL-S	YOOF-S
TARO-S	TICK-S	TORE-S	TURM-S	VELE-S	WALL-S	WHEN-S	WYND-S	YOOP-S
TARP-S	TIDE-S	TORR-S	TURN-S	VELL-S	WAME-S	WHET-S	WYNN-S	YORE-S
TART-S	TIER-S	TORT-S	TUSK-S	VEND-S	WAND-S	WHEW-S	WYTE-S	YORK-S
TASK-S	TIFF-S	TOSA-S	TUTU-S	VENT-S	WANE-S	WHEY-S	XYST-S	YOUK-S
TATE-S	TIFT-S	TOSE-S	TWAE-S	VERB-S	WANG-S	WHID-S	YACK-S	YOUR-S
TATH-S	TIGE-S	TOTE-S	TWAL-S	VERT-S	WANK-S	WHIG-S	YAFF-S	YOWE-S
TATT-S	TIKA-S	TOUK-S	TWAT-S	VEST-S	WANT-S	WHIM-S	YALE-S	YOWL-S
TATU-S	TIKE-S	TOUN-S	TWAY-S	VIAL-S	WAQF-S	WHIN-S	YANG-S	YUCA-S
TAUT-S	TIKI-S	TOUR-S	TWIG-S	VIBE-S	WARD-S	WHIP-S	YANK-S	YUCK-S
TAVA-S	TILE-S	TOUT-S	TWIN-S	VICE-S	WARE-S	WHIR-S	YAPP-S	YUFT-S
TAWA-S	TILL-S	TOZE-S	TWIT-S	VIER-S	WARK-S	WHIT-S	YARD-S	YUGA-S
TAWT-S	TILT-S	TRAD-S	TYMP-S	VIEW-S	WARM-S	WHOP-S	YARN-S	YUKE-S
TAXI-S	TIME-S	TRAM-S	TYNE-S	VILL-S	WARN-S	WICK-S	YARR-S	YUKO-S
TEAD-S	TIND-S	TRAP-S	TYPE-S	VINA-S	WARP-S	WIDE-S	YATE-S	YULE-S
TEAK-S	TINE-S	TRAT-S	TYPO-S	VINE-S	WART-S	WIEL-S	YAUD-S	YUMP-S
TEAL-S	TING-S	TRAY-S	TYRE-S	VINO-S	WASE-S	WILD-S	YAWL-S	YURT-S
TEAM-S	TINK-S	TREE-S	TYRO-S	VINT-S	WASM-S	WILE-S	YAWN-S	ZACK-S
TEAR-S	TINT-S	TREK-S	TZAR-S	VIOL-S	WASP-S	WILI-S	YAWP-S	ZARF-S
TEAT-S	TIPI-S	TRES-S	UDAL-S	VIRE-S	WAST-S	WILL-S	YEAD-S	ZATI-S
TECH-S	TIRE-S	TRET-S	ULVA-S	VIRL-S	WATT-S	WILT-S	YEAN-S	ZEAL-S
TEEL-S	TIRL-S	TREW-S	UMBO-S	VISA-S	WAUK-S	WIMP-S	YEAR-S	ZEBU-S
TEEM-S	TIRO-S	TREY-S	UNAU-S	VISE-S	WAUL-S	WIND-S	YEDE-S	ZEIN-S
TEEN-S	TIRR-S	TRIE-S	UNCE-S	VITA-S	WAUR-S	WINE-S	YEED-S	ZERO-S
TEER-S	TITI-S	TRIG-S	UNCO-S	VIVA-S	WAVE-S	WING-S	YEGG-S	ZEST-S
TEFF-S	TOAD-S	TRIM-S	UNIT-S	VIVE-S	WAWE-S	WINK-S	YELK-S	ZETA-S
TEGG-S	TOCK-S	TRIN-S	URAO-S	VLEI-S	WAWL-S	WINN-S	YELL-S	ZEZE-S
TEGU-S	TOCO-S	TRIO-S	UREA-S	VOAR-S	WEAL-S	WINO-S	YELM-S	ZIFF-S
TEHR-S	TOEA-S	TRIP-S	URGE-S	VOID-S	WEAN-S	WIPE-S	YELP-S	ZILA-S
TEIL-S	TOFF-S	TROD-S	URVA-S	VOLE-S	WEAR-S	WIRE-S	YELT-S	ZIMB-S
TELL-S	TOFT-S	TROG-S	USER-S	VOLK-S	WEED-S	WISE-S	YERD-S	ZINC-S
TEME-S	TOFU-S	TRON-S	UVEA-S	VOLT-S	WEEK-S	WISP-S	YERK-S	ZINE-S
TEMP-S	TOGA-S	TROT-S	VADE-S	VOTE-S	WEEL-S	WIST-S	YESK-S	ZING-S
TEND-S	TOGE-S	TROW-S	VAIL-S	VRIL-S	WEEM-S	WITE-S	YEST-S	ZOBO-S
TENE-S	TOHO-S	TROY-S	VAIR-S	VROW-S	WEEN-S	WITH-S	YETI-S	ZOBU-S
TENT-S	TOIL-S	TRUE-S	VALE-S	VULN-S	WEEP-S	WIVE-S	YETT-S	ZOEA-S
TERF-S	TOKE-S	TRUG-S	VALI-S	WACK-S	WEET-S	WOAD-S	YEUK-S	ZONE-S
TERM-S	TOKO-S	TRYP-S	VAMP-S	WADD-S	WEFT-S	WOCK-S	YEVE-S	ZONK-S
TERN-S	TOLA-S	TSAR-S	VANE-S	WADE-S	WEID-S	WOLD-S	YIKE-S	ZOOM-S
TEST-S	TOLE-S	TUAN-S	VANG-S	WADI-S	WEIL-S	WOLF-S	YILL-S	ZOON-S
TETE-S	TOLL-S	TUBA-S	VANT-S	WADT-S	WEIR-S	WOMB-S	YIRD-S	ZORI-S
TEXT-S	TOLT-S	TUBE-S	VARA-S	WAFF-S	WEKA-S	WONK-S	YIRK-S	ZOUK-S
THAN-S	TOLU-S	TUCK-S	VARE-S	WAFT-S	WELD-S	WONT-S	YITE-S	ZULU-S
THAR-S	TOMB-S	TUFA-S	VASE-S	WAGE-S	WELK-S	WOOD-S	YLEM-S	ZUPA-S
THAW-S	TOME-S	TUFF-S	VAST-S	WAIF-S	WELL-S	WOOF-S	YLKE-S	ZURF-S
THEE-S	TONE-S	TUFT-S	VATU-S	WAIL-S	WELT-S	WOOL-S	YMPE-S	ZYME-S
THEN-S	TONG-S		VAUT-S	WAIN-S	WEMB-S	WOON-S	YOCK-S	
THEW-S	TONK-S			WAIT-S	WEND-S	WORD-S	YOGA-S	

5→6

ABACA-S	ABSIT-S	ADOBE-S	AGIST-S	ALERT-S	ALMAH-S	AMINE-S	ANKER-S
ABAND-S	ABUNA-S	ADOPT-S	AGLET-S	ALEYE-S	ALMEH-S	AMMAN-S	ANKLE-S
ABASE-S	ABUSE-S	ADORE-S	AGOGE-S	ALGIN-S	ALMUG-S	AMMON-S	ANNAL-S
ABATE-S	ABYSM-S	ADORN-S	AGORA-S	ALGUM-S	ALPHA-S	AMNIO-S	ANNAT-S
ABAYA-S	ACCOY-S	ADULT-S	AGREE-S	ALIBI-S	ALTAR-S	AMOUR-S	ANNOY-S
ABBES-S	ACKEE-S	ADVEW-S	AGUTI-S	ALIEN-S	ALTER-S	AMOVE-S	ANNUL-S
ABBEY-S	ACORN-S	AERIE-S	AIDER-S	ALIGN-S	ALURE-S	AMPUL-S	ANODE-S
ABBOT-S	ACTIN-S	AFARA-S	AIOLI-S	ALINE-S	ALWAY-S	AMRIT-S	ANTAR-S
ABCEE-S	ACTON-S	AFEAR-S	AIRER-S	ALIYA-S	AMATE-S	AMUSE-S	ANTIC-S
ABEAR-S	ACTOR-S	AFRIT-S	AISLE-S	ALKIE-S	AMAZE-S	ANANA-S	ANTRE-S
ABELE-S	ACUTE-S	AFTER-S	AIZLE-S	ALKYD-S	AMBAN-S	ANCLE-S	ANVIL-S
ABHOR-S	ADAGE-S	AGAMI-S	AJWAN-S	ALKYL-S	AMBER-S	ANEAR-S	AORTA-S
ABIDE-S	ADAPT-S	AGATE-S	AKENE-S	ALLAY-S	AMBIT-S	ANELE-S	APHID-S
ABLET-S	ADDER-S	AGAVE-S	ALAAP-S	ALLEE-S	AMBLE-S	ANGEL-S	APIOL-S
ABODE-S	ADDIO-S	AGENE-S	ALANG-S	ALLEL-S	AMEBA-S	ANGER-S	APISM-S
ABORD-S	ADDLE-S	AGENT-S	ALAPA-S	ALLEY-S	AMEER-S	ANGLE-S	APNEA-S
ABORT-S	ADEEM-S	AGGER-S	ALARM-S	ALLOD-S	AMEND-S	ANGST-S	APODE-S
ABOUT-S	ADEPT-S	AGGRO-S	ALBUM-S	ALLOT-S	AMENT-S	ANIMA-S	APPAL-S
ABRAY-S	ADIEU-S	AGILA-S	ALDEA-S	ALLOW-S	AMICE-S	ANIME-S	APPAY-S
ABRIN-S	ADMIN-S	AGING-S	ALDER-S	ALLOY-S	AMIDE-S	ANION-S	APPEL-S
ABSEY-S	ADMIT-S		ALEPH-S	ALLYL-S	AMIGO-S	ANISE-S	APPLE-S

APPUI-S	AWNER-S	BEKAH-S	BLOCK-S	BRAKE-S	BURST-S	CERGE-S	CHUFF-S
APPUY-S	AXIOM-S	BELAH-S	BLOKE-S	BRAME-S	BUSSU-S	CERIA-S	CHUMP-S
APRON-S	AXOID-S	BELAY-S	BLOND-S	BRAND-S	BUTTE-S	CERNE-S	CHUNK-S
ARABA-S	AYRIE-S	BELEE-S	BLOOD-S	BRANK-S	BUTYL-S	CESSE-S	CHURL-S
ARAME-S	AZIDE-S	BELGA-S	BLOOM-S	BRAST-S	BUYER-S	CETYL-S	CHURN-S
ARBOR-S	AZINE-S	BELIE-S	BLOOP-S	BRAVE-S	BWANA-S	CHACE-S	CHURR-S
ARDEB-S	AZOTE-S	BELLE-S	BLORE-S	BRAVO-S	BWAZI-S	CHACK-S	CHUSE-S
ARDOR-S	AZOTH-S	BEMAD-S	BLUDE-S	BRAWL-S	BYLAW-S	CHACO-S	CHUTE-S
ARDRI-S	AZURE-S	BEMUD-S	BLUEY-S	BRAWN-S	BYWAY-S	CHAFE-S	CHYLE-S
AREAD-S	AZYME-S	BENET-S	BLUFF-S	BRAZE-S	CABAL-S	CHAFF-S	CHYME-S
ARECA-S	BABEL-S	BENNE-S	BLUID-S	BREAD-S	CABER-S	CHAFT-S	CIBOL-S
AREDE-S	BABOO-S	BENNI-S	BLUNK-S	BREAK-S	CABIN-S	CHAIN-S	CIDER-S
ARENA-S	BABUL-S	BEPAT-S	BLUNT-S	BREAM-S	CABLE-S	CHAIR-S	CIGAR-S
ARETE-S	BACCA-S	BERAY-S	BLURB-S	BREDE-S	CABOB-S	CHALK-S	CIMAR-S
ARETT-S	BACCO-S	BERET-S	BLURT-S	BREED-S	CABOC-S	CHAMP-S	CISCO-S
ARGAN-S	BACON-S	BEROB-S	BOARD-S	BREER-S	CACAO-S	CHANK-S	CITAL-S
ARGIL-S	BADGE-S	BERTH-S	BOART-S	BRERE-S	CACHE-S	CHANT-S	CITER-S
ARGOL-S	BAGEL-S	BERYL-S	BOAST-S	BREVE-S	CADEE-S	CHAPE-S	CITES-S
ARGON-S	BAHUT-S	BESEE-S	BOBAC-S	BRIAR-S	CADET-S	CHARA-S	CIVET-S
ARGOT-S	BAIRN-S	BESET-S	BOBAK-S	BRIBE-S	CADGE-S	CHARD-S	CIVIC-S
ARGUE-S	BAIZE-S	BESIT-S	BOCCA-S	BRICK-S	CADIE-S	CHARE-S	CLACK-S
ARIEL-S	BAJAN-S	BESOM-S	BOCHE-S	BRIDE-S	CADRE-S	CHARK-S	CLADE-S
ARISE-S	BAJRA-S	BESOT-S	BODGE-S	BRIEF-S	CAGOT-S	CHARM-S	CLAIM-S
ARMET-S	BAJRI-S	BETEL-S	BODLE-S	BRIER-S	CAIRD-S	CHARR-S	CLAME-S
ARMIL-S	BAKER-S	BETON-S	BOGAN-S	BRILL-S	CAIRN-S	CHART-S	CLAMP-S
ARMOR-S	BALER-S	BEVEL-S	BOGEY-S	BRINE-S	CALIF-S	CHASE-S	CLANG-S
ARNUT-S	BALOO-S	BEVER-S	BOGIE-S	BRING-S	CALLA-S	CHASM-S	CLANK-S
AROBA-S	BALSA-S	BEVUE-S	BOGLE-S	BRINK-S	CALPA-S	CHAYA-S	CLARO-S
AROID-S	BANCO-S	BEWET-S	BOHEA-S	BRISE-S	CALVE-S	CHEAP-S	CLART-S
AROMA-S	BANDA-S	BEWIG-S	BOING-S	BRISK-S	CAMAN-S	CHEAT-S	CLASP-S
ARRAY-S	BANIA-S	BEZEL-S	BOINK-S	BRIZE-S	CAMAS-S	CHECK-S	CLAUT-S
ARRET-S	BANJO-S	BHANG-S	BOMBE-S	BROAD-S	CAMEO-S	CHEEK-S	CLAVE-S
ARROW-S	BANTU-S	BIBLE-S	BOMBO-S	BROCH-S	CAMEL-S	CHEEP-S	CLEAN-S
ARSON-S	BARBE-S	BIDET-S	BONCE-S	BROCK-S	CAMPO-S	CHEER-S	CLEAR-S
ARTEL-S	BARCA-S	BIDON-S	BONER-S	BROGH-S	CANAL-S	CHEKA-S	CLEAT-S
ARTIC-S	BARDO-S	BIELD-S	BONGO-S	BROIL-S	CANEH-S	CHELA-S	CLECK-S
ASANA-S	BARGE-S	BIGHA-S	BONNE-S	BROKE-S	CANID-S	CHERT-S	CLEEK-S
ASCOT-S	BARON-S	BIGHT-S	BONZE-S	BROND-S	CANNA-S	CHEST-S	CLEEP-S
ASHET-S	BARRE-S	BIGOT-S	BOONG-S	BROOD-S	CANOE-S	CHICA-S	CLEFT-S
ASIDE-S	BARYE-S	BIKER-S	BOORD-S	BROOK-S	CANON-S	CHICK-S	CLEPE-S
ASKER-S	BASAN-S	BIKIE-S	BOOSE-S	BROOL-S	CANTO-S	CHICO-S	CLERK-S
ASPEN-S	BASIC-S	BILBO-S	BOOST-S	BROOM-S	CAPER-S	CHIDE-S	CLEVE-S
ASPER-S	BASIL-S	BILGE-S	BOOTH-S	BROSE-S	CAPLE-S	CHIEF-S	CLICK-S
ASPIC-S	BASIN-S	BIMBO-S	BOOZE-S	BROTH-S	CAPON-S	CHIEL-S	CLIFF-S
ASSAI-S	BASON-S	BINGE-S	BORAK-S	BROWN-S	CAPOT-S	CHILD-S	CLIFT-S
ASSAY-S	BASSE-S	BINGO-S	BORDE-S	BRUIT-S	CAPUL-S	CHILE-S	CLIMB-S
ASSES-S	BASSO-S	BIOME-S	BOREE-S	BRUME-S	CARAP-S	CHILI-S	CLIME-S
ASSET-S	BASTE-S	BIONT-S	BORER-S	BRUNT-S	CARAT-S	CHILL-S	CLINE-S
ASSOT-S	BASTO-S	BIOTA-S	BORGO-S	BRUST-S	CARDI-S	CHIMB-S	CLING-S
ASTER-S	BATHE-S	BIPED-S	BORON-S	BRUTE-S	CARER-S	CHIME-S	CLINK-S
ASTUN-S	BATIK-S	BIPOD-S	BOSOM-S	BUAZE-S	CARES-S	CHIMP-S	CLINT-S
ATMAN-S	BATON-S	BIRLE-S	BOSON-S	BUBAL-S	CARET-S	CHINA-S	CLIPE-S
ATOKE-S	BATTA-S	BIRSE-S	BOSUN-S	BUCHU-S	CAROB-S	CHINE-S	CLOAK-S
ATOLL-S	BAULK-S	BIRTH-S	BOTEL-S	BUCKU-S	CAROL-S	CHINK-S	CLOAM-S
ATONE-S	BAVIN-S	BISON-S	BOTTE-S	BUDGE-S	CAROM-S	CHINO-S	CLOCK-S
ATTAP-S	BAYLE-S	BITER-S	BOUGE-S	BUGLE-S	CARSE-S	CHIRK-S	CLOFF-S
ATTAR-S	BAYOU-S	BLACK-S	BOUGH-S	BUILD-S	CARTA-S	CHIRL-S	CLOKE-S
ATTIC-S	BAZAR-S	BLADE-S	BOULE-S	BUIST-S	CARTE-S	CHIRM-S	CLOMP-S
AUDIO-S	BEANO-S	BLAIN-S	BOULT-S	BULGE-S	CARVE-S	CHIRP-S	CLONE-S
AUDIT-S	BEARD-S	BLAME-S	BOUND-S	BULSE-S	CASCO-S	CHIRR-S	CLONK-S
AUGER-S	BEARE-S	BLAND-S	BOURD-S	BUMBO-S	CASTE-S	CHIRT-S	CLOOP-S
AUGHT-S	BEAST-S	BLANK-S	BOURG-S	BUMPH-S	CATER-S	CHIVE-S	CLOOT-S
AUGUR-S	BEATH-S	BLARE-S	BOURN-S	BUNCE-S	CAULD-S	CHOCK-S	CLOSE-S
AUMIL-S	BEAUT-S	BLAST-S	BOUSE-S	BUNCO-S	CAULK-S	CHOCO-S	CLOTE-S
AUXIN-S	BEBOP-S	BLATT-S	BOVID-S	BUNDU-S	CAUSE-S	CHOIR-S	CLOTH-S
AVAIL-S	BECKE-S	BLAUD-S	BOWAT-S	BUNIA-S	CAVEL-S	CHOKE-S	CLOUD-S
AVALE-S	BEDEL-S	BLAZE-S	BOWEL-S	BUNJE-S	CAVER-S	CHOKO-S	CLOUR-S
AVERT-S	BEDEW-S	BLEAK-S	BOWER-S	BUNKO-S	CAVIE-S	CHOLI-S	CLOUT-S
AVION-S	BEDIM-S	BLEAR-S	BOWET-S	BUNYA-S	CAVIL-S	CHOMP-S	CLOVE-S
AVISE-S	BEDYE-S	BLEAT-S	BOWNE-S	BURAN-S	CAXON-S	CHOOF-S	CLOWN-S
AVISO-S	BEFIT-S	BLEED-S	BOWSE-S	BURET-S	CEASE-S	CHOOK-S	CLOYE-S
AVIZE-S	BEFOG-S	BLEEP-S	BOXER-S	BURGH-S	CEAZE-S	CHOOM-S	CLUCK-S
AVOID-S	BEGAR-S	BLEND-S	BOYAR-S	BURIN-S	CEDAR-S	CHORD-S	CLUMP-S
AVYZE-S	BEGEM-S	BLIMP-S	BRACE-S	BURKA-S	CEILI-S	CHORE-S	CLUNK-S
AWAIT-S	BEGET-S	BLIND-S	BRACK-S	BURKE-S	CELLO-S	CHOSE-S	CLYPE-S
AWAKE-S	BEGIN-S	BLINI-S	BRACT-S	BUROO-S	CELOM-S	CHOTT-S	COACT-S
AWARD-S	BEGUM-S	BLINK-S	BRAID-S	BURQA-S	CENSE-S	CHOUT-S	COAPT-S
AWARN-S	BEIGE-S	BLITE-S	BRAIL-S	BURRO-S	CENTO-S	CHUCK-S	COARB-S
AWETO-S	BEING-S	BLOAT-S	BRAIN-S	BURSE-S	CEORL-S	CHUFA-S	COAST-S

COATE-S	COYPU-S	CUTEY-S	DEUCE-S	DRAFT-S	EGEST-S	ERECT-S	FAVOR-S
COATI-S	COZEN-S	CUTIE-S	DEVEL-S	DRAIL-S	EGGAR-S	ERGON-S	FAYNE-S
COBIA-S	CRACK-S	CUTIN-S	DEVIL-S	DRAIN-S	EGGER-S	ERGOT-S	FAYRE-S
COBLE-S	CRAFT-S	CUVEE-S	DEVOT-S	DRAKE-S	EGRET-S	ERICA-S	FEARE-S
COBRA-S	CRAIG-S	CYCAD-S	DEWAN-S	DRAMA-S	EIDER-S	ERICK-S	FEAST-S
COBZA-S	CRAKE-S	CYCLE-S	DEWAR-S	DRANT-S	EIGHT-S	ERODE-S	FECHT-S
COCCO-S	CRAME-S	CYCLO-S	DHOBI-S	DRAPE-S	EIKON-S	ERROR-S	FEESE-S
COCOA-S	CRAMP-S	CYDER-S	DHOLE-S	DRAWL-S	EISEL-S	ERUCT-S	FEEZE-S
CODER-S	CRANE-S	CYMAR-S	DHOLL-S	DREAD-S	EJECT-S	ERUPT-S	FEIGN-S
CODON-S	CRANK-S	CYNIC-S	DHOTI-S	DREAM-S	ELAND-S	ESCOT-S	FEINT-S
COGIE-S	CRAPE-S	CYTON-S	DIAZO-S	DREAR-S	ELATE-S	ESILE-S	FELID-S
COGUE-S	CRARE-S	DACHA-S	DICER-S	DRECK-S	ELBOW-S	ESKAR-S	FELLA-S
COHAB-S	CRATE-S	DAGGA-S	DICHT-S	DRERE-S	ELCHI-S	ESKER-S	FELON-S
COHOE-S	CRAVE-S	DAINE-S	DICOT-S	DRICE-S	ELDER-S	ESSAY-S	FEMAL-S
COHOG-S	CRAWL-S	DAKER-S	DIENE-S	DRIER-S	ELDIN-S	ESTER-S	FEMME-S
COIGN-S	CRAZE-S	DALLE-S	DIGHT-S	DRIFT-S	ELECT-S	ESTOC-S	FEMUR-S
COLEY-S	CREAK-S	DAMAN-S	DIGIT-S	DRILL-S	ELEMI-S	ESTOP-S	FENCE-S
COLIC-S	CREAM-S	DAMAR-S	DIKER-S	DRINK-S	ELFIN-S	ESTRO-S	FEOFF-S
COLIN-S	CREDO-S	DANCE-S	DILDO-S	DRIVE-S	ELIAD-S	ETAGE-S	FERMI-S
COLOG-S	CREED-S	DANIO-S	DILLI-S	DROIL-S	ELIDE-S	ETAPE-S	FESSE-S
COLON-S	CREEK-S	DARAF-S	DIMER-S	DROIT-S	ELITE-S	ETHAL-S	FESTA-S
COLOR-S	CREEL-S	DARCY-S	DINAR-S	DROLE-S	ELOGE-S	ETHER-S	FETOR-S
COLZA-S	CREEP-S	DARGA-S	DINER-S	DROLL-S	ELOIN-S	ETHIC-S	FETTA-S
COMBE-S	CREME-S	DARIC-S	DINGE-S	DROME-S	ELOPE-S	ETHYL-S	FETWA-S
COMBI-S	CRENA-S	DARRE-S	DINIC-S	DRONE-S	ELPEE-S	ETTIN-S	FEUAR-S
COMBO-S	CREPE-S	DARZI-S	DIODE-S	DROOG-S	ELSIN-S	ETTLE-S	FEVER-S
COMER-S	CREST-S	DATAL-S	DIOTA-S	DROOK-S	ELUDE-S	ETUDE-S	FIBER-S
COMET-S	CREWE-S	DATER-S	DIPSO-S	DROOL-S	ELUTE-S	ETWEE-S	FIBRE-S
COMIC-S	CRICK-S	DAUBE-S	DIRGE-S	DROOP-S	ELVAN-S	EUPAD-S	FIBRO-S
COMMA-S	CRIER-S	DAULT-S	DIRKE-S	DROUK-S	ELVER-S	EUSOL-S	FICHE-S
COMMO-S	CRIME-S	DAUNT-S	DISCO-S	DROVE-S	EMAIL-S	EVADE-S	FICHU-S
COMPO-S	CRIMP-S	DAVEN-S	DISME-S	DROWN-S	EMBAR-S	EVENT-S	FIDGE-S
COMPT-S	CRINE-S	DAVIT-S	DITAL-S	DRUID-S	EMBAY-S	EVERT-S	FIELD-S
CONCH-S	CRISE-S	DAZER-S	DITTO-S	DRUPE-S	EMBED-S	EVICT-S	FIEND-S
CONDO-S	CRISP-S	DEARE-S	DIVAN-S	DRUSE-S	EMBER-S	EVITE-S	FIENT-S
CONEY-S	CRITH-S	DEARN-S	DIVER-S	DRYAD-S	EMBOG-S	EVOKE-S	FIERE-S
CONGA-S	CROAK-S	DEATH-S	DIVOT-S	DRYER-S	EMBOW-S	EXACT-S	FIFER-S
CONGE-S	CROCK-S	DEAVE-S	DIWAN-S	DSOBO-S	EMCEE-S	EXALT-S	FIFTH-S
CONGO-S	CROFT-S	DEBAG-S	DIXIE-S	DSOMO-S	EMEER-S	EXCEL-S	FIGHT-S
CONIA-S	CROMB-S	DEBAR-S	DIZEN-S	DUCAT-S	EMEND-S	EXEAT-S	FILER-S
CONIC-S	CROME-S	DEBEL-S	DODGE-S	DUETT-S	EMMER-S	EXEEM-S	FILET-S
CONIN-S	CRONE-S	DEBIT-S	DOGIE-S	DULIA-S	EMMET-S	EXEME-S	FILLE-S
CONNE-S	CROOK-S	DEBUG-S	DOGMA-S	DULSE-S	EMMEW-S	EXERT-S	FILTH-S
CONTE-S	CROON-S	DEBUT-S	DOHYO-S	DUMBO-S	EMOTE-S	EXILE-S	FINAL-S
CONTO-S	CRORE-S	DECAD-S	DOING-S	DUNCE-S	EMOVE-S	EXINE-S	FINER-S
CONVO-S	CROUP-S	DECAL-S	DOLCE-S	DUOMO-S	EMULE-S	EXIST-S	FIORD-S
COOEE-S	CROUT-S	DECAY-S	DOLMA-S	DUPER-S	EMURE-S	EXODE-S	FIRER-S
COOEY-S	CROWD-S	DECKO-S	DOLOR-S	DURAL-S	ENACT-S	EXPAT-S	FIRST-S
COOMB-S	CROWN-S	DECOR-S	DONAH-S	DURES-S	ENARM-S	EXPEL-S	FIRTH-S
COOPT-S	CROZE-S	DECOY-S	DONEE-S	DUROY-S	ENDEW-S	EXTOL-S	FITTE-S
COPAL-S	CRUCK-S	DEEVE-S	DONGA-S	DURRA-S	ENDOW-S	EXTRA-S	FIVER-S
COPER-S	CRUDE-S	DEFAT-S	DONNE-S	DURUM-S	ENDUE-S	EXUDE-S	FIXER-S
COPRA-S	CRUEL-S	DEFER-S	DONOR-S	DUVET-S	ENEMA-S	EXULT-S	FJORD-S
COPSE-S	CRUET-S	DEGUM-S	DONUT-S	DWALE-S	ENIAC-S	EXURB-S	FLACK-S
CORAL-S	CRUMB-S	DEIGN-S	DOOLE-S	DWALM-S	ENJOY-S	EYRIE-S	FLAFF-S
CORBE-S	CRUMP-S	DEISM-S	DOONA-S	DWANG-S	ENMEW-S	FABLE-S	FLAIL-S
CORER-S	CRUSE-S	DEIST-S	DOORN-S	DWARF-S	ENROL-S	FACER-S	FLAIR-S
COREY-S	CRUST-S	DEKKO-S	DOPER-S	DWAUM-S	ENSEW-S	FACET-S	FLAKE-S
CORGI-S	CRUVE-S	DELAY-S	DORAD-S	DWEEB-S	ENSUE-S	FACIA-S	FLAME-S
CORSE-S	CRWTH-S	DELFT-S	DOREE-S	DWELL-S	ENTER-S	FADER-S	FLAMM-S
CORSO-S	CTENE-S	DELPH-S	DORSE-S	DWILE-S	ENURE-S	FADGE-S	FLANK-S
COSEC-S	CUBEB-S	DELTA-S	DOSEH-S	DWINE-S	ENVOI-S	FAGOT-S	FLARE-S
COSET-S	CUBIC-S	DELVE-S	DOTER-S	DYING-S	ENVOY-S	FAINE-S	FLASK-S
COSTE-S	CUBIT-S	DEMAN-S	DOUAR-S	EAGER-S	EOSIN-S	FAINT-S	FLAWN-S
COTTA-S	CULET-S	DEMIT-S	DOUBT-S	EAGLE-S	EPACT-S	FAITH-S	FLEAM-S
COUGH-S	CUMEC-S	DEMOB-S	DOUGH-S	EAGRE-S	EPHAH-S	FAKER-S	FLECK-S
COUNT-S	CUMIN-S	DEMON-S	DOUMA-S	EARTH-S	EPHOD-S	FAKIR-S	FLEER-S
COUPE-S	CUPEL-S	DEMUR-S	DOURA-S	EASEL-S	EPHOR-S	FALSE-S	FLEET-S
COURB-S	CUPID-S	DENAY-S	DOUSE-S	EASLE-S	EPOCH-S	FANAL-S	FLEME-S
COURE-S	CUPPA-S	DENET-S	DOVER-S	EATER-S	EPODE-S	FANGO-S	FLICK-S
COURT-S	CURAT-S	DENIM-S	DOWAR-S	ECLAT-S	EPOPT-S	FANON-S	FLIER-S
COVEN-S	CURER-S	DEPOT-S	DOWEL-S	EDEMA-S	EPROM-S	FARAD-S	FLIMP-S
COVER-S	CURIA-S	DEPTH-S	DOWER-S	EDGER-S	EQUAL-S	FARCE-S	FLING-S
COVET-S	CURIE-S	DERAY-S	DOWLE-S	EDICT-S	EQUID-S	FARLE-S	FLINT-S
COVEY-S	CURIO-S	DERIG-S	DOWSE-S	EDILE-S	EQUIP-S	FARSE-S	FLIRT-S
COVIN-S	CURSE-S	DERMA-S	DOYEN-S	EDUCE-S	ERASE-S	FATSO-S	FLISK-S
COWAL-S	CURVE-S	DERTH-S	DOZEN-S	EDUCT-S	EQUIP-S	FATWA-S	FLITE-S
COWAN-S	CUSEC-S	DESSE-S	DOZER-S	EEVEN-S	ERBIA-S	FAULT-S	FLOAT-S
COWER-S		DETER-S	DRAFF-S			FAUNA-S	FLOCK-S

FLONG-S	FUGIE-S	GIBER-S	GRAIP-S	GUSTO-S	HIDER-S	ILLTH-S	JNANA-S
FLOOD-S	FUGLE-S	GIGOT-S	GRAMA-S	GUTTA-S	HIGHT-S	IMAGE-S	JOCKO-S
FLOOR-S	FUGUE-S	GIGUE-S	GRAME-S	GUYLE-S	HIJAB-S	IMAGO-S	JODEL-S
FLORA-S	FUMET-S	GILET-S	GRAND-S	GUYOT-S	HIJRA-S	IMARI-S	JOINT-S
FLOTA-S	FUNDI-S	GIMME-S	GRANT-S	GUYSE-S	HIKER-S	IMAUM-S	JOIST-S
FLOTE-S	FURAL-S	GIPPO-S	GRAPE-S	GYELD-S	HILLO-S	IMBAR-S	JOKER-S
FLOUR-S	FUROL-S	GIRON-S	GRAPH-S	GYNAE-S	HIMBO-S	IMBED-S	JORAM-S
FLOUT-S	FUROR-S	GIRTH-S	GRASP-S	GYNIE-S	HINGE-S	IMBUE-S	JORUM-S
FLUFF-S	FURZE-S	GISMO-S	GRATE-S	GYPPO-S	HIPPO-S	IMIDE-S	JOTUN-S
FLUID-S	FUSEE-S	GIUST-S	GRAVE-S	GYRON-S	HIRER-S	IMINE-S	JOUAL-S
FLUKE-S	FUSIL-S	GIVER-S	GRAZE-S	HABIT-S	HITHE-S	IMMEW-S	JOULE-S
FLUME-S	FUTON-S	GLACE-S	GREBE-S	HADJI-S	HIVER-S	IMMIT-S	JOUST-S
FLUMP-S	FUZEE-S	GLADE-S	GRECE-S	HAICK-S	HIZEN-S	IMPEL-S	JOWAR-S
FLUNK-S	FYTTE-S	GLAIK-S	GREED-S	HAJJI-S	HOARD-S	IMPOT-S	JUDGE-S
FLUOR-S	GABLE-S	GLAIR-S	GREEN-S	HAKAM-S	HOAST-S	INARM-S	JUGAL-S
FLURR-S	GADGE-S	GLAND-S	GREET-S	HAKIM-S	HODJA-S	INCLE-S	JUICE-S
FLUTE-S	GADJE-S	GLARE-S	GREGO-S	HALAL-S	HOGAN-S	INCUR-S	JULEP-S
FLYER-S	GADSO-S	GLAUM-S	GREIN-S	HALER-S	HOGEN-S	INDEW-S	JUMAR-S
FLYPE-S	GAFFE-S	GLAUR-S	GRESE-S	HALFA-S	HOICK-S	INDIE-S	JUMBO-S
FLYTE-S	GAITT-S	GLAZE-S	GREVE-S	HALLO-S	HOISE-S	INDOL-S	JUNCO-S
FOEHN-S	GALAH-S	GLEAM-S	GRICE-S	HALMA-S	HOIST-S	INDRI-S	JUNTA-S
FOGEY-S	GALEA-S	GLEAN-S	GRIDE-S	HALON-S	HOKUM-S	INDUE-S	JUNTO-S
FOGLE-S	GALOP-S	GLEBE-S	GRIEF-S	HALSE-S	HOLLA-S	INFER-S	JUPON-S
FOIST-S	GALUT-S	GLEDE-S	GRIFF-S	HALVA-S	HOLLO-S	INGAN-S	JURAT-S
FOLIE-S	GAMAY-S	GLEED-S	GRIFT-S	HALVE-S	HOMER-S	INGLE-S	JUROR-S
FOLIO-S	GAMBA-S	GLEEK-S	GRIKE-S	HAMAL-S	HOMME-S	INGOT-S	KAAMA-S
FONDA-S	GAMBO-S	GLEET-S	GRILL-S	HAMZA-S	HONER-S	INKER-S	KABAB-S
FORAY-S	GAMIN-S	GLENT-S	GRIME-S	HANAP-S	HONEY-S	INKLE-S	KABOB-S
FORCE-S	GAMMA-S	GLIDE-S	GRIND-S	HANCE-S	HONGI-S	INLAY-S	KAHAL-S
FOREL-S	GAMME-S	GLIFF-S	GRIOT-S	HAOMA-S	HONOR-S	INLET-S	KAIAK-S
FORGE-S	GAMUT-S	GLIFT-S	GRIPE-S	HARAM-S	HOOEY-S	INNER-S	KALIF-S
FORME-S	GANJA-S	GLIKE-S	GRISE-S	HAREM-S	HOOKA-S	INORB-S	KALPA-S
FORTE-S	GAPER-S	GLINT-S	GRIST-S	HARIM-S	HOORD-S	INPUT-S	KAMIK-S
FORUM-S	GARBE-S	GLISK-S	GRITH-S	HASTE-S	HOOVE-S	INSET-S	KANEH-S
FOSSA-S	GARBO-S	GLOAT-S	GRIZE-S	HATER-S	HOPER-S	INTER-S	KANGA-S
FOSSE-S	GARRE-S	GLOBE-S	GROAN-S	HAUGH-S	HORDE-S	INTRO-S	KANJI-S
FOUAT-S	GARTH-S	GLOGG-S	GROAT-S	HAULD-S	HORME-S	INULA-S	KANZU-S
FOUET-S	GARUM-S	GLOOM-S	GROIN-S	HAULM-S	HORSE-S	INURE-S	KAPOK-S
FOULE-S	GAUGE-S	GLOOP-S	GROMA-S	HAUNT-S	HORST-S	INURN-S	KAPPA-S
FOUND-S	GAUJE-S	GLOUT-S	GRONE-S	HAUSE-S	HOSTA-S	INWIT-S	KARAT-S
FOUNT-S	GAULT-S	GLOVE-S	GROOF-S	HAVEN-S	HOTEL-S	IPPON-S	KARMA-S
FOUTH-S	GAUNT-S	GLOZE-S	GROOM-S	HAVER-S	HOUFF-S	IRADE-S	KARRI-S
FOWTH-S	GAUZE-S	GLUER-S	GROPE-S	HAVOC-S	HOUGH-S	IROKO-S	KARST-S
FOYER-S	GAVEL-S	GLUME-S	GROUF-S	HAWSE-S	HOUND-S	ISLET-S	KASHA-S
FOYLE-S	GAYAL-S	GLUON-S	GROUP-S	HAYLE-S	HOURI-S	ISSEI-S	KATTI-S
FOYNE-S	GAZAL-S	GLYPH-S	GROUT-S	HAZAN-S	HOUSE-S	ISSUE-S	KAUGH-S
FRACT-S	GAZAR-S	GNARL-S	GROVE-S	HAZEL-S	HOVEL-S	ISTLE-S	KAURI-S
FRAIL-S	GAZER-S	GNARR-S	GROWL-S	HAZER-S	HOVER-S	IXTLE-S	KAVAS-S
FRAIM-S	GAZON-S	GNOME-S	GRUEL-S	HEALD-S	HOWFF-S	IZARD-S	KAYAK-S
FRAME-S	GAZOO-S	GODET-S	GRUFE-S	HEARD-S	HOWRE-S	IZZAT-S	KAYLE-S
FRANC-S	GEARE-S	GODSO-S	GRUME-S	HEARE-S	HULLO-S	JABOT-S	KAZOO-S
FRANK-S	GEBUR-S	GOFER-S	GRUMP-S	HEART-S	HUMAN-S	JAGER-S	KEBAB-S
FRAUD-S	GECKO-S	GOING-S	GRUNT-S	HEAST-S	HUMOR-S	JAGIR-S	KEBOB-S
FREAK-S	GEIST-S	GOLEM-S	GRYCE-S	HEATH-S	HUMPH-S	JALAP-S	KEDGE-S
FREER-S	GEMEL-S	GOLPE-S	GRYDE-S	HEAVE-S	HURRA-S	JAMBE-S	KEEVE-S
FREET-S	GEMOT-S	GOMBO-S	GRYKE-S	HEBEN-S	HURST-S	JAMBO-S	KEFIR-S
FREIT-S	GENET-S	GOMPA-S	GRYPE-S	HECHT-S	HUTIA-S	JAMBU-S	KELIM-S
FREMD-S	GENIE-S	GONAD-S	GUACO-S	HEDGE-S	HUZZA-S	JAPAN-S	KEMBO-S
FREON-S	GENIP-S	GONER-S	GUANA-S	HEEZE-S	HYDRA-S	JAPER-S	KENAF-S
FRERE-S	GENOA-S	GOOSE-S	GUANO-S	HEIST-S	HYDRO-S	JARTA-S	KENDO-S
FRIAR-S	GENOM-S	GOPAK-S	GUARD-S	HEJAB-S	HYENA-S	JARUL-S	KERNE-S
FRIER-S	GENRE-S	GORAL-S	GUAVA-S	HEJRA-S	HYLEG-S	JASEY-S	KERVE-S
FRILL-S	GEODE-S	GORGE-S	GUEST-S	HELLO-S	HYMEN-S	JASPE-S	KESAR-S
FRISK-S	GEOID-S	GORSE-S	GUIDE-S	HELOT-S	HYNDE-S	JAUNT-S	KEVEL-S
FRIST-S	GERAH-S	GOSHT-S	GUILD-S	HELVE-S	HYPER-S	JAVEL-S	KHADI-S
FRITH-S	GERBE-S	GOSSE-S	GUILE-S	HENGE-S	HYSON-S	JAWAN-S	KHAKI-S
FRIZE-S	GERLE-S	GOUGE-S	GUILT-S	HENNA-S	HYTHE-S	JEBEL-S	KHAYA-S
FROCK-S	GERNE-S	GOURA-S	GUIMP-S	HENRY-S	ICHOR-S	JEHAD-S	KHEDA-S
FROND-S	GESSE-S	GOURD-S	GUIRO-S	HEPAR-S	ICING-S	JELAB-S	KHOJA-S
FRONT-S	GESTE-S	GOWAN-S	GUISE-S	HEROE-S	ICKER-S	JELLO-S	KIANG-S
FROST-S	GHAST-S	GRAAL-S	GULAG-S	HERON-S	IDANT-S	JERID-S	KIDDO-S
FROTH-S	GHAUT-S	GRACE-S	GULPH-S	HERSE-S	IDEAL-S	JETON-S	KIDEL-S
FROWN-S	GHAZI-S	GRADE-S	GUMBO-S	HERYE-S	IDIOM-S	JEWEL-S	KIEVE-S
FRUIT-S	GHOST-S	GRAFF-S	GUNGE-S	HEUCH-S	IDIOT-S	JHALA-S	KIGHT-S
FRUMP-S	GHOUL-S	GRAFT-S	GURGE-S	HEUGH-S	IDLER-S	JIBER-S	KIKOI-S
FRUST-S	GHYLL-S	GRAIL-S	GUSLA-S	HEVEA-S	IDYLL-S	JIGOT-S	KILEY-S
FRYER-S	GIANT-S	GRAIN-S	GUSLE-S	HEWER-S	IGAPO-S	JIHAD-S	KILIM-S
FUDGE-S	GIBEL-S	GRAIN-S	GUSLI-S	HEXAD-S	IGLOO-S	JIRGA-S	KIMBO-S
FUERO-S	GIBEL-S	GRAIN-S	GUSLI-S	HEXAD-S	IHRAM-S	JIVER-S	KININ-S

KIOSK-S	LASSI-S	LIVER-S	MAHUA-S	METAL-S	MOTEL-S	NAZIR-S	OCHRE-S
KIPPA-S	LASSO-S	LIVOR-S	MAHWA-S	METER-S	MOTET-S	NEAFE-S	OCKER-S
KIRRI-S	LASSU-S	LIVRE-S	MAIKO-S	METIC-S	MOTIF-S	NEBEK-S	OCTAD-S
KISAN-S	LATEN-S	LLAMA-S	MAILE-S	METIF-S	MOTOR-S	NEBEL-S	OCTAL-S
KITHE-S	LATHE-S	LLANO-S	MAIRE-S	METOL-S	MOTTE-S	NEELD-S	OCTET-S
KLANG-S	LATHI-S	LOAVE-S	MAISE-S	METRE-S	MOTZA-S	NEEMB-S	ODEON-S
KLOOF-S	LATKE-S	LOCAL-S	MAIZE-S	METRO-S	MOULD-S	NEELE-S	ODEUM-S
KNACK-S	LAUCH-S	LOCUM-S	MAJOR-S	MEUSE-S	MOULT-S	NEESE-S	ODISM-S
KNARL-S	LAUGH-S	LODEN-S	MAKAR-S	MEZZE-S	MOUND-S	NEEZE-S	ODIST-S
KNAVE-S	LAUND-S	LODGE-S	MAKER-S	MEZZO-S	MOUNT-S	NEIGH-S	ODIUM-S
KNEAD-S	LAURA-S	LOGAN-S	MALAR-S	MHORR-S	MOURN-S	NEIVE-S	ODOUR-S
KNEEL-S	LAVER-S	LOGIC-S	MALIK-S	MIAOW-S	MOUSE-S	NEPER-S	ODYLE-S
KNELL-S	LAVRA-S	LOGIE-S	MALVA-S	MIASM-S	MOUST-S	NEPIT-S	OFFAL-S
KNIFE-S	LAWIN-S	LOGIN-S	MAMBA-S	MIAUL-S	MOUTH-S	NERKA-S	OFFER-S
KNIVE-S	LAYER-S	LOGON-S	MAMBO-S	MICHE-S	MOVER-S	NERVE-S	OFLAG-S
KNOCK-S	LAZAR-S	LOLOG-S	MAMEE-S	MICRO-S	MOVIE-S	NEUME-S	OGGIN-S
KNOLL-S	LEARE-S	LONER-S	MAMMA-S	MIDGE-S	MOWER-S	NEVEL-S	OGHAM-S
KNOSP-S	LEARN-S	LONGA-S	MANEH-S	MIDST-S	MOWRA-S	NEWEL-S	OGIVE-S
KNOUT-S	LEASE-S	LONGE-S	MANGA-S	MIEVE-S	MOXIE-S	NGAIO-S	OGLER-S
KNOWE-S	LEAST-S	LOOFA-S	MANGE-S	MIGHT-S	MOYLE-S	NGANA-S	OGRES-S
KNOWN-S	LEAVE-S	LOORD-S	MANIA-S	MILER-S	MPRET-S	NICAD-S	OILER-S
KNURL-S	LEAZE-S	LOPER-S	MANNA-S	MILKO-S	MUCIN-S	NICHE-S	OJIME-S
KNURR-S	LEDGE-S	LORAN-S	MANOR-S	MILLE-S	MUCOR-S	NICOL-S	OKAPI-S
KOALA-S	LEDUM-S	LOREL-S	MANSE-S	MILOR-S	MUCRO-S	NIDOR-S	OLDEN-S
KOBAN-S	LEEAR-S	LORIC-S	MANTA-S	MIMER-S	MUDGE-S	NIECE-S	OLDIE-S
KOFTA-S	LEESE-S	LOSEL-S	MANTO-S	MIMIC-S	MUDIR-S	NIEVE-S	OLEIN-S
KOINE-S	LEGER-S	LOSER-S	MANUL-S	MINAR-S	MUDRA-S	NIGER-S	OLEUM-S
KOKER-S	LEGGE-S	LOTAH-S	MAPLE-S	MINCE-S	MUFTI-S	NIGHT-S	OLIVE-S
KOKRA-S	LEMAN-S	LOTTO-S	MAQUI-S	MINER-S	MUIST-S	NIHIL-S	OLLAV-S
KOKUM-S	LEMEL-S	LOUGH-S	MARAE-S	MINGE-S	MUJIK-S	NIKAU-S	OMBRE-S
KOMBU-S	LEMMA-S	LOUND-S	MARAH-S	MINIM-S	MULCT-S	NINJA-S	OMEGA-S
KOORI-S	LEMON-S	LOUPE-S	MARGE-S	MINKE-S	MULEY-S	NINON-S	OMLAH-S
KOPJE-S	LEMUR-S	LOURE-S	MARID-S	MINOR-S	MULGA-S	NINTH-S	OMRAH-S
KOPPA-S	LENTO-S	LOUSE-S	MARLE-S	MIRIN-S	MULSE-S	NISEI-S	ONCER-S
KORMA-S	LEONE-S	LOVER-S	MARON-S	MIRTH-S	MUNGO-S	NISSE-S	ONION-S
KOTOW-S	LEPER-S	LOVEY-S	MAROR-S	MISER-S	MUNTU-S	NITER-S	ONSET-S
KRAAL-S	LEPRA-S	LOVAT-S	MASER-S	MITER-S	MURAL-S	NITON-S	OOBIT-S
KRAFT-S	LESBO-S	LOWAN-S	MASON-S	MITRE-S	MURRA-S	NITRE-S	OOMPH-S
KRAIT-S	LEVEE-S	LOWER-S	MASSA-S	MIXEN-S	MURRE-S	NIXIE-S	OPEPE-S
KRANG-S	LEVEL-S	LOWND-S	MASSE-S	MIXER-S	MURVA-S	NIZAM-S	OPERA-S
KRAUT-S	LEVER-S	LOWNE-S	MATER-S	MIZEN-S	MUSER-S	NOBLE-S	OPINE-S
KRENG-S	LEVIN-S	LOWSE-S	MATIN-S	MNEME-S	MUSET-S	NOINT-S	OPIUM-S
KRILL-S	LIANA-S	LOZEN-S	MATLO-S	MOBLE-S	MUSIC-S	NOISE-S	OPTER-S
KUDZU-S	LIANE-S	LUBRA-S	MATTE-S	MOCHA-S	MUSIT-S	NOMAD-S	OPTIC-S
KUKRI-S	LIANG-S	LUCRE-S	MATZA-S	MODAL-S	MUSSE-S	NONCE-S	ORANG-S
KULAK-S	LIARD-S	LUFFA-S	MATZO-S	MODEL-S	MUSTH-S	NONET-S	ORANT-S
KULAN-S	LIBEL-S	LUGER-S	MAUND-S	MODEM-S	MUTON-S	NOOSE-S	ORATE-S
KURRE-S	LIBER-S	LUMEN-S	MAUVE-S	MODER-S	MVULE-S	NOPAL-S	ORBIT-S
KURTA-S	LIBRA-S	LUNAR-S	MAVEN-S	MOGUL-S	MYALL-S	NORIA-S	ORCIN-S
KWELA-S	LICHI-S	LUNGE-S	MAVIN-S	MOHEL-S	MYNAH-S	NORMA-S	ORDER-S
KYANG-S	LICHT-S	LUNGI-S	MAXIM-S	MOHUR-S	MYOMA-S	NORTH-S	OREAD-S
KYLIE-S	LIEGE-S	LUPIN-S	MAYBE-S	MOIRE-S	MYOPE-S	NOSER-S	ORGAN-S
KYLIN-S	LIFER-S	LUPIN-S	MAYOR-S	MOIST-S	MYRRH-S	NOSEY-S	ORGIA-S
KYLOE-S	LIGAN-S	LURGI-S	MAZER-S	MOLAR-S	NABLA-S	NOTER-S	ORGUE-S
KYNDE-S	LIGER-S	LURVE-S	MAZUT-S	MOLLA-S	NABOB-S	NOULE-S	ORIBI-S
KYTHE-S	LIGGE-S	LUTER-S	MBIRA-S	MOMMA-S	NACHE-S	NOVEL-S	ORIEL-S
LABDA-S	LIGHT-S	LYCEE-S	MEANE-S	MONAD-S	NACHO-S	NOVUM-S	ORLOP-S
LABEL-S	LIGNE-S	LYING-S	MEARE-S	MONAL-S	NACRE-S	NOWAY-S	ORMER-S
LABOR-S	LIKEN-S	LYMPH-S	MEASE-S	MONEY-S	NADIR-S	NOYAU-S	ORPIN-S
LACET-S	LIKER-S	LYRIC-S	MEATH-S	MONTE-S	NAEVE-S	NUBIA-S	ORTHO-S
LADLE-S	LIKIN-S	LYSIN-S	MEDAL-S	MONTH-S	NAGOR-S	NUDGE-S	ORVAL-S
LAGAN-S	LILAC-S	LYSOL-S	MEDIC-S	MOOLA-S	NAHAL-S	NUDIE-S	OSHAC-S
LAGER-S	LIMBO-S	LYSSA-S	MEDLE-S	MOOLI-S	NAIAD-S	NULLA-S	OSIER-S
LAHAR-S	LIMEN-S	LYTHE-S	MEITH-S	MOOVE-S	NAIRA-S	NURSE-S	OTHER-S
LAIGH-S	LIMEY-S	LYTTA-S	MELEE-S	MOPED-S	NAKER-S	NYAFF-S	OTTAR-S
LAIKA-S	LIMIT-S	MACAW-S	MELIC-S	MOPER-S	NALLA-S	NYALA-S	OTTER-S
LAIRD-S	LIMMA-S	MACER-S	MELIK-S	MORAL-S	NAMER-S	NYLON-S	OUBIT-S
LAKER-S	LINAC-S	MACHO-S	MELON-S	MORAS-S	NANCE-S	NYMPH-S	OUCHT-S
LAKIN-S	LINEN-S	MACLE-S	MENGE-S	MORAT-S	NANDU-S	NYSSA-S	OUGHT-S
LAMIA-S	LINER-S	MACON-S	MENSE-S	MORAY-S	NANNA-S	OAKER-S	OUIJA-S
LANCE-S	LINGA-S	MACRO-S	MENTO-S	MOREL-S	NAPOO-S	OAKUM-S	OUNCE-S
LANDE-S	LININ-S	MADAM-S	MEREL-S	MORIA-S	NAPPA-S	OATER-S	OUPHE-S
LAPEL-S	LIPID-S	MADGE-S	MERGE-S	MORNE-S	NAPPE-S	OBANG-S	OUSEL-S
LAPJE-S	LISLE-S	MAFIA-S	MERIL-S	MORON-S	NARCO-S	OBEAH-S	OUTER-S
LAPSE-S	LITER-S	MAFIC-S	MERIT-S	MORPH-S	NASAL-S	OBJET-S	OUZEL-S
LARGE-S	LITHE-S	MAGIC-S	MERLE-S	MORRA-S	NAUNT-S	OCCAM-S	OVATE-S
LARGO-S	LITHO-S	MAGMA-S	MERSE-S	MORRO-S	NAVEL-S	OCCUR-S	OVIST-S
LARUM-S	LITRE-S	MAGOT-S	MESEL-S	MORSE-S	NAVEW-S	OCEAN-S	OVOID-S
LASER-S	LIVEN-S	MAHOE-S	MESON-S	MOSEY-S	NAWAB-S	OCHER-S	OVULE-S

OWCHE-S	PEEVE-S	PLASM-S	PRATT-S	QUACK-S	RAVEL-S	REVEL-S	ROWTH-S
OWLER-S	PEISE-S	PLATE-S	PRAWN-S	QUAFF-S	RAVEN-S	REVET-S	ROYAL-S
OWLET-S	PEIZE-S	PLAYA-S	PREEN-S	QUAIL-S	RAVER-S	REVIE-S	ROYNE-S
OWNER-S	PEKAN-S	PLAZA-S	PREIF-S	QUAIR-S	RAVIN-S	REVUE-S	ROYST-S
OXIDE-S	PEKOE-S	PLEAD-S	PRENT-S	QUAKE-S	RAYAH-S	REWTH-S	ROZET-S
OXIME-S	PELMA-S	PLEAT-S	PRESE-S	QUALM-S	RAYLE-S	RHEUM-S	ROZIT-S
OXLIP-S	PELTA-S	PLEON-S	PREST-S	QUANT-S	RAYNE-S	RHIME-S	RUANA-S
OXTER-S	PENCE-S	PLIER-S	PREVE-S	QUARK-S	RAYON-S	RHINE-S	RUBIN-S
OZEKI-S	PENIE-S	PLING-S	PRIAL-S	QUART-S	RAZEE-S	RHINO-S	RUBLE-S
OZONE-S	PENNE-S	PLINK-S	PRICE-S	QUEAN-S	RAZOO-S	RHOMB-S	RUCHE-S
PACER-S	PERAI-S	PLOAT-S	PRICK-S	QUEEN-S	RAZOR-S	RHONE-S	RUDIE-S
PACHA-S	PERCE-S	PLONG-S	PRIDE-S	QUEER-S	REACT-S	RHUMB-S	RUFFE-S
PADLE-S	PERDU-S	PLONK-S	PRIEF-S	QUELL-S	REALM-S	RHYME-S	RUING-S
PADMA-S	PERIL-S	PLOOK-S	PRIER-S	QUEME-S	REALO-S	RHYNE-S	RULER-S
PADRE-S	PERSE-S	PLOUK-S	PRILL-S	QUENA-S	REAME-S	RIATA-S	RUMAL-S
PAEAN-S	PERVE-S	PLUCK-S	PRIME-S	QUERN-S	REARM-S	RICER-S	RUMBA-S
PAEON-S	PESTO-S	PLUFF-S	PRIMO-S	QUEST-S	REAST-S	RICHT-S	RUMBO-S
PAGAN-S	PETAL-S	PLUMB-S	PRIMP-S	QUEUE-S	REATA-S	RICIN-S	RUMOR-S
PAGER-S	PETAR-S	PLUME-S	PRINK-S	QUEYN-S	REATE-S	RIDER-S	RUPEE-S
PAGLE-S	PETER-S	PLUMP-S	PRINT-S	QUICK-S	REAVE-S	RIDGE-S	RUPIA-S
PAGOD-S	PETRE-S	PLUNK-S	PRION-S	QUIET-S	REBBE-S	RIEVE-S	RURAL-S
PAGRI-S	PEWIT-S	POAKA-S	PRIOR-S	QUIFF-S	REBEC-S	RIFLE-S	RUSMA-S
PAINT-S	PEYSE-S	POAKE-S	PRISE-S	QUILL-S	REBEL-S	RIGHT-S	RUTIN-S
PAIRE-S	PHAGE-S	PODGE-S	PRISM-S	QUILT-S	REBID-S	RIGID-S	RYBAT-S
PAISA-S	PHANG-S	POGGE-S	PRIZE-S	QUINA-S	REBUT-S	RIGOL-S	RYMME-S
PALAY-S	PHARE-S	POILU-S	PROBE-S	QUINE-S	RECAL-S	RIGOR-S	SABER-S
PALET-S	PHASE-S	POIND-S	PROEM-S	QUINT-S	RECAP-S	RILLE-S	SABIN-S
PALKI-S	PHEER-S	POINT-S	PROIN-S	QUIPO-S	RECCE-S	RIMER-S	SABLE-S
PAMPA-S	PHENE-S	POISE-S	PROKE-S	QUIPU-S	RECCO-S	RINSE-S	SABOT-S
PANCE-S	PHEON-S	POKAL-S	PROLE-S	QUIRE-S	RECIT-S	RIPEN-S	SABRA-S
PANDA-S	PHESE-S	POKER-S	PROLL-S	QUIRK-S	RECTO-S	RIPER-S	SABRE-S
PANEL-S	PHIAL-S	POKEY-S	PROMO-S	QUIRT-S	RECUR-S	RISER-S	SADDO-S
PANGA-S	PHOCA-S	POLAR-S	PRONE-S	QUIST-S	REDAN-S	RISHI-S	SADHE-S
PANIC-S	PHONE-S	POLER-S	PRONG-S	QUITE-S	REDIP-S	RIVAL-S	SADHU-S
PANIM-S	PHOTO-S	POLEY-S	PRONK-S	QUOIF-S	REEDE-S	RIVEL-S	SADZA-S
PANNE-S	PIANO-S	POLIO-S	PROOF-S	QUOIN-S	REEST-S	RIVER-S	SAHIB-S
PANTO-S	PICOT-S	POLKA-S	PRORE-S	QUOIT-S	REEVE-S	RIVET-S	SAICE-S
PAPAW-S	PICRA-S	POLYP-S	PROSE-S	QUOLL-S	REFEL-S	RIYAL-S	SAICK-S
PAPER-S	PICUL-S	POMBE-S	PROSO-S	QUONK-S	REFER-S	ROAST-S	SAIGA-S
PAREO-S	PIECE-S	PONCE-S	PROUL-S	QUOTA-S	REFFO-S	ROATE-S	SAINT-S
PARER-S	PIEND-S	PONEY-S	PROVE-S	QUOTE-S	REFIT-S	ROBIN-S	SAITH-S
PAREU-S	PIETA-S	PONGA-S	PROWL-S	QUYTE-S	REGAL-S	ROBLE-S	SAJOU-S
PARGE-S	PIGHT-S	PONGO-S	PROYN-S	RABAT-S	REGAR-S	ROBOT-S	SAKER-S
PARKA-S	PIKER-S	POOJA-S	PRUDE-S	RABBI-S	REGGO-S	RODEO-S	SAKIA-S
PARKI-S	PIKUL-S	POOKA-S	PRUNE-S	RACER-S	REGIE-S	ROGER-S	SALAD-S
PARLE-S	PILAU-S	POORI-S	PRUNT-S	RACHE-S	REGUR-S	ROGUE-S	SALAL-S
PARSE-S	PILAW-S	POORT-S	PRYER-S	RACON-S	REIGN-S	ROIST-S	SALEP-S
PARTI-S	PILER-S	POOVE-S	PRYSE-S	RADAR-S	REIKI-S	ROKER-S	SALET-S
PASEO-S	PILOT-S	POPPA-S	PSALM-S	RADGE-S	REIRD-S	ROLAG-S	SALLE-S
PASHA-S	PILOW-S	PORER-S	PSEUD-S	RADIO-S	REIST-S	ROMAL-S	SALMI-S
PASHM-S	PINGO-S	PORGE-S	PSHAW-S	RADON-S	REIVE-S	ROMAN-S	SALON-S
PASSE-S	PINKO-S	PORNO-S	PSION-S	RAGEE-S	REJIG-S	RONDE-S	SALOP-S
PASTA-S	PINON-S	PORTA-S	PSORA-S	RAGER-S	RELAY-S	RONDO-S	SALPA-S
PASTE-S	PINOT-S	POSER-S	PSYCH-S	RAGGA-S	RELET-S	RONEO-S	SALSA-S
PATEN-S	PINTA-S	POSIT-S	PSYOP-S	RAILE-S	RELIC-S	RONTE-S	SALSE-S
PATER-S	PINTO-S	POSSE-S	PUDGE-S	RAINE-S	RELIE-S	ROOSA-S	SALTO-S
PATIN-S	PIOYE-S	POTIN-S	PUDOR-S	RAIRD-S	REMAN-S	ROOSE-S	SALUE-S
PATIO-S	PIPAL-S	POTOO-S	PUGIL-S	RAISE-S	REMEN-S	ROOST-S	SALVE-S
PATTE-S	PIPER-S	POTTO-S	PUKER-S	RAITA-S	REMIT-S	ROPER-S	SALVO-S
PAUSE-S	PIPIT-S	POUKE-S	PULER-S	RAJAH-S	RENAY-S	ROQUE-S	SAMAN-S
PAVAN-S	PIPUL-S	POULE-S	PULKA-S	RAKEE-S	RENEW-S	ROSET-S	SAMBA-S
PAVEN-S	PIQUE-S	POULP-S	PULSE-S	RAKER-S	RENEY-S	ROSIN-S	SAMBO-S
PAVER-S	PIRAI-S	POULT-S	PUMIE-S	RAMEE-S	RENGA-S	ROSIT-S	SAMFU-S
PAVIN-S	PISTE-S	POUND-S	PUNCE-S	RAMEN-S	RENIG-S	ROTOR-S	SAMPI-S
PAWAW-S	PITON-S	POUPE-S	PUNGA-S	RAMIE-S	RENIN-S	ROUGE-S	SANKO-S
PAYEE-S	PITTA-S	POWAN-S	PUNKA-S	RAMIN-S	RENNE-S	ROUGH-S	SANSA-S
PAYER-S	PIVOT-S	POWER-S	PUNTO-S	RANCE-S	RENTE-S	ROULE-S	SAPAN-S
PEACE-S	PIXEL-S	POWIN-S	PUPIL-S	RANEE-S	REPAY-S	ROUND-S	SAPOR-S
PEARE-S	PIXIE-S	POWND-S	PUREE-S	RANGE-S	REPEL-S	ROUSE-S	SAREE-S
PEARL-S	PIZZA-S	POWRE-S	PURGE-S	RANKE-S	REPOT-S	ROUST-S	SARGE-S
PEASE-S	PLACE-S	POYNT-S	PURIM-S	RAPER-S	REPRO-S	ROUTE-S	SARGO-S
PEAZE-S	PLACK-S	POYSE-S	PURIN-S	RAPHE-S	RERUN-S	ROUTH-S	SARIN-S
PECAN-S	PLAGE-S	PRAAM-S	PURSE-S	RAPID-S	RESAY-S	ROVER-S	SAROD-S
PECKE-S	PLAID-S	PRAHU-S	PUSLE-S	RASSE-S	RESET-S	ROWAN-S	SASIN-S
PEDAL-S	PLAIN-S	PRANA-S	PUZEL-S	RATAN-S	RESIN-S	ROWEL-S	SASSE-S
PEDRO-S	PLAIT-S	PRANG-S	PYGAL-S	RATEL-S	RESIT-S	ROWEN-S	SATAY-S
PEECE-S	PLANE-S	PRANK-S	PYLON-S	RATER-S	RETIE-S	ROWER-S	SATIN-S
PEEOY-S	PLANK-S	PRASE-S	QANAT-S	RATIO-S	RETRO-S	ROWME-S	SATYR-S
PEEPE-S	PLANT-S	PRATE-S	QIBLA-S	RATOO-S	REUSE-S	ROWND-S	SAUBA-S

SAUCE-S	SCULK-S	SHEAL-S	SITAR-S	SLYPE-S	SONNE-S	SPLIT-S	STEER-S
SAUCH-S	SCULL-S	SHEAR-S	SITHE-S	SMACK-S	SONSE-S	SPODE-S	STEIL-S
SAUGH-S	SCULP-S	SHEEL-S	SIVER-S	SMAIK-S	SOOLE-S	SPOIL-S	STEIN-S
SAULT-S	SCURF-S	SHEEN-S	SIXER-S	SMALL-S	SOOTE-S	SPOKE-S	STELE-S
SAUNA-S	SCUSE-S	SHEER-S	SIXTE-S	SMALM-S	SOOTH-S	SPOOF-S	STEME-S
SAUNT-S	SCUTE-S	SHEET-S	SIXTH-S	SMALT-S	SOPOR-S	SPOOK-S	STEND-S
SAUTE-S	SDAYN-S	SHEIK-S	SIZAR-S	SMARM-S	SOREE-S	SPOOL-S	STENT-S
SAVER-S	SDEIN-S	SHELF-S	SIZEL-S	SMART-S	SOREL-S	SPOOM-S	STERE-S
SAVEY-S	SEAME-S	SHELL-S	SIZER-S	SMEAR-S	SORGO-S	SPOON-S	STERN-S
SAVIN-S	SEASE-S	SHEND-S	SKAIL-S	SMEEK-S	SORRA-S	SPOOR-S	STICH-S
SAVOR-S	SEAZE-S	SHEOL-S	SKALD-S	SMELL-S	SOUCE-S	SPOOT-S	STICK-S
SAVOY-S	SEBUM-S	SHERD-S	SKANK-S	SMELT-S	SOUGH-S	SPORE-S	STIFF-S
SAWAH-S	SECCO-S	SHEVA-S	SKART-S	SMILE-S	SOUND-S	SPORT-S	STILB-S
SAWER-S	SEDAN-S	SHIEL-S	SKATE-S	SMIRK-S	SOUSE-S	SPOUT-S	STILE-S
SAYER-S	SEDGE-S	SHIER-S	SKATT-S	SMIRR-S	SOUTH-S	SPRAG-S	STILL-S
SAYID-S	SEDUM-S	SHIFT-S	SKEAN-S	SMITE-S	SOWAR-S	SPRAT-S	STILT-S
SAYON-S	SEGAR-S	SHILL-S	SKEAR-S	SMITH-S	SOWCE-S	SPRAY-S	STIME-S
SCAFF-S	SEGNO-S	SHINE-S	SKEER-S	SMOCK-S	SOWER-S	SPRED-S	STING-S
SCAIL-S	SEGOL-S	SHIRE-S	SKEET-S	SMOKE-S	SOWFF-S	SPREE-S	STINK-S
SCALD-S	SEGUE-S	SHIRK-S	SKEGG-S	SMOKO-S	SOWLE-S	SPREW-S	STINT-S
SCALE-S	SEINE-S	SHIRR-S	SKEIN-S	SMOLT-S	SOWND-S	SPRIG-S	STIPA-S
SCALL-S	SEISE-S	SHIRT-S	SKELF-S	SMOOR-S	SOWNE-S	SPRIT-S	STIPE-S
SCALP-S	SEISM-S	SHITE-S	SKELL-S	SMOOT-S	SOWSE-S	SPROD-S	STIRE-S
SCAMP-S	SEIZE-S	SHIVE-S	SKELM-S	SMORE-S	SOWTH-S	SPROG-S	STIRK-S
SCANT-S	SELAH-S	SHLEP-S	SKELP-S	SMOUT-S	SOYLE-S	SPRUE-S	STIRP-S
SCAPA-S	SELLA-S	SHMEK-S	SKENE-S	SMOWT-S	SPACE-S	SPRUG-S	STIVE-S
SCAPE-S	SELLE-S	SHOAL-S	SKIER-S	SNACK-S	SPADE-S	SPULE-S	STOAT-S
SCARE-S	SELVA-S	SHOAT-S	SKIFF-S	SNAFU-S	SPADO-S	SPUME-S	STOCK-S
SCARF-S	SEMEN-S	SHOCK-S	SKILL-S	SNAIL-S	SPAER-S	SPUNK-S	STOEP-S
SCARP-S	SEMIE-S	SHOER-S	SKIMP-S	SNAKE-S	SPAHI-S	SPURN-S	STOIC-S
SCART-S	SENNA-S	SHOGI-S	SKINK-S	SNARE-S	SPAIN-S	SPURT-S	STOIT-S
SCATH-S	SENSE-S	SHOJI-S	SKIRL-S	SNARK-S	SPALD-S	SPYAL-S	STOKE-S
SCATT-S	SEPAD-S	SHOLA-S	SKIRR-S	SNARL-S	SPALE-S	SPYRE-S	STOLE-S
SCAUD-S	SEPAL-S	SHOOK-S	SKIRT-S	SNATH-S	SPALL-S	SQUAB-S	STOMP-S
SCAUP-S	SEPIA-S	SHOOL-S	SKITE-S	SNEAD-S	SPALT-S	SQUAD-S	STOND-S
SCAUR-S	SEPOY-S	SHOOT-S	SKIVE-S	SNEAK-S	SPANE-S	SQUAT-S	STONE-S
SCEND-S	SERAC-S	SHORE-S	SKLIM-S	SNEAP-S	SPANG-S	SQUAW-S	STONK-S
SCENE-S	SERAI-S	SHORT-S	SKOFF-S	SNECK-S	SPANK-S	SQUEG-S	STOOK-S
SCENT-S	SERGE-S	SHOTE-S	SKRAN-S	SNEER-S	SPARE-S	SQUIB-S	STOOL-S
SCHWA-S	SERIF-S	SHOTT-S	SKRIK-S	SNELL-S	SPARK-S	SQUID-S	STOOP-S
SCION-S	SERIN-S	SHOUT-S	SKULK-S	SNICK-S	SPART-S	SQUIT-S	STOOR-S
SCLIM-S	SERON-S	SHOVE-S	SKULL-S	SNIDE-S	SPASM-S	STACK-S	STOPE-S
SCOFF-S	SEROW-S	SHOYU-S	SKUNK-S	SNIFF-S	SPATE-S	STADE-S	STORE-S
SCOLD-S	SERRA-S	SHRED-S	SKYER-S	SNIFT-S	SPAUL-S	STAFF-S	STORK-S
SCONE-S	SERRE-S	SHREW-S	SKYRE-S	SNIPE-S	SPAWL-S	STAGE-S	STORM-S
SCOOG-S	SERUM-S	SHROW-S	SKYTE-S	SNIRT-S	SPAWN-S	STAIG-S	STOUN-S
SCOOP-S	SERVE-S	SHRUB-S	SLACK-S	SNOEK-S	SPAYD-S	STAIN-S	STOUP-S
SCOOT-S	SETON-S	SHRUG-S	SLADE-S	SNOKE-S	SPEAK-S	STAIR-S	STOUR-S
SCOPA-S	SEVEN-S	SHTUP-S	SLAKE-S	SNOOD-S	SPEAL-S	STAKE-S	STOUT-S
SCOPE-S	SEVER-S	SHUCK-S	SLANE-S	SNOOK-S	SPEAN-S	STALE-S	STOVE-S
SCORE-S	SEWEL-S	SHULE-S	SLANG-S	SNOOL-S	SPEAR-S	STALK-S	STRAD-S
SCORN-S	SEWEN-S	SHUNT-S	SLANT-S	SNOOP-S	SPEAT-S	STALL-S	STRAE-S
SCOUG-S	SEWER-S	SHURA-S	SLATE-S	SNOOT-S	SPECK-S	STAMP-S	STRAG-S
SCOUR-S	SEWIN-S	SHUTE-S	SLAVE-S	SNORE-S	SPEED-S	STAND-S	STRAP-S
SCOUT-S	SEXER-S	SHYER-S	SLEEK-S	SNORT-S	SPEEL-S	STANE-S	STRAW-S
SCOWL-S	SEYEN-S	SIBYL-S	SLEEP-S	SNOUT-S	SPEER-S	STANG-S	STRAY-S
SCOWP-S	SHACK-S	SICKO-S	SLEET-S	SNOWK-S	SPEIR-S	STANK-S	STREP-S
SCRAB-S	SHADE-S	SIDER-S	SLICE-S	SNUFF-S	SPELD-S	STAPH-S	STREW-S
SCRAE-S	SHAFT-S	SIDHA-S	SLICK-S	SOARE-S	SPELK-S	STARE-S	STRIG-S
SCRAG-S	SHAKE-S	SIDLE-S	SLIDE-S	SOBER-S	SPELL-S	STARK-S	STRIP-S
SCRAM-S	SHAKO-S	SIEGE-S	SLIME-S	SOCLE-S	SPELT-S	STARN-S	STROP-S
SCRAN-S	SHALE-S	SIENT-S	SLING-S	SOFAR-S	SPEND-S	STARR-S	STROW-S
SCRAP-S	SHALM-S	SIETH-S	SLINK-S	SOFTA-S	SPERM-S	START-S	STROY-S
SCRAT-S	SHAMA-S	SIEVE-S	SLIPE-S	SOGER-S	SPIAL-S	STATE-S	STRUM-S
SCRAW-S	SHAME-S	SIGHT-S	SLIVE-S	SOKAH-S	SPICA-S	STAVE-S	STRUT-S
SCRAY-S	SHAND-S	SIGIL-S	SLOAN-S	SOKEN-S	SPICE-S	STEAD-S	STUCK-S
SCREE-S	SHANK-S	SIGMA-S	SLOID-S	SOLAH-S	SPICK-S	STEAK-S	STUFF-S
SCREW-S	SHAPE-S	SILEN-S	SLOOM-S	SOLAN-S	SPIEL-S	STEAL-S	STULL-S
SCRIM-S	SHARD-S	SILER-S	SLOOP-S	SOLAR-S	SPIKE-S	STEAM-S	STULM-S
SCRIP-S	SHARE-S	SILVA-S	SLOOT-S	SOLDE-S	SPILE-S	STEAN-S	STUMP-S
SCROD-S	SHARK-S	SIMAR-S	SLOPE-S	SOLER-S	SPILL-S	STEAR-S	STUNT-S
SCROG-S	SHARN-S	SIMUL-S	SLOTH-S	SOLID-S	SPINA-S	STEDD-S	STUPA-S
SCROW-S	SHARP-S	SINEW-S	SLOYD-S	SOLUM-S	SPINE-S	STEDE-S	STUPE-S
SCRUB-S	SHAVE-S	SINGE-S	SLUBB-S	SOLVE-S	SPINK-S	STEED-S	STURT-S
SCRUM-S	SHAWL-S	SIREN-S	SLUIT-S	SOMAN-S	SPIRE-S	STEEK-S	STYLE-S
SCUBA-S	SHAWM-S	SIRIH-S	SLUMP-S	SONAR-S	SPIRT-S	STEEL-S	STYLO-S
SCUFF-S	SHAYA-S	SIROC-S	SLURB-S	SONCE-S	SPITE-S	STEEM-S	STYME-S
SCUFT-S	SHCHI-S	SIRUP-S	SLURP-S	SONDE-S	SPLAT-S	STEEN-S	
	SHEAF-S	SISAL-S	SLUSE-S	SONIC-S	SPLAY-S	STEEP-S	

STYRE-S	TABUN-S	TERNE-S	TOKEN-S	TRULL-S	UNGUM-S	VERSE-S	WATAP-S
STYTE-S	TACAN-S	TERRA-S	TOMAN-S	TRUMP-S	UNHAT-S	VERSO-S	WATER-S
SUBAH-S	TACHE-S	TESLA-S	TONDO-S	TRUNK-S	UNION-S	VERST-S	WAUFF-S
SUBER-S	TACHO-S	TESTE-S	TONER-S	TRUST-S	UNITE-S	VERTU-S	WAUGH-S
SUCRE-S	TAFIA-S	TETRA-S	TONGA-S	TRUTH-S	UNLAW-S	VERVE-S	WAULK-S
SUDOR-S	TAIGA-S	TEWEL-S	TONIC-S	TRYER-S	UNLAY-S	VESPA-S	WAVER-S
SUEDE-S	TAINT-S	TEWIT-S	TONNE-S	TRYST-S	UNLID-S	VESTA-S	WAVEY-S
SUGAR-S	TAIRA-S	THACK-S	TOOTH-S	TSUBA-S	UNMAN-S	VEXER-S	WAXER-S
SUING-S	TAKER-S	THAGI-S	TOPEE-S	TUART-S	UNMEW-S	VEZIR-S	WAZIR-S
SUINT-S	TAKHI-S	THANA-S	TOPEK-S	TUATH-S	UNPAY-S	VIAND-S	WEALD-S
SUITE-S	TAKIN-S	THANE-S	TOPER-S	TUBER-S	UNPEG-S	VICAR-S	WEAMB-S
SUJEE-S	TALAK-S	THANK-S	TOPIC-S	TUFFE-S	UNPEN-S	VIDEO-S	WEAVE-S
SULFA-S	TALAQ-S	THEEK-S	TOQUE-S	TUGRA-S	UNPIN-S	VIFDA-S	WEBER-S
SUMAC-S	TALAR-S	THEFT-S	TORAN-S	TUINA-S	UNRIG-S	VIGIA-S	WECHT-S
SUMPH-S	TALER-S	THEGN-S	TORSE-S	TUISM-S	UNRIP-S	VIGIL-S	WEDGE-S
SUNUP-S	TALMA-S	THEIC-S	TORSK-S	TULIP-S	UNSAY-S	VIGOR-S	WEEKE-S
SUPER-S	TALON-S	THEIR-S	TORSO-S	TULLE-S	UNSET-S	VILLA-S	WEFTE-S
SURAH-S	TALPA-S	THEME-S	TORTE-S	TUMOR-S	UNSEW-S	VINCA-S	WEIGH-S
SURAT-S	TALUK-S	THERE-S	TOTAL-S	TUNER-S	UNTIE-S	VINER-S	WEIRD-S
SURGE-S	TAMAL-S	THERM-S	TOTEM-S	TUNIC-S	UNTIN-S	VINEW-S	WEISE-S
SURRA-S	TAMER-S	THESE-S	TOUGH-S	TUPEK-S	UNWIT-S	VINYL-S	WEIZE-S
SUSHI-S	TAMIN-S	THETA-S	TOUSE-S	TUPIK-S	UNZIP-S	VIOLA-S	WELKE-S
SUTOR-S	TANGA-S	THETE-S	TOUZE-S	TUQUE-S	UPEND-S	VIPER-S	WHACK-S
SUTRA-S	TANGI-S	THICK-S	TOWEL-S	TURBO-S	UPJET-S	VIREO-S	WHANG-S
SWAGE-S	TANGO-S	THIGH-S	TOWER-S	TURME-S	UPLAY-S	VIRGA-S	WHARE-S
SWAIN-S	TANKA-S	THILL-S	TOWSE-S	TUTEE-S	UPPER-S	VIRGE-S	WHARF-S
SWALE-S	TANNA-S	THING-S	TOWZE-S	TUTOR-S	UPRUN-S	VIRTU-S	WHAUP-S
SWAMI-S	TAPER-S	THINK-S	TOXIN-S	TUTTI-S	UPSEE-S	VISIE-S	WHAUR-S
SWAMP-S	TAPET-S	THIOL-S	TOYER-S	TWAIN-S	UPSET-S	VISIT-S	WHEAL-S
SWANK-S	TAPIR-S	THIRD-S	TOZIE-S	TWANG-S	UPSEY-S	VISNE-S	WHEAT-S
SWARD-S	TAPPA-S	THIRL-S	TRACE-S	TWANK-S	UPTAK-S	VISON-S	WHEEL-S
SWARF-S	TARGE-S	THOFT-S	TRACK-S	TWEAK-S	UPTIE-S	VISOR-S	WHEEN-S
SWARM-S	TAROC-S	THOLE-S	TRACT-S	TWEED-S	URALI-S	VISTA-S	WHEFT-S
SWATH-S	TAROK-S	THONG-S	TRADE-S	TWEEL-S	URARI-S	VISTO-S	WHELK-S
SWAYL-S	TAROT-S	THORN-S	TRAIK-S	TWEER-S	URATE-S	VITAL-S	WHELM-S
SWEAL-S	TARRE-S	THORP-S	TRAIL-S	TWEET-S	URENA-S	VIVAT-S	WHELP-S
SWEAR-S	TASAR-S	THOWL-S	TRAIN-S	TWERP-S	URGER-S	VIVDA-S	WHERE-S
SWEAT-S	TASER-S	THRAW-S	TRAIT-S	TWIER-S	URIAL-S	VIVER-S	WHIFF-S
SWEDE-S	TASSE-S	THREE-S	TRAMP-S	TWILL-S	URINE-S	VIXEN-S	WHIFT-S
SWEEL-S	TASTE-S	THRID-S	TRANT-S	TWILT-S	URITE-S	VIZIR-S	WHILE-S
SWEEP-S	TATER-S	THROB-S	TRAPE-S	TWINE-S	URMAN-S	VIZOR-S	WHINE-S
SWEET-S	TATIE-S	THROE-S	TRATT-S	TWINK-S	URSON-S	VOCAB-S	WHIRL-S
SWELL-S	TATOU-S	THROW-S	TRAVE-S	TWIRE-S	URUBU-S	VOCAL-S	WHIRR-S
SWELT-S	TAUBE-S	THRUM-S	TRAWL-S	TWIRL-S	USAGE-S	VODKA-S	WHISK-S
SWERF-S	TAUNT-S	THUJA-S	TREAD-S	TWIRP-S	USHER-S	VOGUE-S	WHIST-S
SWIFT-S	TAUPE-S	THUMB-S	TREAT-S	TWIST-S	USNEA-S	VOICE-S	WHITE-S
SWILL-S	TAVAH-S	THUMP-S	TRECK-S	TWITE-S	USUAL-S	VOILE-S	WHOLE-S
SWING-S	TAVER-S	THUYA-S	TREEN-S	TWOER-S	USURE-S	VOLET-S	WHOOP-S
SWINK-S	TAWER-S	THYME-S	TREMA-S	TWYER-S	USURP-S	VOLTE-S	WHOOT-S
SWIPE-S	TAWSE-S	TIARA-S	TREND-S	TYLER-S	UTTER-S	VOLVA-S	WHORE-S
SWIRE-S	TAXER-S	TIBIA-S	TREST-S	TYPTO-S	UVULA-S	VOLVE-S	WHORL-S
SWIRL-S	TAXOL-S	TICAL-S	TRIAD-S	TYRAN-S	VAGUE-S	VOMER-S	WHORT-S
SWIVE-S	TAXOR-S	TIGER-S	TRIAL-S	TYTHE-S	VAKIL-S	VOMIT-S	WICCA-S
SWONE-S	TAYRA-S	TIGHT-S	TRIBE-S	UDDER-S	VALET-S	VOTER-S	WIDEN-S
SWOON-S	TAZZA-S	TIGON-S	TRICE-S	UHLAN-S	VALOR-S	VOUGE-S	WIDOW-S
SWOOP-S	TEADE-S	TILDE-S	TRICK-S	UHURU-S	VALSE-S	VOWEL-S	WIDTH-S
SWORD-S	TEASE-S	TILER-S	TRIER-S	UKASE-S	VALUE-S	VOWER-S	WIELD-S
SWOUN-S	TEAZE-S	TILTH-S	TRIKE-S	ULCER-S	VALVE-S	VOXEL-S	WIFIE-S
SYBBE-S	TEEND-S	TIMBO-S	TRILL-S	ULEMA-S	VAPOR-S	VOZHD-S	WIGAN-S
SYBIL-S	TEENE-S	TIMER-S	TRINE-S	ULMIN-S	VARAN-S	VRAIC-S	WIGHT-S
SYBOE-S	TEIND-S	TIMON-S	TRIOR-S	ULTRA-S	VAREC-S	VROOM-S	WILGA-S
SYBOW-S	TEMPO-S	TINCT-S	TRIPE-S	ULYIE-S	VARNA-S	VROUW-S	WILJA-S
SYCEE-S	TEMPT-S	TINEA-S	TRITE-S	ULZIE-S	VARVE-S	VULVA-S	WINCE-S
SYLPH-S	TEMSE-S	TINGE-S	TROAD-S	UMBEL-S	VAULT-S	WACKE-S	WINGE-S
SYLVA-S	TENET-S	TITAN-S	TROAT-S	UMBER-S	VAUNT-S	WADER-S	WINZE-S
SYMAR-S	TENIA-S	TITER-S	TROCK-S	UMBRA-S	VAUTE-S	WAFER-S	WIPER-S
SYNCH-S	TENNE-S	TITHE-S	TRODE-S	UMBRE-S	VAWTE-S	WAGER-S	WIRER-S
SYNOD-S	TENNO-S	TITLE-S	TROKE-S	UMIAK-S	VEALE-S	WAGON-S	WITHE-S
SYRAH-S	TENON-S	TITRE-S	TROLL-S	UNARM-S	VEENA-S	WAHOO-S	WIZEN-S
SYREN-S	TENOR-S	TITUP-S	TROMP-S	UNBAG-S	VEGAN-S	WAIFT-S	WODGE-S
SYRUP-S	TENSE-S	TOAST-S	TRONA-S	UNBAR-S	VEGIE-S	WAIST-S	WOLVE-S
SYSOP-S	TENTH-S	TOAZE-S	TRONC-S	UNBED-S	VELAR-S	WAITE-S	WOMAN-S
SYTHE-S	TENUE-S	TODAY-S	TRONE-S	UNCAP-S	VELDT-S	WAIVE-S	WONGA-S
SYVER-S	TEPAL-S	TODDE-S	TROOP-S	UNCLE-S	VENEY-S	WAKEN-S	WONGI-S
TABLA-S	TEPEE-S	TOGUE-S	TROPE-S	UNDAM-S	VENGE-S	WAKER-S	WOOER-S
TABLE-S	TERAI-S	TOILE-S	TROTH-S	UNFIT-S	VENIN-S	WALER-S	WOOLD-S
TABOO-S	TERCE-S	TOISE-S	TROUT-S	UNGAG-S	VENOM-S	WALLA-S	WORLD-S
TABOR-S	TEREK-S	TOKAY-S	TRUCE-S	UNGET-S	VENUE-S	WANZE-S	WORSE-S
	TERFE-S		TRUCK-S	UNGOD-S	VERGE-S	WASTE-S	

WORST-S	WRING-S	XYLYL-S	YARTO-S	YOICK-S	ZAKAT-S	ZIBET-S	ZOMBI-S
WORTH-S	WRIST-S	YACCA-S	YEALM-S	YOJAN-S	ZAMAN-S	ZIGAN-S	ZONDA-S
WOULD-S	WRITE-S	YACHT-S	YEARD-S	YOKEL-S	ZAMBO-S	ZIMBI-S	ZOOEA-S
WOUND-S	WRONG-S	YAGER-S	YEARN-S	YOUNG-S	ZAMIA-S	ZINCO-S	ZOOID-S
WRACK-S	WROOT-S	YAHOO-S	YEAST-S	YOURT-S	ZANJA-S	ZINEB-S	ZORIL-S
WRAST-S	WURST-S	YAKKA-S	YENTA-S	YOUTH-S	ZANTE-S	ZINKE-S	ZORRO-S
WRATH-S	WUSHU-S	YAKOW-S	YERBA-S	YOWIE-S	ZANZE-S	ZIPPO-S	ZUPAN-S
WRAWL-S	XEBEC-S	YAMEN-S	YIELD-S	YRNEH-S	ZEBEC-S	ZIZEL-S	
WREAK-S	XENIA-S	YAPOK-S	YOBBO-S	YUCCA-S	ZEBRA-S	ZLOTY-S	
WRECK-S	XENON-S	YAPON-S	YODEL-S	YULAN-S	ZEBUB-S	ZOCCO-S	
WREST-S	XYLEM-S	YARFA-S	YODLE-S	YUPON-S	ZERDA-S	ZOISM-S	
WRICK-S	XYLOL-S	YARTA-S	YOGIN-S	ZABRA-S	ZHOMO-S	ZOIST-S	

6→7

ABATOR-S	ADJUST-S	ALBEDO-S	AMYTAL-S	ARCADE-S	ASSERT-S	AVOYER-S	BANKER-S
ABDUCE-S	ADLAND-S	ALBERT-S	ANADEM-S	ARCHER-S	ASSIGN-S	AVULSE-S	BANKET-S
ABDUCT-S	ADMIRE-S	ALBINO-S	ANALOG-S	ARCHIL-S	ASSIST-S	AWAKEN-S	BANNER-S
ABELIA-S	ADNOUN-S	ALBITE-S	ANANKE-S	ARCHON-S	ASSIZE-S	AWHAPE-S	BANTAM-S
ABJECT-S	ADORER-S	ALBUGO-S	ANARCH-S	ARCING-S	ASSOIL-S	AWHEEL-S	BANTER-S
ABJURE-S	ADREAD-S	ALCOVE-S	ANATTA-S	ARCSIN-S	ASSORT-S	AWMRIE-S	BANYAN-S
ABLATE-S	ADSORB-S	ALDOSE-S	ANATTO-S	ARCTAN-S	ASSUME-S	AWNING-S	BANZAI-S
ABLAUT-S	ADVENE-S	ALDRIN-S	ANCHOR-S	ARCTIC-S	ASSURE-S	AYWORD-S	BAOBAB-S
ABOLLA-S	ADVENT-S	ALEGAR-S	ANCOME-S	ARDOUR-S	ASTART-S	AZALEA-S	BARAZA-S
ABOUND-S	ADVERB-S	ALEGGE-S	ANEMIA-S	AREOLE-S	ASTERT-S	AZIONE-S	BARBEL-S
ABRADE-S	ADVERT-S	ALERCE-S	ANGICO-S	ARGALA-S	ASTHMA-S	AZOLLA-S	BARBER-S
ABRAID-S	ADVICE-S	ALEVIN-S	ANGINA-S	ARGALI-S	ASTONE-S	BAAING-S	BARBET-S
ABRAZO-S	ADVISE-S	ALEXIA-S	ANGLER-S	ARGAND-S	ASYLUM-S	BABACO-S	BARBIE-S
ABREGE-S	ADWARD-S	ALEXIN-S	ANGORA-S	ARGENT-S	ATABAL-S	BABBLE-S	BAREGE-S
ABROAD-S	AEDILE-S	ALGATE-S	ANICUT-S	ARGHAN-S	ATABEG-S	BABLAH-S	BARGEE-S
ABRUPT-S	AEMULE-S	ALIDAD-S	ANIMAL-S	ARGUER-S	ATABEK-S	BABOON-S	BARITE-S
ABSEIL-S	AERATE-S	ALIGHT-S	ANKLET-S	ARGYLE-S	ATAMAN-S	BACKER-S	BARIUM-S
ABSENT-S	AERIAL-S	ALIPED-S	ANLACE-S	ARIOSO-S	ATAXIA-S	BACKET-S	BARKAN-S
ABSORB-S	AEROBE-S	ALISMA-S	ANLAGE-S	ARISTA-S	ATLATL-S	BACKRA-S	BARKEN-S
ABULIA-S	AETHER-S	ALIYAH-S	ANNEAL-S	ARISTO-S	ATOCIA-S	BADDIE-S	BARKER-S
ABUSER-S	AFFEAR-S	ALKALI-S	ANNEXE-S	ARKITE-S	ATONER-S	BADGER-S	BARLEY-S
ABVOLT-S	AFFECT-S	ALKANE-S	ANNUAL-S	ARKOSE-S	ATRIUM-S	BAETYL-S	BARNEY-S
ACACIA-S	AFFEER-S	ALKENE-S	ANOINT-S	ARMADA-S	ATTACK-S	BAFFLE-S	BAROCK-S
ACAJOU-S	AFFINE-S	ALKYNE-S	ANOMIE-S	ARMFUL-S	ATTAIN-S	BAGFUL-S	BARONG-S
ACANTH-S	AFFIRM-S	ALLEGE-S	ANONYM-S	ARMLET-S	ATTASK-S	BAGGIT-S	BARQUE-S
ACARID-S	AFFORD-S	ALLELE-S	ANORAK-S	ARMOUR-S	ATTEND-S	BAGNIO-S	BARRAT-S
ACATER-S	AFFRAP-S	ALLICE-S	ANOXIA-S	ARMPIT-S	ATTENT-S	BAGUIO-S	BARREL-S
ACCEDE-S	AFFRAY-S	ALLIUM-S	ANSWER-S	ARMURE-S	ATTEST-S	BAGWIG-S	BARRET-S
ACCEND-S	AFFRET-S	ALLUDE-S	ANTARA-S	ARNICA-S	ATTIRE-S	BAHADA-S	BARRIO-S
ACCENT-S	AFGHAN-S	ALLURE-S	ANTHEM-S	AROINT-S	ATTONE-S	BAILEE-S	BARROW-S
ACCEPT-S	AFREET-S	ALMAIN-S	ANTHER-S	AROLLA-S	ATTORN-S	BAILER-S	BARTER-S
ACCITE-S	AGAMID-S	ALMOND-S	ANTIAR-S	AROUSE-S	ATTRAP-S	BAILEY-S	BARTON-S
ACCLOY-S	AGARIC-S	ALMUCE-S	ANTING-S	AROYNT-S	ATTRIT-S	BAILIE-S	BARYON-S
ACCOIL-S	AGEING-S	ALNAGE-S	ANTLER-S	ARPENT-S	ATTUNE-S	BAILLI-S	BARYTA-S
ACCORD-S	AGEISM-S	ALOGIA-S	ANURIA-S	ARRACK-S	AUBADE-S	BAILOR-S	BASALT-S
ACCOST-S	AGEIST-S	ALPACA-S	ANYONE-S	ARREAR-S	AUCUBA-S	BAININ-S	BASHAW-S
ACCREW-S	AGENDA-S	ALPEEN-S	ANYWAY-S	ARREST-S	AUDILE-S	BAITER-S	BASHER-S
ACCRUE-S	AGNAIL-S	ALPINE-S	AORIST-S	ARRIDE-S	AUGITE-S	BAJADA-S	BASKET-S
ACCUSE-S	AGNAME-S	ALSIKE-S	AOUDAD-S	ARRIVE-S	AUGUST-S	BAJREE-S	BASNET-S
ACEDIA-S	AGNATE-S	ALTEZA-S	APACHE-S	ARROBA-S	AUKLET-S	BAKING-S	BASQUE-S
ACETAL-S	AGNISE-S	ALTHEA-S	APEDOM-S	ARROYO-S	AUMAIL-S	BALATA-S	BASSET-S
ACETYL-S	AGNIZE-S	ALUDEL-S	APERCU-S	ARSHIN-S	AUNTER-S	BALBOA-S	BASTER-S
ACHAGE-S	AGOGIC-S	AMADOU-S	APLITE-S	ARSINE-S	AUNTIE-S	BALEEN-S	BASTLE-S
ACHENE-S	AGOUTA-S	AMATOL-S	APLOMB-S	ARTIST-S	AURATE-S	BALKER-S	BASUCO-S
ACHING-S	AGOUTI-S	AMAZON-S	APNOEA-S	ASARUM-S	AURIST-S	BALLAD-S	BATATA-S
ACHKAN-S	AGREGE-S	AMBAGE-S	APOGEE-S	ASCEND-S	AURORA-S	BALLAN-S	BATHER-S
ACKNOW-S	AGRISE-S	AMBLER-S	APOLLO-S	ASCENT-S	AUTEUR-S	BALLAT-S	BATLER-S
ACMITE-S	AGRIZE-S	AMELIA-S	APORIA-S	ASCIAN-S	AUTHOR-S	BALLET-S	BATLET-S
ACQUIT-S	AGRYZE-S	AMENDE-S	APOZEM-S	ASHAME-S	AUTISM-S	BALLON-S	BATOON-S
ACTING-S	AGUISE-S	AMERCE-S	APPAIR-S	ASHLAR-S	AUTUMN-S	BALLOT-S	BATTEL-S
ACTION-S	AGUIZE-S	AMOEBA-S	APPEAL-S	ASHLER-S	AVAILE-S	BALLOW-S	BATTEN-S
ACTURE-S	AHIMSA-S	AMOMUM-S	APPEAR-S	ASHRAM-S	AVATAR-S	BALLUP-S	BATTER-S
ACUMEN-S	AIGLET-S	AMOOVE-S	APPEND-S	ASKANT-S	AVAUNT-S	BALSAM-S	BATTLE-S
ADAGIO-S	AIKIDO-S	AMORCE-S	APPLET-S	ASKARI-S	AVENGE-S	BAMBOO-S	BATTUE-S
ADDEEM-S	AIRGAP-S	AMORET-S	APPORT-S	ASLAKE-S	AVENIR-S	BAMMER-S	BAUBLE-S
ADDEND-S	AIRING-S	AMOUNT-S	APPOSE-S	ASPECT-S	AVENUE-S	BAMPOT-S	BAUERA-S
ADDICT-S	AIRWAY-S	AMPERE-S	APTOTE-S	ASPICK-S	AVIATE-S	BANANA-S	BAWBEE-S
ADDOOM-S	AJOWAN-S	AMPULE-S	ARABIN-S	ASPINE-S	AVIDIN-S	BANDAR-S	BAWBLE-S
ADDUCE-S	AKEDAH-S	AMRITA-S	ARAISE-S	ASPIRE-S	AVOCET-S	BANDIT-S	BAWLER-S
ADDUCT-S	ALALIA-S	AMTMAN-S	ARALIA-S	ASPORT-S	AVOSET-S	BANDOG-S	BAWLEY-S
ADHERE-S	ALARUM-S	AMULET-S	ARAYSE-S	ASSAIL-S	AVOURE-S	BANGER-S	BAXTER-S
ADJOIN-S	ALBATA-S	AMUSER-S	ARBOUR-S	ASSART-S	AVOWAL-S	BANGLE-S	BAYARD-S
ADJURE-S		AMYLUM-S	ARBUTE-S	ASSENT-S	AVOWER-S	BANIAN-S	BAZAAR-S

BEACON-S	BENDER-S	BIONIC-S	BOODLE-S	BROGUE-S	BURNET-S	CAMPER-S	CATENA-S
BEADLE-S	BENNET-S	BIOPIC-S	BOOGIE-S	BROKER-S	BURREL-S	CAMPLE-S	CATGUT-S
BEAGLE-S	BENUMB-S	BIOTIN-S	BOOKIE-S	BROLGA-S	BURROW-S	CANADA-S	CATION-S
BEAKER-S	BENZAL-S	BIRDER-S	BOOMER-S	BRONCO-S	BURSAR-S	CANAPE-S	CATKIN-S
BEAMER-S	BENZIL-S	BIRDIE-S	BOORDE-S	BRONZE-S	BURTON-S	CANARD-S	CATNAP-S
BEANIE-S	BENZOL-S	BIREME-S	BOORKA-S	BROOSE-S	BUSBOY-S	CANCAN-S	CATNEP-S
BEARER-S	BENZYL-S	BIRKIE-S	BOOTEE-S	BROUGH-S	BUSHEL-S	CANCEL-S	CATNIP-S
BEATER-S	BEPELT-S	BIRLER-S	BOOZER-S	BROUZE-S	BUSING-S	CANCER-S	CATSUP-S
BEAVER-S	BEPUFF-S	BIRSLE-S	BOPPER-S	BROWSE-S	BUSKER-S	CANDIE-S	CAUDLE-S
BEBUNG-S	BERATE-S	BISECT-S	BORAGE-S	BROWST-S	BUSKET-S	CANDLE-S	CAUKER-S
BECALL-S	BERLEY-S	BISHOP-S	BORANE-S	BRUISE-S	BUSKIN-S	CANDOR-S	CAUSER-S
BECALM-S	BERLIN-S	BISMAR-S	BORATE-S	BRUNET-S	BUSTEE-S	CANFUL-S	CAUSEY-S
BECKET-S	BERRET-S	BISQUE-S	BORDAR-S	BRUTER-S	BUSTER-S	CANGLE-S	CAUTEL-S
BECKON-S	BERTHA-S	BISTER-S	BORDEL-S	BUBBLE-S	BUSTLE-S	CANGUE-S	CAUTER-S
BECOME-S	BERTHE-S	BISTRE-S	BORDER-S	BUCKER-S	BUTANE-S	CANINE-S	CAVEAT-S
BECURL-S	BESEEM-S	BISTRO-S	BOREEN-S	BUCKET-S	BUTENE-S	CANING-S	CAVERN-S
BEDAUB-S	BESIDE-S	BITING-S	BORIDE-S	BUCKIE-S	BUTLER-S	CANKER-S	CAVIAR-S
BEDAZE-S	BESIGH-S	BITMAP-S	BORING-S	BUCKLE-S	BUTTER-S	CANNEL-S	CAVIER-S
BEDBUG-S	BESING-S	BITTER-S	BORROW-S	BUCKRA-S	BUTTLE-S	CANNER-S	CAVING-S
BEDDER-S	BESMUT-S	BITTIE-S	BORZOI-S	BUDDHA-S	BUTTON-S	CANNON-S	CAVORT-S
BEDECK-S	BESOIN-S	BITTOR-S	BOSBOK-S	BUDDLE-S	BUZZER-S	CANTAR-S	CAWING-S
BEDELL-S	BESORT-S	BITTUR-S	BOSCHE-S	BUDGER-S	BYGONE-S	CANTER-S	CAWKER-S
BEDLAM-S	BESPIT-S	BIZONE-S	BOSKET-S	BUDGET-S	BYLINE-S	CANTLE-S	CAYMAN-S
BEDPAN-S	BESPOT-S	BLAGUE-S	BOSTON-S	BUDGIE-S	BYNAME-S	CANTON-S	CAYUSE-S
BEDRAL-S	BESTAR-S	BLANCO-S	BOTHAN-S	BUFFER-S	BYPATH-S	CANTOR-S	CEDULA-S
BEDROP-S	BESTIR-S	BLAZER-S	BOTHER-S	BUFFET-S	BYPLAW-S	CANULA-S	CELIAC-S
BEDUCK-S	BESTOW-S	BLAZON-S	BOTHIE-S	BUGGAN-S	BYRNIE-S	CANVAS-S	CELLAR-S
BEDUIN-S	BESTUD-S	BLENDE-S	BOTTLE-S	BUGGER-S	BYROAD-S	CANYON-S	CEMBRA-S
BEDUNG-S	BETAKE-S	BLIGHT-S	BOTTOM-S	BUGGIN-S	BYROOM-S	CAPLET-S	CEMENT-S
BEDUST-S	BETEEM-S	BLONDE-S	BOUCHE-S	BUGLER-S	BYWORD-S	CAPLIN-S	CENOTE-S
BEEGAH-S	BETHEL-S	BLOUSE-S	BOUCLE-S	BUGLET-S	BYZANT-S	CAPOTE-S	CENSER-S
BEENAH-S	BETIDE-S	BLOWER-S	BOUGET-S	BUGONG-S	CABALA-S	CAPPER-S	CENSOR-S
BEEPER-S	BETIME-S	BLOWIE-S	BOUGHT-S	BUKSHI-S	CABANA-S	CAPRID-S	CENTAL-S
BEETLE-S	BETISE-S	BLOWSE-S	BOUGIE-S	BULBEL-S	CABBIE-S	CAPSID-S	CENTER-S
BEFALL-S	BETOIL-S	BLOWZE-S	BOULLE-S	BULBIL-S	CABLET-S	CAPTAN-S	CENTRE-S
BEFANA-S	BETRAY-S	BLUDGE-S	BOUNCE-S	BULBUL-S	CABRIE-S	CAPTOR-S	CENTUM-S
BEFLUM-S	BETRIM-S	BLUING-S	BOURNE-S	BULGER-S	CABRIT-S	CARACK-S	CERATE-S
BEFOAM-S	BETTER-S	BLUNGE-S	BOURSE-S	BULGUR-S	CACHET-S	CARACT-S	CEREAL-S
BEFOOL-S	BETTOR-S	BOATEL-S	BOUTON-S	BULKER-S	CACHOU-S	CARAFE-S	CERIPH-S
BEFOUL-S	BEURRE-S	BOATER-S	BOVATE-S	BULLER-S	CACKLE-S	CARBON-S	CERISE-S
BEGGAR-S	BEWAIL-S	BOATIE-S	BOVINE-S	BULLET-S	CACOON-S	CARBOY-S	CERITE-S
BEGIFT-S	BEWARE-S	BOBBIN-S	BOVVER-S	BUMBAG-S	CADDIE-S	CARDER-S	CERIUM-S
BEGILD-S	BEWEEP-S	BOBBLE-S	BOWFIN-S	BUMBLE-S	CADGER-S	CAREEN-S	CERMET-S
BEGIRD-S	BEWRAY-S	BOBCAT-S	BOWGET-S	BUMKIN-S	CADUAC-S	CAREER-S	CEROON-S
BEGNAW-S	BEYOND-S	BOBWIG-S	BOWING-S	BUMMEL-S	CAESAR-S	CAREME-S	CERUSE-S
BEGUIN-S	BEZANT-S	BOCAGE-S	BOWLER-S	BUMMER-S	CAFARD-S	CARIBE-S	CERVID-S
BEGUNK-S	BEZOAR-S	BODACH-S	BOWPOT-S	BUMMLE-S	CAFILA-S	CARINA-S	CESIUM-S
BEHAVE-S	BEZZLE-S	BODDLE-S	BOWSER-S	BUMPER-S	CAFTAN-S	CARLOT-S	CESSER-S
BEHEAD-S	BHAGEE-S	BODEGA-S	BOWWOW-S	BUNDLE-S	CAGOUL-S	CARNAL-S	CESTUI-S
BEHEST-S	BHAJAN-S	BODGER-S	BOWYER-S	BUNGEE-S	CAHIER-S	CARNET-S	CESURA-S
BEHIND-S	BHAJEE-S	BODGIE-S	BOXCAR-S	BUNGEY-S	CAHOOT-S	CARNEY-S	CESURE-S
BEHOLD-S	BHAKTI-S	BODICE-S	BOXFUL-S	BUNGIE-S	CAILLE-S	CARPAL-S	CETANE-S
BEHOOF-S	BHARAL-S	BODING-S	BOXING-S	BUNGLE-S	CAIMAC-S	CARPEL-S	CHACMA-S
BEHOTE-S	BHINDI-S	BODKIN-S	BRACER-S	BUNION-S	CAIMAN-S	CARPER-S	CHADAR-S
BEHOVE-S	BHISTI-S	BODRAG-S	BRAIRD-S	BUNJEE-S	CAIQUE-S	CARPET-S	CHADOR-S
BEHOWL-S	BIBBER-S	BOFFIN-S	BRAISE-S	BUNJIE-S	CAJOLE-S	CARRAT-S	CHAFER-S
BEIGEL-S	BICARB-S	BOGGLE-S	BRAIZE-S	BUNKER-S	CAKING-S	CARREL-S	CHAGAN-S
BEJADE-S	BICKER-S	BOGOAK-S	BRANLE-S	BUNKUM-S	CALCAR-S	CARROT-S	CHAINE-S
BEJANT-S	BICORN-S	BOGONG-S	BRAYER-S	BUNNIA-S	CALICO-S	CARSEY-S	CHAISE-S
BELACE-S	BIDDER-S	BOHUNK-S	BRAZEN-S	BUNSEN-S	CALIGO-S	CARTEL-S	CHAKRA-S
BELATE-S	BIDENT-S	BOILER-S	BRAZIL-S	BUNTAL-S	CALIMA-S	CARTER-S	CHALAN-S
BELAUD-S	BIDING-S	BOLDEN-S	BREARE-S	BUNTER-S	CALIPH-S	CARTON-S	CHALET-S
BELDAM-S	BIFFIN-S	BOLERO-S	BREAST-S	BUNYIP-S	CALKER-S	CARVEL-S	CHANCE-S
BELIEF-S	BIGGIE-S	BOLIDE-S	BREATH-S	BURBLE-S	CALKIN-S	CARVER-S	CHANGE-S
BELIER-S	BIGGIN-S	BOLTER-S	BREESE-S	BURBOT-S	CALLAN-S	CASBAH-S	CHAPEL-S
BELLOW-S	BIGWIG-S	BOMBER-S	BREEZE-S	BURDEN-S	CALLER-S	CASEIN-S	CHAPES-S
BELONG-S	BIKING-S	BONBON-S	BREHON-S	BURDIE-S	CALLET-S	CASERN-S	CHAPKA-S
BELOVE-S	BIKINI-S	BONDER-S	BRENNE-S	BUREAU-S	CALLOW-S	CASHAW-S	CHARET-S
BELTER-S	BILIAN-S	BONDUC-S	BRETON-S	BURGEE-S	CALPAC-S	CASHEW-S	CHARGE-S
BELUGA-S	BILKER-S	BONING-S	BREVET-S	BURGER-S	CALQUE-S	CASING-S	CHARKA-S
BEMAUL-S	BILLET-S	BONISM-S	BREWER-S	BURGLE-S	CALTHA-S	CASINO-S	CHARTA-S
BEMEAN-S	BILLIE-S	BONIST-S	BRIBER-S	BURGOO-S	CALVER-S	CASKET-S	CHASER-S
BEMETE-S	BILLON-S	BONITO-S	BRIDAL-S	BURHEL-S	CAMBER-S	CASQUE-S	CHASSE-S
BEMIRE-S	BILLOW-S	BONNET-S	BRIDGE-S	BURIAL-S	CAMERA-S	CASSIA-S	CHATON-S
BEMOAN-S	BINDER-S	BONNIE-S	BRIDIE-S	BURITI-S	CAMESE-S	CASTER-S	CHATTA-S
BEMOCK-S	BINGER-S	BONSAI-S	BRIDLE-S	BURLAP-S	CAMION-S	CASTLE-S	CHATTI-S
BEMOIL-S	BINGHI-S	BONXIE-S	BRIGUE-S	BURLER-S	CAMISE-S	CASTOR-S	CHAUFE-S
BEMUSE-S	BINGLE-S	BOOBOO-S	BROCHE-S	BURLEY-S	CAMLET-S	CASUAL-S	CHAUFF-S
BENAME-S	BIOGEN-S	BOODIE-S	BROGAN-S	BURNER-S	CAMOTE-S	CATALO-S	CHAUNT-S

CHAZAN-S	CITOLE-S	COMART-S	CORSAC-S	CROTAL-S	DABBER-S	DECAFF-S	DEPUTE-S
CHEESE-S	CITRIN-S	COMATE-S	CORSET-S	CROTON-S	DABBLE-S	DECAMP-S	DERAIL-S
CHEMIC-S	CITRON-S	COMBAT-S	CORVEE-S	CROUPE-S	DACITE-S	DECANE-S	DERATE-S
CHENAR-S	CIVISM-S	COMBER-S	CORVET-S	CROUTE-S	DACKER-S	DECANT-S	DERHAM-S
CHENET-S	CLAMOR-S	COMBLE-S	CORVID-S	CRUISE-S	DACOIT-S	DECARB-S	DERIDE-S
CHEQUE-S	CLAQUE-S	COMEDO-S	CORYMB-S	CRUIVE-S	DACTYL-S	DECARE-S	DERIVE-S
CHERUB-S	CLARET-S	COMFIT-S	CORYZA-S	CRUMEN-S	DADDLE-S	DECCIE-S	DESALT-S
CHERUP-S	CLAUSE-S	COMICE-S	COSECH-S	CRUSET-S	DAEMON-S	DECEIT-S	DESERT-S
CHESIL-S	CLAVER-S	COMING-S	COSHER-S	CRUSIE-S	DAFTAR-S	DECERN-S	DESIGN-S
CHETAH-S	CLAVIE-S	COMMER-S	COSIER-S	CRYING-S	DAFTIE-S	DECIDE-S	DESINE-S
CHEVEN-S	CLEAVE-S	COMMIE-S	COSINE-S	CRYPTO-S	DAGABA-S	DECIME-S	DESIRE-S
CHEVET-S	CLEEVE-S	COMMIT-S	COSMEA-S	CUBAGE-S	DAGGER-S	DECKER-S	DESIST-S
CHEVIN-S	CLERIC-S	COMMON-S	COSSET-S	CUBICA-S	DAGGLE-S	DECKLE-S	DESMAN-S
CHEVRE-S	CLEUCH-S	COMMOT-S	COSSIE-S	CUBISM-S	DAGOBA-S	DECOCT-S	DESMID-S
CHEWER-S	CLEUGH-S	COMPEL-S	COSTAL-S	CUBIST-S	DAHLIA-S	DECODE-S	DESORB-S
CHEWET-S	CLICHE-S	COMPER-S	COSTER-S	CUBOID-S	DAIDLE-S	DECOKE-S	DESPOT-S
CHEWIE-S	CLIENT-S	COMPOT-S	COTISE-S	CUCKOO-S	DAIKER-S	DECREE-S	DESYNE-S
CHIACK-S	CLINIC-S	CONCHE-S	COTTAR-S	CUDDEN-S	DAIKON-S	DECREW-S	DETAIL-S
CHIASM-S	CLIQUE-S	CONCUR-S	COTTER-S	CUDDIE-S	DAIMIO-S	DECTET-S	DETAIN-S
CHIBOL-S	CLITIC-S	CONDER-S	COTTID-S	CUDDIN-S	DAIMON-S	DEDUCE-S	DETECT-S
CHICHA-S	CLIVIA-S	CONDIE-S	COTTON-S	CUDDLE-S	DAKOIT-S	DEDUCT-S	DETENT-S
CHICHI-S	CLOCHE-S	CONDOM-S	COTWAL-S	CUDGEL-S	DALLOP-S	DEEJAY-S	DETENU-S
CHICLE-S	CLOQUE-S	CONDOR-S	COTYLE-S	CUEIST-S	DALTON-S	DEEPEN-S	DETEST-S
CHICON-S	CLOSER-S	CONFAB-S	COUCAL-S	CUESTA-S	DAMAGE-S	DEEPIE-S	DETORT-S
CHIDER-S	CLOSET-S	CONFER-S	COUCHE-S	CUFFIN-S	DAMASK-S	DEFACE-S	DETOUR-S
CHIELD-S	CLOTHE-S	CONFIT-S	COUGAR-S	CUFFLE-S	DAMMAR-S	DEFAME-S	DETUNE-S
CHIGOE-S	CLOUGH-S	CONGEE-S	COULEE-S	CUISSE-S	DAMMER-S	DEFEAT-S	DEUTON-S
CHIGRE-S	CLOVER-S	CONGER-S	COUPEE-S	CUITER-S	DAMPEN-S	DEFECT-S	DEVALL-S
CHIKOR-S	CLUSIA-S	CONGOU-S	COUPER-S	CULLER-S	DAMPER-S	DEFEND-S	DEVEST-S
CHILLI-S	COAITA-S	CONIMA-S	COUPLE-S	CULLET-S	DAMSEL-S	DEFIER-S	DEVICE-S
CHIMER-S	COALER-S	CONINE-S	COUPON-S	CULMEN-S	DAMSON-S	DEFILE-S	DEVISE-S
CHINAR-S	COATEE-S	CONJEE-S	COURSE-S	CULTER-S	DANCER-S	DEFINE-S	DEVOIR-S
CHIRRE-S	COATER-S	CONKER-S	COUSIN-S	CULVER-S	DANDER-S	DEFORM-S	DEVOTE-S
CHISEL-S	COAXER-S	CONNER-S	COUTER-S	CUMBER-S	DANDLE-S	DEFOUL-S	DEVOUR-S
CHITAL-S	COBALT-S	CONOID-S	COUTIL-S	CUMMER-S	DANGER-S	DEFRAG-S	DEVVEL-S
CHITIN-S	COBBER-S	CONSUL-S	COVENT-S	CUMMIN-S	DANGLE-S	DEFRAY-S	DEWANI-S
CHITON-S	COBBLE-S	CONTRA-S	COVERT-S	CUNNER-S	DANTON-S	DEFUSE-S	DEWITT-S
CHOCHO-S	COBNUT-S	CONURE-S	COVING-S	CUPFUL-S	DAPHNE-S	DEFUZE-S	DEWLAP-S
CHOCKO-S	COBURG-S	CONVEY-S	COVYNE-S	CUPOLA-S	DAPPER-S	DEGOUT-S	DEXTER-S
CHOICE-S	COBWEB-S	CONVOY-S	COWAGE-S	CUPPER-S	DAPPLE-S	DEGREE-S	DHARMA-S
CHOKER-S	COCCID-S	COOING-S	COWARD-S	CUPULE-S	DARGLE-S	DEGUST-S	DHARNA-S
CHOKEY-S	COCKER-S	COOKER-S	COWBOY-S	CURARA-S	DARING-S	DEHORN-S	DHOOTI-S
CHOKRA-S	COCKET-S	COOKIE-S	COWPAT-S	CURARE-S	DARKEN-S	DEHORT-S	DHURRA-S
CHOKRI-S	COCKLE-S	COOLER-S	COWPEA-S	CURARI-S	DARKEY-S	DEJECT-S	DIABLE-S
CHOLER-S	COCOON-S	COOLIE-S	COWRIE-S	CURATE-S	DARKIE-S	DELATE-S	DIADEM-S
CHOOSE-S	CODDER-S	COOLTH-S	COYOTE-S	CURDLE-S	DARKLE-S	DELETE-S	DIALOG-S
CHOPIN-S	CODDLE-S	COOMBE-S	COZIER-S	CURFEW-S	DARNEL-S	DELICE-S	DIAPER-S
CHORAL-S	CODGER-S	COOPER-S	CRADLE-S	CURIET-S	DARNER-S	DELICT-S	DIAPIR-S
CHOREA-S	CODING-S	COOSEN-S	CRAPLE-S	CURIUM-S	DARTER-S	DELOPE-S	DIATOM-S
CHOREE-S	CODIST-S	COOSER-S	CRATER-S	CURLER-S	DARTLE-S	DELUDE-S	DIAXON-S
CHOUGH-S	CODLIN-S	COOSIN-S	CRATON-S	CURLEW-S	DARTRE-S	DELUGE-S	DIBBER-S
CHOUSE-S	COELOM-S	COOTIE-S	CRATUR-S	CURPEL-S	DASHER-S	DELVER-S	DIBBLE-S
CHOWRI-S	COERCE-S	COPECK-S	CRAVAT-S	CURRIE-S	DASSIE-S	DEMAIN-S	DICAST-S
CHRISM-S	COEVAL-S	COPIER-S	CRAVEN-S	CURSER-S	DATING-S	DEMAND-S	DICING-S
CHROMA-S	COFFEE-S	COPING-S	CRAVER-S	CURSOR-S	DATIVE-S	DEMARK-S	DICKER-S
CHROME-S	COFFER-S	COPITA-S	CRAYER-S	CURTAL-S	DATURA-S	DEMEAN-S	DICKEY-S
CHROMO-S	COFFIN-S	COPPER-S	CRAYON-S	CURVET-S	DAUBER-S	DEMENT-S	DICKIE-S
CHUKAR-S	COFFLE-S	COPPIN-S	CREACH-S	CUSHAT-S	DAUNER-S	DEMISE-S	DIDDER-S
CHUKKA-S	COGGER-S	COPPLE-S	CREAGH-S	CUSHAW-S	DAUTIE-S	DEMIST-S	DIDDLE-S
CHUKOR-S	COGGIE-S	COPTER-S	CREASE-S	CUSPID-S	DAWDLE-S	DEMOTE-S	DIEDRE-S
CHYACK-S	COGGLE-S	COPULA-S	CREATE-S	CUSSER-S	DAWNER-S	DEMURE-S	DIESEL-S
CHYPRE-S	COHEIR-S	COQUET-S	CRECHE-S	CUSTOM-S	DAWTIE-S	DENGUE-S	DIETER-S
CICADA-S	COHERE-S	CORBAN-S	CREDIT-S	CUTLER-S	DAZZLE-S	DENIAL-S	DIFFER-S
CICALA-S	COHORN-S	CORBEL-S	CREESE-S	CUTLET-S	DEACON-S	DENIER-S	DIGEST-S
CICERO-S	COHORT-S	CORBIE-S	CREMOR-S	CUTTER-S	DEADEN-S	DENNET-S	DIGGER-S
CICUTA-S	COHUNE-S	CORDON-S	CRENEL-S	CUTTLE-S	DEADER-S	DENOTE-S	DIGLOT-S
CIERGE-S	COIGNE-S	CORIUM-S	CREOLE-S	CUTTOE-S	DEAFEN-S	DENTAL-S	DIKAST-S
CIGGIE-S	COINER-S	CORKER-S	CREPON-S	CYANIN-S	DEALER-S	DENTEL-S	DIKKOP-S
CILICE-S	COJOIN-S	CORKIR-S	CRESOL-S	CYBORG-S	DEANER-S	DENTIL-S	DIKTAT-S
CIMIER-S	COLLAR-S	CORMEL-S	CRETIC-S	CYBRID-S	DEARIE-S	DENTIN-S	DILATE-S
CINDER-S	COLLET-S	CORNEA-S	CRETIN-S	CYCLER-S	DEARTH-S	DENUDE-S	DILDOE-S
CINEMA-S	COLLIE-S	CORNEL-S	CREWEL-S	CYGNET-S	DEASIL-S	DEODAR-S	DILUTE-S
CINEOL-S	COLLOP-S	CORNER-S	CRINGE-S	CYMBAL-S	DEBARK-S	DEPART-S	DIMBLE-S
CINQUE-S	COLOUR-S	CORNET-S	CRINUM-S	CYPHER-S	DEBASE-S	DEPEND-S	DIMMER-S
CIPHER-S	COLTER-S	CORONA-S	CRITIC-S	CYPRID-S	DEBATE-S	DEPICT-S	DIMPLE-S
CIRCAR-S	COLUGO-S	COROZO-S	CROCHE-S	CYSTID-S	DEBTEE-S	DEPLOY-S	DIMWIT-S
CIRCLE-S	COLUMN-S	CORPSE-S	CRONET-S	CYTASE-S	DEBTOR-S	DEPONE-S	DINDLE-S
CIRQUE-S	COLURE-S	CORRAL-S	CROOVE-S	CYTODE-S	DEBUNK-S	DEPORT-S	DINGER-S
CITHER-S	COMARB-S	CORRIE-S	CROSSE-S	CZAPKA-S	DECADE-S	DEPOSE-S	DINGEY-S

DINGLE-S	DOODAH-S	DUIKER-S	ELOPER-S	ENLINK-S	ESTEEM-S	FAILLE-S	FIBULA-S
DINNER-S	DOODLE-S	DUMDUM-S	ELSHIN-S	ENLIST-S	ESTRAY-S	FAITOR-S	FICKLE-S
DINNLE-S	DOOFER-S	DUMPER-S	ELTCHI-S	ENLOCK-S	ESTRUM-S	FALCON-S	FICTOR-S
DIOXAN-S	DOOKET-S	DUMPLE-S	ELUANT-S	ENMOVE-S	ETALON-S	FALLAL-S	FIDDLE-S
DIOXIN-S	DOOLIE-S	DUNDER-S	ELUATE-S	ENNAGE-S	ETCHER-S	FALLER-S	FIDGET-S
DIPLOE-S	DOPANT-S	DUNITE-S	ELUDER-S	ENNEAD-S	ETHANE-S	FALLOW-S	FIESTA-S
DIPLON-S	DOPING-S	DUNKER-S	ELUENT-S	ENOUGH-S	ETHENE-S	FALSER-S	FIGURE-S
DIPOLE-S	DOPPER-S	DUNLIN-S	ELUTOR-S	ENRACE-S	ETHNIC-S	FALTER-S	FILFOT-S
DIPPER-S	DOPPIE-S	DUPION-S	EMBACE-S	ENRAGE-S	ETHYNE-S	FAMINE-S	FILING-S
DIRDAM-S	DORADO-S	DUPLET-S	EMBAIL-S	ENRANK-S	ETOILE-S	FANDOM-S	FILLER-S
DIRDUM-S	DORISE-S	DURANT-S	EMBALE-S	ENRING-S	ETRIER-S	FANGLE-S	FILLET-S
DIRECT-S	DORIZE-S	DURBAR-S	EMBALL-S	ENROBE-S	ETYMON-S	FANION-S	FILLIP-S
DIRHAM-S	DORMER-S	DURDUM-S	EMBALM-S	ENROLL-S	EUCAIN-S	FANKLE-S	FILTER-S
DIRHEM-S	DORSAL-S	DURGAN-S	EMBANK-S	ENROOT-S	EUCHRE-S	FANNEL-S	FIMBLE-S
DIRIGE-S	DORSEL-S	DURIAN-S	EMBARK-S	ENSEAL-S	EUNUCH-S	FANNER-S	FINALE-S
DIRNDL-S	DORSER-S	DURION-S	EMBASE-S	ENSEAM-S	EUOUAE-S	FANTAD-S	FINDER-S
DISARM-S	DORTER-S	DURRIE-S	EMBLEM-S	ENSEAR-S	EUPHON-S	FANTOD-S	FINEER-S
DISBAR-S	DOSAGE-S	DUSKEN-S	EMBLIC-S	ENSIGN-S	EUREKA-S	FANTOM-S	FINGAN-S
DISBUD-S	DOSSAL-S	DUSTER-S	EMBOIL-S	ENSILE-S	EVADER-S	FAQUIR-S	FINGER-S
DISCUS-S	DOSSEL-S	DUYKER-S	EMBRUE-S	ENSOUL-S	EVEJAR-S	FARCIN-S	FINIAL-S
DISEUR-S	DOSSER-S	DYBBUK-S	EMBRYO-S	ENSURE-S	EVENER-S	FARDEL-S	FINING-S
DISMAL-S	DOSSIL-S	DYEING-S	EMERGE-S	ENTAIL-S	EVINCE-S	FARDEN-S	FINJAN-S
DISMAN-S	DOTAGE-S	DYNAMO-S	EMETIC-S	ENTAME-S	EVOKER-S	FARINA-S	FINNAC-S
DISMAY-S	DOTANT-S	DYNAST-S	EMETIN-S	ENTICE-S	EVOLUE-S	FARMER-S	FINNAN-S
DISOWN-S	DOTARD-S	DYNODE-S	EMEUTE-S	ENTIRE-S	EVOLVE-S	FARREN-S	FINNER-S
DISPEL-S	DOTING-S	DYVOUR-S	EMIGRE-S	ENTOIL-S	EVOVAE-S	FARROW-S	FIORIN-S
DISPLE-S	DOTTLE-S	DZEREN-S	EMMOVE-S	ENTOMB-S	EVULSE-S	FASCIA-S	FIPPLE-S
DISTIL-S	DOUANE-S	EAGLET-S	EMPALE-S	ENTRAP-S	EVZONE-S	FASTEN-S	FIRING-S
DISUSE-S	DOUBLE-S	EARBOB-S	EMPARE-S	ENTREE-S	EXAMEN-S	FASTER-S	FIRKIN-S
DITHER-S	DOUCET-S	EARCON-S	EMPARL-S	ENVIER-S	EXARCH-S	FATHER-S	FIRLOT-S
DITONE-S	DOUCHE-S	EARFUL-S	EMPART-S	ENWALL-S	EXCAMB-S	FATHOM-S	FIRMAN-S
DITTAY-S	DOUSER-S	EARING-S	EMPIRE-S	ENWIND-S	EXCEED-S	FATSIA-S	FIRMER-S
DIVERT-S	DOUTER-S	EARLAP-S	EMPLOY-S	ENWOMB-S	EXCEPT-S	FATTEN-S	FISCAL-S
DIVEST-S	DOWLNE-S	EARNER-S	EMPUSA-S	ENWRAP-S	EXCIDE-S	FATWAH-S	FISGIG-S
DIVIDE-S	DOWNER-S	EARWIG-S	EMPUSE-S	ENZIAN-S	EXCISE-S	FAUCET-S	FISHER-S
DIVINE-S	DOWSER-S	EATAGE-S	EMULGE-S	ENZONE-S	EXCITE-S	FAUTOR-S	FISSLE-S
DIVING-S	DOWSET-S	EATCHE-S	EMUNGE-S	ENZYME-S	EXCUSE-S	FAVELA-S	FITCHE-S
DIZAIN-S	DOYLEY-S	EATING-S	ENABLE-S	EOLITH-S	EXEMPT-S	FAVISM-S	FITTER-S
DJEBEL-S	DOZING-S	ECARTE-S	ENAMEL-S	EONISM-S	EXHALE-S	FAVOUR-S	FIXATE-S
DOATER-S	DRACHM-S	ECBOLE-S	ENAMOR-S	EPARCH-S	EXHORT-S	FAWNER-S	FIXING-S
DOBBER-S	DRAGEE-S	ECHOER-S	ENCAGE-S	EPAULE-S	EXHUME-S	FEAGUE-S	FIXURE-S
DOBBIE-S	DRAGON-S	ECLAIR-S	ENCALM-S	EPEIRA-S	EXOGEN-S	FECULA-S	FIZGIG-S
DOBBIN-S	DRAPER-S	ECLOSE-S	ENCAMP-S	EPHEBE-S	EXONYM-S	FEDORA-S	FIZZEN-S
DOCENT-S	DRAPET-S	ECONUT-S	ENCASE-S	EPIGON-S	EXOPOD-S	FEEBLE-S	FIZZER-S
DOCKEN-S	DRAUNT-S	ECTYPE-S	ENCAVE-S	EPILOG-S	EXOTIC-S	FEEDER-S	FIZZLE-S
DOCKER-S	DRAWEE-S	ECURIE-S	ENCODE-S	EPIMER-S	EXPAND-S	FEELER-S	FLACON-S
DOCKET-S	DRAWER-S	ECZEMA-S	ENCORE-S	EPOCHA-S	EXPECT-S	FEERIE-S	FLAGON-S
DOCTOR-S	DRAZEL-S	EDGING-S	ENCYST-S	EPONYM-S	EXPEND-S	FEERIN-S	FLAMEN-S
DODDER-S	DREARE-S	EDIBLE-S	ENDART-S	EPOPEE-S	EXPERT-S	FEIJOA-S	FLANGE-S
DODDLE-S	DREDGE-S	EDITOR-S	ENDEAR-S	EQUANT-S	EXPIRE-S	FELINE-S	FLASER-S
DODGER-S	DRIVEL-S	EFFACE-S	ENDING-S	EQUATE-S	EXPORT-S	FELLAH-S	FLAUNE-S
DODKIN-S	DRIVER-S	EFFECT-S	ENDITE-S	EQUIPE-S	EXPOSE-S	FELLER-S	FLAUNT-S
DODMAN-S	DROGER-S	EFFEIR-S	ENDIVE-S	ERASER-S	EXPUGN-S	FELLOE-S	FLAVIN-S
DOFFER-S	DROGUE-S	EFFERE-S	ENDURE-S	ERBIUM-S	EXSECT-S	FELLOW-S	FLAVOR-S
DOGATE-S	DROICH-S	EFFORT-S	ENDURO-S	ERGATE-S	EXSERT-S	FELTER-S	FLAYER-S
DOGGER-S	DROMON-S	EFFRAY-S	ENERVE-S	ERIACH-S	EXTEND-S	FEMALE-S	FLECHE-S
DOGGIE-S	DRONGO-S	EFFUSE-S	ENFACE-S	ERINGO-S	EXTENT-S	FENCER-S	FLEDGE-S
DOLINA-S	DROOME-S	EGENCE-S	ENFANT-S	ERMINE-S	EXTERN-S	FENDER-S	FLEECE-S
DOLINE-S	DROUTH-S	EGGCUP-S	ENFIRE-S	EROTIC-S	EXTINE-S	FENNEC-S	FLENSE-S
DOLLAR-S	DROVER-S	EGGLER-S	ENFOLD-S	ERRAND-S	EXTIRP-S	FENNEL-S	FLEXOR-S
DOLLOP-S	DROWSE-S	EGGNOG-S	ENFORM-S	ERRANT-S	EXTORT-S	FERREL-S	FLIGHT-S
DOLMAN-S	DRUDGE-S	EGOISM-S	ENFREE-S	ERRING-S	EYALET-S	FERRET-S	FLORET-S
DOLMEN-S	DRUPEL-S	EGOIST-S	ENGAGE-S	ERYNGO-S	EYEFUL-S	FERULA-S	FLORIN-S
DOLOUR-S	DRYING-S	EIGHTH-S	ENGAOL-S	ESCAPE-S	EYELET-S	FERULE-S	FLOTEL-S
DOMAIN-S	DUALIN-S	EIRACK-S	ENGILD-S	ESCARP-S	EYELID-S	FESCUE-S	FLOUSE-S
DOMETT-S	DUBBIN-S	EISELL-S	ENGINE-S	ESCHAR-S	EYLIAD-S	FESTAL-S	FLOWER-S
DOMINO-S	DUCKER-S	ELANCE-S	ENGIRD-S	ESCHEW-S	FABLER-S	FESTER-S	FLUATE-S
DONATE-S	DUDDER-S	ELANET-S	ENGLUT-S	ESCORT-S	FABRIC-S	FETTER-S	FLUENT-S
DONDER-S	DUDEEN-S	ELAPSE-S	ENGOBE-S	ESCROC-S	FACADE-S	FETTLE-S	FLUGEL-S
DONGLE-S	DUDISM-S	ELATER-S	ENGORE-S	ESCROL-S	FACIAL-S	FEUTRE-S	FLUTER-S
DONING-S	DUELLO-S	ELCHEE-S	ENGRAM-S	ESCROW-S	FACING-S	FEWMET-S	FLYING-S
DONJON-S	DUENDE-S	ELDING-S	ENGULF-S	ESCUDO-S	FACTOR-S	FEWTER-S	FLYWAY-S
DONKEY-S	DUENNA-S	ELEGIT-S	ENHALO-S	ESLOIN-S	FACTUM-S	FIACRE-S	FODDER-S
DONNAT-S	DUETTO-S	ELENCH-S	ENIGMA-S	ESPADA-S	FADDLE-S	FIANCE-S	FOETOR-S
DONNEE-S	DUFFEL-S	ELEVEN-S	ENISLE-S	ESPIAL-S	FADEUR-S	FIASCO-S	FOGGER-S
DONNOT-S	DUFFER-S	ELEVON-S	ENJAMB-S	ESPRIT-S	FADING-S	FIAUNT-S	FOGLES-S
DONZEL-S	DUFFLE-S	ELICIT-S	ENJOIN-S	ESSIVE-S	FAERIE-S	FIBBER-S	FOGRAM-S
DOOCOT-S	DUGONG-S	ELIXIR-S	ENLACE-S	ESSOIN-S	FAGGOT-S	FIBRIL-S	FOIBLE-S
DOODAD-S	DUGOUT-S	ELOIGN-S	ENLARD-S	ESTATE-S	FAIBLE-S	FIBRIN-S	FOISON-S

FOLATE-S	FUMADO-S	GARRAN-S	GIMMER-S	GORGON-S	GUISER-S	HANDLE-S	HERALD-S
FOLDER-S	FUMAGE-S	GARRET-S	GIMMOR-S	GORING-S	GUITAR-S	HANGAR-S	HERBAL-S
FOLKIE-S	FUMBLE-S	GARRON-S	GINGAL-S	GOSLET-S	GUIZER-S	HANGER-S	HERBAR-S
FOLLOW-S	FUNDER-S	GARROT-S	GINGER-S	GOSPEL-S	GULDEN-S	HANJAR-S	HERDEN-S
FOMENT-S	FUNDIE-S	GARRYA-S	GINGLE-S	GOSSAN-S	GULLER-S	HANKER-S	HERDIC-S
FONDLE-S	FUNKIA-S	GARTER-S	GINNEL-S	GOSSIB-S	GULLET-S	HANKIE-S	HERIOT-S
FONDUE-S	FUNNEL-S	GARUDA-S	GINNER-S	GOSSIP-S	GULLEY-S	HANSEL-S	HERMIT-S
FOODIE-S	FURANE-S	GARVIE-S	GIPSEN-S	GOURDE-S	GULPER-S	HANSOM-S	HERNIA-S
FOOTER-S	FUREUR-S	GASBAG-S	GIRDER-S	GOUTTE-S	GUMNUT-S	HANTLE-S	HEROIC-S
FOOTIE-S	FURFUR-S	GASCON-S	GIRDLE-S	GOVERN-S	GUNITE-S	HAPPEN-S	HEROIN-S
FOOTLE-S	FUROLE-S	GASKET-S	GIRKIN-S	GOWFER-S	GUNNEL-S	HAPTEN-S	HEROON-S
FOOTRA-S	FURORE-S	GASKIN-S	GIRLIE-S	GOWLAN-S	GUNNER-S	HAPTIC-S	HETERO-S
FOOZLE-S	FURROW-S	GASPER-S	GIRNEL-S	GOWPEN-S	GUNSEL-S	HARBOR-S	HETMAN-S
FORAGE-S	FUSAIN-S	GASSER-S	GIRNER-S	GOZZAN-S	GUNTER-S	HARDEN-S	HEWING-S
FORBID-S	FUSION-S	GASTER-S	GITANA-S	GRABEN-S	GUNYAH-S	HAREEM-S	HEXACT-S
FORCAT-S	FUSSER-S	GATEAU-S	GITANO-S	GRADER-S	GURAMI-S	HARELD-S	HEXANE-S
FORCER-S	FUSTET-S	GATHER-S	GIVING-S	GRADIN-S	GURGLE-S	HARKEN-S	HEXENE-S
FOREST-S	FUSTIC-S	GATING-S	GIZZEN-S	GRAILE-S	GURJUN-S	HARLOT-S	HEXING-S
FORGER-S	FUSTOC-S	GAUCHO-S	GLAIVE-S	GRAINE-S	GURLET-S	HARMAN-S	HEXOSE-S
FORGET-S	FUTURE-S	GAUFER-S	GLAMOR-S	GRAITH-S	GURNET-S	HARMEL-S	HEYDAY-S
FORHOO-S	FUZZLE-S	GAUFRE-S	GLANCE-S	GRAKLE-S	GURNEY-S	HARMIN-S	HICCUP-S
FORHOW-S	FYLFOT-S	GAUGER-S	GLAZER-S	GRAMMA-S	GURRAH-S	HARPER-S	HICKEY-S
FORINT-S	GABBER-S	GAUPER-S	GLEAVE-S	GRAMME-S	GUSHER-S	HARROW-S	HIDAGE-S
FORKER-S	GABBLE-S	GAVAGE-S	GLEDGE-S	GRANGE-S	GUSLAR-S	HARTAL-S	HIDDER-S
FORMAT-S	GABBRO-S	GAVIAL-S	GLIDER-S	GRAPLE-S	GUSSET-S	HARTEN-S	HIDING-S
FORMER-S	GABION-S	GAWKER-S	GLIOMA-S	GRAPPA-S	GUSSIE-S	HASLET-S	HIGGLE-S
FORMOL-S	GABLET-S	GAWPER-S	GLOBIN-S	GRATER-S	GUTFUL-S	HASSAR-S	HIGHER-S
FORPET-S	GADDER-S	GAZEBO-S	GLOIRE-S	GRATIN-S	GUTROT-S	HASSLE-S	HIGHTH-S
FORPIT-S	GADGET-S	GAZOON-S	GLORIA-S	GRAVEL-S	GUTSER-S	HASTEN-S	HIJACK-S
FORRAY-S	GADGIE-S	GAZUMP-S	GLOSSA-S	GRAVER-S	GUTTER-S	HATFUL-S	HIJRAH-S
FORSAY-S	GADOID-S	GEEGAW-S	GLOVER-S	GRAYLE-S	GUTTLE-S	HATPEG-S	HINDER-S
FOSSIL-S	GAFFER-S	GEEZER-S	GLOWER-S	GRAZER-S	GUTZER-S	HATPIN-S	HIPPEN-S
FOSSOR-S	GAGAKU-S	GEISHA-S	GLUTEN-S	GREASE-S	GUYLER-S	HATRED-S	HIPPIE-S
FOSTER-S	GAGGER-S	GELADA-S	GLYCIN-S	GREAVE-S	GUZZLE-S	HATTER-S	HIPPIN-S
FOTHER-S	GAGGLE-S	GELDER-S	GLYCOL-S	GREECE-S	GYMBAL-S	HAULER-S	HIRAGE-S
FOURTH-S	GAINER-S	GENDER-S	GNAWER-S	GREESE-S	GYMMAL-S	HAUYNE-S	HIRING-S
FOUSSA-S	GAITER-S	GENEVA-S	GNOMON-S	GREETE-S	GYNNEY-S	HAVING-S	HIRPLE-S
FOUTER-S	GALAGE-S	GENNEL-S	GOALIE-S	GRICER-S	GYPPIE-S	HAWKER-S	HIRSEL-S
FOUTRA-S	GALAGO-S	GENNET-S	GOANNA-S	GRIECE-S	GYPSUM-S	HAWKEY-S	HIRSLE-S
FOUTRE-S	GALENA-S	GENOME-S	GOATEE-S	GRIEVE-S	GYRATE-S	HAWKIE-S	HITHER-S
FOWLER-S	GALERE-S	GENTLE-S	GOBANG-S	GRIFFE-S	HABOOB-S	HAWSER-S	HITTER-S
FOXING-S	GALIOT-S	GENTOO-S	GOBBET-S	GRIGRI-S	HACKEE-S	HAYING-S	HOAXER-S
FRAGOR-S	GALLET-S	GERBIL-S	GOBBLE-S	GRILLE-S	HACKER-S	HAYMOW-S	HOBBIT-S
FRAISE-S	GALLEY-S	GERENT-S	GOBIID-S	GRILSE-S	HACKLE-S	HAYSEL-S	HOBBLE-S
FRAMER-S	GALLON-S	GERMAN-S	GOBLET-S	GRINGO-S	HADDIE-S	HAZARD-S	HOBDAY-S
FRAPPE-S	GALLOP-S	GERMEN-S	GOBLIN-S	GRIPER-S	HADRON-S	HAZING-S	HOBJOB-S
FRATER-S	GALLOW-S	GERMIN-S	GODDEN-S	GRIPPE-S	HAEMIN-S	HAZZAN-S	HOBNOB-S
FRAZIL-S	GALOOT-S	GERUND-S	GODOWN-S	GRISON-S	HAFFET-S	HEADER-S	HOCKER-S
FREEZE-S	GALUTH-S	GETTER-S	GODSON-S	GRIVET-S	HAFFIT-S	HEALER-S	HOCKEY-S
FREMIT-S	GAMBET-S	GEWGAW-S	GODWIT-S	GROCER-S	HAGBUT-S	HEALTH-S	HODDEN-S
FRESCO-S	GAMBIR-S	GEYSER-S	GOFFER-S	GROMET-S	HAGDEN-S	HEARER-S	HODDLE-S
FRIAND-S	GAMBIT-S	GHARRI-S	GOGGLE-S	GROOVE-S	HAGDON-S	HEARSE-S	HOGGER-S
FRICHT-S	GAMBLE-S	GHAZAL-S	GOGLET-S	GROPER-S	HAGGLE-S	HEARTH-S	HOGGET-S
FRIDGE-S	GAMBOL-S	GHAZEL-S	GOITER-S	GROSER-S	HAGLET-S	HEASTE-S	HOGGIN-S
FRIEND-S	GAMETE-S	GHERAO-S	GOITRE-S	GROSET-S	HAIDUK-S	HEATER-S	HOGTIE-S
FRIEZE-S	GAMINE-S	GHESSE-S	GOLDEN-S	GROTTO-S	HAILER-S	HEAUME-S	HOIDEN-S
FRIGHT-S	GAMING-S	GHETTO-S	GOLFER-S	GROUGH-S	HAIQUE-S	HEAVEN-S	HOLDER-S
FRIGOT-S	GAMMER-S	GIAOUR-S	GOLLAN-S	GROUND-S	HAIRDO-S	HEAVER-S	HOLING-S
FRINGE-S	GAMMON-S	GIBBER-S	GOLLAR-S	GROUSE-S	HAIRST-S	HEBONA-S	HOLISM-S
FRIPON-S	GANDER-S	GIBBET-S	GOLLER-S	GROVEL-S	HALIDE-S	HECKLE-S	HOLIST-S
FRISEE-S	GANGER-S	GIBBON-S	GOLLOP-S	GROVET-S	HALITE-S	HECTIC-S	HOLLER-S
FRISKA-S	GANGUE-S	GIBLET-S	GOMBRO-S	GROWER-S	HALLAL-S	HECTOR-S	HOLLOA-S
FRIVOL-S	GANNET-S	GIDGEE-S	GOMOKU-S	GROWTH-S	HALLAN-S	HEDDLE-S	HOLLOW-S
FROISE-S	GANOID-S	GIDJEE-S	GOMUTI-S	GROYNE-S	HALLOA-S	HEDGER-S	HOLMIA-S
FROLIC-S	GANOIN-S	GIGGIT-S	GOMUTO-S	GRUDGE-S	HALLOO-S	HEEHAW-S	HOMAGE-S
FROWST-S	GANSEY-S	GIGGLE-S	GOOBER-S	GRUMPH-S	HALLOW-S	HEELER-S	HOMBRE-S
FRUICT-S	GAOLER-S	GIGLET-S	GOOGLE-S	GRUNGE-S	HALOID-S	HEEZIE-S	HOMING-S
FRYING-S	GAPING-S	GIGLOT-S	GOOGOL-S	GRYFON-S	HALSER-S	HEGIRA-S	HONCHO-S
FUCKER-S	GARAGE-S	GIGOLO-S	GOOLEY-S	GUANGO-S	HALTER-S	HEIFER-S	HONKER-S
FUCOID-S	GARBLE-S	GILCUP-S	GOOLIE-S	GUBBAH-S	HALVAH-S	HEIGHT-S	HONKIE-S
FUDDLE-S	GARCON-S	GILDER-S	GOONDA-S	GUDDLE-S	HALVER-S	HEJIRA-S	HONOUR-S
FUGATO-S	GARDEN-S	GILGAI-S	GOONEY-S	GUENON-S	HAMBLE-S	HELIUM-S	HOODIE-S
FULFIL-S	GARGET-S	GILGIE-S	GOOROO-S	GUFFAW-S	HAMLET-S	HELLER-S	HOODOO-S
FULGOR-S	GARGLE-S	GILLET-S	GOOSEY-S	GUFFIE-S	HAMMAL-S	HELMET-S	HOOFER-S
FULHAM-S	GARIAL-S	GILLIE-S	GOPHER-S	GUGGLE-S	HAMMAM-S	HELPER-S	HOOKAH-S
FULLAM-S	GARJAN-S	GILPEY-S	GOPURA-S	GUIDER-S	HAMMER-S	HEMINA-S	HOOKER-S
FULLAN-S	GARLIC-S	GIMBAL-S	GORGET-S	GUIDON-S	HAMPER-S	HENNER-S	HOOKEY-S
FULLER-S	GARNER-S	GIMLET-S	GORGIA-S	GUILER-S	HAMZAH-S	HENNIN-S	HOOLEY-S
FULMAR-S	GARNET-S	GIMMAL-S	GORGIO-S	GUINEA-S	HANDER-S	HEPTAD-S	HOOPER-S

HOOPOE-S	IGUANA-S	INHOOP-S	ITALIC-S	JOGGER-S	KATHAK-S	KIPPER-S	LANDAU-S
HOORAH-S	ILLIAD-S	INHUME-S	IZZARD-S	JOGGLE-S	KATION-S	KIRBEH-S	LANDER-S
HOORAY-S	ILLIPE-S	INISLE-S	JABBER-S	JOINER-S	KATIPO-S	KIRPAN-S	LANGUE-S
HOOTER-S	ILLITE-S	INJECT-S	JABBLE-S	JOJOBA-S	KEASAR-S	KIRTLE-S	LANGUR-S
HOOVER-S	ILLUDE-S	INJERA-S	JABIRU-S	JOLLEY-S	KEAVIE-S	KISHKE-S	LANNER-S
HOPDOG-S	ILLUME-S	INJURE-S	JACANA-S	JOLTER-S	KEBBIE-S	KISMET-S	LANUGO-S
HOPPER-S	ILLUPI-S	INKPOT-S	JACKAL-S	JORDAN-S	KEBELE-S	KISSEL-S	LAPDOG-S
HOPPLE-S	IMARET-S	INLACE-S	JACKET-S	JOSEPH-S	KEBLAH-S	KISSER-S	LAPFUL-S
HORKEY-S	IMBARK-S	INLAND-S	JAEGER-S	JOSHER-S	KECKLE-S	KITING-S	LAPPEL-S
HORNER-S	IMBASE-S	INLIER-S	JAGGER-S	JOSKIN-S	KEDDAH-S	KITTEN-S	LAPPER-S
HORNET-S	IMBIBE-S	INLOCK-S	JAGHIR-S	JOSSER-S	KEDGER-S	KITTLE-S	LAPPET-S
HORROR-S	IMBOSK-S	INMATE-S	JAGUAR-S	JOSTLE-S	KEEKER-S	KITTUL-S	LAPPIE-S
HORSON-S	IMBRUE-S	INNING-S	JAILER-S	JOTTER-S	KEELER-S	KLAXON-S	LAPTOP-S
HOSIER-S	IMMASK-S	INROAD-S	JAILOR-S	JOTUNN-S	KEELIE-S	KLEPHT-S	LARDER-S
HOSTEL-S	IMMUNE-S	INSEAM-S	JAMBEE-S	JOUNCE-S	KEENER-S	KLUDGE-S	LARDON-S
HOTBED-S	IMMURE-S	INSECT-S	JAMBER-S	JOURNO-S	KEEPER-S	KNAWEL-S	LARGEN-S
HOTPOT-S	IMPACT-S	INSEEM-S	JAMBOK-S	JOWARI-S	KEFFEL-S	KNIGHT-S	LARGES-S
HOTTER-S	IMPAIR-S	INSERT-S	JAMBUL-S	JOWLER-S	KEKSYE-S	KNOWER-S	LARIAT-S
HOTTIE-S	IMPALA-S	INSHIP-S	JAMJAR-S	JUBBAH-S	KELOID-S	KOBANG-S	LARKER-S
HOUDAH-S	IMPALE-S	INSIDE-S	JAMMER-S	JUDDER-S	KELPER-S	KOBOLD-S	LARRUP-S
HOUDAN-S	IMPARK-S	INSIST-S	JAMPAN-S	JUDOGI-S	KELPIE-S	KONFYT-S	LASCAR-S
HOUSEL-S	IMPARL-S	INSOLE-S	JAMPOT-S	JUDOKA-S	KELSON-S	KOODOO-S	LASHER-S
HOWDAH-S	IMPART-S	INSOUL-S	JANDAL-S	JUGFUL-S	KELTER-S	KOOLAH-S	LASING-S
HOWDIE-S	IMPAVE-S	INSPAN-S	JANGLE-S	JUGGLE-S	KELTIE-S	KOPECK-S	LASKET-S
HOWKER-S	IMPAWN-S	INSTAL-S	JANKER-S	JUGLET-S	KELVIN-S	KOPPIE-S	LASQUE-S
HOWLER-S	IMPEDE-S	INSTAR-S	JANSKY-S	JUICER-S	KEMPER-S	KORERO-S	LASSIE-S
HOWLET-S	IMPEND-S	INSTEP-S	JAPING-S	JUJUBE-S	KEMPLE-S	KORKIR-S	LASTER-S
HOYDEN-S	IMPONE-S	INSTIL-S	JARFUL-S	JUMART-S	KENNEL-S	KORORA-S	LATEEN-S
HUBBUB-S	IMPORT-S	INSULA-S	JARGON-S	JUMBAL-S	KENNER-S	KORUNA-S	LATEST-S
HUCKLE-S	IMPOSE-S	INSULT-S	JAROOL-S	JUMBIE-S	KENNET-S	KOSHER-S	LATHEE-S
HUDDLE-S	IMPOST-S	INSURE-S	JARRAH-S	JUMBLE-S	KENTIA-S	KOTWAL-S	LATHER-S
HUMBLE-S	IMPROV-S	INTAKE-S	JARVEY-S	JUMPER-S	KEPHIR-S	KOULAN-S	LATRIA-S
HUMBUG-S	IMPUGN-S	INTEND-S	JARVIE-S	JUNGLE-S	KERNEL-S	KOWHAI-S	LATRON-S
HUMECT-S	IMPUTE-S	INTENT-S	JASPER-S	JUNGLI-S	KERRIA-S	KOWTOW-S	LATTEN-S
HUMHUM-S	INCAGE-S	INTERN-S	JATAKA-S	JUNIOR-S	KERSEY-S	KRAKEN-S	LAUDER-S
HUMITE-S	INCASE-S	INTINE-S	JAUNCE-S	JUNKER-S	KETONE-S	KRATER-S	LAUNCE-S
HUMLIE-S	INCAVE-S	INTOMB-S	JAUNSE-S	JUNKET-S	KETOSE-S	KREESE-S	LAUREL-S
HUMMEL-S	INCEDE-S	INTONE-S	JAWARI-S	JUNKIE-S	KETTLE-S	KUMARA-S	LAVABO-S
HUMMER-S	INCEPT-S	INTRON-S	JAWING-S	JUPATI-S	KEYPAD-S	KUMARI-S	LAVAGE-S
HUMMUM-S	INCEST-S	INTUIT-S	JAZZER-S	JURANT-S	KGOTLA-S	KUMMEL-S	LAVEER-S
HUMOUR-S	INCISE-S	INTUSE-S	JEELIE-S	JURIST-S	KHALAT-S	KUNKAR-S	LAVOLT-S
HUMPEN-S	INCITE-S	INULIN-S	JEERER-S	JUSTLE-S	KHALIF-S	KUNKUR-S	LAWING-S
HUMPER-S	INCLIP-S	INVADE-S	JEMIMA-S	KABALA-S	KHANGA-S	KURGAN-S	LAWYER-S
HUNGER-S	INCOME-S	INVENT-S	JENNET-S	KABAYA-S	KHANUM-S	KURVEY-S	LAXISM-S
HUNKER-S	INCUSE-S	INVERT-S	JERBIL-S	KABELE-S	KHARIF-S	KWACHA-S	LAXIST-S
HUNTER-S	INDABA-S	INVEST-S	JERBOA-S	KABUKI-S	KHILAT-S	KWANZA-S	LAYING-S
HUPPAH-S	INDART-S	INVITE-S	JEREED-S	KACCHA-S	KHILIM-S	KYOGEN-S	LAYOUT-S
HURDEN-S	INDENE-S	INVOKE-S	JERKER-S	KAFILA-S	KHODJA-S	LAAGER-S	LEADEN-S
HURDLE-S	INDENT-S	INWALL-S	JERKIN-S	KAFTAN-S	KHURTA-S	LABIAL-S	LEADER-S
HURLER-S	INDICT-S	INWARD-S	JERQUE-S	KAGOOL-S	KIAUGH-S	LABLAB-S	LEAGUE-S
HURLEY-S	INDIGO-S	INWICK-S	JERSEY-S	KAGOUL-S	KIBBLE-S	LABOUR-S	LEAKER-S
HURRAH-S	INDITE-S	INWIND-S	JESSIE-S	KAIKAI-S	KIBLAH-S	LABRET-S	LEAPER-S
HURRAY-S	INDIUM-S	INWORK-S	JESTEE-S	KAISER-S	KICKER-S	LABRID-S	LEASER-S
HURTER-S	INDOLE-S	INWRAP-S	JESTER-S	KAIZEN-S	KIDDER-S	LACING-S	LEASOW-S
HURTLE-S	INDOOR-S	INYALA-S	JETSAM-S	KAKAPO-S	KIDDLE-S	LACKER-S	LEAVEN-S
HUSHER-S	INDUCE-S	IODATE-S	JETSOM-S	KALIAN-S	KIDLET-S	LACKEY-S	LEAVER-S
HUSKER-S	INDUCT-S	IODIDE-S	JETSON-S	KALIUM-S	KIDNAP-S	LADDER-S	LEBBEK-S
HUSSAR-S	INDULT-S	IODINE-S	JETTON-S	KALMIA-S	KIDNEY-S	LADDIE-S	LECHER-S
HUSSIF-S	INDUNA-S	IODISE-S	JEZAIL-S	KALONG-S	KIDULT-S	LADING-S	LECHWE-S
HUSTLE-S	INFALL-S	IODISM-S	JIBBAH-S	KALPAK-S	KIDVID-S	LAGENA-S	LECTIN-S
HUZOOR-S	INFAME-S	IODIZE-S	JIBBER-S	KAMALA-S	KIERIE-S	LAGGEN-S	LECTOR-S
HYAENA-S	INFANT-S	IOLITE-S	JIGGER-S	KAMELA-S	KIKUYU-S	LAGGER-S	LEDDEN-S
HYBRID-S	INFARE-S	IONISE-S	JIGGLE-S	KAMILA-S	KILERG-S	LAGGIN-S	LEDGER-S
HYDYNE-S	INFECT-S	IONIUM-S	JIGJIG-S	KAMSIN-S	KILLER-S	LAGOON-S	LEEWAY-S
HYLISM-S	INFEFT-S	IONIZE-S	JIGSAW-S	KANAKA-S	KILLUT-S	LAGUNE-S	LEFTIE-S
HYLIST-S	INFEST-S	IONONE-S	JILGIE-S	KANGHA-S	KILTER-S	LAIKER-S	LEGATE-S
HYMNAL-S	INFILL-S	IPECAC-S	JILLET-S	KANTAR-S	KILTIE-S	LAISSE-S	LEGATO-S
HYPATE-S	INFLOW-S	IRENIC-S	JIMJAM-S	KANTEN-S	KIMCHI-S	LALANG-S	LEGEND-S
HYPHEN-S	INFOLD-S	IRONER-S	JINGAL-S	KANTHA-S	KIMMER-S	LALDIE-S	LEGGER-S
HYPNIC-S	INFORM-S	IRRUPT-S	JINGLE-S	KAOLIN-S	KIMONO-S	LALLAN-S	LEGION-S
HYPNUM-S	INFUSE-S	ISABEL-S	JINKER-S	KARAIT-S	KINASE-S	LAMBDA-S	LEGIST-S
HYSSOP-S	INGATE-S	ISATIN-S	JIRBLE-S	KARAKA-S	KINCOB-S	LAMBER-S	LEGLAN-S
IAMBIC-S	INGENU-S	ISLAND-S	JISSOM-S	KARATE-S	KINDER-S	LAMBIE-S	LEGLEN-S
ICECAP-S	INGEST-S	ISOBAR-S	JITNEY-S	KARITE-S	KINDLE-S	LAMENT-S	LEGLET-S
ICICLE-S	INGINE-S	ISOGON-S	JITTER-S	KARSEY-S	KINEMA-S	LAMMER-S	LEGLIN-S
IDEATE-S	INGULF-S	ISOHEL-S	JOANNA-S	KARTER-S	KINGLE-S	LAMMIE-S	LEGUME-S
IGNARO-S	INHALE-S	ISOMER-S	JOBBER-S	KARYON-S	KINKLE-S	LAMPAD-S	LEIGER-S
IGNITE-S	INHAUL-S	ISOPOD-S	JOBBIE-S	KASBAH-S	KINONE-S	LANCER-S	LEIPOA-S
IGNORE-S	INHERE-S	ISSUER-S	JOCKEY-S	KATANA-S	KINRED-S	LANCET-S	LENDER-S

LENGTH-S	LITHIA-S	LUTING-S	MANTLE-S	MEDIAL-S	MILIEU-S	MONGOL-S	MUMBLE-S
LENTIL-S	LITTER-S	LUTIST-S	MANTRA-S	MEDIAN-S	MILKER-S	MONIAL-S	MUMMER-S
LENTOR-S	LITTLE-S	LUVVIE-S	MANTUA-S	MEDICK-S	MILLER-S	MONISM-S	MUMMIA-S
LENVOY-S	LIVING-S	LUXATE-S	MANUAL-S	MEDICO-S	MILLET-S	MONIST-S	MUMPER-S
LEPTON-S	LIZARD-S	LUZERN-S	MANUKA-S	MEDINA-S	MILORD-S	MONKEY-S	MUNDIC-S
LESION-S	LOADEN-S	LYCEUM-S	MANURE-S	MEDIUM-S	MILSEY-S	MONTEM-S	MUNITE-S
LESSEE-S	LOADER-S	LYCHEE-S	MAPPER-S	MEDLAR-S	MILTER-S	MONTRE-S	MUNSHI-S
LESSEN-S	LOAFER-S	LYNAGE-S	MARACA-S	MEDLEY-S	MIMBAR-S	MOOLAH-S	MUNTIN-S
LESSON-S	LOATHE-S	LYRISM-S	MARAUD-S	MEDUSA-S	MIMOSA-S	MOONER-S	MURAGE-S
LESSOR-S	LOBING-S	LYRIST-S	MARBLE-S	MEEKEN-S	MINBAR-S	MOORVA-S	MURDER-S
LETHEE-S	LOBULE-S	LYSINE-S	MARCEL-S	MEEMIE-S	MINCER-S	MOOTER-S	MURENA-S
LETTER-S	LOCALE-S	MACACO-S	MARGAY-S	MEGILP-S	MINDER-S	MOPANE-S	MURINE-S
LETTRE-S	LOCATE-S	MACHAN-S	MARGIN-S	MEGOHM-S	MINGLE-S	MOPANI-S	MURLAN-S
LEUCIN-S	LOCHAN-S	MACKLE-S	MARINA-S	MEGRIM-S	MINING-S	MOPOKE-S	MURLIN-S
LEVANT-S	LOCKER-S	MACOYA-S	MARINE-S	MEINEY-S	MINION-S	MOPPER-S	MURMUR-S
LEVITE-S	LOCKET-S	MACRON-S	MARKER-S	MEINIE-S	MINIUM-S	MOPPET-S	MURRAM-S
LEXEME-S	LOCULE-S	MACULE-S	MARKET-S	MEISHI-S	MINNIE-S	MORALE-S	MURRAY-S
LIAISE-S	LOCUST-S	MADCAP-S	MARKKA-S	MELANO-S	MINNOW-S	MORALL-S	MURREN-S
LIBATE-S	LODGER-S	MADDEN-S	MARLIN-S	MELDER-S	MINTER-S	MOREEN-S	MURREY-S
LIBBER-S	LOFTER-S	MADDER-S	MARMOT-S	MELLAY-S	MINUET-S	MORGAY-S	MURRHA-S
LIBERO-S	LOGGAT-S	MAELID-S	MAROON-S	MELLOW-S	MINUTE-S	MORGEN-S	MURRIN-S
LIBIDO-S	LOGGER-S	MAENAD-S	MARQUE-S	MELTON-S	MINYAN-S	MORGUE-S	MUSANG-S
LIBKEN-S	LOGGIA-S	MAFFIA-S	MARRAM-S	MEMBER-S	MIOMBO-S	MORION-S	MUSCAT-S
LICHEE-S	LOGLOG-S	MAGGOT-S	MARROW-S	MEMOIR-S	MIOTIC-S	MORKIN-S	MUSCID-S
LICHEN-S	LOGOFF-S	MAGIAN-S	MARRUM-S	MENACE-S	MIRAGE-S	MORNAY-S	MUSCLE-S
LICKER-S	LOGOUT-S	MAGILP-S	MARTEL-S	MENAGE-S	MIRITI-S	MORPHO-S	MUSEUM-S
LICTOR-S	LOITER-S	MAGISM-S	MARTEN-S	MENDER-S	MIRROR-S	MORROW-S	MUSHER-S
LIDGER-S	LOLIGO-S	MAGNET-S	MARTIN-S	MENEER-S	MISAIM-S	MORSEL-S	MUSING-S
LIEGER-S	LOLIUM-S	MAGNON-S	MARTYR-S	MENHIR-S	MISCUE-S	MORTAL-S	MUSKEG-S
LIERNE-S	LOLLER-S	MAGNUM-S	MARVEL-S	MENIAL-S	MISERE-S	MORTAR-S	MUSKET-S
LIFTER-S	LOLLOP-S	MAGPIE-S	MARVER-S	MENTEE-S	MISFIT-S	MOSAIC-S	MUSKLE-S
LIGAND-S	LOMENT-S	MAGUEY-S	MASALA-S	MENTOR-S	MISHAP-S	MOSQUE-S	MUSLIN-S
LIGASE-S	LONGAN-S	MAHMAL-S	MASCLE-S	MENYIE-S	MISHIT-S	MOSSIE-S	MUSMON-S
LIGATE-S	LOOFAH-S	MAHOUT-S	MASCON-S	MERCAT-S	MISHMI-S	MOTETT-S	MUSROL-S
LIGGER-S	LOOKER-S	MAHSIR-S	MASCOT-S	MERCER-S	MISKEN-S	MOTHER-S	MUSSEL-S
LIGNIN-S	LOONIE-S	MAIDAN-S	MASHER-S	MERELL-S	MISKEY-S	MOTILE-S	MUSTEE-S
LIGNUM-S	LOOPER-S	MAIDEN-S	MASHIE-S	MERGER-S	MISLAY-S	MOTION-S	MUSTER-S
LIGULA-S	LOOSEN-S	MAIGRE-S	MASHUA-S	MERINO-S	MISSAL-S	MOTIVE-S	MUTANT-S
LIGULE-S	LOOTER-S	MAILER-S	MASJID-S	MERISM-S	MISSAY-S	MOTLEY-S	MUTATE-S
LIGURE-S	LOPPER-S	MAINOR-S	MASKER-S	MERKIN-S	MISSEE-S	MOTMOT-S	MUTINE-S
LIKING-S	LOQUAT-S	MAKING-S	MASLIN-S	MERLIN-S	MISSEL-S	MOTSER-S	MUTISM-S
LIMAIL-S	LORCHA-S	MALATE-S	MASQUE-S	MERLON-S	MISSET-S	MOTTLE-S	MUTTER-S
LIMBEC-S	LORING-S	MALGRE-S	MASSIF-S	MEROME-S	MISTER-S	MOTUCA-S	MUTTON-S
LIMBER-S	LORIOT-S	MALICE-S	MASTER-S	MESAIL-S	MISTLE-S	MOUJIK-S	MUTUAL-S
LIMING-S	LOSING-S	MALIGN-S	MASTIC-S	MESCAL-S	MISUSE-S	MOULIN-S	MUTUCA-S
LIMMER-S	LOTION-S	MALISM-S	MASULA-S	MESETA-S	MITHER-S	MOUSER-S	MUTULE-S
LIMNER-S	LOUDEN-S	MATICO-S	MESSAN-S	MESSAN-S	MITTEN-S	MOUSIE-S	MUTUUM-S
LIMPET-S	LOUNGE-S	MALKIN-S	MATLOW-S	MESTEE-S	MIZZEN-S	MOUSLE-S	MUZHIK-S
LINAGE-S	LOUVER-S	MALLAM-S	MATOKE-S	METAGE-S	MIZZLE-S	MOUSME-S	MUZZLE-S
LINDEN-S	LOUVRE-S	MALLEE-S	MATRIC-S	METATE-S	MNEMON-S	MOUSSE-S	MYELIN-S
LINGAM-S	LOVAGE-S	MALLET-S	MATRON-S	METEOR-S	MOANER-S	MOUTAN-S	MYELON-S
LINGEL-S	LOVING-S	MALLOW-S	MATTER-S	METHOD-S	MOBBIE-S	MOUTER-S	MYGALE-S
LINGER-S	LOWBOY-S	MALMAG-S	MATTIE-S	METHYL-S	MOBBLE-S	MOUTON-S	MYOGEN-S
LINGLE-S	LOWING-S	MALTHA-S	MATURE-S	METIER-S	MOBILE-S	MOWING-S	MYOPIA-S
LINGOT-S	LOWNES-S	MAMMAL-S	MATZAH-S	METOPE-S	MOCKER-S	MOZZIE-S	MYOPIC-S
LINGUA-S	LOZELL-S	MAMMEE-S	MAUGRE-S	METRIC-S	MOCOCK-S	MOZZLE-S	MYOSIN-S
LINHAY-S	LUBBER-S	MAMMER-S	MAULVI-S	MEZAIL-S	MOCUCK-S	MUCATE-S	MYRIAD-S
LINING-S	LUCERN-S	MAMMET-S	MAUMET-S	MEZAIL-S	MODENA-S	MUCHEL-S	MYRTLE-S
LINKER-S	LUCKIE-S	MAMMON-S	MAUVIN-S	MGANGA-S	MODERN-S	MUCKER-S	MYSTIC-S
LINNET-S	LUCUMA-S	MAMZER-S	MAWKIN-S	MIASMA-S	MODIST-S	MUCKLE-S	MZUNGU-S
LINNEY-S	LUCUMO-S	MANAGE-S	MAWMET-S	MICATE-S	MODULE-S	MUCLUC-S	NABBER-S
LINSEY-S	LUGGER-S	MANANA-S	MAXIXE-S	MICHER-S	MOGGAN-S	MUDCAT-S	NACKET-S
LINTEL-S	LUGGIE-S	MANATI-S	MAYDAY-S	MICKEY-S	MOGGIE-S	MUDDER-S	NAGANA-S
LINTER-S	LUGING-S	MANCHE-S	MAYHEM-S	MICKLE-S	MOHAIR-S	MUDDLE-S	NAGARI-S
LINTIE-S	LUMBER-S	MANDIR-S	MAYING-S	MICRON-S	MOHAWK-S	MUDGER-S	NAGGER-S
LIONEL-S	LUMINE-S	MANDOM-S	MAZARD-S	MIDAIR-S	MOIDER-S	MUESLI-S	NAILER-S
LIONET-S	LUMPER-S	MANEGE-S	MAZHBI-S	MIDDAY-S	MOILER-S	MUFFIN-S	NALLAH-S
LIPASE-S	LUNGIE-S	MANGEL-S	MAZOUT-S	MIDDEN-S	MOISER-S	MUFFLE-S	NAMING-S
LIPIDE-S	LUNKER-S	MANGER-S	MAZUMA-S	MIDDLE-S	MOLEST-S	MUFLON-S	NANDOO-S
LIPOID-S	LUNULE-S	MANGLE-S	MEADOW-S	MIDGET-S	MOLINE-S	MUGFUL-S	NANISM-S
LIPPEN-S	LUNYIE-S	MANIAC-S	MEAGRE-S	MIDRIB-S	MOLLAH-S	MUGGEE-S	NANKIN-S
LIPPIE-S	LUPINE-S	MANILA-S	MEALER-S	MIDWAY-S	MOLLIE-S	MUGGER-S	NAPALM-S
LIQUID-S	LURDAN-S	MANIOC-S	MEALIE-S	MIHRAB-S	MOLOCH-S	MUKLUK-S	NAPKIN-S
LIQUOR-S	LURDEN-S	MANITO-S	MIKADO-S	MIKADO-S	MOMENT-S	MULLAH-S	NAPPER-S
LISPER-S	LURKER-S	MANNER-S	MEASLE-S	MIKRON-S	MOMMET-S	MULLER-S	NAPRON-S
LISTEL-S	LUSHER-S	MANOAO-S	MEATHE-S	MILADI-S	MOMZER-S	MULLET-S	NARDOO-S
LISTEN-S	LUSTER-S	MANRED-S	MEAZEL-S	MILAGE-S	MONAUL-S	MULLEY-S	NARROW-S
LISTER-S	LUSTRE-S	MANTEL-S	MEDAKA-S	MILDEN-S	MONETH-S	MULMUL-S	NASARD-S
LITCHI-S	LUTEIN-S	MANTID-S	MEDDLE-S	MILDEW-S	MONGER-S	MULTUM-S	NASION-S

NASUTE-S	NORITE-S	OCTUOR-S	ORISON-S	PAKORA-S	PATRON-S	PERUSE-S	PINKIE-S
NATION-S	NORMAL-S	OCULAR-S	ORMOLU-S	PALACE-S	PATTEN-S	PESADE-S	PINNER-S
NATIVE-S	NORMAN-S	OECIST-S	OROGEN-S	PALAGI-S	PATTER-S	PESANT-S	PINNET-S
NATRON-S	NORSEL-S	OEDEMA-S	OROIDE-S	PALATE-S	PATTLE-S	PESETA-S	PINNIE-S
NATTER-S	NOSEAN-S	OEUVRE-S	ORPHAN-S	PALING-S	PATZER-S	PESEWA-S	PINOLE-S
NATURE-S	NOSHER-S	OFFCUT-S	ORPINE-S	PALKEE-S	PAUNCE-S	PESHWA-S	PINTLE-S
NAUGHT-S	NOSING-S	OFFEND-S	OSCULE-S	PALLAH-S	PAUPER-S	PESTER-S	PIOLET-S
NAUSEA-S	NOSODE-S	OFFICE-S	OSMATE-S	PALLET-S	PAUSER-S	PESTLE-S	PIONER-S
NAUTIC-S	NOSTOC-S	OFFING-S	OSMIUM-S	PALLOR-S	PAVAGE-S	PETARA-S	PIONEY-S
NAVAID-S	NOTATE-S	OFFPUT-S	OSMOSE-S	PALMER-S	PAVANE-S	PETARD-S	PIPAGE-S
NEAFFE-S	NOTICE-S	OFFSET-S	OSMUND-S	PALMIE-S	PAVING-S	PETHER-S	PIPING-S
NEATEN-S	NOTION-S	OGDOAD-S	OSPREY-S	PALOLO-S	PAVIOR-S	PETREL-S	PIPKIN-S
NEBBUK-S	NOUGAT-S	OGLING-S	OSSEIN-S	PALTER-S	PAVISE-S	PETROL-S	PIPPIN-S
NEBECK-S	NOUGHT-S	OHMAGE-S	OSTENT-S	PAMPER-S	PAVONE-S	PETTER-S	PIQUET-S
NEBULA-S	NOUSLE-S	OIKIST-S	OSTLER-S	PANADA-S	PAWNCE-S	PETTLE-S	PIRANA-S
NEBULE-S	NOVENA-S	OILCAN-S	OTTAVA-S	PANAMA-S	PAWNEE-S	PEWTER-S	PIRATE-S
NECTAR-S	NOVICE-S	OILLET-S	OUGLIE-S	PANDAR-S	PAWNER-S	PEYOTE-S	PIRAYA-S
NEEDER-S	NOYADE-S	OILNUT-S	OULONG-S	PANDER-S	PAWPAW-S	PEZANT-S	PIRNIE-S
NEEDLE-S	NOZZER-S	OLEATE-S	OURALI-S	PANDIT-S	PAYING-S	PHEERE-S	PISTIL-S
NEGATE-S	NOZZLE-S	OLEFIN-S	OURARI-S	PANFUL-S	PAYNIM-S	PHEESE-S	PISTOL-S
NEKTON-S	NUANCE-S	OLFACT-S	OUREBI-S	PANGEN-S	PAYOLA-S	PHEEZE-S	PISTON-S
NELSON-S	NUBBIN-S	OLIVER-S	OUSTER-S	PANICK-S	PEACOD-S	PHENOL-S	PITARA-S
NEPETA-S	NUBBLE-S	OLIVET-S	OUTAGE-S	PANISC-S	PEANUT-S	PHENOM-S	PITIER-S
NEPHEW-S	NUCULE-S	OLLAMH-S	OUTBAR-S	PANISK-S	PEAPOD-S	PHENYL-S	PITTER-S
NEREID-S	NUDGER-S	OMELET-S	OUTBID-S	PANTER-S	PEARCE-S	PHIZOG-S	PITURI-S
NERINE-S	NUDISM-S	OMERTA-S	OUTEAT-S	PANTON-S	PEAVEY-S	PHLEGM-S	PIUPIU-S
NERITE-S	NUDIST-S	OMNIUM-S	OUTFIT-S	PANTUN-S	PEBBLE-S	PHLOEM-S	PIZZLE-S
NEROLI-S	NUDNIK-S	ONAGER-S	OUTGUN-S	PANZER-S	PECKER-S	PHOBIA-S	PLACER-S
NERVER-S	NUFFIN-S	ONCOME-S	OUTHIT-S	PAPAIN-S	PECTIN-S	PHOBIC-S	PLACET-S
NESTER-S	NUGGAR-S	ONCOST-S	OUTING-S	PAPAYA-S	PEDALO-S	PHOEBE-S	PLACIT-S
NESTLE-S	NUGGET-S	ONDINE-S	OUTJET-S	PAPISM-S	PEDANT-S	PHONER-S	PLAGUE-S
NETFUL-S	NULLAH-S	ONDING-S	OUTJUT-S	PAPIST-S	PEDDER-S	PHONEY-S	PLAICE-S
NETTLE-S	NUMBAT-S	ONEYER-S	OUTLAW-S	PAPULE-S	PEDDLE-S	PHONIC-S	PLAINT-S
NEURON-S	NUMBER-S	ONEYRE-S	OUTLAY-S	PARADE-S	PEDLAR-S	PHONON-S	PLANER-S
NEUTER-S	NUMDAH-S	ONFALL-S	OUTLER-S	PARAGE-S	PEELER-S	PHOTIC-S	PLANET-S
NEWBIE-S	NUMNAH-S	ONFLOW-S	OUTLET-S	PARAMO-S	PEENGE-S	PHOTON-S	PLANTA-S
NEWELL-S	NUNCIO-S	ONSIDE-S	OUTLIE-S	PARANG-S	PEEPER-S	PHRASE-S	PLAQUE-S
NEWTON-S	NUNCLE-S	ONWARD-S	OUTMAN-S	PARAPH-S	PEEPUL-S	PHREAK-S	PLASMA-S
NHANDU-S	NURDLE-S	ONYCHA-S	OUTPUT-S	PARCEL-S	PEERIE-S	PHYLLO-S	PLATAN-S
NIACIN-S	NURHAG-S	OOCYTE-S	OUTRED-S	PARDAL-S	PEEVER-S	PHYSIC-S	PLATEN-S
NIBBLE-S	NURSER-S	OOLITE-S	OUTRUN-S	PARDON-S	PEEWEE-S	PHYSIO-S	PLATER-S
NICHER-S	NURSLE-S	OOLONG-S	OUTSET-S	PARENT-S	PEEWIT-S	PHYTON-S	PLAYER-S
NICKAR-S	NUTATE-S	OOMIAC-S	OUTSIT-S	PARGET-S	PEINCT-S	PIAFFE-S	PLEASE-S
NICKEL-S	NUTLET-S	OOMIAK-S	OUTSUM-S	PARIAH-S	PELAGE-S	PIAZZA-S	PLEDGE-S
NICKER-S	NUTMEG-S	OOMPAH-S	OUTTOP-S	PARIAL-S	PELHAM-S	PICENE-S	PLENUM-S
NICKUM-S	NUTRIA-S	OORIAL-S	OUTVIE-S	PARING-S	PELITE-S	PICKER-S	PLEUCH-S
NIDGET-S	NUTTER-S	OPAQUE-S	OUTWIN-S	PARKEE-S	PELLET-S	PICKET-S	PLEUGH-S
NIDING-S	NUZZER-S	OPCODE-S	OUTWIT-S	PARKER-S	PELMET-S	PICKLE-S	PLEXOR-S
NIELLO-S	NUZZLE-S	OPENER-S	OVATOR-S	PARKIE-S	PELOID-S	PICNIC-S	PLIGHT-S
NIFFER-S	NYANZA-S	OPERON-S	OVISAC-S	PARKIN-S	PELOTA-S	PIDDLE-S	PLINTH-S
NIGGER-S	NYBBLE-S	OPHITE-S	OXFORD-S	PARLAY-S	PELTER-S	PIDGIN-S	PLONGE-S
NIGGLE-S	NYMPHO-S	OPIATE-S	OXGANG-S	PARLEY-S	PENCEL-S	PIECEN-S	PLOUGH-S
NILGAI-S	OARAGE-S	OPPOSE-S	OXGATE-S	PARLOR-S	PENCIL-S	PIECER-S	PLOVER-S
NILGAU-S	OBDURE-S	OPPUGN-S	OXHEAD-S	PAROLE-S	PENFUL-S	PIERCE-S	PLUNGE-S
NIMMER-S	OBECHE-S	OPTANT-S	OXLAND-S	PARPEN-S	PENNAL-S	PIERID-S	PLURAL-S
NINCOM-S	OBEISM-S	OPTIME-S	OXSLIP-S	PARRAL-S	PENNER-S	PIFFLE-S	PLUTON-S
NINCUM-S	OBEYER-S	OPTION-S	OXTAIL-S	PARREL-S	PENNON-S	PIGEON-S	PNEUMA-S
NIPPER-S	OBIISM-S	ORACHE-S	OXYGEN-S	PARROT-S	PENSEE-S	PIGGIE-S	POCHAY-S
NIPPLE-S	OBJECT-S	ORACLE-S	OXYMEL-S	PARSEC-S	PENSEL-S	PIGGIN-S	POCKET-S
NIPTER-S	OBJURE-S	ORANGE-S	OYSTER-S	PARSER-S	PENSIL-S	PIGLET-S	PODITE-S
NITRYL-S	OBLAST-S	ORATOR-S	OZAENA-S	PARSON-S	PENSUM-S	PIGNUT-S	PODLEY-S
NITWIT-S	OBLATE-S	ORBITA-S	PACHAK-S	PARTAN-S	PENTAD-S	PIGPEN-S	PODSOL-S
NOBBLE-S	OBLIGE-S	ORCEIN-S	PACKER-S	PARTER-S	PENTEL-S	PILAFF-S	PODZOL-S
NOCAKE-S	OBLONG-S	ORCHAT-S	PACKET-S	PARTON-S	PENULT-S	PILAFF-S	POETIC-S
NOCENT-S	OBOIST-S	ORCHEL-S	PADANG-S	PARURE-S	PEOPLE-S	PILFER-S	POFFLE-S
NOCHEL-S	OBSIGN-S	ORCHID-S	PADAUK-S	PASCAL-S	PEPINO-S	PILING-S	POGROM-S
NOCKET-S	OBTAIN-S	ORCHIL-S	PADDER-S	PASEAR-S	PEPLUM-S	PILLAR-S	POINTE-S
NOCTUA-S	OBTEND-S	ORCINE-S	PADDLE-S	PASHIM-S	PEPPER-S	PILLAU-S	POISER-S
NODDER-S	OBTEST-S	ORDAIN-S	PADOUK-S	PASSER-S	PEPSIN-S	PILLOW-S	POISON-S
NODDLE-S	OBTUND-S	ORDEAL-S	PADSAW-S	PASTEL-S	PEPTIC-S	PILULA-S	POLDER-S
NODULE-S	OBVERT-S	ORDURE-S	PAELLA-S	PASTER-S	PERDUE-S	PILULE-S	POLEYN-S
NOGGIN-S	OCCULT-S	OREIDE-S	PAGING-S	PASTIL-S	PERIOD-S	PIMENT-S	POLICE-S
NOMADE-S	OCELOT-S	ORGASM-S	PAGODA-S	PASTOR-S	PERKIN-S	PIMPLE-S	POLING-S
NOMISM-S	OCTANE-S	ORGEAT-S	PAIDLE-S	PATACA-S	PERMIT-S	PINATA-S	POLLAN-S
NONAGE-S	OCTANT-S	ORGONE-S	PAIGLE-S	PATENT-S	PERONE-S	PINCER-S	POLLEN-S
NONANE-S	OCTAVE-S	ORIENT-S	PAINIM-S	PATHIC-S	PERRON-S	PINDER-S	POLLER-S
NOODLE-S	OCTAVO-S	ORIGAN-S	PAIOCK-S	PATINA-S	PERSON-S	PINGER-S	POLYPE-S
NOOKIE-S	OCTETT-S	ORIGIN-S	PAJOCK-S	PATINE-S	PERSUE-S	PINGLE-S	POMACE-S
NOONER-S	OCTROI-S	ORIOLE-S	PAKEHA-S	PATROL-S	PERUKE-S	PINITE-S	POMADE-S

POMELO-S PRAYER-S PULSAR-S QUINIE-S RAPPER-S REEDER-S REPEAT-S REZONE-S
POMMEL-S PREACE-S PULTAN-S QUINOA-S RAPTOR-S REEFER-S REPENT-S RHAPHE-S
POMPEY-S PREAMP-S PULTON-S QUINOL-S RASCAL-S REELER-S REPINE-S RHETOR-S
POMPOM-S PREASE-S PULTUN-S QUINTA-S RASHER-S REFACE-S REPLAN-S RHODIE-S
POMPON-S PRECUT-S PULVER-S QUINTE-S RASPER-S REFECT-S REPLAY-S RHUMBA-S
POMROY-S PREEVE-S PULWAR-S QUINZE-S RASTER-S REFILL-S REPONE-S RHYMER-S
PONCHO-S PREFAB-S PUMELO-S QUIVER-S RASURE-S REFINE-S REPORT-S RHYTHM-S
PONDER-S PREFER-S PUMICE-S QUOIST-S RATBAG-S REFLAG-S REPOSE-S RIBALD-S
PONDOK-S PREIFE-S PUMMEL-S QUOKKA-S RATINE-S REFLET-S REPOST-S RIBAND-S
PONGEE-S PRELIM-S PUMPER-S QUORUM-S RATING-S REFLOW-S REPUGN-S RIBAUD-S
PONGID-S PREMED-S PUNCTO-S QUOTER-S RATION-S REFOOT-S REPULP-S RIBBON-S
PONTIE-S PREMIE-S PUNDIT-S QUOTUM-S RATLIN-S REFORM-S REPURE-S RIBIBE-S
PONTIL-S PREPAY-S PUNKAH-S QWERTY-S RATOON-S REFUEL-S REPUTE-S RIBLET-S
PONTON-S PRESET-S PUNNER-S RABBET-S RATTAN-S REFUGE-S REQUIT-S RIBOSE-S
POODLE-S PRESTO-S PUNNET-S RABBIN-S RATTEN-S REFUND-S RERAIL-S RICHEN-S
POOGYE-S PRETOR-S PUNTEE-S RABBIT-S RATTER-S REFUSE-S REREAD-S RICKER-S
POOJAH-S PREVUE-S PUNTER-S RABBLE-S RATTLE-S REFUTE-S RESALE-S RICKLE-S
POONAC-S PREWYN-S PUPATE-S RACEME-S RATTON-S REGAIN-S RESCUE-S RIDDER-S
POONCE-S PRICER-S PUPPET-S RACING-S RAUNGE-S REGALE-S RESEAL-S RIDDLE-S
POOTER-S PRIEFE-S PURDAH-S RACISM-S RAVAGE-S REGARD-S RESEAT-S RIDGEL-S
POPJOY-S PRIEST-S PURFLE-S RACIST-S RAVINE-S REGENT-S RESEAU-S RIDGER-S
POPLAR-S PRIEVE-S PURGER-S RACKER-S RAVING-S REGEST-S RESECT-S RIDGIL-S
POPLIN-S PRIMER-S PURINE-S RACKET-S RAWING-S REGGAE-S RESEDA-S RIDING-S
POPPER-S PRINCE-S PURISM-S RACOON-S RAYLES-S REGIME-S RESELL-S RIEVER-S
POPPET-S PRISER-S PURIST-S RADDLE-S RAYLET-S REGINA-S RESENT-S RIFFLE-S
POPPIT-S PRISON-S PURLER-S RADIAL-S RAZURE-S REGION-S RESHIP-S RIFLER-S
POPPLE-S PRIVET-S PURLIN-S RADIAN-S RAZZIA-S REGIVE-S RESIDE-S RIGGER-S
POPRIN-S PRIZER-S PURPIE-S RADIUM-S RAZZLE-S REGLET-S RESIGN-S RIGHTO-S
PORGIE-S PROBER-S PURPLE-S RADOME-S READER-S REGRET-S RESILE-S RIGLIN-S
PORISM-S PROBIT-S PURSER-S RAFALE-S REAMER-S REGROW-S RESIST-S RIGOLL-S
PORKER-S PROFIT-S PURSEW-S RAFFIA-S REAPER-S REGULO-S RESKEW-S RIGOUR-S
POROSE-S PROIGN-S PURSUE-S RAFFLE-S REARER-S REHANG-S RESKUE-S RILLET-S
PORTAL-S PROINE-S PURVEY-S RAFTER-S REASON-S REHEAR-S RESOLE-S RINGER-S
PORTER-S PROKER-S PUSHER-S RAGBAG-S REAVER-S REHEAT-S RESORB-S RINSER-S
POSADA-S PROLEG-S PUSSEL-S RAGGEE-S REBACK-S REHEEL-S RESORT-S RIOTER-S
POSEUR-S PROLER-S PUSSER-S RAGGLE-S REBATE-S REITER-S RESTEM-S RIPECK-S
POSING-S PROMPT-S PUTEAL-S RAGING-S REBECK-S REIVER-S RESTER-S RIPPER-S
POSNET-S PROPEL-S PUTELI-S RAGINI-S REBIND-S REJECT-S RESULT-S RIPPLE-S
POSSER-S PROPER-S PUTLOG-S RAGLAN-S REBITE-S REJOIN-S RESUME-S RIPRAP-S
POSSES-S PROPYL-S PUTTEE-S RAGMAN-S REBOIL-S RELATE-S RETAIL-S RISING-S
POSSET-S PROSER-S PUTTER-S RAGOUT-S REBOOT-S RELENT-S RETAIN-S RISKER-S
POSSIE-S PROTEA-S PUTTIE-S RAGTAG-S REBORE-S RELICT-S RETAKE-S RISQUE-S
POSSUM-S PROTON-S PUTURE-S RAGTOP-S REBUFF-S RELIEF-S RETAMA-S RITTER-S
POSTAL-S PROTYL-S PUZZEL-S RAIDER-S REBUKE-S RELIER-S RETARD-S RITUAL-S
POSTER-S PROVER-S PUZZLE-S RAILER-S RECALL-S RELINE-S RETELL-S RIVAGE-S
POSTIE-S PROYNE-S PYCNON-S RAISER-S RECANT-S RELIVE-S RETENE-S RIVLIN-S
POSTIL-S PRUINA-S PYEMIA-S RAISIN-S RECAST-S RELOAD-S RETILE-S RIZARD-S
POTAGE-S PRUINE-S PYGARG-S RAIYAT-S RECEDE-S RELUCT-S RETIME-S RIZZAR-S
POTBOY-S PRUNER-S PYONER-S RAKING-S RECEPT-S RELUME-S RETINA-S RIZZER-S
POTCHE-S PRUSIK-S PYRENE-S RALLYE-S RECIPE-S REMADE-S RETIRE-S RIZZOR-S
POTEEN-S PRYING-S PYRITE-S RAMBLE-S RECITE-S REMAIN-S RETOOL-S ROADIE-S
POTENT-S PSOCID-S PYROLA-S RAMCAT-S RECKON-S REMAKE-S RETORT-S ROAMER-S
POTFUL-S PSYCHE-S PYROPE-S RAMJET-S RECODE-S REMAND-S RETOUR-S ROARER-S
POTGUN-S PSYCHO-S PYTHON-S RAMMER-S RECOIN-S REMARK-S RETREE-S ROBALO-S
POTHER-S PSYLLA-S PYURIA-S RAMPER-S RECORD-S REMBLE-S RETRIM-S ROBBER-S
POTION-S PSYWAR-S QASIDA-S RAMROD-S RECOUP-S REMEAD-S RETUND-S ROBING-S
POTTER-S PTERIN-S QAWWAL-S RAMSON-S RECTOR-S REMEDE-S RETUNE-S ROCHET-S
POTTLE-S PTISAN-S QIGONG-S RANCEL-S RECTUM-S REMEID-S RETURF-S ROCKER-S
POUDER-S PUBLIC-S QINDAR-S RANCHO-S RECULE-S REMIND-S RETURN-S ROCKET-S
POUDRE-S PUCKER-S QINTAR-S RANCOR-S RECURE-S REMINT-S REURGE-S ROCOCO-S
POUFFE-S PUCKLE-S QIVIUT-S RANDAN-S RECUSE-S REMISE-S REVAMP-S RODENT-S
POULPE-S PUDDEN-S QUAERE-S RANDEM-S REDACT-S REMORA-S REVEAL-S RODING-S
POUNCE-S PUDDER-S QUAGGA-S RANDIE-S REDATE-S REMOTE-S REVERB-S ROEMER-S
POURER-S PUDDLE-S QUAHOG-S RANDOM-S REDBUD-S REMUDA-S REVERE-S ROLFER-S
POURIE-S PUEBLO-S QUAICH-S RANDON-S REDCAP-S RENAME-S REVERT-S ROLLER-S
POUSSE-S PUFFER-S QUAIGH-S RANGER-S REDDEN-S RENDER-S REVEST-S ROMAGE-S
POUTER-S PUFFIN-S QUAKER-S RANKER-S REDDER-S RENEGE-S REVEUR-S ROMPER-S
POWDER-S PUGGIE-S QUANGO-S RANKLE-S REDDLE-S RENNET-S REVIEW-S RONDEL-S
POWNEY-S PUGGLE-S QUARTE-S RANSEL-S REDEAL-S RENNIN-S REVILE-S RONYON-S
POWNIE-S PUISNE-S QUARTO-S RANSOM-S REDEEM-S RENOWN-S REVISE-S ROOFER-S
POWTER-S PUKEKO-S QUASAR-S RANTER-S REDEYE-S RENTAL-S REVIVE-S ROOKIE-S
POWWOW-S PULING-S QUAVER-S RANULA-S REDIAL-S RENTER-S REVOKE-S ROOMER-S
POYSON-S PULKHA-S QUEEST-S RANZEL-S REDLEG-S RENVOI-S REVOLT-S ROOMIE-S
PRAISE-S PULLER-S QUELEA-S RAPHIA-S REDOWA-S RENVOY-S REWARD-S ROOTER-S
PRANCE-S PULLET-S QUETHE-S RAPIER-S REDRAW-S REOPEN-S REWIND-S ROOTLE-S
PRANCK-S PULLEY-S QUICHE-S RAPINE-S REDTOP-S REPACK-S REWIRE-S ROPING-S
PRATER-S PULPER-S QUIDAM-S RAPIST-S REDUCE-S REPAIR-S REWORD-S ROQUET-S
PRATIE-S PULPIT-S QUIGHT-S RAPPEE-S REDUIT-S REPAST-S REWORK-S RORTER-S
PRAWLE-S PULQUE-S QUINCE-S RAPPEL-S REEBOK-S REPEAL-S REWRAP-S ROSACE-S

ROSIER-S	SAGGAR-S	SATORI-S	SCRINE-S	SERANG-S	SHOFAR-S	SIPPET-S	SNEATH-S
ROSSER-S	SAGGER-S	SATRAP-S	SCRIPT-S	SERAPE-S	SHOGUN-S	SIPPLE-S	SNEBBE-S
ROSTER-S	SAGOIN-S	SATYRA-S	SCRIVE-S	SERAPH-S	SHOOLE-S	SIRCAR-S	SNEEZE-S
ROSULA-S	SAGUIN-S	SAUCER-S	SCROBE-S	SERDAB-S	SHORAN-S	SIRDAR-S	SNIPER-S
ROTATE-S	SAHIBA-S	SAUGER-S	SCROLL-S	SEREIN-S	SHORER-S	SIRKAR-S	SNIVEL-S
ROTCHE-S	SAIKEI-S	SAULGE-S	SCROOP-S	SERENE-S	SHOTTE-S	SIRRAH-S	SNOOZE-S
ROTGUT-S	SAILER-S	SAULIE-S	SCROWL-S	SERIAL-S	SHOUGH-S	SIRREE-S	SNORER-S
ROTHER-S	SAILOR-S	SAUREL-S	SCRUFF-S	SERINE-S	SHOVEL-S	SISKIN-S	SNUBBE-S
ROTOLO-S	SAIQUE-S	SAVAGE-S	SCRUMP-S	SERIPH-S	SHOVER-S	SISSOO-S	SNUDGE-S
ROTTAN-S	SAITHE-S	SAVANT-S	SCRUNT-S	SERMON-S	SHOWER-S	SISTER-S	SOAKER-S
ROTTEN-S	SAKIEH-S	SAVATE-S	SCRUTO-S	SEROON-S	SHREEK-S	SITCOM-S	SOAPER-S
ROTTER-S	SALAAM-S	SAVINE-S	SCRUZE-S	SEROSA-S	SHREIK-S	SITHEN-S	SOAPIE-S
ROTULA-S	SALADE-S	SAVING-S	SCRYER-S	SERRAN-S	SHRIEK-S	SITREP-S	SOARER-S
ROTUND-S	SALAMI-S	SAVOUR-S	SCRYNE-S	SERVAL-S	SHRIFT-S	SITTAR-S	SOBOLE-S
ROUBLE-S	SALINA-S	SAVVEY-S	SCULLE-S	SERVER-S	SHRIKE-S	SITTER-S	SOCAGE-S
ROUCOU-S	SALINE-S	SAWDER-S	SCULPT-S	SESAME-S	SHRILL-S	SIXAIN-S	SOCCER-S
ROUNCE-S	SALIVA-S	SAWING-S	SCUNGE-S	SESELI-S	SHRIMP-S	SIZING-S	SOCIAL-S
ROUSER-S	SALLAD-S	SAWNEY-S	SCYTHE-S	SESTET-S	SHRINE-S	SIZISM-S	SOCKET-S
ROUTER-S	SALLAL-S	SAWPIT-S	SDAINE-S	SESTON-S	SHRINK-S	SIZIST-S	SODDEN-S
ROVING-S	SALLEE-S	SAWYER-S	SDEIGN-S	SETTEE-S	SHRIVE-S	SIZZLE-S	SODGER-S
ROWING-S	SALLET-S	SAXAUL-S	SEABED-S	SETTER-S	SHROFF-S	SKAITH-S	SODIUM-S
ROZZER-S	SALLOW-S	SAYING-S	SEAHOG-S	SETTLE-S	SHROUD-S	SKARTH-S	SOFFIT-S
RUBATO-S	SALMON-S	SAYYID-S	SEALCH-S	SETULE-S	SHROVE-S	SKATER-S	SOFTEN-S
RUBBER-S	SALOON-S	SAZHEN-S	SEALGH-S	SEWAGE-S	SHTCHI-S	SKELUM-S	SOFTIE-S
RUBBLE-S	SALOOP-S	SCAITH-S	SEALER-S	SEWING-S	SHTETL-S	SKEWER-S	SOIREE-S
RUBINE-S	SALTER-S	SCALAR-S	SEAMER-S	SEXISM-S	SHTICK-S	SKIBOB-S	SOLACE-S
RUBOUT-S	SALUKI-S	SCALER-S	SEANCE-S	SEXIST-S	SHTOOK-S	SKIDOO-S	SOLANO-S
RUBRIC-S	SALUTE-S	SCAMEL-S	SEARAT-S	SEXPOT-S	SHTUCK-S	SKIING-S	SOLDAN-S
RUCKLE-S	SALVER-S	SCAMPI-S	SEARCE-S	SEXTAN-S	SHUFTI-S	SKIVER-S	SOLDER-S
RUCOLA-S	SALVIA-S	SCARAB-S	SEASON-S	SEXTET-S	SIALON-S	SKLATE-S	SOLERA-S
RUDDER-S	SALVOR-S	SCARER-S	SEATER-S	SEXTON-S	SICKEN-S	SKLENT-S	SOLION-S
RUDDLE-S	SAMAAN-S	SCARPA-S	SEAWAY-S	SHACKO-S	SICKIE-S	SKLIFF-S	SOLIVE-S
RUEING-S	SAMARA-S	SCARPH-S	SEBATE-S	SHADOW-S	SICKLE-S	SKREEN-S	SOLLAR-S
RUELLE-S	SAMBAL-S	SCARRE-S	SECANT-S	SHADUF-S	SIDDHA-S	SKRIMP-S	SOLLER-S
RUFFIN-S	SAMBAR-S	SCARTH-S	SECEDE-S	SHAIKH-S	SIDDHI-S	SKRUMP-S	SOLUTE-S
RUFFLE-S	SAMBUR-S	SCATHE-S	SECERN-S	SHAIRN-S	SIDING-S	SKRYER-S	SOLVER-S
RUGGER-S	SAMEKH-S	SCAZON-S	SECKEL-S	SHAKER-S	SIEGER-S	SKYLAB-S	SOMBER-S
RUINER-S	SAMFOO-S	SCERNE-S	SECKLE-S	SHALLI-S	SIENNA-S	SKYWAY-S	SOMBRE-S
RULING-S	SAMIEL-S	SCHELM-S	SECOND-S	SHALOT-S	SIERRA-S	SLAIRG-S	SOMITE-S
RUMBLE-S	SAMITE-S	SCHEME-S	SECRET-S	SHAMAN-S	SIESTA-S	SLALOM-S	SONANT-S
RUMKIN-S	SAMITI-S	SCHISM-S	SECTOR-S	SHAMBA-S	SIFAKA-S	SLATER-S	SONATA-S
RUMMER-S	SAMLET-S	SCHIST-S	SECURE-S	SHAMER-S	SIFFLE-S	SLAVER-S	SONERI-S
RUMOUR-S	SAMLOR-S	SCHIZO-S	SEDATE-S	SHAMOY-S	SIFTER-S	SLAVEY-S	SONNET-S
RUMPLE-S	SAMOSA-S	SCHLEP-S	SEDUCE-S	SHAPER-S	SIGHER-S	SLAYER-S	SONTAG-S
RUNDLE-S	SAMPAN-S	SCHMOE-S	SEEDER-S	SHARER-S	SIGNAL-S	SLEAVE-S	SOOGEE-S
RUNKLE-S	SAMPLE-S	SCHOOL-S	SEEING-S	SHARIA-S	SIGNER-S	SLEAZE-S	SOOGIE-S
RUNLET-S	SAMSHU-S	SCHORL-S	SEEKER-S	SHARIF-S	SIGNET-S	SLEDGE-S	SOOJEY-S
RUNNEL-S	SANCAI-S	SCHOUT-S	SEEMER-S	SHAVER-S	SIGNOR-S	SLEEVE-S	SOOTHE-S
RUNNER-S	SANCHO-S	SCHTIK-S	SEESAW-S	SHAVIE-S	SILAGE-S	SLEIGH-S	SOPITE-S
RUNNET-S	SANDAL-S	SCHUIT-S	SEETHE-S	SHEATH-S	SILANE-S	SLEUTH-S	SORAGE-S
RUNRIG-S	SANDER-S	SCHUYT-S	SEGGAR-S	SHEAVE-S	SILENE-S	SLICER-S	SORBET-S
RUNWAY-S	SANDHI-S	SCILLA-S	SEGHOL-S	SHEEPO-S	SILENT-S	SLIDER-S	SORELL-S
RUPIAH-S	SANGAR-S	SCIROC-S	SEICHE-S	SHEIKH-S	SILICA-S	SLIGHT-S	SORGHO-S
RUSHEE-S	SANJAK-S	SCLAFF-S	SEINER-S	SHEILA-S	SILKEN-S	SLIVER-S	SORNER-S
RUSHER-S	SANNIE-S	SCLATE-S	SEISIN-S	SHEKEL-S	SILKIE-S	SLOGAN-S	SORREL-S
RUSSEL-S	SANNUP-S	SCLAVE-S	SEITEN-S	SHELVE-S	SILLER-S	SLOKEN-S	SORROW-S
RUSSET-S	SANPAN-S	SCLERA-S	SEIZER-S	SHERIA-S	SILVAN-S	SLOUGH-S	SORTER-S
RUSSIA-S	SANSEI-S	SCLERE-S	SEIZIN-S	SHERIF-S	SILVER-S	SLOVEN-S	SORTIE-S
RUSTIC-S	SANTAL-S	SCLIFF-S	SELECT-S	SHERPA-S	SIMIAN-S	SLUDGE-S	SOUARI-S
RUSTLE-S	SANTIR-S	SCONCE-S	SELKIE-S	SHEUCH-S	SIMILE-S	SLUICE-S	SOUPER-S
RUSTRE-S	SANTON-S	SCORER-S	SELLER-S	SHEUGH-S	SIMKIN-S	SMALTO-S	SOUPLE-S
RUTILE-S	SANTUR-S	SCORSE-S	SEMBLE-S	SHEWEL-S	SIMMER-S	SMEATH-S	SOURCE-S
RUTTER-S	SAPELE-S	SCOTER-S	SEMEME-S	SHIBAH-S	SIMNEL-S	SMEETH-S	SOURSE-S
RYOKAN-S	SAPOTA-S	SCOTIA-S	SEMMIT-S	SHIELD-S	SIMOOM-S	SMEGMA-S	SOUTAR-S
RYPECK-S	SAPPAN-S	SCOUSE-S	SEMSEM-S	SHIKAR-S	SIMOON-S	SMEUSE-S	SOUTER-S
SABBAT-S	SAPPER-S	SCOUTH-S	SENATE-S	SHIKSA-S	SIMORG-S	SMIGHT-S	SOVIET-S
SABKHA-S	SAPPLE-S	SCOWTH-S	SENDAL-S	SHIKSE-S	SIMPAI-S	SMILER-S	SOVRAN-S
SACHEM-S	SARAPE-S	SCRAMB-S	SENDER-S	SHINER-S	SIMPER-S	SMILET-S	SOWING-S
SACHET-S	SARDEL-S	SCRAPE-S	SENEGA-S	SHINES-S	SIMPLE-S	SMILEY-S	SOWSSE-S
SACKER-S	SARNEY-S	SCRAWL-S	SENIOR-S	SHINNE-S	SIMURG-S	SMITER-S	SOWTER-S
SACQUE-S	SARNIE-S	SCRAWM-S	SENNET-S	SHIPPO-S	SINDON-S	SMOILE-S	SOZZLE-S
SADDEN-S	SARONG-S	SCRAYE-S	SENNIT-S	SHIRRA-S	SINGER-S	SMOKER-S	SPACER-S
SADDHU-S	SARSEN-S	SCREAK-S	SENSOR-S	SHIVAH-S	SINGLE-S	SMOOTH-S	SPADER-S
SADDLE-S	SARTOR-S	SCREAM-S	SEPHEN-S	SHIVER-S	SINKER-S	SMOUSE-S	SPAHEE-S
SADISM-S	SASHAY-S	SCREED-S	SEPIUM-S	SHIVOO-S	SINNER-S	SMOYLE-S	SPAING-S
SADIST-S	SASINE-S	SCREEN-S	SEPTET-S	SHLOCK-S	SINNET-S	SMUDGE-S	SPALLE-S
SAETER-S	SATARA-S	SCRIBE-S	SEQUEL-S	SHMOCK-S	SINTER-S	SNARER-S	SPARER-S
SAFARI-S	SATEEN-S	SCRIKE-S	SEQUIN-S	SHMUCK-S	SIPHON-S	SNASTE-S	SPARGE-S
SAGENE-S	SATIRE-S	SCRIMP-S	SERAIL-S	SHODER-S	SIPPER-S	SNATHE-S	SPARID-S

SPARKE-S	STANZA-S	STROLL-S	SWARTH-S	TAMPON-S	TELFER-S	THROAT-S	TOILER-S
SPARRE-S	STANZE-S	STROMB-S	SWARVE-S	TANDEM-S	TELLAR-S	THRONE-S	TOILET-S
SPARTH-S	STANZO-S	STROND-S	SWATHE-S	TANGIE-S	TELLEN-S	THRONG-S	TOISON-S
SPATHE-S	STAPLE-S	STROUD-S	SWAYER-S	TANGLE-S	TELLER-S	THROWE-S	TOITOI-S
SPAULD-S	STARER-S	STROUP-S	SWEARD-S	TANGUN-S	TELLIN-S	THRUST-S	TOLING-S
SPAVIE-S	STARVE-S	STROUT-S	SWERVE-S	TANIST-S	TELNET-S	THUGGO-S	TOLLER-S
SPAVIN-S	STATER-S	STRUNT-S	SWEVEN-S	TANKER-S	TELSON-S	THULIA-S	TOLSEL-S
SPAYAD-S	STATIC-S	STUCCO-S	SWINGE-S	TANKIA-S	TEMPEH-S	THWACK-S	TOLSEY-S
SPECIE-S	STATOR-S	STUDIO-S	SWIPER-S	TANNAH-S	TEMPER-S	THWART-S	TOLTER-S
SPEEDO-S	STATUA-S	STUMER-S	SWIVEL-S	TANNER-S	TEMPLE-S	THYMOL-S	TOLUOL-S
SPENCE-S	STATUE-S	STUPID-S	SWIVET-S	TANNIN-S	TENACE-S	THYRSE-S	TOLZEY-S
SPERRE-S	STAYER-S	STUPOR-S	SWOUND-S	TANNOY-S	TENAIL-S	TICKEN-S	TOMBAC-S
SPERSE-S	STAYNE-S	STYLET-S	SWOUNE-S	TANREC-S	TENANT-S	TICKER-S	TOMBAK-S
SPEWER-S	STAYRE-S	STYMIE-S	SWOWND-S	TANTRA-S	TENDER-S	TICKET-S	TOMBOC-S
SPHAER-S	STEALE-S	SUBACT-S	SWOWNE-S	TAPETI-S	TENDON-S	TICKEY-S	TOMBOY-S
SPHEAR-S	STEANE-S	SUBBIE-S	SYLVAN-S	TAPIST-S	TENDRE-S	TICKLE-S	TOMCAT-S
SPHENE-S	STEARE-S	SUBDEW-S	SYLVIA-S	TAPPER-S	TENNER-S	TIDBIT-S	TOMPON-S
SPHERE-S	STEDDE-S	SUBDUE-S	SYMBOL-S	TAPPET-S	TENOUR-S	TIDDLE-S	TOMTIT-S
SPICER-S	STEEVE-S	SUBFEU-S	SYNDET-S	TARAND-S	TENREC-S	TIDING-S	TONEME-S
SPIDER-S	STEMME-S	SUBGUM-S	SYNDIC-S	TARBOY-S	TENSON-S	TIEPIN-S	TONGUE-S
SPIGHT-S	STEPPE-S	SUBLET-S	SYNROC-S	TARCEL-S	TENSOR-S	TIERCE-S	TONING-S
SPIGOT-S	STEREO-S	SUBMIT-S	SYNTAN-S	TARGET-S	TENTER-S	TIEROD-S	TONITE-S
SPILTH-S	STEROL-S	SUBORN-S	SYPHER-S	TARIFF-S	TENURE-S	TIETAC-S	TONKER-S
SPINAR-S	STERVE-S	SUBSET-S	SYPHON-S	TARING-S	TENUTO-S	TIFFIN-S	TONLET-S
SPINEL-S	STEVEN-S	SUBURB-S	SYSTEM-S	TARMAC-S	TENZON-S	TIGLON-S	TONNAG-S
SPINET-S	STEWER-S	SUBWAY-S	TABARD-S	TARPAN-S	TEPHRA-S	TILING-S	TONSIL-S
SPIRAL-S	STIFLE-S	SUCCAH-S	TABERD-S	TARPON-S	TERCEL-S	TILLER-S	TONSOR-S
SPIREA-S	STIGMA-S	SUCCES-S	TABLET-S	TARROW-S	TERCET-S	TILTER-S	TOOART-S
SPIRIC-S	STIGME-S	SUCCOR-S	TABOUR-S	TARSAL-S	TERCIO-S	TIMBAL-S	TOOLER-S
SPIRIT-S	STILET-S	SUCCUS-S	TABRET-S	TARSEL-S	TEREDO-S	TIMBER-S	TOORIE-S
SPITAL-S	STIMIE-S	SUCKEN-S	TACKER-S	TARSIA-S	TERETE-S	TIMBRE-S	TOOTER-S
SPLEEN-S	STINGO-S	SUCKER-S	TACKET-S	TARTAN-S	TERMER-S	TIMING-S	TOOTLE-S
SPLENT-S	STIPEL-S	SUCKET-S	TACKLE-S	TARTAR-S	TERMOR-S	TIMIST-S	TOPPER-S
SPLICE-S	STIRRA-S	SUCKLE-S	TACTIC-S	TASKER-S	TERRET-S	TINAJA-S	TOPPLE-S
SPLIFF-S	STIRRE-S	SUDATE-S	TADDIE-S	TASLET-S	TERRIT-S	TINCAL-S	TORANA-S
SPLINE-S	STIVER-S	SUDDER-S	TAENIA-S	TASSEL-S	TERROR-S	TINDAL-S	TORERO-S
SPLINT-S	STODGE-S	SUDSER-S	TAFFIA-S	TASSET-S	TERTIA-S	TINDER-S	TOROID-S
SPLORE-S	STOGEY-S	SUFFER-S	TAGGEE-S	TASSIE-S	TESTEE-S	TINEID-S	TORPID-S
SPONGE-S	STOGIE-S	SUITOR-S	TAGGER-S	TASTER-S	TESTER-S	TINFUL-S	TORPOR-S
SPOUSE-S	STOKER-S	SUKKAH-S	TAGRAG-S	TATAMI-S	TESTON-S	TINGLE-S	TORQUE-S
SPRAIN-S	STOLON-S	SULFUR-S	TAGUAN-S	TATLER-S	TETHER-S	TINKER-S	TORRET-S
SPRAWL-S	STONER-S	SULPHA-S	TAHINA-S	TATTER-S	TETRAD-S	TINKLE-S	TORSEL-S
SPREAD-S	STONNE-S	SULTAN-S	TAHINI-S	TATTIE-S	TETRYL-S	TINNER-S	TOSHER-S
SPREDD-S	STOOGE-S	SUMACH-S	TAHSIL-S	TATTLE-S	TETTER-S	TINNIE-S	TOSSER-S
SPRING-S	STOOPE-S	SUMMAT-S	TAIAHA-S	TATTOO-S	TEWART-S	TINPOT-S	TOTARA-S
SPRINT-S	STORER-S	SUMMER-S	TAIGLE-S	TATTOW-S	TEWHIT-S	TINSEL-S	TOTTER-S
SPRITE-S	STOREY-S	SUMMIT-S	TAILLE-S	TAUPIE-S	THAIRM-S	TINSEY-S	TOTTIE-S
SPROUT-S	STORGE-S	SUMMON-S	TAILOR-S	TAUTEN-S	THALER-S	TINTER-S	TOUCAN-S
SPRUCE-S	STOUND-S	SUMPIT-S	TAILYE-S	TAUTOG-S	THANAH-S	TIPCAT-S	TOUCHE-S
SPRUIK-S	STOUTH-S	SUNBED-S	TAIPAN-S	TAVERN-S	THANNA-S	TIPPER-S	TOUPEE-S
SPRUIT-S	STOVER-S	SUNBOW-S	TAIVER-S	TAWING-S	THAWER-S	TIPPET-S	TOUPET-S
SPULYE-S	STOWER-S	SUNDAE-S	TAJINE-S	TAWNEY-S	THEAVE-S	TIPPLE-S	TOURER-S
SPUNGE-S	STOWND-S	SUNDER-S	TAKAHE-S	TAWPIE-S	THEINE-S	TIPTOE-S	TOURIE-S
SPURGE-S	STOWRE-S	SUNDEW-S	TAKING-S	TAXING-S	THEISM-S	TIPTOP-S	TOUSER-S
SPURNE-S	STRAFE-S	SUNDOG-S	TALANT-S	TCHICK-S	THEIST-S	TIPULA-S	TOUSLE-S
SPYING-S	STRAFF-S	SUNDRA-S	TALBOT-S	TEACUP-S	THENAR-S	TIRADE-S	TOUTER-S
SQUAIL-S	STRAIK-S	SUNDRI-S	TALCUM-S	TEAGLE-S	THIBET-S	TIRING-S	TOUZLE-S
SQUALL-S	STRAIN-S	SUNGAR-S	TALENT-S	TEAMER-S	THIBLE-S	TIRRIT-S	TOWAGE-S
SQUAME-S	STRAIT-S	SUNHAT-S	TALION-S	TEAPOT-S	THICKO-S	TISANE-S	TOWARD-S
SQUARE-S	STRAKE-S	SUNKET-S	TALKER-S	TEAPOY-S	THIEVE-S	TISICK-S	TOWBAR-S
SQUAWK-S	STRAMP-S	SUNKIE-S	TALKIE-S	TEARER-S	THIRAM-S	TISSUE-S	TOWHEE-S
SQUEAK-S	STRAND-S	SUNRAY-S	TALLAT-S	TEASEL-S	THIRST-S	TITBIT-S	TOWING-S
SQUEAL-S	STRATH-S	SUNSET-S	TALLET-S	TEASER-S	THIVEL-S	TITFER-S	TOWMON-S
SQUIER-S	STREAK-S	SUNTAN-S	TALLOT-S	TEAZEL-S	THORIA-S	TITHER-S	TOWNEE-S
SQUILL-S	STREAM-S	SUPAWN-S	TALLOW-S	TEAZLE-S	THORON-S	TITIAN-S	TOWNIE-S
SQUINT-S	STREEK-S	SUPINE-S	TALMUD-S	TEBBAD-S	THORPE-S	TITLER-S	TOWSER-S
SQUIRE-S	STREEL-S	SUPPER-S	TALUKA-S	TECHIE-S	THOWEL-S	TITOKI-S	TOXOID-S
SQUIRM-S	STREET-S	SUPPLE-S	TALWEG-S	TECHNO-S	THRALL-S	TITTER-S	TOYING-S
SQUIRR-S	STRENE-S	SURBED-S	TAMALE-S	TECKEL-S	THRANG-S	TITTLE-S	TRACER-S
SQUIRT-S	STRIDE-S	SURFER-S	TAMANU-S	TEDDER-S	THRAVE-S	TITTUP-S	TRADER-S
STABLE-S	STRIFE-S	SURFIE-S	TAMARA-S	TEDDIE-S	THREAD-S	TITULE-S	TRANCE-S
STACTE-S	STRIFT-S	SURREY-S	TAMARI-S	TEDIUM-S	THREAP-S	TOCHER-S	TRANSE-S
STADDA-S	STRIKE-S	SURVEW-S	TAMBAC-S	TEEMER-S	THREAT-S	TOCSIN-S	TRAPAN-S
STADIA-S	STRING-S	SURVEY-S	TAMBER-S	TEEPEE-S	THREEP-S	TODDLE-S	TRAUMA-S
STAGER-S	STRIPE-S	SUSLIK-S	TAMINE-S	TEETER-S	THRENE-S	TOECAP-S	TRAVEL-S
STAITH-S	STRIVE-S	SUTLER-S	TAMING-S	TEETHE-S	THRIFT-S	TOERAG-S	TRAYNE-S
STALAG-S	STROAM-S	SUTTEE-S	TAMISE-S	TELEDU-S	THRILL-S	TOETOE-S	TREBLE-S
STAMEN-S	STROBE-S	SUTTLE-S	TAMMAR-S	TELEGA-S	THRIST-S	TOFFEE-S	TREMIE-S
STANCE-S	STROKE-S	SUTURE-S	TAMPER-S	TELESM-S	THRIVE-S	TOGGLE-S	TREMOR-S

TREPAN-S	TUSSER-S	UNGLUE-S	UNTOMB-S	URANIN-S	VERDIN-S	WABAIN-S	WEDGIE-S
TREVIS-S	TUSSLE-S	UNGOWN-S	UNTRIM-S	URANYL-S	VERDIT-S	WABBLE-S	WEEDER-S
TRIAGE-S	TUTSAN-S	UNGYVE-S	UNTUCK-S	URCHIN-S	VERGER-S	WABOOM-S	WEEPER-S
TRICAR-S	TUXEDO-S	UNHAIR-S	UNTUNE-S	UREIDE-S	VERISM-S	WACKER-S	WEEPIE-S
TRICOT-S	TUYERE-S	UNHAND-S	UNTURF-S	UREMIA-S	VERIST-S	WADDIE-S	WEEVER-S
TRIFLE-S	TWAITE-S	UNHANG-S	UNTURN-S	URETER-S	VERMIL-S	WADDLE-S	WEEVIL-S
TRIGON-S	TWEEZE-S	UNHASP-S	UNVAIL-S	URGING-S	VERMIN-S	WADING-S	WEIGHT-S
TRILBY-S	TWELVE-S	UNHEAD-S	UNVEIL-S	URINAL-S	VERREL-S	WADMAL-S	WEIRDO-S
TRIMER-S	TWICER-S	UNHEAL-S	UNWARE-S	URNFUL-S	VERSAL-S	WADMOL-S	WELDER-S
TRIODE-S	TWIGHT-S	UNHELE-S	UNWEAL-S	URNING-S	VERSER-S	WADSET-S	WELDOR-S
TRIPLE-S	TWINER-S	UNHELM-S	UNWILL-S	UROPOD-S	VERSET-S	WAFFLE-S	WELKIN-S
TRIPOD-S	TWINGE-S	UNHIVE-S	UNWIND-S	URTEXT-S	VERSIN-S	WAFTER-S	WELLIE-S
TRISUL-S	TWYERE-S	UNHOOD-S	UNWIRE-S	URTICA-S	VERTUE-S	WAGGLE-S	WELTER-S
TRITON-S	TYCOON-S	UNHOOK-S	UNWIVE-S	USAGER-S	VERVEL-S	WAGGON-S	WESAND-S
TRIUNE-S	TYLOTE-S	UNHOOP-S	UNWORK-S	USANCE-S	VERVEN-S	WAHINE-S	WESTER-S
TRIVET-S	TYMBAL-S	UNHUSK-S	UNWRAP-S	USTION-S	VERVET-S	WAILER-S	WETHER-S
TROADE-S	TYMPAN-S	UNIPED-S	UNYOKE-S	USURER-S	VESPER-S	WAITER-S	WEZAND-S
TROCAR-S	TYPHON-S	UNIPOD-S	UPBEAR-S	USURES-S	VESSEL-S	WAIVER-S	WHACKO-S
TROCHE-S	TYPING-S	UNIQUE-S	UPBIND-S	USWARD-S	VESTAL-S	WAKANE-S	WHALER-S
TROGON-S	TYPIST-S	UNISON-S	UPBLOW-S	UTMOST-S	VEXING-S	WAKIKI-S	WHAMMO-S
TROIKA-S	TYRANT-S	UNITER-S	UPBOIL-S	UTOPIA-S	VIATOR-S	WAKING-S	WHARVE-S
TROMPE-S	TYSTIE-S	UNKING-S	UPBRAY-S	VACATE-S	VIBIST-S	WALISE-S	WHEECH-S
TROPIC-S	TZETSE-S	UNKNIT-S	UPCAST-S	VACUUM-S	VIBRIO-S	WALKER-S	WHEEZE-S
TROTYL-S	UAKARI-S	UNKNOT-S	UPCOIL-S	VAGINA-S	VICTIM-S	WALLAH-S	WHENCE-S
TROUGH-S	UJAMAA-S	UNLACE-S	UPCOME-S	VAHINE-S	VICTOR-S	WALLER-S	WHEUGH-S
TROULE-S	ULICON-S	UNLADE-S	UPCURL-S	VAKEEL-S	VICUNA-S	WALLET-S	WHIDAH-S
TROUPE-S	ULIKON-S	UNLEAD-S	UPDATE-S	VALETA-S	VIDAME-S	WALLIE-S	WHINER-S
TROUSE-S	ULLAGE-S	UNLIKE-S	UPDRAG-S	VALETE-S	VIELLE-S	WALLOP-S	WHINGE-S
TROVER-S	ULLING-S	UNLIME-S	UPDRAW-S	VALINE-S	VIEWER-S	WALLOW-S	WHISHT-S
TROWEL-S	ULSTER-S	UNLINE-S	UPFILL-S	VALISE-S	VIGORO-S	WALNUT-S	WHITEN-S
TRUANT-S	ULTIMA-S	UNLINK-S	UPFLOW-S	VALLEY-S	VIGOUR-S	WAMBLE-S	WHITEY-S
TRUDGE-S	ULTION-S	UNLIVE-S	UPFURL-S	VALLUM-S	VIHARA-S	WAMPEE-S	WHYDAH-S
TRUISM-S	UMBREL-S	UNLOAD-S	UPGANG-S	VALOUR-S	VIKING-S	WAMPUM-S	WICCAN-S
TRYING-S	UMBRIL-S	UNLOCK-S	UPGAZE-S	VALUER-S	VILLAN-S	WANDER-S	WICKED-S
TSAMBA-S	UMLAUT-S	UNLORD-S	UPGROW-S	VALUTA-S	VIMANA-S	WANDOO-S	WICKEN-S
TSETSE-S	UMPIRE-S	UNLOVE-S	UPHANG-S	VAMOSE-S	VIOLER-S	WANGAN-S	WICKER-S
TSOTSI-S	UNBARE-S	UNMAKE-S	UPHAUD-S	VAMPER-S	VIOLET-S	WANGLE-S	WICKET-S
TUBAGE-S	UNBARK-S	UNMASK-S	UPHEAP-S	VANDAL-S	VIOLIN-S	WANGUN-S	WIDDLE-S
TUBBER-S	UNBEAR-S	UNMOOR-S	UPHILL-S	VANNER-S	VIRAGO-S	WANING-S	WIDGET-S
TUBFUL-S	UNBELT-S	UNNAIL-S	UPHOLD-S	VAPOUR-S	VIRGER-S	WANKER-S	WIDGIE-S
TUBING-S	UNBEND-S	UNNEST-S	UPHROE-S	VARECH-S	VIRGIN-S	WANTER-S	WIENIE-S
TUBULE-S	UNBIND-S	UNPACK-S	UPHURL-S	VARIER-S	VIRINO-S	WANTON-S	WIGEON-S
TUCHUN-S	UNBITT-S	UNPICK-S	UPKEEP-S	VARLET-S	VIRION-S	WAPITI-S	WIGGLE-S
TUCKER-S	UNBOLT-S	UNPLUG-S	UPKNIT-S	VARROA-S	VIROID-S	WAPPER-S	WIGWAG-S
TUCKET-S	UNBONE-S	UNPOPE-S	UPLAND-S	VARVEL-S	VIROSE-S	WARBLE-S	WIGWAM-S
TUFFET-S	UNBOOT-S	UNPRAY-S	UPLEAD-S	VASSAL-S	VIRTUE-S	WARDEN-S	WILDER-S
TUFTER-S	UNCAGE-S	UNPROP-S	UPLEAN-S	VATFUL-S	VISAGE-S	WARDER-S	WILLER-S
TUGGER-S	UNCAPE-S	UNRAKE-S	UPLEAP-S	VATTER-S	VISCIN-S	WARDOG-S	WILLET-S
TUGHRA-S	UNCART-S	UNREEL-S	UPLIFT-S	VAUDOO-S	VISCUM-S	WARMER-S	WILLEY-S
TUGRIK-S	UNCASE-S	UNREIN-S	UPLINK-S	VAUNCE-S	VISIER-S	WARMTH-S	WILLIE-S
TUILLE-S	UNCIAL-S	UNREST-S	UPLOAD-S	VAWARD-S	VISILE-S	WARNER-S	WILLOW-S
TULBAN-S	UNCLEW-S	UNROBE-S	UPLOCK-S	VEALER-S	VISION-S	WARPER-S	WILTJA-S
TULWAR-S	UNCLOG-S	UNROLL-S	UPLOOK-S	VECTOR-S	VISITE-S	WARRAN-S	WIMBLE-S
TUMBLE-S	UNCOCK-S	UNROOF-S	UPMAKE-S	VEGGIE-S	VISUAL-S	WARRAY-S	WIMPLE-S
TUMOUR-S	UNCOIL-S	UNROOT-S	UPPING-S	VELETA-S	VITRIC-S	WARREN-S	WINCER-S
TUMULT-S	UNCOLT-S	UNROPE-S	UPRATE-S	VELLET-S	VITTLE-S	WARREY-S	WINCEY-S
TUNDRA-S	UNCOPE-S	UNRULE-S	UPREAR-S	VELLON-S	VIZARD-S	WARSLE-S	WINDAC-S
TUNDUN-S	UNCORD-S	UNSEAL-S	UPREST-S	VELLUM-S	VIZIER-S	WASHER-S	WINDER-S
TUNING-S	UNCORK-S	UNSEAM-S	UPRISE-S	VELOUR-S	VIZSLA-S	WASPIE-S	WINDLE-S
TUNNEL-S	UNCOWL-S	UNSEAT-S	UPRIST-S	VELURE-S	VIZZIE-S	WASTEL-S	WINDOW-S
TUPELO-S	UNCURL-S	UNSEEL-S	UPROAR-S	VELVET-S	VOCULE-S	WASTER-S	WINGER-S
TURACO-S	UNDEAF-S	UNSEEN-S	UPROLL-S	VENDEE-S	VOGUER-S	WATTLE-S	WINKER-S
TURBAN-S	UNDECK-S	UNSELF-S	UPROOT-S	VENDER-S	VOICER-S	WAUCHT-S	WINKLE-S
TURBIT-S	UNDERN-S	UNSHIP-S	UPSEND-S	VENDIS-S	VOIDEE-S	WAUGHT-S	WINNER-S
TURBOT-S	UNDINE-S	UNSHOE-S	UPSHOT-S	VENDOR-S	VOIDER-S	WAUKER-S	WINNLE-S
TUREEN-S	UNDOCK-S	UNSHUT-S	UPSIDE-S	VENDUE-S	VOLLEY-S	WAVING-S	WINNOW-S
TURGOR-S	UNDOER-S	UNSNAP-S	UPSTAY-S	VENEER-S	VOLOST-S	WAXING-S	WINSEY-S
TURION-S	UNDRAW-S	UNSOUL-S	UPSWAY-S	VENEWE-S	VOLUME-S	WAYLAY-S	WINTER-S
TURKEY-S	UNEASE-S	UNSPAR-S	UPTAKE-S	VENGER-S	VOLUTE-S	WEAKEN-S	WINTLE-S
TURNER-S	UNEDGE-S	UNSTEP-S	UPTEAR-S	VENIRE-S	VOMICA-S	WEALTH-S	WIPING-S
TURNIP-S	UNFACT-S	UNSTOP-S	UPTILT-S	VENITE-S	VOMITO-S	WEANEL-S	WIPPEN-S
TURRET-S	UNFAIR-S	UNSTOW-S	UPTOWN-S	VENNEL-S	VOODOO-S	WEANER-S	WIRING-S
TURTLE-S	UNFOLD-S	UNSUIT-S	UPTURN-S	VENTER-S	VOTEEN-S	WEAPON-S	WISARD-S
TUSCHE-S	UNFOOL-S	UNTACK-S	UPWAFT-S	VENTIL-S	VOUDOU-S	WEARER-S	WISDOM-S
TUSHIE-S	UNFORM-S	UNTAME-S	UPWARD-S	VENTRE-S	VOULGE-S	WEASEL-S	WISENT-S
TUSKAR-S	UNFURL-S	UNTEAM-S	UPWELL-S	VENULE-S	VOYAGE-S	WEAVER-S	WISHER-S
TUSKER-S	UNGEAR-S	UNTENT-S	UPWIND-S	VERBAL-S	VOYEUR-S	WEAZEN-S	WISKET-S
TUSSAH-S	UNGILD-S	UNTHAW-S	UPWRAP-S	VERBID-S	VULCAN-S	WEDDER-S	WITGAT-S
TUSSEH-S	UNGIRD-S	UNTILE-S	URACIL-S	VERDET-S	VULGAR-S	WEDELN-S	WITHER-S

WITTER-S	WOOPIE-S	WRITHE-S	YAMMER-S	YIPPER-S	YUMPIE-S	ZENANA-S	ZOMBIE-S
WITTOL-S	WOOSEL-S	WROATH-S	YANKER-S	YNAMBU-S	YUPPIE-S	ZENDIK-S	ZONING-S
WIVERN-S	WORKER-S	WUNNER-S	YANKIE-S	YODLER-S	ZABETA-S	ZENITH-S	ZONULA-S
WIZARD-S	WORMER-S	WURLEY-S	YANQUI-S	YOGINI-S	ZADDIK-S	ZEPHYR-S	ZONULE-S
WIZIER-S	WORRAL-S	WUTHER-S	YAOURT-S	YOGISM-S	ZAFFER-S	ZEREBA-S	ZONURE-S
WOBBLE-S	WORREL-S	WUZZLE-S	YAPOCK-S	YOGURT-S	ZAFFRE-S	ZERIBA-S	ZOOZOO-S
WOGGLE-S	WORRIT-S	WYVERN-S	YAPPER-S	YOJANA-S	ZAMANG-S	ZESTER-S	ZORINO-S
WOLFER-S	WORSEN-S	XEROMA-S	YAPPIE-S	YOKING-S	ZAMBUK-S	ZEUGMA-S	ZOSTER-S
WOLVER-S	WORTLE-S	XYLENE-S	YAQONA-S	YONDER-S	ZANDER-S	ZIGZAG-S	ZYDECO-S
WOMBAT-S	WOUBIT-S	XYLOMA-S	YARPHA-S	YONKER-S	ZAPPER-S	ZILLAH-S	ZYGOMA-S
WOMERA-S	WOWSER-S	XYLOSE-S	YARROW-S	YOPPER-S	ZARAPE-S	ZIMMER-S	ZYGOSE-S
WONDER-S	WRAITH-S	XYSTER-S	YATTER-S	YORKER-S	ZAREBA-S	ZINGEL-S	ZYGOTE-S
WONING-S	WRASSE-S	YABBER-S	YAUPON-S	YORKIE-S	ZARIBA-S	ZINGER-S	ZYMASE-S
WOOBUT-S	WRAXLE-S	YABBIE-S	YAWPER-S	YOWLEY-S	ZARNEC-S	ZINNIA-S	ZYMITE-S
WOODIE-S	WREATH-S	YACKER-S	YELLOW-S	YSHEND-S	ZEALOT-S	ZIPPER-S	ZYMOME-S
WOOFER-S	WRETHE-S	YAFFLE-S	YELPER-S	YTTRIA-S	ZEBECK-S	ZIRCON-S	ZYTHUM-S
WOOING-S	WRIGHT-S	YAGGER-S	YICKER-S	YUCKER-S	ZEBRAS-S	ZITHER-S	
WOOLEN-S	WRITER-S	YAKKER-S	YIKKER-S	YUKATA-S	ZELANT-S	ZODIAC-S	

7→8

ABACTOR-S	ACQUEST-S	AGINNER-S	ALGEBRA-S	AMOROSO-S	ANTLION-S	ARMIGER-S
ABALONE-S	ACQUIRE-S	AGISTER-S	ALGESIA-S	AMOSITE-S	ANTONYM-S	ARMILLA-S
ABANDON-S	ACQUIST-S	AGISTOR-S	ALICANT-S	AMPOULE-S	APADANA-S	ARMLOCK-S
ABATURE-S	ACQUITE-S	AGITATE-S	ALIDADE-S	AMPUTEE-S	APAGOGE-S	ARMOIRE-S
ABDOMEN-S	ACRASIA-S	AGNOMEN-S	ALIENEE-S	AMTRACK-S	APANAGE-S	ARNOTTO-S
ABETTAL-S	ACREAGE-S	AGNOSIA-S	ALIENOR-S	AMYGDAL-S	APATITE-S	AROUSAL-S
ABETTER-S	ACRIDIN-S	AGONISE-S	ALIMENT-S	AMYLASE-S	APEHOOD-S	AROUSER-S
ABETTOR-S	ACROBAT-S	AGONIST-S	ALIZARI-S	AMYLENE-S	APEPSIA-S	ARRAIGN-S
ABIDING-S	ACROGEN-S	AGONIZE-S	ALKANET-S	AMYLOID-S	APHAGIA-S	ARRANGE-S
ABIGAIL-S	ACRONYM-S	AGRAFFE-S	ALLAYER-S	ANAEMIA-S	APHASIA-S	ARRAYAL-S
ABJOINT-S	ACROTER-S	AIDANCE-S	ALLEDGE-S	ANAGOGE-S	APHONIA-S	ARRAYER-S
ABJURER-S	ACRYLIC-S	AILANTO-S	ALLEGER-S	ANAGRAM-S	APLANAT-S	ARREEDE-S
ABLATOR-S	ACTINIA-S	AILERON-S	ALLEGGE-S	ANALYSE-S	APLASIA-S	ARRIAGE-S
ABLEISM-S	ACTINON-S	AILETTE-S	ALLEGRO-S	ANALYST-S	APOCOPE-S	ARRIERO-S
ABORTEE-S	ACTUATE-S	AILMENT-S	ALLHEAL-S	ANALYZE-S	APOSTIL-S	ARRIVAL-S
ABOULIA-S	ACUSHLA-S	AIRBASE-S	ALLONGE-S	ANAPEST-S	APOSTLE-S	ARSENAL-S
ABREACT-S	ADAMANT-S	AIRFLOW-S	ALLONYM-S	ANATASE-S	APOTHEM-S	ARSENIC-S
ABRIDGE-S	ADAPTER-S	AIRFOIL-S	ALLSEED-S	ANCIENT-S	APPARAT-S	ARSHEEN-S
ABROOKE-S	ADAPTOR-S	AIRGLOW-S	ALLURER-S	ANDANTE-S	APPAREL-S	ARSHINE-S
ABSCIND-S	ADDUCER-S	AIRHEAD-S	ALMANAC-S	ANDIRON-S	APPEASE-S	ARTICLE-S
ABSCISE-S	ADENINE-S	AIRHOLE-S	ALMIRAH-S	ANDROID-S	APPERIL-S	ARTISAN-S
ABSCOND-S	ADENOID-S	AIRLIFT-S	ALMONER-S	ANDVILE-S	APPLAUD-S	ARTISTE-S
ABSENCE-S	ADENOMA-S	AIRLINE-S	ALNAGER-S	ANELACE-S	APPLIER-S	ARTWORK-S
ABSINTH-S	ADERMIN-S	AIRLOCK-S	ALODIUM-S	ANEMONE-S	APPOINT-S	ARUGULA-S
ABSOLVE-S	ADHARMA-S	AIRMAIL-S	ALOETIC-S	ANEROID-S	APPOSER-S	ASCARID-S
ABSTAIN-S	ADHERER-S	AIRPORT-S	ALPHORN-S	ANEURIN-S	APPRISE-S	ASCETIC-S
ABTHANE-S	ADHIBIT-S	AIRSHIP-S	ALTERNE-S	ANGEKOK-S	APPRIZE-S	ASCRIBE-S
ABUSAGE-S	ADJOINT-S	AIRSIDE-S	ALTESSE-S	ANGIOMA-S	APPROOF-S	ASEPTIC-S
ABUSION-S	ADJOURN-S	AIRSTOP-S	ALTEZZA-S	ANGLING-S	APPROVE-S	ASHRAMA-S
ABUTTAL-S	ADJUDGE-S	AIRTIME-S	ALTHAEA-S	ANGLIST-S	APPULSE-S	ASINICO-S
ABUTTER-S	ADJUNCT-S	AIRWARD-S	ALTHORN-S	ANILINE-S	APRAXIA-S	ASKANCE-S
ACADEME-S	ADMIRAL-S	AIRWAVE-S	ALUMINA-S	ANIMATE-S	APRICOT-S	ASPERGE-S
ACALEPH-S	ADMIRER-S	AISLING-S	ALUMIUM-S	ANIMISM-S	AQUAFER-S	ASPERSE-S
ACANTHA-S	ADONISE-S	AJUTAGE-S	ALUNITE-S	ANIMIST-S	AQUATIC-S	ASPHALT-S
ACAPNIA-S	ADONIZE-S	AKVAVIT-S	ALVEOLE-S	ANISEED-S	AQUAVIT-S	ASPIRIN-S
ACATOUR-S	ADOPTEE-S	ALAMEDA-S	ALYSSUM-S	ANKLONG-S	AQUIFER-S	ASSAGAI-S
ACCEDER-S	ADOPTER-S	ALAMODE-S	AMALGAM-S	ANKLUNG-S	AQUILON-S	ASSAULT-S
ACCIDIE-S	ADRENAL-S	ALANINE-S	AMANITA-S	ANNATTA-S	ARABICA-S	ASSAYER-S
ACCINGE-S	ADULATE-S	ALANNAH-S	AMARANT-S	ANNATTO-S	ARABISE-S	ASSEGAI-S
ACCLAIM-S	ADVANCE-S	ALBUMEN-S	AMATEUR-S	ANNELID-S	ARABIZE-S	ASSEVER-S
ACCOAST-S	ADVISER-S	ALBUMIN-S	AMATION-S	ANNICUT-S	ARANEID-S	ASSHOLE-S
ACCOMPT-S	ADVISOR-S	ALCAIDE-S	AMBIENT-S	ANNOYER-S	ARAROBA-S	ASSIEGE-S
ACCOUNT-S	AERATOR-S	ALCALDE-S	AMBLING-S	ANNULAR-S	ARBITER-S	ASSIZER-S
ACCOURT-S	AEROBIC-S	ALCAYDE-S	AMBROID-S	ANNULET-S	ARBLAST-S	ASSUAGE-S
ACCRETE-S	AEROSOL-S	ALCAZAR-S	AMENAGE-S	ANODISE-S	ARBORET-S	ASSURED-S
ACCRUAL-S	AFFAIRE-S	ALCHERA-S	AMENDER-S	ANODIZE-S	ARCHIVE-S	ASSURER-S
ACCURSE-S	AFFEARE-S	ALCOHOL-S	AMENTIA-S	ANODYNE-S	ARCHLET-S	ASSWAGE-S
ACCUSAL-S	AFFICHE-S	ALCOPOP-S	AMILDAR-S	ANONYMA-S	ARCHWAY-S	ASTATKI-S
ACCUSER-S	AFFLICT-S	ALCORZA-S	AMMETER-S	ANOSMIA-S	ARCKING-S	ASTEISM-S
ACETATE-S	AFFOORD-S	ALECOST-S	AMMIRAL-S	ANTACID-S	ARCTIID-S	ASTERIA-S
ACETONE-S	AFFORCE-S	ALEMBIC-S	AMMONAL-S	ANTBEAR-S	ARDRIGH-S	ASTERID-S
ACHARYA-S	AFFRONT-S	ALEPINE-S	AMMONIA-S	ANTBIRD-S	AREAWAY-S	ASTHORE-S
ACHIEVE-S	AGAMOID-S	ALERION-S	AMNESIA-S	ANTENNA-S	ARGYRIA-S	ASTILBE-S
ACOLYTE-S	AGELAST-S	ALEURON-S	AMNESIC-S	ANTIENT-S	ARIETTA-S	ASTOUND-S
ACOLYTH-S	AGGRACE-S	ALFALFA-S	AMORISM-S	ANTIGEN-S	ARIETTE-S	ASTRICT-S
ACONITE-S	AGGRADE-S	ALFAQUI-S	AMORIST-S	ANTILOG-S	ARMBAND-S	ASTROID-S
ACOUCHI-S	AGGRATE-S	ALFORJA-S	AMOROSA-S	ANTIQUE-S	ARMHOLE-S	ATABRIN-S

ATAGHAN-S	BACKPAY-S	BASSIST-S	BELTING-S	BIOPHOR-S	BOGYISM-S	BRANTLE-S
ATALAYA-S	BACKSAW-S	BASSOON-S	BELTWAY-S	BIOTITE-S	BOILING-S	BRASERO-S
ATAVISM-S	BACKSET-S	BASTARD-S	BEMEDAL-S	BIOTOPE-S	BOLIVAR-S	BRASIER-S
ATEBRIN-S	BACKSEY-S	BASTIDE-S	BEMOUTH-S	BIOTYPE-S	BOLLARD-S	BRASSET-S
ATELIER-S	BACLAVA-S	BASTING-S	BENCHER-S	BIPLANE-S	BOLLOCK-S	BRASSIE-S
ATHANOR-S	BACONER-S	BASTION-S	BENDING-S	BIRDING-S	BOLONEY-S	BRATTLE-S
ATHEISE-S	BACULUM-S	BATHTUB-S	BENDLET-S	BIRETTA-S	BOLSTER-S	BRAVADO-S
ATHEISM-S	BAFFLER-S	BATISTE-S	BENEFIT-S	BIRLING-S	BOLTING-S	BRAVURA-S
ATHEIST-S	BAGARRE-S	BATTERO-S	BENIGHT-S	BIRLINN-S	BOMBARD-S	BRAWLER-S
ATHEIZE-S	BAGASSE-S	BATTILL-S	BENISON-S	BIRYANI-S	BOMBAST-S	BRAZIER-S
ATHLETA-S	BAGGAGE-S	BATTING-S	BENZENE-S	BISCUIT-S	BOMBORA-S	BREADTH-S
ATHLETE-S	BAGGING-S	BATTUTA-S	BENZINE-S	BISMUTH-S	BONAMIA-S	BREAKER-S
ATISHOO-S	BAGPIPE-S	BAUCHLE-S	BENZOIN-S	BISTORT-S	BONANZA-S	BREATHE-S
ATOMISE-S	BAILIFF-S	BAUDRIC-S	BENZOLE-S	BITTERN-S	BONDAGE-S	BRECCIA-S
ATOMISM-S	BAILLIE-S	BAUXITE-S	BENZOYL-S	BITTOCK-S	BONDING-S	BRECHAM-S
ATOMIST-S	BAINITE-S	BAWCOCK-S	BEPAINT-S	BITTOUR-S	BONESET-S	BREEDER-S
ATOMIZE-S	BAITING-S	BAWDKIN-S	BEPEARL-S	BITUMEN-S	BONFIRE-S	BREVIER-S
ATRESIA-S	BAKLAVA-S	BAWLING-S	BEPROSE-S	BIVALVE-S	BOOBOOK-S	BREWAGE-S
ATROPIA-S	BALADIN-S	BAYONET-S	BEQUEST-S	BIVOUAC-S	BOOKING-S	BREWING-S
ATROPIN-S	BALANCE-S	BAZOOKA-S	BEREAVE-S	BLABBER-S	BOOKLET-S	BREWPUB-S
ATTACHE-S	BALDRIC-S	BAZOUKI-S	BERGAMA-S	BLACKEN-S	BOOMING-S	BRICKIE-S
ATTAINT-S	BALISTA-S	BEADING-S	BERGERE-S	BLADDER-S	BOOMLET-S	BRICOLE-S
ATTEMPT-S	BALKING-S	BEAGLER-S	BERGYLT-S	BLAGGER-S	BOOSTER-S	BRIDLER-S
ATTRACT-S	BALLADE-S	BEAMING-S	BERLINE-S	BLANKET-S	BOOTLEG-S	BRIDOON-S
ATTRIST-S	BALLANT-S	BEAMLET-S	BERSERK-S	BLARNEY-S	BORAZON-S	BRIGADE-S
ATTRITE-S	BALLAST-S	BEANBAG-S	BESAINT-S	BLASTER-S	BORDURE-S	BRIGAND-S
ATTUITE-S	BALLING-S	BEARDIE-S	BESEEKE-S	BLATHER-S	BOREDOM-S	BRIMING-S
AUBERGE-S	BALLIUM-S	BEARING-S	BESHAME-S	BLATTER-S	BORNITE-S	BRIMMER-S
AUCTION-S	BALLOON-S	BEASTIE-S	BESHINE-S	BLAUBOK-S	BORONIA-S	BRINDLE-S
AUDIBLE-S	BALONEY-S	BEATING-S	BESHREW-S	BLAWORT-S	BOROUGH-S	BRINGER-S
AUDIENT-S	BAMBINO-S	BEATNIK-S	BESIEGE-S	BLEATER-S	BORSCHT-S	BRINJAL-S
AUDITOR-S	BANDAGE-S	BEAUFET-S	BESLAVE-S	BLEEDER-S	BORSTAL-S	BRIOCHE-S
AUFGABE-S	BANDANA-S	BEAUFIN-S	BESMEAR-S	BLEEPER-S	BOSCAGE-S	BRIQUET-S
AUGMENT-S	BANDING-S	BEBEERU-S	BESPEAK-S	BLENDER-S	BOSKAGE-S	BRISKEN-S
AUGURER-S	BANDOOK-S	BECASSE-S	BESPEED-S	BLESBOK-S	BOSQUET-S	BRISKET-S
AUGUSTE-S	BANDORA-S	BECHARM-S	BESPICE-S	BLETHER-S	BOTARGO-S	BRISTLE-S
AULNAGE-S	BANDORE-S	BECLOUD-S	BESPORT-S	BLEWART-S	BOTCHER-S	BRISURE-S
AURELIA-S	BANDROL-S	BEDAWIN-S	BESPOUT-S	BLINDER-S	BOTHOLE-S	BRITSKA-S
AUREOLA-S	BANDURA-S	BEDDING-S	BESTAIN-S	BLINKER-S	BOTTEGA-S	BRITTLE-S
AUREOLE-S	BANGING-S	BEDERAL-S	BESTEAD-S	BLINTZE-S	BOTTINE-S	BRITZKA-S
AURICLE-S	BANKING-S	BEDEVIL-S	BESTIAL-S	BLISTER-S	BOTTLER-S	BROADEN-S
AUSPICE-S	BANKSIA-S	BEDIGHT-S	BESTICK-S	BLITHER-S	BOUCHEE-S	BROCADE-S
AUTOCAR-S	BANNOCK-S	BEDIZEN-S	BESTILL-S	BLOATER-S	BOUDOIR-S	BROCAGE-S
AUTOCUE-S	BANQUET-S	BEDOUIN-S	BESTORM-S	BLOCKER-S	BOUILLI-S	BROCARD-S
AUTOMAT-S	BANSHEE-S	BEDPOST-S	BESTREW-S	BLOOMER-S	BOULDER-S	BROCHAN-S
AUTONYM-S	BANTENG-S	BEDROCK-S	BETAINE-S	BLOOPER-S	BOULTER-S	BROCKET-S
AUTOVAC-S	BANTING-S	BEDROOM-S	BETEEME-S	BLOOSME-S	BOUNCER-S	BRODKIN-S
AUXETIC-S	BAPTISE-S	BEDSIDE-S	BETHINK-S	BLOSSOM-S	BOUNDER-S	BROIDER-S
AVARICE-S	BAPTISM-S	BEDSORE-S	BETHUMB-S	BLOTTER-S	BOUQUET-S	BROILER-S
AVENGER-S	BAPTIST-S	BEDTICK-S	BETHUMP-S	BLOUBOK-S	BOURBON-S	BROKAGE-S
AVENTRE-S	BAPTIZE-S	BEDTIME-S	BETITLE-S	BLOUSON-S	BOURDER-S	BROKING-S
AVERAGE-S	BARACAN-S	BEDWARD-S	BETOKEN-S	BLOWGUN-S	BOURDON-S	BROMATE-S
AVIATOR-S	BARBOLA-S	BEDWARF-S	BETREAD-S	BLOWJOB-S	BOURKHA-S	BROMIDE-S
AVIETTE-S	BARBULE-S	BEEFALO-S	BETROTH-S	BLUBBER-S	BOURLAW-S	BROMINE-S
AVIONIC-S	BARCHAN-S	BEEHIVE-S	BETTING-S	BLUCHER-S	BOURREE-S	BROMISM-S
AVOCADO-S	BARGAIN-S	BEELINE-S	BETWEEN-S	BLUDGER-S	BOUTADE-S	BROMMER-S
AWAKING-S	BARGEST-S	BEERAGE-S	BEWHORE-S	BLUECAP-S	BOWHEAD-S	BRONCHO-S
AWLBIRD-S	BARILLA-S	BEFFANA-S	BEZIQUE-S	BLUEING-S	BOWKNOT-S	BRONZER-S
AXINITE-S	BARKHAN-S	BEGGING-S	BHANGRA-S	BLUETTE-S	BOWLDER-S	BROODER-S
AXOLOTL-S	BARMAID-S	BEGHARD-S	BHISTEE-S	BLUFFER-S	BOWLFUL-S	BROTHEL-S
AZIMUTH-S	BARMKIN-S	BEGINNE-S	BIASING-S	BLUNDER-S	BOWLINE-S	BROTHER-S
AZOTISE-S	BAROCCO-S	BEGLOOM-S	BIBCOCK-S	BLUNGER-S	BOWLING-S	BROWNIE-S
AZOTIZE-S	BARONET-S	BEGONIA-S	BIBELOT-S	BLUNKER-S	BOWSHOT-S	BROWSER-S
AZULEJO-S	BARONNE-S	BEGRIME-S	BIBLIST-S	BLUSHER-S	BOWYANG-S	BRUCHID-S
AZURINE-S	BAROQUE-S	BEGUILE-S	BICORNE-S	BLUSHET-S	BOXROOM-S	BRUCINE-S
AZURITE-S	BARRACE-S	BEGUINE-S	BICYCLE-S	BLUSTER-S	BOXWOOD-S	BRUCITE-S
AZYMITE-S	BARRACK-S	BEHIGHT-S	BIDARKA-S	BOARDER-S	BOYCOTT-S	BRUHAHA-S
BABASSU-S	BARRAGE-S	BEHOOVE-S	BIDDING-S	BOASTER-S	BOYHOOD-S	BRUISER-S
BABBITT-S	BARRICO-S	BEIGNET-S	BIFOCAL-S	BOATING-S	BRABBLE-S	BRULYIE-S
BABBLER-S	BARRIER-S	BEJEWEL-S	BIGENER-S	BOBBITT-S	BRACHET-S	BRULZIE-S
BABICHE-S	BARRING-S	BEKNAVE-S	BIGHORN-S	BOBSLED-S	BRACKEN-S	BRUMMER-S
BABUCHE-S	BARWOOD-S	BELABOR-S	BIKEWAY-S	BOBTAIL-S	BRACKET-S	BRUSHER-S
BABUDOM-S	BARYTON-S	BELCHER-S	BILIMBI-S	BODHRAN-S	BRADAWL-S	BRUTING-S
BABUISM-S	BASCULE-S	BELDAME-S	BILLING-S	BODIKIN-S	BRAMBLE-S	BRUXISM-S
BACCARA-S	BASENJI-S	BELGARD-S	BILLION-S	BOGBEAN-S	BRANDER-S	BUBINGA-S
BACKHOE-S	BASHING-S	BELIEVE-S	BILTONG-S	BOGGARD-S	BRANGLE-S	BUBUKLE-S
BACKING-S	BASHLIK-S	BELLHOP-S	BINDING-S	BOGGART-S	BRANSLE-S	BUCCINA-S
BACKLOG-S	BASINET-S	BELOVED-S	BINOCLE-S	BOGGLER-S		BUCKEEN-S
BACKLOT-S	BASOCHE-S		BIOCIDE-S	BOGLAND-S		BUCKING-S

BUCKLER-S	CABOOSE-S	CANTATE-S	CASCADE-S	CHABOUK-S	CHEROOT-S	CINEAST-S
BUCKRAM-S	CACIQUE-S	CANTDOG-S	CASCARA-S	CHADDAR-S	CHERVIL-S	CINEOLE-S
BUCKSAW-S	CACKLER-S	CANTEEN-S	CASERNE-S	CHADDOR-S	CHESNUT-S	CINEREA-S
BUCOLIC-S	CACODYL-S	CANTICO-S	CASHIER-S	CHAFFER-S	CHESSEL-S	CINERIN-S
BUDDING-S	CACOLET-S	CANTINA-S	CASSATA-S	CHAGRIN-S	CHETNIK-S	CIPOLIN-S
BUDGERO-S	CADAVER-S	CANTING-S	CASSAVA-S	CHALAZA-S	CHEWINK-S	CIRCLER-S
BUDWORM-S	CADDICE-S	CANTION-S	CASSINO-S	CHALCID-S	CHIASMA-S	CIRCLET-S
BUFFING-S	CADELLE-S	CANTLET-S	CASSOCK-S	CHALDER-S	CHIBOUK-S	CIRCLIP-S
BUFFOON-S	CADENCE-S	CANTRED-S	CASSONE-S	CHALICE-S	CHICANA-S	CIRCUIT-S
BUGABOO-S	CADENZA-S	CANTREF-S	CASTING-S	CHALLAH-S	CHICANE-S	CISSOID-S
BUGBANE-S	CADMIUM-S	CANTRIP-S	CASTOCK-S	CHALLAN-S	CHICANO-S	CISTERN-S
BUGBEAR-S	CAESIUM-S	CANZONA-S	CASUIST-S	CHALLIE-S	CHICKEN-S	CISTRON-S
BUGGANE-S	CAESURA-S	CAPELET-S	CATALOG-S	CHALONE-S	CHIDING-S	CITADEL-S
BUGGING-S	CAFFEIN-S	CAPELIN-S	CATALPA-S	CHAMADE-S	CHIFFON-S	CITHARA-S
BUGWORT-S	CAFFILA-S	CAPERER-S	CATARRH-S	CHAMBER-S	CHIGGER-S	CITHERN-S
BUILDER-S	CAGOULE-S	CAPITAL-S	CATASTA-S	CHAMFER-S	CHIGNON-S	CITIZEN-S
BUKSHEE-S	CAISSON-S	CAPITAN-S	CATAWBA-S	CHAMISE-S	CHIKARA-S	CITRATE-S
BULGHUR-S	CAITIFF-S	CAPORAL-S	CATBIRD-S	CHAMISO-S	CHIKHOR-S	CITRINE-S
BULGINE-S	CAITIVE-S	CAPPING-S	CATBOAT-S	CHAMLET-S	CHILIAD-S	CITTERN-S
BULIMIA-S	CAJEPUT-S	CAPRATE-S	CATCALL-S	CHAMPAC-S	CHILIOI-S	CLABBER-S
BULIMIC-S	CAJOLER-S	CAPRICE-S	CATCHER-S	CHAMPAK-S	CHILLER-S	CLACHAN-S
BULLACE-S	CAJUPUT-S	CAPSIZE-S	CATCHUP-S	CHANCEL-S	CHILLUM-S	CLACKER-S
BULLBAR-S	CALCINE-S	CAPSTAN-S	CATECHU-S	CHANCER-S	CHIMERA-S	CLADDER-S
BULLBAT-S	CALCITE-S	CAPSULE-S	CATELOG-S	CHANCRE-S	CHIMERE-S	CLADISM-S
BULLDOG-S	CALCIUM-S	CAPTAIN-S	CATERAN-S	CHANGER-S	CHIMLEY-S	CLADIST-S
BULLING-S	CALDERA-S	CAPTION-S	CATERER-S	CHANNEL-S	CHIMNEY-S	CLADODE-S
BULLION-S	CALDRON-S	CAPTIVE-S	CATHEAD-S	CHANNER-S	CHINDIT-S	CLAIMER-S
BULLOCK-S	CALIBER-S	CAPTURE-S	CATHODE-S	CHANOYU-S	CHINKIE-S	CLAMBER-S
BULWARK-S	CALIBRE-S	CAPUCHE-S	CATHOLE-S	CHANSON-S	CHINOOK-S	CLAMOUR-S
BUMBAZE-S	CALICHE-S	CAPUERA-S	CATHOOD-S	CHANTER-S	CHINWAG-S	CLAMPER-S
BUMBLER-S	CALICLE-S	CARABAO-S	CATLING-S	CHANTEY-S	CHIPPER-S	CLANGER-S
BUMMOCK-S	CALIPEE-S	CARABID-S	CATMINT-S	CHANTIE-S	CHIPPIE-S	CLANGOR-S
BUMPING-S	CALIPER-S	CARABIN-S	CATSKIN-S	CHANTOR-S	CHIRPER-S	CLAPNET-S
BUMPKIN-S	CALIVER-S	CARACAL-S	CATSUIT-S	CHAPATI-S	CHIRRUP-S	CLAPPER-S
BUNDOOK-S	CALLANT-S	CARACOL-S	CATTABU-S	CHAPLET-S	CHITTER-S	CLARAIN-S
BUNGLER-S	CALLING-S	CARACUL-S	CATTALO-S	CHAPPAL-S	CHLORAL-S	CLARINO-S
BUNRAKU-S	CALLUNA-S	CARAMEL-S	CATWORM-S	CHAPPIE-S	CHLORIN-S	CLARION-S
BUNTING-S	CALMANT-S	CARANNA-S	CAUDRON-S	CHAPTER-S	CHOBDAR-S	CLARKIA-S
BUOYAGE-S	CALOMEL-S	CARAUNA-S	CAULKER-S	CHARACT-S	CHOCTAW-S	CLASHER-S
BURBLER-S	CALORIC-S	CARAVAN-S	CAULOME-S	CHARADE-S	CHOLENT-S	CLASPER-S
BURDOCK-S	CALORIE-S	CARAVEL-S	CAUSTIC-S	CHARGER-S	CHOLERA-S	CLASSIC-S
BURETTE-S	CALOTTE-S	CARAWAY-S	CAUTION-S	CHARIOT-S	CHOLINE-S	CLATTER-S
BURGAGE-S	CALOYER-S	CARBIDE-S	CAVALLA-S	CHARISM-S	CHONDRE-S	CLAUCHT-S
BURGEON-S	CALPACK-S	CARBINE-S	CAVIARE-S	CHARKHA-S	CHOOKIE-S	CLAUGHT-S
BURGHER-S	CALTRAP-S	CARCAKE-S	CAYENNE-S	CHARLEY-S	CHOOSER-S	CLAVIER-S
BURGHUL-S	CALTROP-S	CARCASE-S	CAZIQUE-S	CHARLIE-S	CHOPINE-S	CLAYPAN-S
BURGLAR-S	CALUMBA-S	CARDECU-S	CEASING-S	CHARMER-S	CHOPPER-S	CLEANER-S
BURNING-S	CALUMET-S	CARDIAC-S	CEDILLA-S	CHARNEL-S	CHORALE-S	CLEANSE-S
BURRELL-S	CALYCLE-S	CARDOON-S	CEDRATE-S	CHARPIE-S	CHORDEE-S	CLEARER-S
BURRHEL-S	CALYPSO-S	CARFARE-S	CEILIDH-S	CHARPOY-S	CHORINE-S	CLEAVER-S
BURRITO-S	CALZONE-S	CARIAMA-S	CEILING-S	CHARQUI-S	CHORISM-S	CLERUCH-S
BURSTER-S	CAMARON-S	CARIBOU-S	CELADON-S	CHARTER-S	CHORIST-S	CLICKER-S
BURTHEN-S	CAMBISM-S	CARIERE-S	CELESTA-S	CHASING-S	CHORIZO-S	CLICKET-S
BURWEED-S	CAMBIST-S	CARIOCA-S	CELESTE-S	CHASTEN-S	CHOROID-S	CLIMATE-S
BUSGIRL-S	CAMBIUM-S	CARIOLE-S	CELLIST-S	CHATTEL-S	CHORTLE-S	CLIMBER-S
BUSHIDO-S	CAMBOGE-S	CARJACK-S	CELLOSE-S	CHATTER-S	CHOWDER-S	CLINGER-S
BUSHING-S	CAMBREL-S	CARLINE-S	CELLULE-S	CHAUFER-S	CHRISOM-S	CLINKER-S
BUSKING-S	CAMBRIC-S	CARLING-S	CEMBALO-S	CHAUMER-S	CHROMEL-S	CLIPART-S
BUSSING-S	CAMELID-S	CARLOAD-S	CENACLE-S	CHAUNCE-S	CHRONIC-S	CLIPPER-S
BUSTARD-S	CAMELOT-S	CARLOCK-S	CENSURE-S	CHAUNGE-S	CHRONON-S	CLIPPIE-S
BUSTIER-S	CAMOGIE-S	CARMINE-S	CENTAGE-S	CHAUVIN-S	CHUCKIE-S	CLITTER-S
BUSTING-S	CAMORRA-S	CARNAGE-S	CENTARE-S	CHAYOTE-S	CHUCKLE-S	CLOBBER-S
BUSTLER-S	CAMPANA-S	CAROCHE-S	CENTAUR-S	CHEAPEN-S	CHUDDAH-S	CLOCKER-S
BUTANOL-S	CAMPHOR-S	CAROMEL-S	CENTAVO-S	CHEAPIE-S	CHUDDAR-S	CLOGGER-S
BUTCHER-S	CAMPION-S	CAROTIN-S	CENTIME-S	CHEATER-S	CHUKKER-S	CLOISON-S
BUTMENT-S	CAMWOOD-S	CAROUSE-S	CENTIMO-S	CHECHIA-S	CHUMLEY-S	CLOSING-S
BUTTOCK-S	CANAKIN-S	CARPARK-S	CENTNER-S	CHECKER-S	CHUNDER-S	CLOSURE-S
BUVETTE-S	CANASTA-S	CARPING-S	CENTRUM-S	CHEEPER-S	CHUNNEL-S	CLOTBUR-S
BUYABLE-S	CANBANK-S	CARPORT-S	CERAMAL-S	CHEERER-S	CHUNNER-S	CLOTTER-S
BUZZARD-S	CANDELA-S	CARRACK-S	CERAMIC-S	CHEERIO-S	CHUNTER-S	CLOTURE-S
BUZZING-S	CANDIDA-S	CARRACT-S	CERASIN-S	CHEETAH-S	CHUPATI-S	CLOUTER-S
BYCOKET-S	CANDOCK-S	CARRECT-S	CERESIN-S	CHEKIST-S	CHUPPAH-S	CLOWDER-S
BYPLACE-S	CANDOUR-S	CARRELL-S	CERUMEN-S	CHELATE-S	CHUTIST-S	CLUBBER-S
BYWONER-S	CANELLA-S	CARRIER-S	CESSION-S	CHELOID-S	CHUTNEY-S	CLUDGIE-S
CABARET-S	CANIKIN-S	CARRION-S	CESSPIT-S	CHELONE-S	CICHLID-S	CLUMBER-S
CABBAGE-S	CANNACH-S	CARTAGE-S	CESTODE-S	CHEMISE-S	CIELING-S	CLUMPER-S
CABBALA-S	CANNULA-S	CARTOON-S	CESTOID-S	CHEMISM-S	CILIATE-S	CLUPEID-S
CABINET-S	CANTALA-S	CARTWAY-S	CEVICHE-S	CHEMIST-S	CIELING-S	CLUSTER-S
CABLING-S	CANTATA-S	CARVING-S	CEVICHE-S	CHEQUER-S	CILIATE-S	CLUTTER-S

CLYSTER-S	COMPAND-S	CONTOUR-S	COUGHER-S	CRIPPLE-S	CURCUMA-S	DATARIA-S
COACHEE-S	COMPARE-S	CONTRAT-S	COUGUAR-S	CRISPER-S	CURETTE-S	DAUBING-S
COACHER-S	COMPART-S	CONTROL-S	COULOIR-S	CRISPIN-S	CURLING-S	DAUNDER-S
COALISE-S	COMPEAR-S	CONTUND-S	COULOMB-S	CRITTER-S	CURRACH-S	DAUNTER-S
COALIZE-S	COMPEER-S	CONTUSE-S	COULTER-S	CRITTUR-S	CURRAGH-S	DAUNTON-S
COALPIT-S	COMPEND-S	CONVENE-S	COUNCIL-S	CROAKER-S	CURRANT-S	DAUPHIN-S
COALTAR-S	COMPERE-S	CONVENT-S	COUNSEL-S	CROCEIN-S	CURRENT-S	DAVIDIA-S
COAMING-S	COMPETE-S	CONVERT-S	COUNTER-S	CROCHET-S	CURRIER-S	DAWCOCK-S
COARSEN-S	COMPILE-S	CONVICT-S	COUPLER-S	CROCKET-S	CURSING-S	DAWDLER-S
COASTER-S	COMPING-S	CONVIVE-S	COUPLET-S	CROFTER-S	CURTAIL-S	DAWNING-S
COATING-S	COMPLIN-S	CONVOKE-S	COUPURE-S	CROMACK-S	CURTAIN-S	DAYMARK-S
COBBLER-S	COMPLOT-S	COOKOUT-S	COURAGE-S	CROODLE-S	CURTANA-S	DAYSACK-S
COCAINE-S	COMPORT-S	COOLANT-S	COURANT-S	CROONER-S	CURTAXE-S	DAYSTAR-S
COCKADE-S	COMPOSE-S	COONCAN-S	COURIER-S	CROPFUL-S	CURTSEY-S	DAYTALE-S
COCKEYE-S	COMPOST-S	COONDOG-S	COURLAN-S	CROPPER-S	CUSHION-S	DAYTIME-S
COCKNEY-S	COMPOTE-S	COONTIE-S	COURSER-S	CROQUET-S	CUSTARD-S	DAZZLER-S
COCKPIT-S	COMPTER-S	COPAIBA-S	COUTURE-S	CROSIER-S	CUSTOCK-S	DEADPAN-S
COCONUT-S	COMPUTE-S	COPAIVA-S	COUVADE-S	CROTTLE-S	CUSTODE-S	DEALING-S
COCOPAN-S	COMRADE-S	COPEPOD-S	COUVERT-S	CROUPER-S	CUSTREL-S	DEASIUL-S
COCOTTE-S	CONACRE-S	COPILOT-S	COVELET-S	CROUPON-S	CUTAWAY-S	DEASOIL-S
COCTION-S	CONCAVE-S	COPPICE-S	COWBANE-S	CROUTON-S	CUTBACK-S	DEBACLE-S
CODEINE-S	CONCEAL-S	COPSHOP-S	COWBELL-S	CROWBAR-S	CUTICLE-S	DEBASER-S
CODETTA-S	CONCEDE-S	COPYCAT-S	COWBIRD-S	CROWDER-S	CUTIKIN-S	DEBATER-S
CODICIL-S	CONCEIT-S	COPYISM-S	COWGIRL-S	CROWDIE-S	CUTLINE-S	DEBITOR-S
CODILLA-S	CONCENT-S	COPYIST-S	COWHAGE-S	CROWNER-S	CUTTING-S	DEBRIDE-S
CODILLE-S	CONCEPT-S	COQUINA-S	COWHAND-S	CROWNET-S	CUTWORK-S	DEBRIEF-S
CODLING-S	CONCERN-S	COQUITO-S	COWHEEL-S	CROZIER-S	CUTWORM-S	DECAGON-S
COEHORN-S	CONCERT-S	CORACLE-S	COWHERB-S	CRUBEEN-S	CUVETTE-S	DECAPOD-S
COELIAC-S	CONCHIE-S	CORANTO-S	COWHERD-S	CRUCIAN-S	CYANATE-S	DECEASE-S
COELOME-S	CONCISE-S	CORBEAU-S	COWHIDE-S	CRUDDLE-S	CYANIDE-S	DECEIVE-S
COEQUAL-S	CONCOCT-S	CORBEIL-S	COWLICK-S	CRUISER-S	CYANINE-S	DECIARE-S
COEXIST-S	CONCORD-S	CORDAGE-S	COWLING-S	CRUISIE-S	CYANISE-S	DECIBEL-S
COFFRET-S	CONCREW-S	CORDIAL-S	COWPOKE-S	CRULLER-S	CYANITE-S	DECIDER-S
COGENCE-S	CONDEMN-S	CORDING-S	COWSHED-S	CRUMBLE-S	CYANIZE-S	DECIDUA-S
COGENER-S	CONDOLE-S	CORDITE-S	COWSLIP-S	CRUMPET-S	CYCLING-S	DECIMAL-S
COGGING-S	CONDONE-S	CORDOBA-S	COWTREE-S	CRUMPLE-S	CYCLIST-S	DECKING-S
COGNATE-S	CONDUCE-S	CORELLA-S	COXCOMB-S	CRUNKLE-S	CYCLOID-S	DECLAIM-S
COGNISE-S	CONDUCT-S	CORIVAL-S	COZENER-S	CRUPPER-S	CYCLONE-S	DECLARE-S
COGNIZE-S	CONDUIT-S	CORKAGE-S	CRABBER-S	CRUSADE-S	CYMBALO-S	DECLINE-S
COHABIT-S	CONDYLE-S	CORNAGE-S	CRACKER-S	CRUSADO-S	CYPRIAN-S	DECODER-S
COHERER-S	CONFECT-S	CORNETT-S	CRACKLE-S	CRUSHER-S	CYSTINE-S	DECOLOR-S
COHIBIT-S	CONFIDE-S	CORNICE-S	CRACOWE-S	CRUSIAN-S	CYSTOID-S	DECORUM-S
COINAGE-S	CONFINE-S	CORNIST-S	CRAMMER-S	CRUZADO-S	CZARDOM-S	DECREET-S
COINING-S	CONFIRM-S	CORNROW-S	CRAMPET-S	CRYOGEN-S	CZARINA-S	DECRIAL-S
COITION-S	CONFORM-S	CORNUTE-S	CRAMPIT-S	CRYONIC-S	CZARISM-S	DECRIER-S
COLIBRI-S	CONFUSE-S	CORNUTO-S	CRAMPON-S	CRYPTON-S	CZARIST-S	DECROWN-S
COLLAGE-S	CONFUTE-S	COROLLA-S	CRANAGE-S	CRYSTAL-S	DABBLER-S	DECRYPT-S
COLLARD-S	CONGEAL-S	CORONAL-S	CRANIUM-S	CUBBING-S	DABSTER-S	DECUMAN-S
COLLATE-S	CONGEST-S	CORONER-S	CRANKLE-S	CUBHOOD-S	DADDOCK-S	DECUPLE-S
COLLECT-S	CONGREE-S	CORONET-S	CRANNOG-S	CUBICLE-S	DAFFING-S	DECURIA-S
COLLEEN-S	CONGRUE-S	CORPORA-S	CRAVING-S	CUCKOLD-S	DAGGING-S	DECURVE-S
COLLEGE-S	CONIFER-S	CORRADE-S	CRAWLER-S	CUDBEAR-S	DAGLOCK-S	DEERLET-S
COLLIDE-S	CONIINE-S	CORRECT-S	CREAMER-S	CUDWEED-S	DAGWOOD-S	DEFACER-S
COLLIER-S	CONJECT-S	CORRIDA-S	CREANCE-S	CUISINE-S	DAKOITI-S	DEFAULT-S
COLLING-S	CONJOIN-S	CORRODE-S	CREASER-S	CUISSER-S	DALLIER-S	DEFENCE-S
COLLOID-S	CONJURE-S	CORRUPT-S	CREATIN-S	CUITTLE-S	DAMBROD-S	DEFENSE-S
COLLUDE-S	CONNECT-S	CORSAGE-S	CREATOR-S	CULCHIE-S	DAMOSEL-S	DEFICIT-S
COLOGNE-S	CONNING-S	CORSAIR-S	CREEPER-S	CULICID-S	DAMOZEL-S	DEFILER-S
COLONEL-S	CONNIVE-S	CORSIVE-S	CREEPIE-S	CULLING-S	DAMPING-S	DEFINER-S
COLONIC-S	CONNOTE-S	CORSLET-S	CREMATE-S	CULLION-S	DANCING-S	DEFLATE-S
COLUMEL-S	CONQUER-S	CORSNED-S	CREMONA-S	CULOTTE-S	DANDLER-S	DEFLECT-S
COMBINE-S	CONSEIL-S	CORTEGE-S	CREOSOL-S	CULPRIT-S	DANELAW-S	DEFORCE-S
COMBING-S	CONSENT-S	CORYPHE-S	CRESSET-S	CULTISM-S	DANGLER-S	DEFRAUD-S
COMBLES-S	CONSIGN-S	COSINES-S	CRESTON-S	CULTIST-S	DANSEUR-S	DEFROCK-S
COMBUST-S	CONSIST-S	COSMISM-S	CRETISM-S	CULTURE-S	DAPHNID-S	DEFROST-S
COMFORT-S	CONSOLE-S	COSMIST-S	CREVICE-S	CULVERT-S	DAPSONE-S	DEFUNCT-S
COMFREY-S	CONSORT-S	COSTARD-S	CRIBBLE-S	CUMARIN-S	DAQUIRI-S	DEGRADE-S
COMIQUE-S	CONSTER-S	COSTEAN-S	CRICKET-S	CUMQUAT-S	DARIOLE-S	DEHISCE-S
COMMAND-S	CONSULT-S	COSTREL-S	CRICOID-S	CUMSHAW-S	DARLING-S	DEICIDE-S
COMMEND-S	CONSUME-S	COSTUME-S	CRIMMER-S	CUNETTE-S	DARNING-S	DEICTIC-S
COMMENT-S	CONTACT-S	COTERIE-S	CRIMPER-S	CUNNING-S	DARRAIN-S	DEIFIER-S
COMMERE-S	CONTAIN-S	COTHURN-S	CRIMPLE-S	CUPCAKE-S	DARRAYN-S	DEISEAL-S
COMMODE-S	CONTECK-S	COTINGA-S	CRIMSON-S	CUPGALL-S	DARSHAN-S	DEJEUNE-S
COMMOTE-S	CONTEMN-S	COTLAND-S	CRINGER-S	CUPHEAD-S	DASHEEN-S	DELAINE-S
COMMOVE-S	CONTEND-S	COTTAGE-S	CRINGLE-S	CUPPING-S	DASHEKI-S	DELAPSE-S
COMMUNE-S	CONTENT-S	COTTIER-S	CRINITE-S	CUPRITE-S	DASHIKI-S	DELATOR-S
COMMUTE-S	CONTEST-S	COTTISE-S	CRINKLE-S	CURACAO-S	DASTARD-S	DELAYER-S
COMPACT-S	CONTEXT-S	COTTOWN-S	CRINOID-S	CURACOA-S	DASYPOD-S	DELIGHT-S
COMPAGE-S	CONTORT-S	COUCHEE-S	CRIOLLO-S	CURATOR-S	DASYURE-S	DELIMIT-S

DELIVER-S	DEXTRAN-S	DISCOER-S	DOGBANE-S	DRILLER-S	EASTING-S	EMBOGUE-S
DELOUSE-S	DEXTRIN-S	DISCORD-S	DOGBOLT-S	DRINKER-S	EASTLIN-S	EMBOSOM-S
DELTOID-S	DHURRIE-S	DISCURE-S	DOGCART-S	DRIZZLE-S	EATABLE-S	EMBOUND-S
DELUDER-S	DIABASE-S	DISDAIN-S	DOGEATE-S	DROGHER-S	EBAUCHE-S	EMBOWEL-S
DEMAINE-S	DIABOLO-S	DISEASE-S	DOGGING-S	DROGUET-S	EBBTIDE-S	EMBOWER-S
DEMAYNE-S	DIADROM-S	DISEDGE-S	DOGGREL-S	DROMOND-S	EBONISE-S	EMBRACE-S
DEMEANE-S	DIAGRAM-S	DISEUSE-S	DOGHOLE-S	DROPLET-S	EBONIST-S	EMBRAID-S
DEMENTI-S	DIAGRID-S	DISFAME-S	DOGSHIP-S	DROPOUT-S	EBONITE-S	EMBRAVE-S
DEMERGE-S	DIALECT-S	DISFORM-S	DOGSKIN-S	DROPPER-S	EBONIZE-S	EMBREAD-S
DEMERIT-S	DIALIST-S	DISGEST-S	DOGSLED-S	DROPPLE-S	ECBOLIC-S	EMBREWE-S
DEMERSE-S	DIALLER-S	DISGOWN-S	DOGTOWN-S	DROSERA-S	ECHAPPE-S	EMBROIL-S
DEMESNE-S	DIALYSE-S	DISGUST-S	DOGTROT-S	DROSTDY-S	ECHELON-S	EMBROWN-S
DEMIGOD-S	DIALYZE-S	DISHELM-S	DOGVANE-S	DROUGHT-S	ECHIDNA-S	EMBRUTE-S
DEMIREP-S	DIAMOND-S	DISHFUL-S	DOGWOOD-S	DROVING-S	ECHOISE-S	EMBRYON-S
DEMOUNT-S	DIAPASE-S	DISHING-S	DOITKIN-S	DROWNER-S	ECHOISM-S	EMERALD-S
DENDRON-S	DIARISE-S	DISHOME-S	DOLLDOM-S	DRUDGER-S	ECHOIST-S	EMETINE-S
DENIZEN-S	DIARIST-S	DISHORN-S	DOLLIER-S	DRUGGER-S	ECHOIZE-S	EMICATE-S
DENTINE-S	DIARIZE-S	DISJECT-S	DOLPHIN-S	DRUGGET-S	ECLIPSE-S	EMIRATE-S
DENTIST-S	DIASTER-S	DISJOIN-S	DOMICIL-S	DRUGGIE-S	ECLOGUE-S	EMITTER-S
DENTURE-S	DIBBLER-S	DISJUNE-S	DOMINEE-S	DRUMBLE-S	ECOCIDE-S	EMOTION-S
DEODAND-S	DICHORD-S	DISLEAF-S	DOMINIE-S	DRUMLIN-S	ECORCHE-S	EMPAIRE-S
DEODATE-S	DICTATE-S	DISLIKE-S	DONATOR-S	DRUMMER-S	ECOTYPE-S	EMPANEL-S
DEONTIC-S	DICTION-S	DISLIMB-S	DONNISM-S	DRYBEAT-S	ECTHYMA-S	EMPAYRE-S
DEPAINT-S	DIDAKAI-S	DISLIMN-S	DONSHIP-S	DUALISM-S	ECTOPIA-S	EMPERCE-S
DEPECHE-S	DIDAKEI-S	DISLINK-S	DOODLER-S	DUALIST-S	ECUELLE-S	EMPEROR-S
DEPLANE-S	DIDDLER-S	DISLOAD-S	DOORMAT-S	DUBBING-S	EDIFICE-S	EMPIRIC-S
DEPLETE-S	DIDICOI-S	DISMASK-S	DOORWAY-S	DUCKING-S	EDIFIER-S	EMPLACE-S
DEPLORE-S	DIDICOY-S	DISMAST-S	DOPATTA-S	DUDGEON-S	EDITION-S	EMPLANE-S
DEPLUME-S	DIEBACK-S	DISMAYL-S	DOPPING-S	DUDHEEN-S	EDUCATE-S	EMPLUME-S
DEPOSAL-S	DIEDRAL-S	DISNEST-S	DORHAWK-S	DUELLER-S	EDUCTOR-S	EMPOWER-S
DEPOSER-S	DIETINE-S	DISOBEY-S	DORLACH-S	DUFFING-S	EELFARE-S	EMPRISE-S
DEPOSIT-S	DIETIST-S	DISPACE-S	DORMANT-S	DUKEDOM-S	EELPOUT-S	EMPTIER-S
DEPRAVE-S	DIFFUSE-S	DISPARK-S	DORNICK-S	DULCIAN-S	EELWORM-S	EMPTION-S
DEPSIDE-S	DIGAMMA-S	DISPART-S	DORTOUR-S	DULCITE-S	EEVNING-S	EMPYEMA-S
DERAIGN-S	DIGGING-S	DISPEND-S	DOSSIER-S	DULCOSE-S	EFFENDI-S	EMULATE-S
DERANGE-S	DIGITAL-S	DISPLAY-S	DOTTREL-S	DULLARD-S	EFFORCE-S	EMULSIN-S
DERIDER-S	DIGLYPH-S	DISPONE-S	DOUBLER-S	DUMAIST-S	EFFULGE-S	EMULSOR-S
DERMOID-S	DIGRAPH-S	DISPORT-S	DOUBLET-S	DUMPBIN-S	EGGHEAD-S	ENABLER-S
DERRICK-S	DILATER-S	DISPOSE-S	DOUBTER-S	DUNGEON-S	EGOTISE-S	ENACTOR-S
DESCALE-S	DILATOR-S	DISPOST-S	DOUCEUR-S	DUNNAGE-S	EGOTISM-S	ENAMOUR-S
DESCANT-S	DILEMMA-S	DISPRED-S	DOUCINE-S	DUNNART-S	EGOTIST-S	ENATION-S
DESCEND-S	DILLING-S	DISPUTE-S	DOULEIA-S	DUNNING-S	EGOTIZE-S	ENCHAFE-S
DESCENT-S	DILUENT-S	DISRANK-S	DOURINE-S	DUNNITE-S	EIDETIC-S	ENCHAIN-S
DESERVE-S	DILUTEE-S	DISRATE-S	DOVECOT-S	DUNNOCK-S	EIGHTVO-S	ENCHANT-S
DESIRER-S	DILUTER-S	DISROBE-S	DOVEKIE-S	DUOTONE-S	EILDING-S	ENCHARM-S
DESKILL-S	DILUTOR-S	DISROOT-S	DOVELET-S	DUPATTA-S	EJECTOR-S	ENCHASE-S
DESKTOP-S	DIMETER-S	DISRUPT-S	DOWAGER-S	DURABLE-S	EKISTIC-S	ENCHEER-S
DESMINE-S	DIMORPH-S	DISSEAT-S	DOWNBOW-S	DURAMEN-S	EKPWELE-S	ENCLASP-S
DESMOID-S	DINETTE-S	DISSECT-S	DOYENNE-S	DURANCE-S	ELASTIC-S	ENCLAVE-S
DESPAIR-S	DINGBAT-S	DISSENT-S	DOZENTH-S	DURESSE-S	ELASTIN-S	ENCLOSE-S
DESPISE-S	DIOCESE-S	DISSERT-S	DRABBER-S	DURMAST-S	ELATION-S	ENCLOUD-S
DESPITE-S	DIOPTER-S	DISTAFF-S	DRABBET-S	DUSTBIN-S	ELATIVE-S	ENCRUST-S
DESPOIL-S	DIOPTRE-S	DISTAIN-S	DRABBLE-S	DUUMVIR-S	ELECTOR-S	ENCRYPT-S
DESPOND-S	DIORAMA-S	DISTEND-S	DRABLER-S	DUVETYN-S	ELECTRO-S	ENDEMIC-S
DESSERT-S	DIORISM-S	DISTICH-S	DRACHMA-S	DVANDVA-S	ELEGIAC-S	ENDERON-S
DESTINE-S	DIORITE-S	DISTILL-S	DRACONE-S	DVORNIK-S	ELEGISE-S	ENDGAME-S
DESTROY-S	DIOXANE-S	DISTORT-S	DRAFTEE-S	DWELLER-S	ELEGIST-S	ENDIRON-S
DETENTE-S	DIOXIDE-S	DISTUNE-S	DRAFTER-S	DWINDLE-S	ELEGIZE-S	ENDOGEN-S
DETENUE-S	DIPHONE-S	DISTURB-S	DRAGGLE-S	DYELINE-S	ELEMENT-S	ENDORSE-S
DETERGE-S	DIPLOMA-S	DISTYLE-S	DRAGNET-S	DYESTER-S	ELEVATE-S	ENDOWER-S
DETINUE-S	DIPLONT-S	DISYOKE-S	DRAGOON-S	DYNAMIC-S	ELFHOOD-S	ENDSHIP-S
DETRACT-S	DIPNOAN-S	DITCHER-S	DRAINER-S	DYSODIL-S	ELFLAND-S	ENDURER-S
DETRAIN-S	DIPPING-S	DIURNAL-S	DRAPIER-S	DYSPNEA-S	ELISION-S	ENERGID-S
DETRUDE-S	DIPTERA-S	DIVERGE-S	DRAPPIE-S	DYSURIA-S	ELITISM-S	ENFELON-S
DEVALUE-S	DIPTYCH-S	DIVERSE-S	DRASTIC-S	EANLING-S	ELITIST-S	ENFEOFF-S
DEVELOP-S	DIREMPT-S	DIVIDER-S	DRAUGHT-S	EARACHE-S	ELLIPSE-S	ENFLAME-S
DEVIANT-S	DISABLE-S	DIVINER-S	DRAWBAR-S	EARDROP-S	ELLWAND-S	ENFORCE-S
DEVIATE-S	DISAVOW-S	DIVISOR-S	DRAWING-S	EARDRUM-S	ELMWOOD-S	ENFRAME-S
DEVILET-S	DISBAND-S	DIVORCE-S	DRAWLER-S	EARFLAP-S	ELOCUTE-S	ENGAGER-S
DEVISAL-S	DISBARK-S	DIVULGE-S	DRAYAGE-S	EARLDOM-S	ELOGIST-S	ENGINER-S
DEVISEE-S	DISCAGE-S	DIZZARD-S	DREADER-S	EARLOBE-S	ELOGIUM-S	ENGLOBE-S
DEVISER-S	DISCANT-S	DJIBBAH-S	DREAMER-S	EARLOCK-S	ELOINER-S	ENGLOOM-S
DEVISOR-S	DISCARD-S	DOATING-S	DREDGER-S	EARMARK-S	ELUSION-S	ENGORGE-S
DEVLING-S	DISCASE-S	DOCKAGE-S	DRESSER-S	EARNEST-S	ELUTION-S	ENGRACE-S
DEVOICE-S	DISCEPT-S	DOCKING-S	DREVILL-S	EARNING-S	ELUVIUM-S	ENGRAFF-S
DEVOLVE-S	DISCERN-S	DOCKISE-S	DRIBBER-S	EARPICK-S	EMANATE-S	ENGRAFT-S
DEVOTEE-S	DISCERP-S	DOCKIZE-S	DRIBBLE-S	EARPLUG-S	EMBATHE-S	ENGRAIL-S
DEWATER-S	DISCIDE-S	DOCQUET-S	DRIBLET-S	EARRING-S	EMBLAZE-S	ENGRAIN-S
		DODGING-S	DRIFTER-S	EARSHOT-S	EMBLOOM-S	ENGRASP-S

ENGRAVE-S	EQUINIA-S	EXCITON-S	FANGLES-S	FIBROID-S	FLECKER-S	FOREGUT-S
ENGUARD-S	ERASION-S	EXCITOR-S	FANNELL-S	FIBROIN-S	FLEECER-S	FORELAY-S
ENGULPH-S	ERASURE-S	EXCLAIM-S	FANNING-S	FIBROMA-S	FLEERER-S	FORELEG-S
ENHANCE-S	ERATHEM-S	EXCLAVE-S	FANTAIL-S	FIBROSE-S	FLESHER-S	FORELIE-S
ENJOYER-S	ERECTER-S	EXCLUDE-S	FANTASM-S	FIBSTER-S	FLETTON-S	FOREPAW-S
ENLARGE-S	ERECTOR-S	EXCRETE-S	FANTAST-S	FICTION-S	FLEURET-S	FORERUN-S
ENLIGHT-S	EREMITE-S	EXCURSE-S	FANTEEG-S	FIDDLER-S	FLEURON-S	FORESAY-S
ENLIVEN-S	EREPSIN-S	EXCUSAL-S	FANZINE-S	FIDDLEY-S	FLEXION-S	FORESEE-S
ENNOBLE-S	ERINITE-S	EXCUSER-S	FARADAY-S	FIDEISM-S	FLEXURE-S	FORETOP-S
ENOUNCE-S	ERMELIN-S	EXECUTE-S	FARAWAY-S	FIDEIST-S	FLICKER-S	FOREVER-S
ENPLANE-S	ERODENT-S	EXEGETE-S	FARCEUR-S	FIEFDOM-S	FLINDER-S	FORFAIR-S
ENPRINT-S	ERODIUM-S	EXEMPLE-S	FARCING-S	FIELDER-S	FLINGER-S	FORFEIT-S
ENQUIRE-S	EROSION-S	EXERGUE-S	FARDAGE-S	FIFTEEN-S	FLIPPER-S	FORFEND-S
ENRANGE-S	EROTEMA-S	EXHAUST-S	FARDING-S	FIGHTER-S	FLITTER-S	FORGING-S
ENRHEUM-S	EROTEME-S	EXHIBIT-S	FARMING-S	FIGMENT-S	FLIVVER-S	FORGIVE-S
ENROUGH-S	EROTISM-S	EXHUMER-S	FARRAGO-S	FIGWORT-S	FLOATEL-S	FORHENT-S
ENROUND-S	ERRATIC-S	EXIGENT-S	FARRIER-S	FILABEG-S	FLOATER-S	FORKFUL-S
ENSHELL-S	ERRHINE-S	EXOCARP-S	FARRUCA-S	FILACER-S	FLOKATI-S	FORLANA-S
ENSLAVE-S	ERUDITE-S	EXODERM-S	FARTHEL-S	FILARIA-S	FLOORER-S	FORLEND-S
ENSNARE-S	ESCALOP-S	EXODIST-S	FARTLEK-S	FILASSE-S	FLOOSIE-S	FORLESE-S
ENSNARL-S	ESCAPEE-S	EXOMION-S	FASCINE-S	FILAZER-S	FLOOZIE-S	FORLORN-S
ENSTAMP-S	ESCAPER-S	EXPANSE-S	FASCISM-S	FILBERD-S	FLORIST-S	FORMANT-S
ENSTEEP-S	ESCHEAT-S	EXPENSE-S	FASCIST-S	FILBERT-S	FLORUIT-S	FORMATE-S
ENSTYLE-S	ESCOLAR-S	EXPIATE-S	FASHION-S	FILCHER-S	FLOTAGE-S	FORMING-S
ENSURER-S	ESCRIBE-S	EXPLAIN-S	FASTING-S	FILEMOT-S	FLOTSAM-S	FORMULA-S
ENSWEEP-S	ESCROLL-S	EXPLANT-S	FATIGUE-S	FILIATE-S	FLOUNCE-S	FORPINE-S
ENTAYLE-S	ESCUAGE-S	EXPLODE-S	FATLING-S	FILIBEG-S	FLOWAGE-S	FORSAKE-S
ENTENTE-S	ESLOYNE-S	EXPLOIT-S	FATTISM-S	FILLING-S	FLUENCE-S	FORSLOE-S
ENTERER-S	ESPARTO-S	EXPLORE-S	FATTIST-S	FILMDOM-S	FLUIDIC-S	FORSLOW-S
ENTERIC-S	ESPOUSE-S	EXPOSAL-S	FAUCHON-S	FILMSET-S	FLUNKEY-S	FORTLET-S
ENTHRAL-S	ESQUIRE-S	EXPOSER-S	FAUNIST-S	FINAGLE-S	FLUSHER-S	FORTUNE-S
ENTHUSE-S	ESSAYER-S	EXPOUND-S	FAVORER-S	FINANCE-S	FLUSTER-S	FORWARD-S
ENTICER-S	ESSENCE-S	EXPULSE-S	FAVRILE-S	FINBACK-S	FLUTINA-S	FORWARN-S
ENTITLE-S	ESSOYNE-S	EXPUNCT-S	FAWNING-S	FINDING-S	FLUTING-S	FORZATO-S
ENTRAIL-S	ESTHETE-S	EXPUNGE-S	FAYENCE-S	FINDRAM-S	FLUTIST-S	FOSSICK-S
ENTRAIN-S	ESTOILE-S	EXPURGE-S	FAZENDA-S	FINESSE-S	FLUTTER-S	FOUDRIE-S
ENTRANT-S	ESTOVER-S	EXSCIND-S	FEASTER-S	FINNACK-S	FLUXION-S	FOUETTE-S
ENTREAT-S	ESTRADE-S	EXTERNE-S	FEATHER-S	FINNOCK-S	FLYBANE-S	FOUGADE-S
ENTRISM-S	ESTREAT-S	EXTRACT-S	FEATURE-S	FIREARM-S	FLYBELT-S	FOULARD-S
ENTRIST-S	ESTREPE-S	EXTRAIT-S	FECHTER-S	FIREBUG-S	FLYBLOW-S	FOULDER-S
ENTRUST-S	ETACISM-S	EXTREAT-S	FEDARIE-S	FIREDOG-S	FLYBOAT-S	FOUMART-S
ENTWINE-S	ETAERIO-S	EXTREME-S	FEDERAL-S	FIREPAN-S	FLYBOOK-S	FOUNDER-S
ENTWIST-S	ETAGERE-S	EXTRUDE-S	FEEDING-S	FIREPOT-S	FLYOVER-S	FOURGON-S
ENVAULT-S	ETALAGE-S	EXUDATE-S	FEEDLOT-S	FIRRING-S	FLYTING-S	FOVEOLA-S
ENVELOP-S	ETCHANT-S	EXURBIA-S	FEELBAD-S	FISHEYE-S	FLYTRAP-S	FOVEOLE-S
ENVENOM-S	ETCHING-S	EYEBALL-S	FEELING-S	FISHGIG-S	FOAMING-S	FOWLING-S
ENVIRON-S	ETHANOL-S	EYEBOLT-S	FEERING-S	FISHING-S	FOGGAGE-S	FOXHOLE-S
ENVYING-S	ETHICAL-S	EYEBROW-S	FELAFEL-S	FISSION-S	FOGHORN-S	FOXSHIP-S
ENWHEEL-S	ETIOLIN-S	EYEHOOK-S	FELICIA-S	FISSURE-S	FOGYDOM-S	FOXTROT-S
EPACRID-S	ETRENNE-S	EYELIAD-S	FELLATE-S	FISTFUL-S	FOGYISM-S	FRACTAL-S
EPAGOGE-S	EUCAINE-S	EYESORE-S	FELSITE-S	FISTULA-S	FOILING-S	FRAMING-S
EPAULET-S	EUCLASE-S	FABLING-S	FELSPAR-S	FITCHET-S	FOISTER-S	FRANION-S
EPEIRID-S	EUCRITE-S	FACONNE-S	FELTING-S	FITCHEW-S	FOLACIN-S	FRAUGHT-S
EPERGNE-S	EUGENIA-S	FACTICE-S	FELUCCA-S	FITMENT-S	FOLDING-S	FRAYING-S
EPHEDRA-S	EUGENIC-S	FACTION-S	FELWORT-S	FITTING-S	FOLIAGE-S	FRAZZLE-S
EPICARP-S	EUGENOL-S	FACTOID-S	FEMITER-S	FIVEPIN-S	FOLIATE-S	FRECKLE-S
EPICEDE-S	EUPHROE-S	FACTURE-S	FENCING-S	FIXTURE-S	FOLIOLE-S	FREEBEE-S
EPICENE-S	EUSTYLE-S	FADAISE-S	FENITAR-S	FIZZGIG-S	FOLKWAY-S	FREEBIE-S
EPICIER-S	EUTEXIA-S	FADDISM-S	FENLAND-S	FIZZING-S	FONDANT-S	FREEDOM-S
EPICISM-S	EVACUEE-S	FADDIST-S	FEOFFEE-S	FLACKER-S	FONDLER-S	FREESIA-S
EPICIST-S	EVANGEL-S	FAGGING-S	FEOFFER-S	FLACKET-S	FONTLET-S	FREEWAY-S
EPICURE-S	EVASION-S	FAHLORE-S	FEOFFOR-S	FLAFFER-S	FOODISM-S	FREEZER-S
EPIDOTE-S	EVENING-S	FAIENCE-S	FERMATA-S	FLAMFEW-S	FOOLING-S	FREIGHT-S
EPIGONE-S	EVENTER-S	FAILING-S	FERMENT-S	FLANEUR-S	FOOTAGE-S	FRESHEN-S
EPIGRAM-S	EVERTOR-S	FAILURE-S	FERMION-S	FLANKER-S	FOOTBAR-S	FRESHER-S
EPILATE-S	EVICTOR-S	FAIRING-S	FERMIUM-S	FLANNEL-S	FOOTBOY-S	FRESHET-S
EPISODE-S	EVIDENT-S	FAIRWAY-S	FERNING-S	FLANNEN-S	FOOTING-S	FRESNEL-S
EPISOME-S	EVIRATE-S	FAITOUR-S	FERRATE-S	FLAPPER-S	FOOTLES-S	FRETSAW-S
EPISTLE-S	EVITATE-S	FALAFEL-S	FERRITE-S	FLASHER-S	FOOTPAD-S	FRIANDE-S
EPITAPH-S	EVOCATE-S	FALBALA-S	FERRUGO-S	FLASKET-S	FOOTROT-S	FRIBBLE-S
EPITHEM-S	EVOLUTE-S	FALCADE-S	FERRULE-S	FLATBED-S	FOOTWAY-S	FRIGATE-S
EPITHET-S	EVOLVER-S	FALCULA-S	FERVOUR-S	FLATLET-S	FOOZLER-S	FRIGGER-S
EPITOME-S	EXACTER-S	FALDAGE-S	FESTOON-S	FLATTEN-S	FOPLING-S	FRIJOLE-S
EPITOPE-S	EXACTOR-S	FALLING-S	FETICHE-S	FLATTER-S	FORAGER-S	FRIPPER-S
EPIZOAN-S	EXAMINE-S	FALLOUT-S	FETLOCK-S	FLAUGHT-S	FORAYER-S	FRISEUR-S
EPOXIDE-S	EXAMPLE-S	FALSISM-S	FETTLER-S	FLAVINE-S	FORBEAR-S	FRISKER-S
EPSILON-S	EXCERPT-S	FANATIC-S	FEUDING-S	FLAVONE-S	FORBODE-S	FRISKET-S
EPURATE-S	EXCHEAT-S	FANCIER-S	FEUDIST-S	FLAVOUR-S	FOREARM-S	FRISSON-S
EQUATOR-S	EXCITER-S	FANFARE-S	FIANCEE-S	FLEAPIT-S	FORECAR-S	FRISURE-S

FRITTER-S	GAMBIST-S	GILDING-S	GOSHAWK-S	GRIZZLE-S	HADROME-S	HAUTEUR-S
FRITURE-S	GAMBLER-S	GILLION-S	GOSLING-S	GROANER-S	HAFFLIN-S	HAVEOUR-S
FRIZZLE-S	GAMBOGE-S	GILTCUP-S	GOSSOON-S	GROCKLE-S	HAFNIUM-S	HAVEREL-S
FROGBIT-S	GAMBREL-S	GIMMICK-S	GOTHITE-S	GROGRAM-S	HAGBOLT-S	HAVIOUR-S
FROGLET-S	GAMELAN-S	GINGALL-S	GOUACHE-S	GROMMET-S	HAGDOWN-S	HAWBUCK-S
FRONTAL-S	GAMINES-S	GINGHAM-S	GOUGERE-S	GROOVER-S	HAGGARD-S	HAWKBIT-S
FRONTON-S	GAMMOCK-S	GINGILI-S	GOURAMI-S	GROSERT-S	HAGGLER-S	HAWKING-S
FROUNCE-S	GANGING-S	GINSENG-S	GOURMET-S	GROUPER-S	HAHNIUM-S	HAYBAND-S
FROWARD-S	GANGREL-S	GINSHOP-S	GOWLAND-S	GROUPIE-S	HAINING-S	HAYCOCK-S
FRUITER-S	GANGSTA-S	GIRAFFE-S	GOWNBOY-S	GROUSER-S	HAIRCUT-S	HAYFORK-S
FRUMPLE-S	GANGWAY-S	GIRASOL-S	GRABBER-S	GROUTER-S	HAIRNET-S	HAYLOFT-S
FRUSTUM-S	GANOINE-S	GIRDING-S	GRABBLE-S	GROWING-S	HAIRPIN-S	HAYRICK-S
FUCHSIA-S	GANTLET-S	GIRDLER-S	GRACKLE-S	GROWLER-S	HALAVAH-S	HAYRIDE-S
FUCKING-S	GARBAGE-S	GIRLOND-S	GRADATE-S	GRUBBER-S	HALBERD-S	HAYSEED-S
FUDDLER-S	GARBLER-S	GIROSOL-S	GRADDAN-S	GRUBBLE-S	HALBERT-S	HAYWARD-S
FUELLER-S	GARBOIL-S	GISARME-S	GRADINE-S	GRUMBLE-S	HALCYON-S	HAYWIRE-S
FUGUIST-S	GARBURE-S	GITTERN-S	GRADUAL-S	GRUMMET-S	HALFLIN-S	HEADAGE-S
FULCRUM-S	GARDANT-S	GIZZARD-S	GRAFTER-S	GRUNION-S	HALFWIT-S	HEADING-S
FULFILL-S	GARIGUE-S	GLACIAL-S	GRAINER-S	GRUNTER-S	HALIBUT-S	HEADRIG-S
FULGOUR-S	GARLAND-S	GLACIER-S	GRAMMAR-S	GRUNTLE-S	HALIDOM-S	HEADSET-S
FULLAGE-S	GARMENT-S	GLADDEN-S	GRANDAD-S	GRYPHON-S	HALIMOT-S	HEADWAY-S
FULMINE-S	GAROTTE-S	GLADDIE-S	GRANDAM-S	GRYSBOK-S	HALLALI-S	HEALING-S
FUMBLER-S	GARPIKE-S	GLADDON-S	GRANDEE-S	GUANACO-S	HALLIAN-S	HEARING-S
FUMETTE-S	GARROTE-S	GLAIRIN-S	GRANDMA-S	GUANINE-S	HALLING-S	HEARKEN-S
FUNDING-S	GARVOCK-S	GLAMOUR-S	GRANDPA-S	GUARANA-S	HALLION-S	HEARSAY-S
FUNERAL-S	GASAHOL-S	GLAZIER-S	GRANFER-S	GUARANI-S	HALLWAY-S	HEARTEN-S
FUNFAIR-S	GASOHOL-S	GLAZING-S	GRANGER-S	GUARDEE-S	HALLYON-S	HEATHEN-S
FUNICLE-S	GASPING-S	GLEANER-S	GRANITA-S	GUAYULE-S	HALOGEN-S	HEATING-S
FUNSTER-S	GASSING-S	GLENOID-S	GRANITE-S	GUDGEON-S	HALTING-S	HEAVING-S
FURFAIR-S	GASTRIN-S	GLIADIN-S	GRANNAM-S	GUERDON-S	HALYARD-S	HEBENON-S
FURIOSO-S	GATEWAY-S	GLIDING-S	GRANNIE-S	GUEREZA-S	HAMMOCK-S	HECKLER-S
FURLANA-S	GAUDGIE-S	GLIMMER-S	GRANOLA-S	GUERITE-S	HAMSTER-S	HECTARE-S
FURLONG-S	GAUFFER-S	GLIMPSE-S	GRANTEE-S	GUESSER-S	HANAPER-S	HEDGING-S
FURNACE-S	GAUGING-S	GLISTEN-S	GRANTER-S	GUESTEN-S	HANDBAG-S	HEDONIC-S
FURRIER-S	GAULTER-S	GLISTER-S	GRANTOR-S	GUICHET-S	HANDCAR-S	HEELING-S
FURRING-S	GAVOTTE-S	GLITTER-S	GRANULE-S	GUIDAGE-S	HANDFUL-S	HEIRDOM-S
FURTHER-S	GAZANIA-S	GLOATER-S	GRAPHIC-S	GUIDING-S	HANDGUN-S	HEISTER-S
FUSAROL-S	GAZELLE-S	GLOBOID-S	GRAPNEL-S	GUILDER-S	HANDJAR-S	HELICON-S
FUSHION-S	GAZETTE-S	GLOBOSE-S	GRAPPLE-S	GUIPURE-S	HANDLER-S	HELIPAD-S
FUSTIAN-S	GAZOOKA-S	GLOBULE-S	GRASPER-S	GUISARD-S	HANDLES-S	HELLIER-S
FUTCHEL-S	GEARING-S	GLONOIN-S	GRASSER-S	GUISING-S	HANDOUT-S	HELLION-S
FUTHARK-S	GEEBUNG-S	GLOSSER-S	GRASSUM-S	GUMBOIL-S	HANDSAW-S	HELPING-S
FUTHORC-S	GEECHEE-S	GLOVING-S	GRATING-S	GUMBOOT-S	HANDSEL-S	HEMIOLA-S
FUTHORK-S	GELATIN-S	GLOZING-S	GRAUPEL-S	GUMDROP-S	HANDSET-S	HEMIONE-S
FUTTOCK-S	GELDING-S	GLUCINA-S	GRAVING-S	GUMMING-S	HANGDOG-S	HEMLOCK-S
GABBARD-S	GEMMATE-S	GLUCOSE-S	GRAVURE-S	GUMMITE-S	HANGING-S	HENBANE-S
GABBART-S	GEMMULE-S	GLUTTON-S	GRAZIER-S	GUMSHOE-S	HANGOUT-S	HENPECK-S
GABBLER-S	GEMSBOK-S	GLYCINE-S	GRAZING-S	GUNBOAT-S	HANUMAN-S	HEPARIN-S
GABELLE-S	GENAPPE-S	GLYCOSE-S	GREASER-S	GUNFIRE-S	HARBOUR-S	HEPATIC-S
GABFEST-S	GENERAL-S	GLYPTIC-S	GREATEN-S	GUNLOCK-S	HARDBAG-S	HEPSTER-S
GADLING-S	GENERIC-S	GNASHER-S	GRECIAN-S	GUNNAGE-S	HARDOKE-S	HEPTANE-S
GADROON-S	GENETIC-S	GNOCCHI-S	GRECQUE-S	GUNNERA-S	HARDTOP-S	HERBAGE-S
GADWALL-S	GENETTE-S	GNOMIST-S	GREENER-S	GUNNING-S	HARICOT-S	HERBIST-S
GAFFING-S	GENIPAP-S	GOBBLER-S	GREENIE-S	GUNPLAY-S	HARLING-S	HERBLET-S
GAGSTER-S	GENISTA-S	GOBURRA-S	GREENTH-S	GUNPORT-S	HARMALA-S	HERDBOY-S
GAHNITE-S	GENITAL-S	GODETIA-S	GREETER-S	GUNROOM-S	HARMINE-S	HERETIC-S
GAINING-S	GENITOR-S	GODHEAD-S	GREGALE-S	GUNSHIP-S	HARMOST-S	HERITOR-S
GAINSAY-S	GENIZAH-S	GODHOOD-S	GREISEN-S	GUNSHOT-S	HAROSET-S	HERLING-S
GALABEA-S	GENLOCK-S	GODLING-S	GREMIAL-S	GUNWALE-S	HARPING-S	HEROINE-S
GALABIA-S	GENTIAN-S	GODROON-S	GREMLIN-S	GURNARD-S	HARPIST-S	HEROISE-S
GALANGA-S	GENTILE-S	GODSEND-S	GRENADE-S	GURUDOM-S	HARPOON-S	HEROISM-S
GALATEA-S	GEOFACT-S	GODSHIP-S	GREYHEN-S	GURUISM-S	HARRIER-S	HEROIZE-S
GALETTE-S	GEOMANT-S	GODWARD-S	GREYING-S	GUTCHER-S	HARSHEN-S	HERRING-S
GALILEE-S	GEORGIC-S	GOGGLER-S	GRIBBLE-S	GUTSFUL-S	HARSLET-S	HERSALL-S
GALIPOT-S	GERBERA-S	GOLDEYE-S	GRICING-S	GUTTATE-S	HARVEST-S	HERSHIP-S
GALLANT-S	GERENUK-S	GOLFING-S	GRIDDER-S	GUZZLER-S	HASSOCK-S	HESSIAN-S
GALLATE-S	GERMAIN-S	GOLIARD-S	GRIDDLE-S	GWINIAD-S	HASTING-S	HETAIRA-S
GALLEON-S	GESTALT-S	GOLLAND-S	GRIEVER-S	GWYNIAD-S	HATBAND-S	HETAIRA-S
GALLIOT-S	GESTAPO-S	GOMBEEN-S	GRIFFIN-S	GYMNAST-S	HATCHEL-S	HEUREKA-S
GALLISE-S	GESTATE-S	GOMERAL-S	GRIFFON-S	GYROCAR-S	HATCHER-S	HEURISM-S
GALLIUM-S	GESTURE-S	GOMERIL-S	GRIFTER-S	HABITAT-S	HATCHET-S	HEXAGON-S
GALLIZE-S	GETAWAY-S	GONDOLA-S	GRIMACE-S	HABITUE-S	HATRACK-S	HEXAPLA-S
GALLNUT-S	GETTING-S	GOPURAM-S	GRINDER-S	HACHURE-S	HATTING-S	HEXAPOD-S
GALLOON-S	GHARIAL-S	GORCOCK-S	GRINNER-S	HACKBUT-S	HATTOCK-S	HEYDUCK-S
GALOCHE-S	GHERKIN-S	GORCROW-S	GRIPPER-S	HACKING-S	HAUBERK-S	HIBACHI-S
GALOPIN-S	GHILGAI-S	GORILLA-S	GRIPPLE-S	HACKLER-S	HAULAGE-S	HICATEE-S
GALUMPH-S	GHILLIE-S	GORMAND-S	GRISKIN-S	HACKLET-S	HAULIER-S	HIDALGA-S
GAMBADO-S	GIGGLER-S	GORSEDD-S	GRISTLE-S	HACKNEY-S	HAUNTER-S	HIDALGO-S
GAMBIER-S	GILBERT-S	GORSOON-S	GRITTER-S	HADDOCK-S	HAUTBOY-S	HIDEOUT-S

HIDLING-S	HUANACO-S	IMPANEL-S	INHAUST-S	ISOBATH-S	JOINING-S	KHANJAR-S
HIGGLER-S	HUFFKIN-S	IMPASSE-S	INHERCE-S	ISOCHOR-S	JOINTER-S	KHEDIVA-S
HIGHBOY-S	HUITAIN-S	IMPASTE-S	INHERIT-S	ISODONT-S	JOLLYER-S	KHEDIVE-S
HIGHWAY-S	HUMDRUM-S	IMPASTO-S	INHIBIT-S	ISOGRAM-S	JONQUIL-S	KHOTBAH-S
HILDING-S	HUMERAL-S	IMPEARL-S	INHUMER-S	ISOHYET-S	JOTTING-S	KHOTBEH-S
HILLOCK-S	HUMIDOR-S	IMPERIL-S	INITIAL-S	ISOKONT-S	JOURNAL-S	KHUTBAH-S
HILLTOP-S	HUMMAUM-S	IMPINGE-S	INJOINT-S	ISOLATE-S	JOURNEY-S	KIBITKA-S
HINDLEG-S	HUMMING-S	IMPLANT-S	INJUNCT-S	ISOLINE-S	JOUSTER-S	KIDDIER-S
HIPPING-S	HUMMOCK-S	IMPLATE-S	INJURER-S	ISOMERE-S	JOYANCE-S	KIDLING-S
HIPSTER-S	HUMOGEN-S	IMPLEAD-S	INKHORN-S	ISOSPIN-S	JUBILEE-S	KIDSKIN-S
HIREAGE-S	HUNDRED-S	IMPLETE-S	INKLING-S	ISOTONE-S	JUDOIST-S	KIKUMON-S
HIRLING-S	HUNTING-S	IMPLODE-S	INKSPOT-S	ISOTOPE-S	JUGGING-S	KILLCOW-S
HIRUDIN-S	HURDLER-S	IMPLORE-S	INKWELL-S	ISOTRON-S	JUGGLER-S	KILLDEE-S
HISSING-S	HURLBAT-S	IMPOSER-S	INLAYER-S	ISOTYPE-S	JUGHEAD-S	KILLICK-S
HISTONE-S	HURLING-S	IMPOUND-S	INNERVE-S	ITACISM-S	JUGULAR-S	KILLING-S
HISTRIO-S	HURTLES-S	IMPREGN-S	INNYARD-S	ITEMISE-S	JUKSKEI-S	KILLJOY-S
HITCHER-S	HUSBAND-S	IMPRESA-S	INQILAB-S	ITEMIZE-S	JUMBLER-S	KILLOCK-S
HOARDER-S	HUSKING-S	IMPRESE-S	INQUERE-S	ITERATE-S	JUMBUCK-S	KILOBAR-S
HOARSEN-S	HUSTLER-S	IMPREST-S	INQUEST-S	IVORIST-S	JUMELLE-S	KILOBIT-S
HOATZIN-S	HUTMENT-S	IMPRINT-S	INQUIET-S	IVRESSE-S	JUNCATE-S	KILOTON-S
HOBBLER-S	HUTTING-S	IMPROVE-S	INQUIRE-S	JACAMAR-S	JUNIPER-S	KINCHIN-S
HOBNAIL-S	HUTZPAH-S	IMPULSE-S	INSANIE-S	JACINTH-S	JUSSIVE-S	KINDLER-S
HOBODOM-S	HYACINE-S	IMPUTER-S	INSCAPE-S	JACKDAW-S	JUSTICE-S	KINDLES-S
HOBOISM-S	HYALINE-S	INBEING-S	INSCULP-S	JACKEEN-S	JUVENAL-S	KINDRED-S
HOEDOWN-S	HYALITE-S	INBREAK-S	INSHELL-S	JACKPOT-S	KABADDI-S	KINETIC-S
HOGBACK-S	HYDATID-S	INBREED-S	INSIDER-S	JACKSIE-S	KABBALA-S	KINFOLK-S
HOGGING-S	HYDRANT-S	INBRING-S	INSIGHT-S	JACOBIN-S	KACHERI-S	KINGCUP-S
HOGHOOD-S	HYDRATE-S	INBURST-S	INSINEW-S	JACONET-S	KACHINA-S	KINGDOM-S
HOGWARD-S	HYDRIDE-S	INCENSE-S	INSNARE-S	JACUZZI-S	KAGOULE-S	KINGLES-S
HOGWEED-S	HYDROID-S	INCHASE-S	INSPECT-S	JADEITE-S	KAHAWAI-S	KINGLET-S
HOISTER-S	HYGIENE-S	INCHPIN-S	INSPIRE-S	JAGHIRE-S	KAINITE-S	KINSHIP-S
HOLDING-S	HYLDING-S	INCISOR-S	INSTALL-S	JALAPIN-S	KAJAWAH-S	KIPPAGE-S
HOLDOUT-S	HYLOIST-S	INCITER-S	INSTANT-S	JALOUSE-S	KAKODYL-S	KIRIMON-S
HOLIDAY-S	HYMNIST-S	INCLASP-S	INSTATE-S	JAMADAR-S	KAMERAD-S	KIRKING-S
HOLLAND-S	HYPERON-S	INCLINE-S	INSTILL-S	JAMBIER-S	KAMICHI-S	KIRKTON-S
HOLMIUM-S	HYPNONE-S	INCLOSE-S	INSULIN-S	JAMBIYA-S	KAMPONG-S	KITCHEN-S
HOLSTER-S	HYPONYM-S	INCLUDE-S	INSURED-S	JAMBONE-S	KAMSEEN-S	KITENGE-S
HOLYDAM-S	HYPOXIA-S	INCOMER-S	INSURER-S	JAMBOOL-S	KANTELA-S	KITHARA-S
HOMAGER-S	IAMBIST-S	INCONNU-S	INSWING-S	JAMDANI-S	KANTELE-S	KITLING-S
HOMEBOY-S	ICEBALL-S	INCRUST-S	INTEGER-S	JAMPANI-S	KAOLINE-S	KLAVIER-S
HOMELYN-S	ICEBERG-S	INCURVE-S	INTERIM-S	JANGLER-S	KARAISM-S	KLINKER-S
HOMINID-S	ICEBOAT-S	INDEXER-S	INTERNE-S	JANITOR-S	KARAKUL-S	KNACKER-S
HOMMOCK-S	ICEPACK-S	INDICAN-S	INTHRAL-S	JANIZAR-S	KARAOKE-S	KNAPPER-S
HOMOLOG-S	ICHNITE-S	INDITER-S	INTONER-S	JANNOCK-S	KARTING-S	KNAPPLE-S
HOMONYM-S	ICONISE-S	INDORSE-S	INTRADA-S	JARGOON-S	KASHMIR-S	KNEADER-S
HOODLUM-S	ICONIZE-S	INDOXYL-S	INTRANT-S	JARRING-S	KASHRUT-S	KNEECAP-S
HOOFROT-S	ICTERIC-S	INDRAFT-S	INTREAT-S	JASMINE-S	KATHODE-S	KNEELER-S
HOOLOCK-S	ICTERID-S	INDUCER-S	INTROIT-S	JAUNTIE-S	KATORGA-S	KNEVELL-S
HOOSGOW-S	IDLESSE-S	INDULGE-S	INTRUDE-S	JAVELIN-S	KATYDID-S	KNICKER-S
HOPBIND-S	IDOLISE-S	INDULIN-S	INTRUST-S	JAWBONE-S	KAYOING-S	KNIFING-S
HOPBINE-S	IDOLISM-S	INDWELL-S	INTWINE-S	JAWFALL-S	KEBBOCK-S	KNITTER-S
HOPEFUL-S	IDOLIST-S	INEARTH-S	INTWIST-S	JAWHOLE-S	KEBBUCK-S	KNITTLE-S
HOPLITE-S	IDOLIZE-S	INERTIA-S	INULASE-S	JAYWALK-S	KEELAGE-S	KNOBBER-S
HOPPING-S	IGARAPE-S	INFANTA-S	INVADER-S	JEEPNEY-S	KEELING-S	KNOBBLE-S
HOPSACK-S	IGNITER-S	INFANTE-S	INVALID-S	JEERING-S	KEELSON-S	KNOCKER-S
HORDEIN-S	IGNORER-S	INFARCT-S	INVEIGH-S	JELLABA-S	KEENING-S	KNOTTER-S
HORDOCK-S	IGUANID-S	INFAUNA-S	INVERSE-S	JEMADAR-S	KEEPING-S	KNOWHOW-S
HORIZON-S	IJTIHAD-S	INFERNO-S	INVITEE-S	JEMIDAR-S	KEEPNET-S	KNUBBLE-S
HORMONE-S	IKEBANA-S	INFIDEL-S	INVITER-S	JEOFAIL-S	KEISTER-S	KNUCKLE-S
HORNBUG-S	ILKADAY-S	INFIELD-S	INVOICE-S	JEOPARD-S	KEITLOA-S	KOFTGAR-S
HORNFUL-S	ILLAPSE-S	INFIMUM-S	INVOLVE-S	JERKING-S	KELLAUT-S	KOKANEE-S
HORNING-S	ILLOGIC-S	INFLAME-S	INWEAVE-S	JERQUER-S	KEMPING-S	KOMATIK-S
HORNIST-S	IMAGINE-S	INFLATE-S	IODURET-S	JESTING-S	KENNING-S	KOUPREY-S
HORNITO-S	IMAGING-S	INFLECT-S	IONISER-S	JETFOIL-S	KERAMIC-S	KREMLIN-S
HORNLET-S	IMAGISM-S	INFLICT-S	IONIZER-S	JIBBING-S	KERATIN-S	KRIMMER-S
HORSING-S	IMAGIST-S	INFORCE-S	IONOMER-S	JIGAJIG-S	KERNING-S	KRULLER-S
HOSANNA-S	IMAMATE-S	INFRACT-S	IPOMOEA-S	JIGAJOG-S	KERNITE-S	KRYPTON-S
HOSPICE-S	IMBATHE-S	INFUSER-S	IRIDISE-S	JIGGING-S	KEROGEN-S	KRYTRON-S
HOSTAGE-S	IMBIBER-S	INGENER-S	IRIDIUM-S	JILLION-S	KERYGMA-S	KUFIYAH-S
HOSTING-S	IMBOSOM-S	INGENUE-S	IRIDIZE-S	JINGLER-S	KESTREL-S	KUMQUAT-S
HOSTLER-S	IMBOWER-S	INGLOBE-S	IRISATE-S	JINGLET-S	KETCHUP-S	KUNZITE-S
HOTHEAD-S	IMBROWN-S	INGOING-S	IRONING-S	JINJILI-S	KEYHOLE-S	KURSAAL-S
HOTLINE-S	IMBRUTE-S	INGRAFT-S	IRONISE-S	JIPYAPA-S	KEYLINE-S	KYANISE-S
HOTSHOT-S	IMBURSE-S	INGRAIN-S	IRONIST-S	JOBBING-S	KEYNOTE-S	KYANITE-S
HOTTING-S	IMITANT-S	INGRATE-S	IRONIZE-S	JOCKNEY-S	KEYWORD-S	KYANIZE-S
HOUSING-S	IMITATE-S	INGROUP-S	ISAGOGE-S	JOGGING-S	KHADDAR-S	LABARUM-S
HOUTING-S	IMMERGE-S	INGULPH-S	ISATINE-S	JOGTROT-S	KHALIFA-S	LABIATE-S
HOWLING-S	IMMERSE-S	INHABIT-S	ISOBARE-S	JOHNNIE-S	KHAMSIN-S	LABROID-S
	IMPAINT-S	INHALER-S	ISOBASE-S	JOINDER-S	KHANATE-S	LACQUER-S

LACQUEY-S	LAYBACK-S	LIMACON-S	LUCERNE-S	MAMMOCK-S	MASSEUR-S	MESQUIT-S
LACTASE-S	LAYETTE-S	LIMBECK-S	LUCIFER-S	MAMMOTH-S	MASTABA-S	MESSAGE-S
LACTATE-S	LAYLOCK-S	LIMEADE-S	LUCIGEN-S	MANACLE-S	MASTICH-S	MESSIAH-S
LACTEAL-S	LAYTIME-S	LIMEPIT-S	LUDSHIP-S	MANAGER-S	MASTIFF-S	MESTIZA-S
LACTONE-S	LAZARET-S	LIMITED-S	LUGEING-S	MANAKIN-S	MASTOID-S	MESTIZO-S
LACTOSE-S	LEADING-S	LIMITER-S	LUGHOLE-S	MANATEE-S	MATADOR-S	METAMER-S
LACUNAR-S	LEAFAGE-S	LIMPING-S	LUGSAIL-S	MANCALA-S	MATCHER-S	METAYER-S
LADANUM-S	LEAFBUD-S	LIMPKIN-S	LUGWORM-S	MANCHET-S	MATELOT-S	METCAST-S
LADETTE-S	LEAFLET-S	LINCHET-S	LULIBUB-S	MANDALA-S	MATINEE-S	METHANE-S
LADRONE-S	LEAGUER-S	LINDANE-S	LUMBAGO-S	MANDATE-S	MATOOKE-S	METHINK-S
LADYBUG-S	LEAKAGE-S	LINEAGE-S	LUMBANG-S	MANDIOC-S	MATRICE-S	METICAL-S
LADYCOW-S	LEANING-S	LINGULA-S	LUMPKIN-S	MANDIRA-S	MATSURI-S	METISSE-S
LADYISM-S	LEARNER-S	LINKAGE-S	LUNATIC-S	MANDOLA-S	MATTING-S	METONYM-S
LADYKIN-S	LEASING-S	LINKBOY-S	LUNCHER-S	MANDORA-S	MATTOCK-S	METOPON-S
LAETARE-S	LEASOWE-S	LINOCUT-S	LUNETTE-S	MANDREL-S	MATTOID-S	METRIST-S
LAGGARD-S	LEASURE-S	LINSANG-S	LUNGFUL-S	MANDRIL-S	MATWEED-S	MEZUZAH-S
LAGGING-S	LEATHER-S	LINSEED-S	LUPULIN-S	MANGLER-S	MATZOON-S	MICELLE-S
LAICISE-S	LEAVING-S	LIONCEL-S	LURCHER-S	MANGOLD-S	MAULGRE-S	MICHING-S
LAICIZE-S	LECTERN-S	LIONISE-S	LURDANE-S	MANHOLE-S	MAUNDER-S	MICROBE-S
LAIRAGE-S	LECTION-S	LIONISM-S	LURKING-S	MANHOOD-S	MAUTHER-S	MICTION-S
LAIRISE-S	LECTURE-S	LIONIZE-S	LUSTRUM-S	MANHUNT-S	MAUVEIN-S	MIDIRON-S
LAIRIZE-S	LECTURN-S	LIQUATE-S	LUTHERN-S	MANIHOC-S	MAUVINE-S	MIDLAND-S
LAKELET-S	LEECHEE-S	LIQUEUR-S	LUTHIER-S	MANIKIN-S	MAWSEED-S	MIDMOST-S
LALLING-S	LEERING-S	LISPING-S	LYCOPOD-S	MANILLA-S	MAWTHER-S	MIDNOON-S
LAMBADA-S	LEEWARD-S	LISPUND-S	LYDDITE-S	MANILLE-S	MAXIMIN-S	MIDRIFF-S
LAMBAST-S	LEFTISM-S	LISTING-S	LYMITER-S	MANIPLE-S	MAXWELL-S	MIDSHIP-S
LAMBERT-S	LEFTIST-S	LITERAL-S	LYMPHAD-S	MANITOU-S	MAYPOLE-S	MIDTERM-S
LAMBKIN-S	LEGATEE-S	LITHATE-S	LYNCHET-S	MANJACK-S	MAYSTER-S	MIDWIFE-S
LAMETER-S	LEGATOR-S	LITHITE-S	LYRICON-S	MANKIND-S	MAYWEED-S	MIDWIVE-S
LAMIGER-S	LEGGING-S	LITHIUM-S	MACADAM-S	MANNITE-S	MAZURKA-S	MIGRANT-S
LAMITER-S	LEGGISM-S	LITTLIN-S	MACAQUE-S	MANNOSE-S	MAZZARD-S	MIGRATE-S
LAMMING-S	LEGHORN-S	LIVELOD-S	MACHAIR-S	MANPACK-S	MEACOCK-S	MILEAGE-S
LAMPERN-S	LEGITIM-S	LIVENER-S	MACHETE-S	MANRENT-S	MEANDER-S	MILFOIL-S
LAMPING-S	LEGROOM-S	LLANERO-S	MACHINE-S	MANSARD-S	MEANING-S	MILKING-S
LAMPION-S	LEGUMIN-S	LOADING-S	MACHREE-S	MANSION-S	MEASURE-S	MILLDAM-S
LAMPOON-S	LEGWEAR-S	LOAFING-S	MACRAME-S	MANTEAU-S	MECONIN-S	MILLIME-S
LAMPREY-S	LEGWORK-S	LOANING-S	MACRAMI-S	MANTEEL-S	MEDACCA-S	MILLING-S
LAMPUKA-S	LEIDGER-S	LOATHER-S	MADDOCK-S	MANTLET-S	MEDALET-S	MILLION-S
LAMPUKI-S	LEISLER-S	LOBBYER-S	MADLING-S	MANTRAM-S	MEDDLER-S	MILLRUN-S
LANDING-S	LEISTER-S	LOBELET-S	MADOQUA-S	MANTRAP-S	MEDIANT-S	MIMMICK-S
LANDLER-S	LEISURE-S	LOBELIA-S	MADRASA-S	MANUMEA-S	MEDIATE-S	MINARET-S
LANEWAY-S	LEKKING-S	LOBSTER-S	MADRONA-S	MANUMIT-S	MEDICAL-S	MINCING-S
LANGAHA-S	LEMMING-S	LOBWORM-S	MADRONE-S	MANURER-S	MEDULLA-S	MINDING-S
LANGREL-S	LEMPIRA-S	LOCKAGE-S	MADRONO-S	MANYATA-S	MEDUSAN-S	MINDSET-S
LANGUET-S	LENDING-S	LOCKFUL-S	MADWORT-S	MAORMOR-S	MEERCAT-S	MINEOLA-S
LANGUOR-S	LENIENT-S	LOCKJAW-S	MADZOON-S	MAPPING-S	MEERKAT-S	MINERAL-S
LANIARD-S	LENTISK-S	LOCKOUT-S	MAESTRO-S	MAPPIST-S	MEETING-S	MINETTE-S
LANOLIN-S	LEOPARD-S	LOCKRAM-S	MAFFICK-S	MARABOU-S	MEGABAR-S	MINEVER-S
LANTANA-S	LEOTARD-S	LODGING-S	MAFFLIN-S	MARBLER-S	MEGABIT-S	MINGLER-S
LANTERN-S	LEPTOME-S	LOGANIA-S	MAGALOG-S	MARCHER-S	MEGAFOG-S	MINIATE-S
LANYARD-S	LESBIAN-S	LOGBOOK-S	MAGENTA-S	MARCONI-S	MEGARAD-S	MINIBAR-S
LAPPING-S	LETTERN-S	LOGGING-S	MAGNATE-S	MAREMMA-S	MEGARON-S	MINICAB-S
LAPSANG-S	LETTING-S	LOGLINE-S	MAGNETO-S	MARGENT-S	MEGASSE-S	MINICAM-S
LAPWING-S	LETTUCE-S	LOGWOOD-S	MAHATMA-S	MARGOSA-S	MEGATON-S	MINIKIN-S
LAPWORK-S	LEUCINE-S	LONGBOW-S	MAHONIA-S	MARIMBA-S	MEISTER-S	MINIVER-S
LARDOON-S	LEUCITE-S	LONGING-S	MAHSEER-S	MARINER-S	MELANGE-S	MINIVET-S
LARMIER-S	LEUCOMA-S	LOOFFUL-S	MAIDISM-S	MARKHOR-S	MELANIN-S	MINNICK-S
LASAGNA-S	LEVATOR-S	LOOKISM-S	MAILBAG-S	MARKING-S	MELILOT-S	MINNOCK-S
LASAGNE-S	LEVERET-S	LOOKOUT-S	MAILING-S	MARLINE-S	MELISMA-S	MINSTER-S
LASHING-S	LEWISIA-S	LOONING-S	MAILLOT-S	MARLING-S	MELLITE-S	MINTAGE-S
LASHKAR-S	LEXICON-S	LOOPING-S	MAILVAN-S	MARMITE-S	MELODIC-S	MINUEND-S
LASSOCK-S	LIAISON-S	LOOTING-S	MAIMING-S	MARMOSE-S	MELTING-S	MIRACLE-S
LASTAGE-S	LIBBARD-S	LOPPING-S	MAINOUR-S	MARPLOT-S	MELTITH-S	MIRADOR-S
LASTING-S	LIBELEE-S	LORDING-S	MAINTOP-S	MARQUEE-S	MEMENTO-S	MIRBANE-S
LATCHET-S	LIBELER-S	LORDKIN-S	MAISTER-S	MARQUES-S	MENACER-S	MISCALL-S
LATENCE-S	LIBERAL-S	LORETTE-S	MAJORAT-S	MARRIER-S	MENDING-S	MISCAST-S
LATERAL-S	LIBRATE-S	LORGNON-S	MALACIA-S	MARSHAL-S	MENFOLK-S	MISDATE-S
LATHING-S	LICENCE-S	LORIMER-S	MALAISE-S	MARTEXT-S	MENORAH-S	MISDEAL-S
LATITAT-S	LICENSE-S	LORINER-S	MALARIA-S	MARTINI-S	MENTHOL-S	MISDEED-S
LATRINE-S	LICHWAY-S	LORRELL-S	MALEATE-S	MARTLET-S	MENTION-S	MISDEEM-S
LATTICE-S	LICKING-S	LOUNDER-S	MALICHO-S	MARYBUD-S	MERCHET-S	MISDIAL-S
LAUGHER-S	LIGGING-S	LOUNGER-S	MALISON-S	MASCARA-S	MERFOLK-S	MISDIET-S
LAUNDER-S	LIGHTEN-S	LOURING-S	MALLARD-S	MASHING-S	MERLING-S	MISDOER-S
LAUWINE-S	LIGHTER-S	LOWLAND-S	MALMSEY-S	MASHLAM-S	MERMAID-S	MISDRAW-S
LAVOLTA-S	LIGNAGE-S	LOWVELD-S	MALTASE-S	MASHLIM-S	MERONYM-S	MISEASE-S
LAWLAND-S	LIGNITE-S	LOXYGEN-S	MALTING-S	MASHLIN-S	MERSION-S	MISFALL-S
LAWSUIT-S	LIGNOSE-S	LOZENGE-S	MALTOSE-S	MASHLUM-S	MESCLUN-S	MISFARE-S
LAXATOR-S	LIGROIN-S	LUBBARD-S	MAMELON-S	MASQUER-S	MESCLUN-S	MISFEED-S
LAYAWAY-S	LIMACEL-S	LUCARNE-S	MAMMOCK-S	MASSAGE-S	MESHING-S	MISFEED-S

MISFILE-S	MONSTER-S	MUMBLER-S	NEMESIA-S	NOWHERE-S	ONANISM-S	OUTGIVE-S
MISFIRE-S	MONTAGE-S	MUMMING-S	NEOLITH-S	NOYANCE-S	ONANIST-S	OUTGOER-S
MISFORM-S	MONTANT-S	MUMMOCK-S	NEONATE-S	NUCLEIN-S	ONCOGEN-S	OUTGROW-S
MISGIVE-S	MONTERO-S	MUNCHER-S	NEPHRON-S	NUCLEON-S	ONDATRA-S	OUTHAUL-S
MISHEAR-S	MONTURE-S	MUNNION-S	NERVINE-S	NUCLIDE-S	ONGOING-S	OUTHIRE-S
MISHMEE-S	MOOCHER-S	MUNSTER-S	NERVULE-S	NULLING-S	ONSTEAD-S	OUTHYRE-S
MISJOIN-S	MOOKTAR-S	MUNTING-S	NERVURE-S	NUMERAL-S	ONYCHIA-S	OUTJEST-S
MISKNOW-S	MOONEYE-S	MUNTJAC-S	NESTFUL-S	NUNATAK-S	OOLAKAN-S	OUTJUMP-S
MISLEAD-S	MOONLET-S	MUNTJAK-S	NESTING-S	NUNDINE-S	OOMIACK-S	OUTLAND-S
MISLIKE-S	MOONSET-S	MUONIUM-S	NETBALL-S	NUNHOOD-S	OOPHYTE-S	OUTLAST-S
MISLIVE-S	MOORAGE-S	MURAENA-S	NETIZEN-S	NUNSHIP-S	OOSPORE-S	OUTLEAP-S
MISLUCK-S	MOORHEN-S	MURGEON-S	NETSUKE-S	NUPTIAL-S	OPALINE-S	OUTLIER-S
MISMAKE-S	MOORILL-S	MURIATE-S	NETTING-S	NURSING-S	OPENING-S	OUTLINE-S
MISMATE-S	MOORING-S	MURLAIN-S	NETWORK-S	NURTURE-S	OPERAND-S	OUTLIVE-S
MISNAME-S	MOORLOG-S	MURRAIN-S	NEURINE-S	NUTCASE-S	OPERANT-S	OUTLOOK-S
MISPLAY-S	MOOTING-S	MURRION-S	NEURISM-S	NUTGALL-S	OPERATE-S	OUTMODE-S
MISRATE-S	MOPHEAD-S	MURTHER-S	NEURITE-S	NUTMEAL-S	OPHIURA-S	OUTMOVE-S
MISREAD-S	MORAINE-S	MUSCONE-S	NEUROMA-S	NUTTING-S	OPINION-S	OUTNAME-S
MISRULE-S	MORDANT-S	MUSETTE-S	NEURONE-S	NUTWOOD-S	OPORICE-S	OUTPACE-S
MISSEEM-S	MORDENT-S	MUSICAL-S	NEUSTON-S	NYLGHAU-S	OPOSSUM-S	OUTPART-S
MISSEND-S	MORELLO-S	MUSIMON-S	NEUTRAL-S	NYMPHET-S	OPPIDAN-S	OUTPEEP-S
MISSILE-S	MORICHE-S	MUSKONE-S	NEUTRON-S	OAKLING-S	OPPOSER-S	OUTPEER-S
MISSION-S	MORISCO-S	MUSKRAT-S	NEWSBOY-S	OARWEED-S	OPSONIN-S	OUTPLAY-S
MISSIVE-S	MORLING-S	MUSTANG-S	NIBBLER-S	OATCAKE-S	OPUNTIA-S	OUTPORT-S
MISSTEP-S	MORMAOR-S	MUSTARD-S	NIBLICK-S	OATMEAL-S	OPUSCLE-S	OUTPOST-S
MISSUIT-S	MORNING-S	MUTAGEN-S	NICTATE-S	OBELISE-S	ORALISM-S	OUTPOUR-S
MISTAKE-S	MOROCCO-S	MUZZLER-S	NIGELLA-S	OBELISK-S	ORARIAN-S	OUTPRAY-S
MISTELL-S	MORPHEW-S	MYALGIA-S	NIGGARD-S	OBELIZE-S	ORARION-S	OUTRACE-S
MISTERM-S	MORPHIA-S	MYALISM-S	NIGGLER-S	OBLIGEE-S	ORARIUM-S	OUTRAGE-S
MISTICO-S	MORRHUA-S	MYELOMA-S	NIGHTIE-S	OBLIGOR-S	ORATION-S	OUTRANK-S
MISTIME-S	MORRICE-S	MYLODON-S	NIHONGA-S	OBLIQUE-S	ORBITAL-S	OUTRATE-S
MISTING-S	MORRION-S	MYNHEER-S	NINEPIN-S	OBSCURE-S	ORBITER-S	OUTRIDE-S
MISTRAL-S	MORSURE-S	MYOGRAM-S	NIOBATE-S	OBSERVE-S	ORCHARD-S	OUTROAR-S
MISTUNE-S	MORTICE-S	MYOSOTE-S	NIOBITE-S	OBTRUDE-S	ORCINOL-S	OUTROOP-S
MISUSER-S	MORTISE-S	MYOTUBE-S	NIOBIUM-S	OBVERSE-S	ORDERER-S	OUTROOT-S
MISWEEN-S	MORWONG-S	MYRBANE-S	NIRVANA-S	OBVIATE-S	ORDINAL-S	OUTROPE-S
MISWEND-S	MOSHING-S	MYRINGA-S	NITERIE-S	OCARINA-S	ORDINAR-S	OUTSAIL-S
MISWORD-S	MOUCHER-S	MYRRHOL-S	NITHING-S	OCCIPUT-S	ORDINEE-S	OUTSELL-S
MISYOKE-S	MOUFLON-S	MYTHISE-S	NITRATE-S	OCCLUDE-S	OREGANO-S	OUTSHOT-S
MITOGEN-S	MOULAGE-S	MYTHISM-S	NITRIDE-S	OCEANID-S	OREWEED-S	OUTSIDE-S
MITZVAH-S	MOULDER-S	MYTHIST-S	NITRILE-S	OCTAGON-S	ORGANZA-S	OUTSIZE-S
MIXTION-S	MOUNTER-S	MYTHIZE-S	NITRITE-S	OCTAPLA-S	ORGIAST-S	OUTSOAR-S
MIXTURE-S	MOURNER-S	NAARTJE-S	NOBBLER-S	OCTETTE-S	ORIFICE-S	OUTSOLE-S
MIZMAZE-S	MOUSAKA-S	NACARAT-S	NOCTUID-S	OCTOPOD-S	ORIGAMI-S	OUTSPAN-S
MOBBING-S	MOUSING-S	NACELLE-S	NOCTULE-S	OCTUPLE-S	ORIGANE-S	OUTSTAY-S
MOBSTER-S	MOUSMEE-S	NACRITE-S	NOCTURN-S	OCULIST-S	OROPESA-S	OUTSTEP-S
MOCHELL-S	MOUTHER-S	NAGAPIE-S	NODDING-S	ODALISK-S	ORPHREY-S	OUTSWIM-S
MOCKAGE-S	MOVABLE-S	NAGMAAL-S	NOGGING-S	ODALLER-S	ORTOLAN-S	OUTTAKE-S
MOCKING-S	MOWBURN-S	NAILING-S	NOMARCH-S	ODDBALL-S	OSMIATE-S	OUTTALK-S
MODELER-S	MOZETTA-S	NAIVETE-S	NOMBRIL-S	ODDMENT-S	OSMUNDA-S	OUTTELL-S
MODELLO-S	MRIDANG-S	NAMASTE-S	NOMINAL-S	ODORANT-S	OSSELET-S	OUTTURN-S
MODICUM-S	MUCHELL-S	NANDINE-S	NOMINEE-S	ODYLISM-S	OSSETER-S	OUTVOTE-S
MODISTE-S	MUCIGEN-S	NANKEEN-S	NONAGON-S	ODYSSEY-S	OSSICLE-S	OUTWALK-S
MOELLON-S	MUDBATH-S	NAPHTHA-S	NONETTE-S	OENOMEL-S	OSTEOMA-S	OUTWARD-S
MOFETTE-S	MUDDLER-S	NARCEEN-S	NONETTO-S	OERSTED-S	OSTIOLE-S	OUTWEAR-S
MOIDORE-S	MUDFLAP-S	NARGILE-S	NONSUIT-S	OESTRUM-S	OTALGIA-S	OUTWEED-S
MOINEAU-S	MUDFLAT-S	NARRATE-S	NOONDAY-S	OFFBEAT-S	OTOCYST-S	OUTWEEP-S
MOISTEN-S	MUDHOLE-S	NARTJIE-S	NOONING-S	OFFENCE-S	OTOLITH-S	OUTWELL-S
MOITHER-S	MUDHOOK-S	NARWHAL-S	NORIMON-S	OFFENSE-S	OTTOMAN-S	OUTWICK-S
MOLERAT-S	MUDIRIA-S	NASHGAB-S	NORLAND-S	OFFEREE-S	OUABAIN-S	OUTWIND-S
MOLIMEN-S	MUDLARK-S	NATRIUM-S	NORTENA-S	OFFERER-S	OUAKARI-S	OUTWING-S
MOLINET-S	MUDPACK-S	NATURAL-S	NORTENO-S	OFFEROR-S	OULAKAN-S	OUTWORK-S
MOLLUSC-S	MUDSCOW-S	NAVARCH-S	NORTHER-S	OFFICER-S	OUSTITI-S	OUVRAGE-S
MOLLUSK-S	MUDWORT-S	NAVARHO-S	NORWARD-S	OFFLOAD-S	OUTBACK-S	OUVRIER-S
MONARCH-S	MUEDDIN-S	NAVARIN-S	NOSEBAG-S	OFFSCUM-S	OUTBRAG-S	OVATION-S
MONARDA-S	MUEZZIN-S	NAVETTE-S	NOSEGAY-S	OFFSIDE-S	OUTBURN-S	OVERACT-S
MONAXON-S	MUFFLER-S	NAYWARD-S	NOSTRIL-S	OFFTAKE-S	OUTCAST-S	OVERAGE-S
MONDAIN-S	MUGGING-S	NAYWORD-S	NOSTRUM-S	OILSKIN-S	OUTCOME-S	OVERALL-S
MONEYER-S	MUGSHOT-S	NEBBICH-S	NOTABLE-S	OKIMONO-S	OUTCROP-S	OVERAWE-S
MONGREL-S	MUGWORT-S	NECKING-S	NOTAEUM-S	OLDSTER-S	OUTDARE-S	OVERBID-S
MONIKER-S	MUGWUMP-S	NECKLET-S	NOTCHEL-S	OLEARIA-S	OUTDATE-S	OVERBUY-S
MONILIA-S	MUKHTAR-S	NECKTIE-S	NOTCHER-S	OLEFINE-S	OUTDOOR-S	OVERDYE-S
MONITOR-S	MULATTA-S	NECROSE-S	NOTELET-S	OLIGIST-S	OUTDURE-S	OVEREAT-S
MONOCLE-S	MULATTO-S	NEEDLER-S	NOTHING-S	OLIVINE-S	OUTEDGE-S	OVEREYE-S
MONOCOT-S	MULLEIN-S	NEEDLES-S	NOTITIA-S	OLOROSO-S	OUTFACE-S	OVERGET-S
MONOFIL-S	MULLION-S	NEGLECT-S	NOURICE-S	OLYCOOK-S	OUTFALL-S	OVERHIT-S
MONOMER-S	MULLOCK-S	NEGLIGE-S	NOURSLE-S	OLYKOEK-S	OUTFLOW-S	OVERJOY-S
MONOPOD-S	MULMULL-S	NEGROID-S	NOUSELL-S	OMICRON-S	OUTFOOT-S	OVERLAP-S
MONSOON-S	MULTURE-S	NELUMBO-S	NOVELLA-S	OMITTER-S	OUTGATE-S	OVERLAY-S

OVERLIE-S	PANDORE-S	PATELLA-S	PERCEPT-S	PIERAGE-S	PLAGIUM-S	POLARON-S
OVERMAN-S	PANDOUR-S	PATHWAY-S	PERCHER-S	PIERCER-S	PLAITER-S	POLECAT-S
OVERNET-S	PANDURA-S	PATIENT-S	PERDURE-S	PIERROT-S	PLANNER-S	POLEMIC-S
OVERPAY-S	PANGENE-S	PATRIAL-S	PEREGAL-S	PIETISM-S	PLANTER-S	POLENTA-S
OVERRED-S	PANGRAM-S	PATRICK-S	PEREIRA-S	PIETIST-S	PLASHET-S	POLITIC-S
OVERREN-S	PANICLE-S	PATRIOT-S	PERFECT-S	PIFFERO-S	PLASMID-S	POLLACK-S
OVERRUN-S	PANNAGE-S	PATROON-S	PERFORM-S	PIFFLER-S	PLASMIN-S	POLLARD-S
OVERSEA-S	PANNICK-S	PATTERN-S	PERFUME-S	PIGBOAT-S	PLASTER-S	POLLING-S
OVERSEE-S	PANNIER-S	PATULIN-S	PERFUSE-S	PIGFEED-S	PLASTIC-S	POLLOCK-S
OVERSET-S	PANNING-S	PAUSING-S	PERGOLA-S	PIGGING-S	PLASTID-S	POLLUTE-S
OVERSEW-S	PANOCHA-S	PAVIOUR-S	PERIAPT-S	PIGHTLE-S	PLATANE-S	POLOIST-S
OVERSOW-S	PANTHER-S	PAVLOVA-S	PERIDOT-S	PIGLING-S	PLATEAU-S	POLONIE-S
OVERTOP-S	PANTILE-S	PAXIUBA-S	PERIGEE-S	PIGMEAT-S	PLATINA-S	POLYGAM-S
OVERUSE-S	PANTINE-S	PAYBACK-S	PERIGON-S	PIGMENT-S	PLATING-S	POLYGON-S
OVICIDE-S	PANTING-S	PAYFONE-S	PERIOST-S	PIGSKIN-S	PLATOON-S	POLYMER-S
OVIDUCT-S	PANTLER-S	PAYMENT-S	PERIQUE-S	PIGSNEY-S	PLATTER-S	POLYNIA-S
OVULATE-S	PANTOUM-S	PAYROLL-S	PERIWIG-S	PIGTAIL-S	PLAUDIT-S	POLYNYA-S
OWRELAY-S	PAPERER-S	PAYSAGE-S	PERJURE-S	PIGWEED-S	PLAYBOY-S	POLYOMA-S
OXALATE-S	PAPILIO-S	PAYSLIP-S	PERLITE-S	PIKELET-S	PLAYLET-S	POLYPOD-S
OXAZINE-S	PAPOOSE-S	PEACHER-S	PERMUTE-S	PILCHER-S	PLAYPEN-S	POMATUM-S
OXBLOOD-S	PAPRIKA-S	PEACOCK-S	PERPEND-S	PILCORN-S	PLEADER-S	POMEROY-S
OXIDANT-S	PARABLE-S	PEAFOWL-S	PERPENT-S	PILCROW-S	PLEASER-S	POMFRET-S
OXIDASE-S	PARACME-S	PEARLER-S	PERRIER-S	PILGRIM-S	PLEATER-S	POMPANO-S
OXIDATE-S	PARAFLE-S	PEARLIN-S	PERSICO-S	PILLAGE-S	PLECTRE-S	POMPELO-S
OXIDISE-S	PARAGON-S	PEASANT-S	PERSIST-S	PILLING-S	PLEDGEE-S	POMPION-S
OXIDIZE-S	PARANYM-S	PEASCOD-S	PERSONA-S	PILLION-S	PLEDGER-S	POMPOON-S
OXONIUM-S	PARAPET-S	PECCAVI-S	PERTAIN-S	PILLOCK-S	PLEDGET-S	PONCEAU-S
OXYTONE-S	PARASOL-S	PECKING-S	PERTAKE-S	PILSNER-S	PLEDGOR-S	PONDAGE-S
OZONISE-S	PARATHA-S	PECTISE-S	PERTURB-S	PIMENTO-S	PLENIPO-S	PONIARD-S
OZONIZE-S	PARBOIL-S	PECTIZE-S	PERUSAL-S	PINBALL-S	PLENIST-S	PONTAGE-S
PABULUM-S	PARDALE-S	PECTOSE-S	PERUSER-S	PINCASE-S	PLEOPOD-S	PONTIFF-S
PACHISI-S	PARDNER-S	PEDDLER-S	PERVADE-S	PINCHER-S	PLEROMA-S	PONTILE-S
PACKAGE-S	PAREIRA-S	PEDICAB-S	PERVERT-S	PINDARI-S	PLEROME-S	PONTOON-S
PACKING-S	PARELLA-S	PEDICEL-S	PESAUNT-S	PINDOWN-S	PLESSOR-S	POOFTAH-S
PACKWAY-S	PARELLE-S	PEDICLE-S	PETCOCK-S	PINFOLD-S	PLEXURE-S	POOFTER-S
PACTION-S	PARFAIT-S	PEDRAIL-S	PETIOLE-S	PINGLER-S	PLICATE-S	POOGYEE-S
PADDING-S	PARGANA-S	PEDRERO-S	PETTING-S	PINGUIN-S	PLISKIE-S	POPADUM-S
PADDLER-S	PARISON-S	PEEKABO-S	PETUNIA-S	PINHEAD-S	PLODDER-S	POPCORN-S
PADDOCK-S	PARITOR-S	PEELING-S	PFENNIG-S	PINHOLE-S	PLONKER-S	POPEDOM-S
PADELLA-S	PARKING-S	PEERAGE-S	PHAEISM-S	PINKING-S	PLOSION-S	POPERIN-S
PADLOCK-S	PARKWAY-S	PEGGING-S	PHAETON-S	PINNACE-S	PLOSIVE-S	POPOVER-S
PAENULA-S	PARLOUR-S	PEISHWA-S	PHALLIN-S	PINNING-S	PLOTTER-S	POPULAR-S
PAEONIC-S	PAROLEE-S	PELICAN-S	PHANTOM-S	PINNOCK-S	PLOTTIE-S	PORIFER-S
PAGEANT-S	PARONYM-S	PELISSE-S	PHASMID-S	PINNULA-S	PLOUTER-S	PORRECT-S
PAGURID-S	PAROTID-S	PELLACH-S	PHEAZAR-S	PINNULE-S	PLOWTER-S	PORRIGO-S
PAILFUL-S	PARPANE-S	PELLACK-S	PHELLEM-S	PINOCLE-S	PLUCKER-S	PORTAGE-S
PAILLON-S	PARPEND-S	PELLOCK-S	PHENATE-S	PINTADO-S	PLUGGER-S	PORTEND-S
PAINTER-S	PARPENT-S	PELORIA-S	PHILTER-S	PINTAIL-S	PLUMAGE-S	PORTENT-S
PAIOCKE-S	PARQUET-S	PELTAST-S	PHILTRE-S	PIONEER-S	PLUMBER-S	PORTICO-S
PAIRIAL-S	PARROCK-S	PELTING-S	PHOBISM-S	PIONING-S	PLUMBUM-S	PORTION-S
PAIRING-S	PARSING-S	PEMICAN-S	PHOBIST-S	PIPEFUL-S	PLUMCOT-S	PORTRAY-S
PAISANO-S	PARSLEY-S	PENANCE-S	PHONATE-S	PIPETTE-S	PLUMIST-S	POSAUNE-S
PAISLEY-S	PARSNEP-S	PENDANT-S	PHONEME-S	PIRAGUA-S	PLUMMET-S	POSEUSE-S
PAJOCKE-S	PARSNIP-S	PENDENT-S	PHOTISM-S	PIRANHA-S	PLUMPEN-S	POSITON-S
PAKAPOO-S	PARTAKE-S	PENFOLD-S	PHRASER-S	PIROGUE-S	PLUMPER-S	POSTAGE-S
PAKFONG-S	PARTIAL-S	PENGUIN-S	PIAFFER-S	PISCINA-S	PLUMULE-S	POSTBAG-S
PAKTONG-S	PARTING-S	PENNANT-S	PIANINO-S	PISCINE-S	PLUNDER-S	POSTEEN-S
PALABRA-S	PARTITA-S	PENNINE-S	PIANISM-S	PISMIRE-S	PLUNGER-S	POSTERN-S
PALADIN-S	PARTLET-S	PENSION-S	PIANIST-S	PISSOIR-S	PLUNKER-S	POSTING-S
PALATAL-S	PARTNER-S	PENTACT-S	PIARIST-S	PISTOLE-S	PLUSAGE-S	POSTURE-S
PALAVER-S	PARTURE-S	PENTANE-S	PIASTRE-S	PITAPAT-S	PLUVIAL-S	POTABLE-S
PALETOT-S	PARVENU-S	PENTENE-S	PIBROCH-S	PITARAH-S	PLYWOOD-S	POTAGER-S
PALETTE-S	PARVISE-S	PENTHIA-S	PICADOR-S	PITCHER-S	POACHER-S	POTASSA-S
PALFREY-S	PASSADE-S	PENTICE-S	PICAMAR-S	PITFALL-S	POCHARD-S	POTCHER-S
PALLONE-S	PASSADO-S	PENTISE-S	PICCOLO-S	PITHEAD-S	POCHOIR-S	POTENCE-S
PALMFUL-S	PASSAGE-S	PENTODE-S	PICKAXE-S	PITPROP-S	POCKARD-S	POTHEEN-S
PALMIET-S	PASSATA-S	PENTOSE-S	PICKEER-S	PITTING-S	POCKPIT-S	POTHOLE-S
PALMIST-S	PASSING-S	PENUCHE-S	PICKING-S	PITTITE-S	PODAGRA-S	POTHOOK-S
PALMTOP-S	PASSION-S	PENUCHI-S	PICKLER-S	PITUITA-S	PODESTA-S	POTICHE-S
PALMYRA-S	PASSIVE-S	PEONAGE-S	PICKMAW-S	PITUITE-S	POETISE-S	POTOROO-S
PALOOKA-S	PASSKEY-S	PEONISM-S	PICOTEE-S	PIVOTER-S	POETIZE-S	POTSHOP-S
PALPATE-S	PASSOUT-S	PEPSINE-S	PICQUET-S	PLACARD-S	POINDER-S	POTTAGE-S
PAMPERO-S	PASTERN-S	PEPTIDE-S	PICRATE-S	PLACATE-S	POINTEL-S	POUFTAH-S
PANACEA-S	PASTIME-S	PEPTISE-S	PICRITE-S	PLACCAT-S	POINTER-S	POUFTER-S
PANACHE-S	PASTING-S	PEPTIZE-S	PICTURE-S	PLACEBO-S	POISSON-S	POULARD-S
PANCAKE-S	PASTURE-S	PEPTONE-S	PIDDLER-S	PLACING-S	POITREL-S	POULDER-S
PANDECT-S	PATAMAR-S	PERAEON-S	PIDDOCK-S	PLACKET-S	POKEFUL-S	POULDRE-S
PANDOOR-S	PATBALL-S	PERCALE-S	PIDGEON-S	PLAFOND-S	POLACCA-S	POULTER-S
PANDORA-S	PATCHER-S	PERCALE-S	PIEBALD-S	PLAFOND-S	POLACRE-S	POUNCET-S

POUNDAL-S	PRIMATE-S	PTYALIN-S	QUETZAL-S	RAPHIDE-S	REDBIRD-S	RENEGUE-S
POUNDER-S	PRIMERO-S	PUCCOON-S	QUEUING-S	RAPLOCH-S	REDCOAT-S	RENEWAL-S
POURING-S	PRIMEUR-S	PUCELLE-S	QUEYNIE-S	RAPPING-S	REDDING-S	RENEWER-S
POURSEW-S	PRIMINE-S	PUDDING-S	QUIBBLE-S	RAPPORT-S	REDHEAD-S	RENNING-S
POURSUE-S	PRIMING-S	PUDDLER-S	QUIBLIN-S	RAPTURE-S	REDNECK-S	RENTIER-S
POUSSIN-S	PRIMMER-S	PUDDOCK-S	QUICKEN-S	RAREBIT-S	REDOUBT-S	REORDER-S
POUTHER-S	PRIMULA-S	PUFFING-S	QUICKIE-S	RASCHEL-S	REDOUND-S	REPAINT-S
POUTING-S	PRINCES-S	PUGGING-S	QUIDDIT-S	RASPING-S	REDPOLL-S	REPAPER-S
PRABBLE-S	PRINTER-S	PUGGREE-S	QUIDDLE-S	RASTRUM-S	REDRAFT-S	REPINER-S
PRACTIC-S	PRISAGE-S	PULDRON-S	QUIESCE-S	RATAFIA-S	REDRIVE-S	REPIQUE-S
PRAETOR-S	PRIVADO-S	PULSATE-S	QUIETEN-S	RATCHET-S	REDROOT-S	REPLACE-S
PRAIRIE-S	PRIVATE-S	PULTOON-S	QUIETER-S	RATFINK-S	REDSKIN-S	REPLANT-S
PRAISER-S	PROBAND-S	PULTURE-S	QUILLAI-S	RATLINE-S	REDUCER-S	REPLETE-S
PRALINE-S	PROBANG-S	PUMPION-S	QUILLET-S	RATLING-S	REDWING-S	REPLICA-S
PRANCER-S	PROBATE-S	PUMPKIN-S	QUILLON-S	RATPACK-S	REDWOOD-S	REPLIER-S
PRANCKE-S	PROBLEM-S	PUNALUA-S	QUILTER-S	RATTEEN-S	REEDBED-S	REPOINT-S
PRANKLE-S	PROCEED-S	PUNCHER-S	QUINCHE-S	RATTING-S	REEDING-S	REPOSAL-S
PRATING-S	PROCTOR-S	PUNNING-S	QUININE-S	RATTLER-S	REEFING-S	REPOSIT-S
PRATTLE-S	PROCURE-S	PUNSTER-S	QUINNAT-S	RATTLIN-S	REELING-S	REPPING-S
PRAUNCE-S	PRODUCE-S	PUPUNHA-S	QUINOID-S	RAVAGER-S	REFEREE-S	REPRIME-S
PRAWLIN-S	PRODUCT-S	PURGING-S	QUINONE-S	RAVELIN-S	REFINER-S	REPRINT-S
PRAYING-S	PROFANE-S	PURITAN-S	QUINTAL-S	RAVENER-S	REFLATE-S	REPRISE-S
PREASSE-S	PROFFER-S	PURLIEU-S	QUINTET-S	RAVIOLI-S	REFLECT-S	REPRIVE-S
PRECEDE-S	PROFILE-S	PURLINE-S	QUITTAL-S	RAWHEAD-S	REFLOAT-S	REPRIZE-S
PRECEPT-S	PROGRAM-S	PURLING-S	QUITTER-S	RAWHIDE-S	REFOUND-S	REPROOF-S
PRECISE-S	PROJECT-S	PURLOIN-S	QUITTOR-S	REACHER-S	REFRACT-S	REPROVE-S
PRECOOK-S	PROLATE-S	PURPORT-S	QUIZZER-S	REACTOR-S	REFRAIN-S	REPRYVE-S
PRECOOL-S	PROLINE-S	PURPOSE-S	QUODLIN-S	READAPT-S	REFRAME-S	REPTILE-S
PREDATE-S	PROLLER-S	PURPURA-S	QUOITER-S	READING-S	REFUGEE-S	REPULSE-S
PREDAWN-S	PROLONG-S	PURPURE-S	RABANNA-S	READMIT-S	REFUSAL-S	REPUNIT-S
PREDIAL-S	PROMISE-S	PURRING-S	RABATTE-S	READOPT-S	REFUSER-S	REQUERE-S
PREDICT-S	PROMMER-S	PURSUAL-S	RABBLER-S	REAGENT-S	REFUTAL-S	REQUEST-S
PREDOOM-S	PROMOTE-S	PURSUER-S	RABBONI-S	REALGAR-S	REFUTER-S	REQUIEM-S
PREEMIE-S	PRONATE-S	PURSUIT-S	RACCOON-S	REALIGN-S	REGALIA-S	REQUIRE-S
PREFACE-S	PRONEUR-S	PURVIEW-S	RACEWAY-S	REALISE-S	REGATTA-S	REQUITE-S
PREFADE-S	PRONOUN-S	PUSHROD-S	RACKETT-S	REALISM-S	REGENCE-S	REQUOTE-S
PREFECT-S	PROOTIC-S	PUSTULE-S	RACKING-S	REALIST-S	REGIMEN-S	REROUTE-S
PREFORM-S	PROPAGE-S	PUTCHER-S	RACLOIR-S	REALIZE-S	REGORGE-S	RESCALE-S
PREHEAT-S	PROPALE-S	PUTCHUK-S	RACQUET-S	REALLIE-S	REGRADE-S	RESCIND-S
PREHEND-S	PROPANE-S	PUTLOCK-S	RADIANT-S	REALLOT-S	REGRANT-S	RESCORE-S
PRELATE-S	PROPEND-S	PUTTIER-S	RADIATA-S	REALTIE-S	REGRATE-S	RESCUER-S
PRELECT-S	PROPENE-S	PUTTING-S	RADIATE-S	REALTOR-S	REGREDE-S	RESEIZE-S
PRELUDE-S	PROPHET-S	PUTTOCK-S	RADICAL-S	REAMEND-S	REGREET-S	RESERVE-S
PREMIER-S	PROPINE-S	PUZZLER-S	RADICEL-S	REARISE-S	REGRIND-S	RESHAPE-S
PREMISE-S	PROPONE-S	PYAEMIA-S	RADICLE-S	REAWAKE-S	REGROUP-S	RESIANT-S
PREMIUM-S	PROPOSE-S	PYCNITE-S	RAFFLER-S	REBADGE-S	REGULAR-S	RESIDER-S
PREMOVE-S	PRORATE-S	PYEBALD-S	RAGBOLT-S	REBATER-S	REHOUSE-S	RESIDUE-S
PREPACK-S	PROSING-S	PYRALID-S	RAGGING-S	REBIRTH-S	REINTER-S	RESINER-S
PREPARE-S	PROSPER-S	PYRAMID-S	RAGHEAD-S	REBLOOM-S	REISSUE-S	RESKILL-S
PREPONE-S	PROTECT-S	PYREXIA-S	RAGMENT-S	REBOUND-S	REJOICE-S	RESOLVE-S
PREPOSE-S	PROTEGE-S	PYROGEN-S	RAGTIME-S	REBRACE-S	REJONEO-S	RESOUND-S
PREPUCE-S	PROTEID-S	PYRRHIC-S	RAGWEED-S	REBUILD-S	REJOURN-S	RESPEAK-S
PREQUEL-S	PROTEIN-S	PYRROLE-S	RAGWORK-S	REBUKER-S	REJUDGE-S	RESPECT-S
PRESAGE-S	PROTEND-S	PYTHIUM-S	RAGWORM-S	RECEIPT-S	RELACHE-S	RESPELL-S
PRESENT-S	PROTEST-S	QABALAH-S	RAGWORT-S	RECEIVE-S	RELAPSE-S	RESPIRE-S
PRESIDE-S	PROTHYL-S	QAWWALI-S	RAILBED-S	RECENSE-S	RELATER-S	RESPITE-S
PRESSER-S	PROTIST-S	QUACKER-S	RAILING-S	RECHART-S	RELATOR-S	RESPOND-S
PRESSIE-S	PROTIUM-S	QUACKLE-S	RAILWAY-S	RECHATE-S	RELAXIN-S	RESPRAY-S
PRESUME-S	PROTORE-S	QUADRAT-S	RAIMENT-S	RECHEAT-S	RELEASE-S	RESTAFF-S
PRETEND-S	PROTYLE-S	QUADRIC-S	RAINBOW-S	RECHECK-S	RELIEVE-S	RESTAGE-S
PRETEST-S	PROULER-S	QUAFFER-S	RAISING-S	RECITAL-S	RELIEVO-S	RESTART-S
PRETEXT-S	PROVAND-S	QUAHAUG-S	RALLIER-S	RECITER-S	RELIGHT-S	RESTATE-S
PRETZEL-S	PROVEND-S	QUAKING-S	RAMAKIN-S	RECLAIM-S	RELIQUE-S	RESTING-S
PREVAIL-S	PROVERB-S	QUANNET-S	RAMBLER-S	RECLAME-S	RELIVER-S	RESTOCK-S
PREVENE-S	PROVIDE-S	QUANTIC-S	RAMEKIN-S	RECLIMB-S	REMANET-S	RESTORE-S
PREVENT-S	PROVINE-S	QUARREL-S	RAMPAGE-S	RECLINE-S	REMANIE-S	RESTYLE-S
PREVERB-S	PROVING-S	QUARTAN-S	RAMPART-S	RECLOSE-S	REMBLAI-S	RESURGE-S
PREVIEW-S	PROVISO-S	QUARTER-S	RAMPICK-S	RECLUSE-S	REMERGE-S	RETABLE-S
PREVISE-S	PROVOKE-S	QUARTET-S	RAMPIKE-S	RECOUNT-S	REMNANT-S	RETAKER-S
PREWARM-S	PROVOST-S	QUARTIC-S	RAMPING-S	RECOURE-S	REMODEL-S	RETHINK-S
PREWARN-S	PROWLER-S	QUASHEE-S	RAMPION-S	RECOVER-S	REMORSE-S	RETICLE-S
PREZZIE-S	PRUNING-S	QUASHIE-S	RAMPIRE-S	RECOWER-S	REMOULD-S	RETINOL-S
PRIBBLE-S	PRURIGO-S	QUASSIA-S	RANCHER-S	RECOYLE-S	REMOUNT-S	RETINUE-S
PRICKER-S	PSALTER-S	QUAYAGE-S	RANCOUR-S	RECRUIT-S	REMOVAL-S	RETIRAL-S
PRICKET-S	PSCHENT-S	QUEENIE-S	RANGOLI-S	RECTION-S	REMOVER-S	RETIREE-S
PRICKLE-S	PSIONIC-S	QUELLER-S	RANKING-S	RECUILE-S	REMUAGE-S	RETIRER-S
PRIGGER-S	PSYCHIC-S	QUERIST-S	RANSACK-S	RECURVE-S	REMUEUR-S	RETITLE-S
PRIMAGE-S	PSYLLID-S	QUESTER-S	RANTING-S	RECYCLE-S	RENAGUE-S	RETRACE-S
	PTARMIC-S	QUESTOR-S	RAOULIA-S	REDBACK-S	RENEGER-S	RETRACT-S

RETRAIN-S	RISSOLE-S	ROWBOAT-S	SALIENT-S	SCALDER-S	SCRIEVE-S	SENATOR-S
RETRAIT-S	RIVERET-S	ROWLOCK-S	SALIGOT-S	SCALING-S	SCROOGE-S	SENDING-S
RETRATE-S	RIVETER-S	ROYALET-S	SALPIAN-S	SCALLOP-S	SCROTUM-S	SENECIO-S
RETREAD-S	RIVIERA-S	ROYSTER-S	SALTANT-S	SCALPEL-S	SCROUGE-S	SENSING-S
RETREAT-S	RIVIERE-S	ROZELLE-S	SALTATE-S	SCALPER-S	SCROWLE-S	SENSISM-S
RETRIAL-S	RIVULET-S	RUBBING-S	SALTCAT-S	SCAMBLE-S	SCROYLE-S	SENSIST-S
RETSINA-S	RIZZART-S	RUBDOWN-S	SALTERN-S	SCAMPER-S	SCRUPLE-S	SEPIOST-S
REUNION-S	ROADING-S	RUBELLA-S	SALTIER-S	SCANDAL-S	SCRYING-S	SEPPUKU-S
REUNITE-S	ROADWAY-S	RUBEOLA-S	SALTING-S	SCANNER-S	SCUCHIN-S	SEPTIME-S
REUTTER-S	ROAMING-S	RUBICON-S	SALTIRE-S	SCANTLE-S	SCUDDER-S	SEPTUOR-S
REVALUE-S	ROARING-S	RUCHING-S	SALUTER-S	SCAPPLE-S	SCUDDLE-S	SEQUENT-S
REVENGE-S	ROASTER-S	RUCTION-S	SALVAGE-S	SCAPULA-S	SCUDLER-S	SEQUOIA-S
REVENUE-S	ROBINIA-S	RUDDOCK-S	SALVETE-S	SCARLET-S	SCUFFLE-S	SERAFIN-S
REVERER-S	ROBOTIC-S	RUDERAL-S	SALVING-S	SCARPER-S	SCULLER-S	SERFAGE-S
REVERIE-S	ROBUSTA-S	RUELLIA-S	SAMADHI-S	SCATOLE-S	SCULPIN-S	SERFDOM-S
REVERSE-S	ROCKIER-S	RUFFIAN-S	SAMBUCA-S	SCATTER-S	SCUMBAG-S	SERIATE-S
REVERSI-S	ROCKING-S	RUFFLER-S	SAMISEN-S	SCAUPER-S	SCUMBER-S	SERICIN-S
REVERSO-S	ROCKLAY-S	RUFIYAA-S	SAMOVAR-S	SCAVAGE-S	SCUMBLE-S	SERICON-S
REVEUSE-S	ROCQUET-S	RUGGING-S	SAMPIRE-S	SCEDULE-S	SCUMMER-S	SERIEMA-S
REVILER-S	RODDING-S	RUINATE-S	SAMPLER-S	SCEPTER-S	SCUNNER-S	SERINGA-S
REVISAL-S	RODEWAY-S	RUINING-S	SAMSARA-S	SCEPTIC-S	SCUPPER-S	SERKALI-S
REVISER-S	RODSTER-S	RULLION-S	SAMSHOO-S	SCEPTRE-S	SCUTAGE-S	SERPENT-S
REVISIT-S	ROEBUCK-S	RULLOCK-S	SANCTUM-S	SCHANSE-S	SCUTTER-S	SERRATE-S
REVISOR-S	ROISTER-S	RUMBLER-S	SANDBAG-S	SCHANZE-S	SCUTTLE-S	SERUEWE-S
REVIVAL-S	ROKELAY-S	RUMMAGE-S	SANDBOY-S	SCHAPPE-S	SCYTALE-S	SERVANT-S
REVIVER-S	ROLFING-S	RUMPLES-S	SANDING-S	SCHEMER-S	SCYTHER-S	SERVEWE-S
REVIVOR-S	ROLLICK-S	RUNAWAY-S	SANDPIT-S	SCHERZO-S	SDEIGNE-S	SERVICE-S
REVOLVE-S	ROLLING-S	RUNBACK-S	SANGOMA-S	SCHISMA-S	SEABANK-S	SERVILE-S
REWEIGH-S	ROLLMOP-S	RUNDALE-S	SANGRIA-S	SCHLEPP-S	SEABIRD-S	SERVING-S
REWRITE-S	ROLLOCK-S	RUNDLET-S	SANICLE-S	SCHLICH-S	SEACOCK-S	SESSION-S
REYNARD-S	ROLLOUT-S	RUNDOWN-S	SANTOUR-S	SCHLOCK-S	SEAFOLK-S	SESTETT-S
RHABDOM-S	ROMAIKA-S	RUNNING-S	SAOUARI-S	SCHMECK-S	SEAFOOD-S	SESTINA-S
RHENIUM-S	ROMANCE-S	RUNNION-S	SAPAJOU-S	SCHMOCK-S	SEAFOWL-S	SESTINE-S
RHIZINE-S	ROMAUNT-S	RUPTURE-S	SAPHEAD-S	SCHMUCK-S	SEAGULL-S	SETBACK-S
RHIZOID-S	ROMNEYA-S	RUSALKA-S	SAPHENA-S	SCHNOOK-S	SEAHAWK-S	SETLINE-S
RHIZOME-S	RONDINO-S	RUSTING-S	SAPLING-S	SCHNORR-S	SEAKALE-S	SETTING-S
RHODIUM-S	RONDURE-S	RUSTLER-S	SAPONIN-S	SCHOLAR-S	SEALANT-S	SETTLER-S
RHODORA-S	RONTGEN-S	RUSTLES-S	SAPPHIC-S	SCHOOLE-S	SEALINE-S	SETTLOR-S
RHUBARB-S	ROOFING-S	RUTTING-S	SAPROBE-S	SCHTICK-S	SEALING-S	SETUALE-S
RHYMIST-S	ROOFTOP-S	RYBAULD-S	SAPSAGO-S	SCHTOOK-S	SEAMAID-S	SETWALL-S
RHYTINA-S	ROOINEK-S	RYEPECK-S	SAPWOOD-S	SCHTUCK-S	SEAMARK-S	SEVENTH-S
RIBBAND-S	ROOMFUL-S	SABATON-S	SARAFAN-S	SCIARID-S	SEAMSET-S	SEVERAL-S
RIBBING-S	ROOSTER-S	SABELLA-S	SARANGI-S	SCIENCE-S	SEAPORT-S	SEVRUGA-S
RIBCAGE-S	ROOTAGE-S	SABKHAH-S	SARCASM-S	SCISSEL-S	SEARING-S	SEXFOIL-S
RIBIBLE-S	ROOTING-S	SABKHAT-S	SARCODE-S	SCISSIL-S	SEASIDE-S	SEXPERT-S
RIBSTON-S	ROOTLES-S	SABREUR-S	SARCOID-S	SCISSOR-S	SEASURE-S	SEXTANT-S
RIBWORK-S	ROOTLET-S	SABURRA-S	SARCOMA-S	SCOFFER-S	SEATING-S	SEXTETT-S
RIBWORT-S	ROPEWAY-S	SACATON-S	SARDANA-S	SCOLDER-S	SEAWARD-S	SEXTILE-S
RICKSHA-S	RORQUAL-S	SACCADE-S	SARDINE-S	SCOLLOP-S	SEAWARE-S	SEXTUOR-S
RICOTTA-S	ROSACEA-S	SACCULE-S	SARKING-S	SCOOPER-S	SEAWEED-S	SEYSURE-S
RIDDLER-S	ROSAKER-S	SACKAGE-S	SARMENT-S	SCOOTER-S	SEAWORM-S	SFUMATO-S
RIDGING-S	ROSALIA-S	SACKBUT-S	SARSDEN-S	SCOPULA-S	SECEDER-S	SHABBLE-S
RIDOTTO-S	ROSEBAY-S	SACKFUL-S	SARSNET-S	SCORING-S	SECLUDE-S	SHACKLE-S
RIEMPIE-S	ROSEBUD-S	SACKING-S	SASHIMI-S	SCORNER-S	SECONDE-S	SHADING-S
RIFFLER-S	ROSEHIP-S	SACRING-S	SATCHEL-S	SCORPER-S	SECRETE-S	SHADOOF-S
RIFLING-S	ROSELLA-S	SACRIST-S	SATIATE-S	SCORSER-S	SECTION-S	SHAFTER-S
RIGGALD-S	ROSELLE-S	SADDLER-S	SATINET-S	SCOTOMA-S	SECULAR-S	SHAITAN-S
RIGGING-S	ROSEOLA-S	SADIRON-S	SATSUMA-S	SCOURER-S	SECULUM-S	SHAKING-S
RIGHTEN-S	ROSETTE-S	SAFFIAN-S	SATYRAL-S	SCOURGE-S	SECURER-S	SHAKUDO-S
RIGHTER-S	ROSIERE-S	SAFFRON-S	SATYRID-S	SCOURIE-S	SEDUCER-S	SHALLON-S
RIGLING-S	ROSOLIO-S	SAFROLE-S	SAUNTER-S	SCOURSE-S	SEEDBED-S	SHALLOP-S
RIMMING-S	ROSTRUM-S	SAGENES-S	SAURIAN-S	SCOUSER-S	SEEDING-S	SHALLOT-S
RINGBIT-S	ROTATOR-S	SAGGARD-S	SAUSAGE-S	SCOWDER-S	SEEDLIP-S	SHALLOW-S
RINGGIT-S	ROTCHIE-S	SAGGING-S	SAUTOIR-S	SCOWRER-S	SEELING-S	SHALWAR-S
RINGING-S	ROTIFER-S	SAGITTA-S	SAVANNA-S	SCOWRIE-S	SEEMING-S	SHAMBLE-S
RINGLET-S	ROTUNDA-S	SAGOUIN-S	SAVARIN-S	SCRAICH-S	SEEPAGE-S	SHAMMER-S
RINGWAY-S	ROUGHEN-S	SAGUARO-S	SAVELOY-S	SCRAIGH-S	SEETHER-S	SHAMPOO-S
RINSING-S	ROUGHER-S	SAHIBAH-S	SAVIOUR-S	SCRAPER-S	SEGMENT-S	SHANTEY-S
RIOTING-S	ROUGHIE-S	SAILING-S	SAWBILL-S	SCRAPIE-S	SEINING-S	SHAPING-S
RIOTISE-S	ROUILLE-S	SAIMIRI-S	SAWBUCK-S	SCRAUCH-S	SEIZING-S	SHARIAT-S
RIOTIZE-S	ROULADE-S	SAKERET-S	SAWDUST-S	SCRAUGH-S	SEIZURE-S	SHARING-S
RIPIENO-S	ROULEAU-S	SAKIYEH-S	SAWMILL-S	SCREEVE-S	SELFING-S	SHARKER-S
RIPOSTE-S	ROUMING-S	SAKSAUL-S	SAXHORN-S	SCREICH-S	SELFISM-S	SHARPEN-S
RIPPIER-S	ROUNDEL-S	SALAMON-S	SAZERAC-S	SCREIGH-S	SELFIST-S	SHARPER-S
RIPPLER-S	ROUNDER-S	SALBAND-S	SCABBLE-S	SCREWER-S	SELTZER-S	SHARPIE-S
RIPPLET-S	ROUNDLE-S	SALCHOW-S	SCAFFIE-S	SCRIBER-S	SELVAGE-S	SHASTER-S
RIPTIDE-S	ROUSTER-S	SALFERN-S	SCAGLIA-S	SCRIECH-S	SEMINAR-S	SHASTRA-S
RISOTTO-S	ROUTINE-S	SALICET-S	SCALADE-S	SCRIECH-S	SEMIPED-S	SHATTER-S
RISPING-S	ROUTING-S	SALICIN-S	SCALADO-S	SCRIENE-S	SEMITAR-S	SHAVING-S

SHAWLEY-S	SIDEBAR-S	SKUTTLE-S	SNICKET-S	SOUROCK-S	SPOOLER-S	STEAMIE-S
SHAWLIE-S	SIDECAR-S	SKYHOOK-S	SNIFFER-S	SOURSOP-S	SPOONEY-S	STEARIN-S
SHEARER-S	SIEVERT-S	SKYJACK-S	SNIFFLE-S	SOUSING-S	SPOORER-S	STEEPEN-S
SHEATHE-S	SIFTING-S	SKYLARK-S	SNIFTER-S	SOUSLIK-S	SPORRAN-S	STEEPER-S
SHEBANG-S	SIGHTER-S	SKYLINE-S	SNIGGER-S	SOUTANE-S	SPORTER-S	STEEPLE-S
SHEDDER-S	SIGMATE-S	SKYSAIL-S	SNIGGLE-S	SOUTHER-S	SPORULE-S	STEERER-S
SHEHITA-S	SIGNAGE-S	SKYWARD-S	SNIPPER-S	SOWBACK-S	SPOTTER-S	STEMBOK-S
SHEIKHA-S	SIGNING-S	SLABBER-S	SNIPPET-S	SPACING-S	SPOUSAL-S	STEMLET-S
SHELLAC-S	SIGNIOR-S	SLACKEN-S	SNIRTLE-S	SPADGER-S	SPOUTER-S	STEMMER-S
SHELLER-S	SIGNORE-S	SLACKER-S	SNOOKER-S	SPAIRGE-S	SPRAINT-S	STEMPEL-S
SHELTER-S	SILENCE-S	SLADANG-S	SNOOPER-S	SPAMMER-S	SPRAYER-S	STEMPLE-S
SHELTIE-S	SILESIA-S	SLAMMER-S	SNOOZER-S	SPANCEL-S	SPREAGH-S	STEMSON-S
SHERBET-S	SILICLE-S	SLANDER-S	SNOOZLE-S	SPANGLE-S	SPREAZE-S	STENCIL-S
SHEREEF-S	SILICON-S	SLANGER-S	SNORING-S	SPANIEL-S	SPREDDE-S	STENGAH-S
SHERIAT-S	SILIQUA-S	SLAPPER-S	SNORKEL-S	SPANKER-S	SPREEZE-S	STENTOR-S
SHERIFF-S	SILIQUE-S	SLASHER-S	SNORTER-S	SPANNER-S	SPRIGHT-S	STEPNEY-S
SHIATSU-S	SILLOCK-S	SLATHER-S	SNOTTER-S	SPARGER-S	SPRINGE-S	STEPPER-S
SHIATZU-S	SILURID-S	SLATING-S	SNOTTIE-S	SPARKIE-S	SPULYIE-S	STEPSON-S
SHICKER-S	SIMARRE-S	SLATTER-S	SNOWCAP-S	SPARKLE-S	SPULZIE-S	STERLET-S
SHICKSA-S	SIMILOR-S	SLEDGER-S	SNUBBER-S	SPAROID-S	SPUNKIE-S	STERNUM-S
SHIDDER-S	SIMITAR-S	SLEEKEN-S	SNUFFER-S	SPARRER-S	SPURNER-S	STEROID-S
SHIFTER-S	SIMPKIN-S	SLEEKER-S	SNUFFLE-S	SPARROW-S	SPURRER-S	STEWARD-S
SHIKARI-S	SIMPLER-S	SLEEPER-S	SNUGGLE-S	SPARTAN-S	SPURREY-S	STEWING-S
SHIMAAL-S	SIMULAR-S	SLEEVER-S	SNUZZLE-S	SPARTHE-S	SPURTLE-S	STEWPAN-S
SHIMMER-S	SIMURGH-S	SLEIGHT-S	SOAKAGE-S	SPASTIC-S	SPURWAY-S	STEWPOT-S
SHIMMEY-S	SINDING-S	SLENTER-S	SOAKING-S	SPATTEE-S	SPUTNIK-S	STIBBLE-S
SHINDIG-S	SINGING-S	SLICING-S	SOARING-S	SPATTER-S	SPUTTER-S	STIBINE-S
SHINGLE-S	SINGLET-S	SLICKEN-S	SOBBING-S	SPATULA-S	SPYHOLE-S	STIBIUM-S
SHIPFUL-S	SINGULT-S	SLICKER-S	SOCAGER-S	SPATULE-S	SQUACCO-S	STICKER-S
SHIPLAP-S	SINKAGE-S	SLIDDER-S	SOCCAGE-S	SPAWNER-S	SQUALOR-S	STICKLE-S
SHIPPEN-S	SINKING-S	SLIDING-S	SOCIATE-S	SPEAKER-S	SQUARER-S	STIDDIE-S
SHIPPER-S	SINOPIA-S	SLIMMER-S	SOCKEYE-S	SPECIAL-S	SQUEEZE-S	STIFFEN-S
SHIPPON-S	SIRGANG-S	SLINGER-S	SOGGING-S	SPECKLE-S	SQUIDGE-S	STIFFIE-S
SHIPWAY-S	SIRLOIN-S	SLINKER-S	SOILAGE-S	SPECTER-S	SQUILLA-S	STIFLER-S
SHIRKER-S	SIRNAME-S	SLINTER-S	SOILING-S	SPECTRE-S	SQUIRES-S	STILLER-S
SHITTAH-S	SIROCCO-S	SLIPPER-S	SOILURE-S	SPEEDER-S	SRADDHA-S	STILTER-S
SHITTIM-S	SITFAST-S	SLIPWAY-S	SOJOURN-S	SPEELER-S	STABBER-S	STINGER-S
SHMOOSE-S	SITTING-S	SLITHER-S	SOLANUM-S	SPELDER-S	STABILE-S	STINKER-S
SHMOOZE-S	SITUATE-S	SLITTER-S	SOLDADO-S	SPELDIN-S	STABLER-S	STINTER-S
SHOCKER-S	SIXAINE-S	SLOBBER-S	SOLDIER-S	SPELLER-S	STACKER-S	STIPEND-S
SHOEING-S	SIXTEEN-S	SLOCKEN-S	SOLFEGE-S	SPELTER-S	STACKET-S	STIPPLE-S
SHOGGLE-S	SIZEISM-S	SLOGGER-S	SOLICIT-S	SPENCER-S	STADDLE-S	STIPULE-S
SHONEEN-S	SIZEIST-S	SLOTTER-S	SOLIDUM-S	SPENDER-S	STADIAL-S	STIRRAH-S
SHOOGIE-S	SIZZLER-S	SLOWING-S	SOLIPED-S	SPERTHE-S	STADIUM-S	STIRRER-S
SHOOGLE-S	SJAMBOK-S	SLUBBER-S	SOLITON-S	SPHAERE-S	STAFFER-S	STIRRUP-S
SHOOTER-S	SKATING-S	SLUGGER-S	SOLOIST-S	SPHEARE-S	STAGGER-S	STISHIE-S
SHOPFUL-S	SKATOLE-S	SLUMBER-S	SOLVATE-S	SPHERIC-S	STAGING-S	STOCKER-S
SHOPHAR-S	SKEETER-S	SLUMMER-S	SOLVENT-S	SPICULE-S	STAINER-S	STODGER-S
SHOPPER-S	SKEGGER-S	SLURPER-S	SOMEONE-S	SPIELER-S	STAITHE-S	STOITER-S
SHORING-S	SKELDER-S	SMACKER-S	SOMEWAY-S	SPIGNEL-S	STALKER-S	STOLLEN-S
SHORTEN-S	SKELLIE-S	SMARAGD-S	SONANCE-S	SPILING-S	STAMINA-S	STOMACH-S
SHORTIE-S	SKELLUM-S	SMARTEN-S	SONDAGE-S	SPILITE-S	STAMMEL-S	STOMPER-S
SHOTGUN-S	SKELTER-S	SMARTIE-S	SONDELI-S	SPILLER-S	STAMMER-S	STONING-S
SHOTPUT-S	SKEPFUL-S	SMASHER-S	SONSHIP-S	SPINAGE-S	STAMPER-S	STONKER-S
SHOTTLE-S	SKEPTIC-S	SMATTER-S	SOOPING-S	SPINDLE-S	STANDEE-S	STOOKER-S
SHOUTER-S	SKIDDER-S	SMEDDUM-S	SOOTHER-S	SPINNER-S	STANDER-S	STOOLIE-S
SHOWGHE-S	SKIDPAN-S	SMELLER-S	SOPHISM-S	SPINNET-S	STANIEL-S	STOOPER-S
SHOWING-S	SKIFFLE-S	SMELTER-S	SOPHIST-S	SPINNEY-S	STANNEL-S	STOPGAP-S
SHRIEVE-S	SKILLET-S	SMICKER-S	SOPPING-S	SPINODE-S	STANYEL-S	STOPING-S
SHRIGHT-S	SKIMMER-S	SMICKET-S	SOPRANO-S	SPINOUT-S	STAPLER-S	STOPOFF-S
SHRIVEL-S	SKIMMIA-S	SMIDGEN-S	SORBATE-S	SPINULE-S	STAPPLE-S	STOPPER-S
SHRIVER-S	SKINFUL-S	SMIDGIN-S	SORBENT-S	SPIRAEA-S	STARDOM-S	STOPPLE-S
SHTETEL-S	SKINKER-S	SMILING-S	SORBITE-S	SPIRANT-S	STARING-S	STORAGE-S
SHUCKER-S	SKINNER-S	SMOKING-S	SOREHON-S	SPIREME-S	STARKEN-S	STOTTER-S
SHUDDER-S	SKIPPER-S	SMOLDER-S	SORGHUM-S	SPIRTLE-S	STARKER-S	STOUTEN-S
SHUFFLE-S	SKIPPET-S	SMOTHER-S	SORNING-S	SPITTER-S	STARLET-S	STOVING-S
SHUNNER-S	SKIRRET-S	SMOUSER-S	SOROBAN-S	SPITTLE-S	STARNIE-S	STOWAGE-S
SHUNTER-S	SKIRTER-S	SMUDGER-S	SORTING-S	SPLICER-S	STARTER-S	STOWING-S
SHUTTER-S	SKITTER-S	SMUGGLE-S	SOSSING-S	SPLODGE-S	STARTLE-S	STRAINT-S
SHUTTLE-S	SKITTLE-S	SMYTRIE-S	SOTTING-S	SPLURGE-S	STASHIE-S	STRAYER-S
SHYSTER-S	SKIVING-S	SNABBLE-S	SOUBISE-S	SPODIUM-S	STATICE-S	STREWER-S
SIAMANG-S	SKOLLIE-S	SNAFFLE-S	SOUFFLE-S	SPOILER-S	STATION-S	STRIATE-S
SIAMESE-S	SKREIGH-S	SNAPPER-S	SOULDAN-S	SPONDEE-S	STATISM-S	STRIDOR-S
SIAMEZE-S	SKRIECH-S	SNARING-S	SOUMING-S	SPONDYL-S	STATIST-S	STRIGIL-S
SIBLING-S	SKRIEGH-S	SNARLER-S	SOUNDER-S	SPONGER-S	STATURE-S	STRIKER-S
SIBSHIP-S	SKUDLER-S	SNEAKER-S	SOUPCON-S	SPONGIN-S	STATUTE-S	STRIVER-S
SICKBED-S	SKULKER-S	SNEERER-S	SOURING-S	SPONSON-S	STEALER-S	STRODLE-S
SIDEARM-S	SKULPIN-S	SNEEZER-S		SPONSOR-S	STEALTH-S	STROKER-S
	SKUMMER-S	SNICKER-S		SPOOFER-S	STEAMER-S	STROOKE-S

STROPHE-S	SULFATE-S	SWEETIE-S	TALIPED-S	TEMPERA-S	THYLOSE-S	TOPLINE-S
STROWER-S	SULFIDE-S	SWELLER-S	TALIPOT-S	TEMPEST-S	THYMINE-S	TOPMAST-S
STRUDEL-S	SULFITE-S	SWELTER-S	TALKING-S	TEMPLAR-S	THYROID-S	TOPONYM-S
STUBBLE-S	SULFONE-S	SWERVER-S	TALLAGE-S	TEMPLET-S	TICKING-S	TOPPING-S
STUDDLE-S	SULLAGE-S	SWIDDEN-S	TALLBOY-S	TEMPTER-S	TICKLER-S	TOPSAIL-S
STUDENT-S	SULPHUR-S	SWIFTER-S	TALLENT-S	TEMPURA-S	TIDDLER-S	TOPSIDE-S
STUDIER-S	SULTANA-S	SWIGGER-S	TALLIER-S	TENDRIL-S	TIDDLEY-S	TOPSOIL-S
STUFFER-S	SUMATRA-S	SWILLER-S	TALLITH-S	TENDRON-S	TIDEWAY-S	TOPSPIN-S
STUMBLE-S	SUMMAND-S	SWIMMER-S	TALOOKA-S	TENONER-S	TIEBACK-S	TORCHER-S
STUMMEL-S	SUMMATE-S	SWINDGE-S	TAMANDU-S	TENSION-S	TIERCEL-S	TORCHON-S
STUMPER-S	SUMMING-S	SWINDLE-S	TAMARAO-S	TENTAGE-S	TIERCET-S	TORDION-S
STUNNER-S	SUMMIST-S	SWINGER-S	TAMARAU-S	TENTFUL-S	TIETACK-S	TORGOCH-S
STURMER-S	SUMPTER-S	SWINGLE-S	TAMARIN-S	TENTIGO-S	TIFFING-S	TORMENT-S
STUSHIE-S	SUNBAKE-S	SWIPPLE-S	TAMASHA-S	TENTING-S	TIGHTEN-S	TORNADE-S
STUTTER-S	SUNBATH-S	SWISHER-S	TAMBOUR-S	TEQUILA-S	TILAPIA-S	TORNADO-S
STYLISE-S	SUNBEAM-S	SWITHER-S	TAMBURA-S	TERBIUM-S	TILLAGE-S	TORPEDO-S
STYLIST-S	SUNBELT-S	SWIZZLE-S	TAMPING-S	TEREBRA-S	TILLING-S	TORRENT-S
STYLITE-S	SUNBIRD-S	SWOBBER-S	TAMPION-S	TERGITE-S	TILLITE-S	TORSADE-S
STYLIZE-S	SUNBURN-S	SWOPPER-S	TANADAR-S	TERMITE-S	TILTING-S	TORSION-S
STYLOID-S	SUNDARI-S	SWORDER-S	TANAGER-S	TERNION-S	TIMARAU-S	TORTONI-S
STYPTIC-S	SUNDECK-S	SWOTTER-S	TANAGRA-S	TERPENE-S	TIMBALE-S	TORTURE-S
STYRENE-S	SUNDIAL-S	SWOZZLE-S	TANBARK-S	TERRACE-S	TIMBREL-S	TORULIN-S
SUASION-S	SUNDOWN-S	SYENITE-S	TANDOOR-S	TERRAIN-S	TINAMOU-S	TOSHACH-S
SUBADAR-S	SUNGLOW-S	SYLPHID-S	TANGELO-S	TERRANE-S	TINCHEL-S	TOSSING-S
SUBAREA-S	SUNLAMP-S	SYLVINE-S	TANGENT-S	TERREEN-S	TINFOIL-S	TOSSPOT-S
SUBATOM-S	SUNRISE-S	SYLVITE-S	TANGHIN-S	TERRENE-S	TINGLER-S	TOSTADA-S
SUBBASE-S	SUNROOF-S	SYMBION-S	TANGLER-S	TERRIER-S	TINHORN-S	TOTIENT-S
SUBBING-S	SUNSPOT-S	SYMBOLE-S	TANGRAM-S	TERRINE-S	TINKLER-S	TOTTING-S
SUBDEAN-S	SUNSUIT-S	SYMITAR-S	TANIWHA-S	TERSION-S	TINNING-S	TOUCHER-S
SUBDUAL-S	SUNTRAP-S	SYMPTOM-S	TANKAGE-S	TERTIAL-S	TINTACK-S	TOUGHEN-S
SUBDUCE-S	SUNWARD-S	SYNAPSE-S	TANKARD-S	TERTIAN-S	TINTING-S	TOUGHIE-S
SUBDUCT-S	SUPPAWN-S	SYNAPTE-S	TANKFUL-S	TESTERN-S	TINTYPE-S	TOURACO-S
SUBDUER-S	SUPPORT-S	SYNCARP-S	TANKING-S	TESTING-S	TINWARE-S	TOURING-S
SUBEDAR-S	SUPPOSE-S	SYNCHRO-S	TANLING-S	TESTOON-S	TIPPING-S	TOURISM-S
SUBEDIT-S	SUPREME-S	SYNCOPE-S	TANNAGE-S	TESTRIL-S	TIPPLER-S	TOURIST-S
SUBERIN-S	SUPREMO-S	SYNDING-S	TANNATE-S	TESTUDO-S	TIPSTER-S	TOURNEY-S
SUBFUSC-S	SURAMIN-S	SYNFUEL-S	TANNING-S	TETANIC-S	TIRASSE-S	TOUSING-S
SUBFUSK-S	SURANCE-S	SYNODAL-S	TANTARA-S	TETRACT-S	TITHING-S	TOWBOAT-S
SUBGOAL-S	SURBASE-S	SYNONYM-S	TANTRUM-S	TETRODE-S	TITLARK-S	TOWLINE-S
SUBHEAD-S	SURBATE-S	SYNOVIA-S	TANYARD-S	TEUCHAT-S	TITLING-S	TOWMOND-S
SUBJECT-S	SURCOAT-S	SYNTAGM-S	TAPERER-S	TEXTILE-S	TITRATE-S	TOWMONT-S
SUBJOIN-S	SURFACE-S	SYNTHON-S	TAPIOCA-S	TEXTURE-S	TITULAR-S	TOWPATH-S
SUBLATE-S	SURFEIT-S	SYRINGA-S	TAPPICE-S	THALWEG-S	TOASTER-S	TOWROPE-S
SUBLIME-S	SURFING-S	SYRINGE-S	TAPPING-S	THANAGE-S	TOASTIE-S	TOXEMIA-S
SUBPLOT-S	SURGEON-S	SYRPHID-S	TAPROOM-S	THANKER-S	TOBACCO-S	TOYSHOP-S
SUBRING-S	SURGING-S	SYSTOLE-S	TAPROOT-S	THANNAH-S	TOCCATA-S	TRACING-S
SUBSERE-S	SURLOIN-S	SYSTYLE-S	TAPSTER-S	THAWING-S	TODDLER-S	TRACKER-S
SUBSIDE-S	SURMISE-S	TABANID-S	TARRIER-S	THEATER-S	TOECLIP-S	TRACTOR-S
SUBSIST-S	SURNAME-S	TABARET-S	TARRING-S	THEATRE-S	TOEHOLD-S	TRADING-S
SUBSOIL-S	SURTOUT-S	TABETIC-S	TARROCK-S	THEORBO-S	TOENAIL-S	TRADUCE-S
SUBSONG-S	SURVEWE-S	TABINET-S	TARSIER-S	THEOREM-S	TOHEROA-S	TRAFFIC-S
SUBSUME-S	SURVIEW-S	TABLIER-S	TARTANA-S	THEORIC-S	TOHUNGA-S	TRAGULE-S
SUBTACK-S	SURVIVE-S	TABLING-S	TARTANE-S	THERIAC-S	TOILING-S	TRAILER-S
SUBTEEN-S	SUSPECT-S	TABLOID-S	TARTARE-S	THERIAN-S	TOISECH-S	TRAINEE-S
SUBTEND-S	SUSPEND-S	TABORER-S	TARTINE-S	THERMAL-S	TOKAMAK-S	TRAINER-S
SUBTEXT-S	SUSPIRE-S	TABORET-S	TARTLET-S	THIAMIN-S	TOLLAGE-S	TRAIPSE-S
SUBTYPE-S	SUSTAIN-S	TABORIN-S	TARWEED-S	THICKEN-S	TOLLING-S	TRAITOR-S
SUBUNIT-S	SWABBER-S	TABRERE-S	TASKING-S	THICKET-S	TOLUATE-S	TRAJECT-S
SUBVERT-S	SWADDLE-S	TACHISM-S	TASSELL-S	THIGGER-S	TOLUENE-S	TRAMCAR-S
SUBZONE-S	SWAGGER-S	TACHIST-S	TASTING-S	THILLER-S	TOMBOLA-S	TRAMMEL-S
SUCCADE-S	SWAGGIE-S	TACHYON-S	TATOUAY-S	THIMBLE-S	TOMBOLO-S	TRAMPER-S
SUCCEED-S	SWALING-S	TACKING-S	TATTING-S	THINKER-S	TOMFOOL-S	TRAMPET-S
SUCCOUR-S	SWALLET-S	TACKLER-S	TATTLER-S	THINNER-S	TOMPION-S	TRAMPLE-S
SUCCUBA-S	SWALLOW-S	TACTION-S	TAUNTER-S	THISTLE-S	TONDINO-S	TRAMWAY-S
SUCCUMB-S	SWAMPER-S	TACTISM-S	TAURINE-S	THORITE-S	TONEPAD-S	TRANCHE-S
SUCKING-S	SWANKER-S	TADPOLE-S	TAVERNA-S	THORIUM-S	TONIGHT-S	TRANECT-S
SUCKLER-S	SWANKEY-S	TAEDIUM-S	TAXICAB-S	THOUGHT-S	TONNAGE-S	TRANGAM-S
SUCRASE-S	SWANKIE-S	TAFFETA-S	TAXIWAY-S	THREAVE-S	TONNEAU-S	TRANGLE-S
SUCRIER-S	SWAPPER-S	TAGGING-S	TEACHER-S	THRIMSA-S	TONNELL-S	TRANKUM-S
SUCROSE-S	SWARMER-S	TAGMEME-S	TEAMING-S	THRIVER-S	TONSURE-S	TRANNIE-S
SUCTION-S	SWASHER-S	TAILARD-S	TEASING-S	THROWER-S	TONTINE-S	TRANSIT-S
SUFFETE-S	SWATTER-S	TAILING-S	TEATIME-S	THRUWAY-S	TOOLBAG-S	TRANSOM-S
SUFFICE-S	SWAYING-S	TAILLES-S	TECHNIC-S	THRYMSA-S	TOOLBAR-S	TRANTER-S
SUFFUSE-S	SWAZZLE-S	TAILLIE-S	TEKTITE-S	THUGGEE-S	TOOLING-S	TRAPEZE-S
SUGGEST-S	SWEARER-S	TAILZIE-S	TELECOM-S	THULITE-S	TOOLKIT-S	TRAPPER-S
SUGGING-S	SWEATER-S	TAKEOUT-S	TELEOST-S	THULIUM-S	TOOTSIE-S	TRAVAIL-S
SUICIDE-S	SWEENEY-S	TALAUNT-S	TELLING-S	THUMPER-S	TOPARCH-S	TRAWLER-S
SUIDIAN-S	SWEEPER-S	TALAYOT-S	TELPHER-S	THUNDER-S	TOPCOAT-S	TRAYBIT-S
SUITING-S	SWEETEN-S	TALIPAT-S	TEMBLOR-S	THWAITE-S	TOPKNOT-S	TRAYFUL-S

TREACLE-S	TROUBLE-S	TWANKAY-S	UNITION-S	UPGRADE-S	VAQUERO-S	VILLAIN-S
TREADER-S	TROUNCE-S	TWASOME-S	UNITISE-S	UPHEAVE-S	VAREUSE-S	VILLEIN-S
TREADLE-S	TROUPER-S	TWATTLE-S	UNITIZE-S	UPHOARD-S	VARIANT-S	VINASSE-S
TREAGUE-S	TROUSER-S	TWEEDLE-S	UNJOINT-S	UPHOIST-S	VARIATE-S	VINEGAR-S
TREASON-S	TROUTER-S	TWEETER-S	UNKNOWN-S	UPHOORD-S	VARIOLA-S	VINTAGE-S
TREATER-S	TRUCAGE-S	TWELFTH-S	UNLEARN-S	UPMAKER-S	VARIOLE-S	VINTNER-S
TREDDLE-S	TRUCKER-S	TWIBILL-S	UNLOOSE-S	UPRAISE-S	VARMENT-S	VIOLATE-S
TREETOP-S	TRUCKIE-S	TWIDDLE-S	UNMOULD-S	UPRIGHT-S	VARMINT-S	VIOLENT-S
TREFOIL-S	TRUCKLE-S	TWIGGER-S	UNMOUNT-S	UPRISAL-S	VARYING-S	VIOLIST-S
TREHALA-S	TRUDGEN-S	TWIGLOO-S	UNNERVE-S	UPROUSE-S	VASSAIL-S	VIOLONE-S
TREILLE-S	TRUDGER-S	TWINING-S	UNNOBLE-S	UPSHOOT-S	VAULTER-S	VIRANDA-S
TREKKER-S	TRUFFLE-S	TWINKLE-S	UNORDER-S	UPSILON-S	VAUNTER-S	VIRANDO-S
TREMBLE-S	TRUMPET-S	TWINSET-S	UNPAINT-S	UPSPEAK-S	VAURIEN-S	VIRELAY-S
TREMOLO-S	TRUNDLE-S	TWINTER-S	UNPANEL-S	UPSPEAR-S	VEDALIA-S	VIRETOT-S
TRENAIL-S	TRUSSER-S	TWIRLER-S	UNPAPER-S	UPSTAGE-S	VEDETTE-S	VIRGATE-S
TRENISE-S	TRUSTEE-S	TWISCAR-S	UNPLACE-S	UPSTAIR-S	VEERING-S	VIRGULE-S
TRENTAL-S	TRUSTER-S	TWISTER-S	UNPLAIT-S	UPSTAND-S	VEGETAL-S	VISCOSE-S
TREPANG-S	TRYPSIN-S	TWISTOR-S	UNPLUMB-S	UPSTARE-S	VEHICLE-S	VISIBLE-S
TRESSEL-S	TRYSAIL-S	TWITTEN-S	UNPLUME-S	UPSTART-S	VEILING-S	VISITEE-S
TRESTLE-S	TRYSTER-S	TWITTER-S	UNPURSE-S	UPSURGE-S	VEINING-S	VISITER-S
TREYBIT-S	TSADDIK-S	TWIZZLE-S	UNQUEEN-S	UPSWARM-S	VEINLET-S	VISITOR-S
TRIARCH-S	TSADDIQ-S	TWOCCER-S	UNQUIET-S	UPSWEEP-S	VELIGER-S	VITAMIN-S
TRIATIC-S	TSARDOM-S	TWOSOME-S	UNQUOTE-S	UPSWELL-S	VELOUTE-S	VITIATE-S
TRIAXON-S	TSARINA-S	TYCHISM-S	UNRAVEL-S	UPSWING-S	VENATOR-S	VITRAGE-S
TRIBADE-S	TSARISM-S	TYLOPOD-S	UNREAVE-S	UPTHROW-S	VENDACE-S	VITRAIN-S
TRIBBLE-S	TSARIST-S	TYPHOID-S	UNREEVE-S	UPTRAIN-S	VENDAGE-S	VITREUM-S
TRIBLET-S	TSIGANE-S	TYPHOON-S	UNRIGHT-S	UPTREND-S	VENERER-S	VITRINE-S
TRIBUNE-S	TSUNAMI-S	TYRANNE-S	UNRIVET-S	UPVALUE-S	VENISON-S	VITRIOL-S
TRIBUTE-S	TUATARA-S	TZADDIK-S	UNROOST-S	UPWHIRL-S	VENTAGE-S	VIVERRA-S
TRICKER-S	TUBBING-S	TZADDIQ-S	UNROUND-S	URAEMIA-S	VENTAIL-S	VOCABLE-S
TRICKLE-S	TUBEFUL-S	UDALLER-S	UNSAINT-S	URALITE-S	VENTANA-S	VOCODER-S
TRICORN-S	TUBFAST-S	UKELELE-S	UNSCALE-S	URANIDE-S	VENTIGE-S	VOGUING-S
TRIDARN-S	TUBULIN-S	UKULELE-S	UNSCREW-S	URANISM-S	VENTING-S	VOICING-S
TRIDENT-S	TUFTING-S	ULICHON-S	UNSENSE-S	URANITE-S	VENTRAL-S	VOIDING-S
TRIDUUM-S	TUGBOAT-S	ULULATE-S	UNSHALE-S	URANIUM-S	VENTURE-S	VOITURE-S
TRIFFID-S	TUGGING-S	UMBRAGE-S	UNSHAPE-S	UREDINE-S	VENTURI-S	VOIVODE-S
TRIFLER-S	TUGHRIK-S	UMBRERE-S	UNSHELL-S	URETHAN-S	VERANDA-S	VOLANTE-S
TRIGGER-S	TUILYIE-S	UNALIST-S	UNSHOOT-S	URETHRA-S	VERBENA-S	VOLPINO-S
TRIGLOT-S	TUILZIE-S	UNAWARE-S	UNSHOUT-S	URGENCE-S	VERDICT-S	VOLTAGE-S
TRIGRAM-S	TUITION-S	UNBEGET-S	UNSINEW-S	URICASE-S	VERDITE-S	VOLUSPA-S
TRILITH-S	TULCHAN-S	UNBEING-S	UNSLING-S	URIDINE-S	VERDURE-S	VOLUTIN-S
TRILOBE-S	TUMBLER-S	UNBLIND-S	UNSNARL-S	URINATE-S	VERISMO-S	VOUCHEE-S
TRIMMER-S	TUMBREL-S	UNBLOCK-S	UNSNECK-S	URODELE-S	VERMEIL-S	VOUCHER-S
TRIMTAB-S	TUMBRIL-S	UNBOSOM-S	UNSPEAK-S	UROLITH-S	VERMELL-S	VOYAGER-S
TRINDLE-S	TUMESCE-S	UNBRACE-S	UNSPELL-S	UROMERE-S	VERNIER-S	VULGATE-S
TRINGLE-S	TUMSHIE-S	UNBUILD-S	UNSTACK-S	UROSOME-S	VERONAL-S	VULTURE-S
TRINKET-S	TUNICIN-S	UNCHAIN-S	UNSTATE-S	USUCAPT-S	VERRUCA-S	VULTURN-S
TRINKUM-S	TUNICLE-S	UNCHARM-S	UNSTEEL-S	USURPER-S	VERRUGA-S	WABBLER-S
TRIOLET-S	TUNNAGE-S	UNCHECK-S	UNSTICK-S	UTENSIL-S	VERSANT-S	WABSTER-S
TRIONYM-S	TUNNING-S	UNCHILD-S	UNSTOCK-S	UTILISE-S	VERSINE-S	WADDING-S
TRIPLET-S	TURACIN-S	UNCLASP-S	UNSTRAP-S	UTILIZE-S	VERSING-S	WADDLER-S
TRIPOLI-S	TURBAND-S	UNCLOAK-S	UNSTRIP-S	UTOPIAN-S	VERSION-S	WADMAAL-S
TRIPPER-S	TURBANT-S	UNCLOSE-S	UNSWEAR-S	UTOPISM-S	VERTIGO-S	WADMOLL-S
TRIPPET-S	TURBINE-S	UNCLOUD-S	UNTHINK-S	UTOPIST-S	VERVAIN-S	WADSETT-S
TRIPPLE-S	TURBITH-S	UNCOVER-S	UNTRACE-S	UTRICLE-S	VESICLE-S	WAFFLER-S
TRIREME-S	TURBOND-S	UNCRATE-S	UNTREAD-S	UTTERER-S	VESSAIL-S	WAFTAGE-S
TRISECT-S	TURDION-S	UNCROWN-S	UNTRUST-S	VACANCE-S	VESTIGE-S	WAFTING-S
TRISEME-S	TURFING-S	UNCTION-S	UNTRUTH-S	VACATUR-S	VESTING-S	WAFTURE-S
TRISHAW-S	TURFITE-S	UNCURSE-S	UNTWINE-S	VACCINE-S	VESTURE-S	WAGERER-S
TRISOME-S	TURMOIL-S	UNDIGHT-S	UNTWIST-S	VACUATE-S	VETERAN-S	WAGONER-S
TRISULA-S	TURNDUN-S	UNDOING-S	UNTYING-S	VACUIST-S	VETIVER-S	WAGTAIL-S
TRITIDE-S	TURNING-S	UNEARTH-S	UNVAILE-S	VACUOLE-S	VETKOEK-S	WAILING-S
TRITIUM-S	TURNKEY-S	UNEQUAL-S	UNVISOR-S	VAGRANT-S	VETTURA-S	WAINAGE-S
TRITONE-S	TURNOFF-S	UNFAITH-S	UNVOICE-S	VAIVODE-S	VIADUCT-S	WAISTER-S
TRIUMPH-S	TURNOUT-S	UNFROCK-S	UNWATER-S	VALANCE-S	VIALFUL-S	WAITING-S
TRIVIUM-S	TURPETH-S	UNGIRTH-S	UNWEAVE-S	VALENCE-S	VIBRATE-S	WAIVODE-S
TRIZONE-S	TURTLER-S	UNGLOVE-S	UNWOMAN-S	VALIANT-S	VIBRATO-S	WAIWODE-S
TROCHEE-S	TUSHKAR-S	UNGUARD-S	UNWORTH-S	VALONEA-S	VICEROY-S	WAKENER-S
TROELIE-S	TUSHKER-S	UNGUENT-S	UNWRITE-S	VALONIA-S	VICIATE-S	WALKING-S
TROLLER-S	TUSKING-S	UNHEART-S	UPBRAID-S	VALUATE-S	VICOMTE-S	WALKWAY-S
TROLLEY-S	TUSSOCK-S	UNHINGE-S	UPBREAK-S	VALVULE-S	VICTUAL-S	WALLABA-S
TROLLOP-S	TUSSORE-S	UNHOARD-S	UPBRING-S	VAMOOSE-S	VIDETTE-S	WALLING-S
TROMINO-S	TUTANIA-S	UNHORSE-S	UPBUILD-S	VAMPING-S	VIDUAGE-S	WALTZER-S
TROMMEL-S	TUTELAR-S	UNHOUSE-S	UPBURST-S	VAMPIRE-S	VIEWING-S	WAMEFUL-S
TROOLIE-S	TUTENAG-S	UNICORN-S	UPCHEER-S	VANDYKE-S	VIHUELA-S	WANGLER-S
TROOPER-S	TUTTING-S	UNIFIER-S	UPCHUCK-S	VANESSA-S	VILAYET-S	WANHOPE-S
TROPISM-S	TUTWORK-S	UNIFORM-S	UPCLIMB-S	VANILLA-S	VILIACO-S	WANIGAN-S
TROPIST-S	TWADDLE-S	UNITARD-S	UPCLOSE-S	VANNING-S	VILIAGO-S	WANNABE-S
TROTTER-S	TWANGLE-S	UNITING-S	UPGOING-S	VANTAGE-S	VILLAGE-S	WANTAGE-S

WANTING-S	WAXWORK-S	WHACKER-S	WHITLOW-S	WISHING-S	WRESTLE-S	ZAMARRA-S
WARATAH-S	WAYBILL-S	WHAISLE-S	WHITRET-S	WISTITI-S	WRIGGLE-S	ZAMARRO-S
WARBLER-S	WAYFARE-S	WHAIZLE-S	WHITTAW-S	WITCHEN-S	WRINGER-S	ZAMBUCK-S
WARDING-S	WAYMARK-S	WHALING-S	WHITTER-S	WITLING-S	WRINKLE-S	ZAMOUSE-S
WARDROP-S	WAYMENT-S	WHAMPLE-S	WHITTLE-S	WITLOOF-S	WRITING-S	ZANELLA-S
WARFARE-S	WAYPOST-S	WHANGAM-S	WHIZZER-S	WITTING-S	WRONGER-S	ZANJERO-S
WARHEAD-S	WAYSIDE-S	WHANGEE-S	WHOLISM-S	WITWALL-S	WRYBILL-S	ZANYISM-S
WARISON-S	WAYWODE-S	WHATNOT-S	WHOLIST-S	WOBBLER-S	WRYNECK-S	ZAPTIAH-S
WARLING-S	WEARING-S	WHATSIT-S	WHOMBLE-S	WOIWODE-S	XANTHAM-S	ZAPTIEH-S
WARLOCK-S	WEASAND-S	WHEEDLE-S	WHOMMLE-S	WOLFING-S	XANTHAN-S	ZAREEBA-S
WARLORD-S	WEATHER-S	WHEELER-S	WHOOBUB-S	WOLFKIN-S	XANTHIN-S	ZARNICH-S
WARMING-S	WEAVING-S	WHEELIE-S	WHOOPEE-S	WOLFRAM-S	XERAFIN-S	ZEALANT-S
WARNING-S	WEAZAND-S	WHEENGE-S	WHOOPER-S	WOLVING-S	XERASIA-S	ZEBRINA-S
WARPATH-S	WEBBING-S	WHEEPLE-S	WHOPPER-S	WONNING-S	XYLENOL-S	ZEBRULA-S
WARPING-S	WEBSITE-S	WHEESHT-S	WHUMMLE-S	WOODCUT-S	XYLITOL-S	ZEBRULE-S
WARRAND-S	WEBSTER-S	WHEEZLE-S	WICKIUP-S	WOODSIA-S	XYLOGEN-S	ZELATOR-S
WARRANT-S	WEBWORM-S	WHERRET-S	WIDENER-S	WOOFTER-S	YACHTER-S	ZEMSTVO-S
WARRIOR-S	WEDDING-S	WHETTER-S	WIDGEON-S	WOOLDER-S	YACHTIE-S	ZEOLITE-S
WARSHIP-S	WEDGING-S	WHICKER-S	WIDOWER-S	WOOLFAT-S	YAKHDAN-S	ZETETIC-S
WARTHOG-S	WEDLOCK-S	WIELDER-S	WIGGING-S	WOOLLEN-S	YAMULKA-S	ZEUXITE-S
WARTIME-S	WEEDING-S	WHIDDER-S	WIGGLER-S	WOOLSEY-S	YAPSTER-S	ZIGANKA-S
WASHDAY-S	WEEKDAY-S	WHIFFER-S	WILDCAT-S	WOOMERA-S	YARDAGE-S	ZILLION-S
WASHING-S	WEEKEND-S	WHIFFET-S	WILDING-S	WOORALI-S	YARDANG-S	ZIMOCCA-S
WASHOUT-S	WEEPING-S	WHIFFLE-S	WIMBREL-S	WOORARA-S	YASHMAK-S	ZINCITE-S
WASHPOT-S	WEFTAGE-S	WHIMPER-S	WINCING-S	WOOSELL-S	YATAGAN-S	ZINCODE-S
WASHRAG-S	WEIGELA-S	WHIMPLE-S	WINDAGE-S	WORDAGE-S	YAWNING-S	ZITHERN-S
WASHTUB-S	WEIGHER-S	WHIMSEY-S	WINDBAG-S	WORDING-S	YCLEEPE-S	ZIZANIA-S
WASSAIL-S	WEIRDIE-S	WHINGER-S	WINDGUN-S	WORKBAG-S	YEALDON-S	ZOCCOLO-S
WASTAGE-S	WELCHER-S	WHINING-S	WINDIGO-S	WORKDAY-S	YEARNER-S	ZOISITE-S
WASTING-S	WELCOME-S	WHIPCAT-S	WINDING-S	WORKING-S	YELLING-S	ZONULET-S
WASTREL-S	WELDING-S	WHIPPER-S	WINDLES-S	WORKTOP-S	YELLOCH-S	ZOOLITE-S
WATCHER-S	WELFARE-S	WHIPPET-S	WINDOCK-S	WORRIER-S	YELPING-S	ZOOLITH-S
WATCHET-S	WELLING-S	WHIPSAW-S	WINDORE-S	WORSHIP-S	YESHIVA-S	ZOONITE-S
WATERER-S	WELSHER-S	WHIRLER-S	WINDROW-S	WORSTED-S	YIELDER-S	ZOOTYPE-S
WATTAGE-S	WENCHER-S	WHIRRET-S	WINGLET-S	WOSBIRD-S	YOBBISM-S	ZORGITE-S
WAULING-S	WENDIGO-S	WHIRTLE-S	WINKING-S	WOUNDER-S	YOGHURT-S	ZORILLE-S
WAULKER-S	WERGILD-S	WHISKER-S	WINKLER-S	WOURALI-S	YOUNGTH-S	ZORILLO-S
WAVELET-S	WESTERN-S	WHISKET-S	WINNING-S	WRANGLE-S	YOUNKER-S	ZYMOGEN-S
WAVERER-S	WESTING-S	WHISKEY-S	WINNOCK-S	WRAPPER-S	YOWLING-S	ZYMOTIC-S
WAVESON-S	WESTLIN-S	WHISPER-S	WIPEOUT-S	WREAKER-S	YPSILON-S	
WAWLING-S	WETBACK-S	WHISTLE-S	WIRETAP-S	WREATHE-S	YTTRIUM-S	
WAXBILL-S	WETLAND-S	WHITHER-S	WIREWAY-S	WRECKER-S	ZABTIEH-S	
WAXWING-S	WETWARE-S	WHITING-S		WRESTER-S	ZAITECH-S	

8→9 *(see page 206)*

BULGINES-S	NERVINES-S	PROCURES-S	SPECKLES-S	TARTINES-S	TYRANNES-S
ESQUIRES-S	PRELATES-S	SPARKLES-S	TARANTAS-S	TRICKLES-S	

2→3

T-AD	T-AN	T-AX	T-EF	T-HE	T-IS	T-OM	T-OR	T-UM	T-WO
T-AE	T-AR	T-AY	T-EL	T-HO	T-IT	T-ON	T-OW	T-UN	T-YE
T-AI	T-AT	T-EA	T-EN	T-ID·	T-OD	T-OO	T-OY	T-UP	
T-AM	T-AW	T-EE	T-ES	T-IN	T-OE	T-OP	T-UG	T-UT	

3→4

T-ACE	T-ANE	T-EAT	T-ENE	T-HIS	T-OES	T-OPS	T-RAT	T-ROW	T-WAS
T-ACH	T-APE	T-ECH	T-ENS	T-HON	T-OFF	T-ORC	T-RAY	T-RUE	T-WAT
T-ACT	T-ARE	T-EEL	T-ERF	T-HUG	T-OFT	T-ORE	T-REE	T-RUG	T-WAY
T-ADS	T-ARS	T-EEN	T-ERN	T-ICE	T-OHO	T-ORS	T-REF	T-RYE	T-WEE
T-AHA	T-ART	T-EFF	T-EST	T-ICH	T-OIL	T-ORT	T-RES	T-SAR	T-WIG
T-AIL	T-ASH	T-EFS	T-HAE	T-IDE	T-OKE	T-OUK	T-RET	T-UGS	T-WIN
T-AIS	T-ASK	T-EGG	T-HAN	T-IDS	T-OLD	T-OUR	T-REW	T-UNS	T-WIT
T-AIT	T-ASS	T-ELD	T-HAT	T-IFF	T-OLE	T-OUT	T-REZ	T-UPS	T-WOS
T-AKE	T-ATE	T-ELL	T-HAW	T-ILL	T-OMS	T-OWN	T-RIG	T-URD	T-YES
T-ALA	T-AVA	T-ELS	T-HEM	T-INK	T-ONE	T-OWT	T-RIM	T-URN	
T-ALE	T-AWA	T-ELT	T-HEN	T-INS	T-ONS	T-OYS	T-RIN	T-UTS	
T-ALL	T-AYS	T-EME	T-HEW	T-IRE	T-OOM	T-RAD	T-RIP	T-UTU	
T-AMP	T-EAR	T-EMS	T-HEY	T-ITS	T-OON	T-RAM	T-ROD	T-WAE	
T-ANA	T-EAS	T-END	T-HIN	T-ODS	T-OPE	T-RAP	T-ROT		

4→5

T-ABID	T-ACHE	T-AGMA	T-AKES	T-ALAS	T-ALLY	T-AMPS	T-ANTI	T-ARED
T-ABLE	T-ACTS	T-AILS	T-AKIN	T-ALES	T-ALMA	T-ANAS	T-APED	T-ARES
T-ACES	T-AFFY	T-AITS	T-ALAR	T-ALKY	T-AMIS	T-ANNA	T-APES	T-ARTS

T-ARTY	T-ELLS	T-HETE	T-INKS	T-OURS	T-RASH	T-RIMS	T-RUES	T-WEET
T-ASAR	T-EMES	T-HEWS	T-IRES	T-OUTS	T-RATS	T-RINE	T-RUGS	T-WICE
T-ASKS	T-ENDS	T-HICK	T-ITCH	T-OWED	T-RAVE	T-RINS	T-RULY	T-WIGS
T-AULD	T-ENES	T-HIGH	T-OAST	T-OWER	T-RAYS	T-RIPE	T-RUMP	T-WILL
T-AUNT	T-EPEE	T-HILL	T-OFFS	T-OWNS	T-READ	T-RIPS	T-RUST	T-WILT
T-AVAS	T-ERAS	T-HING	T-OHOS	T-OWTS	T-RECK	T-RITE	T-RUTH	T-WINE
T-AVER	T-ERES	T-HINS	T-OILS	T-OYER	T-REED	T-ROAD	T-SARS	T-WINK
T-AWED	T-ERNE	T-HOLE	T-OKAY	T-RACE	T-REEN	T-ROCK	T-ULES	T-WINS
T-AWNY	T-ERNS	T-HONG	T-OKES	T-RACK	T-REES	T-RODE	T-URDS	T-WINY
T-AXED	T-ESTS	T-HORN	T-ONER	T-RADE	T-REIF	T-RODS	T-URNS	T-WIRE
T-AXES	T-EUGH	T-HOSE	T-ONES	T-RADS	T-REND	T-ROKE	T-UTUS	T-WIST
T-AXIS	T-HACK	T-HOWL	T-ONUS	T-RAGI	T-REST	T-ROLL	T-WAES	T-WITE
T-AXON	T-HANK	T-HUGS	T-OOMS	T-RAIK	T-RETS	T-ROMP	T-WAIN	T-WITS
T-EACH	T-HAWS	T-HUMP	T-OONS	T-RAIL	T-REWS	T-RONE	T-WANG	
T-EARS	T-HEED	T-ICED	T-OPED	T-RAIN	T-RIAL	T-ROOP	T-WANK	
T-EASE	T-HEFT	T-ICES	T-OPES	T-RAIT	T-RICE	T-ROPE	T-WATS	
T-EATS	T-HEIR	T-ICKY	T-ORCS	T-RAMP	T-RICK	T-ROTS	T-WAYS	
T-EDDY	T-HEME	T-IDES	T-ORES	T-RAMS	T-RIDE	T-ROUT	T-WEAK	
T-EELS	T-HENS	T-ILLS	T-ORTS	T-RANT	T-RIFF	T-ROWS	T-WEED	
T-EFFS	T-HERE	T-ILLY	T-OUCH	T-RAPE	T-RIGS	T-RUCK	T-WEEL	
T-EGGS	T-HERM	T-IMPS	T-OUKS	T-RAPS	T-RILL	T-RUED	T-WEER	

5→6

T-ABLED	T-ASSES	T-ESTER	T-HORNY	T-OORIE	T-RAYNE	T-RONES	T-WANGS
T-ABLES	T-ASSET	T-ETHER	T-HOUGH	T-OPING	T-READS	T-ROOPS	T-WANKS
T-ABLET	T-ASTER	T-HACKS	T-HOWLS	T-OTHER	T-RECKS	T-ROPED	T-WEEDS
T-ACHES	T-AUGHT	T-HALER	T-HUMPS	T-OTTER	T-REENS	T-ROPES	T-WEEDY
T-AGGER	T-AUNTS	T-HANKS	T-ICHES	T-OURIE	T-RENDS	T-ROUGH	T-WEELS
T-AILED	T-AURIC	T-HATCH	T-ICING	T-OUTED	T-RESTS	T-ROULE	T-WEENY
T-AKING	T-AVERS	T-HAWED	T-ICKER	T-OUTER	T-RIALS	T-ROUSE	T-WEEST
T-ALKIE	T-AVERT	T-HEAVE	T-INGLE	T-OWING	T-RICED	T-ROUTS	T-WEETS
T-ALLOT	T-AWING	T-HEFTS	T-INKED	T-OYERS	T-RICES	T-ROVER	T-WIGHT
T-ALLOW	T-AXING	T-HEIRS	T-INKER	T-RACED	T-RICKS	T-ROWED	T-WILLS
T-ALMAS	T-AXMAN	T-HEIST	T-INKLE	T-RACER	T-RIFLE	T-ROWEL	T-WILLY
T-AMBER	T-AXMEN	T-HEMES	T-INNED	T-RACES	T-RILLS	T-RUCKS	T-WILTS
T-AMINE	T-CHICK	T-HENCE	T-INNER	T-RACKS	T-RIMER	T-RUING	T-WINED
T-ANGLE	T-EAGLE	T-HERMS	T-INTER	T-RAIKS	T-RINES	T-RUMPS	T-WINES
T-ANKER	T-EASED	T-HETES	T-IRADE	T-RAILS	T-RIPES	T-RUSTS	T-WINGE
T-ANNAS	T-EASEL	T-HEWED	T-ISSUE	T-RAINS	T-RITES	T-RUSTY	T-WINKS
T-ANNOY	T-EASES	T-HICKS	T-ITCHY	T-RAITS	T-RIVET	T-RUTHS	T-WIRED
T-ANTRA	T-ENDED	T-HIGHS	T-MESES	T-RAMPS	T-ROADS	T-SAMBA	T-WIRES
T-APING	T-ENTER	T-HILLS	T-OASTS	T-RANCE	T-ROCKS	T-UGGED	T-WISTS
T-ARRAS	T-ENURE	T-HINGS	T-OCHER	T-RANTS	T-RODES	T-UPPED	T-WITCH
T-ARROW	T-EPEES	T-HOLED	T-OILED	T-RAPED	T-ROKED	T-URBAN	T-WITES
T-ASHES	T-ERNED	T-HOLES	T-OILER	T-RAPES	T-ROKES	T-URNED	
T-ASKED	T-ERNES	T-HONGS	T-OKAYS	T-RAVEL	T-ROLLS	T-WAINS	
T-ASKER	T-ERROR	T-HORNS	T-ONERS	T-RAVES	T-ROMPS	T-WAITE	

6→7

T-ABLETS	T-ASKING	T-HANKER	T-INNING	T-RAMPER	T-RIFLED	T-ROUPED	T-WATTLE
T-ABLING	T-ASSETS	T-HAWING	T-INTERS	T-RANCED	T-RIFLER	T-ROUSER	T-WEETED
T-ACKERS	T-ASTERS	T-HEATER	T-IRADES	T-RANCES	T-RIFLES	T-ROUSES	T-WEETER
T-ACTION	T-AUNTER	T-HEAVES	T-ISSUED	T-RANSOM	T-RIGGED	T-ROUTER	T-WIDDLE
T-ACTUAL	T-AWNIER	T-HEISTS	T-ISSUES	T-RANTED	T-RIGGER	T-ROVERS	T-WIGGED
T-AFFIES	T-CHICKS	T-HELVES	T-ITCHES	T-RANTER	T-RILLED	T-ROWELS	T-WIGHTS
T-AGGERS	T-EAGLES	T-HEREAT	T-OCHERS	T-RAPING	T-RIMERS	T-ROWING	T-WILLED
T-AILING	T-EARFUL	T-HEREBY	T-OFFISH	T-RAPPED	T-RIMMED	T-RUCKED	T-WILTED
T-ALIPED	T-EARING	T-HEREIN	T-OILERS	T-RAPPER	T-RIPPED	T-RUCKLE	T-WINGED
T-ALKIES	T-EASELS	T-HEREOF	T-OILING	T-RASHED	T-RIPPER	T-RUEING	T-WINGES
T-ALLIED	T-EASING	T-HEREON	T-OMENTA	T-RASHES	T-RIPPLE	T-RUFFLE	T-WINIER
T-ALLIES	T-EDDIES	T-HERETO	T-ONUSES	T-RASSES	T-RIVETS	T-RUMPED	T-WINING
T-ALLOTS	T-ENABLE	T-HERMAE	T-OTTERS	T-RAVELS	T-ROATED	T-RUNDLE	T-WINKED
T-ALLOWS	T-ENDING	T-HETHER	T-OUCHES	T-RAYNES	T-ROCHES	T-RUSTED	T-WINKLE
T-AMBERS	T-ENFOLD	T-HITHER	T-OUGHLY	T-READER	T-ROCKED	T-SAMBAS	T-WINTER
T-AMINES	T-ENSILE	T-HOLING	T-OUTERS	T-REASON	T-ROKING	T-UCKERS	T-WIRING
T-AMISES	T-ENTERS	T-HORNED	T-OUTING	T-RECKED	T-ROLLED	T-UGGING	T-WISTED
T-ANGLED	T-ENURED	T-HUMPED	T-RACERS	T-REDDLE	T-ROLLER	T-UMBLES	T-WITCHY
T-ANGLER	T-ENURES	T-HUMPER	T-RACING	T-REMBLE	T-ROMPED	T-UMBREL	T-WITTED
T-ANGLES	T-ERBIUM	T-ICKERS	T-RACKED	T-RENTAL	T-ROOPED	T-UMBRIL	T-WITTER
T-ANKERS	T-ERNING	T-ILLITE	T-RACKER	T-RIBLET	T-ROPING	T-UNABLE	T-ZADDIK
T-ANNOYS	T-ERRORS	T-INGLES	T-RAIKED	T-RICING	T-ROTTED	T-UPPING	
T-ANTARA	T-ESTATE	T-INKERS	T-RAILED	T-RICKED	T-ROTTER	T-URGENT	
T-ANTRUM	T-ESTERS	T-INKING	T-RAILER	T-RICKER	T-ROUBLE	T-URNING	
T-ARROWS	T-ETHERS	T-INKLED	T-RAINED	T-RICKLE	T-ROUGHS	T-WADDLE	
T-ARTIER	T-HALERS	T-INKLES	T-RAMMED	T-RICKLY	T-ROULES	T-WAITES	
T-ASKERS	T-HANKED	T-INNERS	T-RAMPED	T-RIDENT	T-ROUNCE	T-WANGLE	

7→8

T-ACONITE	T-ENTERED	T-RACKERS	T-REDDLED	T-RIPPLES	T-RUNDLED	T-WIDDLES
T-ACTIONS	T-ERBIUMS	T-RACKING	T-REDDLES	T-ROATING	T-RUNDLES	T-WIGGING
T-ADVANCE	T-HANKERS	T-RAIKING	T-REMBLED	T-ROCKING	T-RUNNION	T-WIGHTED
T-AILERON	T-HANKING	T-RAILERS	T-REMBLES	T-ROLLERS	T-RUSTIER	T-WILLIES
T-ALIPEDS	T-HATCHED	T-RAILING	T-RENDING	T-ROLLING	T-RUSTILY	T-WILLING
T-ALLNESS	T-HATCHER	T-RAINING	T-RENTALS	T-ROMPING	T-RUSTING	T-WILTING
T-ALLOWED	T-HATCHES	T-RAMMING	T-REVISES	T-ROOPING	T-RUTHFUL	T-WINGING
T-ALLYING	T-HEATERS	T-RAMPERS	T-RIBLETS	T-ROSSERS	T-UBEROUS	T-WINIEST
T-ANGLERS	T-HIRLING	T-RAMPING	T-RICKERS	T-ROTTERS	T-UMBRELS	T-WINKING
T-ANGLING	T-HORNIER	T-RANCHES	T-RICKING	T-ROTTING	T-UMBRILS	T-WINKLED
T-ANNATES	T-HORNING	T-RANCING	T-RICKLES	T-ROUBLES	T-URNINGS	T-WINKLER
T-ANNOYED	T-HUMPERS	T-RANSOMS	T-RIFLERS	T-ROUNCES	T-WADDLED	T-WINKLES
T-ANTARAS	T-HUMPING	T-RANTERS	T-RIFLING	T-ROUPING	T-WADDLER	T-WINNING
T-ARRASES	T-ILLITES	T-RANTING	T-RIGGERS	T-ROUSERS	T-WADDLES	T-WINTERS
T-ARROWED	T-INKLING	T-RAPPERS	T-RIGGING	T-ROUTERS	T-WANGLED	T-WISTING
T-ARTIEST	T-INNINGS	T-RAPPING	T-RILLING	T-ROUTING	T-WANGLES	T-WITCHED
T-ASSWAGE	T-ISSUING	T-RASHING	T-RIMMING	T-RUCKING	T-WATTLED	T-WITCHES
T-ASTABLE	T-ITCHIER	T-REACHER	T-RIPPERS	T-RUCKLED	T-WATTLES	T-WITTERS
T-AUNTERS	T-OCHERED	T-READERS	T-RIPPIER	T-RUCKLES	T-WEEDIER	T-WITTING
T-AUTONYM	T-OMENTUM	T-READING	T-RIPPING	T-RUFFLED	T-WEENIES	T-ZADDIKS
T-AWNIEST	T-OTTERED	T-REASONS	T-RIPPLED	T-RUFFLES	T-WEETING	
T-EARLESS	T-RACINGS	T-RECKING	T-RIPPLER	T-RUMPING	T-WIDDLED	

8→9

T-ACONITES	T-ERRORIST	T-HUMBLING	T-REACHERS	T-RUNNIONS	T-WINKLERS
T-ACTUALLY	T-HATCHERS	T-INKLINGS	T-READINGS	T-RUSTIEST	T-WINKLING
T-AILERONS	T-HATCHING	T-ITCHIEST	T-REDDLING	T-RUSTLESS	T-WINNINGS
T-ALLOWING	T-HEREAWAY	T-OCHERING	T-REMBLING	T-RUTHLESS	T-WITCHIER
T-ANGLINGS	T-HEREFROM	T-OTTERING	T-RIMMINGS	T-URGENTLY	T-WITCHING
T-ANNOYING	T-HERENESS	T-RACHITIS	T-RIPPLERS	T-WADDLERS	T-WITTERED
T-ARROWING	T-HEREUNTO	T-RACKINGS	T-RIPPLING	T-WADDLING	T-WITTINGS
T-ARTINESS	T-HEREUPON	T-RAINBAND	T-ROLLINGS	T-WANGLING	T-ZADDIKIM
T-AURIFORM	T-HEREWITH	T-RAINLESS	T-ROUTINGS	T-WATTLING	
T-AUTOLOGY	T-HORNBILL	T-RAMPINGS	T-ROWELLED	T-WEEDIEST	
T-AUTONYMS	T-HORNIEST	T-RAPPINGS	T-RUCKLING	T-WIDDLING	
T-ENTERING	T-HORNLESS	T-RAVELLED	T-RUFFLING	T-WIGHTING	

2→3

AI-T	BI-T	EF-T	GO-T	HO-T	LO-T	NE-T	OR-T	PO-T	TI-T
AN-T	BO-T	EL-T	GU-T	JO-T	MA-T	NO-T	OU-T	RE-T	TO-T
AR-T	DI-T	ES-T	HA-T	KA-T	ME-T	NU-T	OW-T	SI-T	WE-T
BA-T	DO-T	FA-T	HE-T	LA-T	MO-T	OF-T	PA-T	SO-T	WO-T
BE-T	EA-T	GI-T	HI-T	LI-T	NA-T	OP-T	PI-T	TA-T	YE-T

3→4

AIR-T	CAN-T	DOR-T	GAS-T	LAS-T	MOO-T	PIN-T	SAL-T	TEA-T	WAR-T
ARE-T	CAR-T	DOS-T	GEL-T	LEA-T	MOR-T	POO-T	SAN-T	TEL-T	WAS-T
BAH-T	CEL-T	DOW-T	GEN-T	LEE-T	MOT-T	POS-T	SEA-T	TEN-T	WAT-T
BAN-T	CHA-T	DUE-T	GIF-T	LES-T	MUN-T	POT-T	SEC-T	TES-T	WEE-T
BAS-T	CHI-T	EAS-T	GIS-T	LIN-T	MUS-T	PUN-T	SEN-T	TIL-T	WEN-T
BAT-T	COL-T	ECH-T	GOA-T	LIS-T	NET-T	PUT-T	SET-T	TIN-T	WHA-T
BAY-T	COO-T	ERS-T	GUS-T	LOO-T	NEW-T	PYE-T	SEX-T	TIP-T	WHO-T
BEE-T	COS-T	ETA-T	HAE-T	LOS-T	NOT-T	QUA-T	SHE-T	TOO-T	WIS-T
BEL-T	COT-T	EVE-T	HAS-T	LOW-T	NOW-T	RAI-T	SIS-T	TOR-T	WON-T
BEN-T	CUR-T	FAR-T	HEN-T	MAL-T	OBI-T	RAN-T	SKA-T	TOW-T	WOO-T
BIN-T	DAL-T	FAS-T	HEP-T	MAR-T	ONS-T	RAP-T	SKI-T	TWA-T	WOS-T
BIT-T	DAN-T	FEE-T	HES-T	MAS-T	OON-T	RAS-T	SOU-T	UNI-T	YES-T
BOA-T	DAW-T	FEN-T	HIN-T	MAT-T	PAN-T	REF-T	SPA-T	VAN-T	YET-T
BOO-T	DEB-T	FET-T	HIP-T	MEL-T	PAR-T	REN-T	SUE-T	VAS-T	YON-T
BOR-T	DEF-T	FIT-T	HIS-T	MEN-T	PAS-T	RES-T	SUI-T	VAU-T	
BOT-T	DEL-T	FON-T	HOO-T	MIL-T	PEA-T	RIP-T	TAI-T	VEX-T	
BRA-T	DEN-T	FOR-T	HOS-T	MIS-T	PEN-T	RIT-T	TAR-T	VIN-T	
BUN-T	DIE-T	GAN-T	JUS-T	MIX-T	PER-T	ROO-T	TAT-T	VOL-T	
BUS-T	DIN-T	GAR-T	KEN-T	MOA-T	PHO-T	ROW-T	TAU-T	WAD-T	
BUT-T	DIT-T		KEP-T	MOI-T	PIE-T	RUN-T	TAW-T	WAN-T	

4→5

ABLE-T	AVAS-T	BIDE-T	BRAS-T	CAPO-T	CLEF-T	COOS-T	CURS-T	DUET-T
AGAS-T	AVER-T	BLAT-T	BREN-T	CARE-T	CLIP-T	COSE-T	DEAL-T	EARS-T
AGEN-T	BEAU-T	BLUR-T	BURN-T	CHAR-T	CLOU-T	COUR-T	DELF-T	ERGO-T
AMEN-T	BEGO-T	BOAR-T	BURS-T	CHER-T	COME-T	COVE-T	DENE-T	EVEN-T
ANNA-T	BENE-T	BOAS-T	CADE-T	CHOU-T	COMP-T	CRUE-T	DICH-T	EVER-T
ARET-T	BERE-T	BOOS-T	CANS-T	CIVE-T	COOP-T	CRUS-T	DOES-T	EWES-T

EXUL-T	GLEN-T	ISLE-T	MEIN-T	PIER-T	SAIN-T	SKAT-T	SWOP-T	WAIF-T
FACE-T	GOSH-T	JOIN-T	MERI-T	PIPI-T	SAIS-T	SKIN-T	TACE-T	WARS-T
FAIN-T	GRAN-T	JURA-T	MIDS-T	PLAN-T	SALE-T	SLEE-T	TAPE-T	WEES-T
FILE-T	GREE-T	KARA-T	MORA-T	PLEA-T	SAUL-T	SLIP-T	TARO-T	WELK-T
FIRS-T	GRIS-T	KEMP-T	MOTE-T	POOR-T	SAYS-T	SPAR-T	TEMP-T	WHIP-T
FLEE-T	GUES-T	LACE-T	MOUS-T	PRAT-T	SCAN-T	SPUR-T	TENE-T	WRAP-T
FLIT-T	HADS-T	LEAN-T	MUSE-T	QUIN-T	SCAR-T	STAR-T	TRAT-T	YEAS-T
FREE-T	HAUL-T	LEAP-T	NIGH-T	REES-T	SCAT-T	STEN-T	TRES-T	YOUR-T
FRIS-T	HEAR-T	LEAS-T	NONE-T	REIS-T	SHIR-T	STEP-T	TWEE-T	
FUME-T	HECH-T	LIAR-T	OUCH-T	REPO-T	SHOO-T	STOA-T	VALE-T	
GAIT-T	HIGH-T	LICH-T	OVER-T	RICH-T	SHOT-T	STUN-T	VELD-T	
GAUN-T	HOAS-T	MANE-T	PAIN-T	RIVE-T	SHUN-T	SURA-T	VERS-T	
GENE-T	HORS-T	MAYS-T	PALE-T	ROOS-T	SIEN-T	SWAP-T	VIVA-T	
GLEE-T	INGO-T	MEAN-T	PEAR-T	ROSE-T	SIGH-T	SWEE-T	VOLE-T	

5→6

ABLES-T	BUDGE-T	DOUCE-T	GORGE-T	MERES-T	PUCES-T	SILEN-T	TOILE-T
AGHAS-T	BUFFE-T	DOUGH-T	GROVE-T	MIDGE-T	PURES-T	SMILE-T	TRUES-T
ANIGH-T	BUGLE-T	DOWSE-T	HAIRS-T	MILLE-T	PURIS-T	SONNE-T	TUFFE-T
ANKLE-T	CABLE-T	DRAPE-T	HALES-T	MODES-T	RABBI-T	SORES-T	TURBO-T
APPLE-T	CACHE-T	DREAM-T	HAUGH-T	MOLES-T	RAYLE-T	SOUGH-T	TYRAN-T
ASSOT-T	CAPLE-T	DRIES-T	HAULS-T	MOTET-T	RELIC-T	SPINE-T	UNPEN-T
ASTER-T	CATCH-T	DUPLE-T	HEIGH-T	MUTES-T	RENNE-T	SPOIL-T	UNWON-T
BARBE-T	CHARE-T	EAGLE-T	HONES-T	NUDES-T	REPOS-T	STEAL-T	VERSE-T
BARES-T	CLOSE-T	FERES-T	IDLES-T	OCTET-T	RILLE-T	STILE-T	VERVE-T
BARRE-T	COMMO-T	FIDGE-T	JUMAR-T	OLIVE-T	RIPES-T	STYLE-T	WAUGH-T
BASAL-T	COMPO-T	FILLE-T	KAPUT-T	PALES-T	ROQUE-T	SUMMA-T	WAURS-T
BASES-T	CORSE-T	FINES-T	LAMES-T	PARGE-T	ROUGH-T	SURES-T	WEIGH-T
BASSE-T	COVEN-T	FLIES-T	LANCE-T	PATEN-T	RUDES-T	SWEER-T	WHISH-T
BECKE-T	COVER-T	FORES-T	LATEN-T	PEARS-T	SAFES-T	SWEIR-T	WIDES-T
BENNE-T	CRONE-T	FORGE-T	LAXES-T	PIERS-T	SAGES-T	SWIVE-T	WISES-T
BLAES-T	CRUSE-T	FORGO-T	LEARN-T	PIQUE-T	SAIDS-T	TABLE-T	WRIES-T
BLUES-T	CURIE-T	FREES-T	LINGO-T	PLACE-T	SALLE-T	TAMES-T	
BONNE-T	CURVE-T	FROWS-T	LIVES-T	PLAIN-T	SCEAT-T	TAPIS-T	
BOUGE-T	CUTES-T	GABLE-T	LOCUS-T	PLANE-T	SCRIP-T	TARGE-T	
BOUGH-T	DIKAS-T	GADGE-T	LOWES-T	POSSE-T	SCULP-T	TASSE-T	
BREVE-T	DIVER-T	GAMES-T	MALIS-T	PRESE-T	SERES-T	TAVER-T	
BROWS-T	DIVES-T	GARRE-T	MATZO-T	PRIES-T	SHIES-T	TERCE-T	

6→7

ACUTES-T	BUSIES-T	DECREE-T	KINGLE-T	MOLINE-T	RACKET-T	SEXTET-T	TONIES-T
ADJOIN-T	CALLAN-T	DEWLAP-T	LAMBER-T	NOBLES-T	RADGES-T	SHARIA-T	TOWMON-T
AERIES-T	CANTLE-T	DIPLON-T	LANGUE-T	NOSIES-T	RADIAN-T	SHERIA-T	TRIPLE-T
ALKANE-T	CIRCLE-T	DOUBLE-T	LARGES-T	ORGIAS-T	RAGMEN-T	SINGLE-T	TRITES-T
ARCHES-T	CLOSES-T	DROGUE-T	LITHES-T	OVERGO-T	RANKES-T	SLEIGH-T	TURBAN-T
ARTIES-T	COMPOS-T	DROLES-T	LOGIES-T	PALMIE-T	RASHES-T	SNIDES-T	UGLIES-T
ATTAIN-T	CONGES-T	EPAULE-T	LONGES-T	PARPEN-T	REDEAL-T	SPARES-T	UPLEAN-T
ATTASK-T	CONSUL-T	FAINES-T	LOOSES-T	PELTAS-T	REPLAN-T	SPRAIN-T	UPLEAP-T
BABIES-T	CONTES-T	FALSES-T	LOWSES-T	PINIES-T	RICHES-T	STALES-T	VAGUES-T
BALLAN-T	CONTRA-T	FITCHE-T	LUSHES-T	PLEDGE-T	RIPPLE-T	STRAIN-T	WADSET-T
BARGES-T	CORNET-T	FITTES-T	MANCHE-T	POKIES-T	RIZZAR-T	TAIVER-T	WALIES-T
BASSES-T	COSIES-T	FOULES-T	MANTLE-T	POLLEN-T	ROOTLE-T	TEMPLE-T	WARRAN-T
BEDROP-T	COUPLE-T	GASHES-T	MAUVES-T	POSHES-T	ROSIES-T	TENSES-T	WAVIES-T
BEMEAN-T	COZIES-T	GRAVES-T	MEANES-T	POSIES-T	RUBIES-T	THATCH-T	WHEESH-T
BORSCH-T	CROCHE-T	GROSER-T	MEDIAN-T	POUNCE-T	RUNDLE-T	THOUGH-T	WHITES-T
BOSSES-T	CRUDES-T	HACKLE-T	MIGHTS-T	PRONES-T	SABKHA-T	TIDIES-T	WOULDS-T
BRAVES-T	CULVER-T	HOLIES-T	MISHAP-T	QUARTE-T	SESTET-T	TIERCE-T	ZANIES-T
BROUGH-T	DEARES-T	JINGLE-T	MISKEN-T	QUINTE-T	SEXTAN-T	TINIES-T	ZONULE-T

7→8

ANGRIES-T	BRASHES-T	COCKIES-T	DINGIES-T	DUMPIES-T	FRESHES-T	HEAVIES-T
ARTSIES-T	BUDDIES-T	COMBIES-T	DINKIES-T	DUNNIES-T	FUNNIES-T	HEMPIES-T
BACCARA-T	BUGGIES-T	CONGREE-T	DIPLOMA-T	EARLIES-T	FURRIES-T	HENNIES-T
BAGGIES-T	BULLIES-T	CONJOIN-T	DIRTIES-T	EMONGES-T	GAUDIES-T	HIPPIES-T
BALDIES-T	BUSHIES-T	CONTRAS-T	DISJOIN-T	EMPTIES-T	GAWKIES-T	HOOKIES-T
BANDIES-T	BUTCHES-T	CRAZIES-T	DIVINES-T	FANCIES-T	GENTLES-T	HUMBLES-T
BASEMEN-T	CANZONE-T	CROSSES-T	DIZZIES-T	FATTIES-T	GIDDIES-T	HUMPIES-T
BAWDIES-T	CARNIES-T	CUTTIES-T	DODDIES-T	FEEBLES-T	GLOBULE-T	HUNKIES-T
BIRKIES-T	CASEMEN-T	DAFFIES-T	DOGGIES-T	FENNIES-T	GOODIES-T	HUSKIES-T
BITTIES-T	CATTIES-T	DANDIES-T	DOTTIES-T	FERLIES-T	GOOSIES-T	INDICAN-T
BLONDES-T	CHEWIES-T	DEBBIES-T	DOWDIES-T	FICKLES-T	GROSSES-T	INSCULP-T
BLOWIES-T	CHOICES-T	DEMURES-T	DREARES-T	FLAKIES-T	GROUSES-T	IRONIES-T
BODGIES-T	CHOKIES-T	DICKIES-T	DRIBBLE-T	FLASHES-T	GUTTIES-T	JANTIES-T
BONNIES-T	CISSIES-T	DIDDIES-T	DUCKIES-T	FLUSHES-T	HANDCAR-T	JEMMIES-T
BOOKIES-T	CLASSIS-T	DILLIES-T	DUMMIES-T	FOOTIES-T	HAPPIES-T	JERKIES-T

JETTIES-T	MERRIES-T	OUTLEAP-T	PUGGIES-T	SECURES-T	SULKIES-T	TRANCHE-T
JOLLIES-T	MINUTES-T	PALMIES-T	PURPLES-T	SEDATES-T	SUNBURN-T	TRICKLE-T
JUNGLIS-T	MISDEAL-T	PALSIES-T	QUARTET-T	SERENES-T	SUPPLES-T	UNIQUES-T
JUNKIES-T	MISSIES-T	PAPPIES-T	QUINTET-T	SHINIES-T	SURFIES-T	UNLEARN-T
KHALIFA-T	MOODIES-T	PARKIES-T	RAGGIES-T	SHIPMEN-T	SWISHES-T	UTOPIAS-T
KITTLES-T	MOONIES-T	PASSMEN-T	RANDIES-T	SILKIES-T	SYMBION-T	WALLIES-T
LINTIES-T	MOSSIES-T	PASTIES-T	READIES-T	SILLIES-T	TACKIES-T	WASPIES-T
LIPPIES-T	MOUSIES-T	PEERIES-T	REGIMEN-T	SIMPLES-T	TALKIES-T	WEARIES-T
LITTLES-T	MOWBURN-T	PERSICO-T	REMOTES-T	SISSIES-T	TANGIES-T	WEDGIES-T
LOATHES-T	MUDDIES-T	PETTIES-T	RETRAIT-T	SMOKIES-T	TARDIES-T	WEENIES-T
LOOBIES-T	MYLODON-T	PHONIES-T	ROOKIES-T	SOAPIES-T	TARRIES-T	WEEPIES-T
LOONIES-T	NAPPIES-T	PIGGIES-T	ROOMIES-T	SOMBRES-T	TATTIES-T	WHITIES-T
LUCKIES-T	NASTIES-T	PINKIES-T	ROOTIES-T	SOOTHES-T	TAWNIES-T	WITHIES-T
MARABOU-T	NEWSIES-T	PISTOLE-T	ROUNDLE-T	SPANGLE-T	TECHIES-T	WOODIES-T
MARDIES-T	NONUPLE-T	PLUSHES-T	ROWDIES-T	SPARKLE-T	TELETEX-T	YAPPIES-T
MARMOSE-T	NOOKIES-T	PODDIES-T	RUDDIES-T	SPRUCES-T	TIDDIES-T	
MASHIES-T	OCTUPLE-T	POPPIES-T	RUMMIES-T	SQUARES-T	TINNIES-T	
MATURES-T	OPAQUES-T	PORKIES-T	SAFARIS-T	STABLES-T	TOFFIES-T	
MEAGRES-T	ORANGES-T	POTTIES-T	SAVAGES-T	STEEVES-T	TOTTIES-T	
MEALIES-T	OUTBURN-T	PRIVIES-T	SAVVIES-T	STONIES-T	TOWNIES-T	

8→9

AUGUSTES-T	CHOCCIES-T	FRILLIES-T	PLACEMEN-T	SKELLIES-T	SUBLIMES-T
BLOODIES-T	CHUMMIES-T	GLOSSIES-T	POLYGLOT-T	SKILLIES-T	SUPREMES-T
BOLSHIES-T	COMPLAIN-T	GREASIES-T	POURSUIT-T	SNOTTIES-T	SWANKIES-T
BRASSIES-T	CONCISES-T	GREENIES-T	PRECISES-T	SPARKIES-T	TAWDRIES-T
BRICKIES-T	CREEPIES-T	HEARTIES-T	PREPPIES-T	SPOONIES-T	THINGIES-T
BRITTLES-T	CRUMMIES-T	JAUNTIES-T	PRETTIES-T	SPRINGLE-T	TIDDLIES-T
BROWNIES-T	CRUSTIES-T	LANDDROS-T	PRIVATES-T	SPUNKIES-T	TRENDIES-T
BUBBLIES-T	DAINTIES-T	LAVISHES-T	QUEENIES-T	SPURRIES-T	TRUSTIES-T
CABRIOLE-T	DAYDREAM-T	LOVELIES-T	RESTRAIN-T	STANCHES-T	UNTIDIES-T
CHAPPIES-T	DISCOVER-T	MULTIPLE-T	SCANTIES-T	STEADIES-T	VIDEOTEX-T
CHATTIES-T	DISTRAIN-T	OBLIQUES-T	SCURVIES-T	STEAMIES-T	WHEELIES-T
CHERRIES-T	DRUGGIES-T	OBSCURES-T	SEPTUPLE-T	STEGODON-T	WHIMSIES-T
CHILLIES-T	EXTREMES-T	OUTLEARN-T	SEXTUPLE-T	STICKIES-T	WHINNIES-T
CHINKIES-T	FLIMSIES-T	OVERBURN-T	SHEENIES-T	STUBBIES-T	WOBBLIES-T
CHIPPIES-T	FLOPPIES-T	OVERLEAP-T	SHODDIES-T	STUMPIES-T	WOOLLIES-T
CHITTIES-T	FOREMEAN-T	PEARLIES-T	SICKLIES-T	STURDIES-T	WORTHIES-T

2→3
U-DO   U-RE   U-TE

3→4

U-DAL	U-LES	U-NIS	U-PAS	U-SED	U-TIS	U-VAS
U-DOS	U-LEX	U-NIT	U-RES	U-TES	U-VAE	

4→5

U-DALS	U-NITS	U-PLAY	U-RATE	U-REDO	U-RIAL	U-RITE	U-SING	U-TILE
U-NITE	U-PEND	U-PLED	U-REAL	U-RENT	U-RINE	U-SAGE	U-SURE	U-VEAL

5→6

U-LEXES	U-NOWED	U-PLEAD	U-PRISE	U-RESES	U-RUSES	U-SURER
U-LOSES	U-PENDS	U-PLINK	U-PROLL	U-RIALS	U-SABLE	U-SURES
U-NEATH	U-PHANG	U-PLOOK	U-PROSE	U-RINES	U-SAGER	U-SWARD
U-NITER	U-PLAID	U-PRATE	U-RATES	U-RITES	U-SAGES	
U-NITES	U-PLAYS	U-PREST	U-REDIA	U-ROSES	U-SURED	

6→7

U-NEARED	U-PENDED	U-PLINKS	U-PRAISE	U-PRESTS	U-SURING
U-NEATEN	U-PHANGS	U-PLOOKS	U-PRATED	U-PRISES	U-SWARDS
U-NITERS	U-PLEADS	U-PLYING	U-PRATES	U-PROLLS	

7→8
U-PENDING   U-PLAYING   U-PRAISED   U-PRAISES   U-PRATING   U-PRISING   U-PROLLED

8→9

U-PHANGING	U-PLIGHTED	U-PLINKING	U-PROLLING
U-PLEADING	U-PLIGHTER	U-PRAISING	

2→3

| AY-U | EM-U | ME-U | PI-U | TA-U | YO-U |
| EA-U | KY-U | MO-U | SO-U | UT-U | |

3→4

| AIT-U | EME-U | GEN-U | LIE-U | MEN-U | PUD-U | RIM-U | TAP-U | TEG-U | TUT-U |
| BAP-U | FRA-U | GUR-U | MAS-U | MOT-U | RAT-U | TAB-U | TAT-U | THO-U | VAT-U |

4→5

| BANT-U | BUND-U | CORN-U | JAMB-U | MUNT-U | PILA-U | VERT-U |
| BUCK-U | BUSS-U | HAIK-U | LASS-U | PARE-U | QUIP-U | |

5→6

CONGO-U

6→7

MANITO-U   TAMARA-U

2→3

| V-AE | V-AS | V-EE | V-ID | V-IS | V-OR | V-OX | V-UM |
| V-AN | V-AT | V-EX | V-IN | V-OE | V-OW | V-UG | |

3→4

V-AIL	V-ALE	V-ANT	V-ELD	V-ERS	V-IDE	V-INS	V-LEI	V-OLE	V-UGS
V-AIN	V-AMP	V-ARE	V-ELL	V-EST	V-IDS	V-IRE	V-OAR	V-ORS	
V-AIR	V-ANE	V-ARY	V-END	V-ICE	V-ILL	V-ITA	V-OES	V-ROW	

4→5

V-AGUE	V-AMPS	V-AUNT	V-ENDS	V-IBEX	V-IRID	V-OMER	V-ROOM
V-AILS	V-ANES	V-EALE	V-ERST	V-ICED	V-ITAS	V-OMIT	V-ROWS
V-AIRS	V-ANTS	V-EERY	V-ESTS	V-ICES	V-LEIS	V-OUCH	V-ULVA
V-AIRY	V-ARES	V-ELDS	V-ETCH	V-ILLS	V-LIES	V-OWED	
V-ALES	V-ARNA	V-ELLS	V-EXES	V-IRES	V-OARS	V-OWER	

5→6

V-AGILE	V-ALINE	V-ATMAN	V-EALES	V-ENDUE	V-ICING	V-ORANT	V-ULVAS
V-AGUED	V-ALLEY	V-AUNTS	V-EGGED	V-ENTER	V-IZARD	V-OTARY	
V-AGUES	V-ARNAS	V-AUNTY	V-ELATE	V-ERSES	V-OMERS	V-OWING	
V-AILED	V-ASTER	V-AWARD	V-ENDED	V-ERVEN	V-OMITS	V-ROOMS	

6→7

V-ACATES	V-AIRIER	V-ASSAIL	V-EGGING	V-ENDUES	V-ESTRAL	V-IZARDS	V-ROOMED
V-ACUITY	V-ALINES	V-AUNTER	V-ELATED	V-ENTAIL	V-ETCHES	V-OCULAR	
V-AILING	V-ALLEYS	V-AWARDS	V-ENDING	V-ENTERS	V-IBICES	V-OUCHES	

7→8

| V-AGILITY | V-ASSAILS | V-ENATION | V-ENTAYLE | V-ERMINED | V-OTARIES |
| V-AIRIEST | V-AUNTERS | V-ENTAILS | V-ERISTIC | V-IRIDIAN | V-ROOMING |

8→9

V-ACUITIES   V-ENATIONS   V-ENTAYLES   V-IDEOGRAM   V-INDICATE

2→3

| DI-V | GO-V | GU-V | LA-V | RE-V | SO-V |

3→4

CHI-V   DEE-V   MIR-V   PER-V

4→5

OLLA-V

2→3

W-AD	W-AR	W-AW	W-EE	W-EX	W-IN	W-OE	W-OP	W-OX
W-AE	W-AS	W-AX	W-EM	W-HA	W-IS	W-ON	W-OS	W-US
W-AN	W-AT	W-AY	W-EN	W-HO	W-IT	W-OO	W-OW	W-YE

3→4

W-ADD	W-ALE	W-ARM	W-AWE	W-ELD	W-ETA	W-HIM	W-ICH	W-ITS	W-ORD
W-ADS	W-ALL	W-ARS	W-AWL	W-ELK	W-HAM	W-HIN	W-IDE	W-OES	W-ORE
W-AFT	W-AND	W-ART	W-AYS	W-ELL	W-HAP	W-HIP	W-ILL	W-OKE	W-ORT
W-AGE	W-ANE	W-ARY	W-EAN	W-ELT	W-HAT	W-HIT	W-IMP	W-OLD	W-RAP
W-AID	W-ANT	W-ASH	W-EAR	W-EMS	W-HEN	W-HOA	W-INK	W-ONS	W-REN
W-AIL	W-ANY	W-ASP	W-EEK	W-END	W-HET	W-HOP	W-INN	W-OOF	W-RIT
W-AIN	W-ARD	W-ATE	W-EEL	W-ENS	W-HEW	W-HOT	W-INS	W-OON	W-UDS
W-AIT	W-ARE	W-AUK	W-EEN	W-ERE	W-HEY	W-HOW	W-IRE	W-OOS	W-YES
W-AKE	W-ARK	W-AVE	W-EFT	W-EST	W-HID	W-ICE	W-ISH	W-OPS	

4→5

W-ADDS	W-ANNA	W-AVES	W-ELLS	W-HEAR	W-HISH	W-ILLY	W-OULD	W-RICK
W-AGED	W-ANTS	W-AWES	W-ELTS	W-HEAT	W-HISS	W-IMPS	W-OVEN	W-RING
W-AGES	W-ARDS	W-AWLS	W-ENDS	W-HEEL	W-HIST	W-INCH	W-OWED	W-RITE
W-AGON	W-ARED	W-AXED	W-ESTS	W-HEFT	W-HITS	W-INKS	W-OXEN	W-RITS
W-AIDE	W-ARES	W-AXES	W-ETAS	W-HELM	W-HIZZ	W-INNS	W-RACK	W-ROKE
W-AILS	W-ARKS	W-EANS	W-EXES	W-HELP	W-HOLE	W-IRES	W-RAPS	W-RONG
W-AITS	W-ARMS	W-EARS	W-HACK	W-HENS	W-HOOP	W-ITCH	W-RAPT	W-ROOT
W-AKED	W-ARTS	W-ECHT	W-HALE	W-HERE	W-HOOT	W-OLDS	W-RAST	W-ROTE
W-AKES	W-ARTY	W-EDGE	W-HAMS	W-HETS	W-HOPS	W-OMEN	W-RATE	W-RUNG
W-ALES	W-ASHY	W-EDGY	W-HANG	W-HEWS	W-HORE	W-OOFS	W-RATH	W-USES
W-ALLS	W-ASPS	W-EELS	W-HAPS	W-HEYS	W-HOSE	W-OONS	W-REAK	
W-ALLY	W-ATAP	W-EFTS	W-HARE	W-HINS	W-ICKY	W-OOZY	W-RECK	
W-ANDS	W-AUKS	W-ELDS	W-HATS	W-HIPS	W-IDES	W-ORDS	W-RENS	
W-ANES	W-AVER	W-ELKS	W-HEAL	W-HIPT	W-ILLS	W-ORTS	W-REST	

5→6

W-ADDED	W-ANTED	W-EASEL	W-HALER	W-HELPS	W-HOOPS	W-IZARD	W-RETCH
W-ADDLE	W-ARMED	W-EAVES	W-HALES	W-HENCE	W-HOOSH	W-ONNED	W-RICKS
W-AFTER	W-ARRAY	W-EBBED	W-HAMMY	W-HERRY	W-HOOTS	W-ORMER	W-RIGHT
W-AGING	W-ASHEN	W-EDGED	W-HANGS	W-HEUGH	W-ICHES	W-OUBIT	W-RINGS
W-AGONS	W-ASHES	W-EDGES	W-HARES	W-HEWED	W-ICKER	W-OUNDY	W-RITES
W-AILED	W-ASTER	W-EIGHT	W-HEALS	W-HILLY	W-INKED	W-OWING	W-ROOTS
W-AKING	W-ATAPS	W-ELDER	W-HEARE	W-HINGE	W-INKER	W-RACKS	
W-ALLOW	W-AUGHT	W-ENDED	W-HEATS	W-HINNY	W-INKLE	W-RASSE	
W-AMBLE	W-AVERS	W-ESTER	W-HEELS	W-HIPPY	W-INNER	W-RATHS	
W-ANGLE	W-AXING	W-ETHER	W-HEEZE	W-HISTS	W-INTER	W-REAKS	
W-ANKER	W-EANED	W-HACKS	W-HEFTS	W-HOLES	W-ISHES	W-RECKS	
W-ANKLE	W-EARED	W-HALED	W-HELMS	W-HOLLY	W-ITCHY	W-RESTS	

6→7

W-ACKERS	W-ANTING	W-EASELS	W-HAMMED	W-HETHER	W-HIZZED	W-INKING	W-RACKED
W-ADDING	W-APPEND	W-EBBING	W-HANGED	W-HEUGHS	W-HIZZES	W-INKLED	W-RAPPED
W-ADDLED	W-ARLING	W-EDGIER	W-HAPPED	W-HEWING	W-HOLISM	W-INKLES	W-RAPPER
W-ADDLES	W-ARMING	W-EDGING	W-HEELED	W-HIDDER	W-HOLIST	W-INNERS	W-RASSES
W-AFTERS	W-ARRANT	W-EIGHTS	W-HEELER	W-HINGED	W-HOOPED	W-INNING	W-REAKED
W-AILING	W-ARRAYS	W-EIGHTY	W-HEEZED	W-HINGES	W-HOOPER	W-INTERS	W-RECKED
W-ALLIES	W-ARTIER	W-ELDERS	W-HEEZES	W-HIPPED	W-HOOTED	W-ITCHED	W-RESTED
W-ALLOWS	W-ASHERY	W-ELDING	W-HELMED	W-HIPPER	W-HOPPED	W-ITCHES	W-RESTER
W-AMBLED	W-ASHIER	W-ENDING	W-HELPED	W-HISHED	W-HOPPER	W-IZARDS	W-RICKED
W-AMBLES	W-ASSAIL	W-ESTERS	W-HEREAT	W-HISHES	W-ICKERS	W-ONNING	W-RIGHTS
W-AMUSES	W-ASTERS	W-ETHERS	W-HEREBY	W-HISSED	W-IMPISH	W-OOZIER	W-RINGED
W-ANGLED	W-ATTEST	W-HACKED	W-HEREIN	W-HISSES	W-INCHED	W-OOZILY	W-RINGER
W-ANGLER	W-AUGHTS	W-HACKER	W-HEREOF	W-HISTED	W-INCHES	W-ORMERS	W-ROOTED
W-ANGLES	W-EANING	W-HALERS	W-HEREON	W-HITHER	W-INDIGO	W-OUBITS	W-ROUGHT
W-ANKERS	W-EARING	W-HALING	W-HERETO	W-HITTER	W-INKERS	W-OURALI	W-ULLING

7→8

W-ADDLING	W-ARTLESS	W-HACKERS	W-HELPING	W-HISHING	W-HOOPING	W-INNINGS
W-AGELESS	W-ASHIEST	W-HACKING	W-HERRIES	W-HISSING	W-HOOSHED	W-ITCHIER
W-ALLOWED	W-ASSAILS	W-HAMMING	W-HIDDERS	W-HISTING	W-HOOSHES	W-ITCHING
W-AMBLING	W-ASTABLE	W-HANGING	W-HINNIED	W-HITHERS	W-HOOTING	W-OOZIEST
W-ANGLERS	W-EANLING	W-HAPPING	W-HINNIES	W-HITTERS	W-HOPPERS	W-OURALIS
W-ANGLING	W-EARINGS	W-HEELERS	W-HIPPIER	W-HIZZING	W-HOPPING	W-RACKING
W-ANTINGS	W-EDGIEST	W-HEELING	W-HIPPING	W-HOLISMS	W-INCHING	W-RAPPERS
W-ARRAYED	W-EDGINGS	W-HEEZING	W-HIPSTER	W-HOLISTS	W-INDIGOS	W-RAPPING
W-ARTIEST	W-ELDINGS	W-HELMING	W-HIRLING	W-HOOPERS	W-INKLING	W-REAKING

W-RECKING   W-RESTING   W-RETCHES   W-RINGERS   W-ROOTING
W-RESTERS   W-RETCHED   W-RICKING   W-RINGING

8→9
W-ALLOWING   W-ASSAILER   W-HERENESS   W-HIPPINGS   W-HOOSHING   W-RINGINGS
W-AMBLINGS   W-EANLINGS   W-HEREUNTO   W-HIPSTERS   W-HOPPINGS
W-ANGLINGS   W-EDGEWISE   W-HEREUPON   W-HIRLINGS   W-IMPISHLY
W-ARRAYING   W-HACKINGS   W-HEREWITH   W-HITHERED   W-ITCHIEST
W-ASHERIES   W-HEELINGS   W-HINNYING   W-HOLESOME   W-OOZINESS
W-ASSAILED   W-HEREFROM   W-HIPPIEST   W-HOLISTIC   W-RAPPINGS

2→3
BO-W   FA-W   HO-W   KO-W   MA-W   NE-W   PO-W   TA-W   WO-W
DA-W   HA-W   JO-W   LA-W   ME-W   NO-W   RE-W   TE-W   YE-W
DO-W   HE-W   KA-W   LO-W   MO-W   PA-W   SO-W   TO-W   YO-W

3→4
ALE-W   ARE-W   BRO-W   CHE-W   FRO-W   SHE-W   SPA-W   VIE-W
ANE-W   BRA-W   CHA-W   ENE-W   PRO-W   SKA-W   THE-W   WHO-W

4→5
BEDE-W   NAVE-W   PAWA-W   SINE-W   THRO-W
KOTO-W   PAPA-W   PILA-W   SYBO-W   VINE-W

5→6
BURRO-W   HOLLO-W   MISSA-W   PURSE-W   UNCLE-W
HALLO-W   MATLO-W   MORRO-W   REVIE-W

6→7
FITCHE-W

7→8
BUDGERO-W   RICKSHA-W

8→9
KABELJOU-W

2→3
X-IS

4→5
X-ERIC   X-YLEM

5→6
X-YLEMS

6→7
X-EROTIC

2→3
BO-X   HE-X   LA-X   MA-X   MU-X   PA-X   PO-X   SI-X   TA-X   WO-X
FA-X   HO-X   LO-X   MI-X   NO-X   PI-X   RE-X   SO-X   WE-X   YE-X

3→4
APE-X   CRU-X   EAU-X   FLU-X   HOA-X   JEU-X   PRE-X   ULE-X

4→5
BEAU-X   CARE-X   CODE-X   LIMA-X   REDO-X   SORE-X   VITE-X
BORA-X   CHOU-X   LATE-X   MURE-X   SILE-X   VIBE-X

5→6
ADIEU-X   BIJOU-X   BOYAU-X   DUPLE-X

6→7
BATEAU-X   CADEAU-X   GATEAU-X   MINIMA-X   SIMPLE-X
BUREAU-X   COTEAU-X   MILIEU-X   RESEAU-X   TRIPLE-X

7→8
BANDEAU-X   CHAPEAU-X   JAMBEAU-X   PLATEAU-X   ROULEAU-X   TRUMEAU-X
BERCEAU-X   CHATEAU-X   MANTEAU-X   PONCEAU-X   TABLEAU-X
CAMAIEU-X   FABLIAU-X   MORCEAU-X   RONDEAU-X   TONNEAU-X

8→9
FLAMBEAU-X   MULTIPLE-X

2→3
Y-AH   Y-AW   Y-EN   Y-EX   Y-IN   Y-OD   Y-OS   Y-OW   Y-UP
Y-AM   Y-EA   Y-ES   Y-GO   Y-OB   Y-ON   Y-OU   Y-UG   Y-US

3→4
Y-AHS   Y-AWL   Y-EAS   Y-ELL   Y-EST   Y-INS   Y-OLD   Y-OUR   Y-ULE
Y-ALE   Y-AWN   Y-ECH   Y-ELM   Y-EUK   Y-IRK   Y-OOF   Y-OWE   Y-UPS
Y-ARD   Y-BET   Y-EGG   Y-ELT   Y-EVE   Y-OBS   Y-OOP   Y-OWL   Y-WIS
Y-ARE   Y-EAN   Y-ELD   Y-ENS   Y-GOE   Y-ODE   Y-ORE   Y-UGS
Y-ATE   Y-EAR   Y-ELK   Y-ERK   Y-ILL   Y-OKE   Y-OUK   Y-UKE

4→5
Y-ALES   Y-AWNS   Y-EANS   Y-ELKS   Y-EUKS   Y-IRKS   Y-ORES   Y-RAPT   Y-UPON
Y-AMEN   Y-AWNY   Y-EARD   Y-ELLS   Y-EVEN   Y-LIKE   Y-OUKS   Y-RENT
Y-ARDS   Y-BORE   Y-EARN   Y-ELMS   Y-EVES   Y-MOLT   Y-OURN   Y-SAME
Y-AULD   Y-CLAD   Y-EARS   Y-ELTS   Y-EXES   Y-OKES   Y-OURS   Y-TOST
Y-AWED   Y-COND   Y-EAST   Y-ERKS   Y-FERE   Y-OOFS   Y-OWES   Y-UKES
Y-AWLS   Y-DRAD   Y-EGGS   Y-ESTS   Y-ILLS   Y-OOPS   Y-OWLS   Y-ULES

5→6
Y-AGGER   Y-ARROW   Y-BOUND   Y-EARLY   Y-ESTER   Y-OWLED   Y-SHENT
Y-AKKAS   Y-AWING   Y-BRENT   Y-EARNS   Y-EUKED   Y-PIGHT   Y-WROKE
Y-AMENS   Y-AWNED   Y-EANED   Y-EASTS   Y-ICKER   Y-PLAST
Y-ANKER   Y-BLENT   Y-EARDS   Y-ESSES   Y-IRKED   Y-SHEND

6→7
Y-ACKERS   Y-ARROWS   Y-CLEPED   Y-EARNED   Y-EUKING   Y-MOLTEN   Y-SHENDS
Y-AGGERS   Y-AWNIER   Y-EANING   Y-EARNER   Y-ICKERS   Y-OWLING   Y-SLAKED
Y-ANKERS   Y-AWNING   Y-EARDED   Y-EASTED   Y-IRKING   Y-PLIGHT   Y-UCKERS

7→8
Y-ATAGHAN   Y-AWNINGS   Y-CLEEPED   Y-EARDING   Y-EARNERS   Y-EASTING
Y-AWNIEST   Y-BOUNDEN   Y-EANLING   Y-EARLIES   Y-EARNING   Y-OURSELF

8→9
Y-ATAGHANS   Y-CLEEPING   Y-EANLINGS   Y-EARNINGS   Y-RAVISHED   Y-SHENDING

2→3
AN-Y   BE-Y   FA-Y   HA-Y   JO-Y   LO-Y   NA-Y   SH-Y   TA-Y
AR-Y   BO-Y   GO-Y   HE-Y   KA-Y   MA-Y   NO-Y   SO-Y   TO-Y
BA-Y   DA-Y   GU-Y   HO-Y   LA-Y   MO-Y   PA-Y   ST-Y   WE-Y

3→4
ACH-Y   AWA-Y   BUR-Y   COR-Y   DOG-Y   ELM-Y   GAB-Y   ILL-Y   LIN-Y   MIX-Y
AIR-Y   AWN-Y   BUS-Y   COS-Y   DOP-Y   FAD-Y   GAM-Y   INK-Y   LOG-Y   MON-Y
ALA-Y   BOD-Y   CAN-Y   COX-Y   DOR-Y   FOG-Y   GOB-Y   JOE-Y   LOR-Y   MOP-Y
ALL-Y   BOG-Y   CHA-Y   COZ-Y   DOT-Y   FOX-Y   GOE-Y   JUD-Y   MAN-Y   NIX-Y
ARM-Y   BON-Y   CIT-Y   DEF-Y   EAS-Y   FRA-Y   HER-Y   LAC-Y   MAR-Y   NOS-Y
ART-Y   BOX-Y   CON-Y   DEN-Y   EEL-Y   FUM-Y   HUG-Y   LAD-Y   MAT-Y   NOW-Y
ASH-Y   BRA-Y   COP-Y   DEW-Y   EGG-Y   FUR-Y   IFF-Y   LEV-Y   MIR-Y   OAK-Y

OAR-Y	OWL-Y	PIX-Y	QUA-Y	SAG-Y	THE-Y	TON-Y	URD-Y	WAX-Y
OIL-Y	PAL-Y	POS-Y	REN-Y	SEX-Y	TID-Y	TOW-Y	VIN-Y	WIN-Y
OLD-Y	PIN-Y	POX-Y	RIM-Y	SPA-Y	TIN-Y	TUN-Y	WAD-Y	YAW-Y
OOS-Y	PIP-Y	PRE-Y	ROK-Y	TAK-Y	TOD-Y	TWA-Y	WAN-Y	YUK-Y
ORB-Y	PIT-Y	PUN-Y	RUB-Y	TED-Y	TOE-Y	UPS-Y	WAR-Y	

4→5

ABBE-Y	CARD-Y	DURO-Y	GOOS-Y	KILT-Y	MOOD-Y	POLL-Y	SAVE-Y	TOAD-Y
ACID-Y	CARR-Y	DUSK-Y	GORM-Y	KIND-Y	MOOL-Y	PONE-Y	SCAR-Y	TOFF-Y
AGON-Y	CHAR-Y	DUST-Y	GOUT-Y	KINK-Y	MOON-Y	PONG-Y	SEAM-Y	TONE-Y
ALAR-Y	CHEW-Y	DYKE-Y	GRIM-Y	KOOK-Y	MOOR-Y	PONT-Y	SEED-Y	TOSH-Y
ANNO-Y	CHIV-Y	EARL-Y	GRIS-Y	LACE-Y	MOPE-Y	POOF-Y	SEEL-Y	TOSS-Y
ANTS-Y	COAL-Y	EBON-Y	GUCK-Y	LAIR-Y	MOPS-Y	POPS-Y	SEEP-Y	TOWN-Y
ARTS-Y	COBB-Y	EVER-Y	GULF-Y	LANK-Y	MORA-Y	PORK-Y	SERR-Y	TOWS-Y
ATOM-Y	COCK-Y	FAIR-Y	GULL-Y	LARD-Y	MOSE-Y	PORT-Y	SESE-Y	TRIP-Y
ATOP-Y	COLE-Y	FELL-Y	GURL-Y	LARK-Y	MOSS-Y	POSE-Y	SHAD-Y	TUFT-Y
AUNT-Y	COLL-Y	FELT-Y	GUSH-Y	LATH-Y	MOTE-Y	POTT-Y	SHIN-Y	TUMP-Y
BAFF-Y	COMB-Y	FEND-Y	GUST-Y	LAWN-Y	MOTH-Y	POUT-Y	SHOW-Y	TURF-Y
BALD-Y	CONE-Y	FERN-Y	GYPS-Y	LEAD-Y	MOTT-Y	POWN-Y	SILK-Y	TUSH-Y
BALK-Y	CONK-Y	FIER-Y	HAIL-Y	LEAF-Y	MOUS-Y	POZZ-Y	SILL-Y	TUSK-Y
BALL-Y	COOK-Y	FILL-Y	HAIR-Y	LEAK-Y	MUCK-Y	PRAT-Y	SILT-Y	TWIN-Y
BALM-Y	COOL-Y	FILM-Y	HAND-Y	LEAN-Y	MULE-Y	PREX-Y	SINK-Y	UNIT-Y
BAND-Y	COOM-Y	FISH-Y	HANK-Y	LEAR-Y	MUMM-Y	PRIM-Y	SISS-Y	VAIR-Y
BARD-Y	COPS-Y	FIST-Y	HARD-Y	LEER-Y	MUMS-Y	PROS-Y	SLAT-Y	VAST-Y
BARK-Y	CORE-Y	FIZZ-Y	HARP-Y	LEFT-Y	MURK-Y	PUDS-Y	SLIM-Y	VEAL-Y
BARM-Y	CORK-Y	FLAK-Y	HASH-Y	LEZZ-Y	MURL-Y	PUFF-Y	SLOP-Y	VEER-Y
BASS-Y	CORN-Y	FLAM-Y	HAST-Y	LIME-Y	MUSH-Y	PULP-Y	SNAR-Y	VEIL-Y
BATT-Y	COVE-Y	FLAW-Y	HEAD-Y	LINE-Y	MUSK-Y	PUNT-Y	SNIP-Y	VEIN-Y
BAWD-Y	CRAP-Y	FLAX-Y	HEAP-Y	LING-Y	MUSS-Y	PURS-Y	SNOW-Y	VIEW-Y
BEAD-Y	CRUD-Y	FLOR-Y	HEED-Y	LINN-Y	MUST-Y	PUSH-Y	SOAP-Y	WACK-Y
BEAK-Y	CRUS-Y	FLUE-Y	HEFT-Y	LINT-Y	NARK-Y	PUSS-Y	SOFT-Y	WADD-Y
BEAM-Y	CULL-Y	FOAM-Y	HEMP-Y	LOAM-Y	NEED-Y	PUTT-Y	SOIL-Y	WALL-Y
BEEF-Y	CURD-Y	FOOD-Y	HERB-Y	LOFT-Y	NERD-Y	RAGG-Y	SONS-Y	WANE-Y
BEER-Y	CURL-Y	FOOT-Y	HILL-Y	LOLL-Y	NETT-Y	RAIN-Y	SOOT-Y	WANK-Y
BELL-Y	CURN-Y	FORA-Y	HOAR-Y	LOON-Y	NEWS-Y	RAND-Y	SOUP-Y	WANT-Y
BEND-Y	CURR-Y	FORB-Y	HOKE-Y	LOOP-Y	NIFF-Y	RANG-Y	SPEW-Y	WART-Y
BENT-Y	CUSH-Y	FORK-Y	HOLE-Y	LORD-Y	NIRL-Y	RASP-Y	SPIC-Y	WASH-Y
BIGG-Y	CUTE-Y	FORT-Y	HOME-Y	LOSS-Y	NOOK-Y	READ-Y	SPIK-Y	WASP-Y
BILL-Y	DAFF-Y	FROW-Y	HONE-Y	LOUR-Y	NOSE-Y	REAM-Y	SPIN-Y	WAVE-Y
BING-Y	DAIS-Y	FUBS-Y	HONK-Y	LOVE-Y	NOUN-Y	REDD-Y	STAG-Y	WEAR-Y
BITS-Y	DAMP-Y	FUFF-Y	HOOK-Y	LUCK-Y	PACE-Y	REED-Y	STEW-Y	WEED-Y
BITT-Y	DARK-Y	FULL-Y	HORN-Y	LUMP-Y	PALL-Y	REEK-Y	STUD-Y	WEEN-Y
BLOW-Y	DAUB-Y	FUND-Y	HORS-Y	LUSH-Y	PALM-Y	REIF-Y	SUDS-Y	WEEP-Y
BLUE-Y	DEAR-Y	FUNK-Y	HUFF-Y	LUST-Y	PALS-Y	REST-Y	SUET-Y	WELL-Y
BOOB-Y	DEAW-Y	FURR-Y	HULK-Y	MALT-Y	PAND-Y	RICE-Y	SULK-Y	WHIN-Y
BOOK-Y	DECO-Y	FUSS-Y	HULL-Y	MANG-Y	PANS-Y	RIFT-Y	SUNN-Y	WHIT-Y
BOOT-Y	DEED-Y	FUST-Y	HUMP-Y	MARD-Y	PARD-Y	RILE-Y	SURF-Y	WICK-Y
BOSK-Y	DICE-Y	FUZZ-Y	HUNK-Y	MARL-Y	PARK-Y	RIND-Y	TACK-Y	WILL-Y
BOSS-Y	DICK-Y	GALL-Y	HURL-Y	MASH-Y	PARR-Y	RISK-Y	TALC-Y	WIMP-Y
BOTH-Y	DICT-Y	GAME-Y	HUSH-Y	MASS-Y	PART-Y	ROAR-Y	TALK-Y	WIND-Y
BOTT-Y	DIKE-Y	GASP-Y	HUSK-Y	MAST-Y	PAST-Y	ROCK-Y	TALL-Y	WINE-Y
BULK-Y	DILL-Y	GAUD-Y	HUSS-Y	MATE-Y	PATS-Y	ROIL-Y	TANG-Y	WING-Y
BULL-Y	DING-Y	GAUM-Y	IRON-Y	MAWK-Y	PAWK-Y	ROOF-Y	TANK-Y	WISP-Y
BUMP-Y	DINK-Y	GAWK-Y	ITCH-Y	MEAL-Y	PAWN-Y	ROOK-Y	TANS-Y	WITH-Y
BUNG-Y	DIRT-Y	GEEK-Y	JAZZ-Y	MEAN-Y	PEAK-Y	ROOM-Y	TART-Y	WOMB-Y
BUNT-Y	DISH-Y	GENT-Y	JEEL-Y	MEAT-Y	PEAT-Y	ROOP-Y	TATT-Y	WONK-Y
BURL-Y	DITS-Y	GILL-Y	JELL-Y	MEIN-Y	PEON-Y	ROOT-Y	TEAR-Y	WOOD-Y
BURR-Y	DITT-Y	GIMP-Y	JERK-Y	MELT-Y	PERK-Y	ROPE-Y	TECH-Y	WOOF-Y
BUSH-Y	DOLL-Y	GINN-Y	JIFF-Y	MERC-Y	PHON-Y	RORT-Y	TEEN-Y	WORD-Y
BUSK-Y	DOOM-Y	GIPS-Y	JIMP-Y	MESH-Y	PICK-Y	ROUP-Y	TELL-Y	WORM-Y
BUST-Y	DOPE-Y	GIRL-Y	JOKE-Y	MESS-Y	PIET-Y	RUDD-Y	TENT-Y	YAPP-Y
BUTT-Y	DORK-Y	GLAD-Y	JOLL-Y	MICK-Y	PINE-Y	RUMP-Y	TEST-Y	YAWN-Y
BUZZ-Y	DORM-Y	GLOB-Y	JOLT-Y	MIFF-Y	PINK-Y	RUNT-Y	THAW-Y	YEST-Y
CAGE-Y	DORT-Y	GLUE-Y	JOWL-Y	MILK-Y	PION-Y	RUSH-Y	THEW-Y	YOLK-Y
CAKE-Y	DOWD-Y	GOAT-Y	JUMP-Y	MING-Y	PITH-Y	RUST-Y	TICH-Y	YUCK-Y
CALM-Y	DOWN-Y	GOLD-Y	JUNK-Y	MINT-Y	PLAT-Y	SALT-Y	TICK-Y	ZEST-Y
CAMP-Y	DUCK-Y	GOOD-Y	KELL-Y	MISS-Y	PLUM-Y	SAME-Y	TILL-Y	ZINC-Y
CANN-Y	DULL-Y	GOOF-Y	KELP-Y	MIST-Y	POCK-Y	SAND-Y	TINT-Y	ZING-Y
CANT-Y	DUMP-Y	GOOL-Y	KELT-Y	MOCH-Y	POKE-Y	SARK-Y	TIPS-Y	
CARB-Y	DUNG-Y	GOOP-Y	MOLL-Y	POLE-Y		SASS-Y	TIZZ-Y	

5→6

AMBER-Y	BAKER-Y	BEAUT-Y	BLANK-Y	BLOCK-Y	BLOWS-Y	BOOZE-Y	BRAIN-Y
ARMOR-Y	BALLS-Y	BETON-Y	BLASH-Y	BLOKE-Y	BLUES-Y	BOSOM-Y	BRAND-Y
ARROW-Y	BARON-Y	BIELD-Y	BLEAK-Y	BLOOD-Y	BLUID-Y	BOTCH-Y	BRANK-Y
AUGUR-Y	BEACH-Y	BITCH-Y	BLEAR-Y	BLOOM-Y	BOOKS-Y	BOWER-Y	BRASH-Y

BRASS-Y	CREAK-Y	FLUNK-Y	KNACK-Y	POINT-Y	SKILL-Y	STEAM-Y	TREND-Y
BRAWL-Y	CREAM-Y	FLURR-Y	KNURL-Y	PONCE-Y	SKIMP-Y	STEDD-Y	TRESS-Y
BRAWN-Y	CREEK-Y	FLUSH-Y	LAUGH-Y	POUCH-Y	SLANG-Y	STEED-Y	TRICK-Y
BRICK-Y	CREEP-Y	FOLKS-Y	LEACH-Y	PRANK-Y	SLAVE-Y	STEEL-Y	TRIPE-Y
BRIER-Y	CREPE-Y	FORTH-Y	LEMON-Y	PRICE-Y	SLEEK-Y	STEEP-Y	TROLL-Y
BRISK-Y	CRICK-Y	FREAK-Y	LIVER-Y	PRIOR-Y	SLEEP-Y	STEER-Y	TROUT-Y
BROOD-Y	CRIMP-Y	FREET-Y	LOATH-Y	PRISM-Y	SLEET-Y	STICK-Y	TRUST-Y
BROOM-Y	CRISP-Y	FREIT-Y	LOWER-Y	PUNCH-Y	SLIMS-Y	STIFF-Y	TRUTH-Y
BROWN-Y	CROAK-Y	FRIAR-Y	LUNAR-Y	QUALM-Y	SLINK-Y	STILL-Y	TWANG-Y
BROWS-Y	CROUP-Y	FRILL-Y	MANGE-Y	QUEEN-Y	SLOOM-Y	STILT-Y	TWEED-Y
BRUSH-Y	CRUMB-Y	FRISK-Y	MARSH-Y	QUINS-Y	SLOSH-Y	STING-Y	TWEEL-Y
BUNCH-Y	CRUMP-Y	FRIZZ-Y	MAUND-Y	QUIRK-Y	SLUBB-Y	STINT-Y	TWILL-Y
CARSE-Y	CRUST-Y	FROST-Y	MEDLE-Y	RAKER-Y	SLUMP-Y	STOCK-Y	TWIRL-Y
CATCH-Y	CUTES-Y	FROTH-Y	MEREL-Y	REAST-Y	SLUSH-Y	STORE-Y	TWIST-Y
CAUSE-Y	DAINT-Y	FROWS-Y	MIGHT-Y	REECH-Y	SMALM-Y	STORM-Y	UMBER-Y
CHAFF-Y	DEATH-Y	FRUIT-Y	MISER-Y	REEST-Y	SMARM-Y	STOUR-Y	UNRED-Y
CHALK-Y	DINGE-Y	FRUMP-Y	MISSA-Y	REPLA-Y	SMART-Y	STRAW-Y	VAULT-Y
CHANT-Y	DOUGH-Y	GAMES-Y	MONOS-Y	RHEUM-Y	SMEAR-Y	STRIP-Y	VAUNT-Y
CHARR-Y	DRAFF-Y	GHOST-Y	MOTOR-Y	RIVER-Y	SMELL-Y	STUFF-Y	VETCH-Y
CHASM-Y	DRAFT-Y	GLAIR-Y	MOULD-Y	ROOTS-Y	SMILE-Y	STUMP-Y	VICAR-Y
CHEAP-Y	DREAM-Y	GLASS-Y	MOUSE-Y	ROPER-Y	SMIRK-Y	SUGAR-Y	VINER-Y
CHECK-Y	DREAR-Y	GLAUR-Y	MOUTH-Y	ROSET-Y	SMIRR-Y	SWAMP-Y	VOGUE-Y
CHEEK-Y	DRECK-Y	GLEAM-Y	MURRA-Y	ROSIN-Y	SMITH-Y	SWANK-Y	VOLAR-Y
CHEER-Y	DRESS-Y	GLEET-Y	MURRE-Y	ROUGH-Y	SNAIL-Y	SWARD-Y	WAFER-Y
CHERT-Y	DRIFT-Y	GLITZ-Y	NIGHT-Y	RUDER-Y	SNARL-Y	SWART-Y	WARRE-Y
CHEST-Y	DROLL-Y	GLOOM-Y	NITER-Y	SAMEL-Y	SNEAK-Y	SWASH-Y	WATER-Y
CHILL-Y	DROOP-Y	GLOOP-Y	NOMAD-Y	SATIN-Y	SNEER-Y	SWEAT-Y	WAVER-Y
CHINK-Y	DROPS-Y	GLOSS-Y	NOTCH-Y	SAVOR-Y	SNELL-Y	SWEEP-Y	WHACK-Y
CHIRP-Y	DROSS-Y	GNARL-Y	OCCAM-Y	SCALL-Y	SNIFF-Y	SWEET-Y	WHEAT-Y
CHOKE-Y	DROWS-Y	GOOSE-Y	OCHER-Y	SCANT-Y	SNIFT-Y	SWING-Y	WHEEL-Y
CHUFF-Y	DUPER-Y	GOURD-Y	OCHRE-Y	SCARE-Y	SNOOP-Y	SWIPE-Y	WHELK-Y
CHUNK-Y	EARTH-Y	GOWAN-Y	OILER-Y	SCATT-Y	SNOOT-Y	SWIRL-Y	WHIFF-Y
CIDER-Y	EATER-Y	GRAIN-Y	ONION-Y	SCAUR-Y	SNORT-Y	SWISH-Y	WHIMS-Y
CLART-Y	EGGER-Y	GRAPE-Y	ORBIT-Y	SCREW-Y	SNOUT-Y	SYLPH-Y	WHIRL-Y
CLASS-Y	EIGHT-Y	GRASS-Y	OSIER-Y	SCURF-Y	SNUFF-Y	SYRUP-Y	WHIRR-Y
CLIFF-Y	EMBUS-Y	GREED-Y	OWLER-Y	SCUZZ-Y	SOREL-Y	TAWER-Y	WHISK-Y
CLIFT-Y	FAINT-Y	GREEN-Y	PAEON-Y	SEVER-Y	SPACE-Y	TEENS-Y	WHITE-Y
CLING-Y	FAKER-Y	GROUP-Y	PAINT-Y	SHAND-Y	SPARK-Y	THICK-Y	WIELD-Y
CLOUD-Y	FAULT-Y	GROUT-Y	PAPER-Y	SHARN-Y	SPAWN-Y	THING-Y	WINCE-Y
CLUCK-Y	FELON-Y	GROWL-Y	PARLE-Y	SHEAF-Y	SPEAR-Y	THORN-Y	WITCH-Y
CLUMP-Y	FILTH-Y	GRUMP-Y	PATCH-Y	SHEEN-Y	SPECK-Y	THUMB-Y	WOODS-Y
CLUNK-Y	FINER-Y	GUILT-Y	PEACH-Y	SHEEP-Y	SPEED-Y	TIGER-Y	WORTH-Y
COACH-Y	FITCH-Y	HEARS-Y	PEARL-Y	SHEET-Y	SPIFF-Y	TILER-Y	WOUND-Y
COCKS-Y	FLASH-Y	HEART-Y	PETAR-Y	SHELF-Y	SPOOK-Y	TITCH-Y	WRATH-Y
COLON-Y	FLESH-Y	HEATH-Y	PHONE-Y	SHELL-Y	SPOON-Y	TITUP-Y	WRIST-Y
CONCH-Y	FLINT-Y	HITCH-Y	PITCH-Y	SHIFT-Y	SPORT-Y	TOAST-Y	YEAST-Y
CONVO-Y	FLIRT-Y	HORSE-Y	PLASH-Y	SHIRT-Y	SPOSH-Y	TOOTH-Y	YOUTH-Y
COUNT-Y	FLISK-Y	HOUSE-Y	PLONK-Y	SHOAL-Y	SPOUT-Y	TOOTS-Y	
COUTH-Y	FLOAT-Y	HUMUS-Y	PLUCK-Y	SHORT-Y	SPUNK-Y	TOUCH-Y	
CRAFT-Y	FLOSS-Y	HURRA-Y	PLUFF-Y	SINEW-Y	STAGE-Y	TOWER-Y	
CRAMP-Y	FLOUR-Y	JACKS-Y	PLUMP-Y	SKEAR-Y	STALK-Y	TRASH-Y	
CRANK-Y	FLUFF-Y	JAUNT-Y	PLUSH-Y	SKEER-Y	STARR-Y	TREAT-Y	
CRAWL-Y	FLUKE-Y	KECKS-Y	POACH-Y	SKELL-Y	STEAD-Y		

6→7

ANALOG-Y	BURSAR-Y	COSHER-Y	DYVOUR-Y	GINGER-Y	KITSCH-Y	MORASS-Y	PEPPER-Y
ANARCH-Y	BUTLER-Y	COTTON-Y	EPARCH-Y	GINNER-Y	KITTEN-Y	MOTHER-Y	PHLEGM-Y
ARCHER-Y	BUTTER-Y	CRAMES-Y	EUPHON-Y	GOSSIP-Y	LADDER-Y	MOUSER-Y	PICKER-Y
ARMOUR-Y	BUTTON-Y	CREESH-Y	EXARCH-Y	GRAVEL-Y	LATHER-Y	MUMMER-Y	PILFER-Y
AUTUMN-Y	CANKER-Y	CRUNCH-Y	FACTOR-Y	GROCER-Y	LECHER-Y	MUTTON-Y	PILLOW-Y
BALSAM-Y	CANNER-Y	CURSOR-Y	FARMER-Y	GROUCH-Y	LENGTH-Y	NAILER-Y	PLAGUE-Y
BATTER-Y	CARROT-Y	CUTLER-Y	FERRET-Y	GULLER-Y	LITTER-Y	NATTER-Y	PLOVER-Y
BEAVER-Y	CARVER-Y	DACOIT-Y	FIBBER-Y	GUNNER-Y	MAGGOT-Y	NAUGHT-Y	POTHER-Y
BEGGAR-Y	CASTOR-Y	DAUBER-Y	FIDDLE-Y	HACKER-Y	MAPPER-Y	NECTAR-Y	POTTER-Y
BILLOW-Y	CAUTER-Y	DEANER-Y	FIDGET-Y	HAUGHT-Y	MARROW-Y	NIGGER-Y	POWDER-Y
BINDER-Y	CHANCE-Y	DIARCH-Y	FISHER-Y	HEALTH-Y	MARTYR-Y	NOSHER-Y	PREACH-Y
BIOGEN-Y	CHINTZ-Y	DITHER-Y	FLAUNT-Y	HENNER-Y	MASTER-Y	NUGGET-Y	PROBIT-Y
BLIGHT-Y	CHOOSE-Y	DODDER-Y	FLIGHT-Y	HERBAR-Y	MATTER-Y	NURSER-Y	PUCKER-Y
BLOTCH-Y	CHURCH-Y	DODGER-Y	FLOWER-Y	HICCUP-Y	MEADOW-Y	NUTTER-Y	PUFFER-Y
BOILER-Y	CINDER-Y	DOGGER-Y	FORGER-Y	HOGGER-Y	MELLOW-Y	ORANGE-Y	QUARTZ-Y
BRANCH-Y	CIRCUS-Y	DOUGHT-Y	FOUGHT-Y	HONEST-Y	MERCER-Y	ORATOR-Y	QUAVER-Y
BRAVER-Y	CLIQUE-Y	DOWLNE-Y	FRATCH-Y	HOSIER-Y	MILDEW-Y	OROGEN-Y	QUEACH-Y
BREATH-Y	CLOVER-Y	DRAPER-Y	FRATER-Y	JAGGER-Y	MISTER-Y	PALMAR-Y	QUIVER-Y
BREWER-Y	COLOUR-Y	DROICH-Y	FROWST-Y	JASPER-Y	MOCKER-Y	PANICK-Y	RABBIT-Y
BRIBER-Y	COOKER-Y	DROUTH-Y	FURROW-Y	JITTER-Y	MODEST-Y	PARROT-Y	RACKET-Y
BROKER-Y	COOPER-Y	DUDDER-Y	GARGET-Y	JOBBER-Y	MONGER-Y	PAUNCH-Y	RAGGED-Y
BUGGER-Y	COPPER-Y	DYNAST-Y	GEODES-Y	JOINER-Y	MORALL-Y	PEDLAR-Y	RATTER-Y

```
RAUNCH-Y  SCRUMP-Y  SINTER-Y  SQUALL-Y  STRIPE-Y  THRILL-Y  UNREAD-Y  WEIGHT-Y
RECTOR-Y  SCRUNT-Y  SKETCH-Y  SQUASH-Y  SUCCOR-Y  THRIST-Y  UNTENT-Y  WHALER-Y
RIBBON-Y  SEALER-Y  SLAVER-Y  SQUAWK-Y  SUMMAR-Y  THROAT-Y  VALLAR-Y  WILLOW-Y
ROBBER-Y  SENSOR-Y  SLEECH-Y  SQUEAK-Y  SUMMER-Y  TIDDLE-Y  VAPOUR-Y  WINTER-Y
ROCKER-Y  SERVER-Y  SLOUCH-Y  SQUIFF-Y  SUTLER-Y  TINDER-Y  VELVET-Y  WORMER-Y
RUBBER-Y  SHADOW-Y  SLOUGH-Y  SQUIRM-Y  SWARTH-Y  TITTUP-Y  VERMIL-Y  WREATH-Y
RUSSET-Y  SHEATH-Y  SNATCH-Y  SQUISH-Y  SWITCH-Y  TOTTER-Y  VERMIN-Y  YELLOW-Y
SALLOW-Y  SHIVER-Y  SPICER-Y  STAGER-Y  TACKET-Y  TRACER-Y  VICTOR-Y
SATRAP-Y  SHOWER-Y  SPIDER-Y  STARCH-Y  TALLOW-Y  TRICKS-Y  VILLAN-Y
SAVOUR-Y  SHRILL-Y  SPIRIT-Y  STENCH-Y  TANNER-Y  TRIPOD-Y  WASHER-Y
SCRAWL-Y  SHRIMP-Y  SPLASH-Y  STREAK-Y  TATTER-Y  TURNER-Y  WASTER-Y
SCREAK-Y  SHROUD-Y  SPLEEN-Y  STREAM-Y  THIRST-Y  TWITCH-Y  WEALTH-Y
SCRIMP-Y  SIGNOR-Y  SPRAWL-Y  STREET-Y  THREAD-Y  TYMPAN-Y  WEEDER-Y
SCRUFF-Y  SILVER-Y  SPRING-Y  STRING-Y  THRIFT-Y  UNHAND-Y  WEEVIL-Y
```

7→8

```
ADVISOR-Y  CLATTER-Y  FRIPPER-Y  JUGGLER-Y  PUDDING-Y  SHUDDER-Y  THICKET-Y
ANTILOG-Y  CLERUCH-Y  FRUITER-Y  KNACKER-Y  PUPILAR-Y  SLABBER-Y  THUNDER-Y
ANTONYM-Y  CLUSTER-Y  FURRIER-Y  LACUNAR-Y  QUACKER-Y  SLATTER-Y  TITULAR-Y
APOPLEX-Y  COBBLER-Y  GEALOUS-Y  LAMINAR-Y  QUIDDIT-Y  SLEEPER-Y  TOPARCH-Y
AUDITOR-Y  COLLIER-Y  GIMMICK-Y  LEATHER-Y  QUIZZER-Y  SLIDDER-Y  TOPONYM-Y
AXILLAR-Y  CONCEIT-Y  GLIBBER-Y  MERONYM-Y  RAINBOW-Y  SLIPPER-Y  TOURIST-Y
BASTARD-Y  COTTAGE-Y  GLIDDER-Y  METONYM-Y  RECOVER-Y  SLITHER-Y  TRIARCH-Y
BISCUIT-Y  CREAMER-Y  GLIMMER-Y  MILITAR-Y  REFINER-Y  SLOBBER-Y  TRICKER-Y
BLADDER-Y  CRYOGEN-Y  GLITTER-Y  MONARCH-Y  REVISOR-Y  SLUMBER-Y  TRIFFID-Y
BLANKET-Y  CURATOR-Y  GLUTTON-Y  MONITOR-Y  RHUBARB-Y  SMELTER-Y  TRIPPER-Y
BLISTER-Y  CURRANT-Y  GOLIARD-Y  NAVARCH-Y  ROTATOR-Y  SMOTHER-Y  TROLLOP-Y
BLOOMER-Y  CUSHION-Y  GREENER-Y  NOMARCH-Y  RUBBISH-Y  SNIPPET-Y  TUMULAR-Y
BLOSSOM-Y  DASTARD-Y  GRINDER-Y  ORANGER-Y  SACRIST-Y  SNOTTER-Y  TUSSOCK-Y
BLUSTER-Y  DELIVER-Y  GROWLER-Y  ORDINAR-Y  SADDLER-Y  SNUGGER-Y  TUTELAR-Y
BOTCHER-Y  DILATOR-Y  HAPLOID-Y  OUTWEAR-Y  SAFFRON-Y  SOLDIER-Y  TWITTER-Y
BROIDER-Y  DIPLOID-Y  HARMOST-Y  PARADOX-Y  SAMPLER-Y  SOLICIT-Y  UNCLOUD-Y
BULLOCK-Y  DONATOR-Y  HASSOCK-Y  PARONYM-Y  SAVAGER-Y  SPINNER-Y  UNTRUST-Y
BULRUSH-Y  DRAUGHT-Y  HATCHER-Y  PATCHER-Y  SAWDUST-Y  SPLOTCH-Y  UNWATER-Y
BURGLAR-Y  DREAMER-Y  HATCHET-Y  PEACOCK-Y  SCATTER-Y  SPOOFER-Y  UNWORTH-Y
BUTCHER-Y  DROLLER-Y  HEATHER-Y  PEASANT-Y  SCHLEPP-Y  SPUTTER-Y  VAUNTER-Y
CAJOLER-Y  DROUGHT-Y  HEXAPOD-Y  PERCHER-Y  SCHLOCK-Y  SQUELCH-Y  VILLAIN-Y
CANTICO-Y  DRUDGER-Y  HILLOCK-Y  PHANTOM-Y  SCRATCH-Y  STEALTH-Y  VINEGAR-Y
CENTAUR-Y  ENDOGEN-Y  HOMOLOG-Y  PLASTER-Y  SCREECH-Y  STOMACH-Y  WARRANT-Y
CHAFFER-Y  ENGINER-Y  HOMONYM-Y  PLUMBER-Y  SCRUNCH-Y  STRETCH-Y  WHISKER-Y
CHANCER-Y  ENTREAT-Y  HUMMOCK-Y  POLYGAM-Y  SCULLER-Y  SULPHUR-Y  WHISPER-Y
CHEATER-Y  EVANGEL-Y  HYPONYM-Y  POLYGON-Y  SEMINAR-Y  SUNBEAM-Y
CHEVRON-Y  FARRIER-Y  INCISOR-Y  POLYMER-Y  SHATTER-Y  SYNCARP-Y
CHIEFER-Y  FEATHER-Y  JANIZAR-Y  POLYPOD-Y  SHELTER-Y  SYNONYM-Y
CHIRRUP-Y  FLATTER-Y  JEALOUS-Y  PRIGGER-Y  SHIMMER-Y  TABLOID-Y
CIRCUIT-Y  FLUSTER-Y  JEOPARD-Y  PSALTER-Y  SHMALTZ-Y  TASSELL-Y
```

8→9

```
ADULATOR-Y  DEVIATOR-Y  HISTOGEN-Y  OPSIMATH-Y  PROVISOR-Y  TETRAPOD-Y
ALLOPATH-Y  DICTATOR-Y  HUCKSTER-Y  ORTHODOX-Y  PULSATOR-Y  TETRARCH-Y
ANTIPHON-Y  DIRECTOR-Y  HYPERNYM-Y  OSTEOGEN-Y  PUPILLAR-Y  THEOSOPH-Y
ASSERTOR-Y  DISCOVER-Y  IMMODEST-Y  OUTDOORS-Y  RADIATOR-Y  TREACHER-Y
AUXILIAR-Y  EDUCATOR-Y  INCENSOR-Y  OVERWEAR-Y  RAKEHELL-Y  TRIPLOID-Y
BACILLAR-Y  ELEVATOR-Y  INVENTOR-Y  PAPILLAR-Y  SCAPULAR-Y  TRIUMVIR-Y
BIOGRAPH-Y  EMBRACER-Y  JEWELLER-Y  PARAFFIN-Y  SCHMALTZ-Y  UNHEALTH-Y
BLEACHER-Y  ENGRAVER-Y  MAGISTER-Y  PATHOGEN-Y  SCOUTHER-Y  UNTHRIFT-Y
BLIZZARD-Y  EPIGRAPH-Y  MALINGER-Y  PEDERAST-Y  SEIGNIOR-Y  VIBRATOR-Y
BRANCHER-Y  ETHNARCH-Y  MAMILLAR-Y  PENTARCH-Y  SERJEANT-Y  VILLAGER-Y
CALCULAR-Y  EVOCATOR-Y  MANDATOR-Y  PERFUMER-Y  SLAISTER-Y  VISCOUNT-Y
CAPSULAR-Y  EXECUTOR-Y  MEDIATOR-Y  PHOTOGEN-Y  SPLINTER-Y  WHIFFLER-Y
CHANDLER-Y  EXEMPLAR-Y  MEDULLAR-Y  PHYLARCH-Y  SPLUTTER-Y  WHIPCORD-Y
CHICANER-Y  EXPIATOR-Y  MIGRATOR-Y  PISCATOR-Y  SQUEAKER-Y  ZAMINDAR-Y
COLOPHON-Y  FLOURISH-Y  MILLINER-Y  POLYARCH-Y  SQUIRREL-Y  ZEMINDAR-Y
CONTRAST-Y  FORMULAR-Y  MYOGRAPH-Y  POLYMATH-Y  STIPULAR-Y  ZOOMORPH-Y
CREMATOR-Y  GOSSAMER-Y  NARRATOR-Y  POLYONYM-Y  STITCHER-Y
CROTCHET-Y  GRANULAR-Y  NUMMULAR-Y  POLYPHON-Y  SUBAHDAR-Y
CURSITOR-Y  HEPTARCH-Y  OENOPHIL-Y  PREDATOR-Y  SUBLUNAR-Y
DEMOCRAT-Y  HIERARCH-Y  OLIGARCH-Y  PRODITOR-Y  TELEPATH-Y
```

2→3

```
Z-AX   Z-EA   Z-EE   Z-EL   Z-EX   Z-HO   Z-IT   Z-OO   Z-OS
```

3→4

Z-ANY	Z-ELS	Z-ETA	Z-IFF	Z-OBO	Z-OOM	Z-OOS
Z-EAS	Z-EST	Z-HOS	Z-ITS	Z-ONE	Z-OON	Z-OUK

4→5

Z-AMBO	Z-AXES	Z-ETAS	Z-HOMO	Z-OBOS	Z-OOMS	Z-OPPO	Z-UPAS
Z-ANTE	Z-ESTS	Z-EXES	Z-INKY	Z-ONES	Z-OONS	Z-OUKS	

5→6

Z-AMBOS   Z-ANTES   Z-ESTER   Z-HOMOS   Z-INKED

6→7

Z-ESTERS	Z-INKIER	Z-OOGAMY	Z-OOIDAL	Z-OOLOGY
Z-INCITE	Z-INKING	Z-OOGENY	Z-OOLITE	

7→8

Z-INCITES   Z-INKIEST   Z-OOLITES   Z-OOLITIC   Z-OOPHYTE   Z-OOSPORE

8→9

Z-OOGAMIES	Z-OOGENIES	Z-OOLOGIST	Z-OOSPORES
Z-OOGAMOUS	Z-OOLOGIES	Z-OOPHYTES	

2→3

AD-Z   BE-Z   BI-Z   MI-Z   MO-Z   PO-Z   RE-Z

3→4

CHE-Z	FIZ-Z	LEZ-Z	MOZ-Z	PHI-Z	PUT-Z
CHI-Z	JIZ-Z	MIZ-Z	OYE-Z	POZ-Z	ZIZ-Z

4→5

CAPI-Z   CHIZ-Z   FRIZ-Z   GLIT-Z   MILT-Z   SPIT-Z   WHIZ-Z   WOOT-Z

5→6

QUART-Z   SPRIT-Z

Blockers

Blockers are the opposites of hooks – they can't have a letter added either at the front or the end of the word.

Blockers of length two to six letters are given in the lists here. To 'unclutter' the 5- and 6-letter lists, so that you can focus on the more relevant blockers, we have excluded all 5- and 6-letter words ending in -ED, -J, -S, -X, -Y and -Z. It hardly seems necessary to show that words like BAKED, FALAJ, CHIPS, HELIX, DUMMY and TOPAZ are blockers!

2-LETTER WORD BLOCKERS

FY	MY	XU

3-LETTER WORD BLOCKERS

BEZ	FAB	FRY	KEX	MUX	PHS	RAX	SLY	TWP	ZAX
BIZ	FAP	GEY	KOI	NAE	PLY	RHY	SMA	VLY	ZEX
BYS	FAX	GOT	KYE	NOH	POH	SAE	SOX	VOX	ZOA
CLY	FEW	HEX	LEU	NOX	PST	SAX	SWY	WHY	ZUZ
COY	FEZ	HOX	LOX	NTH	PUH	SAZ	TAJ	WOX	
CUZ	FIX	HUH	LUZ	NYS	PYX	SEZ	THY	YEX	
DUX	FLY	IVY	MAE	PAX	QIS	SIX	TUX	YOS	

4-LETTER WORD BLOCKERS

ABBS	BAYS	BUMS	COSS	DIES	DULY	FAIX	FOXY	GHIS	HEMS
ABED	BEDS	BUNS	COSY	DIGS	DUOS	FALX	FOYS	GIBS	HEPS
ABLY	BEEN	BURY	COXY	DIMS	DUPS	FANS	FOZY	GIDS	HEPT
ACHY	BEES	BUSY	COZY	DINS	DUSH	FASH	FRAE	GIED	HISN
ADRY	BEGS	BUYS	CRUX	DISS	DUTY	FAUX	FROM	GIEN	HIYA
AESC	BELS	CAGY	CUBS	DIVS	DYED	FAWS	FUCI	GIES	HOAX
AHEM	BENJ	CAKY	CUED	DIXY	DYES	FEDS	FUDS	GIGS	HOBS
AHOY	BENS	CALX	CUES	DOBS	DZOS	FEET	FUGS	GINS	HODS
AIAS	BEVY	CANY	CURT	DOCS	EASY	FEGS	FUMS	GITS	HOLP
AJAR	BIBS	CAPS	CUSS	DODS	EAUS	FEIS	FUMY	GIZZ	HOLY
AJEE	BIDS	CASH	CWMS	DOEN	EBBS	FENS	FUNS	GJUS	HOMY
ALAE	BIEN	CAUF	DABS	DOGS	ECHO	FETS	FURS	GLEG	HOSS
ALBS	BIGS	CAVY	DADS	DOGY	ECOD	FEUS	FURY	GNUS	HOYS
ALEE	BINS	CAYS	DAES	DOHS	ECUS	FEYS	FUSC	GOAS	HUED
ALIT	BIOS	CEES	DAFT	DOMY	EDDO	FIBS	GABS	GOBS	HUES
ALSO	BISH	CELS	DAGS	DONS	EDHS	FIDS	GABY	GOBY	HUGY
AMOK	BLEW	CEPS	DAHS	DOOS	EHED	FIGS	GADY	GOES	HUIS
ANEW	BOBS	CHEZ	DAKS	DOPS	ELMY	FIKY	GAED	GOEY	HUNG
ANOW	BODS	CHIS	DAMS	DOPY	ELSE	FILS	GAES	GOGO	HUPS
APEX	BODY	CIGS	DANS	DORY	EMUS	FINS	GAGA	GORY	HYED
APTS	BOGS	CITO	DAPS	DOSH	EMYS	FITS	GAGS	GOVS	HYES
AREG	BOGY	CITS	DASH	DOSS	ENOW	FLED	GALS	GOYS	HYPS
AREW	BOHS	CITY	DEAF	DOST	EOAN	FLEX	GAMY	GUBS	IBIS
AROW	BOKS	COAX	DEBS	DOTH	ESPY	FLIX	GANE	GULY	IDEM
AWRY	BONA	COBS	DEEK	DOTS	EUGE	FLUX	GAPS	GUMS	IDLY
AYUS	BOPS	COCH	DEFT	DOTY	EUOI	FOBS	GARE	GUNS	IGAD
BAAS	BORS	CODS	DEFY	DOWF	EVOE	FOCI	GASH	GUPS	ILKA
BABY	BOSH	COFT	DELS	DOXY	EWKS	FOEN	GATS	GURS	INIA
BADE	BOTS	COKY	DEMY	DOZY	EYAS	FOES	GAYS	GUVS	INLY
BADS	BOXY	COLS	DENY	DRAT	EYES	FOGS	GAZY	GYMS	INRO
BAGS	BOYS	COMS	DEUS	DREW	EYNE	FOGY	GEDS	GYNY	IURE
BAMS	BRRR	CONY	DEWS	DUBS	EYRY	FOHS	GEED	GYRI	JABS
BANS	BUBO	COPY	DEWY	DUDS	FADS	FONE	GELS	HATH	JAGS
BAPS	BUBS	CORF	DEYS	DUED	FADY	FONS	GEMS	HAZY	JAKS
BARS	BUDS	CORY	DIBS	DUES	FAGS	FOPS	GENS	HEIL	JAMS
BATS	BUGS	COSH	DIED	DUGS	FAHS	FOUS	GEOS	HELD	JAPS

JARS	KIFS	MAND	NESS	PITY	ROUX	SOCS	THAT	VANS	WYCH
JASS	KILD	MANY	NETS	PIXY	RUBY	SODS	THEY	VATS	WYES
JASY	KINE	MAPS	NEVI	POAS	RUCS	SOGS	THIS	VAUS	WYNS
JAWS	KIRS	MARY	NIDI	POCO	RUNS	SOHO	THUS	VEES	YAKS
JAYS	KISH	MATS	NIDS	POKY	RUTS	SOHS	TICS	VETO	YAPS
JAZY	KISS	MATY	NIED	POMS	RYAS	SOLS	TIDS	VEXT	YAUP
JEED	KNEW	MAWS	NIMS	PONS	RYES	SOME	TIDY	VIAE	YAWS
JEES	KOAS	MAZY	NISI	PONY	RYFE	SOON	TIGS	VIAS	YAWY
JESS	KOBS	MEGS	NIXY	POOH	SABS	SOPS	TILS	VIBS	YBET
JETS	KOND	MELS	NODI	POOS	SACS	SORI	TINS	VIDS	YEAH
JEUX	KOPS	METS	NOES	PORY	SAGS	SOSS	TINY	VIDS	YECH
JEWS	KOSS	MHOS	NOMS	POSY	SAGY	SOTS	TIPT	VIMS	YEPS
JIBS	KOWS	MILS	NOPE	POWS	SAPS	SOVS	TITS	VINS	YEWS
JIGS	KRIS	MINX	NOSH	PRUH	SASH	SOYS	TOBY	VIVO	YGOE
JINX	KYNE	MINY	NOSY	PSST	SAWN	SPED	TODS	VIZY	YINS
JIZZ	KYUS	MIRY	NOTT	PUBS	SAWS	SPRY	TODY	VOES	YIPS
JOBS	LACS	MIXT	NOUS	PUGH	SCRY	STEY	TOED	VOLS	YMPT
JOCO	LACY	MIXY	NOYS	PUGS	SECO	SUBS	TOES	VORS	YOBS
JOES	LANX	MIZZ	NUNS	PUIR	SECS	SUCH	TOEY	VUGS	YOKS
JOGS	LAVS	MNAS	NYAS	PULY	SEEN	SUES	TOGS	VUMS	YOLD
JOKY	LEAL	MOAS	NYED	PUNS	SEES	SUKS	TOLD	WADY	YOND
JORS	LECH	MOBS	OAKY	PUNY	SEGS	SUMS	TONS	WANY	YOWS
JOSH	LEKE	MODS	OBIS	PUPS	SEIK	SUNG	TORN	WARY	YUAN
JOSS	LEKS	MOES	ODDS	PUTS	SELD	SUNS	TOWY	WAVY	YUGS
JOTS	LEPS	MOLY	ODEA	PUTZ	SELS	SUPS	TOYS	WAXY	YUKS
JOWS	LEVA	MOMS	OHMS	PUYS	SEPS	SUQS	TREZ	WEBS	YUKY
JOYS	LEVY	MONY	ONST	PYES	SETS	SUSS	TUGS	WEDS	YUNX
JUDS	LEWD	MOOI	ONYX	QATS	SEWN	SWIZ	TUNY	WEMS	YUPS
JUDY	LIDS	MOPY	OPTS	QUEP	SEWS	SWUM	TUPS	WENS	YWIS
JUGS	LIGS	MOTS	ORFS	RACA	SEXY	SYED	TUTS	WERE	ZAGS
JURE	LINY	MOWN	ORYX	RAHS	SEYS	SYES	TUZZ	WERT	ZANY
JURY	LIRE	MOWS	OYEZ	RAZZ	SHAT	TADS	TWAS	WETS	ZAPS
JUTS	LOBI	MOYS	PADS	RECS	SHMO	TAED	TWOS	WHOA	ZEAS
JYNX	LOCI	MOZZ	PALY	REFS	SHOD	TAES	TYDE	WHOM	ZEDS
KAED	LORN	MUCH	PAPS	REFT	SIBS	TAKS	TYGS	WHOT	ZEKS
KAES	LOST	MUDS	PEDS	REHS	SICH	TAKY	UGLY	WICH	ZELS
KAIS	LUDS	NAIF	PEGS	RELY	SICS	TALI	UNCI	WIFE	ZIGS
KANS	LUVS	NAIN	PEPS	REMS	SIMS	TAMS	UNDO	WILY	ZIPS
KEAS	LYES	NAMS	PHAT	RENY	SINS	TAUS	UNIS	WIRY	ZITE
KEBS	LYMS	NANS	PHEW	REVS	SIPS	TAXA	UPGO	WOES	ZITI
KEDS	LYNX	NAOI	PHIZ	RHOS	SIRS	TEDY	UPSY	WOGS	ZITS
KEFS	MAAS	NAOS	PHOS	RHUS	SITS	TEES	UTAS	WOKS	ZIZZ
KEKS	MACS	NAVY	PIAS	RIPT	SIZY	TEFS	UVAE	WONS	ZOOS
KENS	MADE	NAYS	PIGS	ROED	SKAS	TEGS	UVAS	WOST	
KEPT	MADS	NEFS	PIPS	ROES	SKIS	TELD	VACS	WOWF	
KESH	MAGS	NEKS	PIPY	ROKS	SKOL	TELS	VAES	WOWS	
KETS	MAKS	NEPS	PIRS	ROKY	SKRY	TELT	VAGI	WUDS	
KEYS	MALS	NESH	PISS	ROPY	SOBS	THAE	VAIN	WUSS	

5-LETTER WORD BLOCKERS

(except words ending in -ED, -J, -S, -X, -Y, -Z)

ABACI	AESIR	AINEE	ANTAE	ATRIP	BASHO	BLUER	CALID	CLIPT	CUISH
ABACK	AFALD	AITCH	APACE	AULIC	BASSI	BONZA	CANST	CLOMB	CULCH
ABAFT	AFIRE	ALACK	APAGE	AULOI	BASTA	BOREL	CAPUT	CLOZE	CURCH
ABASH	AFOOT	ALAND	APAID	AURAE	BATCH	BORIC	CARGO	CLUNG	CURSI
ABASK	AFORE	ALBEE	APART	AURAL	BEDAD	BOXEN	CARPI	COMAE	CURST
ABEAM	AFOUL	ALEFT	APAYD	AUREI	BEECH	BRACH	CECAL	COMAL	DATUM
ABLOW	AGAIN	ALGAE	APEAK	AVAST	BEGAD	BRAVA	CECUM	COOST	DAYNT
ABOIL	AGAPE	ALGAL	APEEK	AVIAN	BEGAT	BRAVI	CERCI	CORAM	DEALT
ABORE	AGAST	ALGID	APERT	AWASH	BEGOT	BREEM	CERIC	CORNI	DEDAL
ABOVE	AGGRI	ALIKE	APIAN	AWAVE	BELCH	BREME	CESTI	CORNO	DEERE
ABRAM	AGLEE	ALIVE	APOOP	AWEEL	BELOW	BRULE	CHAVE	COUDE	DEMIC
ABRIM	AGLOW	ALOFT	APORT	AWORK	BENCH	BUCKO	CHERE	COULD	DEMPT
ABUNE	AGONE	ALOHA	APTER	AXIAL	BESAT	BUFFA	CHIAO	COURD	DIACT
ACERB	AGOOD	ALONE	AQUAE	AXILE	BESAW	BUFFI	CHIMO	COXAE	DICTA
ACINI	AGRIN	ALOOF	AREAL	AYELP	BIFID	BUFFO	CHODE	COXAL	DIDST
ACOCK	AHEAD	ALOUD	AREAR	AYGRE	BIGAE	BUILT	CHOTA	COYER	DINGO
ACOLD	AHEAP	ALOWE	AREDD	AYONT	BIRCH	BURNT	CHYND	CRASH	DIRER
ACRID	AHENT	AMAIN	ARERE	AZOIC	BIVIA	BUTCH	CILIA	CREPT	DITCH
ADOWN	AHIGH	AMNIA	ARIOT	AZURN	BLAER	BUXOM	CINCH	CRONK	DOCHT
ADRAD	AHIND	AMONG	AROSE	BAKEN	BLASE	BYSSI	CINCT	CROST	DOEST
ADSUM	AHINT	AMORT	ASKEW	BANAL	BLIST	CABRE	CIPPI	CRUOR	DOETH
ADUNC	AHOLD	AMUCK	ASTIR	BARER	BLIVE	CACTI	CIRRI	CRUSH	DOGGO
ADYTA	AHULL	ANCON	ASWIM	BARIC	BLOWN	CAESE	CIVIL	CUFFO	DOILT
AECIA	AIDOI	ANILE	ATILT	BASER		CAJUN	CLASH	CUING	DOLIA

DOMAL	GAMER	HUTCH	LURID	NOVAE	PUTID	SHORN	SWITH	UNCUT	WHILK
DOTAL	GANCH	HYLIC	LYART	NOXAL	PUTTO	SHOWN	SWOLN	UNDEE	WHIPT
DOWNA	GARNI	HYOID	LYNCH	NUDER	PYOID	SHULN	SWOPT	UNDID	WHOSE
DRANK	GAYER	ICTIC	MADID	NUGAE	PYRAL	SHUSH	SWORE	UNDUE	WHOSO
DRAVE	GEESE	ILEAC	MAIST	NUMEN	QUALE	SIELD	SWORN	UNDUG	WIDER
DRAWN	GELID	ILIAC	MANET	NYING	QUASI	SIGLA	SWUNG	UNETH	WINCH
DRENT	GENAL	IMSHI	MANGO	OATEN	QUAYD	SINCE	SYKER	UNGOT	WINNA
DREST	GENIC	INAPT	MANIC	OBIIT	QUOAD	SKINT	TABID	UNHIP	WISER
DUCAL	GENII	INBYE	MARCH	OBOLI	RABIC	SKOAL	TACET	UNKID	WITAN
DUING	GESSO	INCUT	MARIA	OGMIC	RABID	SLAID	TACIT	UNMET	WOFUL
DUMKA	GEYAN	INEPT	MAYST	OHMIC	RADII	SLAIN	TAGMA	UNRID	WOMEN
DUNCH	GEYER	INERM	MEANT	OHONE	RAGDE	SLASH	TAISH	UNSOD	WOVEN
DUNNO	GHEST	INERT	MEDII	OIDIA	RAMAL	SLEER	TAKEN	UNWET	WOWEE
DUNSH	GIVEN	INFRA	MEINT	OLEIC	RARER	SLEPT	TANTI	UPBYE	WOXEN
DUOMI	GLIAL	INTIL	MENSH	OLPAE	RASTA	SLIER	TANTO	UPRAN	WRAPT
DURST	GLODE	INTRA	MERER	ORGIC	RECTI	SLIPT	TAPEN	URAEI	WRATE
DUTCH	GNASH	INUST	MESAL	OSSIA	REDID	SLISH	TAULD	URDEE	WROTE
DWELT	GNAWN	IODIC	MESIC	OTAKU	REJON	SLUNG	TAXON	UREAL	WROTH
EHING	GOBBI	JEUNE	MESNE	OUTDO	RELIT	SLUNK	TAZZE	UREDO	WRUNG
EIGNE	GOBBO	JINGO	MESTO	OUTGO	RENAL	SLYER	TEACH	UREIC	WRYER
ELMEN	GOIER	JOKOL	MEYNT	OVOLI	RERAN	SMASH	TECTA	URENT	XERIC
EMONG	GONIA	JUGUM	MICRA	OVOLO	RESAT	SMOTE	TELIC	URNAL	XOANA
ENLIT	GONNA	JURAL	MIKRA	OWSEN	RHYTA	SNASH	TEMPI	UTERI	XYLIC
ENORM	GONZO	KACHA	MILCH	PACTA	RIFER	SNUCK	TEPID	UVEAL	XYSTI
EROSE	GOTTA	KAING	MINAE	PAISE	RIMAE	SNUSH	TEUCH	VACUA	YARER
ETYMA	GOYIM	KAMME	MISDO	PAKKA	RONNE	SOCKO	TEUGH	VAGAL	YAULD
EVHOE	GROWN	KEECH	MISGO	PALER	RORAL	SODIC	THAIM	VAIRE	YBORE
EVOHE	GRUFF	KEMPT	MITCH	PALPI	RORIC	SOLDI	THELF	VALID	YCLAD
EWHOW	GRYPT	KIDGE	MODII	PAOLI	RORID	SOLDO	THEMA	VAPID	YCOND
FASTI	GULAR	KINDA	MOLAL	PAOLO	RUBAI	SOPRA	THIEF	VASAL	YDRAD
FATAL	GULCH	KNELT	MOLTO	PAPAL	RUNIC	SORAL	THILK	VATIC	YEVEN
FAUGH	GUMMA	KNISH	MONDO	PAVID	RYPER	SORDA	THINE	VEHME	YEWEN
FAURD	GYRAL	KRONA	MOOSE	PAYSD	SAFER	SORDO	THOLI	VELUM	YFERE
FAVER	HABLE	KYDST	MOTEN	PEART	SAGUM	SOUCT	THOSE	VENAE	YINCE
FAYER	HADAL	LABRA	MOTTO	PENAL	SAIST	SPAKE	THRAE	VENAL	YLIKE
FECAL	HADST	LADEN	MUCID	PEPLA	SALIC	SPARD	THREW	VILDE	YMOLT
FECIT	HAIKU	LAMER	MULCH	PERCH	SAMEN	SPENT	TICCA	VILER	YOGIC
FEHME	HAITH	LARCH	MULSH	PHYLE	SANER	SPRAD	TIDAL	VILLI	YOKUL
FERAL	HANCH	LAWER	MUNCH	PIERT	SAPID	SPUTA	TIKKA	VINAL	YOURN
FERER	HARSH	LAXER	MUSHA	PIEZO	SAYNE	STAID	TIMID	VIOLD	YRAPT
FETAL	HASTA	LAZZI	MUTER	PILCH	SAYST	STASH	TONDI	VIRAL	YRENT
FETCH	HAULT	LAZZO	MYOID	PILEA	SCAND	STEPT	TOPHI	VIRID	YRIVD
FETID	HAUTE	LEANT	NAEVI	PILEI	SCAPI	STOAE	TOPOI	VITAE	YSAME
FEWER	HEAME	LEAPT	NARRE	PILUM	SCENA	STOAI	TORCH	VIVID	YTOST
FEYER	HEMAL	LEASH	NATAL	PINCH	SCUDI	STOLN	TORIC	VOILA	ZAIRE
FILAR	HEWGH	LEGAL	NAVAL	PLENA	SEELD	STONG	TORII	VOLAE	ZILCH
FILCH	HIANT	LEISH	NEGRO	PLESH	SENSA	STOOD	TORSI	VOLTA	ZOEAE
FINCH	HILAR	LEPID	NEIST	POOCH	SENZA	STUMM	TOXIC	VOULU	ZOEAL
FLITT	HILCH	LEPTA	NEMPT	PORAL	SERAL	STUNG	TREFA	VULGO	ZONAE
FLOSH	HILUM	LIART	NEVER	PORCH	SERER	STUNK	TREIF	VYING	ZOPPA
FLOWN	HOING	LIVID	NEWER	POUPT	SERIC	STURE	TRIFF	WACKO	ZOPPO
FLUNG	HOKKU	LOACH	NGWEE	PRESA	SERVO	STYLI	TRILD	WAIDE	ZOWIE
FOCAL	HOOCH	LOAST	NICER	PROUD	SESSA	SUCCI	TRUER	WANLE	ZUZIM
FORDO	HOTCH	LOBAR	NIDAL	PUBIC	SETAE	SULCI	TUBAE	WANNA	ZYGAL
FOUER	HOTEN	LOSEN	NIMBI	PUCER	SHAKT	SURAL	TUBAL	WARST	ZYGON
FRACK	HOVEN	LOTIC	NITID	PUCKA	SHALT	SWACK	TUBAR	WAXEN	ZYMIC
FRATI	HOWBE	LOYAL	NIVAL	PUDIC	SHASH	SWANG	TUMID	WELCH	
FRENA	HOWSO	LUCID	NOMEN	PUKKA	SHERE	SWAPT	TYNDE	WELKT	
FRUSH	HUGER	LUDIC	NOMOI	PULMO	SHEWN	SWARE	TYPAL	WELSH	
FUGAL	HUMIC	LUMME	NOTAL	PUPAE	SHONE	SWEPT	ULNAE	WENCH	
FUNGI	HUMID	LURCH	NOTUM	PUPAL	SHOPE	SWINE	UNAPT	WERSH	
FURTH	HUNCH			PURER			UNBID	WHICH	

6-LETTER WORD BLOCKERS

(except words ending in -ED, -J, -S, -X, -Y, -Z)

ABATTU	ABURST	ADRIFT	AFLAME	AGOING	AKIMBO	AMEBAE	ANGOLA	AORTAL	APTING
ABEIGH	ACETIC	ADROIT	AFLOAT	AGONIC	ALBEIT	AMEBIC	ANIGHT	AORTIC	ARCANA
ABLAZE	ACHIER	ADYTUM	AFRAID	AGOROT	ALDERN	AMIDST	ANNULI	APEMAN	ARCANE
ABLEST	ACIDER	AECIUM	AFRESH	AGUISH	ALEXIC	AMNION	ANODAL	APEMEN	ARCHEI
ABLOOM	ACIDIC	AEFALD	AFRONT	AIDANT	ALGOID	AMORAL	ANODIC	APICAL	ARDENT
ABLUSH	ACKNEW	AERIER	AGAMIC	AIDFUL	ALMOST	ANCILE	ANOMIC	APIECE	AREACH
ABOARD	ACRAWL	AFAWLD	AGAPAE	AIKONA	ALULAE	ANCORA	ANOUGH	APODAL	ARGULI
ABORAL	ACULEI	AFEARD	AGHAST	AIRMAN	ALUMNI	ANEATH	ANOXIC	APPAID	ARGUTE
ABORNE	ACUTER	AFFYDE	AGILER	AIRMEN	ALVINE	ANEMIC	ANYHOW	APPAYD	ARIDER
ABSURD	ADNATE	AFIELD	AGLEAM		AMBUSH	ANETIC	AORTAE	APTEST	ARIGHT

BLOCKERS: 6-Letter Words

ARILLI	BEDASH	BULLAE	COKIER	DENSER	EIDENT	FEUING	FULVID	GREYER	ICONIC
ARIOSI	BEDIDE	BUMALO	COKING	DERING	EIDOLA	FEWEST	FUMIER	GRIPLE	IDLEST
ARISEN	BEDRID	BURSAE	COMODO	DERMAL	EIKING	FEYEST	FUMING	GRUING	IDOLUM
AROUND	BEDYDE	BURSAL	COMOSE	DERMIC	EKUELE	FEYING	FUNEST	GRUTCH	IMIDIC
ARRISH	BEFELD	BUSIER	CONGII	DETACH	ELDEST	FIFING	FUNGAL	GRYSIE	IMMANE
ARTFUL	BEFELL	BUSMAN	CONING	DEVOID	ELMIER	FIKIER	FUNNER	GUNMAN	IMMESH
ASHAKE	BEGILT	BUSMEN	COSING	DEVORE	ELVISH	FIKING	FURCAL	GUNMEN	INANER
ASHINE	BEGIRT	BUYING	COSMIC	DEVOUT	EMBOST	FIKISH	FURDER	GUTTAE	INARCH
ASHORE	BEGONE	BYKING	COSTAE	DEWIER	EMMESH	FILIAL	FUSILE	GUYING	INBENT
ASLANT	BEHALF	BYLIVE	COWING	DEWING	ENARCH	FILOSE	FUSING	GYBING	INBORN
ASLEEP	BEHELD	CABMAN	COWISH	DIACID	ENCASH	FYKING	GAGING	GYLDEN	INCAVI
ASLOPE	BELIKE	CABMEN	COWMAN	DIAMYL	ENGILT	FINEST	GAGMAN	GYMNIC	INCAVO
ASMEAR	BELIVE	CAECAL	COWMEN	DICIER	ENGIRT	FINISH	GAGMEN	GYRANT	INCULT
ASPOUT	BEMATA	CAECUM	COXIER	DICTUM	ENLEVE	FINITE	GAIJIN	GYRING	INDIGN
ASQUAT	BENDEE	CAGIER	COXING	DIKIER	ENMESH	FINSKO	GALANT	GYROSE	INFELT
ASSOTT	BENIGN	CAGING	COYEST	DIKING	ENODAL	FISTIC	GALEAE	GYVING	INFERE
ASTARE	BEREFT	CAKIER	COYING	DINFUL	ENRAPT	FITFUL	GALLIC	HABILE	INFIRM
ASTOOP	BESANG	CALAMI	COYISH	DINING	ENRICH	FIXIVE	GALORE	HADDEN	INGRAM
ASTRUT	BESEEN	CALASH	COZING	DINKER	EOTHEN	FLAMBE	GALOSH	HAEING	INGRUM
ASWARM	BESTAD	CALCIC	CREANT	DINKUM	EPICAL	FLANCH	GAMASH	HAEMAL	INLAID
ASWING	BESUNG	CALLID	CREDAL	DIREST	EPODIC	FLAXEN	GAMEST	HAEMIC	INMESH
ASWIRL	BETING	CALMER	CRIANT	DISCAL	EQUINE	FLEECH	GAMIER	HAIKAI	INMOST
ASWOON	BETOOK	CAMASH	CRIBLE	DISTAL	EREMIC	FLEMIT	GARDAI	HAINCH	INRUSH
ATAXIC	BETROD	CAMSHO	CRISSA	DITTIT	ERENOW	FLENCH	GARISH	HALEST	INTACT
ATHROB	BEWENT	CANIER	CROTCH	DOABLE	ERRATA	FLETCH	GASHER	HALFEN	INTIME
ATOKAL	BEWEPT	CANNAE	CROUCH	DOITIT	ETERNE	FLIEST	GASLIT	HAMATE	INTIRE
ATOMIC	BIAXAL	CANNOT	CROUSE	DOLENT	ETYMIC	FLINCH	GASMAN	HAMOSE	INTOWN
ATONAL	BIFOLD	CANTHI	CRUDER	DOLING	ETYPIC	FLITCH	GASMEN	HAMULI	INWITH
ATONIC	BIFORM	CARMAN	CRURAL	DOLIUM	EURIPI	FLOCCI	GAUNCH	HARDER	INWORN
ATOPIC	BIGGER	CARMEN	CRUTCH	DOMIER	EWGHEN	FLORAE	GAYEST	HARISH	IRATER
ATWAIN	BINATE	CAROLI	CUBING	DOMING	EWKING	FLORAL	GAZIER	HATING	IRIDAL
ATWEEL	BINMAN	CARVEN	CUEING	DOPIER	EXEUNT	FLORID	GAZING	HAULST	IRIDIC
ATWEEN	BINMEN	CATCHT	CULTCH	DORMIE	EXILIC	FLOUSH	GEASON	HAUNCH	IRITIC
ATWIXT	BIRKEN	CATTLE	CULTIC	DORSUM	EXODIC	FLUIER	GEDDIT	HAWKIT	ITERUM
AUBURN	BISSON	CAUDAD	CUMULI	DOSING	EXONIC	FLYEST	GEEING	HAZIER	ITSELF
AVANTI	BITTEN	CAUGHT	CUNEAL	DOTIER	EXTOLD	FLYSCH	GELATO	HEARIE	JACENT
AVERSE	BIVIUM	CAUSAE	CUPMAN	DOTISH	EYEING	FOEMAN	GEMINI	HELIAC	JADING
AVIDER	BLAEST	CAUSAL	CUPMEN	DOUCER	FABBER	FOEMEN	GEMMAE	HELING	JADISH
AVITAL	BLAISE	CAUSEN	CUPRIC	DOURER	FACILE	FOETAL	GEMMAN	HEMPEN	JANTEE
AVOUCH	BLAIZE	CEDARN	CURIAE	DOVIER	FADIER	FOETID	GEMMEN	HEPPER	JEEING
AWARER	BLANCH	CEDING	CURING	DOVING	FAECAL	FOGASH	GENIAL	HETING	JEJUNA
AWATCH	BLATER	CELLAE	CURSAL	DOVISH	FAINER	FOGMAN	GEODIC	HEYING	JEJUNE
AWEIGH	BLEACH	CENDRE	CURTER	DOWING	FAIRER	FOGMEN	GESTIC	HIEING	JEWING
AWHILE	BLENCH	CERCAL	CURULE	DOWIER	FAKING	FOLIAR	GEYEST	HIEMAL	JIBING
AWOKEN	BLOTTO	CERING	CUTCHA	DOZIER	FALLEN	FOLIUM	GIBING	HIKING	JIMPER
AWRACK	BLUEST	CERULE	CYANIC	DREAMT	FAMING	FONDER	GIDDAP	HIPPIC	JINNEE
AWRONG	BLUIER	CHEAPO	CYMOID	DREICH	FAMISH	FONTAL	GIDDUP	HISPID	JIVING
AWSOME	BLUISH	CHELAE	CYMOSE	DRENCH	FARAND	FORANE	GIEING	HISTIE	JOBING
AXEMAN	BOKING	CHICER	CYSTIC	DRIEST	FARFET	FORBYE	GIGMAN	HOAING	JOCOSE
AXEMEN	BOLDER	CHINCH	CYTISI	DRIVEN	FARING	FORDID	GIGMEN	HODMAN	JOCUND
AZONAL	BOLETI	CHIRAL	CYTOID	DROLER	FASCIO	FOREGO	GILDEN	HODMEN	JOKIER
AZONIC	BOLLEN	CHOLIC	DAEDAL	DROMIC	FATTER	FORGAT	GINGKO	HOHING	JOKING
AZOTIC	BONIER	CHORIC	DAEING	DROMOI	FAUCAL	FORGOT	GINKGO	HOLDEN	JOLING
BABIER	BONZER	CHOSEN	DAFTER	DRYISH	FAUNAE	FORMAL	GIUSTO	HOLIER	JOVIAL
BACCAE	BOOING	CHYLDE	DAIMEN	DUDISH	FAUNAL	FORMIC	GLAZEN	HOLMIC	JOWING
BACULA	BOREAL	CIDING	DAMMIT	DUEFUL	FAVELL	FORRAD	GLITCH	HOLPEN	JOYFUL
BADMAN	BOSHTA	CILIUM	DANKER	DUETTI	FAVEST	FORREN	GLOBAL	HOMIER	JOYING
BADMEN	BOSKER	CISTIC	DARKER	DUKING	FAVOSE	FORRIT	GLUIER	HOOROO	JUBATE
BAGMAN	BOSSER	CITING	DAWISH	DULCET	FAXING	FOSSAE	GLUING	HOOTCH	JUGATE
BAGMEN	BOTONE	CITRIC	DAYGLO	DULLER	FAYEST	FOUEST	GLUISH	HOOVEN	JUKING
BALDER	BOWMAN	CLATCH	DAZING	DUMBER	FAYING	FOULER	GLUTEI	HOPING	JUSTER
BALING	BOWMEN	CLECHE	DEAFER	DUMOSE	FAZING	FOVEAE	GNOMAE	HORRID	JYMOLD
BANING	BOXIER	CLENCH	DEARER	DUNNER	FECIAL	FOVEAL	GNOMIC	HOSING	KAEING
BANISH	BOYING	CLEVER	DEAWIE	DUPING	FECUND	FOXIER	GOIEST	HOWZAT	KAPUTT
BARDIC	BOYISH	CLINCH	DEBILE	DURING	FEHMIC	FOZIER	GOLDER	HOXING	KARMIC
BAREST	BRAWER	CLONAL	DEBOSH	DUSKER	FELSIC	FRAENA	GOLOSH	HOYING	KAWING
BARFUL	BREACH	CLONIC	DECANI	DYABLE	FENMAN	FRANCO	GONION	HUDDEN	KEIGHT
BARING	BREECH	CLOVEN	DECENT	DYADIC	FENMEN	FREEST	GOOIER	HUDDUP	KEPPIT
BARISH	BREGMA	CLUING	DEEDER	DYKIER	FEODAL	FRENCH	GORIER	HUGEST	KEYING
BARMAN	BRIGHT	CLUNCH	DEEING	DYKING	FEREST	FRENNE	GOTHIC	HUMERI	KIBOSH
BARMEN	BROKEN	CLUTCH	DEEPER	EADISH	FERIAL	FRENUM	GOTTEN	HYDRIC	KIRSCH
BARREN	BROMIC	CLYING	DEFFER	EASIER	FERINE	FRIGID	GOWDER	HYEING	KLATCH
BASEST	BROOCH	CLYPEI	DEFTER	EASSEL	FERRIC	FROREN	GOYISH	HYETAL	KLOOCH
BASSER	BRUMAL	CNIDAE	DEGAGE	EASSIL	FERVID	FRORNE	GRAVEN	HYMNIC	KNITCH
BATMAN	BRUNCH	COBRIC	DEIDER	ECHINI	FETIAL	FROZEN	GRAVID	HYPHAE	KOUROI
BATMEN	BRUTAL	COCCAL	DEIFIC	ECHOIC	FETING	FRUGAL	GRAYER	HYPHAL	KRONEN
BAYING	BULBAR	COGENT		EFFETE	FETISH	FRUSTA	GREIGE	HYPING	KRONER
BEATEN		COITAL		EGESTA	FEUDAL	FULCRA		HYPOID	KRONOR
BECAME						FULGID		IBIDEM	

KRONUR	LOUPEN	MODULO	OCHONE	PHYLAE	PYKNIC	ROKIER	SEPTUM	SOONER	SYLVAE
KUTCHA	LOUPIT	MONACT	OCREAE	PHYLUM	PYNING	ROOPIT	SEREST	SORDID	SYNING
KVETCH	LOWSER	MONERA	OCTOPI	PICINE	PYXING	ROPIER	SERRAE	SOREST	SYPING
KYBOSH	LOWSIT	MOOING	ODDEST	PICRIC	QUAINT	RORIER	SETOSE	SORING	SYRLYE
LABARA	LUBRIC	MOPIER	ODDISH	PIEING	QUALIA	ROSCID	SEXFID	SOUGHT	TAEING
LABILE	LUCENT	MOPISH	OGAMIC	PIEMAN	QUATCH	ROSEAL	SEXIER	SOURER	TAISCH
LABIUM	LUCKEN	MORBID	OGIVAL	PIEMEN	QUEINT	ROTING	SEXING	SPEECH	TAKIER
LABRUM	LUETIC	MORISH	OGRISH	PIERST	QUENCH	ROUPIT	SHAKEN	SPERST	TALEAE
LACTIC	LUITEN	MORSAL	OIDIUM	PILEUM	QUETCH	RUBATI	SHALOM	SPICAE	TALLER
LAESIE	LUMBAR	MOSHAV	OILMAN	PILOSE	QUINIC	RUBBET	SHAPEN	SPINAE	TALPAE
LAICAL	LUPPEN	MOSING	OILMEN	PINEAL	QUOOKE	RUBBIT	SHAVEN	SPINAL	TAMEST
LAKISH	LURING	MOTIER	OMASAL	PINETA	QUOTHA	RUBIER	SHOLOM	SPINTO	TAPING
LAMEST	LUTTEN	MOUGHT	OMASUM	PINKER	RABATO	RUEFUL	SHOULD	SPLOSH	TAPPIT
LAMIAE	LYFULL	MOZING	ONIRIC	PINNAE	RACIAL	RUGATE	SHRANK	SPOILT	TARNAL
LAMISH	LYSING	MUCOID	ONLINE	PINXIT	RACIER	RUGOSE	SHREWD	SPOKEN	TAUGHT
LANATE	LYTTAE	MULISH	ONRUSH	PIONIC	RADDER	RULIER	SHROWD	SPRACK	TAURIC
LANOSE	MAAING	MUONIC	OPIOID	PIPIER	RADGER	RUMINA	SHRUNK	SPRAID	TAUTER
LARGER	MACING	MURKER	OPTING	PIRNIT	RADISH	RUSHEN	SHTOOM	SPRANG	TAUTIT
LARINE	MADMAN	MUTEST	ORBIER	PITHOI	RAHING	RUSINE	SHTUMM	SPRENT	TAVERT
LAROID	MADMEN	MUTING	ORGANA	PITMAN	RAKISH	RYKING	SHYEST	SPRONG	TAWIER
LARVAE	MAGLEV	MUXING	OSCINE	PITMEN	RAMATE	SACCOI	SHYING	SPRUNG	TAXMAN
LARVAL	MAGYAR	MYSELF	OSTEAL	PLACID	RAMEAL	SACRAL	SHYISH	SPRUSH	TAXMEN
LATENT	MAHZOR	MYTHIC	OSTIAL	PLAGAL	RAMOSE	SACRUM	SIALIC	SPRYER	TEAING
LATHEN	MAINER	MYTHOI	OSTIUM	PLANAR	RAMULI	SADDER	SICCAN	SPUING	TECTUM
LATISH	MALEIC	MYXOMA	OTIOSE	PLANCH	RANCID	SAFEST	SICCAR	SPUTUM	TEDIER
LAWEST	MALIST	NAIANT	OUTATE	PLEACH	RANINE	SAFING	SICKER	STALER	TEEING
LAWFUL	MALLEI	NAIFER	OUTBYE	PLIANT	RAREST	SAGEST	SIDDUR	STALKO	TEGMEN
LAWMAN	MAMMAE	NAIVER	OUTDID	PLICAE	RARING	SAGIER	SILENI	STANCH	TELIAL
LAWMEN	MANENT	NARIAL	OUTSAT	PLICAL	RATHER	SAIDST	SILING	STANCK	TELIUM
LAXEST	MANFUL	NARINE	OUTWON	PLISSE	RATITE	SAIRER	SILVAE	STATAL	TEMENE
LAYMAN	MANQUE	NASTIC	OVERDO	PLONGD	RAUCID	SAKKOI	SIMIAL	STATIM	TENIAE
LAYMEN	MANTIC	NATANT	OVULAR	PODIAL	RAVISH	SALEWD	SINFUL	STEARD	TENSER
LEARNT	MARISH	NAUTCH	OWLISH	POKIER	RAWISH	SALPAE	SINING	STEELD	TERAPH
LEETLE	MASING	NEANIC	OWRIER	POKING	RAXING	SAMIER	SIPING	STELAE	TERATA
LEFTER	MATIER	NEATER	OXALIC	POLISH	REALER	SANCTA	SIRING	STELAR	TERBIC
LENGER	MATZOH	NEBISH	PACTUM	POLYPI	REALIA	SANEST	SISTRA	STEMMA	TERGAL
LENTEN	MAUNNA	NEFAST	PALEAE	POMATO	REBATO	SAPEGO	SITING	STERIC	TERGUM
LENTIC	MAUVER	NERVAL	PALEST	PONENT	RECENT	SAPFUL	SIWASH	STEYER	TERRAE
LERING	MAYEST	NESHER	PALIER	PONTAL	RECHIE	SARING	SIZIER	STINKO	TERSER
LESBIC	MAYHAP	NETHER	PALISH	PONTIC	RECKAN	SATANG	SKEIGH	STITCH	TESTAE
LESSER	MAZIER	NEURAL	PALLAE	POOING	RECTAL	SATING	SKOLIA	STOLEN	THECAE
LETHAL	MEANER	NEWEST	PALLID	POOKIT	REDIAE	SATIVE	SKOOSH	STOLID	THECAL
LEWDER	MEATAL	NEWISH	PALPAL	POPISH	REDONE	SAYEST	SKYIER	STOMAL	THENCE
LIBANT	MEDIAE	NICEST	PAPISH	PORIER	REDREW	SBIRRI	SKYING	STONEN	THETCH
LIBRAE	MEEKER	NICISH	PAPYRI	PORING	REEDEN	SBIRRO	SKYISH	STOUSH	THETIC
LIEDER	MEETER	NIELLI	PARDIE	POSHER	REGAVE	SCALAE	SKYMAN	STRADE	THOLOI
LIEFER	MENSAL	NIOBIC	PARISH	POSIER	REGNAL	SCATCH	SKYMEN	STRATA	THRASH
LIENAL	MENSCH	NIRLIT	PARTIM	POTASH	REHASH	SCEATT	SLATCH	STRATI	THRAWN
LIEVER	MEREST	NIXING	PASSEE	POTATO	REHUNG	SCENIC	SLEEST	STRAWN	THRESH
LIFULL	MERING	NOBBUT	PASSIM	POTING	REKING	SCHEMA	SLIEST	STREWN	THRICE
LIGGEN	MERMAN	NOBLER	PAUSAL	POTMAN	RELAID	SCIENT	SLIVEN	STRIAE	THROVE
LIMBIC	MERMEN	NODOSE	PAWING	POTMEN	RELIDE	SCOLIA	SLOOSH	STRODE	THROWN
LIMPER	MESIAL	NOGAKU	PEARST	POUKIT	RELISH	SCOPAE	SLOWER	STROMA	THRUSH
LIMPID	MESIAN	NOSIER	PEASON	POWWAW	REMOUD	SCORCH	SLUING	STRONG	THYINE
LIMULI	METING	NOSTOI	PECTEN	POXIER	REPAND	SCOTCH	SLYEST	STROVE	THYMIC
LINEAL	MEVING	NOTING	PECTIC	POXING	REPLUM	SCRYDE	SLYISH	STRUCK	THYRSI
LINEAR	MEWING	NOTOUR	PEDATE	PRIMAL	RESAID	SCUTAL	SMALTI	STRUNG	TIBIAE
LINIER	MIGNON	NOULDE	PEEING	PRONER	RESOLD	SCUTCH	SMATCH	STYING	TICING
LINISH	MILDER	NOUNAL	PELTAE	PRONTO	RETIAL	SCUTUM	SMEECH	SUABLE	TIDIER
LIPOMA	MILKEN	NOWISE	PELVIC	PROSIT	RETOLD	SCYPHI	SMIRCH	SUAVER	TIFOSI
LITHIC	MIMING	NOYING	PENIAL	PSEUDO	RETOOK	SEAMAN	SMOOCH	SUBITO	TIFOSO
LITTEN	MIMMER	NUBILE	PENILE	PSORIC	RETRAL	SEAMEN	SMOUCH	SUBMAN	TINEAL
LIVEST	MINIER	NUCHAE	PENMAN	PUCEST	RETROD	SEARCH	SMUTCH	SUBMEN	TINIER
LOBULI	MINISH	NUCHAL	PENMEN	PUDENT	RETUSE	SEARER	SNEESH	SUBSEA	TINING
LOCULI	MIRIER	NUDEST	PENNAE	PUIRER	RHINAL	SECESH	SNIDER	SULCAL	TINMAN
LOGGIE	MIRING	NUKING	PEPFUL	PUKING	RHIZIC	SECUND	SNITCH	SULLEN	TINMEN
LOGIER	MIRKER	NUMINA	PERAEA	PULIER	RHODIC	SEDENT	SOAKEN	SUMMAE	TOEIER
LOGION	MISDID	NUTANT	PERCEN	PUNCTA	RHOTIC	SEDILE	SOBEIT	SUNKEN	TOEING
LOIPEN	MISLIT	OAFISH	PERDIE	PUNIER	RHYTON	SEIKER	SOCMAN	SUNLIT	TOFORE
LOMATA	MISSAE	OAKIER	PERFET	PUNISH	RICHER	SEJANT	SOCMEN	SUPERB	TOLUIC
LOMING	MISSAW	OBESER	PERISH	PUNKER	RICTAL	SELDOM	SODAIC	SURBET	TOMATO
LONGER	MISUST	OBIING	PERITI	PUREST	RIDDEN	SELLAE	SOEVER	SUREST	TOMBIC
LOOING	MITIER	OBITAL	PERTER	PURING	RIFEST	SEMEIA	SOFTER	SUTILE	TOMIAL
LOOSER	MITRAL	OBITER	PETITE	PUTRID	RILIER	SEMPER	SOLEIN	SWATCH	TOMIUM
LOOTEN	MIXIER	OBTECT	PHAEIC	PUTSCH	RILING	SEMPRE	SOLEMN	SWEERT	TONANT
LORATE	MIXING	OCELLI	PHATIC	PUTTEN	RIMOSE	SENILE	SOLGEL	SWEIRT	TONISH
LOTHER	MNEMIC		PHOCAE	PYCNIC	RIPEST	SENSUM	SOLIDI	SWOOSH	TOOMER
LOUCHE	MODISH		PHONAL	PYEING	RODMAN	SEPMAG	SOLING	SYEING	TOPMAN
LOUDER	MODULI				RODMEN	SEPTAL	SOMATA		TOPMEN

TOROSE	TUNIER	UNDREW	UNMEET	UPBORE	UVULAR	VILLAR	WANNER	WISING	YEOMEN
TORRID	TURBID	UNEATH	UNMOWN	UPDREW	VACANT	VINIER	WARIER	WITHAL	YEVING
TORTEN	TURFEN	UNEVEN	UNPAID	UPGONE	VADOSE	VINING	WARING	WITING	YEXING
TOSING	TURGID	UNFELT	UNPENT	UPGREW	VAGILE	VIRENT	WARMAN	WOEFUL	YIPPEE
TOSSEN	TUSSAL	UNFINE	UNREAL	UPGUSH	VAGROM	VIRILE	WARMEN	WOODEN	YPIGHT
TOTHER	TUTMAN	UNFIRM	UNRENT	UPHAND	VAGUER	VIRING	WASHEN	WORSER	YPLAST
TOTING	TUTMEN	UNGAIN	UNROVE	UPHELD	VAINER	VISCID	WAURST	WOWFER	YSHENT
TOWIER	TWEEST	UNGILT	UNRUDE	UPHILD	VALVAL	VISIVE	WAVIER	WOWING	YTTRIC
TOYISH	TWILIT	UNGLAD	UNSAID	UPHUNG	VALVAR	VISTAL	WAXIER	WRENCH	YUKIER
TOYMAN	TYEING	UNGORD	UNSENT	UPLAID	VARSAL	VITTAE	WEAKER	WRETCH	YUKING
TOYMEN	TYKISH	UNGUAL	UNSEWN	UPMOST	VASTER	VIVACE	WETTER	WROKEN	YWROKE
TOZING	TYNING	UNHEWN	UNSHOD	UPPISH	VATMAN	VOGIER	WEXING	WRYEST	ZANIER
TRAGIC	UBIQUE	UNHUNG	UNSOFT	UPROSE	VATMEN	VOLAGE	WEYARD	WRYING	ZAPATA
TRENCH	UGLIER	UNHURT	UNSOLD	UPRUSH	VEDUTA	VOLING	WHATEN	WYTING	ZELOSO
TREPID	UGSOME	UNIFIC	UNSOWN	UPRYST	VEDUTE	VORAGO	WHATNA	XENIAL	ZEROTH
TRIACT	ULNARE	UNITAL	UNSPUN	UPSENT	VEGETE	VORANT	WHATSO	XENIUM	ZIPTOP
TRIBAL	ULTIMO	UNJUST	UNSUNG	UPTOOK	VEHMIC	VORPAL	WHEARE	XOANON	ZOARIA
TRIFID	UMBRAE	UNKENT	UNTOLD	UPTORE	VELOCE	VOTING	WHILOM	XYLOID	ZOETIC
TRILLO	UMBRAL	UNKEPT	UNTORN	UPTORN	VENIAL	VOTIVE	WHILST	XYSTOI	ZONOID
TRINAL	UNBEEN	UNKIND	UNTROD	UPWENT	VENOSE	VULVAE	WHITER	YAKUZA	ZOOEAE
TRISTE	UNBENT	UNLAID	UNWELL	URACHI	VERIER	VULVAL	WHOOSH	YAREST	ZOOEAL
TRITER	UNBORE	UNLASH	UNWEPT	URANIC	VERLIG	VULVAR	WIDEST	YAWING	ZOONAL
TROCHI	UNCINI	UNLEAL	UNWISH	UREDIA	VERMAL	WABBIT	WIDISH	YBLENT	ZOONIC
TROPPO	UNCLAD	UNLICH	UNWIST	UREMIC	VERNAL	WAEFUL	WILFUL	YBOUND	ZUFOLI
TRUEST	UNCOOL	UNLOST	UNWONT	URETIC	VIABLE	WANDLE	WILIER	YBRENT	ZUFOLO
TRUING	UNDEAD	UNMADE	UNWORN	URSINE	VICING	WANIER	WILING	YCLEPT	ZYMOID
TUBATE	UNDEAR	UNMARD	UPBEAT	USABLE	VIDUAL	WANKLE	WIRIER	YEDING	
TUMULI	UNDONE	UNMEEK	UPBLEW	UVULAE	VILEST	WANNEL	WISEST	YEOMAN	

Section Seven

Anagrams

Introduction

The final section is substantial, containing all valid 7-letter and 8-letter words arranged in alphabetical order of their constituent letters.

Suppose you have the seven letters THORCES on your rack. You are sure that there must be a valid 7-letter word there. Just arrange the letters in alphabetical order (CEHORST), then look for CEHORST in the following 7-letter lists; it appears alphabetically ordered between CEHORSS and CEHORSU. You will find that there are six valid anagrams of your seven letters!

Perhaps you have the seven letters CORLINE, and you cannot see a valid 7-letter word. Arrange the letters into alphabetical order (CEILNOR) and check the list here. Lo and behold! The list goes from CEILNOP to CEILNOS, confirming that there is no anagram of those seven letters.

The same method can be used for 8-letter words. All valid 8-letter words have been put into their alphabetically-ordered forms, which themselves have been arranged alphabetically. What anagrams, if any, are there for the eight letters THROUCES? Easy! Put the letters into alphabetical order, check CEHORSTU in the 8-letter list, and you will find that there are two valid words, SCOUTHER and TOUCHERS.

The 7-letter Anagrams list contains over 26,000 words, and the 8-letter list has over 30,000 words. Happy anagram searching!

7-LETTER ANAGRAMS

AAAADNP	APADANA	AAACNRV	CARAVAN	AAAILPS	APLASIA	AABCELN	BALANCE
AAAALTY	ATALAYA	AAACNST	CANASTA	AAAILRS	ARALIAS	AABCELP	CAPABLE
AAABBCL	CABBALA	AAACNTT	CANTATA	AAAILRT	TALARIA		PACABLE
AAABBKL	KABBALA	AAACPST	PATACAS	AAAIMNT	AMANITA	AABCELT	ACTABLE
AAABCCR	BACCARA	AAACRWY	CARAWAY	AAAIPRX	APRAXIA	AABCEMR	MACABRE
AAABCIR	ARABICA	AAACSST	CASSATA	AAAIQRU	AQUARIA	AABCERR	BARRACE
AAABCLS	CABALAS	AAACSSV	CASSAVA	AAAISTX	ATAXIAS	AABCERT	ABREACT
AAABCLV	BACLAVA	AAACSTT	CATASTA	AAAJKST	JATAKAS		CABARET
AAABCMR	CARAMBA	AAADELM	ALAMEDA	AAAJMPS	PAJAMAS	AABCHIR	BRACHIA
AAABCNR	BARACAN	AAADFRY	FARADAY	AAAJMSU	UJAMAAS	AABCHMT	AMBATCH
AAABCNS	CABANAS	AAADHMR	ADHARMA	AAAKKMR	MARKKAA	AABCHNR	BARCHAN
AAABCOR	CARABAO	AAADILX	ADAXIAL	AAAKKNS	KANAKAS	AABCHOR	ABROACH
AAABCTW	CATAWBA	AAADIRT	DATARIA	AAAKKRS	KARAKAS	AABCHSS	CASBAHS
AAABDGS	DAGABAS		RADIATA	AAAKLMS	KAMALAS	AABCILM	CAMBIAL
AAABDHS	BAHADAS	AAADJMR	JAMADAR	AAAKNST	KATANAS	AABCINR	CARABIN
AAABDJS	BAJADAS	AAADLMN	MANDALA	AAALLPT	PALATAL	AABCIOP	COPAIBA
AAABDLM	LAMBADA	AAADLMW	WADMAAL	AAALMSS	MASALAS	AABCITX	TAXICAB
AAABDNN	BANDANA	AAADMNT	ADAMANT		SALAAMS	AABCKLY	LAYBACK
AAABEGL	GALABEA	AAADMRS	ARMADAS	AAALNNT	LANTANA	AABCKNN	CANBANK
AAABFLL	FALBALA		MADRASA	AAALNPT	APLANAT	AABCKPY	BACKPAY
AAABGIL	GALABIA	AAADNPS	PANADAS	AAALRRY	ARRAYAL		PAYBACK
AAABHLQ	QABALAH	AAADNRS	SARDANA	AAALWYY	LAYAWAY	AABCKRR	BARRACK
AAABILX	ABAXIAL	AAADNRT	TANADAR	AAAMMNS	MANANAS	AABCKRS	BACKRAS
AAABKLS	KABALAS	AAAEGLT	GALATEA	AAAMNPS	PANAMAS	AABCKSW	BACKSAW
AAABKLV	BAKLAVA	AAAEGNP	APANAGE	AAAMNRT	AMARANT	AABCLMU	CALUMBA
AAABKSY	KABAYAS	AAAEHLT	ALTHAEA	AAAMNSS	SAMAANS	AABCLPY	CAPABLY
AAABLLW	WALLABA	AAAEIMN	ANAEMIA	AAAMNST	ATAMANS	AABCLSY	SCYBALA
AAABLPR	PALABRA	AAAELMP	PALAMAE	AAAMNTY	MANYATA	AABCMST	TAMBACS
AAABLST	ALBATAS	AAAELSZ	AZALEAS	AAAMORT	TAMARAO	AABCMSU	SAMBUCA
	ATABALS	AAAENST	ANATASE	AAAMPRT	PATAMAR	AABCORT	ABACTOR
	BALATAS	AAAERWY	AREAWAY	AAAMRRZ	ZAMARRA		ACROBAT
AAABMOS	ABOMASA	AAAFFLL	ALFALFA	AAAMRSS	SAMARAS	AABCOTT	CATBOAT
AAABMST	MASTABA	AAAFIRT	RATAFIA		SAMSARA	AABCRSS	SCARABS
AAABNNR	RABANNA	AAAFNRS	SARAFAN	AAAMRST	TAMARAS	AABCSUU	AUCUBAS
AAABNNS	BANANAS	AAAFRWY	FARAWAY	AAAMRTU	TAMARAU	AABCTTU	CATTABU
AAABORR	ARAROBA	AAAGGLN	GALANGA	AAANNSV	SAVANNA	AABDDEN	ABANDED
AAABRSX	ABRAXAS	AAAGHIP	APHAGIA	AAANNTT	ANNATTA	AABDDER	ABRADED
AAABRSZ	BARAZAS	AAAGHLN	LANGAHA	AAANRST	ANTARAS	AABDDIK	KABADDI
	BAZAARS	AAAGHNT	ATAGHAN	AAANRTT	TANTARA	AABDEFL	FADABLE
AAABSTT	BATATAS	AAAGHPR	AGRAPHA		TARTANA	AABDEGN	BANDAGE
AAACCIS	ACACIAS	AAAGINZ	GAZANIA	AAANSTT	ANATTAS	AABDEHS	ABASHED
AAACCLR	CARACAL	AAAGIPT	PATAGIA	AAAOPRZ	PARAZOA	AABDEIS	DIABASE
AAACCRS	CASCARA	AAAGISS	ASSAGAI	AAAPPRT	APPARAT	AABDELL	BALLADE
AAACDLU	ACAUDAL	AAAGLMM	AMALGAM	AAAPPSY	PAPAYAS	AABDELT	ABLATED
AAACDMM	MACADAM	AAAGLMN	NAGMAAL	AAAPRSS	APSARAS		DATABLE
AAACDNS	CANADAS	AAAGLNO	ANALOGA	AAAPSST	PASSATA	AABDEMN	BEADMAN
AAACENP	PANACEA	AAAGLNS	LASAGNA	AAARSST	SATARAS	AABDEMS	SAMBAED
AAACGNT	AGACANT	AAAGLRS	ARGALAS	AAARSTV	AVATARS	AABDENU	BANDEAU
AAACHLZ	CHALAZA	AAAGMMT	MAGMATA	AAARTTU	TUATARA	AABDERS	ABRADES
AAACHNT	ACANTHA	AAAGMNR	ANAGRAM	AAARTXY	ATARAXY	AABDERY	ABRAYED
AAACHRY	ACHARYA	AAAGMNS	SAGAMAN	AABBBOS	BAOBABS	AABDESU	AUBADES
AAACILM	MALACIA	AAAGMTT	TAGMATA	AABBCEG	CABBAGE	AABDGHN	HANDBAG
AAACIMR	CARIAMA	AAAGNNS	NAGANAS	AABBCGY	CABBAGY	AABDGHR	HARDBAG
AAACINP	ACAPNIA	AAAGNPR	PARGANA	AABBCOS	BABACOS	AABDGMO	GAMBADO
AAACINR	ACARIAN	AAAGNRT	TANAGRA	AABBDGR	GABBARD	AABDGNS	SANDBAG
AAACIRS	ACRASIA	AAAGNRU	GUARANA	AABBDHS	HABDABS	AABDGOS	DAGOBAS
AAACJMR	JACAMAR	AAAGNTY	YATAGAN	AABBEGN	BEANBAG	AABDHMS	BADMASH
AAACJNS	JACANAS	AAAHHLV	HALAVAH	AABBELT	BATABLE	AABDHNT	HATBAND
AAACLLV	CAVALLA	AAAHIKW	KAHAWAI	AABBERT	BARBATE	AABDHNY	HAYBAND
AAACLMN	ALMANAC	AAAHIPS	APHASIA	AABBGRT	GABBART	AABDHRS	BARDASH
	MANCALA	AAAHIST	TAIAHAS	AABBHLS	BABLAHS	AABDIIS	BASIDIA
AAACLNT	CANTALA	AAAHJKW	KAJAWAH	AABBLLS	LABLABS	AABDIKR	BIDARKA
AAACLPS	ALPACAS	AAAHLMR	HARMALA	AABBLOR	BARBOLA	AABDILN	BALADIN
AAACLPT	CATALPA	AAAHLNN	ALANNAH	AABBLOS	BALBOAS	AABDIMR	BARMAID
AAACLRZ	ALCAZAR	AAAHMMT	MAHATMA	AABBSST	SABBATS	AABDINS	INDABAS
AAACMNP	CAMPANA	AAAHMRS	ASHRAMA	AABBSSU	BABASSU	AABDINT	TABANID
AAACMRS	MARACAS	AAAHMST	TAMASHA	AABCCEL	ACCABLE	AABDIOT	BIODATA
	MASCARA	AAAHPRT	PARATHA	AABCCER	BACCARE	AABDIRS	ABRAIDS
AAACNNR	CARANNA	AAAHRTW	WARATAH	AABCCET	BACCATE	AABDLLS	BALLADS
AAACNPT	CATAPAN	AAAILLS	ALALIAS	AABCCIR	BRACCIA	AABDLMS	LAMBDAS
AAACNRT	NACARAT	AAAILMR	MALARIA	AABCDIR	CARABID	AABDLNS	SALBAND
AAACNRU	CARAUNA	AAAILNX	ANAXIAL	AABCEKR	BACKARE	AABDLRW	BRADAWL

AABDMNR	ARMBAND
AABDNNO	ABANDON
AABDNOR	BANDORA
AABDNRS	BANDARS
AABDNRU	BANDURA
AABDORS	ABROADS
AABDORV	BRAVADO
AABDRRW	DRAWBAR
AABDRST	BASTARD
	TABARDS
AABDRSU	SUBADAR
AABDRSY	BAYARDS
AABDSTU	DATABUS
AABEELT	EATABLE
AABEEMO	AMOEBAE
AABEERZ	ZAREEBA
AABEFFL	AFFABLE
AABEFFN	BEFFANA
AABEFGU	AUFGABE
AABEFNS	BEFANAS
AABEGGG	BAGGAGE
AABEGGR	GARBAGE
AABEGLR	ALGEBRA
AABEGMR	BERGAMA
	MEGABAR
AABEGMS	AMBAGES
AABEGRR	BAGARRE
	BARRAGE
AABEGSS	BAGASSE
AABEGST	ATABEGS
AABEGSU	ABUSAGE
AABEHLT	HATABLE
AABEHNT	ABTHANE
AABEHRS	EARBASH
AABEHSS	ABASHES
AABEIKN	IKEBANA
AABEILM	AMABILE
	AMIABLE
AABEILS	ABELIAS
AABEILT	LABIATE
AABEIRS	AIRBASE
	ARABISE
AABEIRZ	ARABIZE
AABEJLL	JELLABA
AABEJMU	JAMBEAU
AABEKLM	MAKABLE
AABEKLT	TAKABLE
AABEKNS	SEABANK
AABEKST	ATABEKS
AABELLL	LABELLA
AABELLN	BALNEAL
AABELLO	ABOLLAE
AABELLS	SABELLA
	SALABLE
AABELMN	NAMABLE
AABELMT	TAMABLE
AABELNO	ABALONE
AABELNR	BANALER
AABELPP	PAPABLE
AABELPR	PARABLE
AABELPY	PAYABLE
AABELRT	RATABLE
AABELSS	BALASES
AABELST	ABLATES
	ASTABLE
AABELSV	SAVABLE
AABELSY	SAYABLE
AABELTT	ABETTAL
AABELTU	TABLEAU
	TABULAE
AABELTV	VATABLE
AABELTX	TAXABLE
AABEMNS	BASEMAN
AABEMOS	AMOEBAS
AABENNW	WANNABE
AABENRT	ANTBEAR
AABENTY	ABEYANT
AABERST	ABREAST
AABERSU	BAUERAS
	SUBAREA
AABERSZ	ZAREBAS
AABERTT	RABATTE
	TABARET
AABERTU	ABATURE
AABESTZ	ZABETAS
AABETUX	BATEAUX
AABFFLY	AFFABLY
AABFILU	FABLIAU
AABFLRU	FABULAR
AABGGRS	RAGBAGS
AABGGSS	GASBAGS
AABGHNR	BHANGRA
AABGHNS	GABNASH
	NASHGAB
AABGHSW	BAGWASH
AABGIIL	ABIGAIL
AABGILM	MAILBAG
AABGINR	BARGAIN
AABGINS	ABASING
	BAAINGS
AABGINT	ABATING
AABGRST	RATBAGS
AABHHIS	SAHIBAH
AABHHKS	SABKHAH
AABHHRU	BRUHAHA
AABHISS	SAHIBAS
AABHITT	HABITAT
AABHJNS	BHAJANS
AABHKNR	BARKHAN
AABHKSS	KASBAHS
	SABKHAS
AABHKST	SABKHAT
AABHLRS	BHARALS
AABHLTY	BATHYAL
AABHMSS	SHAMBAS
AABHSSW	BASHAWS
AABIILX	BIAXIAL
AABIJMY	JAMBIYA
AABIKNS	BANKSIA
AABILLR	BARILLA
AABILLS	LABIALS
AABILMN	BIMANAL
AABILOU	ABOULIA
AABILRS	BASILAR
AABILST	BALISTA
AABILSU	ABULIAS
AABIMMR	MARIMBA
AABIMNO	BONAMIA
AABINNS	BANIANS
AABINOU	OUABAIN
AABINRS	ARABINS
AABINRT	ATABRIN
AABINST	ABSTAIN
AABINSW	WABAINS
AABINSZ	BANZAIS
AABIPUX	PAXIUBA
AABIRSZ	ZARIBAS
AABISTT	ABATTIS
AABKNRS	BARKANS
AABKNRT	TANBARK
AABKOOZ	BAZOOKA
AABLLNS	BALLANS
AABLLNT	BALLANT
AABLLNY	BANALLY
AABLLOS	ABOLLAS
AABLLPT	PATBALL
AABLLST	BALLAST
	BALLATS
AABLLSY	SALABLY
AABLLWY	WALLABY
AABLMRU	LABARUM
AABLMSS	BALSAMS
	SAMBALS
AABLMST	LAMBAST
AABLMSY	ABYSMAL
	BALSAMY
AABLNTT	BLATANT
AABLORT	ABLATOR
AABLOSV	LAVABOS
AABLPRU	PABULAR
AABLRST	ARBLAST
AABLRTU	TABULAR
AABLRTY	RATABLY
AABLSST	BASALTS
AABLSSY	ABYSSAL
AABLSTU	ABLAUTS
AABLTTU	ABUTTAL
AABLTXY	TAXABLY
AABMNOT	BOATMAN
AABMNST	BANTAMS
	BATSMAN
AABMORU	MARABOU
AABMRSS	SAMBARS
AABMRTU	TAMBURA
AABMSST	TSAMBAS
AABMSSY	AMBASSY
AABNNOZ	BONANZA
AABNNSY	BANYANS
AABNOST	SABATON
AABORRS	ARROBAS
AABORST	ABATORS
AABORSZ	ABRAZOS
AABOTTY	ATTABOY
AABQSUU	SUBAQUA
AABRRST	BARRATS
AABRRSU	SABURRA
AABRRUV	BRAVURA
AABRSTY	BARYTAS
AABSSSY	SASSABY
AABTTTU	BATTUTA
AACCDEM	MEDACCA
AACCDES	CASCADE
	SACCADE
AACCDIR	CARDIAC
AACCDIS	CICADAS
AACCDSU	CADUACS
AACCEKR	CARCAKE
AACCELO	CLOACAE
AACCENV	VACANCE
AACCERS	CARCASE
AACCEST	SACCATE
AACCHHK	KACHCHA
AACCHIN	CHICANA
AACCHIR	ARCHAIC
AACCHKS	KACCHAS
AACCHLN	CLACHAN
AACCHMP	CHAMPAC
AACCHMS	CHACMAS
AACCHNN	CANNACH
AACCHRT	CHARACT
AACCILM	ACCLAIM
AACCILS	CICALAS
AACCIMS	CAIMACS
AACCIOR	CARIOCA
AACCIRT	ACRATIC
AACCITT	ATACTIC
AACCJKR	CARJACK
AACCKLP	CALPACK
AACCKRR	CARRACK
AACCKRS	CARACKS
AACCLLO	CLOACAL
AACCLLT	CATCALL
AACCLOP	POLACCA
AACCLOR	CARACOL
AACCLPS	CALPACS
AACCLPT	PLACCAT
AACCLRS	CALCARS
AACCLRU	ACCRUAL
	CARACUL
AACCLSU	ACCUSAL
AACCMOS	MACACOS
AACCNNS	CANCANS
AACCNVY	VACANCY
AACCORU	CURACAO
	CURACOA
AACCOST	ACCOAST
AACCOTT	TOCCATA
AACCRRT	CARRACT
AACCRSS	CARCASS
AACCRST	CARACTS
AACDDEL	DECADAL
AACDDER	ARCADED
AACDDHR	CHADDAR
AACDDIN	CANDIDA
AACDEEM	ACADEME
AACDEFL	FALCADE
AACDEFS	FACADES
AACDEHM	CHAMADE
AACDEHR	CHARADE
AACDEHT	CATHEAD
AACDEII	AECIDIA
AACDEIL	ALCAIDE
AACDEIN	AIDANCE
AACDEIS	ACEDIAS
AACDELL	ALCALDE
AACDELN	CANDELA
	DECANAL
AACDELR	CALDERA
AACDELS	SCALADE
AACDELY	ALCAYDE
AACDEMY	ACADEMY
AACDENV	ADVANCE
AACDENZ	CADENZA
AACDEPS	SCAPAED
AACDERS	ARCADES
AACDERV	CADAVER
AACDETU	CAUDATE
AACDETV	VACATED
AACDEUX	CADEAUX
AACDFIR	FARADIC
AACDFRS	CAFARDS
AACDHMR	DRACHMA
AACDHNR	HANDCAR
AACDHRS	CHADARS
AACDIIS	ASCIDIA
AACDILR	RADICAL
AACDINT	ANTACID
AACDINV	VANADIC
AACDIOR	ACAROID
AACDIRS	ACARIDS
	ASCARID
AACDJKW	JACKDAW
AACDKSY	DAYSACK
AACDLNO	CALANDO
AACDLNS	SCANDAL
AACDLOR	CARLOAD
AACDLOS	SCALADO
AACDLPR	PLACARD
AACDMPS	MADCAPS
AACDNRS	CADRANS
	CANARDS
AACDOOV	AVOCADO
AACDRSS	CSARDAS
AACDRSZ	CZARDAS
AACEEGR	ACREAGE
AACEEHR	EARACHE
AACEEHT	CHAETAE
AACEELN	ANELACE
AACEEMR	CAMERAE
AACEENT	CATENAE
AACEERT	ACERATE
AACEETT	ACETATE
AACEFLT	FALCATE
AACEFLU	FACULAE
AACEFMN	FACEMAN
AACEFRR	CARFARE
AACEFRS	CARAFES
AACEGGR	AGGRACE
AACEGHS	ACHAGES
AACEGKP	PACKAGE
AACEGKS	SACKAGE
AACEGNR	CARNAGE
	CRANAGE
AACEGRT	CARTAGE

AACEGSV	SCAVAGE	AACFLRU	FACULAR	AACIMPR	PICAMAR	AACMNOR	CAMARON
AACEHIN	ACHENIA	AACFLTU	FACTUAL	AACIMTY	CYMATIA	AACMNRU	ARCANUM
AACEHIR	ARCHAEI	AACFNST	CAFTANS	AACINNT	CANTINA	AACMNSY	CAYMANS
AACEHLP	ACALEPH	AACFRRU	FARRUCA	AACINOR	CONARIA	AACMORR	CAMORRA
AACEHLR	ALCHERA	AACGHNS	CHAGANS		OCARINA	AACMORS	SARCOMA
AACEHNO	CHOANAE	AACGILL	GLACIAL	AACINPT	CAPITAN	AACMORT	MARCATO
AACEHNP	PANACHE	AACGILM	MAGICAL		CAPTAIN	AACMOSY	MACOYAS
AACEHNR	ACHARNE	AACGILS	SCAGLIA	AACINRS	ARNICAS	AACMRRT	TRAMCAR
AACEHPP	APPEACH	AACGINT	AGNATIC		CARINAS	AACMRSS	SARCASM
AACEHPS	APACHES	AACGIRS	AGARICS	AACINRZ	CZARINA	AACMRST	RAMCATS
AACEHPU	CHAPEAU	AACGIRV	AGRAVIC	AACINSS	ASCIANS		TARMACS
AACEHRT	TRACHEA	AACGLOT	CATALOG		SANCAIS	AACNNOZ	CANZONA
AACEHST	ACHATES	AACGLOU	COAGULA	AACINST	SATANIC	AACNOST	SACATON
AACEHTT	ATTACHE	AACGNOU	GUANACO	AACIOPT	TAPIOCA	AACNPST	CAPSTAN
AACEHTU	CHATEAU	AACHHKR	CHARKHA	AACIOPV	COPAIVA		CAPTANS
AACEIMN	ANAEMIC	AACHHLL	CHALLAH	AACIOST	ATOCIAS		CATNAPS
AACEIMU	CAMAIEU	AACHIKN	KACHINA		COAITAS	AACNRST	ARCTANS
AACEINR	ACARINE	AACHIKR	CHIKARA	AACIQTU	AQUATIC		CANTARS
	CARINAE	AACHILR	RACHIAL	AACIRSS	ASCARIS	AACNRTU	CURTANA
AACEIRV	AVARICE	AACHILT	CALATHI	AACIRST	CARITAS	AACNSSV	CANVASS
	CAVIARE	AACHIMR	MACHAIR	AACIRSV	CAVIARS	AACNSTU	ASCAUNT
AACEKNP	PANCAKE	AACHIMS	CHIASMA	AACISSS	CASSIAS	AACORST	OSTRACA
AACEKNS	ASKANCE	AACHIPS	APHASIC	AACISTT	ASTATIC	AACORTU	ACATOUR
AACEKOT	OATCAKE	AACHIPT	CHAPATI	AACJKLS	JACKALS		AUTOCAR
AACELLN	CANELLA	AACHIRS	ARACHIS	AACJKMN	JACKMAN	AACOTUV	AUTOVAC
AACELLS	SACELLA	AACHIRT	CITHARA		MANJACK	AACPRSS	SCARPAS
AACELLT	LACTEAL	AACHITY	CYATHIA	AACJKSS	JACKASS	AACRRST	CARRATS
AACELMN	MANACLE	AACHKMP	CHAMPAK	AACJOSU	ACAJOUS	AACRRSU	CURARAS
AACELMR	CAMERAL	AACHKNS	ACHKANS	AACKMNP	MANPACK	AACRSTV	CRAVATS
	CARAMEL	AACHKPS	CHAPKAS		PACKMAN	AACRTTT	ATTRACT
	CERAMAL		PACHAKS	AACKMRT	AMTRACK	AACRTUV	VACATUR
AACELMU	MACULAE	AACHKRS	CHAKRAS	AACKNRS	RANSACK	AACRTUY	ACTUARY
AACELNS	ANLACES		CHARKAS	AACKPRR	CARPARK	AACRTWY	CARTWAY
AACELNU	CANULAE	AACHKRT	HATRACK	AACKPRT	RATPACK	AACTUWY	CUTAWAY
	LACUNAE	AACHKSW	KWACHAS	AACKPSZ	CZAPKAS	AADDDEN	ADDENDA
AACELNV	VALANCE	AACHLLN	CHALLAN	AACKPWY	PACKWAY	AADDEGM	DAMAGED
AACELPS	PALACES	AACHLMS	CHASMAL	AACKRRS	ARRACKS	AADDEIL	ALIDADE
AACELPT	PLACATE	AACHLNS	CHALANS	AACKSTT	ATTACKS	AADDEMM	MADAMED
AACELRV	CARAVEL	AACHLPP	CHAPPAL	AACLLNS	CALLANS	AADDENP	DEADPAN
AACELST	ACETALS	AACHLPS	PASCHAL	AACLLNT	CALLANT	AADDEPR	PARADED
	LACTASE	AACHLST	CALTHAS	AACLLNU	CALLUNA	AADDEPT	ADAPTED
AACELTT	LACTATE	AACHLSU	ACUSHLA		LACUNAL	AADDERS	ADREADS
AACELTV	CLAVATE	AACHMNP	CHAPMAN	AACLLOR	CORALLA	AADDERW	AWARDED
AACEMMR	MACRAME	AACHMNS	MACHANS	AACLLSU	CLAUSAL	AADDESX	ADDAXES
AACEMNS	CASEMAN	AACHNOP	PANOCHA	AACLLVY	CAVALLY	AADDGNR	GRADDAN
AACEMNV	CAVEMAN	AACHNOU	HUANACO	AACLMNO	COALMAN		GRANDAD
AACEMPR	PARACME	AACHNPX	PANCHAX	AACLMNT	CALMANT	AADDHKR	KHADDAR
AACEMQU	MACAQUE	AACHNRS	ANARCHS		CLAMANT	AADDHRS	SRADDHA
AACEMRS	CAMERAS	AACHNRV	NAVARCH	AACLMRU	MACULAR	AADDIIK	DIDAKAI
AACEMSS	CAMASES	AACHNRY	ANARCHY	AACLMSU	CALAMUS	AADDIIV	DAVIDIA
AACENPS	CANAPES	AACHNST	ACANTHS	AACLNNU	CANNULA	AADDILS	ALIDADS
AACENRT	CATERAN	AACHNSZ	CHAZANS	AACLNPY	CLAYPAN	AADDLNS	ADLANDS
AACENST	CATENAS	AACHRRT	CATARRH	AACLNRS	CARNALS	AADDNVV	DVANDVA
AACENTT	CANTATE	AACHRST	CHARTAS	AACLNRU	LACUNAR	AADDOSU	AOUDADS
AACENTY	CYANATE	AACHRWY	ARCHWAY	AACLNSU	CANULAS	AADDRST	DASTARD
AACEORS	ROSACEA	AACHSSW	CASHAWS	AACLOPR	CAPORAL	AADDRSW	ADWARDS
AACEPRT	CAPRATE	AACHSTT	CHATTAS	AACLOPT	OCTAPLA	AADDSST	STADDAS
AACEPRU	CAPUERA	AACIILN	ANCILIA	AACLORT	COALTAR	AADEEFR	AFEARED
AACEPRV	PRECAVA		LACINIA		CROTALA	AADEEGH	HEADAGE
AACERSS	CAESARS	AACIINP	APICIAN	AACLORZ	ALCORZA	AADEEMT	EDEMATA
AACERST	ACATERS	AACIINT	ACTINIA	AACLOST	CATALOS	AADEENR	ANEARED
AACERSU	CAESURA	AACIITV	VIATICA		COASTAL	AADEERT	AERATED
AACERSZ	SAZERAC	AACIJLP	JALAPIC	AACLOTT	CATTALO	AADEFFR	AFFEARD
AACERTU	ARCUATE	AACIKLR	CLARKIA	AACLOTV	OCTAVAL	AADEFGL	FALDAGE
AACERWY	RACEWAY	AACIKNN	CANAKIN	AACLPRS	CARPALS	AADEFGR	FARDAGE
AACESTV	CAVEATS	AACILMS	CALIMAS	AACLPRT	CALTRAP	AADEFIS	FADAISE
	VACATES	AACILNR	CLARAIN	AACLPSS	PASCALS	AADEFLU	AEFAULD
AACETTU	ACTUATE		CRANIAL	AACLPSU	PASCUAL	AADEFNZ	FAZENDA
AACETUV	VACUATE	AACILNT	ACTINAL		SCAPULA	AADEFTW	FATWAED
AACFFIL	CAFFILA		ALICANT	AACLRSS	LASCARS	AADEGGR	AGGRADE
AACFILS	CAFILAS	AACILOS	ASOCIAL		RASCALS		GARAGED
	FACIALS	AACILOX	COAXIAL		SCALARS	AADEGHR	RAGHEAD
	FASCIAL	AACILPS	SPACIAL	AACLRST	CASTRAL	AADEGLS	GELADAS
AACFILU	FAUCIAL	AACILPT	CAPITAL	AACLRVY	CALVARY	AADEGMN	AGNAMED
AACFINT	FANATIC		PLACITA		CAVALRY		MANAGED
AACFISS	FASCIAS	AACIMMR	MACRAMI	AACLSSU	CASUALS	AADEGMR	MEGARAD
AACFLLU	FALCULA	AACIMNS	CAIMANS	AACLSTT	SALTCAT	AADEGMS	DAMAGES
AACFLLY	FALLACY		MANIACS	AACLSUV	VASCULA	AADEGNS	AGENDAS
AACFLRT	FRACTAL	AACIMOR	ACROMIA	AACLTTU	TACTUAL	AADEGRT	GRADATE

AADEGRV	RAVAGED	AADGIMM	DIGAMMA	AADLMPS	LAMPADS	AAEEPRT	PATERAE
AADEGRY	DRAYAGE	AADGIMO	AGAMOID	AADLMSW	WADMALS	AAEERST	AERATES
	YARDAGE	AADGIMR	DIAGRAM	AADLNRY	LANYARD	AAEERSW	SEAWARE
AADEGSV	SAVAGED	AADGIMS	AGAMIDS	AADLNSS	SANDALS	AAEERTU	AUREATE
AADEHIR	AIRHEAD	AADGINW	ADAWING	AADLNSU	LANDAUS	AAEERTX	EXARATE
AADEHKS	AKEDAHS	AADGIOS	ADAGIOS	AADLNSV	VANDALS	AAEFFGR	AGRAFFE
AADEHMN	HEADMAN	AADGLLW	GADWALL	AADLPPU	APPLAUD	AAEFFIR	AFFAIRE
AADEHMS	ASHAMED	AADGLMY	AMYGDAL	AADLPRS	PARDALS	AAEFFLL	FALAFEL
AADEHPS	SAPHEAD	AADGLNO	GONADAL	AADLRRU	RADULAR	AAEFFNR	FANFARE
AADEHPW	AWHAPED	AADGLNR	GARLAND	AADMMRS	DAMMARS	AAEFFRS	AFFEARS
AADEHRW	RAWHEAD	AADGLNS	SLADANG	AADMNNS	SANDMAN	AAEFFTT	TAFFETA
	WARHEAD	AADGLRU	GRADUAL	AADMNOR	MADRONA	AAEFGTW	WAFTAGE
AADEHWY	HEADWAY	AADGMNR	GRANDAM		MANDORA	AAEFKLO	OAKLEAF
AADEIKK	KAIAKED		GRANDMA		MONARDA	AAEFLPR	EARFLAP
AADEILR	RADIALE	AADGMNS	GADSMAN		ROADMAN		PARAFLE
AADEILV	AVAILED	AADGMRS	SMARAGD	AADMNRS	MANSARD	AAEFLRS	RAFALES
	VEDALIA	AADGNPR	GRANDPA	AADMNRY	DRAYMAN	AAEFLSV	FAVELAS
AADEIMS	SEAMAID	AADGNPS	PADANGS		YARDMAN	AAEFMRT	FERMATA
AADEINR	ARANEID	AADGNRS	ARGANDS	AADMNSY	DAYSMAN	AAEFQRU	AQUAFER
AADEINS	NAIADES	AADGNRT	GARDANT	AADMNTU	MUTANDA	AAEFRRW	WARFARE
AADEIPS	DIAPASE	AADGNRY	YARDANG		TAMANDU	AAEFRWY	WAYFARE
AADEIRS	ARAISED	AADGOPR	PODAGRA	AADMOQU	MADOQUA	AAEGGLS	GALAGES
AADEIRT	RADIATE	AADGOPS	PAGODAS	AADMORT	MATADOR	AAEGGNO	ANAGOGE
	TIARAED	AADGRSU	GARUDAS	AADMOSU	AMADOUS	AAEGGOP	APAGOGE
AADEITV	AVIATED	AADHILS	DAHLIAS	AADMRSU	MARAUDS	AAEGGRS	GARAGES
AADEITW	AWAITED	AADHIMS	SAMADHI	AADMRSZ	MAZARDS	AAEGGRT	AGGRATE
AADEJMR	JEMADAR	AADHJNR	HANDJAR	AADMRZZ	MAZZARD	AAEGGSV	GAVAGES
AADEKKY	KAYAKED	AADHKNY	YAKHDAN	AADMSYY	MAYDAYS	AAEGHLU	HAULAGE
AADEKLR	KRAALED	AADHLRY	HALYARD	AADNNOT	NOTANDA	AAEGHNT	THANAGE
AADEKLS	ASLAKED	AADHMRS	DHARMAS	AADNNRS	RANDANS	AAEGILR	LAIRAGE
AADEKMR	KAMERAD	AADHNRS	DARSHAN	AADNOPR	PANDORA		REGALIA
AADEKMS	MEDAKAS		DHARNAS	AADNORT	ONDATRA	AAEGILS	ALGESIA
AADELLP	PADELLA	AADHNSW	HANDSAW	AADNORY	ANYROAD	AAEGINP	NAGAPIE
AADELLY	ALLAYED	AADHRSZ	HAZARDS	AADNPRS	PANDARS	AAEGINV	VAGINAE
AADELMO	ALAMODE	AADHRWY	HAYWARD	AADNPRU	PANDURA	AAEGINW	WAINAGE
AADELMR	ALARMED	AADHSWY	WASHDAY	AADNRRW	WARRAND	AAEGIPR	IGARAPE
AADELMX	MALAXED	AADIILR	DIARIAL	AADNRRY	DARRAYN	AAEGIRR	ARRIAGE
AADELNR	ADRENAL	AADIINR	DIARIAN	AADNRSS	NASARDS	AAEGISS	ASSEGAI
AADELNW	DANELAW	AADIIPS	ASPIDIA	AADNRST	ASTRAND	AAEGITT	AGITATE
AADELPR	PARDALE	AADIJMN	JAMDANI		TARANDS	AAEGJTU	AJUTAGE
AADELPT	PALATED	AADIKLY	ILKADAY	AADNRTY	TANYARD	AAEGKNT	TANKAGE
AADELRU	RADULAE	AADILLO	ALODIAL	AADNRVW	VANWARD	AAEGKOS	SOAKAGE
AADELRY	ALREADY	AADILMR	ADMIRAL	AADNRWY	NAYWARD	AAEGLLR	GLAREAL
AADELSS	SALADES		AMILDAR	AADOPRR	PARADOR	AAEGLLT	GALLATE
	SALSAED	AADILNP	PALADIN	AADOPRS	PARADOS		TALLAGE
AADELTU	ADULATE	AADILNR	LANIARD	AADOPRT	ADAPTOR	AAEGLMN	GAMELAN
AADELTY	DAYTALE	AADILPS	APSIDAL	AADOPRX	PARADOX	AAEGLMT	GAMETAL
AADEMNO	ADENOMA	AADILRS	RADIALS	AADOPSS	PASSADO	AAEGLNN	ANLAGEN
AADEMNS	ANADEMS	AADILRT	TAILARD		POSADAS	AAEGLNR	ALNAGER
	MAENADS	AADILST	STADIAL	AADOPTT	DOPATTA	AAEGLNS	ALNAGES
AADEMNT	MANDATE	AADILTV	DATIVAL	AADORWY	ROADWAY		ANLAGES
AADEMSS	AMASSED	AADILWY	WAYLAID	AADOSTT	TOSTADA		GALENAS
AADENNT	ANDANTE	AADIMNR	MANDIRA	AADPSSW	PADSAWS		LAGENAS
AADENRV	VERANDA	AADIMNS	MAIDANS	AADPSSY	SPAYADS		LASAGNE
AADENRW	AWARNED	AADIMOR	DIORAMA	AADPTTU	DUPATTA	AAEGLNU	AULNAGE
AADENST	ANSATED	AADIMOT	DOMATIA	AADQRTU	QUADRAT	AAEGLOP	APOGEAL
AADENSW	WEASAND	AADINRR	DARRAIN	AADRSTU	DATURAS	AAEGLRR	REALGAR
AADENWZ	WEAZAND	AADINRS	RADIANS	AADRSTY	DAYSTAR	AAEGLRS	ALEGARS
AADEPRS	ASPREAD	AADINRT	INTRADA	AADRSVW	VAWARDS		LAAGERS
	PARADES		RADIANT	AADRWWY	WAYWARD	AAEGLST	AGELAST
AADEPRT	ADAPTER	AADINRV	VIRANDA	AAEEFFR	AFFEARE		ALGATES
	READAPT	AADINSV	NAVAIDS	AAEEFGL	LEAFAGE		LASTAGE
AADEPSS	ESPADAS	AADIOSS	QASIDAS	AAEEGKL	LEAKAGE	AAEGLSV	LAVAGES
	PASSADE	AADIRRW	AIRWARD	AAEEGLT	ETALAGE		SALVAGE
AADEPWW	PAWAWED	AADIRSU	SUDARIA		GALEATE	AAEGMNR	MANAGER
AADERRS	ARRASED	AADISST	STADIAS	AAEEGMN	AMENAGE	AAEGMNS	AGNAMES
AADERRY	ARRAYED	AADJLNS	JANDALS	AAEEGRV	AVERAGE		MANAGES
AADERSW	SEAWARD	AADKMRY	DAYMARK	AAEEGST	EATAGES		SAGAMEN
AADERSY	ARAYSED	AADKMSS	DAMASKS	AAEEHRT	HETAERA	AAEGMNT	GATEMAN
AADERTU	AURATED	AADKNRT	TANKARD	AAEEINT	TAENIAE		MAGENTA
AADESSY	ASSAYED	AADKPSU	PADAUKS	AAEEKLS	SEAKALE		MAGNATE
AADFLTW	TWAFALD	AADKRWW	AWKWARD	AAEEKRW	REAWAKE	AAEGMPR	RAMPAGE
AADFNRR	FARRAND	AADLLMR	MALLARD	AAEELMT	MALEATE	AAEGMRT	REGMATA
AADFNST	FANTADS	AADLLNW	LAWLAND	AAEELOR	AREOLAE	AAEGMSS	MASSAGE
AADFRST	DAFTARS	AADLLPU	PALUDAL	AAEELRT	LAETARE	AAEGNNP	PANNAGE
AADGGHR	HAGGARD	AADLLSS	SALLADS	AAEEMNT	EMANATE	AAEGNNT	TANNAGE
AADGGLR	LAGGARD	AADLMNN	LANDMAN		ENEMATA	AAEGNOP	APOGEAN
AADGGRS	SAGGARD	AADLMNO	MANDOLA		MANATEE	AAEGNPT	PAGEANT
AADGHIL	HIDALGA	AADLMNU	LADANUM	AAEEPPS	APPEASE	AAEGNRR	ARRANGE

AAEGNRT	TANAGER	AAEIRST	ARISTAE	AAELTUV	VALUATE	AAFIJST	FAJITAS
AAEGNST	AGNATES		ASTERIA	AAELTVV	VALVATE	AAFIKLS	KAFILAS
AAEGNTV	VANTAGE		ATRESIA	AAELTZZ	ALTEZZA	AAFIKSS	SIFAKAS
AAEGNTW	WANTAGE	AAEIRSX	XERASIA	AAELWWY	WELAWAY	AAFILNT	FANTAIL
AAEGORS	OARAGES	AAEIRTT	ARIETTA	AAEMMMR	MAREMMA	AAFILQU	ALFAQUI
AAEGPRR	PARERGA	AAEIRTV	VARIATE	AAEMMMT	MAMMATE	AAFINNT	INFANTA
AAEGPRS	PARAGES	AAEIRVW	AIRWAVE	AAEMMNU	MANUMEA	AAFINNU	INFAUNA
AAEGPSS	PASSAGE	AAEISTT	SATIATE	AAEMMOT	OMMATEA	AAFINRS	FARINAS
AAEGPSV	PAVAGES	AAEISTV	AVIATES	AAEMNNT	EMANANT	AAFIPRT	PARFAIT
AAEGPSY	PAYSAGE	AAEISTX	ATAXIES	AAEMNPP	PAMPEAN	AAFIRSS	SAFARIS
AAEGQUY	QUAYAGE	AAEJMST	MAATJES	AAEMNPT	PEATMAN	AAFIRUY	RUFIYAA
AAEGRRV	RAVAGER	AAEJNRT	NAARTJE	AAEMNRT	RAMENTA	AAFIRWY	FAIRWAY
AAEGRST	AGRASTE	AAEKKOR	KARAOKE	AAEMNRU	MURAENA	AAFISST	FATSIAS
AAEGRSV	RAVAGES	AAEKLMS	KAMELAS	AAEMNST	NAMASTE	AAFJLLW	JAWFALL
	SAVAGER	AAEKLNS	ALKANES	AAEMNTU	MANTEAU	AAFJLOR	ALFORJA
AAEGRTT	REGATTA	AAEKLNT	ALKANET	AAEMOTZ	METAZOA	AAFKNST	KAFTANS
AAEGSSU	ASSUAGE		KANTELA	AAEMQSU	SQUAMAE	AAFLLLS	FALLALS
	SAUSAGE	AAEKLSS	ASLAKES	AAEMRST	AMEARST	AAFLLTY	FATALLY
AAEGSSV	AVGASES	AAEKMNW	WAKEMAN		RETAMAS	AAFLMPR	FRAMPAL
	SAVAGES	AAEKMRR	EARMARK			AAFLNOR	FORLANA
AAEGSSW	ASSWAGE	AAEKMRS	SEAMARK	AAEMRTU	AMATEUR	AAFLNRU	FURLANA
AAEGSTU	GATEAUS	AAEKNNS	ANANKES	AAEMSSS	AMASSES	AAFLWYY	FLYAWAY
AAEGSTW	WASTAGE	AAEKNSW	AWAKENS	AAENNNT	ANTENNA	AAFMNRT	RAFTMAN
AAEGTTW	WATTAGE		WAKANES	AAENNST	ANNATES	AAFMNST	FANTASM
AAEGTUX	GATEAUX	AAEKPRT	PARTAKE	AAENNSZ	ZENANAS	AAFNRRT	FARRANT
AAEGTWY	GATEWAY	AAEKRSS	KEASARS	AAENNTT	TANNATE	AAFNSTT	FANTAST
	GETAWAY	AAEKRST	KARATES	AAENNTV	VENTANA	AAFNSTY	FANTASY
AAEHHPT	APHTHAE	AAELLLM	LAMELLA	AAENOPS	APNOEAS	AAGGILN	GANGLIA
AAEHILP	APHELIA	AAELLNZ	ZANELLA	AAENOSZ	OZAENAS	AAGGKSU	GAGAKUS
AAEHIRT	HETAIRA	AAELLPR	PARELLA	AAENPRP	PARPANE	AAGGLMO	MAGALOG
AAEHKNT	KHANATE	AAELLPS	PAELLAS	AAENPST	ANAPEST	AAGGLOS	GALAGOS
AAEHKPS	PAKEHAS	AAELLPT	PATELLA		PEASANT	AAGGMNS	MGANGAS
AAEHKST	TAKAHES	AAELLRT	LATERAL			AAGGNOY	ANAGOGY
AAEHKSW	SEAHAWK	AAELLRY	ALLAYER	AAENPSV	PAVANES	AAGGNST	GANGSTA
AAEHLLL	ALLHEAL	AAELMMT	LEMMATA	AAENPSX	PANAXES	AAGGNWY	GANGWAY
AAEHLPX	HEXAPLA	AAELMNT	AMENTAL	AAENPTT	EPATANT	AAGGQSU	QUAGGAS
AAEHLRT	TREHALA	AAELMNU	ALUMNAE	AAENRRT	NARRATE	AAGGRSS	SAGGARS
AAEHLST	ALTHEAS	AAELMOT	OATMEAL	AAENRSS	NARASES	AAGGRST	RAGTAGS
AAEHLTT	ATHLETA	AAELMPT	PALMATE	AAENRST	ANESTRA		TAGRAGS
AAEHMSS	ASHAMES	AAELMST	MALATES	AAENRTT	TARTANE		
AAEHMTT	THEMATA		MALTASE	AAENRTU	NATURAE	AAGHILR	GHARIAL
AAEHNPR	HANAPER		TAMALES		TAUREAN	AAGHKNS	KANGHAS
AAEHNPS	SAPHENA	AAELMSX	MALAXES	AAENRTV	TAVERNA		KHANGAS
AAEHNSY	HYAENAS	AAELMSY	AMYLASE	AAENRUW	UNAWARE	AAGHLNT	GNATHAL
AAEHPRZ	PHEAZAR	AAELNNS	ANNEALS	AAENRUZ	AZUREAN	AAGHLOS	GASAHOL
AAEHPSW	AWHAPES	AAELNOV	VALONEA	AAENSSU	NAUSEAS	AAGHLSZ	GHAZALS
AAEHRSY	HEARSAY	AAELNPT	PLATANE	AAENSSV	VANESSA	AAGHMNN	HANGMAN
AAEHSTT	HASTATE	AAELNPU	PAENULA	AAEORRT	AERATOR	AAGHMNW	WHANGAM
AAEILLX	AXILLAE	AAELNRS	ARSENAL	AAEORRU	AURORAE	AAGHMRS	GRAMASH
AAEILMN	LAMINAE	AAELNST	SEALANT	AAEPPRS	APPEARS	AAGHNRS	ARGHANS
AAEILMS	AMELIAS	AAELNSY	ANALYSE	AAEPPRT	PARAPET		HANGARS
	MALAISE	AAELNTT	TETANAL	AAEPRSS	PASEARS	AAGHQUU	QUAHAUG
AAEILNN	ALANINE	AAELNTZ	ZEALANT		SARAPES	AAGHRSW	WASHRAG
AAEILNO	AEOLIAN	AAELNWY	LANEWAY	AAEPRST	PETARAS	AAGHSTY	SAGATHY
AAEILNT	ANTLIAE	AAELNYZ	ANALYZE	AAEPRSZ	ZARAPES	AAGIKNW	AWAKING
AAEILOR	OLEARIA	AAELORR	AREOLAR	AAEPRTY	PEATARY	AAGIKNZ	ZIGANKA
AAEILPX	EPAXIAL	AAELORU	AUREOLA	AAERRRS	ARREARS	AAGILMY	MYALGIA
AAEILRS	AERIALS	AAELOTX	OXALATE	AAERRRY	ARRAYER	AAGILNN	ANGINAL
AAEILRV	VELARIA	AAELPPR	APPAREL	AAERRSS	ARRASES	AAGILNO	LOGANIA
AAEILSS	ALIASES	AAELPPS	APPEALS	AAERRTT	TARTARE	AAGILNP	PAGINAL
AAEILSV	AVAILES	AAELPPT	PALPATE	AAERSST	SEARATS	AAGILNS	AGNAILS
AAEILSX	ALEXIAS	AAELPPU	PAPULAE	AAERSSY	ARAYSES	AAGILNV	AVALING
AAEIMMT	IMAMATE	AAELPRS	EARLAPS		ASSAYER		VAGINAL
AAEIMNS	AMNESIA	AAELPRT	APTERAL	AAERSTU	AURATES	AAGILNY	ALAYING
	ANEMIAS	AAELPRV	PALAVER	AAERSTW	AWAREST	AAGILOS	ALOGIAS
AAEIMNT	AMENTIA	AAELPSS	PALASES	AAESSTV	SAVATES	AAGILOT	OTALGIA
	ANIMATE	AAELPST	PALATES	AAESSWY	SEAWAYS	AAGILPS	PALAGIS
AAEIMPY	PYAEMIA	AAELPTT	TAPETAL	AAFFIMS	MAFFIAS	AAGILRS	ARGALIS
AAEIMRU	URAEMIA	AAELPTU	PLATEAU	AAFFINS	SAFFIAN		GARIALS
AAEIMTV	AMATIVE	AAELPTY	APETALY	AAFFIRS	AFFAIRS	AAGILSV	GAVIALS
AAEINNO	AEONIAN	AAELRTV	LARVATE		RAFFIAS	AAGILTW	WAGTAIL
AAEINST	TAENIAS	AAELRTZ	LAZARET	AAFFIST	TAFFIAS	AAGIMNO	ANGIOMA
AAEIPPS	APEPSIA	AAELRVY	ALVEARY	AAFFPRS	AFFRAPS	AAGIMNS	MAGIANS
AAEIPRR	PAREIRA	AAELSST	ATLASES	AAFFRSY	AFFRAYS		SIAMANG
AAEIPRS	SPIRAEA	AAELSTT	SALTATE	AAFGHNS	AFGHANS	AAGIMNT	AMATING
AAEIPRT	APTERIA	AAELSTV	VALETAS	AAFGORR	FARRAGO	AAGIMNZ	AMAZING
AAEIPTT	APATITE	AAELSTZ	ALTEZAS	AAFHIKL	KHALIFA	AAGINNS	ANGINAS
AAEIRSS	ARAISES	AAELSUX	ASEXUAL	AAFHLWY	HALFWAY	AAGINNW	WANIGAN
		AAELSWX	SEALWAX	AAFHSTW	FATWAHS	AAGINOS	AGNOSIA
				AAFIILR	FILARIA	AAGINPY	APAYING

AAGINRR	ARRAIGN	AAHILMS	SHIMAAL	AAIILMR	AIRMAIL	AAILPTT	TALIPAT
AAGINRS	NAGARIS	AAHILMT	THALAMI	AAIILPR	PAIRIAL	AAILPZZ	PALAZZI
	SANGRIA	AAHILNT	THALIAN	AAIILPT	TILAPIA	AAILQWW	QAWWALI
	SARANGI	AAHILSY	ALIYAHS	AAIILRZ	ALIZARI	AAILRRV	ARRIVAL
AAGINRT	GRANITA	AAHIMNO	MAHONIA	AAIINNZ	ANZIANI	AAILRST	LARIATS
AAGINRU	GUARANI	AAHIMNZ	HAZANIM	AAIINZZ	ZIZANIA		LATRIAS
AAGINST	AGAINST	AAHIMSS	AHIMSAS	AAIIRVV	VIVARIA	AAILRTV	TRAVAIL
	GITANAS	AAHINOP	APHONIA	AAIJLNP	JALAPIN	AAILRWY	RAILWAY
AAGINSU	IGUANAS	AAHINPR	PIRANHA	AAIJMNP	JAMPANI	AAILSSS	ASSAILS
AAGINSV	VAGINAS	AAHINST	SHAITAN	AAIJNRZ	JANIZAR	AAILSSV	SALIVAS
AAGINSY	GAINSAY		TAHINAS	AAIJNST	TINAJAS		SALVIAS
AAGINTY	ANTIGAY	AAHINTW	TANIWHA	AAIJPPY	JIPYAPA		VASSAIL
AAGIOTT	AGITATO	AAHIPRS	PARIAHS	AAIJRSW	JAWARIS	AAILSSW	WASSAIL
AAGIPRS	AIRGAPS		RAPHIAS	AAIKLLS	ALKALIS	AAILTTT	LATITAT
AAGIPRU	PIRAGUA	AAHIPRT	PITARAH	AAIKLMS	KALMIAS	AAIMMNO	AMMONIA
AAGIRRY	ARGYRIA	AAHIPTZ	ZAPTIAH		KAMILAS	AAIMNNO	OMNIANA
AAGISTT	SAGITTA	AAHIRSS	SHARIAS	AAIKLNS	KALIANS	AAIMNOS	ANOSMIA
AAGJNRS	GARJANS	AAHIRST	SHARIAT	AAIKMNN	MANAKIN	AAIMNOT	AMATION
AAGJRSU	JAGUARS	AAHIRSV	VIHARAS	AAIKMNR	RAMAKIN	AAIMNRS	MARINAS
AAGKOOZ	GAZOOKA	AAHJKNR	KHANJAR	AAIKMOR	ROMAIKA	AAIMNRT	TAMARIN
AAGKORT	KATORGA	AAHJNRS	HANJARS	AAIKMRS	KARAISM	AAIMNST	MANATIS
AAGLLNS	LALANGS	AAHJRRS	JARRAHS	AAIKNST	TANKIAS		STAMINA
AAGLLNT	GALLANT	AAHKKST	KATHAKS	AAIKORU	OUAKARI	AAIMNSV	VIMANAS
AAGLMMS	MALMAGS	AAHKLRS	LASHKAR	AAIKOSY	SOKAIYA	AAIMNTX	TAXIMAN
AAGLMNS	MANGALS	AAHKLST	KHALATS	AAIKPPR	PAPRIKA	AAIMRST	AMRITAS
AAGLNOR	GRANOLA	AAHKMSY	YASHMAK	AAIKRSS	ASKARIS		TAMARIS
AAGLNOS	ANALOGS	AAHKNST	KANTHAS	AAIKRST	KARAITS	AAIMRSU	SAMURAI
AAGLNOY	ANALOGY	AAHKRSS	RAKSHAS	AAIKRSU	UAKARIS	AAIMRTU	TIMARAU
AAGLNPS	LAPSANG	AAHLLLS	HALLALS	AAIKSTT	ASTATKI	AAIMSST	STASIMA
AAGLNRS	RAGLANS	AAHLLNS	HALLANS	AAIKTVV	AKVAVIT	AAIMSTT	TATAMIS
AAGLNRU	ANGULAR		NALLAHS	AAILLLP	PALLIAL	AAIMSTV	ATAVISM
AAGLRUU	ARUGULA	AAHLLOS	HALLOAS	AAILLMM	MAMILLA	AAIMSUV	MAUVAIS
	AUGURAL	AAHLLPS	PALLAHS	AAILLMN	MANILLA	AAINNRU	URANIAN
AAGLRVX	GRAVLAX	AAHLLSW	WALLAHS	AAILLMR	ARMILLA	AAINNRV	NAVARIN
AAGLSST	STALAGS	AAHLLWY	HALLWAY	AAILLMX	MAXILLA		NIRVANA
AAGMMNS	MAGSMAN	AAHLMMS	HAMMALS	AAILLNV	VANILLA	AAINOPS	PAISANO
AAGMMRR	GRAMMAR		MAHMALS	AAILLPP	PAPILLA	AAINORR	ORARIAN
AAGMMRS	GRAMMAS		MASHLAM	AAILLRX	AXILLAR	AAINORV	OVARIAN
AAGMMTU	GUMMATA	AAHLMRS	MARSHAL	AAILLSV	SALIVAL	AAINOSX	ANOXIAS
AAGMNNR	GRANNAM	AAHLMRU	HAMULAR	AAILLUV	ALLUVIA	AAINPPS	PAPAINS
AAGMNOS	SANGOMA	AAHLMST	MALTHAS	AAILLXY	AXIALLY	AAINPRS	PIRANAS
AAGMNPR	PANGRAM	AAHLNPX	PHALANX	AAILMMN	MAILMAN	AAINPST	PATINAS
AAGMNPY	PANGAMY	AAHLNRW	NARWHAL	AAILMMR	AMMIRAL		PINATAS
AAGMNRS	RAGMANS	AAHLPRS	PHRASAL	AAILMMS	MIASMAL		TAIPANS
AAGMNRT	TANGRAM	AAHLPST	ASPHALT	AAILMMX	MAXIMAL	AAINRST	ANTIARS
	TRANGAM		TAPLASH	AAILMNR	LAMINAR		ARTISAN
AAGMNSW	SWAGMAN	AAHLRSS	ASHLARS		RAILMAN		TSARINA
AAGMNSZ	ZAMANGS	AAHLRST	HARTALS	AAILMNS	ALMAINS	AAINRSU	ANURIAS
AAGMOPY	APOGAMY	AAHLRSW	SHALWAR		ANIMALS		SAURIAN
AAGMORS	MARGOSA	AAHMMMS	HAMMAMS		MANILAS	AAINRSV	SAVARIN
AAGMOSU	AGAMOUS	AAHMMNS	MASHMAN	AAILMNT	MATINAL	AAINRTV	VARIANT
AAGMRRY	GRAMARY	AAHMNNU	HANUMAN	AAILMNU	ALUMINA	AAINRTW	ANTIWAR
AAGMRSY	MARGAYS	AAHMNRS	HARMANS	AAILMNV	MAILVAN	AAINSTT	ATTAINS
AAGNNOS	GOANNAS	AAHMNSS	SHAMANS	AAILMPS	IMPALAS	AAINSTV	VANITAS
AAGNNSW	WANGANS	AAHMNTX	XANTHAM	AAILMRT	MARITAL	AAINTTT	ATTAINT
AAGNOPR	PARAGON	AAHMOPR	AMPHORA		MARTIAL	AAINTTU	TUTANIA
AAGNORS	ANGORAS	AAHMQSU	QUAMASH	AAILMSS	ALISMAS	AAIOPRS	APORIAS
AAGNORZ	ORGANZA	AAHMRSS	ASHRAMS		SALAMIS	AAIOPRT	ATROPIA
AAGNPRS	PARANGS	AAHMSST	ASTHMAS	AAILMSU	AUMAILS	AAIORSU	SAOUARI
AAGNRRS	GARRANS	AAHMSSU	MASHUAS	AAILNOT	AILANTO	AAIORTV	AVIATOR
AAGNRSS	SANGARS	AAHMSTZ	MATZAHS	AAILNOV	NOVALIA	AAIPPRS	APPAIRS
AAGNRTV	VAGRANT	AAHNNOS	HOSANNA		VALONIA	AAIPPRU	PUPARIA
AAGNSTU	TAGUANS	AAHNNST	TANNAHS	AAILNPS	SALPIAN	AAIPPTT	PITAPAT
AAGOPSS	SAPSAGO		THANNAS	AAILNPT	PLATINA	AAIPRST	PITARAS
AAGORSU	SAGUARO	AAHNNTX	XANTHAN	AAILNRU	ULNARIA	AAIPRSY	PIRAYAS
AAGOSTU	AGOUTAS	AAHNORT	ATHANOR	AAILNRY	LANIARY	AAIPRTT	PARTITA
AAGPPRS	GRAPPAS	AAHNORV	NAVARHO	AAILNSS	SALINAS	AAIPSZZ	PIAZZAS
AAGRRSY	GARRYAS	AAHNRTX	ANTHRAX	AAILNSY	INYALAS	AAIQSSU	QUASSIA
AAHHLSV	HALVAHS	AAHNRTY	RHATANY	AAILNTV	VALIANT	AAIQTUV	AQUAVIT
AAHHMSZ	HAMZAHS	AAHNSZZ	HAZZANS	AAILORS	ROSALIA	AAIRSST	ARISTAS
AAHHNNT	THANNAH	AAHPPRS	PARAPHS		SOLARIA		TARSIAS
AAHHNPT	NAPHTHA	AAHPRSY	YARPHAS	AAILORU	RAOULIA	AAIRSTT	STRIATA
AAHHNST	THANAHS	AAHPRTW	WARPATH	AAILORV	VARIOLA	AAIRSTY	RAIYATS
AAHIIMT	HIMATIA	AAHPTWY	PATHWAY	AAILOST	SOLATIA	AAIRSWY	AIRWAYS
AAHIKRT	KITHARA	AAHRSSS	HASSARS	AAILPPT	APPALTI	AAIRSZZ	RAZZIAS
AAHILLL	HALLALI	AAHRSST	SHASTRA	AAILPRS	PARIALS	AAITWXY	TAXIWAY
AAHILLN	HALLIAN	AAHRTTW	ATHWART	AAILPRT	PARTIAL	AAJJMRS	JAMJARS
AAHILMR	ALMIRAH	AAHSSSY	SASHAYS		PATRIAL	AAJKLWY	JAYWALK
		AAIIKKS	KAIKAIS	AAILPST	SPATIAL		

AAJKMNR	JARKMAN	AALMSTY	AMYTALS	AAMRSST	MATRASS	ABBDELS	DABBLES
AAJKNSS	SANJAKS	AALMTTU	MULATTA	AAMRSSU	ASARUMS		SLABBED
AAJMNPS	JAMPANS	AALNNRU	ANNULAR	AAMRSTU	SUMATRA	ABBDELW	WABBLED
AAJMNZZ	JAZZMAN	AALNNSU	ANNUALS		TRAUMAS	ABBDERR	DRABBER
AAJMORT	MAJORAT	AALNPRT	PLANTAR	AAMRTWY	TRAMWAY	ABBDERS	DABBERS
AAJMPSY	PYJAMAS	AALNPST	PLANTAS	AAMSSTU	SATSUMA	ABBDERT	DRABBET
			PLATANS	AANNOTT	ANNATTO	ABBDEST	STABBED
AAJNNOS	JOANNAS	AALNPUU	PUNALUA	AANNPSS	SANPANS		TEBBADS
AAJNOSW	AJOWANS	AALNQTU	QUANTAL	AANNSYZ	NYANZAS	ABBDESU	BEDAUBS
AAJNOSY	YOJANAS	AALNRSU	RANULAS	AANOQSY	YAQONAS	ABBDESW	SWABBED
AAJOPSU	SAPAJOU	AALNRTT	LATRANT	AANORST	TORANAS	ABBDGIN	DABBING
AAKKLPS	KALPAKS	AALNRTU	NATURAL	AANOSST	SONATAS	ABBDHIJ	DJIBBAH
AAKKLRU	KARAKUL	AALNSST	SANTALS	AANOSTT	ANATTOS	ABBDILR	LIBBARD
AAKKMOT	TOKAMAK	AALNSTT	SALTANT	AANPPSS	SAPPANS	ABBDINR	RIBBAND
AAKKMRS	MARKKAS		TALANTS	AANPRST	PARTANS	ABBDITY	DABBITY
AAKKOPS	KAKAPOS	AALNSTU	SULTANA		SPARTAN	ABBDLRU	LUBBARD
AAKKSUZ	ZAKUSKA	AALNSTY	ANALYST		TARPANS	ABBDMOR	BOMBARD
AAKLMPU	LAMPUKA	AALNTTU	TALAUNT		TRAPANS	ABBDMOU	BABUDOM
AAKLMRY	MALARKY	AALOPPT	APPALTO	AANPSST	PASSANT	ABBEESW	BAWBEES
AAKLMUY	YAMULKA	AALOPRS	PARASOL	AANQRTU	QUARTAN	ABBEFST	FABBEST
AAKLNOO	OOLAKAN	AALOPSY	PAYOLAS	AANRRSW	WARRANS	ABBEGIR	GABBIER
AAKLNOU	OULAKAN	AALOPVV	PAVLOVA	AANRRTW	WARRANT	ABBEGLR	GABBLER
AAKLOOP	PALOOKA	AALOPZZ	PALAZZO	AANRSTT	RATTANS		GRABBLE
AAKLOOT	TALOOKA	AALORRU	AURORAL		TANTRAS	ABBEGLS	GABBLES
AAKLRSU	KURSAAL	AALORSU	AROUSAL		TARTANS	ABBEGNO	BOGBEAN
	RUSALKA	AALORTX	LAXATOR	AANRUWY	RUNAWAY	ABBEGNU	BUGBANE
AAKLSSU	SAKSAUL	AALOSTT	SALTATO	AANSSTV	SAVANTS	ABBEGRR	GRABBER
AAKLSTU	TALUKAS	AALOSVW	AVOWALS	AANSSTZ	STANZAS	ABBEGRS	GABBERS
AAKLWWY	WALKWAY	AALOTTY	TALAYOT	AANSTTT	STATANT	ABBEGRU	BUGBEAR
AAKMMNR	MARKMAN	AALPPRU	PAPULAR	AANSTUV	AVAUNTS	ABBEHLS	SHABBLE
AAKMNSU	MANUKAS	AALPRRS	PARRALS	AANSWYY	ANYWAYS	ABBEIRS	BARBIES
AAKMOSU	MOUSAKA	AALPRSW	ASPRAWL	AAOORRW	WOORARA	ABBEIST	BABIEST
AAKMRSU	KUMARAS	AALPRSY	PARLAYS	AAOPSST	POTASSA		TABBIES
AAKMRUZ	MAZURKA	AALPSTU	SPATULA		SAPOTAS	ABBEISY	YABBIES
AAKMRWY	WAYMARK	AALQSWW	QAWWALS	AAORRSU	AURORAS	ABBEJLS	JABBLES
AAKNNTU	NUNATAK	AALRSST	TARSALS	AAORRSV	VARROAS	ABBEJRS	JABBERS
AAKNORS	ANORAKS	AALRSTU	AUSTRAL	AAORSTT	TOTARAS	ABBELMR	BRAMBLE
AAKNRST	KANTARS	AALRSTY	ASTYLAR	AAOSTTV	OTTAVAS	ABBELNS	SNABBLE
AAKNSST	ASKANTS		SATYRAL	AAOTTUY	TATOUAY	ABBELOR	BELABOR
AAKNSWZ	KWANZAS	AALSSSV	VASSALS	AAPPSWW	PAWPAWS	ABBELPR	PRABBLE
AAKNTWY	TWANKAY	AALSSTU	ASSAULT	AAPRSST	SATRAPS	ABBELRR	RABBLER
AAKOOPP	PAKAPOO	AALSSUX	SAXAULS	AAPRSTT	ATTRAPS	ABBELRS	BARBELS
AAKOPRS	PAKORAS	AALSTUV	VALUTAS	AAPRSTY	SATRAPY		RABBLES
AAKORST	OSTRAKA	AALSWYY	WAYLAYS	AAQRSSU	QUASARS		SLABBER
AAKPRWY	PARKWAY	AAMMMRY	MAMMARY	AARRSTT	TARTARS	ABBELRU	BARBULE
AAKRTUY	AUTARKY	AAMMNRT	MANTRAM	AARRSWY	WARRAYS	ABBELRW	WABBLER
AAKSSTT	ATTASKS	AAMMNST	AMTMANS	AARSSST	ASSARTS	ABBELSU	BAUBLES
AAKSTTT	ATTASKT	AAMMOTY	MYOMATA	AARSSTT	ASTARTS	ABBELSW	BAWBLES
AAKSTUY	YUKATAS	AAMMRRS	MARRAMS	AARSSTY	SATYRAS		WABBLES
AALLLNS	LALLANS	AAMMRST	RAMSTAM	AASSTTU	STATUAS	ABBELUY	BUYABLE
AALLLSS	SALLALS		TAMMARS	ABBBDEL	BABBLED	ABBEMUZ	BUMBAZE
AALLMMS	MALLAMS	AAMMSUZ	MAZUMAS		BLABBED	ABBENRS	NABBERS
AALLMPU	AMPULLA	AAMNNOY	ANONYMA	ABBBELR	BABBLER	ABBEORS	EARBOBS
AALLNPU	PLANULA	AAMNOOS	MANOAOS		BLABBER	ABBERRS	BARBERS
AALLNSY	NASALLY	AAMNORS	OARSMAN		BRABBLE	ABBERST	BARBETS
AALLORS	AROLLAS	AAMNORT	AMORANT	ABBBELS	BABBLES		RABBETS
AALLOSZ	AZOLLAS	AAMNOSZ	AMAZONS	ABBBITT	BABBITT		STABBER
AALLOTV	LAVOLTA	AAMNOTY	ANATOMY	ABBCDER	CRABBED	ABBERSW	SWABBER
AALLPPY	PAPALLY	AAMNPRT	MANTRAP	ABBCDES	SCABBED	ABBERSY	YABBERS
AALLRUY	AURALLY		RAMPANT	ABBCEHI	BABICHE	ABBESSU	SUBBASE
AALLRVY	VALLARY	AAMNPRY	PARANYM	ABBCEHU	BABUCHE	ABBFIRT	FRABBIT
AALLSTT	ATLATLS	AAMNPSS	PASSMAN	ABBCEIS	CABBIES	ABBGGIN	GABBING
	TALLATS		SAMPANS	ABBCELR	CLABBER	ABBGHSU	GUBBAHS
AALLUVV	VALVULA	AAMNPST	TAPSMAN	ABBCELS	SCABBLE	ABBGIJN	JABBING
AALMMMS	MAMMALS	AAMNPTY	TYMPANA	ABBCERR	CRABBER	ABBGINN	NABBING
AALMMNO	AMMONAL	AAMNRST	ARTSMAN	ABBCIKT	BACKBIT	ABBGINR	BARBING
AALMMNT	MALTMAN		MANTRAS	ABBCIRS	BICARBS	ABBGINT	TABBING
AALMNOS	SALAMON	AAMNSTU	MANTUAS	ABBCOST	BOBCATS	ABBGINU	BUBINGA
AALMNOY	ANOMALY		TAMANUS	ABBCRYY	CRYBABY	ABBGINY	BABYING
AALMNPS	NAPALMS	AAMOORS	AMOROSA	ABBDDEL	DABBLED	ABBGMSU	BUMBAGS
AALMNSU	MANUALS	AAMOPRS	PARAMOS	ABBDDER	DRABBED	ABBGOOU	BUGABOO
AALMORT	ALAMORT	AAMORRZ	ZAMARRO	ABBDEFR	FRABBED	ABBGORS	GABBROS
AALMORY	MAYORAL	AAMORSV	SAMOVAR	ABBDEGL	GABBLED	ABBHIJS	JIBBAHS
AALMOST	AMATOLS	AAMORTY	AMATORY	ABBDEGR	GRABBED	ABBHISY	BABYISH
AALMPRY	PALMARY	AAMOSSS	SAMOSAS	ABBDEIT	TABBIED	ABBHJSU	JUBBAHS
	PALMYRA	AAMOSTT	STOMATA	ABBDEJL	JABBLED	ABBHOOS	BABOOSH
AALMPSS	PLASMAS	AAMOTTU	AUTOMAT	ABBDELR	DABBLER		HABOOBS
AALMRRU	RAMULAR	AAMPRRT	RAMPART		DRABBLE	ABBHRRU	RHUBARB
AALMRSU	ALARUMS	AAMPSSY	AMPASSY		RABBLED	ABBHTTU	BATHTUB
AALMSSU	MASULAS						

ABBIIMN	BAMBINI	ABCEESS	BECASSE	ABCGHIN	BACHING	ABDDEIS	BADDIES
ABBILOR	BILOBAR	ABCEESU	BECAUSE	ABCGHKO	HOGBACK	ABDDELR	BLADDER
ABBILOT	BOBTAIL	ABCEGIR	RIBCAGE	ABCGIKN	BACKING	ABDDELU	BLAUDED
ABBILSU	BUBALIS	ABCEGMO	CAMBOGE	ABCGILN	CABLING	ABDDENR	BRANDED
ABBIMNO	BAMBINO	ABCEGOR	BROCAGE	ABCGINR	BRACING	ABDDEOR	ABORDED
ABBIMSU	BABUISM	ABCEGOS	BOCAGES	ABCGKLO	BACKLOG		BOARDED
ABBINOR	RABBONI		BOSCAGE	ABCGMSU	SCUMBAG	ABDDERW	BEDWARD
ABBINRS	RABBINS	ABCEGSU	CUBAGES	ABCHHII	HIBACHI	ABDDHIS	BADDISH
ABBIRST	RABBITS	ABCEHKO	BACKHOE	ABCHIMT	BATHMIC	ABDDHSU	BUDDHAS
ABBIRTY	RABBITY	ABCEHLU	BAUCHLE	ABCHIOT	COHABIT	ABDDINS	DISBAND
ABBKLOU	BLAUBOK	ABCEHMR	BECHARM	ABCHKOU	CHABOUK	ABDDLLO	ODDBALL
ABBLLRU	BULLBAR		BRECHAM	ABCHKTU	HACKBUT	ABDDMOR	DAMBROD
ABBLLTU	BULLBAT		CHAMBER	ABCHKUW	HAWBUCK	ABDEEFL	FEELBAD
ABBLMRY	BRAMBLY		CHAMBRE	ABCHNOR	BROCHAN	ABDEEGL	BEAGLED
ABBMOOR	BOMBORA	ABCEHOS	BASOCHE	ABCHNRU	BRAUNCH	ABDEEGR	REBADGE
ABBMOOS	BAMBOOS	ABCEHRS	BRACHES	ABCHNRY	BRANCHY	ABDEEHO	OBEAHED
ABBMOST	BOMBAST	ABCEHRT	BRACHET	ABCIILL	BACILLI	ABDEEHS	BEHEADS
ABBNOOS	BABOONS	ABCEHST	BATCHES	ABCIILN	ALBINIC	ABDEEHT	BEATHED
ABBORSS	ABSORBS	ABCEIKT	TIEBACK	ABCIILT	ALBITIC	ABDEEHV	BEHAVED
ABBQSUY	SQUABBY	ABCEILL	ICEBALL	ABCIIMN	MINICAB	ABDEEIR	BEADIER
ABCCCHI	BACCHIC	ABCEILM	ALEMBIC	ABCIIMS	IAMBICS		BEARDIE
ABCCEIR	ACERBIC		CEMBALI	ABCIIOR	CIBORIA	ABDEEJS	BEJADES
	BRECCIA	ABCEILR	CALIBER	ABCIIOT	ABIOTIC	ABDEELM	BELDAME
ABCCEIS	BACCIES		CALIBRE	ABCIJNO	JACOBIN		BEMEDAL
	SEBACIC	ABCEILT	CITABLE	ABCILRS	SCRIBAL		EMBALED
ABCCEOS	BACCOES	ABCEIMO	AMOEBIC	ABCILTU	CUBITAL	ABDEELN	ENABLED
ABCCHII	BACCHII	ABCEINR	CARBINE	ABCIMMS	CAMBISM	ABDEELR	BEDERAL
ABCCHTY	BYCATCH	ABCEINT	CABINET	ABCIMMU	CAMBIUM		BLEARED
ABCCILU	CUBICAL	ABCEIOR	AEROBIC	ABCIMST	CAMBIST	ABDEELS	BEADLES
ABCCIMR	CAMBRIC	ABCEIOT	ICEBOAT	ABCINOT	BOTANIC	ABDEELT	BELATED
ABCCINU	BUCCINA	ABCEIRS	ASCRIBE	ABCIORR	BARRICO		BLEATED
ABCCIOR	BORACIC		CABRIES	ABCIORU	CARIBOU	ABDEELY	BELAYED
	BRACCIO		CARBIES	ABCIOUV	BIVOUAC		DYEABLE
ABCCISU	CUBICAS		CARIBES	ABCIRST	CABRITS	ABDEEMN	BEADMEN
ABCCKOW	BAWCOCK	ABCEISS	ABSCISE	ABCIRTY	BARYTIC		BEDEMAN
ABCCKTU	CUTBACK		SCABIES	ABCISSS	ABSCISS		BENAMED
ABCCOOR	BAROCCO	ABCEITT	TABETIC	ABCJOSU	JACOBUS	ABDEEMR	AMBERED
ABCCOOT	TOBACCO	ABCEJST	ABJECTS	ABCKLLY	BLACKLY		BREAMED
ABCCSUU	SUCCUBA	ABCEKLN	BLACKEN	ABCKLOT	BACKLOT		EMBREAD
ABCDDEU	ABDUCED	ABCEKLR	BLACKER	ABCKMRU	BUCKRAM	ABDEEMS	EMBASED
ABCDEEH	BEACHED	ABCEKNR	BRACKEN	ABCKMUZ	ZAMBUCK	ABDEEMY	EMBAYED
ABCDEEL	BELACED	ABCEKRS	BACKERS	ABCKNNO	BANNOCK	ABDEEMZ	BEMAZED
	DEBACLE		REBACKS	ABCKNRU	RUNBACK	ABDEERS	DEBASER
ABCDEHT	BATCHED	ABCEKRT	BRACKET	ABCKORS	BAROCKS		SABERED
ABCDEHU	DEBAUCH	ABCEKST	BACKETS	ABCKOSW	SOWBACK	ABDEERT	BERATED
ABCDEIK	DIEBACK		BACKSET	ABCKOTU	OUTBACK		BETREAD
ABCDEIN	CABINED		SETBACK	ABCKRSU	BUCKRAS		DEBATER
ABCDEIP	PEDICAB	ABCEKSY	BACKSEY	ABCKSTU	SACKBUT		REBATED
ABCDEIR	CARBIDE	ABCEKTW	WETBACK		SUBTACK	ABDEERW	BEWARED
ABCDEKL	BLACKED	ABCELLS	BECALLS	ABCKSUW	BUCKSAW	ABDEERY	BERAYED
ABCDEKR	REDBACK	ABCELLU	BULLACE		SAWBUCK	ABDEESS	DEBASES
ABCDEOR	BROCADE	ABCELMO	CEMBALO	ABCLMNU	CLUBMAN		SEABEDS
ABCDERS	DECARBS	ABCELMR	CAMBREL	ABCLMOY	CYMBALO	ABDEEST	BESTEAD
ABCDERU	CUDBEAR		CLAMBER	ABCLMSY	CYMBALS		DEBATES
ABCDESU	ABDUCES	ABCELMS	BECALMS	ABCLMSU	BACULUM	ABDEESZ	BEDAZES
ABCDHIO	ICHABOD		SCAMBLE	ABCLNOS	BLANCOS	ABDEETT	ABETTED
ABCDHOR	CHOBDAR	ABCELOP	PLACEBO	ABCLNOY	BALCONY	ABDEFFL	BAFFLED
ABCDHOS	BODACHS	ABCELOV	VOCABLE	ABCLOST	COBALTS	ABDEFLT	FLATBED
ABCDIIS	DIBASIC	ABCELPU	BLUECAP	ABCMORS	COMARBS	ABDEFLU	LEAFBUD
ABCDILR	BALDRIC	ABCELPY	BYPLACE	ABCMOST	COMBATS	ABDEFOR	FORBADE
ABCDINS	ABSCIND	ABCELRU	CURABLE		TOMBACS	ABDEFRW	BEDWARF
ABCDIRS	SCABRID	ABCELST	CABLETS	ABCMRSS	SCRAMBS	ABDEFST	BEDFAST
ABCDIRT	CATBIRD	ABCELSU	BASCULE	ABCNORS	CARBONS	ABDEGGL	BLAGGED
ABCDIRU	BAUDRIC	ABCEMRS	CAMBERS		CORBANS	ABDEGGR	BRAGGED
ABCDISU	SUBACID		CEMBRAS	ABCORRW	CROWBAR	ABDEGHR	BEGHARD
ABCDNOS	ABSCOND	ABCEMSX	EXCAMBS	ABCORSX	BOXCARS	ABDEGIN	BEADING
ABCDOOR	CORDOBA	ABCENOR	BACONER	ABCORSY	CARBOYS	ABDEGIR	ABRIDGE
ABCDORR	BROCARD	ABCENOS	BEACONS	ABCOSSU	BASUCOS		BRIGADE
ABCDSTU	ABDUCTS	ABCENOW	COWBANE	ABCSSTU	SUBACTS	ABDEGLM	GAMBLED
ABCEEHS	BEACHES	ABCENRU	UNBRACE	ABDDDEL	BLADDED	ABDEGLN	BANGLED
ABCEEHU	EBAUCHE	ABCEOOS	CABOOSE	ABDDEEJ	BEJADED	ABDEGLR	BELGARD
ABCEELS	BELACES	ABCEORU	CORBEAU	ABDDEER	BEARDED		GARBLED
ABCEEMR	EMBRACE	ABCERRS	BRACERS		BREADED	ABDEGNO	BONDAGE
ABCEEMS	EMBACES	ABCESSS	ABSCESS	ABDDEES	DEBASED		DOGBANE
ABCEENS	ABSENCE	ABCFIKN	FINBACK	ABDDEET	DEBATED	ABDEGOS	BODEGAS
ABCEERR	ACERBER	ABCFILO	BIFOCAL	ABDDEEZ	BEDAZED	ABDEGRS	BADGERS
	CEREBRA	ABCFIRS	FABRICS	ABDDEIN	ABIDDEN	ABDEHIT	HABITED
	REBRACE	ABCFLOO	COBLOAF		BANDIED	ABDEHLM	HAMBLED
ABCEERU	BERCEAU	ABCFNOS	CONFABS	ABDDEIR	BRAIDED	ABDEHLR	HALBERD

ABDEHOW	BOWHEAD	ABDENTU	UNBATED	ABDMNNO	BONDMAN	ABEELRT	BLEATER
ABDEHRS	BERDASH	ABDEOOT	TABOOED	ABDMRUY	MARYBUD		RETABLE
	BRASHED	ABDEORR	BOARDER	ABDNOOR	ONBOARD	ABEELST	BELATES
ABDEHRT	BREADTH		BROADER	ABDNOPR	PROBAND	ABEELSU	SUEABLE
ABDEHSU	SUBHEAD	ABDEORT	ABORTED	ABDNOSU	ABOUNDS	ABEELSV	BESLAVE
ABDEILP	BIPEDAL		TABORED		BAUSOND	ABEEMNS	BASEMEN
	PIEBALD	ABDEOST	BOASTED	ABDNOSX	SANDBOX		BEMEANS
ABDEILR	BALDIER	ABDEOTU	BOUTADE	ABDNOSY	SANDBOY		BENAMES
	BRAILED	ABDEQSU	BASQUED	ABDNOYY	ANYBODY	ABEEMNT	BEMEANT
	RAILBED	ABDERSS	SERDABS	ABDNRTU	TURBAND	ABEEMRS	BEAMERS
	RIDABLE	ABDERST	DABSTER	ABDOORW	BARWOOD		BESMEAR
ABDEILS	BALDIES		TABERDS	ABDORRS	BORDARS	ABEEMRV	EMBRAVE
	DIABLES	ABDERSU	DAUBERS	ABDORSS	ADSORBS	ABEEMSS	EMBASES
	DISABLE		SUBEDAR	ABDORSY	BYROADS	ABEEMST	EMBASTE
ABDEILT	LIBATED	ABDERSV	ADVERBS	ABDRRSU	DURBARS	ABEENRV	VERBENA
ABDEILU	AUDIBLE	ABDERTY	DRYBEAT	ABDRSTU	BUSTARD	ABEENRY	BEANERY
ABDEIMR	EMBRAID	ABDERUY	DAUBERY	ABDRUZZ	BUZZARD	ABEEORS	AEROBES
ABDEIMS	IMBASED	ABDETTU	ABUTTED	ABEEEGR	BEERAGE	ABEEORT	ABORTEE
ABDEINR	BANDIER	ABDGGIN	BADGING	ABEEELS	SEEABLE	ABEEPST	BESPATE
	BRAINED	ABDGGOR	BOGGARD	ABEEERV	BEREAVE	ABEERRS	BEARERS
ABDEINS	BANDIES	ABDGIIN	ABIDING	ABEEFFL	EFFABLE		BREARES
ABDEINW	BEDAWIN	ABDGILN	BALDING	ABEEFLO	BEEFALO	ABEERRT	REBATER
ABDEIRR	BARDIER	ABDGINN	BANDING	ABEEFTU	BEAUFET		TABRERE
	BRAIDER	ABDGINO	ABODING	ABEEGHR	HERBAGE		TEREBRA
	BRIARED	ABDGINR	BARDING	ABEEGHS	BEEGAHS	ABEERST	BEATERS
	RABIDER		BRIGAND		BHAGEES		BERATES
ABDEIRS	BRAISED	ABDGINT	DINGBAT	ABEEGLL	GABELLE		REBATES
	DARBIES	ABDGINU	DAUBING	ABEEGLR	BEAGLER	ABEERSV	BEAVERS
	SEABIRD	ABDGINW	WINDBAG	ABEEGLS	BEAGLES	ABEERSW	BEWARES
	SIDEBAR	ABDGLNO	BOGLAND	ABEEGRR	GERBERA	ABEERSZ	ZEREBAS
ABDEIRT	TRIBADE	ABDGLUY	LADYBUG	ABEEGRS	ABREGES	ABEERTT	ABETTER
ABDEIRU	DAUBIER	ABDGNOS	BANDOGS		BAREGES	ABEERVY	BEAVERY
ABDEIRW	BAWDIER	ABDGORS	BODRAGS		BARGEES	ABEESST	SEBATES
ABDEISS	BIASSED	ABDHHOS	DOBHASH	ABEEGRU	AUBERGE	ABEESWX	BEESWAX
ABDEIST	BASTIDE	ABDHIIT	ADHIBIT	ABEEGRW	BREWAGE	ABEFFIS	BAFFIES
ABDEISW	BAWDIES	ABDHILS	BALDISH	ABEEHJS	BHAJEES	ABEFFLR	BAFFLER
ABDEJRU	ABJURED	ABDHMOR	RHABDOM	ABEEHMS	BESHAME	ABEFFLS	BAFFLES
ABDEKLN	BLANKED	ABDHMSU	BUDMASH	ABEEHMT	EMBATHE	ABEFFOT	OFFBEAT
ABDEKLU	BAULKED	ABDHMTU	MUDBATH	ABEEHNN	HENBANE	ABEFGIL	FILABEG
ABDEKNR	BRANKED	ABDHNOR	BODHRAN	ABEEHNS	BANSHEE	ABEFGST	GABFEST
ABDEKNU	UNBAKED	ABDHNSU	HUSBAND		BEENAHS	ABEFILN	FINABLE
ABDEKRS	DEBARKS	ABDHOSY	HOBDAYS	ABEEHNT	BENEATH	ABEFILR	FRIABLE
ABDELMR	MARBLED	ABDHRSU	BURDASH	ABEEHRT	BREATHE	ABEFILS	FAIBLES
	RAMBLED		RHABDUS	ABEEHSV	BEHAVES	ABEFILU	FIBULAE
ABDELMS	BEDLAMS	ABDIKNW	BAWDKIN	ABEEIKR	BEAKIER	ABEFILX	FIXABLE
	BELDAMS	ABDIKRS	DISBARK	ABEEILS	BAILEES	ABEFINU	BEAUFIN
ABDELMW	WAMBLED	ABDILMO	BIMODAL	ABEEIMR	BEAMIER	ABEFITY	BEATIFY
ABDELMY	EMBAYLD	ABDILOO	DIABOLO	ABEEINS	BEANIES	ABEFLLS	BEFALLS
ABDELNR	BLANDER	ABDILOR	LABROID	ABEEINT	BETAINE	ABEFLLU	BALEFUL
ABDELOR	LABORED	ABDILOT	TABLOID	ABEEIRT	EBRIATE	ABEFLLY	FLYABLE
ABDELOS	ALBEDOS	ABDILRS	BRIDALS	ABEEIST	BEASTIE	ABEFLNU	BANEFUL
ABDELOT	BLOATED		LABRIDS	ABEEJMS	JAMBEES	ABEFLNY	FLYBANE
ABDELOW	DOWABLE		RIBALDS	ABEEJRS	BAJREES	ABEFLRS	FABLERS
ABDELPU	DUPABLE	ABDILRW	AWLBIRD	ABEEKLR	BLEAKER	ABEFMOS	BEFOAMS
ABDELPY	PYEBALD	ABDILRY	RABIDLY	ABEEKLS	KABELES	ABEFORR	FORBEAR
ABDELRR	DRABLER	ABDILUY	AUDIBLY	ABEEKNT	BETAKEN	ABEFPRS	PREFABS
ABDELRS	BEDRALS	ABDILWY	BAWDILY	ABEEKNV	BEKNAVE	ABEGGIR	BAGGIER
ABDELRU	DURABLE	ABDIMNR	BIRDMAN	ABEEKOP	PEEKABO	ABEGGIS	BAGGIES
ABDELRW	BRAWLED	ABDIMOR	AMBROID	ABEEKPS	BESPAKE	ABEGGLR	BLAGGER
	WARBLED	ABDINOR	INBOARD		BESPEAK	ABEGGMO	GAMBOGE
ABDELST	BALDEST	ABDINRS	RIBANDS	ABEEKRR	BREAKER	ABEGGNU	BUGGANE
	BLASTED	ABDINRT	ANTBIRD	ABEEKRS	BEAKERS	ABEGGRS	BEGGARS
	STABLED	ABDINST	BANDITS	ABEEKST	BETAKES	ABEGGRU	BURGAGE
ABDELSU	BELAUDS	ABDIOSU	BADIOUS	ABEELLY	EYEBALL	ABEGGRY	BEGGARY
ABDELTT	BATTLED	ABDIPRU	UPBRAID	ABEELMM	EMBLEMA	ABEGHNS	SHEBANG
	BLATTED	ABDIRRS	BRAIRDS	ABEELMS	EMBALES	ABEGIMN	BEAMING
ABDEMMO	MAMBOED	ABDIRSU	RIBAUDS	ABEELMT	BEAMLET	ABEGIMR	GAMBIER
ABDEMNO	ABDOMEN		SUBARID	ABEELMZ	EMBLAZE	ABEGIMT	MEGABIT
ABDEMRU	RUMBAED	ABDIRTY	TRIBADY	ABEELNP	PLEBEAN	ABEGINN	BEANING
ABDENOR	BANDORE	ABDKNOO	BANDOOK	ABEELNR	ENABLER	ABEGINO	BEGONIA
	BROADEN	ABDLLNY	BLANDLY	ABEELNS	BALEENS	ABEGINR	BEARING
ABDENOT	BATONED	ABDLLOR	BOLLARD		ENABLES	ABEGINT	BEATING
ABDENOY	NAEBODY	ABDLNOR	BANDROL	ABEELNT	TENABLE	ABEGINY	ABYEING
ABDENPS	BEDPANS	ABDLORY	BROADLY	ABEELNU	NEBULAE	ABEGIPP	BAGPIPE
ABDENRR	BRANDER	ABDLRUY	DURABLY	ABEELOR	EARLOBE	ABEGKOR	BROKAGE
ABDENRU	UNBARED		RYBAULD	ABEELPR	BEPEARL	ABEGKOS	BOSKAGE
ABDENRW	BRAWNED	ABDLRYY	BYRLADY	ABEELQU	EQUABLE	ABEGLMR	GAMBLER
ABDENSS	BADNESS	ABDLSUU	SUBDUAL	ABEELRR	BLEARER		GAMBREL
ABDENSU	SUBDEAN				ERRABLE	ABEGLMS	GAMBLES

ABEGLNR	BRANGLE	ABEILNP	BIPLANE	ABEKNRS	BANKERS	ABELSTT	BATLETS
ABEGLNS	BANGLES	ABEILNS	LESBIAN		BARKENS		BATTELS
ABEGLOR	ALBERGO	ABEILPT	PATIBLE	ABEKNST	BANKETS		BATTLES
ABEGLOT	GLOBATE	ABEILRS	BAILERS	ABEKNSU	SUNBAKE		BLATEST
ABEGLRR	GARBLER	ABEILRT	LIBRATE	ABEKOOR	ABROOKE		TABLETS
ABEGLRS	GARBLES		TABLIER	ABEKPRU	UPBREAK	ABELSTU	SUBLATE
ABEGLST	GABLETS		TRIABLE	ABEKRRS	BARKERS	ABELSTY	BAETYLS
ABEGLSU	BELUGAS	ABEILSS	ABSEILS	ABEKSST	BASKETS		BEASTLY
	BLAGUES		ISABELS	ABELLMN	BELLMAN	ABELSWY	BAWLEYS
ABEGMOR	EMBARGO		LABISES	ABELLMS	EMBALLS	ABELTWY	BELTWAY
ABEGMRU	UMBRAGE	ABEILST	ABLEIST	ABELLNT	NETBALL	ABEMMRS	BAMMERS
ABEGMST	GAMBETS		ALBITES	ABELLOS	LOSABLE	ABEMNOS	AMBONES
ABEGNNT	BANTENG		ASTILBE	ABELLOV	LOVABLE		BEMOANS
ABEGNOS	NOSEBAG		BESTIAL		VOLABLE	ABEMNOT	BOATMEN
ABEGNRS	BANGERS		LIBATES	ABELLRU	RUBELLA	ABEMNRY	BYREMAN
	GRABENS		STABILE		RULABLE		MYRBANE
ABEGNSW	BEGNAWS	ABEILSW	BEWAILS	ABELLST	BALLETS	ABEMNST	BATSMEN
ABEGORR	BEGORRA	ABEILSY	BAILEYS	ABELLTU	BULLATE	ABEMNSU	SUNBEAM
ABEGORS	BORAGES	ABEILSZ	SIZABLE	ABELMMR	MEMBRAL	ABEMNSY	BYNAMES
ABEGORX	GEARBOX	ABEILVV	BIVALVE	ABELMMS	EMBALMS	ABEMORT	BROMATE
ABEGOSZ	GAZEBOS	ABEIMNR	MIRBANE	ABELMNT	BELTMAN	ABEMRST	TAMBERS
ABEGOTT	BOTTEGA	ABEIMNT	AMBIENT		LAMBENT	ABEMSSY	EMBASSY
ABEGOUY	BUOYAGE	ABEIMRR	BARMIER	ABELMNU	ALBUMEN	ABENNOR	BARONNE
ABEGRRU	GARBURE	ABEIMRS	AMBRIES	ABELMOV	MOVABLE	ABENNRS	BANNERS
ABEGRST	BARGEST	ABEIMSS	IMBASES	ABELMRR	MARBLER	ABENORS	BORANES
ABEGSTU	TUBAGES	ABEINOT	NIOBATE		RAMBLER	ABENORT	BARONET
ABEHILR	HIRABLE	ABEINPT	BEPAINT	ABELMRS	AMBLERS		REBOANT
ABEHIMS	BEAMISH	ABEINRT	ATEBRIN		LAMBERS	ABENORW	RAWBONE
ABEHIMT	IMBATHE	ABEINRZ	ZEBRINA		MARBLES	ABENOTY	BAYONET
ABEHIRS	BEARISH	ABEINST	BASINET		RAMBLES	ABENQTU	BANQUET
ABEHISU	BEAUISH		BESAINT	ABELMRT	LAMBERT	ABENRRU	URBANER
ABEHITU	HABITUE		BESTAIN	ABELMSU	BEMAULS	ABENRST	BANTERS
ABEHITZ	ZABTIEH	ABEINTT	TABINET	ABELMSW	WAMBLES	ABENRSU	UNBARES
ABEHKLS	KEBLAHS	ABEIORS	ISOBARE	ABELMTU	MUTABLE		UNBEARS
ABEHKRU	HAUBERK	ABEIOSS	ABIOSES	ABELNOT	NOTABLE	ABENRSY	BARNEYS
ABEHLMS	HAMBLES		ISOBASE	ABELNOY	BALONEY	ABENRSZ	BRAZENS
	SHAMBLE	ABEIOST	BOATIES	ABELNRS	BRANLES	ABENRUX	EXURBAN
ABEHLNU	UNHABLE	ABEIOTV	OBVIATE		BRANSLE	ABENSST	ABSENTS
ABEHLRS	HERBALS	ABEIPST	BAPTISE	ABELNRT	BRANTLE		BASNETS
ABEHLRT	BLATHER	ABEIPTZ	BAPTIZE	ABELNRU	NEBULAR	ABENSTT	BATTENS
	HALBERT	ABEIRRR	BARRIER	ABELNRY	BLARNEY	ABENSTU	BUTANES
ABEHLSS	BLASHES	ABEIRRS	BRASIER	ABELNSU	NEBULAS		SUNBEAT
ABEHNOS	HEBONAS	ABEIRRT	ARBITER	ABELNSZ	BENZALS	ABENSTZ	BEZANTS
ABEHRRS	BRASHER		RAREBIT	ABELNTU	TUNABLE	ABEOOTV	OBOVATE
	HERBARS	ABEIRRW	WARBIER	ABELOPR	ROPABLE	ABEOPRS	SAPROBE
ABEHRRY	HERBARY	ABEIRRZ	BIZARRE	ABELOPT	POTABLE	ABEOPRT	PROBATE
ABEHRSS	BASHERS		BRAZIER	ABELORS	LABROSE	ABEOQRU	BAROQUE
	BRASHES	ABEIRSS	BASSIER	ABELORT	BLOATER	ABEORRS	ARBORES
ABEHRST	BATHERS		BRAISES	ABELORU	RUBEOLA		BRASERO
	BERTHAS		BRASSIE	ABELORW	ROWABLE	ABEORRT	ARBORET
	BREATHS	ABEIRST	BAITERS	ABELOSS	BOLASES		TABORER
ABEHRTY	BREATHY		BARITES	ABELOST	BOATELS	ABEORST	BOASTER
ABEIILL	BAILLIE	ABEIRSX	BRAXIES		OBLATES		BOATERS
ABEIILS	BAILIES	ABEIRSZ	BRAIZES	ABELOSV	ABSOLVE		BORATES
ABEIINT	BAINITE		ZERIBAS	ABELOTW	TOWABLE		SORBATE
ABEIJMR	JAMBIER	ABEIRTT	BATTIER	ABELPRU	PUBERAL	ABEORSU	AEROBUS
ABEIJNS	BASENJI		BIRETTA	ABELQUY	EQUABLY	ABEORSV	BRAVOES
ABEIKLL	LIKABLE	ABEIRTV	VIBRATE	ABELRRS	BARRELS	ABEORSX	BORAXES
ABEIKLR	BALKIER	ABEIRUX	EXURBIA	ABELRRW	BRAWLER	ABEORSY	ROSEBAY
ABEIKLS	SKIABLE	ABEISSS	BIASSES		WARBLER	ABEORSZ	BEZOARS
ABEIKNR	INBREAK	ABEISTT	BATISTE	ABELRSS	BRALESS	ABEORTT	ABETTOR
ABEIKNT	BEATNIK	ABEISUV	ABUSIVE	ABELRST	ALBERTS		BATTERO
ABEIKRR	BARKIER	ABEITUX	BAUXITE		BATLERS		TABORET
	BRAKIER	ABEJMNO	JAMBONE		BLASTER	ABEOSTV	BOVATES
ABEIKWY	BIKEWAY	ABEJMNS	ENJAMBS		LABRETS	ABEPRSU	UPBEARS
ABEILLO	LOBELIA	ABEJMRS	JAMBERS		STABLER	ABEQRSU	BARQUES
ABEILLP	PLIABLE	ABEJMUX	JAMBEUX	ABELRSV	VERBALS	ABEQSSU	BASQUES
ABEILLR	LIBERAL	ABEJNOS	BANJOES	ABELRSW	BAWLERS	ABERRST	BARRETS
ABEILLV	LIVABLE	ABEJNOW	JAWBONE		WARBLES		BARTERS
ABEILMR	BALMIER	ABEJNST	BEJANTS	ABELRSY	BARLEYS	ABERRSU	SABREUR
	MIRABLE	ABEJORS	JERBOAS	ABELRSZ	BLAZERS	ABERRSY	BRAYERS
	REMBLAI	ABEJRRU	ABJURER	ABELRTT	BATTLER	ABERRVY	BRAVERY
ABEILMS	ABLEISM	ABEJRSU	ABJURES		BLATTER	ABERSSS	BRASSES
	EMBAILS	ABEKLLY	BLEAKLY		BRATTLE	ABERSST	BASTERS
	LAMBIES	ABEKLNR	BLANKER	ABELRTW	BLEWART		BESTARS
ABEILMT	LIMBATE	ABEKLNT	BLANKET	ABELRUZ	ZEBRULA		BRASSET
	TIMBALE	ABEKLRS	BALKERS	ABELRVY	BRAVELY		BREASTS
ABEILMX	MIXABLE	ABEKMNS	EMBANKS	ABELSST	BASTLES	ABERSSU	ABUSERS
ABEILMY	BEAMILY	ABEKMRS	EMBARKS		STABLES		SURBASE

ABERSSZ	ZEBRASS		ABGIMST	GAMBIST		ABIILMU	BULIMIA			SJAMBOK
ABERSTT	BATTERS			GAMBITS		ABIILNQ	INQILAB		ABJLMOO	JAMBOOL
	TABRETS		ABGINNN	BANNING		ABIILNS	AIBLINS		ABJLMSU	JAMBULS
ABERSTU	ARBUTES		ABGINNR	BARNING			BILIANS			JUMBALS
	SURBATE		ABGINNT	BANTING		ABIILRY	BILIARY		ABKLLNY	BLANKLY
ABERSTV	BRAVEST		ABGINOS	BAGNIOS		ABIILST	STIBIAL		ABKLRUW	BULWARK
ABERSTW	BRAWEST			GABIONS		ABIILTY	ABILITY		ABKLSSY	SKYLABS
	WABSTER		ABGINOT	BOATING		ABIIMNR	MINIBAR		ABKMNOO	BOOKMAN
ABERSTX	BAXTERS		ABGINRR	BARRING		ABIIMST	IAMBIST		ABKMOST	TOMBAKS
ABERSTY	BARYTES		ABGINRS	SABRING		ABIINNS	BAININS		ABKMSUZ	ZAMBUKS
	BETRAYS		ABGINRV	BRAVING		ABIINOR	ROBINIA		ABKNRSU	UNBARKS
ABERSUU	BUREAUS		ABGINRY	BRAYING		ABIINRY	BIRYANI		ABKNRUU	BUNRAKU
ABERSWY	BEWRAYS		ABGINRZ	BRAZING		ABIIOSS	ABIOSIS		ABKOORS	BOORKAS
ABERTTU	ABUTTER		ABGINSS	BASSING		ABIJLNR	BRINJAL		ABLLLUY	LULLABY
ABERTTY	BATTERY		ABGINST	BASTING		ABIJNOT	ABJOINT		ABLLNOO	BALLOON
ABERUUX	BUREAUX		ABGINSU	ABUSING		ABIJRSU	JABIRUS		ABLLNOS	BALLONS
ABESSST	BASSEST		ABGINTT	BATTING		ABIKKSU	KABUKIS		ABLLOPR	PROBALL
	BASSETS		ABGINTU	TABUING		ABIKLMN	LAMBKIN		ABLLORU	LOBULAR
ABESSSY	ABYSSES		ABGINTY	BAYTING		ABIKLOR	KILOBAR		ABLLOST	BALLOTS
ABESTTU	BATTUES		ABGIOPT	PIGBOAT		ABIKMNR	BARMKIN		ABLLOSW	BALLOWS
ABFFGIN	BAFFING		ABGIOSU	BAGUIOS		ABIKMRS	IMBARKS		ABLLOTY	TALLBOY
ABFFIIL	BAILIFF		ABGKNOS	KOBANGS		ABIKOUZ	BAZOUKI		ABLLPSU	BALLUPS
ABFFLOU	BUFFALO		ABGKOOS	BOGOAKS		ABIKRST	BRITSKA		ABLLRUY	BULLARY
ABFGILN	FABLING		ABGKORW	WORKBAG		ABIKRTZ	BRITZKA		ABLMMOU	BUMMALO
ABFGINR	BARFING		ABGLMNU	LUMBANG		ABILLMN	BILLMAN		ABLMNOU	UMBONAL
ABFGLSU	BAGFULS		ABGLMOS	GAMBOLS		ABILLMU	BALLIUM		ABLMOOT	TOMBOLA
ABFHIST	BATFISH		ABGLMOU	LUMBAGO		ABILLMY	BALMILY		ABLMOPS	APLOMBS
ABFHLSU	BASHFUL		ABGLMSY	GYMBALS		ABILLNP	PINBALL		ABLMOSY	LAMBOYS
ABFIILR	BIFILAR		ABGLOOT	TOOLBAG		ABILLPY	PLIABLY		ABLMOVY	MOVABLY
ABFIIMR	FIMBRIA		ABGLORS	BROLGAS		ABILLSW	SAWBILL		ABLMPUU	PABULUM
ABFILRU	FIBULAR		ABGLORT	RAGBOLT		ABILLSY	SYLLABI		ABLMSTY	TYMBALS
ABFILSU	FIBULAS		ABGLOSU	ALBUGOS		ABILLTT	BATTILL		ABLMTUY	MUTABLY
ABFIMOR	FIBROMA			SUBGOAL		ABILLWX	WAXBILL		ABLNOSZ	BLAZONS
ABFLOTY	FLYBOAT		ABGLRRU	BURGLAR		ABILLWY	WAYBILL		ABLNOTU	BUTANOL
ABFOORT	FOOTBAR		ABGNOPR	PROBANG		ABILMNU	ALBUMIN		ABLNOTY	NOTABLY
ABFSTTU	TUBFAST		ABGNORS	BARONGS		ABILMOX	MAILBOX		ABLNSTU	BUNTALS
ABGGGIN	BAGGING			BROGANS		ABILMST	TIMBALS			TULBANS
ABGGILY	BAGGILY		ABGNOTU	GUNBOAT		ABILNOS	ALBINOS		ABLNTUY	TUNABLY
ABGGINN	BANGING		ABGNOWY	BOWYANG		ABILNOT	BITONAL		ABLOORS	ROBALOS
ABGGINR	BARGING		ABGOORT	BOTARGO		ABILNOZ	BIZONAL		ABLOORT	TOOLBAR
	GARBING		ABGOPST	POSTBAG		ABILNRY	BAIRNLY		ABLOORY	OBOLARY
ABGGIST	BAGGITS		ABGORRU	GOBURRA		ABILOPR	BIPOLAR		ABLOPYY	PLAYBOY
ABGGISW	BAGWIGS		ABGORTU	OUTBRAG			PARBOIL		ABLORST	BORSTAL
ABGGNOS	GOBANGS		ABGOTTU	TUGBOAT		ABILORS	BAILORS		ABLORSU	LABOURS
ABGGNSU	BUGGANS		ABHHISS	SHIBAHS		ABILORT	ORBITAL		ABLORTW	BLAWORT
ABGGORT	BOGGART		ABHHKOT	KHOTBAH		ABILORV	BOLIVAR		ABLORUW	BOURLAW
ABGHILN	BLAHING		ABHHKTU	KHUTBAH		ABILOTU	OBITUAL		ABLOSST	OBLASTS
ABGHINS	BASHING		ABHHSUY	HUSHABY		ABILRRY	LIBRARY		ABLOSTT	TALBOTS
ABGHINT	BATHING		ABHIINT	INHABIT		ABILRSU	BURIALS		ABLOSTV	ABVOLTS
ABGHLOT	HAGBOLT		ABHIKLS	BASHLIK			RAILBUS		ABLOSTX	SALTBOX
ABGHLRU	BURGHAL			KIBLAHS		ABILRSZ	BRAZILS		ABLPRSU	BURLAPS
ABGHOTU	ABOUGHT		ABHIKST	BHAKTIS		ABIMMRS	MIMBARS		ABLPSUY	PLAYBUS
ABGHSTU	HAGBUTS		ABHIKTW	HAWKBIT		ABIMNRS	MINBARS		ABLRSWY	BYRLAWS
ABGIILN	BAILING		ABHILNO	HOBNAIL		ABIMOSS	BIOMASS		ABLRTUU	TUBULAR
ABGIINS	BIASING		ABHILOS	ABOLISH		ABIMPST	BAPTISM		ABMMNOS	MOBSMAN
ABGIINT	BAITING		ABHILTU	HALIBUT			BITMAPS		ABMNSUY	YNAMBUS
ABGIINZ	BAIZING		ABHIMRS	MIHRABS		ABIMRSS	BISMARS		ABMOOSW	WABOOMS
ABGIKLN	BALKING		ABHIMSZ	MAZHBIS		ABIMRST	IMBRAST		ABMOPST	BAMPOTS
ABGIKNN	BANKING		ABHINST	ABSINTH		ABIMRSU	BARIUMS		ABMORTU	TAMBOUR
ABGIKNO	BOAKING		ABHIOPS	PHOBIAS		ABIMRTT	TRIMTAB		ABMOSTU	SUBATOM
ABGIKNR	BARKING		ABHIORS	BOARISH		ABIMTTY	AMBITTY		ABMOSTW	WOMBATS
	BRAKING		ABHIOST	ISOBATH		ABINNSU	BUNNIAS		ABMRSSU	SAMBURS
ABGIKNS	BAKINGS		ABHISTU	HABITUS		ABINOOR	BORONIA		ABNOORS	SOROBAN
	BASKING		ABHKORU	BOURKHA		ABINORT	TABORIN		ABNOORZ	BORAZON
ABGIKNU	BAUKING		ABHKRSU	KURBASH		ABINORW	RAINBOW		ABNOOSS	BASSOON
ABGILLN	BALLING		ABHLMSY	SHAMBLY		ABINOSS	BONSAIS		ABNOOST	BATOONS
ABGILMN	AMBLING		ABHLRTU	HURLBAT		ABINOST	BASTION		ABNORST	BARTONS
	BALMING		ABHMNSU	BUSHMAN			OBTAINS		ABNORSY	BARYONS
	BLAMING		ABHMRSU	RHUMBAS		ABINOSU	ABUSION		ABNORTY	BARYTON
	LAMBING		ABHNOST	BOTHANS		ABINRTV	VIBRANT		ABNOSSU	BONASUS
ABGILMS	GIMBALS		ABHNSTU	SUNBATH		ABIORRS	BARRIOS		ABNOTUY	BUOYANT
ABGILNR	BLARING		ABHORRS	HARBORS		ABIORSS	ISOBARS		ABNRSTU	TURBANS
ABGILNS	SABLING		ABHORRU	HARBOUR		ABIORST	ORBITAS		ABNRTTU	TURBANT
ABGILNT	TABLING		ABHOTUY	HAUTBOY		ABIORTV	VIBRATO		ABNSTYZ	BYZANTS
ABGILNW	BAWLING		ABHPSTY	BYPATHS		ABIPSTT	BAPTIST		ABOOPSX	SOAPBOX
ABGILNZ	BLAZING		ABHRSTU	TARBUSH		ABIRTTY	TRAYBIT		ABOORTW	ROWBOAT
ABGILOR	GARBOIL		ABHSTUW	WASHTUB		ABISSST	BASSIST		ABOOTTW	TOWBOAT
ABGIMMN	BAMMING		ABIIKKT	KIBITKA		ABJJOOS	JOJOBAS		ABORRSU	ARBOURS
ABGIMRS	GAMBIRS		ABIILLS	BAILLIS		ABJKMOS	JAMBOKS			

ABORRSW BARROWS
ABORSTU OUTBARS
    ROBUSTA
    RUBATOS
    TABOURS
ABORSTW TOWBARS
ABORSTY TARBOYS
ABOSTUU AUTOBUS
ABPRSTU ABRUPTS
    UPBRAST
ABPRSUY UPBRAYS
ABRRSSU BURSARS
ABRRSUY BURSARY
ABRRTUY TURBARY
ABRSTUU ARBUTUS
ABSSUWY SUBWAYS
ACCCILY ACYCLIC
ACCDDEE ACCEDED
ACCDDEI CADDICE
ACCDEEN CADENCE
ACCDEER ACCEDER
ACCDEES ACCEDES
ACCDEHK CHACKED
ACCDEHN CHANCED
ACCDEHO COACHED
ACCDEHT CATCHED
ACCDEII ACCIDIE
ACCDEIO ACCOIED
ACCDEIT ACCITED
ACCDEIU CADUCEI
ACCDEKL CACKLED
    CLACKED
ACCDEKO COCKADE
ACCDEKR CRACKED
ACCDENS ACCENDS
ACCDENY CADENCY
ACCDEOT COACTED
ACCDEOY ACCOYED
ACCDERU ACCRUED
    CARDECU
ACCDESU ACCUSED
    SUCCADE
ACCDFIL FLACCID
ACCDHIL CHALCID
ACCDILS SCALDIC
ACCDIOT OCTADIC
ACCDKNO CANDOCK
ACCDKOW DAWCOCK
ACCDLOY ACCOYLD
    CACODYL
ACCDORS ACCORDS
ACCEEHO COACHEE
ACCEELN CENACLE
ACCEENR CREANCE
ACCEERT ACCRETE
ACCEFIT FACTICE
ACCEFLU FELUCCA
ACCEGIN ACCINGE
ACCEGOS SOCCAGE
ACCEHHI CHECHIA
ACCEHIL CALICHE
    CHALICE
ACCEHIM MACCHIE
ACCEHIN CHICANE
ACCEHLN CHANCEL
ACCEHLO COCHLEA
ACCEHNO CONCHAE
ACCEHNR CHANCER
    CHANCRE
ACCEHNS CHANCES
ACCEHNT CATCHEN
ACCEHNU CHAUNCE
ACCEHNY CHANCEY
ACCEHOR CAROCHE
    COACHER
ACCEHOS CHACOES
    COACHES
ACCEHPU CAPUCHE
ACCEHRS CREACHS

ACCEHRT CATCHER
    RECATCH
ACCEHST CACHETS
    CATCHES
ACCEHTU CATECHU
ACCEHXY CACHEXY
ACCEIKP ICEPACK
ACCEILL CALICLE
ACCEILN CALCINE
ACCEILO COELIAC
ACCEILS CALICES
    CELIACS
ACCEILT CALCITE
ACCEIMR CERAMIC
    RACEMIC
ACCEINO COCAINE
    OCEANIC
ACCEINV VACCINE
ACCEIPR CAPRICE
ACCEIPS ICECAPS
    IPECACS
ACCEIPV PECCAVI
ACCEIQU CACIQUE
ACCEIRS CARICES
ACCEIRT CREATIC
ACCEIST ACCITES
    ASCETIC
ACCEKLR CACKLER
    CLACKER
    CRACKLE
ACCEKLS CACKLES
ACCEKMO MEACOCK
ACCEKOP PEACOCK
ACCEKOS SEACOCK
ACCEKPU CUPCAKE
ACCEKRR CRACKER
ACCELLY CALYCLE
ACCELNO CONCEAL
ACCELNS CANCELS
ACCELOR CORACLE
ACCELOT CACOLET
ACCELSU SACCULE
ACCELSY CALYCES
ACCEMNU CACUMEN
ACCENOR CONACRE
ACCENOS ASCONCE
ACCENOV CONCAVE
ACCENPT PECCANT
ACCENRS CANCERS
ACCENST ACCENTS
ACCEOPY CACOEPY
ACCEORW CRACOWE
ACCEPRY PECCARY
ACCEPST ACCEPTS
ACCERRS SCARCER
ACCERRT CARRECT
ACCERSU ACCRUES
    ACCURSE
    ACCUSER
ACCERSW ACCREWS
ACCESSU ACCUSES
ACCFIIP PACIFIC
ACCFILY CALCIFY
ACCGHIN CACHING
    CHACING
ACCHHIS CHICHAS
ACCHHKU KUCHCHA
ACCHIKS CHIACKS
ACCHIMS CHASMIC
ACCHINO CHICANO
ACCHIOT CHAOTIC
ACCHIOU ACOUCHI
ACCHIRS SCRAICH
ACCHJSU JACCHUS
ACCHKOY HAYCOCK
ACCHKSY CHYACKS
ACCHLNO CONCHAL
ACCHLTU CLAUCHT
ACCHNRS SCRANCH

ACCHNRU CRAUNCH
ACCHOPU CAPOUCH
ACCHOSU CACHOUS
ACCHOTW CHOCTAW
ACCHOUY ACOUCHY
ACCHPTU CATCHUP
    UPCATCH
ACCHRRU CURRACH
ACCHRST SCRATCH
ACCHRSU SCRAUCH
ACCHSSU SUCCAHS
ACCIILN ACLINIC
ACCIINT ACTINIC
ACCIIST ASCITIC
    SCIATIC
ACCILLU CALCULI
ACCILMO COMICAL
ACCILMU CALCIUM
ACCILNO CONICAL
    LACONIC
ACCILNY CYNICAL
ACCILOR CALORIC
ACCILOS ACCOILS
    CALICOS
ACCILOV VOCALIC
ACCILRU CRUCIAL
ACCILRY ACRYLIC
ACCILSS CLASSIC
ACCILST CLASTIC
ACCILSU SACCULI
ACCIMOZ ZIMOCCA
ACCINNO CANONIC
ACCINOT CANTICO
ACCINRU CRUCIAN
ACCINSW WICCANS
ACCIOPR CAPROIC
ACCIORS SCORIAC
ACCIPRT PRACTIC
ACCIRRS CIRCARS
ACCIRST ARCTICS
ACCISTT TACTICS
ACCISTU CAUSTIC
    CICUTAS
ACCKLOR CARLOCK
ACCKLRY CRACKLY
ACCKMOR CROMACK
ACCKOSS CASSOCK
ACCKOST CASTOCK
ACCLOSU COUCALS
ACCLOSY ACCLOYS
ACCMOPT ACCOMPT
    COMPACT
ACCMRUU CURCUMA
ACCNNOO COONCAN
ACCNOOP COCOPAN
ACCNOOR RACCOON
ACCNOOS CACOONS
ACCNOTT CONTACT
ACCNOTU ACCOUNT
ACCOPTY COPYCAT
ACCOQSU SQUACCO
ACCORSS CORCASS
    CORSACS
ACCORTU ACCOURT
ACCOSST ACCOSTS
ACCRSTU ACCURST
ACDDDEI CADDIED
ACDDDEL CLADDED
ACDDDEU ADDUCED
ACDDEEF DEFACED
ACDDEER CEDARED
ACDDEES DECADES
ACDDEEY DECAYED
ACDDEIN CANDIED
ACDDEIS CADDIES
ACDDEIU DECIDUA
ACDDELN CANDLED
ACDDELO CLADODE

ACDDELR CLADDER
    CRADLED
ACDDELS SCALDED
ACDDELU CAUDLED
ACDDEMU DUCDAME
ACDDEOP DECAPOD
ACDDERU ADDUCER
ACDDESU ADDUCES
    SCAUDED
ACDDHHU CHUDDAH
ACDDHIS CADDISH
ACDDHKO HADDOCK
ACDDHOR CHADDOR
ACDDHRU CHUDDAR
ACDDIRS DISCARD
ACDDIST ADDICTS
ACDDKMO MADDOCK
ACDDKOP PADDOCK
ACDDSSY CADDYSS
ACDDSTU ADDUCTS
ACDEEES DECEASE
ACDEEFF EFFACED
ACDEEFN ENFACED
ACDEEFR DEFACER
    REFACED
ACDEEFS DEFACES
ACDEEFT FACETED
ACDEEGL GLACEED
ACDEEGN ENCAGED
ACDEEHL LEACHED
ACDEEHP PEACHED
ACDEEHR REACHED
ACDEEHT CHEATED
ACDEEIR DECIARE
ACDEEJT DEJECTA
ACDEEKR CREAKED
ACDEELL CADELLE
ACDEELN CLEANED
    ELANCED
    ENLACED
ACDEELR CLEARED
    CREEDAL
    DECLARE
ACDEELS DESCALE
ACDEELT CLEATED
ACDEELV CLEAVED
ACDEEMN MENACED
ACDEEMR AMERCED
    CREAMED
    RACEMED
ACDEENR ENRACED
ACDEENS DECANES
    ENCASED
ACDEENT ENACTED
ACDEENV ENCAVED
    VENDACE
ACDEEPR CAPERED
    PEARCED
    PREACED
ACDEEPS ESCAPED
ACDEERS CREASED
    DECARES
    SEARCED
ACDEERT CATERED
    CEDRATE
    CERATED
    CREATED
    REACTED
ACDEEST TEDESCA
ACDEETU EDUCATE
ACDEETX EXACTED
ACDEFFH CHAFFED
ACDEFFS DECAFFS
ACDEFHU CHAUFED
ACDEFIN FANCIED
ACDEFIR FARCIED
ACDEFRS SCARFED
ACDEFRT CRAFTED
    FRACTED

Code	Word(s)
ACDEGGL	CLAGGED
ACDEGGR	CRAGGED
ACDEGHN	CHANGED
	GANCHED
ACDEGHR	CHARGED
ACDEGIN	INCAGED
ACDEGIR	CADGIER
ACDEGIS	DISCAGE
ACDEGKO	DOCKAGE
ACDEGLN	CANGLED
	CLANGED
	GLANCED
ACDEGNO	CONGAED
	DECAGON
ACDEGNU	UNCAGED
ACDEGOR	CARGOED
	CORDAGE
ACDEGRS	CADGERS
ACDEHHN	HANCHED
ACDEHHT	HATCHED
ACDEHIN	CHAINED
	ECHIDNA
ACDEHIP	EDAPHIC
ACDEHIR	CHAIRED
ACDEHIX	HEXADIC
ACDEHKL	CHALKED
	HACKLED
ACDEHKR	CHARKED
ACDEHKW	WHACKED
ACDEHLN	LANCHED
ACDEHLR	CHALDER
ACDEHLS	CLASHED
ACDEHLT	LATCHED
ACDEHMP	CHAMPED
ACDEHMR	CHARMED
	MARCHED
ACDEHMS	CHASMED
ACDEHMT	MATCHED
ACDEHNR	ENDARCH
	RANCHED
ACDEHNT	CHANTED
ACDEHOP	POACHED
ACDEHOR	CHORDAE
	ROACHED
ACDEHOT	CATHODE
ACDEHPP	CHAPPED
ACDEHPR	PARCHED
ACDEHPT	PATCHED
ACDEHPU	CUPHEAD
ACDEHRR	CHARRED
ACDEHRS	CRASHED
ACDEHRT	CHARTED
	RATCHED
ACDEHST	SCATHED
ACDEHTT	CHATTED
ACDEHTW	WATCHED
ACDEHTY	YACHTED
ACDEIIR	ACIDIER
ACDEILL	CEDILLA
ACDEILM	CAMELID
	CLAIMED
	DECIMAL
	DECLAIM
	MALICED
	MEDICAL
ACDEILN	INLACED
ACDEILR	DECRIAL
	RADICEL
	RADICLE
ACDEILS	SCAILED
ACDEILT	CITADEL
	DELTAIC
	DIALECT
	EDICTAL
ACDEIMT	MICATED
ACDEIMY	MEDIACY
ACDEINO	OCEANID
ACDEINR	CAIRNED
	CARNIED
ACDEINS	CANDIES
	INCASED
ACDEINV	INCAVED
ACDEINY	CYANIDE
ACDEIPR	EPACRID
ACDEIPS	DISPACE
ACDEIRR	ACRIDER
	CARRIED
ACDEIRS	CARDIES
	DARCIES
	RADICES
	SIDECAR
ACDEIRU	DECURIA
ACDEISS	DISCASE
ACDEIST	ACIDEST
	DACITES
ACDEISV	ADVICES
ACDEITT	DICTATE
ACDEITY	EDACITY
ACDEJLO	CAJOLED
ACDEJNU	JAUNCED
ACDEKLM	MACKLED
ACDEKLN	CLANKED
ACDEKLO	CLOAKED
ACDEKLS	SLACKED
ACDEKLT	TACKLED
	TALCKED
ACDEKLU	CAULKED
ACDEKMS	SMACKED
ACDEKNR	CRANKED
ACDEKNS	SNACKED
ACDEKOR	CROAKED
ACDEKQU	QUACKED
ACDEKRS	DACKERS
ACDEKRT	TRACKED
ACDEKRW	WRACKED
ACDEKST	STACKED
ACDELLS	SCALLED
ACDELMM	CLAMMED
ACDELMP	CAMPLED
	CLAMPED
ACDELMS	MASCLED
ACDELNO	CELADON
ACDELNS	CALENDS
	CANDLES
ACDELNT	CANTLED
ACDELNU	LAUNCED
	UNLACED
ACDELOR	ORACLED
ACDELOS	SOLACED
ACDELOT	LOCATED
ACDELPP	CLAPPED
ACDELPS	CLASPED
	SCALPED
ACDELQU	CALQUED
ACDELRS	CRADLES
	SCALDER
ACDELRT	CLARTED
ACDELRU	CAULDER
ACDELRW	CRAWLED
ACDELSS	CLASSED
	DECLASS
ACDELST	CASTLED
	SCLATED
ACDELSU	CAUDLES
	CEDULAS
ACDELTT	CLATTED
ACDELTU	CLAUTED
ACDEMMR	CRAMMED
ACDEMMS	SCAMMED
ACDEMNU	DECUMAN
ACDEMOR	CAROMED
	COMRADE
ACDEMPR	CRAMPED
ACDEMPS	DECAMPS
	SCAMPED
ACDENNS	SCANNED
ACDENNT	CANDENT
ACDENNU	NUANCED
ACDENOR	ACORNED
	DRACONE
ACDENOS	DEACONS
ACDENPR	PRANCED
ACDENPT	PANDECT
ACDENPU	UNCAPED
	UNPACED
ACDENRS	DANCERS
ACDENRT	CANTRED
	TRANCED
ACDENRU	DURANCE
	UNRACED
ACDENRY	ARDENCY
ACDENSS	ASCENDS
ACDENST	DECANTS
	DESCANT
	SCANTED
ACDENSU	UNCASED
ACDENTU	UNACTED
ACDENUV	VAUNCED
ACDEOPS	PEACODS
	PEASCOD
ACDEOPT	COAPTED
ACDEORR	CORRADE
ACDEORS	SARCODE
ACDEORT	CORDATE
	REDCOAT
ACDEOST	COASTED
ACDEOTT	CODETTA
ACDEOUV	COUVADE
ACDEPPR	CRAPPED
ACDEPRS	REDCAPS
	SCARPED
	SCRAPED
ACDEPSU	SCAUPED
ACDERRS	CARDERS
	SCARRED
ACDERST	REDACTS
	SCARTED
ACDERSU	CRUSADE
	SCAURED
ACDERTT	DETRACT
	TRACTED
ACDERTU	CURATED
	TRADUCE
ACDESTT	SCATTED
ACDFIIY	ACIDIFY
ACDFIOT	FACTOID
ACDGGIN	CADGING
ACDGINN	DANCING
ACDGINO	GONADIC
ACDGINR	CARDING
ACDGKLO	DAGLOCK
ACDGNOT	CANTDOG
ACDGORT	DOGCART
ACDHIIL	CHILIAD
ACDHIOP	PHACOID
ACDHIRY	DIARCHY
ACDHLOR	CHORDAL
	DORLACH
ACDHMRS	DRACHMS
ACDHNOW	COWHAND
ACDHOOT	CATHOOD
ACDHOPR	POCHARD
ACDHORR	ORCHARD
ACDHORS	CHADORS
ACDHRUY	DUARCHY
ACDHRYY	DYARCHY
ACDIIIN	INDICIA
ACDIINN	INDICAN
ACDIINO	CONIDIA
ACDIINR	ACRIDIN
ACDIIOS	ISODICA
ACDIIRS	CIDARIS
	SCIARID
ACDIIRT	ARCTIID
	TRIACID
	TRIADIC
ACDIITY	ACIDITY
ACDIKLS	SKALDIC
ACDILLO	CODILLA
ACDILMO	DOMICAL
ACDILMS	CLADISM
ACDILNO	NODICAL
ACDILNU	DULCIAN
ACDILOP	PLACOID
	PODALIC
ACDILOR	CORDIAL
ACDILOT	COTIDAL
ACDILPU	PALUDIC
ACDILST	CLADIST
ACDILTW	WILDCAT
ACDIMMU	CADMIUM
ACDIMNO	MANDIOC
	MONACID
	MONADIC
	NOMADIC
ACDIMNY	DYNAMIC
ACDINRU	IRACUND
ACDINST	DISCANT
ACDINSW	WINDACS
ACDIOPR	PARODIC
	PICADOR
ACDIORR	CORRIDA
ACDIORS	SARCOID
ACDIORT	ARCTOID
	CAROTID
ACDIOST	DACOITS
ACDIOSZ	ZODIACS
ACDIOTY	DACOITY
ACDIPRS	CAPRIDS
ACDIPSS	CAPSIDS
ACDIQRU	QUADRIC
ACDIRST	DRASTIC
ACDISST	DICASTS
ACDITUV	VIADUCT
ACDJNTU	ADJUNCT
ACDKLOP	PADLOCK
ACDKLSY	SKYCLAD
ACDKMOO	MOCKADO
ACDKMPU	MUDPACK
ACDKOPR	POCKARD
ACDLLOR	COLLARD
ACDLLUY	DUCALLY
ACDLNOR	CALDRON
ACDLNOT	COTLAND
ACDLOWY	LADYCOW
ACDLSTY	DACTYLS
ACDMMNO	COMMAND
ACDMNOP	COMPAND
ACDMOOW	CAMWOOD
ACDMORZ	CZARDOM
ACDMSTU	MUDCATS
ACDNOOR	CARDOON
ACDNORS	CANDORS
ACDNORU	CANDOUR
	CAUDRON
ACDORST	COSTARD
ACDORSU	CRUSADO
ACDORSW	COWARDS
ACDORUZ	CRUZADO
ACDRSTU	CUSTARD
ACDRSUU	CARDUUS
ACEEEPS	ESCAPEE
ACEEEUV	EVACUEE
ACEEFFS	EFFACES
ACEEFHN	ENCHAFE
ACEEFIN	FAIENCE
	FIANCEE
ACEEFMN	FACEMEN
ACEEFNS	ENFACES
ACEEFNY	FAYENCE
ACEEFPR	PREFACE
ACEEFRS	REFACES
ACEEGIL	ELEGIAC
ACEEGNR	ENGRACE
ACEEGNS	ENCAGES
ACEEGNT	CENTAGE

ACEEGSU	ESCUAGE		ACEEMSZ	ECZEMAS
ACEEHHT	CHEETAH		ACEENNP	PENANCE
ACEEHIP	CHEAPIE		ACEENNR	NARCEEN
ACEEHIT	HICATEE		ACEENNT	CANTEEN
	TEACHIE		ACEENNY	CAYENNE
ACEEHIV	ACHIEVE		ACEENOT	ACETONE
ACEEHKS	HACKEES		ACEENRS	CAREENS
ACEEHLR	RELACHE			CASERNE
ACEEHLS	LEACHES			ENRACES
ACEEHLT	CHELATE		ACEENRT	CENTARE
ACEEHMP	EMPEACH			CRENATE
ACEEHMR	MACHREE		ACEENSS	ENCASES
ACEEHMT	MACHETE			SEANCES
ACEEHNN	ENHANCE		ACEENST	CETANES
ACEEHNP	CHEAPEN			TENACES
ACEEHNS	ACHENES		ACEENSV	ENCAVES
	ENCHASE		ACEENTU	CUNEATE
ACEEHOR	OCHREAE		ACEEORS	ACEROSE
ACEEHPP	ECHAPPE		ACEEORT	OCREATE
ACEEHPR	CHEAPER		ACEEOST	ACETOSE
	PEACHER			COATEES
ACEEHPS	PEACHES		ACEEOTV	EVOCATE
ACEEHRR	REACHER		ACEEPRR	CAPERER
ACEEHRS	REACHES		ACEEPRS	ESCAPER
ACEEHRT	CHEATER			PEARCES
	HECTARE			PERCASE
	RECHATE			PREACES
	RECHEAT		ACEEPSS	ESCAPES
	TEACHER		ACEERRS	CAREERS
ACEEHST	EATCHES			CREASER
	ESCHEAT		ACEERRT	CATERER
	TEACHES			RETRACE
ACEEHTT	THECATE			TERRACE
ACEEHTX	EXCHEAT		ACEERSS	CREASES
ACEEILP	CALIPEE			SEARCES
ACEEIMT	EMICATE		ACEERST	CERATES
ACEEINR	CINEREA			CREATES
ACEEINU	EUCAINE			ECARTES
ACEEIRR	CARIERE			SECRETA
ACEEISV	VESICAE		ACEERSU	CESURAE
ACEEJKN	JACKEEN		ACEERTX	EXACTER
ACEEKNP	KNEECAP			EXCRETA
ACEELLN	NACELLE		ACEESSS	ASCESES
ACEELMP	EMPLACE		ACEESST	ECTASES
ACEELMR	RECLAME		ACEFFHI	AFFICHE
ACEELNR	CLEANER		ACEFFHR	CHAFFER
ACEELNS	CLEANSE		ACEFFIN	CAFFEIN
	ELANCES		ACEFFIS	SCAFFIE
	ENLACES		ACEFFOR	AFFORCE
	SCALENE		ACEFFST	AFFECTS
ACEELNT	LATENCE		ACEFGOT	GEOFACT
ACEELNV	ENCLAVE		ACEFHMR	CHAMFER
	VALENCE		ACEFHRS	CHAFERS
ACEELPR	PERCALE		ACEFHSU	CHAUFES
	REPLACE		ACEFIIL	FELICIA
ACEELPT	CAPELET		ACEFILM	MALEFIC
ACEELRR	CLEARER		ACEFILR	FILACER
ACEELRS	ALERCES		ACEFINN	FINANCE
	CEREALS		ACEFINR	FANCIER
	RESCALE		ACEFINS	FANCIES
ACEELRT	TREACLE		ACEFIRS	FARCIES
ACEELRU	CAERULE			FIACRES
ACEELRV	CLEAVER		ACEFITV	FACTIVE
ACEELST	CELESTA		ACEFITY	ACETIFY
ACEELSU	EUCLASE		ACEFKLR	FLACKER
ACEELSV	CLEAVES		ACEFKLT	FLACKET
ACEELVX	EXCLAVE		ACEFLRU	CAREFUL
ACEEMNR	MENACER		ACEFLSU	FECULAS
ACEEMNS	CASEMEN		ACEFNNO	FACONNE
	MENACES		ACEFNRT	CANTREF
ACEEMNT	CEMENTA		ACEFNRU	FURNACE
ACEEMNV	CAVEMEN		ACEFOPR	PROFACE
ACEEMRR	CREAMER		ACEFORR	FORECAR
ACEEMRS	AMERCES		ACEFOTU	OUTFACE
	CAREMES		ACEFRRT	REFRACT
	RACEMES		ACEFRRU	FARCEUR
ACEEMRT	CREMATE			
	MEERCAT			
ACEEMSS	CAMESES			

ACEFRSU	SURFACE		ACEHIMS	CHAMISE
ACEFRTU	FACTURE		ACEHINN	ENCHAIN
	FURCATE		ACEHINS	CHAINES
ACEFSTU	FAUCETS			INCHASE
ACEGHLO	GALOCHE		ACEHINT	CHANTIE
ACEGHNR	CHANGER		ACEHINY	HYACINE
ACEGHNS	CHANGES		ACEHIPP	CHAPPIE
	GANCHES		ACEHIPR	CHARPIE
ACEGHNU	CHAUNGE		ACEHIPT	APHETIC
ACEGHOU	GOUACHE			HEPATIC
ACEGHOW	COWHAGE		ACEHIRR	CHARIER
ACEGHRR	CHARGER		ACEHIRS	CAHIERS
ACEGHRS	CHARGES			CASHIER
	CREAGHS			ERIACHS
ACEGHRT	GERTCHA		ACEHIRT	THERIAC
ACEGHRU	GAUCHER		ACEHIRV	ARCHIVE
ACEGILL	ELLAGIC		ACEHISS	CHAISES
ACEGILN	ANGELIC		ACEHIST	ACHIEST
	ANGLICE			AITCHES
ACEGILP	PELAGIC		ACEHITY	YACHTIE
ACEGILR	GLACIER		ACEHITZ	ZAITECH
	GRACILE		ACEHKLR	HACKLER
ACEGIMO	CAMOGIE		ACEHKLS	HACKLES
ACEGIMR	GRIMACE			SHACKLE
ACEGIMT	GAMETIC		ACEHKLT	HACKLET
ACEGINO	COINAGE		ACEHKNY	HACKNEY
ACEGINP	PEACING		ACEHKRS	HACKERS
ACEGINR	GRECIAN		ACEHKRW	WHACKER
ACEGINS	CEASING		ACEHKRY	HACKERY
	INCAGES		ACEHLLP	PELLACH
ACEGINV	VEGANIC		ACEHLLS	SHELLAC
ACEGINY	GYNECIA		ACEHLMT	CHAMLET
ACEGINZ	CEAZING		ACEHLMY	ALCHEMY
ACEGIRU	GAUCIER		ACEHLNN	CHANNEL
ACEGIRW	GAWCIER		ACEHLNO	CHALONE
ACEGIST	CAGIEST		ACEHLNR	CHARNEL
ACEGKLO	LOCKAGE			LARCHEN
ACEGKLR	GRACKLE		ACEHLNS	LANCHES
ACEGKMO	MOCKAGE		ACEHLOP	EPOCHAL
ACEGKOR	CORKAGE		ACEHLOR	CHOLERA
ACEGLLO	COLLAGE			CHORALE
ACEGLNO	CONGEAL		ACEHLOS	LOACHES
ACEGLNR	CLANGER			OSCHEAL
ACEGLNS	CANGLES		ACEHLOT	CATHOLE
	GLANCES		ACEHLPS	CHAPELS
ACEGLOT	CATELOG		ACEHLPT	CHAPLET
ACEGLOU	CAGOULE		ACEHLPY	CHEAPLY
ACEGMOP	COMPAGE		ACEHLRS	CLASHER
ACEGNOR	ACROGEN			LARCHES
	CORNAGE			RASCHEL
ACEGNOT	COGNATE		ACEHLRT	ARCHLET
ACEGNSU	CANGUES		ACEHLRY	CHARLEY
	UNCAGES		ACEHLSS	CLASHES
ACEGORS	CARGOES			SEALCHS
	CORSAGE		ACEHLST	CHALETS
	SOCAGER			LATCHES
ACEGORU	COURAGE			SATCHEL
ACEGOSS	SOCAGES		ACEHLTT	CHATTEL
ACEGOSW	COWAGES			LATCHET
ACEGOTT	COTTAGE		ACEHMNP	CHAPMEN
ACEGRTU	TRUCAGE		ACEHMNR	ENCHARM
ACEGSTU	SCUTAGE		ACEHMNS	MANCHES
ACEHHLT	HATCHEL		ACEHMNT	MANCHET
ACEHHNS	HANCHES		ACEHMRR	CHARMER
ACEHHRT	HATCHER			MARCHER
ACEHHRU	HACHURE		ACEHMRS	MARCHES
ACEHHRX	HEXARCH			MESARCH
ACEHHST	CHETAHS		ACEHMRT	MATCHER
	HATCHES			REMATCH
ACEHHTT	HATCHET		ACEHMRU	CHAUMER
ACEHIKR	KACHERI		ACEHMSS	SACHEMS
ACEHILL	CHALLIE		ACEHMST	MATCHES
	HELICAL		ACEHMTY	ECTHYMA
ACEHILR	CHARLIE		ACEHNNR	CHANNER
ACEHILT	ALETHIC		ACEHNNT	ENCHANT
	ETHICAL		ACEHNRR	RANCHER
ACEHIMN	MACHINE		ACEHNRS	CHENARS
ACEHIMP	IMPEACH			RANCHES
ACEHIMR	CHIMERA		ACEHNRT	CHANTER

	TRANCHE		CAILLES	ACEINNT	ANCIENT		STATICE
ACEHNSS	SCHANSE	ACEILLX	LEXICAL	ACEINNY	CYANINE		TIETACS
ACEHNST	CHASTEN	ACEILMN	CNEMIAL	ACEINOP	PAEONIC	ACEITTV	CAVETTI
	NATCHES		MELANIC	ACEINOS	ACINOSE	ACEITTX	EXTATIC
ACEHNSZ	SCHANZE	ACEILMR	CALMIER	ACEINOT	ACONITE	ACEITUX	AUXETIC
ACEHNTT	ETCHANT		CLAIMER		ANOETIC	ACEJKMN	JACKMEN
ACEHNTU	UNTEACH		MIRACLE	ACEINPR	CAPRINE	ACEJKOP	PAJOCKE
ACEHNTY	CHANTEY		RECLAIM	ACEINPS	INSCAPE	ACEJKST	JACKETS
ACEHOPR	POACHER	ACEILMS	LIMACES		PINCASE	ACEJLOR	CAJOLER
ACEHOPS	EPOCHAS		MALICES	ACEINRR	CARNIER	ACEJLOS	CAJOLES
	POACHES	ACEILMT	CLIMATE	ACEINRS	ARSENIC	ACEJNOT	JACONET
ACEHORS	CHOREAS		METICAL		CARNIES	ACEJNOY	JOYANCE
	ORACHES	ACEILMX	EXCLAIM		CERASIN	ACEJNSU	JAUNCES
	ROACHES	ACEILMY	MYCELIA	ACEINRT	CANTIER	ACEJNTU	JUNCATE
ACEHOSS	CHAOSES	ACEILNP	CAPELIN		CERTAIN	ACEJPTU	CAJEPUT
ACEHOTY	CHAYOTE		PANICLE		CREATIN	ACEJRTT	TRAJECT
ACEHPPS	SCHAPPE		PELICAN		CRINATE	ACEKKNR	KNACKER
ACEHPRS	EPARCHS	ACEILNR	CARLINE		NACRITE	ACEKLLP	PELLACK
	PARCHES	ACEILNS	INLACES	ACEINSS	CASEINS	ACEKLMS	MACKLES
ACEHPRT	CHAPTER		SANICLE		INCASES	ACEKLNR	CRANKLE
	PATCHER		SCALENI	ACEINST	CANIEST	ACEKLNS	SLACKEN
ACEHPRY	EPARCHY	ACEILNU	CAULINE		CINEAST	ACEKLOR	EARLOCK
	PREACHY	ACEILOR	CALORIE	ACEINSU	EUCAINS	ACEKLPT	PLACKET
ACEHPSS	CHAPESS		CARIOLE	ACEINSV	INCAVES	ACEKLQU	QUACKLE
ACEHPST	PATCHES		COALIER	ACEINSY	CYANISE	ACEKLRS	CALKERS
ACEHQUY	QUEACHY		LORICAE	ACEINTT	NICTATE		LACKERS
ACEHRRS	ARCHERS	ACEILOS	COALISE		TETANIC		SLACKER
ACEHRRT	CHARTER	ACEILOT	ALOETIC	ACEINTV	VENATIC	ACEKLRT	TACKLER
	RECHART	ACEILOZ	COALIZE	ACEINTX	INEXACT	ACEKLRU	CAULKER
ACEHRRX	XERARCH	ACEILPR	CALIPER	ACEINTY	CYANITE	ACEKLST	TACKLES
ACEHRRY	ARCHERY		REPLICA	ACEINYZ	CYANIZE	ACEKLSY	LACKEYS
ACEHRSS	CHASERS	ACEILPS	PLAICES	ACEIOOZ	ZOOECIA	ACEKMNP	PACKMEN
	CRASHES		SPECIAL	ACEIOPT	ECTOPIA	ACEKMRS	SMACKER
	ESCHARS	ACEILPT	PLICATE	ACEIORS	ORACIES	ACEKNOS	NOCAKES
ACEHRST	ARCHEST	ACEILPU	PECULIA		SCORIAE	ACEKNPR	PRANCKE
	CHARETS	ACEILRR	CERRIAL	ACEIORT	EROTICA	ACEKNRS	CANKERS
	CHASTER	ACEILRS	CLARIES	ACEIOST	SOCIATE	ACEKNRY	CANKERY
	RATCHES		ECLAIRS	ACEIOTX	EXOTICA	ACEKNST	NACKETS
ACEHRSU	ARCHEUS		SCALIER	ACEIPPR	EPICARP	ACEKORR	CROAKER
ACEHRSV	VARECHS	ACEILRT	ARTICLE	ACEIPPT	TAPPICE	ACEKPPR	PREPACK
ACEHRSX	EXARCHS		RECITAL	ACEIPRR	CRAPIER	ACEKPRS	PACKERS
ACEHRSY	HYRACES		TALCIER	ACEIPRS	EPACRIS		REPACKS
ACEHRTT	CHATTER	ACEILRU	AURICLE		SCRAPIE	ACEKPST	PACKETS
	RATCHET	ACEILRV	CALIVER		SPACIER	ACEKQRU	QUACKER
ACEHRTW	WATCHER		CLAVIER	ACEIPRT	PARETIC	ACEKRRS	RACKERS
ACEHRTY	YACHTER		VELARIC		PICRATE	ACEKRRT	TRACKER
ACEHRXY	EXARCHY	ACEILRY	CLAYIER	ACEIPST	ASEPTIC	ACEKRSS	SACKERS
ACEHSSS	CHASSES	ACEILSS	SALICES		PACIEST		SCREAKS
ACEHSST	SACHETS	ACEILST	ASTELIC		SPICATE	ACEKRST	RACKETS
	SCATHES		ELASTIC	ACEIPSU	AUSPICE		STACKER
ACEHSSW	CASHEWS		LACIEST	ACEIPSZ	CAPIZES		TACKERS
ACEHSTW	WATCHES		LATICES		CAPSIZE	ACEKRSU	CAUKERS
ACEHSTX	HEXACTS		SALICET	ACEIPTV	CAPTIVE	ACEKRSW	CAWKERS
ACEHTTU	TEUCHAT	ACEILSV	CLAVIES	ACEIQRU	ACQUIRE		WACKERS
ACEHTTW	WATCHET		VESICAL	ACEIQSU	CAIQUES	ACEKRSY	SCREAKY
ACEIILM	CIMELIA	ACEILTT	LATTICE	ACEIQTU	ACQUITE		YACKERS
ACEIILS	LAICISE		TACTILE	ACEIQUZ	CAZIQUE	ACEKRTT	RACKETT
ACEIILT	CILIATE	ACEIMNO	ENCOMIA	ACEIRRR	CARRIER	ACEKRTY	RACKETY
ACEIILZ	LAICIZE	ACEIMNP	PEMICAN	ACEIRRS	CARRIES	ACEKSST	CASKETS
ACEIITV	CAITIVE	ACEIMNR	CARMINE		SCARIER	ACEKSTT	STACKET
	VICIATE	ACEIMNS	AMNESIC	ACEIRRT	CIRRATE		TACKETS
ACEIJKS	JACKSIE		CINEMAS		ERRATIC	ACEKTTY	TACKETY
ACEIKLS	SACLIKE	ACEIMNT	EMICANT	ACEIRRZ	CRAZIER	ACELLMO	CALOMEL
ACEIKLT	CATLIKE		NEMATIC	ACEIRST	CRISTAE	ACELLNU	NUCLEAL
ACEIKMR	KERAMIC	ACEIMOV	VOMICAE		RACIEST	ACELLNY	CLEANLY
ACEIKNT	ANTICKE	ACEIMPR	CAMPIER		STEARIC	ACELLOR	CORELLA
ACEIKOP	PAIOCKE	ACEIMPY	PYAEMIC	ACEIRSU	SAUCIER		OCELLAR
ACEIKPR	EARPICK	ACEIMRT	MATRICE		URICASE	ACELLOS	LOCALES
ACEIKPX	PICKAXE	ACEIMRU	URAEMIC	ACEIRSV	CARVIES	ACELLOT	COLLATE
ACEIKRS	EIRACKS	ACEIMSS	CAMISES		CAVIERS	ACELLPS	SCALPEL
ACEIKRT	TACKIER	ACEIMST	ACMITES		VARICES	ACELLPY	CLYPEAL
ACEIKRW	WACKIER		ETACISM		VISCERA	ACELLRR	CARRELL
ACEIKSS	SEASICK		MICATES	ACEIRSZ	CRAZIES	ACELLRS	CALLERS
ACEIKST	CAKIEST		SEMATIC	ACEIRTT	CATTIER		CELLARS
	TACKIES	ACEIMSU	CAESIUM		CITRATE		RECALLS
ACEIKTT	TIETACK	ACEINNP	PINNACE	ACEISSS	ASCESIS		SCLERAL
ACEILLM	LIMACEL	ACEINNR	CANNIER	ACEISST	ASCITES	ACELLRY	CLEARLY
	MICELLA	ACEINNS	CANINES		ECTASIS	ACELLST	CALLETS
ACEILLS	ALLICES		NANCIES	ACEISTT	CATTIES	ACELMNO	COALMEN

ACELMNS	ENCALMS
ACELMOR	CAROMEL
ACELMOT	CAMELOT
ACELMOU	CAULOME
	LEUCOMA
ACELMPR	CLAMPER
ACELMPS	CAMPLES
ACELMRS	MARCELS
ACELMRY	CAMELRY
ACELMSS	MASCLES
	MESCALS
	SCAMELS
ACELMST	CALMEST
	CAMLETS
ACELMSU	ALMUCES
	MACULES
ACELMTU	CALUMET
ACELNNS	CANNELS
ACELNNU	UNCLEAN
ACELNNY	LYNCEAN
ACELNOR	CORNEAL
ACELNOT	LACTONE
ACELNOZ	CALZONE
ACELNPS	ENCLASP
	SPANCEL
ACELNPT	CLAPNET
ACELNPU	UNPLACE
ACELNRS	LANCERS
	RANCELS
ACELNRT	CENTRAL
ACELNRU	LUCARNE
	NUCLEAR
	UNCLEAR
ACELNRY	LARCENY
ACELNST	CANTLES
	CENTALS
	LANCETS
	SCANTLE
ACELNSU	CENSUAL
	LAUNCES
	UNLACES
	UNSCALE
ACELNTT	CANTLET
ACELNTY	LATENCY
ACELNVY	VALENCY
ACELOPR	POLACRE
ACELOPS	ESCALOP
ACELOPT	POLECAT
ACELOQU	COEQUAL
ACELORS	CLAROES
	COALERS
	ESCOLAR
	ORACLES
ACELORY	CALOYER
ACELOSS	SOLACES
ACELOST	ALECOST
	LACTOSE
	LOCATES
	SCATOLE
	TALCOSE
ACELOSV	ALCOVES
	COEVALS
ACELOTT	CALOTTE
ACELOTU	OCULATE
ACELOTY	ACOLYTE
	COTYLAE
ACELOUV	VACUOLE
ACELPPR	CLAPPER
ACELPPS	SCAPPLE
ACELPRS	CARPELS
	CLASPER
	CRAPLES
	PARCELS
	PLACERS
	SCALPER
ACELPRT	PLECTRA
ACELPRY	PRELACY
ACELPST	CAPLETS
	PLACETS
ACELPSU	CAPSULE
	SPECULA
	UPSCALE
ACELPSY	CYPSELA
ACELPTY	ECTYPAL
ACELQRU	LACQUER
ACELQSU	CALQUES
	CLAQUES
ACELQUY	LACQUEY
ACELRRS	CARRELS
ACELRRU	RAUCLER
ACELRRW	CRAWLER
ACELRSS	SCALERS
	SCLERAS
ACELRST	CARTELS
	CLARETS
	SCARLET
	TARCELS
ACELRSU	CESURAL
	SECULAR
ACELRSV	CALVERS
	CARVELS
	CLAVERS
ACELRTT	CLATTER
ACELRTY	TREACLY
ACELSSS	CLASSES
	SACLESS
ACELSST	CASTLES
	SCLATES
ACELSSU	CLAUSES
ACELSSV	SCLAVES
ACELSTU	CAUTELS
	SULCATE
ACELSTY	ACETYLS
	SCYTALE
ACELSUU	ACULEUS
ACELSUX	EXCUSAL
ACELSXY	CALYXES
ACELTUY	ACUTELY
ACELTXY	EXACTLY
ACEMMRR	CRAMMER
ACEMNOR	CREMONA
	ROMANCE
ACEMNOS	ANCOMES
ACEMNPS	ENCAMPS
ACEMNSU	ACUMENS
ACEMOPR	COMPARE
	COMPEAR
ACEMOPS	POMACES
ACEMORS	AMORCES
ACEMORU	MORCEAU
ACEMOSS	COSMEAS
ACEMOST	CAMOTES
	COMATES
ACEMOSU	MUCOSAE
ACEMPRS	CAMPERS
	SCAMPER
ACEMPRT	CRAMPET
ACEMPST	CAMPEST
ACEMRSS	SCREAMS
ACEMRST	MERCATS
ACEMRSY	CRAMESY
ACEMSSU	CAMUSES
ACEMSTT	METCAST
ACEMSTU	MUCATES
ACENNOS	ANCONES
	SONANCE
ACENNOT	CONNATE
ACENNOY	NOYANCE
ACENNOZ	CANZONE
ACENNRS	SCANNER
ACENNRY	CANNERY
ACENNST	NASCENT
ACENNSU	NUANCES
ACENNTY	TENANCY
ACENOOR	CORONAE
ACENOPT	PATONCE
ACENOPU	PONCEAU
ACENORS	CARNOSE
	COARSEN
	CORNEAS
	EARCONS
	ENACTOR
ACENORT	ENACTOR
ACENOSS	CASSONE
ACENOST	COSTEAN
	OCTANES
ACENOTT	ATTONCE
ACENOTV	CENTAVO
ACENPRR	PRANCER
ACENPRS	PRANCES
ACENPRU	PRAUNCE
ACENPST	CATNEPS
ACENPSU	PAUNCES
	UNCAPES
ACENPSW	PAWNCES
ACENPTT	PENTACT
ACENPTY	PATENCY
ACENRSS	ANCRESS
	CASERNS
ACENRST	CANTERS
	CARNETS
	NECTARS
	RECANTS
	SCANTER
	TANRECS
	TRANCES
ACENRSU	SURANCE
ACENRSV	CAVERNS
	CRAVENS
ACENRSY	CARNEYS
	SCENARY
ACENRSZ	ZARNECS
ACENRTT	TRANECT
ACENRTU	CENTAUR
	UNCRATE
	UNTRACE
ACENRTY	ENCRATY
	NECTARY
ACENSST	ASCENTS
	SECANTS
	STANCES
ACENSSU	UNCASES
	USANCES
ACENSTT	CANTEST
ACENSTU	NUTCASE
ACENSUV	VAUNCES
ACEOOPP	APOCOPE
ACEOOTZ	ECTOZOA
ACEOPRX	EXOCARP
ACEOPST	CAPOTES
	SCOPATE
	TOECAPS
ACEOPSW	COWPEAS
ACEOPTU	OUTPACE
ACEORRS	COARSER
ACEORRT	ACROTER
	CREATOR
	REACTOR
ACEORSS	ROSACES
ACEORST	COASTER
	COATERS
ACEORSU	ACEROUS
	CAROUSE
ACEORSX	COAXERS
ACEORTU	OUTRACE
ACEORTV	OVERACT
ACEORTX	EXACTOR
ACEOSSU	CASEOUS
ACEOSTT	COSTATE
ACEOSTU	ACETOUS
ACEOSTV	AVOCETS
	OCTAVES
ACEOTTV	CAVETTO
ACEOTUU	AUTOCUE
ACEOTUX	COTEAUX
ACEPPRS	CAPPERS
ACEPRRS	CARPERS
	SCARPER
	SCRAPER
ACEPRSS	ESCARPS
	PARSECS
	SCRAPES
	SPACERS
ACEPRST	CARPETS
	PRECAST
	SPECTRA
ACEPRSU	APERCUS
	SCAUPER
ACEPRTU	CAPTURE
ACEPSST	ASPECTS
ACEPSTU	CUSPATE
	TEACUPS
ACEQRTU	RACQUET
ACEQSSU	CASQUES
	SACQUES
ACEQSTU	ACQUEST
ACERRSS	CRASSER
	SCARERS
	SCARRES
ACERRST	CARTERS
	CRATERS
	TRACERS
ACERRSU	CURARES
ACERRSV	CARVERS
	CRAVERS
ACERRSY	CRAYERS
ACERRTT	RETRACT
ACERRTY	TRACERY
ACERRUV	VERRUCA
ACERRVY	CARVERY
ACERSST	ACTRESS
	CASTERS
	RECASTS
ACERSSU	ARCUSES
	CAUSERS
	CESURAS
	SAUCERS
	SUCRASE
ACERSSV	SCARVES
ACERSSY	CARSEYS
	SCRAYES
ACERSTT	SCATTER
ACERSTU	ACTURES
	CAUTERS
	CRUSTAE
	CURATES
ACERSTY	SECTARY
ACERTTT	TETRACT
ACERTTU	CURTATE
ACERTTX	EXTRACT
ACERTTY	CATTERY
ACERTUV	CURVATE
ACERTUX	CURTAXE
ACERTUY	CAUTERY
ACESSTT	STACTES
ACESSTU	CAESTUS
	CUESTAS
ACESSTY	CYTASES
	ECSTASY
ACESSUY	CAUSEYS
	CAYUSES
ACESTTU	ACUTEST
	SCUTATE
ACESTTY	TESTACY
ACESTUY	EUSTACY
ACFFHSU	CHAUFFS
ACFFIIT	CAITIFF
ACFFIKM	MAFFICK
ACFFILT	AFFLICT
ACFFIRT	TRAFFIC
ACFFIRY	FARCIFY
ACFFLSS	SCLAFFS
ACFGHIN	CHAFING
ACFGINR	FARCING
ACFGINS	FACINGS
ACFHIST	CATFISH

ACFHISU	FUCHSIA	ACGILMY	MYALGIC	ACHILLO	LOCHIAL		NOMARCH
ACFHLNU	FLAUNCH	ACGILNN	LANCING	ACHILLP	PHALLIC	ACHMNRU	UNCHARM
ACFHNOU	FAUCHON	ACGILNO	COALING	ACHILLS	CHALLIS	ACHMOPR	CAMPHOR
ACFHRTY	FRATCHY	ACGILNP	PLACING	ACHILLT	THALLIC	ACHMORS	CHROMAS
ACFIILN	FINICAL	ACGILNR	CARLING	ACHILMO	MALICHO	ACHMORZ	MACHZOR
ACFIKNN	FINNACK	ACGILNS	LACINGS	ACHILOR	CHORIAL	ACHMOST	STOMACH
ACFILNO	FOLACIN		SCALING	ACHILOS	SCHOLIA	ACHMSSU	SUMACHS
ACFILRY	CLARIFY	ACGILNT	CATLING	ACHILPS	CALIPHS	ACHMSUW	CUMSHAW
ACFILSS	FISCALS		TALCING	ACHILRS	ARCHILS	ACHNNOS	CHANSON
ACFIMOR	ACIFORM	ACGILNU	CINGULA		CARLISH	ACHNORS	ANCHORS
ACFIMSS	FASCISM		GLUCINA	ACHILRY	CHARILY		ARCHONS
ACFINNS	FINNACS	ACGILNV	CALVING	ACHILST	CHITALS		RANCHOS
ACFINNY	INFANCY	ACGILNW	CLAWING	ACHILSY	CLAYISH	ACHNORT	CHANTOR
ACFINOT	FACTION	ACGILNY	CLAYING	ACHILWY	LICHWAY	ACHNOSS	SANCHOS
ACFINRS	FARCINS	ACGILOS	CALIGOS	ACHIMNO	MANIHOC	ACHNOST	CHATONS
ACFINRT	FRANTIC	ACGILRS	GARLICS	ACHIMOS	CHAMISO	ACHNOSY	ONYCHAS
	INFARCT	ACGIMMN	CAMMING		CHAMOIS	ACHNOTY	TACHYON
	INFRACT	ACGIMNO	COAMING	ACHIMRS	CHARISM	ACHNOUY	CHANOYU
ACFINRY	CARNIFY	ACGIMNP	CAMPING	ACHIMSS	CHIASMS	ACHNOVY	ANCHOVY
ACFIOSS	FIASCOS	ACGIMNU	CAUMING		SCHISMA	ACHNPSS	SCHNAPS
ACFIPRY	CAPRIFY	ACGINNN	CANNING	ACHIMST	MASTICH	ACHNPUY	PAUNCHY
ACFIRSY	SACRIFY	ACGINNR	CRANING		TACHISM	ACHNRTY	CHANTRY
	SCARIFY		RANCING	ACHINNU	UNCHAIN	ACHNRUY	RAUNCHY
ACFISST	FASCIST	ACGINNS	CANINGS	ACHINOP	APHONIC		UNCHARY
ACFKLSU	SACKFUL	ACGINNT	CANTING	ACHINOY	ONYCHIA	ACHNSTU	CANTHUS
ACFLLOY	FOCALLY	ACGINOR	ORGANIC	ACHINPS	SPINACH		CHAUNTS
ACFLNOS	FALCONS	ACGINOS	ANGICOS	ACHINRS	CHINARS		STAUNCH
	FLACONS	ACGINOT	COATING	ACHINRZ	ZARNICH	ACHNSTY	SNATCHY
ACFLNSU	CANFULS		COTINGA	ACHINTX	XANTHIC	ACHOOST	CAHOOTS
ACFLOST	OLFACTS	ACGINOX	COAXING	ACHINUV	CHAUVIN	ACHOPRT	TOPARCH
ACFLRUU	FURCULA	ACGINPP	CAPPING	ACHIOPT	APHOTIC	ACHOPRY	CHARPOY
ACFLTTU	TACTFUL	ACGINPR	CARPING	ACHIORT	CHARIOT	ACHOPSY	POCHAYS
ACFLTUY	FACULTY	ACGINPS	SCAPING		HARICOT	ACHORST	ORCHATS
ACFMSTU	FACTUMS		SPACING	ACHIPPS	SAPPHIC	ACHORSU	AUROCHS
ACFNSTU	UNFACTS	ACGINRS	ARCINGS	ACHIPST	HAPTICS	ACHPRSS	SCARPHS
ACFORST	FACTORS		RACINGS		PATHICS	ACHRSST	SCARTHS
	FORCATS		SACRING		SPATHIC	ACHRSTY	STARCHY
ACFORTY	FACTORY		SCARING	ACHIPTU	CHUPATI	ACHRSUU	URACHUS
ACGGINR	GRACING	ACGINRT	CARTING	ACHIPTW	WHIPCAT	ACHSSTU	CUSHATS
ACGGIOS	AGOGICS		CRATING	ACHIQRU	CHARQUI	ACHSSTY	STACHYS
ACGGRSY	SCRAGGY		TRACING	ACHIQSU	QUAICHS	ACHSSUW	CUSHAWS
ACGHIKN	HACKING	ACGINRV	CARVING	ACHIRRT	TRIARCH	ACHSTUW	WAUCHTS
ACGHIMO	OGHAMIC		CRAVING	ACHIRTU	HAIRCUT	ACHSTUY	CYATHUS
ACGHINR	ARCHING	ACGINRZ	CRAZING	ACHIRTY	CHARITY	ACIIKNN	CANIKIN
	CHAGRIN	ACGINSS	CASINGS	ACHISSS	CHASSIS	ACIIKRS	AIRSICK
	CHARING	ACGINST	ACTINGS	ACHISST	SCAITHS	ACIILMM	MIMICAL
ACGHINS	ACHINGS		CASTING	ACHISTT	CATTISH	ACIILNR	CLARINI
	CASHING	ACGINSU	CAUSING		CHATTIS	ACIILNS	SALICIN
	CHASING		SAUCING		TACHIST		SINICAL
ACGHINT	GNATHIC	ACGINSV	CAVINGS	ACHKKSU	CHUKKAS	ACIILOV	VILIACO
ACGHINW	CHAWING	ACGINSW	CAWINGS	ACHKLST	KLATSCH	ACIILRY	CILIARY
	CHINWAG	ACGINTT	CATTING	ACHKMMO	HAMMOCK	ACIILSS	SILICAS
ACGHIOR	CHORAGI	ACGIRST	GASTRIC	ACHKOPS	HOPSACK	ACIILST	ITALICS
ACGHIPR	GRAPHIC	ACGKMMO	GAMMOCK	ACHKORS	CHOKRAS	ACIILSU	ILIACUS
ACGHIRS	SCRAIGH	ACGKORV	GARVOCK	ACHKOSS	HASSOCK	ACIILSV	CLIVIAS
ACGHLTU	CLAUGHT	ACGLLPU	CUPGALL		SHACKOS	ACIILTY	LAICITY
ACGHNRU	GRAUNCH	ACGLNOR	CLANGOR	ACHKOSW	WHACKOS	ACIIMMN	MINICAM
ACGHOSU	GAUCHOS	ACGLOSU	CAGOULS	ACHKOTT	HATTOCK	ACIIMMS	MIASMIC
ACGHRRU	CURRAGH	ACGNNOR	CRANNOG	ACHKRSU	CHUKARS	ACIIMNR	CRIMINA
ACGHRSU	SCRAUGH	ACGNOOT	OCTAGON	ACHKSTW	THWACKS	ACIIMOT	COMITIA
ACGIILN	ALGINIC	ACGNORS	GARCONS	ACHLLOO	ALCOHOL	ACIIMST	ISMATIC
ACGIITU	AUGITIC	ACGNOSS	GASCONS	ACHLLOR	CHLORAL		ITACISM
ACGIJKN	JACKING	ACGORRY	GYROCAR	ACHLMSY	CHLAMYS	ACIINNO	ANIONIC
ACGIKLN	CALKING	ACGORSU	COUGARS	ACHLMYY	ALCHYMY	ACIINNS	NIACINS
	LACKING	ACGORUU	COUGUAR	ACHLNOS	LOCHANS	ACIINOS	ASINICO
ACGIKNP	PACKING	ACGSTTU	CATGUTS	ACHLNOY	HALCYON	ACIINOV	AVIONIC
ACGIKNR	ARCKING	ACHHIRS	RHACHIS	ACHLNTU	TULCHAN	ACIINPS	PISCINA
	CARKING	ACHHOST	TOSHACH		UNLATCH	ACIINTT	TITANIC
	CRAKING	ACHHPPU	CHUPPAH	ACHLOPR	RAPLOCH	ACIIPPR	PRIAPIC
	RACKING	ACHHTTT	THATCHT	ACHLOPT	POTLACH	ACIIPRT	PIRATIC
ACGIKNS	CAKINGS	ACHIIKM	KAMICHI	ACHLORS	CHORALS	ACIIRST	SATIRIC
	CASKING	ACHIILS	ISCHIAL		LORCHAS	ACIIRTT	TRIATIC
	SACKING	ACHIIMS	CHIASMI		SCHOLAR	ACIJUZZ	JACUZZI
ACGIKNT	TACKING	ACHIIPS	PACHISI	ACHLORT	TROCHAL	ACIKLNS	CALKINS
ACGIKNV	VACKING	ACHIJKS	HIJACKS	ACHLOSW	SALCHOW	ACIKLOR	AIRLOCK
ACGIKNY	YACKING	ACHIJNT	JACINTH	ACHLOTY	ACOLYTH	ACIKLTY	TACKILY
ACGILLN	CALLING	ACHIKRS	RICKSHA	ACHLPST	SPLATCH	ACIKMOO	OOMIACK
ACGILLO	LOGICAL	ACHIKRY	HAYRICK	ACHLTUZ	CHALUTZ	ACIKMPR	RAMPICK
ACGILMN	CALMING	ACHIKSS	SHICKSA	ACHMNOR	MONARCH		

ACIKMPW	PICKMAW	ACIMRSS	RACISMS	ACJKKSY	SKYJACK
ACIKNNP	PANNICK	ACIMRST	MATRICS	ACJKLOW	LOCKJAW
ACIKNPS	PANICKS	ACIMRSZ	CZARISM	ACJKNNO	JANNOCK
ACIKNPY	PANICKY	ACIMSST	MASTICS	ACJKOPS	PAJOCKS
ACIKNRS	NICKARS		MISCAST	ACJKOPT	JACKPOT
ACIKNST	CATKINS	ACIMSTT	TACTISM	ACJLORU	JOCULAR
	CATSKIN	ACINNOT	ACTINON	ACJMNTU	MUNTJAC
ACIKNTT	TINTACK		CANTION	ACJPTUU	CAJUPUT
ACIKOPS	PAIOCKS		CONTAIN	ACKLLOP	POLLACK
ACIKPRT	PATRICK	ACINNOZ	CANZONI	ACKLLOY	LAYLOCK
ACIKPSS	ASPICKS	ACINNST	STANNIC	ACKLLSY	SLACKLY
ACIKRST	KARSTIC	ACINNSY	CYANINS	ACKLMNO	LOCKMAN
ACILLMS	MISCALL	ACINNTU	ANNICUT	ACKLMOR	ARMLOCK
ACILLRY	LYRICAL	ACINOPT	CAPTION		LOCKRAM
ACILLSS	SCILLAS		PACTION	ACKLNOU	UNCLOAK
ACILMNO	LIMACON	ACINOQU	COQUINA	ACKLORW	WARLOCK
ACILMOT	COMITAL	ACINORR	CARRION	ACKLORY	ROCKLAY
ACILMPS	PLASMIC	ACINORS	SARONIC	ACKLOSS	LASSOCK
ACILMSU	MUSICAL	ACINORT	CAROTIN	ACKMMMO	MAMMOCK
ACILNNY	CANNILY	ACINOSS	CAISSON	ACKMMTT	MATTOCK
ACILNOR	CLARINO		CASINOS	ACKNNOW	ACKNOWN
	CLARION		CASSINO	ACKNOSW	ACKNOWS
ACILNOS	OILCANS	ACINOST	ACTIONS	ACKNPRS	PRANCKS
ACILNOU	INOCULA		CATIONS	ACKNPSU	UNPACKS
ACILNOZ	CALZONI	ACINOSU	ACINOUS	ACKNSTU	UNSTACK
ACILNPS	CAPLINS	ACINOSY	SYCONIA		UNTACKS
	INCLASP	ACINOTT	TACTION	ACKOPRR	PARROCK
ACILNPY	PLIANCY	ACINOTU	AUCTION	ACKOPSY	YAPOCKS
ACILNST	TINCALS		CAUTION	ACKORRT	TARROCK
ACILNSU	UNCIALS	ACINPRT	CANTRIP	ACLLLOY	LOCALLY
ACILNTU	LUNATIC	ACINPRY	CYPRIAN	ACLLOOR	COROLLA
ACILNUV	VINCULA	ACINPSS	PANISCS	ACLLOPS	SCALLOP
ACILOPT	COALPIT	ACINPST	CATNIPS	ACLLORS	COLLARS
	OPTICAL	ACINQTU	QUANTIC	ACLLORU	LOCULAR
	TOPICAL	ACINRSS	ARCSINS	ACLLOSU	CALLOUS
ACILORR	RACLOIR	ACINRSU	CRUSIAN	ACLLOSW	CALLOWS
ACILORV	CORIVAL	ACINRTT	TANTRIC	ACLLOVY	VOCALLY
ACILOSS	SOCIALS	ACINRTU	CURTAIN	ACLMNOO	LOCOMAN
ACILOST	STOICAL		TURACIN	ACLMNUY	CALUMNY
ACILOTV	VOLATIC	ACINSTU	ANICUTS	ACLMORS	CLAMORS
	VOLTAIC		NAUTICS	ACLMORU	CLAMOUR
ACILOTX	TOXICAL	ACINSUV	VICUNAS	ACLMSTU	TALCUMS
ACILPRT	CLIPART	ACIOPRS	PROSAIC	ACLMSUU	LUCUMAS
ACILPST	PLACITS	ACIOPRT	APRICOT	ACLMSUY	MASCULY
	PLASTIC		PAROTIC	ACLNOOR	CORONAL
ACILPSU	SPICULA		PATRICO	ACLNOOT	COOLANT
ACILPTY	TYPICAL	ACIOPST	COPITAS	ACLNOOV	VOLCANO
ACILRSU	URACILS	ACIOPTT	APTOTIC	ACLNORU	CORNUAL
ACILRTU	CURTAIL	ACIOPTY	OPACITY		COURLAN
	TRUCIAL	ACIORRS	CORSAIR	ACLNOUV	UNVOCAL
ACILRTY	CLARITY	ACIORSU	CARIOUS	ACLNPSU	UNCLASP
ACILRYZ	CRAZILY		CURIOSA	ACLNRTU	TRUNCAL
ACILSSS	CLASSIS	ACIORTT	RICOTTA	ACLNSTY	SCANTLY
ACILSSU	CLUSIAS	ACIOSST	SCOTIAS	ACLNSUV	VULCANS
ACILSUY	SAUCILY	ACIOSSV	OVISACS	ACLOOPP	ALCOPOP
ACILTTY	CATTILY	ACIPRSY	PISCARY	ACLOPRT	CALTROP
	TACITLY	ACIPRVY	PRIVACY		PROCTAL
ACILTUV	VICTUAL	ACIPSST	SPASTIC	ACLOPRU	COPULAR
ACIMNOP	CAMPION	ACIPSTT	TIPCATS		CUPOLAR
ACIMNOR	MARCONI	ACIPTUY	PAUCITY	ACLOPSU	COPULAS
ACIMNOS	CAMIONS	ACIQRTU	QUARTIC		CUPOLAS
	CONIMAS	ACIQSTU	ACQUIST		SCOPULA
	MANIOCS		ACQUITS	ACLOPSY	CALYPSO
	MASONIC	ACIRRSS	SIRCARS	ACLOPTY	POLYACT
ACIMNRU	CRANIUM	ACIRRST	TRICARS	ACLORRS	CORRALS
	CUMARIN	ACIRRSU	CURARIS	ACLORST	CARLOTS
ACIMNTT	CATMINT	ACIRSST	RACISTS		CROTALS
ACIMOOS	OOMIACS		SACRIST		SCROTAL
ACIMOPT	POTAMIC	ACIRSSU	CUIRASS	ACLORSU	CAROLUS
ACIMOSS	MOSAICS	ACIRSTT	ASTRICT		OCULARS
ACIMOST	MATICOS	ACIRSTU	URTICAS		OSCULAR
	SOMATIC	ACIRSTW	TWISCAR		RUCOLAS
ACIMOSV	VOMICAS	ACIRSTY	SATYRIC	ACLORUV	VOCULAR
ACIMPRT	CRAMPIT	ACIRSTZ	CZARIST	ACLOSST	COSTALS
	PTARMIC	ACISSTT	STATICS	ACLOSTU	LOCUSTA
ACIMPRY	PRIMACY	ACISSTU	CASUIST		TALCOUS
ACIMPSS	SCAMPIS	ACISTTU	CATSUIT	ACLOSTW	COTWALS
	SPASMIC	ACISTUV	VACUIST	ACLPRTY	CRYPTAL
ACIMPST	IMPACTS	ACITUVY	VACUITY	ACLPRUU	CUPULAR

ACLRSSW	SCRAWLS	ACNNNOS	CANNONS		
ACLRSSY	CRASSLY	ACNNNUY	UNCANNY		
ACLRSTU	CRUSTAL	ACNNORY	CANONRY		
	CURTALS	ACNNOST	CANTONS		
ACLRSTY	CRYSTAL	ACNNOSY	CANYONS		
ACLRSWY	SCRAWLY		SONANCY		
ACLSSTU	CUTLASS	ACNNRSY	SCRANNY		
ACMNOPR	CRAMPON	ACNOOPS	POONACS		
ACMNOPY	COMPANY	ACNOORS	CORONAS		
ACMNORS	MACRONS		RACOONS		
ACMNORY	ACRONYM	ACNOORT	CARTOON		
ACMNOSS	MASCONS		CORANTO		
ACMNSTU	SANCTUM	ACNOPSW	SNOWCAP		
ACMOOST	SCOTOMA	ACNORRS	RANCORS		
ACMOPRT	COMPART	ACNORRU	RANCOUR		
ACMOPSS	COMPASS	ACNORST	CANTORS		
ACMOPST	COMPAST		CARTONS		
ACMORST	COMARTS		CONTRAS		
ACMORTW	CATWORM		CRATONS		
ACMOSST	MASCOTS	ACNORSU	NACROUS		
ACMOSTT	TOMCATS	ACNORSY	CRAYONS		
ACMOSTU	MOTUCAS	ACNORTT	CONTRAT		
ACMQTUU	CUMQUAT	ACNORTU	COURANT		
ACMRSSW	SCRAWMS	ACNOSSZ	SCAZONS		
ACMSSTU	MUSCATS	ACNOSTT	OCTANTS		
ACMSTUU	MUTUCAS	ACNOSTU	CONATUS		
ACMSUUV	VACUUMS		NOCTUAS		
			TOUCANS		
		ACNPRSY	SYNCARP		
		ACNRRTU	CURRANT		
		ACNRSTU	UNCARTS		
		ACNRSUY	UNSCARY		
		ACNRSWY	SCRAWNY		
		ACNRTUY	TRUANCY		
		ACOOPRR	CORPORA		
		ACOOPSU	OPACOUS		
		ACOOPTT	TOPCOAT		
		ACOORTU	TOURACO		
		ACOOSTV	OCTAVOS		
		ACOPRRT	CARPORT		
		ACOPRST	CAPTORS		
		ACOPSTU	UPCOAST		
		ACOPSTW	COWPATS		
		ACORRST	CARROTS		
			TROCARS		
		ACORRTT	TRACTOR		
		ACORRTU	CURATOR		
		ACORRTY	CARROTY		
		ACORSST	CASTORS		
		ACORSSU	SARCOUS		
		ACORSTT	COTTARS		
		ACORSTU	SURCOAT		

	TURACOS	ADDEGJU	ADJUDGE	ADDEMNU	MAUNDED	ADDLLRU	DULLARD
ACORSTV	CAVORTS	ADDEGLN	DANGLED	ADDEMOP	POMADED	ADDLOOS	SOLDADO
ACORSTY	CASTORY		GLADDEN	ADDEMRS	MADDERS	ADDLTWY	TWADDLY
ACORSUU	RAUCOUS	ADDEGLR	GLADDER	ADDEMST	MADDEST	ADDMNOS	DODMANS
ACORSYZ	CORYZAS	ADDEGRS	GADDERS	ADDEMUW	DWAUMED		ODDSMAN
ACOSTTU	OUTCAST	ADDEGRU	GUARDED	ADDENOR	ADORNED	ADDMOOS	ADDOOMS
ACOSUUV	VACUOUS	ADDEHIR	DIHEDRA	ADDENOT	DONATED	ADDNNOR	DONNARD
ACPPRSY	SCRAPPY	ADDEHIS	HADDIES		NODATED	ADDOORS	DORADOS
ACPSSTU	CATSUPS	ADDEHKS	KEDDAHS	ADDENOU	DUODENA	ADDOPSY	DASYPOD
	UPCASTS	ADDEHLN	HANDLED	ADDENPU	PUDENDA	ADDORST	DOTARDS
ACPSTUU	USUCAPT	ADDEHOR	HOARDED	ADDENRS	DANDERS	ADDQSUY	SQUADDY
ACRRSTU	CRATURS	ADDEHRS	SHARDED	ADDENRT	DRANTED	ADEEEFY	FEDAYEE
ACRSTTU	TRACTUS	ADDEIIK	DIDAKEI	ADDENRU	DAUNDER	ADEEEMN	DEMEANE
ADDDDEL	DADDLED	ADDEIIS	DAISIED	ADDENSS	SADDENS	ADEEERR	ARREEDE
ADDDDOR	DODDARD	ADDEILL	DALLIED	ADDENSU	ASUDDEN	ADEEERX	EXEDRAE
ADDDEER	DREADED		DIALLED	ADDENSY	SDAYNED	ADEEESW	SEAWEED
ADDDEFL	FADDLED	ADDEILP	PLAIDED	ADDENTU	DAUNTED	ADEEFGU	FEAGUED
ADDDEGL	GLADDED	ADDEILR	DIEDRAL		UNDATED	ADEEFHS	SHEAFED
ADDDEIL	DAIDLED		DRAILED	ADDEOPT	ADOPTED	ADEEFIR	AREFIED
ADDDEIS	DADDIES	ADDEILS	DAIDLES	ADDEORS	DEODARS		FEDARIE
ADDDEIW	WADDIED		LADDIES	ADDEPPR	DRAPPED	ADEEFKR	FREAKED
ADDDELN	DANDLED	ADDEILT	DILATED	ADDEPRS	PADDERS	ADEEFLR	FEDERAL
ADDDELP	PADDLED	ADDEIMR	ADMIRED	ADDEPTU	UPDATED	ADEEFLT	DEFLATE
ADDDELR	RADDLED		MARDIED	ADDERSS	ADDRESS	ADEEFMS	DEFAMES
ADDDELS	DADDLES	ADDEIMS	DIADEMS	ADDERST	ADDREST	ADEEFNS	DEAFENS
	SADDLED	ADDEIMX	ADMIXED		RADDEST	ADEEFPR	PREFADE
ADDDELW	DAWDLED	ADDEINO	ADENOID	ADDERSW	SWARDED	ADEEFRT	DRAFTEE
	WADDLED	ADDEINP	PANDIED	ADDERSY	DRYADES	ADEEFRW	WAFERED
ADDDENO	DEODAND	ADDEINR	DANDIER	ADDERTT	DRATTED	ADEEFST	DEAFEST
ADDDENS	ADDENDS		DRAINED	ADDESST	SADDEST		DEFASTE
ADDDEQU	QUADDED	ADDEINS	DANDIES	ADDESTU	ADUSTED		DEFEATS
ADDDGIN	DADDING		SDAINED		SUDATED		FEASTED
ADDDOOS	DOODADS	ADDEINU	UNAIDED	ADDFHIS	FADDISH	ADEEGGH	EGGHEAD
ADDEEEM	ADEEMED	ADDEINV	INVADED	ADDFIMS	FADDISM	ADEEGGL	ALEGGED
ADDEEFM	DEFAMED		VIDENDA	ADDFINY	DANDIFY	ADEEGGN	ENGAGED
ADDEEGR	DEGRADE	ADDEIOR	RADIOED	ADDFIST	FADDIST	ADEEGLL	ALLEDGE
ADDEEHL	HEALDED	ADDEIOT	TOADIED	ADDGGIN	GADDING		ALLEGED
ADDEEHR	ADHERED	ADDEIOV	AVOIDED	ADDGHIN	HADDING	ADEEGLM	GLEAMED
	REDHEAD	ADDEIPS	PADDIES	ADDGIIR	DIAGRID	ADEEGLN	GLEANED
ADDEEIR	READIED	ADDEIRR	ARRIDED	ADDGILN	ADDLING	ADEEGLR	REGALED
ADDEEIT	IDEATED	ADDEIRT	TARDIED	ADDGIMN	MADDING	ADEEGLT	TEAGLED
ADDEEKN	KNEADED	ADDEIST	TADDIES	ADDGINO	DADOING	ADEEGLU	LEAGUED
ADDEEKR	DAKERED	ADDEISV	ADVISED	ADDGINP	PADDING	ADEEGMN	ENDGAME
ADDEELM	MEDALED	ADDEISW	WADDIES	ADDGINU	DAUDING		MANEGED
ADDEELN	DELENDA	ADDEITU	AUDITED	ADDGINW	DAWDING		MENAGED
ADDEELP	PEDALED	ADDEJLY	JADEDLY		WADDING	ADEEGNR	ANGERED
	PLEADED	ADDEJNU	UNJADED	ADDGIOS	GADOIDS		DERANGE
ADDEELT	DELATED	ADDEJRU	ADJURED	ADDGLNO	GLADDON		ENRAGED
ADDEELY	DELAYED	ADDEKLR	DARKLED	ADDGMNO	GODDAMN		GRANDEE
ADDEEMN	AMENDED	ADDELLU	ALLUDED	ADDGOOS	OGDOADS		GRENADE
ADDEEMR	DREAMED		DUALLED	ADDGOOW	DAGWOOD	ADEEGNT	AGENTED
ADDEEMS	ADDEEMS	ADDELMW	DWALMED	ADDGORW	GODWARD		NEGATED
ADDEENS	DEADENS	ADDELNR	DANDLER	ADDGOSY	DOGDAYS	ADEEGNV	AVENGED
ADDEENV	ADVENED	ADDELNS	DANDLES	ADDHILS	LADDISH		VENDAGE
	DAVENED	ADDELNU	UNLADED	ADDHINP	DAPHNID	ADEEGOT	DOGEATE
ADDEENY	DENAYED	ADDELPP	DAPPLED	ADDHISS	SADDISH		GOATEED
ADDEEOT	DEODATE	ADDELPR	PADDLER		SIDDHAS	ADEEGRR	REGRADE
ADDEERR	DREADER	ADDELPS	PADDLES	ADDHITY	HYDATID	ADEEGRS	DRAGEES
ADDEERS	DEADERS	ADDELRS	LADDERS	ADDHOOS	DOODAHS		GREASED
ADDEERT	DERATED		RADDLES	ADDHSSU	SADDHUS	ADEEGRU	GUARDEE
	REDATED		SADDLER	ADDIINS	DISDAIN	ADEEGRV	GREAVED
ADDEERY	DERAYED	ADDELRT	DARTLED	ADDIKST	TSADDIK	ADEEGRW	RAGWEED
	YEARDED	ADDELRW	DAWDLER	ADDIKSZ	ZADDIKS		WAGERED
ADDEEST	DEADEST		DRAWLED	ADDIKTY	KATYDID	ADEEHIR	HEADIER
	SEDATED		WADDLER	ADDIKTZ	TZADDIK	ADEEHLR	HEDERAL
	STEADED	ADDELRY	DREADLY	ADDILMN	MIDLAND	ADEEHLS	LEASHED
ADDEEVW	ADVEWED		LADDERY	ADDILNY	DANDILY		SHEALED
ADDEFIR	FADDIER	ADDELSS	SADDLES	ADDILOS	DISLOAD	ADEEHLX	EXHALED
ADDEFLS	FADDLES	ADDELST	STADDLE	ADDIMNO	DIAMOND	ADEEHMN	HEADMEN
ADDEFLY	FADEDLY	ADDELSW	DAWDLES	ADDIMOR	DIADROM	ADEEHNN	HENNAED
ADDEFNU	UNFADED		SWADDLE	ADDIMRS	DIRDAMS	ADEEHNS	DASHEEN
ADDEFRT	DRAFTED		WADDLES	ADDIMSY	DISMAYD	ADEEHNV	HAVENED
ADDEFRU	DEFRAUD	ADDELTW	TWADDLE		MIDDAYS	ADEEHPR	EPHEDRA
ADDEFRW	DWARFED	ADDELYZ	DAZEDLY	ADDINOR	ANDROID	ADEEHRR	ADHERER
ADDEGGL	DAGGLED	ADDELZZ	DAZZLED	ADDINRY	DIANDRY		REHEARD
ADDEGGR	DRAGGED	ADDEMMR	DRAMMED	ADDIPRS	DISPRAD	ADEEHRS	ADHERES
ADDEGHO	GODHEAD	ADDEMMW	DWAMMED	ADDIQST	TSADDIQ		HEADERS
ADDEGIL	GLADDIE	ADDEMNS	DEMANDS	ADDIQTZ	TZADDIQ		HEARSED
ADDEGIN	DEADING		MADDENS	ADDIRZZ	DIZZARD		SHEARED

ADEEHRT	EARTHED	ADEELUV	DEVALUE	ADEESST	SEDATES	ADEGGGL	GAGGLED
	HEARTED	ADEEMNR	AMENDER	ADEESSY	ESSAYED	ADEGGHL	HAGGLED
ADEEHRV	HAVERED		ENARMED	ADEESTT	ESTATED	ADEGGHS	SHAGGED
ADEEHRX	EXHEDRA		MEANDER	ADEESTU	SAUTEED	ADEGGIR	DAGGIER
ADEEHST	HEADSET		REAMEND	ADEESTW	SWEATED	ADEGGIS	GADGIES
ADEEHSV	SHEAVED		RENAMED	ADEESTY	YEASTED	ADEGGIU	GAUDGIE
ADEEHSY	HAYSEED	ADEEMNS	AMENDES	ADEESVY	SAVEYED		GUIDAGE
ADEEIJT	JADEITE		DEMEANS	ADEETUX	EXUDATE	ADEGGLR	DRAGGLE
ADEEILM	EMAILED	ADEEMNT	ENTAMED	ADEFFFL	FLAFFED		GARGLED
	LIMEADE	ADEEMNY	DEMAYNE	ADEFFGR	GRAFFED		RAGGLED
ADEEILN	ALIENED	ADEEMOS	OEDEMAS	ADEFFIN	AFFINED	ADEGGLS	DAGGLES
	DELAINE	ADEEMPR	EMPARED	ADEFFIP	PIAFFED		SLAGGED
ADEEILR	LEADIER	ADEEMRR	DREAMER	ADEFFIR	DAFFIER	ADEGGLW	WAGGLED
ADEEILS	AEDILES		REARMED	ADEFFIS	DAFFIES	ADEGGNS	SNAGGED
	DEISEAL	ADEEMRS	REMADES	ADEFFIX	AFFIXED	ADEGGRS	DAGGERS
ADEEILY	EYELIAD		REMEADS	ADEFFLM	MAFFLED	ADEGGRY	RAGGEDY
ADEEIMN	DEMAINE		SMEARED	ADEFFLR	RAFFLED	ADEGGST	GADGETS
ADEEIMT	MEDIATE	ADEEMST	STEAMED	ADEFFLW	WAFFLED		STAGGED
ADEEINN	ADENINE	ADEEMSU	MEDUSAE	ADEFFNY	NYAFFED	ADEGGSW	SWAGGED
ADEEINS	ANISEED	ADEEMSW	MAWSEED	ADEFFQU	QUAFFED	ADEGHIN	HEADING
ADEEIRR	READIER	ADEEMTW	MATWEED	ADEFFST	STAFFED	ADEGHIR	HEADRIG
ADEEIRS	DEARIES	ADEEMWY	MAYWEED	ADEFFUW	WAUFFED	ADEGHIS	HIDAGES
	READIES	ADEENNS	ENNEADS	ADEFGGL	FLAGGED	ADEGHJU	JUGHEAD
ADEEIRW	WEARIED	ADEENNX	ANNEXED	ADEFGGR	FRAGGED	ADEGHLU	LAUGHED
ADEEISS	DISEASE	ADEENPS	SNEAPED	ADEFGLN	FANGLED	ADEGHMO	HOMAGED
	SEASIDE		SPEANED		FLANGED	ADEGHNP	PHANGED
ADEEIST	IDEATES	ADEENRS	DEANERS	ADEFGOR	FORAGED	ADEGHNS	GNASHED
ADEEITV	DEVIATE		ENDEARS	ADEFGOT	FAGOTED		HAGDENS
ADEEJSY	DEEJAYS	ADEENRU	UNEARED	ADEFGOU	FOUGADE	ADEGHNW	WHANGED
ADEEKNR	KNEADER	ADEENRV	RAVENED	ADEFGRS	DEFRAGS	ADEGHPR	GRAPHED
	NAKEDER	ADEENRY	DEANERY	ADEFGRT	GRAFTED	ADEGHST	GHASTED
ADEEKNS	SNEAKED		RENAYED	ADEFHIT	FAITHED	ADEGHUW	WAUGHED
ADEEKNW	WAKENED		YEARNED	ADEFHLS	FLASHED	ADEGILL	GALLIED
ADEEKRS	SKEARED	ADEENST	STANDEE	ADEFHRW	WHARFED	ADEGILN	ALIGNED
ADEEKRW	WREAKED		STEANED	ADEFHST	SHAFTED		DEALING
ADEEKTW	TWEAKED	ADEENSV	ADVENES	ADEFILL	FLAILED		LEADING
ADEEKWY	WEEKDAY	ADEENTT	DENTATE	ADEFILS	DISLEAF	ADEGILO	GEOIDAL
ADEELLS	ALLSEED	ADEEOPT	ADOPTEE	ADEFIMN	INFAMED	ADEGILR	GLADIER
ADEELLY	ALLEYED	ADEEORS	OREADES	ADEFIMS	DISFAME		GLAIRED
ADEELMP	EMPALED	ADEEORW	OARWEED	ADEFINR	FRIANDE	ADEGILS	SILAGED
ADEELMR	EMERALD	ADEEPPR	PAPERED	ADEFINT	DEFIANT	ADEGILT	LIGATED
ADEELMS	MEASLED	ADEEPRS	PREASED		FAINTED		TAIGLED
ADEELMT	MEDALET		SPEARED	ADEFIRS	FRAISED	ADEGILV	GLAIVED
	METALED	ADEEPRT	ADEPTER	ADEFIST	DAFTIES	ADEGINR	AREDING
ADEELMU	AEMULED		PREDATE		FADIEST		DEARING
ADEELMY	YEALMED		TAPERED	ADEFITX	FIXATED		DERAIGN
ADEELNP	DEPLANE	ADEEPRV	DEPRAVE	ADEFKLN	FANKLED		EARDING
ADEELNR	LEARNED		PERVADE		FLANKED		GRADINE
ADEELNS	LEADENS	ADEEPSS	PESADES	ADEFKNR	FRANKED		GRAINED
ADEELNT	EDENTAL	ADEEQRU	QUAERED	ADEFLLN	ELFLAND		READING
	LATENED	ADEEQTU	EQUATED	ADEFLMM	FLAMMED	ADEGINS	AGNISED
ADEELPR	PEARLED	ADEERRR	DREARER	ADEFLNN	FENLAND	ADEGINV	DEAVING
	PLEADER	ADEERRS	DREARES	ADEFLOT	FLOATED		EVADING
ADEELPS	DELAPSE		READERS	ADEFLPP	FLAPPED	ADEGINW	WINDAGE
	ELAPSED		REDSEAR	ADEFLRS	FARDELS	ADEGINY	YEADING
	PLEASED		REREADS	ADEFLRU	DAREFUL	ADEGINZ	AGNIZED
ADEELPT	PLEATED	ADEERRT	RETREAD	ADEFLTT	FLATTED	ADEGIOT	GODETIA
ADEELRS	DEALERS		TREADER	ADEFLTU	DEFAULT	ADEGIRS	AGRISED
	LEADERS	ADEERRV	AVERRED		FAULTED	ADEGIRU	GAUDIER
	REDEALS	ADEERSS	RESEDAS	ADEFMNU	UNFAMED	ADEGIRZ	AGRIZED
ADEELRT	ALERTED	ADEERST	DEAREST	ADEFNRS	FARDENS	ADEGIST	AGISTED
	ALTERED		DERATES	ADEFNSU	UNDEAFS	ADEGISU	AGUISED
	REDEALT		ESTRADE	ADEFNUZ	UNFAZED		GAUDIES
	RELATED		REASTED	ADEFOOS	SEAFOOD	ADEGISV	VISAGED
	TREADLE		REDATES	ADEFORS	FEDORAS	ADEGIUV	VIDUAGE
ADEELRW	LEEWARD		SEDATER	ADEFORV	FAVORED	ADEGIUZ	AGUIZED
ADEELRX	RELAXED		STEARED	ADEFORY	FEODARY	ADEGJLN	JANGLED
ADEELRY	DELAYER		TASERED		FORAYED	ADEGLLU	ULLAGED
	LAYERED	ADEERSV	ADVERSE	ADEFPPR	FRAPPED	ADEGLMN	MANGLED
	RELAYED		EVADERS	ADEFPRR	PREFARD	ADEGLMR	MALGRED
ADEELST	DELATES	ADEERSW	DRAWEES	ADEFRRT	DRAFTER	ADEGLMU	GLAUMED
	STEALED	ADEERTT	ARETTED		REDRAFT	ADEGLNN	ENDLANG
ADEELSV	SLEAVED		TREATED	ADEFRRW	DWARFER	ADEGLNR	DANGLER
ADEELSW	SWEALED	ADEERTV	AVERTED	ADEFRST	STRAFED		GNARLED
ADEELTT	LADETTE		TAVERED	ADEFRSU	FADEURS	ADEGLNS	DANGLES
ADEELTV	VALETED	ADEERTW	DEWATER	ADEFRSW	SWARFED		GLANDES
	VELATED		TARWEED	ADEFRSY	DEFRAYS		SLANGED
ADEELTX	EXALTED		WATERED	ADEFRUY	FEUDARY	ADEGLNT	TANGLED
ADEELTZ	TEAZLED	ADEERVW	WAVERED	ADEFSTT	DAFTEST	ADEGLNU	LANGUED

ADEGLNW	WANGLED	ADEHKNS	SHANKED		DARKIES		SIDEARM
ADEGLOP	GALOPED	ADEHKNT	THANKED	ADEIKRT	TRAIKED	ADEIMRT	READMIT
ADEGLOT	GLOATED	ADEHKOR	HARDOKE	ADEILLR	DALLIER	ADEIMST	MISDATE
ADEGLPU	PLAGUED	ADEHKOT	KATHODE		DIALLER	ADEIMSV	VIDAMES
ADEGLRS	DARGLES	ADEHKRS	SHARKED		RALLIED	ADEIMSX	ADMIXES
ADEGLRU	RAGULED	ADEHLLO	HALLOED	ADEILLS	DALLIES	ADEIMTU	TAEDIUM
ADEGLRY	GRADELY	ADEHLLP	LAPHELD		DISLEAL	ADEIMTY	DAYTIME
ADEGLSS	GLASSED	ADEHLNR	HANDLER		LADDIES	ADEINNN	NANDINE
ADEGMNS	GADSMEN	ADEHLNS	HANDLES		SALLIED		NANNIED
ADEGMNU	GUDEMAN		HANDSEL	ADEILLT	TALLIED	ADEINOR	ANEROID
ADEGMRU	MAUGRED	ADEHLOS	SHOALED	ADEILLV	VIALLED	ADEINOS	ADONISE
ADEGNNO	NONAGED	ADEHLOT	LOATHED	ADEILLY	IDEALLY		ANODISE
ADEGNNU	DUNNAGE	ADEHLPS	PLASHED	ADEILMM	DILEMMA		SODAINE
ADEGNOP	PONDAGE	ADEHLRS	HARELDS	ADEILMP	IMPALED	ADEINOV	NAEVOID
ADEGNOR	GROANED		HERALDS		IMPLEAD	ADEINOX	DIOXANE
ADEGNOS	SONDAGE	ADEHLSS	HASSLED	ADEILMS	MAELIDS	ADEINOZ	ADONIZE
ADEGNOT	TANGOED		SLASHED		MEDIALS		ANODIZE
ADEGNOV	DOGVANE	ADEHLSW	SHAWLED		MISDEAL	ADEINPR	PARDINE
ADEGNOW	GOWANED	ADEHLTY	DEATHLY		MISLEAD	ADEINPS	PANDIES
	WAGONED	ADEHMMS	SHAMMED	ADEILMU	MIAULED		PANSIED
ADEGNPR	PRANGED	ADEHMMW	WHAMMED	ADEILNN	ANNELID		SPAINED
ADEGNPS	SPANGED	ADEHMNR	HERDMAN		LINDANE	ADEINPT	DEPAINT
ADEGNPU	UNPAGED	ADEHMOP	MOPHEAD	ADEILNP	PLAINED		PAINTED
ADEGNRR	GNARRED	ADEHMOR	HADROME	ADEILNS	DENIALS		PATINED
	GRANDER	ADEHMRS	DERHAMS		SNAILED	ADEINRR	DRAINER
ADEGNRS	DANGERS	ADEHMSS	SMASHED	ADEILNU	ALIUNDE		RANDIER
	GANDERS	ADEHNPS	DAPHNES		UNIDEAL	ADEINRS	RANDIES
	GARDENS	ADEHNNS	HANDERS	ADEILNV	ANDVILE		SANDIER
ADEGNRT	DRAGNET		HARDENS	ADEILNX	INDEXAL		SARDINE
	GRANTED	ADEHNRU	UNHEARD	ADEILOR	DARIOLE	ADEINRT	DETRAIN
ADEGNRU	ENGUARD	ADEHNSS	SNASHED	ADEILOS	DEASOIL		TRAINED
	RAUNGED	ADEHNST	HANDSET	ADEILOU	DOULEIA	ADEINRU	UNAIRED
ADEGNST	STANGED	ADEHNSU	UNHEADS	ADEILPP	APPLIED		URANIDE
ADEGNTU	GAUNTED	ADEHNTU	HAUNTED	ADEILPR	PEDRAIL	ADEINRV	INVADER
ADEGNTW	TWANGED	ADEHOOP	APEHOOD		PREDIAL		RAVINED
ADEGNUW	UNWAGED	ADEHOPX	HEXAPOD	ADEILPS	ALIPEDS	ADEINSS	SDAINES
ADEGORW	DOWAGER	ADEHORR	HOARDER		PAIDLES	ADEINST	DETAINS
	WORDAGE	ADEHOST	HOASTED		PALSIED		INSTEAD
ADEGOSS	DOSAGES	ADEHOSX	OXHEADS	ADEILPT	PLAITED		SAINTED
ADEGOST	DOGATES	ADEHPPW	WHAPPED		TALIPED		SATINED
	DOTAGES	ADEHPRS	PHRASED	ADEILQU	QUAILED		STAINED
ADEGOTT	TOGATED		SHARPED	ADEILRR	LARDIER	ADEINSV	INVADES
ADEGOVY	VOYAGED	ADEHPST	HEPTADS	ADEILRS	DERAILS	ADEINSW	DEWANIS
ADEGPRS	GRASPED		SPATHED		REDIALS	ADEINTT	TAINTED
	SPADGER	ADEHPSW	PSHAWED		SIDERAL	ADEINTU	AUDIENT
	SPARGED	ADEHQSU	QUASHED	ADEILRT	DILATER	ADEINTV	DEVIANT
ADEGPRU	UPGRADE	ADEHRRU	HURRAED		TRAILED	ADEINVV	NAVVIED
ADEGPUZ	UPGAZED	ADEHRSS	DASHERS	ADEILRV	VALIDER	ADEIOPS	ADIPOSE
ADEGRRS	GRADERS	ADEHRST	DEARTHS	ADEILRY	READILY	ADEIOPT	OPIATED
	REGARDS		HARDEST	ADEILSS	AIDLESS	ADEIORS	ROADIES
ADEGRSS	GRASSED		HATREDS		DEASILS		SOREDIA
ADEGRST	RADGEST		THREADS	ADEILST	DETAILS	ADEIORX	EXORDIA
ADEGRSU	SUGARED		TRASHED		DILATES	ADEIOST	IODATES
ADEGRTY	GYRATED	ADEHRTW	WRATHED	ADEILSU	AUDILES		TOADIES
	TRAGEDY	ADEHRTY	HYDRATE		DEASIUL	ADEIOSX	OXIDASE
ADEGRUU	AUGURED		THREADY	ADEILSV	DEVISAL	ADEIOSZ	DIAZOES
ADEGRUY	GAUDERY	ADEHSST	STASHED	ADEILSY	DIALYSE	ADEIOTX	OXIDATE
ADEGRYZ	AGRYZED	ADEHSSW	SWASHED		EYLIADS	ADEIOVV	VAIVODE
ADEGSSU	DEGAUSS	ADEHSTW	SWATHED	ADEILYZ	DIALYZE	ADEIOVW	WAIVODE
ADEHHOT	HOTHEAD	ADEHSYY	HEYDAYS	ADEIMMR	MERMAID	ADEIOWW	WAIWODE
ADEHHSS	SHASHED	ADEHUZZ	HUZZAED	ADEIMMS	MISMADE	ADEIPPR	DRAPPIE
ADEHIKS	DASHEKI	ADEIILR	DELIRIA	ADEIMNR	ADERMIN		PREPAID
ADEHIKV	KHEDIVA		IRIDEAL		INARMED	ADEIPPU	APPUIED
ADEHILN	INHALED	ADEIILS	DAILIES	ADEIMNS	DEMAINS	ADEIPRR	DRAPIER
ADEHILP	HELIPAD		LIAISED		MAIDENS		PARRIED
ADEHILS	HALIDES		SEDILIA		MEDIANS		RAPIDER
ADEHILY	HEADILY	ADEIINR	DENARII		MEDINAS	ADEIPRS	ASPIRED
ADEHINP	PINHEAD	ADEIIPR	PERIDIA		SIDEMAN		DESPAIR
ADEHINR	HANDIER	ADEIIRS	AIRSIDE	ADEIMNT	MEDIANT		DIAPERS
ADEHIPP	HAPPIED		DAIRIES	ADEIMNU	UNAIMED		PRAISED
ADEHIPR	RAPHIDE		DIARIES	ADEIMOW	MIAOWED	ADEIPRT	DIPTERA
ADEHIPS	APHIDES		DIARISE	ADEIMPR	DAMPIER		PARTIED
ADEHIPT	PITHEAD	ADEIIRZ	DIARIZE	ADEIMPV	IMPAVED		PIRATED
ADEHIRR	HARDIER	ADEIISS	DAISIES	ADEIMRR	ADMIRER	ADEIPRV	VAPIDER
	HARRIED	ADEIJMR	JEMIDAR		MARDIER	ADEIPSS	APSIDES
ADEHIRS	SHADIER	ADEIKLN	KNAIDEL		MARRIED	ADEIRRS	ARRIDES
ADEHIRW	RAWHIDE	ADEIKLS	SKAILED	ADEIMRS	ADMIRES		RAIDERS
ADEHIRY	HAYRIDE	ADEIKNS	KANDIES		MARDIES	ADEIRRT	TARDIER
	HYDRIAE	ADEIKRS	DAIKERS		MISREAD		TARRIED

ADEIRRV	ARRIVED
ADEIRST	ARIDEST, ASTERID, ASTRIDE, DIASTER, DISRATE, STAIDER, STAIRED, TARDIES, TIRADES
ADEIRSU	RESIDUA
ADEIRSV	ADVISER, VARDIES
ADEIRTT	ATTIRED
ADEIRTV	TARDIVE
ADEIRTY	DIETARY
ADEISSS	DASSIES
ADEISST	DISSEAT, SAIDEST
ADEISSV	ADVISES
ADEISSZ	ASSIZED
ADEISTU	DAUTIES
ADEISTV	AVIDEST, DATIVES, VISTAED
ADEISTW	DAWTIES, WAISTED
ADEISVV	SAVVIED
ADEISWY	WAYSIDE
ADEITWY	TIDEWAY
ADEJMOR	MAJORED
ADEJMRU	MUDEJAR
ADEJNSU	JAUNSED
ADEJNTU	JAUNTED
ADEJOPR	JEOPARD
ADEJRSU	ADJURES
ADEJSSU	JUDASES
ADEKKNS	SKANKED
ADEKLNP	PLANKED
ADEKLNR	RANKLED
ADEKLNS	KALENDS
ADEKLNY	NAKEDLY
ADEKLRS	DARKLES
ADEKLST	SKLATED, STALKED
ADEKLSY	YSLAKED
ADEKLUW	WAULKED
ADEKMRS	DEMARKS
ADEKNPP	KNAPPED
ADEKNPR	PRANKED
ADEKNPS	SPANKED
ADEKNRR	KNARRED
ADEKNRS	DARKENS
ADEKNRU	UNRAKED
ADEKNST	DANKEST
ADEKNSU	UNASKED
ADEKNSW	SWANKED
ADEKNUW	UNWAKED
ADEKNVY	VANDYKE
ADEKPRS	SPARKED
ADEKPSY	KEYPADS
ADEKRST	DARKEST, STARKED
ADEKRSY	DARKEYS
ADELLMS	SMALLED
ADELLMU	MEDULLA
ADELLNR	LANDLER
ADELLNW	ELLWAND
ADELLOR	ODALLER
ADELLOW	ALLOWED
ADELLOY	ALLOYED
ADELLPS	SPALLED
ADELLRU	ALLURED, UDALLER
ADELLST	STALLED
ADELLSU	ALLUDES, ALUDELS
ADELLSV	DEVALLS
ADELMMS	SLAMMED, SMALMED
ADELMNN	LANDMEN
ADELMNR	MANDREL
ADELMNT	MANTLED
ADELMOR	EARLDOM
ADELMOS	DAMOSEL
ADELMOZ	DAMOZEL
ADELMPS	SAMPLED
ADELMRS	MEDLARS
ADELMSS	DAMSELS
ADELNNP	PLANNED
ADELNNU	UNLADEN
ADELNOR	LADRONE
ADELNOS	LOADENS
ADELNOT	TALONED
ADELNOY	YEALDON
ADELNPT	PLANTED
ADELNRS	DARNELS, ENLARDS, LANDERS, SLANDER, SNARLED
ADELNRU	LAUNDER, LURDANE, RUNDALE
ADELNRY	DEARNLY
ADELNSS	SENDALS
ADELNST	DENTALS, SLANTED
ADELNSU	UNLADES, UNLEADS
ADELNTU	LUNATED, UNDEALT
ADELNTW	WETLAND
ADELNUW	UNLAWED
ADELOPR	LEOPARD, PAROLED
ADELOPS	DEPOSAL, PEDALOS
ADELOPT	PLOATED, TADPOLE
ADELORS	LOADERS, ORDEALS, RELOADS
ADELORT	DELATOR, LEOTARD
ADELORU	ROULADE
ADELOSS	ALDOSES, LASSOED
ADELOST	SALTOED
ADELPPP	PLAPPED
ADELPPS	DAPPLES, SAPPLED, SLAPPED
ADELPRS	PEDLARS
ADELPRY	PEDLARY
ADELPST	SPALTED, STAPLED
ADELPSU	UPLEADS
ADELPSW	DEWLAPS, SPAWLED
ADELPSY	SPLAYED
ADELPTT	PLATTED
ADELPTW	DEWLAPT
ADELPTY	ADEPTLY
ADELRRS	LARDERS
ADELRRU	RUDERAL
ADELRRW	DRAWLER
ADELRSS	SARDELS
ADELRST	DARTLES
ADELRSU	LAUDERS
ADELRSW	WARSLED
ADELRSZ	DRAZELS
ADELRTT	RATTLED
ADELRTW	TRAWLED
ADELRTX	DEXTRAL
ADELRTY	LYRATED
ADELRWW	WRAWLED
ADELRWX	WRAXLED
ADELRZZ	DAZZLER
ADELSST	DESALTS
ADELSTT	SLATTED
ADELSTU	AULDEST, SALUTED
ADELSUV	AVULSED
ADELSWY	SWAYLED
ADELSZZ	DAZZLES
ADELTTT	TATTLED
ADELTTW	WATTLED
ADELTUV	VAULTED
ADELTUX	LUXATED
ADELTWZ	WALTZED
ADEMMPS	SPAMMED
ADEMMRS	DAMMERS, SMARMED
ADEMMRT	TRAMMED
ADEMNNS	SANDMEN
ADEMNNU	MUNDANE, UNNAMED
ADEMNOR	MADRONE, ROADMEN
ADEMNOS	DAEMONS, MASONED, MODENAS, MONADES, NOMADES
ADEMNOW	WOMANED
ADEMNPS	DAMPENS
ADEMNRS	MANREDS, RANDEMS, REMANDS
ADEMNRU	DURAMEN, MANURED, MAUNDER, UNARMED
ADEMNRY	DRAYMEN, YARDMEN
ADEMNSS	DESMANS, MADNESS
ADEMNST	TANDEMS
ADEMNSU	MEDUSAN, SUDAMEN
ADEMNSY	DAYSMEN
ADEMNTU	UNMATED, UNTAMED
ADEMOOV	AMOOVED
ADEMOPS	APEDOMS, POMADES
ADEMORS	RADOMES
ADEMOSV	VAMOSED
ADEMOSW	MEADOWS
ADEMOSY	SOMEDAY
ADEMOWY	MEADOWY
ADEMPRS	DAMPERS
ADEMPRT	TRAMPED
ADEMPSS	SPASMED
ADEMPST	DAMPEST, STAMPED
ADEMPSW	SWAMPED
ADEMRRU	EARDRUM
ADEMRST	SMARTED
ADEMRSU	REMUDAS
ADEMRSW	SWARMED
ADEMRTU	MATURED
ADEMSSU	ASSUMED, MEDUSAS
ADEMTTU	MUTATED
ADENNOY	ANNOYED, ANODYNE
ADENNPS	SPANNED
ADENNPT	PENDANT
ADENNST	STANDEN
ADENNSU	DUENNAS
ADENNSW	SWANNED
ADENNWY	DEWANNY
ADENOOP	NAPOOED
ADENOOZ	ENDOZOA
ADENOPR	APRONED, OPERAND, PADRONE, PANDORE
ADENOPS	DAPSONE
ADENOPT	TONEPAD
ADENORT	TORNADE
ADENORU	RONDEAU
ADENOST	ASTONED, DONATES, ONSTEAD
ADENOSU	DOUANES
ADENOSY	NOYADES
ADENOTT	NOTATED
ADENOTZ	ZONATED
ADENPPR	PARPEND
ADENPPS	APPENDS, SNAPPED
ADENPPW	WAPPEND
ADENPRR	PARDNER
ADENPRS	PANDERS
ADENPRU	UNPARED
ADENPRW	PRAWNED, PREDAWN
ADENPST	PEDANTS, PENTADS
ADENPSW	SPAWNED
ADENPSX	EXPANDS, SPANDEX
ADENPSY	DYSPNEA
ADENPUV	UNPAVED
ADENQTU	QUANTED
ADENRRS	DARNERS, ERRANDS, SNARRED
ADENRRW	REDRAWN
ADENRRY	REYNARD
ADENRSS	SANDERS, SARSDEN
ADENRST	ENDARTS, STANDER, STARNED
ADENRSU	ASUNDER, DANSEUR, DAUNERS
ADENRSW	DAWNERS, WANDERS, WARDENS
ADENRSZ	ZANDERS
ADENRTT	TRANTED
ADENRTU	DAUNTER, NATURED, UNRATED, UNTREAD
ADENRTV	VERDANT
ADENRTX	DEXTRAN
ADENRTY	DENTARY, TRAYNED, TYRANED
ADENRUY	UNREADY
ADENSSS	SADNESS
ADENSSU	SUNDAES
ADENSSW	WESANDS
ADENSTT	ATTENDS
ADENSTU	SAUNTED, UNSATED
ADENSTV	ADVENTS
ADENSTY	STAYNED
ADENSUV	UNSAVED
ADENSWY	ENDWAYS
ADENSWZ	WEZANDS
ADENTTU	ATTUNED, NUTATED, TAUNTED
ADENTUV	VAUNTED
ADENTUX	UNTAXED
ADENUWY	UNWAYED
ADEOORT	ODORATE
ADEOPPS	APPOSED, PEAPODS

ADEOPQU	OPAQUED	ADFFHNO	OFFHAND	ADGILOS	DIALOGS
ADEOPRR	EARDROP	ADFFIST	DISTAFF	ADGILSU	GLADIUS
ADEOPRT	ADOPTER	ADFFLNO	FANFOLD	ADGILUY	GAUDILY
	READOPT	ADFFLOO	OFFLOAD	ADGIMMN	DAMMING
ADEOPRV	VAPORED	ADFFOOR	AFFOORD	ADGIMNN	DAMNING
ADEOPSS	SPADOES	ADFFORS	AFFORDS	ADGIMNP	DAMPING
ADEOPST	PODESTA	ADFGGIN	FADGING	ADGIMNR	MRIDANG
ADEORRS	ADORERS	ADFGINN	FANDING	ADGINNR	DARNING
	DROSERA	ADFGINR	FARDING		NARDING
ADEORRW	ARROWED	ADFGINS	FADINGS		RANDING
ADEORST	DOATERS	ADFGLLU	GLADFUL	ADGINNS	SANDING
	ROASTED	ADFHLNU	HANDFUL	ADGINNT	DANTING
	TORSADE	ADFHOOS	SHADOOF	ADGINNW	DAWNING
	TROADES	ADFHSSU	SHADUFS	ADGINOR	ADORING
ADEORSU	AROUSED	ADFILLU	FLUIDAL		GRADINO
ADEORSV	SAVORED	ADFIMNR	FINDRAM		ROADING
ADEORSW	REDOWAS	ADFIMNY	DAMNIFY	ADGINOS	GANOIDS
ADEORTT	ROTATED	ADFINRS	FRIANDS	ADGINOT	DOATING
	TROATED	ADFINRT	INDRAFT	ADGINPP	DAPPING
ADEORTU	OUTDARE	ADFIORS	FORSAID	ADGINPR	DRAPING
ADEORWY	RODEWAY	ADFLLYY	LADYFLY	ADGINPS	SPADING
ADEORYZ	ZEDOARY	ADFLMOO	DAMFOOL	ADGINRR	DARRING
ADEOSTT	TOASTED	ADFLMPU	MUDFLAP	ADGINRS	DARINGS
ADEOTTU	OUTDATE	ADFLMTU	MUDFLAT		GRADINS
ADEOWWY	WAYWODE	ADFLNOP	PLAFOND	ADGINRT	DARTING
ADEPPRS	DAPPERS	ADFLNSY	SANDFLY		TRADING
ADEPPRT	TRAPPED	ADFLORU	FOULARD	ADGINRU	DAURING
ADEPPRW	WRAPPED	ADFMNOS	FANDOMS	ADGINRW	DRAWING
ADEPPST	STAPPED	ADFMOSU	FUMADOS		WARDING
ADEPPSW	SWAPPED	ADFNNOT	FONDANT	ADGINRY	YARDING
ADEPPTU	PUPATED	ADFNOST	FANTODS	ADGINST	DATINGS
ADEPPUY	APPUYED	ADFOOPT	FOOTPAD	ADGINSW	WADINGS
ADEPRRS	DRAPERS	ADFORRW	FORWARD	ADGINTU	DAUTING
	SPARRED		FROWARD	ADGINTW	DAWTING
ADEPRRY	DRAPERY	ADGGGIN	DAGGING	ADGINNY	GWYNIAD
ADEPRSS	ADPRESS	ADGGHNO	HANGDOG	ADGIPRU	PAGURID
	SPADERS	ADGGILN	GADLING	ADGIRSU	GUISARD
	SPREADS	ADGGILR	RIGGALD	ADGIRZZ	GIZZARD
ADEPRST	DEPARTS	ADGGINN	DANGING	ADGLLNO	GOLLAND
	DRAPETS	ADGGINO	GOADING	ADGLMNO	MANGOLD
	PETARDS	ADGGINR	GRADING	ADGLNOO	GONDOLA
ADEPRSY	SPRAYED		NIGGARD	ADGLNOR	GOLDARN
ADEPRTT	PRATTED	ADGGINU	GAUDING	ADGLNOW	GOWLAND
ADEPRTU	UPRATED	ADGHILO	HIDALGO	ADGLNOY	DAYLONG
ADEPSTT	SPATTED	ADGHINN	HANDING	ADGLNRY	GRANDLY
ADEPSTU	UPDATES	ADGHINS	DASHING	ADGLOPS	LAPDOGS
ADEPSZZ	SPAZZED		SHADING	ADGMNOO	GOODMAN
ADEQRSU	SQUARED	ADGHINU	HAUDING	ADGMNOR	GORMAND
ADERRST	DARTERS	ADGHIPR	DIGRAPH	ADGNOOR	DRAGOON
	DARTRES	ADGHIRR	ARDRIGH		GADROON
	RETARDS	ADGHNNU	HANDGUN		
	STARRED	ADGHNOS	HAGDONS	ADGNOOS	GOONDAS
	TRADERS	ADGHNOW	HAGDOWN	ADGNORS	DRAGONS
ADERRSW	DRAWERS	ADGHORW	HOGWARD	ADGNORU	AGROUND
	REDRAWS	ADGHRTU	DRAUGHT	ADGNRRU	GURNARD
	REWARDS	ADGIILN	DIALING	ADGNRSU	DURGANS
	WARDERS		GLIADIN	ADGNRUU	UNGUARD
ADERSSU	ASSURED		LAIDING	ADGORSW	WARDOGS
	RUDASES	ADGIILT	DIGITAL	ADGPRSU	UPDRAGS
ADERSSW	SAWDERS	ADGIIMN	MAIDING	ADHHIRS	HARDISH
	SWEARDS	ADGIINN	DAINING	ADHHISW	WHIDAHS
ADERSTT	STARTED	ADGIINO	GONIDIA	ADHHOSU	HOUDAHS
	TETRADS	ADGIINR	GRADINI	ADHHOSW	HOWDAHS
ADERSTV	ADVERTS		RAIDING	ADHHSWY	WHYDAHS
	STARVED	ADGIINU	IGUANID	ADHIIJT	IJTIHAD
ADERSTW	STEWARD	ADGIINW	GWINIAD	ADHIIKS	DASHIKI
	STRAWED	ADGIIPY	PYGIDIA	ADHIIMS	MAIDISH
	WRASTED	ADGILLN	LADLING	ADHIKNS	DANKISH
ADERSTY	STRAYED	ADGILMN	MADLING	ADHIKRS	DARKISH
ADERSUY	DASYURE	ADGILNN	LANDING	ADHIKSU	HAIDUKS
ADERSVW	DWARVES	ADGILNO	DIGONAL	ADHILMO	HALIDOM
	SWARVED		LOADING	ADHILNY	HANDILY
ADERWWY	WEYWARD	ADGILNR	DARLING	ADHILOP	HAPLOID
ADESSTU	SUDATES		LARDING	ADHILOS	HALOIDS
ADESSTW	WADSETS	ADGILNS	LADINGS	ADHILOY	HOLIDAY
ADESTTU	STATUED		LIGANDS		HYALOID
ADESTTW	SWATTED	ADGILNU	LANGUID	ADHILRY	HARDILY
	WADSETT		LAUDING	ADHILSY	LADYISH
ADFFGIN	DAFFING	ADGILOR	GOLIARD		SHADILY
				ADHIMPS	DAMPISH

	PHASMID	ADIINST	DISTAIN
ADHIMRS	DIRHAMS	ADIINSU	INDUSIA
ADHINOT	ANTHOID		SUIDIAN
ADHINPU	DAUPHIN	ADIINSV	AVIDINS
ADHINSS	SANDHIS	ADIINSZ	DIZAINS
ADHIORS	HAIRDOS	ADIIPRS	DIAPIRS
ADHJKOS	KHODJAS	ADIIPXY	PYXIDIA
ADHKORW	DORHAWK	ADIIQRU	DAQUIRI
ADHKOSU	SHAKUDO	ADIIRST	DIARIST
ADHLLNO	HOLLAND	ADIIRTY	ARIDITY
ADHLMOY	HOLYDAM	ADIITVY	AVIDITY
ADHLMPY	LYMPHAD	ADIJMSS	MASJIDS
ADHMNOO	HOODMAN	ADIJNOS	ADJOINS
	MANHOOD	ADIJNOT	ADJOINT
ADHMNSU	NUMDAHS	ADIKLNY	LADYKIN
ADHNNSU	NHANDUS	ADIKLOS	ODALISK
	UNHANDS	ADIKLPS	KLIPDAS
ADHNNUY	UNHANDY	ADIKMNN	MANKIND
ADHNORS	HADRONS	ADIKMOS	MIKADOS
ADHNORU	UNHOARD	ADIKMSS	DISMASK
ADHNOSU	HOUDANS	ADIKNOS	DAIKONS
ADHNOTU	HANDOUT	ADIKNPS	KIDNAPS
ADHNRSY	SHANDRY		SKIDPAN
ADHNRTY	HYDRANT	ADIKNRS	DISRANK
ADHNRUY	UNHARDY	ADIKOST	DAKOITS
ADHOORR	RHODORA		
ADHOPRT	HARDTOP		
ADHOPRU	UPHOARD		
ADHOSSW	SHADOWS		
ADHOSWY	SHADOWY		
ADHPRSU	PURDAHS		
ADHPSUU	UPHAUDS		
ADHRRSU	DHURRAS		
ADIIILR	IRIDIAL		
ADIIINR	IRIDIAN		
ADIIKOS	AIKIDOS		
ADIIKOT	DAKOITI		
ADIILLS	ILLIADS		
ADIILMS	MILADIS		
	MISDIAL		
	MISLAID		
ADIILNO	LIANOID		
ADIILNV	INVALID		
ADIILOS	SIALOID		
ADIILST	DIALIST		
ADIILUV	DILUVIA		
ADIIMMS	MAIDISM		
ADIIMOS	DAIMIOS		
ADIIMPV	IMPAVID		
ADIIMRS	MIDAIRS		
ADIIMRU	MUDIRIA		
ADIIMSS	MISSAID		
ADIINPR	PINDARI		
	PRIDIAN		

ADIKPRS	DISPARK		ORDAINS	ADLOPSU	UPLOADS		UPWARDS
ADIKSST	DIKASTS		SADIRON	ADLORRW	WARLORD	ADRSSUW	USWARDS
ADIKSTT	DIKTATS	ADINORV	VIRANDO	ADLORSS	DORSALS	ADSSTUW	SAWDUST
ADILLMM	MILLDAM	ADINOSX	DIAXONS	ADLORSU	SUDORAL	AEEEFLR	EELFARE
ADILLSY	DISALLY		DIOXANS	ADLOSSS	DOSSALS	AEEEGKL	KEELAGE
ADILLVY	VALIDLY	ADINOTX	OXIDANT	ADLPSSU	SPAULDS	AEEEGLT	LEGATEE
ADILMNO	MONDIAL	ADINPST	PANDITS	ADMMNOS	MANDOMS	AEEEGNT	TEENAGE
ADILMNR	MANDRIL		SANDPIT	ADMMNSU	SUMMAND	AEEEGPR	PEERAGE
ADILMNU	MAUDLIN	ADINQRS	QINDARS	ADMNOOR	MADRONO	AEEEGPS	SEEPAGE
ADILMOP	DIPLOMA	ADINRRT	TRIDARN	ADMNOOW	WOODMAN	AEEEGRR	EAGERER
ADILMOU	ALODIUM	ADINRST	INDARTS	ADMNOOZ	MADZOON	AEEEGRT	ETAGERE
ADILMOY	AMYLOID	ADINRSU	DURIANS	ADMNOQU	QUONDAM	AEEEILN	ALIENEE
ADILMPS	PLASMID		SUNDARI	ADMNORS	RANDOMS	AEEELRS	RELEASE
ADILMSS	DISMALS	ADINRSW	INWARDS		RODSMAN	AEEELTV	ELEVATE
ADILMSU	DUALISM	ADINRTU	TRIDUAN	ADMNORT	DORMANT	AEEFFLL	FELAFEL
ADILMSY	DISMAYL		UNITARD		MORDANT	AEEFFNS	NEAFFES
	LADYISM	ADINSTT	DISTANT	ADMNOSS	DAMSONS	AEEFFRS	AFFEERS
ADILNNS	INLANDS	ADINSTU	UNSTAID	ADMNOSU	OSMUNDA	AEEFGNT	FANTEEG
ADILNOR	ORDINAL	ADINTTY	DITTANY	ADMNOSY	DYNAMOS	AEEFGRS	SERFAGE
ADILNOS	DOLINAS	ADIOOSW	WOODSIA	ADMNSTU	DUSTMAN	AEEFGSU	FEAGUES
ADILNRS	ALDRINS	ADIOPRS	SPAROID	ADMOORT	DOORMAT	AEEFGTW	WEFTAGE
ADILNRU	DIURNAL	ADIOPRT	PAROTID	ADMOPPU	POPADUM	AEEFHRT	FEATHER
ADILNSS	ISLANDS	ADIOPRV	PRIVADO	ADMORRS	RAMRODS		TEREFAH
ADILNST	TINDALS	ADIORST	ASTROID	ADMORST	STARDOM	AEEFILR	LEAFIER
ADILNSU	DUALINS	ADIORSU	SAUROID		TSARDOM	AEEFILW	ALEWIFE
	SUNDIAL	ADIORSV	ADVISOR	ADMORTW	MADWORT	AEEFIRS	AREFIES
ADILOOV	OVOIDAL	ADIORTU	AUDITOR	ADMRSTU	DURMAST		FAERIES
ADILOOZ	ZOOIDAL	ADIOSVW	DISAVOW		MUSTARD		FREESIA
ADILOPR	DIPOLAR	ADIPRSS	SPARIDS	ADNNOOS	NANDOOS	AEEFISW	SEAWIFE
ADILORT	DILATOR	ADIPRST	DISPART	ADNNOOY	NOONDAY	AEEFLLT	FELLATE
ADILOTU	OUTLAID	ADIRRST	SIRDARS	ADNNORS	RANDONS		LEAFLET
ADILPRY	PYRALID	ADIRRSZ	RIZARDS	ADNNORT	DONNART	AEEFLMN	ENFLAME
	RAPIDLY	ADIRRSU	SARDIUS	ADNNOST	DANTONS	AEEFLMS	FEMALES
ADILPST	PLASTID	ADIRSSW	WISARDS		DONNATS	AEEFLRT	REFLATE
ADILPSY	DISPLAY	ADIRSTY	SATYRID	ADNNOSU	ADNOUNS	AEEFLRW	WELFARE
ADILPTU	PLAUDIT	ADIRSUY	DYSURIA	ADNNOTU	DAUNTON	AEEFLRY	LEAFERY
ADILPVY	VAPIDLY	ADIRSVZ	VIZARDS	ADNNRTU	DUNNART	AEEFLRZ	ALFEREZ
ADILQSU	SQUALID	ADIRSWZ	WIZARDS	ADNNRUW	UNDRAWN	AEEFLSU	EASEFUL
ADILRSZ	LIZARDS	ADIRSZZ	IZZARDS	ADNOOPR	PANDOOR	AEEFLTX	TELEFAX
ADILRTY	TARDILY	ADISSST	SADISTS	ADNOORS	NARDOOS	AEEFMNR	ENFRAME
ADILSTU	DUALIST	ADISSYY	SAYYIDS	ADNOORT	DONATOR		FREEMAN
ADILSTY	STAIDLY	ADISTTY	DITTAYS		ODORANT	AEEFMRR	REFRAME
ADILTUY	DUALITY	ADJKOSU	JUDOKAS		TANDOOR	AEEFMRT	FERMATE
ADIMNNO	MONDAIN	ADJNORS	JORDANS		TORNADO	AEEFOTV	FOVEATE
ADIMNOS	DAIMONS	ADJNORU	ADJOURN	ADNOOSW	WANDOOS	AEEFPPR	FRAPPEE
	DOMAINS	ADJSSTU	ADJUSTS	ADNOPRS	PARDONS	AEEFRRT	FERRATE
ADIMNRS	MANDIRS	ADKKLOY	KAKODYL	ADNOPRU	PANDOUR	AEEFRST	AFREETS
ADIMNSS	DISMANS	ADKLMRU	MUDLARK	ADNOPRV	PROVAND		FEASTER
ADIMNST	MANTIDS	ADKOPSU	PADOUKS	ADNOPST	DOPANTS	AEEFRTU	FEATURE
ADIMOOS	ISODOMA	ADKORWY	WORKDAY	ADNORRW	NORWARD	AEEFRWY	FREEWAY
ADIMORR	MIRADOR	ADKRSWY	SKYWARD	ADNORSW	ONWARDS	AEEGGLL	ALLEGGE
ADIMOST	DIATOMS	ADLLMOW	WADMOLL	ADNORTU	ROTUNDA	AEEGGLR	GREGALE
	MASTOID	ADLLMOY	MODALLY	ADNORWY	NAYWORD	AEEGGLS	ALEGGES
ADIMOTT	MATTOID	ADLLNOW	LOWLAND	ADNOSTT	DOTANTS	AEEGGLT	GATELEG
ADIMPRY	PYRAMID	ADLLNOY	NODALLY	ADNOSTU	ASTOUND	AEEGGNR	ENGAGER
ADIMQSU	QUIDAMS	ADLLOPR	POLLARD	ADNPRUW	UPDRAWN	AEEGGNS	ENGAGES
ADIMRSS	DISARMS	ADLLOPS	DALLOPS	ADNPSTU	UPSTAND	AEEGGOP	EPAGOGE
ADIMRSU	RADIUMS	ADLLORS	DOLLARS	ADNRSST	STRANDS	AEEGGRS	AGREGES
ADIMRSW	MISDRAW	ADLMNOS	ALMONDS	ADNRSSU	SUNDRAS		RAGGEES
ADIMRSY	MYRIADS		DOLMANS	ADNRSTU	DRAUNTS		REGGAES
ADIMSSS	SADISMS	ADLMORU	MODULAR		DURANTS	AEEGGST	TAGGEES
ADIMSST	DISMAST	ADLMOSW	WADMOLS		TUNDRAS	AEEGGSW	GEEGAWS
ADIMSSY	DISMAYS	ADLMSTU	TALMUDS	ADNRSUW	SUNWARD	AEEGHIR	HIREAGE
ADIMSTU	DUMAIST	ADLNNOR	NORLAND		UNDRAWS	AEEGHNW	WHANGEE
	STADIUM	ADLNOOR	LARDOON	ADNSSTY	DYNASTS	AEEGILL	GALILEE
ADIMSWY	MIDWAYS	ADLNOPU	POUNDAL	ADNSTYY	DYNASTY	AEEGILM	MILEAGE
ADINNOP	DIPNOAN	ADLNORS	LARDONS	ADOOPSU	APODOUS	AEEGILN	LINEAGE
ADINNOR	ANDIRON	ADLNORU	NODULAR	ADOOPSW	SAPWOOD	AEEGILP	EPIGEAL
ADINNRS	INNARDS	ADLNOSS	SOLDANS	ADOORWY	DOORWAY	AEEGILW	WEIGELA
ADINNRW	INDRAWN	ADLNOST	DALTONS	ADOOSUV	VAUDOOS	AEEGINP	EPIGEAN
ADINNRY	INNYARD	ADLNOSU	SOULDAN	ADOOWWX	WOODWAX	AEEGINR	REGINAE
ADINNSU	INDUNAS		UNLOADS	ADOPRRW	WARDROP	AEEGINU	EUGENIA
ADINOOP	POINADO	ADLNOSX	OXLANDS	ADORRSU	ARDOURS	AEEGIPR	PIERAGE
ADINOPP	OPPIDAN	ADLNOSY	SYNODAL	ADORSTW	TOWARDS	AEEGISS	AEGISES
ADINOPR	PADRONI	ADLNOTU	OUTLAND	ADORSUU	ARDUOUS		ASSIEGE
	PONIARD	ADLNPSU	UPLANDS	ADORSWY	AYWORDS	AEEGJRS	JAEGERS
ADINOPT	PINTADO	ADLNRSU	LURDANS	ADORTUW	OUTWARD	AEEGLLR	ALLEGER
ADINORR	ORDINAR	ADLNRUY	LAUNDRY	ADOUUVX	VAUDOUX	AEEGLLS	ALLEGES
ADINORS	INROADS	ADLOPRU	POULARD	ADPRSUW	UPDRAWS	AEEGLLZ	GAZELLE

AEEGLMN	GLEEMAN, MELANGE
AEEGLNR	ENLARGE, GENERAL, GLEANER
AEEGLNT	ELEGANT
AEEGLNV	EVANGEL
AEEGLPR	PEREGAL
AEEGLPS	PELAGES
AEEGLRS	GALERES, REGALES
AEEGLRU	LEAGUER, REGULAE
AEEGLRW	LEGWEAR
AEEGLRY	EAGERLY
AEEGLSS	AGELESS, ALGESES
AEEGLST	EAGLETS, LEGATES, TEAGLES, TELEGAS
AEEGLSU	LEAGUES
AEEGLSV	GLEAVES, SELVAGE
AEEGLTT	GALETTE
AEEGLTU	TEGULAE
AEEGLTV	VEGETAL
AEEGMMT	GEMMATE, TAGMEME
AEEGMNR	GERMANE
AEEGMNS	MANEGES, MENAGES
AEEGMNT	GATEMEN
AEEGMRR	MEAGRER
AEEGMRS	MEAGRES
AEEGMRU	REMUAGE
AEEGMSS	MEGASSE, MESSAGE
AEEGMST	GAMETES, METAGES
AEEGNNP	PANGENE
AEEGNNR	ENRANGE
AEEGNNS	ENNAGES
AEEGNOP	PEONAGE
AEEGNPP	GENAPPE
AEEGNRS	ENRAGES
AEEGNRT	GRANTEE, GREATEN, REAGENT
AEEGNRU	RENAGUE
AEEGNRV	AVENGER, ENGRAVE
AEEGNSS	SAGENES, SENEGAS
AEEGNST	NEGATES
AEEGNSV	AVENGES, GENEVAS
AEEGNTT	TENTAGE
AEEGNTV	VENTAGE
AEEGOPS	APOGEES
AEEGORV	OVERAGE
AEEGOST	GOATEES
AEEGPRS	ASPERGE, PRESAGE
AEEGRRS	GREASER
AEEGRRT	GREATER, REGRATE
AEEGRRW	WAGERER
AEEGRSS	GREASES
AEEGRST	ERGATES, RESTAGE
AEEGRSV	GREAVES
AEEGRTU	TREAGUE
AEEGRUZ	GUEREZA
AEEGSSW	SEWAGES
AEEGSTT	GESTATE, TAGETES
AEEGTTZ	GAZETTE
AEEHHNT	HEATHEN
AEEHHRT	HEATHER
AEEHHST	SHEATHE
AEEHHSW	HEEHAWS
AEEHINR	HERNIAE
AEEHIPR	HEAPIER
AEEHIRV	HEAVIER
AEEHIST	ATHEISE
AEEHISV	HEAVIES
AEEHITZ	ATHEIZE
AEEHKNR	HEARKEN
AEEHKNT	THANKEE
AEEHKRU	HEUREKA
AEEHLNT	LETHEAN
AEEHLRS	HEALERS
AEEHLRT	LEATHER
AEEHLRV	HAVEREL
AEEHLSS	LEASHES
AEEHLST	LATHEES
AEEHLSW	AWHEELS
AEEHLSX	EXHALES
AEEHLSY	EYELASH
AEEHLTT	ATHLETE
AEEHMNT	METHANE
AEEHMRS	HAREEMS, MAHSEER
AEEHMRT	ERATHEM, THERMAE
AEEHMST	MEATHES
AEEHMSU	HEAUMES
AEEHNPT	HEPTANE, PHENATE
AEEHNRS	ARSHEEN
AEEHNRT	EARTHEN, HEARTEN
AEEHNST	ETHANES
AEEHNSV	HEAVENS
AEEHNSX	HEXANES
AEEHNTW	WHEATEN
AEEHPRS	RESHAPE, SPHAERE, SPHEARE
AEEHPRT	PREHEAT
AEEHPSS	APHESES, SPAHEES
AEEHPUV	UPHEAVE
AEEHQSU	QUASHEE
AEEHRRS	HEARERS, REHEARS, SHEARER
AEEHRSS	HEARSES
AEEHRST	AETHERS, HEATERS, REHEATS
AEEHRSV	HEAVERS
AEEHRSW	WHEREAS
AEEHRTT	THEATER, THEATRE, THEREAT
AEEHRTV	THREAVE
AEEHRTW	WEATHER, WHEREAT, WREATHE
AEEHSST	HEASTES
AEEHSSV	SHEAVES
AEEHSTV	THEAVES
AEEIIRS	AIERIES
AEEIKLR	LEAKIER
AEEIKPR	PEAKIER
AEEIKSV	KEAVIES
AEEILLR	REALLIE
AEEILMR	MEALIER
AEEILMS	MEALIES
AEEILNP	ALEPINE
AEEILNS	SEALINE
AEEILNT	LINEATE
AEEILPT	EPILATE, PILEATE
AEEILRR	EARLIER, LEARIER
AEEILRS	EARLIES, REALISE
AEEILRT	ATELIER, REALTIE
AEEILRV	LEAVIER, VEALIER
AEEILRZ	REALIZE
AEEILTT	AILETTE
AEEILTV	ELATIVE
AEEIMNR	REMANIE
AEEIMNS	MEANIES, NEMESIA
AEEIMNT	MATINEE
AEEIMNX	EXAMINE
AEEIMPR	EMPAIRE
AEEIMRR	REAMIER
AEEIMRS	SEAMIER, SERIEMA
AEEIMRT	EMIRATE, MEATIER
AEEIMSS	MISEASE, SIAMESE
AEEIMST	STEAMIE
AEEIMSZ	SIAMEZE
AEEIMTT	TEATIME
AEEINPR	PERINEA
AEEINRT	RETINAE, TRAINEE
AEEINST	ETESIAN
AEEINTV	NAIVETE
AEEINVW	INWEAVE
AEEIORT	ETAERIO
AEEIPRR	PEREIRA
AEEIPRS	APERIES, EPEIRAS
AEEIPRT	PEATIER
AEEIPSV	PEAVIES
AEEIPTX	EXPIATE
AEEIRRR	ARRIERE
AEEIRRS	REARISE
AEEIRRT	TEARIER
AEEIRRW	WEARIER
AEEIRST	AERIEST, SERIATE
AEEIRSW	WEARIES
AEEIRTT	ARIETTE, ITERATE
AEEIRTV	EVIRATE
AEEISST	EASIEST
AEEISVV	EVASIVE
AEEITTV	AVIETTE, EVITATE
AEEITUX	EUTEXIA
AEEIUVX	EXUVIAE
AEEJKSS	JAKESES
AEEJMSS	JAMESES
AEEJNST	SEJEANT
AEEJNTU	JAUNTEE
AEEJRSV	EVEJARS
AEEKKNO	KOKANEE
AEEKLLT	LAKELET
AEEKLMN	KEELMAN
AEEKLNS	ALKENES
AEEKLNT	KANTELE
AEEKLPS	PALKEES
AEEKLRS	LEAKERS
AEEKLSV	VAKEELS
AEEKMNS	KAMSEEN
AEEKMNW	WAKEMEN
AEEKMRS	REMAKES
AEEKMRT	MEERKAT
AEEKNNN	NANKEEN
AEEKNRS	SNEAKER
AEEKNRT	RETAKEN
AEEKNRW	WAKENER
AEEKNSW	WEAKENS
AEEKORW	REAWOKE
AEEKPRS	PARKEES, RESPEAK, SPEAKER
AEEKPRT	PERTAKE
AEEKRRT	RETAKER
AEEKRRW	WREAKER
AEEKRST	RETAKES, SAKERET
AEEKRSU	EUREKAS
AEEKSSS	ASKESES
AEEKSTW	WEAKEST
AEELLLS	ALLELES
AEELLMS	MALLEES
AEELLOV	ALVEOLE
AEELLPR	PARELLE
AEELLSS	SALLEES
AEELMNP	EMPANEL, EMPLANE
AEELMNR	REELMAN
AEELMNS	ENAMELS
AEELMNT	MANTEEL
AEELMNV	VELAMEN
AEELMNY	AMYLENE
AEELMPS	EMPALES
AEELMPX	EXAMPLE, EXEMPLA
AEELMRS	MEALERS
AEELMRT	LAMETER
AEELMSS	MEASLES
AEELMSU	AEMULES
AEELMSZ	MEAZELS
AEELMTU	EMULATE
AEELNNP	ENPLANE
AEELNNR	LERNEAN
AEELNPS	ALPEENS, SPELEAN
AEELNRR	LEARNER
AEELNRT	ALTERNE, ENTERAL, ETERNAL
AEELNRW	RENEWAL
AEELNSS	ENSEALS
AEELNST	ELANETS, LATEENS, LEANEST
AEELNSV	ENSLAVE, LEAVENS
AEELNSW	WEANELS
AEELNTY	ENTAYLE
AEELOPR	PAROLEE
AEELORS	AREOLES
AEELORU	AUREOLE
AEELOST	OLEATES
AEELOSW	LEASOWE
AEELPRR	PEARLER
AEELPRS	LEAPERS, PLEASER, RELAPSE, REPEALS
AEELPRT	PLEATER, PRELATE
AEELPRU	PLEURAE
AEELPSS	ELAPSES, PLEASES, SAPELES
AEELPSU	EPAULES
AEELPTT	PALETTE, PELTATE
AEELPTU	EPAULET
AEELQSU	QUELEAS, SEQUELA
AEELRRT	ALERTER, RELATER
AEELRSS	EARLESS, LEASERS, RESALES, RESEALS, SEALERS
AEELRST	ELATERS, REALEST, RELATES

	STEALER
AEELRSU	LEASURE
AEELRSV	LAVEERS
	LEAVERS
	REVEALS
	SEVERAL
	VEALERS
AEELRSX	RELAXES
AEELRSY	SEALERY
AEELRUV	REVALUE
AEELSST	ALTESSE
	STEALES
	TEASELS
AEELSSV	SLEAVES
AEELSSW	AWELESS
	WEASELS
AEELSSZ	SLEAZES
AEELSTU	ELUATES
	SETUALE
AEELSTV	SALVETE
	VALETES
	VELETAS
AEELSTX	LATEXES
AEELSTY	EYALETS
AEELSTZ	TEAZELS
	TEAZLES
AEELSWY	LEEWAYS
AEELTTY	LAYETTE
AEELTVW	WAVELET
AEEMMMS	MAMMEES
AEEMMPY	EMPYEMA
AEEMMRT	AMMETER
	METAMER
AEEMNNO	ANEMONE
AEEMNPS	SPAEMEN
AEEMNPT	PEATMEN
AEEMNRS	RENAMES
AEEMNRT	REMANET
AEEMNSS	ENSEAMS
AEEMNST	ENTAMES
	MEANEST
AEEMNSX	EXAMENS
AEEMOPT	METOPAE
AEEMORT	EROTEMA
AEEMOSW	AWESOME
	WAESOME
AEEMPRS	AMPERES
	EMPARES
AEEMPRT	TEMPERA
AEEMPRY	EMPAYRE
AEEMPSW	WAMPEES
AEEMPTU	AMPUTEE
AEEMQRU	MARQUEE
AEEMRRS	REAMERS
AEEMRSS	SEAMERS
AEEMRST	STEAMER
	TEAMERS
AEEMRSU	MEASURE
AEEMRTY	METAYER
AEEMSSS	SESAMES
AEEMSST	MESETAS
	SEAMSET
AEEMSTT	METATES
AEENNOT	NEONATE
AEENNPT	PENNATE
	PENTANE
AEENNRS	ENSNARE
AEENNRX	REANNEX
AEENNST	NEATENS
AEENNSX	ANNEXES
AEENNTU	UNEATEN
AEENOPR	PERAEON
AEENOSS	ANOESES
AEENOSU	AENEOUS
AEENPST	NEPETAS
	PENATES
	PESANTE
AEENPSW	PAWNEES
AEENPSX	EXPANSE

AEENRRS	EARNERS
AEENRRT	TERRANE
AEENRRV	RAVENER
AEENRRY	YEARNER
AEENRSS	ENSEARS
AEENRST	EARNEST
	EASTERN
	NEAREST
AEENRSW	WEANERS
AEENRTT	ENTREAT
	RATTEEN
	TERNATE
AEENRTV	AVENTRE
	NERVATE
	VETERAN
AEENRUV	UNREAVE
AEENSST	ENTASES
	SATEENS
	SENATES
	SENSATE
	STEANES
AEENSSU	UNEASES
AEENSSV	AVENSES
AEENSSW	WAENESS
AEENSTT	NEATEST
AEENSUV	AVENUES
AEENSWZ	WEAZENS
AEENTTV	NAVETTE
AEENUVW	UNWEAVE
AEEOPRT	OPERATE
AEEORRS	REAROSE
AEEORSS	SEROSAE
AEEORST	ROSEATE
AEEORSV	OVERSEA
AEEORTV	OVERATE
	OVEREAT
AEEORVW	OVERAWE
AEEOSUU	EUOUAES
AEEOSVV	EVOVAES
AEEPPRR	PAPERER
	PREPARE
	REPAPER
AEEPPRS	RAPPEES
AEEPRRS	REAPERS
AEEPRRT	PEARTER
	TAPERER
AEEPRSS	ASPERSE
	PARESES
	PRAESES
	PREASES
	PREASSE
	SERAPES
AEEPRST	REPEATS
AEEPRSZ	SPREAZE
AEEPRTU	EPURATE
AEEPRTY	PEATERY
AEEPRTZ	TRAPEZE
AEEPSSS	ASEPSES
AEEPSST	PESETAS
AEEPSSW	PESEWAS
AEEPSTT	SEPTATE
	SPATTEE
AEEPSVY	PEAVEYS
AEEQRSU	QUAERES
AEEQSTU	EQUATES
AEERRRS	REARERS
AEERRSS	ERASERS
AEERRST	SERRATE
	TEARERS
AEERRSU	ERASURE
AEERRSV	REAVERS
AEERRSW	SWEARER
	WEARERS
AEERRTT	RETRATE
	RETREAT
	TREATER
AEERRTW	WATERER
AEERRVW	WAVERER
AEERSST	RESEATS

	SAETERS
	SEAREST
	SEATERS
	STEARES
	TEASERS
	TESSERA
AEERSSU	RESEAUS
	SEASURE
AEERSSV	ASSEVER
AEERSSY	ESSAYER
AEERSTT	ESTREAT
	RESTATE
AEERSTU	AUSTERE
AEERSTW	SWEATER
AEERSUV	VAREUSE
AEERSUX	RESEAUX
AEERSVW	WEAVERS
AEERTTX	EXTREAT
AEERTWW	WETWARE
AEESSSW	SEESAWS
AEESSTT	ESTATES
AEESSTU	SAUTEES
AEESSTX	TEXASES
AEESSUX	AUXESES
AEESTTT	TESTATE
AEFFFLR	FLAFFER
AEFFGIR	GIRAFFE
AEFFGNR	ENGRAFF
AEFFGRS	GAFFERS
AEFFGRU	GAUFFER
AEFFHST	HAFFETS
AEFFINS	AFFINES
AEFFIPR	PIAFFER
AEFFIPS	PIAFFES
AEFFIST	TAFFIES
AEFFISX	AFFIXES
AEFFKOP	OFFPEAK
AEFFKOT	OFFTAKE
AEFFLLY	FLYLEAF
AEFFLMW	FLAMFEW
AEFFLNS	SNAFFLE
AEFFLRR	RAFFLER
AEFFLRS	RAFFLES
AEFFLRU	FEARFUL
AEFFLRW	WAFFLER
AEFFLSW	WAFFLES
AEFFLSY	YAFFLES
AEFFLTU	FATEFUL
AEFFQRU	QUAFFER
AEFFRST	AFFRETS
	RESTAFF
	STAFFER
AEFFRSY	EFFRAYS
AEFFRSZ	ZAFFERS
	ZAFFRES
AEFFTTY	TAFFETY
AEFGGGO	FOGGAGE
AEFGGMO	MEGAFOG
AEFGGRY	FAGGERY
AEFGILN	FEALING
	FINAGLE
	LEAFING
AEFGILO	FOLIAGE
AEFGILR	FRAGILE
AEFGINR	FEARING
AEFGINT	FEATING
AEFGIRT	FRIGATE
AEFGIRU	REFUGIA
AEFGITU	FATIGUE
AEFGLLU	FULLAGE
AEFGLNS	FANGLES
	FLANGES
AEFGLOT	FLOTAGE
AEFGLOW	FLOWAGE
AEFGLRS	REFLAGS
AEFGLRU	RAGEFUL
AEFGLUZ	GAZEFUL
AEFGMSU	FUMAGES
AEFGNRR	GRANFER

AEFGNRT	ENGRAFT
AEFGOOT	FOOTAGE
AEFGORR	FORAGER
AEFGORS	FORAGES
AEFGORV	FORGAVE
AEFGRRT	GRAFTER
AEFGRSU	GAUFERS
	GAUFRES
AEFHLLS	FELLAHS
AEFHLOR	FAHLORE
AEFHLRS	FLASHER
AEFHLRT	FARTHEL
AEFHLRZ	FAHLERZ
AEFHLSS	FLASHES
AEFHLTU	HATEFUL
AEFHRRT	FARTHER
AEFHRST	FATHERS
	SHAFTER
AEFHRSY	FASHERY
AEFIILT	FILIATE
AEFIIRS	FAIRIES
AEFIJLO	JEOFAIL
AEFIJOS	FEIJOAS
AEFIKLR	FLAKIER
AEFIKLS	FLAKIES
AEFILLS	FAILLES
AEFILMN	FEMINAL
	INFLAME
AEFILMR	FLAMIER
AEFILNS	FINALES
AEFILNT	INFLATE
AEFILNU	INFULAE
AEFILNV	FLAVINE
AEFILOT	FOLIATE
AEFILPT	FLEAPIT
AEFILRR	FLARIER
	FRAILER
AEFILRU	FAILURE
AEFILRV	FAVRILE
AEFILRW	FLAWIER
AEFILRX	FLAXIER
AEFILRZ	FILAZER
AEFILSS	FALSIES
	FILASSE
AEFIMNR	FIREMAN
AEFIMNS	FAMINES
	INFAMES
AEFIMOR	FOAMIER
AEFIMRR	FIREARM
AEFIMRS	MISFARE
AEFINNS	FANNIES
AEFINNT	INFANTE
AEFINNZ	FANZINE
AEFINPR	FIREPAN
AEFINRR	REFRAIN
AEFINRS	INFARES
	SERAFIN
AEFINRT	FAINTER
	FENITAR
AEFINRX	XERAFIN
AEFINST	FAINEST
	NAIFEST
AEFINTX	ANTEFIX
AEFIQRU	AQUIFER
AEFIRRR	FARRIER
AEFIRSS	FRAISES
AEFIRST	FAIREST
AEFIRTT	FATTIER
AEFISST	FIESTAS
AEFISTT	FATTIES
AEFISTX	FIXATES
AEFKLNR	FLANKER
AEFKLNS	FANKLES
AEFKLOS	SEAFOLK
AEFKLRT	FARTLEK
AEFKLST	FLASKET
AEFKLUW	WAKEFUL
AEFKNRR	FRANKER
AEFKORS	FORSAKE

AEFLLNN	FANNELL
	FLANNEL
AEFLLOT	FLOATEL
AEFLLRS	FALLERS
AEFLLSY	FALSELY
AEFLLTT	FLATLET
AEFLLTU	TALEFUL
AEFLLUZ	ZEALFUL
AEFLMNS	FLAMENS
AEFLMOR	FEMORAL
AEFLMUW	WAMEFUL
AEFLMUZ	MAZEFUL
AEFLNNN	FLANNEN
AEFLNNS	FANNELS
AEFLNOV	FLAVONE
AEFLNRS	SALFERN
AEFLNRU	FLANEUR
	FRENULA
	FUNERAL
AEFLNSU	FLAUNES
AEFLNTT	FLATTEN
AEFLOOV	FOVEOLA
AEFLOPW	PEAFOWL
AEFLORS	LOAFERS
	SAFROLE
AEFLORT	FLOATER
	FLOREAT
	REFLOAT
AEFLORY	FORELAY
AEFLOST	FOLATES
AEFLOSW	SEAFOWL
AEFLPPR	FLAPPER
AEFLPRS	FELSPAR
AEFLPRY	PALFREY
AEFLRSS	FALSERS
	FLASERS
AEFLRST	FALTERS
AEFLRSU	EARFULS
	FERULAS
	REFUSAL
AEFLRSY	FLAYERS
AEFLRTT	FLATTER
AEFLRTU	REFUTAL
	TEARFUL
AEFLRZZ	FRAZZLE
AEFLSST	FALSEST
	FESTALS
AEFLSTU	FLUATES
	SULFATE
AEFMNOR	FORAMEN
	FOREMAN
AEFMNRT	RAFTMEN
AEFMNRU	FRAENUM
AEFMORR	FOREARM
AEFMORT	FORMATE
AEFMRRS	FARMERS
	FRAMERS
AEFMRRY	FARMERY
AEFNNRS	FANNERS
AEFNNST	ENFANTS
AEFNOPR	PROFANE
AEFNOPY	PAYFONE
AEFNORR	FORERAN
AEFNRRS	FARRENS
AEFNRSS	FARNESS
AEFNRSU	FURANES
	UNSAFER
AEFNRSW	FAWNERS
AEFNSST	FASTENS
	FATNESS
AEFNSTT	FATTENS
AEFOPRW	FOREPAW
AEFORRV	FAVORER
	OVERFAR
AEFORRY	FORAYER
AEFORSW	FORESAW
AEFORSY	FORESAY
AEFOSST	FATSOES
AEFOSTU	FEATOUS
AEFPPRS	FRAPPES
AEFRRST	FRATERS
	RAFTERS
AEFRRTY	FRATERY
AEFRSSS	FRASSES
AEFRSST	FASTERS
	STRAFES
AEFRSTW	FRETSAW
	WAFTERS
AEFRTUW	WAFTURE
AEFSSTT	FASTEST
AEFSSUV	FAVUSES
AEFSTTT	FATTEST
AEGGGLS	GAGGLES
AEGGGLU	LUGGAGE
AEGGGRS	GAGGERS
AEGGHLR	HAGGLER
AEGGHLS	HAGGLES
AEGGHSW	EGGWASH
AEGGIJR	JAGGIER
AEGGILN	GEALING
	LIGNAGE
AEGGINR	GEARING
	NAGGIER
AEGGINS	AGEINGS
	SIGNAGE
AEGGIOS	ISAGOGE
AEGGIRR	RAGGIER
AEGGIRS	RAGGIES
	SAGGIER
AEGGIRT	TAGGIER
AEGGIRU	GARIGUE
AEGGISW	SWAGGIE
AEGGJRS	JAGGERS
AEGGJRY	JAGGERY
AEGGLNO	AGELONG
AEGGLNR	GANGREL
AEGGLNS	LAGGENS
AEGGLRS	GARGLES
	LAGGERS
	RAGGLES
AEGGLSW	WAGGLES
AEGGMNY	YEGGMAN
AEGGMSS	EGGMASS
AEGGNNU	GUNNAGE
AEGGNRR	GRANGER
AEGGNRS	GANGERS
	GRANGES
	NAGGERS
AEGGNSU	GANGUES
AEGGRRY	RAGGERY
AEGGRSS	AGGRESS
	SAGGERS
	SEGGARS
AEGGRST	GAGSTER
	GARGETS
	STAGGER
	TAGGERS
AEGGRSU	GAUGERS
AEGGRSW	SWAGGER
AEGGRSY	YAGGERS
AEGGRTY	GARGETY
AEGGRWY	WAGGERY
AEGGSWW	GEWGAWS
AEGHHIT	AHEIGHT
AEGHIJR	JAGHIRE
AEGHILN	HEALING
AEGHILR	LAIGHER
AEGHINP	HEAPING
AEGHINR	HEARING
AEGHINT	GAHNITE
	HEATING
AEGHINV	HEAVING
AEGHINZ	GENIZAH
AEGHIRS	HEGIRAS
	HIRAGES
AEGHISS	GEISHAS
AEGHLNO	HALOGEN
AEGHLNT	ALENGTH
AEGHLRU	LAUGHER
AEGHLSS	SEALGHS
AEGHLST	HAGLETS
AEGHLSZ	GHAZELS
AEGHLTW	THALWEG
AEGHMNN	HANGMEN
AEGHMOR	HOMAGER
AEGHMOS	HOMAGES
	OHMAGES
AEGHMSU	MESHUGA
AEGHNOX	HEXAGON
AEGHNRS	GNASHER
	HANGERS
	REHANGS
AEGHNRU	NURAGHE
AEGHNSS	GNASHES
AEGHNST	STENGAH
AEGHOPY	HYPOGEA
AEGHORS	GHERAOS
AEGHOSS	SEAHOGS
AEGHOST	HOSTAGE
AEGHPRS	SPREAGH
AEGHPST	HATPEGS
AEGHRST	GATHERS
AEGHSST	GASHEST
AEGIIMN	IMAGINE
AEGIKLN	LEAKING
	LINKAGE
AEGIKLT	GLAIKET
AEGIKNP	PEAKING
AEGIKNR	REAKING
AEGIKNS	SINKAGE
AEGIKPP	KIPPAGE
AEGIKPR	GARPIKE
AEGIKRW	GAWKIER
AEGIKSW	GAWKIES
AEGILLL	ILLEGAL
AEGILLN	NIGELLA
AEGILLP	PILLAGE
AEGILLS	GALLIES
	GALLISE
AEGILLT	TILLAGE
AEGILLU	LIGULAE
AEGILLV	VILLAGE
AEGILLY	AGILELY
AEGILLZ	GALLIZE
AEGILMN	LEAMING
	MEALING
AEGILMR	GREMIAL
	LAMIGER
AEGILMS	MILAGES
AEGILNN	ANELING
	EANLING
	LEANING
	NEALING
AEGILNP	LEAPING
	PEALING
	PLEAING
AEGILNR	ENGRAIL
	LAERING
	LEARING
	NARGILE
	REALIGN
	REGINAL
AEGILNS	LEASING
	LINAGES
	SEALING
AEGILNT	ATINGLE
	ELATING
	GELATIN
	GENITAL
AEGILNU	LINGUAE
AEGILNV	LEAVING
AEGILNY	ALEYING
AEGILOS	GOALIES
	SOILAGE
AEGILOU	EULOGIA
AEGILPS	PAIGLES
AEGILRR	GLARIER
AEGILRS	GRAILES
AEGILRZ	GLAZIER
AEGILSS	ALGESIS
	LIGASES
	SILAGES
AEGILST	AGILEST
	AIGLETS
	LIGATES
	TAIGLES
AEGILSV	GLAIVES
AEGILTU	GLUTAEI
AEGILTY	EGALITY
AEGIMMR	GAMMIER
AEGIMNN	AMENING
	MEANING
AEGIMNP	PIGMEAN
AEGIMNR	GERMAIN
	MANGIER
	MEARING
	REAMING
AEGIMNS	ENIGMAS
	GAMINES
	MEASING
	SEAMING
AEGIMNT	MINTAGE
	TEAMING
	TEGMINA
AEGIMOS	IMAGOES
AEGIMPR	EPIGRAM
	PRIMAGE
AEGIMPS	MAGPIES
AEGIMPT	PIGMEAT
AEGIMRR	ARMIGER
AEGIMRS	GISARME
	MAIGRES
	MIRAGES
AEGIMRT	MIGRATE
	RAGTIME
AEGIMRU	GAUMIER
AEGIMRY	IMAGERY
AEGIMSS	AGEISMS
AEGIMST	GAMIEST
	SIGMATE
AEGIMSV	MISGAVE
AEGINNO	GANOINE
AEGINNP	NEAPING
	PEANING
AEGINNR	AGINNER
	EARNING
	ENGRAIN
	GRANNIE
	NEARING
AEGINNS	SEANING
AEGINNT	ANTEING
	ANTIGEN
	GENTIAN
AEGINNU	ANGUINE
	GUANINE
AEGINNW	WEANING
AEGINNY	YEANING
AEGINOR	ORIGANE
AEGINOS	AGONIES
	AGONISE
AEGINOZ	AGONIZE
AEGINPP	GENIPAP
AEGINPR	REAPING
AEGINPS	PEASING
	SPAEING
	SPINAGE
AEGINPZ	PEAZING
AEGINRR	ANGRIER
	EARRING
	GRAINER
	RANGIER
	REARING
AEGINRS	ANGRIES
	EARINGS
	ERASING
	GAINERS

GRAINES
REGAINS
REGINAS
SEARING
SERINGA
AEGINRT · GRANITE
GRATINE
INGRATE
TANGIER
TEARING
AEGINRV REAVING
VINEGAR
AEGINRW WEARING
AEGINSS AGNISES
SEASING
AEGINST EASTING
EATINGS
GAINEST
GENISTA
INGATES
INGESTA
SEATING
TANGIES
TEASING
TSIGANE
AEGINSU GUINEAS
AEGINSZ AGNIZES
SEAZING
AEGINTV VINTAGE
AEGINTZ TEAZING
AEGINVW WEAVING
AEGIORT GOATIER
AEGIPPR GAPPIER
AEGIPPS PIPAGES
AEGIPRR GRAPIER
AEGIPRS GASPIER
PRISAGE
SPAIRGE
AEGIRRZ GRAZIER
AEGIRSS AGRISES
GASSIER
AEGIRST AGISTER
GAITERS
STAGIER
STRIGAE
TRIAGES
AEGIRSV GARVIES
GRAVIES
RIVAGES
AEGIRSW EARWIGS
GAWSIER
AEGIRSZ AGRIZES
AEGIRTV VIRGATE
VITRAGE
AEGIRUZ GAUZIER
AEGISST AGEISTS
SAGIEST
AEGISSU AGUISES
AEGISSV VISAGES
AEGISTU AUGITES
AEGISTY GASEITY
AEGISTZ GAZIEST
AEGISUZ AGUIZES
AEGISYZ AZYGIES
AEGJLNR JANGLER
AEGJLNS JANGLES
AEGKKNO ANGEKOK
AEGKLOU KAGOULE
AEGKLRS GRAKLES
AEGKMRY KERYGMA
AEGKRSW GAWKERS
AEGKSST GASKETS
AEGLLLY LEGALLY
AEGLLNO ALLONGE
GALLEON
AEGLLNR LANGREL
AEGLLNS LEGLANS
AEGLLOR ALLEGRO
AEGLLOT TOLLAGE

AEGLLRY ALLERGY
GALLERY
LARGELY
REGALLY
AEGLLST GALLETS
AEGLLSU SEAGULL
SULLAGE
ULLAGES
AEGLLSY GALLEYS
AEGLLTU GLUTEAL
AEGLMNR MANGLER
AEGLMNS MANGELS
MANGLES
AEGLMOR GOMERAL
AEGLMOU MOULAGE
AEGLMPU PLUMAGE
AEGLMRS MALGRES
AEGLMRU MAULGRE
AEGLMSY MYGALES
AEGLNOS ENGAOLS
AEGLNOT TANGELO
AEGLNPR GRAPNEL
AEGLNPS SPANGLE
AEGLNRS ANGLERS
LARGENS
SLANGER
AEGLNRT TANGLER
TRANGLE
AEGLNRU GRANULE
AEGLNRW WANGLER
WRANGLE
AEGLNRY ANGERLY
AEGLNSS GLASSEN
AEGLNST LANGEST
TANGLES
AEGLNSU ANGELUS
LAGUNES
LANGUES
AEGLNSW WANGLES
AEGLNSY LYNAGES
AEGLNTT GANTLET
AEGLNTU LANGUET
AEGLNTW TWANGLE
AEGLNUU UNGULAE
AEGLNUW GUNWALE
AEGLOPR PERGOLA
AEGLORS GAOLERS
AEGLORT GLOATER
LEGATOR
AEGLOSS GLOSSAE
AEGLOST LEGATOS
AEGLOSU GEALOUS
AEGLOSV LOVAGES
AEGLOTV VOLTAGE
AEGLPPR GRAPPLE
AEGLPRS GRAPLES
AEGLPRU EARPLUG
GRAUPEL
AEGLPSU PLAGUES
PLUSAGE
AEGLPUY PLAGUEY
AEGLRRU REGULAR
AEGLRSS LARGESS
AEGLRST LARGEST
AEGLRSV GRAVELS
VERGLAS
AEGLRSY ARGYLES
GRAYLES
AEGLRSZ GLAZERS
AEGLRTU GAULTER
TEGULAR
TRAGULE
AEGLRTY GREATLY
AEGLRVY GRAVELY
AEGLSSS GLASSES
AEGLSSU SAULGES
AEGLSTT GESTALT
AEGLSTW TALWEGS
AEGLTUV VULGATE

AEGLUUY GUAYULE
AEGLUVY VAGUELY
AEGMMNS MAGSMEN
AEGMMRS GAMMERS
GRAMMES
AEGMMRU RUMMAGE
AEGMMSS SMEGMAS
AEGMNNO AGNOMEN
AEGMNOR MEGARON
AEGMNOS MANGOES
AEGMNOT GEOMANT
MAGNETO
MEGATON
MONTAGE
AEGMNPY PYGMEAN
AEGMNRS ENGRAMS
GERMANS
MANGERS
AEGMNRT GARMENT
MARGENT
RAGMENT
AEGMNST MAGNETS
AEGMNSW SWAGMEN
AEGMNTU AUGMENT
MUTAGEN
AEGMOOR MOORAGE
AEGMORS ROMAGES
AEGMOSY GAYSOME
AEGMOXY EXOGAMY
AEGMRSU MAUGRES
MURAGES
AEGMSUY MAGUEYS
AEGMSUZ ZEUGMAS
AEGNNOS NONAGES
AEGNNOT TONNAGE
AEGNNPS PANGENS
AEGNNRT REGNANT
AEGNNRU GUNNERA
AEGNNST GANNETS
AEGNNTT TANGENT
AEGNNTU TUNNAGE
AEGNOOR OREGANO
AEGNOPT PONTAGE
AEGNORR GROANER
ORANGER
AEGNORS ONAGERS
ORANGES
AEGNORW WAGONER
AEGNORY ORANGEY
AEGNOSY NOSEGAY
AEGNOWY WAYGONE
AEGNPRS ENGRASP
AEGNPRT TREPANG
AEGNRRS GARNERS
RANGERS
AEGNRRT GRANTER
REGRANT
AEGNRSS SERANGS
AEGNRST ARGENTS
GARNETS
STRANGE
AEGNRSU RAUNGES
UNGEARS
AEGNRSW GNAWERS
AEGNRTU GAUNTER
AEGNSSY GANSEYS
GAYNESS
AEGNSTT GESTANT
AEGNTTU TUTENAG
AEGOORT ROOTAGE
AEGOPPR PROPAGE
AEGOPRT PORTAGE
POTAGER
AEGOPST GESTAPO
POSTAGE
POTAGES
AEGOPTT POTTAGE
AEGORRT GARROTE
AEGORSS SORAGES

AEGORST ORGEATS
STORAGE
TOERAGS
AEGORTT GAROTTE
AEGORTU OUTRAGE
AEGORUV OUVRAGE
AEGORVY VOYAGER
AEGOSSU GASEOUS
AEGOSTU OUTAGES
AEGOSTW STOWAGE
TOWAGES
AEGOSTX OXGATES
AEGOSVY VOYAGES
AEGOTTU OUTGATE
AEGOTTV GAVOTTE
AEGOTUV OUTGAVE
AEGPRRS GRASPER
SPARGER
AEGPRRY GRAPERY
AEGPRSS GASPERS
SPARGES
AEGPRST PARGETS
AEGPRSU GAUPERS
AEGPRSW GAWPERS
AEGPSSU PEGASUS
AEGPSTU UPSTAGE
AEGPSUZ UPGAZES
AEGRRSS GRASSER
AEGRRST GARRETS
GARTERS
GRATERS
AEGRRSU ARGUERS
AEGRRSV GRAVERS
AEGRRSZ GRAZERS
AEGRRUU AUGURER
AEGRRUV GRAVURE
VERRUGA
AEGRSSS GASSERS
GRASSES
AEGRSST GASTERS
STAGERS
AEGRSSU ARGUSES
SAUGERS
USAGERS
AEGRSTT TARGETS
AEGRSTV GRAVEST
AEGRSTY GRAYEST
GYRATES
STAGERY
AEGRSUV SEVRUGA
AEGRSYZ AGRYZES
AEGSSSU GAUSSES
AEGSTUU AUGUSTE
AEGSTUV VAGUEST
AEGTTTU GUTTATE
AEHHIKS SHEIKHA
AEHHIRS HASHIER
AEHHIST SHEHITA
AEHHLST HEALTHS
AEHHLTY HEALTHY
AEHHNRS HARSHEN
AEHHPRS RHAPHES
AEHHRRS HARSHER
AEHHRST HEARTHS
AEHHSSS SHASHES
AEHHSST SHEATHS
AEHHSTY SHEATHY
AEHIILR HAILIER
AEHIIRR HAIRIER
AEHIJRS HEJIRAS
AEHIKNS HANKIES
AEHIKRS SHAKIER
AEHIKSS SAKIEHS
AEHIKSW HAWKIES
AEHIKSY SAKIYEH
AEHILMN HELIMAN
AEHILMO HEMIOLA
AEHILNR HERNIAL
INHALER

AEHILNS	INHALES
AEHILNY	HYALINE
AEHILOR	AIRHOLE
AEHILRS	HAILERS
	SHALIER
AEHILRT	LATHIER
AEHILRU	HAULIER
AEHILSS	SHEILAS
AEHILST	HALITES
AEHILSW	SHAWLIE
	WHAISLE
AEHILTT	LITHATE
AEHILTY	HYALITE
AEHILUV	VIHUELA
AEHILVY	HEAVILY
AEHILWZ	WHAIZLE
AEHIMMR	HAMMIER
AEHIMNR	HARMINE
AEHIMNS	HAEMINS
	HEMINAS
AEHIMNY	HYMENIA
AEHIMPS	PHAEISM
AEHIMRS	MASHIER
	MISHEAR
AEHIMSS	MASHIES
	MESSIAH
AEHIMST	ATHEISM
AEHINPR	HEPARIN
AEHINPS	INPHASE
AEHINPT	PENTHIA
AEHINRS	ARSHINE
	HERNIAS
AEHINRT	HAIRNET
	INEARTH
	THERIAN
AEHINSS	HESSIAN
AEHINSV	EVANISH
	VAHINES
AEHINSW	WAHINES
AEHIORR	HOARIER
AEHIPPR	HAPPIER
AEHIPPS	HAPPIES
AEHIPPT	EPITAPH
AEHIPRS	HARPIES
	SHARPIE
AEHIPSS	APHESIS
AEHIPSW	PEISHWA
AEHIPTZ	ZAPTIEH
AEHIQSU	HAIQUES
	QUASHIE
AEHIRRR	HARRIER
AEHIRRS	HARRIES
AEHIRSS	ARISHES
	SHERIAS
AEHIRST	HASTIER
	SHERIAT
AEHIRSV	ASHIVER
AEHIRSW	WASHIER
	WEARISH
AEHIRTW	THAWIER
AEHIRWY	HAYWIRE
AEHISST	ASHIEST
	SAITHES
	STASHIE
	TAISHES
AEHISSV	SHAVIES
AEHISTT	ATHEIST
	STAITHE
AEHISTZ	HAZIEST
AEHISVY	YESHIVA
AEHITTW	THWAITE
AEHJLOW	JAWHOLE
AEHKMSS	SAMEKHS
AEHKNRS	HANKERS
	HARKENS
AEHKNRT	THANKER
AEHKOSS	SHAKOES
AEHKPRS	PHREAKS
AEHKRRS	SHARKER
AEHKRSS	SHAKERS
AEHKRSW	HAWKERS
AEHKSWY	HAWKEYS
AEHLLOV	HELLOVA
AEHLLRS	HERSALL
AEHLLYZ	HAZELLY
AEHLMNO	MANHOLE
AEHLMNY	HYMENAL
AEHLMOR	ARMHOLE
AEHLMPS	PELHAMS
AEHLMPW	WHAMPLE
AEHLMRS	HARMELS
AEHLMRT	THERMAL
AEHLMRU	HUMERAL
AEHLMST	HAMLETS
AEHLNOS	ENHALOS
AEHLNOT	ETHANOL
AEHLNRT	ENTHRAL
AEHLNSS	HANSELS
AEHLNST	HANTLES
AEHLNSU	UNHEALS
	UNLEASH
	UNSHALE
AEHLORS	SHOALER
AEHLORT	LOATHER
AEHLOSS	ASSHOLE
AEHLOST	LOATHES
AEHLPRS	SPHERAL
AEHLPSS	HAPLESS
	PLASHES
AEHLPST	PLASHET
AEHLPSY	SHAPELY
AEHLRSS	ASHLERS
	HALSERS
	LASHERS
	SLASHER
AEHLRST	HALTERS
	HARSLET
	LATHERS
	SLATHER
	THALERS
AEHLRSU	HAULERS
AEHLRSV	HALVERS
AEHLRSW	WHALERS
AEHLRTY	EARTHLY
	HARTELY
	HEARTLY
	LATHERY
AEHLRWY	WHALERY
AEHLSSS	HASSLES
	SLASHES
AEHLSST	HASLETS
	HATLESS
AEHLSSY	HAYSELS
AEHLSTT	STEALTH
AEHLSTW	WEALTHS
AEHLSWY	SHAWLEY
AEHLTWY	WEALTHY
AEHMMNS	MASHMEN
AEHMMRS	HAMMERS
	SHAMMER
AEHMMSS	SHAMMES
AEHMMSY	MAYHEMS
AEHMNOR	MENORAH
AEHMNOS	HOSEMAN
AEHMNOT	NATHEMO
AEHMNOY	HAEMONY
AEHMNPY	NYMPHAE
AEHMNRU	HUMANER
AEHMNST	ANTHEMS
	HETMANS
AEHMOPT	APOTHEM
AEHMPRS	HAMPERS
AEHMPTY	EMPATHY
AEHMRSS	MARSHES
	MASHERS
	SHAMERS
	SMASHER
AEHMRST	HAMSTER
AEHMRTU	MAUTHER
AEHMRTW	MAWTHER
AEHMSSS	SMASHES
AEHMSST	SMEATHS
AEHMUZZ	MEZUZAH
AEHNNTU	UNNEATH
AEHNNWY	ANYWHEN
AEHNOPT	PHAETON
	PHONATE
AEHNOPW	WANHOPE
AEHNORS	HOARSEN
AEHNORT	ANOTHER
AEHNPPS	HAPPENS
AEHNPRS	SHARPEN
AEHNPRT	PANTHER
AEHNPST	HAPTENS
AEHNPSU	UNSHAPE
AEHNRSS	HARNESS
AEHNRST	ANTHERS
	HARTENS
	THENARS
AEHNRTU	HAUNTER
	UNEARTH
	UNHEART
	URETHAN
AEHNRTX	NARTHEX
AEHNSSS	SNASHES
AEHNSST	HASTENS
	SNATHES
	SNEATHS
AEHNSSZ	SAZHENS
AEHNSTY	SHANTEY
AEHNSUY	HAUYNES
AEHNTTW	WHATTEN
AEHOORT	TOHEROA
AEHORRS	HOARSER
AEHORST	ASTHORE
	EARSHOT
	HAROSET
AEHORSX	HOAXERS
AEHORUV	HAVEOUR
AEHOSTU	ATHEOUS
AEHPPRS	PERHAPS
AEHPPSU	UPHEAPS
AEHPRRS	HARPERS
	PHRASER
	SHARPER
AEHPRSS	PHRASES
	SERAPHS
	SHAPERS
	SHERPAS
	SPHAERS
	SPHEARS
AEHPRST	SPARTHE
	TEPHRAS
	THREAPS
AEHPRTT	PHATTER
AEHPRTY	THERAPY
AEHPSST	SPATHES
AEHPSSW	PESHWAS
AEHPSTY	HYPATES
AEHQSSU	QUASHES
AEHRRSS	RASHERS
	SHARERS
AEHRRTU	URETHRA
AEHRSST	RASHEST
	SHASTER
	TRASHES
AEHRSSV	SHAVERS
AEHRSSW	HAWSERS
	SWASHER
	WASHERS
AEHRSTT	HATTERS
	RATHEST
	SHATTER
	THREATS
AEHRSTV	HARVEST
	THRAVES
AEHRSTW	THAWERS
	WREATHS
AEHRSVW	WHARVES
AEHRSWY	WASHERY
AEHRSXY	HYRAXES
AEHRTUU	HAUTEUR
AEHRTWY	WREATHY
AEHSSST	STASHES
AEHSSSW	SWASHES
AEHSSTW	SWATHES
AEHSTUX	EXHAUST
AEIIKNT	KAINITE
AEIIKSS	SAIKEIS
AEIILLT	TAILLIE
AEIILNN	ANILINE
AEIILNR	AIRLINE
AEIILNX	EXILIAN
AEIILRR	LAIRIER
AEIILRS	LAIRISE
AEIILRZ	LAIRIZE
AEIILSS	LIAISES
	SILESIA
AEIILST	LAITIES
AEIILSW	LEWISIA
AEIILTZ	TAILZIE
AEIIMNT	INTIMAE
	MINIATE
AEIIMPR	IMPERIA
AEIIMRT	AIRTIME
AEIIMST	AMITIES
	ATIMIES
AEIIMTT	IMITATE
AEIINNS	ASININE
	INSANIE
AEIINQU	EQUINIA
AEIINRR	RAINIER
AEIINRS	SENARII
AEIINRT	INERTIA
AEIINST	ISATINE
AEIINSX	SIXAINE
AEIINTX	AXINITE
AEIIPRR	PRAIRIE
AEIIRRV	RIVIERA
	VAIRIER
AEIIRST	AIRIEST
	IRISATE
AEIITTV	VITIATE
AEIJLNV	JAVELIN
AEIJLRS	JAILERS
AEIJLSZ	JEZAILS
AEIJMMR	JAMMIER
AEIJMMS	JEMIMAS
AEIJMNS	JASMINE
AEIJNRS	INJERAS
AEIJNRT	JANTIER
	NARTJIE
AEIJNST	JANTIES
	TAJINES
AEIJNTU	JAUNTIE
AEIJRSV	JARVIES
AEIJRZZ	JAZZIER
AEIKLNO	KAOLINE
AEIKLNR	LANKIER
AEIKLNU	UNALIKE
AEIKLOT	KEITLOA
AEIKLRR	LARKIER
AEIKLRS	LAIKERS
	SERKALI
AEIKLRT	TALKIER
AEIKLRV	KLAVIER
AEIKLRW	WARLIKE
AEIKLSS	ALSIKES
AEIKLST	LAKIEST
	TALKIES
AEIKMMS	MISMAKE
AEIKMNP	PIKEMAN
AEIKMNR	MANKIER
	RAMEKIN
AEIKMNS	KINEMAS

AEIKMPR	RAMPIKE		REALISM		TALIPES		OSMIATE
AEIKMRW	MAWKIER	AEILMRT	LAMITER	AEILPSY	PAISLEY	AEIMOTX	TOXEMIA
AEIKMSS	KAMISES		MALTIER	AEILQTU	LIQUATE	AEIMOTZ	ATOMIZE
AEIKMST	MISTAKE	AEILMSS	AIMLESS		TEQUILA	AEIMPRR	RAMPIRE
AEIKNRR	NARKIER		MESAILS	AEILRRS	RAILERS	AEIMPRS	IMPRESA
AEIKNRS	SNAKIER		SAMIELS		RERAILS		SAMPIRE
AEIKNRT	KERATIN		SEISMAL	AEILRRT	RETIRAL	AEIMPRT	PRIMATE
AEIKNRW	WANKIER	AEILMSZ	MEZAILS		RETRIAL	AEIMPRV	VAMPIRE
AEIKNSS	KINASES	AEILMTY	LAYTIME		TRAILER	AEIMPSS	IMPASSE
AEIKNST	INTAKES		MEATILY	AEILRSS	AIRLESS		PESSIMA
	KENTIAS	AEILNNY	INANELY		SAILERS	AEIMPST	IMPASTE
	TANKIES	AEILNOP	OPALINE		SERAILS		PASTIME
AEIKNSW	SWANKIE	AEILNOR	AILERON		SERIALS	AEIMPSV	IMPAVES
AEIKNSY	KYANISE		ALERION	AEILRST	REALIST	AEIMPSW	MAPWISE
	YANKIES		ALIENOR		RETAILS	AEIMPSY	PYEMIAS
AEIKNSZ	KAIZENS	AEILNOT	ELATION		SALTIER	AEIMRRR	MARRIER
AEIKNTY	KYANITE		TOENAIL		SALTIRE	AEIMRRS	MARRIES
AEIKNYZ	KYANIZE	AEILNPR	PEARLIN		SLATIER		SIMARRE
AEIKOST	OAKIEST		PLAINER	AEILRSV	REVISAL	AEIMRSS	MASSIER
AEIKPRR	PARKIER		PRALINE	AEILRSW	SWALIER	AEIMRST	IMARETS
AEIKPRS	PARKIES	AEILNPS	ALPINES		WAILERS		MAESTRI
	SPARKIE		SPANIEL	AEILRTT	TERTIAL		MAISTER
AEIKPRW	PAWKIER		SPLENIA	AEILRTU	URALITE		MASTIER
AEIKQRU	QUAKIER	AEILNPT	PANTILE	AEILRTW	WALTIER		MISRATE
AEIKRRS	KERRIAS	AEILNPX	EXPLAIN	AEILRTY	IRATELY		SEMITAR
	SARKIER	AEILNQU	EQUINAL		REALITY		SMARTIE
AEIKRSS	KAISERS	AEILNRS	NAILERS	AEILRVV	REVIVAL	AEIMRSU	UREMIAS
	KARSIES	AEILNRT	ENTRAIL	AEILRVY	VIRELAY	AEIMRSW	AWMRIES
AEIKRST	ARKITES		LATRINE	AEILRWY	WEARILY	AEIMRTU	MURIATE
	KARITES		RATLINE	AEILSSS	LAISSES	AEIMRTW	WARTIME
AEIKRSZ	KARZIES		RELIANT		LASSIES	AEIMSSS	AMISSES
AEIKSSS	ASKESIS		RETINAL	AEILSSU	SAULIES		MESSIAS
AEIKSTT	TAKIEST		TRENAIL	AEILSSV	VALISES	AEIMSST	ASTEISM
AEILLMN	MANILLE	AEILNRV	RAVELIN		VESSAIL		SAMIEST
AEILLNR	RALLINE	AEILNRW	LAWNIER	AEILSSW	WALISES		SAMITES
AEILLOV	ALVEOLI	AEILNRX	RELAXIN	AEILSTU	SITULAE		TAMISES
AEILLPR	PALLIER	AEILNRY	INLAYER	AEILSTV	ESTIVAL	AEIMSSV	MASSIVE
AEILLPS	ILLAPSE		NAILERY	AEILSTW	WALIEST		MAVISES
AEILLRR	RALLIER	AEILNSS	SALINES	AEILSTY	TAILYES	AEIMSSY	MYIASES
AEILLRS	RALLIES		SILANES	AEILSTZ	LAZIEST	AEIMSTT	MATIEST
AEILLRT	LITERAL	AEILNST	EASTLIN	AEILTVY	VILAYET		MATTIES
	TALLIER		ELASTIN	AEILUVX	EXUVIAL	AEIMSTZ	MAZIEST
AEILLRU	RUELLIA		ENTAILS	AEIMMMS	MAMMIES		MESTIZA
AEILLRW	WALLIER		SALIENT	AEIMMNS	MISNAME	AEIMSUV	AMUSIVE
AEILLSS	ALLISES		SLAINTE	AEIMMRS	RAMMIES	AEIMSXX	MAXIXES
	SALLIES		STANIEL	AEIMMRT	MARMITE	AEIMTYZ	AZYMITE
AEILLST	TAILLES		TENAILS	AEIMMST	MISMATE	AEINNNS	NANNIES
	TALLIES	AEILNSU	INSULAE		TAMMIES	AEINNOT	ENATION
AEILLSW	WALLIES		INULASE	AEIMMZZ	MIZMAZE	AEINNPR	PANNIER
AEILLUV	ELUVIAL	AEILNSV	ALEVINS	AEIMNNT	MANNITE	AEINNPT	PANTINE
AEILLVX	VEXILLA		VALINES	AEIMNOR	MORAINE		PINNATE
AEILMMN	MAILMEN	AEILNTU	ALUNITE	AEIMNOS	ANOMIES	AEINNRS	INSANER
AEILMMS	LAMMIES	AEILNTV	VENTAIL	AEIMNOU	MOINEAU		INSNARE
	MELISMA	AEILNUV	UNALIVE	AEIMNRR	MARINER	AEINNRT	ENTRAIN
AEILMNN	LINEMAN		UNVAILE	AEIMNRS	MARINES		TRANNIE
	MELANIN	AEILNUW	LAUWINE		REMAINS	AEINNRU	ANEURIN
AEILMNO	MINEOLA	AEILNVY	NAIVELY		SEMINAR	AEINNSS	SANNIES
AEILMNP	IMPANEL	AEILOPR	PELORIA		SIRNAME		SIENNAS
	MANIPLE	AEILOPS	LEIPOAS	AEIMNRT	MINARET	AEINNST	INANEST
AEILMNR	MANLIER	AEILORV	VARIOLE		RAIMENT	AEINNSZ	ENZIANS
	MARLINE	AEILOST	ISOLATE	AEIMNRV	VERMIAN	AEINNTT	ANTIENT
	MINERAL	AEILOTV	VIOLATE	AEIMNRW	WIREMAN	AEINOPZ	EPIZOAN
	RAILMEN	AEILPPR	APPERIL	AEIMNSS	INSEAMS	AEINORS	ERASION
AEILMNS	ISLEMAN		APPLIER		SAMISEN	AEINORT	OTARINE
	MENIALS		ARIPPLE	AEIMNST	INMATES	AEINOSS	ANOESIS
	SEMINAL	AEILPPS	APPLIES		MAINEST	AEINOST	ATONIES
AEILMNT	AILMENT		LAPPIES		MANTIES	AEINOSV	EVASION
	ALIMENT	AEILPRS	PALSIER		TAMINES	AEINOSZ	AZIONES
AEILMOR	LOAMIER		PARLIES	AEIMNTX	TAXIMEN	AEINOXZ	OXAZINE
AEILMPR	IMPEARL	AEILPRT	PLAITER	AEIMNTY	AMENITY	AEINPPR	NAPPIER
	LEMPIRA		PLATIER		ANYTIME	AEINPPS	NAPPIES
	PALMIER	AEILPRV	PREVAIL	AEIMNUV	MAUVEIN	AEINPRS	RAPINES
AEILMPS	IMPALES	AEILPSS	ESPIALS		MAUVINE	AEINPRT	PAINTER
	PALMIES		LAPISES	AEIMOOP	IPOMOEA		PERTAIN
AEILMPT	IMPLATE		LIPASES	AEIMOPR	EMPORIA		REPAINT
	PALMIET		PALSIES	AEIMORR	ARMOIRE	AEINPSS	ASPINES
AEILMRR	LARMIER	AEILPST	APLITES	AEIMOST	AMOSITE		PANSIES
	MARLIER		PALIEST		ATOMIES	AEINPST	PANTIES
AEILMRS	MAILERS				ATOMISE		PATINES

	SAPIENT	AEIOSTT	OSTIATE		STRIATE
	SPINATE		TOASTIE		TASTIER
AEINPTT	PATIENT	AEIOSTZ	AZOTISE		TERTIAS
AEINPTU	PETUNIA	AEIOTZZ	AZOTIZE	AEIRSTV	TAIVERS
AEINPTY	PANEITY	AEIPPPR	PAPPIER		VASTIER
AEINQTU	ANTIQUE	AEIPPPS	PAPPIES	AEIRSTW	WAISTER
	QUINATE	AEIPPRS	APPRISE		WAITERS
AEINRRS	SIERRAN		SAPPIER		WARIEST
	SNARIER	AEIPPRT	PERIAPT	AEIRSVV	SAVVIER
AEINRRT	RETRAIN	AEIPPRY	YAPPIER	AEIRSWV	WAIVERS
	TERRAIN	AEIPPRZ	APPRIZE	AEIRTTT	ATTRITE
	TRAINER		ZAPPIER		TATTIER
AEINRSS	ARSINES	AEIPPSS	PASPIES		TITRATE
	SARNIES	AEIPPSY	YAPPIES	AEIRTTV	TAIVERT
AEINRST	ANESTRI	AEIPRRS	PARRIES	AEIRTTW	TAWTIER
	ANTSIER		PRAISER	AEIRTTX	EXTRAIT
	NASTIER		RAPIERS	AEIRTUY	AUREITY
	RATINES		RASPIER	AEIRTUZ	AZURITE
	RESIANT		REPAIRS	AEIRTVY	VARIETY
	RETAINS	AEIPRSS	ASPIRES	AEIRWWY	WIREWAY
	RETINAS		PARESIS	AEISSST	SIESTAS
	RETSINA		PRAISES		TASSIES
	STAINER		SPIREAS	AEISSSZ	ASSIZES
	STARNIE	AEIPRST	PARTIES	AEISSUV	SUASIVE
	STEARIN		PASTIER	AEISSUX	AUXESIS
AEINRSV	AVENIRS		PIASTRE	AEISSVV	SAVVIES
	RAVINES		PIRATES	AEISTTT	TATTIES
AEINRTT	INTREAT		PRATIES	AEISTTU	SITUATE
	ITERANT		TRAIPSE	AEISTTV	STATIVE
	NATTIER	AEIPRSU	SPURIAE	AEISTTW	TAWIEST
	NITRATE		UPRAISE		TWAITES
	TARTINE	AEIPRSV	PARVISE	AEISTTY	SATIETY
	TERTIAN	AEIPRSW	WASPIER	AEISTVW	WAVIEST
AEINRTU	RUINATE	AEIPRTT	PARTITE	AEISTWX	WAXIEST
	TAURINE	AEIPRTV	PRIVATE	AEITTTU	ATTUITE
	URANITE	AEIPRTW	WIRETAP	AEITTTV	VITTATE
	URINATE	AEIPRXY	PYREXIA	AEJKMNR	JARKMEN
AEINRTW	TAWNIER	AEIPSSS	ASEPSIS	AEJKNRS	JANKERS
	TINWARE	AEIPSST	PASTIES	AEJLNUV	JUVENAL
AEINRUV	VAURIEN		PATSIES	AEJLOSU	JALOUSE
AEINRUW	UNWARIE		TAPISES		JEALOUS
AEINRUZ	AZURINE	AEIPSSV	PASSIVE	AEJLOUZ	AZULEJO
AEINRVV	VERVAIN		PAVISES	AEJMMRS	JAMMERS
AEINRWY	YAWNIER		SPAVIES	AEJMNZZ	JAZZMEN
AEINSSS	SANSEIS	AEIPSSW	WASPIES	AEJMRST	RAMJETS
	SASINES	AEIPSTT	PATTIES	AEJMSST	JETSAMS
AEINSST	ENTASIS		TAPETIS	AEJMSSY	JESSAMY
	NASTIES	AEIPSTU	TAUPIES	AEJMSTY	MAJESTY
	SESTINA	AEIPSTW	TAWPIES	AEJNNOS	JOANNES
	TANSIES	AEIPTXY	EPITAXY	AEJNORZ	ZANJERO
	TISANES	AEIQRUV	AQUIVER	AEJNSST	JESSANT
AEINSSV	SAVINES	AEIQSSU	SAIQUES	AEJNSSU	JAUNSES
	VINASSE	AEIRRRT	TARRIER	AEJPRSS	JASPERS
AEINSTT	INSTATE	AEIRRSS	ARRISES	AEJPRSY	JASPERY
	SATINET		RAISERS	AEJRSVY	JARVEYS
AEINSTU	AUNTIES		SIERRAS	AEJRSZZ	JAZZERS
	SINUATE	AEIRRST	ARTSIER	AEKKNRS	KRAKENS
AEINSTV	NAIVEST		SERRATI	AEKKRSY	YAKKERS
	NATIVES		TARRIES	AEKLLTU	KELLAUT
	VAINEST		TARSIER	AEKLNPP	KNAPPLE
AEINSTW	AWNIEST	AEIRRSV	ARRIVES	AEKLNPR	PRANKLE
	TAWNIES		VARIERS	AEKLNRS	RANKLES
	WANIEST	AEIRRTT	RATTIER	AEKLNST	ANKLETS
	WANTIES		RETRAIT		ASKLENT
AEINSTZ	ZANIEST		TARTIER		LANKEST
AEINSVV	NAVVIES	AEIRRTW	WARTIER	AEKLNSW	KNAWELS
AEINSWY	ANYWISE	AEIRRTY	RETIARY	AEKLNSY	ALKYNES
AEINTVY	NAIVETY	AEIRRVV	VIVERRA	AEKLORY	ROKELAY
AEINTXY	ANXIETY	AEIRSSS	SASSIER	AEKLOST	SKATOLE
AEIOPRS	SOAPIER	AEIRSST	ARTSIES	AEKLPRS	SPARKLE
AEIOPSS	SOAPIES		SAIREST	AEKLRRS	LARKERS
AEIOPST	ATOPIES		SATIRES	AEKLRST	STALKER
	OPIATES		TIRASSE		TALKERS
AEIOQSU	SEQUOIA	AEIRSSU	SAURIES	AEKLRSW	WALKERS
AEIORRR	ARRIERO	AEIRSSZ	ASSIZER	AEKLRUW	WAULKER
	ROARIER	AEIRSTT	ARTIEST	AEKLSST	LASKETS
AEIORST	OARIEST		ARTISTE		SKLATES
	OTARIES		ATTIRES	AEKLSTU	AUKLETS
AEIORSV	OVARIES		IRATEST	AEKMMNR	MARKMEN

AEKMNOS	SOKEMAN	AELLMNU	LUMENAL
AEKMNSU	UNMAKES	AELLMRS	SMALLER
AEKMOOT	MATOOKE	AELLMST	MALLETS
AEKMOST	MATOKES	AELLMSU	MALLEUS
AEKMPRU	UPMAKER	AELLMSY	MELLAYS
AEKMPSU	UPMAKES		MESALLY
AEKMRRS	MARKERS	AELLMTY	METALLY
	REMARKS	AELLMWX	MAXWELL
AEKMRSS	MASKERS	AELLNOP	PALLONE
AEKMRST	MARKETS	AELLNOR	LLANERO
AEKNNRS	ENRANKS	AELLNOV	NOVELLA
AEKNNST	KANTENS	AELLNOY	ALONELY
AEKNNTU	UNTAKEN	AELLNPY	PENALLY
AEKNPPR	KNAPPER	AELLNRT	ENTRALL
AEKNPRS	SPANKER	AELLNSS	ALLNESS
AEKNPSU	UNSPEAK	AELLNSW	ENWALLS
AEKNPTU	UPTAKEN	AELLNTT	TALLENT
AEKNRRS	RANKERS	AELLNUU	LUNULAE
AEKNRSS	KRANSES	AELLNVY	VENALLY
AEKNRST	RANKEST	AELLORS	ROSELLA
	STARKEN	AELLORT	REALLOT
	TANKERS	AELLORV	OVERALL
AEKNRSU	UNRAKES	AELLPPS	LAPPELS
AEKNRSW	SWANKER	AELLPRU	PLEURAL
	WANKERS		
AEKNRSY	YANKERS		
AEKNRSZ	KRANZES		
AEKNRVY	KNAVERY		
AEKNSSU	ANKUSES		
AEKNSWY	SWANKEY		
AEKORRS	ROSAKER		
AEKORSS	ARKOSES		
	SOAKERS		
AEKOTTU	OUTTAKE		
	TAKEOUT		
AEKPPSU	UPSPAKE		
	UPSPEAK		
AEKPRRS	PARKERS		
AEKPRSS	SPARKES		
AEKPSSY	PASSKEY		
AEKPSTU	UPTAKES		
AEKQRSU	QUAKERS		
AEKQSSU	SQUEAKS		
AEKQSUY	SQUEAKY		
AEKRRST	KARTERS		
	KRATERS		
	STARKER		
AEKRSST	SKATERS		
	STRAKES		
	STREAKS		
	TASKERS		
AEKRSSY	KARSEYS		
AEKRSTY	STREAKY		
AEKRSUW	WAUKERS		
AEKSSSV	KVASSES		

Code	Word(s)
AELLPSS	SPALLES
AELLPST	PALLEST
AELLPTU	PLUTEAL
AELLPTY	PLAYLET
AELLQUY	EQUALLY
AELLRRU	ALLURER
AELLRST	STELLAR, TELLARS
AELLRSU	ALLURES, LAURELS
AELLRSW	WALLERS
AELLRSY	RALLYES
AELLRTY	ALERTLY, ELYTRAL
AELLSST	SALLETS, TASSELL
AELLSSW	LAWLESS
AELLSTT	TALLEST, TALLETS
AELLSTW	SETWALL, SWALLET, WALLESS
AELLSTY	STALELY
AELLSVY	VALLEYS
AELLTUU	ULULATE
AELLUVV	VALVULE
AELMMNO	MAMELON
AELMMNT	MALTMEN
AELMMOY	MYELOMA
AELMMRS	LAMMERS, SLAMMER
AELMMRT	TRAMMEL
AELMMST	STAMMEL
AELMMSY	MALMSEY
AELMNNS	LENSMAN
AELMNOR	ALMONER, NEMORAL
AELMNOS	MELANOS
AELMNOT	LOMENTA, OMENTAL, TELAMON
AELMNPR	LAMPERN
AELMNRU	NUMERAL
AELMNST	LAMENTS, MANTELS, MANTLES
AELMNSU	MENSUAL
AELMNTT	MANTLET
AELMNTU	NUTMEAL
AELMOPR	PLEROMA
AELMOPU	AMPOULE
AELMOPY	MAYPOLE
AELMORS	MORALES
AELMORT	MOLERAT
AELMORU	MORULAE
AELMORV	REMOVAL
AELMOST	MALTOSE
AELMOTT	MATELOT
AELMPRS	EMPARLS, LAMPERS, PALMERS, SAMPLER
AELMPRT	TEMPLAR, TRAMPLE
AELMPRY	LAMPREY
AELMPSS	SAMPLES
AELMPST	AMPLEST
AELMPSU	AMPULES
AELMPTU	PLUMATE
AELMRRS	MARRELS
AELMRSS	ARMLESS
AELMRST	ARMLETS, MARTELS
AELMRSU	MAULERS
AELMRSV	MARVELS
AELMRTT	MARTLET
AELMSST	SAMLETS
AELMSTU	AMULETS
AELNNPR	PLANNER
AELNNPS	PENNALS
AELNNPU	UNPANEL
AELNNRS	ENSNARL, LANNERS
AELNNRT	LANTERN
AELNNRU	UNLEARN
AELNNST	STANNEL
AELNNTU	ANNULET
AELNOPT	POLENTA
AELNORS	ORLEANS
AELNORU	ALEURON
AELNORV	VERONAL
AELNOST	ETALONS
AELNOTV	VOLANTE
AELNOUZ	ZONULAE
AELNPPY	PLAYPEN
AELNPRS	PLANERS, REPLANS
AELNPRT	PANTLER, PLANTER, REPLANT
AELNPRY	PLENARY
AELNPSS	NAPLESS
AELNPST	PLANETS, PLATENS
AELNPSU	UPLEANS
AELNPTU	UPLEANT
AELNPTX	EXPLANT
AELNPTY	APLENTY, PENALTY
AELNQUU	UNEQUAL
AELNRRS	SNARLER
AELNRSS	RANSELS
AELNRST	ANTLERS, RENTALS, SALTERN, STERNAL
AELNRSZ	RANZELS
AELNRTT	TRENTAL
AELNRTV	VENTRAL
AELNRTU	NEUTRAL
AELNRUV	UNRAVEL
AELNSSU	SENSUAL, UNSEALS
AELNSSW	AWNLESS
AELNSSX	LAXNESS
AELNSTT	LATTENS, TALENTS
AELNSTU	ELUANTS, UNLASTE
AELNSTV	LEVANTS
AELNSTY	STANYEL
AELNSTZ	ZELANTS
AELNSUW	UNWEALS
AELNTUV	ENVAULT
AELOORS	AEROSOL, ROSEOLA
AELOPPR	PROPALE
AELOPPX	APOPLEX
AELOPRR	PREORAL
AELOPRS	PAROLES, REPOSAL
AELOPRT	PROLATE
AELOPRV	OVERLAP
AELOPST	APOSTLE, PELOTAS
AELOPSX	EXPOSAL
AELOPTT	PALETOT
AELOPTU	OUTLEAP
AELORRT	REALTOR, RELATOR
AELORSS	OARLESS, SOLERAS
AELORST	OESTRAL
AELORTU	TORULAE
AELORTV	LEVATOR
AELORTY	ROYALET
AELORTZ	ZELATOR
AELORUU	ROULEAU
AELORVY	OVERLAY
AELORWY	OWRELAY
AELOSSS	LASSOES
AELOSSV	SALVOES
AELOSSW	LEASOWS
AELOSTV	SOLVATE
AELOSTZ	ZEALOTS
AELOSUZ	ZEALOUS
AELOSVY	SAVELOY
AELOTTU	TOLUATE
AELOTUV	OVULATE
AELOTVV	VOLVATE
AELPPRS	LAPPERS, RAPPELS, SLAPPER
AELPPRY	REAPPLY
AELPPSS	SAPPLES
AELPPST	APPLETS, LAPPETS, STAPPLE
AELPPSU	APPULSE, PAPULES, UPLEAPS
AELPPTU	UPLEAPT
AELPQSU	PLAQUES
AELPRRS	PARRELS
AELPRST	PALTERS, PLASTER, PLATERS, PSALTER, STAPLER
AELPRSU	PERUSAL, SERPULA
AELPRSW	PRAWLES
AELPRSY	PARLEYS, PARSLEY, PLAYERS, REPLAYS, SPARELY
AELPRTT	PARTLET, PLATTER, PRATTLE
AELPRTY	PEARTLY, PRELATY, PTERYLA
AELPRUY	EPULARY
AELPSSS	SAPLESS
AELPSST	PASTELS, STAPLES
AELPSTT	PATTLES, PELTAST
AELPSTU	PULSATE, PUTEALS, SPATULE
AELPUUV	UPVALUE
AELQRRU	QUARREL
AELQSSU	LASQUES, SQUEALS
AELQTUZ	QUETZAL
AELRRSU	SURREAL
AELRRTT	RATTLER
AELRRTW	TRAWLER
AELRSST	ARTLESS, LASTERS, SALTERS, SLATERS, TARSELS
AELRSSU	SAURELS
AELRSSV	SALVERS, SERVALS, SLAVERS, VERSALS
AELRSSW	WARSLES
AELRSSY	RAYLESS, SLAYERS
AELRSTT	RATTLES, SLATTER, STARLET, STARTLE, TATLERS
AELRSTU	SALUTER
AELRSTV	TRAVELS, VARLETS, VESTRAL
AELRSTW	WASTREL
AELRSTY	RAYLETS
AELRSUV	VALUERS
AELRSVV	VARVELS
AELRSVY	SLAVERY
AELRSWX	WRAXLES
AELRSWY	LAWYERS
AELRSZZ	RAZZLES
AELRTTT	TARTLET, TATTLER
AELRTTU	TUTELAR
AELRTUV	VAULTER
AELRTWZ	WALTZER
AELSSST	TASSELS
AELSSTT	LATESTS, SALTEST, STALEST, TASLETS
AELSSTU	SALUTES, TALUSES
AELSSTV	VESTALS
AELSSTW	WASTELS
AELSSTX	TAXLESS
AELSSUV	AVULSES
AELSSVY	SLAVEYS
AELSSWY	WAYLESS
AELSTTT	TATTLES
AELSTTW	WATTLES
AELSTTY	STATELY, STYLATE
AELSTUX	LUXATES
AELSTWZ	WALTZES
AELSUVY	SUAVELY
AELSWZZ	SWAZZLE
AELTTTW	TWATTLE
AELTTUX	TEXTUAL
AELTUVV	VULVATE
AEMMMRS	MAMMERS
AEMMMST	MAMMETS
AEMMNOT	MOMENTA
AEMMNTU	AMENTUM
AEMMORS	MARMOSE
AEMMPRS	SPAMMER
AEMMRRS	RAMMERS
AEMMRST	STAMMER
AEMMRSY	YAMMERS
AEMMRSZ	MAMZERS
AEMMSTU	MAUMETS, SUMMATE
AEMMSTW	MAWMETS
AEMNNOS	MANNOSE
AEMNNOT	MONTANE
AEMNNOU	NOUMENA
AEMNNRS	MANNERS
AEMNNRT	MANRENT, REMNANT
AEMNNSW	NEWSMAN
AEMNNTU	UNMEANT
AEMNOPR	REPOMAN
AEMNOPS	MOPANES
AEMNOPZ	ZAMPONE
AEMNORS	ENAMORS, MOANERS, OARSMEN
AEMNORU	ENAMOUR, NEUROMA
AEMNORV	OVERMAN
AEMNORY	ROMNEYA
AEMNOSS	MONASES
AEMNOST	MANTOES
AEMNOTT	TOMENTA
AEMNOTU	NOTAEUM, OUTNAME

Code	Words	Code	Words	Code	Words	Code	Words
AEMNPSS	PASSMEN	AEMRSTT	MATTERS		SPAWNER	AEOPRST	ESPARTO
AEMNPST	ENSTAMP		SMATTER	AENPRSZ	PANZERS		PROTEAS
	TAPSMEN	AEMRSTU	MATURES	AENPRTT	PATTERN		SEAPORT
AEMNPSU	PNEUMAS		STRUMAE		REPTANT	AEOPRTT	PORTATE
AEMNPTU	PUTAMEN	AEMRSTW	WARMEST	AENPRUV	PARVENU	AEOPRVY	OVERPAY
AEMNPTY	PAYMENT	AEMRSTY	MASTERY	AENPSST	APTNESS	AEOPRWY	ROPEWAY
AEMNRRU	MANURER		MAYSTER		PATNESS	AEOPSSS	PSOASES
AEMNRST	ARTSMEN		STREAMY		PESANTS	AEOPSTT	APTOTES
	MARTENS	AEMRTTX	MARTEXT	AENPSSY	SYNAPSE		TEAPOTS
	SARMENT	AEMRTTY	MATTERY	AENPSTT	PATENTS	AEOPSTY	TEAPOYS
	SMARTEN	AEMRTUU	TRUMEAU		PATTENS	AEOPSTZ	TOPAZES
AEMNRSU	MANURES	AEMSSSU	ASSUMES	AENPSTU	PEANUTS	AEOQRTU	EQUATOR
	MURENAS	AEMSSUW	WAMUSES		PESAUNT		QUORATE
	SURNAME	AEMSSYZ	ZYMASES	AENPSTW	STEWPAN	AEOQRUV	VAQUERO
AEMNRTU	TRUEMAN	AEMSTTU	MUTATES	AENPSTY	SYNAPTE	AEOQSUU	AQUEOUS
AEMNRTV	VARMENT	AEMSTUV	MAUVEST	AENPSTZ	PEZANTS	AEORRRS	ROARERS
AEMNSSS	MESSANS	AEMSTVZ	ZEMSTVA	AENQSTU	EQUANTS	AEORRSS	SOARERS
AEMNSST	STAMENS	AENNNOS	NONANES	AENRRSS	SERRANS	AEORRST	ROASTER
AEMNSSU	UNSEAMS	AENNNPT	PENNANT		SNARERS	AEORRSU	AROUSER
AEMNSTU	UNTAMES	AENNOPS	PANNOSE	AENRRST	ERRANTS	AEORSSS	SAROSES
	UNTEAMS	AENNORT	NORTENA		RANTERS		SEROSAS
AEMNSTY	AMNESTY	AENNORY	ANNOYER	AENRRSW	WARNERS	AEORSSU	AROUSES
AEMNTWY	WAYMENT	AENNOSS	NOSEANS		WARRENS	AEORSTT	ROTATES
AEMOORW	WOOMERA	AENNOSV	NOVENAS	AENRRTT	TRANTER		TOASTER
AEMOOST	OSTEOMA	AENNOSY	ANYONES	AENRRTY	TERNARY	AEORSUV	AVOURES
AEMOOSV	AMOOVES	AENNOTU	TONNEAU	AENRSSS	SARSENS	AEORSVW	AVOWERS
	VAMOOSE	AENNPRS	SPANNER	AENRSST	SARSNET		OVERSAW
AEMOPPR	PAMPERO	AENNQTU	QUANNET		TRANSES	AEORSVY	AVOYERS
AEMOPSZ	APOZEMS	AENNRST	TANNERS	AENRSSW	ANSWERS	AEORTTU	OUTRATE
AEMORRS	REMORAS	AENNRSV	VANNERS		RAWNESS	AEORTUW	OUTWEAR
	ROAMERS	AENNRTT	ENTRANT	AENRSSY	SARNEYS	AEORTVX	OVERTAX
AEMORRV	OVERARM	AENNRTV	VERNANT	AENRSTT	NATTERS	AEOSSTV	AVOSETS
AEMORST	AMORETS	AENNRTY	TANNERY		RATTENS	AEOSTTU	OUTEATS
	MAESTRO		TYRANNE	AENRSTU	AUNTERS	AEPPRRS	RAPPERS
	OMERTAS	AENNSSW	WANNESS		NATURES	AEPPRRT	TRAPPER
AEMORSU	RAMEOUS	AENNSTT	TANNEST		SAUNTER	AEPPRRW	WRAPPER
AEMORSW	SEAWORM		TENANTS	AENRSTV	SERVANT	AEPPRSS	APPRESS
	WOMERAS	AENNSTW	WANNEST		TAVERNS		SAPPERS
AEMORSX	XEROMAS	AENOOTZ	ENTOZOA		VERSANT	AEPPRST	TAPPERS
AEMOSST	OSMATES	AENOPPR	PROPANE	AENRSTW	STRAWEN	AEPPRSU	PAUPERS
AEMOSSV	VAMOSES	AENOPRS	PERSONA		WANTERS		UPSPEAR
AEMOSTW	TWASOME	AENOPRT	OPERANT	AENRSTY	TRAYNES	AEPPRSW	SWAPPER
AEMOSUZ	ZAMOUSE		PRONATE	AENRSUW	UNSWEAR		WAPPERS
AEMOSWY	SOMEWAY		PROTEAN		UNWARES	AEPPRSY	PREPAYS
AEMOTTZ	MOZETTA	AENOPSU	POSAUNE	AENRTTU	TAUNTER		YAPPERS
AEMPPRS	MAPPERS	AENOPSV	PAVONES	AENRTTY	NATTERY	AEPPRSZ	ZAPPERS
	PAMPERS	AENOPSW	WEAPONS	AENRTUV	VAUNTER	AEPPSTT	TAPPETS
	PREAMPS	AENORRT	ORNATER	AENRTUW	UNWATER	AEPPSTU	PUPATES
AEMPPRY	MAPPERY	AENORRV	OVERRAN	AENRUWY	UNWEARY	AEPQRTU	PARQUET
AEMPRRS	RAMPERS	AENORSS	REASONS	AENSSST	ASSENTS	AEPRRRS	SPARRER
AEMPRRT	TRAMPER	AENORST	ATONERS		SNASTES	AEPRRSS	PARSERS
AEMPRRW	PREWARM		SENATOR	AENSSTU	NASUTES		RASPERS
AEMPRST	EMPARTS		TREASON		UNSEATS		SPARERS
	STAMPER	AENORTV	VENATOR	AENSSTX	SEXTANS		SPARRES
	TAMPERS	AENORXY	ANOREXY	AENSSTY	STAYNES		SPARSER
AEMPRSV	REVAMPS	AENOSSS	SEASONS	AENSSTZ	STANZES	AEPRRST	PARTERS
	VAMPERS	AENOSST	ASTONES	AENSSWY	SAWNEYS		PRATERS
AEMPRSW	SWAMPER	AENOSTT	ATTONES	AENSSXY	SYNAXES	AEPRRSU	PARURES
AEMPRTT	TRAMPET		NOTATES	AENSTTT	ATTENTS		UPREARS
AEMPRTU	TEMPURA	AENOSTU	SOUTANE	AENSTTU	ATTUNES	AEPRRSW	REWRAPS
AEMPSSU	EMPUSAS	AENOSVW	WAVESON		NUTATES		WARPERS
AEMPTTT	ATTEMPT	AENOUUV	NOUVEAU		TAUTENS	AEPRRSY	PRAYERS
AEMPTTU	TAPETUM	AENPPRS	NAPPERS		TETANUS		RESPRAY
AEMQRSU	MARQUES		PARPENS		UNSTATE		SPRAYER
	MASQUER		PARSNEP	AENSTTX	SEXTANT	AEPRRTU	PARTURE
AEMQSSU	MASQUES		SNAPPER	AENSTUX	UNTAXES		RAPTURE
	SQUAMES	AENPPRT	PARPENT	AENSTWY	TAWNEYS	AEPRRTY	PETRARY
AEMRRRY	REMARRY	AENPPRU	UNPAPER	AENTTTU	ATTUENT	AEPRSSS	PASSERS
AEMRRST	SMARTER	AENPRRT	PARTNER	AEOOPPS	PAPOOSE	AEPRSST	PASTERS
AEMRRSU	ARMURES	AENPRRW	PREWARN	AEOOPRS	OROPESA		REPASTS
AEMRRSV	MARVERS	AENPRST	ARPENTS	AEOPPPS	PAPPOSE		SPAREST
AEMRRSW	SWARMER		ENTRAPS	AEOPPRS	APPOSER	AEPRSSU	PAUSERS
	WARMERS		PANTERS	AEOPPRV	APPROVE	AEPRSSY	PESSARY
AEMRRTU	ERRATUM		PARENTS	AEOPPSS	APPOSES	AEPRSTT	PATTERS
	MATURER		PASTERN	AEOPQRU	OPAQUER		SPATTER
AEMRSST	MASTERS		PERSANT	AEOPQSU	OPAQUES		TAPSTER
	STREAMS		TREPANS	AEOPRRT	PRAETOR	AEPRSTU	PASTURE
AEMRSSU	AMUSERS	AENPRSW	ENWRAPS		PRORATE		UPRATES
	MASSEUR		PAWNERS	AEOPRSS	SOAPERS		UPSTARE

	UPTEARS	AFFGSUW	GUFFAWS	AFHIKRS	KHARIFS	AFISSTY	SATISFY
AEPRSTY	YAPSTER	AFFHILN	HAFFLIN	AFHIKUY	KUFIYAH	AFISTTT	FATTIST
AEPRSTZ	PATZERS	AFFHIRS	RAFFISH	AFHILLN	HALFLIN	AFITTUY	FATUITY
AEPRSWY	YAWPERS	AFFHIST	HAFFITS	AFHILSS	FALSISH	AFJLRSU	JARFULS
AEPRSYY	SPRAYEY	AFFILMN	MAFFLIN	AFHILTW	HALFWIT	AFKLNRY	FRANKLY
AEPRTXY	APTERYX	AFFILPS	PILAFFS	AFHIMNU	HAFNIUM	AFKLNTU	TANKFUL
AEPSSTU	PETASUS	AFFILSY	FALSIFY	AFHINOS	FASHION	AFKLOWY	FOLKWAY
AEPSSZZ	SPAZZES	AFFIMRS	AFFIRMS	AFHINTU	UNFAITH	AFLLMPU	PALMFUL
AEPSTTU	UPSTATE	AFFIMST	MASTIFF	AFHIRRS	SHARIFS	AFLLMSU	FULLAMS
AEPSZZZ	PZAZZES	AFFINRU	FUNFAIR	AFHISST	FASTISH	AFLLNOS	ONFALLS
AEQRRSU	SQUARER		RUFFIAN	AFHISSW	SAWFISH	AFLLNSU	FULLANS
AEQRRTU	QUARTER	AFFINTY	TIFFANY	AFHISTT	FATTISH	AFLLOOY	ALOOFLY
AEQRSSU	SQUARES	AFFIORR	FORFAIR	AFHKORY	HAYFORK	AFLLOSW	FALLOWS
AEQRSTU	QUAREST	AFFIRRU	FURFAIR	AFHKRTU	FUTHARK	AFLLOTU	FALLOUT
	QUARTES	AFFIRST	TARIFFS	AFHLMRU	HARMFUL		OUTFALL
AEQRSUV	QUAVERS	AFFNORS	SAFFRON	AFHLMSU	FULHAMS	AFLLPSU	LAPFULS
AEQRTTU	QUARTET	AFFNORT	AFFRONT	AFHLOOS	LOOFAHS	AFLLPUY	PLAYFUL
AEQRUVY	QUAVERY	AFFRSST	STRAFFS	AFHLOTY	HAYLOFT	AFLLUWY	AWFULLY
AERRSST	ARRESTS	AFGGGIN	FAGGING	AFHLSTU	HATFULS	AFLMNOU	MOANFUL
	RASTERS	AFGGINN	FANGING	AFHMOST	FATHOMS	AFLMORU	FORMULA
	STARERS	AFGGOST	FAGGOTS	AFHOOPT	POOFTAH	AFLMORW	WOLFRAM
AERRSSU	ASSURER	AFGHHIS	HAGFISH	AFHOPTU	POUFTAH	AFLMOST	FLOTSAM
	RASURES	AFGHINS	FASHING	AFHORSS	SHOFARS	AFLMRSU	ARMFULS
AERRSTT	RATTERS	AFGHINT	HAFTING	AFIILNS	FINIALS		FULMARS
	RESTART	AFGHIRS	GARFISH	AFIILOR	AIRFOIL	AFLMSTU	MASTFUL
	STARTER	AFGHLSU	GASHFUL	AFIILRT	AIRLIFT	AFLMSUU	FAMULUS
AERRSTY	STRAYER	AFGHLTU	FLAUGHT	AFIILRY	FAIRILY	AFLNORT	FRONTAL
AERRSUZ	RAZURES	AFGHRTU	FRAUGHT	AFIIMOS	MAFIOSI	AFLNOTT	FLOTANT
AERRSWY	WARREYS	AFGIIKN	FAIKING	AFIJNNS	FINJANS	AFLNPSU	PANFULS
AERRTTY	RATTERY	AFGIILN	FAILING	AFIKLOT	FLOKATI	AFLNRTU	RUNFLAT
AERSSST	ASSERTS	AFGIINN	FAINING	AFIKNRT	RATFINK	AFLNSTU	FLAUNTS
	TRASSES	AFGIINR	FAIRING	AFIKNSU	FUNKIAS	AFLNTUY	FLAUNTY
AERSSSU	ASSURES	AFGIINT	FIATING	AFIKRSS	FRISKAS	AFLOOTW	WOOLFAT
	SARUSES	AFGIINW	WAIFING	AFILLMS	MISFALL	AFLORSU	FUSAROL
AERSSSW	WRASSES	AFGIKLN	FLAKING	AFILLNS	INFALLS	AFLORSV	FLAVORS
AERSSTT	ASTERTS	AFGILLN	FALLING	AFILLNY	FINALLY	AFLORUV	FLAVOUR
	STARETS	AFGILMN	FLAMING	AFILLPT	PITFALL	AFLORWW	WARWOLF
	STATERS	AFGILNO	FOALING	AFILLPU	PAILFUL	AFLOSSU	FOSSULA
	TASTERS		LOAFING	AFILLRY	FRAILLY	AFLPRTY	FLYTRAP
AERSSTV	STARVES	AFGILNR	FLARING		VIALFUL	AFLRTUY	TRAYFUL
AERSSTW	WASTERS	AFGILNS	FALSING	AFILLUW	WAILFUL	AFLSTUV	VATFULS
AERSSTY	ESTRAYS	AFGILNT	FATLING	AFILMOR	ALIFORM	AFLSWYY	FLYWAYS
	STAYERS	AFGILNW	FLAWING	AFILMOY	FOAMILY	AFMNOOT	FOOTMAN
	STAYRES	AFGILNY	ANGLIFY	AFILMPY	AMPLIFY	AFMNORT	FORMANT
AERSSUV	VARUSES		FLAYING	AFILMSS	FALSISM	AFMNOST	FANTOMS
AERSSVW	SWARVES	AFGILRU	FIGURAL	AFILNPU	PAINFUL	AFMNRSU	SURFMAN
AERSSWY	SAWYERS	AFGIMNO	FOAMING	AFILNSV	FLAVINS	AFMNRTU	TURFMAN
	SWAYERS	AFGIMNR	FARMING	AFILNTU	FLUTINA	AFMOOSS	SAMFOOS
AERSTTT	STRETTA		FRAMING	AFILNTY	FAINTLY	AFMORST	FARMOST
	TARTEST	AFGIMNY	MAGNIFY	AFILORW	AIRFLOW		FORMATS
	TATTERS	AFGINNN	FANNING	AFILQUY	QUALIFY	AFMORTU	FOUMART
AERSTTU	ASTUTER	AFGINNS	FINGANS	AFILRRY	FRIARLY	AFMOSTT	AFTMOST
	STATURE	AFGINNW	FAWNING	AFILRSZ	FRAZILS	AFMOSTU	SFUMATO
AERSTTV	VATTERS	AFGINNY	FAYNING	AFILRTY	FRAILTY	AFNORRW	FORWARN
AERSTTW	SWATTER	AFGINRR	FARRING	AFILSSY	SALSIFY	AFNSSTU	SUNFAST
	TEWARTS	AFGINRS	FARSING	AFILSTU	FISTULA	AFOOPPR	APPROOF
AERSTTY	YATTERS	AFGINRT	FARTING	AFILSTY	FALSITY	AFOORST	FOOTRAS
AERSTTZ	STARETZ		INGRAFT	AFIMNRS	FIRMANS	AFOORTZ	FORZATO
AERSTUU	AUTEURS		RAFTING	AFIMOOS	MAFIOSO	AFOOTWY	FOOTWAY
AERSTUY	ESTUARY	AFGINRY	FRAYING	AFIMORV	AVIFORM	AFORRSW	FARROWS
AERTTTY	TATTERY	AFGINST	FASTING	AFIMSSS	MASSIFS	AFORRSY	FORRAYS
AERTTUV	VETTURA	AFGINTT	FATTING	AFIMSSV	FAVISMS	AFORSSY	FORSAYS
AESSSTT	TASSETS	AFGINTW	WAFTING	AFIMSTT	FATTISM	AFORSTU	FAUTORS
AESSTTT	ATTESTS	AFGIOTT	FAGOTTI	AFINNNS	FINNANS		FOUTRAS
AESSTTU	STATUES	AFGIRTY	GRATIFY	AFINNOR	FRANION	AFORSUV	FAVOURS
AESSTTV	VASTEST	AFGKNOP	PAKFONG	AFINNOS	FANIONS	AFOSSSU	FOUSSAS
AESSTUV	SUAVEST	AFGKORT	KOFTGAR	AFINNST	INFANTS	AFOSTUU	FATUOUS
AESSTUY	EUSTASY	AFGLLLY	GALLFLY	AFINRSU	UNFAIRS	AFPSTUW	UPWAFTS
AESSVVY	SAVVEYS	AFGLLUY	FUGALLY	AFINSSU	FUSAINS	AGGGGIN	GAGGING
AESTTTU	STATUTE	AFGLNOS	FLAGONS	AFINSTU	FAUNIST	AGGGHIN	HAGGING
	TAUTEST	AFGLRYY	GRAYFLY		FIAUNTS	AGGGIJN	JAGGING
AESTTTW	WATTEST	AFGMNOR	FROGMAN		FUSTIAN	AGGGILN	LAGGING
AFFFGIN	FAFFING	AFGMORS	FOGRAMS		INFAUST	AGGGIMN	MAGGING
AFFGGIN	GAFFING	AFGOOTT	FAGOTTO	AFIORST	FAITORS	AGGGINN	GANGING
AFFGINN	NAFFING	AFGORRS	FRAGORS	AFIORTU	FAITOUR		NAGGING
AFFGINW	WAFFING	AFGOSTU	FUGATOS	AFIORTZ	FORZATI	AGGGINR	RAGGING
AFFGINY	AFFYING	AFHIIRS	FAIRISH	AFIORSU	FAQUIRS	AGGGINS	SAGGING
	YAFFING	AFHIKLS	KHALIFS	AFISSTT	SITFAST	AGGGINT	TAGGING
						AGGGINU	GAUGING

AGGGGINW	WAGGING
AGGGINZ	ZAGGING
AGGHHIS	HAGGISH
AGGHIIL	GHILGAI
AGGHIMN	GINGHAM
AGGHINN	HANGING
AGGHINS	GASHING
AGGHISW	WAGGISH
AGGIIJJ	JIGAJIG
AGGIILS	GILGAIS
AGGIIMN	IMAGING
AGGIINN	GAINING
AGGIINT	GAITING
AGGIJJO	JIGAJOG
AGGIKNW	GAWKING
AGGILLN	GALLING
	GINGALL
AGGILNN	ANGLING
AGGILNO	GAOLING
	GOALING
AGGILNR	GLARING
AGGILNS	GINGALS
	LAGGINS
AGGILNZ	GLAZING
AGGILOS	LOGGIAS
AGGIMMN	GAMMING
AGGIMNN	MANGING
AGGIMNS	GAMINGS
AGGIMNU	GAUMING
AGGINNP	PANGING
AGGINNR	RANGING
AGGINNT	GANTING
	TANGING
AGGINNW	GNAWING
AGGINPP	GAPPING
AGGINPR	GRAPING
	PARGING
AGGINPS	GAPINGS
	GASPING
	PAGINGS
AGGINPU	GAUPING
AGGINPW	GAWPING
AGGINRR	GARRING
AGGINRS	RAGINGS
	SIRGANG
AGGINRT	GRATING
	TARGING
AGGINRU	ARGUING
AGGINRV	GRAVING
AGGINRY	GRAYING
AGGINRZ	GRAZING
AGGINSS	GASSING
AGGINST	GASTING
	GATINGS
	STAGING
AGGINSW	SWAGING
AGGINUV	VAGUING
AGGIORS	GORGIAS
AGGISWW	WIGWAGS
AGGISZZ	ZIGZAGS
AGGLOST	LOGGATS
AGGMNOS	MOGGANS
AGGMORR	GROGRAM
AGGMOST	MAGGOTS
AGGMOTY	MAGGOTY
AGGNOSU	GUANGOS
AGGNOSW	WAGGONS
AGGNOSX	OXGANGS
AGGNPSU	UPGANGS
AGGNRSU	NUGGARS
AGGPRSY	PYGARGS
AGHHIMN	HIGHMAN
AGHHINS	HASHING
AGHHIWY	HIGHWAY
AGHHOSW	HOGWASH
AGHHTUY	HAUGHTY
AGHIILN	HAILING
AGHIINN	HAINING
AGHIINR	HAIRING
AGHIJRS	JAGHIRS
AGHIKNN	HANKING
AGHIKNR	HARKING
AGHIKNS	SHAKING
AGHIKNW	HAWKING
AGHIKSU	KIAUGHS
AGHILLN	HALLING
AGHILNO	HALOING
AGHILNR	HARLING
AGHILNS	HALSING
	LASHING
	SHALING
AGHILNT	HALTING
	LATHING
AGHILNU	HAULING
AGHILNV	HALVING
AGHILNW	WHALING
AGHILRS	LARGISH
AGHILRT	ALRIGHT
AGHILST	ALIGHTS
AGHIMMN	HAMMING
AGHIMNR	HARMING
AGHIMNS	MASHING
	SHAMING
AGHIMNW	HAWMING
AGHIMPS	GAMPISH
AGHINNO	NIHONGA
AGHINNT	TANGHIN
AGHINOR	HOARING
AGHINOX	HOAXING
AGHINPP	HAPPING
AGHINPR	HARPING
AGHINPS	HASPING
	PASHING
	PHASING
	SHAPING
AGHINPT	PATHING
AGHINRS	GARNISH
	RASHING
	SHARING
AGHINRU	NURAGHI
AGHINSS	SASHING
AGHINST	HASTING
	TASHING
AGHINSU	ANGUISH
AGHINSV	HAVINGS
	SHAVING
AGHINSW	HAWSING
	WASHING
AGHINSY	HAYINGS
AGHINSZ	HAZINGS
AGHINTT	HATTING
	TATHING
AGHINTW	THAWING
AGHIOST	GOATISH
AGHIPSW	PIGWASH
AGHIQSU	QUAIGHS
AGHIRRS	GHARRIS
AGHIRST	GRAITHS
AGHIRSU	GUARISH
AGHKOSW	GOSHAWK
AGHLMPU	GALUMPH
AGHLNUY	NYLGHAU
AGHLOOS	GASOHOL
AGHLOSU	GOULASH
AGHLSTU	GALUTHS
AGHLSTY	GHASTLY
AGHNNSU	UNHANGS
AGHNOTU	HANGOUT
	TOHUNGA
AGHNPSU	UPHANGS
AGHNRST	THRANGS
AGHNRSU	NURHAGS
AGHNRUY	AHUNGRY
AGHNSTU	NAUGHTS
AGHNSUY	GUNYAHS
AGHNTUY	NAUGHTY
AGHOQSU	QUAHOGS
AGHORTW	WARTHOG
AGHPTUY	PAUGHTY
AGHRRSU	GURRAHS
AGHRSTU	TUGHRAS
AGHRSTY	GYTRASH
AGHSTUW	WAUGHTS
AGIIJLN	JAILING
AGIIKLN	LAIKING
AGIIKLT	GLAIKIT
AGIIKNP	PAIKING
AGIIKNR	RAIKING
AGIILMN	MAILING
AGIILNN	ALINING
	NAILING
AGIILNR	GLAIRIN
	LAIRING
	RAILING
AGIILNS	AISLING
	NILGAIS
	SAILING
AGIILNT	TAILING
AGIILNV	VAILING
AGIILNW	WAILING
AGIILOV	VILIAGO
AGIILPT	PIGTAIL
AGIILTY	AGILITY
AGIIMMN	MAIMING
AGIIMMS	IMAGISM
AGIIMNN	MAINING
AGIIMOR	ORIGAMI
AGIIMST	IMAGIST
AGIINNP	PAINING
AGIINNR	AIRNING
	INGRAIN
	RAINING
AGIINNS	SAINING
AGIINNW	WAINING
AGIINPR	PAIRING
AGIINRS	AIRINGS
	ARISING
	RAGINIS
	RAISING
	SAIRING
AGIINRT	AIRTING
	RAITING
AGIINSV	AVISING
	VISAING
AGIINTW	WAITING
AGIINTX	TAXIING
AGIINVV	VIVAING
AGIINVW	WAIVING
AGIINVZ	AVIZING
AGIJLNS	JINGALS
AGIJMMN	JAMMING
AGIJNPP	JAPPING
AGIJNPS	JAPINGS
AGIJNPU	JAUPING
AGIJNRR	JARRING
AGIJNSW	JAWINGS
AGIJNZZ	JAZZING
AGIJSSW	JIGSAWS
AGIKKNR	KARKING
AGIKKNY	YAKKING
AGIKLNN	LANKING
AGIKLNO	OAKLING
AGIKLNR	LARKING
AGIKLNS	SLAKING
AGIKLNT	TALKING
AGIKLNW	WALKING
AGIKMNR	MARKING
AGIKMNS	MAKINGS
	MASKING
AGIKNNR	NARKING
	RANKING
AGIKNNS	SNAKING
AGIKNNT	KANTING
	TANKING
AGIKNNU	UNAKING
AGIKNNW	WANKING
AGIKNNY	YANKING
AGIKNOS	SOAKING
AGIKNOY	KAYOING
	OKAYING
AGIKNPR	PARKING
AGIKNQU	QUAKING
AGIKNRS	RAKINGS
	SARKING
AGIKNRT	KARTING
AGIKNSS	GASKINS
AGIKNST	SKATING
	STAKING
	TAKINGS
	TASKING
AGIKNSW	WAKINGS
AGIKNUW	WAUKING
AGILLLN	LALLING
AGILLMN	MALLING
AGILLMU	GALLIUM
AGILLNP	PALLING
AGILLNU	LINGUAL
	LINGULA
AGILLNW	WALLING
AGILLNY	ALLYING
AGILLOR	GORILLA
AGILLOT	GALLIOT
AGILLRU	LIGULAR
AGILLSU	LIGULAS
	LUGSAIL
AGILMMN	LAMMING
AGILMMS	GIMMALS
AGILMNO	LOAMING
AGILMNP	LAMPING
	PALMING
AGILMNR	MARLING
AGILMNS	LINGAMS
	MALIGNS
AGILMNT	MALTING
AGILMNU	MAULING
AGILMOS	GLIOMAS
AGILMPS	MAGILPS
AGILMPU	PLAGIUM
AGILNNO	LOANING
AGILNNP	PLANING
AGILNNR	LARNING
AGILNNS	LINSANG
AGILNNT	TANLING
AGILNOP	GALOPIN
AGILNOR	RANGOLI
AGILNOT	ANTILOG
AGILNOV	LOAVING
AGILNOZ	LAZOING
AGILNPP	LAPPING
	PALPING
AGILNPR	PARLING
AGILNPS	LAPSING
	PALINGS
	SAPLING
AGILNPT	PLATING
AGILNPW	LAPWING
AGILNPY	PLAYING
AGILNRT	RATLING
AGILNRW	WARLING
AGILNRY	ANGRILY
	NARGILY
	RAYLING
AGILNSS	LASINGS
	SIGNALS
AGILNST	ANGLIST
	LASTING
	SALTING
	SLATING
	STALING
AGILNSU	LINGUAS
	NILGAUS
	SALUING
AGILNSV	SALVING
	SLAVING
	VALSING

```
AGILNSW  LAWINGS
         SWALING
AGILNSY  LAYINGS
         SLAYING
AGILNTY  GIANTLY
AGILNUV  VALUING
AGILNUW  WAULING
AGILNVV  VALVING
AGILNWW  WAWLING
AGILNWY  YAWLING
AGILOPT  GALIPOT
AGILORS  GIRASOL
         GLORIAS
AGILORW  AIRGLOW
AGILOST  GALIOTS
         SALIGOT
AGILRSS  SLAIRGS
AGILSTY  STAGILY
AGIMMNR  RAMMING
AGIMMSS  MAGISMS
AGIMNNN  MANNING
AGIMNNO  MOANING
AGIMNNR  RINGMAN
AGIMNNS  NAMINGS
AGIMNOR  ROAMING
AGIMNOT  MOATING
AGIMNOV  AMOVING
AGIMNPP  MAPPING
AGIMNPR  RAMPING
AGIMNPT  TAMPING
AGIMNPV  VAMPING
AGIMNRR  MARRING
AGIMNRS  MARGINS
AGIMNRT  MARTING
         MIGRANT
AGIMNRW  WARMING
AGIMNRY  MYRINGA
AGIMNSS  MASSING
AGIMNST  MASTING
         TAMINGS
AGIMNSU  AMUSING
AGIMNSY  MAYINGS
AGIMNTT  MATTING
AGIMORS  ISOGRAM
AGIMORU  GOURAMI
AGIMOSY  ISOGAMY
AGIMRRT  TRIGRAM
AGIMRSU  GURAMIS
AGIMRTY  TRIGAMY
AGIMSST  STIGMAS
AGIMSWW  WIGWAMS
AGINNNP  PANNING
AGINNNT  TANNING
AGINNNV  VANNING
AGINNNW  WANNING
AGINNOS  GANOINS
AGINNOT  ATONING
AGINNPP  NAPPING
AGINNPS  SPANING
AGINNPT  PANTING
AGINNPW  PAWNING
AGINNRS  SNARING
AGINNRT  RANTING
AGINNRW  WARNING
AGINNRY  YARNING
AGINNST  ANTINGS
         STANING
AGINNSW  AWNINGS
         WANINGS
AGINNTW  WANTING
AGINNWY  YAWNING
AGINNWZ  WANZING
AGINNYZ  ZANYING
AGINOOO  OOGONIA
AGINOPS  SOAPING
AGINORR  ROARING
AGINORS  IGNAROS
         ORIGANS
         SIGNORA

         SOARING
AGINORT  ORATING
         ROATING
AGINOSS  SAGOINS
AGINOST  AGONIST
         GITANOS
AGINOSU  SAGOUIN
AGINOTV  OVATING
AGINOTZ  TOAZING
AGINOVW  AVOWING
AGINPPP  PAPPING
AGINPPR  PARPING
         RAPPING
AGINPPS  SAPPING
AGINPPT  TAPPING
AGINPPW  WAPPING
AGINPPY  YAPPING
AGINPPZ  ZAPPING
AGINPRS  PARINGS
         PARSING
         RASPING
         SPARING
AGINPRT  PARTING
         PRATING
         TRAPING
AGINPRW  WARPING
AGINPRY  PRAYING
AGINPSS  PASSING
         SPAINGS
AGINPST  PASTING
AGINPSU  PAUSING
AGINPSV  PAVINGS
AGINPSY  PAYINGS
         SPAYING
AGINPTT  PATTING
AGINPTU  TAPUING
AGINPWY  YAWPING
AGINRRT  TARRING
AGINRRW  WARRING
AGINRST  GASTRIN
         GRATINS
         RATINGS
         STARING
         TARINGS
AGINRSV  RAVINGS
AGINRSW  RAWINGS
AGINRSY  SIGNARY
         SYRINGA
AGINRTT  RATTING
AGINRTY  GIANTRY
AGINRUW  WAURING
AGINRVY  VARYING
AGINRWY  RINGWAY
AGINRZZ  RAZZING
AGINSSS  ASSIGNS
         SASSING
AGINSSU  SAGUINS
AGINSSV  SAVINGS
AGINSSW  SAWINGS
AGINSSY  SAYINGS
AGINSTT  STATING
         TASTING
AGINSTU  SAUTING
AGINSTV  STAVING
AGINSTW  STAWING
         TAWINGS
         WASTING
AGINSTX  TAXINGS
AGINSTY  STAYING
AGINSVW  WAVINGS
AGINSWX  WAXINGS
AGINSWY  SWAYING
AGINTTT  TATTING
AGINTTU  TATUING
         TAUTING
AGINTTV  VATTING
AGINTTW  TAWTING
AGINTUV  VAUTING
AGINTVW  VAWTING

AGINTXY  TAXYING
AGINTYZ  TZIGANY
AGINVYZ  AVYZING
AGINWWX  WAXWING
AGIORST  AGISTOR
         ORGIAST
AGIORSU  GIAOURS
AGIORSV  VIRAGOS
AGIOSTU  AGOUTIS
AGIRSTU  GUITARS
AGIRTVY  GRAVITY
AGISTTW  WITGATS
AGISTUV  VAGITUS
AGJLRUU  JUGULAR
AGJNOOR  JARGOON
AGJNORS  JARGONS
AGKLNNO  ANKLONG
AGKLNNU  ANKLUNG
AGKLNOS  KALONGS
AGKLOOS  KAGOOLS
AGKLOST  KGOTLAS
AGKLOSU  KAGOULS
AGKMNOP  KAMPONG
AGKNOPT  PAKTONG
AGKNRSU  KURGANS
AGKORRW  RAGWORK
AGLLNOO  GALLOON
AGLLNOS  GALLONS
         GOLLANS
AGLLNTU  GALLNUT
         NUTGALL
AGLLOPS  GALLOPS
AGLLORS  GOLLARS
AGLLOSS  GLOSSAL
AGLLOSW  GALLOWS
AGLLOTT  GLOTTAL
AGLLRYY  GYRALLY
AGLMMSY  GYMMALS
AGLMOPY  POLYGAM
AGLMORS  GLAMORS
AGLMORU  GLAMOUR
AGLNNOS  LONGANS
AGLNOOS  LAGOONS
AGLNORU  LANGUOR
AGLNOSS  SLOGANS
AGLNOST  ALONGST
AGLNOSU  LANUGOS
AGLNOSW  GOWLANS
AGLNPSY  SPANGLY
AGLNPUY  GUNPLAY
AGLNRSU  LANGURS
AGLNTUY  GAUNTLY
AGLOOPY  APOLOGY
AGLOOST  GALOOTS
AGLOSSS  GLOSSAS
AGLOSUV  VALGOUS
AGLRSSU  GUSLARS
AGLRSUU  ARGULUS
AGLRSUV  VULGARS
AGMMNOS  GAMMONS
AGMMORY  MYOGRAM
AGMNNOS  MAGNONS
         SONGMAN
AGMNNOW  GOWNMAN
AGMNORU  ORGANUM
AGMNOST  AMONGST
AGMNSSU  MUSANGS
AGMNSTU  MUSTANG
AGMNSTY  GYMNAST
         SYNTAGM
AGMNSYY  SYNGAMY
AGMOOYZ  ZOOGAMY
AGMOPRR  PROGRAM
AGMOPRU  GOPURAM
AGMORRW  RAGWORM
AGMORSS  ORGASMS
AGMORSY  MORGAYS
AGMOSYZ  ZYGOMAS

AGMPRSU  GRAMPUS
AGMPSUZ  GAZUMPS
AGMRSSU  GRASSUM
AGNNNOO  NONAGON
AGNNOOR  ORGANON
AGNNOST  TONNAGS
AGNNSTU  TANGUNS
AGNNSUW  WANGUNS
AGNOOSZ  GAZOONS
AGNOQSU  QUANGOS
AGNORRS  GARRONS
AGNORRT  GRANTOR
AGNORSS  SARONGS
AGNOSSS  GOSSANS
AGNOSST  SONTAGS
AGNOSTU  NOUGATS
AGNOSZZ  GOZZANS
AGNRSSU  SUNGARS
AGNRTUY  GAUNTRY
AGOPPST  STOPGAP
AGOPRST  RAGTOPS
AGOPRSU  GOPURAS
AGORRST  GARROTS
AGORRTW  RAGWORT
AGORSTU  RAGOUTS
AGOSTTU  TAUTOGS
AGOSUYZ  AZYGOUS
AGSSTUU  AUGUSTS
AHHHISS  HASHISH
AHHIJRS  HIJRAHS
AHHIKSS  SHAIKHS
AHHIKSW  HAWKISH
AHHIMNU  HAHNIUM
AHHIPRS  RHAPHIS
AHHISSV  SHIVAHS
AHHISTT  SHITTAH
AHHKOOS  HOOKAHS
AHHLRSY  HARSHLY
AHHOORS  HOORAHS
AHHOPRS  SHOPHAR
AHHPPSU  HUPPAHS
AHHPTUZ  HUTZPAH
AHHRRSU  HURRAHS
AHIIKRS  SHIKARI
AHIILPS  SILPHIA
AHIILST  LITHIAS
AHIIMNT  THIAMIN
AHIIMSS  SASHIMI
AHIINPR  HAIRPIN
AHIINST  TAHINIS
AHIINTU  HUITAIN
AHIIPRS  AIRSHIP
AHIKLRS  LARKISH
AHIKLST  KHILATS
AHIKLSY  SHAKILY
AHIKMNS  KHAMSIN
AHIKMRS  KASHMIR
AHIKMSW  MAWKISH
AHIKNSS  SNAKISH
AHIKNSV  KNAVISH
AHIKOSW  KOWHAIS
AHIKPRS  PARKISH
AHIKRSS  SHIKARS
AHIKSSS  SHIKSAS
AHIKSST  SKAITHS
AHILLNO  HALLION
AHILLNP  PHALLIN
AHILLRT  ATHRILL
AHILLSS  SHALLIS
AHILLST  TALLISH
AHILLSZ  ZILLAHS
AHILLTT  TALLITH
AHILMMS  MASHLIM
AHILMMY  HAMMILY
AHILMNS  MASHLIN
AHILMOP  OMPHALI
AHILMOS  HOLMIAS
AHILMOT  HALIMOT
AHILMSU  ALUMISH
```

AHILNPS	PLANISH	AHKMORR	MARKHOR	AHNSTUW	UNTHAWS	AIINPRS	ASPIRIN
AHILMPSV	SHRINAL	AHKMOSW	MOHAWKS	AHNSTUY	UNHASTY	AIINPST	PIANIST
AHILNRT	INTHRAL	AHKMRTU	MUKHTAR	AHOORSY	HOORAYS	AIINRSS	RAISINS
AHILNSU	INHAULS	AHKNPSU	PUNKAHS	AHOPRTY	ATROPHY	AIINRTV	VITRAIN
AHILNSY	LINHAYS	AHKRSST	SKARTHS	AHOPSTW	WASHPOT	AIINSST	ISATINS
AHILORY	HOARILY	AHKRSSU	KASHRUS	AHOPTTW	TOWPATH	AIINSSX	SIXAINS
AHILOTY	ALIYOTH	AHKRSTU	KASHRUT	AHORRSW	HARROWS	AIINSTT	TITANIS
AHILPPS	SHIPLAP		KHURTAS	AHORSTT	THROATS		TITIANS
AHILPPY	HAPPILY		TUSHKAR	AHORSTU	AUTHORS	AIINSTV	NAIVIST
AHILPSY	APISHLY	AHLLMOS	MOLLAHS	AHORSTW	WROATHS	AIIPRST	PIARIST
AHILSST	SALTISH		OLLAMHS	AHORTTY	THROATY	AIIPSTW	WAPITIS
	TAHSILS	AHLLMSU	MULLAHS	AHOSTUW	OUTWASH	AIIPTTU	PITUITA
AHILSSV	SLAVISH	AHLLNOS	SHALLON		WASHOUT	AIJJMMS	JIMJAMS
AHILSTU	HALITUS	AHLLNOY	HALLYON	AHPRRTY	PHRATRY	AIJLORS	JAILORS
	THULIAS	AHLLNSU	NULLAHS	AHPRSST	SPARTHS	AIJLSTW	WILTJAS
AHILSTY	HASTILY	AHLLOOS	HALLOOS	AHPSXYY	ASPHYXY	AIJLYZZ	JAZZILY
AHIMMRS	RAMMISH		HOLLOAS	AHQSSUY	SQUASHY	AIJNORT	JANITOR
AHIMNNS	MANNISH	AHLLOPS	SHALLOP	AHRRSUY	HURRAYS	AIJORSW	JOWARIS
AHIMNNU	INHUMAN	AHLLOST	SHALLOT	AHRSSSU	HUSSARS	AIJPSTU	JUPATIS
AHIMNPS	SHIPMAN	AHLLOSW	HALLOWS	AHRSSTT	STRATHS	AIKKMOT	KOMATIK
AHIMNRS	HARMINS		SHALLOW	AHRSSTW	SWARTHS	AIKKSUZ	ZAKUSKI
AHIMOPR	MORPHIA	AHLLOTY	LOATHLY	AHRSTTW	THWARTS	AIKLLNY	LANKILY
AHIMORS	MOHAIRS	AHLLPSU	PHALLUS	AHRSTWY	SWARTHY	AIKLMMN	MILKMAN
AHIMPSS	MISHAPS	AHLLPYY	APHYLLY	AHRTUWY	THRUWAY	AIKLMNN	LINKMAN
	PASHIMS	AHLLRST	THRALLS	AHSSSTU	TUSSAHS	AIKLMNS	MALKINS
AHIMPST	MISHAPT	AHLLSTU	THALLUS	AIIILMT	MILITIA	AIKLMPU	LAMPUKI
AHIMPSV	VAMPISH	AHLMMSU	MASHLUM	AIIILNT	INITIAL	AIKLMSU	KALIUMS
AHIMPSW	WAMPISH	AHLMNPY	NYMPHAL	AIIILVX	LIXIVIA	AIKLNOS	KAOLINS
AHIMRSS	MAHSIRS	AHLMNSY	HYMNALS	AIIIMRS	SAIMIRI	AIKLNSY	SNAKILY
AHIMRST	THAIRMS	AHLMNUY	HUMANLY	AIIKKSW	WAKIKIS	AIKLPWY	PAWKILY
	THRIMSA	AHLMOOS	MOOLAHS	AIIKMMS	SKIMMIA	AIKLRTT	TITLARK
AHIMRSW	WARMISH	AHLMORU	HUMORAL	AIIKMNN	MANIKIN	AIKLSSU	SALUKIS
AHIMTUZ	AZIMUTH	AHLMSTZ	SHMALTZ	AIIKRTT	TRAIKIT	AIKLSSY	SKYSAIL
AHIMTVZ	MITZVAH	AHLMSUU	HAMULUS	AIILLLP	LAPILLI	AIKMSS	IMMASKS
AHINNSW	WANNISH	AHLNOPR	ALPHORN	AIILLMN	LIMINAL	AIKMNNS	KINSMAN
AHINNTX	XANTHIN	AHLNORT	ALTHORN	AIILLMS	LIMAILS	AIKMNSS	KAMSINS
AHINORT	ORTHIAN	AHLORST	HARLOTS	AIILLNV	VILLAIN	AIKMNSW	MAWKINS
AHINOTZ	HOATZIN	AHLOSST	SHALOTS	AIILLQU	QUILLAI	AIKMOOS	OOMIAKS
AHINPST	HATPINS	AHLOSTU	OUTLASH	AIILLUV	ILLUVIA	AIKMPRS	IMPARKS
AHINRSS	ARSHINS	AHLOTUU	OUTHAUL	AIILMMN	MINIMAL	AIKMRSU	KUMARIS
	SHAIRNS	AHLPRSY	SHARPLY	AIILMNO	MONILIA	AIKNNNS	NANKINS
AHINRST	TARNISH	AHLPRUY	HYPURAL	AIILMRS	SIMILAR	AIKNNPS	NAPKINS
AHINRSU	UNHAIRS	AHLPSSU	SULPHAS	AIILMRT	MILITAR	AIKNOST	KATIONS
AHINRSV	VARNISH	AHLPSSY	SPLASHY	AIILMRY	MILIARY	AIKNPRS	KIRPANS
AHINRTY	RHYTINA	AHMMMOT	MAMMOTH	AIILNOS	LIAISON		PARKINS
AHINSTU	INHAUST	AHMMMUU	HUMMAUM	AIILNPT	PINTAIL	AIKNPSS	PANISKS
AHIOOST	ATISHOO	AHMMOSW	WHAMMOS	AIILNPU	NAUPLII	AIKOPST	KATIPOS
AHIOPRU	OPHIURA	AHMNNSU	NUMNAHS	AIILNTU	NAUTILI	AIKORST	TROIKAS
AHIOPXY	HYPOXIA	AHMNNTU	MANHUNT	AIILNTY	ANILITY	AIKRRSS	SIRKARS
AHIORST	THORIAS	AHMNNUU	UNHUMAN	AIILOPP	PAPILIO	AIKRSST	STRAIKS
AHIORUV	HAVIOUR	AHMNOPS	SHOPMAN	AIILORV	RAVIOLI	AILLMNU	LUMINAL
AHIPRST	HARPIST	AHMNOPT	PHANTOM	AIILQSU	SILIQUA	AILLMOT	MAILLOT
AHIPRSU	RUPIAHS	AHMNORY	HARMONY	AIILRTV	TRIVIAL	AILLMPU	PALLIUM
AHIPRSW	WARSHIP	AHMNOSS	HANSOMS		VITRAIL	AILLMSU	ALLIUMS
AHIPSSW	WASPISH	AHMNOSW	SHOWMAN	AIIMMNS	ANIMISM	AILLMSW	SAWMILL
AHIPSWW	WHIPSAW	AHMNRYY	HYMNARY	AIIMMNX	MAXIMIN	AILLMSY	MISALLY
AHIPSWY	SHIPWAY	AHMOOPS	OOMPAHS		MINIMAX	AILLNNO	LANOLIN
AHIRRSS	SHIRRAS		SHAMPOO	AIIMMSS	MISAIMS	AILLNOP	PAILLON
	SIRRAHS	AHMOOSS	SAMSHOO	AIIMNOR	AMORINI	AILLNPY	PLAINLY
AHIRRST	STIRRAH	AHMORRU	MORRHUA	AIIMNPS	PAININS	AILLNST	INSTALL
AHIRSST	HAIRSTS	AHMORST	HARMOST		PIANISM	AILLNSV	VILLANS
AHIRSTT	ATHIRST	AHMOSSY	SHAMOYS	AIIMNPT	IMPAINT	AILLNSW	INWALLS
	RATTISH	AHMOSTU	MAHOUTS		TIMPANI	AILLNVY	VILLANY
	TARTISH	AHMOSWY	HAYMOWS	AIIMNRT	MARTINI	AILLPRS	PILLARS
AHIRSTW	TRISHAW	AHMOTTZ	MATZOTH	AIIMNSS	SIMIANS	AILLPRU	PILULAR
	WRAITHS	AHMRRSU	MURRHAS	AIIMNST	ANIMIST	AILLPSU	PILLAUS
AHISSTT	STAITHS	AHMRSTW	WARMTHS	AIIMNTT	IMITANT		PILULAS
AHISSTU	SHIATSU	AHMRSTY	THRYMSA	AIIMNTU	MINUTIA	AILLPUV	PLUVIAL
	THIASUS	AHMSSSU	SAMSHUS	AIIMNTV	VITAMIN	AILLQSU	SQUILLA
AHISSTW	WHATSIS	AHNOOPR	HARPOON	AIIMPRS	IMPAIRS	AILLRSU	ARILLUS
AHISTTW	WHATSIT	AHNORSS	SHORANS	AIIMPSS	SIMPAIS	AILLSTY	SALTILY
AHISTUZ	SHIATZU	AHNORSX	SAXHORN	AIIMRST	SIMITAR	AILLTVY	VITALLY
AHITTWW	WHITTAW	AHNOTTW	WHATNOT	AIIMSST	SAMITIS	AILLTWW	WITWALL
AHJOOPS	POOJAHS	AHNPPUU	PUPUNHA	AIIMSSY	MYIASIS	AILMMOR	IMMORAL
AHKKSSU	SUKKAHS	AHNPPUY	UNHAPPY	AIINNOP	PIANINO	AILMMSS	MALISMS
AHKLOOS	KOOLAHS	AHNPRXY	PHARYNX	AIINNSZ	ZINNIAS	AILMMSY	MYALISM
AHKLPSU	PULKHAS	AHNPSSU	UNHASPS	AIINNTY	INANITY	AILMMUU	ALUMIUM
AHKMNSU	KHANUMS	AHNSSTU	SUNHATS	AIINOPS	SINOPIA	AILMNNO	NOMINAL
				AIINOTT	NOTITIA	AILMNOP	LAMPION

Column 1

```
AILMNOS  MALISON
         MONIALS
         SOMNIAL
AILMNOY  ALIMONY
AILMNPS  PLASMIN
AILMNPT  IMPLANT
AILMNRS  MARLINS
AILMNRU  MURLAIN
AILMNSS  MASLINS
AILMOPT  OPTIMAL
AILMORS  ORALISM
AILMOST  SOMITAL
AILMPRS  IMPARLS
AILMPRU  PRIMULA
AILMPST  PALMIST
AILMPSY  MISPLAY
AILMRST  MISTRAL
AILMRSU  SIMULAR
AILMSSS  MISSALS
AILMSSX  LAXISMS
AILMSSY  MISLAYS
AILMSTU  ULTIMAS
AILMSUV  MAULVIS
AILNNOT  ANTLION
AILNNPU  PINNULA
AILNNSU  UNNAILS
         UNSLAIN
AILNOPY  POLYNIA
AILNOQU  AQUILON
AILNOSS  SIALONS
AILNOST  TALIONS
AILNOTU  OUTLAIN
AILNPRW  PRAWLIN
AILNPST  PLAINTS
AILNPSX  SALPINX
AILNPTU  NUPTIAL
         PATULIN
         UNPLAIT
AILNPTY  INAPTLY
         PTYALIN
AILNQTU  QUINTAL
AILNRST  RATLINS
AILNRSU  INSULAR
         URINALS
AILNRTT  RATTLIN
AILNSST  INSTALS
AILNSSU  INSULAS
AILNSSV  SILVANS
AILNSTU  UNALIST
AILNSTY  NASTILY
         SAINTLY
AILNSUV  UNVAILS
AILNTTY  NATTILY
AILNTUV  UNVITAL
AILOORS  OORIALS
AILOORW  WOORALI
AILOPST  APOSTIL
         TOPSAIL
AILOPSY  SOAPILY
AILOPTT  TALIPOT
AILOPTV  PIVOTAL
AILOQTU  ALIQUOT
AILORSS  SAILORS
AILORST  TAILORS
AILORSU  OURALIS
AILORTY  ORALITY
AILORUW  WOURALI
AILORUX  UXORIAL
AILORVY  OLIVARY
AILOSSS  ASSOILS
AILOSTU  OUTSAIL
AILOSTX  OXTAILS
AILPPRU  PUPILAR
AILPPSY  PAYSLIP
AILPRSS  SPIRALS
AILPRSU  PARULIS
         UPRISAL
AILPRSY  PYRALIS
AILPSST  PASTILS
```

Column 2

```
         SPITALS
AILPSTU  TIPULAS
AILPSWY  SLIPWAY
AILQSSU  SQUAILS
AILQTTU  QUITTAL
AILQTUY  QUALITY
AILRRVY  RIVALRY
AILRSTT  STARLIT
AILRSTU  RITUALS
         TRISULA
AILRSTY  TRYSAIL
AILRTTU  TITULAR
AILRTUV  VIRTUAL
         VITULAR
AILSSTX  LAXISTS
AILSSUV  VISUALS
AILSSVY  SYLVIAS
AILSSVZ  VIZSLAS
AILSTTY  TASTILY
AILSTUW  LAWSUIT
AILTTTY  TATTILY
AIMMMSU  MUMMIAS
AIMMMUX  MAXIMUM
AIMMNTU  MANUMIT
AIMMORS  AMORISM
AIMMOSS  MIMOSAS
AIMMOST  ATOMISM
AIMNNOS  MANSION
         ONANISM
AIMNNSS  NANISMS
AIMNNSY  MINYANS
AIMNOOR  AMORINO
AIMNOPR  RAMPION
AIMNOPS  MOPANIS
AIMNOPT  MAINTOP
         TAMPION
         TIMPANO
AIMNOPZ  ZAMPONI
AIMNORS  MAINORS
AIMNORT  TORMINA
AIMNORU  MAINOUR
AIMNOST  MANITOS
         STAMNOI
AIMNOTU  MANITOU
         TINAMOU
AIMNPSW  IMPAWNS
AIMNPSY  PAYNIMS
AIMNPTY  TYMPANI
AIMNRRU  MURRAIN
AIMNRST  MARTINS
AIMNRSU  SURAMIN
         URANISM
AIMNRTU  NATRIUM
AIMNRTV  VARMINT
AIMNRUU  URANIUM
AIMNSTT  MATTINS
AIMNSTU  TSUNAMI
AIMNSUV  MAUVINS
AIMNSYZ  ZANYISM
AIMOPST  IMPASTO
AIMOPSY  MYOPIAS
AIMORRU  ORARIUM
AIMORST  AMORIST
AIMORUZ  ZOARIUM
AIMOSTT  ATOMIST
AIMPPSS  PAPISMS
AIMPPST  MAPPIST
AIMPRRY  PRIMARY
AIMPRST  ARMPITS
         IMPARTS
AIMPRSY  PYRAMIS
AIMQRSU  MARQUIS
AIMRSST  TSARISM
AIMRSTU  ATRIUMS
         MATSURI
AIMRSTY  MAISTRY
         SYMITAR
AIMSSSY  MISSAYS
AIMSSTT  STATISM
```

Column 3

```
AIMSSTU  AUTISMS
AINNNST  TANNINS
AINNOPS  SAPONIN
AINNOSS  NASIONS
AINNOST  ANOINTS
         NATIONS
         ONANIST
AINNPSS  INSPANS
AINNPTU  UNPAINT
AINNQTU  QUINNAT
         QUINTAN
AINNRSU  URANINS
AINNRTT  INTRANT
AINNRTU  URINANT
AINNSTT  INSTANT
AINNSTU  UNSAINT
AINNTUY  ANNUITY
AINOOPR  PRONAOI
AINOORR  ORARION
AINOORT  ORATION
AINOOTV  OVATION
AINOPPT  APPOINT
AINOPRS  PARISON
         SOPRANI
AINOPRT  ATROPIN
AINOPSS  PASSION
AINOPTU  OPUNTIA
         UTOPIAN
AINOQSU  QUINOAS
AINORST  AROINTS
         RATIONS
AINORSW  WARISON
AINORTX  TRIAXON
AINOSSU  SANIOUS
         SUASION
AINOSTT  STATION
AINOSUX  ANXIOUS
AINOSVY  SYNOVIA
AINPPRS  PARSNIP
AINPQTU  PIQUANT
AINPRSS  SPINARS
         SPRAINS
AINPRST  SPIRANT
         SPRAINT
AINPRSU  PRUINAS
AINPRSW  INWRAPS
AINPRTU  PURITAN
         UPTRAIN
AINPSST  PTISANS
AINPSSV  SPAVINS
AINQRST  QINTARS
AINQRUY  QUINARY
AINQSTU  ASQUINT
         QUINTAS
AINQSUY  YANQUIS
AINRRTY  TRINARY
AINRRUY  URINARY
AINRSTT  INSTARS
         SANTIRS
         STRAINS
AINRSTT  STRAINT
         TRANSIT
AINRSTU  NUTRIAS
AINRTUY  UNITARY
AINSSTT  TANISTS
AINSSTU  ISSUANT
         SUSTAIN
AINSSXY  SYNAXIS
AINTTVY  TANTIVY
AIOORSS  ARIOSOS
AIOPRRT  AIRPORT
         PARITOR
AIOPRST  AIRSTOP
         PAROTIS
AIOPRSV  PAVIORS
AIOPRTT  PATRIOT
AIOPRTY  TOPIARY
AIOPRUV  PAVIOUR
AIOPSTU  UTOPIAS
```

Column 4

```
AIORRRW  WARRIOR
AIORRSU  OURARIS
AIORRTT  TRAITOR
AIORRTX  ORATRIX
AIORSST  AORISTS
         ARISTOS
         SATORIS
AIORSSU  SOUARIS
AIORSTU  SAUTOIR
AIORSTV  TRAVOIS
         VIATORS
AIORSTY  OSTIARY
AIORSUV  SAVIOUR
         VARIOUS
AIPPRRS  RIPRAPS
AIPPSST  PAPISTS
AIPRSST  RAPISTS
AIPRSTU  UPSTAIR
AIPRSUY  PYURIAS
AIPRTVY  PRAVITY
AIPSSTT  TAPISTS
AIPSSTW  SAWPITS
AIRRSST  STIRRAS
AIRRSZZ  RIZZARS
AIRRTZZ  RIZZART
AIRSSSU  RUSSIAS
AIRSSTT  ARTISTS
         SITTARS
         STRAITS
         TSARIST
AIRSSTU  AURISTS
AIRSTTT  ATTRIST
         ATTRITS
AIRSTTY  YTTRIAS
AIRSTVY  VARSITY
AIRTUVX  VITRAUX
AISSSST  ASSISTS
AISSTTT  STATIST
AISTTVY  VASTITY
AISTUVY  SUAVITY
AJKMNNU  JUNKMAN
AJKMNTU  MUNTJAK
AJKNSSY  JANSKYS
AJLLRUY  JURALLY
AJLNORU  JOURNAL
AJLOORS  JAROOLS
AJLOPPY  JALOPPY
AJMNRUY  JURYMAN
AJMOPST  JAMPOTS
AJMRSTU  JUMARTS
AJNRSTU  JURANTS
AKKKORU  ROKKAKU
AKKLRSY  SKYLARK
AKKNRSU  KUNKARS
AKKOQSU  QUOKKAS
AKLNOSU  KOULANS
AKLNOSX  KLAXONS
AKLOPRW  LAPWORK
AKLOSTW  KOTWALS
AKLOTTU  OUTTALK
AKLOTUW  OUTWALK
AKLPRSY  SPARKLY
AKLRSTY  STARKLY
AKMNORW  WORKMAN
AKMNRTU  TRANKUM
AKMNSSU  UNMASKS
AKMOORT  MOOKTAR
AKMQTUU  KUMQUAT
AKMRSTU  MUSKRAT
AKNORSU  KORUNAS
AKNORSY  KARYONS
         RYOKANS
AKNORTU  OUTRANK
AKOOPRT  PARTOOK
AKOORRS  KORORAS
AKOOSTU  ATOKOUS
AKORRTW  ARTWORK
AKORWWX  WAXWORK
AKQSSUW  SQUAWKS
```

Letters	Anagram(s)
AKQSUWY	SQUAWKY
AKRSSTU	TUSKARS
AKSSWYY	SKYWAYS
ALLLOYY	LOYALLY
ALLMNOP	POLLMAN
ALLMNOT	TOLLMAN
ALLMNOY	ALLONYM
ALLMORS	MORALLS
ALLMORY	MORALLY
ALLMOSS	SLALOMS
ALLMOSW	MALLOWS
ALLMPUU	PLUMULA
ALLMSUU	VALLUMS
ALLNOPS	POLLANS
ALLNOTY	TONALLY
ALLNRUU	LUNULAR
ALLNSTY	SLANTLY
ALLNTUU	ULULANT
ALLOOPS	APOLLOS
	PALOLOS
ALLOOTX	AXOLOTL
ALLOPRS	PALLORS
ALLOPRY	PAYROLL
ALLOPSW	WALLOPS
ALLORSS	SOLLARS
ALLORYY	ROYALLY
ALLOSSW	SALLOWS
ALLOSTT	TALLOTS
ALLOSTV	LAVOLTS
ALLOSTW	TALLOWS
ALLOSWW	SWALLOW
	WALLOWS
ALLOSWY	SALLOWY
ALLOTTY	TOTALLY
ALLOTWY	TALLOWY
ALLOTYY	LOYALTY
ALLPRSU	PLURALS
ALLPSSY	PSYLLAS
ALLQSSU	SQUALLS
ALLQSUY	SQUALLY
ALLRRUY	RURALLY
ALLRSTU	LUSTRAL
ALLSSUY	USUALLY
ALMMSUY	AMYLUMS
ALMNNUY	UNMANLY
ALMNOOP	LAMPOON
ALMNOOT	TOOLMAN
ALMNOOW	WOOLMAN
ALMNORS	NORMALS
ALMNORU	UNMORAL
ALMNORY	ALMONRY
ALMNOSS	SALMONS
ALMNOSU	MONAULS
	SOLANUM
ALMNOWY	WOMANLY
ALMNPSU	SUNLAMP
ALMNRSU	MURLANS
ALMNSUU	ALUMNUS
ALMOOPY	POLYOMA
ALMOPPT	PALMTOP
ALMOPRT	MARPLOT
ALMORRU	MORULAR
ALMORSS	SAMLORS
ALMORST	MORTALS
ALMOSST	SMALTOS
ALMOSTW	MATLOWS
ALMOSXY	XYLOMAS
ALMOTTU	MULATTO
ALMRSTY	SMARTLY
ALMRSUU	RAMULUS
ALMRTUU	TUMULAR
ALMSSUY	ALYSSUM
	ASYLUMS
ALMSTUU	MUTUALS
	UMLAUTS
ALNNRSU	UNSNARL
ALNNSUU	ANNULUS
ALNOOPR	POLARON
ALNOOPT	PLATOON
ALNOORT	ORTOLAN
ALNOOSS	SALOONS
	SOLANOS
ALNOPPY	PANOPLY
ALNOPSS	SPONSAL
ALNOPYY	POLYNYA
ALNORST	LATRONS
ALNORUY	UNROYAL
ALNORUZ	ZONULAR
ALNOSUZ	ZONULAS
ALNPRUY	PLANURY
ALNPTUY	UNAPTLY
ALNPTXY	PLANXTY
ALNRSUY	URANYLS
ALNSSTU	SULTANS
ALNSSVY	SYLVANS
ALNSTUW	WALNUTS
ALNSUUU	UNUSUAL
ALOOPSS	SALOOPS
ALOOPYZ	POLYZOA
ALOORRS	SORORAL
ALOPPRS	POPLARS
ALOPPRU	POPULAR
ALOPPRY	PROPYLA
ALOPPST	LAPTOPS
ALOPRRS	PARLORS
ALOPRRU	PARLOUR
ALOPRST	PATROLS
	PORTALS
ALOPRSU	PARLOUS
ALOPSST	POSTALS
ALOPSSU	SPOUSAL
ALOPSUV	VOLUSPA
ALOPTUY	OUTPLAY
ALOQRRU	RORQUAL
ALOQRSU	SQUALOR
ALOQSTU	LOQUATS
ALORRST	ROSTRAL
ALORRSW	WORRALS
ALORSSU	ROSULAS
ALORSSV	SALVORS
ALORSTU	ROTULAS
ALORSUV	VALOURS
ALORTYY	ROYALTY
ALOSTTU	OUTLAST
ALOSTUW	OUTLAWS
ALOSTUY	LAYOUTS
	OUTLAYS
ALPRRSU	LARRUPS
ALPRSSU	PULSARS
ALPRSSW	SPRAWLS
ALPRSUU	PURSUAL
ALPRSUW	PULWARS
ALPRSWY	SPRAWLY
ALRSTTY	STARTLY
ALRSTUU	SUTURAL
ALRSTUW	TULWARS
AMMMNOS	MAMMONS
AMMMOSU	AMOMUMS
AMMNOOR	MOORMAN
AMMNOOT	MOOTMAN
AMMNRUY	NUMMARY
AMMOORR	MAORMOR
	MORMAOR
AMMOPTU	POMATUM
AMMORST	MARMOTS
AMMPSUW	WAMPUMS
AMMRRSU	MARRUMS
	MURRAMS
AMMRSUY	SUMMARY
AMMSSTU	SUMMATS
AMNNOOX	MONAXON
AMNNORS	NORMANS
AMNNOSW	SNOWMAN
AMNNOSY	ANONYMS
AMNNOTT	MONTANT
AMNNOTY	ANTONYM
AMNNOUW	UNWOMAN
AMNOOPP	POMPANO
AMNOORS	MAROONS
AMNOOTT	OTTOMAN
AMNOOTZ	MATZOON
AMNOPRT	PORTMAN
AMNOPRY	PARONYM
AMNOPST	POSTMAN
	TAMPONS
	TOPSMAN
AMNOPTU	PANTOUM
AMNOPTY	TYMPANO
AMNORSS	RAMSONS
	RANSOMS
AMNORST	MATRONS
	TRANSOM
AMNORSY	MASONRY
	MORNAYS
AMNORTU	ROMAUNT
AMNOSST	STAMNOS
AMNOSTU	AMOUNTS
	MOUTANS
	OUTMANS
AMNPSTY	TYMPANS
AMNPTYY	TYMPANY
AMNQTUU	QUANTUM
AMNRRUY	UNMARRY
AMNRSTU	UNSMART
AMNRTTU	TANTRUM
AMNSTTU	MUTANTS
AMNSTUU	AUTUMNS
AMNTUUY	AUTUMNY
AMOOORS	AMOROSO
AMOOPRT	TAPROOM
AMOORSU	AMOROUS
AMOORSV	MOORVAS
AMORRWY	MARROWY
AMORSST	MATROSS
	STROAMS
AMORSSY	MORASSY
AMOSTUW	OUTSWAM
AMOSTUZ	MAZOUTS
AMOSUYZ	AZYMOUS
AMPRSST	STRAMPS
AMPRSUW	UPSWARM
AMRRSTU	RASTRUM
AMRRSTY	MARTYRS
AMRRSUY	MURRAYS
AMRRTYY	MARTYRY
AMRSTTU	STRATUM
ANNOPRS	NAPRONS
ANNOPST	PANTONS
ANNOPTY	POYNANT
ANNORST	NATRONS
ANNOSST	SANTONS
	SONANTS
ANNOSTW	WANTONS
ANNOSTY	TANNOYS
ANNOTTY	TANTONY
ANNPSSU	SANNUPS
	UNSNAPS
ANNPSTU	PANTUNS
ANNRTYY	TYRANNY
ANNSSTU	SUNTANS
ANNSSTY	SYNTANS
ANOOPRS	PRONAOS
	SOPRANO
ANOOPRT	PATROON
	PRONOTA
ANOORST	RATOONS
ANOORTT	ARNOTTO
ANOPRRS	SPORRAN
ANOPRSS	PARSONS
ANOPRST	PARTONS
	PATRONS
	TARPONS
ANOPRTV	PROVANT
ANOPSTT	OPTANTS
ANOPSTU	OUTSPAN
ANOPSUY	YAUPONS
ANORRSW	NARROWS
ANORSSV	SOVRANS
ANORSTT	ATTORNS
	RATTONS
	ROTTANS
ANORSTU	ROUSANT
	SANTOUR
ANORSTY	AROYNTS
ANORSUU	ANUROUS
	URANOUS
ANORWWY	WAYWORN
ANOSSTZ	STANZOS
AOOPPRS	APROPOS
AOOPRTT	TAPROOT
AOORRST	ORATORS
AOORRSY	ARROYOS
AOORRTT	ROTATOR
AOORRTU	OUTROAR
AOORRTY	ORATORY
AOORSTT	TOOARTS
AOORSTU	OUTSOAR
AOORSTV	OVATORS
AOOSTTT	TATTOOS
AOOSTUZ	AZOTOUS
AOOTXYZ	ZOOTAXY
AOPPPSU	PAPPOUS
AOPPRRT	RAPPORT
AOPPRST	APPORTS
AOPRRST	PARROTS
	RAPTORS
AOPRRSU	UPROARS
AOPRRSW	SPARROW
AOPRRTY	PARROTY
	PORTRAY
AOPRSST	ASPORTS
	PASTORS
AOPRSTU	ASPROUT
AOPRSTW	POSTWAR
AOPRSUV	VAPOURS
AOPRTTU	OUTPART
AOPRTUY	OUTPRAY
AOPRUVY	VAPOURY
AOPSSTU	PASSOUT
AOPSTUY	AUTOPSY
AOPSTWY	WAYPOST
AOQRSTU	QUARTOS
AORRSST	SARTORS
AORRSTW	TARROWS
AORRSWY	SOWARRY
	YARROWS
AORSSST	ASSORTS
AORSSTT	STATORS
AORSSTU	SOUTARS
AORSSUV	SAVOURS
AORSSUY	OSSUARY
	SUASORY
AORSTUY	YAOURTS
AORSUVY	SAVOURY
AORTUVY	AVOUTRY

AOSTTTW	TATTOWS	BBDEIRS	DIBBERS	BBEIRTU	TUBBIER	BBHRSUY	SHRUBBY
AOSTTUY	OUTSTAY	BBDEKNO	KNOBBED	BBEISSU	BUSBIES	BBIIILM	BILIMBI
APPRRUU	PURPURA	BBDELMO	MOBBLED		SUBBIES	BBIILST	BIBLIST
APPRSTY	STRAPPY	BBDELMU	BUMBLED	BBEJORS	JOBBERS	BBIKOSS	SKIBOBS
APPRSUW	UPWRAPS	BBDELNO	NOBBLED	BBEJORY	JOBBERY	BBIKTUZ	KIBBUTZ
APPRSUY	PAPYRUS	BBDELNU	NUBBLED	BBEKLNO	KNOBBLE	BBILLSU	BULBILS
APRSSSU	SURPASS	BBDELOS	BOBSLED	BBEKLNU	KNUBBLE	BBILLUU	LULIBUB
APRSSWY	PSYWARS	BBDELOW	WOBBLED	BBEKLOS	BLESBOK	BBILNOY	NOBBILY
APRSTTU	UPSTART	BBDELRU	BLURBED	BBEKLUU	BUBUKLE	BBIMOSY	YOBBISM
APRSTTY	TAPSTRY		BURBLED	BBEKNOR	KNOBBER	BBINNSU	NUBBINS
APRSUWY	SPURWAY	BBDELSU	SLUBBED	BBEKNSU	NEBBUKS	BBINORS	RIBBONS
APSSTUY	UPSTAYS	BBDENSU	SNUBBED	BBELLSU	BULBELS	BBINORY	RIBBONY
APSSUWY	UPSWAYS	BBDEORS	DOBBERS	BBELMOS	MOBBLES	BBJLOOW	BLOWJOB
AQRTUYZ	QUARTZY	BBDEOSW	SWOBBED	BBELMOT	BOMBLET	BBKLNOY	KNOBBLY
AQSTTUY	SQUATTY	BBDESTU	STUBBED	BBELMRU	BUMBLER	BBKLNUY	KNUBBLY
ARSSTTU	STRATUS	BBDGIIN	DIBBING	BBELMSU	BUMBLES	BBKLOOU	BLOUBOK
BBBDELO	BLOBBED	BBDGINO	DOBBING	BBELNOR	NOBBLER	BBKOOOO	BOOBOOK
	BOBBLED	BBDGINU	DUBBING	BBELNOS	NOBBLES	BBKOOSS	BOSBOKS
BBBDELU	BLUBBED	BBDILRY	DRIBBLY	BBELNSU	NUBBLES	BBLLSUU	BULBULS
	BUBBLED	BBDINOS	DOBBINS	BBELNSY	NYBBLES	BBLOSUU	BULBOUS
BBBEIOS	BOBBIES	BBDINSU	DUBBINS	BBELORS	SLOBBER	BBLSTUY	STUBBLY
BBBEIRS	BIBBERS	BBDKSUY	DYBBUKS	BBELORW	WOBBLER	BBNNOOS	BONBONS
BBBEISU	BUBBIES	BBEEERU	BEBEERU	BBELORY	LOBBYER	BBNOORU	BOURBON
BBBELOS	BOBBLES	BBEEIKS	KEBBIES	BBELOSW	WOBBLES	BBOOOOS	BOOBOOS
BBBELRU	BLUBBER	BBEEIRW	WEBBIER	BBELRRU	BURBLER	BBORSTU	BURBOTS
BBBELSU	BUBBLES	BBEEKLS	LEBBEKS	BBELRSU	BURBLES	BBOSSUY	BUSBOYS
BBBEORY	BOBBERY	BBEELPS	PEBBLES		LUBBERS	BBRSSUU	SUBURBS
BBBGIIN	BIBBING	BBEELSS	EBBLESS		RUBBLES	BCCEIIS	BICCIES
BBBGINO	BOBBING	BBEENSS	SNEBBES		SLUBBER	BCCEILO	ECBOLIC
BBBHIOS	BOBBISH	BBEFILR	FRIBBLE	BBELSTU	STUBBLE	BCCEILU	CUBICLE
BBBHSUU	HUBBUBS	BBEFIRS	FIBBERS	BBEMNSU	BENUMBS	BCCEILY	BICYCLE
BBBINOS	BOBBINS	BBEFIRU	FUBBIER	BBEMORS	BOMBERS	BCCILOU	BUCOLIC
BBBIOTT	BOBBITT	BBEFIRY	FIBBERY	BBENOTW	BOWBENT	BCCINOO	OBCONIC
BBCCIKO	BIBCOCK	BBEFRUY	FUBBERY	BBENRSU	SNUBBER	BCCISUU	SUCCUBI
BBCDEIR	CRIBBED	BBEGIKN	KEBBING	BBENSSU	SNUBBES	BCCMOOX	COXCOMB
BBCDELO	COBBLED	BBEGILR	GLIBBER	BBEOOSY	YOBBOES	BCCMSUU	SUCCUMB
BBCDELU	CLUBBED		GRIBBLE	BBEORRS	ROBBERS	BCDEEHL	BELCHED
BBCEHIN	NEBBICH	BBEGINN	NEBBING	BBEORRY	ROBBERY	BCDEEHN	BENCHED
BBCEILR	CRIBBLE	BBEGINW	WEBBING	BBEORSW	SWOBBER	BCDEEIL	DECIBEL
BBCEIOR	COBBIER	BBEGIOS	GIBBOSE	BBEORYY	YOBBERY	BCDEEKS	BEDECKS
BBCEISU	CUBBIES	BBEGIRS	GIBBERS	BBEPRUW	BREWPUB	BCDEHIR	BIRCHED
BBCEKKO	KEBBOCK	BBEGIST	GIBBETS	BBERRSU	RUBBERS	BCDEHIT	BITCHED
BBCEKKU	KEBBUCK	BBEGLOR	GOBBLER	BBERRUY	RUBBERY	BCDEHNU	BUNCHED
BBCELOR	CLOBBER	BBEGLOS	GOBBLES	BBERSTU	TUBBERS	BCDEHOR	BROCHED
	COBBLER	BBEGLRU	GRUBBLE	BBFGIIN	FIBBING	BCDEHOT	BOTCHED
BBCELOS	COBBLES	BBEGNSU	BEBUNGS	BBFGINO	FOBBING	BCDEHOU	DEBOUCH
BBCELRU	CLUBBER	BBEGOST	GOBBETS	BBFGINU	FUBBING	BCDEIIO	BIOCIDE
BBCEORS	COBBERS	BBEGRRU	GRUBBER	BBGGIIN	GIBBING	BCDEIKR	BRICKED
BBCEOSW	COBWEBS	BBEHINS	NEBBISH	BBGGINO	GOBBING	BCDEIKS	SICKBED
BBCGINO	COBBING	BBEHIOS	HOBBIES	BBGIIJN	JIBBING	BCDEIKT	BEDTICK
BBCGINU	CUBBING	BBEHISU	HUBBIES	BBGIILN	LIBBING	BCDEILM	CLIMBED
BBCHISU	CUBBISH	BBEHLOR	HOBBLER	BBGIINN	NIBBING	BCDEILO	DOCIBLE
BBCINOU	BUBONIC	BBEHLOS	HOBBLES	BBGIINR	BRIBING	BCDEIOS	BODICES
BBCRSUY	SCRUBBY	BBEHMTU	BETHUMB		RIBBING	BCDEIRS	SCRIBED
BBDDEIL	DIBBLED	BBEIILR	RIBIBLE	BBGIJNO	JOBBING	BCDEKLO	BLOCKED
BBDDEIR	DRIBBED	BBEIIMR	IMBIBER	BBGILNO	LOBBING	BCDEKLU	BUCKLED
BBDDERU	DRUBBED	BBEIIMS	IMBIBES	BBGILNU	BULBING	BCDEKOR	BEDROCK
BBDEEIR	DEBBIER	BBEIIRR	RIBBIER	BBGIMNO	BOMBING		BROCKED
BBDEEIS	DEBBIES	BBEIIRS	RIBIBES		MOBBING	BCDEKSU	BEDUCKS
BBDEEIT	EBBTIDE	BBEIJOS	JOBBIES	BBGINNU	NUBBING	BCDELOU	BECLOUD
BBDEELP	PEBBLED	BBEIJRS	JIBBERS	BBGINOO	BOOBING	BCDEMOR	CROMBED
BBDEENS	SNEBBED	BBEIKLS	KIBBLES	BBGINOR	ROBBING	BCDEMRU	CRUMBED
BBDEFLU	FLUBBED	BBEILNR	NIBBLER	BBGINOS	GIBBONS	BCDENOU	BOUNCED
BBDEGIL	GLIBBED	BBEILNS	NIBBLES		SOBBING		BUNCOED
BBDEGLO	GOBBLED	BBEILOS	BILBOES	BBGINRU	RUBBING	BCDEORU	COURBED
BBDEGRU	GRUBBED		LOBBIES	BBGINSU	GUBBINS	BCDESUU	SUBDUCE
BBDEGSU	BEDBUGS	BBEILOT	BIBELOT		SUBBING	BCDHIOR	BICHORD
BBDEHLO	HOBBLED	BBEILPR	PRIBBLE	BBGINTU	TUBBING	BCDHIRU	BRUCHID
BBDEIIM	IMBIBED	BBEILQU	QUIBBLE	BBGIOSU	GIBBOUS	BCDHOOU	CUBHOOD
BBDEIKL	KIBBLED	BBEILRS	LIBBERS	BBGIOSW	BOBWIGS	BCDILOO	COLOBID
BBDEILN	NIBBLED	BBEILRT	TRIBBLE	BBHHIOS	HOBBISH	BCDIOSU	CUBOIDS
BBDEILO	BILOBED	BBEILST	STIBBLE	BBHIMOS	MOBBISH	BCDIORW	COWBIRD
	LOBBIED	BBEILSY	YIBBLES	BBHIOST	HOBBITS	BCDIRSY	CYBRIDS
BBDEILR	DIBBLER	BBEIMOS	MOBBIES	BBHIOSY	YOBBISH	BCDKORU	BURDOCK
	DRIBBLE	BBEINOR	NOBBIER	BBHIRSU	RUBBISH	BCDNOSU	BONDUCS
BBDEILS	DIBBLES	BBEINRU	NUBBIER	BBHISTU	TUBBISH	BCDSTUU	SUBDUCT
BBDEINS	SNIBBED	BBEIOOS	BOOBIES	BBHJOOS	HOBJOBS	BCEEEHN	BEECHEN
BBDEIOS	DOBBIES	BBEIRRS	BRIBERS	BBHNOOS	HOBNOBS	BCEEEHS	BEECHES
BBDEIRR	DRIBBER	BBEIRRY	BRIBERY	BBHOOUW	WHOOBUB		BESEECH

BCEEFIN	BENEFIC	BCEKOSU	BUCKOES		SUBCOOL		INBREED
BCEEGIR	ICEBERG	BCEKOTY	BYCOKET	BCLORTU	CLOTBUR	BDEEINZ	BEDIZEN
BCEEHIP	EPHEBIC	BCEKRSU	BUCKERS	BCMOOST	TOMBOCS	BDEEIRR	BERRIED
BCEEHLR	BELCHER	BCEKSTU	BESTUCK	BCMORSY	CORYMBS		BRIERED
BCEEHLS	BELCHES		BUCKETS	BCMOSTU	COMBUST	BDEEIRS	DERBIES
BCEEHNR	BENCHER	BCELLOW	COWBELL	BCNOORS	BRONCOS	BDEEISS	BESIDES
BCEEHNS	BENCHES	BCELMNU	CLUBMEN	BCNOSTU	COBNUTS	BDEEIST	BETIDES
BCEEHOS	OBECHES	BCELMOS	COMBLES	BCOOSWY	COWBOYS	BDEEIVV	BEVVIED
BCEEHOU	BOUCHEE	BCELMRU	CLUMBER	BCOOTTY	BOYCOTT	BDEEJLS	DJEBELS
BCEEIPS	BESPICE		CRUMBLE	BDDDELU	BUDDLED	BDEEKMO	KEMBOED
BCEEIRS	ESCRIBE	BCELMSU	SCUMBLE	BDDDEOR	BRODDED	BDEEKRU	REBUKED
BCEEKNS	NEBECKS	BCELORS	CORBELS	BDDEEER	REEDBED	BDEELLS	BEDELLS
BCEEKNU	BUCKEEN	BCELOSU	BOUCLES	BDDEEES	SEEDBED	BDEELMR	REMBLED
BCEEKRS	REBECKS	BCELRSU	BECURLS	BDDEEEW	BEDEWED	BDEELMS	SEMBLED
BCEEKST	BECKETS	BCELSSU	CUBLESS	BDDEEIL	BIELDED	BDEELNR	BLENDER
BCEEKSZ	ZEBECKS	BCEMNTU	CUMBENT	BDDEEIR	DEBRIDE	BDEELNS	BLENDES
BCEELOS	ECBOLES	BCEMOOS	COOMBES	BDDEEIS	BEDSIDE	BDEELNT	BENDLET
BCEEMOS	BECOMES	BCEMORS	COMBERS	BDDEEIT	BETIDED	BDEELOV	BELOVED
BCEENOS	OBSCENE	BCEMRSU	CUMBERS		DEBITED	BDEELOW	ELBOWED
BCEENRU	CRUBEEN		SCUMBER	BDDEELN	BLENDED	BDEELRT	TREBLED
BCEFIIS	SEBIFIC	BCENORU	BOUNCER	BDDEERS	BEDDERS	BDEELSS	BLESSED
BCEGIKN	BECKING	BCENOSU	BOUNCES	BDDEETU	DEBUTED	BDEELTT	BLETTED
BCEHINR	BIRCHEN	BCEORSS	SCROBES	BDDEGIN	BEDDING	BDEELZZ	BEZZLED
BCEHINT	BENTHIC	BCEORSU	OBSCURE	BDDEGIR	BRIDGED	BDEEMOS	BESOMED
BCEHIOR	BRIOCHE	BCFSSUU	SUBFUSC	BDDEGLU	BLUDGED	BDEEMOW	EMBOWED
BCEHIRS	BIRCHES	BCGIKNO	BOCKING	BDDEIIR	BIRDIED	BDEEMOX	EMBOXED
BCEHIST	BITCHES	BCGIKNU	BUCKING	BDDEIIS	BIDDIES	BDEEMRU	EMBRUED
BCEHITW	BEWITCH	BCGIMNO	COMBING	BDDEILN	BLINDED		UMBERED
BCEHLRU	BLUCHER	BCGINNU	BUNCING	BDDEILR	BRIDLED	BDEEMSU	BEMUSED
BCEHNSU	BUNCHES	BCGINRU	CURBING	BDDEILU	BUILDED	BDEENOR	ENROBED
BCEHORS	BROCHES	BCGORSU	COBURGS	BDDEINR	BRINDED	BDEENPR	PREBEND
BCEHORT	BOTCHER	BCGORSY	CYBORGS	BDDEIOO	BOODIED	BDEENRS	BENDERS
BCEHORW	COWHERB	BCHIIOT	COHIBIT	BDDEIRR	REDBIRD	BDEEORR	REBORED
BCEHOSS	BOSCHES	BCHIKOU	CHIBOUK	BDDEIRS	BIDDERS	BDEEORS	BEDSORE
BCEHOST	BOTCHES	BCHIKSU	BUCKISH	BDDEIRU	BUDDIER		SOBERED
BCEHOSU	BOUCHES	BCHILOS	CHIBOLS	BDDEISU	BUDDIES	BDEEORW	BOWERED
BCEHRSU	CHERUBS	BCHIMOR	RHOMBIC	BDDELNU	BUNDLED	BDEEOSX	SEEDBOX
BCEHRTU	BUTCHER	BCHINOR	BRONCHI	BDDELOO	BLOODED	BDEERUW	BURWEED
BCEHSTU	BUTCHES	BCHIOPR	PIBROCH	BDDELOS	BODDLES	BDEFFLU	BLUFFED
BCEIIKR	BRICKIE	BCHIOPS	PHOBICS	BDDELOU	DOUBLED	BDEFILR	FILBERD
BCEIISV	VIBICES	BCHLOTY	BLOTCHY	BDDELSU	BUDDLES	BDEFLMU	FUMBLED
BCEIKLM	LIMBECK	BCHNOOR	BRONCHO	BDDENOU	BOUNDED	BDEFLOU	BODEFUL
BCEIKLR	BRICKLE	BCHORST	BORSCHT	BDDEOOR	BROODED	BDEFOOR	FORBODE
BCEIKNR	BRICKEN		BORTSCH	BDDEORU	OBDURED	BDEGGLO	BOGGLED
BCEIKRS	BICKERS	BCIIKLN	NIBLICK	BDDEOTU	DOUBTED	BDEGGOR	BROGGED
BCEIKST	BESTICK	BCIILMU	BULIMIC	BDDERSU	REDBUDS	BDEGHIT	BEDIGHT
BCEIKSU	BUCKIES	BCIILOR	COLIBRI	BDDESUU	SUBDUED	BDEGILN	BINGLED
BCEILMO	EMBOLIC	BCIILSY	SIBYLIC	BDDGIIN	BIDDING	BDEGILO	OBLIGED
BCEILMR	CLIMBER	BCIINOS	BIONICS	BDDGINU	BUDDING	BDEGILS	BEGILDS
	RECLIMB	BCIINOT	BIONTIC	BDDISSU	DISBUDS	BDEGINN	BENDING
BCEILMS	EMBLICS	BCIIOPS	BIOPICS	BDEEEFL	FEEBLED	BDEGINO	BOINGED
	LIMBECS	BCIISTU	BISCUIT	BDEEELL	DELEBLE	BDEGINR	BREDING
BCEILNO	BINOCLE	BCIKNOS	KINCOBS	BDEEELP	BLEEPED	BDEGIOO	BOOGIED
BCEILOR	BRICOLE	BCIKORT	BROCKIT	BDEEELR	BLEEDER	BDEGIOR	BODGIER
	CORBEIL	BCIKOTT	BITTOCK	BDEEELT	BEETLED	BDEGIOS	BODGIES
BCEIMNO	COMBINE	BCILMPU	PLUMBIC	BDEEEMN	BEDEMEN	BDEGIOT	BIGOTED
BCEIMOR	COMBIER		UPCLIMB	BDEEEMT	BEMETED	BDEGIRS	BEGIRDS
	MICROBE	BCILPSU	PUBLICS	BDEEEPS	BESPEED		BRIDGES
BCEIMOS	COMBIES	BCIMSSU	CUBISMS	BDEEERR	BREEDER	BDEGIRU	BRIGUED
BCEINOR	BICORNE	BCINORS	BICORNS		BREEDER	BDEGISU	BUDGIES
BCEINOS	EBONICS	BCINORU	RUBICON	BDEEERZ	BREEZED	BDEGLNU	BLUNGED
BCEINOZ	BENZOIC	BCINSUU	INCUBUS	BDEEEST	DEBTEES		BUNGLED
BCEINRU	BRUCINE	BCIOORT	ROBOTIC	BDEEFIR	BRIEFED	BDEGLRU	BLUDGER
BCEIORS	CORBIES	BCIORST	STROBIC		DEBRIEF		BURGLED
BCEIRRS	SCRIBER	BCIOSTY	SYBOTIC		FIBERED	BDEGLSU	BLUDGES
BCEIRSS	SCRIBES	BCIRRSU	RUBRICS	BDEEGOR	BEGORED	BDEGNSU	BEDUNGS
BCEIRSU	SUBERIC	BCIRTUY	BUTYRIC	BDEEGOY	BOGEYED	BDEGORS	BODGERS
BCEIRTU	BRUCITE	BCISSTU	CUBISTS	BDEEHOV	BEHOVED	BDEGORU	BUDGERO
BCEISST	BISECTS	BCISTUU	CUBITUS	BDEEHRT	BERTHED	BDEGRSU	BUDGERS
BCEJOST	OBJECTS	BCJKMUU	JUMBUCK	BDEEIKN	BEINKED	BDEGSTU	BUDGETS
BCEJSTU	SUBJECT	BCKLLOO	BOLLOCK	BDEEILL	BELLIED	BDEHINS	BEHINDS
BCEKLOR	BLOCKER	BCKLLOU	BULLOCK		DELIBLE	BDEHIRT	BIRTHED
BCEKLRU	BRUCKLE	BCKLNOU	UNBLOCK		LIBELED	BDEHLMU	HUMBLED
	BUCKLER	BCKMMOU	BUMMOCK	BDEEILS	EDIBLES	BDEHLOS	BEHOLDS
BCEKLSU	BUCKLES	BCKMOSU	BUCKSOM	BDEEILV	BEDEVIL	BDEHLSU	BLUSHED
BCEKMOS	BEMOCKS	BCKOTTU	BUTTOCK	BDEEIMR	BEMIRED	BDEHMTU	THUMBED
BCEKNOS	BECKONS	BCLMOOU	COULOMB	BDEEIMT	BEDTIME	BDEHORY	HERDBOY
BCEKORT	BROCKET	BCLMRUY	CRUMBLY		BETIMED	BDEHOST	HOTBEDS
BCEKORU	ROEBUCK	BCLOOSU	COLOBUS	BDEEINR	BENDIER	BDEHRSU	BRUSHED

BDEIIRS BIRDIES / BRIDIES	BDELOOS BOODLES	BDGIINR BIRDING / BRIDING	BEEELPR BLEEPER
BDEIIVV BIVVIED	BDELORS BORDELS	BDGIINS BIDINGS	BEEELST BEETLES
BDEIJLR JIRBLED	BDELORU BOULDER / DOUBLER	BDGIIOO GOBIOID	BEEEMOS BEESOME
BDEIKLN BLINKED	BDELORW BOWLDER	BDGIIOS GOBIIDS	BEEEMRW EMBREWE
BDEIKMO KIMBOED	BDELOST BOLDEST	BDGILOO GLOBOID	BEEEMSS BESEEMS
BDEIKNO BOINKED	BDELOSU BLOUSED / DOUBLES	BDGIMNU DUMBING	BEEEMST BEMETES / BETEEMS
BDEIKRS BRISKED	BDELOSW BLOWSED	BDGINNO BONDING	BEEENNZ BENZENE
BDEILLU BULLIED	BDELOTT BLOTTED / BOTTLED	BDGINNU BUNDING	BEEENTW BETWEEN
BDEILMS DIMBLES	BDELOTU BOULTED / DOUBLET	BDGINOS BODINGS	BEEEPRS BEEPERS
BDEILMW WIMBLED	BDELOWZ BLOWZED	BDGINOY BODYING	BEEEPSW BEWEEPS
BDEILNN BLINNED	BDELRRU BLURRED	BDGLLOU BULLDOG	BEEERSS BREESES
BDEILNR BLINDER / BRINDLE	BDELRTU BLURTED	BDGLOOT DOGBOLT	BEEERSZ BREEZES
BDEILOP LOBIPED	BDELSSU BUDLESS	BDHIINS BHINDIS	BEEERTV BREVETE
BDEILOR BROILED	BDELSTU BUSTLED	BDHINOP HOPBIND	BEEFGIN BEEFING
BDEILOS BOLIDES	BDELSWY LEWDSBY	BDHIOSU BUSHIDO	BEEFGIT BIGFEET
BDEILOX BOLIXED	BDELTTU BUTTLED	BDHIRSY HYBRIDS	BEEFILR FEBRILE
BDEILPP BLIPPED	BDEMNNO BONDMEN	BDHMOOO HOBODOM	BEEFILS BELIEFS
BDEILRR BRIDLER	BDEMNOU EMBOUND	BDHOOOY BOYHOOD	BEEFINT BENEFIT
BDEILRS BIRSLED / BRIDLES	BDEMOOR BEDROOM / BOREDOM / BROOMED	BDIIKNO BODIKIN	BEEFIRR BRIEFER
BDEILRT DRIBLET	BDEMOOS BOSOMED	BDIILMS DISLIMB	BEEFNRU FUNEBRE
BDEILRU BLUDIER / BUILDER / REBUILD	BDEMORS SOMBRED	BDIILOS LIBIDOS	BEEGGNU GEEBUNG
BDEILTZ BLITZED	BDEMSTU DUMBEST	BDIIMRS MIDRIBS	BEEGILL LEGIBLE
BDEIMMR BRIMMED	BDENNOU BOUNDEN / UNBONED	BDIISTT TIDBITS	BEEGILO OBLIGEE
BDEIMNR BIRDMEN	BDENNSU UNBENDS	BDIKNOR BRODKIN	BEEGILS BEIGELS
BDEIMOR BROMIDE	BDENORS BONDERS	BDIKNOS BODKINS	BEEGILU BEGUILE
BDEIMRU IMBRUED	BDENORU BOUNDER / REBOUND / UNROBED	BDILLNY BLINDLY	BEEGIMR BEGRIME
BDEIMTU BITUMED	BDENORW BROWNED	BDILNNU UNBLIND	BEEGINN BEGINNE
BDEINOR INORBED	BDENORZ BRONZED	BDILNUU UNBUILD	BEEGINP BEEPING
BDEINOU BEDOUIN	BDENOST OBTENDS	BDILPUU UPBUILD	BEEGINR BIGENER
BDEINRS BINDERS / REBINDS	BDENOSY BEYONDS	BDILRUY BUIRDLY	BEEGINT BEETING / BEIGNET
BDEINRY BINDERY	BDENOUW UNBOWED	BDILTUY DIBUTYL	BEEGINU BEGUINE
BDEINST BIDENTS	BDENOUX UNBOXED	BDIMNPU DUMPBIN	BEEGLNO ENGLOBE
BDEINSU BEDUINS	BDENRSU BURDENS	BDINNOU INBOUND	BEEGMNO GOMBEEN
BDEIOOS BOODIES	BDENRTU BRUNTED	BDINNSU UNBINDS	BEEGMOU EMBOGUE
BDEIORR BROIDER	BDENSSU SUNBEDS	BDINOOR BRIDOON	BEEGNOS ENGOBES
BDEIORS BORIDES / DISROBE	BDENSTU SUBTEND	BDINPSU UPBINDS	BEEGNSU BUNGEES
BDEIORT DEBITOR / ORBITED	BDENSUY SEBUNDY	BDINRSU SUNBIRD	BEEGNTU UNBEGET
BDEIORV OVERBID	BDEOORR BROODER	BDINSTU DUSTBIN	BEEGRSU BURGEES
BDEIORZ ZEBROID	BDEOORS BOORDES	BDIOOOV OBOVOID	BEEHINS BESHINE
BDEIOSY DISOBEY	BDEOOST BOOSTED	BDIOORU BOUDOIR	BEEHIRR HERBIER
BDEIRRS BIRDERS	BDEOPRS BEDROPS	BDIORSW WOSBIRD	BEEHIST BHISTEE
BDEIRST BESTRID / BISTRED	BDEOPRT BEDROPT	BDIOSSY BYSSOID	BEEHKSU BUKSHEE
BDEIRSU BRUISED / BURDIES	BDEOPST BEDPOST	BDIOSTU OUTBIDS	BEEHLRT BLETHER / HERBLET
BDEIRSV VERBIDS	BDEORRS BORDERS	BDIOSUU DUBIOUS	BEEHLST BETHELS
BDEIRTU BRUITED	BDEORRU BORDURE / BOURDER	BDIRSTU DISTURB	BEEHNNO HEBENON
BDEISSU SUBSIDE	BDEORSS DESORBS	BDISSUY SUBSIDY	BEEHNOS BESHONE
BDEISTU BUISTED / SUBEDIT	BDEORST DEBTORS / STROBED	BDKLOOS KOBOLDS	BEEHOOV BEHOOVE
BDEITUY DUBIETY	BDEORSU OBDURES / ROSEBUD	BDKNOOU BUNDOOK	BEEHOPS EPHEBOS / PHOEBES
BDEJLMU JUMBLED	BDEORSW BROWSED	BDLOOOX OXBLOOD	BEEHORS HERBOSE
BDEJORU OBJURED	BDEORTU DOUBTER / OBTRUDE / OUTBRED / REDOUBT	BDMORUW BUDWORM	BEEHORW BEWHORE
BDEKLNU BLUNKED	BDERSSU SURBEDS	BDNNOUU UNBOUND	BEEHOST BEHOTES
BDEKNOU BUNKOED	BDERSTU BURSTED	BDNOORU BOURDON	BEEHOSV BEHOVES
BDEKNSU DEBUNKS	BDERSUU SUBDUER	BDNOOWW DOWNBOW	BEEHPSU EPHEBUS
BDEKOOR BROOKED	BDERSUY RUDESBY	BDNOPUU UPBOUND	BEEHRST BERTHES / SHERBET
BDELMMU BUMMLED / MUMBLED	BDESSTU BEDUSTS / BESTUDS	BDNORTU TURBOND	BEEHRSW BESHREW
BDELMOO BLOOMED	BDESSUU SUBDUES	BDNORUW RUBDOWN	BEEHRTY THEREBY
BDELMPU PLUMBED	BDESSUW SUBDEWS	BDNOSTU OBTUNDS	BEEHRWY WHEREBY
BDELMRU DRUMBLE / RUMBLED	BDFIIOR FIBROID	BDOOOWX BOXWOOD	BEEHSST BEHESTS
BDELMTU TUMBLED	BDFIISU FIDIBUS	BDORSWY BYWORDS	BEEHSTY BHEESTY
BDELNOR BLONDER	BDFIORS FORBIDS	BEEEEFR FREEBEE	BEEIJLU JUBILEE
BDELNOS BLONDES / BOLDENS	BDGGINO BODGING	BEEEEKS BESEEKE	BEEILLR LIBELER
BDELNRU BLUNDER	BDGGINU BUDGING	BEEEEMT BETEEME	BEEILLS BELLIES
BDELNSU BUNDLES	BDGIINN BINDING	BEEEFIR BEEFIER / FREEBIE	BEEILNR BERLINE
BDELNTU BLUNTED		BEEEFLR FEEBLER	BEEILOS OBELISE
BDELOOP BLOOPED		BEEEFLS FEEBLES	BEEILOZ OBELIZE
		BEEEFTW WEBFEET	BEEILRS BELIERS
		BEEEGIS BESIEGE	BEEILTT BETITLE
		BEEEGRR BERGERE	BEEIMRS BEMIRES / BIREMES
		BEEEHIV BEEHIVE	BEEIMST BETIMES
		BEEEHNS SHEBEEN	BEEINNS BENNIES
		BEEEHPS EPHEBES	BEEINNZ BENZINE
		BEEEILL LIBELEE	BEEINOS EBONIES / EBONISE
		BEEEILN BEELINE	
		BEEEILV BELIEVE	
		BEEEIRR BEERIER	
		BEEEJLW BEJEWEL	
		BEEEKLS KEBELES	

BEEINOT	EBONITE	BEERRWY	BREWERY		OBEYING	BEHMOTU	BEMOUTH
BEEINOZ	EBONIZE	BEERSSU	REBUSES	BEGINRR	BRINGER	BEHMPTU	BETHUMP
BEEINPR	PEBRINE		SUBSERE	BEGINRS	BINGERS	BEHNORS	BREHONS
BEEINRT	BENTIER	BEERSTT	BETTERS	BEGINRW	BREWING	BEHNOST	BENTHOS
BEEINRZ	ZEBRINE	BEERSTV	BREVETS	BEGINSS	BESINGS	BEHNRTU	BURTHEN
BEEINSW	NEWBIES	BEERSTW	BESTREW		BIGNESS	BEHOORT	THEORBO
BEEIORS	EBRIOSE		WEBSTER	BEGINST	BESTING	BEHORRT	BROTHER
BEEIQUZ	BEZIQUE	BEERTTU	BURETTE	BEGINSU	BEGUINS	BEHORST	BOSHTER
BEEIRRS	BERRIES	BEESSTU	BUSTEES		BUNGIES		BOTHERS
BEEIRRV	BREVIER	BEETTUV	BUVETTE	BEGINTT	BETTING	BEHORSU	HERBOUS
BEEIRST	REBITES	BEFFLRU	BLUFFER	BEGIOOS	BOOGIES	BEHORTT	BETROTH
BEEIRTY	EBRIETY	BEFFPSU	BEPUFFS	BEGIOSU	BOUGIES	BEHRRSU	BRUSHER
BEEISST	BETISES	BEFFRSU	BUFFERS	BEGIRSU	BRIGUES	BEHRSSU	BRUSHES
BEEISTT	BETTIES		REBUFFS		RUGBIES	BEIIKLR	RIBLIKE
BEEISTW	WEBSITE	BEFFSTU	BUFFETS	BEGISSU	GIBUSES	BEIIKRR	BIRKIER
BEEISVV	BEVVIES	BEFGIIL	FILIBEG	BEGKMOS	GEMSBOK	BEIIKRS	BIRKIES
BEEJNSU	BUNJEES	BEFGIRU	FIREBUG	BEGKNSU	BEGUNKS	BEIILLS	BILLIES
BEEKNOT	BETOKEN	BEFGIST	BEGIFTS	BEGLLOU	GLOBULE	BEIILRS	RISIBLE
BEEKOPS	BESPOKE	BEFHOOS	BEHOOFS	BEGLMOO	BEGLOOM	BEIILSV	VISIBLE
BEEKORS	REEBOKS	BEFILMS	FIMBLES	BEGLMRU	GRUMBLE	BEIINOT	NIOBITE
BEEKRRS	BERSERK	BEFILOS	FOIBLES	BEGLNOS	BELONGS	BEIINRR	BRINIER
BEEKRSU	REBUKES	BEFILPY	PLEBIFY	BEGLNRU	BLUNGER	BEIINST	STIBINE
BEELLMN	BELLMEN	BEFILRT	FILBERT		BUNGLER	BEIIOTT	BIOTITE
BEELLOT	LOBELET	BEFILRY	BRIEFLY	BEGLNSU	BLUNGES	BEIIRRS	BIRSIER
BEELMMS	EMBLEMS	BEFILSU	FUSIBLE		BUNGLES	BEIIRST	BITSIER
BEELMNT	BELTMEN	BEFINOR	BONFIRE	BEGLOOS	GLOBOSE	BEIIRTT	BITTIER
BEELMOW	EMBOWEL	BEFIORS	FIBROSE	BEGLOOT	BOOTLEG	BEIISTT	BITTIES
BEELMRS	REMBLES	BEFIORX	FIREBOX	BEGLOST	GOBLETS	BEIISVV	BIVVIES
BEELMRT	TREMBLE	BEFIRST	FIBSTER	BEGLOSU	GLEBOUS	BEIJLRS	JERBILS
BEELMSS	SEMBLES	BEFIRSU	FUBSIER	BEGLRSU	BUGLERS		JIRBLES
BEELNNO	ENNOBLE	BEFIRVY	VERBIFY		BULGERS	BEIJMSU	JUMBIES
BEELNOZ	BENZOLE	BEFITUX	TUBIFEX		BURGLES	BEIJNSU	BUNJIES
BEELNSU	NEBULES	BEFLLTY	FLYBELT	BEGLRTY	BERGYLT	BEIKLNR	BLINKER
BEELOSV	BELOVES	BEFLMRU	FUMBLER	BEGLSTU	BUGLETS	BEIKLNS	LIBKENS
BEELOTY	EYEBOLT	BEFLMSU	BEFLUMS	BEGNNUU	UNBEGUN	BEIKLOR	BLOKIER
BEELPST	BEPELTS		FUMBLES	BEGNORU	BURGEON	BEIKLOS	OBELISK
BEELRST	BELTERS	BEFLOOS	BEFOOLS	BEGNOSY	BYGONES	BEIKLRS	BILKERS
	TREBLES	BEFLOSU	BEFOULS	BEGNOTU	UNBEGOT	BEIKLRU	BULKIER
BEELRSY	BERLEYS	BEFLTUU	TUBEFUL	BEGNSUY	BUNGEYS	BEIKNRS	BRISKEN
BEELRUZ	ZEBRULE	BEFOORR	FORBORE	BEGOORS	GOOBERS	BEIKOOR	BOOKIER
BEELSSS	BLESSES	BEFOOTW	WEBFOOT	BEGORSU	BROGUES	BEIKOOS	BOOKIES
BEELSZZ	BEZZLES	BEFSSUU	SUBFEUS	BEGOSTU	BOUGETS		BOOKSIE
BEELTTU	BLUETTE	BEGGGIN	BEGGING	BEGOSTW	BOWGETS	BEIKORS	BOSKIER
BEEMMRS	MEMBERS	BEGGIIS	BIGGIES	BEGRRSU	BURGERS	BEIKRRS	BRISKER
BEEMNPT	BENEMPT	BEGGINO	BEGOING	BEGRSSU	BURGESS	BEIKRST	BRISKET
BEEMNRY	BYREMEN	BEGGIOR	BOGGIER	BEHHKOT	KHOTBEH	BEILLMN	BILLMEN
BEEMORW	EMBOWER	BEGGIRU	BUGGIER	BEHIITX	EXHIBIT	BEILLRR	BRILLER
BEEMOSS	MEBOSES	BEGGIST	BIGGEST	BEHIKNT	BETHINK	BEILLRU	BULLIER
BEEMOSX	EMBOXES	BEGGISU	BUGGIES	BEHIKRS	KIRBEHS	BEILLST	BESTILL
BEEMRRU	UMBRERE	BEGGLOR	BOGGLER	BEHILMS	BLEMISH		BILLETS
BEEMRSU	EMBRUES	BEGGLOS	BOGGLES	BEHILMT	THIMBLE	BEILLSU	BULLIES
BEEMRTU	EMBRUTE	BEGGRSU	BUGGERS	BEHILOS	BOLSHIE	BEILMNR	NIMBLER
BEEMSSU	BEMUSES	BEGGRUY	BUGGERY	BEHILRT	BLITHER	BEILMOR	EMBROIL
BEENNRS	BRENNES	BEGHHIT	BEHIGHT	BEHILST	THIBLES	BEILMOS	BEMOILS
BEENNST	BENNETS	BEGHINT	BENIGHT	BEHILSU	HELIBUS		EMBOILS
BEENORS	BOREENS	BEGHISS	BESIGHS	BEHINOP	HOPBINE		MOBILES
	ENROBES	BEGHITT	BETIGHT	BEHIOST	BOTHIES	BEILMRS	LIMBERS
BEENOST	BONESET	BEGHRRU	BURGHER	BEHIOTW	HOWBEIT	BEILMRT	TIMBREL
BEENRRT	BRENTER	BEGIILR	BILGIER	BEHIRRT	REBIRTH	BEILMRW	WIMBREL
BEENSTU	BUTENES	BEGIINN	INBEING	BEHIRST	HERBIST	BEILMSU	SUBLIME
	SUBTEEN	BEGIINS	BINGIES	BEHIRSU	BUSHIER	BEILMSW	WIMBLES
BEEOOST	BOOTEES	BEGIKMN	KEMBING	BEHISSU	BUSHIES	BEILNOO	OBELION
BEEOPRS	BEPROSE	BEGILLN	BELLING	BEHISTT	THIBETS	BEILNOW	BOWLINE
BEEORRS	REBORES	BEGILLY	LEGIBLY	BEHLLOP	BELLHOP	BEILNRS	BERLINS
	SOBERER	BEGILNO	IGNOBLE	BEHLMOW	WHOMBLE	BEILNSY	BYLINES
			INGLOBE	BEHLMRU	HUMBLER	BEILNSZ	BENZILS
BEEORRU	BOURREE	BEGILNS	BINGLES	BEHLMSU	HUMBLES	BEILNTZ	BLINTZE
BEEORSV	OBSERVE	BEGILNT	BELTING	BEHLOOT	BOTHOLE	BEILOOR	LOOBIER
	OBVERSE	BEGILNU	BLUEING	BEHLORT	BROTHEL	BEILOOS	LOOBIES
	VERBOSE		BULGINE	BEHLOSW	BEHOWLS	BEILOQU	OBLIQUE
BEEORSY	OBEYERS	BEGILNY	BELYING	BEHLRRU	BURRHEL	BEILORR	BROILER
BEEORWY	EYEBROW	BEGILOS	OBLIGES	BEHLRSU	BLUSHER	BEILORS	BOILERS
BEEOSST	OBESEST	BEGILRS	GERBILS		BURHELS		LIBEROS
BEEPRRV	PREVERB	BEGILRT	GILBERT	BEHLSSU	BLUSHES		REBOILS
BEEQSTU	BEQUEST	BEGILRU	BULGIER		BUSHELS	BEILORT	TRILOBE
BEERRST	BERRETS	BEGILST	GIBLETS	BEHLSTU	BLUSHET	BEILORW	BLOWIER
BEERRSU	BEURRES	BEGINNU	UNBEING	BEHMNSU	BUSHMEN	BEILORY	BOILERY
BEERRSV	REVERBS	BEGINOS	BIOGENS	BEHMOOY	HOMEBOY	BEILOST	BETOILS
BEERRSW	BREWERS	BEGINOY	BIOGENY	BEHMORS	HOMBRES	BEILOSW	BLOWIES

BEILOSX	BOLIXES
BEILRRS	BIRLERS
BEILRRU	BURLIER
BEILRSS	BIRSLES
	RIBLESS
BEILRST	BLISTER
	BRISTLE
	RIBLETS
BEILRTT	BRITTLE
	TRIBLET
BEILRTU	REBUILT
BEILRTY	LIBERTY
BEILRUY	BRULYIE
BEILRUZ	BRULZIE
BEILSSS	BLISSES
BEILSST	BITLESS
BEILSTU	BLUIEST
	SUBTILE
BEILSTW	BLEWITS
BEILSTZ	BLITZES
BEIMMRR	BRIMMER
BEIMNOR	BROMINE
BEIMNTU	BITUMEN
BEIMORW	IMBOWER
BEIMOSS	OBEISMS
BEIMOSZ	ZOMBIES
BEIMPRU	BUMPIER
BEIMRST	BETRIMS
	TIMBERS
	TIMBRES
BEIMRSU	ERBIUMS
	IMBRUES
	IMBURSE
BEIMRTU	IMBRUTE
	TERBIUM
BEINNOR	BONNIER
BEINNOS	BENISON
	BONNIES
BEINNOZ	BENZOIN
BEINNSU	BUNNIES
BEINORT	BORNITE
BEINORW	BROWNIE
BEINOSS	BESOINS
BEINOST	BONIEST
	EBONIST
BEINOSV	BOVINES
BEINOSX	BONXIES
BEINOSZ	BIZONES
BEINOTT	BOTTINE
BEINRSU	RUBINES
	SUBERIN
BEINRSY	BYRNIES
BEINRTT	BITTERN
BEINRTU	BUNTIER
	TRIBUNE
	TURBINE
BEINSSY	BYSSINE
BEIOOPT	BIOTOPE
BEIOORZ	BOOZIER
BEIOOST	BOOTIES
BEIOPTY	BIOTYPE
BEIORRT	ORBITER
BEIORSS	BOSSIER
	RIBOSES
BEIORST	ORBIEST
	SORBITE
BEIORSU	BOUSIER
	OUREBIS
BEIOSSU	SOUBISE
BEIOSTT	BOTTIES
BEIOSTX	BOXIEST
BEIOSTY	OBESITY
BEIPPSU	BUPPIES
BEIPSST	BESPITS
BEIPSSU	PUBISES
BEIQRTU	BRIQUET
BEIQSSU	BISQUES
BEIRRRU	BURRIER
BEIRRSU	BRISURE
	BRUISER
BEIRSST	BESTIRS
	BISTERS
	BISTRES
BEIRSSU	BRUISES
BEIRSTT	BITTERS
BEIRSTU	BUSTIER
	RUBIEST
BEIRTTU	TRIBUTE
BEIRTTY	TREYBIT
BEIRUZZ	BUZZIER
BEISSTU	BUSIEST
BEISTTU	BUTTIES
BEITTWX	BETWIXT
BEJJSUU	JUJUBES
BEJLMRU	JUMBLER
BEJLMSU	JUMBLES
BEJLOSS	JOBLESS
BEJORSU	OBJURES
BEKLNRU	BLUNKER
BEKLOOT	BOOKLET
BEKLRSU	BULKERS
BEKMNOO	BOOKMEN
BEKMOST	STEMBOK
BEKNNOW	BEKNOWN
BEKNORS	BONKERS
BEKNORU	UNBROKE
BEKNRSU	BUNKERS
BEKOPRU	UPBROKE
BEKORRS	BROKERS
BEKORRY	BROKERY
BEKOSST	BOSKETS
BEKRSSU	BUSKERS
	BUSKETS
BELLORR	BORRELL
BELLOSU	BOULLES
	LOBULES
	SOLUBLE
BELLOSW	BELLOWS
BELLOUV	VOLUBLE
BELLRRU	BURRELL
BELLRSU	BULLERS
BELLSTU	BULLETS
BELMMOO	EMBLOOM
BELMMRU	MUMBLER
BELMMSU	BUMMELS
	BUMMLES
	MUMBLES
BELMNOS	NOMBLES
BELMNOU	NELUMBO
BELMNSU	NUMBLES
BELMOOR	BLOOMER
	REBLOOM
BELMOOS	BLOOSME
BELMOOT	BOOMLET
BELMOPR	PROBLEM
BELMORT	TEMBLOR
BELMOSU	EMBOLUS
BELMOSY	SYMBOLE
BELMPRU	PLUMBER
BELMRRU	RUMBLER
BELMRSU	LUMBERS
	RUMBLES
	SLUMBER
	UMBRELS
BELMRTU	TUMBLER
	TUMBREL
BELMRTY	TREMBLY
BELMSTU	STUMBLE
	TUMBLES
BELNNOU	UNNOBLE
BELNNTU	UNBLENT
BELNOOY	BOLONEY
BELNOST	NOBLEST
BELNOSZ	BENZOLS
BELNOYZ	BENZOYL
BELNRTU	BLUNTER
BELNSSU	UNBLESS
BELNSTU	SUNBELT
	UNBELTS
	UNBLEST
BELNSYZ	BENZYLS
BELOOPR	BLOOPER
BELOORS	BOLEROS
BELOOSS	SOBOLES
BELOPSU	PUEBLOS
BELORST	BOLSTER
	BOLTERS
	LOBSTER
BELORSU	ROUBLES
BELORSW	BLOWERS
	BOWLERS
BELORSY	SOBERLY
BELORTT	BLOTTER
	BOTTLER
BELORTU	BOULTER
	TROUBLE
BELOSSU	BLOUSES
	BOLUSES
BELOSSW	BLOWSES
BELOSTT	BOTTLES
BELOSTU	BOLETUS
BELOSWZ	BLOWZES
BELRRSU	BURLERS
	BURRELS
BELRSTU	BLUSTER
	BUSTLER
	BUTLERS
	SUBTLER
BELRSUY	BURLEYS
BELRTUY	BUTLERY
BELSSTU	BUSTLES
	SUBLETS
BELSTTU	BUTTLES
BELSTUU	TUBULES
BEMMNOS	MOBSMEN
BEMMOOS	EMBOSOM
BEMMORR	BROMMER
BEMMRRU	BRUMMER
BEMMRSU	BUMMERS
BEMMSTU	BUMMEST
BEMNORW	EMBROWN
BEMNORY	EMBRYON
BEMNOST	ENTOMBS
BEMNOSU	UMBONES
BEMNOSW	ENWOMBS
BEMNPTY	BYNEMPT
BEMNRSU	NUMBERS
BEMNSTU	NUMBEST
BEMNTTU	BUTMENT
BEMOORS	BOOMERS
BEMORRS	SOMBRER
BEMORSS	SOMBERS
	SOMBRES
BEMORST	BESTORM
	MOBSTER
BEMORSU	UMBROSE
BEMORSY	EMBRYOS
BEMORUX	BUXOMER
BEMORWW	WEBWORM
BEMOTUY	MYOTUBE
BEMPRSU	BUMPERS
BEMSSTU	BESMUTS
BEMSSUU	SUBSUME
BENNORU	UNBORNE
BENNORW	NEWBORN
BENNORZ	BRONZEN
BENNOST	BONNETS
BENNOSU	UNBONES
BENNSSU	BUNSENS
BENOPRR	PREBORN
BENOPRU	UPBORNE
BENORRW	BROWNER
BENORRZ	BRONZER
BENORST	BRETONS
	SORBENT
BENORSU	BOURNES
	UNROBES
BENORSZ	BRONZES
BENORWY	BYWONER
BENOSSU	BONUSES
BENOSUX	UNBOXES
BENOSUZ	SUBZONE
BENOSWY	NEWSBOY
BENRRSU	BURNERS
BENRSTU	BRUNETS
	BUNTERS
	BURNETS
	BURSTEN
BEOORSS	BROOSES
BEOORST	BOOSTER
	REBOOTS
BEOORSZ	BOOZERS
BEOPPRS	BOPPERS
BEOPRRS	PROBERS
BEOPRRV	PROVERB
BEOPRST	BESPORT
BEOPSST	BESPOTS
BEOPSTU	BESPOUT
BEOQSTU	BOSQUET
BEOQSUY	OBSEQUY
BEOQTUU	BOUQUET
BEORRSS	RESORBS
BEORRSW	BROWSER
BEORSST	BESORTS
	SORBETS
	STROBES
BEORSSU	BOURSES
BEORSSW	BOWSERS
	BROWSES
BEORSTT	BETTORS
BEORSTU	OBTUSER
BEORSTV	OBVERTS
BEORSUU	UBEROUS
BEORSUZ	BROUZES
	SUBZERO
BEORSVV	BOVVERS
BEORSWY	BOWYERS
BEORUVY	OVERBUY
BEOSSST	BOSSEST
BEOSSTT	OBTESTS
BEOSSTW	BESTOWS
BEPRRTU	PERTURB
BEPRTUY	PUBERTY
BEPSTUY	SUBTYPE
BEQRSUU	BRUSQUE
BERRSTU	BRUTERS
	BURSTER
BERSSTU	BUSTERS
BERSTTU	BUTTERS
BERSTUV	SUBVERT
BERSUZZ	BUZZERS
BERTTUY	BUTTERY
BESSSTU	SUBSETS
BESTTUX	SUBTEXT
BFFGIIN	BIFFING
BFFGINO	BOFFING
BFFGINU	BUFFING
BFFIINS	BIFFINS
BFFINOS	BOFFINS
BFFLLUY	BLUFFLY
BFFNOOU	BUFFOON
BFGIOOT	BIGFOOT
BFGIORT	FROGBIT
BFHILSU	LUBFISH
BFHIRSU	FURBISH
BFHISTU	TUBFISH
BFIILRS	FIBRILS
BFIINOR	FIBROIN
BFIINRS	FIBRINS
BFILMRU	BRIMFUL
BFIMOYZ	ZOMBIFY
BFINOSW	BOWFINS
BFIORSU	FIBROUS
BFIRTUY	BRUTIFY
BFKLOOU	BOOKFUL

BFKLOOY	FLYBOOK	BGILOOY	BIOLOGY	BHIOPSS	BISHOPS
BFKSSUU	SUBFUSK	BGILRSU	BUSGIRL	BHIOPST	PHOBIST
BFLLOUW	BOWLFUL	BGIMMNU	BUMMING	BHIOSWZ	SHOWBIZ
BFLLOWY	BLOWFLY	BGIMNNU	NUMBING	BHIRSTU	BRUTISH
	FLYBLOW	BGIMNOO	BOOMING	BHIRTTU	TURBITH
BFLOSUX	BOXFULS	BGIMNOT	TOMBING	BHKNOSU	BOHUNKS
BFLSTUU	TUBFULS	BGIMNOW	WOMBING	BHLRSUU	BULRUSH
BFOOOTY	FOOTBOY	BGIMNPU	BUMPING	BHMOORS	RHOMBOS
BGGGIIN	BIGGING	BGIMOSY	BOGYISM	BHMORSU	RHOMBUS
BGGGINO	BOGGING	BGINNOS	BONINGS	BHMUUZZ	HUMBUZZ
BGGGINU	BUGGING	BGINNOU	BOUNING	BHOOSTW	BOWSHOT
BGGHIIS	BIGGISH	BGINNOW	BOWNING	BHOOSWX	SHOWBOX
BGGIILN	BILGING	BGINNRU	BURNING	BIIIKNS	BIKINIS
BGGIINN	BINGING	BGINNTU	BUNTING	BIIKLOT	KILOBIT
BGGIINS	BIGGINS	BGINOOS	BOOSING	BIILLNO	BILLION
BGGIISW	BIGWIGS	BGINOOT	BOOTING	BIILLOU	BOUILLI
BGGILNO	GLOBING	BGINOOZ	BOOZING	BIILLTW	TWIBILL
BGGILNU	BUGLING	BGINOPP	BOPPING	BIILNNR	BIRLINN
	BULGING	BGINOPR	PROBING	BIILNQU	QUIBLIN
BGGINNO	BONGING	BGINORS	BORINGS	BIILOSU	BILIOUS
BGGINNU	BUNGING		ROBINGS	BIILSVY	VISIBLY
BGGINOU	BOUGING		SORBING	BIIMNOU	NIOBIUM
BGGINSU	BUGGINS	BGINOSS	BOSSING	BIIMNSU	MINIBUS
BGGNOOS	BOGONGS		OBSIGNS	BIIMOSS	OBIISMS
BGGNOSU	BUGONGS	BGINOSU	BOUSING	BIIMSTU	STIBIUM
BGHHIOY	HIGHBOY	BGINOSW	BOWINGS	BIINOST	BIOTINS
BGHIINS	BINGHIS		BOWSING	BIIORSV	VIBRIOS
BGHILST	BLIGHTS	BGINOSX	BOXINGS	BIIOSUV	BIVIOUS
BGHILTY	BLIGHTY	BGINOTT	BOTTING	BIIRSTU	BURITIS
BGHINOO	BOOHING	BGINOUY	BUOYING	BIISSTV	VIBISTS
	HOBOING	BGINPRU	BURPING	BIISTTT	TITBITS
BGHINOR	BIGHORN		UPBRING	BIJNOSU	SUBJOIN
BGHINSU	BUSHING	BGINRRU	BURRING	BIKLLUY	BULKILY
BGHLRUU	BULGHUR	BGINRSU	SUBRING	BIKLNOY	LINKBOY
	BURGHUL	BGINRTU	BRUTING	BIKLRSY	BRISKLY
BGHMSUU	HUMBUGS	BGINRUY	BURYING	BIKMNPU	BUMPKIN
BGHNORU	HORNBUG		RUBYING	BIKMNSU	BUMKINS
BGHOORU	BOROUGH	BGINSSU	BUSINGS	BIKMOSS	IMBOSKS
BGHORSU	BROUGHS		BUSSING	BIKNSSU	BUSKINS
BGHORTU	BROUGHT	BGINSTU	BUSTING	BIKORRW	RIBWORK
BGHOSTU	BOUGHTS		TUBINGS	BILLNOS	BILLONS
BGIIKLN	BILKING	BGINSUY	BUSYING	BILLNOU	BULLION
BGIIKNS	BIKINGS	BGINTTU	BUTTING	BILLOOY	LOOBILY
BGIILLN	BILLING	BGINUZZ	BUZZING	BILLOSW	BILLOWS
BGIILMN	LIMBING	BGIORTY	BIGOTRY	BILLOUV	VOLUBIL
BGIILNO	BOILING	BGIOSSS	GOSSIBS	BILLOWY	BILLOWY
BGIILNR	BIRLING	BGKLOOO	LOGBOOK	BILLRWY	WRYBILL
BGIILNS	SIBLING	BGKORSY	GRYSBOK	BILMNOR	NOMBRIL
BGIIMNR	BRIMING	BGLMRUY	GRUMBLY	BILMOSU	LIMBOUS
BGIIMNU	IMBUING	BGLNOOS	OBLONGS	BILMPUY	BUMPILY
BGIINNN	BINNING	BGLNOOW	LONGBOW	BILMRSU	UMBRILS
BGIINNR	BRINING	BGLNOUW	BLOWGUN	BILMRTU	TUMBRIL
	INBRING	BGLOOSU	GLOBOUS	BILMSUU	BULIMUS
BGIINRR	BIRRING	BGLOSSU	BUGLOSS	BILNNOY	BONNILY
BGIINRT	RINGBIT	BGLRSUU	BULGURS	BILNTUU	BUTULIN
BGIINST	BITINGS	BGMOORS	GOMBROS		UNBUILT
BGIINTT	BITTING	BGMOOTU	GUMBOOT	BILOOYZ	BOOZILY
BGIKLNU	BULKING	BGMSSUU	SUBGUMS	BILOPSU	UPBOILS
BGIKNNO	BONKING	BGNOOWY	GOWNBOY	BILOSSU	SUBSOIL
BGIKNNU	BUNKING	BGNOSSU	SUBSONG	BILOSSY	BOSSILY
BGIKNOO	BOOKING	BGOORSU	BURGOOS	BILPTUU	UPBUILT
BGIKNOR	BROKING	BGORTUW	BUGWORT	BILRSTY	BRISTLY
BGIKNRU	BURKING	BHIIINT	INHIBIT		TRILBYS
BGIKNSU	BUSKING	BHIINRS	BRINISH	BILRTTY	BRITTLY
BGILLNO	BOLLING	BHIIPSS	SIBSHIP	BILRTUY	TILBURY
BGILLNU	BULLING	BHIISST	BHISTIS	BIMMOOS	IMBOSOM
BGILMNO	MOBLING	BHIKOOS	BOOKISH		MIOMBOS
BGILMOU	GUMBOIL	BHIKSSU	BUKSHIS	BIMMORS	BROMISM
BGILNOS	GLOBINS	BHILLSU	BULLISH	BIMNORS	MISBORN
	GOBLINS	BHILOTU	HOLIBUT	BIMNORW	IMBROWN
	LOBINGS	BHILPSU	PUBLISH	BIMNOSS	BONISMS
BGILNOT	BILTONG	BHIMOOR	RHOMBOI	BIMNOST	INTOMBS
	BOLTING	BHIMOOS	HOBOISM	BIMNOSU	OMNIBUS
BGILNOW	BLOWING	BHIMOPS	PHOBISM	BIMNOSY	SYMBION
	BOWLING	BHIMORT	THROMBI	BIMRSUX	BRUXISM
BGILNOY	IGNOBLY	BHIMSTU	BISMUTH	BIMSSSU	SUBMISS
BGILNRU	BURLING	BHINRSU	BURNISH	BIMSSTU	SUBMITS
BGILNSU	BLUINGS	BHIOOPR	BIOPHOR	BINNOSU	BUNIONS
BGILOOR	OBLIGOR	BHIOORS	BOORISH	BINOORS	BONSOIR
				BINOOST	BONITOS
				BINOOSU	NIOBOUS
				BINORST	RIBSTON
				BINOSST	BONISTS
				BINPSUY	BUNYIPS
				BINRSTU	INBURST
				BINSTTU	UNBITTS
				BINSTUU	SUBUNIT
				BIOORSZ	BORZOIS
				BIOOSST	OBOISTS
				BIOOSUV	OBVIOUS
				BIOPRST	PROBITS
				BIOPRTY	PROBITY
				BIORRTU	BURRITO
				BIORRTW	RIBWORT
				BIORSST	BISTROS
				BIORSTT	BISTORT
					BITTORS
				BIORSUU	RUBIOUS
				BIORTTU	BITTOUR
				BIOSTUW	WOUBITS
				BIRSTTU	BITTURS
					TURBITS
				BISSSTU	SUBSIST
				BJNOORU	BONJOUR
				BKMNSUU	BUNKUMS
				BKNOOTW	BOWKNOT
				BKNORSY	SKYBORN
				BKOORWX	WORKBOX
				BLLNTUY	BLUNTLY
				BLLOSUU	LOBULUS
				BLLOUVY	VOLUBLY
				BLMMPUU	PLUMBUM
				BLMNPUU	UNPLUMB
				BLMOOOT	TOMBOLO
				BLMOORW	LOBWORM
				BLMOOSS	BLOSSOM
				BLMOSSY	SYMBOLS
				BLMRSUY	SLUMBRY
				BLMSTUY	STUMBLY
				BLNNOUW	UNBLOWN
				BLNOOSU	BLOUSON
				BLNOPUW	UPBLOWN
				BLNOSTU	UNBOLTS
				BLOOOTX	TOOLBOX
				BLOOQUY	OBLOQUY
				BLOOSWY	LOWBOYS
				BLOPSTU	SUBPLOT
				BLOPSUW	UPBLOWS
				BMNOOSU	UNBOSOM
				BMNORUW	MOWBURN
				BMNOSTU	UNTOMBS
				BMOOORX	BOXROOM
				BMOORSY	BYROOMS
				BMOOSTT	BOTTOMS
				BMOOSTY	TOMBOYS
				BMORSST	STROMBS
				BMORSUU	BRUMOUS
					UMBROUS
				BNNRSUU	SUNBURN
				BNNRTUU	UNBURNT
				BNOOSST	BOSTONS
				BNOOSTU	BOUTONS
					UNBOOTS
				BNOOTTY	BOTTONY
				BNORSSU	SUBORNS
				BNORSTU	BURTONS
				BNORSUU	BURNOUS
				BNORTUU	OUTBURN
				BNOSSUW	SUNBOWS
				BNOSTTU	BUTTONS
				BNOTTUY	BUTTONY
				BOOPSTW	BOWPOTS
				BOOPSTX	POSTBOX
				BOOPSTY	POTBOYS
				BOORRSW	BORROWS
				BOOSTUW	WOOBUTS
				BOOSWWW	BOWWOWS
				BOPSSTU	POSTBUS

Code	Word(s)
BORRSUW	BURROWS
BORSSTW	BROWSTS
BORSTTU	TURBOTS
BORSTUU	RUBOUTS
BORSTXY	BOSTRYX
BPRSTUU	UPBURST
CCCDIOO	COCCOID
CCCDIOS	COCCIDS
CCCNOOT	CONCOCT
CCDEEER	RECCEED
CCDEEHK	CHECKED
CCDEEIO	ECOCIDE
CCDEEIR	RECCIED
CCDEEIS	DECCIES
CCDEEKL	CLECKED
CCDEENO	CONCEDE
CCDEENY	DECENCY
CCDEEOR	COERCED
CCDEESU	SUCCEED
CCDEHIN	CINCHED
CCDEHKO	CHOCKED
CCDEHKU	CHUCKED
CCDEHNO	CONCHED
CCDEHOU	COUCHED
CCDEIIT	DEICTIC
CCDEIKL	CLICKED
CCDEIKR	CRICKED
CCDEILR	CIRCLED
CCDEIMO	COMEDIC
CCDEIOS	CODICES
CCDEKLO	CLOCKED
	COCKLED
CCDEKLU	CLUCKED
CCDEKOR	CROCKED
CCDELOU	OCCLUDE
CCDENOO	CONCEDO
CCDENOS	SCONCED
CCDENOU	CONDUCE
CCDEOST	DECOCTS
CCDHIIL	CICHLID
CCDIILO	CODICIL
CCDIILU	CULICID
CCDIIOR	CRICOID
CCDILOY	CYCLOID
CCDKLOU	CUCKOLD
CCDNOOR	CONCORD
CCDNOTU	CONDUCT
CCEEGNO	COGENCE
CCEEHIV	CEVICHE
CCEEHKR	CHECKER
	RECHECK
CCEEHOR	ECORCHE
CCEEHOU	COUCHEE
CCEEHRS	CRECHES
	SCREECH
CCEEILN	LICENCE
CCEEINR	ECCRINE
CCEEINS	SCIENCE
CCEEIRS	RECCIES
CCEEIRV	CREVICE
CCEEKOY	COCKEYE
CCEELRY	RECYCLE
CCEENRY	RECENCY
CCEEORS	COERCES
CCEERSY	SECRECY
CCEFNOT	CONFECT
CCEGNOY	COGENCY
CCEHHIS	CHICHES
CCEHIKN	CHICKEN
CCEHIKU	CHUCKIE
CCEHILS	CHICLES
	CLICHES
CCEHILU	CULCHIE
CCEHIMS	CHEMICS
CCEHINO	CONCHIE
CCEHINS	CINCHES
CCEHINT	TECHNIC
CCEHIOR	CHOICER
	CHOREIC
CCEHIOS	CHOICES
CCEHIRS	SCREICH
	SCRIECH
CCEHIST	CHICEST
	HECTICS
CCEHKLU	CHUCKLE
CCEHKMS	SCHMECK
CCEHKNU	UNCHECK
CCEHKOR	CHOCKER
CCEHLOS	CLOCHES
CCEHLRU	CLERUCH
CCEHLSU	CLEUCHS
	CULCHES
CCEHNOS	CONCHES
CCEHORS	CROCHES
CCEHORT	CROCHET
CCEHOSS	COSECHS
CCEHOSU	COUCHES
CCEHRSU	CURCHES
CCEHSTU	CUTCHES
CCEIILS	CILICES
	ICICLES
CCEIIMS	CIMICES
CCEIIPS	PICCIES
CCEIIRT	ICTERIC
CCEIIST	CECITIS
CCEIKLR	CLICKER
CCEIKLT	CLICKET
CCEIKOR	COCKIER
CCEIKOS	COCKIES
CCEIKRT	CRICKET
CCEIKRY	CRICKEY
CCEILOT	COCTILE
CCEILRR	CIRCLER
CCEILRS	CIRCLES
	CLERICS
CCEILRT	CIRCLET
CCEILSU	CULICES
CCEILSY	CYLICES
CCEILTU	CUTICLE
CCEIMNO	MECONIC
CCEIMOS	COMICES
CCEIMOT	COMETIC
CCEIMST	SMECTIC
CCEINOR	CORNICE
	CROCEIN
CCEINOS	CONCISE
CCEINOT	CONCEIT
CCEINRT	CENTRIC
CCEIOPP	COPPICE
CCEIOPT	ECTOPIC
CCEIORS	CICEROS
CCEIORT	ORECTIC
CCEIOSS	CISCOES
CCEIPST	SCEPTIC
CCEIRST	CRETICS
CCEISSU	SUCCISE
CCEJNOT	CONJECT
CCEKLOR	CLOCKER
CCEKLOS	COCKLES
CCEKNOT	CONTECK
CCEKNOY	COCKNEY
CCEKOPS	COPECKS
CCEKOPT	PETCOCK
CCEKORS	COCKERS
CCEKORT	CROCKET
CCEKOST	COCKETS
CCELLOT	COLLECT
CCELNOY	CYCLONE
CCELNUY	LUCENCY
CCELRSY	CYCLERS
CCENNOR	CONCERN
CCENNOT	CONCENT
	CONNECT
CCENOPT	CONCEPT
CCENORT	CONCERT
CCENORW	CONCREW
CCENOSS	SCONCES
CCEOOTT	COCOTTE
CCEOPRT	PERCOCT
CCEORRT	CORRECT
CCEORSS	ESCROCS
	SOCCERS
CCEORTW	TWOCCER
CCEOSSU	SUCCOSE
CCESSSU	SUCCESS
CCFIRUY	CRUCIFY
CCFLOSU	FLOCCUS
CCGHINO	GNOCCHI
CCGIINS	SICCING
CCGIKNO	COCKING
CCGILNY	CYCLING
CCGKOOR	GORCOCK
CCHHIIS	CHICHIS
CCHHIIT	ICHTHIC
CCHHLIS	SCHLICH
CCHHOOS	CHOCHOS
CCHHRUY	CHURCHY
CCHIIST	STICHIC
CCHIKST	SCHTICK
	TCHICKS
CCHILOR	CHLORIC
CCHIMOR	CHROMIC
CCHINOR	CHRONIC
CCHINOS	CHICONS
CCHINSU	SCUCHIN
CCHIORY	CHICORY
CCHIOTW	COWITCH
CCHIPSU	HICCUPS
CCHIPSY	PSYCHIC
CCHIPUY	HICCUPY
CCHIRST	SCRITCH
CCHKLOS	SCHLOCK
CCHKMOS	SCHMOCK
CCHKMSU	SCHMUCK
CCHKOOS	CHOCKOS
CCHKOSY	COCKSHY
CCHKPUU	UPCHUCK
CCHKSTU	SCHTUCK
CCHNRSU	SCRUNCH
CCHNRUY	CRUNCHY
CCHOSTU	SUCCOTH
CCIIILS	SILICIC
CCIILNS	CLINICS
CCIILPR	CIRCLIP
CCIILST	CLITICS
CCIINPS	PICNICS
CCIIRST	CRITICS
CCIIRTU	CIRCUIT
CCIISTY	SICCITY
CCIKLOW	COWLICK
CCIKLOY	COCKILY
	COLICKY
CCIKOPT	COCKPIT
CCILNOO	COLONIC
CCILNOU	COUNCIL
CCILOOP	PICCOLO
CCILSTY	CYCLIST
CCIMOTY	MYCOTIC
CCINOOT	COCTION
CCINORY	CRYONIC
CCINOTV	CONVICT
CCIOORS	SIROCCO
CCIOPTU	OCCIPUT
CCIORSS	SCIROCS
CCIPRTY	CRYPTIC
CCIRSUY	CIRCUSY
CCKMOOS	MOCOCKS
CCKMOSU	MOCUCKS
CCKNOSU	UNCOCKS
CCKOOSU	CUCKOOS
CCKOSTU	CUSTOCK
CCLMSUU	MUCLUCS
CCLOOOZ	ZOCCOLO
CCLOPSY	CYCLOPS
CCLOSTU	OCCULTS
CCMOOOR	MOROCCO
CCNOOOS	COCOONS
CCNOOPU	PUCCOON
CCNOOTU	COCONUT
CCNOPUY	CONCUPY
CCNORSU	CONCURS
CCNOSSU	CONCUSS
CCOOORS	ROCOCOS
CCORSSU	SUCCORS
CCORSUU	SUCCOUR
CCORSUY	SUCCORY
CCOSSTU	STUCCOS
CCOSSUU	SUCCOUS
CCSSSUU	SUCCUSS
CDDDEEI	DECIDED
CDDDEEO	DECODED
CDDDEEU	DEDUCED
CDDDELO	CLODDED
	CODDLED
CDDDELU	CUDDLED
CDDDERU	CRUDDED
CDDDSOU	SCUDDED
CDDEEER	DECREED
	RECEDED
CDDEEES	SECEDED
CDDEEII	DEICIDE
CDDEEIN	INCEDED
CDDEEIR	DECIDER
	DECRIED
CDDEEIS	DECIDES
CDDEEIX	EXCIDED
CDDEEKL	DECKLED
CDDEEKO	DECKOED
	DECOKED
CDDEENO	ENCODED
CDDEENS	DESCEND
	SCENDED
CDDEEOR	DECODER
	RECODED
CDDEEOS	DECODES
CDDEEOY	DECOYED
CDDEERU	REDUCED
CDDEESU	DEDUCES
	SEDUCED
CDDEEUW	CUDWEED
CDDEHIL	CHILDED
CDDEHIN	CHIDDEN
CDDEHIT	DICHTED
	DITCHED
CDDEHNU	DUNCHED
CDDEHOU	DOUCHED
CDDEIIS	DISCIDE
CDDEINU	INDUCED
CDDEIOS	DISCOED
CDDEISU	CUDDIES
CDDELOS	CODDLES
	SCOLDED
CDDELOU	CLOUDED
CDDELRU	CRUDDLE
	CURDLED
CDDELSU	CUDDLES
	SCUDDLE
CDDENSU	CUDDENS
CDDEORS	CODDERS
CDDEORW	CROWDED
CDDERSU	SCUDDER
CDDESTU	DEDUCTS
CDDGINO	CODDING
CDDHIOR	DICHORD
CDDIIIO	DIDICOI
CDDIIOS	DISCOID
CDDIIOY	DIDICOY
CDDIIRU	DRUIDIC
CDDIKOP	PIDDOCK
CDDINSU	CUDDINS
CDDIORS	DISCORD
CDDKOPU	PUDDOCK
CDDKORU	RUDDOCK
CDEEEFL	FLEECED
CDEEEFN	DEFENCE
CDEEEHK	CHEEKED

CDEEEHL	LEECHED
CDEEEHP	CHEEPED
	DEPECHE
CDEEEHR	CHEERED
	REECHED
CDEEEHS	CHEESED
CDEEEIP	EPICEDE
CDEEEIV	DECEIVE
CDEEEJT	EJECTED
CDEEEKL	CLEEKED
CDEEELP	CLEEPED
CDEEELT	ELECTED
CDEEEPR	PRECEDE
CDEEERS	CREESED
	DECREES
	RECEDES
	SECEDER
CDEEERT	DECREET
	ERECTED
CDEEESS	SECEDES
CDEEESX	EXCEEDS
CDEEFHT	FETCHED
CDEEFII	EDIFICE
CDEEFKL	FLECKED
CDEEFLT	DEFLECT
CDEEFOR	DEFORCE
CDEEFST	DEFECTS
CDEEGIR	GRIECED
CDEEGNO	CONGEED
CDEEHIS	DEHISCE
CDEEHIV	CHEVIED
CDEEHKL	HECKLED
CDEEHLT	LETCHED
CDEEHLW	WELCHED
CDEEHMS	SCHEMED
CDEEHNW	WENCHED
CDEEHOR	CHORDEE
	COHERED
	OCHERED
CDEEHPR	PERCHED
CDEEHRT	RETCHED
CDEEHRU	EUCHRED
CDEEHST	CHESTED
CDEEIIT	EIDETIC
CDEEILN	DECLINE
CDEEILP	PEDICEL
	PEDICLE
CDEEILS	DELICES
CDEEIMN	ENDEMIC
CDEEIMS	DECIMES
CDEEINO	CODEINE
CDEEINR	CEDRINE
CDEEINS	INCEDES
CDEEINT	ENTICED
CDEEINV	EVINCED
CDEEIOS	DIOCESE
CDEEIOV	DEVOICE
CDEEIPR	PIERCED
CDEEIPT	PEDETIC
CDEEIRR	DECRIER
CDEEIRS	DECRIES
CDEEIRT	RECITED
	TIERCED
CDEEIST	DECEITS
CDEEISV	DEVICES
CDEEISX	EXCIDES
	EXCISED
CDEEITV	EVICTED
CDEEITX	EXCITED
CDEEJNO	CONJEED
CDEEJST	DEJECTS
CDEEKKL	KECKLED
CDEEKLR	CLERKED
CDEEKLS	DECKLES
CDEEKNR	REDNECK
CDEEKNS	SNECKED
CDEEKOS	DECOKES
CDEEKPS	SPECKED
CDEEKRS	DECKERS
CDEEKRT	TRECKED
CDEEKRW	WRECKED
CDEELMM	CLEMMED
CDEELOS	ECLOSED
CDEELPU	CUPELED
	DECUPLE
CDEELPY	YCLEPED
CDEELRU	RECULED
	ULCERED
CDEELSU	SCEDULE
	SECLUDE
CDEELUX	EXCLUDE
CDEENOR	ENCORED
CDEENOS	ENCODES
	SECONDE
CDEENOZ	COZENED
CDEENRS	DECERNS
	SCERNED
CDEENRT	CENTRED
	CREDENT
CDEENST	DESCENT
	SCENTED
CDEEOOY	COOEYED
CDEEOPR	COPERED
	PROCEED
CDEEORS	RECODES
CDEEORV	COVERED
CDEEORW	COWERED
CDEEOST	CESTODE
	TEDESCO
CDEEOTV	COVETED
CDEERRU	RECURED
	REDUCER
CDEERSS	SCREEDS
CDEERST	CRESTED
CDEERSU	RECUSED
	REDUCES
	RESCUED
	SECURED
	SEDUCER
CDEERSW	DECREWS
	SCREWED
CDEERTU	ERUCTED
CDEERUV	DECURVE
CDEESSU	SEDUCES
CDEESSY	ECDYSES
CDEESTT	DECTETS
	DETECTS
CDEESUX	EXCUSED
CDEFFHU	CHUFFED
CDEFFIL	CLIFFED
CDEFFLU	CUFFLED
CDEFFOS	SCOFFED
CDEFFSU	SCUFFED
CDEFHIL	FILCHED
CDEFHIN	FINCHED
CDEFHOO	CHOOFED
CDEFIIT	DEFICIT
CDEFIKL	FICKLED
	FLICKED
CDEFILT	CLIFTED
CDEFINO	CONFIDE
CDEFKLO	FLOCKED
CDEFKOR	DEFROCK
	FROCKED
CDEFNTU	DEFUNCT
CDEFOSU	FOCUSED
CDEFRTU	FRUCTED
CDEFSUU	FUCUSED
CDEGGHU	CHUGGED
CDEGGLO	CLOGGED
	COGGLED
CDEGGOS	SCOGGED
CDEGGSU	SCUGGED
CDEGHLU	GULCHED
CDEGHOU	COUGHED
CDEGIKN	DECKING
CDEGILU	CLUDGIE
CDEGINO	COIGNED
CDEGINR	CRINGED
CDEGINU	EDUCING
CDEGIOR	ERGODIC
CDEGLSU	CUDGELS
CDEGNSU	SCUNGED
CDEGOOS	SCOOGED
CDEGORS	CODGERS
CDEGOSU	SCOUGED
CDEHHIL	HILCHED
CDEHHIT	HITCHED
CDEHHNU	HUNCHED
CDEHHOT	HOTCHED
CDEHHTU	HUTCHED
CDEHIIL	CEILIDH
CDEHIIV	CHIVIED
CDEHIKN	CHINKED
CDEHIKO	HOICKED
CDEHIKR	CHIRKED
CDEHIKT	THICKED
CDEHILL	CHILLED
CDEHILO	CHELOID
	HELCOID
CDEHILP	DELPHIC
CDEHILR	CHILDER
	CHIRLED
CDEHILS	CHIELDS
CDEHILT	LICHTED
CDEHIMR	CHIRMED
CDEHIMT	MITCHED
CDEHINN	CHINNED
CDEHINO	HEDONIC
CDEHINP	PINCHED
CDEHINW	WINCHED
CDEHIOR	CHOIRED
CDEHIOW	COWHIDE
CDEHIPP	CHIPPED
CDEHIPR	CHIRPED
CDEHIPT	PITCHED
CDEHIQU	QUICHED
CDEHIRR	CHIRRED
CDEHIRS	CHIDERS
	HERDICS
CDEHIRT	CHIRTED
	DITCHER
	RICHTED
CDEHIST	DITCHES
CDEHISU	DUCHIES
CDEHITT	CHITTED
CDEHITW	WITCHED
CDEHIVV	CHIVVED
CDEHIZZ	CHIZZED
CDEHKOS	SHOCKED
CDEHKSU	SHUCKED
CDEHKUY	HEYDUCK
CDEHLMU	MULCHED
CDEHLNU	LUNCHED
CDEHLNY	LYNCHED
CDEHLOT	CLOTHED
CDEHLRU	LURCHED
CDEHMMU	CHUMMED
CDEHMNU	MUNCHED
CDEHMOO	MOOCHED
CDEHMOP	CHOMPED
CDEHMOR	CHROMED
CDEHMOU	MOUCHED
CDEHNOR	CHONDRE
CDEHNOT	NOTCHED
CDEHNPU	PUNCHED
CDEHNRU	CHUNDER
	CHURNED
CDEHNSU	DUNCHES
CDEHNSY	SYNCHED
CDEHOPP	CHOPPED
CDEHOPT	POTCHED
CDEHOPU	POUCHED
CDEHORT	TORCHED
CDEHORW	CHOWDER
	COWHERD
CDEHOSU	CHOUSED
	DOUCHES
	HOCUSED
CDEHOSW	COWSHED
CDEHOTU	TOUCHED
CDEHOUV	VOUCHED
CDEHPSY	PSYCHED
CDEHRRU	CHURRED
CDEHRSU	CRUSHED
CDEHSSU	DUCHESS
CDEHSTU	DUTCHES
CDEHSTY	SCYTHED
CDEIIKR	DICKIER
CDEIIKS	DICKIES
CDEIIMR	DIMERIC
CDEIINS	INCISED
	INDICES
CDEIINT	IDENTIC
	INCITED
CDEIIOR	ERICOID
CDEIIOV	OVICIDE
CDEIIRT	DICTIER
	ICTERID
CDEIIST	DEISTIC
	DICIEST
CDEIISU	SUICIDE
CDEIJST	DISJECT
CDEIKLN	CLINKED
CDEIKLP	PICKLED
CDEIKLS	SICKLED
	SLICKED
CDEIKLT	TICKLED
CDEIKMS	MEDICKS
CDEIKNS	DICKENS
	SNICKED
CDEIKNZ	ZINCKED
CDEIKOS	DOCKISE
CDEIKOY	YOICKED
CDEIKOZ	DOCKIZE
CDEIKPR	PRICKED
CDEIKRR	DERRICK
CDEIKRS	DICKERS
	SCRIKED
CDEIKRT	TRICKED
CDEIKRU	DUCKIER
CDEIKRW	WRICKED
CDEIKST	STICKED
CDEIKSU	DUCKIES
CDEIKSW	WICKEDS
CDEIKSY	DICKEYS
CDEILLO	CODILLE
	COLLIDE
	COLLIED
CDEILLU	CULLIED
CDEILMO	MELODIC
CDEILNU	INCLUDE
	NUCLIDE
CDEILOO	OCELOID
CDEILOP	POLICED
CDEILOR	DOCILER
CDEILPP	CLIPPED
CDEILPS	SPLICED
CDEILPU	CLUPEID
CDEILRU	LUCIDER
CDEILST	DELICTS
CDEILSU	SLUICED
CDEILTU	DUCTILE
	DULCITE
CDEIMNO	DEMONIC
CDEIMOR	DORMICE
CDEIMOS	MEDICOS
CDEIMOT	DEMOTIC
CDEIMPR	CRIMPED
CDEIMPU	PUMICED
CDEIMSU	MISCUED
CDEINOS	CONDIES
	SECONDI
CDEINOT	CTENOID
	DEONTIC
	NOTICED

CDEINOU	DOUCINE	CDELOST	COLDEST	CDFIOSU	FUCOIDS	CDNOORS	CONDORS
CDEINOZ	ZINCODE	CDELOSU	DULCOSE	CDGHIIN	CHIDING		CORDONS
CDEINPR	PRINCED	CDELOSW	SCOWLED	CDGIINO	GONIDIC	CDNORSU	UNCORDS
CDEINRS	CINDERS	CDELOTT	CLOTTED	CDGIINS	DICINGS	CDOOOPT	OCTOPOD
	DISCERN	CDELOTU	CLOUTED		DISCING	CDOOOST	DOOCOTS
	RESCIND	CDELOUY	DOUCELY	CDGIINT	DICTING	CDOORRY	CORRODY
CDEINRU	INDUCER	CDELPSU	SCULPED	CDGIKNO	DOCKING	CDOORST	DOCTORS
CDEINRY	CINDERY	CDELRSU	CURDLES	CDGIKNU	DUCKING	CDOOTUW	WOODCUT
CDEINSU	CUNDIES		SCUDLER	CDGILNO	CODLING	CDOPRTU	PRODUCT
	INCUDES	CDELRUY	CRUDELY	CDGINNO	CONDIGN	CDOSTUY	CUSTODY
	INCUSED	CDEMMNO	COMMEND	CDGINOR	CORDING	CEEEEGH	GEECHEE
	INDUCES	CDEMMOO	COMMODE	CDGINOS	CODINGS	CEEEEHL	LEECHEE
CDEINSX	EXSCIND	CDEMMSU	SCUMMED	CDGINRU	CURDING	CEEEFLR	FLEECER
CDEINTT	TINCTED	CDEMNNO	CONDEMN	CDGINTU	DUCTING	CEEEFLS	FLEECES
CDEINTU	UNCITED	CDEMNOP	COMPEND	CDGNOOO	COONDOG	CEEEGNR	REGENCE
CDEIOPR	PERCOID	CDEMOOS	COMEDOS	CDHIIMO	DOCHMII	CEEEGNS	EGENCES
CDEIOPT	PICOTED	CDEMOPT	COMPTED	CDHIINT	CHINDIT	CEEEGRS	GREECES
CDEIORS	DISCOER	CDEMORU	DECORUM	CDHIIST	DISTICH	CEEEHIR	REECHIE
CDEIORT	CORDITE	CDEMPRU	CRUMPED	CDHILLY	CHILDLY	CEEEHKS	KEECHES
CDEIORV	DIVORCE	CDENNOO	CONDONE	CDHILNU	UNCHILD	CEEEHLS	ELCHEES
CDEIORW	CROWDIE	CDENNOT	CONTEND	CDHILOS	COLDISH		LEECHES
CDEIOST	CESTOID	CDENOOR	CROONED	CDHINOR	CHONDRI	CEEEHNR	ENCHEER
	COTISED	CDENOOS	SECONDO	CDHIOOR	CHOROID	CEEEHPR	CHEEPER
CDEIPRS	CRISPED	CDENOPU	POUNCED		OCHROID	CEEEHRR	CHEERER
	DISCERP		UNCOPED	CDHIORS	DROICHS	CEEEHRS	REECHES
CDEIPRT	PREDICT	CDENORS	CONDERS		ORCHIDS	CEEEHSS	CHEESES
CDEIPST	DEPICTS		CORSNED	CDHIORY	DROICHY	CEEEINP	EPICENE
	DISCEPT		SCORNED	CDHIPTY	DIPTYCH	CEEEIPR	CREEPIE
CDEIRRU	CURDIER	CDENORW	CROWNED	CDHKOOR	HORDOCK	CEEEIRV	RECEIVE
	CURRIED		DECROWN	CDIIIOT	IDIOTIC	CEEELLU	ECUELLE
CDEIRST	CREDITS	CDENOSS	SECONDS	CDIIJRU	JURIDIC	CEEELPY	YCLEEPE
	DIRECTS	CDENOST	DOCENTS	CDIILLY	IDYLLIC	CEEELST	CELESTE
CDEIRSU	CRUISED	CDENOTU	COUNTED	CDIILMO	DOMICIL	CEEELSV	CLEEVES
	DISCURE	CDENPUY	PUDENCY	CDIINOR	CRINOID	CEEEMPR	EMPERCE
CDEIRSV	CERVIDS	CDENRUU	UNCURED	CDIINOT	DICTION	CEEENRS	RECENSE
	SCRIVED	CDENRUY	DUNCERY	CDIINOZ	ZINCOID	CEEENSS	ESSENCE
CDEIRTV	VERDICT	CDEOOPP	COPEPOD	CDIINST	INDICTS	CEEEPRR	CREEPER
CDEISST	DISSECT	CDEOOPS	OPCODES	CDIIORS	CIRSOID	CEEERRT	ERECTER
CDEISSY	ECDYSIS		SCOOPED	CDIIOSS	CISSOID	CEEERSS	CREESES
CDEITUX	EXCUDIT	CDEOOPT	COOPTED	CDIIOTY	IDIOTCY	CEEERST	SECRETE
CDEJNOU	JOUNCED	CDEOORR	CORRODE	CDIKNOR	DORNICK	CEEERSV	SCREEVE
CDEKKNO	KNOCKED	CDEOORV	VOCODER	CDIKNOW	WINDOCK	CEEERTX	EXCRETE
CDEKLNO	CLONKED	CDEOOST	SCOOTED	CDILLOO	COLLOID	CEEETUX	EXECUTE
CDEKLNU	CLUNKED	CDEOOTV	DOVECOT	CDILLUY	LUCIDLY	CEEFFNO	OFFENCE
CDEKLOW	WEDLOCK	CDEOPPR	CROPPED	CDILNOS	CODLINS	CEEFFOR	EFFORCE
CDEKLPU	PLUCKED	CDEOPRS	CORPSED	CDILOTU	DULOTIC	CEEFFOS	COFFEES
CDEKLRU	RUCKLED	CDEOPRU	CROUPED	CDIMMOU	MODICUM	CEEFFST	EFFECTS
CDEKLSU	SCULKED		PRODUCE	CDIMNOO	MONODIC	CEEFHIR	CHIEFER
	SUCKLED	CDEOPSU	SCOUPED	CDIMNSU	MUNDICS	CEEFHIT	FETICHE
CDEKMOS	SMOCKED	CDEOPSW	SCOWPED	CDIMOSU	MUSCOID		FITCHEE
CDEKNOS	DOCKENS	CDEOQTU	DOCQUET	CDIMSSU	MUSCIDS	CEEFHLS	FLECHES
CDEKNRU	DRUCKEN	CDEORRS	RECORDS	CDINOOS	CONOIDS	CEEFHRT	FECHTER
CDEKNSU	SUNDECK	CDEORRW	CROWDER	CDINOOT	ODONTIC	CEEFHST	FETCHES
	UNDECKS	CDEORSS	CROSSED	CDINOSY	SYNODIC	CEEFINV	VENEFIC
CDEKOOR	CROOKED		SCORSED	CDINOTU	CONDUIT	CEEFIRR	FIERCER
CDEKORS	DOCKERS	CDEORSU	COURSED		NOCTUID	CEEFKLR	FLECKER
CDEKORT	TROCKED		SCOURED	CDINSSY	SYNDICS		FRECKLE
CDEKOST	DOCKETS		SOURCED	CDINSTU	INDUCTS	CEEFLNU	FLUENCE
	STOCKED	CDEORSW	SCOWDER	CDIOOTT	COTTOID	CEEFLRT	REFLECT
CDEKRSU	DUCKERS	CDEORTU	COURTED	CDIOPSS	PSOCIDS	CEEFNNS	FENNECS
CDEKRTU	TRUCKED		EDUCTOR	CDIORSV	CORVIDS	CEEFNOR	ENFORCE
CDELLOU	COLLUDE	CDEORUU	DOUCEUR	CDIOSST	CODISTS	CEEFNRS	FENCERS
CDELLSU	SCULLED	CDEOSSU	ESCUDOS	CDIOSTT	COTTIDS	CEEFPRT	PERFECT
CDELMOP	CLOMPED	CDEOSTU	CUSTODE	CDIOSTY	CYSTOID		PREFECT
CDELMPU	CLUMPED		DOUCEST	CDIOTUV	OVIDUCT	CEEFRST	REFECTS
CDELMSU	MUSCLED		DOUCETS	CDIPRSY	CYPRIDS	CEEFSSU	FESCUES
CDELMTU	MULCTED		SCOUTED	CDIPSSU	CUSPIDS	CEEGHIN	EECHING
CDELNOO	CONDOLE	CDEOSTY	CYTODES	CDIRSUY	DYSURIC	CEEGINR	CREEING
CDELNOU	ENCLOUD	CDEOSYZ	ZYDECOS	CDIRTUY	CRUDITY		ENERGIC
CDELNOW	CLOWNED	CDEPRSU	SPRUCED	CDISSSU	DISCUSS		GENERIC
CDELNOY	CONDYLE	CDEPRTY	DECRYPT	CDISSTY	CYSTIDS	CEEGINT	GENETIC
CDELOOR	COLORED	CDERRSU	SCURRED	CDKNNOU	DUNNOCK	CEEGINU	EUGENIC
	CROODLE	CDERSTU	CRUDEST	CDKNOSU	UNDOCKS	CEEGIRS	CIERGES
	DECOLOR		CRUSTED	CDLNOUU	UNCLOUD		GRIECES
CDELOPP	CLOPPED	CDERSUZ	SCRUZED	CDLOOPY	LYCOPOD	CEEGKOS	GECKOES
CDELOPU	COUPLED	CDFHIOS	CODFISH	CDMMOOO	COMMODO	CEEGLLO	COLLEGE
CDELORS	SCOLDER	CDFIILU	FLUIDIC	CDMNOOS	CONDOMS	CEEGLNT	NEGLECT
CDELORU	CLOURED	CDFILUY	DULCIFY	CDMOSUW	MUDSCOW	CEEGLOU	ECLOGUE
CDELORW	CLOWDER	CDFIOOT	OCTOFID	CDNNOTU	CONTUND	CEEGNOR	COGENER

	CONGREE	CEEIINR	EIRENIC	CEEKRRW	WRECKER	CEEPPRT	PERCEPT
CEEGNOS	CONGEES	CEEIIPR	EPICIER	CEELLLU	CELLULE		PRECEPT
CEEGNRU	URGENCE	CEEIJOR	REJOICE	CEELLNO	COLLEEN	CEEPPRU	PREPUCE
CEEGNRY	REGENCY	CEEIKLT	CLEEKIT	CEELLOS	CELLOSE	CEEPRSS	PRECESS
CEEGORT	CORTEGE	CEEIKNT	NECKTIE	CEELLPU	PUCELLE	CEEPRST	RECEPTS
CEEGQRU	GRECQUE	CEEIKPR	PICKEER	CEELMNT	CLEMENT		RESPECT
CEEHHSW	WHEECHS	CEEILLM	MICELLE	CEELMOO	COELOME		SCEPTER
CEEHILN	ELENCHI	CEEILNO	CINEOLE	CEELMOT	TELECOM		SCEPTRE
CEEHILS	HELICES	CEEILNR	RECLINE	CEELMOW	WELCOME		SPECTER
	LICHEES	CEEILNS	LICENSE	CEELNOS	ENCLOSE		SPECTRE
CEEHILV	VEHICLE		SELENIC	CEELNPS	PENCELS	CEEPRTX	EXCERPT
CEEHIMR	CHIMERE		SILENCE	CEELNRS	CRENELS	CEEPSTX	EXCEPTS
CEEHIMS	CHEMISE	CEEILNU	LEUCINE	CEELNRT	LECTERN		EXPECTS
CEEHINR	INHERCE	CEEILPS	ECLIPSE	CEELNRU	LUCERNE	CEEPSTY	ECTYPES
CEEHINS	CHINESE	CEEILRT	RETICLE	CEELORS	CREOLES	CEERRSU	RECURES
CEEHIOR	CHEERIO		TIERCEL		RECLOSE		RESCUER
CEEHIOS	ECHOISE	CEEILRU	RECUILE	CEELORT	ELECTOR		RESCURE
CEEHIOZ	ECHOIZE	CEEILST	SECTILE		ELECTRO		SECURER
CEEHIRT	ETHERIC	CEEILSV	VESICLE	CEELORY	RECOYLE	CEERRSW	SCREWER
	HERETIC	CEEILTU	LEUCITE	CEELOSS	ECLOSES	CEERRUV	RECURVE
	TECHIER	CEEIMNT	CENTIME	CEELOSU	COULEES	CEERSSS	CESSERS
CEEHIRW	CHEWIER	CEEIMRS	MERCIES	CEELOTU	ELOCUTE		CRESSES
CEEHISS	SEICHES	CEEIMST	EMETICS	CEELOTV	COVELET	CEERSST	CRESSET
CEEHIST	TECHIES	CEEINNS	INCENSE	CEELPRT	PLECTRE		RESECTS
CEEHISV	CHEVIES	CEEINOS	SENECIO		PRELECT		SECRETS
CEEHISW	CHEWIES	CEEINPR	PERCINE	CEELRSS	SCLERES	CEERSSU	CERUSES
CEEHKLR	HECKLER	CEEINPS	PICENES	CEELRST	TERCELS		CESURES
CEEHKLS	HECKLES		PIECENS	CEELRSU	RECLUSE		RECUSES
CEEHKNP	HENPECK	CEEINPT	PENTICE		RECULES		RESCUES
CEEHKST	KETCHES	CEEINRS	CERESIN	CEELRSW	CREWELS		SECURES
CEEHLNO	CHELONE		SCRIENE	CEELRTU	LECTURE	CEERSTT	TERCETS
	ECHELON		SINCERE	CEELRTY	ERECTLY	CEERSUX	EXCURSE
CEEHLNS	ELENCHS	CEEINRT	ENTERIC	CEELSST	SELECTS		EXCUSER
CEEHLNU	LEUCHEN		ENTICER	CEELTTU	LETTUCE	CEERTTU	CURETTE
CEEHLOW	COWHEEL	CEEINRV	CERVINE	CEEMMOR	COMMERE	CEESSTX	EXSECTS
CEEHLRS	LECHERS	CEEINST	ENTICES	CEEMNOW	NEWCOME	CEESSUX	EXCUSES
CEEHLRW	WELCHER	CEEINSV	EVINCES	CEEMNRU	CERUMEN	CEETTUV	CUVETTE
CEEHLRY	CHEERLY	CEEIOPT	PICOTEE	CEEMNST	CEMENTS	CEFFIOR	OFFICER
	LECHERY	CEEIORT	COTERIE	CEEMOPR	COMPEER	CEFFIOS	OFFICES
CEEHLSS	CHESSEL	CEEIPRR	CREPIER		COMPERE	CEFFISU	SUFFICE
CEEHLST	LETCHES		PIERCER	CEEMOPT	COMPETE	CEFFLOS	COFFLES
CEEHLSW	LECHWES	CEEIPRS	PIECERS	CEEMRRS	MERCERS	CEFFLSU	CUFFLES
	WELCHES		PIERCES	CEEMRRY	MERCERY		SCUFFLE
CEEHLSY	LYCHEES		PRECISE		REMERCY	CEFFORS	COFFERS
	SLEECHY		RECIPES	CEEMRST	CERMETS		SCOFFER
CEEHMRS	SCHEMER	CEEIPRT	RECEIPT	CEEMSTU	TUMESCE	CEFFORT	COFFRET
CEEHMRT	MERCHET	CEEIPRU	EPICURE	CEEMSTY	MYCETES	CEFFSTU	SUFFECT
CEEHMSS	SCHEMES	CEEIPSS	SPECIES	CEENNOU	ENOUNCE	CEFGINN	FENCING
CEEHNPU	PENUCHE	CEEIPST	PECTISE	CEENNOV	CONVENE	CEFHILR	FILCHER
CEEHNRW	WENCHER	CEEIPTZ	PECTIZE	CEENNRT	CENTNER	CEFHILS	FILCHES
CEEHNST	CHENETS	CEEIQSU	QUIESCE	CEENOPT	POTENCE	CEFHILY	CHIEFLY
	TENCHES	CEEIRRT	RECITER	CEENORS	ENCORES	CEFHINS	FINCHES
CEEHNSV	CHEVENS	CEEIRSS	CERISES		NECROSE	CEFHIRY	CHIEFRY
CEEHNSW	WENCHES	CEEIRST	CERITES	CEENORZ	COZENER	CEFHIST	FITCHES
	WHENCES		RECITES	CEENOST	CENOTES	CEFHITT	FITCHET
CEEHORR	COHERER		TIERCES	CEENPRS	SPENCER	CEFHITW	FITCHEW
CEEHORS	CHOREES	CEEIRSU	ECURIES	CEENPSS	SPENCES	CEFHLTU	FUTCHEL
	COHERES	CEEIRSV	SCRIEVE	CEENRSS	CENSERS	CEFIILT	FICTILE
	ECHOERS		SERVICE		SCERNES	CEFIIOR	ORIFICE
CEEHORT	TROCHEE	CEEIRTT	TIERCET		SCREENS	CEFIITV	FICTIVE
CEEHOUV	VOUCHEE	CEEIRTU	EUCRITE		SECERNS	CEFIKLR	FICKLER
CEEHPRR	PERCHER	CEEIRTX	EXCITER	CEENRST	CENTERS		FLICKER
CEEHPRS	PERCHES	CEEISSX	EXCISES		CENTRES	CEFIKLS	FICKLES
CEEHPRU	UPCHEER	CEEISTX	EXCITES		TENRECS	CEFILNT	INFLECT
CEEHQRU	CHEQUER	CEEITTZ	ZETETIC	CEENRSU	CENSURE	CEFILNU	FUNICLE
CEEHQSU	CHEQUES	CEEJNOS	CONJEES	CEENRSY	SCENERY	CEFILRU	LUCIFER
CEEHQUY	QUEECHY	CEEJORT	EJECTOR	CEENTTU	CUNETTE	CEFIMOR	COMFIER
CEEHRST	ETCHERS	CEEJRST	REJECTS	CEEOPST	PECTOSE	CEFIMRY	MERCIFY
	RETCHES	CEEKKLS	KECKLES	CEEOPSU	COUPEES	CEFINNO	CONFINE
CEEHRSU	EUCHRES	CEEKKSS	KECKSES	CEEOPTY	ECOTYPE	CEFINOR	CONIFER
CEEHRSV	CHEVRES	CEEKLNT	NECKLET	CEEORRS	RESCORE		INFORCE
CEEHRSW	CHEWERS	CEEKLPS	SPECKLE	CEEORRT	ERECTOR	CEFINST	INFECTS
CEEHRSY	CREESHY	CEEKLSS	SECKELS	CEEORRU	RECOURE	CEFIPSY	SPECIFY
CEEHRTU	TEUCHER		SECKLES	CEEORRV	RECOVER	CEFIRSS	SFERICS
CEEHSSS	CHESSES	CEEKLST	TECKELS	CEEORRW	RECOWER	CEFIRTY	CERTIFY
CEEHSSW	ESCHEWS	CEEKOSS	COKESES	CEEORSU	CEREOUS		RECTIFY
CEEHSTV	CHEVETS	CEEKOSY	SOCKEYE	CEEORSV	CORVEES	CEFISSU	FICUSES
	VETCHES	CEEKPRS	PECKERS	CEEORTW	COWTREE	CEFKLOT	FETLOCK
CEEHSTW	CHEWETS	CEEKPRY	RYEPECK	CEEOTTT	OCTETTE	CEFKLRY	FRECKLY
						CEFKRSU	FUCKERS

CEFLNOU	FLOUNCE	CEGNRUY	URGENCY
CEFLNUY	FLUENCY	CEGNSSU	SCUNGES
CEFMORY	COMFREY	CEGNSTY	CYGNETS
CEFNORS	CONFERS	CEGOORS	SCROOGE
CEFNORU	FROUNCE	CEGORRS	GROCERS
CEFNOSS	CONFESS	CEGORRY	GROCERY
CEFNOST	CONFEST	CEGORSU	SCOURGE
CEFNOSU	CONFUSE		SCROUGE
CEFNOTU	CONFUTE	CEHHILS	HILCHES
CEFOPRS	FORCEPS	CEHHIRS	CHERISH
CEFORRS	FORCERS		SHRIECH
CEFORRT	CROFTER	CEHHIRT	HITCHER
CEFORSS	FRESCOS	CEHHIST	HITCHES
CEFORSU	REFOCUS	CEHHNSU	HUNCHES
CEFOSSU	FOCUSES	CEHHOOS	HOOCHES
CEFRSUW	CURFEWS	CEHHOST	HOTCHES
CEFSSUU	FUCUSES		SHOCHET
CEGGHIR	CHIGGER	CEHHSSU	SHEUCHS
CEGGIIS	CIGGIES	CEHHSTU	HUTCHES
CEGGIKN	GECKING	CEHIIKN	CHINKIE
CEGGIOR	GEORGIC	CEHIINR	HIRCINE
CEGGIOS	COGGIES	CEHIINS	NICEISH
CEGGLOR	CLOGGER	CEHIINT	ICHNITE
CEGGLOS	COGGLES	CEHIIPP	CHIPPIE
CEGGORS	COGGERS	CEHIIRT	ITCHIER
CEGGPSU	EGGCUPS		TICHIER
CEGHILN	LECHING	CEHIISV	CHIVIES
CEGHINO	ECHOING		VICHIES
CEGHINP	PECHING	CEHIKNT	CHETNIK
CEGHINT	ETCHING		KITCHEN
CEGHINW	CHEWING		THICKEN
CEGHIOR	CHOREGI	CEHIKNW	CHEWINK
CEGHIOS	CHIGOES	CEHIKOO	CHOOKIE
CEGHIRS	CHIGRES	CEHIKOR	CHOKIER
	SCREIGH	CEHIKOS	CHOKIES
CEGHITU	GUICHET	CEHIKPS	PECKISH
CEGHLSU	CLEUGHS	CEHIKRS	SHICKER
	GULCHES		SKRIECH
CEGHORU	COUGHER	CEHIKRT	THICKER
CEGHRTU	GUTCHER	CEHIKRW	WHICKER
CEGIILN	CEILING	CEHIKST	CHEKIST
	CIELING	CEHIKSY	HICKEYS
CEGIINP	PIECING	CEHIKTT	THICKET
CEGIKKN	KECKING	CEHILLR	CHILLER
CEGIKNN	NECKING	CEHILMY	CHIMLEY
CEGIKNP	PECKING	CEHILNO	CHOLINE
CEGIKNR	RECKING		HELICON
CEGIKRU	GUCKIER	CEHILNS	LICHENS
CEGILNP	CLEPING		LINCHES
CEGILNR	CLINGER	CEHILNT	LINCHET
	CRINGLE		TINCHEL
CEGILNU	CLUEING	CEHILPR	PILCHER
	LUCIGEN	CEHILPS	PILCHES
CEGILNW	CLEWING	CEHILRT	LICHTER
CEGILNY	GLYCINE	CEHILRV	CHERVIL
CEGIMNU	MUCIGEN	CEHILSS	CHESILS
CEGINNR	CERNING		CHISELS
CEGINNS	CENSING	CEHILST	ELTCHIS
	SCENING	CEHILSZ	ZILCHES
CEGINOS	COGNISE	CEHILTY	LECYTHI
	COIGNES		TECHILY
CEGINOZ	COGNIZE	CEHIMMS	CHEMISM
CEGINPR	PERCING	CEHIMNY	CHIMNEY
CEGINRR	CRINGER	CEHIMOR	MOCHIER
CEGINRS	CRINGES		MORICHE
CEGINRW	CREWING	CEHIMOS	ECHOISM
CEGINSS	CESSING	CEHIMRS	CHIMERS
CEGIRRS	GRICERS		MICHERS
CEGKLNO	GENLOCK	CEHIMRT	THERMIC
CEGKLOR	GROCKLE	CEHIMST	CHEMIST
CEGLNOO	COLOGNE		MITCHES
CEGLOOY	ECOLOGY	CEHINOP	CHOPINE
CEGLOSU	GLUCOSE		PHOCINE
CEGLOSY	GLYCOSE	CEHINOR	CHORINE
CEGNNOO	ONCOGEN	CEHINOT	HENOTIC
CEGNORS	CONGERS	CEHINOX	CHOENIX
CEGNORU	CONGRUE	CEHINPR	NEPHRIC
CEGNORY	CRYOGEN		PHRENIC
CEGNOST	CONGEST		PINCHER

CEHINPS	PINCHES	CEHLPSS	SCHLEPS
	SPHENIC	CEHLPSU	PLEUCHS
CEHINPU	PENUCHI	CEHLQSU	SQUELCH
CEHINQU	QUINCHE	CEHLRRU	LURCHER
CEHINRS	NICHERS	CEHLRSU	LURCHES
	RICHENS	CEHMNRU	MUNCHER
CEHINRT	CITHERN	CEHMNSU	MUNCHES
CEHINST	ETHNICS	CEHMOOR	MOOCHER
	STHENIC	CEHMOOS	MOOCHES
CEHINSU	ECHINUS	CEHMORS	CHROMES
CEHINSV	CHEVINS	CEHMORU	MOUCHER
CEHINTW	WITCHEN	CEHMOSS	SCHMOES
CEHIOPS	HOSPICE	CEHMOSU	MOUCHES
CEHIOPT	POTICHE	CEHMSTU	HUMECTS
CEHIORS	COHEIRS		MUTCHES
	HEROICS	CEHNNRU	CHUNNER
CEHIORT	ROTCHIE	CEHNOOR	COEHORN
	THEORIC	CEHNORT	NOTCHER
CEHIOST	ECHOIST	CEHNORV	CHEVRON
	TOISECH	CEHNOST	NOTCHES
CEHIOTU	COUTHIE		TECHNOS
CEHIPPR	CHIPPER	CEHNOSU	COHUNES
CEHIPRR	CHIRPER	CEHNPRU	PUNCHER
CEHIPRS	CERIPHS		UNPERCH
	CIPHERS	CEHNPST	PSCHENT
	SPHERIC	CEHNPSU	PUNCHES
CEHIPRT	PITCHER	CEHNRSU	RUNCHES
CEHIPST	CHIPSET	CEHNRTU	CHUNTER
	PITCHES	CEHNSTU	CHESNUT
CEHIQSU	QUICHES	CEHNSTY	STENCHY
CEHIRRS	CHIRRES	CEHNSUU	EUNUCHS
CEHIRRT	RICHTER	CEHNTUY	CHUTNEY
CEHIRST	CITHERS	CEHOOPS	POOCHES
	ESTRICH	CEHOORS	CHOOSER
	RICHEST		SOROCHE
CEHIRSU	CUSHIER	CEHOORT	CHEROOT
CEHIRSZ	SCHERZI	CEHOOSS	CHOOSES
CEHIRTT	CHITTER	CEHOOSY	CHOOSEY
CEHISSU	CUISHES	CEHOPPR	CHOPPER
CEHISTT	TITCHES	CEHOPRS	PORCHES
CEHISTW	WITCHES	CEHOPRT	POTCHER
CEHISZZ	CHIZZES	CEHOPRY	CORYPHE
CEHKKRU	CHUKKER	CEHOPST	POTCHES
CEHKLMO	HEMLOCK	CEHOPSU	POUCHES
CEHKLSU	HUCKLES	CEHORRT	TORCHER
CEHKORS	CHOKERS	CEHORRS	COSHERS
	HOCKERS	CEHORST	HECTORS
	SHOCKER		ROCHETS
CEHKOSY	CHOKEYS		ROTCHES
	HOCKEYS		TOCHERS
CEHKPTU	KETCHUP		TORCHES
CEHKRSU	SHUCKER		TROCHES
CEHKSTU	KUTCHES	CEHORSU	CHOREUS
CEHKSTY	SKETCHY	CEHORSY	COSHERY
CEHLLMO	MOCHELL	CEHORSZ	SCHERZO
CEHLLMU	MUCHELL	CEHORTU	COUTHER
CEHLLNS	SCHNELL		RETOUCH
CEHLLOY	YELLOCH		TOUCHER
CEHLMOR	CHROMEL	CEHORTW	WOTCHER
CEHLMSS	SCHELMS	CEHORUV	VOUCHER
CEHLMSU	MUCHELS	CEHOSSU	CHOUSES
	MULCHES		HOCUSES
CEHLMSZ	SCHMELZ	CEHOSTU	TOUCHES
CEHLMUY	CHUMLEY	CEHOSUV	VOUCHES
CEHLNNU	CHUNNEL	CEHPRSU	CHERUPS
CEHLNOS	NOCHELS	CEHPRSY	CHYPRES
CEHLNOT	CHOLENT		CYPHERS
	NOTCHEL	CEHPRTU	PUTCHER
CEHLNRU	LUNCHER	CEHPSSY	PSYCHES
CEHLNSU	LUNCHES	CEHQSTU	QUETSCH
CEHLNSY	LYNCHES	CEHRRSU	CRUSHER
CEHLNTY	LYNCHET	CEHRSSU	CRUSHES
CEHLOOS	SCHOOLE	CEHRSTT	STRETCH
CEHLORS	CHOLERS	CEHRSTY	SCYTHER
	ORCHELS	CEHSSTU	TUSCHES
CEHLORT	CHORTLE	CEHSSTY	SCYTHES
CEHLOST	CLOTHES	CEIIJRU	JUICIER
CEHLPPS	SCHLEPP	CEIIKLS	SICLIKE
		CEIIKMS	MICKIES

CEIIKNT	KINETIC
CEIIKPR	PICKIER
CEIIKQU	QUICKIE
CEIIKSS	SICKIES
CEIIKST	EKISTIC
	ICKIEST
	TICKIES
CEIIKSW	WICKIES
CEIILLS	SILICLE
CEIILNN	INCLINE
CEIILPP	CLIPPIE
CEIILPT	PELITIC
CEIILST	ELICITS
CEIILTV	LEVITIC
CEIIMMT	MIMETIC
CEIIMNR	CRIMINE
CEIIMNS	MENISCI
CEIIMOT	MEIOTIC
CEIIMPR	EMPIRIC
CEIIMPS	EPICISM
CEIIMRS	CIMIERS
CEIIMSS	SEISMIC
CEIIMTT	TITMICE
CEIINNO	CONIINE
	INCONIE
CEIINNR	CINERIN
CEIINOR	ONEIRIC
CEIINOS	ICONISE
CEIINOV	INVOICE
CEIINOZ	ICONIZE
CEIINPS	PISCINE
CEIINRS	IRENICS
	SERICIN
	SIRENIC
CEIINRT	CITRINE
	CRINITE
	INCITER
	NERITIC
CEIINRZ	ZINCIER
CEIINSS	ICINESS
	INCISES
CEIINST	INCITES
CEIINSU	CUISINE
CEIINTZ	CITIZEN
	ZINCITE
CEIIOPZ	EPIZOIC
CEIIPPR	PIPERIC
CEIIPRR	PRICIER
CEIIPRS	SPICIER
CEIIPRT	PICRITE
CEIIPST	EPICIST
CEIIRSS	CISSIER
CEIIRST	ERISTIC
	RICIEST
CEIIRSU	CRUISIE
CEIISSS	CISSIES
CEIISVV	CIVVIES
CEIITUV	UVEITIC
CEIJNST	INJECTS
CEIJRSU	JUICERS
CEIJSTU	JUSTICE
CEIKKNR	KNICKER
CEIKKRS	KICKERS
CEIKLMS	MICKLES
CEIKLNR	CLINKER
	CRINKLE
CEIKLNS	NICKELS
	SLICKEN
CEIKLPR	PICKLER
	PRICKLE
CEIKLPS	PICKLES
CEIKLRS	LICKERS
	RICKLES
	SLICKER
CEIKLRT	TICKLER
	TRICKLE
CEIKLRU	LUCKIER
CEIKLSS	SICKLES
CEIKLST	STICKLE
	TICKLES
CEIKLSU	LUCKIES
CEIKLSY	KYLICES
CEIKMRS	SMICKER
CEIKMRU	MUCKIER
CEIKMST	SMICKET
CEIKMSY	MICKEYS
CEIKNOR	CONKIER
CEIKNQU	QUICKEN
CEIKNRS	NICKERS
	SNICKER
CEIKNSS	SICKENS
CEIKNST	SNICKET
	TICKENS
CEIKNSW	WICKENS
CEIKOOS	COOKIES
CEIKOPR	POCKIER
CEIKORR	CORKIER
	ROCKIER
CEIKOST	COKIEST
CEIKPRR	PRICKER
CEIKPRS	PICKERS
	RIPECKS
	SPICKER
CEIKPRT	PRICKET
CEIKPRY	PICKERY
CEIKPST	PICKETS
	SKEPTIC
CEIKQRU	QUICKER
CEIKRRS	RICKERS
CEIKRRT	TRICKER
CEIKRSS	SCRIKES
CEIKRST	RICKETS
	STICKER
	TICKERS
CEIKRSW	WICKERS
CEIKRSY	YICKERS
CEIKRTU	TRUCKIE
CEIKRTY	RICKETY
CEIKRUY	YUCKIER
CEIKSST	SICKEST
CEIKSTT	TICKETS
CEIKSTW	WICKETS
CEIKSTY	TICKEYS
CEILLNO	LIONCEL
CEILLNU	NUCELLI
CEILLOR	COLLIER
CEILLOS	COLLIES
CEILLST	CELLIST
CEILLSU	CULLIES
CEILMOP	COMPILE
	POLEMIC
CEILMPR	CRIMPLE
CEILNNU	NUCLEIN
CEILNOP	PINOCLE
CEILNOS	CINEOLS
	CONSEIL
	INCLOSE
CEILNOT	LECTION
CEILNOX	LEXICON
CEILNPS	PENCILS
	SPLENIC
CEILNST	CLIENTS
	LECTINS
	STENCIL
CEILNSU	LEUCINS
CEILNTU	CUTLINE
	TUNICLE
CEILOOS	COOLIES
CEILOPR	PELORIC
CEILOPS	POLICES
CEILOPT	TOECLIP
CEILORS	RECOILS
CEILORT	CORTILE
CEILORU	URCEOLI
CEILOSS	OSSICLE
CEILOST	CITOLES
CEILPPR	CLIPPER
	CRIPPLE
CEILPRS	SPLICER
CEILPSS	SPLICES
CEILPSU	SPICULE
CEILQSU	CLIQUES
CEILQUY	CLIQUEY
CEILRRU	CURLIER
CEILRSS	SLICERS
CEILRSV	CLIVERS
CEILRSY	CLERISY
CEILRTT	CLITTER
CEILRTU	UTRICLE
CEILSSS	SCISSEL
CEILSSU	SLUICES
CEILTTU	CUITTLE
CEIMMOS	COMMIES
CEIMMRR	CRIMMER
CEIMNNO	MECONIN
CEIMNOR	INCOMER
CEIMNOS	INCOMES
	MESONIC
CEIMNOT	CENTIMO
	ENTOMIC
	TONEMIC
CEIMNRS	CREMSIN
	MINCERS
CEIMNRU	MINCEUR
	NUMERIC
CEIMNYZ	ENZYMIC
CEIMOOR	COOMIER
CEIMOPT	METOPIC
CEIMOQU	COMIQUE
CEIMORR	MORRICE
CEIMORT	MORTICE
CEIMOTT	TOTEMIC
CEIMOTV	VICOMTE
CEIMOTX	TOXEMIC
CEIMPRR	CRIMPER
CEIMPRS	SPERMIC
CEIMPSU	PUMICES
CEIMRST	CRETISM
	METRICS
CEIMRSU	CERIUMS
	MURICES
CEIMSSU	CESIUMS
	MISCUES
CEINNOS	CONINES
CEINNOV	CONNIVE
CEINOOT	COONTIE
CEINOPR	PERICON
	PONCIER
	PORCINE
CEINOPT	ENTOPIC
	NEPOTIC
CEINORR	CORNIER
CEINORS	COINERS
	CRINOSE
	CRONIES
	ORCEINS
	ORCINES
	RECOINS
	SERICON
CEINORT	RECTION
CEINORU	COENURI
	NOURICE
CEINORV	CORVINE
CEINORY	ORIENCY
CEINOSS	CESSION
	COSINES
CEINOST	NOTICES
	SECTION
CEINOSV	NOVICES
CEINOTT	ENTOTIC
	TONETIC
CEINOTX	EXCITON
CEINOUV	UNVOICE
CEINOVV	CONVIVE
CEINPRS	PINCERS
	PRINCES
CEINPRY	CYPRINE
CEINPST	INCEPTS
	INSPECT
	PECTINS
	PEINCTS
CEINPTY	PYCNITE
CEINQSU	CINQUES
	QUINCES
CEINRRU	CURNIER
CEINRSS	SCRINES
CEINRST	CISTERN
	CRETINS
CEINRSV	CRIVENS
CEINRSW	WINCERS
CEINRTT	CITTERN
CEINRUV	INCURVE
CEINSST	INCESTS
	INSECTS
CEINSSU	INCUSES
CEINSTY	CYSTINE
CEINSWY	WINCEYS
CEINTTX	EXTINCT
CEINVVY	VIVENCY
CEIOOPR	OPORICE
CEIOOST	COOTIES
CEIOPPS	COPPIES
CEIOPRS	COPIERS
	COPSIER
	PERSICO
CEIOPST	POETICS
CEIOPSU	PICEOUS
CEIORRS	CIRROSE
	CORRIES
	CROSIER
CEIORRU	COURIER
CEIORRZ	CROZIER
CEIORSS	COSIERS
CEIORST	EROTICS
	TERCIOS
CEIORSU	SCOURIE
CEIORSV	CORSIVE
	VOICERS
CEIORSW	COWRIES
	SCOWRIE
CEIORSZ	COZIERS
CEIORTT	COTTIER
CEIORTV	EVICTOR
CEIORTX	EXCITOR
	XEROTIC
CEIOSSS	COSSIES
CEIOSST	COSIEST
	COTISES
	OECISTS
CEIOSSV	VISCOSE
CEIOSTT	COTTISE
CEIOSTV	COSTIVE
CEIOSTX	COEXIST
	COXIEST
	EXOTICS
CEIOSTY	SOCIETY
CEIOSTZ	COZIEST
CEIPPST	PEPTICS
CEIPQTU	PICQUET
CEIPRRS	CRISPER
	PRICERS
CEIPRSS	SPICERS
CEIPRST	TRICEPS
CEIPRSY	SPICERY
CEIPRTU	CUPRITE
	PICTURE
CEIPRTY	PYRETIC
CEIPRXY	PYREXIC
CEIPSSS	SCEPSIS
CEIPSST	CESSPIT
CEIQRSU	CIRQUES
CEIRRRU	CURRIER
CEIRRSU	CRUISER

	CURRIES
	SUCRIER
CEIRRTT	CRITTER
CEIRRTU	RECRUIT
CEIRRTX	RECTRIX
CEIRRUV	CURVIER
CEIRSSU	CRUISES
	CRUSIES
	CUISSER
CEIRSSV	SCRIVES
CEIRSTT	TRISECT
CEIRSTU	CUITERS
	CURIETS
	ICTERUS
CEIRSTW	TWICERS
CEIRSUV	CRUIVES
	CURSIVE
CEIRTTU	CUTTIER
CEIRTTX	TECTRIX
CEISSSU	CUISSES
CEISSTU	CESTUIS
	CUEISTS
	CUTISES
	ICTUSES
CEISTTU	CUTTIES
CEJKNOY	JOCKNEY
CEJKOSY	JOCKEYS
CEJNOOS	COJONES
CEJNORU	CONJURE
CEJNOSU	JOUNCES
	JUNCOES
CEJOPRT	PROJECT
CEKKLNU	KNUCKLE
CEKKNOR	KNOCKER
CEKKOPS	KOPECKS
CEKLLOP	PELLOCK
CEKLLRY	CLERKLY
CEKLMNO	LOCKMEN
CEKLMSU	MUCKLES
CEKLNOS	ENLOCKS
	SLOCKEN
CEKLNRU	CRUNKLE
CEKLORS	LOCKERS
CEKLOST	LOCKETS
CEKLPRU	PLUCKER
CEKLPSU	PUCKLES
CEKLRSU	RUCKLES
	SUCKLER
CEKLRTU	TRUCKLE
CEKLSSU	SUCKLES
CEKMORS	MOCKERS
CEKMORY	MOCKERY
CEKMRSU	MUCKERS
CEKNNSU	UNSNECK
CEKNOOV	CONVOKE
CEKNORR	CRONKER
CEKNORS	CONKERS
	RECKONS
CEKNORT	TROCKEN
CEKNOST	NOCKETS
CEKNRWY	WRYNECK
CEKNSSU	SUCKENS
CEKOOPR	PRECOOK
CEKOOPW	COWPOKE
CEKOORR	CROOKER
CEKOORS	COOKERS
CEKOORY	COOKERY
CEKOPST	POCKETS
CEKORRS	CORKERS
	ROCKERS
CEKORRY	ROCKERY
CEKORST	RESTOCK
	ROCKETS
	STOCKER
CEKOSST	SOCKETS
CEKPRSU	PUCKERS
CEKPRSY	RYPECKS
CEKPRUY	PUCKERY
CEKRRTU	TRUCKER
CEKRSSU	SUCKERS
CEKRSTU	TUCKERS
CEKRSUY	YUCKERS
CEKSSTU	SUCKETS
CEKSTTU	TUCKETS
CELLMOU	COLUMEL
CELLNOO	COLONEL
CELLORS	ESCROLL
CELLOST	COLLETS
CELLOSU	LOCULES
	OCELLUS
CELLOSY	CLOSELY
CELLRRU	CRULLER
CELLRSU	CRUELLS
	CULLERS
	SCULLER
CELLRUY	CRUELLY
CELLSSU	SCULLES
CELLSTU	CULLETS
CELMMSU	MESCLUM
CELMNOO	LOCOMEN
	MONOCLE
CELMNSU	CULMENS
	MESCLUN
CELMOOS	COELOMS
CELMOPS	COMPELS
CELMOPX	COMPLEX
CELMORS	CORMELS
CELMPRU	CLUMPER
	CRUMPLE
CELMSSU	MUSCLES
CELMSUU	SECULUM
CELMSUY	LYCEUMS
CELNNOU	NUCLEON
CELNNSU	NUNCLES
CELNOOS	COLONES
	CONSOLE
CELNORS	CORNELS
CELNOSU	COUNSEL
	UNCLOSE
CELNOTU	NOCTULE
CELNRSU	LUCERNS
CELNRTU	LECTURN
CELNSUU	NUCLEUS
	NUCULES
CELNSUW	UNCLEWS
CELOOPR	PRECOOL
CELOORS	COOLERS
	CREOSOL
CELOOST	COOLEST
	OCELOTS
CELOPPS	COPPLES
CELOPRU	COUPLER
CELOPSU	COUPLES
	OPUSCLE
	UPCLOSE
CELOPTU	COUPLET
	OCTUPLE
CELOQSU	CLOQUES
CELORSS	CLOSERS
	CRESOLS
	ESCROLS
CELORST	COLTERS
	CORSLET
	COSTREL
	LECTORS
CELORSU	CLOSURE
	COLURES
CELORSV	CLOVERS
CELORSW	SCROWLE
CELORSY	SCROYLE
CELORTT	CLOTTER
	CROTTLE
CELORTU	CLOTURE
	CLOUTER
	COULTER
CELORVY	CLOVERY
CELOSST	CLOSEST
	CLOSETS
CELOSSU	OSCULES
CELOSTY	COTYLES
CELOSUV	VOCULES
CELOTTU	CULOTTE
CELPRSU	CURPELS
	SCRUPLE
CELPSUU	CUPULES
CELPSUY	CLYPEUS
CELRRSU	CURLERS
CELRSTU	CLUSTER
	CULTERS
	CUSTREL
	CUTLERS
	RELUCTS
CELRSTY	CLYSTER
CELRSUV	CULVERS
CELRSUW	CURLEWS
CELRTTU	CLUTTER
CELRTUU	CULTURE
CELRTUV	CULVERT
CELRTUY	CRUELTY
	CUTLERY
CELSTTU	CUTLETS
	CUTTLES
	SCUTTLE
CEMMNOT	COMMENT
CEMMNOU	COMMUNE
CEMMOOT	COMMOTE
CEMMOOV	COMMOVE
CEMMORS	COMMERS
CEMMOTU	COMMUTE
CEMMRSU	CUMMERS
	SCUMMER
CEMNNOT	CONTEMN
CEMNOOP	COMPONE
CEMNOOS	ONCOMES
CEMNOOY	ECONOMY
CEMNOSU	CONSUME
	MUSCONE
CEMNRSU	CRUMENS
CEMNRTU	CENTRUM
CEMNSTU	CENTUMS
CEMOOPS	COMPOSE
CEMOOPT	COMPOTE
CEMOOTU	OUTCOME
CEMOPRS	COMPERS
CEMOPRT	COMPTER
CEMOPSU	UPCOMES
CEMOPTU	COMPUTE
CEMORRS	CREMORS
CEMOSSU	COMUSES
	MUSCOSE
CEMOSSY	MYCOSES
CEMOSTU	COSTUME
CEMPRRU	CRUMPER
CEMPRTU	CRUMPET
CEMRRUY	MERCURY
CEMRSTU	RECTUMS
CEMSSUU	MUCUSES
CENNOOT	CONNOTE
CENNORS	CONNERS
CENNOST	CONSENT
	NOCENTS
CENNOTT	CONTENT
CENNOTV	CONVENT
CENNRSU	CUNNERS
	SCUNNER
CENOOPS	POONCES
CENOORR	CORONER
	CROONER
CENOORS	CEROONS
CENOORT	CORONET
CENOOSS	COOSENS
CENOPRS	CREPONS
CENOPSU	POUNCES
	UNCOPES
CENOPSY	SYNCOPE
CENOPTU	POUNCET
CENOPTY	POTENCY
CENOQRU	CONQUER
CENORRS	CORNERS
	SCORNER
CENORRW	CROWNER
CENORSS	CENSORS
CENORST	CONSTER
	CORNETS
	CRESTON
	CRONETS
CENORSU	CONURES
	ROUNCES
CENORTT	CORNETT
CENORTU	CORNUTE
	COUNTER
	RECOUNT
	TROUNCE
CENORTV	CONVERT
CENORTW	CROWNET
CENORUV	UNCOVER
CENOSSY	COYNESS
CENOSTT	CONTEST
CENOSTU	CONTUSE
	ECONUTS
CENOSTV	COVENTS
CENOSVY	CONVEYS
	COVYNES
CENOTTX	CONTEXT
CENPRTY	ENCRYPT
CENPTUX	EXPUNCT
CENRRTU	CURRENT
CENRSSY	SCRYNES
CENRSTU	ENCRUST
CENRSUU	UNCURSE
CENRSUW	UNSCREW
CENRTUY	CENTURY
CENSSTY	ENCYSTS
CEOOPRS	COOPERS
	SCOOPER
CEOOPRY	COOPERY
CEOORSS	COOSERS
CEOORST	SCOOTER
CEOORSV	CROOVES
CEOOSTY	COYOTES
	OOCYTES
CEOPPRR	CROPPER
CEOPPRS	COPPERS
CEOPPRY	COPPERY
CEOPRRS	SCORPER
CEOPRRT	PORRECT
CEOPRRU	CROUPER
	PROCURE
CEOPRSS	CORPSES
	PROCESS
CEOPRST	COPTERS
CEOPRSU	COUPERS
	CROUPES
	RECOUPS
CEOPRTT	PROTECT
CEOPRUU	COUPURE
CEOQRTU	CROQUET
	ROCQUET
CEOQSTU	COQUETS
CEORRSS	CROSSER
	RECROSS
	SCORERS
	SCORSER
CEORRST	RECTORS
CEORRSU	COURSER
	CRUORES
	SCOURER
CEORRSW	SCOWRER
CEORRSY	SORCERY
CEORRTY	RECTORY
CEORSSS	CROSSES
	SCORSES
CEORSST	CORSETS
	COSTERS
	ESCORTS
	SCOTERS

	SECTORS
CEORSSU	COURSES
	SCOURSE
	SCOUSER
	SOURCES
	SUCROSE
CEORSSW	ESCROWS
CEORSTT	COTTERS
CEORSTU	COUTERS
	CROUTES
	SCOUTER
CEORSTV	CORVETS
	COVERTS
	VECTORS
CEORTUU	COUTURE
CEORTUV	COUVERT
CEOSSST	COSSETS
CEOSSSU	SCOUSES
CEOSSSY	SYCOSES
CEOSTTT	OCTETTS
CEOSTTU	CUTTOES
CEPPRRU	CRUPPER
CEPPRSU	CUPPERS
	SCUPPER
CEPRRSU	SPRUCER
CEPRSSU	PERCUSS
	SPRUCES
CEPRSSY	CYPRESS
CEPRSTU	PRECUTS
CEPRSTY	SCEPTRY
CEPSSTU	SUSPECT
CERRSSU	CURSERS
CERRSSY	SCRYERS
CERSSSU	CUSSERS
CERSSTU	CRUSETS
CERSSUZ	SCRUZES
CERSTTU	CURTEST
	CUTTERS
	SCUTTER
CERSTUV	CURVETS
CERSTUY	CURTESY
	CURTSEY
CESSUZZ	SCUZZES
CFFGINO	COFFING
CFFGINU	CUFFING
CFFHINO	CHIFFON
CFFIIRT	TRIFFIC
CFFILSS	SCLIFFS
CFFINOS	COFFINS
CFFINSU	CUFFINS
CFFMOSU	OFFSCUM
CFFOSTU	OFFCUTS
CFFRSSU	SCRUFFS
CFFRSUY	SCRUFFY
CFGIINO	COIFING
CFGIKNU	FUCKING
CFGINOR	FORCING
CFHILYY	CHYLIFY
CFHIMYY	CHYMIFY
CFHIOSW	COWFISH
CFHIRST	FRICHTS
CFHORTU	FUTHORC
CFIIIMR	MIRIFIC
CFIIIVV	VIVIFIC
CFIIKNY	FINICKY
CFIILNT	INFLICT
CFIIMNO	OMNIFIC
CFIINOT	FICTION
CFIINOY	ICONIFY
CFIINYZ	ZINCIFY
CFIIOSS	OSSIFIC
CFIKNNO	FINNOCK
CFIKOSS	FOSSICK
CFILORS	FROLICS
CFILORU	FLUORIC
CFIMNOR	CONFIRM
CFIMOST	COMFITS
CFINOST	CONFITS
CFIORST	FICTORS

CFIORSY	SCORIFY
CFIRSTU	FRUICTS
CFISSTU	FUSTICS
CFKLLOU	LOCKFUL
CFKNORU	UNFROCK
CFKOTTU	FUTTOCK
CFLMRUU	FULCRUM
CFLNORY	CORNFLY
CFLNOUX	CONFLUX
CFLNOUY	FLOUNCY
CFLOPRU	CROPFUL
CFLPSUU	CUPFULS
CFMNOOR	CONFORM
CFMOORT	COMFORT
CFOSSTU	FUSTOCS
CFOSSUU	FUSCOUS
CGGGINO	COGGING
CGGIINR	GRICING
CGGORSY	SCROGGY
CGHHOSU	CHOUGHS
CGHIIMN	CHIMING
	MICHING
CGHIINN	CHINING
	INCHING
	NICHING
CGHIINR	RICHING
CGHIINT	ITCHING
CGHIINV	CHIVING
CGHIKNO	CHOKING
	HOCKING
CGHILPY	GLYPHIC
CGHINNO	CHIGNON
CGHINOR	OCHRING
CGHINOS	COSHING
CGHINRU	RUCHING
CGHINSU	CHUSING
CGHIOSY	GOYISCH
CGHLOSU	CLOUGHS
CGHOORT	TORGOCH
CGHORUY	GROUCHY
CGIIJNU	JUICING
CGIIKKN	KICKING
CGIIKLN	LICKING
CGIIKMM	GIMMICK
CGIIKNN	NICKING
CGIIKNP	PICKING
CGIIKNR	RICKING
CGIIKNS	SICKING
CGIIKNT	TICKING
CGIIKNW	WICKING
CGIILLO	ILLOGIC
CGIILNO	COILING
CGIILNP	CLIPING
CGIILNS	SLICING
CGIIMMN	MINCING
CGIIMNR	CRIMING
CGIINNO	COINING
CGIINNR	CRINING
CGIINNW	WINCING
CGIINNZ	ZINCING
CGIINOR	GIRONIC
CGIINOV	VOICING
CGIINPR	PRICING
CGIINPS	SPICING
CGIINRT	TRICING
CGIKLNO	CLOKING
	LOCKING
CGIKMNO	MOCKING
CGIKMNU	MUCKING
CGIKNNO	CONKING
	NOCKING
CGIKNOO	COOKING
CGIKNOR	CORKING
	ROCKING
CGIKNOS	SOCKING
CGIKNOT	TOCKING
CGIKNOY	YOCKING
CGIKNPU	KINGCUP
CGIKNRU	RUCKING

CGIKNSU	SUCKING
CGIKNTU	TUCKING
CGIKNUY	YUCKING
CGILLNO	COLLING
CGILLNU	CULLING
CGILMNU	CULMING
CGILNNO	CLONING
CGILNNU	UNCLING
CGILNOO	COOLING
CGILNOS	CLOSING
CGILNOT	COLTING
CGILNOW	COWLING
CGILNPY	CLYPING
CGILNRU	CURLING
CGILNSY	GLYCINS
CGILORW	COWGIRL
CGILOTT	GLOTTIC
CGILPSU	GILCUPS
CGILPTU	GILTCUP
CGILPTY	GLYPTIC
CGIMNOO	COOMING
CGIMNOP	COMPING
CGIMNOR	CROMING
CGIMNOS	COMINGS
CGINNNO	CONNING
CGINNNU	CUNNING
CGINNOP	PONCING
CGINNOR	CORNING
CGINNOS	CONSIGN
CGINNPU	PUNCING
CGINNSY	SYNCING
CGINOOP	COOPING
CGINOOS	COOINGS
CGINOPP	COPPING
CGINOPS	COPINGS
	COPSING
	SCOPING
CGINOPU	COUPING
CGINOPW	COWPING
CGINOPY	COPYING
CGINORS	SCORING
CGINORU	COURING
CGINORW	CROWING
CGINORY	GYRONIC
CGINOST	COSTING
	GNOSTIC
CGINOSU	CONGIUS
	SOUCING
CGINOSV	COVINGS
CGINOSW	SOWCING
CGINPPU	CUPPING
CGINRRU	CURRING
CGINRSU	CURSING
CGINRSY	CRYINGS
	SCRYING
CGINRUV	CURVING
CGINSSU	CUSSING
	SCUSING
CGINTTU	CUTTING
CGIOOOS	GIOCOSO
CGIOTYZ	ZYGOTIC
CGKLNOU	GUNLOCK
CGLLOSY	GLYCOLS
CGLNOSU	UNCLOGS
CGLOOSU	COLUGOS
CGNOOSU	CONGOUS
CGOORRW	GORCROW
CHHIKOR	CHIKHOR
CHHINOR	RHONCHI
CHHINTU	UNHITCH
CHHIRST	SHRITCH
CHHISST	SHTCHIS
CHHISTY	ICHTHYS
CHHNOOS	HONCHOS
CHHRTTU	THRUTCH
CHIIILO	CHILIOI
CHIIKMS	KIMCHIS
CHIIKNN	KINCHIN

CHIIKSS	SICKISH
CHIILLS	CHILLIS
CHIILST	LITCHIS
CHIIMSU	ISCHIUM
CHIINNP	INCHPIN
CHIINST	CHITINS
CHIIOPT	OPHITIC
CHIIOST	STICHOI
CHIKLLO	HILLOCK
CHIKLTY	THICKLY
CHIKNOO	CHINOOK
CHIKORS	CHIKORS
	CHOKRIS
CHIKORY	HICKORY
CHIKOST	THICKOS
CHIKPSU	PUCKISH
CHIKSST	SCHTIKS
	SHTICKS
CHIKSTY	KITSCHY
CHILLMU	CHILLUM
CHILLTY	LICHTLY
CHILNOR	CHLORIN
CHILNOU	ULICHON
CHILNSY	LYCHNIS
CHILOOS	COOLISH
CHILORS	ORCHILS
CHILOST	COLTISH
CHILSTU	CULTISH
CHIMNPY	NYMPHIC
CHIMOPR	MORPHIC
CHIMORS	CHORISM
	CHRISOM
CHIMRRY	MYRRHIC
CHIMRSS	CHRISMS
CHIMSSS	SCHISMS
CHIMSTY	TYCHISM
CHINOOR	CHORION
CHINOPS	CHOPINS
	PHONICS
CHINOST	CHITONS
CHINOSU	CUSHION
CHINPSY	HYPNICS
CHINQSU	SQUINCH
CHINRSU	URCHINS
CHINTUW	UNWITCH
CHINTYZ	CHINTZY
CHIOOPR	POCHOIR
CHIOORS	ISOCHOR
CHIOORZ	CHORIZO
CHIOPRT	TROPHIC
CHIOPST	PHOTICS
CHIOPXY	HYPOXIC
CHIORST	CHORIST
	OSTRICH
CHIORSW	CHOWRIS
CHIOSST	STICHOS
CHIOSSZ	SCHIZOS
CHIPRRU	CHIRRUP
CHIPRRY	PYRRHIC
CHIPSSY	PHYSICS
CHIQSTU	SQUITCH
CHIRRSU	CURRISH
CHIRSTY	CHRISTY
CHISSST	SCHISTS
CHISSTU	SCHUITS
CHISTTU	CHUTIST
CHISTWY	SWITCHY
CHITTWY	TWITCHY
CHKLOOO	HOOLOCK
CHKLOOT	KLOOTCH
CHKLOSS	SHLOCKS
CHKMMOO	HOMMOCK
CHKMMOU	HUMMOCK
CHKMOSS	SHMOCKS
CHKMSSU	SHMUCKS
CHKNOOS	SCHNOOK
CHKOOST	SCHTOOK
CHKORSU	CHUKORS
CHKPTUU	PUTCHUK

CHKSSTU	SHTUCKS	CIIOSUV	VICIOUS	CIMNRSU	CRINUMS
CHLMOOS	MOLOCHS	CIIPRSS	SPIRICS	CIMOORS	MORISCO
CHLOOSS	SCHOOLS	CIIPRTY	PYRITIC	CIMOOST	OSMOTIC
CHLOOST	COOLTHS	CIIRSTV	VITRICS	CIMOPSY	COPYISM
CHLOPST	SPLOTCH	CIIRTVX	VICTRIX		MISCOPY
CHLORSS	SCHORLS	CIJNNOO	CONJOIN		MYOPICS
CHLORTY	CHOLTRY	CIJNNTU	INJUNCT	CIMORSU	CORIUMS
CHLOSSS	SCHLOSS	CIJNOOS	COJOINS	CIMOSST	COSMIST
CHLOSUY	SLOUCHY	CIKKLLO	KILLOCK		SITCOMS
CHMOORS	CHROMOS	CIKLLOP	PILLOCK	CIMOSSY	MYCOSIS
CHMOOST	SCHTOOM	CIKLLOR	ROLLICK	CIMOTYZ	ZYMOTIC
CHMOOSZ	SCHMOOZ	CIKLLOS	SILLOCK	CIMPRSS	SCRIMPS
CHMOSUY	CHYMOUS	CIKLLOW	KILLCOW	CIMPRSY	SCRIMPY
CHNNOOR	CHRONON	CIKLLSY	SLICKLY	CIMRSSU	CRISSUM
CHNNOSU	NONSUCH	CIKLLUY	LUCKILY	CIMRSUU	CURIUMS
CHNOOPS	PONCHOS	CIKLMSU	MISLUCK	CIMSSTY	MYSTICS
CHNOORS	COHORNS	CIKLMSY	SMICKLY	CIMSSUV	VISCUMS
CHNOORT	TORCHON	CIKLNOS	INLOCKS	CINNNOU	INCONNU
CHNORRS	SCHNORR	CIKLNRY	CRINKLY	CINNORU	UNICORN
CHNORSY	SYNCHRO	CIKLOPZ	ZIPLOCK	CINNOSU	NUNCIOS
CHNORTU	COTHURN	CIKLORY	ROCKILY	CINNOTU	UNCTION
CHNOTUU	UNCOUTH	CIKLPRY	PRICKLY	CINNSUU	UNCINUS
CHNSTUU	TUCHUNS	CIKLQUY	QUICKLY	CINOOPS	OPSONIC
CHOOPPS	COPSHOP	CIKLRTY	TRICKLY	CINOORS	CORONIS
CHOORST	COHORTS	CIKLSTU	LUSTICK	CINOOSS	COOSINS
CHOORSU	OCHROUS	CIKMNNO	MINNOCK	CINOPPS	COPPINS
CHOPSSY	PSYCHOS	CIKMNSU	NICKUMS	CINOPRX	PRINCOX
CHORSTU	TROCHUS	CIKNNOP	PINNOCK	CINORRT	TRICORN
CHOSSTU	SCHOUTS	CIKNNOW	WINNOCK	CINORSS	INCROSS
	SCOUTHS	CIKNPSU	UNPICKS	CINORST	CISTRON
CHOSSTW	SCOWTHS	CIKNSTU	UNSTICK		CITRONS
CHPSSUY	SCYPHUS	CIKOPPT	POCKPIT		CORNIST
CHRRSUU	CHURRUS	CIKORRS	CORKIRS	CINORSZ	ZIRCONS
CHSSTUY	SCHUYTS	CIKOTUW	OUTWICK	CINORTU	RUCTION
CIIILLT	ILLICIT	CIKRSTY	TRICKSY	CINOSST	CONSIST
CIIILNV	INCIVIL	CILLNOS	COLLINS		TOCSINS
CIIIMNR	CRIMINI	CILLNOU	CULLION	CINOSSU	COUSINS
CIIINPT	INCIPIT	CILLOOR	CRIOLLO	CINOSTU	SUCTION
CIIKKLL	KILLICK	CILLOPY	POLLICY	CINOSUZ	ZINCOUS
CIIKMMM	MIMMICK	CILMNOP	COMPLIN	CINRSTU	INCRUST
CIIKMNN	MINNICK	CILMSTU	CULTISM	CIOOPRT	PORTICO
CIIKNSW	INWICKS	CILNOOR	ORCINOL		PROOTIC
CIIKNTU	CUTIKIN	CILNOOS	CLOISON	CIOOPSU	COPIOUS
CIIKPUW	WICKIUP		SCOLION	CIOOQTU	COQUITO
CIIKSST	TISICKS	CILNOPR	PILCORN	CIOORST	OCTROIS
CIIKSTT	STICKIT	CILNORY	LYRICON	CIOORSU	CORIOUS
CIILLTY	LICITLY	CILNOSU	ULICONS	CIOPRST	TROPICS
CIILLVY	CIVILLY		UNCOILS	CIOPSTY	COPYIST
CIILNOP	CIPOLIN	CILNOTU	LINOCUT	CIOQRSU	CROQUIS
CIILNOS	SILICON	CILNOXY	XYLONIC	CIORRSU	CIRROUS
CIILNPS	INCLIPS	CILNPSU	INSCULP	CIORSSS	SCISSOR
CIILNUV	UNCIVIL		SCULPIN	CIORSTT	TRICOTS
CIILOOT	OOLITIC	CILNPTU	UNCLIPT	CIORSTU	CITROUS
CIILOPT	POLITIC	CILNSTU	LINCTUS	CIORSTV	VICTORS
CIILORT	CORTILI	CILOOPT	COPILOT	CIORSUU	CURIOUS
CIILOST	COLITIS	CILOORU	COULOIR	CIORTVY	VICTORY
	SOLICIT	CILOOSS	COLOSSI	CIOSSSY	SYCOSIS
CIILPSY	SPICILY	CILOOST	SCIOLTO	CIOSSUV	VISCOUS
CIILSSS	SCISSIL	CILOPRW	PILCROW	CIPRSST	SCRIPTS
CIIMMRY	MIMICRY	CILOPRY	PYLORIC	CIPRSSU	PRUSSIC
CIIMNNO	NIMONIC	CILOPSU	UPCOILS	CIPRTTY	TRYPTIC
CIIMNOT	MICTION	CILOPSW	COWSLIP	CIPSTTY	STYPTIC
CIIMOST	MIOTICS	CILORST	LICTORS	CIRRTTU	CRITTUR
	MISTICO	CILOSTU	COUTILS	CIRSSTU	RUSTICS
	SOMITIC		OCULIST	CIRTUVY	CURVITY
CIIMOTT	MITOTIC	CILPRSY	CRISPLY	CISSTUY	CYTISUS
CIIMOTV	MOTIVIC	CILPRTU	CULPRIT	CJNORUY	CONJURY
CIIMSSV	CIVISMS	CILRRSU	SCURRIL	CKKLNUY	KNUCKLY
CIIMSTV	VICTIMS	CILRSUU	SURCULI	CKLLMOU	MULLOCK
CIINNTU	TUNICIN	CILSTTU	CULTIST	CKLLOOP	POLLOCK
CIINOOT	COITION	CIMMNSU	CUMMINS	CKLLOOR	ROLLOCK
CIINOPS	PSIONIC	CIMMOSS	COSMISM	CKLLORU	RULLOCK
CIINORS	INCISOR	CIMMOST	COMMITS	CKLNOSU	UNLOCKS
CIINPRS	CRISPIN	CIMNNOS	NINCOMS	CKLNUUY	UNLUCKY
CIINQTU	QUINTIC	CIMNNSU	NINCUMS	CKLOOOY	OLYCOOK
CIINRST	CITRINS	CIMNOOR	MORONIC	CKLOORW	ROWLOCK
CIINSSV	VISCINS		OMICRON	CKLOOTU	LOCKOUT
CIINTUY	UNICITY	CIMNORS	CRIMSON	CKLOPSU	UPLOCKS
CIIORST	SORITIC		MICRONS	CKLOPTU	PUTLOCK

CKMMMOU	MUMMOCK
CKNORSU	UNCORKS
CKNOSTU	UNSTOCK
CKNSTUU	UNSTUCK
	UNTUCKS
CKOOOTU	COOKOUT
CKOORSU	SOUROCK
CKOPTTU	PUTTOCK
CKORTUW	CUTWORK
CKOSSTU	TUSSOCK
CLLMOSU	MOLLUSC
CLLOOPS	COLLOPS
	SCOLLOP
CLLORSS	SCROLLS
CLLOSUU	LOCULUS
CLMNOSU	COLUMNS
CLMOOPT	COMPLOT
CLMOPTU	PLUMCOT
CLMOSUU	LUCUMOS
	OSCULUM
CLMSUUU	CUMULUS
CLNOORT	CONTROL
CLNOOSS	CONSOLS
CLNOSSU	CONSULS
CLNOSTU	CONSULT
	UNCOLTS
CLNOSUW	UNCOWLS
CLNRSUU	UNCURLS
CLOORSU	COLOURS
CLOORUY	COLOURY
CLORSSW	SCROWLS
CLORSSY	CROSSLY
CLORSUY	CORYLUS
CLORTUY	COURTLY
CLOSSTU	LOCUSTS
CLPRSUU	UPCURLS
CLPSSTU	SCULPTS
CMMNOOS	COMMONS
CMMOOST	COMMOTS
CMMRSUY	SCRUMMY
CMNOOOT	MONOCOT
CMNOOPY	COMPONY
CMNOPTU	PUNCTUM
CMOOPRT	COMPORT
CMOOPST	COMPOST
	COMPOTS
CMOORSU	CORMOUS
CMOOSTY	SCOTOMY
CMORSTU	SCROTUM
CMORTUW	CUTWORM
CMOSSTU	CUSTOMS
CMPRSSU	SCRUMPS
CMPRSUY	SCRUMPY
CNNOPSY	PYCNONS
CNNORTU	NOCTURN
CNNORUW	UNCROWN
CNOOPPR	POPCORN
CNOOPRU	CROUPON
CNOOPSU	COUPONS
	SOUPCON
CNOORRW	CORNROW
CNOORST	CONSORT
	CROTONS
CNOORTT	CONTORT
CNOORTU	CONTOUR
	CORNUTO
	CROUTON ·
CNOOSST	NOSTOCS
	ONCOSTS
CNOOSTT	COTTONS
CNOOSTY	TYCOONS
CNOOSUU	NUCUOUS
CNOOSVY	CONVOYS
CNOOTTW	COTTOWN
CNOOTTY	COTTONY
CNOPRTY	CRYPTON
CNOPSTU	PUNCTOS
CNORSSU	UNCROSS
CNORSSY	SYNROCS

CNORTUY	COUNTRY	DDEEELT	DELETED	DDEELSU	DELUDES	DDEGRTU	TRUDGED
CNRSSTU	SCRUNTS	DDEEEMN	EMENDED	DDEEMMO	MODEMED	DDEHIRS	HIDDERS
CNRSTUY	SCRUNTY	DDEEEMR	REMEDED	DDEEMOT	DEMOTED		REDDISH
COOORSZ	COROZOS	DDEEENT	TEENDED	DDEEMRU	DEMURED		SHIDDER
COOPRRT	PROCTOR	DDEEENW	ENDEWED	DDEENOP	DEPONED	DDEHIRT	THIRDED
COOPRSS	SCROOPS	DDEEEPS	SPEEDED	DDEENOT	DENOTED	DDEHIRW	WHIDDER
COOPRTU	OUTCROP	DDEEEST	DEEDEST	DDEENOW	ENDOWED	DDEHIRY	HYDRIDE
COOPSTU	OCTOPUS		STEEDED	DDEENOZ	DOZENED	DDEHLOS	HODDLES
COORSTU	OCTUORS	DDEEESX	DESEXED	DDEENPS	DEPENDS	DDEHLRU	HURDLED
COORSUU	ROUCOUS	DDEEFGL	FLEDGED	DDEENPU	UPENDED	DDEHLSU	HUDDLES
COOSTTY	OTOCYST	DDEEFII	DEIFIED	DDEENRS	REDDENS	DDEHNOS	HODDENS
COPRRTU	CORRUPT		EDIFIED	DDEENRT	TRENDED	DDEHNOU	HOUNDED
COPRSTY	CRYPTOS	DDEEFIL	DEFILED	DDEENRU	ENDURED	DDEHNRU	HUNDRED
COPRSUU	CUPROUS		FIELDED	DDEENST	STENDED	DDEHNSU	DUNSHED
CORRSSU	CURSORS	DDEEFIN	DEFINED	DDEENSU	DENUDES	DDEHRSU	SHUDDER
CORRSUY	CURSORY	DDEEFLU	DEEDFUL		DUDEENS	DDEHRSY	SHREDDY
CORSSTU	SCRUTOS	DDEEFNS	DEFENDS		DUENDES	DDEIIKR	KIDDIER
DDDDEIL	DIDDLED	DDEEFSU	DEFUSED	DDEENSY	DESYNED	DDEIIKS	KIDDIES
DDDEEGR	DREDGED	DDEEFUZ	DEFUZED	DDEENTU	DETUNED	DDEIIMS	MIDDIES
DDDEEHL	HEDDLED	DDEEGGL	GLEDGED	DDEEOPS	DEPOSED	DDEIINT	INDITED
DDDEEIR	DERIDED	DDEEGIN	DEEDING	DDEEORR	ORDERED	DDEIINV	DIVINED
DDDEELM	MEDDLED		DEIGNED	DDEEORV	DOVERED	DDEIIOS	IODIDES
DDDEELP	PEDDLED	DDEEGIS	DISEDGE	DDEEORW	DOWERED		IODISED
DDDEELR	REDDLED	DDEEGLP	PLEDGED	DDEEOTV	DEVOTED	DDEIIOX	DIOXIDE
DDDEELS	SLEDDED	DDEEGLS	SLEDGED	DDEEOTX	DETOXED	DDEIIOZ	IODIZED
DDDEELU	DELUDED	DDEEGLU	DELUGED	DDEEPRS	PEDDERS	DDEIIRT	DIRTIED
DDDEEMO	DEMODED	DDEEGNU	UNEDGED		SPREDDE		TIDDIER
DDDEENS	SNEDDED	DDEEGRR	DREDGER	DDEEPTU	DEPUTED	DDEIIRV	DIVIDER
DDDEENU	DENUDED	DDEEGRS	DREDGES	DDEERRS	REDDERS	DDEIIST	STIDDIE
DDDEERU	UDDERED	DDEEHLS	HEDDLES	DDEERSS	DRESSED		TIDDIES
DDDEEST	STEDDED	DDEEHNU	DUDHEEN	DDEERST	REDDEST	DDEIISV	DIVIDES
DDDEFIL	FIDDLED	DDEEHRS	SHEDDER		TEDDERS	DDEIISW	WIDDIES
DDDEFLU	FUDDLED	DDEEILS	SLEIDED	DDEERSW	WEDDERS	DDEIITT	DITTIED
DDDEGII	GIDDIED	DDEEILV	DEVILED	DDEERTU	DETRUDE	DDEIIZZ	DIZZIED
DDDEGLU	GUDDLED	DDEEILW	WIELDED	DDEESST	STEDDES	DDEIKLN	KINDLED
DDDEGRU	DRUDGED	DDEEILY	DEEDILY	DDEETTU	DUETTED	DDEIKLS	KIDDLES
DDDEHIW	WHIDDED		YIELDED	DDEFGIR	FRIDGED	DDEIKNR	KINDRED
DDDEHLO	HODDLED	DDEEIMP	IMPEDED	DDEFILR	FIDDLER	DDEIKRS	KIDDERS
DDDEHLU	HUDDLED	DDEEIMS	DEMISED	DDEFILS	FIDDLES		SKIDDER
DDDEHTU	THUDDED		MISDEED	DDEFILY	FIDDLEY	DDEILLO	DOLLIED
DDDEIIK	KIDDIED	DDEEINS	DESINED	DDEFIRT	DRIFTED	DDEILLR	DRILLED
DDDEIIR	DIDDIER		NEDDIES	DDEFLNO	FONDLED	DDEILLU	ILLUDED
DDDEIIS	DIDDIES		SDEINED	DDEFLOO	FLOODED	DDEILMP	DIMPLED
DDDEIIV	DIVIDED	DDEEINT	ENDITED	DDEFLRU	FUDDLER	DDEILMS	MIDDLES
DDDEIKS	SKIDDED		TEINDED	DDEFLSU	FUDDLES	DDEILNN	DINNLED
DDDEILM	MIDDLED	DDEEINW	INDEWED	DDEFNOR	FRONDED	DDEILNS	DINDLES
DDDEILN	DINDLED		WIDENED	DDEFNOU	FOUNDED		SLIDDEN
DDDEILP	PIDDLED	DDEEINX	INDEXED	DDEFORS	FODDERS	DDEILNW	DWINDLE
DDDEILR	DIDDLER	DDEEINZ	DIZENED	DDEGGRU	DRUGGED	DDEILOR	DROILED
	RIDDLED	DDEEIOV	VIDEOED		GRUDGED	DDEILOS	DILDOES
DDDEILS	DIDDLES	DDEEIPR	PREDIED	DDEGHIT	DIGHTED	DDEILOT	DELTOID
DDDEILT	TIDDLED	DDEEIPS	DEPSIDE	DDEGIIR	GIDDIER	DDEILPR	PIDDLER
DDDEILW	WIDDLED	DDEEIRR	DERIDER	DDEGIIS	GIDDIES	DDEILPS	DISPLED
DDDEIMU	MUDDIED		REDDIER	DDEGILR	GIRDLED		PIDDLES
DDDEIOR	DODDIER		RIDERED		GLIDDER	DDEILPU	DUPLIED
DDDEIOS	DODDIES	DDEEIRS	DERIDES		GRIDDLE	DDEILQU	QUIDDLE
DDDEIRS	DIDDERS		DESIRED	DDEGIMO	DEMIGOD	DDEILRR	RIDDLER
DDDEIRU	DUDDIER		DIEDRES	DDEGINR	GRINDED	DDEILRS	RIDDLES
	RUDDIED		RESIDED		REDDING		SLIDDER
DDDELMU	MUDDLED	DDEEIRV	DERIVED	DDEGINT	TEDDING	DDEILRT	TIDDLER
DDDELNO	NODDLED	DDEEIRW	WEIRDED	DDEGINW	WEDDING	DDEILST	TIDDLES
DDDELOO	DOODLED	DDEEIST	DEIDEST	DDEGINY	EDDYING	DDEILSW	WIDDLES
DDDELOP	PLODDED		TEDDIES	DDEGIOR	DODGIER	DDEILTU	DILUTED
DDDELOS	DODDLES	DDEEISV	DEVISED	DDEGIRR	GRIDDER	DDEILTW	TWIDDLE
DDDELOT	TODDLED	DDEEKKO	DEKKOED	DDEGLOS	DOGSLED	DDEILTY	LYDDITE
DDDELPU	PUDDLED	DDEELLU	DUELLED	DDEGLSU	GUDDLES		TIDDLEY
DDDELRU	RUDDLED	DDEELLW	DWELLED	DDEGMOS	DODGEMS	DDEIMMU	DUMMIED
DDDENOS	SNODDED	DDEELMO	MODELED	DDEGMSU	SMUDGED	DDEIMNS	MIDDENS
DDDEOPR	PRODDED	DDEELMR	MEDDLER	DDEGNOS	GODDENS	DDEIMNU	MUEDDIN
DDDEOQU	QUODDED	DDEELMS	MEDDLES		GODSEND	DDEIMOO	MOODIED
DDDEORS	DODDERS	DDEELNO	OLDENED	DDEGNOU	DUDGEON	DDEIMOR	DERMOID
DDDEORY	DODDERY	DDEELNS	LEDDENS	DDEGNSU	SNUDGED	DDEIMOS	DESMOID
DDDEPSU	SPUDDED	DDEELOP	DELOPED	DDEGORS	DODGERS	DDEIMRU	MUDDIER
DDDERSU	DUDDERS	DDEELPR	PEDDLER		GORSEDD	DDEIMSS	DESMIDS
DDDERUY	DUDDERY	DDEELPS	PEDDLES	DDEGORY	DODGERY	DDEIMST	MIDDEST
DDDESTU	STUDDED		SPELDED	DDEGOSS	GODDESS	DDEIMSU	DEDIMUS
DDDGINO	DODDING	DDEELRS	REDDLES	DDEGOST	STODGED		MUDDIES
DDEEEIR	DEEDIER	DDEELRT	TREDDLE	DDEGRRU	DRUDGER	DDEINOP	POINDED
DDEEELN	NEEDLED	DDEELRU	DELUDER	DDEGRSU	DRUDGES	DDEINOS	NODDIES

DDEINOT	DENTOID		DDENOSY	DYNODES		DEEEHNS	SHEENED		DEEERST	REESTED
DDEINPS	DISPEND		DDENOUW	WOUNDED		DEEEHPS	PHEESED			STEERED
DDEINRU	UNDRIED		DDENPSU	PUDDENS		DEEEHPZ	PHEEZED		DEEERSV	DESERVE
DDEINST	DISTEND		DDENRSU	DUNDERS		DEEEHRS	SHEERED			SEVERED
DDEINSW	SWIDDEN		DDENSTU	STUDDEN		DEEEHST	SEETHED		DEEERSW	SEWERED
DDEIOPR	PODDIER		DDEOOPR	DROOPED			SHEETED			SWEERED
DDEIOPS	PODDIES		DDEOORU	ODOURED		DEEEHTT	TEETHED			WEEDERS
DDEIORS	DORISED		DDEOORW	REDWOOD		DEEEHWZ	WHEEZED		DEEERTV	EVERTED
	SODDIER		DDEOPPR	DROPPED		DEEEIJL	JEELIED		DEEERTW	TWEERED
DDEIORV	OVERDID		DDEORSW	DROWSED		DEEEIMR	EMERIED		DEEERTX	EXERTED
DDEIORW	DOWDIER			SWORDED		DEEEINR	NEEDIER		DEEERWY	WEEDERY
DDEIORZ	DORIZED		DDEPRSS	SPREDDS		DEEEIPS	DEEPIES		DEEESSX	DESEXES
DDEIOST	TODDIES		DDEPRSU	PUDDERS		DEEEIRR	REEDIER		DEEESTV	STEEVED
DDEIOSW	DOWDIES		DDERRSU	RUDDERS		DEEEIRS	SEEDIER		DEEESTW	SWEETED
DDEIOTT	DITTOED		DDERSSU	SUDDERS		DEEEIRW	WEEDIER		DEEETTV	VEDETTE
DDEIOWW	WIDOWED		DDGGINO	DODGING		DEEEISV	DEVISEE		DEEETTW	TWEETED
DDEIPPR	DRIPPED			GODDING		DEEEJNU	DEJEUNE		DEEETWZ	TWEEZED
DDEIPRS	DISPRED		DDGHINO	HODDING		DEEEJRS	JEREEDS		DEEFFFO	FEOFFED
DDEIPSU	PUDDIES		DDGHOOO	GODHOOD		DEEEKLN	KNEELED		DEEFFIN	EFFENDI
DDEIRRS	RIDDERS		DDGIIKN	KIDDING		DEEEKLS	SLEEKED		DEEFFOR	OFFERED
DDEIRRU	RUDDIER		DDGIILY	GIDDILY		DEEEKMS	SMEEKED		DEEFFST	DEFFEST
DDEIRSU	RUDDIES		DDGIINR	RIDDING		DEEEKNW	WEEKEND		DEEFFSU	EFFUSED
DDEISSU	DISUSED		DDGIMNU	MUDDING		DEEEKRS	KREESED		DEEFGGL	FLEGGED
DDEISTU	STUDIED		DDGINNO	NODDING			SKEERED		DEEFGIN	FEEDING
DDEJRSU	JUDDERS		DDGINOP	PODDING		DEEELMS	MESELED			FEIGNED
DDEKMOU	DUKEDOM		DDGINOR	RODDING		DEEELNR	NEEDLER		DEEFGIP	PIGFEED
DDEKOOR	DROOKED		DDGINOS	SODDING		DEEELNS	NEEDLES		DEEFGLS	FLEDGES
DDEKORU	DROUKED		DDGINOT	TODDING		DEEELPS	SPEELED		DEEFGRU	REFUGED
DDELLOR	DROLLED		DDGINPU	PUDDING		DEEELPT	DEPLETE		DEEFHLS	FLESHED
DDELMOU	MOULDED		DDGINRU	RUDDING		DEEELRT	DEERLET			SHELFED
DDELMPU	DUMPLED		DDGINUW	WUDDING		DEEELRV	LEVERED		DEEFHLU	HEEDFUL
DDELMRU	MUDDLER		DDGOOOW	DOGWOOD		DEEELST	DELETES		DEEFHRS	FRESHED
DDELMSU	MUDDLES		DDHIISS	SIDDHIS			SLEETED		DEEFIIR	DEIFIER
DDELNOO	NOODLED		DDHIKSU	KIDDUSH			STEELED			EDIFIER
DDELNOS	NODDLES		DDHIORY	HYDROID		DEEELSV	SLEEVED			REIFIED
DDELNOU	LOUNDED		DDIIKSV	KIDVIDS		DEEELSW	SWEELED		DEEFIIS	DEIFIES
	NODULED		DDIILOP	DIPLOID		DEEELTW	TWEEDLE			EDIFIES
DDELNOW	LOWNDED		DDIIQTU	QUIDDIT			TWEELED		DEEFILN	ENFILED
DDELNRU	NURDLED		DDIKNOS	DODKINS		DEEELTX	TELEXED		DEEFILR	DEFILER
	RUNDLED		DDILMUY	MUDDILY		DEEEMMW	EMMEWED			FERLIED
DDELOOR	DOODLER		DDILNRS	DIRNDLS		DEEEMNW	ENMEWED			FIELDER
	DROOLED		DDILOSY	DYSODIL		DEEEMRS	DEMERSE		DEEFILS	DEFILES
DDELOOS	DOODLES		DDILOWY	DOWDILY			EMERSED		DEEFIMS	MISFEED
DDELOOW	WOOLDED		DDILRUY	RUDDILY			REDEEMS		DEEFINR	DEFINER
DDELOPR	PLODDER		DDILTWY	TWIDDLY			REMEDES			ENFIRED
DDELORT	TODDLER		DDIMRSU	DIRDUMS		DEEEMRT	METERED			FENDIER
DDELORW	WORLDED		DDIMSSU	DUDISMS		DEEEMST	STEEMED			REFINED
DDELOST	TODDLES		DDINOST	SNODDIT		DEEENPR	PREENED		DEEFINS	DEFINES
DDELOTT	DOTTLED		DDIORTU	TURDOID		DEEENPS	DEEPENS		DEEFINT	FEINTED
DDELPRU	PUDDLER		DDLLMOO	DOLLDOM		DEEENQU	QUEENED		DEEFINX	ENFIXED
DDELPSU	PUDDLES		DDMMSUU	DUMDUMS		DEEENRS	NEEDERS		DEEFIRR	FERRIED
DDELRSU	RUDDLES		DDMNOOR	DROMOND			SERENED		DEEFIRS	DEFIERS
DDELSTU	STUDDLE		DDMRSUU	DURDUMS			SNEERED		DEEFIRT	FETIDER
DDEMMRU	DRUMMED		DDORSTY	DROSTDY		DEEENRT	ENTERED		DEEFIRZ	FRIEZED
DDEMMSU	SMEDDUM		DEEEEMX	EXEEMED		DEEENRV	ENERVED		DEEFLLU	FUELLED
DDEMNOS	ODDSMEN		DEEEFFR	EFFERED		DEEENRW	RENEWED		DEEFLNS	FLENSED
DDEMNOT	ODDMENT		DEEEFLR	FLEERED		DEEENRY	RENEYED		DEEFLNU	NEEDFUL
DDEMNOU	MOUNDED		DEEEFLT	FLEETED		DEEENST	STEENED		DEEFLOT	FEEDLOT
DDEMRSU	MUDDERS		DEEEFNR	ENFREED		DEEENSV	VENDEES		DEEFLTT	FETTLED
DDENNOR	DENDRON		DEEEFNS	DEFENSE		DEEENSW	ENSEWED		DEEFMOR	FREEDOM
	DONNERD		DEEEFRS	FEEDERS		DEEENSZ	SNEEZED		DEEFNRS	FENDERS
DDENOOS	SNOODED		DEEEFRV	FEVERED		DEEENTT	DETENTE		DEEFNRU	UNFREED
DDENOPS	DESPOND		DEEEGKL	GLEEKED		DEEENTU	DETENUE		DEEFNUU	UNFEUED
DDENOPU	POUNDED		DEEEGLP	PLEDGEE		DEEENTV	EVENTED		DEEFORV	OVERFED
DDENOPW	POWNDED		DEEEGLT	GLEETED		DEEEORW	OREWEED		DEEFORZ	DEFROZE
DDENORS	DONDERS		DEEEGMR	DEMERGE		DEEEOTV	DEVOTEE		DEEFRSU	REFUSED
	NODDERS			EMERGED		DEEEPRS	SPEEDER		DEEFRSW	SWERFED
	SNODDER		DEEEGNP	PEENGED			SPEERED		DEEFRTT	FRETTED
DDENORT	TRODDEN		DEEEGNR	GREENED		DEEEPRT	PETERED		DEEFRTU	FEUTRED
DDENORU	REDOUND			RENEGED		DEEEPRU	EPERDUE			REFUTED
	ROUNDED		DEEEGRR	REGREDE		DEEEPRV	PREEVED		DEEFSSU	DEFUSES
	UNDERDO		DEEEGRS	DEGREES		DEEEPSS	PEDESES		DEEFSTT	DEFTEST
DDENORW	DROWNED		DEEEGRT	DETERGE		DEEEPST	DEEPEST		DEEFSUZ	DEFUZES
	ROWNDED			GREETED			STEEPED		DEEGGIS	GIDGEES
	WONDRED		DEEEGST	EGESTED		DEEEQRU	QUEERED		DEEGGLS	GLEDGES
DDENOSS	ODDNESS		DEEEHKT	THEEKED		DEEERRS	REEDERS		DEEGHIN	HEEDING
	SODDENS		DEEEHLS	SHEELED		DEEERRV	REVERED			NEIGHED
DDENOSU	SOUNDED		DEEEHLW	WHEEDLE		DEEERSS	SEEDERS		DEEGHIR	HEDGIER
DDENOSW	SOWNDED			WHEELED					DEEGHIW	WEIGHED

Key	Word(s)
DEEGHOW	HOGWEED
DEEGHRS	HEDGERS
DEEGHSS	GHESSED
DEEGIJS	GIDJEES
DEEGIKR	KEDGIER
DEEGILN	DELEING
DEEGILR	GELIDER
	LEDGIER
	LEIDGER
DEEGIMN	DEEMING
DEEGINN	ENGINED
	NEEDING
DEEGINR	DREEING
	ENERGID
	GREINED
	REEDING
	REIGNED
DEEGINS	SDEIGNE
	SEEDING
DEEGINV	DEEVING
DEEGINW	WEEDING
DEEGINY	YEEDING
DEEGIPW	PIGWEED
DEEGIRS	SEDGIER
DEEGIRV	DIVERGE
	GRIEVED
DEEGIRW	WEDGIER
DEEGIST	EDGIEST
DEEGISW	WEDGIES
DEEGJRU	REJUDGE
DEEGKRS	KEDGERS
DEEGLMU	EMULGED
DEEGLNS	LEGENDS
DEEGLNT	GENTLED
	GLENTED
DEEGLOY	GOLDEYE
DEEGLPR	PLEDGER
DEEGLPS	PLEDGES
DEEGLPT	PLEDGET
DEEGLRS	GELDERS
	LEDGERS
	REDLEGS
	SLEDGER
DEEGLSS	SLEDGES
DEEGLSU	DELUGES
DEEGMNU	EMUNGED
	GUDEMEN
DEEGNNO	ENDOGEN
DEEGNNR	GRENNED
DEEGNOR	ENGORED
DEEGNRS	GENDERS
DEEGNSU	DENGUES
	UNEDGES
DEEGOOS	SOOGEED
DEEGORR	ROGERED
DEEGOSY	GEODESY
DEEGOTU	OUTEDGE
DEEGRRU	REURGED
DEEGSSU	GUESSED
DEEGSTU	GUESTED
DEEHIKV	KHEDIVE
DEEHILS	SHIELED
DEEHILT	LETHIED
DEEHINR	INHERED
DEEHIRR	HERRIED
DEEHIST	HEISTED
DEEHITV	THIEVED
DEEHKLW	WHELKED
DEEHLLO	HELLOED
DEEHLLS	SHELLED
DEEHLMW	WHELMED
DEEHLNU	UNHELED
DEEHLOV	HOVELED
DEEHLPW	WHELPED
DEEHLSV	SHELVED
DEEHLSW	WELSHED
DEEHMNR	HERDMEN
DEEHMNS	MENSHED
DEEHMRU	RHEUMED
DEEHMUX	EXHUMED
DEEHNOY	HONEYED
DEEHNPR	PREHEND
DEEHNRS	HERDENS
DEEHNUY	UNHEEDY
DEEHORV	HOVERED
DEEHPRS	SPHERED
DEEHRSS	HERDESS
DEEHRSU	USHERED
DEEHRSW	SHREWED
DEEHRTW	WRETHED
DEEHTTW	WHETTED
DEEIINT	DIETINE
DEEIIPR	EPEIRID
DEEIIRW	WEIRDIE
DEEIIST	DEITIES
DEEIJLL	JELLIED
DEEIJMM	JEMMIED
DEEIJTT	JETTIED
DEEIKLL	KILLDEE
DEEIKLN	LIKENED
DEEIKNS	ENSKIED
DEEIKOV	DOVEKIE
DEEILNO	ELOINED
DEEILNR	RELINED
DEEILNS	ENISLED
	ENSILED
	LINSEED
DEEILNV	LIVENED
DEEILNY	DYELINE
	NEEDILY
DEEILPR	REPLIED
DEEILPS	SEEDLIP
	SPIELED
DEEILRS	RESILED
DEEILRT	RETILED
DEEILRV	DELIVER
	RELIVED
	REVILED
DEEILRW	WIELDER
DEEILRY	YIELDER
DEEILSS	DIESELS
	IDLESSE
DEEILSY	EYELIDS
	SEEDILY
DEEILTU	DILUTEE
DEEILTV	DEVILET
DEEIMMS	MISDEEM
DEEIMMW	IMMEWED
DEEIMNO	DOMINEE
DEEIMNR	ERMINED
DEEIMNS	DESMINE
	SIDEMEN
DEEIMNT	DEMENTI
DEEIMPR	DEMIREP
DEEIMPS	IMPEDES
	SEMIPED
DEEIMPT	EMPTIED
DEEIMRS	REMEIDS
	REMISED
DEEIMRT	DEMERIT
	DIMETER
	MERITED
	MITERED
	RETIMED
DEEIMRX	REMIXED
DEEIMSS	DEMISES
DEEIMTT	EMITTED
DEEINNP	PENNIED
DEEINNS	INDENES
DEEINNT	DENTINE
DEEINNU	ENNUIED
DEEINNZ	DENIZEN
DEEINOR	ORDINEE
DEEINPR	REPINED
	RIPENED
DEEINRR	DERNIER
	NERDIER
DEEINRS	DENIERS
	NEREIDS
	RESINED
DEEINRU	UREDINE
DEEINRW	WIDENER
DEEINRX	INDEXER
DEEINSS	DESINES
DEEINST	DESTINE
	ENDITES
	STEINED
DEEINSV	ENDIVES
DEEINSW	ENDWISE
	SINEWED
DEEINSX	INDEXES
DEEINTT	DINETTE
DEEINTU	DETINUE
DEEINTV	EVIDENT
DEEINVW	VINEWED
DEEINVX	INVEXED
DEEINWZ	WIZENED
DEEIOPS	EPISODE
	POESIED
DEEIOPT	EPIDOTE
DEEIOPX	EPOXIDE
DEEIORS	OREIDES
	OSIERED
DEEIOSV	VOIDEES
DEEIPPT	PEPTIDE
DEEIPRS	PREDIES
	PRESIDE
	SPEIRED
DEEIPRT	TEPIDER
DEEIPRV	DEPRIVE
	PRIEVED
DEEIPRX	EXPIRED
DEEIPSS	DESPISE
	PEDESIS
DEEIPST	DESPITE
DEEIQRU	QUERIED
DEEIQTU	QUIETED
DEEIRRS	DERRIES
	DESIRER
	RESIDER
	SERRIED
DEEIRRT	RETIRED
	RETRIED
	TIREDER
DEEIRRV	REDRIVE
	RIVERED
DEEIRRW	REWIRED
	WEIRDER
DEEIRSS	DESIRES
	RESIDES
DEEIRST	DIETERS
	REISTED
DEEIRSU	RESIDUE
	UREIDES
DEEIRSV	DERIVES
	DEVISER
	DIVERSE
	REVISED
DEEIRTU	ERUDITE
DEEIRTV	RIVETED
	VERDITE
DEEIRVV	REVIVED
DEEISSU	DISEUSE
DEEISSV	DEVISES
DEEISTT	TEDIEST
DEEISTW	DEWIEST
DEEISTX	EXISTED
DEEITTV	VIDETTE
DEEJNOY	ENJOYED
DEEJQRU	JERQUED
DEEKKRT	TREKKED
DEEKLLN	KNELLED
DEEKLPS	SKELPED
DEEKLRS	SKELDER
DEEKNOT	TOKENED
DEEKORV	REVOKED
DEEKPPS	SKEPPED
DEEKPRU	PERUKED
DEEKRRS	SKERRED
DEEKRSU	RESKUED
DEELLMS	SMELLED
DEELLNS	SNELLED
DEELLPS	SPELLED
DEELLQU	QUELLED
DEELLRU	DUELLER
DEELLRW	DWELLER
DEELLRY	ELDERLY
DEELLST	STELLED
DEELLSW	SWELLED
DEELMNO	LEMONED
DEELMOR	MODELER
	REMODEL
DEELMPT	TEMPLED
DEELMPU	DEPLUME
DEELMRS	MELDERS
DEELMRU	RELUMED
DEELMST	SMELTED
DEELMSY	MEDLEYS
DEELMTT	METTLED
DEELNRS	LENDERS
	SLENDER
DEELNSS	ENDLESS
DEELNST	DENTELS
	NESTLED
DEELNSW	WEDELNS
DEELNSY	DENSELY
DEELNTT	NETTLED
DEELOPP	PEOPLED
DEELOPR	DEPLORE
DEELOPS	DELOPES
DEELOPV	DEVELOP
DEELOPX	EXPLODE
DEELORS	RESOLED
DEELORU	URODELE
DEELORV	LOVERED
DEELORW	LOWERED
DEELOSU	DELOUSE
DEELOTV	DOVELET
DEELOTW	TOWELED
DEELOVV	DEVOLVE
	EVOLVED
DEELPRS	SPELDER
DEELPRU	PRELUDE
DEELPST	PESTLED
DEELPTT	PETTLED
DEELRRU	RULERED
DEELRSU	ELUDERS
DEELRSV	DELVERS
DEELRSW	WELDERS
DEELRUV	VELURED
DEELSTT	SETTLED
DEELSTU	TELEDUS
DEELSTW	LEWDEST
	SWELTED
DEELSUV	EVULSED
DEELSVV	DEVVELS
DEELTUX	EXULTED
DEELVXY	VEXEDLY
DEEMMOV	EMMOVED
DEEMMST	STEMMED
DEEMNOV	ENMOVED
	VENOMED
DEEMNOY	MONEYED
DEEMNRS	MENDERS
DEEMNST	DEMENTS
DEEMNTU	UNMETED
DEEMNUW	UNMEWED
DEEMORS	EMERODS
DEEMORV	REMOVED
DEEMORX	EXODERM
DEEMOSS	DEMOSES
DEEMOST	DEMOTES
DEEMOSY	MOSEYED
DEEMPRS	PREMEDS
DEEMPTT	TEMPTED
DEEMRRU	DEMURER

DEEMRSU	DEMURES / RESUMED
DEENNOR	ENDERON
DEENNOS	DONNEES
DEENNOT	TENONED
DEENNOY	DOYENNE
DEENNOZ	ENZONED
DEENNPT	PENDENT
DEENNST	DENNETS / STENNED
DEENNTZ	TENDENZ
DEENNUY	ENNUYED
DEENOOR	RONEOED
DEENOPR	REPONED
DEENOPS	DEPONES / SPONDEE
DEENOPT	PENTODE
DEENORS	ENDORSE
DEENORT	ERODENT
DEENORW	ENDOWER
DEENORZ	REZONED
DEENOST	DENOTES
DEENPPR	PERPEND
DEENPRS	SPENDER
DEENPRT	PRENTED / PRETEND
DEENPSX	EXPENDS
DEENRRS	RENDERS
DEENRRU	ENDURER
DEENRSS	REDNESS / SENDERS
DEENRST	STERNED / TENDERS / TENDRES
DEENRSU	ENDURES / ENSURED
DEENRSV	VENDERS
DEENRSZ	DZERENS
DEENRTU	DENTURE / RETUNED / TENURED
DEENRTV	VENTRED
DEENSST	DENSEST
DEENSSY	DESYNES
DEENSTT	DETENTS / STENTED
DEENSTU	DETENUS / DETUNES
DEENSTX	EXTENDS
DEENSUV	VENDUES
DEENSUW	UNSEWED
DEENSUX	UNSEXED
DEENUVX	UNVEXED
DEEOPRR	PEDRERO
DEEOPRS	DEPOSER / REPOSED
DEEOPRW	POWERED
DEEOPSS	DEPOSES / SPEEDOS
DEEOPSX	EXPOSED / PODEXES
DEEORRR	ORDERER / REORDER
DEEORRS	REREDOS
DEEORRV	OVERRED / REDROVE
DEEORST	OERSTED / ROSETED / TEREDOS
DEEORTT	OTTERED / TETRODE
DEEORTW	TOWERED
DEEORTX	OXTERED
DEEORTZ	ROZETED
DEEORUV	OVERDUE
DEEORVY	OVERDYE
DEEOSTV	DEVOTES
DEEOSTX	DETOXES
DEEOTUW	OUTWEED
DEEPPPR	PREPPED
DEEPPST	STEPPED
DEEPRRS	SPERRED
DEEPRRU	PERDURE / REPURED
DEEPRSS	DEPRESS / PRESSED / SPERSED
DEEPRST	PRESTED
DEEPRSU	PERDUES / PERSUED / PERUSED
DEEPRTU	ERUPTED / REPUTED
DEEPRUV	PREVUED
DEEPSTU	DEPUTES
DEEQSTU	QUESTED
DEERRSS	DRESSER / REDRESS / DRESSES / DESSERT / TRESSED
DEERSSU	DURESSE
DEERSTV	STERVED / VERDETS
DEERSTW	STREWED / WRESTED
DEERSTX	DEXTERS
DEERSTY	DYESTER
DEERSVW	SWERVED
DEERTTU	UTTERED
DEERTUX	EXTRUDE
DEESSTT	DETESTS
DEESSTV	DEVESTS
DEESTTT	STETTED
DEFFFLU	FLUFFED
DEFFHIW	WHIFFED
DEFFHOU	HOUFFED
DEFFHOW	HOWFFED
DEFFIKS	SKIFFED
DEFFILP	PIFFLED
DEFFILR	RIFFLED
DEFFILS	SIFFLED
DEFFIMO	FIEFDOM
DEFFINS	SNIFFED
DEFFIOS	OFFSIDE
DEFFIRS	DIFFERS
DEFFIST	STIFFED
DEFFISU	DIFFUSE
DEFFKOS	SKOFFED
DEFFLMU	MUFFLED
DEFFLPU	PLUFFED
DEFFLRU	RUFFLED
DEFFLSU	DUFFELS / DUFFLES
DEFFNOR	FORFEND
DEFFNOS	OFFENDS
DEFFNSU	SNUFFED
DEFFOPU	POUFFED
DEFFORS	DOFFERS
DEFFOSW	SOWFFED
DEFFRSU	DUFFERS
DEFFSTU	DUFFEST / STUFFED
DEFGGIR	FRIGGED
DEFGGLO	FLOGGED
DEFGGOR	FROGGED
DEFGINN	FENDING
DEFGINR	FRINGED
DEFGINU	FEUDING
DEFGINY	DEFYING
DEFGIOR	FIREDOG
DEFGIRS	FRIDGES
DEFGIRT	GRIFTED
DEFGIRU	FIGURED
DEFGIST	FIDGETS
DEFGITY	FIDGETY
DEFGRTU	GRUFTED
DEFHIRS	REDFISH
DEFHIST	SHIFTED
DEFHLOO	ELFHOOD
DEFHLSU	FLUSHED
DEFHORT	FROTHED
DEFHRSU	FRUSHED
DEFIILN	INFIDEL / INFIELD
DEFIIMS	FIDEISM
DEFIIMW	MIDWIFE
DEFIINU	UNIFIED
DEFIINX	INFIXED
DEFIIST	FIDEIST
DEFIKLS	FLISKED
DEFIKRS	FRISKED
DEFILLO	FOLLIED
DEFILLR	FRILLED
DEFILMP	FLIMPED
DEFILNR	FLINDER
DEFILNU	UNFILDE / UNFILED
DEFILOO	FOLIOED
DEFILPP	FLIPPED
DEFILRT	FLIRTED / TRIFLED
DEFILRU	DIREFUL
DEFILSS	FISSLED
DEFILST	STIFLED
DEFILSU	SULFIDE
DEFILTT	FLITTED
DEFILXY	FIXEDLY
DEFILZZ	FIZZLED
DEFIMOR	DEIFORM
DEFINRS	FINDERS / FRIENDS
DEFINRU	UNFIRED
DEFINST	SNIFTED
DEFINSU	FUNDIES / INFUSED
DEFINSY	DENSIFY
DEFINUX	UNFIXED
DEFINUY	UNDEIFY
DEFIOOS	FOODIES
DEFIOQU	QUOIFED
DEFIORU	FOUDRIE
DEFIOST	FOISTED
DEFIPRY	PERFIDY
DEFIRRT	DRIFTER
DEFIRST	FRISTED
DEFIRTT	FRITTED
DEFIRTU	FRUITED
DEFIRZZ	FRIZZED
DEFISTU	FEUDIST
DEFISTW	SWIFTED
DEFKLNU	FLUNKED
DEFLLOU	DOLEFUL
DEFLLUW	DEWFULL
DEFLMPU	FLUMPED
DEFLNOO	ONEFOLD
DEFLNOP	PENFOLD
DEFLNOR	FONDLER / FORLEND
DEFLNOS	ENFOLDS / FONDLES
DEFLNOT	TENFOLD
DEFLNRU	DERNFUL
DEFLOOR	FLOORED
DEFLOOT	FOOTLED
DEFLOOZ	FOOZLED
DEFLOPP	FLOPPED
DEFLORS	FOLDERS
DEFLORU	FLOURED / FOULDER
DEFLOSS	FLOSSED
DEFLOSU	DEFOULS / FLOUSED
DEFLOTU	FLOUTED
DEFLPRU	PURFLED
DEFLRRU	FLURRED
DEFLRUU	DUREFUL
DEFLUZZ	FUZZLED
DEFMNUU	UNFUMED
DEFMORS	DEFORMS / SERFDOM
DEFMPRU	FRUMPED
DEFNOOR	FORDONE
DEFNORT	FRONTED
DEFNORU	FOUNDER / REFOUND
DEFNORW	FROWNED
DEFNOST	FONDEST
DEFNOSU	FONDUES
DEFNRSU	FUNDERS / REFUNDS
DEFOOPR	PROOFED
DEFOOPS	SPOOFED
DEFOORS	DOOFERS / FORDOES
DEFORST	DEFROST / FROSTED
DEFORTU	FOUTRED
DEGGGIL	GIGGLED
DEGGGIR	GRIGGED
DEGGGLO	GOGGLED
DEGGGLU	GLUGGED / GUGGLED
DEGGGOR	GROGGED
DEGGHIL	HIGGLED
DEGGHIN	HEDGING
DEGGHIW	WHIGGED
DEGGHOS	SHOGGED
DEGGIJL	JIGGLED
DEGGIKN	KEDGING
DEGGILN	GELDING / NIGGLED
DEGGILW	WIGGLED
DEGGINS	EDGINGS / SNIGGED
DEGGINW	WEDGING
DEGGIOR	DOGGIER
DEGGIOS	DOGGIES
DEGGIPR	PRIGGED
DEGGIRS	DIGGERS
DEGGIRT	TRIGGED
DEGGIRU	DRUGGIE
DEGGISW	SWIGGED
DEGGITW	TWIGGED
DEGGJLO	JOGGLED
DEGGJLU	JUGGLED
DEGGKSU	SKUGGED
DEGGLOO	GOOGLED
DEGGLOR	DOGGREL
DEGGLOS	SLOGGED
DEGGLOT	TOGGLED
DEGGLPU	PLUGGED / PUGGLED
DEGGLRU	GURGLED
DEGGLSU	SLUGGED
DEGGMSU	SMUGGED
DEGGNOO	DOGGONE
DEGGNOS	SNOGGED
DEGGNOU	GUDGEON
DEGGNSU	SNUGGED
DEGGOPR	PROGGED
DEGGORS	DOGGERS
DEGGORT	TROGGED
DEGGORY	DOGGERY
DEGGOSS	DOGGESS
DEGGRRU	DRUGGER
DEGGRSU	GRUDGES
DEGGRTU	DRUGGET
DEGHHOU	HOUGHED
DEGHILN	HINDLEG
DEGHILT	DELIGHT / LIGHTED
DEGHINN	HENDING
DEGHINR	HERDING

DEGHINT	NIGHTED	DEGINNY	DENYING	DEGMOOR	GROOMED	DEHIORS	RHODIES
DEGHINW	WHINGED	DEGINOP	PIDGEON	DEGMPRU	GRUMPED	DEHIORT	THEROID
DEGHIOT	HOGTIED	DEGINOR	ERODING	DEGMRSU	MUDGERS	DEHIOST	HOISTED
DEGHIPT	PIGHTED		GROINED		SMUDGER	DEHIOSU	HIDEOUS
DEGHIRT	GIRTHED		IGNORED	DEGMSSU	SMUDGES	DEHIOSV	DOVEISH
	RIGHTED		NEGROID	DEGNNOU	DUNGEON	DEHIOSW	HOWDIES
DEGHIST	SIGHTED		REDOING	DEGNOPR	PRONGED	DEHIOTU	HIDEOUT
DEGHITW	WIGHTED	DEGINOS	DINGOES	DEGNOPS	SPONGED	DEHIPPS	SHIPPED
DEGHLOO	DOGHOLE	DEGINOW	WENDIGO	DEGNORU	GUERDON	DEHIPPW	WHIPPED
DEGHNOT	THONGED		WIDGEON		UNDERGO	DEHIRRS	SHIRRED
DEGHORR	DROGHER		WONGIED		UNGORED	DEHIRRU	DHURRIE
DEGHORU	ROUGHED	DEGINRR	GRINDER	DEGNORW	WRONGED		HURRIED
DEGHOST	GHOSTED		REGRIND	DEGNOTU	TONGUED	DEHIRRW	WHIRRED
DEGHOSU	SOUGHED	DEGINRS	DINGERS	DEGNRSU	GERUNDS	DEHIRST	DITHERS
DEGIIKR	KIDGIER		ENGIRDS		NUDGERS		SHIRTED
DEGIILL	GILLIED	DEGINRU	DUNGIER	DEGNRTU	GRUNTED	DEHIRSU	HURDIES
DEGIILN	EILDING	DEGINRW	REDWING		TRUDGEN	DEHIRSV	DERVISH
	ELIDING		WRINGED	DEGNRUU	UNURGED		SHRIVED
DEGIINR	DINGIER	DEGINRY	YERDING	DEGNSSU	SNUDGES	DEHIRTV	THRIVED
DEGIINS	DINGIES	DEGINSS	DESIGNS	DEGNUVY	UNGYVED	DEHIRTW	WRITHED
DEGIINT	DIETING		SDEIGNS	DEGOORV	GROOVED	DEHIRTY	DITHERY
	EDITING	DEGINST	NIDGETS	DEGOOST	STOOGED	DEHISSW	SWISHED
	IGNITED		STEDING	DEGOPRU	GROUPED		WHISSED
DEGIIPS	GIPSIED		STINGED	DEGORRS	DROGERS	DEHISTT	SHITTED
DEGIIRR	RIDGIER	DEGINSU	GUNDIES	DEGORSS	GROSSED	DEHISTW	WHISTED
	RIGIDER		SUEDING		SODGERS	DEHISVV	SHIVVED
DEGIIRS	DIRIGES	DEGINSW	SWINDGE	DEGORST	STODGER	DEHIWZZ	WHIZZED
DEGIISW	WIDGIES		SWINGED	DEGORSU	DROGUES	DEHLLOO	HOLLOED
DEGIJLN	JINGLED	DEGINSY	DINGEYS		GOURDES	DEHLLOU	HULLOED
DEGIKLO	GODLIKE		DYEINGS		GROUSED	DEHLMOU	MUDHOLE
DEGILLR	GRILLED	DEGINTW	TWINGED	DEGORTU	DROGUET	DEHLMSU	MULSHED
DEGILLU	GULLIED	DEGINUX	EXUDING		GROUTED	DEHLOOS	SHOOLED
DEGILLY	GELIDLY	DEGIOOR	GOODIER	DEGOSST	STODGES	DEHLOOT	TOEHOLD
DEGILMN	MEDLING	DEGIOOS	GOODIES	DEGOSTU	DEGOUTS	DEHLOPP	HOPPLED
	MELDING		SOOGIED	DEGOSTW	GOWDEST	DEHLORS	HOLDERS
	MINGLED	DEGIOPR	PODGIER	DEGRRTU	TRUDGER	DEHLORW	WHORLED
DEGILNN	LENDING	DEGIORR	GRODIER	DEGRSTU	TRUDGES	DEHLOSS	SLOSHED
DEGILNO	GLENOID	DEGIORT	GOITRED	DEGSSTU	DEGUSTS	DEHLOST	SLOTHED
DEGILNP	PINGLED	DEGIPPR	GRIPPED	DEHHISW	WHISHED	DEHLRRU	HURDLER
DEGILNS	DINGLES	DEGIPRU	PUDGIER	DEHHMPU	HUMPHED	DEHLRSU	HURDLES
	ELDINGS	DEGIPSY	GYPSIED	DEHHOOS	HOOSHED	DEHLRTU	HURTLED
	ENGILDS	DEGIQSU	SQUIDGE	DEHHSSU	SHUSHED	DEHLSSU	SLUSHED
	SINGLED	DEGIRRS	GIRDERS	DEHIINN	HINNIED	DEHLSTU	HUSTLED
DEGILNT	GLINTED		RIDGERS	DEHIIPS	PIEDISH	DEHMNOO	HOODMEN
	TINGLED	DEGIRRU	DURGIER	DEHIIRS	DISHIER	DEHMOPR	MORPHED
DEGILNU	ELUDING	DEGIRSS	DIGRESS	DEHIKRS	SHIRKED	DEHMORU	HUMORED
	INDULGE	DEGIRSU	GUIDERS		SHRIKED	DEHMOST	METHODS
DEGILNV	DELVING	DEGIRTT	GRITTED	DEHIKSW	WHISKED	DEHMOTU	MOUTHED
	DEVLING	DEGISST	DIGESTS	DEHILLO	HILLOED	DEHMPTU	THUMPED
DEGILNW	WELDING		DISGEST	DEHILLS	SHILLED	DEHNNSU	SHUNNED
DEGILOR	GLORIED	DEGISTU	GIUSTED	DEHILMS	DISHELM	DEHNOOR	HONORED
	GODLIER	DEGISTW	WIDGETS	DEHILNP	DELPHIN	DEHNOOW	HOEDOWN
	GOLDIER	DEGKLSU	KLUDGES	DEHILPR	HIRPLED	DEHNOPU	UNHOPED
DEGILOU	OUGLIED	DEGLMMO	GLOMMED	DEHILRS	HIRSLED	DEHNORS	DEHORNS
DEGILRR	GIRDLER	DEGLMOO	GLOOMED	DEHILRT	THIRLED	DEHNORT	NORTHED
DEGILRS	GILDERS	DEGLMOU	MOGULED	DEHILRW	WHIRLED		THONDER
	GIRDLES	DEGLNNO	ENDLONG	DEHILSS	SHIELDS		THORNED
	GLIDERS	DEGLNOP	PLONGED	DEHILTY	DIETHYL		THRONED
	GRISLED	DEGLNOS	DONGLES	DEHIMMS	SHIMMED		
	LIDGERS		GOLDENS	DEHIMMW	WHIMMED	DEHNOSU	UNSHOED
	RIDGELS	DEGLNOU	LOUNGED	DEHIMNU	INHUMED	DEHNOSY	HOYDENS
DEGILRU	GUILDER	DEGLNPU	PLUNGED	DEHIMOR	HEIRDOM	DEHNOTZ	DOZENTH
DEGILRW	WERGILD	DEGLNSU	GULDENS	DEHIMOS	DISHOME	DEHNRSU	HURDENS
DEGILUV	DIVULGE	DEGLNUU	UNGLUED	DEHIMOT	ETHMOID	DEHNRTU	THUNDER
DEGIMNN	MENDING		UNGULED	DEHIMRS	DIRHEMS	DEHNSSU	DUNSHES
DEGIMNS	SMIDGEN	DEGLOOP	GLOOPED	DEHIMRU	HUMIDER		SNUSHED
DEGIMPU	GUIMPED	DEGLOPR	PLEDGOR	DEHIMST	SMITHED	DEHNSSY	YSHENDS
DEGIMST	MIDGETS	DEGLOPS	SPLODGE	DEHINNS	SHINNED	DEHNSTU	SHUNTED
DEGINNN	DENNING	DEGLORS	LODGERS	DEHINNT	THINNED	DEHNSYY	HYDYNES
DEGINNP	PENDING	DEGLORW	GROWLED	DEHINOP	DIPHONE	DEHOOPT	PHOTOED
DEGINNR	GRINNED	DEGLOSS	GLOSSED		PHONIED	DEHOOPW	WHOOPED
	RENDING		GODLESS	DEHINOR	HORDEIN	DEHOOST	SOOTHED
DEGINNS	ENDINGS	DEGLOST	GOLDEST	DEHINOS	HOIDENS	DEHOOSW	WOOSHED
	SENDING	DEGLOTU	GLOUTED	DEHINPS	ENDSHIP	DEHOOTT	TOOTHED
DEGINNT	DENTING	DEGLSSU	SLUDGES	DEHINRS	HINDERS	DEHOOTW	WHOOTED
	TENDING	DEGLTTU	GLUTTED		SHRINED	DEHOPPS	SHOPPED
DEGINNU	ENDUING		GUTTLED	DEHINRU	UNHIRED	DEHOPPW	WHOPPED
DEGINNV	VENDING	DEGLUZZ	GUZZLED	DEHINUV	UNHIVED	DEHORSS	SHODERS
DEGINNW	WENDING	DEGMNOO	GOODMEN	DEHIOOS	HOODIES	DEHORST	DEHORTS
							SHORTED

DEHORSV	SHROVED	
DEHORSW	SHROWED	
DEHORTT	TROTHED	
DEHORTW	WORTHED	
DEHOSTT	SHOTTED	
DEHOSTU	SHOUTED	
	SOUTHED	
DEHOSTW	SOWTHED	
DEHPTTU	PHUTTED	
DEIIIRS	IRIDISE	
DEIIIRZ	IRIDIZE	
DEIIJMM	JIMMIED	
DEIIKLS	DISLIKE	
DEIIKNR	DINKIER	
DEIIKNS	DINKIES	
	KINDIES	
DEIIKST	DIKIEST	
DEIILLR	DILLIER	
DEIILLS	DILLIES	
DEIILLW	WILLIED	
DEIILMP	IMPLIED	
DEIILMT	DELIMIT	
	LIMITED	
DEIILNS	INISLED	
DEIILOS	DOILIES	
	IDOLISE	
DEIILOZ	IDOLIZE	
DEIILPS	LIPIDES	
DEIILRV	LIVIDER	
DEIIMMX	IMMIXED	
DEIIMNO	DOMINIE	
DEIIMRT	TIMIDER	
DEIIMST	MISDIET	
	STIMIED	
DEIIMSZ	MIDSIZE	
DEIIMVW	MIDWIVE	
DEIINOS	IODINES	
	IONISED	
DEIINOT	EDITION	
	TENIOID	
DEIINOZ	IONIZED	
DEIINRR	RINDIER	
DEIINRS	INSIDER	
DEIINRT	INDITER	
	NITRIDE	
DEIINRU	URIDINE	
DEIINRV	DIVINER	
DEIINRW	WINDIER	
DEIINSS	INSIDES	
DEIINST	INDITES	
	TINEIDS	
DEIINSV	DIVINES	
DEIINTV	INVITED	
DEIIORT	DIORITE	
DEIIORV	IVORIED	
DEIIOSS	IODISES	
DEIIOSX	OXIDISE	
DEIIOSZ	IODIZES	
DEIIOXZ	OXIDIZE	
DEIIPPR	DIPPIER	
DEIIPRS	PIERIDS	
DEIIPRT	RIPTIDE	
DEIIRRT	DIRTIER	
DEIIRST	DIRTIES	
	DITSIER	
DEIIRTT	TRITIDE	
DEIIRTZ	DITZIER	
DEIIRVV	VIVIDER	
DEIIRZZ	DIZZIER	
DEIISTT	DIETIST	
	DITTIES	
	TIDIEST	
DEIISTV	VISITED	
DEIISVV	DIVVIES	
DEIISZZ	DIZZIES	
DEIIVZZ	VIZZIED	
DEIJLLO	JOLLIED	
DEIJNOR	JOINDER	
DEIJNOT	JOINTED	
DEIJNRU	INJURED	
DEIJNSU	DISJUNE	
DEIJOST	JOISTED	
DEIJTTU	JUTTIED	
DEIKKNS	SKINKED	
DEIKLLS	DESKILL	
	SKILLED	
DEIKLNP	PLINKED	
DEIKLNR	KINDLER	
DEIKLNS	KINDLES	
DEIKLNT	TINKLED	
DEIKLNW	WINKLED	
DEIKLOR	RODLIKE	
DEIKLOS	KELOIDS	
DEIKLRS	SKIRLED	
DEIKLRT	KIRTLED	
DEIKLST	KIDLETS	
DEIKLTT	KITTLED	
DEIKMMS	SKIMMED	
DEIKMPS	SKIMPED	
DEIKMRS	SMIRKED	
DEIKNNS	SKINNED	
DEIKNOV	INVOKED	
DEIKNPR	PRINKED	
DEIKNRR	DRINKER	
DEIKNRS	KINDERS	
	KINREDS	
	REDSKIN	
DEIKNST	DINKEST	
	KINDEST	
DEIKNSW	SWINKED	
DEIKNSY	KIDNEYS	
DEIKNSZ	ZENDIKS	
DEIKNTT	KNITTED	
DEIKNTW	TWINKED	
DEIKORR	DORKIER	
DEIKOSY	DISYOKE	
DEIKPPS	SKIPPED	
DEIKQRU	QUIRKED	
DEIKRRS	SKIRRED	
DEIKRST	SKIRTED	
DEIKRSU	DUIKERS	
	DUSKIER	
DEIKSTY	DYKIEST	
DEILLMO	MODELLI	
DEILLMU	ILLUMED	
DEILLNW	INDWELL	
DEILLOR	DOLLIER	
DEILLOS	DOLLIES	
DEILLOV	LIVELOD	
DEILLPR	PRILLED	
DEILLPS	SPILLED	
DEILLQU	QUILLED	
DEILLRR	DRILLER	
DEILLRT	TRILLED	
DEILLRU	DULLIER	
DEILLRV	DREVILL	
DEILLSS	LIDLESS	
DEILLST	STILLED	
DEILLSU	ILLUDES	
	SULLIED	
DEILLSW	SWILLED	
DEILLTW	TWILLED	
DEILMMP	PLIMMED	
DEILMMS	SLIMMED	
DEILMNS	MILDENS	
DEILMNU	LUMINED	
	UNLIMED	
DEILMOP	IMPLODE	
DEILMOS	SMOILED	
DEILMOY	MYELOID	
DEILMPP	PIMPLED	
DEILMPS	DIMPLES	
	MISPLED	
	SIMPLED	
DEILMPW	WIMPLED	
DEILMST	MILDEST	
	MISTLED	
DEILMSW	MILDEWS	
DEILMWY	MILDEWY	
DEILMXY	MIXEDLY	
DEILMZZ	MIZZLED	
DEILNNS	DINNLES	
DEILNNU	UNLINED	
DEILNOO	EIDOLON	
DEILNOS	DOLINES	
	INDOLES	
	SONDELI	
DEILNOT	LENTOID	
DEILNOU	UNOILED	
DEILNPP	NIPPLED	
DEILNPS	SPELDIN	
	SPINDLE	
	SPLINED	
DEILNRT	TENDRIL	
	TRINDLE	
DEILNST	DENTILS	
DEILNSW	SWINDLE	
	WINDLES	
DEILNSY	SNIDELY	
DEILNTU	DILUENT	
	UNTILED	
DEILNTW	INDWELT	
	WINTLED	
DEILNUV	UNLIVED	
DEILOOS	DOOLIES	
DEILOPS	DESPOIL	
	DIPLOES	
	DIPOLES	
	PELOIDS	
	SOLIPED	
	SPOILED	
DEILOPT	PILOTED	
DEILORS	SOLDIER	
	SOLIDER	
DEILORT	DOILTER	
DEILOSY	DOYLIES	
DEILOTU	OUTLIED	
DEILPPR	RIPPLED	
DEILPPS	SIPPLED	
	SLIPPED	
DEILPPT	TIPPLED	
DEILPPU	UPPILED	
DEILPRT	TRIPLED	
DEILPRU	PRELUDI	
DEILPSS	DISPELS	
	DISPLES	
DEILPSU	DUPLIES	
DEILPTY	TEPIDLY	
DEILQTU	QUILTED	
DEILRRU	LURIDER	
DEILRSS	SLIDERS	
DEILRSV	DRIVELS	
DEILRSW	SWIRLED	
	WILDERS	
DEILRTU	DILUTER	
DEILRTW	TWIRLED	
DEILRTY	TIREDLY	
DEILRVY	DEVILRY	
DEILRWY	WEIRDLY	
DEILRWZ	WRIZLED	
DEILRZZ	DRIZZLE	
DEILSTT	STILTED	
DEILSTU	DILUTES	
DEILSTW	WILDEST	
DEILSTY	DISTYLE	
DEILSZZ	SIZZLED	
DEILTTT	TITTLED	
DEILTTU	TITULED	
DEILTTW	TWILTED	
DEIMMMU	MUMMIED	
DEIMMOT	TOMMIED	
DEIMMPR	PRIMMED	
DEIMMRS	DIMMERS	
DEIMMRT	MIDTERM	
	TRIMMED	
DEIMMRU	DUMMIER	
	IMMURED	
DEIMMST	DIMMEST	
DEIMMSU	DUMMIES	
	MEDIUMS	
DEIMNNU	MINUEND	
DEIMNOP	IMPONED	
DEIMNOR	MINORED	
DEIMNOS	MISDONE	
DEIMNPS	IMPENDS	
DEIMNRS	MINDERS	
	REMINDS	
DEIMNRU	UNRIMED	
DEIMNSS	DIMNESS	
	MISSEND	
DEIMNST	MINDSET	
DEIMNSW	MISWEND	
DEIMNTU	MINUTED	
	MUNITED	
	MUTINED	
DEIMNUX	UNMIXED	
DEIMOOR	DOOMIER	
	MOIDORE	
	MOODIER	
DEIMOOS	MOODIES	
DEIMOPS	IMPOSED	
DEIMORS	MISDOER	
	MOIDERS	
DEIMORU	ERODIUM	
DEIMOSS	MISDOES	
DEIMOST	DOMIEST	
	MODISTE	
	MOISTED	
DEIMOTT	OMITTED	
DEIMOTV	MOTIVED	
	VOMITED	
DEIMPPR	PRIMPED	
DEIMPRT	DIREMPT	
DEIMPRU	DUMPIER	
	UMPIRED	
DEIMPSU	DUMPIES	
DEIMPTU	IMPUTED	
DEIMRRS	SMIRRED	
DEIMRSW	MISDREW	
DEIMRUU	UREDIUM	
DEIMSST	DEMISTS	
DEIMSSU	MISUSED	
DEIMSTT	SMITTED	
DEIMSTU	MUISTED	
	TEDIUMS	
DEIMSTY	STYMIED	
DEINNNU	NUNDINE	
DEINNOO	ONIONED	
DEINNOP	PINNOED	
DEINNOR	ENDIRON	
DEINNOS	ONDINES	
DEINNOT	INTONED	
	NOINTED	
DEINNRS	DINNERS	
DEINNRU	DUNNIER	
	INURNED	
DEINNST	DENTINS	
	INDENTS	
	INTENDS	
DEINNSU	DUNNIES	
	UNDINES	
DEINNSW	ENWINDS	
DEINNTU	DUNNITE	
DEINNTW	TWINNED	
DEINOPR	POINDER	
	PROINED	
DEINOPS	DISPONE	
	SPINODE	
DEINOPT	POINTED	
DEINOQU	QUOINED	
DEINORR	DRONIER	
DEINORS	DONSIER	
	INDORSE	
	ROSINED	
DEINORU	DOURINE	

DEINORW	DOWNIER, WINDORE
DEINOSS	ONSIDES
DEINOST	DITONES, STONIED
DEINPPS	SNIPPED
DEINPRS	PINDERS
DEINPRT	PRINTED
DEINPST	STIPEND
DEINPSU	UNIPEDS, UNSPIDE, UNSPIED
DEINPUW	UNWIPED
DEINRST	TINDERS
DEINRSU	INSURED
DEINRSV	VERDINS
DEINRSW	REWINDS, WINDERS
DEINRTT	TRIDENT
DEINRTU	INTRUDE, TURDINE, UNTIRED, UNTRIDE, UNTRIED
DEINRTX	DEXTRIN
DEINRTY	TINDERY
DEINRUW	UNWIRED
DEINSST	DISNEST, DISSENT, SNIDEST
DEINSSV	VENDISS
DEINSSW	WINDSES
DEINSTT	DENTIST, DISTENT, STINTED
DEINSTU	DISTUNE, DUNITES
DEINSTY	DENSITY, DESTINY
DEINSUZ	UNSIZED
DEINUVW	UNWIVED
DEIOORS	OROIDES
DEIOORW	WOODIER
DEIOOST	OSTEOID
DEIOOSW	WOODIES
DEIOOVV	VOIVODE
DEIOOWW	WOIWODE
DEIOPPP	POPPIED
DEIOPPS	DOPPIES
DEIOPRS	PERIODS
DEIOPRT	DIOPTER, DIOPTRE, PERIDOT, PROTEID
DEIOPRV	PROVIDE
DEIOPSS	DISPOSE
DEIOPST	DEPOSIT, DOPIEST, PODITES, POSITED, SOPITED, TOPSIDE
DEIOPSV	VESPOID
DEIOPTT	TIPTOED
DEIOPTV	PIVOTED
DEIOQTU	QUOITED
DEIORRT	DORTIER
DEIORRW	ROWDIER, WORDIER, WORRIED
DEIORSS	DORISES, DOSSIER
DEIORST	EDITORS, ROISTED, ROSITED, SORTIED, STEROID, STORIED, TIERODS, TRIODES
DEIORSV	DEVISOR, DEVOIRS, VISORED, VOIDERS
DEIORSW	DOWRIES, ROWDIES, WEIRDOS
DEIORSZ	DORIZES
DEIORTT	DOTTIER
DEIORTU	ETOURDI, IODURET, OUTRIDE
DEIORTZ	ROZITED
DEIORVZ	VIZORED
DEIORWW	WIDOWER
DEIOSTT	DOTIEST, STOITED
DEIOSTU	OUTSIDE, TEDIOUS
DEIOSTV	DOVIEST
DEIOSTW	DOWIEST
DEIOSTX	EXODIST
DEIOSTZ	DOZIEST
DEIOSUV	DEVIOUS
DEIOTUV	OUTVIED
DEIPPPU	PUPPIED
DEIPPQU	QUIPPED
DEIPPRS	DIPPERS
DEIPPRT	TRIPPED
DEIPPSU	DUPPIES
DEIPRSS	SPIDERS
DEIPRST	SPIRTED, STRIPED
DEIPRSU	PUDSIER, SIRUPED
DEIPRSY	SPIDERY
DEIPSSU	UPSIDES
DEIPSTT	SPITTED
DEIPSTU	DISPUTE
DEIPSXY	PYXIDES
DEIPTTU	PUTTIED, TITUPED
DEIQRSU	SQUIRED
DEIQRTU	QUIRTED
DEIQTTU	QUITTED
DEIQUZZ	QUIZZED
DEIRRST	STIRRED
DEIRRSU	DRUSIER, DURRIES
DEIRRSV	DRIVERS
DEIRRUX	DRUXIER
DEIRSST	DISSERT, STRIDES
DEIRSSU	DISEURS, SUDSIER
DEIRSTU	DUSTIER, REDUITS, STUDIER
DEIRSTV	DIVERTS, STRIVED, VERDITS
DEISSST	DESISTS
DEISSSU	DISUSES
DEISSTU	STUDIES, TISSUED
DEISSTV	DIVESTS
DEISTTW	DEWITTS, TWISTED
DEISWZZ	SWIZZED
DEITTTW	TWITTED
DEJLOST	JOSTLED
DEJLSTU	JUSTLED
DEJOSTU	JOUSTED
DEKKLSU	SKULKED
DEKKNSU	SKUNKED
DEKLLNO	KNOLLED
DEKLNOP	PLONKED
DEKLNPU	PLUNKED
DEKLNRU	KNURLED, RUNKLED
DEKLRSU	SKUDLER
DEKNNRU	DRUNKEN
DEKNOOS	SNOOKED
DEKNOPR	PRONKED
DEKNOQU	QUONKED
DEKNOSW	SNOWKED
DEKNOSY	DONKEYS
DEKNOTT	KNOTTED
DEKNOTU	KNOUTED
DEKNOUY	UNYOKED
DEKNPSU	SPUNKED
DEKNRRU	DRUNKER
DEKNRSU	DUNKERS
DEKNRTU	TRUNKED
DEKNSSU	DUSKENS
DEKOOPS	SPOOKED
DEKOOST	DOOKETS, STOOKED
DEKOOTW	KOTOWED
DEKOPST	DESKTOP
DEKORST	STROKED
DEKORWY	KEYWORD
DEKOSSU	KUDOSES
DEKRSUY	DUYKERS
DEKSSTU	DUSKEST
DELLMOO	MODELLO
DELLOOW	WOOLLED
DELLOPR	PROLLED, REDPOLL
DELLORR	DROLLER
DELLORT	TROLLED
DELLOSU	DUELLOS
DELLOVW	LOWVELD
DELLSTU	DULLEST
DELMMSU	SLUMMED
DELMNOS	DOLMENS
DELMOOS	SLOOMED
DELMOOW	ELMWOOD
DELMORS	SMOLDER
DELMORU	MOULDER, REMOULD
DELMOSU	MODULES, MOUSLED
DELMOSY	SMOYLED
DELMOTT	MOTTLED
DELMOTU	MOULTED
DELMOUV	VOLUMED
DELMPPU	PLUMPED
DELMPRU	RUMPLED
DELMPSU	DUMPLES, SLUMPED
DELMUZZ	MUZZLED
DELNOOS	NOODLES, SNOOLED
DELNORS	RONDELS
DELNORT	ENTROLD
DELNORU	LOUNDER, ROUNDEL, ROUNDLE
DELNOSS	OLDNESS
DELNOSU	LOUDENS, NODULES, NOUSLED
DELNOSW	DOWLNES
DELNOSZ	DONZELS
DELNOTY	NOTEDLY
DELNOUV	UNLOVED
DELNOWY	DOWLNEY
DELNPRU	PLUNDER
DELNRSU	LURDENS, NURDLES, NURSLED, RUNDLES
DELNRTU	RUNDLET, TRUNDLE
DELNRUU	UNRULED
DELNSSU	DULNESS
DELNUWY	UNWELDY
DELNUZZ	NUZZLED
DELOOPP	PLEOPOD
DELOOPS	POODLES, SPOOLED
DELOORT	ROOTLED
DELOORW	WOOLDER
DELOOST	STOOLED
DELOOTT	TOOTLED
DELOPPP	PLOPPED, POPPLED
DELOPPR	DROPPLE
DELOPPS	SLOPPED
DELOPPT	TOPPLED
DELOPRS	POLDERS
DELOPRT	DROPLET
DELOPRU	POULDER, POULDRE, PROULED
DELOPRW	PROWLED
DELOPSU	SOUPLED
DELOPSY	DEPLOYS, PODLEYS
DELOPTT	PLOTTED
DELORRY	ORDERLY
DELORSS	DORSELS, RODLESS, SOLDERS
DELORST	DROLEST, OLDSTER, STRODLE
DELORSW	WELDORS
DELORSY	YODLERS
DELORTT	DOTTLER, DOTTREL
DELORTU	TROULED
DELORUV	LOUVRED
DELOSSS	DOSSELS
DELOSSU	DULOSES
DELOSTT	DOTTLES, SLOTTED
DELOSTU	LOUDEST, OULDEST, TOUSLED
DELOSYY	DOYLEYS
DELOSZZ	SOZZLED
DELOTUV	VOLUTED
DELOTUZ	TOUZLED
DELPPRU	PURPLED
DELPPSU	SUPPLED
DELPRSU	DRUPELS, SLURPED
DELPSSU	PLUSSED
DELPSTU	DUPLETS
DELPSUY	SPULYED
DELPUZZ	PUZZLED
DELRRSU	SLURRED
DELRSTU	LUSTRED, RUSTLED, STRUDEL
DELRTTU	TURTLED
DELSSTU	TUSSLED
DELSTTU	SUTTLED
DELUWZZ	WUZZLED
DEMMRRU	DRUMMER
DEMMSTU	STUMMED
DEMNOOR	MORENDO
DEMNOOW	WOODMEN
DEMNORS	MODERNS, RODSMEN
DEMNORT	MORDENT
DEMNORU	MOURNED
DEMNORY	DEMONRY
DEMNOST	ENDMOST
DEMNOTU	DEMOUNT, MOUNTED
DEMNOUV	UNMOVED
DEMNSTU	DUSTMEN
DEMOOPP	POPEDOM

DEMOOPR	PREDOOM	DENOSTT	SNOTTED	DEORTTU	TUTORED	DGGINRY	GRYDING
DEMOOPS	SPOOMED	DENOSTU	DEUTONS	DEORTUU	OUTDURE	DGGNOSU	DUGONGS
DEMOORS	DROOMES		SNOUTED	DEOSSSW	SOWSSED	DGHHOOO	HOGHOOD
	SMOORED	DENOSUW	SWOUNED	DEOSSTW	DOWSETS	DGHIILN	HIDLING
DEMOORT	MOTORED	DENPRSU	SPURNED	DEOSSYY	ODYSSEY		HILDING
DEMOORV	VROOMED	DENPRTU	PRUDENT	DEOSTTT	STOTTED	DGHIINS	DISHING
DEMOOSS	OSMOSED		PRUNTED	DEOSTTU	DUETTOS		HIDINGS
DEMOOST	SMOOTED		UPTREND		TESTUDO		SHINDIG
DEMOOTT	MOTTOED	DENPSSU	SUSPEND	DEOSTTW	SWOTTED	DGHILNO	HOLDING
DEMOOTU	OUTMODE		UPSENDS	DEOSTUU	DUTEOUS	DGHILNY	HYLDING
DEMOPRT	TROMPED	DENRSSU	SUNDERS	DEOSTUX	TUXEDOS	DGHILOS	GOLDISH
DEMOPST	STOMPED		UNDRESS	DEPRRSU	SPURRED	DGHILPY	DIGLYPH
DEMORRS	DORMERS	DENRSSY	DRYNESS	DEPRRUY	PRUDERY	DGHINOO	HOODING
DEMORRU	RUMORED	DENRSTU	RETUNDS	DEPRSTU	SPURTED	DGHINOR	HORDING
DEMORST	STORMED	DENRSUU	UNSURED	DEPRSUU	PURSUED	DGHINSU	DUSHING
DEMOSSU	SMOUSED	DENSSTY	SYNDETS		USURPED	DGHINTU	UNDIGHT
DEMOSTT	DOMETTS	DENSSUW	SUNDEWS	DEPRSUY	SYRUPED	DGHIOOS	GOODISH
DEMOSTU	MOUSTED	DENSTTU	STUDENT	DERRSTU	RUSTRED	DGHIOPS	DOGSHIP
	SMOUTED		STUNTED	DERSSSU	SUDSERS		GODSHIP
DEMOSTY	MODESTY	DENTUVY	DUVETYN	DERSSTU	DUSTERS	DGHOOPS	HOPDOGS
DEMPRSU	DUMPERS	DEOOPPS	OPPOSED		TRUSSED	DGHORTU	DROUGHT
DEMPRTU	TRUMPED	DEOOPRS	SPOORED	DERSTTU	STURTED	DGHOTUY	DOUGHTY
DEMPSTU	STUMPED	DEOOPRT	TORPEDO		TRUSTED	DGIIKLN	KIDLING
DEMRRSU	MURDERS		TROOPED	DERSTTY	TRYSTED	DGIIKNN	DINKING
	SMURRED	DEOOPST	STOOPED	DERSTUU	SUTURED		KINDING
DEMSTTU	SMUTTED	DEOOPSW	SWOOPED	DFFGINO	DOFFING	DGIIKNR	DIRKING
DENNORT	DONNERT	DEOOPSX	EXOPODS	DFFGINU	DUFFING	DGIIKNS	DISKING
	TENDRON	DEOORRT	REDROOT	DFFIIMR	MIDRIFF	DGIILLN	DILLING
DENNORU	ENROUND	DEOORST	ROOSTED	DFFIIRT	TRIFFID	DGIILNO	LOIDING
DENNOST	STONNED	DEOORTU	OUTRODE	DFFIMOR	DIFFORM	DGIILNR	DIRLING
	TENDONS	DEOORTW	WROOTED	DFFLOOU	FOODFUL	DGIILNS	SIDLING
DENNOTU	UNNOTED	DEOOSTT	TOOTSED	DFGGIIN	FIDGING		SLIDING
	UNTONED	DEOOSTU	OUTDOES	DFGGINU	FUDGING	DGIILNW	WILDING
DENNOUW	ENWOUND	DEOPPPR	PROPPED	DFGHIOS	DOGFISH	DGIILRS	RIDGILS
	UNOWNED	DEOPPQU	QUOPPED	DFGIINN	FINDING	DGIILRY	RIGIDLY
DENNOUZ	UNZONED	DEOPPRR	DROPPER	DFGIINY	DIGNIFY	DGIIMMN	DIMMING
DENNRSU	UNDERNS	DEOPPRS	DOPPERS	DFGILNO	FOLDING	DGIIMMN	MINDING
DENNSTU	DUNNEST	DEOPPST	STOPPED	DFGINNO	FONDING	DGIIMNS	SMIDGIN
	STUNNED	DEOPPSW	SWOPPED	DFGINNU	FUNDING	DGIIMOP	PIGMOID
DENNTUU	UNTUNED	DEOPRRU	PROUDER	DFGINOR	FORDING	DGIIMOS	SIGMOID
DENOOPS	SNOOPED	DEOPRST	DEPORTS	DFGINOU	FUNGOID	DGIINNN	DINNING
	SPOONED		REDTOPS	DFGMOOY	FOGYDOM	DGIINNR	RINDING
DENOOSS	NOSODES		SPORTED	DFHILSU	DISHFUL	DGIINNS	NIDINGS
DENOOST	SNOOTED	DEOPRSU	POUDERS	DFHIMSU	MUDFISH		SINDING
	STOODEN		POUDRES	DFILMMO	FILMDOM	DGIINNT	DINTING
DENOOSW	SWOONED	DEOPRSW	POWDERS	DFILMNU	MINDFUL		TINDING
DENOOSZ	SNOOZED	DEOPRTU	TROUPED	DFILNOP	PINFOLD	DGIINNU	INDUING
DENOOTU	DUOTONE	DEOPRWY	POWDERY	DFILNOS	INFOLDS	DGIINNW	DWINING
	OUTDONE	DEOPSST	DESPOTS	DFILOSX	SIXFOLD		WINDING
DENOOUW	UNWOOED	DEOPSSU	SPOUSED	DFILOTW	TWIFOLD	DGIINOS	INDIGOS
DENOPPR	PROPEND	DEOPSTT	SPOTTED	DFILTUU	DUTIFUL	DGIINOV	VOIDING
DENOPPU	UNPOPED	DEOPSTU	SPOUTED	DFIMNUY	MUNDIFY	DGIINOW	WINDIGO
DENOPRS	PONDERS	DEOPTTY	TYPTOED	DFIMOOS	FOODISM	DGIINPP	DIPPING
	RESPOND	DEOQRTU	TORQUED	DFIMORS	DISFORM	DGIINPR	PRIDING
DENOPRT	PORTEND	DEORRSS	DORSERS	DFLMOOU	DOOMFUL	DGIINPS	PIDGINS
	PROTEND	DEORRST	DORTERS	DFLNOSU	UNFOLDS	DGIINPU	PINGUID
DENOPRU	POUNDER		RODSTER	DFLOOTW	TWOFOLD	DGIINRS	RIDINGS
	UNROPED	DEORRSU	ORDURES	DFLOPRY	DROPFLY	DGIINRT	DIRTING
DENOPRV	PROVEND	DEORRSV	DROVERS	DFLOTWY	TWYFOLD	DGIINRV	DRIVING
DENOPRY	PROYNED	DEORRSW	REWORDS	DFNNOUU	UNFOUND	DGIINRY	YIRDING
DENOPSU	UNPOSED		SWORDER	DFNORUY	FOUNDRY	DGIINSS	DISSING
DENOPTY	POYNTED	DEORSSS	DOSSERS	DFOORSX	OXFORDS		SIDINGS
DENOPUX	EXPOUND		DROSSES	DGGGIIN	DIGGING	DGIINST	TIDINGS
DENORRU	RONDURE	DEORSSU	DOUSERS	DGGGINO	DOGGING	DGIINSV	DIVINGS
	ROUNDER	DEORSSW	DOWSERS	DGGHIOS	DOGGISH	DGIINTT	DITTING
	UNORDER		DROWSES	DGGIILN	GILDING	DGIINTY	DIGNITY
DENORRW	DROWNER	DEORSTT	DETORTS		GLIDING		TIDYING
DENORST	RODENTS	DEORSTU	DETOURS	DGGIINN	DINGING	DGIIORT	TIGROID
	SNORTED		DOUREST	DGGIINR	GIRDING	DGIJOSU	JUDOGIS
DENORSU	ENDUROS		DOUTERS		GRIDING	DGIKMNO	KINGDOM
	RESOUND		OUTREDS		RIDGING	DGIKNNU	DUNKING
	SOUNDER		ROUSTED	DGGIINU	GUIDING	DGIKNNY	KYNDING
	UNDOERS	DEORSTW	STROWED	DGGIJNU	JUDGING	DGIKNOO	DOOKING
DENORSV	VENDORS		WORSTED	DGGILNO	GODLING	DGIKNOS	DOGSKIN
DENORSW	DOWNERS	DEORSTY	DESTROY		LODGING	DGIKNSU	DUSKING
	WONDERS		ROYSTED	DGGIMNU	MUDGING	DGILLNO	DOLLING
DENORSY	YONDERS		STROYED	DGGINNO	DONGING	DGILLNU	DULLING
DENORUW	REWOUND	DEORSUV	DEVOURS	DGGINNU	DUNGING	DGILLOY	GODLILY
	WOUNDER	DEORTTT	TROTTED		NUDGING	DGILMNO	MOLDING

DGILNOR GIRLOND
         LORDING
DGILNOY YODLING
DGILNSU UNGILDS
DGILNYY DYINGLY
DGILOST DIGLOTS
DGILRUY GUILDRY
DGIMNOO DOOMING
DGIMNPU DUMPING
DGIMOPY PYGMOID
DGINNNO DONNING
DGINNNU DUNNING
DGINNOP PONDING
DGINNOR DRONING
DGINNOS DONINGS
         ONDINGS
DGINNOU UNDOING
DGINNOW DOWNING
DGINNSY SYNDING
DGINNTU DUNTING
         TUNDING
DGINNUW WINDGUN
DGINNUY UNDYING
DGINOOW WOODING
DGINOPP DOPPING
DGINOPS DOPINGS
         PONGIDS
DGINORR DORRING
DGINORS RODINGS
DGINORT DORTING
DGINORV DROVING
DGINORW WORDING
DGINOSS DOSSING
DGINOST DOTINGS
DGINOSU DOUSING
         GUIDONS
DGINOSW DISGOWN
         DOWSING
DGINOSZ DOZINGS
DGINOTT DOTTING
DGINOTU DOUTING
DGINPPU DUPPING
DGINRSU UNGIRDS
DGINRSY DRYINGS
DGINSSU SUDSING
DGINSTU DUSTING
DGIOPRY PRODIGY
DGIOSTW GODWITS
DGISSTU DISGUST
DGLNOUY UNGODLY
DGLOOOW LOGWOOD
DGLOPSY SPLODGY
DGLOSYY DYSLOGY
DGMOPRU GUMDROP
DGMORUU GURUDOM
DGNOOOR GODROON
DGNOORS DRONGOS
DGNOOSS GODSONS
DGNOOSW GODOWNS
DGNOOTW DOGTOWN
DGNORSU GROUNDS
DGNOSSU SUNDOGS
DGOORTT DOGTROT
DGOSTUU DUGOUTS
DHIILNS HIDLINS
DHIILOT LITHOID
DHIILSW WILDISH
DHIIMMS DIMMISH
DHIIMNO HOMINID
DHIIMPS MIDSHIP
DHIINRU HIRUDIN
DHIIOPX XIPHOID
DHIIORZ RHIZOID
DHIIOST HISTOID
DHIKSSU DUSKISH
DHILLOS DOLLISH
DHILLSU DULLISH
DHILMUY HUMIDLY

DHILNOP DOLPHIN
DHILOST DOLTISH
DHILOSU LOUDISH
DHILPSU LUDSHIP
DHILPSY SYLPHID
DHILRTY THIRDLY
DHIMOPR DIMORPH
DHIMORU HUMIDOR
         RHODIUM
DHIMPSU DUMPISH
DHINNOS DONNISH
DHINNSU DUNNISH
DHINOPS DONSHIP
DHINOPY HYPNOID
DHINORS DISHORN
         DRONISH
DHIOOST DHOOTIS
DHIOPTY TYPHOID
DHIORSW WORDISH
DHIORTY THYROID
DHIPRSU PRUDISH
DHIPRSY SYRPHID
DHKMOOU MUDHOOK
DHKORSY DROSHKY
DHLMOOU HOODLUM
DHLOOTU HOLDOUT
DHLOPSU UPHOLDS
DHMMRUU HUMDRUM
DHMNOYY HYMNODY
DHNNOOU NUNHOOD
DHNOOSU UNHOODS
DHOOOOS HOODOOS
DHOOPRU UPHOORD
DHOORSU RHODOUS
DHOPRSU PUSHROD
DHORSSU SHROUDS
DHORSTU DROUTHS
DHORSUY HYDROUS
         SHROUDY
DHORTUY DROUTHY
DHORXYY HYDROXY
DIIIMRU IRIDIUM
DIIIMSV DIVISIM
DIIINPS INSIPID
DIIJNOS DISJOIN
DIIKKNS KIDSKIN
DIIKLNS DISLINK
DIIKNOT DOITKIN
DIILLST DISTILL
DIILLVY LIVIDLY
DIILMNS DISLIMN
DIILMOO MODIOLI
DIILMOS IDOLISM
DIILMTY TIMIDLY
DIILNNU INDULIN
DIILNWY WINDILY
DIILOPS LIPOIDS
DIILOST IDOLIST
DIILQSU LIQUIDS
DIILRSU SILURID
DIILRTY DIRTILY
DIILSST DISTILS
DIILVVY VIVIDLY
DIILYZZ DIZZILY
DIIMNOR MIDIRON
DIIMNSU INDIUMS
DIIMORS DIORISM
DIIMOSS IODISMS
DIIMSSS DISMISS
DIIMSTW DIMWITS
DIIMSUV VIDIMUS
DIINNOT TONDINI
DIINNSW INWINDS
DIINOQU QUINOID
DIINORS SORDINI
DIINOSX DIOXINS
DIIOPRS SPIROID
DIIORSV DIVISOR
         VIROIDS

DIITUVY VIDUITY
DIJOSTU JUDOIST
DIKKOPS DIKKOPS
DIKLNOR LORDKIN
DIKLSTU KIDULTS
DIKLSUY DUSKILY
DIKNNSU NUDNIKS
DIKNORV DVORNIK
DIKOORT DROOKIT
DIKOOSS SKIDOOS
DIKORTU DROUKIT
DILLOSY SOLIDLY
DILLPSY PSYLLID
DILLRUY LURIDLY
DILMNRU DRUMLIN
DILMOOY MOODILY
DILMORS MILORDS
DILMOST MISTOLD
DILMOSU SOLIDUM
DILMOSY ODYLISM
DILMTUY TUMIDLY
DILNNSU DUNLINS
DILNOOS OODLINS
DILNOPS DIPLONS
DILNOPT DIPLONT
DILNOQU QUODLIN
DILNORT INTROLD
DILNOSU UNSOLID
DILNOXY INDOXYL
DILNPSU LISPUND
DILNPSY SPINDLY
DILNSTU INDULTS
DILORTU DILUTOR
DILORWY ROWDILY
         WORDILY
DILOSSS DOSSILS
DILOSSU DULOSIS
         SOLIDUS
DILOSTY STYLOID
DILRYZZ DRIZZLY
DILSTUY DUSTILY
DIMMOST MIDMOST
DIMNNOO MIDNOON
DIMNNOS DONNISM
DIMNNOT DINMONT
DIMNOOS DOMINOS
DIMNOPU IMPOUND
DIMNSSU NUDISMS
DIMOPSU SPODIUM
DIMORSW MISWORD
DIMOSST MODISTS
DIMOSSU SODIUMS
DIMOSSW WISDOMS
DIMRTUU TRIDUUM
DIMRUUV DUUMVIR
DINNOOR RONDINO
DINNOOT TONDINO
DINNOPW PINDOWN
DINNOSS SINDONS
DINNOUW INWOUND
DINNSUW UNWINDS
DINOORS INDOORS
         SORDINO
DINOORT TORDION
DINOOST ISODONT
DINOPSU DUPIONS
         UNIPODS
DINORSU DURIONS
DINORTU TURDION
DINORWW WINDROW
DINOSSW DISOWNS
DINOSWW WINDOWS
DINOTUW OUTWIND
DINPSTU PUNDITS
DINPSUW UPWINDS
DINRSSU SUNDRIS
DINSSTU NUDISTS
DIOOPSS ISOPODS
DIOORST DISROOT

         TOROIDS
DIOORTT RIDOTTO
DIOOSTX TOXOIDS
DIOPRST DISPORT
         TORPIDS
         TRIPODS
DIOPRTY TRIPODY
DIOPSST DISPOST
DIORRST STRIDOR
DIORSTT DISTORT
DIOSSTU STUDIOS
DIOSUUV VIDUOUS
DIPRSTU DISRUPT
DIPSSTU STUPIDS
DIRSTUY SURDITY
DJNNOOS DONJONS
DKNNRUU UNDRUNK
DKNOOPS PONDOKS
DKOOOOS KOODOOS
DKOOOSZ ODZOOKS
DLLOOPS DOLLOPS
DLLORWY WORLDLY
DLMNOOY MYLODON
DLMNOUU UNMOULD
DLMOSUU MODULUS
DLNOPRU PULDRON
DLNOPSY SPONDYL
DLNORSU UNLORDS
DLNORUY ROUNDLY
DLNOSUY SOUNDLY
DLOOPPY POLYPOD
DLOOPSS PODSOLS
DLOOPSZ PODZOLS
DLOOPTY TYLOPOD
DLOOPUY DUOPOLY
DLOOPWY PLYWOOD
DLOORSU DOLOURS
DLOOSTU OUTSOLD
DLOOTTU OUTTOLD
DLOPRUY PROUDLY
DLOSTUW WOULDST
DMNOOOP MONOPOD
DMNOORS DROMONS
DMNOOTW TOWMOND
DMNOSSU OSMUNDS
DMORTUW MUDWORT
DNNOOST DONNOTS
DNNORUU UNROUND
DNNORUW RUNDOWN
DNNOSUU UNSOUND
DNNOUUW UNWOUND
DNNRTUU TURNDUN
DNNSTUU TUNDUNS
DNOORTU OROTUND
DNOOTUW NUTWOOD
DNOPUUW UPWOUND
DNORSST STRONDS
DNORSTU ROTUNDS
DNOSSTU STOUNDS
DNOSSTW STOWNDS
DNOSSUW SWOUNDS
DNOSSWW SWOWNDS
DOOOOSV VOODOOS
DOOORSU ODOROUS
DOOORTU OUTDOOR
DOOPRSU UROPODS
DOOPRSY PROSODY
DOOPRTU DROPOUT
DOOPSTU UPSTOOD
DOORRTU DORTOUR
DOOSUUV VOUDOUS
DORSSTU STROUDS
DORSUVY DYVOURS
DORUVYY DYVOURY
EEEEFRR REFEREE
EEEEGTX EXEGETE
EEEENTT ENTETEE
EEEEPST TEEPEES

EEEEPSW	PEEWEES
EEEFFFO	FEOFFEE
EEEFFOR	OFFEREE
EEEFFRS	EFFERES
EEEFGRU	REFUGEE
EEEFHRS	SHEREEF
EEEFIRS	FEERIES
EEEFLRR	FLEERER
EEEFLRS	FEELERS
EEEFLRT	FLEETER
EEEFMNR	FREEMEN
EEEFNRS	ENFREES
EEEFORS	FORESEE
EEEFRRS	REEFERS
EEEFRRZ	FREEZER
EEEFRSZ	FREEZES
EEEGHNW	WHEENGE
EEEGIKR	GEEKIER
EEEGILS	ELEGIES, ELEGISE
EEEGILZ	ELEGIZE
EEEGINP	EPIGENE
EEEGINR	GREENIE
EEEGIPR	PERIGEE
EEEGLMN	GLEEMEN
EEEGLNT	GENTEEL
EEEGMRR	REMERGE
EEEGMRS	EMERGES
EEEGNPR	EPERGNE
EEEGNPS	PEENGES
EEEGNRR	GREENER, RENEGER
EEEGNRS	RENEGES
EEEGNRU	RENEGUE
EEEGNRV	REVENGE
EEEGNSS	GENESES
EEEGNTT	GENETTE
EEEGRRT	GREETER, REGREET
EEEGRSS	GREESES
EEEGRST	GREETES
EEEGRSZ	GEEZERS
EEEGRUX	EXERGUE
EEEHILW	WHEELIE
EEEHISZ	HEEZIES
EEEHLNW	ENWHEEL
EEEHLPW	WHEEPLE
EEEHLRS	HEELERS, REHEELS
EEEHLRW	WHEELER
EEEHLST	LETHEES
EEEHLWZ	WHEEZLE
EEEHNST	ETHENES
EEEHNSX	HEXENES
EEEHPRS	PHEERES
EEEHPSS	PHEESES
EEEHPSZ	PHEEZES
EEEHRRS	SHEERER
EEEHRST	SEETHER
EEEHSST	SEETHES
EEEHSTT	ESTHETE, TEETHES
EEEHSWZ	WHEEZES
EEEIJLS	JEELIES
EEEIKLS	KEELIES
EEEIKRR	REEKIER
EEEILRR	LEERIER
EEEILRS	SEELIER
EEEILRV	RELIEVE
EEEILST	EELIEST
EEEIMMS	MEEMIES
EEEIMNS	ENEMIES
EEEIMNT	EMETINE
EEEIMPR	PREEMIE
EEEIMRS	EMERIES
EEEIMRT	EREMITE
EEEINQU	QUEENIE
EEEINRT	TEENIER
EEEINRW	WEENIER
EEEINSW	WEENIES
EEEIPRR	PEERIER
EEEIPRS	PEERIES, SEEPIER
EEEIPRW	WEEPIER
EEEIPSU	EPUISEE
EEEIPSW	WEEPIES
EEEIRRT	RETIREE
EEEIRRV	REVERIE
EEEIRST	EERIEST
EEEIRSV	VEERIES
EEEIRSZ	RESEIZE
EEEISTW	SWEETIE
EEEJNPY	JEEPNEY
EEEJPRS	JEEPERS
EEEJRRS	JEERERS
EEEJSST	JESTEES
EEEKKRS	KEEKERS
EEEKLLU	UKELELE
EEEKLMN	KEELMEN
EEEKLNR	KNEELER
EEEKLNS	SLEEKEN
EEEKLPW	EKPWELE
EEEKLRS	KEELERS, SLEEKER
EEEKMNS	MEEKENS
EEEKMST	MEEKEST
EEEKNPT	KEEPNET
EEEKNRS	KEENERS
EEEKNST	KEENEST
EEEKPRS	KEEPERS
EEEKRSS	KREESES, SEEKERS
EEEKRST	SKEETER
EEELMNR	REELMEN
EEELMNT	ELEMENT
EEELMPX	EXEMPLE
EEELMSX	LEXEMES
EEELNST	STELENE
EEELNSV	ELEVENS
EEELPRS	PEELERS, SLEEPER, SPEELER
EEELPRT	REPLETE
EEELPST	STEEPLE
EEELRRS	REELERS
EEELRSV	SLEEVER
EEELRTV	LEVERET
EEELSSS	LESSEES
EEELSST	TELESES
EEELSSV	SLEEVES
EEELSSY	EYELESS
EEELSTX	TELEXES
EEELSTY	EYELETS
EEELTTX	TELETEX
EEEMMSS	SEMEMES
EEEMNRS	MENEERS
EEEMNSS	NEMESES
EEEMNST	MENTEES
EEEMORT	EROTEME
EEEMRSS	SEEMERS
EEEMRST	TEEMERS
EEEMRTX	EXTREME
EEEMSST	ESTEEMS, MESTEES
EEEMSTT	MEETEST
EEEMSTU	EMEUTES
EEENNPT	PENTENE
EEENNRT	ETRENNE
EEENNTT	ENTENTE
EEENPRT	TERPENE
EEENPRV	PREVENE
EEENPSS	PENSEES
EEENPST	ENSTEEP, STEEPEN
EEENPSW	ENSWEEP
EEENPSX	EXPENSE
EEENRRS	SERENER, SNEERER
EEENRRT	ENTERER, TERREEN, TERRENE
EEENRRV	VENERER
EEENRRW	RENEWER
EEENRSS	SERENES
EEENRST	ENTREES, RETENES
EEENRSV	ENERVES, EVENERS, VENEERS
EEENRSZ	SNEEZER
EEENRTV	EVENTER
EEENRTX	EXTERNE
EEENRUV	REVENUE, UNREEVE
EEENSSZ	SNEEZES
EEENSTV	EVENEST
EEENSTW	SWEETEN
EEENSTX	EXTENSE
EEENSVW	VENEWES
EEENSWY	SWEENEY
EEEOPPS	EPOPEES
EEEORSV	OVERSEE
EEEORSY	EYESORE
EEEORVY	OVEREYE
EEEPPRS	PEEPERS
EEEPRSS	PEERESS
EEEPRST	ESTREPE, STEEPER
EEEPRSV	PEEVERS, PREEVES
EEEPRSW	SWEEPER, WEEPERS
EEEPRSZ	SPREEZE
EEEQRRU	QUEERER, REQUERE
EEEQSUZ	SQUEEZE
EEERRRV	REVERER
EEERRST	RETREES, STEERER
EEERRSV	RESERVE, REVERES, REVERSE, SEVERER
EEERSSS	SEERESS
EEERSTT	TEETERS, TERETES
EEERSTV	STEEVER
EEERSTW	SWEETER
EEERSUV	REVEUSE
EEERSUW	SERUEWE
EEERSVW	SERVEWE, WEEVERS
EEERTTW	TWEETER
EEESSTT	SETTEES, TESTEES
EEESSTV	STEEVES
EEESTTW	WEETEST
EEESTWZ	TWEEZES
EEFFFNO	ENFEOFF
EEFFFOR	FEOFFER
EEFFORR	OFFERER
EEFFOST	TOFFEES
EEFFSSU	EFFUSES
EEFFSTU	SUFFETE
EEFGILN	FEELING, FLEEING
EEFGINR	FEERING, FREEING, REEFING
EEFGINS	FEESING
EEFGINZ	FEEZING
EEFGLLU	GLEEFUL
EEFGLOR	FORELEG
EEFGLOS	SOLFEGE
EEFGRSU	REFUGES
EEFHIRS	HEIFERS
EEFHIRT	HEFTIER
EEFHISY	FISHEYE
EEFHLNS	ENFLESH
EEFHLRS	FLESHER, HERSELF
EEFHLSS	FLESHES
EEFHNRS	FRESHEN
EEFHORT	THEREOF
EEFHORW	WHEREOF
EEFHRRS	FRESHER, REFRESH
EEFHRSS	FRESHES
EEFHRST	FRESHET
EEFIIRR	FIERIER
EEFIIRS	REIFIES
EEFILLS	FELLIES
EEFILLX	FLEXILE
EEFILNO	OLEFINE
EEFILNS	FELINES
EEFILOR	FORELIE
EEFILRR	FERLIER
EEFILRS	FERLIES, RELIEFS
EEFILRT	FELTIER, FERTILE
EEFILST	FELSITE, LEFTIES, LIEFEST
EEFIMNR	FIREMEN
EEFIMRT	FEMITER
EEFINNR	FENNIER
EEFINNS	FENNIES
EEFINRR	FERNIER, REFINER
EEFINRS	ENFIRES, FEERINS, FINEERS, REFINES
EEFINRT	FEINTER
EEFINSS	FINESSE
EEFINSX	ENFIXES
EEFIPRS	PREIFES, PRIEFES
EEFIRRS	FERRIES
EEFIRRT	FERRITE
EEFIRSS	FRISEES
EEFIRSZ	FRIEZES
EEFISTV	FESTIVE
EEFLLOS	FELLOES
EEFLLRS	FELLERS
EEFLLRU	FUELLER
EEFLLST	FELLEST
EEFLLTY	FLEETLY
EEFLMTU	TEEMFUL
EEFLNNO	ENFELON
EEFLNNS	FENNELS
EEFLNOS	ONESELF
EEFLNRS	FRESNEL
EEFLNSS	FLENSES
EEFLOOV	FOVEOLE
EEFLORS	FORLESE
EEFLRRS	FERRELS
EEFLRRU	FERRULE
EEFLRST	FELTERS, REFLETS, TELFERS
EEFLRSU	FERULES, REFUELS
EEFLRTT	FETTLER
EEFLRTU	FLEURET
EEFLRUX	FLEXURE
EEFLSTT	FETTLES, LEFTEST
EEFLSUY	EYEFULS
EEFMNOR	FOREMEN

EEFMNRT FERMENT
EEFMOTT MOFETTE
EEFMPRU PERFUME
EEFMSTW FEWMETS
EEFMTTU FUMETTE
EEFNORT OFTENER
EEFNORZ ENFROZE
EEFNRRY FERNERY
EEFNRTV FERVENT
EEFNSSW FEWNESS
EEFORRV FOREVER
EEFORRZ REFROZE
EEFOTTU FOUETTE
EEFPRRS PREFERS
EEFPRSU PERFUSE
EEFRRST FERRETS
EEFRRSU REFUSER
EEFRRTU REFUTER
EEFRRTY FERRETY
EEFRSST FESTERS
EEFRSSU REFUSES
EEFRSTT FETTERS
EEFRSTU FEUTRES
        REFUTES
EEFRSTW FEWTERS
EEFSSTU FETUSES
EEGGGLR GLEGGER
EEGGHTU THUGGEE
EEGGILN GLEEING
        NEGLIGE
EEGGILR LEGGIER
EEGGINR GREEING
EEGGIPS PEGGIES
EEGGIST EGGIEST
EEGGISV VEGGIES
EEGGKRS SKEGGER
EEGGLRS EGGLERS
        LEGGERS
EEGGMNY YEGGMEN
EEGGMSU MUGGEES
EEGGNOR ENGORGE
EEGGNOY GEOGENY
EEGGORR REGORGE
EEGGORU GOUGERE
EEGGPRU PUGGREE
EEGHILN HEELING
EEGHINT THEEING
EEGHINY HYGIENE
EEGHINZ HEEZING
EEGHIRW REWEIGH
        WEIGHER
EEGHLNU LEUGHEN
EEGHNRT GREENTH
EEGHNRY GREYHEN
EEGHRTU TEUGHER
EEGHSSS GHESSES
EEGIIRS GRIESIE
EEGIJLN JEELING
EEGIJNR JEERING
EEGIKKN KEEKING
EEGIKLN KEELING
EEGIKNN KEENING
        KNEEING
EEGIKNP KEEPING
        PEEKING
EEGIKNR REEKING
EEGIKNS SEEKING
EEGIKNT KITENGE
EEGILLS GELLIES
EEGILNP LEEPING
        PEELING
EEGILNR LEERING
        REELING
EEGILNS LEESING
        SEELING
EEGILNT GENTILE
EEGILOS ELOGIES
EEGILRS LEIGERS
        LIEGERS

EEGILRV VELIGER
EEGILST ELEGIST
        ELEGITS
EEGIMMR GEMMIER
        IMMERGE
EEGIMNR MEERING
        REGIMEN
EEGIMNS SEEMING
EEGIMNT MEETING
        TEEMING
EEGIMNX EXEMING
EEGIMRS EMIGRES
        REGIMES
        REMIGES
EEGINNP PEENING
EEGINNR ENGINER
        INGENER
EEGINNS ENGINES
        NEESING
        SNEEING
EEGINNT TEENING
EEGINNU GENUINE
        INGENUE
EEGINNV EEVNING
        EVENING
EEGINNW ENEWING
        WEENING
EEGINNZ NEEZING
EEGINOP EPIGONE
EEGINOS SOIGNEE
EEGINPP PEEPING
EEGINPR PEERING
        PREEING
EEGINPS SEEPING
EEGINPV PEEVING
EEGINPW WEEPING
EEGINRS GREISEN
EEGINRT GENTIER
        INTEGER
        TEERING
        TREEING
EEGINRV REEVING
        REGIVEN
        VEERING
EEGINSS GENESIS
        SEEINGS
EEGINSW SEEWING
        SWEEING
EEGINTV VENTIGE
EEGINTW WEETING
EEGINTX EXIGENT
EEGIOST EGOTISE
        GOETIES
EEGIOTZ EGOTIZE
EEGIRRV GRIEVER
EEGIRSS SIEGERS
EEGIRSV GRIEVES
        REGIVES
EEGIRTT TERGITE
EEGIRTU GUERITE
EEGISTV VESTIGE
EEGKNOR KEROGEN
EEGKNRU GERENUK
EEGLLNS LEGLENS
EEGLLSS LEGLESS
EEGLLST LEGLETS
EEGLMMU GEMMULE
EEGLMSU EMULGES
        LEGUMES
EEGLNNS GENNELS
EEGLNOR ERELONG
EEGLNOU EUGENOL
EEGLNOZ LOZENGE
EEGLNRT GENTLER
EEGLNRY GREENLY
EEGLNST GENTLES
        LENGEST
EEGLRST REGLETS
EEGLRTY TELERGY

EEGMMRY GEMMERY
EEGMNOS EMONGES
        GENOMES
EEGMNRS GERMENS
EEGMNST SEGMENT
EEGMNSU EMUNGES
EEGMRRS MERGERS
EEGNNST GENNETS
EEGNOPS PONGEES
EEGNORS ENGORES
        NEGROES
EEGNOSX EXOGENS
EEGNPUX EXPUNGE
EEGNRSS NEGRESS
EEGNRST GERENTS
        REGENTS
EEGNRSV VENGERS
EEGNSSU GENUSES
        NEGUSES
EEGNSTU GUESTEN
EEGOOPY POOGYEE
EEGOOSS SOOGEES
EEGOPRT PROTEGE
EEGORTV OVERGET
EEGOSSS GESSOES
EEGPRUX EXPURGE
EEGRRSS REGRESS
EEGRRST REGRETS
EEGRRSU RESURGE
        REURGES
EEGRRSV VERGERS
EEGRSST REGESTS
EEGRSSU GUESSER
EEGRSSY GEYSERS
EEGRSTT GETTERS
EEGRSTU GESTURE
EEGRSTY GREYEST
EEGSSSU GUESSES
EEHHRTT THETHER
EEHHRTW WHETHER
EEHHSTW WHEESHT
EEHILLR HELLIER
EEHILMN HELIMEN
EEHILPS EPHELIS
EEHILRS LEISHER
EEHILRW WHILERE
EEHILST SHELTIE
EEHILSX HELIXES
EEHIMMS MISHMEE
EEHIMNO HEMIONE
EEHIMPR HEMPIER
EEHIMPS HEMPIES
EEHIMPT EPITHEM
EEHIMRS MESHIER
EEHINNR HENNIER
EEHINNS HENNIES
EEHINOR HEROINE
EEHINRR ERRHINE
EEHINRS HENRIES
        INHERES
EEHINRT NEITHER
        THEREIN
EEHINRW WHEREIN
EEHINST THEINES
EEHIORS HEROISE
EEHIORZ HEROIZE
EEHIPRT PRITHEE
EEHIPSV PEEVISH
EEHIPTT EPITHET
EEHIRRS HERRIES
EEHIRSS HEIRESS
        HERISSE
EEHIRST HEISTER
EEHIRSV SHRIEVE
EEHIRTW THEWIER
EEHIRWY WHEYIER
EEHISTV THIEVES
EEHKLOY KEYHOLE
EEHKLSS SHEKELS

EEHKOOY EYEHOOK
EEHKRSS SHREEKS
EEHLLMP PHELLEM
EEHLLNS ENSHELL
EEHLLRS HELLERS
        SHELLER
EEHLMMW WHEMMLE
EEHLMST HELMETS
EEHLNSU UNHELES
EEHLPRS HELPERS
EEHLPRT TELPHER
EEHLPSS PLESHES
EEHLRST SHELTER
EEHLRSW WELSHER
EEHLRSY SHEERLY
EEHLSSU HUELESS
EEHLSSV SHELVES
EEHLSSW SHEWELS
        WELSHES
EEHLSTT SHTETEL
EEHLSTV THELVES
EEHMNOP PHONEME
EEHMNOS HOSEMEN
EEHMNRU ENRHEUM
EEHMNRY MYNHEER
EEHMNSS MENSHES
EEHMORT THEOREM
EEHMPST TEMPEHS
EEHMRUX EXHUMER
EEHMSST SMEETHS
EEHMSUX EXHUMES
EEHNNOS SHONEEN
EEHNNRS HENNERS
EEHNNRY HENNERY
EEHNOPT POTHEEN
EEHNORT THEREON
EEHNORW NOWHERE
        WHEREON
EEHNPSS SEPHENS
        SPHENES
EEHNPSW NEPHEWS
EEHNRST THRENES
EEHNSST NESHEST
EEHNSTU ENTHUSE
EEHNSTV SEVENTH
EEHNSTY ETHYNES
EEHOOPW WHOOPEE
EEHOPRU EUPHROE
EEHOPSS SHEEPOS
EEHORST HETEROS
EEHORSU REHOUSE
EEHORSW WHERESO
EEHORTT THERETO
EEHORTW WHERETO
EEHORVW WHOEVER
        WHOEVER
EEHOSST ETHOSES
EEHOSSX HEXOSES
EEHOSTW TOWHEES
EEHPPST HEPPEST
EEHPRSS SPHERES
EEHPRST HEPSTER
        PETHERS
        SPERTHE
        THREEPS
EEHPRTY PRYTHEE
EEHQSTU QUETHES
EEHRRSW WERSHER
EEHRRTW WHERRET
EEHRRSU RUSHEES
EEHRSTT TETHERS
EEHRSTW WETHERS
        WRETHES
EEHRSTZ HERTZES
EEHRTTW WHETTER
EEHRVWY WHYEVER
EEIIKRS KIERIES
EEIILRV VEILIER
EEIIMNS MEINIES

EEIIMPR	RIEMPIE		RELIEVO	EEIMRRR	MERRIER		SIXTEEN
EEIIMRT	EMERITI	EEILOST	ESTOILE	EEIMRRS	MERRIES	EEINSTY	SYENITE
EEIIMST	ITEMISE		ETOILES	EEIMRRT	TRIREME	EEIOPPT	EPITOPE
EEIIMTZ	ITEMIZE	EEILOTZ	ZEOLITE	EEIMRSS	MESSIER	EEIOPSS	POESIES
EEIINRT	ERINITE	EEILPRR	REPLIER		MISERES	EEIOPST	POETISE
	NITERIE	EEILPRS	REPLIES		REMISES	EEIOPSX	EPOXIES
EEIINRV	VEINIER		SPIELER	EEIMRST	MEISTER	EEIOPTZ	POETIZE
EEIINSW	WIENIES	EEILPRT	PERLITE		METIERS	EEIORRS	ROSIERE
EEIINTV	INVITEE		REPTILE		RETIMES	EEIORSS	SOIREES
EEIIPST	PIETIES	EEILPRU	PUERILE		TREMIES	EEIORSV	EROSIVE
EEIIRRV	RIVIERE	EEILPSS	PELISSE		TRISEME	EEIOSST	ISOETES
EEIIRVW	VIEWIER	EEILPST	EPISTLE	EEIMRSX	REMIXES	EEIOSTT	TOEIEST
EEIISST	SEITIES		PELITES	EEIMRTT	EMITTER	EEIPPPR	PEPPIER
EEIISTV	VISITEE	EEILQRU	RELIQUE		TERMITE	EEIPPST	PEPTISE
EEIJKRR	JERKIER	EEILRRS	RELIERS	EEIMSSS	MISSEES	EEIPPTT	PIPETTE
EEIJKRS	JERKIES	EEILRRV	RELIVER		SEMISES	EEIPPTZ	PEPTIZE
EEIJLLS	JELLIES		REVILER	EEIMSST	METISSE	EEIPQRU	PERIQUE
EEIJMMR	JEMMIER	EEILRSS	RESILES	EEINNNP	PENNINE		REPIQUE
EEIJMMS	JEMMIES	EEILRST	LEISTER	EEINNPS	PENNIES	EEIPQSU	EQUIPES
EEIJNNS	JENNIES		RETILES	EEINNRS	NERINES	EEIPRRR	PERRIER
EEIJRRS	JERRIES		STERILE	EEINNRT	INTERNE	EEIPRRS	PERRIES
EEIJRTT	JETTIER	EEILRSU	LEISURE	EEINNRU	NEURINE		REPRISE
EEIJSSS	JESSIES	EEILRSV	RELIVES	EEINNRV	ENRIVEN		RESPIRE
EEIJSTT	JETTIES		REVILES		INNERVE	EEIPRRV	REPRIVE
EEIKLLS	KELLIES		SERVILE		NERVINE	EEIPRRZ	REPRIZE
	SKELLIE	EEILRTT	RETITLE	EEINNRW	WENNIER	EEIPRSS	PRESSIE
EEIKLNY	KEYLINE	EEILSSS	SESELIS	EEINNST	INTENSE	EEIPRST	RESPITE
EEIKLPS	KELPIES		SESSILE		TENNIES	EEIPRSV	PREVISE
EEIKLPT	PIKELET	EEILSST	TELESIS	EEINNTW	ENTWINE		PRIEVES
EEIKLSS	SELKIES		TIELESS	EEINNTZ	NETIZEN	EEIPRSW	SPEWIER
EEIKLST	KELTIES	EEILSSU	ILEUSES	EEINOPR	PEREION	EEIPRSX	EXPIRES
	SLEEKIT	EEILSSW	LEWISES		PIONEER		PREXIES
EEIKMNP	PIKEMEN	EEILSSX	LEXISES	EEINOPS	PEONIES	EEIPRTT	PETTIER
EEIKNRT	KERNITE		SILEXES	EEINPPS	PEPSINE	EEIPRVW	PREVIEW
EEIKNSS	ENSKIES	EEILSTV	LEVITES	EEINPNR	REPINER	EEIPRZZ	PREZZIE
	KINESES		LIEVEST	EEINPRS	EREPSIN	EEIPSTT	PETTIES
EEIKPRR	PERKIER	EEILSTX	SEXTILE		REPINES	EEIPSTW	PEEWITS
EEIKPRS	PESKIER	EEILSUV	ELUSIVE	EEINPRT	INEPTER	EEIQRRU	REQUIRE
EEIKRST	KEISTER	EEILSVW	WEEVILS	EEINPRZ	PRENZIE	EEIQRSU	ESQUIRE
EEIKRSY	SKIEYER	EEILSZZ	LEZZIES	EEINPSS	PENISES		QUERIES
EEIKSST	SEIKEST	EEILTTX	TEXTILE	EEINPST	PENTISE	EEIQRTU	QUIETER
EEIKSTT	STEEKIT	EEILVWY	WEEVILY	EEINPSV	PENSIVE		REQUITE
EEIKTTT	TEKTITE	EEIMMNS	IMMENSE		VESPINE	EEIRRRT	RETIRER
EEILLMT	MELLITE	EEIMMRS	IMMERSE	EEINQRU	ENQUIRE		TERRIER
EEILLNS	NELLIES	EEIMMSS	MIMESES		INQUERE	EEIRRSS	SERRIES
EEILLPS	ELLIPSE		MISSEEM	EEINQTU	QUIETEN		SIRREES
EEILLRS	LEISLER	EEIMNNO	NOMINEE	EEINQUY	QUEYNIE	EEIRRST	ETRIERS
EEILLRT	TREILLE	EEIMNNT	EMINENT	EEINRRS	RESINER		REITERS
EEILLRV	EVILLER	EEIMNOS	SEMEION	EEINRRT	INERTER		RESTIER
EEILLSS	EISELLS	EEIMNRS	ERMINES		REINTER		RETIRES
EEILLST	TELLIES	EEIMNRV	MINEVER		RENTIER		RETRIES
EEILLSV	VIELLES	EEIMNRW	WIREMEN		TERRINE		TERRIES
EEILLSW	WELLIES	EEIMNSS	INSEEMS	EEINRRV	NERVIER	EEIRRSV	REIVERS
EEILMNN	LINEMEN		MISSEEN		VERNIER		REVERSI
EEILMNR	ERMELIN		NEMESIS	EEINRSS	SEINERS		REVISER
EEILMNS	ISLEMEN		SIEMENS		SEREINS		RIEVERS
EEILMPT	IMPLETE	EEIMNST	EMETINS		SERINES	EEIRRSW	REWIRES
EEILMRT	MELTIER	EEIMNSW	MISWEEN	EEINRST	ENTIRES	EEIRRTV	RIVERET
EEILMRV	VERMEIL	EEIMNSY	MEINEYS		ENTRIES		RIVETER
EEILMST	ELMIEST		MENYIES		NERITES	EEIRRTW	REWRITE
EEILNNO	LEONINE	EEIMNTT	MINETTE		TRENISE	EEIRRVV	REVIVER
EEILNNT	LENIENT	EEIMOPS	EPISOME	EEINRSV	ENVIERS	EEIRSSU	REISSUE
EEILNNV	ENLIVEN	EEIMOPT	EPITOME		INVERSE	EEIRSSV	IVRESSE
EEILNOR	ELOINER	EEIMORS	ISOMERE		VENIRES		REVISES
EEILNPS	PENSILE	EEIMOSS	MEIOSES		VERSINE	EEIRSSZ	SEIZERS
EEILNRS	LIERNES	EEIMOTV	EMOTIVE	EEINRSW	NEWSIER	EEIRSTT	TESTIER
	RELINES	EEIMPRR	PREMIER	EEINRTT	NETTIER	EEIRSTU	SUETIER
EEILNRV	LIVENER		REPRIME		TENTIER	EEIRSTV	RESTIVE
EEILNSS	ENISLES	EEIMPRS	EMPIRES	EEINRTU	NEURITE		SIEVERT
	ENSILES		EMPRISE		RETINUE		STIEVER
	SENSILE		EPIMERS		REUNITE		VERIEST
	SILENES		IMPRESE		UTERINE	EEIRSTW	STEWIER
EEILNST	SETLINE		PREMIES	EEINSST	SEITENS	EEIRSTZ	ZESTIER
	TENSILE		PREMISE		SESTINE	EEIRSUZ	SEIZURE
EEILNTT	ENTITLE		SPIREME	EEINSSV	SENVIES	EEIRSVV	REVIVES
EEILNTV	VEINLET	EEIMPRT	EMPTIER	EEINSSW	NEWSIES	EEIRSVW	REVIEWS
EEILOPT	PETIOLE	EEIMPST	EMPTIES	EEINSTV	TENSIVE		VIEWERS
EEILORT	TROELIE		SEPTIME		VENITES	EEIRTVV	VETIVER
EEILORV	OVERLIE	EEIMQRU	REQUIEM	EEINSTX	EXTINES	EEISSSV	ESSIVES

EEISSTX	SEXIEST	
EEISTVX	VITEXES	
EEITUXZ	ZEUXITE	
EEJKRRS	JERKERS	
EEJLLMU	JUMELLE	
EEJLRWY	JEWELRY	
EEJNNST	JENNETS	
EEJNOOO	REJONEO	
EEJNORS	REJONES	
EEJNORY	ENJOYER	
EEJPRRU	PERJURE	
EEJQRRU	JERQUER	
EEJQRSU	JERQUES	
EEJRSST	JESTERS	
EEJRSSY	JERSEYS	
EEKKOTV	VETKOEK	
EEKKRRT	TREKKER	
EEKKSSY	KEKSYES	
EEKLLNV	KNEVELL	
EEKLLSY	SLEEKLY	
EEKLLUU	UKULELE	
EEKLMPS	KEMPLES	
EEKLMRZ	KLEZMER	
EEKLNNS	KENNELS	
EEKLNOS	KEELSON	
EEKLNRS	KERNELS	
EEKLPRS	KELPERS	
EEKLRST	KELTERS	
	KESTREL	
	SKELTER	
EEKLSSY	KEYLESS	
EEKLSTT	KETTLES	
EEKMNOS	SOKEMEN	
EEKMPRS	KEMPERS	
EEKNNRS	KENNERS	
EEKNNST	KENNETS	
EEKNOSS	KENOSES	
EEKNOST	KETONES	
EEKNOTY	KEYNOTE	
EEKNRSS	SKREENS	
EEKNSTU	NETSUKE	
EEKOPRS	RESPOKE	
EEKORSV	EVOKERS	
	REVOKES	
EEKOSSS	SEKOSES	
EEKOSST	KETOSES	
EEKPPSU	UPKEEPS	
EEKPRSU	PERUKES	
EEKRSST	STREEKS	
EEKRSSU	RESKUES	
EEKRSSW	RESKEWS	
	SKEWERS	
EEKRSSY	KERSEYS	
EEKSSTW	SKEWEST	
EELLMRS	MERELLS	
	SMELLER	
EELLMRV	VERMELL	
EELLNOV	NOVELLE	
EELLNRS	SNELLER	
EELLNST	TELLENS	
EELLNSW	NEWELLS	
EELLORS	ROSELLE	
EELLORZ	ROZELLE	
EELLPRS	RESPELL	
	SPELLER	
EELLPST	PELLETS	
EELLQRU	QUELLER	
EELLRSS	RESELLS	
	SELLERS	
EELLRST	RETELLS	
	TELLERS	
EELLRSU	RUELLES	
EELLRSW	SWELLER	
EELLSTV	VELLETS	
EELMMOP	POMMELE	
EELMMPU	EMPLUME	
EELMNNS	LENSMEN	
EELMNOO	OENOMEL	
EELMOPR	PLEROME	

EELMOPT	LEPTOME	
EELMORW	EELWORM	
EELMOST	OMELETS	
EELMPRS	SEMPLER	
EELMPST	PELMETS	
	STEMPEL	
	STEMPLE	
	TEMPLES	
EELMPTT	TEMPLET	
EELMRST	SMELTER	
EELMRSU	LEMURES	
	RELUMES	
EELMSST	TELESMS	
EELMSTT	METTLES	
	STEMLET	
EELNNSV	VENNELS	
EELNOPV	ENVELOP	
EELNOSV	ELEVONS	
EELNOSY	ESLOYNE	
EELNOTT	NOTELET	
EELNOTU	TOLUENE	
EELNPSS	PENSELS	
	SPLEENS	
EELNPST	PENTELS	
EELNPSY	SPLEENY	
EELNQUY	QUEENLY	
EELNRST	RELENTS	
	SLENTER	
EELNRSU	UNREELS	
EELNRTT	LETTERN	
EELNRUV	NERVULE	
EELNSSS	LESSENS	
EELNSST	NESTLES	
EELNSSU	UNSEELS	
EELNSTT	NETTLES	
	TELNETS	
EELNSTU	ELUENTS	
	UNSTEEL	
EELNSTY	ENSTYLE	
	TENSELY	
EELNSUV	VENULES	
EELNSXY	XYLENES	
EELNTTU	LUNETTE	
EELOPPS	PEOPLES	
EELOPRS	ELOPERS	
	LEPROSE	
EELOPRX	EXPLORE	
EELOPSS	ELOPSES	
EELOPTU	EELPOUT	
EELORSS	RESOLES	
EELORSV	RESOLVE	
EELORTT	LORETTE	
EELORVV	EVOLVER	
	REVOLVE	
EELOSSS	LOESSES	
EELOSST	OSSELET	
	TELOSES	
	TOELESS	
EELOSTT	TELEOST	
EELOSUV	EVOLUES	
EELOSVV	EVOLVES	
EELOTUV	EVOLUTE	
	VELOUTE	
EELPPRX	PERPLEX	
EELPPSU	PEEPULS	
EELPQRU	PREQUEL	
EELPRST	PELTERS	
	PETRELS	
	RESPELT	
	SPELTER	
EELPRSU	REPULSE	
EELPRSY	SLEEPRY	
	YELPERS	
EELPRTZ	PRETZEL	
EELPRUX	PLEXURE	
EELPRVY	REPLEVY	
EELPSST	PESTLES	
EELPSTT	PETTLES	
EELPSTY	STEEPLY	

EELPSUX	EXPULSE	
EELQRUY	QUEERLY	
EELQSSU	SEQUELS	
EELRRSV	VERRELS	
EELRRVY	REVELRY	
EELRSST	STREELS	
	TRESSEL	
EELRSSU	RULESSE	
EELRSTT	LETTERS	
	LETTRES	
	SETTLER	
	STERLET	
	TRESTLE	
EELRSTV	SVELTER	
EELRSTW	SWELTER	
	WELTERS	
	WRESTLE	
EELRSTY	RESTYLE	
	TERSELY	
EELRSTZ	SELTZER	
EELRSUV	VELURES	
EELRSVV	VERVELS	
EELSSSU	USELESS	
EELSSSV	VESSELS	
EELSSSX	SEXLESS	
EELSSTT	SETTLES	
EELSSTU	SETULES	
EELSSUV	EVULSES	
EELSTUY	EUSTYLE	
EELSTVV	VELVETS	
EELSTVW	TWELVES	
EELSTWY	SWEETLY	
EELTVVY	VELVETY	
EEMMNOT	MEMENTO	
EEMMORS	MEROMES	
EEMMOSU	MOUSMEE	
EEMMOSV	EMMOVES	
EEMMRST	STEMMER	
EEMMSSS	SEMSEMS	
EEMMSST	STEMMES	
EEMNNOV	ENVENOM	
EEMNNSW	NEWSMEN	
EEMNOOS	SOMEONE	
EEMNOOY	MOONEYE	
EEMNOPR	REPOMEN	
EEMNORS	MOREENS	
EEMNORY	MONEYER	
EEMNOST	TEMENOS	
	TONEMES	
EEMNOSV	ENMOVES	
EEMNPTU	UMPTEEN	
EEMNRTU	TRUEMEN	
EEMNSYZ	ENZYMES	
EEMOOSW	WOESOME	
EEMOPRR	EMPEROR	
EEMOPRT	TEMPORE	
EEMOPRV	PREMOVE	
EEMOPRW	EMPOWER	
EEMOPST	METOPES	
EEMORRS	REMORSE	
	ROEMERS	
EEMORRT	REMOTER	
EEMORRU	UROMERE	
EEMORRV	REMOVER	
EEMORST	METEORS	
	REMOTES	
EEMORSV	REMOVES	
EEMPRRT	PRETERM	
EEMPRSS	EMPRESS	
EEMPRST	TEMPERS	
EEMPRSU	PRESUME	
	SUPREME	
EEMPRTT	TEMPTER	
EEMPRTU	PERMUTE	
EEMPSSU	EMPUSES	
EEMPSTT	TEMPEST	
EEMPSTX	EXEMPTS	
EEMRRST	TERMERS	

EEMRRUU	REMUEUR	
EEMRSST	RESTEMS	
EEMRSSU	RESUMES	
EEMRSUX	MUREXES	
EEMSSSU	SMEUSES	
EEMSSTU	MUSTEES	
EEMSTTU	MUSETTE	
EENNORT	ENTERON	
	TENONER	
EENNORU	NEURONE	
EENNOSS	ONENESS	
EENNOSZ	ENZONES	
EENNOTT	NONETTE	
EENNOTY	NEOTENY	
EENNPRS	PENNERS	
EENNQUU	UNQUEEN	
EENNRST	RENNETS	
	TENNERS	
EENNRUV	UNNERVE	
EENNSST	SENNETS	
EENNSSU	UNSEENS	
	UNSENSE	
EENNSSW	NEWNESS	
EENOPPR	PREPONE	
	PROPONE	
EENOPPT	PEPTONE	
EENOPRS	OPENERS	
	PERONES	
	REOPENS	
	REPONES	
EENOPST	OPENEST	
	PENTOSE	
	POSTEEN	
	POTEENS	
EENORRV	OVERREN	
EENORSY	ONEYERS	
	ONEYRES	
EENORSZ	REZONES	
EENORTV	OVERNET	
EENOSSY	ESSOYNE	
	NOYESES	
EENOSTV	VENTOSE	
	VOTEENS	
EENOSTW	TOWNEES	
EENOSVZ	EVZONES	
EENPPRT	PERPENT	
EENPRST	PRESENT	
	REPENTS	
	SERPENT	
EENPRSY	PYRENES	
EENPRTV	PREVENT	
EENPSTU	PUNTEES	
EENPSTW	ENSWEPT	
EENPSTY	STEPNEY	
EENQSTU	SEQUENT	
EENRRST	RENTERS	
	STERNER	
EENRRSU	ENSURER	
EENRRSV	NERVERS	
EENRRUV	NERVURE	
EENRSST	NESTERS	
	RESENTS	
	STRENES	
EENRSSU	ENSURES	
EENRSTT	TENTERS	
	TESTERN	
EENRSTU	NEUTERS	
	RETUNES	
	TENURES	
	TUREENS	
EENRSTV	VENTERS	
	VENTRES	
EENRSTW	WESTERN	
EENRSTX	EXTERNS	
EENRSTY	STYRENE	
	YESTERN	
EENRSVV	VERVENS	
EENRTUV	VENTURE	
EENSSST	SETNESS	

EENSSSY	SYNESES	EEPRTTX	PRETEXT
EENSSTT	TENSEST	EEPSSTT	SEPTETS
EENSSTV	STEVENS	EEPSTTU	PUTTEES
EENSSTW	WETNESS	EEPSTTY	TYPESET
EENSSUV	VENUSES	EEQRRUY	EQUERRY
EENSSUX	UNSEXES	EEQRSTU	QUESTER
EENSSVW	SWEVENS		REQUEST
EENSTTX	EXTENTS	EEQSSTU	QUEESTS
EENSTTY	TEENTSY	EEQSUYZ	SQUEEZY
EENSTUW	UNSWEET	EERRSST	RESTERS
EENSTVY	SEVENTY	EERRSSV	SERVERS
EEOOPRS	OPEROSE		VERSERS
EEOOSTT	TOETOES	EERRSTT	TERRETS
EEOPPRS	PREPOSE	EERRSTU	URETERS
EEOPPTU	OUTPEEP	EERRSTV	REVERTS
EEOPRRV	REPROVE	EERRSTW	STREWER
EEOPRSS	REPOSES		WRESTER
EEOPRSX	EXPOSER	EERRSUV	REVEURS
EEOPRTT	TREETOP	EERRSVW	SWERVER
EEOPRTU	OUTPEER	EERRSVY	SERVERY
EEOPSSS	SPEOSES	EERRTTU	REUTTER
EEOPSST	POETESS		UTTERER
EEOPSSU	ESPOUSE	EERRTTY	RETTERY
	POSEUSE	EERSSST	TRESSES
EEOPSSX	EXPOSES	EERSSTT	SETTERS
EEOPSTU	TOUPEES		STREETS
EEOPSTY	PEYOTES		TERSEST
EEOPTUW	OUTWEEP		TESTERS
EEOQRTU	REQUOTE	EERSSTV	REVESTS
EEORRST	RESTORE		STERVES
EEORRSV	REVERSO		VERSETS
EEORRTU	REROUTE	EERSSTW	STEWERS
EEORRTV	EVERTOR		WESTERS
EEORRTW	REWROTE	EERSSTX	EXSERTS
EEORSST	OSSETER	EERSSTZ	ZESTERS
	STEREOS	EERSSUY	SEYSURE
EEORSSX	SOREXES	EERSSVW	SWERVES
	XEROSES	EERSTTT	STRETTE
EEORSTT	ROSETTE		TETTERS
EEORSTV	ESTOVER	EERSTTU	TRUSTEE
	OVERSET	EERSTTY	STREETY
EEORSTX	XEROTES	EERSTUV	VERSUTE
EEORSTY	ESOTERY		VERTUES
EEORSUV	OEUVRES		VESTURE
	OVERUSE	EERSTUY	TUYERES
EEORSVW	OVERSEW	EERSTVV	VERVETS
EEORTUV	OUVERTE	EERSTWY	TWYERES
EEPPPRS	PEPPERS	EERSUVW	SURVEWE
EEPPPRY	PEPPERY	EERTTUX	TEXTURE
EEPPRST	STEPPER	EESSSTT	SESTETS
EEPPSST	STEPPES		TSETSES
EEPPSTU	STEEPUP	EESSTTT	SESTETT
EEPPSUW	UPSWEEP	EESSTTU	SUTTEES
EEPPSUY	EUPEPSY	EESSTTX	SEXTETS
EEPRRSS	PRESSER	EESSTTY	STEYEST
	REPRESS	EESSTTZ	TZETSES
	SPERRES	EESTTTW	WETTEST
EEPRRSU	PERUSER	EESTTTX	SEXTETT
	REPURES	EFFFIRU	FUFFIER
EEPRRTV	PERVERT	EFFFOOR	FEOFFOR
EEPRRVY	REPRYVE	EFFGIJN	JEFFING
EEPRSSS	PRESSES	EFFGINR	REFFING
	SPERSES	EFFGIRS	GRIFFES
EEPRSST	PESTERS	EFFGORS	GOFFERS
	PRESETS	EFFGRRU	GRUFFER
EEPRSSU	PERSUES	EFFHILW	WHIFFLE
	PERUSES	EFFHIRS	SHERIFF
EEPRSSV	VESPERS	EFFHIRU	HUFFIER
EEPRSSW	SPEWERS	EFFHIRW	WHIFFER
EEPRSSX	EXPRESS	EFFHITW	WHIFFET
EEPRSTT	PERTEST	EFFHLSU	SHUFFLE
	PETTERS	EFFIIJS	JIFFIES
	PRETEST	EFFIIMR	MIFFIER
EEPRSTU	PERTUSE	EFFIINR	NIFFIER
	REPUTES	EFFIIST	FIFTIES
EEPRSTW	PEWTERS		IFFIEST
EEPRSTX	EXPERTS		STIFFIE
	SEXPERT	EFFIKLS	SKIFFLE
EEPRSUV	PREVUES		

EFFILLU	LIFEFUL	EFGLOSS	FOGLESS
EFFILNO	OFFLINE	EFGMNOR	FROGMEN
EFFILNS	SNIFFLE	EFGNOOR	FORGONE
EFFILPR	PIFFLER	EFGOORS	FORGOES
EFFILPS	PIFFLES	EFGORRS	FORGERS
EFFILRR	RIFFLER	EFGORRU	FERRUGO
EFFILRS	RIFFLES	EFGORRY	FORGERY
EFFILRY	FIREFLY	EFGORST	FORGETS
EFFILSS	SIFFLES	EFGORSW	GOWFERS
EFFINRS	NIFFERS	EFGORTU	FOREGUT
	SNIFFER	EFHIINS	FINEISH
EFFINST	INFEFTS	EFHIIRS	FISHIER
	STIFFEN	EFHIJSW	JEWFISH
EFFIOPR	PIFFERO	EFHILMS	FLEMISH
EFFIORT	FORFEIT		HIMSELF
	TOFFIER	EFHILSS	SELFISH
EFFIOST	TOFFIES	EFHILST	LEFTISH
EFFIPRU	PUFFIER	EFHILTY	HEFTILY
EFFIRRT	TRIFFER	EFHINNS	FENNISH
EFFIRST	RESTIFF	EFHIRSS	FISHERS
	STIFFER		SERFISH
EFFLMRU	MUFFLER		SHERIFS
EFFLMSU	MUFFLES	EFHIRST	SHIFTER
EFFLNSU	SNUFFLE	EFHIRSY	FISHERY
EFFLOPS	POFFLES	EFHISUW	HUSWIFE
EFFLOSU	SOUFFLE	EFHLLPU	HELPFUL
EFFLRRU	RUFFLER	EFHLLSY	FLESHLY
EFFLRSU	RUFFLES	EFHLNSU	UNFLESH
EFFLRTU	FRETFUL	EFHLOOX	FOXHOLE
	TRUFFLE	EFHLOPU	HOPEFUL
EFFNRSU	SNUFFER	EFHLOSS	FLOSHES
EFFNRUU	UNRUFFE	EFHLRSU	FLUSHER
EFFOORR	OFFEROR	EFHLRSY	FRESHLY
EFFOPRR	PROFFER	EFHLSSU	FLUSHES
EFFOPSU	POUFFES	EFHLSTY	THYSELF
EFFORST	EFFORTS	EFHLTTW	TWELFTH
EFFOSST	OFFSETS	EFHNORT	FORHENT
EFFPRSU	PUFFERS	EFHOORS	HOOFERS
EFFPRUY	PUFFERY	EFHORST	FOTHERS
EFFRSSU	SUFFERS	EFHRRTU	FURTHER
EFFRSTU	STUFFER	EFHRSSU	FRUSHES
EFFSSUU	SUFFUSE	EFIIKST	FIKIEST
EFFSTTU	TUFFETS	EFIILLS	FILLIES
EFGGIOR	FOGGIER	EFIILMR	FILMIER
EFGGIRR	FRIGGER	EFIILMS	MISFILE
EFGGIRU	FUGGIER	EFIILRT	FITLIER
EFGGIRY	FIGGERY	EFIILRY	FIERILY
EFGGORS	FOGGERS	EFIILSS	FISSILE
EFGHIMS	GEMFISH	EFIIMRS	MISFIRE
EFGHINT	HEFTING	EFIINNR	FINNIER
EFGHIRT	FIGHTER	EFIINPV	FIVEPIN
	FREIGHT	EFIINRT	NIFTIER
EFGILLN	FELLING	EFIINRU	UNIFIER
EFGILMN	FLEMING	EFIINSU	UNIFIES
EFGILNR	FLINGER	EFIINSX	INFIXES
EFGILNS	SELFING	EFIIRRR	FIRRIER
EFGILNT	FELTING	EFIIRRT	RIFTIER
EFGILNX	FLEXING	EFIIRST	FISTIER
EFGILNY	FLEYING	EFIIRZZ	FIZZIER
EFGILRU	GULFIER	EFIISSV	FISSIVE
EFGIMNT	FIGMENT	EFIJLLY	JELLIFY
EFGINNP	PFENNIG	EFIJLOR	FRIJOLE
EFGINNR	FERNING	EFIJLOT	JETFOIL
EFGINOR	FOREIGN	EFIKLOS	FOLKIES
EFGINRS	FINGERS	EFIKLRU	FLUKIER
	FRINGES	EFIKNRU	FUNKIER
EFGINRU	GUNFIRE	EFIKORR	FORKIER
EFGINSS	FESSING	EFIKRRS	FRISKER
EFGINTT	FETTING	EFIKRST	FRISKET
EFGINTW	WEFTING	EFILLMS	MISFELL
EFGIOOR	GOOFIER	EFILLOO	FOLIOLE
EFGIORV	FORGIVE	EFILLOS	FOLLIES
EFGIRRT	GRIFTER	EFILLRS	FILLERS
EFGIRSU	FIGURES		REFILLS
EFGLLSU	FLUGELS	EFILLST	FILLETS
EFGLNSU	ENGULFS	EFILLUW	WILEFUL
EFGLNTU	FULGENT	EFILMNU	FULMINE
EFGLORS	GOLFERS	EFILMOT	FILEMOT
EFGLORT	FROGLET	EFILMSS	SELFISM

EFILMST	FILMSET		FRISURE
	LEFTISM		FURRIES
EFILNOS	OLEFINS		SURFIER
EFILNOX	FLEXION	EFIRRTT	FRITTER
EFILNSS	FINLESS	EFIRRTU	FRITURE
EFILOOS	FLOOSIE		FRUITER
	FOLIOSE		TURFIER
EFILOOZ	FLOOZIE	EFIRRTY	TERRIFY
EFILOPR	PROFILE	EFIRRUZ	FURZIER
EFILORR	FLORIER	EFIRSST	SIFTERS
EFILORT	LOFTIER		STRIFES
	TREFOIL	EFIRSSU	FISSURE
EFILOSX	SEXFOIL		FUSSIER
EFILPPR	FLIPPER		SURFIES
EFILPPS	FIPPLES	EFIRSTT	FITTERS
EFILPPU	PIPEFUL		TITFERS
EFILPRS	PILFERS	EFIRSTU	FUSTIER
EFILPRY	PILFERY		SURFEIT
EFILQUY	LIQUEFY	EFIRSTW	SWIFTER
EFILRRS	RIFLERS	EFIRSUX	FIXURES
EFILRRT	TRIFLER	EFIRSVY	VERSIFY
EFILRST	FILTERS	EFIRSZZ	FIZZERS
	LIFTERS		FRIZZES
	STIFLER	EFIRTTU	TUFTIER
	TRIFLES		TURFITE
EFILRTT	FLITTER	EFIRTUV	FURTIVE
EFILRTU	FLUTIER	EFIRTUX	FIXTURE
	FUTILER	EFIRUZZ	FUZZIER
EFILRVV	FLIVVER	EFISTTT	FITTEST
EFILRZZ	FRIZZLE	EFISTTY	TESTIFY
EFILSSS	FISSLES	EFJLSTU	JESTFUL
EFILSST	SELFIST	EFKLMNO	MENFOLK
	STIFLES	EFKLMOR	MERFOLK
EFILSTT	LEFTIST	EFKLNUY	FLUNKEY
EFILSTU	FLUIEST	EFKLOPU	POKEFUL
	SULFITE	EFKLPSU	SKEPFUL
EFILSZZ	FIZZLES	EFKORRS	FORKERS
EFILUVX	FLUXIVE	EFLLOST	FLOTELS
EFIMMRU	FERMIUM	EFLLOSW	FELLOWS
EFIMNOR	FERMION	EFLLRSU	FULLERS
EFIMNTT	FITMENT	EFLLSTU	FULLEST
EFIMOST	FOMITES	EFLMOSU	FULSOME
EFIMRRS	FIRMERS	EFLMPRU	FRUMPLE
EFIMRST	FIRMEST	EFLMSUU	MUSEFUL
	FREMITS	EFLNNSU	FUNNELS
EFIMSTU	FUMIEST	EFLNORT	FORLENT
EFIMTTU	FUMETTI	EFLNORU	FLEURON
EFINNOR	INFERNO	EFLNORY	FELONRY
EFINNRS	FINNERS	EFLNOSU	SULFONE
EFINNRU	FUNNIER	EFLNOTT	FLETTON
EFINNSU	FUNNIES		FONTLET
EFINOPR	FORPINE	EFLNPSU	PENFULS
EFINRST	SNIFTER	EFLNSSU	FULNESS
EFINRSU	INFUSER		UNSELFS
EFINRUY	REUNIFY	EFLNSTU	FLUENTS
EFINSST	FITNESS		NESTFUL
	INFESTS		NETFULS
EFINSSU	INFUSES	EFLNSUY	SYNFUEL
EFINSUX	UNFIXES	EFLNTTU	TENTFUL
EFINSZZ	FIZZENS	EFLNTUU	TUNEFUL
EFIOOPR	POOFIER	EFLOORR	FLOORER
EFIOORR	ROOFIER		FORLORE
EFIOORT	FOOTIER	EFLOORS	FORSLOE
EFIOORW	WOOFIER	EFLOORY	FOOLERY
EFIOOST	FOOTIES	EFLOORZ	FOOZLER
EFIOPRR	PORIFER	EFLOOST	FOOTLES
EFIOPRT	FIREPOT	EFLOOSZ	FOOZLES
EFIORRT	ROTIFER	EFLORRS	ROLFERS
EFIORRW	FROWIER	EFLORST	FLORETS
EFIORSS	FROISES		LOFTERS
EFIORST	FOISTER	EFLORSU	FUROLES
	FORTIES		OURSELF
EFIOSST	SOFTIES	EFLORSW	FLOWERS
EFIOSTX	FOXIEST		FOWLERS
EFIOSTZ	FOZIEST		REFLOWS
EFIPPRR	FRIPPER		WOLFERS
EFIPRTY	PETRIFY	EFLORSX	FLEXORS
EFIRRRU	FURRIER	EFLORTT	FORTLET
EFIRRSU	FRISEUR	EFLORTW	FELWORT

EFLORVY	FLYOVER	EGGGILS	GIGGLES
	OVERFLY	EGGGINP	PEGGING
EFLORWW	WERWOLF	EGGGINV	VEGGING
EFLORWY	FLOWERY	EGGGLOR	GOGGLER
EFLOSSS	FLOSSES	EGGGLOS	GOGGLES
EFLOSSU	FLOUSES	EGGGLSU	GUGGLES
EFLOSTU	FOULEST	EGGGNOS	EGGNOGS
EFLOTUW	OUTFLEW	EGGHILR	HIGGLER
EFLPRSU	PURFLES	EGGHILS	HIGGLES
EFLPRUY	PREYFUL	EGGHINP	PEGHING
EFLPSTU	PESTFUL	EGGHIRT	THIGGER
EFLRSTU	FLUSTER	EGGHLOS	SHOGGLE
	FLUTERS	EGGHORS	HOGGERS
	RESTFUL	EGGHORY	HOGGERY
EFLRTTU	FLUTTER	EGGHOST	HOGGETS
EFLSTUZ	ZESTFUL	EGGIILS	GILGIES
EFLSUZZ	FUZZLES	EGGIINS	SIEGING
EFMNOOT	FOOTMEN	EGGIIPR	PIGGIER
EFMNORS	ENFORMS	EGGIIPS	PIGGIES
EFMNOST	FOMENTS	EGGIJLS	JIGGLES
EFMNRSU	SURFMEN	EGGIJRS	JIGGERS
EFMNRTU	TURFMEN	EGGILLN	GELLING
EFMOORZ	ZOEFORM	EGGILMS	LEGGISM
EFMOPRR	PERFORM	EGGILNN	LENGING
	PREFORM	EGGILNR	NIGGLER
EFMOPRT	POMFRET	EGGILNS	GINGLES
EFMORRS	FORMERS		NIGGLES
	REFORMS		SNIGGLE
EFMOTTU	FUMETTO	EGGILNU	LUGEING
EFMPRUY	PERFUMY	EGGILNY	GLEYING
EFMRTUY	FURMETY	EGGILRS	LIGGERS
EFNNORT	FORNENT	EGGILRW	WIGGLER
EFNNOTU	UNOFTEN		WRIGGLE
EFNNSTU	FUNNEST	EGGILST	GIGLETS
EFNOOST	FESTOON	EGGILSU	LUGGIES
EFNORRU	FORERUN	EGGILSW	WIGGLES
EFNORTU	FORTUNE	EGGIMMN	GEMMING
EFNORTW	FORWENT	EGGIMNN	MENGING
EFNORUZ	UNFROZE	EGGIMNR	GERMING
EFNOSST	SOFTENS		MERGING
EFNRSTU	FUNSTER	EGGIMOS	MOGGIES
EFOOPRR	REPROOF	EGGIMRU	MUGGIER
EFOOPRS	SPOOFER	EGGINNR	GERNING
EFOOPRT	FORETOP	EGGINNS	GINSENG
	POOFTER	EGGINNV	VENGING
EFOORRS	ROOFERS	EGGINRS	GINGERS
EFOORST	FOETORS		NIGGERS
	FOOTERS		SNIGGER
	REFOOTS	EGGINRU	GRUEING
EFOORSW	WOOFERS		GUNGIER
EFOORTW	WOOFTER	EGGINRV	VERGING
EFOPPRY	FOPPERY	EGGINRW	GREWING
EFOPRSS	PROFESS	EGGINRY	GINGERY
EFOPRST	FORPETS		GREYING
EFOPRSU	PROFUSE		NIGGERY
EFOPRTU	POUFTER	EGGINSS	GESSING
EFOPRTY	TORPEFY	EGGINTT	GETTING
EFORRSU	FERROUS	EGGINTW	TWIGGEN
	FURORES	EGGIORS	SOGGIER
EFORRTY	TORREFY	EGGIPRR	PRIGGER
EFORRUV	FERVOUR	EGGIPRU	PUGGIER
EFORSST	FORESTS	EGGIPRY	PIGGERY
	FOSTERS	EGGIPSU	PUGGIES
EFORSSU	FOURSES	EGGIRRS	RIGGERS
EFORSTU	FOUTERS	EGGIRRT	TRIGGER
	FOUTRES	EGGIRRU	RUGGIER
EFOSSTT	SOFTEST	EGGIRSW	SWIGGER
EFOSTWW	WOWFEST	EGGIRTW	TWIGGER
EFPRTUY	PUTREFY	EGGIRUV	VUGGIER
EFPSTUY	STUPEFY	EGGIRWY	WIGGERY
EFRRSSU	SURFERS	EGGJLOS	JOGGLES
EFRRSTU	RETURFS	EGGJLRU	JUGGLER
EFRRSUU	FUREURS	EGGJLSU	JUGGLES
EFRSSSU	FUSSERS	EGGJORS	JOGGERS
EFRSTTU	TUFTERS	EGGLMSU	SMUGGLE
EFRSTUU	FUTURES	EGGLNSU	SNUGGLE
EFSSTTU	FUSTETS	EGGLOOS	GOOGLES
EGGGILN	LEGGING	EGGLOOY	GEOLOGY
EGGGILR	GIGGLER	EGGLORS	LOGGERS

	SLOGGER	EGHIRSS SIGHERS	EGIINTV EVITING	EGILNRT RINGLET
EGGLOST	GOGLETS	EGHIRST SIGHTER	EGIINTX EXITING	TINGLER
	TOGGLES	EGHIRSU GUSHIER	EGIINVW VIEWING	TRINGLE
EGGLOSW	WOGGLES	EGHIRSY GREYISH	EGIINWZ WEIZING	EGILNRY RELYING
EGGLPRU	PLUGGER	EGHIRTT TIGHTER	EGIIPPS GIPPIES	EGILNSS SINGLES
EGGLPSU	PUGGLES	EGHISTW WEIGHTS	EGIIPRW PERIWIG	EGILNST GLISTEN
EGGLRSU	GURGLES	EGHITWY WEIGHTY	EGIIPSS GIPSIES	LESTING
	LUGGERS	EGHLLOU LUGHOLE	EGIJKNR JERKING	SINGLET
	SLUGGER	EGHLMPS PHLEGMS	EGIJLLN JELLING	TINGLES
EGGMRSU	MUGGERS	EGHLMPY PHLEGMY	EGIJLNR JINGLER	EGILNSU LUNGIES
	SMUGGER	EGHLNOR LEGHORN	EGIJLNS JINGLES	SLUEING
EGGNOOY	GEOGONY	EGHLNPU ENGULPH	EGIJLNT JINGLET	EGILNSW SLEWING
EGGNRSU	GRUNGES	EGHLNST LENGTHS	EGIJNOS JINGOES	SWINGLE
	SNUGGER	EGHLNTY LENGTHY	EGIJNST JESTING	EGILNSZ ZINGELS
EGGNSTU	NUGGETS	EGHLOOS SHOOGLE	EGIJNTT JETTING	EGILNTT ETTLING
EGGNTUY	NUGGETY	EGHLOSS SEGHOLS	EGIKKLN LEKKING	LETTING
EGGORST	GORGETS	EGHLPSU PLEUGHS	EGIKLNS KINGLES	EGILNTU ELUTING
EGGORTY	TOGGERY	EGHMMOS MEGOHMS	EGIKLNT KINGLET	EGILNTW WELTING
EGGPRUY	PUGGERY	EGHMNOU HUMOGEN	EGIKLNW WELKING	WINGLET
EGGRRSU	RUGGERS	EGHMOSU GUMSHOE	EGIKLRS KILERGS	EGILNVY LEVYING
EGGRSTU	TUGGERS	EGHNORU ENROUGH	EGIKMNP KEMPING	EGILOOS GOOLIES
EGGSSTU	SUGGEST	ROUGHEN	EGIKNNN KENNING	OLOGIES
EGHHIMN	HIGHMEN	EGHNOSU ENOUGHS	EGIKNNR KERNING	EGILOPS EPILOGS
EGHHIRS	HIGHERS	EGHNOTU TOUGHEN	EGIKNNT KENTING	EGILORS GLOIRES
EGHHIST	EIGHTHS	EGHNRSU HUNGERS	EGIKNOV EVOKING	GLORIES
	HEIGHTS	EGHOPRS GOPHERS	EGIKNPP KEPPING	EGILOSS GLIOSES
	HIGHEST	EGHORRU ROUGHER	EGIKNPR PERKING	EGILOST ELOGIST
EGHHOSW	SHOWGHE	EGHORTU TOUGHER	EGIKNRV KERVING	LOGIEST
EGHHSSU	SHEUGHS	EGHOSTT GHETTOS	EGIKNRY YERKING	EGILOSU OUGLIES
EGHHSUW	WHEUGHS	EGHOSUU HUGEOUS	EGIKNST KESTING	EGILPPR GRIPPLE
EGHIILL	GHILLIE	EGHRSSU GUSHERS	EGIKNSW SKEWING	EGILPST PIGLETS
EGHIINR	HEIRING	EGHRTUY THEURGY	EGIKNSY YESKING	EGILPSY GILPEYS
EGHIINT	NIGHTIE	EGIIJLS JILGIES	EGIKNUY YEUKING	EGILRRU GURLIER
EGHIINV	INVEIGH	EGIIKLW WIGLIKE	EGILLMN MELLING	EGILRSS GRILSES
EGHIKNR	GHERKIN	EGIILLS GILLIES	EGILLNO LOGLINE	EGILRST GLISTER
EGHIKRS	SKREIGH	EGIILMT LEGITIM	EGILLNS LEGLINS	GRISTLE
	SKRIEGH	EGIILNR LEIRING	LINGELS	EGILRSU GUILERS
EGHILLN	HELLING	LINGIER	LINGLES	LIGURES
EGHILMN	HELMING	EGIILNS SEILING	SELLING	LURGIES
EGHILNP	HELPING	EGIILNT LIGNITE	EGILLNT TELLING	EGILRSY GREISLY
EGHILNR	HERLING	EGIILNV VEILING	EGILLNW WELLING	GRIESLY
EGHILNS	SHINGLE	EGIILNX EXILING	EGILLNY YELLING	GRISELY
EGHILNT	ENLIGHT	EGIILPS GILPIES	EGILLOS GOLLIES	EGILRTT GLITTER
	LIGHTEN	EGIILRS GIRLIES	EGILLRS GRILLES	EGILRTY TIGERLY
EGHILNV	HELVING	EGIIMMN MEINING	EGILLST GILLETS	EGILRUV VIRGULE
EGHILPT	PIGHTLE	EGIIMNP IMPINGE	EGILLSU GULLIES	EGILRZZ GRIZZLE
EGHILRT	LIGHTER	EGIIMNR MINGIER	LIGULES	EGILSST LEGISTS
	RELIGHT	EGIIMNT ITEMING	EGILMMN LEMMING	EGILSSW WIGLESS
EGHILSS	SLEIGHS	EGIIMNV MIEVING	EGILMMR GLIMMER	EGILSTU GLUIEST
EGHILST	SLEIGHT	EGIIMPR GIMPIER	EGILMNR GREMLIN	UGLIEST
EGHIMMN	HEMMING	EGIIMRR GRIMIER	MERLING	EGILSTZ GLITZES
EGHIMNS	MESHING	EGIIMPS PIGMIES	MINGLER	EGIMMRR GRIMMER
EGHIMNT	THEMING	EGIIMSV MISGIVE	EGILMNS MINGLES	EGIMMRS GIMMERS
EGHIMPT	EMPIGHT	EGIINNP PEINING	EGILMNT MELTING	MEGRIMS
EGHINNN	HENNING	EGIINNR GINNIER	EGILMNU EMULING	EGIMMRU GUMMIER
EGHINNT	HENTING	REINING	LEGUMIN	EGIMMTU GUMMITE
EGHINNU	UNHINGE	EGIINNS INGINES	EGILMNW MEWLING	EGIMNNN NEMNING
EGHINOS	SHOEING	INSIGNE	EGILMNY YELMING	EGIMNNO OMENING
EGHINPS	HESPING	SEINING	EGILMOR GOMERIL	EGIMNNR RINGMEN
	PHESING	EGIINNV VEINING	EGILMOU ELOGIUM	EGIMNNS MENSING
EGHINRR	HERRING	EGIINOP EPIGONI	EGILMPS GLIMPSE	EGIMNOS MISGONE
EGHINRT	RIGHTEN	EGIINPS PEISING	MEGILPS	EGIMNOT EMOTING
EGHINRW	WHINGER	PIGSNIE	EGILMST GIMLETS	MITOGEN
EGHINRY	HERYING	EGIINPZ PEIZING	EGILNNS GINNELS	EGIMNOV EMOVING
EGHINST	NIGHEST	EGIINRR GIRNIER	EGILNOP ELOPING	EGIMNOW MEOWING
EGHINSW	HEWINGS	EGIINRT IGNITER	EGILNOS ELOIGNS	EGIMNPR IMPREGN
	SHEWING	TIERING	LEGIONS	PERMING
	WHINGES	TIGRINE	LIGNOSE	EGIMNPT PIGMENT
EGHINSX	HEXINGS	EGIINRV REIVING	LINGOES	TEMPING
EGHINTT	TIGHTEN	RIEVING	EGILNOT LENTIGO	EGIMNQU QUEMING
EGHINWW	WHEWING	EGIINRW WEIRING	EGILNPP LEPPING	EGIMNRS GERMINS
EGHIOOS	SHOOGIE	WINGIER	EGILNPR PINGLER	EGIMNRT METRING
EGHIORS	OGREISH	EGIINRZ ZINGIER	EGILNPS PINGLES	TERMING
EGHIORU	ROUGHIE	EGIINSS SEISING	SPIGNEL	EGIMNRU EMURING
EGHIOST	HOGTIES	EGIINST IGNITES	EGILNPT PELTING	EGIMNSS MESSING
EGHIOTT	GOTHITE	EGIINSV SIEVING	EGILNPY YELPING	EGIMNST STEMING
EGHIOTU	TOUGHIE	VISEING	EGILNRS GIRNELS	TEMSING
EGHIOTV	EIGHTVO	EGIINSW WEISING	LINGERS	EGIMNSU MEUSING
EGHIRRT	RIGHTER	EGIINSZ SEIZING	SLINGER	EGIMNSW MEWSING

EGIMORR	GORMIER		SIGNERS	EGJLNSU	JUNGLES	EGNNTUU	UNGUENT
EGIMOSS	EGOISMS		SINGERS	EGJLSTU	JUGLETS	EGNOOPS	PONGOES
	MISGOES	EGINRST	RESTING	EGKLORW	LEGWORK	EGNOORS	ORGONES
EGIMOST	EGOTISM		STINGER	EGKMSSU	MUSKEGS		OROGENS
EGIMPSY	PYGMIES	EGINRSU	REUSING	EGKNOSY	KYOGENS	EGNOORY	OROGENY
EGIMSST	STIGMES		RUEINGS	EGLLORS	GOLLERS	EGNOOST	GENTOOS
EGINNNP	PENNING		SIGNEUR	EGLLRSU	GULLERS	EGNOOSY	GOONEYS
EGINNNR	RENNING	EGINRSV	SERVING	EGLLRTU	GULLERY	EGNOOTU	OUTGONE
EGINNNY	YENNING		VERSING	EGLLSTU	GULLETS	EGNOOYZ	ZOOGENY
EGINNOP	OPENING	EGINRSW	SWINGER	EGLLSUY	GULLEYS	EGNOPRS	SPONGER
EGINNPU	PENGUIN		WINGERS	EGLMMRU	GLUMMER	EGNOPRY	PROGENY
EGINNRR	GRINNER	EGINRSY	SYRINGE	EGLMNOO	ENGLOOM		PYROGEN
EGINNRS	ENRINGS	EGINRSZ	ZINGERS	EGLMNOR	MONGREL	EGNOPSS	SPONGES
	GINNERS	EGINRTT	GITTERN	EGLMOOR	LEGROOM	EGNOPSW	GOWPENS
EGINNRT	RENTING		RETTING	EGLNNSU	GUNNELS	EGNORRW	WRONGER
	RINGENT	EGINRTU	TRUEING	EGLNOOY	NEOLOGY	EGNORSS	ENGROSS
	TERNING	EGINRTV	VERTING	EGLNOPS	PLONGES	EGNORSU	SURGEON
EGINNRU	ENURING	EGINRTY	RETYING	EGLNORU	LOUNGER	EGNORSV	GOVERNS
EGINNRV	NERVING	EGINRVV	REVVING	EGLNOST	LONGEST	EGNORSY	ERYNGOS
EGINNRY	GINNERY	EGINRVY	REVYING	EGLNOSU	LOUNGES		GROYNES
	RENYING	EGINSST	INGESTS	EGLNOUV	UNGLOVE	EGNORUY	YOUNGER
EGINNSS	ENSIGNS		SIGNETS	EGLNOXY	LOXYGEN	EGNOSSY	GONYSES
	SENSING	EGINSSW	SEWINGS		XYLOGEN	EGNOSTU	TONGUES
EGINNST	NESTING		SWINGES	EGLNOYZ	LOZENGY	EGNOSXY	OXYGENS
	SENTING	EGINSTT	SETTING	EGLNPRU	PLUNGER	EGNPRSU	REPUGNS
	TENSING		TESTING	EGLNPSU	PLUNGES	EGNPSSU	SPUNGES
EGINNSU	ENSUING	EGINSTU	GUNITES	EGLNRTU	GRUNTLE	EGNPSUX	EXPUGNS
	GUNNIES	EGINSTV	VESTING	EGLNSSU	GUNLESS	EGNRRTU	GRUNTER
	INGENUS	EGINSTW	STEWING		GUNSELS	EGNRSTU	GUNTERS
EGINNSW	NEWSING		TWINGES	EGLNSTU	ENGLUTS		GURNETS
EGINNSY	GYNNIES		WESTING		GLUTENS		SURGENT
EGINNTT	NETTING	EGINSTZ	ZESTING	EGLNSUU	UNGLUES	EGNRSUY	GURNEYS
	TENTING	EGINSVX	VEXINGS	EGLOOSY	GOOLEYS	EGNRSYY	SYNERGY
EGINNTV	VENTING	EGINSWY	SWEYING	EGLOPRS	PROLEGS	EGNRTTU	GRUTTEN
EGINNVY	ENVYING	EGINSZZ	GIZZENS	EGLOPSS	GOSPELS		TURGENT
EGINOPR	PERIGON	EGINTTV	VETTING	EGLORRW	GROWLER	EGNSUVY	UNGYVES
	PONGIER	EGINTTW	WETTING	EGLORSS	GLOSSER	EGOOPSY	POOGYES
EGINOPS	EPIGONS	EGIOOPR	GOOPIER	EGLORSU	REGULOS	EGOORRV	GROOVER
	PIGEONS	EGIOORS	GOOSIER	EGLORSV	GLOVERS	EGOORSV	GROOVES
	PINGOES	EGIOOSS	GOOSIES		GROVELS	EGOORSY	GOOSERY
EGINORR	IGNORER		SOOGIES	EGLORSW	GLOWERS	EGOORTU	OUTGOER
EGINORS	ERINGOS	EGIOOST	GOOIEST	EGLOSSS	GLOSSES	EGOORTV	OVERGOT
	IGNORES	EGIOPRS	PORGIES	EGLOSST	GOSLETS	EGOOSST	STOOGES
	REGIONS		SERPIGO	EGLOSUV	VOULGES	EGOOSSY	GOOSEYS
	SIGNORE	EGIOPRU	GROUPIE	EGLPRSU	GULPERS	EGOOSTU	OUTGOES
EGINORT	GENITOR		PIROGUE		SPLURGE	EGOPRRS	GROPERS
EGINORV	OVERING	EGIORRS	GORSIER	EGLRSTU	GURLETS	EGOPRRU	GROUPER
EGINORZ	ZEROING	EGIORST	GOITERS	EGLRSUU	REGULUS		REGROUP
EGINOSU	IGNEOUS		GOITRES	EGLRSUY	GUYLERS	EGORRSS	GROSERS
EGINOSW	WIGEONS		GORIEST	EGLRSYY	GRYSELY		GROSSER
EGINOSY	ISOGENY	EGIORTU	GOUTIER		GRYSELY	EGORRST	GROSERT
EGINOTT	TENTIGO	EGIORTV	VERTIGO	EGLRUZZ	GUZZLER	EGORRSU	GROUSER
EGINOTV	VETOING	EGIORTZ	ZORGITE	EGLSSTU	GUTLESS	EGORRSW	GROWERS
EGINPPP	PEPPING	EGIORUV	VOGUIER	EGLSTUU	GLUTEUS	EGORRTU	GROUTER
EGINPPR	REPPING	EGIOSST	EGOISTS	EGLSUZZ	GUZZLES	EGORRUY	ROGUERY
EGINPPS	PIGPENS		STOGIES	EGMMORT	GROMMET	EGORSSS	GROSSES
EGINPRS	PERSING	EGIOSTT	EGOTIST	EGMMRRU	GRUMMER	EGORSST	GROSETS
	PINGERS	EGIOSTV	VOGIEST	EGMMRTU	GRUMMET		STORGES
	SPRINGE	EGIOTUV	OUTGIVE	EGMNNOS	SONGMEN	EGORSSU	GROUSES
EGINPRU	PUERING	EGIPPPR	GRIPPER	EGMNNOW	GOWNMEN	EGORSTV	GROVETS
EGINPRV	PERVING	EGIPPRS	GRIPPES	EGMNORS	MONGERS	EGORSUV	VOGUERS
	PREVING	EGIPPSU	GUPPIES		MORGENS	EGORTUW	OUTGREW
EGINPRY	PREYING	EGIPPSY	GYPPIES	EGMNORU	MURGEON	EGOSSTY	STOGEYS
EGINPSS	GIPSENS	EGIPRRS	GRIPERS	EGMNORY	MONGERY	EGOSSYZ	ZYGOSES
EGINPSU	SPUEING	EGIPRUU	GUIPURE	EGMNOST	EMONGST	EGOSTTU	GOUTTES
EGINPSW	SPEWING	EGIPSSY	GYPSIES	EGMNOSY	MYOGENS	EGOSTYZ	ZYGOTES
EGINPSY	ESPYING	EGIRRSU	GURRIES	EGMNOYZ	ZYMOGEN	EGPRRSU	PURGERS
	PEYSING		SURGIER	EGMNSTU	NUTMEGS	EGPRSSU	SPURGES
	PIGSNEY	EGIRRSV	VIRGERS	EGMORST	GROMETS	EGPRSUU	UPSURGE
EGINPTT	PETTING	EGIRRTT	GRITTER	EGMORSU	GRUMOSE	EGRRSUY	SURGERY
EGINPYY	EPIGYNY	EGIRSST	TIGRESS		MORGUES	EGRSSTU	GUTSERS
EGINQUU	QUEUING	EGIRSSU	GUISERS	EGMORTU	GOURMET	EGRSSUY	GYRUSES
EGINRRS	ERRINGS	EGIRSTU	GUSTIER	EGNNORT	RONTGEN	EGRSTTU	GUTTERS
	GIRNERS		GUTSIER	EGNNOSU	GUENONS	EGRSTUZ	GUTZERS
	RINGERS	EGIRSTV	GRIVETS	EGNNPTU	PUNGENT	EGSSSTU	GUSSETS
	SERRING	EGIRSUZ	GUIZERS	EGNNRSU	GUNNERS	EHHIKSS	SHEIKHS
EGINRRW	WRINGER	EGIRTTU	GUTTIER	EGNNRUY	GUNNERY	EHHILLS	HELLISH
EGINRSS	INGRESS	EGISSSU	GUSSIES	EGNNSYY	GYNNEYS	EHHIPRS	HERSHIP
	RESIGNS	EGISTTU	GUTTIES			EHHIRST	HITHERS

EHHIRSU	HUSHIER		PHILTRE	EHIORRT	HERITOR	EHLMMUW	WHUMMLE
EHHIRTT	THITHER	EHILRRW	WHIRLER	EHIORSS	HOSIERS	EHLMNOT	MENTHOL
EHHIRTW	WHITHER	EHILRSS	HIRSELS	EHIORST	HERIOTS	EHLMNOY	HOMELYN
EHHISSW	WHISHES		HIRSLES		HOISTER	EHLMNSU	UNHELMS
EHHISWY	WHEYISH	EHILRST	SLITHER		SHORTIE	EHLMOOS	HOLESOM
EHHNPSY	HYPHENS	EHILRSU	HURLIES		TOSHIER	EHLMOPS	PHLOEMS
EHHOOSS	HOOSHES		LUSHIER	EHIORSU	HOUSIER	EHLMSSU	MULSHES
EHHORTT	THOTHER	EHILRSV	SHRIVEL	EHIORSW	SHOWIER	EHLMSTY	METHYLS
EHHRSSU	HUSHERS	EHILRTU	LUTHIER	EHIORSY	HOSIERY	EHLNOPS	PHENOLS
EHHSSSU	SHUSHES	EHILRTW	WHIRTLE	EHIORTT	THORITE	EHLNORT	HORNLET
EHIILLR	HILLIER	EHILSSS	SLISHES	EHIORTU	OUTHIRE	EHLNPSY	PHENYLS
EHIILTT	LITHITE	EHILSTT	LISTETH		ROUTHIE	EHLNRTU	LUTHERN
EHIIMSS	MEISHIS		LITHEST	EHIORTV	OVERHIT	EHLNTTY	TENTHLY
EHIINNS	HINNIES		THISTLE	EHIOSTT	HOTTIES	EHLOOPT	POTHOLE
EHIINRS	SHINIER	EHILSTV	THIVELS	EHIOSTY	ISOHYET	EHLOOSS	SHOOLES
EHIINRT	INHERIT	EHILSTW	WHISTLE	EHIPPRS	SHIPPER	EHLOOSY	HOOLEYS
EHIINRW	WHINIER	EHILTTU	THULITE	EHIPPRW	WHIPPER	EHLOPPS	HOPPLES
EHIINRZ	RHIZINE	EHILTTW	WHITTLE	EHIPPST	HIPPEST	EHLOPSX	PHLOXES
EHIINSS	SHINIES	EHILTWY	WHITELY	EHIPPTW	WHIPPET	EHLOPSY	SPYHOLE
EHIIPPR	HIPPIER	EHIMMRS	SHIMMER	EHIPRSS	RESHIPS	EHLORST	HOLSTER
EHIIPPS	HIPPIES	EHIMMSY	SHIMMEY		SERIPHS		HOSTLER
EHIIPRT	PITHIER	EHIMNPS	SHIPMEN	EHIPRST	HIPSTER	EHLORSW	HOWLERS
EHIIRST	HIRSTIE	EHIMNRS	MENHIRS	EHIPRSU	PUSHIER	EHLORTY	HELOTRY
EHIIRTW	WHITIER	EHIMNRU	INHUMER	EHIPRSW	WHISPER	EHLOSSS	SLOSHES
	WITHIER		RHENIUM	EHIPSTT	PETTISH	EHLOSST	HOSTELS
EHIISST	STISHIE	EHIMNSU	INHUMES	EHIPSZZ	PHIZZES	EHLOSSU	HOUSELS
EHIISTW	WHITIES	EHIMNTY	THYMINE	EHIRRSS	SHERRIS	EHLOSSV	SHOVELS
	WITHIES	EHIMORS	HEROISM	EHIRRSU	HURRIES	EHLOSTT	LOTHEST
EHIJNNO	JOHNNIE		MOREISH		RUSHIER		SHOTTLE
EHIKKSS	KISHKES	EHIMORT	MOITHER	EHIRRSV	SHRIVER	EHLOSTW	HOWLETS
EHIKLRU	HULKIER		MOTHIER	EHIRRTV	THRIVER		THOWELS
EHIKMNT	METHINK	EHIMORZ	RHIZOME	EHIRRTW	WHIRRET	EHLOSTY	THYLOSE
EHIKNOS	HONKIES	EHIMOST	HOMIEST	EHIRSSW	SHIVERS	EHLPRSU	PLUSHER
EHIKNRS	KERNISH	EHIMPRU	HUMPIER		SHRIVES	EHLPSSU	PLUSHES
EHIKNRT	RETHINK	EHIMPRW	WHIMPER	EHIRSSW	SWISHER	EHLRRSU	HURLERS
	THINKER	EHIMPSU	HUMPIES		WISHERS	EHLRSSU	LUSHERS
EHIKNRU	HUNKIER	EHIMRST	HERMITS	EHIRSTT	HITTERS	EHLRSTU	HURTLES
EHIKNSS	KNISHES		MITHERS		TITHERS		HUSTLER
EHIKNSU	HUNKIES	EHIMRSU	HEURISM	EHIRSTU	HIRSUTE	EHLRSUY	HURLEYS
EHIKOOR	HOOKIER		MUSHIER	EHIRSTV	THRIVES	EHLSSSU	SLUSHES
EHIKOOS	HOOKIES	EHIMRTY	THYMIER	EHIRSTW	SWITHER	EHLSSTT	SHTETLS
EHIKOST	HOKIEST	EHIMSST	THEISMS		WITHERS	EHLSSTU	HUSTLES
EHIKPRS	KEPHIRS	EHIMSTU	HUMITES		WRITHES		LUSHEST
EHIKRRS	SHIRKER		TUMSHIE	EHIRSTZ	ZITHERS		SLEUTHS
EHIKRSS	SHREIKS	EHIMSTY	MYTHISE	EHIRSVY	SHIVERY	EHLSTTU	SHUTTLE
	SHRIEKS	EHIMSWY	WHIMSEY	EHIRTTW	WHITRET	EHMMRSU	HUMMERS
	SHRIKES	EHIMTYZ	MYTHIZE		WHITHER	EHMNOOR	HORMONE
EHIKRSU	HUSKIER	EHINNNS	HENNINS	EHIRWZZ	WHIZZER		MOORHEN
EHIKRSW	WHISKER	EHINNRT	THINNER	EHISSSU	HUSSIES	EHMNOPS	PHENOMS
EHIKSSS	SHIKSES	EHINNSS	SHINNES	EHISSSW	SWISHES		SHOPMEN
EHIKSSU	HUSKIES	EHINNSW	WENNISH		WHISSES	EHMNOST	MONETHS
EHIKSTW	WHISKET	EHINOPR	PHONIER	EHISSTT	THEISTS	EHMNOSW	SHOWMEN
EHIKSWY	WHISKEY	EHINOPS	PHONIES	EHISSTU	STUSHIE	EHMNPSU	HUMPENS
EHILLMN	HILLMEN	EHINOPX	PHOENIX		TUSHIES	EHMNPTY	NYMPHET
EHILLNO	HELLION	EHINORR	HORNIER	EHISTTW	TEWHITS	EHMNTTU	HUTMENT
EHILLNS	INSHELL	EHINORS	HEROINS		WETTISH	EHMOOSS	SHMOOSE
EHILLOS	HOLLIES		INSHORE		WHITEST	EHMOOSW	SOMEHOW
EHILLRS	RELLISH	EHINOST	HISTONE	EHISTWY	WHITEYS	EHMOOSZ	SHMOOZE
EHILLRT	THILLER	EHINOSU	HEINOUS	EHISUZZ	HUZZIES	EHMOPRW	MORPHEW
EHILLRU	HULLIER	EHINPPS	HIPPENS	EHISWZZ	WHIZZES	EHMORST	MOTHERS
EHILLTY	LITHELY		SHIPPEN	EHJOPSS	JOSEPHS		SMOTHER
EHILMPW	WHIMPLE	EHINPSS	HIPNESS	EHJORSS	JOSHERS	EHMORTU	MOUTHER
EHILMSU	HELIUMS	EHINRSS	SHINERS	EHKLNOS	LOKSHEN	EHMORTY	MOTHERY
	HUMLIES		SHRINES	EHKLPST	KLEPHTS	EHMOSWY	SOMEWHY
EHILMTT	MELTITH	EHINRSV	SHRIVEN	EHKNORS	HONKERS	EHMPRSU	HUMPERS
EHILMUW	UMWHILE	EHINRSW	WHINERS	EHKNRSU	HUNKERS	EHMPRTU	THUMPER
EHILNOP	PINHOLE	EHINRTV	THRIVEN	EHKNSSU	HUNKSES	EHMRRSY	RHYMERS
EHILNOT	HOTLINE	EHINRTW	WRITHEN	EHKOORS	HOOKERS	EHMRRTU	MURTHER
	NEOLITH	EHINRTZ	ZITHERN	EHKOOSY	HOOKEYS	EHMRSSU	MUSHERS
EHILNPS	PLENISH	EHINSSS	SHINESS	EHKORSS	KOSHERS	EHMRSUU	HUMERUS
EHILNSS	ELSHINS	EHINSST	SITHENS	EHKORSW	HOWKERS	EHMSSUU	HUMUSES
EHILOOR	HOOLIER	EHINSTW	WHITENS	EHKORSY	HORKEYS	EHNNOPR	NEPHRON
EHILOPT	HOPLITE	EHINSTZ	ZENITHS	EHKRSSU	HUSKERS	EHNNOPY	HYPNONE
EHILOSS	ISOHELS	EHINSUV	UNHIVES	EHKRSTU	TUSHKER	EHNNRSU	SHUNNER
EHILOST	EOLITHS	EHIOPPR	HOPPIER	EHLLNSU	UNSHELL	EHNNSTU	UNSHENT
	HOLIEST	EHIOPRS	ROSEHIP	EHLLOOS	HOLLOES	EHNNSUW	UNSHEWN
	HOSTILE	EHIOPST	ETHIOPS	EHLLORS	HOLLERS	EHNOORS	HEROONS
EHILPRS	HIRPLES		OPHITES	EHLMMOW	WHOMMLE		ONSHORE
EHILPRT	PHILTER	EHIORRS	HORSIER	EHLMMSU	HUMMELS		SOREHON

EHNOPRS	PHONERS	EHRSSTY	SHYSTER	EIILPPR	LIPPIER	EIINRTV	INVITER
EHNOPRY	HYPERON		THYRSES	EIILPPS	LIPPIES		VITRINE
EHNOPSU	EUPHONS	EHRSTTU	SHUTTER	EIILPST	SPILITE	EIINRTW	TWINIER
EHNOPSY	PHONEYS	EHRSTTW	STREWTH	EIILQSU	SILIQUE	EIINSSS	SEISINS
EHNOPUY	EUPHONY	EHRSTUW	WUTHERS	EIILRST	RILIEST	EIINSSZ	SEIZINS
EHNORRS	HORNERS	EHRSTUY	TUSHERY		SILTIER	EIINSTT	SITTINE
EHNORRT	HORRENT	EHRTTTY	THRETTY	EIILRSX	ELIXIRS		TINIEST
	NORTHER	EHSSSTU	TUSSEHS	EIILSSV	VISILES	EIINSTU	UNITIES
EHNORRY	HERONRY	EIIILRV	RILIEVI	EIILSTT	ELITIST		UNITISE
EHNORSS	NOSHERS	EIIILST	ILEITIS	EIILSTU	UTILISE	EIINSTV	INVITES
EHNORST	HORNETS	EIIINPR	RIPIENI	EIILSTW	WILIEST		VINIEST
	SHORTEN	EIIJMMS	JIMMIES	EIILTUY	TUILYIE	EIINSTW	WINIEST
	THRENOS	EIIJMPR	JIMPIER	EIILTUZ	TUILZIE	EIINTUV	UNITIVE
	THRONES	EIIKKNR	KINKIER		UTILIZE	EIINTUZ	UNITIZE
EHNORSU	UNHORSE	EIIKLLP	LIPLIKE	EIILTXY	EXILITY	EIIORST	RIOTISE
EHNORSY	NOSHERY	EIIKLMR	MILKIER	EIIMMRS	MIMSIER	EIIORSV	IVORIES
EHNOSST	HOTNESS	EIIKLMS	MISLIKE	EIIMMSS	MIMESIS	EIIORTZ	RIOTIZE
EHNOSSU	UNSHOES	EIIKLPS	PLISKIE	EIIMMST	MISTIME	EIIOSTZ	ZOISITE
EHNOSTT	SHOTTEN	EIIKLRS	SILKIER	EIIMMSX	IMMIXES	EIIPPPR	PIPPIER
EHNOSTY	HONESTY	EIIKLSS	SILKIES	EIIMNNS	MINNIES	EIIPPRR	RIPPIER
EHNOSUU	UNHOUSE	EIIKLST	KILTIES	EIIMNPR	PRIMINE	EIIPPRT	TIPPIER
EHNPRSY	PHRENSY	EIIKNPR	PINKIER	EIIMNRT	INTERIM	EIIPPRZ	ZIPPIER
EHNRSTU	HUNTERS	EIIKNPS	PINKIES		MINTIER	EIIPPST	PIPIEST
	SHUNTER	EIIKNRS	SINKIER		TERMINI	EIIPPSY	YIPPIES
	UNHERST	EIIKNRZ	ZINKIER	EIIMNRV	MINIVER	EIIPRRS	SPIRIER
EHNRTWY	WRYTHEN	EIIKNSS	KINESIS	EIIMNST	MINIEST	EIIPRRT	TRIPIER
EHNSSSU	SNUSHES	EIIKNST	INKIEST	EIIMNTV	MINIVET	EIIPRRV	PRIVIER
EHNSSSY	SHYNESS	EIIKPRS	SPIKIER	EIIMNTY	NIMIETY	EIIPRST	PITIERS
EHOOOPS	HOOPOES	EIIKPSS	PISKIES	EIIMOSS	MEIOSIS		TIPSIER
EHOOPRS	HOOPERS	EIIKRRS	RISKIER	EIIMPRS	PISMIRE	EIIPRSV	PRIVIES
EHOOPRW	WHOOPER	EIIKRSV	SKIVIER		PRIMSIE	EIIPRSW	SWIPIER
EHOOPTY	OOPHYTE	EIIKSTT	KITTIES	EIIMPRW	WIMPIER		WISPIER
EHOORST	HOOTERS	EIILLMM	MILLIME	EIIMPST	PIETISM	EIIPSTT	PIETIST
	SHOOTER	EIILLMT	LIMELIT	EIIMPTY	IMPIETY	EIIPTTT	PITTITE
	SOOTHER	EIILLNV	VILLEIN	EIIMRSS	MISSIER	EIIPTTU	PITUITE
EHOORSV	HOOVERS	EIILLPS	ILLIPES	EIIMRST	MIRIEST	EIIRRTZ	RITZIER
EHOOSST	SOOTHES	EIILLRS	SILLIER		MISTIER	EIIRSSS	SISSIER
EHOOSSW	WOOSHES	EIILLRT	TILLIER		RIMIEST	EIIRSSV	VISIERS
EHOPPRS	HOPPERS	EIILLSS	SILLIES	EIIMSSS	MISSIES	EIIRSTV	REVISIT
	SHOPPER	EIILLST	ILLITES	EIIMSST	STIMIES		STIVIER
EHOPPRT	PROPHET	EIILLSW	WILLIES	EIIMSSV	MISSIVE		VISITER
EHOPPRW	WHOPPER	EIILLTT	TILLITE	EIIMSSZ	SIZEISM	EIIRSTW	WIRIEST
EHOPRRY	ORPHREY	EIILLTV	VITELLI	EIIMSTT	MITIEST	EIIRSVZ	VIZIERS
EHOPRST	POTHERS	EIILMNV	MILVINE	EIIMSTX	MIXIEST	EIIRSWZ	WIZIERS
	STROPHE	EIILMPR	IMPERIL	EIINNNP	NINEPIN	EIIRTTW	WITTIER
	THORPES	EIILMPS	IMPLIES	EIINNNS	NINNIES	EIISSSS	SISSIES
EHOPRSU	UPHROES	EIILMPT	LIMEPIT	EIINNPS	PINNIES	EIISSTV	VISITES
EHOPRTU	POUTHER	EIILMRR	MIRLIER	EIINNQU	QUININE	EIISSTX	SIXTIES
EHOPRTY	POTHERY	EIILMRS	MILREIS	EIINNRT	TINNIER	EIISSTZ	SIZEIST
EHOPRUY	EUPHORY		SLIMIER	EIINNST	INTINES		SIZIEST
EHOPSSS	SPOSHES	EIILMRT	LIMITER		TINNIES	EIISTTT	TITTIES
EHOPSST	POSHEST	EIILMSS	MISSILE	EIINNSW	INSINEW	EIISTUV	UVEITIS
EHORRSS	SHORERS		SIMILES	EIINNTV	INVENIT	EIISTZZ	TIZZIES
EHORRST	RHETORS	EIILMST	ELITISM	EIINNTW	INTWINE	EIISVZZ	VIZZIES
	ROTHERS		LIMIEST	EIINOPR	RIPIENO	EIJKKSU	JUKSKEI
	SHORTER		LIMITES	EIINORR	IRONIER	EIJKNPR	PERJINK
EHORRTW	THROWER	EIILMSU	MILIEUS	EIINORS	IONISER		PREJINK
EHORSST	TOSHERS	EIILMSV	MISLIVE		IRONIES	EIJKNRS	JERKINS
EHORSSV	SHOVERS	EIILMUX	MILIEUX		IRONISE		JINKERS
	SHROVES	EIILNNS	LINNIES		NOISIER	EIJKNRU	JUNKIER
EHORSSW	SHOWERS	EIILNOS	ELISION	EIINORZ	IONIZER	EIJKNSU	JUNKIES
EHORSTT	HOTTERS		ISOLINE		IRONIZE	EIJKOST	JOKIEST
EHORSTU	SHOUTER		LIONISE	EIINOSS	IONISES	EIJLLNY	INJELLY
	SOUTHER	EIILNOT	ETIOLIN	EIINOSZ	IONIZES	EIJLLOR	JOLLIER
EHORSTW	THROWES	EIILNOV	OLIVINE	EIINPPR	NIPPIER	EIJLLOS	JOLLIES
EHORSTX	EXHORTS	EIILNOZ	LIONIZE	EIINPRS	INSPIRE	EIJLLST	JILLETS
EHORSWY	SHOWERY	EIILNPS	SPLENII		PIRNIES	EIJLORT	JOLTIER
EHORTUY	OUTHYRE	EIILNRR	NIRLIER		SNIPIER	EIJLORW	JOWLIER
EHOSSST	HOSTESS	EIILNRS	INLIERS		SPINIER	EIJMPRU	JUMPIER
EHOSSTT	SHOTTES	EIILNRT	LINTIER	EIINPST	PINIEST	EIJMPST	JIMPEST
EHOSTTT	HOTTEST		NITRILE		PINITES	EIJNNOS	ENJOINS
EHOTTTW	WOTTETH	EIILNSS	INISLES		TIEPINS	EIJNORS	JOINERS
EHPRSSU	PUSHERS	EIILNST	LINIEST	EIINQRU	INQUIRE		REJOINS
EHPRSSY	SYPHERS		LINTIES	EIINQSU	QUINIES	EIJNORT	JOINTER
EHPRSYZ	ZEPHYRS	EIILORR	ROILIER	EIINQTU	INQUIET	EIJNORY	JOINERY
EHPRTTU	TURPETH	EIILORS	SOILIER	EIINRTT	NITRITE	EIJNOST	JONTIES
EHPRTUW	UPTHREW	EIILORV	RILIEVO		NITTIER	EIJNPRU	JUNIPER
EHRRSSU	RUSHERS	EIILOST	IOLITES		TINTIER	EIJNRRU	INJURER
EHRRSTU	HURTERS		OILIEST			EIJNRSU	INJURES

EIJNSTY	JITNEYS	EIKNOSS	KENOSIS
EIJRSTT	JITTERS	EIKNOSV	INVOKES
EIJRTTY	JITTERY	EIKNPRS	PERKINS
EIJSSUV	JUSSIVE	EIKNPST	PINKEST
EIJSTTU	JUTTIES	EIKNPSU	SPUNKIE
EIKKLNR	KLINKER	EIKNRSS	SINKERS
EIKKLNS	KINKLES	EIKNRST	SKINTER
EIKKNRS	SKINKER		STINKER
EIKKOOR	KOOKIER		TINKERS
EIKKRSY	YIKKERS	EIKNRSW	WINKERS
EIKKRUY	YUKKIER	EIKNRTT	KNITTER
EIKLLNW	INKWELL		TRINKET
EIKLLOS	SKOLLIE	EIKNSSU	SUNKIES
EIKLLRS	KILLERS	EIKNSTT	KITTENS
	RESKILL	EIKNTTY	KITTENY
EIKLLST	SKILLET	EIKNTUZ	KUNZITE
EIKLMMN	MILKMEN	EIKOORR	ROOKIER
EIKLMNN	LINKMEN	EIKOORS	ROOKIES
EIKLMNR	KREMLIN	EIKOPPS	KOPPIES
EIKLMRS	MILKERS	EIKOPRR	PORKIER
EIKLNNS	ENLINKS	EIKOPRS	PORKIES
EIKLNRS	LINKERS	EIKOPST	POKIEST
	SLINKER	EIKORST	ROKIEST
EIKLNRT	TINKLER	EIKORSY	YORKIES
EIKLNRW	WINKLER	EIKOSST	KETOSIS
	WRINKLE	EIKPPRS	KIPPERS
EIKLNSS	KINLESS		SKIPPER
	SILKENS	EIKPPST	SKIPPET
EIKLNST	LENTISK	EIKPRSY	SPIKERY
	TINKLES	EIKPSSS	SKEPSIS
EIKLNSU	SUNLIKE	EIKRRSS	RISKERS
	UNLIKES	EIKRRST	SKIRRET
EIKLNSV	KELVINS		SKIRTER
EIKLNSW	WELKINS		STRIKER
	WINKLES	EIKRSSS	KISSERS
EIKLNSY	SKYLINE	EIKRSST	STRIKES
EIKLNTT	KNITTLE	EIKRSSV	SKIVERS
EIKLNTU	NUTLIKE	EIKRSTT	SKITTER
EIKLNTW	TWINKLE	EIKRSTU	TURKIES
EIKLOOP	PLOOKIE		TUSKIER
EIKLOPU	PLOUKIE	EIKSSTW	WISKETS
EIKLORY	YOLKIER	EIKSSTY	SKYIEST
EIKLOTY	TOYLIKE	EIKSTUY	YUKIEST
EIKLPRY	PERKILY	EILLLOS	LOLLIES
EIKLPSY	PESKILY	EILLMNU	MULLEIN
EIKLRST	KILTERS	EILLMOS	MOLLIES
	KIRTLES	EILLMOT	MELILOT
EIKLRSU	SULKIER	EILLMOU	MOUILLE
EIKLRTT	KITTLER	EILLMRS	MILLERS
EIKLSSS	KISSELS	EILLMST	MILLETS
EIKLSSU	SULKIES		MISTELL
EIKLSTT	KITTLES	EILLMSU	ILLUMES
	SKITTLE	EILLNNP	PENNILL
EIKMMRR	KRIMMER	EILLNOS	LIONELS
EIKMMRS	KIMMERS		NIELLOS
	SKIMMER	EILLNSS	ILLNESS
EIKMNNS	KINSMEN	EILLNST	LENTILS
EIKMNOR	MONIKER		LINTELS
EIKMNRS	MERKINS		TELLINS
EIKMNSS	MISKENS	EILLOPS	POLLIES
EIKMNST	MISKENT	EILLORU	ROUILLE
EIKMNSW	MISKNEW	EILLORW	LOWLIER
EIKMORS	IRKSOME	EILLORZ	ZORILLE
	SMOKIER	EILLOST	OILLETS
EIKMOSS	SMOKIES	EILLOSV	VILLOSE
EIKMOSY	MISYOKE	EILLOSW	WOLLIES
EIKMRRU	MURKIER	EILLPRS	SPILLER
EIKMRSS	KIRMESS	EILLPSS	LIPLESS
EIKMRST	MIRKEST	EILLPSU	PILULES
EIKMRSU	MUSKIER	EILLQTU	QUILLET
EIKMSST	KISMETS	EILLRSS	SILLERS
EIKMSSY	MISKEYS	EILLRST	RILLETS
EIKNNOS	KINONES		STILLER
EIKNNRS	SKINNER		TILLERS
EIKNOOR	NOOKIER		TRELLIS
	ROOINEK	EILLRSW	SWILLER
EIKNOOS	NOOKIES		WILLERS
EIKNOPS	PINKOES	EILLRTT	LITTLER
EIKNORW	WONKIER	EILLSST	LISTELS

EILLSSU	SULLIES	EILNORR	LORINER
EILLSTT	LITTLES	EILNORS	NEROLIS
EILLSTU	TUILLES	EILNORT	RETINOL
EILLSTW	WILLEST	EILNOSS	ESLOINS
	WILLETS		INSOLES
EILLSWY	WILLEYS		LESIONS
EILMMNO	MOLIMEN		LIONESS
EILMMRS	LIMMERS	EILNOST	ENTOILS
	SLIMMER		LIONETS
EILMMRU	LUMMIER		ONLIEST
EILMNOS	MOLINES	EILNOSU	ELUSION
EILMNOT	MOLINET	EILNOTU	ELUTION
EILMNRS	LIMNERS		OUTLINE
	MERLINS	EILNOTV	VIOLENT
EILMNSS	SIMNELS	EILNOTW	TOWLINE
EILMNSU	EMULSIN	EILNOVV	INVOLVE
	LUMINES	EILNPPS	LIPPENS
	UNLIMES		NIPPLES
EILMNSY	MYELINS	EILNPRS	PILSNER
EILMOOS	MOOLIES	EILNPRU	PURLINE
EILMOPR	IMPLORE	EILNPSS	PENSILS
EILMORR	LORIMER		SPINELS
EILMORS	MOILERS		SPLINES
EILMORT	MOTLIER	EILNPST	PINTLES
EILMOSS	LIMOSES		PLENIST
	LISSOME	EILNPSU	LUPINES
	SMOILES		SPINULE
EILMOST	MOTILES	EILNPTY	INEPTLY
EILMPPS	PIMPLES	EILNPUV	VULPINE
EILMPPU	PLUMPIE	EILNRST	LINTERS
EILMPRS	PRELIMS		SLINTER
	SIMPLER		SNIRTLE
EILMPRU	LUMPIER	EILNRSV	SILVERN
	PLUMIER	EILNRTY	INERTLY
EILMPRY	PRIMELY	EILNRVY	NERVILY
EILMPSS	SIMPLES	EILNSSS	SINLESS
EILMPST	LIMPEST	EILNSST	ENLISTS
	LIMPETS		LISTENS
EILMPSU	IMPULSE		SILENTS
EILMPSW	WIMPLES		TINSELS
EILMPSX	SIMPLEX	EILNSSU	INSULSE
EILMPTY	EMPTILY		SILENUS
EILMRRU	MURLIER	EILNSSV	SNIVELS
EILMRRY	MERRILY	EILNSSY	LINSEYS
EILMRSS	RIMLESS		LYSINES
	SMILERS	EILNSTU	LUTEINS
EILMRST	MILTERS		UNTILES
EILMRSU	MISRULE		UTENSIL
EILMRSV	VERMILS	EILNSTV	VENTILS
EILMRSY	MISERLY	EILNSTW	WESTLIN
EILMRTY	LYMITER		WINTLES
EILMRVY	VERMILY	EILNSUV	UNLIVES
EILMSSS	MISSELS		UNVEILS
EILMSST	MISTLES	EILNSUY	LUNYIES
	SMILETS	EILNSVY	SYLVINE
EILMSSU	MUESLIS	EILNVXY	VIXENLY
EILMSSY	MESSILY	EILOOPR	LOOPIER
	MILSEYS	EILOORS	ORIOLES
	SMILEYS	EILOORT	TROOLIE
EILMSTT	SMITTLE	EILOOST	OOLITES
EILMSTZ	MILTZES		OSTIOLE
EILMSZZ	MIZZLES		STOOLIE
EILMUUV	ELUVIUM	EILOOTZ	ZOOLITE
EILNNPU	PINNULE	EILOPRS	SLOPIER
EILNNST	LINNETS		SPOILER
EILNNSU	UNLINES	EILOPRT	POITREL
EILNNSW	WINNLES		POLITER
EILNNSY	LINNEYS	EILOPST	PIOLETS
EILNOOP	POLONIE		PISTOLE
EILNOOR	LOONIER	EILOPSU	PILEOUS
EILNOOS	LOONIES	EILOPSV	PLOSIVE
EILNOOV	VIOLONE	EILOPTT	PLOTTIE
EILNOPP	PLENIPO	EILOPTX	EXPLOIT
EILNOPR	PROLINE	EILORRS	LORRIES
EILNOPS	EPSILON	EILORRU	LOURIER
	PINOLES	EILORSS	LORISES
EILNOPT	POINTEL		LOSSIER
	PONTILE		RISSOLE
	TOPLINE	EILORST	LOITERS

	TOILERS	EILSUVV	LUVVIES		PROMISE	EINNOST	INTONES
EILORSU	LOUSIER	EILSWZZ	SWIZZLE	EIMOPRV	IMPROVE		TENSION
	SOILURE	EILTWZZ	TWIZZLE	EIMOPSS	IMPOSES	EINNOSV	VENISON
EILORSV	OLIVERS	EIMMMOS	MOMMIES		MOPSIES	EINNOTT	NONETTI
	VIOLERS	EIMMMST	MIMMEST	EIMOPST	MOPIEST		TONTINE
EILORTT	TORTILE	EIMMMSU	MUMMIES		OPTIMES	EINNOVW	INWOVEN
	TRIOLET	EIMMNRS	NIMMERS	EIMORRW	WORMIER	EINNPRS	PINNERS
EILORTU	OUTLIER	EIMMNSU	IMMUNES	EIMORSS	ISOMERS		SPINNER
EILOSSV	SOLIVES	EIMMOPS	POMMIES		MOISERS	EINNPRT	ENPRINT
EILOSTT	LITOTES	EIMMORS	MEMOIRS		MOSSIER	EINNPST	PINNETS
	TOILETS	EIMMOST	TOMMIES	EIMORST	EROTISM		SPINNET
EILOSTU	OUTLIES	EIMMPRR	PRIMMER		MOISTER		TENPINS
EILOSTV	OLIVETS	EIMMPRU	PREMIUM		MORTISE	EINNPSY	SPINNEY
	VIOLETS	EIMMRRT	TRIMMER		TRISOME	EINNRRU	RUNNIER
EILOSTW	OWLIEST	EIMMRRU	RUMMIER	EIMORSU	MOUSIER	EINNRSS	SINNERS
EILOTUV	OUTLIVE	EIMMRSS	MERISMS	EIMORSV	VERISMO	EINNRST	INTERNS
EILPPRR	RIPPLER		SIMMERS	EIMORTT	MOTTIER		TINNERS
EILPPRS	RIPPLES	EIMMRST	MISTERM		OMITTER	EINNRSU	SUNNIER
	SLIPPER	EIMMRSU	IMMURES	EIMOSSS	MOSSIES		UNREINS
EILPPRT	RIPPLET		MUMSIER	EIMOSST	MITOSES		UNRISEN
	TIPPLER		RUMMIES		SOMITES	EINNRSW	WINNERS
	TRIPPLE	EIMMRSW	SWIMMER	EIMOSSU	MOUSIES	EINNRTV	VINTNER
EILPPRU	PULPIER	EIMMRSZ	ZIMMERS	EIMOSTT	MOTIEST	EINNRUV	UNRIVEN
EILPPSS	PIPLESS	EIMMRUY	YUMMIER		TITMOSE	EINNSST	SENNITS
	SIPPLES	EIMMSST	SEMMITS	EIMOSTU	TIMEOUS		SINNETS
EILPPST	STIPPLE	EIMMSTU	TUMMIES	EIMOSTV	MOTIVES	EINNSSY	SINSYNE
	TIPPLES	EIMMSTZ	TZIMMES	EIMOSTZ	MESTIZO	EINNSTT	INTENTS
EILPPSW	SWIPPLE	EIMNNOT	MENTION	EIMOSZZ	MOZZIES	EINNSTU	TUNNIES
EILPRSS	LISPERS	EIMNOOR	IONOMER	EIMPRRS	PRIMERS	EINNSTV	INVENTS
EILPRST	SPIRTLE		MOONIER	EIMPRRU	IMPURER	EINNSUW	UNSINEW
	TRIPLES	EIMNOOS	MOONIES		PRIMEUR	EINNTUW	UNTWINE
EILPRTT	TRIPLET		NOISOME	EIMPRSS	IMPRESS	EINOOPZ	EPIZOON
EILPRTX	TRIPLEX	EIMNOOT	EMOTION		PREMISS	EINOORS	EROSION
EILPRUU	PURLIEU	EIMNOOX	EXOMION		SIMPERS	EINOOST	ISOTONE
EILPSST	STIPELS	EIMNOPS	IMPONES	EIMPRST	IMPREST	EINOOSZ	OZONISE
EILPSTT	SPITTLE		PEONISM		PERMITS	EINOOTZ	ZOONITE
EILPSTU	PULIEST	EIMNOPT	EMPTION	EIMPRSU	RUMPIES	EINOOZZ	OZONIZE
	PUTELIS		PIMENTO		SPUMIER	EINOPPR	POPERIN
	STIPULE	EIMNORS	MERINOS		UMPIRES		PROPINE
EILPSUY	SPULYIE		MERSION	EIMPRTU	IMPUTER	EINOPPS	PEPINOS
EILPSUZ	SPULZIE	EIMNOSS	EONISMS		TUMPIER	EINOPRS	ORPINES
EILPSZZ	PIZZLES	EIMNOST	MOISTEN	EIMPSST	MISSTEP		PIONERS
EILPTTY	PETTILY		MONTIES	EIMPSSU	SEPIUMS		PROINES
EILQRTU	QUILTER	EIMNOSW	WINSOME	EIMPSTU	IMPETUS	EINOPRT	POINTER
EILQRUU	LIQUEUR	EIMNOTY	OMNEITY		IMPUTES		PROTEIN
EILQTUY	QUIETLY		OMNIETY	EIMPSUY	YUMPIES		PTERION
EILRRSU	LURRIES	EIMNPST	PIMENTS	EIMQSTU	MESQUIT		REPOINT
	SURLIER	EIMNPTU	PINETUM	EIMRRST	RETRIMS	EINOPRV	PROVINE
EILRRTW	TWIRLER	EIMNQSU	MESQUIN		TRIMERS	EINOPSS	SPINOSE
EILRSST	LISTERS	EIMNRRU	MURRINE	EIMRRSU	MURRIES	EINOPST	POINTES
EILRSSV	SILVERS	EIMNRST	ENTRISM	EIMRSST	MISTERS		PONTIES
	SLIVERS		MINSTER		SMITERS	EINOPSW	POWNIES
EILRSTT	LITTERS		MINTERS	EIMRSSU	MISUSER	EINOPSY	PIONEYS
	SLITTER		REMINTS		MUSSIER	EINOQUX	EQUINOX
	STILTER	EIMNRSU	MURINES		SURMISE	EINORRS	IRONERS
	TESTRIL		NEURISM	EIMRSSV	VERISMS	EINORSS	ORNISES
	TILTERS	EIMNRSV	VERMINS	EIMRSTT	METRIST		SENIORS
	TITLERS	EIMNRTU	MINUTER	EIMRSTU	MUSTIER		SONERIS
EILRSTU	LUSTIER	EIMNRVY	VERMINY	EIMRSTY	MISTERY		SONSIER
	RULIEST	EIMNSSS	SENSISM		SMYTRIE	EINORST	NORITES
	RUTILES	EIMNSST	MISSENT	EIMRTUV	VITREUM		ORIENTS
EILRSUW	WURLIES	EIMNSSU	MINUSES	EIMRTUX	MIXTURE		STONIER
EILRSVY	SILVERY	EIMNSTT	MITTENS	EIMRUZZ	MUZZIER		TERSION
EILRSZZ	SIZZLER		SMITTEN	EIMSSST	MISSETS		TRIONES
EILRTTY	LITTERY	EIMNSTU	MINUETS	EIMSSSU	MISUSES	EINORSU	URINOSE
	TRITELY		MINUTES	EIMSSSX	SEXISMS	EINORSV	RENVOIS
EILRTUV	RIVULET		MISTUNE	EIMSSTY	STYMIES		VERSION
EILSSTT	STILETS		MUNITES	EIMSTYZ	ZYMITES	EINORSW	SNOWIER
EILSSTW	WITLESS		MUTINES	EINNNOS	NONNIES	EINORTT	TRITONE
EILSSTY	STYLISE	EIMNSTW	MISWENT	EINNNRS	RENNINS	EINORTU	ROUTINE
EILSSVW	SWIVELS	EIMNSZZ	MIZZENS	EINNOOS	IONONES	EINORTW	TOWNIER
EILSSZZ	SIZZLES	EIMNUZZ	MUEZZIN	EINNOPS	PENSION	EINORTZ	TRIZONE
EILSTTT	TITTLES	EIMOORR	MOORIER	EINNOQU	QUINONE	EINOSSS	ESSOINS
EILSTTU	TITULES		ROOMIER	EINNORT	INTONER		OSSEINS
EILSTTV	VITTLES	EIMOORS	ROOMIES		TERNION		SESSION
EILSTTY	STYLITE	EIMOPPR	MOPPIER	EINNORU	NOUNIER	EINOSST	NOSIEST
	TESTILY		POMPIER		REUNION		SONTIES
EILSTVY	SYLVITE	EIMOPRR	PRIMERO	EINNORV	ENVIRON		STONIES
EILSTYZ	STYLIZE	EIMOPRS	IMPOSER	EINNOSS	SONNIES	EINOSSU	SINUOSE

EINOSTT	SNOTTIE / TONIEST / TONITES
EINOSTW	TOWNIES
EINOSUV	ENVIOUS / NIVEOUS / VEINOUS
EINOTTT	TOTIENT
EINPPRS	NIPPERS / SNIPPER
EINPPSS	PEPSINS
EINPPST	SNIPPET
EINPPSW	WIPPENS
EINPRRT	PRINTER / REPRINT
EINPRRU	UNRIPER
EINPRSS	SNIPERS
EINPRST	NIPTERS / PTERINS
EINPRSU	PRUINES / PURINES / UPRISEN
EINPRTU	REPUNIT
EINPSST	INSTEPS / SPINETS
EINPSSU	PUISNES / SUPINES
EINPSTT	SPITTEN
EINPSTU	PUNIEST / PUNTIES
EINPTTY	TINTYPE
EINQRUU	UNIQUER
EINQRUY	ENQUIRY
EINQSSU	SEQUINS
EINQSTU	INQUEST / QUINTES
EINQSUU	UNIQUES
EINQSUZ	QUINZES
EINQTTU	QUINTET
EINQTUU	UNQUIET
EINRRSS	RINSERS
EINRRSU	INSURER / RUINERS
EINRRTU	RUNTIER
EINRSST	INSERTS / SINTERS
EINRSSU	INSURES / SUNRISE
EINRSSV	VERSINS
EINRSTT	ENTRIST / STINTER / TINTERS
EINRSTU	TRIUNES / UNITERS
EINRSTV	INVERTS / STRIVEN
EINRSTW	TWINERS / WINTERS
EINRSTY	SINTERY
EINRSUW	UNWIRES / UNWISER
EINRSWV	WIVERNS
EINRSWY	SWINERY
EINRTTU	NUTTIER
EINRTTW	TWINTER / WRITTEN
EINRTUV	UNRIVET / VENTURI
EINRTUW	UNWRITE
EINRTWY	WINTERY
EINSSST	SENSIST
EINSSSU	SINUSES
EINSSSY	SYNESIS
EINSSTU	INTUSES
EINSSTV	INVESTS
EINSSTW	WISENTS / WITNESS
EINSSTY	TINSEYS
EINSSUW	SUNWISE
EINSSWY	WINSEYS
EINSTTU	TUNIEST
EINSTTW	ENTWIST / TWINSET
EINSTTY	TENSITY
EINSUVW	UNWIVES
EINTTTW	TWITTEN
EINTTUY	TENUITY
EIOOPRR	ROOPIER
EIOOPRV	POOVIER
EIOOPST	ISOTOPE
EIOOPSW	WOOPIES
EIOORRT	ROOTIER / ROOTIES / SOOTIER / TOORIES
EIOORWZ	WOOZIER
EIOOSST	OOSIEST
EIOOSTT	TOOTSIE
EIOOSTZ	OOZIEST
EIOPPPR	POPPIER
EIOPPPS	POPPIES
EIOPPRS	SOPPIER
EIOPPSS	POPSIES
EIOPRRS	PROSIER
EIOPRRT	PIERROT / PORTIER / PORIEST / REPOSIT / RIPOSTE / ROPIEST
EIOPRSU	POURIES / SOUPIER
EIOPRSX	PROXIES
EIOPRTT	POTTIER
EIOPRTU	POUTIER
EIOPRTV	PIVOTER
EIOPSSS	POSSIES
EIOPSST	POSIEST / POSTIES / SEPIOST / SOPITES / TIPTOES
EIOPSTT	POTTIES
EIOPSTU	PITEOUS
EIOPSTX	POXIEST
EIOPSTY	ISOTYPE
EIOPSZZ	POZZIES
EIOPTUW	WIPEOUT
EIOQRTU	QUOITER
EIORRRS	SORRIER
EIORRRT	RORTIER
EIORRRW	WORRIER
EIORRSS	ORRISES / ROSIERS
EIORRST	RIOTERS / ROISTER / RORIEST
EIORRSV	REVISOR
EIORRSW	WORRIES
EIORRUV	OUVRIER
EIORRVV	REVIVOR
EIORSST	ROSIEST / SORITES / SORTIES / STORIES / TOSSIER
EIORSSU	SERIOUS
EIORSSV	VIROSES
EIORSSX	XEROSIS
EIORSTT	STOITER
EIORSTU	OURIEST / TOURIES / TOUSIER
EIORSTV	TORSIVE
EIORSTW	OWRIEST / TOWSIER
EIORTTT	TOTTIER
EIORTTU	TOUTIER
EIORTTV	TORTIVE / VIRETOT
EIORTUV	VOITURE
EIORTUZ	TOUZIER
EIORTWZ	TOWZIER
EIOSSTV	SOVIETS / STOVIES
EIOSTTT	TOTTIES
EIOSTTU	TOUSTIE
EIOSTTW	TOWIEST
EIOSTUV	OUTVIES
EIOSTUZ	OUTSIZE
EIPPPSU	PUPPIES
EIPPRRS	RIPPERS
EIPPRRT	TRIPPER
EIPPRSS	SIPPERS
EIPPRST	TIPPERS
EIPPRSU	PURPIES
EIPPRSY	YIPPERS
EIPPRSZ	ZIPPERS
EIPPRTT	TRIPPET
EIPPSST	SIPPETS
EIPPSTT	TIPPETS
EIPPSUY	YUPPIES
EIPQSTU	PIQUETS
EIPRRSS	PRISERS
EIPRRSU	PURSIER
EIPRRSZ	PRIZERS
EIPRRTU	PURTIER
EIPRRTY	TRIPERY
EIPRRUV	UPRIVER
EIPRSST	ESPRITS / PERSIST / PRIESTS / SITREPS / SPRITES / STIRPES / STRIPES / TRIPSES
EIPRSSU	SUSPIRE / UPRISES
EIPRSSW	SWIPERS
EIPRSTT	PITTERS / SPITTER
EIPRSTU	PERITUS / PUIREST
EIPRSTV	PRIVETS
EIPRSTX	EXTIRPS
EIPRSTY	PYRITES / STRIPEY
EIPRSUU	EURIPUS
EIPRTTU	PUTTIER
EIPRUVW	PURVIEW
EIPSSSU	PUSSIES
EIPSSTZ	SPITZES
EIPSTTU	PUTTIES
EIQRSSU	RISQUES / SQUIERS / SQUIRES
EIQRSTU	QUERIST / REQUITS
EIQRSUV	QUIVERS
EIQRTTU	QUITTER
EIQRUVY	QUIVERY
EIQRUZZ	QUIZZER
EIQSTUU	QUIETUS
EIQSUZZ	QUIZZES
EIRRRST	STIRRER
EIRRSST	STIRRES
EIRRSTT	RITTERS / TERRITS
EIRRSTU	RUSTIER
EIRRSTV	STRIVER
EIRRSTW	WRITERS
EIRRSZZ	RIZZERS
EIRRTTU	RUTTIER
EIRSSST	RESISTS / SISTERS
EIRSSSU	ISSUERS / RISUSES
EIRSSTT	SITTERS
EIRSSTV	STIVERS / STRIVES / TREVISS / VERISTS
EIRSSUU	USURIES
EIRSSUV	VIRUSES
EIRSTTT	STRETTI / TITTERS / TRITEST
EIRSTTU	TERTIUS
EIRSTTV	TRIVETS
EIRSTTW	TWISTER / WITTERS
EIRSTUV	VIRTUES
EIRSUVV	SURVIVE
EIRSUVW	SURVIEW
EIRTTTW	TWITTER
EISSSTU	TISSUES
EISSSTW	SWITSES
EISSSTX	SEXISTS
EISSTTY	TYSTIES
EISSTUV	TUSSIVE
EISSTVW	SWIVETS
EISSWZZ	SWIZZES
EISTTTU	TUTTIES
EJJMNUU	JEJUNUM
EJKMNNU	JUNKMEN
EJKNRSU	JUNKERS
EJKNSTU	JUNKETS
EJKOORY	JOOKERY
EJKORUY	JOUKERY
EJLLORY	JOLLYER
EJLLOSY	JOLLEYS
EJLORST	JOLTERS
EJLORSW	JOWLERS
EJLOSST	JOSTLES
EJLOSSY	JOYLESS
EJLSSTU	JUSTLES
EJMNRUY	JURYMEN
EJMOSST	JETSOMS
EJMPRSU	JUMPERS
EJNORRU	REJOURN
EJNORUY	JOURNEY
EJNOSST	JETSONS
EJNOSTT	JETTONS
EJOORVY	OVERJOY
EJOOSSY	SOOJEYS
EJORSSS	JOSSERS
EJORSTT	JOTTERS
EJORSTU	JOUSTER
EJOSTTU	OUTJEST / OUTJETS
EJPRRUY	PERJURY
EJSSTTU	JUSTEST
EKKLOOY	OLYKOEK
EKKLRSU	SKULKER
EKKOPSU	PUKEKOS
EKLLMSU	SKELLUM
EKLLRRU	KRULLER
EKLMMSU	KUMMELS
EKLMSSU	MUSKLES / SKELUMS
EKLNOPR	PLONKER
EKLNORS	SNORKEL
EKLNOSS	KELSONS / SLOKENS
EKLNPRU	PLUNKER
EKLNRSU	LUNKERS / RUNKLES
EKLNSST	SKLENTS
EKLOORS	LOOKERS
EKLRRSU	LURKERS

EKLSTTU	SKUTTLE	ELLOPTU	POLLUTE	ELNOPRY	PRONELY	ELOPSTT	POTTLES
EKLSTUZ	KLUTZES	ELLORRS	ROLLERS	ELNOPST	LEPTONS	ELOPSTU	TUPELOS
EKMMRSU	SKUMMER	ELLORRT	TROLLER	ELNOPSY	POLEYNS	ELORRSS	SORRELS
EKMNORW	WORKMEN	ELLORSS	SOLLERS	ELNOPTU	OPULENT	ELORRSW	WORRELS
EKMNORY	MONKERY		SORRELLS	ELNORSS	NORSELS	ELORSSS	LESSORS
EKMNOSU	MUSKONE	ELLORST	TOLLERS	ELNORST	LENTORS	ELORSST	OSTLERS
EKMNOSY	MONKEYS	ELLORTY	TROLLEY	ELNORSU	NOURSLE		STEROLS
EKMNPTU	UNKEMPT	ELLORVY	LOVERLY	ELNORTY	ELYTRON		TORSELS
EKMOOPS	MOPOKES	ELLOSST	TOLSELS	ELNOSSS	LESSONS	ELORSSV	SOLVERS
EKMORSS	SMOKERS	ELLOSTU	OUTSELL		SONLESS	ELORSTT	SETTLOR
EKMRSTU	MURKEST	ELLOSVY	VOLLEYS	ELNOSST	TELSONS		SLOTTER
EKMSSTU	MUSKETS	ELLOSWY	YELLOWS	ELNOSSU	ENSOULS		TOLTERS
EKNNOST	NEKTONS	ELLOTTU	OUTTELL		NOUSLES	ELORSTU	ELUTORS
EKNOORS	SNOOKER	ELLOTUW	OUTWELL				OUTLERS
EKNOPSU	UNSPOKE	ELLOVWY	VOWELLY	ELNOSSV	SLOVENS		TROULES
EKNORST	STONKER	ELLOWYY	YELLOWY	ELNOSSW	LOWNESS	ELORSTV	REVOLTS
	STROKEN	ELLPRSU	PULLERS	ELNOSTT	TONLETS	ELORSTW	TROWELS
	TONKERS	ELLPSTU	PULLETS	ELNOSTU	LENTOUS		WORTLES
EKNORSW	KNOWERS	ELLPSUW	UPSWELL	ELNOSTV	SOLVENT	ELORSUV	LOUVERS
EKNORSY	YONKERS		UPWELLS	ELNOSUV	UNLOVES		LOUVRES
EKNORTT	KNOTTER	ELLPSUY	PULLEYS	ELNOSUZ	ZONULES		VELOURS
EKNORTW	NETWORK	ELMMOPS	POMMELS	ELNOSVY	LENVOYS	ELORSUY	ELUSORY
EKNORUY	YOUNKER	ELMMORT	TROMMEL	ELNOSZZ	NOZZLES	ELORSVW	WOLVERS
EKNOSUY	UNYOKES	ELMMPSU	PUMMELS	ELNOTUZ	ZONULET	ELORTTY	LOTTERY
EKNPSTU	PUNKEST	ELMMPTU	PLUMMET	ELNOTVY	NOVELTY	ELORTVY	OVERTLY
EKNRTUY	TURNKEY	ELMMRSU	SLUMMER	ELNPSST	SPLENTS	ELOSSTU	LOTUSES
EKNSSTU	SUNKETS	ELMMSTU	STUMMEL	ELNPSTU	PENULTS		SOLUTES
EKOOPRT	PERTOOK	ELMNOOT	MOONLET	ELNRSSU	NURSLES		TOUSLES
EKOOPRV	PROVOKE		TOOLMEN	ELNRSTU	RUNLETS	ELOSSTW	LOWSEST
EKOORRS	KOREROS	ELMNOOW	WOOLMEN	ELNRSTY	STERNLY		SLOWEST
EKOORRY	ROOKERY	ELMNORS	MERLONS	ELNRSUU	UNRULES	ELOSSTY	SYSTOLE
EKOORST	STOOKER	ELMNOST	LOMENTS	ELNRSUZ	LUZERNS		TOLSEYS
	STROOKE		MELTONS	ELNSSSU	SUNLESS		TOYLESS
EKOPPSU	UPSPOKE	ELMNOSY	MYELONS	ELNSSSY	SLYNESS		TYLOSES
EKOPRRS	PORKERS	ELMNOTU	MOULTEN	ELNSTTU	NUTLETS	ELOSSXY	XYLOSES
	PROKERS	ELMNOTY	YMOLTEN	ELNSUZZ	NUZZLES	ELOSSZZ	SOZZLES
EKOPRUY	KOUPREY	ELMNPPU	PLUMPEN		SNUZZLE	ELOSTTU	OUTLETS
EKORRST	STROKER	ELMNPSU	PLENUMS	ELOOPRS	LOOPERS	ELOSTTY	TYLOTES
EKORRSW	REWORKS	ELMNPUU	UNPLUME		SPOOLER	ELOSTUU	LUTEOUS
	WORKERS	ELMOOPP	POMPELO	ELOORST	LOOTERS	ELOSTUV	VOLUTES
EKORRSY	YORKERS	ELMOOPS	POMELOS		RETOOLS	ELOSTUZ	TOUZLES
EKORSST	STOKERS	ELMOORT	TREMOLO		ROOTLES	ELOSTYZ	TOLZEYS
	STROKES	ELMOPRY	POLYMER		TOOLERS	ELOSWYY	YOWLEYS
EKPPSUU	SEPPUKU	ELMOPSU	PLUMOSE	ELOORTT	ROOTLET	ELOSWZZ	SWOZZLE
EKPRSSY	KRYPSES		PUMELOS	ELOOSST	LOOSEST	ELPPRRU	PURPLER
EKRRSSY	SKRYERS				LOTOSES	ELPPRSU	PULPERS
EKRSSTU	TUSKERS	ELMOPSY	EMPLOYS	ELOOSSW	WOOSELS		PURPLES
EKRSTUY	TURKEYS	ELMORSS	MORSELS	ELOOSTT	TOOTLES		REPULPS
EKRSUVY	KURVEYS	ELMORSU	EMULSOR	ELOOSTU	OUTSOLE		SUPPLER
ELLLORR	LORRELL	ELMOSST	MOLESTS	ELOOSWY	WOOLSEY	ELPPSSU	SUPPLES
ELLLORS	LOLLERS	ELMOSSU	MOUSLES	ELOPPPS	POPPLES	ELPQSUU	PULQUES
ELLLOSZ	LOZELLS	ELMOSSY	SMOYLES	ELOPPRS	LOPPERS	ELPRRSU	PURLERS
ELLMNOO	MOELLON	ELMOSTT	MOTTLES		PROPELS		SLURPER
ELLMNOP	POLLMEN	ELMOSTY	MOTLEYS	ELOPPST	STOPPLE	ELPRSTU	SPURTLE
ELLMNOT	TOLLMEN	ELMOSUU	EMULOUS		TOPPLES	ELPRSUV	PULVERS
ELLMOOR	MORELLO	ELMOSUV	VOLUMES	ELOPPSU	POULPES	ELPRTUU	PULTURE
ELLMOSW	MELLOWS	ELMOSXY	OXYMELS	ELOPPSY	POLYPES	ELPRUZZ	PUZZLER
ELLMOWY	MELLOWY	ELMOSZZ	MOZZLES	ELOPRRS	PROLERS	ELPSSSU	PLUSSES
ELLMPUU	PLUMULE	ELMPPRU	PLUMPER	ELOPRRU	PROULER		PUSSELS
ELLMRSU	MULLERS	ELMPPSU	PEPLUMS	ELOPRRW	PROWLER	ELPSSUU	LUPUSES
ELLMSTU	MULLETS	ELMPRSU	LUMPERS	ELOPRRY	PYRROLE	ELPSSUY	SPULYES
ELLMSUV	VELLUMS		RUMPLES	ELOPRSS	PLESSOR	ELPSTUU	PLUTEUS
ELLMSUY	MULLEYS	ELMPRUY	PLUMERY		SPLORES		PUSTULE
ELLNNOT	TONNELL	ELMRSTY	MYRTLES	ELOPRST	PETROLS	ELPSUZZ	PUZZELS
ELLNOOW	WOOLLEN	ELMRTUU	MULTURE	ELOPRSU	LEPROUS		PUZZLES
ELLNOPS	POLLENS	ELMRTUY	ELYTRUM		PELORUS	ELRRSTU	RUSTLER
ELLNOPT	POLLENT	ELMRUZZ	MUZZLER		PERLOUS	ELRRTTU	TURTLER
ELLNORS	ENROLLS	ELMSSSU	MUSSELS		SPORULE	ELRSSSU	RUSSELS
ELLNOST	STOLLEN		SUMLESS	ELOPRSV	PLOVERS	ELRSSTU	LUSTERS
ELLNOSU	NOUSELL	ELMSTUU	MUTULES	ELOPRSX	PLEXORS		LUSTRES
ELLNOSV	VELLONS	ELMSUZZ	MUZZLES	ELOPRSY	LEPROSY		RESULTS
ELLNOSW	SWOLLEN	ELNNOPU	NONUPLE	ELOPRTT	PLOTTER		RUSTLES
ELLNOXY	XYLENOL	ELNNOSS	NELSONS	ELOPRTU	PLOUTER		SUTLERS
ELLNPSU	UNSPELL	ELNNRSU	RUNNELS		POULTER		ULSTERS
ELLNSUU	LUNULES	ELNNSTU	TUNNELS	ELOPRTW	PLOWTER	ELRSTTU	TURTLES
ELLOOSW	WOOSELL	ELNOOSS	LOOSENS	ELOPRTY	PROTYLE	ELRSTTY	TETRYLS
ELLOOSY	LOOSELY	ELNOOSU	UNLOOSE	ELOPRVY	OVERPLY	ELRSTUY	SUTLERY
ELLOPRR	PROLLER	ELNOOSW	WOOLENS		PLOVERY	ELRSTWY	SWELTRY
ELLOPRS	POLLERS	ELNOOSZ	SNOOZLE	ELOPSST	TOPLESS	ELRSUWY	WURLEYS
		ELNOPRU	PLEURON	ELOPSSU	SOUPLES		

ELRTTUY UTTERLY
ELRTUUV VULTURE
ELSSSTU TUSSLES
ELSSTTU SUTTLES
ELSSTTY STYLETS
ELSSTYY SYSTYLE
ELSUWZZ WUZZLES
EMMMOST MOMMETS
EMMMRSU MUMMERS
EMMMRUY MUMMERY
EMMNNOS MNEMONS
EMMNOOR MONOMER
         MOORMEN
EMMNOOT MOOTMEN
EMMNORY MERONYM
EMMNOST MOMENTS
         MONTEMS
EMMNOTU OMENTUM
EMMNOTY METONYM
EMMOPRR PROMMER
EMMORSZ MOMZERS
EMMOSSU MOUSMES
EMMOSYZ ZYMOMES
EMMPRSU MUMPERS
EMMRRSU RUMMERS
EMMRSSU SUMMERS
EMMRSTU RUMMEST
EMMRSUY SUMMERY
EMMSSUU MUSEUMS
EMNNOOR MONERON
EMNNOSW SNOWMEN
EMNOOPT METOPON
EMNOORS MOONERS
EMNOORT MONTERO
EMNOOSS MONOSES
EMNOOST MOONSET
EMNOOSY NOYSOME
EMNOOTY ENOMOTY
EMNOPRT PORTMEN
EMNOPST POSTMEN
         TOPSMEN
EMNOPSY EPONYMS
EMNORRU MOURNER
EMNORSS SERMONS
EMNORST MENTORS
         MONSTER
         MONTRES
EMNORTT TORMENT
EMNORTU MONTURE
         MOUNTER
         REMOUNT
EMNOSST STEMSON
EMNOSTU UNSMOTE
EMNOSTY ETYMONS
EMNOSXY EXONYMS
EMNPSSU PENSUMS
EMNRRSU MURRENS
EMNRSSU RUMNESS
EMNRSTU MUNSTER
         STERNUM
EMOOPRT PROMOTE
EMOOPRY POMEROY
EMOORRS MOROSER
         ROOMERS
EMOORST MOOTERS
EMOORSU UROSOME
EMOOSSS OSMOSES
EMOOSTT MOOTEST
         MOTTOES
         TOOMEST
EMOOSTW TWOSOME
EMOOSTY MYOSOTE
         TOYSOME
EMOOTUV OUTMOVE
EMOPPRS MOPPERS
EMOPPST MOPPETS
EMOPPSY POMPEYS
EMOPRRS ROMPERS
EMOPRST STOMPER
         TROMPES
EMOPRSU SUPREMO
EMOPSSU MOPUSES
EMOPSSY MYOPSES
EMOQSSU MOSQUES
EMORRST TERMORS
         TREMORS
EMORRSU MORSURE
EMORRSW WORMERS
EMORRWY WORMERY
EMORSST MOTSERS
EMORSSU MOUSERS
         SMOUSER
EMORSTU MOUTERS
         OESTRUM
EMORSUY MOUSERY
EMOSSSU MOUSSES
         SMOUSES
EMOSSYZ ZYMOSES
EMOSTTT MOTETTS
EMOSTVZ ZEMSTVO
EMPPRSU PUMPERS
EMPRSTU STUMPER
         SUMPTER
EMPRTTU TRUMPET
EMRRSTU STURMER
EMRRSUY MURREYS
EMRSSTU ESTRUMS
         MUSTERS
         STUMERS
EMRSTTU MUTTERS
EMRSTYY MYSTERY
EMSSSTY SYSTEMS
ENNNOPS PENNONS
ENNNRUY NUNNERY
ENNOORS NOONERS
ENNOORT NORTENO
ENNOOTT NONETTO
ENNORST STONERN
ENNORSU NEURONS
ENNORSW RENOWNS
ENNORTU NEUTRON
ENNOSST SONNETS
         STONNES
         TENSONS
ENNOSSW NOWNESS
ENNOSTU NEUSTON
ENNOSTW NEWTONS
ENNOSTZ TENZONS
ENNOUVW UNWOVEN
ENNPRSU PUNNERS
ENNPSTU PUNNETS
         UNSPENT
ENNRRSU RUNNERS
ENNRSTU RUNNETS
         STUNNER
ENNRSUW WUNNERS
ENNSSTU UNNESTS
ENNSTTU UNTENTS
ENNSTUU UNTUNES
ENNTTUY UNTENTY
ENOOPPR PROPONE
ENOOPRS OPERONS
         SNOOPER
ENOOPSY SPOONEY
ENOORSS SEROONS
ENOORST ENROOTS
ENOORSU ONEROUS
ENOORSZ SNOOZER
ENOOSST SOONEST
ENOOSSZ SNOOZES
ENOOSTT TESTOON
ENOOSTU UNSOOTE
ENOOTXY OXYTONE
ENOPPSU UNPOPES
ENOPRRS PERRONS
ENOPRRU PRONEUR
ENOPRSS PERSONS
ENOPRST POSTERN
         PRONEST
ENOPRSU UNROPES
ENOPRSY PROYNES
         PYONERS
ENOPRTT PORTENT
ENOPRTY ENTROPY
ENOPSST POSNETS
         STEPSON
ENOPSTT POTENTS
ENOPSWY POWNEYS
ENOQTUU UNQUOTE
ENORRSS SNORERS
         SORNERS
ENORRST SNORTER
ENORRTT TORRENT
ENORRUV OVERRUN
ENORSSS SENSORS
ENORSST STONERS
         TENSORS
ENORSSW WORSENS
ENORSSY SENSORY
ENORSTT ROTTENS
         SNOTTER
         STENTOR
ENORSTU TENOURS
         TONSURE
ENORSTY TYRONES
ENORSUV NERVOUS
         UNSWORE
ENORSUZ ZONURES
ENORSVY RENVOYS
ENORSZZ NOZZERS
ENORTUW UNWROTE
ENORTUY TOURNEY
ENOSSST SESTONS
ENOSSTT OSTENTS
         TESTONS
ENOSSTU OUTNESS
         TONUSES
ENOSSTW TWONESS
ENOSSTX SEXTONS
ENOSSUW SWOUNES
ENOSSWW SWOWNES
ENOSTTU STOUTEN
         TENUTOS
ENOSTUU TENUOUS
ENOTTUW OUTWENT
ENPRRSU PRUNERS
         SPURNER
ENPRSSU SPURNES
ENPRSTU PUNSTER
         PUNTERS
ENPRSUU UNPURSE
ENPRSWY PREWYNS
ENPSSSU SUSPENS
ENPSSTU UNSTEPS
ENPSTTU STUPENT
ENPSTUW UNSWEPT
ENRRSSU NURSERS
ENRRSTU RETURNS
         TURNERS
ENRRSUU UNSURER
ENRRSUY NURSERY
ENRRTUU NURTURE
         UNTRUER
ENRRTUY TURNERY
ENRSSTU UNRESTS
ENRSSWY WRYNESS
ENRSTTU ENTRUST
         NUTTERS
ENRSUZZ NUZZERS
ENRSVWY WYVERNS
ENRTTUY NUTTERY
ENSSSTU SUNSETS
EOOOPRS OOSPORE
EOOPPRS OPPOSER
         PROPOSE
EOOPPSS OPPOSES
EOOPPRV POPOVER
         SPOORER
EOOPRRT PROTORE
         TROOPER
EOOPRSS POROSES
EOOPRST POOREST
         POOTERS
         STOOPER
EOOPRTU OUTROPE
EOOPRTV OVERTOP
EOOPRTW TOWROPE
EOOPRVY POOVERY
EOOPRYZ ZOOPERY
EOOPSST STOOPES
EOOPTYZ ZOOTYPE
EOORRST ROOSTER
         ROOTERS
         TOREROS
EOORSSS SOROSES
EOORSTT TOOTERS
EOORSVW OVERSOW
EOORTUW OUTWORE
EOOSSSU OSSEOUS
EOOSSTT TOOTSES
EOOSTWZ WOOTZES
EOOTTUV OUTVOTE
EOPPPRS POPPERS
EOPPPST POPPETS
EOPPRRS PROPERS
         PROSPER
EOPPRSS OPPRESS
         PORPESS
EOPPRST STOPPER
         TOPPERS
EOPPRSU PURPOSE
EOPPRSW SWOPPER
EOPPRSY PYROPES
         YOPPERS
EOPPSSU SUPPOSE
EOPRRSS PRESSOR
         PROSERS
EOPRRST PORTERS
         PRETORS
         REPORTS
         SPORTER
EOPRRSU POURERS
EOPRRSV PROVERS
EOPRRTU TROUPER
EOPRSSS POSSERS
EOPRSST PORTESS
         POSTERS
         PRESTOS
         REPOSTS
EOPRSSU POSEURS
         SEROPUS
         SOUPERS
EOPRSSW PROWESS
EOPRSSY OSPREYS
         PYROSES
EOPRSTT POTTERS
         PROTEST
         SPOTTER
EOPRSTU PETROUS
         POSTURE
         POUTERS
         PROTEUS
         SEPTUOR
         SPOUTER
         TROUPES
EOPRSTW POWTERS
EOPRSTX EXPORTS
EOPRSUU POURSUE
         UPROUSE
EOPRSUW POURSEW
EOPRTTY POTTERY
EOPRTUY EUTROPY
EOPRTVY POVERTY
EOPSSSS POSSESS
EOPSSST POSSETS
EOPSSSU POUSSES

	SPOUSES
EOPSSTX	SEXPOTS
EOPSTTU	OUTSTEP
	TOUPETS
EOPSTTW	STEWPOT
EOPTTUW	OUTWEPT
EOQRSTU	QUESTOR
	QUOTERS
	ROQUETS
	TORQUES
EORRRST	RORTERS
	TERRORS
EORRSSS	ROSSERS
EORRSST	RESORTS
	ROSTERS
	SORTERS
	STORERS
EORRSSU	ROUSERS
EORRSTT	RETORTS
	ROTTERS
	TORRETS
EORRSTU	RETOURS
	ROUSTER
	ROUTERS
	TOURERS
	TROUSER
EORRSTV	TROVERS
EORRSTW	STROWER
EORRSTY	ROYSTER
EORRSZZ	ROZZERS
EORRTTT	TROTTER
EORRTTU	TORTURE
	TROUTER
EORSSST	TOSSERS
EORSSSU	SOURSES
EORSSTU	ESTROUS
	OESTRUS
	OUSTERS
	SOUREST
	SOUTERS
	TOUSERS
	TROUSES
	TUSSORE
EORSSTV	STOVERS
	VOTRESS
EORSSTW	SOWTERS
	STOWERS
	STOWRES
	TOWSERS
EORSSTY	OYSTERS
	STOREYS
EORSSTZ	ZOSTERS
EORSSWW	WOWSERS
EORSTTT	STOTTER
	STRETTO
	TOTTERS
EORSTTU	STOUTER
	TOUTERS
EORSTTW	SWOTTER
EORSTTX	EXTORTS
EORSTTY	ROSETTY
EORSTUX	SEXTUOR
EORSUVY	VOYEURS
EORTTTY	TOTTERY
EOSSSST	STOSSES
EOSSSSW	SOWSSES
EOSSTTU	OUTSETS
EOSTTTW	WOTTEST
EPPPSTU	PUPPETS
EPPRRTU	PRERUPT
EPPRRUU	PURPURE
EPPRSSU	SUPPERS
EPPSTUW	UPSWEPT
EPRRRSU	SPURRER
EPRRSSU	PURSERS
EPRRSUU	PURSUER
	USURPER
EPRRSUY	SPURREY
EPRRTUU	RUPTURE
EPRSSSU	PUSSERS
EPRSSTU	UPRESTS
EPRSSTY	SPRYEST
EPRSSUU	PURSUES
EPRSSUW	PURSEWS
EPRSTTU	PUTTERS
	SPUTTER
EPRSTUU	PUTURES
EPRSUVY	PURVEYS
EQRSTWY	QWERTYS
ERRSSTU	RUSTRES
	TRUSSER
ERRSSUU	USURERS
ERRSSUY	SURREYS
ERRSTTU	RUTTERS
	TRUSTER
	TURRETS
ERRSTTY	TRYSTER
ERSSSTU	RUSSETS
	TRUSSES
	TUSSERS
ERSSSUU	USURESS
ERSSTTU	TUTRESS
ERSSTUU	SUTURES
ERSSTUY	RUSSETY
ERSSTXY	XYSTERS
ERSSUVW	SURVEWS
ERSSUVY	SURVEYS
ERSTTTU	STUTTER
ERSTTUX	URTEXTS
FFFGINU	FUFFING
FFGGINO	GOFFING
FFGHINU	HUFFING
FFGIIMN	MIFFING
FFGIINN	NIFFING
FFGIINR	GRIFFIN
FFGIINT	TIFFING
FFGILNU	LUFFING
FFGIMNU	MUFFING
FFGINOR	GRIFFON
FFGINOS	OFFINGS
FFGINPU	PUFFING
FFGINRU	RUFFING
FFGLOOS	LOGOFFS
FFGLRUY	GRUFFLY
FFHHISU	HUFFISH
FFHIISY	FISHIFY
FFHIKNU	HUFFKIN
FFHILSU	FISHFUL
FFHILTY	FIFTHLY
FFHILUY	HUFFILY
FFHIMSU	MUFFISH
FFHIOST	TOFFISH
FFHORSS	SHROFFS
FFIILMY	MIFFILY
FFIINST	TIFFINS
FFIISUZ	ZIFFIUS
FFIKLSS	SKLIFFS
FFILLLU	FULFILL
FFILLSU	FULFILS
FFILOST	FILFOTS
FFILOUZ	ZUFFOLI
FFILPSS	SPLIFFS
FFILPUY	PUFFILY
FFILRTY	FRITFLY
FFILSTU	FISTFUL
FFILSTY	STIFFLY
FFIMNSU	MUFFINS
FFINNSU	NUFFINS
FFINOPT	PONTIFF
FFINPSU	PUFFINS
FFINRSU	RUFFINS
FFIORTY	FORTIFY
FFIOSST	SOFFITS
FFIQSUY	SQUIFFY
FFIRTUY	FRUTIFY
FFKLORU	FORKFUL
FFLLOOU	LOOFFUL
FFLNSUY	SNUFFLY
FFLOOUZ	ZUFFOLO
FFLOSTY	FYLFOTS
FFNORTU	TURNOFF
FFOOPST	STOPOFF
FFOPSTU	OFFPUTS
FFRRSUU	FURFURS
FGGGIIN	FIGGING
FGGGINO	FOGGING
FGGGINU	FUGGING
FGGHIIS	FISHGIG
FGGIINT	GIFTING
FGGIISS	FISGIGS
FGGIISZ	FIZGIGS
FGGIIZZ	FIZZGIG
FGGILNO	GOLFING
FGGILNU	FUGLING
	GULFING
FGGILOY	FOGGILY
FGGINOO	GOOFING
FGGINOR	FORGING
FGGINOW	GOWFING
FGHIINS	FISHING
FGHILST	FLIGHTS
FGHILSU	SIGHFUL
FGHILTY	FLIGHTY
FGHIMNU	HUMFING
FGHINOO	HOOFING
FGHINOU	HOUFING
FGHINOW	HOWFING
FGHIOSY	FOGYISH
FGHIRST	FRIGHTS
FGHNOOR	FOGHORN
FGHORUY	FROUGHY
FGHOTUY	FOUGHTY
FGIIKNN	FINKING
	KNIFING
FGIIKNR	FIRKING
FGIIKNS	FISKING
FGIILLN	FILLING
FGIILMN	FILMING
FGIILNO	FOILING
FGIILNR	RIFLING
FGIILNS	FILINGS
FGIILNT	FLITING
	LIFTING
FGIILNX	FLIXING
FGIILNY	LIGNIFY
FGIIMNR	FIRMING
FGIINNO	FOINING
FGIINNS	FININGS
FGIINRR	FIRRING
FGIINRS	FIRINGS
FGIINRT	RIFTING
FGIINRY	NIGRIFY
FGIINRZ	FRIZING
FGIINST	FISTING
	SIFTING
FGIINSX	FIXINGS
FGIINSY	SIGNIFY
FGIINTT	FITTING
	TIFTING
FGIINZZ	FIZZING
FGIKLNU	FLUKING
FGIKNNU	FUNKING
FGIKNOR	FORKING
FGILLNU	FULLING
FGILNOO	FOOLING
FGILNOP	FOPLING
FGILNOR	ROLFING
FGILNOT	LOFTING
FGILNOU	FOULING
FGILNOW	FLOWING
	FOWLING
	WOLFING
FGILNOY	FOYLING
FGILNPY	FLYPING
FGILNRU	FURLING
FGILNSU	INGULFS
FGILNSY	FLYINGS
FGILNTU	FLUTING
FGILNTY	FLYTING
FGILNUX	FLUXING
FGILOOY	GOOFILY
FGILORY	GLORIFY
FGIMNOR	FORMING
FGIMOSY	FOGYISM
FGINNNO	FONNING
FGINNNU	FUNNING
FGINNOY	FOYNING
FGINOOR	ROOFING
FGINOOT	FOOTING
FGINOOW	WOOFING
FGINOPU	POUFING
FGINORT	FORTING
FGINOST	SOFTING
FGINOSW	SOWFING
FGINOSX	FOXINGS
FGINRRU	FURRING
FGINRSU	SURFING
FGINRSY	FRYINGS
FGINRTU	TURFING
FGINSSU	FUSSING
FGINSTU	FUSTING
FGINTTU	TUFTING
FGINUZZ	FUZZING
FGIORST	FRIGOTS
FGIORTW	FIGWORT
FGISTUU	FUGUIST
FGJLSUU	JUGFULS
FGLLNUU	LUNGFUL
FGLMSUU	MUGFULS
FGLNORU	FURLONG
FGLNOSU	SONGFUL
FGLNPUU	UPFLUNG
FGLOOUY	UFOLOGY
FGLORSU	FULGORS
FGLORUU	FULGOUR
FGLOTUY	GOUTFLY
FGLSTUU	GUSTFUL
	GUTFULS
	GUTSFUL
FGNOORU	FOURGON
FGNORSY	GRYFONS
FGNOSUU	FUNGOUS
FHIILMS	FILMISH
FHIINPS	PINFISH
FHILLSU	FULLISH
FHILOOS	FOOLISH
FHILOSW	WOLFISH
FHILPSU	SHIPFUL
FHILPTU	PITHFUL
FHILSUW	WISHFUL
FHINOSU	FUSHION
FHINRSU	FURNISH
FHINSSU	SUNFISH
FHIOOST	OOFTISH
FHIOPPS	FOPPISH
FHIOPSX	FOXSHIP
FHIORRY	HORRIFY
FHIOSST	SOFTISH
FHIPPSU	PUPFISH
FHIRSST	SHRIFTS
FHIRSTT	THRIFTS
FHIRTTY	THRIFTY
FHIRTUY	THURIFY
FHISSSU	HUSSIFS
FHISSTU	SHUFTIS
FHKORTU	FUTHORK
FHLNORU	HORNFUL
FHLNSUU	UNFLUSH
FHLOOSY	SHOOFLY
FHLOPSU	SHOPFUL
FHLPSUU	PUSHFUL
FHLRTUU	HURTFUL
	RUTHFUL
FHOOORS	FORHOOS
FHOOORT	HOOFROT
FHOOOTT	HOTFOOT

FHOORSW	FORHOWS	FIORSUU	FURIOUS	GGHIINN	HINGING	GGINOPU	UPGOING
FHORSTU	FOURTHS	FIOSTTU	OUTFITS		NIGHING	GGINOQS	QIGONGS
FIIIKNN	FINIKIN	FIPPUYY	YUPPIFY	GGHIINS	SIGHING	GGINORS	GORINGS
FIIKNRS	FIRKINS	FIRSSTT	STRIFTS	GGHIIPS	PIGGISH		GRINGOS
FIIKNYZ	ZINKIFY	FKLORUW	WORKFUL	GGHIIRS	RIGGISH	GGINORU	ROGUING
FIILLMO	MILFOIL	FKNOSTY	KONFYTS	GGHIITT	THIGGIT		ROUGING
FIILLNS	INFILLS	FKOOORS	FORSOOK	GGHIMSU	MUGGISH	GGINORW	GROWING
FIILLPS	FILLIPS	FLLOOSW	FOLLOWS	GGHINNO	HONGING	GGINOUV	VOGUING
FIILLSU	FUSILLI	FLLOPTU	PLOTFUL	GGHINOS	HOGGINS	GGINPPY	GYPPING
FIILNOT	TINFOIL		TOPFULL	GGHINSU	GUSHING	GGINPRU	PURGING
FIILNTY	NIFTILY	FLLOSUU	SOULFUL	GGHIPSU	PUGGISH	GGINRSU	SURGING
FIILPTU	PITIFUL	FLLOUWY	WOFULLY	GGHLOSY	SHOGGLY		URGINGS
FIIMMNU	INFIMUM	FLLSTUU	LUSTFUL	GGHORSU	GROUGHS	GGINSTU	GUSTING
FIIMSST	MISFITS	FLMMOUX	FLUMMOX	GGHOSTU	THUGGOS		GUTSING
FIINORS	FIORINS	FLMNOOU	MOUFLON	GGIIILN	GINGILI	GGINTTU	GUTTING
FIINOSS	FISSION	FLMNOSU	MUFLONS	GGIIJJS	JIGJIGS	GGIOORS	GORGIOS
FIINRTY	NITRIFY	FLMOOOT	TOMFOOL	GGIIKNN	KINGING	GGIPRSY	SPRIGGY
FIIPSTY	TIPSIFY	FLMOORS	FORMOLS	GGIILLN	GILLING	GGLLOOS	LOGLOGS
FIIRTVY	VITRIFY	FLMOORU	ROOMFUL	GGIILNP	PIGLING	GGLOOOS	GOOGOLS
FIJLLOY	JOLLIFY	FLNOORR	FORLORN	GGIILNR	RIGLING	GGNOORS	GORGONS
FIJSTUY	JUSTIFY	FLNOOSU	UNFOOLS	GGIILNU	GUILING	GHHHIIS	HIGHISH
FIKKLNO	KINFOLK	FLNOOSW	ONFLOWS	GGIIMMN	MINGING	GHHHIST	HIGHTHS
FIKLLSU	SKILFUL	FLNRSUU	UNFURLS	GGIIMNP	GIMPING	GHHIINS	HISHING
FIKLNOW	WOLFKIN		URNFULS	GGIIMNR	GRIMING	GHHINSU	HUSHING
FIKLNSU	SKINFUL	FLOORSW	FORSLOW	GGIINNN	GINNING	GHHIRST	SHRIGHT
FIKLRSU	RISKFUL	FLOOTUW	OUTFLOW	GGIINNO	INGOING	GHHORTU	THROUGH
FIKNNOS	FINNSKO	FLOPSTU	POTFULS	GGIINNP	PINGING	GHHOSSU	SHOUGHS
FILLLUW	WILLFUL	FLOPSUW	UPFLOWS	GGIINNR	GIRNING	GHHOTTU	THOUGHT
FILLMOY	MOLLIFY	FLOSUUV	FULVOUS		RINGING	GHIIKNO	HOIKING
FILLNUY	NULLIFY	FLPRSUU	UPFURLS	GGIINNS	SIGNING	GHIIKNT	KITHING
FILLOTU	TOILFUL	FLRSSUU	SULFURS		SINGING	GHIILLN	HILLING
FILLOTY	LOFTILY	FMNORSU	UNFORMS	GGIINNT	TINGING	GHIILNR	HIRLING
FILLPSU	UPFILLS	FMRSTUU	FRUSTUM	GGIINNW	WINGING	GHIILNT	HILTING
FILLSTU	LISTFUL	FNNNUUY	UNFUNNY	GGIINNZ	ZINGING		LITHING
FILMNOO	MONOFIL	FNNOORT	FRONTON	GGIINPR	GRIPING	GHIILNW	WHILING
FILMSTU	MISTFUL	FNNOORW	FORWORN	GGIINPS	PIGGINS	GHIILRS	GIRLISH
FILNNUY	FUNNILY	FNOORSU	SUNROOF	GGIINRS	GRISING	GHIINNS	SHINING
FILNORS	FLORINS		UNROOFS	GGIINRT	GIRTING	GHIINNT	HINTING
FILNOSW	INFLOWS	FNOPRTU	UPFRONT		RINGGIT		NITHING
FILNOUX	FLUXION	FNRSTUU	UNTURFS	GGIINSU	GUISING	GHIINNW	WHINING
FILNSTU	TINFULS	FNSTTUU	UNSTUFT	GGIINSV	GIVINGS	GHIINOS	HOISING
FILNTUY	UNFITLY	FOOOPRT	ROOFTOP	GGIIRRS	GRIGRIS	GHIINPP	HIPPING
FILOOTW	WITLOOF	FOOORTT	FOOTROT	GGIJNSU	JUGGINS	GHIINPS	PISHING
FILORST	FIRLOTS	FOOOTTU	OUTFOOT	GGILLNU	GULLING	GHIINPT	PITHING
	FLORIST	FOORSSS	FOSSORS	GGILNNO	LONGING	GHIINRS	HIRINGS
FILORSV	FRIVOLS	FOORTTX	FOXTROT	GGILNNU	LUNGING	GHIINSS	HISSING
FILORTU	FLORUIT	FORRSUW	FURROWS	GGILNOS	GOSLING	GHIINST	HISTING
FILORTY	TRIFOLY	FORRUWY	FURROWY		OGLINGS		INSIGHT
FILOSSS	FOSSILS	FORSSTW	FROWSTS	GGILNOV	GLOVING		SHITING
FILPPUY	PULPIFY	FORSTWY	FROWSTY	GGILNOW	GLOWING		SITHING
FILPSTU	UPLIFTS	GGGGIIN	GIGGING		GOWLING	GHIINSW	WISHING
FILRSTY	FIRSTLY	GGGHINO	HOGGING	GGILNOZ	GLOZING	GHIINTT	HITTING
FILRYZZ	FRIZZLY	GGGHINU	HUGGING	GGILNPU	GULPING		TITHING
FILSSUY	FUSSILY	GGGIIJN	JIGGING	GGILNRU	GURLING	GHIINTW	WHITING
FILSTTU	FLUTIST	GGGIILN	LIGGING	GGILNSU	LUGINGS		WITHING
FILSTUW	WISTFUL	GGGIINP	PIGGING	GGILNUY	GUYLING	GHIINZZ	HIZZING
FILSTUY	FUSTILY	GGGIINR	RIGGING		UGLYING	GHIIRST	TIGRISH
FILSTWY	SWIFTLY	GGGIINT	TIGGING	GGILOOS	GIGOLOS	GHIJNOS	JOSHING
FILUYZZ	FUZZILY	GGGIINW	WIGGING	GGILOST	GIGLOTS	GHIKLNU	HULKING
FIMMMUY	MUMMIFY	GGGIINZ	ZIGGING	GGILOSY	SOGGILY	GHIKNNO	HONKING
FIMMORS	MISFORM	GGGIIST	GIGGITS	GGILRWY	WRIGGLY	GHIKNOO	HOOKING
FIMNORS	INFORMS	GGGIJNO	JOGGING	GGIMMNU	GUMMING	GHIKNOW	HOWKING
FIMNORU	UNIFORM	GGGIJNU	JUGGING	GGIMNOR	GORMING	GHIKNST	KNIGHTS
FIMOORV	OVIFORM	GGGILNO	LOGGING	GGIMNPU	GUMPING	GHIKNSU	HUSKING
FIMORRT	TRIFORM	GGGILNU	LUGGING	GGIMNPY	GYMPING	GHIKNTY	KYTHING
FIMORTY	MORTIFY	GGGIMNU	MUGGING	GGIMNSU	MUGGINS	GHIKRTU	TUGHRIK
FIMRTUY	FURMITY	GGGINNO	GONGING	GGINNNU	GUNNING	GHILLNU	HULLING
FIMSTYY	MYSTIFY		NOGGING	GGINNOO	ONGOING	GHILLSU	GULLISH
FINOOSS	FOISONS	GGGINOR	GORGING	GGINNOP	PONGING	GHILLTY	LIGHTLY
FINOPRS	FRIPONS	GGGINOS	SOGGING	GGINNOR	GRONING	GHILNOS	HOLINGS
FINOPTY	PONTIFY	GGGINOT	TOGGING	GGINNOS	NOGGINS		LONGISH
FINORSS	FRISSON	GGGINOU	GOUGING	GGINNOT	TONGING	GHILNOT	THOLING
FINORST	FORINTS	GGGINPU	PUGGING	GGINNOW	GOWNING	GHILNOW	HOWLING
FINOSSU	FUSIONS	GGGINRU	RUGGING	GGINNRU	GURNING	GHILNPU	INGULPH
FIOORSU	FURIOSO	GGGINSU	SUGGING	GGINOPO	POGOING	GHILNRU	HURLING
FIOPRST	FORPITS	GGGINTU	TUGGING	GGINOOS	GOOSING	GHILNSU	LUSHING
	PROFITS	GGHHIIN	HIGHING	GGINOPR	GORPING		SHULING
FIOPRSY	PROSIFY	GGHHIOS	HOGGISH			GROPING	GHILNSY	SHINGLY
FIOPSTX	POSTFIX	GGHIIJS	JIGGISH			PORGING	GHILNTY	NIGHTLY

GHILPST	PLIGHTS	GHNOSSU	SHOGUNS	GIILNOT	TOILING		WIPINGS
GHILPTY	YPLIGHT	GHNOSTU	GUNSHOT	GIILNPP	LIPPING		WISPING
GHILRTY	RIGHTLY		NOUGHTS	GIILNPS	LISPING	GIINPTT	PITTING
GHILSST	SLIGHTS		SHOTGUN		PILINGS	GIINPTY	PITYING
GHILSTY	SIGHTLY	GHNOTUY	YOUNGTH		SPILING	GIINQRU	QUIRING
GHILTTY	TIGHTLY	GHOOOSW	HOOSGOW	GIILNRS	RIGLINS	GIINQTU	QUITING
GHILTWY	WIGHTLY	GHOORSS	SORGHOS	GIILNRT	TIRLING	GIINRRS	SIRRING
GHIMMNU	HUMMING	GHORSTU	TROUGHS	GIILNST	LISTING	GIINRRT	TIRRING
GHIMNNY	HYMNING	GHORSTW	GROWTHS		SILTING	GIINRSS	RISINGS
GHIMNOS	GNOMISH	GHORTUW	WROUGHT		STILING	GIINRST	STIRING
	HOMINGS	GHORTUY	YOGHURT		TILINGS		TIRINGS
	MOSHING	GHOSTUU	OUTGUSH	GIILNSV	LIVINGS	GIINRSV	VIRGINS
GHIMNPU	HUMPING	GIIJKNN	JINKING		SLIVING	GIINRSW	WIRINGS
GHIMNRY	RHYMING	GIIJLNT	JILTING	GIILNTT	TILTING	GIINRTT	RITTING
GHIMNSU	MUSHING	GIIJNNO	JOINING		TITLING	GIINRTW	TWIRING
GHIMRSU	SIMURGH	GIIJNNX	JINXING	GIILNTW	WILTING		WRITING
GHIMSST	SMIGHTS	GIIKKNN	KINKING		WITLING	GIINSST	SISTING
GHIMSTT	MIGHTST	GIIKKNR	KIRKING	GIILOSS	GLIOSIS	GIINSSU	ISSUING
GHINNOP	PHONING	GIIKLLN	KILLING	GIILOST	OLIGIST	GIINSSW	WISSING
GHINNOR	HORNING	GIIKLMN	MILKING	GIILRST	STRIGIL	GIINSSZ	SIZINGS
GHINNOS	NOSHING	GIIKLNN	INKLING	GIIMMNN	NIMMING	GIINSTT	SITTING
GHINNOT	NOTHING		KILNING	GIIMMNR	RIMMING	GIINSTU	SUITING
GHINNTU	HUNTING		LINKING	GIIMMNS	MININGS	GIINSTV	STIVING
GHINOOP	HOOPING	GIIKLNR	LIRKING	GIIMNNT	MINTING	GIINSTW	WISTING
GHINOOS	SHOOING	GIIKLNS	LIKINGS	GIIMNPP	PIMPING	GIINSVW	SWIVING
GHINOOT	HOOTING		SILKING	GIIMNPR	PRIMING	GIINTTT	TITTING
GHINOOV	HOOVING	GIIKLNT	KILTING	GIIMNRT	MITRING	GIINTTW	WITTING
GHINOPP	HOPPING		KITLING	GIIMNRV	MIRVING	GIINVYZ	VIZYING
GHINOPS	GINSHOP	GIIKNNO	OINKING	GIIMNSS	MISSING	GIINZZZ	ZIZZING
	POSHING	GIIKNNP	PINKING	GIIMNST	MISTING	GIJKNNU	JUNKING
GHINORS	HORSING	GIIKNNR	RINKING		SMITING	GIJKNOO	JOOKING
	SHORING	GIIKNNS	SINKING		STIMING	GIJKNOU	JOUKING
GHINORW	WHORING	GIIKNNT	TINKING		TIMINGS	GIJLLNO	JOLLING
GHINOST	HOSTING	GIIKNNV	KNIVING	GIINNNP	PINNING	GIJLNOT	JOLTING
	TOSHING	GIIKNNW	WINKING	GIINNNR	RINNING	GIJLNOU	JOULING
GHINOSU	HOUSING	GIIKNNZ	ZINKING	GIINNNS	INNINGS	GIJLNOW	JOWLING
GHINOSV	SHOVING	GIIKNPP	KIPPING		SINNING	GIJLNSU	JUNGLIS
GHINOSW	SHOWING	GIIKNPS	PIGSKIN	GIINNNT	TINNING	GIJMNPU	JUMPING
GHINOTT	HOTTING		SPIKING	GIINNNW	WINNING	GIJNOTT	JOTTING
	TONIGHT	GIIKNRS	GIRKINS	GIINNOP	OPINING	GIJNSTU	JUSTING
GHINOTU	HOUTING		GRISKIN		PIONING	GIJNTTU	JUTTING
	THOUING		KRISING	GIINNOR	IRONING	GIKKNNO	KONKING
GHINPPU	HUPPING		RISKING		ROINING	GIKKNOO	KOOKING
GHINPPY	HYPPING	GIIKNRY	YIRKING	GIINNOS	NOISING	GIKKNOY	YOKKING
GHINPSU	GUNSHIP	GIIKNSS	KISSING	GIINNOT	OINTING	GIKLNOO	LOOKING
	PUSHING		SKIINGS	GIINNPP	NIPPING	GIKLNOP	POLKING
GHINRSU	RUSHING	GIIKNST	KISTING	GIINNPS	SNIPING	GIKLNRU	LURKING
GHINRTU	HURTING		KITINGS	GIINNPU	PINGUIN	GIKLNSU	LUSKING
	UNGIRTH		SKITING	GIINNRS	RINSING		SULKING
	UNRIGHT	GIIKNSV	SKIVING	GIINNRT	TRINING	GIKMNOS	SMOKING
GHINSTU	TUSHING		VIKINGS	GIINNRU	INURING	GIKMNSU	MUSKING
GHINTTU	HUTTING	GIIKNTT	KITTING		RUINING	GIKNNNO	KONNING
GHINTTY	TYTHING	GIILLLN	LILLING		URINING	GIKNNOP	PONKING
GHIOPSZ	PHIZOGS	GIILLMN	MILLING	GIINNSW	INSWING	GIKNNOS	SNOKING
GHIORST	RIGHTOS	GIILLNN	NILLING	GIINNTT	TINTING	GIKNNOT	TONKING
GHIORSU	ROGUISH	GIILLNO	GILLION	GIINNTU	UNITING	GIKNNOW	KNOWING
GHIOSUV	VOGUISH	GIILLNP	PILLING	GIINNTV	VINTING	GIKNNOZ	ZONKING
GHIPRST	SPRIGHT	GIILLNR	RILLING	GIINNTW	TWINING	GIKNNSU	UNKINGS
GHIPRTU	UPRIGHT	GIILLNT	LILTING	GIINOPS	POISING	GIKNOOP	POOKING
GHIPSST	SPIGHTS		TILLING	GIINORS	ORIGINS	GIKNOOR	ROOKING
GHIPTTU	UPTIGHT	GIILLNW	WILLING		SIGNIOR	GIKNOPR	PROKING
GHIQSTU	QUIGHTS	GIILMNN	LIMNING		SIGNORI	GIKNOPU	POUKING
GHIRSTW	WRIGHTS	GIILMNO	MOILING	GIINORT	RIOTING	GIKNORT	TROKING
GHISTTW	TWIGHTS	GIILMNP	LIMPING	GIINOSY	YOGINIS	GIKNORW	WORKING
GHLMOOO	HOMOLOG	GIILMNS	LIMINGS	GIINPPP	PIPPING	GIKNORY	YORKING
GHLOOSY	SHOOGLY		SLIMING	GIINPPR	RIPPING	GIKNOST	STOKING
GHLOPSU	PLOUGHS		SMILING	GIINPPS	PIPINGS	GIKNOSY	YOKINGS
GHLORUY	ROUGHLY	GIILMNT	MILTING		SIPPING	GIKNOTU	TOUKING
GHLOSSU	SLOUGHS	GIILMPR	PILGRIM	GIINPPT	TIPPING	GIKNOUY	YOUKING
GHLOSTY	GHOSTLY	GIILMRY	GRIMILY	GIINPPY	YIPPING	GIKNRSY	SKRYING
GHLOSUY	SLOUGHY	GIILNNN	LINNING	GIINPPZ	ZIPPING		SKYRING
GHLOTUY	TOUGHLY	GIILNNR	NIRLING	GIINPQU	PIQUING	GIKNSTU	TUSKING
GHMORSU	SORGHUM	GIILNNS	LIGNINS	GIINPRS	PRISING	GIKNSTY	SKYTING
GHMOSTU	MUGSHOT		LININGS		RISPING	GIKRSTU	TUGRIKS
GHMPRSU	GRUMPHS	GIILNNY	INLYING		SPIRING	GILLLNO	LOLLING
GHNOPRY	GRYPHON	GIILNOR	LIGROIN	GIINPRZ	PRIZING	GILLLNU	LULLING
GHNORST	THRONGS		ROILING	GIINPSS	PISSING	GILLMNU	MULLING
GHNORUU	UNROUGH	GIILNOS	SILOING	GIINPST	SPITING	GILLNNU	NULLING
			SOILING	GIINPSW	SWIPING	GILLNOP	POLLING

GILLNOR	ROLLING
GILLNOT	TOLLING
GILLNPU	PULLING
GILLNSU	ULLINGS
GILLNUW	WULLING
GILLNYY	LYINGLY
GILLOOS	LOLIGOS
GILLORS	RIGOLLS
GILMNOO	LOOMING
	MOOLING
GILMNOR	MORLING
GILMNOT	MOLTING
GILMNOY	MOYLING
GILMNPU	LUMPING
	PLUMING
GILMNRU	MURLING
GILMNSU	LIGNUMS
GILNNOO	GLONOIN
	LOONING
GILNNOU	LOUNING
GILNNOW	LOWNING
GILNNRU	NURLING
GILNNSU	UNSLING
GILNNTU	LUNTING
GILNNUV	VULNING
GILNOOP	LOOPING
	POOLING
GILNOOS	LOOSING
	SOLOING
	SOOLING
GILNOOT	LOOTING
	TOOLING
GILNOPP	LOPPING
GILNOPR	PROLING
GILNOPS	POLINGS
	SLOPING
GILNOPT	POLTING
GILNOPU	LOUPING
GILNOPW	PLOWING
GILNORS	LORINGS
GILNORU	LOURING
GILNOSS	LOSINGS
GILNOST	LINGOTS
	TIGLONS
	TOLINGS
GILNOSU	LOUSING
GILNOSV	LOVINGS
	SOLVING
GILNOSW	LOWINGS
	LOWSING
	SLOWING
	SOWLING
GILNOTT	LOTTING
GILNOTU	LOUTING
GILNOTW	LOWTING
GILNOVV	VOLVING
GILNOVW	WOLVING
GILNOWY	YOWLING
GILNPPU	PULPING
GILNPRU	PURLING
GILNPSU	PLUSING
	PULINGS
	PULSING
	PUSLING
GILNPUY	UPLYING
GILNRSU	RULINGS
GILNSTU	LUSTING
	LUTINGS
	SINGULT
GILNSTY	STYLING
GILNVYY	VYINGLY
GILOORS	GIROSOL
GILOOTW	TWIGLOO
GILORTT	TRIGLOT
GILORTY	TRILOGY
GILOSTT	GLOTTIS
GILRSTY	GRISTLY
GILRTUY	LITURGY
GILRYZZ	GRIZZLY
GIMMMNU	MUMMING
GIMMNPU	MUMPING
GIMMNRY	RYMMING
GIMMNSU	SUMMING
GIMMNUV	VUMMING
GIMMORS	GIMMORS
GIMNNOO	MOONING
GIMNNOR	MORNING
GIMNOOP	MOOPING
GIMNOOR	MOORING
	ROOMING
GIMNOOS	SOOMING
GIMNOOT	MOOTING
	TOOMING
GIMNOOV	MOOVING
GIMNOOZ	ZOOMING
GIMNOPP	MOPPING
GIMNOPR	ROMPING
GIMNOPU	MOUPING
GIMNOPY	YOMPING
GIMNORS	SMORING
GIMNORU	ROUMING
GIMNORW	WORMING
GIMNOSS	MOSSING
GIMNOST	GNOMIST
GIMNOSU	MOUSING
	SOUMING
GIMNOSW	MOWINGS
	SOWMING
GIMNPPU	PUMPING
GIMNPRU	RUMPING
GIMNPSU	IMPUGNS
	SPUMING
GIMNPTU	TUMPING
GIMNPUY	YUMPING
GIMNSSU	MUSINGS
	MUSSING
GIMNSTU	MUSTING
GIMNSTY	STYMING
GIMORSS	SIMORGS
GIMOSSY	YOGISMS
GIMOSTU	GOMUTIS
GIMRSSU	SIMURGS
GIMRSUU	GURUISM
GINNNOO	NOONING
GINNNOR	RONNING
GINNNOW	WONNING
GINNNPU	PUNNING
GINNNRU	RUNNING
GINNNSU	SUNNING
GINNNTU	TUNNING
GINNOOS	NOOSING
GINNOOW	WOONING
GINNOPS	SPONGIN
GINNOPY	PONYING
GINNORS	SNORING
	SORNING
GINNORU	GRUNION
GINNORW	INGROWN
GINNORY	ROYNING
GINNOSS	NOSINGS
GINNOST	STONING
	TONINGS
GINNOSW	SNOWING
	WONINGS
GINNOSZ	ZONINGS
GINNOTW	WONTING
GINNPRU	PRUNING
GINNPTU	PUNTING
GINNRSU	NURSING
	URNINGS
GINNRTU	TURNING
GINNSTU	TUNINGS
GINNTTU	NUTTING
GINNTUY	UNTYING
GINOOPP	POOPING
GINOOPR	ROOPING
GINOOPS	SOOPING
GINOOPT	POOTING
GINOORS	ROOSING
GINOORT	ROOTING
GINOOSS	ISOGONS
GINOOST	SOOTING
GINOOSW	WOOINGS
GINOOTT	TOOTING
GINOPPP	POPPING
GINOPPS	SOPPING
GINOPPT	TOPPING
GINOPPU	POUPING
GINOPPW	WOPPING
GINOPRS	PROIGNS
	PROSING
	ROPINGS
GINOPRT	PORTING
	TROPING
GINOPRU	INGROUP
	POURING
	ROUPING
GINOPRV	PROVING
GINOPRW	POWRING
GINOPSS	POSINGS
	POSSING
GINOPST	POSTING
	STOPING
GINOPSY	POYSING
GINOPTT	POTTING
GINOPTU	POUTING
GINOQTU	QUOTING
GINORRT	RORTING
GINORRV	VORRING
GINORSS	GRISONS
	INGROSS
	SIGNORS
GINORST	ROSTING
	SORTING
	STORING
	TRIGONS
GINORSU	ROUSING
	SOURING
GINORSV	ROVINGS
GINORSW	ROWINGS
	WORSING
GINORSY	ROSYING
	SIGNORY
GINORTT	ROTTING
GINORTU	ROUTING
	TOURING
GINORTW	ROWTING
	TROWING
GINOSSS	SOSSING
GINOSST	STINGOS
	TOSSING
GINOSSU	SOUSING
GINOSSW	SOWINGS
	SOWSING
GINOSTT	SOTTING
GINOSTU	OUSTING
	OUTINGS
	TOUSING
GINOSTV	STOVING
GINOSTW	STOWING
	TOWINGS
	TOWSING
GINOSTY	TOYINGS
GINOTTT	TOTTING
GINOTTU	TOUTING
GINOTTW	TOWTING
	WOTTING
GINOTUW	OUTWING
GINOTUZ	TOUZING
GINOTWZ	TOWZING
GINPPPU	PUPPING
GINPPSU	SUPPING
	UPPINGS
GINPPTU	TUPPING
GINPRRU	PURRING
GINPRSS	SPRINGS
GINPRSU	PURSING
GINPRSY	PRYINGS
	PRYSING
	SPRINGY
GINPSSY	SPYINGS
GINPSTU	PIGNUTS
	STUPING
GINPSTY	TYPINGS
GINPSUW	UPSWING
GINPTTU	PUTTING
GINPTUY	UPTYING
GINQTUY	QUYTING
GINRRSU	RUNRIGS
GINRSST	STRINGS
GINRSTU	RUSTING
GINRSTY	STRINGY
	STYRING
	TRYINGS
GINRSUU	USURING
GINRTTU	RUTTING
GINSSSU	SUSSING
GINSTTU	TUTSING
GINSTTY	STYTING
GINTTTU	TUTTING
GIOOPRR	PORRIGO
GIOORSV	VIGOROS
GIOPRRU	PRURIGO
GIOPSSS	GOSSIPS
GIOPSST	SPIGOTS
GIOPSSY	GOSSIPY
GIORRSU	RIGOURS
GIORSUV	VIGOURS
GIOSSYZ	ZYGOSIS
GISWWYY	WYSIWYG
GJNOOSU	GOUJONS
GJNRSUU	GURJUNS
GJOORTT	JOGTROT
GKMOOSU	GOMOKUS
GLLOOPS	GOLLOPS
GLMNOOS	MONGOLS
GLMOOOR	MOORLOG
GLMOOYY	MYOLOGY
GLMORUW	LUGWORM
GLNNOOR	LORGNON
GLNNSUU	UNSLUNG
GLNOOOS	OOLONGS
GLNOOOY	NOOLOGY
GLNOOPR	PROLONG
GLNOOPY	POLYGON
GLNOOSU	OULONGS
GLNORWY	WRONGLY
GLNOSUW	SUNGLOW
GLNOTTU	GLUTTON
GLNOUYY	YOUNGLY
GLNPSUU	UNPLUGS
GLOOORY	OROLOGY
GLOOOTY	OTOLOGY
GLOOOYZ	ZOOLOGY
GLOORUY	UROLOGY
GLOOSTU	LOGOUTS
GLOPSTU	PUTLOGS
GLORSSY	GROSSLY
GLPRSUY	SPLURGY
GMMOSUU	GUMMOUS
GMMPUUW	MUGWUMP
GMNNOOS	GNOMONS
GMNOORU	GUNROOM
GMNOORW	MORWONG
GMNSTUU	GUMNUTS
GMNSUUZ	MZUNGUS
GMOOPRS	POGROMS
GMOOSTU	GOMUTOS
GMORSUU	GRUMOUS
GMORTUW	MUGWORT
GMPSSUY	GYPSUMS
GMRUYYZ	ZYMURGY
GNNORUW	UNGROWN
GNNORYY	GYRONNY
GNNOSUW	UNGOWNS

GNNRUUW	UNWRUNG	HILOSST	HOLISTS	HKOOSST	SHTOOKS	IIKNPPS	PIPKINS
GNOOORS	GORSOON	HILOSSW	SLOWISH	HKORSWY	WORKSHY	IIKNSSS	SISKINS
GNOOOSS	GOSSOON	HILOSTU	LOUTISH	HLLOOSW	HOLLOWS	IIKOSST	OIKISTS
GNOOOYZ	ZOOGONY	HILOSTW	WHOLIST	HLLOPSY	PHYLLOS	IIKOSTT	TITOKIS
GNOORST	TROGONS	HILOSTY	HYLOIST	HLMNOTY	MONTHLY	IILLLSY	SILLILY
GNOPPSU	OPPUGNS	HILOSVW	WOLVISH	HLMNPYY	NYMPHLY	IILLMNO	MILLION
GNOPRTU	GUNPORT	HILOSWY	SHOWILY	HLMORRY	MYRRHOL	IILLMSY	SLIMILY
GNOPRUW	UPGROWN	HILOTWW	WHITLOW	HLMOSTY	THYMOLS	IILLNOP	PILLION
GNOPSTU	POTGUNS	HILPRUW	UPWHIRL	HLOOSTY	SOOTHLY	IILLNOZ	ZILLION
GNOSTUU	OUTGUNS	HILPSST	SPILTHS	HLOPRTY	PROTHYL	IILLNST	INSTILL
GOOOORS	GOOROOS	HILSSTY	HYLISTS	HLORSTY	SHORTLY	IILLNTT	LITTLIN
GOORSTT	GROTTOS		STYLISH	HLOTUYY	YOUTHLY	IILLPSU	ILLUPIS
GOORTUW	OUTGROW	HILSTTY	THISTLY	HLPRSUU	SULPHUR	IILMNOS	LIONISM
GOPRSUW	UPGROWS	HILSTXY	SIXTHLY		UPHURLS	IILMORS	SIMILOR
GORRSTU	TURGORS	HIMMPSU	MUMPISH	HMMMSUU	HUMMUMS	IILMOSS	LIMOSIS
GORSTTU	GUTROTS	HIMMRSU	RUMMISH	HMMNOOY	HOMONYM	IILMSTU	STIMULI
	ROTGUTS	HIMMSTY	MYTHISM	HMMOOSU	HOUMMOS	IILMSTY	MISTILY
GORSTUY	YOGURTS	HIMNOOS	MOONISH	HMMRTUY	THRUMMY	IILNNSU	INSULIN
HHIIPPS	HIPPISH	HIMNSSU	MUNSHIS	HMNOPSY	NYMPHOS		INULINS
HHIISTW	WHITISH	HIMNSTY	HYMNIST	HMNOPYY	HYPONYM	IILNORS	SIRLOIN
HHIMRTY	RHYTHMI	HIMOORS	MOORISH	HMNPSUY	HYPNUMS	IILNOSV	VIOLINS
HHINORS	HORNISH	HIMOPRS	ROMPISH	HMOOPRS	MORPHOS	IILNOSY	NOISILY
HHIORSW	WHORISH	HIMOPSS	SOPHISM	HMOOSST	SMOOTHS	IILNPPY	NIPPILY
HHIOSTT	HOTTISH	HIMOPST	PHOTISM	HMORSUU	HUMOURS	IILNPUV	PULVINI
HHISSTW	WHISHTS	HIMORTU	THORIUM	HMSTUYZ	ZYTHUMS	IILNRSV	RIVLINS
HHMMSUU	HUMHUMS	HIMOTTY	TIMOTHY	HNNOOPS	PHONONS	IILNSST	INSTILS
HHMRSTY	RHYTHMS	HIMPRSS	SHRIMPS	HNNORSU	UNSHORN	IILOPRT	TRIPOLI
HHOOSTT	HOTSHOT	HIMPRSY	SHRIMPY	HNNOSTY	SYNTHON	IILOPST	PILOTIS
HIIIKRS	RIKISHI	HIMPRTU	TRIUMPH	HNNOSUW	UNSHOWN	IILORTV	VITRIOL
HIIJKNS	HIJINKS	HIMPTUY	PYTHIUM	HNOOPST	PHOTONS	IILOSTV	VIOLIST
HIIKLMS	KHILIMS	HIMRSTY	RHYMIST	HNOOPSU	UNHOOPS	IILPRVY	PRIVILY
HIIKNPS	KINSHIP	HIMSSTU	ISTHMUS	HNOOPTY	TYPHOON	IILPSST	PISTILS
	PINKISH	HIMSTTY	MYTHIST	HNOORSS	HORSONS	IILPSTY	TIPSILY
HIILMTU	LITHIUM	HINNNSU	NUNNISH	HNOORST	THORONS	IILTTUY	UTILITY
HIILPST	SHILPIT	HINNORT	TINHORN	HNOORSU	HONOURS	IILTTWY	WITTILY
HIILPTY	PITHILY	HINNOST	TONNISH	HNOOSTU	UNSHOOT	IIMMMNU	MINIMUM
HIILRTT	TRILITH	HINNPSU	NUNSHIP	HNOPSSY	SYPHONS	IIMMNSU	MINIMUS
HIIMMSS	MISHMIS	HINOOPS	INHOOPS	HNOPSTY	PHYTONS		MINIUMS
HIIMPSW	WIMPISH	HINOORT	HORNITO		PYTHONS	IIMNNOS	MINIONS
HIIMSSS	MISSISH	HINOORZ	HORIZON		TYPHONS	IIMNOSS	MISSION
HIIMSST	MISHITS	HINOOST	INSOOTH	HNORTUW	UNWORTH	IIMNOSU	IONIUMS
HIIMSTT	SHITTIM	HINOPPS	SHIPPON	HNOSTUU	UNSHOUT		NIMIOUS
HIINORS	ROINISH	HINOPSS	SIPHONS	HNRTTUU	UNTRUTH	IIMNOTX	MIXTION
HIINPPS	HIPPINS		SONSHIP	HNSSTUU	UNSHUTS	IIMNPRT	IMPRINT
HIINPSS	INSHIPS	HINORST	HORNIST	HOOPPST	POTSHOP	IIMOPSU	IMPIOUS
HIINSSW	SWINISH	HINORSU	NOURISH	HOOPRST	PORTHOS	IIMOSST	MITOSIS
HIIOPRZ	RHIZOPI	HINORSY	ROYNISH	HOOPSTT	HOTPOTS	IIMOSSU	SIMIOUS
HIIORST	HISTRIO	HINOSSW	SNOWISH	HOOPSTU	UPSHOOT	IIMRTTU	TRITIUM
HIISTTT	TITTISH	HINOSTW	TOWNISH	HOOPSTY	TOYSHOP	IIMRTUV	TRIVIUM
HIKLSSU	LUSKISH	HINPSSU	UNSHIPS	HOORRRS	HORRORS	IIMSSSZ	SIZISMS
HIKLSUY	HUSKILY	HINPTUW	UNWHIPT	HOORRST	ORTHROS	IIMSSTT	TIMISTS
HIKMNOS	MONKISH	HINRSTU	RUNTISH	HOORSUZ	HUZOORS	IIMSSTU	MISSUIT
HIKMRSU	MURKISH	HIOOPRS	POORISH	HOOSTTU	OUTSHOT	IINNOOP	OPINION
HIKMSUZ	MUZHIKS	HIOOSSV	SHIVOOS	HOPRTUW	UPTHROW	IINNOPS	PINIONS
HIKNNOR	INKHORN	HIOPPPS	POPPISH	HOPSSSY	HYSSOPS	IINNOTU	UNITION
HIKNNTU	UNTHINK	HIOPPSS	SHIPPOS	HOPSSTU	UPSHOTS	IINOPSS	ISOSPIN
HIKNRSS	SHRINKS	HIOPRSW	WORSHIP	HOPSTTU	SHOTPUT		SINOPIS
HIKOORS	ROOKISH	HIOPSST	SOPHIST	HOPSTUY	TYPHOUS	IINORST	IRONIST
HILLOPT	HILLTOP	HIOPSSY	PHYSIOS	HORSTUU	OUTRUSH	IINORSV	VIRINOS
HILLOPY	LYOPHIL	HIOPSTU	UPHOIST	HOSSTTU	STOUTHS		VIRIONS
HILLPSU	UPHILLS	HIORSSU	SOURISH	HRSSTTU	THRUSTS	IINORTT	INTROIT
HILLRSS	SHRILLS	HIORSTY	HISTORY	HRSSTUY	THYRSUS	IINOSSV	VISIONS
HILLRST	THRILLS	HIOSSTT	SOTTISH	IIIJJLN	JINJILI	IINOSUV	INVIOUS
HILLRSY	SHRILLY	HIOSTTU	OUTHITS	IIIKMNN	MINIKIN	IINOTTU	TUITION
HILLRTY	THRILLY	HIOTTUW	OUTWITH	IIIMRST	MIRITIS	IINPPPS	PIPPINS
HILMMOU	HOLMIUM		WITHOUT	IIISTTW	WISTITI	IINQRUY	INQUIRY
HILMOPS	LOMPISH	HIQSSUY	SQUISHY	IIJLLNO	JILLION	IINRTTY	TRINITY
	PHLOMIS	HIRSSTT	THIRSTS	IIJMNOS	MISJOIN	IINSSST	INSISTS
HILMOSS	HOLISMS		THRISTS	IIJNNOT	INJOINT	IINSTTU	INTUITS
HILMOSW	WHOLISM	HIRSTTU	RUTTISH	IIKKLNY	KINKILY	IINSTTW	INTWIST
HILMPSU	LUMPISH	HIRSTTY	THIRSTY	IIKLLMY	MILKILY		NITWITS
HILMSSY	HYLISMS		THRISTY	IIKLLSY	SILKILY	IIOOSTT	TOITOIS
HILMSUY	MUSHILY	HKKLOOZ	KOLKHOZ	IIKLMNP	LIMPKIN	IIOPRSS	PISSOIR
HILMTUU	THULIUM	HKKOOSY	SKYHOOK	IIKLNOS	OILSKIN	IIORSSV	VIROSIS
HILNNTY	NINTHLY	HKKOSTU	SUKKOTH	IIKLPSY	SPIKILY	IIORSTV	IVORIST
HILNPST	PLINTHS	HKNOOSU	UNHOOKS	IIKLRSY	RISKILY		VISITOR
HILOOTT	OTOLITH	HKNOOWW	KNOWHOW	IIKMNOR	KIRIMON	IIOSTTU	OUSTITI
HILOOTZ	ZOOLITH	HKNSSUU	UNHUSKS	IIKMNPS	SIMPKIN	IIPPSUU	PIUPIUS
HILORTU	UROLITH	HKOOOPT	POTHOOK	IIKMNSS	SIMKINS	IIPRSST	SPIRITS

7-LETTER ANAGRAMS

Column 1

	TRIPSIS
IIPRSTU	PITURIS
IIPRSTY	SPIRITY
IIPRTVY	PRIVITY
IIQSTUV	QIVIUTS
IIRRSTT	TIRRITS
IISSSTZ	SIZISTS
IJKLLOY	KILLJOY
IJKMOSU	MOUJIKS
IJKNOSS	JOSKINS
IJLLLOY	JOLLILY
IJLLOTY	JOLLITY
IJLMPUY	JUMPILY
IJLNOQU	JONQUIL
IJLNOTY	JOINTLY
IJMOSSS	JISSOMS
IJNNOTU	UNJOINT
IJNORSU	JUNIORS
IJRSSTU	JURISTS
IKKMNOU	KIKUMON
IKKNORT	KIRKTON
IKKORRS	KORKIRS
IKKSUUY	KIKUYUS
IKLLSTU	KILLUTS
IKLLSUY	SULKILY
IKLMNPU	LUMPKIN
IKLMOOS	LOOKISM
IKLMOSY	SMOKILY
IKLMRUY	MURKILY
IKLMSUY	MUSKILY
IKLNNSU	UNLINKS
IKLNOOS	SKOLION
IKLNOOT	KILOTON
IKLNOSU	ULIKONS
IKLNPSU	SKULPIN
	UPLINKS
IKLNRWY	WRINKLY
IKLOTTU	TOOLKIT
IKLOSSU	SOUSLIK
IKLSSSU	SUSLIKS
IKLSTTU	KITTULS
IKMNOOO	OKIMONO
IKMNOOS	KIMONOS
IKMNORS	MIKRONS
	MORKINS
IKMNOSW	MISKNOW
IKMNPPU	PUMPKIN
IKMNRSU	RUMKINS
IKMNRTU	TRINKUM
IKMOOST	MISTOOK
IKMOSSU	KOUMISS
IKMPRSS	SKRIMPS
IKNNPTU	UNPINKT
IKNNSTU	UNKNITS
IKNOOST	ISOKONT
IKNOPST	INKPOTS
	INKSPOT
IKNORSW	INWORKS
IKNPSTU	SPUTNIK
	UPKNITS
IKPRSSU	PRUSIKS
	SPRUIKS
IKPRSSY	KRYPSIS
ILLLOWY	LOWLILY
ILLMNOU	MULLION
ILLMNRU	MILLRUN
ILLMOOR	MOORILL
ILLMOSU	LOLIUMS
ILLMPUY	LUMPILY
ILLMSUU	LIMULUS
ILLNOQU	QUILLON
ILLNORU	RULLION
ILLNPUU	LUPULIN
ILLNSUW	UNWILLS
ILLNTUY	NULLITY
ILLOORZ	ZORILLO
ILLOPRY	PILLORY
ILLOPSW	PILLOWS
ILLOPWY	PILLOWY

Column 2

ILLOSUV	VILLOUS
ILLOSUY	LOUSILY
ILLOSWW	WILLOWS
ILLOTXY	XYLITOL
ILLOUVV	VOLVULI
ILLOWWY	WILLOWY
ILLPPUY	PULPILY
ILLPSUV	PULVILS
ILLQSSU	SQUILLS
ILLRSUY	SURLILY
ILLSTUY	LUSTILY
ILMMRUY	RUMMILY
ILMMSSU	MIMULUS
ILMNOOT	MOONLIT
ILMNOSU	MOULINS
ILMNRSU	MURLINS
ILMNSSU	MUSLINS
ILMOORY	ROOMILY
ILMOOSS	MOLOSSI
ILMORTU	TURMOIL
ILMOSTY	MOISTLY
ILMPSTU	PLUMIST
ILMRSSY	LYRISMS
ILMSTUY	MUSTILY
ILMUYZZ	MUZZILY
ILNNSUY	SUNNILY
ILNOOPS	PLOSION
ILNOOPV	VOLPINO
ILNOOSS	SOLIONS
ILNOOST	LOTIONS
	SOLITON
ILNOPPS	POPLINS
ILNOPRU	PURLOIN
ILNOPST	PONTILS
ILNOPSU	UPSILON
ILNOPSY	YPSILON
ILNOQSU	QUINOLS
ILNORST	NOSTRIL
ILNORSU	SURLOIN
ILNORTU	TORULIN
ILNOSST	TONSILS
ILNOSSU	INSOULS
ILNOSTU	OILNUTS
	ULTIONS
ILNOSTY	STONILY
ILNOSWY	SNOWILY
ILNOTUV	VOLUTIN
ILNPRSU	PURLINS
ILNPSST	SPLINTS
ILNPSTU	UNSPILT
ILNRSTY	NITRYLS
ILNSSTU	INSULTS
ILNTTUY	NUTTILY
ILOOORS	ROSOLIO
ILOOPST	POLOIST
	TOPSOIL
ILOORST	LORIOTS
ILOORTY	OLITORY
ILOOSST	SOLOIST
ILOOSTY	SOOTILY
ILOOWYZ	WOOZILY
ILOPPSY	SOPPILY
ILOPRSY	PROSILY
ILOPSST	PISTOLS
	POSTILS
ILOPSSX	OXSLIPS
ILOPSTT	SPOTLIT
ILOPSUY	PIOUSLY
ILOQRSU	LIQUORS
ILORRSY	SORRILY
ILOSSTY	TOSSILY
	TYLOSIN
ILOSTTW	WITTOLS
ILPPSTU	PULPITS
ILPSTTU	UPTILTS
ILRSSTU	TRISULS
ILRSSTY	LYRISTS
ILRSTUY	RUSTILY
ILSSTTU	LUTISTS

Column 3

ILSSTTY	STYLIST
IMMNOSS	MONISMS
	NOMISMS
IMMNOSU	MUSIMON
	OMNIUMS
IMMNOUU	MUONIUM
IMMOOSS	SIMOOMS
IMMOPTU	OPTIMUM
IMMOSSU	OSMIUMS
IMMSSTU	MUTISMS
	SUMMIST
	SUMMITS
IMNNNOU	MUNNION
IMNNOOR	NORIMON
IMNNOSW	MINNOWS
IMNNSTU	MUNTINS
IMNOOPP	POMPION
IMNOOPT	TOMPION
IMNOORR	MORRION
IMNOORS	MORIONS
IMNOORT	MONITOR
	TROMINO
IMNOOSS	MONOSIS
	SIMOONS
IMNOOST	MOTIONS
IMNOOSU	OMINOUS
IMNOOSY	ISONOMY
IMNOOUX	OXONIUM
IMNOPPU	PUMPION
IMNORRU	MURRION
IMNORTY	TRIONYM
IMNOSST	MONISTS
IMNOSSY	MYOSINS
IMNOSVY	VISNOMY
IMNRRSU	MURRINS
IMNRSTU	UNTRIMS
IMOOPRX	PROXIMO
IMOOSSS	OSMOSIS
IMOOSSU	OSMIOUS
IMOOSTV	VOMITOS
IMOPRSS	PORISMS
IMOPRST	IMPORTS
	TROPISM
IMOPRSV	IMPROVS
IMOPRTU	PROTIUM
IMOPSST	IMPOSTS
IMOPSTU	UTOPISM
IMORRRS	MIRRORS
IMORSTU	TOURISM
IMORSTY	TRISOMY
IMOSSYZ	ZYMOSIS
IMOSTTT	TOMTITS
IMOSTUV	VOMITUS
IMOSTUW	OUTSWIM
IMPRSSU	PURISMS
IMPSSTU	SUMPITS
IMQRSSU	SQUIRMS
IMQRSUY	SQUIRMY
IMRSSTU	SISTRUM
	TRISMUS
	TRUISMS
IMRTTUY	YTTRIUM
INNNORU	RUNNION
INNOOPS	OPSONIN
INNOOST	NOTIONS
INNORST	INTRONS
INNOSSU	UNISONS
INNOSTU	NONSUIT
INNOSWW	WINNOWS
INNQSUY	SQUINNY
INOOPRT	PORTION
INOOPSS	POISONS
	POISSON
INOOPST	OPTIONS
	POSITON
	POTIONS
INOORSS	ORISONS
INOORST	ISOTRON
	NITROSO

Column 4

	TORSION
INOORSZ	ZORINOS
INOORTT	TORTONI
INOOSST	TOISONS
INOOSUX	NOXIOUS
INOPPRS	POPRINS
INOPRSS	PRISONS
INOPSST	PISTONS
INOPSSU	POUSSIN
	SPINOUS
INOPSTT	TINPOTS
INOPSTU	SPINOUT
INORSTT	TRITONS
INORSTU	NITROUS
	TURIONS
INORSUU	RUINOUS
	URINOUS
INORSUV	UNVISOR
INOSSTU	USTIONS
INOSSUU	SINUOUS
INOSTUW	OUTWINS
INPRSST	SPRINTS
INPRSTU	TURNIPS
	UNSTRIP
INPRSTY	TRYPSIN
INQSSTU	SQUINTS
INRSTTU	INTRUST
INSSTUU	SUNSUIT
	UNSUITS
INSTTUW	UNTWIST
INTTUWY	UNWITTY
IOOPRSS	POROSIS
IOOPRSV	PROVISO
IOOPSTY	ISOTOPY
IOORSSS	SOROSIS
IOORSTT	RISOTTO
IOORSTU	RIOTOUS
IOOSSSS	SISSOOS
IOPPPRT	PITPROP
IOPPPST	POPPITS
IOPPRST	RIPSTOP
IOPPRSY	PYROSIS
IOPRSTT	PROTIST
	TROPIST
IOPSTTU	UTOPIST
IOQRTTU	QUITTOR
IOQSSTU	QUOISTS
IORRSTW	WORRITS
IORRSZZ	RIZZORS
IORRTTX	TORTRIX
IORSSTU	SUITORS
	TSOURIS
IORSTTU	TOURIST
IORSTTW	TWISTOR
IOSSSTT	TSOTSIS
IOSSTTU	OUTSITS
IOSTTUW	OUTWITS
IPRRSTU	IRRUPTS
	STIRRUP
IPRSSTU	PURISTS
	SPRUITS
	UPRISTS
IPRSTUU	PURSUIT
IPSSSTY	STYPSIS
IPSSTTY	TYPISTS
IPSTTTU	TITTUPS
IPTTTUY	TITTUPY
IQRRSSU	SQUIRRS
IQRSSTU	SQUIRTS
JMOPTUU	OUTJUMP
JNNOSTU	JOTUNNS
JNOORSU	JOURNOS
	SOJOURN
JOOPPSY	POPJOYS
JOSTTUU	OUTJUTS
KKLMSUU	MUKLUKS
KKNRSUU	KUNKURS

KLLMOSU	MOLLUSK		PULTONS	MNOTTUY	MUTTONY	NORSTUU	OUTRUNS
KLOOOTU	LOOKOUT	LNOSSUU	UNSOULS	MOOOTYZ	ZOOTOMY	NORTTUU	OUTTURN
	OUTLOOK	LNPSTUU	PULTUNS	MOOPPSU	POMPOUS		TURNOUT
KLOOPSU	UPLOOKS	LNRTUUV	VULTURN	MOOPRSY	POMROYS	NOSSTUW	UNSTOWS
KMPRSSU	SKRUMPS	LNRTUUY	UNTRULY	MOOPSSU	OPOSSUM	NPRSTUU	UPTURNS
KNNNOUW	UNKNOWN	LOOOORS	OLOROSO	MOOPSTT	TOPMOST	NRSSTTU	STRUNTS
KNNOSTU	UNKNOTS	LOOORST	ROTOLOS	MOORRSW	MORROWS	NRSSTUU	STURNUS
KNOOPTT	TOPKNOT	LOOSSTV	VOLOSTS	MOOSTTU	OUTMOST		UNTRUSS
KNOPRTY	KRYPTON	LOPPRSY	PROPYLS	MOPPRST	PROMPTS	NRSTTUU	UNTRUST
KNORRTY	KRYTRON	LOPPSUU	PULPOUS	MOPSSSU	POSSUMS	OOOORPT	POTOROO
KNORSUW	UNWORKS	LOPPSUY	POLYPUS	MOPSSUU	SPUMOUS	OOOOSZZ	ZOOZOOS
KOOOTTU	OUTTOOK	LOPRSTY	PROTYLS	MOQRSUU	QUORUMS	OOOPRTU	OUTROOP
KOOPRTW	WORKTOP	LOPRSUY	PYLORUS	MOQSTUU	QUOTUMS	OOORTTU	OUTROOT
KOORTUW	OUTWORK	LOPRTUY	POULTRY	MORRSTU	ROSTRUM	OOPRRST	TORPORS
KOOSSUU	SOUKOUS	LORSTTY	TROTYLS	MORRSUU	RUMOURS	OOPRSSU	SOURSOP
KOOSTWW	KOWTOWS	LORSTUU	TORULUS	MORSTUU	TUMOURS	OOPRSTU	PORTOUS
KORTTUW	TUTWORK	LOSTTUY	STOUTLY	MOSSTTU	UTMOSTS		UPROOTS
LLLMMUU	MULMULL	LPRSSUU	SURPLUS	MOSSTUU	OUTSUMS	OOPRSTV	PROVOST
LLLOOPS	LOLLOPS	MMNOSSU	MUSMONS	MOSTUUW	OUTSWUM	OOPRTTU	OUTPORT
LLMMSUU	MULMULS		SUMMONS	NNNSUUY	UNSUNNY	OOPRTUU	OUTPOUR
LLMOOPR	ROLLMOP	MMOOPPS	POMPOMS	NNOOOPT	PONTOON	OOPSSTT	TOSSPOT
LLMPPUY	PLUMPLY	MMOOSTT	MOTMOTS	NNOOPRU	PRONOUN	OOPSTTU	OUTPOST
LLNORSU	UNROLLS	MMOPSTY	SYMPTOM	NNOOPSS	SPONSON		OUTTOPS
LLOOPRT	TROLLOP	MMRRSUU	MURMURS	NNOOPST	PONTONS	OOPSWWW	POWWOWS
LLOORTU	ROLLOUT	MMSTUUU	MUTUUMS	NNOORSY	RONYONS	OORRSSW	SORROWS
LLOOSTU	TOLUOLS	MNNOOOS	MONSOON	NNORSUW	UNSWORN	OORSTUU	ROUTOUS
LLOPRSU	UPROLLS	MNNOSYY	SYNONYM	NNOSSUY	UNSONSY	OPPRRTU	PURPORT
LLORSST	STROLLS	MNNOTUU	UNMOUNT	NNOSTYY	SYNTONY	OPPRSTU	SUPPORT
LMMSTUU	MULTUMS	MNOOOPP	POMPOON	NNRSTUU	UNTURNS	OPPRSTY	STROPPY
LMOORSU	ORMOLUS	MNOOOYZ	ZOONOMY	NOOPRSS	SPONSOR	OPPRSUY	PYROPUS
LMOOSTY	TOYLSOM	MNOOPPS	POMPONS	NOOPRST	PROTONS	OPRSSTU	SPROUTS
LMOPSUU	PLUMOUS	MNOOPST	TOMPONS	NOOPSSY	POYSONS		STROUPS
LMORSSU	MUSROLS	MNOOPTY	TOPONYM	NOORSST	TONSORS		STUPORS
LMRSTUU	LUSTRUM	MNOORSU	UNMOORS	NOORSTU	UNROOST	OPSTTUU	OUTPUTS
LMSTTUU	TUMULTS	MNOOSTU	MOUTONS		UNROOTS	ORSSTTU	STROUTS
LMSTUUU	TUMULUS	MNOOSTW	TOWMONS	NOORTUW	OUTWORN	ORSSUUU	USUROUS
LNNOPSU	NONPLUS	MNOOSUY	ONYMOUS	NOPPRSU	UNPROPS	ORSTTUU	SURTOUT
LNOOPTU	PULTOON	MNOOTTW	TOWMONT	NOPSSTU	SUNSPOT		
LNOOSST	STOLONS	MNORSTU	NOSTRUM		UNSTOPS		
LNOPSTU	PLUTONS	MNOSTTU	MUTTONS	NOPSTUW	UPTOWNS		

8-LETTER ANAGRAMS

AAAACCRR CARACARA
AAAACJRR JARARACA
AAAACNRS ANASARCA
AAAADMTV AMADAVAT
AAAADNPS APADANAS
AAAADTVV AVADAVAT
AAAAHJMR MAHARAJA
AAAAIMPR ARAPAIMA
AAAAIRTX ATARAXIA
AAAAJKRR JARARAKA
AAAAKKMT TAKAMAKA
AAAAKKNT KATAKANA
AAAALSTY ATALAYAS
AAAAMMTT MATAMATA
AAAARSS SASARARA
AAABBCLS CABBALAS
AAABBELT ABATABLE
AAABBHKL KABBALAH
AAABBILT ABBATIAL
AAABBKLS KABBALAS
AAABCCRS BACCARAS
AAABCCRT BACCARAT
AAABCHLS CALABASH
AAABCHMU MACAHUBA
AAABCINT ANABATIC
AAABCIRS ARABICAS
AAABCITT CIABATTA
AAABCLSV BACLAVAS
AAABCNRR BARRACAN
         BARRANCA
AAABCNRS BARACANS
AAABCNRU CARNAUBA
AAABCORS CARABAOS
AAABCPRY CAPYBARA
AAABCSTW CATAWBAS
AAABDEST DATABASE
AAABDKNT DATABANK
AAABDLMS LAMBADAS
AAABDNNN BANDANNA
AAABDNNS BANDANAS
AAABDNRS SARABAND
AAABDNRT ABRADANT
AAABEGHL GALABEAH
AAABEGLL GALLABEA
AAABEGLS GALABEAS
AAABEHNR HABANERA
AAABEHRT BARATHEA
AAABEMPR PARABEMA
AAABENSS ANABASES
AAABFLLS FALBALAS
AAABGHIL GALABIAH
AAABGILL GALLABIA
AAABGILS GALABIAS
AAABGLOR ALGAROBA
AAABGMNQ MBAQANGA
AAABGRTU RUTABAGA
AAABHLQS QABALAHS
AAABILTT BATTALIA
AAABINSS ANABASIS
AAABIPSS PIASSABA
AAABKLSV BAKLAVAS
AAABKPSS BAASSKAP
AAABLLSW WALLABAS
AAABLMOS ABOMASAL
AAABLOPR PARABOLA
AAABLPRS PALABRAS
AAABMSST MASTABAS
AAABNNRS RABANNAS
AAABORRS ARAROBAS
AAACCELN CALCANEA
AAACCEPR CARAPACE
AAACCILR CALCARIA

AAACCIMM CAIMACAM
AAACCLRS CARACALS
AAACCRSS CASCARAS
AAACCRTT CATARACT
AAACDEIM ACADEMIA
AAACDEQU AQUACADE
AAACDETU ACAUDATE
AAACDILR CALDARIA
AAACDINR ACARIDAN
AAACDKLY LACKADAY
AAACDMMS MACADAMS
AAACDNNO ANACONDA
AAACDNRS SANDARAC
AAACDOTV ADVOCAAT
AAACEGNT AGACANTE
AAACEGTU AGUACATE
AAACEHIN ACHAENIA
AAACEHLT CALATHEA
AAACEHLZ CHALAZAE
AAACELNT ANALECTA
AAACELST CATALASE
AAACENNP PANACEAN
AAACENPS PANACEAS
AAACEPRV PRAECAVA
AAACGINT CAATINGA
AAACGLSW SCALAWAG
AAACGMNP CAMPAGNA
AAACHILZ CHALAZIA
AAACHIPS APHASIAC
AAACHLNR ANARCHAL
AAACHLSZ CHALAZAS
AAACHNST ACANTHAS
AAACHRSY ACHARYAS
AAACILMN MANIACAL
AAACILMR CALAMARI
AAACILMS MALACIAS
AAACILRV CALVARIA
AAACILSY CALISAYA
AAACIMRS CARIAMAS
AAACINPS ACAPNIAS
AAACINTV CAVATINA
AAACIPSU SAPUCAIA
AAACIRRS SACRARIA
AAACIRSS ACRASIAS
AAACIRTX ATARAXIC
AAACJMRS JACAMARS
AAACKMRT TAMARACK
AAACLLSV CAVALLAS
AAACLMNS ALMANACS
         MANCALAS
AAACLMRY CALAMARY
AAACLNST CANTALAS
AAACLPST CATALPAS
AAACLRST ALCATRAS
AAACLRSZ ALCAZARS
AAACMNPS CAMPANAS
AAACMRSS MACASSAR
         MASCARAS
AAACMRSU AMARACUS
AAACNNRS CARANNAS
AAACNPST CATAPANS
AAACNRST NACARATS
AAACNRSU CARAUNAS
AAACNRSV CARAVANS
AAACNSST CANASTAS
AAACNSTT CANTATAS
AAACRRWY CARRAWAY
AAACRSWY CARAWAYS
AAACSSST CASSATAS
AAACSSSV CASSAVAS
AAACSSTT CATASTAS
AAACSTWY CASTAWAY

AAADEGNP APANAGED
AAADELMS ALAMEDAS
         SALAAMED
AAADENTV VANADATE
AAADEPRT TAPADERA
AAADFRSY FARADAYS
AAADGIMM GAMMADIA
AAADGLMY AMYGDALA
AAADHMRS ADHARMAS
         MADRASAH
AAADHNRT THANADAR
AAADIILR RADIALIA
AAADILRU ADULARIA
AAADIMNY ADYNAMIA
AAADIRST DATARIAS
         RADIATAS
AAADJMRS JAMADARS
AAADKLMN KALAMDAN
AAADKRRV AARDVARK
AAADLMNQ QALAMDAN
AAADLMNS MANDALAS
AAADLMSW WADMAALS
AAADMNST ADAMANTS
AAADMNTU TAMANDUA
AAADMORT MATADORA
AAADMRSS MADRASAS
         MADRASSA
AAADNRSS SARDANAS
AAADNRST TANADARS
AAAEGISS ASSEGAAI
AAAEGLMX MALAXAGE
AAAEGLRT ALTARAGE
AAAEGLST GALATEAS
AAAEGNPP APPANAGE
AAAEGNPS APANAGES
AAAEGRST GASTRAEA
AAAEHLST ALTHAEAS
AAAEHMNT ANATHEMA
AAAEHNPS ANAPHASE
AAAEIMNS ANAEMIAS
AAAEKKRT KARATEKA
AAAEKTWY TAKEAWAY
AAAELMMN ANALEMMA
AAAELMPT PALAMATE
AAAELMTX MALAXATE
AAAELRTV LAVATERA
AAAENNSS ANANASES
AAAENOPR PARANOEA
AAAENPRV PARAVANE
AAAENPST ANAPAEST
AAAENSST ANATASES
AAAEPRST SEPARATA
AAAERSWY AREAWAYS
AAAERTWY TEARAWAY
AAAFFLLS ALFALFAS
AAAFINST FANTASIA
AAAFINUV AVIFAUNA
AAAFIRST RATAFIAS
AAAFNRSS SARAFANS
AAAFRSWY FARAWAYS
AAAGGLLN GALANGAL
AAAGGLNS GALANGAS
AAAGGLOP GALAPAGO
AAAGHINR HIRAGANA
AAAGHIPR AGRAPHIA
AAAGHIPS APHAGIAS
AAAGHLNS LANGAHAS
AAAGHNST ATAGHANS
AAAGHNTY YATAGHAN
AAAGILPT PATAGIAL
AAAGILRT ALIGARTA
AAAGIMMT GAMMATIA

AAAGINRR AGRARIAN
AAAGINSZ GAZANIAS
AAAGISSS ASSAGAIS
AAAGLMMS AMALGAMS
AAAGLMNS NAGMAALS
AAAGLNSS LASAGNAS
AAAGLRRW WARRAGAL
AAAGLRST ASTRAGAL
AAAGMNRS ANAGRAMS
AAAGMPRR PARAGRAM
AAAGNOPR ARAPONGA
AAAGNPRS PARASANG
         PARGANAS
AAAGNPRU ARAPUNGA
AAAGNRST TANAGRAS
AAAGNRSU GUARANAS
AAAGNSTY YATAGANS
AAAHHLSV HALAVAHS
AAAHIKSW KAHAWAIS
AAAHIMNR MAHARANI
AAAHIMNS SHAMIANA
AAAHIMRT HAMARTIA
AAAHINPR RAPHANIA
AAAHIPSS APHASIAS
AAAHJKSW KAJAWAHS
AAAHKMNS KHANSAMA
AAAHKRSS RAKSHASA
AAAHLMRS HARMALAS
AAAHLNNS ALANNAHS
AAAHMMST MAHATMAS
AAAHMNRT AMARANTH
AAAHMRSS ASHRAMAS
AAAHMSST TAMASHAS
AAAHNNSV SAVANNAH
AAAHNOPR ANAPHORA
AAAHNSTY ATHANASY
AAAHPRST PARATHAS
AAAHRSTW WARATAHS
AAAHTTWY THATAWAY
AAAIINPR APIARIAN
AAAIKKMM KAIMAKAM
AAAILLMR MALARIAL
AAAILLPT PALATIAL
AAAILMNR MALARIAN
AAAILMRS MALARIAS
AAAILMSV MALVASIA
AAAILNRU AULARIAN
AAAILPRV PARAVAIL
AAAILPSS APLASIAS
AAAILRST SALARIAT
AAAIMMQQ QAIMAQAM
AAAIMMST MASAMATA
AAAIMNST AMANITAS
AAAINNRR RANARIAN
AAAINOPR PARANOIA
AAAINQRU AQUARIAN
AAAIPRSX APRAXIAS
AAAIPSSV PIASSAVA
AAAKKTZZ KAZATZKA
AAAKMNRS NAMASKAR
AAAKOSWY SOAKAWAY
AAALLPRX PARALLAX
AAALLPST PALATALS
AAALNNPT PLATANNA
AAALNNST LANTANAS
AAALNPRT RATAPLAN
AAALNPST APLANATS
AAALNRTT TARLATAN
AAALPRST SATRAPAL
AAALRRSY ARRAYALS
AAALSWYY LAYAWAYS
AAAMNOPR PANORAMA

AAAMNRRY YARRAMAN	AABCDHKR HARDBACK	AABCKSWY SWAYBACK	AABDHLLN HANDBALL
AAAMNRST AMARANTS	AABCDIIS DIABASIC	AABCLLLO COALBALL	AABDHLLR HARDBALL
AAAMNSTY MANYATAS	AABCDINT ABDICANT	AABCLLLY BALLCLAY	AABDHNST HATBANDS
AAAMNTTY MANYATTA	AABCDIRS CARABIDS	AABCLLPY PLACABLY	AABDHNSY HAYBANDS
AAAMORST TAMARAOS	AABCDKLN BACKLAND	AABCLMSU CALUMBAS	AABDHRSU SUBAHDAR
AAAMOTTU AUTOMATA	AABCDKRW BACKWARD	AABCLNUU CUNABULA	AABDIILS BASIDIAL
AAAMPRST PATAMARS	DRAWBACK	AABCLRRY CARBARYL	AABDIKRS BIDARKAS
AAAMRRSZ ZAMARRAS	AABCDKRY BACKYARD	AABCMSSU SAMBUCAS	AABDILLN BALLADIN
AAAMRSSS SAMSARAS	AABCDNRR BRANCARD	AABCNORR BARRANCO	AABDILNS BALADINS
AAAMRSTU TAMARAUS	AABCEENY ABEYANCE	AABCORST ABACTORS	AABDIMNO ABDOMINA
AAAMRTTU TRAUMATA	AABCEERS SCARABEE	ACROBATS	AABDIMNR MADBRAIN
AAAMRTZZ RAZMATAZ	AABCEERT ACERBATE	AABCOSTT CATBOATS	AABDIMRS BARMAIDS
AAANNSSV SAVANNAS	AABCEGOT CABOTAGE	AABCRSTT ABSTRACT	AABDINNR RAINBAND
AAANNSTT ANNATTAS	AABCEHNR BARCHANE	AABCSTTU CATTABUS	AABDINST TABANIDS
AAANOPRZ PARAZOAN	AABCEILM AMICABLE	AABDDEGN BANDAGED	AABDKNNS SANDBANK
AAANORSY SAYONARA	AABCEIMN AMBIANCE	AABDDEHN HEADBAND	AABDLLRY BALLADRY
AAANPRTV PARAVANT	AABCEINR CARABINE	AABDDEIR ABRAIDED	AABDLLUY LAUDABLY
AAANQTUU AQUANAUT	AABCEIRT BACTERIA	AABDDELL BALLADED	AABDLMNU LABDANUM
AAANRSTT TANTARAS	AABCEITT CIABATTE	AABDDENR BRANDADE	AABDLMNY DAMNABLY
TARANTAS	AABCEKLM CLAMBAKE	AABDDESS BADASSED	AABDLNPT PLATBAND
TARTANAS	AABCEKLR LACEBARK	AABDDIKS KABADDIS	AABDLNSS SALBANDS
AAAORSWY SOARAWAY	AABCELLP PLACABLE	AABDDLNS BADLANDS	AABDLORR LARBOARD
AAAPPRST APPARATS	AABCELLR CABALLER	AABDDMOR DAMBOARD	AABDLORY ADORABLY
AAAPSSST PASSATAS	AABCELLS SCALABLE	AABDEEHL BEHEADAL	AABDLRSW BRADAWLS
AAARSTTU TUATARAS	AABCELNR BALANCER	AABDEELR READABLE	AABDMNNS BANDSMAN
AAASTWYY STAYAWAY	BARNACLE	AABDEELT DATEABLE	AABDMNNY BANDYMAN
AABBBDEK KABABBED	AABCELNS BALANCES	DEALBATE	AABDMNRS ARMBANDS
AABBCDEG CABBAGED	AABCELOR ALBACORE	AABDEELV EVADABLE	AABDNNOS ABANDONS
AABBCDKN BACKBAND	AABCELPR CAPABLER	AABDEERY BAYADERE	AABDNNTU ABUNDANT
AABBCDRS SCABBARD	AABCELRT BRACTEAL	AABDEGIN BADINAGE	AABDNORS BANDORAS
AABBCEGS CABBAGES	AABCELWY CABLEWAY	AABDEGIR BIGARADE	AABDNRRY BARNYARD
AABBCEIS ABBACIES	AABCEMRV VAMBRACE	AABDEGLR GRADABLE	AABDNRSU BANDURAS
AABBCEKR BAREBACK	AABCENYY ABEYANCY	AABDEGNS BANDAGES	AABDORSV BRAVADOS
AABBCEKT BACKBEAT	AABCERRS BARRACES	AABDEHHI DAHABIEH	AABDORWY BROADWAY
AABBCINR BARBICAN	AABCERST ABREACTS	AABDEHKR HARDBAKE	WAYBOARD
AABBCIRR BARBARIC	CABARETS	AABDEHMR HARDBEAM	AABDRRSS BRASSARD
AABBCIST SABBATIC	AABCERTT CABRETTA	AABDEILN BALADINE	AABDRRSW DRAWBARS
AABBCORS BARBASCO	AABCESSU ABACUSES	AABDEIOU ABOIDEAU	AABDRSST BASTARDS
AABBDENS BASEBAND	AABCFIIL BIFACIAL	AABDEIRS ARABISED	AABDRSSU SUBADARS
AABBDERT BARBATED	AABCFKLL BACKFALL	AABDEIRZ ARABIZED	AABDRSTY BASTARDY
AABBDGRS GABBARDS	AABCFKLT FLATBACK	AABDEISS DIABASES	AABEEGKR BREAKAGE
AABBEELR BEARABLE	AABCFKST FASTBACK	AABDEJLL DJELLABA	AABEEGNT ABNEGATE
AABBEELT BEATABLE	AABCHILR BRACHIAL	AABDEJNX BANJAXED	AABEEHLL HEALABLE
AABBEGNS BEANBAGS	AABCHINR BRANCHIA	AABDEKRY DAYBREAK	AABEEHLT HATEABLE
AABBEILL BAILABLE	AABCHKLS BACKLASH	AABDELLS BALLADES	AABEEHMR HARAMBEE
AABBEKLN BANKABLE	AABCHKRS SHABRACK	AABDELLT BALLATED	AABEEKLM MAKEABLE
AABBELLM BLAMABLE	AABCHKSW BACKWASH	AABDELLU LAUDABLE	AABEEKLT TAKEABLE
AABBELLS BASEBALL	AABCHLOO COOLABAH	AABDELMN DAMNABLE	AABEEKMT BAKEMEAT
AABBELRY BEARABLY	AABCHMRY CHAMBRAY	AABDELMS BALSAMED	MAKEBATE
AABBEORT BAREBOAT	AABCHNRS BARCHANS	AABDELOR ADORABLE	AABEEKRW BAKEWARE
AABBGRST GABBARTS	AABCIILS BASILICA	AABDELPR PARABLED	AABEELLS LEASABLE
AABBHKSU BABUSHKA	AABCIKLT TAILBACK	AABDELPT BALDPATE	SALEABLE
AABBIILL BILABIAL	AABCILLR BACILLAR	AABDELRS BASELARD	AABEELMN AMENABLE
AABBILRT BARBITAL	AABCILMS BALSAMIC	AABDELRT TRADABLE	NAMEABLE
AABBIRSU BABIRUSA	CABALISM	AABDELRW DRAWABLE	AABEELMT TAMEABLE
AABBLLMY BLAMABLY	AABCILMY AMICABLY	AABDELRY READABLY	AABEELPT TAPEABLE
AABBLORS BARBOLAS	AABCILNN CANNIBAL	AABDELSW SAWBLADE	AABEELRS ERASABLE
AABBLSSU SUBBASAL	AABCILNO ANABOLIC	AABDEMNS BEADSMAN	AABEELRT RATEABLE
AABBMMOZ ZAMBOMBA	AABCILST BASALTIC	AABDENTU UNABATED	TEARABLE
AABBSSSU BABASSUS	CABALIST	AABDENUX BANDEAUX	AABEELRW WEARABLE
AABCCCHI BACCHIAC	AABCINNN CANNABIN	AABDENVW WAVEBAND	AABEELST EATABLES
AABCCEHK BACKACHE	AABCINNR CINNABAR	AABDEORS SEABOARD	AABEEMPR ABAMPERE
AABCCELS CASCABEL	AABCINNS CANNABIS	AABDEORT TEABOARD	AABEENNW WANNABEE
AABCCERT BRACCATE	AABCINRS CARABINS	AABDERRT TABERDAR	AABEENOR ANAEROBE
AABCCHIN BACCHIAN	AABCINSU BANAUSIC	AABDERRW BEARWARD	AABEERRT ABERRATE
AABCCHIS BISCACHA	AABCIOPS COPAIBAS	AABDERTT RABATTED	AABEERSZ ZAREEBAS
AABCCHIZ BIZCACHA	AABCIRSS BRASSICA	AABDERTV VARTABED	AABEERTT TRABEATE
AABCCHKT BACKCHAT	AABCISSS ABSCISSA	AABDERWY WAYBREAD	AABEFFNS BEFFANAS
AABCCHNT BACCHANT	AABCISTX TAXICABS	AABDESSS BADASSES	AABEFGSU AUFGABES
AABCCINN CANNABIC	AABCKKLT TALKBACK	AABDFHLN FAHLBAND	AABEFLLL FLABELLA
AABCCKKP BACKPACK	AABCKLNO LOANBACK	AABDGHNS HANDBAGS	AABEFLMU FLAMBEAU
AABCCKLP BLACKCAP	AABCKLPY PLAYBACK	AABDGHRS HARDBAGS	AABEGGGS BAGGAGES
AABCCKLW CLAWBACK	AABCKLSY LAYBACKS	AABDGINN ABANDING	AABEGGRS GARBAGES
AABCCMOT CATACOMB	AABCKNNS CANBANKS	AABDGINR ABRADING	AABEGHLN HANGABLE
AABCDEIN ABIDANCE	AABCKPRT BRATPACK	AABDGMOS GAMBADOS	AABEGHNR BERGHAAN
AABCDEIT ABDICATE	AABCKPSY BACKPAYS	AABDGNOV VAGABOND	AABEGILN GAINABLE
AABCDELL CABALLED	PAYBACKS	AABDGNSS SANDBAGS	AABEGINR ABEARING
AABCDELN BALANCED	AABCKRRS BARRACKS	AABDGORR GARBOARD	AABEGLLL GLABELLA
AABCDHKN BACKHAND	AABCKSSW BACKSAWS	AABDGOTU GADABOUT	AABEGLRS ALGEBRAS

```
AABEGLRT GLABRATE        AABELOVW AVOWABLE        AABILRVY VARIABLY        AACCDIRS CARDIACS
AABEGLRU ARGUABLE        AABELPPT TAPPABLE        AABILSST BALISTAS        AACCDOVY ADVOCACY
AABEGMNR BARGEMAN        AABELPRS PARABLES        AABIMMRS MARIMBAS        AACCEELT CALCEATE
AABEGMNY MANGABEY                 SPARABLE        AABIMNNO BONAMANI        AACCEENT CETACEAN
AABEGMRS BERGAMAS        AABELPSS PASSABLE        AABIMNOS BONAMIAS        AACCEFLO COALFACE
         MEGABARS        AABELRST ARBALEST        AABIMNRU MANUBRIA        AACCEGOR ACCORAGE
AABEGMRT BREGMATA        AABELRTY BETRAYAL        AABIMORS AMBROSIA        AACCEGRU CARUCAGE
AABEGMTT GAMBETTA                 RATEABLY        AABIMRSU SIMARUBA        AACCEHIX CACHEXIA
AABEGNOR BARONAGE        AABELSTT ABETTALS        AABINNPR BRAINPAN        AACCEILN CALCANEI
AABEGORT ABROGATE                 STATABLE        AABINORS ABRASION        AACCEIRR CERCARIA
AABEGOST SABOTAGE                 TASTABLE        AABINOSU OUABAINS        AACCEKRS CARCAKES
AABEGRRS BAGARRES        AABELSTW WASTABLE        AABINRST ATABRINS        AACCELOR CARACOLE
         BARRAGES        AABELTTU TABULATE                 BARTISAN        AACCELPT PLACCATE
AABEGSSS BAGASSES        AABELTUX TABLEAUX        AABINRTZ BARTIZAN        AACCELRR CARCERAL
AABEGSSU ABUSAGES        AABENNSW WANNABES        AABINSST ABSTAINS        AACCENRT CARCANET
AABEHIRR HERBARIA        AABENRRT ABERRANT        AABIORRS SORBARIA        AACCENSV VACANCES
AABEHKLS SHAKABLE        AABENRST ANTBEARS        AABIORTT ABATTOIR        AACCERSS CARCASES
AABEHLMS SHAMABLE                 RATSBANE        AABIOSSY BIOASSAY        AACCERTU ACCURATE
AABEHLOT OATHABLE        AABEORRT ARBORETA        AABIPSUX PAXIUBAS                 CARUCATE
AABEHLPS SHAPABLE        AABEORST RABATOES        AABIRTUY RUBAIYAT        AACCFGOO CACAFOGO
AABEHLPT ALPHABET       AABERSSU SUBAREAS        AABJLMNO JAMBOLAN        AACCFILR FARCICAL
AABEHLRW WARHABLE        AABERSTT RABATTES        AABKLLPR BALLPARK        AACCGILT GALACTIC
AABEHLSW WASHABLE                 TABARETS        AABKMNNS BANKSMAN        AACCHILL CAILLACH
AABEHNST ABTHANES        AABERSTU ABATURES        AABKNRST TANBARKS        AACCHILP PACHALIC
AABEIKNS IKEBANAS        AABESZZZ BAZAZZES        AABKOOSZ BAZOOKAS        AACCHINR ANARCHIC
AABEILLM MAILABLE        AABFILUX FABLIAUX        AABKOPRS SOAPBARK                 CHARACIN
AABEILLS ISABELLA        AABFLLST FASTBALL        AABLLMOR BALMORAL        AACCHINS CHICANAS
         SAILABLE        AABFLOTT FALTBOAT        AABLLNST BALLANTS        AACCHISV VISCACHA
AABEILNR INARABLE                 FLATBOAT        AABLLPPY PALPABLY        AACCHIVZ VIZCACHA
AABEILNS BANALISE        AABGGNOT TABOGGAN        AABLLPST PATBALLS        AACCHLNS CLACHANS
AABEILNZ BANALIZE        AABGGRRT BRAGGART        AABLLSST BALLASTS        AACCHLOR CHARCOAL
AABEILRS RAISABLE        AABGHINS ABASHING        AABLLSTU BLASTULA        AACCHLOT CACHALOT
AABEILRV VARIABLE        AABGHNRS BHANGRAS        AABLLUVY VALUABLY        AACCHLRS CLARSACH
AABEILST BALISTAE        AABGHNSS NASHGABS        AABLMNOR ABNORMAL        AACCHMNO COACHMAN
         LABIATES        AABGIILS ABIGAILS        AABLMNTU AMBULANT        AACCHMPS CHAMPACS
         SATIABLE        AABGILMS MAILBAGS        AABLMRSU LABARUMS        AACCHNNS CANNACHS
AABEILTV ABLATIVE        AABGILNT ABLATING        AABLMSST LAMBASTS        AACCHNOR CORANACH
AABEINOZ ZABAIONE        AABGIMNS SAMBAING        AABLNTTT BLATTANT        AACCHRST CHARACTS
AABEINRT RABATINE        AABGINRS BARGAINS        AABLORST ABLATORS        AACCIINV VACCINIA
AABEINST BASANITE        AABGINRY ABRAYING        AABLOTUY LAYABOUT        AACCIIST SCIATICA
AABEIOTU ABOITEAU        AABGLLLO GOALBALL        AABLPSSY PASSABLY        AACCILMS ACCLAIMS
AABEIRSS AIRBASES        AABGLLRY BALLYRAG        AABLRRSU SABURRAL        AACCILNV VACCINAL
         ARABISES        AABGLMNU GALBANUM        AABLRSST ARBLASTS        AACCILRU ACICULAR
AABEIRSV ABRASIVE        AABGLRUY ARGUABLY        AABLRSUU SUBAURAL        AACCILTT TACTICAL
AABEIRSZ ARABIZES        AABGMORR BAROGRAM        AABLSTTU ABUTTALS        AACCIMNU CACUMINA
AABEIRTU AUBRETIA        AABGNORZ GARBANZO        AABMMOSU ABOMASUM        AACCIORS CARIOCAS
         AUBRIETA        AABHHISS SAHIBAHS        AABMNNOO BONAMANO        AACCIORU CARIACOU
AABEJLLS JELLABAS        AABHHKSS SABKHAHS        AABMNOTW BATWOMAN        AACCIPTY CAPACITY
AABEJMUX JAMBEAUX        AABHHORU BROUHAHA        AABMNRTU RAMBUTAN        AACCIRTY CARYATIC
AABEJNSX BANJAXES        AABHHRSU BRUHAHAS        AABMORSU MARABOUS        AACCJKRS CARJACKS
AABEKLLT TALKABLE        AABHIINU BAUHINIA        AABMORTU MARABOUT        AACCJKRW CRACKJAW
AABEKLLW WALKABLE        AABHIJMY JAMBIYAH                 TAMBOURA        AACCJORU CARCAJOU
AABEKMNR BRAKEMAN        AABHILTU HABITUAL        AABMOSSU ABOMASUS                 CARJACOU
AABEKNSS SEABANKS        AABHINST HABITANS        AABMRSTU TAMBURAS        AACCKLPS CALPACKS
AABEKPRR PARBREAK        AABHINTT HABITANT        AABNNOST ABSONANT        AACCKORT COATRACK
AABEKRRS BARESARK        AABHIRST TABASHIR        AABNNOSZ BONANZAS        AACCKRRS CARRACKS
AABELLMT MEATBALL        AABHISTT HABITATS        AABNOSST SABATONS        AACCLLRU CALCULAR
AABELLNO LOANABLE        AABHKNRS BARKHANS        AABORRRT BARRATOR        AACCLLST CATCALLS
AABELLPP PALPABLE        AABHKSST SABKHATS        AABORSTT BAROSTAT        AACCLMNY CLAMANCY
AABELLPS LAPSABLE        AABHLLSW WASHBALL        AABRRRTY BARRATRY        AACCLOPS POLACCAS
AABELLPY PLAYABLE        AABHNOTU AUTOBAHN        AABRRSST BRASSART        AACCLORS CARACOLS
AABELLSS SABELLAS        AABHQSSU SQUABASH        AABRRSSU SUBARRAS        AACCLPRS CALCSPAR
AABELLSV SALVABLE        AABHRRSU SURBAHAR        AABRRSUV BRAVURAS        AACCLPST PLACCATS
AABELLSY SALEABLY        AABIJMSY JAMBIYAS        AABSTTTU BATTUTAS        AACCLRSU ACCRUALS
AABELLUV VALUABLE        AABIKNSS BANKSIAS        AACCCDIS SACCADIC                 CARACULS
AABELMNY AMENABLY        AABILLLY LABIALLY        AACCCFIO FOCACCIA                 SACCULAR
AABELMST BLASTEMA        AABILLRS BARILLAS        AACCCHHU CACHUCHA        AACCLSSU ACCUSALS
         LAMBASTE        AABILLST BALLISTA        AACCCRUY ACCURACY        AACCORSU CURACAOS
AABELMSU AMUSABLE        AABILMNS BAILSMAN        AACCDDES CASCADED                 CURACOAS
AABELMTU AMBULATE        AABILMNU BIMANUAL        AACCDEIM ACADEMIC        AACCOSST ACCOASTS
AABELNNT TANNABLE        AABILNNU BIANNUAL        AACCDELO ACCOLADE        AACCOSTT STACCATO
AABELNOS ABALONES        AABILNOR BARONIAL        AACCDEMS MEDACCAS                 STOCCATA
AABELNPS ANABLEPS        AABILNOT ABLATION        AACCDENU CADUCEAN                 TOCCATAS
AABELNPT PANTABLE        AABILNRU BINAURAL        AACCDERR RACECARD        AACCRRST CARRACTS
AABELNRY BALNEARY        AABILNTY BANALITY        AACCDERS CARCASED        AACDDEIL DAEDALIC
AABELNST BANALEST        AABILOSU ABOULIAS                 CARDCASE        AACDDENV ADVANCED
AABELOPR PARABOLE        AABILOTT BOATTAIL        AACCDESS CASCADES        AACDDETU CAUDATED
AABELORR ARBOREAL        AABILRRT ARBITRAL                 SACCADES        AACDDHRS CHADDARS
AABELOSV LAVABOES        AABILRST ARBALIST        AACCDHIR CHARACID        AACDDILN CANDIDAL
```

AACDDINS CANDIDAS
AACDEEHH HEADACHE
AACDEEHR AREACHED
　　　　　HEADRACE
AACDEEHS HEADCASE
AACDEELS ESCALADE
AACDEEMS ACADEMES
AACDEEPS ESCAPADE
AACDEEST ESTACADE
AACDEETU ECAUDATE
AACDEFHR HARDFACE
AACDEFLS FALCADES
AACDEFLT FALCATED
AACDEGGR AGGRACED
AACDEGKP PACKAGED
AACDEGMR DECAGRAM
AACDEHHY HEADACHY
AACDEHIN HACIENDA
AACDEHLN CHALANED
AACDEHLP CEPHALAD
AACDEHMR DRACHMAE
AACDEHMS CHAMADES
AACDEHRS CHARADES
AACDEHRT CATHEDRA
AACDEHST CATHEADS
AACDEHTT ATTACHED
AACDEILS ALCAIDES
　　　　　SIDALCEA
AACDEIMN MAENADIC
AACDEIMS CAMISADE
AACDEINR CANARIED
　　　　　RADIANCE
AACDEINS AIDANCES
AACDEIRT RADICATE
AACDEJNT ADJACENT
AACDEKNP PANCAKED
AACDEKNS ASKANCED
AACDEKTT ATTACKED
AACDELLS ALCALDES
AACDELMN MANACLED
AACDELNR CALENDAR
　　　　　LANDRACE
AACDELNS CANDELAS
AACDELNV VALANCED
AACDELOS ESCALADO
AACDELPT PLACATED
AACDELRS CALDERAS
AACDELSS SCALADES
AACDELSY ALCAYDES
AACDELTT LACTATED
AACDELTV CLAVATED
AACDENSV ADVANCES
　　　　　CANVASED
AACDENSZ CADENZAS
AACDENTU ADUNCATE
AACDENTV TADVANCE
AACDEOPS ESCAPADO
AACDEOTU AUTOCADE
AACDEOTV ADVOCATE
AACDEPRS SCARPAED
AACDEQUY ADEQUACY
AACDERST CADASTRE
AACDERSV CADAVERS
AACDERTU ARCUATED
AACDETTU ACTUATED
AACDETUV VACUATED
AACDGINR ARCADING
　　　　　CARANGID
　　　　　CARDIGAN
AACDHHKR HARDHACK
AACDHIIS DICHASIA
AACDHILL CHILLADA
AACDHILR DIARCHAL
AACDHIMR DRACHMAI
AACDHINP HANDICAP
AACDHINR ARACHNID
AACDHKRT HARDTACK
AACDHLNP HANDCLAP
AACDHLOT CATHODAL

AACDHLRY CHARLADY
AACDHMMR DRAMMACH
AACDHMRS DRACHMAS
AACDHNRS HANDCARS
AACDHNRT HANDCART
AACDHPRS CRASHPAD
AACDIINS ASCIDIAN
AACDILLP PALLADIC
AACDILMT DALMATIC
AACDILMU CALADIUM
AACDILNO DIACONAL
AACDILNR CARDINAL
AACDILNU DULCIANA
AACDILOZ ZODIACAL
AACDILRR RAILCARD
AACDILRS RADICALS
AACDIMNO MANDIOCA
AACDIMNY ADYNAMIC
AACDIMOS CAMISADO
AACDIMRT DRAMATIC
AACDINRT RADICANT
　　　　　TRIDACNA
AACDINRY RADIANCY
AACDINST ANTACIDS
AACDIOTU AUTACOID
AACDIRSS ASCARIDS
AACDIRTY CARYATID
AACDITUY AUDACITY
AACDJKSW JACKDAWS
AACDJQRU JACQUARD
AACDKLLN LACKLAND
AACDKSSY DAYSACKS
AACDLNSS SCANDALS
AACDLORS CARLOADS
AACDLORT CARTLOAD
AACDLOSS SCALADOS
AACDLPRS PLACARDS
AACDLRTY DACTYLAR
AACDMMOR CARDAMOM
AACDMMRU CARDAMUM
AACDMNNO MANCANDO
AACDMNOR CARDAMON
AACDOOSV AVOCADOS
AACDORRT CARTROAD
AACEEFIT FACETIAE
AACEEFLP PALEFACE
AACEEGIR ACIERAGE
　　　　　AGACERIE
AACEEGLR CLEARAGE
AACEEGLV CLEAVAGE
AACEEGRS ACREAGES
AACEEHLP ACALEPHE
AACEEHLT LEACHATE
AACEEHRS AREACHES
　　　　　EARACHES
AACEEHRT TRACHEAE
AACEEIMT EMACIATE
AACEEINN ENCAENIA
AACEEIRT ACIERATE
AACEEKRT CARETAKE
AACEELNS ANELACES
AACEELRT LACERATE
AACEELST ESCALATE
AACEELTU ACULEATE
AACEEMRT MACERATE
　　　　　RACEMATE
AACEEMST CASEMATE
AACEENNT CATENANE
AACEENTT CATENATE
AACEEPRV PRECAVAE
AACEEPSS SEASCAPE
AACEERSU CAESURAE
AACEERTV ACERVATE
AACEESTT ACETATES
AACEETUV EVACUATE
AACEETVX EXCAVATE
AACEFFIN AFFIANCE
AACEFHLP HALFPACE
AACEFIST FASCIATE

AACEFRRS CARFARES
AACEFRST SEACRAFT
AACEFRSX CARFAXES
AACEFRTT ARTEFACT
AACEGGRS AGGRACES
AACEGHNT CHANTAGE
AACEGILN ANGELICA
AACEGILT GLACIATE
AACEGINR CANAIGRE
AACEGINY GYNAECIA
AACEGIOP APOGAEIC
AACEGIRR CARRIAGE
AACEGIRV VICARAGE
AACEGKPR PACKAGER
AACEGKPS PACKAGES
AACEGKRT TRACKAGE
AACEGKSS SACKAGES
AACEGLNY LANCEGAY
AACEGNRS CARNAGES
　　　　　CRANAGES
AACEGRST CARTAGES
AACEGRSV SCAVAGER
AACEGSSV SCAVAGES
AACEHILL ACHILLEA
　　　　　HELIACAL
AACEHILN ACHENIAL
AACEHILP PHACELIA
AACEHIMR CHIMAERA
AACEHIMT HAEMATIC
AACEHIRS ARCHAISE
AACEHIRT THERIACA
AACEHIRZ ARCHAIZE
AACEHLNT CALANTHE
AACEHLNU EULACHAN
AACEHLPS ACALEPHS
AACEHLRS ALCHERAS
AACEHLRT TRACHEAL
AACEHLRX EXARCHAL
AACEHLSS CALASHES
AACEHLST ALCAHEST
AACEHMNP CAMPHANE
AACEHMRS MARCHESA
AACEHMSS CAMASHES
AACEHMST SCHEMATA
AACEHNPS PANACHES
AACEHPRT RACEPATH
AACEHPUX CHAPEAUX
AACEHRSS CHARASES
AACEHRSU ARCHAEUS
AACEHRTT REATTACH
AACEHSTT ATTACHES
AACEHTUX CHATEAUX
AACEIILN LACINIAE
AACEIINT ACTINIAE
AACEIIRV CAVIARIE
AACEIKMT KAMACITE
AACEILLM CAMELLIA
AACEILLN ALLIANCE
　　　　　CANAILLE
AACEILMN ANALCIME
　　　　　CALAMINE
AACEILMT CALAMITE
AACEILNS CANALISE
AACEILNT ANALCITE
　　　　　LAITANCE
AACEILNU ACAULINE
AACEILNV VALIANCE
AACEILNZ CANALIZE
AACEILOP ALOPECIA
AACEILRT TAILRACE
AACEILRV CAVALIER
AACEILST SALICETA
AACEIMNS AMNESIAC
AACEIMRS MACARISE
　　　　　MESARAIC
AACEIMRZ MACARIZE
AACEIMTT CATAMITE
AACEIMUX CAMAIEUX
AACEINRS CANARIES

AACEINRT CARINATE
AACEINRV VARIANCE
AACEINST ESTANCIA
AACEIOPR CAPOEIRA
AACEIPPS PAPACIES
AACEIPRS AIRSPACE
AACEIPRT APRICATE
AACEIPSS CAPIASES
AACEIPTT APATETIC
　　　　　CAPITATE
AACEIRSV AVARICES
　　　　　CAVIARES
AACEIRTV VICARATE
AACEITTV ACTIVATE
　　　　　CAVITATE
AACEJLTU JACULATE
AACEKKLW CAKEWALK
AACEKNPS PANCAKES
AACEKNSS ASKANCES
AACEKOST OATCAKES
AACEKRTT ATTACKER
AACELLMR MARCELLA
AACELLNS CANELLAS
AACELLOT ALLOCATE
AACELLST CASTELLA
　　　　　LACTEALS
AACELLTY ALLEYCAT
AACELMNP PLACEMAN
AACELMNS MANACLES
AACELMRS CARAMELS
　　　　　CERAMALS
AACELMTU MACULATE
AACELNNU CANNULAE
AACELNOR LECANORA
AACELNPR PARLANCE
AACELNPT PLACENTA
AACELNRT LACERANT
AACELNRY ARCANELY
AACELNST ANALECTS
AACELNSV VALANCES
AACELNTU LACUNATE
　　　　　TENACULA
AACELOST CATALOES
AACELOSU ACAULOSE
AACELPST PLACATES
AACELPSU SCAPULAE
AACELRSU CAESURAL
AACELRSV CARAVELS
AACELRWY CLEARWAY
AACELSST LACTASES
AACELSTT LACTATES
AACELSTY CATALYSE
AACELTTY CATTLEYA
AACELTYZ CATALYZE
AACEMMRS MACRAMES
AACEMNOR AMORANCE
AACEMNPS SPACEMAN
AACEMNST CAMSTANE
AACEMPRS PARACMES
AACEMQSU MACAQUES
AACEMRSS MASSACRE
AACEMSSS CAMASSES
AACENOTU OCEANAUT
AACENPRS PANCREAS
AACENPST PASTANCE
AACENPSU SAUCEPAN
AACENRST CANASTER
　　　　　CATERANS
AACENRTT REACTANT
AACENRTY CATENARY
AACENRVZ CZAREVNA
AACENSSV CANVASSE
AACENSTT CANTATES
　　　　　CASTANET
AACENSTY CYANATES
AACENTUV EVACUANT
AACEOPRT CAPROATE
AACEORSS ROSACEAS
AACEORSU ARACEOUS

AACEOSST SEACOAST	AACHIMNP CHINAMPA	AACILNTT TANTALIC	AACLNNSU CANNULAS
AACEPRST CAPRATES	AACHIMNR CHAIRMAN	AACILNTU NAUTICAL	AACLNOPR COPLANAR
AACEPRSU CAPUERAS	AACHIMNS SHAMANIC	AACILNTY ANALYTIC	AACLNOTT OCTANTAL
AACERSSS RASCASSE	AACHIMNT MATACHIN	AACILNUV NAVICULA	AACLNPSY CLAYPANS
AACERSSU CAESURAS	AACHIMNZ CHAZANIM	AACILNVY VALIANCY	AACLNRSU LACUNARS
AACERSSZ SAZERACS	AACHIMRR ARMCHAIR	AACILPRU PIACULAR	AACLNRUY LACUNARY
AACERSTT CASTRATE	AACHIMRS ARCHAISM	AACILPST APLASTIC	AACLNTVY VACANTLY
AACERSWY RACEWAYS	CHARISMA	CAPITALS	AACLOOPT TAPACOLO
AACERTTT TRACTATE	MACHAIRS	AACILPSZ CAPSIZAL	AACLOPRS CAPORALS
AACESSSV CAVASSES	AACHIMSS CHIASMAS	AACILPTU CAPITULA	AACLOPST OCTAPLAS
AACESSTT SCEATTAS	AACHIMST CATHISMA	AACILPTY ATYPICAL	AACLOPTU TAPACULO
AACESTTU ACTUATES	AACHINNT ACANTHIN	AACILQRU ACQUIRAL	AACLORRU ORACULAR
AACESTUV VACUATES	AACHINRT CANTHARI	AACILRTY ALACRITY	AACLORST COALTARS
AACESUWY CAUSEWAY	AACHINSW CHAINSAW	AACILRUU AURICULA	AACLORSU CAROUSAL
AACFFILS CAFFILAS	AACHIPST CHAPATIS	AACILSTT STATICAL	AACLORSZ ALCORZAS
AACFGRST CRAGFAST	AACHIPTT CHAPATTI	AACILSTY SALACITY	AACLORUV VACUOLAR
AACFHMST CAMSHAFT	AACHIRST ARCHAIST	AACIMMNO AMMONIAC	AACLOSTT CATTALOS
AACFILLY FACIALLY	CITHARAS	AACIMMRS MACARISM	AACLPPRT CLAPTRAP
AACFILOS FASCIOLA	AACHIRTX TAXIARCH	MACRAMIS	AACLPRST CALTRAPS
AACFINST FANATICS	AACHKMPS CHAMPAKS	MARASMIC	AACLPRSU CAPSULAR
AACFIRRT AIRCRAFT	AACHKPSS SCHAPSKA	AACIMNOR MACARONI	SCAPULAR
AACFIRST FRASCATI	AACHKRST HATRACKS	MAROCAIN	AACLPRTY CALYPTRA
AACFIRTT ARTIFACT	AACHKSTY HAYSTACK	AACIMNOT ANATOMIC	AACLPSSU SCAPULAS
AACFISST FASCISTA	AACHLLNS CHALLANS	AACIMORT AROMATIC	AACLPTTU CATAPULT
AACFJKLP FLAPJACK	AACHLMNO MONACHAL	AACIMPRS PICAMARS	AACLRSTU CLAUSTRA
AACFKLPT FLATPACK	AACHLMOS CHLOASMA	AACINNST CANTINAS	AACLRSUV VASCULAR
AACFLLSU FALCULAS	AACHLORT THORACAL	AACINOPR PARANOIC	AACLRTUX CURTALAX
AACFLRST FRACTALS	AACHLPPS CHAPPALS	AACINOPT CAPITANO	AACLSSTT SALTCATS
AACFRRSU FARRUCAS	AACHLSSU ACUSHLAS	PACATION	AACLSTTY CATALYST
AACGGINO ANAGOGIC	AACHLSTU CALATHUS	AACINORS OCARINAS	AACLSTUY CASUALTY
AACGGIOP APAGOGIC	AACHMMNR MARCHMAN	AACINORT RAINCOAT	AACMNOOR MACAROON
AACGHIPR AGRAPHIC	AACHMNNR RANCHMAN	AACINOTV VACATION	AACMNORS CAMARONS
AACGHIRR CHIRAGRA	AACHMNTW WATCHMAN	AACINPST CAPITANS	MASCARON
AACGHLLO AGALLOCH	AACHMNUY NAUMACHY	CAPTAINS	AACMNPRY RAMPANCY
AACGHNOR CHARANGO	AACHMORT ACHROMAT	AACINPTY CAPITAYN	AACMORRS CAMORRAS
AACGHOPZ GAZPACHO	TRACHOMA	AACINQTU ACQUAINT	AACMRRST TRAMCARS
AACGHORU GUACHARO	AACHMPRT CHAMPART	AACINRST ARCANIST	AACMRSSS SARCASMS
AACGIIMN MAGICIAN	AACHMPRY PHARMACY	AACINRSZ CZARINAS	AACNNOSZ CANZONAS
AACGIINR GARCINIA	AACHNOPS PANOCHAS	AACINSTZ STANZAIC	AACNOSST SACATONS
AACGILLO ALOGICAL	AACHNOSU HUANACOS	AACIOPST TAPIOCAS	AACNOTTY CATATONY
AACGILLS GLACIALS	AACHNPRS SARPANCH	AACIOPSV COPAIVAS	AACNPSST CAPSTANS
AACGILLU ALGUACIL	AACHNRST TRASHCAN	AACIPRTY RAPACITY	AACNRSTT TRANSACT
AACGILNO ANALOGIC	AACHNRSV NAVARCHS	AACIQSTU AQUATICS	AACNRSTU CURTANAS
AACGILNV GALVANIC	AACHNRVY NAVARCHY	AACIRRTT TARTARIC	AACOORTX TOXOCARA
AACGILOX COXALGIA	AACHNSTU ACANTHUS	AACIRSTT CASTRATI	AACOPRSU ACARPOUS
AACGILRT TRAGICAL	AACHOPPR APPROACH	AACIRSTZ CZARITSA	AACOPRTU AUTOCARP
AACGILSS SCAGLIAS	AACHORTU RACAHOUT	AACJKLPS SLAPJACK	AACOPSTV POSTCAVA
AACGIMMT MAGMATIC	AACHOTTU TACAHOUT	AACJKMNS MANJACKS	AACORRTV VARACTOR
AACGIMMN MANGANIC	AACHRRST CATARRHS	AACJKOOR JACKAROO	AACORSTT CASTRATO
AACGIMNP CAMPAIGN	AACHRSWY ARCHWAYS	AACKKNPS KNAPSACK	AACORSTU ACATOURS
PANGAMIC	AACHRTUY AUTARCHY	AACKLNPS KNAPSCAL	AUTOCARS
AACGIMOP APOGAMIC	AACIILMN ANIMALIC	AACKLOWY LOCKAWAY	AACORTTU ACTUATOR
AACGIMRR MARGARIC	AACIILMO MAIOLICA	AACKMNPS MANPACKS	AUTOCRAT
AACGIMUU GUAIACUM	AACIILRV VICARIAL	AACKMNRT TRACKMAN	AACOSTUV AUTOVACS
AACGINOT CONTAGIA	AACIIMNT ANIMATIC	AACKMNST TACKSMAN	AACRSTUV VACATURS
AACGINPS SCAPAING	AACIINPR PICARIAN	AACKMRST AMTRACKS	AACRSTWY CARTWAYS
AACGINTV VACATING	AACIINPT CAPITANI	AACKNRSS RANSACKS	AACSTUWY CUTAWAYS
AACGISTY SAGACITY	AACIINST ACTINIAS	AACKORWY ROCKAWAY	AADDDEEH DEADHEAD
AACGLMOU GLAUCOMA	AACIJLMO MAJOLICA	AACKPRRS CARPARKS	AADDDEER ADREADED
AACGLOST CATALOGS	AACIJNOP JAPONICA	AACKPRST RATPACKS	AADDDERW ADWARDED
AACGMNRS CRAGSMAN	AACIKLMS MAILSACK	AACKPSWY PACKWAYS	AADDDGNR GRANDDAD
AACGNOSU GUANACOS	AACIKLRS CLARKIAS	AACKRTWY TRACKWAY	AADDEGGR AGGRADED
AACGNRVY VAGRANCY	AACIKMNW MACKINAW	AACLLMMU MACALLUM	AADDEGRT GRADATED
AACHHIKR KACHAHRI	AACIKNNS CANAKINS	AACLLMRY LACRYMAL	AADDEHHR HARDHEAD
AACHHKRS CHARKHAS	AACIKRTU AUTARKIC	AACLLNRY CARNALLY	AADDEHLN HEADLAND
AACHHLLS CHALLAHS	AACILLMR LACRIMAL	AACLLNST CALLANTS	AADDEHMN HANDMADE
AACHHTWY HATCHWAY	AACILLMT CLIMATAL	AACLLNSU CALLUNAS	AADDEHRZ HAZARDED
AACHIIMR MARIACHI	AACILLPY APICALLY	AACLLRRY CARRYALL	AADDEILN DEDALIAN
AACHIKNR CHINKARA	AACILLRY RACIALLY	AACLLRSY RASCALLY	AADDEILS ALIDADES
AACHIKNS KACHINAS	AACILMNT CALAMINT	AACLLSSU CLAUSULA	AADDEIRT RADIATED
AACHIKRS CHIKARAS	CLAIMANT	AACLLSUY CASUALLY	AADDEKMS DAMASKED
AACHILLP CALIPHAL	AACILMOR ACROMIAL	CAUSALLY	AADDELTU ADULATED
AACHILLR RACHILLA	AACILMOT ATOMICAL	AACLLTUY ACTUALLY	AADDEMNT MANDATED
AACHILMS CHAMISAL	AACILMTY CALAMITY	AACLMNNS CLANSMAN	AADDEMRU MARAUDED
AACHILMT THALAMIC	AACILNOR CONARIAL	AACLMNSS CLASSMAN	AADDEMRY DAYDREAM
AACHILNP CHAPLAIN	AACILNRS CLARAINS	AACLMNST CALMANTS	AADDENPR PANDARED
AACHILPS CALIPASH	AACILNRV CARNIVAL	AACLMRRU MACRURAL	AADDENPS DEADPANS
AACHILRV ARCHIVAL	AACILNST ALICANTS	AACLNNOT CANTONAL	
AACHIMNN CHAINMAN		AACLNNRU CANNULAR	

AADDGNRS GRADDANS	AADEGLMN MAGDALEN	AADEJNNP JAPANNED	AADGGIMN DAMAGING
GRANDADS	AADEGLMY AMYGDALE	AADEKLLN LAKELAND	AADGGLNN GANGLAND
AADDGNRU GRADUAND	AADEGLNS SELADANG	AADEKLNR KALENDAR	AADGGLRS LAGGARDS
AADDHHRS SHRADDHA	AADEGLSV SALVAGED	AADEKMNR MANDRAKE	AADGGRSS SAGGARDS
AADDHIMN HANDMAID	AADEGMPR RAMPAGED	AADEKMRS KAMERADS	AADGGRST STAGGARD
AADDHKRS KHADDARS	AADEGMRS MEGARADS	AADEKNST ASKANTED	AADGHILS HIDALGAS
AADDHRSS SRADDHAS	AADEGMSS MASSAGED	AADEKSTT ATTASKED	AADGHIPR DIAGRAPH
AADDIIKS DIDAKAIS	AADEGNRR ARRANGED	AADELLPP APPALLED	AADGHRTU HATGUARD
AADDIISV DAVIDIAS	AADEGNTV VANTAGED	AADELLPS PADELLAS	AADGIINS GAINSAID
AADDILNO DIANODAL	AADEGPSS PASSAGED	AADELLRT DATALLER	AADGILLR GAILLARD
AADDKMMO MOKADDAM	AADEGRST GRADATES	AADELLWY WELLADAY	GALLIARD
AADDLLNY LANDLADY	AADEGRSV SAVEGARD	AADELMNP NAPALMED	AADGILMR MADRIGAL
AADDLNRW LANDWARD	AADEGRSY DRAYAGES	AADELMNR ALDERMAN	AADGILNO DIAGONAL
AADDLNRY YARDLAND	YARDAGES	MALANDER	GONADIAL
AADDMMQU MUQADDAM	AADEGRTU GRADUATE	AADELMNS DALESMAN	AADGILNS SALADING
AADDNRST STANDARD	AADEGSSU ASSUAGED	LEADSMAN	AADGIMMN MADAMING
AADDNRWY YARDWAND	AADEGSSW ASSWAGED	AADELMOS ALAMODES	AADGIMMS DIGAMMAS
AADDNSVV DVANDVAS	AADEHHOR HOARHEAD	AADELMPT PALMATED	AADGIMNR MRIDANGA
AADDRSST DASTARDS	AADEHILR HEADRAIL	AADELMRU ALARUMED	AADGIMOS AGAMOIDS
AADDRSTY DASTARDY	RAILHEAD	AADELMYZ AMAZEDLY	AADGIMPR PARADIGM
AADEEFFR AFFEARED	AADEHIRR DIARRHEA	AADELNRS ADRENALS	AADGIMRS DIAGRAMS
AADEEGHR HEADGEAR	AADEHIRS AIRHEADS	AADELNST EASTLAND	AADGIMRT GRADATIM
AADEEGHS HEADAGES	AADEHKMR HEADMARK	AADELNSW DANELAWS	AADGINPR PARADING
AADEEGLR LAAGERED	AADEHLLL HALALLED	AADELNSY ANALYSED	AADGINPT ADAPTING
AADEEGLT GALEATED	AADEHLLO HALLOAED	AADELNYZ ANALYZED	AADGINRR DARRAIGN
AADEEGMN AMENAGED	AADEHLMP HEADLAMP	AADELPPT PALPATED	AADGINRU GUARDIAN
ENDAMAGE	AADEHLNR ANHEDRAL	AADELPRS PARDALES	AADGINRW AWARDING
AADEEGRV AVERAGED	AADEHLPS SLAPHEAD	AADELPRY PARLAYED	AADGIQRU QUADRIGA
AADEEHMT MEATHEAD	AADEHLRS ASHLARED	AADELRSY SALEYARD	AADGLLSW GADWALLS
AADEEIRT ERADIATE	AADEHMNS HEADSMAN	AADELRTU RADULATE	AADGLMOR MALGRADO
AADEEIRW AWEARIED	AADEHMST MASTHEAD	AADELRTV LARVATED	AADGLMSY AMYGDALS
AADEEKNW AWAKENED	AADEHNPS SANDHEAP	AADELRTY DAYTALER	AADGLNRS GARLANDS
AADEEKRW REAWAKED	AADEHNRV VERANDAH	AADELSTT SALTATED	AADGLNSS SLADANGS
AADEELNN ANNEALED	AADEHPPR PARAPHED	AADELSTU ADULATES	AADGLOPR PODAGRAL
AADEELPP APPEALED	AADEHPSS SAPHEADS	AADELSTY DAYTALES	AADGLRSU GRADUALS
AADEELTV ALVEATED	AADEHRRW HARDWARE	AADELTUV VALUATED	AADGMNOR DRAGOMAN
AADEEMNT EMANATED	AADEHRSS HARASSED	AADEMNOS ADENOMAS	AADGMNOS GOADSMAN
AADEEMOT OEDEMATA	AADEHRSW RAWHEADS	AADEMNPS SPADEMAN	AADGMNRS DRAGSMAN
AADEEMRR DEMERARA	WARHEADS	AADEMNST MANDATES	GRANDAMS
AADEENPT TAPENADE	AADEHSSY SASHAYED	AADEMNUZ UNAMAZED	GRANDMAS
AADEENTT ANTEDATE	AADEHSTT HASTATED	AADEMORT MATADORE	AADGMRSS SMARAGDS
AADEEPPR APPEARED	AADEHSWY HEADWAYS	AADEMRRU MARAUDER	AADGNNQU QUANDANG
AADEEPPS APPEASED	AADEILMS MALADIES	AADEMRSS MADRASES	AADGNPRS GRANDPAS
AADEEPRS PASEARED	AADEILMU AUMAILED	AADEMSSS ADMASSES	AADGNRST GARDANTS
AADEEQTU ADEQUATE	AADEILNT DENTALIA	AADENNST ANDANTES	AADGNRSY YARDANGS
AADEFFLT AFFLATED	AADEILPR PRAEDIAL	AADENRRT NARRATED	AADGNRTU GUARDANT
AADEFFNR FANFARED	AADEILPS PALISADE	AADENRRW WARRANED	AADGNRUV VANGUARD
AADEFFRY AFFRAYED	AADEILPT LAPIDATE	AADENRSV VERANDAS	AADGOPRS PODAGRAS
AADEFGLS FALDAGES	AADEILRS SALARIED	AADENRTT TARTANED	AADGRRUW GURDWARA
AADEFGRS FARDAGES	AADEILSS ASSAILED	AADENSSW WEASANDS	AADHHIPS PADISHAH
AADEFHLT FLATHEAD	AADEILSV VEDALIAS	AADENSWZ WEAZANDS	AADHIINP APHIDIAN
AADEFHST HEADFAST	AADEILTV VALIDATE	AADENTUV AVAUNTED	AADHILLR HALLIARD
AADEFHTW FATWAHED	AADEIMNN AMANDINE	AADEOPRT TAPADERO	AADHILNR HANDRAIL
AADEFIRS FARADISE	AADEIMNP PANDEMIA	AADEOPST ADESPOTA	AADHILRV HAVILDAR
SAFARIED	AADEIMNR MARINADE	AADEORRT AERODART	AADHIMSS SAMADHIS
AADEFIRZ FARADIZE	AADEIMNT ANIMATED	AADEPRST ADAPTERS	AADHINRR HARRIDAN
AADEFISS FADAISES	DIAMANTE	READAPTS	AADHJNRS HANDJARS
AADEFLLR FALDERAL	AADEIMPZ DIAZEPAM	AADEPSSS PASSADES	AADHKNSY YAKHDANS
AADEFLRY DEFRAYAL	AADEIMRV MARAVEDI	AADEQRTU QUADRATE	AADHLMOY DALMAHOY
AADEFLTT FALDETTA	AADEIMSS SEAMAIDS	AADERRRW REARWARD	AADHLNPY HANDPLAY
AADEFNSZ FAZENDAS	AADEIMST DIASTEMA	AADERRWY WARRAYED	AADHLNSW WASHLAND
AADEFRRW WARFARED	AADEINRR DARRAINE	AADERSST ASSARTED	AADHLRSY HALYARDS
AADEFRWY WAYFARED	AADEINRS ARANEIDS	AADERSSW SEAWARDS	AADHMNNY HANDYMAN
AADEGGRS AGGRADES	AADEINRT DENTARIA	AADERSTT ASTARTED	AADHMNOU OMADHAUN
AADEGGRT AGGRATED	RAINDATE	AADERSTW EASTWARD	AADHNRSS DARSHANS
AADEGGRU GUARDAGE	AADEINTT ATTAINED	RADWASTE	AADHNSSW HANDSAWS
AADEGHLN DANELAGH	AADEIPPR APPAIRED	AADERUVY AYURVEDA	AADHNSTT HATSTAND
AADEGHRS RAGHEADS	AADEIPRS PARADISE	AADFGNNO FANDANGO	AADHRRTW THRAWARD
RHAGADES	AADEIPSS DIAPASES	AADFGRSU SAUFGARD	AADHRRYZ HAZARDRY
AADEGILL DIALLAGE	AADEIPSU DIAPAUSE	AADFHNST HANDFAST	AADHRSWY HAYWARDS
AADEGILT GLADIATE	AADEIPTV ADAPTIVE	AADFIINT INTIFADA	AADHSSWY WASHDAYS
AADEGINR AREADING	AADEIRST DATARIES	AADFIMRS FARADISM	AADIJMNS JAMDANIS
DRAINAGE	RADIATES	AADFINRU UNAFRAID	AADIKLLO ALKALOID
GARDENIA	AADEIRTV VARIATED	AADFLLLN LANDFALL	AADIKLLR KILLADAR
AADEGINT INDAGATE	AADEISST DIASTASE	AADFLORW AARDWOLF	AADIKLRY KAILYARD
AADEGITT AGITATED	AADEISTT SATIATED	AADFLOTX TOADFLAX	AADIKLSY ILKADAYS
AADEGITV DIVAGATE	AADEITVW VIEWDATA	AADFLOWY FOLDAWAY	AADIKMNS DAMASKIN
AADEGJTU ADJUTAGE	AADEJMPY PYJAMAED	AADFMRRY FARMYARD	AADILLLO ALLODIAL
AADEGLLT TALLAGED	AADEJMRS JEMADARS	AADGGHRS HAGGARDS	AADILLNR LANDRAIL

AADILLPR	PALLIARD
AADILLRS	SILLADAR
AADILLRY	RADIALLY
AADILMNN	MAINLAND
AADILMNO	DOMAINAL
	DOMANIAL
AADILMNP	PLAIDMAN
AADILMRS	ADMIRALS
	AMILDARS
AADILNOR	ORDALIAN
AADILNPR	PRANDIAL
AADILNPS	PALADINS
AADILNRS	LANIARDS
AADILNTT	DILATANT
AADILOPS	PALISADO
AADILORR	RAILROAD
AADILPRS	PARDALIS
AADILPRY	LAPIDARY
AADILRRS	RISALDAR
AADILRST	TAILARDS
AADILSST	STADIALS
AADIMNNR	MANDARIN
AADIMNRS	MANDIRAS
AADIMNRT	TAMARIND
AADIMNRY	DAIRYMAN
	MAINYARD
AADIMNRZ	ZAMINDAR
AADIMNSS	DAMASSIN
AADIMNSU	SUDAMINA
AADIMNUV	VANADIUM
AADIMORS	DIORAMAS
AADIMSTZ	SAMIZDAT
AADINNOT	ADNATION
AADINOPR	PARANOID
AADINOPS	DIAPASON
AADINOPT	ADAPTION
AADINRRS	DARRAINS
AADINRRW	AIRDRAWN
AADINRST	INTRADAS
	RADIANTS
AADINRSV	VIRANDAS
AADIOPRS	DIASPORA
AADIORRT	RADIATOR
AADIPSUY	UPADAISY
AADIRRSW	AIRWARDS
AADIRRSY	DISARRAY
AADJNTTU	ADJUTANT
AADJNTUV	ADJUVANT
AADKLMNR	LANDMARK
AADKLNPR	PARKLAND
AADKLRTU	TALUKDAR
AADKMNRS	DARKMANS
AADKMRSY	DAYMARKS
AADKNRST	TANKARDS
AADKORWY	WORKADAY
AADKPRRW	PARKWARD
AADLLMRS	MALLARDS
AADLLNSW	LAWLANDS
AADLMNNS	LANDSMAN
AADLMNOR	MANDORLA
AADLMNOS	MANDOLAS
AADLMNSS	LANDMASS
AADLMNSU	LADANUMS
AADLMNUU	LAUDANUM
AADLNOPR	PARLANDO
AADLNOPS	SOAPLAND
AADLNOST	SALTANDO
AADLNRSY	LANYARDS
AADLORST	LOADSTAR
AADLORTU	ADULATOR
AADLPPRW	WALDRAPP
AADLPPSU	APPLAUDS
AADMMNOW	MADWOMAN
AADMMNSU	MANDAMUS
AADMNORS	MADRONAS
	MANDORAS
	MONARDAS
	ROADSMAN
AADMNORT	MANDATOR

AADMNRSS	MANSARDS
AADMNSTU	TAMANDUS
AADMOPPP	PAPPADOM
AADMOQSU	MADOQUAS
AADMORRT	TRAMROAD
AADMORST	MATADORS
AADMRSZZ	MAZZARDS
AADNOPRS	PANDORAS
AADNORST	ONDATRAS
AADNORTY	DONATARY
AADNOSUV	VANADOUS
AADNOSWY	NOWADAYS
AADNPRSU	PANDURAS
AADNQRSU	QUADRANS
AADNQRTU	QUADRANT
AADNQRUY	QUANDARY
AADNRRSW	WARRANDS
AADNRRSY	DARRAYNS
AADNRSTY	TANYARDS
AADNRSWY	NAYWARDS
AADOPPRR	PARADROP
AADOPRST	ADAPTORS
AADOPRXY	PARADOXY
AADOPSSS	PASSADOS
AADOPSTT	DOPATTAS
AADOPSUY	PADUASOY
AADORSVY	SAVOYARD
AADORSWY	ROADWAYS
AADOSSTT	TOSTADAS
AADPSTTU	DUPATTAS
AADQRSTU	QUADRATS
AADRSSTY	DAYSTARS
AAEEEHRT	HETAEARE
AAEEFFRS	AFFEARES
AAEEFGLS	LEAFAGES
AAEEFRRS	SEAFARER
AAEEGILN	ALIENAGE
AAEEGILP	EPIGAEAL
AAEEGINP	EPIGAEAN
AAEEGKLS	LEAKAGES
AAEEGLLN	ENALLAGE
AAEEGLST	ETALAGES
AAEEGMNS	AMENAGES
AAEEGMPR	AMPERAGE
AAEEGMTY	METAYAGE
AAEEGNRS	SANGAREE
AAEEGRST	STEARAGE
AAEEGRSV	AVERAGES
AAEEGRTW	WATERAGE
AAEEHIMR	HAEREMAI
AAEEHPRT	HEARTPEA
AAEEHRTW	WHEATEAR
AAEEHRWY	HEREAWAY
AAEEILNT	ALIENATE
AAEEINTT	TAENIATE
AAEEJMNP	JAMPANEE
AAEEKLSS	SEAKALES
AAEEKLTW	LATEWAKE
AAEEKMNS	NAMESAKE
AAEEKNRW	REAWAKEN
AAEEKPRT	PARAKEET
AAEEKPSS	SEASPEAK
AAEEKQSU	SEAQUAKE
AAEEKRSW	REAWAKES
AAEELLLM	LAMELLAE
AAEELLMT	MALLEATE
AAEELLPT	PATELLAE
AAEELMST	MALEATES
AAEELNNR	ANNEALER
	LERNAEAN
AAEELNPS	SEAPLANE
	SPELAEAN
AAEELNPU	PAENULAE
AAEELORT	AREOLATE
AAEELRST	LAETARES
AAEELRTU	LAUREATE
AAEELSST	ELASTASE
AAEELTUV	EVALUATE
AAEELVWY	WAYLEAVE

AAEEMNPT	NAMETAPE
AAEEMNST	EMANATES
	MANATEES
AAEEMPRS	PARAMESE
AAEENNNT	ANTENNAE
AAEENPRT	PARANETE
AAEENRRS	ARRASENE
AAEENRST	ARSENATE
	SERENATA
AAEENRTT	ANTEATER
AAEENSTU	NAUSEATE
AAEEPPRR	APPEARER
	RAPPAREE
	REAPPEAR
AAEEPPRS	APPEASER
AAEEPPSS	APPEASES
AAEEPRST	ASPERATE
	SEPARATE
AAEEPSTT	ASEPTATE
AAEERRWW	REWAREWA
AAEERSSW	SEAWARES
AAEERSTT	STEARATE
AAEERSTW	SEAWATER
AAEERSWX	EARWAXES
AAEFFGRS	AGRAFFES
AAEFFGST	STAFFAGE
AAEFFIRS	AFFAIRES
AAEFFLLS	FALAFELS
AAEFFLPR	PARAFFLE
AAEFFNRS	FANFARES
AAEFFSTT	TAFFETAS
AAEFGHRW	WHARFAGE
AAEFGINR	AFEARING
AAEFGITT	FATIGATE
AAEFGLLL	FLAGELLA
AAEFGLOT	FLOATAGE
AAEFGRTU	FRAUTAGE
AAEFGSTW	WAFTAGES
AAEFILTY	FAYALITE
AAEFIMRR	AIRFRAME
AAEFINNT	FAINEANT
AAEFINNU	INFAUNAE
AAEFINPU	EPIFAUNA
AAEFINTX	ANTEFIXA
AAEFLMTT	FLATMATE
AAEFLPRS	EARFLAPS
	PARAFLES
AAEFLRTW	FLATWARE
AAEFMRST	FERMATAS
AAEFORSU	AQUAFERS
AAEFRRRW	WARFARER
AAEFRRSW	WARFARES
AAEFRRWY	WAYFARER
AAEFRSWY	WAYFARES
AAEGGINR	GRAINAGE
AAEGGIOT	AGIOTAGE
AAEGGLNR	LANGRAGE
AAEGGLNU	LANGUAGE
AAEGGNOS	ANAGOGES
AAEGGNOW	WAGONAGE
AAEGGNRY	GARGANEY
AAEGGOPR	PARAGOGE
AAEGGOPS	APAGOGES
AAEGGRST	AGGRATES
AAEGHLNP	PHALANGE
AAEGHLSU	HAULAGES
AAEGHMRX	HEXAGRAM
AAEGHMSS	GAMASHES
AAEGHNRU	HARANGUE
AAEGHNST	THANAGES
AAEGHOPY	HYPOGAEA
AAEGILLR	GALLERIA
AAEGILLT	ALLIGATE
AAEGILNP	PELAGIAN
AAEGILNR	REGALIAN
AAEGILNT	AGENTIAL
	ALGINATE
AAEGILRS	GASALIER
	LAIRAGES

	REGALIAS
AAEGILSS	ALGESIAS
AAEGILSX	GALAXIES
AAEGILTT	TAILGATE
AAEGIMNO	EGOMANIA
AAEGIMNP	PIGMAEAN
AAEGIMNS	MAGNESIA
AAEGIMNZ	MAGAZINE
AAEGIMRR	MARRIAGE
AAEGIMRT	GEMATRIA
	MARITAGE
AAEGINNR	ANEARING
AAEGINPS	NAGAPIES
	PAGANISE
AAEGINPT	PAGINATE
AAEGINPZ	PAGANIZE
AAEGINRS	ANGARIES
AAEGINRT	AERATING
AAEGINST	SAGINATE
AAEGINSW	WAINAGES
AAEGINTV	NAVIGATE
	VAGINATE
AAEGIPRS	IGARAPES
AAEGIPRU	PERIAGUA
AAEGIRRS	ARRIAGES
AAEGIRSV	VAGARIES
AAEGISSS	ASSEGAIS
AAEGISTT	AGITATES
AAEGIVWY	GIVEAWAY
AAEGJSTU	AJUTAGES
AAEGKNST	TANKAGES
AAEGKOSS	SOAKAGES
AAEGLLMS	SMALLAGE
AAEGLLPR	PELLAGRA
AAEGLLSS	GALLEASS
AAEGLLST	GALLATES
	STALLAGE
	TALLAGES
AAEGLLTU	GLUTAEAL
AAEGLMNS	GAMELANS
AAEGLMNV	GAVELMAN
AAEGLNOU	ANALOGUE
AAEGLNPP	LAGNAPPE
AAEGLNPT	PLANTAGE
AAEGLNRS	ALNAGERS
AAEGLNRU	AULNAGER
AAEGLNSS	LASAGNES
AAEGLNSU	AULNAGES
AAEGLNTU	ANGULATE
AAEGLOSV	AASVOGEL
AAEGLRRS	REALGARS
	RESALGAR
AAEGLRRW	WARRAGLE
AAEGLRST	AGRESTAL
AAEGLRTY	LEGATARY
AAEGLSST	AGELASTS
	LASTAGES
AAEGLSSV	SALVAGES
AAEGLSVY	SAVAGELY
AAEGLTUV	VAULTAGE
AAEGMMNR	ENGRAMMA
AAEGMMPY	PYGMAEAN
AAEGMNRS	MANAGERS
AAEGMNRV	GRAVAMEN
AAEGMNST	MAGENTAS
	MAGNATES
AAEGMORR	AEROGRAM
AAEGMORS	SAGAMORE
AAEGMPRS	RAMPAGES
AAEGMPRU	RAMPAUGE
AAEGMRRV	MARGRAVE
AAEGMRRY	GRAMARYE
AAEGMRST	MEGASTAR
AAEGMRTU	AGERATUM
AAEGMSSS	MASSAGES
AAEGMTTW	MEGAWATT
AAEGNNOP	NEOPAGAN
AAEGNNPS	PANNAGES
AAEGNNST	TANNAGES

AAEGNPST	PAGEANTS		ALKALISE	AAEIPRST	ASPIRATE		PATERNAL
AAEGNRRR	ARRANGER	AAEIKLLZ	ALKALIZE		PARASITE		PRENATAL
AAEGNRRS	ARRANGES	AAEIKMRR	KRAMERIA		SEPTARIA	AAELNPRW	WARPLANE
AAEGNRST	STARAGEN	AAEILLLU	ALLELUIA	AAEIPRTT	PATRIATE	AAELNPST	PLATANES
	TANAGERS	AAEILLMM	MAMILLAE	AAEIPRTZ	TRAPEZIA		PLEASANT
AAEGNRTU	RUNAGATE	AAEILLMR	ARMILLAE	AAEIPRXY	APYREXIA	AAELNPSU	PAENULAS
AAEGNSTT	STAGNATE	AAEILLMX	MAXILLAE	AAEIPSTT	APATITES	AAELNRSS	ARSENALS
AAEGNSTV	VANTAGES	AAEILLPP	PAPILLAE	AAEIQRTU	TAQUERIA	AAELNRSY	ANALYSER
AAEGNSTW	WANTAGES	AAEILLPT	PALLIATE	AAEIRRRT	TERRARIA	AAELNRTT	ALTERANT
AAEGNTUV	VAUNTAGE	AAEILLRT	ARILLATE	AAEIRSST	ASTERIAS		ALTERNAT
AAEGORRT	ARROGATE	AAEILLRY	AERIALLY		ATRESIAS	AAELNRTX	RELAXANT
AAEGORTT	AEGROTAT	AAEILLTT	TALLIATE	AAEIRSSX	XERASIAS	AAELNRYZ	ANALYZER
AAEGPPRW	WRAPPAGE	AAEILLTV	ALLATIVE	AAEIRSTT	ARIETTAS	AAELNSST	SEALANTS
AAEGPSSS	PASSAGES	AAEILMNT	ALAIMENT		ARISTATE	AAELNSSV	ENVASSAL
AAEGPSSY	PAYSAGES		LAMINATE	AAEIRSTV	VARIATES	AAELNSSY	ANALYSES
AAEGQSUY	QUAYAGES	AAEILMNV	VELAMINA	AAEIRSVW	AIRWAVES	AAELNSTZ	ZEALANTS
AAEGRRSV	RAVAGERS	AAEILMRT	MATERIAL	AAEIRTTZ	ZARATITE	AAELNSWY	LANEWAYS
AAEGRSTT	REGATTAS	AAEILMSS	MALAISES	AAEISSTT	SATIATES	AAELNSYZ	ANALYZES
AAEGRSVY	SAVAGERY	AAEILNNS	ALANINES	AAEITTVX	TAXATIVE	AAELORSU	AUREOLAS
AAEGSSSU	ASSUAGES		ANNALISE	AAEJLNOP	JALAPENO	AAELORTY	ALEATORY
	SAUSAGES	AAEILNNZ	ANNALIZE	AAEJNNPR	JAPANNER	AAELOSTX	OXALATES
AAEGSSSW	ASSWAGES	AAEILNPR	AIRPLANE	AAEJNRST	NAARTJES	AAELPPRS	APPARELS
AAEGSSTV	SAVAGEST	AAEILNPT	PALATINE	AAEJNRTZ	JAZERANT	AAELPPST	PALPATES
AAEGSSTW	TASSWAGE	AAEILNRU	AURELIAN	AAEJRSSW	SWARAJES	AAELPPSU	APPLAUSE
	WASTAGES	AAEILNRV	VALERIAN	AAEKKORS	KARAOKES	AAELPRST	PALESTRA
AAEGSTTW	WATTAGES	AAEILNSS	NASALISE	AAEKLMRY	MALARKEY	AAELPRSV	PALAVERS
AAEGSTWY	GATEWAYS	AAEILNSZ	NASALIZE	AAEKLNRS	LARNAKES	AAELPRSY	PARALYSE
	GETAWAYS	AAEILNTT	ANTLIATE	AAEKLNST	ALKANETS	AAELPRTT	TETRAPLA
AAEHIIRT	HETAIRAI	AAEILNTV	AVENTAIL		KANTELAS	AAELPRYZ	PARALYZE
	HETAIRIA	AAEILORS	OLEARIAS	AAEKMRRS	EARMARKS	AAELPSTU	PLATEAUS
AAEHILMN	HIELAMAN	AAEILPPS	PAPALISE	AAEKMRSS	SEAMARKS	AAELPSTV	PALSTAVE
AAEHILNP	APHELIAN	AAEILPPZ	PAPALIZE	AAEKNPRT	PARTAKEN	AAELPTUV	VAPULATE
AAEHILNT	ANTHELIA	AAEILPRT	PARIETAL	AAEKORTY	AKARYOTE	AAELPTUX	PLATEAUX
AAEHILPR	PARHELIA	AAEILPST	STAPELIA	AAEKPRRT	PARTAKER	AAELRSTZ	LAZARETS
AAEHIMNT	ANTHEMIA	AAEILRRT	ARTERIAL	AAEKPRST	PARTAKES	AAELRTUV	VELATURA
	HAEMATIN	AAEILRSS	ASSAILER	AAEKSSSV	KAVASSES	AAELRUZZ	ZARZUELA
AAEHINPT	APHANITE		SALARIES		VAKASSES	AAELRWYY	WAYLAYER
AAEHINST	ASTHENIA	AAEILRSU	AURELIAS	AAELLLMR	LAMELLAR	AAELSSTT	SALTATES
AAEHIPST	APATHIES	AAEILRTV	VARIETAL	AAELLLPR	PARALLEL	AAELSTUV	VALUATES
AAEHIRST	HETAIRAS	AAEILSTV	AESTIVAL	AAELLMPU	AMPULLAE	AAELSTZZ	ALTEZZAS
AAEHKLST	ALKAHEST		SALIVATE	AAELLNPU	PLANULAE	AAEMMMRS	MAREMMAS
AAEHKMRY	HAYMAKER	AAEILSTX	SAXATILE	AAELLNSZ	ZANELLAS	AAEMMNRT	ARMAMENT
AAEHKNST	KHANATES	AAEILTVX	LAXATIVE	AAELLORV	ALVEOLAR	AAEMMNSU	MANUMEAS
AAEHKSSW	SEAHAWKS	AAEIMMST	IMAMATES	AAELLPRS	PARELLAS	AAEMMSTT	STEMMATA
AAEHLLLS	ALLHEALS	AAEIMNOT	METANOIA	AAELLPRT	PATELLAR	AAEMNOSW	SEAWOMAN
AAEHLMNT	METHANAL	AAEIMNPR	PEARMAIN	AAELLPST	PATELLAS	AAEMNOTZ	METAZOAN
AAEHLMNW	WHALEMAN	AAEIMNPT	IMPANATE	AAELLRST	LATERALS	AAEMNPRS	SPEARMAN
AAEHLMSY	SEALYHAM	AAEIMNRR	MARINERA	AAELLRSY	ALLAYERS	AAEMNPRT	PARAMENT
AAEHLMTU	HAMULATE	AAEIMNRT	ANIMATER	AAELLUVV	VALVULAE	AAEMNRST	SARMENTA
AAEHLNTX	EXHALANT		MARINATE	AAELLWWY	WELLAWAY		SEMANTRA
AAEHLPRX	HEXAPLAR	AAEIMNRZ	MAZARINE	AAELLWYY	ALLEYWAY	AAEMNRSU	MURAENAS
AAEHLPSX	HEXAPLAS	AAEIMNSS	AMNESIAS	AAELMMNO	MELANOMA	AAEMNRTT	ATRAMENT
AAEHLPUV	UPHEAVAL	AAEIMNST	AMENTIAS	AAELMMTU	MALAMUTE	AAEMNRTW	WATERMAN
AAEHLRST	TREHALAS		ANIMATES	AAELMNOT	MALONATE	AAEMNSST	NAMASTES
AAEHLRTT	THEATRAL	AAEIMOPR	PAROEMIA	AAELMNPT	PLATEMAN	AAEMNSTU	MANTEAUS
AAEHLSTT	ATHLETAS	AAEIMOTX	TOXAEMIA	AAELMNRT	MATERNAL	AAEMNTUX	MANTEAUX
AAEHMNPY	NYMPHAEA	AAEIMPSY	PYAEMIAS	AAELMNSS	SALESMAN	AAEMORTT	AMARETTO
AAEHMNRS	SHAREMAN	AAEIMRSU	URAEMIAS	AAELMNST	TALESMAN		TERATOMA
	SHEARMAN	AAEIMSUV	MAUVAISE	AAELMNSW	WEALSMAN	AAEMORTX	XEROMATA
AAEHMNRT	EARTHMAN	AAEINNTT	ANTENATI	AAELMNSY	SEAMANLY	AAEMOSTT	STEATOMA
AAEHMOPR	AMPHORAE	AAEINORT	AERATION	AAELMOST	OATMEALS	AAEMOTTU	AUTOMATE
AAEHMORT	ATHEROMA	AAEINORX	ANOREXIA	AAELMPRT	MALAPERT	AAEMPPSS	PAMPASES
AAEHNPRS	HANAPERS	AAEINPRS	PANARIES	AAELMPRX	EXAMPLAR	AAEMPTTU	AMPUTATE
AAEHNPSS	SAPHENAS	AAEINRRW	RAINWEAR	AAELMPSS	LAMPASES	AAEMQSTU	SQUAMATE
AAEHNPST	PHEASANT	AAEINRST	ANTISERA		LAMPASSE	AAEMRRTU	ARMATURE
AAEHNPSY	SYNAPHEA		ARTESIAN	AAELMPST	PLATEASM	AAEMRSTU	AMATEURS
AAEHNTTX	XANTHATE		RESINATA	AAELMPTV	VAMPLATE	AAEMRTTU	MATURATE
AAEHPRSZ	PHEAZARS	AAEINRTT	REATTAIN	AAELMPTY	PLAYMATE	AAENNNST	ANTENNAS
AAEHRRSS	HARASSER	AAEINRTU	INAURATE	AAELMRSY	LAMASERY	AAENNOTT	ANNOTATE
AAEHRSSS	HARASSES	AAEINRTZ	ATRAZINE	AAELMRTT	MALTREAT	AAENNSTT	STANNATE
AAEHRSSY	HEARSAYS	AAEINSTT	ASTATINE	AAELMSST	MALTASES		TANNATES
AAEHRTWX	EARTHWAX		SANITATE	AAELMSSY	AMYLASES	AAENNSTU	NAUSEANT
AAEIIKNS	AKINESIA		TANAISTE	AAELNNNT	ANTENNAL	AAENNSTV	VENTANAS
AAEIIMRV	VIRAEMIA	AAEINSTV	SANATIVE	AAELNNOT	NEONATAL	AAENORRU	AUROREAN
AAEIIPRS	APIARIES	AAEINTTT	TITANATE	AAELNNTU	ANNULATE	AAENORST	ANOESTRA
AAEIIRSV	AVIARIES	AAEIPPRS	APPRAISE	AAELNOSS	SEASONAL	AAENORSU	ARANEOUS
AAEIKKMZ	KAMIKAZE	AAEIPPSS	APEPSIAS	AAELNOSV	VALONEAS	AAENORTU	AERONAUT
AAEIKLLN	ALKALINE	AAEIPRRS	PAREIRAS	AAELNPRS	PRENASAL	AAENOSST	ASSONATE
AAEIKLLS	ALKALIES	AAEIPRSS	SPIRAEAS	AAELNPRT	PARENTAL	AAENPPRS	PARPANES

Column 1

```
AAENPPRT APPARENT
         TRAPPEAN
AAENPRTY PRYTANEA
AAENPSST ANAPESTS
         PEASANTS
AAENPSTT ANTEPAST
AAENPSTY PEASANTY
AAENRRSS NARRASES
AAENRRST NARRATES
AAENRSTT TARTANES
AAENRSTV TAVERNAS
         TSAREVNA
AAENRSUW UNAWARES
AAENSSSV VANESSAS
AAENTTTT ATTENTAT
AAEOPSTT APOSTATE
AAEORRST AERATORS
AAEORSTT AEROSTAT
AAEORTTV ROTAVATE
AAEPPRST PARAPETS
AAEPPSTT APPESTAT
AAEPSWXX PAXWAXES
AAEPSZZZ PAZAZZES
AAERRRSY ARRAYERS
AAERRSST TARRASES
AAERRSTT TARTARES
AAERRTTT TARTRATE
AAERSSSY ASSAYERS
AAERSTTU SATURATE
AAERTWWY WATERWAY
AAFFILRT TAFFRAIL
AAFFINPR PARAFFIN
AAFFINSS SAFFIANS
AAFFLPST PALSTAFF
AAFFLSTU AFFLATUS
AAFFNNOR FANFARON
AAFGILNO GOLFIANA
AAFGINTW FATWAING
AAFGLLNU LANGLAUF
AAFGLNRT FLAGRANT
AAFGNRRT FRAGRANT
AAFGORRS FARRAGOS
AAFHHIKL KHALIFAH
AAFHIKLS KHALIFAS
AAFHIKLT KHALIFAT
         KHILAFAT
AAFHIRST AIRSHAFT
AAFHRSUU HAUSFRAU
AAFIILLM FAMILIAL
AAFIILLR FILARIAL
AAFIILMR FAMILIAR
AAFIILRS FILARIAS
AAFIINST FISTIANA
AAFIKLLY ALKALIFY
AAFILLNR RAINFALL
AAFILLUV AVAILFUL
AAFILMST FATALISM
AAFILNNU INFAUNAL
AAFILNST FANTAILS
AAFILOPR PARAFOIL
AAFILQSU ALFAQUIS
AAFILSTT FATALIST
AAFILTTY FATALITY
AAFIMNOR FORAMINA
AAFINNRS SAFRANIN
AAFINNST INFANTAS
AAFINNSU INFAUNAS
AAFINRRW WARFARIN
AAFINSTU FAUSTIAN
AAFIPRST PARFAITS
AAFIRSST SAFARIST
AAFIRSUY RUFIYAAS
AAFIRSWY FAIRWAYS
AAFJLLSW JAWFALLS
AAFJLORS ALFORJAS
AAFLLPRT PRATFALL
AAFLLPST SPATFALL
AAFLMORV LAVAFORM
AAFLNORS FORLANAS
```

Column 2

```
         SAFRONAL
AAFLNOTT FLOATANT
AAFLNRSU FURLANAS
AAFLSTWY FLATWAYS
AAFMNRST RAFTSMAN
AAFMNSST FANTASMS
AAFNPPRT FRAPPANT
AAFNSSTT FANTASTS
AAGGGINR GARAGING
AAGGILNR GANGLIAR
AAGGIMNN MANAGING
AAGGIMNR MARAGING
AAGGINRV RAVAGING
AAGGINSV SAVAGING
AAGGIRST GARAGIST
AAGGITTW GIGAWATT
AAGGLLLY LALLYGAG
AAGGLMOS MAGALOGS
AAGGMNNS GANGSMAN
AAGGNSST GANGSTAS
AAGGNSWY GANGWAYS
AAGHHINS SHANGHAI
AAGHILNN HANGNAIL
AAGHILPY HYPALGIA
AAGHILRS GHARIALS
         HARIGALS
AAGHIMNS ASHAMING
AAGHIMRT TAGHAIRM
AAGHINPS PAGANISH
AAGHINPW AWHAPING
AAGHIPRR AIRGRAPH
AAGHIRSV VAGARISH
AAGHKMNY GYMKHANA
AAGHLNPY ANAGLYPH
AAGHLOSS GASAHOLS
AAGHMNOY MAHOGANY
AAGHMNSW WHANGAMS
AAGHNOPR AGRAPHON
AAGHOPPR APOGRAPH
AAGHQSUU QUAHAUGS
AAGHRRTU ARRAUGHT
AAGHRSSW WASHRAGS
AAGIIKKN KAIAKING
AAGIILMN IMAGINAL
AAGIILNS ALIASING
AAGIILNV AVAILING
AAGIIMST ASTIGMIA
AAGIINRS ARAISING
AAGIINTV AVIATING
AAGIINTW AWAITING
AAGIKKNY KAYAKING
AAGIKLNO KAOLIANG
AAGIKLNR KRAALING
AAGIKLNS ASLAKING
AAGIKMRS SKIAGRAM
AAGIKNSW AWAKINGS
AAGIKNSZ ZIGANKAS
AAGILLNY ALLAYING
AAGILLSS GALLIASS
AAGILLTV GALLIVAT
AAGILLUZ ALGUAZIL
AAGILMMR MAILGRAM
AAGILMNO MAGNOLIA
AAGILMNR ALARMING
         MARGINAL
AAGILMNX MALAXING
AAGILMOT GLIOMATA
AAGILMSY MYALGIAS
AAGILNOS LOGANIAS
AAGILNOT GALTONIA
AAGILNPT PALATING
AAGILNRR LARRIGAN
AAGILNSS SALSAING
AAGILNUV VAGINULA
AAGILOOP APOLOGIA
AAGILOST OTALGIAS
AAGILPRY PLAGIARY
AAGILRRW WARRIGAL
AAGILSTT SAGITTAL
```

Column 3

```
AAGILSTW WAGTAILS
AAGIMMRR MARIGRAM
AAGIMNNO AGNOMINA
AAGIMNOS ANGIOMAS
AAGIMNPS PAGANISM
AAGIMNRR MARGARIN
AAGIMNSS AMASSING
         SIAMANGS
AAGIMNSY GYMNASIA
AAGIMPTU PATAGIUM
AAGIMSSV SAVAGISM
AAGIMSTT STIGMATA
AAGINNNY NANNYGAI
AAGINNOT AGNATION
AAGINNRW AWARNING
AAGINNSW WANIGANS
AAGINNSY SYNANGIA
AAGINNTV VAGINANT
AAGINNTW AWANTING
AAGINOSS AGNOSIAS
AAGINPPY APPAYING
AAGINPRU PAGURIAN
AAGINPWW PAWAWING
AAGINRRS ARRAIGNS
AAGINRRY ARRAYING
AAGINRSS SANGRIAS
         SARANGIS
AAGINRST GRANITAS
AAGINRSU GUARANIS
AAGINRSY ARAYSING
AAGINSST ASSIGNAT
AAGINSSU GAUSSIAN
AAGINSSY ASSAYING
         GAINSAYS
AAGIORTT AGITATOR
AAGIPRSU PIRAGUAS
AAGIRRSY ARGYRIAS
AAGIRSTV GRAVITAS
         STRAVAIG
AAGISSTT SAGITTAS
AAGKNOOR KANGAROO
AAGKOOSZ GAZOOKAS
AAGKORST KATORGAS
AAGLLMOY ALLOGAMY
AAGLLNOO LAGOONAL
AAGLLNRY LARYNGAL
AAGLLNST GALLANTS
AAGLLOPY POLYGALA
AAGLMNSS GLASSMAN
AAGLNNOO ANALOGON
AAGLNORS GRANOLAS
AAGLNPSS LAPSANGS
AAGLNQUU AQUALUNG
AAGLNRRU GRANULAR
AAGLOPRY PARALOGY
AAGLRRUW WARRAGUL
AAGLRSTU GASTRULA
AAGLRSUU ARUGULAS
AAGMMRRS GRAMMARS
AAGMNNOR NANOGRAM
AAGMNNRS GRANNAMS
AAGMNOPZ ZAMPOGNA
AAGMNORT MARTAGON
AAGMNOSS SANGOMAS
AAGMNPRS PANGRAMS
AAGMNRST TANGRAMS
         TRANGAMS
AAGMNRTU ARMGAUNT
AAGMNSSW SWAGSMAN
AAGMNSTY SYNTAGMA
AAGMORSS MARGOSAS
AAGMOTUY AUTOGAMY
AAGMOTYZ ZYGOMATA
AAGMRSST MATGRASS
AAGNNSTT STAGNANT
AAGNOPRS PARAGONS
AAGNOPRT TRAGOPAN
AAGNORRT ARROGANT
         TARRAGON
```

Column 4

```
AAGNORSZ ORGANZAS
AAGNORTU ARGONAUT
AAGNRSTV VAGRANTS
AAGNRTUY GUARANTY
AAGNRTYZ ZYGANTRA
AAGOPSSS SAPSAGOS
AAGORSSS SARGASSO
AAGOSSUU SAGUAROS
AAGRSSTU SASTRUGA
AAGRSTUZ ZASTRUGA
AAHHKMRS HASHMARK
AAHHMMSS SHAMMASH
AAHHNNST THANNAHS
AAHHNPST NAPHTHAS
AAHIIKRT TARAKIHI
AAHIJPRS RAJASHIP
AAHIKLPS PASHALIK
AAHIKRST KITHARAS
AAHILLLS HALLALIS
AAHILLNS HALLIANS
AAHILMNR HARMALIN
AAHILMRS ALMIRAHS
AAHILMSS SHIMAALS
AAHILNNT INHALANT
AAHILNOT HALATION
AAHILPSY PHYSALIA
AAHIMNOS MAHONIAS
AAHIMNPS PASHMINA
AAHIMNZZ HAZZANIM
AAHINOPS APHONIAS
AAHINPRS PIRANHAS
AAHINRTU HAURIANT
AAHINSST SHAITANS
AAHINSTW TANIWHAS
AAHIPRST PITARAHS
AAHIPSTZ ZAPTIAHS
AAHIPSXY ASPHYXIA
AAHIRSST SHARIATS
AAHJKNRS KHANJARS
AAHKLLMR HALLMARK
AAHKLRSS LASHKARS
AAHKMOTW TOMAHAWK
AAHKMSSY YASHMAKS
AAHKRSSW SAWSHARK
AAHLLLOO HALLALOO
AAHLLOPT ALLOPATH
AAHLLSWY HALLWAYS
AAHLMMSS MASHLAMS
AAHLMOOS MASOOLAH
AAHLMRSS MARSHALS
AAHLMSTU THALAMUS
AAHLNRSW NARWHALS
AAHLPSST ASPHALTS
AAHLRSSW SHALWARS
AAHMNNSU HANUMANS
AAHMNORT MARATHON
AAHMNOST HOASTMAN
AAHMNOTX XANTHOMA
AAHMNPST PHANTASM
AAHMNRST TRASHMAN
AAHMNSTX XANTHANS
AAHMRSST STRAMASH
AAHNNOSS HOSANNAS
AAHNNSTX XANTHANS
AAHNORST ATHANORS
AAHNORSV NAVARHOS
AAHNPSTY PHANTASY
AAHOPRTU AUTOHARP
AAHPRSTW WARPATHS
AAHPSTWY PATHWAYS
AAHRRTTW THRAWART
AAHRSSST SHASTRAS
AAIIILMR MILIARIA
AAIIIMNR NIRAMIAI
AAIIKKNN KINAKINA
AAIILMNS MAINSAIL
AAIILMRS AIRMAILS
AAIILNRZ ALIZARIN
AAIILNUX UNIAXIAL
```

AAIILPRR RIPARIAL	SANTALIN	AAINPRTZ PARTIZAN	AALMNTUU AUTUMNAL
AAIILPRS PAIRIALS	AAILNOPS SALOPIAN	AAINQRTU QUATRAIN	AALMOOSS MASSOOLA
AAIILPST TILAPIAS	AAILNOPT TALAPOIN	AAINQTTU AQUATINT	AALMOPSX AXOPLASM
AAIILRSZ ALIZARIS	AAILNORT NOTARIAL	AAINRRSS SARRASIN	AALMOSTT STOMATAL
AAIILRTX TRIAXIAL	RATIONAL	AAINRRSZ SARRAZIN	AALMOTXY XYLOMATA
AAIILRUX AUXILIAR	AAILNOST AILANTOS	AAINRSST ARTISANS	AALMPPSU PASPALUM
AAIILTXY AXIALITY	AAILNOSV VALONIAS	TSARINAS	AALMPRSY PALMYRAS
AAIIMMNT MAINTAIN	AAILNOTV LAVATION	AAINRSSU SAURIANS	AALMPSTY PLATYSMA
AAIIMNPX PANMIXIA	AAILNPRU PLANURIA	AAINRSSV SAVARINS	AALMQSUU SQUAMULA
AAIINOTV AVIATION	AAILNPSS SALPIANS	AAINRSTV VARIANTS	AALMSTTU MULATTAS
AAIINPRR RIPARIAN	AAILNPST PLATINAS	AAINRSTY SANITARY	AALNNOPT PANTALON
AAIINPZZ PIAZZIAN	AAILNQTU ALIQUANT	AAINSSSS ASSASSIN	AALNNPUU PUNALUAN
AAIINRST INTARSIA	AAILNSSY ANALYSIS	AAINSTTT ANTISTAT	AALNNRSU ANNULARS
AAIINSZZ ZIZANIAS	AAILNSTV VALIANTS	ATTAINTS	AALNNTUU LUNANAUT
AAIIOPST APOSITIA	AAILNSTY NASALITY	AAINSTTU TUTANIAS	AALNOPRT PATRONAL
AAIIORTZ ZOIATRIA	AAILNTTT LATITANT	AAINSTTY SATANITY	AALNPSUU PUNALUAS
AAIIPRST APIARIST	AAILNTTY NATALITY	AAIOPRRT TROPARIA	AALNRRTY ARRANTLY
AAIIRSTV AVIARIST	AAILORRS RASORIAL	AAIOPRST ATROPIAS	AALNRSTU NATURALS
AAIIRSTW WISTARIA	AAILORRV VARIOLAR	AAIOPRSU PAROUSIA	AALNSSTT SALTANTS
AAIIRTVX AVIATRIX	AAILORSS ROSALIAS	AAIOPSTU AUTOPSIA	AALNSSTU SULTANAS
AAIJLNPS JALAPINS	AAILORSU RAOULIAS	AAIORSSU SAOUARIS	AALNSSTY ANALYSTS
AAIJMNPS JAMPANIS	AAILORSV VARIOLAS	AAIORSTV AVIATORS	AALNSTTU TALAUNTS
AAIJNRSZ JANIZARS	AAILPPRU PUPARIAL	AAIORTUZ AZOTURIA	TANTALUS
AAIJNRYZ JANIZARY	AAILPPST PAPALIST	AAIPPSTT PITAPATS	AALOPPRV APPROVAL
AAIJPPSY JIPYAPAS	AAILPRST PARTIALS	AAIPRSSX SPARAXIS	AALOPRSS PARASOLS
AAIKKNOS SKOKIAAN	PATRIALS	AAIPRSTT PARTITAS	AALOPRST PASTORAL
AAIKLNST NASTALIK	TRIAPSAL	AAIQRSTU AQUARIST	AALOPSVV PAVLOVAS
AAIKMNNS MANAKINS	AAILPSTT TALIPATS	AAIQSSSU QUASSIAS	AALORSSU AROUSALS
AAIKMNRS RAMAKINS	AAILQRSU SQUARIAL	AAIQSTUV AQUAVITS	AALORSTX LAXATORS
AAIKMNST ANTIMASK	AAILQSWW QAWWALIS	AAIRSSTT TSARITSA	AALORTUV VALUATOR
AAIKMORS ROMAIKAS	AAILRRSV ARRIVALS	AAIRSTWY STAIRWAY	AALORTVY LAVATORY
AAIKMRSS KARAISMS	AAILRSTV TRAVAILS	AAISTWXY TAXIWAYS	AALOSTTY TALAYOTS
AAIKMRST TAMARISK	AAILRSVY SALIVARY	AAJKLSWY JAYWALKS	AALPRSTU PASTURAL
AAIKNNTT ANTITANK	AAILRSWY RAILWAYS	AAJMMORR MARJORAM	SPATULAR
AAIKORSU OUAKARIS	AAILSSSV VASSAILS	AAJMORST MAJORATS	AALPSSTU SPATULAS
AAIKPPRS PAPRIKAS	AAILSSSW WASSAILS	AAJOPSSU SAPAJOUS	AALRRTTY TARTARLY
AAIKSSTT ASTATKIS	AAILSSTY STAYSAIL	AAKKLRSU KARAKULS	AALRSSTY SATYRALS
AAIKSSTV SVASTIKA	AAILSTTT LATITATS	AAKKMOST TOKAMAKS	AALRSSVY VASSALRY
AAIKSSTW SWASTIKA	AAIMMNOS AMMONIAS	AAKLMPSU LAMPUKAS	AALRSTTW STALWART
AAIKSTVV AKVAVITS	AAIMMNST MAINMAST	AAKLMRUY YARMULKA	AALRSTUY SALUTARY
AAILLLUV ALLUVIAL	AAIMMRSU SAMARIUM	AAKLMSUY YAMULKAS	AALSSSTU ASSAULTS
AAILLMMM MAMMILLA	AAIMNORT ANIMATOR	AAKLNOOS OOLAKANS	AAMMNPRS RAMPSMAN
AAILLMMR MAMILLAR	MONTARIA	AAKLNOSU OULAKANS	AAMMNRST MANTRAMS
AAILLMNS MANILLAS	TAMANOIR	AAKLOOPS PALOOKAS	AAMMOTXY MYXOMATA
AAILLMNT MANTILLA	AAIMNORW AIRWOMAN	AAKLOOST TALOOKAS	AAMMRSSU MARASMUS
AAILLMNY ANIMALLY	AAIMNOSS ANOSMIAS	AAKLPRTY KALYPTRA	AAMMNOSY ANONYMAS
AAILLMRS ARMILLAS	AAIMNOST AMATIONS	AAKLRSSU KURSAALS	AAMNPRST MANTRAPS
AAILLNOV VALLONIA	AAIMNPRZ MARZIPAN	RUSALKAS	AAMNPRSY PARANYMS
AAILLNSV VANILLAS	AAIMNPTU PUTAMINA	AAKLSSSU SAKSAULS	AAMNQSUW SQUAWMAN
AAILLPPR PAPILLAR	AAIMNRRT TRIMARAN	AAKLSWWY WALKWAYS	AAMOORSS AMOROSAS
AAILLRRY ARILLARY	AAIMNRRU RANARIUM	AAKMMNRS MARKSMAN	AAMOPRRU PARAMOUR
AAILLRXY AXILLARY	AAIMNRST TAMARINS	AAKMOSSU MOUSAKAS	AAMORRSZ ZAMARROS
AAILMMRS ALARMISM	AAIMNSST MANTISSA	MOUSSAKA	AAMORSSV SAMOVARS
AMMIRALS	SATANISM	AAKMRSUZ MAZURKAS	AAMORSTT STROMATA
AAILMNNT LAMANTIN	STAMINAS	AAKMRSWY WAYMARKS	AAMOSTTU AUTOMATS
AAILMNOP PALAMINO	AAIMNSTU AMIANTUS	AAKNNSTU NUNATAKS	AAMPRRST RAMPARTS
AAILMNOR MANORIAL	AAIMNSTY MAINSTAY	AAKNSTWY TWANKAYS	AAMRSSST SMARTASS
MORAINAL	AAIMOPRS MARIPOSA	AAKOOPPS PAKAPOOS	AAMRSSTU SUMATRAS
AAILMNOX MONAXIAL	AAIMPRST PASTRAMI	AAKPRSWY PARKWAYS	AAMRSTWY TRAMWAYS
AAILMNPS PANISLAM	AAIMPRSU MARSUPIA	AALLLSTY LAYSTALL	AAMSSSTU SATSUMAS
AAILMNRU MANURIAL	AAIMQRUU AQUARIUM	AALLMNST STALLMAN	AANNOSST ASSONANT
AAILMNRY LAMINARY	AAIMRRSY MISARRAY	AALLMNTY TALLYMAN	AANNOSTT ANNATTOS
AAILMNST STAMINAL	AAIMRRTY MARTYRIA	AALLMNUY MANUALLY	AANNRSTY STANNARY
TALISMAN	AAIMRSTU TIMARAUS	AALLMSST SMALLSAT	AANOOPPX OPOPANAX
AAILMNSU ALUMINAS	AAIMSSTV ATAVISMS	AALLNNUY ANNUALLY	AANOOPRZ PARAZOON
AAILMNSV MAILVANS	AAINNOPV PAVONIAN	AALLNPRU PLANULAR	AANOPRTY ANATROPY
NAVALISM	AAINNOST SONATINA	AALLNRTY TARNALLY	AANORRRT NARRATOR
AAILMOPT LIPOMATA	AAINNOTT NATATION	AALLOORW WALLAROO	AANORSTY SANATORY
AAILMORR ARMORIAL	AAINNRSV NAVARINS	AALLORSU ALLOSAUR	AANORTTY NATATORY
AAILMPPS PAPALISM	NIRVANAS	AALLOSTV LAVOLTAS	AANPRSST SPARTANS
AAILMPRT PRIMATAL	AAINNRTU NUTARIAN	AALLPRST PLASTRAL	AANQRSTU QUARTANS
AAILMRST ALARMIST	AAINNSST NAISSANT	AALLRUVV VALVULAR	AANRRSTW WARRANTS
ALASTRIM	AAINNSSY SANNYASI	AALMMNOS AMMONALS	AANRRTTY TARTANRY
AAILMTTU ULTIMATA	AAINOPSS PAISANOS	AALMNORT MATRONAL	AANRRTWY WARRANTY
AAILNNOT NATIONAL	AAINORRS ORARIANS	AALMNORU MONAURAL	AANRSTTU SATURANT
AAILNNPT PLAINANT	ROSARIAN	AALMNOSS SALAMONS	AANRSUWY RUNAWAYS
PLANTAIN	AAINOTTX TAXATION	AALMNOWY LAYWOMAN	AAOORRSW WOORARAS
AAILNNRU LUNARIAN	AAINPRST ASPIRANT	AALMNPTY TYMPANAL	AAOPSSST POTASSAS
AAILNNST ANNALIST	PARTISAN	AALMNTTU TANTALUM	AAOPSSTY APOSTASY

AAORSSTT STAROSTA	ABBDHIRT BIRDBATH	ABBHILSY SHABBILY	ABCDEIIT DIABETIC
AAORSUVV VAVASOUR	ABBDHOOY BABYHOOD	ABBHRRSU RHUBARBS	ABCDEIKS BACKSIDE
AAORSVVY VAVASORY	ABBDILNO BAILBOND	ABBHRRUY RHUBARBY	DIEBACKS
AAOSTTUY TATOUAYS	ABBDILRS LIBBARDS	ABBHSTTU BATHTUBS	ABCDEILR CALIBRED
AAOSTWWY STOWAWAY	ABBDINRS RIBBANDS	ABBIINOT BIBATION	ABCDEIPS PEDICABS
AARSTTUY STATUARY	ABBDLRSU LUBBARDS	ABBILLOT BOATBILL	ABCDEIRS ASCRIBED
ABBBCDEO CABOBBED	ABBDNORW BROWBAND	ABBILLSU SILLABUB	CARBIDES
ABBBDEEK KEBABBED	ABBEEINR BEARBINE	ABBILOST BIOBLAST	ABCDEISS ABSCISED
ABBBDEEL BEDABBLE	ABBEEJRR JABBERER	BOBTAILS	ABCDEKLO BLOCKADE
ABBBDEKO KABOBBED	ABBEEJRS BEJABERS	ABBIMNOS BAMBINOS	ABCDEKLV BACKVELD
ABBBDELR BRABBLED	ABBEENOR BAREBONE	ABBIMSSU BABUISMS	ABCDEKNN NECKBAND
ABBBEILR BABBLIER	ABBEEQRU BARBEQUE	ABBINORS RABBONIS	ABCDEKNU UNBACKED
ABBBELRS BABBLERS	ABBEERTT BARBETTE	ABBINORX BRAINBOX	ABCDEKRS REDBACKS
BLABBERS	ABBEESSS ABBESSES	ABBIRRTY RABBITRY	ABCDELMS SCAMBLED
BRABBLES	ABBEFILR FLABBIER	ABBIRSUU SUBURBIA	ABCDELNO BLANCOED
ABBBGILN BABBLING	ABBEGIST GABBIEST	ABBKLOSU BLAUBOKS	ABCDELOO CABOODLE
BLABBING	ABBEGLRR GRABBLER	ABBLLLOW BLOWBALL	ABCDEMOT COMBATED
ABBBISTT BABBITTS	ABBEGLRS GABBLERS	ABBLLRSU BULLBARS	ABCDEMRS SCRAMBED
ABBBOSTU SUBABBOT	GRABBLES	ABBLLSTU BULLBATS	ABCDENRU UNBRACED
ABBCDELS SCABBLED	ABBEGNOS BOGBEANS	ABBLLSUY SYLLABUB	ABCDENTU ABDUCENT
ABBCDERS SCRABBED	ABBEGNSU BUGBEANS	ABBLOPRY PROBABLY	ABCDEORS BROCADES
ABBCDKNO BACKBOND	ABBEGRRS GRABBERS	ABBMOORS BOMBORAS	ABCDERSU CUDBEARS
ABBCEERU BARBECUE	ABBEGRSU BUGBEARS	ABBMOSST BOMBASTS	ABCDESTU SUBACTED
ABBCEGIR CRIBBAGE	ABBEHILS BABELISH	ABBNRSUU SUBURBAN	ABCDGINU ABDUCING
ABBCEHIS BABICHES	ABBEHIRS SHABBIER	ABBOSSTY BOBSTAYS	ABCDHKLO HOLDBACK
ABBCEHOU BABOUCHE	ABBEHLSS SHABBLES	ABCCDEHO CABOCHED	ABCDHORS CHOBDARS
ABBCEHSU BABUCHES	ABBEHORT BATHROBE	ABCCDHIK DABCHICK	ABCDIILO BIOCIDAL
ABBCEHTU BATHCUBE	ABBEILMS BABELISM	ABCCEEHN BECHANCE	DIABOLIC
ABBCEIKT BACKBITE	ABBEILNU BUBALINE	ABCCEELP PECCABLE	ABCDIIMY CYMBIDIA
ABBCEILR BARBICEL	ABBEILOT BILOBATE	ABCCEEOR CABOCEER	ABCDIIRT TRIBADIC
ABBCEIRR CRABBIER	ABBEILRS SLABBIER	ABCCEILY CELIBACY	ABCDIKLR BALDRICK
ABBCEIRS SCABBIER	ABBEILST BISTABLE	ABCCEIRS BRECCIAS	ABCDIKLS BACKSLID
ABBCEKLU BLUEBACK	ABBEINTT TABBINET	ABCCEIRT BACTERIC	ABCDIKRU BAUDRICK
ABBCEKNO BACKBONE	ABBEIRRT RABBITER	ABCCEKMO COMEBACK	ABCDILLR BIRDCALL
ABBCEKNU BUCKBEAN	ABBEISSW SWABBIES	ABCCESUU SUCCUBAE	ABCDILOU CUBOIDAL
ABBCELLU CLUBABLE	ABBEKLOO BOOKABLE	ABCCHISU BACCHIUS	ABCDILRS BALDRICS
ABBCELRS CLABBERS	ABBELMRS BRAMBLES	ABCCHNOO CABOCHON	ABCDINSS ABSCINDS
SCRABBLE	ABBELNSS SNABBLES	ABCCIKKK KICKBACK	ABCDIRST CATBIRDS
ABBCELRU CURBABLE	ABBELOOT BOOTABLE	ABCCIKKP PICKBACK	ABCDIRSU BAUDRICS
ABBCELSS SCABBLES	ABBELOPR PROBABLE	ABCCIKOR ABRICOCK	SUBACRID
ABBCERRS CRABBERS	ABBELORS BELABORS	ABCCILOR CARBOLIC	ABCDKNOW BACKDOWN
ABBCGINR CRABBING	ABBELORU BELABOUR	ABCCILOT COBALTIC	ABCDKOPR BACKDROP
ABBCGINS SCABBING	ABBELPRS PRABBLES	ABCCIMRS CAMBRICS	ABCDKORW BACKWORD
ABBCGIOR GABBROIC	ABBELQSU SQUABBLE	ABCCINOR CARBONIC	ABCDLLNU CLUBLAND
ABBCIILL BIBLICAL	ABBELRRS RABBLERS	ABCCINSU BUCCINAS	ABCDNOSS ABSCONDS
ABBCIINR RABBINIC	ABBELRSS SLABBERS	ABCCKLLO BALLCOCK	ABCDOORS CORDOBAS
ABBCIKRT BRICKBAT	ABBELRSU BARBULES	ABCCKLOX CLACKBOX	ABCDOPRU CUPBOARD
ABBCILRY CRABBILY	ABBELRSW WABBLERS	ABCCKOOT COCKBOAT	ABCDORRS BROCARDS
ABBCKLOY BLACKBOY	ABBELRSY SLABBERY	ABCCKOSW BAWCOCKS	ABCDORTU ABDUCTOR
ABBDDEEL BEDDABLE	ABBELSUY BUYABLES	ABCCKSTU CUTBACKS	ABCDORUY OBDURACY
ABBDDEEU BEDAUBED	ABBEMOOR AEROBOMB	ABCCOORS BAROCCOS	ABCEEEFK BEEFCAKE
ABBDDEIL BIDDABLE	ABBEMOSX BOMBAXES	ABCCOOST TOBACCOS	ABCEEFNT BENEFACT
ABBDDELR DRABBLED	ABBEMSUZ BUMBAZES	ABCCSSUU SUCCUBAS	ABCEEHIR BEACHIER
ABBDEEJR JABBERED	ABBEORRS ABSORBER	ABCDDEER DECARBED	ABCEEHLM BECHAMEL
ABBDEERR BARBERED	REABSORB	ABCDDEOR BROCADED	ABCEEHLN ALEBENCH
ABBDEERT RABBETED	ABBEORTW BROWBEAT	ABCDDETU ABDUCTED	ABCEEHLR BLEACHER
ABBDEERY YABBERED	ABBEQRSU SQUABBER	ABCDEEFK FEEDBACK	ABCEEHLS BLEACHES
ABBDEGLR GRABBLED	ABBERRRY BARBERRY	ABCDEEHL BLEACHED	ABCEEHLW CHEWABLE
ABBDEIRR DRABBIER	ABBERRYY BAYBERRY	ABCDEEHR BERDACHE	ABCEEHRS BREACHES
ABBDEIRT RABBITED	ABBERSST STABBERS	BREACHED	ABCEEHSU EBAUCHES
ABBDELMO BABELDOM	ABBERSSW SWABBERS	ABCDEEJT ABJECTED	ABCEEILT CELIBATE
ABBDELMR BRAMBLED	ABBESSSU SUBBASES	ABCDEEKR REBACKED	CITEABLE
ABBDELNS SNABBLED	ABBFGINR FRABBING	ABCDEELL BECALLED	ABCEEIMN AMBIENCE
ABBDELRR DRABBLER	ABBFILLY FLABBILY	ABCDEELM BECALMED	ABCEELOV EVOCABLE
ABBDELRS DABBLERS	ABBGGILN GABBLING	ABCDEELS DEBACLES	ABCEELRR CEREBRAL
DRABBLES	ABBGGINR GRABBING	ABCDEELU EDUCABLE	ABCEELRT BRACELET
ABBDEMUZ BUMBAZED	ABBGIJLN JABBLING	ABCDEEMR CAMBERED	ABCEEMRR EMBRACER
ABBDENRU UNBARBED	ABBGILNR RABBLING	EMBRACED	ABCEEMRS EMBRACES
ABBDEORS ABSORBED	ABBGILNS SLABBING	ABCDEEMX EXCAMBED	ABCEENSS ABSENCES
ABBDEQSU SQUABBED	ABBGILNU BAUBLING	ABCDEENO BEACONED	ABCEERRS REBRACES
ABBDERRS DRABBERS	ABBGILNW WABBLING	ABCDEERR REBRACED	ABCEERST ACERBEST
ABBDERST DRABBEST	ABBGINST STABBING	ABCDEETU ABDUCTEE	ABCEERUX BERCEAUX
DRABBETS	ABBGINSU BUBINGAS	ABCDEGIR BIRDCAGE	ABCEESSS BECASSES
ABBDFOOY BABYFOOD	ABBGINSW SWABBING	CAGEBIRD	ABCEFIIT BEATIFIC
ABBDGILN DABBLING	ABBGINTY TABBYING	ABCDEHLN BLANCHED	ABCEFIKL BACKFILE
ABBDGINR DRABBING	ABBGOOSU BUGABOOS	ABCDEHLU BAUCHLED	ABCEFIKR BACKFIRE
ABBDGIOR GABBROID	ABBHIIMS BIMBASHI	ABCDEHNR BRANCHED	ABCEFINO BONIFACE
ABBDHIJS DJIBBAHS		ABCDEHOR BROACHED	ABCEGHIN BEACHING
ABBDHIRS DRABBISH		ABCDEHOS CABOSHED	ABCEGILN BELACING

ABCEGIMN EMBACING	SETBACKS	ABCIINSS ABSCISIN	ABDDEEEH BEHEADED
ABCEGIRS RIBCAGES	ABCEKSSY BACKSEYS	ABCIIORS ISOBARIC	ABDDEEGG DEBAGGED
ABCEGKLL BLACKLEG	ABCEKSTW WETBACKS	ABCIIRST TRIBASIC	ABDDEEGR BADGERED
ABCEGKLO BLOCKAGE	ABCELLPU CULPABLE	ABCIISTY BASICITY	REBADGED
ABCEGKMU MEGABUCK	ABCELLSU BUCELLAS	ABCIITUX BAUXITIC	ABDDEEHS BEDASHED
ABCEGKOR BROCKAGE	BULLACES	ABCIJNOS JACOBINS	ABDDEEKR DEBARKED
ABCEGMOS CAMBOGES	ABCELMNY LAMBENCY	ABCIKKLL KICKBALL	ABDDEELU BELAUDED
ABCEGNOR BONGRACE	ABCELMOS CEMBALOS	ABCIKLST BACKLIST	ABDDEERR DEBARRED
ABCEGORS BROCAGES	ABCELMRS CAMBRELS	ABCIKNPS BACKSPIN	ABDDEEST BEDSTEAD
ABCEGOSS BOSCAGES	CLAMBERS	ABCILLRU LUBRICAL	BESTADDE
ABCEHITT BATHETIC	SCAMBLER	ABCILLSU BACILLUS	ABDDEGIR ABRIDGED
ABCEHKOS BACKHOES	SCRAMBLE	ABCILLSY SYLLABIC	BRIGADED
ABCEHKTW BETHWACK	ABCELMSS SCAMBLES	ABCILMMO CIMBALOM	ABDDEHMO HEBDOMAD
ABCEHLNS BLANCHES	ABCELNOT BALCONET	ABCILMSU SUBCLAIM	ABDDEHOY HOBDAYED
ABCEHLOR BACHELOR	ABCELNUU NUBECULA	ABCILNPU PUBLICAN	ABDDEILS DISABLED
ABCEHLSU BAUCHLES	ABCELOOT BOOTLACE	ABCILOOR COOLIBAR	ABDDEILU BUDDLEIA
CHASUBLE	ABCELOPS PLACEBOS	ABCILOSY SOCIABLY	ABDDEINR BRANDIED
ABCEHLTU LEACHTUB	ABCELORT BROCATEL	ABCILRRU RUBRICAL	ABDDEINS SIDEBAND
ABCEHMOT HECATOMB	ABCELOST OBSTACLE	ABCIMMSS CAMBISMS	ABDDEIRR BRAIRDED
ABCEHMRS BECHARMS	ABCELOSV VOCABLES	ABCIMMSU CAMBIUMS	ABDDELRS BLADDERS
BRECHAMS	ABCELOTU BLUECOAT	ABCIMORR MICROBAR	ABDDELRY BLADDERY
CHAMBERS	ABCELPSU BLUECAPS	ABCIMRTU UMBRATIC	ABDDENNU UNBANDED
ABCEHNRR BRANCHER	ABCELPSY BYPLACES	ABCIMSST CAMBISTS	ABDDENOU ABOUNDED
ABCEHNRS BRANCHES	ABCELRSW BESCRAWL	ABCINORU CONURBIA	ABDDEORS ADSORBED
ABCEHOOT COHOBATE	ABCELRTT BRACTLET	ABCINRVY VIBRANCY	ABDDERSW BEDWARDS
ABCEHOPU PABOUCHE	ABCELSSU BASCULES	ABCIORRS BARRICOS	ABDDGILN BLADDING
ABCEHORR BROACHER	ABCEMORS CRAMBOES	ABCIORSU CARIBOUS	ABDDHIOR RHABDOID
ABCEHORS BROACHES	ABCENORS BACONERS	ABCIOSSU SCABIOUS	ABDDILMO LAMBDOID
ABCEHORU BAROUCHE	ABCENOSW COWBANES	ABCIOSUV BIVOUACS	ABDDILRY LADYBIRD
ABCEHOSS BASOCHES	ABCENOUY BUOYANCE	ABCIRSTT ABSTRICT	ABDDIMNO BONDMAID
ABCEHRST BRACHETS	ABCENRSU UNBRACES	ABCJKOOT JACKBOOT	ABDDINSS DISBANDS
ABCEHRTT BRATCHET	ABCENTUX EXCUBANT	ABCKKORW BACKWORK	ABDDIRRY YARDBIRD
ABCEIKKL KICKABLE	ABCEOOSS CABOOSES	ABCKLLOS BALLOCKS	ABDDLLOS ODDBALLS
ABCEIKLR CRABLIKE	ABCEORSU CORBEAUS	ABCKLOPT BLACKTOP	ABDDMORS DAMBRODS
ABCEIKST TIEBACKS	ABCEOSUX SAUCEBOX	ABCKLOST BACKLOTS	ABDEEEFN BEDEAFEN
ABCEILLR CRIBELLA	ABCERRTU CARBURET	ABCKLOSW SLOWBACK	ABDEEEMN BEMEANED
ABCEILLS ICEBALLS	ABCESSTU SUBCASTE	ABCKLOTU BLACKOUT	ABDEEERV BEAVERED
ABCEILLT BALLETIC	ABCESTUU SUBACUTE	ABCKMOOR BACKROOM	BEREAVED
ABCEILMS ALEMBICS	ABCFIKLL BACKFILL	ABCKMORR BROCKRAM	ABDEEFIT TABEFIED
ABCEILNN BINNACLE	ABCFIKLT BACKLIFT	ABCKMOSS MOSSBACK	ABDEEFLM FLAMBEED
ABCEILNU BACULINE	LIFTBACK	ABCKMOST BACKMOST	ABDEEFLS FEELBADS
ABCEILOR ALBICORE	ABCFIKNS FINBACKS	ABCKMRSU BUCKRAMS	ABDEEFMO BEFOAMED
CABRIOLE	ABCFILOS BIFOCALS	ABCKMSUZ ZAMBUCKS	ABDEEGGL BEDAGGLE
ABCEILOS SOCIABLE	ABCFKLLU FULLBACK	ABCKNNOS BANNOCKS	ABDEEGGR BEGGARED
ABCEILRS CALIBERS	ABCFKOST SOFTBACK	ABCKNRSU RUNBACKS	ABDEEGHR HERBAGED
CALIBRES	ABCGGIMO GAMBOGIC	ABCKNRTU TURNBACK	ABDEEGNW BEGNAWED
ABCEILTT BITTACLE	ABCGHINT BATCHING	ABCKOORU BUCKAROO	ABDEEGRS REBADGES
ABCEILTU BACULITE	ABCGHKOS HOGBACKS	ABCKOPST BACKSTOP	ABDEEGRU BEDEGUAR
ABCEIMST BETACISM	ABCGIINN CABINING	ABCKORUY BUCKAYRO	ABDEEHMS BESHAMED
ABCEINOO COENOBIA	ABCGIKLN BLACKING	ABCKOSSW SOWBACKS	ABDEEHMT EMBATHED
ABCEINRS CARBINES	ABCGIKNS BACKINGS	ABCKOSTU OUTBACKS	ABDEEHNO BONEHEAD
ABCEINST CABINETS	ABCGILNS CABLINGS	ABCKSSTU SACKBUTS	ABDEEHRT BREATHED
ABCEINTU INCUBATE	ABCGKLOS BACKLOGS	SUBTACKS	ABDEEHSS BEDASHES
ABCEIORS AEROBICS	ABCGLNOX CLANGBOX	ABCKSSUW BUCKSAWS	ABDEEHST BETHESDA
ABCEIORT BORACITE	ABCGMSSU SCUMBAGS	SAWBUCKS	ABDEEHTT BEHATTED
ABCEIOST ICEBOATS	ABCHHIIS HIBACHIS	ABCLLNOR CORNBALL	ABDEEILM EMBAILED
ABCEIRRT CRIBRATE	ABCHIIPS BIPHASIC	ABCLLPUY CULPABLY	ABDEEILN DENIABLE
ABCEIRRS ASCRIBES	ABCHIKLS BLACKISH	ABCLMOOO COLOBOMA	ABDEEILR RIDEABLE
ABCEIRSW CRABWISE	ABCHIKRS BRACKISH	ABCLMOSY CYMBALOS	ABDEEILS ABSEILED
ABCEIRTT BRATTICE	ABCHILMO CHOLIAMB	ABCLMSUU BACULUMS	ABDEEILT DELIBATE
ABCEIRTY ACERBITY	ABCHILOO COOLIBAH	ABCLMSUY SCYBALUM	ABDEEILW BEWAILED
ABCEISSS ABSCISES	ABCHIMOR CHORIAMB	ABCLNORY CARBONYL	ABDEEIRS BEARDIES
ABSCISSE	ABCHIMRU BRACHIUM	ABCLORXY CARBOXYL	ABDEEIRT EBRIATED
ABCEISST ASBESTIC	ABCHINOR BRONCHIA	ABCLOSUV SUBVOCAL	ABDEEIST BEADIEST
ABCEISTT TABETICS	ABCHIOOR BORACHIO	ABCLSSSU SUBCLASS	DIABETES
ABCEJLTY ABJECTLY	ABCHIOST COHABITS	ABCLSUUU SUBUCULA	ABDEEITU BEAUTIED
ABCEKKRU BUCKRAKE	ABCHIRRT TRIBRACH	ABCMOORT MOBOCRAT	ABDEEJMN ENJAMBED
ABCEKKSW SKEWBACK	ABCHKLOT HACKBOLT	ABCNNORU CONURBAN	ABDEEKMN EMBANKED
ABCEKLLO LOCKABLE	ABCHKMPU HUMPBACK	ABCNORTY CORYBANT	ABDEEKMR BEDMAKER
ABCEKLMO MOCKABLE	ABCHKOOP CHAPBOOK	ABCNOUYY BUOYANCY	EMBARKED
ABCEKLNS BLACKENS	ABCHKOSU CHABOUKS	ABCORRSS CROSSBAR	ABDEEKNR BARKENED
ABCEKLOO COOKABLE	ABCHKSTU HACKBUTS	ABCORRSW CROWBARS	BEDARKEN
ABCEKLPU PALEBUCK	ABCHKSUW HAWBUCKS	ABCORRTU TURBOCAR	ABDEEKNV BEKNAVED
ABCEKLST BLACKEST	ABCHMOTX MATCHBOX	ABCORSSU SCABROUS	ABDEELLL LABELLED
ABCEKNRS BRACKENS	ABCHNORS BROCHANS	ABCOSSTU SUBCOSTA	ABDEELLM EMBALLED
ABCEKOOS BOOKCASE	ABCHOTWX WATCHBOX	ABCOSTTU COTTABUS	ABDEELLT BALLETED
CASEBOOK	ABCIIMNS MINICABS	ABCRSTTU SUBTRACT	ABDEELLW WELDABLE
ABCEKRST BRACKETS	ABCIINOT CIBATION	ABDDDEEM BEMADDED	ABDEELMM EMBALMED
ABCEKSST BACKSETS		ABDDDEET ADDEBTED	ABDEELMS BELDAMES

BEMEDALS	ABDEHLOT BOLTHEAD	ABDEMNNS BANDSMEN	ABDIINOS OBSIDIAN
ABDEELMU BEMAULED	ABDEHLRS HALBERDS	ABDEMNNY BANDYMEN	ABDIINTT BANDITTI
ABDEELMZ EMBLAZED	ABDEHMRU RHUMBAED	ABDEMNOS ABDOMENS	ABDIIRTY RABIDITY
ABDEELNT BANDELET	ABDEHMSU AMBUSHED	ABDEMRTU DRUMBEAT	ABDIKLNR BLINKARD
ABDEELRS BEDERALS	ABDEHNTU UNBATHED	UMBRATED	ABDIKNSW BAWDKINS
ABDEELRZ BLAZERED	ABDEHORR ABHORRED	ABDENNOS NOSEBAND	ABDIKRSS DISBARKS
ABDEELSV BESLAVED	HARBORED	ABDENOOT BATOONED	ABDILOOS DIABOLOS
ABDEELTT BATTELED	ABDEHOSW BESHADOW	ABDENORS BANDORES	ABDILORS LABROIDS
TABLETED	BOWHEADS	BROADENS	ABDILOST BLASTOID
ABDEELZZ BEDAZZLE	ABDEHRST BREADTHS	ABDENORW RAWBONED	TABLOIDS
ABDEEMNO BEMOANED	ABDEHSSU SUBHEADS	ABDENORY BONEYARD	ABDILOTY TABLOIDY
ABDEEMNS BEADSMEN	ABDEIIRT DIATRIBE	ABDENOTW DOWNBEAT	ABDILRRY RIBALDRY
BEDESMAN	ABDEIKMR IMBARKED	ABDENRRS BRANDERS	ABDILRSW AWLBIRDS
ABDEEMRR EMBARRED	ABDEIKNU BAUDEKIN	ABDENRRU UNBARRED	ABDILRZZ BLIZZARD
ABDEEMRS EMBREADS	ABDEILMN MANDIBLE	ABDENRSS DRABNESS	ABDILSTU SUBTIDAL
ABDEEMRV EMBRAVED	ABDEILNR BILANDER	ABDENRST BANDSTER	ABDIMORS AMBROIDS
ABDEENNR BANNERED	ABDEILNT BIDENTAL	ABDENRTU BREADNUT	ABDINOTY ANTIBODY
ABDEENRT BANTERED	ABDEILNY DENIABLY	TURBANED	ABDINRST ANTBIRDS
ABDEENRZ BRAZENED	ABDEILOV VOIDABLE	ABDENSSU SUBDEANS	ABDINRTY BANDITRY
ABDEENST ABSENTED	ABDEILPS PIEBALDS	ABDENTTU DEBUTANT	ABDIOSUU SUBAUDIO
ABDEENTT BATTENED	ABDEILRS RAILBEDS	ABDEOPRT PROBATED	ABDIPRSU UPBRAIDS
ABDEEPRS BESPREAD	ABDEILRT LIBRATED	ABDEORRS BOARDERS	ABDIRRUY RIBAUDRY
ABDEEPTT BEPATTED	ABDEILRV DRIVABLE	ABDEORRU ARBOURED	ABDKLNOO BOOKLAND
ABDEERRT BARTERED	ABDEILRY DIABLERY	ABDEORRW WARDROBE	ABDKNOOS BANDOOKS
ABDEERRY RYEBREAD	ABDEILSS DISABLES	ABDEORST BROADEST	ABDLLNOS SLOBLAND
ABDEERSS DEBASERS	ABDEILST BALDIEST	ABDEORSW SOWBREAD	ABDLLORS BOLLARDS
ABDEERST BETREADS	ABDEILSU AUDIBLES	ABDEORTU OBDURATE	ABDLNORS BANDROLS
BREASTED	ABDEILTU DUTIABLE	TABOURED	ABDLRSUU SUBDURAL
DEBATERS	ABDEIMNR BRIDEMAN	ABDEOSTU BOUTADES	ABDLRSUY ABSURDLY
ABDEERTT BATTERED	ABDEIMOO AMOEBOID	ABDEPRUY UPBRAYED	RYBAULDS
DRABETTE	ABDEIMOR AMBEROID	ABDEPSSY BYPASSED	ABDLSSUU SUBDUALS
ABDEERTY BETRAYED	ABDEIMRR IMBARRED	ABDERRSU ABSURDER	ABDLSTUU SUBADULT
ABDEERWY BEWRAYED	ABDEIMRS EMBRAIDS	ABDERSST DABSTERS	ABDMNNOS BONDSMAN
ABDEESST BASSETED	ABDEINOR DEBONAIR	ABDERSSU SUBEDARS	ABDMNOUW MAWBOUND
BESTEADS	ABDEINOT OBTAINED	SURBASED	ABDMOOPR MOPBOARD
ABDEFLLO FOLDABLE	ABDEINRS BRANDIES	ABDERSTU SURBATED	ABDMRSUY MARYBUDS
ABDEFLNU FUNDABLE	BRANDISE	ABDERSTW BEDSTRAW	ABDNOPRS PROBANDS
UNFABLED	ABDEINST BANDIEST	ABDERSTY DRYBEATS	ABDNORSU BAUDRONS
ABDEFLOR FORDABLE	ABDEINSU UNBIASED	ABDFLOOT FOLDBOAT	ABDNORUY BOUNDARY
ABDEFLST FLATBEDS	ABDEINSW BEDAWINS	ABDFNORU FUNBOARD	ABDNOSSY SANDBOYS
ABDEFLSU LEAFBUDS	ABDEINTU UNBAITED	ABDGGORS BOGGARDS	ABDNRSTU TURBANDS
ABDEFNRU FABURDEN	ABDEIOTV OBVIATED	ABDGHINR HANGBIRD	ABDOORSW BARWOODS
ABDEFRSW BEDWARFS	ABDEIPST BAPTISED	ABDGIINR BRAIDING	ABDOORTU OUTBOARD
ABDEGGIL DIGGABLE	ABDEIPTZ BAPTIZED	ABDGIINS ABIDINGS	ABDOOSSW BASSWOOD
ABDEGGNU UNBAGGED	ABDEIRSS SEABIRDS	ABDGILNR BARDLING	ABDRSSTU BUSTARDS
ABDEGHRS BEGHARDS	SIDEBARS	ABDGILNU BLAUDING	ABDRSUZZ BUZZARDS
ABDEGIJN BEJADING	ABDEIRST BARDIEST	ABDGIMRU GUIMBARD	ABEEEFRS FREEBASE
ABDEGILN BLINDAGE	BRAIDEST	ABDGINNR BRANDING	ABEEEGRS BARGEESE
ABDEGILU GUIDABLE	RABIDEST	ABDGINNS BANDINGS	BEERAGES
ABDEGIMT GAMBITED	TRIBADES	ABDGINNY BANDYING	ABEEEGRV BEVERAGE
ABDEGINO GABIONED	ABDEIRSW BAWDRIES	ABDGINOR ABORDING	ABEEEHTT HEBETATE
ABDEGINR BEARDING	DAWBRIES	BOARDING	ABEEENRT TENEBRAE
BREADING	ABDEIRTV VIBRATED	ABDGINRS BRIGANDS	ABEEENRV BEREAVEN
ABDEGINS BEADINGS	ABDEISST BASTIDES	ABDGINST DINGBATS	ABEEENST ABSENTEE
DEBASING	ABDEISSU DISABUSE	ABDGINSU DAUBINGS	ABEEERRT TEREBRAE
ABDEGINT DEBATING	ABDEISTU DAUBIEST	ABDGINSW WINDBAGS	ABEEERSV BEREAVES
ABDEGINZ BEDAZING	ABDEISTW BAWDIEST	ABDGLNOS BOGLANDS	ABEEFFTU BEAUFFET
ABDEGIRR ABRIDGER	ABDEITTU DUBITATE	ABDGLOOR LOGBOARD	ABEEFILS FEASIBLE
ABDEGIRS ABRIDGES	ABDEJNOW JAWBONED	ABDGLSUY LADYBUGS	ABEEFIST TABEFIES
BRIGADES	ABDEKLSW SKEWBALD	ABDHHSSU SHADBUSH	ABEEFLLL FELLABLE
ABDEGLNR BRANGLED	ABDEKNNU UNBANKED	ABDHIIST ADHIBITS	ABEEFLLN BEFALLEN
ABDEGLOT GLOBATED	ABDEKNRU UNBARKED	DISHABIT	ABEEFLOS BEEFALOS
ABDEGLRS BELGARDS	ABDEKNSU SUNBAKED	ABDHILLN HANDBILL	ABEEFORR FOREBEAR
ABDEGLRY BADGERLY	ABDEKOOR ABROOKED	ABDHILNS BLANDISH	ABEEFSTU BEAUFETS
ABDEGMRU UMBRAGED	ABDEKORY KEYBOARD	ABDHINRS BRANDISH	ABEEGHRS HERBAGES
ABDEGNOR BONDAGER	ABDELLOT BALLOTED	ABDHIORS BROADISH	ABEEGHRT BERTHAGE
ABDEGNOS BONDAGES	ABDELMNU UNBLAMED	ABDHIPRS BARDSHIP	ABEEGINR BAREGINE
DOGBANES	ABDELNOR BANDEROL	ABDHIRTY BIRTHDAY	BERGENIA
ABDEGOPR PEGBOARD	ABDELNOZ BLAZONED	ABDHKNOO HANDBOOK	ABEEGIRV VERBIAGE
ABDEGRSU SUBGRADE	ABDELNRY BYLANDER	ABDHLORW BLOWHARD	ABEEGLLR GABELLER
ABDEHILL BILLHEAD	ABDELNSS BALDNESS	ABDHLOSW SHADBLOW	ABEEGLLS GABELLES
ABDEHILS DISHABLE	ABDELNST BLANDEST	ABDHMORS RHABDOMS	ABEEGLRS BEAGLERS
ABDEHIMT IMBATHED	ABDELORU LABOURED	ABDHMOTU BADMOUTH	ABEEGLTT GETTABLE
ABDEHINS BANISHED	ABDELOSV ABSOLVED	ABDHMSTU MUDBATHS	ABEEGMNR BARGEMEN
ABDEHITU HABITUDE	ABDELPSY PYEBALDS	ABDHNORS BODHRANS	ABEEGMTY MEGABYTE
ABDEHKLU BULKHEAD	ABDELRRS DRABLERS	ABDHNSSU HUSBANDS	ABEEGOSZ GAZEBOES
ABDEHLLN HANDBELL	ABDELRSU DURABLES	ABDIILLR BILLIARD	ABEEGRRS GERBERAS
ABDEHLLU BULLHEAD	ABDELRTT BRATTLED	ABDIIMNR MIDBRAIN	ABEEGRST ABSTERGE
ABDEHLMS SHAMBLED	ABDELSTU SUBLATED	ABDIIMSU BASIDIUM	ABEEGRSU AUBERGES

```
ABEEGRSW BREWAGES
ABEEGTTU BAGUETTE
ABEEHILR HIREABLE
ABEEHINT THEBAINE
ABEEHLLP HELPABLE
ABEEHLLR BEERHALL
         HAREBELL
ABEEHLSV BEHALVES
ABEEHMSS BESHAMES
ABEEHMST EMBATHES
ABEEHNNS HENBANES
ABEEHNPP BEHAPPEN
ABEEHNSS BANSHEES
ABEEHNTT HEBETANT
ABEEHQTU BEQUEATH
ABEEHRRT BREATHER
ABEEHRST BREATHES
         HARTBEES
ABEEIKLL LIKEABLE
ABEEIKRS BAKERIES
ABEEIKST BEAKIEST
ABEEILLR RELIABLE
ABEEILLV LEVIABLE
         LIVEABLE
ABEEILMS BELAMIES
ABEEILNP PLEBEIAN
ABEEILNU BANLIEUE
ABEEILNV ENVIABLE
ABEEILPX EXPIABLE
ABEEILRR BLEARIER
ABEEILRT LIBERATE
ABEEILST SEABLITE
ABEEILSV EVASIBLE
ABEEILSZ SEIZABLE
         SIZEABLE
ABEEILTV EVITABLE
ABEEILVW VIEWABLE
ABEEIMRT AMBERITE
ABEEIMST BEAMIEST
ABEEINST BETAINES
ABEEINTY AYENBITE
ABEEIPRS BEPRAISE
ABEEIRTT BATTERIE
ABEEIRTV BREVIATE
ABEEISST BEASTIES
ABEEISSV ABESSIVE
ABEEISTU BEAUTIES
ABEEITUX BEAUXITE
ABEEJMOR JAMBOREE
ABEEKLOT KEELBOAT
ABEEKLST BLEAKEST
ABEEKMNR BRAKEMEN
         EMBANKER
ABEEKNSV BEKNAVES
ABEEKOOP PEEKABOO
ABEEKOPS PEEKABOS
ABEEKPSS BESPEAKS
ABEEKRRS BREAKERS
ABEEKRST BESTREAK
ABEELLLS SELLABLE
ABEELLLT TELLABLE
ABEELLOT BALLOTEE
ABEELLOV LOVEABLE
ABEELLSY EYEBALLS
ABEELLTT LETTABLE
ABEELMMR EMBALMER
         EMMARBLE
ABEELMOV MOVEABLE
ABEELMPR PREAMBLE
ABEELMRT ATREMBLE
ABEELMSS ASSEMBLE
         BEAMLESS
ABEELMST BEAMLETS
ABEELMSZ EMBLAZES
ABEELMTT EMBATTLE
ABEELNOP BEANPOLE
         OPENABLE
ABEELNRS ENABLERS
ABEELNRT RENTABLE

ABEELNTU TUNEABLE
ABEELOPR OPERABLE
         ROPEABLE
ABEELOPS POSEABLE
ABEELORS EARLOBES
ABEELORX EXORABLE
ABEELPRS BEPEARLS
ABEELRST BLEAREST
         BLEATERS
         RETABLES
ABEELRSU REUSABLE
ABEELRSV BESLAVER
ABEELRTT BATTELER
ABEELRTU BATELEUR
         BLEUATRE
ABEELSSS BASELESS
ABEELSST BATELESS
ABEELSSU SUBLEASE
ABEELSSV BESLAVES
ABEELSTT TESTABLE
ABEEMMNR MEMBRANE
ABEEMMRU BUMMAREE
ABEEMNOR BEMOANER
ABEEMNST BASEMENT
ABEEMNTT ABETMENT
         BATEMENT
ABEEMRSS BESMEARS
ABEEMRSV EMBRAVES
ABEENNRT BANNERET
ABEENNRU EBURNEAN
ABEENNTU UNBEATEN
ABEENORS SEABORNE
ABEENOTZ BENZOATE
ABEENRRR BARRENER
ABEENRRT BANTERER
ABEENRSS BARENESS
ABEENRSV VERBENAS
ABEENSSS BASENESS
ABEEORRV OVERBEAR
ABEEORST ABORTEES
         REBATOES
ABEEORTV OVERBEAT
ABEEPRRY PEABERRY
ABEERRRT BARTERER
ABEERRST REBATERS
         TABRERES
         TEREBRAS
ABEERRTT BARRETTE
         BATTERER
ABEERRTV VERTEBRA
ABEERRTY BETRAYER
         TEABERRY
ABEERSTT ABETTERS
ABEERSTU SUBERATE
ABEESZZZ BEZAZZES
ABEFFLRS BAFFLERS
ABEFFOST OFFBEATS
ABEFGILS FILABEGS
ABEFGLLR BERGFALL
ABEFGSST GABFESTS
ABEFHILS FISHABLE
ABEFHOOT HOOFBEAT
ABEFIIMR FIMBRIAE
ABEFILLL FALLIBLE
ABEFILLM FILMABLE
ABEFILLR FIREBALL
ABEFILLT LIFTABLE
ABEFILOT LIFEBOAT
ABEFILRS BARFLIES
ABEFILSU FABULISE
ABEFILSY FEASIBLY
ABEFILUZ FABULIZE
ABEFINSU BEAUFINS
ABEFIRRT FIREBRAT
ABEFITUY BEAUTIFY
ABEFLLMU BLAMEFUL
ABEFLLTU TABLEFUL
ABEFLMOR FORMABLE
ABEFLNRU FUNEBRAL

ABEFLNSY FLYBANES
ABEFMRSU SUBFRAME
ABEFOORT BAREFOOT
ABEFORRS FORBEARS
ABEGGHLU HUGGABLE
ABEGGILN BEAGLING
ABEGGIST BAGGIEST
ABEGGITY GIGABYTE
ABEGGLLU LUGGABLE
ABEGGLRS BLAGGERS
ABEGGLRY BEGGARLY
ABEGGMOS GAMBOGES
ABEGGNSU BUGGANES
ABEGGRSU BURGAGES
ABEGHILP PHILABEG
ABEGHILR ALBERGHI
ABEGHINO OBEAHING
ABEGHINT BEATHING
ABEGHINV BEHAVING
ABEGHNSS SHEBANGS
ABEGHORR BEGORRAH
ABEGHRRY HAGBERRY
ABEGHRST BARGHEST
ABEGIIMS BIGAMIES
ABEGIKNR BREAKING
ABEGIKNT BETAKING
ABEGILMN EMBALING
ABEGILNN ENABLING
ABEGILNR BLEARING
ABEGILNS SINGABLE
ABEGILNT BELATING
         BLEATING
         TANGIBLE
ABEGILNY BELAYING
ABEGILOT OBLIGATE
ABEGIMNN BENAMING
ABEGIMNR BREAMING
ABEGIMNS BEAMINGS
         EMBASING
ABEGIMNY EMBAYING
ABEGIMRS GAMBIERS
ABEGIMST MEGABITS
ABEGIMUX GIAMBEUX
ABEGINOR ABORIGEN
ABEGINOS BEGONIAS
ABEGINRS BEARINGS
         SABERING
ABEGINRT BERATING
         REBATING
ABEGINRW BEWARING
ABEGINRY BERAYING
ABEGINST BEATINGS
ABEGINTT ABETTING
ABEGINTW WINGBEAT
ABEGIOSS BIOGASES
ABEGIPPR BAGPIPER
ABEGIPPS BAGPIPES
ABEGKORS BROKAGES
         GROSBEAK
ABEGKOSS BOSKAGES
ABEGLLLU GULLABLE
ABEGLLOR BARGELLO
ABEGLMRS GAMBLERS
         GAMBRELS
ABEGLNRS BRANGLES
ABEGLORW GROWABLE
ABEGLRRS GARBLERS
ABEGLRUU BLAGUEUR
ABEGLSTU GUSTABLE
ABEGMNOS GAMBESON
ABEGMORT BERGAMOT
ABEGMRSU UMBRAGES
ABEGNNST BANTENGS
ABEGNOSS NOSEBAGS
ABEGNRST BANGSTER
ABEGNRTU BURGANET
ABEGNSTU SUBAGENT
ABEGOORS BARGOOSE
ABEGOSTT BOTTEGAS

ABEGOSUY BUOYAGES
ABEGRRSU GARBURES
ABEGRRUV BURGRAVE
ABEGRSST BARGESTS
ABEGSSTU SUBSTAGE
ABEHILLR HAIRBELL
ABEHILNR HIBERNAL
ABEHILRS BLASHIER
ABEHILTT TITHABLE
ABEHIMOS OBEAHISM
ABEHIMST IMBATHES
ABEHINSS BANISHES
ABEHINST ABSINTHE
ABEHIOPU EUPHOBIA
ABEHIORV BEHAVIOR
ABEHIRRS BRASHIER
ABEHISTU HABITUES
ABEHISTZ ZABTIEHS
ABEHJORS JOBSHARE
ABEHKLLW HAWKBELL
ABEHKNOR HORNBEAK
ABEHKRSU HAUBERKS
ABEHLLRT BETHRALL
ABEHLMMU HUMMABLE
ABEHLMSS SHAMBLES
ABEHLNOT BENTHOAL
ABEHLOTY HYLOBATE
ABEHLRST BLATHERS
         HALBERTS
ABEHLSSS BASHLESS
ABEHMNOR HORNBEAM
ABEHMOOR REHOBOAM
ABEHMSSU AMBUSHES
ABEHNSTU SUNBATHE
ABEHORRR ABHORRER
         HARBORER
ABEHORST BATHORSE
ABEHOSST BATHOSES
ABEHOSTX HATBOXES
ABEHOSXY HAYBOXES
ABEHRSST BRASHEST
ABEIILLS BAILLIES
ABEIILMT IMITABLE
ABEIILNN BIENNIAL
ABEIILNV INVIABLE
ABEIILPT PITIABLE
ABEIILRR LIBRAIRE
ABEIILRS BISERIAL
ABEIILST ALBITISE
         SIBILATE
ABEIILTV VITIABLE
ABEIILTZ ALBITIZE
ABEIINRR BRAINIER
ABEIINRS BINARIES
ABEIINST BAINITES
ABEIJLTU JUBILATE
ABEIJMNN BENJAMIN
ABEIJMRS JAMBIERS
ABEIJNSS BASENJIS
ABEIKLLN BALKLINE
         LINKABLE
ABEIKLNS BLANKIES
ABEIKLSS KISSABLE
ABEIKLST BALKIEST
ABEIKNRR BRANKIER
ABEIKNRS BEARSKIN
         INBREAKS
ABEIKNST BEATNIKS
ABEIKRST BARKIEST
         BRAKIEST
         BREASKIT
ABEIKSWY BIKEWAYS
ABEILLLT TILLABLE
ABEILLLW WILLABLE
ABEILLMM LIMBMEAL
ABEILLNT LIBELANT
ABEILLOS ISOLABLE
         LOBELIAS
ABEILLOV VIOLABLE
```

ABEILLQU	LIQUABLE	ABEINRTU	BRAUNITE	ABELMNST	SEMBLANT	ABENORTT	BETATRON

ABEILLQU LIQUABLE
ABEILLRR BRAILLER
ABEILLRS BALLSIER
　　　　　LIBERALS
ABEILLRY BERYLLIA
　　　　　BLEARILY
　　　　　RELIABLY
ABEILLST BASTILLE
ABEILLTT TILTABLE
ABEILMNS BAILSMEN
ABEILMNT BAILMENT
ABEILMOR BROMELIA
ABEILMRR MARBLIER
ABEILMRS REMBLAIS
ABEILMRW WAMBLIER
ABEILMSS ABLEISMS
　　　　　MISSABLE
ABEILMST BALMIEST
　　　　　TIMBALES
ABEILNNW WINNABLE
ABEILNOP OPINABLE
ABEILNPS BIPLANES
ABEILNPT PINTABLE
ABEILNRS RINSABLE
ABEILNRU RUINABLE
ABEILNSS ALBINESS
　　　　　LESBIANS
ABEILNST INSTABLE
ABEILNSU SABULINE
ABEILNTV BIVALENT
ABEILNUV UNVIABLE
ABEILNVY ENVIABLY
ABEILPPT TIPPABLE
ABEILPRT PARTIBLE
ABEILPRZ PRIZABLE
ABEILPSS PASSIBLE
ABEILPST EPIBLAST
ABEILRRU REBURIAL
ABEILRRW BRAWLIER
ABEILRST LIBRATES
　　　　　TABLIERS
ABEILRTW WRITABLE
ABEILSST ASTILBES
　　　　　BESTIALS
　　　　　STABILES
ABEILSSU ISSUABLE
　　　　　SUASIBLE
ABEILSTU SUITABLE
ABEILSTY BEASTILY
ABEILSUX BISEXUAL
ABEILSVV BIVALVES
ABEIMNRS MIRBANES
ABEIMNST AMBIENTS
ABEIMRST BARMIEST
ABEIMRSU AUMBRIES
ABEIMRTV AMBIVERT
　　　　　VERBATIM
ABEIMSSU IAMBUSES
ABEINNOS BESONIAN
ABEINNOZ BEZONIAN
ABEINNRR BRANNIER
ABEINNRU INURBANE
ABEINORR AIRBORNE
ABEINORS BARONIES
ABEINORT BARITONE
　　　　　OBTAINER
ABEINOST BOTANIES
　　　　　BOTANISE
　　　　　NIOBATES
　　　　　OBEISANT
ABEINOTZ BOTANIZE
ABEINPST BEPAINTS
ABEINQSU BASQUINE
ABEINRRW BRAWNIER
ABEINRST ATEBRINS
　　　　　BANISTER
ABEINRSU ANBURIES
　　　　　URBANISE
ABEINRSZ ZEBRINAS

ABEINRTU BRAUNITE
　　　　　URBANITE
ABEINRUZ URBANIZE
ABEINSST BASINETS
　　　　　BASSINET
　　　　　BESAINTS
　　　　　BESTAINS
ABEINSSU UNBIASES
ABEINSTT TABINETS
ABEINTTU INTUBATE
ABEIORSS ISOBARES
ABEIORST SABOTIER
ABEIORTV ABORTIVE
ABEIOSSS ISOBASES
ABEIOSTV OBVIATES
ABEIPSST BAPTISES
ABEIPSTZ BAPTIZES
ABEIRRRS BARRIERS
ABEIRRSS BRASIERS
　　　　　BRASSIER
ABEIRRST ARBITERS
　　　　　RAREBITS
ABEIRRSZ BRAZIERS
ABEIRRTT BRATTIER
ABEIRRVY BREVIARY
ABEIRSSS BRASSIES
ABEIRSTT BIRETTAS
ABEIRSTV VIBRATES
ABEIRSTW WARBIEST
ABEIRSTY BESTIARY
　　　　　SYBARITE
ABEIRSUX EXURBIAS
ABEIRTTY YTTERBIA
ABEISSST BASSIEST
ABEISSTT BATISTES
ABEISTTT BATTIEST
ABEISTUX BAUXITES
ABEISZZZ BIZAZZES
ABEITTTU TITUBATE
ABEJKLOU KABELJOU
ABEJLMPU JUMPABLE
ABEJMNOS JAMBONES
ABEJMOOR JEROBOAM
ABEJNOSW JAWBONES
ABEJOSWX JAWBOXES
ABEJRRSU ABJURERS
ABEKLMOS SMOKABLE
ABEKLNOW KNOWABLE
ABEKLNRY BANKERLY
ABEKLNST BLANKEST
　　　　　BLANKETS
ABEKLNTY BLANKETY
ABEKLORW WORKABLE
ABEKLRSS BARKLESS
ABEKMNNS BANKSMEN
ABEKNSSU SUNBAKES
ABEKNSSY SNEAKSBY
ABEKOORS ABROOKES
ABEKOORY YEARBOOK
ABEKORTU OUTBREAK
ABEKPRSU UPBREAKS
ABEKRSTY BASKETRY
ABELLLMU LABELLUM
ABELLLOR ROLLABLE
ABELLLOT TOLLABLE
ABELLLSY SYLLABLE
ABELLMOR OMBRELLA
ABELLMRU UMBELLAR
　　　　　UMBRELLA
ABELLNOS BONSELLA
ABELLNOT BALLONET
ABELLNRU RUBELLAN
ABELLNST NETBALLS
ABELLOSV SOLVABLE
ABELLOTU LOBULATE
ABELLRSU RUBELLAS
ABELLRVY VERBALLY
ABELMNNO NOBLEMAN
ABELMNOZ EMBLAZON

ABELMNST SEMBLANT
ABELMNSU ALBUMENS
ABELMOOT MOOTABLE
ABELMOSV MOVABLES
ABELMOVY MOVEABLY
ABELMPTU PLUMBATE
ABELMRRS MARBLERS
　　　　　RAMBLERS
ABELMRST LAMBERTS
ABELMSSY ASSEMBLY
ABELNNOR BANNEROL
ABELNNRU RUNNABLE
ABELNORZ BLAZONER
ABELNOST NEOBLAST
　　　　　NOTABLES
ABELNOSY BALONEYS
ABELNQTU BLANQUET
ABELNRSS BRANSLES
ABELNRST BRANTLES
ABELNRSY BLARNEYS
ABELNRUY URBANELY
ABELNRYZ BRAZENLY
ABELNSTU UNSTABLE
ABELNSTY ABSENTLY
ABELNSUU UNUSABLE
ABELOPRT PORTABLE
ABELOPRU POURABLE
ABELOPRV PROVABLE
ABELOPST POTABLES
ABELOPTT TABLETOP
ABELOQTU QUOTABLE
ABELORRU LABOURER
ABELORST BLOATERS
　　　　　SORTABLE
　　　　　STORABLE
ABELORSU RUBEOLAS
ABELORSV ABSOLVER
ABELOSSU SABULOSE
ABELOSSV ABSOLVES
ABELOSTU ABSOLUTE
ABELOSTW BESTOWAL
ABELPRTU PUBERTAL
ABELQSUU SUBEQUAL
ABELRRSW BRAWLERS
　　　　　WARBLERS
ABELRRTU BARRULET
ABELRSST BLASTERS
　　　　　STABLERS
ABELRSSY LABRYSES
ABELRSTT BATTLERS
　　　　　BLATTERS
　　　　　BRATTLES
ABELRSTU BALUSTER
ABELRSTW BLEWARTS
ABELRSUZ ZEBRULAS
ABELRTTU BURLETTA
　　　　　REBUTTAL
ABELSSTT STABLEST
ABELSSTU SUBLATES
ABELSTUU SUBULATE
ABELSTWY BELTWAYS
ABELTTUU TUBULATE
ABEMMNOO MOONBEAM
ABEMNOTU UMBONATE
ABEMNOTW BATWOMEN
ABEMNPRU PENUMBRA
ABEMNRSY MYRBANES
ABEMNSSU SUNBEAMS
ABEMNSTU SUBMENTA
ABEMNSUY SUNBEAMY
ABEMNTTU ABUTMENT
ABEMORRS EMBRASOR
ABEMORST BROMATES
ABEMORSU AMBEROUS
ABEMORTZ BAROMETZ
ABENNORS BARONNES
ABENOPSU SUBPOENA
ABENORSS BARONESS
ABENORST BARONETS

ABENORTT BETATRON
ABENORTV BEVATRON
ABENORTY BARYTONE
ABENOSSW SAWBONES
ABENOSTY BAYONETS
ABENQSTU BANQUETS
ABENRRYZ BRAZENRY
ABENRSTU UNBRASTE
　　　　　URBANEST
ABEOPRSS SAPROBES
ABEOPRST PROBATES
ABEOQRSU BAROQUES
ABEORRSS BRASEROS
ABEORRST ARBORETS
　　　　　TABORERS
ABEORSST BOASTERS
　　　　　SORBATES
ABEORSSY ROSEBAYS
ABEORSTT ABETTORS
　　　　　BATTEROS
　　　　　TABORETS
ABEORSTU SABOTEUR
ABEORTTU OBTURATE
　　　　　TABOURET
ABEORTUV OUTBRAVE
ABEOSSST ASBESTOS
ABEOSTUV SUBOVATE
ABEPRRTU ABRUPTER
ABEPSSSY BYPASSES
ABEQRSUU ARQUEBUS
ABERRSSU SABREURS
ABERRTYY TAYBERRY
ABERRWXY WAXBERRY
ABERSSST BRASSETS
ABERSSSU SURBASES
ABERSSTU ABSTRUSE
　　　　　SURBATES
ABERSSTW WABSTERS
ABERSTTU ABUTTERS
ABERTTUY BUTYRATE
ABESSTTU SUBSTATE
ABFFGILN BAFFLING
ABFFIILS BAILIFFS
ABFFLLPU PUFFBALL
ABFFNOTU BOUFFANT
ABFGILNS FABLINGS
ABFGLLOO GOOFBALL
ABFGORUU FAUBOURG
ABFHIIST BAITFISH
ABFHILLS FISHBALL
ABFHINNO INFOBAHN
ABFHIORS BOARFISH
ABFIILLR FIBRILLA
ABFILLLY FALLIBLY
ABFILNSU BASINFUL
ABFILSTU FABULIST
ABFIMORS FIBROMAS
ABFJORSU FRABJOUS
ABFKLLOR KORFBALL
ABFLLOOT FOOTBALL
ABFLLOST SOFTBALL
ABFLOSTU BOASTFUL
ABFLOSTY FLYBOATS
ABFLOSUU FABULOUS
ABFNORTU TURBOFAN
ABFOORST FOOTBARS
ABFSSTTU TUBFASTS
ABGGGILN BLAGGING
ABGGGINR BRAGGING
ABGGGINS BAGGINGS
ABGGIJNN JINGBANG
ABGGILMN GAMBLING
ABGGILNR GARBLING
ABGGINNS BANGINGS
ABGGNOOT TOBOGGAN
ABGGORST BOGGARTS
ABGHHILL HIGHBALL
ABGHIINT HABITING
ABGHILMN HAMBLING

ABGHINRS BRASHING
ABGHINSS BASHINGS
ABGHINWZ WHIZBANG
ABGHIOPR BIOGRAPH
ABGHLOST HAGBOLTS
ABGHMORU BROUGHAM
ABGIILNR BRAILING
ABGIILNS SAIBLING
ABGIILNT LIBATING
ABGIILOT OBLIGATI
ABGIIMNS IMBASING
ABGIIMST BIGAMIST
ABGIINNO BIGNONIA
ABGIINNR BRAINING
ABGIINOR ABORIGIN
ABGIINRS BRAISING
ABGIINSS BIASINGS
         BIASSING
ABGIINST BAITINGS
ABGIJNRU ABJURING
ABGIKLNN BLANKING
ABGIKLNS BALKINGS
ABGIKLNU BAULKING
ABGIKNNR BRANKING
ABGIKNNS BANKINGS
ABGILLMN LAMBLING
ABGILLNS BALLINGS
ABGILMNR MARBLING
         RAMBLING
ABGILMNS AMBLINGS
ABGILMNW WAMBLING
ABGILNNT BANTLING
ABGILNOR LABORING
ABGILNOT BLOATING
         OBLIGANT
ABGILNRT BRATLING
ABGILNRW BRAWLING
         WARBLING
ABGILNST BLASTING
         STABLING
         TABLINGS
ABGILNSW BAWLINGS
ABGILNTT BATTLING
         BLATTING
ABGILNTY TANGIBLY
ABGILOOT OBLIGATO
ABGILORS GARBOILS
ABGILORW BRIGALOW
ABGIMMNO MAMBOING
ABGIMNRU RUMBAING
ABGIMOSU BIGAMOUS
         SUBIMAGO
ABGIMSST GAMBISTS
ABGINNOR ABORNING
ABGINNOT BATONING
ABGINNRU UNBARING
ABGINNRX BANXRING
ABGINNST BANTINGS
ABGINOOT TABOOING
ABGINORT ABORTING
         TABORING
ABGINOST BOASTING
         BOATINGS
         BOSTANGI
ABGINRRS BARRINGS
ABGINRST BRASTING
ABGINSST BASTINGS
ABGINSTT BATTINGS
ABGINSTW BATSWING
ABGINTTU ABUTTING
ABGIOPST PIGBOATS
ABGKORSW WORKBAGS
ABGLLLOY GLOBALLY
ABGLLORU GLOBULAR
ABGLLRUY BULLYRAG
ABGLMNSU LUMBANGS
ABGLMOSU LUMBAGOS
ABGLNOOT LONGBOAT

ABGLNOUW BUNGALOW
ABGLOOST TOOLBAGS
ABGLOOTY BATOLOGY
ABGLORST RAGBOLTS
ABGLORSU GLABROUS
ABGLOSSU SUBGOALS
ABGLRRSU BURGLARS
ABGLRRUY BURGLARY
ABGMNOOR GAMBROON
ABGNOPRS PROBANGS
ABGNORSU OSNABURG
ABGNOSTU GUNBOATS
ABGNOSWY BOWYANGS
ABGOORST BOTARGOS
ABGOPSST POSTBAGS
ABGORRSU GOBURRAS
ABGORSTU OUTBRAGS
ABGOSTTU TUGBOATS
ABHHKOST KHOTBAHS
ABHHKSTU KHUTBAHS
ABHHRSTU HATBRUSH
ABHIINRS BRAINISH
ABHIINST INHABITS
ABHIIORZ RHIZOBIA
ABHIKLOR KOHLRABI
ABHIKLSS BASHLIKS
ABHIKSTW HAWKBITS
ABHILLPT PITHBALL
ABHILNOS HOBNAILS
ABHILNOT BIATHLON
ABHILOPS BASOPHIL
ABHILRTW WHIRLBAT
ABHILSST STABLISH
ABHILSTU HALIBUTS
ABHIMMST BATHMISM
ABHINSST ABSINTHS
ABHIOSST ISOBATHS
ABHIOSTU HAUTBOIS
ABHIRSTT BRATTISH
ABHKLSUW BUSHWALK
ABHKORSU BOURKHAS
         KOURBASH
ABHLLMOT MOTHBALL
ABHLLOOY BALLYHOO
ABHLORTW WHORLBAT
ABHLOSWW WASHBOWL
ABHLPSUY SUBPHYLA
ABHLRSTU HURLBATS
ABHLSSTU SALTBUSH
ABHMNOTY BOTHYMAN
ABHMNSUU SUBHUMAN
ABHMOORT BATHROOM
ABHNSSTU SUNBATHS
ABHOORST TARBOOSH
ABHOOSTW SHOWBOAT
ABHORRSU HARBOURS
ABHORSTU TARBOUSH
ABHOSTUY HAUTBOYS
ABHSSTUW WASHTUBS
ABIIINRY BIRIYANI
ABIIKKST KIBITKAS
ABIIKLSS BASILISK
ABIILLMR MILLIBAR
ABIILLTY LABILITY
ABIILMNO BINOMIAL
ABIILMNS ALBINISM
ABIILMSU BULIMIAS
ABIILNOT LIBATION
ABIILNQS INQILABS
ABIILNRZ BRAZILIN
ABIILNST SIBILANT
ABIILPTY PITIABLY
ABIIMNOT AMBITION
ABIIMNRS MINIBARS
ABIIMSST IAMBISTS
ABIINORS ROBINIAS
ABIINRSY BIRYANIS
ABIIRSSV VIBRISSA
ABIJLNRS BRINJALS

ABIJLNTU JUBILANT
ABIJNOOT JOBATION
ABIJNOST ABJOINTS
         BANJOIST
ABIKLMNS LAMBKINS
         LAMBSKIN
ABIKLNRY BYRLAKIN
ABIKLORS KILOBARS
ABIKMNNR BRINKMAN
ABIKMNRS BARMKINS
ABIKNORR IRONBARK
ABIKOSUZ BAZOUKIS
ABIKRSST BRITSKAS
ABIKRSTZ BRITZKAS
         BRITZSKA
ABILLLPY PLAYBILL
ABILLMSU BALLIUMS
ABILLNPS PINBALLS
ABILLOVY VIOLABLY
ABILLRTY TRIBALLY
ABILLSSW SAWBILLS
ABILLSTT BATTILLS
ABILLSWX WAXBILLS
ABILLSWY WAYBILLS
ABILMNOU OLIBANUM
ABILMNSU ALBUMINS
ABILMOPS BIOPLASM
ABILMOTU BUMALOTI
ABILNOOT LOBATION
         OBLATION
ABILNORU UNILOBAR
ABILNOTU ABLUTION
         ABUTILON
ABILNRTU TRIBUNAL
         TURBINAL
ABILOPRS PARBOILS
ABILOPST BIOPLAST
ABILORST ORBITALS
         STROBILA
ABILORSV BOLIVARS
ABILORTY LIBATORY
ABILPSSY PASSIBLY
ABILRSSY BRASSILY
ABILRSUV SUBVIRAL
ABILSSUY ISSUABLY
ABILSTUY SUITABLY
ABIMMNOO MAINBOOM
ABIMNOSU BIMANOUS
ABIMNRTU TAMBURIN
ABIMORSU BIRAMOUS
ABIMPSST BAPTISMS
ABIMRSST STRABISM
ABIMRSTT TRIMTABS
ABINOORS BORONIAS
ABINOORT ABORTION
ABINORST TABORINS
ABINORSW RAINBOWS
ABINORTU TABOURIN
ABINORWY RAINBOWY
ABINOSST BASTIONS
ABINOSSU ABUSIONS
ABINOSTT BOTANIST
ABINRTUY URBANITY
ABINTTTU TITUBANT
ABIOPRSU BIPAROUS
ABIOPSTU SUBTOPIA
ABIORRST ARBORIST
ABIORRTV VIBRATOR
ABIORSTV VIBRATOS
ABIORTUY OBITUARY
ABIPSSTT BAPTISTS
ABIRRSTU AIRBURST
ABIRSSUZ SUBSIZAR
ABIRSTTY TRAYBITS
ABISSSST BASSISTS
ABJKMOSS SJAMBOKS
ABJLMOOS JAMBOOLS
ABKKMOOR BOOKMARK
ABKLLNOR BANKROLL

ABKLOOPY PLAYBOOK
ABKLRSUW BULWARKS
ABKNOPST STOPBANK
ABKNPRTU BANKRUPT
ABKNRSUU BUNRAKUS
ABKOORTW WORKBOAT
ABKOOSTT KOTTABOS
ABLLMOOR BALLROOM
ABLLMOPW BLOWLAMP
ABLLNOOS BALLOONS
ABLLNOSW SNOWBALL
ABLLORST BORSTALL
ABLLOSTY TALLBOYS
ABLLRTUY BRUTALLY
ABLLSSUY SYLLABUS
ABLMNRUU ALBURNUM
         LABURNUM
ABLMOOST TOMBOLAS
ABLMOSTY MYOBLAST
ABLMPSUU PABULUMS
ABLNORYZ BLAZONRY
ABLNOSTU BUTANOLS
ABLNOSUZ SUBZONAL
ABLNRSUU SUBLUNAR
ABLNSUUY UNUSABLY
ABLOORST TOOLBARS
ABLOORTY OBLATORY
ABLOOSTT BOOTLAST
ABLOOSTZ ZOOBLAST
ABLOPRSU SUBPOLAR
ABLOPRVY PROVABLY
ABLOPSUU PABULOUS
ABLOPSYY PLAYBOYS
ABLOQTUY QUOTABLY
ABLORSST BORSTALS
ABLORSSU SUBSOLAR
ABLORSTW BLAWORTS
ABLORSUW BOURLAWS
ABLOSSUU SABULOUS
ABLOSTTU SUBTOTAL
ABLPRTUY ABRUPTLY
ABMNTTUY BUTTYMAN
ABMORSTU TAMBOURS
ABMOSSTU SUBATOMS
ABNOORRT ROBORANT
ABNOORSS SOROBANS
ABNOORSZ BORAZONS
ABNOOSSS BASSOONS
ABNORSTY BARYTONS
ABNORTUU RUNABOUT
ABNOSSSU BONASSUS
ABNRSTTU TURBANTS
ABOORRSU ARBOROUS
ABOORSTW ROWBOATS
ABOOSTTW TOWBOATS
ABORSSTU ROBUSTAS
ACCCDIIO COCCIDIA
ACCCENPY PECCANCY
ACCCFIIL CALCIFIC
ACCCHILO COLCHICA
ACCCIIPR CAPRICCI
ACCCILLY CYCLICAL
ACCCIOPU CAPUCCIO
ACCDDEEN ACCENDED
         CADENCED
ACCDDEIS CADDICES
ACCDDEOR ACCORDED
ACCDDIIT DIDACTIC
ACCDEENS CADENCES
ACCDEENT ACCENTED
ACCDEEPT ACCEPTED
ACCDEERS ACCEDERS
ACCDEERT ACCRETED
ACCDEERU CARDECUE
ACCDEERW ACCREWED
ACCDEESS ACCESSED
ACCDEGIN ACCEDING
         ACCINGED
ACCDEHIK CHIACKED

ACCDEHIL	CHALICED		CHEMICAL
ACCDEHIN	CHICANED	ACCEHILP	CEPHALIC
ACCDEHKY	CHYACKED	ACCEHILS	CALICHES
ACCDEHLT	CLATCHED		CHALICES
ACCDEHNR	CRANCHED	ACCEHILT	HECTICAL
ACCDEHNU	CHAUNCED	ACCEHIMN	MECHANIC
ACCDEIIS	ACCIDIES	ACCEHIMS	SACHEMIC
ACCDEILN	CALCINED	ACCEHINO	ANECHOIC
ACCDEILU	CAUDICLE	ACCEHINR	CHANCIER
ACCDEILY	DELICACY		CHICANER
ACCDEINT	ACCIDENT	ACCEHINS	CHICANES
ACCDEIRT	ACCREDIT	ACCEHIOS	COACHIES
ACCDEISU	CAUDICES	ACCEHIRT	CATCHIER
ACCDEKLR	CRACKLED	ACCEHLNS	CHANCELS
ACCDEKOS	COCKADES	ACCEHLOR	COCHLEAR
ACCDELLY	CALYCLED	ACCEHLOT	CATECHOL
ACCDELOY	ACCLOYED	ACCEHLST	CLATCHES
ACCDENOR	CONACRED	ACCEHMNO	COACHMEN
ACCDENOV	CONCAVED	ACCEHNNO	CHACONNE
ACCDEORR	ACCORDER	ACCEHNNY	CYNANCHE
ACCDEOST	ACCOSTED	ACCEHNOR	CHARNECO
ACCDERSU	ACCURSED		ENCROACH
	CARDECUS	ACCEHNOT	CONCHATE
ACCDESSU	SUCCADES	ACCEHNRS	CHANCERS
ACCDESUU	CADUCEUS		CHANCRES
	CAUCUSED		CRANCHES
ACCDGHOO	COACHDOG	ACCEHNRY	CHANCERY
ACCDHIIR	DIARCHIC	ACCEHNSU	CHAUNCES
ACCDHILS	CHALCIDS	ACCEHOPT	CACHEPOT
ACCDHIMO	DOCHMIAC	ACCEHORS	CAROCHES
ACCDHIOT	CATHODIC		COACHERS
ACCDHLOR	CLOCHARD	ACCEHPSU	CAPUCHES
ACCDIIST	DICASTIC	ACCEHRST	CATCHERS
ACCDIITY	DICACITY		CRATCHES
ACCDILOY	CALYCOID	ACCEHSST	SCATCHES
ACCDILTY	DACTYLIC	ACCEHSTU	CATECHUS
ACCDINOR	CANCROID	ACCEIIST	CAECITIS
	DRACONIC	ACCEIKPS	ICEPACKS
ACCDIOOR	CORACOID	ACCEILLN	CANCELLI
ACCDIORS	SARCODIC	ACCEILLR	CLERICAL
ACCDIOST	STICCADO	ACCEILLS	CALICLES
ACCDITUY	CADUCITY	ACCEILLU	CAULICLE
ACCDKNOS	CANDOCKS	ACCEILLV	CLAVICLE
ACCDKOSW	DAWCOCKS	ACCEILNS	CALCINES
ACCDLOSY	CACODYLS		SCENICAL
ACCDOOST	STOCCADO	ACCEILNT	CANTICLE
ACCDOOXY	CACODOXY	ACCEILNV	CLAVECIN
ACCDOSUU	CADUCOUS	ACCEILNY	CALYCINE
ACCEEHIT	HICCATEE	ACCEILOS	CALICOES
ACCEEHLO	COCHLEAE		COELIACS
ACCEEHOS	COACHEES	ACCEILRV	CERVICAL
ACCEEHRT	CETERACH	ACCEILST	CALCITES
ACCEEHST	SEECATCH	ACCEIMOS	OCCAMIES
ACCEEILR	CELERIAC	ACCEIMRS	CERAMICS
ACCEEILS	ECCLESIA	ACCEINNR	CANCRINE
ACCEEKLN	NECKLACE	ACCEINOS	COCAINES
ACCEELNR	CLARENCE	ACCEINSV	VACCINES
ACCEELNS	CENACLES	ACCEINTU	CUNEATIC
ACCEELOS	COALESCE	ACCEIOPR	CECROPIA
ACCEELRT	CALCRETE	ACCEIOTV	COACTIVE
ACCEENNS	NASCENCE	ACCEIPRS	CAPRICES
ACCEENPR	CREPANCE	ACCEIPRT	PRACTICE
ACCEENRS	CREANCES	ACCEIPSV	PECCAVIS
ACCEENST	ACESCENT	ACCEIQSU	CACIQUES
ACCEEORT	CROCEATE	ACCEIRRR	RICERCAR
ACCEEPRT	ACCEPTER	ACCEIRSU	CURACIES
ACCEERST	ACCRETES	ACCEIRTU	CRUCIATE
ACCEESSS	ACCESSES	ACCEISST	ASCETICS
ACCEFFIY	EFFICACY	ACCEISTT	ECSTATIC
ACCEFILS	FASCICLE	ACCEKLNR	CRACKNEL
ACCEFIST	FACTICES	ACCEKLRS	CACKLERS
ACCEFLSU	FELUCCAS		CLACKERS
ACCEGINS	ACCINGES		CRACKLES
ACCEGKMO	GAMECOCK	ACCEKMOS	MEACOCKS
ACCEGOSS	SOCCAGES	ACCEKOPS	PEACOCKS
ACCEHHIS	CHECHIAS	ACCEKOPY	PEACOCKY
ACCEHHKO	CHECHAKO	ACCEKOSS	SEACOCKS
ACCEHIKP	CHICKPEA	ACCEKPSU	CUPCAKES
ACCEHILM	ALCHEMIC	ACCEKRRS	CRACKERS

ACCELLSY	CALYCLES	ACCHRSSU	SCRAUCHS
ACCELLUY	CALYCULE	ACCHRSTY	SCRATCHY
ACCELMNY	CYCLAMEN	ACCIIIOT	OITICICA
ACCELNOS	CONCEALS	ACCIILLN	CLINICAL
ACCELNOV	CONCLAVE	ACCIILMT	CLIMATIC
ACCELNRU	CARUNCLE	ACCIILRT	CRITICAL
ACCELORS	CORACLES	ACCIIMNN	CINNAMIC
ACCELOST	CACOLETS	ACCIINNO	ANICONIC
ACCELRSY	SCARCELY	ACCIINNP	PICCANIN
ACCELSSU	SACCULES	ACCIINOT	ACONITIC
ACCELWYY	CYCLEWAY	ACCIIPST	PASTICCI
ACCENNSY	NASCENCY	ACCIIRTX	CICATRIX
ACCENORR	CORNACRE	ACCIJKMR	JIMCRACK
ACCENORS	CONACRES	ACCIKLOT	COCKTAIL
ACCENORT	ACCENTOR	ACCIKNST	CANSTICK
ACCENOST	COSECANT	ACCIKOPR	APRICOCK
ACCENOSU	CONCAUSE	ACCIKPRT	PRACTICK
ACCENOSV	CONCAVES	ACCILLUY	CALYCULI
ACCEOPRT	ACCEPTOR	ACCILMOS	COSMICAL
ACCEOPTU	OCCUPATE	ACCILMOX	CACOMIXL
ACCEORSS	ARCCOSES	ACCILMSU	CALCIUMS
ACCEORST	ECTOSARC	ACCILNOT	CICLATON
ACCEORSW	CRACOWES	ACCILNOV	VOLCANIC
ACCEORTU	ACCOUTER	ACCILNUV	VULCANIC
	ACCOUTRE	ACCILORS	CALORICS
ACCEOSSS	SACCOSES	ACCILORT	CORTICAL
ACCERRST	CARRECTS	ACCILPRY	CAPRYLIC
ACCERSST	SCARCEST	ACCILRRU	CIRCULAR
ACCERSSU	ACCURSES	ACCILRSY	ACRYLICS
	ACCUSERS	ACCILSSS	CLASSICS
ACCESSTU	CACTUSES	ACCIMNOS	MOCCASIN
ACCESSUU	CAUCUSES	ACCIMNTU	CANTICUM
ACCFHLTY	CATCHFLY	ACCIMORR	MICROCAR
ACCFIILT	LACTIFIC	ACCIMORU	COUMARIC
ACCFIKLL	CALFLICK	ACCIMOSZ	ZIMOCCAS
ACCFLNOO	CONFOCAL	ACCIMPSU	CAPSICUM
ACCFOORT	COFACTOR	ACCIMSTY	CYMATICS
ACCGHIKN	CHACKING	ACCINOOS	OCCASION
ACCGHINN	CHANCING	ACCINOOT	COACTION
ACCGHINO	COACHING	ACCINORT	NARCOTIC
ACCGHINT	CATCHING	ACCINORV	CAVICORN
ACCGHIOR	CHORAGIC	ACCINOST	CANTICOS
ACCGIINT	ACCITING	ACCINOTY	CANTICOY
ACCGIKLN	CACKLING		CYANOTIC
	CLACKING	ACCINRSU	CRUCIANS
ACCGIKMR	GIMCRACK	ACCIOPST	SPICCATO
ACCGIKNR	CRACKING	ACCIORST	ACROSTIC
ACCGINOT	COACTING	ACCIORSY	ISOCRACY
ACCGINOY	ACCOYING	ACCIOSTT	STICCATO
ACCGINRU	ACCRUING	ACCIOSTU	ACOUSTIC
ACCGINSU	ACCUSING	ACCIPRST	PRACTICS
ACCGLOOY	CACOLOGY	ACCIRSTY	SCARCITY
ACCHHITT	CHITCHAT	ACCISSTU	CAUSTICS
ACCHHMOS	CAMSHOCH	ACCKKRSU	RUCKSACK
ACCHIIRT	RACHITIC	ACCKLORS	CARLOCKS
ACCHIIST	CHIASTIC	ACCKMMRU	CRUMMACK
ACCHILNO	CHALONIC	ACCKMORS	CROMACKS
ACCHILOR	ORICHALC	ACCKOOOT	COCKATOO
ACCHILOT	CATHOLIC	ACCKOPRT	CRACKPOT
ACCHINNO	CINCHONA	ACCKOSSS	CASSOCKS
ACCHINOS	CHICANOS	ACCKOSST	CASTOCKS
ACCHINPU	CAPUCHIN	ACCLLOSU	OCCLUSAL
ACCHIORT	THORACIC	ACCLLSUU	CALCULUS
	TROCHAIC	ACCLSSUU	SACCULUS
ACCHIOSU	ACOUCHIS	ACCMOPST	ACCOMPTS
ACCHIRRT	CARRITCH		COMPACTS
ACCHIRSS	SCRAICHS	ACCMOSTU	ACCUSTOM
ACCHKLOR	CHARLOCK	ACCMRSUU	CURCUMAS
ACCHKOSY	HAYCOCKS	ACCNNOOS	COONCANS
ACCHLOOT	CACHOLOT	ACCNOOPS	COCOPANS
ACCHLSTU	CLAUCHTS	ACCNOOTU	OCCOANUT
ACCHMORS	CASCHROM	ACCNOPTU	OCCUPANT
ACCHNNUY	UNCHANCY	ACCNORTT	CONTRACT
ACCHNOOR	CORONACH	ACCNOSTT	CONTACTS
ACCHNOTU	COUCHANT	ACCNOSTU	ACCOUNTS
ACCHORTU	CARTOUCH	ACCOPSTY	COPYCATS
ACCHOSTW	CHOCTAWS	ACCOQSSU	SQUACCOS
ACCHPSTU	CATCHUPS	ACCORRTY	CARRYCOT
ACCHRRSU	CURRACHS		

ACCORSTU ACCOURTS	FRESCADE	ACDEEOPS PEASECOD	ACDEHLRS CHALDERS
ACDDDEIT ADDICTED	ACDEEFRY FEDERACY	ACDEEORT DECORATE	ACDEHMST SMATCHED
ACDDDETU ADDUCTED	ACDEEGLY DELEGACY	ACDEEOTV EVOCATED	ACDEHNOR ANCHORED
ACDDDKOS DADDOCKS	ACDEEGNR ENGRACED	ACDEEPPR RECAPPED	RONDACHE
ACDDEEES DECEASED	ACDEEHIV ACHIEVED	ACDEEPRS ESCARPED	ACDEHNPU PAUNCHED
ACDDEEHT DETACHED	ACDEEHKO COKEHEAD	ACDEEPRT CARPETED	ACDEHNRU RAUNCHED
ACDDEEIT DEDICATE	ACDEEHLP PLEACHED	ACDEEPST ASPECTED	ACDEHNST SNATCHED
ACDDEEIU DECIDUAE	ACDEEHLT CHELATED	ACDEERRS SCAREDER	STANCHED
ACDDEEKR DACKERED	ACDEEHMR DEMARCHE	ACDEERRT CRATERED	ACDEHNSU UNCASHED
ACDDEELR DECLARED	ACDEEHNN ENHANCED	RETRACED	ACDEHNTU CHAUNTED
ACDDEELS DESCALED	ACDEEHNR ENARCHED	TERRACED	ACDEHORT CHORDATE
ACDDEEMP DECAMPED	ACDEEHNS ENCASHED	ACDEERSS CARESSED	ACDEHORW COWHEARD
ACDDEENR CREDENDA	ENCHASED	ACDEERST CEDRATES	ACDEHOST CATHODES
ACDDEENS ASCENDED	ACDEEHPR PREACHED	ACDEESTU EDUCATES	ACDEHOUV AVOUCHED
ACDDEENT DECADENT	ACDEEHRS SEARCHED	ACDEESUX CAUDEXES	ACDEHPPS SCHAPPED
DECANTED	ACDEEHSS CHASSEED	ACDEESUY CAUSEYED	ACDEHPRS SCARPHED
ACDDEERT REDACTED	ACDEEHST DETACHES	ACDEFFHU CHAUFFED	ACDEHPRU UPCHEARD
ACDDEETU EDUCATED	ACDEEIIP EPICEDIA	ACDEFFLS SCLAFFED	ACDEHPST DESPATCH
ACDDEGIS DISCAGED	ACDEEILT DELICATE	ACDEFFOR AFFORCED	ACDEHPSU CUPHEADS
ACDDEHIK DICKHEAD	ACDEEIMR MEDICARE	ACDEFGIN DEFACING	ACDEHQTU QUATCHED
ACDDEIIL DEICIDAL	ACDEEIMT DECIMATE	ACDEFHLN FLANCHED	ACDEHRST STARCHED
ACDDEIIM MEDICAID	EMICATED	ACDEFIIL DEIFICAL	ACDEHTUW WAUCHTED
ACDDEILU DECIDUAL	MEDICATE	ACDEFIIP PACIFIED	ACDEIILS LAICISED
ACDDEINR CANDIDER	ACDEEINN DECENNIA	ACDEFILN CANFIELD	ACDEIILZ LAICIZED
RIDDANCE	ENNEADIC	ACDEFILR FRICADEL	ACDEIIMU AECIDIUM
ACDDEINT DEDICANT	ACDEEINR DERACINE	ACDEFINN FINANCED	ACDEIINR ACRIDINE
ACDDEINY CYANIDED	ACDEEINU AUDIENCE	ACDEFLOT OLFACTED	ACDEIINS SCIAENID
ACDDEIPS DISPACED	ACDEEINV DEVIANCE	ACDEFNRU FURNACED	ACDEIINT ACTINIDE
ACDDEISS CADDISES	ACDEEIPS DISPEACE	ACDEFORT FACTORED	DIACTINE
DISCASED	ACDEEIRS DECIARES	ACDEFOTU OUTFACED	INDICATE
ACDDEISU DECIDUAS	ACDEEJKT JACKETED	ACDEFRSU SURFACED	ACDEIINU INDUCIAE
ACDDEITT DICTATED	ACDEEKLR LACKERED	ACDEFRTU FURCATED	ACDEIIST ACIDIEST
ACDDEKLO DEADLOCK	ACDEEKLY LACKEYED	ACDEGGRS SCRAGGED	ACDEIITV CAVITIED
ACDDEKOR RADDOCKE	ACDEEKNR CANKERED	ACDEGHLO GALOCHED	VATICIDE
ACDDELOS CLADODES	ACDEEKPR REPACKED	ACDEGHNU CHAUNGED	VICIATED
ACDDELRS CLADDERS	ACDEEKPT PACKETED	GAUNCHED	ACDEIJNU JAUNDICE
ACDDENTU ADDUCENT	ACDEEKRS SCREAKED	ACDEGIIL ALGICIDE	ACDEIKNP PANICKED
ACDDEOPS DECAPODS	ACDEEKRT RACKETED	ACDEGIKM MAGICKED	ACDEIKNT ANTICKED
ACDDEORR CORRADED	ACDEELLR CELLARED	ACDEGIMR DECIGRAM	ACDEILLM MEDALLIC
ACDDEORW COWARDED	RECALLED	GRIMACED	ACDEILLN DECLINAL
ACDDERSU ADDUCERS	ACDEELLS CADELLES	ACDEGINU GUIDANCE	ACDEILLS CEDILLAS
CRUSADED	ACDEELMN ENCALMED	ACDEGINY DECAYING	ACDEILLV CAVILLED
ACDDERTU TRADUCED	ACDEELMP EMPLACED	ACDEGIRS DISGRACE	ACDEILMN MEDCINAL
ACDDGILN CLADDING	ACDEELNR CALENDER	ACDEGISS DISCAGES	ACDEILMO CAMELOID
ACDDGINU ADDUCING	ENCRADLE	ACDEGIST CADGIEST	MELODICA
ACDDGINY CADDYING	ACDEELNS CLEANSED	ACDEGKOS DOCKAGES	ACDEILMS CAMELIDS
ACDDHHSU CHUDDAHS	ACDEELNT LANCETED	ACDEGLOU CLOUDAGE	DECIMALS
ACDDHIIO DIADOCHI	ACDEELNV ENCLAVED	ACDEGNOS DECAGONS	DECLAIMS
ACDDHIMR DIDRACHM	ACDEELPR REPLACED	ACDEGNRU UNGRACED	MEDICALS
ACDDHKOS HADDOCKS	ACDEELRR DECLARER	ACDEGORS CORDAGES	ACDEILMT CLIMATED
SHADDOCK	ACDEELRS DECLARES	ACDEGOTT COTTAGED	MALEDICT
ACDDHORS CHADDORS	RESCALED	ACDEHHIN HAINCHED	ACDEILMX CLIMAXED
ACDDHRSU CHUDDARS	ACDEELRT CLARETED	ACDEHHNU HAUNCHED	ACDEILNP PANICLED
ACDDIIOR CARDIOID	DECRETAL	ACDEHHRU HACHURED	ACDEILOS COALISED
ACDDILNY CANDIDLY	TREACLED	ACDEHHTT THATCHED	ACDEILOZ COALIZED
ACDDILTY DIDACTYL	ACDEELRV CALVERED	ACDEHIIP APHICIDE	ACDEILPR PLACIDER
ACDDINNU UNCANDID	CLAVERED	ACDEHIJK HIJACKED	ACDEILPS DISPLACE
ACDDINSY DISCANDY	ACDEELSS DECLASSE	ACDEHILR HERALDIC	ACDEILPT PLICATED
ACDDIRSS DISCARDS	DESCALES	ACDEHILT DITHECAL	ACDEILRS DECRIALS
ACDDKLNO DOCKLAND	ACDEEMNP ENCAMPED	ACDEHIMN MACHINED	RADICELS
ACDDKMOS MADDOCKS	ACDEEMRS SCREAMED	ACDEHIMS SCHIEDAM	RADICLES
ACDDKOPS PADDOCKS	ACDEEMRT CREMATED	ACDEHINR INARCHED	ACDEILRT ARTICLED
ACDDKORY DOCKYARD	ACDEENNP PENANCED	ACDEHINS ECHIDNAS	ACDEILRU AURICLED
ACDDORTU ADDUCTOR	ACDEENNT TENDANCE	INCHASED	RADICULE
ACDEEEFT DEFECATE	ACDEENNY CAYENNED	ACDEHIRS RACHIDES	ACDEILST CITADELS
ACDEEEKS SEEDCAKE	ACDEENOT ANECDOTE	ACDEHIRT THRIDACE	DIALECTS
ACDEEEMR REEDMACE	ACDEENRS ASCENDER	TRACHEID	ACDEILTT LATTICED
ACDEEENR CAREENED	REASCEND	ACDEHIRV ARCHIVED	ACDEIMNO COMEDIAN
ACDEEENT ANTECEDE	ACDEENRT CANTERED	ACDEHIST SCAITHED	DAEMONIC
ACDEEERR CAREERED	CRENATED	ACDEHISU CHIAUSED	DEMONIAC
ACDEEERS DECREASE	DECANTER	ACDEHKLO HEADLOCK	ACDEIMNP PANDEMIC
ACDEEESS DECEASES	NECTARED	ACDEHKLS SHACKLED	ACDEIMPT IMPACTED
SEEDCASE	RECANTED	ACDEHKNU UNHACKED	ACDEIMRT DERMATIC
ACDEEFFT AFFECTED	ACDEENRV CAVERNED	ACDEHKOV HAVOCKED	TIMECARD
ACDEEFHN ENCHAFED	CRAVENED	ACDEHKRU ARCHDUKE	ACDEINNR CRANNIED
ACDEEFIL CALEFIED	ACDEENRY CARNEYED	ACDEHKTW THWACKED	ACDEINOP CANOPIED
ACDEEFIN DEFIANCE	ACDEENRZ CREDENZA	ACDEHLNP PLANCHED	ACDEINOS DIOCESAN
ACDEEFPR PREFACED	ACDEENSV VENDACES	ACDEHLNR CHANDLER	OCEANIDS
ACDEEFRS DEFACERS	ACDEENTT DANCETTE	ACDEHLNU LAUNCHED	ACDEINOT ACTIONED

ACDEINOV VOIDANCE	ENDOSARC	CHLORDAN	ACDIRSST DRASTICS
ACDEINPT PEDANTIC	ACDENORT CARTONED	CHONDRAL	ACDIRSTT DISTRACT
PENTADIC	ACDENORY CRAYONED	ACDHLORS DORLACHS	ACDISTUV VIADUCTS
ACDEINRR RANCIDER	DEACONRY	ACDHMORU MOUCHARD	ACDJNSTU ADJUNCTS
ACDEINRT CRINATED	ACDENOSY CYANOSED	ACDHNORW CHAWDRON	ACDKLOPS PADLOCKS
DICENTRA	ACDENOTU OUTDANCE	ACDHNOSW COWHANDS	ACDKMMOR DRAMMOCK
ACDEINSS ACIDNESS	UNCOATED	ACDHOOST CATHOODS	ACDKMPSU MUDPACKS
ACDEINST DISTANCE	ACDENPPU UNCAPPED	ACDHOOTW WOODCHAT	ACDKOPRS POCKARDS
ACDEINSY CYANIDES	ACDENPRU PRAUNCED	ACDHOPRS POCHARDS	ACDLLORS COLLARDS
CYANISED	ACDENPST PANDECTS	ACDHORRS ORCHARDS	ACDLNNOR CORNLAND
ACDEINTT NICTATED	ACDENRST CANTREDS	ACDHORSY DYSCHROA	ACDLNOPR CROPLAND
ACDEINVY DEVIANCY	ACDENRSU DURANCES	ACDIIILN INDICIAL	ACDLNORS CALDRONS
ACDEINYZ CYANIZED	ACDENRTU UNCARTED	ACDIIIPR DIAPIRIC	ACDLNORU CAULDRON
ACDEIOPS DIASCOPE	UNCRATED	ACDIIJLU JUDICIAL	ACDLNORY CONDYLAR
ACDEIORS IDOCRASE	UNDERACT	ACDIILMS DISCLAIM	ACDLNOST COTLANDS
ACDEIORT CERATOID	UNTRACED	ACDIILNO CONIDIAL	ACDLOORT DOCTORAL
ACDEIORV COVARIED	ACDENRVY VERDANCY	ACDIILNS SCALDINI	ACDLORWY COWARDLY
ACDEIOSS ACIDOSES	ACDENSST DESCANTS	ACDIILSU SUICIDAL	ACDLOSWY LADYCOWS
ACDEIOSU EDACIOUS	ACDENSUU UNCAUSED	ACDIILTY CALIDITY	ACDMMNOO COMMANDO
ACDEIPPT TAPPICED	ACDENTTY DANCETTY	DIALYTIC	ACDMMNOS COMMANDS
ACDEIPRS EPACRIDS	ACDEOPRU CROUPADE	ACDIIMNO DAIMONIC	ACDMNOPS COMPANDS
ACDEIPSS DISPACES	ACDEOPRY COPYREAD	ACDIIMOR CORMIDIA	ACDMNORY DORMANCY
SPADICES	ACDEOPSS PEASCODS	DIORAMIC	MORDANCY
ACDEIPST SPICATED	ACDEOPTT CAPOTTED	ACDIIMOT DIATOMIC	ACDMOOPR MACROPOD
ACDEIPSZ CAPSIZED	ACDEOPTU OUTPACED	ACDIIMSU ASCIDIUM	ACDMOOSW CAMWOODS
ACDEIPTV CAPTIVED	ACDEORRS CORRADES	ACDIINNS INDICANS	ACDMORSZ CZARDOMS
ACDEIQRU ACQUIRED	ACDEORRT REDACTOR	ACDIINNT INDICANT	ACDNOORR RONCADOR
ACDEIRSS SIDECARS	ACDEORSS SARCODES	ACDIINOP PINACOID	ACDNOORS CARDOONS
ACDEIRST ACRIDEST	ACDEORST REDCOATS	ACDIINOT ACTINOID	ACDNOORV CORDOVAN
ACDEIRSU DECURIAS	ACDEORSU CAROUSED	DIATONIC	ACDNOOTU DUCATOON
ACDEIRTT TETRACID	ACDEORTU EDUCATOR	ACDIINPY PYCNIDIA	ACDNORRW WARDCORN
TETRADIC	OUTRACED	ACDIINRS ACRIDINS	ACDNORSU CANDOURS
ACDEISSS DISCASES	ACDEORTV CAVORTED	ACDIIOSS ACIDOSIS	CAUDRONS
ACDEISTT DICTATES	ACDEOSTT CODETTAS	ACDIIRSS SCIARIDS	ACDNOSTW DOWNCAST
ACDEKLNR CRANKLED	COSTATED	ACDIIRST ARCTIIDS	ACDNOSUU ADUNCOUS
ACDEKLQU QUACKLED	ACDEOSUV COUVADES	CARDITIS	ACDOOPPR PODOCARP
ACDEKNPR PRANCKED	ACDEPPRS SCRAPPED	ACDIIRTY ACRIDITY	ACDOOPTY OCTAPODY
ACDEKNPU UNPACKED	ACDEPRTU CAPTURED	ACDIISST SADISTIC	ACDOORST OSTRACOD
ACDEKNRU UNRACKED	ACDEQTUU AQUEDUCT	ACDIKMOO COOKMAID	SCORDATO
ACDEKNTU UNTACKED	ACDERRSU CRUSADER	ACDIKRRY RICKYARD	ACDOPRST POSTCARD
ACDEKOST STOCKADE	ACDERRTU TRADUCER	ACDILLOS CODILLAS	ACDORRWY COWARDRY
ACDELLNU UNCALLED	ACDERSSU CRUSADES	ACDILLOU CAUDILLO	ACDORSST COSTARDS
ACDELLOR CAROLLED	ACDERSTT DETRACTS	LODICULA	ACDORSSU CRUSADOS
COLLARED	SCRATTED	ACDILLPY PLACIDLY	ACDORSUZ CRUZADOS
ACDELLOT COLLATED	ACDERSTU TRADUCES	ACDILMOR DROMICAL	ACDRSSTU CUSTARDS
ACDELMOR CLAMORED	ACDERTUV CURVATED	ACDILMSS CLADISMS	ACDRSTTU DUSTCART
ACDELMSU MUSCADEL	ACDFFHNU HANDCUFF	ACDILNOO CONOIDAL	ACEEEFRR CAREFREE
ACDELNOO CANOODLE	ACDFFIRT DIFFRACT	ACDILNOS SCALDINO	ACEEEGLN ELEGANCE
ACDELNOR COLANDER	ACDFFLOS SCAFFOLD	ACDILNSU DULCIANS	ACEEEGRS CARGEESE
ACDELNOS CELADONS	ACDFIILU FIDUCIAL	ACDILNSY SYNDICAL	ACEEEIPR EARPIECE
ACDELNPU UNPLACED	ACDFILOU FUCOIDAL	ACDILNUU NUDICAUL	ACEEEKNT NECKATEE
ACDELNRY CALENDRY	ACDFIOST FACTOIDS	ACDILOPY POLYACID	ACEEELMR CAMELEER
ACDELNST SCANTLED	ACDGHOTW WATCHDOG	ACDILORS CORDIALS	ACEEENRS ENCREASE
ACDELNSU UNSCALED	ACDGIILO DIALOGIC	ACDILOUV OVIDUCAL	ACEEENSV EVANESCE
ACDELOPT CLODPATE	ACDGILNN CANDLING	ACDILPSU CUSPIDAL	ACEEEPSS ESCAPEES
ACDELOPU CUPOLAED	ACDGILNR CRADLING	ACDILSST CLADISTS	ACEEERRT RECREATE
ACDELORV OVERCLAD	ACDGILNS SCALDING	ACDILSTW WILDCATS	ACEEERTT ETCETERA
ACDELOTU OCULATED	ACDGILNU CAUDLING	ACDIMMSU CADMIUMS	ACEEERTX EXECRATE
ACDELPPS SCAPPLED	ACDGIMOT DOGMATIC	ACDIMNOO MONOACID	ACEEESUV EVACUEES
ACDELRSS SCALDERS	ACDGINNS DANCINGS	ACDIMNOS MANDIOCS	ACEEFFIN CAFFEINE
ACDELRSW SCRAWLED	ACDGINNY CANDYING	ACDIMNSU MUSCADIN	ACEEFFRT AFFECTER
ACDELRSY SACREDLY	ACDGINSU SCAUDING	SCANDIUM	ACEEFHNS ENCHAFES
ACDELSTU CAULDEST	ACDGIOPR PODAGRIC	ACDIMNSY DYNAMICS	ACEEFILM MALEFICE
SULCATED	ACDGKLOS DAGLOCKS	ACDIMOSY DOCIMASY	ACEEFILS CALEFIES
ACDEMMRS SCRAMMED	ACDGNOST CANTDOGS	ACDINOPS SPONDAIC	ACEEFINS FAIENCES
ACDEMNOR ROMANCED	ACDGORST DOGCARTS	ACDINORS SARDONIC	FIANCEES
ACDEMNSU DECUMANS	ACDHIILS CHILIADS	ACDINORT TORNADIC	ACEEFKOR ECOFREAK
ACDEMOPR COMPADRE	ACDHIINT TACHINID	ACDINORW CORDWAIN	ACEEFLPU PEACEFUL
COMPARED	ACDHIKOR CHOKIDAR	ACDINSST DISCANTS	ACEEFLSS FACELESS
ACDEMORS COMRADES	ACDHILPR PILCHARD	ACDINSTY DYNASTIC	ACEEFNSY FAYENCES
ACDEMORT DEMOCRAT	ACDHILPS CLAPDISH	ACDINTUY ADUNCITY	ACEEFPRS PREFACES
ACDEMRSW SCRAWMED	ACDHINOR HADRONIC	ACDIOPRS PICADORS	ACEEFPRT PERFECTA
ACDEMUUV VACUUMED	RHODANIC	SPORADIC	PRAEFECT
ACDENNNO CANNONED	ACDHINRY DINARCHY	ACDIORRS CORRIDAS	ACEEFRSU FARCEUSE
ACDENNOR ORDNANCE	ACDHINSW SANDWICH	ACDIORSS SARCOIDS	ACEEGHNR ENCHARGE
ACDENNOT CANTONED	ACDHIOPS SCAPHOID	ACDIORTT DICTATOR	ACEEGHNX EXCHANGE
ACDENNST SCANDENT	ACDHIORY HYRACOID	ACDIOSTY DYSTOCIA	ACEEGHRR RECHARGE
ACDENOPR ENDOCARP	ACDHIPST DISPATCH	ACDIPRST ADSCRIPT	ACEEGILS ELEGIACS
ACDENORS DRACONES	ACDHLNOR CHALDRON	ACDIQRSU QUADRICS	LEGACIES

ACEEGINS	AGENCIES
ACEEGKNR	NECKGEAR
ACEEGKRW	WRECKAGE
ACEEGLNY	ELEGANCY
ACEEGLPU	PUCELAGE
ACEEGNOZ	COZENAGE
ACEEGNRS	ENGRACES
ACEEGNRY	REAGENCY
ACEEGNST	CENTAGES
ACEEGNSV	SCAVENGE
ACEEGORR	RACEGOER
ACEEGORV	COVERAGE
ACEEGSSU	ESCUAGES
ACEEHHST	CHEETAHS
ACEEHILR	LEACHIER
ACEEHINT	ECHINATE
ACEEHIPR	PEACHIER
ACEEHIPS	CHEAPIES
ACEEHIPT	PETECHIA
ACEEHIRV	ACHIEVER
	CHIVAREE
ACEEHIST	HICATEES
ACEEHISV	ACHIEVES
ACEEHITV	ATCHIEVE
ACEEHKNS	SKEECHAN
ACEEHKTT	HACKETTE
ACEEHLMP	EMPLEACH
ACEEHLOS	SHOELACE
ACEEHLPS	PLEACHES
ACEEHLRS	RELACHES
ACEEHLSS	LACHESES
ACEEHLST	CHELATES
ACEEHLSW	ESCHEWAL
ACEEHLTV	CHEVALET
ACEEHMNP	CAMPHENE
ACEEHMNR	MENARCHE
ACEEHMRS	CASHMERE
	MACHREES
	MARCHESE
ACEEHMST	MACHETES
ACEEHNNR	ENHANCER
ACEEHNNS	ENHANCES
ACEEHNPS	CHEAPENS
ACEEHNRS	ENARCHES
ACEEHNRV	REVANCHE
ACEEHNSS	ENCASHES
	ENCHASES
ACEEHORT	OCHREATE
ACEEHPPS	ECHAPPES
ACEEHPRR	PREACHER
ACEEHPRS	PEACHERS
	PREACHES
ACEEHPRT	ETHERCAP
ACEEHPST	CHEAPEST
ACEEHQSU	QUEACHES
ACEEHRRS	REACHERS
	RESEARCH
	SEARCHER
ACEEHRRT	TREACHER
ACEEHRSS	SEARCHES
ACEEHRST	CHEATERS
	HECTARES
	RECHATES
	RECHEATS
	TEACHERS
ACEEHRTT	CATHETER
ACEEHRTY	CHEATERY
ACEEHSST	ESCHEATS
ACEEHSTX	CATHEXES
	EXCHEATS
ACEEIKNP	PEACENIK
ACEEIKRR	CREAKIER
ACEEILLM	MICELLAE
ACEEILMN	CAMELINE
ACEEILMT	EMETICAL
ACEEILNP	CAPELINE
ACEEILNR	CINEREAL
	RELIANCE
ACEEILNS	SALIENCE

ACEEILPS	CALIPEES
	ESPECIAL
ACEEILRS	ESCALIER
ACEEILRV	RECEIVAL
ACEEIMOT	ACOEMETI
ACEEIMRR	CREAMIER
	REARMICE
ACEEIMRS	CASIMERE
	RACEMISE
ACEEIMRT	CEMITARE
ACEEIMRZ	RACEMIZE
ACEEIMST	EMICATES
ACEEINNR	NARCEINE
ACEEINPS	SAPIENCE
ACEEINPT	PATIENCE
ACEEINRT	CINEREAS
	INCREASE
	RESIANCE
ACEEINRT	CENTIARE
	CREATINE
	INCREATE
	ITERANCE
ACEEINST	CINEASTE
ACEEINSU	EUCAINES
ACEEINTV	ENACTIVE
ACEEINTX	EXITANCE
ACEEIPST	SPECIATE
ACEEIRRS	CARIERES
	CREASIER
ACEEIRSU	CAUSERIE
ACEEIRSW	WISEACRE
ACEEIRTV	CREATIVE
	REACTIVE
ACEEISTV	VESICATE
ACEEJKNS	JACKEENS
ACEEKLMR	MACKEREL
ACEEKLRW	EELWRACK
ACEEKMPT	EMPACKET
ACEEKNPS	KNEECAPS
ACEEKNRW	NECKWEAR
ACEEKRRT	RACKETER
ACEELLNS	NACELLES
ACEELLNT	LANCELET
ACEELLOT	OCELLATE
ACEELLPT	CAPELLET
ACEELLRR	CELLARER
ACEELLRT	CELLARET
ACEELMNO	CAMELEON
ACEELMNP	PLACEMEN
ACEELMPS	EMPLACES
ACEELMRS	RECLAMES
	SCLEREMA
ACEELNPT	PENTACLE
ACEELNRR	LARCENER
ACEELNRS	CLEANERS
	CLEANSER
ACEELNRU	CERULEAN
ACEELNSS	CLEANSES
ACEELNST	CLEANEST
	LATENCES
ACEELNSU	NUCLEASE
ACEELNSV	ENCLAVES
	VALENCES
ACEELNTT	TENTACLE
ACEELNTU	NUCLEATE
ACEELOPS	ESCALOPE
ACEELORS	ESCAROLE
ACEELORT	RELOCATE
ACEELOSV	VOCALESE
ACEELPRR	REPLACER
ACEELPRS	PERCALES
	REPLACES
ACEELPST	CAPELETS
ACEELPSY	CYPSELAE
ACEELPTU	PECULATE
ACEELPTY	CLYPEATE
ACEELRRS	CLEARERS
ACEELRSS	CARELESS
	RESCALES

ACEELRST	CLEAREST
	SCELERAT
	TREACLES
ACEELRSV	CLEAVERS
ACEELRTT	RACLETTE
ACEELRTU	ULCERATE
ACEELRTV	CERVELAT
ACEELRTX	EXCRETAL
ACEELSST	CELESTAS
ACEELSSU	EUCLASES
ACEELSTT	TELECAST
ACEELSVX	EXCLAVES
ACEEMNNS	SCENEMAN
ACEEMNOT	MECONATE
ACEEMNPS	SPACEMEN
ACEEMNRS	MENACERS
ACEEMNST	CASEMENT
ACEEMOPR	CAMPOREE
ACEEMOPT	COPEMATE
ACEEMORS	RACEMOSE
ACEEMORV	OVERCAME
ACEEMRRS	CREAMERS
	SCREAMER
ACEEMRRY	CREAMERY
ACEEMRST	CREMATES
	MEERCATS
ACEENNPS	PENANCES
ACEENNRS	NARCEENS
ACEENNRT	ENTRANCE
ACEENNST	CANTEENS
ACEENNSY	CAYENNES
ACEENORT	CAROTENE
ACEENOST	ACETONES
	NOTECASE
ACEENPRR	PARCENER
ACEENPRT	PERCEANT
ACEENRRT	RECANTER
	RECREANT
ACEENRSS	CASERNES
ACEENRST	CENTARES
	REASCENT
	SARCENET
ACEENRTU	ENACTURE
	UNCREATE
ACEEORST	CREASOTE
ACEEOSTT	ECOSTATE
ACEEOSTV	EVOCATES
ACEEPPRS	CAPERERS
ACEEPRSS	ESCAPERS
ACEEPRTT	ETTERCAP
ACEEPRTU	PERACUTE
ACEEPRTX	EXCERPTA
ACEEPSSU	AUCEPSES
ACEEPSST	SPECTATE
ACEERRSS	CREASERS
ACEERRST	CATERERS
	RETRACES
	TERRACES
ACEERRSU	ECRASEUR
ACEERRTU	CREATURE
ACEERRUV	VERRUCAE
ACEERSSS	CARESSES
ACEERSST	CATERESS
	CERASTES
ACEERSSU	SURCEASE
ACEERSSV	CREVASSE
ACEERSTX	EXACTERS
ACEERTTU	ERUCTATE
ACEESSST	ECSTASES
ACEESSTT	CASSETTE
ACEESTTX	EXACTEST
ACEFFGIN	EFFACING
ACEFFHIR	CHAFFIER
ACEFFHIS	AFFICHES
ACEFFHRS	CHAFFERS
ACEFFHRU	CHAUFFER
ACEFFHRY	CHAFFERY
ACEFFIMS	CAFFEISM
ACEFFINS	CAFFEINS

ACEFFISS	SCAFFIES
ACEFFORS	AFFORCES
ACEFGINN	ENFACING
ACEFGINR	REFACING
ACEFGINT	FACETING
ACEFGLRU	GRACEFUL
ACEFGOST	GEOFACTS
ACEFHLNS	FLANCHES
ACEFHMRS	CHAMFERS
ACEFHORU	FAROUCHE
ACEFHRST	FRATCHES
ACEFHRSU	CHAUFERS
ACEFIILS	FELICIAS
ACEFIIPR	PACIFIER
ACEFIIPS	PACIFIES
ACEFIIRT	ARTIFICE
ACEFILLY	FACILELY
ACEFILOP	EPIFOCAL
ACEFILOS	FASCIOLE
	FOCALISE
ACEFILOZ	FOCALIZE
ACEFILRS	FILACERS
ACEFIMPR	CAMPFIRE
ACEFINNS	FINANCES
ACEFINRS	FANCIERS
ACEFINRX	CARNIFEX
ACEFINSS	FASCINES
ACEFINST	FANCIEST
ACEFIOSS	FIASCOES
ACEFIRRT	CRAFTIER
ACEFIRTT	TRIFECTA
ACEFIRTY	FERACITY
ACEFISST	FACTISES
ACEFKLRS	FLACKERS
ACEFKLST	FLACKEST
ACEFLLSS	CALFLESS
ACEFLMNO	FLAMENCO
ACEFLNOR	FALCONER
ACEFLNOT	CONFLATE
	FALCONET
ACEFLNRY	CRANEFLY
ACEFLORS	ALFRESCO
ACEFLRTU	FULCRATE
ACEFLRUU	FURCULAE
ACEFMNOO	MOONFACE
ACEFNNOS	FACONNES
ACEFNORV	CONFERVA
ACEFNPRT	PENCRAFT
ACEFNRST	CANTREFS
ACEFNRSU	FURNACES
ACEFOOPT	FOOTPACE
ACEFOPST	POSTFACE
ACEFORRS	FORECARS
ACEFORST	FORECAST
ACEFORSX	CARFOXES
ACEFOSTU	OUTFACES
ACEFRRST	REFRACTS
ACEFRRSU	FARCEURS
	SURFACER
ACEFRRTU	FRACTURE
ACEFRSSU	SURFACES
ACEFRSTU	FACTURES
ACEGGILN	CAGELING
	GLACEING
ACEGGILR	CLAGGIER
ACEGGINN	ENCAGING
ACEGGIOP	EPAGOGIC
ACEGGIRR	CRAGGIER
ACEGHILN	LEACHING
ACEGHILT	LICHGATE
ACEGHINP	PEACHING
ACEGHINR	REACHING
ACEGHINT	CHEATING
	TEACHING
ACEGHLOS	GALOCHES
ACEGHLRS	SCHLAGER
ACEGHLRU	RUGELACH
ACEGHLTY	LYCHGATE
ACEGHMMU	CHUMMAGE

ACEGHMOR	ECHOGRAM
	GRAMOCHE
ACEGHNRS	CHANGERS
ACEGHNSU	CHAUNGES
	GAUNCHES
ACEGHOSU	GOUACHES
ACEGHOSW	COWHAGES
ACEGHRRS	CHARGERS
ACEGHRTU	RECAUGHT
ACEGHSTU	GAUCHEST
ACEGIIMP	EPIGAMIC
ACEGIINV	VICINAGE
ACEGIKNR	CREAKING
ACEGILLO	COLLEGIA
ACEGILLR	ALLERGIC
ACEGILMU	MUCILAGE
ACEGILNN	CLEANING
	ELANCING
	ENLACING
ACEGILNR	CLEARING
ACEGILNT	CLEATING
ACEGILNV	CLEAVING
ACEGILNW	LACEWING
ACEGILOS	CALIGOES
ACEGILRS	GLACIERS
ACEGILRV	CLAVIGER
ACEGILRY	GLYCERIA
ACEGILSS	GLACISES
ACEGILST	GELASTIC
ACEGIMMT	TAGMEMIC
ACEGIMMN	MENACING
ACEGIMNR	AMERCING
	CREAMING
ACEGIMNT	MAGNETIC
ACEGIMOS	CAMOGIES
ACEGIMOX	EXOGAMIC
ACEGIMRS	GRIMACES
ACEGIMTY	MEGACITY
ACEGINNO	CANOEING
ACEGINNR	ENRACING
ACEGINNS	ENCASING
ACEGINNT	ENACTING
ACEGINNV	ENCAVING
ACEGINOS	COINAGES
ACEGINOY	GYNOECIA
ACEGINPR	CAPERING
	PEARCING
	PREACING
ACEGINPS	ESCAPING
ACEGINRS	CREASING
	GRECIANS
	SEARCING
ACEGINRT	CATERING
	CITRANGE
	CREATING
	REACTING
ACEGINSS	CAGINESS
	CEASINGS
ACEGINTX	EXACTING
ACEGIOTT	COGITATE
ACEGIPRS	SPAGERIC
ACEGIRST	AGRESTIC
ACEGISTU	GAUCIEST
ACEGISTW	GAWCIEST
ACEGKLOS	LOCKAGES
ACEGKLOV	GAVELOCK
ACEGKLRS	GRACKLES
ACEGKMOS	MOCKAGES
ACEGKORS	CORKAGES
ACEGKORW	CAGEWORK
ACEGKRTU	TRUCKAGE
ACEGLLNO	COLLAGEN
ACEGLLOS	COLLAGES
ACEGLNOS	CONGEALS
ACEGLNRS	CLANGERS
ACEGLOST	CATELOGS
ACEGLOSU	CAGOULES
ACEGMNOY	GEOMANCY

ACEGMNRS	CRAGSMEN
ACEGMOPS	COMPAGES
ACEGMORS	SCARMOGE
ACEGMRRY	GRAMERCY
ACEGNNOY	CYANOGEN
ACEGNNTY	TANGENCY
ACEGNORS	ACROGENS
	CORNAGES
ACEGNOST	COGNATES
ACEGNSSY	CAGYNESS
ACEGOORS	CARGOOSE
ACEGOPRY	GEOCARPY
ACEGORSS	CORSAGES
	SOCAGERS
ACEGORST	ESCARGOT
ACEGORSU	COURAGES
ACEGORTT	COTTAGER
ACEGORTY	CATEGORY
ACEGOSTT	COTTAGES
ACEGOTTY	COTTAGEY
ACEGRSTU	TRUCAGES
ACEGSSTU	SCUTAGES
ACEHHINS	HAINCHES
ACEHHIRR	HIERARCH
ACEHHIST	SHECHITA
ACEHHLST	HATCHELS
ACEHHLSU	SHAUCHLE
ACEHHMNN	HENCHMAN
ACEHHNRT	ETHNARCH
ACEHHNSU	HAUNCHES
ACEHHPRT	HEPTARCH
ACEHHRST	HATCHERS
ACEHHRSU	HACHURES
ACEHHRTT	THATCHER
ACEHHRTY	HATCHERY
	THEARCHY
ACEHHSTT	HATCHETS
	THATCHES
ACEHHTTY	HATCHETY
ACEHIIMS	ISCHEMIA
ACEHIIRT	HIERATIC
ACEHIJKR	HIJACKER
ACEHIKLP	KEPHALIC
ACEHIKLR	CHALKIER
	HACKLIER
ACEHIKLW	LICHWAKE
ACEHIKRS	KACHERIS
ACEHIKRW	WHACKIER
ACEHILLS	CHALLIES
ACEHILLT	HELLICAT
ACEHILMN	INCHMEAL
ACEHILMO	CHOLEMIA
ACEHILMP	IMPLEACH
ACEHILMS	CAMELISH
ACEHILNP	CEPHALIN
ACEHILNT	CHAINLET
	CHATLINE
	ETHNICAL
ACEHILOR	HALICORE
	HEROICAL
ACEHILPR	PARHELIC
ACEHILRS	CHARLIES
ACEHILST	ETHICALS
ACEHILTT	ATHLETIC
	THETICAL
ACEHIMMS	CHAMMIES
ACEHIMNN	CHAINMEN
ACEHIMNP	CAMPHINE
ACEHIMNR	CHAIRMEN
ACEHIMNS	MACHINES
ACEHIMNT	ANTHEMIC
ACEHIMNU	ACHENIUM
ACEHIMPR	CAMPHIRE
ACEHIMPT	EMPATHIC
	EMPHATIC
ACEHIMRS	CHASMIER
	CHIMERAS
	MARCHESI
ACEHIMRT	RHEMATIC

ACEHIMSS	CHAMISES
ACEHIMST	MISTEACH
	TACHISME
ACEHIMTT	THEMATIC
ACEHINNS	ENCHAINS
ACEHINOT	INCHOATE
ACEHINRS	INARCHES
ACEHINRV	VACHERIN
ACEHINSS	INCHASES
ACEHINST	ASTHENIC
	CHANTIES
ACEHINSY	HYACINES
	SYNECHIA
ACEHIOPR	POACHIER
ACEHIOST	TOISEACH
ACEHIPPR	CHAPPIER
ACEHIPPS	CHAPPIES
ACEHIPRS	ASPHERIC
	CHARPIES
	PARCHESI
	SERAPHIC
ACEHIPRT	CHAPITER
	PATCHIER
	PHREATIC
ACEHIPST	HEPATICS
	PASTICHE
ACEHIPTT	PATHETIC
ACEHIPTW	WHITECAP
ACEHIRRR	CHARRIER
ACEHIRRS	CASHIERS
	RACHISES
ACEHIRST	CHARIEST
	STICHERA
	THERIACS
ACEHIRSU	EUCHARIS
ACEHIRSV	ARCHIVES
ACEHIRSW	ARCHWISE
ACEHIRTT	CHATTIER
	THEATRIC
ACEHISST	CHASTISE
	TAISCHES
ACEHISSU	CHIAUSES
ACEHISTT	CHATTIES
	TACHISTE
ACEHISTX	CATHEXIS
ACEHISTY	YACHTIES
ACEHISTZ	ZAITECHS
ACEHKLOV	HAVELOCK
ACEHKLPR	KREPLACH
ACEHKLRS	HACKLERS
ACEHKLSS	SHACKLES
ACEHKLST	HACKLETS
	KLATCHES
ACEHKLTY	LATCHKEY
ACEHKMPU	MUCKHEAP
ACEHKNSY	HACKNEYS
ACEHKOSS	SHACKOES
ACEHKOSW	WHACKOES
ACEHKOTU	TUCKAHOE
ACEHKRSW	WHACKERS
ACEHKRTW	THWACKER
ACEHLLMO	MALLECHO
ACEHLLOR	ORCHELLA
ACEHLLPS	PELLACHS
ACEHLLSS	SHELLACS
ACEHLLSU	HALLUCES
ACEHLMOT	CHAMELOT
ACEHLMST	CHAMLETS
ACEHLNNS	CHANNELS
ACEHLNOS	CHALONES
ACEHLNOU	EULACHON
ACEHLNPS	PLANCHES
ACEHLNPT	PLANCHET
ACEHLNRS	CHARNELS
ACEHLNRU	LAUNCHER
	RELAUNCH
ACEHLNST	STANCHEL
ACEHLNSU	LAUNCHES
ACEHLORS	CHOLERAS

	CHORALES
ACEHLORT	CHELATOR
	CHLORATE
	TROCHLEA
ACEHLORU	LEACHOUR
ACEHLOST	CATHOLES
	ESCHALOT
ACEHLPRT	CHAPTREL
ACEHLPRY	CHAPELRY
ACEHLPSS	CHAPLESS
ACEHLPST	CHAPLETS
ACEHLRSS	CLASHERS
	RASCHELS
ACEHLRST	ARCHLETS
ACEHLRSY	CHARLEYS
ACEHLRTU	ARCHLUTE
	TRAUCHLE
ACEHLSSS	CASHLESS
ACEHLSST	SATCHELS
	SLATCHES
ACEHLSTT	CHATTELS
	LATCHETS
ACEHLSTY	CHASTELY
ACEHMMNR	MARCHMEN
ACEHMNNR	RANCHMEN
ACEHMNRS	ENCHARMS
ACEHMNRT	MERCHANT
ACEHMNSS	CHESSMAN
ACEHMNST	MANCHETS
ACEHMNTW	WATCHMEN
ACEHMORT	CHROMATE
ACEHMPRS	CHAMPERS
ACEHMRRS	CHARMERS
	MARCHERS
ACEHMRST	MATCHERS
ACEHMRSU	CHAUMERS
ACEHMSST	SMATCHES
ACEHMSTU	MUSTACHE
ACEHMSTY	ECTHYMAS
ACEHNNOP	PANCHEON
ACEHNNPT	PENCHANT
ACEHNNRS	CHANNERS
ACEHNNST	ENCHANTS
ACEHNOPR	CANEPHOR
	CHAPERON
ACEHNOPT	CENOTAPH
ACEHNORR	RANCHERO
ACEHNORT	ANCHORET
ACEHNPRT	PENTARCH
ACEHNPRU	UNPREACH
ACEHNPSU	PAUNCHES
ACEHNRRS	RANCHERS
ACEHNRSS	ARCHNESS
ACEHNRST	CHANTERS
	SNATCHER
	STANCHER
	TRANCHES
ACEHNRSU	RAUNCHES
ACEHNRTT	TRANCHET
ACEHNRTU	CHAUNTER
ACEHNSSS	SCHANSES
ACEHNSST	CHASTENS
	SNATCHES
	STANCHES
ACEHNSSZ	SCHANZES
ACEHNSTT	ETCHANTS
ACEHNSTU	NAUTCHES
	UNCHASTE
ACEHNSTY	CHANTEYS
ACEHNSTZ	SCHANTZE
ACEHOPRR	REPROACH
ACEHOPRS	POACHERS
ACEHORRS	HORSECAR
ACEHORRV	OVERARCH
ACEHORST	CHAROSET
	THORACES
ACEHORTT	THEOCRAT
ACEHORTU	OUTREACH
ACEHOSSW	SHOWCASE

ACEHOSTU	CATHOUSE
	SOUTACHE
ACEHOSTY	CHAYOTES
ACEHOSUV	AVOUCHES
ACEHPPSS	CHAPPESS
	SCHAPPES
ACEHPRST	CHAPTERS
	PATCHERS
ACEHPRSU	PURCHASE
ACEHPRTY	PATCHERY
	PETCHARY
ACEHQSTU	QUATCHES
ACEHRRST	CHARTERS
	RECHARTS
	STARCHER
ACEHRRTT	TETRARCH
ACEHRSST	STARCHES
ACEHRSSU	CHASSEUR
ACEHRSTT	CHATTERS
	RATCHETS
ACEHRSTW	WATCHERS
ACEHRSTY	YACHTERS
ACEHRTTY	TRACHYTE
ACEHSSSU	CHAUSSES
ACEHSSTT	CHASTEST
ACEHSSTW	SWATCHES
ACEHSTTU	CATHETUS
	TEUCHATS
ACEHSTTW	WATCHETS
ACEHTTUZ	ZUCHETTA
ACEIILMN	LIMACINE
ACEIILNR	IRENICAL
ACEIILNS	SALICINE
ACEIILSS	LAICISES
ACEIILST	CILIATES
	SILICATE
ACEIILSZ	LAICIZES
ACEIIMRV	VIRAEMIC
ACEIIMSS	ASEISMIC
ACEIIMTU	MAIEUTIC
ACEIINPS	PISCINAE
ACEIINRS	RIANCIES
ACEIINST	CANITIES
ACEIINTV	INACTIVE
ACEIINTZ	ANTICIZE
ACEIIPRS	PIRACIES
ACEIIRRT	CRITERIA
ACEIIRSV	VICARIES
ACEIISTU	ACUITIES
ACEIISTV	CAITIVES
	CAVITIES
	VICIATES
ACEIITTV	VITICETA
ACEIJKSS	JACKSIES
ACEIJMST	MAJESTIC
ACEIJNRR	JERRICAN
ACEIKKNR	KNACKIER
ACEIKLRT	TALCKIER
ACEIKLRY	CREAKILY
ACEIKMNN	NICKNAME
ACEIKMRS	KERAMICS
ACEIKMRV	MAVERICK
ACEIKNPS	CAPESKIN
ACEIKNRR	CRANKIER
ACEIKNRS	SKINCARE
ACEIKOPS	PAIOCKES
ACEIKORR	CROAKIER
ACEIKPRS	EARPICKS
ACEIKPSX	PICKAXES
ACEIKRRV	VRAICKER
ACEIKSTT	TACKIEST
	TIETACKS
ACEIKSTW	WACKIEST
ACEILLLT	CLITELLA
ACEILLMR	MICELLAR
	MILLRACE
ACEILLMS	LIMACELS
ACEILLMT	METALLIC
ACEILLMY	MYCELIAL
ACEILLNT	CLIENTAL
ACEILLOP	CALLIOPE
ACEILLOR	ROCAILLE
ACEILLOS	LOCALISE
ACEILLOT	TEOCALLI
ACEILLOZ	LOCALIZE
ACEILLPR	CALLIPER
ACEILLPS	ALLSPICE
ACEILLPY	EPICALLY
ACEILLRV	CAVILLER
ACEILLSS	SCALLIES
ACEILMMO	CAMOMILE
ACEILMMR	CLAMMIER
ACEILMNN	CLINAMEN
ACEILMNO	COALMINE
ACEILMNP	MANCIPLE
ACEILMNS	MESCALIN
ACEILMOS	CAMISOLE
ACEILMPS	MISPLACE
ACEILMPT	PELMATIC
ACEILMRS	CLAIMERS
	MIRACLES
	RECLAIMS
ACEILMRT	METRICAL
ACEILMST	CALMIEST
	CLEMATIS
	CLIMATES
	METICALS
ACEILMSU	MUSICALE
ACEILMSX	CLIMAXES
	EXCLAIMS
ACEILMTU	AMULETIC
ACEILNNP	PANNICLE
	PINNACLE
ACEILNNR	ENCRINAL
ACEILNOR	ACROLEIN
	CREOLIAN
	LONICERA
ACEILNPS	CAPELINS
	PANICLES
	PELICANS
ACEILNPT	PECTINAL
	PLANETIC
ACEILNRS	CARLINES
ACEILNRT	CLARINET
ACEILNSS	SANICLES
ACEILNSU	AESCULIN
	LUNACIES
ACEILNSY	SALIENCY
ACEILOPR	CAPRIOLE
ACEILOPT	POETICAL
ACEILORR	CARRIOLE
ACEILORS	CALORIES
	CARIOLES
ACEILORT	EROTICAL
	LORICATE
ACEILORV	ARVICOLE
ACEILOSS	COALISES
ACEILOST	ALOETICS
	COALIEST
	SOCIETAL
ACEILOSV	VOCALISE
ACEILOSZ	COALIZES
ACEILOTV	LOCATIVE
ACEILPPY	PIPECLAY
ACEILPRS	CALIPERS
	REPLICAS
	SPIRACLE
ACEILPRT	PARTICLE
	PRELATIC
ACEILPRU	PECULIAR
ACEILPSS	SLIPCASE
	SPECIALS
ACEILPST	PLICATES
ACEILPSU	SPICULAE
ACEILPTY	ETYPICAL
ACEILPXY	EPICALYX
ACEILRRT	CLARTIER
ACEILRRW	CRAWLIER
ACEILRSS	CLASSIER
ACEILRST	ALTRICES
	ARTICLES
	RECITALS
	SELICTAR
ACEILRSU	AURICLES
ACEILRSV	CALIVERS
	CLAVIERS
	VISCERAL
ACEILRTT	TRACTILE
ACEILRTV	VERTICAL
ACEILRTY	LITERACY
ACEILSST	ELASTICS
	SALICETS
	SCALIEST
ACEILSTT	LATTICES
	TALCIEST
ACEILSTY	CLAYIEST
ACEILSUV	VESICULA
ACEILTVY	ACTIVELY
ACEIMMNP	PEMMICAN
ACEIMMOS	SEMICOMA
ACEIMMRS	RACEMISM
ACEIMNOR	CORAMINE
ACEIMNPS	PEMICANS
ACEIMNRS	CARMINES
ACEIMNRU	MANICURE
ACEIMNSS	AMNESICS
ACEIMNST	SEMANTIC
ACEIMNSU	SEMUNCIA
ACEIMNSY	SYCAMINE
ACEIMOPT	POEMATIC
ACEIMOTX	TOXAEMIC
ACEIMOTZ	METAZOIC
ACEIMPRR	CRAMPIER
	MERICARP
ACEIMPSS	ESCAPISM
ACEIMPST	CAMPIEST
	CAMPSITE
ACEIMPTU	PUMICATE
ACEIMRST	CERAMIST
	MATRICES
ACEIMRTT	TREMATIC
ACEIMRTU	MURICATE
ACEIMSST	ETACISMS
ACEIMSSU	CAESIUMS
ACEINNOS	CANONISE
ACEINNOT	ENACTION
ACEINNOZ	CANONIZE
ACEINNPS	PINNACES
ACEINNRS	CRANNIES
ACEINNST	ANCIENTS
	CANNIEST
	INSTANCE
ACEINNSU	NUISANCE
ACEINNSY	CYANINES
ACEINNTU	UNCINATE
ACEINOPR	APOCRINE
	CAPONIER
	PROCAINE
ACEINOPS	CANOPIES
	CAPONISE
	PAEONICS
ACEINOPZ	CAPONIZE
ACEINORS	SCENARIO
ACEINORT	ACTIONER
	ANORETIC
	CREATION
	REACTION
ACEINORV	VERONICA
ACEINORX	ANOREXIC
ACEINOST	ACONITES
	CANOEIST
ACEINOTT	TACONITE
ACEINOTV	CONATIVE
ACEINOTX	EXACTION
ACEINPSS	INSCAPES
	PINCASES
ACEINPTT	PITTANCE
ACEINPUY	PICAYUNE
ACEINRRU	CURARINE
ACEINRRY	CINERARY
ACEINRSS	ARSENICS
	CERASINS
	RACINESS
ACEINRST	CANISTER
	CARNIEST
	CISTERNA
	CREATINS
	NACRITES
	SCANTIER
ACEINRTT	INTERACT
ACEINRTV	NAVICERT
ACEINRTX	XERANTIC
ACEINRVY	VICENARY
ACEINSST	CINEASTS
	SCANTIES
ACEINSSU	ISSUANCE
ACEINSSY	CYANISES
ACEINSTT	CANTIEST
	NICTATES
	TETANICS
ACEINSTV	CISTVAEN
	VESICANT
ACEINSTY	CYANITES
ACEINSYZ	CYANISEZ
ACEINTTU	TUNICATE
ACEINTTX	EXCITANT
ACEINTTY	TENACITY
ACEINTUV	UNACTIVE
ACEIOPRT	OPERATIC
ACEIOPST	ECTOPIAS
ACEIORSV	COVARIES
	VARICOSE
ACEIOSST	SOCIATES
ACEIOSSU	CAESIOUS
ACEIOSTT	OSCITATE
ACEIOTVV	VOCATIVE
ACEIPPRR	CRAPPIER
	PERICARP
ACEIPPRS	EPICARPS
ACEIPPST	TAPPICES
ACEIPRRS	PERISARC
ACEIPRSS	SCRAPIES
ACEIPRST	CRAPIEST
	CRISPATE
	PICRATES
	PRACTISE
ACEIPRTV	PRACTIVE
ACEIPRTY	APYRETIC
ACEIPSST	ASEPTICS
	ESCAPIST
	SPACIEST
ACEIPSSU	AUSPICES
ACEIPSSZ	CAPSIZES
ACEIPSTV	CAPTIVES
ACEIQRSU	ACQUIRES
ACEIQSTU	ACQUITES
ACEIQSUZ	CAZIQUES
ACEIRRRS	CARRIERS
	SCARRIER
ACEIRRST	ERRATICS
ACEIRRSU	CURARISE
ACEIRRSW	AIRSCREW
ACEIRRTT	RETRAICT
ACEIRRTX	CREATRIX
ACEIRRTY	RETIRACY
ACEIRRUZ	CURARIZE
ACEIRSST	SCARIEST
ACEIRSSU	SCAURIES
	URICASES
ACEIRSSV	VICARESS
ACEIRSTT	CITRATES
	CRISTATE
	SCATTIER
ACEIRSTU	SURICATE
ACEIRSTZ	CRAZIEST

ACEIRTTU	URTICATE
ACEIRTTV	TRACTIVE
ACEIRTUV	CURATIVE
ACEIRTVY	VERACITY
ACEISSSS	CASSISES
ACEISSST	ECSTASIS
ACEISSSU	SAUCISSE
ACEISSTT	STATICES
ACEISSTU	SAUCIEST
	SUITCASE
ACEISTTT	CATTIEST
ACEISTTU	EUSTATIC
ACEISTTW	SCAWTITE
ACEISTUX	AUXETICS
ACEJKOOR	JACKEROO
ACEJKOPS	PAJOCKES
ACEJLORS	CAJOLERS
ACEJLORY	CAJOLERY
ACEJMRST	SCRAMJET
ACEJNNOO	JONCANOE
ACEJNOST	JACONETS
ACEJNOSY	JOYANCES
ACEJNRRY	JERRYCAN
ACEJNSTU	JUNCATES
ACEJPSTU	CAJEPUTS
ACEJRSTT	TRAJECTS
ACEKKNRS	KNACKERS
ACEKKNRY	KNACKERY
ACEKLLPS	PELLACKS
ACEKLNRS	CRANKLES
ACEKLNSS	SLACKENS
ACEKLNTU	UNTACKLE
ACEKLORS	EARLOCKS
ACEKLORV	LAVEROCK
ACEKLPRS	SPRACKLE
ACEKLPST	PLACKETS
ACEKLQSU	QUACKLES
ACEKLRSS	SLACKERS
ACEKLRST	TACKLERS
ACEKLRSU	CAULKERS
ACEKLSSS	SACKLESS
ACEKLSST	SLACKEST
ACEKMNRT	TRACKMEN
ACEKMNST	TACKSMEN
ACEKMRSS	SMACKERS
ACEKNNOW	ACKNOWNE
ACEKNPRS	PRANCKES
ACEKNPRU	UNPACKER
ACEKOORT	CARETOOK
ACEKOORW	COOKWARE
ACEKOPRW	CAPEWORK
ACEKORRS	CROAKERS
ACEKORRV	OVERRACK
ACEKORSW	CASEWORK
ACEKPPRS	PREPACKS
ACEKPSSY	SKYSCAPE
ACEKQRSU	QUACKERS
ACEKQRUY	QUACKERY
ACEKRRST	TRACKERS
ACEKRRTY	RACKETRY
ACEKRSST	STACKERS
ACEKRSTT	RACKETTS
ACEKRSTU	RUCKSEAT
ACEKSSTT	STACKETS
ACEKSSUW	WAESUCKS
ACELLLRU	CELLULAR
ACELLMOS	CALOMELS
ACELLMSU	SACELLUM
ACELLNRU	NUCELLAR
ACELLOPS	COLLAPSE
	ESCALLOP
ACELLORR	CAROLLER
ACELLORS	CORELLAS
ACELLORV	COVERALL
	OVERCALL
ACELLORW	CALLOWER
ACELLOST	COLLATES
ACELLOSW	COLESLAW
ACELLOTU	LOCULATE

ACELLPSS	SCALPELS
ACELLRRS	CARRELLS
ACELLRTY	RECTALLY
ACELLSSU	CALLUSES
ACELLSSW	CLAWLESS
ACELLSTU	SCUTELLA
ACELLTWY	CETYWALL
ACELMMOU	MAMELUCO
ACELMNNS	CLANSMEN
ACELMNOR	AMELCORN
ACELMNRU	CRUMENAL
ACELMNSS	CALMNESS
	CLASSMEN
ACELMOPT	COMPLEAT
ACELMORS	CAROMELS
	SCLEROMA
ACELMORY	CLAYMORE
ACELMOST	CAMELOTS
	MOLECAST
ACELMOSU	CAULOMES
	LEUCOMAS
	MACULOSE
ACELMPRS	CLAMPERS
ACELMPSY	ECLAMPSY
ACELMSSU	LACMUSES
ACELMSTU	CALUMETS
	MUSCATEL
ACELMSUU	SAECULUM
ACELMTUU	CUMULATE
ACELNNRS	SCRANNEL
ACELNORV	NOVERCAL
ACELNOST	LACTONES
ACELNOSU	LACUNOSE
ACELNOSZ	CALZONES
ACELNOTV	COVALENT
ACELNOVY	CONVEYAL
ACELNPSS	ENCLASPS
	SPANCELS
ACELNPST	CLAPNETS
ACELNPSU	UNPLACES
ACELNRSU	LUCARNES
ACELNRVY	CRAVENLY
ACELNSST	SCANTLES
ACELNSSU	SCALENUS
	UNSCALES
ACELNSTT	CANTLETS
ACELNSTY	SECANTLY
ACELOPPU	POPULACE
ACELOPRS	PARCLOSE
	POLACRES
ACELOPRT	PECTORAL
ACELOPRU	OPERCULA
ACELOPSS	ESCALOPS
ACELOPST	POLECATS
ACELOPTU	COPULATE
	OUTPLACE
ACELOPTY	CALOTYPE
ACELOQSU	COEQUALS
ACELORRT	RECTORAL
ACELORSS	ESCOLARS
	LACROSSE
ACELORST	SECTORAL
ACELORSU	CAROUSEL
ACELORSY	CALOYERS
	COARSELY
ACELOSST	ALECOSTS
ACELOSTU	LACTEOUS
	LOCUSTAE
	OSCULATE
ACELOSTY	ACOLYTES
ACELOSUV	VACUOLES
ACELPPRS	CLAPPERS
	SCRAPPLE
ACELPPSS	SCAPPLES
ACELPRSS	CLASPERS

	SCALPERS
ACELPRST	SCEPTRAL
	SPECTRAL
ACELPRSU	SPECULAR
ACELPSSU	CAPSULES
ACELPTUU	CUPULATE
ACELPTUY	EUCALYPT
ACELQRSU	LACQUERS
ACELQRUU	CLAQUEUR
ACELQSUY	LACQUEYS
ACELRRSW	CRAWLERS
	SCRAWLER
ACELRSSS	SCARLESS
ACELRSST	SCARLETS
ACELRSSU	SECULARS
ACELRSTT	CLATTERS
	SCRATTLE
ACELRSTU	RAUCLEST
ACELRTTU	CULTRATE
ACELRTTY	CLATTERY
ACELSSTT	TACTLESS
ACELSSTY	SCYTALES
ACELSSUX	EXCUSALS
ACEMMOTY	MYCETOMA
ACEMMRRS	CRAMMERS
ACEMNORR	ROMANCER
ACEMNORS	CREMONAS
	ROMANCES
ACEMNOST	CAMSTONE
ACEMNPSS	CAMPNESS
ACEMNRUY	NUMERACY
ACEMNSSU	MANCUSES
ACEMOORS	ACROSOME
ACEMOOST	COMATOSE
ACEMOPRS	COMPARES
	COMPEARS
	MESOCARP
ACEMORRT	CREMATOR
ACEMORSY	SYCAMORE
ACEMORTY	COMETARY
ACEMORUX	MORCEAUX
ACEMPRSS	SCAMPERS
ACEMPRST	CRAMPETS
ACEMPSSU	CAMPUSES
ACEMSSTT	METCASTS
ACENNNOU	ANNOUNCE
ACENNOSS	CANONESS
	SONANCES
ACENNOSY	NOYANCES
ACENNOTT	CONTENANT
ACENNOTV	COVENANT
ACENNOTZ	CANZONET
ACENNPRY	PERNANCY
ACENNRSS	SCANNERS
ACENNSUY	SEACUNNY
ACENOORT	CORONATE
ACENOOTZ	ECTOZOAN
ACENOPRT	PORTANCE
ACENOPST	CAPSTONE
ACENOPSU	PONCEAUS
ACENOPUX	PONCEAUX
ACENOQTU	COTQUEAN
ACENORRW	CAREWORN
ACENORSS	COARSENS
	NARCOSES
ACENORST	ANCESTOR
	ENACTORS
	SARCONET
	SORTANCE
ACENORSU	CARNEOUS
	NACREOUS
ACENORTT	CONTRATE
ACENORTU	COURANTE
	OUTRANCE
ACENORUY	EUCARYON
ACENOSSS	CASSONES
ACENOSST	CONTESSA
	COSTEANS
ACENOSSV	CAVESSON

ACENOSSY	CYANOSES
ACENOSTT	CONSTATE
ACENOSTV	CENTAVOS
ACENOTTU	TOUCANET
ACENPRRS	PRANCERS
ACENPRSU	ENCARPUS
	PRAUNCES
ACENPSTT	PENTACTS
ACENPTTU	PUNCTATE
ACENRSST	CRANTSES
ACENRSSU	SURANCES
ACENRSTT	TRANECTS
	TRANSECT
ACENRSTU	CENTAURS
	RECUSANT
	UNCRATES
	UNTRACES
ACENRSTY	ANCESTRY
ACENRTTU	TRUNCATE
ACENRTUY	CENTAURY
	CYANURET
ACENSSTT	SCANTEST
ACENSSTU	NUTCASES
ACENSSTW	NEWSCAST
ACEOOPPS	APOCOPES
ACEOOPSU	POACEOUS
ACEOORTV	EVOCATOR
	OVERCOAT
ACEOPPRS	COPPERAS
ACEOPRRT	RECAPTOR
ACEOPRSX	EXOCARPS
ACEOPRTT	ATTERCOP
ACEOPSTU	OUTPACES
ACEORRST	ACROTERS
	CREATORS
	REACTORS
ACEORRSU	CAROUSER
ACEORRTT	RETROACT
ACEORRVW	OVERCRAW
ACEORSST	COARSEST
	COASTERS
ACEORSSU	CAROUSES
ACEORSTT	SECTATOR
ACEORSTU	OUTRACES
ACEORSTV	OVERCASTS
	OVERCAST
ACEORSTX	EXACTORS
ACEORTUY	EUCARYOT
ACEOSTTU	OUTCASTE
ACEOSTUU	AUTOCUES
ACEPRRSS	SCARPERS
	SCRAPERS
ACEPRRTU	CAPTURER
ACEPRSSU	SCAUPERS
ACEPRSTU	CAPTURES
	PRESCUTA
ACEPSTTY	TYPECAST
ACEQRSTU	RACQUETS
ACEQSSTU	ACQUESTS
ACERRSTT	RETRACTS
ACERRSUV	VERRUCAS
ACERSSST	CRASSEST
ACERSSSU	SUCRASES
ACERSSTT	SCATTERS
ACERSTTT	TETRACTS
ACERSTTU	CRUSTATE
ACERSTTX	EXTRACTS
ACERSTTY	SCATTERY
ACERSTUX	CURTAXES
ACFFGHIN	CHAFFING
ACFFHNOR	CHAFFRON
ACFFIILO	OFFICIAL
ACFFIIST	CAITIFFS
ACFFIKMS	MAFFICKS
ACFFILNU	FANCIFUL
ACFFILST	AFFLICTS
ACFFIRST	TRAFFICS
ACFFLOSW	SCOFFLAW
ACFGHINU	CHAUFING

ACFGIIMN MAGNIFIC	ACGHHIJK HIGHJACK	ACGIKNOR CROAKING	ACGINRTT TRACTING
ACFGIIPR CAPRIFIG	ACGHHINN HANCHING	ACGIKNPS PACKINGS	ACGINRTU CURATING
ACFGIKNR FRACKING	ACGHHINT HATCHING	ACGIKNQU QUACKING	ACGINSST CASTINGS
ACFGINNY FANCYING	ACGHIINR CHAIRING	ACGIKNRS ARCKINGS	ACGINSTT SCATTING
ACFGINRS FARCINGS	ACGHIKLN CHALKING	RACKINGS	ACGIOORS GRACIOSO
SCARFING	HACKLING	ACGIKNRT TRACKING	ACGIORST ORGASTIC
ACFGINRT CRAFTING	ACGHIKNR CHARKING	ACGIKNRW WRACKING	ACGIORSU GRACIOUS
FRACTING	ACGHIKNS HACKINGS	ACGIKNSS SACKINGS	ACGIPRSY SPAGYRIC
ACFGITUY FUGACITY	ACGHIKNW WHACKING	ACGIKNST STACKING	ACGJLNOU CONJUGAL
ACFGKNOP PACKFONG	ACGHILNN LANCHING	TACKINGS	ACGKMMOS GAMMOCKS
ACFGLNOR CORNFLAG	ACGHILNS CLASHING	ACGIKPRS GRIPSACK	ACGKORSV GARVOCKS
ACFHHINW HAWFINCH	ACGHILNT LATCHING	ACGILLNS CALLINGS	ACGLLPSU CUPGALLS
ACFHILNO FALCHION	ACGHILNU LAUCHING	ACGILMMN CLAMMING	ACGLMOUU COAGULUM
ACFHILNU FAULCHIN	ACGHILNY ACHINGLY	ACGILMNP CAMPLING	ACGLNORS CLANGORS
ACFHILOS COALFISH	ACGHILOR OLIGARCH	CLAMPING	ACGLNORU CLANGOUR
ACFHINOU FAUCHION	ACGHIMNP CHAMPING	ACGILNNT CANTLING	ACGLOORY ARCOLOGY
ACFHIRSS SCARFISH	ACGHIMNR CHARMING	ACGILNNU LAUNCING	ACGLOSUU GLAUCOUS
ACFHIRSW CRAWFISH	MARCHING	UNLACING	ACGLSSTU CUTGLASS
ACFHIRSY CRAYFISH	ACGHIMNT MATCHING	ACGILNOR ORACLING	ACGNNOOT CONTANGO
ACFHISSU FUCHSIAS	ACGHINNR RANCHING	ACGILNOS SOLACING	ACGNNORS CRANNOGS
ACFHLMRU CHARMFUL	ACGHINNT CHANTING	ACGILNOT LOCATING	ACGNOOST OCTAGONS
ACFHLTUW WATCHFUL	ACGHINNU UNACHING	ACGILNPP CLAPPING	ACGNORST CONGRATS
ACFHMNOR CHAMFRON	ACGHINOP POACHING	ACGILNPS CLASPING	ACGORRSY GYROCARS
ACFHNOSU FAUCHONS	ACGHINOR ROACHING	PLACINGS	ACGORSSW COWGRASS
ACFIILST FISTICAL	ACGHINPP CHAPPING	SCALPING	ACGORSUU COUGUARS
ACFIILSV SALVIFIC	ACGHINPR PARCHING	ACGILNQU CALQUING	ACGPPSUU SCUPPAUG
ACFIILTY FACILITY	ACGHINPT NIGHTCAP	ACGILNRS CARLINGS	ACHHILPT PHTHALIC
ACFIIMPS PACIFISM	PATCHING	ACGILNRT CLARTING	ACHHINTW WHINCHAT
ACFIIMSS FASCISMI	ACGHINRR CHARRING	ACGILNRW CRAWLING	ACHHINTY HYACINTH
ACFIIPST PACIFIST	ACGHINRS CHAGRINS	ACGILNSS CLASSING	ACHHIPPR HIPPARCH
ACFIISST FASCISTI	CRASHING	SCALINGS	ACHHLMOS MASHLOCH
ACFIKLNS CALFSKIN	ACGHINRT CHARTING	ACGILNST CASTLING	ACHHLNOR RHONCHAL
ACFIKNNS FINNACKS	RATCHING	CATLINGS	ACHHLPRY PHYLARCH
ACFILLSY FISCALLY	ACGHINRU CHURINGA	SCLATING	ACHHLSUY SHAUCHLY
ACFILNOR FORNICAL	NURAGHIC	ACGILNSU GLUCINAS	ACHHNTTU NUTHATCH
ACFILNOS FOLACINS	ACGHINSS CHASINGS	ACGILNTT CLATTING	UNTHATCH
ACFILORT TRIFOCAL	ACGHINST SCATHING	ACGILNTU CLAUTING	ACHHOSST TOSHACHS
ACFILRTY CRAFTILY	ACGHINSW CHINWAGS	ACGILRSU SURGICAL	ACHHPPSU CHUPPAHS
ACFILSSY CLASSIFY	ACGHINTT CHATTING	ACGIMMNR CRAMMING	ACHHPTUZ CHUTZPAH
ACFILSTU SULFATIC	ACGHINTW WATCHING	ACGIMMNS SCAMMING	ACHIIKMS KAMICHIS
ACFIMNRU FRANCIUM	ACGHINTY YACHTING	ACGIMNOR CAROMING	ACHIILMS CHILIASM
ACFIMOSS FASCISMO	ACGHIPRS GRAPHICS	ACGIMNOS COAMINGS	ACHIILST CHILIAST
ACFIMSSS FASCISMS	ACGHIQTU ACQUIGHT	ACGIMNPR CRAMPING	ACHIINRT TRICHINA
ACFINORT FRACTION	ACGHIRSS SCRAIGHS	ACGIMNPS SCAMPING	ACHIIPSS PACHISIS
ACFINOST FACTIONS	ACGHLLOR GRALLOCH	ACGIMNSY GYMNASIC	ACHIIRST RACHITIS
ACFINRST INFARCTS	ACGHLOOY CHAOLOGY	SYNGAMIC	ACHIIRSU ISCHURIA
INFRACTS	ACGHLSTU CLAUGHTS	ACGIMORS ORGASMIC	ACHIJKPW WHIPJACK
ACFINSTY SANCTIFY	ACGHNTUU UNCAUGHT	ACGINNNS SCANNING	ACHIJNST JACINTHS
ACFIOSTU FACTIOUS	ACGHORSU CHORAGUS	ACGINNNU NUANCING	ACHIKKNS KNACKISH
ACFIRTUY FURACITY	ACGHPTUU UPCAUGHT	ACGINNPR PRANCING	ACHIKKSW KICKSHAW
ACFISSST FASCISTS	ACGHRRSU CURRAGHS	ACGINNPU UNCAPING	ACHIKLLW HICKWALL
ACFKLORS FORSLACK	ACGHRSSU SCRAUGHS	ACGINNRT TRANCING	ACHIKLPT CHALKPIT
ACFKLOST LOCKFAST	ACGIILMN CLAIMING	ACGINNRU UNCARING	ACHIKNOP PACHINKO
ACFKLRUW WRACKFUL	MALICING	ACGINNRY CARNYING	ACHIKRSS RICKSHAS
ACFKLSSU SACKFULS	ACGIILNN INLACING	ACGINNST CANTINGS	ACHIKRSW RICKSHAW
ACFKOSTT FATSTOCK	ACGIILNO LOGICIAN	SCANTING	ACHIKRSY HAYRICKS
ACFLMNOO MOONCALF	ACGIILNS SCAILING	ACGINNSU UNCASING	ACHIKSSS SHICKSAS
ACFLNORY FALCONRY	ACGIIMNT MICATING	ACGINNUV VAUNCING	ACHILLOR ORCHILLA
ACFLOOPS FOOLSCAP	ACGIIMOS ISOGAMIC	ACGINOPT COAPTING	ACHILLRT CLITHRAL
ACFLORSU SCROFULA	ACGIIMST SIGMATIC	ACGINORY CONGIARY	ACHILMOP OMPHALIC
ACFLRRUU FURCULAR	ACGIINNS INCASING	ACGINOST AGNOSTIC	ACHILMOS MALICHOS
ACFMOTTU FACTOTUM	ACGIINNV INCAVING	COASTING	ACHILMRS CHRISMAL
ACFNRSTU FRUCTANS	ACGIINRT GRANITIC	COATINGS	ACHILMTY MYTHICAL
ACGGGILN CLAGGING	ACGIIPRS SPAGIRIC	COTINGAS	ACHILNNS CLANNISH
ACGGHINN CHANGING	ACGIJJKO JICKAJOG	ACGINPPR CRAPPING	ACHILNOO HOOLICAN
GANCHING	ACGIJLNO CAJOLING	ACGINPPS CAPPINGS	ACHILNOS LICHANOS
ACGGHINR CHARGING	ACGIJNNU JAUNCING	ACGINPRS CARPINGS	ACHILNPS CLANSHIP
ACGGIINN INCAGING	ACGIKLMN MACKLING	SCARPING	ACHILOPR RHOPALIC
ACGGIINT GIGANTIC	ACGIKLNN CLANKING	SCRAPING	ACHILORT ACROLITH
ACGGIIOS ISAGOGIC	ACGIKLNO CLOAKING	ACGINPSS SPACINGS	ACHILPSY PHYSICAL
ACGGILNN CANGLING	ACGIKLNS SLACKING	ACGINPSU SCAUPING	ACHILPTY PATCHILY
CLANGING	ACGIKLNT TACKLING	ACGINRRS SCARRING	ACHILRUY CHYLURIA
GLANCING	TALCKING	ACGINRRY CARRYING	ACHILRVY CHIVALRY
ACGGINNO CONGAING	ACGIKLNU CAULKING	ACGINRSS SACRINGS	ACHILSWY LICHWAYS
ACGGINNU UNCAGING	ACGIKLRY GARLICKY	ACGINRST SCARTING	ACHIMMOS MACHISMO
ACGGINOR CARGOING	ACGIKMNS SMACKING	TRACINGS	ACHIMMST MISMATCH
ACGGIOOR CORAGGIO	ACGIKNNR CRANKING	ACGINRSU SCAURING	ACHIMNNW WINCHMAN
ACGGLNOU GLUCAGON	ACGIKNNS SNACKING	ACGINRSV CARVINGS	ACHIMNOP CHAMPION
ACGGLRSY SCRAGGLY		CRAVINGS	ACHIMNOR CHOIRMAN

```
         HARMONIC   ACHNOSUY CHANOYUS   ACIKMPST MAPSTICK   ACIMNORY ACRIMONY
ACHIMNOS MANIHOCS   ACHNPPSS SCHNAPPS   ACIKMPSW PICKMAWS   ACIMNOSS MOCASSIN
ACHIMNPT PITCHMAN   ACHNRSTU UNSTARCH   ACIKNNPS PANNICKS   ACIMNOST MONASTIC
ACHIMOPR AMPHORIC   ACHNRSYY SYNARCHY   ACIKNSST CATSKINS   ACIMNOTU ACONITUM
ACHIMOSS CHAMISOS   ACHNRTUY CHAUNTRY   ACIKNSTT TINTACKS   ACIMNPTY TYMPANIC
         ISOCHASM   ACHOORTY CHAYROOT   ACIKPRST PATRICKS   ACIMNRSU CRANIUMS
ACHIMPSS SCAMPISH   ACHOPRST TOPARCHS   ACILLLOP POLLICAL            CUMARINS
ACHIMRSS CHARISMS   ACHOPRSY CHARPOYS   ACILLMMY CLAMMILY   ACIMNSTT CATMINTS
ACHIMRST CHARTISM   ACHOPRTY TOPARCHY   ACILLMOS LOCALISM   ACIMOOST SCOTOMIA
ACHIMSSS SCHISMAS   ACHOTTUW OUTWATCH   ACILLMSS MISCALLS   ACIMORST ACROTISM
ACHIMSST MASTICHS   ACHRSTTU STRAUCHT   ACILLNOO COLONIAL   ACIMORSY CRAMOISY
         TACHISMS   ACIIILMN INIMICAL   ACILLNOR CARILLON   ACIMOSST ACOSMIST
ACHIMSSU CHIASMUS   ACIIILNV CIVILIAN   ACILLNOS SCALLION            MASSICOT
ACHIMTUY CYATHIUM   ACIIKNNN CANNIKIN   ACILLOQU COQUILLA   ACIMOSTT MASTICOT
ACHINNOP PANCHION   ACIIKNNS CANIKINS   ACILLORT CLITORAL            STOMATIC
ACHINNSU UNCHAINS   ACIIKPRT PAITRICK   ACILLORY COLLYRIA   ACIMPRST CRAMPITS
ACHINOPR PAROCHIN   ACIILLSU SILICULA   ACILLOST LOCALIST            PTARMICS
ACHINORT ANORTHIC   ACIILLTV VILLATIC   ACILLOSY SOCIALLY   ACIMRRSY MISCARRY
ACHINOSY ONYCHIAS   ACIILMNR CRIMINAL   ACILLOTY LOCALITY   ACIMRSSZ CZARISMS
ACHINOTZ HOACTZIN   ACIILNOR IRONICAL   ACILMNOP COMPLAIN   ACIMSSST MISCASTS
ACHINRSZ ZARNICHS   ACIILNOT TALIONIC   ACILMNOS LACONISM   ACIMSSTT TACTISMS
ACHINSUV CHAUVINS   ACIILNPT PLATINIC            LIMACONS   ACINNOOT CONATION
ACHIORSS COARSISH   ACIILNSS SALICINS   ACILMOOS SCOLIOMA            INTONACO
ACHIORST CHARIOTS   ACIILOSV VILIACOS   ACILMOPR PROCLAIM   ACINNORR NARICORN
         HARICOTS   ACIILRTT TRITICAL   ACILMOPT COMPITAL   ACINNOSS SCANSION
ACHIORTV TOVARICH   ACIILRTU URALITIC   ACILMOSV VOCALISM   ACINNOST ACTINONS
ACHIPPSS SAPPHICS   ACIILSST SILASTIC   ACILMPTU PLACITUM            CANONIST
ACHIPRRT PARRITCH   ACIILSTV SILVATIC   ACILMSSS CLASSISM            CANTIONS
ACHIPSTU CHUPATIS   ACIIMMNS MINICAMS   ACILMSSU MUSICALS            CONTAINS
ACHIPSTW WHIPCATS   ACIIMNOR MORAINIC   ACILMSTY MYSTICAL            SANCTION
ACHIPTTU CHUPATTI   ACIIMNOS SIMONIAC   ACILMTUY ULTIMACY   ACINNOTU CONTINUA
ACHIQRSU CHARQUIS   ACIIMNOT AMNIOTIC   ACILNOOT LOCATION   ACINNRTY TYRANNIC
ACHIRRST TRIARCHS   ACIIMNST ACTINISM   ACILNOOV VOCALION   ACINNSTU ANNICUTS
ACHIRRTY TRIARCHY   ACIIMNSU MUSICIAN   ACILNOPS SALPICON   ACINNSTY INSTANCY
ACHIRSTT CHARTIST   ACIIMNTU ACTINIUM   ACILNOPT PLATONIC   ACINOOPR PICAROON
         STRAICHT   ACIIMNTY IMITANCY   ACILNORS CLARINOS   ACINOOTV VOCATION
ACHIRSTU HAIRCUTS            INTIMACY            CLARIONS   ACINOPPT PANOPTIC
ACHISSTT TACHISTS            MINACITY   ACILNORT CILANTRO   ACINOPRS PARSONIC
ACHISTTY CHASTITY   ACIIMOTT AMITOTIC            CONTRAIL   ACINOPST CAPTIONS
ACHKMMOS HAMMOCKS   ACIIMPRT PRIMATIC   ACILNOSU UNSOCIAL            PACTIONS
ACHKMORS SHAMROCK   ACIIMPRV VAMPIRIC   ACILNOUV UNIVOCAL   ACINOPTU ACUPOINT
ACHKNNUU NUNCHAKU   ACIIMRST SCIMITAR   ACILNPSS INCLASPS   ACINOQSU COQUINAS
ACHKNOOT CANTHOOK   ACIIMRTU MURIATIC            SCALPINS   ACINORRS CARRIONS
ACHKOPSS HOPSACKS   ACIIMSST ITACISMS   ACILNRSU CISLUNAR   ACINORRT CONTRAIR
ACHKOSSS HASSOCKS   ACIIMSTV ACTIVISM   ACILNRUY CULINARY   ACINORSS NARCOSIS
ACHKOSSY HASSOCKY   ACIIMTUV VIATICUM            URANYLIC   ACINORST CANTORIS
ACHKOSTT HATTOCKS   ACIINNOT INACTION   ACILNSTU LUNATICS            CAROTINS
ACHLLOOS ALCOHOLS            NICOTIAN            SULTANIC   ACINORTT TRACTION
ACHLLORS CHLORALS   ACIINNQU CINQUAIN   ACILNSTY SCANTILY   ACINOSSS CAISSONS
ACHLLORY CHORALLY   ACIINNTT INCITANT   ACILOPRT TROPICAL            CASSINOS
ACHLMSTZ SCHMALTZ   ACIINNTY CANINITY   ACILOPST COALPITS   ACINOSSY CYANOSIS
ACHLNOOU OULACHON   ACIINOPT OPTICIAN   ACILORRS RACLOIRS   ACINOSTT OSCITANT
ACHLNOSY HALCYONS   ACIINORZ ZIRCONIA   ACILORRV CORRIVAL            TACTIONS
ACHLNSTU TULCHANS   ACIINOSS ASINICOS   ACILORST CALORIST   ACINOSTU ANTICOUS
ACHLNSTY STANCHLY   ACIINOSV AVIONICS   ACILORSV CORIVALS            AUCTIONS
ACHLOPRS RAPLOCHS   ACIINOTT CITATION   ACILORTV VORTICAL            CAUTIONS
ACHLOPRT CALTHROP   ACIINPSS PISCINAS   ACILORYZ ZIRCALOY   ACINOSTW WAINSCOT
ACHLOPRY POLYARCH   ACIINRSS NARCISSI   ACILOSTV VOCALIST   ACINOSWX COXSWAIN
ACHLOPTT POTLATCH   ACIINRSU URANISCI   ACILOTVY VOCALITY   ACINOTTX TOXICANT
ACHLORSS SCHOLARS   ACIINRTU URANITIC   ACILPRST CLIPARTS   ACINPQUY PIQUANCY
ACHLOSSW SALCHOWS   ACIIOPST APOSITIC   ACILPRSU SPICULAR   ACINPRST CANTRIPS
ACHLOSTY ACOLYTHS   ACIIORST AORISTIC   ACILPRTU PICTURAL   ACINPRSY CYPRIANS
ACHLOTWX WAXCLOTH   ACIIORTV VICTORIA   ACILPSST PLASTICS   ACINPSTY SYNAPTIC
ACHMNORS MONARCHS   ACIIPPST PAPISTIC   ACILRSTU CURTAILS   ACINQSTU QUANTICS
         NOMARCHS   ACIIRSTT ARTISTIC            RUSTICAL   ACINRSSU CRUSIANS
ACHMNORY MONARCHY            TRIATICS   ACILRTUV CULTIVAR   ACINRSTU CURTAINS
         NOMARCHY   ACIISTTU AUTISTIC            CURVITAL            SATURNIC
ACHMNRSU UNCHARMS   ACIISTTV ACTIVIST   ACILSSST CLASSIST            TURACINS
ACHMNRTU TRUCHMAN   ACIITTVY ACTIVITY   ACILSTUV VICTUALS   ACINRTTU TACITURN
ACHMOPRS CAMPHORS   ACIITVVY VIVACITY   ACILSTVY SYLVATIC            URTICANT
ACHMORTU OUTMARCH   ACIJKKPS SKIPJACK   ACIMMOSS ACOSMISM   ACINSTTY SANCTITY
ACHMOSST STOMACHS   ACIJKSTW STICKJAW   ACIMMTUY CYMATIUM            SCANTITY
ACHMOSTY STOMACHY   ACIJSUZZ JACUZZIS   ACIMNNNO CINNAMON   ACINSTYY SYNCYTIA
ACHMOTTU OUTMATCH   ACIKLMST MALSTICK   ACIMNOOR ACROMION   ACIOOPST SCOTOPIA
ACHMSSUW CUMSHAWS   ACIKLNRY CRANKILY   ACIMNOPS CAMPIONS   ACIOOTYZ ZOOCYTIA
ACHNNORU UNANCHOR   ACIKLORS AIRLOCKS   ACIMNORS MARCONIS   ACIOPRST APRICOTS
ACHNNOSS CHANSONS   ACIKLORY CROAKILY   ACIMNORT ROMANTIC            PISCATOR
ACHNORST CHANTORS   ACIKMOOS OOMIACKS   ACIMNORU CONARIUM   ACIOPRTT PROTATIC
ACHNOSTY TACHYONS   ACIKMPRS RAMPICKS            COUMARIN   ACIOPRTY POTICARY
```

ACIOPSST POTASSIC
ACIOPSSU SPACIOUS
ACIOPSTU CAPTIOUS
ACIOPTTU AUTOPTIC
ACIORRSS CORSAIRS
ACIORSSU SCARIOUS
ACIORSTT RICOTTAS
ACIORTTY ATROCITY
         CITATORY
ACIORTVY VORACITY
ACIOSTUU CAUTIOUS
ACIPRRUU PIRARUCU
ACIPSSST SPASTICS
ACIQRSTU QUARTICS
ACIQSSTU ACQUISTS
ACIRRTTX TRACTRIX
ACIRRTUX CURATRIX
ACIRSSST SACRISTS
ACIRSSTT ASTRICTS
ACIRSSTW TWISCARS
ACIRSSTY SACRISTY
ACIRSSTZ CZARISTS
ACISSSTU CASUISTS
ACISSTTU CATSUITS
ACISSTUV VACUISTS
ACISTTUY ASTUCITY
ACJKKSSY SKYJACKS
ACJKLOSW LOCKJAWS
ACJKNNOS JANNOCKS
ACJKOPST JACKPOTS
ACJMNSTU MUNTJACS
ACJPSTUU CAJUPUTS
ACKKMOPR POCKMARK
ACKKORRW RACKWORK
ACKLLOPS POLLACKS
ACKLLOSY LAYLOCKS
ACKLLPSU SKULLCAP
ACKLMNOS LOCKSMAN
ACKLMORS ARMLOCKS
         LOCKRAMS
ACKLNOSU UNCLOAKS
ACKLOOPW WOOLPACK
ACKLOOSW WOOLSACK
ACKLORSW WARLOCKS
ACKLORSY ROCKLAYS
ACKLOSSS LASSOCKS
ACKMMMOS MAMMOCKS
ACKMNOST STOCKMAN
ACKMNRTU TRUCKMAN
ACKMOSTT MATTOCKS
ACKNSSTU UNSTACKS
ACKOPRRS PARROCKS
ACKOPRRT TRAPROCK
ACKORRST TARROCKS
ACKORSTW CATWORKS
ACLLLNOY CLONALLY
ACLLMNOU COLUMNAL
ACLLMORU CORALLUM
ACLLOORS COROLLAS
ACLLOORT COLLATOR
ACLLOOSS COLOSSAL
ACLLOPSS SCALLOPS
ACLLORUY OCULARLY
ACLLRTUU CULTURAL
ACLMMNOU COMMUNAL
ACLMNOOO COOLAMON
ACLMNORU COLUMNAR
ACLMNORY NORMALCY
ACLMORSU CLAMOURS
ACLMORTU CROTALUM
ACLMPRSU SCALPRUM
ACLMRSUU MUSCULAR
ACLMSUUV VASCULUM
ACLNOORS CORONALS
ACLNOORT COLORANT
ACLNOOST COOLANTS
ACLNOPSY SYNCOPAL
ACLNORSU CONSULAR
         COURLANS

ACLNORTU CALUTRON
ACLNOSTU CONSULTA
         OSCULANT
ACLNPSSU UNCLASPS
ACLNPTUU PUNCTUAL
ACLNSSUY UNCLASSY
ACLOOPPS ALCOPOPS
ACLOOPRR CORPORAL
ACLOPRST CALTROPS
ACLOPRXY XYLOCARP
ACLOPSSU SCOPULAS
ACLOPSSY CALYPSOS
ACLOPSUU OPUSCULA
ACLORRTU TORCULAR
ACLOSSTU OUTCLASS
ACLRSSTY CRYSTALS
ACMMNOSY SCAMMONY
ACMMNOYY MYOMANCY
ACMNOOPR MONOCARP
ACMNOORR CROMORNA
ACMNOORT MONOCRAT
ACMNOOYZ ZOOMANCY
ACMNOPRS CRAMPONS
ACMNORSY ACRONYMS
ACMNSSTU SANCTUMS
ACMOOPRS COPROSMA
ACMOOSST SCOTOMAS
ACMOPRST COMPARTS
ACMORSTW CATWORMS
         WORMCAST
ACMORSTY COSTMARY
ACMQSTUU CUMQUATS
ACNNNORY CANNONRY
ACNNOSTT CONSTANT
ACNOOORT OCTAROON
ACNOORRY CORONARY
ACNOORST CARTOONS
         CORANTOS
         OSTRACON
ACNOORSU CANOROUS
ACNOORTY OCTONARY
ACNOPSSW SNOWCAPS
ACNORRSU RANCOURS
ACNORRTY CONTRARY
ACNORSTT CONTRAST
         CONTRATS
ACNORSTU COURANTS
ACNORTTU TURNCOAT
ACNORTUY NOCTUARY
ACNPRSSY SYNCARPS
ACNPRSUY SPRAUNCY
ACNPRSYY SYNCARPY
ACNRRSTU CURRANTS
ACNRRTUY CURRANTY
ACOOPRRS CORPORAS
ACOOPRST TOPCOATS
ACOORSTU TOURACOS
ACOPRRST CARPORTS
ACOPRRTT PROTRACT
ACORRSTT TRACTORS
ACORRSTU CURATORS
ACORRTUY CURATORY
ACORSSTU SURCOATS
ACORSSUW CURASSOW
ACORSSWY CROSSWAY
ACORSTTY CRYOSTAT
ACOSSTTU OUTCASTS
ACPSSTUU USUCAPTS
ADDDEEEM ADDEEMED
ADDDEEEN DEADENED
ADDDEEGR DEGRADED
ADDDEEIM DIADEMED
ADDDEELR LADDERED
ADDDEEMN DEMANDED
         MADDENED
ADDDEENR DANDERED
         REDDENDA
ADDDEENS SADDENED
ADDDEEPS SEPADDED

ADDDEGJU ADJUDGED
ADDDELSW SWADDLED
ADDDELTW TWADDLED
ADDDEMNU ADDENDUM
ADDDEMOO ADDOOMED
ADDDENOS DEODANDS
ADDDENRU DEUDDARN
ADDDEORS ADDORSED
ADDDGILN DADDLING
ADDEEEFN DEAFENED
ADDEEEFT DEFEATED
ADDEEEJY DEEJAYED
ADDEEELN LEADENED
ADDEEEMN DEMEANED
ADDEEEMR REMEADED
ADDEEENR DEADENER
         ENDEARED
ADDEEFIL DEFILADE
ADDEEFIM MADEFIED
ADDEEFLT DEFLATED
ADDEEFNU UNDEAFED
ADDEEFPR PREFADED
ADDEEFRY DEFRAYED
ADDEEFTT DEFATTED
ADDEEGLL ALLEDGED
ADDEEGLN DANEGELD
ADDEEGNR DANGERED
         DERANGED
         GARDENED
ADDEEGRR REGARDED
         REGRADED
ADDEEGRS DEGRADES
ADDEEGSS DEGASSED
ADDEEHLR HERALDED
ADDEEHLY ALDEHYDE
ADDEEHNR HARDENED
ADDEEHNU UNHEADED
ADDEEHRS REDHEADS
ADDEEHRT THREADED
ADDEEIKR DAIKERED
ADDEEILN DEADLINE
ADDEEILR DEADLIER
         DERAILED
         REDIALED
ADDEEILT DETAILED
ADDEEIMT MEDIATED
ADDEEINT DETAINED
ADDEEIPR DIAPERED
ADDEEISS DISEASED
ADDEEIST STEADIED
ADDEEITV DEVIATED
ADDEEKMR DEMARKED
ADDEEKNR DARKENED
ADDEELLM MEDALLED
ADDEELLP PEDALLED
ADDEELLV DEVALLED
ADDEELNO LOADENED
ADDEELNP DEPLANED
ADDEELNR ENLARDED
ADDEELNU UNLEADED
ADDEELOR RELOADED
ADDEELPS DELAPSED
ADDEELRT TREADLED
ADDEELST DESALTED
ADDEELUV DEVALUED
ADDEEMNN DEMANNED
ADDEEMNP DAMPENED
ADDEEMNR DAMNEDER
         DEMANDER
         REMANDED
ADDEENPP APPENDED
ADDEENPR PANDERED
ADDEENPX EXPANDED
ADDEENRR DARNEDER
ADDEENRT ENDARTED
ADDEENRU DAUNERED
ADDEENRW DAWNERED
         WANDERED
         WARDENED

ADDEENSS DEADNESS
ADDEENTT ATTENDED
         DENTATED
ADDEENTU DENUDATE
ADDEEOST DEODATES
ADDEEPRT DEPARTED
         PREDATED
ADDEEPRV DEPRAVED
         PERVADED
ADDEERRS DREADERS
ADDEERRT RETARDED
ADDEERRW REWARDED
         WARDERED
ADDEERSW SAWDERED
ADDEERTV ADVERTED
ADDEFFOR AFFORDED
ADDEFIIL LADIFIED
ADDEFILY LADYFIED
ADDEFIST FADDIEST
ADDEFLRU DREADFUL
ADDEFRSU DEFRAUDS
ADDEGGLR DRAGGLED
ADDEGHOS GODHEADS
ADDEGILO DIALOGED
ADDEGILS GLADDIES
ADDEGINR DREADING
ADDEGIRS DISGRADE
ADDEGJSU ADJUDGES
ADDEGLNS GLADDENS
ADDEGLST GLADDEST
ADDEGNRU UNGRADED
ADDEGPRU UPGRADED
ADDEHHIN HINDHEAD
ADDEHILR DIHEDRAL
ADDEHMRU DRUMHEAD
ADDEHNNU UNHANDED
ADDEHNSU UNDASHED
         UNSHADED
ADDEHORW HEADWORD
ADDEHOSW SHADOWED
ADDEHPRU PURDAHED
ADDEHRTY HYDRATED
ADDEIIKS DIDAKEIS
ADDEIIRS DIARISED
ADDEIIRZ DIARIZED
ADDEIITV ADDITIVE
ADDEIJNO ADJOINED
ADDEILNS ISLANDED
         LANDSIDE
ADDEILNT TIDELAND
ADDEILRS DIEDRALS
ADDEILSY DIALYSED
ADDEILYZ DIALYZED
ADDEIMOS SODAMIDE
ADDEIMRS DISARMED
         MISDREAD
ADDEIMST MISDATED
ADDEIMSY DISMAYED
ADDEIMTT ADMITTED
ADDEINOR ORDAINED
ADDEINOS ADENOIDS
         ADONISED
         ANODISED
ADDEINOZ ADONIZED
         ANODIZED
ADDEINRT INDARTED
ADDEINST DANDIEST
ADDEIOPR PARODIED
ADDEIORS ROADSIDE
         SIDEROAD
ADDEIOTX OXIDATED
ADDEIPPR DIDAPPER
ADDEIPRS DISPREAD
ADDEIPSS DIPSADES
ADDEIQSU SQUADDIE
ADDEIRST DISRATED
ADDEIRSW SIDEWARD
ADDEIRVZ VIZARDED
ADDEISSU DISSUADE

```
ADDEISSW SWADDIES
ADDEJSTU ADJUSTED
ADDEKNVY VANDYKED
ADDELLOR DOLLARED
ADDELMOS DOLMADES
ADDELNOU DUODENAL
         UNLOADED
ADDELNPU PUDENDAL
ADDELNRS DANDLERS
ADDELNSU UNSADDLE
ADDELOPU UPLOADED
ADDELPRS PADDLERS
ADDELRSS SADDLERS
ADDELRST STRADDLE
ADDELRSW DAWDLERS
         SWADDLER
         WADDLERS
ADDELRSY SADDLERY
ADDELRTW TWADDLER
ADDELSST STADDLES
ADDELSSW SWADDLES
ADDELSTW TWADDLES
ADDEMMNU UNDAMMED
ADDEMNNU UNDAMNED
ADDEMNPU UNDAMPED
ADDENNOT DANTONED
ADDENOPR PARDONED
ADDENORU UNADORED
ADDENPRU UNDRAPED
ADDENRST STRANDED
ADDENRSU DAUNDERS
ADDENRTU DRAUNTED
         UNTRADED
ADDENRUW UNWARDED
ADDEORTU OUTDARED
ADDEOTTU OUTDATED
ADDEPRSU SUPERADD
ADDFFILO DAFFODIL
ADDFFINR DANDRIFF
ADDFFNRU DANDRUFF
ADDFGILN FADDLING
ADDFIMSS FADDISMS
ADDFISST FADDISTS
ADDGGILN GLADDING
ADDGIILN DAIDLING
ADDGIIRS DIAGRIDS
ADDGILNN DANDLING
ADDGILNP PADDLING
ADDGILNR RADDLING
ADDGILNS SADDLING
ADDGILNW DAWDLING
         WADDLING
ADDGINPS PADDINGS
ADDGINQU QUADDING
ADDGINSW WADDINGS
ADDGINWY WADDYING
ADDGLNOS GLADDONS
ADDGMRUU MUDGUARD
ADDGOOSW DAGWOODS
ADDGORSW GODWARDS
ADDHHLNO HANDHOLD
ADDHIMOO MAIDHOOD
ADDHINPS DAPHNIDS
ADDHINRW HINDWARD
ADDHINSY DANDYISH
ADDHIOTY HYDATOID
ADDHISTY HYDATIDS
ADDHLOOY LADYHOOD
ADDHOORW HARDWOOD
ADDIIKMZ ZADDIKIM
ADDIILUV DIVIDUAL
ADDIINOT ADDITION
ADDIINSS DISDAINS
ADDIINTV DIVIDANT
ADDIKSST TSADDIKS
ADDIKSTY KATYDIDS
ADDIKSTZ TZADDIKS
ADDILLNW WILDLAND
ADDILMNS MIDLANDS

ADDILNNW LANDWIND
ADDILOSS DISLOADS
ADDIMNOS DIAMONDS
ADDIMNSY DANDYISM
ADDIMORS DIADROMS
ADDINNOR ORDINAND
ADDINORS ANDROIDS
         DISADORN
ADDINQUY QUIDDANY
ADDINRWW WINDWARD
ADDIQSST TSADDIQS
ADDIQSTZ TZADDIQS
ADDIRSZZ DIZZARDS
ADDKNRRU DRUNKARD
ADDLLNOR LANDLORD
ADDLLRSU DULLARDS
ADDLNNOW DOWNLAND
ADDLNOOW DOWNLOAD
         WOODLAND
ADDLNORS LANDDROS
ADDLOOSS SOLDADOS
ADDMOOSY DOOMSDAY
ADDNOPWY PANDOWDY
ADDNORWW DOWNWARD
ADDOORWW WOODWARD
ADDOORWY WOODYARD
ADDOPSSY DASYPODS
ADEEEFFR AFFEERED
ADEEEFNY FEDAYEEN
ADEEEFRT FEDERATE
ADEEEGLT DELEGATE
ADEEEGNR RENEGADE
ADEEEGNT TEENAGED
ADEEEGPS GAPESEED
ADEEEGRS DEGREASE
ADEEEHHW HEEHAWED
ADEEEHRT REHEATED
ADEEEHRX EXHEDRAE
ADEEEHSY EYESHADE
ADEEEINT DETAINEE
ADEEEKNW WEAKENED
ADEEELNS ENSEALED
ADEEELNV LEAVENED
ADEEELRS RELEASED
         RESEALED
ADEEELRV LAVEERED
         REVEALED
ADEEELST TEASELED
ADEEELSW WEASELED
ADEEELTV ELEVATED
ADEEELTZ TEAZELED
ADEEEMNS DEMEANES
         ENSEAMED
ADEEEMNT EMENDATE
ADEEEMRU EMERAUDE
ADEEENNT NEATENED
ADEEENRS ENSEARED
         SERENADE
ADEEENTT ATTENDEE
         EDENTATE
ADEEENWZ WEAZENED
ADEEEPRS RAPESEED
ADEEEPRT REPEATED
ADEEERRS ARREEDES
ADEEERST RESEATED
ADEEESSW SEAWEEDS
         SEESAWED
ADEEFFIR EFFRAIDE
ADEEFHNR FREEHAND
ADEEFHOR FOREHEAD
ADEEFHRT FATHERED
ADEEFILN ENFILADE
ADEEFIMS MADEFIES
ADEEFINR FREDAINE
ADEEFIOR FOEDARIE
ADEEFIRR RAREFIED
ADEEFIRS FEDARIES
ADEEFIRY REAEDIFY

ADEEFLLT FELLATED
ADEEFLMN ENFLAMED
ADEEFLOR FREELOAD
ADEEFLRR DEFERRAL
ADEEFLRS FEDERALS
ADEEFLRT DEFLATER
         FALTERED
         REFLATED
ADEEFLSS FADELESS
ADEEFLST DEFLATES
ADEEFMNR ENFRAMED
         FREEDMAN
ADEEFMRR REFRAMED
ADEEFNRU UNFEARED
ADEEFNSS DEAFNESS
ADEEFNST FASTENED
ADEEFNTT FATTENED
ADEEFORR FOREREAD
ADEEFORT FOREDATE
ADEEFPRS PREFADES
ADEEFRRT RAFTERED
ADEEFRRY DEFRAYER
         FEDERARY
ADEEFRST DRAFTEES
ADEEFRTU FEATURED
ADEEGGHS EGGHEADS
ADEEGGJR JAGGEDER
ADEEGGLL ALLEGGED
ADEEGGRR RAGGEDER
ADEEGHOR GHERAOED
ADEEGHRT GATHERED
ADEEGIMN ADEEMING
ADEEGINR REGAINED
ADEEGIRS DISAGREE
ADEEGISS ASSIEGED
ADEEGLLS ALLEDGES
ADEEGLLT GALLETED
ADEEGLNO ENGAOLED
ADEEGLNR ENLARGED
         LARGENED
ADEEGLNT DANEGELT
ADEEGLSV SELVAGED
ADEEGMMT GEMMATED
ADEEGMNR GENDARME
ADEEGMNS ENDGAMES
ADEEGMNY MEGADYNE
ADEEGMOP MEGAPODE
ADEEGMOS MEGADOSE
ADEEGMSS MESSAGED
ADEEGNNR ENDANGER
         ENRANGED
ADEEGNNV VENDANGE
ADEEGNOR RENEGADO
ADEEGNRR GARDENER
         GARNERED
ADEEGNRS DERANGES
         GRANDEES
         GRENADES
ADEEGNRU DUNGAREE
         RENAGUED
         UNGEARED
ADEEGNRV ENGRAVED
ADEEGNSS AGEDNESS
ADEEGNSV VENDAGES
ADEEGORT DEROGATE
ADEEGOST DOGEATES
ADEEGOTW GOATWEED
ADEEGPRS ASPERGED
         PRESAGED
ADEEGPRT PARGETED
ADEEGRRR REGARDER
ADEEGRRS REGRADES
ADEEGRRT GARRETED
         GARTERED
         REGRATED
ADEEGRRU REDARGUE
ADEEGRSS DRESSAGE
ADEEGRST RESTAGED
ADEEGRSU GUARDEES

ADEEGRSW RAGWEEDS
ADEEGRTT TARGETED
ADEEGSSS DEGASSES
ADEEGSTT GESTATED
ADEEGSWY EDGEWAYS
ADEEGTTZ GAZETTED
ADEEHHRS REHASHED
ADEEHHST SHEATHED
ADEEHILN HEADLINE
ADEEHILS DEISHEAL
ADEEHIRT DEATHIER
ADEEHISS EADISHES
ADEEHIST ATHEISED
         HEADIEST
ADEEHISV ADHESIVE
ADEEHITZ ATHEIZED
ADEEHKNR HANKERED
         HARKENED
ADEEHKWW HAWKWEED
ADEEHLLW WELLHEAD
ADEEHLNO ENHALOED
ADEEHLNR REHANDLE
ADEEHLNU UNHEALED
ADEEHLRS ASHLERED
ADEEHLRT HALTERED
         LATHERED
ADEEHLSS HEADLESS
ADEEHMMR HAMMERED
ADEEHMNN MENHADEN
ADEEHMNS HEADSMEN
ADEEHMNT ANTHEMED
ADEEHMPR HAMPERED
ADEEHNOT HEADNOTE
ADEEHNPP HAPPENED
ADEEHNRR HARDENER
ADEEHNRT ADHERENT
         HARTENED
         THREADEN
ADEEHNSS DASHEENS
ADEEHNST HASTENED
ADEEHNTU UNHEATED
ADEEHOPR HEADROPE
ADEEHORS SOREHEAD
ADEEHORV OVERHEAD
ADEEHPPU UPHEAPED
ADEEHPRS EPHEDRAS
         RESHAPED
ADEEHPUV UPHEAVED
ADEEHRRS ADHERERS
         REDSHARE
ADEEHRRT THREADER
ADEEHRST HEADREST
ADEEHRSW WASHERED
ADEEHRTT HATTERED
         THREATED
ADEEHRTW WREATHED
ADEEHSST HEADSETS
ADEEHSSY HAYSEEDS
ADEEIILS IDEALISE
ADEEIILZ IDEALIZE
ADEEIITV IDEATIVE
ADEEIJMR JEREMIAD
ADEEIJRS JADERIES
ADEEIJST JADEITES
ADEEIKLS LAKESIDE
ADEEILLO OEILLADE
ADEEILLR REALLIED
ADEEILMN ENDEMIAL
ADEEILMR REMEDIAL
ADEEILMS LIMEADES
ADEEILMV MEDIEVAL
ADEEILNS DELAINES
ADEEILNT ENTAILED
         LINEATED
ADEEILPR PEDALIER
ADEEILPT DEPILATE
         EPILATED
         PILEATED
ADEEILRR DERAILER
```

RERAILED	ADEELLRT TELLARED	ADEEMNSY DEMAYNES	ADEEPRSW PERSWADE
ADEEILRS REALISED	ADEELLRV RAVELLED	ADEEMNTU UNTEAMED	ADEEPRSZ SPREAZED
SIDEREAL	ADEELLSS ALLSEEDS	ADEEMNTW METEWAND	ADEEPRTT PATTERED
ADEEILRT RETAILED	LEADLESS	ADEEMORS SEADROME	ADEEPRTU DEPURATE
ADEEILRZ REALIZED	ADEELLTY ELATEDLY	ADEEMORT MODERATE	EPURATED
ADEEILSS DEISEALS	ADEELMNO LEMONADE	ADEEMPPR PAMPERED	ADEEPRTZ TRAPEZED
IDEALESS	ADEELMNP EMPLANED	ADEEMPRT EMPARTED	ADEEPSST STAPEDES
ADEEILST LEADIEST	ADEELMNR ALDERMEN	TAMPERED	ADEEPSTT ADEPTEST
ADEEILSV DISLEAVE	ADEELMNS DALESMEN	ADEEMPRY REVAMPED	ADEEPSWY SPEEDWAY
ADEEILSY EYELIADS	EMENDALS	ADEEMPRY EMPAYRED	ADEEQRTU DETRAQUE
ADEEIMNR REMAINED	LEADSMEN	ADEEMPST STAMPEDE	ADEEQRUV QUAVERED
ADEEIMNS DEMAINES	ADEELMNT LAMENTED	STEPDAME	ADEERRRT RETARDER
INSEAMED	ADEELMOS SOMEDEAL	ADEEMRRS DREAMERS	ADEERRRW REREWARD
ADEEIMNT DEMENTIA	ADEELMPR EMPARLED	ADEEMRRV MARVERED	REWARDER
ADEEIMNX EXAMINED	ADEELMPX EXAMPLED	ADEEMRRY DREAMERY	ADEERRST ARRESTED
ADEEIMPR EMPAIRED	ADEELMRS DEMERSAL	ADEEMRST MASTERED	DREAREST
ADEEIMRR DREAMIER	EMERALDS	STREAMED	RETREADS
ADEEIMRS MADERISE	ADEELMST MEDALETS	ADEEMRSU MEASURED	SERRATED
ADEEIMRT DIAMETER	ADEELMTU EMULATED	ADEEMRTT MATTERED	TREADERS
REMEDIAT	ADEELNNP ENPLANED	ADEEMRTY METEYARD	ADEERRSV ADVERSER
ADEEIMRZ MADERIZE	ADEELNNU UNANELED	ADEEMSSW MAWSEEDS	ADEERRTT RETRATED
ADEEIMSS SIAMESED	ADEELNOR OLEANDER	ADEEMSTW MATWEEDS	ADEERRTW REDWATER
ADEEIMST MEDIATES	ADEELNPS DEPLANES	ADEEMSWY MAYWEEDS	ADEERRWY WARREYED
ADEEIMSZ SIAMEZED	ADEELNPU UPLEANED	ADEENNRS ENSNARED	ADEERSST ASSERTED
ADEEIMTT MEDITATE	ADEELNRT ANTLERED	ADEENNRU UNEARNED	ESTRADES
ADEEINNS ADENINES	ADEELNRV LAVENDER	ADEENNTT TENANTED	ADEERSTT ASTERTED
ANDESINE	ADEELNSU UNLEASED	ADEENNUW UNWEANED	RESTATED
ADEEINPR PINDAREE	UNSEALED	ADEENNUY UNYEANED	ADEERSTW DEWATERS
ADEEINPT DIAPENTE	ADEELNSV ENSLAVED	ADEENOPW WEAPONED	TARWEEDS
ADEEINRS ARSENIDE	ADEELNTT TALENTED	ADEENORS REASONED	WASTERED
DENARIES	ADEELNTU UNELATED	ADEENORV ENDEAVOR	ADEERSTY ESTRAYED
DRAISENE	ADEELNTV LEVANTED	ADEENORY AERODYNE	ADEERTTT TATTERED
NEARSIDE	ADEELNTY ENTAYLED	ADEENOSS SEASONED	ADEERTTY YATTERED
ADEEINRT DETAINER	ADEELOPS PEDALOES	ADEENOST ENDOSTEA	ADEERTWW WARTWEED
RETAINED	ADEELORU AUREOLED	ADEENOTT DENOTATE	ADEERVYY EVERYDAY
ADEEINSS ANISEEDS	ADEELORV OVERLADE	DETONATE	ADEESSSS ASSESSED
ADEEINST ANDESITE	ADEELOST DESOLATE	ADEENPRT PARENTED	ADEESSTT SEDATEST
ADEEIPRR REPAIRED	ADEELOSW LEASOWED	ADEENPRU UNREAPED	ADEESTTT ATTESTED
ADEEIPRS AIRSPEED	ADEELPPR LAPPERED	ADEENPRX EXPANDER	ADEESTUX EXUDATES
ADEEIPTX EXPIATED	ADEELPPT LAPPETED	ADEENPTT PATENTED	ADEESVVY SAVVEYED
ADEEIRRR DREARIER	ADEELPPU UPLEAPED	PATTENED	ADEFFGUW GUFFAWED
ADEEIRST READIEST	ADEELPRS PLEADERS	ADEENRRW WANDERER	ADEFFIMR AFFIRMED
SERIATED	RELAPSED	ADEENRSS DEARNESS	ADEFFIRR DRAFFIER
SIDERATE	ADEELPRT PALTERED	ADEENRSU UNDERSEA	ADEFFIRT TARIFFED
STEADIER	ADEELPRY PARLEYED	ADEENRSW ANSWERED	ADEFFIST DAFFIEST
ADEEIRSV READVISE	REPLAYED	ADEENRTT ATTENDER	ADEFFLNS SNAFFLED
ADEEIRTT ITERATED	ADEELPSS DELAPSES	NATTERED	ADEFFRST STRAFFED
ADEEIRTV DERIVATE	ADEELPST PEDESTAL	RATTENED	ADEFGGOT FAGGOTED
EVIRATED	ADEELPTY PEDATELY	ADEENRTU DENATURE	ADEFGIIS GASIFIED
TAIVERED	ADEELQSU SQUEALED	ADEENRTV AVENTRED	ADEFGILN FINAGLED
ADEEISSS DISEASES	ADEELRRR LARDERER	ADEENRUV UNREAVED	ADEFGILO FOLIAGED
SEASIDES	ADEELRRT TREADLER	ADEENSST ASSENTED	ADEFGILS GADFLIES
ADEEISST STEADIES	ADEELRST TREADLES	STANDEES	GASFIELD
ADEEISSV ADESSIVE	ADEELRSV SLAVERED	ADEENSSU DANSEUSE	ADEFGIMN DEFAMING
ADEEISTV DEVIATES	ADEELRSW LEEWARDS	ADEENSTU UNSEATED	ADEFGIRT DRIFTAGE
SEDATIVE	ADEELRSY DELAYERS	ADEENTTU TAUTENED	ADEFGIRU ARGUFIED
ADEEITTV EVITATED	ADEELRTV TRAVELED	ADEENTTV VENDETTA	ADEFGITU FATIGUED
ADEEITVW TIDEWAVE	ADEELRUV REVALUED	ADEEOPPR PADERERO	ADEFGLOT GATEFOLD
ADEEKMRR REMARKED	ADEELSST DATELESS	ADEEOPRT OPERATED	ADEFGLRU FELDGRAU
ADEEKMRT MARKETED	TASSELED	ADEEOPST ADOPTEES	ADEFGNOR FRONDAGE
ADEEKNNR ENRANKED	ADEELSTT LADETTES	ADEEORRV OVERREAD	ADEFGOSU FOUGADES
ADEEKNPW KNAPWEED	ADEELSTY SEDATELY	ADEEORSW OARWEEDS	ADEFHILS DEALFISH
ADEEKNRS KNEADERS	ADEELSUV DEVALUES	ADEEORVW OVERAWED	ADEFHILY HAYFIELD
ADEEKNST NAKEDEST	ADEEMMMR MAMMERED	ADEEPPRR DAPPERER	ADEFHIMS FAMISHED
ADEEKQSU SQUEAKED	ADEEMMRY YAMMERED	PREPARED	ADEFHKOR FORKHEAD
ADEEKRST STREAKED	ADEEMMSS MESDAMES	ADEEPPRW WAPPERED	ADEFHLTU DEATHFUL
ADEEKSWY WEEKDAYS	ADEEMMXY MYXEDEMA	ADEEPRRS SPREADER	ADEFHMOT FATHOMED
ADEELLLP LAPELLED	ADEEMNNR MANNERED	ADEEPRRT DEPARTER	ADEFHNOR FOREHAND
ADEELLMT METALLED	REMANNED	ADEEPRRU UPREARED	ADEFHOST SOFTHEAD
ADEELLMU MEDULLAE	ADEEMNOR DEMEANOR	ADEEPRSS ASPERSED	ADEFIILR AIRFIELD
ADEELLNP PANELLED	ENAMORED	PREASSED	ADEFIILS LADIFIES
ADEELLNW ENWALLED	ADEEMNPS SPADEMEN	REPASSED	SALIFIED
ADEELLNY LEADENLY	ADEEMNRS AMENDERS	ADEEPRST PEDERAST	ADEFIILT FILIATED
ADEELLPR PEDALLER	MEANDERS	PREDATES	ADEFIIMR RAMIFIED
PREDELLA	REAMENDS	REPASTED	ADEFIINS SANIFIED
ADEELLPT PALLETED	ADEEMNSS SEEDSMAN	TRAPESED	ADEFIIRT RATIFIED
PETALLED	ADEEMNST STAMENED	ADEEPRSU PERSUADE	ADEFIIRU AURIFIED
ADEELLQU EQUALLED	ADEEMNSU UNSEAMED	ADEEPRSV DEPRAVES	ADEFILMN INFLAMED
ADEELLRS SARDELLE		PERVADES	ADEFILNR FILANDER

ADEFILNT INFLATED	ADEGHNNU UNHANGED	ADEGJNOR JARGONED
ADEFILOR FORELAID	ADEGHNRT THRANGED	ADEGKLOY DEKALOGY
ADEFILOT FOLIATED	ADEGHOOP PAGEHOOD	ADEGLLNU GLANDULE
ADEFILSS DISLEAFS	ADEGHORT GOATHERD	UNGALLED
ADEFILSY LADYFIES	ADEGHRTU DAUGHTER	ADEGLLOP GALLOPED
ADEFIMPR FIREDAMP	ADEGHTUW WAUGHTED	ADEGLLOR GOLLARED
ADEFIMRS MISFARED	ADEGIILN GLIADINE	ADEGLLOW GALLOWED
ADEFIMSS DISFAMES	ADEGIILP DIPLEGIA	ADEGLMOR GLAMORED
ADEFINRR INFRARED	ADEGIIMN IMAGINED	ADEGLMOS GLADSOME
ADEFINRS FRIANDES	ADEGIIMS DIGAMIES	ADEGLMPU PLUMAGED
ADEFINRU UNFAIRED	ADEGIINT IDEATING	ADEGLMRU MAULGRED
ADEFINYZ DENAZIFY	ADEGIITT DIGITATE	ADEGLMUY AMYGDULE
ADEFIORS FORESAID	ADEGIJSW JIGSAWED	ADEGLNOY GONDELAY
ADEFIRRT DRAFTIER	ADEGIKNN KNEADING	ADEGLNPS SPANGLED
ADEFLLLU LADLEFUL	ADEGIKNR DAKERING	ADEGLNRS DANGLERS
ADEFLLNS ELFLANDS	ADEGILLO GLADIOLE	GLANDERS
ADEFLLOW FALLOWED	ADEGILLP PILLAGED	ADEGLNRW WRANGLED
ADEFLLUY FEUDALLY	ADEGILLR GRILLADE	ADEGLNSS GLADNESS
ADEFLMRU DREAMFUL	ADEGILLS GALLISED	ADEGLNTW TWANGLED
ADEFLNNS FENLANDS	ADEGILLZ GALLIZED	ADEGLNUZ UNGLAZED
ADEFLNOR FORELAND	ADEGILMN MALIGNED	ADEGLOPP GALOPPED
ADEFLNRU DEARNFUL	MEDALING	ADEGLPPR GRAPPLED
ADEFLNTU FLAUNTED	ADEGILNO GALENOID	ADEGMMNO GAMMONED
ADEFLNUU UNFEUDAL	ADEGILNP PEDALING	ADEGMMRU RUMMAGED
ADEFLNUW UNFLAWED	PLEADING	ADEGMNOS GOADSMEN
ADEFLORT DEFLATOR	ADEGILNR DANGLIER	ADEGMNOT MONTAGED
ADEFLORV FLAVORED	DEARLING	ADEGMNOY ENDOGAMY
ADEFLPRS FELDSPAR	DRAGLINE	ADEGMNRS DRAGSMEN
ADEFLPSU SPADEFUL	ADEGILNS DEALINGS	ADEGMORS ORGASMED
ADEFLRTU TRADEFUL	LEADINGS	ADEGMORW WORDGAME
ADEFLRTW LEFTWARD	SIGNALED	ADEGMPUZ GAZUMPED
ADEFLRZZ FRAZZLED	ADEGILNT DELATING	ADEGNNOR ANDROGEN
ADEFLSTU DEFAULTS	ADEGILNY DELAYING	DRAGONNE
SULFATED	ADEGILOS GOLIASED	ADEGNNPU UNPANGED
ADEFMNRU UNFRAMED	ADEGILOU DIALOGUE	ADEGNNSU DUNNAGES
ADEFMORT FORMATED	ADEGILRS SLAIRGED	ADEGNOPS PONDAGES
ADEFMOSU FAMOUSED	ADEGILSS GLISSADE	ADEGNOPU POUNDAGE
FUMADOES	ADEGILST GLADIEST	ADEGNORT DRAGONET
ADEFNNNU UNFANNED	ADEGILSV DISGAVEL	ADEGNOSS SONDAGES
ADEFNOPR PROFANED	ADEGIMMN AMENDING	ADEGNOSV DOGVANES
ADEFNSST DAFTNESS	ADEGIMNR DREAMING	ADEGNPUY PYENGADU
ADEFOOSS SEAFOODS	MARGINED	ADEGNRRU GRANDEUR
ADEFORRR FORRADER	ADEGIMOR IDEOGRAM	ADEGNRST DRAGNETS
FOREWARD	ADEGIMRT MIGRATED	GRANDEST
ADEFORRY FORRAYED	ADEGIMST SIGMATED	ADEGNRSU ENGUARDS
ADEFORUV FAVOURED	ADEGINNV ADVENING	ADEGNRUU UNARGUED
ADEFPTUW UPWAFTED	DAVENING	ADEGNRUZ GAZUNDER
ADEFRRST DRAFTERS	ADEGINNY DENAYING	UNGRAZED
REDRAFTS	ADEGINOR ORGANDIE	ADEGOORY GOODYEAR
ADEFRSTW DWARFEST	ADEGINOS AGONISED	ADEGOPPR PROPAGED
ADEFSSTT STEDFAST	DIAGNOSE	ADEGOPPR PROGRADE
ADEGGGNU UNGAGGED	ADEGINOZ AGONIZED	ADEGORRT GARROTED
ADEGGIRR DRAGGIER	ADEGINPU ANGUIPED	ADEGORST GOADSTER
ADEGGIST DAGGIEST	ADEGINRR DREARING	ADEGORSW DOWAGERS
ADEGGISU GAUDGIES	ADEGINRS DERAIGNS	WORDAGES
GUIDAGES	GRADINES	ADEGORTT GAROTTED
ADEGGJLY JAGGEDLY	READINGS	ADEGORTU OUTRAGED
ADEGGLRS DRAGGLES	ADEGINRT DERATING	RAGOUTED
ADEGGLRY RAGGEDLY	GRADIENT	ADEGPRRU UPGRADER
ADEGGMOY DEMAGOGY	REDATING	ADEGPRSS SPADGERS
ADEGGNOW WAGGONED	TREADING	ADEGPRSU UPGRADES
ADEGGNUU UNGAUGED	ADEGINRY DERAYING	ADEGPSTU UPSTAGED
ADEGGOPY PEDAGOGY	READYING	ADEGRRST DRAGSTER
ADEGGPRS SPRAGGED	YEARDING	ADEGRSSU GRADUSES
ADEGGRTY GADGETRY	ADEGINSS ASSIGNED	ADEGTTTU GUTTATED
ADEGHHOS HOGSHEAD	ADEGINST SEDATING	ADEHHIPR RHAPHIDE
ADEGHILN HEALDING	STEADING	ADEHHIPS HEADSHIP
ADEGHILT ALIGHTED	ADEGINSW WINDAGES	ADEHHIST SHITHEAD
ADEGHINR ADHERING	ADEGINTV VINTAGED	ADEHHNTU HEADHUNT
HEADRING	ADEGINVW ADVEWING	ADEHHOOR HOORAHED
ADEGHINS HEADINGS	ADEGINYZ ZYGAENID	ADEHHOST HEADSHOT
SHEADING	ADEGIORT ERGATOID	HOTHEADS
ADEGHIRS GARISHED	ADEGIOST GODETIAS	ADEHHRRU HURRAHED
HEADRIGS	ADEGIPRS SPAIRGED	ADEHHRST THRASHED
ADEGHIRT GRAITHED	ADEGIRWY RIDGEWAY	ADEHIITZ THIAZIDE
ADEGHJSU JUGHEADS	ADEGISSU DISUSAGE	ADEHIKLV KHEDIVAL
ADEGHLNO HEADLONG	ADEGISTU GAUDIEST	ADEHIKNS SKINHEAD
ADEGHLOS GALOSHED	ADEGISUV VIDUAGES	ADEHIKSS DASHEKIS
		ADEHIKST SKAITHED

ADEHIKSV KHEDIVAS
ADEHILLP PHIALLED
PILLHEAD
ADEHILNR HARDLINE
ADEHILNU UNHAILED
ADEHILPS HELIPADS
ADEHILSV LAVISHED
ADEHILSW WHAISLED
ADEHILWZ WHAIZLED
ADEHIMRS MISHEARD
ADEHIMRY HYDREMIA
ADEHINOP DIAPHONE
ADEHINOS ADHESION
ADEHINPS DEANSHIP
PINHEADS
ADEHINPU DAUPHINE
ADEHINRU UNHAIRED
ADEHINSS SHANDIES
ADEHINST HANDIEST
ADEHINSV VANISHED
ADEHIOTT ATHETOID
ADEHIPRS RAPHIDES
ADEHIPSS PISSHEAD
ADEHIPST PITHEADS
SIDEPATH
ADEHIRSS RADISHES
ADEHIRST HAIRSTED
HARDIEST
ADEHIRSV RAVISHED
ADEHIRSW RAWHIDES
ADEHIRSY HAYRIDES
ADEHIRVW HIVEWARD
ADEHISST SHADIEST
ADEHJLOT JOLTHEAD
ADEHKLNU LUNKHEAD
ADEHKNRS REDSHANK
ADEHKNSU UNSHAKED
ADEHKORW HEADWORK
ADEHKOST KATHODES
ADEHLLOO HALLOOED
HOLLOAED
ADEHLLOW HALLOWED
ADEHLLRT THRALLED
ADEHLLRW HELLWARD
ADEHLMNO HOMELAND
ADEHLMOY HOLYDAME
ADEHLNRS HANDLERS
ADEHLNSS HANDLESS
HANDSELS
ADEHLNST SHETLAND
ADEHLNSU UNHALSED
UNLASHED
UNSHALED
ADEHLOOR HORDEOLA
ADEHLOPS ASPHODEL
PHOLADES
ADEHLPSS SPLASHED
ADEHLRRY HERALDRY
ADEHMNNY HANDYMEN
ADEHMNOS HANDSOME
ADEHMNOT METHADON
THANEDOM
ADEHMNRS HERDSMAN
ADEHMNRU UNHARMED
ADEHMNSU UNSHAMED
ADEHMOOP OOMPAHED
ADEHMOOR HEADROOM
ADEHMOPS MOPHEADS
ADEHMORS HADROMES
ADEHMORW HOMEWARD
ADEHMOST HEADMOST
ADEHMOSU MADHOUSE
ADEHMOSY SHAMOYED
ADEHNOPR ORPHANED
ADEHNOPT PHONATED
ADEHNORV HANDOVER
OVERHAND
ADEHNOSS SANDSHOE

ADEHNOSU SEAHOUND
ADEHNPSU UNHASPED
        UNSHAPED
ADEHNPTU UNPATHED
ADEHNRSS HARDNESS
ADEHNRSU UNSHARED
ADEHNRSW SWANHERD
ADEHNRTU UNTHREAD
ADEHNSST HANDSETS
ADEHNSSU SUNSHADE
        UNSHADES
ADEHNSUV UNSHAVED
ADEHNSUW UNWASHED
ADEHNTTU UNHATTED
ADEHNTTW UNTHAWED
ADEHOOPS APEHOODS
ADEHOORW HAREWOOD
ADEHOORY HOORAYED
ADEHOPRS RHAPSODE
ADEHOPST POTASHED
ADEHOPSX HEXAPODS
ADEHOPXY HEXAPODY
ADEHORRS HOARDERS
ADEHORRW HARROWED
ADEHORSW SHADOWER
ADEHORTT THROATED
ADEHORTU AUTHORED
ADEHQSSU SQUASHED
ADEHRRUY HURRAYED
ADEHRSTY HYDRATES
ADEHRTTW THWARTED
ADEIILMN LIMNAEID
ADEIILMS IDEALISM
        MILADIES
ADEIILPR PERIDIAL
ADEIILRS LAIRISED
ADEIILRZ LAIRIZED
ADEIILST IDEALIST
ADEIILTV DILATIVE
ADEIILTY IDEALITY
ADEIIMMS MISAIMED
ADEIIMNN INDAMINE
ADEIIMNR MERIDIAN
ADEIIMNT MINIATED
ADEIIMPR IMPAIRED
ADEIIMTT IMITATED
ADEIINNS SANIDINE
ADEIINOT IDEATION
        TAENIOID
ADEIINRS DRAISINE
ADEIINRT DAINTIER
ADEIINRU UREDINIA
ADEIINST ADENITIS
        DAINTIES
ADEIINUV INDUVIAE
ADEIIPRR PERRADII
        PRAIRIED
ADEIIPRS PRESIDIA
ADEIIPST STAPEDII
ADEIIRSS AIRSIDES
        DIARISES
ADEIIRST IRISATED
ADEIIRSZ DIARIZES
ADEIITTV TIDIVATE
        VITIATED
ADEIITUV AUDITIVE
ADEIJMRS JEMIDARS
ADEIKLLO KELOIDAL
ADEIKLLY LADYLIKE
ADEIKLSW SIDEWALK
ADEIKMMS IMMASKED
ADEIKMPR IMPARKED
ADEIKMRT TIDEMARK
ADEIKNSY KYANISED
ADEIKNYZ KYANIZED
ADEIKORT KERATOID
ADEIKRST STRAIKED
ADEILLMY MEDIALLY
ADEILLNU UNALLIED

ADEILLNW INWALLED
ADEILLOR ARILLODE
ADEILLPR PALLIDER
ADEILLPS ILLAPSED
        SPADILLE
ADEILLRS DALLIERS
        DIALLERS
ADEILLRT TRIALLED
ADEILLRV RIVALLED
ADEILLSW SIDEWALL
ADEILMMS DILEMMAS
ADEILMNP PLAIDMEN
ADEILMNU UNMAILED
ADEILMNY MAIDENLY
ADEILMOS DAMOISEL
ADEILMPP PALMIPED
ADEILMPR IMPARLED
ADEILMPS IMPLEADS
        MISPLEAD
ADEILMPT IMPLATED
ADEILMRY DREAMILY
ADEILMSS MAIDLESS
        MISDEALS
        MISLEADS
ADEILMST MEDALIST
        MISDEALT
ADEILMSY DYSMELIA
ADEILNNR INLANDER
ADEILNNS ANNELIDS
        LINDANES
ADEILNNU UNNAILED
ADEILNOP PALINODE
ADEILNOS NODALISE
ADEILNOT DELATION
ADEILNOZ NODALIZE
ADEILNPT PANTILED
ADEILNPU PALUDINE
ADEILNRS ISLANDER
ADEILNSU UNSAILED
ADEILNSV ANDVILES
ADEILNTU UNTAILED
ADEILNTV DIVALENT
ADEILNUV UNVAILED
ADEILOPS EPISODAL
        OPALISED
        SEPALOID
ADEILOPT PETALOID
ADEILOPZ OPALIZED
ADEILOQU ODALIQUE
ADEILORS DARIOLES
        SOLIDARE
        SOREDIAL
ADEILORT IDOLATER
        TAILORED
ADEILORV OVERLAID
ADEILORX EXORDIAL
ADEILOSS ASSOILED
        DEASOILS
ADEILOST DIASTOLE
        ISOLATED
        SODALITE
        SOLIDATE
ADEILOSU DOULEIAS
ADEILOTT DATOLITE
ADEILOTV DOVETAIL
        VIOLATED
ADEILPPP PEDIPALP
ADEILPRS PEDRAILS
        PREDIALS
ADEILPRT DIPTERAL
        TRIPEDAL
ADEILPRU EPIDURAL
ADEILPRV DEPRIVAL
ADEILPSS DESPISAL
ADEILPST TALIPEDS
ADEILPTU PLAUDITE
ADEILQSU SQUAILED
ADEILQTU LIQUATED
ADEILRRY DREARILY

ADEILRST DILATERS
        LARDIEST
ADEILRSU RESIDUAL
ADEILRSY DIALYSER
ADEILRTT DETRITAL
ADEILRTY DIELYTRA
ADEILRVY VARIEDLY
ADEILRYZ DIALYZER
ADEILSSU DEASIULS
ADEILSSV DEVISALS
ADEILSSY DIALYSES
ADEILSTV VALIDEST
ADEILSTY DIASTYLE
        STEADILY
ADEILSUV DISVALUE
ADEILSXY DYSLEXIA
ADEILSYZ DIALYZES
ADEILTTU ALTITUDE
        LATITUDE
ADEIMMNS MISNAMED
ADEIMMNU UNMAIMED
ADEIMMRS MERMAIDS
ADEIMMST MISMATED
ADEIMNNO DEMONIAN
ADEIMNOT DOMINATE
        NEMATOID
ADEIMNOZ NOMADIZE
ADEIMNPW IMPAWNED
ADEIMNRR MANRIDER
ADEIMNRS ADERMINS
        SIRNAMED
ADEIMNRY DAIRYMEN
ADEIMNRZ ZEMINDAR
ADEIMNSS SIDESMAN
ADEIMNST MEDIANTS
        TIDESMAN
ADEIMNSU MAUNDIES
ADEIMNSY DYNAMISE
ADEIMNTY DYNAMITE
ADEIMNYZ DYNAMIZE
ADEIMORR AIRDROME
ADEIMORT MEDIATOR
ADEIMOSS SESAMOID
ADEIMOST ATOMISED
ADEIMOTZ ATOMIZED
ADEIMPRR RAMPIRED
ADEIMPRT IMPARTED
ADEIMPRV VAMPIRED
ADEIMPST DAMPIEST
        IMPASTED
ADEIMRRS ADMIRERS
        DISARMER
ADEIMRSS MISREADS
        SIDEARMS
ADEIMRST MARDIEST
        MISRATED
        READMITS
ADEIMRTU MURIATED
ADEIMSST MISDATES
ADEIMSTU TAEDIUMS
ADEIMSTY DAYTIMES
ADEINNNS NANDINES
ADEINNOT ANOINTED
        ANTINODE
ADEINNPT PINNATED
ADEINNPU UNPAINED
ADEINNRS INSNARED
ADEINNRZ RENDZINA
ADEINNSU UNSAINED
ADEINNSX DISANNEX
ADEINNTU INUNDATE
ADEINOPT ANTIPODE
ADEINORR ORDAINER
        REORDAIN
ADEINORS ANEROIDS

        DONARIES
ADEINORT AROINTED
        DERATION
        ORDINATE
        RATIONED
ADEINORU DOUANIER
ADEINOSS ADONISES
        ANODISES
ADEINOSX DIOXANES
ADEINOSZ ADONIZES
        ANODIZES
ADEINOST ASTONIED
        SEDATION
ADEINOTT ANTIDOTE
        TETANOID
ADEINOTV DONATIVE
ADEINPPX APPENDIX
ADEINPRS SPRAINED
ADEINPRT DIPTERAN
ADEINPRU UNPAIRED
        UNREPAID
ADEINPST DEPAINTS
ADEINPSV SPAVINED
ADEINQTU ANTIQUED
ADEINRRS DRAINERS
        SERRANID
ADEINRSS ARIDNESS
        SARDINES
ADEINRST DETRAINS
        RANDIEST
        STRAINED
ADEINRSU DENARIUS
        UNRAISED
        URANIDES
ADEINRSV INVADERS
        SANDIVER
ADEINRSY SYNEDRIA
ADEINRTT NITRATED
ADEINRTU DATURINE
        INDURATE
        RUINATED
        URINATED
ADEINRUV UNVARIED
ADEINRVY VINEYARD
ADEINSST SANDIEST
ADEINSSV AVIDNESS
ADEINSSW WINDASES
ADEINSTT INSTATED
ADEINSTU AUDIENTS
        SINUATED
ADEINSTV DEVIANTS
ADEINSTY DESYATIN
ADEIOPRS DIASPORE
        PARODIES
ADEIOPRV OVERPAID
ADEIOPST DIOPTASE
ADEIOPTV ADOPTIVE
ADEIORRT ADROITER
ADEIORST ASTEROID
ADEIORTT TERATOID
ADEIORTV DEVIATOR
ADEIOSSX OXIDASES
ADEIOSTX OXIDATES
ADEIOSTZ AZOTISED
ADEIOSVV VAIVODES
ADEIOSVW WAIVODES
ADEIOSWW WAIWODES
ADEIOTZZ AZOTIZED
ADEIPPRS APPRISED
        DRAPPIES
ADEIPPRZ APPRIZED
ADEIPRRS DRAPIERS
ADEIPRSS DISPAIRS
ADEIPRST DIPTERAS
        RAPIDEST
        SPIRATED
        TARSIPED
        TRAIPSED
ADEIPRSU UPRAISED

ADEIPRTU EUPATRID	ADELMOSS DAMOSELS	ADEMNOPT TAMPONED	ADENRSTU DAUNTERS
ADEIPSTV VAPIDEST	ADELMOSZ DAMOZELS	ADEMNORS MADRONES	TRANSUDE
ADEIPTTU APTITUDE	ADELMOTU MODULATE	RANSOMED	UNTREADS
ADEIQRRU QUARRIED	ADELMPRT TRAMPLED	ROADSMEN	ADENRSTX DEXTRANS
ADEIQSUY QUAYSIDE	ADELMRRU DEMURRAL	ADEMNOTU AMOUNTED	ADENRSUY UNDERSAY
ADEIRRSW SWARDIER	ADELMSUY AMUSEDLY	OUTNAMED	ADENRTTU TRUANTED
ADEIRRTW TAWDRIER	ADELMTUU UMLAUTED	ADEMNPSS DAMPNESS	ADENRTTY TYRANTED
ADEIRRWW WIREDRAW	ADELNNNU UNNANELD	ADEMNRRU UNDERARM	ADENRUWY UNDERWAY
ADEIRRZZ RIZZARED	ADELNNOT LENTANDO	UNMARRED	ADENSTTU UNSTATED
ADEIRSST ASTERIDS	ADELNOPR PONDERAL	ADEMNRSU DURAMENS	UNTASTED
DIASTERS	ADELNORS LADRONES	MAUNDERS	ADENSTUW UNWASTED
DISASTER	SOLANDER	SURNAMED	ADENSTUY UNSTAYED
DISRATES	ADELNORU UNLOADER	ADEMNRTU UNDREAMT	UNSTEADY
ADEIRSSU RADIUSES	URODELAN	ADEMNRUW UNWARMED	ADENSUWY UNSWAYED
SUDARIES	ADELNORV OVERLAND	ADEMNSSU MEDUSANS	ADEOOPSS APODOSES
ADEIRSSV ADVISERS	RONDAVEL	ADEMNSUU UNAMUSED	ADEOORRT TOREADOR
ADEIRSTT STRAITED	ADELNOSY YEALDONS	ADEMOORT MODERATO	ADEOOTTT TATTOOED
STRIATED	ADELNPRS SPANDREL	ADEMOOST STOMODEA	ADEOPPRV APPROVED
TARDIEST	ADELNPRU PENDULAR	ADEMOOSV VAMOOSED	ADEOPRRT PARROTED
ADEIRSTW TAWDRIES	UNDERLAP	ADEMOPST STAMPEDO	PREDATOR
ADEIRTTT ATTRITED	UPLANDER	ADEMORRT MORTARED	PRORATED
TITRATED	ADELNPRY PANDERLY	ADEMORRU ARMOURED	ADEOPRRU UPROARED
ADEIRVWY DRIVEWAY	ADELNPSY DYSPNEAL	ADEMORRW MARROWED	ADEOPRST ADOPTERS
ADEISSST ASSISTED	ADELNPUY UNPLAYED	ADEMORST STROAMED	ASPORTED
DISSEATS	ADELNRSS SLANDERS	ADEMORTW WARDMOTE	READOPTS
ADEISSTT DISTASTE	ADELNRSU LAUNDERS	ADEMPRST STRAMPED	ADEOPRTT TETRAPOD
STAIDEST	LURDANES	ADEMRRSU EARDRUMS	ADEOPRUV VAPOURED
ADEISSWY SIDEWAYS	RUNDALES	ADEMRRTY MARTYRED	ADEOPSST PODESTAS
WAYSIDES	ADELNRTY ARDENTLY	ADENNNTU UNTANNED	ADEOPSTT DESPOTAT
ADEISTTU SITUATED	ADELNRUY UNDERLAY	ADENNOSY ANODYNES	POSTDATE
ADEISTWY TIDEWAYS	ADELNSTU UNSALTED	ADENNOTU UNATONED	ADEORRSS DROSERAS
ADEITTTU ATTITUDE	ADELNSTW WETLANDS	ADENNOTW WANTONED	ADEORRST ROADSTER
ATTUITED	ADELNTUU UNDULATE	ADENNOTY TANNOYED	ADEORRTW TARROWED
ADEJLOSU JALOUSED	ADELNUUV UNVALUED	ADENNPST PENDANTS	ADEORRVW OVERDRAW
ADEJMRRU JUMARRED	ADELNUZZ UNDAZZLE	ADENNRRU UNDERRAN	ADEORSST ASSORTED
ADEJOPRS JEOPARDS	ADELOORV OVERLOAD	ADENNRRY TYRANNED	TORSADES
ADEJOPRY JEOPARDY	ADELOOWW WOODWALE	ADENNRUW UNWARNED	ADEORSTU OUTDARES
ADEJRSTU ADJUSTER	ADELOOPR PROPALED	ADENNSTU ASTUNNED	ADEORSTX EXTRADOS
READJUST	ADELOPPR PROPALED	ADENNTUW UNWANTED	ADEORSUV SAVOURED
ADEKLMRY MARKEDLY	ADELOPRT PROLATED	ADENOOPS EPANODOS	ADEORSWY RODEWAYS
ADEKLNOX KLAXONED	ADELOPSS DEPOSALS	ADENOORT RATOONED	ADEORTTU OUTRATED
ADEKLNPP KNAPPLED	ADELOPST TADPOLES	ADENOORW WANDEROO	ADEOSSTT ASSOTTED
ADEKLNPR PRANKLED	ADELOPSU PALUDOSE	ADENOPRR PARDONER	ADEOSTTU OUTDATES
ADEKLNSU UNSLAKED	ADELOPSY SEPALODY	ADENOPRS OPERANDS	ADEOSWWY WAYWODES
ADEKLPRS SPARKLED	ADELOPTY PETALODY	PANDORES	ADEOTTTW TATTOWED
ADEKMNRU UNMARKED	ADELORRV OVERLARD	ADENOPRT PRONATED	ADEPPRST STRAPPED
ADEKMNSU UNMASKED	ADELORSS ROADLESS	ADENOPRX EXPANDOR	ADEPRRTU RAPTURED
ADEKMORS DARKSOME	ADELORST DELATORS	ADENOPSS DAPSONES	ADEPRSTU PASTURED
ADEKNNSS DANKNESS	LEOTARDS	SPADONES	UPSTARED
ADEKNRSS DARKNESS	LODESTAR	ADENOPST TONEPADS	ADEPSTUY UPSTAYED
ADEKNSVY VANDYKES	ADELORSU ROULADES	ADENOPSU UNSOAPED	ADEPSUWY UPSWAYED
ADEKQSUW SQUAWKED	ADELOSSW DOWLASES	ADENOPSY DYSPNOEA	ADEQSTTU SQUATTED
ADELLMOR MORALLED	ADELOSTV SOLVATED	ADENORRW NARROWED	ADERRSSW WARDRESS
ADELLMOS SLALOMED	ADELOTUV OVULATED	ADENORST TORNADES	ADERRSTT REDSTART
ADELLMRU MEDULLAR	ADELOTUW OUTLAWED	ADENORTT ATTORNED	ADERSSSU ASSUREDS
ADELLMSU MEDULLAS	ADELOVWY AVOWEDLY	ADENORTY AROYNTED	ADERSSTW STEWARDS
ADELLNNU ANNULLED	ADELPPRY DAPPERLY	ADENORUX RONDEAUX	ADERSSUY DASYURES
ADELLNPS SPENDALL	ADELPRRU LARRUPED	ADENOSST ONSTEADS	ADERSTTU STATURED
ADELLNRS LANDLERS	ADELPRSW SPRAWLED	ADENOTUY AUTODYNE	ADERSTUX SURTAXED
ADELLNSS LANDLESS	ADELPRTT PRATTLED	ADENOUVW UNAVOWED	ADERSTWW WESTWARD
ADELLNSW ELLWANDS	ADELPSTT SPLATTED	ADENPPRS PARPENDS	ADESSTTW WADSETTS
WALLSEND	ADELPSTU PULSATED	ADENPPSU UNSAPPED	ADFFGIIR GIRAFFID
ADELLNUW UNWALLED	ADELPUUV UPVALUED	ADENPPTU UNTAPPED	ADFFGINS DAFFINGS
ADELLOPW WALLOPED	ADELRRSU RUDERALS	ADENPRRS PARDNERS	ADFFHIRS DRAFFISH
ADELLORS ODALLERS	ADELRRSW DRAWLERS	ADENPRSU UNSPARED	ADFFISST DISTAFFS
ADELLOSW SALLOWED	ADELRRTU ULTRARED	ADENPRSW PREDAWNS	ADFFLOOS OFFLOADS
ADELLOTT ALLOTTED	ADELRSTT STARTLED	ADENPRTU DEPURANT	ADFFLRUU FRAUDFUL
TOTALLED	ADELRSZZ DAZZLERS	ADENPRTY PEDANTRY	ADFFNOST STANDOFF
ADELLOTV LAVOLTED	ADELRTUY ADULTERY	ADENPRUW UNWARPED	ADFFOORS AFFOORDS
ADELLOTW TALLOWED	ADELSTTY STATEDLY	ADENPRUY UNDERPAY	ADFGINNU UNFADING
ADELLOWW WALLOWED	ADELTTTW TWATTLED	UNPRAYED	ADFGINRS FARDINGS
ADELLQSU SQUALLED	ADEMMNOW MADWOMEN	ADENPSSY DYSPNEAS	ADFGINRT DRAFTING
ADELLRSU UDALLERS	ADEMMSTU SUMMATED	ADENQRSU SQUANDER	ADFGINRW DWARFING
ADELLTUU ULULATED	ADEMNNNU UNMANNED	ADENRRSY REYNARDS	ADFHIOST TOADFISH
ADELMNNS LANDSMEN	ADEMNNOU UNMOANED	ADENRRTU UNTARRED	ADFHIRSW DWARFISH
ADELMNOS LODESMAN	ADEMNNRU MUNDANER	ADENRRWY WARDENRY	ADFHLNSU HANDFULS
ADELMNRS MANDRELS	UNDERMAN	ADENRSSS SARSDENS	ADFHLOST HOLDFAST
ADELMOOW WOODMEAL	ADEMNOOR MAROONED	ADENRSST STANDERS	ADFHOOSS SHADOOFS
ADELMORS EARLDOMS	ADEMNOPR POMANDER	ADENRSSU DANSEURS	

ADFIILPY LAPIDIFY	ADGIINSV ADVISING	ADGNRSUU UNGUARDS	INDUVIAL
ADFILLLN LANDFILL	ADGIINSW GWINIADS	ADGOOPRS GOSPODAR	ADIILOPP DIPLOPIA
ADFILLMN FILMLAND	ADGIINTU AUDITING	ADGOPRSU PODARGUS	ADIILRST DISTRAIL
ADFILLNW WINDFALL	ADGIJNRU ADJURING	ADGORTUU OUTGUARD	ADIILSST DIALISTS
ADFILMNO MANIFOLD	ADGIKLNR DARKLING	ADHHIPRS HARDSHIP	ADIILSSY DIALYSIS
ADFIMNRS FINDRAMS	ADGILLNU ALLUDING	ADHHNRTY HYDRANTH	ADIILTVY VALIDITY
ADFIMRSW DWARFISM	DUALLING	ADHIIJST IJTIHADS	ADIIMMSS MAIDISMS
ADFINORZ FORZANDI	ADGILLNW WINDGALL	ADHIIKSS DASHIKIS	ADIIMPSU ASPIDIUM
ADFINRST INDRAFTS	ADGILLNY DALLYING	ADHIINOP OPHIDIAN	ADIIMRSU MUDIRIAS
ADFIORSV DISFAVOR	ADGILMNS MADLINGS	ADHIINRW WHINIARD	ADIINNOT NIDATION
ADFKLLNO FOLKLAND	ADGILMNW DWALMING	ADHILLMO HOLLIDAM	ADIINOTU AUDITION
ADFLLNOW DOWNFALL	ADGILMOR MARIGOLD	ADHILLNS SANDHILL	ADIINPRS PINDARIS
ADFLMNOR LANDFORM	ADGILNNS LANDINGS	ADHILLOP PHALLOID	ADIINRST DISTRAIN
ADFLMNOY MANYFOLD	SANDLING	ADHILLOT THALLOID	ADIINSST DISTAINS
ADFLMOPR FRAMPOLD	ADGILNNU UNLADING	ADHILMOO HOMALOID	ADIINSSU SUIDIANS
ADFLMPSU MUDFLAPS	ADGILNOS LOADINGS	ADHILMOS HALIDOMS	ADIIOPRS SPORIDIA
ADFLMSTU MUDFLATS	ADGILNPP DAPPLING	ADHILNST HANDLIST	ADIIOPRT TAPIROID
ADFLNOPS PLAFONDS	ADGILNRS DARLINGS	ADHILOPS SHIPLOAD	ADIIORST TARSIOID
ADFLOOWY FLOODWAY	ADGILNRT DARTLING	ADHILOPY HAPLOIDY	ADIIPRTU TRIPUDIA
ADFLORSU FOULARDS	ADGILNRW DRAWLING	ADHILOSY HOLIDAYS	ADIIPRTY RAPIDITY
ADFMRSTU STUDFARM	ADGILNRY DARINGLY	ADHILPSY LADYSHIP	ADIIPSTY SAPIDITY
ADFNNOST FONDANTS	ADGILNZZ DAZZLING	ADHIMNOS ADMONISH	ADIIPTVY VAPIDITY
ADFNOORZ FORZANDO	ADGILOOS SOLIDAGO	ADHIMNOU HUMANOID	ADIIQRSU DAQUIRIS
ADFOOPST FOOTPADS	ADGILOPR PRODIGAL	ADHIMOPP AMPHIPOD	ADIIRSST DIARISTS
ADFORRSW FORWARDS	ADGILORS GOLIARDS	ADHIMPSS PHASMIDS	ADIIRSTT DISTRAIT
FROWARDS	ADGILORY GOLIARDY	ADHIMRTY MYRIADTH	TRIADIST
ADGGGILN DAGGLING	GYROIDAL	ADHINPSU DAUPHINS	ADIJNOST ADJOINTS
ADGGGINR DRAGGING	ADGIMMNR DRAMMING	ADHINRWY WHINYARD	ADIKKRRW KIRKWARD
ADGGGINS DAGGINGS	ADGIMMNW DWAMMING	ADHINSST STANDISH	ADIKKRRY KIRKYARD
ADGGHNOS HANGDOGS	ADGIMNNU MAUNDING	ADHINSTU DIANTHUS	ADIKLNPS LANDSKIP
ADGGILNN DANGLING	ADGIMNOP POMADING	ADHIOSTY TOADYISH	ADIKLNSY LADYKINS
ADGGILNS GADLINGS	ADGIMNPS DAMPINGS	ADHIPRSW WARDSHIP	ADIKLOSS ODALISKS
ADGGILRS RIGGALDS	ADGIMNRS MRIDANGS	ADHIPRSY SHIPYARD	ADIKMNNS MANKINDS
ADGGINRS NIGGARDS	ADGIMNRY MARDYING	ADHIPSTY DISPATHY	ADIKMSSS DISMASKS
ADGGINRU GUARDING	ADGIMNUW DWAMING	ADHIRTWW WITHDRAW	ADIKNNNU DUNNAKIN
ADGGLRSU SLUGGARD	ADGIMOSU DIGAMOUS	ADHKNORW HANDWORK	ADIKNNST INKSTAND
ADGHHILN HIGHLAND	ADGINNOR ADORNING	ADHKORSW DORHAWKS	ADIKNPSS SKIDPANS
ADGHHIOR HIGHROAD	ADGINNOT DONATING	ADHKOSSU SHAKUDOS	ADIKNRSS DISRANKS
ADGHILNN HANDLING	ADGINNPY PANDYING	ADHLLNOS HOLLANDS	ADIKNRST STINKARD
ADGHILOS HIDALGOS	ADGINNRS DARNINGS	ADHLMORT THRALDOM	ADIKPRSS DISPARKS
ADGHILPY DIAGLYPH	ADGINNRT DRANTING	ADHLMOSY HOLYDAMS	ADILLLPY PALLIDLY
ADGHILTY DAYLIGHT	ADGINNSS SANDINGS	ADHLMPSY LYMPHADS	ADILLMMS MILLDAMS
ADGHINOR HOARDING	ADGINNST STANDING	ADHLNORW WALDHORN	ADILLMNR MANDRILL
ADGHINPR HANDGRIP	ADGINNSW DAWNINGS	ADHMNOOS MANHOODS	ADILLMOU ALLODIUM
ADGHINSS SHADINGS	ADGINNSY SDAYNING	ADHNNOOR HONORAND	ADILLMOV VILLADOM
ADGHIPRS DIGRAPHS	ADGINNTU DAUNTING	ADHNORSU UNHOARDS	ADILLMSY DISMALLY
ADGHIRRS ARDRIGHS	ADGINOOP POIGNADO	ADHNOSTU HANDOUTS	ADILLNPS LANDSLIP
ADGHITTW TIGHTWAD	ADGINOOR RIGADOON	THOUSAND	ADILLOOP POLOIDAL
ADGHLNNO LONGHAND	ADGINOPT ADOPTING	ADHNOSUW UNSHADOW	ADILLOPS SPADILLO
ADGHNNSU HANDGUNS	ADGINORS ROADINGS	ADHNRSTY HYDRANTS	ADILLOSW DISALLOW
ADGHNOSW HAGDOWNS	ADGINOST DOATINGS	ADHOOPRS HOSPODAR	ADILLOSY DISLOYAL
ADGHOOPR ODOGRAPH	ADGINOTY TOADYING	ADHOORRS RHODORAS	ADILLRWY WILLYARD
ADGHORSW HOGWARDS	ADGINPPR DRAPPING	ADHOORSW ROADSHOW	ADILLSTY DISTALLY
ADGHPSYY DYSPHAGY	ADGINPTU UPDATING	ADHOORYZ HYDROZOA	ADILMMOS MODALISM
ADGHRSTU DRAUGHTS	ADGINRST TRADINGS	ADHOPRST HARDTOPS	ADILMNNO MANDOLIN
ADGHRTUY DRAUGHTY	ADGINRSW DRAWINGS	POTSHARD	ADILMNOS SALMONID
ADGIILLN DIALLING	SWARDING	ADHOPRSU UPHOARDS	ADILMNRS MANDRILS
ADGIILLO GLADIOLI	WARDINGS	ADHOPRSY RHAPSODY	ADILMOOR MODIOLAR
ADGIILNO GONIDIAL	ADGINRTY TARDYING	ADHORSTU TOADRUSH	ADILMOPS DIPLOMAS
ADGIILNP PLAIDING	ADGINSTU ADUSTING	ADHORSWY SHOWYARD	ADILMOPT DIPLOMAT
ADGIILNR DRAILING	SUDATING	ADHPSTYY DYSPATHY	ADILMOPY OLYMPIAD
ADGIILNS GLIADINS	ADGINSWY GWYNIADS	ADIIINRV VIRIDIAN	ADILMORU ORDALIUM
ADGIILNT DILATING	ADGIPRSU PAGURIDS	ADIIIQRU DAIQUIRI	ADILMOST MODALIST
ADGIILPY PYGIDIAL	ADGIRSZZ GIZZARDS	ADIIKLMM MILKMAID	ADILMOSU ALODIUMS
ADGIILST DIGITALS	ADGKOOSZ GADZOOKS	ADIIKLST TAILSKID	ADILMOSY AMYLOIDS
ADGIILTY ALGIDITY	ADGLLNOS GOLLANDS	ADIIKNOP PINAKOID	ADILMOTY MODALITY
ADGIIMNR ADMIRING	ADGLMNOS MANGOLDS	ADIIKNST ANTISKID	ADILMPSS PLASMIDS
ADGIIMNX ADMIXING	ADGLNOOS GONDOLAS	ADIIKOST DAKOITIS	ADILMPSU PALUDISM
ADGIIMST DIGAMIST	ADGLNOSW GOWLANDS	ADIILLMR MILLIARD	ADILMSSU DUALISMS
ADGIINNR DRAINING	ADGLOORY GARDYLOO	ADIILLNY IDYLLIAN	ADILMSSY DISMAYLS
ADGIINNS SDAINING	ADGMNORS GORMANDS	ADIILLOR ARILLOID	LADYISMS
ADGIINNV INVADING	ADGMNORU GOURMAND	ADIILLUV DILUVIAL	ADILNNNU NUNDINAL
ADGIINNY DIGYNIAN	ADGNNOQU QUANDONG	ADIILMSS MISDIALS	ADILNNSU DISANNUL
ADGIINOR RADIOING	ADGNNORS GRANDSON	ADIILNOT DILATION	ADILNOOR DOORNAIL
ADGIINOV AVOIDING	ADGNNRYY GYNANDRY	ADIILNSU INDUSIAL	ADILNOOV VINDALOO
ADGIINRR ARRIDING	ADGNOORS DRAGOONS	ADIILNSV INVALIDS	ADILNOPY PALINODY
ADGIINRY DAIRYING	GADROONS	ADIILNSW WINDSAIL	ADILNORS ORDINALS
ADGIINSU IGUANIDS	ADGNRRSU GURNARDS	ADIILNTY DAINTILY	ADILNOTY NODALITY
		ADIILNUV DILUVIAN	ADILNPRS SPANDRIL

ADILNPST	DISPLANT	ADINRRST	TRIDARNS
ADILNRSU	DIURNALS	ADINRSSU	SUNDARIS
ADILNRWY	INWARDLY	ADINRSTU	UNITARDS
ADILNSSU	SUNDIALS	ADINRUVZ	UNVIZARD
ADILNSSW	WINDLASS	ADIOOPSS	APODOSIS
ADILOOPZ	DIPLOZOA	ADIOOSSW	WOODSIAS
ADILOORT	IDOLATOR	ADIOPRSS	SPAROIDS
	TOROIDAL	ADIOPRST	PARODIST
ADILOPRT	TRIPODAL		PAROTIDS
ADILOPSS	DISPOSAL	ADIOPRSV	PRIVADOS
ADILOQSU	SQUALOID	ADIOPRTY	PODIATRY
ADILORST	DILATORS	ADIOPSTY	DYSTOPIA
ADILORSY	SOLIDARY	ADIORRTT	TRADITOR
ADILORTY	ADROITLY	ADIORSST	ASTROIDS
	DILATORY	ADIORSSV	ADVISORS
	IDOLATRY	ADIORSTT	STRADIOT
ADILOSTY	SODALITY	ADIORSTU	AUDITORS
ADILPPSY	DISAPPLY	ADIORSVY	ADVISORY
ADILPRSY	PYRALIDS	ADIORTUY	AUDITORY
ADILPSST	PLASTIDS	ADIOSSVW	DISAVOWS
ADILPSSY	DISPLAYS	ADIPRRTU	PURTRAID
ADILPSTU	PLAUDITS	ADIPRSST	DISPARTS
ADILRTWY	TAWDRILY	ADIRRWYZ	WIZARDRY
ADILRWYZ	WIZARDLY	ADIRSSTY	SATYRIDS
ADILSSTU	DUALISTS	ADIRSSUY	DYSURIAS
ADIMMNOO	AMMONOID	ADJNORSU	ADJOURNS
ADIMMNOS	MONADISM	ADJORSTU	ADJUSTOR
	NOMADISM	ADKKLOSY	KAKODYLS
ADIMMNSY	DYNAMISM	ADKLMRSU	MUDLARKS
ADIMMOST	AMIDMOST	ADKLOORW	WOODLARK
ADIMMOTU	DOMATIUM		WORKLOAD
ADIMNNOS	MONDAINS	ADKMOORR	DARKROOM
ADIMNNOT	DOMINANT	ADKNORTU	OUTDRANK
ADIMNOOR	MAINDOOR	ADKNRSTU	STUNKARD
ADIMNOST	DONATISM	ADKORSWY	WORKDAYS
	SAINTDOM	ADKRSSWY	SKYWARDS
ADIMNOWW	WIDOWMAN	ADLLLOOY	DOOLALLY
ADIMNRSW	MISDRAWN	ADLLMOSW	WADMOLLS
ADIMNRSY	MISANDRY	ADLLNOSW	LOWLANDS
ADIMNSTY	DYNAMIST	ADLLOPRS	POLLARDS
ADIMOPRY	MYRIAPOD	ADLLORSY	DORSALLY
ADIMOPSY	SYMPODIA	ADLMNOOR	MOORLAND
ADIMORRS	MIRADORS	ADLMNORY	RANDOMLY
ADIMOSST	MASTOIDS	ADLMNOSS	MOSSLAND
ADIMOSTT	MATTOIDS	ADLMOORU	MALODOUR
ADIMOSTY	TOADYISM	ADLMOPRW	MOLDWARP
ADIMPRSY	PYRAMIDS	ADLMOPSY	PSALMODY
ADIMRSSW	MISDRAWS	ADLNNORS	NORLANDS
ADIMRSUU	SUDARIUM	ADLNNOTW	TOWNLAND
ADIMSSST	DISMASTS	ADLNNTUU	UNDULANT
ADIMSSTU	DUMAISTS	ADLNOORS	LARDOONS
	STADIUMS	ADLNOPRT	PORTLAND
ADINNNTU	INUNDANT	ADLNOPRU	PAULDRON
ADINNOOT	DONATION	ADLNOPSU	POUNDALS
	NODATION	ADLNOPWY	DOWNPLAY
ADINNOPS	DIPNOANS	ADLNORWY	ONWARDLY
ADINNORS	ANDIRONS	ADLNOSSU	SOULDANS
ADINNORT	ORDINANT	ADLNOSSY	SYNODALS
ADINNOTU	NUDATION	ADLNOSTU	OUTLANDS
ADINNRSY	INNYARDS	ADLOORWW	WOOLWARD
ADINOOPS	ISOPODAN	ADLOPRSU	POULARDS
ADINOOPT	ADOPTION	ADLOPRWY	WORDPLAY
ADINOORT	TANDOORI	ADLOPSUU	PALUDOUS
ADINOOTT	DOTATION	ADLOQSUW	OLDSQUAW
ADINOPPS	OPPIDANS	ADLORRSW	WARLORDS
ADINOPRR	RAINDROP	ADLORTWY	TOWARDLY
ADINOPRS	PONIARDS	ADLPRUWY	UPWARDLY
ADINOPST	PINTADOS	ADMMNOOS	DOOMSMAN
ADINORRS	ORDINARS	ADMMNSSU	SUMMANDS
ADINORRY	ORDINARY	ADMMNTUU	MUTANDUM
ADINORSS	SADIRONS	ADMNNORY	MONANDRY
ADINORST	INTRADOS	ADMNNOSU	SOUNDMAN
ADINORSU	DINOSAUR	ADMNNOTU	NOTANDUM
ADINORTU	DURATION	ADMNOOOT	ODONTOMA
ADINOSTU	SUDATION	ADMNOORS	DOORSMAN
ADINOSTX	OXIDANTS		MADRONOS
ADINOSTY	DYSTONIA	ADMNOOST	MASTODON
ADINPSST	SANDPITS	ADMNOOSW	WOODSMAN
		ADMNOOSZ	MADZOONS

ADMNORST	DORMANTS		STEERAGE
	MORDANTS	AEEEGRSW	SEWERAGE
ADMNORSW	SANDWORM	AEEEGTTV	VEGETATE
	SWORDMAN	AEEEHLRT	ETHEREAL
ADMNOSSU	OSMUNDAS	AEEEHMPR	EPHEMERA
ADMNPPSU	SANDPUMP	AEEEHNRS	ENHEARSE
ADMOORRW	WARDROOM	AEEEHRRS	REHEARSE
ADMOORST	DOORMATS	AEEEHRRT	REHEATER
ADMOPPPU	POPPADUM	AEEEHSTT	AESTHETE
ADMOPPSU	POPADUMS	AEEEILNS	ALIENEES
ADMORSST	STARDOMS	AEEEIMNX	EXAMINEE
	TSARDOMS	AEEEIRST	EATERIES
ADMORSTW	MADWORTS	AEEEJNTT	JEANETTE
ADMRSSTU	DURMASTS	AEEEKKPS	KEEPSAKE
	MUSTARDS	AEEEKMSS	KAMEESES
ADNNOOSY	NOONDAYS	AEEEKMSZ	KAMEEZES
ADNNORTY	DYNATRON	AEEEKNRW	WEAKENER
ADNNOSTU	DAUNTONS	AEEELLST	TELESALE
ADNNRSTU	DUNNARTS	AEEELNRV	VENEREAL
ADNOOPRS	PANDOORS	AEEELNST	SELENATE
	SPADROON	AEEELPRR	REPEALER
ADNOOQRU	QUADROON	AEEELQSU	SEQUELAE
ADNOORST	DONATORS	AEEELRRS	RELEASER
	ODORANTS	AEEELRRV	REVEALER
	TANDOORS	AEEELRSS	RELEASES
	TORNADOS	AEEELRST	TEASELER
ADNOORTY	DONATORY	AEEELRSW	WEASELER
ADNOOSVW	ADVOWSON	AEEELSSS	EASELESS
ADNOPRSU	PANDOURS	AEEELSTV	ELEVATES
ADNOPRSV	PROVANDS	AEEEMMRT	METAMERE
ADNOQRSU	SQUADRON	AEEEMNST	EASEMENT
ADNORRSW	NORWARDS	AEEEMPRS	PERMEASE
ADNORSTU	ROTUNDAS	AEEEMPRT	PERMEATE
ADNORSTW	SANDWORT	AEEENNRV	VENEREAN
ADNORSWY	NAYWORDS	AEEENPTT	PATENTEE
ADNORSXY	SARDONYX	AEEENRST	SERENATE
ADNORTUW	UNTOWARD	AEEENRTT	ENTERATE
ADNORWWY	WANWORDY	AEEENRTV	ENERVATE
ADNOSSTU	ASTOUNDS		VENERATE
ADNOSTTU	OUTSTAND	AEEEPRRT	REPARTEE
	STANDOUT		REPEATER
ADNPSSTU	UPSTANDS	AEEEPSTW	SWEETPEA
ADNRSSUW	SUNWARDS	AEEERRST	ARRESTEE
ADOOPRRT	TRAPDOOR	AEEERSST	TESSERAE
ADOOPRSU	SAUROPOD	AEEFFLLS	FELAFELS
ADOOPSSW	SAPWOODS	AEEFFLRT	TAFFEREL
ADOORSWY	DOORWAYS	AEEFFNRT	AFFERENT
ADOPRRSW	WARDROPS	AEEFGILR	FILAGREE
ADOPRSSW	PASSWORD	AEEFGIRR	FERRIAGE
ADOPSSSU	SOAPSUDS	AEEFGIRS	FEGARIES
ADORRSTU	DARTROUS	AEEFGLSU	FUSELAGE
ADORSTUW	OUTWARDS	AEEFGNST	FANTEEGS
ADORSTUY	SUDATORY	AEEFGRSS	SERFAGES
ADORTUVY	ADVOUTRY	AEEFGSTW	WEFTAGES
ADPRRTUY	PURTRAYD	AEEFHIRS	SHEAFIER
ADRSSTTU	STARDUST	AEEFHLLS	SELFHEAL
ADSSSTUW	SAWDUSTS	AEEFHRST	FEATHERS
ADSSTUWY	SAWDUSTY	AEEFHRTY	FEATHERY
AEEEELRS	RELEASEE	AEEFIINR	INFERIAE
AEEEFLRS	EELFARES	AEEFIKLL	LEAFLIKE
AEEEFRRW	FREEWARE	AEEFIKRR	FREAKIER
AEEEFRTY	AFTEREYE	AEEFIKRS	FAKERIES
AEEEGKLS	KEELAGES	AEEFIKRW	WAKERIFE
AEEEGLLS	LEGALESE	AEEFILMN	FILENAME
AEEEGLNR	GENERALE	AEEFILNR	FLANERIE
AEEEGLRT	EGLATERE	AEEFILRS	SERAFILE
	REGELATE	AEEFILRT	FRAILTEE
	RELEGATE	AEEFILST	FEALTIES
AEEEGLRV	LEVERAGE		LEAFIEST
AEEEGLST	LEGATEES	AEEFIPSW	SPAEWIFE
AEEEGLSV	SELVAGEE	AEEFIRRS	RAREFIES
AEEEGLTV	VEGELATE	AEEFIRSS	FREESIAS
AEEEGNRT	GENERATE	AEEFISST	SAFETIES
	RENEGATE	AEEFKMNT	FAKEMENT
	TEENAGER	AEEFKOPR	FOREPEAK
AEEEGPRS	PEERAGES	AEEFLLMR	FEMERALL
AEEEGPSS	SEEPAGES	AEEFLLMT	FLAMELET
AEEEGRST	EAGEREST	AEEFLLNV	EVENFALL
	ETAGERES	AEEFLLRW	FAREWELL

```
AEEFLLSS LEAFLESS
AEEFLLST FELLATES
         LEAFLETS
AEEFLMNS ENFLAMES
AEEFLMOS FLEASOME
AEEFLMSS FAMELESS
AEEFLNRU FUNEREAL
AEEFLOOV FOVEOLAE
AEEFLORV OVERLEAF
AEEFLRRR REFERRAL
AEEFLRRS FEARLESS
AEEFLRST REFLATES
AEEFLRSW WELFARES
AEEFMNOR FOREMEAN
         FORENAME
AEEFMNRS ENFRAMES
AEEFMORS FEARSOME
AEEFMRRS REFRAMES
AEEFMRTY FEMETARY
AEEFNRST FASTENER
         FENESTRA
AEEFNRTT FATTENER
AEEFNSSS SAFENESS
AEEFOSTU FEATEOUS
AEEFRRST FERRATES
AEEFRSST FEASTERS
AEEFRSTU FEATURES
AEEFRSWY FREEWAYS
AEEFTTUV FAUVETTE
AEEGGHIW WEIGHAGE
AEEGGINR AGREEING
AEEGGIRV AGGRIEVE
AEEGGLLS ALLEGGES
AEEGGLOU AEGLOGUE
AEEGGLRS GREGALES
AEEGGNNR GANGRENE
AEEGGNOS GASOGENE
AEEGGNOZ GAZOGENE
AEEGGNRS ENGAGERS
AEEGGOPS EPAGOGES
AEEGGPRU PUGGAREE
AEEGHIRS HIREAGES
AEEGHIRT HERITAGE
AEEGHLOT HELOTAGE
AEEGHLRS SHEARLEG
AEEGHLRW RAGWHEEL
AEEGHMPR GRAPHEME
AEEGHNRS SHAGREEN
AEEGHNSW WHANGEES
AEEGHRRT GATHERER
         REGATHER
AEEGIINR AEGIRINE
AEEGIIRT AEGIRITE
AEEGIIST GAIETIES
AEEGILLS GALILEES
         LEGALISE
AEEGILLZ LEGALIZE
AEEGILMN LIEGEMAN
AEEGILMR GLEAMIER
AEEGILMS MILEAGES
AEEGILNR ALGERINE
AEEGILNS ENSILAGE
         LINEAGES
AEEGILNT GALENITE
         GELATINE
         LEGATINE
AEEGILNV INVEAGLE
AEEGILPR PERIGEAL
AEEGILRS GASELIER
AEEGILST ELEGIAST
AEEGILSW WEIGELAS
AEEGILTV LEVIGATE
AEEGIMNR GERMAINE
AEEGIMNT GEMINATE
AEEGIMRS GAMESIER
AEEGIMRT EMIGRATE
         REMIGATE
AEEGINPR PERIGEAN
AEEGINRR REGAINER

AEEGINRS GESNERIA
AEEGINRT GRATINEE
AEEGINRZ RAZEEING
AEEGINSS ASSIGNEE
AEEGINST SAGENITE
AEEGINSU EUGENIAS
AEEGINSV ENVISAGE
AEEGINTV AGENTIVE
         NEGATIVE
AEEGINTX EXIGEANT
AEEGIPQU EQUIPAGE
AEEGIPRS PIERAGES
AEEGIRRS GREASIER
AEEGIRSS GREASIES
AEEGIRTT AIGRETTE
AEEGIRTV ERGATIVE
AEEGISSS ASSIEGES
AEEGLLNR ALLERGEN
AEEGLLRS ALLEGERS
AEEGLLSZ GAZELLES
AEEGLMNS MELANGES
AEEGLMNV GAVELMEN
AEEGLMRT TELEGRAM
AEEGLMRY MEAGRELY
AEEGLNNR ENLARGEN
AEEGLNOS GASOLENE
AEEGLNOT ELONGATE
AEEGLNRR ENLARGER
AEEGLNRS ENLARGES
         GENERALS
         GLEANERS
AEEGLNSV EVANGELS
AEEGLNVY EVANGELY
AEEGLOST SEGOTALE
AEEGLPRS PEREGALS
AEEGLRSS EELGRASS
         GEARLESS
         LARGESSE
AEEGLRSU LEAGUERS
AEEGLRSW LEGWEARS
AEEGLRTU REGULATE
AEEGLRUX EXERGUAL
AEEGLSST GATELESS
AEEGLSSV SELVAGES
AEEGLSSW WAGELESS
AEEGLSSY EYEGLASS
AEEGLSTT GALETTES
AEEGLSTV VEGETALS
AEEGLTTU TUTELAGE
AEEGLTUV EVULGATE
AEEGMMOS GAMESOME
AEEGMMST GEMMATES
         TAGMEMES
AEEGMNOR ARGEMONE
AEEGMNRS AGREMENS
AEEGMNRT AGREMENT
AEEGMNSS GAMENESS
         MAGNESES
AEEGMNTT TEGMENTA
AEEGMNTZ GAZEMENT
AEEGMOST SOMEGATE
AEEGMRST GAMESTER
         MEAGREST
AEEGMRSU REMUAGES
AEEGMSSS MEGASSES
         MESSAGES
AEEGMSSU MESSUAGE
AEEGNNNO ENNEAGON
AEEGNNPS PANGENES
AEEGNNRS ENRANGES
AEEGNNRT GENERANT
AEEGNNRU ENRAUNGE
AEEGNNRV ENGRAVEN
AEEGNOPS PEONAGES
AEEGNPPS GENAPPES
AEEGNRRT ETRANGER
AEEGNRRV ENGRAVER
AEEGNRST ESTRANGE

         GRANTEES
         GREATENS
         REAGENTS
         SEGREANT
         SERGEANT
         STERNAGE
AEEGNRSU RENAGUES
AEEGNRSV AVENGERS
         ENGRAVES
AEEGNRTU GAUNTREE
AEEGNSSS SAGENESS
AEEGNSTT TENTAGES
AEEGNSTV VENTAGES
AEEGNTTV VEGETANT
AEEGOPRV OVERPAGE
AEEGOPSS SAPEGOES
AEEGORSV OVERAGES
AEEGORVV OVERGAVE
AEEGOSTX GEOTAXES
AEEGPRRS ASPERGER
         PRESAGER
AEEGPRRT PARGETER
AEEGPRSS ASPERGES
         PRESAGES
AEEGRRRT REGRATER
AEEGRRSS GREASERS
AEEGRRST REGRATES
AEEGRRSW WAGERERS
AEEGRSST RESTAGES
AEEGRSTT GREATEST
AEEGRSTU TREAGUES
AEEGRSTW STREWAGE
AEEGRSUZ GUEREZAS
AEEGSSTT GESTATES
AEEGSTTZ GAZETTES
AEEHHHSS HASHEESH
AEEHHIRT HEATHIER
AEEHHNST ENSHEATH
         HEATHENS
AEEHHOOP PAHOEHOE
AEEHHRSS REHASHES
AEEHHRST HEATHERS
AEEHHRTY HEATHERY
AEEHHSST SHEATHES
AEEHIKRS SHIKAREE
AEEHILNP ELAPHINE
AEEHILRS SHIRALEE
AEEHILRT ETHERIAL
AEEHIMPT EPITHEMA
AEEHINRS INHEARSE
AEEHINRT ATHERINE
AEEHIPST APHETISE
         HEAPIEST
         HEPATISE
AEEHIPTT HEPATITE
AEEHIPTZ APHETIZE
         HEPATIZE
AEEHIRRS HEARSIER
AEEHIRRT EARTHIER
         HEARTIER
AEEHIRSS ASHERIES
AEEHIRST HEARTIES
AEEHIRSV SHIVAREE
AEEHIRTW WHEATIER
AEEHISST ATHEISES
         ESTHESIA
AEEHISTT ATHETISE
         HESITATE
AEEHISTV HEAVIEST
AEEHISTZ ATHEIZES
AEEHITTZ ATHETIZE
AEEHKLLR RAKEHELL
AEEHKLLU KEELHAUL
AEEHKNRS HEARKENS
AEEHKRSU HEUREKAS
AEEHLLSS SEASHELL
AEEHLMNW WHALEMEN
         WHEELMAN
AEEHLMNY HYMENEAL

AEEHLMOS HEALSOME
AEEHLMPT HELPMATE
AEEHLNOS ENHALOES
AEEHLNPT ELEPHANT
AEEHLNRT LEATHERN
AEEHLNSS HALENESS
AEEHLNVY HEAVENLY
AEEHLORS ARSEHOLE
AEEHLORV OVERHALE
AEEHLPST PLEASETH
AEEHLPTT TELEPATH
AEEHLRST HALTERES
         LEATHERS
AEEHLRSV HAVERELS
AEEHLRTT HEARTLET
AEEHLRTY LEATHERY
AEEHLSST HATELESS
AEEHLSTT ATHLETES
AEEHLTTY ETHYLATE
AEEHMMRR HAMMERER
AEEHMNNY HYMENEAN
AEEHMNRS SHAREMEN
         SHEARMEN
AEEHMNRT EARTHMEN
AEEHMNST METHANES
AEEHMNTX EXANTHEM
AEEHMPSS EMPHASES
AEEHMRSS MAHSEERS
AEEHMRST ERATHEMS
AEEHMRTY ERYTHEMA
AEEHMSST MATHESES
AEEHMTUX EXHUMATE
AEEHNNSS SNEESHAN
AEEHNNTX XANTHENE
AEEHNOPR EARPHONE
AEEHNPST HEPTANES
         PHENATES
         STEPHANE
AEEHNRSS ARSHEENS
AEEHNRST HASTENER
         HEARTENS
AEEHNRSU UNHEARSE
AEEHNRTT HATERENT
         THREATEN
AEEHNRTU URETHANE
AEEHNRTW WATERHEN
         WREATHEN
AEEHNRWY ANYWHERE
AEEHNSST ANTHESES
AEEHNSTU UNEATHES
AEEHNSTW ENSWATHE
AEEHORRV OVERHEAR
AEEHORSS SEAHORSE
         SEASHORE
AEEHORTV OVERHEAT
AEEHPRRS REPHRASE
AEEHPRSS RESHAPES
         SPHAERES
         SPHEARES
AEEHPRST PREHEATS
         SPREATHE
AEEHPSUV UPHEAVES
AEEHQSSU QUASHEES
AEEHRRSS SHEARERS
AEEHRRTU URETHRAE
AEEHRRTW WREATHER
AEEHRSTT THEATERS
         THEATRES
AEEHRSTV THREAVES
AEEHRSTW WEATHERS
         WREATHES
AEEHRTVW WHATEVER
AEEHSTTW SAWTEETH
AEEIIMRT METAIRIE
AEEIISST ASEITIES
AEEIKKLW LIKEWAKE
AEEIKLMU LEUKEMIA
AEEIKLPT TAPELIKE
AEEIKLRW WEAKLIER
```

```
AEEIKLST LEAKIEST
AEEIKLVW WAVELIKE
AEEIKMMR MERIMAKE
AEEIKMNT KETAMINE
AEEIKNRS SNEAKIER
AEEIKNRT ANKERITE
         KREATINE
AEEIKNSS AKINESES
AEEIKPST PEAKIEST
AEEIKRRS RAKERIES
         SKEARIER
AEEILLNT TENAILLE
AEEILLRS REALLIES
AEEILLST LEALTIES
AEEILMMN MELAMINE
AEEILMMT MEALTIME
AEEILMNT MELANITE
AEEILMRS ALMERIES
         MEASLIER
AEEILMRT EREMITAL
         MATERIEL
         REALTIME
AEEILMST MEALIEST
AEEILMSV MALVESIE
AEEILMTZ METALIZE
AEEILNNS SELENIAN
AEEILNPR PERINEAL
AEEILNPS ALEPINES
         PENALISE
         SEPALINE
AEEILNPT PETALINE
         TAPELINE
AEEILNPZ PENALIZE
AEEILNRT ELATERIN
         ENTAILER
         TREENAIL
AEEILNSS SEALINES
AEEILNTV ELVANITE
         VENTAILE
AEEILORT AEROLITE
AEEILOTT ETIOLATE
AEEILPRR PEARLIER
AEEILPRS ESPALIER
         PEARLIES
AEEILPRT PEARLITE
AEEILPST EPILATES
AEEILPSW PALEWISE
AEEILQSU EQUALISE
AEEILQUX EXEQUIAL
AEEILQUZ EQUALIZE
AEEILRRS REALISER
AEEILRRT RETAILER
AEEILRRZ REALIZER
AEEILRSS REALISES
AEEILRST ATELIERS
         EARLIEST
         LEARIEST
         REALTIES
AEEILRSV VELARISE
AEEILRSY YEARLIES
AEEILRSZ REALIZES
         SLEAZIER
AEEILRTT LATERITE
         LITERATE
AEEILRTV LEVIRATE
         RELATIVE
AEEILRVW LIVEWARE
         REVIEWAL
AEEILRVZ VELARIZE
AEEILSST ASTELIES
AEEILSTT AILETTES
AEEILSTV ELATIVES
         LEAVIEST
         VEALIEST
AEEILSVW ALEWIVES
AEEILTTV LEVITATE
AEEIMMNT MEANTIME
AEEIMNRS REMANIES
AEEIMNRX EXAMINER

AEEIMNSS NEMESIAS
AEEIMNST MATINEES
         SEMINATE
AEEIMNSX EXAMINES
AEEIMNUV MAUVEINE
AEEIMOSS AMEIOSES
AEEIMPRS EMPAIRES
AEEIMRRS SMEARIER
AEEIMRSS SERIEMAS
AEEIMRST EMIRATES
         REAMIEST
         STEAMIER
AEEIMRTV VIAMETER
AEEIMSSS MISEASES
         SIAMESES
AEEIMSST SEAMIEST
         STEAMIES
AEEIMSSZ SIAMEZES
AEEIMSTT ESTIMATE
         ETATISME
         MEATIEST
         TEATIMES
AEEIMSTW TEAMWISE
AEEINNRS ANSERINE
AEEINOPS PAEONIES
AEEINPRS NAPERIES
AEEINPRT APERIENT
AEEINPTT PIANETTE
AEEINRRS REARISEN
AEEINRRT RETAINER
AEEINRSS SENARIES
AEEINRST ARSENITE
         RESINATE
         STEARINE
         TRAINEES
AEEINRSU UNEASIER
AEEINSSS EASINESS
AEEINSSV VAINESSE
AEEINSTT ANISETTE
         TETANIES
         TETANISE
AEEINSTV NAIVETES
AEEINSVW INWEAVES
AEEINTTZ TETANIZE
AEEIOOPP EPOPOEIA
AEEIORST ETAERIOS
AEEIPPRR PAPERIER
AEEIPPSS APEPSIES
AEEIPPST APPETISE
AEEIPPSU EUPEPSIA
AEEIPPTT APPETITE
AEEIPPTZ APPETIZE
AEEIPRRR REPAIRER
AEEIPRRS PEREIRAS
         SPEARIER
AEEIPRST PETARIES
AEEIPRTV PERVIATE
AEEIPSST EPITASES
AEEIPSTT PEATIEST
AEEIPSTX EXPIATES
AEEIQRSU QUEASIER
AEEIQRUZ QUEAZIER
AEEIQSTU EQUISETA
AEEIRRSS REARISES
AEEIRRST ARTERIES
         REASTIER
AEEIRRTT RETRAITE
AEEIRRTW WATERIER
AEEIRRVW WAVERIER
AEEIRSST SERIATES
AEEIRSTT ARIETTES
         ITERATES
         TEARIEST
         TREATIES
         TREATISE
AEEIRSTV EVIRATES
AEEIRSTW SWEATIER
         TAWERIES
         WEARIEST

AEEIRSTY YEASTIER
AEEIRSVV AVERSIVE
AEEISSTX EXTASIES
AEEISSVW SEAWIVES
AEEISTTT ETATISTE
         STEATITE
AEEISTTV AVIETTES
         ESTIVATE
         EVITATES
AEEISTUX EUTAXIES
         EUTEXIAS
AEEITTUX EUTAXITE
AEEITUVX EXUVIATE
AEEJLNPT JETPLANE
AEEJLOSU JEALOUSE
AEEJNRST SERJEANT
AEEJOPRT PEJORATE
AEEKKLWY LYKEWAKE
AEEKKNOS KOKANEES
AEEKKPSY KEEPSAKY
AEEKLLST LAKELETS
         SKELETAL
AEEKLMRT TELEMARK
AEEKLMSS MAKELESS
AEEKLNST KANTELES
AEEKLSSW WAKELESS
AEEKLSTY EYESTALK
AEEKMNSS KAMSEENS
AEEKMORV MAKEOVER
AEEKMRRR REMARKER
AEEKMRRT MARKETER
AEEKMRST MEERKATS
AEEKNNNS NANKEENS
AEEKNORW REAWOKEN
AEEKNPRT PERTAKEN
AEEKNPSU SNEAKUP
AEEKNPSW NEWSPEAK
AEEKNRSS SNEAKERS
AEEKNRSW WAKENERS
AEEKNSSW WEAKNESS
AEEKORRV OVERRAKE
AEEKORST KERATOSE
         KREASOTE
AEEKORTV OVERTAKE
         TAKEOVER
AEEKPRSS RESPEAKS
         SPEAKERS
AEEKPRST PERTAKES
AEEKQRSU SQUEAKER
AEEKRRST RETAKERS
         STREAKER
AEEKRRSW WREAKERS
AEEKRSST SAKERETS
AEELLLTT TELLTALE
AEELLMMS MAMSELLE
AEELLNOV NOVELLAE
AEELLOSV ALVEOLES
AEELLOTT ALLOTTEE
AEELLPRS PARELLES
AEELLPTT PLATELET
AEELLPTY TELEPLAY
AEELLRRT TERRELLA
AEELLSST SATELLES
         TESSELLA
AEELLSSZ ZEALLESS
AEELLSTT STELLATE
AEELLSWY WEASELLY
AEELLTVV VALVELET
AEELMMTU MALEMUTE
AEELMNPS EMPANELS
         EMPLANES
         ENSAMPLE
AEELMNPT PLATEMEN
AEELMNSS LAMENESS
         MANELESS
         NAMELESS
         SALESMEN
AEELMNST MANTEELS
         STEELMAN

         TALESMEN
AEELMNSW WEALSMEN
AEELMNSY AMYLENES
AEELMNTT MANTELET
AEELMNTV LAVEMENT
AEELMOTT MATELOTE
AEELMPRX EXEMPLAR
AEELMPRY EMPYREAL
AEELMPSX EXAMPLES
AEELMPTT PALMETTE
         TEMPLATE
AEELMRST LAMETERS
AEELMSSS SEAMLESS
AEELMSST MATELESS
         MEATLESS
         TAMELESS
AEELMSTU EMULATES
AEELNNPS ENPLANES
AEELNNRT LANNERET
AEELNNSS LEANNESS
AEELNOPR PERONEAL
AEELNOPT ANTELOPE
AEELNORU ALEURONE
AEELNPPS SPALPEEN
AEELNPSS PALENESS
AEELNQSU SQUALENE
AEELNRRS LEARNERS
AEELNRSS REALNESS
AEELNRST ALTERNES
AEELNRSV ENSLAVER
AEELNRSW RENEWALS
AEELNRTV LEVANTER
         RELEVANT
AEELNRTX EXTERNAL
AEELNSST LATENESS
AEELNSSV ENSLAVES
         VANELESS
AEELNSTY ENTAYLES
AEELNTUV EVENTUAL
AEELNTVY VENTAYLE
AEELOPRS PAROLEES
AEELOPRV OVERLEAP
AEELORRS RELEASOR
AEELORST OLEASTER
AEELORSU AUREOLES
AEELORTT TOLERATE
AEELORTV ELEVATOR
AEELORTW TOLEWARE
AEELOSSW LEASOWES
AEELOTTT TEETOTAL
AEELPRRS PEARLERS
         RELAPSER
AEELPRRT PALTERER
AEELPRSS PLEASERS
         RELAPSES
AEELPRST PLEATERS
         PRELATES
AEELPRSU PLEASURE
         SERPULAE
AEELPRSV VESPERAL
AEELPRTY PTERYLAE
AEELPSST SPATLESE
         TAPELESS
AEELPSTT PALETTES
AEELPSTU EPAULETS
AEELPSTV SEPTLEVA
AEELQRSU SQUEALER
AEELRRST RELATERS
AEELRRSV REVERSAL
         SLAVERER
AEELRRTU URETERAL
AEELRRTV TRAVELER
AEELRSST STEALERS
         TEARLESS
         TESSERAL
AEELRSSU LEASURES
AEELRSSV SEVERALS
AEELRSSW WARELESS
AEELRSTT ALERTEST
```

AEELRSTU RESALUTE	AEENORVW OVENWARE	AEERRSVW WAVERERS	AEFGMNOR FORGEMAN
AEELRSTY EASTERLY	AEENOTTU OUTEATEN	AEERSSSS REASSESS	AEFGMNRT FRAGMENT
AEELRSUV REVALUES	AEENPPTT APPETENT	AEERSSSU SEASURES	AEFGNNOT FONTANGE
AEELRSVY AVERSELY	AEENPQTU PETANQUE	AEERSSSV ASSEVERS	AEFGNORT FRONTAGE
AEELSSST ALTESSES	AEENPSSX EXPANSES	AEERSSSY ESSAYERS	AEFGNRRS GRANFERS
SATELESS	AEENRRRW WARRENER	AEERSSTT ESTREATS	AEFGNRST ENGRAFTS
SEATLESS	AEENRRSS RARENESS	RESTATES	AEFGOOPT FOOTPAGE
AEELSSTU SETUALES	AEENRRST TERRANES	AEERSSTW SWEATERS	AEFGOORT FOOTGEAR
AEELSSTV SALVETES	AEENRRSV RAVENERS	AEERSSTZ ERSATZES	AEFGOOST FOOTAGES
AEELSVW WAVELESS	AEENRRSW ANSWERER	AEERSSUU URAEUSES	AEFGORRS FORAGERS
AEELSTTY LAYETTES	REANSWER	AEERSSUV VAREUSES	AEFGORTT FROTTAGE
AEELSTVW WAVELETS	AEENRRSY YEARNERS	AEERSTTT ATTESTER	AEFGOSSU FOUGASSE
AEEMMNRS MERESMAN	AEENRRTT NATTERER	AEERSTTX EXTREATS	AEFGRRST GRAFTERS
AEEMMNTZ MAZEMENT	AEENRRTV TAVERNER	AEERSTWW WETWARES	AEFHIKRS FREAKISH
AEEMPPSY EMPYEMAS	AEENRSSS SEARNESS	AEERTTTZ TERZETTA	AEFHIKSW WEAKFISH
AEEMMRST AMMETERS	AEENRSST ASSENTER	AEERVWYY EVERYWAY	AEFHILLN FELLAHIN
METAMERS	EARNESTS	AEESSSSS ASSESSES	AEFHILLT TEFILLAH
AEEMMSST MESSMATE	SARSENET	AEFFFLRS FLAFFERS	AEFHILOR FORHAILE
AEEMNNOS ANEMONES	AEENRSSX XERANSES	AEFFGIRS GIRAFFES	AEFHILOX HEXAFOIL
AEEMNNRT REMANENT	AEENRSTT ENTREATS	AEFFGNRS ENGRAFFS	AEFHILRS FLASHIER
AEEMNNSS MEANNESS	RATTEENS	AEFFGRSU GAUFFERS	AEFHIMSS FAMISHES
AEEMNORV OVERNAME	AEENRSTV AVENTRES	SUFFRAGE	AEFHLMSU SHAMEFUL
AEEMNORZ ARMOZEEN	VETERANS	AEFFHIKY KAFFIYEH	AEFHLORS FAHLORES
AEEMNOSW SEAWOMEN	AEENRSUV UNREAVES	AEFFILRW WAFFLIER	AEFHLRSS FLASHERS
AEEMNPRS SPEARMEN	AEENRTTV ANTEVERT	AEFFILUV EFFLUVIA	AEFHLRST FARTHELS
AEEMNPRT PETERMAN	AEENRTTX EXTERNAT	AEFFIMRR AFFIRMER	AEFHLRTY FATHERLY
AEEMNPRY EMPYREAN	EXTRANET	REAFFIRM	AEFHLSST FLASHEST
AEEMNPTV PAVEMENT	AEENRTTY ENTREATY	AEFFIPRS PIAFFERS	AEFHMNRS FRESHMAN
AEEMNRST REMANETS	AEENRTUV AVENTURE	AEFFKLRU FREAKFUL	AEFHNRSW FERNSHAW
AEEMNRSW MENSWEAR	AEENSTTV NAVETTES	AEFFKOST OFFTAKES	AEFHRRST SHAFTERS
AEEMNRTU NUMERATE	AEENSUVW UNWEAVES	AEFFLMSW FLAMFEWS	AEFHRSTT FARTHEST
AEEMNRTV AVERMENT	AEEOPRRT PATERERO	AEFFLNSS SNAFFLES	AEFIILMS FAMILIES
AEEMNRTW WATERMEN	PERORATE	AEFFLNTU AFFLUENT	AEFIILNS FINALISE
AEEMNRUV MANEUVER	AEEOPRST OPERATES	AEFFLRRS RAFFLERS	AEFIILNZ FINALIZE
AEEMNRVY EVERYMAN	PROTEASE	AEFFLRSW WAFFLERS	AEFIILSS SALIFIES
AEEMNSSS SAMENESS	AEEOPRTT OPERETTA	AEFFLSTU FEASTFUL	AEFIILST FILIATES
AEEMNSST TAMENESS	AEEORRSU REAROUSE	SUFFLATE	AEFIIMNS INFAMIES
AEEMNSTU MANSUETE	AEEORRSW SOWARREE	AEFFLSUX AFFLUXES	INFAMISE
AEEMORST EROTEMAS	AEEORRTV OVERRATE	AEFFMRSU EARMUFFS	AEFIIMNZ INFAMIZE
AEEMPPRR PAMPERER	AEEORRVW OVERWEAR	AEFFNNSS NAFFNESS	AEFIIMRS RAMIFIES
AEEMPRRT TAMPERER	AEEORRVY OVERYEAR	AEFFNORT AFFRONTE	AEFIINRT FAINTIER
AEEMPRST TEMPERAS	AEEORSSV OVERSEAS	AEFFORST AFFOREST	AEFIINSS SANIFIES
AEEMPRSY EMPAYRES	AEEORSTV OVEREATS	AEFFQRSU QUAFFERS	AEFIINST FAINITES
AEEMPRTT ATTEMPER	AEEORSVW OVERAWES	AEFFRSST RESTAFFS	AEFIIPRT APERITIF
AEEMPSTU AMPUTEES	AEEPPRRR PREPARER	STAFFERS	AEFIIRRS FRIARIES
AEEMQRRU REMARQUE	AEEPPRRS PAPERERS	AEFGGGOS FOGGAGES	AEFIIRRT RATIFIER
AEEMQRSU MARQUEES	PREPARES	AEFGGILR FLAGGIER	AEFIIRST RATIFIES
AEEMQTTU MAQUETTE	REPAPERS	AEFGGINU FEAGUING	AEFIIRSU AURIFIES
AEEMRRST REMASTER	AEEPPRRT PARTERRE	AEFGGMOS MEGAFOGS	AEFIITVX FIXATIVE
STREAMER	AEEPRRST TAPERERS	AEFGHINR HANGFIRE	AEFIJLOS JEOFAILS
AEEMRRSU MEASURER	AEEPRRTT PATTERER	AEFGHINS SHEAFING	AEFIKLST FLAKIEST
AEEMRSST MASSETER	AEEPRRTU APERTURE	AEFGHOSS FOGASHES	AEFIKMRR FIREMARK
SEAMSTER	AEEPRSSS ASPERSES	AEFGHTTU FUGHETTA	AEFIKRUW WAUKRIFE
STEAMERS	PREASSES	AEFGIIRS GASIFIER	AEFILLOT FELLATIO
AEEMRSSU MEASURES	REPASSES	AEFGIISS GASIFIES	AEFILLRW FIREWALL
REASSUME	AEEPRSST TRAPESES	AEFGIKNR FREAKING	AEFILMNR INFLAMER
AEEMRSTT TEAMSTER	AEEPRSSZ SPREAZES	AEFGILNS FINAGLES	RIFLEMAN
AEEMRSTY METAYERS	AEEPRSTT PEARTEST	AEFGILOS FOLIAGES	AEFILMNS FLAMINES
AEEMSSST SEAMSETS	AEEPRSTU EPURATES	AEFGILRR FRAGILER	INFLAMES
AEEMSSSU MASSEUSE	SUPERATE	AEFGIMTU FUMIGATE	MISFALNE
AEEMSSTU MEATUSES	AEEPRSTZ TRAPEZES	AEFGINRW WAFERING	AEFILMNT FILAMENT
AEEMSTTU AMUSETTE	AEEPSSTT SPATTEES	AEFGINRY AREFYING	AEFILMST FLAMIEST
AEENNOST NEONATES	AEEQRRUV QUAVERER	AEFGINST FEASTING	AEFILMSY MAYFLIES
AEENNPST PENTANES	AEERRRST ARRESTER	AEFGINTU FANTIGUE	AEFILMTY FEMALITY
AEENNRSS ENSNARES	REARREST	AEFGIRRU ARGUFIER	AEFILNNR INFERNAL
NEARNESS	AEERRSST ASSERTER	AEFGIRST FRIGATES	AEFILNOR FORELAIN
AEENNRTU ENAUNTER	REASSERT	AEFGIRSU ARGUFIES	AEFILNOT OLEFIANT
AEENNRTV REVENANT	SERRATES	AEFGIRTU FIGURATE	AEFILNPS LIFESPAN
AEENNRUX ANNEXURE	TERRASES	FRUITAGE	AEFILNRU FRAULEIN
AEENNSSS SANENESS	AEERRSSU ERASURES	AEFGISTU FATIGUES	AEFILNST INFLATES
AEENNSST NEATNESS	REASSURE	AEFGLLOP FLAGPOLE	AEFILNSV FLAVINES
AEENOORT AEROTONE	AEERRSSW SWEARERS	AEFGLLSU FULLAGES	AEFILOOR AEROFOIL
AEENOPRS PERAEONS	AEERRSTT RETRATES	AEFGLMNU FUGLEMAN	AEFILORS FORESAIL
PERSONAE	RETREATS	AEFGLMOP MEGAFLOP	AEFILORT FLOATIER
AEENORRS REASONER	TREATERS	AEFGLNSS FANGLESS	AEFILOST FOLIATES
AEENORSS SEASONER	AEERRSTU AUSTERER	AEFGLORW GAREFOWL	AEFILPPR FLAPPIER
AEENORST RESONATE	TREASURE	AEFGLOST FLOTAGES	AEFILPST FLEAPITS
AEENORTV OVERNEAT	AEERRSTV TRAVERSE	AEFGLOSW FLOWAGES	AEFILRST FLARIEST
RENOVATE	AEERRSTW WATERERS	AEFGLRTU GRATEFUL	FRAILEST

AEFILRSU FAILURES	AEFLNNNS FLANNENS	AEFRSSTW FRETSAWS	AEGHILRU LAUGHIER
AEFILRSV FAVRILES	AEFLNNOT FONTANEL	AEFRSTUW WAFTURES	AEGHILST LAIGHEST
AEFILRSZ FILAZERS	AEFLNOPR FOREPLAN	AEGGGILN ALEGGING	AEGHIMPS MAGESHIP
AEFILRTT FILTRATE	AEFLNOPT PANTOFLE	AEGGGINN ENGAGING	AEGHINNT NAETHING
AEFILRTU FAULTIER	AEFLNORS FARNESOL	AEGGGLSU LUGGAGES	AEGHINNV HAVENING
FILATURE	AEFLNOSV FLAVONES	AEGGHIRS SHAGGIER	AEGHINRS HEARINGS
AEFILRUW WEARIFUL	AEFLNRSS SALFERNS	AEGGHISS HAGGISES	HEARSING
AEFILSSS FILASSES	AEFLNRSU FLANEURS	AEGGHLRS HAGGLERS	SHEARING
AEFILSTT FLATTIES	FUNERALS	AEGGHMSU MESHUGGA	AEGHINRT EARTHING
AEFILSTU FISTULAE	AEFLNRTU FLAUNTER	AEGGHOPY GEOPHAGY	HEARTING
AEFILSTV FESTIVAL	AEFLNSST FLATNESS	AEGGHORU ROUGHAGE	INGATHER
AEFILSTW FLATWISE	AEFLNSTT FLATTENS	AEGGIJST JAGGIEST	AEGHINRV HAVERING
FLAWIEST	AEFLNSUY UNSAFELY	AEGGIKNR KNAGGIER	AEGHINST GAHNITES
AEFILSTX FLAXIEST	AEFLOOSV FOVEOLAS	AEGGILLN ALLEGING	HEATINGS
AEFILTUU FAUTEUIL	AEFLOPRT TERAFLOP	AEGGILLR GRILLAGE	AEGHINSV HEAVINGS
AEFIMMMR MAMMIFER	AEFLOPRY FOREPLAY	AEGGILMN GLEAMING	SHEAVING
AEFIMNST MANIFEST	AEFLOPSW PEAFOWLS	AEGGILNN GLEANING	AEGHINSZ GENIZAHS
AEFIMORR AERIFORM	AEFLORSS SAFROLES	AEGGILNR GANGLIER	AEGHINTT GNATHITE
AEFIMORT FORMIATE	AEFLORST FLOATERS	REGALING	AEGHIOPS ESOPHAGI
AEFIMOST FOAMIEST	FORESTAL	AEGGILNS LIGNAGES	AEGHIPPR EPIGRAPH
AEFIMRRS FIREARMS	REFLOATS	AEGGILNT TEAGLING	AEGHIPRT GRAPHITE
AEFIMRRW FIRMWARE	AEFLORSU FUSAROLE	AEGGILNU LEAGUING	AEGHIRRS GHARRIES
AEFIMRSS MISFARES	AEFLORSY FORELAYS	AEGGILRS SLAGGIER	AEGHIRSS GARISHES
AEFINNSS FAINNESS	AEFLORTW FLEAWORT	AEGGILRW WAGGLIER	AEGHLNOS HALOGENS
AEFINNST INFANTES	AEFLOSSU FOSSULAE	AEGGIMNN MANEGING	AEGHLOPY HYPOGEAL
AEFINNSZ FANZINES	AEFLOSSW SEAFOWLS	MENAGING	AEGHLOSS GALOSHES
AEFINOPR PINAFORE	AEFLOSTT FALSETTO	AEGGIMRT GREGATIM	AEGHLOTX HEXAGLOT
AEFINORS FARINOSE	AEFLPPRS FLAPPERS	AEGGINNR ANGERING	AEGHLRSU LAUGHERS
AEFINPRS FIREPANS	AEFLPPRY FLYPAPER	ENRAGING	AEGHLRTU LAUGHTER
AEFINRRS REFRAINS	AEFLPRSS FELSPARS	AEGGINNT AGENTING	AEGHLRTY LETHARGY
AEFINRRU UNFAIRER	AEFLPRSY PALFREYS	NEGATING	AEGHLSTW THALWEGS
AEFINRRZ FRANZIER	AEFLPSUU PAUSEFUL	AEGGINNV AVENGING	AEGHMNOP PHENOGAM
AEFINRSS FAIRNESS	AEFLRSSU REFUSALS	AEGGINRS GEARINGS	AEGHMOPT APOTHEGM
SANSERIF	AEFLRSTT FATTRELS	GREASING	AEGHMORS HOMAGERS
SERAFINS	FLATTERS	SNAGGIER	AEGHNNST HANGNEST
AEFINRST FENITARS	AEFLRSTU REFUTALS	AEGGINRV GREAVING	AEGHNOPT HEPTAGON
AEFINRSX XERAFINS	AEFLRSZZ FRAZZLES	AEGGINRW WAGERING	PATHOGEN
AEFINSTT FAINTEST	AEFLRTTU AFLUTTER	AEGGINSS SIGNAGES	AEGHNOPY HYPOGEAN
AEFIORTV FAVORITE	AEFLRTTY FLATTERY	AEGGINST NAGGIEST	AEGHNORV HANGOVER
AEFIQRSU AQUIFERS	AEFLSSTU FLATUSES	AEGGIOPR ARPEGGIO	OVERHANG
AEFIRRRS FARRIERS	SULFATES	GEROPIGA	AEGHNOSX HEXAGONS
AEFIRRRY FARRIERY	AEFLSTTT FLATTEST	AEGGIOSS ISAGOGES	AEGHNPSW SPANGHEW
AEFIRRST FRATRIES	AEFLSTTU TASTEFUL	AEGGIQRU QUAGGIER	AEGHNRSS GNASHERS
AEFIRSTW WASTRIFE	AEFLSTUW WASTEFUL	AEGGIRRT RAGGIEST	AEGHNSST STENGAHS
AEFIRTUX FIXATURE	AEFMNRRY FERRYMAN	AEGGIRSU GARIGUES	AEGHOPPR PROPHAGE
AEFISTTT FATTIEST	AEFMNRST RAFTSMEN	AEGGIRWY EARWIGGY	AEGHOPPY APOPHYGE
AEFKLMRY FLYMAKER	AEFMORRS FOREARMS	AEGGISST SAGGIEST	AEGHOPXY EXOPHAGY
AEFKLNRS FLANKERS	AEFMORRT REFORMAT	AEGGISSW SWAGGIES	AEGHORST SHORTAGE
AEFKLOSS SEAFOLKS	AEFMORST FOREMAST	AEGGISTT TAGGIEST	AEGHOSST HOSTAGES
AEFKLRST FARTLEKS	FORMATES	AEGGLNRS GANGRELS	AEGHPRSS SPREAGHS
AEFKLRUW WREAKFUL	AEFMORVW WAVEFORM	AEGGLORY GARGOYLE	AEGHPRTU UPGATHER
AEFKLSST FLASKETS	AEFMOSSU FAMOUSES	AEGGLRST STRAGGLE	AEGIILLU AIGUILLE
AEFKLSTT TALKFEST	AEFNNSTU UNFASTEN	AEGGMNNS GANGSMEN	AEGIILMN EMAILING
AEFKNORS FORSAKEN	AEFNOPRR PROFANER	AEGGMORR ERGOGRAM	AEGIILMR REMIGIAL
AEFKNRST FRANKEST	AEFNOPRS PROFANES	AEGGMORT MORTGAGE	AEGIILNN ALIENING
AEFKOPRS FORSPEAK	AEFNOPSY PAYFONES	AEGGNNSU GUNNAGES	AEGIILNR GAINLIER
AEFKORRW WORKFARE	AEFNORRW FOREWARN	AEGGNORV OVERGANG	AEGIILRR GLAIRIER
AEFKORSS FORSAKES	AEFNORST SEAFRONT	AEGGNORW WAGGONER	AEGIILTT LITIGATE
AEFLLMMU FLAMMULE	AEFNRRST TRANSFER	AEGGNRRS GRANGERS	AEGIIMNR IMAGINER
AEFLLNNS FANNELLS	AEFNRRUY FUNERARY	AEGGNRST GANGSTER	MIGRAINE
FLANNELS	AEFNSSST FASTNESS	AEGGOPRU GROUPAGE	AEGIIMNS IMAGINES
AEFLLNNU UNFALLEN	AEFNSSTU UNSAFEST	AEGGRSST GAGSTERS	AEGIIMTT MITIGATE
AEFLLORV OVERFALL	AEFNSTUY UNSAFETY	STAGGERS	AEGIINNN NENNIGAI
AEFLLORW FALLOWER	AEFOORTW FOOTWEAR	AEGGRSSW SWAGGERS	AEGIINNR ARGININE
AEFLLOST FLOATELS	AEFOPRRT FOREPART	AEGHIJRS JAGHIRES	AEGIINRR GRAINIER
AEFLLPRT PRATFELL	AEFOPRST FOREPAST	AEGHILLM MEGILLAH	AEGIIRRT IRRIGATE
AEFLLPTU PLATEFUL	AEFOPRSW FOREPAWS	AEGHILLS SHIGELLA	AEGIISTV VESTIGIA
AEFLLRUW AWFULLER	AEFORRSV FAVORERS	AEGHILMT MEGALITH	AEGIJLNR JANGLIER
AEFLLRUX FLEXURAL	AEFORRSW FORESWEAR	AEGHILNR NARGHILE	AEGIKLNS LINKAGES
AEFLLSSW FLAWLESS	AEFORRSY FORAYERS	NARGILEH	AEGIKLNW WEAKLING
AEFLLSST FLATLETS	AEFORRUV FAVOURER	AEGHILNS HEALINGS	AEGIKMNR REMAKING
AEFLLSTY FESTALLY	AEFORRWY FOREWARY	LEASHING	AEGIKNNS SNEAKING
AEFLMNOT MATFELON	AEFORSSY FORESAYS	SHEALING	AEGIKNNW WAKENING
AEFLMORU FORMULAE	AEFORSTW FORWASTE	AEGHILNT ATHELING	AEGIKNPS SPEAKING
FUMAROLE	SOFTWARE	AEGHILNX EXHALING	AEGIKNRS SKEARING
AEFLMOSS FOAMLESS	AEFORSTY FORESTAY	AEGHILPS SHAGPILE	AEGIKNRT RETAKING
AEFLMOTU FLAMEOUT	AEFOSTUU FEATUOUS	AEGHILRT LITHARGE	AEGIKNRW WREAKING
AEFLMPRR FRAMPLER	AEFOSTUV VOUTSAFE	THIRLAGE	AEGIKNSS SINKAGES
AEFLMSUW WAMEFULS	AEFPRSST PRESSFAT		AEGIKNTW TWEAKING

AEGIKPPS	KIPPAGES		
AEGIKPRS	GARPIKES		
AEGIKSTW	GAWKIEST		
AEGILLMS	LEGALISM		
AEGILLNS	NIGELLAS		
AEGILLNU	LINGULAE		
AEGILLNY	GENIALLY		
AEGILLPR	PILLAGER		
AEGILLPS	PILLAGES		
	SPILLAGE		
AEGILLRU	GUERILLA		
AEGILLRV	VILLAGER		
AEGILLSS	GALLISES		
AEGILLST	LEGALIST		
	STILLAGE		
	TILLAGES		
AEGILLSV	VILLAGES		
AEGILLSZ	GALLIZES		
AEGILLTU	LIGULATE		
AEGILLTY	LEGALITY		
AEGILMMR	AGLIMMER		
	LAMMIGER		
AEGILMNP	EMPALING		
AEGILMNR	GERMINAL		
	MALIGNER		
	MALINGER		
AEGILMNS	MEASLING		
AEGILMNT	LIGAMENT		
	METALING		
AEGILMNU	AEMULING		
AEGILMNY	YEALMING		
AEGILMRS	GREMIALS		
	LAMIGERS		
	REGALISM		
AEGILMRX	LEXIGRAM		
AEGILNNR	LEARNING		
AEGILNNS	EANLINGS		
	LEANINGS		
AEGILNNT	GANTLINE		
	LATENING		
AEGILNNU	UNGENIAL		
AEGILNNW	WEANLING		
AEGILNNY	YEANLING		
AEGILNOR	GERANIOL		
	REGIONAL		
AEGILNOS	GASOLINE		
AEGILNOT	GELATION		
	LEGATION		
AEGILNPR	PEARLING		
AEGILNPS	ELAPSING		
	PLEASING		
AEGILNPT	PLEATING		
AEGILNRR	GNARLIER		
AEGILNRS	ENGRAILS		
	NARGILES		
	REALIGNS		
	SALERING		
	SANGLIER		
	SIGNALER		
	SLANGIER		
AEGILNRT	ALERTING		
	ALTERING		
	INTEGRAL		
	RELATING		
	TANGLIER		
	TRIANGLE		
AEGILNRX	RELAXING		
AEGILNRY	LAYERING		
	RELAYING		
	YEARLING		
AEGILNSS	GAINLESS		
	GLASSINE		
	LEASINGS		
	SEALINGS		
AEGILNST	EASTLING		
	GELATINS		
	GENITALS		
	STEALING		
AEGILNSV	LEAVINGS		
	SLEAVING		
AEGILNSW	SWEALING		
AEGILNTV	VALETING		
AEGILNTX	EXALTING		
AEGILNTZ	TEAZLING		
AEGILNUV	VAGINULE		
AEGILOPS	SPOILAGE		
AEGILOPT	PILOTAGE		
AEGILORS	GASOLIER		
	GIRASOLE		
	SERAGLIO		
AEGILOSS	GOLIASES		
	SOILAGES		
AEGILOST	OTALGIES		
AEGILPPS	SLIPPAGE		
AEGILPPU	PUPILAGE		
AEGILPRU	PLAGUIER		
AEGILRRU	GLAURIER		
AEGILRSS	GLASSIER		
AEGILRST	GLARIEST		
	REGALIST		
AEGILRSY	GREASILY		
AEGILRSZ	GLAZIERS		
AEGILRTT	AGLITTER		
AEGILRTU	LIGATURE		
AEGILRTY	REGALITY		
AEGILSTZ	GLAZIEST		
AEGIMMST	GAMMIEST		
AEGIMNNR	ENARMING		
	RENAMING		
AEGIMNNS	MEANINGS		
AEGIMNNT	ENTAMING		
AEGIMNPR	EMPARING		
AEGIMNRR	REARMING		
AEGIMNRS	GERMAINS		
	SMEARING		
AEGIMNRT	EMIGRANT		
AEGIMNRU	GERANIUM		
	MAUNGIER		
AEGIMNSS	GAMINESS		
AEGIMNST	MANGIEST		
	MINTAGES		
	STEAMING		
	TEAMINGS		
AEGIMNSV	VEGANISM		
AEGIMOOS	OOGAMIES		
AEGIMORR	ARMIGERO		
AEGIMORS	GORAMIES		
AEGIMORW	WAGMOIRE		
AEGIMPRS	EPIGRAMS		
	PRIMAGES		
AEGIMPRU	UMPIRAGE		
AEGIMPST	PIGMEATS		
AEGIMQRU	QUAGMIRE		
AEGIMRRS	ARMIGERS		
AEGIMRRT	RAGTIMER		
AEGIMRSS	GISARMES		
AEGIMRST	MAGISTER		
	MIGRATES		
	RAGTIMES		
	STERIGMA		
AEGIMSST	SIGMATES		
AEGIMSSU	MISUSAGE		
AEGIMSTU	GAUMIEST		
AEGINNNX	ANNEXING		
AEGINNOS	GANOINES		
AEGINNOT	NEGATION		
AEGINNPS	SNEAPING		
	SPEANING		
AEGINNRS	AGINNERS		
	EARNINGS		
	ENGRAINS		
	GRANNIES		
AEGINNRV	RAVENING		
AEGINNRY	RENAYING		
	YEARNING		
AEGINNST	ANTIGENS		
	GENTIANS		
	STEANING		
AEGINNSU	GUANINES		
	SANGUINE		
AEGINORR	ORANGIER		
AEGINORS	IGNAROES		
	ORGANISE		
	ORIGANES		
AEGINORZ	ORGANIZE		
AEGINOSS	AGONISES		
AEGINOSZ	AGONIZES		
AEGINPPR	PAPERING		
AEGINPPS	GENIPAPS		
AEGINPRS	PREASING		
	SPEARING		
AEGINPRT	TAPERING		
AEGINPRY	REPAYING		
AEGINPSS	SPINAGES		
AEGINQTU	EQUATING		
AEGINRRS	EARRINGS		
	GRAINERS		
AEGINRRV	AVERRING		
AEGINRSS	REASSIGN		
	SEARINGS		
	SERINGAS		
AEGINRST	ANGRIEST		
	ASTRINGE		
	GANISTER		
	GANTRIES		
	GRANITES		
	INGRATES		
	RANGIEST		
	REASTING		
	STEARING		
	TASERING		
AEGINRSV	VINEGARS		
AEGINRSW	SWEARING		
	WEARINGS		
AEGINRSY	RESAYING		
AEGINRTT	ARETTING		
	TREATING		
AEGINRTV	AVERTING		
	TAVERING		
	VINTAGER		
AEGINRTW	TWANGIER		
	WATERING		
AEGINRVW	WAVERING		
AEGINRVY	VINEGARY		
AEGINRWY	WEARYING		
AEGINSST	EASTINGS		
	GENISTAS		
	GIANTESS		
	SEATINGS		
	TEASINGS		
	TSIGANES		
AEGINSSY	ESSAYING		
AEGINSTT	ESTATING		
	TANGIEST		
AEGINSTU	SAUTEING		
AEGINSTV	VINTAGES		
AEGINSTW	SWEATING		
AEGINSTY	YEASTING		
AEGINSVW	WEAVINGS		
AEGINSVY	SAVEYING		
AEGIOPRR	PROGERIA		
AEGIORSS	ARGOSIES		
AEGIORSV	VIRAGOES		
AEGIOSTT	GOATIEST		
AEGIOSTU	AGOUTIES		
AEGIOSTX	GEOTAXIS		
AEGIPPRT	GRIPTAPE		
AEGIPPST	GAPPIEST		
AEGIPRSS	PRISAGES		
	SPAIRGES		
AEGIPRST	GRAPIEST		
AEGIPRTY	PTERYGIA		
AEGIPSST	GASPIEST		
AEGIQRSU	SQUIRAGE		
AEGIRRSS	GRASSIER		
AEGIRRSU	SUGARIER		
AEGIRRSZ	GRAZIERS		
AEGIRRTY	ARGYRITE		
AEGIRSST	AGISTERS		
AEGIRSTT	STRIGATE		
AEGIRSTV	VIRGATES		
	VITRAGES		
AEGIRSUU	AUGURIES		
AEGISSST	GASSIEST		
AEGISSTT	STAGIEST		
AEGISSTW	GAWSIEST		
AEGISTUZ	GAUZIEST		
AEGJLNRS	JANGLERS		
AEGJLTUU	JUGULATE		
AEGKKKNO	ANGEKKOK		
AEGKKNOS	ANGEKOKS		
AEGKLOSU	KAGOULES		
AEGKMNRU	GUNMAKER		
AEGKMRSY	KERYGMAS		
AEGLLLMU	GLUMELLA		
AEGLLNOS	ALLONGES		
	GALLEONS		
AEGLLNOV	LONGEVAL		
AEGLLNPS	LANGSPEL		
AEGLLNRS	LANGRELS		
AEGLLOPR	GALLOPER		
AEGLLORS	ALLEGROS		
AEGLLORV	OVERGALL		
AEGLLORY	ALLEGORY		
AEGLLOSS	GOALLESS		
AEGLLOST	TOLLAGES		
AEGLLRVY	GRAVELLY		
AEGLLSSU	GALLUSES		
	SEAGULLS		
	SULLAGES		
AEGLMNNO	MANGONEL		
AEGLMNRS	MANGLERS		
AEGLMNSS	GLASSMEN		
AEGLMNTU	GUNMETAL		
AEGLMORS	GOMERALS		
AEGLMOSU	MOULAGES		
AEGLMOTV	MEGAVOLT		
AEGLMPSU	PLUMAGES		
AEGLMRSU	MAULGRES		
AEGLMSSU	GAUMLESS		
AEGLNNPT	PLANGENT		
AEGLNNTU	UNTANGLE		
AEGLNOPT	GANTLOPE		
AEGLNORY	YEARLONG		
AEGLNOST	TANGELOS		
AEGLNPRS	GRAPNELS		
	SPANGLER		
	SPRANGLE		
AEGLNPSS	PANGLESS		
	SPANGLES		
AEGLNPST	SPANGLET		
AEGLNRRW	WRANGLER		
AEGLNRSS	SLANGERS		
AEGLNRST	STRANGLE		
	TANGLERS		
	TRANGLES		
AEGLNRSU	GRANULES		
AEGLNRSW	WANGLERS		
	WRANGLES		
AEGLNRSY	LARYNGES		
AEGLNRUY	GUNLAYER		
AEGLNSTT	GANTLETS		
AEGLNSTU	LANGUETS		
AEGLNSTW	TWANGLES		
AEGLNSUW	GUNWALES		
AEGLNTTU	GAUNTLET		
AEGLNTUU	UNGULATE		
AEGLOOOZ	ZOOGLOEA		
AEGLOOPU	APOLOGUE		
AEGLOORY	AEROLOGY		
AEGLOPRS	PERGOLAS		
AEGLORST	GLOATERS		
	LEGATORS		
AEGLORSU	GLAREOUS		
AEGLORTU	OUTGLARE		
AEGLORTV	TRAVELOG		

AEGLORTW	WATERLOG		TUTENAGS
AEGLORTY	GEOLATRY	AEGOORST	ROOTAGES
AEGLOSSW	GALOWSES	AEGOORSV	VORAGOES
AEGLOSTV	VOLTAGES	AEGOOSWY	WAYGOOSE
AEGLOSUY	GEALOUSY	AEGOPPRS	PROPAGES
AEGLPPRS	GRAPPLES	AEGOPPST	STOPPAGE
AEGLPRSU	EARPLUGS	AEGOPPSU	SUPPEAGO
	GRAUPELS	AEGOPRST	PORTAGES
AEGLPSSU	PLUSAGES		POTAGERS
	PLUSSAGE	AEGOPRTU	PORTAGUE
AEGLRRSU	REGULARS	AEGOPSST	GESTAPOS
AEGLRRUV	VULGARER		POSTAGES
AEGLRSTU	GAULTERS	AEGOPSSU	SPOUSAGE
	GESTURAL	AEGOPSTT	GATEPOST
	TRAGULES		POTTAGES
AEGLRTUY	ARGUTELY	AEGORRRT	REGRATOR
AEGLSSTT	GESTALTS	AEGORRST	GARROTES
AEGLSSUV	VALGUSES	AEGORRTT	GAROTTER
AEGLSTUU	GLUTAEUS		GAROTTE
AEGLSTUV	VULGATES	AEGORSSS	SARGOSES
AEGLSUUY	GUAYULES	AEGORSST	STORAGES
AEGMMNOR	GAMMONER	AEGORSTT	GAROTTES
AEGMMRRU	RUMMAGER	AEGORSTU	OUTRAGES
AEGMMRSU	RUMMAGES	AEGORSUV	OUVRAGES
AEGMNNOS	AGNOMENS	AEGORSVY	VOYAGERS
AEGMNNOT	MAGNETON	AEGORTTU	TUTORAGE
AEGMNORS	MEGARONS	AEGORUVY	VOYAGEUR
AEGMNORV	MANGROVE	AEGOSSTW	STOWAGES
AEGMNOST	GEOMANTS	AEGOSSYZ	AZYGOSES
	MAGNETOS	AEGOSTTU	OUTGATES
	MEGATONS	AEGOSTTV	GAVOTTES
	MONTAGES	AEGPRRSS	GRASPERS
AEGMNOSX	MAGNOXES		SPARGERS
AEGMNOXY	XENOGAMY	AEGPSSTU	UPSTAGES
AEGMNRST	GARMENTS	AEGPSSUU	GAUPUSES
	MARGENTS	AEGPSSUW	GAWPUSES
	RAGMENTS	AEGQRTUU	TRUQUAGE
AEGMNRTU	ARGUMENT	AEGRRSSS	GRASSERS
AEGMNSSW	SWAGSMEN	AEGRRSUU	AUGURERS
AEGMNSSY	GAMYNESS	AEGRRSUV	GRAVURES
AEGMNSTU	AUGMENTS		VERRUGAS
	MUTAGENS	AEGRSSSU	SARGUSES
AEGMOORS	MOORAGES	AEGRSSUV	SEVRUGAS
AEGMOPRW	GAPEWORM	AEGRSTTY	STRATEGY
AEGMORSS	GOSSAMER	AEGRSTUU	AUGUSTER
AEGMPSTU	STUMPAGE	AEGSSTUU	AUGUSTES
AEGNNOPT	PENTAGON	AEGSTTTU	GUTTATES
AEGNNOST	TONNAGES	AEHHHIST	SHEHITAH
AEGNNPRT	PREGNANT	AEHHIKSS	SHEIKHAS
AEGNNRSU	GUNNERAS	AEHHIMTW	HAMEWITH
AEGNNRTY	GANNETRY	AEHHIPSW	PEISHWAH
AEGNNSTT	TANGENTS	AEHHISST	HASHIEST
AEGNNSTU	TUNNAGES		SHEHITAS
AEGNOORS	OREGANOS	AEHHISVY	YESHIVAH
AEGNOPRR	PARERGON	AEHHLNTU	UNHEALTH
AEGNOPST	PONTAGES	AEHHNRSS	HARSHENS
AEGNORRS	GROANERS	AEHHNRSW	HERNSHAW
AEGNORRY	ORANGERY	AEHHORST	HAROSETH
AEGNORST	ORANGEST	AEHHRRST	THRASHER
	RAGSTONE	AEHHRSST	HARSHEST
	STONERAG		THRASHES
AEGNORSW	WAGONERS	AEHIIKLR	HAIRLIKE
AEGNORTT	TETRAGON	AEHIIKRT	TERAKIHI
AEGNORTY	NEGATORY	AEHIIKST	SHIITAKE
AEGNORUV	VARGUENO	AEHIILMO	HEMIOLIA
AEGNOSSY	NOSEGAYS	AEHIILNR	HAIRLINE
AEGNOTUY	AUTOGENY	AEHIILST	HAILIEST
AEGNPRSS	ENGRASPS	AEHIIMNT	THIAMINE
AEGNPRST	TREPANGS	AEHIIMOP	HEMIOPIA
AEGNPRYY	PANEGYRY	AEHIINNT	IANTHINE
AEGNRRST	GRANTERS	AEHIINTZ	THIAZINE
	REGRANTS	AEHIIRST	HAIRIEST
	STRANGER	AEHIKKLW	HAWKLIKE
AEGNRSTU	STRAUNGE	AEHIKLLT	LATHLIKE
AEGNRSYY	ASYNERGY	AEHIKLNP	KEPHALIN
AEGNSSST	GASTNESS	AEHIKNSS	SNEAKISH
AEGNSSSY	SYNGASES	AEHIKSST	SHAKIEST
AEGNSTTU	GAUNTEST	AEHIKSSY	SAKIYEHS
		AEHILLNT	THALLINE

AEHILMNY	HYMENIAL	AEHINSSZ	HAZINESS
AEHILMOS	HEMIOLAS	AEHINSTT	HESITANT
AEHILMOT	HALIMOTE	AEHINSTW	INSWATHE
AEHILMSW	LIMEWASH	AEHINTTT	ANTITHET
AEHILNOP	APHELION	AEHIOPRS	APHORISE
AEHILNRS	INHALERS	AEHIOPRU	EUPHORIA
AEHILNRU	INHAULER	AEHIOPRZ	APHORIZE
AEHILNSY	HYALINES	AEHIORRV	OVERHAIR
AEHILNTX	ANTHELIX	AEHIORST	HOARIEST
AEHILNTZ	ZENITHAL	AEHIORTU	THIOUREA
AEHILORS	AIRHOLES	AEHIPPRS	PAPISHER
	SHOALIER		SAPPHIRE
AEHILORT	AEROLITH	AEHIPPSS	PAPISHES
AEHILPRS	PLASHIER	AEHIPPST	EPITAPHS
AEHILRSS	HAIRLESS		HAPPIEST
AEHILRSU	HAULIERS		PEATSHIP
AEHILRSV	LAVISHER	AEHIPRRS	PHRASIER
	SHRIEVAL	AEHIPRRT	RATHRIPE
AEHILRTY	HEARTILY	AEHIPRSS	PARISHES
AEHILSST	SHALIEST		SHARPIES
AEHILSSV	LAVISHES	AEHIPRTT	THREAPIT
AEHILSSW	SHAWLIES	AEHIPSSW	PEISHWAS
	WHAISLES	AEHIPSTZ	ZAPTIEHS
AEHILSTT	LATHIEST	AEHIPSWW	WASHWIPE
	LITHATES	AEHIQSSU	QUASHIES
AEHILSTY	HYALITES	AEHIRRRS	HARRIERS
AEHILSUV	VIHUELAS	AEHIRRSS	ARRISHES
AEHILSWZ	WHAIZLES	AEHIRRST	TRASHIER
AEHIMMSS	SHAMMIES	AEHIRRSV	RAVISHER
AEHIMMST	HAMMIEST	AEHIRRTW	WRATHIER
AEHIMMSW	WHAMMIES	AEHIRSST	SHERIATS
AEHIMNNU	INHUMANE	AEHIRSSV	RAVISHES
AEHIMNRS	HARMINES	AEHIRSSW	SWASHIER
	SHIREMAN	AEHIRSTU	THESAURI
AEHIMNSS	SHAMISEN	AEHIRSTW	SWATHIER
AEHIMNSU	HUMANISE		WATERISH
AEHIMNTU	INHUMATE	AEHIRSTY	HYSTERIA
AEHIMNUZ	HUMANIZE	AEHIRSWY	HAYWIRES
AEHIMPRS	SAMPHIRE	AEHISSST	STASHIES
	SERAPHIM	AEHISSSW	SIWASHES
AEHIMPRT	TERAPHIM	AEHISSSY	ESSAYISH
AEHIMPRX	XERAPHIM	AEHISSTT	ATHEISTS
AEHIMPSS	EMPHASIS		HASTIEST
	MISSHAPE		STAITHES
	PHAEISMS	AEHISSTU	HIATUSES
AEHIMPST	MATESHIP	AEHISSTW	WASHIEST
	SHIPMATE	AEHISSVY	YESHIVAS
AEHIMRRS	MARSHIER	AEHISTTW	THAWIEST
AEHIMRSS	MARISHES		THWAITES
	MISHEARS	AEHJLOSW	JAWHOLES
AEHIMSSS	MESSIAHS	AEHJNNOS	JOHANNES
AEHIMSST	ATHEISMS	AEHKMOPW	MOPEHAWK
	MASHIEST	AEHKNNSU	UNSHAKEN
	MATHESIS	AEHKNRST	THANKERS
AEHINNSS	SHANNIES	AEHKNSWW	NEWSHAWK
AEHINNTX	XANTHEIN	AEHKRRSS	SHARKERS
	XANTHINE	AEHLLLTY	LETHALLY
AEHINOPS	APHONIES	AEHLLMOP	LAMPHOLE
AEHINOPU	EUPHONIA	AEHLLNRT	ENTHRALL
AEHINPRS	HEPARINS	AEHLLRSS	HERSALLS
	PARISHEN	AEHLMMNS	HELMSMAN
	SERAPHIN	AEHLMNOS	MANHOLES
AEHINPRT	PERIANTH	AEHLMNOT	METHANOL
AEHINPST	PENTHIAS	AEHLMNUY	HUMANELY
	THESPIAN	AEHLMORS	ARMHOLES
AEHINRRS	SHARNIER	AEHLMPPT	PAMPHLET
AEHINRSS	ARSHINES	AEHLMPSW	WHAMPLES
AEHINRST	HAIRNETS	AEHLMRSS	HARMLESS
	INEARTHS	AEHLMRST	THERMALS
	THERIANS	AEHLMRSU	HUMERALS
AEHINRSV	ENRAVISH	AEHLNOST	ETHANOLS
	VANISHER	AEHLNPRS	SHRAPNEL
AEHINRSW	SHERWANI	AEHLNPTY	ENTHALPY
AEHINRTU	HAURIENT	AEHLNRST	ENTHRALS
AEHINRTW	TARWHINE	AEHLNSST	NATHLESS
AEHINSSS	HESSIANS	AEHLNSSU	UNLASHES
AEHINSST	ANTHESIS		UNSHALES
	SHANTIES	AEHLNSTY	NAYTHLES
AEHINSSV	VANISHES	AEHLNTUZ	HAZELNUT

AEHLOPRT PLETHORA	AEHORSST ASTHORES	AEIIMSTT IMITATES	AEIKMMSS MISMAKES
AEHLORST LOATHERS	EARSHOTS	AEIINNRS SIRENIAN	AEIKMNRS RAMEKINS
AEHLORSY HOARSELY	HAROSETS	AEIINNSS INSANIES	AEIKMNST MANKIEST
AEHLORUV OVERHAUL	HOARSEST	AEIINNTV INNATIVE	MISTAKEN
AEHLOSSS ASSHOLES	AEHORSSW SAWHORSE	AEIINOTT NOTITIAE	AEIKMPRS RAMPIKES
AEHLOSST SHOALEST	AEHORSTT RHEOSTAT	AEIINPRT PAINTIER	AEIKMPSS MISSPEAK
AEHLOSTT LOATHEST	AEHORSTX THORAXES	AEIINPST PIANISTE	AEIKMSST MISTAKES
AEHLPPRT THRAPPLE	AEHORSUV HAVEOURS	AEIINQSU EQUINIAS	AEIKMSTW MAWKIEST
AEHLPRSS SPLASHER	AEHORSVW OVERWASH	AEIINRRV RIVERAIN	AEIKNPRR PRANKIER
AEHLPSSS SPLASHES	AEHORSWY HORSEWAY	AEIINRSS AIRINESS	AEIKNRST KERATINS
AEHLPSST PATHLESS	AEHPRRSS PHRASERS	AEIINRST INERTIAS	NARKIEST
PLASHETS	SHARPERS	RAINIEST	AEIKNRSW SWANKIER
AEHLPSTU SULPHATE	AEHPRSST SHARPEST	AEIINRSY YERSINIA	AEIKNRTW KNITWEAR
AEHLRRTU URETHRAL	SPARTHES	AEIINSST ISATINES	AEIKNSST SNAKIEST
AEHLRSSS SLASHERS	AEHPRSUX HARUSPEX	SANITIES	AEIKNSSW SWANKIES
AEHLRSST HARSLETS	AEHPRSUY EUPHRASY	SANITISE	AEIKNSSY KYANISES
SLATHERS	AEHPSTTT PHATTEST	AEIINSSX SIXAINES	AEIKNSTV KISTVAEN
AEHLSSTT STEALTHS	AEHQRSSU SQUASHER	AEIINSTV VANITIES	AEIKNSTW WANKIEST
AEHLSSTW THAWLESS	AEHQSSSU SQUASHES	AEIINSTX AXINITES	AEIKNSTY KYANITES
AEHLSSWY SHAWLEYS	AEHRRSTU URETHRAS	AEIINSTZ SANITIZE	AEIKNSYZ KYANIZES
AEHLSTTY STEALTHY	AEHRRSTY TRASHERY	AEIINSVV INVASIVE	AEIKPRRS SPARKIER
AEHMMRSS SHAMMERS	AEHRRTTW THWARTER	AEIINTTT TITANITE	AEIKPRSS SPARKIES
AEHMNNPY NYMPHEAN	AEHRSSST SHASTERS	AEIINTTU UINTAITE	AEIKPRST PARKIEST
AEHMNOPR MORPHEAN	AEHRSSSW SWASHERS	AEIIPRRS PRAIRIES	AEIKPSTW PAWKIEST
AEHMNORS HORSEMAN	AEHRSSTT SHATTERS	AEIIPRST PARITIES	AEIKQSTU QUAKIEST
MENORAHS	AEHRSSTV HARVESTS	AEIIPRSW PAIRWISE	AEIKRSST ASTERISK
SHOREMAN	AEHRSTTY SHATTERY	AEIIPRTZ TRAPEZII	SARKIEST
AEHMNOST HOASTMEN	AEHRSTUU HAUTEURS	AEIIPRZZ PIZZERIA	AEILLLMO MALLEOLI
AEHMNOSU HOUSEMAN	AEHSSTUX EXHAUSTS	AEIIPSST EPITASIS	AEILLLNY LINEALLY
AEHMNPRU PREHUMAN	AEIIINTT INITIATE	AEIIRRST RARITIES	AEILLMNS MANILLES
AEHMNRST TRASHMEN	AEIIIRRT RETIARII	AEIIRRSV RIVIERAS	AEILLMSY MESIALLY
AEHMNSTU HUMANEST	AEIIKLNT KALINITE	AEIIRRTT IRRITATE	AEILLNNO LANOLINE
AEHMOPRT METAPHOR	AEIIKNRS KAISERIN	AEIIRSSS SIRIASES	AEILLNNS NAINSELL
AEHMOPST APOTHEMS	AEIIKNSS AKINESIS	AEIIRSST IRISATES	AEILLNNU UNLINEAL
AEHMOSTW SOMEWHAT	AEIIKNST KAINITES	SATIRISE	AEILLNOR ALLERION
AEHMPRST HAMPSTER	AEIIKRTY TERIYAKI	AEIIRSTV VAIRIEST	AEILLNPS SPLENIAL
AEHMRSSS SMASHERS	AEIILLMR MILLIARE	AEIIRSTW WISTERIA	AEILLNQU QUINELLA
AEHMRSST HAMSTERS	AEIILLRS RAILLIES	AEIIRSTZ SATIRIZE	AEILLNRY LINEARLY
AEHMRSTU MAUTHERS	AEIILLST TAILLIES	AEIIRSVV VIVARIES	AEILLNSS NAILLESS
AEHMRSTW MAWTHERS	AEIILLTV ILLATIVE	AEIIRTTT TRITIATE	SENSILLA
AEHMSSSU SHAMUSES	AEIILMNN MAINLINE	AEIIRTVZ VIZIRATE	AEILLNVY VENIALLY
AEHMSTTY AMETHYST	AEIILMNS ALIENISM	AEIISTTV VITIATES	AEILLOTV VOLATILE
AEHMSUZZ MEZUZAHS	AEIILMPR IMPERIAL	AEIISTVZ IZVESTIA	AEILLPPR APPERILL
AEHNNPRU NENUPHAR	AEIILMTT MILITATE	AEIITTTV TITIVATE	AEILLPSS ILLAPSES
AEHNNPSU UNSHAPEN	AEIILNNS ANILINES	AEIITTVV VITATIVE	AEILLPST PALLIEST
AEHNNSUV UNSHAVEN	AEIILNQU AQUILINE	AEIJLMSS MAJLISES	PASTILLE
AEHNNSUW UNWASHEN	AEIILNRR AIRLINER	AEIJLNSV JAVELINS	AEILLQTU TEQUILLA
AEHNOOPT HANEPOOT	AEIILNRS AIRLINES	AEIJLOPS JALOPIES	AEILLRRS RALLIERS
AEHNOPRT HAPTERON	SNAILIER	AEIJLOSU JALOUSIE	AEILLRRY RAILLERY
AEHNOPST PHAETONS	AEIILNRT INERTIAL	AEIJMMST JAMMIEST	AEILLRSS RAILLESS
PHONATES	AEIILNST ALIENIST	AEIJMNSS JASMINES	AEILLRST LITERALS
STANHOPE	LITANIES	AEIJNRST NARTJIES	TALLIERS
AEHNOPSW WANHOPES	AEIILPPT TAILPIPE	AEIJNRTU JAUNTIER	AEILLRSU RUELLIAS
AEHNOPXY XENOPHYA	AEIILPRT LIPARITE	AEIJNSTT JANTIEST	AEILLRSY SERIALLY
AEHNOQTU HAQUETON	AEIILRSS LAIRISES	AEIJNSTU JAUNTIES	AEILLRTU TAILLEUR
AEHNORSS HOARSENS	AEIILRST LAIRIEST	AEIJORST JAROSITE	AEILLSSS SAILLESS
AEHNPRSS SHARPENS	LISTERIA	AEIJPSSS JASPISES	AEILLSST TAILLESS
AEHNPRST PANTHERS	AEIILRSV RIVALISE	AEIJSTZZ JAZZIEST	AEILLSTW WALLIEST
AEHNPSSU UNSHAPES	AEIILRSZ LAIRIZES	AEIKKLLW LIKEWALK	AEILLSUV ALLUSIVE
AEHNRSSS RASHNESS	AEIILRTT LITERATI	AEIKKLPR PARKLIKE	AEILLSYZ SLEAZILY
AEHNRSTU HAUNTERS	AEIILRVZ RIVALIZE	AEIKKMNO KAKIEMON	AEILLTUZ LAZULITE
UNEARTHS	AEIILSSS SILESIAS	AEIKLLSS KILLASES	AEILMMNS MELANISM
UNHEARTS	AEIILSSW LEWISIAS	AEIKLNNP PANNIKEL	AEILMMNT IMMANTLE
URETHANS	AEIILSTV VITALISE	AEIKLNOS KAOLINES	AEILMMNY IMMANELY
AEHNSSTT THATNESS	AEIILSTX LAXITIES	AEIKLNSS SEALSKIN	AEILMMOR MEMORIAL
AEHNSSTW WHATNESS	AEIILSTZ TAILZIES	AEIKLNST LANKIEST	AEILMMOT IMMOLATE
AEHNSSTY SHANTEYS	AEIILTVZ VITALIZE	AEIKLNSW SWANLIKE	AEILMMRT TRILEMMA
AEHNSTUW UNSWATHE	AEIIMMRT MARITIME	AEIKLNSY SNEAKILY	AEILMMSS MELISMAS
AEHOORST TOHEROAS	AEIIMMSX MAXIMISE	AEIKLOST KEITLOAS	AEILMNNO MINNEOLA
AEHOPPRS PROPHASE	AEIIMMXZ MAXIMIZE	AEIKLPRT TRAPLIKE	AEILMNNP IMPANNEL
AEHOPRSS PHAROSES	AEIIMNST MINIATES	AEIKLPSS KALPISES	AEILMNNS LINESMAN
AEHOPRST POTSHARE	AEIIMNSZ SIMAZINE	AEIKLRSS SERKALIS	MELANINS
AEHOPSST PATHOSES	AEIIMNTT INTIMATE	AEIKLRST LARKIEST	AEILMNOS LAMINOSE
POTASHES	AEIIMNTU MINUTIAE	STALKIER	MINEOLAS
SPATHOSE	AEIIMNTV VITAMINE	STARLIKE	SEMOLINA
AEHOPSTT HEATSPOT	AEIIMOSS AMEIOSIS	AEIKLRSV KLAVIERS	AEILMNPS IMPANELS
AEHOQRUU HUAQUERO	AEIIMPRR IMPAIRER	AEIKLRTW WARTLIKE	MANIPLES
AEHORRSV OVERRASH	AEIIMRST AIRTIMES	AEIKLSSS SAIKLESS	AEILMNRS MARLINES
AEHORRSW WARHORSE	SERIATIM	AEIKLSTT TALKIEST	MINERALS

AEILMNRT	TERMINAL	
	TRAMLINE	
AEILMNRU	LEMURIAN	
AEILMNSS	ISLESMAN	
AEILMNST	AILMENTS	
	ALIMENTS	
	MANLIEST	
AEILMOPR	PROEMIAL	
AEILMORS	MORALISE	
AEILMORZ	MORALIZE	
AEILMOST	LOAMIEST	
AEILMPRS	IMPEARLS	
	LEMPIRAS	
AEILMPRV	PRIMEVAL	
AEILMPSS	PESSIMAL	
AEILMPST	IMPLATES	
	PALMIEST	
	PALMIETS	
	PETALISM	
	SEPTIMAL	
AEILMPTY	PLAYTIME	
AEILMQRU	QUALMIER	
AEILMRRS	LARMIERS	
AEILMRSS	REALISMS	
AEILMRST	LAMITERS	
	MARLIEST	
AEILMRSY	SMEARILY	
AEILMRTT	REMITTAL	
AEILMRUV	VELARIUM	
AEILMSSX	SMILAXES	
AEILMSTT	MALTIEST	
	METALIST	
	SMALTITE	
AEILMSTU	SIMULATE	
AEILMSTY	LAYTIMES	
	STEAMILY	
AEILMTTU	MUTILATE	
	ULTIMATE	
AEILNNOS	SOLANINE	
AEILNNRT	INTERNAL	
AEILNNSY	INSANELY	
AEILNNTY	INNATELY	
AEILNOPS	OPALINES	
AEILNOPT	ANTIPOLE	
AEILNOPU	POULAINE	
AEILNORS	AILERONS	
	ALERIONS	
	ALIENORS	
AEILNORT	ORIENTAL	
	RELATION	
	TAILERON	
AEILNORV	OVERLAIN	
AEILNOST	ELATIONS	
	INSOLATE	
	TOENAILS	
AEILNOTT	TONALITE	
AEILNPRS	PEARLINS	
	PRALINES	
AEILNPRT	TRIPLANE	
AEILNPSS	PAINLESS	
	SPANIELS	
AEILNPST	PANTILES	
	PLAINEST	
AEILNPSX	EXPLAINS	
AEILNPTT	TINPLATE	
AEILNRRS	SNARLIER	
AEILNRSS	RAINLESS	
AEILNRST	ENTRAILS	
	LATRINES	
	RATLINES	
	TRENAILS	
AEILNRSU	LUNARIES	
AEILNRSV	RAVELINS	
AEILNRSX	RELAXINS	
AEILNRSY	INLAYERS	
	SNAILERY	
AEILNRTT	RATTLINE	
AEILNRTU	AUNTLIER	
	RETINULA	
	TENURIAL	
AEILNRTV	INTERVAL	
AEILNRTY	INTERLAY	
AEILNSST	EASTLINS	
	ELASTINS	
	SALIENTS	
	STANIELS	
AEILNSSU	INULASES	
AEILNSSZ	LAZINESS	
AEILNSTU	ALUNITES	
	INSULATE	
AEILNSTV	VENTAILS	
AEILNSTW	LAWNIEST	
AEILNSUV	UNVAILES	
AEILNSUW	LAUWINES	
AEILNSUY	UNEASILY	
AEILNTVY	NATIVELY	
	VENALITY	
AEILNUVV	UNIVALVE	
AEILOORV	OVARIOLE	
AEILOPPT	OPPILATE	
AEILOPRS	PELORIAS	
	POLARISE	
AEILOPRT	EPILATOR	
	PETIOLAR	
AEILOPRZ	POLARIZE	
AEILOPST	SPOLIATE	
AEILORSS	SOLARISE	
AEILORST	SOTERIAL	
	VALORISE	
	VARIOLES	
	VOLARIES	
AEILORSY	ROYALISE	
AEILORSZ	SOLARIZE	
AEILORTT	LITERATO	
AEILORTV	VIOLATER	
AEILORVZ	VALORIZE	
AEILORYZ	ROYALIZE	
AEILOSST	ISOLATES	
AEILOSSX	OXALISES	
AEILOSTT	TOTALISE	
AEILOSTV	VIOLATES	
AEILOTTV	VOLITATE	
AEILOTTZ	TOTALIZE	
AEILPPQU	APPLIQUE	
AEILPPRS	APPERILS	
	APPLIERS	
AEILPRRS	REPRISAL	
AEILPRRT	PALTRIER	
AEILPRST	PILASTER	
	PLAISTER	
	PLAITERS	
AEILPRSV	PREVAILS	
AEILPRSW	SLIPWARE	
AEILPRXY	PYREXIAL	
AEILPSST	PALSIEST	
AEILPSSY	PAISLEYS	
AEILPSTT	PLATIEST	
AEILPSTY	PTYALISE	
AEILPSUV	PLAUSIVE	
AEILPTYZ	PTYALIZE	
AEILQRSU	SQUAILER	
AEILQRTU	QUARTILE	
	REQUITAL	
AEILQSTU	LIQUATES	
	TEQUILAS	
AEILQSUY	QUEASILY	
AEILQTUY	EQUALITY	
AEILRRST	RETIRALS	
	RETRIALS	
	TRAILERS	
AEILRRSU	RURALISE	
AEILRRTT	RATTLIER	
AEILRRTY	LITERARY	
AEILRRUZ	RURALIZE	
AEILRSST	REALISTS	
	SALTIERS	
	SALTIRES	
	SLAISTER	
AEILRSSV	REVISALS	
	RIVALESS	
AEILRSTT	TERTIALS	
AEILRSTU	URALITES	
AEILRSVV	REVIVALS	
AEILRSVY	VIRELAYS	
AEILRTTY	ALTERITY	
AEILRTUZ	LAZURITE	
AEILRTVV	TRIVALVE	
AEILRTXZ	ZELATRIX	
AEILSSSV	VESSAILS	
AEILSSTT	SALTIEST	
	SLATIEST	
AEILSSTW	SWALIEST	
AEILSTTW	WALTIEST	
AEILSTVY	VILAYETS	
AEIMMMRZ	MAMZERIM	
AEIMMNNT	IMMANENT	
AEIMMNOT	AMMONITE	
AEIMMNSS	MISNAMES	
AEIMMPRS	SPAMMIER	
AEIMMPST	PSAMMITE	
AEIMMRRS	SMARMIER	
AEIMMRST	MARMITES	
AEIMMRTU	IMMATURE	
AEIMMSST	MISMATES	
AEIMMSZZ	MIZMAZES	
AEIMNNOT	NOMINATE	
AEIMNNRS	REINSMAN	
AEIMNNST	MANNITES	
AEIMNOPT	PTOMAINE	
AEIMNORS	MORAINES	
AEIMNORW	AIRWOMEN	
AEIMNORZ	ARMOZINE	
AEIMNOST	SOMNIATE	
AEIMNOSU	MOINEAUS	
AEIMNOSW	WOMANISE	
AEIMNOTZ	MONAZITE	
AEIMNOWZ	WOMANIZE	
AEIMNPRZ	PRIZEMAN	
AEIMNQRU	RAMEQUIN	
AEIMNRRS	MARINERS	
AEIMNRRV	RIVERMAN	
AEIMNRSS	SEMINARS	
	SIRNAMES	
AEIMNRST	MINARETS	
	RAIMENTS	
AEIMNRSU	ANEURISM	
AEIMNRSY	SEMINARY	
AEIMNRTT	MARTINET	
AEIMNRTU	RUMINATE	
AEIMNRTW	WARIMENT	
AEIMNRTY	TYRAMINE	
AEIMNSSS	SAMISENS	
AEIMNSST	MANTISES	
	MATINESS	
AEIMNSSU	ANIMUSES	
AEIMNSSZ	MAZINESS	
AEIMNSUV	MAUVEINS	
	MAUVINES	
AEIMNTTU	MATUTINE	
AEIMNTVZ	VIZAMENT	
AEIMOOPS	IPOMOEAS	
AEIMOPSX	APOMIXES	
AEIMOPTT	OPTIMATE	
AEIMORRS	ARMOIRES	
	ARMORIES	
AEIMORST	AMORTISE	
	ATOMISER	
AEIMORTT	AMORETTI	
AEIMORTZ	AMORTIZE	
	ATOMIZER	
AEIMOSST	AMITOSES	
	AMOSITES	
	ATOMISES	
	OSMIATES	
AEIMOSTX	TOXEMIAS	
AEIMOSTZ	ATOMIZES	
AEIMOTTV	MOTIVATE	
AEIMPRRS	RAMPIRES	
AEIMPRRT	IMPARTER	
AEIMPRSS	IMPRESAS	
	SAMPIRES	
AEIMPRST	APTERISM	
	PRIMATES	
AEIMPRSV	VAMPIRES	
AEIMPRSW	SWAMPIER	
AEIMPRTU	APTERIUM	
AEIMPSSS	IMPASSES	
AEIMPSST	IMPASTES	
	PASTIMES	
AEIMQRSU	MARQUISE	
AEIMRRRS	MARRIERS	
AEIMRRSS	SIMARRES	
AEIMRSST	ASTERISM	
	MAISTERS	
	MISRATES	
	SEMITARS	
	SMARTIES	
AEIMRSSY	EMISSARY	
AEIMRSTT	MISTREAT	
	TERATISM	
AEIMRSTU	MURIATES	
	SEMITAUR	
AEIMRSTW	WARTIMES	
AEIMRSTX	MATRIXES	
AEIMRSTY	SYMITARE	
AEIMRSWW	SWIMWEAR	
AEIMSSST	ASTEISMS	
	MASSIEST	
AEIMSSTT	MASTIEST	
	MISSTATE	
AEIMSSTZ	MESTIZAS	
AEIMSTYZ	AZYMITES	
AEIMTTUV	MUTATIVE	
AEINNNOX	ANNEXION	
AEINNOPV	PAVONINE	
AEINNORS	RAISONNE	
AEINNORT	ANOINTER	
	INORNATE	
AEINNOST	ENATIONS	
AEINNOTT	INTONATE	
AEINNOTV	INNOVATE	
	VENATION	
AEINNPRS	PANNIERS	
AEINNPST	PANTINES	
AEINNRRT	INERRANT	
AEINNRSS	INSNARES	
AEINNRST	ENTRAINS	
	TRANNIES	
AEINNRSU	ANEURINS	
	UNARISEN	
AEINNRSW	SWANNIER	
AEINNRTT	INTRANET	
AEINNSST	INSANEST	
AEINNSSV	VAINNESS	
AEINNSSZ	ZANINESS	
AEINNSTT	ANTIENTS	
	STANNITE	
AEINNTUV	UNNATIVE	
AEINOPPT	ANTIPOPE	
AEINOPRT	ATROPINE	
AEINOPST	SAPONITE	
AEINOPSZ	EPIZOANS	
AEINOPTZ	TOPAZINE	
AEINOQTU	EQUATION	
AEINORRT	ANTERIOR	
AEINORRW	IRONWARE	
AEINORSS	ERASIONS	
	SENSORIA	
AEINORST	ANOESTRI	
	ARSONITE	
	NOTARIES	
	NOTARISE	
	ROSINATE	
AEINORSV	AVERSION	
AEINORTT	TENTORIA	

AEINORTZ	NOTARIZE	AEINSSVW	WAVINESS		ARTSIEST	AEKORTUY	EUKARYOT
AEINOSST	ASSIENTO	AEINSSWX	WAXINESS		STRIATES	AEKOSTTU	OUTTAKES
	ASTONIES	AEINSTTT	NATTIEST	AEIRSSTV	TRAVISES		TAKEOUTS
AEINOSSV	EVASIONS	AEINSTTV	TASTEVIN	AEIRSSTW	WAISTERS	AEKPPSSU	UPSPEAKS
AEINOSSX	SAXONIES	AEINSTTW	TAWNIEST		WAITRESS	AEKPSSSU	PASSKEYS
AEINOSTV	STOVAINE	AEINSTUV	SUIVANTE		WASTRIES	AEKQRSUW	SQUAWKER
AEINOSTX	SAXONITE	AEINSTWY	YAWNIEST	AEIRSTTT	ATTRITES	AEKRRSST	STARKERS
AEINOSXZ	OXAZINES	AEINSUVV	VESUVIAN		RATTIEST	AEKRSSTT	STARKEST
AEINOTVX	VEXATION	AEINTTUU	AUTUNITE		TARTIEST	AELLLORY	LOYALLER
AEINPPRS	SNAPPIER	AEIOPPST	APPOSITE		TITRATES	AELLLRTU	TELLURAL
AEINPPST	NAPPIEST	AEIOPRRT	PRIORATE	AEIRSTTW	WARTIEST	AELLLSUV	VULSELLA
AEINPRRT	TERRAPIN	AEIOPRSV	VAPORISE	AEIRSTTX	EXTRAITS	AELLMNOZ	MANZELLO
AEINPRRU	UNREPAIR	AEIOPRTX	EXPIATOR	AEIRSTUZ	AZURITES	AELLMNST	STALLMEN
AEINPRST	PAINTERS	AEIOPRVZ	VAPORIZE	AEIRSTVY	VESTIARY	AELLMNTY	MENTALLY
	PANTRIES	AEIOPSST	SOAPIEST	AEIRSWWY	WAYWISER		TALLYMEN
	PERTAINS	AEIOPTTV	OPTATIVE		WIREWAYS	AELLMORR	MORALLER
	PINASTER	AEIOQSSU	SEQUOIAS	AEIRTTTW	ATWITTER	AELLMORT	MARTELLO
	PRISTANE	AEIORRRS	ARRIEROS	AEISSSST	SASSIEST	AELLMOTY	TOMALLEY
	REPAINTS	AEIORRST	ROARIEST	AEISSSTW	TISWASES	AELLMPUU	PLUMULAE
AEINPRSU	UNPRAISE		ROTARIES	AEISSSTY	ESSAYIST	AELLMRSY	MERSALYL
AEINPRSW	SPAWNIER	AEIORSSV	SAVORIES	AEISSTTT	TASTIEST	AELLMSST	SMALLEST
AEINPRTT	TRIPTANE	AEIORSTV	VIATORES	AEISSTTU	SITUATES	AELLMSWX	MAXWELLS
AEINPRTU	PAINTURE		VOTARIES	AEISSTTV	VASTIEST	AELLNOPS	PALLONES
AEINPRTX	EXPIRANT	AEIORSVW	AVOWRIES	AEISSTVV	SAVVIEST	AELLNOPV	VOLPLANE
AEINPSST	STEAPSIN	AEIORTTV	ROTATIVE	AEISSTWZ	TIZWASES	AELLNORS	LLANEROS
AEINPSTT	PATIENTS	AEIOSSTT	TOASTIES	AEISTTTT	TATTIEST	AELLNOSV	NOVELLAS
	SUPINATE	AEIOSSTZ	AZOTISES	AEISTTTU	ATTUITES	AELLNOWW	ENWALLOW
AEINPSTY	EPINASTY	AEIOSTZZ	AZOTIZES	AEISTTTW	TAWTIEST	AELLNPRU	PRUNELLA
AEINPTTY	ANTITYPE	AEIPPPST	PAPPIEST	AEJLNSUV	JUVENALS	AELLNPSS	PLANLESS
AEINQRTU	QUAINTER	AEIPPRRS	APPRISER	AEJLOSSU	JALOUSES	AELLNPTT	PLANTLET
AEINQSTU	ANTIQUES	AEIPPRRT	TRAPPIER	AEJLOSUY	JEALOUSY	AELLNPTU	PLANTULE
	QUANTISE	AEIPPRRZ	APPRIZER	AEJLOSUZ	AZULEJOS	AELLNRUY	NEURALLY
AEINQTTU	EQUITANT	AEIPPRSS	APPRISES	AEJNORSZ	ZANJEROS		UNREALLY
AEINQTUZ	QUANTIZE	AEIPPRST	PERIAPTS	AEKKLLWY	LYKEWALK	AELLNRVY	VERNALLY
AEINRRST	RESTRAIN	AEIPPRSZ	APPRIZES	AEKKMNOO	KAKEMONO	AELLNSST	TALLNESS
	RETRAINS	AEIPPSST	SAPPIEST	AEKKOSSS	SAKKOSES	AELLNSTT	TALLENTS
	STRAINER	AEIPPSTY	YAPPIEST	AEKLLLSTU	KELLAUTS	AELLNTTY	LATENTLY
	TERRAINS	AEIPPSTZ	ZAPPIEST	AEKLMRUW	LUKEWARM	AELLNTUU	LUNULATE
	TRAINERS	AEIPQRTU	PRATIQUE	AEKLMRUY	YARMULKE	AELLOPRS	REPOSALL
	TRANSIRE	AEIPRRRS	SPARRIER	AEKLNNSS	LANKNESS	AELLOPRW	WALLOPER
AEINRRTV	VERATRIN	AEIPRRSS	PRAISERS	AEKLNOSY	ANKYLOSE	AELLORRY	ROYALLER
AEINRRTW	INTERWAR	AEIPRRSY	SPRAYIER	AEKLNPPS	KNAPPLES	AELLORSS	ROSELLAS
AEINRRUW	UNWARIER	AEIPRRTV	PRIVATER	AEKLNPRS	PRANKLES	AELLORST	REALLOTS
AEINRSST	ARTINESS	AEIPRSST	PASTRIES	AEKLOPTY	KALOTYPE	AELLORSV	OVERALLS
	RESIANTS		PIASTRES	AEKLORSY	ROKELAYS	AELLORSW	SALLOWER
	RETSINAS		RASPIEST	AEKLORTV	OVERTALK	AELLORWW	WALLOWER
	SNARIEST		TRAIPSES	AEKLOSST	SKATOLES	AELLOSUV	ALVEOLUS
	STAINERS	AEIPRSSU	UPRAISES		STALKOES	AELLPSTY	PLAYLETS
	STARNIES	AEIPRSSV	PARVISES	AEKLPRRS	SPARKLER	AELLQRSU	SQUALLER
	STEARINS	AEIPRSTV	PRIVATES	AEKLPRSS	SPARKLES	AELLRRSU	ALLURERS
AEINRSSU	SENARIUS	AEIPRSTW	WIRETAPS	AEKLPRST	SPARKLET	AELLRRTY	RETRALLY
AEINRSSW	WARINESS	AEIPRSTY	ASPERITY	AEKLRSST	STALKERS	AELLRTTY	LATTERLY
AEINRSSX	XERANSIS	AEIPRSVY	VESPIARY	AEKLRSUW	WAULKERS	AELLRTVY	TREVALLY
AEINRSTT	INTREATS	AEIPRSXY	PYREXIAS	AEKMMNRS	MARKSMEN	AELLRWYY	LAWYERLY
	NITRATES	AEIPSSST	PASTIES	AEKMNRSU	UNMASKER	AELLSSST	SALTLESS
	STRAITEN	AEIPSSSV	PASSIVES	AEKMOOST	MATOOKES		TASSELLS
	TARTINES	AEIPSSTT	PASTIEST	AEKMOPRT	TOPMAKER	AELLSSTW	SETWALLS
	TERTIANS	AEIPSSTW	WASPIEST	AEKMORTW	TEAMWORK		SWALLETS
AEINRSTU	RUINATES	AEIPSZZZ	PIZAZZES		WORKMATE	AELLSSTY	TASSELLY
	TAURINES	AEIPTTUV	PUTATIVE	AEKMPRRV	VERKRAMP	AELLSTUU	ULULATES
	URANITES	AEIQRRRU	QUARRIER	AEKMPRSU	UPMAKERS	AELLSUVV	VALVULES
	URINATES	AEIQRRSU	QUARRIES	AEKNNRSS	RANKNESS	AELLSUXY	SEXUALLY
AEINRSTW	TINWARES	AEIQRRTU	QUARTIER	AEKNORRV	OVERRANK	AELMMNOS	MAMELONS
AEINRSUV	VAURIENS	AEIRRRST	STARRIER	AEKNORUY	EUKARYON	AELMMORW	MEALWORM
AEINRSUZ	AZURINES		TARRIERS	AEKNOTTU	OUTTAKEN	AELMMOSY	MYELOMAS
	SUZERAIN	AEIRRSST	TARSIERS	AEKNPPRS	KNAPPERS	AELMMRSS	SLAMMERS
AEINRSVV	VERVAINS	AEIRRSSY	SISERARY	AEKNPRSS	SPANKERS	AELMMRST	STRAMMEL
AEINRSZZ	SNAZZIER	AEIRRSTT	RETRAITS	AEKNPSSU	UNSPEAKS		TRAMMELS
AEINRTTU	TAINTURE		STRAITER	AEKNRSST	STARKENS	AELMMSST	STAMMELS
AEINRTUV	VAUNTIER		TARRIEST	AEKNRSSW	SWANKERS	AELMMSSY	MALMSEYS
AEINSSST	SAINTESS	AEIRSTTW	STRAWIER	AEKNRSTZ	KRANTZES	AELMNNOU	NOUMENAL
	SESTINAS	AEIRRSVV	VIVERRAS	AEKNSSTW	SWANKEST	AELMNNRY	MANNERLY
AEINSSSV	VINASSES	AEIRRTTT	RETRAITT	AEKNSSWY	SWANKEYS	AELMNNTU	UNMANTLE
AEINSSTT	ANTSIEST	AEIRRTTY	TERTIARY	AEKOPSTU	OUTSPEAK	AELMNOPS	NEOPLASM
	INSTATES	AEIRRVWY	RIVERWAY		SPEAKOUT		PLEONASM
	NASTIEST	AEIRSSST	TIRASSES	AEKORRSS	ROSAKERS	AELMNORS	ALMONERS
	SATINETS	AEIRSSSZ	ASSIZERS	AEKORRWW	WORKWEAR	AELMNOST	SALMONET
	TITANESS	AEIRSSTT	ARTISTES	AEKORSSS	KAROSSES	AELMNOSU	MELANOUS
				AEKORSTV	OVERTASK	AELMNOWY	LAYWOMEN

AELMNOYY YEOMANLY
AELMNPRS LAMPERNS
AELMNRSU MENSURAL
         NUMERALS
AELMNSTT MANTLETS
AELMNSTU NUTMEALS
AELMOOPT OMOPLATE
AELMOORS SALEROOM
AELMOPRR PREMOLAR
AELMOPRS PLEROMAS
AELMOPRT PROMETAL
         TEMPORAL
AELMOPSU AMPOULES
AELMOPSX EXOPLASM
AELMOPSY MAYPOLES
         PLAYSOME
AELMOPTT METAPLOT
         PALMETTO
AELMORST MOLERATS
AELMORSU RAMULOSE
AELMORSV REMOVALS
AELMORTU EMULATOR
AELMOSSS MOLASSES
AELMOSST MALTOSES
AELMOSTT MATELOTS
AELMOSTY ATMOLYSE
AELMOTVZ MAZELTOV
AELMOTYZ ATMOLYZE
AELMPRRT TRAMPLER
AELMPRSS SAMPLERS
AELMPRST TEMPLARS
         TRAMPLES
AELMPRSY LAMPREYS
         SAMPLERY
AELMPSUX AMPLEXUS
AELMQSUU SQUAMULE
AELMRSTT MALTSTER
         MARTLETS
AELMRSTY MASTERLY
AELMRTUY MATURELY
AELMSSST MASTLESS
AELNNNPU UNPANNEL
AELNNOOP NAPOLEON
AELNNOOX NALOXONE
AELNNORU NEURONAL
AELNNOSU ANNULOSE
AELNNPRS PLANNERS
AELNNPSU UNPANELS
AELNNRSS ENSNARLS
AELNNRST LANTERNS
AELNNRSU UNLEARNS
AELNNRTU UNLEARNT
AELNNSST STANNELS
AELNNSTU ANNULETS
AELNOOTZ ENTOZOAL
AELNOPRS PERSONAL
         PSORALEN
AELNOPST LAPSTONE
         PLEONAST
         POLENTAS
AELNORSU ALEURONS
AELNORSV VERONALS
AELNORTT TETRONAL
         TOLERANT
AELNORTU OUTLEARN
AELNORTY ORNATELY
AELNOSTV VOLANTES
AELNPPSY PLAYPENS
         SPYPLANE
AELNPRST PANTLERS
         PLANTERS
         REPLANTS
AELNPRSU PURSLANE
         SUPERNAL
AELNPRTY PLENARTY
AELNPSSS SPANLESS
AELNPSSU SPANSULE
AELNPSTX EXPLANTS
AELNPTTU PETULANT

AELNPTTY PATENTLY
AELNQSUU UNEQUALS
AELNRRSS SNARLERS
AELNRRTY ERRANTLY
AELNRRUV NERVULAR
AELNRSST SALTERNS
AELNRSTT SLATTERN
         TRENTALS
AELNRSTU NEUTRALS
AELNRSTV VENTRALS
AELNRSUV UNRAVELS
AELNRSVY SYLVANER
AELNRSXY LARYNXES
AELNRUWY UNWARELY
AELNSSST SALTNESS
AELNSSTY STANYELS
AELNSTUV ENVAULTS
AELNSUUX UNSEXUAL
AELNTTUX EXULTANT
AELOOPRZ ZOOPERAL
         ROSEOLAS
AELOORTZ ZOOLATER
AELOPPRS PROLAPSE
         PROPALES
         SAPROPEL
AELOPPSU PAPULOSE
AELOPPTU POPULATE
AELOPPXY APOPLEXY
AELOPQUY OPAQUELY
AELOPRRV REPROVAL
AELOPRSS REPOSALS
AELOPRST PETROSAL
         PROLATES
AELOPRSU LEAPROUS
AELOPRSV OVERLAPS
AELOPRVY OVERPLAY
AELOPSSS SOAPLESS
AELOPSST APOSTLES
AELOPSSU ESPOUSAL
         SEPALOUS
AELOPSSX EXPOSALS
AELOPSTT PALETOTS
AELOPSTU OUTLEAPS
         PETALOUS
AELOPTTU OUTLEAPT
AELORRST REALTORS
         RELATORS
AELORSTU ROSULATE
AELORSTV LEVATORS
AELORSTY ROYALETS
AELORSTZ ZELATORS
AELORSUU ROULEAUS
AELORSVY OVERLAYS
AELORSWY OWRELAYS
AELORTTV VARLETTO
AELORTYZ ZEALOTRY
AELORUUX ROULEAUX
AELOSSTV SOLVATES
AELOSSTY ASYSTOLE
AELOSSVY SAVELOYS
AELOSTTU TOLUATES
AELOSTTW WASTELOT
AELOSTUV OVULATES
AELOSTUY AUTOLYSE
AELOTUUV OUTVALUE
AELOTUYZ AUTOLYZE
AELPPRSS SLAPPERS
AELPPSST STAPPLES
AELPPSSU APPULSES
AELPRRSW SPRAWLER
AELPRRTT PRATTLER
AELPRSST PLASTERS
         PSALTERS
         STAPLERS
AELPRSSU PERUSALS
AELPRSSY PARSLEYS
         SPARSELY
AELPRSTT PARTLETS

         PLATTERS
         PRATTLES
         SPLATTER
         SPRATTLE
AELPRSTU APLUSTRE
AELPRSTY PLASTERY
         PSALTERY
AELPSSSS PASSLESS
AELPSSTT PELTASTS
AELPSSTU PULSATES
         SPATULES
AELPSUUV UPVALUES
AELQRRSU QUARRELS
AELQRSUY SQUARELY
AELQSTUZ QUETZALS
AELRRSTT RATTLERS
         STARTLER
AELRRSTW TRAWLERS
AELRRTVY VARLETRY
AELRSSST STARLESS
AELRSSTT SLATTERS
         STARLETS
         STARTLES
AELRSSTU SALUTERS
AELRSSTW WARTLESS
         WASTRELS
AELRSSUW WALRUSES
AELRSTTT TARTLETS
         TATTLERS
AELRSTTU LUSTRATE
         TUTELARS
AELRSTTY SLATTERY
AELRSTUV VAULTERS
         VESTURAL
AELRSTWZ WALTZERS
AELRSUVY SURVEYAL
AELRTTTW TWATTLER
AELRTTUX TEXTURAL
AELRTTUY TUTELARY
AELSSSTU SALTUSES
AELSSSTY STAYLESS
AELSSWZZ SWAZZLES
AELSTTTW TWATTLES
AELSTTUY ASTUTELY
AEMMMOTU OMMATEUM
AEMMMRTY MAMMETRY
AEMMNNOY MONEYMAN
AEMMNPRS RAMPSMEN
AEMMNRRY MERRYMAN
AEMMNRTU RAMENTUM
AEMMORSS MARMOSES
AEMMORST MARMOSET
AEMMPRSS SPAMMERS
AEMMRSST STAMMERS
AEMMRTUY MAUMETRY
AEMMRTWY MAWMETRY
AEMMSSTU SUMMATES
AEMMSSUW WAMMUSES
AEMNNOPW PENWOMAN
AEMNNORT ORNAMENT
AEMNNOSS MANNOSES
AEMNNRST MANRENTS
         REMNANTS
AEMNOORR MAROONER
AEMNOORT ANTEROOM
AEMNOORY AERONOMY
AEMNOOTZ METAZOON
AEMNOPRS PROSEMAN
AEMNOPRT EMPATRON
AEMNOPRW MANPOWER
AEMNORRS RANSOMER
AEMNORST MONSTERA
         STOREMAN
AEMNORSU ENAMOURS
         NEUROMAS
AEMNORSV OVERMANS
         OVERSMAN
AEMNORSY ROMNEYAS

AEMNORTT TORMENTA
AEMNORTU ROUTEMAN
AEMNORTY MONETARY
AEMNORYY YEOMANRY
AEMNOSTU NOTAEUMS
         OUTNAMES
         SEAMOUNT
AEMNPRSS PRESSMAN
AEMNPRSU SUPERMAN
AEMNPSST ENSTAMPS
         PASSMENT
AEMNPSTU SPUMANTE
AEMNPSTY PAYMENTS
AEMNQSUW SQUAWMEN
AEMNRRSU MANURERS
AEMNRRUY NUMERARY
AEMNRSST SARMENTS
         SMARTENS
AEMNRSSU SURNAMES
AEMNRSSW WARMNESS
AEMNRSTU ANESTRUM
         MENSTRUA
         TRANSUME
AEMNRSTV VARMENTS
AEMNRSTW TRANSMEW
         TREWSMAN
AEMNRSUY ANEURYSM
AEMNSTWY WAYMENTS
AEMOOPST POMATOES
AEMOORSW WOOMERAS
AEMOORTT AMORETTO
AEMOOSST MAESTOSO
         OSTEOMAS
AEMOOSSV VAMOOSES
AEMOOSTT TOMATOES
AEMOOSTU AUTOSOME
AEMOOTTY TOMATOEY
AEMOPPRS PAMPEROS
AEMOPRTW POMWATER
         TAPEWORM
AEMOQSSU SQUAMOSE
AEMORRRU ARMOURER
AEMORRST REARMOST
AEMORRSY ROSEMARY
AEMORSSS MORASSES
AEMORSST MAESTROS
AEMORSSW SEAWORMS
AEMORSSY MAYORESS
AEMORSTV OVERMAST
AEMORSVW OVERSWAM
AEMORTTU TAUTOMER
AEMOSSTT EASTMOST
AEMOSSTW TWASOMES
AEMOSSUZ ZAMOUSES
AEMOSSWY SOMEWAYS
AEMOSTTZ MOZETTAS
AEMOTTZZ MOZZETTA
AEMPRRST TRAMPERS
AEMPRRSW PREWARMS
AEMPRRSY SPERMARY
AEMPRSST STAMPERS
AEMPRSSW SWAMPERS
AEMPRSTT TRAMPETS
AEMPRSTU TEMPURAS
         UPSTREAM
AEMPSSUW MAWPUSES
         WAMPUSES
AEMPSTTT ATTEMPTS
AEMQRSSU MARQUESS
         MASQUERS
AEMRRSSW SWARMERS
AEMRRTUV VERATRUM
AEMRSSSU MASSEURS
AEMRSSTT MATTRESS
         SMARTEST
         SMATTERS
AEMRSSTY MAYSTERS
AEMRSTTU MATUREST
         TESTAMUR

AEMRSTTX MARTEXTS	AENRSTTU TAUNTERS	AEPPRSSU UPSPEARS	AFFLORTU FORFAULT
AEMRTUUX TRUMEAUX	AENRSTUV VAUNTERS	AEPPRSSW SWAPPERS	AFFLRRUU FURFURAL
AEMSTTTU TESTATUM	AENRSTUW UNWATERS	AEPQRSTU PARQUETS	AFFNORSS SAFFRONS
AENNNPST PENNANTS	AENRSTWY STERNWAY	AEPRRRSS SPARRERS	AFFNORST AFFRONTS
AENNNTTU UNTENANT	AENRTUVY VAUNTERY	AEPRRSSY RESPRAYS	AFFNORSY SAFFRONY
AENNOPRT PATRONNE	AENRTUWY UNWATERY	SPRAYERS	AFFNRRUU FURFURAN
AENNOPST PENTOSAN	AENSSSTV VASTNESS	AEPRRSTU PARTURES	AFGGGILN FLAGGING
AENNOPUW UNWEAPON	AENSSSTW WASTNESS	RAPTURES	AFGGGINR FRAGGING
AENNORST NORTENAS	AENSSTTU TAUTNESS	AEPRSSST SPARSEST	AFGGGINS FAGGINGS
RESONANT	UNSTATES	TRESPASS	AFGGILNN FANGLING
AENNORSU UNREASON	AENSSTTX SEXTANTS	AEPRSSTT SPATTERS	FLANGING
AENNORSY ANNOYERS	AENSSTXY SYNTAXES	TAPSTERS	AFGGILOP GIGAFLOP
AENNORTW WANTONER	AEOOPPPS PAPPOOSE	AEPRSSTU PASTURES	AFGGINOR FORAGING
AENNORVY NOVENARY	AEOOPPSS PAPOOSES	UPSTARES	AFGGINOT FAGOTING
AENNOSSU UNSEASON	AEOOPRRT OPERATOR	AEPRSSTY YAPSTERS	AFGGINRT GRAFTING
AENNOSTU TONNEAUS	AEOOPRRS OROPESAS	AEPRSTTU STUPRATE	AFGHIINT FAITHING
AENNOTUX TONNEAUX	AEOOPSTT POTATOES	AEPRSTTY TAPESTRY	AFGHILLN HALFLING
AENNPRSS SPANNERS	AEOORRST SORORATE	AEPRSTUX SUPERTAX	AFGHILNS FLASHING
AENNPSSU PANNUSES	AEOORTTT TATTOOER	AEPRTUVY PYRUVATE	AFGHILNT FANLIGHT
AENNQSTU QUANNETS	AEOORTTV ROTOVATE	AEPSSSSU PASSUSES	AFGHILPS FLAGSHIP
AENNRSTT ENTRANTS	AEOPPRRV APPROVER	AEQRRSSU SQUARERS	AFGHINRT FARTHING
AENNRSTY TYRANNES	AEOPPRSS APPOSERS	AEQRRSTU QUARTERS	AFGHINRW WHARFING
AENNRSWY SWANNERY	AEOPPRSV APPROVES	AEQRSSTU SQUAREST	AFGHINST SHAFTING
AENNRTTY TENANTRY	AEOPQRTU PAROQUET	AEQRSTTU QUARTETS	AFGHIOST GOATFISH
AENOOPST TEASPOON	AEOPQSTU OPAQUEST	SQUATTER	AFGHLLUU LAUGHFUL
AENOORRT RATOONER	AEOPRRRT PARROTER	AEQRSTUZ QUARTZES	AFGHLNSU FLASHGUN
AENOPPRS PROPANES	AEOPRRST PRAETORS	AEQRTTTU QUARTETT	AFGHLSTU FLAUGHTS
AENOPRSS PERSONAS	PRORATES	AERRSSSU ASSURERS	GHASTFUL
RESPONSA	AEOPRRTV OVERPART	AERRSSTT RESTARTS	AFGHRSTU FRAUGHTS
AENOPRST OPERANTS	AEOPRRUV VAPOURER	STARTERS	AFGIILLN FLAILING
PRONATES	AEOPRRVW WRAPOVER	AERRSSTU SERRATUS	AFGIILNS FAILINGS
AENOPRTT PATENTOR	AEOPRSST ESPARTOS	AERRSSTY STRAYERS	AFGIIMNN INFAMING
AENOPRWY WEAPONRY	PORTASES	AERRSTUY TREASURY	AFGIINNT FAINTING
AENOPSSU POSAUNES	PROTASES	AERSSSST STRASSES	AFGIINRS FAIRINGS
AENORRRW NARROWER	SEAPORTS	AERSSSTY SATYRESS	FRAISING
AENORRST ANTRORSE	AEOPRSSU ASPEROUS	AERSSTTU STATURES	AFGIINTX FIXATING
AENORSST ASSENTOR	AEOPRSSV OVERPASS	AERSSTTW SWATTERS	AFGIKLNN FANKLING
SENATORS	AEOPRSTT PROSTATE	AERSSTUX SURTAXES	FLANKING
TREASONS	AEOPRSTU APTEROUS	AERSSTXY STYRAXES	AFGIKNNR FRANKING
AENORSTT ORNATEST	AEOPRSTV OVERPAST	AERSTTUV VETTURAS	AFGIKORT KOFTGARI
AENORSTV VENATORS	AEOPRSVY OVERPAYS	AERSTTVY TRAVESTY	AFGILLNS FALLINGS
AENORSTW STONERAW	AEOPRSWY ROPEWAYS	AERTTUXY TEXTUARY	AFGILLNT FLATLING
AENORSUV RAVENOUS	AEOPRTWX WATERPOX	AESSSTTU STATUSES	AFGILMMN FLAMMING
AENORTTX TETRAXON	AEOPSSST POTASSES	AESSTTTU ASTUTEST	AFGILMNO FLAMINGO
AENORTTY ATTORNEY	AEOPTTUY AUTOTYPE	STATUTES	AFGILNOS LOAFINGS
AENOSSTU SOUTANES	AEOQRSTU EQUATORS	AFFFFINN NIFFNAFF	AFGILNOT FLOATING
AENOSSTZ STANZOES	QUAESTOR	AFFFGILN FLAFFING	AFGILNPP FLAPPING
AENOSSUU NAUSEOUS	AEOQRSUV VAQUEROS	AFFGGINR GRAFFING	AFGILNST FATLINGS
AENOSSVW WAVESONS	AEOQRTTU TORQUATE	AFFGGINS GAFFINGS	AFGILNTT FLATTING
AENPPRSS PARSNEPS	AEOQRTUZ QUATORZE	AFFGHIRT AFFRIGHT	AFGILNTU FAULTING
SNAPPERS	AEORRRST ARRESTOR	AFFGIINP PIAFFING	AFGILORW GAIRFOWL
AENPPRST PARPENTS	ASSORTER	AFFGIINX AFFIXING	AFGILSSY GLASSIFY
AENPRRSU UNPAPERS	ORATRESS	AFFGIIRT GRAFFITI	AFGIMNOS FOAMINGS
AENPRRST PARTNERS	ROASTERS	AFFGILMN MAFFLING	AFGIMNRS FARMINGS
AENPRRSW PREWARNS	AEORRSSU AROUSERS	AFFGILNR RAFFLING	FRAMINGS
AENPRSSW SPAWNERS	AEORRSTT ROSTRATE	AFFGILNW WAFFLING	AFGIMNTU FUMIGANT
AENPRSTT PASTERNS	AEORRTUV AVOUTRER	AFFGIMRS MISGRAFF	AFGIMORS GASIFORM
PATTERNS	AEORRTZZ TERRAZZO	AFFGINNY NYAFFING	AFGIMRST MISGRAFT
TRANSEPT	AEORSSSS ASSESSOR	AFFGINQU QUAFFING	AFGINNNS FANNINGS
AENPRSTU PERSAUNT	AEORSSTT STRATOSE	AFFGINST STAFFING	AFGINNSW FAWNINGS
AENPRSUV PARVENUS	TOASTERS	AFFGINUW WAUFFING	AFGINORV FAVORING
AENPSSSY SYNAPSES	AEORSSTV VOTARESS	AFFGIORT GRAFFITO	AFGINORY FORAYING
AENPSSTU PESAUNTS	AEORSSTX STORAXES	AFFHILNS HAFFLINS	AFGINPPR FRAPPING
AENPSSTW STEWPANS	AEORSTTT ATTESTOR	AFFHILST FLATFISH	AFGINRST INGRAFTS
WASPNEST	TESTATOR	AFFHILTU FAITHFUL	STRAFING
AENPSSTY SYNAPTES	AEORSTTU OUTRATES	AFFIINTY AFFINITY	AFGINRSW SWARFING
AENPSSTZ SPETSNAZ	OUTSTARE	AFFILMNS MAFFLINS	AFGINRSY FRAYINGS
AENPSTZZ SPETZNAZ	AEORSTUW OUTSWEAR	AFFILSUX SUFFIXAL	AFGINRTU FIGURANT
AENQRRTU QUARTERN	OUTWEARS	AFFIMSST MASTIFFS	AFGINSST FASTINGS
AENQSTTU QUESTANT	AEORSTVY OVERSTAY	AFFINORR FORFAIRN	AFGINSTW WAFTINGS
AENRRRTY ERRANTRY	AEORSUVW WAVEROUS	AFFINOSU AFFUSION	AFGINSUY SANGUIFY
AENRRSTT TRANTERS	AEORSVWY OVERSWAY	AFFINRSU FUNFAIRS	AFGKNOPS PAKFONGS
AENRSSST SARSNETS	AEORTUWY OUTWEARY	RUFFIANS	AFGKORST KOFTGARS
AENRSSTT TARTNESS	AEORTVXY VEXATORY	AFFIORRS FORFAIRS	AFGLLNOT FLATLONG
AENRSSTU ANESTRUS	AEPPPSSU PAPPUSES	AFFIPSTT TIPSTAFF	AFGLLRUU FUGURAL
SAUNTERS	AEPPRRST STRAPPER	AFFIRRSU FURFAIRS	AFGLLRUY FRUGALLY
AENRSSTV SERVANTS	TRAPPERS	AFFLLOOT FOOTFALL	AFGLLSSU GLASSFUL
VERSANTS	AEPPRRSW WRAPPERS	AFFLLTUU FAULTFUL	AFGLLSTU GASTFULL
AENRSSUW UNSWEARS		AFFLOOOT FOALFOOT	AFGLNNOO GONFALON

Code	Word(s)	Code	Word(s)	Code	Word(s)	Code	Word(s)
AFGLNORU	GROANFUL	AFIMNORT	NATIFORM	AGGGINNS	GANGINGS	AGGINPSS	GASPINGS
AFGLNOUW	WAGONFUL	AFIMNOSU	INFAMOUS		SNAGGING	AGGINPUZ	UPGAZING
AFGNNNOO	GONFANON	AFIMORRU	AURIFORM	AGGGINRS	RAGGINGS	AGGINRSS	GRASSING
AFGOORTZ	ZOOGRAFT	AFIMORRV	VARIFORM	AGGGINSS	SAGGINGS		SIRGANGS
AFHIILRS	FRAILISH	AFIMORSV	VASIFORM	AGGGINST	STAGGING	AGGINRST	GRATINGS
AFHIILSS	SAILFISH	AFIMSSTT	FATTISMS		TAGGINGS	AGGINRSU	SUGARING
AFHIIMST	MISFAITH	AFINNORS	FRANIONS	AGGGINSU	GAUGINGS	AGGINRSV	GRAVINGS
AFHIINST	FAINTISH	AFINNOTU	FOUNTAIN	AGGGINSW	SWAGGING	AGGINRSZ	GRAZINGS
AFHIKSUY	KUFIYAHS	AFINNRTY	INFANTRY	AGGGIYZZ	ZIGZAGGY	AGGINRTY	GYRATING
AFHILLNS	HALFLINS	AFINOPSY	SAPONIFY	AGGHIILS	GHILGAIS	AGGINRUU	AUGURING
AFHILLSW	WALLFISH	AFINQTUY	QUANTIFY	AGGHILNU	LAUGHING	AGGINRYZ	AGRYZING
AFHILLSY	FLASHILY	AFINRSTX	TRANSFIX	AGGHILST	GASLIGHT	AGGINSSS	GASSINGS
AFHILSST	SALTFISH	AFINSSTU	FAUNISTS	AGGHILSY	SHAGGILY	AGGINSST	STAGINGS
AFHILSTT	FLATTISH		FUSTIANS	AGGHIMNO	HOMAGING	AGGIRTUZ	ZIGGURAT
AFHILSTW	HALFWITS	AFIORSTU	FAITOURS	AGGHIMNS	GINGHAMS	AGGKLNNU	GANGKLUNG
AFHIMNST	MANSHIFT	AFIORSTZ	SFORZATI	AGGHINNP	PHANGING	AGGLLLOY	LOLLYGAG
AFHIMNSU	HAFNIUMS	AFIRSTTY	STRATIFY	AGGHINNS	GNASHING	AGGLLOOY	ALGOLOGY
AFHINOSS	FASHIONS	AFISSSTT	SITFASTS		HANGINGS	AGGLMOOR	LOGOGRAM
AFHIOSSU	FASHIOUS	AFISSTTT	FATTISTS	AGGHINNW	WHANGING	AGGLOORY	AGROLOGY
AFHIRSST	STARFISH	AFKLNOTU	OUTFLANK	AGGHINPR	GRAPHING	AGGLRSTY	STRAGGLY
AFHKLNTU	THANKFUL	AFKLNSTU	TANKFULS	AGGHINST	GHASTING	AGGMORRS	GROGRAMS
AFHKORSX	FOXSHARK	AFKLOSWY	FOLKWAYS	AGGHINUW	WAUGHING	AGGNUWZZ	ZUGZWANG
AFHKORSY	HAYFORKS	AFKMOORT	FOOTMARK	AGGIIJJS	JIGAJIGS	AGHHIILT	HIGHTAIL
AFHKRSTU	FUTHARKS	AFLLLORY	FLORALLY	AGGIILNN	ALIGNING	AGHHINSS	SHASHING
AFHLLOTU	LOATHFUL	AFLLLUWY	LAWFULLY	AGGIILNR	GLAIRING	AGHHISWY	HIGHWAYS
AFHLOSTU	OUTFLASH	AFLLMNUY	MANFULLY	AGGIILNS	SILAGING	AGHHLOTU	ALTHOUGH
AFHLOSTY	HAYLOFTS	AFLLMORY	FORMALLY	AGGIILNT	LIGATING	AGHIILNN	INHALING
AFHLRTUW	WRATHFUL	AFLLMPSU	PALMFULS		TAIGLING	AGHIINNS	HAININGS
AFHNOOST	FANTOOSH	AFLLNOSW	SNOWFALL	AGGIILNV	GINGIVAL	AGHIIPRR	HAIRGRIP
AFHOOPST	POOFTAHS	AFLLNUUW	UNLAWFUL	AGGIIMNS	IMAGINGS	AGHIIRTT	AIRTIGHT
AFHOOPTT	FOOTPATH	AFLLOSTU	FALLOUTS	AGGIINNR	GRAINING	AGHIJNRT	NIGHTJAR
AFHOPSTU	POUFTAHS		OUTFALLS	AGGIINNS	AGNISING	AGHIKNNS	SHANKING
AFIIKMRS	FAKIRISM	AFLLRTUY	ARTFULLY		GAININGS	AGHIKNNT	THANKING
AFIILLLY	FILIALLY	AFLLSTUW	WASTFULL	AGGIINNZ	AGNIZING	AGHIKNRS	SHARKING
AFIILLNU	UNFILIAL	AFLMNORU	UNFORMAL	AGGIINRS	AGRISING	AGHIKNSS	SHAKINGS
AFIILMMS	FAMILISM	AFLMOPRT	PLATFORM	AGGIINRZ	AGRIZING	AGHIKNSW	HAWKINGS
AFIILMNS	FINALISM	AFLMORRU	FORMULAR	AGGIINST	AGISTING	AGHILLNO	HALLOING
AFIILNRU	UNIFILAR	AFLMORSU	FORMULAS	AGGIINSU	AGUISING	AGHILLNS	HALLINGS
AFIILNST	FINALIST	AFLMORSW	WOLFRAMS	AGGIINUZ	AGUIZING	AGHILLNT	ALLNIGHT
AFIILNTY	FINALITY	AFLMORTU	FOULMART	AGGIJJOS	JIGAJOGS	AGHILMTY	ALMIGHTY
AFIILORS	AIRFOILS	AFLMORTW	FLATWORM	AGGIJLNN	JANGLING	AGHILNOO	HOOLIGAN
AFIILRST	AIRLIFTS	AFLMOSST	FLOTSAMS	AGGILLNS	GINGALLS	AGHILNOS	SHOALING
AFIIMRSY	FAIRYISM	AFLMOSUY	FAMOUSLY	AGGILLNU	ULLAGING	AGHILNOT	LOATHING
AFIINNOS	SAINFOIN	AFLNOPRU	APRONFUL	AGGILLNY	GALLYING	AGHILNPS	PLASHING
	SINFONIA	AFLNORST	FRONTALS	AGGILMNN	MANGLING	AGHILNRS	HARLINGS
AFIINOTX	FIXATION	AFLNRTUU	UNARTFUL	AGGILMNO	GLOAMING		RINGHALS
AFIIORRT	TRIFORIA	AFLNTUUV	VAUNTFUL	AGGILMNR	MALGRING	AGHILNRY	NARGHILY
AFIKLNNR	FRANKLIN	AFLNTUUY	UNFAULTY	AGGILMNU	GLAUMING	AGHILNSS	HASSLING
AFIKLORT	FORKTAIL	AFLOOSTW	WOOLFATS	AGGILNNO	GANGLION		LASHINGS
AFIKLOST	FLOKATIS	AFLORSSU	FUSAROLS	AGGILNNR	GNARLING		SLANGISH
AFIKNRST	RATFINKS	AFLORSUV	FLAVOURS	AGGILNNS	ANGLINGS		SLASHING
AFIKRSTY	KARSTIFY	AFLOSTUU	FLATUOUS		SLANGING	AGHILNST	HALTINGS
AFILLLOT	FLOTILLA	AFLPRSTY	FLYTRAPS	AGGILNNT	GNATLING		LATHINGS
AFILLMSS	MISFALLS	AFLRSTTU	STARTFUL		TANGLING	AGHILNSU	LANGUISH
AFILLNPU	PLAINFUL	AFLRSTUY	TRAYFULS	AGGILNNW	WANGLING	AGHILNSW	SHAWLING
AFILLPST	PITFALLS	AFMNNORT	FRONTMAN	AGGILNOP	GALOPING		WHALINGS
AFILLPSU	PAILFULS	AFMNORST	FORMANTS	AGGILNOT	GLOATING	AGHILRSY	GARISHLY
AFILLSUV	VIALFULS	AFMOOPRR	PROFORMA		GOATLING	AGHILRTY	GRAITHLY
AFILLTUY	FAULTILY	AFMORSTU	FOUMARTS	AGGILNPU	PLAGUING	AGHILSUY	AGUISHLY
AFILMNOR	FORMALIN	AFMORTUY	FUMATORY	AGGILNPY	GAPINGLY	AGHIMMNS	SHAMMING
	INFORMAL	AFMOSSTU	SFUMATOS	AGGILNRY	GRAYLING	AGHIMMNW	WHAMMING
AFILMOPR	PALIFORM	AFNORRSW	FORWARNS		RAGINGLY	AGHIMNSS	MASHINGS
AFILMSSS	FALSISMS	AFOOPPRS	APPROOFS	AGGILNSS	GLASSING		SMASHING
AFILNORT	FLATIRON	AFOOPRRT	RATPROOF	AGGILNSZ	GLAZINGS	AGHIMNTY	THIGAMMY
	INFLATOR	AFOORSTZ	FORZATOS	AGGIMNRU	MAUGRING	AGHIMPRU	GRAPHIUM
AFILNPPT	FLIPPANT		SFORZATO	AGGINNOR	GROANING	AGHINNOS	NIHONGAS
AFILNRUY	UNFAIRLY	AFOOSTWY	FOOTWAYS	AGGINNOT	TANGOING	AGHINNSS	SNASHINGS
AFILNSTU	FLUTINAS	AFORSTTW	FORSWATT	AGGINNOW	WAGONING	AGHINNST	TANGHINS
	INFLATUS	AFOSSTUU	FASTUOUS	AGGINNPR	PRANGING	AGHINNTU	HAUNTING
AFILORSW	AIRFLOWS	AGGGGILN	GAGGLING	AGGINNPS	SPANGING	AGHINNTY	ANYTHING
AFILORTY	FILATORY	AGGGHILN	HAGGLING	AGGINNRR	GNARRING	AGHINOST	HOASTING
AFILRSTU	FISTULAR	AGGGHINS	SHAGGING	AGGINNRT	GRANTING	AGHINPPW	WHAPPING
AFILSSTU	FISTULAS	AGGGILNN	GANGLING	AGGINNRU	RAUNGING	AGHINPPY	HAPPYING
AFILSTTU	FLAUTIST	AGGGILNR	GARGLING	AGGINNST	STANGING	AGHINPRS	HARPINGS
AFIMMNOR	MANIFORM		RAGGLING	AGGINNTU	GAUNTING		PHRASING
AFIMMORR	RAMIFORM	AGGGILNS	LAGGINGS	AGGINNTW	TWANGING		SHARPING
AFIMNOPR	NAPIFORM		SLAGGING	AGGINOVY	VOYAGING	AGHINPSW	PSHAWING
AFIMNORR	RANIFORM	AGGGILNW	WAGGLING	AGGINPRS	GRASPING	AGHINQSU	QUASHING
					SPARGING		

AGHINRRU HURRAING	AGIIMNOW MIAOWING	AGILLNRU ALLURING	AGILNRWW WRAWLING
AGHINRRY HARRYING	AGIIMNPV IMPAVING	LINGULAR	AGILNRWX WRAXLING
AGHINRSS SHARINGS	AGIIMNSS AMISSING	AGILLNRY NARGILLY	AGILNSST ANGLISTS
AGHINRST TRASHING	AGIIMNST GIANTISM	RALLYING	LASTINGS
AGHINRTW THRAWING	AGIIMNTT MITIGANT	AGILLNST STALLING	SALTINGS
WRATHING	AGIIMORS ORIGAMIS	AGILLNSU LINGULAS	SLATINGS
AGHINSST HASTINGS	AGIIMSST IMAGISTS	AGILLNSW WALLINGS	AGILNSSV SALVINGS
STASHING	AGIINNPS SPAINING	AGILLNSY SALLYING	AGILNSSW SWALINGS
AGHINSSV SHAVINGS	AGIINNPT PAINTING	SIGNALLY	AGILNSTT SLATTING
AGHINSSW SWASHING	AGIINNRS INGRAINS	SLANGILY	AGILNSTU SALUTING
WASHINGS	AGIINNRT TRAINING	AGILLNTY TALLYING	AGILNSUV AVULSING
AGHINSTT HATTINGS	AGIINNRV RAVINING	AGILLOOR GILLAROO	AGILNSUW WAULINGS
AGHINSTW SWATHING	AGIINNST SAINTING	AGILLOPT GALLIPOT	AGILNSVY SAVINGLY
THAWINGS	SATINING	AGILLORS GORILLAS	AGILNSWW WAWLINGS
AGHINUZZ HUZZAING	STAINING	AGILLOST GALLIOTS	AGILNSWY SWAYLING
AGHIPRRT TRIGRAPH	AGIINNSW SWAINING	AGILLPRY PLAYGIRL	AGILNTTT TATTLING
AGHIRSTT STRAIGHT	AGIINNTT TAINTING	AGILLPUY PLAGUILY	AGILNTTW WATTLING
AGHISSTW SIGHTSAW	AGIINOPT OPIATING	AGILLSSU LUGSAILS	AGILNTUV VAULTING
AGHKOSSW GOSHAWKS	AGIINORS SIGNORIA	AGILLSSY GLASSILY	AGILNTUX LUXATING
AGHLLMPU GALLUMPH	AGIINORT RIGATONI	AGILMMNS LAMMINGS	AGILNTWZ WALTZING
AGHLMOOR HOLOGRAM	AGIINPRS ASPIRING	SLAMMING	AGILOORS GLORIOSA
AGHLMPSU GALUMPHS	PAIRINGS	SMALMING	AGILOOXY AXIOLOGY
AGHLNOSU SHOGUNAL	PRAISING	AGILMNNT MANTLING	AGILOPST GALIPOTS
AGHLNSUY NYLGHAUS	AGIINPRT PIRATING	AGILMNPS LAMPINGS	AGILORSS GIRASOLS
AGHLOOSS GASOHOLS	AGIINRRV ARRIVING	SAMPLING	AGILORSW AIRGLOWS
AGHMMOOY HOMOGAMY	AGIINRSS RAISINGS	AGILMNQU QUALMING	AGILOSST SALIGOTS
AGHMNPSU SPHAGNUM	AGIINRTT ATTIRING	AGILMNRS MARLINGS	AGILSYYZ SYZYGIAL
AGHMOOPY OMOPHAGY	AGIINSSZ ASSIZING	AGILMNST MALTINGS	AGIMMNPS SPAMMING
AGHMOPRY MYOGRAPH	AGIINSTV VISTAING	AGILMOPR LIPOGRAM	AGIMMNRS SMARMING
AGHNNSTU SHANTUNG	AGIINSTW WAITINGS	AGILMORS ALGORISM	AGIMMNRT TRAMMING
AGHNOORS SHAGROON	AGIISSTV VISAGIST	AGILMPSU PLAGIUMS	AGIMMOSY MISOGAMY
AGHNOSTU HANGOUTS	AGIJMNOR MAJORING	AGILNNNP PLANNING	AGIMMNNOS MASONING
TOHUNGAS	AGIJNNSU JAUNSING	AGILNNOP PANGOLIN	AGIMMNOW WOMANING
AGHNPRSY SYNGRAPH	AGIJNNTT TJANTING	AGILNNOS LOANINGS	AGIMMNRU MANURING
AGHNTTUU UNTAUGHT	AGIJNNTU JAUNTING	AGILNNPT PLANTING	UNARMING
AGHOOPYZ ZOOPHAGY	AGIJNRRS JARRINGS	AGILNNRS SNARLING	AGIMNNTU UNTAMING
AGHOPSSW SWAGSHOP	AGIKKNNS SKANKING	AGILNNSS LINSANGS	AGIMNOOV AMOOVING
AGHORSTW WARTHOGS	AGIKLMOR KILOGRAM	AGILNNST SLANTING	AGIMNORS ORGANISM
AGHRSTTU STRAUGHT	AGIKLNNP PLANKING	TANLINGS	ROAMINGS
AGIIILNS LIAISING	AGIKLNNR RANKLING	AGILNNUW UNLAWING	AGIMNORU ORIGANUM
AGIIINNS INSIGNIA	AGIKLNOS OAKLINGS	AGILNNUY UNGAINLY	AGIMNORY AGRIMONY
AGIIKLNS SKAILING	AGIKLNST SKLATING	UNLAYING	AGIMNOSV VAMOSING
AGIIKNRT TRAIKING	STALKING	AGILNOOO OOGONIAL	AGIMNPPS MAPPINGS
AGIILLOV VILLAGIO	TALKINGS	AGILNOOS ISOGONAL	AGIMNPRS RAMPINGS
VILLIAGO	AGIKLNSW WALKINGS	AGILNOPR PAROLING	AGIMNPRT TRAMPING
AGIILMNP IMPALING	AGIKLNTY TAKINGLY	AGILNOPS GALOPINS	AGIMNPSS SPASMING
AGIILMNS MAILINGS	AGIKLNUW WAULKING	AGILNOPT PLOATING	AGIMNPST STAMPING
MISALIGN	AGIKLORY KILOGRAY	AGILNORS RANGOLIS	TAMPINGS
AGIILMNU MIAULING	AGIKMNNU UNMAKING	AGILNORT TRIGONAL	AGIMNPSV VAMPINGS
AGIILNNP PLAINING	AGIKMNPU UPMAKING	AGILNOSS GLOSSINA	AGIMNPSW SWAMPING
AGIILNNS NAILINGS	AGIKMNRS MARKINGS	LASSOING	AGIMNRRY MARRYING
SNAILING	AGIKNNPP KNAPPING	AGILNOST ANTILOGS	AGIMNRST MIGRANTS
AGIILNNU INGUINAL	AGIKNNPR PRANKING	SALTOING	SMARTING
AGIILNNY INLAYING	AGIKNNRR KNARRING	AGILNOTY ANTILOGY	AGIMNRSW SWARMING
AGIILNOR ORIGINAL	AGIKNNRS RANKINGS	AGILNPPP PLAPPING	WARMINGS
AGIILNOT INTAGLIO	AGIKNNRU UNRAKING	AGILNPPS LAPPINGS	AGIMNRSY MYRINGAS
LIGATION	AGIKNNST TANKINGS	SAPPLING	AGIMNRTU MATURING
TAGLIONI	AGIKNNSW SWANKING	SLAPPING	AGIMNSSU ASSUMING
AGIILNOX GLOXINIA	AGIKNOSS SOAKINGS	AGILNPPY APPLYING	AGIMNSTT MATTINGS
AGIILNPT PLAITING	AGIKNOST GOATSKIN	AGILNPRS SPARLING	AGIMNTTU MUTATING
AGIILNQU QUAILING	AGIKNOSY KAYOINGS	SPRINGAL	AGIMORRT MIGRATOR
AGIILNRS GLAIRINS	AGIKNPRS PARKINGS	AGILNPSS SAPLINGS	AGIMORSS ISOGRAMS
RAILINGS	SPARKING	AGILNPST PLATINGS	AGIMORSU GOURAMIS
AGIILNRT RINGTAIL	AGIKNPTU UPTAKING	SPALTING	AGIMQRUY QUAGMIRY
TRAILING	AGIKNQSU QUAKINGS	STAPLING	AGIMRRST TRIGRAMS
AGIILNRV VIRGINAL	AGIKNRSS SARKINGS	AGILNPSW LAPWINGS	AGINNNNY NANNYING
AGIILNSS AISLINGS	AGIKNRST KARTINGS	SPAWLING	AGINNNOY ANNOYING
SAILINGS	STARKING	AGILNPSY PALSYING	AGINNNPS PANNINGS
AGIILNST TAILINGS	AGIKNSST SKATINGS	SPLAYING	SPANNING
AGIILNSW WAILINGS	TASKINGS	AGILNPTT PLATTING	AGINNNST TANNINGS
AGIILNTT LITIGANT	AGILLLNS LALLINGS	AGILNPUY UPLAYING	AGINNNSV VANNINGS
AGIILNTV VIGILANT	AGILLMNS SMALLING	AGILNRST RATLINGS	AGINNNSW SWANNING
AGIILORU OLIGURIA	AGILLMNU MULLIGAN	STARLING	AGINNOOP NAPOOING
AGIILOSV VILIAGOS	AGILLMNY MALIGNLY	AGILNRSU SINGULAR	AGINNOPR APRONING
AGIILPST PIGTAILS	AGILLMSU GALLIUMS	AGILNRSW WARLINGS	AGINNOPT POIGNANT
AGIILTVY VAGILITY	AGILLNOW ALLOWING	WARSLING	AGINNORT IGNORANT
AGIIMMNS MAIMINGS	AGILLNOY ALLOYING	AGILNRTT RATTLING	AGINNOST ASTONING
AGIIMMSS IMAGISMS	AGILLNPS SPALLING	AGILNRTW TRAWLING	AGINNOTT NOTATING
AGIIMNNR INARMING		AGILNRVY RAVINGLY	AGINNPPS SNAPPING

AGINNPRW PRAWNING	STARINGS	AGMOPRSU GOPURAMS	AHILPSSY PHYSALIS
AGINNPST PANTINGS	AGINRSSU ASSURING	AGMORRSW RAGWORMS	AHILRSTY TRASHILY
AGINNPSW SPAWNING	AGINRSSY SYRINGAS	AGMRSSSU GRASSUMS	AHILRTWY WRATHILY
WINGSPAN	AGINRSTT RATTINGS	AGNNNOOS NONAGONS	AHIMMNSU HUMANISM
AGINNPUY UNPAYING	STARTING	AGNNOOPT POONTANG	AHIMMORZ MAHZORIM
AGINNQTU QUANTING	AGINRSTV STARVING	AGNNOQTU QUANTONG	AHIMMOSV MOSHAVIM
AGINNRRS SNARRING	AGINRSTW STRAWING	AGNORRST GRANTORS	AHIMNOST HOISTMAN
AGINNRSS SNARINGS	WRASTING	AGNORTUY NUGATORY	AHIMNOSW WOMANISH
AGINNRST RANTINGS	AGINRSTY STRAYING	AGNPPRSU UPSPRANG	AHIMNSTU HUMANIST
STARNING	AGINRSVW SWARVING	AGOORRTY ROGATORY	AHIMNTUY HUMANITY
AGINNRSW WARNINGS	AGINRSVY VARYINGS	AGOORTUY AUTOGYRO	AHIMOPRS APHORISM
AGINNRTT TRANTING	AGINRSWY RINGWAYS	AGOPPSST STOPGAPS	MORPHIAS
AGINNRTU NATURING	AGINSSTT TASTINGS	AGORRSSW GROSSART	AHIMPPSS SAPPHISM
AGINNRTY TRAYNING	AGINSSTW WASTINGS	ROTGRASS	AHIMPRST TRAMPISH
TYRANING	AGINSSWY SWAYINGS	AGORRSTW RAGWORTS	AHIMRSST SMARTISH
AGINNSTU SAUNTING	AGINSTTT TATTINGS	AGORRTYY GYRATORY	THRIMSAS
UNSATING	AGINSTTW SWATTING	AGORSTTY GYROSTAT	AHIMSTUZ AZIMUTHS
AGINNSTW WANTINGS	AGINSVVY SAVVYING	AHHIKLSS SHASHLIK	AHIMSTVZ MITZVAHS
AGINNSTY STAYNING	AGINSWWX WAXWINGS	AHHILNPT PHTHALIN	AHINNNSY NANNYISH
AGINNSUY UNSAYING	AGIOORSU ORAGIOUS	AHHILOST HAILSHOT	AHINNOPT ANTIPHON
AGINNSWY YAWNINGS	AGIOORSZ GRAZIOSO	AHHILPSW WHIPLASH	AHINNSTX XANTHINS
AGINNTTU ATTUNING	AGIOORTU AUTOGIRO	AHHIMMSS MISHMASH	AHINOPRU OPHIURAN
NUTATING	AGIOORTU AUTOGIRO	AHHIMNSU HAHNIUMS	AHINORST TRAHISON
TAUNTING	AGIOPPRT AGITPROP	AHHIPRSS SHARPISH	AHINOSST ASTONISH
AGINNTUV VAUNTING	AGIOPRUY UROPYGIA	AHHISSTT SHITTAHS	AHINOSTZ HOATZINS
AGINNTUX UNTAXING	AGIORRTT GRATTOIR	AHHKRSTU KASHRUTH	AHINPPSS SNAPPISH
AGINNVVY NAVVYING	AGIORSST AGISTORS	AHHLMRTY RHYTHMAL	AHINPRST TRANSHIP
AGINOORT ROGATION	ORGIASTS	AHHLNOPT NAPHTHOL	AHINQSUV VANQUISH
AGINOPPS APPOSING	AGIRSSTU SASTRUGI	AHHMPRRU HARRUMPH	AHINRSTY RHYTINAS
AGINOPQU OPAQUING	AGIRSTUZ ZASTRUGI	AHHNORTW HAWTHORN	AHINSSTU INHAUSTS
AGINOPRV VAPORING	AGIRTTUY GRATUITY	AHHOPRSS SHOPHARS	AHIOOPPT PHOTOPIA
AGINORRS GARRISON	AGJLRSUU JUGULARS	AHHOPSTU APHTHOUS	AHIOOSST ATISHOOS
ROARINGS	AGJNOORS JARGOONS	AHIIKRSS SHIKARIS	AHIOPRST APHORIST
AGINORRW ARROWING	AGJNOPST JOGPANTS	AHIILLNPS PLAINISH	AHIOPRSU OPHIURAS
AGINORSS ASSIGNOR	AGKLNNOS ANKLONGS	AHIILOST HALIOTIS	AHIOPSXY HYPOXIAS
SOARINGS	AGKLNNSU ANKLUNGS	AHIILPTW WHIPTAIL	AHIORSTV TOVARISH
AGINORST ORGANIST	AGKMMORY KYMOGRAM	AHIILRTY HILARITY	AHIORSUV HAVIOURS
ROASTING	AGKMNOPS KAMPONGS	AHIIMNOT HIMATION	AHIOSTWY HOISTWAY
AGINORSU AROUSING	AGKNOPST PAKTONGS	AHIIMNST ISTHMIAN	AHIPPSST SAPPHIST
AGINORSV SAVORING	AGKORRSW RAGWORKS	THIAMINS	AHIPRSST HARPISTS
AGINORTT ROTATING	AGLLLNOW LONGWALL	AHIIMSSS SASHIMIS	AHIPRSSW WARSHIPS
TROATING	AGLLMOPW GLOWLAMP	AHIINOPT PHOTINIA	AHIPSSWW WHIPSAWS
AGINORTV GRAVITON	AGLLNOOS GALLOONS	AHIINPRS HAIRPINS	AHIPSSWY SHIPWAYS
AGINORTY GYRATION	NUTGALLS	AHIINPST ANTISHIP	AHIQRSSU SQUARISH
ORGANITY	AGLLRUVY VULGARLY	AHIINSST SAINTISH	AHIRRSST STIRRAHS
AGINOSST AGONISTS	AGLMOOTY ATMOLOGY	AHIINSSW SWAINISH	AHIRSSTT STARTISH
AGINOSSU SAGOUINS	AGLMOPSY POLYGAMS	AHIINSTU HUITAINS	AHIRSSTW TRISHAWS
AGINOSTT TANGOIST	AGLMOPYY POLYGAMY	AHIIOPST HOSPITIA	AHISSSTU SHIATSUS
TOASTING	AGLMORSU GLAMOURS	AHIIPRSS AIRSHIPS	AHISSTTW WHATSITS
AGINPPRS RAPPINGS	AGLNORSU LANGUORS	AHIKLNRS RINKHALS	AHISSTUZ SHIATZUS
AGINPPRT TRAPPING	AGLNOSST GLASNOST	AHIKLRSY RAKISHLY	AHISTTWW WHITTAWS
AGINPPRW WRAPPING	AGLNOSWY LONGWAYS	AHIKMNSS KHAMSINS	AHKMORRS MARKHORS
AGINPPST STAPPING	AGLNPSUY GUNPLAYS	AHIKMRSS KASHMIRS	AHKMRSTU MUKHTARS
TAPPINGS	AGLNRUUV UNVULGAR	AHIKNPRS PRANKISH	AHKNOTUY THANKYOU
AGINPPSW SWAPPING	AGLNSSSU SUNGLASS	AHIKPRSS SPARKISH	AHKRSSTU KASHRUTS
AGINPPTU PUPATING	AGLNSTUY YGLAUNST	AHILLMOU HALLOUMI	TUSHKARS
AGINPPUY APPUYING	AGLOOPST GOALPOST	AHILLMPS PHALLISM	AHLLNOOS SHALLOON
AGINPRRS SPARRING	AGLOOTUY AUTOLOGY	AHILLMSS SMALLISH	AHLLNOSS SHALLONS
AGINPRRY PARRYING	AGLOPRSS LOPGRASS	AHILLMTU THALLIUM	AHLLNOSY HALLYONS
AGINPRSS SPRAINGS	AGLORSSY GLOSSARY	AHILLNOS HALLIONS	AHLLNOUW UNHALLOW
RASPINGS	AGLPSSSY SPYGLASS	AHILLNPS PHALLINS	AHLLOPSS SHALLOPS
AGINPRST PARTINGS	AGLRTTUU GUTTURAL	AHILLNRT INTHRALL	AHLLOSST SHALLOTS
PRATINGS	AGLSTUUY AUGUSTLY	AHILLNTW WANTHILL	AHLLOSSW SHALLOWS
AGINPRSW WARPINGS	AGMMNOOR MONOGRAM	AHILLSTT TALLITHS	AHLLOSTU THALLOUS
AGINPRSY PRAYINGS	NOMOGRAM	AHILLSVY LAVISHLY	AHLLPRYY PHYLLARY
SPRAYING	AGMMNOOY MONOGAMY	AHILMMSS MASHLIMS	AHLMMOPY LYMPHOMA
AGINPRTT PRATTING	AGMMOORT TOMOGRAM	AHILMNSS MASHLINS	AHLMMSSU MASHLUMS
AGINPRTU UPRATING	AGMMORSY MYOGRAMS	AHILMOPT PHILAMOT	AHLMNOOR HORMONAL
AGINPRTY PARTYING	AGMNOOPR PORNOMAG	AHILMOST HALIMOTS	AHLMOOPS OMPHALOS
AGINPSSS PASSINGS	AGMNOORS SONOGRAM	MAILSHOT	AHLMOPTY POLYMATH
AGINPSST PASTINGS	AGMNOORY AGRONOMY	AHILMQSU QUALMISH	AHLMSTYZ SHMALTZY
AGINPSSU PAUSINGS	AGMNORST ANGSTROM	AHILNOPS SIPHONAL	AHLNNORT LANTHORN
AGINPSTT SPATTING	AGMNSSTU MUSTANGS	AHILNOPT OLIPHANT	AHLNOPRS ALPHORNS
AGINPSZZ SPAZZING	AGMNSSTY GYMNASTS	AHILNORT HORNTAIL	AHLNORST ALTHORNS
AGINQRSU SQUARING	SYNTAGMS	AHILNRST INTHRALS	AHLOPSST SLAPSHOT
AGINRRST STARRING	AGMOOOSU OOGAMOUS	AHILOPST HOSPITAL	AHLORRTY HARLOTRY
TARRINGS	AGMOOPRY POROGAMY	AHILOSTU HALITOUS	AHLOSTUU OUTHAULS
AGINRRTY TARRYING	AGMOPRRS PROGRAMS	AHILPPSS SHIPLAPS	AHLRSTUY LATHYRUS
AGINRSST GASTRINS			

AHLRTTWY THWARTLY	MILITARY	AIKKMOST KOMATIKS	AILMNPST IMPLANTS
AHMMMOST MAMMOTHS	AIILMSTV VITALISM	AIKKNOTY KANTIKOY	AILMNPTU PLATINUM
AHMMMSUU HUMMAUMS	AIILNOPV PAVILION	AIKKRTUZ ZIKKURAT	AILMNRSU MURLAINS
AHMMNSTU HUNTSMAN	AIILNOSS LIAISONS	AIKLLLMW WALKMILL	AILMNRUY LUMINARY
MANHUNTS	AIILNOSV VISIONAL	AIKLLMRR RILLMARK	AILMNSTU SIMULANT
AHMNOPST PHANTOMS	AIILNPST ALPINIST	AIKLLMUW WAUKMILL	AILMOORS SAILROOM
AHMNOPTY PHANTOMY	PINTAILS	AIKLMPSU LAMPUKIS	AILMOORT MOTORAIL
AHMOOPSS SHAMPOOS	TAILSPIN	AIKLMPTU KALUMPIT	MOTORIAL
AHMOORSW WASHROOM	AIILNSTY SALINITY	AIKLNPST LANTSKIP	AILMOPRX PROXIMAL
AHMOOSSS SAMSHOOS	AIILOPPS PAPILIOS	AIKLOSUV SOUVLAKI	AILMORSS ORALISMS
AHMORRST SHORTARM	AIILORSV RAVIOLIS	AIKLOTTW KILOWATT	SOLARISM
AHMORRSU MORRHUAS	AIILQSSU SILIQUAS	AIKLRSTT TITLARKS	AILMORST MORALIST
AHMORSST HARMOSTS	AIILRSTT TRIALIST	AIKLSSSY SKYSAILS	AILMORSU SOLARIUM
AHMORSTY HARMOSTY	AIILRTTY TRIALITY	AIKMMNOO MAKIMONO	AILMORSY ROYALISM
AHMORTTW TAMWORTH	AIILRTVY RIVALITY	AIKMNOOY YAKIMONO	AILMORTY MOLARITY
AHMOSTTW MOSTWHAT	AIILSTTV VITALIST	AIKMORSS KOMISSAR	MORALITY
AHMPSTYY SYMPATHY	AIILTTVY VITALITY	AIKNNOOS NAINSOOK	AILMOSTU SOLATIUM
AHMQSSUU MUSQUASH	AIIMMNNY MINYANIM	AIKNNSSW SWANSKIN	AILMOSTV VOLTAISM
AHMRSSTY THRYMSAS	AIIMMNSS ANIMISMS	AIKNORST SKIATRON	AILMPPSY MISAPPLY
AHNNSTYY SYNANTHY	AIIMMNSX MAXIMINS	AIKNORTY KARYOTIN	AILMPRSU PRIMULAS
AHNOOPRS HARPOONS	AIIMMNTY IMMANITY	AIKNOSTT STOTINKA	AILMPSST PALMISTS
AHNOOPSU APHONOUS	AIIMMSTX MAXIMIST	AIKRSSTY SATYRISK	PSALMIST
AHNOORRY HONORARY	AIIMNNOS INSOMNIA	AILLLNOO LINALOOL	AILMPSSY MISPLAYS
AHNOPPSW PAWNSHOP	AIIMNPSS PIANISMS	AILLMMSY SMALMILY	AILMPSTY PTYALISM
AHNOPPSY PANSOPHY	SINAPISM	AILLMNQU QUILLMAN	AILMRRSU RURALISM
AHNOPSST SNAPSHOT	AIIMNPST IMPAINTS	AILLMOST MAILLOTS	AILMRSST MISTRALS
AHNORSSX SAXHORNS	AIIMNPSX PANMIXIS	MISALLOT	AILMRSSU SIMULARS
AHNORTWW WANWORTH	AIIMNRST MARTINIS	AILLMOTY MOLALITY	SURMISAL
AHNOSTTW WHATNOTS	AIIMNSST ANIMISTS	AILLMPRY PRIMALLY	AILMRSTU ALTRUISM
AHNOSTUX XANTHOUS	SAINTISM	AILLMSSW SAWMILLS	MURALIST
AHNPPSUU PUPUNHAS	SAMNITIS	AILLMUUV ALLUVIUM	ULTRAISM
AHOOPTYZ ZOOPATHY	AIIMNSTT IMITANTS	AILLNNOS LANOLINS	AILNNOOT NOTIONAL
AHOOSSTY SOOTHSAY	TITANISM	AILLNOPP PAPILLON	AILNNOST ANTLIONS
AHOOSTTW SAWTOOTH	AIIMNSTV NATIVISM	AILLNOPS PAILLONS	AILNNOSU UNISONAL
AHOPSSTW WASHPOTS	VITAMINS	AILLNOST STALLION	AILNNOTU LUNATION
AHOPSTTW TOWPATHS	AIIMNTTU TITANIUM	AILLNOSU ALLUSION	AILNNPSU PINNULAS
AHOPSTUW SOUTHPAW	AIIMOPSX APOMIXIS	AILLNOUV ALLUVION	AILNNPTU UNPLIANT
AHOSSTUW WASHOUTS	AIIMORTT IMITATOR	AILLNPTY PLIANTLY	AILNOOPT OPTIONAL
AHOSSTUY SOUTHSAY	TIMARIOT	AILLNSST INSTALLS	AILNOOST SOLATION
AHRSTUWY THRUWAYS	AIIMOSST AMITOSIS	AILLOQTU TOQUILLA	AILNOPRU UNIPOLAR
AIIILLVX LIXIVIAL	AIIMPPRS PRIAPISM	AILLORSY SAILORLY	AILNOPSY POLYNIAS
AIIILMST MILITIAS	AIIMPRTY IMPARITY	AILLORTT LITTORAL	AILNOPTY PONYTAIL
AIIILNST INITIALS	AIIMRSST SIMITARS	TORTILLA	AILNOQSU AQUILONS
AIIILRVZ VIZIRIAL	AIIMRSTU TIRAMISU	AILLOSTY LOYALIST	AILNORTZ TRIZONAL
AIIIMRSS SAIMIRIS	AIIMRUVV VIVARIUM	AILLPPRU PUPILLAR	AILNOSSS SASSOLIN
AIIIRSSS SIRIASIS	AIIMSSTT MASTITIS	AILLPPSU SUPPLIAL	AILNOSUV AVULSION
AIIJKMOT KOMITAJI	AIINNOPS PIANINOS	AILLPRSY SPIRALLY	AILNOSVY SYNOVIAL
AIIJNRTX JANITRIX	AIINNOSV INVASION	AILLPRTY PALTRILY	AILNOTTV VOLITANT
AIIKKSUY SUKIYAKI	AIINNQTU QUINTAIN	AILLPSUV PLUVIALS	AILNOTTY TONALITY
AIIKLLST SILKTAIL	AIINNSTY INSANITY	AILLPSWY SPILLWAY	AILNOTUX LUXATION
AIIKLNRR LARRIKIN	AIINOOSV AVOISION	AILLQSSU SQUILLAS	AILNPPSY SNAPPILY
AIIKMMSS SKIMMIAS	AIINORTT ANTIRIOT	AILLRSTY RALLYIST	AILNPRSU PURSLAIN
AIIKMNNN MANNIKIN	TRITONIA	AILLRTUY RITUALLY	AILNPRSW PRAWLINS
AIIKMNNS MANIKINS	AIINOSTT NOTITIAS	AILLRTWY WILLYART	AILNPRUV PULVINAR
AIIKNNNP PANNIKIN	AIINPRSS ASPIRINS	AILLSTWW WITWALLS	AILNPSTU NUPTIALS
AIIKORTY YAKITORI	AIINPSST PIANISTS	AILLSUVY VISUALLY	PATULINS
AIIKTTZZ TZATZIKI	AIINRRTT IRRITANT	AILMMNOO MONOMIAL	UNPLAITS
AIILLLMT MILLTAIL	AIINRSTV VITRAINS	AILMMNUU ALUMINUM	AILNPSTY PTYALINS
AIILLLUV ILLUVIAL	AIINSTTV NATIVIST	AILMMOOR MAILROOM	AILNPSUU NAUPLIUS
AIILLMRY MILLIARY	VISITANT	AILMMORS MORALISM	AILNPTTU TULIPANT
AIILLNNV VANILLIN	AIINTTVY NATIVITY	AILMMORT IMMORTAL	AILNQRTU TRANQUIL
AIILLNOP POLLINIA	AIIORRST SARTORII	AILMMRSY SMARMILY	AILNQSTU QUINTALS
AIILLNOT ILLATION	AIIORSTT AORTITIS	AILMMSSY MYALISMS	AILNQTUY QUAINTLY
AIILLNSV VILLAINS	AIIORSTV OVARITIS	AILMMSTU SUMMITAL	AILNRSTT RATTLINS
AIILLNVY VILLAINY	AIIORTTV VITIATOR	AILMMSUU ALUMIUMS	AILNRSTU LUNARIST
AIILLPRS SLIPRAIL	AIIPRRST AIRSTRIP	AILMNNOS NOMINALS	AILNRTTU RUTILANT
SPIRILLA	AIIPRSST PIARISTS	AILMNNOT MANNITOL	AILNRUWY UNWARILY
AIILLQSU QUILLAIS	AIIPRVVY VIVIPARY	AILMNNTU LUMINANT	AILNSSTU STUNSAIL
AIILLWWW WILLIWAW	AIIPSTTU PITUITAS	AILMNOOP PALOMINO	UNALISTS
AIILMNOS MONILIAS	AIIRSSTT SATIRIST	AILMNOOR MONORAIL	AILNSTTU LUTANIST
AIILMNOT LIMATION	AIISSSTY SYSSITIA	AILMNOOS MOONSAIL	AILNSTUU NAUTILUS
MILTONIA	AIJKKNOU KINKAJOU	AILMNOOT MOTIONAL	AILOOPRT TROOPIAL
AIILMNPS ALPINISM	AIJLLOOR JILLAROO	AILMNOPR PROLAMIN	AILOORRS SORORIAL
AIILMNPT PALMITIN	AIJLLOVY JOVIALLY	AILMNOPS LAMPIONS	AILOORST ISOLATOR
AIILMRTT MILITART	AIJLNTUY JAUNTILY	AILMNOPT PILOTMAN	AILOORSW WOORALIS
AIILMPUV IMPLUVIA	AIJMORTY MAJORITY	AILMNOPY PALIMONY	AILOORTV VIOLATOR
AIILMRST MISTRIAL	AIJNOPPY POPINJAY	AILMNORT TORMINAL	AILOPRRV PROVIRAL
TRIALISM	AIJNORST JANITORS	AILMNOSS MALISONS	AILOPRSU PLIOSAUR
AIILMRTY LIMITARY		AILMNPSS PLASMINS	AILOPRTU TROUPIAL

AILOPRTY POLARITY
AILOPRUY POLYURIA
AILOPSST APOSTILS
         TOPSAILS
AILOPSTT TALIPOTS
AILORSST SOLARIST
AILORSTU SUTORIAL
AILORSTY ROYALIST
         SOLITARY
AILORSUW WOURALIS
AILORTTU TUTORIAL
AILORTUV OUTRIVAL
AILOSSTU OUTSAILS
AILOTTTY TOTALITY
AILPPRUY PUPILARY
AILPPSSY PAYSLIPS
AILPRSUS UPRISALS
AILPRSTU STIPULAR
AILPSSWY SLIPWAYS
AILPSTUY PLAYSUIT
AILQSTTU QUITTALS
AILRRSTU RURALIST
AILRRSTY STARRILY
AILRRTUY RURALITY
AILRSSTU TRISULAS
AILRSSTY TRYSAILS
AILRSTTU ALTRUIST
         TITULARS
         ULTRAIST
AILRSTTY STRAITLY
AILRSUVV SURVIVAL
AILRTTUY TITULARY
AILSSTUW LAWSUITS
AIMMMNOU AMMONIUM
AIMMNORT MORTMAIN
AIMMNSTU MANUMITS
AIMMORSS AMORISMS
AIMMOSST ATOMISMS
         SOMATISM
AIMMOSSU MIASMOUS
AIMMRRSY MISMARRY
AIMMRSUU MASURIUM
AIMNNOSS MANSIONS
         ONANISMS
AIMNNOTU MOUNTAIN
AIMNNOTY ANTIMONY
         ANTINOMY
AIMNNRTU RUMINANT
AIMNOOOZ ZOONOMIA
AIMNOOTY MYOTONIA
AIMNOPRS RAMPIONS
AIMNOPST MAINTOPS
         TAMPIONS
AIMNOQRU MAROQUIN
AIMNORSU MAINOURS
AIMNORTY MINATORY
AIMNOSST STASIMON
AIMNOSTU MANITOUS
         TINAMOUS
AIMNOTTU MUTATION
AIMNPRYY PAYNIMRY
AIMNPSTU SUMPITAN
AIMNRRSU MURRAINS
AIMNRSSU SURAMINS
         URANISMS
AIMNRSTT TRANSMIT
AIMNRSTU NATRIUMS
         NATURISM
AIMNRSTV VARMINTS
AIMNRSUU URANIUMS
AIMNSSTU TSUNAMIS
AIMNSSYZ ZANYISMS
AIMOPRRS PROSAISM
AIMOPRST ATROPISM
AIMOPSST IMPASTOS
AIMOPSSY SYMPOSIA
AIMORRST ARMORIST
AIMORRSU ORARIUMS
         ROSARIUM

AIMORRUV VARIORUM
AIMORSST AMORISTS
AIMORSSU OSSARIUM
AIMOSSTT ATOMISTS
         SOMATIST
AIMPPRUU PUPARIUM
AIMPPSST MAPPISTS
AIMPRSTY PARTYISM
AIMRSSST TSARISMS
AIMRSSTU MATSURIS
AIMRSSTY SYMITARS
AIMRSTTU STRIATUM
AIMRTTUY MATURITY
AIMSSSTT STATISMS
AINNNOST SANTONIN
AINNOOTT NOTATION
AINNOOTV NOVATION
AINNOOTZ ZONATION
AINNOPSS SAPONINS
AINNOSST ONANISTS
AINNOTTU NUTATION
AINNPSTU UNPAINTS
AINNQSTU QUINNATS
AINNRSTT INTRANTS
AINNRSTU INSURANT
AINNRSTY TYRANNIS
AINNSSTT INSTANTS
AINNSSTU UNSAINTS
AINNSTTY NYSTATIN
AINOOPTT POTATION
AINOORRS ORARIONS
AINOORST ORATIONS
AINOORTT ROTATION
AINOOSTT OSTINATO
AINOOSTV OVATIONS
AINOOTTV OTTAVINO
AINOPPRT PARPOINT
AINOPPST APPOINTS
AINOPPTU PUPATION
AINOPRSS PARISONS
AINOPRST ATROPINS
AINOPRTV PROVIANT
AINOPSSS PASSIONS
AINOPSTT POSTNATI
AINOPSTU OPUNTIAS
         UTOPIANS
AINOPSTW SWAPTION
AINOQRSU NARQUOIS
AINORRSW WARRISON
AINORRTU URINATOR
AINORSST ARSONIST
AINORSSW WARISONS
AINORSTT STRONTIA
AINORSTU SUTORIAN
AINORSTX TRIAXONS
AINORTVY VANITORY
AINOSSSU SUASIONS
AINOSSTT STATIONS
AINOSSVY SYNOVIAS
AINOSTTU TITANOUS
AINPPRSS PARSNIPS
AINPPRTT TRIPPANT
AINPRSST SPIRANTS
         SPRAINTS
AINPRSTU PURITANS
         UPTRAINS
AINPSSSY SYNAPSIS
AINPSSTU PUISSANT
AINQTTUY QUANTITY
AINRSSTT STRAINTS
         TRANSITS
AINRSTTU ANTIRUST
         NATURIST
AINRSTTY TANISTRY
AINSSSTU SUSTAINS
AIOOORRT ORATORIO
AIOORSUV OVARIOUS
AIOPRRST AIRPORTS
         PARITORS

AIOPRRTT PORTRAIT
AIOPRSST AIRSTOPS
         PROSAIST
         PROTASIS
AIOPRSTT PATRIOTS
AIOPRSUV PAVIOURS
AIOPSTTU UTOPIAST
AIORRRSW WARRIORS
AIORRSTT TRAITORS
AIORRSTV VARISTOR
AIORRTWY RYOTWARI
AIORSSTU SAUTOIRS
AIORSSUV SAVIOURS
AIORSTTV VOTARIST
AIORSTUV VIRTUOSA
AIOSSSTY ISOSTASY
AIPPRSTY PAPISTRY
AIPRSSTU UPSTAIRS
AIPRSSTY SPARSITY
AIRRSTTY ARTISTRY
AIRRSTZZ RIZZARTS
AIRSSSTT TSARISTS
AIRSSTTT ATTRISTS
AISSSTTT STATISTS
AJKMNSTU MUNTJAKS
AJKNNOOU JUNKANOO
AJLNORSU JOURNALS
AJMRSTUY JURYMAST
AJORRTUY JURATORY
AKKLRSSY SKYLARKS
AKLLMRUY MULLARKY
AKLMNOOW MOONWALK
AKLNNOPT PLANKTON
AKLOPRSW LAPWORKS
AKLOSTTU OUTTALKS
AKLOSTUW OUTWALKS
AKLPRRSU LARKSPUR
AKMMNOOR MONOMARK
AKMNRSTU TRANKUMS
AKMOORST MOOKTARS
AKMOPRST POSTMARK
AKMQSTUU KUMQUATS
AKMRSSTU MUSKRATS
AKNOORST OSTRAKON
AKNOOUYZ YOKOZUNA
AKNOPSTW SWANKPOT
AKNORSTU OUTRANKS
AKOPRRTW PARTWORK
AKORRSTW ARTWORKS
AKORSWWX WAXWORKS
ALLLPRUY PLURALLY
ALLMNORY NORMALLY
ALLMNOSY ALLONYMS
ALLMORTY MORTALLY
ALLMOUWY MULLOWAY
ALLMPRUU PLUMULAR
ALLMTUUY MUTUALLY
ALLNORSS LASSLORN
ALLOOSTX AXOLOTLS
ALLOPRSY PAYROLLS
ALLOPSTY POSTALLY
ALLORSST ALLSORTS
ALLORTWW WALLWORT
ALLOSSWW SWALLOWS
ALLRUUVY UVULARLY
ALMMNRUU NUMMULAR
ALMMORTW MALTWORM
ALMNOOPS LAMPOONS
ALMNORTY MATRONLY
ALMNOSSU SOLANUMS
ALMNPSSU SUNLAMPS
ALMOOPRY PLAYROOM
ALMOOPSY POLYOMAS
ALMOPPST LAMPPOST
         PALMTOPS
ALMOPRST MARPLOTS
ALMORSUU RAMULOUS
ALMOSTTU MULATTOS

ALMPSSTY SYMPLAST
ALMRTUUY TUMULARY
ALMSSSUY ALYSSUMS
ALNNOOPR NONPOLAR
ALNNOTWY WANTONLY
ALNNRSSU UNSNARLS
ALNOOPPR PROPANOL
ALNOOPRS POLARONS
ALNOOPRT PORTOLAN
         PRONOTAL
ALNOOPST PLATOONS
ALNOOPXY POLYAXON
ALNOOPYZ POLYZOAN
ALNOORST ORTOLANS
ALNOPRST PLASTRON
ALNOPRTU PORTULAN
ALNOPSYY POLYNYAS
ALNORRWY NARROWLY
ALNORSVY SOVRANLY
ALNPPSTU SUPPLANT
ALNRRTUU NURTURAL
ALOOPPRS PROPOSAL
ALOOPRST POSTORAL
ALOOPRTU UPROOTAL
ALOORSUV VALOROUS
ALOORTYZ ZOOLATRY
ALOPPRSU POPULARS
ALOPPRYY POLYPARY
ALOPPSSU SUPPOSAL
ALOPPSUU PAPULOUS
ALOPRRSU PARLOURS
         SPORULAR
ALOPRSTT PORTLAST
ALOPRSTU POSTURAL
         PULSATOR
ALOPRSTY PASTORLY
ALOPSSSU SPOUSALS
ALOPSSUV VOLUSPAS
ALOPSTUU PATULOUS
ALOPSTUY OUTPLAYS
ALOQRRSU RORQUALS
ALOQRSSU SQUALORS
ALORRSUY SURROYAL
ALORSTTW SALTWORT
ALORSUVY SAVOURLY
ALORTUWY OUTLAWRY
ALOSSTTU OUTLASTS
ALPPSTUY PLATYPUS
ALPRSSUU PURSUALS
ALPRSTUU PUSTULAR
AMMNOORT MOTORMAN
AMMNPTUY TYMPANUM
AMMOORRS MAORMORS
         MORMAORS
AMMOPSTU POMATUMS
AMNNOOSX MONAXONS
AMNNOOTT MONTANTO
AMNNORSW MANSWORN
AMNNORSY MANSONRY
AMNNOSTT MONTANTS
AMNNOSTW TOWNSMAN
AMNNOSTY ANTONYMS
AMNNOSUW UNWOMANS
AMNNOTTU MOUNTANT
AMNNOTYY ANTONYMY
AMNNPSTU PUNTSMAN
AMNNSTTU STUNTMAN
AMNOOPPS POMPANOS
AMNOOSTT OTTOMANS
AMNOOSTZ MATZOONS
AMNOOTUY AUTONOMY
AMNOOTWY TOYWOMAN
AMNOOTXY TAXONOMY
AMNOPRSY PARONYMS
AMNOPRYY PARONYMY
AMNOPSTU PANTOUMS
AMNORSST TRANSOMS
AMNORSTU ROMAUNTS
AMNOSTUY AUTONYMS

AMNOTTUY	TAUTONYM
AMNRSTTU	TANTRUMS
AMOOORSS	AMOROSOS
AMOOPRST	TAPROOMS
AMOORRTY	MORATORY
AMOORSTZ	SMORZATO
AMOORTWY	MOTORWAY
AMOOSSTU	ASTOMOUS
AMOOTTUY	AUTOTOMY
AMOPRRST	MARSPORT
AMOPRSXY	PAROXYSM
AMOQSSUU	SQUAMOUS
AMORRTUY	MORTUARY
AMORSTTU	OUTSMART
AMORTTUY	MUTATORY
AMPRSSUW	UPSWARMS
AMRRSSTU	RASTRUMS
ANNOORST	SONORANT
ANNOSSTU	STANNOUS
ANNPRSUY	SPUNYARN
ANOOPRRT	PRONATOR
ANOOPRSS	SOPRANOS
ANOOPRST	PATROONS
ANOORSTT	ARNOTTOS
ANOORSUU	ANOUROUS
ANOPPPRT	PROPPANT
ANOPRRSS	SPORRANS
ANOPRSTU	STROUPAN
ANOPRTTU	TRAPUNTO
ANOPSSTU	OUTSPANS
ANOQRSSU	SQUARSON
ANORSSTU	SANTOURS
ANORSTVY	SOVRANTY
ANPPSSUW	SUPPAWNS
ANPRSSTU	SUNTRAPS
	UNSTRAPS
ANPRSTUU	PURSUANT
ANRRTTUY	TRUANTRY
ANRSSTYY	SYNASTRY
AOOOPRST	SOAPROOT
AOOOPRTZ	PROTOZOA
AOOPPRSY	APOSPORY
AOOPRSSU	SAPOROUS
AOOPRSTT	TAPROOTS
AOOPRSTU	ATROPOUS
AOOPRSTW	SOAPWORT
AOOPRSUV	VAPOROUS
AOOPRTTY	POTATORY
AOORRSTT	ROTATORS
AOORRSTU	OUTROARS
AOORRTTY	ROTATORY
AOORSSTU	OUTSOARS
AOORSSUV	SAVOROUS
AOPPRRST	RAPPORTS
AOPPRSST	PASSPORT
AOPRRRTY	PARROTRY
AOPRRSSW	SPARROWS
AOPRRSTY	PORTRAYS
AOPRRTUY	POURTRAY
AOPRSSTT	STARSPOT
AOPRSTTU	OUTPARTS
AOPRSTTY	PYROSTAT
AOPRSTUY	OUTPRAYS
AOPSSSTU	PASSOUTS
AOPSSTWY	WAYPOSTS
AORRSTTW	STARWORT
AORRTTWW	WARTWORT
AORSSTTU	STRATOUS
AORSSTTY	STAROSTY
AOSSTTUY	OUTSTAYS
APPPRSUU	PURPURAS
APRSSTTU	UPSTARTS
APRSSUWY	SPURWAYS
BBBCEOWY	COBWEBBY
BBBDEEKO	KEBOBBED
BBBDEEOR	BEROBBED
BBBEILOR	BOBBLIER
BBBEILRU	BUBBLIER
BBBEILSU	BUBBLIES
BBBEINOT	BOBBINET
BBBELRSU	BLUBBERS
BBBGILNO	BLOBBING
	BOBBLING
BBBGILNU	BLUBBING
	BUBBLING
BBBHNOOY	HOBNOBBY
BBBHOOUU	HUBBUBOO
BBBIOSTT	BOBBITTS
BBCCIKOS	BIBCOCKS
BBCDEILR	CRIBBLED
BBCDERSU	SCRUBBED
BBCDIMOY	BOMBYCID
BBCEHINS	NEBBICHS
BBCEHIRU	CHUBBIER
BBCEILRS	CRIBBLES
	SCRIBBLE
BBCEILRU	CLUBBIER
BBCEIOST	COBBIEST
BBCEKKOS	KEBBOCKS
BBCEKKSU	KEBBUCKS
BBCEKLUU	BLUEBUCK
BBCELORS	CLOBBERS
	COBBLERS
BBCELORY	COBBLERY
BBCELRSU	CLUBBERS
BBCEMNOU	BUNCOMBE
BBCERRSU	SCRUBBER
BBCGIINR	CRIBBING
BBCGILNO	COBBLING
BBCGILNU	CLUBBING
BBCGINSU	CUBBINGS
BBCHILSU	CLUBBISH
BBCHKOOS	BOSCHBOK
BBCILMSU	CLUBBISM
BBCILRSY	SCRIBBLY
BBCILSTU	CLUBBIST
BBDDEEMO	DEMOBBED
BBDDEILR	DRIBBLED
BBDDENUU	UNDUBBED
BBDEEGIR	GIBBERED
BBDEEGIT	GIBBETED
BBDEEIJR	JIBBERED
BBDEEIST	DEBBIEST
	EBBTIDES
BBDEEMNU	BENUMBED
BBDEENUW	UNWEBBED
BBDEEOPP	BEBOPPED
BBDEERRU	RUBBERED
BBDEERSU	SUBBREED
BBDEFILR	FRIBBLED
BBDEGLRU	GRUBBLED
BBDEHORT	THROBBED
BBDEHRSU	SHRUBBED
BBDEILLN	BELLBIND
BBDEILQU	QUIBBLED
BBDEILRR	DRIBBLER
BBDEILRS	DIBBLERS
	DRIBBLES
BBDEILRT	DRIBBLET
BBDEILRU	BLUEBIRD
BBDEINOR	RIBBONED
BBDEINRU	UNRIBBED
BBDEIOQU	SQUIBBED
BBDEIRRS	DRIBBERS
BBDEKLNO	KNOBBLED
BBDEKLNU	KNUBBLED
BBDELOSS	BOBSLEDS
BBDELSTU	STUBBLED
BBDENRUU	UNRUBBED
BBDGIILN	DIBBLING
BBDGIINR	DRIBBING
BBDGINRU	DRUBBING
BBDGINSU	DUBBINGS
BBDIKMUY	DYBBUKIM
BBDOSUYY	BUSYBODY
BBEEEMSX	BEMBEXES
BBEEERSU	BEBEERUS
BBEEHINS	NEBBISHE
BBEEHLOW	BOBWHEEL
BBEEIIRR	BERIBERI
BBEEILPR	PEBBLIER
	PLEBBIER
BBEEIMSX	BEMBIXES
BBEEIMTT	BIMBETTE
BBEEIRRS	BERBERIS
BBEEISTW	WEBBIEST
BBEELLLU	BLUEBELL
BBEFILRR	FRIBBLER
BBEFILRS	FRIBBLES
BBEFISTU	FUBBIEST
BBEGIIST	GIBBSITE
BBEGILNP	PEBBLING
BBEGILOR	GLOBBIER
BBEGILRS	GRIBBLES
BBEGILRY	GLIBBERY
BBEGILST	GLIBBEST
BBEGINNS	SNEBBING
BBEGINSW	WEBBINGS
BBEGIRRU	GRUBBIER
BBEGLORS	GOBBLERS
BBEGLRSU	GRUBBLES
BBEGRRSU	GRUBBERS
BBEHLORS	HOBBLERS
BBEIILRS	RIBIBLES
BBEIIMRS	IMBIBERS
BBEIIRST	RIBBIEST
BBEIKNOR	KNOBBIER
BBEIKNRU	KNUBBIER
BBEILLNO	BONIBELL
BBEILNRS	NIBBLERS
BBEILNRU	NUBBLIER
BBEILORS	SLOBBIER
BBEILORW	WOBBLIER
BBEILOST	BIBELOTS
BBEILOSW	WOBBLIES
BBEILPRS	PRIBBLES
BBEILQRU	QUIBBLER
BBEILQSU	QUIBBLES
BBEILRRU	RUBBLIER
BBEILRRY	BILBERRY
BBEILRST	STIBBLER
BBEILRSU	SLUBBIER
BBEILSST	STIBBLES
BBEIMOST	BOMBSITE
BBEIMRSU	BRUMBIES
BBEINORS	SNOBBIER
BBEINOST	NOBBIEST
BBEINRSU	SNUBBIER
BBEINSTU	NUBBIEST
BBEIRSTU	STUBBIER
	SUBTRIBE
BBEISSTU	STUBBIES
BBEISTTU	TUBBIEST
BBEKLNOS	KNOBBLES
BBEKLNSU	KNUBBLES
BBEKLOSS	BLESBOKS
BBEKLSUU	BUBUKLES
BBEKNOOT	BONTEBOK
BBEKNORS	KNOBBERS
BBELLRUY	LUBBERLY
BBELMOST	BOMBLETS
BBELMRSU	BUMBLERS
BBELNORS	NOBBLERS
BBELORSS	SLOBBERS
BBELORSW	WOBBLERS
BBELORSY	LOBBYERS
	SLOBBERY
BBELRRSU	BURBLERS
BBELRSSU	SLUBBERS
BBELSTTU	STUBBLES
BBENORSY	SNOBBERY
BBENRSSU	SNUBBERS
BBEORSSW	SWOBBERS
BBEPRSUW	BREWPUBS
BBFGILNU	FLUBBING
BBGGIILN	GLIBBING
BBGGILNO	GOBBLING
BBGGINRU	GRUBBING
BBGHILNO	HOBBLING
BBGIIIMN	IMBIBING
BBGIIJNS	JIBBINGS
BBGIIKLN	KIBBLING
BBGIILMN	BLIMBING
BBGIILNN	NIBBLING
BBGIINNS	SNIBBING
BBGIINRS	RIBBINGS
BBGIJNOS	JOBBINGS
BBGILMNO	MOBBLING
BBGILMNU	BUMBLING
BBGILNNO	NOBBLING
BBGILNNU	NUBBLING
BBGILNOW	WOBBLING
BBGILNOY	LOBBYING
BBGILNRU	BLURBING
	BURBLING
BBGILNSU	SLUBBING
BBGIMNOS	MOBBINGS
BBGINNSU	SNUBBING
BBGINOSS	SOBBINGS
BBGINOSW	SWOBBING
BBGINRSU	RUBBINGS
BBGINSSU	SUBBINGS
BBGINSTU	STUBBING
	TUBBINGS
BBHILOSS	SLOBBISH
BBHIMOSY	HOBBYISM
BBHINOSS	SNOBBISH
BBHINSSU	SNUBBISH
BBHIOOSY	BOOBYISH
BBHIORTY	HOBBITRY
BBHIOSTY	HOBBYIST
BBHIRSUY	RUBBISHY
BBHOOSUW	WHOOBUBS
BBHRSSUU	SUBSHRUB
BBIIILMS	BILIMBIS
BBIILSST	BIBLISTS
BBIKLLOO	BILLBOOK
BBIKLNOO	BOBOLINK
BBILLOYY	BILLYBOY
BBILLSUU	LULIBUBS
BBILOSTY	LOBBYIST
BBILOSUU	BIBULOUS
BBIMNOSS	SNOBBISM
BBIMOOSY	BOOBYISM
BBIMOSSY	YOBBISMS
BBINORRY	RIBBONRY
BBJLOOSW	BLOWJOBS
BBKLOOSU	BLOUBOKS
BBKOOOOS	BOOKOOOS
BBNOORSU	BOURBONS
BBNORSTU	STUBBORN
BCCDEILY	BICYCLED
BCCDHIKO	DOBCHICK
BCCDIKOR	COCKBIRD
BCCEEIRR	CEREBRIC
BCCEHIRU	CHERUBIC
BCCEIIIS	CICISBEI
BCCEIILO	LIBECCIO
BCCEIIOS	CICISBEO
BCCEILOS	ECBOLICS
BCCEILRU	CRUCIBLE
BCCEILSU	CUBICLES
BCCEILSY	BICYCLES
BCCEMRUU	CUCUMBER
BCCIIMOR	MICROBIC
BCCIISTU	CUBISTIC
BCCILMOU	COLUMBIC
BCCILOOR	BROCCOLI
BCCILOSU	BUCOLICS
BCCIRTUU	CUCURBIT
BCCMOOSX	COXCOMBS
BCCMSSUU	SUCCUMBS
BCCSSUUU	SUCCUBUS

BCDDEEEK BEDECKED	BCEEIRTT BRETTICE	BCEKLNUU UNBUCKLE	BCINOSSU SUBSONIC
BCDDEEKU BEDUCKED	BCEEKNSU BUCKEENS	BCEKLORS BLOCKERS	BCINOSTU SUBTONIC
BCDDEHIL CHILDBED	BCEELLOT BELLCOTE	BCEKLRSU BUCKLERS	BCINOSUU INCUBOUS
BCDDESUU SUBDUCED	BCEELOOR BORECOLE	BCEKMSTU STEMBUCK	BCIOORST ROBOTICS
BCDEEEHR BREECHED	BCEELRTU TUBERCLE	BCEKOORU BUCKEROO	BCIORRSU CRIBROUS
BCDEEEHR BLENCHED	BCEEMNRU ENCUMBER	BCEKORST BROCKETS	BCIORSST CROSSBIT
BCDEEHLN BLENCHED	BCEEMRRU CEREBRUM	BCEKORSU ROEBUCKS	BCJKMSUU JUMBUCKS
BCDEEHOU DEBOUCHE	CUMBERER	BCEKOSTY BYCOKETS	BCKKOOOO COOKBOOK
BCDEEIKR BICKERED	BCEENORS OBSCENER	BCELLOSW COWBELLS	BCKLLOOS BOLLOCKS
BCDEEILR CREDIBLE	BCEENRSU CRUBEENS	BCELMOSS COMBLESS	BCKLLOSU BULLOCKS
BCDEEILS DECIBELS	BCEEPRTY CYBERPET	BCELMRSU CLUMBERS	BCKLLOUY BULLOCKY
BCDEEILU EDUCIBLE	BCEERSTU SUBERECT	CRUMBLES	BCKLNOSU SUNBLOCK
BCDEEINT BENEDICT	BCEERSXY CYBERSEX	BCELMSSU SCUMBLES	UNBLOCKS
BCDEEIPS BESPICED	BCEFFIIR FEBRIFIC	BCELORTU CLOTEBUR	BCKMMOSU BUMMOCKS
BCDEEIRS DESCRIBE	BCEFHISU SUBCHIEF	BCELRSSU CURBLESS	BCKOOOPY COPYBOOK
ESCRIBED	BCEFILOR FORCIBLE	BCEMRSSU SCUMBERS	BCKOSTTU BUTTOCKS
BCDEEIST BISECTED	BCEGHILN BELCHING	BCENORSU BOUNCERS	BCLMOORU CLUBROOM
BCDEEJOT OBJECTED	BCEGHINN BENCHING	BCEORRSU OBSCURER	BCLMOOSU COULOMBS
BCDEEKMO BEMOCKED	BCEGIINO BIOGENIC	BCEORRWY COWBERRY	BCLOORTU CLUBROOT
BCDEEKNO BECKONED	BCEGIMNO BECOMING	BCEORSSU OBSCURES	BCLORSTU CLOTBURS
BCDEEKTU BUCKETED	BCEGLNOO CONGLOBE	BCFIIMOR MORBIFIC	BCMORSSU CUMBROUS
BCDEELOR CORBELED	BCEHIIRT BITCHIER	BCFIIORT FIBROTIC	BCMOSSTU COMBUSTS
BCDEELRU BECURLED	BCEHIMRS BESMIRCH	BCFILORY FORCIBLY	BCOORSSW CROSSBOW
BCDEEMRU CUMBERED	BCEHIMRU CHERUBIM	BCFIMORU CUBIFORM	BCOOSTTY BOYCOTTS
BCDEEORV BEDCOVER	BCEHINRU BUNCHIER	BCFSSSUU SUBFUSCS	BCORSTTU OBSTRUCT
BCDEEOTT OBTECTED	CHERUBIN	BCGHIINR BIRCHING	BCRSSTUU SUBCRUST
BCDEHINS DISBENCH	BCEHIORS BRIOCHES	BCGHIINT BITCHING	BDDDEEEM EMBEDDED
BCDEHLOT BLOTCHED	BCEHIORT BOTCHIER	BCGHINNU BUNCHING	BDDDEEIM IMBEDDED
BCDEHOOR BROOCHED	BCEHIRST BRITCHES	BCGHINOR BROCHING	BDDDEEIR DEBRIDED
BCDEIIOS BIOCIDES	BCEHIRTY BITCHERY	BCGHINOT BOTCHING	BDDDEEMU BEMUDDED
BCDEIITU DECUBITI	BCEHLOST BLOTCHES	BCGHINTU BUTCHING	BDDDEENU UNBEDDED
BCDEIKRR REDBRICK	BCEHLRSU BLUCHERS	BCGIIKNR BRICKING	BDDDENUU UNBUDDED
BCDEIKSS SICKBEDS	BCEHMSTU BESMUTCH	BCGIILMN CLIMBING	BDDEEELL DEBELLED
BCDEIKST BEDTICKS	BCEHNRSU BRUNCHES	BCGIINRS SCRIBING	BDDEEERS REEDBEDS
BCDEILRY CREDIBLY	BCEHOORS BROOCHES	BCGIKLNO BLOCKING	BDDEEESS SEEDBEDS
BCDEIMNO COMBINED	BCEHORRU BROCHURE	BCGIKLNU BUCKLING	BDDEEFLU BEFUDDLE
BCDEINOU ICEBOUND	BCEHORSS BROSCHES	BCGIKNSU BUCKINGS	BDDEEGGU DEBUGGED
BCDEKOOO CODEBOOK	BCEHORST BOTCHERS	BCGIMNOR CROMBING	BDDEEGIL BEGILDED
BCDEKORS BEDROCKS	BCEHORSW COWHERBS	BCGIMNOS COMBINGS	BDDEEGIR BEGIRDED
BCDEKOSS BEDSOCKS	BCEHORTY BOTCHERY	BCGIMNRU CRUMBING	BDDEEGNU BEDUNGED
BCDELMRU CRUMBLED	BCEHRSTU BUTCHERS	BCGINNOU BOUNCING	BDDEEGTU BUDGETED
BCDELMSU SCUMBLED	BCEHRTUY BUTCHERY	BUNCOING	BDDEEHOS DEBOSHED
BCDELOSU BECLOUDS	BCEHSTTU BUTCHEST	BCGINORU COURBING	BDDEEIMM BEDIMMED
BCDEMNOU UNCOMBED	BCEIIKLN ICEBLINK	BCHIILTY BITCHILY	BDDEEIMO EMBODIED
BCDENRUU UNCURBED	BCEIIKRR BRICKIER	BCHIIOST COHIBITS	BDDEEINR REBIDDEN
BCDEORSU OBSCURED	BCEIIKRS BRICKIES	BCHIISSU HIBISCUS	BDDEEINT INDEBTED
BCDESSUU SUBDUCES	BCEIILMS MISCIBLE	BCHIKLOS BLOCKISH	BDDEEINW BINDWEED
BCDHIRSU BRUCHIDS	BCEIILNV VINCIBLE	BCHIKOSU CHIBOUKS	BDDEEIRS BIRDSEED
BCDHOOSU CUBHOODS	BCEIIMRS IMBRICES	BCHIOORY CHOIRBOY	DEBRIDES
BCDHORSU SUBCHORD	BCEIINRS INSCRIBE	BCHIOPRS PIBROCHS	BDDEEISS BEDSIDES
BCDIIMOR BROMIDIC	BCEIKLMS LIMBECKS	BCHKNORU BUCKHORN	BDDEEKNU DEBUNKED
BCDIIPSU BICUSPID	BCEIKLOO BOOKLICE	BCHKOSTU BUCKSHOT	BDDEELMU BEMUDDLE
BCDIKLLU DUCKBILL	BCEIKLOR BLOCKIER	BCHLRSUU CLUBRUSH	BDDEELNO BOLDENED
BCDILMOY MOLYBDIC	BCEIKSST BESTICKS	BCHNOORS BRONCHOS	BDDEENNU UNBENDED
BCDILORU COLUBRID	BCEILMRS CLIMBERS	BCHNORSU BRONCHUS	BDDEENOT OBTENDED
BCDIMORS SCOMBRID	RECLIMBS	BCHORSST BORSCHTS	BDDEENRU BURDENED
BCDINRUU RUBICUND	BCEILNOS BINOCLES	BCIIILMU UMBILICI	BDDEEORR BORDERED
BCDIORSW COWBIRDS	BCEILNRU RUNCIBLE	BCIIKLNS NIBLICKS	BDDEEORS DESORBED
BCDKORSU BURDOCKS	BCEILORS BRICOLES	BCIILLSY SIBYLLIC	BDDEEOSS DEBOSSED
BCDSSTUU SUBDUCTS	CORBEILS	BCIILMRU LUMBRICI	BDDEESSU DEBUSSED
BCEEEFIN BENEFICE	BCEILOTU TUBICOLE	BCIILMSU BULIMICS	BDDEESTU BEDUSTED
BCEEEFKN NECKBEEF	BCEILPRU REPUBLIC	BCIILORS COLIBRIS	BDDEESUW SUBDEWED
BCEEEHRS BREECHES	BCEIMNOS COMBINES	BCIIMNOO BIONOMIC	BDDEGINS BEDDINGS
BCEEENRS BESCREEN	BCEIMORS MICROBES	BCIIMORU CIBORIUM	BDDEIIMO IMBODIED
BCEEERSU BERCEUSE	BCEIMOST COMBIEST	BCIIMRSS SCRIBISM	BDDEILNR BRINDLED
BCEEFILN FENCIBLE	BCEIMOSW COMBWISE	BCIINORV VIBRONIC	BDDEILOO BLOODIED
BCEEGIRS ICEBERGS	BCEIMRRU CRUMBIER	BCIIORST SORBITIC	BDDEINNU UNBIDDEN
BCEEHKSU BUCKSHEE	BCEINORS BICORNES	BCIISSTU BISCUITS	BDDEINOU UNBODIED
BCEEHLNS BLENCHES	BCEINORU BOUNCIER	BCIISTUY BISCUITY	BDDEINRU UNDERBID
BCEEHLRS BELCHERS	BCEINOVX BICONVEX	BCIKKNSU BUCKSKIN	BDDEIORS DISORBED
BCEEHNRS BENCHERS	BCEINRSU BRUCINES	BCIKLOOT BOOTLICK	DISROBED
BCEEHNRU UNBREECH	BCEIOOPS BIOSCOPE	BCIKORRW CRIBWORK	BDDEIOWY WIDEBODY
BCEEHOSU BOUCHEES	BCEIORRS CRIBROSE	BCIKOSTT BITTOCKS	BDDEIRRS REDBIRDS
BCEEIILM IMBECILE	BCEIORST BISECTOR	BCILLPUY PUBLICLY	BDDEISSU SUBSIDED
BCEEINOT CENOBITE	BCEIRRSS SCRIBERS	BCILMOSY SYMBOLIC	BDDEISTU BUDDIEST
BCEEIOSX ICEBOXES	BCEIRSTU BRUCITES	BCILMPSU UPCLIMBS	BDDELMRU DRUMBLED
BCEEIPSS BESPICES	BCEJOORT OBJECTOR	BCILNOUY BOUNCILY	BDDENOTU OBTUNDED
BICEPSES	BCEJSSTU SUBJECTS	BCIMORSU MICROBUS	BDDEORTU OBTRUDED
BCEEIRSS ESCRIBES	BCEKLNOT BLONCKET	BCINORSU RUBICONS	BDDGIINS BIDDINGS

BDDGILNU BUDDLING	BDEEILMO BEMOILED	REBUTTED	BDEINOSU BEDOUINS
BDDGINOR BRODDING	EMBOILED	BDEESSSU DEBUSSES	BDEINRSU BURNSIDE
BDDGINSU BUDDINGS	BDEEILMR LIMBERED	BDEFIIRU RUBIFIED	BDEINRTU TURBINED
BDDGOOSY DOGSBODY	BDEEILNV VENDIBLE	BDEFILRS FILBERDS	UNDERBIT
BDDHIIRY DIHYBRID	BDEEILOR ERODIBLE	BDEFILSU SUBFIELD	BDEINRUU UNBURIED
BDDINOOW WOODBIND	REBOILED	BDEFINRR FERNBIRD	BDEINTTU UNBITTED
BDEEEEMS BESEEMED	BDEEILOS OBELISED	BDEFIORS FIBROSED	BDEIOORR BROODIER
BDEEEEMT BETEEMED	BDEEILOT BETOILED	BDEFOORS FORBODES	BDEIORRS BROIDERS
BDEEEGIS BESIEGED	BDEEILOZ OBELIZED	BDEGHILT BLIGHTED	BDEIORRY BROIDERY
BDEEEGMM BEGEMMED	BDEEILRW BEWILDER	BDEGHIRT BEDRIGHT	BDEIORSS DISROBES
BDEEEGNO EDGEBONE	BDEEILSV BEDEVILS	BDEGHIST BEDIGHTS	BDEIORST DEBITORS
BDEEEGRU BUDGEREE	BDEEILTT BETITLED	BDEGIILN BIELDING	BDEIORSV OVERBIDS
BDEEEHTU HEBETUDE	BDEEIMNR BRIDEMEN	BDEGIINT BETIDING	BDEIOSSY DISOBEYS
BDEEEILV BELIEVED	BDEEIMOS EMBODIES	DEBITING	BDEIOSUX SUBOXIDE
BDEEEINS BENISEED	BDEEIMRT TIMBERED	BDEGILNN BLENDING	BDEIRSSU DISBURSE
BDEEELLR REBELLED	BDEEIMST BEDTIMES	BDEGILNO INGLOBED	BDEISSSU SUBSIDES
BDEEELLV BEVELLED	BDEEIMSU EMBUSIED	BDEGINOS OBSIGNED	BDEISSTU SUBEDITS
BDEEELMM EMBLEMED	BDEEINOS EBONISED	BDEGINTU DEBUTING	BDEKLMOO BLOKEDOM
BDEEELPT BEPELTED	BDEEINOT OBEDIENT	BDEGIOST BODGIEST	BDEKNOOU UNBOOKED
BDEEELRS BLEEDERS	BDEEINOZ EBONIZED	BDEGLMRU GRUMBLED	BDELLOOR BORDELLO
BDEEELUW BLUEWEED	BDEEINRS INBREEDS	BDEGLNOU BLUDGEON	DOORBELL
BDEEEMMR MEMBERED	BDEEINST BENDIEST	BDEGLRSU BLUDGERS	BDELLOUZ BULLDOZE
BDEEEMNS BEDESMEN	BDEEINSW BENDWISE	BDEGORRY DOGBERRY	BDELMOOS BLOOSMED
BDEEEMRW EMBREWED	BDEEINSZ BEDIZENS	BDEGORSU BUDGEROS	BDELMRSU DRUMBLES
BDEEENTT BENETTED	BDEEIORU BOUDERIE	BDEGORUW BUDGEROW	BDELMRUU DELUBRUM
BDEEEPSS BESPEEDS	BDEEIRRU REBURIED	BDEHIKOS KIBOSHED	BDELMSTU STUMBLED
BDEEERRS BREEDERS	BDEEIRST BESTRIDE	BDEHILMT THIMBLED	BDELNNOU UNNOBLED
BDEEERRV REVERBED	BDEEISTU BESUITED	BDEHIOPS BISHOPED	BDELNNUU UNBUNDLE
BDEEERTT BETTERED	BDEEKNRU BUNKERED	BDEHKOSY KYBOSHED	BDELNOSS BOLDNESS
BDEEERTV BREVETED	BDEEKORR BROKERED	BDEHLMOW WHOMBLED	BDELNOST BLONDEST
BDEEETTW BEWETTED	BDEELLOW BELLOWED	BDEHLSUV BUSHVELD	BDELNOTU UNBOLTED
BDEEFFPU BEPUFFED	BOWELLED	BDEHORSY HERDBOYS	BDELNOUU UNDOUBLE
BDEEFFRU BUFFERED	BDEELLRU BULLERED	BDEIIKLR BIRDLIKE	BDELNOUW UNBLOWED
REBUFFED	BDEELLRY REDBELLY	BDEIIKTZ KIBITZED	BDELNRSU BLUNDERS
BDEEFFTU BUFFETED	BDEELMNO EMBOLDEN	BDEIILRU BLUIDIER	BDELOORV OVERBOLD
BDEEFGGO BEFOGGED	BDEELMPU BEPLUMED	BDEIILTY DEBILITY	BDELORSU BOULDERS
BDEEFGIT BEGIFTED	BDEELMRT TREMBLED	BDEIIMOS IMBODIES	DOUBLERS
BDEEFILR BELFRIED	BDEELMRU LUMBERED	BDEIKMOS IMBOSKED	BDELORSW BOWLDERS
BDEEFINN BEFINNED	BDEELNNO ENNOBLED	BDEIKNOR BRODEKIN	BDELORTU TROUBLED
BDEEFINR BEFRIEND	BDEELNRS BLENDERS	BDEIKNSU BUSKINED	BDELOSTU DOUBLETS
BDEEFIRS DEBRIEFS	BDEELNST BENDLETS	BDEILLMU BDELLIUM	BDELPSUU SUBDUPLE
BDEEFIRU RUBEFIED	BDEELNTU UNBELTED	BDEILLOW BILLOWED	BDEMNNOS BONDSMEN
BDEEFITT BEFITTED	BDEELORU REDOUBLE	BDEILLOX BOLLIXED	BDEMNOSU EMBOUNDS
BDEEFLOO BEFOOLED	BDEELOSU BESOULED	BDEILMOS SEMIBOLD	BDEMNOTU UNTOMBED
BDEEFLOU BEFOULED	BDEELOSV BELOVEDS	BDEILMSU SUBLIMED	BDEMNSSU DUMBNESS
BDEEFOOR FOREBODE	BDEELRTU BUTLERED	BDEILNOU UNILOBED	BDEMOORS BEDROOMS
BDEEFSUU SUBFEUED	BDEEMNOT BODEMENT	BDEILNOY BODYLINE	BOREDOMS
BDEEGGIW BEWIGGED	ENTOMBED	BDEILNRS BLINDERS	BDEMOOSY SOMEBODY
BDEEGGMO EMBOGGED	BDEEMNOW ENWOMBED	BRINDLES	BDEMOOTT BOTTOMED
BDEEGGNU UNBEGGED	BDEEMNRU NUMBERED	BDEILNRU UNBRIDLE	BDEMSSUU SUBSUMED
BDEEGGRU BEGRUDGE	BDEEMORR EMBORDER	BDEILNST BLINDEST	BDENNOUY YBOUNDEN
BUGGERED	BDEEMORS SOMBERED	BDEILNVY VENDIBLY	BDENNRUU UNBURDEN
BDEEGHIS BESIGHED	BDEEMOSS EMBOSSED	BDEILOOR BLOODIER	UNBURNED
BDEEGILN BLEEDING	BDEEMPRU BUMPERED	BDEILOOS BLOODIES	BDENOOTU UNBOOTED
BDEEGILU BEGUILED	BDEEMRTU EMBRUTED	BDEILOPU UPBOILED	BDENOOTW BENTWOOD
BDEEGIMR BEGRIMED	BDEEMSSU EMBUSSED	BDEILOQU OBLIQUED	BDENORSU BOUNDERS
BDEEGINR BREEDING	BDEENNOT BONNETED	BDEILORT TRILOBED	REBOUNDS
BDEEGINW BEDEWING	BDEENOUY UNOBEYED	BDEILORV LOVEBIRD	SUBORNED
BDEEGINY BEDYEING	BDEENPRS PREBENDS	BDEILOSS BODILESS	BDENOTTU BUTTONED
BDEEGKNU BEGUNKED	BDEEOORT REBOOTED	BDEILOSW DISBOWEL	BDENRSUU UNBRUSED
BDEEGLNO BELONGED	BDEEOPRS BEPROSED	BDEILRRS BRIDLERS	BDENRUUY UNDERBUY
ENGLOBED	BDEEOPRW BEPOWDER	BDEILRST BRISTLED	BDENSSTU SUBTENDS
BDEEGMOU EMBOGUED	BDEEORRR BORDERER	DRIBLETS	BDEOORRS BROODERS
BDEEHLNO BEHOLDEN	BDEEORRS RESORBED	BDEILRSU BUILDERS	BDEOORRW BORROWED
BDEEHLOR BEHOLDER	BDEEORSS BEDSORES	REBUILDS	BDEOOTUX OUTBOXED
BDEEHLOW BEHOWLED	BDEEORST BESORTED	BDEILSTU BLUDIEST	BDEOPSST BEDPOSTS
BDEEHOOV BEHOOVED	BESTRODE	BDEIMNOT INTOMBED	BDEORRSU BORDURES
BDEEHORT BOTHERED	BDEEORSV OBSERVED	BDEIMNSU NIMBUSED	BOURDERS
BDEEHORW BEWHORED	BDEEORTU OUTBREED	BDEIMNUU UNIMBUED	SUBORDER
BDEEHOSS DEBOSHES	BDEEORTV OBVERTED	BDEIMORR IMBORDER	BDEORRTU OBTRUDER
BDEEIILN INEDIBLE	BDEEOSSS DEBOSSES	MORBIDER	BDEORRUW BURROWED
BDEEIILR BIELDIER	OBSESSED	BDEIMORS BROMIDES	BDEORSSU ROSEBUDS
BDEEIIPT BEPITIED	BDEEOSST BETOSSED	BDEIMORY EMBRYOID	BDEORSTU DOUBTERS
BDEEIKRS KERBSIDE	BDEEOSTT BESOTTED	BDEIMOSS IMBOSSED	OBTRUDES
BDEEIKSS BEKISSED	OBTESTED	BDEIMRSU IMBURSED	REDOUBTS
BDEEILLL LIBELLED	BDEEOSTW BESTOWED	BDEIMRTU IMBRUTED	BDERSSUU SUBDUERS
BDEEILLT BILLETED	BDEERSUW BURWEEDS	BDEINOOS NOBODIES	BDERSTUU SUBTRUDE
BDEEILLU ELUDIBLE	BDEERTTU BUTTERED	BDEINOOW WOODBINE	BDFFIPRU PUFFBIRD
			BDFGNOOU FOGBOUND

BDFIIORS FIBROIDS	BDLNOOWW BLOWDOWN	BEEGILLR GERBILLE	BEEIMRTT EMBITTER
BDFILLLO BILLFOLD	BDLOOOSX OXBLOODS	BEEGILNP BLEEPING	BEEIMSSU EMBUSIES
BDFINORU UNFORBID	BDMOORRS SMORBROD	BEEGILNT BEETLING	BEEINNSS BEINNESS
BDFINRRU FURIBUND	BDMORSUW BUDWORMS	BEEGILOS OBLIGEES	BEEINNSZ BENZINES
BDFIRRSU SURFBIRD	BDNNOOTU BUNODONT	BEEGILRU BEGUILER	BEEINORT TENEBRIO
BDFLOTUU DOUBTFUL	BDNOORSU BOURDONS	BEEGILSU BEGUILES	BEEINOSS EBONISES
BDGGIINR BRIDGING	BDNOOSWW DOWNBOWS	BEEGIMNT BEMETING	BEEINOST BETONIES
BDGGILNU BLUDGING	BDNOOTUU OUTBOUND	BEEGIMRS BEGRIMES	EBONITES
BDGIILLN BLINDING	BDNORSTU TURBONDS	BEEGINNR BEGINNER	BEEINOSZ EBONIZES
BDGIILNR BRIDLING	BDNORSUW RUBDOWNS	BENIGNER	BEEINPRS PEBRINES
BDGIILNU BUILDING	BDOOOSWX BOXWOODS	BEEGINNS BEGINNES	BEEINRSS NEBRISES
BDGIINNS BINDINGS	BDORUWZZ BUZZWORD	BEEGINRR BREERING	BEEINRTT REBITTEN
BDGIINRS BIRDINGS	BEEEEFLN ENFEEBLE	BEEGINRS BIGENERS	BEEINSTT BENTIEST
BDGIINRW BIRDWING	BEEEEFRS FREEBEES	BEEGINRZ BREEZING	BEEIOQSU OBSEQUIE
BDGILNNU BUNDLING	BEEEEKSS BESEEKSS	BEEGINST BEIGNETS	BEEIORSS SOBERISE
BDGILNOO BLOODING	BEEEEMST BETEEMES	BEEGINSU BEGUINES	BEEIORSW BOWERIES
BDGILNOU DOUBLING	BEEEENRT TEREBENE	BEEGINSW BEESWING	BEEIORSZ SOBERIZE
BDGILOOS GLOBOIDS	BEEEENRZ EBENEZER	BEEGKLUY KEYBUGLE	BEEIORTV OVERBITE
BDGINNOS BONDINGS	BEEEFIRS FREEBIES	BEEGLNOR BELONGER	BEEIOSUZ BEZIQUES
BDGINNOU BOUNDING	BEEEFIST BEEFIEST	BEEGLNOS ENGLOBES	BEEIRRSU REBURIES
UNBODING	BEEEFLSS FEBLESSE	BEEGMNOS GOMBEENS	BEEIRRSV BREVIERS
BDGINOOR BROODING	BEEEFLST FEEBLEST	BEEGMOSU EMBOGUES	BEEIRRTT BITTERER
BDGINOOY BOODYING	BEEEGILN BELEEING	BEEGMRSU SUBMERGE	BEEIRSSU SUBERISE
BDGINORS BIRDSONG	BEEEGINS BESEEING	BEEGNOOW WOBEGONE	BEEIRSSW BREWISES
SONGBIRD	BEEEGIRS BESIEGER	BEEGNOTT BEGOTTEN	BEEIRSTU UBERTIES
BDGINORU OBDURING	BEEEGISS BESIEGES	BEEGNRSU SUBGENRE	BEEIRSUZ SUBERIZE
BDGINOTU DOUBTING	BEEEGRRS BERGERES	BEEGNSTU UNBEGETS	BEEISSTW WEBSITES
BDGINSUU SUBDUING	BEEEGRTT BEGETTER	BEEHHMOT BEHEMOTH	BEEKMOPR PEMBROKE
BDGLLOSU BULLDOGS	BEEEHIST BHEESTIE	BEEHINSS BESHINES	BEEKNOPS BESPOKEN
BDGLOOST DOGBOLTS	BEEEHISV BEEHIVES	NEBISHES	BEEKNOST BETOKENS
BDGNRUUY BURGUNDY	BEEEHLRT HERBELET	BEEHIRST HERBIEST	STEENBOK
BDHIIPRW WHIPBIRD	BEEEHLWW WEBWHEEL	BEEHISST BHISTEES	BEEKRRSS BERSERKS
BDHIMOOR RHOMBOID	BEEEHNSS SHEBEENS	BEEHKSSU BUKSHEES	BEEKRRSU REBUKERS
BDHIMORT BIRTHDOM	BEEEILLL LIBELLEE	BEEHLOOR BOREHOLE	BEELLORW BELLOWER
BDHIMSUU SUBHUMID	BEEEILLS LIBELEES	BEEHLOVY BEHOVELY	REBELLOW
BDHINOPS HOPBINDS	BEEEILNS BEELINES	BEEHLRSS HERBLESS	BEELLOST LOBELETS
BDHIORST BIRDSHOT	BEEEILRV BELIEVER	BEEHLRST BLETHERS	BEELMMOP BEPOMMEL
BDHIOSSU BUSHIDOS	BEEEILSV BELIEVES	HERBLETS	BEELMNNO NOBLEMEN
BDHMOOOS HOBODOMS	BEEEINST EBENISTE	BEEHNNOS HEBENONS	BEELMOSW EMBOWELS
BDHNRSUU UNSHRUBD	BEEEIRRZ BREEZIER	BEEHNOOP NEOPHOBE	BEELMRRT TREMBLER
BDHOOOSY BOYHOODS	BEEEIRST BEERIEST	BEEHNRRT BRETHREN	BEELMRRU LUMBERER
BDIIINRS BRINDISI	BEEEJLSW BEJEWELS	BEEHOOSV BEHOOVES	BEELMRST TREMBLES
BDIIKNOS BODIKINS	BEEELLRR REBELLER	BEEHORSW BEWHORES	BEELNNOS ENNOBLES
BDIILMSS DISLIMBS	BEEELLRT BELLETER	BEEHRSST SHERBETS	BEELNOSS BONELESS
BDIILOQU OBLIQUID	BEEELLRV BEVELLER	BEEHRSSW BESHREWS	NOBLESSE
BDIIMRUU RUBIDIUM	BEEELMNS ENSEMBLE	BEEIILNZ ZIBELINE	BEELNOSU BLUENOSE
BDIKNORS BRODKINS	BEEELMRS RESEMBLE	BEEIINOS EBIONISE	BEELNOSZ BENZOLES
BDILLOOY BLOODILY	BEEELMSY BESEEMLY	BEEIINOZ EBIONIZE	BEELNSSU BLUENESS
BDILMORY MORBIDLY	BEEELMZZ EMBEZZLE	BEEIINRT BENITIER	BEELNTUY BUTYLENE
BDILNNSU SUNBLIND	BEEELPRS BLEEPERS	BEEIIPST BEPITIES	BEELOOST OBSOLETE
UNBLINDS	BEEEMMRR REMEMBER	BEEIIRRR BRIERIER	BEELOQRU BRELOQUE
BDILNOWW WINDBLOW	BEEEMNSU UNBESEEM	BEEIIRSS IBERISES	BEELORVW OVERBLEW
BDILNPRU PURBLIND	BEEEMRSW EMBREWES	BEEIISTU UBIETIES	BEELOSTW STEELBOW
BDILNSUU UNBUILDS	BEEENNSZ BENZENES	BEEIISTZ BITESIZE	BEELOSTY EYEBOLTS
BDILPSUU UPBUILDS	BEEENSST SEBESTEN	BEEIJLSU JUBILEES	BEELPRUV BUPLEVER
BDILRTUY TURBIDLY	BEEENSTW BETWEENS	BEEIJSTU BEJESUIT	BEELRSSV VERBLESS
BDIMNORU MORIBUND	BEEEPPPR BEPEPPER	BEEIKLTU TUBELIKE	BEELRSUZ ZEBRULES
BDIMNPSU DUMPBINS	BEEEPRST BEPESTER	BEEIKSSS BEKISSES	BEELSSTU TUBELESS
BDIMOOSS DISBOSOM	BEEERSST BRETESSE	BEEILLLR LIBELLER	BEELSTTU BLUETTES
BDIMOSTU MISDOUBT	BEEERSTT BESETTER	BEEILLNO LOBELINE	BEEMNRRU NUMBERER
BDINNRUW WINDBURN	BEEESSST TSESSEBE	BEEILLRS LIBELERS	RENUMBER
BDINOORS BRIDOONS	BEEFFLMU BEMUFFLE	BEEILLTT BELITTLE	BEEMOPRT OBTEMPER
BDINORSW SNOWBIRD	BEEFGILN FEEBLING	BEEILMOS EMBOLIES	BEEMORRS SOMBERER
BDINRSSU SUNBIRDS	BEEFGINR BEFRINGE	BEEILMPR PERIBLEM	BEEMORSS EMBOSSER
BDINRTUU UNTURBID	BEEFHILS FEEBLISH	BEEILNNS BLENNIES	BEEMORSW EMBOWERS
BDINSSTU DUSTBINS	BEEFILLT LIFEBELT	BEEILNRS BERLINES	BEEMOSSS EMBOSSES
BDIOORSU BOUDOIRS	BEEFILLX FLEXIBLE	BEEILNSS SENSIBLE	BEEMQSUU EMBUSQUE
BDIOORTY BOTRYOID	BEEFILNU UNBELIEF	BEEILNST STILBENE	BEEMRRSU UMBRERES
BDIORSSW WOSBIRDS	BEEFILRS BELFRIES	TENSIBLE	BEEMRSSU SUBMERSE
BDIOSTUY BODYSUIT	BEEFINST BENEFITS	BEEILNSU NEBULISE	BEEMRSTU EMBRUTES
BDIRSSTU DISTURBS	BEEFIRST BRIEFEST	BEEILNUZ NEBULIZE	BEEMRTTU UMBRETTE
BDKNOOOR DOORKNOB	BEEFIRSU RUBEFIES	BEEILOSS OBELISES	BEEMRTUZ ZERUMBET
BDKNOOSU BUNDOOKS	BEEFLORW BEFLOWER	BEEILOSZ OBELIZES	BEEMSSSU EMBUSSES
BDKOOSTU STUDBOOK	BEEFNORR FREEBORN	BEEILOTV LOVEBITE	BEENORTU BOUNTREE
BDLLSTUU BULLDUST	BEEFNRTU UNBEREFT	BEEILRRT TERRIBLE	BEENORTV VERBOTEN
BDLNOOOU DOUBLOON	BEEGGNSU GEEBUNGS	BEEILRSU BLUESIER	BEENOSST BONESETS
BDLNOOUY UNBLOODY	BEEGHLMR BERGMEHL	BEEILRYZ BREEZILY	BEENOSTU TUBENOSE
	BEEGIILL ELIGIBLE	BEEILSTT BETITLES	BEENPRST BESPRENT
	BEEGIILX EXIGIBLE	BEEIMRRU UMBRIERE	BEENRSTT BRENTEST

BEENRSTW	BESTREWN	BEGHIOST	GOBSHITE	BEHIISTX	EXHIBITS	BEIIOPSS	BIOPSIES
BEENRTTU	BRUNETTE	BEGHIRRT	BRIGHTER	BEHIKLOS	BLOKEISH	BEIIORST	ORBITIES
BEENSSTU	SUBTEENS	BEGHLNOU	BUNGHOLE	BEHIKNST	BETHINKS	BEIIOSTT	BIOTITES
	SUBTENSE	BEGHNOTU	BOUGHTEN	BEHIKOSS	KIBOSHES	BEIIRSST	BIRSIEST
BEEOORRT	BOORTREE	BEGHOSTU	BESOUGHT	BEHILLOS	SHOEBILL	BEIISSTT	BITSIEST
BEEOORRV	OVERBORE	BEGHOSUU	BUGHOUSE	BEHILLTY	BLITHELY	BEIISTUZ	SUBITIZE
BEEOORTT	BEETROOT	BEGHRRSU	BURGHERS	BEHILMRW	WHIMBREL	BEIJLMRU	JUMBLIER
BEEOPRSS	BEPROSES	BEGIIISS	SIGISBEI	BEHILMST	THIMBLES	BEIJMOSU	JUMBOISE
BEEORRSS	BOURREES	BEGIILLN	LIBELING	BEHILNPY	BIPHENYL	BEIJMOUZ	JUMBOIZE
BEEORRSV	OBSERVER	BEGIILLY	ELIGIBLY	BEHILORR	HORRIBLE	BEIJNORW	BIJWONER
	VERBOSER	BEGIILST	BILGIEST	BEHILORS	BOLSHIER	BEIKLMOW	WOMBLIKE
BEEORRTU	BOURTREE	BEGIIMNR	BEMIRING	BEHILOSS	BOLSHIES	BEIKLNRS	BLINKERS
BEEORSST	SOBEREST	BEGIIMNT	BETIMING	BEHILRST	BLITHERS	BEIKLOSS	OBELISKS
BEEORSSU	SUBEROSE	BEGIINNS	INBEINGS	BEHILRTU	THURIBLE	BEIKLOST	BLOKIEST
BEEORSSV	OBSERVES	BEGIINRT	REBITING	BEHILSTT	BLITHEST	BEIKLOTY	KILOBYTE
	OBVERSES	BEGIINRZ	ZINGIBER	BEHIMNOO	BONHOMIE	BEIKLSTU	BULKIEST
BEEORSTU	TUBEROSE	BEGIIOSS	SIGISBEO	BEHIMRTU	THUMBIER	BEIKMNNR	BRINKMEN
BEEORSTW	BESTOWER	BEGIKMNO	KEMBOING	BEHINNOS	SHINBONE	BEIKNRRY	INKBERRY
BEEORSWY	EYEBROWS	BEGIKNRU	REBUKING	BEHINOPS	HOPBINES	BEIKNRSS	BRISKENS
BEEOSSSS	OBSESSES	BEGILLLU	GULLIBLE	BEHINOSW	WISHBONE	BEIKOORS	BOOKSIER
BEEOSSST	BETOSSES	BEGILLNU	BULLGINE	BEHIOOPR	BIOPHORE	BEIKOORT	BROOKITE
BEEPRRSU	SUPERBER	BEGILLNY	BELLYING	BEHIRRST	REBIRTHS	BEIKOOST	BOOKIEST
BEEPRRSV	PREVERBS	BEGILMNR	REMBLING	BEHIRRSU	BRUSHIER	BEIKOSST	BOSKIEST
BEEPRSTY	PRESBYTE	BEGILMNS	SEMBLING	BEHIRSST	HERBISTS	BEIKRSST	BRISKEST
BEEQSSTU	BEQUESTS	BEGILNNY	BENIGNLY	BEHIRSSU	HUBRISES		BRISKETS
BEERRSTW	BREWSTER	BEGILNOR	IGNOBLER	BEHIRSSY	HYBRISES		
BEERRTTU	REBUTTER	BEGILNOS	INGLOBES	BEHISSTU	BUSHIEST	BEILLMSS	LIMBLESS
BEERSSSU	SUBSERES	BEGILNOV	BELOVING	BEHKOSSY	KYBOSHES	BEILLMSU	SEMIBULL
BEERSSTW	BESTREWS	BEGILNOW	ELBOWING	BEHLLOOT	BOLTHOLE	BEILLNTU	BULLETIN
	WEBSTERS	BEGILNRT	TREBLING	BEHLLOOW	BLOWHOLE	BEILLORS	BROLLIES
BEERSSUV	SUBSERVE	BEGILNSS	BLESSING	BEHLLOPS	BELLHOPS	BEILLOSU	LIBELOUS
	SUBVERSE		GLIBNESS	BEHLLPSU	BELLPUSH	BEILLOSX	BOLLIXES
BEERSTTU	BURETTES	BEGILNST	BELTINGS	BEHLMOSW	WHOMBLES	BEILLRST	BRILLEST
BEESTTUV	BUVETTES	BEGILNSU	BLUEINGS	BEHLMSTU	HUMBLEST	BEILLSST	BESTILLS
BEFFLRSU	BLUFFERS		BULGINES	BEHLOOPY	HYPOBOLE	BEILLSTU	BULLIEST
BEFFLSTU	BLUFFEST	BEGILNTT	BLETTING		LYOPHOBE	BEILMMOS	EMBOLISM
BEFGIILL	FILLIBEG	BEGILNUW	BLUEWING	BEHLOOST	BOTHOLES	BEILMNOR	BROMELIN
BEFGIILS	FILIBEGS	BEGILNZZ	BEZZLING	BEHLORST	BROTHELS	BEILMNOU	NOBELIUM
BEFGIINR	BRIEFING	BEGILRST	GILBERTS	BEHLOSSU	SLOEBUSH	BEILMNRU	UNLIMBER
BEFGIRSU	FIREBUGS	BEGILSTU	BULGIEST	BEHLRRSU	BURRHELS	BEILMNST	NIMBLEST
BEFHILSU	BLUEFISH	BEGIMNOS	BESOMING	BEHLRSSU	BLUSHERS	BEILMNUU	NEBULIUM
BEFIIRSU	RUBIFIES	BEGIMNOW	EMBOWING	BEHLSSTU	BLUSHETS	BEILMOOR	BLOOMIER
BEFILLXY	FLEXIBLY	BEGIMNOX	EMBOXING	BEHMNNOY	BOTHYMEN	BEILMORS	EMBROILS
BEFILMOR	FORELIMB	BEGIMNRU	EMBRUING	BEHMOOOX	HOMEOBOX	BEILMPTU	PLUMBITE
BEFILOST	BOTFLIES		UMBERING	BEHMOOSY	HOMEBOYS	BEILMRRU	RUMBLIER
BEFILOUY	LIFEBUOY	BEGIMNSU	BEMUSING	BEHMOOSTU	BEMOUTHS	BEILMRSS	BRIMLESS
BEFILRST	FILBERTS	BEGIMOST	MISBEGOT	BEHMPSTU	BETHUMPS	BEILMRST	TIMBRELS
BEFINORS	BONFIRES	BEGIMOSY	BOGEYISM	BEHNNOUY	HONEYBUN	BEILMRSU	SUBLIMER
BEFIORSS	FIBROSES	BEGINNNR	BRENNING	BEHNRSTU	BURTHENS	BEILMRSW	WIMBRELS
BEFIORTT	FOREBITT	BEGINNNU	UNBENIGN	BEHOOOST	BOOTHOSE	BEILMSSU	SUBLIMES
BEFIRSST	FIBSTERS	BEGINNOR	ENROBING	BEHOOORST	THEORBOS	BEILNNTU	BUNTLINE
BEFISSTU	FUBSIEST		RINGBONE	BEHOOSUY	HOUSEBOY	BEILNOPS	BONSPIEL
BEFLLLUY	BELLYFUL	BEGINNSU	UNBEINGS	BEHORRST	BROTHERS	BEILNOSW	BOWLINES
BEFLLSTY	FLYBELTS	BEGINOOS	BESOGNIO	BEHORSSU	ROSEBUSH	BEILNOVY	BOVINELY
BEFLMRSU	FUMBLERS	BEGINORR	REBORING	BEHORSTT	BETROTHS	BEILNSSY	SENSIBLY
BEFLORUW	FURBELOW	BEGINORS	SOBERING	BEHRRSSU	BRUSHERS	BEILNSTZ	BLINTZES
BEFLSTUU	TUBEFULS	BEGINORW	BOWERING	BEIIIKRST	MINIBIKE	BEILOORV	OVERBOIL
BEFNOORR	FORBORNE	BEGINRRS	BRINGERS	BEIIKRST	BIRKIEST	BEILOOST	LOOBIEST
BEFNOSSY	FYNBOSES	BEGINRRY	BERRYING	BEIIKRTZ	KIBITZER	BEILOPPW	BLOWPIPE
BEFORRXY	FOXBERRY	BEGINRSW	BREWINGS	BEIIKSTZ	KIBITZES	BEILOPSS	POSSIBLE
BEGGGINS	BEGGINGS	BEGINSTT	BETTINGS	BEIILMMO	IMMOBILE	BEILOQRU	OBLIQUER
BEGGIINN	BINGEING	BEGKMOSS	GEMSBOKS	BEIILMOS	MOBILISE	BEILOQSU	OBLIQUES
BEGGILRU	BLUGGIER	BEGLLOSU	GLOBULES	BEIILMOZ	MOBILIZE	BEILORRS	BROILERS
BEGGINOY	BOGEYING	BEGLLOTU	GLOBULET	BEIILMSU	BULIMIES	BEILORST	STROBILE
BEGGIOST	BOGGIEST	BEGLMOOS	BEGLOOMS	BEIILNRS	RINSIBLE		TRILOBES
BEGGISTU	BUGGIEST	BEGLMRRU	GRUMBLER	BEIILOPR	PERIBOLI	BEILORSW	BLOWSIER
BEGGLORS	BOGGLERS	BEGLMRSU	GRUMBLES	BEIILRST	TRILBIES	BEILORTT	BLOTTIER
BEGGOOOS	GOOSEGOB	BEGLNOUW	BLUEGOWN	BEIILRTT	LIBRETTI		LIBRETTO
BEGHHIST	BEHIGHTS	BEGLNRSU	BLUNGERS	BEIILRUZ	BRUILZIE	BEILORWZ	BLOWZIER
BEGHIILP	PHILIBEG		BUNGLERS	BEIILSSV	VISIBLES	BEILOSSY	BIOLYSES
BEGHILRT	BLIGHTER	BEGLOOSS	GLOBOSES	BEIILSTT	STILBITE	BEILOSTW	BLOWIEST
	THERBLIG	BEGLOOST	BOOTLEGS	BEIIMNNR	RENMINBI	BEILRRTT	BRITTLER
BEGHINOR	NEIGHBOR	BEGLRSTY	BERGYLTS	BEIIMNOS	EBIONISM	BEILRRTY	TERRIBLY
BEGHINOT	BEHOTING	BEGNOORU	BOURGEON	BEIIMRTT	IMBITTER	BEILRSST	BLISTERS
BEGHINOV	BEHOVING	BEGNORSU	BURGEONS	BEIINORS	BRIONIES		BRISTLES
BEGHINRT	BERTHING	BEGNORTU	BURGONET	BEIINOST	NIOBITES	BEILRSTT	BRITTLES
	BRIGHTEN	BEGNSSUU	SUBGENUS	BEIINRST	BRINIEST		TRIBLETS
BEGHINST	BENIGHTS	BEGPRSUU	SUPERBUG	BEIINSST	STIBINES	BEILRSTU	BURLIEST
		BEHHKOST	KHOTBEHS	BEIINSTT	STIBNITE		

SUBTILER	BEKLOOOR BOOKLORE	BEMNORSY EMBRYONS	BFOOOSTY FOOTBOYS
BEILRSTY BLISTERY	BEKLOORT BROOKLET	BEMNSTTU BUTMENTS	BGGGILNO BOGGLING
BEILRSUY BRULYIES	BEKLOOSS BOOKLESS	BEMNTTUY BUTTYMEN	BGGGINOR BROGGING
BEILRSUZ BRULZIES	BEKLOOST BOOKLETS	BEMOORRS SOMBRERO	BGGGINSU BUGGINGS
BEILRTTY BITTERLY	BEKLORUV OVERBULK	BEMORSST BESTORMS	BGGIILNN BINGLING
BEILSTTU SUBTITLE	BEKMOOPS SPEKBOOM	MOBSTERS	BGGIILNO OBLIGING
BEIMMRRS BRIMMERS	BEKMOSST STEMBOKS	SOMBREST	BGGIILNY GIBINGLY
BEIMNORS BROMINES	BEKNNORU UNBROKEN	BEMORSSU MORBUSES	BGGIINNO BOINGING
BEIMNSSU NIMBUSES	BEKNOOOT NOTEBOOK	BEMORSWW WEBWORMS	BGGIINNR BRINGING
BEIMNSTU BITUMENS	BEKNOPRU UPBROKEN	BEMOSTUX BUXOMEST	BGGIINRU BRIGUING
BEIMOORR BROOMIER	BEKOOORV OVERBOOK	BEMOSTUY MYOTUBES	BGGILNNU BLUNGING
BEIMOORS BOSOMIER	BEKOORST BOOKREST	BEMSSSUU SUBSUMES	BUNGLING
RIBOSOME	BEKOORTU OUTBROKE	BENNNOTU UNBONNET	BGGILNRU BURGLING
BEIMORRV OVERBRIM	BEKOOTTX TEXTBOOK	BENNOOTU BOUTONNE	BGGINOOT TOBOGGIN
BEIMORSW IMBOWERS	BELLMORT MORTBELL	BENORRSU SUBORNER	BGHHIORW HIGHBROW
BEIMORTY BIOMETRY	BELLMORU UMBRELLO	BENORRSZ BRONZERS	BGHHIOSY HIGHBOYS
BEIMORYZ RIBOZYME	BELLMRUY LUMBERLY	BENORRUV OVERBURN	BGHIINRT BIRTHING
BEIMOSSS IMBOSSES	BELLNOSU BULLNOSE	BENORSST SORBENTS	BGHILMNU HUMBLING
BEIMPSTU BUMPIEST	BELLNTUY TUNBELLY	BENORSTU RUBSTONE	BGHILNSU BLUSHING
BEIMRSSU IMBURSES	BELLORTW BELLWORT	BENORSTW BESTROWN	BGHILRTY BRIGHTLY
BEIMRSTU IMBRUTES	BELLRRSU BURRELLS	BROWNEST	BGHIMNTU THUMBING
RESUBMIT	BELMMOOS EMBLOOMS	BENORSUU BURNOUSE	BGHIMOTU BIGMOUTH
TERBIUMS	BELMMRSU MUMBLERS	BENORSWY BYWONERS	BGHINORS BIGHORNS
BEINNOSS BENISONS	BELMNOSU NELUMBOS	BENORTTU REBUTTON	BGHINRSU BRUSHING
BONINESS	BELMOORS BLOOMERS	BENOSSUZ SUBZONES	BGHINSSU BUSHINGS
BEINNOST BONNIEST	REBLOOMS	BENOSSWY NEWSBOYS	BGHIORSU BROGUISH
BEINNOSZ BENZOINS	BELMOORY BLOOMERY	BENRRSUY SUNBERRY	BGHLRSUU BURGHLURS
BEINNRYZ ZEBRINNY	BELMOOSS BLOOSMES	BENSSSUY BUSYNESS	BURGHULS
BEINORRW BROWNIER	BELMOOST BOOMLETS	BEOORRRW BORROWER	BGHNORSU HORNBUGS
BEINORRZ BRONZIER	BELMOPRS PROBLEMS	REBORROW	BGHNOTUU UNBOUGHT
BEINORST BORNITES	BELMORST TEMBLORS	BEOORRVW OVERBROW	BGHOOPTU BOUGHPOT
RIBSTONE	BELMORSY SOMBRELY	BEOORSST BOOSTERS	BGHOORSU BOROUGHS
BEINORSW BROWNIES	BELMORUW RUMBELOW	BEOORSTY BOTRYOSE	BGIIJLNR JIRBLING
BEINORSY BRYONIES	BELMOSST TOMBLESS	BEOOSTUX OUTBOXES	BGIIKLNN BLINKING
BEINORTZ BRONZITE	BELMOSSY SYMBOLES	BEOOTTZZ BOZZETTO	BGIIKMNO KIMBOING
BEINOSST EBONISTS	BELMPRSU PLUMBERS	BEOPRRSV PROVERBS	BGIIKNNO BOINKING
BEINOSSX BOXINESS	BELMPRUY PLUMBERY	BEOPRSST BESPORTS	BGIIKNRS BRISKING
BEINOSTT BOTTINES	BELMRRSU RUMBLERS	BEOPSSTU BESPOUTS	BGIILLNS BILLINGS
BEINOSTU BOUNTIES	BELMRRUY MULBERRY	BEOQSSTU BOSQUETS	BGIILMNW WIMBLING
BEINRRSY NISBERRY	BELMRSSU SLUMBERS	BEOQSTUU BOUQUETS	BGIILNNN BLINNING
BEINRSSU SUBERINS	BELMRSTU STUMBLER	BEORRSSW BROWSERS	BGIILNOR BROILING
BEINRSTT BITTERNS	TUMBLERS	BEORRSTU ROBUSTER	BGIILNOS BOILINGS
BEINRSTU TRIBUNES	TUMBRELS	BEORSSSU SORBUSES	BGIILNOX BOLIXING
TURBINES	BELMRSUY SLUMBERY	BEORSSUU SUBEROUS	BGIILNPP BLIPPING
BEINRSUU UNBURIES	BELMSSTU STUMBLES	BEORSTTU TUBEROUS	BGIILNRS BIRLINGS
BEINSSSU BUSINESS	BELNNOSU UNNOBLES	BEORSUVY OVERBUSY	BIRSLING
BEINSTTU BUNTIEST	BELNOOSY BOLONEYS	OVERBUYS	BRISLING
BEIOOPST BIOTOPES	BELNOSUU NEBULOUS	BEOSSTTU OBTUSEST	BGIILNSS SIBLINGS
BEIOORST ROBOTISE	BELNOSYZ BENZOYLS	BEPRRSTU PERTURBS	BGIILNTZ BLITZING
BEIOORTZ ROBOTIZE	BELNSSTU SUNBELTS	BEPSSTUY SUBTYPES	BGIIMMNR BRIMMING
BEIOOSSV OVIBOSES	BELNSTUU UNSUBTLE	BEQRRSUU BRUSQUER	BGIIMNRS BRIMINGS
BEIOOSTZ BOOZIEST	BELOOPRS BLOOPERS	BERRSSTU BURSTERS	BGIIMNRU IMBRUING
BEIOPSTY BIOTYPES	BELOORSW ROSEBOWL	BERRSTUU SURREBUT	BGIINNOR INORBING
BEIOQTUU BOUTIQUE	BELOORVW OVERBLOW	BERSSTTU BUTTRESS	BGIINNRS INBRINGS
BEIORRST ORBITERS	BELOOSST BOOTLESS	BERSSTUV SUBVERST	BGIINORT ORBITING
BEIORRSU BOURSIER	BELOOTUV OBVOLUTE	SUBVERTS	BGIINRST RINGBITS
BEIORRSW BROWSIER	BELORRTU TROUBLER	BESSSSUY BYSSUSES	BGIINRSU BRUISING
BEIORRTU ROBURITE	BELORSST BOLSTERS	BESSTTUX SUBTEXTS	BGIINRTU BRUITING
BEIORSST SORBITES	BELORSSW BROWLESS	BFFGILNU BLUFFING	BGIINSTU BUISTING
BEIORSTY SOBRIETY	BELORSTT BLOTTERS	BFFGINSU BUFFINGS	BGIINVVY BIVVYING
BEIOSSST BOSSIEST	BOTTLERS	BFFNOOSU BUFFOONS	BGIJLMNU JUMBLING
BEIOSSSU SOUBISES	BELORSTU BOULTERS	BFFNOSUX SNUFFBOX	BGIJNORU OBJURING
BEIOSSTU BOUSIEST	TROUBLES	BFGILMNU FUMBLING	BGIKLNNU BLUNKING
BEIOTTZZ BOZZETTI	BELOSTUY OBTUSELY	BFGIORST FROGBITS	BGIKNNOU BUNKOING
BEIQRSTU BRIQUETS	BELPRSUY SUPERBLY	BFGLLORU BULLFROG	BGIKNOOR BROOKING
BEIRRSSU BRISURES	BELRSSTU BLUSTERS	BFHILOSW BLOWFISH	BGIKNOOS BOOKINGS
BRUISERS	BUSTLERS	BFHLLSUU BLUSHFUL	BGIKNORS BROKINGS
BEIRRSTU BURRIEST	BELRSTUY BLUSTERY	BFIINORS FIBROINS	BGIKNSSU BUSKINGS
BEIRRTTU TRIBUTER	BELSSTTU SUBTLEST	BFIIORSS FIBROSIS	BGILLNOU GLOBULIN
BEIRSSTU BUSTIERS	BELSSTUY SUBSTYLE	BFILLSSU BLISSFUL	BGILLNSU BULLINGS
BEIRSTTU TRIBUTES	BELSTTUY SUBTLETY	BFIMNORU NUBIFORM	BGILLNUY BULLYING
BEIRSTTY TREYBITS	BEMMOOSS EMBOSOMS	BFIMORTU TUBIFORM	BGILMMNU BUMMLING
BEISSTTU BUSTIEST	BEMMORRS BROMMERS	BFINORYZ BRONZIFY	MUMBLING
BEISTUZZ BUZZIEST	BEMMRRSU BRUMMERS	BFIORSTT FROSTBIT	BGILMNOO BLOOMING
BEJKOOST JESTBOOK	BEMNNSSU NUMBNESS	BFKLOOSY FLYBOOKS	BGILMNPU PLUMBING
BEJLMRSU JUMBLERS	BEMNOORT TROMBONE	BFKSSSUU SUBFUSKS	BGILMNRU RUMBLING
BEJORTTU TURBOJET	BEMNORSW EMBROWNS	BFLLOSUW BOWLFULS	BGILMNTU TUMBLING
BEKLNORY BROKENLY		BFLLOSWY FLYBLOWS	BGILMORY GORBLIMY
BEKLNRSU BLUNKERS		BFLOORSU SUBFLOOR	BGILMOSU GUMBOILS

BGILNNOS SNOBLING	BHLOOOTT TOLBOOTH	BLMNPSUU UNPLUMBS	CCDEIIRT CRICETID
BGILNNTU BLUNTING	BHLRSUUY BULRUSHY	BLMOOOST TOMBOLOS	CCDEIIST DEICTICS
BGILNOOP BLOOPING	BHMNTTUU THUMBNUT	BLMOOOTY LOBOTOMY	CCDEILOS SCOLECID
BGILNORY BORINGLY	BHMOPTTU THUMBPOT	BLMOORSW LOBWORMS	CCDEINOR CORNICED
BGILNOST BILTONGS	BHMORSTU THROMBUS	BLMOOSSS BLOSSOMS	CCDEINOS CONCISED
BOLTINGS	BHNOSSUW SNOWBUSH	BLMOOSSY BLOSSOMY	CCDEINOT OCCIDENT
BGILNOSU BLOUSING	BHOOSSTW BOWSHOTS	BLMOPSUU PLUMBOUS	CCDEIOPP COPPICED
BGILNOSW BOWLINGS	BIIKLOST KILOBITS	BLNOOSSU BLOUSONS	CCDEIOPU OCCUPIED
BGILNOTT BLOTTING	BIIKNOOT BOOTIKIN	BLOOSSTY SLYBOOTS	CCDEKNOU UNCOCKED
BOTTLING	BIILLMOR MORBILLI	BLOPSSTU SUBPLOTS	CCDELNOU CONCLUDE
BGILNOTU BOULTING	BIILLNOS BILLIONS	BLORSTUY ROBUSTLY	CCDELORU OCCLUDER
BGILNRRU BLURRING	BIILLOSU BOUILLIS	BLOSTUUU TUBULOUS	CCDELOSU OCCLUDES
BGILNRTU BLURTING	BIILSTTW TWIBLITS	BMNOOSSU UNBOSOMS	CCDELOTU OCCULTED
BGILNSTU BUSTLING	BIILMOTY MOBILITY	BMNORSUW MOWBURNS	CCDENOOO COCOONED
BGILNTTU BUTTLING	BIILNNRS BIRLINNS	BMNORTUW MOWBURNT	CCDENOSU CONDUCES
BGILOORS OBLIGORS	BIILNOOV OBLIVION	BMOOORSX BOXROOMS	CCDEORRU OCCURRED
BGILRSSU BUSGIRLS	BIILNOTY NOBILITY	BMOORSSU SOMBROUS	CCDEORSU SUCCORED
BGIMNOOR BROOMING	BIILNQSU QUIBLINS	BMOORTTY BOTTOMRY	CCDEOSTU STUCCOED
BGIMNOOS BOOMINGS	BIILNTUY NUBILITY	BMORSSTU STROMBUS	CCDHIIKP DIPCHICK
BOSOMING	BIILORST STROBILI	BNNOTTUU UNBUTTON	CCDHIILO CICHLOID
BGIMNORS SOMBRING	BIILOSSU SIBILOUS	BNNRSSUU SUNBURNS	CCDHIILS CICHLIDS
BGIMNPSU BUMPINGS	BIILOSSY BIOLYSIS	BNNRSTUU SUNBURNT	CCDHIIOR DICHROIC
BGIMOSSY BOGYISMS	BIILSTTW WITBLITS	BNOOOSTW SNOWBOOT	CCDHINOO CONCHOID
BGINNNOU UNBONING	BIIMMNSY NIMBYISM	BNOOOSUY SONOBUOY	CCDIILOS CODICILS
BGINNORU UNROBING	BIIMMOSZ ZOMBIISM	BNOORTUW BROWNOUT	CCDIILSU CULICIDS
BGINNORW BROWNING	BIIMNOSU NIOBIUMS	BNORRUUW UNBURROW	CCDIINOO CONOIDIC
BGINNORZ BRONZING	BIIMSSTU STIBIUMS	BNORSTUU OUTBURNS	CCDIINOS SCINCOID
BGINNOUX UNBOXING	BIINRSTU BURINIST	BNORTTUU OUTBURNT	CCDIINST DISCINCT
BGINNRSU BURNINGS	BIIQTUUY UBIQUITY	BNRSSTUU SUNBURST	CCDIIORS CRICOIDS
BGINNRTU BRUNTING	BIIRSSTU BURSITIS	BORSTTUU OUTBURST	CCDIIORT DICROTIC
BGINNSTU BUNTINGS	BIJNOSSU SUBJOINS	BPRSSTUU UPBURSTS	CCDILOSY CYCLOIDS
BGINOOST BOOSTING	BIKLNOSY LINKBOYS	CCCDIILY DICYCLIC	CCDINOTU CONDUCTI
BGINORST STROBING	BIKMNPSU BUMPKINS	CCCEEILT ECLECTIC	CCDKLOSU CUCKOLDS
BGINORSW BROWSING	BIKOOUUZ BOUZOUKI	CCCEGOSY COCCYGES	CCDKOOOW WOODCOCK
BGINPRSU UPBRINGS	BIKORRSW RIBWORKS	CCCEHIOR CHOCCIER	CCDNOORS CONCORDS
BGINRSSU SUBRINGS	BILLMSUY BULLYISM	CCCEHIOS CHOCCIES	CCDNOSTU CONDUCTS
BGINRSTU BRUSTING	BILLNOOU BOUILLON	CCCEIIRT ECCRITIC	CCEEGINR RECCEING
BRUTINGS	BILLNOSU BULLIONS	CCCEILNY ENCYCLIC	CCEEGNOS COGENCES
BURSTING	BILLRSWY WRYBILLS	CCCEILUY EUCYCLIC	CCEEHINZ ZECCHINE
BGINSSSU BUSSINGS	BILMMPSU PLUMBISM	CCCHIORY CHICCORY	CCEEHISV CEVICHES
BGINSSTU BUSTINGS	BILMNORS NOMBRILS	CCCIINSU SUCCINIC	CCEEHKNS SCHNECKE
BGINSUZZ BUZZINGS	BILMOSTU BOTULISM	CCCILNOY CYCLONIC	CCEEHKRS CHECKERS
BGKLOOOS LOGBOOKS	BILMRSTU TUMBRILS	CCCILOPY CYCLOPIC	RECHECKS
BGKNOOOS SONGBOOK	BILNOSUU NUBILOUS	CCCINSTU SUCCINCT	CCEEHLNS CLENCHES
BGKORSSY GRYSBOKS	BILNSTUU TUBULINS	CCCIOORS SCIROCCO	CCEEHORS ECORCHES
BGLNOOSW LONGBOWS	BILOORST SORBITOL	CCCNOOST CONCOCTS	CCEEHOSU COUCHEES
BGLNOSUW BLOWGUNS	BILOPSSY POSSIBLY	CCDDEENO CONCEDED	CCEEHRSY SCREECHY
BGLOORYY BRYOLOGY	BILORSST BRISTOLS	CCDDEEOT DECOCTED	CCEEIILS CICELIES
BGMOOSTU GUMBOOTS	BILOSSSU SUBSOILS	CCDDELOU OCCLUDED	CCEEIIST CECITIES
BGNOOSWY GOWNBOYS	BIMMOOSS IMBOSOMS	CCDDENOU CONDUCED	CCEEILNR ENCIRCLE
BGNOSSSU SUBSONGS	BIMMORSS BROMISMS	CCDEEENR CREDENCE	CCEEILNS LICENCES
BGOPRSSU SUBGROUP	BIMNORSW IMBROWNS	CCDEEHIL CLICHEED	CCEEILNT ELENCTIC
BGORSTUW BUGWORTS	BIMNOSSY SYMBIONS	CCDEEHLN CLENCHED	CCEEILPY EPICYCLE
BHIIINST INHIBITS	BIMNOSTY SYMBIONT	CCDEEILN LICENCED	CCEEILRT ELECTRIC
BHIIKRSS BRISKISH	BIMNRRUU MUIRBURN	CCDEEINS SCIENCED	CCEEIMNU ECUMENIC
BHIILMPS BLIMPISH	BIMNRUUV VIBURNUM	CCDEEIOP CODPIECE	CCEEINOR CICERONE
BHIIMRST MISBIRTH	BIMOSSTY SYBOTISM	CCDEEIOS ECOCIDES	CCEEINOV CONCEIVE
BHIIOPRT PROHIBIT	BIMRSSUX BRUXISMS	CCDEEKOR COCKERED	CCEEINSS SCIENCES
BHIIPSSS SIBSHIPS	BINOORST ISOBRONT	CCDEEKOY COCKEYED	CCEEIORV COERCIVE
BHIKLLOO BILLHOOK	BINORSST RIBSTONS	CCDEELRY RECYCLED	CCEEIPSS SPECCIES
BHILLNOR HORNBILL	BINRSSTU INBURSTS	CCDEENOR CONCEDER	CCEEIRSS ECCRISES
BHILLPUW BULLWHIP	BINSSTUU SUBUNITS	CCDEENOS CONCEDES	CCEEIRSV CERVICES
BHILLSTU BULLSHIT	BIOPRRSU SUBPRIOR	CCDEESSU SUCCEEDS	CRESCIVE
BHILNSTU BLUNTISH	BIOPRSTW BOWSPRIT	CCDEHHRU CHURCHED	CREVICES
BHILORRY HORRIBLY	BIORRSTU BURRITOS	CCDEHIKT TCHICKED	CCEEITTU EUTECTIC
BHILOSTU HOLIBUTS	BIORRSTW RIBWORTS	CCDEHILN CLINCHED	CCEEKLOR COCKEREL
BHILOSYY BOYISHLY	BIORSSTT BISTORTS	CCDEHIPU HICCUPED	CCEEKOSY COCKEYES
BHIMNORT THROMBIN	BIORSTTU BITTOURS	CCDEHKLU CHUCKLED	CCEELMNY CLEMENCY
BHIMOOPR BIOMORPH	BIORSTUY BISTOURY	CCDEHLTU CLUTCHED	CCEELOSS SCOLECES
BHIMOOSS HOBOISMS	BIOSTTUY OBTUSITY	DECLUTCH	CCEELRSY RECYCLES
BHIMOPSS PHOBISMS	BIRRSTTU SUBTRIST	CCDEHNRU CRUNCHED	CCEEMMNO COMMENCE
BHIMSSTU BISMUTHS	BISSSSTU SUBSISTS	CCDEHORS SCORCHED	CCEEMMOR COMMERCE
BHINOPSU UNBISHOP	BKKOOORW BOOKWORK	CCDEHORT CROTCHED	CCEEMOPS COMPESCE
BHINORSW BROWNISH	WORKBOOK	CCDEHORU CROUCHED	CCEENNOS ENSCONCE
BHIOOPRS BIOPHORS	BKMOOORW BOOKWORM	CCDEHOST SCOTCHED	CCEENORT CONCRETE
BHIOPSST PHOBISTS	BKMOORUZ ZOMBORUK	CCDEHRTU CRUTCHED	CCEENRST CRESCENT
BHIRSTTU TURBITHS	BKNOOSTW BOWKNOTS	CCDEHSTU SCUTCHED	CCEFIIPS SPECIFIC
BHKNOOOR HORNBOOK	BLLLLOOY LOBLOLLY	CCDEIILO CLEIDOIC	CCEFIRRU CRUCIFER
BHKOOOPS BOOKSHOP	BLMMPSUU PLUMBUMS	CCDEIINO COINCIDE	CCEFLLOU FLOCCULE

CCEFLOOS	FLOCCOSE		
CCEFNOST	CONFECTS		
CCEGHIKN	CHECKING		
CCEGHIOR	CHOREGIC		
CCEGIKLN	CLECKING		
CCEGILOO	ECOLOGIC		
CCEGILRY	GLYCERIC		
CCEGINNO	CONGENIC		
CCEGINOR	COERCING		
CCEGINRY	RECCYING		
CCEGNOOS	COGNOSCE		
CCEHHINS	CHINCHES		
CCEHHRSU	CHURCHES		
CCEHIIMR	CHIMERIC		
CCEHIIMS	ISCHEMIC		
CCEHIINZ	ZECCHINI		
CCEHIKNS	CHICKENS		
CCEHIKSU	CHUCKIES		
CCEHILNR	CLINCHER		
CCEHILNS	CLINCHES		
CCEHILOR	CHOLERIC		
CCEHILOY	CHOICELY		
CCEHILSU	CULCHIES		
CCEHINOR	CORNICHE		
	ENCHORIC		
CCEHINOS	CONCHIES		
CCEHINOZ	ZECCHINO		
CCEHINST	TECHNICS		
CCEHIORT	RICOCHET		
CCEHIOST	CHOICEST		
CCEHIRSS	SCREICHS		
	SCRIECHS		
CCEHKLSU	CHUCKLES		
CCEHKMSS	SCHMECKS		
CCEHKMSU	CHECKSUM		
CCEHKNSU	UNCHECKS		
CCEHKOTU	CHECKOUT		
CCEHLMOR	CROMLECH		
CCEHLNNU	UNCLENCH		
CCEHLNSU	CLUNCHES		
CCEHLRSU	CLERUCHS		
CCEHLRUY	CLERUCHY		
CCEHLSTU	CLUTCHES		
	CULTCHES		
CCEHNRSU	CRUNCHES		
CCEHORRS	SCORCHER		
CCEHORSS	SCORCHES		
CCEHORST	CROCHETS		
	CROTCHES		
CCEHORSU	CROUCHES		
CCEHORTT	CROTCHET		
CCEHOSST	SCOTCHES		
CCEHRSTU	CRUTCHES		
	SCUTCHER		
CCEHRTUY	CUTCHERY		
CCEHSSTU	SCUTCHES		
CCEIIKLN	NICKELIC		
CCEIILLN	ENCLITIC		
CCEIILNU	CULICINE		
CCEIILOR	LICORICE		
CCEIILPT	ECLIPTIC		
CCEIILST	SCILICET		
CCEIILTU	LEUCITIC		
CCEIINNR	ENCRINIC		
CCEIINOR	CICERONI		
CCEIIRRT	CIRCITER		
CCEIIRSS	ECCRISIS		
CCEIIRST	ICTERICS		
CCEIIRTT	RECTITIC		
CCEIIRTU	EUCRITIC		
CCEIKLRS	CLICKERS		
CCEIKLRU	CLUCKIER		
CCEIKLST	CLICKETS		
CCEIKORS	COCKSIER		
CCEIKOST	COCKIEST		
CCEIKRST	CRICKETS		
CCEILMOO	COELOMIC		
CCEILMOP	COMPLICE		
CCEILNOR	CORNICLE		
CCEILNUY	UNICYCLE		
CCEILOSS	SCOLICES		
CCEILRRS	CIRCLERS		
CCEILRRU	CURRICLE		
CCEILRST	CIRCLETS		
CCEILRSY	CRESYLIC		
CCEILRTY	TRICYCLE		
CCEILRUU	CURLICUE		
CCEILSTU	CUTICLES		
CCEIMNOO	ECONOMIC		
	ONCOMICE		
CCEIMOST	COSMETIC		
CCEIMRRU	MERCURIC		
CCEINNOS	INSCONCE		
CCEINNOV	CONVINCE		
CCEINOOR	COERCION		
CCEINOPT	CONCEPTI		
CCEINORS	CONCISER		
	CORNICES		
	CROCEINS		
CCEINORT	CONCERTI		
	NECROTIC		
CCEINOSS	CONCISES		
CCEINOST	CONCEITS		
CCEINOTT	CONCETTI		
	TECTONIC		
CCEINOTY	CONCEITY		
CCEINPRT	PRECINCT		
CCEINRTU	CINCTURE		
CCEINSTY	SYNECTIC		
CCEIOORT	CROCOITE		
CCEIOOTX	ECOTOXIC		
CCEIOOTZ	ECTOZOIC		
CCEIOPPS	COPPICES		
CCEIOPRT	ECTROPIC		
CCEIOPRU	OCCUPIER		
CCEIOPSU	OCCUPIES		
CCEIORST	CORTICES		
CCEIPSST	SCEPTICS		
CCEIRRSU	CIRCUSES		
CCEJNOST	CONJECTS		
CCEKLORS	CLOCKERS		
CCEKNOST	CONTECKS		
CCEKNOSY	COCKNEYS		
CCEKOPST	PETCOCKS		
CCEKORRY	CROCKERY		
CCEKORST	CROCKETS		
CCEKORSU	COCKSURE		
CCELLOST	COLLECTS		
CCELMOPT	COMPLECT		
CCELNOSY	CYCLONES		
CCELOPSY	CYCLOPES		
CCELOSSY	CYCLOSES		
CCELSSUY	CYCLUSES		
CCENNORS	CONCERNS		
CCENNOST	CONCENTS		
	CONNECTS		
CCENOORT	CONCERTO		
CCENOOTT	CONCETTO		
CCENOPST	CONCEPTS		
CCENORST	CONCERTS		
CCENORSW	CONCREWS		
CCENORTY	CORNETCY		
CCENRRUY	CURRENCY		
CCEOOORR	COROCORE		
CCEOORSU	CROCEOUS		
CCEOOSTT	COCOTTES		
CCEOPRUY	REOCCUPY		
CCEORRST	CORRECTS		
CCEORSSU	CROCUSES		
CCEORSTU	STUCCOER		
CCEORSTW	TWOCCERS		
CCESSSUU	CUSCUSES		
CCFIINOR	CORNIFIC		
CCFIIRUX	CRUCIFIX		
CCFIKNOY	COCKNIFY		
CCFILLOU	FLOCCULI		
CCFILNOT	CONFLICT		
CCFKLOOT	COCKLOFT		
CCFLOOOO	LOCOFOCO		
CCGHHIOU	HICCOUGH		
CCGHIINN	CINCHING		
CCGHIKNO	CHOCKING		
CCGHIKNU	CHUCKING		
CCGHINNO	CONCHING		
CCGHINOS	GNOCCHIS		
CCGHINOU	COUCHING		
CCGIIKLN	CLICKING		
CCGIIKNR	CRICKING		
CCGIILNR	CIRCLING		
CCGIKLNO	CLOCKING		
	COCKLING		
CCGIKLNU	CLUCKING		
CCGIKNOR	CROCKING		
CCGILLOY	GLYCOLIC		
CCGILNOY	GLYCONIC		
CCGILNSY	CYCLINGS		
CCGILOSU	GLUCOSIC		
CCGINNOS	SCONCING		
CCGINOTW	TWOCCING		
CCGKOORS	GORCOCKS		
CCHHIITY	ICHTHYIC		
CCHHILSS	SCHLICHS		
CCHHINOT	CHTHONIC		
CCHHLRUY	CHURCHLY		
CCHHNRUU	UNCHURCH		
CCHIINUZ	ZUCCHINI		
CCHIIORT	ORCHITIC		
CCHIKMPU	CHIPMUCK		
CCHIKSST	SCHTICKS		
CCHINORS	CHRONICS		
CCHINOSU	SCUCHION		
CCHINSSU	SCUCHINS		
CCHIPSSY	PSYCHICS		
CCHKLOSS	SCHLOCKS		
CCHKLOSY	SCHLOCKY		
CCHKMOSS	SCHMOCKS		
CCHKMSSU	SCHMUCKS		
CCHKOOST	COCKSHOT		
CCHKOPTU	PUTCHOCK		
CCHKOSTU	COCKSHUT		
CCHKPSUU	UPCHUCKS		
CCHKSSTU	SCHTUCKS		
CCHLNTUU	UNCLUTCH		
CCHNRSUY	SCRUNCHY		
CCIIKNPY	PICNICKY		
CCIILPRS	CIRCLIPS		
CCIIMNSY	CYNICISM		
CCIINNSU	CICINNUS		
CCIINORZ	ZIRCONIC		
CCIIRSTU	CIRCUITS		
CCIIRTUY	CIRCUITY		
CCIKKLOP	LOCKPICK		
	PICKLOCK		
CCIKLOSW	COWLICKS		
CCIKNOPR	PRINCOCK		
CCIKOPRS	CROPSICK		
CCIKOPST	COCKPITS		
CCILNOOS	COLONICS		
CCILNOSU	COUNCILS		
CCILNSUY	SUCCINYL		
CCILOOPS	PICCOLOS		
CCILORUU	CURCULIO		
CCILOSSY	CYCLOSIS		
CCILSSTY	CYCLISTS		
CCIMNRUU	CURCUMIN		
CCINOOST	COCTIONS		
CCINOPRT	PROCINCT		
CCINOPSY	SYNCOPIC		
CCINORSY	CRYONICS		
CCINOSTV	CONVICTS		
CCIOOPST	SCOTOPIC		
CCIOORSS	SIROCCOS		
CCIOOTXY	OXYTOCIC		
CCIOPSTU	OCCIPUTS		
CCIRSSUY	CIRCUSSY		
CCJNNOTU	CONJUNCT		
CCKKLMUU	MUCKLUCK		
CCKMMORU	CRUMMOCK		
CCKMOOOR	MOORCOCK		
CCKNORTU	TURNCOCK		
CCKOOPST	STOPCOCK		
CCKOPRSU	COCKSPUR		
CCKOSSTU	CUSTOCKS		
CCLLOTUY	OCCULTLY		
CCLMOOPU	COCOPLUM		
CCLNOOOR	CONCOLOR		
CCLOOOSZ	ZOCCOLOS		
CCLOORSU	OCCLUSOR		
CCMOOORS	MOROCCOS		
CCNOOPSU	PUCCOONS		
CCNOORSU	CONCOURS		
CCNOOSTU	COCONUTS		
CCOOOORR	COROCORO		
CCOOSSUU	COUSCOUS		
CCOOTTUU	TUCOTUCO		
CCORSSTU	CROSSCUT		
CCORSSUU	SUCCOURS		
CCOTTUUU	TUCUTUCO		
CCRSUUUU	SURUCUCU		
CDDDEETU	DEDUCTED		
CDDDEIIS	DISCIDED		
CDDDELRU	CRUDDLED		
CDDDELSU	SCUDDLED		
CDDDIIOY	DIDDICOY		
CDDEEEEX	EXCEEDED		
CDDEEEFN	DEFENCED		
CDDEEEFT	DEFECTED		
CDDEEEIV	DECEIVED		
CDDEEEJT	DEJECTED		
CDDEEENR	DECERNED		
CDDEEENT	DECEDENT		
CDDEEEPR	PRECEDED		
CDDEEERS	SCREEDED		
CDDEEERW	DECREWED		
CDDEEETT	DETECTED		
CDDEEFOR	DEFORCED		
CDDEEHIS	DEHISCED		
CDDEEHIT	CHEDDITE		
CDDEEHNR	DRENCHED		
CDDEEIIS	DEICIDES		
CDDEEIKR	DICKERED		
CDDEEILN	DECLINED		
CDDEEILP	PEDICLED		
CDDEEINR	CINDERED		
CDDEEIOV	DEVOICED		
CDDEEIPT	DEPICTED		
CDDEEIRS	DECIDERS		
	DESCRIED		
CDDEEIRT	CREDITED		
	DIRECTED		
CDDEEKNU	UNDECKED		
CDDEEKOT	DOCKETED		
CDDEEKUW	DUCKWEED		
CDDEELMO	COMEDDLE		
CDDEELPU	DECUPLED		
CDDEELSU	SCEDULED		
	SECLUDED		
CDDEELUX	EXCLUDED		
CDDEELUY	DEUCEDLY		
CDDEENOS	SECONDED		
CDDEENSS	DESCENDS		
CDDEEORR	RECORDED		
CDDEEORS	DECODERS		
CDDEERUV	DECURVED		
CDDEESUW	CUDWEEDS		
CDDEFIIO	CODIFIED		
CDDEFINO	CONFIDED		
CDDEGIIN	DECIDING		
CDDEGINO	DECODING		
CDDEGINU	DEDUCING		
CDDEHIOW	COWHIDED		
CDDEHISU	CHUDDIES		
CDDEIINT	INDICTED		
CDDEIISS	DISCIDES		
CDDEIKOS	DOCKISED		
	DOCKSIDE		

CDDEIKOZ DOCKIZED	CDEEERRS SCREEDER	CDEEIITT DIETETIC	CDEEKPRU PUCKERED
CDDEILLO COLLIDED	CDEEERSS RECESSED	CDEEIJNT INJECTED	CDEEKRSU SUCKERED
CDDEILNU INCLUDED	SECEDERS	CDEEIJOR REJOICED	CDEEKRTU TUCKERED
CDDEILOR CLODDIER	CDEEERST DECREETS	CDEEIKLN NICKELED	CDEELLPU CUPELLED
CDDEILRU CUDDLIER	RESECTED	CDEEIKMY MICKEYED	CDEELMOW WELCOMED
CDDEINTU INDUCTED	SECRETED	CDEEIKNR NICKERED	CDEELNOS ENCLOSED
CDDEIORV DIVORCED	CDEEERSV SCREEVED	CDEEIKNS SICKENED	CDEELNPU PEDUNCLE
CDDEIRRU CRUDDIER	CDEEERTX EXCRETED	CDEEIKNV INVECKED	CDEELNTY DECENTLY
CDDEIRSU DISCURED	CDEEERTX EXCRETED	CDEEIKPT PICKETED	CDEELNUW UNCLEWED
CDDEKNOU UNDOCKED	CDEEESTX EXSECTED	CDEEIKRR DRECKIER	CDEELOOW LOCOWEED
CDDELLOU COLLUDED	CDEEETUX EXECUTED	CDEEIKRW WICKEDER	CDEELOPU DECOUPLE
CDDELNOO CONDOLED	CDEEFFOR COFFERED	WICKERED	CDEELORS RECLOSED
CDDELOOR CROODLED	EFFORCED	CDEEIKRY YICKERED	CDEELORV CLOVERED
CDDELRSU CRUDDLES	CDEEFHLN FLENCHED	CDEEIKTT TICKETED	CDEELORY RECOYLED
CDDELSSU SCUDDLES	CDEEFHLT FLETCHED	CDEEILNP PENDICLE	CDEELOST CLOSETED
CDDEMNOU DUNCEDOM	CDEEFIIL ICEFIELD	CDEEILNR RECLINED	CDEELOTU ELOCUTED
CDDENNOO CONDONED	CDEEFIIS EDIFICES	CDEEILNS DECLINES	CDEELPRU PRECLUDE
CDDENOOR CORDONED	CDEEFIIT FETICIDE	LICENSED	CDEELPSU DECUPLES
CDDENORU UNCORDED	CDEEFINT INFECTED	SILENCED	CDEELRTU LECTURED
CDDEOORR CORRODED	CDEEFKLR FRECKLED	CDEEILNT DENTICLE	RELUCTED
CDDEOORT DOCTORED	CDEEFKOR FOREDECK	CDEEILNU NUCLEIDE	CDEELRUX EXCLUDER
CDDEOPRU PRODUCED	CDEEFLST DEFLECTS	CDEEILOR RECOILED	CDEELSSU SCEDULES
CDDERSSU SCUDDERS	CDEEFNNU UNFENCED	CDEEILPS ECLIPSED	SECLUDES
CDDGHILO GODCHILD	CDEEFNOR ENFORCED	PEDICLES	CDEELSUX EXCLUDES
CDDGILNO CLODDING	CDEEFORS DEFORCES	PEDICLES	CDEEMOPR COMPERED
CODDLING	FRESCOED	CDEEILRS SCLEREID	CDEEMOPT COMPETED
CDDGILNU CUDDLING	CDEEFORT DEFECTOR	CDEEILRT DERELICT	CDEEMORT ECTODERM
CDDGINRU CRUDDING	CDEEGIIR REGICIDE	CDEEILRU RECUILED	CDEEMSTU TUMESCED
CDDGINSU SCUDDING	CDEEGINO GENOCIDE	CDEEIMNR ENDERMIC	CDEENNOS CONDENSE
CDDHIIRY DIHYDRIC	CDEEGINR RECEDING	CDEEIMNS ENDEMICS	CDEENNOU DENOUNCE
CDDHILOS CLODDISH	CDEEGINS SECEDING	CDEEIMOR MEDIOCRE	ENOUNCED
CDDHIORS DICHORDS	CDEEGIOS GEODESIC	CDEEIMOS COMEDIES	CDEENNOV CONVENED
CDDIIIOS DIDICOIS	CDEEGIOT GEODETIC	CDEEIMPR PREMEDIC	CDEENNPY PENDENCY
CDDIIOSY DIDICOYS	CDEEGNOR CONGREED	CDEEIMRS MISCREED	CDEENNTU UNDECENT
CDDIISTY DYTISCID	CDEEHHSU SHEUCHED	CDEEIMRV DECEMVIR	CDEENNTY TENDENCY
CDDIKOPS PIDDOCKS	CDEEHHTT THETCHED	CDEEINNS INCENSED	CDEENOOS COOSENED
CDDIORSS DISCORDS	CDEEHIKL HELIDECK	CDEEINNT INDECENT	CDEENORR CORNERED
CDDKOPSU PUDDOCKS	CDEEHILN LICHENED	CDEEINOR RECOINED	CDEENORS CENSORED
CDDKORSU RUDDOCKS	CDEEHILP CHELIPED	CDEEINOS CODEINES	NECROSED
CDDMMOUU MOCUDDUM	CDEEHINR ENRICHED	CDEEINPR PINCERED	SECONDER
CDDOOORW CORDWOOD	INHERCED	CDEEINPS DISPENCE	CDEENORT CENTRODE
CDEEEFFT EFFECTED	NICHERED	CDEEINPT DEPEINCT	CDEENOSS SECONDES
CDEEEFHL FLEECHED	RICHENED	INCEPTED	CDEENOTX COEXTEND
CDEEEFNS DEFENCES	CDEEHIOS ECHOISED	PEINCTED	CDEENOVX CONVEXED
CDEEEFRT REFECTED	CDEEHIOZ ECHOIZED	PENTICED	CDEENOVY CONVEYED
CDEEEHHW WHEECHED	CDEEHIPR CIPHERED	CDEEINTU INDUCTEE	CDEENPRU PRUDENCE
CDEEEHLR LECHERED	DECIPHER	CDEEINTV INVECTED	CDEENRSU CENSURED
CDEEEHMS SMEECHED	CDEEHIRR CHERRIED	CDEEIORV DIVORCEE	CDEENRUV VERECUND
CDEEEHPS DEPECHES	DREICHER	CDEEIOSS DIOCESES	CDEENSST DESCENTS
SPEECHED	CDEEHISS DEHISCES	CDEEIOSV DEVOICES	CDEENSSU CENSUSED
CDEEEHRS CREESHED	CDEEHIST TEDESCHI	CDEEIPRS PRECISED	CDEENSTY ENCYSTED
CDEEEHST TEDESCHE	CDEEHITW ITCHWEED	CDEEIPRT DECREPIT	CDEEOOPR COOPERED
CDEEEHSW ESCHEWED	CDEEHKST SKETCHED	DEPICTER	CDEEOOPR COPPERED
CDEEEINP PIECENED	CDEEHKTV KVETCHED	CDEEIPRU PEDICURE	CDEEORRR RECORDER
CDEEEINV EVIDENCE	CDEEHLMO LEECHDOM	CDEEIPST PECTISED	CDEEORRS RESCORED
CDEEEIPS EPICEDES	CDEEHLQU QUELCHED	CDEEIPTZ PECTIZED	CDEEORRU RECOURED
CDEEEIRV DECEIVER	CDEEHLSU SCHEDULE	CDEEIQSU QUIESCED	CDEEORST CORSETED
RECEIVED	CDEEHMTU HUMECTED	CDEEIRRS DECRIERS	ESCORTED
CDEEEISV DECEIVES	CDEEHNQU QUENCHED	CDEEIRRT DIRECTER	SECTORED
CDEEEJRT REJECTED	CDEEHNRR DRENCHER	REDIRECT	CDEEORSW ESCROWED
CDEEEKNW NECKWEED	CDEEHNRS DRENCHES	CDEEIRSS DESCRIES	CDEEORTT DETECTOR
CDEEELLX EXCELLED	CDEEHNRT TRENCHED	CDEEIRST DISCREET	CDEEORTV CORVETED
CDEEELOS COLESEED	CDEEHNRW WRENCHED	DISCRETE	VECTORED
CDEEELPY YCLEEPED	CDEEHNST STENCHED	CDEEIRSU DECURIES	CDEEOSST CESTODES
CDEEELST DESELECT	CDEEHNUW UNCHEWED	CDEEIRSV DESCRIVE	COSSETED
SELECTED	CDEEHORS CHORDEES	SCRIEVED	CDEEOSTT ESCOTTED
CDEEELUX EXCLUDEE	COSHERED	SERVICED	CDEEPRST SCEPTRED
CDEEEMNT CEMENTED	CDEEHORT HECTORED	CDEEIRTU CUITERED	CDEERRRU RECURRED
CDEEEMPR EMPERCED	TOCHERED	CDEEJKOY JOCKEYED	CDEERRSU CURSEDER
CDEEENNT TENDENCE	CDEEHPRU CHERUPED	CDEEKLNO ENLOCKED	REDUCERS
CDEEENOS SECONDEE	CDEEHPRY CYPHERED	CDEEKLPS SPECKLED	
CDEEENRS RECENSED	CDEEHQTU QUETCHED	CDEEKMRU MUCKERED	CDEERRUV RECURVED
SCREENED	CDEEHRTW WRETCHED	CDEEKNOR RECKONED	CDEERSSU SEDUCERS
SECERNED	CDEEHSSU DUCHESSE	CDEEKNRS REDNECKS	CDEERSUV DECURVES
CDEEENRT CENTERED	CDEEIILT ELICITED	CDEEKNRU UNRECKED	CDEERSUX EXCURSED
DECENTER	CDEEIIMN MEDICINE	CDEEKOPT POCKETED	CDEERTTU CURETTED
CDEEEPRS PRECEDES	CDEEIIMP EPIDEMIC	CDEEKORT ROCKETED	CDEERTUV CURVETED
CDEEEPTX EXCEPTED	CDEEIINT INDICTEE	CDEEKORW ROCKWEED	CDEFFINO COFFINED
EXPECTED	CDEEIIST EIDETICS	CDEEKOST SOCKETED	
	CDEEIISV DECISIVE		

CDEFFISU SUFFICED	SCHOOLED	CDEILMMS SCLIMMED	CDEIPRTU PICTURED
CDEFFLSU SCUFFLED	CDEHLORT CHORTLED	CDEILMOP COMPILED	CDEIPSST DISCEPTS
CDEFHILN FLINCHED	CDEHLOSU SLOUCHED	COMPLIED	CDEIRRSU SCURRIED
CDEFHIMO CHIEFDOM	CDEHMOOS SMOOCHED	CDEILMOS MELODICS	CDEIRSSU DISCURES
CDEFHIRT FRICHTED	CDEHMOSU SMOUCHED	CDEILMPR CRIMPLED	CDEIRSTU CRUDITES
CDEFIIIL FILICIDE	CDEHMSTU SMUTCHED	CDEILMRU DULCIMER	CURDIEST
CDEFIIIT CITIFIED	CDEHNOOP CHENOPOD	CDEILMSY DYSMELIC	CURTSIED
CDEFIIOR CODIFIER	CDEHNORS CHONDRES	CDEILNOS INCLOSED	CDEIRSTV VERDICTS
CDEFIIOS CODIFIES	CDEHNRSU CHUNDERS	CDEILNOU UNCOILED	CDEISSST DISSECTS
CDEFIIST DEFICITS	CDEHOORR RHEOCORD	CDEILNRY CYLINDER	CDEISSSU DISCUSES
CDEFIITY CITYFIED	CDEHORSU CHORUSED	CDEILNSU INCLUDES	CDEJNORU CONJURED
CDEFINNO CONFINED	CDEHORSW CHOWDERS	NUCLIDES	CDEKKLNU KNUCKLED
CDEFINNU INFECUND	COWHERDS	UNSLICED	CDEKLMOR CLERKDOM
CDEFINOR CONFIDER	CDEHOSSU HOCUSSED	CDEILOOW WOODLICE	CDEKLMOU DUCKMOLE
INFORCED	CDEHOSSW COWSHEDS	CDEILOPS SCOPELID	CDEKLNOU UNLOCKED
CDEFINOS CONFIDES	CDEHSSSU SCHUSSED	CDEILOPU CLUPEOID	CDEKLNRU CRUNKLED
CDEFINOX CONFIXED	CDEIIILS SILICIDE	UPCOILED	CDEKLOPU UPLOCKED
CDEFKORS DEFROCKS	CDEIIIMT IMTICIDE	CDEILORS SCLEROID	CDEKLORY YELDROCK
CDEFLNOU FLOUNCED	CDEIIIOS IDIOCIES	CDEILORU CLOUDIER	CDEKLOSW WEDLOCKS
CDEFLORY FORCEDLY	CDEIIIRV VIRICIDE	CDEILORV COVERLID	CDEKLRTU TRUCKLED
CDEFNORU FROUNCED	CDEIIITV VITICIDE	CDEILOSS DISCLOSE	CDEKNOOU UNCOOKED
UNFORCED	CDEIIKKS SIDEKICK	CDEILOST DOCILEST	CDEKNOOV CONVOKED
CDEFNOSU CONFUSED	CDEIIKLS SICKLIED	CDEILPPR CRIPPLED	CDEKNORU UNCORKED
CDEFNOTU CONFUTED	CDEIIKMM MIMICKED	CDEILPSU CLUPEIDS	CDEKNSSU SUNDECKS
CDEFNSTU DEFUNCTS	CDEIIKNR CIDERKIN	CDEILRTY DIRECTLY	CDEKNSSU UNSUCKED
CDEFOSSU FOCUSSED	CDEIIKNW INWICKED	CDEILSTU DULCITES	CDEKNTUU UNTUCKED
CDEGHORU GROUCHED	CDEIIKRS DRICKSIE	LUCIDEST	CDELLNUU UNCULLED
CDEGHRTU GRUTCHED	CDEIIKRT DICKTIER	CDEILSXY DYSLEXIC	CDELLOOP CLODPOLE
CDEGIINN INCEDING	CDEIIKST DICKIEST	CDEILTTU CUITTLED	CDELLORS SCROLLED
CDEGIINX EXCIDING	STICKIED	CDEIMMOX COMMIXED	CDELLORU COLLUDER
CDEGIKNO DECKOING	CDEIILMO DOMICILE	CDEIMOOW WOODMICE	CDELLOSU COLLUDES
DECOKING	CDEIILNN INCLINED	CDEIMORT MORTICED	CDELLOTU CLOUDLET
CDEGIKNS DECKINGS	CDEIILNO INDOCILE	CDEIMOST DOMESTIC	CDELMNOO MONOCLED
CDEGILSU CLUDGIES	CDEIILOT IDIOLECT	CDEIMPRS SCRIMPED	CDELMNOU COLUMNED
CDEGINNO ENCODING	CDEIILPS DISCIPLE	CDEINNOU UNCOINED	CDELMPRU CRUMPLED
CDEGINNS SCENDING	CDEIILPU PEDICULI	CDEINNOV CONNIVED	CDELNOOS CONDOLES
CDEGINOR RECODING	PULICIDE	CDEINOOS COOSINED	CONSOLED
CDEGINOS COGNISED	CDEIILRU RIDICULE	CDEINOOZ ENDOZOIC	CDELNOSS COLDNESS
CDEGINOY DECOYING	CDEIIMOS DIOECISM	CDEINORR CORDINER	CDELNOSU ENCLOUDS
CDEGINOZ COGNIZED	CDEIIMRT DIMETRIC	CDEINORS CONSIDER	UNCLOSED
CDEGINRU REDUCING	CDEIINNT INCIDENT	CDEINORT CENTROID	CDELNOSY CONDYLES
CDEGINRY DECRYING	CDEIINOS DECISION	DOCTRINE	SECONDLY
CDEGINSU SEDUCING	ICONISED	CDEINORU DECURION	CDELNOTU UNCOLTED
CDEGINSY DYSGENIC	CDEIINOV INVOICED	CDEINOST DEONTICS	CDELNOUW UNCOWLED
CDEGNORU CONGRUED	CDEIINOZ ICONIZED	CDEINOSU DOUCINES	CDELNRUU UNCURLED
CDEGOORS SCROOGED	CDEIINRT INDIRECT	CDEINOSZ ZINCODES	CDELOORS CROODLES
CDEGORSU SCOURGED	CDEIIOPR PERIODIC	CDEINOTU EDUCTION	DECOLORS
SCROUGED	CDEIIOPS EPISODIC	CDEINOUV UNVOICED	CDELOORU COLOURED
CDEGORSW SCROWDGE	CDEIIOPT EPIDOTIC	CDEINOUV CONVIVED	DECOLOUR
CDEHIILO HELICOID	CDEIIOSV OVICIDES	CDEINPRS PRESCIND	CDELOPSU UPCLOSED
CDEHIILS CEILIDHS	CDEIIPRR CIRRIPED	CDEINPRU UNPRICED	CDELOPTU OCTUPLED
CDEHIIMO HOMICIDE	CDEIIRST ICTERIDS	CDEINPSY DYSPNEIC	CDELORSS CORDLESS
CDEHIIMR CHIMERID	CDEIIRTU DIURETIC	CDEINRRU INCURRED	SCOLDERS
CDEHIINO ECHINOID	CDEIIRUV VIRUCIDE	CDEINRSS DISCERNS	CDELORSU CLOSURED
CDEHIIVV CHIVVIED	CDEIISSU SUICIDES	RESCINDS	CDELORSW CLOWDERS
CDEHIKOS HOICKSED	CDEIISTT DICTIEST	CDEINRSU INDUCERS	SCROWLED
CDEHIKRW HERDWICK	CDEIJNOO COJOINED	CDEINRUV INCURVED	CDELORTU CLOTURED
CDEHILMR MERCHILD	CDEIJSST DISJECTS	CDEINSSX EXSCINDS	CDELOSSU DULCOSES
CDEHILNR CHILDREN	CDEIKLNO INLOCKED	CDEINSTY SYNDETIC	CDELOSTU LOCUSTED
CDEHILOR CHLORIDE	CDEIKLNR CRINKLED	CDEIOORS CORODIES	CDELPRSU SCRUPLED
CDEHILOS CHELOIDS	CDEIKLNU UNLICKED	CDEIOPRT DEPICTOR	CDELPRUU UPCURLED
CDEHILRT ELDRITCH	CDEIKLOS SIDELOCK	CDEIOPST DESPOTIC	CDELPSTU SCULPTED
CDEHIMOT METHODIC	CDEIKLPR PRICKLED	CDEIORRT CREDITOR	CDELRSSU SCUDLERS
CDEHIMRS SMIRCHED	CDEIKLRT TRICKLED	DIRECTOR	CDELRSUY CURSEDLY
CDEHINNR INDRENCH	CDEIKLST STICKLED	CDEIORRV DIVORCER	CDELRTUU CULTURED
CDEHINOS HEDONICS	CDEIKLWY WICKEDLY	CDEIORSS DISCOERS	CDELSSTU DUCTLESS
CDEHINQU QUINCHED	CDEIKMSU MUSICKED	CDEIORST CORDITES	CDELSTTU SCUTTLED
CDEHINST SNITCHED	CDEIKNPU UNPICKED	CDEIORSU DISCOURE	CDEMMNOO COMMONED
CDEHIOOR OCHIDORE	CDEIKNTU TUNICKED	CDEIORSV DISCOVER	CDEMMNOS COMMENDS
CDEHIOSW COWHIDES	CDEIKOSS KOSSDIES	DIVORCES	CDEMMNOU COMMUNED
CDEHIOTY THEODICY	CDEIKOSY YOICKSED	CDEIORSW CROWDIES	CDEMMOOS COMMODES
CDEHIQTU QUITCHED	CDEIKOSZ DOCKIZES	CDEIORSY DECISORY	CDEMMOOV COMMOVED
CDEHIRST DITCHERS	CDEIKRRS DERRICKS	CDEIORTU OUTCRIED	CDEMMOTU COMMUTED
CDEHISTT STITCHED	CDEIKSTU DUCKIEST	CDEIOSST CESTOIDS	CDEMMRSU SCRUMMED
CDEHISTW SWITCHED	CDEILLOR COLLIDER	CDEIOSTT COTTISED	CDEMNNOS CONDEMNS
CDEHITTW TWITCHED	CDEILLOS CODILLES	CDEIPRSS DISCERPS	CDEMNOOW COMEDOWN
CDEHKLSU SHELDUCK	COLLIDES	CDEIPRST PREDICTS	CDEMNOPS COMPENDS
CDEHKSUY HEYDUCKS	CDEILLOU LODICULE	SCRIPTED	CDEMNOSU CONSUMED
CDEHLOOS DESCHOOL	CDEILLPU PELLUCID	CDEIPRSY CYPRIDES	CDEMNOTU DOCUMENT

CDEMNSUU	SECUNDUM	CDHILOOS	DOLICHOS
CDEMOOPS	COMPOSED	CDHIMOSU	DOCHMIUS
CDEMOPTU	COMPUTED	CDHINNOR	CHONDRIN
CDEMORSU	DECORUMS	CDHIOOPW	WOODCHIP
CDEMOSTU	COSTUMED	CDHIOORS	CHOROIDS
	CUSTOMED	CDHIOORT	TROCHOID
CDEMPRSU	SCRUMPED	CDHIOPRW	WHIPCORD
CDENNOOS	CONDONES	CDHIOPRY	HYDROPIC
CDENNOOT	CONNOTED	CDHIOPSY	PSYCHOID
CDENNOST	CONTENDS	CDHIORRT	TRICHORD
CDENNOUY	UNCOYNED	CDHIOSUV	DISVOUCH
CDENOORT	CREODONT	CDHIPSTY	DIPTYCHS
CDENOOST	SECODONT	CDHKOORS	HORDOCKS
CDENOOTT	COTTONED	CDHLOOPY	COPYHOLD
CDENOOVY	CONVOYED	CDHNORSU	CHONDRUS
CDENORSS	CORSNEDS	CDHOORRU	UROCHORD
CDENORTU	CORNUTED	CDIIIMNU	INDICIUM
	TROUNCED	CDIIIORT	DIORITIC
CDENOSTU	CONTUSED	CDIIKPST	DIPSTICK
CDENRSUU	UNCURSED	CDIILMOS	DOMICILS
CDENRTUU	UNDERCUT	CDIILOTY	DOCILITY
CDENRUUV	UNCURVED	CDIILTUY	LUCIDITY
CDEOOPPS	COPEPODS	CDIIMNOU	CONIDIUM
CDEOOPRS	SCROOPED		ONCIDIUM
CDEOOPST	POSTCODE	CDIINOOS	ISODICON
CDEOORRS	CORRODES		ONISCOID
CDEOORSU	DECOROUS	CDIINORS	CRINOIDS
CDEOORSV	VOCODERS	CDIINOST	DICTIONS
CDEOOSTV	DOVECOTS	CDIINPRY	CYPRINID
CDEOPRRU	PROCURED	CDIINSTT	DISTINCT
	PRODUCER	CDIIOORS	SORICOID
CDEOPRSU	PRODUCES	CDIIOPRT	DIOPTRIC
CDEOQSTU	DOCQUETS	CDIIORSU	SCIUROID
CDEORRSW	CROWDERS	CDIIOSSS	CISSOIDS
CDEORSST	DOCTRESS	CDIIPTUY	CUPIDITY
CDEORSSU	SCOURSED		PUDICITY
CDEORSSW	SCOWDERS	CDIIRSTT	DISTRICT
CDEORSTU	EDUCTORS	CDIJNSTU	DISJUNCT
	SEDUCTOR	CDIKKNOW	KICKDOWN
CDEORSUU	DOUCEURS	CDIKNORS	DORNICKS
CDEOSSTU	CUSTODES	CDIKNOSW	WINDOCKS
CDEPRSTY	DECRYPTS		WINDSOCK
CDEPRUUV	UPCURVED	CDILLOOS	COLLOIDS
CDERSTTU	DESTRUCT	CDILLOTU	DULCITOL
CDFIILSU	FLUIDICS	CDILLOUY	CLOUDILY
CDFIKMNU	MINDFUCK	CDILOOPS	PODSOLIC
CDFIKORS	DISFROCK	CDILOORS	DISCOLOR
CDFNNOOU	CONFOUND	CDILOORT	LORDOTIC
CDGHIILN	CHILDING	CDILOOTY	COTYLOID
CDGHIINS	CHIDINGS	CDILOSST	DISCLOST
CDGHIINT	DICHTING	CDILOSTY	SCOLYTID
	DITCHING	CDIMMOSU	MODICUMS
CDGHINNU	DUNCHING	CDIMOORT	MICRODOT
CDGHINOR	CHORDING	CDINNQUU	QUIDNUNC
CDGHINOU	DOUCHING	CDINOOOR	CORONOID
CDGIINNU	INDUCING	CDINORSW	DISCROWN
CDGIINOS	DISCOING	CDINORTU	INDUCTOR
CDGIKLNU	DUCKLING	CDINOSTU	CONDUITS
CDGIKLOR	GRIDLOCK		DISCOUNT
CDGIKNOS	DOCKINGS		NOCTUIDS
CDGIKNSU	DUCKINGS	CDINOSTY	DYSTONIC
CDGILNOS	CODLINGS	CDIOOPRS	PROSODIC
	SCOLDING	CDIOORRR	CORRIDOR
CDGILNOU	CLOUDING	CDIOPRSU	CUSPIDOR
CDGILNRU	CURDLING	CDIOSSTY	CYSTOIDS
CDGINORS	CORDINGS	CDIOSTUV	OVIDUCTS
CDGINORW	CROWDING	CDJLNOUY	JOCUNDLY
CDGNOOOS	COONDOGS	CDKMMORU	DRUMMOCK
CDHHIILS	CHILDISH	CDKNNOSU	DUNNOCKS
CDHIILTW	TWICHILD	CDKOOORW	CORKWOOD
CDHIINST	CHINDITS	CDLLLOOP	CLODPOLL
CDHIIOST	CHORIOID	CDLNOSUU	UNCLOUDS
CDHIIORT	HIDROTIC	CDLNOUUY	UNCLOUDY
	TRICHOID	CDLOOOTW	COLTWOOD
CDHIIOSZ	SCHIZOID	CDLOOPSY	LYCOPODS
CDHIISST	DISTICHS	CDLOORTY	DOCTORLY
CDHILNSU	UNCHILDS	CDLOOSTU	OUTSCOLD
CDHILOOP	CHILOPOD	CDMNOOPU	COMPOUND
		CDMNORUU	CORUNDUM

CDMOSSUW	MUDSCOWS	CEEEMNRT	CEMENTER
CDNNOOOT	CONODONT		CEREMENT
CDNNOSTU	CONTUNDS	CEEEMPRS	EMPERCES
CDOOOPST	OCTOPODS	CEEEMRTY	CEMETERY
CDOORRUY	CORDUROY	CEEENNPT	TENPENCE
CDOOSTUW	WOODCUTS	CEEENNST	SENTENCE
CDOPRSTU	PRODUCTS	CEEENPRS	PRESENCE
CDORSSUW	CUSSWORD	CEEENPRT	PRETENCE
CEEEEGHS	GEECHEES	CEEENQSU	SEQUENCE
CEEEEHLS	LEECHEES	CEEENRRS	SCREENER
CEEEELST	SELECTEE	CEEENRRT	RECENTER
CEEEEPRS	PRECEESE		RECENTRE
CEEEFFIR	EFFIERCE	CEEENRSS	RECENSES
CEEEFFRT	EFFECTER	CEEENSSS	ESSENCES
CEEEFHLS	FLEECHES	CEEENSST	CENTESES
CEEEFILR	FLEECIER	CEEEPRRS	CREEPERS
CEEEFINR	ENFIERCE	CEEEPRTX	EXPECTER
CEEEFLRS	FLEECERS	CEEERRST	ERECTERS
CEEEFNOR	CONFEREE	CEEERRSV	SCREEVER
CEEEGIMN	EMCEEING	CEEERRTX	EXCRETER
CEEEGINS	EGENCIES	CEEERSSS	RECESSES
CEEEGINX	EXIGENCE	CEEERSST	SECRETES
CEEEGITX	EXEGETIC		SESTERCE
CEEEGMNR	MERGENCE	CEEERSSU	CEREUSES
CEEEGNRS	REGENCES	CEEERSSV	SCREEVES
CEEEGNRV	VERGENCE	CEEERSTX	EXCRETES
CEEEHIKR	CHEEKIER	CEEERTTV	CREVETTE
CEEEHIRR	CHEERIER	CEEERTUX	EXECUTER
	REECHIER	CEEESSSX	EXCESSES
CEEEHIRS	CHEESIER	CEEESTUX	EXECUTES
CEEEHLRV	CHEVEREL	CEEFFNOS	OFFENCES
CEEEHLSS	SLEECHES	CEEFFORS	EFFORCES
CEEEHMSS	SMEECHES	CEEFFORT	EFFECTOR
CEEEHNNP	PENNEECH	CEEFGILN	FLEECING
CEEEHNRS	ENCHEERS	CEEFHIKR	KERCHIEF
CEEEHPRS	CHEEPERS	CEEFHIRY	CHIEFERY
CEEEHPSS	SPEECHES	CEEFHISS	CHIEFESS
CEEEHRRS	CHEERERS	CEEFHIST	CHIEFEST
CEEEHRSS	CREESHES		FETICHES
	SECESHER	CEEFHLNS	FLENCHES
CEEEHRSW	ESCHEWER	CEEFHLRT	FLETCHER
CEEEHRVY	CHEVERYE	CEEFHLRU	CHEERFUL
CEEEHSSS	SECESHES	CEEFHLST	FLETCHES
CEEEIJTV	EJECTIVE	CEEFHRST	FECHTERS
CEEEIKRR	CREEKIER	CEEFIINT	INFICETE
CEEEILNN	LENIENCE	CEEFILRT	TELFERIC
CEEEILNS	LICENSEE	CEEFILRY	FIERCELY
CEEEILNT	TELECINE	CEEFINPP	FIPPENCE
CEEEILRS	CELERIES	CEEFINRT	FRENETIC
CEEEILRT	ERECTILE	CEEFIPRT	PERFECTI
CEEEILTV	CLEVEITE	CEEFIRST	FIERCEST
	ELECTIVE	CEEFKLRS	FLECKERS
CEEEIMNN	EMINENCE		FRECKLES
CEEEIMPR	EMPIERCE	CEEFKLSS	FECKLESS
CEEEIMRR	REREMICE	CEEFLNOR	FLORENCE
CEEEINNT	ENCEINTE	CEEFLNSU	FLUENCES
CEEEINPR	PIECENER	CEEFLNTU	FECULENT
CEEEINPS	EPICENES	CEEFLRST	REFLECTS
CEEEINRS	CERESINE	CEEFNORR	CONFRERE
CEEEINSS	ESNECIES		ENFORCER
CEEEIPRR	CREEPIER		RENFORCE
	CREPERIE	CEEFNORS	ENFORCES
CEEEIPRS	CREEPIES	CEEFNRVY	FERVENCY
CEEEIPRV	PERCEIVE	CEEFOPRR	PERFORCE
CEEEIRRV	RECEIVER	CEEFOPRT	PERFECTO
CEEEIRSV	RECEIVES	CEEFORRS	FRESCOER
CEEEIRSX	EXERCISE	CEEFORSS	FRESCOES
CEEEIRTV	ERECTIVE	CEEFPRST	PERFECTS
CEEEJRRT	REJECTER		PREFECTS
CEEEKNNP	PENNEECK	CEEGHIKN	CHEEKING
CEEELLNR	CRENELLE	CEEGHILN	LEECHING
CEEELLSU	ECUELLES	CEEGHINP	CHEEPING
CEEELPSY	YCLEEPES	CEEGHINR	CHEERING
CEEELRRV	CLEVERER		REECHING
CEEELRST	RESELECT	CEEGHINS	CHEESING
CEEELRTT	ELECTRET	CEEGHLOW	COGWHEEL
	TERCELET	CEEGIJNT	EJECTING
CEEELSST	CELESTES	CEEGIKLN	CLEEKING
CEEEMNNS	SCENEMEN	CEEGILNP	CLEEPING

CEEGILNT ELECTING
CEEGILOT ECLOGITE
CEEGILRS CLERGIES
CEEGILRT TELERGIC
CEEGIMNS MISCEGEN
CEEGINOO COOEEING
CEEGINOR EROGENIC
CEEGINPR CREEPING
CEEGINRS CREESING
    GENERICS
CEEGINRT ERECTING
    GENTRICE
CEEGINST GENETICS
CEEGINSU EUGENICS
CEEGINXY EXIGENCY
CEEGIORX EXOERGIC
CEEGLLOR COLLEGER
CEEGLLOS COLLEGES
CEEGLNST NEGLECTS
CEEGLOSU ECLOGUES
CEEGMMOR COMMERGE
CEEGNNOO ONCOGENE
CEEGNNOR CONGENER
CEEGNNPU PUNGENCE
CEEGNORS COGENERS
    CONGREES
CEEGNORT CONGREET
    COREGENT
CEEGNORV CONVERGE
CEEGNOTY ECTOGENY
CEEGNRSU URGENCES
CEEGNRVY VERGENCY
CEEGORST CORTEGES
CEEGQRSU GRECQUES
CEEHHMNN HENCHMEN
CEEHHSTT THETCHES
CEEHIIST ETHICISE
CEEHIITZ ETHICIZE
CEEHIKLY CHEEKILY
CEEHIKNW CHEEWINK
CEEHILLN CHENILLE
CEEHILLV CHEVILLE
CEEHILRT TELECHIR
CEEHILRV CHEVERIL
CEEHILRW CLERIHEW
CEEHILRY CHEERILY
CEEHILSV VEHICLES
CEEHILSW SWELCHIE
CEEHIMMS CHEMMIES
CEEHIMRS CHIMERES
CEEHIMRT HERMETIC
CEEHIMSS CHEMISES
CEEHINOR COINHERE
CEEHINPR ENCIPHER
CEEHINPT PHENETIC
CEEHINRS ENRICHES
    INHERCES
CEEHINST SITHENCE
CEEHINSX CHENIXES
CEEHINTT ENTHETIC
CEEHIORS CHEERIOS
CEEHIOSS ECHOISES
CEEHIOSV COHESIVE
CEEHIOSZ ECHOIZES
CEEHIPRT HERPETIC
CEEHIRRR CHERRIER
CEEHIRRS CHERRIES
CEEHIRRT CHERTIER
CEEHIRSS RICHESSE
CEEHIRST CHESTIER
    HERETICS
CEEHIRTT TETCHIER
CEEHIRTU HEURETIC
CEEHIRTV VETCHIER
CEEHISTT TECHIEST
CEEHISTW CHEWIEST
CEEHKLRS HECKLERS
CEEHKNPS HENPECKS
CEEHKRST SKETCHER

CEEHKRTV KVETCHER
CEEHKSST SKETCHES
CEEHKSTV KVETCHES
CEEHLNOS CHELONES
    ECHELONS
CEEHLNOT ENCLOTHE
CEEHLNPU PENUCHLE
CEEHLNSU ELENCHUS
CEEHLORT RECLOTHE
CEEHLOSS ECHOLESS
CEEHLOSW COWHEELS
CEEHLQSU QUELCHES
CEEHLRSW WELCHERS
CEEHLSSS CHESSELS
CEEHMNOR CHROMENE
CEEHMNSS CHESSMEN
    MENSCHES
CEEHMORT COMETHER
CEEHMRSS SCHEMERS
CEEHMRST MERCHETS
CEEHNNOW NOWHENCE
CEEHNNRT ENTRENCH
CEEHNORT COHERENT
CEEHNORV CHEVERON
CEEHNPSU PENUCHES
CEEHNQRU QUENCHER
CEEHNQSU QUENCHES
CEEHNRRT RETRENCH
    TRENCHER
CEEHNRST TRENCHES
CEEHNRSW WENCHERS
    WRENCHES
CEEHRTTU TEUCHTER
CEEHNSST STENCHES
CEEHOPRY CORYPHEE
CEEHOPTT POCHETTE
CEEHORRS COHERERS
    COSHERER
CEEHORRT HECTORER
    TORCHERE
CEEHORSS ORCHESES
CEEHORST TROCHEES
CEEHOSUV VOUCHEES
CEEHPRRS PERCHERS
CEEHPRRY PERCHERY
CEEHPRSU UPCHEERS
CEEHPSST SPETCHES
CEEHQRSU CHEQUERS
CEEHQSTU QUETCHES
CEEHRSTW WRETCHES
CEEHRTTU TEUCHTER
CEEHSTTU TEUCHEST
CEEIIMPR EPIMERIC
CEEIIMRT EREMITIC
CEEIINRT ICTERINE
CEEIINST NICETIES
CEEIINVV EVINCIVE
CEEIIPRS EPICIERS
CEEIIRST SERICITE
CEEIJNOT EJECTION
CEEIJORR REJOICER
CEEIJORS REJOICES
CEEIJRUV VERJUICE
CEEIKKSS KECKSIES
CEEIKLNN NECKLINE
CEEIKLPR PICKEREL
CEEIKNRS SICKENER
CEEIKNST NECKTIES
CEEIKPRS PICKEERS
    SPECKIER
CEEIKPRT PICKETER
CEEILLLP PELLICLE
CEEILLMS MICELLES
CEEILLNT LENTICEL
    LENTICLE
CEEILMOR COMELIER
CEEILMPS SEMPLICE
CEEILNNT CENTINEL
CEEILNNY LENIENCY
CEEILNOS CINEOLES

CEEILNOT COTELINE
    ELECTION
CEEILNOV VIOLENCE
CEEILNPX CINEPLEX
CEEILNRR RECLINER
CEEILNRS LICENSER
    RECLINES
    SILENCER
CEEILNRU CERULEIN
CEEILNRV VERNICLE
CEEILNSS ENCLISES
    LICENSES
    SILENCES
CEEILNSU LEUCINES
CEEILORR RECOILER
CEEILOSS SOLECISE
CEEILOSZ SOLECIZE
CEEILPSS ECLIPSES
CEEILQSU LIQUESCE
CEEILRST RETICLES
    SCLERITE
    TIERCELS
CEEILRSU CISELEUR
    CISELURE
    RECUILES
CEEILRSV VERSICLE
CEEILRTU RETICULE
CEEILRTY CELERITY
CEEILSSV CLEVISES
    VESICLES
    VICELESS
CEEILSTT TELESTIC
    TESTICLE
CEEILSTU LEUCITES
CEEIMMPY EMPYEMIC
CEEIMMRS MESMERIC
CEEIMNNY EMINENCY
CEEIMNPS SPECIMEN
CEEIMNST CENTIMES
CEEIMORT METEORIC
CEEIMSTT SMECTITE
CEEINNOT NEOTENIC
CEEINNRS INCENSER
CEEINNRT INCENTRE
CEEINNSS INCENSES
    NICENESS
CEEINNST NESCIENT
CEEINORR ENCIERRO
CEEINORT ERECTION
    NEOTERIC
CEEINORV OVERNICE
CEEINORX EXOCRINE
CEEINOSS SENECIOS
CEEINOST ICESTONE
    SEICENTO
CEEINOTV EVECTION
CEEINPRT PRENTICE
CEEINPST PECTINES
    PENTICES
CEEINPSX SIXPENCE
CEEINRRS SINCERER
CEEINRSS CERESINS
    SCRIENES
CEEINRST CENTRIES
    ENTERICS
    ENTICERS
    SCIENTER
    SECRETIN
CEEINRSU INSECURE
    SINECURE
CEEINRTT RETICENT
CEEINRTU CENTIURE
    ENURETIC
CEEINSST CENTESIS
CEEINSTY CYSTEINE
CEEIOPPR PERICOPE
CEEIOPPS EPISCOPE
CEEIOPST ECTOPIES
    PICOTEES

CEEIORST COTERIES
    ESOTERIC
CEEIORSX EXORCISE
CEEIORTT EROTETIC
CEEIORTX EXOTERIC
CEEIORXZ EXORCIZE
CEEIOSTV COVETISE
CEEIPPRT PRECEPIT
CEEIPPTU EUPEPTIC
CEEIPRRS PIERCERS
    PRECISER
CEEIPRSS PRECISES
CEEIPRST CREPIEST
    RECEIPTS
CEEIPRSU EPICURES
CEEIPSST PECTISES
CEEIPSTZ PECTIZES
CEEIQSSU QUIESCES
CEEIRRSS CERRISES
CEEIRRST RECITERS
CEEIRRSW SCREWIER
CEEIRRTU URETERIC
CEEIRSSV SCRIEVES
    SERVICES
CEEIRSTT TIERCETS
CEEIRSTU CERUSITE
    CUTESIER
    EUCRITES
CEEIRSTV VERTICES
CEEIRSTX EXCITERS
CEEIRSVX CERVIXES
CEEISSST CITESSES
CEEISTTZ ZETETICS
CEEISUVX EXCUSIVE
CEEJKOTT JOCKETTE
CEEJORRT REJECTOR
CEEJORST EJECTORS
CEEKKNPS KENSPECK
CEEKLNST NECKLETS
CEEKLPSS SPECKLES
CEEKLRSS CLERKESS
    RECKLESS
CEEKNORR RECKONER
CEEKNRSU SUCKENER
CEEKORRT CORKTREE
    ROCKETER
CEEKOSSY SOCKEYES
CEEKOSTT SOCKETTE
CEEKPRSY RYEPECKS
CEEKRRSW WRECKERS
CEELLLSU CELLULES
CEELLMOU MOLECULE
CEELLNOS COLLEENS
CEELLNOU NUCLEOLE
CEELLORT RECOLLET
CEELLOSS CELLOSES
CEELLPSU PUCELLES
CEELLRRU CRUELLER
CEELLRVY CLEVERLY
CEELLSSU CLUELESS
CEELMOOS COELOMES
CEELMOPT COMPLETE
CEELMORW WELCOMER
CEELMOST TELECOMS
CEELMOSW WELCOMES
CEELMRTU ELECTRUM
CEELNNOP PENONCEL
CEELNNOT CENTONEL
CEELNOPU OPULENCE
CEELNORS ENCLOSER
CEELNORT ELECTRON
CEELNORU ENCOLURE
CEELNOSS ENCLOSES
CEELNPTU CENTUPLE
CEELNRST LECTERNS
CEELNRSU LUCERNES
CEELNRTU RELUCENT
CEELNRTY RECENTLY
CEELNSTU ESCULENT

CEELORSS	CORELESS	CEEORSTX	CORTEXES
	RECLOSES	CEEORTTV	CORVETTE
	SCLEROSE	CEEORTUX	EXECUTOR
CEELORST	CORSELET	CEEOSSST	CESTOSES
	ELECTORS	CEEOSTTT	OCTETTES
	ELECTROS	CEEPPRST	PERCEPTS
	SELECTOR		PRECEPTS
CEELORSY	RECOYLES	CEEPPRSU	PREPUCES
CEELORTV	COVERLET	CEEPRRSU	PRECURSE
CEELOSSU	COLEUSES	CEEPRSST	RESPECTS
CEELOSTU	ELOCUTES		SCEPTERS
CEELOSTV	COVELETS		SCEPTRES
CEELPRST	PLECTRES		SPECTERS
	PRELECTS		SPECTRES
CEELRRTU	LECTURER	CEEPRSTX	EXCERPTS
CEELRSST	LECTRESS	CEERRSST	RECTRESS
CEELRSSU	CURELESS	CEERRSSU	RESCUERS
	RECLUSES		SECURERS
CEELRSTU	LECTURES	CEERRSSW	SCREWERS
CEELRSTY	SECRETLY	CEERRSUV	RECURVES
CEELRSUY	SECURELY	CEERRTUZ	CREUTZER
CEELSTTU	LETTUCES	CEERSSST	CRESSETS
CEEMMNTU	CEMENTUM	CEERSSTU	SECUREST
CEEMMORS	COMMERES	CEERSSTW	SETSCREW
CEEMNORR	CREMORNE	CEERSSUX	EXCURSES
CEEMNORW	NEWCOMER		EXCUSERS
CEEMNORY	CEREMONY	CEERSTTU	CURETTES
CEEMNOYZ	COENZYME	CEERTUXY	EXECUTRY
CEEMNRSU	CERUMENS	CEESTTUV	CUVETTES
CEEMOORV	OVERCOME	CEFFHIRU	CHUFFIER
CEEMOORW	OWRECOME	CEFFIILR	CLIFFIER
CEEMOPRS	COMPEERS	CEFFIORS	OFFICERS
	COMPERES	CEFFIORU	COIFFEUR
CEEMOPST	COMPETES		COIFFURE
CEEMOSSS	COSMESES	CEFFIRSU	SUFFICER
CEEMSSTU	TUMESCES	CEFFISSU	SUFFICES
CEENNORT	CRETONNE	CEFFLORU	FORCEFUL
CEENNORU	RENOUNCE	CEFFLRSU	SCUFFLER
CEENNORV	CONVENER	CEFFLSSU	SCUFFLES
CEENNOST	CENTONES	CEFFORSS	SCOFFERS
CEENNOSV	CONVENES	CEFFORST	COFFRETS
CEENNRST	CENTNERS	CEFGHINT	FECHTING
CEENOPST	POTENCES		FETCHING
CEENOPTW	TWOPENCE	CEFGIKLN	FLECKING
CEENORSS	NECROSES	CEFGINNS	FENCINGS
CEENORSV	CONSERVE	CEFGLNUY	FULGENCY
	CONVERSE	CEFHIIMS	MISCHIEF
CEENORSZ	COZENERS	CEFHILNR	FLINCHER
CEENORTT	TRECENTO	CEFHILNS	FLINCHES
CEENORVY	CONVEYER	CEFHILRS	FILCHERS
	RECONVEY	CEFHILRT	FLICHTER
CEENOSVX	CONVEXES	CEFHILST	FLITCHES
CEENPPTU	TUPPENCE	CEFHINSU	FUCHSINE
CEENPRSS	SPENCERS	CEFHISTT	FITCHETS
CEENPSSU	SUSPENCE	CEFHISTU	FUCHSITE
CEENRSSU	CENSURES	CEFHISTW	FITCHEWS
CEENRSTU	UNSECRET	CEFHLSSY	FLYSCHES
CEENSSSU	CENSUSES	CEFHLSTU	CHESTFUL
CEENSTTU	CUTENESS		FUTCHELS
CEENSTTU	CUNETTES	CEFIIIST	CITIFIES
CEEOORRW	ORECROWE	CEFIILRT	CLIFTIER
CEEOORST	CREOSOTE	CEFIILST	FELSITIC
CEEOPRRT	RECEPTOR	CEFIILTY	FELICITY
CEEOPRTX	EXCEPTOR	CEFIIOPR	OPIFICER
CEEOPRTY	CEROTYPE	CEFIIORS	ORIFICES
CEEOPSST	PECTOSES	CEFIIPRT	PETRIFIC
CEEOPSTY	ECOTYPES	CEFIIRRT	FERRITIC
CEEOQTTU	COQUETTE		TERRIFIC
CEEORRRS	SORCERER	CEFIISTY	CITYFIES
CEEORRSS	RESCORES	CEFIKLOR	FIRELOCK
CEEORRST	ERECTORS	CEFIKLRS	FLICKERS
CEEORRSU	RECOURES	CEFIKLST	FICKLEST
	RECOURSE	CEFILLLO	FOLLICLE
	RESOURCE	CEFILMRU	CRIMEFUL
CEEORRSV	RECOVERS		MERCIFUL
CEEORRSW	RECOWERS	CEFILNOT	FLECTION
CEEORRVY	RECOVERY	CEFILNST	INFLECTS
CEEORSTW	COWTREES	CEFILNSU	FUNICLES
		CEFILOUV	VOICEFUL

CEFILRSU	LUCIFERS	CEGIINPR	PIERCING
CEFIMOST	COMFIEST	CEGIINRT	RECITING
CEFINNOR	CONFINER	CEGIINSS	GNEISSIC
CEFINNOS	CONFINES	CEGIINSX	EXCISING
CEFINORS	FORENSIC	CEGIINTV	EVICTING
	FORINSEC	CEGIINTX	EXCITING
	FORNICES	CEGIIOST	EGOISTIC
	INFORCES	CEGIJLOU	LOGJUICE
CEFINORT	INFECTOR	CEGIKKLN	KECKLING
CEFINOSX	CONFIXES	CEGIKLNR	CLERKING
CEFINOTT	CONFETTI		RECKLING
CEFIOPRS	FORCIPES	CEGIKNNS	NECKINGS
CEFIORTY	FEROCITY		SNECKING
CEFIRRSU	SCURFIER	CEGIKNPS	PECKINGS
CEFIRSTU	FRUTICES		SPECKING
CEFIRTUV	FRUCTIVE	CEGIKNRT	TRECKING
CEFKLLOS	ELFLOCKS	CEGIKNRW	WRECKING
CEFKLOOR	FORELOCK	CEGIKSTU	GUCKIEST
CEFKLOST	FETLOCKS	CEGILMMN	CLEMMING
CEFKLRUW	WRECKFUL	CEGILNOO	NEOLOGIC
CEFLLOSU	FLOSCULE	CEGILNOS	ECLOSING
CEFLNOSU	FLOUNCES	CEGILNPU	CUPELING
CEFLNRUU	FURUNCLE	CEGILNRS	CLINGERS
CEFLNSTU	SCENTFUL		CRINGLES
CEFMORSY	COMFREYS	CEGILNRU	RECULING
CEFNORSU	FROUNCES		ULCERING
CEFNOSSU	CONFUSES	CEGILNRY	GLYCERIN
CEFNOSTU	CONFUTES	CEGILNSU	LUCIGENS
CEFORRST	CROFTERS	CEGILNSY	GLYCINES
CEFORSTU	FRUCTOSE	CEGILNTU	CULTIGEN
CEFOSSSU	FOCUSSES	CEGIMNOY	MYOGENIC
CEGGHIRS	CHIGGERS	CEGIMNSU	MUCIGENS
CEGGILOO	GEOLOGIC	CEGIMNUY	GYNECIUM
CEGGILOR	COGGIER	CEGINNOR	ENCORING
	COGGLIER	CEGINNOZ	COZENING
CEGGILRS	SCRIGGLE	CEGINNRS	SCERNING
CEGGINNO	CONGEING	CEGINNRT	CENTRING
CEGGINOO	GEOGONIC	CEGINNST	SCENTING
CEGGIORS	GEORGICS	CEGINNSY	ENSIGNCY
	SCROGGIE	CEGINOOP	GEOPONIC
CEGGLNOY	GLYCOGEN	CEGINOOR	OROGENIC
CEGGLORS	CLOGGERS	CEGINOOY	COOEYING
CEGHHINT	HECHTING	CEGINOOZ	ZOOGENIC
CEGHIINY	HYGIENIC	CEGINOPR	COPERING
CEGHIKLN	HECKLING	CEGINOPY	PYOGENIC
CEGHIKNT	KETCHING	CEGINORT	GERONTIC
CEGHILNT	LETCHING	CEGINORV	COVERING
CEGHILNW	WELCHING	CEGINORW	COWERING
CEGHILST	GLITCHES	CEGINOSS	COGNISES
CEGHIMNS	SCHEMING	CEGINOSZ	COGNIZES
CEGHINNW	WENCHING	CEGINOTV	COVETING
CEGHINOR	COHERING	CEGINRRS	CRINGERS
	OCHERING	CEGINRRU	RECURING
CEGHINPR	PERCHING	CEGINRST	CRESTING
CEGHINRT	RETCHING	CEGINRSU	RECUSING
CEGHINRU	EUCHRING		RESCUING
CEGHINST	CHESTING		SCUNGIER
	ETCHINGS		SECURING
CEGHINVY	CHEVYING	CEGINRSW	SCREWING
CEGHIRSS	SCREIGHS	CEGINRSY	SYNERGIC
CEGHIRTU	THEURGIC	CEGINRTU	ERUCTING
CEGHISTU	GUICHETS	CEGINSUX	EXCUSING
CEGHMRUY	CHEMURGY	CEGIRSTU	SCUTIGER
CEGHNORS	GROSCHEN	CEGKLNOS	GENLOCKS
CEGHORSU	CHOREGUS	CEGKLORS	GROCKLES
	COUGHERS	CEGLLOOU	COLLOGUE
	GROUCHES	CEGLLORY	GLYCEROL
CEGHRSTU	GRUTCHES	CEGLLRYY	GLYCERYL
	GUTCHERS	CEGLNOOS	COLOGNES
CEGIILNR	CLINGIER	CEGLNOTY	COGENTLY
CEGIILNS	CEILINGS	CEGLOOOY	OECOLOGY
	CIELINGS	CEGLOOTY	CETOLOGY
CEGIILNT	GENTILIC	CEGLOSSU	GLUCOSES
CEGIILOP	EPILOGIC	CEGLOSSY	GLYCOSES
CEGIILOS	LOGICISE	CEGMNNOO	COGNOMEN
CEGIILOZ	LOGICIZE	CEGNNOOS	ONCOGENS
CEGIINNT	ENTICING	CEGNNPUY	PUNGENCY
CEGIINNV	EVINCING	CEGNOOTY	GONOCYTE
		CEGNORSS	CONGRESS

```
CEGNORSU CONGRUES              HELICONS            SPITCHER   CEHNSTUY CHUTNEYS
         SCROUNGE     CEHILNPY PHENYLIC   CEHIPSST CHIPSETS   CEHOOORZ ZOOCHORE
CEGNORSY CRYOGENS     CEHILNSS CHINLESS   CEHIQSTU QUITCHES   CEHOORSS CHOOSERS
CEGNORYY CRYOGENY     CEHILNST LINCHETS   CEHIRSST STRICHES            SOROCHES
CEGNOSST CONGESTS              TINCHELS   CEHIRSTT CHITTERS   CEHOORST CHEROOTS
CEGOORSS SCROOGES     CEHILORT CHLORITE            RICHTEST   CEHOORSU OCHEROUS
CEGORRSU SCOURGER              CLOTHIER            STITCHER            OCHREOUS
         SCROUGER     CEHILORY HEROICLY   CEHIRSTY HYSTERIC   CEHOOSUW COWHOUSE
CEGORSSU SCOURGES     CEHILPRS PILCHERS   CEHIRTTW TWITCHER   CEHOPPRS CHOPPERS
         SCROUGES     CEHILPTY PHYLETIC   CEHIRTWY WITCHERY   CEHOPPRY PROPHECY
CEHHIIRT HITCHIER     CEHILRSV CHERVILS   CEHISSTT STITCHES   CEHOPRST POTCHERS
CEHHINPY HYPHENIC     CEHILSTT LICHTEST   CEHISSTU CUSHIEST   CEHOPRSY CORYPHES
CEHHIRST HITCHERS     CEHILSTW SWITCHEL   CEHISSTW SWITCHES   CEHORRST TORCHERS
CEHHNORU HURCHEON     CEHILTTY TETCHILY   CEHISSUW SUCHWISE   CEHORSSU CHORUSES
CEHHOOST HOOTCHES     CEHIMMRU CHUMMIER   CEHISTTW TWITCHES   CEHORSSZ SCHERZOS
CEHHOPTY HYPOTHEC     CEHIMMSS CHEMISMS   CEHKKRSU CHUKKERS   CEHORSTU SCOUTHER
CEHIIKNR CHINKIER     CEHIMMSU CHUMMIES   CEHKLLOS SKELLOCH            TOUCHERS
CEHIIKNS CHINKIES     CEHIMNNW WINCHMEN   CEHKLMOS HEMLOCKS   CEHORSTW SCOWTHER
CEHIILLR CHILLIER     CEHIMNOP PHONEMIC   CEHKLOOS KLOOCHES   CEHORSUV VOUCHERS
CEHIILLS CHILLIES     CEHIMNOR CHOIRMEN   CEHKLORS SHERLOCK   CEHOSSSU HOCUSSES
CEHIILMO HEMIOLIC     CEHIMNPT PITCHMEN   CEHKNPUY KEYPUNCH   CEHOSTTU COUTHEST
CEHIILNN LICHENIN     CEHIMNSY CHIMNEYS   CEHKORSS SHOCKERS   CEHOTTUZ ZUCHETTO
CEHIILNT LECITHIN     CEHIMOOT HOMEOTIC   CEHKPSTU KETCHUPS   CEHPRSTU PUTCHERS
CEHIILOT EOLITHIC     CEHIMORS MORICHES   CEHKRSSU SHUCKERS   CEHPSSTU PUTSCHES
CEHIIMOP HEMIOPIC     CEHIMORT CHROMITE   CEHKRSTU HUCKSTER   CEHRRSSU CRUSHERS
CEHIIMOS ISOCHEIM              TRICHOME   CEHLLMOS MOCHELLS   CEHRSSTY SCYTHERS
         ISOCHIME     CEHIMOSS ECHOISMS   CEHLLMSU MUCHELLS   CEHRSTTY STRETCHY
CEHIIMPT MEPHITIC     CEHIMOST MOCHIEST            SCHELLUM   CEHSSSSU SCHUSSES
CEHIIMST ETHICISM     CEHIMRSS SMIRCHES   CEHLLOSY YELLOCHS   CEIIILSV CIVILISE
CEHIINST ICHNITES     CEHIMSST CHEMISTS   CEHLLOUY LOUCHELY   CEIIILVZ CIVILIZE
CEHIIPPR CHIPPIER     CEHINNRT INTRENCH   CEHLMNOU HOMUNCLE   CEIIIMNT CIMINITE
CEHIIPPS CHIPPIES     CEHINOOS COHESION   CEHLMORS CHROMELS   CEIIINSS SINICISE
CEHIIPRR CHIRPIER     CEHINOPS CHOPINES   CEHLMSUY CHUMLEYS   CEIIINSV INCISIVE
CEHIIPRT PITCHIER     CEHINOPT PHONETIC   CEHLNNOU LUNCHEON   CEIIINSZ SINICIZE
CEHIIRST CHRISTIE     CEHINOPU EUPHONIC   CEHLNNSU CHUNNELS   CEIIJSTU JUICIEST
CEHIIRTT CHITTIER     CEHINORS CHORINES   CEHLNOST CHOLENTS   CEIIKLMR LIMERICK
         TITCHIER     CEHINORT NOTCHIER            NOTCHELS   CEIIKLRS SICKLIER
         TRICHITE     CEHINORU UNHEROIC   CEHLNOTU UNCLOTHE   CEIIKLRT TICKLIER
CEHIIRTW WITCHIER     CEHINOSY HYOSCINE   CEHLNRSU LUNCHERS   CEIIKLSS SICKLIES
CEHIISTT CHITTIES     CEHINOTY ONYCHITE   CEHLNSTY LYNCHETS   CEIIKMMR MIMICKER
         ETHICIST     CEHINPRS PINCHERS   CEHLOOSS SCHOOLES   CEIIKNRZ ZINCKIER
         ITCHIEST     CEHINPRU PUNCHIER   CEHLORST CHORTLES   CEIIKNSS KINESICS
         THEISTIC              UNCIPHER   CEHLORSU SLOUCHER   CEIIKNST KINETICS
         TICHIEST     CEHINPSU PENUCHIS   CEHLORTY HECTORLY   CEIIKPST PICKIEST
CEHIISVV CHIVVIES     CEHINQSU QUINCHES   CEHLOSSU SLOUCHES   CEIIKQSU QUICKIES
CEHIKLPT KLEPHTIC     CEHINRSS RICHNESS   CEHLOSTU SELCOUTH   CEIIKRRT TRICKIER
CEHIKLRS CLERKISH     CEHINRST CHRISTEN   CEHLPPSS SCHLEPPS   CEIIKRST STICKIER
CEHIKLSU SUCHLIKE              CITHERNS   CEHLPPSY SCHLEPPY   CEIIKSST EKISTICS
CEHIKMOS HOMESICK              SNITCHER   CEHLQSUY SQUELCHY            STICKIES
CEHIKNRU CHUNKIER     CEHINRTU RUTHENIC   CEHLRRSU LURCHERS   CEIILLMT MELLITIC
CEHIKNST CHETNIKS     CEHINSST SNITCHES   CEHLSTUY LECYTHUS   CEIILLOP POLLICIE
         KITCHENS     CEHINSTW WITCHENS   CEHMNRSU MUNCHERS   CEIILLPT ELLIPTIC
         KNITCHES     CEHINSTZ CHINTZES   CEHMNRTU TRUCHMEN   CEIILLSS SILICLES
         THICKENS     CEHIOORS CHOOSIER   CEHMNSSU MUCHNESS   CEIILLSU SILICULE
CEHIKNSW CHEWINKS              ISOCHORE   CEHMOORS MOOCHERS   CEIILMNT LIMNETIC
CEHIKOOS CHOOKIES     CEHIOPPR CHOPPIER   CEHMOOSS SMOOCHES   CEIILMOT CIMOLITE
CEHIKOSS HOICKSES     CEHIOPRS SOPHERIC   CEHMOOSZ SCHMOOZE   CEIILNNS INCLINES
CEHIKOST CHOKIEST     CEHIOPRU EUPHORIC   CEHMORSU MOUCHERS   CEIILNOS ISOCLINE
         THICKOES              POUCHIER   CEHMORUV OVERMUCH            SILICONE
CEHIKRSS KIRSCHES     CEHIOPSS HOSPICES   CEHMOSSU SMOUCHES   CEIILNQU CLINIQUE
         SHICKERS     CEHIOPST POSTICHE   CEHMSSTU SMUTCHES   CEIILNSS ENCLISIS
         SKRIECHS              POTICHES   CEHNNNOU NUNCHEON   CEIILOPP EPIPLOIC
CEHIKRSW WHICKERS     CEHIORRT RHETORIC   CEHNNOPU PUNCHEON            EPIPOLIC
CEHIKSST CHEKISTS              TORCHIER   CEHNNOSU NONESUCH   CEIILOPS POLICIES
         KITSCHES     CEHIORSS CHORISES            UNCHOSEN   CEIILORT ELICITOR
CEHIKSTT THICKEST              ORCHESIS   CEHNNRSU CHUNNERS   CEIILOTZ ZEOLITIC
         THICKETS              ORCHISES   CEHNOORS COEHORNS   CEIILPPS CLIPPIES
         THICKSET     CEHIORST ROTCHIES            SCHOONER   CEIILPRT PERLITIC
CEHIKTTY THICKETY              THEORICS   CEHNOPTU PUTCHEON   CEIILPRU PIRLICUE
CEHILLRS CHILLERS     CEHIORSW CHOWRIES   CEHNORST NOTCHERS   CEIILPTX EXPLICIT
         SCHILLER     CEHIORTT TROCHITE   CEHNORSV CHEVRONS   CEIILPTY PYELITIC
CEHILLST CHILLEST     CEHIORTU COUTHIER   CEHNORTU CHOUNTER   CEIILQRU CLIQUIER
CEHILMMS SCHIMMEL              TOUCHIER   CEHNORVY CHEVRONY   CEIILRSU SLUICIER
CEHILMSY CHIMLEYS     CEHIOSST ECHOISTS   CEHNPRSU PUNCHERS   CEIILRTV VERTICIL
CEHILMTY METHYLIC              TOISECHS   CEHNPSST PSCHENTS   CEIILSSS SCISSILE
CEHILNOP PHENOLIC     CEHIPPRS CHIPPERS   CEHNRSTU CHUNTERS   CEIIMNOT EMICTION
         PINOCHLE     CEHIPRRS CHIRPERS   CEHNSSSU SUCHNESS   CEIIMOPT EPITOMIC
CEHILNOR CHLORINE     CEHIPRSS SPHERICS   CEHNSSTU CHESNUTS   CEIIMORS ISOMERIC
CEHILNOS CHOLINES     CEHIPRST PITCHERS   CEHNSTTU CHESTNUT   CEIIMOST COMITIES
```

```
                   SEMIOTIC
CEIIMPRR  CRIMPIER
CEIIMPRS  EMPIRICS
CEIIMPSS  EPICISMS
CEIIMRRT  TRIMERIC
CEIIMRST  MERISTIC
          TRISEMIC
CEIINNOP  NEPIONIC
CEIINNOR  IRENICON
CEIINNOS  CONIINES
          OSCININE
CEIINNOT  NICOTINE
CEIINNRS  CINERINS
CEIINNRT  INTRINCE
CEIINNST  INSCIENT
CEIINOPS  EPINOSIC
CEIINOPT  EPITONIC
CEIINORS  RECISION
          SORICINE
CEIINOSS  ICONISES
CEIINOSV  INVOICES
CEIINOSX  EXCISION
CEIINOSZ  ICONIZES
CEIINOTV  EVICTION
CEIINPSS  PISCINES
CEIINRSS  SERICINS
CEIINRST  CITRINES
          CRINITES
          INCITERS
CEIINRSU  INCISURE
          SCIURINE
CEIINRTU  NEURITIC
CEIINSSU  CUISINES
CEIINSTU  CUTINISE
CEIINSTY  CYTISINE
          SYENITIC
CEIINSTZ  CITIZENS
          ZINCIEST
          ZINCITES
CEIINTUZ  CUTINIZE
CEIIOPRS  IRISCOPE
CEIIOPRT  PERIOTIC
CEIIOPTT  PICOTITE
CEIIOSTV  SOVIETIC
CEIIPRRS  CRISPIER
CEIIPRST  PICRITES
          PRICIEST
CEIIPSST  EPICISTS
          SPICIEST
CEIIQRTU  CRITIQUE
CEIIRSSU  CRUISIES
CEIIRSTT  RECTITIS
CEIIRSTV  VERISTIC
CEIISSST  CISSIEST
CEIISTVV  VIVISECT
CEIJNORT  INJECTOR
CEIJNOUV  CUNJEVOI
CEIJRSTU  JUSTICER
CEIJSSTU  JUSTICES
CEIKKNRS  KNICKERS
CEIKKRRS  SKERRICK
CEIKLNPS  SPICKNEL
CEIKLNRS  CLINKERS
          CRINKLES
CEIKLNRU  CLUNKIER
CEIKLNSS  SLICKENS
CEIKLSOV  LOVESICK
CEIKLPRS  PICKLERS
          PRICKLES
CEIKLPRU  PLUCKIER
CEIKLRSS  SLICKERS
CEIKLRST  STICKLER
          STRICKLE
          TICKLERS
          TRICKLES
CEIKLRSY  SICKERLY
CEIKLRTT  TRICKLET
CEIKLSST  SLICKEST
          STICKLES

CEIKLSTU  LUCKIEST
CEIKMNOR  MONICKER
CEIKMOPT  IMPOCKET
CEIKMORS  OCKERISM
CEIKMRSS  SMICKERS
CEIKMRSU  MUSICKER
CEIKMSST  SMICKETS
CEIKMSTU  MUCKIEST
CEIKNNSU  INSUCKEN
CEIKNOST  CONKIEST
CEIKNOTY  CYTOKINE
CEIKNQSU  QUICKENS
CEIKNRSS  SNICKERS
CEIKNRST  STRICKEN
CEIKNRSU  UNSICKER
CEIKNSSS  SICKNESS
CEIKNSST  SNICKETS
CEIKOPST  POCKIEST
CEIKORRS  ROCKIERS
CEIKORST  CORKIEST
          ROCKIEST
          STOCKIER
CEIKOSSY  YOICKSES
CEIKPRRS  PRICKERS
CEIKPRST  PRICKETS
CEIKPSST  SKEPTICS
          SPICKEST
CEIKQSTU  QUICKEST
          QUICKSET
CEIKRRST  TRICKERS
CEIKRRTY  TRICKERY
CEIKRSST  STICKERS
CEIKRSTU  TRUCKIES
CEIKRTTY  RICKETTY
CEIKSTUY  YUCKIEST
CEILLNOS  LIONCELS
CEILLNOU  NUCLEOLI
CEILLOPS  POLLICES
CEILLOQU  COQUILLE
CEILLORS  COLLIERS
          ORSELLIC
CEILLORY  COLLIERY
CEILLOTU  COUTILLE
CEILLRTU  TELLURIC
CEILLSST  CELLISTS
CEILLSSU  CULLISES
CEILMMUY  MYCELIUM
CEILMNOP  COMPLINE
CEILMNOT  MONTICLE
CEILMOPR  COMPILER
          COMPLIER
CEILMOPS  COMPILES
          COMPLIES
          POLEMICS
CEILMOSS  SOLECISM
CEILMOSU  COLISEUM
CEILMPRS  CRIMPLES
CEILMPRU  CLUMPIER
CEILMPUU  PECULIUM
CEILMRSU  CLUMSIER
          MUSCLIER
CEILMTUU  LUTECIUM
CEILNNOT  CONTLINE
CEILNNSU  NUCLEINS
CEILNNSY  SYNCLINE
CEILNOOS  COLONIES
          COLONISE
          ECLOSION
CEILNOOZ  COLONIZE
CEILNOPR  PERCOLIN
          REPLICON
CEILNOPS  PINOCLES
CEILNOPT  LEPTONIC
CEILNORS  INCLOSER
          LICENSOR
CEILNOSS  CONSEILS
          INCLOSES
CEILNOST  LECTIONS
CEILNOSU  LEUCOSIN

CEILNOSX  LEXICONS
CEILNPRY  PRINCELY
CEILNRTU  LINCTURE
CEILNRUV  CULVERIN
CEILNSST  STENCILS
CEILNSTU  CUTLINES
          TUNICLES
CEILNSUU  UNSLUICE
CEILOPRT  PETROLIC
CEILOPRV  PROCLIVE
CEILOPST  TOECLIPS
CEILOPTU  EPULOTIC
          POULTICE
CEILOPTY  EPICOTYL
CEILORST  CLOISTER
          COISTREL
          COSTLIER
          CREOLIST
CEILORTT  CLOTTIER
CEILORTY  CRYOLITE
CEILOSSS  OSSICLES
CEILOSST  SOLECIST
          SOLSTICE
CEILOSSU  COULISSE
CEILOTVY  VELOCITY
CEILPPRS  CLIPPERS
          CRIPPLES
CEILPRSS  SPLICERS
CEILPRSU  SURPLICE
CEILPRUU  PURLICUE
CEILPSSU  SPICULES
CEILRRSU  SCURRILE
CEILRSTT  CLITTERS
CEILRSTU  CURLIEST
          UTRICLES
CEILSSSS  SCISSELS
CEILSTTU  CUITTLES
CEIMMNNO  MNEMONIC
CEIMMNOU  ENCOMIUM
          MECONIUM
CEIMMORT  RECOMMIT
CEIMMOSX  COMMIXES
CEIMMRRS  CRIMMERS
CEIMMRRU  CRUMMIER
CEIMMRSU  CRUMMIES
          SCUMMIER
CEIMMRSY  MERYCISM
CEIMNNOO  ENCOMION
CEIMNNOS  MECONINS
CEIMNNOY  NEOMYCIN
CEIMNOOT  EMOTICON
CEIMNOPT  PENTOMIC
CEIMNOPY  EPONYMIC
CEIMNORS  CREMOSIN
          INCOMERS
          SERMONIC
CEIMNORT  INTERCOM
CEIMNOST  CENTIMOS
CEIMNRST  CENTRISM
CEIMNSSU  MENISCUS
CEIMOOST  COOMIEST
CEIMOOUZ  ZOOECIUM
CEIMOPRS  COMPRISE
CEIMOQSU  COMIQUES
CEIMORRS  MORRICES
CEIMORRT  MORTICER
CEIMORST  MORTICES
CEIMORSX  EXORCISM
CEIMORSY  ISOCRYME
CEIMORTY  EMICTORY
CEIMOSSS  COSMESIS
CEIMOSTV  VICOMTES
CEIMPRRS  CRIMPERS
CEIMPRRU  CRUMPIER
CEIMRRSU  SCRIMURE
CEIMRRTU  TURMERIC
CEIMRSST  CRETISMS
CEIMSSTY  SYSTEMIC
CEINNNOT  INNOCENT

CEINNNOU  INCONNUE
CEINNORS  INCENSOR
CEINNORU  NEURONIC
CEINNORV  CONNIVER
CEINNOSV  CONNIVES
CEINNOTU  CONTINUE
CEINOOST  COONTIES
CEINOOTZ  ENTOZOIC
          ENZOOTIC
CEINOPPR  CORNPIPE
CEINOPRS  CONSPIRE
          INCORPSE
CEINOPRT  ENTROPIC
          INCEPTOR
CEINOPRV  PROVINCE
CEINOPST  PONCIEST
CEINOPTT  ENTOPTIC
CEINOPTU  UNPOETIC
CEINORRS  RESORCIN
CEINORRT  TRICORNE
CEINORSS  NECROSIS
          SERICONS
CEINORST  CORNIEST
          RECTIONS
CEINORSU  NOURICES
          ROUNCIES
CEINORTT  CONTRITE
          CORNETTI
CEINORTU  NEUROTIC
CEINORTV  CONTRIVE
CEINOSSS  COSINESS
          CESSIONS
CEINOSST  SECTIONS
CEINOSSX  COXINESS
CEINOSTT  CENTOIST
          STENOTIC
CEINOSTU  COUNTIES
CEINOSTX  EXCITONS
CEINOSTY  CYTOSINE
CEINOSUV  UNVOICES
CEINOSVV  CONVIVES
CEINPRSS  PRINCESS
CEINPSST  INSPECTS
CEINPSTY  PYCNITES
CEINRSST  CISTERNS
CEINRSTT  CENTRIST
          CITTERNS
CEINRSTU  CURNIEST
CEINRSUV  INCURVES
CEINRSVV  CRIVVENS
CEINRTTU  INTERCUT
          TINCTURE
CEINSSTY  CYSTINES
CEIOOPRS  OPORICES
CEIOOTUV  OUTVOICE
CEIOOTXX  EXOTOXIC
CEIOPPRS  CROPPIES
CEIOPPSY  EPISCOPY
CEIOPRRU  CROUPIER
CEIOPRSS  PERSICOS
CEIOPRST  PERSICOT
CEIOPRSU  PRECIOUS
CEIOPRTU  EUTROPIC
          OUTPRICE
CEIOPSST  COPSIEST
CEIOPSSU  SPECIOUS
CEIORRSS  CROSIERS
CEIORRSU  COURIERS
CEIORRSZ  CROZIERS
CEIORRTU  COURTIER
CEIORRUZ  CRUZEIRO
CEIORSST  CROSSTIE
CEIORSSU  SCOURIES
CEIORSSV  CORSIVES
CEIORSSW  CORSSWIE
CEIORSSX  SIXSCORE
CEIORSTT  COTTIERS
CEIORSTU  CITREOUS
          OUTCRIES
```

CEIORSTV	EVICTORS
	VORTICES
CEIORSTX	EXCITORS
	EXORCIST
CEIORSVY	VICEROYS
CEIORTTU	TOREUTIC
CEIOSSSV	VISCOSES
CEIOSSTT	COTTISES
CEIOSSTU	COITUSES
CEIOSSTX	COEXISTS
CEIPQSTU	PICQUETS
CEIPRRSS	CRISPERS
CEIPRRST	RESCRIPT
CEIPRSST	CRISPEST
CEIPRSTU	CREPITUS
	CUPRITES
	PICTURES
	PIECRUST
CEIPSSST	CESSPITS
CEIRRRSU	CURRIERS
	SCURRIER
CEIRRSSU	CRUISERS
	SCURRIES
	SUCRIERS
CEIRRSTT	CRITTERS
	RESTRICT
	STRICTER
CEIRRSTU	CRUSTIER
	RECRUITS
CEIRRSUV	SCURVIER
CEIRSSSU	CUISSERS
	SCISSURE
CEIRSSTT	TRISECTS
CEIRSSTU	CITRUSES
	CRUSTIES
	CURTSIES
	RICTUSES
CEIRSSTV	VICTRESS
CEIRSSUV	SCURVIES
CEIRSTTU	TUTRICES
CEIRSTUV	CURVIEST
CEIRSTUY	SECURITY
CEIRSUZZ	SCUZZIER
CEISSSSU	CISSUSES
CEISSSTU	CISTUSES
CEISTTTU	CUTTIEST
CEJKNOSY	JOCKNEYS
CEJLOOSY	JOCOSELY
CEJNORRU	CONJURER
CEJNORSU	CONJURES
CEJNRTUU	JUNCTURE
CEJNSSUU	JUNCUSES
CEJOPRST	PROJECTS
CEKKLNSU	KNUCKLES
CEKKNORS	KNOCKERS
CEKLLOOV	LOVELOCK
CEKLLOPS	PELLOCKS
CEKLLSSU	LUCKLESS
CEKLMNOS	LOCKSMEN
CEKLNOSS	SLOCKENS
CEKLNOST	STENLOCK
CEKLNRSU	CRUNKLES
CEKLOORV	OVERLOCK
CEKLOPST	LOCKSTEP
CEKLPRSU	PLUCKERS
CEKLRRTU	TRUCKLER
CEKLRSSU	SUCKLERS
CEKLRSTU	TRUCKLES
CEKMNOST	STOCKMEN
CEKMNRTU	TRUCKMEN
CEKNNSSU	UNSNECKS
CEKNOOSV	CONVOKES
CEKNOPST	PENSTOCK
CEKNORST	CRONKEST
CEKNORTU	COKERNUT
CEKNOSTU	UNSOCKET
CEKNRSWY	WRYNECKS
CEKOOORV	OVERCOOK
CEKOOPRS	PRECOOKS

CEKOOPSW	COWPOKES
CEKOORST	CROOKEST
CEKOPRST	SPROCKET
CEKORRTY	ROCKETRY
CEKORSST	RESTOCKS
	STOCKERS
CEKRRSTU	TRUCKERS
CEKRSSUU	RUCKUSES
CELLMOSU	COLUMELS
CELLNOOS	COLONELS
CELLNSUU	NUCELLUS
CELLNTUU	LUCULENT
CELLOOQU	COLLOQUE
CELLORSS	ESCROLLS
CELLOSSY	CLOYLESS
CELLRRSU	CRULLERS
CELLRSUY	SCULLERY
CELMMSSU	MESCLUMS
CELMNOOS	MONOCLES
CELMNOTY	CLOYMENT
CELMNOUY	UNCOMELY
CELMNSSU	MESCLUNS
CELMNTUU	MUCULENT
CELMOOOT	LOCOMOTE
CELMOOSY	CLOYSOME
CELMOPSU	COMPULSE
CELMOPSY	SYMPLOCE
CELMOSUU	CUMULOSE
CELMPRSU	CLUMPERS
	CRUMPLES
CELMPRTU	PLECTRUM
CELMPSUU	SPECULUM
CELMSSUU	SECULUMS
CELNNOSU	NUCLEONS
CELNNOTY	NOCENTLY
CELNNOUV	UNCLOVEN
CELNOORS	CONSOLER
CELNOORT	CONTROLE
CELNOORU	ENCOLOUR
CELNOOSS	CONSOLES
	COOLNESS
CELNOOVV	CONVOLVE
CELNOPRT	PLECTRON
CELNOPUU	UNCOUPLE
CELNORTW	CROWNLET
CELNORWY	CLOWNERY
CELNOSSU	CLONUSES
	COUNSELS
	UNCLOSES
CELNOSTU	NOCTULES
CELNOSUV	CONVULSE
CELNOSVY	SOLVENCY
CELNOVXY	CONVEXLY
CELNPTUU	PUNCTULE
CELNRSTU	LECTURNS
CELOOPRS	PRECOOLS
CELOOPSS	CESSPOOL
CELOORRU	COLOURER
CELOORSS	CREOSOLS
CELOORTW	COLEWORT
CELOORVY	OVERCLOY
CELOPRSU	COUPLERS
CELOPRSU	OPUSCLES
	UPCLOSES
CELOPSTU	COUPLETS
	OCTUPLES
CELOPSUU	OPUSCULE
CELOPTTU	OCTUPLET
CELORSST	CORSLETS
	COSTRELS
	CROSSLET
CELORSSU	CLOSURES
	SCLEROUS
CELORSSW	SCROWLES
CELORSSY	SCROYLES
CELORSTT	CLOTTERS
	CROTTLES
CELORSTU	CLOTURES

	CLOUTERS
	COULTERS
CELORSTY	COYSTREL
CELORSUU	ULCEROUS
	URCEOLUS
CELORSUY	CROUSELY
CELORTTU	COURTLET
CELORTVY	COVERTLY
CELOSTTU	CULOTTES
CELPRRSU	SCRUPLER
CELPRSSU	SCRUPLES
CELPRSUY	SPRUCELY
CELRSSTU	CLUSTERS
	CUSTRELS
CELRSSTY	CLYSTERS
CELRSTTU	CLUTTERS
	SCUTTLER
CELRSTUU	CULTURES
CELRSTUV	CULVERTS
CELRSTUY	CLUSTERY
CELSSTTU	SCUTTLES
CELSSTUU	CULTUSES
CEMMNOOR	COMMONER
CEMMNOOY	COMMONEY
CEMMNOOS	CONSOMME
CEMMNOST	COMMENTS
CEMMOOST	COMMOTES
CEMMOOSV	COMMOVES
CEMMORTU	COMMUTER
CEMMOSTU	COMMUTES
CEMNORSU	CONSUMER
	MUCRONES
CEMNOSSU	CONSUMES
	MUSCONES
CEMNRSTU	CENTRUMS
CEMOOPRS	COMPOSER
CEMOOPSS	COMPOSES
CEMOOPST	COMPOTES
CEMOORSY	SYCOMORE
CEMOOSSS	COSMOSES
CEMOOSTU	OUTCOMES
CEMOOSTY	CYTOSOME
CEMOPRSS	COMPRESS
CEMOPRST	COMPTERS
CEMOPRTU	COMPUTER
CEMOPSTU	COMPOTUS
CEMORSSU	CORMUSES
CEMORSTU	COSTUMER
	CUSTOMER
CEMOSSTU	COSTUMES
CEMPRSTU	CRUMPEST
	CRUMPETS
	SPECTRUM
CENNOORV	CONVENOR
CENNOOST	CONNOTES
CENNORRT	CORRNENT
CENNORTU	NOCTURNE
CENNOSST	CONSENTS
CENNOSTT	CONTENTS
CENNOSTV	CONVENTS
CENNRSSU	SCUNNERS
CENOOOTZ	ECTOZOON
CENOORRS	CORONERS
	CROONERS
CENOORST	CORONETS
CENOORSU	CORNEOUS
CENOORTT	CORNETTO
CENOORVY	CONVEYOR
CENOPRSY	NECROPSY
CENOPRSY	PYCNOSES
	SYNCOPES
CENOPSTU	POUNCETS
CENOQRSU	CONQUERS

CENOQSTU	CONQUEST
CENORRSS	SCORNERS
CENORRSW	CROWNERS
CENORRTU	TROUNCER
CENORSST	CONSTERS
	CRESTONS
CENORSTT	CORNETTS
CENORSTU	CORNUTES
	COUNTERS
	RECOUNTS
	TROUNCES
CENORSTV	CONVERTS
CENORSTW	CROWNETS
CENORSUU	CERNUOUS
	COENURUS
CENORSUV	UNCOVERS
CENORSUY	CYNOSURE
CENOSSTT	CONTESTS
CENOSSTU	CONTUSES
	COUNTESS
CENOSTTX	CONTEXTS
CENPRSTY	ENCRYPTS
CENPRTUU	PUNCTURE
CENPSTUX	EXPUNCTS
CENRRSTU	CURRENTS
CENRSSTU	CURTNESS
	ENCRUSTS
CENRSSUU	UNCURSES
CENRSSUW	UNSCREWS
CEOOOPST	OTOSCOPE
CEOOPRRV	OVERCROP
CEOOPRSS	SCOOPERS
CEOOPSWX	COWPOXES
CEOORRVW	OVERCROW
CEOORSST	SCOOTERS
CEOOSTUV	COVETOUS
CEOPPRRS	CROPPERS
CEOPPRST	PROSPECT
CEOPPRRU	PROCURER
CEOPPRSS	SCORPERS
CEOPRRST	PORRECTS
CEOPRRSU	CROUPERS
	PROCURES
CEOPRSTT	PROTECTS
CEOPRSTW	SCREWTOP
CEOPRSUU	COUPURES
	CUPREOUS
CEOQRSTU	CROQUETS
	ROCQUETS
CEOQRTUY	COQUETRY
CEORRSSS	SCORSERS
CEORRSSU	COURSERS
	CURSORES
	SCOURERS
CEORRSSW	SCOWRERS
CEORRSTY	CORSETRY
CEORSSST	CROSSEST
CEORSSSU	SCOURSES
	SCOUSERS
	SUCROSES
CEORSSTU	SCOUTERS
CEORSSUV	CORVUSES
CEORSTUU	COUTURES
CEORSTUV	COUVERTS
CEORSTUY	COURTESY
CEOSSSTU	COSTUSES
CEOSSTTU	COTTUSES
CEPPRRSU	CRUPPERS
CEPPRSSU	SCUPPERS
CEPPRTUU	UPPERCUT
CEPRSSTU	SPRUCEST
CEPRSSUY	CYPRUSES
CEPRSTUU	CUTPURSE
CEPSSSTU	SUSPECTS
CERSSSUU	RUSCUSES
CERSSTTU	SCUTTERS
CERSSTUY	CURTSEYS
CERSSUUX	EXCURSUS

CFFGHINU CHUFFING	CGHHINTU HUTCHING	CGIIKNPS PICKINGS	CGILORSW COWGIRLS
CFFGILNU CUFFLING	CGHIIKNN CHINKING	CGIIKNRS SCRIKING	CGILPSTU GILTCUPS
CFFGINOS SCOFFING	CGHIIKNO HOICKING	CGIIKNRT TRICKING	CGILPSTY GLYPTICS
CFFGINSU SCUFFING	CGHIIKNR CHIRKING	CGIIKNRW WRICKING	CGIMMNSU SCUMMING
CFFHINOS CHIFFONS	CGHIIKNT THICKING	CGIIKNST STICKING	CGIMNNOO GNOMONIC
CFFIRTUY FRUCTIFY	CGHIILLN CHILLING	TICKINGS	ONCOMING
CFFMOSSU OFFSCUMS	CGHIILNR CHIRLING	CGIILLOS ILLOGICS	CGIMNOPS COMPINGS
CFGHIILN FILCHING	CGHIILNT LICHTING	CGIILMNO LOGICISM	CGIMNOPT COMPTING
CFGHINOO CHOOFING	CGHIIMNR CHIRMING	CGIILNOP POLICING	CGIMNOPU UPCOMING
CFGIIKLN FICKLING	CGHIIMNS MICHINGS	CGIILNPP CLIPPING	CGIMNPRU CRUMPING
FLICKING	CGHIIMNT MITCHING	CGIILNPS SPLICING	CGIMRRUY MICRURGY
CFGIKLNO FLOCKING	CGHIINNN CHINNING	CGIILNSS SLICINGS	CGINNNOS CONNINGS
CFGIKNOR FROCKING	CGHIINNP PINCHING	CGIILNSU SLUICING	CGINNNSU CUNNINGS
CFGIKNSU FUCKINGS	CGHIINNW WINCHING	CGIILOST LOGICIST	CGINNOOR CROONING
CFGINORT CROFTING	CGHIINOR CHOIRING	LOGISTIC	CGINNOPU POUNCING
CFGINOSU FOCUSING	CGHIINPP CHIPPING	CGIILRTU LITURGIC	UNCOPING
CFHIINOO FINOCHIO	CGHIINPR CHIRPING	CGIIMNNO INCOMING	CGINNORS SCORNING
CFHIIORR HORRIFIC	CGHIIPTT PITCHING	CGIIMMNS MINCINGS	CGINNORW CROWNING
CFHIKORS ROCKFISH	CGHIINQU QUICHING	CGIIMNPR CRIMPING	CGINNOSS CONSIGNS
CFHILPTY FLYPITCH	CGHIINRR CHIRRING	CGIIMNPU PUMICING	CGINNOTU COUNTING
CFHIMOSS SCOMFISH	CGHIINRT CHIRTING	CGIIMNSU MISCUING	CGINOOPS SCOOPING
CFHIMSSU SCUMFISH	RICHTING	CGIINNOS COININGS	CGINOOPT COOPTING
CFHLOPUU POUCHFUL	CGHIINTT CHITTING	CGIINNOT NOTICING	CGINOOST SCOOTING
CFHORSTU FUTHORCS	CGHIINTW WITCHING	CGIINNPR PRINCING	CGINOOTV COGNOVIT
CFIIILSY SILICIFY	CGHIINVV CHIVVING	CGIINNSU INCUSING	CGINOPPR CROPPING
CFIIKNYZ ZINCKIFY	CGHIINVY CHIVYING	CGIINNSW WINCINGS	CGINOPRS CORPSING
CFIILNST INFLICTS	CGHIINZZ CHIZZING	CGIINNTT TINCTING	CGINOPRU CROUPING
CFIILNUU FUNICULI	CGHIKNNU CHUNKING	CGIINOOS ISOGONIC	CGINOPSU SCOUPING
CFIILOPR PROLIFIC	CGHIKNOS SHOCKING	CGIINOPT PICOTING	CGINOPSW SCOWPING
CFIILPSU PULSIFIC	CGHIKNSU SHUCKING	CGIINORT TRIGONIC	CGINORSS CROSSING
CFIIMNOS SOMNIFIC	CGHILMNU MULCHING	CGIINOST COTISING	SCORINGS
CFIIMORT MORTIFIC	CGHILNNU LUNCHING	CGIINOSV VOICINGS	SCORSING
CFIINOPT PONTIFIC	CGHILNNY LYNCHING	CGIINPRS CRISPING	CGINORSU COURSING
CFIINOPT FRICTION	CGHILNOT CLOTHING	CGIINRSU CRUISING	SCOURING
CFIINOST FICTIONS	CGHILNRU LURCHING	CGIINRSV SCRIVING	SOURCING
CFIKLSTU STICKFUL	CGHIMMNU CHUMMING	CGIJNNOU JOUNCING	CGINORTU COURTING
CFIKNNOS FINNOCKS	CGHIMNNU MUNCHING	CGIKKNNO KNOCKING	CGINOSTU SCOUTING
CFIKOSSS FOSSICKS	CGHIMNOO MOOCHING	CGIKLNNO CLONKING	CGINPPSU CUPPINGS
CFIKPSTU PUCKFIST	CGHIMNOP CHOMPING	CGIKLNNU CLUNKING	CGINPRSU SPRUCING
CFILMOOR COLIFORM	CGHIMNOR CHROMING	CGIKLNOR ROCKLING	CGINRRSU SCURRING
CFILRSUU SULFURIC	CGHIMNOU MOUCHING	CGIKLNPU PLUCKING	CGINRRUY CURRYING
CFIMNOOR CONIFORM	CGHIMNPU CHUMPING	CGIKLNRU RUCKLING	CGINRSSU CURSINGS
CFIMNORS CONFIRMS	CGHIMPSY SPHYGMIC	CGIKLNSU SCULKING	CGINRSSY SCRYINGS
CFIMNORU UNCIFORM	CGHINNOS CHIGNONS	SUCKLING	CGINRSTU CRUSTING
CFINNOTU FUNCTION	CGHINNOT NOTCHING	CGIKMNOS MOCKINGS	CGINRSUZ SCRUZING
CFKLLOSU LOCKFULS	CGHINNPU PUNCHING	SMOCKING	CGINSTTU CUTTINGS
CFKNORSU UNFROCKS	CGHINNRU CHURNING	CGIKNOOR CROOKING	CGKLNOSU GUNLOCKS
CFKOSTTU FUTTOCKS	CGHINNSY SYNCHING	CGIKNORS ROCKINGS	CGKNOSTU GUNSTOCK
CFLLOPRU CROPFULL	CGHINOOS CHOOSING	CGIKNORT TROCKING	CGLLOSYY GLYCOSYL
CFLMRSUU FULCRUMS	CGHINOPP CHOPPING	CGIKNOST STOCKING	CGLMOOYY MYCOLOGY
CFLNOORT CORNLOFT	CGHINOPU POUCHING	CGIKNPSU KINGCUPS	CGLNOOOY ONCOLOGY
CFLNORSU SCORNFUL	CGHINOPT POTCHING	CGIKNRTU TRUCKING	CGLOOOTY TOCOLOGY
CFLOOPSU SCOOPFUL	CGHINORT TORCHING	CGIKNSSU SUCKINGS	CGLOOTYY CYTOLOGY
CFLOPRSU CROPFULS	CGHINOSU CHOUSING	CGIKNSTU GUNSTICK	CGMNNOOR MONGCORN
CFMNOORS CONFORMS	HOCUSING	CGILLNOS COLLINGS	CGMNNORU MUNGCORN
CFMOORST COMFORTS	CGHINOTU TOUCHING	CGILLNOY COLLYING	CGOORRSW GORCROWS
CFNNOORT CONFRONT	CGHINOUV VOUCHING	CGILLNSU CULLINGS	CHHIIKST THICKISH
CFOOORTW CROWFOOT	CGHINPSY PSYCHING	SCULLING	CHHIILTY HITCHILY
CFRSTUUU USUFRUCT	CGHINPTU PINCHGUT	CGILLNUY CULLYING	CHHIIPST PHTHISIC
CGGGHINU CHUGGING	CGHINRRU CHURRING	CGILMNOP CLOMPING	CHHIKORS CHIKHORS
CGGGILNO CLOGGING	CGHINRSU CRUSHING	CGILMNPU CLUMPING	CHHILRSU CHURLISH
COGGLING	RUCHINGS	CGILMNSU MUSCLING	CHHIMRTY RHYTHMIC
CGGGINOS COGGINGS	CGHINSTY SCYTHING	CGILMNTU MULCTING	CHHNORSU RHONCHUS
SCOGGING	CGHNOOSU SOUCHONG	CGILMNUU CINGULUM	CHHOOPTT HOTCHPOT
CGGGINSU SCUGGING	CGHOORST TORGOCHS	GLUCINUM	CHIIILOS CHILIOIS
CGGHILNU GULCHING	CGIIILNT LIGNITIC	CGILNNOW CLOWNING	CHIIKLST TICKLISH
CGGHINOU COUGHING	CGIIINNS INCISING	CGILNOOR COLORING	CHIIKNNS KINCHINS
CGGIILNN CLINGING	CGIIINNT INCITING	CGILNOOY COOINGLY	CHIIKRST TRICKISH
CGGIINNO COIGNING	CGIIKLNN CLINKING	CGILNOPP CLOPPING	CHIILLLY CHILLILY
CGGIINNR CRINGING	CGIIKLNP PICKLING	CGILNOPU COUPLING	CHIILMSY HYLICISM
CGGIINRS GRICINGS	CGIIKLNS LICKINGS	CGILNORU CLOURING	CHIILNNP LINCHPIN
CGGILRSY SCRIGGLY	SLICKING	CGILNOSS CLOSINGS	CHIILOST HOLISTIC
CGGINNSU SCUNGING	CGIIKLNT TICKLING	CGILNOSW COWLINGS	CHIILPRY CHIRPILY
CGGINOOS SCOOGING	CGIIKMMS GIMMICKS	SCOWLING	CHIILQSU CLIQUISH
CGGINOSU SCOUGING	CGIIKMMY GIMMICKY	CGILNOTT CLOTTING	CHIILSTY HYLICIST
CGHHIILN HILCHING	CGIIKNNS SNICKING	CGILNOTU CLOUTING	CHIIMPRU PICHURIM
CGHHIINT HITCHING	CGIIKNNZ ZINCKING	CGILNPSU SCULPING	CHIINNPS INCHPINS
CGHHINNU HUNCHING	CGIIKNOY YOICKING	CGILNRSU CURLINGS	CHIINOPS SIPHONIC
CGHHINOT HOTCHING	CGIIKNPR PRICKING	CGILOORU UROLOGIC	CHIINORT ORNITHIC

CHIIORSS CHORISIS	CHNOORST TORCHONS	CIIPRRTU PRURITIC	CIMMOSSS COSMISMS
CHIIORST HISTORIC	CHNORRSS SCHNORRS	CIIPRSTU PURISTIC	CIMNOOOZ ZOONOMIC
ORCHITIS	CHNORSSY SYNCHROS	CIIRSTTU TRUISTIC	CIMNOORS OMICRONS
CHIIPPRU HIPPURIC	CHNORSTU COTHURNS	CIISSTTY CYSTITIS	CIMNOORU CORONIUM
CHIIRSTT TRISTICH	CHOOORYZ ZOOCHORY	CIJNNOOS CONJOINS	CIMNOPRT COMPRINT
CHIKLLOS HILLOCKS	CHOOPPSS COPSHOPS	CIJNNOOT CONJOINT	CIMNORSS CRIMSONS
CHIKLLOY HILLOCKY	CHOOPSTU OCTOPUSH	CIJNNOTU JUNCTION	CIMNORSY CRONYISM
CHIKMNNU MUNCHKIN	CIIIKNTU CUITIKIN	CIJNNSTU INJUNCTS	CIMNOSTU MISCOUNT
CHIKMNPU CHIPMUNK	CIIILMPT IMPLICIT	CIJOOSTY JOCOSITY	CIMNOSUY SYCONIUM
CHIKMNTU MUTCHKIN	CIIILMSU SILICIUM	CIKKLLOS KILLOCKS	CIMOOOTZ ZOOTOMIC
CHIKNNOP PHINNOCK	CIIILPST SPILITIC	CIKLLOPR KILLCROP	CIMOORSS MORISCOS
CHIKNOOS CHINOOKS	CIIILSTV CIVILIST	CIKLLOPS PILLOCKS	CIMOPSSY COPYISMS
CHIKOPTY KYPHOTIC	CIIILTVY CIVILITY	CIKLLORS ROLLICKS	CIMOSSST COSMISTS
CHIKORST TROCHISK	CIIIMNSV INCIVISM	CIKLLOSS SILLOCKS	CIMOSTUU MUTICOUS
CHIKPSYY PHYSICKY	CIIINNOS INCISION	CIKLLOSW KILLCOWS	CIMOSTUY MUCOSITY
CHILLMSU CHILLUMS	CIIINTVY VICINITY	CIKLLPUY PLUCKILY	CIMOSTYZ ZYMOTICS
CHILLOOT OILCLOTH	CIIJRSTU JURISTIC	CIKLMSSU MISLUCKS	CINNNOSU INCONNUS
CHILMOPS COMPLISH	CIIKKLLS KILLICKS	CIKLNOST LINSTOCK	CINNOOSS SCOINSON
CHILMOSU SCHOLIUM	CIIKLLSY SICKLILY	CIKLOSTY STOCKILY	CINNOOST SCONTION
CHILNPNY LYNCHPIN	CIIKLOPT POLITICK	CIKMNNOS MINNOCKS	CINNOOTU CONTINUO
CHILNOOS SCHOLION	CIIKLPST LIPSTICK	CIKMOORS SICKROOM	CINNORSU UNICORNS
CHILNORS CHLORINS	CIIKLRTY TRICKILY	CIKMOPST MOPSTICK	CINNOSTU UNCTIONS
CHILNOSU ULICHONS	CIIKLSTY STICKILY	CIKNNOOS COONSKIN	CINNOSTY SYNTONIC
CHILNOSW CLOWNISH	CIIKMMMS MIMMICKS	CIKNNOPS PINNOCKS	CINNQUUX QUINCUNX
CHILOOOZ HOLOZOIC	CIIKMNNS MINNICKS	CIKNNOSW WINNOCKS	CINOOOTZ ZOONOTIC
CHILOOPT HOLOPTIC	CIIKNOOT COOTIKIN	CIKNSSTU UNSTICKS	CINOOPRS SCORPION
CHILOSYY COYISHLY	CIIKNSTU CUTIKINS	CIKOPPST POCKPITS	CINOOPRT PROTONIC
CHILOTUY TOUCHILY	CIIKPSUW WICKIUPS	CIKOSSTT STOCKIST	CINOOSUV COVINOUS
CHIMMORU CHROMIUM	CIILLNOP POLLINIC	CIKOSTUW OUTWICKS	CINOOTXY OXYTOCIN
CHIMNOOR HORMONIC	CIILMOPY IMPOLICY	CILLMNOR CORNMILL	CINOPSSY PYCNOSIS
CHIMNOSU INSOMUCH	CIILMOSS SCIOLISM	CILLMSUY CLUMSILY	CINOPSTY SYNOPTIC
CHIMNOUY ONYCHIUM	CIILMQSU CLIQUISM	CULLYISM	CINORRST TRICORNS
CHIMOORU MOUCHOIR	CIILMRSY LYRICISM	CILLNOOT COTILLON	CINORSST CISTRONS
CHIMORSS CHORISMS	CIILNOOT NOCTILIO	CILLNORS INSCROLL	CORNISTS
CHRISOMS	CIILNOPS CIPOLINS	CILLNOSU CULLIONS	CINORSTT CONTRIST
CHIMORST CHRISTOM	PSILOCIN	SCULLION	CINORSTU RUCTIONS
CHIMPSSY PSYCHISM	CIILNOSS SILICONS	CILLOOOT OCOTILLO	CINORSUY COUSINRY
CHIMSSTY TYCHISMS	CIILOOPT POLITICO	CILLOORS CRIOLLOS	CINOSSST CONSISTS
CHINOORT ORTHICON	CIILOOTZ ZOOLITIC	CILMNOPS COMPLINS	CINOSSTU SUCTIONS
CHINOPTY HYPNOTIC	CIILOPPT POPLITIC	CILMNOPU PULMONIC	CINOSTUV VISCOUNT
PYTHONIC	CIILOPST POLITICS	CILMNOUU INOCULUM	CINRSSTU INCRUSTS
TYPHONIC	PSILOTIC	CILMNUUV VINCULUM	CINRSTTU INSTRUCT
CHINORTU COTHURNI	CIILORST CLITORIS	CILMOORS MISCOLOR	CINRSTUY SCRUTINY
CHINOSSU CUSHIONS	COISTRIL	CILMOPSY OLYMPICS	CIOOPRST PORTICOS
CHINOSTZ SCHIZONT	CIILOSST SCIOLIST	CILMPRSY SCRIMPLY	PROOTICS
CHINOSUY CUSHIONY	SOLICITS	CILMPSUU SPICULUM	CIOOPTYZ ZOOTYPIC
CHINSTTU UNSTITCH	CIILOSTY SOLICITY	CILMSSTU CULTISMS	CIOOQSTU COQUITOS
CHIOOPPT PHOTOPIC	CIILOSVV SLIVOVIC	CILNOORS ORCINOLS	CIOORRWW WORRICOW
CHIOOPRS POCHOIRS	CIILRSTY LYRICIST	CILNOORU UNICOLOR	CIOORSSU SCORIOUS
CHIOORSS ISOCHORS	CIILRTUU UTRICULI	CILNOOSS CLOISONS	CIOOSSTU STOCIOUS
CHIOORSU ICHOROUS	CIILSSSS SCISSILS	CILNOOST COLONIST	CIOPSSTY COPYISTS
CHIOORSZ CHORIZOS	CIIMNOOS ISONOMIC	CILNOOTU LOCUTION	CIORRSTU CURSITOR
CHIOORTT ORTHOTIC	CIIMNOST MICTIONS	CILNOPRS PILCORNS	CIORSSSS SCISSORS
CHIOPRST STROPHIC	MONISTIC	CILNOPTU PLUTONIC	CIPPRRUU PURPURIC
CHIOPSTY HYPOCIST	NOMISTIC	CILNORSY LYRICONS	CIPSSTTY STYPTICS
CHIORSSS CROSSISH	CIIMORST TRISOMIC	CILNOSTU LINOCUTS	CIRRSTTU CRITTURS
CHIORSST CHORISTS	CIIMOSST MISTICOS	CILNOSUY COUSINLY	CJNOORRU CONJUROR
CHIPRRSU CHIRRUPS	STOICISM	CILNPSSU INSCULPS	CJRSUUUU SUCURUJU
CHIPRRSY PYRRHICS	CIIMRSTY MYRISTIC	SCULPINS	CKKNOOTU KNOCKOUT
CHIPRRUY CHIRRUPY	CIINNSTT INSTINCT	CILNPSTU INSCULPT	CKKOORRW ROCKWORK
CHIPRTTY TRIPTYCH	CIINNSTU TUNICINS	CILOOPST COPILOTS	CKLLMOSU MULLOCKS
CHIPSSTY PSYCHIST	CIINOOST COITIONS	CILOOPYZ POLYZOIC	CKLLOOPS POLLOCKS
CHIRRSSU SCIRRHUS	ISOTONIC	CILOORRT TRICOLOR	CKLLOORS ROLLOCKS
CHISSTTU CHUTISTS	CIINOOTZ ZOONITIC	CILOORST CORTISOL	CKLLORSU RULLOCKS
CHKLOOOS HOOLOCKS	CIINOPSS PSIONICS	CILOORSU COULOIRS	CKLMMOSU SLUMMOCK
CHKMMOOS HOMMOCKS	CIINOPSU OPINICUS	CILOOSSU SCIOLOUS	CKLOOOSY OLYCOOKS
CHKMMOUS HUMMOCKS	CIINORSS INCISORS	CILOPPRY PROPYLIC	CKLOORSW ROWLOCKS
CHKMMOUY HUMMOCKY	CIINORST CROSTINI	CILOPRSW PILCROWS	CKLOOSTU LOCKOUTS
CHKNOOSS SCHNOOKS	CIINORSY INCISORY	CILOPSSW COWSLIPS	CKLOPSTU PUTLOCKS
CHKNORSU CORNHUSK	CIINOSSS SCISSION	CILORSTY COYSTRIL	CKMMMOSU MUMMOCKS
CHKOOSST SCHTOOKS	CIINOSTT STICTION	CILOSSTU OCULISTS	CKMNOOOR MOONROCK
CHKPSTUU PUTCHUKS	CIINOTTY TONICITY	CILOSSTY SYSTOLIC	CKMOOOOR COOKROOM
CHLNOOOP COLOPHON	CIINPRSS CRISPINS	CILOSSUU LUSCIOUS	CKNOSSTU UNSTOCKS
CHLOORSU CHLOROUS	CIINPSTU SINCIPUT	CILPRSTU CULPRITS	CKNRSTUU UNSTRUCK
CHLOPSTY SPLOTCHY	CIIOOPST ISOTOPIC	CILPSSTU SCULPSIT	CKOOOSTU COOKOUTS
CHLORTUY CHOULTRY	CIIOPRST PORISTIC	CILRSTTY STRICTLY	CKOOPSTT STOCKPOT
CHMNOORT CORNMOTH	CIIOQTUX QUIXOTIC	CILRSTUY CRUSTILY	CKOORSSU SOUROCKS
CHMNORRU CRUMHORN	CIIORRWW WIRRICOW	CILRSUVY SCURVILY	CKOPSTTU PUTTOCKS
CHNNOORS CHRONONS	CIIOTTXY TOXICITY	CILSSTTU CULTISTS	CKORSTUW CUTWORKS

CKOSSSTU TUSSOCKS	DDDEIIMS SMIDDIED	DDEEGMMU DEGUMMED	DDEEOPRT DEPORTED
CKOSSTUY TUSSOCKY	DDDEIINV DIVIDEND	DDEEGOPS GODSPEED	DDEEOPRW POWDERED
CLLLOOPT CLOTPOLL	DDDEIIST DIDDIEST	DDEEGRRS DREDGERS	DDEEORRW REWORDED
CLLMOSSU MOLLUSCS	STIDDIED	DDEEGSTU DEGUSTED	DDEEORTT DETORTED
CLLOOPSS SCOLLOPS	DDDEILNU UNLIDDED	DDEEHILS SHIELDED	DDEEORTU DETOURED
CLLOOQUY COLLOQUY	DDDEILNW DWINDLED	DDEEHINR HINDERED	DDEEORUV DEVOURED
CLMMNOOY COMMONLY	DDDEILQU QUIDDLED	DDEEHIRT DITHERED	DDEEORVY OVERDYED
CLMOOOTY COLOTOMY	DDDEILRS DIDDLERS	DDEEHISS EDDISHES	DDEEPPRU PERDURED
CLMOOPST COMPLOTS	DDDEILTW TWIDDLED	DDEEHNOR DEHORNED	DDEEPRSS SPREDDES
CLMOPSTU PLUMCOTS	DDDEIMOS DISMODED	DDEEHNSU DUDHEENS	DDEERRUV VERDURED
CLNOORST CONTROLS	DDDEINOR DENDROID	DDEEHORT DEHORTED	DDEERSTU DETRUDES
CLNOORTU CONTROUL	DDDEINRU UNDERDID	DDEEHRRS SHREDDER	DDEERTUX EXTRUDED
COUNTROL	DDDEIOST DODDIEST	DDEEHRSS SHEDDERS	DDEFFISU DIFFUSED
CLNOSSTU CONSULTS	DDDEIQSU SQUIDDED	DDEEIINT INEDITED	DDEFIIIN NIDIFIED
CLNOSTUY UNCOSTLY	DDDEISTU DUDDIEST	DDEEIIRV REDIVIDE	DDEFIILM MIDFIELD
CLOOOPRT PROTOCOL	DDDENORW DROWNDED	DDEEILLV DEVILLED	DDEFIILR FIDDLIER
CLOORTUY LOCUTORY	DDDGIILN DIDDLING	DDEEILMN MILDENED	DDEFIIMO MODIFIED
CLOOSSSU COLOSSUS	DDDIIOOR DORIDOID	DDEEILMW MILDEWED	DDEFIIMW MIDWIFED
CLOPRSTU SCULPTOR	DDEEEEMR REDEEMED	DDEEILRW WILDERED	DDEFILNO INFOLDED
CLRSSUUU SURCULUS	DDEEEENP DEEPENED	DDEEIMNP IMPENDED	DDEFILRS FIDDLERS
CMMNNOOU UNCOMMON	DDEEEFLX DEFLEXED	DDEEIMNR REMINDED	DDEFILSY FIDDLEYS
CMNOOOST MONOCOTS	DDEEEFNR DEFENDER	DDEEIMOR MOIDERED	DDEFLNOU UNFOLDED
CMNOOOTY ONCOTOMY	DDEEEFRR DEFERRED	DDEEIMSS MISDEEDS	DDEFLRSU FUDDLERS
CMNOORRW CORNWORM	DDEEEGLR LEDGERED	DDEEIMST DEMISTED	DDEFLRUU UDDERFUL
CMNOPSTU CONSUMPT	DDEEEGMR DEMERGED	DDEEIMTT DEMITTED	DDEFNNUU UNFUNDED
CMOOPRST COMPORTS	DDEEEGNR DEGENDER	DDEEINNR DINNERED	DDEGGINR DREDGING
CMOOPSST COMPOSTS	GENDERED	DDEEINNT INDENTED	DDEGGLOY DOGGEDLY
CMOPRSUX SCRUMPOX	DDEEEGRR REGREDED	INTENDED	DDEGGNOO DOGGONED
CMORSSTU SCROTUMS	DDEEEGRT DETERGED	DDEEINRT DENDRITE	DDEGHILN HEDDLING
CMORSTUW CUTWORMS	DDEEEHLW WHEELDED	DDEEINST DESTINED	DDEGHINS SHEDDING
CNNOOORT CONTORNO	DDEEEHNU UNHEEDED	DDEEINTU UNEDITED	DDEGIINR DERIDING
CNNORSTU NOCTURNS	DDEEEIMR REMEDIED	DDEEIOPR PERIODED	DDEGIIST GIDDIEST
CNNORSUW UNCROWNS	REMEDIED	DDEEIPPR REDIPPED	DDEGILMN MEDDLING
CNOOOORT OCTOROON	DDEEEIST DEEDIEST	DDEEIPRS PRESIDED	DDEGILNP PEDDLING
CNOOPPRS POPCORNS	STEEDIED	DDEEIPRV DEPRIVED	DDEGILNR REDDLING
CNOOPRSU CROUPONS	DDEEELLV DEVELLED	DDEEIPSS DEPSIDES	DDEGILNS SLEDDING
CNOOPSSU SOUPCONS	DDEEELNW WEDELNED	DESPISED	DDEGILNU DELUDING
CNOORRSW CORNROWS	DDEEELPT DEPLETED	DDEEIRRS DERIDERS	INDULGED
CNOORRTY CRYOTRON	DDEEELSS DEEDLESS	DDEEIRST REDDIEST	UNGILDED
CNOORSST CONSORTS	DDEEELTW TWEEDLED	DDEEIRSV DIVERSED	DDEGILOS DISLODGE
CNOORSTT CONTORTS	DDEEEMNT DEMENTED	DDEEIRTV DIVERTED	DDEGILRS GRIDDLES
CNOORSTU CONTOURS	DDEEEMRS DEMERSED	DDEEISST DESISTED	DDEGILRY GLIDDERY
CORNUTOS	DDEEENNU UNNEEDED	STEDDIES	DDEGILST GLIDDEST
CROUTONS	DDEEENPX EXPENDED	DDEEISTV DIVESTED	DDEGILUV DIVULGED
OUTSCORN	DDEEENRR RENDERED	DDEEITTW DEWITTED	DDEGIMOS DEMIGODS
CNOOSTTW COTTOWNS	DDEEENRT TENDERED	DDEEJLLO JODELLED	DDEGINNS SNEDDING
CNOPRSTY CRYPTONS	DDEEENSU UNSEEDED	DDEEKNSU DUSKENED	DDEGINNU DENUDING
CNOSTUUU UNCTUOUS	DDEEENTT DENETTED	DDEELLMO MODELLED	DDEGINRS REDDINGS
COOOPSYZ ZOOSCOPY	DDEEENTX EXTENDED	DDEELLOW DOWELLED	DDEGINRU UNGIRDED
COOPRRST PROCTORS	DDEEENUW UNWEEDED	DDEELLOY YODELLED	DDEGINST STEDDING
COOPRSTU OUTCROPS	DDEEERRT DETERRED	DDEELMPU DEPLUMED	DDEGINSW SWINDGED
COOPRSUU CROUPOUS	DDEEERST DESERTED	DDEELMRS MEDDLERS	WEDDINGS
COOPRSUY UROSCOPY	DDEEERSV DESERVED	DDEELNOU LOUDENED	DDEGINUU UNGUIDED
COORRWWY WORRYCOW	DDEEESTT DETESTED	DDEELOPR DEPLORED	DDEGIOST DODGIEST
COORSSTU OUTCROSS	DDEEESTV DEVESTED	POLDERED	DDEGIQSU SQUIDGED
COOSSTTY OTOCYSTS	DDEEFFIR DIFFERED	DDEELOPX EXPLODED	DDEGIRRS GRIDDERS
COPRRSTU CORRUPTS	DDEEFFNO OFFENDED	DDEELOPY DEPLOYED	DDEGLOPS SPLODGED
DDDDEEIR DIDDERED	DDEEFGIT FIDGETED	DDEELORS SOLDERED	DDEGLOSS DOGSLEDS
DDDDEEOR DODDERED	DDEEFINR FRIENDED	DDEELOSU DELOUSED	DDEGNORU GROUNDED
DDDEEEFN DEFENDED	DDEEFINU UNDEFIDE	DDEELOVV DEVOLVED	UNDERDOG
DDDEEENP DEPENDED	UNDEFIED	DDEELPRS PEDDLERS	DDEGNOSS GODSENDS
DDDEEENR REDDENED	DDEEFLNO ENFOLDED	DDEELPRU PRELUDED	DDEGNOSU DUDGEONS
DDDEEENU UNDEEDED	DDEEFLOU DEFOULED	DDEELRST TREDDLES	DDEGORSS GORSEDDS
DDDEEERW WEDDERED	DDEEFMOR DEFORMED	DDEELRSU DELUDERS	DDEGRRSU DRUDGERS
DDDEEFOR FODDERED	DDEEFNRU REFUNDED	DDEEMNOR ENDODERM	DDEGRRUY DRUDGERY
DDDEEGIS DISEDGED	UNDERFED	DDEEMRRU DEMURRED	DDEHILNY HIDDENLY
DDDEEHRS SHREDDED	DDEEFORR FODDERER	MURDERED	DDEHIMOS DISHOMED
DDDEEIST STEDDIED	DDEEGGIR DERIGGED	DDEENNOR DONNERED	DDEHINNU UNHIDDEN
DDDEEJRU JUDDERED	DDEEGGOR DOGGEDER	DDEENNOY ENDODYNE	DDEHINOR DIHEDRON
DDDEELRT TREDDLED	DDEEGHNU UNHEDGED	DDEENNTU UNTENDED	DDEHIORS SHODDIER
DDDEENOR DONDERED	DDEEGILN ENGILDED	DDEENOPR PERDENDO	DDEHIOSS SHODDIES
REDDENDO	DDEEGINR ENRIDGED	PONDERED	DDEHIRSS SHIDDERS
DDDEENOS SODDENED	DDEEGINS DESIGNED	DDEENOPW PONDWEED	DDEHIRSW WHIDDERS
DDDEENUW UNWEDDED	SDEIGNED	DDEENORS ENDORSED	DDEHIRSY HYDRIDES
DDDEEORR DODDERER	DDEEGIRV DIVERGED	DDEENORW WONDERED	DDEHNOOU UNHOODED
DDDEEPRU PUDDERED	DDEEGISS DISEDGES	DDEENOSS ENDOSSED	DDEHNPUU UPHUDDEN
DDDEERTU DETRUDED	DDEEGIST DIGESTED	DDEENPRS SPREDDEN	DDEHNRSU HUNDREDS
DDDGNOOU UNGODDED	DDEEGJRU REJUDGED	DDEENRSU SUNDERED	DDEHOOOO HOODOOED
DDDEHIRT THRIDDED	DDEEGLNO GOLDENED	DDEENRTU RETUNDED	

Letters	Word(s)
DDEHOOSW	WOODSHED
DDEHORSU	SHROUDED
DDEHRSSU	SHUDDERS
DDEHRSUY	SHUDDERY
DDEIIIRS	IRIDISED
DDEIIIRZ	IRIDIZED
DDEIIKLS	DISLIKED
DDEIIKRS	KIDDIERS
DDEIILNR	DIELDRIN
DDEIILOS	IDOLISED
DDEIILOZ	IDOLIZED
DDEIILRT	TIDDLIER
DDEIILST	TIDDLIES
DDEIIMSS	SMIDDIES
DDEIIMVW	MIDWIVED
DDEIINRT	NITRIDED
DDEIINTU	UNTIDIED
DDEIIOPS	DIOPSIDE
	DIPODIES
DDEIIOST	ODDITIES
DDEIIOSX	DIOXIDES
	OXIDISED
DDEIIOXZ	OXIDIZED
DDEIIRSV	DIVIDERS
DDEIIRUV	REDUVIID
DDEIISST	STIDDIES
DDEIISTT	TIDDIEST
DDEIKNRS	KINDREDS
DDEIKOSY	DISYOKED
DDEIKRSS	SKIDDERS
DDEILMOP	IMPLODED
DDEILMOV	DEVILDOM
DDEILMSU	MUDSLIDE
DDEILNPS	SPINDLED
	SPLENDID
DDEILNRT	TRINDLED
DDEILNRU	UNRIDDLE
DDEILNSW	DWINDLES
	SWINDLED
DDEILOPS	DISPLODE
	LOPSIDED
DDEILOST	DELTOIDS
DDEILOSY	DYSODILE
DDEILPRS	PIDDLERS
DDEILPRU	PUDDLIER
DDEILQRU	QUIDDLER
DDEILQSU	QUIDDLES
DDEILRRS	RIDDLERS
DDEILRSS	SLIDDERS
DDEILRST	STRIDDLE
	TIDDLERS
DDEILRSY	SLIDDERY
DDEILRTW	TWIDDLER
DDEILRZZ	DRIZZLED
DDEILSTW	TWIDDLES
DDEILSTY	LYDDITES
	TIDDLEYS
DDEIMMNU	UNDIMMED
DDEIMNNU	UNMINDED
DDEIMNSU	MUEDDINS
DDEIMNUV	VIDENDUM
DDEIMORS	DERMOIDS
DDEIMOSS	DESMOIDS
DDEIMOSU	MEDUSOID
DDEIMSTU	MUDDIEST
DDEINNRU	UNRIDDEN
DDEINNTU	UNDINTED
DDEINOPS	DISPONED
DDEINORS	INDORSED
DDEINOSW	DISENDOW
	DISOWNED
	DOWNSIDE
DDEINOWW	WINDOWED
DDEINPPU	UNDIPPED
DDEINPSS	DISPENDS
DDEINRST	STRIDDEN
DDEINRTU	INTRUDED
DDEINSST	DISTENDS
DDEINSSW	SWIDDENS
DDEINSTU	DISTUNED
DDEIOPRS	DROPSIED
DDEIOPRV	PROVIDED
DDEIOPSS	DISPOSED
DDEIOPST	PODDIEST
DDEIORRS	DISORDER
	SORDIDER
DDEIOSST	SODDIEST
DDEIOSTW	DOWDIEST
DDEIPRSS	DISPREDS
DDEIPRSU	SPUDDIER
DDEIPSTU	DISPUTED
DDEIRSSU	DRUIDESS
DDEIRSTU	RUDDIEST
	STURDIED
DDEKMOSU	DUKEDOMS
DDELLNUU	UNDULLED
DDELMRSU	MUDDLERS
DDELNORU	UNLORDED
DDELNRTU	TRUNDLED
DDELNSUY	SUDDENLY
DDELOORS	DOODLERS
DDELOPRS	PLODDERS
DDELORST	STRODDLE
	STRODLED
	TODDLERS
DDELOSYY	DYSODYLE
DDELPRSU	PUDDLERS
DDELSSTU	STUDDLES
DDEMMSSU	SMEDDUMS
DDEMNOOU	UNDOOMED
DDEMNOST	ODDMENTS
DDEMNOUU	DUODENUM
DDEMNPUU	PUDENDUM
DDEMOOTU	OUTMODED
DDENNORS	DENDRONS
DDENNOSU	UNSODDEN
DDENOPSS	DESPONDS
DDENORSU	REDOUNDS
DDENORTU	ROTUNDED
DDENORUW	UNWORDED
DDENOSST	SNODDEST
DDENOSTU	STOUNDED
DDENOSTW	STOWNDED
DDENOSUW	SWOUNDED
DDENOTTU	DONUTTED
DDENSTUY	SUDDENTY
DDEOOOVV	VOODOOED
DDEOORSW	REDWOODS
DDEOORWW	ROWDEDOW
DDEOOUUV	VOUDOUED
DDEORTUU	OUTDURED
DDFGIILN	FIDDLING
DDFGILNU	FUDDLING
DDFIIOSU	FIDDIOUS
DDFMNOUU	DUMFOUND
DDGGIINY	GIDDYING
DDGGILNU	GUDDLING
DDGGINOS	DODGINGS
DDGGINRU	DRUDGING
DDGHIINW	WHIDDING
DDGHILNO	HODDLING
DDGHILNU	HUDDLING
DDGHINTU	THUDDING
DDGHOOOS	GODHOODS
DDGIIINV	DIVIDING
DDGIIKNS	SKIDDING
DDGIIKNY	KIDDYING
DDGIILMN	MIDDLING
DDGIILNN	DINDLING
DDGIILNP	PIDDLING
DDGIILNR	RIDDLING
DDGIILNT	TIDDLING
DDGIILNW	WIDDLING
DDGILMNU	MUDDLING
DDGILNNO	NODDLING
DDGILNOO	DOODLING
DDGILNOP	PLODDING
DDGILNOT	TODDLING
DDGILNPU	PUDDLING
DDGILNRU	RUDDLING
DDGIMNUY	MUDDYING
DDGIMRSU	DRUDGISM
DDGINNOS	NODDINGS
	SNODDING
DDGINOPR	PRODDING
DDGINOQU	QUODDING
DDGINORS	RODDINGS
DDGINPSU	PUDDINGS
	SPUDDING
DDGINPUY	PUDDINGY
DDGINRUY	RUDDYING
DDGINSTU	STUDDING
DDGOOOSW	DOGWOODS
DDHILOSY	SHODDILY
DDHIORSY	HYDROIDS
DDHIOSWY	DOWDYISH
DDHLLOOO	DOLLHOOD
DDIIIIVV	DIVIDIVI
DDIILOPY	DIPLOIDY
DDIIMMUY	DIDYMIUM
DDIIMRSU	DRUIDISM
	SIDDURIM
DDIINOPU	DUPONDII
DDIIQSTU	QUIDDITS
DDIIQTUY	QUIDDITY
DDILOOWW	WILDWOOD
DDILORSY	SORDIDLY
DDILOSSY	DYSODILS
DDIMOSUY	DIDYMOUS
DDIMOSWY	DOWDYISM
DDINNOWW	DOWNWIND
DDINOOOT	ODONTOID
DDINOOWW	WOODWIND
DDLLMOOS	DOLLDOMS
DDLMORSU	DOLDRUMS
DDMNOORS	DROMONDS
DDOORWWY	ROWDYDOW
DDORSSTY	DROSTDYS
DEEEEFRR	REFEREED
DEEEEFRZ	DEFREEZE
DEEEEGKR	KEDGEREE
DEEEEHLR	REHEELED
DEEEEKMN	MEEKENED
DEEEELTY	EYELETED
DEEEEMRR	REDEEMER
DEEEEMST	ESTEEMED
DEEEENRV	VENEERED
DEEEERTT	TEETERED
DEEEFFIR	EFFEIRED
DEEEFINR	FINEERED
	NEEDFIRE
	REDEFINE
DEEEFIPT	TEPEFIED
DEEEFIRW	FIREWEED
DEEEFLLR	REFELLED
DEEEFLPT	DEEPFELT
DEEEFLRT	FELTERED
	TELFERED
DEEEFLRX	REFLEXED
DEEEFLSX	DEFLEXES
DEEEFMNR	FREEDMEN
DEEEFNRT	DEFERENT
DEEEFNSS	DEFENSES
DEEEFNST	ENFESTED
DEEEFORV	OVERFEED
DEEEFRRR	DEFERRER
	REFERRED
DEEEFRRT	FERRETED
DEEEFRST	FESTERED
DEEEFRTT	FETTERED
DEEEFRTW	FEWTERED
DEEEGHNW	WHEENGED
DEEEGILS	ELEGISED
DEEEGILZ	ELEGIZED
DEEEGIPR	PEDIGREE
DEEEGIRR	GREEDIER
DEEEGISS	DIEGESES
DEEEGISW	EDGEWISE
DEEEGLPS	PLEDGEES
DEEEGLSS	EDGELESS
DEEEGLSV	SELVEDGE
DEEEGMRR	DEMERGER
	REMERGED
DEEEGMRS	DEMERGES
DEEEGNNR	ENGENDER
DEEEGNRU	RENEGUED
DEEEGNRV	REVENGED
DEEEGRRS	REGREDES
DEEEGRST	DETERGES
DEEEGRTT	GETTERED
DEEEHHSW	WHEESHED
DEEEHKRS	SHREEKED
DEEEHLMT	HELMETED
DEEEHLPW	WHEEPLED
DEEEHLRW	WHEEDLER
DEEEHLSS	HEEDLESS
DEEEHLSW	WHEEDLES
DEEEHLWZ	WHEEZLED
DEEEHMMS	EMMESHED
DEEEHMNS	ENMESHED
DEEEHRTT	TETHERED
DEEEIKLS	SEEDLIKE
DEEEILNR	NEEDLIER
DEEEILNS	SELENIDE
DEEEILRV	RELIEVED
DEEEILTV	DELETIVE
DEEEILVW	WEEVILED
DEEEIMNS	INSEEMED
DEEEIMRS	REMEDIES
DEEEINRR	REINDEER
DEEEINRS	NEREIDES
DEEEINST	NEEDIEST
DEEEINSX	ENDEIXES
DEEEINTV	EVENTIDE
DEEEIPRS	SPEEDIER
DEEEIPTX	EXPEDITE
DEEEIRRR	DERRIERE
DEEEIRSS	DIERESES
DEEEIRST	REEDIEST
DEEEIRSZ	RESEIZED
DEEEIRTW	TWEEDIER
DEEEIRVW	REVIEWED
DEEEISST	SEEDIEST
	STEEDIES
DEEEISSV	DEVISEES
DEEEISTW	WEEDIEST
DEEEJLLW	JEWELLED
DEEEJNRU	DEJEUNER
DEEEJNSU	DEJEUNES
DEEEKNSW	WEEKENDS
DEEEKOPW	POKEWEED
DEEEKRST	STREEKED
DEEEKRSW	SKEWERED
	SKEWERED
DEEELLLV	LEVELLED
DEEELLNT	DENTELLE
DEEELLNV	NEVELLED
DEEELLNW	NEWELLED
DEEELLPR	REPELLED
DEEELLPT	PELLETED
DEEELLPX	EXPELLED
DEEELLRT	TELLERED
DEEELLRV	REVELLED
DEEELMOS	SOMEDELE
DEEELNPU	UNPEELED
DEEELNRS	NEEDLERS
DEEELNRT	RELENTED
DEEELNRU	UNREELED
DEEELNSS	LESSENED
	NEEDLESS
	SELDSEEN
DEEELNSU	UNSEELED
DEEELOPV	DEVELOPE
DEEELPRT	PELTERED
	REPLETED

DEEELPST	DEPLETES	DEEFFINS	EFFENDIS
	STEEPLED	DEEFFINT	INFEFTED
DEEELRSS	REDELESS	DEEFFNOR	OFFENDER
DEEELRST	DEERLETS		REOFFEND
	STREELED	DEEFFRSU	SUFFERED
DEEELRTT	LETTERED	DEEFGILR	FLEDGIER
DEEELRTW	TWEEDLER	DEEFGINR	FINGERED
	WELTERED	DEEFGINS	FEEDINGS
DEEELSSS	SEEDLESS	DEEFGIPS	PIGFEEDS
DEEELSSW	WEEDLESS	DEEFGIUW	GUDEWIFE
DEEELSTW	TWEEDLES	DEEFGLNU	ENGULFED
DEEELTVV	VELVETED	DEEFGLOO	FEELGOOD
DEEEMNNT	NEEDMENT	DEEFGLUW	GULFWEED
DEEEMNSS	DEMESNES	DEEFHIMU	HUMEFIED
	SEEDSMEN	DEEFHINT	HINDFEET
DEEEMPRT	TEMPERED	DEEFHLOR	FREEHOLD
DEEEMPTX	EXEMPTED	DEEFHLRS	FELDSHER
DEEEMRRU	MURDEREE	DEEFHORT	FOTHERED
DEEEMRSS	DEMERSES	DEEFIILN	FEDELINI
DEEEMRST	DEEMSTER		LENIFIED
DEEENNRT	ENTENDER	DEEFIINT	DEFINITE
DEEENNUW	UNWEENED	DEEFIIRS	DEIFIERS
DEEENOPR	REOPENED		EDIFIERS
DEEENORS	ENDORSEE		FIRESIDE
DEEENPRT	REPENTED	DEEFIIRV	VERIFIED
	REPETEND	DEEFILLR	REFILLED
DEEENPRU	UNPEERED	DEEFILLT	FILLETED
DEEENPRV	PREVENED	DEEFILMS	MEDFLIES
DEEENPRX	EXPENDER	DEEFILNX	INFLEXED
DEEENPSS	DEEPNESS	DEEFILPR	PILFERED
DEEENRRR	RENDERER	DEEFILRS	DEFILERS
DEEENRRT	TENDERER		FIELDERS
DEEENRRV	REVEREND	DEEFILRT	FILTERED
DEEENRST	RESENTED	DEEFIMSS	MISFEEDS
DEEENRTT	TENTERED	DEEFIMTU	TUMEFIED
DEEENRTU	NEUTERED	DEEFINRR	INFERRED
DEEENRTX	EXTENDER	DEEFINRS	DEFINERS
DEEENRUV	REVENUED	DEEFINRZ	FRENZIED
	UNREEVED	DEEFINSS	FINESSED
DEEENSSS	SEEDNESS	DEEFINST	FENDIEST
DEEENSTT	DETENTES		INFESTED
DEEENSTU	DETENUES	DEEFIORS	FORESIDE
DEEENSTX	DENTEXES	DEEFIORT	FOETIDER
DEEENSUV	VENDEUSE	DEEFIPRX	PREFIXED
DEEEOPRR	PEDERERO	DEEFIRRV	FERVIDER
DEEEORVY	OVEREYED	DEEFIRTT	REFITTED
DEEEOSTV	DEVOTEES	DEEFISTT	FETIDEST
DEEEPPPR	PEPPERED	DEEFLLNU	UNFELLED
DEEEPRSS	SPEEDERS	DEEFLNOR	FORELEND
DEEEPRST	ESTREPED	DEEFLNSU	UNSELFED
	PESTERED	DEEFLNTU	DEFLUENT
DEEEPRSZ	SPREEZED	DEEFLORW	DEFLOWER
DEEEPRTX	EXPERTED		FLOWERED
DEEEQRRU	REQUERED		REFLOWED
DEEEQSUZ	SQUEEZED	DEEFLOST	FEEDLOTS
DEEERRRV	VERDERER	DEEFLPSU	SPEEDFUL
DEEERRST	DESERTER	DEEFLRUX	REFLUXED
DEEERRSV	DESERVER	DEEFMNOR	ENFORMED
	RESERVED	DEEFMNOT	FOMENTED
	REVERSED	DEEFMORR	DEFORMER
DEEERRTV	REVERTED		REFORMED
DEEERSSV	DESERVES	DEEFMORS	FREEDOMS
DEEERSTT	RESETTED	DEEFMPRU	PERFUMED
	SETTERED	DEEFNORZ	DEFROZEN
	STREETED	DEEFNOST	SOFTENED
DEEERSTV	REVESTED	DEEFNRRU	REFUNDER
DEEERSTW	WESTERED	DEEFNSST	DEFTNESS
DEEERSTX	EXSERTED	DEEFOORT	REFOOTED
DEEERSUW	SERUEWED	DEEFORST	DEFOREST
DEEERSVW	SERVEWED		FORESTED
DEEERTTT	TETTERED		FOSTERED
DEEERTTV	REVETTED	DEEFORTU	FOUTERED
DEEESTTU	SUEDETTE	DEEFPRSU	PERFUSED
DEEESTTV	VEDETTES	DEEFRRTU	RETURFED
DEEFFGLU	EFFULGED	DEEGGHHO	HEDGEHOG
DEEFFGOR	GOFFERED	DEEGGHIP	HEDGEPIG
DEEFFINR	NIFFERED	DEEGGIJR	JIGGERED
			REJIGGED
		DEEGGINR	GINGERED

	NIGGERED	DEEGLNOR	GOLDENER
	RENIGGED	DEEGLNOU	ENGOULED
DEEGGIRR	DREGGIER	DEEGLNOZ	LOZENGED
DEEGGLOR	DOGGEREL	DEEGLNRY	LEGENDRY
DEEGGNOR	ENGORGED	DEEGLOPR	PLEDGEOR
DEEGGNPU	UNPEGGED	DEEGLOPS	DOGSLEEP
DEEGGORR	REGORGED	DEEGLORV	GROVELED
DEEGGQSU	SQUEGGED	DEEGLORW	GLOWERED
DEEGGRRU	RUGGEDER	DEEGLOSY	GOLDEYES
DEEGHHIR	HIGHERED	DEEGLPRS	PLEDGERS
DEEGHHSU	SHEUGHED	DEEGLPST	PLEDGETS
DEEGHILS	SLEIGHED	DEEGLRSS	SLEDGERS
DEEGHIST	HEDGIEST	DEEGMNRU	DUNGMERE
DEEGHITW	WEIGHTED	DEEGNNOS	ENDOGENS
DEEGHNRU	HUNGERED	DEEGNNOY	ENDOGENY
DEEGHOPR	GOPHERED	DEEGNORV	GOVERNED
DEEGHOPS	SHEEPDOG	DEEGNPRU	REPUGNED
DEEGHORW	HEDGEROW	DEEGNPUX	EXPUGNED
DEEGHOSW	HOGWEEDS		EXPUNGED
DEEGHOTT	DOGTEETH	DEEGOSTU	OUTEDGES
DEEGIINN	INDIGENE	DEEGOTUW	GOUTWEED
DEEGIISS	DIEGESIS	DEEGPRUX	EXPURGED
DEEGIKST	KEDGIEST	DEEGRRSU	RESURGED
DEEGILMO	LIEGEDOM	DEEGRSTU	GESTURED
DEEGILMP	IMPLEDGE	DEEGRTTU	GUTTERED
DEEGILMT	GIMLETED	DEEGSSTU	GUSSETED
DEEGILNN	NEEDLING	DEEHHIRT	HITHERED
DEEGILNO	ELOIGNED	DEEHHNPY	HYPHENED
	LEGIONED	DEEHHPRS	SHEPHERD
DEEGILNR	ENGIRDLE	DEEHHRST	THRESHED
	LINGERED	DEEHHRSU	HUSHERED
	REEDLING	DEEHIKRS	SHREIKED
	SEEDLING		SHRIEKED
DEEGILNS	SEEDLING	DEEHIKSV	KHEDIVES
DEEGILNT	DELETING	DEEHILNS	ENSHIELD
DEEGILRS	LEIDGERS	DEEHILRS	RELISHED
DEEGILRW	WEREGILD		SHIELDER
DEEGILRY	GREEDILY	DEEHILSV	DISHEVEL
DEEGILST	GELIDEST	DEEHIMMS	IMMESHED
	LEDGIEST	DEEHIMNS	INMESHED
DEEGIMMR	IMMERGED	DEEHIMRT	MITHERED
DEEGIMNN	EMENDING	DEEHINRR	HINDERER
DEEGIMNR	REMEDING	DEEHINRS	DRISHEEN
DEEGIMRU	DEMIURGE	DEEHINST	DISTHENE
DEEGINNR	ENRINGED	DEEHINTW	WHITENED
DEEGINNS	ENSIGNED	DEEHIORS	HEROISED
DEEGINNT	TEENDING	DEEHIORZ	HEROIZED
DEEGINNW	ENDEWING	DEEHIPRS	HESPERID
DEEGINOP	PIGEONED		PERISHED
DEEGINPS	SPEEDING	DEEHIRRS	REDSHIRE
DEEGINRS	DESIGNER	DEEHIRRT	DITHERER
	ENERGIDS	DEEHIRSV	SHIVERED
	REDESIGN		SHRIEVED
	REEDINGS	DEEHIRSW	SHREWDIE
	RESIGNED	DEEHIRTW	WITHERED
DEEGINSS	DINGESES	DEEHIRTY	HEREDITY
	EDGINESS	DEEHKLPS	HELPDESK
	SDEIGNES	DEEHKNOS	KEESHOND
	SEEDINGS	DEEHKNRU	HUNKERED
DEEGINST	INGESTED	DEEHKORS	KOSHERED
	SIGNETED	DEEHLLOR	HOLLERED
	STEEDING	DEEHLLOV	HOVELLED
DEEGINSW	WEEDINGS	DEEHLMMW	WHEMMLED
DEEGINSX	DESEXING	DEEHLMNU	UNHELMED
DEEGINZZ	GIZZENED	DEEHLMSW	WHELMESH
DEEGIOST	EGOTISED	DEEHLNPU	UNHELPED
DEEGIOTZ	EGOTIZED	DEEHLORV	OVERHELD
DEEGIPSW	PIGWEEDS		VERDELHO
DEEGIRST	DIGESTER	DEEHLPPS	SHLEPPED
	ESTRIDGE	DEEHLSTU	SLEUTHED
DEEGIRSU	GUDESIRE	DEEHMNRS	HERDSMEN
DEEGIRSV	DIVERGES	DEEHMORT	MOTHERED
DEEGISST	SEDGIEST	DEEHNOPY	PHONEYED
DEEGISTW	WEDGIEST	DEEHNORR	DEERHORN
DEEGJPRU	PREJUDGE		DEHORNER
DEEGJRSU	REJUDGES	DEEHNORT	DETHRONE
DEEGLLOR	GOLLERED		THRENODE
DEEGLLRU	GRUELLED	DEEHNPRS	PREHENDS
DEEGLLUY	GULLEYED	DEEHNSTU	ENTHUSED

DEEHOORV HOOVERED	LOITERED	INQUERED	DEEIRRSU RUDERIES
DEEHOPRT POTHERED	DEEILOTT TOILETED	DEEINQSU SEQUINED	DEEIRRSV REDRIVES
DEEHORRT DEHORTER	DEEILPSS SEEDLIPS	DEEINRRT INTERRED	DEEIRRTV VERDITER
DEEHORSU REHOUSED	DEEILPST EPISTLED	TRENDIER	DEEIRRWW WIREDREW
DEEHORSW SHOWERED	DEEILPSU EPULIDES	DEEINRRV REDRIVEN	DEEIRRZZ RIZZERED
DEEHORTT HOTTERED	DEEILPSY SPEEDILY	DEEINRSS DIRENESS	DEEIRSST EDITRESS
DEEHORTX EXHORTED	DEEILRSU LEISURED	DEEINRST INSERTED	RESISTED
DEEHPRSY SYPHERED	DEEILRSV DELIVERS	NERDIEST	SISTERED
DEEHRRSW SHREWDER	DESILVER	RESIDENT	DEEIRSSU DIURESES
DEEHRTUW WUTHERED	SILVERED	SINTERED	REISSUED
DEEIILNS SIDELINE	SLIVERED	TRENDIES	RESIDUES
DEEIILRV LIVERIED	DEEILRSW WIELDERS	DEEINRSU UREDINES	DEEIRSSV DEVISERS
DEEIILRW WIELDIER	DEEILRSY YIELDERS	DEEINRSW WIDENERS	DISSERVE
DEEIIMRS DIMERISE	DEEILRTT LITTERED	DEEINRSX INDEXERS	DISSEVER
DEEIIMRZ DIMERIZE	RETITLED	DEEINRTU REUNITED	DIVERSES
DEEIIMST ITEMISED	DEEILRVY DELIVERY	DEEINRTV INVERTED	DEEIRSTT TIREDEST
DEEIIMTZ ITEMIZED	DEEILSSS IDLESSES	DEEINRTW WINTERED	DEEIRSTU ERUDITES
DEEIINST DIETINES	DEEILSST TIDELESS	DEEINRTX DEXTRINE	SURETIED
DEEIINSX ENDEIXIS	DEEILSSV DEVILESS	DEEINSST DESTINES	DEEIRSTV VERDITES
DEEIIPRS EPEIRIDS	DEEILSTU DILUTEES	DEEINSSV VENDISES	DEEIRSTW WEIRDEST
DEEIIRSS DIERESIS	DEEILSTV DEVILETS	DEEINSSW DEWINESS	DEEIRTTT TITTERED
DEEIIRST SIDERITE	DEEILSUV DELUSIVE	WIDENESS	DEEIRTTV RIVETTED
DEEIIRSV DERISIVE	DEEILTUY YULETIDE	DEEINSTT DINETTES	DEEIRTTW WITTERED
DEEIIRSW WEIRDIES	DEEIMMNS ENDEMISM	DEEINSTU DETINUES	DEEISSSU DISEUSES
DEEIISSS DISSEISE	DEEIMMRS IMMERSED	DEEINSTV EVIDENTS	DEEISTTV VIDETTES
DEEIISSW SIDEWISE	SIMMERED	INVESTED	DEEJKNTU JUNKETED
DEEIISSZ DISSEIZE	DEEIMMSS MISDEEMS	DEEINSUZ UNSEIZED	DEEJPRRU PERJURED
DEEIJNNO ENJOINED	DEEIMNOR DOMINEER	DEEINTUV DUVETINE	DEEJPTTU UPJETTED
DEEIJNOR REJOINED	DOMINEES	DEEINUVW UNVIEWED	DEEKLNOS SLOKENED
DEEIJRTT JITTERED	DEEIMNOZ DEMONIZE	DEEIOPRT PERIDOTE	DEEKLNST SKLENTED
DEEIKKRY YIKKERED	DEEIMNPT PEDIMENT	DEEIOPRX PEROXIDE	DEEKLRSS SKELDERS
DEEIKLLR KILLDEER	DEEIMNRR REMINDER	DEEIOPSS EPISODES	DEEKMNOY MONKEYED
DEEIKLLS KILLDEES	DEEIMNRT REMINTED	DEEIOPST EPIDOTES	DEEKNNNU UNKENNED
SKELLIED	DEEIMNRV VERMINED	POETISED	DEEKNOTW KNOTWEED
DEEIKLNN ENKINDLE	DEEIMNSS DESMINES	DEEIOPSX EPOXIDES	DEEKNOTY KEYNOTED
ENLINKED	SIDESMEN	DEEIOPTZ POETIZED	DEEKORRW REWORKED
DEEIKLNR REKINDLE	DEEIMNST DEMENTIS	DEEIORRV OVERRIDE	DEEKRUVY KURVEYED
DEEIKLNS SILKENED	SEDIMENT	DEEIORSV OVERSIDE	DEELLMOR MODELLER
DEEIKLOV DOVELIKE	TIDESMEN	DEEIORTU ETOURDIE	DEELLMOW MELLOWED
DEEIKLSW SILKWEED	DEEIMNTT MITTENED	DEEIOTVX VIDEOTEX	DEELLNOP POLLENED
DEEIKMSY MISKEYED	DEEIMOST TEDISOME	DEEIPPQU EQUIPPED	DEELLNOR ENROLLED
DEEIKNRS DEERSKIN	DEEIMPRR PERIDERM	DEEIPPRZ ZIPPERED	DEELLORW ROWELLED
DEEIKNRT TINKERED	REPRIMED	DEEIPPST PEPTIDES	DEELLORY YODELLER
DEEIKNTT KITTENED	DEEIMPRS DEMIREPS	PEPTISED	DEELLOTW TOWELLED
DEEIKOSV DOVEKIES	PREMISED	DEEIPPTT PIPETTED	DEELLOTX EXTOLLED
DEEIKPPR KIPPERED	SIMPERED	DEEIPPTZ PEPTIZED	DEELLOVW VOWELLED
DEEIKRSU DUKERIES	DEEIMPRX PREMIXED	DEEIPQRU REPIQUED	DEELLOVY VOLLEYED
DEEIKRSV SKIVERED	DEEIMPSS SEMIPEDS	DEEIPQTU PIQUETED	DEELLOWY YELLOWED
DEEIKSTT DISKETTE	DEEIMRSS DERMISES	DEEIPRRS REPRISED	DEELLPUW UPWELLED
DEEILLMP IMPELLED	DEEIMRST DEMERITS	RESPIRED	DEELLRSU DUELLERS
MILLEPED	DEMISTER	DEEIPRRV REPRIVED	DEELLRSW DWELLERS
DEEILLNO NIELLOED	DIMETERS	DEEIPRRZ REPRIZED	DEELLSSW WELDLESS
DEEILLOR ORIELLED	MISTERED	DEEIPRSS DESPISER	DEELLSUX DUXELLES
DEEILLPR PERILLED	DEEIMRTT REMITTED	DISPERSE	DEELMMPU EMPLUMED
DEEILLRT TILLERED	DEEIMSSU MEDIUSES	PRESIDES	DEELMNOO MELODEON
TREDILLE	DEEINNRS SINNERED	DEEIPRST PRIESTED	DEELMNOS LODESMEN
DEEILLRV RIVELLED	DEEINNRT INDENTER	RESPITED	DEELMNTU UNMELTED
DEEILLWY WILLEYED	INTENDER	DEEIPRSU DUPERIES	DEELMNTW WELDMENT
DEEILMOS MELODIES	INTERNED	DEEIPRSV DEPRIVES	DEELMOOS DOLESOME
MELODISE	DEEINNRU UNREINED	PREVISED	DEELMOPR EMPOLDER
DEEILMOZ MELODIZE	DEEINNRV INNERVED	DEEIPRTT PITTERED	DEELMOPY EMPLOYED
DEEILMPT IMPLETED	DEEINNST DENTINES	PRETTIED	DEELMORS MODELERS
DEEILNOS ESLOINED	DESINENT	DEEIPRTX EXTIRPED	REMODELS
DEEILNOT DELETION	DEEINNSZ DENIZENS	DEEIPSSS DESPISES	DEELMOST MOLESTED
ENTOILED	DEEINNTV INVENTED	DEEIPSST DESPITES	DEELMOSU DUELSOME
DEEILNPP LIPPENED	DEEINNTW ENTWINED	SIDESTEP	DEELMPSU DEPLUMES
DEEILNRU UNDERLIE	DEEINNUV UNENVIED	DEEIPSTT TEPIDEST	DEELMRUY DEMURELY
DEEILNSS IDLENESS	DEEINOPS DISPONEE	DEEIPSTU DEPUTIES	DEELNNTU TUNNELED
LINSEEDS	DEEINORS ORDINEES	DEPUTISE	DEELNOOS LOOSENED
DEEILNST ENLISTED	DEEINORT ORIENTED	DEEIPTUZ DEPUTIZE	DEELNORT REDOLENT
LINTSEED	DEEINOST SIDENOTE	DEEIQRRU REQUIRED	DEELNORV OVERLEND
LISTENED	DEEINOSV NOSEDIVE	DEEIQRTU REQUITED	DEELNOSS LESSONED
TINSELED	DEEINPPR NIPPERED	DEEIQRUV QUIVERED	DEELNOSU ENSOULED
DEEILNSY DYELINES	DEEINPSS DISPENSE	DEEIQTUU QUIETUDE	DEELNOSY ESLOYNED
DEEILNTT ENTITLED	PIEDNESS	DEEIRRSS DERRIES	DEELNPRS RESPLEND
DEEILNUV UNVEILED	DEEINPST PENTISED	DESIRERS	DEELNRTU UNDERLET
DEEILOPT LEPIDOTE	DEEINPSU UNESPIED	DRESSIER	DEELNRTY TENDERLY
PETIOLED	DEEINQRU ENQUIRED	RESIDERS	DEELNSSW LEWDNESS
DEEILORT DOLERITE		DEEIRRST DESTRIER	DEELNSTY ENSTYLED

DEELOORT RETOOLED	DEENNRTU UNTENDER	DEEORSTT ROSETTED	DEFHIOOW WIFEHOOD
DEELOPPR LOPPERED	DEENNRUV UNNERVED	TETRODES	DEFHLOOS ELFHOODS
DEELOPRS DEPLORES	DEENNSSU NUDENESS	DEEORSTX DEXTROSE	SELFHOOD
DEELOPRX EXPLODER	UNSENSED	DEEORSTY STOREYED	DEFHLOSU FLOUSHED
EXPLORED	DEENNSTU UNNESTED	DEEORSUV OVERUSED	DEFHOOOR FORHOOED
DEELOPRY REDEPLOY	DEENNTTU UNNETTED	DEEORSVY OVERDYES	DEFHOORS SERFHOOD
DEELOPSV DEVELOPS	UNTENTED	DEEORTTT TOTTERED	DEFHOORW FORHOWED
DEELOPSX EXPLODES	DEENNTUV UNVENTED	DEEORTTX EXTORTED	DEFIIILV VILIFIED
DEELORRS SOLDERER	DEENOORT ENROOTED	DEEORTUV DEVOUTER	DEFIIIMN MINIFIED
DEELORSU URODELES	DEENOORV OVERDONE	DEEOSSUX EXODUSES	DEFIIINS NIDIFIES
DEELORSV RESOLVED	DEENOORW WOODENER	DEEOSTUW OUTWEEDS	DEFIIIVV VIVIFIED
DEELORTT DOTTEREL	DEENOPPR PREPONED	DEEOSTUX TUXEDOES	DEFIILLN INFILLED
TOLTERED	DEENOPPR PONDERER	DEEPPRSU SUPPERED	DEFIILLO OILFIELD
DEELORTV REVOLTED	DEENOPSS SPONDEES	DEEPRRSU PERDURES	DEFIILLP FILLIPED
DEELORTY DELETORY	DEENOPST PENTODES	DEEPRRVY REPRYVED	DEFIILLW WILDLIFE
DEELORUV LOUVERED	DEENORRS ENDORSER	DEEPRSTU PERTUSED	DEFIILMS MISFIELD
DEELORVV REVOLVED	DEENORRW WONDERER	DEEPRSUW PURSEWED	MISFILED
DEELOSSU DELOUSES	DEENORSS ENDORSES	DEEPRSUY PSEUDERY	DEFIILNS INFIDELS
DEELOSTV DOVELETS	DEENORST ERODENTS	DEEPRTTU PUTTERED	INFIELDS
DEELOSVV DEVOLVES	DEENORSW ENDOWERS	DEEPRUVY PURVEYED	DEFIILRW WILDFIRE
DEELOTUV EVOLUTED	WORSENED	DEERRSSS DRESSERS	DEFIILSU FLUIDISE
DEELPPRU REPULPED	DEENORTU DEUTERON	DEERRSUV VERDURES	DEFIILTY FIDELITY
DEELPRSS SPELDERS	DEENOSSS ENDOSSES	DEERRTTU TURRETED	DEFIILUZ FLUIDIZE
DEELPRSU PRELUDES	DEENOSST STENOSED	DEERRTUX EXTRUDER	DEFIIMNO OMNIFIED
REPULSED	DEENPPRS PERPENDS	DEERSSST DESSERTS	DEFIIMNU MUNIFIED
DEELPRTU DRUPELET	DEENPRSS SPENDERS	STRESSED	DEFIIMOR MODIFIER
DEELPRUV PULVERED	DEENRRSU ENDURERS	DEERSSSU DURESSES	DEFIIMOS MODIFIES
DEELPRUX DUPLEXER	SUNDERER	DEERSSTU RUSSETED	DEFIIMRS MISFIRED
DEELPSUX DUPLEXES	DEENRRTU RETURNED	DEERSSTY DYESTERS	DEFIIMSS FIDEISMS
EXPULSED	DEENRRSU RUDENESS	DEERSSUV SUVERSED	DEFIIMSW MIDWIFES
DEELPTTY PETTEDLY	DEENRSTU DENTURES	DEERSTUV VESTURED	DEFIINOT NOTIFIED
DEELRSTU LUSTERED	SEDERUNT	DEERSTUX EXTRUDES	DEFIINTU FINITUDE
RESULTED	UNDERSET	DEERSUVW SURVEWED	DEFIINTY IDENTIFY
ULSTERED	UNDESERT	DEERSUVY SURVEYED	DEFIIOSS OSSIFIED
DEELRSTW LEWDSTER	DEENRSUU UNDERUSE	DEERTTUX TEXTURED	DEFIIOTV VIDEOFIT
WRESTLED	DEENRSUV UNVERSED	DEFFHILW WHIFFLED	DEFIIPRU PURIFIED
DEELRSTY RESTYLED	DEENRTUV VENTURED	DEFFHLSU SHUFFLED	DEFIIPSS FISSIPED
DEEMMORS MESODERM	DEENSSSY SYNDESES	DEFFHORS SHROFFED	DEFIIPTY TYPIFIED
DEEMMRRU DUMMERER	DEENSTTU UNTESTED	DEFFILNS SNIFFLED	DEFIIRRT DRIFTIER
DEEMMRSU SUMMERED	DEENTTUV UNVETTED	DEFFILOV FIVEFOLD	DEFIISST FIDEISTS
DEEMNNRU UNDERMEN	DEENTTUW UNWETTED	DEFFIMOS FIEFDOMS	DEFILLNU UNFILLED
DEEMNNTU TENENDUM	DEENTUVY DUVETYNE	DEFFIORS OFFSIDER	DEFILLPU UPFILLED
DEEMNOOS MOONSEED	DEEOORRV OVERDOER	DEFFIOSS OFFSIDES	DEFILMNU FULMINED
DEEMNOQU QUEENDOM	OVERRODE	DEFFIRSU DIFFUSER	UNFILMED
DEEMNORR MODERNER	DEEOORSV OVERDOES	DEFFISSU DIFFUSES	DEFILNNO NINEFOLD
DEEMNORS SERMONED	OVERDOSE	DEFFISUX SUFFIXED	DEFILNRS FLINDERS
DEEMNORT ENTODERM	DEEOPPRS PREPOSED	DEFFLNSU SNUFFLED	DEFILNRU UNRIFLED
DEEMNOSS DEMONESS	DEEOPPST ESTOPPED	DEFFLRTU TRUFFLED	URNFIELD
ENMOSSED	DEEOPRRR PREORDER	DEFFNORS FORFENDS	DEFILNRY FRIENDLY
DEEMOORT ODOMETER	DEEOPRRS PEDREROS	DEFFSSUU SUFFUSED	DEFILOPR PROFILED
DEEMOPPY POMPEYED	DEEOPRRT REPORTED	DEFFSTUY DYESTUFF	DEFILORR FLORIDER
DEEMOPRV PREMOVED	DEEOPRRV REPROVED	DEFGGILN FLEDGING	DEFILORU FLUORIDE
DEEMOPST DEEPMOST	DEEOPRSS DEPOSERS	DEFGHILT FLIGHTED	DEFILOTU OUTFIELD
DEEMOQRU QUEERDOM	DEEOPRST POSTERED	DEFGHIRT FRIGHTED	DEFILPRU PRIDEFUL
DEEMORRT TREMORED	REEDSTOP	DEFGIILN DEFILING	DEFILPTU UPLIFTED
DEEMORST MODESTER	REPOSTED	FIELDING	DEFILRRU FLURRIED
DEEMORSW WORMSEED	DEEOPRTT POTTERED	DEFGIILU UGLIFIED	DEFILRVY FERVIDLY
DEEMORSX EXODERMS	REPOTTED	DEFGIINN DEFINING	DEFILRZZ FRIZZLED
DEEMORTU MOUTERED	DEEOPRTW POWTERED	DEFGIINY DEIFYING	DEFILSSU SULFIDES
UDOMETER	DEEOPRTX EXPORTED	EDIFYING	DEFIMNOR INFORMED
DEEMPRST DEMPSTER	DEEOPRUZ DOUZEPER	DEFGIIRR FRIGIDER	DEFIMORY REMODIFY
DEEMPRSU PRESUMED	DEEOPSST POSSETED	DEFGILNU INGULFED	DEFIMRRU DRUMFIRE
DEEMPRTU PERMUTED	DEEOPSSU ESPOUSED	DEFGILTY GIFTEDLY	DEFINNRU REINFUND
DEEMRRRU DEMURRER	DEEOQRTU REQUOTED	DEFGINSU DEFUSING	UNFRIEND
MURDERER	ROQUETED	FEUDINGS	DEFINOPR FORPINED
DEEMRSTU DEMUREST	DEEORRRS ORDERERS	DEFGINTU UNGIFTED	DEFINORW FOREWIND
MUSTERED	REORDERS	DEFGINUZ DEFUZING	DEFINSTU UNSIFTED
DEEMRTTU MUTTERED	DEEORRRV VERDEROR	DEFGIOOW GOODWIFE	DEFINTTU UNFITTED
DEEMSSTY SYSTEMED	DEEORRST RESORTED	DEFGIORS FIREDOGS	DEFIOORW FIREWOOD
DEENNNOP PENNONED	RESTORED	DEFGJORU FORJUDGE	DEFIOPRT PROFITED
DEENNNPU UNPENNED	ROSTERED	DEFGMOOY FOGEYDOM	DEFIORRU FROIDEUR
DEENNOPT DEPONENT	DEEORRSV OVERREDS	DEFGNORU UNFORGED	DEFIORSU FOUDRIES
DEENNOPU UNOPENED	DEEORRTT RETORTED	DEFGOOSX DOGFOXES	DEFIOTXY DETOXIFY
DEENNORS ENDERONS	DEEORRTU REROUTED	DEFHIIMU HUMIFIED	DEFIRRST DRIFTERS
DEENNORW RENOWNED	RETOURED	DEFHIINS FIENDISH	DEFIRSSU FRISSURE
DEENNOSS DONENESS	DEEORRUV DEVOURER	FINISHED	DEFISSTU FEUDISTS
DEENNOST SONNETED	DEEORRVW OVERDREW	DEFHILLO LIFEHOLD	DEFKLORY FORKEDLY
DEENNOSY DOYENNES	DEEORSST OERSTEDS	DEFHILSS DISFLESH	DEFLLOOR FOLDEROL
DEENNPST PENDENTS		DEFHINSU UNFISHED	DEFLLOOW FOLLOWED

DEFLMPRU	FRUMPLED
DEFLNOOU	UNFOOLED
DEFLNOPS	PENFOLDS
DEFLNORS	FONDLERS
	FORLENDS
DEFLNORU	FLOUNDER
	UNFOLDER
DEFLNRUU	UNFURLED
DEFLNSSU	FUNDLESS
DEFLOORS	FORSLOED
DEFLOORT	FORETOLD
DEFLOORV	OVERFOLD
DEFLOOSS	FOODLESS
DEFLOPUW	UPFLOWED
DEFLORSU	FOULDERS
DEFLPRUU	UPFURLED
DEFLRSUU	SULFURED
DEFMNORU	UNFORMED
DEFMOOOR	FOREDOOM
DEFMORSS	SERFDOMS
DEFNNORT	FRONDENT
DEFNNOSS	FONDNESS
DEFNOOPS	SPOONFED
DEFNOORS	FRONDOSE
DEFNOORU	UNROOFED
DEFNOORV	OVERFOND
DEFNOOTU	UNFOOTED
DEFNOPRS	FORSPEND
DEFNORRU	FRONDEUR
DEFNORSU	FOUNDERS
	REFOUNDS
DEFNORTU	FORTUNED
DEFNORUV	OVERFUND
DEFNOSSW	DOWFNESS
DEFNRRUU	UNDERFUR
	UNFURRED
DEFNRTUU	UNTURFED
DEFOORRW	FOREWORD
DEFOOTUX	OUTFOXED
DEFORRUW	FURROWED
DEFORSST	DEFROSTS
DEFORSTW	FROWSTED
DEGGGIIT	GIGGITED
DEGGGILN	GLEDGING
DEGGHINS	HEDGINGS
DEGGHLOS	SHOGGLED
DEGGHRSU	SHRUGGED
DEGGIINN	DEIGNING
DEGGILNP	PLEDGING
DEGGILNS	GELDINGS
	SLEDGING
	SNIGGLED
DEGGILNU	DELUGING
DEGGILRW	WRIGGLED
DEGGINNU	UNEDGING
DEGGINRU	UNRIGGED
DEGGINSW	WEDGINGS
DEGGINUW	UNWIGGED
DEGGIORS	DISGORGE
DEGGIOST	DOGGIEST
DEGGIPRS	SPRIGGED
DEGGIRRU	DRUGGIER
DEGGIRST	STRIGGED
DEGGIRSU	DRUGGIES
DEGGLMSU	SMUGGLED
DEGGLNSU	SNUGGLED
DEGGLORS	DOGGRELS
DEGGLRUY	RUGGEDLY
DEGGNOOR	DOGGONER
DEGGNORU	UNGORGED
DEGGNOSU	GUDGEONS
DEGGRRSU	DRUGGERS
DEGGRSTU	DRUGGETS
DEGHIILL	GHILLIED
DEGHIINS	DINGHIES
DEGHIKNT	KNIGHTED
DEGHILNS	HINDLEGS
	SHINGLED
DEGHILOU	OUGHLIED

DEGHILPT	PLIGHTED
DEGHILST	DELIGHTS
	SLIGHTED
DEGHINNS	SHENDING
DEGHINNU	UNHINGED
DEGHIOOS	SHOOGIED
DEGHIORU	DOUGHIER
DEGHIPST	DESPIGHT
	SPIGHTED
DEGHIQTU	QUIGHTED
DEGHITTW	TWIGHTED
DEGHLNOR	HORNGELD
DEGHLOOS	DOGHOLES
	GOLOSHED
	SHOOGLED
DEGHLOPU	PLOUGHED
DEGHLOSU	SLOUGHED
DEGHMOSU	GUMSHOED
DEGHMPRU	GRUMPHED
DEGHNORT	THRONGED
DEGHNORY	HYDROGEN
DEGHORRS	DROGHERS
DEGHPSUU	UPGUSHED
DEGIIIRS	RIGIDISE
DEGIIIRZ	RIGIDIZE
DEGIIIST	DIGITISE
DEGIIITZ	DIGITIZE
DEGIIKST	KIDGIEST
DEGIILNR	GRIDELIN
DEGIILNS	EILDINGS
	SIDELING
DEGIILNT	DILIGENT
DEGIILNV	DEVILING
DEGIILNW	WIELDING
DEGIILNY	YIELDING
DEGIILTY	GELIDITY
DEGIIMNP	IMPEDING
	IMPINGED
DEGIIMNS	DEMISING
DEGIIMSU	MISGUIDE
DEGIINNR	NIDERING
DEGIINNS	DESINING
	SDEINING
DEGIINNT	ENDITING
	INDIGENT
	TEINDING
DEGIINNW	INDEWING
	WIDENING
DEGIINNX	INDEXING
DEGIINNZ	DIZENING
DEGIINOS	INDIGOES
DEGIINOV	VIDEOING
DEGIINRS	DESIRING
	RESIDING
	RINGSIDE
DEGIINRT	DIRIGENT
DEGIINRV	DERIVING
	VIRGINED
DEGIINRW	WEIRDING
DEGIINST	DINGIEST
	INDIGEST
DEGIINSV	DEVISING
DEGIIRST	RIDGIEST
	RIGIDEST
DEGIISSU	DISGUISE
DEGIJMSU	MISJUDGE
DEGIKKNO	DEKKOING
DEGIKLNU	DUKELING
DEGIKNNU	UNKINGED
DEGILLNU	DUELLING
DEGILLNW	DWELLING
DEGILMNO	MODELING
DEGILMPS	GLIMPSED
DEGILNNO	OLDENING
DEGILNNS	LENDINGS
DEGILNOP	DELOPING
	DIPLOGEN
DEGILNOS	GLENOIDS

	SIDELONG
DEGILNPS	SPELDING
DEGILNRU	INDULGER
DEGILNRY	YELDRING
DEGILNSU	INDULGES
DEGILNSV	DEVLINGS
DEGILNSW	SWINGLED
	WELDINGS
DEGILNWY	WINGEDLY
DEGILOOR	GOODLIER
DEGILOOY	IDEOLOGY
DEGILOST	GODLIEST
	GOLDIEST
DEGILOSZ	GOLDSIZE
DEGILPSU	PULSIDGE
DEGILRRS	GIRDLERS
DEGILRSU	GUILDERS
	SLUDGIER
DEGILRSW	WERGILDS
DEGILRZZ	GRIZZLED
DEGILSUV	DIVULGES
DEGIMMNO	MODEMING
DEGIMNNS	MENDINGS
DEGIMNOS	SMIDGEON
DEGIMNOT	DEMOTING
DEGIMNPU	IMPUGNED
DEGIMNRU	DEMURING
DEGIMNSS	SMIDGENS
DEGIMOOT	GOODTIME
DEGIMOOY	GEOMYOID
DEGIMRSU	SMUDGIER
DEGINNNU	UNENDING
DEGINNOP	DEPONING
DEGINNOT	DENOTING
DEGINNOW	ENDOWING
DEGINNOZ	DOZENING
DEGINNPS	SPENDING
DEGINNPU	UPENDING
DEGINNRT	TRENDING
DEGINNRU	ENDURING
	UNRINGED
DEGINNSS	SENDINGS
DEGINNST	STENDING
DEGINNSU	UNSIGNED
DEGINNSY	DESYNING
DEGINNTU	DETUNING
	UNTINGED
DEGINNUW	UNWINGED
DEGINOPR	PROIGNED
DEGINOPS	DEPOSING
	DISPONGE
	PIDGEONS
DEGINORR	ORDERING
DEGINORS	NEGROIDS
DEGINORU	GUERIDON
DEGINORV	DOVERING
DEGINORW	DOWERING
DEGINOSW	WENDIGOS
	WIDGEONS
DEGINOTV	DEVOTING
DEGINOTX	DETOXING
DEGINPRS	SPRINGED
DEGINPRY	PREDYING
DEGINPSU	DISPUNGE
DEGINPTU	DEPUTING
DEGINRRS	GRINDERS
	REGRINDS
DEGINRRY	GRINDERY
DEGINRSS	DRESSING
DEGINRST	STRINGED
DEGINRSW	REDWINGS
DEGINRSY	SYNERGID
	SYRINGED
DEGINSSU	DINGUSES
DEGINSSW	SWINDGES
DEGINSTU	DUNGIEST
DEGINTTU	DUETTING
DEGIOORS	GOODSIRE
DEGIOOST	GOODIEST

DEGIOPRR	PORRIDGE
DEGIOPSS	GOSSIPED
DEGIOPST	PODGIEST
DEGIORRU	GOURDIER
DEGIORST	GRODIEST
	STODGIER
DEGIPSTU	PUDGIEST
DEGIQSSU	SQUIDGES
DEGIRRTU	TURGIDER
DEGIRSTU	DURGIEST
DEGISSST	DISGESTS
DEGJMNTU	JUDGMENT
DEGLLNOY	GOLDENLY
DEGLLOOP	GOLLOPED
DEGLLOSS	GOLDLESS
DEGLMNOT	LODGMENT
DEGLMOOY	DEMOLOGY
DEGLNOUV	UNGLOVED
DEGLNRTU	GRUNTLED
DEGLOOPY	PEDOLOGY
DEGLOOUU	DUOLOGUE
DEGLOPRS	PLEDGORS
DEGLOPSS	SPLODGES
DEGLPRSU	SPLURGED
DEGMMNUU	UNGUMMED
DEGMRSSU	SMUDGERS
DEGNNORU	GROUNDEN
DEGNNOSU	DUNGEONS
DEGNNOUW	UNGOWNED
DEGNOORS	DRONGOES
DEGNOOSS	GOODNESS
DEGNOOST	STEGODON
DEGNOPPU	OPPUGNED
DEGNORRU	GROUNDER
	REGROUND
DEGNORSU	GUERDONS
DEGNORTU	TRUDGEON
DEGNORUU	UNROUGED
DEGNORYY	GYRODYNE
DEGNPRUU	UNPURGED
DEGNRSTU	TRUDGENS
DEGORSST	STODGERS
DEGORSTU	DROGUETS
DEGPRSUU	UPSURGED
DEGRRSTU	TRUDGERS
DEHHILTW	WITHHELD
DEHHISTW	WHISHTED
DEHHMRTY	RHYTHMED
DEHHOOSW	WHOOSHED
DEHIILLS	HILLSIDE
DEHIILLW	WHILLIED
DEHIILSV	DEVILISH
DEHIILNS	LINISHED
DEHIIMMS	SHIMMIED
DEHIIMNS	MINISHED
DEHIIMRU	MUDIRIEH
DEHIIMST	DITHEISM
	SMITHIED
DEHIINNS	SHINNIED
DEHIINNW	WHINNIED
DEHIINSS	SHINDIES
DEHIIRRW	WHIRRIED
DEHIIRST	DISHERIT
DEHIISST	DISHIEST
DEHIISTT	DITHEIST
	STITHIED
DEHIJMNO	DEMIJOHN
DEHIKMOS	SHEIKDOM
DEHIKPSU	DUKESHIP
DEHILLOP	PHELLOID
DEHILLRS	SHRILLED
DEHILLRT	THRILLED
DEHILMOS	DEMOLISH
DEHILMPW	WHIMPLED
DEHILMSS	DISHELMS
DEHILMTY	DIMETHYL
DEHILNOR	INHOLDER
DEHILNPY	DIPHENYL
DEHILOOR	HELIODOR

DEHILOOS	DHOOLIES
DEHILOPS	POLISHED
DEHILPSU	SULPHIDE
DEHILPSY	SYLPHIDE
DEHILRTW	WRITHLED
DEHILSTW	WHISTLED
DEHILTTW	WHITTLED
DEHIMNOS	HEDONISM
DEHIMORS	HEIRDOMS
DEHIMOSS	DISHOMES
DEHIMPRS	SHRIMPED
DEHIMPSY	DEMYSHIP
DEHIMSTU	HUMIDEST
DEHIMSTY	MYTHISED
DEHIMTYZ	MYTHIZED
DEHINOOP	INHOOPED
DEHINOPR	NEPHROID
DEHINOPS	DIPHONES
	SIPHONED
	SPHENOID
DEHINORS	HORDEINS
DEHINOST	HEDONIST
DEHINPSS	ENDSHIPS
DEHINPSU	PUNISHED
DEHINSUW	UNWISHED
DEHIOOVW	WIVEHOOD
DEHIOPRS	SPHEROID
DEHIOPRT	TROPHIED
DEHIORRR	HORRIDER
DEHIORSS	DISHORSE
	HIDROSES
DEHIORTU	OUTHIRED
DEHIORTW	WORTHIED
DEHIORTY	THYREOID
DEHIOSSU	DISHOUSE
DEHIOSSW	SIDESHOW
DEHIOSTU	HIDEOUTS
DEHIPSSU	PSEUDISH
DEHIQSSU	SQUISHED
DEHIRRSU	DHURRIES
DEHIRSTT	THIRSTED
	THRISTED
DEHIRTWW	WITHDREW
DEHKLNOU	ELKHOUND
DEHKNOOU	UNHOOKED
DEHKNSUU	UNHUSKED
DEHKOOSS	SKOOSHED
DEHLLOOW	HOLLOWED
DEHLLOPY	PHYLLODE
DEHLMMOW	WHOMMLED
DEHLMMUW	WHUMMLED
DEHLMORY	HYDROMEL
DEHLMOSU	MUDHOLES
DEHLNOOW	DOWNHOLE
DEHLOOOW	WOODHOLE
DEHLOOPT	POTHOLED
DEHLOORV	HOLDOVER
	OVERHOLD
DEHLOOSS	HOODLESS
	SLOOSHED
DEHLOOST	TOEHOLDS
DEHLOOSW	WOOLSHED
DEHLOPRU	UPHOLDER
DEHLOPSS	SPLOSHED
DEHLORSU	SHOULDER
DEHLPRUU	UPHURLED
DEHLRRSU	HURDLERS
DEHLRSWY	SHREWDLY
DEHLSTTU	SHUTTLED
DEHMMRTU	THRUMMED
DEHMNOOY	HOMODYNE
DEHMNRUY	UNRHYMED
DEHMOORW	WHOREDOM
DEHMOOSS	SHMOOSED
DEHMOOST	SMOOTHED
DEHMOOSZ	SHMOOZED
DEHMOPRY	HYPODERM
DEHMORUU	HUMOURED
DEHNNTUU	UNHUNTED

DEHNOOPU	UNHOOPED
DEHNOORU	HONOURED
DEHNOOSW	HOEDOWNS
DEHNOPSY	SYPHONED
DEHNORSU	ENSHROUD
	UNHORSED
DEHNORSY	ENHYDROS
DEHNORTY	THRENODY
DEHNOSTZ	DOZENTHS
DEHNOSUU	UNHOUSED
DEHNRSTU	THUNDERS
DEHNRTUY	THUNDERY
DEHOOOPP	POPEHOOD
DEHOOPRT	THEROPOD
DEHOOSSW	SWOOSHED
DEHOPRST	POTSHERD
DEHORRST	REDSHORT
DEHORTUY	OUTHYRED
DEHOSSTU	STOUSHED
DEHPPSTU	SHTUPPED
DEHPRSSU	SPRUSHED
DEHPRSUU	UPRUSHED
DEHRRSTU	DRUTHERS
DEHRSTTU	THRUSTED
DEIIIMST	DIMITIES
DEIIINSV	DIVINISE
DEIIINVZ	DIVINIZE
DEIIIRSS	IRIDISES
DEIIIRSZ	IRIDIZES
DEIIIRTV	VIRIDITE
DEIIISVV	DIVISIVE
DEIIKLMS	MISLIKED
DEIIKLNR	KINDLIER
DEIIKLNS	DISLIKEN
DEIIKLNV	DEVILKIN
DEIIKLSS	DISLIKES
DEIIKNST	DINKIEST
DEIIKSVV	SKIVVIED
DEIILLMP	MILLIPED
DEIILLMT	TIDEMILL
DEIILLST	DILLIEST
DEIILMPR	DIMPLIER
DEIILMRU	DELIRIUM
DEIILMST	DELIMITS
	LIMITEDS
DEIILMSV	DEVILISM
	MISLIVED
DEIILNNU	INDULINE
DEIILNOS	LIONISED
DEIILNOZ	LIONIZED
DEIILNPV	VILIPEND
DEIILNVY	DIVINELY
DEIILOPS	PLOIDIES
DEIILORS	IDOLISER
DEIILORZ	IDOLIZER
DEIILOSS	IDOLISES
DEIILOSZ	IDOLIZES
DEIILPRT	TRIPLIED
DEIILPSS	SIDESLIP
DEIILRST	REDISTIL
DEIILSTU	UTILISED
DEIILSTV	LIVIDEST
DEIILTUY	TUILYIED
DEIILTUZ	TUILZIED
	UTILIZED
DEIIMMRS	DIMERISM
DEIIMMST	MISTIMED
DEIIMMTT	IMMITTED
DEIIMNOS	DOMINIES
DEIIMNRT	DIRIMENT
DEIIMNTU	MUTINIED
DEIIMNUV	VENIDIUM
DEIIMPRU	PERIDIUM
DEIIMSST	MISDIETS
DEIIMSTT	TIMIDEST
DEIIMSVW	MIDWIVES
DEIINNOP	PINIONED
DEIINNPP	PINNIPED
DEIINNTW	INTWINED

DEIINNUV	UNDIVINE
DEIINORS	DERISION
	IRONISED
	RESINOID
DEIINORT	RETINOID
DEIINORZ	IRONIZED
DEIINOST	EDITIONS
	SEDITION
DEIINOSV	VISIONED
DEIINPPW	WINDPIPE
DEIINPRS	INSPIRED
DEIINPRT	INTREPID
DEIINPRY	PYRIDINE
DEIINPTU	UNPITIED
DEIINQRU	INQUIRED
DEIINQSU	QUINSIED
	SQUINIED
DEIINRSS	INDRISES
	INSIDERS
DEIINRST	DISINTER
	INDITERS
	NITRIDES
	RINDIEST
DEIINRSU	DISINURE
	URIDINES
DEIINRSV	DIVINERS
DEIINRTU	UNTIDIER
DEIINSST	INSISTED
	TIDINESS
DEIINSTU	DISUNITE
	NUDITIES
	UNITISED
	UNTIDIES
DEIINSTV	DIVINEST
DEIINSTW	WINDIEST
DEIINTTU	INTUITED
DEIINTTY	IDENTITY
DEIINTUZ	UNITIZED
DEIIOPRS	PRESIDIO
DEIIOPRT	DIPTEROI
DEIIOPZZ	PEZIZOID
DEIIORST	DIORITES
DEIIORSX	OXIDISER
DEIIORTX	TRIOXIDE
DEIIORTY	IODYRITE
DEIIORXZ	OXIDIZER
DEIIOSSX	OXIDISES
DEIIOSXZ	OXIDIZES
DEIIPPRR	DRIPPIER
DEIIPPST	DIPPIEST
DEIIPRST	RIPTIDES
	SPIRITED
DEIIPRSZ	DISPRIZE
DEIIPTTY	TEPIDITY
DEIIQSTU	DISQUIET
DEIIRSSU	DIURESIS
DEIIRSTT	DIRTIEST
	TRITIDES
DEIISSTT	DIETISTS
	DITSIEST
DEIISTTZ	DITZIEST
DEIISTVV	VIVIDEST
DEIISTZZ	DIZZIEST
DEIJNORS	JOINDERS
DEIJNSSU	DISJUNES
DEIKKLNO	KLONDIKE
DEIKLLSS	DESKILLS
DEIKLMMS	SKLIMMED
DEIKLMNU	UNMILKED
DEIKLNNU	UNLINKED
DEIKLNRS	KINDLERS
DEIKLNRW	WRINKLED
DEIKLNSS	KINDLESS
DEIKLNTW	TWINKLED
DEIKLSSS	DISKLESS
DEIKLSTT	SKITTLED
DEIKMOSY	MISYOKED
DEIKMPRS	SKRIMPED
DEIKNNPU	UNPINKED

DEIKNNRU	UNKINDER
DEIKNNSS	KINDNESS
DEIKNORV	OVERKIND
DEIKNORW	INWORKED
DEIKNRRS	DRINKERS
DEIKNRSS	REDSKINS
DEIKNSSU	UNKISSED
DEIKORSS	DROSKIES
DEIKORST	DORKIEST
DEIKOSSY	DISYOKES
DEIKPRSU	PRUSIKED
	SPRUIKED
DEIKRRSU	SKURRIED
DEIKRSVY	SKYDIVER
DEIKSSTU	DUSKIEST
DEILLMNU	UNMILLED
DEILLNSW	INDWELLS
DEILLNTU	UNTILLED
DEILLNUW	UNWILLED
DEILLOOV	LIVELOOD
DEILLOPW	PILLOWED
DEILLORR	LORDLIER
DEILLORS	DOLLIERS
DEILLOSV	LIVELODS
DEILLOWW	WILLOWED
DEILLRRS	DRILLERS
DEILLRSV	DREVILLS
DEILLSTU	DUELLIST
	DULLIEST
DEILMNOO	MELODION
DEILMNSS	MILDNESS
	MINDLESS
DEILMNSU	MUSLINED
DEILMOOT	DOLOMITE
DEILMOPR	IMPLORED
	IMPOLDER
DEILMOPS	IMPLODES
DEILMORU	LEMUROID
	MOULDIER
DEILMOST	MELODIST
DEILMOSU	EMULSOID
DEILMPPU	PLUMIPED
DEILMPSU	DISPLUME
	IMPULSED
DEILMPTU	MULTIPED
DEILMRRU	DRUMLIER
DEILMRSU	MISRULED
DEILMSSY	DEMISSLY
DEILNNOT	INDOLENT
DEILNOOS	SOLENOID
DEILNOPT	TOPLINED
DEILNORS	DISENROL
DEILNOSS	SONDELIS
DEILNOSU	DELUSION
	INSOULED
	UNSOILED
DEILNOTU	OUTLINED
DEILNOVV	INVOLVED
DEILNPRS	SPELDRIN
DEILNPRU	UNDERLIP
DEILNPSS	SPELDINS
	SPINDLES
DEILNPST	SPLINTED
DEILNRSS	RINDLESS
DEILNRST	SNIRTLED
	TENDRILS
	TRINDLES
DEILNRSW	SWINDLER
DEILNRTY	TRENDILY
DEILNSSV	VILDNESS
DEILNSSW	SWINDLES
	WILDNESS
	WINDLESS
DEILNSTU	DILUENTS
	INSULTED
	UNLISTED
DEILNTTU	UNTITLED
DEILNTUY	UNITEDLY
DEILNUWY	UNWIELDY

DEILOOPS	POOLSIDE		
DEILOOPW	WOODPILE		
DEILOPPY	POLYPIDE		
DEILOPRU	PRELUDIO		
DEILOPSS	DESPOILS		
	SOLIPEDS		
DEILOQRU	LIQUORED		
DEILORSS	SOLDIERS		
DEILORST	STOLIDER		
DEILORSU	SOULDIER		
DEILORSY	SOLDIERY		
DEILOSST	SOLIDEST		
DEILOSSV	DISSOLVE		
DEILOSTT	DOILTEST		
DEILOSTU	SOLITUDE		
DEILOTUV	OUTLIVED		
DEILPPRT	TRIPPLED		
DEILPPST	STIPPLED		
DEILPPSU	SUPPLIED		
DEILPPTU	PULPITED		
DEILPSTT	SPLITTED		
DEILPSTU	STIPULED		
DEILPSUY	SPULYIED		
DEILPSUZ	SPULZIED		
DEILPTTU	UPTILTED		
DEILRSTU	DILUTERS		
	LURIDEST		
DEILRSVY	DIVERSLY		
DEILRSZZ	DRIZZLES		
DEILRTVY	DEVILTRY		
DEILSSTY	DISTYLES		
	STYLISED		
DEILSTUY	SEDULITY		
DEILSTYZ	STYLIZED		
DEILSWZZ	SWIZZLED		
DEILTWZZ	TWIZZLED		
DEIMMNOS	DEMONISM		
DEIMMOST	IMMODEST		
DEIMMPST	MISDEMPT		
DEIMMRST	MIDTERMS		
DEIMMSTU	DUMMIEST		
DEIMNNOS	MISDONNE		
DEIMNNOU	UNMONIED		
DEIMNNSU	MINUENDS		
DEIMNOOS	DOMINOES		
	MONODIES		
DEIMNOOT	DEMOTION		
	MOTIONED		
DEIMNOOX	MONOXIDE		
DEIMNOPT	PIEDMONT		
DEIMNORT	DORMIENT		
DEIMNOST	DEMONIST		
DEIMNOTW	DOWNTIME		
DEIMNOWW	WIDOWMEN		
DEIMNPRU	UNPRIMED		
DEIMNPSS	MISSPEND		
DEIMNPTU	IMPUDENT		
DEIMNRTU	RUDIMENT		
DEIMNSSS	MISSENDS		
DEIMNSST	MINDSETS		
DEIMNSSU	UNMISSED		
DEIMNSSW	MISWENDS		
DEIMNSTU	MISTUNED		
DEIMOORS	MOIDORES		
DEIMOOSS	SODOMIES		
	SODOMISE		
DEIMOOST	DOOMIEST		
	MOODIEST		
	SODOMITE		
DEIMOOSZ	SODOMIZE		
DEIMOPRS	PROMISED		
DEIMOPRT	IMPORTED		
DEIMOPRV	IMPROVED		
DEIMORRR	MIRRORED		
DEIMORRS	MISORDER		
	MORRISED		
DEIMORSS	MISDOERS		
DEIMORST	MORTISED		
DEIMORSU	DIMEROUS		
	ERODIUMS		
	SOREDIUM		
DEIMORUX	EXORDIUM		
DEIMOSST	MODISTES		
DEIMOSTT	DEMOTIST		
DEIMPRST	DIREMPTS		
DEIMPSTU	DUMPIEST		
DEIMQRSU	SQUIRMED		
DEIMRSSU	SURMISED		
DEIMRSUU	RESIDUUM		
DEINNNOU	INNUENDO		
DEINNNPU	UNPINNED		
DEINNNSU	NUNDINES		
DEINNNTU	UNTINNED		
DEINNOOT	NOONTIDE		
DEINNORS	ENDIRONS		
DEINNORU	UNIRONED		
DEINNOWW	WINNOWED		
DEINNPRU	UNDERPIN		
DEINNRUU	UNINURED		
DEINNRUV	UNDRIVEN		
DEINNSTU	DUNNIEST		
	DUNNITES		
DEINOOPS	POISONED		
DEINOOPW	PINEWOOD		
DEINOOSZ	OZONISED		
DEINOOTV	DEVOTION		
DEINOOZZ	OZONIZED		
DEINOPPR	PROPINED		
DEINOPPW	DOWNPIPE		
DEINOPRS	DISPONER		
	POINDERS		
	PRISONED		
DEINOPRV	PROVINED		
DEINOPRY	PYRENOID		
DEINOPSS	DISPONES		
	DOPINESS		
	SPINODES		
DEINOPSU	UNPOISED		
DEINOPTW	DEWPOINT		
DEINORSS	INDORSES		
DEINORST	DRONIEST		
DEINORSU	DOURINES		
	SOURDINE		
DEINORSW	DISOWNER		
	WINDOERS		
	WINDROSE		
DEINORTT	INTORTED		
DEINORVW	OVERWIND		
DEINOSST	DONSIEST		
DEINOSSV	VOIDNESS		
DEINOSSZ	DOZINESS		
DEINOSTW	DOWNIEST		
DEINOSWZ	DOWNSIZE		
DEINOTTU	DUETTINO		
DEINPPRU	UNRIPPED		
DEINPPUZ	UNZIPPED		
DEINPRST	SPRINTED		
DEINPRTU	TURNIPED		
DEINPRUZ	UNPRIZED		
DEINPSST	STIPENDS		
DEINQSTU	SQUINTED		
DEINRRTU	INTRUDER		
DEINRSSU	INSUREDS		
	SUNDRIES		
DEINRSTT	STRIDENT		
	TRIDENTS		
DEINRSTU	INTRUDES		
DEINRSTX	DEXTRINS		
DEINRTUW	UNDERWIT		
DEINSSST	DISNESTS		
	DISSENTS		
DEINSSSY	SYNDESIS		
DEINSSTT	DENTISTS		
DEINSSTU	DISTUNES		
DEINSTUU	UNSUITED		
DEINTTUW	UNWITTED		
DEIOOPRR	DROOPIER		
DEIOORSW	WOODSIER		
DEIOOSTW	WOODIEST		
DEIOOSVV	VOIVODES		
DEIOOSWW	WOIWODES		
DEIOPRRV	PROVIDER		
DEIOPRSS	DISPOSER		
	DROPSIES		
DEIOPRST	DIOPTERS		
	DIOPTRES		
	DIPTEROS		
	PERIDOTS		
	PROTEIDS		
	RIPOSTED		
DEIOPRSV	DISPROVE		
	PROVIDES		
DEIOPRSW	DROPWISE		
DEIOPSSS	DISPOSES		
DEIOPSST	DEPOSITS		
	TOPSIDES		
DEIORRRT	TORRIDER		
DEIORRSS	DROSSIER		
DEIORRSW	DROWSIER		
DEIORRSY	DERISORY		
DEIORRTU	OUTRIDER		
DEIORRTW	WORRITED		
DEIORRZZ	RIZZORED		
DEIORSSS	DOSSIERS		
DEIORSST	STEROIDS		
DEIORSSU	DESIROUS		
DEIORSSV	DEVISORS		
DEIORSTT	DORTIEST		
DEIORSTU	IODURETS		
	OUTRIDES		
	OUTSIDER		
	SUITORED		
DEIORSTW	ROWDIEST		
	WORDIEST		
DEIORSWW	WIDOWERS		
DEIORTUV	OUTDRIVE		
DEIOSSTU	OUTSIDES		
DEIOSSTX	EXODISTS		
DEIOSTUZ	OUTSIZED		
DEIPPRST	STRIPPED		
DEIPPTTU	TITUPPED		
DEIPRRTU	IRRUPTED		
	PUTRIDER		
DEIPRSSU	DISPURSE		
	SUSPIRED		
DEIPRSTU	DISPUTER		
	STUPIDER		
DEIPRSTZ	SPRITZED		
DEIPSSTU	DISPUTES		
	PUDSIEST		
DEIPTTTU	TITTUPED		
DEIQRRSU	SQUIRRED		
DEIQRSTU	SQUIRTED		
DEIRRSTU	STURDIER		
DEIRSSST	DISSERTS		
	DISTRESS		
DEIRSSTU	DIESTRUS		
	DRUSIEST		
	STUDIERS		
	STURDIES		
DEIRSSUY	DYSURIES		
DEIRSTTU	DETRITUS		
DEIRSTUX	DRUXIEST		
DEIRSUVV	SURVIVED		
DEISSSTU	SUDSIEST		
DEISSTTU	DUSTIEST		
DEISTTTU	DUETTIST		
DEJLOOOR	JORDELOO		
DEJOOPPY	POPJOYED		
DEKKLNOY	KLONDYKE		
DEKLNOOU	UNLOOKED		
DEKLOOPU	UPLOOKED		
DEKLRSSU	SKUDLERS		
DEKLSTTU	SKUTTLED		
DEKMPRSU	SKRUMPED		
DEKNORUW	UNWORKED		
DEKNRSTU	DRUNKEST		
DEKNRSUY	UNDERSKY		
DEKNSSSU	DUSKNESS		
DEKOOPRV	PROVOKED		
DEKOOTWW	KOWTOWED		
DEKOPSST	DESKTOPS		
DEKORSWY	KEYWORDS		
DELLLOOP	LOLLOPED		
DELLMOOS	MODELLOS		
DELLMOSW	SWELLDOM		
DELLNOPU	UNPOLLED		
DELLNORU	UNROLLED		
DELLNORW	ROWNDELL		
DELLNPUU	UNPULLED		
DELLNSSU	DULLNESS		
DELLOPRS	REDPOLLS		
DELLOPRU	UPROLLED		
DELLOPTU	POLLUTED		
DELLORRY	DROLLERY		
DELLORSS	LORDLESS		
DELLORST	DROLLEST		
	STROLLED		
DELLOSVW	LOWVELDS		
DELLOTUW	OUTDWELL		
DELMNOOV	NOVELDOM		
DELMNORY	MODERNLY		
DELMNOSU	UNSELDOM		
DELMNOTW	MELTDOWN		
DELMNPUU	PENDULUM		
	UNPLUMED		
DELMOOSW	ELMWOODS		
DELMORSS	SMOLDERS		
DELMORSU	MOULDERS		
	REMOULDS		
	SMOULDER		
DELMOSTY	MODESTLY		
DELMRTUU	MULTURED		
DELMTTUU	TUMULTED		
DELNOOSU	NODULOSE		
	UNLOOSED		
DELNOOSZ	SNOOZLED		
DELNOOWY	WOODENLY		
DELNOPPU	UNLOPPED		
DELNOPRS	SPLENDOR		
DELNORSU	LOUNDERS		
	NOURSLED		
	ROUNDELS		
	ROUNDLES		
	UNSOLDER		
DELNORTU	ROUNDLET		
DELNORYY	YONDERLY		
DELNOSSU	LOUDNESS		
DELNOSUU	UNDULOSE		
	UNSOULED		
DELNOSUV	UNSOLVED		
DELNPRSU	PLUNDERS		
DELNRRTU	TRUNDLER		
DELNRSTU	RUNDLETS		
	TRUNDLES		
DELNSUZZ	SNUZZLED		
DELOOPPS	PLEOPODS		
DELOORRV	OVERLORD		
DELOORRW	WORDLORE		
DELOORSS	LORDOSES		
DELOORSV	OVERSOLD		
DELOORSW	WOOLDERS		
DELOORTY	ROOTEDLY		
DELOORUV	OVERLOUD		
DELOOSSW	WOODLESS		
DELOPPRS	DROPPLES		
DELOPPST	STOPPLED		
DELOPRST	DROPLETS		
DELOPRSU	POULDERS		
	POULDRES		
DELOPSTU	POSTLUDE		
DELORSST	OLDSTERS		
	STRODLES		
DELORSSW	WORDLESS		

DELORSTT	DOTTRELS
DELORSUY	DELUSORY
DELOSSUU	SEDULOUS
DELOSTTT	DOTTLEST
DELOTTUW	OUTDWELT
DELOTUVY	DEVOUTLY
DELRSSTU	STRUDELS
DELSSSTU	DUSTLESS
DEMMNOOO	MONOMODE
DEMMNOOS	DOOMSMEN
DEMMNOSU	SUMMONED
DEMMNSUU	UNSUMMED
DEMMRRSU	DRUMMERS
DEMMRRUU	MURMURED
DEMMRSTU	STRUMMED
DEMNNOSU	SOUNDMEN
DEMNOOOP	MONOPODE
DEMNOOPT	TOMPONED
DEMNOORS	DOORSMEN
DEMNOORU	UNMOORED
DEMNOOSW	WOODSMEN
DEMNORST	MORDENTS
DEMNORSW	SWORDMEN
DEMNORSY	SYNDROME
DEMNORUW	UNWORMED
DEMNOSTU	DEMOUNTS
	MUDSTONE
DEMOOPPS	POPEDOMS
DEMOOPPR	PRODROME
DEMOOPPS	PREDOOMS
DEMOOPRT	PROMOTED
DEMOORST	DOOMSTER
DEMOORSU	DORMOUSE
DEMOORTY	ODOMETRY
DEMOOSTU	OUTMODES
DEMOOTUV	OUTMOVED
DEMOPPRT	PROMPTED
DEMOPSSU	POSSUMED
DEMORRUU	RUMOURED
DEMPRSTU	DUMPSTER
DENNNSUU	UNSUNNED
DENNOOOZ	ENDOZOON
DENNORST	TENDRONS
DENNORSU	ENROUNDS
DENNOTUW	UNWONTED
DENNPRUU	UNPRUNED
DENNRTUU	UNTURNED
DENOOOTW	WOODNOTE
DENOOOVW	OVENWOOD
DENOOPPR	PROPONED
DENOOPRS	PRODNOSE
DENOOPSY	POYSONED
DENOORTU	UNROOTED
DENOOSSW	WOODNESS
DENOOSTU	DUOTONES
DENOPPRS	PROPENDS
DENOPRSS	RESPONDS
DENOPRST	PORTENDS
	PROTENDS
DENOPRSU	POUNDERS
DENOPRSV	PROVENDS
DENOPRUV	UNPROVED
DENOPSTU	OUTSPEND
	UNPOSTED
DENOPSTW	STEWPOND
DENOPSUX	EXPOUNDS
DENOQTUU	UNQUOTED
DENORRSU	RONDURES
	ROUNDERS
	UNORDERS
DENORRSW	DROWNERS
DENORRTU	ROTUNDER
DENORRUU	ROUNDURE
DENORSSU	DOURNESS
	RESOUNDS
	SOUNDERS
DENORSTU	ROUNDEST
	TONSURED

	UNSORTED
DENORSUU	UNROUSED
	UNSOURED
DENORSUW	WOUNDERS
DENORTTU	UNROTTED
DENORTUW	UNDERTOW
DENOSSTU	SOUNDEST
DENOSTUW	UNSTOWED
DENPRSTU	UPTRENDS
DENPRSUU	UNPURSED
DENPRTUU	UPTURNED
DENPSSSU	SUSPENDS
DENRRTUU	NURTURED
DENRSSSU	SUNDRESS
DENRSTTU	STRUNTED
DENSSTTU	STUDENTS
DENSTUVY	DUVETYNS
DEOOORSW	ROSEWOOD
DEOOOSWW	WOODWOSE
DEOOPPRS	PROPOSED
DEOOPPRT	PTEROPOD
DEOOPRRV	PROVEDOR
DEOOPRST	DOORSTEP
	TORPEDOS
DEOOPRTU	UPROOTED
DEOOPWWW	POWWOWED
DEOORRST	REDROOTS
DEOORRSW	SORROWED
DEOORRVW	OVERWORD
DEOORRWW	OWREWORD
DEOOPPRS	DROPPERS
DEOPPRST	STROPPED
DEOPPRSU	PURPOSED
DEOPPSSU	SUPPOSED
DEOPRRTU	PROTRUDE
DEOPRSTU	POSTURED
	PROUDEST
	SPROUTED
DEOPRSUU	POURSUED
	UPROUSED
DEORRSST	RODSTERS
DEORRSSW	SWORDERS
DEORRTTU	TORTURED
DEORSSTY	DESTROYS
DEORSTTU	STROUTED
DEORSTUU	OUTDURES
DEORSTUV	OVERDUST
DEORSTUX	DEXTROUS
DEOSSSYY	ODYSSEYS
DEOSSTTU	TESTUDOS
DEPPSSYY	DYSPEPSY
DEPRRTUU	RUPTURED
DEQRSUUY	SURQUEDY
DERSTTTU	STRUTTED
DFFGINSU	DUFFINGS
DFFIILUY	FLUIDIFY
DFFIIMRS	MIDRIFFS
DFFIIRST	TRIFFIDS
DFFIIRTY	TRIFFIDY
DFFLOORU	FOURFOLD
DFFOORUW	WOODRUFF
DFGGHIOT	DOGFIGHT
DFGGIINR	FRIDGING
DFGHILOS	GOLDFISH
DFGIIIRY	RIGIDIFY
DFGIILRY	FRIGIDLY
DFGIINRT	DRIFTING
DFGILNNO	FONDLING
DFGILNOO	FLOODING
DFGILNOS	FOLDINGS
DFGINNOU	FOUNDING
DFGINNSU	FUNDINGS
DFGINOOR	FORDOING
DFGMOOSY	FOGYDOMS

DFHIIMUY	HUMIDIFY
DFHILSSU	DISHFULS
DFHIMRSU	DRUMFISH
DFHINOOT	HINDFOOT
DFHLOOOT	FOOTHOLD
DFHNOOUX	FOXHOUND
DFIIINVY	DIVINIFY
DFIILMTU	MULTIFID
DFIILOSY	SOLIDIFY
DFIILTUY	FLUIDITY
DFIINPRT	DRIFTPIN
DFIKNOOS	SKINFOOD
DFILLOOT	FLOODLIT
DFILLORY	FLORIDLY
DFILLOWW	WILDFOWL
DFILMMOS	FILMDOMS
DFILNOPS	PINFOLDS
DFIMOOOR	IODOFORM
DFIMOOSS	FOODISMS
DFIMORSS	DISFORMS
DFINRSUW	WINDSURF
DFIOOPRS	DISPROOF
DFLNOOWW	DOWNFLOW
DFLOPRUU	PROUDFUL
DFNOOPRU	PROFOUND
DFOOOORW	WOODROOF
DFOOOSTW	SOFTWOOD
DGGGIINS	DIGGINGS
DGGGINOS	DOGGINGS
DGGGINRU	DRUGGING
	GRUDGING
DGGHIINT	DIGHTING
DGGIILNR	GIRDLING
	RIDGLING
DGGIILNS	GILDINGS
	GLIDINGS
DGGIINNR	GRINDING
DGGIINNW	WINGDING
DGGIINRS	GIRDINGS
	RIDGINGS
DGGINSU	GUIDINGS
DGGIMNSU	SMUDGING
DGGINNSU	SNUDGING
DGGINOST	STODGING
DGGINRTU	TRUDGING
DGGIRSTU	DRUGGIST
DGHHOOOS	HOGHOODS
DGHIILNS	HILDINGS
	HILDINGS
DGHIIMNT	MIDNIGHT
DGHIIMST	MISDIGHT
DGHIINNW	HINDWING
DGHIINPS	SPHINGID
DGHIINRT	THIRDING
DGHIINSS	DISHINGS
	SHINDIGS
DGHIISST	DISSIGHT
DGHIKNOO	KINGHOOD
DGHILNOS	HOLDINGS
DGHILNRU	HURDLING
DGHILNSY	HYLDINGS
DGHILOOR	GIRLHOOD
DGHILPSY	DIGLYPHS
DGHINNOU	HOUNDING
DGHINNSU	DUNSHING
DGHINSTU	UNDIGHTS
DGHIOORS	DROOGISH
DGHIOPSS	DOGSHIPS
	GODSHIPS
DGHNOTUU	DOUGHNUT
DGHOOOTT	DOGTOOTH
DGHORSTU	DROUGHTS
DGHORTUY	DROUGHTY
DGIIIMRS	DIRIGISM
DGIIINNT	INDITING
DGIIINNV	DIVINING
DGIIINOS	IODISING

DGIIINOZ	IODIZING
DGIIIRTY	RIGIDITY
DGIIKLNN	KINDLING
DGIIKLNS	KIDLINGS
DGIIKNNR	DRINKING
DGIILLNR	DRILLING
DGIILLNS	DILLINGS
DGIILLNU	ILLUDING
DGIILLOU	LIGULOID
DGIILMNP	DIMPLING
DGIILNNN	DINNLING
DGIILNOR	DROILING
DGIILNOS	DISLOIGN
DGIILNPS	DISPLING
DGIILNSS	SLIDINGS
DGIILNSW	WILDINGS
DGIILNTU	DILUTING
DGIIMNNS	MINDINGS
DGIIMNOS	MISDOING
DGIIMNOU	GONIDIUM
DGIIMNSS	SMIDGINS
DGIIMPUY	PYGIDIUM
DGIINNOP	POINDING
DGIINNRW	WINDRING
DGIINNSS	SINDINGS
DGIINNSW	WINDINGS
DGIINORR	GRIDIRON
DGIINORS	DORISING
DGIINORZ	DORIZING
DGIINOSV	VOIDINGS
DGIINOSW	WINDIGOS
DGIINOTT	DITTOING
DGIINOWW	WIDOWING
DGIINPPR	DRIPPING
DGIINPPS	DIPPINGS
DGIINRST	STRIDING
DGIINRTY	DIRTYING
DGIINSSU	DISUSING
DGIINTTY	DITTYING
DGIINYZZ	DIZZYING
DGIKLOOY	KIDOLOGY
DGIKMNOS	KINGDOMS
DGIKNOOR	DROOKING
DGIKNOOW	KINGWOOD
DGIKNORU	DROUKING
DGIKNOSS	DOGSKINS
DGILLNOR	DROLLING
	LORDLING
DGILLNOY	DOLLYING
DGILLOOW	GOODWILL
DGILMNOU	MOULDING
DGILMNPU	DUMPLING
DGILMSUY	SMUDGILY
DGILNNOO	NOODLING
DGILNNOU	LOUNDING
DGILNNOW	LOWNDING
DGILNNRU	NURDLING
DGILNOOR	DROOLING
DGILNOOW	WOOLDING
DGILNORS	GIRLONDS
	LORDINGS
DGILNORY	YOLDRING
DGILNOTY	DOTINGLY
DGILNPUY	DUPLYING
DGILOOTW	GILTWOOD
DGILOPSU	SOLPUGID
DGILOSTY	STODGILY
DGILRTUY	TURGIDLY
DGIMMNRU	DRUMMING
DGIMMNUY	DUMMYING
DGIMNNOU	MOUNDING
DGIMNOOY	MOODYING
DGINNNSU	DUNNINGS
DGINNOOS	SNOODING
DGINNOPU	POUNDING
DGINNOPW	POWNDING
DGINNORU	ROUNDING
DGINNORW	DROWNING
	ROWNDING

DGINNOSU	SOUNDING	DHJOPRSU	JODHPURS
	UNDOINGS	DHKMNOOO	MONKHOOD
DGINNOSW	SOWNDING	DHKMOOSU	MUDHOOKS
DGINNOUW	WOUNDING	DHLLOPYY	PHYLLODY
DGINNSSY	SYNDINGS	DHLMOOSU	HOODLUMS
DGINNSUW	WINDGUNS	DHLOOORT	ROOTHOLD
DGINOOPR	DROOPING	DHLOOSTU	HOLDOUTS
DGINOOPS	SPONGOID	DHLORXYY	HYDROXYL
DGINOOTU	OUTDOING	DHLOSSTU	SHOULDST
DGINOPPR	DROPPING	DHMMRSUU	HUMDRUMS
DGINOPPS	DOPPINGS	DHMNOOOT	HOMODONT
DGINORSV	DROVINGS	DHMOOPPU	PUMPHOOD
DGINORSW	DROWSING	DHMORTUY	DRYMOUTH
	SWORDING	DHNNOOSU	NUNHOODS
	WORDINGS	DHNOOSWW	SHOWDOWN
DGINOSSW	DISGOWNS	DHNORSUU	UNSHROUD
DGINOSUY	DIGYNOUS	DHNOSTUW	SHUTDOWN
DGINSTUY	STUDYING	DHOOOPRT	ORTHOPOD
DGISSSTU	DISGUSTS	DHOOORTX	ORTHODOX
DGLOOOPY	PODOLOGY	DHOOPRSU	UPHOORDS
DGLOOOSW	LOGWOODS	DHOORSUW	WOODRUSH
DGLOOOSY	DOSOLOGY	DHOPRSSU	PUSHRODS
DGLOOOXY	DOXOLOGY	DHOPRSYY	HYDROPSY
DGMOPRSU	GUMDROPS	DIIIKMNS	MINIDISK
DGMOPSYY	GYPSYDOM	DIIILLQU	ILLIQUID
DGMORSUU	GURUDOMS	DIIILTVY	LIVIDITY
DGNNORUU	UNGROUND	DIIIMOST	IDIOTISM
DGNOOORS	GODROONS	DIIIMRSU	IRIDIUMS
DGNOOSTW	DOGTOWNS	DIIIMTTY	TIMIDITY
DGNOOTYZ	ZYGODONT	DIIINOSV	DIVISION
DGOORSTT	DOGTROTS	DIIINTVY	DIVINITY
DHHILOTW	WITHHOLD	DIIIPRST	DISPIRIT
DHIIIMNS	DIMINISH	DIIIRTVY	VIRIDITY
DHIIIOST	HISTIOID	DIIITVVY	VIVIDITY
	IDIOTISH	DIIJNOSS	DISJOINS
DHIILOSS	SOLIDISH	DIIJNOST	DISJOINT
DHIIMNOO	HOMINOID	DIIKKNSS	KIDSKINS
DHIIMNOS	HOMINIDS	DIIKLNSS	DISLINKS
DHIIMPSS	MIDSHIPS	DIIKNOST	DOITKINS
DHIIMTUY	HUMIDITY	DIILLMNR	MILLRIND
DHIINPSW	WINDSHIP	DIILLMNW	WINDMILL
DHIINTWW	WITHWIND	DIILLMPY	LIMPIDLY
DHIIOPRU	OPHIURID	DIILLQUY	LIQUIDLY
DHIIORSS	HIDROSIS	DIILLSST	DISTILLS
DHIIORSZ	RHIZOIDS	DIILLSTY	IDYLLIST
DHIKNOOW	HOODWINK	DIILMNSS	DISLIMNS
DHIKORSY	HYDROSKI	DIILMOSS	IDOLISMS
DHILLNOW	DOWNHILL		SOLIDISM
DHILLOPY	PHYLLOID	DIILMOTY	MYTILOID
DHILLORS	DROLLISH	DIILMUUV	DILUVIUM
DHILLOST	TOLLDISH	DIILNNSU	INDULINS
DHILMOPY	LYMPHOID	DIILNOTU	DILUTION
DHILMOSY	MODISHLY	DIILNOUV	DILUVION
DHILNOPS	DOLPHINS	DIILNOXY	XYLOIDIN
DHILOPRS	LORDSHIP	DIILNTUY	UNTIDILY
DHILOPSS	SLIPSHOD	DIILOPRT	TRIPLOID
DHILORRY	HORRIDLY	DIILOPSY	YPSILOID
DHILPSSU	LUDSHIPS	DIILORSU	SILUROID
DHILPSSY	SYLPHIDS	DIILOSST	IDOLISTS
DHIMNOST	HINDMOST		SOLIDIST
DHIMNOSU	UNMODISH	DIILOSTY	SOLIDITY
DHIMOOOY	OMOHYOID	DIILQSUU	LIQUIDUS
DHIMOOSS	MISSHOOD	DIILRSSU	SILURIDS
DHIMOPPY	HIPPYDOM	DIIMNNOO	DOMINION
DHIMOPRS	DIMORPHS	DIIMNNSU	UNDINISM
DHIMORSU	HUMIDORS	DIIMNORS	MIDIRONS
	RHODIUMS	DIIMNSSU	INDUSIUM
DHINOORS	DISHONOR	DIIMOPRS	PRISMOID
DHINOPSS	DONSHIPS	DIIMORSS	DIORISMS
DHINORSS	DISHORNS	DIIMPUXY	PYXIDIUM
DHINORSU	ROUNDISH	DIIMRUUV	DUUMVIRI
DHIOOPRZ	RHIZOPOD	DIIMTTUY	TUMIDITY
DHIOPRSU	PROUDISH	DIINNOSU	DISUNION
DHIOPSTY	TYPHOIDS	DIINOQSU	QUINOIDS
DHIORSTY	THYROIDS	DIINOSSU	SINUSOID
	THYRSOID	DIINSTUY	DISUNITY
DHIORSWY	ROWDYISH	DIIOPRTY	PITYROID
DHIPRSSY	SYRPHIDS		
DIIORSSV	DIVISORS	DIOPRSST	DISPORTS
DIJOSSTU	JUDOISTS	DIOPSSST	DISPOSTS
DIKLMOOW	MILKWOOD	DIORRSST	STRIDORS
DIKLNNUY	UNKINDLY	DIORRSTT	DISTORTS
DIKLNORS	LORDKINS	DIOSSTUU	STUDIOUS
DIKLRUUU	DURUKULI	DIPRSSTU	DISRUPTS
DIKNOOSW	WOODSKIN	DIRRSSTU	DISTRUST
DIKNORSV	DVORNIKS	DKNORTUU	OUTDRUNK
DIKNORTU	OUTDRINK	DKOOORWW	WOODWORK
DIKOOSTU	DITOKOUS	DKORSTUW	STUDWORK
DILLMNOP	MILLPOND	DLLMORSU	SLUMLORD
DILLOSTY	STOLIDLY	DLLNORUY	UNLORDLY
DILLPSSY	PSYLLIDS	DLMNOOSY	MYLODONS
DILMNOOS	SMILODON	DLMNOOTY	MYLODONT
DILMNORW	LINDWORM	DLMNOSUU	UNMOULDS
DILMNRSU	DRUMLINS	DLMORSUY	SMOULDRY
DILMOOSU	MODIOLUS	DLNOOPRU	POULDRON
DILMOSSU	SOLIDUMS	DLNOOSUU	NODULOUS
DILMOSSY	ODYLISMS	DLNOPRSU	PULDRONS
DILNOPST	DIPLONTS	DLNOPSSY	SPONDYLS
DILNOPSU	LISPOUND	DLNORTUY	ROTUNDLY
DILNOQSU	QUODLINS	DLNOSUUU	UNDULOUS
DILNOXSY	INDOXYLS	DLOOOORS	DOLOROSO
DILNOUWY	WOUNDILY	DLOOORSU	DOLOROUS
DILNPSSU	LISPUNDS	DLOOPPSY	POLYPODS
DILOOPPY	POLYPOID	DLOOPPUW	PULPWOOD
DILOOPRY	DROOPILY	DLOOPPYY	POLYPODY
DILOORSS	LORDOSIS	DLOOPSTY	TYLOPODS
DILOOSUY	ODIOUSLY	DLOOPSWY	PLYWOODS
DILOOTUV	VOLUTOID	DMNNOOOT	MONODONT
DILOPRTY	TORPIDLY	DMNOOOPS	MONOPODS
DILORRTY	TORRIDLY	DMNOOSTW	DOWNMOST
DILORSTU	DILUTORS		TOWMONDS
DILORSWY	DROWSILY	DMOOORWW	WOODWORM
DILOSSTY	STYLOIDS		WORMWOOD
DILPRTUY	PUTRIDLY	DMOPPPUU	PUPPODUM
DILPSTUY	STUPIDLY	DMOPPPUY	PUPPYDOM
DILRSTUY	STURDILY	DMORSTUW	MUDWORTS
DIMMNORY	MYRMIDON	DMPPPUUY	MUDPUPPY
DIMMOOSU	ISODOMUM	DNNOOPRU	PUNDONOR
DIMMOSST	MIDMOSTS	DNNORSUU	UNROUNDS
DIMNNOOS	MIDNOONS	DNNORSUW	RUNDOWNS
DIMNNOSS	DONNISMS	DNNORTUW	DOWNTURN
DIMNNOST	DINMONTS	DNNOSSUW	SUNDOWNS
DIMNOOOS	ISODOMON	DNNRSTUU	TURNDUNS
DIMNOOST	MONODIST	DNOOPPRU	PROPOUND
DIMNOPSU	IMPOUNDS	DNOOPRSW	SNOWDROP
DIMNOSTU	DISMOUNT	DNOOPRUW	DOWNPOUR
DIMNOSUW	UNWISDOM	DNOORSUW	WONDROUS
DIMOOPRR	PRODROMI	DNOOSTUW	NUTWOODS
DIMOOPRY	MYRIOPOD	DNOOSTWW	STOWDOWN
DIMOPRSU	MISPROUD	DNOOTUUW	OUTWOUND
DIMOPSSU	SPODIUMS	DNOPRSSU	SUNDROPS
DIMORSSW	MISWORDS	DNORRSSU	SURROUND
DIMORSWY	ROWDYISM	DNORSSUY	UNDROSSY
DIMOSTUY	DUMOSITY	DOOOPRST	DOORPOST
DIMRSTUU	TRIDUUMS		DOORSTOP
DIMRSUUV	DUUMVIRS	DOOORSTU	OUTDOORS
DINNOORS	RONDINOS	DOOOSTTU	OUTSTOOD
DINNOOST	TONDINOS	DOOPRSTU	DROPOUTS
DINNOPSW	PINDOWNS	DOOPSWWY	POWSOWDY
DINOOORW	IRONWOOD	DOORRSTU	DORTOURS
DINOOPSU	DIPNOOUS	DOORRSUU	ORDUROUS
DINOORST	TORDIONS	DOORSSUU	SUDOROUS
DINOORSU	NIDOROUS	EEEEFNRZ	ENFREEZE
DINOOSST	ISODONTS	EEEEFRRS	REFEREES
DINOOSTT	ODONTIST	EEEEFRRZ	REFREEZE
DINOOSTY	NODOSITY	EEEEGGRR	GREEGREE
DINORSTU	STURNOID	EEEEGQSU	SQUEEGEE
	TURDIONS	EEEEGSSX	EXEGESES
DINORSWW	WINDROWS	EEEEGSTX	EXEGETES
DINOSTUW	OUTWINDS	EEEELLPX	EXPELLEE
DINPRTUY	PUNDITRY	EEEELMST	TELESEME
DINRSTUY	INDUSTRY	EEEELNSV	SLEEVEEN
DIOOPRRT	PRODITOR	EEEENRRV	VENEERER
DIOOPRRV	PROVIDOR	EEEEPPSW	PEESWEEP
DIOORSST	DISROOTS	EEEEPRRV	REPREEVE
DIOORSTT	RIDOTTOS	EEEEPTTW	PEETWEET
		EEEFFFOS	FEOFFEES

EEEFFLOR FOREFEEL	EEEHIRSS HERESIES	EEEINSSW SWEENIES	EEELSTVY STEEVELY
EEEFFLTY EFFETELY	EEEHIRST ETHERISE	EEEINSTT TEENIEST	EEELTTTX TELETEXT
EEEFFNRT EFFERENT	SHEETIER	EEEINSTW TWEENIES	EEEMMNRS MERESMEN
EEEFFORS OFFEREES	EEEHIRTZ ETHERIZE	WEENIEST	EEEMMRUZ MEZEREUM
EEEFFORT FOREFEET	EEEHIRWZ WHEEZIER	EEEINTUX EUXENITE	EEEMNNTT TENEMENT
EEEFFRVW FEVERFEW	EEEHKLNO KNEEHOLE	EEEIPRRV REPRIEVE	EEEMNORZ MEZEREON
EEEFGRSU REFUGEES	EEEHLMNW WHEELMEN	EEEIPRST PEERIEST	EEEMNPRT PETERMEN
EEEFHRSS SHEREEFS	EEEHLMPT HELPMEET	STEEPIER	EEEMNRST ETRENNES
EEEFIPRR REPRIEFE	EEEHLNSW ENWHEELS	EEEIPRSW SWEEPIER	EEEMNRVY EVERYMEN
EEEFIPST TEPEFIES	EEEHLNTV ELEVENTH	EEEIPSST SEEPIEST	EEEMNSST MEETNESS
EEEFIRRT FREETIER	EEEHLNTY ETHYLENE	EEEIPSTW WEEPIEST	EEEMORRV EVERMORE
EEEFLRRS FLEERERS	EEEHLNXY HEXYLENE	EEEIQSUX EXEQUIES	EEEMORST EROTEMES
EEEFLRSX REFLEXES	EEEHLOPW WEEPHOLE	EEEIRRST REESTIER	STEREOME
EEEFLSST FEETLESS	EEEHLPSW WHEEPLES	RETIREES	EEEMORTV OVERTEEM
EEEFLSTT FLEETEST	EEEHLRSW WHEELERS	EEEIRRSV REREVISE	EEEMPRRT TEMPERER
EEEFNNPY PENNYFEE	EEEHLSWZ WHEEZLES	REVERIES	EEEMPRSS EMPRESSE
EEEFNORS FORESEEN	EEEHMMSS EMMESHES	EEEIRRTV RETRIEVE	EEEMPSSY EMPYESES
EEEFNRRT REFERENT	EEEHMNSS ENMESHES	EEEIRRVW REVIEWER	EEEMRRTX EXTREMER
EEEFNRSS FREENESS	EEEHMNTV VEHEMENT	EEEIRSST STEERIES	EEEMRSST SEMESTER
EEEFNRTT ENFETTER	EEEHNNPT NEPENTHE	EEEIRSSV SEVERIES	EEEMRSTX EXTREMES
EEEFNRUZ UNFREEZE	EEEHNNQU HENEQUEN	EEEIRSSZ RESEIZES	EEENNOPR NEOPRENE
EEEFORRV OVERFREE	EEEHNPRS ENSPHERE	EEEIRTVX EXERTIVE	EEENNPST PENTENES
EEEFORSS FORESEES	EEEHNRSS HERENESS	EEEISSTW SWEETIES	EEENNRST ETRENNES
EEEFRRRT FERRETER	EEEHNRVW WHENEVER	EEEJLLRW JEWELLER	EEENNRUV UNEVENER
EEEFRRSZ FREEZERS	EEEHNSSS SNEESHES	EEEJNPSY JEEPNEYS	EEENNSSV EVENNESS
EEEGGILN NEGLIGEE	EEEHORST SHOETREE	EEEKLLSU UKELELES	EEENNSTT ENTENTES
EEEGGIRS EGGERIES	EEEHPRSS HERPESES	EEEKLNNR ENKERNEL	EEENOPRR REOPENER
EEEGHINT EIGHTEEN	EEEHPRST SPREETHE	EEEKLNRS KNEELERS	EEENORSV OVERSEEN
EEEGHLRS SHEERLEG	EEEHRRVW WHEREVER	EEEKLNSS SLEEKENS	EEENORVW OVERWEEN
EEEGHNSW WHEENGES	EEEHRSST SEETHERS	EEEKLPSW EKPWELES	EEENORVY EVERYONE
EEEGIKST GEEKIEST	SHEEREST	EEEKLRSS SLEEKERS	EEENPPRS PREPENSE
EEEGILMN LIEGEMEN	EEEHSSTT ESTHETES	EEEKLSST SLEEKEST	EEENPRRT REPENTER
EEEGILNV ENVEIGLE	EEEIKLMS MISLEEKE	EEEKMNRS KERMESSE	EEENPRST PRETENSE
LEVEEING	EEEIKLRS SKEELIER	EEEKNNSS KEENNESS	TERPENES
EEEGILPS ESPIEGLE	SLEEKIER	EEEKNORS KEROSENE	EEENPRSV PREVENES
EEEGILRT GLEETIER	EEEIKLSW WEEKLIES	EEEKNORV OVERKNEE	EEENPSST ENSTEEPS
EEEGILSS ELEGISES	EEEILRSZ SLEEZIER	EEEKNPST KEEPNETS	STEEPENS
EEEGILSZ ELEGIZES	EEEIKRRS SKEERIER	EEEKOPRV OVERKEEP	EEENPSSW ENSWEEPS
EEEGIMNX EXEEMING	EEEIKRST KEEKIEST	EEEKRSST SKEETERS	EEENPSSX EXPENSES
EEEGINNR ENGINEER	EEEILLRV REVEILLE	EEELLLRV LEVELLER	EEENRRSS SNEERERS
EEEGINRR GREENIER	EEEILMRS SEEMLIER	EEELLNQU QUENELLE	EEENRRST ENTERERS
EEEGINRS ENERGIES	EEEILNNO EOLIENNE	EEELLPRR REPELLER	RESENTER
ENERGISE	EEEILNPR PELERINE	EEELLRRT RETELLER	TERREENS
GREENIES	EEEILNRY EYELINER	EEELLRRV REVELLER	TERRENES
EEEGINRV ENGRIEVE	EEEILNST SELENITE	EEELMNST ELEMENTS	EEEMNRSV REVENERS
EEEGINRZ ENERGIZE	EEEILPRS SLEEPIER	STEELMEN	VENERERS
EEEGIPRS PERIGEES	EEEILRRV RELIEVER	EEELMOPP EMPEOPLE	EEENRRSW RENEWERS
EEEGISSX EXEGESIS	EEEILRST LEERIEST	EEELMOPY EMPLOYEE	EEENRRTU RETURNEE
EEEGISTV EGESTIVE	SLEETIER	EEELMORT TELOMERE	EEENRRTV REVERENT
EEEGITVV VEGETIVE	STEELIER	EEELMOTT OMELETTE	EEENRSSU ENURESES
EEEGLMOS GLEESOME	EEEILRSV RELIEVES	EEELMPSX EXEMPLES	EEENRSSZ SNEEZERS
EEEGLNRT GREENLET	EEEILRSZ SLEEZIER	EEELMRTU MULETEER	EEENRSTV EVENTERS
EEEGMNRT EMERGENT	EEEILSST SEELIEST	EEELMSSS SEEMLESS	EEENRSTX EXTERNES
EEEGMNRU MERENGUE	EEEILSSW ELSEWISE	EEELMSST TEEMLESS	EEENRSTY YESTREEN
EEEGMORT GEOMETER	EEEILSTV TELEVISE	EEELNOPV ENVELOPE	EEENRSUV REVENUES
EEEGMRRS REMERGES	EEEILTVW TELEVIEW	EEELNOSV NOVELESE	UNREEVES
EEEGNNRS SENGREEN	EEEIMNRU MEUNIERE	EEELNQTU QUEENLET	EEENSSTW SWEETENS
EEEGNPRS EPERGNES	EEEIMNST EMETINES	EEELNRSW NEWSREEL	TWEENESS
EEEGNRRS GREENERS	EEEIMPRR PREMIERE	EEELNRSY SERENELY	EEENSSWY SWEENEYS
RENEGERS	EEEIMPRS EMPERIES	EEELNRTV NERVELET	EEEOPRRV OVERPEER
EEEGNRRU RENEGUER	EMPERISE	EEELOPPR REPEOPLE	EEEORRSV OVERSEER
EEEGNRRV REVENGER	PREEMIES	EEELOPRT PETROLEE	EEEORRST EROTESES
EEEGNRRY GREENERY	EEEIMPRZ EMPERIZE	EEELORST SLOETREE	EEEORSSV OVERSEES
EEEGNRST GREENEST	EEEIMRRS MISERERE	EEELPRSS PEERLESS	EEEORSSY EYESORES
EEEGNRSU RENEGUES	EEEIMRST EREMITES	SLEEPERS	EEEORSVY OVEREYES
EEEGNRSV REVENGES	EEEIMRTT REMITTEE	SPEELERS	EEEPPPRR PEPPERER
EEEGNSTT GENETTES	EEEINNNT NINETEEN	EEELPRST REPLETES	EEEPPSTU STEEPEUP
EEEGOPRT PROTEGEE	EEEINNRT INTERNEE	EEELPRSY SLEEPERY	EEEPRRST PESTERER
EEEGRRST GREETERS	EEEINQRU QUEENIER	EEELPSST STEEPLES	EEEPRRSU REPERUSE
REGREETS	EEEINQSU QUEENIES	EEELRRTT LETTERER	EEEPRRSV PERVERSE
EEEGRSSS EGRESSES	EEEINQTU QUEENITE	EEELRSST TREELESS	PRESERVE
EEEGRSUX EXERGUES	EEEINRRS SNEERIER	EEELRSSV SLEEVERS	EEEPRRTW PEWTERER
EEEHHSSW WHEESHES	EEEINRSS EERINESS	EEELRSTT RESETTLE	EEEPRSST ESTREPES
EEEHILRW EREWHILE	EEEINRST ETERNISE	EEELRSTV LEVERETS	STEEPERS
WHEELIER	TEENSIER	VERSELET	EEEPRSSW SWEEPERS
EEEHILSW WHEELIES	EEEINRSV VENERIES	EEELRSVY SEVERELY	EEEPRSSZ SPREEZES
EEEHINRS SHEENIER	EEEINRSZ SNEEZIER	EEELRTVV VELVERET	EEEPSSTT STEEPEST
EEEHINSS SHEENIES	EEEINRTT REINETTE	EEELSSTW WEETLESS	EEEPSTTT SEPTETTE
EEEHIPRS SHEEPIER	TEENTIER		
	EEEINRTZ ETERNIZE		

EEEQRRSU	REQUERES
EEEQRRUV	VERQUERE
EEEQRSTU	QUEEREST
EEEQRSUZ	SQUEEZER
EEEQSSUZ	SQUEEZES
EEERRRSV	REVERERS
	REVERSER
EEERRSST	STEERERS
EEERRSSV	RESERVES
	REVERSES
EEERRSTT	RESETTER
EEERSSTV	SEVEREST
EEERSSUV	REVEUSES
EEERSSUW	SERUEWES
EEERSSVW	SERVEWES
EEERSTTW	TWEETERS
EEERSTVX	VERTEXES
EEERSTWZ	TWEEZERS
EEESSTTT	SESTETTE
EEESSTTV	STEEVEST
EEESSTTW	SWEETEST
EEESTTTX	SEXTETTE
EEFFFGLU	GEFUFFLE
EEFFFKLU	KEFUFFLE
EEFFFNOS	ENFEOFFS
EEFFFORS	FEOFFERS
EEFFGIIS	EFFIGIES
EEFFGINR	EFFERING
EEFFGIRR	GREFFIER
EEFFGLSU	EFFULGES
EEFFHIKY	KEFFIYEH
EEFFINST	FIFTEENS
EEFFISUV	EFFUSIVE
EEFFLNTU	EFFLUENT
EEFFLORT	FOREFELT
EEFFLSUX	EFFLUXES
EEFFNOSS	OFFENSES
EEFFORRS	OFFERERS
EEFFORSX	FORFEXES
EEFFRRSU	SUFFERER
EEFFSSTU	SUFFETES
EEFGIILR	FILIGREE
EEFGILNR	FLEERING
EEFGILNS	FEELINGS
EEFGILNT	FLEETING
EEFGINNP	PFENNIGE
EEFGINRR	REFRINGE
EEFGINRS	FEERINGS
	REEFINGS
EEFGINRV	FEVERING
EEFGINRZ	FREEZING
EEFGIRRU	REFIGURE
EEFGLMNU	FUGLEMEN
EEFGLNRY	GREENFLY
EEFGLNUV	VENGEFUL
EEFGLORS	FORELEGS
EEFGLOSS	SOLFEGES
EEFGMNOR	FORGEMEN
EEFGNOOR	FOREGONE
EEFGOORR	FOREGOER
EEFGOORS	FOREGOES
EEFHILLR	HELLFIRE
EEFHILRS	FLESHIER
	SHELFIER
EEFHIMSU	HUMEFIES
EEFHIRSV	FEVERISH
EEFHIRTY	ETHERIFY
EEFHISST	FETISHES
EEFHISSY	FISHEYES
EEFHISTT	HEFTIEST
EEFHLLWY	FLYWHEEL
EEFHLMOT	HOMEFELT
EEFHLMST	THEMSELF
EEFHLRSS	FLESHERS
EEFHMNRS	FRESHMEN
EEFHMORR	HEREFROM
EEFHNORT	FOREHENT
EEFHNRSS	FRESHENS
EEFHORRT	THEREFOR
EEFHORRW	WHEREFOR
EEFHORSW	FORESHEW
EEFHRRSS	FRESHERS
EEFHRSST	FRESHEST
	FRESHETS
EEFIIKLL	LIFELIKE
EEFIIKLW	WIFELIKE
EEFIIKRS	FIKERIES
EEFIILLN	LIFELINE
EEFIILMT	LIFETIME
EEFIILNS	LENIFIES
EEFIILRW	WIFELIER
EEFIIMMN	FEMININE
EEFIIMNS	FEMINISE
EEFIIMNZ	FEMINIZE
EEFIINRS	FINERIES
EEFIIRRT	FREITIER
EEFIIRRV	VERIFIER
EEFIIRST	FEISTIER
	FERITIES
	FIERIEST
EEFIIRSV	VERIFIES
EEFIKLRS	SERFLIKE
EEFIKNNP	PENKNIFE
EEFILLMT	TELEFILM
EEFILLSS	LIFELESS
EEFILMNR	RIFLEMEN
EEFILMOS	LIFESOME
EEFILMST	FISTMELE
EEFILNOS	FELONIES
	OLEFINES
EEFILNSS	FINELESS
EEFILNUV	NIEVEFUL
EEFILORS	FORELIES
EEFILPRR	PILFERER
EEFILRRT	FERTILER
EEFILRSS	FIRELESS
EEFILRST	FERLIEST
EEFILRSU	FUSILEER
EEFILSST	FELSITES
EEFILSSW	WIFELESS
EEFILSTT	FELTIEST
EEFIMORT	FORETIME
EEFIMRST	FEMITERS
EEFIMSTU	TUMEFIES
EEFINNSS	FINENESS
EEFINNST	FENNIEST
EEFINORV	OVERFINE
EEFINRRS	REFINERS
EEFINRRY	REFINERY
EEFINRSS	FINESSER
	RIFENESS
EEFINRST	FERNIEST
EEFINRSU	REINFUSE
EEFINRSZ	FRENZIES
EEFINSSS	FINESSES
EEFINSTT	FEINTEST
EEFIORSX	ORIFEXES
EEFIPRSX	PREFIXES
EEFIRRST	FERRITES
EEFIRRTT	FRETTIER
EEFIRSTT	FRISETTE
EEFIRSTY	ESTERIFY
EEFKNORW	FOREKNEW
EEFLLNSS	FELLNESS
EEFLLORT	FORETELL
EEFLLORV	OVERFELL
EEFLLRSU	FUELLERS
EEFLLRXY	REFLEXLY
EEFLLSSS	SELFLESS
EEFLMNSU	MENSEFUL
EEFLMORU	FUMEROLE
EEFLNNOS	ENFELONS
EEFLNORT	FORELENT
EEFLNORW	ENFLOWER
EEFLNOST	FELSTONE
EEFLNRSS	FRESNELS
EEFLNRTU	REFLUENT
EEFLNSSS	SELFNESS
EEFLNSSU	SENSEFUL
EEFLNTUV	EVENTFUL
EEFLOOSV	FOVEOLES
EEFLOPTT	POLTFEET
EEFLORRW	FLOWERER
	REFLOWER
EEFLORSS	FORLESES
EEFLORTV	LEFTOVER
EEFLORTW	FLOWERET
EEFLORVW	OVERFLEW
EEFLORWW	WEREWOLF
EEFLOSUX	FLEXUOSE
EEFLRRSU	FERRULES
EEFLRSTT	FETTLERS
EEFLRSTU	FLEURETS
EEFLRSUX	FLEXURES
	REFLUXES
EEFMNORT	FOMENTER
EEFMNRRY	FERRYMEN
EEFMNRST	FERMENTS
EEFMORRR	REFORMER
EEFMOSTT	MOFETTES
EEFMPRRU	PERFUMER
EEFMPRSU	PERFUMES
EEFMSTTU	FUMETTES
EEFNNORS	ENFROSEN
EEFNNORZ	ENFROZEN
EEFNORRZ	REFROZEN
EEFNORST	ENFOREST
	SOFTENER
EEFNORTU	FOURTEEN
EEFNORTW	FOREWENT
EEFNOSTT	OFTENEST
EEFNQRTU	FREQUENT
EEFNRTTU	UNFETTER
EEFOORRT	ROOFTREE
EEFORRST	FORESTER
	FOSTERER
	REFOREST
EEFORRSU	FERREOUS
EEFORRSV	FOREVERS
EEFORRTY	FERETORY
EEFORSUV	FEVEROUS
EEFOSSTT	FOSSETTE
EEFOSSTU	FOETUSES
EEFOSTTU	FOUETTES
EEFPRSSU	PERFUSES
EEFRRSSU	REFUSERS
EEFRRSTU	REFUTERS
EEGGGLST	GLEGGEST
EEGGHLLS	EGGSHELL
EEGGHLOR	HOGGEREL
EEGGHMSU	MESHUGGE
EEGGHSTU	THUGGEES
EEGGIJRR	REJIGGER
EEGGIKLN	GLEEKING
EEGGIKNR	GREEKING
EEGGILNR	LEGERING
EEGGILNS	NEGLIGES
EEGGILNT	GLEETING
EEGGILST	LEGGIEST
EEGGIMNR	EMERGING
EEGGINNP	PEENGING
EEGGINNR	GREENING
	RENEGING
EEGGINRS	GREESING
EEGGINRT	GREETING
EEGGINST	EGESTING
EEGGINSU	SEGUEING
EEGGKRSS	SKEGGERS
EEGGLOOR	GEOLOGER
EEGGNORS	ENGORGES
EEGGORRS	REGORGES
EEGGORSU	GOUGERES
EEGGPRRS	PREGGERS
EEGGPRSU	PUGGREES
EEGGQRSU	SQUEGGER
EEGHHINT	HEIGHTEN
EEGHIIST	EIGHTIES
EEGHIKNT	THEEKING
EEGHIKRS	SKEIGHER
EEGHILNS	HEELINGS
	SHEELING
EEGHILNW	WHEELING
EEGHILRS	SLEIGHER
EEGHINNS	SHEENING
EEGHINPS	PHEESING
EEGHINPT	PHENGITE
EEGHINPZ	PHEEZING
EEGHINRS	GREENISH
	SHEERING
EEGHINST	SEETHING
	SHEETING
EEGHINSY	HYGIENES
EEGHINTT	TEETHING
EEGHINWZ	WHEEZING
EEGHIOTT	GOETHITE
EEGHIRSW	REWEIGHS
	WEIGHERS
EEGHISST	SIGHTSEE
EEGHISTY	EYESIGHT
EEGHLNNT	LENGTHEN
EEGHMNOY	HEGEMONY
EEGHNNRU	ENHUNGER
EEGHNOOP	GEOPHONE
EEGHNOPS	PHOSGENE
EEGHNOPY	HYPOGENE
EEGHNRST	GREENTHS
EEGHNRSY	GREYHENS
EEGHNSSU	HUGENESS
EEGHOPTY	GEOPHYTE
EEGHORTT	TOGETHER
EEGHOSTT	GHETTOES
EEGHSTTU	TEUGHEST
EEGIILNR	LINGERIE
EEGIILNV	INVEIGLE
EEGIIMNS	GEMINIES
EEGIINTV	GENITIVE
EEGIIOST	EGOITIES
EEGIJLNY	JEELYING
EEGIJNRS	JEERINGS
EEGIKLNN	KNEELING
EEGIKLNS	KEELINGS
	SLEEKING
EEGIKLOT	EKLOGITE
EEGIKMNS	SMEEKING
EEGIKNNS	KEENINGS
EEGIKNPS	KEEPINGS
EEGIKNRS	KREESING
	SKEERING
EEGIKNST	KITENGES
	STEEKING
EEGILNOR	ELOIGNER
EEGILNPS	PEELINGS
	SLEEPING
	SPEELING
EEGILNRR	LINGERER
EEGILNRS	LEERINGS
	REELINGS
EEGILNRU	REGULINE
EEGILNRV	LEVERING
EEGILNSS	SEELINGS
EEGILNST	GENTILES
	SLEETING
	STEELING
EEGILNSV	SLEEVING
EEGILNSW	SWEELING
EEGILNTW	TWEELING
EEGILNTX	TELEXING
EEGILOPU	EPILOGUE
EEGILOSS	GELOSIES
EEGILOSU	EULOGIES
	EULOGISE
EEGILOUZ	EULOGIZE
EEGILQSU	SQUILGEE
EEGILRSU	REGULISE
EEGILRSV	VELIGERS
EEGILRTV	VERLIGTE

EEGILRTY LEGERITY	EEGINTTW TWEETING	EEHILMNU HELENIUM	EEHLLRSS SHELLERS
EEGILRUZ REGULIZE	EEGINTUX TEGUEXIN	EEHILMOR HOMELIER	EEHLMMNS HELMSMEN
EEGILSST ELEGISTS	EEGIOPSU EPIGEOUS	EEHILNOP NEOPHILE	EEHLMMSW WHEMMLES
EEGIMMNW EMMEWING	EEGIORST ERGOTISE	EEHILORT HOTELIER	EEHLMOOS HOLESOME
EEGIMMRS IMMERGES	EEGIORTZ ERGOTIZE	EEHILOSS HELIOSES	EEHLMOSS HOMELESS
EEGIMMST GEMMIEST	EEGIORVV OVERGIVE	EEHILRSS HEIRLESS	EEHLNOTT TELETHON
EEGIMNNS MENINGES	EEGIOSST EGOTISES	RELISHES	EEHLOPSS HOPELESS
EEGIMNNW ENMEWING	EEGIOSTZ EGOTIZES	EEHILRSV SHELVIER	EEHLORST HOSTELER
EEGIMNRS REGIMENS	EEGIPRST PRESTIGE	EEHILSST LEISHEST	EEHLORSV SHOVELER
EEGIMNRT METERING	EEGIRRST REGISTER	SHELTIES	EEHLOSSS SHOELESS
REGIMENT	EEGIRRSV GRIEVERS	EEHILSSV HIVELESS	EEHLPPRS SHLEPPER
EEGIMNRU MERINGUE	EEGIRSTT GRISETTE	EEHILWYZ WHEEZILY	EEHLPRSU SPHERULE
EEGIMNRY EMERYING	TERGITES	EEHIMMSS MISHMEES	EEHLRSST SHELTERS
EEGIMNSS SEEMINGS	EEGIRSTU GUERITES	MISHMEES	EEHLRSSW WELSHERS
EEGIMNST MEETINGS	EEGISSTV VESTIGES	EEHIMNOS HEMIONES	EEHLRSTY SHELTERY
STEEMING	EEGJORSU GOUJEERS	EEHIMNRS SHIREMEN	EEHLSSTT SHTETELS
EEGIMNSU EUGENISM	EEGKNORS KEROGENS	EEHIMNSS INMESHES	EEHLSSTW THEWLESS
EEGINNPR PREENING	EEGKNRSU GERENUKS	EEHIMPRS EMPERISH	EEHMMOPR MORPHEME
EEGINNQU QUEENING	EEGLMMSU GEMMULES	EEHIMPST EPITHEMS	EEHMMORT OHMMETER
EEGINNRS ENGINERS	EEGLMNOP EMPLONGE	HEMPIEST	EEHMNOOS MOONSHEE
INGENERS	EEGLMNTU EMULGENT	EEHIMQUV VEHMIQUE	EEHMNOPS PHONEMES
SERENING	EEGLMOSS GLOSSEME	EEHIMRRU RHEUMIER	EEHMNORS HORSEMEN
SNEERING	EEGLNNTU UNGENTLE	EEHIMRST ERETHISM	SHOREMEN
EEGINNRT ENTERING	EEGLNOPY POLYGENE	ETHERISM	EEHMNOSU HOUSEMEN
EEGINNRV ENERVING	EEGLNOSU EUGENOLS	EEHIMRTT THERMITE	EEHMNOSW SOMEWHEN
EEGINNRW RENEWING	EEGLNOSZ LOZENGES	EEHIMSST MESHIEST	EEHMNRSU ENRHEUMS
EEGINNRY ENGINERY	EEGLNOTY TELEGONY	EEHINNQU HENEQUIN	EEHMNRSY MYNHEERS
RENEYING	EEGLNSTT GENTLEST	EEHINNRS ENSHRINE	EEHMOORT RHEOTOME
EEGINNST STEENING	EEGLORRV GROVELER	EEHINNRT INHERENT	EEHMOOSS HOMEOSES
EEGINNSU INGENUES	EEGMMOSU GEMMEOUS	EEHINNSS SNEESHIN	EEHMORST THEOREMS
UNSEEING	EEGMNOST EMONGEST	EEHINNST HENNIEST	EEHMORVW WHOMEVER
EEGINNSV EEVNINGS	GEMSTONE	EEHINORS HEROINES	EEHMRSUX EXHUMERS
EVENINGS	EEGMNSST SEGMENTS	EEHINORT ETHERION	EEHMSSTY METHYSES
EEGINNSW ENSEWING	EEGMNTTU TEGUMENT	EEHINPRS INSPHERE	EEHNNORT ENTHRONE
EEGINNSZ SNEEZING	EEGMORSU GRUESOME	EEHINPRT NEPHRITE	EEHNNOSS SHONEENS
EEGINNTV EVENTING	EEGMORTY GEOMETRY	PREHNITE	EEHNNPPU UNHEPPEN
EEGINOOS OOGENIES	EEGNNORT ROENTGEN	TREPHINE	EEHNNSSS NESHNESS
EEGINOPR PERIGONE	EEGNNOSS GONENESS	EEHINRRS ERRHINES	EEHNNSTU UNNETHES
EEGINOPS EPIGONES	EEGNNOSV EVENSONG	EEHINRTT THIRTEEN	EEHNOPRU HEREUPON
EEGINORR ERIGERON	EEGNOORV ENGROOVE	EEHINRTW WHITENER	EEHNOPST POSHTEEN
EEGINORS ERINGOES	OVERGONE	EEHIOPPS HOSEPIPE	POTHEENS
EEGINORV VIROGENE	EEGNOOST OSTEOGEN	EEHIORSS HEROISES	EEHNOPTY HYPNOTEE
EEGINOST EGESTION	EEGNOPTY GENOTYPE	EEHIORST ISOTHERE	NEOPHYTE
EEGINPRS SPEERING	EEGNORST ESTROGEN	THEORIES	EEHNORST HONESTER
SPREEING	EEGNORSU GENEROUS	THEORISE	EEHNORSW HERONSEW
EEGINPRT PETERING	EEGNORSY ERYNGOES	EEHIORSZ HEROIZES	NOWHERES
EEGINPRU PUREEING	EEGNPRUX EXPUNGER	EEHIORTZ THEORIZE	EEHNORTU HEREUNTO
EEGINPRV PREEVING	EEGNPSUX EXPUNGES	EEHIPPST PSEPHITE	EEHNORTV OVERHENT
EEGINPST STEEPING	EEGNRSSY GREYNESS	EEHIPPTY EPIPHYTE	EEHNPRSU UNSPHERE
EEGINPSW SWEEPING	EEGNRSTU GUERNSEY	EEHIPRRS PERISHER	EEHNRTTU UNTETHER
WEEPINGS	EEGNSSTU GUESTENS	SPHERIER	EEHNSSTU ENTHUSES
EEGINQRU QUEERING	EEGOOPSY POOGYEES	EEHIPRSS PERISHES	EEHNSSTV SEVENTHS
EEGINQUU QUEUEING	EEGOORSV OVERGOES	EEHIPRST TREESHIP	EEHOOPRS OOSPHERE
EEGINRRS RESIGNER	EEGOPRST PROTEGES	EEHIPRTT PERTHITE	EEHOOPSW WHOOPEES
EEGINRRV REVERING	EEGOPRSU SUPEREGO	TEPHRITE	EEHOORSV OVERSHOE
EEGINRSS GREISENS	EEGORRST OSTREGER	THREEPIT	EEHOPRSU EUPHROES
EEGINRST GENTRIES	EEGORRVW OVERGREW	EEHIPSST STEEPISH	EEHOPRVY OVERHYPE
INTEGERS	EEGORSSS OGRESSES	EEHIPSTT EPITHETS	EEHORRTX EXHORTER
REESTING	EEGORSTU UROSTEGE	EEHIPSUU EUPHUISE	EEHORSSU REHOUSES
STEERING	EEGORSTV OVERGETS	EEHIPUUZ EUPHUIZE	EEHORSVW WHOSEVER
STREIGNE	EEGPRSUX EXPURGES	EEHIQRSU QUEERISH	EEHORTTU THEREOUT
EEGINRSU SEIGNEUR	EEGRRSSU RESURGES	EEHIRRSS SHERRIES	EEHORTUW WHEREOUT
EEGINRSV SEVERING	EEGRSSSU GUESSERS	EEHIRRSV SHIVERER	EEHPRSST HEPSTERS
VEERINGS	EEGRSSTU GESTURES	EEHIRRSW WHERRIES	SPERTHES
EEGINRSW SEWERING	EEHHIPSS SHEEPISH	EEHIRSST HEISTERS	EEHPRSTY PHYSETER
EEGINRTU GENITURE	EEHHIRTW HEREWITH	EEHIRSSV SHRIEVES	EEHRRSTW WHERRETS
EEGINRTV EVERTING	EEHHLRST THRESHEL	EEHIRSSX RHEXISES	EEHRSSSU REHUSSES
EEGINRTW TWEERING	EEHHRRST THRESHER	EEHIRSTT ETHERIST	USHERESS
EEGINRTX EXERTING	EEHHRSST THRESHES	EEHIRTVY THIEVERY	EEHRSSTW WERSHEST
GENETRIX	EEHHSSTW WHEESHTS	EEHISSTW SWEETISH	EEHRSTTW WHETTERS
EEGINSSS GNEISSES	EEHIIKLV HIVELIKE	EEHISTTW THEWIEST	EEIIKLLR LIKELIER
EEGINSSU GENIUSES	EEHIKLMO HOMELIKE	EEHISTWY WHEYIEST	EEIIKLPP PIPELIKE
EEGINSTT GENTIEST	EEHIKLRW WHELKIER	EEHKLOSY KEYHOLES	EEIIKLSW LIKEWISE
EEGINSTU EUGENIST	EEHIKRRS SHRIEKER	EEHKOOSY EYEHOOKS	EEIILLMM MILLIEME
EEGINSTV STEEVING	EEHILLMS SHLEMIEL	EEHLLMPS PHELLEMS	EEIILLMT MELILITE
VENTIGES	EEHILLNP HELPLINE	EEHLLMSS HELMLESS	EEIILLOP EOLIPILE
EEGINSTW SWEETING	EEHILLRS HELLIERS	EEHLLNSS ENSHELLS	EEIILLRV LIVELIER
EEGINSTX EXIGENTS	SHELLIER	EEHLLORV HOVELLER	EEIILMNT ILMENITE
EEGINTTV VIGNETTE		EEHLLPSS HELPLESS	

```
                  MELINITE
                  TIMELINE
EEIILMRT  TIMELIER
EEIILMSS  EMISSILE
EEIILNPP  PIPELINE
EEIILNST  LENITIES
EEIILNTV  LENITIVE
EEIILORS  OILERIES
EEIILRST  TILERIES
EEIILRSV  LIVERIES
EEIILSTV  LEVITIES
                  VEILIEST
EEIILSTW  LEWISITE
EEIIMMTT  MIMETITE
EEIIMNOT  MEIONITE
EEIIMNST  ENMITIES
EEIIMOST  MOIETIES
EEIIMPRS  RIEMPIES
EEIIMRSS  MISERIES
EEIIMSST  ITEMISES
EEIIMSSV  EMISSIVE
EEIIMSTZ  ITEMIZES
EEIINNST  NINETIES
EEIINORT  ERIONITE
EEIINPPR  PIPERINE
EEIINPRS  PINERIES
EEIINPRV  VIPERINE
EEIINRRV  RIVERINE
EEIINRSS  RESINISE
                  SIRENISE
EEIINRST  ERINITES
                  NITERIES
EEIINRSV  VINERIES
EEIINRSW  SINEWIER
                  WINERIES
EEIINRSZ  RESINIZE
                  SIRENIZE
EEIINRTT  INTERTIE
                  RETINITE
EEIINSSV  INESSIVE
EEIINSTT  ENTITIES
EEIINSTV  INVITEES
                  VEINIEST
EEIIORSS  OSIERIES
EEIIPRSX  EXPIRIES
EEIIPRTT  EPITRITE
EEIIQSTU  EQUITIES
EEIIQTUV  QUIETIVE
EEIIRRSV  RIVIERES
EEIIRRTV  TIRRIVEE
EEIIRSTV  VERITIES
EEIISSTV  VISITEES
EEIISTVW  VIEWIEST
EEIJKRST  JERKIEST
EEIJLMSS  MEJLISES
EEIJLNNU  JULIENNE
EEIJLNRT  JETLINER
EEIJLNUV  JUVENILE
EEIJMMST  JEMMIEST
EEIJNNOR  ENJOINER
EEIJSTTT  JETTIEST
EEIKLLRS  SKELLIER
EEIKLLRY  KYRIELLE
EEIKLLSS  SKELLIES
EEIKLNSS  LIKENESS
EEIKLNST  NESTLIKE
EEIKLNSY  KEYLINES
EEIKLORS  ROSELIKE
EEIKLORT  LORIKEET
EEIKLPST  PIKELETS
                  SPIKELET
EEIKLRST  TRISKELE
EEIKMRSS  KERMISES
EEIKNORS  KEROSINE
EEIKNRRT  TINKERER
EEIKNRST  KERNITES
EEIKOQUV  EQUIVOKE
EEIKPPPR  KIPPERER
EEIKPRST  PERKIEST

EEIKPSST  PESKIEST
EEIKRRSS  SKERRIES
EEIKRRST  KEISTERS
EEIKSSTY  SKIEYEST
EEIKSTTT  TEKTITES
EEILLMPR  IMPELLER
EEILLMRS  SMELLIER
EEILLMRU  RELLUME
EEILLMST  MELLITES
EEILLNOR  LONELIER
EEILLNSY  SENILELY
EEILLNVV  VENVILLE
EEILLORS  ORSEILLE
EEILLORV  LOVELIER
EEILLOSV  LOVELIES
EEILLPSS  ELLIPSES
EEILLPSY  SLEEPILY
EEILLRSS  LEISLERS
EEILLRST  TREILLES
EEILLSSV  VEILLESS
EEILLSTV  EVILLEST
EEILLTVY  VELLEITY
EEILLVWY  WEEVILLY
EEILMNNS  LINESMEN
EEILMNNU  ENLUMINE
EEILMNOP  PEMOLINE
EEILMNOR  LEMONIER
EEILMNRS  ERMELINS
EEILMNRU  LEMURINE
                  RELUMINE
EEILMNSS  ISLESMEN
EEILMNSU  SELENIUM
                  SEMILUNE
EEILMOPS  POLEMISE
EEILMOPZ  POLEMIZE
EEILMORT  MOTELIER
EEILMOST  MESOLITE
                  MISLETOE
EEILMPST  IMPLETES
EEILMPSX  IMPLEXES
EEILMRST  TERMLIES
EEILMRSV  VERMEILS
EEILMSST  TIMELESS
EEILMSTT  MELTIEST
EEILMSUV  EMULSIVE
EEILNNST  LENIENTS
                  SENTINEL
EEILNNSV  ENLIVENS
EEILNOPR  LEPORINE
EEILNORS  ELOINERS
EEILNOST  NOSELITE
EEILNOSV  NOVELISE
EEILNOVZ  NOVELIZE
EEILNPPZ  ZEPPELIN
EEILNPRS  PILSENER
EEILNPRU  PERILUNE
EEILNPRV  REPLEVIN
EEILNPST  PLENTIES
EEILNRSS  REINLESS
EEILNRST  LISTENER
                  SILENTER
EEILNRSV  LIVENERS
EEILNRTT  NETTLIER
EEILNRTY  ENTIRELY
                  LIENTERY
EEILNRUV  UNVEILER
EEILNSST  SETLINES
EEILNSSV  EVILNESS
                  VILENESS
EEILNSTT  ENTITLES
EEILNSTV  VEINLETS
EEILOPRS  PELORIES
EEILOPST  PETIOLES
EEILORRT  LOITERER
EEILORRV  OVERLIER
EEILORRW  LOWERIER
EEILORST  LITEROSE
                  TROELIES
EEILORSV  OVERLIES

                  RELIEVOS
                  VOLERIES
EEILORSW  OWLERIES
EEILORVV  OVERLIVE
                  OVERVEIL
EEILOSST  ESTOILES
EEILOSTW  OWELTIES
EEILOSTZ  ZEOLITES
EEILOSVW  VOWELISE
EEILOTTT  TOILETTE
EEILOVWZ  VOWELIZE
EEILPPSS  PIPELESS
EEILPPSY  EPILEPSY
EEILPRRS  REPLIERS
EEILPRSS  SPIELERS
EEILPRST  EPISTLER
                  PELTRIES
                  PERLITES
                  REPTILES
EEILPSSS  PELISSES
EEILPSST  EPISTLES
EEILPSSU  EPULISES
EEILPSSV  PELVISES
EEILPSTY  EPISTYLE
EEILQRSU  RELIQUES
EEILRRSV  RELIVERS
                  REVILERS
EEILRSST  LEISTERS
                  RITELESS
                  TIRELESS
EEILRSSU  LEISURES
EEILRSSV  SERVILES
EEILRSSW  WIRELESS
EEILRSTT  RETITLES
EEILSSTW  WITELESS
EEILSSTX  SEXTILES
EEILSSVW  VIEWLESS
EEILSTTX  TEXTILES
EEILSTVY  STIEVELY
EEIMMNRS  IMMENSER
EEIMMORS  MEMORIES
                  MEMORISE
EEIMMORZ  MEMORIZE
EEIMMOST  SOMETIME
EEIMMRSS  IMMERSES
EEIMMRST  MERISTEM
                  MIMESTER
                  MISMETRE
EEIMMRSU  EUMERISM
EEIMMSSS  MISSEEMS
EEIMNNOS  NOMINEES
EEIMNNRS  REINSMEN
EEIMNOPS  EPISEMON
EEIMNORS  EMERSION
EEIMNORT  TIMONEER
EEIMNORV  VOMERINE
EEIMNOST  MONETISE
                  SEMITONE
EEIMNOTX  XENOTIME
EEIMNOTZ  MONETIZE
EEIMNPRU  PERINEUM
EEIMNPRZ  PRIZEMEN
EEIMNPST  SEPIMENT
EEIMNQSU  MESQUINE
EEIMNRRT  TERMINER
EEIMNRRV  RIVERMEN
EEIMNRSV  MINEVERS
EEIMNRTU  MUTINEER
EEIMNRTV  VIREMENT
EEIMNSSW  MISWEENS
EEIMNSTT  MINETTES
EEIMOPRS  PROMISEE
                  REIMPOSE
EEIMOPSS  EPISOMES
EEIMOPST  EPITOMES
                  EPSOMITE
EEIMORSS  ISOMERES
EEIMORST  TIRESOME
EEIMORTV  OVERTIME

EEIMORTX  OXIMETER
EEIMOSSW  SOMEWISE
EEIMOSSX  EXOMISES
EEIMPPRS  EPISPERM
EEIMPRRS  PREMIERS
                  REPRIMES
                  SIMPERER
EEIMPRSS  EMPRISES
                  IMPRESES
                  IMPRESSE
                  MESPRISE
                  PREMISES
                  SPIREMES
EEIMPRST  EMPTIERS
EEIMPRSX  PREMIXES
EEIMPRSZ  MESPRIZE
EEIMPSST  SEPTIMES
EEIMPSSY  EMPYESIS
EEIMPSTT  EMPTIEST
EEIMQRSU  REQUIEMS
EEIMQSTU  MESQUITE
EEIMRRST  MERRIEST
                  TRIREMES
EEIMRRTT  REMITTER
                  TRIMETER
EEIMRSST  MEISTERS
                  TRISEMES
EEIMRSTT  EMITTERS
                  TERMITES
EEIMRSTU  EMERITUS
EEIMRTTY  TEMERITY
EEIMSSST  MESSIEST
                  METISSES
EEINNNPS  PENNINES
EEINNPTT  PENITENT
EEINNRST  INTENSER
                  INTERNES
EEINNRSU  NEURINES
EEINNRSV  INNERVES
                  NERVINES
EEINNRTT  RENITENT
EEINNRUX  XENURINE
EEINNSST  TENNISES
EEINNSTT  SENTIENT
EEINNSTW  ENTWINES
                  WENNIEST
EEINNSTZ  NETIZENS
EEINOPPR  PEPERINO
                  PEPERONI
EEINOPRS  ISOPRENE
                  PIONEERS
EEINORRT  REORIENT
EEINORSS  ESSOINER
EEINORST  SEROTINE
EEINORSV  EVERSION
EEINORTT  TENORITE
EEINORTX  EXERTION
EEINOSST  ESSONITE
EEINOSTT  NOISETTE
                  TEOSINTE
EEINPPSS  PEPSINES
EEINPRRS  REPINERS
EEINPRSS  EREPSINS
                  RIPENESS
EEINPRSU  PENURIES
                  RESUPINE
EEINPRTX  INEXPERT
EEINPSST  PENTISES
EEINPSTT  INEPTEST
                  SPINETTE
EEINQRRU  ENQUIRER
EEINQRSU  ENQUIRES
                  INQUERES
                  SQUIREEN
EEINQSTU  QUIETENS
EEINQSUY  QUEYNIES
EEINRRSS  RESINERS
EEINRRST  INSERTER
                  REINSERT
```

```
         REINTERS
         RENTIERS
         TERRINES
EEINRRSU REINSURE
EEINRRSV VERNIERS
EEINRRTV INVERTER
EEINRRTX INTERREX
EEINRSST INTERESS
         SENTRIES
         TRENISES
EEINRSSU ENURESIS
EEINRSSV INVERSES
         VERSINES
EEINRSTT INERTEST
         INTEREST
         STERNITE
EEINRSTU ESURIENT
         NEURITES
         RETINUES
         REUNITES
EEINRSTV NERVIEST
         REINVEST
         SERVIENT
         SIRVENTE
EEINRSTX INTERSEX
EEINRSTY SERENITY
EEINRSUV UNIVERSE
EEINRSWW NEWSWIRE
EEINRTTY ENTIRETY
         ETERNITY
EEINSSST SESTINES
EEINSSSW WISENESS
EEINSSTW NEWSIEST
EEINSSTX SIXTEENS
EEINSSTY SYENITES
EEINSTTT NETTIEST
         TENTIEST
EEINSTTW TENTWISE
         TWENTIES
EEINSTTX EXISTENT
EEIOPPRS EPISPORE
         POPERIES
EEIOPPST EPITOPES
EEIOPRRT PORTIERE
EEIOPRRV OVERRIPE
EEIOPRST POETRIES
EEIOPSST POETISES
EEIOPSTZ POETIZES
EEIORRRS ORRERIES
EEIORRSS ROSERIES
         ROSIERES
EEIORRTV OVERTIRE
EEIORRTW TOWERIER
EEIORRTX EXTERIOR
EEIORRUV OUVRIERE
EEIORSST EROTESIS
EEIORSSX OREXISES
EEIORSVW OVERWISE
EEIORSVZ OVERSIZE
EEIORVVW OVERVIEW
EEIORVWW WIREWOVE
EEIPPPRR PREPPIER
EEIPPPRS PREPPIES
EEIPPPST PEPPIEST
EEIPPRRS PERSPIRE
EEIPPRTY PERIPETY
EEIPPSST PEPTISES
EEIPPSTT PIPETTES
EEIPPSTZ PEPTIZES
EEIPQRSU PERIQUES
         REPIQUES
EEIPRRRS PERRIERS
EEIPRRSS REPRISES
         RESPIRES
EEIPRRSV REPRIVES
EEIPRRSZ REPRIZES
EEIPRRTT PRETERIT

         PRETTIER
EEIPRSSS PRESSIES
EEIPRSST RESPITES
EEIPRSSV PREVISES
EEIPRSTT PRETTIES
EEIPRSTY PERSEITY
EEIPRSVW PREVIEWS
EEIPRSZZ PREZZIES
EEIPRTUV ERUPTIVE
EEIPSSSS SPEISSES
EEIPSSTW SPEWIEST
         STEPWISE
EEIPSTTT PETTIEST
EEIQRRRU REQUIRER
EEIQRRSU REQUIRES
EEIQRRTU REQUITER
EEIQRRUV VERQUIRE
EEIQRSSU ESQUIRES
EEIQRSTU QUIETERS
         REQUITES
EEIQRSTW QWERTIES
EEIQRTUY QUEERITY
EEIQSSSU ESQUISSE
EEIQSTTU QUIETEST
EEIRRRST RETIRERS
         TERRIERS
EEIRRSST TRESSIER
EEIRRSSV REVERSIS
         REVISERS
EEIRRSTV REVERIST
         RIVERETS
         RIVETERS
EEIRRSTW REWRITES
EEIRRSVV REVIVERS
EEIRRTTT TITTERER
EEIRSSSU REISSUES
EEIRSSSV IVRESSES
EEIRSSTT RESTIEST
EEIRSSTU SURETIES
EEIRSSTV SIEVERTS
         TREVISES
         VESTRIES
EEIRSSUZ SEIZURES
EEIRSTTU SUETTIER
EEIRSTUV VETIVERS
EEIRSTVY SEVERITY
EEIRTTTZ TERZETTI
EEISSTTT TESTIEST
EEISSTTU SUETIEST
EEISSTTV STIEVEST
EEISSTTW STEWIEST
EEISSTTZ ZESTIEST
EEISTTTX TETTIXES
EEISTUXZ ZEUXITES
EEJJLNUY JEJUNELY
EEJKMOOS JOKESOME
EEJLLMSU JUMELLES
EEJLLORY JOLLEYER
EEJLPSTU PULSEJET
EEJNOORS REJONEOS
EEJNORSY ENJOYERS
EEJPRRRU PERJURER
EEJPRRSU PERJURES
EEJPRSTU SUPERJET
EEJQRRSU JERQUERS
EEKKORWW WORKWEEK
EEKKOSTV VETKOEKS
EEKKRRST TREKKERS
EEKLLNRY KERNELLY
EEKLLNSV KNEVELLS
EEKLLSUU UKULELES
EEKLNNNU UNKENNEL
EEKLNOSS KEELSONS
EEKLNOST SKELETON
EEKLNOSV VELSKOEN
EEKLRSST KESTRELS
         SKELTERS
EEKNOPRS RESPOKEN
EEKNOSTY KEYNOTES

         KEYSTONE
EEKNSSSW SKEWNESS
EEKNSSTU NETSUKES
EEKOORST KREOSOTE
EEKOPRTV OVERKEPT
EEKORSTV OVERKEST
EEKRRTUZ KREUTZER
EELLMORW MELLOWER
EELLMPTU PLUMELET
EELLMRSS SMELLERS
EELLMRSV VERMELLS
EELLNORR ENROLLER
EELLNOUV NOUVELLE
EELLNPRU PRUNELLE
EELLNRSU SULLENER
EELLNSST SNELLEST
EELLNSSW WELLNESS
EELLNSTU ENTELLUS
EELLOPSS ELLOPSES
EELLORSS ROSELLES
EELLORST SOLLERET
EELLORSV OVERSELL
EELLORSZ ROZELLES
EELLORTX EXTOLLER
EELLORVY VOLLEYER
EELLORWY YELLOWER
EELLOSSV LOVELESS
EELLOSUV LEVULOSE
EELLPRSS RESPELLS
         SPELLERS
EELLQRSU QUELLERS
EELLRSSU RULELESS
EELLRSSW SWELLERS
EELLSSTU TELLUSES
EELLSSTW SWELLEST
EELMMPSU EMPLUMES
EELMMPUX EXEMPLUM
EELMNOOS LONESOME
         OENOMELS
EELMNORS SOLEMNER
EELMNSUY UNSEEMLY
EELMNTTU TEMULENT
EELMNTUY UNMEETLY
EELMOOSV LOVESOME
EELMOPRS PLEROMES
EELMOPRY EMPLOYER
EELMOPST LEPTOMES
EELMOPSY POLYSEME
EELMORST MOLESTER
EELMORSW EELWORMS
EELMORTY MOTLEYER
         REMOTELY
EELMOSSV MOVELESS
EELMOTVW TWELVEMO
EELMPPRU EMPURPLE
EELMPSST SEMPLEST
         STEMPELS
         STEMPLES
EELMPSTT TEMPLETS
EELMRRTU MURRELET
EELMRSST SMELTERS
         TERMLESS
EELMRSTY SMELTERY
EELMRTUX LUXMETER
EELMSSST STEMLESS
EELMSSTT STEMLETS
EELNNOSS LONENESS
EELNNRTU TUNNELER
EELNNUVY UNEVENLY
EELNOORS LOOSENER
EELNOPPU UNPEOPLE
EELNOPRT PETRONEL
EELNOPSV ENVELOPS
EELNOPTY POLYTENE
EELNOQTU ELOQUENT
EELNORST ENTRESOL
EELNORTT TELETRON
EELNORTV OVERLENT
EELNOSSS NOSELESS

         SOLENESS
EELNOSST NOTELESS
         TONELESS
EELNOSSU SELENOUS
EELNOSSY ESLOYNES
EELNOSSZ ZONELESS
EELNOSTT NOTELETS
EELNOSTU TOLUENES
EELNOTVV EVOLVENT
EELNRSST SLENTERS
EELNRSTT LETTERNS
EELNRSUV NERVULES
EELNSSSW NEWSLESS
EELNSSTT TENTLESS
EELNSSTU TUNELESS
         UNSTEELS
EELNSSTY ENSTYLES
EELNSSUV UNSELVES
EELNSTTU LUNETTES
         UNSETTLE
EELOPPSS PEPLOSES
EELOPPST ESTOPPEL
EELOPRRX EXPLORER
EELOPRSX EXPLORES
EELOPRTT TELEPORT
EELOPSTU EELPOUTS
         OUTSLEEP
         SLEEPOUT
EELOQRUY REQUOYLE
EELORRSV RESOLVER
EELORRTV REVOLTER
EELORRUV OVERRULE
EELORRVV REVOLVER
EELORSSS ROSELESS
EELORSSV RESOLVES
EELORSTT LORETTES
EELORSTU RESOLUTE
EELORSVV EVOLVERS
         REVOLVES
EELORTTU ROULETTE
EELORTUV REVOLUTE
EELOSSST OSSELETS
EELOSSSU SOLEUSES
EELOSSTT TELEOSTS
EELOSSTU SETULOSE
EELOSSTV VOTELESS
EELOSSTX SEXTOLET
EELOSTUV EVOLUTES
         VELOUTES
EELPPSSU PEPLUSES
EELPPSTU SEPTUPLE
EELPQRSU PREQUELS
EELPRSST SPELTERS
EELPRSSU REPULSES
EELPRSTZ PRETZELS
EELPRSUX PLEXURES
EELPRTXY EXPERTLY
EELPSSUX EXPULSES
         PLEXUSES
EELPSTUX SEXTUPLE
EELRRSTW WRESTLER
EELRSSST RESTLESS
         TRESSELS
EELRSSTT SETTLERS
         STERLETS
         TRESTLES
EELRSSTW SWELTERS
         WRESTLES
EELRSSTY RESTYLES
         TYRELESS
EELRSSTZ SELTZERS
EELRSTWY WESTERLY
EELSSTTV SVELTEST
EELSSTTX TEXTLESS
EELSSTUY EUSTYLES
EEMMNNOY MONEYMEN
EEMMNOOP MENOPOME
EEMMNOST MEMENTOS
EEMMNOTV MOVEMENT
```

EEMMNRRY MERRYMEN	EENOPSST PENTOSES	EEORRTUV OVERTURE	EFFINOSU EFFUSION
EEMMOORS MEROSOME	POSTEENS	TROUVERE	EFFINRSS SNIFFERS
EEMMOSSU MOUSMEES	EENORRSV OVERRENS	EEORSSST OSSETERS	EFFINRSU SNUFFIER
EEMMRSST STEMMERS	EENORRTT ROTTENER	EEORSSTT ROSETTES	EFFINSST STIFFENS
EEMMNOPW PENWOMEN	EENORRSS SORENESS	EEORSSTV ESTOVERS	EFFIOPRS PIFFEROS
EEMNNOSV ENVENOMS	EENORSSU NEUROSES	OVERSETS	EFFIORST FORFEITS
EEMNOOSS SOMEONES	EENORSTT ONSETTER	EEORSSUV OVERUSES	EFFIOSTT TOFFIEST
EEMNOOSY MOONEYES	EENORSTV OVERNETS	EEORSSVW OVERSEWS	EFFIPSTU PUFFIEST
EEMNOPRS PROSEMEN	EENORSTX EXTENSOR	EEORSTVX VORTEXES	EFFIQRSU SQUIFFER
EEMNORRS SERMONER	EENORSVW OVERSEWN	EEORTTTZ TERZETTO	EFFIRSTT TRIFFEST
EEMNORST SERMONET	EENORTVW OVERWENT	EEOSSSVW VOWESSES	EFFIRSTU STUFFIER
STOREMEN	EENOSSST STENOSES	EEOSSTTT SESTETTO	EFFISSTT STIFFEST
EEMNORSU MOUNSEER	EENOSSSY ESSOYNES	EEPPRSST STEPPERS	EFFISSUX SUFFIXES
EEMNORSV OVERSMEN	EENPPRST PERPENTS	EEPPSSUW UPSWEEPS	EFFLMNUU UNMUFFLE
EEMNORSY MONEYERS	EENPRSST PERTNESS	EEPQRRUU PERRUQUE	EFFLMRSU MUFFLERS
EEMNORTU ROUTEMEN	PRESENTS	EEPRRSSS PRESSERS	EFFLNRSU SNUFFLER
EEMNPRSS PRESSMEN	SERPENTS	EEPRRSSU PERUSERS	EFFLNRUU UNRUFFLE
EEMNPRSU SUPERMEN	EENPRSSU PURENESS	PRESSURE	EFFLNSSU SNUFFLES
EEMNPRTU ERUMPENT	EENPRSTT STREPENT	EEPRRSTV PERVERTS	EFFLOSSU SOUFFLES
UNTEMPER	EENPRSTV PREVENTS	EEPRRSVY REPRYVES	EFFLRRSU RUFFLERS
EEMNRSTU MUENSTER	EENPSSSU SUSPENSE	EEPRSSTT PRETESTS	EFFLRSTU TRUFFLES
EEMNRSTW TREWSMEN	EENPSSTY STEPNEYS	EEPRSSTX SEXPERTS	EFFNRSSU SNUFFERS
EEMNSSTU MUTENESS	EENPSTTU PETUNTSE	EEPRSTTU UPSETTER	EFFOOORT FOREFOOT
TENESMUS	EENPTTUZ PETUNTZE	EEPRSTTX PRETEXTS	EFFOORRS OFFERORS
EEMNSTTV VESTMENT	EENQSSTU SEQUENTS	EEQRSSTU QUESTERS	EFFOPRRS PROFFERS
EEMOORRV MOREOVER	EENRRRTU RETURNER	REQUESTS	EFFORRUV OVERRUFF
EEMOORTT ROOMETTE	EENRRSSU ENSURERS	EERRSSTU TRESSURE	EFFRSSTU STUFFERS
EEMOOSSX EXOSMOSE	EENRRSTV RENVERST	EERRSSTW STREWERS	EFFSSSUU SUFFUSES
EEMOPRRS EMPERORS	EENRRSUV NERVURES	WRESTERS	EFGGGILN FLEGGING
PREMORSE	EENRRTUV VENTURER	EERRSSVW SWERVERS	EFGGIINN FEIGNING
EEMOPRSV PREMOVES	EENRSSSU SURENESS	EERRSTTU REUTTERS	EFGGILOS SOLFEGGI
EEMOPRSW EMPOWERS	EENRSSTT STERNEST	UTTERERS	EFGGINRU REFUGING
EEMOQTTU MOQUETTE	TESTERNS	EERRSTUV VESTURER	EFGGIORR FROGGIER
EEMORRSS REMORSES	EENRSSTU TRUENESS	EERRSTVY REVESTRY	EFGGIOST FOGGIEST
EEMORRSU UROMERES	EENRSSTW WESTERNS	EERRSUVY RESURVEY	EFGGIRRS FRIGGERS
EEMORRSV REMOVERS	EENRSSTY STYRENES	EERSSSST STRESSES	EFGGISTU FUGGIEST
EEMORRTU MOUTERER	EENRSTUV VENTURES	EERSSSTU ESTRUSES	EFGGORRY FROGGERY
OUTREMER	EEOOPRST PROTEOSE	EERSSSUY SEYSURES	EFGHILNS FLESHING
EEMORSST SOMERSET	EEOOPRSX EXOSPORE	EERSSTTU TRUSTEES	SHELFING
EEMORSTT REMOTEST	EEOOPRTZ ZOETROPE	EERSSTUV VESTURES	EFGHINRS FRESHING
EEMORSTU TEMEROUS	EEOORRVW OVERWORE	EERSSUVW SURVEWES	EFGHINRT FRIGHTEN
EEMOTTTU TEETOTUM	EEOPPRRR PROPERER	EERSTTTU UTTEREST	EFGHIOSY FOGEYISH
EEMPRRSU PRESUMER	EEOPPRSS PORPESSE	EERSTTUX TEXTURES	EFGHIRST FIGHTERS
SUPREMER	PREPOSES	EESSSTTT SESTETTS	FREIGHTS
EEMPRSST SEMPSTER	EEOPPSTU OUTPEEPS	EESSTTTX SEXTETTS	EFGHNOTU FOUGHTEN
EEMPRSSU PRESUMES	EEOPRRRT REPORTER	EFFFGINO FEOFFING	EFGIILNU FIGULINE
SUPREMES	EEOPRRRV REPROVER	EFFFILRU FLUFFIER	EFGIILSU UGLIFIES
EEMPRSTT TEMPTERS	EEOPRRSU REPOSURE	EFFFISTU FUFFIEST	EFGIIMNS MISFEIGN
EEMPRSTU PERMUTES	EEOPRRSV REPROVES	EFFFOORS FEOFFORS	EFGIINNR ENFIRING
EEMPSSTT TEMPESTS	EEOPRRTT POTTERER	EFFGILRU GRIEFFUL	INFRINGE
EEMPSSTY EMPTYSES	EEOPRRTX EXPORTER	EFFGINOR OFFERING	REFINING
EEMRRSTU MUSTERER	EEOPRSSS ESPRESSO	EFFGINSU EFFUSING	EFGIINNT FEINTING
EEMRRSUU REMUEURS	EEOPRSST PORTESSE	EFFGRSTU GRUFFEST	EFGIINNX ENFIXING
EEMRRTTU MUTTERER	EEOPRSSU ESPOUSER	EFFHIIRW WHIFFIER	EFGIINRR FRINGIER
EEMSSTTU MUSETTES	REPOUSSE	EFFHIISW FISHWIFE	EFGIINRU FIGURINE
EENNNOSS NONSENSE	EEOPRSSX EXPOSERS	EFFHIITT FIFTIETH	EFGIINRY REIFYING
EENNNPTY TENPENNY	EXPRESSO	EFFHILRW WHIFFLER	EFGIINRZ FRIEZING
EENNOORT ROTENONE	EEOPRSTT TREETOPS	EFFHILSW WHIFFLES	EFGIITUV FUGITIVE
EENNOPSS OPENNESS	EEOPRSTV OVERSTEP	EFFHIRSS SHERIFFS	EFGIKNOR FOREKING
EENNOPTX EXPONENT	EEOPRSTY SEROTYPE	EFFHIRSW WHIFFERS	EFGILLNO LIFELONG
EENNORRW RENOWNER	EEOPRSUX EXPOSURE	EFFHISTU HUFFIEST	EFGILLNU FUELLING
EENNORST TENONERS	EEOPRTVY OVERTYPE	EFFHISTW WHIFFETS	EFGILLUU GUILEFUL
EENNORSU NEURONES	EEOPSSSU ESPOUSES	EFFHLRSU SHUFFLER	EFGILMOR FILMGOER
EENNOSTT NONETTES	POSEUSES	EFFHLSSU SHUFFLES	EFGILNNS FLENSING
EENNQSUU UNQUEENS	EEOPSSTW SWEETSOP	EFFHOORS OFFSHORE	EFGILNOR FLORIGEN
EENNRSUV UNNERVES	EEOPSTUW OUTWEEPS	EFFIIMST MIFFIEST	EFGILNRS FLINGERS
EENNSSSU UNSENSES	EEOQRSTU REQUOTES	EFFIINRS SNIFFIER	EFGILNRY FERLYING
EENNSSTX NEXTNESS	EEOQRTTU ROQUETTE	EFFIINSS IFFINESS	EFGILNSS SELFINGS
EENOORST ROESTONE	EEORRRST RESORTER	EFFIINST NIFFIEST	EFGILNST FELTINGS
EENOORTV OVERTONE	RESTORER	EFFIIPRS SPIFFIER	EFGILNTT FETTLING
EENOPPRS PREPONES	RETRORSE	EFFIISST STIFFIES	EFGILSTU GULFIEST
PROPENES	EEORRRTT RETORTER	EFFIKLSS SKIFFLES	EFGIMNST FIGMENTS
PROPENSE	EEORRSST RESTORES	EFFILNRS SNIFFLER	EFGIMOSY FOGEYISM
EENOPPST PEPTONES	EEORRSSV REVERSOS	EFFILNSS SNIFFLES	EFGIMRUU REFUGIUM
EENOPRSS RESPONSE	EEORRSTU REROUTES	EFFILORT FORELIFT	EFGINNPR PFENNING
EENOPRST PROTENSE	EEORRSTV EVERTORS	EFFILPRS PIFFLERS	EFGINNPS PFENNIGS
EENOPRSU PERONEUS	EEORRSTX EXTRORSE	EFFILPRU PLUFFIER	EFGINNRS FERNINGS
EENOPRTT ENTREPOT	EEORRTTT TOTTERER	EFFILRRS RIFFLERS	EFGINORV FORGIVEN
EENOPRXY PYROXENE		EFFILRSU SIFFLEUR	EFGINORW FOREWING

EFGINPUY PINGUEFY	EFIILNTY FELINITY	EFILOPRR PROFILER	EFIRRSTT FRITTERS
EFGINRRY FERRYING	FINITELY	EFILOPRS PROFILES	EFIRRSTU FRITURES
EFGINRSU GUNFIRES	EFIILOQU FILIOQUE	EFILORRU FLOURIER	FRUITERS
REFUSING	EFIILRRT FLIRTIER	EFILORSS FLOSSIER	FURRIEST
EFGINRSW SWERFING	EFIILRSU FUSILIER	EFILORST FLORIEST	EFIRRTUY FRUITERY
EFGINRTT FRETTING	EFIILSTT FITLIEST	TREFOILS	EFIRSSSU FISSURES
EFGINRTU FEUTRING	EFIIMMNS FEMINISM	EFILORTU FLUORITE	EFIRSSTU SURFEITS
REFUTING	EFIIMNOS FISNOMIE	EFILOSSX SEXFOILS	SURFIEST
EFGINRTY GENTRIFY	OMNIFIES	EFILOSTT LOFTIEST	EFIRSSTW SWIFTERS
EFGIOOST GOOFIEST	EFIIMNRR INFIRMER	EFILOSTU OUTFILES	EFIRSTTU TURFIEST
EFGIOPTT PETTIFOG	EFIIMNST FEMINIST	EFILPPRS FLIPPERS	TURFITES
EFGIORSV FORGIVES	EFIIMNSU MUNIFIES	EFILPPST FLIPPEST	EFIRSTUX FIXTURES
EFGIRRST GRIFTERS	EFIIMNTY FEMINITY	EFILPPSU PIPEFULS	EFIRSTUZ FURZIEST
EFGLOOVX FOXGLOVE	EFIIMRSS MISFIRES	EFILPRTU UPLIFTER	EFISSSTU FUSSIEST
EFGLORST FROGLETS	EFIINNST FINNIEST	EFILPSTU SPITEFUL	EFISSTTU FUSTIEST
EFGLRSUU SURGEFUL	EFIINORR INFERIOR	EFILRRST TRIFLERS	EFISSTTW SWIFTEST
EFGLSSTU SLUGFEST	EFIINORT NOTIFIER	EFILRRSU FLURRIES	EFISTTTU TUFTIEST
EFGNOSST SONGFEST	EFIINOST NOTIFIES	EFILRSST RIFTLESS	EFISTUZZ FUZZIEST
EFGNSSUU FUNGUSES	EFIINPSV FIVEPINS	STIFLERS	EFKLLOOR FOLKLORE
EFGORRSU FERRUGOS	EFIINPSX SPINIFEX	EFILRSTT FLITTERS	EFKLMNOS MENFOLKS
EFGORSTU FOREGUTS	EFIINRRT FERRITIN	EFILRSTW FEWTRILS	EFKLMORS MERFOLKS
EFHHIRSS FRESHISH	EFIINRST SNIFTIER	EFILRSVV FLIVVERS	EFKLNSUY FLUNKEYS
EFHIILRT FILTHIER	EFIINRSU UNIFIERS	EFILRSZZ FRIZZLES	EFKLOPSU POKEFULS
EFHIILST TILEFISH	EFIINRSY RESINIFY	EFILRTTU FRUITLET	EFKLORUW FLUEWORK
EFHIIMSU HUMIFIES	EFIINSTT NIFTIEST	EFILSSST SELFISTS	EFKLPSSU SKEPFULS
EFHIINRS FINISHER	EFIINSUV INFUSIVE	EFILSSTT LEFTISTS	EFKNOORW FOREKNOW
EFHIINSS FINISHES	EFIIOSSS OSSIFIES	EFILSSTU SULFITES	EFKOOPRS FORSPOKE
EFHIIPPS PIPEFISH	EFIIPRRU PURIFIER	EFILSTTU FLUTIEST	EFKORRTW FRETWORK
EFHIIPRS FIRESHIP	EFIIPRST SPITFIRE	FUTILEST	EFLLLOOW WOOLFELL
EFHIIRST SHIFTIER	EFIIPRSU PURIFIES	EFILSTTW SWIFTLET	EFLLLOWY FELLOWLY
EFHIISST FISHIEST	EFIIPRTY TYPIFIER	EFIMMRSU FERMIUMS	EFLLLPSU SPELLFUL
EFHILRSU FLUSHIER	EFIIPSTY TYPIFIES	EFIMNORR INFORMER	EFLLNSSU FULLNESS
EFHILTWY WHITEFLY	EFIIRRST FIRRIEST	REINFORM	EFLLNTUY FLUENTLY
EFHIOOOR FORHOOIE	EFIIRRTU FRUITIER	RENIFORM	EFLLOORW FOLLOWER
EFHIOPRS FORESHIP	EFIIRRZZ FRIZZIER	EFIMNORS ENSIFORM	EFLLOOTW FOOTWELL
EFHIORRT FROTHIER	EFIIRSTT RIFTIEST	FERMIONS	EFLLORUV OVERFULL
EFHIORSS ROSEFISH	EFIIRTUV FRUITIVE	EFIMNRSS FIRMNESS	EFLLOUWY WOEFULLY
EFHIORSV OVERFISH	EFIIRVVY REVIVIFY	EFIMNSTT FITMENTS	EFLLRUUY RUEFULLY
EFHIORTT FORTIETH	EFIISSTT FISTIEST	EFIMORRT RETIFORM	EFLLSUUY USEFULLY
EFHIPRSS SERFSHIP	EFIISTZZ FIZZIEST	EFIMORRW FIREWORM	EFLMMRUY FLUMMERY
EFHIPRSU FURPHIES	EFIJLORS FRIJOLES	EFIMORST SETIFORM	EFLMNRUU FRENULUM
EFHIRRTU THURIFER	EFIJLOST JETFOILS	EFIMOSTT OFTTIMES	EFLMORRY FORMERLY
EFHIRSST SHIFTERS	EFIKLNSU FLUNKIES	EFIMPRRU FRUMPIER	EFLMORSS FORMLESS
EFHISSTU SHUFTIES	EFIKLOOR ROOFLIKE	EFIMRSTU FREMITUS	EFLMORSU FULSOMER
EFHKLNOU FUNKHOLE	EFIKLORS FOLKSIER	EFINNORS INFERNOS	EFLMPRSU FRUMPLES
EFHLLLSU SHELLFUL	EFIKLSTU FLUKIEST	EFINNSTU FUNNIEST	EFLNOOSU FELONOUS
EFHLNORS HORNFELS	EFIKNNOS FINNESKO	EFINOPRS FORPINES	EFLNORSU FLEURONS
EFHLOOSS HOOFLESS	EFIKNORS FORESKIN	EFINOPTX PONTIFEX	EFLNORTT FRONTLET
EFHLOOSX FOXHOLES	EFIKNRSU REFUSNIK	EFINORRT FRONTIER	EFLNOSSU FOULNESS
EFHLOPSU HOPEFULS	EFIKNSTU FUNKIEST	EFINORSU REFUSION	SULFONES
EFHLORSY HORSEFLY	EFIKORRW FIREWORK	EFINOSSX FOXINESS	EFLNOSTT FLETTONS
EFHLOSSU FLOUSHES	EFIKORST FORKIEST	EFINOSSZ FOZINESS	FONTLETS
EFHLOSUU HOUSEFUL	EFIKRRSS FRISKERS	EFINRSST SNIFTERS	EFLNOSTY STONEFLY
EFHLOSUY HOUSEFLY	EFIKRSST FRISKETS	EFINRSSU INFUSERS	EFLNSSTU NESTFULS
EFHLRSSU FLUSHERS	EFILLLNU FLUELLIN	EFINRTTU UNFITTER	EFLNSSUY SYNFUELS
EFHLSSTU FLUSHEST	EFILLMSU SMILEFUL	EFIOOPST POOFIEST	EFLNSTTU TENTFULS
EFHLSTTW TWELFTHS	EFILLOOS FOLIOLES	EFIOORST ROOFIEST	EFLNSUUU UNUSEFUL
EFHNORST FORHENTS	EFILLORV OVERFILL	EFIOOSTT FOOTIEST	EFLOORRS FLOORERS
EFHOORSW FORESHOW	EFILLRUY IREFULLY	EFIOOSTW WOOFIEST	EFLOORSS FORSLOES
EFHORRTY FROTHERY	EFILLSTY STELLIFY	EFIOPRRS PORIFERS	ROOFLESS
EFHRRSTU FURTHERS	EFILLTUY FUTILELY	EFIOPRRT PROFITER	EFLOORSW FORESLOW
EFHRSTTU FURTHEST	EFILMNSU FULMINES	EFIOPRST FIREPOTS	EFLOORSZ FOOZLERS
EFIIILRV VILIFIER	EFILMOST FILEMOTS	EFIORRST FROSTIER	EFLOORTU FOOTRULE
EFIIILSV VILIFIES	EFILMRSS FIRMLESS	ROTIFERS	EFLOORVW OVERFLOW
EFIIIMNS MINIFIES	EFILMSSS SELFISMS	EFIORRSW FROWSIER	EFLOOSST FOOTLESS
EFIIINNT INFINITE	EFILMSST FILMSETS	EFIORRTT RETROFIT	EFLOPRUW POWERFUL
EFIIIRVV VIVIFIER	LEFTISMS	EFIORRWZ FROWZIER	EFLORRUY RYEFLOUR
EFIIISTX FIXITIES	EFILMSUY EMULSIFY	EFIORSST FOISTERS	EFLORSTT FORTLETS
EFIIISVV VIVIFIES	EFILNNTU INFLUENT	EFIORSTU FOUSTIER	EFLORSTW FELWORTS
EFIIKLRS FLISKIER	EFILNORU FLUORINE	EFIORSTW FROWIEST	EFLORSUY YOURSELF
EFIIKRRS FRISKIER	EFILNOSU NOISEFUL	EFIPPRRS FRIPPERS	EFLORSVY FLYOVERS
EFIILLNT TEFILLIN	EFILNOSX FLEXIONS	EFIPPRRY FRIPPERY	EFLOSUUX FLEXUOUS
EFIILLRR FRILLIER	EFILNRTT FLITTERN	EFIPRRUY REPURIFY	EFLPRSSU PRESSFUL
EFIILLRS FRILLIES	EFILNSUX INFLUXES	EFIPRSTU SUPERFIT	EFLPRSUU PURSEFUL
EFIILMRS FLIMSIER	EFILNUWY UNWIFELY	EFIPRTTY PRETTIFY	EFLRSSTU FLUSTERS
EFIILMSS FLIMSIES	EFILOOSS FLOOSIES	EFIRRRSU FURRIERS	EFLRSTTU FLUTTERS
MISFILES	EFILOOSZ FLOOZIES	EFIRRRUY FURRIERY	EFLRSTUU FRUSTULE
EFIILMST FILMIEST	EFILOPPR FLOPPIER	EFIRRSSU FRISEURS	EFLRSTUY FLUSTERY
EFIILNRT FLINTIER	EFILOPPS FLOPPIES	FRISURES	EFMNNORT FRONTMEN

EFMNORTY	FROMENTY
EFMNRTUY	FRUMENTY
	FURMENTY
EFMOORST	FOREMOST
EFMOORSU	FOURSOME
EFMOPRRS	PERFORMS
	PREFORMS
EFMOPRST	POMFRETS
EFNNOOOR	FORENOON
EFNNORST	FORNENST
EFNNORUZ	UNFROZEN
EFNOOOTT	FOOTNOTE
EFNOOPRT	PENTROOF
EFNOOSST	EFTSOONS
	FESTOONS
EFNOPRST	FORSPENT
EFNORRST	RENFORST
EFNORRSU	FORERUNS
EFNORSTU	FORTUNES
EFNOSSST	SOFTNESS
EFNRSSTU	FUNSTERS
EFOOORST	FOOTSORE
EFOOPRRS	REPROOFS
EFOOPRSS	SPOOFERS
EFOOPRST	FORETOPS
	POOFTERS
EFOOPRSY	SPOOFERY
EFOOPSTT	FOOTSTEP
EFOORRSW	FORSWORE
EFOORSTT	FOOTREST
EFOORSTW	WOOFTERS
EFOOSTUX	OUTFOXES
EFOPRRSU	PROFUSER
EFOPRSTU	POUFTERS
EFORRSST	FORTRESS
EFORRSTW	FROWSTER
EFORRSTY	FORESTRY
EFORRSUV	FERVOURS
EFORRTTU	FROTTEUR
EFORSSST	FOSTRESS
EGGGIILR	GIGGLIER
EGGGILNS	LEGGINGS
EGGGILOR	GOGGLIER
EGGGILRS	GIGGLERS
EGGGINPS	PEGGINGS
EGGGIORR	GROGGIER
EGGGLORS	GOGGLERS
EGGGNNOR	RONGGENG
EGGGOOOS	GOOSEGOG
EGGGORRY	GROGGERY
EGGHIINN	NEIGHING
EGGHIINW	WEIGHING
EGGHILRS	HIGGLERS
EGGHINSS	GHESSING
EGGHIRST	THIGGERS
EGGHLOSS	SHOGGLES
EGGHRTUY	THUGGERY
EGGIIJLR	JIGGLIER
EGGIILNR	NIGGLIER
EGGIILRW	WIGGLIER
EGGIINNN	ENGINING
EGGIINNR	GREINING
	REIGNING
EGGIINNS	SINGEING
EGGIINNT	TINGEING
EGGIINNW	WINGEING
EGGIINRV	GRIEVING
	REGIVING
EGGIIPST	PIGGIEST
EGGIIRTW	TWIGGIER
EGGIKNOS	GINGKOES
	GINKGOES
EGGILLNY	GINGELLY
EGGILMNU	EMULGING
EGGILMSS	LEGGISMS
EGGILNNO	LONGEING
EGGILNNT	GENTLING
	GLENTING
EGGILNNU	LUNGEING

EGGILNRS	NIGGLERS
	SNIGGLER
EGGILNRU	GRUELING
EGGILNRY	GINGERLY
EGGILNSS	SNIGGLES
EGGILNSU	LUGEINGS
EGGILOOS	GOOGLIES
EGGILQSU	SQUIGGLE
EGGILRRW	WRIGGLER
EGGILRSW	WIGGLERS
	WRIGGLES
EGGIMNNU	EMUNGING
EGGIMORS	SMOGGIER
EGGIMSTU	MUGGIEST
EGGINNNR	GRENNING
EGGINNOR	ENGORING
EGGINNSS	GINSENGS
EGGINORR	GORGERIN
	ROGERING
EGGINOUV	VOGUEING
EGGINRRU	GRUNGIER
	REURGING
EGGINRSS	GRESSING
	SNIGGERS
EGGINRSY	GREYINGS
EGGINSSU	GUESSING
EGGINSTT	GETTINGS
EGGINSTU	GUESTING
	GUNGIEST
EGGIOSST	SOGGIEST
EGGIPRRS	PRIGGERS
EGGIPRRY	PRIGGERY
EGGIPSTU	PUGGIEST
EGGIRRST	TRIGGERS
EGGIRSSW	SWIGGERS
EGGIRSTT	TRIGGEST
EGGIRSTU	RUGGIEST
	STUGGIER
EGGIRSTW	TWIGGERS
EGGISTUV	VUGGIEST
EGGJLRSU	JUGGLERS
EGGJLRUY	JUGGLERY
EGGLMOOY	GEMOLOGY
EGGLMRSU	SMUGGLER
EGGLMSSU	SMUGGLES
EGGLNSSU	SNUGGLES
EGGLORSS	SLOGGERS
EGGLORUY	GURGOYLE
EGGLPRSU	PLUGGERS
EGGLRSSU	SLUGGERS
EGGLRSTU	STRUGGLE
EGGMNTUY	NUTMEGGY
EGGMSSTU	SMUGGEST
EGGNOOST	GEOGNOST
EGGNOOSY	GEOGNOSY
EGGNORST	GONGSTER
EGGNRSUY	SNUGGERY
EGGNSSTU	SNUGGEST
EGGOORSU	GORGEOUS
EGGSSSTU	SUGGESTS
EGHHILTY	EIGHTHLY
EGHHINSS	HIGHNESS
EGHHOSSW	SHOWGHES
EGHIILLS	GHILLIES
EGHIILNR	HIRELING
EGHIILNS	SHEILING
	SHIELING
EGHIIMRT	MIGHTIER
EGHIINNR	INHERING
EGHIINRT	THINGIER
EGHIINST	HEISTING
	NIGHTIES
	THINGIES
EGHIINSV	INVEIGHS
EGHIINTV	THIEVING
EGHIIRST	TIGERISH
EGHIKNRS	GHERKINS
EGHIKRSS	SKREIGHS
	SKRIEGHS

EGHILLNO	HELLOING
EGHILLNS	SHELLING
EGHILMNW	WHELMING
EGHILNNU	UNHELING
EGHILNOV	HOVELING
EGHILNPS	HELPINGS
EGHILNPT	PENLIGHT
EGHILNPW	WHELPING
EGHILNRS	HERLINGS
	SHINGLER
EGHILNSS	SHINGLES
EGHILNST	ENLIGHTS
	LIGHTENS
EGHILNSV	SHELVING
EGHILNSW	WELSHING
EGHILNUW	GLUHWEIN
EGHILORT	REGOLITH
EGHILOSU	OUGHLIES
EGHILPRT	PLIGHTER
EGHILPST	PIGHTLES
EGHILRST	LIGHTERS
	RELIGHTS
	SLIGHTER
EGHILSST	SLEIGHTS
EGHILSTT	LIGHTEST
EGHIMNNS	MENSHING
EGHIMNSS	MESHINGS
EGHIMNUX	EXHUMING
EGHIMPRU	GRUMPHIE
EGHIMSTT	MIGHTEST
EGHINNOY	HONEYING
EGHINNSS	NIGHNESS
EGHINNST	SENNIGHT
EGHINNSU	UNHINGES
EGHINORT	THROEING
EGHINORV	HOVERING
EGHINOSS	SHOEINGS
EGHINOST	HISTOGEN
EGHINOSU	GINHOUSE
EGHINPRS	SPHERING
EGHINPSS	SPHINGES
EGHINQTU	QUETHING
EGHINRRS	HERRINGS
EGHINRRU	HUNGRIER
EGHINRRY	HERRYING
EGHINRST	RIGHTENS
EGHINRSU	USHERING
EGHINRSW	SHREWING
	WHINGERS
EGHINRTW	WRETHING
EGHINSTT	SHETTING
	TIGHTENS
EGHINTTW	WHETTING
EGHIOOSS	SHOOGIES
EGHIOPSU	PISHOGUE
EGHIORST	GHOSTIER
EGHIORSU	ROUGHIES
EGHIOSTT	GOTHITES
EGHIOSTU	TOUGHIES
EGHIOSTV	EIGHTVOS
EGHIOTUW	OUTWEIGH
EGHIQRTU	REQUIGHT
EGHIRRST	RIGHTERS
EGHIRSST	SIGHTERS
EGHIRSTT	RIGHTEST
	STREIGHT
EGHISSTU	GUSHIEST
EGHISTTT	TIGHTEST
EGHLLOSU	LUGHOLES
EGHLMNOP	PHLEGMON
EGHLNORS	LEGHORNS
EGHLNPSU	ENGULPHS
EGHLNRUY	HUNGERLY
EGHLOOOR	HOROLOGE
EGHLOORY	RHEOLOGY
EGHLOOSS	GOLOSHES
	SHOOGLES
EGHLOOTY	ETHOLOGY

	THEOLOGY
EGHLOPRU	PLOUGHER
EGHMNOOY	HOMOGENY
EGHMNORS	GEMSHORN
EGHMNOSU	HUMOGENS
EGHMOPUY	HYPOGEUM
EGHMOSSU	GUMSHOES
EGHNOOPT	PHOTOGEN
EGHNOOTY	THEOGONY
EGHNORSU	ENROUGHS
	ROUGHENS
EGHNORUV	OVERHUNG
EGHNOSTU	TOUGHENS
EGHNOSUU	GUNHOUSE
EGHNRSTT	STRENGTH
EGHOOOSW	HOOSEGOW
EGHORRSU	ROUGHERS
EGHORRTW	REGROWTH
EGHORSTU	ROUGHEST
EGHOSTTU	TOUGHEST
EGHPSSUU	UPGUSHES
EGIIINSV	VISIEING
EGIIJLNR	JINGLIER
EGIIKLLO	KILLOGIE
EGIIKLNN	LIKENING
EGIIKLNR	KINGLIER
EGIILMMN	IMMINGLE
EGIILMST	LEGITIMS
EGIILNNO	ELOINING
EGIILNNR	RELINING
EGIILNNS	ENISLING
	ENSILING
EGIILNNU	LINGUINE
EGIILNNV	LIVENING
EGIILNOR	RELIGION
EGIILNPS	SPIELING
EGIILNRS	RESILING
EGIILNRT	GIRTLINE
	RETILING
	TINGLIER
	TIRELING
EGIILNRV	RELIVING
	REVILING
EGIILNST	LIGNITES
	LINGIEST
EGIILNSV	VEILINGS
EGIILNSW	WISELING
EGIILRRS	GRISLIER
EGIILRTU	GUILTIER
EGIILRTZ	GLITZIER
EGIIMMNW	IMMEWING
EGIIMNNU	INGENIUM
EGIIMNOS	IGNOMIES
EGIIMNPS	IMPINGES
EGIIMNRS	REMISING
EGIIMNRT	MERITING
	MITERING
	RETIMING
EGIIMNRX	REMIXING
EGIIMNST	MINGIEST
EGIIMNSV	MISGIVEN
EGIIMNTT	EMITTING
EGIIMOPT	IMPETIGO
EGIIMORR	GRIMOIRE
EGIIMPST	GIMPIEST
EGIIMRST	GRIMIEST
	TIGERISM
EGIIMSSV	MISGIVES
EGIINNPR	REPINING
	RIPENING
EGIINNRS	RESINING
EGIINNSS	SEININGS
EGIINNST	GINNIEST
	STEINING
EGIINNSV	VEININGS
EGIINNSW	SINEWING
EGIINNVW	VINEWING
EGIINNWZ	WIZENING
EGIINOPR	PEIGNOIR

EGIINORS	SEIGNIOR	EGILMNRU	RELUMING
EGIINPRS	SPEIRING	EGILMNST	MELTINGS
EGIINPRV	PRIEVING		SMELTING
EGIINPRX	EXPIRING	EGILMNSU	LEGUMINS
EGIIPNSS	PIGSNIES	EGILMOOR	GLOOMIER
EGIINQTU	QUIETING	EGILMORS	GOMERILS
EGIINRRT	RETIRING	EGILMOSU	ELOGIUMS
EGIINRRW	REWIRING	EGILMOUU	EULOGIUM
EGIINRST	GIRNIEST	EGILMPRU	GLUMPIER
	IGNITERS	EGILMPSS	GLIMPSES
	REISTING	EGILNNST	NESTLING
	STINGIER	EGILNNTT	NETTLING
	STRIGINE	EGILNOPP	PEOPLING
EGIINRSU	SIGNIEUR		POPELING
EGIINRSV	REVISING	EGILNORS	RESOLING
EGIINRSW	RINGWISE	EGILNORW	LOWERING
	SWINGIER	EGILNOSS	LIGNOSES
EGIINRTU	INTRIGUE	EGILNOSU	LIGNEOUS
EGIINRTV	RIVETING	EGILNOSW	LONGWISE
EGIINRTX	GENITRIX	EGILNOTW	TOWELING
EGIINRVV	REVIVING	EGILNOVV	EVOLVING
EGIINSSZ	SEIZINGS	EGILNPRS	PINGLERS
EGIINSTW	WINGIEST		SPERLING
EGIINSTX	EXISTING		SPRINGLE
EGIINSTZ	ZINGIEST	EGILNPRY	REPLYING
EGIINSVW	VIEWINGS	EGILNPSS	SPIGNELS
EGIIPPRR	GRIPPIER	EGILNPST	PELTINGS
EGIIPRSW	PERIWIGS		PESTLING
EGIIPSST	PIGSTIES	EGILNPSY	YELPINGS
EGIIRRTT	GRITTIER	EGILNPTT	PETTLING
EGIITUXY	EXIGUITY	EGILNRRU	RULERING
EGIJKNRS	JERKINGS	EGILNRRY	ERRINGLY
EGIJLLNY	JELLYING	EGILNRSS	RINGLESS
EGIJLNRS	JINGLERS		SLINGERS
EGIJLNRU	JUNGLIER	EGILNRST	LINGSTER
EGIJLNST	JINGLETS		RINGLETS
EGIJMMNY	JEMMYING		STERLING
EGIJNNOY	ENJOYING		TINGLERS
EGIJNQRU	JERQUING		TRINGLES
EGIJNSST	JESTINGS	EGILNRSW	NEWSGIRL
EGIJNTTY	JETTYING	EGILNRUV	VELURING
EGIKKLNS	LEKKINGS	EGILNSSS	SIGNLESS
EGIKKNRT	TREKKING	EGILNSST	GLISTENS
EGIKLNOS	SONGLIKE		SINGLETS
EGIKLNPS	SKELPING	EGILNSSU	UGLINESS
EGIKLNSS	KINGLESS	EGILNSSW	SWINGLES
EGIKLNST	KINGLETS		WINGLESS
EGIKMNPS	KEMPINGS	EGILNSTT	LETTINGS
EGIKNNNS	KENNINGS		SETTLING
EGIKNNOT	TOKENING	EGILNSTW	SWELTING
EGIKNNRS	KERNINGS		WINGLETS
EGIKNNSY	ENSKYING	EGILNSUV	EVULSING
EGIKNORV	OVERKING	EGILNTUX	EXULTING
	REVOKING	EGILNVXY	VEXINGLY
EGIKNPPS	SKEPPING	EGILOOOS	OOLOGIES
EGIKNRRS	SKERRING	EGILOOPR	GLOOPIER
EGIKNRSU	RESKUING	EGILOORR	GROOLIER
EGILLMNS	SMELLING	EGILOOSU	ISOLOGUE
EGILLNNS	SNELLING	EGILOOTY	ETIOLOGY
EGILLNOS	LOGLINES	EGILORRW	GROWLIER
EGILLNOV	LIVELONG	EGILORSS	GLOSSIER
EGILLNPS	SPELLING	EGILORTY	GYROLITE
EGILLNQU	QUELLING	EGILOSSS	GLOSSIES
EGILLNST	STELLING	EGILOSST	ELOGISTS
	TELLINGS	EGILOSTU	EULOGIST
EGILLNSW	SWELLING	EGILPPRS	GRIPPLES
	WELLINGS	EGILRRZZ	GRIZZLER
EGILLNSY	YELLINGS	EGILRSST	GLISTERS
EGILLNTU	GLUTELIN		GRISTLES
EGILLOOR	GLORIOLE	EGILRSTT	GLITTERS
EGILMMNS	LEMMINGS	EGILRSTU	GURLIEST
EGILMMRS	GLIMMERS	EGILRSUV	VIRGULES
EGILMMRY	GLIMMERY	EGILRSZZ	GRIZZLES
EGILMNNO	LEMONING	EGILRTTY	GLITTERY
EGILMNPU	IMPLUNGE	EGIMMNNO	EMMOVING
EGILMNRS	GREMLINS	EGIMMNST	STEMMING
	MERLINGS	EGIMMRST	GRIMMEST
	MINGLERS	EGIMMSTU	GUMMIEST
			GUMMITES

EGIMNNNO	MIGNONNE	EGINPRRU	REPURING
EGIMNNOV	ENMOVING	EGINPRSS	PRESSING
	VENOMING		SPERSING
EGIMNNUW	UNMEWING		SPRINGES
EGIMNORS	NEGROISM	EGINPRST	PRESTING
EGIMNORV	REMOVING	EGINPRSU	PERSUING
EGIMNOST	MITOGENS		PERUSING
EGIMNOSU	GEMINOUS	EGINPRTU	ERUPTING
EGIMNOSY	MOSEYING		REPUTING
EGIMNPRS	IMPREGNS	EGINPRUV	PREVUING
EGIMNPRU	IMPUGNER	EGINPRYY	PERIGYNY
EGIMNPST	PIGMENTS	EGINPSSY	PIGSNEYS
EGIMNPTT	TEMPTING	EGINPSTT	PETTINGS
EGIMNPTY	EMPTYING		SPETTING
EGIMNRSS	GRIMNESS	EGINQRUY	QUERYING
EGIMNRSU	RESUMING	EGINQSTU	QUESTING
EGIMNRUY	ERYNGIUM	EGINQSUU	QUEUINGS
EGIMORST	ERGOTISM	EGINRRST	RESTRING
	GORMIEST		RINGSTER
EGIMOSST	EGOTISMS		STRINGER
EGIMOSTW	TWIGSOME	EGINRRSW	WRINGERS
EGIMPRRU	GRUMPIER	EGINRRSY	SERRYING
EGIMNNOT	TENONING	EGINRRTY	RETRYING
EGINNNOZ	ENZONING	EGINRSST	RESTINGS
EGINNNRS	RENNINGS		STINGERS
EGINNNST	STENNING		TRESSING
EGINNNUY	ENNUYING		TRIGNESS
EGINNOOR	RONEOING	EGINRSSV	SERVINGS
EGINNOPR	REPONING		VERSINGS
EGINNOPS	OPENINGS	EGINRSSW	SWINGERS
EGINNORT	NITROGEN	EGINRSSY	SYRINGES
EGINNORV	VIGNERON	EGINRSTT	GITTERNS
EGINNORZ	REZONING	EGINRSTV	STERVING
EGINNPRT	PRENTING	EGINRSTW	STREWING
EGINNPSU	PENGUINS		WRESTING
EGINNRRS	GRINNERS	EGINRSVW	SWERVING
EGINNRRU	UNERRING	EGINRTTU	UTTERING
EGINNRST	STERNING	EGINSSTT	SETTINGS
EGINNRSU	ENSURING		TESTINGS
EGINNRTU	RETUNING	EGINSSTV	VESTINGS
EGINNRTV	VENTRING	EGINSSTW	STEWINGS
EGINNSSS	SENSINGS		WESTINGS
EGINNSST	NESTINGS	EGINSTTT	STETTING
EGINNSTT	NETTINGS	EGIOOPST	GOOPIEST
	STENTING	EGIOORRV	GROOVIER
	TENTINGS	EGIOOSST	GOOSIEST
EGINNSTV	VENTINGS	EGIOPRSU	GROUPIES
EGINNSUW	UNSEWING		PIROGUES
EGINNSUX	UNSEXING	EGIOPRTU	PORTIGUE
EGINNSVY	ENVYINGS	EGIORRTT	GROTTIER
EGINOORV	INGROOVE	EGIORRTU	GROUTIER
EGINOPRS	PERIGONS	EGIORSST	GORSIEST
	REPOSING		STRIGOSE
	SPONGIER	EGIORSSU	GRISEOUS
EGINOPRW	POWERING	EGIORSTU	GOUSTIER
EGINOPRY	PIGEONRY	EGIORSTV	VERTIGOS
EGINOPST	PONGIEST	EGIORSTY	OYSTRIGE
EGINOPSX	EXPOSING	EGIORSTZ	ZORGITES
EGINOPSY	POESYING	EGIORSUV	GRIEVOUS
EGINORRS	IGNORERS	EGIOSSTT	EGOTISTS
EGINORSS	GORINESS	EGIOSTTU	GOUTIEST
	SIGNORES	EGIOSTUV	OUTGIVES
EGINORST	GENITORS		VOGUIEST
	ROSETING	EGIOSUUX	EXIGUOUS
EGINORSY	SEIGNORY	EGIPPRRS	GRIPPERS
EGINORTT	OTTERING	EGIPRSUU	GUIPURES
EGINORTU	OUTREIGN	EGIRRSTT	GRITTERS
	ROUTEING	EGIRRSTY	REGISTRY
EGINORTW	TOWERING	EGIRSSTU	SURGIEST
EGINORTX	OXTERING	EGIRSTTT	GRITTEST
EGINORTZ	ROZETING	EGISSTTU	GUSTIEST
EGINORVW	OVERWING		GUTSIEST
EGINOSTT	TENTIGOS	EGISSYYZ	SYZYGIES
EGINOTUV	OUTGIVEN	EGISTTTU	GUTTIEST
EGINPPPR	PREPPING	EGJLNORU	JONGLEUR
EGINPPRS	REPPINGS	EGJLNOTU	JELUTONG
EGINPPST	STEPPING	EGKLORSW	LEGWORKS
EGINPRRS	SPERRING	EGLLMORW	GROMWELL
	SPRINGER	EGLLOOPY	PELOLOGY

EGLMMSTU GLUMMEST
EGLMNOOS ENGLOOMS
         LONGSOME
EGLMNOOY MENOLOGY
EGLMNORS MONGRELS
EGLMNSSU GLUMNESS
EGLMOORS LEGROOMS
EGLMOPRU PROMULGE
EGLMORSS GORMLESS
EGLNNOOR LONGERON
EGLNNOSS LONGNESS
EGLNNTUY UNGENTLY
EGLNOOOY OENOLOGY
EGLNOOPR PROLONGE
EGLNOOPY PENOLOGY
EGLNOORV OVERLONG
EGLNOPYY POLYGENY
EGLNORSU LOUNGERS
EGLNORUU LONGUEUR
EGLNOSSS SONGLESS
EGLNOSUV UNGLOVES
EGLNOSXY LOXYGENS
         XYLOGENS
EGLNPRSU PLUNGERS
EGLNRSTU GRUNTLES
EGLNRTUY URGENTLY
EGLOOORY OREOLOGY
EGLOOPRU PROLOGUE
EGLOOPTY LOGOTYPE
EGLOORSY SEROLOGY
EGLOOSXY SEXOLOGY
EGLOPRTU GROUPLET
EGLORRSW GROWLERS
EGLORRWY GROWLERY
EGLORSSS GLOSSERS
EGLORSUU RUGULOSE
EGLORSUY RUGOSELY
EGLPRSSU SPLURGES
EGLRSUZZ GUZZLERS
EGLSSUUV VULGUSES
EGMMORST GROMMETS
EGMMOSSU GUMMOSES
EGMMRSTU GRUMMEST
         GRUMMETS
EGMNNOOY MONOGENY
         NOMOGENY
EGMNNOSW GOWNSMEN
EGMNOOOS MONGOOSE
EGMNOORY MEROGONY
EGMNOOSU MUNGOOSE
EGMNORSU MURGEONS
EGMNOSYZ ZYMOGENS
EGMNRSSU GRUMNESS
EGMNSSSU SMUGNESS
EGMORSTU GOURMETS
EGNNOOTY ONTOGENY
EGNNORST RONTGENS
EGNNOSTU GUNSTONE
EGNNOTTU UNGOTTEN
EGNNSSSU SNUGNESS
EGNNSTTU TUNGSTEN
EGNNSTUU UNGUENTS
EGNOORRV GOVERNOR
EGNOPPRU OPPUGNER
EGNOPRSS SPONGERS
EGNOPRSY PYROGENS
EGNORRST STRONGER
EGNORRSW WRONGERS
EGNORSST SONGSTER
EGNORSSU SURGEONS
EGNORSTT TONGSTER
EGNORSTU STURGEON
EGNORSTW WRONGEST
EGNOSTUY YOUNGEST
EGNPRSUU SUPERGUN
EGNRRSTU GRUNTERS
         RESTRUNG
EGOOPRRU PROROGUE
EGOORRSV GROOVERS

EGOORRVW OVERGROW
EGOORSTT GROTTOES
EGOORSTU OUTGOERS
EGOPRRSS PROGRESS
EGOPRRSU GROUPERS
         REGROUPS
EGOPSSUY GYPSEOUS
EGORRSST GROSERTS
EGORRSSU GROUSERS
EGORRSTU GROUTERS
EGORSSST GROSSEST
EGORSSTU GROUSEST
EGPRSSUU UPSURGES
EHHIIPRS HEIRSHIP
EHHIISTV THIEVISH
EHHILMNT HELMINTH
EHHILOST SHITHOLE
EHHINOPT THIOPHEN
EHHIOPRS HEROSHIP
EHHIORTT HITHERTO
EHHIPRSS HERSHIPS
EHHIRSSW SHREWISH
EHHIRSTW WHITHERS
EHHISSTU HUSHIEST
EHHLOOST SHOTHOLE
EHHNOORS SHOEHORN
EHHOOPST THEOSOPH
EHHOOSSW WHOOSHES
EHHOOSTU OUTHOUSE
EHHORSTU SHOUTHER
EHHRSSTU THRUSHES
EHIIKLPT PITHLIKE
EHIIKLPW WHIPLIKE
EHIIKSSW WHISKIES
EHIILLST HILLIEST
EHIILLSW WHILLIES
EHIILMOS HOMILIES
EHIILNRS LINISHER
EHIILNSS LINISHES
EHIILOSS HELIOSIS
EHIILRRW WHIRLIER
EHIILRSV LIVERISH
EHIILSTT LITHITES
EHIIMMRW WHIMMIER
EHIIMMSS SHIMMIES
EHIIMNOS HOMINIES
EHIIMNNS MINISHES
EHIIMRSW WHIMSIER
EHIIMSST SMITHIES
EHIIMSSW WHIMSIES
EHIINNOS INHESION
EHIINNQU HENIQUIN
EHIINNRS INSHRINE
EHIINNRW WHINNIER
EHIINNSS SHINNIES
EHIINNSW WHINNIES
EHIINRRT HIRRIENT
EHIINRST INHERITS
EHIINRSZ RHIZINES
EHIINSST SHINIEST
         SHINTIES
EHIINSTW WHINIEST
EHIINSVX VIXENISH
EHIIPPRW WHIPPIER
EHIIPPST HIPPIEST
EHIIPRSV VIPERISH
EHIIPSTT PITHIEST
EHIIRRST SHIRTIER
EHIIRRSW WHIRRIES
EHIIRRTX HERITRIX
EHIIRSSU HUISSIER
EHIIRSSW SWISHIER
EHIIRSTT SHITTIER
         THIRTIES
EHIISSST STISHIES
EHIISSTT STITHIES
EHIISTTW WHITIEST

         WITHIEST
EHIISTTX SIXTIETH
EHIJNNOS JOHNNIES
EHIKLNOS SINKHOLE
EHIKLOSY YOKELISH
EHIKLOTY LEKYTHOI
EHIKLRSU RUSHLIKE
EHIKLSTU HULKIEST
EHIKMNST METHINKS
EHIKNORS SHONKIER
EHIKNRRS SHRINKER
EHIKNRST RETHINKS
         THINKERS
EHIKNSTU HUNKIEST
EHIKOOST HOOKIEST
EHIKOPRS POKERISH
EHIKRRSS SHIRKERS
EHIKRSSW WHISKERS
EHIKRSWY WHISKERY
EHIKSSTU HUSKIEST
EHIKSSTW WHISKETS
EHIKSSWY WHISKEYS
EHILLLMO MOLEHILL
EHILLMOY HOMELILY
EHILLNOS HELLIONS
EHILLNSS INSHELLS
EHILLOPY LYOPHILE
EHILLPTY PHYLLITE
EHILLRRS SHRILLER
EHILLRRT THRILLER
EHILLRST THILLERS
EHILLRTY LITHERLY
EHILLSSW SWELLISH
EHILLSTU HULLIEST
EHILMOOR HEIRLOOM
EHILMOST HELOTISM
EHILMPSW WHIMPLES
EHILMPSY SYMPHILE
EHILMQUU UMQUHILE
EHILMSTT MELTITHS
EHILNOOP OENOPHIL
EHILNOPS PINHOLES
EHILNORU UNHOLIER
EHILNOSS HOLINESS
EHILNOST HOTLINES
         NEOLITHS
EHILNOSV NOVELISH
EHILNOTX XENOLITH
EHILNPSY SYLPHINE
EHILNSWY NEWISHLY
EHILOOPZ ZOOPHILE
EHILOOST HOOLIEST
EHILOPRS PILHORSE
         POLISHER
EHILOPRT HELIPORT
EHILOPSS POLISHES
EHILOPST HELISTOP
         HOPLITES
         ISOPLETH
EHILORSS SLOSHIER
EHILORTY RHYOLITE
EHILPRST PHILTERS
         PHILTRES
EHILPRSU PLUSHIER
EHILPRSY SYLPHIER
EHILPSSS SHIPLESS
EHILPSST PITHLESS
         THLIPSES
EHILPSTU SULPHITE
EHILRRSW WHIRLERS
EHILRSST SLITHERS
         THRISSEL
EHILRSSU SLUSHIER
EHILRSSV SHRIVELS
EHILRSTT THRISTLE
EHILRSTU LUTHIERS
EHILRSTW WHIRTLES
         WHISTLER
EHILRSTY SLITHERY

EHILRTTW WHITTLER
EHILRTTY TRIETHYL
EHILSSTT THISTLES
EHILSSTU LUSHIEST
EHILSSTW WHISTLES
EHILSTTU THULITES
EHILSTTW WHITTLES
EHIMMNUY HYMENIUM
EHIMMRSS SHIMMERS
EHIMMRSY SHIMMERY
EHIMMSSY SHIMMEYS
EHIMNOPR MORPHINE
EHIMNORT THERMION
EHIMNOST HOISTMEN
EHIMNOSU HEMIONUS
EHIMNOTT MONTEITH
EHIMNPRS PHRENISM
EHIMNPST SHIPMENT
EHIMNRRU MURRHINE
EHIMNRRY MYRRHINE
EHIMNRSU INHUMERS
         RHENIUMS
EHIMNSTY THYMINES
EHIMOOSS HOMEOSIS
EHIMOOST SMOOTHIE
EHIMOPRS SOPHERIM
EHIMOPSS PHIMOSES
EHIMORSS HEROISMS
EHIMORST ISOTHERM
         MOITHERS
EHIMORSZ RHIZOMES
EHIMORTU MOUTHIER
EHIMOSTT MOTHIEST
EHIMPPSS PSEPHISM
EHIMPRRS SHRIMPER
EHIMPRSU MURPHIES
EHIMPRSW WHIMPERS
EHIMPSTU HUMPIEST
         HUMPTIES
         TUMPHIES
EHIMPSUU EUPHUISM
EHIMPTTU UMPTIETH
EHIMRSST SMITHERS
EHIMRSSU HEURISMS
EHIMRSTY SMITHERY
EHIMSSTU MUSHIEST
         TUMSHIES
EHIMSSTY METHYSIS
         MYTHISES
EHIMSSWY WHIMSEYS
EHIMSTTY THYMIEST
EHIMSTYZ MYTHIZES
EHINNRST THINNERS
EHINNSST THINNESS
EHINNSSU SUNSHINE
EHINNSTT THINNEST
EHINOPPR HORNPIPE
EHINOPRT TRIPHONE
EHINOPST PHONIEST
         SIPHONET
EHINORRT THORNIER
EHINORSS HERISSON
EHINORST HORNIEST
EHINOSST HISTONES
EHINOSTU OUTSHINE
EHINPPSS SHIPPENS
EHINPRSU PUNISHER
EHINPSSU PUNISHES
EHINPSSX SPHINXES
EHINRRSU INRUSHES
EHINRSTZ ZITHERNS
EHINSSST THISNESS
EHINSSUW UNWISHES
EHIOOPSW WHOOPSIE
EHIOORTT TOOTHIER
EHIOOSST STOOSHIE
EHIOPPPS POPESHIP
EHIOPPRS SHOPPIER
EHIOPPST HOPPIEST

```
         POETSHIP
EHIOPRSS ROSEHIPS
         SPOSHIER
EHIOPRST TROPHIES
EHIOPTTW WHITEPOT
EHIORRST HERITORS
EHIORRTU ROUTHIER
EHIORRTW WORTHIER
EHIORSST HOISTERS
         HORSIEST
         HOSTRIES
         SHORTIES
EHIORSTT THEORIST
         THORITES
EHIORSTU OUTHIRES
EHIORSTV OVERHITS
EHIORSTW WORTHIES
EHIORTUY YOUTHIER
EHIORTWZ HOWITZER
EHIOSSTT TOSHIEST
EHIOSSTU HOUSIEST
EHIOSSTW SHOWIEST
EHIOSSTY ISOHYETS
EHIOSTVY YESHIVOT
EHIPPRSS SHIPPERS
EHIPPRSW WHIPPERS
EHIPPSSU HIPPUSES
EHIPPSTW WHIPPETS
EHIPQSUY PHYSIQUE
EHIPRSST HIPSTERS
         THRIPSES
EHIPRSSW WHISPERS
EHIPRSTW WHIPSTER
EHIPRSWY WHISPERY
EHIPSSTU PUSHIEST
EHIPSTUU EUPHUIST
EHIQSSSU SQUISHES
EHIRRSSV SHRIVERS
EHIRRSTT THIRSTER
EHIRRSTV THRIVERS
EHIRRSTW WHIRRETS
EHIRRTTU TRUTHIER
EHIRSSSW SWISHERS
EHIRSSTU RUSHIEST
EHIRSSTW SWITHERS
EHIRSTTW WHITRETS
         WHITSTER
         WHITTERS
EHIRSWZZ WHIZZERS
EHIRTTTW WHITTRET
EHISSSTU STUSHIES
EHISSSTW SWISHEST
EHISSTUW THUSWISE
EHISSUVW HUSWIVES
EHKLOSTY LEKYTHOS
EHKMOORW HOMEWORK
EHKMORSU HUMORESK
EHKNNRSU SHRUNKEN
EHKOOSSS SKOOSHES
EHKOPSSY KYPHOSES
EHKRSSTU TUSHKERS
EHLLMOPY PHYLLOME
EHLLNSSU UNSHELLS
EHLLNSTU NUTSHELL
EHLLOOOP LOOPHOLE
EHLLOORW HOLLOWER
EHLMMOSW WHOMMLES
EHLMMSUW WHUMMLES
EHLMNOST MENTHOLS
EHLMNOSY HOMELYNS
EHLMNOTU MOLEHUNT
EHLMNOUY UNHOMELY
EHLMOORW WORMHOLE
EHLMORTY MOTHERLY
EHLNOPSU SULPHONE
EHLNORSS HORNLESS
EHLNORST HORNLETS
EHLNOSTY HONESTLY

EHLNRSTU LUTHERNS
EHLNSSSU LUSHNESS
         SHUNLESS
EHLOOPRT PORTHOLE
         POTHOLER
EHLOOPST POTHOLES
EHLOOPTY HOLOTYPE
EHLOOSSS SLOOSHES
EHLOPPRT THROPPLE
EHLOPRTY PROTHYLE
EHLOPSSS SPLOSHES
EHLOPSSY SPYHOLES
EHLORSST HOLSTERS
         HOSTLERS
EHLORSTT THROSTLE
EHLORSTY HOSTELRY
EHLORTTT THROTTLE
EHLOSSTT SHOTTLES
EHLOSSTW THOWLESS
EHLOSSTY THYLOSES
EHLPSSTU PLUSHEST
EHLRSSTU HURTLESS
         HUSTLERS
         RUTHLESS
EHLSSTTU SHUTTLES
EHMMRRTU THRUMMER
EHMMSSUU HUMMUSES
EHMNNSTU HUNTSMEN
EHMNOORS HORMONES
         MOORHENS
EHMNOOST SMOOTHEN
EHMNOOTY THEONOMY
EHMNOPSU HOMESPUN
EHMNPRYY HYPERNYM
EHMNPSTY NYMPHETS
EHMNSTTU HUTMENTS
EHMOOOTZ ZOOTHOME
EHMOOPTY HOMOTYPE
EHMOORST SMOOTHER
EHMOOSSS SHMOOSES
EHMOOSSZ SHMOOZES
EHMOPRSW MORPHEWS
EHMORSST SMOTHERS
EHMORSTU MOUTHERS
EHMORSTY SMOTHERY
EHMORTUV VERMOUTH
EHMOSSUU HOUMUSES
EHMOTUZZ MEZUZOTH
EHMPRSTU THUMPERS
EHMRRSTU MURTHERS
EHMRTUYY EURYTHMY
EHNNOPRS NEPHRONS
EHNNOPSY HYPNONES
EHNNORRT NORTHERN
EHNNORTU UNTHRONE
EHNNOSTU UNHONEST
EHNNRSSU SHUNNERS
EHNOOPTY HONEYPOT
EHNOORRU HONOURER
EHNOORSS SOREHONS
EHNOORSW WHORESON
EHNOORTW HONEWORT
EHNOOSSW SNOWSHOE
EHNOOSTU OUTSHONE
EHNOPRSY HYPERONS
EHNOPSSS POSHNESS
EHNOPSSY HYPNOSES
EHNORRST NORTHERS
EHNORSST SHORTENS
EHNORSSU ONRUSHES
         UNHORSES
EHNORSTT THORNSET
EHNORSTU SOUTHERN
EHNOSSUU UNHOUSES
EHNOSTUU NUTHOUSE
EHNRSSTU HUNTRESS
         SHUNTERS
EHNSSSTU THUSNESS
EHOOPRSW WHOOPERS

EHOOPRTY ORTHOEPY
EHOOPSTU HOUSETOP
         POTHOUSE
EHOOPSTY OOPHYTES
EHOOPTYZ ZOOPHYTE
EHOORSST ORTHOSES
         SHOOTERS
         SOOTHERS
EHOORSTV OVERSHOT
EHOOSSSW SWOOSHES
EHOOSSTT SOOTHEST
EHOOSTUU OUTHOUSE
EHOPPRSS SHOPPERS
EHOPPRST PROPHETS
EHOPPRSW WHOPPERS
EHOPPRSY PROPHESY
EHOPRRSY ORPHREYS
EHOPRSST STROPHES
EHOPRSTU POUTHERS
EHOPRSTY TROPHESY
EHOPRTUY EUTROPHY
EHOPSSTY PHYTOSES
EHORRSTW THROWERS
EHORRSTY HERSTORY
EHORSSTT SHORTEST
EHORSSTU SHOUTERS
         SOUTHERS
EHORSTUY OUTHYRES
EHOSSSTU STOUSHES
EHPRSSSU SPRUSHES
EHPRSSUU UPRUSHES
EHPRSTTU TURPETHS
EHPSSTUY TYPHUSES
EHRRSTTU THRUSTER
EHRSSSTY SHYSTERS
EHRSSTTU SHUTTERS
EIIILMSS SIMILISE
EIIILMSZ SIMILIZE
EIIILPPR LIRIPIPE
EIIIMMNS MINIMISE
EIIIMMNZ MINIMIZE
EIIIRRTV TIRRIVIE
EIIIRSST IRITISES
EIIJKNRT JIRKINET
EIIJMPST JIMPIEST
EIIJNRSU INJURIES
EIIKKLLM MILKLIKE
EIIKKNST KINKIEST
EIIKLLMN LIMEKILN
EIIKLLNO LIONLIKE
EIIKLLRS SKILLIER
EIIKLLSS SKILLIES
EIIKLMRS MISLIKER
EIIKLMSS MISLIKES
EIIKLMST MILKIEST
EIIKLNRS SLINKIER
EIIKLNRT TINKLIER
EIIKLPSS PLISKIES
EIIKLRTT KITTLIER
EIIKLSST SILKIEST
EIIKMPRS SKIMPIER
EIIKMRRS SMIRKIER
EIIKNNRS SKINNIER
EIIKNNSS INKINESS
EIIKNNSW WINESKIN
EIIKNPST PINKIEST
EIIKNSST SINKIEST
EIIKNSTZ ZINKIEST
EIIKPPRS SKIPPIER
EIIKPSST SPIKIEST
EIIKQRRU QUIRKIER
EIIKRRST RISKIEST
EIIKSSTV SKIVIEST
EIIKSSVV SKIVVIES
EIILLLVY LIVELILY
EIILLMMR MILLIREM
EIILLMMS MILLIMES
EIILLMNR MILLINER
EIILLMNS SLIMLINE

EIILLMNU ILLUMINE
EIILLNST NIELLIST
EIILLNSU SUILLINE
EIILLNSV VILLEINS
EIILLNTV VITELLIN
EIILLPSS ELLIPSIS
EIILLRST STILLIER
EIILLSST SILLIEST
EIILLSTT TILLIEST
         TILLITES
EIILLSTW TWILLIES
EIILLSUV ILLUSIVE
EIILMNNT LINIMENT
EIILMNOT LIMONITE
EIILMNSS LIMINESS
EIILMOPT IMPOLITE
EIILMPPR PIMPLIER
EIILMPRS IMPERILS
EIILMPST LIMEPITS
EIILMRSS SLIMSIER
EIILMRST LIMITERS
         MIRLIEST
EIILMRZZ MIZZLIER
EIILMSSS MISSILES
EIILMSST ELITISMS
         SLIMIEST
EIILMSSV MISLIVES
EIILMSTT MISTITLE
EIILMSTY MYELITIS
EIILNNOT LENITION
EIILNOSS ELISIONS
         ISOLINES
         LIONISES
         OILINESS
EIILNOST ETIOLINS
EIILNOSV OLIVINES
EIILNOSZ LIONIZES
EIILNOTT TOILINET
EIILNQTU QUINTILE
EIILNRST NIRLIEST
         NITRILES
EIILNSSW WILINESS
EIILNSTT LINTIEST
EIILNSTY SENILITY
EIILNSVY SYLVIINE
EIILNTTU INTITULE
EIILNTUV VITULINE
EIILOPST PISOLITE
         POLITIES
EIILORST ROILIEST
EIILORTT TROILITE
EIILOSST SOILIEST
EIILOTVV VOLITIVE
EIILPPRR RIPPLIER
EIILPPRS SLIPPIER
EIILPPST LIPPIEST
EIILPRST TRIPLIES
EIILPRSU PLURISIE
EIILPSST PITILESS
         SPILITES
EIILPSTY PYELITIS
EIILPSUZ SPUILZIE
EIILQSSU SILIQUES
EIILRRSW SWIRLIER
EIILRRTW TWIRLIER
EIILRSTT STILTIER
EIILRSTU UTILISER
EIILRTUZ UTILIZER
EIILSSTT ELITISTS
         SILTIEST
EIILSSTU ULITISES
         UTILISES
EIILSTUY TUILYIES
EIILSTUZ TUILZIES
         UTILIZES
EIIMMNNO MENOMINI
EIIMMNNT IMMINENT
         MINIMENT
EIIMMNSU IMMUNISE
```

EIIMMNTU	IMMINUTE	EIINQRSU	INQUIRES	EIKKNRSS	SKINKERS	EIKRSSTT	SKITTERS
EIIMMNUZ	IMMUNIZE	EIINQSSU	QUINSIES	EIKKOOST	KOOKIEST	EIKRSSTU	TURKISES
EIIMMPRU	IMPERIUM		SQUINIES	EIKKSTUY	YUKKIEST	EIKSSTTU	TUSKIEST
EIIMMRSW	SWIMMIER	EIINQSTU	INQUIETS	EIKLLMSS	MILKLESS	EILLLOVY	LOVELILY
EIIMMSSS	SEISMISM	EIINQTUY	EQUINITY	EIKLLNSW	INKWELLS	EILLLPUV	PULVILLE
EIIMMSST	MIMSIEST		INEQUITY	EIKLLNUY	UNLIKELY	EILLMNOU	LINOLEUM
	MISTIMES	EIINRRTW	WINTRIER	EIKLLORV	OVERKILL	EILLMNQU	QUILLMEN
EIIMNOPT	PIMIENTO	EIINRRST	SINISTER	EIKLLOSS	SKOLLIES	EILLMNSU	MULLEINS
EIIMNOSS	EMISSION	EIINRSSW	WIRINESS	EIKLLRSS	RESKILLS	EILLMOPS	PLIMSOLE
	SIMONIES	EIINRSTT	NITRITES	EIKLLSSS	SKILLESS	EILLMOST	MELILOTS
EIIMNOSV	VISNOMIE		STINTIER	EIKLLSST	SKILLETS	EILLMPSS	MISSPELL
EIIMNOTV	MONITIVE	EIINRSTU	NEURITIS	EIKLMNOS	MOLESKIN		PSELLISM
EIIMNPRS	PRIMINES	EIINRSTV	INVITERS	EIKLMNRS	KREMLINS	EILLMPTU	MULTIPLE
EIIMNRSS	MIRINESS		VINTRIES	EIKLNOOR	OERLIKON	EILLMSST	MISTELLS
EIIMNRST	INTERIMS		VITRINES	EIKLNOPR	PLONKIER	EILLMUVX	VEXILLUM
	MINISTER	EIINSSSZ	SIZINESS	EIKLNOSW	SNOWLIKE	EILLNOPY	EPYLLION
EIIMNRSV	MINIVERS	EIINSSTU	UNITISES	EIKLNPRS	SPRINKLE	EILLNOST	STELLION
EIIMNRTT	INTERMIT	EIINSTTT	TINTIEST	EIKLNRRU	KNURLIER	EILLNOTU	LUTEOLIN
EIIMNRTX	INTERMIX		TINTIEST	EIKLNRSS	SLINKERS	EILLNPUU	LUPULINE
EIIMNSTT	MINTIEST	EIINSTTW	TWINIEST	EIKLNRST	LINKSTER	EILLNSTY	SILENTLY
EIIMNSTU	MUTINIES	EIINSTUZ	UNITIZES		STRINKLE		TINSELLY
EIIMNSTV	MINIVETS	EIIOPRRS	PRIORIES		TINKLERS	EILLNSVY	SNIVELLY
EIIMOPRX	MIREPOIX	EIIOPSTV	POSITIVE	EIKLNRSW	WINKLERS	EILLNUVY	UNLIVELY
EIIMOPST	OPTIMISE	EIIORRST	RIOTRIES		WRINKLES	EILLOORW	WOOLLIER
EIIMOPTZ	OPTIMIZE	EIIORSST	RIOTISES	EIKLNRTW	TWINKLER	EILLOOSW	WOOLLIES
EIIMOSSV	OMISSIVE	EIIORSTZ	RIOTIZES	EIKLNSSS	SKINLESS	EILLOPTY	POLITELY
EIIMOSTY	MOYITIES	EIIOSSTT	OSTEITIS	EIKLNSST	LENTISKS	EILLORST	TRILLOES
EIIMOSUX	EXIMIOUS		OTITISES	EIKLNSSY	SKYLINES		TROLLIES
EIIMOTVV	VOMITIVE	EIIOSSTZ	ZOISITES	EIKLNSTT	KNITTLES	EILLORSU	ROUILLES
EIIMPRRS	PRIMSIER	EIIOTTTV	TOTITIVE	EIKLNSTW	TWINKLES	EILLORSZ	ZORILLES
EIIMPRSS	MISPRISE	EIIPPPST	PIPPIEST	EIKLOOPR	PLOOKIER	EILLOSSS	SOILLESS
	PISMIRES	EIIPPRRS	RIPPIERS	EIKLOORT	ROOTLIKE	EILLOSST	TOILLESS
EIIMPRSZ	MISPRIZE	EIIPPRRT	TRIPPIER	EIKLOPRU	PLOUKIER	EILLOSTW	LOWLIEST
EIIMPSST	PIETISMS	EIIPPSTT	TIPPIEST	EIKLOPRW	PILEWORK	EILLPRSS	SPILLERS
EIIMPSTW	WIMPIEST	EIIPPSTZ	ZIPPIEST	EIKLOSTY	YOLKIEST	EILLQSTU	QUILLETS
EIIMQSTU	QUIETISM	EIIPRRSS	PRISSIER	EIKLSSTT	SKITTLES	EILLRSST	STILLERS
EIIMRRRS	SMIRRIER	EIIPRRST	STRIPIER	EIKLSSTU	SULKIEST	EILLRSSW	SWILLERS
EIIMRSTT	METRITIS	EIIPRRTW	TRIPWIRE	EIKLSTTT	KITTLEST	EILLRSTT	TESTRILL
EIIMRSTW	MISWRITE	EIIPRSST	SPIRIEST	EIKMMRRS	KRIMMERS	EILLRSVY	SILVERLY
EIIMSSSS	MISSISES	EIIPRSTT	RISPETTI	EIKMMRSS	SKIMMERS	EILLSSST	LISTLESS
EIIMSSST	MISSIEST		TRIPIEST	EIKMNORS	MONIKERS	EILLSSTT	STILLEST
EIIMSSSV	MISSIVES	EIIPRSTU	PURITIES	EIKMNOST	TOKENISM	EILLSTTT	LITTLEST
EIIMSSSZ	SIZEISMS	EIIPRSTV	PRIVIEST	EIKMNOSU	MOUSEKIN	EILLSTUV	VITELLUS
EIIMSSTT	MISTIEST	EIIPRSTY	PYRITISE	EIKMOPSS	MISSPOKE	EILMMNOS	MOLIMENS
EIINNNPS	NINEPINS	EIIPRSVV	SPIVVIER	EIKMOSST	SMOKIEST	EILMMPRU	PLUMMIER
EIINNOOR	ONIONIER	EIIPRTYZ	PYRITIZE	EIKMOSSY	MISYOKES	EILMMRSS	SLIMMERS
EIINNOSU	UNIONISE	EIIPSSTT	PIETISTS	EIKMRSTU	MURKIEST	EILMMRSU	SLUMMIER
EIINNOSV	ENVISION		STIPITES	EIKMSSSU	KUMISSES	EILMMSST	SLIMMEST
EIINNOUZ	UNIONIZE	EIIPSSTW	SWIPIEST	EIKMSSTU	MUSKIEST	EILMMSTU	LUMMIEST
EIINNPSS	SPINNIES		WISPIEST	EIKNNOST	INKSTONE	EILMNOPT	PILOTMEN
EIINNQSU	QUININES	EIIPSTTT	PITTIEST	EIKNNPSS	PINKNESS	EILMNOST	MOLINETS
EIINNRTV	INVERTIN	EIIPSTTU	PITUITES	EIKNNRSS	SKINNERS	EILMNOSU	EMULSION
EIINNSST	TININESS	EIIQSTTU	QUIETIST	EIKNOORS	ROOINEKS	EILMNOSV	NOVELISM
EIINNSSW	INSINEWS	EIIRRSTW	WRISTIER	EIKNOOST	NOOKIEST	EILMNOTU	MOULINET
EIINNSTT	TINNIEST	EIIRRSTW	WRISTIER	EIKNORTT	KNOTTIER	EILMNOTY	MYLONITE
EIINNSTW	INTWINES	EIIRRSTZ	RITZIEST	EIKNOSTW	WONKIEST	EILMNPSS	LIMPNESS
EIINOPRS	RIPIENOS	EIIRSSSS	SISSIEST	EIKNPRSU	SPUNKIER	EILMNPSU	SPLENIUM
EIINOPRT	POINTIER	EIIRSSTZ	SIZEISTS	EIKNPRTU	TURNPIKE	EILMNRST	MINSTREL
EIINOPST	SINOPITE	EIIRSSTV	STIVIEST	EIKNPSSU	SPUNKIES	EILMNSSS	SLIMNESS
EIINOPTT	PETITION	EIISTTTW	WITTIEST	EIKNRRTU	RETURNIK	EILMNSSU	EMULSINS
EIINORRT	INTERIOR	EIJJNTUY	JEJUNITY	EIKNRSST	STINKERS	EILMNSTU	MUSLINET
EIINORSS	IONISERS	EIJKKSSU	JUKSKEIS	EIKNRSTT	KNITTERS	EILMNTUY	MINUTELY
	IRONISES	EIJKNSTU	JUNKIEST		TRINKETS		UNTIMELY
EIINORST	IRONIEST	EIJLLOST	JOLLIEST	EIKNSSSU	UNKISSES	EILMOOPS	LIPOSOME
EIINORSV	REVISION	EIJLOSTW	JOWLIEST	EIKNSSTT	SKINTEST	EILMOORS	SLOOMIER
	VISIONER	EIJMNPSS	JIMPNESS	EIKNSTUZ	KUNZITES	EILMOOST	TOILSOME
EIINORSZ	IONIZERS	EIJMPSTU	JUMPIEST	EIKOOPRS	SPOOKIER	EILMOPRR	IMPLORER
	IRONIZES	EIJNORST	JOINTERS	EIKOORST	ROOKIEST	EILMOPRS	IMPLORES
EIINOSST	NOISIEST	EIJNORTU	JOINTURE	EIKOPPRW	PIPEWORK		PELORISM
EIINOSTV	NOVITIES	EIJNOSTT	JETTISON	EIKOPRST	PORKIEST	EILMOPST	POLEMIST
EIINPPRS	SNIPPIER	EIJNPRSU	JUNIPERS	EIKOPRSV	OVERSKIP	EILMORRS	LORIMERS
EIINPPST	NIPPIEST	EIJNRRSU	INJURERS	EIKORRWW	WIREWORK	EILMOSTT	MOTLIEST
EIINPRRS	INSPIRER	EIJSSSUV	JUSSIVES	EIKPPRSS	SKIPPERS	EILMOSUV	VOLUMISE
EIINPRSS	INSPIRES	EIKKLNRS	KLINKERS	EIKPPSST	SKIPPETS	EILMOUVZ	VOLUMIZE
EIINPRST	PRISTINE			EIKPRRSU	SPRUIKER	EILMPPRU	IMPURPLE
EIINPSST	SNIPIEST			EIKRRSST	SKIRRETS		PLUMPIER
	SPINIEST				SKIRTERS	EILMPRSS	SIMPLERS
EIINPTUV	PUNITIVE				STRIKERS	EILMPRSU	SLUMPIER
EIINQRRU	INQUIRER			EIKRRSSU	SKURRIES	EILMPRUY	IMPURELY

```
EILMPSST MISSPELT
         SIMPLEST
EILMPSSU IMPULSES
EILMPSTU LUMPIEST
         PLUMIEST
EILMRSSU MISRULES
EILMRSSY REMISSLY
EILMRSTU MURLIEST
EILMRSTY LYMITERS
EILMSSTU LITMUSES
EILMSUUV ELUVIUMS
EILMTTUU LUTETIUM
EILMTTUY MULTEITY
EILNNOST INSOLENT
EILNNOSW SNOWLINE
EILNNOTV VINOLENT
EILNNPSU PINNULES
EILNNTTY INTENTLY
EILNOOPP EPIPLOON
EILNOOPS POLONIES
         POLONISE
EILNOOPZ POLONIZE
EILNOOST LOONIEST
         OILSTONE
EILNOOSV VIOLONES
EILNOPPS PLENIPOS
EILNOPPY POLYPINE
EILNOPRS PROLINES
EILNOPRT TOPLINER
EILNOPRU NEUROPIL
EILNOPSS EPSILONS
EILNOPST POINTELS
         PONTILES
         TOPLINES
EILNOPTU UNPOLITE
EILNORRS LORINERS
EILNORRT RITORNEL
EILNORST RETINOLS
EILNORTT TROTLINE
EILNORTW TOWNLIER
EILNOSSU ELUSIONS
EILNOSSW LEWISSON
EILNOSTU ELUTIONS
         OUTLINES
EILNOSTV NOVELIST
         VIOLENTS
EILNOSTW TOWLINES
EILNOSUV EVULSION
EILNOSVV INVOLVES
EILNOTUV INVOLUTE
EILNOTXY XYLONITE
EILNOTYZ ZYLONITE
EILNPRSS PILSNERS
EILNPRST SPLINTER
EILNPRSU PURLINES
EILNPSST PLENISTS
EILNPSSU SPINULES
         SPLENIUS
EILNPSUY SUPINELY
EILNQUUY UNIQUELY
EILNRRUU UNRULIER
EILNRSST SLINTERS
         SNIRTLES
EILNRSTU INSULTER
         LUSTRINE
EILNRSTY TINSELRY
EILNRTUV VIRULENT
EILNRTWY WINTERLY
EILNSSTT TINTLESS
EILNSSTU UTENSILS
EILNSSTW WESTLINS
EILNSSVY SYLVINES
EILNSTTU LUTENIST
EILNSUWY UNWISELY
EILOOPRR POORLIER
EILOOPST LOOPIEST
EILOOPTZ ZOPILOTE
EILOORST TROOLIES
EILOORTV OVERTOIL

EILOOSST OSTIOLES
         STOOLIES
EILOOSTZ ZOOLITES
EILOPPPR POPPLIER
EILOPPRS SLOPPIER
EILOPPTY POLYPITE
EILOPRRT PORTLIER
EILOPRSS SPOILERS
EILOPRST POITRELS
EILOPRSU PERILOUS
EILOPRSV OVERSLIP
EILOPRTW PILEWORT
EILOPSSS PSILOSES
EILOPSST PISTOLES
         PTILOSES
         SLOPIEST
EILOPSSV PLOSIVES
EILOPSTT PISTOLET
         PLOTTIES
         POLITEST
EILOPSTX EXPLOITS
EILOPSUV PLUVIOSE
EILORRTU ULTERIOR
EILORSSS RISSOLES
EILORSSU SOILURES
EILORSTT TRIOLETS
EILORSTU LOURIEST
         OUTLIERS
EILORSZZ SOZZLIER
EILORTTY TOILETRY
EILOSSST LOSSIEST
EILOSSTU LOUSIEST
EILOSTTT STILETTO
EILOSTUV OUTLIVES
         SOLUTIVE
EILPPPRY PREPPILY
EILPPRRS RIPPLERS
EILPPRRT TRIPPLER
EILPPRRU PURPLIER
EILPPRSS SLIPPERS
EILPPRST RIPPLETS
         STIPPLER
         TIPPLERS
         TRIPPLES
EILPPRSU PERIPLUS
         SUPPLIER
EILPPRSY SLIPPERY
EILPPRTU PULPITER
EILPPSST STIPPLES
EILPPSSU SUPPLIES
EILPPSSW SWIPPLES
EILPPSTU PULPIEST
EILPRSST SPIRTLES
EILPRSTT SPLITTER
         TRIPLETS
EILPRSTY PRIESTLY
         SPRITELY
EILPRSUU PURLIEUS
EILPRSUY PLEURISY
EILPRTTY PRETTILY
EILPSSTT SPITTLES
EILPSSTU STIPULES
EILPSSUY SPULYIES
EILPSSUZ SPULZIES
EILQRRSU SQUIRREL
EILQRSTU QUILTERS
EILQRSUU LIQUEURS
EILQRSUY SQUIRELY
EILQSTUU LUSTIQUE
EILRRSSU SLURRIES
EILRRSTU SULTRIER
EILRRSTW TWIRLERS
EILRRTWY WRITERLY
EILRSSST STIRLESS
EILRSSTT SLITTERS
         STILTERS
         TESTRILS
EILRSSTU SURLIEST
EILRSSTY SISTERLY

EILRSSZZ SIZZLERS
EILRSTTU SURTITLE
EILRSTTW WRISTLET
EILRSTTZ STRELITZ
EILRSTUV RIVULETS
EILRSUUX LUXURIES
EILSSSTY STYLISES
EILSSTTU LUSTIEST
EILSSTTY STYLITES
EILSSTUU LITUUSES
EILSSTVY SYLVITES
EILSSTYZ STYLIZES
EILSSWZZ SWIZZLES
EILSTWZZ TWIZZLES
EIMMMNOT IMMOMENT
EIMMMORZ MOMZERIM
EIMMNNOT MONIMENT
EIMMNNTU MUNIMENT
EIMMNORS MISNOMER
EIMMOPRU EMPORIUM
EIMMOPST METOPISM
EIMMOSTT TOTEMISM
EIMMPRRS PRIMMERS
EIMMPRST PRIMMEST
EIMMPRSU PREMIUMS
EIMMPSSU PESSIMUM
EIMMRRST TRIMMERS
EIMMRSST MISTERMS
EIMMRSSW SWIMMERS
EIMMRSTT TRIMMEST
EIMMRSTU RUMMIEST
EIMMSSTU MUMSIEST
EIMMSTUY YUMMIEST
EIMNNOOT NOONTIME
EIMNNOPT IMPONENT
EIMNNOST MENTIONS
EIMNNOTT OINTMENT
EIMNNOUY EUONYMIN
EIMNOOPS EMPOISON
EIMNOORS IONOMERS
         MOONRISE
EIMNOORT REMOTION
EIMNOORV OMNIVORE
EIMNOOSS MONOSIES
EIMNOOST EMOTIONS
         MOONIEST
EIMNOOSX EXOMIONS
EIMNOPRT ORPIMENT
EIMNOPSS PEONISMS
EIMNOPST EMPTIONS
         NEPOTISM
         PIMENTOS
EIMNOPTT IMPOTENT
EIMNORSS MERSIONS
EIMNORSU INERMOUS
         MONSIEUR
EIMNORSW WINSOMER
EIMNORTY ENORMITY
EIMNOSST MOISTENS
EIMNPRSS PRIMNESS
EIMNPSST MISSPENT
EIMNPSTU NUMPTIES
EIMNRSST ENTRISMS
         MINSTERS
         TRIMNESS
EIMNRSSU NEURISMS
EIMNRSTU TERMINUS
EIMNRSTY ENTRYISM
         MISENTRY
EIMNSSSS SENSISMS
EIMNSSTU MISTUNES
EIMNSTTU MINUTEST
EIMNSUZZ MUEZZINS
EIMOORST MOORIEST
         MOTORISE
         ROOMIEST
EIMOORTZ MOTORIZE
EIMOPPRR IMPROPER
EIMOPPST MOPPIEST

EIMOPRRS PRIMEROS
         PRIMROSE
         PROMISER
EIMOPRRT IMPORTER
         REIMPORT
EIMOPRRV IMPROVER
EIMOPRSS IMPOSERS
         PROMISES
EIMOPRST IMPOSTER
EIMOPRSV IMPROVES
EIMOPRUU EUROPIUM
EIMOPSTY PEYOTISM
EIMOQSTU MISQUOTE
EIMORRSS MORRISES
EIMORRST MORTISER
         STORMIER
EIMORRTT REMITTOR
EIMORRWW WIREWORM
EIMORSST EROTISMS
         MORTISES
         TRISOMES
EIMORSSV VERISMOS
EIMORSTT OMITTERS
EIMORSTU MISROUTE
         MOISTURE
EIMORSTW MISWROTE
         WORMIEST
EIMORSTY ISOMETRY
EIMORSVW OVERSWIM
EIMOSSST MOSSIEST
EIMOSSTT MOISTEST
EIMOSSTU MOUSIEST
EIMOSSTZ MESTIZOS
EIMOSTTT MOTTIEST
         TOTEMIST
EIMOSTTU TITMOUSE
EIMPRRSU PRIMEURS
EIMPRSST IMPRESTS
EIMPRSSU PRIMUSES
EIMPRSTU IMPUREST
         IMPUTERS
         STUMPIER
EIMPSSST MISSTEPS
EIMPSSTU SPUMIEST
         STUMPIES
EIMPSSTY EMPTYSIS
EIMPSTTU TUMPIEST
EIMQSSTU MESQUITS
EIMQSTUY MYSTIQUE
EIMRRRSU SMURRIER
EIMRRSST SURMISER
EIMRRSSU MISUSERS
         SURMISES
EIMRSSTT METRISTS
EIMRSSTY SMYTRIES
EIMRSSUU MIURUSES
EIMRSTTU SMUTTIER
EIMRSTUV VITREUMS
EIMRSTUX MIXTURES
EIMSSSSU MISUSES
EIMSSSTU MUSSIEST
EIMSSTTU MUSTIEST
EIMSTUZZ MUZZIEST
EINNOOTX NEOTOXIN
EINNOPSS PENSIONS
EINNOQSU QUINONES
EINNORST INTONERS
         TERNIONS
EINNORSU REUNIONS
EINNORSV ENVIRONS
EINNORTT TONTINER
EINNORTU NEUTRINO
EINNORTV INVENTOR
         NOVERINT
EINNORWW WINNOWER
EINNOSSS NOSINESS
EINNOSST TENSIONS
EINNOSSV VENISONS
```

```
EINNOSTT TINSTONE        EINPRRST PRINTERS        EIOPSSTU SOUPIEST        EIRTTTWY TWITTERY
         TONTINES                 REPRINTS        EIOPSSTY ISOTYPES        EIRTTUWZ WURTZITE
EINNOSTU NOUNIEST                 SPRINTER        EIOPSTTT POTTIEST        EISSSSTU TUSSISES
EINNPRSS SPINNERS        EINPRRTU PRURIENT        EIOPSTTU POUTIEST        EJLLORSY JOLLYERS
EINNPRST ENPRINTS        EINPRSST SPINSTER        EIOPSTTY PEYOTIST        EJLOPSTU PULSOJET
EINNPRSY SPINNERY        EINPRSTU REPUNITS        EIOPSTUW WIPEOUTS        EJMOPRUV OVERJUMP
EINNPSST SPINNETS                 UNPRIEST        EIOQRSTU QUOITERS        EJNORRSU REJOURNS
EINNPSSU PUNINESS                 UNRIPEST        EIORRRST ERRORIST        EJNORSUY JOURNEYS
EINNPSSY SPINNEYS        EINPRTTU INPUTTER        EIORRRSW WORRIERS        EJNRSTUU UNJUSTER
EINNPSXY SIXPENNY        EINPSTTX SPINTEXT        EIORRRTU ROTURIER        EJNSSSTU JUSTNESS
EINNRSTU RUNNIEST        EINPSTTY TINTYPES        EIORRSST RESISTOR        EJOORSVY OVERJOYS
         STURNINE        EINQRSTU SQUINTER                 ROISTERS        EJORSSTU JOUSTERS
EINNRSTV VINTNERS        EINQSSTU INQUESTS                 SORRIEST        EJOSSTTU OUTJESTS
EINNRTTU NUTRIENT        EINQSTTU QUINTETS        EIORRSSV REVISORS        EKKLOOSY OLYKOEKS
EINNSSTU SUNNIEST        EINQSTUU UNIQUEST        EIORRSTT RORTIEST        EKKLRSSU SKULKERS
EINNSSUW UNSINEWS                 UNQUIETS        EIORRSTU STOURIER        EKKMORSY KROMESKY
EINNSTUW UNTWINES        EINQTTTU QUINTETT        EIORRSTV SERVITOR        EKLLMSSU SKELLUMS
EINOOPRS POISONER        EINRRSSU INSURERS        EIORRSUV OUVRIERS        EKLLOSSY KYLLOSES
         SNOOPIER        EINRSSST INSTRESS        EIORRSVV REVIVORS        EKLLRRSU KRULLERS
         SPOONIER        EINRSSSU SUNRISES        EIORRSVY REVISORY        EKLNOOOR ONLOOKER
EINOOPSS SPOONIES        EINRSSTT ENTRISTS        EIORRTTU TROUTIER        EKLNOPRS PLONKERS
EINOORSS EROSIONS                 STINTERS        EIORSSTT STOITERS        EKLNORSS SNORKELS
EINOORST SNOOTIER        EINRSSXY SYRINXES        EIORSSTY SEROSITY        EKLNOSST KNOTLESS
EINOORSZ OZONISER        EINRSTTU RUNTIEST        EIORSTTU TOUSTIER        EKLNPRSU PLUNKERS
         SNOOZIER        EINRSTTW TWINTERS                 TUTORISE        EKLOOORV OVERLOOK
EINOORZZ OZONIZER        EINRSTTY ENTRYIST        EIORSTTV VIRETOTS        EKLOOPSW SLOWPOKE
EINOOSST ISOTONES        EINRSTUV UNRIVETS        EIORSTUV VIRTUOSE        EKLORSSW WORKLESS
EINOOSSZ OOZINESS                 VENTURIS                 VITREOUS        EKLSSSTU TUSKLESS
         OZONISES        EINRSTUW UNWRITES                 VOITURES        EKLSSTTU SKUTTLES
EINOOSZZ ZOONITES        EINRTUUV UNVIRTUE        EIORTTUZ TUTORIZE        EKMMORSU MURKSOME
EINOOSZZ OZONIZES        EINSSSST SENSISTS        EIOSSSTT TOSSIEST        EKMMRSSU SKUMMERS
EINOOTXX EXOTOXIN        EINSSTTW ENTWISTS        EIOSSTTU TOUSIEST        EKMNOSSU MUSKONES
EINOPPRS POPERINS                 TWINSETS        EIOSSTTW TOWSIEST        EKMOOPRR MOREPORK
         PROPINES        EINSSTUW UNWISEST        EIOSSTUZ OUTSIZES        EKMOORSW WORKSOME
EINOPRRS PRISONER        EINSSTUX UNSEXIST        EIOSTTTT TOTTIEST        EKMOOSSS KOSMOSES
EINOPRSS PORINESS        EINSSTXY SYNTEXIS        EIOSTTTU TOUTIEST        EKMRSTUY MUSKETRY
         PRESSION        EINSTTTU NUTTIEST        EIOSTTUZ TOUZIEST        EKNNOPSU UNSPOKEN
         ROPINESS        EINSTTTW TWITTENS        EIOSTTWZ TOWZIEST        EKNOOPRW OPENWORK
EINOPRST POINTERS        EIOOPPRS PORPOISE        EIPPRRST STRIPPER        EKNOORSS SNOOKERS
         PROTEINS        EIOOPPST OPPOSITE                 TRIPPERS        EKNOORST STROOKEN
         REPOINTS        EIOOPRST PORTOISE        EIPPRRTY TRIPPERY        EKNOPPSU UPSPOKEN
EINOPRSU PRUINOSE                 ROOPIEST        EIPPRSTT TRIPPETS        EKNORSST STONKERS
EINOPRSV OVERSPIN        EIOOPSST ISOTOPES        EIPQRSTU QUIPSTER        EKNORSTW NETWORKS
         PROVINES        EIOOPSTV POOVIEST        EIPRRRSU SPURRIER        EKNORSUY YOUNKERS
EINOPRTU ERUPTION        EIOORRSS SORORISE        EIPRRSSU SPURRIES        EKNRSTUY TURNKEYS
EINOPSTT NEPOTIST        EIOORRST ROOTSIER                 SURPRISE        EKOOORTV OVERTOOK
EINOQSTU QUESTION        EIOORRSZ SORORIZE        EIPRRSTZ SPRITZER        EKOOPRRV PROVOKER
EINOQTTU QUOTIENT        EIOORSTT ROOTIEST        EIPRRSUY SYRUPIER        EKOOPRRW ROPEWORK
EINORRST INTRORSE                 TORTOISE        EIPRSSST PERSISTS        EKOOPRSV PROVOKES
         SNORTIER        EIOOSSTT SOOTIEST        EIPRSSSU SUSPIRES        EKOOPRSY SPOOKERY
EINORRTV INVERTOR                 TOOTSIES        EIPRSSTT SPITTERS        EKOOPSTU OUTSPOKE
EINORSSS ROSINESS        EIOOSTWZ WOOZIEST                 TIPSTERS        EKOORRVW OVERWORK
EINORSST TERSIONS        EIOPPPST POPPIEST        EIPRSSTU PURSIEST        EKOORSST STOOKERS
EINORSSU NEUROSIS        EIOPPRTW PIPEWORT        EIPRSSTZ SPRITZES                 STROOKES
         RESINOUS        EIOPPSST SOPPIEST        EIPRSTTU PURTIEST        EKOPRSTU UPSTROKE
EINORSSV VERSIONS        EIOPRRSS PRIORESS                 PUTTIERS        EKOPRSUY KOUPREYS
EINORSTT SNOTTIER        EIOPRRST PIERROTS        EIPRSUVW PURVIEWS        EKORRSST STROKERS
         TENORIST                 SPORTIER        EIPRSVVY SPIVVERY        EKORRUVY KURVEYOR
         TRITONES        EIOPRRSU SUPERIOR        EIPSSTXY PTYXISES        EKORSSTU KURTOSES
EINORSTU ROUTINES        EIOPRRTV OVERTRIP        EIQRRSTU SQUIRTER        EKPPSSUU SEPPUKUS
         SNOUTIER        EIOPRSST PERIOSTS        EIQRSSSU SQUIRESS        ELLLMOWY MELLOWLY
EINORSTV INVESTOR                 PROSIEST        EIQRSSTU QUERISTS        ELLLNSUY SULLENLY
EINORSTY TYROSINE                 REPOSITS        EIQRSTTU QUITTERS        ELLLORRS LORRELLS
EINORSTZ TRIZONES                 RIPOSTES        EIQRSUZZ QUIZZERS        ELLMNOOS MOELLONS
EINORSUV SOUVENIR                 TRIPOSES        EIQRUYZZ QUIZZERY        ELLMNOSY SOLEMNLY
EINORTTU RITENUTO        EIOPRSTT PORTIEST        EIQSSUZZ SQUIZZES        ELLMNOTY MOLTENLY
EINOSSSS SESSIONS                 RISPETTO        EIRRRSST STIRRERS        ELLMNPUY LUMPENLY
EINOSSST SONSIEST                 SPOTTIER        EIRRSSTV STRIVERS        ELLMOORS MORELLOS
         STENOSIS        EIOPRSTU ROUPIEST        EIRRSTTU TRUSTIER        ELLMPSUU PLUMULES
EINOSSTT SNOTTIES                 SPOUTIER        EIRSSSTU SUITRESS        ELLNNOST TONNELLS
         STONIEST        EIOPRSTV PIVOTERS                 TSURISES        ELLNNSSU NULLNESS
EINOSSTW SNOWIEST                 SPORTIVE        EIRSSTTU RUSTIEST        ELLNOORV LOVELORN
EINOSTTT TOTIENTS        EIOPRSUV PERVIOUS                 TRUSTIES        ELLNOOSW WOOLLENS
EINOSTTW TOWNIEST                 PREVIOUS        EIRSSTTW TWISTERS        ELLNOPRU PRUNELLO
EINOSTUU TENUIOUS                 VIPEROUS        EIRSSUVV SURVIVES        ELLNOSST STOLLENS
EINOSTVY VENOSITY        EIOPRTTT TRIPTOTE        EIRSSUVW SURVIEWS        ELLNOSSU NOUSELLS
EINPPRSS SNIPPERS        EIOPRTTY PETITORY        EIRSTTTU RUTTIEST        ELLNOSVY SLOVENLY
EINPPSST SNIPPETS        EIOPRTUZ OUTPRIZE        EIRSTTTW TWITTERS        ELLNOSXY XYLENOLS
EINPPSTY SNIPPETY        EIOPSSST SEPIOSTS        EIRSTTUX TUTRIXES
```

ELLNOUVY	UNLOVELY	ELOORSTT	ROOTLETS		NEMOROUS	ENOPRRSU	PRONEURS
ELLNPSSU	UNSPELLS	ELOORSTU	TORULOSE	EMNOORSW	NEWSROOM	ENOPRSST	POSTERNS
ELLOOSSW	WOOSELLS	ELOORSUV	OVERSOUL	EMNOORTY	NOOMETRY	ENOPRSTT	PORTENTS
ELLOPRRS	PROLLERS	ELOOSSST	SOOTLESS	EMNOOSST	MOONSETS	ENOPRTUW	UPTOWNER
ELLOPRST	POLLSTER	ELOOSSTU	OUTSOLES	EMNOOSUV	VENOMOUS	ENOPSSST	STEPSONS
ELLOPRTU	POLLUTER	ELOOSSWY	WOOLSEYS	EMNOOTTY	TENOTOMY	ENOPSSSY	SYNOPSES
ELLOPRUV	PULLOVER	ELOOSVVX	VOLVOXES	EMNOOTUV	OUTVENOM	ENOPSTTU	OUTSPENT
ELLOPSST	PLOTLESS	ELOPPRRY	PROPERLY	EMNOOTWY	TOYWOMEN	ENOQSTUU	UNQUOTES
ELLOPSTU	POLLUTES	ELOPPSST	STOPPLES	EMNORRSU	MOURNERS	ENORRSST	SNORTERS
ELLORRST	STROLLER	ELOPRRSU	PROULERS	EMNORSST	MONSTERS	ENORRSTT	TORRENTS
	TROLLERS	ELOPRRSW	PROWLERS	EMNORSTT	SORTMENT	ENORRSUV	OVERRUNS
ELLORSTY	TROLLEYS	ELOPRRSY	PYRROLES		TORMENTS	ENORRTUU	TOURNURE
ELLOSSSU	SOULLESS	ELOPRRTY	PORTERLY	EMNORSTU	MONTURES	ENORRTUV	OVERTURN
ELLOSSTU	OUTSELLS	ELOPRSSS	PLESSORS		MOUNTERS		TURNOVER
ELLOSTTU	OUTTELLS	ELOPRSSU	SPORULES		REMOUNTS	ENORSSSU	SOURNESS
ELLOSTUW	OUTSWELL	ELOPRSTT	PLOTTERS	EMNORSUU	NUMEROUS	ENORSSTT	SNOTTERS
	OUTWELLS	ELOPRSTU	PLOUTERS	EMNOSSST	STEMSONS		STENTORS
ELLPPSUY	SUPPLELY		POULTERS	EMNOSSUY	EUONYMUS	ENORSSTU	TONSURES
ELLPSSUW	UPSWELLS	ELOPRSTW	PLOWTERS	EMNRSSTU	MUNSTERS	ENORSSTU	STENTOUR
ELLSSSTU	LUSTLESS	ELOPRSTY	PROSTYLE		STERNUMS	ENORSTTY	SNOTTERY
ELMMNOTU	LOMENTUM		PROTYLES	EMNRSSUU	NUMEROUS	ENORSTUV	VENTROUS
ELMMNOTY	MOMENTLY	ELOPRSUV	OVERPLUS	EMOOPRRT	PROMOTER	ENORSTUY	TOURNEYS
ELMMORST	TROMMELS	ELOPRSYY	PYROLYSE	EMOOPRST	PROMOTES	ENOSSSUU	SENSUOUS
ELMMOSUX	LUMMOXES	ELOPRXYY	PYROXYLE	EMOOPRSY	POMEROYS	ENOSSTTU	STOUTENS
ELMMPSTU	PLUMMETS	ELOPRYYZ	PYROLYZE		PYROSOME	ENPRRSSU	SPURNERS
ELMMRSSU	SLUMMERS	ELOPSSST	SPOTLESS	EMOOPRSZ	ZOOSPERM	ENPRSSSY	SPRYNESS
ELMMRSTU	STRUMMEL		STOPLESS	EMOOPSSU	ESPUMOSO	ENPRSSTU	PUNSTERS
ELMMRSUY	SUMMERLY	ELOPSSUU	OPULUSES	EMOORSST	MOROSEST	ENPRSSUU	PRUNUSES
ELMMSSTU	STUMMELS	ELOPSTTU	OUTSLEPT	EMOORSSU	UROSOMES		UNPURSES
ELMNNOSU	UNSOLEMN	ELORSSTT	SETTLORS	EMOORTYZ	ZOOMETRY	ENPRTTUY	UNPRETTY
ELMNOOOP	MONOPOLE		SLOTTERS	EMOOSSTW	TWOSOMES	ENRRRTUU	NURTURER
ELMNOOSS	MOONLESS	ELORSTUY	SOUTERLY	EMOOSSTY	MYOSOTES	ENRRSTUU	NURTURES
ELMNOOST	MOONLETS		UROSTYLE	EMOOSTUV	OUTMOVES	ENRSSTTU	STUNTERS
ELMNOPSU	PULMONES	ELORTTTU	TROUTLET	EMOPPRRT	PROMPTER	ENRSSTUU	UNSUREST
ELMNPPSU	PLUMPENS	ELOSSSTY	SYSTOLES	EMOPRSST	STOMPERS	ENRSTTUU	UNTRUEST
ELMNPSUU	UNPLUMES	ELOSSTUU	SETULOUS	EMOPRSSU	SPERMOUS	EOOOPRSS	OOSPORES
ELMNUUZZ	UNMUZZLE	ELOSSWZZ	SWOZZLES		SUPREMOS		SOPOROSE
ELMOOPPS	POMPELOS	ELPPRSTU	PURPLEST	EMORRRUU	RUMOURER	EOOOPRSZ	ZOOSPORE
ELMOOPSY	POLYSOME	ELPPSSTU	SUPPLEST	EMORRSSU	MORSURES	EOOOPRTZ	ZOOTROPE
ELMOORST	TREMOLOS	ELPRSSLU	SLURPERS	EMORRSSU	SMOUSERS	EOOPPRRS	PROPOSER
ELMOORSY	MOROSELY	ELPRSSSU	SPURLESS	EMORSSTU	OESTRUMS	EOOPPRSS	OPPOSERS
ELMOPRSY	POLYMERS	ELPRSSTU	SPURTLES		STRUMOSE		PROPOSES
ELMOPRTY	METOPRYL	ELPRSTTU	SPLUTTER	EMORSUVW	OVERSWUM	EOOPPRSV	POPOVERS
ELMOPRYY	POLYMERY	ELPRSTUU	PULTURES	EMOSSTTW	WESTMOST	EOOPPSST	POSTPOSE
ELMOPSYY	POLYSEMY	ELPRSUZZ	PUZZLERS	EMOSSTVZ	ZEMSTVOS	EOOPPTTY	TOPOTYPE
ELMORSSU	EMULSORS	ELPSSTUU	PUSTULES	EMPRRTUY	TRUMPERY	EOOPRRSS	SPOORERS
ELMOSYYZ	LYSOZYME	ELRRSSTU	RUSTLERS	EMPRSSTU	STUMPERS	EOOPRRST	PROTORES
ELMPPRSU	PLUMPERS	ELRRSTTU	TURTLERS		SUMPTERS		TROOPERS
ELMPPSTU	PLUMPEST	ELRSSSTU	RUSTLESS	EMPRSSUU	RUMPUSES	EOOPRRTU	OUTROPER
ELMPRSSU	RUMPLESS	ELRSSTUY	SLUTTERY	EMPRSTTU	STRUMPET		UPROOTER
ELMRRTUU	MULTURER	ELRSTUUV	VULTURES		TRUMPETS	EOOPRSST	STOOPERS
ELMRSTUU	MULTURES	ELSSSTUY	STYLUSES	EMRRSSTU	STURMERS	EOOPRSTU	OUTROPES
ELMRSUZZ	MUZZLERS	ELSSSTYY	SYSTYLES	ENNOOORT	TENOROON		PORTEOUS
ELNNOOSU	UNLOOSEN	EMMMNOTU	MOMENTUM	ENNOOOTZ	ENTOZOON	EOOPRSTV	OVERPOST
ELNNOPTU	NONUPLET	EMMNNOTU	MONUMENT	ENNOOPPT	OPPONENT		OVERTOPS
ELNOOSST	SOLONETS	EMMNOORS	MONOMERS	ENNOORST	NORTENOS		STOPOVER
ELNOOSSU	UNLOOSES	EMMNOORT	MOTORMEN	ENNOOSTT	NONETTOS	EOOPRSTW	TOWROPES
ELNOOSSZ	SNOOZLES	EMMNORSU	SUMMONER	ENNOPRSU	UNPERSON	EOOPRTUW	OUTPOWER
ELNOOSTZ	SOLONETZ	EMMNORSY	MERONYMS	ENNOPRUV	UNPROVEN	EOOPSTYZ	ZOOTYPES
ELNOPTTY	POTENTLY	EMMNORYY	MERONYMY	ENNOPTWY	TWOPENNY	EOORRRSW	SORROWER
ELNORSSU	NOURSLES	EMMNOSTY	METONYMS	ENNORSST	STERNSON	EOORRSST	ROOSTERS
ELNORSTU	TURNSOLE	EMMNOTTU	TOMENTUM	ENNORSTU	NEUTRONS	EOORSSTU	OESTROUS
ELNORSVY	SLOVENRY	EMMNOTYY	METONYMY	ENNORTTU	UNROTTEN	EOORSSVW	OVERSOWS
ELNORTTY	ROTTENLY	EMMOOORS	ROOMSOME	ENNOSSTU	NEUSTONS	EOORSSTUW	OUTSWORE
ELNOSSSW	SLOWNESS	EMMOPRRS	PROMMERS		SUNSTONE	EOORTTUV	OUTVOTER
	SNOWLESS	EMMOPTTY	POMMETTY	ENNPPTUY	TUPPENNY	EOOSTTUV	OUTVOTES
ELNOSSTV	SOLVENTS	EMMRRRUU	MURMURER	ENNRSSTU	STUNNERS	EOPPRSRS	PROSPERS
ELNOSSTW	TOWNLESS		REMURMUR	ENOOOSSZ	ZOONOSES	EOPPRRTY	PROPERTY
	WONTLESS	EMMRSTYY	SYMMETRY	ENOOPPRS	PROPONES	EOPPRSST	STOPPERS
ELNOSTUZ	ZONULETS	EMMNNOOU	NOUMENON	ENOOPPST	POSTPONE	EOPPRSSU	PURPOSES
ELNPPSSU	UNSUPPLE	EMMNOOOT	MONOTONE	ENOOPRSS	POORNESS		SUPPOSER
ELNPRTUU	PURULENT	EMMNOSTW	TOWNSMEN		SNOOPERS	EOPPRSSW	SWOPPERS
ELNSSUZZ	SNUZZLES	EMMNPSTU	PUNTSMEN	ENOOPSSY	SPOONEYS	EOPPRSSU	SUPPOSES
ELOOPRSS	SPOOLERS	EMMNSTTU	STUNTMEN	ENOOPSST	POTSTONE	EOPRRSST	PORTRESS
ELOOPRSU	SUPERLOO	EMMOOPST	METOPONS	ENOORRVW	OVERWORN		SPORTERS
ELOOPRUW	OWERLOUP	EMMNOOPY	MONOTYPE	ENOORSSZ	SNOOZERS	EOPRRSTU	POSTURER
ELOOPSSS	SESSPOOL	EMMNOORST	MESOTRON	ENOORSVW	OVERSOWN		TROUPERS
ELOORSST	ROOTLESS		MONTEROS	ENOOSSTT	TESTOONS	EOPRRUVY	PURVEYOR
		EMMNOORSU	ENORMOUS	ENOOSTXY	OXYTONES	EOPRSSTT	PROTESTS
				ENOPPRRU	UNPROPER		

	SPOTTERS
EOPRSSTU	POSTURES
	SEPTUORS
	SPOUTERS
EOPRSSUU	POURSUES
	UPROUSES
EOPRSSUW	POURSEWS
EOPSSTTU	OUTSTEPS
EOPSSTTW	STEWPOTS
EOQRSSTU	QUESTORS
EORRRTTU	TORTURER
EORRSSST	STRESSOR
	TROSSERS
EORRSSTU	ROUSTERS
	TROUSERS
EORRSSTW	STROWERS
	TROWSERS
EORRSSTY	ROYSTERS
EORRSTTT	TROTTERS
EORRSTTU	TORTURES
	TROUTERS
EORRSUVY	SURVEYOR
EORRTUUV	TROUVEUR
EORSSSTU	TUSSORES
EORSSTTT	STOTTERS
EORSSTTU	TUTORESS
EORSSTTW	SWOTTERS
EORSSTUX	SEXTUORS
EORSTTUW	OUTWREST
EORSTUUV	VERTUOUS
EOSSTTTU	STOUTEST
EPPPRTUY	PUPPETRY
EPPRRSSU	SUPPRESS
EPPRSSUY	SUPERSPY
EPRRRSSU	SPURRERS
EPRRSSUU	PURSUERS
	USURPERS
EPRRSSUY	SPURREYS
EPRRSTUU	RUPTURES
EPRSSTTU	SPUTTERS
EPRSTTUY	SPUTTERY
EQRRTUUU	TRUQUEUR
ERRSSSTU	TRUSSERS
ERRSSTTU	TRUSTERS
ERRSSTTY	TRYSTERS
ERRSTTTU	STRUTTER
ERSSTTTU	STUTTERS
FFFGILNU	FLUFFING
FFFMOOTU	FOOTMUFF
FFGGIILN	GLIFFING
FFGHIINW	WHIFFING
FFGHINOU	HOUFFING
FFGHINOW	HOWFFING
FFGHIRSU	GRUFFISH
FFGIIKNS	SKIFFING
FFGIILNP	PIFFLING
FFGIILNR	RIFFLING
FFGIILNS	SIFFLING
FFGIINNS	SNIFFING
FFGIINPS	SPIFFING
FFGIINRS	GRIFFINS
FFGIINST	STIFFING
	TIFFINGS
FFGIKNOS	SKOFFING
FFGILMNU	MUFFLING
FFGILNPU	PLUFFING
FFGILNRU	RUFFLING
FFGINNSU	SNUFFING
FFGINOPU	POUFFING
FFGINORS	GRIFFONS
FFGINOSW	SOWFFING
FFGINPSU	PUFFINGS
FFGINSTU	STUFFING
FFHIISST	STIFFISH
FFHIISTY	FIFTYISH
FFHIKNSU	HUFFKINS
FFHIOPSS	SPOFFISH
FFHIRSSU	SURFFISH
FFHOOOST	OFFSHOOT
FFIILMOR	FILIFORM
FFIILNSY	SNIFFILY
FFIILNTY	FLINTIFY
FFIINOOS	SOFFIONI
FFIKLRSU	FRISKFUL
FFILLLSU	FULFILLS
FFILLTUY	FITFULLY
FFILRTUU	FRUITFUL
FFILSSTU	FISTFULS
FFILSTUY	STUFFILY
FFIMORSU	FUSIFORM
FFINOPRT	OFFPRINT
FFINOPST	PONTIFFS
FFKLORSU	FORKFULS
FFLLOOSU	LOOFFULS
FFLMNOOU	MOUFFLON
FFLNOTUU	FOUNTFUL
FFLORRUU	FURFUROL
FFNORSTU	TURNOFFS
FFNSTUUY	UNSTUFFY
FFOOPSST	STOPOFFS
FGGGIINR	FRIGGING
FGGGILNO	FLOGGING
FGGGINOR	FROGGING
FGGHIINT	FIGHTING
FGGHIISS	FISHGIGS
FGGHINTU	GUNFIGHT
FGGIILNN	FLINGING
FGGIINNR	FRINGING
FGGIINRT	GRIFTING
FGGIINRU	FIGURING
FGGIISZZ	FIZZGIGS
FGGILNOR	FROGLING
FGGILNOS	GOLFINGS
FGGINOOR	FORGOING
FGGINORS	FORGINGS
FGHIIKNS	KINGFISH
FGHIINSS	FISHINGS
FGHIINST	SHIFTING
FGHILLTU	LIGHTFUL
FGHILMTU	MIGHTFUL
FGHILNSU	FLUSHING
FGHILRTU	RIGHTFUL
FGHINORT	FROTHING
FGHINRSU	FRUSHING
FGHIOPST	GIFTSHOP
FGHIOTTU	OUTFIGHT
FGHLORUU	FURLOUGH
FGHNOORS	FOGHORNS
FGHNOTUU	UNFOUGHT
FGIIINNX	INFIXING
FGIIKLNS	FLISKING
FGIIKNNS	KNIFINGS
FGIIKNRS	FRISKING
FGIILLNR	FRILLING
FGIILLNS	FILLINGS
FGIILNOO	FOLIOING
FGIILNOS	FOILINGS
FGIILNPP	FLIPPING
FGIILNRS	RIFLINGS
FGIILNRT	FLIRTING
	TRIFLING
FGIILNSS	FISSLING
FGIILNST	STIFLING
FGIILNTT	FLITTING
FGIILNZZ	FIZZLING
FGIINNST	SNIFTING
FGIINNSU	INFUSING
FGIINNUX	UNFIXING
FGIINNUY	UNIFYING
FGIINOST	FOISTING
FGIINRRS	FIRRINGS
FGIINRST	FRISTING
FGIINRTT	FRITTING
FGIINRTU	FRUITING
FGIINRZZ	FRIZZING
FGIINSST	SIFTINGS
FGIINSTT	FITTINGS
FGIINSTW	SWIFTING
FGIINSZZ	FIZZINGS
FGIIRSTU	FIGURIST
FGIKLNNU	FLUNKING
FGILLNOW	WOLFING
FGILLNOY	FOLLYING
FGILMNPU	FLUMPING
FGILNNTU	GUNFLINT
FGILNOOR	FLOORING
FGILNOOS	FOOLINGS
FGILNOOT	FOOTLING
FGILNOOZ	FOOZLING
FGILNOPP	FLOPPING
FGILNOPS	FOPLINGS
FGILNORS	ROLFINGS
FGILNORU	FLOURING
FGILNSTU	FLUTINGS
FGILNSTY	FLYTINGS
FGILNUZZ	FUZZLING
FGIMNORS	FORMINGS
FGIMNPRU	FRUMPING
FGIMOSSY	FOGYISMS
FGINNORT	FRONTING
FGINNORW	FROWNING
FGINOOPR	PROOFING
FGINOOPS	SPOOFING
FGINOORS	ROOFINGS
FGINOOST	FOOTINGS
FGINORST	FROSTING
FGINORTU	FOUTRING
FGINRRSU	FURRINGS
FGINRSTU	SURFINGS
FGINRSTU	TURFINGS
FGINSTTU	TUFTINGS
FGIORSTW	FIGWORTS
FGISSTUU	FUGUISTS
FGLLMOOU	GLOOMFUL
FGLLNSUU	LUNGFULS
FGLNORSU	FURLONGS
FGLNORUW	WRONGFUL
FGLOOOST	FOOTSLOG
FGLORSUU	FULGOURS
FGLSSTUU	GUTSFULS
FGNOORSU	FOURGONS
FGNOORTU	UNFORGOT
FHHOORST	SHOFROTH
FHIIKLMS	MILKFISH
FHIIKNSS	FISHSKIN
FHIILLTY	FILTHILY
FHIILRST	FLIRTISH
FHIILSTY	SHIFTILY
FHIKLLLO	HILLFOLK
FHIKMNOS	MONKFISH
FHIKNORT	FORTHINK
FHILLOOT	FOOTHILL
FHILMPSU	LUMPFISH
FHILMRTU	MIRTHFUL
FHILORSU	FLOURISH
FHILORTY	FROTHILY
FHILPSSU	SHIPFULS
FHIMPRSU	FRUMPISH
FHINOSSU	FUSHIONS
FHINRTTU	UNTHRIFT
FHIOOPTT	PHOTOFIT
FHIOPSSX	FOXSHIPS
FHIORSTY	FORTYISH
FHKORSTU	FUTHORKS
FHLLLOTU	LOTHFULL
FHLLOSTU	SLOTHFUL
FHLMOTUU	MOUTHFUL
FHLNORSU	HORNFULS
FHLOOSTU	SOOTHFUL
FHLOOTTU	TOOTHFUL
FHLOPSSU	SHOPFULS
FHLORTTU	TROTHFUL
FHLORTUW	WORTHFUL
FHLORTUY	FOURTHLY
FHLOSTUU	OUTFLUSH
FHLOTUUY	YOUTHFUL
FHLRTTUU	TRUTHFUL
FHOOORST	FORSOOTH
	HOOFROTS
FIIINNTY	INFINITY
FIIKLRSY	FRISKILY
FIILLMOS	MILFOILS
FIILLMSY	FLIMSILY
FIILLMTU	MULTIFIL
FIILLNTY	FLINTILY
FIILMNRY	INFIRMLY
FIILMOPR	PILIFORM
FIILMPSY	SIMPLIFY
FIILNOST	TINFOILS
FIILTTUY	FUTILITY
FIIMMNSU	INFIMUMS
FIIMOPRS	PISIFORM
FIIMOSTY	MOISTIFY
FIINNOSU	INFUSION
FIINORTU	FRUITION
FIINOSSS	FISSIONS
FIINTUXY	UNFIXITY
FIIQUYZZ	QUIZZIFY
FIKKLNOS	KINFOLKS
	KINSFOLK
FIKLLLSU	SKILLFUL
FIKLNOSW	WOLFSKIN
	WOLFSKIN
FIKLNSSU	SKINFULS
FIKNORSW	FORSWINK
FILLLUWY	WILFULLY
FILLNSUY	SINFULLY
	SULFINYL
FILLNUUW	UNWILFUL
FILLOPPY	FLOPPILY
FILLOPSU	SPOILFUL
FILMNOOS	MONOFILS
FILMOPRS	SLIPFORM
FILMORRY	LYRIFORM
FILMOSSU	MOFUSSIL
FILNOSUX	FLUXIONS
FILOOSTW	WITLOOFS
FILORSST	FLORISTS
FILORSTU	FLORUITS
FILORSTY	FROSTILY
FILRSTTU	TRISTFUL
FILSSTTU	FLUTISTS
FILSTTUY	STULTIFY
FIMMNOOR	OMNIFORM
FIMMORRU	MURIFORM
FIMMORSS	MISFORMS
FIMNORSU	UNIFORMS
FIMOPRRY	PYRIFORM
FIMORTUY	FUMITORY
FIMOSTUY	FUMOSITY
FIMRSTUU	FUTURISM
FINORSSS	FRISSONS
FINORSUY	INFUSORY
FIOORSSU	FURIOSOS
FIORTTUY	FORTUITY
FIRSTTUU	FUTURIST
FIRTTUUY	FUTURITY
FJLLOUYY	JOYFULLY
FJLNOUUY	UNJOYFUL
FKKLOORW	WORKFOLK
FKKOORTW	KOFTWORK
FKLMOOOT	FOLKMOOT
FKLNRTUU	TRUNKFUL
FKMOORRW	FORMWORK

```
FKNORSUW FORSWUNK
FKOOORTW FOOTWORK
FLLOOPUW UPFOLLOW
FLMNOOSU MOUFLONS
FLMNORUU MOURNFUL
FLMOOORW MOORFOWL
FLMOOOST TOMFOOLS
FLMOORSU ROOMFULS
FLMORSTU STORMFUL
FLNOOPSU SPOONFUL
FLNOORRS FORLORNS
FLNOOSTU SNOOTFUL
FLNOOTUW OUTFLOWN
FLOOOPTT POLTFOOT
FLOOPTTY TOPLOFTY
FLOORSSW FORSLOWS
FLOOSTUW OUTFLOWS
FLOPRSTU SPORTFUL
FLORTTUU TROUTFUL
FLRSTTUU TRUSTFUL
FMNOOOOR MOONROOF
FMRSSTUU FRUSTUMS
FNNOOORT FRONTOON
FNNOORST FRONTONS
FNOOORTW FOOTWORN
FNOOPRSU SUNPROOF
FNOORRSW FORSWORN
FNOORSSU SUNROOFS
FNOORTUW OUTFROWN
FOOOPRST ROOFTOPS
FOOOPSTT FOOTPOST
FOOORSTT FOOTROTS
FOOOSTTU OUTFOOTS
FOORSTTX FOXTROTS
GGGGIILN GIGGLING
GGGGIINR GRIGGING
GGGGILNO GOGGLING
GGGGILNU GLUGGING
         GUGGLING
GGGGINOR GROGGING
GGGHIILN HIGGLING
GGGHIINT THIGGING
GGGHIINW WHIGGING
GGGHINOS HOGGINGS
         SHOGGING
GGGIIJLN JIGGLING
GGGIIJNS JIGGINGS
GGGIILNN NIGGLING
GGGIILNS LIGGINGS
GGGIILNW WIGGLING
GGGIINPR PRIGGING
GGGIINPS PIGGINGS
GGGIINRS RIGGINGS
GGGIINRT TRIGGING
GGGIINSW SWIGGING
         WIGGINGS
GGGIINTW TWIGGING
GGGIJLNO JOGGLING
GGGIJLNU JUGGLING
GGGIJNOS JOGGINGS
GGGIJNSU JUGGINGS
GGGIKNSU SKUGGING
GGGILNOO GOOGLING
GGGILNOS LOGGINGS
         SLOGGING
GGGILNOT TOGGLING
GGGILNPU PLUGGING
         PUGGLING
GGGILNRU GURGLING
GGGILNSU SLUGGING
GGGIMNSU MUGGINGS
         SMUGGING
GGGINNOS NOGGINGS
         SNOGGING
GGGINNSU SNUGGING
GGGINOPR PROGGING
GGGINORT TROGGING
GGGINOSS SOGGINGS

GGGINPSU PUGGINGS
GGGINRSU RUGGINGS
GGGINSSU SUGGINGS
GGGINSTU TUGGINGS
GGHHIINT HIGHTING
GGHHINOU HOUGHING
GGHIILNT LIGHTING
GGHIINPT PIGHTING
GGHIINRT GIRTHING
         RIGHTING
GGHIINST SIGHTING
GGHIINTW WIGHTING
GGHIIPRS PRIGGISH
GGHILSSU SLUGGISH
GGHIMSTU THUGGISM
GGHINORU ROUGHING
GGHINOST GHOSTING
GGHINOSU SOUGHING
GGHINOTY HOGTYING
GGIIILNS GINGILIS
GGIIINNT IGNITING
GGIIJLNN JINGLING
GGIIKLNN KINGLING
GGIILLNR GRILLING
GGIILLNY GILLYING
GGIILMNN MINGLING
GGIILMNY GINGLYMI
GGIILNNP PINGLING
GGIILNNS SINGLING
         SLINGING
GGIILNNT GLINTING
         TINGLING
GGIILNPS PIGLINGS
GGIILNRS RIGLINGS
GGIIMNOS MISGOING
GGIIMNPU GUIMPING
GGIINNNR GRINNING
GGIINNOR GROINING
         IGNORING
GGIINNOS INGOINGS
GGIINNOW WONGIING
GGIINNRS RINGINGS
GGIINNRW WRINGING
GGIINNSS SIGNINGS
         SINGINGS
GGIINNST STINGING
GGIINNSW SWINGING
GGIINNTW TWINGING
GGIINNUV UNGIVING
GGIINPPR GRIPPING
GGIINPSY GIPSYING
GGIINRST RINGGITS
GGIINSSU GUISINGS
GGIINSTU GIUSTING
GGIIRRSS GRISGRIS
GGILLNUY GULLYING
GGILLOOW GOLLIWOG
GGILMNNO GLOMMING
GGILMNOO GLOOMING
GGILNNOP PLONGING
GGILNNOS LONGINGS
GGILNNOU LOUNGING
GGILNNPU PLUNGING
GGILNNUU UNGLUING
GGILNOOP GLOOPING
GGILNORW GROWLING
GGILNORY GLORYING
GGILNOSS GLOSSING
         GOSLINGS
GGILNOSV GLOVINGS
GGILNOSZ GLOZINGS
GGILNOTU GLOUTING
GGILNTTU GLUTTING
         GUTTLING
GGILNUZZ GUZZLING
GGILQSUY SQUIGGLY
GGIMMNSU GUMMINGS

GGIMNOOR GROOMING
GGIMNPRU GRUMPING
GGINNNSU GUNNINGS
GGINNOOS ONGOINGS
GGINNOPR PRONGING
GGINNOPS SPONGING
GGINNORW WRONGING
GGINNOSS SINGSONG
GGINNOTU TONGUING
GGINNRTU GRUNTING
GGINNUVY UNGYVING
GGINOORV GROOVING
GGINOOST STOOGING
GGINOOTU OUTGOING
GGINOPRS PROGGINS
GGINOPRU GROUPING
GGINOPSU UPGOINGS
GGINORSS GROSSING
GGINORSU GROUSING
GGINORSW GROWINGS
GGINORTU GROUTING
GGINOSUV VOGUINGS
GGINPRSU PURGINGS
GGINPSYY GYPSYING
GGINRSSU SURGINGS
GGLLOOWY GOLLYWOG
GHHIILST LIGHTISH
GHHIINSW WHISHING
GHHIIRST RIGHTISH
GHHIISTT TIGHTISH
GHHILOSU GHOULISH
GHHIMNPU HUMPHING
GHHIMOST HIGHMOST
GHHINOOS HOOSHING
GHHINSSU SHUSHING
GHHIORSU ROUGHISH
GHHIOSTU TOUGHISH
GHHIRSST SHRIGHTS
GHHOORTU THOROUGH
GHHOSTTU THOUGHTS
GHIIJNOS JINGOISH
GHIIKNNT THINKING
GHIIKNPS KINGSHIP
GHIIKNRS SHIRKING
         SHRIKING
GHIIKNSW WHISKING
GHIILLNO HILLOING
GHIILLNS SHILLING
GHIILMST MISLIGHT
GHIILMTY MIGHTILY
GHIILNPR HIRPLING
GHIILNRS HIRLINGS
         HIRSLING
GHIILNRT THIRLING
GHIILNRW WHIRLING
GHIILNST TINGLISH
GHIILNTW WHITLING
GHIILTTW TWILIGHT
GHIIMMNS SHIMMING
GHIIMMNW WHIMMING
GHIIMNNU INHUMING
GHIIMNST SMITHING
GHIINNNS SHINNING
GHIINNNT THINNING
GHIINNNY HINNYING
GHIINNRS SHRINING
GHIINNST NITHINGS
GHIINNSW WHININGS
GHIINNUV UNHIVING
GHIINOST HOISTING
GHIINPPS HIPPINGS
         SHIPPING
GHIINPPW WHIPPING
GHIINRRS SHIRRING
GHIINRRW WHIRRING
GHIINRST SHIRTING
GHIINRSV SHRIVING
GHIINRTV THRIVING
GHIINRTW WRITHING

GHIINSSS HISSINGS
GHIINSST INSIGHTS
GHIINSSW SWISHING
         WHISSING
         WISHINGS
GHIINSTT SHITTING
         TITHINGS
GHIINSTW WHISTING
         WHITINGS
GHIINSVV SHIVVING
GHIINWZZ WHIZZING
GHIIORSV VIGORISH
GHIIRSTT RIGHTIST
GHIKLNTY KNIGHTLY
GHIKLSTY SKYLIGHT
GHIKNNTU UNKNIGHT
GHIKNSSU HUSKINGS
GHIKRSTU TUGHRIKS
GHILLNOO HOLLOING
GHILLNOU HULLOING
GHILLOTW LOWLIGHT
GHILLSTY SLIGHTLY
GHILMNSU MULSHING
GHILNOOS SHOOLING
GHILNOPP HOPPLING
GHILNOPS LONGSHIP
GHILNOPY HOPINGLY
GHILNOSS SLOSHING
GHILNOST SLOTHING
GHILNOSU HOUSLING
GHILNOSW HOWLINGS
GHILNPSU INGULPHS
GHILNRSU HURLINGS
GHILNRTU HURTLING
GHILNRUY HUNGRILY
GHILNSSU SLUSHING
GHILNSTU HUSTLING
         SUNLIGHT
GHILORSW SHOWGIRL
GHILPRTY TRIGLYPH
GHIMMNSU HUMMINGS
GHIMNOPR MORPHING
GHIMNOPU GUMPHION
GHIMNORU HUMORING
GHIMNOSS MOSHINGS
GHIMNOTU MOUTHING
GHIMNPTU THUMPING
GHIMNSTU GUNSMITH
GHIMRSSU SIMURGHS
GHINNNSU SHUNNING
GHINNOOR HONORING
GHINNOPY PHONYING
GHINNORS HORNINGS
GHINNORT NORTHING
         THORNING
         THRONING
GHINNOST NOTHINGS
GHINNSSU SNUSHING
GHINNSTU HUNTINGS
         SHUNTING
GHINOOPT PHOTOING
GHINOOPW WHOOPING
GHINOOST SHOOTING
         SOOTHING
GHINOOSW WOOSHING
GHINOOTT TOOTHING
GHINOOTW WHOOTING
GHINOPPS HOPPINGS
         SHOPPING
GHINOPPW WHOPPING
GHINOPSS GINSHOPS
GHINORSS HORSINGS
         SHORINGS
GHINORST SHORTING
GHINORSV SHROVING
GHINORSW SHROWING
GHINORTT TROTHING
GHINORTW INGROWTH
```

THROWING	GIIKMMNS SKIMMING	GIILNSTT SLITTING	GIINORST RIOTINGS
WORTHING	GIIKMNPS SKIMPING	STILTING	ROISTING
GHINOSST HOSTINGS	GIIKMNRS SMIRKING	TILTINGS	ROSITING
GHINOSSU HOUSINGS	GIIKNNNS SKINNING	TITLINGS	GIINORSV VISORING
GHINOSSW SHOWINGS	GIIKNNOV INVOKING	GIILNSTU LINGUIST	GIINORTZ ROZITING
GHINOSTT HOTTINGS	GIIKNNPR PRINKING	GIILNSTW WITLINGS	GIINORVZ VIZORING
SHOTTING	GIIKNNPS PINKINGS	GIILNSTY STINGILY	GIINOSTT STOITING
TONIGHTS	GIIKNNSS SINKINGS	GIILNSZZ SIZZLING	GIINPPQU QUIPPING
GHINOSTU HOUTINGS	GIIKNNSW SWINKING	GIILNTTT TITTLING	GIINPPRT TRIPPING
SHOUTING	WINKINGS	GIILNTTU TITULING	GIINPPST TIPPINGS
SOUTHING	GIIKNNTT KNITTING	GIILNTTW TWILTING	GIINPRSS RISPINGS
GHINOSTW SOWTHING	GIIKNNTW TWINKING	GIILOSST OLIGISTS	GIINPRST SPIRTING
GHINOSUY YOUNGISH	GIIKNPPS SKIPPING	GIILPSTU PUGILIST	STRIPING
GHINOTTU OUTNIGHT	GIIKNPSS PIGSKINS	GIILRSST STRIGILS	GIINPRSU SIRUPING
GHINPSSU GUNSHIPS	GIIKNQRU QUIRKING	GIIMMNPR RIMMING	UPRISING
GHINPTTU PHUTTING	GIIKNRRS SKIRRING	GIIMMNRS RIMMINGS	GIINPSTT PITTINGS
GHINRRUY HURRYING	GIIKNRSS GRISKINS	GIIMMNRT TRIMMING	SPITTING
GHINRSTU UNGIRTHS	GIIKNRST SKIRTING	GIIMMNRU IMMURING	GIINPTTU TITUPING
UNRIGHTS	STRIKING	GIIMMNSW SWIMMING	GIINQRSU SQUIRING
GHINSSTU HUSTINGS	GIIKNSSV SKIVINGS	GIIMNNOP IMPONING	GIINQRTU QUIRTING
GHINSTTU HUTTINGS	GIILLMNS MILLINGS	GIIMNNOR MINORING	GIINQTTU QUITTING
SHUTTING	GIILLMNU ILLUMING	GIIMNNOY IGNOMINY	GIINQUZZ QUIZZING
GHIORTTU OUTRIGHT	GIILLNOS GILLIONS	GIIMNNTU MINUTING	GIINRRST STIRRING
GHIOSTTU OUTSIGHT	GIILLNPR PRILLING	MUNITING	GIINRSTV STRIVING
GHIPRSST SPRIGHTS	GIILLNPS PILLINGS	MUTINING	GIINRSTW WRITINGS
GHIPRSTU UPRIGHTS	SPILLING	GIIMNOPS IMPOSING	GIINSSSW SWISSING
GHIPRSUU GURUSHIP	GIILLNQU QUILLING	GIIMNOST MOISTING	GIINSSTT SITTINGS
GHLMOOOS HOMOLOGS	GIILLNRT TRILLING	GIIMNOTT OMITTING	GIINSSTU SUITINGS
GHLMOOOY HOMOLOGY	GIILLNST STILLING	GIIMNOTV MOTIVING	TISSUING
GHLNOOOR LONGHORN	TILLINGS	VOMITING	GIINSTTW TWISTING
GHLNOORU HOURLONG	GIILLNSW SWILLING	GIIMNPPR PRIMPING	WITTINGS
GHLNORSU SLUGHORN	GIILLNTT LITTLING	GIIMNPRS PRIMINGS	GIINSWZZ SWIZZING
GHLNOTYY YONGTHLY	GIILLNTW TWILLING	GIIMNPRU UMPIRING	GIINTTTW TWITTING
GHLOOORY HOROLOGY	GIILLNWY WILLYING	GIIMNPTU IMPUTING	GIIORRST RIGORIST
GHLORTUU TURLOUGH	GIILLOPW POLLIWIG	GIIMNRRS SMIRRING	GIIPRSTZ SPRITZIG
GHMORSSU SORGHUMS	GIILLPSW PIGSWILL	GIIMNSST MISTINGS	GIJKLNOY JOKINGLY
GHMOSSTU MUGSHOTS	GIILLTUY GUILTILY	GIIMNSSU MISUSING	GIJLLNOY JOLLYING
GHMPSSUU SPHYGMUS	GIILLTYZ GLITZILY	GIIMNSSW SWINGISM	GIJLNOST JOSTLING
GHNOPRSY GRYPHONS	GIILMMNP PLIMMING	GIIMNSTT SMITTING	GIJLNSTU JUNGLIST
GHNOPYYY HYPOGYNY	GIILMMNS SLIMMING	GIIMNSTU MUISTING	JUSTLING
GHNOSSTU GUNSHOTS	GIILMNNU LUMINING	GIIMNSTY STIMYING	GIJNOSTT JOTTINGS
SHOTGUNS	UNLIMING	GIIMORRS RIGORISM	GIJNOSTU JOUSTING
GHNOSTUU UNSOUGHT	GIILMNOS SMOILING	GIINNNOO ONIONING	GIJNTTUY JUTTYING
GHNOSTUY YOUNGTHS	GIILMNPS LIMPINGS	GIINNNOT INTONING	GIKKLNSU SKULKING
GHOOOSSW HOOSGOWS	SIMPLING	NOINTING	GIKKNNSU SKUNKING
GHOORTUY YOGHOURT	GIILMNPW WIMPLING	GIINNNPS PINNINGS	GIKLLNNO KNOLLING
GHOPRTUW UPGROWTH	GIILMNPY IMPLYING	SPINNING	GIKLNNOP PLONKING
GHORSTUY YOGHURTS	GIILMNSS SMILINGS	GIINNNRU INURNING	GIKLNNPU PLUNKING
GIIILMNT LIMITING	GIILMNST MISTLING	GIINNNST TINNINGS	GIKLNNRU KNURLING
GIIILNNS INISLING	GIILMNZZ MIZZLING	GIINNNSW WINNINGS	RUNKLING
GIIILNNU LINGUINI	GIILMPRS PILGRIMS	GIINNNTW TWINNING	GIKLNNUY UNKINGLY
GIIILOTV VITILIGO	GIILMPSU PUGILISM	GIINNOPR PROINING	GIKLNOPR PORKLING
GIIIMMNX IMMIXING	GIILMNNU UNLINING	GIINNOPS PIONINGS	GIKLNRSU LURKINGS
GIIINNOS IONISING	GIILNNPP NIPPLING	GIINNOQU QUOINING	GIKLORRW WORKGIRL
GIIINNOT IGNITION	GIILNNPS SPLINING	GIINNORS IRONINGS	GIKMNOSS SMOKINGS
GIIINNOZ IONIZING	GIILNNTU UNTILING	NIGROSIN	GIKNNOOS SNOOKING
GIIINNTV INVITING	GIILNNTW TWINLING	ROSINING	GIKNNOPR PRONKING
GIIINSTV VISITING	WINTLING	GIINNORT IGNITRON	GIKNNOQU QUONKING
GIIJMMNY JIMMYING	GIILNNUV UNLIVING	GIINNPPS SNIPPING	GIKNNOST STONKING
GIIJMNOS JINGOISM	GIILNOPS SPOILING	GIINNPRT PRINTING	GIKNNOSW SNOWKING
GIIJNNOS JOININGS	GIILNOPT PILOTING	GIINNPSS SNIPINGS	GIKNNOTT KNOTTING
GIIJNNOT JOINTING	GIILNORS LIGROINS	GIINNPSU PINGUINS	GIKNNOTU KNOUTING
GIIJNNRU INJURING	GIILNOSS SOILINGS	GIINNRSS RINSINGS	GIKNNOUY UNYOKING
GIIJNOST JINGOIST	GIILNOST TOILINGS	GIINNRSU INSURING	GIKNNPSU SPUNKING
JOISTING	GIILNPPR RIPPLING	RUININGS	GIKNNRTU TRUNKING
GIIKKLNP KINGKLIP	GIILNPPS SIPPLING	GIINNRTU UNTIRING	GIKNOOPS SPOOKING
GIIKKNNS SKINKING	SLIPPING	GIINNRUW UNWIRING	GIKNOOST STOOKING
GIIKKNRS KIRKINGS	GIILNPPT TIPPLING	GIINNSSW INSWINGS	GIKNOOTW KOTOWING
GIIKLLNS KILLINGS	GIILNPRS SPIRLING	GIINNSTT STINTING	GIKNOPST KINGPOST
SKILLING	GIILNPRT TRIPLING	TINTINGS	GIKNORRW RINGWORK
GIIKLMNS MILKINGS	GIILNPSS LISPINGS	GIINNSTU UNITINGS	GIKNORST STROKING
GIIKLNPR PLINKING	SPILINGS	GIINNSTW TWININGS	GIKNORSW WORKINGS
GIIKLNNS INKLINGS	GIILNQSU QUISLING	GIINNUVW UNWIVING	GIKNSSTU TUSKINGS
SLINKING	GIILNQTU QUILTING	GIINOPST POSITING	GILLMOOY GLOOMILY
GIIKLNNT TINKLING	GIILNRSW SWIRLING	SOPITING	GILLNNSU NULLINGS
GIIKLNNW WINKLING	GIILNRTW TWIRLING	GIINOPTV PIVOTING	GILLNOPR PROLLING
GIIKLNRS SKIRLING	GIILNRVY VIRGINLY	GIINOQTU QUOITING	GILLNOPS POLLINGS
GIIKLNST KITLINGS	GIILNSST LISTINGS	GIINORSS SIGNIORS	GILLNORS ROLLINGS
GIIKLNTT KITTLING			GILLNORT TROLLING

Code	Word(s)
GILLNOST	TOLLINGS
GILLNOSY	LOSINGLY
GILLNOVY	LOVINGLY
GILLNPUY	PULINGLY
GILLNSUY	SULLYING
GILLOOPW	POLLIWOG
GILLOPRY	POLLYWIG
GILLORVY	GILLYVOR
GILLOSSY	GLOSSILY
GILMMNSU	SLUMMING
GILMMTUY	MULTIGYM
GILMNOOS	SLOOMING
GILMNOPY	MOPINGLY
GILMNORS	MORLINGS
GILMNORT	MORTLING
GILMNOSS	MOSLINGS
GILMNOSU	MOUSLING
GILMNOSY	SMOYLING
GILMNOTT	MOTTLING
GILMNOTU	MOULTING
GILMNOUV	VOLUMING
GILMNOVY	MOVINGLY
GILMNPPU	PLUMPING
GILMNPRU	RUMPLING
GILMNPSU	SLUMPING
GILMNSUY	MUSINGLY
GILMNUZZ	MUZZLING
GILMOOSY	MISOLOGY
GILMPRUY	GRUMPILY
GILNNOOS	GLONOINS
	LOONINGS
	SNOOLING
GILNNOSU	NOUSLING
GILNNOTW	TOWNLING
GILNNOUV	UNLOVING
GILNNRSU	NURSLING
GILNNSSU	UNSLINGS
GILNNUZZ	NUZZLING
GILNOOPS	LOOPINGS
	SPOOLING
GILNOORT	ROOTLING
GILNOOST	LOOTINGS
	STOOLING
	TOOLINGS
GILNOOTT	TOOTLING
GILNOOVY	VINOLOGY
GILNOOWY	WOOINGLY
GILNOPPP	PLOPPING
	POPPLING
GILNOPPS	LOPPINGS
	SLOPPING
GILNOPPT	TOPPLING
GILNOPRU	PROULING
GILNOPRW	PROWLING
GILNOPSU	SOUPLING
GILNOPSY	POSINGLY
	SPONGILY
GILNOPTT	PLOTTING
GILNORSU	LOURINGS
GILNORTU	TROULING
GILNORVY	ROVINGLY
GILNOSSW	SLOWINGS
GILNOSTT	SLOTTING
GILNOSVW	WOLVINGS
GILNOSWY	YOWLINGS
GILNOSZZ	SOZZLING
GILNOTUY	OUTLYING
GILNOTUZ	TOUZLING
GILNPPRU	PURPLING
GILNPPSU	SUPPLING
GILNPRSU	PURLINGS
	SLURPING
	SPURLING
GILNPRYY	PRYINGLY
GILNPSSU	PLUSSING
GILNPUZZ	PUZZLING
GILNRSSU	SLURRING
GILNRSTU	LUSTRING
	RUSTLING
GILNRTTU	TURTLING
GILNRTYY	TRYINGLY
GILNSSTU	SINGULTS
	TUSSLING
GILNSTTU	SUTTLING
GILNTUUY	UNGUILTY
GILNUWZZ	WUZZLING
GILOOORS	ROSOGLIO
GILOOOST	OOLOGIST
GILOORSS	GIROSOLS
GILOORSU	GLORIOUS
GILOORVY	VIROLOGY
GILOOSSS	ISOGLOSS
GILOOSTW	TWIGLOOS
GILOOSTY	SITOLOGY
GILORSTT	TRIGLOTS
GILOSTUY	GULOSITY
GIMMMNSU	MUMMINGS
GIMMMNUY	MUMMYING
GIMMNOTY	TOMMYING
GIMMNSSU	SUMMINGS
GIMMNSTU	STUMMING
GIMMOSSU	GUMMOSIS
GIMNNORS	MORNINGS
GIMNNORU	MOURNING
GIMNNOTU	MOUNTING
GIMNNOUV	UNMOVING
GIMNNSTU	MUNTINGS
GIMNOOOU	OOGONIUM
GIMNOOPS	SPOOMING
GIMNOORS	MOORINGS
	SMOORING
GIMNOORT	MOTORING
GIMNOORV	VROOMING
GIMNOOSS	OSMOSING
GIMNOOST	MOOTINGS
	SMOOTING
GIMNOPRT	TROMPING
GIMNOPST	STOMPING
GIMNOPTU	GUMPTION
GIMNORRU	RUMORING
GIMNORRW	RINGWORM
GIMNORST	STORMING
GIMNORSU	ROUMINGS
GIMNOSST	GNOMISTS
GIMNOSSU	MOUSINGS
	SMOUSING
	SOUMINGS
GIMNOSTU	MOUSTING
	SMOUTING
GIMNOSYY	MISOGYNY
GIMNPRTU	TRUMPING
GIMNPSTU	STUMPING
GIMNRRSU	SMURRING
GIMNSTTU	SMUTTING
GIMPSSYY	GYPSYISM
GIMRSSUU	GURUISMS
GINNNOOS	NOONINGS
GINNNOST	STONNING
GINNNOSW	WONNINGS
GINNNPSU	PUNNINGS
GINNNRSU	RUNNINGS
GINNNSTU	STUNNING
	TUNNINGS
GINNNTUU	UNTUNING
GINNOOPS	SNOOPING
	SPOONING
GINNOOST	SNOOTING
GINNOOSW	SWOONING
GINNOOSZ	SNOOZING
GINNOPSU	UNPOPING
GINNOPRU	UNROPING
GINNOPRY	PROYNING
GINNOPSS	SPONGINS
GINNOPSY	PYONINGS
GINNOPTU	GUNPOINT
GINNOPTY	POYNTING
GINNORSS	SNORINGS
	SORNINGS
GINNORST	SNORTING
GINNORSU	GRUNIONS
GINNOSST	STONINGS
GINNOSTT	SNOTTING
GINNOSTU	SNOUTING
	STOUNING
GINNOSTY	STONYING
GINNOSUW	SWOUNING
GINNPRSU	PRUNINGS
	SPURNING
GINNRSSU	NURSINGS
GINNRSTU	TURNINGS
	UNSTRING
GINNSTTU	NUTTINGS
	STUNTING
GINNSTUY	UNTYINGS
GINOOPPS	OPPOSING
GINOOPRS	SPOORING
GINOOPRT	TROOPING
GINOOPSS	SOOPINGS
GINOOPST	STOOPING
GINOOPSW	SWOOPING
GINOORST	ROOSTING
	ROOTINGS
GINOORTW	WROOTING
GINOOSTT	TOOTSING
GINOPPPR	PROPPING
GINOPPQU	QUOPPING
GINOPPSS	SOPPINGS
GINOPPST	STOPPING
	TOPPINGS
GINOPPSW	SWOPPING
GINOPRSS	PROSINGS
GINOPRST	SPORTING
GINOPRSU	INGROUPS
	POURINGS
GINOPRSV	PROVINGS
GINOPRTU	TROUPING
GINOPSST	POSTINGS
	SIGNPOST
	STOPINGS
GINOPSSU	SPOUSING
GINOPSTT	SPOTTING
GINOPSTU	POUTINGS
	SPOUTING
GINOPTTY	TYPTOING
GINORRWY	WORRYING
GINORSST	SORTINGS
GINORSSU	SOURINGS
GINORSTU	ROUSTING
	ROUTINGS
	TOURINGS
GINORSTW	STROWING
	WORSTING
GINORSTY	ROYSTING
	STORYING
	STROYING
GINORTTT	TROTTING
GINORTTU	TROUTING
	TUTORING
GINOSSSS	SOSSINGS
GINOSSST	TOSSINGS
GINOSSSU	SOUSINGS
GINOSSSW	SOWSSING
GINOSSTT	SOTTINGS
GINOSSTU	TOUSINGS
GINOSSTV	STOVINGS
GINOSSTW	STOWINGS
GINOSTTT	STOTTING
	TOTTINGS
GINOSTTW	SWOTTING
GINOSTUW	OUTSWING
	OUTWINGS
	SPURRING
GINPRSTU	SPURTING
GINPRSUU	PURSUING
	USURPING
GINPRSUY	SYRUPING
GINPSSUW	UPSWINGS
GINPSTTU	PUTTINGS
GINPTTUY	PUTTYING
GINRSSTU	RUSTINGS
	TRUSSING
GINRSTTU	RUTTINGS
	STURTING
	TRUSTING
GINRSTTY	TRYSTING
GINRSTUU	SUTURING
GINSTTTU	TUTTINGS
GIOOPRRS	PORRIGOS
GIOORRSU	RIGOROUS
GIOORSTU	GOITROUS
GIOORSUV	VIGOROUS
GIOPRRSU	PRURIGOS
GIOPRSSY	GOSSIPRY
GIOPRSTU	GROUPIST
GIORSTUY	RUGOSITY
GJOORSTT	JOGTROTS
GKLOOOTY	TOKOLOGY
GLLOOPTY	POLYGLOT
GLLOOPWY	POLLYWOG
GLLOOXYY	XYLOLOGY
GLMNOOOT	MONOGLOT
GLMNOOOY	MONOLOGY
	NOMOLOGY
GLMNRTUU	NGULTRUM
GLMOOOPY	POMOLOGY
GLMOOORS	MOORLOGS
GLMOOYYZ	ZYMOLOGY
GLMORSUW	LUGWORMS
GLNNOORS	LORGNONS
GLNOOOSY	NOSOLOGY
GLNOOOTY	ONTOLOGY
GLNOOPRS	PROLONGS
GLNOOPSY	POLYGONS
GLNOOPYY	POLYGONY
GLNOPYYY	POLYGYNY
GLNORSTY	STRONGLY
	STRONGYL
GLNORTUW	LUNGWORT
GLNOSSUW	SUNGLOWS
GLNOSTTU	GLUTTONS
GLNOTTUY	GLUTTONY
GLOOOPSY	POSOLOGY
GLOOOPTY	OPTOLOGY
	TOPOLOGY
GLOOORUY	OUROLOGY
GLOOPSSY	GOSSYPOL
GLOOPTYY	TYPOLOGY
GLOORSUU	ORGULOUS
GMMPSUUW	MUGWUMPS
GMNOOOOY	MONOGONY
GMNOOYYY	MONOGYNY
GMNOORSU	GUNROOMS
GMNOORSW	MORWONGS
GMORSTUW	MUGWORTS
GNNPRSUU	UNSPRUNG
GNNRSTUU	UNSTRUNG
GNOOORSS	GORSOONS
GNOOOSSS	GOSSOONS
GNOORSUW	WRONGOUS
GNOORTUW	OUTGROWN
GNOPRSTU	GUNPORTS
GNPPRSUU	UPSPRUNG
GOORSTUW	OUTGROWS
GOORTTUW	GOUTWORT
HHIILOPT	THIOPHIL
HHIINNST	THINNISH
HHIIPSST	PHTHISIS
HHILPSSY	SYLPHISH
HHIMNPSY	NYMPHISH
HHIMPSSU	SUMPHISH

HHINOOSW NOHOWISH	HIMOPSSS SOPHISMS	HOOPSSTU UPSHOOTS	IILRSSTU SILURIST
HHIORSST SHORTISH	HIMOPSST PHOTISMS	HOOPSSTY TOYSHOPS	IILSTUUV UVULITIS
HHKKSSUU KHUSKHUS	HIMORSTU HUMORIST	HOORTTUW OUTWORTH	IILSTUVV UVLVITIS
HHMRSTUY RHYTHMUS	THORIUMS	HOOSSTTU OUTSHOTS	IIMMNTUY IMMUNITY
HHOOPPRS PHOSPHOR	HIMOTTVZ MITZVOTH	HOPPRRYY PORPHYRY	IIMMOPST OPTIMISM
HHOOSSTT HOTSHOTS	HIMPRSTU TRIUMPHS	HOPRRSUY PYRRHOUS	IIMMOPSU OPIUMISM
HIIILMNS NIHILISM	HIMPSTUY PYTHIUMS	HOPRSTUW UPTHROWS	IIMMSTTU MITTIMUS
HIIILNST NIHILIST	HIMRSSTY RHYMISTS	HOPSSTTU SHOTPUTS	IIMNNOOT MONITION
HIIILNTY NIHILITY	HIMSSTTY MYTHISTS	HPRSTTUU UPTHRUST	IIMNNOSU UNIONISM
HIIINRST RHINITIS	HINNORST TINHORNS	IIIJJLNS JINJILIS	IIMNNOTU MUNITION
HIIKMNRS MISTHINK	HINNPSSU NUNSHIPS	IIIKLNPS SPILIKIN	IIMNOOSS OMISSION
HIIKMRSS SKIRMISH	HINNSSUY SUNSHINY	IIIKMNNS MINIKINS	IIMNOPRS IMPRISON
HIIKNPSS KINSHIPS	HINOORST HORNITOS	IIILLMNP MINIPILL	IIMNOPST MISPOINT
HIIKOPRS PIROSHKI	HINOORSZ HORIZONS	IIILLMNU ILLINIUM	IIMNORTT INTROMIT
HIIKOPRZ PIROZHKI	HINOPPSS SHIPPONS	IIILLNOS ILLISION	IIMNORTY MINORITY
HIIKQRSU QUIRKISH	HINOPSSS SONSHIPS	IIILMRSV VIRILISM	IIMNOSSS MISSIONS
HIIKSSTT SKITTISH	HINOPSSY HYPNOSIS	IIILMUVX LIXIVIUM	IIMNOSST SIMONIST
HIILMMSS SLIMMISH	HINOPSTW TOWNSHIP	IIILRTVY VIRILITY	IIMNOSTX MIXTIONS
HIILMOST HOMILIST	HINORSST HORNISTS	IIIMMMNS MINIMISM	IIMNPRST IMPRINTS
HIILMPSU SILPHIUM	HINORTXY THYROXIN	IIIMMNST INTIMISM	MISPRINT
HIILMPSY IMPISHLY	HIOOOPRZ ZOOPHORI	MINIMIST	IIMNPTUY IMPUNITY
HIILMSTU LITHIUMS	HIOOPRTT POORTITH	IIIMMPRS IMPRIMIS	IIMNRSTY MINISTRY
HIILMSWY WHIMSILY	HIOORRST ORTHOSIS	IIIMNSTT INTIMIST	IIMOPSTT OPTIMIST
HIILMTUY HUMILITY	HIOOSSTT SHOOTIST	IIIMNTTY INTIMITY	IIMOSSTY MYOSITIS
HIILPSST THLIPSIS	HIOPRSSW WORSHIPS	IIINORRS IRRISION	IIMOTTVY MOTIVITY
HIILPSSY SYPHILIS	HIOPRSUZ RHIZOPUS	IIINPRST INSPIRIT	IIMPRTUY IMPURITY
HIILRSTT TRILITHS	HIOPSSST SOPHISTS	IIINQTUY INIQUITY	IIMRRTUV TRIUMVIR
HIILRSTY SHIRTILY	HIOPSSTU UPHOISTS	IIINSSTU SINUITIS	IIMRSTTU TRITIUMS
HIILSSTT STILTISH	HIOPSSTY PHYTOSIS	IIIOSTTU OUISTITI	IIMRSTUV TRIVIUMS
HIIMNSTT TINSMITH	HIORRSSY SORRYISH	IIISSTTW WISTITIS	IIMSSSTU MISSUITS
HIIMOPSS PHIMOSIS	HIOSSTTU STOUTISH	IIJLLNOS JILLIONS	IIMSSTUW SWIMSUIT
HIIMSSTT SHITTIMS	HIPPPSUY PUPPYISH	IIJMNOSS MISJOINS	IINNOOPS OPINIONS
HIINORST HISTRION	HIPSUYZZ ZIZYPHUS	IIJNNOST INJOINTS	IINNOPPT PINPOINT
HIINPSTW TWINSHIP	HKKOOSSY SKYHOOKS	IIJNNSTU NINJITSU	IINNOPTU PUNITION
HIIORSST HISTRIOS	HKMNORRU KRUMHORN	IIKLLNOS SKILLION	IINNOSTU INUSTION
HIIPPQSU QUIPPISH	HKNOORRW HORNWORK	IIKLMNPS LIMPKINS	UNIONIST
HIIKMNSU MINSHUKU	HKNOOSWW KNOWHOWS	IIKLMPSY SKIMPILY	UNITIONS
HIKNNORS INKHORNS	HKOOOPST POTHOOKS	IIKLNOSS OILSKINS	IINNPSST TINSNIPS
HIKNNSTU UNTHINKS	HKOOPRSW WORKSHOP	IIKLQRUY QUIRKILY	IINNSTTU TINNITUS
HIKNOTTU OUTTHINK	HLLLOOWY HOLLOWLY	IIKMNNOO MONOKINI	IINOOPST POSITION
HIKOOPSS SPOOKISH	HLLMNOOU MONOHULL	IIKMNORS KIRIMONS	IINOPSSS ISOSPINS
HIKOPSSY KYPHOSIS	HLLOPPRY PROPHYLL	IIKMNPSS SIMPKINS	IINORSST IRONISTS
HILLMSUY MULISHLY	HLMOOSTY SMOOTHLY	IIKNOSTT STOTINKI	IINORSTT INTROITS
HILLNOUY UNHOLILY	HLMOORSY MYRRHOLS	IILLLPUV PULVILLI	IINOSTTU TUITIONS
HILLOPST HILLTOPS	HLNOOPPY POLYPHON	IILLMNOS MILLIONS	IINOSTVY VINOSITY
HILMMOSU HOLMIUMS	HLOPRSTY PROTHYLS	IILLMRTU TRILLIUM	IINRTTUY TRIUNITY
HILMNOOT MONOLITH	HLPRSSUU SULPHURS	IILLMUUV ILLUVIUM	IINSSTTW INTWISTS
HILMOOPT PHILOMOT	HLPRSUUY SULPHURY	IILLNOOR ORILLION	IIOOPSTV OVIPOSIT
HILMOPSY MOPISHLY	HMMNOOSY HOMONYMS	IILLNOPS PILLIONS	IIOOSTTY OTIOSITY
HILMOSSW WHOLISMS	HMMNOOYY HOMONYMY	IILLNORT TRILLION	IIOPRRTY PRIORITY
HILMPPSU PLUMPISH	HMMOORSU MUSHROOM	IILLNOST STILLION	IIOPRSSS PISSOIRS
HILMPSY SYMPHILY	HMMRSTUU HUMSTRUM	IILLNOSU ILLUSION	IIORRRSY IRRISORY
HILMSTUU THULIUMS	HMNOOOST MOONSHOT	IILLNOSZ ZILLIONS	IIORSSTV IVORISTS
HILNOPSU UNPOLISH	HMNOOOTY HOMOTONY	IILLNSST INSTILLS	VISITORS
HILNOSTY TONISHLY	HMNOORRW HORNWORM	IILLNSTT LITTLINS	IIORSTUV VIRTUOSI
HILOOPYZ ZOOPHILY	HMNOOSTU UNSMOOTH	IILLOPUV PULVILIO	IIOSSTTU OUSTITIS
HILOOSTT OTOLITHS	HMNOPSYY HYPONYMS	IILMMPSS SIMPLISM	IIPRSSTU SPIRITUS
HILOOSTZ ZOOLITHS	SYMPHONY	IILMMSSU SIMULIUM	IJKLLOSY KILLJOYS
HILOOTTY TOOTHILY	HMNOPYYY HYPONYMY	IILMNORT MIRLITON	IJLNOQSU JONQUILS
HILOPPSY POPISHLY	HMOOOPRZ ZOOMORPH	IILMNOSS LIONISMS	IJNNOSTU UNJOINTS
HILORSTU UROLITHS	HMOOORSW SHOWROOM	IILMNSTU LUMINIST	IJNNSTUU NINJUTSU
HILORTWY WORTHILY	HMOOPTYY HOMOTYPY	IILMORSS SIMILORS	IKKLNORW LINKWORK
HILOSSTW WHOLISTS	HMOORSUU HUMOROUS	IILMORST TROILISM	IKKLNOSY KOLINSKY
HILOSSTY HYLOISTS	HNNOSSTY SYNTHONS	IILMOTTY MOTILITY	IKKMNOSU KIKUMONS
THYLOSIS	HNOOOOPR OOPHORON	IILMPSST SIMPLIST	IKKNORST KIRKTONS
HILOSTWW WHITLOWS	HNOOPRSW SHOPWORN	IILMRSSY MISSILRY	IKKORSSY SIKORSKY
HILOSTYY TOYISHLY	HNOOPSTY TYPHOONS	IILNNOOT NOLITION	IKLLOOTV KILOVOLT
HILPPRSU PURPLISH	HNOORRTW HORNWORT	IILNNSSU INSULINS	IKLLOSSY KYLLOSIS
HILPPSUY UPPISHLY	HNOORSTU SOUTHRON	IILNOOST INOSITOL	IKLMNPSU LUMPKINS
HILPRSUW UPWHIRLS	HNOOSSTU UNSHOOTS	IILNOOTV VOLITION	IKLMOOSS LOOKISMS
HILSSTTU SLUTTISH	HNOPRTUW UPTHROWN	IILNORSS SIRLOINS	IKLMORSW SILKWORM
HIMMOPRU PHORMIUM	HNORSTUW UNWORTHS	IILOOPPR LIRIPOOP	IKLMORTW MILKWORT
HIMMSSTY MYTHISMS	HNORTUWY UNWORTHY	IILOPRST TRIPOLIS	IKLNOOST KILOTONS
HIMNOPRX PHORMINX	HNOSSTUU UNSHOUTS	IILOPSSS PSILOSIS	IKLNOPST SLIPKNOT
HIMNOPSY PHISNOMY	HNRSTTUU UNTRUTHS	IILOPSST PTILOSIS	IKLNPSSU SKULPINS
HIMNSSTY HYMNISTS	HOOOSTTU OUTSHOOT	IILOPSTY PILOSITY	IKLOOPSY SPOOKILY
HIMOOPRS ISOMORPH	HOOPPSST POTSHOPS	IILORSTT TROILIST	IKLOOSTT TOOLKITS
HIMOPRSW SHIPWORM	HOOPPSTY PHOTOPSY	IILORSTV VITRIOLS	IKLOSSSU SOUSLIKS
HIMOPRWW WHIPWORM	HOOPRRST PORTHORS	IILOSSTV VIOLISTS	IKMNNOSW MISKNOWN

IKMNOOOS	OKIMONOS	ILOOSSST	SOLOISTS	INOPPSST	TOPSPINS	LLOOPRTY	TROLLOPY

IKMNOOOS OKIMONOS
IKMNOSSW MISKNOWS
IKMNPPSU PUMPKINS
IKMNRSTU TRINKUMS
IKNNOPSY PONYSKIN
IKNNRSTU TURNSKIN
IKNOOPRT PINKROOT
IKNOORRW IRONWORK
IKNOOSST ISOKONTS
IKNOPSST INKSPOTS
IKNOPSTW TOWNSKIP
IKNPSSTU SPUTNIKS
IKORSSTU KURTOSIS
ILLLMOPS PLIMSOLL
ILLLMPPU PULPMILL
ILLLOOPP LOLLIPOP
ILLMNOSU MULLIONS
ILLMNRSU MILLRUNS
ILLMOORS MOORILLS
ILLMOPRW PILLWORM
ILLMOSSY LISSOMLY
ILLMPTUY MULTIPLY
ILLNOQSU QUILLONS
ILLNORSU RULLIONS
ILLNPSUU LUPULINS
ILLOOPRW POORWILL
ILLOORSZ ZORILLOS
ILLOPPSS SLIPSLOP
ILLOPPSY SLOPPILY
ILLOPRTW PILLWORT
ILLOPRXY PROLIXLY
ILLORSTU TROLLIUS
ILLORSUY ILLUSORY
ILLOSTXY XYLITOLS
ILLOTTWY WITTOLLY
ILLRSTUY SULTRILY
ILMNOOPS POLONISM
ILMNOOPU POLONIUM
ILMNOSUU LUMINOUS
ILMOPPSU POPULISM
ILMORSTU TURMOILS
ILMORSTY STORMILY
ILMOSTUV VOLUMIST
ILMOSTUY TIMOUSLY
ILMPPTUU PULPITUM
ILMPSSTU PLUMISTS
ILMPSTUY STUMPILY
ILMSSTUU STIMULUS
ILMSTTUY SMUTTILY
ILNOOPSS PLOSIONS
ILNOOPSV VOLPINOS
ILNOOPSY SPOONILY
ILNOOSST SOLITONS
ILNOOSTU SOLUTION
ILNOOSTY SNOOTILY
ILNOOTUV VOLUTION
ILNOPRSU PURLOINS
ILNOPSSU UPSILONS
ILNOPSSW SNOWSLIP
ILNOPSSY YPSILONS
ILNOPSTU UNSPOILT
ILNORSST NOSTRILS
ILNORSSU SURLOINS
ILNORSTU TORULINS
ILNORSTY NITROSYL
ILNORTXY NITROXYL
ILNOSSTW STOWLINS
ILNOSTTY SNOTTILY
ILNOSTUV VOLUTINS
ILNPSUUV PULVINUS
ILOOORSS ROSOLIOS
ILOOPPRS PROPOLIS
ILOOPSST POLOISTS
         TOPSOILS
ILOORSTU RISOLUTO

ILOOSSST SOLOISTS
ILOPPSTU POPULIST
ILOPRSTY SPORTILY
ILOPSTTY SPOTTILY
ILOPSUUV PLUVIOUS
ILOQRTUU LOQUITUR
ILPPRTUY PULPITRY
ILRSTTUY TRUSTILY
ILRSTUUX LUXURIST
ILSSSTTY STYLISTS
IMMNOSSU MUSIMONS
IMMNOSUU MUONIUMS
IMMOORTU MOTORIUM
IMMRSTUY SUMMITRY
IMMSSSTU SUMMISTS
IMNNNOSU MUNNIONS
IMNNOORS NORIMONS
IMNNOOTT MONOTINT
IMNNOSUU NUMINOUS
IMNOOPPS POMPIONS
IMNOOPST TOMPIONS
IMNOOPSU OPSONIUM
IMNOORRS MORRIONS
IMNOORST MONITORS
         TROMINOS
IMNOORTY MONITORY
IMNOORVY OMNIVORY
IMNOOSUX OXONIUMS
IMNOPPSU PUMPIONS
IMNORRSU MURRIONS
IMNORSTY TRIONYMS
IMNOSTUU MUTINOUS
IMNRSTUU UNTRUISM
IMOOPRRS PROMISOR
IMOOPRST IMPOSTOR
IMOOQSTU MOSQUITO
IMOORSTT MOTORIST
IMOORSTU SUMOTORI
         TIMOROUS
IMOORSTY MOROSITY
IMOORTVY VOMITORY
IMOOSSTY MYOSOTIS
IMOPRRSY PRIMROSY
IMOPRSST TROPISMS
IMOPRSTU PROTIUMS
IMOPSSTU UTOPISMS
IMORSSTU TOURISMS
IMORSTTU TUTORISM
IMOSSTUW OUTSWIMS
IMPPPSUY PUPPYISM
IMRSSTTU MISTRUST
IMRSSTTY MISTRYST
IMRSTTUY YTTRIUMS
INNNORSU RUNNIONS
INNNORTU TRUNNION
INNNOSTY SYNTONIN
INNOOPSS OPSONINS
         SPONSION
INNOOPSU UNPOISON
INNOORST NOTORNIS
INNOPRSU UNPRISON
INNOSSTU NONSUITS
INOOOSSZ ZOONOSIS
INOOOTXZ ZOOTOXIN
INOOPRST PORTIONS
         POSITRON
         SORPTION
INOOPSSS POISSONS
INOOPSST POSITONS
INOOPSTT SPITTOON
INOOPTTU OUTPOINT
INOORSST ISOTRONS
         TORSIONS
INOORSTT TORTONIS
INOORSTY SONORITY

INOPPSST TOPSPINS
INOPRTTU PRINTOUT
INOPRTUY PUNITORY
INOPSSSU POUSSINS
INOPSSSY SYNOPSIS
INOPSSTU SPINOUTS
INORSSUV UNVISORS
INPPRRUU PURPURIN
INPRSSTU UNSTRIPS
INPRSSTY TRYPSINS
INPRSTTU TURNSPIT
INRSSTTU INTRUSTS
INSSSTUU SUNSUITS
INSSTTUW UNTWISTS
IOOPRRSV PROVISOR
IOOPRSSV PROVISOS
IOOPRSSY ISOSPORY
IOOPRSTY ISOTROPY
         POROSITY
IOORRSTY SORORITY
IOORRTTT TROTTOIR
IOORSSTT RISOTTOS
IOORSSUV VOUSSOIR
IOORSTTU TORTIOUS
IOORSTUV VIRTUOSO
IOORSUUX UXORIOUS
IOOSSTTU STOTIOUS
IOPPPRST PITPROPS
IOPRRSUV PROVIRUS
IOPRSSTT PROTISTS
         TROPISTS
IOPRSSUU SPURIOUS
IOPRSTTU OUTSTRIP
IOPRSTUU POURSUIT
IOPRSTUY PYRITOUS
IOPRSUVX POXVIRUS
IOPSSTTU UTOPISTS
IOQRSTTU QUITTORS
IOQRTUXY QUIXOTRY
IORRSUVV SURVIVOR
IORSSTTU TOURISTS
IORSSTTW TWISTORS
IORSSUUU USURIOUS
IORSTTUY TOURISTY
         YTTRIOUS
IORSTUUV VIRTUOUS
IPRRSSTU STIRRUPS
IPRRSTUU PRURITUS
IPRSSTUU PURSUITS
JLNSTUUY UNJUSTLY
JLOOSUYY JOYOUSLY
JMOPSTUU OUTJUMPS
JNNOORRU NONJUROR
JNOORSSU SOJOURNS
JNOOSUUY UNJOYOUS
KKNOORTW KNOTWORK
KKOOSSUU KOUSKOUS
KLLMNSUU NUMSKULL
KLLMOSSU MOLLUSKS
KLNORSTY KLYSTRON
KLOOORWW WOOLWORK
KLOOOSTU LOOKOUTS
         OUTLOOKS
KLOOPRSW SLOPWORK
KMOOORRW WORKROOM
KNNNOSUW UNKNOWNS
KNOOPSTT TOPKNOTS
KNOPRSTY KRYPTONS
KNORRSTY KRYTRONS
KOOPRSTW WORKTOPS
KOORSTUW OUTWORKS
KORSTTUW TUTWORKS
LLLMMSUU MULMULLS
LLMOOPRS ROLLMOPS
LLOOPRST TROLLOPS

LLOOPRTY TROLLOPY
LLOORSTU ROLLOUTS
LLOSUUVV VOLVULUS
LMNOOOPY MONOPOLY
LMNOOPYY POLYONYM
LMOOOORT TOOLROOM
LMOOPSYY POLYSOMY
LMOORSWW SLOWWORM
LMOOSSSU MOLOSSUS
LMOPPRTY PROMPTLY
LMRSSTUU LUSTRUMS
LNOOOPRT POLTROON
LNOOOPYZ POLYZOON
LNOOPPRY PROPYLON
LNOOPSTU PULTOONS
LNRSTUUV VULTURNS
LOOOORSS OLOROSOS
LOOPPSUU POPULOUS
LOOPPSUY POLYPOUS
LORSSTUU LUSTROUS
MMOPSSTY SYMPTOMS
MNNOOOSS MONSOONS
MNNOOOTY MONOTONY
MNNOOSSY SYNONYMS
MNNOSTUU UNMOUNTS
MNNOSYYY SYNONYMY
MNOOOPPS POMPOONS
MNOOORTW MOONWORT
MNOOORXY OXYMORON
MNOOPRTU PRONOTUM
MNOOPSTY TOPONYMS
MNOOPTYY TOPONYMY
MNOOSTTW TOWMONTS
MNORSSTU NOSTRUMS
MNORSTUU SURMOUNT
MOOOPRRT PROMOTOR
MOOORRTW TOMORROW
MOOPSSSU OPOSSUMS
MOORRSUU RUMOROUS
MOORSTUU TUMOROUS
MOORSTUY UROSTOMY
MORRSSTU ROSTRUMS
MORSSTUU STRUMOUS
MSSTTUUU TSUTSUMU
NNOOOPST PONTOONS
         SPONTOON
NNOOPRSU PRONOUNS
NNOOPSSS SPONSONS
NOOOPPRS PROSOPON
NOOORSSU SONOROUS
NOOPRSSS SPONSORS
NOORSSTU UNROOSTS
NOORSTUW OUTSWORN
NOPSSSTU SUNSPOTS
NORSTTUU OUTTURNS
         TURNOUTS
NRSSTTUU UNTRUSTS
NRSTTUUY UNTRUSTY
OOOOPRST POTOROOS
OOOPRSSU OSPOROUS
OOOPRSTU OUTROOPS
OOORSTTU OUTROOTS
OOPRSSTU SOURSOPS
OOPRSSTV PROVOSTS
OOPRSTTU OUTPORTS
         OUTSPORT
OOPRSTUU OUTPOURS
OOPSSSTT TOSSPOTS
OOPSSTTU OUTSPOTS
OORSTTUU TORTUOUS
OPPRRSTU PURPORTS
OPPRSSTU SUPPORTS
OPRSSSUU SOURPUSS
ORSSTTUU SURTOUTS
RRSSSUUU SUSURRUS